THE RANDOM HOUSE CROSSWORD PUZZLE DICTIONARY

SECOND EDITION

Books published by The Ballantine Publishing Group are available at quantity discounts on bulk purchases for premium, educational, fund-raising, and special sales use. For details, please call 1-800-733-3000.

Published by Ivy Books:

THE RANDOM HOUSE HANDY CROSSWORD BOOK #1
THE RANDOM HOUSE HANDY CROSSWORD BOOK #2
THE RANDOM HOUSE HANDY CROSSWORD BOOK #3
THE RANDOM HOUSE HANDY CROSSWORD BOOK #4
THE RANDOM HOUSE HANDY CROSSWORD BOOK #5
THE RANDOM HOUSE HANDY CROSSWORD BOOK #6
THE RANDOM HOUSE HANDY CROSSWORD BOOK #7

THE RANDOM HOUSE CROSSWORD PUZZLE DICTIONARY

SECOND EDITION

IVY BOOKS • NEW YORK

Ivy Books
Published by Ballantine Books
Copyright © 1994 by Random House, Inc

Prepared for Random House, Inc., by Sachem Publishing Associates, Inc., Stephen F. Elliott, President: Elizabeth J. Jewell, Managing Editor.

http://www.randomhouse.com

ISBN 0-8041-1349-1

This edition published by arrangement with Random House, Inc.

Manufactured in the United States of America

First Ballantine Books Edition: April 1995

10 9 8 7

PREFACE

Although various word games and puzzles have existed almost since the beginnings of language, the modern crossword puzzle is a 20th-century innovation. The first newspaper crossword appeared on December 21, 1913, in the New York *World* and this new type of word puzzle quickly captured the public's fancy. Within a decade, crossword puzzles were featured in most American newspapers, and they soon became the rage in England as well. Since the 1920s, crossword puzzles have been a standard feature of daily newspapers and have proved enormously popular when collected in book form.

Now found in almost every language and in variations ranging from theme puzzles to diagramless puzzles, crosswords are available for almost any age and vocabulary level. Those who solve crossword puzzles invariably relish the challenge of completing a puzzle, of "getting it right." When faced with a clue they cannot answer, they resist "cheating"—looking at the puzzle's solution. One way out of this difficulty is to consult a reference work, yet neither a dictionary nor an encyclopedia nor an almanac contains the necessary information in a useful, quick-reference format. A standard dictionary might give a few synonyms for a word, an encyclopedia would give information about countries or historical figures, and an almanac usually has information about sports figures or the Academy awards, but only a crossword puzzle dictionary combines in one handy volume the information that might be found in all three. Equally important, it does so without extraneous information and with the convenience of an arrangement by the number of letters in each word.

The Random House Crossword Puzzle Dictionary, drawing on the resources of the Random House dictionaries and thesauruses, with research into a host of other topics, answers the need of crossword puzzlers for one single-purpose reference work. In addition to general vocabulary and synonyms, there are entries covering history; the natural and physical sciences; literature; music, painting, and other arts; religion; mythology; sports; popular culture; and current affairs, among others. And there are special entries with detailed information on the continents and countries of the world, states of the United States, U.S. presidents, the months of the year, and other facts of special interest.

While *The Random House Crossword Puzzle Dictionary*'s primary purpose is to meet the needs of the growing numbers of people who find crosswords both relaxing and challenging, even a cursory glance will demonstrate the book's usefulness as a reference for trivia buffs. From who won the Academy Award for best actress in 1970 (Glenda Jackson) to the name of a coffee grown in Jamaica (Blue Mountain), it's all here.

A volume of this scope is necessarily the work of many researchers, editors, and proof-readers. We would like to acknowledge the invaluable contributions made by Julianna Arbo, Suzanne Stone Burke, Francine Esposito, Gretchen Ferrante, Jan Jamilkowski, Rebecca Lyon, Julie E. Marsh, Blaine Merritt, Laurie Romanik, Christine Lindberg Stevens, and Diane Bell Surprenant; and by Patricia W. Ehresmann, Typographic Director and Production Manager, Random House, Inc., and Rita Rubin, Administrative Assistant.

HOW TO USE
THIS BOOK

The main entries in *The Random House Crossword Puzzle Dictionary* are words or phrases likely to appear as crossword puzzle clues. Each entry consists of a clue word or phrase and a list of answer words, arranged first by the number of letters in each word and then alphabetically. For example, if the main entry—**banal**—is the clue for a five-letter answer, the answer—"trite"—will be found alphabetically listed under the five-letter answer words. For phrases, such as **contracted form**, the answer could be "digest," "summary," or "synopsis." Entries may also contain indented subheads and secondary subheads. If, for instance, the clue is a phrase, like **cotton fabric**, the word **cotton** will be found as a main entry in the dictionary, and **fabric** will be found as a subhead under it, with such possible answer words as "terry," "poplin," and "gingham." In some cases, the answers can be found in more than one place. For example, if the clue is **Mexican coin**, the answer could be found by looking under the main entry **Mexico** and the subhead **monetary unit**, or by looking under the main entry **coin/currency** and the subhead **of Mexico**.

Longer entries are set off in highlighted boxes so they can be found more quickly. All continents and countries of the world, states of the United States, presidents of the United States, and months of the year appear in boxed items, as do many other major entries.

There are also cross references for alternate spellings (**Epicaste** *see* **7** Jocasta) and very closely related items (**Epeans** *see* **5** Epeus—a look at **Epeus** reveals that *Epeans* are descendants of this king of the Peloponnesus).

The main entries, subheads, secondary subheads, and numbers all appear in boldface type; the answer words are in regular roman type. Most punctuation and accent marks have been omitted, since they are not used in puzzle answers; occasionally, apostrophes and other marks have been included in answers to make them more readable.

THE RANDOM HOUSE CROSSWORD PUZZLE DICTIONARY

SECOND EDITION

A

aardvark
also: 7 ant bear 8 anteater
family: 15 Orycteropodidae
species: 15 Orycteropus afer
order: 13 Tubulidentata
native to: 6 Africa
food: 4 ants 8 termites
name comes from: 9 Africaans
meaning: 8 earth hog, earth pig

Aaron
brother: 5 Moses
father: 5 Amram
mother: 8 Jochebed
sister: 6 Miriam
son: 5 Abihu, Nadab 7 Eleazar, Ithamar
wife: 8 Elisheba
successor: 7 Eleazar
deathplace: 3 Hor 8 Mount Hor
priestly descendant of: 8 Aaronite
set up: 10 golden calf

Aaron, Henry (Hank)
sport: 8 baseball
position: 10 outfielder
record: 8 homeruns
team: 13 Atlanta Braves 15 Milwaukee Braves 16 Milwaukee Brewers

Aaron's Rod 21 miraculously blossomed
yielded: 7 almonds
herb: 21 Thermopsis caroliniana

Aatam *see* 4 Pima
Ab 16 fifth Hebrew month
Abaddon 4 hell 8 Appolyon
abaft 6 behind 11 to the rear of 12 to the stern of

Abagtha 6 eunuch
served: 9 Ahasuerus

abandon 4 dash, drop, elan, jilt, junk, quit, stop 5 ardor, cease, forgo, gusto, leave, let go, scrap, verve, waive 6 desert, give up, spirit 7 discard, forfeit, forsake, freedom 8 abdicate, evacuate, forswear, get rid of, renounce, run out on 9 animation, cast aside, repudiate, surrender 10 depart from, enthusiasm, exuberance, relinquish, wantonness 11 discontinue, impetuosity, leave behind, spontaneity, unrestraint 12 immoderation, intemperance, recklessness, withdraw from 13 impulsiveness

abandoned 4 lewd, wild 5 loose 6 impure, jilted, sinful, vacant, wanton, wicked 7 debased, immoral 8 cast away, degraded, deserted, desolate, forsaken, marooned, rejected, unchaste 9 cast aside, debauched, discarded, dissolute, neglected, reprobate, shameless 10 dissipated, left behind, licentious, profligate, unoccupied 11 unrepentant 12 disreputable, incorrigi-ble, irreformable, relinquished, un-principled 13 irreclaimable

abandon oneself to 7 yield to 8 give in to, give up to 9 indulge in

Abantes
tribe: 7 Euboean

Abaris
origin: 5 Greek
form: 4 sage

Abas
mentioned in: 5 Iliad
king of: 7 Argolis
father: 6 Celeus 7 Lynceus 9 Eurydamas
mother: 8 Metanira 12 Hypermnestra
wife: 6 Aglaia
son: 7 Proetus 8 Acrisius
daughter: 7 Idomene
changed into: 4 bird 6 lizard
mocked: 7 Demeter
protected by: 11 magic shield
companion: 8 Diomedes
killed by: 8 Diomedes

a bas 8 down with 11 to the bottom

abase 4 mock 5 shame 6 debase, defame, demean, humble, malign, vilify 7 cheapen, degrade, mortify, put down, vitiate 8 badmouth, belittle, besmirch, bring low, cast down, disgrace, dishonor 9 denigrate, devaluate, discredit, downgrade, humiliate 13 bring down a peg, cut down to size

abash 4 dash 5 daunt 6 deject, dismay 7 depress 8 dispirit 9 discomfit, embarrass 10 discompose, disconcert, discourage, dishearten

abashed 3 shy 5 cowed, fazed 7 ashamed, bashful, crushed, daunted, humbled, subdued 8 confused, dismayed, overawed 9 chagrined, mortified 10 bewildered, confounded, humiliated, nonplussed, taken aback 11 dumbfounded, embarrassed, intimidated 12 disconcerted, disheartened 13 self-conscious

abashment 3 awe 6 wonder 9 confusion 12 discomfiture, discomposure 13 embarrass-ment 14 disconcertment

abate 3 ebb 4 cool, dull, ease, fade, slow, wane 5 allay, blunt, lower, quell, quiet, slack 6 dampen, go down, lessen, pacify, recede, reduce, soften, soothe, temper, weaken 7 assuage, curtail, decline, dwindle, fall off, lighten, mollify, relieve, slacken, subside 8 decrease, diminish, fade away, fall away, mitigate, moderate, palliate, restrain, restrict, slack off, slow down, taper off 9 alleviate

abatement 3 cut, ebb 5 break 6 ebbing, waning 8 decrease, discount, soothing 9 lessening, reduction, weakening 10 con-

Abba

cession, mitigation, moderation, slackening, subsidence 11 assuagement, curtailment 13 mollification

Abba
means: 6 father

Abbe Faria
character in: 21 The Count of Monte Cristo
author: 5 Dumas (pere)

abbey 6 cenoby, chapel, church, friary, priory 7 convent, nunnery 8 cloister, seminary 9 cathedral, hermitage, monastery

Abbey, Edwin Austin
born: 14 Philadelphia PA
artwork: 21 Quest of the Golden Grail 23 The Quest for the Holy Grail 37 Richard Duke of Gloucester and the Lady Anne

Abbott, Bud
real name: 14 William A Abbott
partner: 11 Lou Costello
born: 12 Asbury Park NJ
roles: 11 Who's on First 12 Buck Privates 13 Hold that Ghost 33 Abbott and Costello Meet Frankenstein

abbreviate 3 cut 4 clip, trim 6 reduce 7 abridge, curtail, cut down, shorten 8 boil down, compress, condense, contract, cut short, diminish, truncate 9 summarize, synopsize

abbreviated 5 brief, short 7 limited, summary 8 abridged 9 condensed, curtailed, shortened 10 compressed, summarized

abbreviation 5 brief 6 digest 7 cutting, pruning, summary 8 abstract, clipping, synopsis, trimming 9 lessening, reduction, short form 10 abridgment, diminution, shortening 11 abstraction, compression, contraction, curtailment, cut-down form, reduced form 12 condensation 13 condensed form, shortened form 14 compressed form, contracted form

Abderus
father: 6 Hermes
killed by: 5 mares 13 Diomedes mares

abdicate 4 cede, quit 5 forgo, waive, yield 6 abjure, give up, resign 7 abandon 8 abnegate, renounce 9 surrender 10 relinquish 15 vacate the throne

abdomen 3 gut, pot 5 belly, tummy 6 paunch, venter 7 stomach 8 pot belly 9 bay window 11 breadbasket, epigastrium 14 visceral cavity

Abdon 11 Hebrew judge
father: 5 Micah 6 Achbor, Jehiel 7 Shashak
city of: 5 Asher

abduct 5 seize, steal 6 kidnap 7 bear off 8 carry off, take away 10 run off with 11 make off with

Abduction from the Harem, The
also: 25 Die Entführung aus dem Serail
opera by: 6 Mozart
character: 5 Osmin 6 Blonde 8 Belmonte, Pedrillo 9 Constanze 10 Pasha Selim

Abdul-Jabbar, Kareem
formerly: 11 Lew Alcindor 22 Lewis Ferdinand Alcindor
sport: 10 basketball
position: 6 center
team: 8 LA Lakers 10 UCLA Bruins 14 Milwaukee Bucks 16 Los Angeles Lakers
shot: 7 sky hook

Abednego
companion: 6 Daniel
friend: 8 Meschach, Shadrach
former name: 7 Azariah

Abel
father: 4 Adam
mother: 3 Eve
brother: 4 Cain, Seth
killer: 4 Cain

Abel, Niels Henrik
field: 11 mathematics
nationality: 9 Norwegian
theorem: 8 binomial
theory of: 19 elliptical functions

Abe Lincoln in Illinois
author: 14 Robert Sherwood
director: 12 John Cromwell
cast: 10 Alan Baxter, Mary Howard, Ruth Gordon (Mary Todd Lincoln) 11 Dorothy Tree, Minor Watson 12 Gene Lockhart 13 Howard da Silva, Raymond Massey (Abraham Lincoln)

Abelmeholah
home of: 6 Elisha

aberrance 6 oddity 7 anomaly 8 rambling, straying 9 wandering 10 aberration 11 abnormality, peculiarity 12 eccentricity, irregularity 13 nonconformity

aberrant 3 odd 7 unusual 8 abnormal, atypical, peculiar, uncommon 9 anomalous, eccentric, irregular

aberration 5 lapse, quirk 6 lunacy, oddity 7 anomaly, madness 8 delusion, illusion, insanity, mutation, rambling, straying 9 aberrance, aberrancy, curiosity, departure, deviation, exception, wandering 10 digression, distortion, divergence 11 abnormality, derangement, incongruity, mental lapse, peculiarity, singularity, strangeness 12 eccentricity, idiosyncrasy, irregularity, unconformity 13 hallucination, nonconformity, self-deception

abet 3 aid 4 back, goad, help, spur, urge 5 egg on 6 assist, incite, lead on, second, uphold, urge on 7 advance, endorse, promote, support, sustain 8 advocate, join with, sanction 9 encourage, instigate

abettor 4 ally 6 cohort 7 partner 9 accessory, associate, colleague 10 accomplice 11 confederate 12 collaborator

ab extra 11 from outside, from without

abeyance 5 delay, on ice, pause 6 hiatus, recess 7 latency 8 deferral, dormancy, inaction 9 cessation, remission 10 quiescence, suspension 11 adjournment 12 intermission, postponement 13 in cold storage, on a back burner, waiting period 14 discontinuance

abhor 4 hate, shun 5 scorn 6 detest, eschew, loathe 7 despise, disdain, dislike 8 execrate, recoil at 9 abominate, can't stand, shudder at 10 shrink from 11 can't stomach 12 be revolted by 13 be nauseated by, find repulsive

abhorred 5 hated 8 despised, detested, disliked 10 abominated

abhorrence 4 hate 5 odium, scorn 6 hatred 7 disdain, disgust, dislike 8 aversion, contempt, distaste, loathing 9 antipathy, revulsion 10 repugnance 11 abomination

abhorrent 4 foul, vile 6 odious 7 hateful 8 accursed 9 execrable, loathsome, repellent, repugnant, repulsive, revolting 10 abominable, despicable, disgusting, nauseating

Abiathar
　companion: 5 David
　father: 9 Ahimelech
　banished to: 7 Anatoth
　conspired to overthrow: 5 David

abide 3 sit 4 bear, last, live, stay, stop 5 brook, dwell, stand, tarry, visit 6 accept, endure, linger, remain, reside, suffer 7 sojourn, stomach 8 stand for, submit to, tolerate

abide by 4 obey 6 follow 8 accede to, adhere to, submit to 9 conform to 10 comply with 11 go along with

abiding 4 fast, firm 6 steady 7 durable, eternal, lasting 8 constant, enduring, unending 9 immutable, permanent, steadfast 10 changeless, continuing, unchanging, unshakable 11 everlasting 12 indissoluble, wholehearted 13 unquestioning

Abidjan
　capital of: 10 Ivory Coast

Abigail
　husband: 5 David, Nabal
　brother: 5 David

Abihu
　father: 8 Aaron
　mother: 8 Elisheba
　brother: 5 Nadab 7 Eleazar, Ithamar
　killed with: 5 Nadab
　accompanied to Mt Sinai: 5 Moses

Abijah
　father: 8 Rehoboam
　grandfather: 7 Solomon
　grandmother: 6 Naamah

ability 4 bent, gift 5 flair, knack, power, skill 6 acumen, genius, talent 7 faculty, knowhow, mind for 8 aptitude, capacity, facility 9 adeptness, expertise, potential 10 adroitness, capability, competence 11 proficiency 12 potentiality 13 qualification

Abimelech
　king of: 5 Gerar
　means: 15 the father is king
　father: 6 Gideon 8 Abiathar
　brother: 6 Jotham
　army commander: 7 Phichol

ab initio 16 from the beginning

Abinoam
　father: 4 Saul
　son: 5 Barak

ab intra 10 from inside, from within

Abishag
　comforted: 5 David

abject 3 low 4 base, mean, vile 6 sordid 7 ignoble 8 complete, cringing, hopeless, horrible, terrible, thorough, wretched 9 groveling, miserable 10 deplorable, despicable, spiritless 11 inescapable 12 contemptible

abjuration 7 refusal 8 eschewal 9 rejection 10 abnegation, disclaimer, retraction 11 repudiation 12 renunciation

abjure 6 desert, give up, recant, reject 7 abandon, disavow 8 disallow, disclaim, forswear, renounce 9 repudiate 10 relinquish

ablaze 5 afire, eager, fiery 6 aflame, alight, ardent, fervid, on fire, red-hot 7 blazing, burning, excited, fervent, flaming, flushed, glowing, ignited, zealous 8 feverish, hopped-up, in flames, turned-on 10 passionate, switched-on 11 conflagrant, impassioned, intoxicated

able 3 apt, fit 4 good 5 adept 6 adroit, expert, fitted 7 capable, equal to, learned 8 adequate, skillful, talented 9 competent, effective, efficient, masterful, practiced, qualified 10 proficient 11 experienced 12 accomplished

able-bodied 5 beefy, hardy, husky, lusty, thewy 6 brawny, hearty, robust, rugged, strong, sturdy 8 athletic, muscular, powerful, stalwart, vigorous 9 herculean, strapping, well-built 15 broad-shouldered

ablution 4 bath, wash 7 bathing, washing 8 cleaning, lavation 9 cleansing 12 purification 13 ritual washing 17 ceremonial washing

Abnaki (Wabanaki)
　language family: 9 Algonkian 10 Algonquian
　tribe: 6 Micmac 8 Malecite 9 Penobscot 13 Norridgewock, Passamaquoddy
　location: 5 Maine 6 Canada, Quebec 7 Old Town 9 Norumbega 10 New England 12 New Brunswick

abnegate 5 forgo, waive 6 abjure, eschew, give up, refuse 7 abstain, forbear 8 renounce 9 repudiate 10 relinquish 11 deny oneself

abnegation 7 refusal 8 eschewal, giving up 9 rejection, sacrifice, surrender 10 abstinence, continence, forbearing, self-denial, temperance 11 forbearance, resignation 12 renunciation 14 relinquishment

Abner
　commanded: 9 Saul's army
　father: 3 Ner
　cousin: 4 Saul

abnormal 3 odd 4 rare 5 queer, weird 7 bizarre, curious, deviant, strange, unusual 8 aberrant, atypical, deformed, freakish, peculiar, uncommon 9 anomalous, eccentric, grotesque, irregular, monstrous, unheard of, unnatural 10 inordinate, outlandish, unexpected 11 exceptional 12 unaccustomed 13 extraordinary 14 unconventional

abnormality 6 oddity 7 anomaly 9 aberrance, curiosity, deformity, deviation 10 aberration, perversion 11 peculiarity 12 eccentricity, idiosyncrasy, irregularity, malformation, unconformity

abode 3 pad 4 home, nest 5 house 7 address, habitat, lodging 8 domicile, dwelling 9 residence 10 habitation 13 dwelling place 14 living quarters

abolish 3 end 5 annul, erase, quash 6 cancel, repeal, revoke 7 blot out, nullify, rescind, squelch, vitiate, wipe out 8 abrogate, set aside, stamp out 9 eliminate, eradicate, extirpate, repudiate, terminate 10 annihilate, do away with, extinguish, invalidate, obliterate, put an end to 11 exterminate 18 declare null and void

abolishment 7 voiding 8 recision 9 abolition, annulment 10 extinction, rescinding, revocation 11 destruction, eradication 12 cancellation 13 doing away with, nullification

abolition 6 ending, repeal 9 annulment, vitiation 10 abrogation, extinction, rescinding, retraction, revocation 11 abolishment, dissolution, elimination, eradication, recantation, repudiation, termination 12 cancellation, invalidation 13 nullification

abominable 4 base, evil, foul, vile 5 awful, lousy 6 cursed, horrid, odious 7 hateful, heinous, hellish 8 accursed, damnable, horrible, infamous, terrible, wretched 9 abhorrent, atrocious, execrable, loathsome, miserable, repellent, repugnant, repulsive, revolting 10 deplorable, despicable, detestable, disgusting, unsuitable, villainous 11 ignominious 12 contemptible, disagreeable 13 reprehensible

abominate 4 hate 5 abhor, scorn 6 detest, loathe 7 despise 8 execrate 9 can't stand 10 recoil from, shrink from 11 can't stomach 12 be revolted by 13 find repugnant, find repulsive

abomination 4 evil, hate 6 hatred, horror, plague 7 bugbear, disgust, torment 8 anathema, aversion, disgrace, loathing 9 annoyance, antipathy, bete noire, obscenity, revulsion 10 abhorrence, affliction, defilement, repugnance 11 detestation

aboriginal 5 first, prime 6 native 7 ancient, endemic, primary 8 earliest, original, primeval 9 primitive 10 indigenous, primordial 13 autochthonous

aborigine 6 native 16 indigenous person 18 original inhabitant 19 primitive inhabitant

abort 3 end 4 fail, halt, stop 7 call off 8 miscarry 9 terminate

abortion 6 ending, fiasco 7 failure, halting 8 disaster 10 calling off 11 miscarriage, termination 16 fruitless attempt 19 unsuccessful attempt

abortive 4 vain 6 futile 7 sterile, useless 8 bootless 9 fruitless, nonviable, worthless 10 profitless, unavailing, unfruitful 11 ineffective, ineffectual, unrewarding 12 unproductive, unprofitable, unsuccessful 13 inefficacious

abound 4 gush, teem 5 swarm 6 thrive 7 run wild 8 be filled, be rich in, flourish, overflow 9 be flooded, luxuriate, spill over 10 be numerous 11 be plentiful, superabound, proliferate

abounding 4 rich, rife 5 ample 6 lavish, plenty 7 profuse, replete, teeming 8 abundant, brimming, swarming 9 bounteous, bountiful 11 overflowing, running over 14 more than enough

about 2 in, of, on 4 near 5 astir, circa 6 abroad, almost, around, circum, nearby, nearly 7 close to 9 proximate, regarding 10 concerning, in regard to 13 approximately, connected with 14 associated with

about-face 5 shift 6 switch 7 reverse 8 reversal 9 disavowal, turnabout, volte-face 10 retraction, rightabout, turnaround 11 recantation 13 change of heart 14 tergiversation

above 4 atop, over 5 aloft, north, supra 6 before, beyond, dorsal, excess, heaven, higher 7 earlier 8 in heaven, overhead, superior, upstairs 9 exceeding 10 surpassing

above all 4 most 9 most of all 10 especially 12 particularly

aboveboard 4 just, open 5 blunt, frank, moral, plain 6 candid, direct, honest, public, square 7 artless, ethical, sincere, upright 8 revealed, straight, truthful, virtuous 9 disclosed, guileless, ingenuous, righteous 10 forthright, foursquare 11 unconcealed 12 on the up and up, plain-dealing, out in the open 13 square-dealing, undissembling 15 straightforward 16 straightshooting

ab ovo 10 from the egg 16 from the beginning

abracadabra 5 charm, magic, spell 6 voodoo 7 sorcery 8 exorcism 10 hocus-pocus, invocation, magic spell, mumbo-jumbo, open sesame, witchcraft 11 incantation

abrade 3 rub 4 file, fray, fret, rasp 5 chafe, erode, grate, grind 6 scrape 8 irritate, wear down

Abraham
former name: 5 Abram
founded: 12 Hebrew nation
father: 5 Terah
wife: 5 Sarah, Sarai 7 Keturah
brother: 5 Haran, Nahor
son: 5 Isaac 6 Midian 7 Ishmael
nephew: 3 Lot
birthplace: 15 Ur of the Chaldees
received: 17 law of circumcision
sacrificed Isaac at: 6 Moriah
burial place: 6 Hebron
tomb buried in: 9 Machpelah

Abraham Lincoln
author: 12 Carl Sandburg

Abraham's bosom 6 heaven

Abram *see 7* Abraham

Abramovitz, Max
architect of: 13 ALCOA Building (Pittsburgh PA, with Wallace Harrison) **15** Avery Fisher Hall (Lincoln Center NYC)

Abrams, Creighton
served in: 4 WWII **10** Vietnam War
rank: 16 army chief of staff

abrasion 6 lesion, scrape **7** chafing, erosion, grating, rubbing, scratch **8** friction, scouring, scraping **11** excoriation, scraped spot

abrasive 5 harsh, nasty, rough, sharp **6** biting, coarse **7** caustic, chafing, cutting, galling, grating, hurtful, rasping **8** annoying **10** irritating **11** excoriating **16** grinding material, scouring material, scraping material

abreast 6 in rank **7** aligned **10** side by side **11** in alignment

abridge 3 cut **4** trim **5** limit **6** digest, lessen, reduce **7** curtail, cut down, shorten **8** compress, condense, decrease, diminish, pare down, restrict, take away, truncate **9** scale down, telescope **10** abbreviate

abridgment 6 digest **8** decrease **9** lessening, reduction, restraint **10** diminution, limitation, truncation **11** curtailment, diminishing, restriction **12** abbreviation, condensation **13** condensed form, shortened form

abroad 3 out **4** rife **5** astir, forth **7** at large, outside **8** overseas **9** all around **10** out of doors **13** in circulation, out of the house, round and about **15** making the rounds, out in the open air, out of the country

abrogate 3 end **4** junk, undo, void **5** annul, quash **6** abjure, cancel, negate, recall, repeal, revoke **7** abolish, nullify, rescind, retract, reverse, vitiate **8** dissolve, override, renounce, set aside, throw out, withdraw **9** repudiate, terminate **10** do away with, invalidate, put an end to **11** countermand

abrogation 6 repeal **7** junking **8** recision, reneging, reversal **9** abolition, annulment **10** rescinding, retraction, revocation **11** abolishment, going back on, repudiation **12** cancellation **13** nullification

abrupt 4 curt, rude **5** blunt, brisk, crisp, gruff, hasty, quick, rapid, rough, sharp, sheer, short, steep, swift **6** sudden **7** brusque, uncivil **8** impolite **9** impulsive **10** unexpected, unforeseen, ungracious **11** precipitate, precipitous, unannounced, unlooked for **12** discourteous **13** instantaneous, unanticipated, unceremonious

Absalom
father: 5 David
mother: 6 Maacah
sister: 5 Tamar
brother: 7 Solomon **8** Adonijah
half-brother: 7 Amnon
defeated at: 6 Gilead
killed by: 4 Joab

Absalom, Absalom!
author: 15 William Faulkner
character: 5 Henry **6** Judith **10** Charles Bon **13** Rosa Coldfield **14** Quentin Compson, Shreve McCannon **16** Goodhue Coldfield **19** Colonel Thomas Sutpen **20** Ellen Coldfield Sutpen

Absalom and Achitophel
author: 10 John Dryden

abscond 3 fly **4** flee, skip **5** split **6** escape, run off, vanish **7** make off, run away, take off **8** steal off **9** disappear, steal away **10** take flight

absence 3 cut **4** lack, want **6** dearth **7** truancy **8** scarcity **10** deficiency, scantiness **11** absenteeism, nonpresence **12** nonexistence **13** insufficiency, nonappearance, nonattendance **14** unavailability

Absence of Malice
director: 13 Sydney Pollack
based on story by: 11 Kurt Luedtke
cast: 10 Bob Balaban, Paul Newman, Sally Field **13** Melinda Dillon
setting: 5 Miami

absent 3 cut, out **4** away, gone **5** blank, empty, vague **6** dreamy, musing, truant, vacant **7** faraway, missing, out of it, removed, unaware **8** heedless, keep away, stay away, tuned out **9** not appear, not show up, oblivious **10** distracted, nonpresent, not present, out to lunch, play truant, unthinking **11** inattentive, preoccupied, unconscious **12** nonattendant

absentee 6 no show, truant **10** nonpresent **11** nonattendee, nonpresence **12** nonattendant **13** nonattendance

absenteeism 5 hooky **7** truancy **11** nonpresence **13** nonappearance **19** absence without cause

absent-minded 5 blank, vague **6** dreamy **9** oblivious **10** abstracted, distracted **11** preoccupied **14** out in left field **17** out of it

Absent Without Leave
author: 12 Heinrich Böll

absinthe
ingredient: 8 licorice, wormwood **9** aromatics, star anise
color: 11 yellow green
substitute: 4 Ouzo **6** Pastis, Pernod **8** Anisette

absolute 4 full, pure, real, sure **5** sheer, total, utter **7** certain, genuine, perfect, supreme **8** complete, decisive, definite, outright, positive, reliable, thorough **9** confirmed, out-and-out, unbounded, unlimited **10** conclusive, consummate, infallible, undeniable **11** unequivocal, unmitigated, unqualified **12** unrestrained, unrestricted **13** unadulterated, unconditional **14** unquestionable **17** through and through

Absolute, Sir Anthony
character in: 9 The Rivals
author: 8 Sheridan

absolutely 5 truly **6** indeed, really, wholly **7** utterly **8** entirely **9** certainly, decidedly **10** completely, definitely, positively, thoroughly **11** indubitably, undoubtedly **13** unequivocally **14** unquestionably **15** unconditionally **17** without limitation

absolution 5 mercy 6 pardon 7 amnesty, release 9 acquittal, clearance, quittance, remission 10 indulgence, liberation 11 deliverance, exculpation, exoneration, forgiveness, vindication 12 dispensation

absolve 4 free 5 clear, loose 6 acquit, exempt, pardon, shrive 7 deliver, forgive, release, set free 9 discharge, exculpate, exonerate, vindicate 10 excuse from 13 find not guilty, judge innocent

absolved 5 freed 6 exempt, spared 7 cleared, excused 8 forgiven, pardoned, released, relieved 9 acquitted 10 discharged, exonerated, vindicated 13 found innocent

absorb 3 fix 5 rivet 6 arrest, digest, engage, enwrap, ingest, occupy, soak up, suck up, take up 7 consume, drink in, engross, immerse 8 sponge up 9 fascinate, preoccupy, swallow up 10 assimilate 11 incorporate

absorbed 4 deep 8 immersed, involved, soaked up, sucked up 9 blotted up, engrossed

absorbent 6 porous, spongy 7 osmotic, thirsty 8 bibulous, pervious 9 permeable 10 absorptive, penetrable 12 assimilative

absorbing 8 engaging, exciting 9 thrilling 10 engrossing, intriguing 11 captivating, fascinating, interesting

abstain 5 avoid, forgo 6 desist, eschew, refuse, resist 7 decline, forbear, refrain

abstainer 3 dry 7 ascetic 10 nondrinker, self-denier, teetotaler

abstemious 3 dry 5 sober 7 ascetic, austere, sparing, spartan 8 teetotal 9 abstinent, continent, temperate 10 forbearing 11 abstentious, self-denying, straitlaced, teetotaling 12 nonindulgent 15 selfdisciplined

abstention 7 refusal 8 eschewal 9 avoidance, desisting, eschewing 10 abstaining, refraining, resistance 11 forbearance, holding back 13 nonindulgence 14 denying oneself 16 nonparticipation

abstinence 8 chastity, sobriety 10 abstention, continence, discipline, self-denial, temperance 11 forbearance, self-control 13 nonindulgence, self-restraint

abstinent 3 dry 5 sober 6 chaste 8 celibate, virginal 9 continent 10 abstemious, forbearing

abstract 4 take 5 brief 6 arcane, digest, precis, remote, remove, resume, subtle 7 abridge, extract, general, isolate, obscure, outline, summary, take out 8 abstruse, compress, condense, esoteric, profound, separate, synopsis, withdraw 9 imaginary, recondite, summarize, synopsize, theoretic, unapplied, visionary 10 abridgment, conceptual, dissociate, indefinite, intangible 11 generalized, impractical, nonspecific, theoretical 12 condensation, hypothetical, intellectual 14 recapitulation

abstruse 4 deep 6 arcane, remote, subtle 7 complex, obscure 8 abstract, esoteric, profound, puzzling 9 enigmatic, recondite 10 perplexing 11 complicated 12 unfathomable 16 incomprehensible

absurd 4 wild 5 crazy, funny, inane, kooky, silly 6 screwy, stupid 7 asinine, comical, foolish, idiotic 8 farcical 9 illogical, laughable, ludicrous, senseless 10 irrational, ridiculous 11 nonsensical 12 preposterous, unreasonable

absurdity 6 drivel, idiocy 7 fallacy, inanity 8 delusion, nonsense 9 asininity, falsehood, silliness 10 buffoonery 11 comicalness, foolishness 13 irrationality 14 ridiculousness 15 unbelievability 16 unreasonableness

Absyrtus see 8 Apsyrtus

Abu Dhabi
   capital of: 18 United Arab Emirates

Abuja
   capital of: 7 Nigeria

abundance 4 glut, heap 5 flood 6 bounty, excess, plenty, wealth 7 surfeit, surplus 8 plethora, richness 9 plenitude, profusion, repletion 10 cornucopia 11 copiousness, full measure, sufficiency

abundant 4 rich, rife 5 ample 6 enough, galore, lavish, plenty 7 copious, profuse, replete, teeming 8 brimming, prolific 9 abounding, bounteous, bountiful, luxuriant 10 sufficient

ab urbe condita 24 from the founding of the city

abuse 4 harm, hurt, slur 5 curse, scold 6 berate, carp at, defame, deride, ill-use, injure, injury, insult, malign, misuse, rail at, revile, tirade, vilify 7 assault, bawl out, beating, carping, censure, cruelty, cursing, exploit, harming, insults, railing, slander, torment, upbraid 8 badmouth, belittle, berating, denounce, derision, diatribe, illtreat, maltreat, mistreat, reproach, ridicule, scolding, sneering, torments 9 castigate, criticism, criticize, denigrate, disparage, excoriate, invective 10 belittling, defamation, impose upon, imposition, oppression, speak ill of, upbraiding 11 castigation 12 exploitation, maltreatment, mistreatment, vilification 13 disparagement, misemployment, tongue-lashing 14 inveigh against, misapplication 15 take advantage of

abusive 4 rude, vile 5 cruel, gross, harsh 7 harmful, hurtful, obscene 8 critical, improper, reviling, scornful 9 injurious, insulting, maligning, offensive, vilifying 10 censorious, defamatory, derogatory, scurrilous, slanderous 11 acrimonious, castigating, deprecatory, disparaging, foulmouthed 12 vituperative

abusive word 5 curse 6 insult 7 epithet 9 blasphemy, expletive, invective, obscenity

abut 4 join, meet 5 touch 6 adjoin, border

abutment 4 prop, stay 5 brace, union 7 contact, meeting, support 8 buttress, junction, shoulder, touching 9 adjacency

abutting 6 next to 7 joining, meeting 8 adjacent, touching 9 bordering 10 contiguous, juxtaposed 12 conterminous

abysmal 4 deep, vast 7 endless, extreme, immense 8 complete, enormous, profound, thorough, unending 9 boundless 10 bottomless, incredible, stupendous 12 unfathomable, unbelievable, unimaginable
abyss 4 gulf, void 5 depth, gorge, gully, nadir 7 fissure 8 crevasse 9 vast chasm 13 bottomless pit
Abyssinia *see* 8 Ethiopia
Acacallis
   father: 5 Minos
   mother: 8 Pasiphae
   son: 11 Amphithemis
acacia
   family: 6 legume 11 leguminosae
   also called: 5 thorn 6 mimosa, wattle
academic 4 moot 6 remote, school 7 bookish, erudite, general, learned 8 abstract, educated, pedantic, studious 9 scholarly 10 collegiate, scholastic, university 11 conjectural, educational, liberal-arts, presumptive, speculative, theoretical 12 hypothetical, ivory-towered, nontechnical, not practical 13 nonvocational, suppositional 14 nonspecialized 18 college-preparatory
Academus
   origin: 8 Arcadian
   owned: 6 estate
   located in: 6 Athens
   served as meeting place for: 12 philosophers
Academy Award
   also called: 5 Oscar
   1927-28:
   actor: 12 Emil Jannings
   actress: 11 Janet Gaynor
   director: 12 Frank Borzage 14 Lewis Milestone
   picture: 5 Wings
   1928-29:
   actor: 12 Warner Baxter
   actress: 12 Mary Pickford
   director: 10 Frank Lloyd
   picture: 14 Broadway Melody
   1929-30:
   actor: 12 George Arliss
   actress: 12 Norma Shearer
   director: 14 Lewis Milestone
   picture: 25 All Quiet on the Western Front
   1930-31:
   actor: 15 Lionel Barrymore
   actress: 13 Marie Dressler
   director: 12 Norman Taurog
   picture: 8 Cimarron
   1931-32:
   actor: 12 Fredric March
   actress: 10 Helen Hayes
   director: 12 Frank Borzage
   picture: 10 Grand Hotel
   1932-33:
   actor: 15 Charles Laughton
   actress: 16 Katharine Hepburn
   director: 10 Frank Lloyd
   picture: 9 Cavalcade
   1934:
   actor: 10 Clark Gable

   actress: 16 Claudette Colbert
   director: 10 Frank Capra
   picture: 18 It Happened One Night
   1935:
   actor: 14 Victor McLaglen
   actress: 10 Bette Davis
   director: 8 John Ford
   picture: 17 Mutiny on the Bounty
   1936:
   actor: 8 Paul Muni
   actress: 11 Luise Rainer
   director: 10 Frank Capra
   picture: 16 The Great Ziegfeld
   1937:
   actor: 12 Spencer Tracy
   actress: 11 Luise Rainer
   director: 10 Leo McCarey
   picture: 15 Life of Emile Zola
   1938:
   actor: 12 Spencer Tracy
   actress: 10 Bette Davis
   director: 10 Frank Capra
   picture: 20 You Can't Take It with You
   1939:
   actor: 11 Robert Donat
   actress: 11 Vivien Leigh
   director; 13 Victor Fleming
   picture: 15 Gone with the Wind
   1940:
   actor: 12 James Stewart
   actress: 12 Ginger Rogers
   director: 8 John Ford
   picture: 7 Rebecca
   1941:
   actor: 10 Gary Cooper
   actress: 12 Joan Fontaine
   director: 8 John Ford
   picture: 19 How Green Was My Valley
   1942:
   actor: 11 James Cagney
   actress: 11 Greer Garson
   director: 12 William Wyler
   picture: 10 Mrs Miniver
   1943:
   actor: 9 Paul Lukas
   actress: 13 Jennifer Jones
   director: 13 Michael Curtiz
   picture: 10 Casablanca
   1944:
   actor: 10 Bing Crosby
   actress: 13 Ingrid Bergman
   director: 10 Leo McCarey
   picture: 10 Going My Way
   1945:
   actor: 10 Ray Milland
   actress: 12 Joan Crawford
   director: 11 Billy Wilder
   picture: 14 The Lost Weekend
   1946:
   actor: 12 Fredric March
   actress: 17 Olivia de Havilland
   director: 12 William Wyler
   picture: 22 The Best Years of Our Lives
   1947:
   actor: 12 Ronald Colman
   actress: 12 Loretta Young
   director: 9 Elia Kazan

picture: 19 Gentleman's Agreement
1948:
actor: 15 Laurence Olivier
actress: 9 Jane Wyman
director: 10 John Huston
picture: 6 Hamlet
1949:
actor: 17 Broderick Crawford
actress: 17 Olivia de Havilland
director: 17 Joseph L Mankiewicz
picture: 14 All the King's Men
1950:
actor: 10 Jose Ferrer
actress: 12 Judy Holliday
director: 17 Joseph L Mankiewicz
picture: 11 All About Eve
1951:
actor: 14 Humphrey Bogart
actress: 11 Vivien Leigh
director: 13 George Stevens
picture: 17 An American in Paris
1952:
actor: 10 Gary Cooper
actress: 12 Shirley Booth
director: 8 John Ford
picture: 19 Greatest Show on Earth
1953:
actor: 13 William Holden
actress: 13 Audrey Hepburn
director: 13 Fred Zinnemann
picture: 18 From Here to Eternity
1954:
actor: 12 Marlon Brando
actress: 10 Grace Kelly
director: 9 Elia Kazan
picture: 15 On the Waterfront
1955:
actor: 14 Ernest Borgnine
actress: 11 Anna Magnani
director: 11 Delbert Mann
picture: 5 Marty
1956:
actor: 10 Yul Brynner
actress: 13 Ingrid Bergman
director: 13 George Stevens
picture: 26 Around the World in Eighty
Days
1957:
actor: 12 Alec Guinness
actress: 14 Joanne Woodward
director: 9 David Lean
picture: 23 The Bridge on the River Kwai
1958:
actor: 10 David Niven
actress: 12 Susan Hayward
director: 16 Vincente Minnelli
picture: 4 Gigi
1959:
actor: 14 Charlton Heston
actress: 14 Simone Signoret
director: 12 William Wyler
picture: 6 Ben-Hur
1960:
actor: 13 Burt Lancaster
actress: 15 Elizabeth Taylor
director: 11 Billy Wilder
picture: 12 The Apartment

1961:
actor: 16 Maximilian Schell
actress: 11 Sophia Loren
director: 10 Robert Wise 13 Jerome
Robbins
picture: 13 West Side Story
1962:
actor: 11 Gregory Peck
actress: 12 Anne Bancroft
director: 9 David Lean
picture: 16 Lawrence of Arabia
1963:
actor: 13 Sidney Poitier
actress: 12 Patricia Neal
director: 14 Tony Richardson
picture: 8 Tom Jones
1964:
actor: 11 Rex Harrison
actress: 12 Julie Andrews
director: 11 George Cukor
picture: 10 My Fair Lady
1965:
actor: 9 Lee Marvin
actress: 13 Julie Christie
director: 10 Robert Wise
picture: 15 The Sound of Music
1966:
actor: 12 Paul Scofield
actress: 15 Elizabeth Taylor
director: 13 Fred Zinnemann
picture: 17 A Man for All Seasons
1967:
actor: 10 Rod Steiger
actress: 16 Katharine Hepburn
director: 11 Mike Nichols
picture: 19 In the Heat of the Night
1968:
actor: 14 Cliff Robertson
actress: 15 Barbra Streisand 16 Katharine Hepburn
director: 12 Sir Carol Reed
picture: 6 Oliver!
1969:
actor: 9 John Wayne
actress: 11 Maggie Smith
director: 15 John Schlesinger
picture: 14 Midnight Cowboy
1970:
actor: 12 George C Scott
actress: 13 Glenda Jackson
director: 17 Franklin Schaffner
picture: 6 Patton
1971:
actor: 11 Gene Hackman
actress: 9 Jane Fonda
director: 15 William Friedkin
picture: 19 The French Connection
1972:
actor: 12 Marlon Brando
actress: 11 Liza Minnelli
director: 8 Bob Fosse
picture: 12 The Godfather
1973:
actor: 10 Jack Lemmon
actress: 13 Glenda Jackson
director: 13 George Roy Hill
picture: 8 The Sting

1974:
actor: 9 Art Carney
actress: 12 Ellen Burstyn
director: 18 Francis Ford Coppola
picture: 12 The Godfather (Part II)
1975:
actor: 13 Jack Nicholson
actress: 14 Louise Fletcher
director: 11 Milos Forman
picture: 25 One Flew Over the Cuckoo's Nest
1976:
actor: 10 Peter Finch
actress: 11 Faye Dunaway
director: 13 John G Avildsen
picture: 5 Rocky
1977:
actor: 15 Richard Dreyfuss
actress: 11 Diane Keaton
director: 10 Woody Allen
picture: 9 Annie Hall
1978:
actor: 9 Jon Voight
actress: 9 Jane Fonda
director: 13 Michael Cimino
picture: 13 The Deer Hunter
1979:
actor: 13 Dustin Hoffman
actress: 10 Sally Field
director: 12 Robert Benton
picture: 14 Kramer vs Kramer
1980:
actor: 12 Robert De Niro
actress: 11 Sissy Spacek
director: 13 Robert Redford
picture: 14 Ordinary People
1981:
actor: 10 Henry Fonda
actress: 16 Katharine Hepburn
director: 12 Warren Beatty
picture: 14 Chariots of Fire
1982:
actor: 11 Ben Kingsley
actress: 11 Meryl Streep
director: 19 Richard Attenborough
picture: 6 Gandhi
1983:
actor: 12 Robert Duvall
actress: 15 Shirley MacLaine
director: 12 James L Brooks
picture: 17 Terms of Endearment
1984:
actor: 14 F Murray Abraham
actress: 10 Sally Field
director: 11 Milos Forman
picture: 7 Amadeus
1985:
actor: 11 William Hurt
actress: 13 Geraldine Page
director: 13 Sydney Pollack
picture: 11 Out of Africa
1986:
actor: 10 Paul Newman
actress: 12 Marlee Matlin
director: 11 Oliver Stone
picture: 7 Platoon
1987:
actor: 14 Michael Douglas
actress: 4 Cher
director: 18 Bernardo Bertolucci
picture: 14 The Last Emperor
1988:
actor: 13 Dustin Hoffman
actress: 11 Jodie Foster
director: 13 Barry Levinson
picture: 7 Rain Man
1989:
actor: 14 Daniel Day-Lewis
actress: 12 Jessica Tandy
director: 11 Oliver Stone
picture: 16 Driving Miss Daisy
1990:
actor: 11 Jeremy Irons
actress: 10 Kathy Bates
director: 12 Kevin Costner
picture: 16 Dances With Wolves
1991:
actor: 14 Anthony Hopkins
actress: 11 Jodie Foster
director: 13 Jonathan Demme
picture: 20 The Silence of the Lambs
1992:
actor: 8 Al Pacino
actress: 12 Emma Thompson
director: 13 Clint Eastwood
picture: 10 Unforgiven
1993:
actor: 8 Tom Hanks
actress: 11 Holly Hunter
director: 15 Steven Spielberg
picture: 14 Schindler's List

Acanthopolis
  type: 8 dinosaur 10 ornithopod
Acastus
  member of: 9 Argonauts
  father: 6 Pelias
  mother: 10 Phylomache
  sister: 8 Alcestis
  wife: 8 Cretheis
  daughter: 7 Sterope 8 Laodemia, Sthenele
Acawai, Akawai
  language family: 7 Cariban
  location: 7 Guianas 12 South America
Accad
  kingdom of: 6 Nimrod
  location: 13 Plain of Shinar
  captured by: 6 Sargon (I)
Acca Larentia
  form: 7 goddess
  corresponds to: 6 Dea Dia
accede 5 admit, grant 6 accept, permit 7 abide by, agree to, approve, concede, defer to, endorse, inherit, yield to 8 assent to, submit to 9 acquiesce, conform to, consent to, succeed to 10 comply with, concur with 11 acknowledge, subscribe to, surrender to
accede to the throne 4 keep 5 claim, usurp 6 ascend 7 possess, succeed 8 take over 9 be crowned 15 ascend the throne
accelerando
  music: 15 becoming quicker

accelerate 4 rush, spur 5 hurry, impel 6 hasten, step up 7 advance, augment, further, promote, quicken, speed up 8 expedite 9 intensify 10 facilitate, to go faster 11 pick up speed, precipitate

accelerator 3 gas 4 goad, prod, spur 8 gas pedal 13 encouragement

accent 4 hint, tone 5 drawl, touch, twang 6 detail, stress 7 feature 8 emphasis, ornament, tonality, trimming 9 adornment, emphasize, highlight, punctuate, spotlight, underline 10 accentuate, inflection, intonation, modulation, underscore 11 enunciation 12 articulation 13 embellishment, primary stress, pronunciation

accentuate 6 accent, stress 7 feature, point up 9 emphasize, punctuate, underline 10 underscore

accentuation 6 accent, stress 8 emphasis

accept 3 buy 4 avow, bear 5 admit 6 assume 7 agree to, fall for, swallow 8 accede to, assent to 9 consent to, undertake 11 acknowledge, go along with

acceptable 4 fair, good, so-so 6 proper, worthy 8 adequate, passable, suitable 9 agreeable, allowable, tolerable 10 admissible 12 satisfactory

acceptable person
Latin: 12 persona grata

acceptance 6 belief, taking 7 consent, receipt 8 approval, sanction 9 accepting, agreement, receiving, reception 10 concession, permission 11 affirmation, approbation, endorsement, recognition 12 acquiescence, confirmation 14 acknowledgment 15 stamp of approval

accepted 5 usual 6 common, normal 7 regular 8 approved, standard 9 confirmed, customary, universal 10 acceptable, agreed upon 11 established, time-honored 12 acknowledged, conventional

access 3 way 4 path, road 5 entry 6 avenue, course, entree 7 gateway, passage 8 entrance 10 admittance, an approach, passageway

accessible 5 handy, ready 6 at hand, nearby, on hand 8 possible 9 available, reachable 10 attainable, obtainable 11 within reach 12 approachable

accession 7 seizure 9 induction 10 arrogation, assumption, investment, taking over, usurpation 11 inheritance 12 inauguration, installation

accessory 4 plus 6 accent, cohort, detail 7 adjunct, partner 8 addition 9 adornment, assistant, associate, auxiliary, colleague, component, extension 10 accomplice, attachment, complement, decoration, supplement 11 confederate, contributor 13 accompaniment

accident 4 fate, luck 5 crash, fluke, wreck 6 chance, mishap 7 smashup 8 fortuity 9 collision, mischance 10 misfortune 11 good fortune, serendipity 12 happenstance, misadventure

accidental 6 chance, random 9 haphazard, unplanned, unwitting 10 fortuitous, incidental, unexpected, unforeseen

acclaim 4 hail, laud 5 cheer, exalt, extol, honor, kudos 6 bravos, praise, salute 7 applaud, commend, ovation 8 applause, cheering, eulogize, plaudits 9 celebrate, rejoicing 10 compliment, enthusiasm 11 acclamation, endorsement

acclamation 6 cheers, homage 7 acclaim, hurrahs, ovation, tribute 8 cheering, hosannas, plaudits 9 adulation 10 salutation 11 approbation

acclimate 5 adapt, inure 6 adjust 8 accustom 9 get used to, habituate, reconcile 11 accommodate 16 become seasoned to

acclimation 9 seasoning 10 adaptation, adjustment 11 habituation

acclimatize 5 adapt 6 attune 8 accustom 9 acclimate, get used to

acclivity 4 hill, rise 6 ascent 9 elevation 11 upward slope

accolade 5 award, honor, prize 6 praise, trophy 7 acclaim, tribute 8 citation 10 admiration, compliment, decoration 11 recognition, testimonial 12 commendation

accommodate 3 aid, fit 4 help, hold 5 adapt, board, house, lodge, put up 6 adjust, assist, billet, modify, oblige, supply 7 bed down, conform, contain, furnish, provide, quarter, shelter 8 accustom 9 acclimate, entertain, get used to, harmonize, lend a hand, reconcile

accommodating 4 kind 6 polite 7 helpful 8 gracious, obliging, yielding 9 courteous 10 hospitable, neighborly 11 considerate 12 conciliatory

accommodation 5 rooms 7 concord, housing 8 lodgings, quarters 9 agreement 10 adjustment, compromise, settlement 12 arrangements 14 reconciliation

accommodative 8 friendly 9 appeasing, pacifying, placatory 10 mollifying 11 peacemaking, reconciling 12 conciliatory

accompaniment 6 escort 7 support 8 ornament 9 accessory, adornment 10 incidental

accompany 5 guard, usher 6 attend, back up, convoy, escort, follow 7 conduct, support 8 chaperon

accomplice 4 aide, ally 5 crony 6 cohort, helper, stooge 7 abettor, comrade, partner 8 henchman, sidekick 9 accessory, assistant, associate, colleague, supporter 11 confederate, participant, subordinate 12 collaborator 13 co-conspirator 14 partner-in-crime

accomplish 2 do 6 attain, finish 7 achieve, execute, fulfill, get done, perform, produce, realize 8 carry out, complete, expedite, knock off 9 succeed at 10 bring about

accomplished 3 apt 4 able, deft, fine 6 adroit, expert, gifted, proved, proven 7 capable, eminent, skilled 8 accepted, effected, existing, finished, masterly, polished, realized, seasoned, skillful, talented 9 brilliant, completed, concluded, practiced, qualified 10 cultivated, proficient 11 consummated, established, experienced, well-trained

accomplishment 3 act 4 deed, feat, gift 5 skill 6 talent 7 exploit, success, triumph, victory 9 execution 10 attainment, capability 11 achievement, carrying out, culmination, fulfillment, proficiency, realization, tour de force 12 consummation

accord 4 cede, give, jibe 5 agree, allow, award, grant, match, tally 6 bestow, concur, render, square, tender, unison 7 concede, concert, conform, harmony, present, rapport 8 be in tune, bequeath, sympathy 9 agreement, harmonize, unanimity, vouchsafe 10 accordance, be in unison, comply with, conformity, consonance, correspond, uniformity 11 concurrence, go along with 19 mutual understanding

accordant 4 like 7 similar 8 parallel 10 consistent 11 homogeneous

accordingly 2 so 4 ergo, then, thus 5 hence 6 thence, whence 8 suitably 9 as a result, therefore, wherefore, whereupon 11 conformably, in due course, in which case 12 consequently 15 correspondingly

accost 3 nab 4 hail, halt, stop 5 greet 6 call to, salute, waylay 7 address, solicit 8 approach, confront 10 buttonhole 11 proposition

accouchement 10 childbirth 11 confinement

accoucheur 12 obstetrician 25 assistant during childbirth

accoucheuse 7 midwife 25 assistant during childbirth

account 3 use 4 deem, hold, note, rank, rate, sake, tale 5 basis, books, cause, count, gauge, honor, judge, merit, score, story, think, value, weigh, worth 6 esteem, import, reason, reckon, record, regard, report, repute, view as 7 believe, clarify, dignity, explain, grounds, history, justify, recital, version 8 appraise, consider, estimate, megillah, standing 9 calculate, chronicle, narration, narrative, statement 10 accounting, commentary, illuminate, importance

accountable 6 guilty, liable 7 at fault, to blame 8 beholden, culpable 9 obligated 10 answerable, chargeable 11 blameworthy, responsible

accountant 3 CPA 7 actuary, auditor 10 bookkeeper 25 certified public accountant

account for 6 excuse 7 explain, justify 9 answer for

accounting 5 cause 6 answer, motive, reason 7 warrant 10 motivation 11 explanation

account rendered
French: 11 compte rendu

accoutrements 4 gear 7 apparel 8 supplies 9 equipment, trappings 11 accessories, furnishings 13 paraphernalia

Accra, Akkra
   capital of: 5 Ghana

accredit 6 assign, credit 7 ascribe, certify, empower, endorse, license 8 sanction 9 attribute, authorize, guarantee 10 commission 19 officially recognize 22 furnish with credentials

accredited 8 ascribed, assigned, endorsed, licensed 9 authentic, certified, empowered 10 attributed, authorized, recognized, sanctioned 12 commissioned 20 officially recognized

accretion 4 rise 6 growth 7 accrual 8 addition, increase 9 expansion, extension, increment 10 supplement 11 enlargement 12 accumulation, augmentation 13 amplification

accrue 4 grow 5 add up, amass 6 pile up 7 build up, collect 8 increase 10 accumulate

accumulate 4 grow 5 amass, hoard 6 accrue, garner, gather, heap up, pile up, save up 7 collect, store up 8 assemble, cumulate 9 aggregate 10 congregate 14 gather together

accumulation 4 heap, mass, pile 5 hoard, stack, stock, store 6 pile-up, supply 7 accrual 8 amassing, hoarding 9 acquiring, gathering, stockpile 10 assemblage, collecting, collection 11 aggregation 13 agglomerating 14 conglomeration

accuracy 5 truth 6 verity 8 fidelity 9 exactness, precision 10 exactitude 11 correctness 12 accurateness, faithfulness

accurate 4 true 5 exact, right 7 careful, correct, perfect, precise 8 faithful, truthful, unerring 9 authentic, faultless 10 meticulous, scrupulous 11 punctilious 12 without error

accursed 4 base, foul, vile 6 cussed, horrid, odious 7 hellish 8 damnable, horrible, infamous 9 abhorrent, atrocious, execrable, loathsome, revolting 10 abominable, despicable, detestable, disgusting 12 contemptible

accusation 6 charge 8 citation 9 complaint 10 allegation, imputation, indictment 11 insinuation 13 incrimination

accuse 4 cite 5 blame 6 charge, indict 7 arraign, upbraid 8 reproach 10 take to task 13 call to account 22 lodge a complaint against

accuser 8 attacker 11 complainant 13 finger pointer

accustomed 3 set 5 fixed, prone, trite, usual 6 cliche, common, inured, normal, used to, wonted 7 general, given to, regular, routine 8 everyday, expected, familiar, habitual, hardened, ordinary, seasoned 9 customary, hackneyed, ingrained, prevalent, well-known 10 acclimated, habituated, prevailing 11 commonplace, established 12 conventional, familiarized

ace 2 A-1 3 top 4 star 5 crack, super 6 expert, master, tip-top, victor, winner 8 champion, medalist, terrific, top-rated 9 excellent, first-rate, headliner 10 first-class 11 crackerjack, outstanding 12 front-ranking

Aceldama
   means: 12 field of blood
   purchased by: 5 Judas

Acerbas see 8 Sychaeus

acerbity 7 acidity, sarcasm 8 acridity, acrimony, pungency, sourness, tartness 9 nastiness, sharpness 10 bitterness 11 astringency, brusqueness 12 irascibility

aces 2 A-1 4 fine, tops 5 great, prime, super 6 grade-A, superb, tip-top 8 peerless, superior, terrific, top-notch 9 excellent, first-rate, marvelous, matchless, superfine, wonderful 10 first-class, tremendous 11 outstanding, superlative 13 extraordinary

Acesius
epithet of: 6 Apollo
means: 6 healer

Acessamenus
origin: 8 Thracian
mentioned in: 5 Iliad
form: 4 king

Acetes
origin: 6 Lydian
duty: 8 helmsman
protected by: 8 Dionysus

Achaeus
founder of: 6 Achaea
father: 6 Xuthus
mother: 6 Creusa
brother: 3 Ion

Achan
punishment: 13 stoned to death

Acharnians
author: 12 Aristophanes
character: 7 Demigod 8 Lamachus 11 Dikaiopolis

Achates
mentioned in: 6 Aeneid
companion of: 6 Aeneas
position: 11 armorbearer

ache 4 hurt, need, pain, pang, want 5 covet, crave, mourn, smart, throb, yearn 6 be sore, desire, grieve, hanker, hunger, lament, sorrow, suffer, twinge 7 agonize, long for 10 soreness 10 discomfort

Achech
origin: 8 Egyptian
form: 8 creature
body of: 4 lion
wings of: 4 bird

Achelous
form: 3 god
habitat: 5 river
father: 7 Oceanus
mother: 6 Tethys
daughter: 6 Sirens 8 Castalia 10 Callirrhoe
defeated by: 8 Hercules
struggled over: 8 Deianira

Acheron
river in: 5 Hades
ferryman: 6 Charon
carries: 4 dead

Acheson, Dean
author of: 20 Present at the Creation

a cheval 7 by horse 11 on horseback

achieve 2 do 3 get, win 4 earn, gain 5 reach 6 attain, effect, finish, obtain 7 acquire, fulfill, procure, realize 8 arrive at,

carry out, complete, dispatch 9 succeed in 10 accomplish, bring about, effectuate 11 bring to pass

achievement 3 act 4 coup, deed, fear 5 skill 6 effort 7 command, exploit, mastery 9 expertise 10 attainment 11 acquirement, fulfillment, realization, tour de force 14 accomplishment

achieve recognition 6 arrive, make it 7 succeed 8 make good 10 be somebody 11 reach the top

Achilles
mentioned in: 5 Iliad
father: 6 Peleus
mother: 6 Thetis
foster father: 7 Phoenix
grandfather: 6 Aeacus
teacher: 6 Chiron
charioteer: 9 Automedon
friend: 9 Patroclus
warrior in: 9 Trojan War
vulnerability: 4 heel
killed: 6 Hector
killed by: 5 Paris

Achish
king of: 4 Gath
gave refuge to: 5 David

Achomawi
language family: 5 Hokan
location: 8 Pit River 10 California 12 Shasta County
related to: 8 Atsugewi

Achsah
father: 5 Caleb
grandfather: 9 Jephunneh
husband: 7 Othniel

acid 4 sour, tart 5 acrid, harsh, nasty, sharp 6 biting, bitter, ironic 7 acerbic, caustic, crabbed, cutting, pungent 8 scalding, scathing, stinging, vinegary 9 acidulous, irascible, sarcastic, satirical, vitriolic 10 astringent, vinegarish 11 acrimonious

acidity 8 acerbity, pungency, sourness, tartness 9 sharpness 10 bitterness 11 astringency 13 nonalkalinity

Acis
lover: 7 Galatea
killed by: 10 Polyphemus

Acis and Galatea
opera by: 6 Handel

Acis et Galatee
opera by: 5 Lully

acknowledge 3 own 5 admit, allow, grant, yield 6 accede, accept, answer, assent, concur 7 concede, confess, own up to, reply 8 call upon, thank for 9 recognize, respond to

acknowledged 7 acceded 8 accepted, admitted, answered, called on, conceded 9 replied to 10 agreed upon, called upon, recognized, thanked for 11 established, responded to

acknowledgment 5 reply 6 answer, credit, thanks 8 response 9 admission, gratitude 10 concession, confession 11 affirmation, recognition 12 appreciation, recognizance

acme 4 apex, peak 5 crest, crown 6 apogee, climax, height, heyday, summit, zenith 8 pinnacle 9 flowering, high point 11 culmination 12 highest point
Latin: 11 ne plus ultra

Acmon
companion: 8 Diomedes
changed into: 4 bird
defied: 9 Aphrodite

acolyte 3 fan 6 helper, novice 7 admirer, devotee, groupie 8 adherent, altar boy, follower 9 assistant, attendant

Acoma
language family: 6 Pueblo
location: 3 Ako 4 Acus 8 Valencia 9 New Mexico
noted for: 7 pottery

acorn
from: 3 oak
shape: 8 balanoid

a couvert 9 sheltered 10 under cover

acquaint 4 meet, tell 6 advise, inform, notify, reveal 7 apprise 8 disclose 9 divulge to, enlighten, introduce, make aware 11 familiarize

acquaintance 8 dealings 9 awareness, knowledge 10 cognizance, friendship 11 association, conversance, familiarity 12 relationship

acquiesce 5 admit, agree, allow, bow to, grant, yield 6 accede, assent, comply, concur, give in, submit 7 concede, conform, consent 10 capitulate, fall in with 13 resign oneself 16 reconcile oneself

acquiescence 5 leave 7 consent 8 approval, giving in, sanction 10 permission, submission 11 concurrence

acquiescent 7 willing 8 amenable, yielding 9 agreeable 10 submissive

acquire 3 get, win 4 earn, gain 6 attain, obtain, pick up, secure 7 achieve, capture, procure, realize 9 cultivate

acquirement 4 gain 5 prize 7 earning 10 attainment, obtainment, possession 11 achievement, acquisition, procurement

acquisition 4 gain 5 prize 8 property, purchase 10 attainment, obtainment, possession 11 achievement, acquirement, procurement

acquisitive 6 greedy 7 selfish 8 covetous, grasping 10 avaricious, possessive 13 materialistic

acquit 3 act 5 clear 6 behave, excuse, exempt, let off, pardon 7 absolve, comport, conduct, deliver, release, relieve, set free 8 liberate, reprieve 9 discharge, exculpate, exonerate, vindicate

Acraea
epithet of: 9 Aphrodite
means: 6 height

acre
one-fourth: 4 rood
one-half: 3 erf 5 erven
two-thirds: 5 cover
ten: 6 decare 7 hectare
one hundred: 7 hectare
one hundred twenty: 4 hide

Acres, Bob
character in: 9 The Rivals
author: 8 Sheridan

acrid 4 acid 5 harsh, nasty, sharp 6 biting, bitter, ironic, smelly 7 burning, caustic, pungent 8 stinging 9 sarcastic, satirical, vitriolic 10 irritating, malodorous 11 acrimonious 12 foul-smelling

acrimonious 4 sour 5 nasty, testy 6 bitchy, biting, bitter 7 caustic, cutting, peevish 8 venomous, spiteful 9 corrosive, irascible, rancorous, sarcastic, splenetic, vitriolic 10 ill-natured

acrimony 5 anger, scorn, spite 6 animus, rancor, spleen 7 ill will 8 asperity, derision 9 animosity, hostility, malignity 10 antagonism, bitterness, malignancy 12 hard feelings, spitefulness

Acrisius
king of: 5 Argos
father: 4 Abas
mother: 6 Aglaia
twin brother: 7 Proetus
daughter: 5 Danae
grandson: 7 Perseus
killed by: 7 Perseus

acrophobia
fear of: 7 heights

acrostic 6 cipher, puzzle 7 acronym

act 2 do 3 bit, gig, law 4 bill, deed, do it, fake, feat, move, play, pose, show, skit, step, work 5 edict, enact, feign, front, order, put-on 6 action, affect, behave, decree, stance 7 execute, exploit, go about, mandate, measure, operate, perform, portray, posture, press on, routine, statute 8 carry out, function, pretense, put forth, simulate 9 enactment, ordinance, represent 10 pretension, resolution 11 achievement, affectation, counterfeit, impersonate, legislation, performance, pretend to be 14 accomplishment

Actaeon
form: 6 hunter
father: 9 Aristaeus
mother: 7 Autonoe
changed into: 4 stag
transformed by: 5 Diana
killed by: 6 hounds
killed at: 9 Gargaphia

acting 5 drama 6 deputy, ersatz, pro tem 7 interim, theater 8 the stage 9 dramatics, simulated, surrogate, temporary 10 dramaturgy, stagecraft, substitute, the theater 11 dramatic art, officiating, provisional, thespianism 12 stage playing

actinium
chemical symbol: 2 Ac

action 3 act 4 deed, feat, move, step, suit, work 5 force, power 6 battle, combat, effect, effort, motion 7 exploit, process, warfare 8 activity, conflict, endeavor, exertion, fighting, movement, progress 9 adventure, execution, influence, operation 10 enterprise, excitement, performing, production 11 achievement, functioning, performance, prosecution 14 accomplishment

Actis
father: 6 Helius
mother: 5 Rhoda
crime: 10 fratricide
taught: 9 astrology
fled to: 5 Egypt
memorial: 16 Colossus of Rhodes

activate 4 stir 5 drive, impel, start 6 prompt, propel, turn on 7 actuate 8 energize, mobilize, motivate, vitalize 9 stimulate

activated 5 drive 7 started 8 impelled, in action, in effect, turned on 9 effective, energized, mobilized, operative, vitalized 10 stimulated 11 in operation

active 4 busy, spry 5 agile, alert, alive, peppy, quick 6 acting, at work, frisky, lively, nimble 7 engaged, in force, on the go, working, zealous 8 animated, diligent, forceful, occupied, spirited, vigorous 9 ambitious, assertive, effectual, energetic, gogetting, operative, sprightly, strenuous 10 aggressive, productive 11 functioning, imaginative, industrious 12 enterprising 13 indefatigable

active person 4 doer 6 dynamo 7 hustler 8 activist, go-getter

activist 4 doer 6 zealot 7 apostle 8 advocate, exponent 9 proponent, supporter

activity 4 fuss, stir 6 action, bustle, flurry, hustle, tumult 7 project, pursuit, venture 8 endeavor, exercise, exertion, function, goings on, movement, vivacity 9 agitation, animation, avocation, commotion 10 assignment, enterprise, hurly-burly, liveliness, occupation 11 undertaking 13 sprightliness

act of the faith
Spanish: 8 auto da fe, auto de fe

act of war 4 raid 6 attack, strike 7 assault, offense 8 invasion 10 aggression, hostile act

actor 3 ham 4 doer, star 6 player, walk on 7 starlet, trouper 8 thespian 9 bit player, performer 11 functionary, participant, perpetrator 14 dramatic artist 15 supporting actor
type: 4 hero 7 feature, leading 9 character 10 supporting

Actor
king of: 6 Phthia
father: 8 Myrmidon
mother: 8 Pasidice
brother: 6 Augeas
son: 7 Cteatus, Eurytus

actual 4 real, sure, true 7 certain, current, factual, genuine, present 8 bona fide, concrete, existent, existing, physical, tangible 9 authentic, confirmed, corporeal 10 legitimate, prevailing, true-to-life, verifiable

actuality 4 fact, life 5 being, truth 6 effect, living, verity 7 reality 8 existing 9 existence, plain fact, substance 10 brutal fact 11 point of fact

actually 5 truly 6 indeed, in fact, really, verily 9 genuinely, literally
Latin: 7 ex facto

actually existing
Latin: 6 in esse 7 de facto

actuary 5 clerk 9 tabulator 12 statistician

actuate 4 move, stir 5 cause, drive, impel, rouse 6 arouse, excite, incite, induce, prompt 7 animate, inspire, trigger 8 activate, motivate 9 influence, instigate, stimulate 10 bring about

acumen 6 wisdom 7 insight 8 keenness, sagacity 9 acuteness, ingenuity, smartness 10 astuteness, cleverness, perception, shrewdness 11 discernment 12 intelligence, perspicacity 13 sound judgment 15 clearheadedness

acute 4 keen 5 sharp 6 clever, fierce, peaked, severe 7 intense, very bad 8 critical, piercing, powerful 9 agonizing, ingenious, intuitive, sensitive, very great 10 discerning, perceptive 11 distressing, penetrating 12 excruciating, needleshaped 14 discriminating

acuteness 6 acumen 8 keenness 9 sharpness, smartness 10 astuteness, cleverness, shrewdness

acute suffering 5 agony 7 anguish, torment, torture 8 distress

adage 3 saw 4 quip, wise 5 axiom, maxim, motto 6 cliche, dictum, old saw, saying, truism 7 epigram, precept, proverb 8 aphorism 9 platitude 11 observation

adagio
music: 4 slow

Adah
also: 9 Bashemath
husband: 4 Esau 6 Lamech
son: 5 Jabal, Jubal 7 Eliphaz

Adam
wife: 3 Eve
son: 4 Abel, Cain, Seth
home: 4 Eden
grandson: 4 Enas 5 Enoch

adamant 3 set 4 firm 5 fixed, rigid, tough 7 uptight 8 obdurate, resolute, stubborn 9 immovable, insistent, unbending 10 determined, hard as rock, inexorable, inflexible, unyielding 12 intransigent 14 uncompromising

Adamas
ally of: 7 Trojans
plotted against: 10 Antilochus
thwarted by: 8 Poseidon

Adamawa-Eastern
language family: 16 Niger-Kordofanian
group: 10 Niger-Congo
includes: 5 Sango, Zande

Adam Bede
author: 11 George Eliot
character: 8 Seth Bede 11 Dinah Morris, Hetty Sorrel 12 Martin Poyser 17 Arthur Donnithorne

Adams, Henry
author of: 6 Esther 9 Democracy 14 Chapters of Erie 24 History of the United States (Under the Jefferson and Adams Administration), The Education of Henry Adams 26 Mont-Saint Michel and

Chartres **34** The Degradation of the Democratic Dogma

Adams, John
nickname: **19** Atlas of Independence
presidential rank: **6** second
party: **10** Federalist
state represented: **2** MA
defeated: **9** Jefferson
vice president: **9** Jefferson
cabinet:
state: **8** (John) Marshall **9** (Timothy) Pickering
treasury: **6** (Samuel) Dexter **7** (Oliver) Wolcott
war: **6** (Samuel) Dexter **7** (James) McHenry
attorney general: **3** (Charles) Lee
navy: **8** (Benjamin) Stoddert
born: **2** MA **9** Braintree
town now called: **6** Quincy
died/buried: **6** Quincy
education: **7** Harvard
religion: **9** Unitarian
author: **18** Discourses on Davila **20** Thoughts on Government
political career: **13** vice president **24** First Continental Congress **25** Second Continental Congress
minister: **11** Netherlands **12** Great Britain
civilian career: **6** lawyer
notable events of lifetime/term: **9** XYZ Affair
act: **9** Judiciary **16** Alien and Sedition
father: **4** John
mother: **7** Susanna (Boylston)
siblings: **5** Elihu **13** Peter Boylston
wife: **7** Abigail (Smith)
children: **7** Charles, Susanna **10** John Quincy (6th president) **13** Abigail Amelia **14** Thomas Boylston

Adams, John Quincy
nickname: **14** Old Man Eloquent
presidential rank: **5** sixth
party: **4** Whig **10** Federalist **20** Democratic-Republican
state represented: **2** MA
defeated: **4** (Henry) Clay **7** (Andrew) Jackson **8** (William H) Crawford
vice president: **7** (John C) Calhoun
cabinet:
state: **4** (Henry) Clay
treasury: **4** (Richard) Rush
war: **6** (Peter Buell) Porter **7** (James) Barbour
attorney general: **4** (William) Wirt
navy: **8** (Samuel Lewis) Southard
born: **2** MA **9** Braintree
town now called: **6** Quincy
died: **2** DC **10** Washington
buried: **2** MA **6** Quincy
education:
studied in: **5** Paris **9** Amsterdam **11** Latin School
University of: **6** Leyden
College: **7** Harvard
religion: **9** Unitarian

author: **7** Memoirs **14** Eulogy to Monroe, The Adams Papers **17** Eulogy to Lafayette **18** Letters from Silesia
political career: **8** US Senate **19** Massachusetts Senate **24** US House of Representatives
secretary of: **5** state
minister: **6** Russia **7** Prussia **8** Portugal **11** Netherlands **12** Great Britain
civilian career: **6** lawyer
notable events of lifetime/term: **19** Pan-American Congress **20** Tariff of Abominations
father: **4** John
mother: **7** Abigail (Smith)
siblings: **7** Abigail, Charles, Susanna **14** Thomas Boylston
wife: **6** Louisa (Catherine Johnson)
children: **4** John **14** Charles Francis **15** Louisa Catherine **16** George Washington

Adams, Parson
character in: **13** Joseph Andrews
author: **8** Fielding

Adams, Richard
author of: **4** Maia **7** Shardik **12** Girl in a Swing **13** The Plague Dogs, Watership Down

Adam's Rib
director: **11** George Cukor
script by: **10** Ruth Gordon **11** Garson Kanin
cast: **8** Tom Ewell **9** Jean Hagen **10** David Wayne **12** Judy Holliday, Spencer Tracy **16** Katharine Hepburn

Adapa
origin: **8** Akkadian
form: **4** sage
forfeits: **4** food **5** water **11** immortality
offered by: **3** Anu
patron: **2** Ea

adapt 3 fit **4** suit **5** alter, frame, shape **6** adjust, change, modify, rework **7** conform, convert, fashion, make fit, remodel, reshape **8** attune to **9** acclimate, harmonize, recompose, reconcile, transform **10** assimilate, coordinate **11** accommodate, acculturate **12** make suitable

adaptable 6 pliant, usable **7** unrigid **8** amenable, flexible, obliging **9** alterable, compliant, easygoing, malleable, tractable **10** adjustable, applicable, changeable, openminded **11** conformable, serviceable **13** accommodating, accommodative

adaptation 5 shift **6** change **8** revision **9** refitting, reshaping, reworking **10** adjustment, alteration, conversion, remodeling **12** modification **13** metamorphosis

Adar 18 twelfth Hebrew month

add 4 join **5** affix, sum up, total **6** append, attach, join on, reckon, tack on **7** combine, compute, count up, enlarge, include **8** figure up, increase **9** calculate, enlarge by **10** increase by, supplement

Addams, Frankie
character in: **19** A Member of the Wedding
author: **15** Carson McCullers

Addams Family, The
character: 5 Gomez, Lurch 7 Pugsley 8 Morticia 9 Grandmama, Wednesday 11 Uncle Fester
cast: 9 John Astin 10 Lisa Loring, Ted Cassidy 11 Blossom Rock 12 Carolyn Jones, Jackie Coogan 13 Ken Weatherwax

add details 6 expand 7 clarify 9 elaborate, embellish 13 particularize
added 5 extra 6 joined 7 totaled 8 appended, attached, computed, included, joined on, reckoned, summed up, tacked on 9 counted up 10 additional, enlarged by, enumerated 11 increased by 13 supplementary
addendum 7 codicil 8 addition 9 appendage 10 attachment, postscript, supplement 12 afterthought
addict 3 fan, nut 4 buff, head, hook, user 5 freak, hound 6 junkie, submit, turn on, votary 7 acolyte, devotee, druggie, habitue 8 adherent 9 dope fiend, indulge in, surrender
addiction 5 craze, mania, quirk 6 fetish, hangup 8 fixation 9 cocainism, obsession 10 alcoholism, compulsion, dipsomania, morphinism 11 barbiturism, enslavement 12 addictedness, enthrallment 13 preoccupation
adding machine
invented by: 6 Pascal 9 Burroughs
Addis Ababa
capital of: 8 Ethiopia
Addison, Joseph
author of: 4 Cato 9 The Tatler 12 The Spectator 13 The Freeholder
co-author: 13 Richard Steele
addition 4 wing 5 annex, extra 6 adding 7 adjunct, joining 8 addendum, additive, annexing, increase, totaling 9 adjoining, appendage, appending, attaching, embracing, expansion, extending, extension, including, increment, reckoning, summation, summing up 10 counting up, increasing 11 enlargement, enumeration 12 appurtenance, augmentation, encompassing
additional 5 added, extra, spare 7 added on 8 appended 12 over-and-above 13 supplementary
additional feature 5 extra 7 adjunct 10 attachment, complement, supplement 12 appurtenance 13 accompaniment
additive 5 extra 8 addition 10 adulterant, supplement 12 augmentation, preservative
addle 5 mix up 6 muddle 7 confuse, nonplus, stupefy 8 befuddle
addled 5 silly 7 foolish, mixed-up, muddled 8 confused 9 befuddled, nonplused 10 nonplussed
add on 5 affix 6 append, attach, tack on 7 include 10 increase by
address 4 talk 5 greet, orate 6 salute, speech, talk to 7 lecture, oration, speak to, write to 8 dwelling, locality, location 9 discourse, statement

Address to the Deil
author: 11 Robert Burns
add to 6 expand, extend, pad out 7 amplify, augment, bolster, enlarge 8 compound, increase, lengthen 10 strengthen, stretch out, supplement
Ade, George
author of: 13 Fables in Slang 15 The College Widow 17 The County Chairman
Aden
capital of: 10 South Yemen
adept 3 apt 4 able, good 6 adroit, expert, gifted, master 7 skilled 8 skillful 9 dexterous, ingenious, masterful, practiced 10 proficient 12 accomplished
adequacy 7 fitness 11 sufficiency 16 satisfactoriness
adequate 3 fit 4 so-so 5 ample 6 enough 7 fitting 8 passable, suitable 9 tolerable 10 sufficient 12 satisfactory
a deux 6 for two 10 two at a time
ad extremum 6 at last 7 finally 12 to the extreme
ad fin 8 at the end 12 toward the end
adhere 3 fix 4 glue, hold, keep 5 cling, paste, stick 6 be true, cement, cleave, fasten, glue on, keep to 7 abide by, be loyal, stand by 8 maintain 9 stick fast 10 be constant, be faithful
adherence 6 fealty 7 loyalty 8 adhesion, devotion, fidelity 9 constancy, keeping to, obedience 10 allegiance, attachment, observance, stickiness 12 adhesiveness, faithfulness
adherent 3 fan 4 ally 5 gummy, pupil 6 sticky, viscid 7 acolyte, devotee, viscous 8 adhering, adhesive, advocate, champion, clinging, disciple, follower, partisan, sticking, upholder 9 supporter
adhesion 9 adherence 10 attachment, sticking to
adhesive 4 glue 5 epoxy, gummy, paste 6 cement, gummed, mortar, solder, sticky 7 stickum 8 adherent, adhering, clinging, sticking 12 mucilaginous, rubber cement
ad hoc 17 with respect to this 18 for this purpose only
ad hominem 8 to the man 17 against an opponent 20 appealing to prejudice
adieu 4 by-by, ciao, ta-ta 5 adios, aloha 6 bye-bye, goodby, so long 7 a demain, cheerio, goodbye, good day 8 a bientot, au revoir, farewell, godspeed, toodle-oo 10 take it easy 11 leavetaking, see you later, valediction 14 Auf Wiedersehen
ad infinitum 9 endlessly 10 infinitely, to infinity, unendingly 11 boundlessly, ceaselessly, limitlessly, unceasingly 12 continuously, interminably, without limit
ad initium 14 at the beginning
ad interim 13 in the meantime
adios 4 by-by, ciao, ta-ta 5 adieu, aloha 6 bye-bye, goodby, so long 7 a demain, cheerio, goodbye, good day 8 a bientot, au revoir, farewell, godspeed, toodle-oo 10 take it easy 11 leavetaking, see you later, valediction 14 Auf Wiedersehen

adjacency 5 union 7 contact, meeting 8 abutment, junction, touching 11 proximation 13 juxtaposition

adjacent 6 beside, next to 8 abutting, touching 9 bordering, proximate 10 contiguous, juxtaposed, next door to, tangential 12 conterminous

adjoining 6 joined 7 joining 8 next-door, touching 9 connected 10 contiguous 14 interconnected

adjourn 3 end 4 move 5 close 6 put off, recess, remove, repair 7 dismiss, suspend 8 break off, dissolve, postpone, withdraw 9 depart for, interrupt 11 discontinue

adjournment 6 recess 7 removal 8 abeyance 9 dismissal 10 suspension 12 postponement

adjudge 4 rule 5 judge 6 decide, decree, ordain, rule on, settle, umpire 7 referee 8 consider 9 arbitrate, determine, pronounce 10 adjudicate

adjudicate 4 rule 5 judge 6 settle 7 adjudge 9 arbitrate

adjunct 9 accessory, auxiliary, secondary 10 complement, incidental, subsidiary, supplement 12 appurtenance

adjuration 4 oath, plea, suit 6 appeal 8 advising, entreaty 12 supplication

adjure 3 beg 5 plead 6 charge, enjoin, exhort 7 beseech, command, entreat, implore, solicit 8 appeal to, petition 9 importune 10 supplicate

adjust 3 fix, set 4 move 5 adapt, alter, order 6 attune, change, modify 7 conform 8 accustom, regulate 9 acclimate, reconcile 11 accommodate

adjustable 7 movable 9 adaptable, alterable 11 rectifiable, regulatable 12 controllable

adjusting 8 adapting, altering 9 modifying 10 regulating 11 acclimating, controlling

adjusting device 5 lever, tuner, valve 6 handle 7 adapter 8 governor 9 modulator, regulator 11 control knob

adjustment 6 fixing 7 control, setting 8 adapting, focusing 9 adjusting, alignment, regulator 10 alteration, regulating, regulation, settlement, settling in 11 acclimation, orientation 12 modification 13 justification, rectification, straightening 14 reconciliation

adjutant 4 aide 9 assistant, right hand 10 aide-de-camp 12 right-hand man

ad-lib 6 make up 9 improvise 11 extemporize 13 improvisation 14 speak impromptu 15 speak off the cuff 21 speak extemporaneously 23 extemporaneous wisecrack

ad loc, ad locum 10 at the place, to the place

Admah
  destroyed with: 5 Sodom 6 Zeboim 8 Gomorrah

ad majorem Dei gloriam 23 for the greater glory of God

Admete
  father: 10 Eurystheus
  received: 12 golden girdle
  belonged to: 4 Ares

  received from: 8 Hercules
  stolen from: 9 Hippolyte

Admeto, Re di Tessaglia
  also: 21 Admetus King of Thessaly
  opera by: 6 Handel

Admetus
  king of: 8 Thessaly
  member of: 9 Argonauts
  father: 6 Pheres
  wife: 8 Alcestis

administer 3 run 4 boss, give 5 apply 6 direct, govern, manage, tender 7 oversee 8 dispense 9 supervise 11 preside over, superintend 12 administrate

administering 7 bossing, running, tending 8 managing 9 directing, executing 10 dispensing, governance, overseeing 11 carrying out, supervising, supervision 14 administration, superintending

administrate 3 run 6 direct, govern, manage 9 supervise 10 administer 11 superintend

administration 5 brass 8 officers 9 execution, governing, tendering 10 executives, government, leadership, management, overseeing 11 application 12 dispensation, distribution 13 administering, governing body 15 superintendence

administrative 9 executive 10 management, managerial 11 supervisory 14 organizational

administrative head 7 manager 8 chairman, director 9 executive, president 10 supervisor 13 administrator 14 superintendent

admirable 6 worthy 8 laudable 9 estimable, venerable 11 commendable 12 praiseworthy

Admirable Crichton, The
  author: 12 James M Barrie

admiration 5 honor 6 esteem, praise 7 respect 8 approval 10 high regard, veneration 11 high opinion 12 commendation

admire 5 prize, value 6 esteem, praise 7 respect

admirer 3 fan 5 swain 6 suitor, votary 7 acolyte, devotee 8 adherent, advocate, champion, disciple, follower, partisan 9 attendant 10 aficionado

admissible 7 allowed 8 passable 9 allowable, permitted, tolerable, tolerated 10 acceptable, admittable, legitimate 11 permissible

admission 3 fee 5 entry 6 access, assent, charge, entree, tariff, ticket 8 entrance 10 admittance, concession, confession, profession 11 affirmation, declaration, entrance fee 14 acknowledgment

admit 3 let 5 allow, grant, let in, own up 6 induct, invest, permit 7 appoint, concede, confess, declare, profess, receive, welcome 8 let enter 11 acknowledge

admittable 7 allowed 9 allowable, permitted, tolerable, tolerated 10 acceptable, admissible 11 permissible

admittance 5 entry 6 access, entree 7 ingress 8 entrance 9 admission

admixture 4 mess 5 blend 6 jumble, medley 7 amalgam, melange, mixture 8 compound, mishmash 9 composite, confusion, potpourri 10 commixture, hodgepodge, salmagundi 11 combination, commingling, gallimaufry 12 amalgamation, intermixture 13 intermingling 14 conglomeration

admonish 4 warn 5 chide, scold 6 advise, enjoin, rebuke, tip off 7 caution, censure, chasten, counsel, reprove, upbraid 8 reproach 9 criticize, reprimand 10 put on guard, take to task 11 remonstrate 13 call to account 16 rap on the knuckles

admonition 6 advice, rebuke 7 chiding, warning 8 reproach, scolding 9 reprimand 11 mild reproof 12 remonstrance 16 rap on the knuckles

admonitor 7 advisor 9 counselor 10 admonisher

Adnah
  deserted from: 4 Saul
  deserted to: 5 David
  fought against: 10 Amalekites
  commander for: 10 Jehosaphat

ado 4 fuss, stir, to-do 5 furor 6 bother, bustle, flurry, fracas, furore, hubbub, pother, racket, tumult, uproar 7 flutter, trouble, turmoil 9 agitation, commotion, confusion 10 hurlyburly

adobe 3 mud 4 clay, silt, tile 5 brick, marly 6 earthy 7 clayish 13 sun-dried brick

adolescence 5 teens, youth 7 puberty 10 pubescence

adolescent 3 lad 4 lass, teen 5 minor, youth 6 boyish, callow, lassie 7 babyish, girlish, puerile 8 childish, immature, juvenile, teenager, young man, youthful 9 fledgling, pubescent, schoolboy, stripling, young teen 10 schoolgirl, sophomoric, young woman 11 undeveloped

Adolf Hitler 9 der Fuhrer 10 der Fuehrer

Adonai 3 God 6 my Lord

Adonia
  event: 8 festival
  honors: 6 Adonis

Adonijah
  father: 5 David
  mother: 7 Haggith
  brother: 5 Amnon 7 Absalom, Chileab
  executed by: 7 Solomon
  conspired to overthrow: 5 David

Adonis
  represents: 15 vegetation cycle
  father: 7 Cinyras
  mother: 6 Myrrha, Smyrna
  favorite of: 9 Aphrodite
  killed by: 4 boar
  festival in honor of: 6 Adonia

adopt 3 use 4 take 6 accept, affect, assume, choose, employ, follow, take up 7 approve, embrace, espouse, utilize 9 conform to 11 acknowledge, appropriate

adorable 6 divine 7 darling, likable, lovable, winsome 8 charming, engaging, fetching, pleasing, precious 9 appealing 10 delightful 11 captivating 12 irresistible

adoration 5 honor 7 worship 8 devotion 9 adulation, reverence 10 exaltation, veneration, worshiping 11 idolization 13 glorification, magnification

adore 4 like, love 5 exalt, fancy, prize 6 admire, dote on, revere 7 cherish, glorify, idolize, worship 8 hold dear, venerate

adorer 3 fan 5 lover 7 admirer 8 follower 9 worshiper

adorn 5 array 6 bedeck 7 bejewel, deck out, furbish 8 beautify, decorate, ornament 9 embellish

adornment 6 attire, finery 7 jewelry 8 ornament 10 decoration 13 embellishment, ornamentation

ad patres 4 dead

Adrammelech 13 Sepharvite god
  father: 11 Sennacherib
  killed: 11 Sennacherib

Adrastea
  also: 7 Nemesis
  origin: 5 Greek
  goddess of: 17 divine retribution
  father: 9 Melisseus
  reared: 4 Zeus
  entrusted by: 4 Rhea

Adrastos *see* 8 Adrastus

Adrastus
  also: 8 Adrastos
  king of: 5 Argos
  son: 8 Aegialus
  leader of: 18 Seven against Thebes
  companions: 6 Tydeus 8 Capaneus 9 Polynices 10 Amphiaraus, Hippomedon 13 Parthenopaeus
  horse: 5 Arion

ad rem 9 pertinent 15 straightforward 17 without digression

Adrian, Edgar Douglas
  field: 8 medicine 10 physiology
  nationality: 7 British
  discovered function of: 10 nerve cells
  awarded: 10 Nobel Prize

Adriana
  character in: 17 The Comedy of Errors
  author: 11 Shakespeare

adrift 4 lost 5 at sea 6 afloat, aweigh 8 confused, drifting, unmoored, unstable 9 perplexed, uncertain, unsettled 10 bewildered, irresolute, unanchored

adroit 3 apt 4 deft 5 slick 6 artful, clever, expert, facile, nimble 7 cunning, skilled 8 skillful 9 dexterous, masterful 10 proficient

adroitness 7 aptness 8 deftness, facility 9 dexterity, handiness 10 cleverness 11 proficiency 12 skillfulness
  French: 11 savoir-faire

adulation 7 fawning 8 flattery 9 adoration 11 fulsomeness 13 fulsome praise

adulatory 7 fulsome 8 admiring 10 flattering 13 complimentary

adult 3 big, man 5 elder, of age, woman 6 father, granny, mature, mother, parent, senior 7 grandma, grandpa, grownup, oldster 8 seasoned 9 developed, full-grown 11 experienced, grandfather, grandmother 13 senior citizen

adulterate 3 cut 4 thin 5 water 9 water down 10 depreciate 11 contaminate

adulterated 3 cut 6 impure, watery 7 debased, diluted, thinned, watered 8 doctored, weakened 11 watered down

adultery 9 carnality, cuckoldry 10 unchastity 11 fornication, promiscuity 14 unfaithfulness 17 marital infidelity 18 illicit intercourse 21 extramarital relations

adulthood 8 maturity, ripeness 10 full growth 11 age of reason

adumbrate 3 dim 6 darken, sketch 7 obscure, outline 8 intimate 9 prefigure 10 foreshadow, overshadow

adumbrated 3 dim 5 murky 7 shadowy 8 darkened 9 intimated 10 indistinct, prefigured 12 foreshadowed, overshadowed

advance 3 pre 4 gain, pass, step 5 add to, offer, prior 6 assign, binder, growth, move up, pay now, propel, send up 7 bring up, forward, further, improve, in front, lay down, press on, proffer, promote, upgrade, up front 8 foremost, increase, multiply, overture, previous, progress 9 go forward, promotion 10 furthering, move onward, prepayment, put up front 11 advancement, down payment, improvement, preliminary, proposition 12 breakthrough, bring forward, pay on account

advanced 7 extreme, far gone, radical 10 avant-garde 12 farther along, further along 14 industrialized

advanced in years 3 old 4 aged 5 hoary, older 7 ancient, antique, elderly 8 outmoded 9 senescent, venerable 10 antiquated, gray-haired

advancement 4 rise 5 boost 9 bettering, elevation, promotion 10 betterment, forwarding 11 improvement, progression

Advancement of Learning
    author: 12 Francis Bacon

advance slowly 4 inch 5 crawl, creep

advantage 3 aid 4 boon, edge, help 5 asset, clout 6 profit 7 benefit, comfort, service, success, support 8 blessing 9 dominance, upper hand 10 precedence 11 convenience, superiority

advantageous 6 useful 7 helpful 8 enviable, superior, valuable 9 favorable, fortunate 10 auspicious, beneficial, dominating, profitable

advent 5 onset, start 6 coming 7 arrival 9 appearing, beginning, emergence, opening up 10 appearance, occurrence 12 commencement

adventitious 5 alien 6 exotic 7 foreign, strange 9 adventive, extrinsic 10 accidental

adventure 5 quest 7 emprise, venture 8 escapade 10 enterprise 11 undertaking

adventurer 4 hero 7 heroine 8 romantic, vagabond 9 buccaneer, daredevil 11 giant-killer 12 dragonslayer, swashbuckler 16 soldier of fortune

Adventures of Robin Hood, The
    director: 13 Michael Curtiz 15 William Keighley

    cast: 8 Alan Hale (Little John) 10 Errol Flynn (Robin Hood) 11 Claude Rains (Prince John) 13 Basil Rathbone 17 Olivia de Havilland (Lady Marion)
    Oscar for: 5 score (Erich Wolfgang Korngold)

Adventures of Sherlock Holmes
    author: 16 (Sir) Arthur Conan Doyle
    character: 9 Mrs Hudson 10 Irene Adler 12 Dr John Watson 13 Mycroft Holmes 14 Sherlock Holmes 17 Inspector Lestrade, Professor Moriarty 21 Baker Street Irregulars

adventuresome 4 bold 6 daring 9 audacious, daredevil 11 adventurous

adventurous 4 bold 5 brave, risky 6 daring 7 valiant 8 intrepid, perilous 9 audacious, dangerous, hazardous 10 courageous 11 challenging, venturesome

adventurousness 6 daring 8 audacity, boldness 11 intrepidity

ad verbum 8 verbatim 9 to the word

adversary 3 foe 5 enemy, rival 8 opponent 10 antagonist, competitor

adverse 7 harmful, hostile 8 contrary, inimical, negative, opposing 9 difficult, injurious 10 pernicious, unfriendly 11 detrimental, unfavorable 12 antagonistic, unpropitious

adversity 3 woe 5 trial 6 mishap 7 bad luck, trouble 8 calamity, disaster, distress, hardship 9 suffering 10 affliction, illfortune, misfortune 11 catastrophe, tribulation

advertise 4 show, tout 5 vaunt 6 reveal 7 display 8 proclaim 9 broadcast, publicize 11 noise abroad

advertisement 5 blurb, flier, pitch, promo 6 notice, poster, want ad 7 leaflet, placard, trailer 8 circular, handbill 9 billboard, broadside, throwaway 10 commercial 12 announcement, classified ad, public notice

advice 4 news, view, word 6 report 7 account, counsel, message, opinion, tidings 8 guidance 10 advisement, suggestion 11 information 12 intelligence, notification 13 communication 14 recommendation

advisable 3 fit 4 best, wise 5 smart, sound 6 proper, seemly 7 fitting, prudent 8 a good bet, suitable 9 expedient, judicious 13 recommendable

advise 4 tell, urge, warn 6 enjoin, exhort, inform, notify, report 7 apprise, caution, commend, counsel, suggest 8 admonish 9 encourage, make known, recommend, suggest to 10 give notice 11 communicate

advise against 8 dissuade 10 discourage, disincline

advisement 5 study 7 thought 12 deliberation 13 consideration

adviser, advisor 4 aide 5 coach, guide, tutor 6 mentor 7 monitor, teacher 8 director 9 admonisher, assistant, counselor, preceptor, surrogate 10 consultant, idea person, instructor

advisory 7 guiding, warning **10** admonitory, cautionary, counseling **11** informative, instructive **12** consultative, consultatory **13** informational

advisory board 7 cabinet, council **8** ministry

advocaat
   type: **7** liqueur
   origin: **7** Holland

advocacy 5 aegis **7** backing, defense, support **8** auspices, espousal **9** patronage, promotion **10** furthering, supporting **11** advancement, endorsement, pressing for, propagation, sponsorship **12** championship **14** campaigning for, recommendation

advocate 4 back, urge **5** favor **6** advise, backer, lawyer, patron **7** advance, apostle, counsel, endorse, espouse, further, pleader, promote, propose, push for, support **8** argue for, attorney, believer, champion, defender, press for, promoter, upholder **9** apologist, barrister, counselor, encourage, prescribe, propagate, proponent, recommend, solicitor, spokesman, supporter **10** mouthpiece, stand up for **11** campaign for, speak out for **12** legal adviser, propagandist, spokesperson **13** attorney-at-law

advocatus diaboli 14 devil's advocate

adz 2 ax **3** axe **5** addis **7** hatchet

Aeacides
   descendants of: **6** Aeacus

Aeacus
   form: **5** judge
   habitat: **5** Hades
   father: **4** Zeus
   mother: **6** Aegina
   brother: **12** Rhadamanthys
   wife: **6** Endeis
   son: **6** Peleus, Phocus **7** Telamon
   grandson: **8** Achilles

Aechmagoras
   father: **8** Hercules
   mother: **6** Phialo

Aedon
   father: **9** Pandareus
   sister: **8** Chelidon
   husband: **11** Polytechnus
   transformed into: **11** nightingale
   transformed by: **4** Zeus

Aeetes
   king of: **7** Colchis
   custodian of: **12** Golden Fleece
   father: **6** Helios
   mother: **5** Perse
   sister: **5** Circe **8** Pasiphae
   wife: **5** Idyia **9** Asterodea
   son: **8** Absyrtus, Apsyrtus
   daughter: **5** Medea **9** Chalciope

Aegaeon see **8** Briareus

Aegean Sea
   branch of: **13** Mediterranean
   islands: **5** Chios, Crete, Samos **6** Euboea, Lesbos, Rhodes **8** Cyclades **10** Dodecanese **16** Northern Sporades
   rivers into: **6** Struma, Vardar **7** Maritsa **8** Menderes

   surrounding countries: **6** Greece, Turkey

Aegeon
   character in: **17** The Comedy of Errors
   author: **11** Shakespeare

Aegeria see **6** Egeria

Aegesta see **6** Egesta

Aegeus
   king of: **6** Athens
   son: **6** Medeus **7** Theseus

Aegialeus
   father: **8** Adrastus
   killed by: **8** Laodamas

Aegicores
   father: **3** Ion

Aegimius
   king of: **5** Doris **7** Dorians
   father: **5** Dorus
   son: **5** Dymas **9** Pamphylus

Aegina
   father: **6** Asopus
   mother: **6** Metope
   son: **6** Aeacus
   abducted by: **4** Zeus

Aeginaea
   epithet of: **7** Artemis
   means: **11** goat goddess

Aegiochus
   epithet of: **4** Zeus
   means: **11** aegis bearer

Aegipan
   form: **3** god **4** goat
   related to: **3** Pan

Aegir
   origin: **6** Nordic
   form: **5** giant
   god of: **3** sea
   wife: **3** Ran

aegis 4 wing **5** favor, guard **6** surety **7** backing, shelter, support **8** advocacy, auspices, guaranty **9** patronage **10** protection **11** sponsorship **12** championship, guardianship

Aegis
   form: **6** shield
   shield of: **4** Zeus **6** Athena

Aegisthus
   father: **8** Thyestes
   mother: **7** Pelopia
   cousin: **9** Agamemnon
   daughter: **7** Erigone
   seduced: **12** Clytemnestra
   killed by: **7** Orestes

Aegle
   member of: **8** Heliades **10** Hesperides
   mother of: **6** Graces

Aegyptus
   king of: **5** Egypt
   father: **5** Belus
   twin brother: **6** Danaus
   number of sons: **5** fifty

Aella
   form: **6** Amazon
   gift: **9** swiftness
   killed by: **8** Hercules

Aello
   member of: **7** Harpies

aelurophobia
  fear of: 4 cats
Aemilia
  character in: 17 The Comedy of Errors
  author: 11 Shakespeare
Aeneas
  hero of: 4 Troy
  father: 8 Anchises
  mother: 5 Venus
  grandfather: 5 Capys
  son: 5 Iulus 7 Silvius 8 Ascanius
  ancestor of: 6 Romans
Aeneas Silvius
  king of: 9 Alba Longa
Aeneid
  author: 6 Virgil
  character: 4 Gyas 5 Amata, Dares, Ni-
    sus 6 Arruns, Iarbas, Lausus, Pallas,
    Salius, Turnus 7 Acestes, Allecto,
    Camilla, Celaeno, Drances, Evander,
    Harpies, Helenus, Juturna, Latinus,
    Lavinia, Tarchon, Trojans, Venulus, Vir-
    bius 8 Ascanius, Entellus, Euryalus, Mes-
    sapus 9 Cloanthus, Mezentius, Mnes-
    theus, Palinurus, Sergestus 10 An-
    dromache 12 Cumaean Sibyl
  gods: 4 Juno 5 Diana, Venus 6 Vulcan 7
    Jupiter, Neptune
  Queen of Carthage: 4 Dido
  Aeneas' father: 8 Anchises
  Aeneas' mother: 9 Aphrodite
  Aeneas' wife: 6 Creusa
  Aeneas' son: 5 Iulus
  Aeneas meets in underworld: 6 Charon
    8 Cerberus 9 Palinurus
  parts of the underworld: 7 Elysium 8
    Tartarus 9 Ivory Gate
  river: 4 Styx 5 Lethe
  Aeneas plucks: 11 Golden Bough
  Aeneas visits: 5 Crete, Delos 6 Latium,
    Sicily, Thrace 8 Carthage
Aenius
  ally of: 4 Troy
  killed by: 8 Achilles
Aeolides
  descendants of: 6 Aeolus
Aeolus
  ruler of: 5 winds
  founder of: 8 Aeolians
  father: 6 Hellen
  mother: 6 Orseis
  brother: 5 Dorus 6 Xuthus
  wife: 7 Enarete
  son: 5 Deion 6 Magnes 7 Athamas,
    Misenus 8 Cretheus, Macareus, Perieres,
    Sisyphus 9 Salmoneus
  daughter: 6 Calyce, Canace 7 Alcyone 8
    Cleobule, Perimede, Pisidice
aerate 3 air 9 ventilate 10 mix with air 11
  expose to air
aerial 3 air 4 airy 5 by air, lofty 6 dreamy,
  flying, unreal 7 antenna, elusive, soaring,
  tenuous 8 airborne, ethereal, fanciful, in
  the air 9 ephemeral, imaginary, visionary
  10 by aircraft, from the air, of aircraft 11 atmospheric, impractical, wind-created 13
  unsubstantial 15 capable of flight

aerobatic group 10 Blue Angels
aeronautics 6 flight, flying 8 aviation
Aerope
  father: 7 Catreus, Cerheus
  husband: 6 Atreus 10 Plisthenes
  sister: 9 Clymene
  son: 8 Menelaus 9 Agamemnon
aerophobia
  fear of: 6 flying
aeroplane 5 plane 8 aircraft, airplane
Aesacus
  father: 5 Priam
  lover: 8 Hesperia
Aeschylus
  author of: 8 Oresteia 9 Agamemnon,
    Choephori (The Libation-bearers),
    Eumenides 11 The Persians 13 The Sup-
    pliants 15 Prometheus Bound 16 The
    House of Atreus 18 Seven Against
    Thebes
Aesculapius
  origin: 5 Roman
  god of: 7 healing 8 medicine
  corresponds to: 9 Asclepius
Aesepus
  mother: 9 Abarbarea
  twin brother: 7 Pedasus
  fought in: 9 Trojan War
  killed by: 8 Euryalus
Aesir
  also: 4 Asar
  origin: 12 Scandinavian
  leader: 4 Odin 5 Othin
  home: 6 Asgard
  conflicting with: 5 Vanir
aesthetic see 8 Esthetic
Aesyetes
  son: 7 Antenor
Aethalides
  member of: 9 Argonauts
  father: 6 Hermes
  trait: 6 memory
Aether
  origin: 5 Greek
  personifies: 3 air, sky
Aetheria
  member of: 8 Heliades
  father: 6 Helius
  mother: 7 Clymene
Aethra
  father: 8 Pittheus
  son: 7 Theseus
Aethylla
  brother: 5 Priam
Aetolus
  founder of: 7 Aetolia
  father: 8 Endymion
  brother: 5 Epeus, Paeon
  wife: 6 Pronoe
  son: 7 Calydon, Pleuron
  killed: 8 Laodocus
Afars and the Issas see 8 Djibouti
affability 9 geniality 10 amiability, cordiality
  11 sociability 12 friendliness, pleasantness
  13 compatibility

affable 4 open, warm 5 civil 6 genial 7 amiable, cordial 8 friendly, gracious, mannerly, pleasant, sociable 9 agreeable, congenial, courteous, easygoing 10 compatible 11 good-humored, good-natured

affair 5 amour, event, party 6 effort, matter 7 concern, episode, liaison, pursuit, romance, shindig 8 activity, business, function, incident, interest, intrigue, occasion 9 adventure, festivity, happening, operation 10 love affair, occurrence, proceeding 11 celebration, transaction, undertaking 12 circumstance, relationship 14 social function 15 social gathering

affaire d'honneur 4 duel 13 affair of honor

affect 4 fake, move, stir 5 act on, adopt, alter, fancy, feign, put on, touch 6 assume, change, modify, regard 7 embrace, concern, imitate, impress 8 interest, relate to, simulate 9 impinge on, influence, pertain to, pretend to 10 tend toward 11 counterfeit

affectation 4 airs, sham 5 put-on 6 facade 8 false air, pretense 10 pretension 11 insincerity 13 artificiality, false mannerism

affected 4 vain 5 moved, phony, sorry, upset 6 harmed, unreal 7 assumed, changed, grieved, injured, pompous, stirred, studied, touched 8 impaired, mannered, troubled 9 acted upon, afflicted, concerned, conceited, contrived, impressed, pertinent, sorrowful, unnatural 10 artificial, distressed, influenced, interested, not genuine 11 pretentious 12 vainglorious

affectedness 4 airs 7 hauteur, tension 9 formality 10 constraint 11 haughtiness, pretensions 12 affectations 15 pretentiousness

affection 4 love 6 liking, malady, warmth 7 ailment, disease, illness 8 disorder, fondness, sickness 10 proclivity, tenderness

affectionate 4 fond, warm 6 ardent, caring, doting, loving, tender 11 warmhearted 13 demonstrative, tenderhearted

affectionate term 7 pet name 8 nickname 9 sobriquet 10 endearment

Affery
   character in: 12 Little Dorrit
   author: 7 Dickens

affettuoso
   music: 8 tenderly

affiance 6 engage, pledge 7 betroth 13 engage to marry 15 solemnly promise

affiancing 5 troth 8 pledging 9 betrothal 10 engagement

affiche 6 poster 12 public notice

affidavit 4 oath 8 document 11 affirmation 14 sworn statement

affiliate 3 arm 4 ally, join, part 5 merge, unite 6 branch 7 chapter, connect, consort 8 division 9 associate, colleague 10 amalgamate, fraternize 11 incorporate, subdivision 12 band together

affiliated 6 allied, joined, united 9 connected 10 associated 12 incorporated

affiliation 5 union 8 alliance 10 connection 11 association 12 relationship

affinity 4 bent 5 fancy 6 liking 7 leaning, rapport 8 fondness, homology, likeness, penchant, relation, sympathy, tendency 10 connection, partiality, proclivity, propensity, similarity 11 inclination, parallelism 13 compatibility

affirm 4 aver, avow, hold 5 claim 6 allege, assert, ratify, uphold 7 approve, confirm, contend, declare, endorse, profess, support, sustain, warrant 8 maintain, proclaim, validate

affirmation 6 avowal 7 consent 8 approval 11 declaration, endorsement 12 confirmation, ratification 13 certification

affirmative 3 yes 8 emphatic, positive 9 affirming, approving, assenting, ratifying 10 conclusive, concurring, confirming 11 affirmatory, categorical 12 confirmatory 13 corroborative

affix 3 fix, tag 4 glue, seal 5 add on, paste, put on, set to, stick to 6 attach, fasten, tack on

afflict 5 beset 6 plague 7 oppress, torment 8 distress

afflicted 6 cursed 7 plagued 8 affected, troubled 9 tormented 10 distressed

affliction 4 pain 5 curse, trial 6 misery, ordeal 7 anguish, torment, trouble 8 calamity, distress, hardship 9 adversity 10 misfortune, oppression 11 tribulation 12 wretchedness

affluence 5 money 6 plenty, riches, wealth 7 success 10 prosperity 14 prosperousness, successfulness

affluent 4 rich 6 loaded 7 moneyed, wealthy, well-off 8 well-to-do 9 well-fixed 10 prosperous, well-heeled

afford 4 bear, give, lend, risk 5 grant, offer, yield 6 chance, impart, manage, supply 7 command, furnish, provide, support, sustain

affray 4 fray 5 brawl, melee 6 fracas 7 contest, scuffle 8 conflict 9 encounter 11 altercation

affright 4 fear 5 alarm, dread, panic, scare 6 dismay, fright, horror, terror 8 frighten

affront 4 slur 5 abuse, wrong 6 injury, insult, offend, slight 7 offense, outrage, provoke, put-down 8 disgrace, dishonor, ignominy, rudeness 9 indignity, insolence 11 discourtesy, humiliation 12 ill-treatment, impertinence 13 mortification 16 contemptuousness

afghan 5 shawl, throw 7 blanket 8 covering, coverlet

Afghanistan
   other name: 6 Ariana, Aryana
   capital/largest city: 5 Kabul
   others: 3 Rui 4 Jurm, Nani, Wama 5 Asmar, Balkh, Doshi, Farah, Herat, Kunar, Makur, Maruf, Matun, Pahra, Tagab, Tulak, Urgan 6 Chaman, Gardez, Ghazni, Haibak, Kunduz, Nauzad, Panjao, Rustak, Sangan, Sarobi, Tukzar, Washir 7 Andkhui, Baghlan, Bamiyan, Dilaram, Ghurian, Girishk 8 Charikar, Faizabad, Kandahar 9 Jalalabad 10

Daulatabad, Pul-i-Khumri, Shibarghan 12
Mazar-i-Sharif
government:
parliament: 10 Loya-Jirgah
leader: 4 amir, emir 5 ameer 6
sharif, sherif
measure: 3 paw, sir 5 jerib, karoh 6
khurds 7 kharwar
monetary unit: 3 pul 5 abaze, riyal, rupee 6 abbasi, amania 7 afghani
weight: 3 pau, paw, ser, sir
lake: 13 Hamud-i-Helmand
mountain: 3 Koh 5 Safeo 6 Chagai, Pamirs 7 Nowshak 8 Koh-i-Baba, Safed
Koh, Sulaiman 9 Himalayas, Hindu Kush
11 Khwaja Amran, Paropamisus
highest point: 9 Istoro Nal
river: 4 Lora, Oxus 5 Cabul, Indus, Kabul, Kunar 6 Kokcha, Kunduz 7 Hari Rud,
Helmand, Helmund, Murghab, Taleqan 8
Amu Darya, Farah Rud, Harut Rud,
Khash Rud 9 Arghandab
sea: 5 Darya
physical feature:
desert: 8 Registan
panhandle: 6 Wakhan
pass: 6 Khyber
wind: 9 Afghanets
people: 5 Aimak, Aymak, Kafir, Nuris 6
Baloch, Baluch, Chahar, Durani, Hasara,
Hazara, Kaffir, Kirgiz, Pathan, Tajiks, Uz-
beks 7 Beluchi, Belucki, Ghilzai, Pakhton,
Pakhtun, Pashtun, Pukhtun, Pushtun,
Sistani, Taimani, Taimuri 8 Jamshidi, Siah
Push 9 Firuzkuhi, Safed Push, Safid
Push
dynasty: 8 Barakzai
leader: 5 Najib 7 Mohmand 10 Najibullah
12 Babrak Karmal 14 Hafizullah Amin 17
Mohammad Zahir Shah, Mohammed
Daoud Khan 18 Burhanuddin Rabbani
Noor Mohammed Taraki
language: 4 Dari 5 Farsi 6 Afghan,
Pashto, Pushtu 7 Balochi, Baluchi, Persian
religion: 5 Islam
place:
dam: 6 Boghra 7 Kajakai 9 Arghandab
feature:
clothing: 7 chaderi
coat: 6 chapan
dance: 5 attan
game: 8 buz-kashi
guest room: 5 hujra
hat: 7 karakul
head-cloth: 7 chawdar
house with tower: 4 qala
medicinal plant: 9 asafetida
wrestling: 6 ghosai
food:
potluck meal: 6 sohbat
aficionado 3 fan, nut 5 freak, pupil 7 devotee, pursuer, student 8 disciple
afield 5 amiss 6 abroad, astray 10 off the
mark 11 out of the way 16 off the right
track

afire 5 fiery 6 ablaze, aflame, alight, ardent,
fervid, fuming, on fire 7 blazing, burning,
fervent, flaming, flaring, glowing, ignited,
smoking, zealous 8 afflicker, in flames, inspired 10 flickering, smoldering
afloat 5 at sea 6 adrift, wafted 7 sailing,
wafting 8 drifting, floating
afoot 5 astir 8 underway 10 in the works
a fortiori 10 all the more
afraid 5 sorry 6 scared 7 alarmed, anxious,
chicken, fearful, panicky, unhappy 8 cowardly, timorous 9 regretful, terrified 10
apologetic, frightened 11 lily-livered 12 apprehensive, disappointed, fainthearted 13
anxiety-ridden, panic-stricken 14 chicken-
hearted, chicken-livered, terror-stricken
Afreet
  also: 5 Afrit
  origin: 7 Arabian
  form: 5 demon
afresh 4 anew 5 again 11 from scratch 16
from the beginning
  Latin: 6 de novo
Africa
  country: 4 Chad, Mali, Togo 5 Benin,
Congo, Egypt, Gabon, Ghana, Kenya,
Libya, Niger, Sudan, Zaire 6 Angola,
Gambia, Guinea, Malawi, Rwanda,
Uganda, Zambia 7 Algeria, Burundi,
Comoros, Eritrea, Lesotho, Liberia, Mo-
rocco, Namibia, Nigeria, Reunion, Sene-
gal, Somalia, Tunisia 8 Botswana, Cam-
eroon, Djibouti, Ethiopia, Tanzania,
Zimbabwe 9 Cape Verde, The Gambia,
Mauritius, Swaziland 10 Ivory Coast,
Madagascar, Mauritania, Mozambique,
Seychelles 11 Burkina Faso, Sierra
Leone, South Africa 13 Guinea-Bissau 13
Canary Islands, Western Sahara 15
South-West Africa 16 Equatorial Guinea
18 Sao Tome and Principe 22 Central Af-
rican Republic
  people: 2 Ga 3 Ibo, Kru, Luo, San, Tiv,
Yao 4 Arab, Beja, Bobo, Boer, Fang,
Hutu, Kota, Kuba, Luba, Nuba, Nuer,
Nupe, Teda, Tibu, Zulu 5 Bemba, Dinka,
Galla, Hausa, Kamba, Makua, Masai,
Mende, Mongo, Negro, Pygmy, Rundi,
Serer, Shona, Sotho, Swazi, Temne, Ti-
gre, Tutsi, Wolof, Xhosa 6 Bateke, Ber-
ber, Fulani, Herero, Ibibjo, Kikuyu, Mau
Mau, Nubian, Ovambo, Rwanda, Senufo,
Sidamo, Somali, Tswana, Tuareg, Yo-
ruba, Watusi 7 Ashanti, Baganda, Bam-
bara, Bushmen, Chaamba, Makonde,
Mashoma, Ndebele, Nilotic, Oshogbo,
Songhai, Turkana 8 Khoikhoi, Mangbetu,
Matabele 9 Africaner, Hottentot
  desert: 5 Namib 6 Sahara 8 Kalahari
  island: 5 Bioko, Pemba 6 Canary 7
Comoros, Madeira, Mayotte, Reunion 8
St Helena, Zanzibar 9 Ascension, Cape
Verde, Mauritius 10 Madagascar, Sey-
chelles
  ancient people/empire: 3 Oyo 4 Kush,
Mali, Toro 5 Aksum, Benin, Ghana,
Kongo, Mossi, Nubia, Wadai 6 Ankole,

Tekrur 7 Ashanti, Buganda, Bunyoro, Dahomey, Songhai 8 Baguirmi, Carthage 10 Kanem-Bornu, Monomotapa 11 Ife and Benin
ancient city: 5 Kilwa, Meroe 8 Timbuktu
language: 4 Afar, Peul, Teda 5 Bantu, Bemba, Click, Hausa, Masai, Wolof 6 Arabic, Berber, French, Kanuri, Tsonga 7 Amharic, Khoisan, Lingala, Nilotic, Songhai, Swahili, Turkana 8 Cushitic, Mandingo 9 Afrikaans
river: 4 Juba, Nile, Sudd 5 Congo, Kasai, Niger 6 Kwango, Orange, Ubangi 7 Senegal, Zambezi 8 Blue Nile 9 White Nile
lake: 4 Chad, Kivu, Tana 5 Assal, Nyasa 6 Albert, Edward, Kariba, Malawi, Nassar, Red Sea, Rudolf 8 Victoria 10 Tanganyika 12 Chott Melrhir
falls: 8 Victoria
mountain/mountain range: 3 Air 4 Bihu, Meru 5 Atlas, Elgon, Kenya 6 Hoggar 7 Ahaggar, Crystal, Tibesti, Toubkal 8 Cameroon 9 Emi Koussi, Munchinga, Ruwenzori 10 Futa Jallon 11 Drakensberg, Kilimanjaro 13 Tibesti Massif
lowest point: 17 Qattari Depression
mineral/natural resource: 3 oil, tin 4 gold 5 ivory 6 cloves, copper, rubber 7 diamond, palm oil, uranium
disease: 4 AIDS 7 malaria 9 bilharzia 11 yellow fever 16 sleeping sickness
homeland: 5 Venda 6 Ciskei 8 Transkei 14 Bophuthatswana
game reserve: 5 Tsavo 6 Kruger 8 Amboseli 9 Serengeti
tree: 4 cork, teak 5 cedar, ebony, olive 6 acacia, baobab, okoume, rubber 7 juniper, oil palm 8 date palm, mahogany, tamarisk 10 silk-cotton
animal: 4 lion 5 bongo, hippo, hyena, zebra 6 jackal, monkey 7 buffalo, cheetah, giraffe, gorilla, leopard, wild pig 8 aardvark, antelope, elephant 9 crocodile 10 chimpanzee, rhinoceros 11 wildebeeste 12 hippopotamus
bird: 5 heron, stork 6 falcon 7 bustard, ostrich, pelican 8 flamingo, hornbill 10 kingfisher
fly: 6 tsetse
snake: 5 cobra, mamba 6 python

Africaine, L'
also: 14 The African Girl
opera by: 9 Meyerbeer

African Queen, The
director: 10 John Huston
cast: 12 Robert Morley 14 Humphrey Bogart 16 Katharine Hepburn
setting: 5 Congo
Oscar for: 5 actor (Bogart)

Afrit see 6 Afreet

after 4 next, post 5 later 6 behind 9 afterward, following 10 conclusion, subsequent, succeeding

aftereffect 6 result 11 consequence

After Hours
director: 14 Martin Scorsese
cast: 12 Griffin Dunne 15 Rosanna Arquette

Afterlife
god of: 4 Gwyn

aftermath 6 payoff, result, sequel, upshot 7 outcome 8 follow-up, offshoot 9 byproduct 11 consequence

afterpart 4 back, tail 6 far end 7 back end, rear end, tail end 8 backside, hind part 9 posterior

after the fact 4 late 5 tardy 7 belated, delayed, too late 10 behindhand, behind time

After the Fall
author: 12 Arthur Miller

after this, therefore because of it
Latin: 21 post hoc ergo propter hoc
describes: 14 logical fallacy

afterword 4 coda 8 addendum, epilogue 10 conclusion

Agacles
king of: 9 Myrmidons

Agag
king of: 10 Amalekites
captured by: 4 Saul
killed by: 6 Samuel

again 4 also, anew, more 7 besides 8 moreover, once more 10 in addition, repetition 11 another time, duplication, furthermore 12 additionally
Latin: 6 de novo

against 7 adverse, opposed 8 conflict, contrary, opposite 10 opposition 11 unfavorable

against an opponent
Latin: 9 ad hominem

Against Our Will
author: 16 Susan Brownmiller

against the property
Latin: 5 in rem
describes: 15 legal proceeding

against the thing
Latin: 5 in rem

Agamede
father: 6 Augeas
husband: 6 Mulius
gift: 7 healing
healed with: 5 herbs

Agamemnon
author: 9 Aeschylus
mentioned in: 5 Iliad
king of: 7 Mycenae
leader of: 6 Greeks
fought in: 9 Trojan War
father: 6 Atreus
brother: 8 Menelaus
sister: 8 Anaxibia
wife: 12 Clytemnestra
daughter: 7 Electra 9 Iphigenia 12 Chrysothemis
son: 7 Orestes
cousin: 9 Aegisthus
captive: 9 Cassandra
Clytemnestra's lover: 9 Aegisthus
killed by: 12 Clytemnestra

Aganippe 8 fountain
 location: 6 Greece 7 Helicon
 sacred to: 5 Muses
Aganus
 father: 5 Paris
 mother: 5 Helen
agape 4 agog 6 amazed, gaping 8 wide
 open 9 awestruck, stupefied 10 astonished, dumbstruck, spellbound 11 dumbfounded 12 wonderstruck 13 flabbergasted
Agassiz, Jean Louis Rodolphe
 field: 7 zoology
 worked on: 7 fossils 8 glaciers 14 classification
Agastrophus
 father: 5 Paeon
 killed by: 8 Diomedes
agate
 species: 6 quartz
 variety of: 10 chalcedony
 type: 3 eye 4 moss, onyx, ring 9 landscape 13 fortification
 source: 4 Ider 6 Brazil 7 Uruguay 9
 Oberstein 14 Rio Grande de Sul
Agathon
 father: 5 Priam
Agathyrsus
 father: 8 Hercules
Agave
 father: 6 Cadmus
 mother: 8 Harmonia
 sister: 3 Ino 6 Semele 7 Autonoe
 husband: 6 Echion
 son: 8 Pentheus
age 3 eon, era 4 date 5 epoch, phase, ripen
 6 mature, mellow, period, season 7 develop, forever, make old 8 life span, lifetime 9 adulthood, a long time, grow older,
 seniority 10 generation, millennium 11
 stage of life, stage of time
 French: 6 siecle
aged 3 old 4 ripe 6 mature, mellow 7 ancient, as old as, elderly, ripened 8 enduring, grown old 9 developed, full-grown,
 long-lived
Agee, James
 author of: 10 Agee on Film 17 A Death
 in the Family 23 Let Us Now Praise Famous Men
 screenwriter for: 15 The African Queen
 19 The Night of the Hunter
Agelaus
 mentioned in: 5 Iliad 7 Odyssey
 occupation: 8 herdsman
 father: 8 Hercules, Phradmon
 mother: 7 Omphale
 courted: 8 Penelope
 raised: 5 Paris
 employer: 5 Priam
ageless 7 classic, eternal 8 enduring, timeless
agency 5 force, means, power 6 action, bureau, charge 8 activity 9 influence, mediation, operation 10 department, instrument
 12 intervention 15 instrumentality
agenda 6 docket 7 program 8 schedule 9
 timetable

Agenor
 mentioned in: 5 Iliad
 king of: 9 Phoenicia
 father: 7 Antenor 8 Poseidon
 mother: 5 Libya 6 Theano
 twin brother: 5 Belus
 wife: 10 Telephassa
 son: 5 Cilix 6 Cadmus 7 Phoenix
 daughter: 6 Europa
 gift: 7 bravery
agent 4 doer 5 cause, envoy, force, means,
 mover, power 6 agency, author, deputy,
 worker 7 vehicle 8 advocate, emissary, executor, operator 9 go-between, performer
 10 instrument, negotiator 11 perpetrator 12
 intermediary, practitioner 14 representative
Age of Innocence, The
 author: 12 Edith Wharton
 character: 10 May Welland 12 Ellen
 Olenska 13 Newland Archer
age-old 4 aged 7 ancient, antique, very old
 9 venerable
agglomerate 4 clot, mass 5 amass, bunch,
 clump, rally 6 gather, heap up, muster, pile
 up 7 cluster, collect 8 assemble, condense, mobilize 10 accumulate, collection
 12 accumulation, conglomerate, heap together, lump together 14 conglomeration
 15 gather into a mass
agglomeration 4 heap, mass, pile 5 bunch,
 clump 7 cluster 10 collection 12 accumulation 14 conglomeration
aggrandize 5 bloat, exalt, widen 6 beef up,
 blow up, dilate, expand, extend, puff up,
 step up 7 amplify, broaden, build up, distend, enhance, enlarge, inflate, magnify,
 stretch 8 escalate, increase 9 intensify 10
 strengthen
aggrandizement 8 increase, widening 9
 expansion, extension 10 broadening, escalation, exaltation, stepping up 11 enhancement, enlargement 13 amplification,
 magnification 15 intensification
aggravate 3 vex 4 rile 5 anger, annoy 6
 nettle, worsen 7 affront, inflame 8
 heighten, increase, irritate 9 intensify,
 make worse 10 exacerbate, exasperate
aggravating 7 irksome 9 inflaming, vexatious, worsening 10 irritating 11 heightening 12 exacerbating, exasperating, intensifying
aggregate 3 mix 4 mass 5 blend, union 7
 mixture 8 amassing, compound 9 composite, gathering, summation 10 collection
 11 combination 12 accumulation, conglomerate 14 conglomeration
aggregation 3 mob 4 army, band, bevy,
 crew, gang, host, mass, pack 5 crowd,
 horde, swarm 6 throng 7 cluster 9 multitude 10 collection
aggression 4 raid 7 assault, offense 8 act
 of war, invasion 9 hostility, pugnacity 11 viciousness 12 belligerence 13 combativeness
aggressive 4 bold 5 harsh, pushy 7 dynamic, hostile, intense, vicious, warlike,
 warring, zealous 8 forceful, militant 9 am-

bitious, assailant, assertive, attacking, combative, energetic 10 pugnacious 11 belligerent, competitive, contentious, quarrelsome 12 antagonistic, enterprising 13 self-assertive 15 tending to attack

aggressiveness 9 hostility, pugnacity 10 antagonism 12 belligerence 13 combativeness

aggressor 7 invader 8 attacker 9 assailant 11 belligerent 12 antagonistic

aggrieved 3 sad 4 hurt 5 stung 6 abused, pained 7 injured, put upon, tearful, wounded, wronged 8 grieving, mournful, offended, saddened, troubled 9 affronted, disturbed, sorrowful 10 distressed, illtreated, maltreated, persecuted 11 imposed upon 13 grief-stricken

aghast 6 amazed 7 shocked, stunned 8 appalled 9 astounded, horrified, terrified 10 astonished, fear-struck, frightened 12 horror-struck 13 thunderstruck

agile 4 keen, spry 5 alert, fleet, lithe, quick, swift 6 active, clever, limber, nimble, supple 8 athletic, graceful 9 dexterous

agility 8 alacrity, spryness 9 dexterity, quickness, swiftness 10 limberness, nimbleness 12 gracefulness

agitate 3 jar, mix 4 beat, goad, rock, stir 5 alarm, churn, shake, upset 6 excite, foment, stir up, work up 7 disturb, provoke, shake up, trouble 8 disquiet

agitated 6 uneasy 7 anxious, frantic, nervous 8 confused, seething 9 disturbed, perturbed, unsettled 10 disquieted, distracted, distraught 11 discomfited, discomposed 12 disconcerted

agitation 7 anxiety 9 confusion 10 discomfort, uneasiness 11 disquietude, distraction, nervousness 12 discomfiture, discomposure, perturbation

agitato
  music: 8 agitated

agitator 7 inciter 8 fomentor, inflamer, provoker 9 firebrand 10 incendiary, instigator 11 provocateur 12 rabble-rouser, troublemaker 13 mischief-maker, revolutionary 16 agent provocateur

Aglaia
  member of: 6 Graces
  father: 7 Jupiter
  mother: 8 Eurynome
  sister: 6 Thalia 10 Euphrosyne
  husband: 4 Abas
  son: 7 Proteus 8 Acrisius
  daughter: 7 Idomene

Aglauros see 8 Agraulos

Aglaus
  father: 8 Thyestes
  mother: 5 Naiad
  killed by: 6 Atreus

aglow 4 warm 5 fiery 6 ablaze, red-hot 7 blazing, glowing, radiant, shining

Agnes Grey
  author: 10 Anne Bronte
  character: 8 Mr Weston 13 Rosalie Murray

agnostic 5 pagan 7 atheist, doubter, heathen, heretic, infidel, skeptic 10 empiricist, free spirit, secularist, unbeliever 11 disbeliever, freethinker, nonbeliever 14 doubting Thomas

ago 4 gone, over, past 5 since 6 gone by 7 earlier 8 backward 15 retrospectively

agog 5 astir 7 excited 8 thrilled, worked up 9 awestruck 10 enthralled 11 openmouthed

Agon
  ballet by: 10 Stravinsky

agonize 5 labor, sweat, worry 6 strain, suffer 7 anguish, wrestle 8 struggle

agonizing 6 severe 7 painful, racking 8 grievous, worrying 9 suffering, torturous 10 tormenting, unbearable 11 distressing, intolerable, unendurable 12 excruciating, insufferable

agony 3 woe 4 pain 5 trial 6 effort, misery, sorrow, strain, throes 7 anguish, anxiety, torment, torture 8 distress, striving, struggle 9 suffering 10 affliction 11 tribulation

Agony and the Ecstasy, The
  author: 11 Irving Stone

Agoraea
  epithet of: 6 Athena
  means: 16 of the marketplace

Agoraeus
  epithet of: 4 Zeus 6 Hermes
  means: 16 of the marketplace

agoraphobia
  fear of: 10 open spaces

Agraeus
  epithet of: 6 Apollo
  means: 6 hunter

agrarian 5 rural 7 farming 8 pastoral 11 agronomical, crop-raising 12 agricultural

Agraulos
  also: 8 Aglauros
  father: 7 Actaeus
  husband: 7 Cecropa
  daughter: 9 Pandrosos

agree 4 jibe 5 admit, allow, chime, grant, match, tally 6 accede, accept, accord, assent, concur, settle, square 7 concede, conform, consent, support 8 coincide, side with 9 harmonize, subscribe 10 correspond, think alike

agreeable 7 fitting 8 amenable, in accord, pleasant, pleasing, suitable 9 approving, complying, congenial 10 acceptable, concurring, consenting, gratifying 11 appropriate
  German: 9 gemutlich

agreeableness 7 amenity 9 geniality 10 amiability 11 sociability 12 pleasantness

agreed
  French: 7 d'accord

agreed upon 6 common, normal 8 accepted, approved 9 confirmed, customary 10 acceptable 11 established 12 acknowledged

agreement 4 deal, pact 6 accord 7 analogy, bargain, compact, concert, concord, harmony, promise 8 affinity, alliance, contract, covenant 10 accordance, compliance, conformity, settlement, similarity 11 arrangement, concordance, conformance 13 compatibility 14 correspondence

agricultural 4 farm 5 rural 7 farming 8 agrarian 9 gardening 11 agronomical, crop-raising 13 nonindustrial

agriculture 7 farming, tillage 8 agronomy 9 geoponics, husbandry 10 agronomics 11 crop-raising, cultivation 15 market gardening

Agriculture
    god of: 4 Dago 5 Dagan, Dagon, Picus 6 Saturn 12 Bonus Eventus
    goddess of: 5 Ceres 6 Brigit, Dea Dia, Vacuna

Agriope *see* 8 Eurydice

Agrius
    member of: 8 Gigantes
    form: 7 centaur
    mother: 5 Circe
    father: 8 Odysseus
    son: 9 Thersites
    attacked: 8 Hercules

agronomics 7 farming, tillage 8 agronomy 9 geoponics 11 agriculture, crop-raising

agronomy 7 farming 9 gardening, husbandry 11 agriculture, cultivation

Agrotera
    epithet of: 7 Artemis
    means: 8 huntress

aground 5 stuck 6 ashore 7 beached 8 grounded, stranded 9 foundered

ague 5 chill, fever 7 malaria, shivers 12 sweating fits

Aguecheek, Sir Andrew
    character in: 12 Twelfth Night
    author: 11 Shakespeare

Agyius
    epithet of: 6 Apollo
    means: 15 god of the streets

Ah, But Your Land Is Beautiful
    author: 9 Alan Paton

Ah! Wilderness
    author: 12 Eugene O'Neill

Ahab
    character in: 8 Moby Dick
    author: 8 Melville

Ahab
    father: 4 Omri
    wife: 7 Jezebel
    son: 7 Ahaziah
    daughter: 8 Athaliah
    opposed: 6 Elijah
    killed by: 4 Aram

Ahasuerus
    known as: 6 Xerxes 8 Cyaxares
    wife: 6 Esther
    divorced: 6 Vashti
    son: 6 Darius
    eunuchs: 6 Biztha, Carcas, Zethar 7 Abagtha, Harbona, Mehuman
    servant: 7 Abagtha
    conqueror of: 7 Nineveh

Ahaz
    father: 6 Jotham

Ahaziah
    father: 4 Ahab 7 Jehoram
    mother: 7 Jezebel 8 Athaliah
    uncle: 7 Jehoram
    defeated by: 6 Hazael
    killed by: 4 Jehu
    died at: 7 Megiddo

ahead of time 5 early 6 before, in time, sooner 7 betimes, earlier 9 before now, in advance 10 beforehand, in good time 13 before the fact

Ahib 16 first Hebrew month

Ahiezer
    father: 11 Ammishaddai

Ahimelech
    father: 6 Ahitub
    son: 8 Abiathar
    killed by: 4 Saul
    friend: 8 Ahuzzath

Ahithophel
    counseled: 5 David
    rebelled with: 7 Absalom
    granddaughter: 9 Bathsheba

Ahuzzath
    friend: 9 Abimelech
    visited: 5 Isaac

Aias *see* 4 Ajax

aid 4 abet, alms, dole, help 5 serve 6 assist, foster, relief 7 advance, charity, further, promote, subsidy, support, sustain 8 donation, minister 9 allowance 10 assistance, contribute, facilitate 11 accommodate, helping hand 12 contribution

Aida
    opera by: 5 Verdi
    character: 4 Aida 6 Ramfis 7 Amneris, Radames 8 Amonasro, Rhadames

aide 5 gofer 6 deputy, helper 7 abettor, acolyte 8 adherent, adjutant, follower, retainer, sidekick 9 assistant, associate, auxiliary, man Friday 10 aide-de-camp, apprentice, girl Friday, lieutenant 11 helping hand, subordinate 12 right-hand man

aide-de-camp 4 aide 6 helper 8 adjutant 9 assistant, man Friday, right hand 12 right-hand man

aide memoire 4 memo, note 10 memorandum

aider 4 aide 6 helper 7 abettor 9 assistant 11 helping hand

Aidos
    origin: 5 Greek
    personifies: 10 conscience

Aiken, Conrad Potter
    author of: 6 Ushant 10 Blue Voyage 12 Reviewer's ABC 14 The Charnel Rose 15 Earth Triumphant

Aiken, Howard H
    field: 11 mathematics
    designed: 15 digital computer

ail 4 pain 5 annoy, be ill, upset, worry 6 be sick, bother, sicken 7 afflict, make ill, trouble 8 be infirm, be unwell, distress 12 be indisposed, fail in health

ailing 3 ill 4 sick 6 infirm, sickly, unwell 8 delicate

ailment 6 malady 7 disease, illness 8 disorder, sickness, weakness 9 complaint, infection, infirmity 10 affliction, disability, discomfort 13 indisposition

ailurophobia
  fear of: 4 cats

aim 3 try 4 beam, goal, mean, plan, seek, want, wish 5 essay, focus, level, point, sight, slant 6 aiming, design, desire, direct, intend, intent, object, scheme, strive, target 7 attempt, be after, purpose, take aim, train on 8 ambition, aspire to, endeavor 9 intention 10 aspiration, have in mind, have in view, work toward 11 have an eye to, line of sight 12 marksmanship

aim at 4 seek 6 pursue, target 8 aspire to, shoot for

aimless 6 chance, random 7 erratic, wayward 8 unguided 9 frivolous, haphazard, hit-or-miss, pointless, unfocus(s)ed 10 accidental, rudderless, undirected 11 purposeless, unorganized 12 inconsistent, unsystematic 13 directionless, unpredictable 14 indiscriminate

aine 5 elder 6 eldest

Ainsworth, William Harrison
  author of: 8 Boscobel, Crichton, Rookwood 9 Guy Fawkes 10 Old St Paul's 12 Jack Sheppard 13 Windsor Castle 16 The Flitch of Bacon, The Tower of London 17 The Miser's Daughter, The South Sea Bubble 20 The Lancashire Witches

Ainu
  language spoken in: 8 Hokkaido, Sakhalin

air, airs 3 lay, sky 4 aura, look, mood, puff, song, tell, tone, tune, vent, waft, wind 5 blast, carol, ditty, draft, ozone, style, swank, utter, voice, whiff 6 aerate, ballad, breath, breeze, expose, manner, melody, reveal, spirit, strain, zephyr 7 declare, display, divulge, exhibit, express, feeling, hauteur, quality 8 ambience, disclose, pretense, proclaim 9 arrogance, publicize, ventilate 10 appearance, atmosphere, make public 11 haughtiness, pretensions 12 affectations, affectedness, stratosphere 16 superciliousness
  god of: 5 Enlil
  goddess of: 6 Ninlil

airborne 5 aloft 6 aerial 8 in flight 12 off the ground

aircraft 3 jet, SST 4 bird 5 blimp, crate, plane 6 copter, glider 7 balloon, chopper, prop-jet, zeppelin 8 airplane, jumbo jet 10 helicopter, whirlybird

air current 4 puff, wind 5 blast, draft, whiff 6 breeze, zephyr 11 breath of air

airdrome, aerodrome 7 airbase, airport, jet base 8 airfield 11 flying field 12 landing field

airfield 7 air base, airport, jet base 8 airstrip 11 flying field 12 landing field, landing strip

airfoil
  insect: 4 wing

airless 8 stifling 10 overheated, sweltering 16 poorly ventilated

airplane 3 jet 4 bird 5 crate, plane 7 airship, prop-jet 8 aircraft 9 aeroplane 11 flying jenny 19 heavier-than-air craft 20 propeller-driven plane
  invented by:
    automatic pilot: 6 Sperry
    jet engine: 5 Ohain
    with motor: 12 Wilbur Wright 13 Orville Wright 14 Wright Brothers
    hydro: 7 Curtiss
  first: 5 Flyer
  part: 3 fin 4 flap, nose, tail, wing 5 cabin, cargo, pylon 6 rudder 7 aileron, cockpit, turbine 8 elevator, fuel tank, fuselage, throttle, turbofan, turbojet 9 empennage, propeller, turboprop 10 flight deck, power plant, stabilizer 11 landing gear 13 undercarriage
  kind: 3 MIG 4 Zero 5 Eagle, Gotha, Piper, Sabre 6 Boeing, Cessna, Fokker, Mirage 7 Concorde, Piper Cub 10 Beechcraft, Dornier Do-X 11 Piper Navajo 12 Lockheed Vega, Sopwith Camel 13 Boeing Clipper, Messerschmitt, Piper Cherokee, Super Fortress 14 Cessna Citation, Flying Fortress, Grumman Hellcat, Stratofortress 15 Hawker Hurrican 16 De Havilland Comet
  variation: 3 SST 4 STOL, VTOL 5 blimp, drone, VSTOL 6 bomber, glider 7 airship, fighter 8 zeppelin 10 hang glider, helicopter, supersonic
  battle: 8 dog fight

airport 5 field 7 air base, jet base 8 airdrome, airfield, airstrip 9 aerodrome 11 flying field 12 landing field, landing strip

airship 5 blimp 7 balloon 9 dirigible 19 lighter-than-air craft

airship, rigid dirigible
  invented by: 8 Zeppelin

airstrip 6 runway 12 landing field, landing strip

air weapon
  German: 9 Luftwaffe

airy 5 light, merry, sunny, windy 6 breezy, cheery, drafty, dreamy, jaunty, lively 8 cheerful, ethereal, fanciful, gossamer, illusory, spacious 9 idealized, imaginary, sprightly 10 frolicsome, immaterial 11 unrealistic 12 lighthearted, light-of-heart 13 unsubstantial 14 well-ventilated

aisle 3 way 4 lane, path, walk 5 alley 6 avenue 7 passage, walkway 8 cloister, corridor 10 ambulatory, passageway

Aius Locutius
  form: 5 voice
  warned: 6 Romans
  warned of: 14 Gallic invasion

ajar 4 open 5 agape 6 gaping 8 unclosed 10 partly open

Ajax
  also: 4 Aias
  called: 9 Great Ajax 10 Oilean Ajax 11 Locrian Ajax 13 Ajax the Lesser 14 Telamonian Ajax

king of: 7 Locrius
father: 6 Oileus 7 Telamon
mother: 6 Periboea
brother: 6 Teucer
author: 9 Sophocles
character: 8 Achilles, Odysseus 9 Agamemnon
son: 9 Eurysaces
slave: 8 Tecmessa
seer: 7 Calchas
rescued body of: 8 Achilles
violated shrine of: 6 Athena
killed in: 9 shipwreck

Akela
character in: 14 The Jungle Books
author: 7 Kipling
Akeldama *see* 8 Aceldama

Akh
origin: 8 Egyptian
transfiguration of: 4 dead

Akihito
position: 7 emperor 11 crown prince
reign name: 6 Heisei 17 Establishing Peace
family:
father: 5 Showa 8 Hirohito
mother: 6 Nagako
wife: 7 Michiko
children: 4 Hito 8 Narahito
schools: 6 Oxford 9 Gakushuin

akin 3 kin 4 like 5 alike 6 allied 7 kindred, related, similar, uniform 8 agreeing, parallel 9 analogous, congenial, connected, identical 10 affiliated, comparable, resembling 11 correlative 13 corresponding 14 consanguineous

Akkad *see* 5 Accad

Akutagawa, Ryunosuke
author of: 5 Kappa 8 Rashomon 13 The Hell Screen

a la 9 in honor of 13 in the manner of

Alabama
abbreviation: 2 AL 3 Ala
nickname: 6 Cotton 12 Heart of Dixie, Yellowhammer
capital: 10 Montgomery
largest city: 10 Birmingham
others: 5 Selma 6 Athens, Dothan, Marion, Mobile 7 Decatur, Gadsden 8 Anniston 10 Huntsville, Tuscaloosa
colleges: 5 Miles 6 Auburn 7 Alabama 8 Tuskegee 9 Talladega 10 Huntingdon
explorer: 12 Herman DeSoto
feature:
festival: 11 Azalea Trail
statue: 6 Vulcan
tribe: 5 Creek 6 Tohome 7 Alabamu, Alibamu, Koasati 8 Tuskegee
people: 8 Joe Louis 9 Hank Aaron, Hugo Black 10 Willie Mays 11 Helen Keller, Nat King Cole 13 George Wallace, William C Handy, William Gorgas
lake: 12 Guntersville
land rank: 11 twenty-ninth
physical feature:
gulf: 6 Mexico
highest point: 6 Cheaha

highlands: 11 Appalachian
river: 3 Pea 5 Coosa 6 Mobile 7 Alabama 9 Tombigbee, Tennessee 10 Tallapoosa 13 Chattahoochee
state admission: 12 twenty-second
state bird: 7 flicker 12 yellowhammer
state fish: 6 tarpon
state flower: 8 camellia 9 goldenrod
state motto: 21 We Dare Defend Our Rights
state song: 7 Alabama
state tree: 20 southern longleaf pine

Alabama, Alibamu
language family: 9 Muskogean
location: 5 Texas 9 Louisiana 10 Polk County 12 Alabama River
related to: 7 Koasati

alacrity 4 zeal 6 fervor 7 agility, avidity 8 dispatch 9 alertness, briskness, eagerness, readiness 10 enthusiasm, liveliness, nimbleness, promptness 11 willingness 13 sprightliness

Aladdin
character in: 27 Arabian Nights' Entertainments

Al Aiun, El Aalun
capital of: 13 Western Sahara

a la mode 12 in the fashion, in the style of 13 in the manner of

Alarcon, Pedro Antonio de
author: 10 The Scandal 12 Captain Venom 14 El Nino de la Bola 19 The Three-Cornered Hat

alarm 4 fear 5 alert, panic, scare 6 appall, dismay, fright, terror, war cry 7 agitate, disturb, terrify, trouble, unnerve, warning 8 affright, distress, frighten 9 agitation, hue and cry, misgiving 11 trepidation 12 apprehension, perturbation 13 consternation

alarmed 6 afraid, scared 7 anxious, fearful, panicky, worried 8 dismayed 9 concerned, terrified 10 frightened 12 apprehensive 13 panic-stricken 14 terror-stricken

alarming 5 awful, dread 7 fearful 8 dreadful 10 horrifying, terrifying 11 frightening, hair-raising

alas
expresses: 4 pity 5 grief 6 sorrow 7 concern 9 weariness 11 unhappiness 12 wretchedness

Alaska
abbreviation: 2 AK 4 Alas
nickname: 9 Great Land, Sourdough 12 Last Frontier 20 Land of the Midnight Sun
capital: 6 Juneau
largest city: 9 Anchorage
others: 4 Nome 5 Sitka 6 Barrow, Kodiak 7 Cordova, Douglas, Skagway 9 Fairbanks, Ketchikan
feature: 5 Alcan 13 Alaska Highway
national park: 13 Mount McKinley
tribe: 3 Han 5 Aleut, Haida 6 Ahtena, Akkhas, Eskimo, Karluk, Tetlin 7 Amerind, Ingalik, Kayukon, Khotana, Kutchin, Tanaina, Tlingit, Tlinkit, Venetie 9 Tsimshian, Unakalett
island: 4 Adak, Atka 5 Aleut 6 Kodiak,

Unimak 7 Diomede, Nunivak 8 Aleutian,
Pribilof 9 Alexander
lake: 6 Naknek 7 Iliamna 8 Becharof 9
Teshekpuk
land rank: 5 first
mountain: 3 Ada 4 Muir 5 Coast 6
Alaska, Brooks 7 Foraker, St Elias 8
Aleutian, Wrangell 9 Blackburn
highest point: 8 McKinley
physical feature:
bay: 7 Glacier, Prudhoe
channel: 9 Gastineau
glacier: 9 Malaspina
pass: 8 Chilkoot
rapids: 10 Whitehorse
sea: 6 Arctic 8 Beaufort
strait: 6 Bering
river: 5 Kobuk, Yukon 6 Copper, Noatak,
Tanana 7 Koyukuk, Susitna 8 Colville 9
Kuskokwim, Matanuska, Porcupine
state admission: 10 forty-ninth
state bird: 15 willow ptarmigan
state fish: 10 king salmon
state flower: 11 forget-me-not
state motto: 16 North to the Future
state song: 11 Alaska's Flag
state symbol: 9 bald eagle
state tree: 11 sitka spruce
Aleskan Adventures
author: 8 Rex Beach
Alastor
epithet of: 4 Zeus 5 demon 11 avenging
god
means: 7 avenger
father: 13 Neleus of Pylos
brother: 6 Nestor
wife: 9 Harpalyce
killed by: 8 Hercules
Albach-Retty, Rosemarie
real name of: 13 Romy Schneider
Albania
other name: 8 Shqiperi 9 Shqiprija,
Shqyptare
capital/largest city: 6 Tirana, Tirane
others: 3 Opp 4 Fier, Klos, Puka, Puke 5
Berat, Dukat, Korce, Kruje, Pecin, Peqin,
Qukes, Rubic, Spash, Vlore 6 Avlona,
Bitsan, Dardhe, Durres, Karaje, Preshe,
Valona 7 Chimara, Coritza, Durazzo, El-
basan, Koritsa, Preyesa, Scutari,
Shkoder 8 Tepeleni 11 Gjirokaster
monetary unit: 3 lek 5 franc 6 qintar 7
quintar
island: 6 Saseno
lake: 4 Ulze 5 Matia, Ohrid 6 Prespa 7
Ochrida, Scutari, Shkoder 8 Ohridsko
mountain: 5 Shala 6 Pindus 8 Koritnjk
12 Albanian Alps
highest point: 10 Mount Korab
river: 3 Mat 4 Arta, Drin 5 Byene, Erzen,
Seman 6 Bojana, Bojane, Vijosa, Vijosa,
Vijose 7 Drin-i-ci, Shkumbi
sea: 6 Ionian 8 Adriatic
physical feature:
bay: 5 Vlore
cape: 6 Glossa

gulf: 4 Drin
lagoon: 10 Kara Vastas
peninsula: 6 Balkan
promontory: 13 acroceraunium
strait: 7 Otranto
wind: 4 bora
people: 3 Geg 4 Cham, Gheg, Gueg,
Tosk 6 Arnaut, Arnout 8 Illyrian, Skipetar
king: 3 Zog 9 Ahmet Zogu
leader: 4 Alia 5 Hoxha 7 Berisha 10
Scanderbeg, Skenderbeg 13 Bishop Fan
Noli
language: 3 Geg 4 Cham, Gheg, Hish,
Tosk 5 Greek 8 Albanian
religion: 5 Islam 7 Bektash 13 Roman
Catholic 15 Eastern Orthodox
place:
square: 10 Skenderbeg
feature:
lute: 6 luhata
soldier: 7 palikar
stone house: 4 kula
food:
cheese: 8 kackaval
Albanian
language family: 12 Indo-European
spoken in: 7 Balkans
Albee, Edward
author of: 3 Box 7 All Over 8 Seascape,
Zoo Story 9 Tiny Alice 10 The Sandbox
16 A Delicate Balance, The American
Dream 18 The Lady from Dubuque 21
The Ballad of the Sad Cafe, The Death of
Bessie Smith 25 Who's Afraid of Virginia
Woolf?
identified with: 18 theater of the absurd
Albeniz, Isaac
born: 5 Spain 9 Camprodon
composer of: 6 Iberia 12 The Magic
Opal 13 Henry Clifford
Alberich
origin: 8 Teutonic
king of: 6 dwarfs
possessed treasure of: 8 Niblungs 9 Nibelungs
also possessed: 9 Tarnkappe
Albert, Eddie
real name: 21 Eddie Albert Heimberger
wife: 5 Margo
born: 12 Rock Island IL
roles: 8 Oklahoma 10 Brother Rat,
Green Acres 11 Room Service 12 Roman
Holiday 16 The Longest Day 16 The
Heartbreak Kid 19 The Boys from Syracuse
Alberta
abbreviation: 4 Alta
capital/largest city: 8 Edmonton
others: 7 Calgary, Reddeer 10 Leth-
bridge 11 Medicine Hat
lakes: 5 Banff, Claire 6 Jasper 8
Waterton 9 Athabasca 11 Lesser Slave
rivers: 3 Bow 4 Milk 6 Oldman, Wapiti 9
Athabasca 12 Saskatchewan
religion: 13 Roman Catholic 20 United
Church of Canada 22 Anglican Church of
Canada

people: 5 Dutch 6 French, German 7 British, English 9 Ukrainian 12 Scandinavian

Albert Herring
opera by: 7 Britten

Alberti, Leon Battista
architect of: 15 Palazzo Rucellai 18 Church of Sant' Andrea, Temple Malatestiano 20 Church of San Sebastian 25 Church of Santa Maria Novello

Albertosaurus
type: 8 dinosaur, theropod
period: 10 Cretaceous

Albertson, Jack
born: 8 Malden MA
roles: 14 Chico and the Man 15 The Sunshine Boys 18 Days of Wine and Roses, The Subject Was Roses

album 2 LP 4 book 6 record 8 register 9 portfolio, scrapbook

Albunea
origin: 5 Roman
form: 5 nymph
habitat: 8 fountain

Alcaeus
father: 9 Androgeus
mother: 9 Andromeda
grandfather: 5 Minos
brother: 9 Sthenelus

Alcaids
descendants of: 7 Alcaeus

Alcandre
husband: 7 Polybus
received: 5 Helen 8 Menelaus

Alceste
opera by: 5 Gluck

Alcestis
author: 9 Euripides
character: 6 Apollo 7 Admetus 8 Heracles, Thanatos

Alcestis
father: 6 Pellas
mother: 8 Anaxibia 10 Phylomache
husband: 7 Admetus
son: 7 Eumelus 8 Hippasus
returned from: 5 Hades
returned by: 8 Hercules

Alchemist, The
author: 9 Ben Jonson
character: 4 Face 5 Surly 6 Dapper, Subtle 7 Ananias, Drugger, Kastril, Lovewit 9 Dol Common 10 Dame Pliant 16 Sir Epicure Mammon 20 Tribulation Wholesome

alchemy 5 magic 7 sorcery 8 wizardry 10 conversion, witchcraft 11 magic appeal 13 transmutation 17 medieval chemistry
god of: 6 Hermes

Alcides see 8 Hercules

Alcidice
husband: 10 Salmoneaus
daughter: 4 Tyro

Alcimede
father: 8 Phylacus
mother: 7 Clymene
husband: 5 Aeson
son: 5 Jason

Alcimedon
origin: 8 Arkadian
mentioned in: 5 Iliad
father: 7 Laerces
daughter: 6 Philao
captain of: 9 Myrmidons

Alcina
opera by: 6 Handel
character: 6 Alcina 8 Ruggiero

Alcindor, Lew
former name of: 17 Kareem Abdul-Jabbar

Alcinous
origin: 5 Greek
mentioned in: 7 Odyssey
king of: 10 Phaeacians
father: 10 Nausithous
mother: 8 Periboea
brother: 8 Rhexenor
wife: 5 Arete
son: 8 Laodamas
daughter: 8 Nausicaa
niece: 5 Arete

Alcis
father: 10 Antipoenus
sister: 9 Androclea

Alcithoe
father: 6 Minyas
mocked: 8 Dionysus

Alcmaeon
father: 10 Amphiaraus
mother: 8 Eriphyle
brother: 11 Amphilochus
wife: 10 Callirrhoe
son: 7 Acarnan 10 Amphoterus
daughter: 9 Tisiphone
commanded: 7 Thebans

Alcmaon
father: 7 Thestor
wounded by: 7 Glaucus
killed by: 8 Sarpedon

Alcmene
father: 9 Electryon
mother: 5 Anaxo
husband: 10 Amphitryon 12 Rhadamanthys
twin sons: 8 Hercules, Iphicles

alcohol 3 ale 4 beer, wine 5 drink 6 liquor 7 whiskey 9 the bottle
Latin: 9 aqua vitae

alcoholic 3 sot 4 hard, lush, soak 5 drunk, rummy, souse, toper 6 barfly, boozer, strong 7 guzzler, imbiber, tippler 8 drunkard 9 distilled, fermented, inebriate 10 spirituous 11 dipsomaniac, hard drinker, inebriating, inebriative, whiskey head 12 intoxicating

alcoholism 3 DT's 9 oenomania 10 dipsomania 12 intemperance 15 delirium tremens

Alcon
form: 6 archer, Trojan 7 warrior
aided: 8 Hercules
wounded: 8 Odysseus
abducted: 13 Geryons cattle
killed by: 8 Odysseus

Alcott, Louisa May
  author of: 7 Jo's Boys 9 Little Men 11 Little Women 12 Eight Cousins, Flower Fables 15 Aunt Jo's Scrap-Bag 18 An Old-Fashioned Girl

alcove 3 bay 4 nook 5 niche 6 corner, recess 7 cubicle, opening 11 compartment

Alcyone
  also: 7 Halcyon
  father: 6 Aeolus
  husband: 4 Ceyx
  son: 6 Anthas
  transformed into: 10 kingfisher

Alcyoneus
  form: 5 giant
  hurled: 5 stone
  victim: 8 Hercules
  killed by: 8 Hercules

Alda, Alan
  born: 9 New York NY
  father: 10 Robert Alda
  real name: 15 Alfonso D'Abruzzo
  roles: 4 MASH 9 Paper Lion 12 Sweet Liberty 13 Betsy's Wedding, Hawkeye Pierce 14 The Four Seasons 16 Same Time Next Year, The Mephisto Waltz

Alden, Roberta
  character in: 17 An American Tragedy
  author: 7 Dreiser

al dente 10 to the tooth

alder 5 Alnus
  varieties: 3 Red 5 Black, Hazel, White, Witch 6 Oregon, Smooth, Yellow 7 Italian, Seaside 8 Japanese, Mountain, Speckled 9 Caucasian 10 Manchurian 13 American green, European green

Aldiss, Brian W
  author of: 7 Non-Stop 9 Greybeard 13 The Saliva Tree 19 Frankenstein Unbound, The Billion Year Spree, The Eighty Minute Hour

ale 4 beer, brew 5 stout 12 malt beverage 15 English festival

Alea
  epithet of: 6 Athena
  means: 9 sanctuary

Alebion
  father: 8 Poseidon
  brother: 8 Dercynus
  killed by: 8 Hercules

Alecto
  member of: 6 Furies

alehouse 3 pub 6 saloon, tavern 7 taproom 11 public house

Aleichem, Sholom
  author of: 12 The Great Fair 14 Tevye's Daughter

Alembert, Jean le Rond d'
  field: 11 mathematics
  nationality: 6 French
  studied: 13 fluid dynamics 18 celestial mechanics 28 partial differential equations

Aleph and Other Stories
  author: 15 Jorge Luis Borges

alert 4 warn, wary 5 alarm, aware, quick, siren 6 active, inform, lively, nimble, notify, signal 7 careful, heedful, on guard, warning 8 diligent, forewarn, keen-eyed, vigilant, watchful 9 attentive, observant, sprightly, wideawake 10 perceptive 11 intelligent

alertness 8 alacrity, dispatch 9 awareness, readiness, vigilance 10 liveliness 12 watchfulness

Alethia
  origin: 5 Greek
  personifies: 5 truth

Aleus
  king of: 5 Tegea
  father: 7 Aphidas
  brother: 6 Pereus
  cousin: 6 Neaera
  wife: 6 Neaera
  son: 7 Cepheus 8 Lycurgus 10 Amphidamas
  daughter: 4 Auge

Aleut
  language family: 6 Eskimo
  tribe: 4 Atka 8 Unalaska
  location: 6 Alaska 15 Shumagin Islands 17 Aleutian Peninsula
  noted for: 7 hunting

Aleutians
  islands: 3 Fox, Rat 4 Near 9 Andreanof 25 Islands of the Four Mountains
  state: 6 Alaska
  people: 6 Aleuts
  language: 5 Atkan 9 Unalaskan

Alexander, Jane
  real name: 11 Jane Quigley
  born: 8 Boston MA
  roles: 9 Testament 17 The Great White Hope 18 Eleanor and Franklin 19 All the President's Men

Alexander's Feast
  author: 10 John Dryden

Alexander the Great
  battle: 5 Issus 9 Gaugamela
  birthplace: 5 Pella
  conquered: 6 Darius, Persia
  father: 8 Philip II
  founded: 10 Alexandria
  friend: 11 Hephaestion
  general: 7 Cleitus 8 Philotas 9 Parmenion
  horse: 10 Bucephalus
  mother: 8 Olympias
  nationality: 10 Macedonian
  tutor: 9 Aristotle
  wife: 6 Roxana

Alexandra see 9 Cassandra

Alexandrinus 16 Greek unical codex

alexandrite
  species: 11 chrysoberyl
  source: 8 Sri Lanka
  color: 3 red 5 green

Alexiares
  father: 8 Hercules
  mother: 4 Hebe

Alexicacus
  epithet of: 6 Apollo
  means: 13 averter of evil
Alfader *see* 7 Alfadir
Alfadir
  also: 7 Alfader
  origin: 12 Scandinavian
  epithet of: 4 Odin 5 Othin
Alfheim
  origin: 12 Scandinavian
  dwelling place of: 5 elves
  location: 11 above ground
Alfie
  director: 12 Lewis Gilbert
  based on play by: 12 Bill Naughton
  cast: 12 Michael Caine 14 Shelley Winters
alga, algae 6 fungus 8 pond scum
  contains: 4 agar 5 algin 11 carrageenan, chlorophyll
  type: 3 red 5 brown, green 9 blue-green, euglenids 11 golden-brown, yellow-green 15 dinoflagellates
  forms: 4 kelp 5 dulse 7 diatoms, seaweed 8 plankton, rockweed 9 Irish moss, stonewort
Alger, Horatio
  author of: 10 Ragged Dick 11 Tattered Tom 12 Luck and Pluck
Algeria
  other name: 7 Algerie, Numidia, Pomaria 9 al-Djazair
  capital/largest city: 7 Algiers
  others: 4 Bona, Bone, Oran 5 Aflou, Arzew, Batna, Blida, Medea, Saida, Setif, Tenes 6 Abadla, Annaba, Aumale, Barika, Bechar, Bejaia, Benoud, Biskra, Bougie, Dellys, Djanet, Djelfa, Dzioua, Eloued, Frenda, Guelma, Skikda 7 Boghari, Mascara, Miliana, Negrine, Nemours, Ouargla, Tebessa, Tlemcen 8 Ghardaia, Laghouat 9 Touggourt 11 Constantine 12 Sidi-bel-abbes
  division: 4 Oran 6 Annaba 7 Algiers 11 Constantine
  leader: 3 bey, dey 6 disawa 9 beylerbey
  measure: 3 pik 5 rebis, tarri 6 termin
  monetary unit: 5 dinar 7 centime
  weight: 4 rotl
  lake: 5 Hodna 6 Sabkha 7 Cherqui, Fedjadj, Meirhir 10 Azzel Matti, Mekerrhane
  mountain: 5 Aissa, Atlas, Aures, Dahra 6 Chelia 7 Ahaggar, Kabylia, Mouydir 8 Djurjura Djurdjura, Tell Atlas 12 Saharan Atlas
  highest point: 5 Tahat
  river: 6 Shelif 7 Cheliff 8 Medjerda 15 Cheliffmedjerda
  sea: 13 Mediterranean
  physical feature: 14 Tropic of Cancer
  desert: 6 Sahara
  giant sand dune: 3 erg
  grass: 4 diss 7 esparto
  hill: 4 tell
  oasis: 4 Mzab
  oil field: 7 Edjeleh, El Gassi 10

Zarzaitine 13 Hassi Messaoud (happy spring), Tiguentourine
  plain: 7 Cheliff, Mitidja
  rocky plateau: 7 hammada
  salt basin: 5 chott, shatt
  wind: 7 sirocco
  people: 4 Arab 6 Berber, Kabyle, Shawia, Tuareg 7 Haratin
  author: 3 Dib 5 Camus, Fanon 6 Yacine
  leader: 9 Bendjedid 10 Abd al-Qadir, Abd-al-Kadir,   Abd-el-Kader   11 Boumedienne 13 Ahmed Ben Bella
  ruler: 8 Jugurtha 9 Masinissa
  language: 6 Arabic, Berber, French, Zenata 7 Senhaja
  religion: 5 Islam
  place:
  monastery: 5 Ribat
  ruins: 7 Djemila
  feature:
  camel: 6 mehari
  cavalry man: 5 spahi 6 spahee
  commune: 5 setif
  dwelling: 6 gourbi
  French settler/landowner: 5 colon 8 piednoir
  holy man: 8 marabout
  kingdom: 7 Numidia
  native quarter: 6 casbah, kasbah
  pirate: 7 corsair
  ship: 5 xebec, zebec
  slum: 10 bidonville
  food:
  dish: 8 couscous
  fruit drink: 5 syrop
  seasoning: 4 mint 5 anise, cumin 6 cloves, fennel, ginger, pepper 7 parsley, pimento 8 cinnamon 9 coriander
Algiers
  Arabic: 8 al-Jazair
  building: 11 Great Mosque
  capital of: 7 Algeria
  center of city: 6 Casbah
  French: 5 Alger
  hills: 5 Sahel
  Roman: 7 Icosium
  ruled by: 5 Turks 6 French 7 Berbers 10 Free French 14 Barbary Pirates
  sea: 13 Mediterranean
Algonkian-Mosan
  language branches: 5 Mosan 7 Kutenai 15 Algonkian-Ritwan
Algonkian-Ritwan
  language family: 14 Algonkian-Mosan
  subgroup: 3 Fox 4 Cree, Sauk 5 Wiyot, Yurok 6 Ojibwa 7 Abenaki, Arapaho, Mohican 8 Cheyenne, Delaware, Menomini 9 Blackfoot
Algonkin, Algonquin
  language family: 9 Algonkian 10 Algonquian
  tribe: 7 Abitibi 8 Algonkin 9 Nipissing 11 Temiscaming
  location: 6 Canada 11 Ottawa River
  spirit of nature: 7 Manitou

Algonquian, Algonkian
    tribe: 3 Fox, Sac 4 Cree, Innu, Sauk 5 Miami 6 Abnaki, Atsina, Micmac, Ojibwa, Ottawa, Pequot 7 Arapaho, Mahican, Mohegan, Mohican, Ojibway, Shawnee 8 Algonkin, Cheyenne, Chippawa, Delaware, Haaninin, Iliniwek, Illinois, Kickapoo, Menomini, Merrimac, Powhatan, Puyallop 9 Algonquin, Blackfeet, Blackfoot, Massasoit, Menominee, Menomonie, Mesquakie, Pennacook, Penobscot, Pokanoket, Twightwee, Wampanoag 10 Leni-Lenape, Potawatomi 11 Gros Ventres 12 Narragansett 17 Montagnais-Naskapi

algophobia
    fear of: 4 pain

Algum 13 red sandalwood

Ali, Muhammad
    formerly: 11 Cassius Clay
    sport: 6 boxing
    class: 11 heavyweight
    won: 8 Olympics 16 heavyweight title

alias 9 pseudonym 11 assumed name, nom de guerre

Ali Baba
    character in: 27 Arabian Nights' Entertainments

Alibamu see 7 Alabama

alibi 3 out 6 excuse 7 pretext 11 explanation 13 justification

Alice Adams
    author: 15 Booth Tarkington
    character: 6 Mr Lamb 11 Virgil Adams, Walter Adams 13 Arthur Russell, Mildred Palmer

Alice's Adventures in Wonderland
    author: 12 Lewis Carroll
    character: 5 Alice 7 Duchess 9 Mad Hatter, March Hare 10 Mock Turtle 11 Cheshire Cat, White Rabbit 12 King of Hearts 13 Queen of Hearts

Alice Sit-by-the-Fire
    author: 12 James M Barrie

alien 6 exotic, remote, unlike 7 distant, foreign, opposed, strange 8 contrary, newcomer, outsider, stranger 9 different, estranged, foreigner, immigrant, not native, outlander, separated, unrelated 10 dissimilar, outlandish 11 conflicting, incongruous, unconnected 12 incompatible, inconsistent 13 contradictory
    German: 9 Auslander

alienate 7 divorce 8 estrange, separate, turn away

alienation 5 exile 7 divorce 9 isolation 10 separation, withdrawal 13 repulsiveness

alight 4 land 6 get off 7 deplane, descend, detrain, get down 8 come down, dismount 9 climb down, disembark, thump down, touch down

align 4 ally, even, join, side 6 even up, line up 9 affiliate, associate 10 straighten

alignment 7 allying, evening 9 evening up 13 straightening

alike 4 akin, even, same 5 equal 6 evenly 7 equally, kindred, uniform 8 of a piece, parallel 9 analogous, identical, similarly, uniformly 10 equivalent, synonymous 11 homogeneous, identically 13 corresponding

Alisande (Sandy)
    character in: 36 A Connecticut Yankee in King Arthur's Court
    author: 5 Twain

alive 4 spry 5 alert, aware, eager, quick, vital 6 active, extant, lively, living, viable 7 animate, in force, not dead 8 animated, possible, spirited, vigorous 9 breathing, energetic, operative, vivacious 10 subsisting, unquenched 11 above ground, in existence, in operation 14 unextinguished

alive to 5 alert, awake, aware 7 heedful, mindful 8 watchful 9 attentive, conscious, wide-awake

alkaline 5 salty 7 antacid 9 nonacidic

alkaloid 7 alkaline, codeine, quinine 8 morphine, nicotine 16 colorless complex

all 4 each, full, very 5 any of, every, fully, total, utter, whole 6 each of, entire, to a man, utmost, wholly 7 highest, perfect, totally, utterly 8 any one of, complete, entirely, everyone, greatest, the sum of, the total, the whole 9 every item 10 altogether, completely, every one of, everything, the total of, the whole of 11 every member, every part of, exceedingly, the entirety

All About Eve
    director: 17 Joseph L Mankiewicz
    cast: 10 Anne Baxter, Bette Davis 11 Celeste Holm, Gary Merrill 12 Thelma Ritter 13 George Sanders, Marilyn Monroe
    Oscar for: 7 picture 8 director 10 screenplay 15 supporting actor (George Sanders)

Allan-a-Dale, Alan-a-Dale
    character in: 9 Robin Hood

allargando
    music: 13 getting slower

all around 6 abroad 7 all over 10 everywhere, far and wide 15 making the rounds

all-around 5 broad 6 adroit, gifted 8 flexible 9 adaptable, many-sided, versatile 11 well-rounded 12 ambidextrous, multifaceted 13 comprehensive

allay 4 calm, dull, ease, hush 5 blunt, check, quell, quiet, slake 6 lessen, pacify, quench, reduce, smooth, soften, soothe, subdue 7 appease, assuage, lighten, mollify, relieve, slacken 8 diminish, mitigate, moderate 9 alleviate, put to rest 14 cause to subside

all but 6 almost, nearly 7 close to 8 not quite 10 not far from, very nearly 14 except everyone, within an inch of 16 everything except

all by oneself 5 alone 7 unaided 9 on one's own 10 unassisted 13 unaccompanied

all-consuming 3 hot 5 fiery 6 ardent, fervid, raging, red-hot 7 burning, fanatic, fervent, frantic, glowing, intense, zealous 8 frenzied 10 passionate 11 impassioned

allegation 5 claim **6** avowal, charge **9** assertion, statement **10** accusation, contention, indictment, profession **11** declaration

allege 3 say **4** aver, avow **5** claim, state **6** accuse, affirm, assert, charge, impugn, impute **7** contend, declare, profess **8** maintain

allegiance 6 fealty, homage **7** loyalty **8** devotion, fidelity **9** adherence, constancy, deference, obedience **12** faithfulness

allegory 5 fable **7** parable

allegro
  music: 4 fast

all-embracing 5 broad **6** all-out **7** general, overall **8** complete, sweeping, thorough **9** expansive, extensive, universal, unlimited **10** exhaustive, widespread **11** far-reaching, wide-ranging **12** all-inclusive, encyclopedic **13** comprehensive

Allen, Arabella
  character in: 14 Pickwick Papers
  author: 7 Dickens

Allen, Ethan
  served in: 16 Revolutionary War
  commander of: 17 Green Mountain Boys
  captured: 15 Fort Ticonderoga

Allen, Fred
  real name: 20 John Florence Sullivan
  born: 11 Cambridge MA
  roles: 11 What's My Line **16** The Fred Allen Show

Allen, Steve
  real name: 12 Stephen Allen
  wife: 12 Jayne Meadows
  nickname: 10 Mr Midnight
  born: 9 New York NY
  roles: 13 I've Got a Secret **14** The Tonight Show

Allen, William Hervey
  author of: 7 Israfel **14** Anthony Adverse

Allen, Woody
  author of: 11 Getting Even, Side Effects **15** Without Feathers
  real name: 22 Allen Stewart Konigsberg
  wife: 12 Louise Lasser
  born: 10 Brooklyn NY
  roles: 5 Zelig **7** Bananas, Sleeper **9** Annie Hall, Manhattan **16** Stardust Memories **19** Hannah and Her Sisters
  director of: 5 Zelig **7** Bananas, Sleeper **9** Annie Hall (Oscar), Interiors, Manhattan **16** Stardust Memories **19** Hannah and Her Sisters **20** The Purple Rose of Cairo

alleviate 4 dull, ease, quit **5** abate, allay, blunt, check, slake **6** lessen, quench, reduce, soften, subdue, temper **7** assuage, lighten, mollify, relieve, slacken **8** diminish, mitigate, moderate

alleviation 6 easing, relief **9** lessening **10** palliation

alley 4 lane **5** byway **7** passage, pathway **10** passageway **16** narrow back street

Alley Oop
  creator: 14 Vincent T Hamlin
  character:
  girlfriend: 4 Oola

dinosaur: 5 Dinny
king: 6 Guzzle
scientist: 8 Dr Wonmug
place:
  kingdom of: 3 Moo
  author: 10 John Dryden

All for Love
  author: 10 John Dryden
  character: 6 Antony, Caesar **7** Octavia **9** Cleopatra, Dolabella, Ventidius

All God's Chillun Got Wings
  author: 12 Eugene O'Neill
  character: 6 Mickey **9** Jim Harris **10** Ella Downey

alliance 4 pact **5** union **6** league, treaty **7** compact, company **9** agreement, coalition, concordat **10** federation **11** affiliation, association, confederacy, partnership **13** confederation **15** entente cordiale

allied 4 akin, like **5** alike, joint **6** united **7** cognate, kindred, related, similar **8** combined **9** corporate, federated **10** affiliated, associated, resembling **11** amalgamated **12** incorporated

all in 4 beat **5** spent, tired, weary **6** bushed, done in, pooped **7** drained, wearied, worn out **8** dog tired, fatigued, tired out **9** bone weary, dead tired, exhausted, played out

all in all 5 in sum **10** on the whole **20** when all is said and done

all-inclusive 5 broad **6** all-out, entire **7** general, overall **8** absolute, complete, sweeping, thorough **9** expansive, extensive, universal, unlimited **10** altogether, exhaustive, widespread **11** far-reaching, wide-ranging **12** all-embracing **13** comprehensive

All in the Family
  character: 10 Joey Stivic, Mike Stivic (Meathead) **11** Edith Bunker (Dingbat) **12** Archie Bunker **18** Gloria Bunker Stivic
  cast: 9 Rob Reiner **13** Jean Stapleton **14** Carroll O'Connor, Sally Struthers
  spinoffs: 5 Maude **12** Archie's Place **13** The Jeffersons

allocate 5 allot, allow **6** assign, budget **7** earmark **8** set aside **9** apportion, designate **11** appropriate

allocation 5 quota, share **7** measure, portion **8** division **9** allotment, meting out **10** dealing out **11** consignment, designation **12** apportioning, dispensation, distribution **13** apportionment

Allosaurus see 10 Antrodemus

allot 5 allow, grant **6** assign **7** appoint, consign, dole out, earmark, give out, mete out, provide **8** allocate, dispense, divide up **9** apportion, parcel out **10** distribute, portion out

allotment 5 grant, quota, share **6** ration **7** measure, portion **9** allowance **10** allocation **11** consignment **12** dispensation **13** apportionment, appropriation

all-out 5 broad, total **7** full-out, maximum **8** complete, sweeping, thorough **9** extensive, full-scale **11** unqualified, unremitting **12** all-embracing, all-inclusive **13** comprehensive, thoroughgoing

all over 5 ended, kaput 8 finished 9 concluded 10 everywhere 11 universally

All Over
   author: 11 Edward Albee

allow 3 let 4 give 5 allot, grant 6 assign, permit 7 agree to, approve, concede, provide 8 allocate, sanction 9 authorize

allowable 7 allowed 8 accepted 9 permitted, tolerable, tolerated 10 acceptable, admissible, admittable, authorized, sanctioned 11 permissible

allowance 5 grant 6 bounty, income, ration 7 annuity, payment, pension, stipend, subsidy 8 discount 9 allotment, deduction, reduction 10 concession 11 subtraction

allow to go 4 free 5 let go 6 excuse 7 dismiss, release, set free 8 liberate 9 discharge

allow to pass
   French: 13 laissez passer

alloy 3 mix 5 admix, blend 6 commix, dilute, fusion, impair 7 amalgam, combine, mixture 8 compound, intermix 9 admixture, composite, synthesis 10 adulterate, commixture, interblend 12 conglomerate

alloyed 5 mixed 6 impure 7 debased

All Quiet on the Western Front
   author: 18 Erich Maria Remarque
   character: 6 Muller, Tjaden 10 Paul Baumer 11 Albert Kropp, Haie Westhus 20 Stanislaus Katczinsky (Kat)
   director: 14 Lewis Milestone
   cast: 8 Lew Ayres 12 Louis Wolheim 14 Russell Gleason
   setting: 3 WWI
   Oscar for: 7 picture

all right 2 OK 3 yes 4 fair, hale, safe, well 6 hearty 7 healthy 8 properly, unharmed 9 certainly, correctly, uninjured 10 absolutely, acceptably, unimpaired 14 satisfactorily
   Spanish: 5 bueno

All Said and Done
   author: 16 Simone de Beauvoir

allspice
   botanical name: 7 pimenta, p dioica 12 p officinalis
   also called: 7 pimento
   origin: 7 Jamaica 16 Caribbean Islands
   flavor: 5 clove 6 nutmeg 8 cinnamon
   use: 6 baking

Allston, Washington
   born: 10 Waccamaw SC
   artwork: 9 The Deluge 13 Uriel in the Sun 16 Belshazzar's Feast, Moonlit Landscape 20 Spanish Girl in Reverie

All's Well That Ends Well
   author: 18 William Shakespeare
   character: 5 Diana 6 Helena 7 Bertram 8 Parolles 12 King of France 14 Duke of Florence 19 Countess of Rousillon

All That Jazz
   director: 8 Bob Fosse
   cast: 9 Ben Vereen 11 Ann Reinking, Cliff Gorman, Roy Scheider 12 Jessica Lange, Leland Palmer

All the King's Men
   author: 16 Robert Penn Warren
   character: 10 Jack Burden, Judge Irwin, Sadie Burke 11 Adam Stanton, Willie Stark 12 Annie Stanton
   director: 12 Robert Rossen
   cast: 9 Joanne Dru, John Derek 11 John Ireland 17 Broderick Crawford 19 Mercedes McCambridge
   Oscar for: 5 actor (Crawford) 7 picture 17 supporting actress (McCambridge)

all the more
   Latin: 9 a fortiori

All the President's Men
   author: 11 Bob Woodward 13 Carl Bernstein
   subject: 16 Watergate scandal
   newspaper: 14 Washington Post
   director: 11 Alan J Pakula
   cast: 10 Jack Warden 11 Hal Holbrook 12 Jason Robards, Martin Balsam 13 Dustin Hoffman (Carl Bernstein), Jane Alexander, Robert Redford (Bob Woodward)
   Oscar for: 12 screenwriter 15 supporting actor (Robards)

all the same 5 alike 7 however, uniform 8 unvaried 9 identical 11 homogeneous

all together 7 en masse, in a body 8 as a group, in a group, in unison
   French: 12 tout ensemble

all told 5 in sum, total 6 in toto 7 totally 8 as a whole 10 altogether

allude 4 hint 5 refer 7 mention, speak of, suggest 8 intimate 9 touch upon

allure 4 bait, lure 5 charm, tempt 6 entice, lead on, seduce 7 attract, beguile, enchant, glamour 8 intrigue 9 captivate, fascinate 10 attraction, enticement, temptation 11 enchantment, fascination

allurement 4 draw, lure 5 charm 9 magnetism 10 attraction 11 fascination

alluring 4 sexy 8 charming, enticing, magnetic 10 attractive 11 fascinating

allusion 4 hint 7 mention 9 reference 10 suggestion

Allworthy, Squire
   character in: 8 Tom Jones
   author: 8 Fielding

ally 5 unite 6 league 7 combine, partner 8 confrere 9 accessory, affiliate, associate, colleague 10 accomplice, join forces 11 confederate 12 band together, bind together, collaborator, join together

Allyson, June
   real name: 11 Ella Geisman
   husband: 10 Dick Powell
   born: 9 New York NY
   roles: 8 Good News 9 Interlude, The Shrike 11 Little Women 12 My Man Godfrey 16 The Stratton Story 18 The Glen Miller Story

Almagest
   author: 7 Ptolemy
   title means: 11 the greatest
   subject: 9 astronomy

Al Maghrib see 7 Morocco
almandite
  species: 6 garnet
  color: 3 red
Almaviva, Count and Countess
  author: 12 Beaumarchais
  characters in: 18 The Barber of Seville
  19 The Marriage of Figaro
Almayer's Folly
  author: 12 Joseph Conrad
almighty 7 supreme 8 absolute, infinite 9 sovereign, unlimited 10 invincible, omnipotent 11 all-powerful 12 transcendent
Almira
  opera by: 6 Handel
almond 12 Prunus dulcis
  varieties: 4 Wild 5 Earth, Green, Sweet 6 Bitter, Desert, Indian 8 Tropical 9 Flowering 12 Dwarf Russian
  candy: 8 marzipan
  liqueur: 6 orgeat 7 ratafia
almost 5 about 6 all but, nearly 7 close to 8 not quite, well-nigh 9 just about 10 not far from, very nearly 11 practically, on the verge of 13 approximately 14 within an inch of
almost alike 5 close 7 similar 10 resembling 11 approaching, much the same 15 nearly identical
alms 3 aid 4 dole, gift 5 mercy 6 relief 7 charity, handout, largess, present, subsidy, tribute 8 donation, gratuity, offering, pittance 9 baksheesh 10 assistance 11 benefaction, beneficence 12 contribution
almshouse 6 asylum 9 poorhouse, workhouse
almsman 5 tramp 6 beggar 9 mendicant 10 panhandler
Almug 13 red sandalwood
aloft 2 up 5 above, way up 6 high up, on high 7 skyward 8 in the air, in the sky, overhead 10 heavenward
Aloha state
  nickname of: 6 Hawaii
Aloidae
  name: 4 Otus 9 Ephialtes
  form: 5 giant
  father: 8 Poseidon
  mother: 9 Iphimedia
  raised by: 6 Aloeus
alone 4 only, sole 6 lonely, single, singly, solely, unique 7 forlorn, unaided 8 deserted, desolate, forsaken, isolated, lonesome, peerless, singular, solitary, uniquely 9 abandoned, matchless, nonpareil, separated, unmatched, unrivaled 10 friendless, separately, singularly, solitarily, unassisted, unattended, unequalled, unescorted 11 unsurpassed, without help 12 incomparable, unchaperoned, unparalleled, without peers 13 unaccompanied, without others 14 single-handedly
  Latin: 4 sola 5 solus
  French: 4 seul
along 2 on 4 over 6 beside, during, onward 7 abreast, forward, through

alongside 2 at, by 6 beside, next to 7 abreast, close by 9 at the side 10 parallel to 12 collaterally, parallelwise 13 equidistantly
aloof 4 cold, cool 5 above, apart 6 chilly, formal, remote 7 distant, haughty, high-hat 8 detached, reserved 10 unsociable 11 at a distance, indifferent, standoffish, unconcerned 12 uninterested, unresponsive 13 unsympathetic 14 unapproachable
aloofness 7 reserve 8 coldness, coolness 9 formality 10 detachment, remoteness 11 haughtiness 12 indifference 13 unsociability 15 standoffishness
Alope
  father: 7 Cercyon
  son: 10 Hippothous
  attacked by: 8 Poseidon
Alopecus
  origin: 7 Spartan
  form: 6 prince
aloud 7 audibly
alphabet 4 ABCs 6 schema 7 grammar, letters 8 elements 9 rudiments, tablature 10 characters, principles 13 writing system
Alphesiboea
  also: 7 Arsinoe
  form: 5 nymph
  father: 4 Bias 7 Phegeus 9 Leucippus
  mother: 9 Philodice
  husband: 8 Alcmaeon
  son: 6 Adonis
  rejected: 8 Dionysus
  nurse for: 7 Orestes
Alpheus
  father: 7 Oceanus
  mother: 6 Tethys
  loved: 8 Arethusa
  changed into: 5 river
Alphonse and Gaston
  creator: 14 Frederick Opper
  saying: 22 After you my dear Alphonse, No after you my dear Gaston
alpine 5 alpen, lofty 6 aerial 8 elevated, snow-clad, towering 9 subalpine 10 alpestrine, sky-kissing, snow-capped 11 cloud-capped, mountainous 13 cloud-piercing, cloud-touching 14 heaven-touching
Alps, Alpine
  country: 5 Italy 6 France 7 Austria, Germany 10 Yugoslavia 11 Switzerland 13 Liechtenstein
  range: 6 Carnic, Graian, Julian, Otztal 7 Bernese, Cottian, Pennine 8 Bavarian, Ligurian, Maritime, Rhaetian 9 Dolomites, Lepontine 10 Hohe Tauern
  peak: 4 Rosa 5 Eiger, Monch 8 Jungfrau 10 Karawanken, Matterhorn, Piz Bernina 13 Grossglockner
  highest point: 5 Blanc
  pass: 7 Brenner, Simplon, Splugen, Stelvio 9 Semmering 10 St Gotthard 14 Great St Bernard
  lake: 4 Como 6 Alpine, Geneva 7 Lucerne 8 Maggiore 9 Constance
  resort: 7 Zermatt 8 Chamonix, Salzburg, St Moritz 9 Innsbruck 13 Berchtesgaden

wind: 6 foehns

already 5 early, so far 6 before 8 formerly, hitherto, until now 10 heretofore, previously

already seen
   French: 6 deja vu

also 3 and, too 4 more, plus 5 extra 6 as well 7 besides 8 moreover 9 including 10 in addition 12 additionally

Altaic
   language branches: 6 Turkic 8 Tungusic 9 Mongolian

altar 5 bomos 6 hestia, scribis 7 eschara 8 credence 9 holy table, prothesis 10 Lord's table

Altar
   constellation of: 3 Ara

Altdorfer, Albrecht
   born: 7 Germany 10 Regensburg
   artwork: 16 Susanna at the Bath 20 St George and the Dragon, Susannah and the Elders 24 Landscape with a Footbridge 39 The Battle of Alexander and Darius on the Issus

alter 4 vary 5 amend 6 change, modify, recast, revise 7 convert, remodel 9 transform 13 make different

alterable 7 unfixed 8 variable 9 adaptable 10 adjustable, changeable, modifiable 11 convertible

alteration 6 change 10 adjustment, conversion, remodeling 12 modification 13 transmutation 14 transformation

altercation 3 row 4 spat 5 brawl, broil, fight, melee, scene 6 affray, fracas, rumpus, scrape 7 discord, dispute, quarrel, scuffle 8 argument 9 bickering, wrangling 10 falling-out 11 controversy 12 disagreement

alter ego 4 twin 5 match 6 double 9 duplicate, other self, semblable 10 complement, other image, second self, simulacrum 11 counterpart 12 Doppelganger

alternate 3 sub 4 vary 5 alter, proxy 6 backup, change, deputy, rotate, second 7 another, standby, stand-in 9 surrogate, take turns 10 every other, reciprocal, substitute, successive, understudy 11 alternating, consecutive, every second, interchange, intersperse, pinch hitter

alternative 6 choice, option, way out 8 recourse 9 selection 10 substitute 11 other choice

Altes
   origin: 5 Greek
   mentioned in: 5 Iliad
   king of: 7 Leleges
   daughter: 7 Laothoe

Aithaea
   father: 8 Thestius
   brother: 9 Plexippus
   husband: 6 Oeneus
   son: 6 Toxeus, Tydeus 8 Meleager
   daughter: 5 Gorge 8 Deianira

Althaemenes
   father: 7 Catreus
   sister: 9 Apemosyne
   killed: 7 Catreus 9 Apemosyne

although 3 but, yet 4 even 5 still 7 however 11 nonetheless 12 nevertheless 15 notwithstanding

altitude 4 apex 6 height, vertex, zenith 8 eminence, tallness 9 elevation, loftiness, sublimity 10 prominence

Altman, Robert
   director of: 4 MASH 9 Nashville

altogether 5 fully, in all, in sum, quite 6 in toto, wholly 7 all told, totally, utterly 8 all in all, as a whole, entirely 9 in general, out and out, perfectly 10 absolutely, completely, in sum total, on the whole; thoroughly 12 all inclusive, collectively

altruism 7 charity 10 generosity 11 benevolence 12 philanthropy, public spirit 13 unselfishness 14 bigheartedness, charitableness 15 humanitarianism

altruistic 8 generous 9 unselfish 10 benevolent, charitable 12 humanitarian, largehearted 13 philanthropic 14 public-spirited

aluminum
   chemical symbol: 2 Al

alumnus 8 graduate 12 male graduate 13 former student

Alverio, Rosita Dolores
   real name of: 10 Rita Moreno

always 7 forever 8 evermore 9 eternally, every time, regularly 10 for all time, invariably 11 continually, incessantly, perpetually, unceasingly 12 consistently 13 everlastingly, unremittingly 14 forever and ever

Amadan
   origin: 5 Irish
   form: 5 fairy

Amadeus
   director: 11 Milos Forman
   cast: 8 Tom Hulce (Wolfgang Amadeus Mozart) 14 F Murray Abraham (Antonio Salieri)
   choreography: 10 Twyla Tharp
   Oscar for: 5 actor (Abraham) 7 picture 8 director

Amadis of Gaul
   author: 16 Garcia de Montalvo
   character: 6 Oriana, Perion 7 Elisena 8 Garinter, Lisuarte

Amado, Jorge
   author of: 14 Tent of Miracles 15 Home Is the Sailor 19 Shepherds of the Night 24 Gabriela Clove and Cinnamon 25 Dona Flor and Her Two Husbands 30 The Two Deaths of Quincas Wateryell

Amahl and the Night Visitors
   opera by: 7 Menotti

Amalek
   father: 7 Eliphaz
   mother: 6 Timnah
   grandfather: 4 Esau
   descendant of: 9 Amalekite

amalgam 5 alloy, blend, combo, union 6 fusion, league, merger 7 joining, mixture 8 alliance, compound, mishmash 9 admixture, composite 10 assemblage, commixture 11 combination 12 amalgamation, intermixture

amalgamate 3 mix 4 fuse 5 blend, merge, unify, unite 7 combine 8 coalesce, federate 9 commingle, integrate 10 synthesize 11 consolidate, incorporate 12 join together

Amalthaea
   form: 4 goat 5 nymph
   raised: 4 Zeus

Amarcord ·
   director: 15 Federico Fellini
   cast: 10 Bruno Zanin, Magali Noel 13 Pupella Maggio

amaretto
   type: 7 liqueur
   origin: 5 Italy
   flavor: 6 almond
   with vodka: 9 Godmother

Amaryllis
   character in: 9 Ecologues
   author: 6 Virgil
   represented: 11 shepherdess

Amarynceus
   origin: 5 Greek
   mentioned in: 5 Iliad
   king of: 7 Messene
   ruled: 4 Elis
   ruled with: 6 Augeas
   killed by: 6 Nestor

Amasa
   father: 6 Jether
   mother: 7 Abigail
   uncle: 5 David
   commander for: 5 David 7 Absalom
   killed by: 4 Joab

amass 6 gather, heap up, pile up 7 acquire, collect, compile, round up 8 assemble 10 accumulate

amassing 7 heaping, piling 8 piling up 9 aggregate, compiling, gathering 10 assemblage, assembling, collecting 11 compilation 12 accumulating

Amata
   husband: 7 Latinus
   daughter: 7 Lavinia

amateur 4 tyro 6 novice 7 dabbler 8 beginner, hobbyist, inexpert, neophyte 9 greenhorn, unskilled 10 dilettante, unpolished 13 inexperienced 14 unprofessional 15 nonprofessional

amateurish 5 inept 6 clumsy 7 awkward 8 inexpert, mediocre 9 unskilled, untrained 10 unskillful 11 incompetent, ineffective, unpracticed 13 inexperienced 14 unaccomplished, unprofessional

amatory 3 hot 4 fond, sexy 6 ardent, doting, erotic, loving, sexual, steamy, tender 7 adoring, amorous, devoted, fervent, sensual, sexed-up 8 lovesick, romantic, yearning 9 libidinal, loverlike, rapturous 10 infatuated, lascivious, passionate 11 impassioned, languishing

amaxophobia
   fear of: 7 driving 8 vehicles

amaze 3 awe 4 daze, stun 5 shock 7 astound, stagger, stupefy 8 astonish, surprise 9 dumbfound 11 flabbergast

amazement 3 awe 5 shock 6 wonder 8 surprise 9 disbelief 11 incredulity 12 astonishment, bewilderment, stupefaction

Amaziah
   father: 5 Joash
   opposed: 7 Jehoash
   captured at: 11 Bethshemesh
   killed at: 7 Lachish

Amazon
   occupation: 7 warrior
   sex: 6 female
   queen: 9 Hippolyta

amazonite
   species: 8 feldspar

Amazonomachia
   battle between: 6 Greeks 7 Amazons

ambassador 5 agent, envoy 6 consul, deputy, legate, nuncio 7 attache, courier 8 diplomat, emissary, minister 9 go-between 11 diplomatist 12 intermediary 13 consul general 14 representative

Ambassadors, The
   author: 10 Henry James
   character: 8 Strether, Waymarsh 10 Mrs Newsome 11 Mamie Pocock, Sarah Pocock 12 Maria Gostrey 15 Chadwick Newsome 17 Comtesse de Vionnet

amber
   formed from: 5 resin
   color: 6 yellow
   Greek: 8 elektron

ambiance 3 air 4 aura, mood, tone 5 tenor 6 spirit, flavor, milieu, temper 7 climate, setting 9 character 10 atmosphere 11 environment 12 surroundings

ambiguity 9 vagueness 11 uncertainty 12 abstruseness, doubtfulness, equivocation 14 indefiniteness
   French: 13 double entente

ambiguous 5 vague 7 cryptic, unclear 8 doubtful, puzzling 9 enigmatic, equivocal, uncertain 10 indefinite, misleading

ambition 3 aim 4 goal, hope, plan, push, zeal 5 dream, drive 6 design, desire, intent 7 longing, purpose 8 striving, yearning 9 objective 10 aspiration

ambitious 4 avid 5 eager 6 ardent, intent 7 arduous, zealous 8 aspiring, desirous 9 difficult, energetic, grandiose, strenuous 10 determined 11 industrious 12 enterprising

ambivalent 5 mixed 7 warring 8 clashing, confused, opposing, wavering 9 equivocal, undecided, unfocused 10 wishy-washy 11 conflicting, fluctuating, vacillating 13 contradictory

amble 6 ramble, stroll 7 meander, saunter 15 wander aimlessly

Ambler, Eric
   author of: 11 The Levanter 12 A Kind of Auger 13 The Care of Time 14 The Nightcomers, Uncommon Danger 15 Journey Into Fear, The Dark Frontier 16 The Light of the Day 19 A Coffin for Dimitrios 22 The Siege of the Villa Lipp

Ambling Alp, The
   nickname of: 12 Primo Carnera

ambrosial 5 balmy **8** fragrant, luscious, perfumed **9** delicious **13** sweet-smelling

ambrosia of the gods 4 food **5** drink **6** nectar **7** perfume

ambulance chaser 4 beak **6** lawyer **8** attorney **9** counselor **10** mouthpiece **12** legal advisor

ambulatory 6 mobile, moving **7** walking **10** up and about **11** peripatetic

ambush 4 trap **5** blind, cover **6** attack, entrap, hiding, lay for, waylay **7** assault **8** hideaway, surprise **9** ambuscade **11** concealment, hiding place **13** stalking-horse

Ameche, Don
  real name: 17 Dominic Felix Amici
  born: 9 Kenosha WI
  roles: 6 Cocoon (Oscar) **13** Heaven Can Wait, Moon Over Miami, Silk Stockings **14** That Night in Rio **16** Down Argentine Way **18** The Three Musketeers **29** The Story of Alexander Graham Bell

Amelia
  author: 13 Henry Fielding
  character: 10 Dr Harrison **11** Mrs Atkinson **12** Miss Matthews **19** Captain William Booth

ameliorate 4 heal, help, mend **5** amend, fix up **6** better, perk up, pick up, reform, remedy, revise **7** advance, correct, improve, patch up, promote, rectify **8** palliate, progress **9** come along, get better **10** grow better **11** improve upon

ameliorative 8 remedial **9** improving **10** corrective, palliative **11** therapeutic **12** compensatory

amen 5 truly **6** it is so, so be it, verily **8** hear hear **9** let it be so, yes indeed **11** so shall it be **17** would that it were so

Amen
  also: 4 Amon **5** Ammon
  origin: 8 Egyptian
  king of: 4 gods
  worshiped at: 6 Thebes
  personifies: 3 air **6** breath
  represented by: 3 ram **5** goose
  patron of: 6 Thebes
  corresponds to: 4 Jove, Zeus **6** Amen Ra, Amon Ra **7** Jupiter

amenable 4 open **7** cordial, willing **8** obliging, yielding **9** agreeable, tractable **10** open-minded, responsive, submissive **11** acquiescent, complaisant, cooperative, persuadable, sympathetic **17** favorably disposed

amend 3 fix **4** mend **5** alter, emend **6** better, change, modify, polish, reform, remedy, revise **7** correct, develop, enhance, improve, perfect, rectify

amendment 6 change, reform **7** adjunct **8** addition, revision **10** alteration, correction, emendation **11** improvement **12** modification **13** rectification

amends 7 apology, defense, payment, redress **8** requital **9** atonement, expiation **10** recompense, reparation **11** explanation, restitution, restoration, retribution, vindica-

tion **12** compensation, satisfaction **13** justification, peace offering **14** acknowledgment **15** indemnification

amenity, amenities 8 civility, mildness, niceties **9** geniality, gentility **10** affability, amiability, courtesies, gentleness, politeness, refinement **11** gallantries, good manners **12** friendliness, graciousness, pleasantness **13** agreeableness

Amen Ra
  also: 6 Amon Ra
  origin: 8 Egyptian
  god of: 8 universe
  corresponds to: 4 Amen, Amon, Jove, Zeus **5** Ammon **7** Jupiter

America
  author: 19 Stephen Vincent Benet

America, North
  country: 4 Cuba **5** Haiti **6** Belize, Canada, Mexico, Panama **8** Honduras **9** Costa Rica, Guatemala, Nicaragua **10** El Salvador **12** United States **17** Dominican Republic
  island: 5 Banks **6** Baffin, Kodiak **7** Bahamas, Bermuda **8** Victoria **9** Alexander, Anticosti, Ellesmere, Greenland, Vancouver **10** Aleutians, Cape Breton, Long Island, West Indies **11** Southampton **12** Newfoundland, Prince Edward **13** Prince of Wales **14** Queen Charlotte
  mountain: 5 Coast, Rocky **6** Brooks **7** Cascade **8** Mackenzie **10** Bitterroot **11** Appalachian **12** Sierra Nevada
  highest point: 8 McKinley
  lowest point: 11 Death Valley
  river: 3 Red **4** Ohio **5** Yukon **6** Copper, Fraser, Hudson, Nelson **8** Arkansas, Colorado, Columbia, Delaware, Missouri **9** Mackenzie **10** Coppermine, Sacramento, San Joaquin, St Lawrence **11** Connecticut, Mississippi
  lake: 4 Erie **5** Huron **6** Carson, Walker **7** Nipigon, Ontario **8** Manitoba, Michigan, Reindeer, Superior, Winnipeg **9** Athabasca, Champlain, Great Bear, Great Salt **10** Great Slave **11** Yellowstone
  animal: 3 bat, rat **4** bear, lynx, puma, wolf **5** bison, moose, skunk **6** beaver, musk ox **7** bighorn, caribou **8** sewellel **9** pronghorn, white goat
  bird: 4 hawk **5** eagle, snipe **8** bobwhite, woodcock, wood ibis **9** blue heron, ptarmigan
  sea: 6 Bering **7** Chukchi, Lincoln **8** Beaufort **9** Caribbean
  religion: 7 Judaism **10** Protestant **13** Roman Catholic **27** Eastern Orthodox Christianity
  people: 6 Eskimo **8** European **12** African Negro **14** American Indian
  language: 6 French **7** English, Spanish

America, South
  country: 4 Peru **5** Chile **6** Brazil, Guyana **7** Bolivia, Ecuador, Uruguay **8** Colombia, Paraguay, Suriname **9** Argentina, Venezuela

city: 4 Lima 5 Quito 6 Bogota, Recife 7 Caracas 8 Salvador, Santiago, Sao Paulo 10 Montevideo 11 Buenos Aires, Porto Alegre 12 Rio de Janeiro 13 Belo Horizonte

island: 6 Chiloe, Chonos, Marajo 9 Galapagos 10 Wellington 11 Madre de Dios 13 Juan Fernandez, Reina Adelaida 14 Tierra del Fuego

sea: 9 Caribbean

lake: 5 Patos, Poopo, Mirim 6 Viedma 8 Titicaca 9 Maracaibo, San Martin 10 Concepcion

mountain: 6 Andes 9 Pakaraima 12 Monte Fitz Roy 14 Cerro Aconcagua, Monte Sarmiento 15 Serra dos Parecis 16 Monte San Valentin, Serra do Espinhaco

highest point: 9 Aconcagua

lowest point: 15 Peninsula Valdes

river: 3 Ica 4 Beni, Iaco, Jari, Meta, Napo 5 Abuna, Cauca, Chico, Iriri, Ituxi, Jurua, Jutai, Negro, Palma, Pardo, Purus, Tiete, Tigre, Xingu 6 Amazon, Arauca, Branco, Chubut, Cumina, Curaco, Cuyuni, Grande, Gurupi, Iguacu, Japura, Javari, Mamore, Maroni, Mortes, Parana, Salado, Vaupes 7 Bermejo, Caqueta, Deseado, Guapore, Jamunda, Juruena, Madeira, Mapuera, Maranon, Orinoco, Oyapock, Ucayali, Vichada 8 Amazonas, Araguaia, Colorado, Guaviare, Jamachim, Paraguay, Parnaiba, Putumayo, Tapajoz, Urubamba, Uruguay 9 Essequibo, Jaguaribe, Paranaiba, Saladillo, Sao Manuel, Tocantins 10 Courantyne 12 Sao Francisco

animal: 3 bat 4 bear, deer 5 llama, sloth, tapir 6 alpaca, monkey, ocelot, weasel 7 opossum, peccary, raccoon 8 capybara, javelina 9 armadillo

bird: 3 owl 4 hawk, rhea 5 eagle 6 condor, falcon, jabiru 7 hoatzin 8 flamingo 11 hummingbird

people: 6 Indian 7 African, Chibcha, Mestizo, Mulatto, Spanish 10 Araucanian, Portuguese

religion: 7 Judaism 10 Protestant 13 Roman Catholic

language: 5 Dutch 7 English, Spanish 10 Portuguese

American, The
author: 10 Henry James
character: 8 Mrs Bread 10 Mr Tristram 11 Mrs Tristram 12 Noemie Nioche 13 Count Valentin 14 Claire de Cintre 17 Christopher Newman 25 Marquis Urbain de Bellegarde
setting: 5 Paris

American Caesar
author: 17 William Manchester

American Claimant, The
author: 9 Mark Twain

American Dreams
author: 11 Studs Terkel

American Graffiti
director: 11 George Lucas
cast: 9 Paul Le Mat, Ron Howard 10 Candy Clark 11 Wolfman Jack 12 Harrison Ford 13 Cindy Williams 15 Richard Dreyfuss 17 MacKenzie Phillips

American in Paris, An
director: 16 Vincente Minnelli
cast: 8 Nina Foch 9 Gene Kelly 11 Leslie Caron, Oscar Levant 14 Georges Guetary
score: 14 George Gershwin
Oscar for: 7 picture

Americanization of Emily
director: 12 Arthur Hiller
script by: 14 Paddy Chayefsky
cast: 11 James Coburn, James Garner 12 Julie Andrews 13 Melvyn Douglas

American Tragedy, An
author: 15 Theodore Dreiser
character: 12 Roberta Alden 14 Clyde Griffiths, Sondra Finchley 15 Samuel Griffiths

America's Sweetheart
nickname of: 12 Mary Pickford

amethyst
species: 6 quartz
color: 6 purple
month: 8 February

Amfortas
leader of: 7 knights
in search of: 9 holy grail

ami, amie 6 friend

amiability 10 good nature, kindliness 12 agreeability, friendliness, pleasantness

amiable 6 genial, kindly, polite 7 affable, cordial, winning 8 amicable, charming, engaging, friendly, gracious, obliging, pleasant, pleasing, sociable 9 agreeable, congenial 10 attractive 11 good-natured

amicability 5 amity 7 concord 8 good will 9 affection 10 cordiality, friendship 12 friendliness 14 neighborliness

amicable 4 kind 5 civil 6 kindly, polite 7 amiable, cordial 8 amenable, friendly, sociable 9 agreeable, courteous, peaceable 10 benevolent, harmonious, neighborly 11 kindhearted

Amici, Dominic Felix
real name of: 9 Don Ameche

amicus curiae 17 a friend of the court

amigo, amiga 6 friend

Amis, Kingsley
author of: 8 Ending Up, Lucky Jim 10 Colonel Sun, Jake's Thing 11 I Like It Here, The Green Man 16 One Fat Englishman, Take A Girl Like You 18 Russian Hide-and-Seek, The Anti-Death League 20 That Uncertain Feeling

amiss 4 awry 5 askew, false, wrong 6 astray, faulty 7 falsely, mixed-up, off base, wrongly 8 faultily, improper, mistaken, untoward 9 erroneous, incorrect, out of line 10 fallacious, improperly, mistakenly, out of order, unsuitable, unsuitably, untowardly 11 erroneously, incorrectly 12 inaccurately 13 inappropriate 15 inappropriately

Amittai
 son: 5 Jonah
amity 6 accord 7 concord, harmony 8 good will, sympathy 9 agreement 10 cordiality, fellowship, fraternity, friendship 11 brotherhood, cooperation 13 understanding
Ammishaddai
 son: 7 Ahiezer
Ammon
 father: 3 Lot
 descendants: 9 Ammonites
Ammonite god 6 Molech, Moloch
ammunition 4 ammo, arms 5 shell 6 bullet, rocket 7 missile, torpedo 9 artillery, cartridge, small arms 11 iron rations 13 powder and shot
ammunition dump 7 arsenal 8 magazine 18 military storehouse, munitions warehouse
amnesia 4 daze 5 fugue 6 stupor 7 agnosia 8 blackout 9 memory gap 11 anterograde, trance state
amnesty 6 pardon 8 immunity, reprieve 10 absolution 11 forgiveness 14 reconciliation
amoeba, ameba 4 dyad, germ, mold 5 spore, virus 6 fungus 7 ciliate, microbe 8 bacteria, reovirus 9 bacterium, echovirus 13 microorganism
 part: 7 nucleus 8 membrane 9 pseudopod 10 protoplasm 11 food vacuole 18 contractile vacuole
 reproduction by: 7 fission
amok *see* 5 amuck
Amon *see* 4 Amen
among 2 at 3 mid 4 amid, with 6 amidst 7 amongst, between, betwixt 12 in the midst of
among other persons
 Latin: 10 inter alios
among others 8 attended, escorted, in a crowd, in a group, together 11 accompanied
among other things
 Latin: 9 inter alia
among themselves
 Latin: 7 inter se
Amon Ra *see* 6 Amen Ra
Amopaon
 mentioned in: 5 Iliad
 form: 7 warrior
 army: 6 Trojan
 killed by: 6 Teucer
Amor *see* 5 Cupid
Amore dei Tre Re, L'
 opera by: 10 Montemezzi
Amoretti
 author: 13 Edmund Spenser
amorous 4 fond 6 ardent, doting, loving, tender 8 enamored, lovesick 10 passionate 11 impassioned 12 affectionate
amorousness 4 love 5 ardor 6 warmth 7 passion
amor patriae 10 patriotism 13 love of country

amorphous 5 vague 8 formless, unshapen 9 anomalous, shapeless, undefined 11 nondescript 12 undelineated 13 characterless, indeterminate
Amos
 father: 4 Naum
Amos 'n' Andy
 character: 8 Lightnin' 9 Amos Jones, Andy Brown 13 George (the King Fish) Stevens 15 Sapphire Stevens
 cast: 8 Tim Moore 13 Ernestine Wade, Horace Stewart 14 Alvin Childress 15 Spencer Williams
amount 3 sum 4 bulk, mass 5 total 6 extent, volume 7 measure 8 quantity, sum total 9 aggregate, magnitude
amour 6 affair 7 liaison, romance 8 intrigue 10 love affair
amour propre 8 self-love 10 self-esteem 11 self-respect
Ampelos
 form: 5 satyr
Ampere, Andre-Marie
 field: 7 physics 11 mathematics
 nationality: 6 French
 founded: 15 electrodynamics 16 electromagnetism
Amphiaraus
 father: 6 Oicles
 mother: 12 Hypermnestra
 wife: 8 Eriphyle
 son: 8 Alcmaeon 11 Amphilochus
 daughter: 9 Demonassa
 member: 18 Seven against Thebes
 charioteer: 5 Baton
amphibian 8 seaplane 10 hydroplane, vertebrate 14 aerohydroplane
 kind: 4 frog, newt, toad 9 caecilian 10 salamander
 young: 6 larvae 7 tadpole 8 polliwog
Amphidamas
 king of: 7 Cythera
 father: 5 Aleus
 brother: 7 Cepheus
 member of: 9 Argonauts
Amphilochus
 form: 4 seer
 father: 10 Amphiaraus
 mother: 8 Eriphyle
 brother: 8 Alcmaeon
Amphimachus
 origin: 5 Greek
 mentioned in: 5 Iliad
 chief of: 6 Epeans
 father: 13 Cteatus of Elis
 killed by: 6 Hector
Amphimarus
 father: 8 Poseidon
 son: 5 Linus
 vocation: 8 musician
Amphinome
 form: 6 maiden
 father: 6 Pelias
 sister: 6 Evadne
 deceived by: 5 Medea
 killed: 6 Pelias

Amphinomus
  suitor of: 8 Penelope
Amphion
  father: 4 Zeus
  mother: 7 Antiope
  twin brother: 6 Zethus
  wife: 5 Niobe
  daughter: 7 Chloris
  built: 11 Theban walls
Amphisbaena
  form: 7 serpent
  number of heads: 3 two
amphitheater 4 bowl 5 arena 7 gallery, stadium 8 coliseum 10 auditorium
  Roman: 9 Colosseum
Amphithemis
  also: 7 Garamas
  father: 6 Apollo
  mother: 9 Acacaelis
  son: 8 Nausamon 9 Caphaurus
Amphitrite
  origin: 5 Greek
  goddess of: 3 sea
  father: 6 Nereus
  mother: 5 Doris
  husband: 8 Poseidon
Amphitruo (Amphitryon)
  author: 7 Plautus
  character: 4 Zeus 7 Alcmena, Jupiter, Mercury 10 Amphitryon
Amphitryon
  father: 7 Alcaeus
  grandfather: 7 Perseus
  uncle: 9 Electryon, Sthenelus
  wife: 7 Alcmene
  son: 8 Iphicles
  daughter: 8 Perimede
Amphitryon 38
  author: 13 Jean Giraudoux
Amphius
  ally of: 7 Trojans
amphora 3 jar, jug, urn 4 vase
Amphoterus
  father: 8 Alcmaeon
  mother: 10 Callirrhoe
  brother: 7 Acarnan
ample 3 big 4 huge, vast, wide 5 broad, large, roomy 6 enough, plenty 7 copious, immense, roomy 8 abundant, adequate, extended, generous, spacious 9 bountiful, capacious, expansive, extensive, outspread, plentiful 10 commodious, sufficient, voluminous 11 substantial 12 satisfactory 14 more than enough
amplification 7 raising 8 increase, widening 9 expansion, extension 10 developing, filling out, increasing 11 added detail, development, elaboration, enlargement, expatiation, fleshing out, heightening, lengthening, rounding out 12 augmentation 13 magnification 14 aggrandizement 15 supplementation
amplify 5 add to, raise, widen 6 deepen, expand, extend 7 augment, broaden, develop, enlarge, fill out 8 complete, heighten, increase, lengthen 9 elaborate

(on), expatiate, intensify 10 illustrate, strengthen, supplement
amplitude 4 bulk, mass, size 5 range, reach, scope, sweep, width 6 extent, volume 7 bigness, breadth, compass, expanse 8 fullness, plethora, richness, vastness 9 abundance, dimension, largeness, magnitude, plenitude, profusion 11 copiousness 12 completeness, spaciousness 13 capaciousness
amply 5 fully 6 richly 8 lavishly 9 copiously, liberally, profusely 10 abundantly, adequately, completely, generously, thoroughly 11 bountifully, plentifully 12 sufficiently, unstintingly 14 satisfactorily
amputate 5 sever 6 cut off, excise, lop off, remove 9 dismember
Ampycides
  epithet of: 6 Mopsus
  means: 12 son of Ampycus
Amram
  father: 4 Bani 6 Dishon
  son: 5 Aaron, Moses
  daughter: 6 Miriam
Amsterdam
  airport: 8 Schiphol
  canal: 11 Herengracht 13 Keizersgracht, Prinsengracht
  capital of: 7 Holland 11 Netherlands
  landmark: 8 Oude Kerk 10 Nieuwe Kerk
  museum: 7 Van Gogh 9 Stedelijk 11 Rijksmuseum
  nickname: 16 Venice of the North
  waters: 6 Amstel 7 IJ River 9 Zuiderzee 10 Ijsselmeer 13 North Sea
amuck 4 amok, nuts 6 wildly 7 berserk, bonkers 8 crackers, insanely 9 in a frenzy 10 frenziedly, maniacally 11 ferociously, murderously 14 uncontrollably
amulet 5 charm 6 fetish 8 talisman 10 lucky piece
Amulius
  father: 5 Proca
  brother: 7 Numitor
amuse 5 cheer 6 absorb, divert, occupy, please 7 beguile, engross, enliven, gladden 8 interest 9 entertain
amusement 3 fun 4 game, play 5 hobby, revel 7 delight, pastime 8 pleasure 9 avocation, diversion, enjoyment, merriment 10 recreation 11 distraction 13 entertainment
amusing 5 droll, funny, witty 7 comical, waggish 8 cheering, farcical, humorous, pleasant, pleasing 9 absorbing, beguiling, diverting 10 delightful, engrossing 11 interesting, pleasurable 12 entertaining
Amy, Gilbert
  composer of: 9 Alpha-Beth 10 Epigrammes, Mouvements 11 Antiphonies 12 Trajectories
Amyclas
  father: 7 Amphion 10 Lacedaemon
  mother: 5 Niobe 6 Sparta
Amymone
  father: 6 Danaus
  son: 8 Nauplius
  lover: 8 Poseidon

Amyntor
 king of: 8 Ormenium
 father: 7 Ormenus
 wife: 8 Cleobule
 son: 7 Phoenix
 daughter: 9 Astydamia
 concubine: 6 Phthia
 killed by: 8 Hercules

Amythaon
 father: 4 Tyro
 mother: 8 Cretheus
 wife: 7 Idomene
 son: 4 Bias 8 Melampus

An
 origin: 8 Sumerian
 god of: 6 heaven
 corresponds to: 3 Anu

Anadyomene see 9 Aphrodite

anagram 4 code 6 cipher

Anakim 11 giant people

analects 8 extracts 9 gleanings 10 miscellany, selections 11 collectanea, miscellanea

Analects of Confucius, The
 author: 9 Confucius

analeptic 9 stimulant 11 restorative

analgesic 4 drug 6 opiate 7 anodyne 8 narcotic 10 anesthetic, painkiller

analogous 4 akin, like 7 similar 8 parallel 10 comparable, equivalent 11 correlative 13 corresponding

analogy 6 simile 8 likeness, metaphor 10 comparison, similarity, similitude 11 correlation, equivalence, parallelism, resemblance 14 correspondence

analysis 4 test 5 assay, brief, study 6 digest, precis, review, search 7 breakup, inquiry, outline, summary, therapy 8 abstract, judgment, synopsis, thinking 9 appraisal, breakdown, diagnosis, partition, reasoning, reduction 10 dissection, estimation, evaluation, resolution, separation 11 examination, observation, speculation 12 dissociation 13 investigation, psychotherapy 14 interpretation, psychoanalysis

analyst 5 judge 6 shrink, tester 8 examiner, observer 9 appraiser, estimator, evaluator 12 headshrinker, investigator 13 psychoanalyst

analytic, analytical 7 logical, testing 8 rational, studious 9 inquiring, organized, searching 10 diagnostic, systematic 14 problem-solving

analyze 5 assay, judge, study 6 search 7 examine 8 appraise, consider, diagnose, evaluate, question 9 reason out 11 investigate 12 think through

Anammelech 13 Sepharvite god

Ananais
 father: 8 Nebedeus
 wife: 8 Sapphira
 sent to: 4 Paul, Saul
 lied to: 5 Peter

anarchist 5 rebel 8 mutineer, nihilist 9 insurgent, terrorist 11 syndicalist 13 revolutionary

anarchy 5 chaos 6 utopia 8 disorder 11 lawlessness 13 the millennium 19 absence of government

Anastasia
 director: 13 Anatole Litvak
 cast: 10 Helen Hayes, Yul Brynner 12 Akim Tamiroff 13 Ingrid Bergman
 Oscar for: 7 actress (Bergman)

anathema 3 ban 5 curse, taboo 7 censure 11 abomination, malediction 12 condemnation, denunciation, proscription 13 unmentionable 15 excommunication

Anathema
 author: 14 Leonid Andreyev

anathematize 4 damn 7 accurse, condemn 8 execrate, maledict 9 abominate 13 excommunicate 17 hold in abomination

Anatolia see 7 Armenia

Anatolian
 language family: 12 Indo-European
 spoken in: 9 Asia Minor
 spoken by: 8 Hittites

anatomist 12 morphologist
 American: 5 Allen, Evans 7 Herrick 8 Stockard
 Arabian: 8 Avicenna
 British: 4 Owen 5 Hooke 6 Harvey
 Dutch: 10 Swammerdam
 French: 6 Buffon, Cuvier
 German: 5 Wolff 7 Schwann
 Greek: 5 Galen 9 Aristotle 10 Herophilus 12 Erasistratus
 Italian: 8 Malpighi
 Scottish: 5 Brown

anatomize 7 analyze, dissect 18 separate into pieces

anatomy 4 body 8 analysis 9 structure 10 dissection 11 examination

Anatomy Lesson, The
 author: 10 Philip Roth

Anatomy of a Murder
 director: 13 Otto Preminger
 cast: 8 Eve Arden 9 Lee Remick 10 Ben Gazzara 12 George C Scott, James Stewart, Kathryn Grant 14 Arthur O'Connell
 score: 13 Duke Ellington

Anatomy of Melancholy, The
 author: 12 Robert Burton

Anatosaurus
 type: 8 dinosaur 10 ornithopod
 period: 10 Cretaceous
 characteristic: 10 duck-billed
 location: 12 North America

Anax
 member of: 8 Gigantes
 son: 8 Asterius

Anaxarete
 form: 8 princess

Anaxibia
 father: 6 Atreus
 mother: 6 Aerope
 brother: 8 Menelaus 9 Agamemnon
 husband: 6 Nestor 9 Strophius
 son: 7 Pylades

Anaximander
  field: 11 mathematics
  nationality: 5 Greek
  doctrine: 11 single-world
  first: 22 geometric universe model
Ancaeus
  father: 8 Poseidon
  member: 9 Argonauts
  ship: 4 Argo
  vocation: 8 helmsman
  gift: 8 strength
ancestor 8 begetter, forebear 9 precursor, prototype 10 antecedent, forefather, forerunner, procreator, progenitor 11 predecessor
ancestry 4 line, race 5 house, stock 6 family, origin 7 descent, lineage 8 heredity, pedigree 9 ancestors, blood line, genealogy, parentage 10 derivation, extraction, family tree 11 progenitors
Anchesmius see 4 Zeus
Anchiale
  form: 5 nymph
Anchinoe
  father: 5 Nilus
  husband: 5 Belus
  son: 6 Danaus 8 Aegyptus
Anchisaurus
  type: 8 dinosaur
  location: 17 Connecticut Valley
Anchises
  prince of: 4 Troy
  father: 5 Capys
  mother: 8 Themiste
  grandfather: 9 Assaracus
  uncle: 8 Laomedon
  brother: 7 Laocoon
  son: 5 Lyrus 6 Aeneas
anchor 3 fix 4 hook, moor 5 affix, basis 6 fasten, secure 7 bulwark, defense, mooring, support 8 mainstay, security 9 safeguard 10 foundation 12 ground tackle
anchorage 3 key 4 bund, dock, pier, port, quay, slip 5 berth, haven, jetty, wharf 6 harbor, marina 7 dockage, mooring, seaport 9 harborage, roadstead
ancient 3 old 4 aged 5 hoary, Greek, olden, passe, Roman 6 age-old, bygone, old hat, remote 7 antique, archaic, very old 8 long past, obsolete, outmoded, primeval, timeworn 9 classical, out-of-date, primitive 10 antiquated, fossilized, Greco-Roman 11 obsolescent, prehistoric 12 old-fashioned, out-of-fashion
ancientness 8 great age 9 antiquity 11 advanced age
ancient times 9 antiquity 10 days of yore 12 the Golden Age
Ancile
  origin: 5 Roman
  form: 6 shield
  given to: 13 Numa Pompilius
  given by: 4 Mars
  purpose: 10 protection
  copied by: 8 Mamurius

ancillary 5 minor 7 adjunct 8 inferior 9 accessory, auxiliary, dependent, secondary 10 additional, subsidiary 11 subordinate, subservient 12 contributory 13 supplementary
Ancius
  form: 7 centaur
Ancus Marcius
  king of: 4 Rome
and 3 too 4 also, more, plus 10 in addition
andante
  music: 4 even 14 moderately slow
Andean
  language family: 16 Andean-Equatorial
  group: 3 Ona 6 Aymara, Yahgan, Zaparo 7 Quechua 10 Araucanian
Andean-Equatorial
  language branch: 6 Andean 10 Equatorial
Andersen, Hans Christian
  author of: 10 Thumbelina 11 The Red Shoes 12 The Snow Queen, The Swineherd, The Tinder Box 14 The Nightingale 15 The Ugly Duckling 16 The Little Mermaid 18 The Little Match Girl 20 The Princess and the Pea 21 The Emperor's New Clothes 22 The Steadfast Tin Soldier 25 The Shepherdess and the Sweep
Anderson, Frances Margaret
  real name of: 14 Judith Anderson
Anderson, Judith
  real name: 23 Frances Margaret Anderson
  born: 8 Adelaide 9 Australia
  roles: 5 Medea 6 Hamlet, Salome 7 Macbeth, Rebecca 8 Kings Row 16 Cat on a Hot Tin Roof
Anderson, Maxwell
  author of: 7 High Tor 8 Key Largo 9 Winterset 11 Valley Forge 14 Both Your Houses, Lost in the Stars, Mary of Scotland, What Price Glory? 17 Elizabeth the Queen 20 Knickerbocker Holiday
Anderson, Sherwood
  author of: 9 Poor White 12 Beyond Desire, Dark Laughter, Horses and Men 13 Many Marriages, Winesburg Ohio 15 Death in the Woods 18 The Triumph of the Egg
Anderson, Sparky (George Lee)
  sport: 8 baseball
  position: 7 manager
  team: 9 Minnesota 14 Cincinnati Reds
Andersonville
  author: 15 MacKinlay Kantor
Andersson, Bibi
  born: 6 Sweden 9 Stockholm
  roles: 14 The Seventh Seal 16 Wild Strawberries 19 Scenes from a Marriage 20 Smiles of a Summer Night
Andes
  Spanish: 20 Cordillera de los Andes
  peak: 6 Pissis, Sajama, Sorata 7 Illampu 8 Cotopaxi, Illimani 9 Huascaran 10 Chimborazo 14 Cristobal Colon
  highest point: 9 Aconcagua

volcano: 6 Sangay, Tolima 8 Cotopaxi 10 Tungurahua

country: 4 Peru 5 Chile 6 Panama 7 Bolivia, Ecuador 8 Colombia 9 Argentina, Venezuela

river: 5 Cauca 6 Amazon, Parana 7 Orinoco, Ucayali 9 Magdalena

lake: 5 Poopo 8 Titicaca

animal: 5 llama 6 alpaca, condor, huemul 10 chinchilla

And I Worked at the Writer's Trade
author: 13 Malcolm Cowley

Andorra
other name: 13 Valls d'Andorra 16 Valleys of Andorra

capital/largest city: 14 Andorra-la-Vella

others: 3 Pal 5 Ramio 6 Ordino, Soldeu 7 Canillo, Certers 9 La Massana 11 Les Escaldes 16 San Julian de Loria

division: 6 Encamp, Ordino 7 Andorra, Camillo 9 La Massana, Sant Julia

heads of state: 13 Bishop of Urgel (Spain) 17 President of France

head of government: 11 First Syndic

monetary unit: 5 franc 6 peseta

lake: 11 Engolasters

mountain: 6 d'Etats 8 l'Estanyo, Pyrenees 10 Cataperdis

highest point: 11 Como Pedrosa

river: 6 Ariege, Valira

people: 7 Catalan 8 Andosian

language: 6 French 7 Catalan, Spanish

religion: 13 Roman Catholic

place: 12 Casa de la Vall

Moorish ruin: 4 Ceca, Meka

feature:
co-princes' representative: 7 vigueer, viguier
fiesta: 13 Bal de Morratxa
food payment to bishop: 9 la quistia

Andorra-la-Vella
capital of: 7 Andorra

and others 3 etc 4 et al 6 et alii 7 and so on 8 et cetera 10 and so forth, and the rest

And Quiet Flows the Don
author: 15 Mikhail Sholokov

character: 6 Piotra 7 Bunchuk, Natalia 14 Gregor Melekhov 16 Aksinia Astakhova

Andrea del Sarto
real name: 32 Andrea Domenico d'Agnolo di Francesco

born: 5 Italy 8 Florence

artwork: 7 Caritas 9 A Young Man 16 Birth of the Virgin, Journey of the Magi 19 Madonna of the Harpies, Portrait of a Sculptor

Andrea del Sarto
author: 14 Robert Browning

Andress, Ursula
husband: 9 John Derek

born: 5 Bern 11 Switzerland

roles: 3 She 4 Dr No 12 Casino Royale, Four for Texas

Andrew 7 apostle
brother: 6 Peter, Simon

Andrews, Dana
real name: 17 Carver Dana Andrews

brother: 12 Steve Forrest

born: 9 Collins MS

roles: 5 Laura 9 State Fair 12 Elephant Walk 13 A Walk in the Sun, Ox-Bow Incident 15 Two for the Seesaw 22 The Best Years of Our Lives

Andrews, Julie
real name: 19 Julia Elizabeth Wells

husband: 12 Blake Edwards

born: 7 England 14 Walton-on-Thames

roles: 10 My Fair Lady 11 Mary Poppins (Oscar) 14 Victor Victoria 15 The Sound of Music

Andreyev, Leonid Nikolaevich
author of: 3 S O S 5 Savva 7 Lazarus, Silence 8 Anathema 10 To the Stars 11 The Red Laugh 12 The Life of Man 16 He Who Gets Slapped 18 Love of One's Neighbor 19 Seven That Were Hanged

Andria
author: 7 Terence

Androclea
father: 18 Antipoenus of Thebes

Androcles
origin: 5 Roman

position: 5 slave

Androcles and the Lion
author: 17 George Bernard Shaw

Androgeus
father: 5 Minos

mother: 8 Pasiphae

son: 7 Alcaeus 9 Sthenelus

battled: 6 Athens

androgenous 14 hermaphroditic

Andromache
father: 6 Eetion

husband: 6 Hector

son: 6 Pielus 8 Astyanax, Molossus, Pergamus 9 Cestrinus

author: 9 Euripides

character: 6 Peleus, Thetis 7 Orestes 8 Menelaus

mistress of: 11 Neoptolemus

rival: 8 Hermione

son: 8 Molossus

setting: 8 Thessaly

Andromaque
author: 18 Jean Baptiste Racine

character:
son: 8 Astyanax
king: 7 Pyrrhus
setting: 6 Epirus

Andromeda
father: 7 Cepheus

mother: 10 Cassiopeia

husband: 7 Perseus

son: 6 Mestor, Perses 7 Alcaeus, Heleius 9 Electryon, Sthenelus

daughter: 10 Gorgophone

rescued from: 10 sea monster

rescued by: 7 Perseus

Andromeda Strain, The
author: 15 Michael Crichton

androphobia
fear of: 3 men

Androsphinx
form: 6 sphinx
head of: 3 man

and so forth 3 etc 7 and so on 8 et cetera
9 and others 10 and the rest

and so on 3 etc 8 et cetera 9 and others 10
and so forth, and the rest

And Then There Were None
director: 9 Rene Clair
based on novel by: 14 Agatha Christie
cast: 11 Roland Young 12 Louis Hayward, Walter Huston 15 Barry Fitzgerald
remade as: 16 Ten Little Indians

and thou, Brutus
Latin: 9 et tu Brute
spoken by: 12 Julius Caesar

Andvari
origin: 6 Nordic
form: 5 dwarf

Andy Capp
creator: 14 Reginald Smythe
character: 5 Vicar
wife: 3 Flo
plays: 7 snooker

Andy Griffith Show, The
character: 10 Andy Taylor, Barney Fife,
Goober Pyle, Helen Crump, Opie Taylor
11 Floyd Lawson 12 Otis Campbell 13
Aunt Bee Taylor, Howard Sprague
cast: 8 Hal Smith 9 Don Knotts, Ron
(Ronny) Howard 10 Jack Dodson 12
Andy Griffith, Anita Corsaut, Howard
McNear 13 Frances Bavier, George
Lindsey
setting: 8 Mayberry
Andy's job: 7 sheriff

anecdote 4 tale, yarn 5 story 6 sketch 12
brief account, reminiscence

anemic, anaemic 3 wan 4 dull, pale, weak
5 quiet 6 feeble, pallid 7 subdued 9 colorless 11 thin-blooded 13 characterless

anemone 4 lily 5 plant 6 flower

Anemotis
epithet of: 6 Athena
means: 5 winds

Anesidora
epithet of: 7 Demeter
means: 15 sender up of gifts

anesthesia, anaesthesia, anesthesis 6
stupor 8 numbness 11 insentience 13 loss
of feeling 15 unconsciousness

anesthetic, anaesthetic 4 drug 5 ether, local 6 caudal, opiate, spinal 7 general 8
narcotic, procaine 9 analgesic, enflurane,
halothane, lidocaine, peridural 10 chloro-
form, isoflurane, painkiller, tetracaine, thiopental 11 acupuncture, laughing gas 12 ni-
trous oxide 15 sodium pentothal

anesthetize 4 dope, drug, numb 6 deaden,
sedate

anew 5 again, newly 6 afresh 8 once more
9 over again 11 from scratch
Latin: 6 de novo

a new order of the ages is born
Latin: 17 novus ordo seclorum
author: 6 Virgil
work: 8 Eclogues

motto of: 11 US great seal

angel 3 gem 4 doll 5 jewel, power, saint 6
cherub, patron, seraph, throne, virtue 7
sponsor 8 cherabim, seraphim, treasure 9
archangel 10 benefactor, domination 11
underwriter 12 principality 14 celestial being, heavenly spirit, messenger of God 15
financial backer

Angel, fallen 5 Satan 6 Azazel 7 Lucifer

angelic 4 good, pure 5 ideal 6 divine, lovely
7 saintly 8 adorable, beatific, cherubic,
ethereal, heavenly, innocent, seraphic 9
angel-like, beautiful, celestial, rapturous,
spiritual 10 entrancing 11 enrapturing

Angelic Doctor
nickname of: 15 St Thomas Aquinas

Angelico, Fra
real name: 13 Guido di Pietro
born: 7 Vicchio 14 Castell Vecchio
artwork: 12 Annunciation 15 Madonna
Annalena 19 Descent from the Cross 21
Coronation of the Virgin 29 Madonna of
the Linen Drapers' Guild

Angelo
character in: 17 Measure for Measure
author: 11 Shakespeare

Angel of Fire, The
also: 13 The Fiery Angel
opera by: 9 Prokofiev

anger 3 ire, vex 4 bile, fury, gall, rage, rile
5 annoy, chafe, pique, wrath 6 choler, dander, enmity, enrage, hatred, madden, nettle, rankle, ruffle, spleen, temper 7 incense, inflame, outrage, provoke, umbrage 8 acrimony, embitter, irritate,
vexation 9 animosity, annoyance, displease, hostility, hot temper, ill temper,
infuriate, petulance 10 antagonism, antagonize, exacerbate, exasperate, irritation,
resentment 11 displeasure, indignation 12
exasperation, make bad blood 14 disapprobation 15 get one's dander up 16
cause ill feelings 18 ruffle one's feathers

Anger
author: 9 May Sarton

Angerboda
also: 9 Angrbodha, Angurboda
origin: 12 Scandinavian
form: 8 giantess
children: 3 Hel 6 Fenrir, Fenris 11 Iormungandr, Jormungandr 14 Midgard Serpent

Angerona
origin: 5 Roman
goddess of: 7 anguish

angle 4 bend, cusp, edge, side, turn 5 focus, slant 6 aspect, corner 7 outlook 8 position 9 viewpoint 10 divergence, standpoint 11 perspective, point of view
kind: 5 acute, right 6 obtuse 8 straight
point: 6 vertex
measure: 7 degrees

angled 4 bent 6 fished 7 crooked, slanted 8
diverged

Anglo-Frisian
language family: 12 Indo-European
branch: 8 Germanic
group: 15 Western Germanic
language: 7 English, Frisian

Angola
other name: 7 Bakongo 20 Portuguese
West Africa
capital/largest city: 6 Luanda
others: 5 Dundo 6 Ambriz, Huambo,
Lobito 7 Cabinda, Kampala, Malange,
Malanje, Salazar 8 Benguela, Cassinga,
Vila Luso 9 Ambrizete, Mocamedes 10
Mossamedes, Nova Lisboa, Silva Porto
division: 3 Bie 4 Uige 5 Huila, Lunda,
Zaire 6 Cunene, Huambo, Luanda,
Moxico 7 Cabinda, Malanje 8 Benguela 9
Cuanza Sul, Mocamedes 11 Cuanza
Norte 13 Cuando Cubango
monetary unit: 6 escudo, macuta, macute 7 angolar, centavo
mountain: 5 Chela 6 Loviti 16 Humpata
Highlands
highest point: 4 Moco
river: 4 Cuvo 5 Congo, Cuito, Longa 6
Cassai, Coanza, Cuando, Cuanza,
Cunene, Kunene, Kwango, Kwanza,
Luando 7 Chiumbe, Cubango, Zambezi
11 Lungue-Bungo
sea: 6 Indian 8 Atlantic
physical feature:
basin: 8 Okavango
desert: 9 Mocamedes
falls: 15 Catarata Ruacana, Duque de
Braganca
plain: 8 Planalto
plateau: 4 Rand 5 Huila 11 Benguela
Bie, Lunda Divide
people: 5 Bantu, Kongo, Lundu 6
Chokwe, Herero, Mbundu, Ovambo 7
Bakongo, Kangela, Kikongo 8 Kimbundu,
Kwangare 9 Ovinbundu 12 Nyaneka-
Humbi
leader: 13 Agostinho Neto 20 Jose
Eduardo dos Santos
language: 5 Bantu 8 Kimbundu,
Oumbundu 9 Ovimbundu 10 Portuguese
religion: 7 animism 10 Protestant 13 Roman Catholic
place:
fortress: 9 Sao Miguel
feature:
mahogany: 5 khaya
weed: 6 archil

Angrbodha see 9 Angerboda

angry 3 mad 5 huffy, irate, riled, vexed 6
fuming, galled, piqued, raging 7 annoyed,
boiling, burnt up, enraged, furious, hateful,
hostile, nettled 8 incensed, inflamed, offended, outraged, petulant, provoked 9 affronted, indignant, irascible, irritated, resentful, splenetic, turbulent 10 displeased,
embittered, infuriated 11 acrimonious, exasperated, ill-tempered 12 antagonistic

angst 5 dread 6 unease 7 anxiety 10 foreboding, uneasiness 12 apprehension

angstrom
abbreviation: 1 A

Angstrom, Anders Jon
field: 7 physics 9 astronomy
founded: 12 spectroscopy
mapped: 11 solar system
angstrom unit: 17 wavelength of light

anguish 3 woe 4 pain 5 agony, grief 6 misery, sorrow 7 anxiety, despair, remorse,
torment 8 distress 9 heartache, suffering

Anguish
goddess of: 8 Angerona

anguished 6 pained 7 anxious, fearful 9
tormented 10 distressed 11 heartbroken

angular 4 bent, bony, lank, lean 5 gaunt,
lanky, spare 6 jagged 7 crooked, scrawny
8 rawboned 13 sharp-cornered

Angurboda see 9 Angerboda

Angus Og
origin: 5 Irish
god of: 4 love 5 youth 6 beauty

Anicetus
father: 8 Hercules
mother: 4 Hebe

animadversion 4 flak 7 nagging, quibble 9
aspersion, criticism, pestering 12 faultfinding 14 censoriousness

animal 3 pet 5 beast, brute 6 mammal 8
creature, nonhuman, organism 9 quadruped
group: 4 bird, fish, worm 6 insect, mammal, sponge 7 primate, reptile, rotifer 8
ruminant 9 amphibian 10 vertebrate 12
invertebrate

Animal Crackers
director: 13 Victor Heerman
cast: 5 Chico, Harpo, Zeppo 7 Groucho
11 Lillian Roth 12 Marx Brothers 14 Margaret Dumont
song: 25 Hooray for Captain Spaulding

Animal Farm
author: 12 George Orwell
character: 5 Boxer 7 Mr Jones 8 Napoleon, Snowball

Animals in that Country, The
author: 14 Margaret Atwood

animate 4 fire, goad, move, stir, urge, warm
5 alive, impel, set on 6 arouse, excite, fire
up, incite, moving, prompt, spur on, vivify,
work up 7 actuate, enliven, inspire, provoke, quicken 8 activate, energize, vitalize
9 instigate, make alive, stimulate 10 invigorate, make lively 11 add spirit to 12
give energy to

animated 3 gay, hot 4 airy 5 brisk, quick,
vivid 6 active, ardent, blithe, breezy, bright,
elated, lively 7 buoyant, dynamic, fervent,
glowing, vibrant, zealous, zestful 8 exciting, spirited, sportive, vigorous 9 ebullient,
energetic, sprightly, vivacious 10 passionate 12 invigorating

animation 3 vim 4 fire, glow, life, zest 5 ardor, verve, vigor 6 action, gaiety, spirit 7
elation 8 activity, alacrity, buoyancy, vibrancy, vitality, vivacity 9 alertness, briskness, eagerness, good cheer 10 brightness, ebullience, enthusiasm, excitement,

liveliness 12 exhilaration, sportiveness 13 sprightliness

animosity 4 hate 5 anger 6 enmity, hatred, malice, rancor, strife 7 dislike, ill will 8 acrimony 9 antipathy, hostility, malignity 10 antagonism, bitterness, resentment 11 malevolence 14 unfriendliness

animus 5 anger, spite, venom 6 enmity, hatred, malice, rancor 7 disdain, dislike, ill will 8 acrimony, bad blood 9 animosity, antipathy, hostility 10 antagonism, bitterness, ill feeling, resentment 12 hard feelings

anise
botanical name: 16 Pimpinella Anisum
origin: 5 Egypt, India 13 Mediterranean
flavor: 8 licorice
use: 5 cakes, fruit, rolls 7 cookies
plant with similar flavor: 9 star anise
legend:
safeguards against: 7 evil eye 10 nightmares 11 indigestion
antidote to: 12 scorpion bite

anisette
type: 7 liqueur
origin: 6 France
flavor: 5 anise
drink: 17 Suissesse cocktail
with gin: 8 Snowball 11 Bachio Punch
substitute for: 8 Absinthe

Ankylosaurus
type: 8 dinosaur 10 ornithopod
location: 12 North America
period: 10 Cretaceous
characteristic: 7 armored

Anna
husband: 5 Tobit
daughter: 4 Mary
sister: 4 Dido
corresponds to: 11 Anna Perenna
died by: 8 drowning

Annabel Lee
author: 13 Edgar Allan Poe

Anna Christie
author: 12 Eugene O'Neill
character: 6 Marthy 8 Mat Burke 19 Chris Christopherson
ship: 14 Simeon Winthrop

Anna Karenina
author: 10 Leo Tolstoy
character: 12 Count Vronsky 13 Alexei Karenin 15 Konstantin Levin 19 Kitty Shcherbatskaya 20 Prince Stepan Oblonsky
setting: 6 Moscow, Russia 12 St Petersburg
director: 13 Clarence Brown
cast: 9 May Robson 10 Greta Garbo (Anna Karenina) 13 Basil Rathbone (Karenin), Frederic March (Vronsky) 16 Maureen O'Sullivan 18 Freddie Bartholomew
earlier film version: 4 Love

annals 7 history, minutes, records 8 archives 9 registers 10 chronicles, chronology 13 yearly records 15 historical rolls 20 chronological records

Annam see 7 Vietnam

Anna Marie
character in: 16 Giants of the Earth
author: 7 Rolvaag

Anna of the Five Towns
author: 13 Arnold Bennett

Anna Perenna
origin: 5 Roman
goddess of: 9 longevity

anneal 6 harden, temper 7 toughen

Anne of Geierstein (or, The Maiden of the Mist)
author: 14 Sir Walter Scott

annex 3 add 4 grab, join 5 affix, merge, seize 6 adjoin, append, attach, tack on 7 acquire, connect, subjoin 8 addition 9 appendage 10 attachment 11 appropriate, expropriate, incorporate

Annfwn
also: 5 Annwn
origin: 5 Welsh
means: 8 paradise

Annie Hall
director: 10 Woody Allen
cast: 9 Carol Kane, Paul Simon 10 Woody Allen 11 Diane Keaton, Tony Roberts 13 Shelley Duvall 15 Colleen Dewhurst
Oscar for: 7 actress (Keaton), picture 8 director (Allen) 10 screenplay

annihilate 3 end 5 erase, waste 7 abolish, destroy, wipe out 8 decimate, demolish, lay waste 9 eradicate, extirpate, liquidate 10 extinguish, obliterate 11 exterminate

annihilation 9 abolition, wiping out 11 destruction, extirpation, laying waste, liquidation 12 obliteration 13 extermination

anniversary 4 fete 7 holiday, name day 8 birthday, feast day 9 centenary 10 centennial 11 bicentenary, celebration 12 bicentennial 13 commemoration, golden jubilee 16 sesquicentennial

Ann-Margret
real name: 16 Ann-Margret Olsson
husband: 10 Roger Smith
born: 6 Sweden 9 Valsjobyn
roles: 5 Tommy 12 Bye-Bye Birdie 15 Carnal Knowledge

anno mundi 19 in the year of the world

anno regni 19 in the year of the reign

annotate 5 gloss 6 remark 7 comment, explain, expound 8 construe, footnote 9 elucidate, explicate, interpret 10 commentate

annotation 4 note 5 gloss 6 remark 7 comment 8 exegesis, footnote 10 commentary, marginalia 11 elucidation, explication, observation

announce 5 augur 6 herald, reveal, signal 7 betoken, declare, divulge, give out, portend, presage, publish, signify, trumpet 8 disclose, foretell, proclaim 9 advertise, broadcast, harbinger 10 promulgate 11 disseminate

announcement 9 broadcast, statement 11 declaration 12 proclamation

annoy 3 irk, nag, tax, vex 4 gall, rile 5 harry, tease, worry 6 badger, bother, harass, heckle, hector, nettle, pester, plague, ruffle 7 disturb, provoke, torment, trouble 8 distract, irritate 10 exasperate 13 inconvenience

annoyance 6 bother 8 irritant, nuisance, vexation 10 irritation 11 distraction, disturbance

annoyed 5 irked, upset, vexed 9 disturbed, irritated, perturbed 11 discomposed 12 disconcerted

Ann Sothern Show, The
  character: 6 Johnny 10 Olive Smith 11 James Devery, Katy O'Connor 13 Jason Macauley
  cast: 9 Don Porter 10 Ann Sothern, Ann Tyrrell 11 Ernest Truex 12 Jack Mullaney

annual 4 weed 5 plant 6 flower, serial 7 gazette, journal, reports 8 bulletin, magazine, notebook, periodic 9 vegetable 10 periodical, record book

annuity 6 income 7 pension, stipend 9 allowance

annul 4 undo, void 6 cancel, negate, recall, repeal, revoke 7 abolish, nullify, rescind, retract, reverse 8 abrogate, dissolve 10 invalidate

annulment 6 recall, repeal 7 undoing, voiding 8 reversal 9 abolition 10 abrogation, retraction, revocation 11 dissolution, repudiation 12 cancellation, invalidation 13 nullification

annus mirabilis 13 year of wonders

Annwn *see* 6 Annfwn

anodyne 4 balm 6 solace 7 comfort 9 comforter 10 palliative

anoint 3 oil 5 crown 6 ordain 8 put oil on 9 pour oil on

Anointed One 5 Jesus 7 Messiah

anomalous 3 odd 7 bizarre, strange 8 abnormal, atypical, peculiar 9 irregular, monstrous 11 incongruous 12 out of keeping

anomaly 6 oddity, rarity 9 deviation 10 aberration 11 abnormality, incongruity, peculiarity 12 eccentricity, irregularity 18 exception to the rule

anon 4 soon, then 5 again, later 7 by and by, shortly 8 tomorrow 9 afterward, presently 10 before long 11 immediately, in the future

anonymous 7 unnamed 8 nameless, unsigned 12 unidentified 13 bearing no name 14 unacknowledged 19 of unknown authorship

anoplura
  class: 8 hexopoda
  phylum: 10 arthropoda
  group: 11 sucking lice

another 4 else, more 5 extra, other 7 further, renewed 9 accessory, otherwise 10 additional 12 supplemental 13 something else, supplementary 14 different thing

Anouilh, Jean
  author of: 6 Becket 8 Antigone, Eurydice, Leocadia, L'hermine 11 Dear Antoine 14 Time Remembered 15 Le Bal des Voleurs, Thieves' Carnival 16 Point of Departure, Ring Round the Moon 19 Waltz of the Toreadors 20 L'Invitation au Chateau 23 Traveller Without Luggage

answer 3 say 4 fill, meet, suit 5 reply, serve, solve, write 6 be like, rejoin, retort 7 conform, fulfill, react to, resolve, respond 8 be enough, response, solution 9 be similar, rejoinder 10 be adequate, correspond, pass muster, resolution 11 acknowledge, explanation 12 be correlated, be equivalent, be sufficient, do well enough 14 acknowledgment, be satisfactory

answerable 6 liable 8 beholden 10 chargeable 11 accountable, responsible

Answer as a Man
  author: 14 Taylor Caldwell

ant
  caste: 4 male 5 queen 6 worker 7 soldier
  kind: 3 red 4 army, fire 5 dairy, thief 6 beggar, farmer, velvet, weaver 7 formica, janitor, pharaoh 8 honeypot, mushroom 9 Argentine, carpenter, cornfield, harvester, legionary 10 leaf cutter 11 little black 12 fungus grower, odorous house, southern fire 13 mound building 14 Texas harvester
  group of: 6 colony

Antaea
  epithet of: 4 Rhea 6 Cybele 7 Demeter
  means: 6 prayer

Antaeus
  form: 5 giant
  father: 8 Poseidon
  mother: 2 Ge
  gift: 13 invincibility
  power derived from: 5 Earth
  crushed by: 8 Hercules
  crushed in: 3 air
  home: 6 Africa

antagonism 5 spite 6 animus, enmity, hatred, rancor, strife 7 discord, dislike, rivalry 8 aversion, clashing, conflict, friction 9 animosity, antipathy, hostility 10 bitterness, dissension, opposition, resentment 11 detestation

antagonist 3 foe 5 enemy, rival 7 opposer 8 attacker, opponent 9 adversary, assailant, disputant 10 competitor, contestant

antagonistic 7 hostile 8 contrary, inimical 9 rancorous 10 antisocial, unfriendly 11 belligerent 12 antipathetic, disputatious

antagonize 5 repel 6 offend 8 alienate, estrange

Antagoras
  occupation: 8 shepherd
  home: 3 Cos
  challenged: 8 Hercules

Antananarivo, Tananarive
  capital of: 10 Madagascar

Antarctica
  division: 10 Wilkes Land 13 Marie Byrd Land, Queen Maud Land 14 Edith Ronne Land 17 Ellsworth Highland
  island: 4 Ross 5 Peter, Scott 6 Biscoe, Hearst 7 Ballery, Charcot 8 Adelaide, Elephant 9 Alexander, Joinville, Roosevelt

10 Coronation, King George 11 South Orkney 13 South Shetland
mountain: 8 Sentinel 9 Pensacola 14 Transantarctic 23 Executive Committee Range
valley: 6 Wright
river: 4 Onyx
natural resource/mineral: 4 coal
plant life: 4 moss 5 algae, fungi 6 lichen, pollen 8 bacteria
animal: 4 lice, mite, tick 5 whale 7 fur seal 8 ross seal 9 crabeater 11 weddell seal, wingless fly
bird: 4 skua 6 fulmar, petrel 7 penguin 10 cape pigeon
sea: 4 Ross 5 Davis 6 Scotia 7 Weddell 8 Amundsen 14 Bellingshausen

ante 3 bet, pot 5 stake, wager 12 beginning bet

anteater 5 sloth 7 echidna 8 aardvark 9 armadillo

antecede 7 precede, predate 8 go before, preexist 10 anticipate

ante Christum 12 before Christ
. **abbreviation:** 2 AC

antedate 7 precede, predate 8 antecede, go before 9 come first 10 anticipate 12 happen before

Antediluvian 14 before the flood

antediluvian 7 antique, archaic 8 obsolete 10 antiquated

antelope 8 ruminant
family: 7 Bovidae
kind: 3 doe, gnu 4 buck, deer, fawn, kudu, oryx, roan 5 bongo, eland, moose, sable 6 dik-dik, duiker, impala, lechwe, nilgai 7 gazelle, gemsbok, gerenuk 8 bluebuck, bontebok, steinbok 9 blackbuck, sitatunga, springbok, waterbuck 10 four-horned 12 Klipspringer
habitat: 4 Asia 6 Africa

Antelope State
nickname of: 8 Nebraska

antenna 6 aerial, feeler

anterior 5 front, prior 7 forward, in front 8 previous 9 precedent 10 antecedent 12 placed before

Anteros
brother: 4 Eros
avenger of: 14 unrequited love

Antevorta
also: 6 Prorsa 7 Porrima
form: 5 nymph
member of: 7 Camenae
gift: 8 prophecy

Anthas
father: 8 Poseidon
mother: 7 Alcyone

Anthea
epithet of: 4 Hera
means: 7 flowery

Antheil, George
born: 9 Trenton NJ
autobiography: 13 Bad Boy of Music
composer of: 7 Volpone 12 Helen Retires, Jazz Symphony 13 Sonata Sauvage, Transatlantic 14 Airplane Sonata 15 Ballet Mecanique

anthem 4 hymn, song 5 carol, ditty, music, paean, psalm 6 ballad, sacred 7 cantata 8 doxology 11 church music

Anthesteria
origin: 5 Greek
festival of: 4 wine 6 spring 7 flowers

Antheus
father: 7 Antenor
killed by: 5 Paris

anthology 6 choice, digest 7 garland 8 analects, chapbook, extracts, treasury 9 gleanings, scrapbook 10 collection, compendium, miscellany, selections 11 collectanea, compilation, florilegium, miscellanea 15 commonplace book

Anthony Adverse
author: 18 William Hervey Allen

anthophobia
fear of: 7 flowers

anthropologist
American: 4 Boas, Mead 5 Lowie, Sapir 6 Geertz, Linton, Morgan 7 Kroeber 8 Benedict
British: 5 Leach, Tylor 6 Fortes, Leakey, Rivers 14 Evans-Pritchard, Radcliffe-Brown
French: 5 Mauss 8 Durkheim 11 Levi-Strauss
Polish: 10 Malinowski

anthropology
term: 4 myth 6 custom, ritual 7 culture, kinship 8 artifact 9 ethnology, evolution, field work 11 ethnography 16 natural selection
type/related study: 5 legal, urban 6 social 7 applied, medical 8 cultural, economic, physical 9 political 11 linguistics 12 human ecology 13 psychological 19 structural-symbolist
famous study: 3 San 4 Kung 7 Eskimos, Samoans, Tasaday 10 Aborigines 16 Pacific Islanders

anthropophobia
fear of: 6 people

Antia
husband: 7 Proetus
daughter: 7 Lysippe
slandered by: 11 Bellerophon

antibiotic 4 drug 5 venom 6 poison 8 curative 9 antidotal, antitoxic, pesticide 10 wonder drug 11 insecticide, miracle drug
kind: 8 neomycin, subtilin 9 mycomycin 10 ampicillin, penicillin 12 erythromycin

antic, antics 5 larks, sport 6 pranks, tricks 9 escapades 10 buffoonery, skylarking, tomfoolery 11 shenanigans 12 clownishness, monkeyshines 14 practical jokes

anticipate 5 await 6 expect 7 count on, foresee, long for, look for, predict 8 envision, forecast, foretell 9 pin hope on 10 look toward 13 look forward to

anticipation 4 hope 10 expectancy 11 expectation, preparation

anticlimax 7 letdown 8 comedown 14 disappointment

antidote 4 cure 6 remedy 9 antitoxin 10 antipoison, corrective 12 counteragent, countervenom 13 counterpoison 14 countermeasure

Antigone
author: 9 Sophocles 11 Jean Anouilh
character: 6 Ismene 8 Tiresias
father: 7 Oedipus
mother: 7 Jocasta
brother: 8 Eteocles 9 Polynices
sister: 6 Ismene
uncle: 5 Creon
cousin/lover: 6 Haemon
defied: 5 Creon

Antigua and Barbuda
capital/largest city: 7 St John's
government:
member of: 26 West Indies Associated States
head of state: 14 British monarch 15 governor-general
island: 4 Long 5 Guana 7 Antigua, Barbuda, Redonda
highest point: 9 Boggy Peak
sea: 9 Caribbean
physical feature:
cove: 5 Royal
harbor/harbour: 7 English
people: 7 African, British 8 Lebanese 10 Portuguese
language: 7 English
religion: 8 Anglican, Moravian 13 Roman Catholic
feature: 15 Nelson's Dockyard

anti-intellectual 5 yahoo 7 lowbrow 9 ignoramus, vulgarian 10 illiterate, philistine

Antilochus
father: 6 Nestor
brother: 11 Thrasymedes
friend: 8 Achilles

Antimachus
origin: 5 Greek
mentioned in: 5 Iliad
chieftain of: 7 Trojans

antimony
chemical symbol: 2 Sb

Antinous
suitor of: 8 Penelope
killed by: 8 Odysseus

Antiochus
father: 8 Hercules
mother: 4 Meda

Antiope
form: 6 Amazon
father: 7 Nycteus
sister: 9 Hippolyte
son: 6 Zethus 7 Amphion 10 Hippolytus
mistress of: 7 Theseus

antipathetic 6 averse 7 hostile 8 inimical 9 rancorous 11 ill-disposed

antipathy 6 enmity, rancor 7 disgust, dislike, ill will 9 aversion, distaste, loathing 9 animosity, hostility, repulsion 10 abhorrence, antagonism, repugnance 14 unfriendliness

Antiphas
father: 7 Laocoon

Antiphates
origin: 5 Greek
mentioned in: 5 Iliad 7 Odyssey
father: 8 Melampus
chief of: 10 Laestrygon
occupation: 7 warrior 9 chieftain
killed by: 8 Leonteus

Antipholus
character in: 17 The Comedy of Errors
author: 11 Shakespeare

antiphony 6 chorus 7 refrain 8 response

Antiphus
origin: 5 Greek
mentioned in: 5 Iliad 7 Odyssey
form: 5 nymph
father: 5 Priam 10 Talaemenes
half-brother: 4 Isus
ally of: 4 Troy
devoured by: 10 Polyphemus

antipode 8 contrary, opposite 10 antithesis

Antipoenus
daughter: 5 Alcis 9 Androclea
home: 6 Thebes
descendant of: 6 Sparti

Antiquary, The
author: 14 Sir Walter Scott

antiquated 5 dated, passe 7 antique, archaic 8 obsolete, outdated, outmoded 9 out-of-date 11 obsolescent 12 old-fashioned

antique 3 old 5 curio, relic 6 rarity 7 bibelot, trinket 9 objet d'art 10 antiquated, memorabile 11 memorabilia

antiquities 6 relics 8 artifact 9 monuments

antiquity 7 oldness 8 great age 11 ancientness 12 ancient times

antiseptic 7 aseptic, sterile 8 germ-free 9 germicide 10 germ killer 11 bactericide 12 disinfectant, prophylactic

antisocial 7 asocial, hostile 8 menacing, retiring, unsocial 9 alienated 10 disruptive, rebellious, unfriendly, unsociable 11 belligerent, sociopathic 12 antagonistic, misanthropic

antithesis 7 inverse, reverse 8 antipode, contrary, contrast, converse, opposite

antithetical 6 contrary, opposing, opposite 10 discrepant, refutatory 11 conflicting, disagreeing 13 contradictory 14 countervailing, irreconcilable

antitoxin 5 serum 8 antidote 9 antivenom 12 counteragent 13 counterpoison

antler 4 horn, knob, rack 5 spike 6 shovel 8 deerhorn, troching
part: 3 bay 4 brow 5 crown, royal

ant lion
also: 8 lacewing 9 doodlebug
kind: 6 owlfly 9 dusty wing, mantidfly 12 spongillafly 13 brown lacewing, giant lacewing, green lacewing 14 beaded lacewing 15 ithonid lacewing 16 pleasing lacewing

Antonello da Messina
born: 5 Italy 7 Messina
artwork: 8 Ecce Homo 11 Three Angels 13 Il Condottiere (Portrait of a Man), Sal-

vador Mundi **21** Saint Jerome in his
Study

Antonio
  character in: 12 Twelfth Night **19** The
  Merchant of Venice
  author: 11 Shakespeare

Antonioni, Michelangelo
  director of: 6 Blowup **8** The Night **10**
  The Eclipse **12** The Adventure, The Passenger **14** Zabriskie Point

Antony, Mark
  also: 14 Marcus Antonius
  member of: 11 triumvirate
  other triumvirs: 7 Lepidus **8** Octavian
  (Caesar Augustus)
  lover: 9 Cleopatra
  cousin: 12 Julius Caesar
  wife: 7 Octavia
  battle: 6 Actium **8** Philippi **9** Pharsalus
  invaded: 7 Parthia
  died by: 7 suicide

Antony and Cleopatra
  author: 18 William Shakespeare
  character: 7 Octavia **9** Cleopatra **10**
  Mark Antony **14** Octavius Caesar
  setting: 5 Egypt
  Cleopatra bitten by: 3 asp

antonym 8 opposite **10** antithesis
  abbreviation: 3 ant

Antrodemus
  type: 8 dinosaur, therapod
  also called: 10 Allosaurus
  period: 8 Jurassic **10** Cretaceous

Anu
  origin: 8 Akkadian
  god of: 6 heaven
  corresponds to: 2 An

Anubis
  origin: 8 Egyptian
  god of: 5 tombs **9** embalming
  weigher of: 15 hearts of the dead
  represented by head of: 6 jackal

Anunnaki
  origin: 8 Sumerian
  member of: 14 divine assembly
  assembly headed by: 2 An **5** Enlil

anvil 5 block, incus **9** converter **11** trans-
former

anxiety 4 fear **5** alarm, angst, dread, worry
6 unease **7** anguish, concern, tension **8**
disquiet, distress, suspense **9** misgiving **10**
foreboding, solicitude, uneasiness **11** disquietude, fretfulness **12** apprehension

anxiety-ridden 7 anxious, fearful, nervous
10 distraught **11** worried sick **12** apprehensive

anxious 4 avid, keen **5** eager, tense **6** ardent, intent, uneasy **7** alarmed, earnest,
fearful, fervent, fretful, itching, uptight,
wanting, worried, zealous **8** desirous, troubled, yearning **9** anguished, concerned,
disturbed, expectant, impatient **10** disquieted, distressed **11** overwrought **12** apprehensive

any 3 all, one **4** each, lone, sole, some **5**
every **6** single, unique **8** anything, singular,
solitary **9** something **10** individual, quanti-
fier

anybody 3 any **6** anyone **8** anything

anyhow *see* **6** anyway

anything 3 any **4** some **5** aught **6** anyone **7**
anybody

anyway 6 anyhow **8** sloppily **9** at any rate,
in any case **10** carelessly, in any event, regardless **11** haphazardly, just the same,
nonetheless **12** nevertheless **13** indifferently **14** without concern

anywhere 8 anyplace, wherever **11** where-
soever

Aoede
  muse of: 4 song

Ao-men *see* **5** Macao

A-1 3 ace **4** aces, fine, tops **5** great, prime,
super **6** choice, grade-A, superb, tip-top **7**
capital **8** sterling, superior, top-notch **9** excellent, first-rate, superfine **10** first-class,
tremendous **11** crackerjack, outstanding,
superlative

Aornis
  tributary of: 4 Styx

Aornum
  entrance to: 5 Hades
  used by: 7 Orpheus

Aotearoa *see* **10** New Zealand

apace 4 fast **7** flat-out, hastily, quickly, rapidly, swiftly **8** speedily **9** posthaste **10** at
top speed **11** double-quick, on the double
12 lickety-split **13** expeditiously, precipitately **18** hell bent for leather

Apache
  language family: 10 Athabascan, Athapaskan
  band: 9 Jacarilla, Mescalero, San Carlos
  13 White Mountain
  location: 7 Arizona **8** Oklahoma **9** New
  Mexico
  leader: 7 Cochise **8** Geronimo
  noted for: 8 basketry

apart 4 afar **5** alone, aloof, aside **6** cut off **7**
asunder, distant **8** by itself, divorced, isolated, separate **9** by oneself, into parts, to
one side **10** into pieces, separately

apartment 3 pad **4** flat **5** rooms, suite

Apartment, The
  director: 11 Billy Wilder
  cast: 10 Jack Lemmon, Ray Walston **13**
  Fred MacMurray **15** Shirley MacLaine
  Oscar for: 7 picture

apathetic 4 cold **7** unmoved **9** impassive,
unfeeling **10** disengaged, impossible,
phlegmatic, spiritless **11** emotionless, indifferent, passionless, uncommitted, unconcerned, unemotional **12** uninterested, unresponsive

apathy 8 coolness, lethargy, numbness **9**
lassitude, unconcern **11** impassivity,
inattention, passiveness **12** indifference **13**
impassibility, lack of feeling **14** lack of interest **15** emotionlessness **16** unresponsiveness

apatite
 source: 5 Burma, Mogok
Apatosaurus *see* 12 Brontosaurus
ape 4 copy, echo, mock 5 mimic 6 follow, mirror, monkey, parody, parrot 7 emulate, imitate, primate 8 travesty 9 burlesque 10 caricature
 family: 8 Pongidae
 combining form: 8 pithecus
 study of: 11 pithecology
 kind: 6 gibbon 7 gorilla, siamang 9 orangutan 10 chimpanzee
 famous: 8 Godzilla, King Kong
Apemius
 epithet of: 4 Zeus
 means: 13 averter of ills
Apemosyne
 father: 7 Catreus
 brother: 11 Althaemenes
 ravished by: 6 Hermes
 killed by: 11 Althaemenes
Apepi *see* 7 Apophis
apercu 6 glance 7 glimpse, insight, outline, summary
aperture 3 gap 4 hole, rent, rift, slit, slot 5 chink, cleft, space 6 breach 7 fissure, opening, orifice 10 interstice
apex 3 cap, tip 4 acme, peak 5 crest, crown 6 apogee, climax, height, summit, vertex, zenith 8 pinnacle 11 culmination 12 consummation, highest point 13 crowning point
Aphareus
 king of: 8 Messenia
 father: 8 Perieres
 mother: 10 Gorgophone
 grandfather: 7 Perseus
 brother: 5 Leucippus
 wife: 5 Arene
 son: 4 Ides 7 Lynceus
aphasic 4 dumb, mute 12 inarticulate 17 incapable of speech
Aphesius
 epithet of: 4 Zeus
 means: 8 releaser
aphid
 variety: 3 pea 4 pine, rose 5 apple, grape, peach, tulip 6 cereal, cotton, potato, spruce 7 adelgid, cabbage 8 pear root 9 elm woolly, plant lice, water lily 10 gall-making, phylloxera
Aphidas
 father: 5 Arcas
 son: 5 Aleus
aphorism 5 adage, axiom, maxim 6 dictum, old saw, saying, slogan, truism 7 epigram, proverb 8 apothegm
aphrodisiac 4 sexy 6 carnal, erotic 7 fleshly, philter, raunchy 8 prurient 9 cantharis 10 love potion 11 cantharides, magic potion, stimulating
Aphrodite
 also: 6 Urania 7 Cyprian, Paphian 8 Cytherea 10 Anadyomene
 origin: 5 Greek
 goddess of: 4 love 6 beauty
 husband: 10 Hephaestus
 lover: 4 Ares
 son: 5 Lyrus 6 Deimos, Phobus, Rhodus 7 Priapus
 daughter: 8 Harmonia
 corresponds to: 5 Venus
 epithet: 6 Acraea, Scotia 7 Doritis, Erycina, Limenia 8 Melaenis, Nymphaea, Pandemos 9 Migonitis 11 Aphrogeneia, Apostrophia
Aphrogeneia
 epithet of: 9 Aphrodite
 means: 8 foam born
Apia
 capital of: 12 Western Samoa
apiary 4 hive 7 beehive
apiece 4 each 9 severally 12 individually, respectively
a pied 6 on foot 7 walking
Apis
 origin: 8 Egyptian
 also: 3 Hap 4 Hapi
 form: 4 bull
 from: 7 Memphis
 father: 6 Apollo 9 Phoroneus
 mother: 8 Teledice
 sister: 5 Niobe
 nephew: 5 Argus
 rid Argos of: 8 serpents
 killed by: 7 Aetolus
 worshipped at: 7 Memphis
aplomb 5 poise 7 balance 8 calmness, coolness 9 composure, sang-froid, stability 10 confidence, equanimity 11 intrepidity, savoir faire 13 self-assurance, self-composure 14 self-confidence, self-possession 16 level-headedness 16 imperturbability
Apocalypse Now
 director: 18 Francis Ford Coppola
 based on: 15 Heart of Darkness
 novel by: 12 Joseph Conrad
 cast: 11 Martin Sheen 12 Marlon Brando, Robert Duvall 16 Frederick Forrest
 setting: 7 Vietnam
apocalyptic 4 dire 7 ominous 8 oracular 9 far-seeing, ill-boding, ill-omened, prescient, prophetic, revealing 10 disclosing, eye-opening, foreboding, portentous, predictive, revelatory 11 prophetical 12 inauspicious, revelational 15 prognosticative
apocryphal 7 dubious 8 disputed, doubtful, mythical, spurious 10 fabricated, fictitious, unofficial, unverified 11 unauthentic, uncanonical 12 questionable, unauthorized 14 probably untrue 15 unauthenticated, unsubstantiated
apogee 3 top 4 acme, apex, peak 5 crest, crown 6 climax, summit, vertex, zenith 8 meridian, pinnacle 9 high point 11 culmination 12 highest point
Apollo
 also: 7 Phoebus, Pythius 9 Musagetes
 origin: 5 Greek, Roman
 god of: 5 light, music 6 beauty, poetry 7 healing 8 prophecy
 father: 4 Zeus
 mother: 4 Leto
 twin sister: 7 Artemis

sons: 5 Iamus 8 Laodocus 9 Aristaeus, Asclepius, Philammon 10 Polypoetes
corresponds to: 5 Paeon 8 Hyperion
epithet: 6 Loxias 7 Acesius, Agraeus, Agyieus, Carneus, Phyteus, Spodius 8 Grynaeus 9 Parnopius, Smintheus 10 Alexicacus, Archegetes, Boedromius, Delphinius 11 Argyrotoxus, Epibaterius 12 Platanistius

Apollyon 4 hell 7 Abaddon

apologetic 5 sorry 8 contrite, penitent 9 defensive, regretful 10 excusatory, mitigatory, remorseful 11 exonerative, extenuatory, vindicatory 12 apologetical 13 justificatory, making excuses 15 self-reproachful

Apologia pro Vita Sua
    author: 15 John Henry Newman (Cardinal)

Apologie for Poetrie (Defense for Poetry)
    author: 15 Sir Philip Sidney

apologist 7 pleader 8 advocate, defender 9 supporter

apologize 9 beg pardon 11 make apology 13 express regret

apology 6 excuse 7 defense 11 explanation, vindication 13 begging pardon, justification

Apomyius
    epithet of: 4 Zeus
    means: 14 averter of flies

Apophis
    also: 5 Apepi
    form: 7 serpent
    habitat: 8 darkness
    destroyed daily by: 4 Dawn

Apophthegms New and Old
    author: 12 Francis Bacon

apostasy 7 atheism, perfidy 8 unbelief 9 defection, disbelief, recreancy 10 disloyalty, infidelity, irreligion 11 godlessness 13 double-dealing

apostate 6 bolter 7 heretic, seceder, traitor 8 defector, deserter, recanter, recusant, renegade, turncoat 9 dissenter, dissident, turnabout 10 backslider 13 nonconformist, tergiversator

apostle 5 envoy 6 zealot 7 pioneer, witness 8 activist, advocate, disciple, emissary, exponent, preacher 9 messenger, proponent, supporter 10 evangelist, missionary, propagator 12 propagandist, proselytizer, spokesperson

Apostle, The
    author: 10 Sholem Asch

Apostles 4 John, Jude, Levi, Paul 5 Jacob, James, Peter, Simon 6 Andrew, Philip, Thomas 7 Matthew 8 Barnabas, Matthias 9 Nathanael, Thaddaeus 11 Bartholomew 12 James the Less 13 Judas Iscariot
    apostle to the Gentiles: 4 Paul
    apostle to the English: 9 Augustine
    apostle to the Irish: 7 Patrick
    apostle to the Goths: 7 Ulfilas
    apostle to the Germans: 8 Boniface
    apostle to the French: 5 Denis
    apostle to the American Indians: 9 John Eliot

Apostrophia
    epithet of: 9 Aphrodite
    means: 24 rejecter of sinful passions

apothegm 5 adage, axiom, maxim, motto 6 dictum 7 epigram, proverb 8 aphorism 9 catchword

apotheosis 7 epitome, essence 9 elevation 10 embodiment, exaltation 11 deification 12 canonization, consecration, enshrinement, idealization, quintessence 13 dignification, glorification, magnification 15 immortalization

Appalachian Spring
    ballet by: 7 Copland

appall 4 stun 5 abash, alarm, repel, shock 6 dismay, offend, revolt, sicken 7 disgust, horrify, outrage, terrify, unnerve 8 frighten, nauseate 10 dishearten

appalled 6 aghast 7 alarmed, shocked 8 dismayed, outraged, repelled, revolted 9 disgusted, horrified, nauseated

appalling 4 dire, grim 5 awful 6 horrid 7 fearful, ghastly 8 alarming, dreadful, horrible, horrific, shocking, terrible 9 dismaying, frightful, repellent, repulsive, revolting, sickening 10 abominable, disgusting, horrifying, nauseating, outrageous, terrifying 11 frightening, intolerable 12 insufferable 13 disheartening

apparatus 4 gear 5 gismo, setup, tools 6 device, gadget, outfit, system, tackle 7 machine 8 material, utensils 9 appliance, equipment, machinery, materials, mechanism 10 implements 11 contraption, contrivance, instruments 12 organization 13 paraphernalia

apparatus criticus 8 exegesis 10 annotation 11 elucidation, explication 14 interpretation

apparel 4 duds, garb, gear, togs 5 array, dress, habit, robes 6 attire 7 clothes, costume, raiment, threads, vesture 8 clothing, garments 9 equipment, trappings, vestments 13 accoutrements

appareled 4 clad 5 robed 6 garbed, suited 7 attired, clothed, covered, dressed

apparent 4 open 5 clear, overt, plain 6 likely, marked, patent 7 blatant, evident, obvious, seeming, visible 8 clear-cut, distinct, manifest, probable 10 clear as day, ostensible, presumable 11 conspicuous, discernible, perceivable, perceptible, self-evident, unequivocal 12 unmistakable 14 understandable

apparently
    Latin: 7 ex facie

apparition 5 ghost, shade, spook 6 spirit, wraith 7 phantom, specter 8 phantasm, presence, revenant 10 phenomenon 13 manifestation 15 materialization

appeal 3 beg, SOS 4 plea, pull, suit 5 apply, charm, plead, sue to, tempt 6 adjure, allure, engage, entice, excite, invite, invoke 7 attract, beseech, entreat, implore, request, solicit 8 call upon, charisma, entreaty, interest, petition 9 fascinate 10 adjuration, attraction, supplicate 11 fascination 12 solicitation, supplication

appealing 7 likable, lovable 8 adjuring, charming, engaging, enticing, fetching, inviting, pleading, pleasing, tempting 10 attractive, entreating, requesting, soliciting 11 charismatic, petitioning 12 irresistible, supplicating

appear 4 look, seem, show 5 arise 6 crop up, emerge, loom up, show up, turn up 7 be clear, be plain, come out, perform, surface 8 be patent 9 be evident, be obvious 10 be apparent, be manifest 11 be published, come to light, materialize

appearance 4 look 5 guise, image 6 advent, aspect, coming 7 arrival, pretext 8 pretense 9 appearing, emergence, showing up, turning up 10 impression 11 outward show 13 manifestation 15 materialization

appear at 6 attend, show up 9 perform at

appease 4 calm, dull, ease, lull 5 abate, allay, blunt, quell, quiet, slake, still 6 pacify, quench, solace, soothe, temper 7 assuage, compose, mollify, placate, relieve, satisfy 8 mitigate 9 alleviate 10 conciliate, propitiate 11 accommodate

appeasement 6 easing 7 abating, dulling 8 allaying, blunting, giving in 9 abatement, assuasion, quenching 10 mitigation, submission 11 alleviation, assuagement 12 conciliation, pacification, propitiation, satisfaction 13 accommodation, gratification, mollification

appellation 3 tag 4 name 5 title 6 handle 7 epithet, moniker 8 cognomen 9 sobriquet 11 designation, nom de guerre

append 3 add 4 join 5 affix 6 attach, hang on, tack on 7 subjoin, suspend 10 supplement

appendage 3 arm, leg 4 limb, tail 6 branch, feeler, member 7 adjunct 8 addition, offshoot, tentacle 9 accessory, auxiliary, extension, extremity 10 attachment, supplement

appendix 7 codicil 8 addendum, addition 10 back matter, postscript, supplement

appertain 7 apply to, concern, refer to 8 bear upon, be part of, belong to, inhere in, relate to 9 touch upon

appetite 4 zest 5 gusto 6 desire, hunger, liking, relish, thirst 7 craving, passion, stomach 8 fondness, penchant, yearning 10 proclivity 11 inclination

appetizer 6 canape, dainty, savory, tidbit 8 aperitif, cocktail, delicacy 9 antipasto 11 bonne bouche, hors d'oeuvre

appetizing 6 savory 8 alluring, enticing, inviting, tempting 9 appealing, palatable, succulent 10 attractive 11 tantalizing 13 mouth-watering

applaud 4 clap, hail, laud 5 extol 6 praise 7 acclaim, commend 8 eulogize 10 compliment 12 congratulate

applaudable 8 laudable 9 admirable, desirable, excellent 11 commendable, meritorious, outstanding 12 praiseworthy

applause 5 kudos 6 praise 7 acclaim, ovation 8 approval, clapping, plaudits 9 accolades 11 compliments

apple 5 Malus 15 Malus Sylvestris

   varieties/fruit: 4 Crab, Lodi 6 Pippin 7 Baldwin, Stayman, Winesap 8 Ben Davis, Cortland, Jonathan, McIntosh 9 Delicious 10 Rome Beauty 11 Granny Smith, Gravenstein, Northern Spy, Summer Rambo 12 Grimes Golden, York Imperial 13 Yellow Newtown 14 Stayman Winesap 15 Yellow Delicious 17 Esopus Spitzenberg, Yellow Transparent 19 Rhode Island Greening

   varieties/tree: 2 Wi 3 Kai, Kau, Sea, Wax 4 Cane, Java, Jew's, Pond, Rose, Star 5 Adam's, Baked, Belle, Blade, Chess, Conch, Malay, Melon, Thorn 6 Balsam, Indian, Mammee, Possum 7 Chinese, Custard, Dead Sea, Mexican 8 Elephant, Kangaroo, Otaheite, Paradise, Peruvian 11 Soulard crab, Toringo crab 12 Siberian crab

   beverage: 5 cider 8 Calvados 9 Applejack

apple brandy

   drink: 8 Jack Rose 12 Jack-in-the-Box

   with rum: 6 Bolero 8 Apple Pie

applejack

   type: 6 brandy

   origin: 6 Canada 10 New England

   flavor: 10 apple cider

   drink: 11 Frozen Apple 13 Harvard Cooler

Apple of discord

   color: 6 golden

   thrown by: 4 Eris

   awarded to: 9 Aphrodite

   awarded by: 5 Paris

   inscription: 13 for the fairest

apple of one's eye 11 pride and joy 15 light of one's life

applesauce 3 rot 4 bull, bunk 5 hokum, hooey 6 bunkum 7 baloney, hogwash, spinach 8 tommyrot 9 poppycock 12 fiddlesticks 13 horsefeathers 16 stuff and nonsense

Apples of the Hesperides

   color: 6 golden

   given to: 4 Hera

   kept by: 5 Ladon 10 Hesperides

appliance 4 gear 6 device 7 fixture, machine 9 apparatus, equipment, implement, mechanism 11 contraption, contrivance

applicable 3 apt, fit 6 useful 7 apropos, fitting, germane 8 relevant, suitable 9 adaptable, befitting, pertinent

applicant 7 hopeful 8 aspirant, claimant 9 candidate, job seeker, suppliant 10 petitioner

application 4 balm, form, suit, wash 5 claim, salve 6 appeal, lotion 7 request, unguent 8 dressing, entreaty, industry, ointment, petition, poultice, solution 9 assiduity, attention, diligence, emollient, putting on, relevance 10 commitment, dedication, pertinence 11 germaneness, persistence, requisition, suitability 12 appositeness, perseverance, solicitation 13 attentiveness

Appling, Luke (Lucius Benjamin)
nickname: 16 Old Aches and Pains
sport: 8 baseball
position: 9 shortstop
team: 15 Chicago White Sox

apply 3 fit, use 4 suit 5 adapt, lay on, put on, refer 6 devote, direct, employ, relate 7 address, pertain, request, utilize 8 dedicate, exercise, petition, practice, spread on 9 implement

apply oneself 6 attend 10 buckle down 13 give oneself to 15 give it all one has 16 put one's heart into

appoint 3 fix, set 4 name 5 equip 6 assign, choose, engage, fit out, select, settle, supply 7 arrange, furnish, provide 8 decide on, delegate, deputize, nominate 9 designate, determine, establish, prescribe 10 commission

appointment 3 job 4 date, post, spot 5 berth, place 6 naming, office 7 meeting, station 8 choosing, position 9 placement, selection, situation 10 assignment, engagement, nomination, rendezvous 11 designation, meeting time 13 commissioning

Appointment in Samarra
author: 9 John O'Hara
character: 8 Al Grecco, Caroline 11 Harry Reilly 13 Julian English

appointments 4 gear 6 outfit 8 equipage 9 equipment, furniture 11 furnishings 13 accoutrements

apportion 5 allot, share 6 divide, ration 7 consign, deal out, dole out, mete out, prorate 8 allocate, disperse 9 parcel out, partition 10 measure out

apportioning 8 alloting, dividing 9 doling out, meting out 10 allocating, consigning, dealing out, dispensing 12 distributing

apportionment 5 quota 6 ration 7 measure, portion 8 division 9 allotment 10 allocation 11 consignment 12 distribution, pro rata share

apposite 3 apt 7 apropos, fitting, germane 8 material, relevant, suitable 9 pertinent 10 applicable 11 appropriate

appositeness 9 relevance 10 pertinence 11 germaneness 15 appropriateness

appraisal 8 estimate, judgment 9 valuation 10 assessment, evaluation 14 estimated value

appraise 5 assay, judge, value 6 assess, review, size up 7 examine, inspect 8 evaluate

appreciable 7 evident, obvious 8 clear-cut, definite 10 detectable, noticeable, pronounced 11 discernible, perceivable, perceptible, significant, substantial 12 recognizable 13 ascertainable

appreciate 4 like 5 prize, savor, value 6 admire, esteem, relish 7 cherish, enhance, improve, inflate, realize, respect 8 perceive, treasure 9 recognize 10 compre-

hend, sympathize, understand 11 acknowledge

appreciation 4 rise 6 growth, liking, regard, relish, thanks 7 advance 8 sympathy 9 awareness, elevation, gratitude 10 admiration, cognizance 12 gratefulness, thankfulness 13 comprehension, understanding

apprehend 3 bag, nab, see 4 know 5 catch, grasp, seize, sense 6 arrest, collar 7 capture, discern, realize 8 perceive 9 recognize 10 comprehend, understand 12 take prisoner 15 take into custody

apprehension 5 alarm, dread, worry 6 arrest, dismay 7 anxiety, capture, concern, seizure 8 disquiet, distress, mistrust 9 misgiving, suspicion 10 foreboding, perception, uneasiness 11 premonition 12 presentiment 13 comprehension, understanding 16 apprehensiveness

apprehensive 6 afraid, scared, uneasy 7 alarmed, anxious, fearful, jittery, nervous, worried 9 concerned, misgiving 10 disquieted, distressed, suspicious 11 distrustful

apprehensiveness 5 dread, worry 6 dismay 7 anxiety 9 misgiving 10 foreboding, uneasiness 12 apprehension

apprentice 4 tyro 5 pupil 6 novice 7 learner, student 8 beginner, neophyte 19 indentured assistant

apprise 4 tell 6 advise, inform, notify 8 disclose 9 enlighten 10 make aware

approach 3 way 4 come, near, road 5 begin, equal, match 6 access, avenue, be like, method, system 7 advance, compare, passage, solicit 8 attitude, come near, draw near, embark on, gain upon, initiate, resemble, set about, sound out 9 come close, enter upon, procedure, technique, undertake 10 move toward, passageway 11 approximate

approachable 9 available, reachable 10 accessible

approbation 6 praise 7 acclaim, support 8 applause, approval, sanction 9 laudation 10 acceptance, compliment 11 endorsement 12 commendation, ratification 14 congratulation

appropriate 3 apt 4 take 5 allot 6 assign, proper, seemly 7 apropos, correct, earmark, fitting, germane 8 allocate, relevant, set apart, suitable 9 apportion, befitting, belonging, congruous, opportune, pertinent 10 confiscate, to the point, well-chosen, well-suited 11 expropriate 12 to the purpose 14 characteristic

appropriateness 7 aptness, fitness 9 congruity, propriety, relevance 10 pertinence 11 correctness, suitability

appropriation 6 taking 9 allotment 10 allocation, arrogation, usurpation 12 confiscation 13 expropriation, money set aside 16 misappropriation

approval 5 favor, leave 6 esteem, liking, regard 7 acclaim, consent, license, mandate, respect 8 sanction 9 agreement 10 acceptance, admiration, compliance, permission 11 approbation, concurrence, countenance, endorsement, good opinion 12 acquiescence, appreciation, confirmation 13 authorization 14 acknowledgment

approve 4 like, pass 5 allow 6 accept, affirm, defend, esteem, permit, praise, ratify, second, uphold 7 condone, confirm, endorse, respect, sustain 8 accede to, advocate, assent to, concur in, sanction 9 authorize, consent to 10 appreciate 11 countenance, go along with, rubber-stamp, subscribe to

approved 8 official 9 canonical 10 authorized, sanctioned

approving 9 endorsing, favorable 10 concurring 11 affirmative, sanctioning 12 appreciative

approximate 5 guess, rough 6 reckon 7 inexact, verge on 8 approach, border on, estimate, look like, relative, very near 9 estimated

approximately 5 circa 6 almost, around 7 close to 9 generally, just about 10 more or less, not far from, very nearly

appurtenance 4 wing 5 annex, extra 7 adjunct 8 addendum, addition 9 accessory, appendage, extension 10 attachment

Apres-midi d'un Faune, L' (The Afternoon of a Faun)
  author: 16 Stephane Mallarme

April
  event: 11 Black Monday (13)
  flower: 5 daisy 8 sweet pea
  French: 5 Avril
  gem: 7 diamond
  German: 5 April
  holiday: 6 Easter 11 All Fool's Day (1) 13 April Fool's Day (1)
  Italian: 6 Aprile
  Latin: 7 Aprilis
  number of days: 6 thirty
  origin of name: 4 aper (wild boar) 6 aparas (following) 7 aperire (to open) 9 Aphrodite
  place in year:
    Gregorian: 6 fourth
    Roman: 6 second
  saying: 24 April is the cruellest month 27 April showers bring May flowers
  Spanish: 5 Abril
  zodiac signs: 5 Aries 6 Taurus

April Fool's Day
  French: 9 April Fish

a priori 4 theory 7 opinion 11 of reasoning

apron 3 bib 5 smock 8 covering 10 stagefront

apropos 3 apt 5 seemly 7 correct, fitting, germane, related 8 relevant, suitable 9 befitting, congruous, opportune, pertinent 10 applicable, to the point, well-suited 11 appropriate 12 just the thing

apry
  type: 7 liqueur
  origin: 6 France
  flavor: 7 apricot

Apsyrtus
  also: 8 Absyrtus
  father: 6 Aeetes
  sister: 5 Medea
  killed by: 5 Medea

apt 5 prone 6 bright, clever, gifted, liable, likely, proper, seemly 7 apropos, fitting, germane, given to 8 inclined, relevant, suitable 9 befitting, congruous, opportune, pertinent 10 disposed to, well-suited 11 appropriate, intelligent, predisposed

aptitude 4 bent, gift, turn 5 flair, knack, skill 6 genius, talent 7 ability, faculty, leaning 8 capacity, facility, penchant, tendency 9 endowment, proneness, quickness 10 capability, cleverness, proclivity, propensity 11 inclination, proficiency 12 predilection 14 predisposition

aptness 4 bent, gift 5 flair, knack 6 talent 7 ability, faculty 8 aptitude, facility 11 suitability 15 appropriateness

Apuleius
  author of: 12 The Golden Ass 13 Metamorphoses

aqua 4 blue 5 water 6 bluish 9 turquoise 10 aquamarine 12 greenish-blue

aquamarine 4 aqua, blue 5 beryl 9 turquoise 12 greenish-blue
  color: 9 blue-green

aquaphobia
  fear of: 5 water

aquarelle 10 watercolor

Aquarius
  symbol: 11 water bearer 12 water-carrier
  planet: 6 Saturn, Uranus
  rules: 5 hopes 7 friends
  born: 7 January 8 February

aquatic 6 marine 7 abyssal, fluvial, neritic, oceanic, pelagic 8 littoral 9 thalassic 10 fluviatile, lacustrine

aquavit
  type: 6 spirit
  origin: 11 Scandinavia
  flavor: 4 dill 7 caraway 9 coriander
  drink: 5 Glogg

aqua vitae 7 alcohol 11 water of life

aqueduct 4 duct, race 7 channel, conduit 11 watercourse 18 artificial waterway

aqueous 4 damp 5 moist 6 liquid, serous, watery 7 hydrous 8 waterish 9 lymphatic

Aqueus
  epithet of: 4 Zeus
  means: 6 watery

Aquilo see 6 Boreas

Aquinas, St Thomas
  nickname: 13 Angelic Doctor
  followers: 8 Thomists
  author of: 15 Summa Theologica 21 Summa Totius Theologiae 34 Summa Catholicae Fidei contra Gentiles

Arab
  clothing: 3 fez 4 veil
  country: 4 Iraq, Oman 5 Egypt, Libya, Qatar, Sudan, Syria, Yemen 6 Jordan, Kuwait 7 Algeria, Bahrain, Lebanon, Morocco, Tunisia 11 Saudi Arabia 18 United Arab Emirates

habitat: 6 desert
Holy City: 5 Mecca 6 Medina
language: 6 Arabic
people: 7 Semitic
religion: 6 Muslim 7 Islamic
tribe: 4 Kurd 6 Berber, Nubian, Tuareg

Arabella
opera by: 7 (Richard) Strauss

Arabia
ancient name: 14 Jazirat al-Arab
ancient people: 6 Sabean 8 Egyptian 10 Babylonian
bounded by: 5 Syria 6 Jordan, Red Sea 10 Gulf of Aden, Gulf of Oman 11 Indian Ocean, Persian Gulf
country: 4 Oman 5 Qatar, Yemen 6 Kuwait 11 Saudi Arabia 18 United Arab Emirates
highest peak: 11 Jabal Shayib
holy book: 5 Koran
Holy City: 5 Mecca 6 Medina
island: 7 Bahrain, Socotra 9 Laccadive
language: 6 Arabic
mineral/natural resource: 3 oil 4 goat 5 sheep, wheat 6 barley, millet 7 iron ore, granite 8 porphyry 9 manganese, petroleum
nomadic tribe: 5 Maaza 6 Ababda
prophet: 8 Muhammad
religion: 6 Muslim 7 Islamic
river: 4 Nile, Oxus 5 Indus 6 Tigris 9 Euphrates
sea: 3 Red 7 Arabian 11 Persian Gulf 13 Mediterranean

Arabian Nights
director: 17 Pier Paolo Pasolini
based on: 20 Thousand and One Nights
cast: 11 Franco Citti 13 Ninetto Davoli 14 Ines Pellegrina

Arabian Nights' Entertainments, The (The Thousand and One Nights)
author: 7 unknown
storyteller: 12 Scheherazade

Arabic
national language in: 4 Iraq 5 Syria 6 Jordan 7 Lebanon 11 North Africa 16 Arabian Peninsula
also spoken in: 6 Israel 12 North America, South America 17 Soviet Central Asia, Sub-Saharan Africa
language of: 5 Koran

arable 6 fecund 7 fertile 8 farmable, fruitful, plowable, tillable 10 cultivable, productive

Arachne
origin: 6 Lydian
challenged: 6 Athena
contest: 7 weaving
changed into: 6 spider

arachnid
class: 4 mite, tick 6 spider 8 scorpion 13 daddy-long-legs
phylum: 9 Arthropod
pairs of legs: 4 four
respiratory organ: 12 pulmonary sac, tracheal tube
dwelling: 4 land 5 water

body part: 15 anterior prosoma 20 posterior opisthosoma
way of feeding: 8 parasite, predator 9 scavenger

arachnophobia
fear of: 7 spiders

Aram *see* 5 Syria

Aramis
character in: 18 The Three Musketeers
author: 5 Dumas (pere)

Arapaho
language family: 9 Algonkian 10 Algonquian
tribe: 6 Atsine 11 Gros Ventres 15 Northern Arapaho, Southern Arapaho
location: 6 Plains 8 Colorado, Red River
related to: 8 Cheyenne
ceremony: 8 sun dance

Aras
first king of: 8 Phliasia

Arawak
language family: 8 Arawakan
tribe: 5 Taino 6 Igneri, Lucayo
location: 4 Cuba 5 Haiti 6 Guyana 8 Antilles, Colombia 9 Venezuela 12 South America

Arawakan
tribe: 6 Arawak 8 Boriquen 9 Borinquen

Arawn
lord of: 6 Annfwn

arbiter 5 judge 6 pundit, umpire 7 referee 9 authority 10 arbitrator 11 connoisseur

arbitrary 6 chance, random 7 summary, willful 8 absolute, despotic, fanciful, personal 9 frivolous, imperious, unlimited, whimsical 10 autocratic, capricious, peremptory, subjective 12 inconsistent, uncontrolled, unrestrained

arbitrate 5 judge 6 decide, settle, umpire 7 adjudge, mediate, referee 9 reconcile 10 adjudicate 12 bring to terms 13 sit in judgment

Arbitration, The
author: 8 Menander

arbitrator 5 judge 6 umpire 7 arbiter, referee 8 mediator 9 go-between, moderator 10 negotiator 11 adjudicator 12 intermediary

arbor 5 bower, folly, kiosk 6 gazebo, grotto 7 pergola 8 pavilion 9 belvedere 10 shaded walk 11 summerhouse

arc 3 bow 4 arch 5 curve 8 crescent, half-moon 10 semicircle

arcade 6 loggia, piazza 7 archway, areaway, gallery, skywalk 8 cloister, overpass 9 breezeway, colonnade, peristyle, underpass

Arcadia, The
author: 15 Sir Philip Sidney
character: 5 Mopsa 6 Pamela 7 Dametas, Gynecia, Zelmane 8 Basilius, Cecropia, Pyrocles 9 Amphialus, Musidorus, Philoclea, Plexistus

Arcadian stag *see* 8 Cerynean

Arcanan
  father: 8 Alcmaeon
  mother: 10 Callirrhoe
  brother: 10 Amphoterus

arcane 6 mystic, occult 7 obscure 8 abstruse, esoteric, hermetic, mystical 9 enigmatic, recondite 10 mysterious

Arcas
  father: 4 Zeus
  mother: 8 Callisto
  wife: 5 Erato
  son: 6 Elatus
  ancestor of: 9 Arcadians
  set among: 5 stars
  placed by: 4 Zeus

Arce
  father: 7 Thaumas
  sister: 4 Iris 7 Harpies
  Zeus took: 5 wings
  aided: 6 Titans

Arcesius
  father: 4 Zeus
  mother: 8 Euryodia
  son: 7 Laertes
  grandson: 8 Odysseus

arch 3 arc, bow, sly 4 bend, dome, main, span, wily 5 chief, curve, major, saucy, vault 7 cunning, primary, roguish 8 bow shape 9 curvature, designing, principal 10 curved span 11 mischievous

archaeologist
  American: 7 Bingham 8 Douglass, Stephens
  British: 5 Evans 6 Carter, Childe, Layard, Leakey, Petrie, Wooley 7 Lubbock, Ventris, Wheeler 9 Rawlinson 10 Pitt-Rivers 13 Caton-Thompson
  Danish: 7 Thomsen, Worsaae
  French: 5 Botta 8 Cousteau 11 Champollion
  German: 5 Conze 7 Curtius 8 Dorpfeld, Koldewey 9 Grotefend 10 Schliemann 11 Winckelmann
  Italian: 8 Fiorelli
  Swedish: 4 Geer 9 Montelius

archaic 5 passe 6 bygone 7 ancient, antique 8 obsolete 9 out-of-date 10 antiquated 11 obsolescent 12 old-fashioned

archangel 5 Satan, Uriel 7 Gabriel, Michael, Raphael

arched 4 bent 5 bowed 6 curved

Archegetes
  epithet of: 6 Apollo
  means: 7 founder

Archelaus
  father: 7 Temenus
  descendant of: 8 Hercules

Archelochus
  mentioned in: 5 Iliad
  father: 7 Antenor
  mother: 6 Theano
  killed by: 14 Telamonian Ajax

Archemorus *see* 8 Opheltes

archenemy 3 foe 7 archfoe, bugbear, nemesis, scourge 8 opponent 9 adversary, assailant, noire noire, combatant, disputant 10 antagonist

archeology
  term: 3 dig 6 midden 9 earthwork 11 burial mound 17 aerial photography
  type: 7 salvage 8 American, medieval 9 classical, text-aided 10 Egyptology, industrial, underwater 11 Assyriology, prehistoric 12 Mesopotamian
  ages: 4 Iron 6 Bronze
  Old Stone Age: 11 Paleolithic
  Middle Stone Age: 10 Mesolithic
  New Stone Age: 9 Neolithic
  dating method: 5 cross 8 absolute, carbon-14 13 geochronology 16 dendrochronology 18 thermoluminescence 28 potassium-argon varved deposits
  site/artifact: 2 Ur 4 Giza, Troy 5 Copan, Crete, Delos, Minos 6 Amarna, Carnac, Nimrud, Nippur, Tiryns 7 Alalakh, Babylon, Ephesus, Knossos, Mycenae, Nineveh, Olympia, Pompeii, Rio Azul 8 Behistun, Kuyunjik, Pergamum, pyramids 9 Arikamedu, Hissarlik, Khorsabad, New Grange, Tarquinia, Woodhenge 10 Carchemish, Persepolis, Samothrace, Stonehenge 11 Herculaneum, Machu Picchu, Mohenjodaro 12 Easter Island, Hadrian's Wall, Olduvai Gorge, Rosetta Stone 13 Avebury Circle, Zimbabwe Ruins 14 Dead Sea Scrolls, Laocoon statues 15 temple of Artemis 16 Valley of the Kings 18 Ostrava-Petrokovice, Royal Palace of Minos
  tomb: 11 Tutankhamen 15 Ch'in Shih Huang Ti

Archeptolemus
  mentioned in: 5 Iliad
  father: 7 Iphitus
  charioteer of: 6 Hector

archer 6 bowman 8 spearman
  famous: 5 Cupid 9 Robin Hood 11 William Tell

Archer
  constellation of: 11 Sagittarius

Archer, Isabel
  character in: 18 The Portrait of a Lady
  author: 5 James

Archer, Miles
  character in: 16 The Maltese Falcon
  author: 7 Hammett

Archer, Newland
  character in: 17 The Age of Innocence
  author: 7 Wharton

Archer in Jeopardy
  author: 13 Ross MacDonald

archery
  athlete: 10 Linda Myers, Luanne Ryon 11 Darrell Pace

archetypal 5 model 7 classic 8 original 9 classical, exemplary 10 definitive, prototypal, protypical

archetype 5 model 7 classic 8 exemplar, original 9 prototype 12 prime example

Archias
  founder of: 8 Syracuse
  location: 6 Sicily
  descendant of: 8 Hercules

Archie
  creator: 10 Bob Montana 13 John Goldwater
  character: 5 Betty, Moose 6 Reggie 7 Sabrina 8 Big Ethel, Veronica 11 Mr Weatherby 12 Jughead Jones
  place: 9 Riverdale

Archimago
  character in: 15 The Faerie Queene
  author: 7 Spenser

Archipenko, Alexsandr
  born: 4 Kiev 6 Russia
  artwork: 8 Medranos 9 Gondolier, Medrano II, Pregnancy, The Bather 11 Boxing Match 12 Archipentura, Walking Woman 15 Geometric Statue 18 Wilhelm Furtwangler 19 Woman Combing Her Hair

architect 6 author, shaper 7 creator, deviser, founder, planner 8 designer, engineer 9 artificer, contriver, draftsman, innovator 10 instigator, originator, prime mover 13 master builder 16 building designer
  name 3 Pei 4 Hunt, Mead, Pope, Root, Wren 5 Hoban, Jones, Le Vau, McKim, Mills, Roche, Stone, Tange, White, Wyatt 6 Breuer, Fuller, Owings, Smirke, Wright 7 Bernini, Burnham, Gilbert, Gropius, Johnson, Latrobe, Mansart, Merrill, Renwick 8 Bramante, Harrison, Palladio, Saarinen, Skidmore, Sullivan, Yamasaki 9 Jefferson 10 Richardson 11 Le Corbusier 12 Brunelleschi, Michelangelo 14 Mies van der Rohe 15 Hardouin-Mansart
  legendary first: 8 Daedalus
  designed: 18 Minotaur's Labyrinth
  Roman: 9 Vitruvius

architecture 5 style 6 design 11 structuring 12 construction 14 architectonics 16 structural design

archives 6 annals, museum, papers 7 library, records 9 documents 10 chronicles, depository 11 memorabilia

arctic 3 icy 5 gelid, polar 6 bitter, frigid, frozen 7 glacial, ice-cold 8 freezing, icebound 9 North Pole 10 frostbound 11 far-northern, hyperborean 13 septentrional

Arden, Eve
  real name: 13 Eunice Quedens
  born: 12 Mill Valley CA
  roles: 13 Mildred Pierce, Our Miss Brooks

ardent 4 keen 5 eager, fiery, lusty 6 fierce 7 earnest, fervent, intense, zealous 8 feverish, spirited, vehement 10 passionate 11 impassioned, tempestuous 12 enthusiastic

ardor 4 love, zeal 5 gusto, verve, vigor 6 fervor, spirit 7 feeling, passion, rapture 8 devotion 9 eagerness, intensity, vehemence 10 enthusiasm, excitement, fierceness 11 amorousness 12 feverishness

Ardrey, Robert
  author of: 17 The Social Contract

arduous 4 hard 5 heavy, tough 6 severe, tiring, trying 7 onerous 8 toilsome, vigorous 9 difficult, energetic, fatiguing, Herculean, laborious, strenuous, wearisome 10 burdensome, exhausting, formidable 11 troublesome

arduousness 5 trial 8 tough job 10 difficulty, rough going, uphill work 12 hard sledding, toilsomeness 13 laboriousness, wearisomeness

area 4 turf, zone 5 arena, field, range, realm, scope, space, tract 6 domain, extent, region, sphere 7 expanse, portion, section, stretch, terrain 8 district, locality, precinct, province 9 territory

Areithous
  origin: 5 Greek
  mentioned in: 5 Iliad
  king of: 7 Arcadia
  son: 10 Menesthius
  nickname: 7 maceman
  weapon: 8 iron mace
  killed by: 8 Lycurgus

Areius *see* 5 Areus

arena 4 area, bowl, ring 5 field, lists, realm, scene, stage 6 circus, domain, sector, sphere 7 stadium, theater 8 coliseum, platform, province 9 gymnasium, territory 10 hippodrome 11 battlefield, marketplace 12 amphitheater, battleground, playing field

Arendt, Hannah
  author of: 10 On Violence 12 On Revolution 13 Life of the Mind 17 The Human Condition 19 Crises of the Republic, Eichmann in Jerusalem 27 The Origins of Totalitarianism

Arene
  son: 4 Idas 7 Lynceus

Arensky, Anton Stepanovich (Antony)
  born: 6 Russia 8 Novgorod
  composer of: 7 Tempest 13 Egyptian Night 18 Variations on Legend

Areopagitica
  author: 10 John Milton

Ares
  also: 8 Theritas
  origin: 5 Greek
  god of: 3 war
  father: 4 Zeus
  mother: 4 Hera
  sister: 4 Hebe
  son: 5 Molus 6 Cycnus, Deimos, Phobos, Tereus 8 Diomedes, Eurytion, Meleager, Oenomaus, Phlegyas, Thestius 10 Ascalaphus
  daughter: 7 Alcippe 8 Harmonia 9 Melanippe 11 Penthesilea
  nurse: 5 Thero
  corresponds to: 4 Mars
  epithet: 8 Enyalius 14 Gynaecothoenas

Arete
  father: 8 Rhexenor
  husband: 8 Alcinous
  daughter: 8 Nausicaa
  personifies: 7 courage

Arethusa
 form: 5 nymph
 changed into: 6 spring
 saved from: 7 Alpheus
Aretus
 father: 5 Priam
 killed by: 9 Automedon
Areus
 also: 6 Areius
 father: 4 Bias
 mother: 4 Pero
 brother: 6 Talaus 8 Leodocus
 member of: 9 Argonauts
 epithet of: 4 Zeus
 means: 7 warlike
Are You There, God? It's Me, Margaret
 author: 9 Judy Blume
Argades
 father: 3 Ion
Argeiphontes
 also: 11 Argiphontes
 epithet of: 6 Hermes
 means: 13 slayer of Argus
argent 5 white 6 silver 7 shining, silvery
Argentina
 name means: 6 silver
 capital/largest city: 11 Buenos Aires
 others: 4 Acha, Azul, Goya, Oran, Puan,
 Rosa 5 Jujuy, Junin, Lanus, Lujan,
 Metan, Monte, Salta, Tigre 6 Parana,
 Rufino, Zarate 7 Bolivar, Caseros, Cordoba, Dolores, Formosa, LaBanda,
 LaPlata, LaRioja, Mendoza, Neuquen,
 Posadas, Quilmes, Rafaela, Rosario, San
 Juan, Santa Fe, Tucuman 9 Catamarca,
 Rio Cuerto 10 Avellaneda, Corrientes 11
 Bahai Blanca, Mar del Plata, Resistencia
 17 Santiago del Estero 20 San Carlos de
 Bariloche
 division: 5 Andes, Chaco, Pampa 9
 Patagonia 11 Mesopotamia 14 Tierra del
 Fuego
 measure: 4 sino 5 legua 6 cuadra, lastre
 7 manzana
 monetary unit: 4 peso 7 centavo 9 argentino
 weight: 4 last 5 libra 7 quintal 8 tonelada
 island: 14 Tierra del Fuego
 lake: 6 Viedma 7 Cardiel, Fagnano, Musters 11 Buenos Aires, Mar Chiquita,
 Nahuel Huapi
 mountain: 4 Toro 5 Andes, Chato,
 Laudo, Potro 6 Bonete, Conico, Pissis,
 Rincon 8 Famatina, Murallon, Olivares,
 Tronador, Zapaleri 9 Aconcagua,
 Tupungato 10 Cordillera 13 Ojos del Salado 15 Cerro Mercedario, Sierra de Cordoba
 highest point: 9 Aconcagua
 river: 4 Sali 5 Atuel, Chico, Coyle, Dulce,
 Limay, Negro, Plata, Teuco 6 Blanco,
 Chubut, Cuarto, Flores, Grande, Iguazu,
 Parana, Quinto, Salado 7 Bermejo,
 Deseado, Iguassu, Mendoza, Tercero,
 Tunuyan, Uruguay 8 Colorado, Paraguay,
 Picomayo, Senguerr 9 Pilcomayo
 sea: 8 Atlantic

 physical feature:
 falls: 6 Grande, Iguazu 7 Iguassu
 lowland: 5 chaco
 plains: 6 pampas
 plateau: 4 Puna 6 Parana
 salt flat: 14 Salinas Grandes
 volcano: 5 Lanin, Maipo 6 Domuyo 7
 Peteroa
 wind: 5 Zonda 7 Pampero
 people: 3 Api 4 Lule 5 Vejoz 6 Abipon,
 Vilela 7 Guarani, Puelche, Ranquel,
 Taluhet 8 Querandi, Querendy
 artist: 6 Borges
 author: 4 Wast 6 Banchs, Borges 7
 Lugones 9 Guiraldes, Hernandez 10
 Echeverria
 leader: 4 Roca 5 Illia, Menem, Mitre,
 Peron, Rosas 6 Videla 7 Urquiza 8
 Aramburu, Belgrano, Eva Peron,
 Frondici, Galtieri 9 San Martin, Sarmiento
 11 Isabel Peron
 language: 7 Spanish
 religion: 13 Roman Catholic
 place:
 opera house: 11 Teatro Colon
 world's southernmost town: 7 Ushuaia
 feature:
 bird: 6 chunga
 cowboy: 6 gaucho 7 vaquero
 dance: 5 samba, tango, zamba 6 cuando, gaucho 7 milonga 9 chacarera
 farm: 6 quinta
 knife: 5 facon
 metal straw: 8 bombilla
 ranch: 8 estancia
 school smock: 9 delantale
 shawl: 6 poncho
 trousers: 9 bombachas
 weapon: 4 bola
 food:
 cocktail: 7 clarito
 dish: 4 luna 7 criollo, puchero 8 chivitos,
 empanada 10 parrillada
Arges
 member of: 8 Cyclopes
Argia
 also: 5 Aegia
 father: 7 Oceanus
 mother: 6 Tethys
 husband: 7 Polybus
 son: 5 Argus
Argiope
 form: 5 nymph
 father: 8 Teuthras
 husband: 6 Agenor 8 Telephus
 son: 6 Cadmus
 daughter: 6 Europa
Argiphontes see 12 Argeiphontes
Argive
 pertaining to: 5 Argos
Argo
 ship of: 4 Argo
argon
 chemical symbol: 2 Ar

Argonauts
  searchers for: 12 Golden Fleece
  leader: 5 Jason
  ship: 4 Argo
  sailed to: 7 Colchis

argot 4 cant 5 idiom, lingo, slang 6 jargon, patois 10 vernacular

arguable 7 at issue 9 debatable 10 disputable 12 questionable 13 controversial, problematical

argue 4 hold, show 5 claim, imply, plead 6 assert, bicker, debate, denote, evince, reason 7 contend, display, dispute, exhibit, express, point to, quarrel, quibble, wrangle 8 indicate, maintain, manifest 11 demonstrate, expostulate, remonstrate

argument 3 row 4 case, gist, plot, spat, tiff 5 clash, fight, story 6 debate, reason 7 dispute, outline, quarrel, summary 8 abstract, contents, squabble, synopsis 9 bickering, imbroglio 10 war of words 11 altercation, central idea, controversy, embroilment 12 disagreement

argumentation 6 debate 7 dispute 8 argument 10 discussion

argumentative 5 testy 7 peevish, scrappy 8 contrary, petulant, snappish 9 combative, fractious, litigious, querulous 11 belligerent, contentious, quarrelsome 12 cantankerous, disputatious

Argus
  form: 5 giant
  father: 7 Phrixus
  mother: 9 Chalciope
  builder of: 4 Argo
  number of eyes: 10 one hundred
  epithet: 8 Panoptes

Argyra
  form: 5 nymph
  habitat: 6 spring
  loved: 8 Selemnus

Argyrotoxus
  epithet of: 6 Apollo
  means: 18 lord of the silver bow

aria 3 air 4 solo, song, tune 6 melody, number 7 arietta, excerpt, section 9 selection 10 canzonetta 13 aria cantabile

Aria
  form: 5 nymph
  son: 7 Miletus
  fathered by: 6 Apollo

Ariadna see 7 Ariadne

Ariadne
  also: 7 Ariadna
  father: 5 Minos
  mother: 8 Pasiphae
  husband: 8 Dionysus
  son: 8 Oenopion
  gave thread to: 7 Theseus
  deserted by: 7 Theseus

Ariadne auf Naxos
  also: 14 Ariadne on Naxos
  opera by: 7 (Richard) Strauss
  character: 7 Bacchus, Theseus 8 Composer 10 Zerbinetta

Ariana see 11 Afghanistan

Ariane et Barbe-Bleu
  also: 19 Ariadne and Bluebeard
  opera by: 5 Dukas
  character: 7 Ariadne 9 Bluebeard

Arianrhod
  origin: 5 Welsh
  form: 7 goddess
  brother: 7 Gwydion
  mistress of: 7 Gwydion
  son: 14 Llew Llew Gyffes
  cursed: 14 Llew Llew Gyffes

arid 3 dry 4 dull 5 vapid 6 barren, dreary, jejune 7 dried-up, parched, tedious 8 lifeless, pedantic 9 colorless, dry as dust, waterless 10 desertlike, uninspired 13 unimaginative, uninteresting 15 drought-scourged

aridity 6 dearth 7 drought, dryness 8 aridness, dullness 10 barrenness 12 lifelessness, rainlessness 17 unimaginativeness

aridness 6 dearth 7 aridity, drought, dryness 8 dullness 10 barrenness 12 lifelessness, rainlessness 17 unimaginativeness

arid region 6 desert 9 wasteland 16 barren wilderness

Ariel
  author: 11 Shakespeare, Sylvia Plath
  character in: 10 The Tempest

Aries
  symbol: 3 ram
  planet: 4 Mars
  rules: 11 personality
  born: 5 April, March

Arimaspians
  member of: 9 Scythians
  number of eyes: 3 one

Arion
  form: 11 winged horse
  father: 8 Poseidon
  mother: 7 Demeter

Ariosto, Ludovico
  author of: 14 Orlando Furioso

Arisbe
  father: 6 Teucer
  husband: 5 Priam 8 Dardanus, Hyrtacus

arise 4 dawn, go up, rise, wake 5 awake, begin, climb, ensue, get up, mount, occur, set in, start 6 appear, ascend, crop up, emerge, result, wake up 7 emanate, stand up 8 commence, spring up, stem from 9 originate 11 come to light

Aristaeus
  origin: 5 Greek
  god of: 9 husbandry 10 beekeeping, winemaking
  father: 6 Apollo
  mother: 6 Cyrene
  wife: 7 Autonoe
  son: 7 Actaeon
  caused death of: 8 Eurydice

aristocracy 5 elite 6 gentry 7 peerage, society 8 nobility 9 beau monde 10 patricians, upper class, upper crust 11 high society

aristocrat 4 duke, earl, lady, lord, peer 5 noble 7 Brahmin, duchess, grandee, marquis 8 countess, marquess, nobleman 9 blue blood, gentleman, patrician 10 noblewoman 11 gentlewoman 12 silk stocking

aristocratic 5 noble, regal, royal 6 lordly, titled 7 courtly, genteel, refined 8 highborn, highbred, wellborn 9 dignified, patrician 10 of high rank, upper-class 11 blue-blooded, gentlemanly 12 silk-stocking 13 of gentle blood

Aristodemus
    member of: 10 Heraclidae
    father: 12 Aristomachus
    son: 7 Procles 11 Eurysthenes
    killed by: 9 lightning

Aristomachus
    member of: 10 Heraclidae
    son: 7 Temenus 11 Aristodemus, Cresphontes
    granddaughter: 8 Hyrnetho
    invaded: 12 Peloponnesus

Aristophanes
    author of: 6 Plutus 8 The Birds, The Frogs, The Peace, The Wasps 9 The Clouds 10 Lysistrata, The Knights 13 Ecclesiazusae, The Acharnians

Aristotle
    author of: 7 Physics, Poetics 8 On Plants, Politics, Rhetoric, Sophisms 9 On the Soul 10 Generation 11 Metaphysics 12 On the Heavens 14 Parts of Animals, Prior Analytics 17 Nicomachean Ethics 18 Posterior Analytics 23 On Beginning and Perishing

Arizona
    abbreviation: 2 AZ 4 Ariz
    nickname: 11 Grand Canyon
    capital/largest city: 7 Phoenix
    others: 3 Ajo 4 Eloy, Mesa, Naco, Yuma 5 Globe, Leupp, Tempe 6 Bisbee, McNary, Salome, Toltec, Tucson 7 Cortaro 8 Chandler, Glendale, Prescott 9 Flagstaff 10 Scottsdale
    college: 11 Grand Canyon 12 Southwestern
    explorer: 8 Coronado 12 Marcos de Niza
    feature:
        dam: 6 Hoover 8 Coolidge 9 Roosevelt
        national park: 11 Grand Canyon 15 Petrified Forest
    tribe: 4 Hano, Hopi, Pima 6 Apache, Navaho, Navajo, Papago
    people: 7 Cochise 8 Geronimo 14 Barry Goldwater
    lake: 4 Mead 6 Havasu, Mohave, Mormon, Powell 9 Roosevelt
    land rank: 5 sixth
    mountain: 5 White 6 Lemmon 7 Hualpai 8 Mazatzal 9 Baldy Peak 13 Santa Catalina
    highest point: 13 Humphreys Peak
    physical feature:
        canyon: 5 Grand
        desert: 6 Sonora 7 Painted
        forest: 9 Petrified
    river: 4 Gila, Salt, Zuni 5 Verde 6 Puerco

8 Colorado 12 Bill Williams 14 Little Colorado
    state admission: 11 forty-eighth
    state bird: 10 cactus wren
    state flower: 13 saguaro cactus
    state motto: 11 God Enriches
    state song: 7 Arizona
    state tree: 9 palo verde

ark 3 box 4 ship 5 barge, chest 8 flatboat 9 houseboat 10 Noah's boat

Arkansas
    abbreviation: 2 AR 3 Ark
    nickname: 4 Bear 9 Bowie Land 17 Land of Opportunity
    capital/largest city: 10 Little Rock
    others: 3 Coy, Cuy, Keo, Ola, Roe, Ulm 4 Alma, Bono, Casa, Dell, Diaz, Moro 5 Enola, Perla, Rondo 6 Alicia, Camden 8 El Dorado 9 Fort Smith, Jonesboro, Pine Bluff, Texarkana 10 Hot Springs 11 Blytheville 12 Fayetteville
    feature:
        national park: 10 Hot Springs
    tribe: 5 Caddo, Osage 6 Quapaw 7 Choctaw, Wichita 8 Cherokee
    people: 8 Alan Ladd 10 Dick Powell 11 Bill Clinton 16 Douglas MacArthur
    lake: 6 Beaver, Chicot, Conway, Nimrod 7 Greeson, Norfork 8 Maumelle, Ouachita 10 Bull Shoals 11 Greers Ferry 12 Blue Mountain
    land rank: 13 twenty-seventh
    mountain: 4 Blue 5 Ozark 6 Boston, Gaylor 7 Fourche 8 Magazine, Ouachita
    highest point: 8 Magazine
    river: 3 Red 5 Black, White 6 Saline 7 Buffalo, Current 8 Arkansas, Cossatot, Ouachita 9 St Francis 11 Mississippi
    state admission: 11 twenty-fifth
    state bird: 11 mockingbird
    state flower: 12 apple blossom
    state motto: 13 (Let) The People Rule
    state song: 8 Arkansas
    state tree: 13 shortleaf pine

Arkin, Alan
    born: 9 New York NY
    roles: 7 Catch-22 13 Wait Until Dark 27 Last of the Red-Hot Lovers 23 The Heart Is a Lonely Hunter 40 The Russians Are Coming The Russians Are Coming

Ark of the Covenant
    gold covering: 9 mercy seat 12 propitiatory

arm, arms 4 guns 5 brace, crest, equip, prime 6 branch, outfit, sector 7 forearm, fortify, prepare, protect, section, weapons 8 armament, blazonry, division, firearms, insignia, materiel, offshoot, ordnance, weaponry 9 appendage, make ready, upper limb 10 coat of arms, department, detachment, obtain arms, projection, strengthen, take up arms 12 anterior limb 13 prepare for war 14 heraldic emblem 18 furnish with weapons

armada 4 navy 5 fleet 8 flotilla, squadron 10 escadrille

armadillo
  family: 11 Dasypodidae
  order: 8 Edentata
  body: 5 armor 6 plates
  habitat: 12 South America, United States
    14 Central America
  habit: 9 nocturnal
Armageddon 8 doomsday 11 final battle 13
  great conflict
  author: 8 Leon Uris
armagnac
  type: 6 brandy 7 liqueur
  origin: 6 France
armament 4 arms, guns 7 weapons 8 ordnance, weaponry 9 equipment, munitions
  10 outfitting 13 military might 16 warmaking machine
Armenia
  other name: 5 Minni 6 Urartu 8 Anatolia
  former name: 31 Armenian Soviet Socialist Republic
  capital/largest city: 6 Erivan 7 Yerevan
  ancient capital: 3 Ani 8 Artashat,
    Artaxata
  others: 3 Van 5 Sivas 7 Trabzon 9
    Kirovakan, Leninakan, Trabizond 13
    Bitlisarzurum
  head of state: 9 President
  monetary unit: 5 ruble
  lake: 3 Van 5 Sevan, Urmia 8 Urumiyah
  mountain: 6 Ararat, Taurus 7 Aladagh 8
    Karabakh
  highest peak: 12 Mount Aragats
  river: 3 Ara 4 Aras, Kura 5 Araks, Cyrus,
    Halys, Zanga 6 Araxes, Razdan, Tigris 9
    Euphrates 10 Kizil-Irmak
  physical feature:
  volcano: 7 Aragats
  people: 5 Armen, Ermyn, Gomer, Hadji
  apostle: 7 Gregory
  gypsy: 5 bosha
  hero: 4 haik 6 vartan
  leader: 26 Levon Akopovich Ter
    Petrosyan
  me: 3 ara
  saint: 5 Sahak 6 Mesrop
  language: 7 Russian 8 Armenian
  religion: 16 Armenian Orthodox
  feature:
  cap: 6 calpac
  fortress: 7 erebuni
  game: 7 barbout
  kingdom: 6 Urartu, Vannic 7 Cilicia,
    Sophene 8 Ardsruni
  food:
  bread: 4 peda
  cucumber: 4 guta
  dish: 7 lahvosh 9 paraghatz, sou-boreg
Armenian
  language family: 12 Indo-European
  spoken in: 4 USSR 6 Russia 7 Armenia
Armida
  opera by: 5 Gluck, Haydn, Lully 6
    Dvorak 7 Rossini 10 Eszterhazy
Armies 7 Sabaoth
Armies of the Night
  author: 12 Norman Mailer

armistice 5 peace, truce 9 cease-fire 23
  suspension of hostilities
armlet 6 bangle 8 bracelet, ornament
arm of the sea 5 bight, firth, fjord (flord), inlet 6 strait 7 channel, estuary, narrows
armoire 8 cupboard, wardrobe 12 clothespress
armor 4 mail 5 chain 6 shield 7 bulwark 10
  coat of mail, protection 11 suit of armor 18
  protective covering
armorial bearings 4 arms 5 crest 10 coat
  of arms, escutcheon
armory 7 arsenal 9 arms depot 13 ordnance depot
Arms and the Man
  author: 17 George Bernard Shaw
arms depot 6 armory 7 arsenal 13 ordnance depot 18 military storehouse
Armstrong, Henry
  sport: 6 boxing
  class: 11 lightweight 12 welterweight
army 3 mob 4 band, bevy, crew, gang,
  host, mass, pack 5 crowd, force, horde,
  swarm 6 legion, throng, troops 7 legions,
  militia 8 military, soldiers, soldiery 9 land
  force, multitude 10 land forces 11 aggregation, fighting men 12 congregation 13
  military force 15 military machine
Arnaeus
  also: 4 Irus
  origin: 5 Greek
  mentioned in: 7 Odyssey
  form: 6 beggar 9 errandboy
  errandboy for: 16 Penelopes suitors
Arne
  author: 20 Bjornstjerne Bjornson
Arne
  son: 6 Aeolus 7 Boeotus
  foster father: 9 Desmontes
Arne, Thomas Augustine
  born: 6 London 7 England
  composer of: 6 Alfred, Judith 8
    Rosamond, Tom Thumb 10 Artaxerxes
    14 Love in a Village, Thomas and Sally
Arness, James
  real name: 12 James Aurness
  brother: 11 Peter Graves
  born: 13 Minneapolis MN
  roles: 8 Gunsmoke 10 Matt Dillon
Arnold, Matthew
  author of: 7 Thyrsis 10 Dover Beach 15
    Sohrab and Rustum, The Scholar-Gypsy
    16 Empedocles on Etna 17 Culture and
    Anarchy, Essays in Criticism 18 On
    Translating Homer
Arnold, Roseanne see 8 Roseanne
aroma 4 odor 5 savor, scent, smell 7 bouquet 9 fragrance, redolence
aromatic 5 spicy 7 odorous, piquant, pungent, scented 8 fragrant, perfumed, redolent 11 odoriferous
around 4 near 5 about, circa 10 encircling,
  on all sides, roundabout 11 surrounding
Around the World in Eighty Days
  author: 10 Jules Verne
  director: 15 Michael Anderson

character: 11 Phileas Fogg 12 Passepartout
cast: 10 Cantinflas, David Niven 12 Robert Newton 15 Marlene Dietrich, Shirley MacLaine
score: 11 Victor Young
Oscar for: 5 score 7 picture

arouse 3 fan 4 goad, move, spur, warm, whet 5 pique, rouse, waken 6 awaken, bestir, excite, foment, foster, heat up, incite, kindle, stir up, wake up 7 provoke, quicken, sharpen 8 summon up 9 stimulate

Arowhena
character in: 7 Erewhon
author: 6 Butler

arpeggio 5 chord, scale 8 flourish 13 musical device

arraign 6 accuse, charge, impute, indict 7 censure 8 denounce 9 criticize

arrange 4 file, plan, plot, pose, rank, sort 5 adapt, array, fix up, group, order, range, score 6 assort, design, devise, lay out, line up, map out, set out, settle 7 agree to, marshal, prepare, provide 8 classify, contrive, organize, schedule 9 methodize 11 orchestrate, systematize

arrangement 5 order 8 arraying, disposal, grouping, ordering 10 assortment 12 distribution, organization 13 methodization 14 categorization, classification 15 systematization
German: 9 Ausgleich

arrangements 5 plans, score, terms 7 compact 8 measures 9 agreement 10 adaptation, provisions, settlement 12 preparations 13 orchestration

arrant 4 rank 5 utter 7 extreme 8 flagrant, outright, thorough 9 confirmed, downright, egregious, notorious, out-and-out 11 undisguised, unmitigated 13 thoroughgoing

array 4 deck, garb, pose, rank, robe, show, wrap 5 adorn, align, dress, group, order, place, range 6 attire, bedeck, clothe, deploy, finery, fit out, outfit, parade, set out, supply 7 apparel, arrange, display, marshal, raiment 8 clothing, garments, organize 9 pageantry 10 assortment, collection, exhibition, marshaling 11 arrangement, disposition

arrears 5 debit 9 liability 10 balance due, obligation, unpaid debt 11 overdue debt 12 indebtedness 15 outstanding debt

arrest 3 end, fix, nab 4 bust, halt, hold, slow, stay, stop 5 block, catch, check, delay, pinch, rivet, roust, seize, stall 6 absorb, collar, detain, engage, hinder, occupy, retard, secure 7 attract, capture, engross, inhibit, seizure, slowing, staying 8 blocking, checking, hold back, restrain, stoppage, stopping, suppress 9 apprehend, interrupt, retention 10 inhibiting 11 holding back 12 apprehension, take prisoner

Arrhenius, Svante August
field: 7 physics 9 chemistry
nationality: 7 Swedish
theory of: 24 electrolytic dissociation

arriere pensee 12 hidden motive 17 mental reservation

arrival 5 corner 6 advent, coming 7 entrant, visitor 8 approach, arriving, entrance, newcomer, visitant 10 appearance

arrive 4 come, near 5 get to, occur, reach 6 appear, befall, happen, show up, turn up 7 succeed 8 approach, make good

arrivederci, a rivederci 7 goodbye 8 farewell 16 until we meet again

arrogance 5 scorn 6 egoism, vanity 7 bluster, conceit, disdain, swagger 8 contempt 9 assurance, insolence, loftiness, vainglory 10 lordliness, pretension 11 braggadocio, haughtiness, presumption 13 imperiousness 14 self-importance

arrogant 4 vain 6 lordly 7 haughty, pompous 8 insolent, scornful 9 conceited, imperious 10 disdainful, egoistical, swaggering 11 egotistical, overbearing, overweening, pretentious 12 contemptuous, presumptuous, self-assuming, supercilious, vainglorious 13 high-and-mighty, self-important

arrogate 5 adopt, claim, seize, usurp 6 assume 7 preempt 8 take over 10 commandeer 11 appropriate

arrogation 6 taking 7 seizure 10 assumption, usurpation 12 confiscation 13 appropriation, expropriation

arrow 3 bow 4 bolt, dart 5 shaft 7 pointer 9 direction 12 pointed shaft

Arrow
constellation of: 7 Sagitta

Arrowsmith
author: 13 Sinclair Lewis
character: 10 Leora Tozer 11 Max Gottlieb 12 Terry Wickett 14 Capitola McGurk 15 Gustaf Sondelius 16 Martin Arrowsmith 18 Dr Almus Pickerbaugh

arroyo 4 wadi 5 gorge, gully 6 ravine, trench

arsenal 6 armory 7 weapons 8 magazine 9 arms depot 11 arms factory 13 ordnance depot 14 ammunition dump

arsenic
chemical symbol: 2 As

Arsenic and Old Lace
director: 10 Frank Capra
cast: 9 Cary Grant 10 Jack Carson, Peter Lorre 13 Josephine Hull, Priscilla Lane, Raymond Massey

Arsinoe see 11 Alphesiboea

Arsinous
son: 8 Aecamede

Arsippe
father: 6 Minyas
mocked: 8 Dionysus

ars longa, vita brevis 20 art is long life is short

Ars Poetica
author: 5 Homer

art, arts 5 craft, knack, skill 6 genius 7 finesse, mastery, methods 8 artistry, facility, strategy 9 dexterity, expertise, technique 10 fine points, humanities, principles, subtleties, virtuosity
> **goddess of:** 6 Athena, Athene, Pallas, Saitis 7 Minerva 11 Tritogeneia 12 Pallas Athena 18 Alalcomenean Athena

Artacia
> **origin:** 5 Greek
> **mentioned in:** 7 Odyssey
> **means:** 6 spring
> **in the land of:** 10 Laestrygon

Artegall
> **character in:** 15 The Faerie Queene
> **author:** 7 Spenser

Artemis
> **also:** 7 Cynthia 9 Astratela
> **origin:** 5 Greek
> **form:** 6 virgin 7 goddess 8 huntress
> **habitat:** 4 moon
> **mother:** 4 Leto
> **twin brother:** 6 Apollo
> **companion:** 4 Opis 5 Oread
> **corresponds to:** 5 Diana 6 Phoebe, Selene 11 Britomartis
> **epithet:** 6 Orthia 7 Eurippa, Laphria, Limnaea, Pyronia 8 Aeginaea, Agrotera, Calliste, Caryatis, Daphnaea 9 Hemerasia, Lygodesma 10 Polymastus 11 Leucophryne

Artemision
> **shrine of:** 7 Artemis

artery 3 way 4 path, road, vein 5 aorta 6 street 7 channel, highway 11 blood vessel
artful 3 apt, sly 4 able, deft, foxy, wily 5 adept, quick, sharp, smart 6 adroit, astute, clever, crafty, gifted, shifty, shrewd, subtle, tricky 7 cunning, knowing, politic 8 masterly, scheming, skillful, talented 9 deceitful, deceptive, designing, dexterous, ingenious, inventive, strategic, underhand 10 contriving, diplomatic, proficient 11 imaginative, machinating, maneuvering, resourceful 12 disingenuous
artfulness 5 guile 6 deceit 7 cunning, slyness 8 artifice, foxiness, scheming, subtlety, trickery, wiliness 10 craftiness 11 machination

Arthur
> **director:** 11 Steve Gordon
> **cast:** 11 Dudley Moore, John Gielgud 12 Liza Minnelli 19 Geraldine Fitzgerald
> **Oscar for:** 15 supporting actor (Gielgud)

Arthur
> **began:** 10 Round Table
> **father:** 14 Uther Pendragon
> **half-sister:** 11 Morgan le Fay
> **home:** 7 Camelot
> **island:** 6 Avalon
> **knights:** 3 Kay 6 Gareth, Gawain 7 Geraint 8 Bedivere, Lancelot, Percival, Tristram 9 Launcelot
> **knights sought:** 9 Holy Grail
> **mother:** 7 Igraine, Ygaerne
> **nephew:** 6 Modred
> **sword:** 9 Excalibur

> **given by:** 13 Lady of the Lake
> **wife:** 9 Guinevere
> **wizard:** 6 Merlin

Arthur, Chester Alan
> **nickname:** 4 Chet 16 The Gentleman Boss
> **presidential rank:** 11 twenty-first
> **party:** 10 Republican
> **state represented:** 2 NY
> **defeated:** 5 no-one
> **succeeded upon death of:** 8 Garfield
> **vice president:** 4 none
> **cabinet:**
>> **state:** 6 (James Gillespie) Blaine 13 (Frederick Theodore) Frelinghuysen
>> **treasury:** 6 (Charles James) Folger, (William) Windom 7 (Walter Quintin) Gresham 9 (Hugh) McCulloch
>> **war:** 7 (Robert Todd) Lincoln
>> **attorney general:** 8 (Benjamin Harris) Brewster, (Isaac Wayne) MacVeagh
>> **navy:** 4 (William Henry) Hunt 8 (William Eaton) Chandler
>> **postmaster general:** 4 (Timothy Otis) Howe 5 (Thomas Lemuel) James 6 (Frank) Hatton 7 (Walter Quinton) Gresham
>> **interior:** 6 (Henry Moore) Teller 8 (Samuel Jordan) Kirkwood
> **born:** 2 VT (or Canada) 9 Fairfield
> **died:** 2 NY 11 New York City
> **buried:** 2 NY 6 Albany
> **education:**
>> **college:** 5 Union
>> **studied:** 3 law
> **religion:** 12 Episcopalian
> **interests:** 8 good food (an epicure) 13 salmon fishing
> **political career:** 13 vice president 26 customs collector for New York
> **civilian career:** 6 lawyer 7 teacher
> **military service:** 8 Civil War
> **quartermaster general of:** 12 state militia (New York)
> **notable events of lifetime/term:** 5 Panic (of 1883)
> **Act:** 9 Pendleton 16 Chinese Exclusion 19 Edmunds Anti-Polygamy
> **father:** 7 William
> **mother:** 7 Malvina (Stone)
> **siblings:** 4 Jane, Mary 6 Almeda, George, Regina 7 Malvina, William 8 Ann Eliza
> **wife:** 5 Ellen (Lewis Herndon)
> **nickname:** 4 Nell
> **children:** 11 Chester Alan 12 Ellen Herndon 19 William Lewis Herndon

artichoke 14 Cynara Scolymus
> **varieties:** 5 Globe 7 Chinese 8 Japanese 9 Jerusalem 14 White Jerusalem

article 4 item, part, term 5 count, essay, paper, piece, point, story, theme, thing 6 clause, detail, matter, object, review, sketch 7 portion, product, proviso, write-up 8 division 9 commodity, condition, paragraph, provision, substance 10 commentary, particular 11 proposition, stipulation

articulate 4 join 5 hinge, state, utter, voice 6 convey, facile, fluent, hook up 7 connect, enounce, express 8 eloquent, organize 9 enunciate, formulate, pronounce 10 enunciated, expressive, meaningful, speechlike 12 intelligible

articulation 5 hinge, joint 7 diction 8 juncture 9 elocution, utterance 10 connection 11 enunciation 13 pronunciation

artifact 4 tool 7 manmade 9 arrowhead

artifice 4 hoax, ruse, trap, wile 5 blind, dodge, feint, guile, trick 6 deceit, device, tactic 7 cunning, slyness 8 foxiness, intrigue, maneuver, scheming, trickery, wiliness 9 deception, duplicity, falsehood, imposture, ingenuity, invention, stratagem 10 artfulness, cleverness, craftiness, subterfuge 11 contrivance, machination 13 inventiveness

artificer 7 artisan, deviser 9 contriver, craftsman

artificial 4 fake, mock, sham 5 false, phony, stagy 6 ersatz, forced 7 feigned, labored, manmade, stilted 8 affected, mannered, specious, spurious 9 imitation, insincere, pretended, simulated, synthetic, unnatural 10 factitious, non-natural, theatrical 12 counterfeit 12 manufactured

artillery 6 cannon 7 big guns 8 ordnance 11 mounted guns

artisan 6 master 9 craftsman 10 technician 14 handicraftsman

art is long life is short
Latin: 18 ars longa vita brevis

artist 6 expert, master 8 virtuoso

artistic 7 elegant, stylish 8 graceful, handsome, tasteful 9 aesthetic, exquisite 10 attractive

artistic ability 6 talent 7 mastery 8 artistry 10 virtuosity

artistry 5 taste, touch 6 talent 7 mastery 10 virtuosity 11 proficiency, sensibility 14 accomplishment

artless 4 open, pure, true 5 crude, frank, naive, plain 6 candid, honest, humble, simple 7 natural, sincere 8 innocent, trusting 9 guileless, ingenuous, primitive, unadorned 10 inartistic, lacking art, unaffected, untalented 11 open-hearted, undesigning 13 unpretentious 15 straightforward, unself-conscious, unsophisticated

artlessness 6 candor 7 honesty, naivete 8 openness 9 frankness, sincerity 10 simplicity 11 naturalness 13 guilelessness, ingenuousness 14 unaffectedness

art object
French: 9 objet d'art

Art of Living, The
author: 11 John Gardner

Art of Love, The (Ars Amatoria)
author: 4 Ovid

arty 6 dainty 7 foppish 8 affected, highbrow, overnice, precious 9 dandified, overblown 10 effeminate 11 overrefined, pretentious 12 artsy-craftsy, bluestocking, high-sounding

Aruns
killer of: 7 Camilla

Arval
also: 13 Arval Brothers 14 Fratres Arvales
priests of: 6 Dea Dia
number of priests: 6 twelve

Arval Brothers see 5 Arval

Aryan
modern name: 13 Indo-European
origin: 10 North India 11 Central Asia
family of languages: 5 Hindi 7 Bengali, Panjabi 9 Sinhalese
religion: 8 Hinduism
originated: 11 caste system

Aryana see 11 Afghanistan

as 4 that, when 5 while 7 because, equally

Asa
father: 6 Abijah
grandfather: 8 Rehoboam
grandmother: 6 Maacah
deposed: 6 Maacah
defeated: 6 Baasha

as above
Latin: 7 ut supra

as a group 7 en masse, in a body 8 as a whole, together 11 all together

as a matter of form
Latin: 8 pro forma

Asar see 5 Aesir

as a result 2 so 5 due to 7 because 9 therefore, wherefore, whereupon 11 accordingly 12 consequently 13 in consequence

as a whole 8 all in all 10 altogether 19 all things considered
French: 6 en bloc

as below
Latin: 7 ut infra

Ascalabus
form: 5 youth
mocked: 7 Demeter
changed into: 6 lizard

Ascalaphus
occupation: 6 sentry 8 gardener
location: 10 underworld
father: 4 Ares
brother: 8 Ialmenus
member of: 9 Argonauts
killed by: 9 Deiphobus
changed into: 3 owl
changed by: 7 Demeter

Ascanius
also: 5 Iulus
father: 6 Aeneas
mother: 6 Creusa
founder of: 9 Alba Longa

ascend 4 rise 5 climb, mount, scale 7 inherit 9 succeed to

ascendancy, ascendance 4 edge, rule, sway 5 power, reign 7 command, control, mastery 8 whip hand 9 advantage, authority, dominance, influence, supremacy, upper hand 10 domination, leadership 11 preeminence, sovereignty, superiority 12 predominance

ascension 6 ascent, rising 7 scaling 8 climbing, mounting 10 ascendancy

ascent 4 rise 5 climb, grade, slope 6 rising 7 advance, incline, scaling, upgrade 8 climbing, gradient, mounting, progress 9 ascension 11 advancement, progression

ascertain 5 learn 6 detect, verify 7 certify, find out, unearth 8 discover 9 determine, establish, ferret out

ascertainable 10 detectable 11 discernible, perceivable, perceptible

ascetic 3 nun 4 monk, yogi 5 fakir, stern 6 hermit, strict 7 austere, dervish, eremite, recluse, solitary 9 abstainer, anchorite, religious 10 abstemious, flagellant, self-denier 11 self-denying 13 self-mortifier 14 self-mortifying

Asch, Sholem
   author of: 4 Mary 5 Moses 8 A Village 10 The Apostle, The Prophet 11 The Nazarene, Three Cities 15 Song of the Valley 17 The God of Vengeance

Asclepiade
   descendants of: 9 Asclepius

Asclepius
   origin: 5 Greek
   god of: 7 healing 8 medicine
   father: 6 Apollo
   mother: 7 Coronis
   wife: 6 Epione
   son: 7 Machaon 10 Podalirius
   daughter: 4 Iaso 6 Hygeia
   nurse: 6 Trygon
   corresponds to: 11 Aesculapius
   epithet: 8 Cotyleus

ascribe 6 assign, credit, impute, relate 7 trace to 8 accredit, charge to 9 attribute

Ascus
   form: 5 giant
   helped: 8 Lycurgus
   chained: 8 Dionysus

asea 4 lost 6 addled, adrift 7 puzzled 8 confused 10 bewildered

Asenath
   father: 10 Potipherah
   husband: 6 Joseph
   son: 7 Ephraim 8 Manasseh

Asgard
   home of: 4 Asar 5 Aesir
   origin: 12 Scandinavian
   connected to earth by: 7 bifrost 13 rainbow bridge
   location of: 8 Valhalla

ash 4 dust 6 cinder 7 residue 12 powdered lava
   family: 5 olive
   genus: 8 Fraxinus
   climatic zone: 17 northern temperate
   varieties: 3 Pop, Red, Sea 4 Blue 5 Black, Green, Manna, Texas, Wafer, Water, White 6 Alpine, Ground, Shamel, Syrian, Velvet 7 Arizona, Modesto, Prickly 8 Carolina, Stinking 9 Evergreen, Flowering 10 Manchurian, Montebello 18 Yellow-topped mallee
   use: 4 fuel 6 timber 7 barrels 8 landscape 9 furniture 10 motor parts, sport goods
   most common species: 8 white ash

ashamed 3 shy 7 abashed, bashful, prudish 9 chagrined, mortified, squeamish 10 chapfallen, distressed, humiliated, shamefaced 11 crestfallen, discomfited, embarrassed 12 disconcerted 13 guilt-stricken 18 conscience-stricken

Ashby, Hal
   director of: 10 Being There, Coming Home

ashen 3 wan 4 gray, pale 5 livid, pasty 6 anemic, leaden, pallid 8 blanched

Asher
   father: 5 Jacob
   mother: 6 Zilpah
   brother: 3 Dan, Gad 4 Levi 5 Judah 6 Joseph, Reuben, Simeon 7 Zebulun 8 Benjamin, Issachar, Nephtali
   sister: 5 Dinah
   city in: 8 Manasseh
   descendant of: 8 Asherite

Ashkenaz
   father: 6 Japhet
   mother: 5 Gomer

Ashley, Lady Brett
   character in: 15 The Sun Also Rises
   author: 9 Hemingway

ashore 6 on land 7 aground 9 on dry land

Ashton-Warner, Sylvia
   author of: 5 Three 6 Myself 7 Teacher 8 Spinster 10 Greenstone

Ashtoreth
   origin: 7 Semitic
   corresponds to: 6 Inanna, Ishtar 7 Astarte, Mylitta

Ash-Wednesday
   author: 7 T S Eliot

ashy 3 wan 4 pale 5 ashen, pasty, white 6 pallid, sallow 7 ghastly, ghostly 8 blanched 9 colorless

Asia
   country: 4 Iran, Iraq, Laos, Oman 5 Burma, China, India, Japan, Macao, Nepal, Qatar, Syria, Tibet, Yemen 6 Bhutan, Brunei, Cyprus, Israel, Jordan, Russia, Sikkim, Taiwan, Turkey 7 Armenia, Bahrain, Georgia, Kashmir, Lebanon, Myanmar, Vietnam 8 Cambodia, Hong Kong, Malaysia, Maldives, Mongolia, Pakistan, Sri Lanka, Thailand 9 Indonesia, Kirghizia, Singapore 10 Azerbaijan, Bangladesh, Kazakhstan, Kyrgyzstan, North Korea, South Korea, Tajikistan, Uzbekistan 11 Afghanistan, Saudi Arabia 12 North Vietnam, South Vietnam, Turkmenistan 13 Inner Mongolia 14 Papua New Guinea 15 Sinkiang-Uighur 18 United Arab Emirates
   desert: 4 Gobi, Thar 6 Syrian 7 Arabian, Karakum 8 Kyzylkum 10 Takla Makan
   island: 5 Kuril, Japan 6 Taiwan 7 Hai-nan 8 Sri Lanka 9 Indonesia: 3 Aru 4 Java, Sulu 5 Ceram, Sumba, Timor 6 Borneo, Flores 7 Celebes, Sumatra 8 Moluccas,

Tanimbar 9 Halmahera, New Guinea 11 Philippines

ancient people/empire: 4 Elam, Thai 5 Akkad, Aryan, Indus, Khmer, Media, Shang 6 Mongol, Ohoman, Semite 7 Amorite, Assyria, Hwang Ho, Parthia, Persian 8 Sumerian 9 Babylonia, Dravidian, Sassanian 11 Hephthalite, Mesopotamia

ancient city: 2 Ur 5 Pagan, Sumer 6 Anyang 7 Ayuthia, Harappa 8 Mandalay 12 Mohenjo-daro

ancient leader: 5 Asoka, Kassi 6 Darius 9 Anawratha, Zoroaster 13 Cyrus the Great 17 Alexander the Great

religion: 5 Islam 6 Muslim, Shinto, Taoism 7 Jainism, Judaism 8 Buddhism, Hinduism 12 Christianity, Confucianism 13 Protestantism 16 Roman Catholicism

language: 5 Hindi 6 Arabic, French 7 Chinese, English, Russian, Spanish

Chinese dialects: 2 Wu 3 Min 5 Hakka 8 Mandarin 9 Cantonese

river: 2 Ob 3 Amu, Hsi, Syr 4 Amur, Lena 5 Indus 6 Ganges, Mekong, Tigris 7 Hwang Ho, Salween, Yangtze, Yenisei 9 Euphrates, Irrawaddy 11 Brahmaputra 16 Tigris-Euphrates

lake: 6 Baikal 7 Aral Sea 8 Balkhash 10 Caspian Sea

mountain/mountain range: 5 Altai, Urals 6 Kunlon, Pamirs, Taurus, Zagros 8 Caucasus, Sulaiman, Tien Shan 9 Himalayas, Hindu Kush, Karakoram 10 Arakan Yoma

highest point: 12 Mount Everest

lowest point: 7 Dead Sea

mineral/natural resources: 3 oil, tin 4 coal, mica, talc, zinc 7 bauxite, iron ore, mercury 8 chromium, graphite, selenium, tungsten 9 manganese 10 natural gas

largest city: 8 Shanghai

vegetation: 3 fir, sal 4 moss, pine, teak 5 larch 6 bamboo, lichen, spruce 8 ironwood

animal: 3 elk, yak 4 bear, wolf 5 camel, panda, sable, takin, tiger 6 ermine, kuland 7 markhor 8 antelope, elephant, reindeer 9 arctic fox, polar bear

people: 4 Huis, Kurd, Thai, Turk 5 Aryan, Khmer, Malay, Tungu 6 Buryat, Chuang, Kalmyk, Mongol, Semite, Vighor 7 Baluchi, Burmese, Chinese, Chukchi, Persian, Russian, Tadzhik, Tibetan 8 Armenian, Filipino, Japanese 9 Dravidian 10 Han Chinese, Indonesian, Vietnamese

aside 4 away 5 apart 6 aslant, beside 7 whisper

As I Lay Dying
author: 15 William Faulkner
character:
Bundren family: 4 Anse, Cash, Darl 5 Addie, Jewel 9 Dewey Dell

Asimov, Isaac
author of: 6 I Robot 10 Foundation (trilogy) 12 Caves of Steel, Robots of Dawn 17 The Gods Themselves

character: 12 Elijah Bailey 13 R Daneel Olivaw

asinine 5 silly 6 absurd, insane, stupid 7 foolish, idiotic, moronic, witless 9 brainless, imbecilic, senseless 10 half-witted, irrational, muddlehead, ridiculous 11 lamebrained, thickheaded, thick-witted 12 dunderheaded, feeble-minded, simpleminded, thick-skulled

asininity 5 folly 8 dumbness 9 silliness, stupidity 10 imbecility 11 doltishness, foolishness 16 simplemindedness

as it should be
French: 11 comme il faut

Asius
origin: 5 Greek
mentioned in: 5 Iliad
king of: 7 Percote
father: 8 Hyrtacus
killed by: 9 Idomeneus

ask 3 beg, bid, sue 4 call, pump, quiz, seek, urge 5 apply, claim, grill, plead, press, query 6 appeal, charge, demand, desire, expect, invite, summon 7 beseech, entreat, implore, inquire, request, solicit 8 petition, question, sound out 10 supplicate 11 interrogate

Ask
origin: 6 Nordic
first: 3 man
made from: 7 ash tree
made by: 4 gods

askance 11 skeptically 12 disdainfully, suspiciously 13 distrustfully, mistrustfully 14 disapprovingly

askew 4 awry 6 aslant 7 crooked 8 cockeyed, lopsided, sleeping 9 crookedly

Askkimey *see* 6 Eskimo

aslant 4 awry 5 askew 7 crooked 8 cockeyed, lopsided 9 crookedly, obliquely, slantwise

asleep 6 dozing 7 napping 10 slumbering 13 taking a siesta 14 dead to the world

as much as this
Latin: 8 quoad hoc

Asner, Ed
born: 12 Kansas City KS
roles: 5 Roots 8 Lou Grant 14 Rich Man Poor Man 18 Mary Tyler Moore Show

asocial 8 unsocial 9 nonsocial, reclusive 10 antisocial 12 misanthropic

Asopus
form: 3 god
habitat: 5 river
father: 7 Oceanus
mother: 6 Tethys
wife: 6 Metope
son: 7 Ismenus, Pelagon
number of daughters: 6 twenty

asparagus
varieties: 4 Cape 6 Common, Garden, Smilax 7 Cossack 8 Prussian, Sprenger

aspect 3 air 4 look, side 5 angle, facet, point 7 feature 10 appearance 13 consideration

aspen 7 Populus
varieties: 7 Chinese, Quaking **8** European, Japanese **9** Trembling **12** Large-toothed

asperity 5 rigor **6** rancor **8** acrimony, hardship, severity **9** harshness, hostility, roughness **10** difficulty

Aspern Papers, The
author: 10 Henry James

aspersion 4 slur **5** abuse, smear **7** calumny, censure, obloquy, railing, slander **8** reproach, reviling **10** defamation, detraction **11** deprecation **12** vilification **13** disparagement

Asphalius see **8** Poseidon

Asphodel Fields
meadow of: 10 dead heroes

asphyxiate 5 choke **6** stifle **7** smother **9** suffocate **11** strangulate

aspirant 7 hopeful, nominee **9** applicant, candidate **10** competitor, contestant

aspiration 3 end **4** hope, mark, wish **6** design, desire, intent, object **7** craving, longing, purpose **8** ambition, daydream, endeavor, yearning **9** hankering, intention, objective

aspire 4 seek **5** aim at, covet, crave **6** desire, pursue **7** hope for, long for, pine for, wish for **8** yearn for **9** pant after **10** hunger over **11** hanker after, thirst after

ass 4 dolt, fool, jerk **5** booby, burro, dunce, idiot, moron, ninny **6** donkey, dum-dum, nitwit **7** half-wit, jackass **8** bonehead, imbecile, lunkhead, numskull **9** blockhead, lamebrain **10** dunderhead, nincompoop **11** male jackass

assail 5 fly at **6** attack **7** assault, lunge at, set upon **9** pitch into **11** descend upon

assailant 6 mugger **8** assailer, attacker, molester **9** aggressor, assaulter

assailer 8 attacker **9** aggressor, assailant, assaulter

Assamese
language family: 12 Indo-European
branch: 11 Indo-Iranian
group: 5 Indic
spoken in: 5 (northern) India

Assaracus
origin: 5 Greek
mentioned in: 5 Iliad
father: 4 Tros
son: 5 Capys
founder of: 10 royal house

assassin 6 hit man, killer, slayer **8** murderer **11** executioner

assassinate 4 kill, slay **6** murder, rub out **7** bump off **9** do to death, liquidate **10** put to death **11** exterminate

assault 4 push, raid **5** drive, fly at, foray, lunge, sally, siege, storm **6** assail, attack, charge, invade, strike, thrust **7** besiege, bombard, lunge at, offense, set upon **8** fall upon, invasion, storming, strike at, thrust at **9** assailing, lash out at, onslaught **10** aggression **11** bombardment

assaulter 6 mugger **8** assailer, attacker **9** aggressor, assailant

assay 3 try **4** rate, test **5** essay, prove **6** assess **7** analyze, attempt **8** appraise, endeavor, estimate, evaluate **9** undertake

assemblage 4 body, heap, herd, mass, pack, pile **5** batch, bunch, clump, flock, group, stock, store **6** throng **7** cluster, company **8** assembly, conclave **9** aggregate, amassment, gathering **10** collection **11** aggregation **12** accumulation, congregation

assemble 4 join, meet **5** amass, flock, rally **6** gather, heap up, muster, pile up, summon **7** collect, compile, connect, convene, convoke, marshal, round up **9** construct, fabricate **10** accumulate, congregate **11** fit together, put together **12** call together, come together **13** bring together, group together

assembly 4 body, herd, mass, pack **5** crowd, flock, group, troop **6** throng **7** cluster, company, council **8** conclave, congress **9** aggregate, gathering **10** assemblage, collection **11** aggregation, convocation, legislature **12** congregation

assembly hall 8 auditory **10** auditorium **11** concert hall, lecture hall, meeting hall

assent 5 agree, allow, grant, yield **6** accept, accord, comply, concur, permit **7** approve, concede, consent, defer to **8** approval, sanction **9** acquiesce, admission, agreement **10** acceptance, compliance, concession, fall in with **11** affirmation, approbation, concurrence, endorsement, recognition, subscribe to **12** acquiescence, confirmation, ratification, verification **13** corroboration **14** acknowledgment

assent to 4 okay **5** allow **6** accept, permit **7** approve **8** sanction, say yes to **9** agree with, authorize **11** acquiesce to, go along with

assert 4 aver, avow **5** argue, claim, state, swear **6** accent, affirm, avouch, insist, stress, uphold **7** advance, contend, declare, profess **8** advocate, maintain, propound, set forth **9** emphasize **10** put forward

assertion 5 claim **6** avowal, dictum **8** argument, averment **9** statement, upholding **10** allegation, contention **11** declaration, maintaining **12** protestation

assertion without proof
Latin: 9 ipse dixit

assertive 5 pushy **8** cocksure, decisive, emphatic, forceful, positive **9** confident, insistent, outspoken **10** aggressive **11** domineering, self-assured **12** strong-willed

assertiveness 10 insistence **11** forwardness **12** cocksureness, forcefulness, positiveness **13** agressiveness, outspokenness **14** self-confidence

assess 3 tax **4** levy **5** judge, value **6** charge **8** appraise, consider, estimate, evaluate, look over

assessment 3 fee, tax **4** dues, fine, rate, toll **5** levy, impost, tariff **8** judgment **9** appraisal **10** estimation, evaluation

asset 3 aid **4** boon, help, plus **7** benefit, service **9** advantage

assets 4 cash 5 goods, means, money 6 wealth 7 capital, effects 8 property, reserves 9 resources 10 belongings 11 possessions

asseverate 4 aver, avow 5 state, swear 6 affirm, assert, attest, avouch, insist 7 certify, contend, declare, protect 8 maintain, proclaim 9 emphasize, pronounce
as shown below
  Latin: 7 ut infra

assiduity 8 industry, tenacity 9 diligence 10 dedication, doggedness 11 application, persistence 13 determination

assiduous 6 dogged 7 earnest 8 constant, diligent, sedulous, tireless, untiring 9 laborious, steadfast, tenacious 10 determined, persistent, unflagging 11 hardworking, industrious, persevering, unremitting 13 indefatigable

assign 3 fix, set 4 give, name 5 allot, grant 6 charge, choose, invest 7 appoint, consign, entrust, mete out, specify 8 allocate, delegate, dispense, set apart 9 apportion, designate, determine, prescribe, stipulate 10 commission, distribute

assignation 4 date 5 tryst 7 meeting 10 rendezvous 11 appointment

assignment 3 job 4 duty, post, task 5 chore 6 lesson 8 exercise, homework 9 allotment 10 allocation, commission 11 appointment, designation 12 distribution 13 apportionment

assimilate 6 absorb, digest, imbibe, ingest, take in 9 integrate 10 metabolize 11 incorporate

Assiniboine, Assiniboin
  language family: 6 Siouan
  location: 9 Minnesota 12 Lake Winnipeg, Saskatchewan
  related to: 7 Dakotas

assist 3 aid 4 abet, hand, help 5 boost, serve 6 back up, uphold, wait on 7 benefit, support, sustain 9 cooperate, lend a hand, reinforce 11 accommodate, collaborate, helping hand

assistance 3 aid 4 alms, help 6 relief 7 charity, service, stipend, subsidy, support 10 sustenance 11 cooperation, helping hand 12 contribution 13 collaboration, reinforcement 16 financial support

assistant 3 aid 4 aide, ally 5 aider 6 helper 7 partner 8 adjutant, co-worker, sidekick 9 accessory, associate, auxiliary, colleague, subaltern, supporter 10 accomplice, apprentice, cooperator, lieutenant 11 confederate, helping hand, subordinate 12 collaborator 15 second-in-command

associate 3 mix, pal, tie 4 ally, bind, chum, club, join, link, mate, pair, peer, yoke 5 buddy, crony, merge, unite 6 allied, couple, fellow, friend, hobnob, league, mingle, relate 7 combine, comrade, connect, consort, hang out, partner, related 8 confrere, co-worker, identify, intimate, sidekick 9 affiliate, colleague, companion, confidant, correlate, pal around, rub elbows, run around 10 accomplice, affiliated, fraternize

11 confederate, subordinate 12 collaborator

associated 6 allied, joined, united 9 connected 10 affiliated 11 amalgamated

association 3 tie 4 body, bond, club, meld 5 blend, group, union 6 clique, league 7 combine, company, linkage, mixture, society 8 alliance, intimacy, mingling, relation 9 coalition, community, relations, syndicate 10 assemblage, connection, federation, fellowship, fraternity, friendship, membership 11 affiliation, camaraderie, combination, confederacy, corporation, correlation, familiarity, partnership 12 acquaintance, friendliness, organization, relationship 13 collaboration, companionship, confederation, participation 14 fraternization, identification

assorted 5 mixed 6 motley, sundry, varied 7 diverse, various 9 different 11 diversified 13 heterogeneous, miscellaneous

assortment 5 array, stock, store 6 medley, motley 7 melange, mixture, sorting, variety 8 grouping, quantity 9 arranging, assorting, diversity, potpourri, selection 10 collection, hodgepodge, miscellany 11 arrangement, classifying, disposition 14 classification, conglomeration
as stated below
  Latin: 7 ut infra

assuage 4 calm, ease 5 allay, quiet, still 6 lessen, pacify, soften, soothe, temper 7 appease, lighten, mollify, relieve 8 mitigate, tone down 9 alleviate 14 take the edge off

assuagement 6 easing, relief, solace 7 comfort 8 blunting, easement 9 abatement, lessening, tempering 10 mitigation 11 appeasement 13 mollification

assume 4 take 5 fancy, guess, infer, judge, seize, think, usurp 6 accept, deduce, gather, take on, take up 7 believe, imagine, presume, suppose, surmise, suspect 8 arrogate, shoulder, take over, theorize 9 postulate, speculate, undertake 10 commandeer, conjecture, understand 11 appropriate, expropriate, hypothesize 14 take for granted

assumed 4 fake 5 bogus, false, phony 6 made-up 8 presumed, supposed 9 falsified 10 fictitious 11 make-believe, presupposed, pseudonymic 12 pseudonymous

assumed name 5 alias 7 pen name 9 pseudonym 13 false identity
  French: 10 nom de plume 11 nom de guerre

assuming 4 bold 5 nervy, pushy 6 brazen, cheeky 7 forward, haughty 8 arrogant, insolent 9 audacious, presuming 11 overbearing 12 presumptuous 13 self-assertive

assumption 6 belief, taking, theory 7 premise, seizure 8 assuming, taking on, taking up 9 accepting, postulate 10 acceptance, arrogation, hypothesis, usurpation 11 postulation, presumption, shouldering, supposition, undertaking 13 appropriating 14 presupposition

assurance 3 vow **4** oath **5** poise **6** binder, pledge **7** promise **8** averment, boldness, coolness, sureness, warranty **9** certainty, certitude, guarantee **10** confidence, profession **11** affirmation, assuredness, word of honor **12** self-reliance **14** aggressiveness, self-confidence, self-possession

assure 5 vow to **6** clinch, ensure, secure **7** confirm, promise **8** pledge to **9** guarantee **11** make certain **14** give one's word to

assured 4 sure **5** fixed **6** poised, secure **7** certain, settled **8** positive **9** confident, undoubted **10** dependable, guaranteed **11** indubitable, irrefutable **12** indisputable **13** self-confident, self-possessed **14** unquestionable

Astaire, Fred
  real name: 19 Frederick Austerlitz
  partner: 12 Ginger Rogers
  born: 7 Omaha NE
  roles: 6 Top Hat **9** Funny Face, Let's Dance, Swing Time **10** Holiday Inn **12** Easter Parade, Royal Wedding, Shall We Dance **14** The Gay Divorcee

Astarte
  origin: 7 Semitic
  goddess of: 9 fertility **12** reproduction
  habitat: 4 moon
  corresponds to: 6 Inanna, Ishtar **7** Mylitta **9** Ashtoreth

aster 12 Callistephus
  varieties: 4 Tree **5** Black, China, Heath **6** Annual, Golden, Mojave, Stoke's **7** Italian **8** Blue-wood **9** Tartarian, White wood **10** New England **11** White upland

Asteria
  form: 8 Titaness
  father: 5 Coeus
  mother: 6 Phoebe
  sister: 4 Leto
  husband: 6 Perses
  son: 8 Paropeus
  daughter: 6 Hecate
  changed into: 5 Delos **6** island

Asterion
  also: 8 Asterius
  father: 7 Cometes
  member of: 9 Argonauts

Asterius
  also: 8 Asterion
  form: 5 giant **8** minotaur
  king of: 5 Crete
  father: 4 Anax **8** Tectamus **10** Cretan Bull, Hyperasius
  mother: 8 Pasiphae
  wife: 6 Europa
  adopted sons: 5 Minos **8** Sarpedon **12** Rhadamanthys
  daughter: 5 Crete
  member of: 9 Argonauts

astern 3 aft **5** abaft **6** behind **9** to the rear

Asterodia
  form: 5 nymph
  type of nymph: 9 Caucasian

asteroid 6 debris **9** meteorite, planetoid

Asteropaeus
  origin: 5 Greek
  mentioned in: 5 Iliad
  father: 7 Pelegon
  ally of: 4 Troy
  killed by: 8 Achilles

Asterope *see* **7** Sterope

astir 2 up **5** afoot, awake **6** active, roused **8** in motion, out of bed **10** up and about

astonish 4 daze, stun **5** amaze, shock **6** dazzle **7** astound, confuse, perplex, stagger, startle, stupefy **8** bewilder, confound, dumfound, surprise **9** electrify, overwhelm, take aback **10** strike dumb **11** flabbergast **15** make one's eyes pop **18** take one's breath away

astonishing 7 amazing **8** dazzling, shocking, striking **9** confusing, startling **10** astounding, impressive, perplexing, staggering, stupefying, surprising **11** bewildering, confounding **12** breathtaking, electrifying, overpowering, overwhelming

astonishment 3 awe **5** shock **6** wonder **8** surprise **9** amazement, confusion **10** perplexity, wonderment **12** bewilderment, stupefaction

Astor, Mary
  real name: 28 Lucille Vasconcellos Langhanke
  born: 8 Quincy IL
  roles: 6 Marmee **11** Little Women, The Great Lie **15** Meet Me in St Louis **16** The Maltese Falcon **17** The Palm Beach Story **18** The Prisoner of Zenda

astound 4 daze, stun **5** amaze, shock **6** dazzle **7** stagger, startle, stupefy **8** astonish, dumfound, surprise, take back **9** electrify, overwhelm **10** strike dumb **11** flabbergast **15** make one's eyes pop **18** take one's breath away

Astrabacus
  origin: 5 Greek **7** Spartan
  form: 6 prince
  found: 11 wooden image
  hidden by: 7 Orestes
  co-finder: 8 Alopecus

Astraea
  also: 6 Astrea
  goddess of: 7 justice
  father: 4 Zeus
  mother: 6 Themis

Astraeus
  form: 5 Titan
  consort of: 3 Eos
  father of: 4 wind **5** stars

astral 6 starry **9** celestial **12** astronomical

astraphobia
  fear of: 9 lightning

Astrateia *see* **7** Artemis

astray 3 off **5** amiss **6** afield **10** off the mark **12** off the course **16** off the right track

Astrea *see* **7** Astraea

astringent 4 acid, keen, sour, tart **5** brisk, sharp, stern, tonic **6** biting, severe **7** acerbic, austere, bracing, puckery, styptic **8** curative, incisive, piercing, salutary, stabbing,

astrology 6 Zodiac 9 horoscopy, starcraft 10 astromancy, astrometry, stargazing 11 genethliacs 13 mathematicals 14 astrodiagnosis

belief in: 8 siderism

term: 4 sign 5 house, trine 6 alnath, apheta, aspect 7 almuten, anareta, mansion, mundane, sextile 8 alkahest, nativity, quartile, synastry 9 planetary 10 opposition 11 conjunction

astronomer 4 Bode, Gold 5 Adams, Baade, Bayer, Bethe, Gould, Hoyle, Royer 6 Bessel, Halley, Hubble, Jansky, Kepler, Newton, Piazzi 7 Bradley, Celcius, Galileo, Huggins, Huygens, Kapteyn, Laplace, Ptolemy, Russell, Shapley, Slipher 8 Angstrom, Einstein, Herschel, Hevelius, Lacaille, Lemaitre, Mercator 9 Eddington, Leverrier 10 Copernicus, Hipparchus, Tycho Brahe 11 Aristarchus, Hertzsprung 13 Petrus Apianus

astronomy

term: 5 comet, orbit 6 apogee, meteor, nebula, parsec, quasar 7 azimuth, eclipse, equinox, perigee, transit 8 aphelion, asteroid, ecliptic, meridian, solstice 9 meteorite, satellite 10 perihelion, precession 11 declination, occultation 12 perturbation, spectroscopy 16 celestial equator

type/related study: 9 cosmogony, cosmology 10 astrometry, photometry 12 astrophysics 18 celestial mechanics

see also: 4 star

Astrophel and Stella

author: 15 Sir Philip Sidney

astute 3 sly 4 able, foxy, keen, wily 5 acute, sharp, smart 6 adroit, artful, bright, clever, crafty, shrewd, subtle 7 cunning, knowing, politic 9 designing, sagacious 10 discerning, keen-minded, perceptive 11 calculating, intelligent, penetrating 13 Machiavellian, perspicacious

astuteness 6 acumen 8 keenness 9 acuteness, smartness 10 cleverness, shrewdness 12 perspicacity

Astyanax

also: 11 Scamandrius

father: 6 Hector 9 Strophius

mother: 10 Andromache

thrown from: 11 Trojan walls

thrown by: 6 Greeks

slain by: 8 Menelaus

Astydamia

father: 7 Amyntor

husband: 7 Acastus

daughter: 8 Laodamia

abducted by: 8 Hercules

Asuncion

capital of: 8 Paraguay

asunder 4 rent 5 apart 8 in pieces, to shreds 9 torn apart 11 broken apart

asylum 4 home 5 haven 6 harbor, refuge 7 retreat, shelter 8 madhouse, preserve 9 almshouse, orphanage, poorhouse, sanctuary 10 sanatorium, sanitarium 11 institution 13 children's home, state hospital 14 mental hospital 15 place of immunity 17 mental institution 23 eleemosynary institution

Asynjur

origin: 12 Scandinavian

goddesses of: 4 Asar 5 Aesir

leader: 3 Fri 5 Frigg, Frija 6 Frigga

As You Like It

author: 18 William Shakespeare

character: 5 Celia (Aliena) 6 Audrey, Jaques, Oliver 7 Orlando 8 Rosalind (Ganymede) 9 Frederick 10 Touchstone

Atabyrian see 4 Zeus

at a distance 4 afar, away 5 above, aloof, apart 6 far off 9 separated

Atala

author: 21 Francois Chateaubriand

Atalanta

also: 8 Atalante

form: 6 virgin 8 huntress

father: 5 Iasus

mother: 7 Clymene

son: 13 Parthenopaeus

wounded: 14 Calydonian boar

lost race to: 10 Hippomenes

Atalanta in Calydon

author: 24 Algernon Charles Swinburne

Atalante see 8 Atalanta

at any rate 6 anyhow, anyway 9 in any case 10 in any event

at cross purposes 7 counter, opposed 8 contrary, converse, inimical, opposite 9 disparate 10 at variance, discordant 11 conflicting 12 antithetical, incompatible 13 contradictory

Ate

origin: 5 Greek

form: 7 goddess

personifies: 12 recklessness 16 divine punishment

at ease 4 calm, cool 6 at rest, serene 7 content, relaxed, unmoved 8 composed 9 at leisure, confident, unruffled 10 complacent, nonchalant, unbothered, untroubled 11 comfortable, unconcerned

a tergo 9 at the back 10 from behind

at fault 6 guilty 8 culpable 10 implicated 11 blameworthy, responsible

at full length

Latin: 9 in extenso

Athabascan, Athapascan (Slave Indians)

language family: 10 Athabascan, Athapaskan

location: 6 Canada 14 Great Slave Lake

dominated by: 4 Cree

related to: 9 Chipewyan

tribe: 4 Dine 5 Slave 6 Apache, Navaho, Navajo 9 Mescalero 10 Athabascan

Athaliah

father: 4 Ahab

mother: 7 Jezebel

husband: 7 Jehoram

son: 7 Ahaziah

Athalie

author: 18 Jean Baptiste Racine

Athamas
king of: 6 Thebes
father: 6 Aeolus
wife: 3 Ino 7 Nephele
son: 5 Ptous 6 Leucon 7 Phrixus 8 Learchus 10 Melicertes
daughter: 5 Helle

at hand 4 near, nigh 5 close, handy, on tap, ready 6 nearby 7 close by 8 imminent 9 available, impending 10 accessible, convenient 11 at one's elbow, forthcoming 14 at one's disposal 15 within arm's reach

atheism 8 apostasy, unbelief 9 disbelief 10 irreligion 11 godlessness

atheist 7 infidel 10 unbeliever 11 disbeliever, nonbeliever 13 godless person

Athena
also: 6 Athene, Pallas, Saitis 11 Tritogeneia 12 Pallas Athena 18 Alalcomenean Athena
origin: 5 Greek
goddess of: 4 arts 6 wisdom 7 warfare 9 fertility
father: 4 Zeus 6 Triton
mother: 5 Metis
sprang from head of: 4 Zeus
raised by: 12 Alalcomeneus
symbol: 3 owl
corresponds to: 7 Minerva
epithet: 4 Alea 5 Meter, Xenia 6 Ergane, Itonia, Polias 7 Agoraea, Cissaea, Paeonia, Pronaus, Pronoea 8 Anemotis, Poliates, Zosteria 9 Oxyderces, Parthenia, Poliuchus, Promachus 10 Axiopoenus, Chalinitis, Cyparissia 11 Promachorma

Athens
capital of: 6 Greece
Greek: 7 Athinai
hills: 9 Acropolis 14 Hagios Georgios
landmark: 4 Stoa 9 Areopagus, Parthenon 10 Erechtheum, Propylaeum 17 Theater of Dionysus
marketplace: 5 Agora
mountain: 6 Parnes 8 Aigaleos, Hymettus 10 Pentelikon
named for: 6 Athena
port: 7 Piraeus
river: 7 Ilissus
sea: 6 Aegean 11 Saronic Gulf
square: 8 Syntagma (Constitution)
Athens Graces 4 Auxe 8 Hegemone

athirst 4 avid, keen 5 eager 6 raring 7 longing, panting 9 yearning

athlete 4 jock 8 champion 9 contender, sportsman 10 contestant, game player

athletic 5 burly, hardy, husky, manly 6 brawny, robust, strong, sturdy, virile 8 muscular, powerful, stalwart, vigorous 9 masculine, strapping 10 able-bodied

athletics 5 games 6 sports 8 exercise 9 exercises 10 gymnastics

at home 6 at ease, inside, shut in 7 indoors 8 confined 10 in the house 11 comfortable
French: 4 chez

Athos
character in: 18 The Three Musketeers
author: 5 Dumas (pere)

athwart 6 across 7 astride 8 sideways, sidewise 9 crossways, crosswise 12 transversely

Atlanta
baseball team: 6 Braves
basketball team: 5 Hawks
football team: 7 Falcons

Atlantean
pertaining to: 5 Atlas

Atlantic
pertaining to: 10 Titan Atlas

Atlantic City
director: 10 Louis Malle
cast: 8 Kate Reid 13 Burt Lancaster, Michel Piccoli, Susan Sarandon

at large 5 astir, loose 6 abroad 8 as a whole, at length 9 at liberty, in general 10 on the loose, unconfined 11 out and about 13 in circulation 14 around and about 15 making the rounds

Atlas
form: 5 Titan
father: 7 Iapetus
mother: 7 Clymene
brother: 9 Menoetius 10 Epimetheus, Prometheus
wife: 7 Pleione
daughters: 6 Hyades 7 Calypso 8 Pleiades 10 Hesperides
supported: 3 sky
identified with: 14 Atlas Mountains

Atlas Shrugged
author: 7 Ayn Rand
character: 8 John Galt 11 Hank Reardon 12 Dagny Taggart, James Taggart

at last
Latin: 10 ad extremum

at leisure 4 idle 7 off duty 8 inactive 9 at liberty 10 unemployed, unoccupied

Atli
origin: 12 Scandinavian
sister: 8 Brynhild
wife: 6 Gudrun, Kudrun 7 Guthrun
killed by: 6 Gudrun, Kudrun 7 Guthrun
represents: 6 Atilla

atmosphere 3 air 4 aura, feel, mood, tone 5 color 6 spirit 7 feeling, quality 8 ambience 11 environment 12 surroundings

atmospheric 3 air 4 airy 8 ethereal

at odds 6 unlike 8 contrary 9 different 10 at variance, discordant, discrepant, dissimilar 11 contrasting

at odds with 9 counter to 10 contrary to 14 at variance with

atom 3 bit, dot, jot 4 iota, mite, mote, whit 5 crumb, grain, scrap, shred, speck, trace 6 morsel, tittle 7 smidgen 8 fragment, particle 9 scintilla 10 smithereen

atomic 6 cobalt 7 fission, neutron, nuclear, uranium 8 hydrogen 9 molecular, plutonium, subatomic, unseeable 10 impalpable 11 fissionable, microcosmic, microscopic, superatomic 13 imperceptible, indiscernible, infinitesimal, thermonuclear

atom part 6 proton 7 neutron 8 electron

at once
French: 11 tout de suite

atone 6 pay for, redeem, repent, shrive 7 expiate 9 make up for 10 compensate, recompense, remunerate 12 do penance for 13 make amends for 17 make reparation for

atonement 6 amends, shrift 7 penance, redress 9 expiation 10 recompense, redemption, reparation, repentance 12 compensation, satisfaction 14 penitential act

at one's disposal 5 handy 6 at hand, on hand 9 available 10 accessible, convenient 11 at one's elbow, ready for use 13 at one's service

at one's elbow 5 handy 6 at hand, nearby 9 available 10 accessible, convenient

Atrax
  father: 6 Peneus

at rest 5 quiet, still 6 asleep, at ease, serene 7 at peace, content 8 in repose 9 quiescent 10 motionless

Atreus
  father: 6 Pelops
  mother: 10 Hippodamia
  sister: 6 Nicippe
  wife: 6 Aerope
  son: 8 Menelaus 9 Agamemnon 10 Plisthenes
  daughter: 8 Anaxibia
  killed: 6 Aglaus

Atridae
  descendants of: 6 Atreus
  family name of: 8 Anaxibia, Menelaus 9 Agamemnon 10 Plisthenes

atrium 4 hall 6 cavity 7 auricle 8 entrance 13 Roman entrance

atrocious 3 bad, low 4 dark, evil, rude, vile 5 black, cruel 6 brutal, savage, tawdry, vulgar 7 heinous, hellish, inhuman, uncouth, vicious 8 dreadful, enormous, fiendish, flagrant, grievous, horrible, infamous, infernal, pitiless, ruthless, terrible 9 barbarous, execrable, merciless, monstrous, nefarious, tasteless 10 diabolical, outrageous, villainous

atrociousness 6 infamy 7 cruelty 8 enormity, vileness 9 barbarity, brutality, depravity 11 heinousness, viciousness 13 monstrousness, offensiveness 14 outrageousness

atrocity 6 horror 7 outrage 8 enormity, savagery, villainy 9 barbarism, barbarity, brutality 10 inhumanity 11 heinousness

atrophy 7 decline 8 decaying, drying up 9 lack of use, withering 10 emaciation, shriveling 11 wasting away 12 degeneration 13 deterioration

Atropos
  member of: 5 Fates
  cuts thread of: 4 life

Atsina (Gros Ventres; Haaninin)
  language family: 9 Algonkian 10 Algonquian
  location: 6 Canada 7 Montana 9 Milk River 12 Saskatchewan 13 Missouri River
  related to: 7 Arapaho

attach 3 fix 4 join 5 affix, allot, annex 6 append, assign, couple, detail, secure 7 connect, destine, earmark 8 allocate, be fond of, fasten to, make fast 9 affiliate, associate, designate

attache 4 aide 5 envoy 6 consul 8 adjutant, diplomat, emissary, minister 9 assistant 10 ambassador, vice consul 11 diplomatist, subordinate 12 ambassadress 13 consul general

attachment 4 bond, love 6 fixing, liking, regard 7 adjunct, fixture, respect 8 addendum, addition, affinity, affixing, appendix, coupling, devotion, fondness, securing 9 accessory, affection, appendage, attaching, fastening 10 connection, friendship, supplement, tenderness 12 predilection

attack 3 fit 4 damn, go at 5 abuse, blame, fault, fly at, onset, spasm, spell 6 assail, charge, impugn, strike, stroke, tackle 7 assault, censure, lunge at, offense, seizure 8 denounce, fall upon, invasion, paroxysm 9 criticism, criticize, denigrate, disparage, incursion, offensive, onslaught, pitch into, undertake 10 aggression, impugnment 11 denigration 13 disparagement

attacker 6 mugger 7 accuser 8 assailer, opponent 9 adversary, aggressor, assailant 10 antagonist 11 belligerent

attain 3 win 4 earn, gain, reap 5 reach 6 effect, obtain, secure 7 achieve, acquire, procure, realize 10 accomplish

attainable 6 at hand 9 available, reachable 10 accessible, achievable, realizable 11 within reach

attainment 5 skill 6 talent 7 earning, gaining, getting, mastery, success, winning 8 securing 9 acquiring, attaining, obtaining, procuring 10 competence 11 achievement, acquirement, acquisition, fulfillment, procurement, proficiency, realization 14 accomplishment

attempt 3 aim, try 4 seek 5 essay 6 attack, effort, hazard, strive, tackle, work at 7 assault, venture 8 endeavor 9 have a go at, onslaught, undertake 11 undertaking 12 make an effort, take a crack at, take a whack at

Attenborough, Richard
  director of: 6 Gandhi (Oscar) 12 Young Winston 13 A Bridge Too Far

attend 4 go to, heed, mark, mind, note 5 serve, usher, visit 6 convoy, escort, follow, show up, squire, tend to 7 care for, conduct, observe, oversee, service 8 appear at, consider, frequent, harken to, listen to, wait upon 9 accompany 11 superintend
  French: 4 oyez
  cry used by: 10 court crier
  preceded: 12 proclamation

attendance 4 gate 5 crowd, house 8 audience, presence 10 appearance, assemblage, being there

attendant 3 aid 6 escort, flunky, helper, lackey, menial 7 related, servant 8 adherent, chaperon, follower 9 accessory, assistant, companion, underling 10 associated, consequent 12 accompanying

attention 4 care, heed, mind, note, suit 5 court 6 homage, notice, regard, wooing 7 concern, respect, service, thought 8 civility, courtesy, devotion, wariness 9 alertness, deference, diligence, vigilance 10 observance, politeness 11 assiduities, compliments, gallantries 12 deliberation 13 concentration, consideration, contemplation 14 thoughtfulness

attentive 5 alert, awake 6 intent, polite 7 devoted, heedful, mindful, zealous 8 diligent, obliging 9 courteous, dedicated, listening, observant, wide awake 10 respectful, thoughtful 11 considerate, deferential, painstaking 13 accommodating

attentiveness 7 concern 8 devotion, industry 9 alertness, attention, diligence 10 commitment, dedication 11 application, devotedness, heedfulness, mindfulness 14 thoughtfulness

attenuate 6 dilute, impair, lessen, reduce, weaken 7 draw out, spin out 8 decrease, diminish, enervate, enfeeble 9 water down 10 adulterate

attest 4 show 5 prove 6 affirm, assert, assure, evince, verify 7 bear out, certify, confirm, declare, display, exhibit, support, swear to, testify, warrant 8 vouch for 11 bear witness, corroborate, demonstrate 12 substantiate

attestation 9 testimony 10 deposition 11 declaration

at the back
  Latin: 6 a tergo

at the beginning
  Latin: 9 ad initium

at the bottom
  French: 6 au fond

At the Edge of the Body
  author: 9 Erica Jong

at the end
  Latin: 5 ad fin

at the place
  Latin: 5 ad loc 7 ad locum

At the Sign of the Reine Pedauque
  author: 13 Anatole France

attic 4 loft 6 garret 7 mansard 8 cockloft 9 clerestory
  French: 7 grenier
  German: 9 Dachboden
  Spanish: 9 guardilla

attire 3 don 4 duds, garb, gown, robe, togs 5 array, dress 6 bedeck, clothe, finery, fit out, invest, outfit, rig out 7 apparel, clothes, costume, deck out, raiment, turn out 8 clothing, garments, glad rags, wardrobe 9 vestments 11 habiliments

Attis
  also: 4 Atys
  form: 5 youth
  home: 7 Phrygia
  loved: 6 Cybele
  driven mad by: 6 Cybele

attitude 3 air 4 pose 6 manner, stance 7 outlook, posture 8 demeanor, position 11 disposition, frame of mind, perspective, point of view

attorney 4 beak 6 lawyer 7 counsel 8 advocate 9 barrister, counselor, solicitor 10 mouthpiece 12 legal adviser 14 member of the bar 15 ambulance chaser

attract 4 draw, lure, pull 5 cause, charm, evoke 6 allure, beckon, entice, induce, invite 7 bewitch, enchant, provoke 8 appeal to, interest 9 captivate, fascinate 11 precipitate

attraction 4 lure, pull 5 charm 6 allure, appeal 7 glamour 8 affinity, charisma, tendency 9 magnetism 10 enticement, inducement, temptation 11 captivation, enchantment, fascination 12 drawing power

attractive 4 chic, fair 6 lovely, pretty 7 elegant, likable, sightly, winning 8 alluring, becoming, charming, engaging, enticing, fetching, handsome, inviting, pleasant, pleasing, tasteful, tempting 9 agreeable, appealing, beautiful, seductive 10 bewitching, delightful, enchanting 11 captivating, charismatic, fascinating

attractiveness 5 charm 6 beauty 9 good looks 11 pulchritude 12 handsomeness

attribute 4 gift 5 facet, grace, lay to, trait 6 aspect, assign, credit, impute, talent, virtue 7 ability, ascribe, blame on, cause by, faculty, feature, quality, trace to 8 charge to, property 9 character, endowment, set down to 10 account for, attainment, derive from, saddle with 11 acquirement, bring home to, distinction 14 accomplishment, characteristic

attrition 4 loss 7 erosion 8 abrasion, decrease, friction, grinding, scraping 9 reduction 10 decimation 11 wearing away, wearing down 14 disintegration

attune 5 adapt 6 adjust, tailor 8 accustom 9 acclimate 11 acclimatize

attune to 3 fit 5 adapt 6 adjust 7 conform 9 harmonize 11 accommodate

at variance 7 counter, opposed 8 contrary, converse, inimical, opposite 9 disparate 10 discordant 11 conflicting 12 antithetical, incompatible 13 contradictory 15 at cross purposes

Atwood, Margaret
  author of: 8 Survival 9 Surfacing 10 Bodily Harm, Lady Oracle 11 Second Words 13 Life Before Man, Power Politics, The Circle Game 23 The Animals in That Country

at work 4 busy 5 in use 6 active 7 engaged, working 8 occupied

Atymnius
  mentioned in: 5 Iliad
  companion of: 8 Sarpedon
  killed by: 10 Antilochus

atypical 7 unusual 8 abnormal, contrary, uncommon 9 anomalous, irregular, unnatural, untypical 10 nontypical 11 uncustomary, unlooked for 12 out of keeping 16 unrepresentative

Augeas
king of: 6 Epeans
realm: 4 Elis
member of: 9 Argonauts
brother: 5 Actor
son: 7 Eurytus, Phyleus 10 Agasthenes
daughter: 7 Agamede
grandson: 9 Polyxenus

auger 4 bore 5 drill 6 pierce 10 boring tool

aught 3 all, zip 4 love, nada, null, zero 6 naught 7 a cipher, nothing 8 goose egg 11 horse collar

augment 5 add to, boost, raise, swell, widen 6 deepen, expand, extend 7 amplify, build up, enlarge, inflate, magnify 8 flesh out, heighten, increase, lengthen 9 intensify

augmentation 5 boost, extra, raise 8 addition, increase, swelling, widening 9 deepening, expansion, extension, inflation 10 supplement 11 elaboration, enlargement, heightening, lengthening 13 amplification, magnification 15 intensification

augur 4 bode, seer 6 herald, oracle 7 diviner, portend, predict, presage, promise, prophet, signify 8 forecast, foretell, forewarn, intimate, prophesy 9 be a sign of 10 be an omen of, foreshadow, soothsayer 13 prognosticate 14 prognosticator

augury 4 omen, sign 5 token 6 herald 7 auspice, portent, promise, warning 8 prophecy 9 harbinger, precursor, sortilege 10 divination, forerunner, indication 11 forewarning, soothsaying 14 fortunetelling 15 prognostication

august 5 grand, lofty, noble, regal 6 solemn, superb 7 eminent, exalted, stately, sublime, supreme 8 glorious, imposing, majestic 9 dignified, estimable, grandiose, venerable 10 impressive, monumental 11 high-ranking, illustrious, magnificent 12 awe-inspiring 13 distinguished

August
  Anglo-Saxon: 10 Weod-Monath
  characteristic: 7 dog days
  flower: 5 poppy
  French: 4 Aout
  gem: 7 peridot 8 sardonyx 9 carnelian
  German: 6 August
  holiday:
  England/Scotland: 11 Harvest Home (1)
  Italian: 6 Agosto
  number of days: 9 thirty-one
  original name: 8 Sextilis 12 Metageitnion
  origin of name: 6 Augere (Latin to open) 8 Augustus (Roman emperor)
  place in year:
  Roman: 5 sixth
  Gregorian: 6 eighth
  Spanish: 6 Agosto
  zodiac sign: 3 Leo 5 Virgo

Augustine, St (of Hippo)
  author of: 10 Civitas Dei 11 Confessions, Enchiridion 12 The City of God

augustness 7 dignity, majesty 8 eminence, nobility 9 loftiness 11 distinction 13 monumentality 15 illustriousness

August 1914
  author: 23 Aleksandr Solzhenitsyn Jr

au naturel 4 nude 8 uncooked 15 in a natural state

Auntie Mame
  author: 13 Patrick Dennis

Aunt Jo's Scrap-Bag
  author: 15 Louisa May Alcott

Aunt Julia and the Scriptwriter
  author: 16 Mario Vargas Llosa

au pair 4 maid 5 nanny 9 governess 13 mother's helper

aura 3 air 4 feel, mood 5 aroma 7 essence, feeling, quality 8 ambience 9 character, emanation 10 atmosphere, suggestion

Aura
  companion of: 7 Artemis
  bore: 5 twins
  fathered by: 9 Dionysius
  changed into: 6 spring
  changed by: 4 Zeus

au revoir 7 goodbye 8 farewell 16 until we meet again

Aurness, James
  real name of: 11 James Arness

Aurora
  origin: 5 Roman
  goddess of: 4 dawn
  corresponds to: 3 Eos

Aurora Leigh
  author: 24 Elizabeth Barrett Browning

Ausgleich 10 compromise 11 arrangement 12 equalization

Auslander 5 alien 9 foreigner, outlander

auspice 4 omen, sign 6 augury 7 portent, warning 10 indication 15 prognostication

auspices 4 care 5 aegis 6 charge 7 control, support 8 advocacy, guidance 9 authority, influence, patronage 10 protection 11 countenance, sponsorship 12 championship

auspicious 4 good 5 happy, lucky 6 benign, timely 7 hopeful 9 favorable, fortunate, opportune, promising, red-letter 10 felicitous, heartening, propitious, reassuring, successful 11 encouraging

Austen, Jane
  author of: 4 Emma 10 Persuasion 13 Mansfield Park 15 Northanger Abbey 17 Pride and Prejudice 19 Sense and Sensibility

austere 5 rigid, spare, stark, stern 6 chaste, severe, simple, strict 7 ascetic, Spartan 8 rigorous 10 abstemious, forbidding 11 self-denying, strait-laced

Austerlitz, Frederick
  real name of: 11 Fred Astaire

Australia
  other name: 9 Down Under
  name means: 19 unknown southern land
  capital: 8 Canberra
  largest city: 6 Sydney
  others: 3 Ayr 4 Yass 5 Dubbo, Perth 6 Albury, Cairns, Casino, Coburg, Darwin,

Hobart **7** Bendigo, Geelong, Kogarah, Mildura, Mitcham, Whyalla **8** Adelaide, Ballarat, Bathurst, Brighton, Brisbane, Essendon, Randwick, Ringwood **9** Melbourne, Newcastle, Port Pirie, Toowoomba **10** Broken Hill, Kalgoorlie, Waggawagga, Wollongong **11** Collingwood, Rockhampton **12** Alice Springs

division: 8 Tasmania, Victoria **10** Queensland **13** New South Wales **14** South Australia **16** Western Australia **17** Northern Territory **26** Australian Capital Territory

head of state: 14 British monarch **15** governor general

measure: 4 arna, naut, saum

monetary unit: 4 dump, tray, zack **5** pound **6** dollar **8** shilling

island: 4 Cato, King **5** Cocos, Green, Timor **6** Barrow, Koolan **7** Coringa, Keeling, Neptune, Norfolk **8** Flinders, Kangaroo, Lacepede, Melville, Rottnest, Tasmania, Thursday **9** Admiralty

lake: 4 Eyre **5** Carey, Cowan, Frome, Moore, Wells **6** Austin, Barlee, Bulloo, Dundas, Harris, Mackay **7** Amadeus, Blanche, Everard, Torrens **8** Carnegie, Gairdner **9** MacDonald **10** Yammayamma **14** Disappointment

mountain: 3 Ise **4** Blue, Olga, Ossa, Zeil **5** Bruce, Snowy **6** Cradle, Doreen, Garnet, Gawler, Magnet, Morgan **7** Bongong, Gregory, Herbert **8** Augustus, Brockman, Cuthbert, Jusgrave, Mulligan, Surprise **9** Murchison, Woodroffe **14** Australian Alps **15** New England Range **18** Great Dividing Range

highest point: 9 Kosciusko

river: 3 Hay **4** Avon, Daly, Swan, Yule **5** Bullo, Comet, Drava, Naomi, Paroo, Roper, Yarra **6** Barcoo, Barwon, Bulloo, Culgoa, Degrey, Hunter, Isaacs, Murray, Norman **7** Darling, Derwent, Fitzroy, Georges, Gilbert, Lachlan, Staaten, Warrego **8** Belyando, Brisbane, Burdekin, Clarence, Drysdale, Flinders, Gascoyne, Georgina, Mitchell, Thompson, Victoria, Weeribee, Wooramel **9** Ashburton, Fortescue, Hawksbury, MacKenzie, Macquarie, Murchison, Saltwater **10** Diamantina, Shoalhaven **12** Murrambidgee

sea: 5 Coral, Timor **6** Indian, Tasman **7** Arafura, Pacific

physical feature:

bay: **5** Bight, Shark **6** Botany **7** Moreton **11** Port Phillip

cape: **4** Howe, York **5** Byron **9** Southeast

channel: **5** Cowal **9** Anabranch, Billabong

desert: **6** Arunta, Gibson, Stuart, Tanami **7** Simpson **10** Great Sandy **13** Great Victoria

gulf: **8** Spencers **9** Van Dieman **11** Carpentaria **15** Joseph Bonaparte **20** Great Australian Bight

peninsula: **4** Eyre

reef: **12** Great Barrier

strait: **4** Bass

people: 3 Abo **4** Koko, Mara, Wong **5** Anzac, Binge, Dieri, Maori, Myall **6** Aranda, Arunta, Aussie, Binghi, Digger, Kipper, Papuan **7** Arawong, Ilpirra **8** Antipode, Barkinji, Billijim, Euahlayi, Warragal, Warrigal **9** Aborigine **10** Australoid, Melanesian, Sandgroper

actor: **9** Judy Davis, Mel Gibson, Paul Hogan **10** Bryan Brown

author: **4** West **5** White **7** Russell **10** Richardson

explorer: **4** Bass, Cook **6** Mawson, Tasman **7** Wilkins

leader: **4** Holt **5** Hawke **7** Keating, Menzies, Whitlam

nurse: **11** Sister Kenny

language: 7 English

religion: 7 Judaism **8** Anglican **10** Protestant **13** Roman Catholic

place: 7 outback **9** billabong **11** back country

aborigine area: **9** Arhemland

beach: **5** Manly

dam: **4** Hume

possession: 12 Cocos Islands **13** Norfolk Island **16** Christmas Islands

feature:

animal: **5** dingo **6** kelpie **7** wallaby **8** anteater, kangaroo **9** koala bear **18** duckbilled platypus

bird: **3** emu **10** kookaburra

cowboy: **6** waddie **8** jackaroo

dance: **6** dreher

flower: **7** boronia, fuchsia, waratah **9** coachwood **12** kangaroo paws

game: **3** sye **10** tambaroora

tree: **3** gum **10** eucalyptus

weapon: **5** kiley, kyley **7** wommera **9** boomerang

food: **3** kai **6** tucker

cake: **6** damper **7** brownie

dish: **8** coolamon

drink: **9** arkaloola

fruit: **5** nonda **7** kumquat **11** desertlemon

Austria

other name: 10 Osterreich

name means: 12 eastern state

capital/largest city: 6 Vienna

others: 4 Enns, Graz, Lech, Linz, Ried, Wels **5** Krems, Steyr, Traun **6** Leoben **7** Bregenz, Modling, Spittal, Villach **8** Bad Ischl, Dornbirn, Salzburg **9** Innsbruck, Semmering **10** Kapfenberg, Klagenfurt **11** Sankt Polten **14** Wiener Neustadt

division: 5 Tirol, Tyrol **6** Istria, Styria, Triest **7** Bohemia, Galicia, Moravia, Silesia **8** Bukowina, Dalmatia, Earniola, Gradisca **9** Earinthia **10** Burgenland, Vorarlberg **12** Lower Austria, Upper Austria

Roman province: **6** Raetia **7** Noricum **8** Pannonia

government:
legislature: 9 Bundesrat, Reichsrat 10 Herrenhaus, Reichsrath
head of government: 10 Chancellor
other leader: 7 emperor 12 burgomeister
measure: 4 fass, fuss, joch, mass, muth, yoke 5 halbe, linie, meile, metze, pfiff, punkt 6 achtel, becher, leipoa, seidel 7 dlafter, viertel 8 dreiling 12 futtermassel
monetary unit: 4 lira 5 crown, ducat, krone 6 florin, gulden, heller, zehner 8 albertin, groschen, kreutzer 9 schilling
weight: 4 marc, unze 5 denat, karch, stein 7 centner, pfennig 8 vierling 9 quantchen
lake: 6 Almsee 7 Fertoto, Mondsee 8 Bodensee, Traunsee 9 Constance 10 Neusiedler
mountain: 4 Alps 6 Stubai, Tirols, Tyrols 8 Eisenerz, Rhatikon 9 Dolomites, Kitzbuhel 10 Hohe Tauern 14 Silvretta Group
highest point: 13 Grossglockner
river: 3 Inn, Mur 4 Drau, Elbe, Enns, Iser, Kamp, Lech, Murz, Raab 5 Donau, Drava, Drave, March, Salza, Thaya, Traun 6 Danube, Moldau
physical feature:
basin: 7 Styrian
canal: 6 Danube
mountain pass: 7 Brenner
wind: 6 Foehen
woods: 6 Vienna
people: 5 Poles 6 Croats, Czechs 7 Germans, Gypsies 8 Slovenes 10 Hungarians
botanist: 6 Mendel
composer: 5 Haydn 6 Czerny, Mahler, Mozart, Webern 7 Amadeus, Strauss 8 Bruckner, Schubert 9 Beethoven 10 Schoenberg
emperor: 7 Charles, Francis 9 Ferdinand, Habsburgs, Hapsburgs 10 Franz Josef
philosopher: 12 Wittgenstein
psychiatrist: 5 Adler, Freud, Reich
statesman: 10 Metternich 12 Kurt Waldheim
language: 5 Czech 6 German, Magyar 8 Croatian 9 Slovenian
religion: 7 Judaism 10 Protestant 13 Roman Catholic
place:
boulevard: 3 Kai 11 Ringstrasse
cathedral: 9 St Stephen
city hall: 7 Rathaus
fortress: 13 Hochosterwitz, Hohensalzburg
imperial palace: 7 Hofburg
monastery: 4 Melk 8 Gottweig 14 Klosterneuburg
museum: 6 Mozart 9 Johanneum
people's garden: 11 Volksgarten
resort: 5 Baden 7 Bregenz 8 Bad Ischl 9 Innsbruck, Semmering
feature: 8 yodelers 11 ice grottoes
clothing: 5 loden 10 lederhosen

dance: 5 waltz 6 dreher 7 landler 13 schuhplattler 14 grand polonaise
festival: 8 Salzburg
horse: 10 Lippizaner
pastry shop: 12 konditoreien
food:
breaded veal cutlet: 15 Wiener schnitzel
cake: 11 linzer torte, sacher torte
cookie: 7 kipferl
roll: 10 golatschen

Austroasiatic
language subfamily: 5 Khasi, Munda 8 Annamite, Mon-Khmer 9 Palaung-Wa 10 Nicobarese 11 Semang-Sakai 13 Annamite-Muong
spoken in: 5 Burma, India 7 Nicobar, Vietnam 8 Cambodia, Malaysia 9 Kampuchea

authentic 4 pure, real, true 5 valid 6 actual 7 factual, genuine 8 accurate, attested, bona fide, faithful, original, reliable, verified 9 veritable 10 accredited, dependable, legitimate 11 trustworthy 12 unquestioned 13 authoritative, unadulterated
authenticate 6 attest, avouch, verify 7 certify, confirm, endorse, warrant 8 document, validate, vouch for 9 guarantee 11 corroborate 12 substantiate
authenticated 7 genuine 8 attested, verified 9 validated 10 accredited, vouched for 13 substantiated
authentication 7 voucher 10 validation 11 certificate 12 verification 13 authorization, certification
author 4 poet 5 maker 6 father, framer, writer 7 creator, founder, planner 8 essayist, inventor, novelist, producer 9 initiator, innovator, organizer 10 originator, playwright, prime mover 16 short-story writer
see author under each country
authoritarian 5 harsh 6 severe, strict, tyrant 7 austere, fascist 8 autocrat, dogmatic, martinet 9 by the book, by the rule 10 inflexible, tyrannical, unyielding 11 dictatorial, doctrinaire 12 disciplinary, rule follower 14 disciplinarian, little dictator, uncompromising
authoritative 5 sound, valid 6 lordly, ruling 7 factual, learned 8 arrogant, decisive, dogmatic, imposing, official, reliable 9 authentic, masterful, scholarly, sovereign 10 autocratic, commanding, definitive, dependable, imperative, impressive, peremptory, sanctioned, tyrannical 11 dictatorial, trustworthy 14 administrative
authoritativeness 6 belief 9 authority 10 conviction 11 credibility 14 conclusiveness
authorities 6 expert, police, pundit 7 scholar 10 mastermind, specialist 11 connoisseur, officialdom 12 powers that be
authority 4 rule, sway 5 clout, force, might, power 6 esteem, weight 7 command, control, respect 8 dominion, prestige, strength 9 influence, supremacy 10 domination, importance 12 jurisdiction 14 administration

authorization 7 license 8 approval, sanction 10 commission, imprimatur, permission 11 entitlement 12 confirmation, legalization 13 accreditation, certification

authorize 5 allow 6 enable, invest, permit 7 approve, certify, charter, confirm, empower, entitle, license, warrant 8 accredit, sanction, vouch for 9 give leave 10 commission

authorized 8 approved, official 9 canonical 10 sanctioned

Autobiography of Alice B Toklas
  author: 13 Gertrude Stein

Autobiography of Miss Jane Pittman, The
  author: 13 Ernest J Gaines

autochthonous 5 first 6 native, primal 7 ancient 8 earliest, original, primeval 10 aboriginal, indigenous, primordial

autocracy 7 czarism, tyranny 8 autarchy, monarchy 9 Caesarism, despotism, Hitlerism, kaiserism, monocracy, Stalinism 10 absolutism 11 Bonapartism 12 dictatorship 14 tyrannical rule 15 totalitarianism 16 absolute monarchy

autocrat 5 ruler 6 despot, tyrant 7 monarch 8 dictator, overlord 13 absolute ruler

autocratic 6 despotic 9 czaristic, imperious, tyrannous 10 iron-handed, oppressive, repressive, tyrannical 11 dictatorial, monarchical 13 authoritarian

auto da fe, auto de fe 13 act of the faith 17 burning of heretics
  from: 18 Spanish Inquisition

autograph 4 mark, sign 5 x-mark 9 John Henry, signature 11 endorsement, handwriting, inscription, John Hancock 16 countersignature

Autolycus
  character in: 14 The Winter's Tale
  author: 11 Shakespeare

Autolycus
  form: 5 thief
  father: 6 Hermes
  mother: 6 Chione
  half-brother: 9 Philammon
  wife: 9 Amphithea
  daughter: 8 Anticlea
  grandson: 8 Odysseus
  gift: 12 invisibility 13 shape changing

automated 9 automatic 10 mechanical, mechanized 15 machine-operated

automatic 6 reflex 7 natural, routine 8 electric, habitual, inherent, unwilled 9 automated 10 mechanical, push-button, self-acting, self-moving 11 instinctive, involuntary, spontaneous, unconscious 12 uncontrolled 13 nonvolitional, self-operating 14 self-propelling

automaton 4 pawn, tool 5 patsy, robot 6 puppet, stooge 7 android, cat's-paw, fall guy, machine 10 fantoccino, marionette

Automedon
  charioteer of: 8 Achilles

automobile
  invented by:
    differential gear: 4 Benz
    electric: 8 Morrison
    gasoline: 6 Duryea 7 Daimler
    muffler: 5 Maxim
    self-starter: 9 Kettering
  see also: car

Automobile state
  nickname of: 8 Michigan

Autonoe
  father: 6 Cadmus
  mother: 8 Harmonia
  sister: 3 Ino 5 Agave 6 Semele
  husband: 9 Aristaeus
  son: 7 Actaeon
  daughter: 6 Macris

autonomous 4 free 9 sovereign 11 independent, self-reliant 13 self-governing 14 self-determined, self-sufficient

autonomy 7 freedom 8 home rule, self-rule 10 liberation 11 sovereignty 12 independence 14 self-government 17 self-determination

auto racing
  driver: 6 A J Foyt 7 Al Unser 8 Tom Sneva 9 Niki Lauda 10 Bobby Unser, Juan Fangio 11 Jack Brabham 12 Bobby Allison, Janet Guthrie, Richard Petty 13 Jackie Stewart, Mario Andretti 14 Barney Oldfield, Cale Yarborough, Craig Breedlove 16 Johnny Rutherford

Autry, Gene
  horse: 8 Champion
  born: 7 Tioga TX
  roles: 11 Melody Ranch 16 The Singing Cowboy 19 Tumbling Tumbleweeds 22 Springtime in the Rockies

autumn 4 fall 11 harvest time 12 Indian summer 15 autumnal equinox

auxiliary 6 backup, helper 7 partner, reserve 9 accessory, ancillary, assistant, associate, companion, emergency, secondary 10 accomplice, subsidiary, supplement 11 subordinate 13 supplementary

avail 2 aid, use 4 help 5 serve 6 assist, profit 7 benefit, purpose, service, success, utilize 9 advantage 10 usefulness

available 4 free, open 5 handy, on tap 6 at hand, on hand 9 in reserve 10 accessible, convenient, obtainable

avalanche 4 heap, mass, pile 5 flood 6 deluge 7 barrage, cascade, torrent 8 blizzard 9 cataclysm, rockslide, snowslide 10 earthslide, inundation 11 bombardment

Avalon
  island of: 8 Paradise
  burial place for: 6 heroes 10 King Arthur

avant-garde 7 leaders 8 pioneers, vanguard 10 innovators 11 forerunners, originators, tastemakers 12 advance guard, trailblazers, trendsetters

avarice 5 greed 6 penury 8 rapacity, venality 9 parsimony 10 greediness, stinginess 11 miserliness 12 covetousness, graspingness 13 money-grubbing, niggardliness, penny-pinching 15 close-fistedness

Ave Maria 8 Hail Mary

avenge 5 repay 6 injure, punish 7 revenge 9 retaliate

Avengers, The
 character: 8 Emma Peel, Tara King 9 John (Jonathan) Steed
 cast: 9 Diana Rigg 12 Linda Thorson 13 Patrick Macnee

avenue 3 way 4 gate, path, road 5 means, route 6 access, chance, course, outlet 7 gateway, parkway, passage, pathway 8 approach 9 boulevard, concourse, direction, esplanade 10 passageway 11 opportunity 12 thoroughfare

aver 4 avow 5 state, swear 6 affirm, assert, avouch, insist, verify 7 certify, contend, declare, profess, protest 8 maintain, proclaim 9 emphasize, guarantee, pronounce, represent 10 asseverate

average 3 par 4 fair, mean, norm, so-so 5 ratio, usual 6 common, medial, median, medium, normal, not bad 7 the rule, typical 8 mediocre, midpoint, moderate, ordinary, passable, standard, standing, the usual 9 tolerable 10 mean amount 11 indifferent, rank and file 12 run-of-the-mill

averment 5 claim 6 avowal 8 argument 9 assertion, assurance 10 allegation, contention, profession 11 affirmation

averse 5 loath 7 opposed 8 inimical 9 reluctant, unwilling 10 indisposed, unamenable 11 disinclined, ill-disposed, unfavorable 12 antipathetic, recalcitrant

aversion 6 hatred, horror 7 disgust, dislike 8 distaste, loathing 9 animosity, antipathy, hostility, prejudice, repulsion, revulsion 10 abhorrence, opposition, reluctance, repugnance 11 detestation 13 unwillingness 14 disinclination

avert 4 turn 5 avoid, deter, shift 7 beat off, deflect, fend off, keep off, prevent, ward off 8 preclude, stave off, turn away 9 forestall, frustrate, keep at bay, sidetrack 11 nip in the bud

aviary 4 cage 9 birdhouse, enclosure

aviation 6 flight, flying 11 aeronautics 12 aerodynamics

aviator, aviatrix 4 bird 5 flyer, pilot 6 airman, fly-boy 7 birdman

avid 4 keen 5 eager, rabid 6 ardent, greedy, hungry 7 anxious, devoted, fanatic, intense, zealous 8 covetous, desirous, grasping 9 rapacious, voracious 10 avaricious, insatiable 11 acquisitive 12 enthusiastic

avidity 4 zeal 5 greed 6 fervor, hunger 8 rapacity, voracity 9 eagerness 10 enthusiasm, fanaticism, greediness 12 covetousness 15 acquisitiveness

Avignon Papacy 15 Babylonian Exile 19 Babylonian Captivity

avocado 9 dark green 13 alligator pear, tropical fruit
 origin: 6 Mexico 12 South America 14 Central America
 family: 9 Lauraceae
 used to make: 9 guacamole

avocation 5 hobby 7 pastime 8 sideline 9 diversion 10 recreation 11 distraction 13 entertainment

Avogadro, Amedeo
 field: 7 physics 9 chemistry
 nationality: 7 Italian
 formulated: 19 molecular hypothesis

avoid 4 shun 5 avert, dodge, elude, evade, skirt 6 escape, eschew 7 boycott, forbear, forsake 8 sidestep 10 fight shy of 11 refrain from 12 steer clear of

avoidance 7 eluding, evasion 8 shirking, shunning, skirting

avoid the issue 4 duck 5 dodge, evade, hedge, stall 10 equivocate 17 beat around the bush

a votre sante 12 to your health

avouch 5 argue, swear 6 affirm 7 declare 8 advocate, maintain

avow 4 own 4 aver 5 admit, state, swear 6 affirm, assert, reveal 7 confess, declare, profess 8 announce, disclose, proclaim 11 acknowledge

avowal 4 word 8 averment 9 admission, assertion, assurance, statement 10 confession, profession 11 affirmation, declaration 12 proclamation, protestation 14 acknowledgment

avowed 5 sworn 8 admitted, declared 9 confessed, professed 12 acknowledged, self-declared 14 self-proclaimed

await 6 attend, expect 7 look for 10 anticipate

awake 5 alert, aware, spark 6 arouse, awaken, bestir, excite, incite 7 alive to, heedful, inspire, mindful, provoke 8 openeyed, vigilant, watchful 9 attentive, conscious, stimulate

Awake and Sing!
 author: 13 Clifford Odets

awaken 3 fan 4 fire 6 arouse, excite, kindle, revive, stir up 9 stimulate

awakening 7 arising, arousal 8 sparking, stirring 11 stimulation

award 4 give 5 allot, allow, grant, honor, medal, prize 6 accord, assign, bestow, decree, trophy 7 appoint, concede, laurels, tribute 8 citation, confer on 10 decoration

aware 6 with it 7 alert to, alive to, awake to, mindful 8 apprised, informed, sensible, sentient 9 cognizant, conscious, tuned in to 10 conversant 11 enlightened 12 familiar with 13 knowledgeable

awareness 9 acuteness, alertness, appraisal, knowledge 10 cognizance, perception 11 familiarity, information, mindfulness, realization, recognition, sensibility 12 acquaintance 13 consciousness, understanding

away 3 far 4 gone 6 absent, at once, way off 8 distance 9 elsewhere

awe 3 cow 4 fear 5 abash, alarm, amaze, dread, panic, shock 6 dismay, fright, horror, terror, wonder 7 perturb, quaking, respect, terrify 8 astonish, disquiet, frighten 9 abashment, adoration, amazement, quivering, reverence, solemnity, trembling

10 exaltation, intimidate, veneration **11** disquietude, trepidation **12** apprehension, astonishment, perturbation **13** consternation

awe-inspiring 5 giant, grand, great, noble **6** august, mighty **7** eminent, exalted, mammoth, sublime, supreme, titanic **8** colossal, enormous, gigantic, glorious, imposing, majestic, wondrous **9** excessive **10** impressive, incredible, monumental, prodigious, stupendous, tremendous **11** astonishing, extravagant, illustrious, magnificent, spectacular **12** breathtaking, overwhelming

awesome 6 solemn **7** amazing, fearful **8** alarming, dreadful, fearsome, majestic, wondrous **9** inspiring **10** formidable, perturbing, stupefying, terrifying **11** astonishing, disquieting, frightening, magnificent **12** breathtaking, intimidating, overwhelming

awestruck 6 humble **8** overcome **11** reverential

awful 3 bad, low **4** base, dire, mean, ugly **5** lousy **6** solemn **7** amazing, awesome, fearful, ghastly, heinous, hideous **8** alarming, dreadful, fearsome, gruesome, horrible, majestic, shocking, terrible, wondrous **9** appalling, frightful, monstrous, revolting **10** deplorable, despicable, formidable, horrendous, horrifying, stupefying, terrifying, unpleasant **11** displeasing, disquieting, distressing, redoubtable **12** awe-inspiring, contemptible, disagreeable **13** reprehensible

awfully 4 very **5** quite **8** horribly, terribly **9** extremely, immensely **10** dreadfully **11** excessively **13** exceptionally

awkward 5 inept, clumsy, touchy, trying **7** unhandy **8** bungling, delicate, inexpert, ticklish, ungainly, unwieldy **9** difficult, graceless, maladroit **10** blundering, cumbersome, unpleasant, unskillful **11** troublesome **12** embarrassing, inconvenient, unmanageable **13** disconcerting, uncomfortable, uncoordinated

    French: 6 gauche

Awkward Age, The
    author: 10 Henry James

awkwardness 9 gaucherie **10** clumsiness, difficulty, ineptitude **12** ungainliness, unwieldiness **13** embarrassment, inconvenience

awl 4 nail **6** gimlet **11** leather tool, sharp device

awning 4 hood **6** canopy **7** marquee **8** covering, sunshade

awry 5 amiss, askew, wrong **6** astray, uneven **7** crooked, twisted **8** unevenly **9** crookedly, obliquely **11** out of kilter

axe, ax 3 can **4** chop, fire, oust, sack **5** let go, split **6** bounce, cut out, delete, remove **7** cut down, dismiss **8** get rid of, tomahawk **9** discharge, terminate **11** send packing
    type: 4 pick **6** poleax **7** hatchet **8** tomahawk

Axe, The
    author: 12 Sigrid Undset

Axelrod, Julius
    field: 9 chemistry
    studied: 24 nerve-impulse transmission
    awarded: 10 Nobel Prize

axiom 3 law **5** basic **7** precept **9** postulate, principle **10** assumption **14** fundamental law

axiomatic 5 banal, given **6** cliche **7** assumed **8** accepted, manifest **9** apodictic **10** aphoristic **11** self-evident **12** demonstrable, epigrammatic, indisputable, unquestioned **13** incontestable, platitudinous

Axiopoenus
    epithet of: 6 Athena
    means: 12 just requital

axis 4 stem **5** pivot, shaft **7** compact, entente, spindle **8** alliance **9** alignment, coalition **10** center line **11** affiliation **12** pivotal point **13** confederation **14** line of rotation, line of symmetry

axle 3 bar, pin **5** shaft, wheel **7** spindle **8** crossbar **10** turning bar

ayah 4 maid **5** nurse

aye 3 yea, yes **11** affirmative

Aykroyd, Dan
    born: 6 Canada, Ottawa **7** Ontario
    roles: 12 Ghostbusters **13** Doctor Detroit, Trading Places **16** The Blues Brothers, Driving Miss Daisy, The Great Outdoors **17** Saturday Night Live

Aymara
    location: 4 Peru **7** Bolivia **12** South America

Ayres, Lew
    wife: 8 Lola Lane **12** Ginger Rogers
    born: 13 Minneapolis MN
    roles: 7 Holiday, The Kiss **9** Dr Kildare **25** All Quiet on the Western Front

azalea 12 Rhododendron
    varieties: 4 Cork, Mock, Snow **5** Coast, Dwarf, Early, Flame, Hiryu, Hoary, Luchu, Royal, Sims's, Swamp, Sweet, Torch **6** Alpine, Balsam, Clammy, Indian, Korean, Kurume, Kyushu, Oconee, Pontic, Smooth, Spider, Summer, Yellow **7** Alabama, Chinese, Maries's, Mt Amagi, Oldham's, Western **8** Five-leaf, Japanese, Piedmont, Rusticum, Yodogawa **9** Kirishima, Mayflower, Pink-shell, Roseshell, Wild-thyme **10** Cumberland, Macranthum, Plum-leaved, White swamp **11** Gable hybrid, Ghent hybrid, Molle hybrid **12** Arnold hybrid, Florida flame, Sander hybrid **13** Indicum hybrid **15** Glenn Dale hybrid, Kaempferi hybrid, Knapp Hill hybrid **16** Rutherford hybrid **24** Rusticum Flore Pleno hybrid

Azan
    father: 5 Arcas
    mother: 5 Erato

Azariah
    also: 6 Uzziah
    father: 4 Jehu **5** Ethan **6** Nathan **7** Hilkiah, Jehoram, Johanan **11** Jehoshaphat
    son: 4 Joel
    known as: 8 Abednego

companion: 6 Daniel
friend: 7 Meshach 8 Shadrach
succeeded: 5 Zadok
Azazel 9 scapegoat 11 fallen angel
Azerbaijan
  capital/largest city: 4 Baku
  others 9 Kirovabad
  division 24 Nagorno-Karabakh Territory
  29 Nakhichevan Autonomous Republic
  head of state: 9 president
  government: 8 republic
  monetary unit: 5 manat
  mountain: 8 Caucasus
  sea: 7 Caspian
  people: 5 Azeri 11 Azerbaijani
  language: 6 Turkic
  religion: 6 Muslim
Aziz, Dr
  character in: 15 A Passage to India
  author: 7 Forster
Aztec (Nahua, Mexica)
  language family: 7 Nahuatl 10 Uto-
  Aztecan
  location: 6 Mexico, Puebla 8 Guerrero,
  Veracruz 9 Guatemala, Michoacan 11
  Lake Texcoco 14 Central America
  leader: 9 Montezuma
  worshipped: 12 Quetzalcoatl
  capital: 12 Tenochtitlan
Azuela, Mariano
  author of: 8 The Flies 9 The Bosses 12
  The Underdogs 26 Trials of a Respectable Family
azure 5 lapis 6 cobalt 7 sky blue 8 cerulean
  9 clear blue, cloudless 11 lapis lazuli

B

Baade, Walter
  field: 9 astronomy
  discovered: 15 Hidalgo asteroid
Baal 3 god 5 deity
Baal Merodach *see* 6 Marduk
Babbage, Charles
  field: 11 mathematics
  nationality: 7 British, English
  first: 15 actuarial tables
  inventor of: 13 adding machine 18 calculating machine
  invented forerunner of: 15 digital computer
  planned: 10 calculator
Babbitt 9 bourgeois 10 conformist, middlebrow, philistine
Babbitt
  author: 13 Sinclair Lewis
  character: 11 Myra Babbitt, Seneca Deane 12 Paul Riesling 15 Mrs Tanis Judique 22 George Folansbee Babbitt
babble 5 coo, din, gab, hum 4 blab, talk 5 prate 6 burble, clamor, drivel, gabble, gibber, gurgle, hubbub, jabber, murmur 7 blabber, blather, chatter, prattle, twaddle 8 chitchat, rattle on 9 jabbering, murmuring 14 chitter-chatter
babbling 6 drivel, hubbub 7 blabber, twaddle 8 burbling, gabbling, gurgling, nonsense 9 clamoring, gibberish, jabbering, murmuring
babe 3 tot 4 baby 5 child 6 infant
babe in arms 4 baby 6 infant 7 neonate, newborn
babe in the woods 8 innocent 9 fledgling, greenhorn 10 tenderfoot
babel, Babel 3 din 6 bedlam, clamor, hubbub, tumult, uproar 7 turmoil 9 confusion 10 hullabaloo 11 pandemonium
Babel, Isaac
  author of: 9 Benia Krik 11 Odessa Tales 13 The Red Cavalry
Babe Ruth
  nickname of: 16 George Herman Ruth
Babe the Blue Ox
  character in: 10 Paul Bunyan
baboon 6 monkey
  breeding: 9 year round
  characteristic: 4 mane, pads 6 muzzle
  diet: 6 plants 8 scorpion 12 small animals
  dwelling: 5 Egypt, Sudan 6 Africa, Arabia 7 Somalia 8 Ethiopia
  family: 15 cercopithecidae
  habitat: 5 hills 6 plains
  largest genus: 6 Chacma
  most sacred: 6 Anobis
  smallest genus: 7 Western

babushka 4 baba, veil 5 scarf, stole 8 kerchief
baby 3 wee 4 babe, tiny 5 dwarf, humor, pygmy, small, spoil, young 6 bantam, coddle, coward, infant, little, midget, minute, pamper, petite 7 crybaby, indulge, neonate 8 dwarfish, sniveler 9 miniature, youngster 10 babe in arms, diminutive 11 mollycoddle, overindulge, pocket-sized
Baby
  nickname of: 12 Lauren Bacall
baby carriage 4 cart, pram 6 cradle 12 perambulator
babyish 7 puerile 8 childish, immature, juvenile 9 infantile
babylike 3 wee 4 tiny 5 small 9 infantile 10 diminutive
Babylonian Captivity 13 Avignon Papacy 15 Babylonian Exile
Babylonian god 3 Bel 6 Marduk
Babylonian Mythology
  chief of gods: 6 Marduk 8 Merodach 12 Baal Merodach
  demon: 6 Namtar
  goddess of air: 6 Ninlil
  goddess of death: 10 Ereshkigal
  goddess of love/war/ fertility: 6 Ananna, Inanna, Ishtar 7 Astarte, Mylitta 9 Ashtoreth
  god of air: 5 Enlil
  god of dead: 6 Nergal
  god of fire: 5 Ishum
  god of heaven: 2 An 3 Anu
  god of moon: 3 Sin
  god of pastures/vegetation: 6 Dumuzi
  god of pestilence: 4 Irra
  god of shepherds: 6 Tammuz
  god of sun: 3 Utu 7 Shamash
  god of wisdom: 4 Enki
  hero: 5 Ninib 7 Ninurta
  king: 9 Gilgamesh
  king of gods: 5 Enlil
  mother of gods: 5 Nammu
  queen of heaven: 6 Ishtar
  world of dead: 3 Kur
Baby Roo
  character in: 13 Winnie-the-Pooh
  author: 5 Milne
Baby Snookums
  character in: 12 The Newlyweds
Bacall, Lauren
  real name: 15 Betty Joan Perske
  husband: 12 Jason Robards 14 Humphrey Bogart
  nickname: 4 Baby
  born: 9 New York NY
  roles: 8 Applause, Key Largo 11 Dark Passage, The Big Sleep 12 Cactus

Flower **16** To Have and Have Not **22** How
to Marry a Millionaire

Bacchae
  form: **11** priestesses
  attendants of: **7** Bacchus
  participants in: **11** Bacchanalia

Bacchae, The
  author: **9** Euripides
  character: **4** Zeus **5** Agave **6** Cadmus,
  Semele **8** Dionysus, Pentheus, Tiresias

bacchanal 4 orgy **5** feast, revel, spree **6**
frolic **7** carouse, debauch, revelry, wassail
8 carnival, carousal, festival **10** debauchery, Saturnalia **11** merrymaking

Bacchanalia
  festival honoring: **7** Bacchus

Bacchant
  priest who worships: **7** Bacchus

Bacchante
  also: **6** Thyiad
  priestess who worships: **7** Bacchus

Bacchus
  also: **5** Evius **8** Dionysus
  god of: **4** wine **5** drama **9** fertility
  father: **4** Zeus
  mother: **6** Semele
  son: **6** Phlias **7** Narcaus, Priapus **8**
  Oenopion
  epithet: **6** Lyaeus **7** Bromius, Cresius **8**
  Thyoneus, Triambus **9** Pyrigenes **11**
  Dithyrambus, Mitrephorus

Bach, Carl (Karl) Philipp Emanuel
  born: **6** Weimar **7** Germany
  father: **19** Johann Sebastian Bach
  composer of: **14** Prussian Sonata **19**
  Wurtembergian Sonata

Bach, Johann Sebastian
  born: **7** Germany **8** Eisenach
  composer of: **8** Chaconne **10** Giant
  Fugue, Inventions, Magnificat, Wedge
  Fugue **11** Dorian Fugue, Fiddle Fugue,
  Little Fugue **12** Corelli Fugue, French
  Suites, Fuga alla Giga, German Suites,
  St Anne's Fugue **13** Coffee Cantata, En-
  glish Suites, St John Passion **14** Alla
  Breve Fugue, Easter Oratorio, Peasant
  Cantata, Wedding Cantata **15** Jesu
  Meine Freude, Musical Offering **16** St
  Matthew Passion, The Art of the Fugue
  17 Christmas Oratorio **18** Goldberg Varia-
  tions **20** Brandenburg Concertos **22** The
  Well-Tempered Clavier **24** The Wise and
  Foolish Virgins **30** The Dispute Between
  Phoebus and Pan

Bach, Richard
  author of: **25** Jonathan Livingston
  Seagull

bachelor 6 single **9** single man, unmarried
12 unmarried man

Bachelor Father
  character: **9** Peter Tong **10** Kelly Gregg
  12 Bentley Gregg **13** Ginger Farrell
  cast: **10** Sammee Tong **12** John Forsythe
  14 Noreen Corcoran **17** Bernadette Withers

bachelorhood 8 celibacy **13** baccalaureate
14 unmarried state

bacillus 3 bug **4** germ **7** microbe **8** pathogen **9** bacterium **13** microorganism

Bacis
  origin: **8** Boeotian
  form: **7** prophet

back 3 aid, ebb **4** abet, gone, help, hind,
late, past, rear, tail **5** after, guard, minor,
rural, spine, tardy **6** affirm, assist, attest,
behind, bygone, caudal, dorsal, dorsum,
far end, former, hinder, hold up, praise, recede, recoil, remote, retire, return, revert,
second, succor, tergal, uphold, verify **7** belated, bolster, certify, confirm, delayed, distant, earlier, elapsed, endorse, expired, far
side, finance, not paid, overdue, promote,
protect, rear end, rebound, retract, retreat,
reverse, sponsor, support, sustain, tail
end, warrant **8** advocate, backbone, hind
part, hindmost, maintain, move away, obsolete, previous, sanction, secluded, turn
tail, validate, vouch for, withdraw **9** afterpart, encourage, in arrears, out-of-date,
patronize, posterior, reinforce, subsidize
10 retrogress, testify for, underwrite, un-
traveled **11** bear witness, corroborate,
countenance, countrified, countryside, farthermost, furthermost, reverse side, undeveloped, unimportant, unpopulated **12**
beat a retreat, hindquarters, spinal column, substantiate **13** take sides with

back away from 7 back off **11** retreat from
12 draw back from, withdraw from

backbiter 5 scold **6** carper, critic **7** reviler **8**
vilifier **9** slanderer

backbiting 5 abuse, catty **6** gossip, malice
7 abusive, calumny, gossipy, hurtful, obloquy, slander **8** libeling, reviling **9** aspersion, cattiness, censuring, contumely,
injurious, invective, malicious, maligning,
vilifying **10** belittling, bitchiness, calumnious, defamation, defamatory, derogating,
detracting, detraction, scandalous, scurrility, slanderous, traduction **11** badmouthing,
denigrating, deprecating, disparaging, tra-
ducement **12** backstabbing, calumniation, vilification, vituperation **13** disparagement, maliciousness **16** scandal-
mongering

backbone 4 grit, guts, sand **5** basis, chine,
nerve, pluck, spine, spunk **6** dorsum, mettle, spirit **7** bravery, courage, resolve **8**
firmness, mainstay, strength, tenacity **9**
character, fortitude, manliness, vertebrae
10 foundation, resolution **11** intrepidity **12**
resoluteness, spinal column **13** dauntlessness, steadfastness **15** vertebral column
19 strength of character

back-country 4 farm **5** rural **6** rustic **7** farming **10** provincial

back down 7 back off **8** draw back, move
away **9** withdrawn

backdrop 4 flat **7** curtain, scenery **10** background

backer 4 ally **5** angel **6** patron **7** sponsor **8**
adherent, advocate, champion, follower,
investor, promoter **9** financier, guarantor,
supporter **10** well-wisher **11** underwriter

backfire 4 flop, miss 5 crash 6 fizzle, go awry 8 backlash, lay an egg, miscarry, ricochet 9 boomerang 10 bounce back, disappoint 11 come to grief, fall through 12 come to naught 13 come to nothing

background 3 set 4 past, rear 5 flats 6 milieu 7 context, history, rearing, setting 8 backdrop, breeding, distance, heritage, training 9 education, grounding, landscape, life story 10 experience, upbringing 11 antecedents, credentials, environment, mise-en-scene, preparation 13 circumstances

backhanded 7 awkward 8 reversed 9 insincere

backing 3 aid 4 core, help 5 aegis 6 succor 7 support 8 advocacy, interior, sanction 9 patronage, prompting 10 assistance, inner layer, sustenance 11 championing, cooperation, endorsement, helping hand, sponsorship 13 encouragement

backlash 4 flop, snag 5 crash, ravel 6 fizzle, go away, recoil 7 rebound 8 backfire, kick back, miscarry, ricochet, snap back 9 animosity, boomerang, hostility, reversion 10 antagonism, bounce back, opposition, resistance 11 come to grief, fall through 12 come to naught 13 come to nothing, counteraction, recalcitrance

backlog 5 hoard, stock, store 6 assets, excess, supply 7 nest egg, reserve, savings 9 abundance, amassment, inventory, reservoir, stockpile 12 accumulation 13 reserve supply 14 superabundance

back matter 5 index 8 addendum, appendix 10 supplement 12 bibliography

back off 7 retreat 8 back down, pull back, withdraw

backpack 4 hike, load 5 pouch 6 bundle 8 knapsack

backside 3 can 4 buns, butt, duff, prat, rear, rump, seat, tail 5 fanny 6 behind, bottom, settee, setter, sitter 7 keister, rear end 8 buttocks, derriere 9 fundament, posterior

backslide 5 lapse 6 revert 7 relapse 10 recurrence, regression 11 deteriorate 14 slip from virtue

back street 5 alley, byway 8 alleyway 13 secondary road

Back Street
  director:
    1941 version: 15 Robert Stevenson
    1961 version: 11 David Miller
  based on story by: 11 Fannie Hurst
  cast:
    1932 version: 9 John Boles 10 Irene Dunne
    1941 version: 12 Charles Boyer 16 Margaret Sullavan
    1961 version: 9 John Gavin, Vera Miles 12 Susan Hayward

back talk 3 jaw, lip 4 gall, guff, rude, sass 5 cheek 8 pertness, rudeness 9 impudence, insolence, sassiness, sauciness 12 impertinence

Back to the Future
  director: 14 Robert Zemeckis
  cast: 11 Lea Thompson, Michael J Fox 16 Christopher Lloyd

backup 6 second 7 reserve, standby, stand-in 9 alternate, auxiliary, emergency, secondary 10 substitute, understudy 11 pinch-hitter 13 supplementary

back up 4 abet 6 assist, uphold 9 reinforce 11 corroborate

backward, backwards 3 shy 4 dull, slow 5 dense, tardy, timid, wrong 6 behind, ebbing, remiss, toward 7 bashful, impeded, laggard, messily, reverse, the rear 8 inverted, rearward, receding, reserved, retarded, reticent, reversed, sluggish 9 in retreat, in reverse, inside out, returning, slow-paced, to the past, to the rear, withdrawn 10 disorderly, improperly, regressive, retreating, retrograde, slow-witted, topsy-turvy, upside down 11 chaotically, undeveloped, withdrawing 12 wrong side out 13 retrogressive 15 uncommunicative
  French: 9 en arriere

backwash 4 burg, wake 6 result, sticks, upshot 7 boonies, outcome 8 frontier, tank town 9 aftermath, backwater, boondocks, provinces, upcountry 10 hinterland 11 aftereffect, backcountry, consequence

backwater 3 ebb 5 slack 7 retreat, reverse 8 holdback, stagnant, withdraw

backwoods 5 rural, wilds 6 rustic, simple, sticks 7 boonies, country 8 woodland 9 boondocks, rural area 10 hinterland, provincial 11 back-country, countryside, hinterlands 15 unsophisticated

bacon 3 pig 4 pork 6 gammon 8 porkslab 10 smoked pork 11 porkbellies
  measure: 6 rasher

Bacon, Francis
  author of: 6 Essays 11 New Atlantis 12 Novum Organum 14 Maxims of the Law 16 Instauratio Magna 17 History of Henry VII 18 De Sapientia Veterum 20 Apophthegms New and Old 21 Advancement of Learning 25 Reading on the Statute of Uses

Bacon, Francis
  born: 6 Dublin 7 Ireland
  artwork: 15 Henrietta Moraes 35 Three Studies at the Base of a Crucifixion 44 Studies After Velazquez' Portrait of Pope Innocent X

Bacon, Henry
  architect of: 15 Lincoln Memorial

bacteria 3 bug 4 germ 5 virus 7 microbe 8 bacillus, pathogen 13 microorganism

bactericide 9 germicide 10 antiseptic, germ killer 12 disinfectant

bacteriologist
  American: 4 Reed
  British: 7 Fleming
  German: 4 Koch 7 Behring, Ehrlich 10 Wassermann
  Japanese: 7 Noguchi 8 Kitasato

bad 3 ill, sad, sin **4** base, dire, evil, foul, glum, grim, mean, poor, rank, sick, sour, vile **5** acrid, acute, angry, awful, cross, false, fetid, grave, harsh, lousy, moldy, nasty, risky, sorry, unfit, wrong **6** ailing, bitter, crimes, faulty, gloomy, guilty, infirm, odious, putrid, rancid, rotten, severe, sickly, sinful, touchy, tragic, turned, unwell, wicked, wrongs **7** baneful, beastly, corrupt, decayed, harmful, hurtful, immoral, joyless, lacking, naughty, not good, noxious, painful, searing, serious, spoiled, tainted, unsound, useless **8** below par, contrite, criminal, dreadful, grievous, inferior, menacing, mildewed, offenses, polluted, terrible, troubled, villainy, wretched **9** agonizing, dangerous, defective, deficient, erroneous, frightful, hazardous, imperfect, incorrect, injurious, irascible, irritable, loathsome, miserable, nefarious, obnoxious, offensive, regretful, repugnant, repulsive, revolting, sad events, sickening, troubling, unethical, unhealthy, unnerving, unwelcome, valueless **10** calamitous, decomposed, deplorable, detestable, disastrous, disgusting, distressed, disturbing, fallacious, immorality, inadequate, indisposed, melancholy, misfortune, nauseating, not correct, perfidious, putrescent, remorseful, second-rate, unpleasant, villainous, wickedness **11** detrimental, discouraged, distasteful, distractive, distressing, ineffective, inefficient, opprobrious, regrettable, substandard, troublesome, unpalatable **12** contaminated, disagreeable, discouraging, disreputable, excruciating, questionable, unprincipled, unproductive **13** below standard, disappointing, disheartening, harmful things, nonproductive, reprehensible, shorttempered **14** disappointment **15** disadvantageous, under the weather **18** conscience-stricken

bad faith 7 perfidy, treason **8** betrayal **9** falseness, treachery, two timing **10** disloyalty **11** double-cross **13** breach of faith, double-dealing **14** unfaithfulness

badge 4 mark, seal, sign **5** brand, stamp, token **6** device, emblem, ensign, shield, symbol **7** earmark **8** hallmark, insignia **9** medallion

badger 3 nag, vex **4** bait, goad **5** annoy, beset, bully, chafe, harry, hound, tease **6** coerce, harass, hector, nettle, pester, plague **7** provoke, torment, trouble **8** irritate **9** persecute
   group of: 4 cete

Badger State
   nickname of: 9 Wisconsin

badinage 5 chaff **6** banter, joking **7** jesting, joshing, kidding, ragging, ribbing, waggery **8** chaffing, raillery, repartee, word play

bad judgment 5 folly **10** imprudence **11** foolishness **12** carelessness **13** senselessness **15** thoughtlessness **16** shortsightedness, unperceptiveness

bad luck 6 mishap **7** ill wind **8** bad break **9** adversity, mischance **10** ill fortune, misfortune

badly 5 wrong **6** basely, poorly, sorely, vilely **7** acutely, greatly, ineptly, not well, wrongly **8** faultily, horribly, severely, shoddily, sinfully, sloppily, terribly, very much, wickedly **9** corruptly, extremely, immorally, intensely, unsoundly **10** carelessly, criminally, dreadfully, improperly, wretchedly **11** defectively, deficiently, desperately, erroneously, exceedingly, frightfully, imperfectly, incorrectly, nefariously, offensively, unethically **12** disreputably, inadequately, villainously **13** incompetently, in the worst way **16** unsatisfactorily

bad manners 8 rudeness **9** surliness **10** incivility **11** boorishness, discourtesy **12** impoliteness

bad mark 4 blot **7** demerit **9** poor grade

badminton
   racket: 10 battledore
   racket used to hit: 4 bird **7** shuttle **11** shuttlecock
   Indian version: 5 poona
   stroke: 4 drop **5** clear, smash **7** service **13** backhand drive, forehand drive

badmouthing 5 barbs **7** insults, slander **9** criticism, insulting **10** slandering **11** criticizing

bad taste 9 crudeness, vulgarity **10** coarseness, garishness, tawdryness

bad tasting 4 sour **5** nasty **6** bitter **7** spoiled **9** medicinal, revolting **10** disgusting **11** unpalatable

bad-tempered 5 cross, testy **6** grumpy **7** grouchy **8** choleric, churlish **9** difficult, irascible, irritable **10** ill-natured **11** acrimonious **12** disagreeable

bad times 4 bust **5** slump **9** hard times, recession **10** depression

bad turn 4 harm, hurt **5** wrong **6** injury **7** ill turn **8** disfavor **9** injustice **10** disservice **11** discourtesy

Baekleland, Leo Hendrik
   field: 9 chemistry
   invented: 8 Bakelite **32** artificial light photographic paper

Baer, Max (Maximillian Adalbert)
   nickname: 17 Livermore Larruper
   sport: 6 boxing
   class: 11 heavyweight

Baeyer, Johann Friedrich Wilhelm Adolph von
   field: 9 chemistry
   nationality: 6 German
   synthesized: 6 indigo
   discovered: 13 phthalein dyes
   awarded: 10 Nobel Prize

baffle 3 bar **4** daze, dull, foil, stop **5** amaze, check, stump **6** deaden, muddle, puzzle, reduce, thwart **7** astound, confuse, inhibit, mystify, nonplus, perplex **8** astonish, befuddle, bewilder, confound, dumfound, minimize, restrain, surprise **10** disconcert

baffling 7 elusive 8 puzzling 9 confusing, enigmatic 10 mysterious, mystifying, perplexing 11 confounding 16 incomprehensible

bag 3 get, sag 4 hunt, kill, sack, take, trap 5 bulge, catch, droop, pouch, purse, shoot, snare 6 bundle, entrap, obtain, packet 7 acquire, capture, collect, ensnare 8 paper bag, protrude, suitcase 10 receptacle

bagatelle 6 trifle 7 nothing, trinket 10 knickknack, light music 11 unimportant

baggage 4 bags, gear 5 grips 6 trunks 7 bundles, effects, luggage, valises 8 movables, packages 9 apparatus, equipment, suitcases, trappings 10 belongings 11 impedimenta 13 accoutrements, paraphernalia

baggy 4 limp 5 loose, slack 6 droopy, flabby, puffed 7 bloated, bulbous, flaccid, paunchy, sagging, swollen 9 unpressed, unshapely 12 loose-fitting

Baghdad
capital of: 4 Iraq
founder: 8 (Caliph) al-Mansur
landmark:
minaret: 10 Suq al-Ghazi
mosque: 8 Madrasah 14 al-Mustansiriya
means: 8 God-given
river: 6 Tigris

Bagheera
character in: 14 The Jungle Books
author: 7 Kipling

bagnio 4 bath, stew 5 house 6 bordel, prison 7 brothel 8 bordello, cathouse 10 bawdy house, fancy house, whorehouse 13 sporting house 14 house of ill fame 16 house of ill repute 19 house of prostitution

Bagnold, Enid
author of: 14 National Velvet, The Chalk Garden 23 The Chinese Prime Minister

Bagstock, Joe
character in: 12 Dombey and Son
author: 7 Dickens

Bahamas
capital/largest city: 6 Nassau
others: 8 Freeport 9 Rock Sound 10 George Town 11 Mastic Point 12 Spanish Wells
head of state: 14 British monarch 15 governor general
island: 3 Cat 4 Long 5 Berry, Exuma 6 Andros, Bimini, Caicos, Rum Cay 7 Crooked, Harbour, Watling 9 Eleuthera, Mayaguana 10 Great Abaco 11 Grand Bahama, Great Inagua, Great Ragged, San Salvador 13 New Providence
sea: 8 Atlantic 9 Caribbean
physical feature:
strait: 7 Florida
swamp: 8 mangrove
people: 5 black 7 Haitian
language: 6 Creole 7 English
religion: 12 Christianity
place:
harbor: 9 Governors
naval base: 9 Mayaguana
feature:

key: 3 cay
native: 5 conch

Bahrain
capital/largest city: 6 Manama
others: 5 Rifaa 7 Jidhafs 8 Muharraq
head of state/government: 4 emir
monetary unit: 4 fils 5 dinar
island: 5 Hawar, Jidda 6 Sitrah 7 Bahrain 9 Umm Nassan 10 al-Muharraq 11 An Nabi Salih
physical feature:
gulf: 7 Bahrain, Persian
people: 4 Arab 6 Indian 7 Persian 8 American, European 9 Pakistani
ruling family: 9 al-Khalifa
language: 4 Urdu 5 Farsi 6 Arabic 7 English, Persian
religion: 5 Islam

bail 3 dip 4 bond, lade 5 ladle, scoop, spoon 6 surety 9 guarantee 11 post bond for

bailiff 6 deputy 8 marshall, overseer 9 assistant, constable 12 court officer

bailiwick 4 area, beat, turf 5 arena, orbit, place, realm 6 domain, sphere 7 compass 8 dominion, province 9 territory 10 department 12 neighborhood

Baird, Spencer Fullerton
field: 7 zoology
authority on: 5 birds 7 mammals
established: 30 US Commission of Fish and Fisheries
laboratory at: 11 Woods Hole MA

bait 3 vex 4 lure, ride, worm 5 annoy, bribe, harry, hound, tease, worry 6 allure, badger, come-on, harass, heckle, hector, magnet, needle 7 provoke, torment 9 put bait on, tantalize 10 allurement, antagonize, attraction, enticement, inducement, temptation

bake 3 fry 4 boil, burn, cook, sear, stew 5 grill, roast, saute, toast 6 braise, pan-fry, scorch, simmer 7 parboil, swelter

Baked Bean State
nickname of: 13 Massachusetts

Baker, Norma Jean Mortenson
real name of: 13 Marilyn Monroe

Baking
goddess of: 6 Fornax

Balaam
father: 4 Beor
brother: 4 Bela
lived at: 4 Aram 6 Pethor
commanded by: 5 Balak
killed by: 6 Israel

Balak
father: 6 Zippor
commanded: 6 Balaam

Balakiref, Mily
born: 6 Russia 13 Nijni-Novgorod
member of: 7 Kutchka, The Five
composer of: 6 Russia, Tamara, Thamar 7 Islamey 8 King Lear (overture)

balance, balances 3 pay 4 cool, mean, rest 5 poise, ratio, scale, sum up, tally, total, tot up, weigh 6 aplomb, equate, offset, parity, ponder, reckon, scales, set off,

square, steady, weight 7 compare, compute, harmony, opinion, reflect, remnant, residue 8 cogitate, consider, contrast, coolness, equality, estimate, evaluate, judgment, leftover, level off, parallel, presence, symmetry 9 appraisal, calculate, composure, equipoise, juxtapose, make level, remainder, stability, stabilize 10 amount owed, comparison, counteract, deliberate, equanimity, evaluation, keep steady, neutralize, proportion, steadiness 11 equilibrium 12 counterpoise, equalization, middle ground 13 compensate for, consideration, judiciousness 14 amount credited, self-possession, unflappability 15 level-headedness 16 imperturbability
constellation of: 5 Libra

balanced 4 fair, just 9 equitable, impartial 12 unprejudiced 13 disinterested

balance out 6 cancel, offset 9 make up for 10 neutralize 13 compensate for 14 counterbalance

Balanchine, George
choreographer of: 4 Agon 6 Jewels 8 Episodes, Ivesiana, Serenade 15 Concerto Barocco 16 Allegro Brillante

balcony 4 deck 5 boxes, foyer, loges 6 loggia 7 portico, terrace, veranda 9 mezzanine

bald 4 bare, flat, open 5 blunt, naked, plain, stark, utter 6 barren, simple, smooth 7 denuded, obvious 8 flagrant, glabrous, hairless, outright, treeless 9 depilated, out-and-out, unadorned 11 categorical, undisguised, unqualified, unvarnished 12 without cover 13 unembellished, unequivocable 15 straightforward

Balder
also: 5 Baldr 6 Baldur
origin: 6 Nordic
god of: 6 beauty 8 radiance
father: 4 Odin 5 Othin
mother: 3 Fri 5 Frigg, Frija 6 Frigga
twin brother: 5 Hoder, Hodur
killed by: 5 Hoder, Hodur

balderdash 3 rot 4 bosh, bull, bunk 5 crock, trash 6 bunkum, drivel, hot air 7 twaddle 8 buncombe, claptrap, flummery, nonsense, tommyrot 9 gibberish, poppycock 10 double-talk, tomfoolery 11 obfuscation 16 stuff and nonsense

baldheaded 8 hairless 9 baldpated, depilated 10 skin-headed 11 chrome-domed

Baldr
see: 6 Balder

Baldung Grien, Hans
born: 6 Alsace 10 Weyersheim
artwork: 9 Todentanz 17 Death and the Maiden 19 Death Kissing a Maiden 21 The Bewitched Stable Boy 24 Rest on the Flight into Egypt

Baldur
see: 6 Balder

Baldwin, James
author of: 13 Giovanni's Room, The Amen Corner 14 Another Country 15 Just Above My Head, The Fire Next Time 17 Going to Meet the Man, Nobody Knows My Name, No Name in the Street 21 Blues for Mister Charlie, Go Tell It on the Mountain

bale 4 case, load, pack 6 bundle, packet, parcel 7 package 11 bound bundle

balefire 6 beacon 9 watchfire 10 signal fire

baleful 3 icy 4 cold, dire, evil 6 deadly, malign 7 baneful, furious, harmful, hurtful, ominous 8 sinister, spiteful, venomous 9 malicious, malignant 10 malevolent 11 cold-hearted, threatening

Balfe, Michael William
born: 6 Dublin 7 Ireland
composer of: 15 The Bohemian Girl, The Maid of Artois 17 I rivali di se stessi 18 The Siege of Rochelle

Balfour, David
character in: 9 Kidnapped
author: 9 Stevenson

Bali
province of: 9 Indonesia
capital: 8 Denpasar
city: 10 Singaraja
island: 11 Lesser Sunda
highest peak: 6 Agoeng
climate: 3 dry 7 monsoon
tree: 8 waringin
animal: 4 deer 5 tiger
people: 7 Malayan
religion: 8 Hinduism
agriculture: 3 pig 4 corn, rice 6 cattle, coffee 7 tobacco

Balius
horse of: 8 Achilles
gift: 11 immortality

balk 3 bar 4 foil, shun 5 block, check, demur, evade, shirk, spike, stall 6 baffle, defeat, derail, eschew, hinder, impede, recoil, refuse, resist, stymie, thwart 7 inhibit, prevent 8 draw back, hang back, hesitate, obstruct 9 forestall, frustrate 10 shrink from

Balkan 16 Forested mountain
agriculture: 5 grain 6 cotton, grapes, olives 7 tobacco
ancient people: 4 Slav 5 Greek, Roman 8 Illyrian, Thracian
language: 9 Slovenian 10 Macedonian 14 Serbo-Croatian
mountain: 6 Balkan, Massif 7 Rhodope 10 Carpathian 11 Dinaric Alps 13 Transylvanian
religion: 5 Islam 8 Orthodox 13 Roman Catholic
river: 6 Danube, Morava, Vardar
sea boundary: 5 Black 6 Aegean, Ionian 8 Adriatic 13 Mediterranean
state: 6 Greece, Turkey 7 Albania, Romania 8 Bulgaria 10 Yugoslavia

balky 6 mulish, ornery, unruly 7 restive, wayward, willful 8 contrary, perverse, stubborn 9 fractious, obstinate, pigheaded 10 rebellious, refractory 11 disobedient, intractable 12 recalcitrant, unmanageable

ball 3 hop, orb 4 prom, shot 5 dance, globe 6 pellet, soiree, sphere 7 bullets, globule 8 spheroid 9 cotillion, promenade 11 projectiles

Ball, Lucille
  husband: 9 Desi Arnaz
  children: 4 Desi 5 Lucie
  born: 11 Jamestown NY
  roles: 9 Here's Lucy, I Love Lucy 11 The Lucy Show

Balla, Giacomo
  born: 5 Italy, Turin
  artwork: 8 The Sewer 11 The Mad Woman 18 Speeding Automobile 20 Rhythm of the Violinist 22 Dynamism of a Dog on a Leash 26 The Street Light— Study of Light 29 Mercury Passing in Front of the Sun 40 Swifts Paths of Movement and Dynamic Sequences

ballad 3 lay 4 song 5 carol, ditty 6 chanty 8 folk song 12 rhyming story 13 narrative poem 14 narrative verse

Ballad of Reading Gaol, The
  author: 10 Oscar Wilde

Ballads and Poems
  author: 19 Stephen Vincent Benet

ballast 6 weight 7 balance, control 9 equipoise 10 ballasting, dead weight, makeweight, stabilizer 12 counterpoise 13 counterweight 14 counterbalance 19 stabilizing material

Ballesteros, Severiano
  nickname: 4 Seve
  sport: 4 golf
  nationality: 7 Spanish

ballet 4 Agon 5 Manon, Rodeo 6 Apollo, Parade 7 Giselle, Orpheus 8 Coppelia, Episodes, Ivesiana, Les Noces, Serenade, Swan Lake, The Doves 9 Anastasia, Fancy Free, Interplay, Petrushka, The Jewels 10 La Sylphide, Petrouchka 11 Billy the Kid, Lilac Garden, Soccer Dance, Symphony in C, The Firebird 12 Pillar of Fire, Sailor's Dance, Spring Waters, The Partisans 13 The Nutcracker 14 Romeo and Juliet 15 Concerto Barocco, Fall River Legend, The Rite of Spring 16 Allegro Brillante, La Fille Mal Gardee, Specter of the Rose 17 The Sleeping Beauty 18 Raymonda Variations 19 The Afternoon of a Faun, The Four Temperaments 24 Stravinsky Violin Concerto
  ballet company: 5 Kirov, Royal 7 Bolshoi, Joffrey 9 Mariinsky, Maryinsky 11 New York City 13 Ballets Russes 20 Dance Theater of Harlem 21 American Ballet Theater 22 National Ballet of Canada
  choreographer: 9 Hanya Holm, Lev Ivanov 10 John Weaver 11 Jules Perrot 12 Agnes de Mille, Igor Moiseyev, Marius Petipa, Michel Fokine 13 Jean Dauberval, Jerome Robbins, Leonid Massine 15 Arthur Saint-Leon 16 George Balanchine, Kenneth MacMillan 18 August Bournonville, Bronislava Nijinska,

Jean Georges Noverre, Sir Frederick Ashton
  chorus: 8 ensemble 13 corps de ballet
  dancer: 9 Karen Kain 10 Anton Dolin, Marie Lieta, Serge Lifar 11 Allegra Kent, Anna Pavlova, Anthony Blum, Lucile Grahn, Lynn Seymour, Nadia Nerina 12 Fanny Cerrito, Marie Camargo, Peter Martins 13 Alicia Markova, Andre Eglevsky, Anthony Dowell, Carlotta Grisi, Frank Augustyn, Galina Ulanova, Margot Fonteyn, Marie Taglioni, Melissa Hayden, Patricia Neary, Rudolf Nureyev 14 Arthur Mitchell, Cynthia Gregory, Edward Villella, Gelsey Kirkland, Leonide Massine, Maria Tallchief, Suzanne Farrell, Vaslav Nijinsky 15 Jacques D'Amboise, Martine Van Hamel, Maya Plisetskaya, Natalia Makarova, Patricia McBride, Tamara Karsavina 16 Antoinette Sibley, Olga Spessivtseva 17 Alexandra Danilova, Marina Kondratieva 18 Mikhail Baryshnikov
  fast movement: 7 allegro
  first ballet: 22 Ballet Comique de la Reine
  impresario: 12 Marie Rambert 15 Ninette de Valois, Sergei Diaghilev
  kick: 9 battement
  modern dancer/choreographer: 8 Ted Shawn 9 Eliot Feld 10 Mary Wigman, Paul Draper, Twyla Tharp 11 Anna Sokolow, Antony Tudor, Eric Hawkins, Ruth St Denis 12 Martha Graham 13 Alwin Nikolais, Doris Humphrey, Isadora Duncan 14 Charles Weidman 15 Merce Cunningham
  position/step: 4 jete, plie, tour 5 saute 6 releve 7 en avant, fouette, on point, pas seul, turnout 8 batterie, cabriole, en dedans, en dehors, glissade 9 arabesque, developpe, en arriere, entrechat, pas de chat, pas-de-deux, pirouette 10 demipointe, port de bras, tour en l'air 11 rond de jambe, terre-a-terre 12 pas de bourree, saut de basque 17 changement de pieds
  principal female dancer: 9 ballerina 14 prima ballerina
  principal male dancer: 12 danseur noble
  skirt: 4 tutu
  slow movement: 6 adagio
  term: 4 coda 5 barre 6 ballon 14 divertissement

Ball of Fat
  author: 15 Guy de Maupassant

balloon 4 grow 5 belly, bloat 6 billow, blow up, dilate, expand 7 distend, enlarge, fill out, inflate, puff out 8 increase, swell out 9 inflation 10 pouch, sac

ballot 4 poll, vote 5 slate 6 ticket, voting 7 polling 13 round of voting 16 list of candidates

ballyhoo 4 hype, puff, push, tout 6 herald, hoopla 7 buildup, promote, puffery, trumpet 8 proclaim 9 advertise, promotion, publicity, publicize 10 hullabaloo, propaganda 11 advertising 15 public relations

balm 5 cream, salve 6 balsam, lotion, solace 7 anodyne, comfort, unguent 8 curative, narcotic, ointment, sedative 9 comforter, emollient 10 palliative 11 restorative 12 tranquilizer

balmy 3 odd 4 calm, fair, mild, soft, warm 5 bland, kooky, weird 6 easing, gentle 7 calming, clement, summery 8 aromatic, fragrant, perfumed, pleasant, redolent, soothing 9 agreeable, ambrosial, eccentric, temperate 10 refreshing, salubrious

Balnibari
  fictional land in: 16 Gulliver's Travels
  author: 5 Swift

baloney 3 rot 4 bull, bunk 5 hokum, hooey, stuff 6 bunkum, hot air, humbug 7 hogwash, sausage, spinach 8 claptrap, nonsense, tommyrot 9 poppycock 10 applesauce 11 foolishness

Baloo
  character in: 14 The Jungle Books
  author: 7 Kipling

balsam 3 fir 4 balm 5 cream, salve 7 unguent 8 ointment 9 Impatiens
  varieties: 2 He 3 Fir, She 4 Rose, Wild 6 Garden 8 Zanzibar

Balsam, Martin
  born: 9 New York NY
  roles: 6 Psycho 7 Catch-22 15 A Thousand Clowns, On the Waterfront

Baltic
  language family: 12 Indo-European
  group: 11 Balto-Slavic
  subgroup: 7 Latvian 10 Lithuanian

Baltimore
  baseball team: 7 Orioles
  football team: 5 Stars

Baltimore, David
  field: 12 microbiology
  studied: 11 animal cells 13 viral genetics
  awarded: 10 Nobel Prize

Balto-Slavic
  language family: 12 Indo-European
  branch: 6 Baltic, Slavic

baluster 4 post, rail 6 column, pillar 7 support, upright 8 pilaster

balustrade 7 railing 8 baluster, banister, handrail

Balzac, Honore de
  author of: 7 Gobseck 10 La Vendetta 11 Cousin(e) Bette 12 Father Goriot, Le Cousin Pons, Le Pere Goriot 13 Lost Illusions 14 Eugenie Grandet, The Human Comedy 15 The Wild Ass's Skin 16 La Comedie Humaine 23 The Physiology of Marriage

Bamako
  capital of: 4 Mali

Bambi
  author: 11 Felix Salten
  character: 6 Faline, Flower 7 Thumper

bamboo 4 Sasa 7 Bambusa 9 Shibataea 10 Pseudosasa 11 Arundinaria 13 Phyllostachys 14 Chimonobambusa 15 Semiarundinaria

varieties: 4 Moso 5 Arrow, Black, Dwarf, Giant, Hardy, Hedge, Henon, Meyer, Pygmy, Simon, Stake 6 Buddha, Common, Forage, Oldham, Sacred, Sickle, Square, Tonkin 7 Allgold, Beechey, Mexican 8 Calcutta, Feathery, Heavenly, Narihira 9 Canebrake, Castillon 10 Redberried, Square-stem 11 Punting-pole 12 Alphonse Karr, Yellow-groove 13 Dwarf fern-leaf, Fern-leaf hedge, Oriental hedge 14 Chinese-goddess 16 Dwarf white-stripe 17 Silver-stripe hedge 18 Stripe-stem fern-leaf

bamboozle 3 con, gyp 4 coax, dupe, fool, gull, hoax, lure, rook, take 5 cheat, cozen, trick 6 delude 7 beguile, deceive, defraud, mislead, swindle 8 hoodwink 9 victimize

ban 3 bar 5 debar, taboo 6 banish, enjoin, forbid 7 barring, embargo, exclude 8 disallow, prohibit, stoppage, suppress 9 exclusion, interdict, proscribe, restraint 10 banishment, censorship 11 forbiddance, prohibition, restriction 12 interdiction, proscription

banal 4 dull 5 corny, stale, stock, tired, trite, vapid 6 jejune 7 humdrum, insipid, prosaic 8 bromidic, everyday, ordinary, shopworn 9 hackneyed 10 pedestrian, threadbare, unexciting, unoriginal 11 commonplace, stereotyped 12 cliche-ridden, conventional 13 platitudinous, unimaginative, uninteresting

banality 6 cliche 7 bromide 9 platitude, staleness, triteness 10 insipidity

banana 4 Musa
  varieties: 3 Fe'i 4 Fehi, Koae 5 Dwarf 6 Edible 7 Chinese 9 Flowering 10 Abyssinian, Ladyfinger 12 Canary Island, Chinese dwarf
  similar to: 8 plantain

Bananas
  director: 10 Woody Allen
  cast: 10 Woody Allen 12 Howard Cosell, Louise Lasser 15 Carlos Montalban

Bancroft, Anne
  real name: 23 Anna Maria Louise Italiano
  husband: 9 Mel Brooks
  born: 7 Bronx NY
  roles: 11 Mrs Robinson, The Graduate 15 The Pumpkin Eater, The Turning Point, Two for the Seesaw 16 The Miracle Worker (Oscar)

band 3 set 4 belt, body, club, crew, gang, hoop, join, pack, ring, sash 5 bunch, crowd, group, junta, party, strap, strip, swath, thong, troop, unite 6 caucus, circle, clique, collar, fillet, gather, girdle, league, ribbon, streak, stripe, throng 7 bandeau, binding, circlet, company, society 8 assembly, cincture, ensemble 9 multitude, orchestra, surcingle 10 fellowship, sisterhood 11 association, brotherhood, confederacy, consolidate 13 confederation

bandage 4 bind 5 dress 7 binding, plaster 8 compress, dressing

bandanna, bandana 5 scarf 8 kerchief 10 silk square 11 neckerchief 12 handkerchief

Bandar Seri Begawan
  capital of: 6 Brunei

bandeau 3 bra 4 band 6 fillet 7 binding, circlet 9 brassiere

bandit 4 thug 5 crook, thief 6 badman, outlaw, robber 7 brigand, burglar, footpad, ladrone 8 blackleg 9 desperado, road agent 10 highwayman

bandleader 6 master 7 maestro 8 director 9 conductor
  famous: 11 Glenn Miller, Tommy Dorsey 12 Lawrence Welk

Band of Merry Men
  followers of: 9 Robin Hood

band together 5 unify, unite 6 league 7 combine 10 join forces 11 consolidate

bandy 4 swap 5 trade 6 barter 7 shuffle 8 exchange 9 toss about 11 interchange 16 toss back and forth

bandying 4 swap 5 trade 8 exchange 9 tit for tat 10 quid pro quo 11 give and take

bane 3 woe 4 ruin 5 curse, toxin, venom 6 blight, burden, canker, plague, poison 7 scourge, torment, tragedy 8 calamity, disaster, downfall, nuisance 9 destroyer, detriment, ruination 10 affliction 13 pain in the neck 14 thorn in the side 16 fly in the ointment

baneful 4 evil 6 deadly, malign, woeful 7 harmful, noxious 8 venomous 9 injurious, malignant, poisonous 10 malevolent 11 destructive

bang 3 box, hit, pop, rap, tap 4 beat, blow, boom, clap, cuff, kick, lick, slam, slap, sock 5 burst, clout, crash, knock, smack, thump, whack 6 buffet, charge, report, thrill, thwack, wallop 7 delight 8 good time, headlong, pleasure, suddenly 9 enjoyment, explosion 10 crashingly, excitement

Bangkok, Bankok
  also: 9 Krung Thep
  capital of: 8 Thailand
  landmark: 5 Wat Po 11 Grand Palace 16 Wat Emerald Buddha
  means: 12 City of Angels
  nickname: 15 Venice of the East
  port: 8 Klongtoi
  river: 10 Chao Phraya

Bangladesh
  other name: 10 East Bengal 12 East Pakistan
  capital/largest city: 5 Dacca
  others: 6 Khulna, Sylhet 7 Comilla, Jessore, Rangpur, Saidpur 8 Jamalpur, Rajshahi 9 Madaripur 10 Chittagong 11 Narayanganj 12 Brahmanbaria
  monetary unit: 4 taka 5 paisa
  island: 10 Sundarbans
  mountain: 15 Chittagong Hills
  highest point: 10 Keokradong
  river: 5 Padna 6 Ganges, Meghna 10 Burhi Ganga, Karnaphuli 11 Brahmaputra
  physical feature:
  bay: 6 Bengal
  people: 7 Bengali

  guerrillas: 11 muktibahini
  leader: 6 Ershad 11 Ziaur Rahman 19 Sheikh Mujibur Rahman
  language: 6 Bihari 7 Bengali, English
  religion: 5 Hindu, Islam
  feature:
  clothing: 4 sari 5 lungi

bangle 3 fob 5 chain, charm 6 armlet, bauble, gewgaw, tinsel 7 bibelot, fribble, trinket 8 bracelet, gimcrack, ornament, wristlet 10 knickknack 11 junk jewelry 14 costume jewelry

Bangui
  capital of: 22 Central African Republic

banish 3 ban, bar 4 drop, oust 5 eject, erase, evict, exile, expel 6 deport, dispel, outlaw, reject, remove 7 cast out, discard, dismiss, exclude, put away, shut out, turn out 8 cast away, dislodge, drive out, get rid of, send away, shake off 9 discharge, eliminate, eradicate, extradite 13 excommunicate 14 send to Coventry

banished person 5 exile 6 emigre, pariah 7 outcast 8 deportee, expellee 10 expatriate 14 deported person 15 displaced person

banishment 3 ban 5 exile 6 ouster 7 removal 8 eviction 9 dismissal, exclusion, expulsion 11 deportation 12 expatriation 14 transportation 15 excommunication

Banjo Eyes
  nickname of: 11 Eddie Cantor

Banjul, Bathurst
  capital of: 9 The Gambia

bank 3 bar, row, tip 4 dike, dune, edge, file, flat, fund, heap, hill, keep, line, mass, pile, rank, reef, rise, save, side, tier, tilt 5 amass, array, brink, chain, knoll, mound, ridge, shelf, shoal, shore, slant, slope, stack, store, train 6 barrow, line up, margin, pile up, series, strand, string, supply 7 deposit, parapet, reserve, savings, shallow, terrace 8 keyboard, sandbank 9 exchequer, reservoir, stockpile 10 depository, embankment, repository, storehouse, succession 12 accumulation, trust company 14 savings and loan

Bank Dick, The
  director: 10 Eddie Cline
  cast: 8 W C Fields 9 Una Merkel 15 Cora Witherspoon

Bankhead, Tallulah
  father: 16 William B Bankhead
  born: 12 Huntsville AL
  roles: 8 Lifeboat 14 The Little Foxes 17 The Skin of Our Teeth

banknote 4 bill 9 greenback 11 certificate, legal tender 12 currency note, treasury note 17 silver certificate

bank of pity
  French: 11 mont-de-piete
  literal name for: 10 pawnbroker

bankrupt 5 broke 6 busted, failed, ruined 8 depleted, indigent, in the red, wiped out 9 destitute, exhausted, insolvent, penniless 12 impoverished, without funds

Bankruptcy, A
author: 20 Bjornstjerne Bjornson
Banks, Ernie
nickname: 5 Mr Cub
sport: 8 baseball
noted for: 7 hitting
team: 11 Chicago Cubs
banner 4 flag 6 burgee, colors, ensign, record 7 leading, notable, pendant, pennant, winning 8 standard, streamer 9 red-letter 10 profitable 11 outstanding 14 most successful
Bannock
language family: 10 Shoshonean
location: 5 Idaho
banquet 4 dine 5 feast, revel 6 dinner, repast 9 symposium
Banquo
character in: 7 Macbeth
author: 11 Shakespeare
bantam 3 hen, wee 4 cock, fowl, tiny 5 dwarf, pygmy, runt, small, teeny, weeny 6 little, midget, minute, petite 7 chicken, dwarfed, rooster, stunted 9 miniature 10 diminutive, pocket-size, teeny-weeny 11 Lilliputian, pocket-sized
banter 3 kid, rib 4 dish, josh, mock, ride, twit 5 chaff, jolly, taunt, tease 6 joking, needle 7 jesting, joshing, kidding, ragging, ribbing, teasing, waggery 8 badinage, chaffing, raillery, repartee, word play
Banting, Frederick Grant
field: 8 medicine
nationality: 8 Canadian
extracted: 7 insulin
awarded: 10 Nobel Prize
Bantu
means: 9 the people
dwelling: 6 Africa
tribe: 5 Xosas, Zulus 6 Swazis 7 Basutos, Kalanga
baptism 9 beginning, immersion, sacrament 10 initiation, sprinkling 11 christening 12 introduction, purification 13 rite of passage 16 spiritual rebirth
baptize 3 dub 4 name 8 christen
bar 3 ban, pub, rib, rod 4 band, bank, beam, belt, bolt, cake, curb, flat, line, lock, oust, pale, pole, rail, reef, snag, spar, spit, stay, stop 5 block, catch, check, court, debar, eject, evict, exile, expel, forum, ingot, jimmy, lever, limit, shelf, shoal, slice, sprit, stake, stick, strip, taboo 6 banish, enjoin, fasten, forbid, impede, lounge, paling, ribbon, saloon, secure, streak, stripe, stroke, tavern 7 barrier, block up, canteen, cast out, close up, crowbar, exclude, grating, lock out, measure, prevent, sandbar, shallow, shut out, taproom 8 alehouse, crossbar, disallow, judgment, obstacle, obstruct, preclude, prohibit, restrain, restrict, tribunal 9 barricade, blackball, blacklist, hindrance, long table, lunchroom, restraint, speakeasy 10 constraint, crosspiece, impediment, injunction, limitation 11 obstruction, public house, restriction 14 cocktail

lounge, serving counter, stumbling block 15 legal profession
Bara, Theda
real name: 16 Theodosia Goodman
nickname: 7 The Vamp
born: 12 Cincinnati OH
roles: 6 Carmen, Salome 7 Camille 8 The Vixen 9 Cleopatra 13 A Fool There Was, Madame Du Barry
Barabbas 6 robber 8 murderer
Barak
father: 7 Abinoam
summoned by: 7 Deborah
defeated: 6 Sisera
barb 3 cut, dig, nib 4 cusp, jibe, snag, spur, tine 5 point, prong, spike 6 insult 7 affront, barbule, bristle, prickle, putdown, sarcasm, spicule 9 complaint, criticism 11 badmouthing
Barbados
capital/largest city: 10 Bridgetown
others: 7 Oistins 8 Boscabel, Crab Hill, Hastings, Holetown, Portland, Worthing 9 Bathsheba 10 Martin's Bay 11 Belleplaine 12 Speightstown
school: 10 Codrington
head of state: 14 British monarch 15 governor general
mountain: 6 Chalky
highest point: 7 Hillaby
river: 12 Constitution
sea: 8 Atlantic 9 Caribbean
physical feature:
bay: 4 Foul, Long 8 Carlisle
beach: 5 Crane
gully: 12 Welchman Hall
hill: 10 Cherry Tree
point: 5 North, South 6 Ragged 8 Harrison, Kitridge
people: 5 Bajan 9 Barbadian
leader: 5 Adams
language: 7 English
religion: 8 Anglican
place:
airport: 7 Seawell
castle: 8 Sam Lords
church: 7 St Johns
feature:
sea crab: 7 shagger
barbarian 4 boor, hood, lout, punk 5 alien, bully, crude, rowdy, tough, yahoo 6 savage, vandal 7 boorish, hoodlum, lowbrow, peasant, ruffian, uncouth 8 hooligan 9 ignoramus, outlander, roughneck, vulgarian 10 delinquent, illiterate, philistine, provincial, troglodyte, uncultured 11 knownothing 12 uncultivated 15 unsophisticated 16 anti-intellectual
barbaric 4 rude, wild 5 crude 6 coarse, savage, vulgar 7 boorish, uncouth, untamed 9 barbarian, barbarous 10 unpolished 11 ill-mannered, uncivilized
barbarism 7 cruelty 8 savagery 9 brutality 10 inhumanity 11 viciousness
barbarity 7 cruelty 9 brutality 10 savageness 12 ruthlessness

barbarous 4 mean 5 crass, crude, cruel, harsh, rough 6 brutal, coarse, vulgar 7 inhuman, vicious 8 barbaric, impolite 10 outrageous

barber 3 cut 4 trim 5 dress, shave, style 7 arrange, stylist, tonsure 10 haircutter 11 hairdresser

Barber, Samuel
  born: 13 West Chester PA
  composer of: 7 Vanessa 10 Dover Beach 16 Adagio for Strings 17 Capricorn Concerto 19 Anthony and Cleopatra, The School for Scandal

Barber of Seville, The
  author: 12 Beaumarchais
  opera by: 7 Rossini
  character: 6 Bazile, Figaro, Rosine, Rosina 8 Almaviva, Bartholo 9 Dr Bartolo 13 Count Almaviva

barbette 5 mound 7 bastion, rampart 8 platform 9 earthwork 10 breastwork

barbiturate 8 euphoria, hypnotic, sedative 10 depressive 13 anesthesiatic 14 barbituric acid
  kind: 7 seconal 10 thiopental 11 amobarbital 12 secobarbital 13 phenobarbital

barbule 4 barb 11 feather part

Barchester Towers
  author: 15 Anthony Trollope
  sequel to: 9 The Warden
  character: 7 Mr Slope, Mrs Bold 8 Mr Arabin 9 Dr Proudie, Mr Harding 10 Mrs Proudie 11 Mr Quiverful 13 Canon Stanhope 17 Archdeacon Grantly 18 Signora Vesey-Neroni

bard 4 poet 5 rhymer, writer 8 epic poet, minstrel, poetizer 9 poetaster, rhymester, troubador, versifier 10 poet-singer 13 narrative poet

Bardell, Mrs
  character in: 14 Pickwick Papers
  author: 7 Dickens

Bardot, Brigitte
  husband: 10 Roger Vadim
  born: 5 Paris 6 France
  roles: 18 And God Created Woman

bare 4 bald, mere, nude, open, show, thin, void, worn 5 basic, blank, empty, naked, offer, plain, scant, stark, strip 6 denude, divest, expose, meager, peeled, reveal, simple, unclad, unmask, unveil, vacant 7 austere, exposed, hapless, uncover, undrape, undress, unrobed 8 disrobed, in the raw, marginal, stripped 9 endurable, essential, unadorned, unclothed, uncolored, uncovered, undressed, unsheathe 10 elementary, just enough, threadbare 11 fundamental, supportable, undecorated, undisguised, unvarnished 12 unelaborated, unornamented 13 unembellished 15 straightforward

barefaced 4 bald, bold, flip 5 brash, fresh, sassy 6 brazen, cheeky, snotty 7 forward 8 flippant, impudent, insolent, palpable 9 shameless, unabashed 11 transparent

barefoot 6 unshod 8 shoeless 9 discalced 10 unsandaled 11 discalceate

Barefoot Boy
  author: 21 John Greenleaf Whittier

Barefoot in the Park
  director: 8 Gene Saks
  based on play by: 9 Neil Simon
  cast: 9 Jane Fonda 12 Charles Boyer 13 Robert Redford

barely 4 just 6 almost, hardly 7 faintly, scantly 8 meagerly, only just, scarcely, slightly 9 almost not, just about, sparingly 10 no more than 20 by the skin of one's teeth

bareness 6 nudity 9 bleakness, emptiness, nakedness 10 barrenness

Baresark
  origin: 12 Scandinavian
  form: 7 warrior
  trait: 7 courage

Baretta
  character: 7 Rooster 11 Billy Truman, (Det) Tony Baretta, (Lt) Hal Brubaker
  cast: 8 Tom Ewell 11 Robert Blake 12 Edward Grover 15 Michael D Roberts
  Tony's pet: 8 cockatoo
  named: 4 Fred

barfly 3 sot 4 lush, soak 5 drunk, rummy, souse, toper 7 tippler 8 drunkard 9 alcoholic 11 dipsomaniac

bargain 4 deal, pact 5 steal 6 accord, barter, dicker, haggle, higgle, pledge, treaty 7 compact, entente, good buy, promise 8 contract, covenant, good deal 9 agreement, negotiate 10 settlement 11 arrangement, transaction 13 understanding
  French: 9 bon marche

bargain for 6 expect 7 foresee 8 envision, reckon on 11 contemplate

barge 4 bust, scow, ship 6 launch, vessel 7 freight, intrude

barium
  chemical symbol: 2 Ba

bark 3 bay, cry, rub, yap, yip 4 flay, hide, howl, hull, husk, peel, rind, roar, skin, woof, yell, yelp 5 crust, scale, shout, strip 6 abrade, arf-arf, bellow, bow-wow, casing, cry out, holler, scrape 7 howling 8 covering, periderm 9 sheathing

Barker, Lex
  real name: 25 Alexander Crichlow Barker Jr
  wife: 10 Arlene Dahl, Lana Turner
  born: 5 Rye NY
  roles: 6 Tarzan 11 La Dolce Vita

Barkis
  character in: 16 David Copperfield
  author: 7 Dickens

Barkley, Catherine
  character in: 15 A Farewell to Arms
  author: 9 Hemingway

Barlach, Ernst
  born: 5 Wedel 7 Germany 8 Holstein
  artwork: 9 Expellees 10 Seated Girl, Singing Man 11 Man in a Stock 13 Mater Dolorosa 14 Crippled Beggar, The Hovering One 16 Man Drawing a Sword 25 The Community of the Holy Ones

barn 4 mews **6** corral, stable

Barnabas
  companion: 4 Paul

Barnaby Jones
  character: 7 J R (Jedediah Romano)
  Jones **8** Lt Biddle **10** Betty Jones
  cast: 9 Mark Shera **10** Buddy Ebsen,
  John Carter **13** Lee Meriwether

Barnaby Rudge
  author: 14 Charles Dickens
  character: 8 Mrs Rudge **9** Miss Miggs **10**
  John Willet **11** Dolly Varden **12** Emma
  Haredale **13** Edward Chester, Gabriel
  Varden **14** Reuben Haredale, Simon
  Tappertit, Sir John Chester **16** Dennis the
  Hangman, Geoffrey Haredale
  subject: 11 Gordon riots

Barnard, Christiaan
  field: 7 surgery **8** medicine
  nationality: 12 South African
  performed first: 15 heart transplant

Barnard, Edward Emerson
  field: 9 astronomy
  named for him: 12 red dwarf star

Barnes, Jake
  character in: 15 The Sun Also Rises
  author: 9 Hemingway

Barney Google
  creator: 11 Billy DeBeck
  character: 11 Snuffy Smith
  baby: **5** Bunky
  horse: **3** Spark Plug

Barney Miller
  character: 8 (Det) Phil Fish **9** (Det) Ron
  Harris **10** (Det Wojo) Wojohowicz, (Det)
  Nick Yamana, (Officer) Carl Levitt **14** Inspector Luger, (Det) Arthur Dietrich
  cast: 7 Jack Soo **8** Ron Carey, Ron
  Glass **9** Abe Vigoda, Hal Linden **11** Maxwell Gail **12** James Gregory **15** Steve
  Landesberg

Barnstock *see* **9** Branstock

Baroja y Nessi, Pio
  author of: 15 Caesar or Nothing **23** The
  Struggle for Existence **26** Memorias de
  un Hombre de Accion

barometer
  invented by: 10 Torricelli

baroque 6 florid, ornate **10** flamboyant **11**
extravagant

Barrack-Room Ballads
  author: 14 Rudyard Kipling

barracks 3 BOQ **4** base, camp **7** lodging **8**
garrison

barrage 5 blast, burst, salvo, spray **6** ack-
ack, deluge, shower, stream, volley **7** battery, torrent **8** shelling **9** cannonade, fusillade **10** outpouring **11** bombardment

barrel 3 keg, tub, tun, vat **4** butt, cask,
drum, tube **8** hogshead
  abbreviation: 3 bbl

barren 3 dry **4** arid, dull **5** stale, waste **6**
farrow, futile **7** austere, prosaic, sterile,
useless **8** depleted, desolate, infecund **9**
fruitless, infertile **10** lackluster, unfruitful **11**
ineffectual, uninspiring, unrewarding **12**

unproductive **13** uninformative, uninstructive, uninteresting

barrenness 8 bareness **9** bleakness, emptiness **10** desolation

barren wilderness 6 desert **9** wasteland

barricade 5 block, fence **7** barrier, bulwark,
rampart **8** blockade, obstacle, obstruct **10**
impediment **11** obstruction

Barrie, Sir James M
  author of: 7 The Will **8** Mary Rose, Peter
  Pan **10** Dear Brutus **13** Quality Street **15**
  Margaret Ogilvie, The Wedding Guest **17**
  Alice Sit-By-the-Fire, The Little Minister
  18 A Kiss for Cinderella, The Twelve-
  Pound Look **19** What Every Woman
  Knows **20** Shall We Join the Ladies?,
  The Admirable Crichton
  character: 8 Peter Pan **10** Tinkerbell **11**
  Captain Hook
  Darling children: **4** John **5** Wendy **7** Mi-
  chael
  nurse/Newfoundland dog: **4** Nana
  setting: **14** Never-Never Land

barrier 3 bar **4** moat, wall **5** ditch, fence,
hedge **6** hurdle, trench **7** rampart **8** blockade, handicap, obstacle **9** barricade, hindrance **10** difficulty, impediment, limitation
11 obstruction, restriction **13** fortification
14 stumbling block

Barrier, The
  author: 8 Rex Beach

barring 3 but **4** save **6** except, saving **7** besides **9** excepting, excluding, other than **11**
exclusive of

barrister 6 lawyer **7** counsel **8** advocate,
attorney **9** counselor **10** mouthpiece **13**
attorney-at-law

barroom 3 bar, pub, **6** bistro, lounge, saloon, tavern **7** taproom

barrow 4 heap, pile **5** mound **7** tumulus **8**
handcart, pushcart **11** wheelbarrow

Barrow, Joe Louis
  real name of: 8 Joe Louis

Barry, Gene
  real name: 11 Eugene Klass
  born: 9 New York NY
  roles: 9 Burke's Law **11** Thunder Road
  12 Bat Masterson **16** The Name of the
  Game **17** The War of the Worlds

Barry, John
  served in: 16 Revolutionary War
  commander of ship: 7 Raleigh **8** Alliance **9** Effingham, Lexington
  ship captured: 6 Edward

Barry, Redmond
  character in: 11 Barry Lyndon
  author: 9 Thackeray

Barry, Sir Charles
  architect of: 8 Cliveden **14** City Art Gallery (Manchester) **18** Houses of Parliament (London)

Barry Lyndon
  author: 25 William Makepeace Thackeray
  character: 12 Redmond Barry **14** Lord
  Bullingdon **17** Lady Honoria Lyndon

(Countess of Lyndon) 19 Chevalier de
Balibari
  director: 14 Stanley Kubrick
  cast: 9 Ryan O'Neal 11 Hardy Kruger 12
  Patrick Magee 14 Marisa Berenson
Barrymore, Ethel
  real name: 14 Ethel Mae Blythe
  brother: 4 John 6 Lionel
  born: 14 Philadelphia PA
  roles: 11 A Doll's House 14 The Corn Is
  Green 16 Portrait of Jennie 19 Trelawney
  of the Wells 21 None But the Lonely
  Heart, Rasputin and the Empress
Barrymore, John
  real name: 10 John Blythe
  brother: 6 Lionel
  sister: 5 Ethel
  son: 17 John Drew Barrymore
  daughter: 14 Diana Barrymore
  nickname: 12 Great Profile
  born: 14 Philadelphia PA
  roles: 6 Hamlet 7 Don Juan 8 Moby Dick,
  Svengali 9 Richard IV 10 Grand Hotel 11
  Beau Brummel 13 Dinner at Eight 17 Dr
  Jekyll and Mr Hyde 21 Rasputin and the
  Empress
Barrymore, Lionel
  real name: 12 Lionel Blythe
  brother: 4 John
  sister: 5 Ethel
  born: 14 Philadelphia PA
  roles: 7 The Jest 9 A Free Soul (Oscar),
  Dr Kildare 11 Dr Gillespie 13 Peter Ib-
  bitson, The Copperhead 21 Rasputin and
  the Empress
Barsabbas see 6 Joseph
Barstad, John
  character in: 16 A Tale of Two Cities
  author: 7 Dickens
Bart, Lily
  character in: 15 The House of Mirth
  author: 7 Wharton
barter 4 swap 5 trade 8 exchange 11 interchange
Bartered Bride, The
  opera by: 7 Smetana
  character: 5 Jenik, Kecal, Micha, Vasek
  7 Marenka
Barth, John
  author of: 7 Chimera 12 Giles Goat-Boy
  15 The End of the Road 16 The Floating
  Opera, The Sot-Weed Factor 17 Lost in
  the Funhouse
Barthelme, Donald
  author of: 7 Sadness 8 City Life 9 Great
  Days, Snow White 12 Sixty Stories 13
  The Dead Father 15 Guilty Pleasures 18
  Come Back Dr Caligari 33 Unspeakable
  Practices Unnatural Acts
Bartholdi, Frederic-Auguste
  born: 6 Alsace, Colmar
  artwork: 13 Lion of Belfort 26 Liberty Enlightening the World (Statue of Liberty)
Bartholo, Dr
  character in: 18 The Barber of Seville 19
  The Marriage of Figaro
  author: 12 Beaumarchais

Bartholomew 7 apostle
  also called: 9 Nathanael
Bartholomew Fair
  author: 9 Ben Jonson
Bartok, Bela
  born: 7 Hungary 15 Nagyszentmiklos
  composer of: 9 Wrestling 11 Mikro-
  kosmos 12 Divertimento 14 Cantata
  Profana 15 The Wooden Prince 20 Duke
  Bluebeard's Castle 21 The Miraculous
  Mandarin
Bartolommeo, Fra
  born: 5 Italy 8 Florence
  real name: 31 Bartolommeo di Pagolo
  del Fattorino
  artwork: 5 Jonah 6 Isaiah 13 Salvator
  Mundi 15 The Last Judgment 17 Vision of
  St Bernard 24 Madonna della Misericordia 30 The Mystic Marriage of St Catherine
Barton, Benjamin Smith
  field: 6 botany
  noted for first American: 14 botany
  textbook
Bartram, John
  field: 6 botany
  noted for first American: 12 hybrid
  plants
Baruch
  father: 5 Judah 6 Neriah
  friend and scribe of: 8 Jeremiah
basal 3 key 4 easy 5 basic, vital 6 simple 7
  initial, minimal, primary 8 cardinal 9 beginning, essential, intrinsic, necessary 10 elementary, lower-level, simplified 11 fundamental, rudimentary 12 prerequisite 13
  indispensable
bas bleu 12 bluestocking
base 3 bad, bed, key, low 4 camp, core,
  foul, mean, post, root, vile 5 basis, dirty,
  gross, heart, petty, place, stand 6 abject,
  billet, bottom, craven, ground, impure, locate, scurvy, sinful, sneaky, sordid, source,
  vulgar, wicked 7 alloyed, corrupt, debased,
  essence, found on, ignoble, immoral, install, model on, scrubby, situate, station,
  support 8 backbone, cowardly, degraded,
  depraved, garrison, infamous, inferior,
  pedestal, rudiment, shameful, spurious,
  unworthy 9 dastardly, dissolute, establish,
  faithless, insidious, nefarious, principle 10
  degenerate, derive from, despicable, detestable, evil-minded, foundation, groundwork, iniquitous, villainous 11 adulterated,
  disgraceful, ignominious, poor quality,
  scoundrelly 12 black-hearted, contemptible, dishonorable, disreputable, installation, substructure, underpinning, unprincipled 13 discreditable, reprehensible
baseball
  term: 3 bag, ERA, fan, RBI, run 4 balk,
  base, bunt, bush 5 choke, curve, error,
  fungo, liner, pop-up, slide 6 assist, batter, cellar, double, dugout, duster, inning,
  on deck, relief (pitcher), rookie, single,
  slider, triple, umpire, windup 7 blooper,
  bullpen, catcher, cleanup, fly ball, home

run, infield, pickoff, pitcher, rhubarb, run-down, shutout, slugger 8 bean ball, changeup, grounder, keystone, no hitter, outfield, pitchout, southpaw, spitball 9 bleachers, brushback, grand slam, hot corner, infielder, line drive, sacrifice, shortstop 10 bush league, gopher ball, infield fly, outfielder, passed ball 11 bases loaded, knuckleball, pinch hitter, triple crown, World Series 12 Texas leaguer 16 designated hitter, earned run average

Hall of Fame:

1936: 4 Cobb (Ty), Ruth (Babe) 6 Wagner (Honus) 7 Johnson (Walter) 9 Mathewson (Christy)

1937: 4 Mack (Connie) 5 Young (Cy) 6 Lajoie (Nap), McGraw (John), Wright (George) 7 Johnson (Ban), Speaker (Tris) 8 Bulkeley (Morgan)

1938: 8 Chadwick (Henry) 9 Alexander (Grover) 10 Cartwright (Alexander)

1939: 5 Anson (Cap), Ewing (Buck) 6 Gehrig (Lou), Keeler (Willie), Sisler (George) 7 Collins (Eddie) 8 Comiskey (Charlie), Cummings (Candy), Spalding (Albert) 9 Radbourne (Old Hoss)

1942: 7 Hornsby (Rogers)

1944: 7 Kenesaw (M. Landis)

1945: 5 Duffy (Hugh), Kelly (King) 6 Clarke (Fred) 7 Collins (Jimmy), O'Rourke (Jim) 8 Jennings (Hughey), Robinson (Wilbert) 9 Bresnahan (Roger), Brouthers (Dan), Delahanty (Ed)

1946: 5 Evers (Johnny), Plank (Eddie), Walsh (Ed) 6 Chance (Frank), Tinker (Joe) 7 Burkett (Jesse), Chesbro (Jack), Waddell (Rube) 8 Griffith (Clark), McCarthy (Tommy) 9 McGinnity (Joe)

1947: 5 Grove (Lefty) 6 Frisch (Frankie) 7 Hubbell (Carl) 8 Cochrane (Mickey)

1948: 7 Pennock (Herb), Traynor (Pie)

1949: 5 Brown (Mordecai) 7 Nichols (Kid) 9 Gehringer (Charlie)

1951: 3 Ott (Mel) 4 Foxx (Jimmie)

1952: 5 Waner (Paul) 8 Heilmann (Harry)

1953: 4 Dean (Dizzy), Klem (Bill) 6 Barrow (Ed), Bender (Chief), Wright (Harry) 7 Simmons (Al), Wallace (Bobby) 8 Connolly (Tom)

1954: 5 Terry (Bill) 6 Dickey (Bill)

1955: 5 Baker (Frank), Lyons (Ted), Vance (Dazzy) 6 Schalk (Ray) 8 DiMaggio (Joe), Hartnett (Gabby) 10 Maranville (Rabbit)

1956: 6 Cronin (Joe) 9 Greenberg (Hank)

1957: 8 Crawford (Sam), McCarthy (Joe)

1959: 8 Wheat (Zach)

1961: 5 Carey (Max) 8 Hamilton (Billy)

1962: 5 Roush (Edd) 6 Feller (Bob) 8 Robinson (Jackie) 9 McKechnie (Bill)

1963: 4 Rice (Sam), Eppa (Rixey) 5 Flick (Elmer) 8 Clarkson (John)

1964: 4 Ward (Monte) 5 Faber (Red), Keefe (Tim) 6 Grimes (Burleigh), Manush (Heinie) 7 Appling (Luke), Huggins (Miller)

1965: 6 Galvin (Pud)

1966: 7 Stengel (Casey) 8 Williams (Ted)

1967: 5 Waner (Lloyd) 6 Rickey (Branch) 7 Ruffing (Red)

1968: 6 Cuyler (Kiki), Goslin (Goose) 7 Medwick (Joe)

1969: 4 Hoyt (Waite) 6 Musial (Stan) 9 Coveleski (Stan) 10 Campanella (Roy)

1970: 5 Combs (Earle), Frick (Ford) 6 Haines (Jesse) 8 Boudreau (Lou)

1971: 5 Paige (Satchel), Hafey (Chick), Weiss (George) 6 Hooper (Harry), Kelley (Joe) 7 Beckley (Jake) 8 Bancroft (Dave), Marquard (Rube)

1972: 4 Wynn (Early) 5 Berra (Yogi), Gomez (Lefty) 6 Gibson (Josh), Koufax (Sandy), Youngs (Ross) 7 Leonard (Buck) 8 Harridge (Will)

1973: 5 Evans (Billy), Irvin (Monte), Kelly (George), Spahn (Warren), Welch (Mickey) 8 Clemente (Roberto)

1974: 4 Bell (Cool Papa), Ford (Whitey) 6 Conlan (Jocko), Mantle (Mickey) 8 Thompson (Sam) 9 Bottomley (Jim)

1975 5 Kiner (Ralph) 6 Harris (Bucky), Herman (Billy) 7 Averill (Earl), Johnson (Judy)

1976: 5 Lemon (Bob) 6 Connor (Roger) 7 Hubbard (Cal), Roberts (Robin) 9 Lindstrom (Fred) 10 Charleston (Oscar)

1977: 5 Banks (Ernie), Lloyd (Pop), Lopez (Al), Rusie (Amos) 6 Dihigo (Martin), Sewell (Joe)

1978: 4 Joss (Addie) 7 Mathews (Eddie) 8 MacPhail (Larry)

1979: 4 Mays (Willie) 5 Giles (Warren) 6 Wilson (Hack)

1980: 5 Klein (Chuck) 6 Kaline (Al), Snider (Duke), Yawkey (Tom)

1981: 4 Mize (Johnny), Foster (Rube), Gibson (Bob)

1982: 5 Aaron (Hank) 7 Jackson (Travis) 8 Chandler (Happy), Robinson (Frank)

1983: 4 Kell (George) 6 Alston (Walter) 8 Marichal (Juan), Robinson (Brooks)

1984: 5 Reese (Pee Wee) 7 Ferrell (Rick) 8 Aparicio (Luis), Drysdale (Don) 9 Killebrew (Harmon)

1985: 5 Brock (Lou) 7 Vaughan (Arky), Wilhelm (Hoyt) 9 Slaughter (Enos)

1986: 5 Doerr (Bobby) 7 McCovey (Willie) 8 Lombardi (Ernie)

1987: 6 Hunter (Jim "Catfish") 8 Williams (Billy) 9 Dandridge (Ray)

1988: 8 Stargell (Willie)

1989: 6 Bench (Johnny) 7 Barlick (Al) 11 Yastrzemski (Carl) 12 Schoendienst (Red)

1990: 6 Morgan (Joe), Palmer (Jim)

1991: 5 Carew (Rod), Perry (Gaylord), Veeck (Bill) 7 Jenkins (Ferguson), Lazzeri (Tony)

1992: 5 Seaver (Tom) 7 Fingers (Rollie), McGowan (Bill) 9 Newhouser (Hal)

1993: 7 Jackson (Reggie)

1994: 7 Carlton (Steve), Rizzuto (Phil "Scooter") 8 Durocher (Leo)

other player/coach: 7 Jim Rice 8 Pete

Rose, Vida Blue 9 Alvin Dark, Bowie Kuhn, Gil Hodges, Hank Bauer, Luis Tiant, Nellie Fox, Nolan Ryan, Ralph Houk, Ron Guidry, Ted Turner, Tommy John 10 Boog Powell, Earl Weaver, Maury Wills, Roger Maris, Sparky Lyle 11 Billy Martin, Dave Kingman, Frank Thomas, George Brett, Mark Fidrych, Mike Schmidt, Rich Gossage 12 Graig Nettles, Dave Winfield, Dennis McLain, Dick Williams, Elston Howard, Ken Griffey Jr, Tommy Lasorda 13 Rocky Colavito, Thurman Munson, Walter O'Malley 14 Keith Hernandez, Peter Ueberroth, Sparky Anderson 15 Rickey Henderson 16 Darryl Strawberry 18 Fernando Valenzuela, George Steinbrenner

baseball leagues
   National: 11 Chicago Cubs, New York Mets 13 Atlanta Braves, Houston Astros, Montreal Expos 14 Cincinnati Reds, San Diego Padres 16 St Louis Cardinals 17 Los Angeles Dodgers, Pittsburgh Pirates 18 San Francisco Giants 20 Philadelphia Phillies
   American: 9 Oakland A's 12 Boston Red Sox, Texas Rangers 13 Detroit Tigers 14 Minnesota Twins, New York Yankees 15 Chicago White Sox, Seattle Mariners, Toronto Blue Jays 16 Baltimore Orioles, California Angels, Cleveland Indians, Kansas City Royals, Milwaukee Brewers

baseball team
   Atlanta: 6 Braves
   stadium: 7 Atlanta–Fulton County
   Baltimore: 7 Orioles
   stadium: 11 Camden Yards
   Boston: 6 Red Sox
   stadium: 10 Fenway Park
   California: 6 Angels
   stadium: 7 Anaheim
   Chicago: 4 Cubs
   stadium: 12 Wrigley Field
   Chicago: 8 White Sox
   stadium: 12 Comiskey Park
   Cleveland: 7 Indians
   stadium: 11 Jacobs Field
   Cincinnati: 4 Reds
   stadium: 10 Riverfront
   Colorado: 7 Rockies
   stadium: 10 Coors Field
   Detroit: 6 Tigers
   stadium: 5 Tiger
   Florida: 7 Marlins
   stadium: 9 Joe Robbie
   Houston: 6 Astros
   stadium: 9 Astrodome
   Kansas City: 6 Royals
   stadium: 8 Kauffman
   Los Angeles: 7 Dodgers
   stadium: 6 Dodger 18 Los Angeles Coliseum
   Milwaukee: 7 Brewers
   stadium: 6 County
   Minnesota: 5 Twins

stadium: 12 Metropolitan 24 Hubert H Humphrey Metrodome
   Montreal: 5 Expos
   stadium: 7 Olympic
   New York: 4 Mets
   stadium: 4 Shea
   New York: 7 Yankees
   stadium: 6 Yankee
   Oakland: 2 A's
   stadium: 7 Oakland
   Philadelphia: 8 Phillies
   stadium: 8 Veterans
   Pittsburgh: 7 Pirates
   stadium: 11 Three Rivers
   St Louis: 9 Cardinals
   stadium: 13 Busch Memorial
   San Diego: 6 Padres
   stadium: 10 Jack Murphy
   San Francisco: 6 Giants
   stadium: 15 Candlestick Park
   Seattle: 8 Mariners
   stadium: 8 Kingdome
   Texas: 7 Rangers
   stadium: 11 The Ballpark
   Toronto: 8 Blue Jays
   stadium: 7 SkyDome

baseless 7 unsound 9 unfactual, unfounded 10 groundless, ungrounded 11 unjustified, unsupported 12 without basis 13 unjustifiable 14 uncorroborated 15 unsubstantiated

basement 5 below 6 bottom, cellar 15 underground room

baseness 7 lowness 8 meanness, vileness 9 depravity 11 ignobleness 14 iniquitousness 16 contemptibleness

base of operations
   Greek: 6 pou sto

bash 4 blow 5 blast, clout, crack, knock, party, whack 7 clopper 8 wingding 9 bacchanal

Bashemath *see* 4 Adah

bashful 3 shy 5 timid 6 demure, modest 8 blushing, reserved, reticent, retiring, sheepish, skittish, timorous 9 diffident, shrinking, uncertain 10 shamefaced 11 constrained, unconfident

bashfulness 7 shyness 10 diffidence 12 sheepishness 14 self-effacement 15 unassertiveness

basic 3 key 4 base, core 5 prime, vital 7 bedrock, primary 8 rudiment 9 essential, intrinsic 10 elementary, foundation 11 fundamental, rudimentary 12 foundational, prerequisite, underpinning

basically
   French: 6 au fond

basic ideas 6 basics 7 essence, factors, origins 8 elements, features 9 rudiments 10 principles 11 foundations

basic need 9 essential, necessity, requisite, vital part 10 key element, sine qua non

basic part 4 unit 7 element 9 component 10 ingredient 11 constituent 13 building block

basic quality 6 nature 7 essence 9 principle, substance 12 quintessence

basics 8 elements 9 rudiments 10 principles 11 nitty-gritty 12 fundamentals

basil
  also called: 6 tulasi
  botanical name: 6 Ocimum 8 O minimum 10 O basilicum
  means: 5 royal 6 kingly, lizard (basilisk)
  nickname: 14 kiss-me-Nicholas
  origin: 5 India
  sacred to: 6 Vishnu 7 Krishna, Lakshmi
  symbol of: 4 hate, love
  use: 10 vegetables

basilica 6 church 10 house of God 14 house of worship

Basilisk
  form: 6 dragon

basin 3 pan, tub, vat 4 bowl, dale, dell, font, glen, sink 5 gulch, gully, stoup 6 crater, hollow, lavabo, ravine, tureen, valley 7 dishpan, washtub 8 lavatory, sinkhole, washbowl 9 porringer, washbasin, washstand 10 depression, finger bowl

basis, bases 4 base, root 6 ground 7 bedrock 9 essential, principle 10 foundation, touchstone 11 cornerstone, fundamental 12 underpinning 13 starting point

bask 5 revel, savor 6 relish, wallow 7 delight 8 sunbathe 9 luxuriate 11 warm oneself 12 soak up warmth, toast oneself

basket 5 crate 6 barrel, hamper 7 carrier, pannier 8 bassinet, canister

basketball
  term: 3 key 4 dunk, hoop, pick, post, trap, zone 5 court, guard, lay-up, pivot, point, press, steal 6 assist, basket, center 7 dribble, forward, palming, rebound, referee 8 charging, hook shot, jump shot, sixth man, turnover 9 backboard, backcourt, fast break, field goal, free throw, give-and-go, traveling 11 goal tending, pick-and-roll 12 three-pointer

Hall of Fame:
  1959: 5 Allen (Phog; Forrest Clare), Hyatt (Charles), Mikan (George), Olsen (Harold), Stagg (Amos Alonzo), Tower (Oswald) 6 Gulick (Luther), Hickox (Edward), Morgan (Ralph) 7 Carlson (Henry), Kennedy (Matthew) 8 Luisetti (Hank), Meanwell (Walter E), Naismith (James), Schommer (John) 15 Original Celtics
  1960: 5 Blood (Ernest) 6 Hanson (Victor), Keaney (Frank), Murphy (Charles), Porter (Henry), Wooden (John) 7 Hepbron (George), Lambert (Ward) 8 Macauley (Ed) 9 McCracken (Branch)
  1961: 4 Hoyt (George) 5 Sachs (Leonard), Tobey (David), Walsh (David) 6 Keogan (George), O'Brien (John), Roosma (John) 7 Kurland (Bob), Phillip (Andy), Quigley (Ernest), Trester (Arthur), Wachter (Edward) 8 Borgmann (Bernhard) 9 Steinmetz (Christian) 10 DeBernardi (Forrest), Schabinger (Arthur) 14 Buffalo Germans
  1962: 4 Page (Harlan) 6 Sedran (Barney), St John (Lynn) 8 Thompson (John)

9 McCracken (Jack) 10 Morgenweck (Frank)
  1963: 4 Reid (William) 7 Gruenig (Robert) 11 New York Rens
  1964: 4 Bunn (John) 5 Irish (Ned), Jones (R William) 6 Foster (Harold), Holman (Nat) 7 Russell (John) 8 Loeffler (Kenneth)
  1965: 5 Brown (Walter) 6 Hinkle (Paul), Hobson (Howard), Mokray (William)
  1966: 4 Dean (Everett) 8 Lapchick (Joe)
  1967: 3 Bee (Clair) 4 Cann (Howard), Gill (Amory) 6 Julian (Alvin)
  1968: 3 Iba (Hank; Henry P) 4 Rupp (Adolph F) 6 Taylor (Charles H) 7 Denhart (Henry G) 8 Auerbach (Red; Arnold J)
  1969: 6 Davies (Bob) 9 Carnevale (Bernard L)
  1970: 5 Cousy (Bob) 6 Pettit (Bob) 10 Saperstein (Abe)
  1971: 5 Wells (W R Clifford) 6 Diddle (Edgar A) 7 Douglas (Robert L) 8 Endacott (Paul), Friedman (Max), Gottlieb (Edward)
  1972: 5 Drake (Bruce) 6 Ripley (Elmer H), Wooden (John) 7 Beckman (John), Lonborg (Arthur C), Schayes (Dolph)
  1973: 6 Fisher (Harry A) 7 Schmidt (Ernest) 8 Podoloff (Maurice)
  1974: 6 Liston (Emil) 7 Brennan (Joseph), Russell (Bill) 9 Vandivier (Robert)
  1975 4 Gola (Tom) 6 Krause (Edward W) 7 Litwack (Harry), Sharman (Bill)
  1976: 4 Gale (Lauren) 6 Baylor (Elgin), Cooper (Charles T) 7 Johnson (Wiliam C), McGuire (Frank)
  1977: 5 Fulks (Joe), Hagan (Cliff) 6 Arizin (Paul) 7 Pollard (Jim) 8 Nucatola (John P)
  1978: 5 Barry (Sam; Justin M), Meyer (Raymond J) 6 Hickey (Edgar S), Newell (Peter F) 7 Enright (James E) 8 McLendon (John B) 11 Chamberlain (Wilt)
  1979: 4 West (Jerry) 5 Lucas (Jerry) 7 Shelton (Everett), Shirley (J Dallas) 8 Harrison (Lester) 9 Robertson (Oscar)
  1980: 4 Hepp (Ferenc) 6 Barlow (Thomas B) 7 Kennedy (J Walter) 9 McCutchan (Arad A)
  1981: 4 Case (Everett N), Duer (Alva O), Reed (Willis) 5 Greer (Hal) 6 Gaines (Clarence E), Martin (Slater), Ramsey (Frank)
  1982: 5 Leith (Lloyd R), Smith (Dean E), Wilke (Louis G) 6 Twyman (Jack) 7 Bradley (Bill) 11 DeBusschere (Dave)
  1983: 5 Fagan (Clifford B), Jones (Sam) 6 Steitz (Edward S) 7 Gardner (Jack) 8 Havlicek (John)
  1984: 4 Wade (L Margaret) 5 Cervi (Al) 6 Abbott (Senda Berenson), Teague (Bertha F) 8 Anderson (W Harold), Harshman (Marv K), Thurmond (Nate)
  1985–1986: 5 Watts (Stanley H) 6 Taylor (Fred R) 7 Holzman (Red), Mihalik (Red)

8 Heinsohn (Tom) 10 Cunningham (Billy)
1986–1987: 5 Barry (Rick) 6 Wanzer
(Bobby) 7 Frazier (Walt) 8 Houbregs
(Robert J), Maravich (Pete)
1987–1988: 6 Miller (Ralph H), Unseld
(Wes) 9 McDermott (Robert), Lovelette
(Clyde)
1988–1989: 5 Gates (William "Pop"),
Jones (K C) 7 Wilkens (Lenny)
1989–1990 4 Bing (Dave) 5 Hayes (Elvin)
6 Monroe (Earl) 8 Johnston (Neil)
1990–1991: 6 Cowens (Dave), Knight
(Bobby), O'Brien (Lawrence F) 8 Fleisher
(Lawrence), Gallatin (Harry) 9 Archibald
(Nate), Stankovic (Borislav)
1991–1992: 5 Belov (Sergei), White
(Nera) 6 Lanier (Bob), Ramsay (Jack) 7
Hawkins (Connie), McGuire (Al) 8
Woolpert (Phillip) 10 Carnesecca (Louie)
13 Harris-Stewart (Lusia)
1992–1993: 5 Issel (Dan) 6 Erving (Ju-
lius), Meyers (Ann), Murphy (Calvin),
Walton (Bill) 7 Bellamy (Walter), McGuire
(Dick) 9 Semjonova (Uljana)
1994: 4 Crum (Denny), Daly (Charles J)
6 Rubini (Cesare) 9 Jeannette (Buddy) 11
Blazejowski (Carol)
other player/coach: 8 Pat Riley 9 Bob
McAdoo, Larry Bird 10 Danny Ainge 11
Alex English, Bernard King, Bill Lambeer,
Dick Barnett, James Worthy, Kevin
McHale, Lew Alcindor, Moses Malone 12
George Gervin, Isaiah Thomas, Larry
Johnson, Patrick Ewing, Robert Parish 13
David Robinson, Earvin (Magic) Johnson,
Michael Jordan, Scottie Pippen, Terry
Cummings 14 Charles Barkley, Hakeem
Olajuwon, Shaquille O'Neal 17 Kareem
Abdul-Jabbar
basketball team
league: 3 NBA 29 National Basketball
Association
Atlanta: 5 Hawks
Boston: 7 Celtics
Charlotte: 7 Hornets
Chicago: 5 Bulls
Cleveland: 9 Cavaliers
Dallas: 9 Mavericks
Denver: 7 Nuggets
Detroit: 7 Pistons
Golden State: 8 Warriors
Houston: 7 Rockets
Indiana: 6 Pacers
Los Angeles: 6 Lakers 8 Clippers
Miami: 4 Heat
Milwaukee: 5 Bucks
Minnesota: 12 Timberwolves
New Jersey: 4 Nets
New York: 14 Knickerbockers
Orlando: 5 Magic
Philadelphia: 8 76ers 13 Seventy-Sixers
Phoenix: 4 Suns
Portland: 12 Trail Blazers
Sacramento: 5 Kings
San Antonio: 5 Spurs
Seattle: 11 SuperSonics

Utah: 4 Jazz
Washington: 7 Bullets
Basque
language spoken in: 5 Italy, Spain 6
France
bas-relief
Italian: 12 basso-rilievo
bass 3 low 4 alto 5 basso 7 harmony 8 baritone, bass clef
bass
types: 3 sea 4 rock 5 black 6 calico 7
striped, sunfish
characteristic: 10 forked-tail 12 spiny-
finned
Bassanio
character in: 19 The Merchant of Venice
author: 11 Shakespeare
basso-rilievo 9 bas-relief
Bast, Jacky and Leonard
characters in: 10 Howard's End
author: 9 E M Forster
bastard 6 impure 8 inferior, spurious 9 imperfect, irregular, love child 12 natural
child 17 illegitimate child
bastardize 6 debase, weaken 7 degrade 9
downgrade
baste 3 sew 4 drip 5 roast 6 cudgel, flavor,
stitch, thrash 15 temporary stitch
bastinado 4 beat, blow, cane, drub 5 whale
7 beating 8 drubbing
bastion 4 fort 5 tower 6 pillar 7 bulwark, citadel, rampart 8 barbette, fortress 10
breastwork, stronghold
bat 3 hit, rod 4 cane, clip, club, cuff, mace,
slug, sock 5 baton, billy, knock, smack,
staff, stick, whack 6 buffet, cudgel, mallet,
strike, thwack, wallop 7 clobber 8 bludgeon 9 blackjack, truncheon 10 shillelagh
batch 3 lot 5 bunch, crowd, group, stock 6
amount, number 8 quantity 9 aggregate 10
collection
Bates, Alan
born: 7 England 9 Allestree 10 Derbyshire
roles: 8 The Fixer 10 Georgy Girl 12
King of Hearts 13 Zorba the Greek 16 An
Unmarried Woman 22 Far From the Madding Crowd
Bates, Miss
character in: 4 Emma
author: 6 Austen
Bateson, William
field: 7 biology
nationality: 7 British
founded: 8 genetics
bath 3 dip, tub 4 wash 5 sauna 6 douche,
shower 7 washing 8 ablution, lavement 9
cleansing, immersion, steam bath 10 irri-
gation
type: 2 hip 4 sitz 5 steam 6 shower,
sponge 7 Turkish bath
bathe 3 dip, tub, wet 4 lave, soak, wash 5
douse 6 douche, shower, sponge 7
cleanse 8 irrigate
bathing 3 dip, tub 6 laving, plunge 7 washing 8 swimming 9 ablutions, immersion

bathos 4 corn, mush **5** slush **8** schmaltz **9** mushiness, soppiness **10** maudlinism, slushiness **11** false pathos, mawkishness **14** sentimentalism, sentimentality

bathroom 2 W C **3** can, loo **4** head, john **5** biffy **6** toilet **7** commode, latrine **8** facility, lavatory, men's room, restroom, washroom **10** ladies' room, powder room **11** water closet **14** little boys' room **15** little girls' room

Bathsheba
  also: 8 Bathshua
  father: 5 Eliam
  husband: 5 David, Uriah
  son: 7 Solomon
  grandfather: 10 Ahithophel

Bathshua see **9** Bathsheba

Bathurst
  see: Banjul

Batia
  form: 5 nymph
  father: 6 Teucer
  husband: 8 Dardanus
  son: 12 Erichthonius

Batman
  character: 6 Alfred **7** Egghead, King Tut **8** Catwoman, The Joker **10** Bruce Wayne (Batman), Chief O'Hara, The Penguin, The Riddler **11** Dick Grayson (Robin) **13** Barbara Gordon (Batgirl) **17** Aunt Harriet Cooper **24** Police Commissioner Gordon
  cast: 8 Adam West, Burt Ward **9** John Astin **10** Alan Napier, Eartha Kitt, Madge Blake **11** Cesar Romero, Julie Newmar, Victor Buono, Yvonne Craig **12** Frank Gorshin, Neil Hamilton, Stafford Repp, Vincent Price **13** Lee Meriwether **15** Burgess Meredith
  city: 10 Gotham City
  nickname: 9 Boy Wonder **10** Dynamic Duo **13** Caped Crusader
  gimmick: 6 Batlab **8** Batphone **9** Batmobile, Batsignal

Bat Masterson
  cast: 9 Gene Barry

baton 3 bat, rod **4** club, mace, wand **5** billy, crook, staff, stick **6** cudgel, fasces **7** crosier, scepter, war club **8** bludgeon, caduceus **9** billy club, truncheon **10** nightstick, shillelagh

Baton
  charioteer of: 10 Amphiaraus

batter 4 beat, lash, maul **5** break, crush, pound, smash, smite **6** beat up, buffet, mangle, pummel **7** clobber, shatter

battercake 6 waffle **7** biscuit, pancake

battered 4 shot **6** beat-up, ruined, shabby **8** decrepit **11** dilapidated **12** disreputable

battery 3 set **4** army, band, pack, team **5** block, cadre, force, group, suite, troop **6** caning, cannon, convoy, legion, lineup, outfit, series **7** beating, brigade, company, hitting, hurting, maiming, phalanx, section **8** armament, cannonry, clubbing, division, drubbing, flogging, ordnance, squadron, whipping, wounding **9** cudgeling, spearhead, strapping, thrashing

battle 3 war **4** bout, duel, feud, fray, meet **5** argue, brawl, clash, fight, siege **6** action, affray, combat, debate, engage, tussle **7** contend, contest, crusade, dispute, quarrel, warfare **8** campaign, conflict, skirmish, struggle **9** agitation, encounter, firefight **10** engagement **11** altercation, controversy **13** confrontation

Battle, final
  place: 10 Armageddon

battle cry 6 war cry **8** Geronimo, war whoop **9** Rebel yell

Battle Cry
  author: 8 Leon Uris

battlefield 5 arena, lists **8** the front, war arena **9** front line **10** battle line, no man's land **11** battlefront **12** battleground

battleground 5 arena, lists **11** battlefield, battlefront

Battle of the Books
  author: 13 Jonathan Swift

battle-ready 5 armed **7** arrayed **8** prepared **9** fortified

battleship 4 Iowa **5** Maine **6** Oregon **7** carrier, warship **8** Missouri **9** Ironsides, New Jersey, Wisconsin **10** bluish-gray **11** Dreadnought **12** Constitution
  first: 7 Gloire
  largest: 6 Yamato

Battus
  ruler of: 5 Libya
  form: 7 peasant
  witness to: 11 cattle theft
  thief: 6 Hermes
  turned to: 5 stone
  cured of: 16 speech impediment

batty 4 nuts **5** crazy, loony, queer, wacko, wacky **6** cuckoo, crazed **7** bat-like, cracked

bauble 3 toy **4** bead **6** geegaw, trifle **7** trinket **8** gimcrack, ornament

Baucis
  form: 7 peasant
  home: 7 Phrygia
  husband: 8 Philemon
  offered hospitality to: 4 Zeus **6** Hermes

Baudelaire, Charles
  author of: 13 Flowers of Evil **14** Les Fleurs du Mal

Baugh, Sammy
  nickname: 13 Slinging Sammy
  sport: 8 football
  position: 11 quarterback
  team: 18 Washington Redskins

Bauhin, Gaspard
  field: 6 botany
  nationality: 5 Swiss
  devised: 14 binomial system
  described: 14 ileocecal valve

Baum, Lyman Frank
  author of: 13 The (Wonderful) Wizard of Oz **18** Father Goose His Book, Mother Goose in Prose

Baum, Vicki
  author of: 8 Shanghai **10** Grand Hotel, Grand Opera **12** Men Never Know **13** A Tale from Bali, And Life Goes On

Baumer, Paul
 character in: 25 All Quiet on the Western Front
 author: 8 Remarque
Baumgarner, James
 real name of: 11 James Garner
Bauto
 nurse of: 6 Celeus
bawdy 4 blue, lewd, sexy 5 dirty, gross, lusty 6 coarse, earthy, ribald, risque, sexual, vulgar 7 raunchy 8 immodest, improper, indecent, off-color 10 indecorous, indelicate, licentious, suggestive
bawdy house 7 brothel 8 bordello, cathouse 10 fancy house, whorehouse 13 sporting house 14 house of ill fame 16 house of ill repute 19 house of prostitution
bawl 3 cry 4 call, howl, roar, wail, weep, yell, yowl 5 shout 6 bellow, clamor, cry out, squall 7 blubber, call out
bawling out 6 rebuke 7 censure, chiding, reproof 8 reproach, scolding 9 reprimand 10 chewing out, upbraiding 11 castigation, reprobation 12 dressing-down, remonstrance 13 tongue-lashing
bawl out 5 scold 6 berate, rail at, rebuke, yell at 7 censure, chew out, reprove, upbraid 8 admonish, reproach 9 castigate, dress down, reprimand 10 take to task, tongue-lash 14 read the riot act
Bax, Arnold Edward Trevor
 born: 6 London 7 England
 composer of: 8 Tintagel 13 November Woods 14 Mater Ora Filium 15 The Garden of Fand 27 Overture to a Picaresque Comedy
Baxter, Anne
 grandfather: 16 Frank Lloyd Wright
 born: 14 Michigan City IN
 roles: 8 Applause 11 All About Eve 13 The Razor's Edge
Baxter, Jody
 character in: 11 The Yearling
 author: 8 Rawlings
Baxter, William Sylvanus
 character in: 9 Seventeen
 author: 10 Tarkington
bay 3 cry, yap 4 bank, bark, cove, gulf, howl, nook, road, yelp 5 basin, bayou, bight, fiord, firth, inlet, niche, sound 6 alcove, bellow, clamor, lagoon, recess, strait 7 barking, estuary, howling, narrows, yapping, yelling, yelping 9 bellowing 11 compartment 13 natural harbor
bay (at bay) 7 trapped 8 cornered
bay leaf
 botanical name: 12 Pimenta acris
 expression: 16 to win one's laurels
 from tree: 9 bay laurel
 transformation of: 6 Daphne
 tree sacred to: 6 Apollo
 laurel berries called: 10 bacca lauri
 source of: 13 baccalaureate
 gives gift of: 8 prophecy
 helps girls win back: 12 errant lovers
 origin: 5 Italy
 protects against: 5 death 6 poison 7 sorcery 11 evil spirits
 symbol of: 7 victory (laurel wreath)
 use: 4 fish, fowl, meat, soup, stew
bayou 4 slew 5 creek, inlet, marsh, river, swamp 6 outlet, slough, stream 9 backwater 13 stagnant marsh
Bayou State
 nickname of: 9 Louisiana 11 Mississippi
Bay Psalm Book
 author: 9 John Eliot
Bay State
 nickname of: 13 Massachusetts
bazaar, bazar 4 fair, mart 6 market 8 carnival, exchange 11 charity fair, charity sale, marketplace
Bazile
 character in: 18 The Barber of Seville
 author: 12 Beaumarchais
Bazzard, Deputy
 character in: 22 The Mystery of Edwin Drood
 author: 7 Dickens
B C
 creator: 10 Johnny Hart
 character: 3 Tor 4 Grog 5 Peter 8 anteater 10 Clumsy Carp 11 the Fat Broad
 poet: 5 Wiley
 era: 11 Neanderthal, prehistoric
be 4 last, live, stay 5 exist, occur 6 befall, endure, happen, remain 7 persist, subsist 8 continue 9 be present, take place 10 come to pass
be absent 4 miss 12 fail to attend
beach 5 coast, shore 6 strand 8 littoral, seashore 10 water's edge
Beach, Rex
 author of: 6 The Net 7 Oh Shoot 8 Pardners 9 Going Some 10 Jungle Gold, The Barrier 11 Don Careless, The Spoilers 12 Son of the Gods 13 The Goose Woman, The Ne'er-do-well 15 The Auction Block 17 Alaskan Adventures
beached 7 aground 8 grounded, stranded 11 shipwrecked 12 washed ashore
beacon 4 beam 5 light 6 pharos, signal 7 seamark 8 bale-fire, landmark 9 watch fire 10 lighthouse, watchtower 11 lighted buoy
bead 3 dot 4 blob, drop, pill 5 speck 6 bubble, pellet 7 droplet, globule 8 particle, spherule
be adequate 2 do 6 answer 8 be enough 10 pass muster 12 be sufficient, do well enough 14 be satisfactory
be afraid of 4 fear 5 dread 7 cower 8 cringe at 10 shrink from
beak 3 neb, tip 4 bill, nose, pike, prow 5 lorum, snout, spout 7 process, rostrum, snozzle 8 hooknose 9 headmaster, proboscis 10 magistrate
beaker 3 cup 5 glass 6 vessel 9 container
beam 3 ray 4 emit, glow, prop, spar, stud 5 brace, glare, gleam, glint, joist, shine, width 6 girder, rafter, streak, stream, timber 7 breadth, expanse, glimmer, glitter, radiate, trestle 8 transmit 9 broadcast, radiation

bean 9 Phaseolus
varieties: 3 Goa, Pea, Soy, Wax, Yam 4 Jack, Lima, Moth, Mung, Rice, Seim, Snap, Soja, Soya, Tick, Wild 5 Azuki, Black, Broad, Civet, Coral, Field, Green, Horse, Lubia, Pinto, Salad, Screw, Sewee, Sieva, Snail, Sword, Tonka 6 Butter, Castor, Common, French, Indian, Kaffir, Kidney, Lablab, Locust, Manila, Mescal, Nicker, Potato, Romano, Runner, Sacred, String, Tepary, Velvet, Winged, Wonder 7 Cluster, English, Sarawak, Windsor 8 Bovanist, Bush lima, Carolina, Cherokee, European, Egyptian, Hyacinth, Yard-long 9 Algarroba, Asparagus, Bonavista, Dwarf lima, Java glory 10 Dwarf sieva, Giant stock, Hottentot's 12 Italian queen, Scarlet flame 13 African locust, Florida velvet, Scarlet runner 14 Dutch case-knife 16 White Dutch runner

be a party to 3 aid 4 abet 7 support 9 connive in 11 cooperate in 13 be accessory to, participate in

be apparent 6 appear 7 be clear, be plain 8 be patent 9 be evident, be obvious 10 be manifest

bear 4 bend, drop, give, haul, have, lead, push, show, take, tend, tote, turn, wear 5 abide, admit, allow, apply, brace, brave, bring, brook, carry, curve, drive, force, hatch, press, refer, spawn, stand, whelp, yield 6 affect, aim for, convey, convoy, create, endure, escort, go with, harbor, invite, permit, relate, render, suffer, take on, uphold 7 bolster, cherish, concern, conduct, contain, deliver, develop, deviate, display, diverge, exhibit, pertain, possess, produce, stomach, support, sustain, undergo, warrant 8 bear down, engender, generate, maintain, manifest, shoulder, submit to, tolerate, transfer, underpin 9 accompany, appertain, encourage, germinate, hold close, propagate, put up with, reproduce, touch upon, transport 10 bring forth, keep in mind 11 give birth to, hold up under

bear
combining form: 4 arct, ursi 5 arcto
constellation: 4 ursa 9 ursa major, ursa minor
family: 7 Ursidae
group of: 6 sleuth
kind: 3 sun 5 black, brown, koala, malay, panda, polar, sloth 6 kodiak, wombat 7 grizzly 9 roachback, silvertip 10 spectacled, thalarctos
male: 4 boar
mythological: 8 Callisto
order: 9 carnivora
young: 3 cub

beard 4 dare, defy, face, trap 5 brave 6 corner 7 stubble 8 bristles, confront, whiskers 10 bring to bay 16 five-o'clock shadow

bearded 5 bushy, hairy 6 shaggy 7 bristly, hirsute 8 unshaven 9 whiskered 11 bewhiskered

bear down 4 push 5 press 13 apply pressure

bear down upon 6 assail, attack, come at 7 assault 11 descend upon

Beardsley, Aubrey Vincent
born: 7 England 8 Brighton
artwork: 6 Salome 10 Lysistrata 12 Morte d'Arthur

Beard's Roman Women
author: 14 Anthony Burgess

bearer 5 Atlas 6 holder, porter 7 carrier 8 conveyer, producer 9 messenger 13 beast of burden 16 one holding a check
Spanish: 8 escudero, portador

bear fruit 4 bear 6 mature 7 develop, prosper 8 fructify

bearing 3 air 4 mien, port 5 sense 6 import, manner 7 concern, meaning 8 attitude, behavior, breeding, carriage, demeanor, presence, relation 9 producing, reference, relevance 10 conception, connection, deportment, importance, pertinence 11 application, association, comportment, germination, giving birth, procreation, propagation, reproducing 12 relationship, reproduction, significance 13 applicability

bearing no name 7 unnamed 8 unsigned 9 anonymous

bearings 3 way 6 course 8 position 9 direction 11 orientation 16 sense of direction

bearish 3 cross, gruff, surly, testy 6 crusty, sullen 7 brusque, crabbed, grouchy 8 churlish 9 crotchety, irascible 10 ill-humored, out of sorts 11 ill-tempered, pessimistic 12 cantankerous

bear off 5 seize, steal 6 abduct, convey, kidnap

bear out 5 prove 6 verify 7 confirm 11 corroborate 12 substantiate

Bear State
nickname of: 8 Arkansas

bear up under 4 bear, take 5 abide, brave, brook, stand 6 endure, suffer 7 stomach, undergo, weather 9 go through, withstand

bear witness 4 back 6 attest 7 confirm, testify 9 corroborate, demonstrate 12 give evidence, substantiate

beast 3 cad, cur, pig, rat 4 ogre 5 brute, swine 6 animal, mammal, savage 8 creature 9 barbarian, quadruped

beastly 3 bad 4 vile 5 awful, cruel, gross, lousy, nasty 6 brutal, coarse, savage 7 bestial, brutish, inhuman, swinish 8 degraded, dreadful, terrible 9 barbarous, loathsome, monstrous 10 abominable, deplorable, disgusting, unpleasant 12 contemptible, disagreeable

beat 3 bat, hit, mix, rap, tap, way 4 area, bang, best, blow, cane, club, drub, flap, flog, flop, lick, maul, path, rout, slap, time, whip, zone 5 clout, count, crush, flail, knock, meter, outdo, pound, pulse, punch, quake, quell, realm, repel, route, shake, smack, smite, strap, throb, whack 6 accent, batter, course, defeat, domain, hammer, master, pummel, quiver, rhythm, rounds, stress, strike, stroke, subdue, switch, thrash, thwack, twitch, wallop 7 cadence, circuit, clobber, conquer, destroy, eclipse, flutter, pulsate, put down, repulse, scourge, shellac, surpass, trounce, vibrate, win over **8** overcome, vanquish **9** excel over, fluctuate, go pit-a-pat, overpower, palpitate, pulsation, territory **10** win out over **11** predominate, prevail over, triumph over **14** stir vigorously

beat a retreat 6 beat it **7** back off **8** turn tail, withdraw **10** high tail it

beat around the bush 5 dodge, evade, hedge, stall **10** equivocate, mince words

beatific 4 rapt **6** divine, serene **7** angelic, exalted, saintly, sublime **8** blissful, ecstatic, glorious, heavenly **9** rapturous **10** enraptured **14** transcendental

beat it 2 go **3** out **4** away, scat, shoo **5** be off, leave, scram **6** begone, cut out, depart, get out, go away **7** get lost, vamoose **10** hit the road, make tracks

beatitude 5 bliss **7** ecstasy, rapture **8** euphoria, felicity **10** exaltation **11** blessedness, exaltedness, saintliness **13** transcendence **15** transfiguration

be at loggerheads 5 clash **7** quarrel **8** disagree

be at odds 4 differ **7** dispute, diverge **8** conflict, disagree

beat rhythmically 3 rap, tap **4** drum **6** tattoo **7** pulsate

Beatrice
    character in: 12 Divine Comedy
    author: 5 Dante

Beatrice
    character in: 19 Much Ado About Nothing
    author: 11 Shakespeare

Beatrice et Benedict
    opera by: 7 Berlioz

Beat the Clock
    host: 10 Bud Collyer

Beattie, Ann
    author of: 11 Distortions **14** Falling in Place **15** The Burning House **19** Secrets and Surprises **20** Chilly Scenes of Winter

Beatty, Warren
    real name: 11 Warren Beaty
    sister: 15 Shirley MacLaine
    born: 10 Richmond VA
    roles: 4 Reds **11** All Fall Down **13** Heaven Can Wait **16** Bonnie and Clyde **18** Splendor in the Grass **24** The Roman Spring of Mrs Stone
    director of: 4 Reds (Oscar)

beat up 3 mug **4** lick, maul, whip **6** batter, pummel **7** assault, clobber

beat-up 4 shot **6** shabby **7** worn-out **8** battered **10** broken-down **11** dilapidated

Beaty, Shirley MacLean
    real name of: 15 Shirley MacLaine

Beaty, Warren
    real name of: 12 Warren Beatty

beau, beaux 3 fop, guy, nob **4** buck, dude, love, stud, toff **5** blade, dandy, flame, lover, Romeo, spark, swain, swell, wooer **6** adorer, escort, fellow, fiance, garcon, squire, steady, suitor **7** admirer, beloved, courter, coxcomb, cupidon, Don Juan, gal-

lant, playboy **8** cavalier, courtier, gay blade, Lothario, paramour, popinjay, true love, young man **9** betrothed, boyfriend, courtesan, gentleman, inamorato, ladies' man **10** sweetheart, young blood **15** gentleman caller, gentleman friend
    nickname of: 14 George Brummell

Beauchamp's Career
    author: 14 George Meredith

Beau Geste
    author: 6 P C Wren **15** Christopher Wren
    director: 14 William Wellman
    cast: 10 Gary Cooper, Ray Milland **12** Brian Donlevy, Susan Hayward **13** Robert Preston
    silent version starred: 12 Ronald Colman
    setting: 19 French Foreign Legion

Beaumarchais, Pierre Augustin Caron de
    author of: 18 The Barber of Seville **19** The Marriage of Figaro

beau monde 5 elite **6** gentry **7** society **10** upper class, upper crust **11** aristocracy, high society **15** beautiful people

Beaumont, Ned
    character in: 11 The Glass Key
    author: 7 Hammett

Beauregard, P G T (Pierre Gustave Toutant)
    served in: 8 Civil War
    side: 11 Confederate
    rank: 7 general
    ordered firing on: 8 Ft Sumter
    battle: 7 Bull Run

beaut 4 lulu **5** daisy, dandy **6** beauty **7** stunner **8** knockout **10** good-looker

beautification 9 adornment **10** decoration **13** embellishment, ornamentation

beautiful 4 fair, fine **5** bonny, great **6** comely, lovely, pretty, seemly, superb, worthy **7** radiant **8** alluring, gorgeous, handsome, pleasing, splendid, very good **9** admirable, beauteous, enjoyable, estimable, excellent, exquisite, first-rate, ravishing, wonderful **10** attractive, stupendous **11** captivating, commendable, fine-looking, good-looking, resplendent **15** pulchritudinous

beautify 4 do up **5** adorn, grace **7** dress up, enhance, gussy up, improve **8** ornament **9** embellish, glamorize

beauty 4 boon, doll **5** asset, beaut, belle, grace, Venus **6** eyeful, looker **7** benefit, feature, goddess, stunner **8** knockout, radiance, splendor **9** advantage, good looks, good thing **10** attraction, excellence, good-looker, loveliness **11** pulchritude **12** handsomeness, magnificence, resplendence **14** attractiveness
    goddess of: 6 Graces **7** Gratiae **9** Aphrodite, Charities
    god of: 5 Baldr **6** Apollo, Balder, Baldur **7** Angus Og, Phoebus, Pythias **9** Musagetes

Beauvoir, Simone de
    author of: 12 The Mandarins, The Second Sex **14** A Very Easy Death, All Said

and Done, The Coming of Age, The Prime of Life 17 Ethics of Ambiguity 22 The Force of Circumstance 25 Memoirs of a Dutiful Daughter 34 Brigitte Bardot and the Lolita Syndrome

beaver
young: 3 kit

Beaver State
nickname of: 6 Oregon

be blessed with 3 own 4 have 5 enjoy 7 possess 16 have the benefit of

because 2 so 3 for 4 that, then, thus 5 cause, hence, since 6 whence 7 whereas 8 inasmuch 9 therefore 10 seeing that 11 considering

Bechuanaland
now called: 8 Botswana

Bechuanland see 8 Botswana

beck 3 bid 4 call 7 bidding, summons 9 summoning

Becket
author: 11 Jean Anouilh 18 Alfred Lord Tennyson
director: 14 Peter Glenville
cast: 11 John Gielgud, Peter O'Toole (King Henry II) 13 Richard Burton (Becket)

Beckett, Samuel
author of: 4 Not I, Play, Watt 6 Embers, Molloy 7 Endgame 8 That Time 9 Footfalls, Happy Days 10 Malone Dies 11 All that Fall, The Lost Ones 13 The Unnameable 15 Waiting for Godot 16 Mercier and Camier 20 Murphy Krapp's Last Tape 25 Stories and Texts for Nothing

Beckmann, Max
born: 7 Germany, Leipzig
artwork: 6 Kasbek 7 Perseus 8 Acrobats, The Night 9 The Actors 11 View of Genoa 12 Charnel House, The Argonauts, The Departure 13 Blindman's Buff, Family Picture 14 Double Portrait 17 David and Bathsheba 18 Odysseus and Calypso 19 Sinking of the Titanic 20 Destruction of Messina 22 The Descent from the Cross

beckon 4 call, coax, draw, lure, pull 6 allure, entice, invite, motion, signal, summon, wave at, wave on 7 attract, gesture 11 gesticulate 14 crook a finger at

be clear 6 appear 7 be plain 8 be patent 9 be evident, be obvious 10 be apparent, be manifest

becloud 3 fog 4 blur, hide, veil 5 befog, cloud 6 muddle, screen, shroud 7 confuse, cover up, eclipse, obscure 8 confound, make hazy, overcast 9 obfuscate 10 camouflage, overshadow 14 make indistinct

become 3 get 4 grow, suit, turn 6 go with 7 enhance, flatter, get to be 8 come to be 9 agree with, begin to be 10 complement 11 be reduced to, turn out to be

become apparent 4 dawn, loom 5 arise 6 appear, crop up, emerge, turn up 7 develop, surface

become bigger 4 grow 5 swell 6 expand 7 develop, enlarge, inflate 8 increase

become irrational 5 break, crack 7 crack up 9 break down, fall apart, go berserk 10 go to pieces 11 lose control 12 lose one's mind

become one 3 wed 4 fuse 5 blend, marry, merge, unite 7 combine 8 coalesce 10 amalgamate 11 consolidate

become seasoned to 5 adapt, inure 6 adjust 8 accustom 9 acclimate, get used to, habituate 15 learn to live with

become smaller 6 lessen, shrink 7 decline, dwindle, shrivel 8 decrease, diminish

become visible 4 loom, show 6 appear, crop up, emerge, show up, turn up 7 surface 11 come to light 12 come into view

becoming 3 apt, fit 4 meet 6 pretty, proper, seemly, worthy 7 fitting 8 suitable 9 befitting, congenial, congruous, enhancing, in keeping 10 attractive, compatible, consistent, flattering, harmonious 11 appropriate, good-looking

Becquerel, Antoine Henri
field: 7 physics
nationality: 6 French
discovered: 13 radioactivity
awarded: 10 Nobel Prize

bed 3 cot, hay 4 band, bank, base, belt, bunk, crib, lode, plot, sack, seam, zone 5 berth, floor, layer, patch 6 bottom, cradle, pallet 7 deposit, stratum 8 bedstead 10 foundation

bedazzle 4 daze 6 dazzle 7 astound, confuse, enchant, fluster, nonplus, stagger, stupefy 8 befuddle, bewilder, confound, dumfound 9 captivate, overpower, overwhelm 10 disconcert 11 flabbergast 19 sweep one off one's feet

bed chamber 7 bedroom, boudoir

bed down 5 sleep 7 lie down, sack out 8 doss down 10 hit the hay, settle down 11 accommodate, hit the sack

bedeck 4 deck, trim 5 adorn, array 7 garnish 8 decorate, ornament 9 embellish

be deficient in 4 fail, lack, want 7 be scant 9 be short of 10 have too few

be deprived of 4 lack, lose, want

be deserving of 4 earn, rate 5 merit 7 deserve 10 be worthy of 12 be entitled to

bedevil 3 dog 5 annoy, hound, worry 6 badger, harass, pester, plague 9 beleaguer

be devoted to 4 love 5 adore 6 dote on 7 cherish 8 be fond of

bedim 4 blur 6 darken 7 obscure

Bedivere
character in: 16 Arthurian romance

bedizen 5 adorn, array 6 bedeck, rig out 7 bejewel, costume

bedlam 5 chaos 6 tumult, uproar 7 turmoil 8 madhouse 11 pandemonium

bed of justice
French: 12 lit de justice

Bedouin, Beduin
 also: 4 Absi, Arab 5 nomad 7 bedawee
 Arabic: 6 badawi
 means: 13 desert dweller
 found in: 5 Egypt, Syria 6 Arabia 11
  North Africa
 religion: 5 Islam
bedraggled 4 limp 5 dirty, dowdy, messy,
 seedy, soggy, tacky, tatty 6 blowsy, frowsy,
 frumpy, matted, ragtag, sloppy, soiled, untidy 7 unkempt 8 frumpish, sluttish, tattered 10 disarrayed, disordered, disheveled, slatternly, threadbare 11 disarranged
 13 draggletailed 14 down-at-the-heels,
 out-at-the-elbows
bedridden 7 invalid 8 disabled, immobile
 13 incapacitated
bedroom 7 boudoir, chamber 10 bedchamber
bedspread 5 quilt 8 bedcover, coverlet 9
 comforter
bedstead 3 bed 8 bed frame 10 four poster
bee
 caste: 5 drone, queen 6 worker
 classification: 6 social 8 solitary
 communication: 13 dance language
 family: 6 Apidae 7 Apoidea 8 Bombidae
  10 Andrenidae, Halictidae 11 Meliponi-
  dae, Xylocopidae 12 Megachilidae
 group of: 5 grist, swarm
 order: 11 Hymenoptera
 scent: 10 pheromones
 variety: 5 mason, miner 6 alkali, cuckoo
  8 burrower, honeybee 9 bumblebee, carpenter, plasterer 10 leaf-cutter 11 yellow-
  faced
beech 5 Fagus
 varieties: 4 Blue 5 Water 6 Copper, Purple 7 Cut-leaf, Weeping 8 American,
  European, Fern-leaf, Japanese
Beedle, William Franklin, Jr,
 real name of: 13 William Holden
beef 4 heft, kick, meat 5 brawn, gripe, steer
 6 cattle, grouch, grouse 7 grumble 8 complain 9 bellyache, complaint, criticize, find
 fault
Beef State
 nickname of: 8 Nebraska
beefy 5 bulky, burly, hefty 6 brawny, robust
 8 thickset 9 strapping
beehive 4 hive 6 apiary 9 busy place 10
 powerhouse
Beehive State
 nickname of: 4 Utah
Beekeeping
 god of: 9 Aristaeus
Beelzebub
 character in: 12 Paradise Lost
 author: 6 Milton
be enough 2 do 6 answer 7 suffice
be entitled to 4 rate 5 merit 7 deserve 10
 be worthy of 13 be deserving of
beer 3 ale, keg, mum 4 bier, bock, brew,
 dark, faro, flip, gail, grog, gyle, hops, kvas,
 malt, mild, quas, scud, suds 5 chang,
 chica, draft, grout, kvass, lager, light,
 quass, scuds, stout, weiss 6 bitter, chicha,

 double, gatter, porter, spruce, stingo,
 swanky, swipes, wallop, zythum 7 bottled,
 cerveza, pangasi, pharaoh, Pilsner, tankard, taplash, tapwort 8 bock beer,
 cervisia, near beer, pilsener 10 malt liquor
 add to beer: 7 krausen
 bad/inferior beer: 4 tack 5 belch 6
  swanky 7 taplash
 brand: 5 Beck's, Coors, Pabst, Piels 6
  Miller, Molson, Stroh's 7 Schlitz 8 Bud
  Light, Michelob 9 Budweiser, Lowenbrau
  10 Miller Lite, Molson Gold 13 Guinness
  Stout 15 Pabst Blue Ribbon
 cask: 4 butt
 cup: 3 mug 4 toby 5 glass, stein 6 flagon,
  seidel 7 tankard 8 schooner 9 blackjack
 hot beer and gin: 4 purl
 ingredient: 4 hops, malt 5 yeast 6 barley
 maker: 6 brewer 8 brewster, maltster
 mythological inventor: 9 Gambrinus
 quantity of: 3 keg 4 case 7 six-pack
 small beer: 4 tiff 5 grout
 sour beer: 4 kuas, kvas 5 quash, quass
  8 beeregar
 thin beer: 6 pritch, swipes
 Tibetan beer: 5 chang
 warm beer and oatmeal: 6 storry
 with whiskey: 11 Boilermaker
beer-bust 4 toot 5 binge, drunk, spree 6
 bender 8 carousal 9 bacchanal
Beery, Noah
 brother: 7 Wallace
 son: 6 Noah Jr
 born: 12 Kansas City MO
 roles: 7 Lord Jim, The Dove 9 Beau
  Geste 10 The Sea Wolf 14 The Mark of
  Zorro
Beery, Wallace
 brother: 4 Noah
 nephew: 6 Noah Jr
 wife: 13 Gloria Swanson
 born: 12 Kansas City MO
 roles: 8 The Champ (Oscar) 9 The Bowery, Viva Villa 10 Grand Hotel 11 The Big
  House 13 Dinner at Eight 14 Treasure Island 15 The Mighty Barnum 16 A Message to Garcia
beet 12 Beta vulgaris
 varieties: 3 Red, Sea 4 Leaf, Wild 5 Sugar 6 Garden, Yellow 7 Spinach
Beethoven, Ludwig van
 born: 4 Bonn 7 Germany
 composer of: 5 Laube (sonata) 6 Egmont, Eroica (symphony no 3), Spring
  (sonata) 7 Fidelio, Leonore 8 Coriolan,
  Dramatic (sonata), Kreutzer (sonata),
  Pastoral (symphony no 6), The Storm 9
  Moonlight (sonata), Pastorale (sonata),
  Waldstein (sonata) 10 Bagatellen, Great
  Fugue (no 133), Pathetique (sonata),
  Spirit Trio 11 Grosse Fugue (no 133),
  Harp Quartet (no 74), Namensfeier 12
  Appassionata (sonata), Archduke Trio,
  Konig Stephan 13 Hammerklavier (so-
  nata), Missa Solemnis 15 Emperor Con-
  certo (No 5) 16 Christus am Olberg, The
  Mount of Olives, The Ruins of Athens 17

Die Ruinen von Athen, Die Weihe des Hauses 18 An die ferne Geliebte, Rage over a Lost Penny 20 Rasoumoffsky Quartets (no 59) 24 The Creatures of Prometheus 25 Die Geschopfe des Prometheus

beetle
variety: 3 bog, may, sap 4 bark, bean, flea, leaf, mold, moss, pill, rove, sand, stag 5 cedar, click, flour, grain, marsh, penny, tiger, water 6 beaver, diving, flower, fungus, ground, hister, lizard, spider, weevil 7 bessbug, blister, burying, carrion, firefly, goldbug, goliath, ladybug, soldier 8 elephant, glowworm, hercules, Japanese, ladybird, tortoise 9 ant loving, bombadier, burrowing, checkered, fruitworm, goldsmith, grassroot, scavenger, tumblebug, whirligig 10 deathwatch, false clown, longhorned, mammal nest, shiptimber 11 reticulated, trout stream 12 antlike stone, lightning bug 13 feather winged, horseshoe crab

Beetle Bailey
creator/artist: 9 Dik Browne 10 Mort Walker 12 Bob Gustafson
character: 5 Cosmo, Plato 6 Killer, Lt Flap, Lt Fuzz 10 Miss Buxley 12 Gen Halftrack 17 Sgt Orville Snorkel
chef: 6 Cookie
place: 10 Camp Swampy

be evident 6 appear 7 be clear, be plain 8 be patent 9 be obvious 10 be apparent, be manifest

befall 5 ensue, occur 6 betide, chance, follow, happen 10 come to pass 11 materialize

befitting 3 apt, fit 5 right 6 decent, proper, seemly 8 becoming, relevant, suitable 11 appropriate

be fond of 6 dote on 11 be devoted to 12 be in love with

before 3 ere, yet 5 afore, ahead, prior 6 rather, sooner 7 already, earlier, vis-a-vis 8 erewhile, until now 9 in advance, in front of, in sight of 10 face-to-face, previously

before Christ
abbreviation: 2 BC
Latin: 2 AC 12 ante Christum

beforehand 6 in time, sooner 7 earlier 9 in advance 11 ahead of time

before now 6 in time, sooner 7 earlier 9 in advance

before the fact 6 in time 9 in advance 10 beforehand 11 ahead of time

before the public
Latin: 11 coram populo

befoul 4 soil 5 dirty, smear, stain, sully, taint 6 defile, poison 7 blacken, corrupt, pollute, tarnish 8 besmirch 9 desecrate 11 contaminate

befriend 4 help 6 assist, defend, succor, uphold 7 comfort, embrace, help out, protect, stand by, stick by, support, sustain, welcome 8 side with 9 give aid to, look after 10 minister to 11 consort with 13 associate with 14 fraternize with, sympathize with 17 take under one's wing

be friends 7 consort 9 associate, pal around 10 fraternize

befringe 3 hem 4 bind, edge, trim 6 border 7 festoon 8 decorate

befuddle 4 daze 5 addle, mix up 6 baffle, muddle, puzzle, rattle 7 confuse, fluster, perplex, stupefy 8 bewilder, confound, unsettle 9 disorient, inebriate, make drunk, make tipsy 10 intoxicate, make groggy 11 disorganize

beg 3 bum, sue 4 pray, shun 5 avert, avoid, cadge, dodge, evade, mooch, parry, plead, shirk 6 escape, eschew, hustle, sponge 7 beseech, entreat, fend off, implore, solicit 8 appeal to, petition, sidestep 9 importune, panhandle 10 supplicate

beg, bey 4 lord 6 prince 8 governor

beget 3 get 4 sire 5 breed, cause, spawn 6 effect, father, lead to 7 produce 8 engender, generate, occasion, result in 9 call forth, procreate, propagate 10 bring about, give rise to

begetter 4 sire 6 father 7 creator 9 generator 10 progenitor

beggar 3 bum, guy 4 chap 5 devil, tramp 6 baffle, fellow 7 almsman, moocher, sponger, surpass 8 be beyond 9 challenge, mendicant 10 panhandler

Beggar's Opera, The
author: 7 Lazarus

Beggar's Opera, The
author: 7 John Gay
form: 11 ballad opera
character: 6 Lockit 10 Lucy Lockit 12 Polly Peachum 15 Captain Macheath

begin 5 arise, found, start 6 be born, crop up, emerge, launch, set out 8 break out, commence, embark on, initiate 9 establish, institute, introduce, originate, undertake 10 burst forth, inaugurate 11 set in motion 16 take the first step

beginner 4 babe, tyro 6 author, father, novice, rookie 7 creator, founder, learner, starter, student 8 freshman, neophyte 9 fledgling, greenhorn, initiator, organizer 10 apprentice, originator, prime mover, tenderfoot 11 inaugurator 14 babe in the woods

beginning 3 new 4 germ, seed 5 birth, onset, start 6 embryo, novice, origin, outset, source, spring 7 kickoff, student, untried 8 neophyte, zero hour 9 embryonic, inception, incipient, launching 10 foundation, wellspring 11 preliminary, springboard 12 commencement, fountainhead, inauguration, introduction 13 inexperienced, starting point
Latin: 12 terminus a quo

Beginning of Wisdom, The
author: 19 Stephen Vincent Benet

Beginnings
god of: 5 Janus

begone 3 out 4 away, scat, shoo 5 be off, leave, scram 6 beat it, depart, get out, go away 7 get lost, vamoose

begonia
  varieties: 3 Rex, Wax 4 Fern, King, Star, Wild 5 Hardy, Trout 6 Bamboo, Kidney, Shrimp, Winter, Zigzag 7 Bedding, Dewdrop, Elm-leaf, Eyelash, Fuchsia, Leopard, Lily-pad, Swedish 8 Climbing, Fernleaf, Fire-king, Lorraine, Palm-leaf, Pond-lily, Star-leaf, Trailing 9 Alder-leaf, Angel-wing, Beefsteak, Calla-lily, Christmas, Crazy-leaf, Grape-leaf, Grapevine, Hollyhock, Holly-leaf, Honey-bear, Ironcross, Maple-leaf, Miniature, Pennywort, Trout-leaf, Whirlpool 10 Bronze-leaf, Castor-bean, Finger-leaf, Guinea-wing, Seersucker, Strawberry 11 Fairy-carpet, Lettuce-leaf, Painted-leaf 12 Bloomingfool, Elephant's Ear, Metallic-leaf 13 Peanut-brittle 14 Hybrid tuberous, Nasturtium-leaf, Youth-and-old-age 15 Winter-flowering 16 Manda's woolly-bear, Philodendron-leaf 17 Miniature pond-lily 18 Trailing watermelon

beg pardon 6 excuse 9 apologize 13 express regret, say one is sorry

be grateful 9 be obliged 10 appreciate, be beholden, be thankful 11 be obligated

begrime 4 soil 5 dirty, muddy, smear, stain, sully 6 smudge, soot up 7 besmear, tarnish

begrimed 5 dirty, grimy, muddy 6 filthy, grubby, soiled 7 unclean 8 unwashed 9 tarnished

begrudge 4 envy 5 covet 6 grudge, resent 11 be jealous of, hold against

beguile 4 dupe, hoax, lull, lure 5 amuse, charm, cheat, cheer, trick 6 delude, divert, occupy, please 7 bewitch, deceive, enchant, ensnare 8 distract, hoodwink 9 bamboozle, captivate, entertain 10 lead astray

beguiling 7 winning, winsome 8 charming, magnetic 9 appealing, disarming 10 bewitching, entrancing 11 captivating 12 ingratiating, irresistible

behalf 3 aid, for 4 part, side 5 favor 7 benefit, by proxy, defense, in aid of, support 8 interest

Behan, Brendan
  author of: 10 Borstal Boy, The Hostage 12 The Scarperer 14 The Quare Fellow 25 Confessions of an Irish Rebel

be handed down 4 pass 7 descend 11 be inherited

behave 3 act 13 acquit oneself, deport oneself 14 comport oneself, conduct oneself, control oneself

behavior 4 acts 5 deeds 6 action, habits, manner 7 actions, bearing, conduct, control 8 activity, attitude, demeanor, practice, reaction, response 9 operation 10 deportment 11 comportment, functioning, performance, self-control

behead 9 decollate 10 decapitate, guillotine 15 bring to the block

behest 4 fiat 5 edict, order, say-so 6 charge, decree, ruling 7 bidding, command, dictate, mandate 9 direction, ultimatum 10 injunction 11 instruction

behind 4 rump, seat, slow 5 abaft, after, fanny 8 backward, buttocks, in back of 9 fundament, in arrears 11 to the rear of 12 hindquarters

behind closed doors 7 sub rosa 8 in secret, secretly 9 in private, privately

behindhand 4 late, slow 5 tardy 7 belated 8 backward 10 unpunctual

behind the times 5 passe 7 archaic 9 out-of-date 10 antiquated 12 old-fashioned

behind time 4 late, slow 5 tardy 7 belated, delayed 12 after the fact

behold 3 see 4 heed, look, mark, note, scan, view 5 watch 6 attend, gaze at, look at, notice, regard, survey 7 discern, examine, inspect, observe, stare at, witness 8 look upon 10 scrutinize 11 contemplate 12 pay attention

beholden 5 bound 6 liable 7 obliged 8 indebted 9 obligated 10 answerable, in one's debt 11 accountable, responsible 15 under obligation

behold the man
  Latin: 8 ecce homo
  said by: 13 Pontius Pilate
  spoken of: 6 Christ

behoove 4 suit 5 be apt, befit 6 become, be wise 7 benefit 8 be proper 9 be fitting 11 be advisable, be necessary 13 be appropriate 14 be advantageous

Behring, Emil Adolph von
  field: 12 bacteriology
  nationality: 6 German
  developed: 19 diphtheria antitoxin
  awarded: 10 Nobel Prize

beige 3 tan 4 ecru, fawn 6 greige 8 brownish

be ill 3 ail 6 be sick 8 be unwell 12 be indisposed 13 be in ill health

be in a class with 5 equal, match 6 be up to 7 compare 8 approach 10 be as good as 11 compete with 12 be comparable, be on a par with 13 hold a candle to 14 bear comparison

being 4 core, life, soul 5 human 6 living, mortal, nature, person, psyche, spirit 7 essence, persona, reality 8 creature, existing 9 actuality, existence 10 individual, occurrence 11 subsistence

be inherited 4 pass 7 descend 12 be handed down

be in short supply 4 lack, want 8 be scanty, be scarce 9 fall short

be intemperate 7 carouse, debauch 9 dissipate 11 overindulge

be in tune 4 jibe 5 agree, match, tally 6 accord, square 7 conform 9 harmonize

Beirut, Beyrouth
  capital of: 7 Lebanon
  Phoenician name: 7 Berytus
  sea: 13 Mediterranean
  settled by: 11 Phoenicians
  square: 15 Place des Martyrs

be jealous of 4 envy 6 resent 8 begrudge

Bekesy, Georg von
  field: 7 physics
  researched: 3 ear 7 cochlea, hearing
  awarded: 10 Nobel Prize

Bel 3 god 5 deity

Bela
  father: 4 Beor
  brother: 6 Balaam

belabor 6 rehash, repeat 7 dwell on 9 reiterate 11 pound away at 12 hammer away at, recapitulate 14 beat a dead horse, go on and on about

Bel-Ami
  author: 15 Guy de Maupassant

Belarus
  other name: 10 Belorussia 11 Byelorussia, White Russia
  capital/largest city: 5 Minsk
  head of state: 9 president
  government: 8 republic
  monetary unit: 5 ruble
  river: 5 Dvina 7 Dnieper
  physical feature: 13 Pripet Marshes
  people: 12 Byelorussian

Belasco, David
  author of: 7 DuBarry 15 Madame Butterfly 21 The Return of Peter Grimm 22 The Girl of the Golden West

belated 4 late, slow 5 tardy 6 behind 7 delayed, overdue, past due 8 deferred 10 behindhand, behind time, unpunctual 12 after the fact

belch 4 burp, emit, gush, spew, vent 5 eject, eruct, erupt, expel, issue, spout, spurt, vomit 7 cough up, issuing 8 disgorge, ejection, emission, eruption 9 discharge, roar forth, send forth 10 eructation

Belch, Sir Toby
  character in: 12 Twelfth Night
  author: 11 Shakespeare

beleaguer 3 vex 5 annoy 6 assail, badger, bother, harass, hector, pester, plague 7 besiege, bombard 8 blockade, surround

bel-esprit 3 wit 12 intellectual

belfry 4 dome 5 spire 7 steeple 9 bell tower, campanile

Belgian Congo see 5 Zaire

Belgium
  other name: 13 Gallia Belgica 15 Cockpit of Europe 16 Koninkrijk Belgie 17 Royaume de Belgique
  capital/largest city: 8 Brussels 9 Bruxelles
  others: 2 As 3 Aat, Ans, Ath, Hal, Huy, Mol, Spa 4 Aath, Amay, Asse, Boom, Bree, Doel, Gaud, Geel, Genk, Gent, Hoei, Lier, Looz, Mons, Vise, Waha, Zele 5 Aalst, Alost, Arlon, Ciney, Ecklo, Essen, Eupen, Evere, Genck, Ghent, Heist, Ieper, Jette, Jumet, Liege, Namur, Ronse, Tielt, Uccle, Vorst, Wezet, Ynoir, Ypres 6 Aarlen, Anvers, Bergen, Bilzen, Bruges, Deume, Izegem, Leuven, Lierre, Merxem, Opwijk, Ostend 7 Antwerp, Ardooie, Berchem, Brabant, Hainaut, Herstal, Hoboken, Ixelles, Leliven, Limburg,

Louvain, Malmedy, Mechlin, Roulers, Seraing, Tournai 8 Bastogne, Courtrai, Doorwick, Flanders, Kortrijk, Mouscron, Turnhout, Verviers, Waterloo 9 Antwerpen, Charleroi 10 Anderlecht, Borgerhout, Luxembourg, Quatrebras, Schaerbeek
  school: 7 Louvain
  division: 5 Liege, Namur 7 Antwerp, Brabant, Hainaut, Limburg 8 Flanders, Wallonia
  head of state: 4 king
  measure: 3 vat 4 aune, pied 5 carat 6 perche 8 boisseau
  monetary unit: 5 belga, franc 7 brabant, centime, crocard
  weight: 4 last 5 carat, livre 6 charge 7 chariot 8 esterlin
  mountain: 8 Ardennes
  highest point: 16 Signal de Botrange
  river: 3 Lys 4 Dyle, Leie, Maas, Mark, Yser 5 Boucq, Demer, Lesse, Meuse, Nethe, Rupel, Senne 6 Dender, Escaut, Manjel, Ourthe, Sambre, Semois, Vesdre, Warche 7 Ambleve, Schelde, Scheldt
  sea: 5 North
  physical feature:
  canal: 4 Yser 5 Union 6 Albert 7 Campine
  cave: 7 Furfooz 8 Grenelle
  forest: 8 Ardennes
  plateau: 8 Hohevenn
  people: 4 Remi 6 Nervii 7 Belgian, Fleming, Flemish 8 Walloons 9 Bellovaci
  artist: 5 Ensor 6 Rubens 7 Delvaux, Van Dyke, Van Eyck 8 Brueghal, Magritte
  author: 6 Coster 7 Simenon 9 Verhaeren 10 Conscience, Ghelderode 11 Maeterlinck
  composer: 6 Franck
  king: 6 Albert 7 Leopold 8 Baudouin
  leader: 5 Spaak 9 Tindemans
  language: 5 Dutch 6 French, German 7 Flemish
  religion: 13 Roman Catholic
  place:
  battleground: 5 Bulge 8 Waterloo
  breadhouse: 9 Broodhuis
  castle: 5 Steen
  cathedral: 5 Ghent 13 Saint Rombauts
  city hall: 12 Hotel de Ville
  home for elderly women: 9 Beguinage
  museum: 9 Beaux Arts
  palace: 10 Gruuthuuse
  features:
  horse: 9 Brabancon
  lace: 5 fichu 6 Bruges 7 Malines, Mechlin 8 Brussels
  lawn bowling: 6 boules
  linen: 7 brabant
  musical instrument: 8 carillon
  religious procession: 9 Holy Blood
  tapestry: 9 oudenarde
  food:
  cheese: 9 Limburger
  gingerbread: 12 pain d'espices
  raisin bread: 8 cramique

soup: 9 Waterzooi

Belgrade, Beograd
capital of: 10 Yugoslavia
landmark:
fortress: 10 Kalemegdan
parliament house: 9 Skupstina
name means: 11 white forest
river: 4 Sava 6 Danube
Roman fort: 10 Singidinum
Serbian: 7 Beograd

Belial
character in: 12 Paradise Lost
author: 6 Milton

belie 4 defy, deny, mask 5 cloak 6 betray, negate, refute 7 conceal, falsify, gainsay 8 disguise, disprove 9 repudiate 10 camouflage, contradict, controvert, invalidate 12 misrepresent

belief 4 view 5 faith, guess, trust 6 theory 7 feeling, opinion 8 judgment, reliance 9 assurance, certitude, deduction, inference 10 assumption, conclusion, confidence, conviction, firm notion, hypothesis, impression, persuasion 11 expectation, presumption, supposition

beliefs 5 canon, creed, dogma, faith, tenet 6 ethics, gospel, morals 8 doctrine, morality 9 principle, teachings 10 conviction, persuasion

believable 8 credible, knowable, possible 9 plausible, thinkable 10 acceptable, convincing, imaginable, supposable 11 conceivable, perceivable

believe 4 hold 5 guess, infer, judge, think, trust 6 assume, credit, deduce, rely on 7 count on, fall for, imagine, presume, suppose, surmise, suspect, swallow, swear by 8 be sure of, consider, depend on, maintain, theorize 9 speculate 10 conjecture, presuppose, put faith in 11 hypothesize

believe in 5 trust 6 accept, esteem 7 approve, go in for, respect 11 have faith in 16 have confidence in

Believe It or Not
author: 13 Robert L Ripley

believer 7 admirer 8 advocate, disciple, partisan 9 supporter 16 faithful adherent

be like 5 equal, match 8 approach, resemble

Bel-Imperia
character in: 17 The Spanish Tragedy
author: 3 Kyd

Belinda
character in: 16 The Rape of the Lock
author: 4 Pope

belittle 5 knock, scorn 6 deride, malign 7 disdain, put down, run down, sneer at 8 minimize, mitigate, play down, pooh-pooh 9 deprecate, disparage, underrate 10 depreciate, undervalue 11 make light of 13 underestimate 16 cast aspersions on

belittling 5 snide 10 derogatory 11 deprecating, disparaging, unfavorable 12 depreciating 15 uncomplimentary

Belize
other name: 15 British Honduras
capital: 8 Belmopan

largest city/former capital: 10 Belize City
head of state: 13 prime minister 14 British monarch 15 governor-general
monetary unit: 6 dollar
island: 8 Turneffe
mountain range: 4 Maya
highest point: 12 Victoria Peak
river: 3 New 4 Moho 6 Belize, Monkey
sea: 9 Caribbean
physical feature:
gulf: 8 Honduras
peninsula: 7 Yucatan
swamp: 8 mangrove
people: 5 Mayan 6 Indian, Syrian 7 African, Chinese 15 Spanish-American
language: 7 English

bell 4 gong, peal 5 chime 6 tocsin 7 ringing 8 carillon 16 tintinnabulation

Bell, Alexander Graham
born: 8 Scotland
inventor of: 9 telephone 14 record cylinder
saying: 24 Mr Watson come here I want you

Bellamann, Henry
author of: 8 King's Row

Bellamy, Edward
author of: 8 Equality 15 Looking Backward

Bellamy, Ralph
born: 9 Chicago IL
roles: 11 Ellery Queen, Mike Barnett 13 The Awful Truth 14 Detective Story 15 Man Against Crime, State of the Union 19 Sunrise at Campobello

Bellarius
character in: 9 Cymbeline
author: 11 Shakespeare

Bellaston, Lady
character in: 8 Tom Jones
author: 8 Fielding

bell buoy 5 float 6 signal 13 channel marker

belle 4 star 5 queen 6 beauty 7 charmer 12 heart-stopper

Belle Dame Sans Merci, La
author: 9 John Keats

Bellefleur
author: 15 Joyce Carol Oates

Belle Helene, La
also: 14 Beautiful Helen
operetta by: 9 Offenbach

Bellerophon
form: 4 hero
brother: 8 Deliades
son: 11 Hippolochus
home: 7 Corinth
rode: 7 Pegasus
killed: 7 Chimera

Bell for Adano, A
author: 10 John Hersey
director: 9 Henry King
cast: 10 John Hodiak 11 Gene Tierney 13 William Bendix

bellicose see 11 belligerent

belligerence, belligerency 9 animosity, hostility, pugnacity 10 aggression, antagonism 11 bellicosity 12 warmongering 13 combativeness 14 aggressiveness, unfriendliness

belligerent 7 fighter, hostile, martial, warlike, warring 8 attacker, inimical 9 adversary, aggressor, bellicose, combatant, combative, irascible, irritable, truculent 10 aggressive, antagonist, pugnacious, unfriendly 11 bad-tempered, contentious, quarrelsome 12 antagonistic, cantankerous

belligerent state 3 foe 5 enemy 9 aggressor 13 hostile nation

Bellini, Gentile
born: 5 Italy 6 Venice
father: 6 Jacopo
brother: 8 Giovanni
artwork: 24 The Miracle of the True Cross 26 A Procession in St Mark's Square, The Miracle at Ponte di Lorenzo 27 St Mark Preaching in Alexandria 38 A Procession of Relics in the Piazza San Marco

Bellini, Giovanni (Giambellino)
born: 5 Italy 6 Venice
father: 6 Jacopo
brother: 7 Gentile
artwork: 8 St Jerome 16 Venus with a Mirror 18 St Francis in Ecstasy, The Madonna and Child 19 Allegory of Purgatory, The Agony in the Garden, The Barberini Madonna

Bellini, Jacopo
born: 5 Italy 6 Venice
son: 7 Gentile 8 Giovanni
artwork: 11 Crucifixion 16 Christ on the Cross 35 The Madonna and Child with Lionello d'Este

Bellini, Vincenzo
born: 5 Italy 7 Catania
composer of: 5 Norma, Zaira 8 Il Pirata 9 I Puritani 11 La Straniera 12 La Sonnambula 15 Bianca e Fernando

Bell Jar, The
author: 11 Sylvia Plath

Bellona
origin: 5 Roman
goddess of: 3 war
husband: 4 Mars
brother: 4 Mars
corresponds to: 4 Enyo

bellow 4 bawl, roar, yell 5 shout, whoop 6 holler, scream, shriek

Bellow, Saul
author of: 6 Herzog 13 Dean's December, Humboldt's Gift, Mosby's Memoirs 15 The Last Analysis 16 Mr Sammler's Planet 18 To Jerusalem and Back 25 The Adventures of Augie March

Bellows, George Wesley
born: 10 Columbus OH
artwork: 8 Lady Jean 11 Billy Sunday, Edith Cavell, Floating Ice, Up the Hudson 12 Forty-Two Kids 13 Men of the Docks

14 Rain on the River, Stag at Sharkey's 16 The Cliff Dwellers 18 Emma and her Children 21 Both Members of This Club

Bells Are Ringing
director: 16 Vincente Minnelli
cast: 9 Fred Clark 10 Dean Martin 12 Judy Holliday
song: 10 Just in Time 13 The Party's Over

Bells in Winter
author: 13 Czeslaw Milosz

Bells of St Mary's, The
director: 10 Leo McCarey
cast: 10 Bing Crosby (Father O'Malley) 12 Henry Travers 13 Ingrid Bergman
sequel to: 10 Going My Way
song: 20 Aren't You Glad You're You

bell tower 5 spire 6 belfry 7 steeple 9 campanile

Belluschi, Pietro
architect of: 21 Bank of America Building (San Francisco) 22 Juilliard School of Music (NYC) 31 Pan American World Airways Building (NYC, with Gropius)

bellwether 4 lead 5 doyen, guide, pilot 6 leader 8 director, shepherd 9 conductor, guidepost, precursor 10 forerunner, pacesetter 14 standard-bearer

belly 3 gut, yen 4 guts 5 taste, tummy 6 bowels, depths, desire, hunger, liking, paunch, vitals 7 abdomen, insides, midriff, stomach 8 appetite, interior, recesses 11 breadbasket

bellyache 4 beef, kick 5 gripe 6 grouch, grouse, squawk 7 grumble 8 complain 9 tummy ache 11 stomach ache 12 upset stomach

belong 6 go with 7 concern 8 attach to, be held by, be part of 9 be owned by, pertain to 10 be allied to 11 be a member of 12 be included in 15 be connected with, be the property of

belongings 4 gear, junk 5 goods, stuff 6 things 7 effects 8 movables 11 possessions 13 accoutrements, paraphernalia 16 personal property

beloved 4 beau, dear, love, wife 5 loved, lover 6 adored, fiance, spouse, steady 7 admired, darling, dearest, fiancee, husband, revered 8 endeared, esteemed, loved one, precious 9 betrothed, boyfriend, cherished, respected, treasured 10 girlfriend, sweetheart

below 4 less 5 lower, under 6 in hell 7 beneath, on earth, short of 8 inferior, unworthy 9 at a low ebb, downwards 10 downstairs, downstream, second-rate, underneath 11 at a discount, at the foot of, indifferent, subordinate, underground

below par 3 bad 4 poor 8 inferior 9 imperfect 10 second-rate 11 below average, not up to snuff

below standard 3 bad 4 poor 5 lousy 6 faulty, shoddy 8 below par, inferior, slipshod, terrible 9 imperfect 10 second-rate 12 not up to snuff

Belshazzar
 father: 9 Nabonidus 14 Nebuchadnezzar
belt 4 area, band, land, sash, zone 5 cinch, layer, strip 6 circle, girdle, region, stripe 7 country 8 district, encircle 9 waistband 10 cummerbund
Belteshazzar
 Babylonian name of: 6 Daniel
 friend: 7 Meshach 8 Abednego, Shadrach
Belus
 king of: 7 Chemmis
 father: 8 Poseidon
 mother: 5 Libya
 twin brother: 6 Agenor
 wife: 8 Anchinoe
 son: 6 Danaus 8 Aegyptus
 daughter: 4 Dido
Belushi, John
 born: 9 Chicago IL
 roles: 9 Neighbors 11 Animal House 16 The Blues Brothers 17 Saturday Night Live
be manifest 6 appear 7 be clear, be plain 8 be patent 9 be evident, be obvious 10 be apparent
bemoan 3 rue 5 mourn 6 bewail, lament, regret 7 cry over 8 weep over 9 whine over 10 grieve over
bemused 5 dazed, fuzzy 7 muddled, stunned 8 confused 9 engrossed, stupefied 10 bewildered, dull-witted, thoughtful 11 preoccupied 12 absent-minded
be nauseated by 4 hate 5 abhor 6 detest, loathe 7 despise 8 execrate 9 abominate 11 can't stomach 13 be disgusted by, find repulsive, find revolting, find sickening
Benbow, Horace
 character in: 9 Sanctuary
 author: 8 Faulkner
Ben Casey
 character: 12 Dr David Zorba, Dr Ted Hoffman 13 Nick Kanavaras 14 Dr Maggie Graham
 cast: 8 Sam Jaffe 10 Nick Dennis 12 Harry Landers, Vince Edwards 14 Bettye Ackerman
bench 3 pew 4 seat 5 board, court, stool, table 6 settee 7 counter, take out, trestle 8 sideline, tribunal 9 judiciary, workbench, worktable 10 second team 11 judge's chair, substitutes 12 second string
Benchley, Peter
 author of: 4 Jaws 7 The Deep
Benchley, Robert
 author of: 14 From Bed to Worse 21 Benchley Beside Himself, My Ten Years in a Quandary
benchmark 4 norm 5 gauge, guide, model 7 example, measure 8 exemplar, paradigm, standard 9 criterion, principle, prototype, reference, yardstick 10 touchstone
bend 3 arc, bow 4 flex, hook, lean, loop, mold, sway, turn, warp, wind 5 crook, curve, defer, force, shape, stoop, twist, yield 6 accede, attend, buckle, coerce, compel, crouch, give in, relent, submit 7

bow down, contort, control, succumb 9 genuflect, influence, surrender 10 buckle down, capitulate 11 make crooked
Bend in the River, The
 author: 9 V S Naipaul
Bendix, William
 born: 9 New York NY
 roles: 8 Hostages, Lifeboat 11 The Hairy Ape 13 A Bell for Adano 14 The Life of Riley 16 Guadalcanal Diary, The Babe Ruth Story
bend to one's own will 4 tame 5 break, train 6 master, subdue 8 overcome 10 discipline 12 show who's boss 18 have under one's thumb
beneath 5 below, lower, under 9 covered by 10 inferior to, underneath, unworthy of 11 subordinate, underground 16 below one's dignity
Benedick
 character in: 19 Much Ado About Nothing
 author: 11 Shakespeare
benedictine
 type: 6 brandy, cognac 7 liqueur
 flavor: 4 herb
 with brandy: 5 B and B
 with bourbon: 9 Twin Hills 13 Brighton Punch
 with whiskey: 10 Frisco Sour
benediction 6 prayer 7 benison 8 blessing 10 invocation 12 consecration 13 closing prayer
benefaction 4 alms, gift 5 grant 7 charity 8 bestowal, donation, offering 9 endowment 10 almsgiving 12 contribution, dispensation, philanthropy
benefactor 5 angel, donor 6 backer, friend, helper, patron 7 sponsor 8 upholder 9 supporter 11 contributor 14 fairy godmother
beneficent 6 benign, kindly 7 liberal 8 generous, salutary 10 beneficial, benevolent, charitable 11 magnanimous 13 philanthropic
beneficial 6 useful 7 good for, healing, helpful 8 valuable 9 favorable, healthful 10 productive, profitable, propitious 12 advantageous, contributive
beneficiary 4 heir 7 grantee, heiress, legatee 8 receiver 9 inheritor, recipient
benefit 3 aid, use 4 gain, good, help 5 asset, avail, serve, value, worth 6 assist, behalf, better, profit 7 advance, be aided, service 8 be helped, be served, blessing, interest 9 advantage, do good for 10 be useful to, betterment, profit from 13 charity affair 18 charity performance
Benet, Stephen Vincent
 author of: 7 America 8 Tiger Joy 11 Western Star 14 John Brown's Body, Thirteen O'Clock, Young Adventure 16 Five Men and Pompey 19 Tales Before Midnight, The Headless Horseman 20 The Beginning of Wisdom 24 The Devil and Daniel Webster

benevolence 7 charity 8 good will, kindness 9 benignity 10 compassion, generosity, kindliness, liberality 13 bountifulness 14 charitableness 15 humanitarianism, kindheartedness

benevolent 3 kin 6 benign, humane, tender 7 liberal 8 generous 9 benignant, bounteous, bountiful, unselfish 10 bighearted, charitable 11 considerate, kindhearted, warmhearted 12 humanitarian 13 compassionate, philanthropic

Bengali
  language family: 12 Indo-European
  branch: 11 Indo-Iranian
  group: 5 Indic
  spoken in: 5 (northern) India

Ben-Hur
  author: 10 Lew Wallace
  character: 4 Iras, Isas 5 Jesus 6 Esther 7 Messala 9 Balthasar, Simonides 11 Judah Ben-Hur
  director: 12 William Wyler
  cast: 11 Jack Hawkins, Stephen Boyd 12 Hugh Griffith 14 Charlton Heston (Judah Ben-Hur)
  setting: 9 Palestine
  Oscar for: 5 actor (Heston) 7 picture 8 director 14 cinematography 15 supporting actor (Griffith)

benighted 4 dumb 5 crude, unhip 8 backward, ignorant, untaught 9 primitive, untutored 10 illiterate, uncultured, uneducated, uninformed, unlettered, unschooled 11 empty-headed, know-nothing, uncivilized 12 uncultivated 13 unenlightened

benign 4 good, kind, mild, nice, soft 5 balmy, lucky 6 genial, gentle, humane, kindly, tender 7 affable 8 gracious, harmless, pleasant, salutary 9 favorable, healthful, innocuous, temperate 10 auspicious, benevolent, propitious 11 encouraging, kindhearted, soft-hearted 13 tenderhearted

benignant 4 kind 6 benign, humane, kindly, tender 9 forgiving 10 benevolent 11 kindhearted 13 compassionate, tenderhearted

benignity 8 good will, kindness 10 compassion, kindliness 11 benevolence 15 kindheartedness

Benin
  other name: 17 Republic of Dahomey
  capital: 9 Porto-Novo
  largest city: 7 Cotonou
  others: 4 Pobe 5 Kandi, Kerou, Ketou, Porga 6 Abomey, Ouidah 7 Parakou, Savalou 8 Aplahoue
  government: 30 Military Council of the Revolution
  monetary unit: 5 franc 7 centime
  lake: 5 Aheme 6 Nokoue
  mountain: 7 Atakora
  river: 4 Mono 5 Niger, Oueme 6 Couffo
  sea: 8 Atlantic
  physical feature:
  gulf: 6 Guinea
  plains: 6 Borgou
  people: 3 Fon, Pla 4 Adja, Aizo, Mina,

Peul 5 Pedah, Peuhl, Somba 6 Bariba, Fulani, Yoruba 8 Pilapila 9 Dahomeyan
  language: 3 Fon 5 Dendi 6 Bariba, French, Fulani, Yoruba
  religion: 5 Islam 6 tribal 7 animism 13 Roman Catholic
  food:
  tapioca: 4 gari

Benito Cereno
  author: 14 Herman Melville

Benjamin
  father: 5 Jacob
  mother: 6 Rachel
  also known as: 6 Benoni
  brother: 3 Dan, Gad 4 Levi 5 Asher, Judah 6 Joseph, Reuben, Simeon 7 Zebulun 8 Issachar, Naphtali
  sister: 5 Dinah
  descendant of: 11 Benjaminite

Bennet family
  characters in: 17 Pride and Prejudice
  members: 4 Jane, Mary 5 Kitty, Lydia 9 Elizabeth
  author: 6 Austen

Bennett, Arnold
  author of: 8 Accident 10 Clayhanger, Lord Raingo, Milestones, These Twain 11 Buried Alive 13 Hilda Lessways, Riceyman Steps 15 The Old Wives' Tale 18 Anna of the Five Towns

Benny, Jack
  real name: 16 Benjamin Kubelsky
  born: 10 Waukegan IL
  roles: 12 Charley's Aunt 13 Jack Benny Show, To Be or Not To Be 16 Artists and Models

Benoni *see* 8 Benjamin

Benson
  character: 5 Kraus 12 (Lt Gov) Benson DuBois 13 (Gov) Eugene Gatling
  cast: 10 James Noble 11 Inga Swenson 15 Robert Guillaume

bent 4 bias, gift, mind 5 bowed, flair, knack 6 angled, arched, curved, genius, liking, talent 7 ability, aptness, crooked, faculty, hunched, leaning, stooped, twisted 8 aptitude, capacity, facility, fondness, penchant, tendency 9 contorted, endowment 10 attraction, partiality, proclivity, propensity 11 disposition, inclination 12 predilection 14 predisposition

bent into folds 6 fluted, ridged 7 creased, grooved, pleated 8 crinkled, furrowed, puckered, wrinkled 10 corrugated

Benton, Robert
  director of: 14 Kramer vs Kramer (Oscar) 16 Places in the Heart

Benton, Thomas Hart
  born: 8 Neosho MO
  artwork: 7 Bubbles 8 Boomtown 9 Homestead 12 American Life 13 Arts of the West, Cotton Pickers 14 Threshing Wheat 19 Louisiana Rice Fields, The Lord Is My Shepherd

Benue-Congo
  language family: 16 Niger-Kordofanian
  group: 10 Niger-Congo

includes: 3 Tiv 4 Zulu 5 Bantu, Jukun 6 Chwana, Nyanja 7 Kikongo, Luganda, Swahili

benumb 4 daze, dull 5 blunt 6 deaden 7 stupefy 15 make insensitive

Benvolio
character in: 14 Romeo and Juliet
author: 11 Shakespeare

Benz, Karl
nationality: 6 German
inventor of: 22 electric ignition engine 26 differential gear automobile
built first practical: 10 automobile

be obvious 6 appear 7 be clear, be plain 8 be patent 9 be evident 10 be apparent, be manifest

be off 2 go 5 leave, scram 6 beat it, begone, cut out, depart, go away, set out 8 set forth, withdraw 10 make tracks

be of one mind 5 agree 6 accord, concur 10 think alike 11 see eye to eye

be of use 3 aid 4 help 5 serve 6 assist 7 benefit

be on a par with 5 equal 6 be up to 7 compare 10 be as good as 12 be comparable 14 be in a class with

be on the sick list 3 ail 5 be ill 6 be sick 8 be unwell 12 be indisposed 13 be in ill health 17 be under the weather

Beor
son: 4 Bela 6 Balaam

Beothuk (Red Indians)
location: 6 Canada 12 Newfoundland
intermixed with: 7 Naskapi

Beowulf
author: 7 unknown
character: 4 Finn 5 Breca, Hnaef, Oslaf, Scyld 6 Wiglaf 7 Guthlaf, Hengest, Higelac, Hrethel, Unferth 8 Aeschere, Heardred, Hondscio, Hrothgar 9 Hildeburh
great hall: 6 Heorot
monster: 7 Grendel 14 Grendel's mother
tribe: 5 Danes, Geats 8 Frisians
Beowulf tears from Grendel: 3 arm

bequeath 4 will 5 endow, leave 6 impart 7 consign 8 hand down

bequest 6 legacy 8 bestowal 9 endowment 10 settlement 11 inheritance

be part of 4 form 6 make up 8 belong to 9 appertain, pertain to 10 constitute

be patent 6 appear 7 be clear, be plain 9 be evident, be obvious 10 be apparent, be manifest

be pertinent to 4 bear 5 apply, refer 6 affect, relate 7 concern, pertain 9 appertain, touch upon

be plain 6 appear 7 be clear 8 be patent 9 be evident, be obvious 10 be apparent, be manifest

be pleased with 4 like 5 favor 7 approve

berate 5 scold 6 rail at, rebuke 7 bawl out, chew out, reprove, upbraid 8 reproach 9 castigate, criticize, reprimand 10 take to task, tongue-lash

Berber
language family: 11 Afro-asiatic 13 Hamito-Semitic
spoken in: 6 Sahara 11 North Africa

Berchta see 7 Perchta

bereave 3 rob 5 strip 6 divest 7 deprive 10 dispossess

Berecyntia see 6 Cybele

Berenice's Hair
constellation of: 13 Coma Berenices

be resigned to 6 accept 8 tolerate

Beret
character in: 16 Giants of the Earth
author: 7 Rolvaag

be revolted by 4 hate 5 abhor 6 detest, loathe 7 despise 8 execrate 9 abominate 10 recoil from, shrink from 11 can't stomach 13 find repulsive

berg 4 floe 7 glacier, iceberg, icefloe
South African: 8 mountain
French: 4 neve 5 serac

Berg, Alban
born: 6 Vienna 7 Austria
composer of: 4 Lulu 7 Wozzeck

Bergen, Candace
father: 11 Edgar Bergen
born: 14 Beverly Hills CA
roles: 8 The Group 15 Carnal Knowledge

Berger, Thomas
author of: 7 The Feud 9 Neighbors 10 Vital Parts 11 Killing Time 12 Little Big Man, Sneaky People 15 Regiment of Women

Bergman, Ingmar
director of: 14 The Seventh Seal 16 Cries and Whispers, Wild Strawberries 17 Fanny and Alexander 19 Scenes from a Marriage 20 Smiles of a Summer Night

Bergman, Ingrid
born: 6 Sweden 9 Stockholm
roles: 8 Gaslight (Oscar) 9 Anastasia (Oscar), Joan of Arc, Notorious 10 Casablanca, Intermezzo, Spellbound 17 A Woman Called Golda, The Bells of St Mary's 19 For Whom the Bell Tolls 24 Murder on the Orient Express 25 The Inn of the Sixth Happiness

Berith, Berit, Brith, Brit 8 covenant 12 circumcision

Berle, Milton
real name: 15 Milton Berlinger
nickname: 11 Uncle Miltie 12 Mr Television
born: 9 New York NY
roles: 17 The Texaco Star Hour 18 Who's Minding the Mint 23 Always Leave Them Laughing

Berlin (East, West)
landmark: 14 Humboldt Castle 15 Gruenwald Castle 16 Berlin Opera House, Markisches Museum 21 Scharlottenburg Castle 29 Kaiser-Wilhelm-Gedachtniskirche
river: 5 Spree
square: 14 Alexander-Platz

Berlin, Elaine
real name of: 9 Elaine May

Berlinger, Milton
  real name of: 11 Milton Berle
Berlioz, (Louis) Hector
  born: 6 France 13 La Cote St Andre
  composer of: 6 Rob Roy, Te Deum 7
  Requiem, 8 Herminie, King Lear,
  Waverley 9 Cleopatra, Nuits d'Ete 10 Le
  Corsaire, Les Troyens, The Trojans 11
  Sardanapale 13 Harold in Italy 14 Les
  Francs Juges, Romeo and Juliet 16
  Benvenuto Cellini, Damnation of Faust,
  Le Carnaval Romain, L'Enfance du Christ
  18 Beatrice and Benedict 20 Symphonie
  Fantastique 28 Symphonie Funebre et
  Triomphale
Bermuda
  other name: 13 Somers Islands
  capital/largest city: 8 Hamilton
  others: 8 St George
  head of state: 14 British monarch 15
  governor general
  island: 4 Boaz 5 Coney 7 Bermuda, Ireland, Watford 8 Somerset, St Davids 9 St
  Georges
  highest point: 8 Town Hill
  sea: 8 Atlantic
  physical feature:
  harbor: 6 Castle
  hill: 5 Gibbs
  people:
  discoverer: 14 Juan de Bermudez
  language: 7 English
  religion: 8 Anglican 10 Protestant 15
  Church of England
  feature:
  dancers: 6 Gombey
Bern
  capital of: 11 Switzerland
  landmark: 10 Clock Tower 12 Nydegg
  Church
  river: 4 Aare
Bernard, Henriette-Rosine
  real name of: 14 Sarah Bernhardt
Bernhardt, Sarah
  real name: 22 Henriette-Rosine Bernard
  nickname: 11 Divine Sarah
  born: 5 Paris 6 France
  roles: 6 Phedre 7 Hernani, Ruy Blas 8
  King Lear 14 Queen Elizabeth 17 La
  Dame aux Camelias
Bernini, Gianlorenzo (Giovanni Lorenzo)
  born: 5 Italy 6 Naples
  father: 6 Pietro
  artwork: 7 Montoya 8 Louis XIV,
  Vigevano 10 Bellarmine, St Longinus 13
  Cathedra Petri, Francis I d'Este, The Assumption 15 Apollo and Daphne 18
  Costanza Buonarelli 19 The Rape of Proserpina 21 Saints Andrew and Thomas,
  The Ecstasy of St Theresa 24 Blessed
  Lodovica Albertoni 25 Aeneas Anchises
  and Ascanius
  architect of: 12 Santa Bibiana 16 Piazza
  of St Peter's (Rome) 19 Palazzo Monteci-
  torio 21 Sant' Andrea al Quirinale 22 Palazzo Chigi-Odescalchi 23 Fountain of

the Four Rivers 24 Santa Maria dell'
Assunzione
Bernoulli, Daniel
  field: 11 mathematics
  nationality: 5 Swiss
  theory of: 5 gases 6 fluids 18 Bernoulli's
  Equation
Bernstein, Carl
  author of: 12 The Final Days (with Bob
  Woodward) 19 All the President's Men
  (with Bob Woodward)
  newspaper reporter for: 14 Washington
  Post
Bernstein, Leonard
  born: 10 Lawrence MA
  composer of: 4 Mass 7 Candide, Kaddish 8 Jeremiah 9 Facsimile, Fancy Free,
  On the Town 13 West Side Story, Wonderful Town 15 The Age of Anxiety, Trouble in Tahiti 16 Chichester Psalms
Beroe
  father: 6 Adonis
  mother: 9 Aphrodite
  nurse of: 6 Semele
Berowne
  character in: 16 Love's Labour's Lost
  author: 11 Shakespeare
Berra, Yogi (Lawrence Peter Berra)
  sport: 8 baseball
  position: 5 coach 7 catcher
  team: 14 New York Yankees
berry 3 egg 4 seed 5 fruit, grain, grape 6
dollar, kernel, tomato, banana 7 currant 8
allspice, bayberry, mulberry 9 blueberry,
cranberry, raspberry 10 blackberry, gooseberry, peppercorn, strawberry 11 boysen-
berry, huckleberry, pomegranate 12 check-
erberry
  poisonous: 9 baneberry
Berryman, John
  author of: 8 Recovery 9 Delusions 11
  Love and Fame 12 77 Dream Songs 13
  The Dream Songs 16 Berryman's Sonnets 19 The Freedom of the Poet 21 His
  Toy His Dream His Rest 26 Homage to
  Mistress Bradstreet
berserk 4 amok, wild 5 crazy 6 insane 7
frantic, violent 8 demented, deranged,
frenzied, maniacal, wild-eyed 9 desperate
10 distracted, distraught 12 out of control
Berserker
  origin: 6 Nordic
  form: 7 warrior
berth 3 bed, job 4 bunk, dock, pier, post,
quay, slip, spot 5 haven, niche, place,
wharf 6 billet, employ, office 8 position 9
anchorage, situation 11 appointment 12
resting place 13 sleeping place
Berthollet, Claude Louis
  field: 9 chemistry
  nationality: 6 French
  researched: 7 ammonia 8 chlorine
Bertram
  character in: 20 All's Well That Ends
  Well
  author: 11 Shakespeare

Bertram family
  characters in: 13 Mansfield Park
  members: 3 Tom 5 Julia, Maria 6
    Edmund 9 Sir Thomas
  author: 6 Austen
beryl
  color: 5 green 6 yellow
Berzelius, Jons Jakob
  field: 9 chemistry
  nationality: 7 Swedish
  developed: 15 chemical symbols
  discovered: 6 cerium 7 silicon, thorium 8
    selenium, titanium 9 zirconium
  founded: 15 modern chemistry
be satisfactory 2 do 6 answer 7 suffice 8
  be enough 10 be adequate, pass muster
  12 be sufficient, do well enough
be scant 4 lack, want 8 be skimpy 9 fall
  short 14 be insufficient 15 be in short supply
beseech 3 beg 4 pray 6 adjure 7 entreat,
  implore 9 plead with 10 supplicate
beset 3 dog, set 4 bead, deck, stud 5 annoy, array, hem in, hound, worry 6 assail,
  badger, harass, pester, plague 7 bedevil,
  besiege, set upon 8 surround 9 beleaguer,
  embellish
be sick 3 ail 5 be ill 8 be unwell 12 be indisposed 13 be in ill health
beside 2 by 4 near 5 saved 6 except,
  nearby, unless 7 abreast, barring, without
  8 let alone 9 adjoining, alongside, aside
  from, other than 10 on a par with, side by
  side 12 compared with, in addition to
beside oneself 4 wild 6 elated, joyful, joyous, raging 7 berserk, exalted, frantic, furious, ranting 8 agitated, blissful, distrait, ecstatic, frenetic, frenzied 9 delirious, in a
  frenzy, overjoyed, rapturous 10 distracted,
  distraught, distressed, enraptured 11 carried away, overwrought, transported 13 out
  of one's wits
besides 3 but 4 also, save 6 as well, except, saving 7 barring 8 moreover 9 accepting, excluding, other than 11 exclusive
  of, furthermore
besiege 3 dog 5 annoy, beset, hound 6 assail, badger, harass, pester, plague 7 assault, bedevil 9 beleaguer 10 lay siege to
besmear 4 soil 5 dirty, muddy, smear, stain,
  sully 6 mess up, slop up, smudge 7 begrime, tarnish 8 besmirch
besmeared 5 dirty, grimy, messy 6 grubby,
  smudgy 7 muddied, sullied 8 begrimed 10
  besmirched
besmirch 4 soil 5 smear, stain, sully, taint 6
  defame, defile 7 blacken, corrupt, debauch, degrade, slander, tarnish 8 discolor, disgrace, dishonor 9 discredit
besotted 5 drunk 6 sodden, soused,
  wasted, zapped, zonked 7 smashed 9
  plastered 10 inebriated, infatuated 11 intoxicated 17 under the influence 20 three
  sheets to the wind

bespangle 3 dot 4 gild, star, stud 5 adorn,
  jewel 6 bedeck 7 dress up, festoon, garnish 8 decorate, ornament 9 embellish 10
  illuminate
bespatter 4 blot, soil, spot 5 decry, dirty, libel, smear, stain, sully, taint 6 debase, defame, defile, smudge, splash 7 condemn,
  slander, smotter, tarnish 8 denounce, reproach 9 deprecate, fling dirt 10 calumniate, disapprove
Bessemer, Sir Henry
  nationality: 7 English
  inventor of manufacturing process for:
    5 steel
best 3 top 4 most, pick 5 cream, elite 6
  choice, finest, nicest, utmost 7 hardest,
  largest 8 foremost, greatest, superior, top-
  notch 9 greetings, loveliest, most fully,
  most of all, unequaled, unrivaled 10 unexcelled 11 compliments, unsurpassed 13
  most competent, most desirable, most excellent 14 highest quality, kindest regards
Best, Charles Herbert
  field: 10 physiology
  nationality: 8 Canadian
  discovered: 7 insulin
best group 3 top 5 cream, elite 6 choice 9
  chosen few 10 select body 14 cream of
  the crop, creme de la creme
bestial 5 cruel 6 brutal, savage 7 beastly 8
  barbaric, depraved, inhumane, ruthless 9
  barbarous, merciless
bestir 4 goad, spur, stir, urge 5 rouse,
  speed 6 arouse, excite, hasten 7 quicken
  8 activate 9 get moving
bestir oneself 5 rouse 8 be active 9 make
  haste 10 get up early, lose no time 11
  keep moving 15 make short work of 19
  seize the opportunity
bestow 3 use 4 give, mete 5 apply, award,
  grant, lay on, spend 6 accord, confer, devote, donate, employ, expend, impart, occupy, render 7 consign, consume, deal
  out, deliver, hand out, present, utilize 8
  dispense, give away 9 apportion 10 settle
  upon, turn over to
bestowal 4 alms, gift 5 bonus, favor, grant
  6 reward 7 charity, present, tribute 8 donation, gratuity, offering 9 endowment 10
  conferment, recompense 11 benefaction
  12 contribution, dispensation
best society
  French: 10 grand monde
Best Years of Our Lives, The
  director: 12 William Wyler
  based on story by: 15 MacKinlay Kantor
  script: 14 Robert Sherwood
  cast: 8 Myrna Loy 11 Dana Andrews 12
    Teresa Wright, Virginia Mayo 13 Frederic
    March, Harold Russell 15 Hoagy
    Carmichael
  Oscar for: 5 actor (March) 7 picture 8 di-
    rector
be sufficient 6 answer 7 suffice 8 be
  enough 10 be adequate, pass muster 12
  do well enough 14 be satisfactory

bet 4 ante, risk **5** stake, wager **6** chance, gamble, hazard, plunge **7** venture **8** make a bet **9** speculate **11** speculation

bete noir 5 bogey **6** plague **7** bugaboo, bugbear **8** anathema, bogeyman **9** annoyance **10** black beast

be thankful 8 thank God **10** appreciate **11** thank heaven **19** thank one's lucky stars

Bethe, Hans Albrecht
   field: 7 physics
   developed: 8 atom bomb
   awarded: 10 Nobel Prize

be the same 5 agree, equal, match **6** equate **7** balance **11** be identical

Bethuel
   son: 5 Laban

betide 4 fall **5** occur **6** befall, chance, happen **10** come to pass

betimes 5 early **10** in good time

betoken 4 show **5** augur **6** attest, denote **7** portend, presage, signify **8** foretell

betray 4 dupe, fink, jilt, show, tell **5** rat on, trick **6** expose, reveal, squeal, tell on, unmask **7** abandon, deceive, divulge, lay bare, let down, let slip, sell out, two-time, uncover, violate **8** blurt out, disclose, give away **9** play Judas **10** be disloyal **11** double-cross **12** be unfaithful **13** inform against, play false with **14** break faith with

betrayal 7 perfidy, telling, treason **8** bad faith, sedition, trickery **9** chicanery, deception, duplicity, falseness, treachery, two-timing, violation **10** disclosure, disloyalty, divulgence, revelation **11** double-cross **13** breach of faith, double-dealing **14** unfaithfulness

betrayal of trust 7 falsity, perfidy **8** apostasy, cheating **9** falseness, recreancy **10** disloyalty, infidelity **11** inconstancy **13** deceitfulness, double-dealing, faithlessness **14** unfaithfulness

Betrayer 13 Judas Iscariot

betroth 6 commit, engage, pledge **7** espouse, promise **8** affiance, contract

betrothal 5 troth **8** espousal **10** affiancing, betrothing, engagement

betrothed 6 fiancé **7** engaged, fiancée **8** promised **9** affianced

Bettelheim, Bruno
   author of: 15 Love Is Not Enough **16** The Informed Heart **20** The Uses of Enchantment

better 3 top **4** more **5** finer, outdo, raise **6** bigger, enrich, exceed, fitter, larger, longer, refine, uplift **7** advance, elevate, enhance, farther, forward, further, greater, improve, mending, promote, surpass, upgrade **8** heighten, improved, increase, outstrip, stronger, superior **9** cultivate, healthier, improving **10** preferable, recovering, strengthen **11** more healthy, progressing

bettering 9 elevation **10** betterment **11** advancement, improvement

betterment 4 good **6** reform **7** benefit **8** revision **9** advantage, amendment, promotion **10** correction, enrichment **11** advancement, improvement **12** amelioration,

regeneration **13** rectification **14** reconstruction

better than average 2 A-1 **3** A-OK **4** aces, fine, good, tops **5** great, prime, super **6** choice, grade-A, superb **7** capital, special **8** peerless, sterling, superior, terrific, topnotch **9** excellent, first-rate, marvelous, matchless, wonderful **10** first-class, inimitable, preeminent, remarkable, tremendous **11** exceptional, outstanding, superlative **12** incomparable **13** extraordinary

between 4 amid **5** among, entre **6** amidst, atwixt, shared **7** betwixt, joining **9** in the midst **10** connecting

between ourselves
   French: 9 entre nous
   Latin: 8 inter nos

Between the Battles
   author: 20 Bjornstjerne Bjornson

between themselves
   Latin: 7 inter se

between us 9 entre nous, privately **14** confidentially **15** between you and me **16** between me and thee, between ourselves

betwixt and between 4 so-so **7** average **8** confused **9** in between, undecided **14** halfway between **21** neither one nor the other

Beulah, Land of
   place in: 16 Pilgrim's Progress
   author: 6 Bunyan

be unlike 4 vary **6** differ **7** deviate, diverge **8** conflict, disagree **12** be at variance, be discordant, be dissimilar

be unwell 3 ail **5** be ill **6** be sick **12** be indisposed **13** be in ill health

be unwilling to pursue
   Latin: 13 nolle prosequi

bevel 4 blow, cant, ream, tool **5** angle, bezel, miter, mitre, slant, slope, snape, splay **6** aslant **7** incline, oblique **8** slanting

beverage 3 ade, ale, cup, nog, pop, tea **4** beer, brew, dram, grog, milk, soda, soup, wine **5** broth, cider, cocoa, draft, drink, juice, julep, lager, leban, punch, toddy, water **6** bishop, coffee, cordial, eggnog, liquid, liquor, potion **7** limeade, seltzer, spirits, wassail **8** aperitif, cocktail, highball, lemonade, libation, potation **9** champagne, chocolate, orangeade

Beverley, Constance de
   character in: 7 Marmion
   author: 5 Scott

Beverly Hillbillies, The
   character: 11 Jed Clampett **12** Jane Hathaway, Jethro Bodine **14** Granny Clampett, Milton Drysdale **16** Ellie May Clampett
   cast: 9 Irene Ryan, Max Baer Jr, Nancy Kulp **10** Buddy Ebsen **12** Donna Douglas **13** Raymond Bailey

Beverly Hills Cop
   director: 11 Martin Brest
   cast: 11 Eddie Murphy **13** Judge Reinhold, Lisa Eilbacher

bevy 4 band, body, herd, host, pack **5** brood, covey, crowd, drove, flock, group, horde, party, shoal, swarm **6** clutch, flight, gaggle, school, throng 7 company, coterie 9 gathering, multitude 10 assemblage, collection

bewail 3 rue 5 mourn 6 bemoan, lament, regret 7 cry over, deplore 8 moan over, weep over 10 grieve over

beware 4 mind 6 be wary 7 look out 8 take care, take heed 9 be careful 11 take warning, watch out for 12 be on the alert, guard against 15 take precautions

beware of the dog
  Latin: 9 cave canem

bewhiskered 5 bushy, hairy 6 shaggy 7 bearded, bristly, hirsute 8 unshaven 11 mustachioed

bewilder 5 addle, mix up 6 baffle, bemuse, muddle, puzzle 7 confuse, fluster, mystify, nonplus, perplex, stupefy 8 befuddle 10 disconcert

bewildered 7 at a loss, up a tree 8 all at sea, confused 9 perplexed 10 confounded, nonplussed 12 disconcerted

bewilderment 9 confusion 10 perplexity, puzzlement 11 frustration 13 mystification

bewitch 4 jinx 5 charm, spook 6 turn on 7 bedevil, beguile, delight, enchant 8 entrance 9 captivate, enrapture, fascinate 12 cast a spell on 14 put under a spell

bewitched 7 charmed, seduced 8 beguiled 9 bedeviled, enchanted, entranced 10 captivated, enraptured, fascinated, spellbound 11 under a spell

Bewitched
  character: 6 Endora, Serena 7 Maurice 9 Aunt Clara, Esmerelda, Larry Tate 11 Uncle Arthur 12 Abner Kravitz 13 Gladys Kravitz 14 Darrin Stephens 15 Tabitha Stephens 16 Samantha Stephens
  cast: 8 Dick York 9 Paul Lynde 10 David White 11 Dick Sargent, Marion Lorne, Sandra Gould 12 George Tobias, Maurice Evans 13 Alice Ghostley 14 Agnes Moorehead 19 Elizabeth Montgomery

bewitching 8 alluring, charming, enticing, fetching, tempting 9 appealing, beguiling, disarming, seductive 10 enchanting, entrancing 11 captivating, fascinating 12 irresistible

be worthy of 4 earn, rate 5 merit 7 deserve

bey, beg 4 lord 6 prince 8 governor

beyond 2 by 4 over, past 5 above, later, ultra 6 abroad, except, yonder 7 beneath, besides, farther, further, outside, passing 8 superior 9 exceeding, hereafter 10 out of range, out of reach 11 at a distance, in addition to

Beyond Desire
  author: 15 Maxwell Anderson

beyond hope 8 hopeless 9 desperate 10 despairing

Beyond Human Power
  author: 20 Bjornstjerne Bjornson

beyond one's means 10 immoderate 11 extravagant 15 too high on the hog

beyond question 4 sure 6 surely 7 certain, decided, settled 9 certainly, decidedly 10 absolutely, positively 12 without doubt

Bharat (Varsha) see 5 India

Bhot see 5 Tibet

Bhutan
  other name: 7 Druk-Yul 15 Kingdom of Bhutan, Land of the Dragon
  capital/largest city: 6 Thimbu 7 Thimphu
  others: 4 Paro 12 Phuntsholing 14 Wangdu Phedrang
  government:
  assembly: 7 Tsongdu
  head of state/ government:
  hereditary king: 10 dragon king, druk gyalpo
  other leader:
  spiritual leader: 10 dharma raja
  temporal ruler: 7 deb raja
  monetary unit: 5 paisa, rupee 8 chetrums, ngultrum
  mountain: 5 Black 9 Himalayas 10 Chomo Lhari
  highest point: 10 Kula Kangri
  river: 4 Kuru, Paro 5 Machu, Manas, Pachu, Torsa 6 Amochu, Raidak, Tongsa 7 Sankosh, Thinchu
  physical feature:
  plain: 5 Duars
  people: 5 Monpa 6 Bhutia 7 Tibetan 8 Assamese, Nepalese
  dragon people: 7 Drukpas
  language: 5 Hindi, Lhoke 7 Tibetan 8 Dzongkha, Nepalese
  religion: 15 Tibetan Buddhism
  place:
  fortress (dzong): 4 Paro 6 Bya Kar, Tongsa 8 Tashi Cho
  feature:
  pony: 6 Tangun

Bia
  origin: 5 Greek
  personifies: 5 force
  father: 11 Titan Pallas
  mother: 4 Styx
  brother: 5 Zelos 6 Cratus
  sister: 4 Nike

Biadice
  husband: 8 Cretheus

Bianca
  character in: 19 The Taming of the Shrew
  author: 11 Shakespeare

Bianchi, Mose
  born: 5 Italy, Milan
  artwork: 11 Snow in Milan 21 Return from the Festival

bias 4 bent, sway 5 angle, slant 7 bigotry, feeling, leaning 8 tendency 9 fixed idea, prejudice, proneness 10 narrow view, partiality, predispose, proclivity, propensity, unfairness 11 inclination, intolerance 12 diagonal line, one-sidedness, predilection 13 preconception 16 narrow-mindedness, preconceived idea

Bias
  father: 8 Amythaon
  mother: 7 Idomene
  brother: 8 Melampus

wife: 4 Pero 10 Iphianassa
   son: 6 Talaus
   daughter: 8 Anaxibia
   secured: 6 cattle
   cattle owned by: 8 Phylacus
biased 6 unfair, unjust 7 bigoted, slanted 8 inclined 9 arbitrary 10 intolerant, prejudiced 11 close-minded, opinionated 12 narrow-minded
bibelot 5 curio 7 trinket 8 ornament 9 objet d'art
bible 5 guide 6 manual 8 handbook 9 authority, guidebook 13 reference book
Bible 6 Gospel 7 the Book 8 good book, Holy Writ 10 Scriptures 11 bibliotheca, the Good Book 13 holy scripture 14 Holy Scriptures, sacred writings
Bible, books of
   Old Testament: 3 Job 4 Amos, Ezra, Joel, Osee, Ruth 5 Hosea, Jonah, Jonas, Josue, Kings, Micah, Nahum, Tobit 6 Abdias, Aggeus, Baruch, Daniel, Esdras, Esther, Exodus, Haggai, Isaiah, Isaias, Joshua, Judges, Judith, Psalms, Samuel, Sirach, Tobias, Wisdom 7 Ezekiel, Genesis, Habacuc, Malachi, Micheas, Numbers, Obadiah 8 Ezechiel, Habakkuk, Jeremiah, Jeremias, Nehemiah, Proverbs 9 Leviticus, Maccabees, Machabees, Malachias, Sophonias, Zacharias, Zechariah, Zephaniah 10 Chronicles 11 Deuteronomy, Song of Songs 12 Ecclesiastes, Lamentations 13 Paralipomenon, Song of Solomon 15 Ecclesiasticus 19 Canticle of Canticles
   New Testament: 4 Acts, John, Jude, Luke, Mark 5 James, Peter 6 Romans 7 Hebrews, Matthew, Timothy 9 Ephesians, Galatians 10 Colossians, Revelation 11 Corinthians, Philippians 13 Thessalonians, Titus Philemon
   first five books called: 3 Law 5 Torah 10 Pentateuch
   first seven books called: 10 Heptateuch
Bible scholar 7 biblist 9 biblicist
Bible version 6 The Way 7 Vulgate 8 Peshitta 9 Gutenberg, Jerusalem, King James 10 New English 11 New American, Rheims-Douay 14 The Living Bible 15 American revised, revised standard
Biblical animal 7 unicorn
Biblical gemstone 6 ligure 7 sardius 8 sardonyx
Biblical instrument 7 sackbut
Biblical length
   reed: 9 six cubits
Biblical measure 3 cab, cor 4 epah, omet, reed, seah 5 cubit, epheh, homer 6 shekel 9 half homer
Biblical personage 9 patriarch
Biblical plant 6 hyssop 12 Rose of Sharon
Biblical precept
   Hebrew: 7 mitsvah, mitzvah
Biblical tree 5 algum, almug 6 storax 7 juniper 8 sycamire 10 gopherwood 11 shittim wood 12 opobalsammum 13 red sandalwood

Biblical weed 4 tare 6 darnel
Biblical weight 6 talent
Biblicist 12 Bible scholar
Bibliotheca 5 Bible 14 sacred writings
Biblist 12 Bible scholar
Bickel, Ernest Frederick McIntyre
   real name of: 13 Frederic March
bicker 4 spar, spat 5 argue, fight 6 haggle 7 dispute, quarrel, wrangle 8 disagree, squabble
bickering 4 spat 5 fight 7 arguing, dispute, quarrel 8 argument, fighting 9 wrangling 10 quarreling, squabbling 12 disagreement
Bickford, Charles
   born: 11 Cambridge MA
   roles: 12 Anna Christie 13 Johnny Belinda 16 Song of Bernadette 18 The Farmer's Daughter
bicycle 4 bike, ride 5 cycle, moped 10 two-wheeler
   invented by: 7 Starley
Bicycle Thief, The
   director: 14 Vittorio De Sica
   cast: 14 Lianella Carell 18 Lamberto Maggiorani
bid 3 ask, say, try 4 call, tell, wish 5 greet, offer, order 6 beckon, charge, demand, direct, effort, enjoin, insist, invite, ordain, summon, tender 7 attempt, command, proffer, propose, request, require 8 call upon, endeavor, instruct, offering, proposal 10 invitation
bidding 4 beck, call 5 offer, order 6 behest, charge, demand, offers 7 command, dictate, mandate, request, summons 8 offering, proposal 9 direction, summoning, tendering 10 injunction, invitation, proffering 11 instruction
bide 4 stay, wait 5 abide, dwell, stand, tarry 6 endure, linger, remain, suffer 8 tolerate 9 put up with
Bierce, Ambrose
   author of: 15 Can Such Things Be? 16 In the Midst of Life 19 The Devil's Dictionary
Bierstadt, Albert
   born: 7 Germany 8 Solingen
   artwork: 11 Laramie Park 13 Mount Corcoran 17 The Rocky Mountains 20 Discovery of the Hudson, Storm on the Matterhorn 21 Sunrise Yosemite Valley 22 Settlement of California 31 Thunderstorm in the Rocky Mountains
bifocal lenses
   invented by: 8 Franklin
Bifrost
   origin: 12 Scandinavian
   form: 6 bridge
   bridge of: 4 gods
   made of: 7 rainbow
   from: 6 Asgard
   to: 5 earth
bifurcate 4 fork 5 split 6 branch, divide 7 diverge 8 separate
big 3 top 4 head, high, huge, just, kind, main, vast 5 adult, ample, bulky, chief, great, grown, heavy, husky, large, major,

noble, prime, vital **6** heroic, humane, mature **7** eminent, grown-up, haughty, hulking, immense, leading, liberal, mammoth, massive, notable, pompous, sizable, weighty **8** abundant, arrogant, boastful, bragging, colossal, enormous, generous, gigantic, gracious, princely **9** conceited, grandiose, honorable, important, momentous, prominent, strapping **10** benevolent, chivalrous, high-minded, monumental, prodigious **11** magnanimous, pretentious, significant, substantial **12** considerable **13** consequential

Big Apple
  nickname of: **11** New York City
Big Bend State
  nickname of: **9** Tennessee
Big Chill, The
  director: **14** Laurence Kasdan
  cast: **10** Kevin Kline **11** William Hurt
Big Daddy
  character in: **16** Cat on a Hot Tin Roof
  author: **8** Williams
Big E
  nickname of: **10** Elvin Hayes
Bigfoot 4 Yeti **9** Sasquatch **17** Abominable Snowman
big guns 4 VIPs **5** brass **6** cannon **7** bigwigs, top dogs **8** big shots, ordnance **9** artillery **14** heavy artillery, high mucky-mucks **15** important people
bighearted 6 lavish **7** liberal **8** generous, handsome, princely, prodigal **9** bounteous, bountiful, unselfish **10** beneficent, benevolent, charitable, free-handed, openhanded, unstinting **11** magnanimous, open-hearted **12** humanitarian
bight 3 bay **4** bend, cave, road
Biglow Papers
  author: **18** James Russell Lowell
Big Money, The
  author: **13** John Dos Passos
bigness 4 bulk **8** enormity, hugeness **9** amplitude, great size, greatness, largeness, magnitude **11** massiveness
Big O, The
  nickname of: **14** Oscar Robertson
bigoted 6 biased **10** intolerant, prejudiced **12** closed-minded, narrow-minded
bigotry 4 bias **6** racism **9** prejudice **10** unfairness **11** intolerance **14** discrimination **16** closed-mindedness, narrow-mindedness
Big Parade, The
  director: **9** King Vidor
  cast: **11** John Gilbert, Renee Adoree **14** Hobart Bosworth
big shot 3 VIP **4** name **5** mogul, nabob, wheel **6** big gun, bigwig, fat cat, tycoon **7** big deal, magnate, notable **8** somebody **9** big cheese, dignitary, personage **13** highmuck-a-muck, wheeler-dealer
Big Six
  nickname of: **16** Christy Mathewson
Big Sky, The
  author: **11** A B Guthrie Jr

Big Sky State
  nickname of: **7** Montana
Big Sleep, The
  author: **15** Raymond Chandler
  director: **11** Howard Hawks
  cast: **12** Elisha Cook Jr, Lauren Bacall **13** Dorothy Malone, Martha Vickers **14** Humphrey Bogart (Philip Marlowe)
  setting: **10** Los Angeles
Big Train
  nickname of: **13** Walter Johnson
Big Valley, The
  character: **11** Nick Barkley **12** Audra Barkley, Heath Barkley **13** Jarrod Barkley **15** Victoria Barkley
  cast: **9** Lee Majors **10** Linda Evans, Peter Breck **11** Richard Long **15** Barbara Stanwyck
bigwig 3 vip **7** big shot, notable **9** dignitary, personage
bikini 8 two-piece **11** bathing suit
  topless: **8** monokini
  type: **6** string
Bikini 5 atoll **9** Namu islet **10** West Pacific **15** Marshall Islands
Bilah, Bilhah
  concubine of: **5** Jacob
  son: **3** Dan **8** Maphtali, Naphtali
  served: **6** Rachel
Bildad
  friend: **3** Job **5** Elihu **6** Zophar **7** Eliphaz
bile 4 gall, rage **5** anger, venom, wrath **6** choler, spleen
bilge 3 rot **4** bosh, bull, bunk, tosh **5** hooey, tripe **6** drivel, humbug, jabber, piffle **7** baloney, hogwash, rubbish, twaddle **8** malarkey, nonsense **9** gibberish **10** balderdash **11** foolishness, jabberwocky **13** horsefeathers **16** stuff and nonsense
bilious 4 sick **5** angry, cross, huffy, nasty, testy **6** crabby, cranky, grumpy, queasy, sickly, touchy **7** grouchy, peevish **8** bilelike, greenish, nauseous, petulant, snappish **9** irritable, sickening **10** ill-humored, out of sorts **11** ill-tempered **12** cantankerous **13** short-tempered **15** green at the gills
bilk 3 gyp **4** dupe, gull, rook, take **5** cheat, cozen, trick **6** fleece, rip off **7** deceive, defraud, swindle **8** hoodwink **9** bamboozle, victimize
bill 3 act, fee, law **4** card, chit, list **5** tally **6** agenda, charge, decree, docket, poster, roster, ticket **7** account, catalog, charges, invoice, leaflet, measure, placard, program, statute **8** banknote, brochure, bulletin, calendar, circular, handbill, proposal, register, schedule **9** greenback, inventory, ordinance, reckoning, statement **10** regulation **12** treasury note **13** advertisement **17** silver certificate
billet 3 job **4** base, bunk, camp, digs, note, post **5** berth, house, lodge, place, put up **6** letter, office **7** bed down, lodging, quarter, shelter **8** domicile, dwelling, lodgment, position, quarters **9** residence, situation **11**

accommodate, appointment 13 accommodation

billfold *see* 6 wallet

billiards
player: 11 Willie Hoppe 13 Minnesota Fats, Willie Mosconi

Bill of Divorcement, A
director: 11 George Cukor
cast: 11 Billie Burke 13 John Barrymore 16 Katharine Hepburn

billow 4 roll, wave 5 belly, cloud, crest, surge, swell 6 puff up 7 balloon, breaker

Billy Budd
author: 14 Herman Melville
character: 8 Claggart 11 Captain Vere

billyclub 3 bat 5 billy, stick 8 bludgeon 9 truncheon

bin 3 box 4 cart, crib, silo 5 crate, frame, hatch 6 barrel, basket, bunker, hamper, holder, trough, vessel 9 container, inclosure 10 receptacle

binate 4 dual 6 double 7 coupled, two fold 14 growing in pairs

bind 3 rim, tie 4 edge, gird, glue, join, lash, rope, trim, wrap 5 affix, chafe, cover, cramp, force, frame, hitch, paste, stick, strap, tie up, truss 7 attach, border, coerce, compel, encase, fasten, fringe, oblige, secure, swathe 7 bandage, confine, require 8 encumber, obligate 9 prescribe 11 necessitate

binder 4 glue, roux 5 paste 6 cement 8 notebook 9 assurance, guarantee 11 down payment 12 earnest money 17 looseleaf notebook

binding 4 band, face, tape 5 valid 6 edging, ribbon 7 styptic 8 fastener, ligative 9 stringent 10 compulsory, obligatory, peremptory 12 constricting

binge 3 jag 4 bust, orgy, tear, toot 5 blast, drunk, fling, revel, spree 6 bender 7 carouse 8 beer-bust, carousal 11 bacchanalia 12 drunken spree

Bingham, George Caleb
born: 15 Augusta County VA
artwork: 13 Stump Speaking 17 The Trapper's Return 18 Verdict of the People 19 The Jolly Flatboatman 20 Raftsmen Playing Cards 31 Fur Traders Descending the Missouri

Bingley, Mr
character in: 17 Pride and Prejudice
author: 6 Austen

biochemist 17 biological chemist
American: 4 Cori 5 Bloch, Moore, Ochoa 7 Axelrod, Lipmann 8 Kornberg
English: 5 Krebs 6 Porter, Sanger 8 Mitchell
French: 5 Monod 7 Duclaux
German: 5 Lynen

biogenesis
discoverer: 12 Louis Pasteur

biography 3 bio 4 life, vita 6 memoir 7 account, history 9 life story

biologist
American: 6 Carson, Yerkes 7 Burbank 8 Delbruck

British: 6 Darwin, Huxley 7 Bateson, Medawar
French: 5 Jacob, Monod 7 Lamarck
German: 7 Schwann
Swiss: 6 Haller

biology
branch: 6 botany 7 zoology
classification: 15 Carolus Linnaeus

birch 6 Betula
varieties: 3 Low, Red 4 Fire, Gray 5 Black, Canoe, Dwarf, Paper, River, Swamp, Sweet, Water, White 6 Cherry, Yellow 7 Monarch 8 Mahogany, Old-field 10 West Indian 13 European white, Japanese white, Young's weeping 14 Japanese cherry

Birches
author: 11 Robert Frost

bird
anatomy: 3 bec, neb, nib 4 beak, bill, cere, crop, lora, lore, mala, nape, rump, tail, tuft, wing 5 alula, crest, crown, flank, larum, lorum, pilea, rosta 6 breast, gullet, pecten, pileum, pinion, syrinx, tarsus 7 ambiens, crissum, gizzard, rostrum 8 gigerium, pectines, scapular 9 auchenium, gastraeum 10 cordylanus
aquatic/water: 3 auk, cob, ern, mew 4 cobb, coot, duck, erne, gony, gull, ibis, loon, rail, shag, skua, sora, swan, teal, tern 5 booby, cahow, crane, diver, goose, grebe, heron, murre, ousel, rotch, snipe, solan, stilt, stork 6 avocet, curlew, cygnet, dipper, fulmar, gannet, godwit, hagdon, jabiru, jacana, osprey, petrel, plover, puffin, rotche, scoter, wigeon 7 anhinga, bidcock, bittern, bustard, dovekey, dovekie, finfoot, mallard, moorhen, pelican, penguin, seriema, skimmer, widgeon 8 alcatras, baldpate, dabchick, flamingo, murrelet, umbrette 9 albatross, baptornis, cormorant, gallinule, guillemot, kittiwake, phalarope, snakebird, spoonbill 10 gaviformes, kingfisher, shearwater, sheathbill, yellowlegs 13 whooping crane
bird cage/home: 4 cote, mews, nest 5 roost 6 aviary, volary, volery 7 rookery
bird of freedom: 9 bald eagle
bird of ill-omen: 5 raven
bird of Jove: 5 eagle
bird of June: 7 peacock
bird of Minerva: 3 owl
bird of peace: 4 dove
bird of prey: 3 owl 4 gled, hawk, kite 5 buteo, eagle, glead, glede, harpy, saker 6 condor, elanet, elenet, falcon, musket, osprey, raptor 7 buzzard, goshawk, harrier, kestrel, stooper, vulture 8 caracara 9 accipiter, gyrfalcon, peregrine 11 accipitrine, lammergeier
bird of wonder/rebirth: 7 phoenix
carrion-eater: 4 aura 5 urubu 6 condor 7 buzzard, vulture
class: 4 Aves
combining form: 3 avi 4 orni 5 ornis 6 ornith 7 ornitho 8 ornithes
crow family: 3 daw, jay, kae 4 crow, rook

5 crake, raven 6 chough, corbie, magpie 7 corvine, jackdaw

duck family: 4 clee, coot, lory, smew, teal, wood 5 eider, goose 6 scoter 7 gadwall, mallard, Muscovy, pintail, pochard 8 baldpate, redshank, shoveler 9 merganser 10 bufflehead, canvasback

extinct: 3 auk, jib, moa 4 dodo, jibi, mamo 5 didus 8 Diatryma 9 aepyornis, apatornis, gastornis, hespornis, solitaire 11 archaeornis

flightless: 3 emu, ihi, moa 4 dodo, gorb, kagu, kiwi, rhea, weka 5 nandu 6 callow, kakapo, moorup, ratite, takahe 7 apteryx, horling, ostrich, peacock, penguin, roatelo 8 notornis 9 cassowary

game: 4 duck, guan, rail, sora, teal 5 brant, goose, quail, snipe 6 chukar, colima, grouse, pigeon, plover, turkey 7 bustard, chicken, flapper, gadwall, mallard, pintail, prairie, widgeon 8 baldpate, bobwhite, moorfowl, pheasant, shoveler, tragopan, wildfowl, woodcock 9 merganser, partridge, ptarmigan 10 canvasback

group of birds: 3 nye 4 bank, bevy, cast, nide, sord 5 aerie, brood, covey, drove, flock, plump 6 covert, flight, gaggle, litter, spring

largest: 7 ostrich 11 lammergeier

legendary: 3 roc 6 simurg 7 phoenix, simurgh 9 feng-huang, feng-hwang

loss of feathers: 7 molting

smallest: 11 hummingbird

nocturnal: 3 owl 5 cahow, owlet, potoo 7 bullbat, dorhawk 8 guacharo, nightjar 9 nighthawk, thickknee 10 goatsucker 11 nightingale

pet: 4 myna 5 mynah 6 canary, parrot, pigeon 8 cockatoo, lovebird, parakeet

plumage: 8 ptilosis

poultry: 3 hen 4 duck 5 goose 6 pigeon, turkey 7 chicken, rooster 8 pheasant 14 Cornish game hen

talking: 4 myna 5 mynah 6 parrot

wingless: 4 kiwi, weka 7 apteryx

young: 4 eyas, gull 5 chick, piper, poult, squab 6 gorlin, pullus 7 flapper, nestler 8 birdikin, nestling 9 fledgling

of Africa: 4 coly, fink, taha, tock 5 crane, paauw 6 barbet, bulbul, cuckoo, jabiru, quelea, whidah 7 courser, finfoot, marabou, ostrich, touraco 8 hornbill, oxpecker, parakeet, umbrette 9 beefeater, broadbill, francolin, napecrest, trochilus 10 hammerhead, weaverbird

of Antarctic/Arctic: 3 auk 4 gull, knot, skua, xema 5 brant, murre, rotch 6 dunlin, falcon, fulmar, jaeger, rotche 7 dovekey, dovekie, penguin 8 grayling 9 guillemot, gyrfalcon, ptarmigan 10 sheathbill

of Asia: 4 kora, myna, ruff, smew 5 mynah, pewit, pitta 6 bulbul, chua, drongo, dunlin, hoopoe, linnet 7 boobook, courser, hill tit, lapwing, peacock, sirgang 8 accentor, dotterel, hornbill, leaf bird, parakeet, tragopan, wheatear 9 brambling, francolin, muted swan

of Australia: 3 emu 4 kahu, kiwi, koel, koil, lory 5 arara, galah, lowan, pitta 6 drongo, leipoa 7 boobook, bustard, figbird, grinder, waybung 8 bellbird, bushlark, cockatoo, ganggang, lorikeet, lyrebird, megapode, manucode, morepork, parakeet, platypus 9 bowerbird, cassowary, coachwhip, cockatiel, frogmouth, pardalote, thornbird 10 kookaburra

of Central America: 4 guan, ibis 5 booby, macaw 6 barbet, jabiru, quezal, toucan 7 bittern, cotinga, jacamar, quetzal, tinamou 8 curassow, puffbird, troupial

of Cuba: 6 trogon 8 tocororo 14 bee hummingbird

of England: 4 kite, rook 9 cormorant 11 carrion crow

of Europe: 3 dar, mag, mew, nun 4 clee, gled, mall, merl, pope, rook, ruff, shag, smew, wren 5 amsel, crake, egret, finch, glede, merle, ousel, ouzel, pewit, pipit, stilt, stork, swift, tarin, terek, whaup 6 cuckoo, dunlin, godwit, grouse, hoopoe, linnet, martin, merlin, missel, redleg, roller, siskin, thrush 7 bittern, bustard, jackdaw, kestrel, lapwing, martlet, ortolan, redwing, ruddock, skylark, sparrow, starnel, wagtail, wryneck 8 bee eater, blackcap, brantail, daychick, dotterel, garganey, nightjar, nuthatch, peesweep, redstart, reedling, starling, throstle, wheatear, whimbrel, whinchat, whinshat, woodcock 9 brambling, chaffinch, crossbill, field fare, gallinule, sheldrake, stonechat 10 chiffchaff, goatsucker, kingfisher, lammergeier, turtledove 11 lammergeier, nightingale, wallcreeper 12 capercaillie

of Hawaii: 2 io 3 iwa, ava, ioa, iwa, poe 4 nene, iiwi, koae, mamo, moho, omao 6 parson 9 frigate

of India: 4 baya, kala, koel, koil 5 sarus, shama 6 argala, bulbul, homrai, luggar 7 peacock 8 adjutant, amadavat, pheasant, tragopan 11 red hornbill

of Jamaica: 7 vervain

of Java: 7 sparrow 8 rice bird 9 fruit dove

of Madagascar: 6 drongo 7 anhinga, kirombo, roatelo

of Mexico: 6 jacana

of New Guinea: 9 cassowary 14 bird of paradise

of New Zealand: 3 ihi, kea, moa, poe, tui 4 huia, kaka, kaki, kiwi, koko, kuku, ruru, titi, weka 6 kakapo 7 apteryx 8 morepork, notornis

of North America: 3 ani, auk, tit 4 coot, crow, dove, ibis, lark, loon, pape, rook, sora, stib, swan, tern, wamp, wren 5 booby, brant, colin, crane, egret, finch, grebe, junco, murre, quail, robin, snipe, swift, veery, vireo 6 chebec, cuckoo, curlew, darter, dunlin, fulmar, grouse, hagdon, magpie, martin, oriole, phoebe, plover, shrike, thrush, towhee, turkey, verdin, willet 7 anhinga, bittern, blue jay, catbird, flicker, goshawk, grackle, lapwing, pelican, sparrow, swallow, tanager, warbler 8 bluebird, bobolink, bobwhite, cardinal, grosbeak, killdeer, nuthatch, poorwill, starling, thrasher, titmouse, wheatear 9 blackbird, chickadee, crossbill, goldfinch, gyrfalcon, nighthawk, partridge, sandpiper, snakebird 10 bufflehead, kingfisher, meadowlark, woodpecker 11 hummingbird, mockingbird 12 whippoorwill

of South America: 3 ara, hia 4 anna, guan, jacu, loro, mitu, rhea, soco, toco, yeni 5 egret, macaw, potoo, sylph 6 barbet, chatja, chunga, cracid, jabiru, motmot, sappho, toucan 7 cariama, cotinga, hoatzin, jacamar, limpkin, manakin, seriema, tinamou, warrior 8 boatbill, caracara, curassow, guacharo, hoactzin, screamer, tapacolo, tapaculo, terutero, troupial 9 campanero, trumpeter 11 scarlet ibis

of West India: 3 ani 4 tody

Bird, Larry
　　sport: 10 basketball
　　position: 7 forward
　　team: 13 Boston Celtics

Birdman of Alcatraz
　　director: 17 John Frankenheimer
　　cast: 10 Karl Malden 12 Edmond O'Brien, Neville Brand, Thelma Ritter 13 Burt Lancaster (Robert Stroud)

Bird of Paradise
　　constellation of: 4 Apus

Birds, The
　　author: 12 Aristophanes
　　character: 4 Iris 5 Meton 8 Basileia, Cinesias 9 Euelpides 10 King Tereus, Prometheus 12 Peithetairos

Birds, The
　　director: 15 Alfred Hitchcock
　　based on story by: 15 Daphne du Maurier
　　cast: 9 Rod Taylor 11 Tippi Hedren 12 Jessica Tandy 16 Suzanne Pleshette
　　setting: 10 California

Birds Fall Down, The
　　author: 15 Dame Rebecca West

Birkin, Rupert
　　character in: 11 Women in Love
　　author: 8 Lawrence

Birmingham
　　football team: 9 Stallions

Birmingham, Stephen
　　author of: 8 Our Crowd 11 The Grandees 14 The Right People 15 Life at the Dakota

Birnbaum, Nathan
　　real name of: 11 George Burns

birth 5 blood, start, stock 6 family, origin, source, strain 7 bearing, descent, genesis, lineage 8 ancestry, breeding, delivery 9 beginning, being born, emergence, genealogy, inception, parentage 10 background, beginnings, childbirth, derivation, extraction 11 confinement, parturition 12 commencement

Birth of a Nation, The
　　director: 10 D W Griffith
　　cast: 8 Mae Marsh 11 Lillian Gish 14 Henry B Walthall

Birth of Tragedy, The
　　author: 18 Friedrich Nietzsche

birthstones
　　January: 6 garnet
　　February: 8 amethyst
　　March: 6 jasper 10 aquamarine, bloodstone
　　April: 7 diamond 8 sapphire
　　May: 5 agate 7 emerald
　　June: 5 pearl 7 emerald 9 moonstone 11 alexandrite
　　July: 4 onyx, ruby 8 star ruby
　　August: 7 peridot 8 sardonyx 9 carnelian
　　September: 8 sapphire 10 chrysolite 12 star sapphire
　　October: 4 opal 5 beryl 10 aquamarine, tourmaline
　　November: 5 topaz
　　December: 4 ruby 6 zircon 9 turquoise

biscuit 3 bun 4 cake, roll 5 cooky, scone, wafer 6 bisque, cookie, muffin, parking, simnel 7 cracker, dogbone 8 hardtack, zwieback 9 pale-brown 10 crisp bread, quick bread 15 unglazed pottery

bisect 5 cross, split 8 cut in two 9 cut in half, intersect

bishop 4 abba, pope 5 punch 6 cleric, despot, priest 7 pontiff, prelate, primate 8 overseer 9 clergyman, patriarch 10 chesspiece, high priest
　　of Rome: 4 pope
　　Greek: 9 episkopos
　　means: 8 overseer
　　district: 7 diocese
　　headdress: 5 miter, mitre

Bismarck, Otto von
　　nickname: 14 Iron Chancellor
　　unified: 7 Germany
　　chancellor/minister for: 15 Emperor William I
　　policy: 12 "iron and blood"

bison 4 urus 6 wild ox, wisent 7 aurochs, buffalo
　　native to: 6 Europe 12 North America

Bissau
　　capital of: 12 Guinea-Bissau

Bisset, Jacqueline
　　real name: 22 Jacqueline Fraser Bisset
　　born: 7 England 9 Weybridge
　　roles: 5 Class 7 Airport, The Deep 11 Day for Night 12 Anna Karenina 16 The Mephisto Waltz 24 Murder on the Orient Express

bistro 3 bar 4 cafe 6 tavern 7 cabaret 9 nightclub 10 supper club
　　French: 9 estaminet

bit 3 dab 4 chip, drop, iota, mite, snip, whit 5 crumb, grain, pinch, scrap, shred, speck, spell, trace 6 dollop, moment, morsel, paring, trifle 7 droplet, granule, shaving, smidgen 8 fragment, particle 9 short time 10 short while, small piece, smithereen, sprinkling

type: 5 auger, drill 6 gimlet, wimble 7 bradawl 11 brace and bit

bitch 3 nag 5 botch, brood, cheat, fault, shrew, spoil, witch, whine 6 kvetch, virago 7 blunder, bungle, grouse 8 complain, harridan 9 complaint, female dog, termagant

bitchy 4 mean 5 catty, cruel, nasty 6 wicked 7 hateful, vicious 8 spiteful 9 heartless, malicious 10 backbiting, malevolent, vindictive

bite 3 bit, dab, dig, nip 4 gnaw, grip, snip 5 champ, crumb, gnash, prick, scrap, shred, smart, speck, sting, taste 6 morsel, nibble, pierce 7 eat into 8 mouthful, stinging, take hold 10 small piece, tooth wound 12 small portion

biting 5 harsh, sharp 6 bitter 7 caustic, cutting, mordant, nipping 8 piercing, scathing, smarting, stinging 9 sarcastic, trenchant, withering 12 sharp-tongued

Biton
   father: 7 Cydippe

bit player 5 extra 6 walk on 14 minor character

bitte 6 please 12 you're welcome 14 I beg your pardon

bitter 4 acid, mean, sour, tart 5 acrid, angry, cruel, harsh, sharp 6 biting, morose, severe, sullen 7 acerbic, caustic, crabbed, painful 8 grievous, piercing, scornful, smarting, spiteful, stinging, wretched 9 rancorous, resentful 10 astringent 11 distressing

bitterness 5 anger, scorn, spite 6 animus, rancor, spleen 7 ill will 8 acerbity, acrimony, sourness 9 animosity, harshness, hostility, malignity, sharpness 10 antagonism, malignancy 11 astringency 12 hard feelings, spitefulness 14 unpleasantness

bitters
   type: 6 spirit
   flavor: 6 orange 7 gentian
   brand: 9 Angostura

bivalve 4 clam 5 pinna 6 cockle, mussel, mollusk, scallop 8 mollusca 9 pelecypod 13 lamellibranch

bivouac 4 camp 5 tents 10 campground, encampment

bizarre 3 odd 5 kinky, kooky, queer, weird 7 strange, unusual 8 freakish 9 fantastic, grotesque 10 outlandish

Bizet, Georges
   real name: 26 Alexandre Cesar Leopold Bizet
   born: 5 Paris 6 France
   composer of: 4 Roma (suite) 6 Carmen, Patrie 8 Djamileh 11 Don Procopio, L'Arlesienne 12 Jeux d'enfants, Pearl Fishers 14 Children's Games 15 Ivan the Terrible 16 Le Docteur Miracle 18 The Fair Maid of Perth

Biztha 6 eunuch

Bjornson, Bjornstjerne
   author of: 4 Arne 7 The King 8 Magnhild 9 A Happy Boy, In God's Way, Lame Hulda, The Editor 10 King Sverre 11 A Bankruptcy, The Bankrupt 12 Sigurd Slembe 14 Arnljot Gelline, Beyond Our Power 15 The Fisher Maiden, The Newly Married 16 Beyond Human Might, Sigurd the Bastard 17 Between the Battles 20 Mary Stuart in Scotland 24 Paul Lange and Tora Parsberg 27 Flags Are Flying in Town and Port

blab 3 rat 6 babble, tattle 7 blabber, prattle 9 tell tales 13 spill the beans 20 let the cat out of the bag

blabber 3 gab, gas, yak 4 blab, bull 5 prate 6 babble, drivel, gabble, gibber, gossip, jabber 7 blather, chatter, palaver, prattle, twaddle 8 blah-blah, chitchat, idle talk 9 jabbering 10 mumbo-jumbo 12 gobbledegook 14 chitter-chatter

blabbermouth 6 gabber, gossip, prater 7 blabber 8 bigmouth, busybody, gossiper, informer, jabberer, liverlip, prattler, quidnunc 9 chatterer 10 chatterbox, talebearer, tattletale 11 rumormonger 12 gossipmonger 13 scandalmonger

black, Black 3 bad, dim, jet 4 dark, evil, grim, inky 5 angry, ebony, murky, Negro, raven, sable 6 dismal, gloomy, somber, sullen, wicked 7 colored, furious, hostile, stygian, sunless, swarthy 8 moonless 9 coal-black, lightless, nefarious, unlighted 10 calamitous 11 dark-skinned, threatening 12 Afro-American 13 unilluminated

Black Arrow, The
   author: 20 Robert Louis Stevenson

blackball 3 ban, bar, cut 4 snub 5 debar 6 banish, outlaw, reject 7 boycott, exclude, keep out, shut out 8 pass over, turndown 9 blacklist, ostracize, proscribe 11 vote against 12 cold-shoulder 14 send to Coventry

black beast
   French: 9 bete noire

blackberry 5 Rubus
   variety: 4 Sand 5 Swamp 7 Cut-leaf, Pacific, Running, Sow-teat 9 Evergreen 13 Parsley-leaved 18 Evergreen thornless

Blackberry Winter
   author: 12 Margaret Mead

blackbird 4 crow 5 raven, slave 6 thrush 7 cowbird, grackle, redwing 8 song bird 9 slave ship 11 slave trader 17 kidnapped islander, plantation laborer
   kind: 9 red-winged 12 yellow-headed
   family: 8 Turdidae 9 Icteridae

Blackboard Jungle, The
   director: 13 Richard Brooks
   based on novel by: 10 Evan Hunter
   cast: 9 Glenn Ford, Vic Morrow 11 Anne Francis 12 Louis Calhern, Paul Mazursky, Richard Kiley 13 Sidney Poitier 14 Warner Anderson

Black Boy
   author: 13 Richard Wright

blacken 5 libel, smear, stain, sully 6 befoul, darken, defame, defile, revile, vilify 7 slander, tarnish 8 besmirch, disgrace, dishonor 9 denigrate, discredit 10 stigmatize

Blackfoot, Blackfeet
 language family: 9 Algonkian 10 Algonquian
 tribe: 6 Bloods, Kainah, Piegan, Pikuni 7 Siksika
 location: 6 Canada 7 Alberta, Montana 12 Saskatchewan

blackguard 3 cad, rat, SOB 5 knave, louse, rogue, scamp 6 rascal 7 bastard, villain 9 miscreant, scoundrel

blackhearted 4 base, vile 6 sinful, wicked 7 ignoble 10 despicable, evil-minded, villainous 11 scoundrelly 12 unprincipled 13 reprehensible

blackjack
 also known as: 9 twenty-one
 French: 9 vingt-et-un
 play against: 6 dealer
 additional card: 3 hit

Black Lamb and Grey Falcon
 author: 15 Dame Rebecca West

Black Land, The see 5 Egypt

blackleg 7 cheater 8 swindler 9 trickster

blacklist 3 ban, bar 4 shun 5 debar 6 reject 7 exclude, lock out, shut out 8 preclude 9 blackball, ostracize

blacklisting 7 boycott 8 spurning 9 exclusion, ostracism, rejection 12 blackballing

black magic 7 sorcery 10 witchcraft

blackmail 5 force 6 coerce, extort, payoff 7 squeeze, tribute 8 threaten 9 extortion, hush money, shakedown

black mark 4 blot 5 stain 6 bruise 7 blemish, demerit 9 contusion

Blackmore, Richard Doddridge
 author of: 10 Lorna Doone 11 Springhaven 13 The Maid of Sker

black mountain see 10 Montenegro

Black Narcissus
 author: 11 Rumer Godden
 director: 13 Michael Powell 17 Emeric Pressburger
 cast: 4 Sabu 11 David Farrar, Deborah Kerr, Jean Simmons
 setting: 9 Himalayas

blackness 4 dark 5 gloom, shade 7 dimness 8 darkness

Blackpool, Stephen
 character in: 9 Hard Times
 author: 7 Dickens

Black Prince, The
 author: 11 Iris Murdoch

Blackstone, Sir William
 author of: 12 Commentaries (on the Laws of England)

Black Uhlan
 nickname of: 12 Max Schmeling

Blackwater State
 nickname of: 8 Nebraska

Blackwell, Elizabeth
 first American: 11 woman doctor

bladder 3 bag, sac 4 cyst 5 pouch 7 blister, pustule, saccule, utricle 10 receptacle

blade 4 leaf 5 frond, knife, razor, sword 6 cutter, needle, switch 7 scalpel 10 sled runner 11 cutting edge, skate runner

blah 4 bosh, dull, flat, guff, so-so 5 bland, ho-hum, hooey, vapid 6 boring, bunkum, dreary, hot air, humbug 7 blather, eyewash, humdrum, nothing, tedious, twaddle 8 claptrap, lifeless, listless, nonsense 9 gibberish 10 balderdash, monotonous, pedestrian 11 uninspiring 13 characterless, unimaginative, uninteresting, unstimulating

Blaik, Earl H
 sport: 8 football
 position: 5 coach
 team: 4 Army 9 Dartmouth
 military rank: 7 colonel

Blair, Eric Arthur
 real name of: 12 George Orwell

Blake, Robert
 real name: 28 Michael James Vijencio Gubitosi
 born: 8 Nutley NJ
 roles: 7 Baretta, Our Gang 8 Red Ryder 11 In Cold Blood 12 Little Beaver 23 Tell Them Willie Boy Is Here 24 The Treasure of Sierra Madre

Blake, William
 born: 6 London 7 England
 author of: 6 Milton, Tiriel 9 Jerusalem 13 The Book of Thel 14 Prophetic Books 15 The Book of Urigen 16 Songs of Innocence 17 Songs of Experience 21 Little Lamb Who Made Thee 23 Marriage of Heaven and Hell, Tiger Tiger Burning Bright
 artwork: 6 Milton 9 Book of Job, Jerusalem 11 The Four Zoas 12 Book of Urizen, Divine Comedy 16 Songs of Innocence 17 Songs of Experience 23 Marriage of Heaven and Hell

blamable 10 censurable, deplorable, punishable, reprovable 11 blameworthy 12 reproachable 13 reprehensible

Blamauer, Karoline
 real name of: 10 Lotte Lenya

blame 4 onus 5 fault, guilt 6 accuse, burden, charge, rebuke 7 censure, condemn, reproof, reprove 8 reproach 9 castigate, criticism, criticize, liability 10 accusation, disapprove 11 castigation, culpability 12 condemnation, denunciation, remonstrance 13 find fault with, recrimination 14 accountability, responsibility 15 hold responsible

blameless 5 clear 8 innocent, spotless 9 guiltless, not guilty, unspotted, unstained, unsullied, untainted 10 inculpable, not at fault, unblamable 11 unblemished, uncorrupted 13 unimpeachable 14 irreproachable, not responsible

blameless in life
 Latin: 12 integer vitae

blame on 7 trace to 8 charge to 9 set down to 11 attribute to 14 lay at the door of

blameworthy 8 blamable 10 censurable, deplorable, punishable, reprovable 12 reproachable 13 reprehensible

blanch 4 fade 6 bleach, whiten 7 lighten 8 turn pale

blanched 3 wan 4 pale 5 ashen, faded 6 chalky, pallid 8 bleached 9 bloodless

bland 4 blah, calm, dull, even, flat, mild 5 balmy, quiet, vapid 6 benign, smooth 7 calming, humdrum, nothing, prosaic, tedious 8 moderate, peaceful, soothing, tiresome, tranquil 9 peaceable, temperate, unruffled 10 monotonous, unexciting, untroubled 11 uninspiring 13 nonirritating, uninteresting, unstimulating

blandish 4 coax, lure, urge 5 charm, tempt 6 cajole, entice, prompt 7 blarney, flatter, wheedle 8 inveigle, persuade

blandishment, blandishments 7 blarney, coaxing 8 cajolery, flattery 9 sweet talk, wheedling 12 ingratiation, inveiglement

Blandois, Monsieur
  character in: 12 Little Dorrit
  author: 7 Dickens

blank 3 gap 4 dull, idle, void 5 clean, clear, empty, inane, plain, space 6 futile, hollow, unused, vacant, vacuum, wasted 7 useless, vacancy, vacuous 8 unmarked 9 emptiness, fruitless, valueless, worthless 10 empty space, hollowness, profitless 11 meaningless, thoughtless, unrewarding 12 inexpressive 14 expressionless

blanket 4 coat, film 5 cloak, cover, quilt, throw 6 afghan, carpet, mantle, veneer 7 coating, overlay 8 covering, coverlet 9 comforter

blare 4 honk, peal, roar 5 blast 6 bellow, scream 7 resound, trumpet

blarney 4 fibs, line 5 pitch, spiel 6 hot air 7 coaxing, fawning, snow job, stories 8 cajolery, flattery 9 hyperbole, wheedling 10 inveigling, overpraise, sweet words 12 exaggeration, honeyed words 13 blandishments, overstatement

blasé 4 full 5 bored, jaded 6 gorged 7 glutted 9 apathetic, satisfied, saturated, surfeited, unexcited, unmovable 10 insouciant, nonchalant, spiritless, world-weary 11 indifferent, unconcerned 12 uninterested 14 unenthusiastic

Blasko, Bela
  real name of: 10 Bela Lugosi

blaspheme 5 curse, swear 6 revile 7 profane 10 take in vain

blasphemous 7 godless, impious, profane, ungodly 10 irreverent 11 irreligious 12 sacrilegious

blasphemy 7 cursing, impiety 8 swearing 9 profanity, sacrilege 11 impiousness, irreverence, profanation

blast 4 bomb, boom, bore, gale, gust, honk, peal, roar, rush, toot 5 blare, bleat, burst, level, shell, surge 6 bellow, blow up, report, scream, shriek 7 explode, resound, torpedo 8 dynamite, eruption 9 discharge, explosion, loud noise 10 detonation 11 sound loudly

blasting material 3 TNT 8 dynamite 9 explosive

blatant 4 loud 5 cheap, clear, crass, crude, gross, harsh, noisy, overt 6 brazen, coarse, tawdry, vulgar 7 blaring, glaring, obvious, uncouth 8 flagrant, piercing, unsubtle 9 clamorous, deafening, obtrusive, offensive, prominent, tasteless, ungenteel, unrefined 10 indelicate, unpolished 11 conspicuous, ill-mannered, undignified 12 ear-splitting, unmistakable

blather 4 stir 7 chatter, prattle 8 nonsense 9 commotion

Blatty, William P
  author of: 11 The Exorcist

Blaue Reiter 10 Blue Riders
  group of: 13 German artists

blaze 3 ray 4 beam, burn, fire, glow, rush 5 blast, burst, flame, flare, flash, glare, gleam, shine 6 flames 7 glisten, glitter, shimmer, torrent 8 eruption, outbreak, outburst, radiance 9 explosion 10 brightness, brilliance, effulgence 12 resplendence 13 conflagration

blazer 4 coat 6 jacket 12 sports jacket

blazing 3 hot 5 fiery, afire 6 firing, on fire 7 burning, flaming, flaring, glaring, glowing, intense, shining 8 bursting, bleaming, shooting, shouting 9 brilliant

Blazing Saddles
  director: 9 Mel Brooks
  cast: 9 Mel Brooks 10 Alex Karras, Dom DeLuise, Gene Wilder 11 Slim Pickens 12 Harvey Korman, Madeline Kahn 13 Cleavon Little, John Hillerman 15 David Huddleston

blazon 5 blare, boast 7 trumpet 8 proclaim 10 coat of arms, make public 16 armorial bearings

blazonry 4 arms 5 crest 6 blazon 8 insignia 10 coat of arms 14 heraldic emblem 16 heraldic bearings

bleach 4 fade 6 blanch, whiten 7 lighten, wash out 8 make pale

bleak 3 icy, raw 4 bare, cold, grim 5 chill 6 barren, biting, bitter, dismal, dreary, frosty, gloomy, somber, wintry 7 nipping 8 desolate, piercing 9 cheerless, windswept 10 depressing, forbidding 11 distressing, unpromising 13 weather-beaten

Bleak House
  author: 14 Charles Dickens
  character: 2 Jo (the crossing sweeper) 4 Nemo 5 Guppy, Krook 6 Bucket, Guster 7 Snagsby 8 Ada Clare, Chadband 9 Miss Flite 10 Mrs Jellyby, Turveydrop 11 Dr Woodcourt, Lady Dedlock, Tulkinghorn 12 John Jarndyce 13 Captain Rawdon 14 Harold Skimpole 15 Esther Summerson, Richard Carstone 19 Sir Leicester Dedlock
  satire of: 3 law 6 courts 8 chancery
  case: 19 Jarndyce and Jarndyce

bleakness 8 bareness, grimness 10 barrenness, desolation, dreariness, gloominess 13 cheerlessness

bleat 3 baa, cry, maa 5 whine 7 whimper

bleb 6 bubble 7 blister

bleed 3 run, tap 4 leak, soak 5 drain, valve 6 fleece, suffer 7 diffuse, extract, 8 let blood 9 draw blood, sacrifice 10 hemorrhage, overcharge 12 phlebotomize

Blefuscu
fictional land in: 16 Gulliver's Travels
author: 5 Swift

blemish 3 mar, zit 4 blot, blur, flaw, mark, spot 5 spoil, stain, sully, taint 6 blotch, defect, smirch, smudge 7 tarnish 9 disfigure 12 imperfection 13 disfigurement

blend 3 mix 4 fuse 5 merge, unite 6 fusion, go well, merger, mingle 7 amalgam, combine, mixture 8 coalesce, compound, mergence, mingling 9 harmonize 10 amalgamate, complement, concoction 11 combination, incorporate, intermingle

bless 4 give 5 endow, favor, grace, guard, honor 6 anoint, bestow, hallow, oblige, ordain 7 baptize, benefit, protect, support 8 dedicate, sanctify 9 watch over 10 consecrate

blessed 4 holy 5 happy, lucky 6 adored, graced, joyful, joyous, sacred 7 endowed, favored, revered 8 blissful, hallowed 9 fortunate, venerated, wonderful 10 felicitous, sanctified 11 consecrated

Blessed Damozel, The
author: 20 Dante Gabriel Rossetti

blessedness 5 bliss 8 felicity 9 beatitude 11 saintliness

blessing 4 gain, gift, good 5 favor, grace, leave 6 bounty, profit, regard 7 backing, benefit, consent, support 8 approval, sanction 9 advantage, hallowing 10 dedication, good wishes, invocation, permission 11 benediction, concurrence, good fortune 12 consecration, thanksgiving 14 sanctification

blessings 4 joys 5 gifts 6 favors 7 success 8 benefits, delights 10 advantages 11 good fortune

Blifil, Master
character in: 8 Tom Jones
author: 8 Fielding

Bligh, Captain William
character in: 17 Mutiny on the Bounty
authors: 4 Hall 8 Nordhoff

blight 3 pox, rot 4 harm, kill, ruin, rust 5 blast, crush, curse, decay, smash, spoil, wreck 6 cancer, canker, dry rot, fungus, injure, mildew, plague, thwart, wither 7 cripple, destroy, scourge, shrivel 8 demolish 9 frustrate 10 affliction, corruption, pestilence 12 plant disease 13 contamination

Blimber, Dr
character in: 12 Dombey and Son
author: 7 Dickens

blind 3 dull, ruse 5 cover, dodge, front, shade 6 hidden, insane, obtuse, screen 7 obscure, pretext, unaware 8 disguise, heedless, ignorant, mindless, unseeing 9 concealed, deception, senseless, sightless, sun shield, unfeeling, unknowing, unmindful, unnoticed 10 camouflage, insouciant, irrational, masquerade, neglectful, subterfuge, unthinking 11 inattentive, incognizant, indifferent, insensitive, smoke screen, unconcerned, unconscious, unobservant, unobserving 12 imperceptive, uncontrolled, undiscerning, uninterested, un-

noticeable, unperceptive, unreasonable 13 unenlightened 14 uncontrollable 15 uncomprehending

blind alley 7 closure, dead-end, impasse 8 blockade, cul-de-sac, dead lock, no escape 9 hindrance, stone wall 10 impassable, standstill 11 obstruction

blinder 4 hood 5 blind, shade 6 screen 7 blinker 9 blindfold

blindfold 6 darken 7 bandage, blinder, obscure 8 covering heedless, reckless 11 strike blind

blind seer 8 Tiresias

blink 4 wink 5 flash, shine, waver 6 falter, flinch, squint 7 flicker, glimmer, shimmer, sparkle, twinkle 9 nictitate, vacillate

blinker(s) 3 eye 6 peeper 7 blinder, flasher, goggles 8 black eye 13 warning signal

blintz, blintze 4 blin 5 crepe 6 blints 7 pancake

blip 3 dot, tap 4 spot 5 bleep, image 6 censor 7 replace

bliss 3 joy 4 glee 6 heaven, luxury 7 delight, ecstasy, rapture 8 gladness, paradise 9 happiness 10 exaltation, jubilation 12 exhilaration

blissful 5 happy 6 divine, joyful, joyous 7 blessed, sublime 8 beatific, ecstatic, glorious, heavenly 9 rapturous

blithe 3 gay 4 airy, glad 5 buxom, happy, jolly, merry, sunny 6 casual, cheery, jaunty, jovial, joyous, lively 7 gleeful, radiant 8 carefree, careless, cheerful, debonair, exaltant, heedless, mirthful, uncaring 9 ebullient, sprightly, unfeeling, unmindful 10 blithesome, frolicking 11 indifferent, insensitive, thoughtless, unconcerned, unconscious 12 light-hearted 13 inconsiderate

Blithedale Romance, The
author: 18 Nathaniel Hawthorne

blithesome 3 gay 5 light, merry, sunny 6 breezy, jaunty, lively 7 buoyant 8 animated, carefree, cheerful 11 free and easy

Blixen-Finecke, Karen
real name of: 11 Isak Dinesen

blizzard 4 blow, gale 5 blast 6 flurry, squall 7 tempest 8 snowfall 9 snowstorm 11 winter storm

Blizzard State
nickname of: 11 South Dakota

bloat 5 swell 6 blow up, dilate, expand, puff up 7 balloon, distend, enlarge, inflate

blob 4 daub, drop, mass 7 globule, splotch

bloc 4 body, ring, wing 5 cabal, group, union 6 clique 7 combine, faction 8 alliance 9 coalition 11 combination

Bloch, Ernest
born: 6 Geneva 11 Switzerland
composer of: 7 Macbeth, Solomon 8 Baal Shem, Schelomo 13 Sacred Service 14 Avodath Hakdesh, Israel Symphony 16 American Symphony 19 Concerto Symphonique 20 Voice in the Wilderness

block 3 bar, jam 4 cube, form, halt, mold 5 brick, check, choke, shape 6 hinder, impede, re-form, square, stop up, thwart 7 barrier, prevent, reshape 8 blockade, blockage, obstacle, obstruct 9 hindrance 10 impediment 11 obstruction 12 interference

blockade 3 bar, dam 4 dike 5 block, check, levee 6 hurdle 7 barrier, parapet, rampart 8 blockage, obstacle, obstruct, stockade, stoppage 9 barricade, hindrance, roadblock 10 checkpoint, earthworks, impediment 11 obstruction, restriction 13 fortification

blockage 3 jam 8 obstacle 9 hindrance 10 impediment 11 obstruction

blockhead 3 ass 4 clod, dolt, fool, yutz 5 booby, dummy, dunce, idiot, klutz, moron, ninny 6 dum-dum, nitwit 7 fathead, halfwit, jackass 8 bonehead, dumb-dumb, dumm kopf, imbecile, lunkhead, mushhead, numskull 9 harebrain, lamebrain, simpleton 10 chowerhead, dunderhead, nincompoop, noodlehead 12 featherbrain

block out 3 hew 5 carve 6 chisel, devise, map out, sculpt, sketch 7 outline 8 indicate 9 formulate

block up 3 bar 4 clog 6 stop up 7 brick up 9 barricade

blond, blonde 4 fair, gold, pale 5 light 6 flaxen, golden, yellow 8 light tan 9 yellowish 10 fair-haired 11 fair-skinned 12 lightcolored

Blonde Bombshell
nickname of: 10 Jean Harlow

Blondell, Joan
husband: 8 Mike Todd 10 Dick Powell
born: 9 New York NY
roles: 8 The Champ 11 Blonde Crazy, Gold Diggers, The Blue Veil 14 Blondie Johnson, The Public Enemy 20 A Tree Grows in Brooklyn

Blondie
creator: 9 Chic Young
character:
husband: 15 Dagwood Bumstead
children: 6 Cookie 9 Alexander 12 Baby Dumpling
boss: 6 Julius 9 Mr Dithers
boss's wife: 4 Cora
neighbor: 11 Herb Woodley 14 Tootsie Woodley
dog: 5 Daisy

blood 4 gore 5 birth, stock 6 family, source, spirit, temper 7 descent, lineage, passion 8 ancestry, heritage, vitality 9 lifeblood 10 extraction, family line, vital fluid, vital force 11 temperament 13 consanguinity 14 vital principle

Blood, field of 8 Aceldama

Blood, Sweat and Tears
author: 17 Winston S Churchill

bloodless 4 pale 5 ashen 6 anemic, pallid 7 insipid 8 blanched, lifeless, peaceful 9 colorless, deathlike, washed out

bloodline 6 family 8 ancestry, pedigree 9 genealogy 10 family tree

Bloodline
author: 13 Sidney Sheldon

bloodshed 4 gore 6 murder, pogrom 7 carnage, killing, slaying 8 butchery, massacre 9 blood bath, blood feud, slaughter 10 mass murder 12 bloodletting, manslaughter 15 spilling of blood

Bloodsmoor Romance, A
author: 15 Joyce Carol Oates

bloodstone
month: 5 March

blood system
part: 5 blood, liver 6 spleen 9 lymph node 10 bone marrow

bloodthirsty 5 cruel 6 bloody, brutal, fierce, savage 7 bestial, demonic, inhuman, vicious 8 barbaric, demoniac, fiendish, pitiless, ruthless 9 atrocious, barbarous, cutthroat, heartless, homicidal, merciless, murdering, murderous 10 demoniacal, sanguinary 11 sanguineous

blood vessel 4 vein 5 aorta 6 artery 7 carotid 9 capillary
prefix: 5 angio

Blood Wedding
author: 19 Federico Garcia Lorca

bloody 3 red 4 gory, rude, vevy 5 cruel, lurid 6 cursed, damned 7 crimson, scarlet 8 bleeding 9 merciless, murderous 10 sanguinary

Bloody Shame see 10 Virgin Mary (drink)

bloom 3 bud 4 glow, grow, zest 5 flare, flush, prime, shine, vigor 6 beauty, flower, heyday, luster, sprout, thrive 7 blossom, burgeon, develop, prosper, succeed 8 fare well, flourish, fructify, radiance, rosiness, strength 9 bear fruit, flowerage, flowering, germinate 10 blossoming 11 florescence, flourishing

Bloom, Claire
real name: 11 Claire Blume
husband: 10 Rod Steiger
born: 6 London 7 England
roles: 6 Charly 9 Limelight 10 Richard III 15 Look Back in Anger 26 The Spy Who Came in from the Cold

Bloom, Leopold and Molly
characters in: 7 Ulysses
author: 5 Joyce

bloomers 8 knickers, trousers 9 plus fours, underwear 10 underpants 15 knickerbockers

blooming 3 fit 4 pert, rosy 5 utter 6 abloom, robust, strong 7 healthy 8 vigorous 9 healthful 10 blossoming 11 flourishing 12 efflorescent, fit as a fiddle 15 picture of health

blooper 4 goof, slip 5 boner, botch, error, fluff, gaffe, lapse 6 bobble, booboo, slip-up 7 blunder, mistake, screwup

blossom 4 grow 5 bloom 6 flower, thrive 7 burgeon, develop 8 flourish, progress

Blossomed miraculously 9 Aaron's rod

blossoming 5 bloom 8 blooming, thriving 9 flowering 10 burgeoning, developing 11 florescence, flourishing

blot 3 dry 4 flaw, mark, spot 5 smear, stain, taint 6 absorb, blotch, remove, smirch, smudge, soak up, stigma, take up 7 bad mark, blemish, splotch 8 besmirch 13 discoloration

blotch 4 blot, mark, spot 7 splotch

Blot on the 'Scutcheon, The
author: 14 Robert Browning

blot out 5 erase 6 remove, rub out 7 abolish, eclipse, expunge 9 eliminate, eradicate 10 obliterate

blotting out 7 eclipse, erasing 9 expunging, wiping out 11 eradicating, eradication 12 annihilation, obliterating, obliteration 13 overshadowing

blouse 4 coat 5 drape, tunic, shirt, smock 6 camise, billow 7 blouson 8 casaquin

blow 3 box, hit, jab, pop 4 bang, bash, belt, cuff, gale, gust, honk, jolt, play, puff, sock, toot, wind 5 blast, burst, clout, crack, knock, punch, shock, smack, sound, storm, thump, upset, whack 6 exhale, rebuff, squall, wallop 7 breathe, explode, tempest, tragedy, whistle 8 calamity, disaster, expel air, reversal 9 detriment, windstorm 10 affliction, misfortune 11 catastrophe 14 disappointment

blow from the hand
French: 10 coup de main

blowhard 6 gascon 7 boaster, bragger, egotist 8 braggart 9 big talker 11 braggadocio

blow of mercy
French: 11 coup de grace

blow out 5 burst 7 rupture 10 extinguish

blowsy, blowzy 5 messy 6 frowzy, mussed, sloppy, untidy 7 unkempt 10 disarrayed, disheveled, disordered, disorderly, in disorder 11 disarranged

blow up 5 bloat, burst 6 billow, dilate, expand 7 balloon, distend, enlarge, explode, inflate, puff out 8 dynamite, swell out 12 lose one's cool 14 lose one's temper

Blowup
director: 21 Michelangelo Antonioni
cast: 8 Verushka 10 Sarah Miles 13 David Hemmings 15 Vanessa Redgrave

blowy 5 gusty, windy 6 breezy 7 squally 8 blustery

blubber 3 cry, fat, sob 4 bawl, flab, wail, weep 6 boohoo

Blubber
author: 9 Judy Blume

bludgeon 3 bat, hit 4 club 5 billy, clout, stick 6 cudgel 7 clobber 9 billyclub, truncheon

blue 3 low, sad 4 aqua, down, navy 5 azure 6 bluish, cobalt, gloomy, indigo, morose 7 doleful 8 cerulean, dejected, downcast, sapphire 9 depressed, turquoise 10 aquamarine, despondent, melancholy 11 downhearted, lapis lazuli, ultra-marine 12 disconsolate 14 down in the dumps, down in the mouth

Blue Angel, The
director: 17 Josef von Sternberg
based on novel by: 12 Heinrich Mann
cast: 10 Kurt Gerron 12 Emil Jannings 15 Marlene Dietrich (Lola-Lola)
song: 18 Falling in Love Again

Bluebeard
characteristic: 9 many wives

bluebell 9 Mertensia 18 Mertensia Virginica 21 Campanula rotundifolia
variety: 7 English, Spanish 8 Virginia 10 Australian, California 11 Clanwilliam

blueberry 9 Vaccinium
variety: 3 Low 4 Male 5 Swamp 7 Lowbush, Sourtop, Western 8 Creeping, Elliott's, Highbush, Low sweet 9 Late sweet, Rabbit-eye 10 Velvet-leaf 13 Black highbush

blueblood 4 peer 5 noble 8 nobleman 9 patrician, socialite 10 aristocrat, noblewoman 14 peer of the realm

blue-blooded 5 noble, regal, royal 6 titled 7 courtly 8 highbred, wellborn 9 patrician 10 upper-class 12 aristocratic, of royal blood

blue bloods 5 elite 8 nobility 9 haut monde 10 patricians 11 aristocracy, high society 14 creme de la creme

bluegrass 3 Poa
varieties: 3 Big 4 Wood 5 Rough, Texas 6 Annual, Canada 7 Bulbous, English 8 Kentucky, Sandberg 10 Rough-stalk

Bluegrass State
nickname of: 8 Kentucky

Blue Hen State
nickname of: 8 Delaware

Blue Knight, The
author: 14 Joseph Wambaugh

Blue Law State
nickname of: 11 Connecticut

blue-pencil 3 cut 4 edit, trim 6 censor, cut out, delete, digest, reduce 7 abridge, shorten 8 boil down, condense, pare down 9 expurgate 10 abbreviate

blueprint 4 plan 5 chart 6 design, scheme 7 diagram 9 schematic

Blue Riders
German: 11 Blaue Reiter
group of: 7 artists

blues 5 dumps 8 doldrums 10 depression, low spirits, melancholy 11 despondency

bluestocking
French: 7 bas bleu

bluff 3 lie 4 bank, bold, crag, curt, dupe, fake, fool, hoax, liar, open, peak, sham 5 blunt, boast, cliff, faker, frank, fraud, ridge, rough 6 abrupt, candid, crusty, delude, direct, humbug 7 bluffer, boaster, brusque, deceive, fake out, mislead, pretend 8 bragging, headland, headlong, palisade, pretense 9 bamboozle, deception, idle boast, outspoken, precipice, pretender 10 escarpment, forthright, promontory, subterfuge 11 braggadocio, counterfeit, plainspoken 13 unceremonious, straightforward

bluffer 5 bluff, faker, fraud, phony 6 humbug 9 pretender

bluish 7 off-blue 12 somewhat blue

Blume, Claire
real name of: 11 Claire Bloom

Blume, Judy
author of: 5 Wifey 6 Deenie 7 Blubber, Forever 19 Then Again Maybe I Won't 22 It's Not the End of the World 26 Tales of

a Fourth Grade Nothing 27 Are You
There God? It's Me Margaret

Blumenbach, Johann Friedrich
field: 7 anatomy 10 physiology
nationality: 6 German
father of: 20 physical anthropology

blunder 4 goof, slip 5 boner, error, gaffe 6
booboo, bumble, bungle, slip up 7 faux
pas, mistake, stagger, stumble 8 flounder
9 gaucherie 11 impropriety, make a
booboo 12 indiscretion

blunt 4 curt, dull, numb, open 5 frank,
rough, thick 6 abrupt, benumb, candid, deaden, dulled, soften, weaken 7
brusque, lighten, stupefy 8 edgeless, explicit, mitigate, moderate, tactless 9 outspoken, unpointed 10 to the point 11 insensitive, unsharpened 15 straightforward

bluntness 6 candor 10 directness 14 forthrightness 15 plainspokenness

blur 3 dim, fog, run 4 blot, haze, veil 5 bedim, befog, cloud, smear 6 blotch, darken,
smudge, spread 7 becloud, obscure,
splotch 9 confusion, obscurity

blurb 2 ad 4 rave, spot 5 brief 10 commercial 13 advertisement

blurred 3 dim 5 vague 6 blurry 7 smeared
10 ill-defined, indefinite, indistinct

blurt out 5 blab, sing 7 confess, divulge, let
slip 8 give away 9 come clean

blush 5 color, flush 6 redden 7 grow red,
turn red 8 rosy tint 9 reddening

blushing 3 coy, red 4 rosy 5 fresh, timid 6
demure, modest 7 colored, bashful,
flushed, glowing 8 blooming, sheepish 9
rosaceous 10 embarrassed 11 flourishing

bluster 4 brag, crow, rant 5 bluff, boast,
bully, gloat, noise, storm 7 bombast, bravado, crowing, protest, ranting, swagger 8
boasting, gloating, threaten 9 noisy talk 10
swaggering 14 boisterousness

blustery 5 blowy, gusty, windy 6 breezy 7
squally

Blythe, Ethel Mae
real name of: 14 Ethel Barrymore

Blythe, John
real name of: 13 John Barrymore

Blythe, Lionel
real name of: 15 Lionel Barrymore

Boadicea
Latin name: 8 Boudicca
queen of: 5 Iceni
husband: 10 Prasutagus
ruled: 7 Norfolk (England)
fought: 6 Romans
died: 7 suicide

Boanerges
means: 13 sons of thunder
name given to: 4 John 5 James

boar
group of: 7 sounder

board 3 bed 4 deal, feed, food, slat 5 enter,
get on, house, lodge, meals, panel, plank,
put up 6 batten, billet, embark, go onto 7
council, quarter 8 tribunal 9 clapboard, directors 10 daily meals

board game 4 Clue, Life, ludo 5 chess 7
Othello 8 checkers, cribbage, dominoes,
draughts, fanorona, Monopoly, Scrabble 9
Alquerque 10 backgammon 14 Trivial Pur-
suit 15 Chinese checkers
Egyptian: 5 Senat
Korean: 5 Nyout, Pa-tok
Indian: 7 pachisi 8 parchesi, shatranj 9
ashtapada 10 shaturanga
Japanese: 2 Go 3 I-go 5 Sho-gi
Chinese: 6 Ma-jong, wei-ch'i 7 Ma-jongg
Swedish: 6 tablut

boast 4 brag, crow, have 5 vaunt 6 flaunt 7
contain, exhibit, possess, show off, talk big
15 blow one's own horn

boaster 6 gascon 7 bragger, egotist 8 blowhard, braggart 9 big talker 11 braggadocio

boastful 5 cocky 7 crowing, pompous,
swollen 8 bragging, cocksure, inflated,
puffed up, vaunting 9 conceited 11 braggadocio, exaggerated, pretentious 12 vainglorious

boastfulness 7 conceit, egotism 8 bragging 9 cockiness, immodesty, pomposity,
vainglory 10 self-praise 11 braggadocio 12
cocksureness

boastful soldier
Latin: 14 miles gloriosus

boat 4 ship 5 craft 6 vessel

Boaz
father: 5 Salma 6 Salmon
wife: 4 Ruth
son: 4 Obed
kinsman of: 5 Naomi 9 Elimelech

bob 3 cut, hop, nod 4 clip, crop, dock, duck,
leap, trim 5 dance, shear 6 bounce 7
shorten

Bobadill
character in: 19 Every Man in His
Humour
author: 6 Jonson

bobbin 3 pin 4 coil, cord, reel 5 quill, spool
6 piping 7 ratchet, spindle, torchon 8 cylinder

bobcat 3 cat 4 lynx 7 wildcat

Bob Cummings Show, The
later name: 11 Love That Bob
character: 10 Bob Collins 14 Chuck
MacDonald 15 Charmaine (Shultzy)
Shultz 17 Margaret MacDonald
cast: 9 Ann B Davis 11 Bob Cummings
13 Dwayne Hickman 14 Rosemary De-
Camp

Bob Newhart Show, The
character: 12 Elliot Carlin, Emily Hartley,
Howard Borden 13 Jerry. Robinson, Rob-
ert (Bob) Hartley 20 Carol Kester
Bondurant
cast: 9 Bill Daily, Jack Riley 11 Peter
Bonerz 13 Marcia Wallace 16 Suzanne
Pleshette

Boccaccio, Giovanni
author of: 10 Filostrato, Filocopo 11 Life
of Dante 12 The Decameron

Boccherini, Luigi
  born: 5 Italy, Lucca
  composer of: 8 La Divina 9 The Aviary
  10 Clementina 11 L'Uccelliera

Boccioni, Umberto
  born: 5 Italy 12 Reggio Emilia 16 Reggio
  di Calabria
  artwork: 10 Elasticity 12 The City Rises
  15 Charge of Lancers 18 Dynamism of a
  Cyclist, The Forces of a Street 21 Fusion
  of Head and Window 30 Unique Forms of
  Continuity in Space

Bock, Hier
  field: 6 botany
  nationality: 6 German
  founded: 12 modern botany
  classified: 6 plants
  author of: 15 Neu Kreutterbuch

Bocklin, Arnold
  born: 5 Basel 7 Germany
  artwork: 13 Pan in the Reeds 16 The
  Isle of the Dead

Bod see 5 Tibet

bode 4 omen 5 augur 6 herald 7 betoken,
  ominate, point to, portend, predict, presage, signify 8 forecast, foretell, precurse 9
  foreshadow, prefigure

bodega 9 warehouse 12 grocery store

bodice 3 top 5 stays, waist 6 bolero, corset,
  girdle 7 corsage 8 camisole, corselet 9
  stomacher 10 underwaist

bodily 8 corporal, physical

Bodily Harm
  author: 14 Margaret Atwood

bodkin 3 awl 4 pick, tool 5 auger, borer,
  drill, point, probe 6 dagger, lancet, needle,
  reamer 7 hair pin, piercer 8 puncheon, stiletto

body 3 mob 4 bloc, bulk, form, mass 5 being, build, force, frame, group, shape, stiff,
  thing, torso, trunk 6 corpse, figure, league,
  person, throng 7 cadaver, carcass, combine, council, faction, remains, society 8
  assembly, cohesion, congress, deceased,
  main part, majority, physique, quantity 9
  coalition, multitude, stiffness, thickness 10
  federation 11 brotherhood, consistency 13
  confederation

Body and Soul
  director: 12 Robert Rossen
  cast: 10 Anne Revere 11 Hazel Brooks,
  Lilli Palmer 12 John Garfield 13 William
  Conrad

bodybuilder 12 Charles Atlas 20 Arnold
  Schwarzenegger

Boedromius
  epithet of: 6 Apollo
  means: 7 rescuer

Boeotus
  father: 8 Poseidon
  mother: 4 Arne

Boer, Boor 6 farmer 9 Afrikaner
  language: 9 Afrikaans
  ancestry: 5 Dutch
  inhabitants of: 9 Transvaal 11 South Africa 15 Orange Free State

Boethius, Anicius Manlius Severinus
  also called: 5 Boece
  author of: 23 Consolation of Philosophy

Boffin
  character in: 15 Our Mutual Friend
  author: 7 Dickens

bog 3 fen 4 mire, sink 5 marsh, swamp 6
  morass 7 be stuck 8 quagmire, wetlands 9
  marshland, swampland

Bogaerde, Derek Van den
  real name of: 11 Dirk Bogarde

Bogarde, Dirk
  real name: 19 Derek Van den Bogaerde
  born: 6 London 7 England 9 Hempstead
  roles: 6 Victim 7 Darling 10 The Servant
  13 Death in Venice 14 Song Without End,
  The Night Porter 16 A Tale of Two Cities

Bogart, Humphrey
  nickname: 5 Bogie
  wife: 12 Lauren Bacall
  born: 9 New York NY
  roles: 8 Key Largo 10 Casablanca, High
  Sierra 11 The Big Sleep 14 The Caine
  Mutiny 15 The African Queen (Oscar) 16
  The Maltese Falcon, To Have and Have
  Not 18 The Petrified Forest 27 The Treasure of the Sierra Madre

Bogdanovich, Peter
  director of: 4 Mask 9 Paper Moon 18
  The Last Picture Show

boggle 3 shy 4 balk, muff 5 botch, demure,
  hover, waver 6 bungle, shrink, wobble 7
  blunder, stumble 8 flounder, frighten, hesitate, hold back 9 overwhelm 11 make a
  mess of

boggy 3 wet 4 soft 5 foggy, mossy, soggy 6
  marshy, spongy, swampy 7 squashy

Bogie
  nickname of: 14 Humphrey Bogart

Bogota
  capital of: 8 Colombia

bogus 4 fake, sham 5 dummy, false, phony
  6 ersatz, forged, pseudo 7 feigned, pretend 8 spurious 9 imitation, simulated, synthetic 10 artificial, fraudulent 11 counterfeit, make-believe

Boheme, La
  also: 12 Bohemian Life
  opera by: 7 Puccini
  character: 4 Mimi 7 Colline, Musetta,
  Rodolfo 8 Marcello 9 Schaunard

bohemian, Bohemian 6 hippie 7 beatnik
  10 unorthodox 13 nonconformist 14 unconventional

Bohr, Niels
  field: 7 physics
  nationality: 6 Danish
  developed: 8 atom bomb 13 quantum
  theory, uranium theory

Boiardo, Matteo Maria
  author of: 17 Orlando Innamorato

boil 4 brew, burn, foam, fume, rage, rant,
  rave, sore, stew, toss 5 chafe, churn, froth,
  storm 6 bubble, fester, quiver, seethe, simmer, sizzle, well up 7 abscess, bristle, parboil, pustule, smolder 8 furuncle 9 carbuncle, fulminate

boil down 3 cut 6 reduce 7 abridge, cut down, shorten 8 condense, contract 10 abbreviate

boiler 6 copper, geyser, heater, kettle 7 alembic, caldron, furnace

Boilermaker, the
nickname of: 20 James Jackson Jeffries

boisterous 4 loud, wild 5 noisy, rowdy 6 unruly 9 clamorous, out-of-hand 10 disorderly, uproarious 12 obstreperous, uncontrolled, unrestrained

boite, boite de nuit 7 cabaret 9 nightclub

Bojer, Johan
author of: 12 Folk by the Sea, The Emigrants 14 The Great Hunger, The Power of a Lie 16 Last of the Vikings

bold 3 hot 4 loud, rude 5 brash, brave, fiery, fresh, saucy, vivid 6 brazen, cheeky, daring, flashy, heroic 7 defiant, forward, valiant 8 colorful, creative, fearless, impudent, insolent, intrepid, spirited, stalwart, striking, unafraid, valorous 9 audacious, daredevil, dauntless 10 courageous 11 eye-catching, imaginative, impertinent, indomitable, lionhearted, unshrinking 12 stouthearted 13 adventuresome

boldfaced 5 brash, saucy 6 brassy, brazen 7 forward 8 immodest, impudent, insolent 9 audacious, barefaced, shameless, unabashed

boldness 4 grit 5 nerve, pluck, spunk 6 daring, mettle 7 bravery, courage 8 audacity 9 brashness, hardihood 10 brazenness 13 audaciousness, determination, self-assurance 14 courageousness 15 adventurousness

Bolger, Ray
born: 12 Dorchester MA
roles: 9 Scarecrow 10 On Your Toes 13 The Wizard of Oz, Where's Charley

Bolivia
named for: 12 Simon Bolivar
capital:
administrative: 5 La Paz
legal: 5 Sucre
largest city: 5 La Paz
others: 4 Icla, Itau, Mojo, Saya, Yaco, Yato, Yura 5 Cliza, Llica, Oruro, Quime, Uyuni, Zongo 6 Guaqui, Potosi, Tiraja, Tupiza 8 Pulacayo 9 Santa Cruz 10 Chuquisaca, Cochabamba 11 Vallegrande, Villa Montes
school: 6 Xavier 8 St Andrew 12 San Francisco
division: 6 Valles 7 Oriente, Valleys 8 Montanas 9 Altiplano
measure: 6 league 7 celemin
monetary unit: 7 centavo 13 peso boliviano
weight: 5 libra, marco
lake: 5 Poopo 7 Allagas, Coipasa, Rogagua 8 Titicaca 10 Desaguader
mountain: 4 Jara 5 Andes, Cusco, Cuzco 6 Pupuya, Sajama, Sorata, Sunsas 7 Illampu 8 Illimani, Mururata, Sansimon, Santiago, Zapaleri 12 Eastern Range, Western Range 18 Cordillera Oriental 20 Cordillera Occidental
highest point: 8 Ancohuma
river: 4 Beni, Yata 5 Abuna, Lauca, Orton 6 Blanco, Ichilo, Itenez, Madidi, Mamore, Mizque, Yacuma 7 Guapore, Machupo 8 Inambari, Itonamas 9 Pilcomayo, Rio Grande, San Miguel 11 Desaguadero, Madre de Dios
physical features:
lowlands: 6 Llanos
plateau: 9 Altiplano
swamp: 6 Izozog
valley: 5 Yunga
volcano: 7 Ollague
people: 6 Aymara 7 mestizo, Quechua
author: 7 Mendoza 8 Arguedas 11 Costa du Reis
leader: 5 Busch, Sucre 6 Candia, Ortuno, Zamora 7 Bolivar 9 Melgarejo, Paz Zamora, Santa Cruz 10 Barrientos, Estenssoro
language: 6 Aymara 7 Quechua, Spanish
religion: 13 Roman Catholic
place:
church: 9 St Francis, St Michael 10 San Lorenzo
monument: 11 La Coronilla
ruins: 10 Tiahuanaco
tower: 6 Chulpa
feature:
animal: 5 llama 6 alpaca, vicuna
bar/club: 7 boliche
boat: 5 balsa
dance/song: 5 cueca 7 huainos, pasillo 8 morenada 9 taquirari 10 palla-palla 11 cacharpayas, waka-tokonis
devil dance: 8 Diablado
guitar: 8 charango
skirt: 7 pollera
wind instrument: 4 kena, sicu 5 erque, quena, tarka 6 pututu 9 pinquillo
food:
chicken dish: 14 picante de pollo
corn: 4 mote
corn drink: 3 api 14 chicha taratena
dish: 11 plato paceno 14 sajta de gallina
dried meat: 7 charque
pancakes: 7 bunulos
potato: 5 chuno

Bolkonsky, Andrei
character in: 11 War and Peace
author: 7 Tolstoy

Boll, Heinrich
author of: 8 The Clown 12 The Safety Net 18 Absent Without Leave 21 Group Portrait With Lady 27 The Lost Honor of Katharina Blum 28 Missing Persons and Other Essays

bolster 3 aid 4 help 5 add to, brace 6 assist, cradle, hold up, pillow, prop up, uphold 7 cushion, shore up, support, sustain 8 buttress, maintain, shoulder 9 reinforce 10 strengthen

bolster one's spirits 5 cheer 7 cheer up, comfort, hearten 8 inspirit 9 buoy one up, encourage

bolt 3 bar, fly, peg, pin, rod, run 4 dart, dash, flee, gulp, jump, leap, lock, roll, rush, tear, wolf 5 bound, brand, catch, dowel, flash, hurry, latch, rivet, scoot, shaft, speed 6 fasten, gobble, hasten, hurtle, length, secure, spring, sprint, stroke 8 fastener 12 swallow whole

bolt down 4 wolf 5 scarf 6 devour, gobble 8 gulp down

bomb 3 dud, egg 4 bust, fail, flop, mine 5 lemon 6 fiasco, fizzle 7 bombard, grenade, failure, washout

bombard 5 beset, hound, shell, worry 6 assail, attack, batter, harass, pepper, pester, strafe 7 assault, barrage, besiege 8 fire upon 9 cannonade

bombardment 5 blitz, siege 7 air raid, assault, barrage, bombing 10 blitzkrieg

bombast 3 pad 4 puff, rant 6 cotton 7 bluster, fustian, palaver 8 boasting, flummery, rhapsody, tall talk, verbiage 9 bavardage 10 balderdash 12 braggadocio, exaggeration 13 magniloquence, overstatement 14 grandiloquence 17 sesquipedalianism

bombastic 5 tumid, windy, wordy 6 padded, turgid 7 pompous, verbose 8 inflated 12 magniloquent 13 grandiloquent

Bombay
   area: 7 Trombay 8 Salsette 12 Bombay Island
   called: 14 Gateway to India
   creek: 7 Bassein
   landmark: 9 High Court 13 Taj Mahal Hotel 14 Gateway of India 16 Victoria Terminus 17 Rajabai Clock Tower
   rock formation: 10 Deccan Trap
   sea: 7 Arabian

Bona Dea
   also: 5 Fauna
   origin: 5 Roman
   goddess of: 8 chastity 9 fertility
   worshipped by: 5 women
   father: 6 Faunus
   brother: 6 Faunus
   husband: 6 Faunus

bona fide 4 real, true 5 legal 6 actual, honest, lawful 7 genuine, sincere 9 authentic, honorable 10 legitimate 11 in good faith

bon ami 5 lover 10 good friend

bonanza 8 gold mine, windfall

Bonanza
   character: 3 Ben 4 Adam, Hoss 5 Candy 7 Hop Sing 9 Little Joe
   family: 10 Cartwright
   cast: 10 Dan Blocker 11 David Canary, Lorne Greene 13 Michael Landon, Victor Sen Yung 14 Pernell Roberts
   ranch: 9 Ponderosa

Bonanza State
   nickname of: 7 Montana

bon appetit 14 hearty appetite

Bonario
   character in: 7 Volpone
   author: 6 Jonson

bonbon 5 candy, sweet 7 fondant 9 sweetmeat 10 confection, sugar candy 13 confectionery 14 chocolate cream

bond, bonds 3 tie 4 cord, knot, link, rope 5 irons, scrip, union 6 chains, pledge 7 compact, fetters, promise 8 affinity, bindings, manacles, security, shackles 9 agreement, guarantee, handcuffs 10 allegiance, attachment, connection, fastenings, obligation 11 certificate, stipulation

Bond, James
   actor: 10 Roger Moore 11 Sean Connery 12 Peter Sellers 13 George Lazenby, Timothy Dalton
   appears in: 4 Dr No 9 Moonraker, Octopussy 10 Goldfinger 11 Thunderball 12 A View To A Kill 13 Live and Let Die 15 For Your Eyes Only 16 The Spy Who Loved Me, You Only Live Twice 18 Diamonds Are Forever, From Russia with Love, Never Say Never Again, The Living Daylights 22 The Man with the Golden Gun 26 On Her Majesty's Secret Service
   author: 10 Ian Fleming
   drink: 12 vodka martini 16 shaken not stirred
   employer: 3 MI-6 20 British Secret Service
   foe: 7 Blofeld, SPECTRE
   office staff: 1 M, Q 14 Miss Moneypenny
   university: 6 Oxford
   wife: 5 Tracy

bondage 4 yoke 6 chains 7 fetters, serfdom, slavery 8 shackles 9 captivity, servitude, vassalage 11 enslavement

bone
   comprise: 8 skeleton
   contain: 6 marrow 9 cartilage 11 blood vessel
   fitted together by: 5 joint
   held by: 8 ligament
   pulled by: 6 muscle
   specific: 3 rib 4 ulna 5 femur, skull, tibia 6 carpal, fibula, pelvis, radius, sacrum, tarsal 7 humerus, patella, scapula, sternum 8 clavicle, vertebra 9 vertebrae

bone chilling 3 icy 4 cold 5 harsh, sharp 6 arctic, biting, bitter, frigid 7 cutting, glacial 8 piercing, stinging 11 penetrating 15 teeth-chattering

bonehead 3 ass 4 clod, dolt, fool 5 booby, dunce, idiot, moron, ninny 6 dimwit, nitwit 7 fathead, half-wit 8 dumb-dumb, imbecile, lunkhead 9 blockhead, lamebrain, numbskull 10 dunderhead, nincompoop 11 chowderhead

boner 4 goof, slip 5 error 6 boo-boo, slip-up 7 blooper, blunder, mistake

boneyard 4 dump 7 ossuary 8 Boot Hill, cemetery, junkyard 9 graveyard 10 churchyard 12 burial ground 13 burying ground

Bonheur, Rosa
   real name: 19 Marie Rosalie Bonheur
   born: 6 France 8 Bordeaux
   artwork: 12 The Horse Fair 23 Ploughing in the Nivernais

bonjour 5 hello 7 good day
Bonjour Tristesse
  author: 14 Francoise Sagan
bon marche 7 bargain
bon mot 4 quip 7 epigram 9 witticism
Bonn
  capital of: 11 West Germany
  landmark: 10 Bundeshaus 11 Munster-kerk
  museum: 18 Ludwig van Beethoven
  river: 5 Rhine
  Roman fort: 15 Castra Bonnensia
Bonnard, Pierre
  born: 6 France 16 Fontenay-aux-Roses
  artwork: 8 Intimist, Luncheon 9 The Review 13 Nude in the Bath, The Open Window, Women with a Dog 14 After the Shower, Farm at Le Cannet 16 The Breakfast Room 17 The Terrasse Family 22 Figure Before a Fireplace
bonne amie 5 lover 6 friend 10 good friend
bonne nuit 9 good night
bonnet 3 cap, hat 4 cowl, hood, sail 5 cover, toque 7 chapeau, commode 8 headgear 9 headdress
Bonnie and Clyde
  director: 10 Arthur Penn
  cast: 11 Faye Dunaway (Bonnie Parker), Gene Hackman 12 Warren Beatty (Clyde Barrow) 15 Michael J Pollard
bonny 4 fair 6 comely, lovely, pretty, seemly 7 winning, winsome 8 engaging, fetching, handsome, pleasing 9 beautiful, exquisite, ravishing 10 attractive
bon soir 9 good night 11 good evening
bonus 4 gift 5 prize 6 bounty, reward 7 benefit, premium 8 dividend, gratuity 10 honorarium
Bonus Eventus
  also: 7 Eventus
  origin: 5 Roman
  god of: 4 luck 10 prosperity 11 agriculture
bon vivant 7 epicure, gourmet 8 gourmand, sybarite 10 gastronome
bony 4 lean 5 gaunt, lanky, spare 6 skinny 7 angular, scrawny 11 full of bones 12 skin-and-bones
boo 3 pan 4 hiss 5 taunt 6 deride, heckle, revile 7 catcall 8 ridicule 9 criticize, shout down 11 give the bird 16 give the raspberry
boo-boo 4 goof, slip 5 boner, error 6 slip-up 7 blunder, mistake
boobtube 2 TV 3 box 8 idiot box 13 television set
booby 4 bird, dope, fool 5 dummy, dunce, idiot, moron, ninny 6 dimwit, gannet, nitwit 7 fathead, halfwit 8 bonehead, dumb-dumb, imbecile, lunkhead, numskull 9 blockhead, lamebrain, simpleton 10 nincompoop 11 chowderhead
Booby, Lady
  character in: 13 Joseph Andrews
  author: 8 Fielding

boodle 4 loot, swag 5 booty, bribe, crowd, graft, group 7 plunder 10 collection 11 stolen goods
Boog
  nickname of: 10 John Powell
boohoo 3 cry, sob 4 bawl, weep 7 blubber 9 shed tears
book 4 bill, file, list, note, opus, post, tome 5 album, enter, index, slate 6 accuse, charge, engage, enroll, indict, insert, line up, record, tablet, volume 7 catalog, procure, program, put down, reserve 8 mark down, notebook, register, schedule, treatise 9 bound work, write down 10 arrange for 11 publication, written work 16 make reservations
bookish 7 erudite, learned, stilted 8 academic, educated, informed, literary, pedantic, studious, well-read 9 scholarly 11 pedagogical, impractical 12 intellectual
bookkeeper 5 clerk 7 auditor 10 accountant 11 comptroller
booklet 5 folio 7 leaflet, program 8 brochure, circular, pamphlet
Book of Common Prayer
  author: 10 Joan Didion
Book of Lights, The
  author: 10 Chaim Potok
Book of Manuel
  author: 13 Julio Cortazar
Book of Odes
  author: 9 Confucius
Book of psalms 12 psalter
Book of Sand, The
  author: 15 Jorge Luis Borges
Book of the Duchess, The
  author: 15 Geoffrey Chaucer
boom 3 bar 4 bang, beam, gain, grow, push, roar, spar 5 blast, boost, shaft, spurt 6 growth, rumble, thrive, thrust, upturn 7 advance, develop, prosper, thunder, upsurge 8 flourish, increase 9 expansion, good times
Boom Boom
  nickname of: 15 Bernie Geoffrion
boomerang 5 kalie, kiley, kylie, wango 6 atlatl, recoil 7 rebound, womerah, woomera 8 backfire, ricochet, trombush 9 bound back, solitaire 10 projectile
Boomer State
  nickname of: 8 Oklahoma
boon 3 fun, gay 4 gift 5 favor, jolly, merry 6 kindly 7 benefit, bequest 8 blessing, donation, offering, pleasant 9 advantage, congenial, convivial, endowment 11 full of cheer, good-natured
boon companion 3 pal 4 chum 5 buddy, crony 6 friend 7 comrade 8 confrere, intimate 9 confidant 10 bosom buddy
boondocks 4 bush, veld 6 Podunk, sticks 7 boonies, country, outback 8 frontier 9 backwater, backwoods, provinces 10 hinterland 11 backcountry, countryside 12 squaresville 13 nowheresville 14 wide open spaces

Boone, Richard
  born: 12 Los Angeles CA
  roles: 5 Medic 6 Hombre 7 Paladin 8 The Alamo 11 The Shootist 12 Ten Wanted Men, The Desert Fox 17 Have Gun Will Travel

boonies 6 sticks 7 country 9 backwoods, boondocks, provinces 10 hinterland 11 countryside

boor 3 oaf 4 hick, lout, rube 5 brute, churl, yokel 6 rustic 7 bumpkin, hayseed, peasant 9 vulgarian 10 clodhopper, philistine 11 guttersnipe

boorish 4 rude 5 crude 6 coarse, gauche, oafish, rustic, vulgar 7 loutish, uncouth 9 unrefined 10 unpolished 11 peasantlike

boorishness 8 rudeness 9 surliness, vulgarity 10 bad manners, coarseness, incivility, oafishness 12 churlishness, impoliteness

boost 4 hike, laud, lift, plug, push, rise 5 add to, extol, heave, hoist, pitch, raise, shove 6 expand, foster, free ad, growth, pickup, praise, upturn, urge on 7 acclaim, advance, develop, elevate, enlarge, forward, further, improve, nurture, promote, root for, support, sustain, upsurge, upswing 8 addition, applause, good word, increase, propound 9 expansion, increment, promotion 10 compliment, give a leg up, stick up for 11 development, enlargement, improvement, speak well of

boot
  French: 9 chaussure

booth 3 pen 4 coop, nook, tent 5 hutch, stall, stand, table 7 counter 9 cubbyhole, enclosure 11 compartment

Booth, Shirley
  real name: 15 Thelma Booth Ford
  born: 9 New York NY
  roles: 5 Hazel 13 The Matchmaker 19 Come Back Little Sheba (Oscar)

bootleg 5 hooch 7 illegal, illicit 8 unlawful 9 moonshine 12 football play

bootless 6 futile 7 useless 11 ineffective, ineffectual 12 unproductive, unprofitable

bootlick 4 fawn 5 toady 6 cringe, grovel 7 flatter, truckle

bootmaker 7 cobbler 9 shoemaker

booty 4 gain, loot 5 prize 6 boodle, spoils 7 pillage, plunder, takings 8 pickings, winnings

booze 4 bout, soak 5 drink, hooch, spree 6 guzzle, liquor, tipple 7 alcohol, spirits, swizzle 8 cocktail 10 intoxicant 14 drink like a fish
  type: 3 gin, rum, rye 4 beer, wine 5 vodka 6 scotch 7 bourbon, whiskey

boozer 3 sot 4 lush 5 drunk, souse, toper 7 tippler 8 drunkard 9 alcoholic, inebriate 11 hard drinker

bordello, bordel 4 stew 5 house 6 bagnio 7 brothel 8 cathouse 10 bawdy house, fancy house, whorehouse 13 sporting house 14 house of ill fame 16 house of ill repute 19 house of prostitution

border 3 hem, rim 4 abut, bind, brim, curb, edge, join, line, pale, trim 5 brink, flank, frame, limit, skirt, touch, verge 6 adjoin, fringe, margin 8 befringe, be next to, boundary, frontier, outskirt 9 extremity, perimeter, periphery 13 circumference

borderline 4 open 5 vague 7 halfway, inexact, obscure, unclear 8 marginal 9 ambiguous, equivocal, uncertain, undecided, unsettled 10 ambivalent, indefinite 11 indefinable, problematic 13 indeterminate

bore 4 drag, drip, sink, tire 5 drill, drive, weary 6 burrow, pierce, tunnel 7 caliber, exhaust, fatigue, wear out 8 gouge out 9 hollow out 10 wet blanket 14 inside diameter

Boreadae
  decendants of: 6 Boreas

Boreal
  pertaining to: 6 Boreas

Boreas
  origin: 5 Greek
  personifies: 9 north wind
  father: 8 Astraeus
  mother: 3 Eos
  twin sons: 5 Zetes 6 Calais
  daughter: 6 Chione 9 Cleopatra

bored 5 jaded 7 wearied 12 discontented, uninterested

boredom 6 tedium 8 doldrums, dullness, monotony 9 weariness 11 tediousness
  French: 5 ennui

Borges, Jorge Luis
  author of: 8 The Aleph 10 Labyrinths 11 Dreamtigers 13 The Book of Sand 18 A Personal Anthology, In Praise of Darkness 19 Doctor Brodie's Report, Fervor of Buenos Aires 25 A Universal History of Infamy

Borghild
  origin: 12 Scandinavian
  mentioned in: 8 Volsunga
  husband: 7 Sigmund

Borgia, Alfonso de 16 Pope Callistus III

Borgia, Rodrigo de 15 Pope Alexander VI

Borglum, (John) Gutzon
  born: 10 Bear Lake ID
  artwork: 7 Lincoln 18 Mt Rushmore Memorial, The Mares of Diomedes

Borgnine, Ernest
  real name: 18 Ermes Effron Borgnine
  wife: 11 Ethel Merman
  born: 8 Hamden CT
  roles: 5 Marty (Oscar) 8 Barabbas 11 McHale's Navy 12 The Wild Bunch 13 The Dirty Dozen 17 Bad Day at Black Rock 18 From Here to Eternity 20 The Poseidon Adventure

boring 4 dull, flat 5 stale 6 tiring 7 humdrum, insipid, tedious 8 tiresome 9 wearisome 10 monotonous, unexciting 11 repetitious 13 uninteresting

boring tool 3 bit 5 auger, drill 11 brace and bit

Borinquen see 10 Puerto Rico
Boriquen, Borinquen
  language family: 8 Arawakan
  location: 10 Puerto Rico
  related to: 5 Taino
Boris Godunov
  author: 16 Alexander Pushkin
  opera by: 10 Mussorgsky 12 Shostakovich 14 Rimsky-Korsakov
  character: 6 Dmitri, Feodor, Maryna 7
  Gregory, Grigory 8 Basmanov, Otrepyev
born 6 innate 7 natural 9 delivered, intuitive
  12 brought forth
Born, Max
  field: 7 physics
  nationality: 7 British
  worked on: 13 quantum theory
  awarded: 10 Nobel Prize
borne 6 afloat, braved 7 carried, endured 9
  put up with, tolerated 11 gone through,
  went through 12 given birth to
Borneo
  other name: 10 Kalimantan
  largest city: 12 Bandjermasin
  others: 5 Kumai 6 Sambas, Sampit 7
  Malinau, Pagatan, Sanggau, Sintang,
  Tarakan 8 Ketapang 9 Pontianak 10
  Balikpapan
  division of island:
  independent: 6 Brunei
  Malaysian state: 5 Sabah 7 Sarawak
  part of Indonesia: 10 Kalimantan
  measure: 7 gantang
  weight: 4 para 6 chapah
  mountain: 4 Iran, Raja 5 Saran 6
  Kapuas, Muller, Nijaan, Tebang 8
  Kinibalu, Schwaner
  highest point: 8 Kinabalu
  river: 4 Arut, Iwan 5 Bahau, Berau,
  Kajan, Padas, Pawan 6 Barito, Kapuas,
  Rajang, Sebuku 7 Kahajan, Mahakam,
  Mendawi 8 Pembuang
  sea: 4 Java, Sulu 7 Celebes 10 South
  China
  physical feature:
  bay: 5 Adang, Kumai 6 Sampit
  cape: 3 Aru 4 Datu 5 Lojar 6 Puting,
  Sambar 7 Selatan
  port: 4 Miri 5 Balik, Papan 6 Brunei 9
  Pontianak 12 Bandjermasin
  strait: 8 Macassar
  people: 4 Iban 5 Bukat, Dajak, Dayak,
  Dusan, Malay, Punan 6 Illano 7 Bakatan,
  Chinese, Illanum
  language: 5 Malay 6 tribal 7 Chinese,
  English
  religion: 5 Islam 7 animism 12 Christianity
  feature:
  tree: 5 kapor, kapur 7 billian
Born Yesterday
  director: 11 George Cukor
  cast: 12 Judy Holliday 13 William Holden
  17 Broderick Crawford
  Oscar for: 7 actress (Holliday)

Borodin, Alexander
  born: 6 Russia 12 St Petersburg
  member of: 7 The Five
  composer of: 8 Bogatyri 10 Prince Igor
  25 In the Steppes of Central Asia
boron
  chemical symbol: 1 B
borough 4 burg, town 5 borgo, shire 6
  county, parish 7 village 8 district, precinct,
  province, township 12 municipality
  of New York City: 5 Bronx 6 Queens 8
  Brooklyn 9 Manhattan 12 Staten Island
Borromini, Francesco
  architect of: 10 San Carlino 17 Palazzo
  Falconieri 20 Sant' Ivo della Sapienza 23
  Oratory of San Filippo Neri 24 Collegio di
  Propaganda Fide 26 San Carlo alle
  Quattro Fontane (Rome)
borrow 3 get, use 4 copy, take 5 filch, steal,
  usurp 6 obtain, pilfer, pirate 7 acquire 10
  commandeer, plagiarize, take on loan 11
  appropriate
Borrow, George Henry
  author of: 8 Lavengro 9 Romany Rye,
  Wild Wales 10 The Zincali 15 The Bible in
  Spain
Bors
  character in: 16 Arthurian romance
Bosch, Hieronymus
  real name: 13 Jerome van Aken 14
  Jerome van Aeken 17 Jeroen Anthois-
  zoon
  artwork: 7 Hay-Wain 11 Ship of Fools 14
  The Crucifixion 19 Adoration of the Kings
  21 The Crowning with Thorns 26 The
  Garden of Earthly Delights
bosh 3 rot 4 bunk 6 bunkum, drivel 7 twaddle 8 claptrap, nonsense, tommyrot 10 balderdash, tomfoolery 11 foolishness 16 stuff
  and nonsense
bosky 5 bushy, drunk, shaded, tipsy, treed
  6 wooded
Bosnia-Herzegovina
  capital/largest city: 8 Sarajevo
  others: 4 Neum 5 Tuzla 6 Citluk, Kupres,
  Lenica, Mostar 8 Prijedor 9 Banja Luka,
  Bijeljina 10 Srebrenica 12 Bosanski Brod,
  Siroki Brijeg
  head of state: 9 president
  monetary unit: 5 dinar
  mountain: 11 Dinaric Alps
  river: 3 Una 4 Sava 5 Bosna, Drina,
  Vrbas 7 Neretva
  sea: 8 Adriatic
  people: 4 Serb 5 Croat 6 Muslim 8 Yugoslav
  language: 13 Serbo Croatian
  religion: 11 Sunni Muslim 15 Serbian Orthodox
bosom 4 bust, core, dear, soul 5 chest,
  close, heart, midst 6 breast, center, spirit 7
  beloved, nucleus 8 intimate 9 cherished 11
  inner circle
bosom buddy 4 chum 5 crony 6 cohort 7
  best pal, comrade 8 alter ego, intimate,
  sidekick 9 companion, confidant 10 best
  friend

bosomy 5 busty, buxom 6 zaftig 11 full-figured 13 large-breasted

boss 4 head, push 5 chief, order 6 leader, master 7 command, foreman, kingpin, manager 8 employer 9 big cheese, executive 10 supervisor 13 administrator 14 superintendent

bossy 3 cow 9 imperious 10 commanding, tyrannical 11 dictatorial, domineering

Boston
  airport: 5 Logan
  area: 7 Back Bay 10 Bunker Hill, Fenway Park 11 Faneuil Hall 14 Kennedy Library, Old North Church
  baseball team: 6 Red Sox
  basketball team: 7 Celtics
  dish: 10 baked beans
  hockey team: 6 Bruins
  landmark: 10 Beacon Hill
  leader: 7 Brahmin
  nickname: 8 Bean town
  river: 7 Charles

Bostonians, The
  author: 10 Henry James

Boston Strong Boy
  nickname of: 13 John L. Sullivan

Boswell, James
  author of: 22 The Life of Samuel Johnson

botanist
  American: 6 Barton, Torrey 7 Bartram
  Austrian: 6 Mendel
  Dutch: 7 DeVries
  German: 4 Bock, Cohn
  Scottish: 5 Brown
  Swedish: 8 Linnaeus
  Swiss: 6 Bauhin

botch 3 err, mar 4 blow, fail, flop, flub, goof, hash, mess, muff, ruin 5 spoil 6 bungle, foul up, fumble 7 blunder, butcher, failure, louse up 8 butchery 9 mismanage 11 make a mess of

bother 3 ado, irk, nag, tax, try, vex 4 care, drag, fret, fuss, load, onus, stir 5 annoy, harry, trial, upset, worry 6 dismay, flurry, harass, pester, racket, rumpus, strain, stress, tumult 7 attempt, disturb, problem, trouble 8 disquiet, distress, hardship, headache, irritate, nuisance, vexation 9 aggravate, commotion, hindrance 10 affliction, difficulty, impediment, irritation 11 aggravation, disturbance, encumbrance 12 make an effort 13 inconvenience, pain in the neck 14 responsibility

bothersome 6 taxing, vexing 8 annoying 9 worrisome 10 disturbing 11 aggravating, disquieting, distressing, troublesome 12 inconvenient

Botswana
  other name: 12 Bechuanaland
  capital/largest city: 8 Gaborone 9 Gáberones
  others: 5 Kanye, Orapa, Tsane 6 Serowe 7 Lobatse, Lobotsi, Mochudi, Palapye, Thamaga 10 Molepolole 11 Francistown, Selebi-Pikwe
  monetary unit: 4 pula, rand

  lake: 3 Dow, Xau 5 Ngami
  highest point: 11 Tsodilo Hill
  river: 4 Nata, Okwa 5 Chobe, Nosob 6 Cuando, Molopo, Shashi 7 Cubango, Limpopo 8 Botletle, Okovango 9 Okovanggo
  physical feature:
  desert: 8 Kalahari
  salt pans: 10 Makarikari
  swamp: 8 Okavango
  people: 5 Bantu 6 Tswana 7 Bakatla, Bakwena, Bushman 8 Bamalete, Baralong, Batawana, Batlokwa, Botswana 10 Bamangwato 11 Bangwaketse
  language: 5 Bantu, Click 6 Tswana 7 English, Khoisan 8 Setswana
  religion: 7 animism 10 Protestant 12 Christianity

Botticelli, Sandro
  real name: 30 Alessandro di Mariano dei Filipepi
  born: 5 Italy 8 Florence
  artwork: 12 Birth of Venus 14 Mystic Nativity 16 Calumny of Apelles 18 Adoration of the Magi 22 Pallas Subduing a Centaur 25 The Madonna of the Magnificat

bottle 3 jar 4 vial 5 flask, phial 6 carafe, flagon, vessel 7 canteen

bottleneck 3 bar, jam 4 clog, stop 5 block 6 detour 7 barrier, embolus 8 blockage, embolism, gridlock, obstacle, stoppage, thrombus 10 congestion, impediment, infarction 11 costiveness, obstruction

bottom 3 can 4 base, core, foot, gist, root, rump, seat, sole 5 basis, belly, cause, fanny, heart, lower 6 center, deeper, depths, ground, lowest, origin, source, spring 7 deepest, essence 8 backside, buttocks, pedestal, riverbed 9 beginning, fundament, principle, rudiments, substance, underpart, underside 10 foundation, mainspring, wellspring 12 quintessence

Bottom
  character in: 21 A Midsummer Night's Dream
  author: 11 Shakespeare

bottomless 4 deep 7 abysmal 8 profound 11 measureless 12 immeasurable, unfathomable

Boucher, Francois
  born: 5 Paris 6 France
  artwork: 9 The Rising 13 Madame Boucher, Reclining Girl 16 Evening Landscape, Rinaldo and Armida, The Toilet of Venus 17 Chinese Tapestries, The Triumph of Venus 18 The Setting of the Sun

boudoir 7 bedroom 10 bedchamber 12 dressing room

bough 4 limb 6 branch

bougie 3 dip, wax 5 light, taper 6 candle, cierge, tallow

boulder, bowlder 3 nob 4 crag, knob, rock 5 block, stone 6 gibber 7 dornick 8 megalith

boulevard 6 avenue 7 parkway 9 concourse

bouleversement 7 turmoil 9 confusion, upsetting 11 overturning

bounce 3 bob, hop, pep 4 bump, life 5 bound, thump, verve, vigor 6 energy, jounce, recoil, spirit 7 rebound 8 dynamism, ricochet, vitality, vivacity 9 animation 10 liveliness

bouncing 3 big 4 full 5 jolly, large, lusty, plump 6 chubby, lively, robust, strong 7 healthy 8 animated, vigorous 12 in good health

bound 3 bob, orb, rim 4 area, edge, jump, leap, line, mark, pale, romp, sure, tied 5 dance, fated, hedge, limit, orbit, range, realm, vault 6 border, bounce, define, domain, doomed, forced, fringe, gambol, liable, prance, region, spring, tied up 7 certain, compass, confine, covered, encased, enclosed, flounce, going to, in bonds, limited, obliged, rebound, secured, trussed, wrapped 8 beholden, boundary, confined, destined, district, encircle, fastened, province, required, resolute, resolved, surround, tethered 9 bailiwick, committed, demarcate, extremity, periphery, territory 10 determined, restrained 11 demarcation 12 circumscribe

Boundaries
  god of: 8 Terminus

boundary 3 rim 4 edge, line, pale 6 border, margin 7 barrier 8 frontier, landmark 9 extremity, periphery 11 demarcation 12 dividing line

boundary line 4 edge 5 bound 6 border 8 sideline

bounder 3 cad, rat 4 heel 5 knave, louse, rogue 6 rascal, rotter 7 caitiff, dastard, villain 9 scoundrel 10 blackguard

Bounderby, Mr
  character in: 9 Hard Times
  author: 7 Dickens

boundless 4 vast 7 endless, immense 8 infinite, unending 9 limitless, perpetual, unbounded, unlimited 10 without end 11 everlasting, measureless 12 immeasurable, incalculable, unrestricted 13 inexhaustible

bounteous, bountiful 4 free, full, rich 5 ample, large 6 lavish 7 copious, liberal, profuse, teeming 8 abundant, generous, prolific 9 abounding, plenteous, plentiful, unsparing 10 beneficent, benevolent, charitable, munificent, unstinting 11 magnanimous, overflowing

Bountiful, Lady
  character in: 17 The Beaux Stratagem
  author: 8 Farquhar

bountifulness 10 liberality, generosity 11 benevolence, magnanimity, munificence 14 charitableness 15 humanitarianism

bounty 3 aid 4 gift, help 5 bonus, favor, grant 6 giving, reward 7 charity, present, tribute 8 bestowal, donation, gratuity 9 endowment 10 almsgiving, assistance, generosity, liberality, recompense 11 benefaction, benevolence, munificence 12 contribution, philanthropy 14 charitableness, openhandedness

bouquet 4 odor 5 aroma, scent, spray 7 essence, garland, nosegay, perfume 9 fragrance 11 boutonniere

bouquet garni
  ingredient: 5 basil, thyme 6 celery, savory 7 bay leaf, chervil, parsley 8 rosemary, tarragon

bourbon
  variety of: 7 whiskey
  origin: 7 America
  ingredient: 4 corn
  type: 7 blended 8 straight
  drink: 9 Mint Julep 10 Boston Sour 11 John Collins 12 Old Fashioned
  with Benedictine: 9 Twin Hills
  with brandy and Benedictine: 13 Brighton Punch
  with Cointreau: 10 Temptation
  with rum: 14 Artillery Punch
  with sloe gin: 9 Black Hawk
  with Southern Comfort: 14 Blended Comfort
  with triple sec: 10 Chapel Hill
  with vermouth: 9 Allegheny

bourgeois 6 square 7 Babbitt, burgher 8 commoner, ordinary 11 middle-class 12 conventional 13 unimaginative

Bourgeois Gentleman, The
  author: 7 Moliere
  character: 6 Lucile, Nicole 7 Cleonte, Dorante 8 Covielle, Dorimene 14 Madame Jourdain 16 Monsieur Jourdain

Bourget, Charles Joseph Paul
  author of: 11 The Disciple 12 A Cruel Enigma 14 The Night Cometh

Bourgh, Lady Catherine de
  character in: 17 Pride and Prejudice
  author: 6 Austen

Bourjaily, Vance
  author of: 11 The Violated 14 The End of My Life 18 Brill Among the Ruins 22 Now Playing at Canterbury

Bourne Identity, The
  author: 12 Robert Ludlum

bout 4 fray, term, tilt, turn 5 brush, clash, cycle, fight, match, set-to, siege, spell, spree 6 affair, battle, course, period, series 7 contest, go-round, scuffle, session, tourney 8 conflict, interval, skirmish, struggle 9 encounter 10 contention, engagement 11 boxing match, embroilment

boutonniere 4 posy 7 nosegay 16 buttonhole flower

bow 3 arc 4 bend, knot, prow, stem 5 agree, curve, defer, front, stoop, yield 6 archer, comply, curtsy, give in, kowtow, relent, salaam, submit, weapon 7 concede, succumb, crescent 9 acquiesce, genuflect, surrender 10 capitulate, forward end 12 genuflection, knuckle under

Bow, Clara
  nickname: 6 It Girl
  born: 10 Brooklyn NY
  roles: 2 It 7 Mantrap 12 The Wild Party

bowdlerize 6 censor 9 expurgate 10 bluepencil

bow down 5 yield 6 give in, submit 9 surrender 10 capitulate 12 knuckle under

bowed 4 bent 6 arched, curved, nodded 7 hunched, stooped

bowels 3 gut, pit 4 core, guts, womb 5 abyss, belly, bosom, heart, midst 6 depths, hollow, vitals 7 innards, insides, stomach, viscera 8 entrails, interior, recesses 10 intestines 11 vital organs 13 innermost part

Bowen, Elizabeth
  author of: 8 Eva Trout, The Hotel 10 To the North 11 Bowen's Court, Little Girls, The Cat Jumps 12 A World of Love 15 The Heat of the Day, The House in Paris 18 The Death of the Heart

Bowen's Court
  author: 14 Elizabeth Bowen

bower 4 jack, joker, nook 5 arbor 6 alcove, anchor, pandal 7 bedroom, chamber, cottage, enclose, retreat, sanctum, shelter 8 dwelling, snuggery

Bowie, David
  real name: 16 David Robert Jones
  born: 6 London 7 England
  roles: 9 Cat People, The Hunger 20 The Man Who Fell to Earth 24 Merry Christmas Mr Lawrence

Bowie Land, Bowie State
  nickname of: 8 Arkansas

bowl 4 boat 5 arena, basin 6 cavity, hollow, tureen, valley, vessel 7 dishful, helping, portion, stadium 8 coliseum, deep dish 9 container, porringer 10 depression, receptacle 12 amphitheater

bowler 11 Earl Anthony

bowling
  variation: 7 tenpins 8 duckpins, fivepins 10 candlepins
  term: 4 miss 5 frame, spare, split 6 strike 10 gutterball
  perfect score: 12 three hundred

bow-shape 3 arc 4 arch, bend 5 curve 9 curvature

bow to 5 yield 6 give in, give up, submit 9 acquiesce

box 3 bat, hit, rap 4 belt, cuff, slap, spar 5 booth, caddy, chest, crate, fight, punch, stall, whack 6 buffet, carton, coffer, strike, thwack 8 thumping 9 container 10 receptacle 11 compartment 13 exchange blows

boxer 7 Max Baer 8 Joe Louis 10 Barney Ross, Gene Tunney, Joe Frazier, Joe Walcott, Leon Spinks 11 Archie Moore, Jack Dempsey, Jack Johnson, Jake LaMotta, Larry Holmes, Muhammad Ali, Sonny Liston 12 Benny Leonard, James Corbett, John Sullivan, Johnny Dundee, Max Schmeling, Mickey Walker, Primo Carnera, Roberto Duran, Thomas Hearns 13 Carmen Basilio, Ezzard Charles, George Foreman, James Jeffries, Rocky Graziano, Rocky Marciano 14 Bob Fitzsimmons, Floyd Patterson, Henry Armstrong 15 Maxie Rosenbloom, Sugar Ray Leonard 16 Sugar Ray Robinson

boy 3 lad 5 youth 8 man child 9 male child, stripling, youngster
  French: 6 garcon

Boy
  character in: 6 Tarzan
  author: 9 Burroughs

boycott 5 spurn 6 reject 7 exclude 8 spurning 9 blackball, blacklist, exclusion, ostracism, ostracize, rejection 12 blackballing, blacklisting

Boyd, James
  author of: 5 Drums 8 Long Hunt 9 Roll River 10 Marching On

Boyd, William
  born: 13 Hendrysburg OH
  roles: 15 Hopalong Cassidy

Boyer, Charles
  born: 6 Figeac, France
  roles: 7 Algiers 8 Conquest, Gaslight 10 Back Street 11 Lost Horizon 16 The Garden of Allah 19 All This and Heaven Too

boyfriend 3 man 4 beau, date 5 flame, lover, swain, wooer 6 escort, fellow, old man, squire, steady, suitor 7 admirer, beloved, Don Juan 8 cavalier, Lothario, paramour, truelove, young man 9 companion, inamorato 10 sweetheart 15 gentleman caller

boyish 5 boyey, fresh 6 callow, tender 7 boylike, puerile 8 childish, immature, innocent, juvenile, youthful 9 childlike 10 sophomoric

Boylan, Blazes
  character in: 7 Ulysses
  author: 5 Joyce

Boyle, Robert
  field: 9 chemistry
  nationality: 7 British
  father of: 9 chemistry
  advocated: 20 experimental approach
  established: 9 Boyle's Law

boylike 5 fresh, young 6 boyish, callow 7 puerile 8 childish, immature, innocent, juvenile, youthful 9 childlike

Boys Town
  director: 12 Norman Taurog
  cast: 9 Henry Hull 12 Mickey Rooney, Spencer Tracy (Father Flanagan)
  Oscar for: 5 actor (Tracy)
  sequel: 13 Men of Boys Town

Boy Wonder
  nickname of: 5 Robin 6 Mel Ott

brace 3 duo 4 pair, prop, stay 5 shore, strut, truss 6 bracer, couple, hold up, prop up, steady 7 bolster, bracket, fortify, prepare, shore up, support, sustain, twosome 8 buttress 9 reinforce, stanchion 10 strengthen 13 reinforcement

bracelet 6 armlet, bangle

bracer 10 stiff drink, stimulator, wristguard 11 invigorator 12 strengthener, strong drink

Brachiosaurus
  type: 8 dinosaur, sauropod
  location: 10 East Africa 12 United States
  period: 8 Jurassic

bracing 8 arousing, reviving 10 energizing, fortifying, refreshing 11 restorative, stimulating 12 exhilarating, invigorating 13 strengthening

Brack, Judge
  character in: 11 Hedda Gabler
  author: 5 Ibsen

bracken 4 fern 5 brake, brush, ferns 10 underbrush 11 undergrowth

bracket 4 prop, rank, stay 5 brace, class, group, range, shore, strut, truss 6 prop up, status 7 shore up, support 8 category, classify, division, grouping 9 designate, stanchion 10 categorize 11 designation 14 classification

brackish 4 salt 5 briny, salty 6 saline

Bracknell, Lady Augusta
  character in: 27 The Importance of Being Earnest
  author: 5 Wilde

bract 4 leaf

Bradbury, Ray
  author of: 13 Dandelion Wine, Fahrenheit 451 17 The Illustrated Man 20 The Martian Chronicles 27 Something Wicked This Way Comes

Bradford, Barbara Taylor
  author of: 17 A Woman of Substance

Bradford, Richard
  author of: 15 Red Sky at Morning

Bradley, Bill (William Warren)
  nickname: 10 Dollar Bill
  sport: 10 basketball
  team: 13 New York Knicks
  elected: 7 Senator
  from: 9 New Jersey

Bradstreet, Anne
  author of: 35 The Tenth Muse Lately Sprung Up in America

Brady Bunch, The
  character: 3 Jan 4 Greg 5 Alice, Bobby, Cindy, Peter 6 Marcia 9 Mike Brady 10 Carol Brady
  cast: 8 Eve Plumb 9 Ann B Davis 10 Robert Reed, Susan Olsen 13 Barry Williams 14 Mike Lookinland 16 Maureen McCormick 17 Christopher Knight, Florence Henderson

brag 4 crow 5 boast, vaunt 7 big talk, crowing, talk big 8 boasting, bragging 10 exaggerate, self-praise 12 boastfulness, exaggeration 15 blow one's own horn 19 pat oneself on the back

Brage see 5 Bragi

Bragg, William Henry and William Lawrence
  field: 7 physics
  nationality: 7 British
  determined: 16 crystal structure
  by: 15 X-ray diffraction
  established: 9 Bragg's Law
  awarded: 10 Nobel Prize

braggadocio 5 pride 6 egoism, vanity 7 bluster, conceit, swagger 9 cockiness, vainglory 10 pretension 14 self-importance

braggart 7 boaster, bragger 8 blowhard 9 big talker

Bragi
  also: 5 Brage
  origin: 6 Nordic
  god of: 5 music 6 poetry
  father: 4 Odin 5 Othin
  wife: 4 Idun 5 Iduna, Ithun 6 Ithunn
  mother: 3 Fri 5 Frigg, Frija 6 Frigga

Brahe, Tycho
  field: 9 astronomy
  nationality: 6 Danish
  built: 11 observatory

Brahman
  country: 5 India
  religion: 8 Hinduism
  system: 5 caste
  rank: 7 highest
  function: 6 leader, priest 7 teacher

Brahms, Johannes
  born: 7 Germany, Hamburg
  composer of: 7 Rinaldo 10 Rain Sonata 11 Triumphlied, Volkslieder 12 Thuner-Sonate 13 German Requiem, Song of Destiny, Song of Triumph 14 Schicksalslied, Song of the Fates, Tragic Overture 15 Gesang der Parzen, Hungarian Dances 19 Liebeslieder Waltzes, Meistersinger Sonata 24 Academic Festival Overture 31 Variations on the St Anthony Chorale

braid 4 knit, lace 5 plait, ravel, twine, twist, weave 7 entwine, wreathe 9 interlace 10 intertwine

brain
  part: 7 medulla 8 cerebrum 9 pituitary 10 cerebellum

brainchild 8 creation 9 invention 12 original work 15 imaginative work

brainless 6 genius 9 smartness 10 brightness, brilliance, cleverness 12 intelligence

brainless 4 dumb 6 stupid 7 asinine, foolish, idiotic, moronic, witless 8 mindless 9 imbecilic 10 half-witted 11 lamebrained 12 feeble-minded, simple-minded

brain power 4 mind 9 intellect 12 intelligence 14 mental capacity

Brainworm
  character in: 19 Every Man in His Humour
  author: 6 Jonson

brainy 5 smart 6 bright, clever 9 brilliant 11 intelligent

brake 4 curb, drag, halt, rein, slow, stay, stop 5 check 6 arrest 7 control 9 restraint 10 constraint 11 reduce speed

Bramante, Donato
  architect of: 9 Tempietto 14 Belvedere Court (the Vatican), Palazzo Caprini 19 Santa Maria della Pace 21 Santa Maria della Grazie

bramble 4 bush, vine 5 rough, shrub 7 thicket 8 prickers 13 raspberry bush 14 blackberry bush

Bramble, Matthew
  character in: 14 Humphry Clinker
  author: 8 Smollett

Bran
origin: 5 Welsh
king of: 7 Britain
habitat: 3 sea
saint in: 12 Christianity
brother: 9 Evnissyen 10 Manawyddan
sister: 7 Branwen
head buried in: 6 London

branch 3 arm, leg 4 fork, limb, part, wing 5 bough, prong, spray 6 agency, bureau, divide, feeder, member, office, ramify 7 channel, chapter, diverge, radiate, section, segment 8 division, offshoot, separate, shoot off 9 bifurcate, component, extension, tributary 10 department 11 subdivision 12 ramification

branched 6 forked, parted 7 divided 8 extended 9 spread out

Branchus
father: 6 Apollo
power of: 6 augury
power given by: 6 Apollo

Brancusi, Constantin
born: 7 Romania 13 Pestisani Gorj
artwork: 4 Fish 7 Chimera, The Kiss, The Seal 9 Sorceress 10 Adam and Eve, Prometheus 11 Bird in Space, Prodigal Son 12 Flying Turtle, Sleeping Muse 13 Endless Column 20 Sculpture for the Blind

brand 4 blot, kind, make, mark, sear, sign, slur, sort, spot, type 5 class, grade, label, smear, stain, stamp, taint 6 burn in, emblem, smirch, stigma 7 blemish, quality, variety 8 besmirch, disgrace 9 discredit, trademark 10 imputation, stigmatize 11 manufacture

brandish 4 wave 5 shake, swing, wield 6 flaunt, waggle 7 display, exhibit, show off 8 flourish

brand new 5 fresh, young 6 unused

Brando, Marlon
born: 7 Omaha NE
roles: 8 Sayonara 10 The Wild One, Viva Zapata 12 Julius Caesar, The Godfather (Oscar refused) 13 Apocalypse Now 15 On the Waterfront (Oscar) 16 Last Tango in Paris 17 Mutiny on the Bounty 21 A Streetcar Named Desire

brandy 6 cognac, grappa, kahlua, kirsch, metaxa 8 Calvados, Tia Maria 9 applejack, Slivovitz 12 Grand Marnier, Peter Heering 14 forbidden fruit
French: 8 eau de vie

Brangwen, Ursula and Gudrun
characters in: 11 Women in Love
author: 8 Lawrence

Branstock
also: 9 Barnstock
origin: 12 Scandinavian
mentioned in: 8 Volsunga
form: 3 oak 4 tree
location: 7 Volsung
house of: 7 Volsung
Odin (Othin) thrusts: 4 Gram 5 sword

Brant, Captain Adam
character in: 22 Mourning Becomes Electra
author: 6 O'Neill

Branwen
origin: 5 Welsh
brother: 4 Bran
husband: 10 Matholwych
son killed by: 9 Evnissyen

Braque, Georges
born: 6 France 18 Argenteuil sur Seine
artwork: 7 Atelier, Grand Nu (Great Nude), The Echo 8 The Table 13 The Portuguese 14 Man with a Guitar 16 Violin and Palette, Violin and Pitcher 18 Woman with a Mandolin

brash 4 bold, rash, rude 5 fresh, hasty, sassy 6 brazen, cheeky, madcap 7 forward 8 careless, heedless, impudent, reckless 9 foolhardy, impetuous, imprudent, know-it-all 10 incautious 11 impertinent, precipitous, smart-alecky 12 unconsidered 13 overconfident

brashness 4 gall 5 brass, cheek, nerve 8 audacity, boldness, chutzpah, temerity 10 brazenness, effrontery 11 forwardness, presumption

Brasilia
capital of: 6 Brazil

brass 4 gall, sand, VIPs 5 cheek, nerve 8 audacity, boldness, chutzpah, officers, temerity 9 impudence 10 brazenness, effrontery 11 forwardness, presumption

Brass, Sampson
character in: 19 The Old Curiosity Shop
author: 7 Dickens

brass instrument 4 tuba 5 bugle 6 cornet 7 trumpet 8 trombone 9 euphonium 10 French horn, sousaphone
ancient: 3 lur 7 Alphorn, buisine, serpent 10 ophicleide

brass tacks 4 crux, meat 7 details 9 realities, substance 10 essentials 11 nitty-gritty 15 sum and substance

brassy 4 bold 5 brash, cocky, sassy, saucy 6 brazen 7 forward 8 arrogant, impudent, insolent, overbold 9 barefaced, outspoken, shameless, unabashed 10 unblushing 11 impertinent

brat 3 imp 4 chit 5 whelp 6 hoyden, rascal 9 rude child 12 spoiled child

Brauhaus 6 tavern 7 brewery

Brautigan, Richard
author of: 15 Sombrero Fallout 18 The Hawkline Monster 21 Trout Fishing in America 38 The Pill Versus the Springhill Mine Disaster

bravado 7 big talk, blowing, bluster, bombast, bravura, crowing, puffery, swagger 8 boasting, bragging 9 cockiness 10 swaggering 11 braggadocio 12 boastfulness 13 show of courage

brave 4 bear, dare, defy, face, game, take 5 abide, brook, gutsy, stand 6 breast, endure, gritty, heroic, plucky, spunky, suffer 7 doughty, stomach, sustain, undergo, valiant, weather 8 confront, fearless, intrepid, stalwart, tolerate, unafraid, valorous 9 challenge, dauntless, outbrazen, put up with, stand up to, undaunted, withstand 10 courageous 11 lionhearted, unflinching, unshrinking 12 stouthearted

brave deed 4 feat 7 exploit 9 heroic act 11 achievement

Brave New World
- **author:** 12 Aldous Huxley
- **character:** 4 John 11 Bernard Marx 12 Lenina Crowne, Mustapha Mond

bravery 4 grit 5 pluck, spunk, valor 6 daring, mettle, spirit 7 courage, heroism 8 audacity, boldness 11 intrepidity 12 fearlessness 13 dauntlessness

Bravo, The
- **author:** 19 James Fenimore Cooper

brawl 3 row 4 fray, tiff 5 broil, clash, fight, melee, scrap, set-to 6 battle, fracas, ruckus, rumpus, uproar 7 dispute, quarrel, wrangle 8 squabble 9 imbroglio 11 altercation, embroilment

brawn 5 might, power 7 muscles, stamina 8 strength 9 beefiness, huskiness 10 robustness, ruggedness, sturdiness 19 muscular development

brawny 5 burly, husky 6 mighty, robust, rugged, strong, sturdy 8 muscular, powerful 9 strapping

Bray, Madeline
- **character in:** 16 Nicholas Nickleby
- **author:** 7 Dickens

brazen 4 bold, open 5 brash, saucy 6 brassy, cheeky 7 forward 8 arrogant, immodest, impudent, insolent 9 audacious, barefaced, boldfaced, shameless, unabashed

brazenness 4 gall 5 brass, cheek, nerve 8 audacity, boldness, chutzpah 9 impudence 10 effrontery, fowardness 11 presumption

Brazil
- **capital:** 8 Brasilia
- **former capital:** 12 Rio de Janeiro
- **largest city:** 8 Sao Paulo
- **others:** 5 Bahia, Belem 6 Recife, Sabara, Santos 7 Vitoria 8 Salvador 9 Ouro Preto, Paranagua 10 Diamantina 11 Porto Alegre 13 Belo Horizonte, Cruzeiro do Sul
- **school:**
- **junior high:** 7 ginasio
- **senior high:** 7 colegio
- **measure:** 2 pe 4 moio, sack, vara 5 braca, legoa, milha, tonel 6 canada, cuarto, quarto, tarefa 7 garrafa 8 alqueire
- **monetary unit:** 3 joe 4 reis 5 dobra 7 centara, halfjoe, milreis 8 cruzeiro
- **weight:** 3 bag 4 onca 5 libra 6 arroba, oitava 7 quilate, quintal 8 tonelada
- **island:** 6 Maraca, Marajo 7 Bananal, Cardoso, Caviana, Mexiana 8 Comprida
- **lake:** 4 Aima, Feia 5 Mirim 13 Logo dos Platos
- **mountain:** 3 Mar 5 Geral, Organ, Piaui 6 Acarai, Gurupi, Parima, Urucum 7 Amambai, Carajas, Gradaus, Oragaos, Roraima 8 Bandeira, Itatiaja, Roncador, Tombador 9 Pacaraima, Sugar Loaf 10 Tumuc-Humac
- **highest point:** 7 Neblina
- **river:** 3 Apa, Ica 4 Doce, Geio, Ivai, Jari, Para, Paru, Sono, Tefe 5 Abuna, Anaua, Apore, Capim, Claro, Corua, Icana, Iriri, Itapi, Jurua, Jutai, Manso, Negro, Pardo, Piaui, Preto, Tiete, Turvo, Urubu, Verde, Xingu 6 Ajuana, Amazon, Arinos, Balsas, Branco, Canuma, Contas, Cuiaba, Demini, Grajau, Grande, Gurupi, Ibicui, Iguacu, Japura, Javari, Mearim, Mortes, Mucuri, Parana, Purpus, Ronuro, Sangue, Tacutu, Tibagi, Uatuma, Uaupes 7 Corumba, Iguassu, Madeira, Madiera, Orinoco, Paraiba, Sucuriu, Tapajos, Taquari, Teodoro, Uruguai, Uruguay, Velhass 8 Araguaia, Padauiri, Paracatu, Paraguay, Parnaiba, Solimoes, Tarauaca 9 Tocantins 12 Sao Francisco
- **sea:** 8 Atlantic
- **physical feature:**
- **bay:** 9 All Saints
- **cape:** 4 Frio 6 Blanco, Buzios, Gurupy, Orange 7 Saotome 8 Saoroque
- **dam:** 6 Furnas 7 Peixoto
- **estuary:** 4 Para
- **rain forest:** 5 selva
- **waterfall:** 6 Guaira, Iguacu 7 Iguassu 11 Paulo Afonso
- **people:** 2 Ge 4 Anta 5 Acroa, Arara, Araua, Bravo, Carib, Guana, Negro 6 Arawak, Caraja 7 Carayan, Javahai, Tariana 8 Botocudo, Chambioa 9 Caucasian, mamelucos, mulattoes 10 Portuguese 11 Tupi-Guarani
- **architect:** 8 Niemeyer
- **artist:** 6 Segall 9 Portinari 10 Cavalcenti
- **author:** 5 Amado, Bilac, Ramos 6 Freyre
- **composer:** 10 Villalobos
- **discoverer:** 6 Cabral
- **leader:** 6 Aranha, Branco, Collor, Franco, Geisel, Medici, Vargas 7 Goulart
- **sculptor:** 11 Aleijadinho
- **language:** 10 Portuguese
- **religion:** 10 Protestant 13 Roman Catholic
- **place:**
- **beach:** 7 Ipanema 9 Boa Viagem 10 Copacabana
- **feature:**
- **bird:** 4 mitu 6 mitua
- **dance:** 5 frevo, samba 6 maxixe 9 bossa nova
- **fish:** 7 piranha
- **gourd:** 4 cuia
- **plantation:** 7 fazenda
- **slums:** 7 favelas
- **tree:** 5 icica 6 ucuuba 7 arariba
- **food:**
- **dish:** 6 vatapa 8 feijoada
- **dried salted beef:** 7 charque
- **drink:** 4 acai 9 cafezinho
- **tea:** 4 mate
- **turtle soup:** 16 cas quinho de mucua

Brazil
  director: 12 Terry Gilliam
  cast: 8 Ida Lowry 9 Kim Greist 12 Robert
  De Niro 13 Jonathan Pryce
Brazilian Bombshell
  nickname of: 13 Carmen Miranda
Brazzaville
  capital of: 5 Congo
breach 3 gap 4 gash, hole, rent, rift, slit 5
  break, chink, cleft, crack, split 7 crevice,
  failure, fissure, neglect, opening, rupture 8
  defiance, trespass 9 disregard, violation
  10 infraction 11 dereliction 12 disobedience, infringement 13 noncompliance,
  nonobservance, transgression
breach of faith 7 perfidy 8 bad faith, betrayal 9 falseness, treachery, two-timing 10
  disloyalty 11 double-cross 13 double-
  dealing
breach of order 4 riot 6 fracas, mutiny,
  ruckus, uproar 7 turmoil 8 uprising 9
  commotion, rebellion 10 dissension 11 disturbance, pandemonium 18 disturbance of
  peace
breach of trust 7 falsity, perfidy 9 falseness, treachery 10 disloyalty, infidelity 13
  deceitfulness, double-dealing
bread 3 rye 4 food, pita 5 bucks, dough,
  money, wheat 6 staple 9 sourdough 10
  livelihood, sustenance 11 staff of life 12
  pumpernickel
bread and butter 3 job 6 career, living 7
  calling 8 business, vocation 9 life's work
  10 livelihood 14 means of support
Bread and Wine
  author: 13 Ignazio Silone
breadbasket 3 gut 5 belly, tummy 6 paunch
  7 abdomen, labonza, midriff, Midwest,
  stomach 11 solar plexus
breadth 4 area, size, span 5 range, reach,
  scope, width 6 extent, spread 7 compass,
  expanse, measure, stretch 8 latitude,
  wideness 9 broadness 10 dimensions 13
  extensiveness
break 3 cap, end, fly, gap, off, run, top 4
  beat, bust, chip, dash, defy, flee, gash,
  halt, hole, rend, rent, rest, rift, rive, ruin,
  snap, stop, tame, tear, tell 5 burst, cease,
  cleft, crack, crush, erupt, excel, lapse, occur, outdo, pause, sever, shirk, smash,
  split, train 6 appear, better, breach,
  chance, cleave, detach, divide, escape,
  exceed, happen, hiatus, ignore, inform,
  lessen, master, powder, recess, reveal,
  soften, subdue, sunder, weaken 7 control,
  cushion, destroy, disobey, divulge, eclipse,
  fissure, fortune, give out, lighten, neglect,
  opening, pull off, respite, run away, rupture, shatter, surpass, suspend, tear off, violate, wipe out 8 announce, bankrupt,
  burst out, cracking, demolish, diminish,
  disclose, disjoint, division, fracture, fragment, go beyond, interval, outstrip, overcome, proclaim, renege on, separate, shut
  down, slip away, splinter 9 dismember, disregard, granulate, interlude, interrupt,
  make a dash, pulverize, splitting, tran-

scend 10 discipline, disconnect, fall back
  on, fly the coop, fracturing, impoverish, infringe on, make public, overshadow, separation, shattering, take flight, wrench away
  11 discontinue, get away from, opportunity,
  pay no heed to 12 be derelict in, disintegrate, intermission, interruption, make a
  getaway, stroke of luck 13 strap for funds
  14 bend to one's will, take the force of 15
  take to one's heels
breakable 5 frail, shaky 6 flimsy 7 brittle,
  crumbly, fragile 8 delicate
break apart 7 crumble, shatter 8 collapse 9
  fall apart 12 disintegrate, fall to pieces
breakdown 6 mishap 7 crackup, decline,
  failure 8 analysis, collapse, disorder, division 12 detailed list 13 deterioration 14
  categorization
break down 6 divide 7 dissect 8 collapse,
  separate 9 decompose 11 deteriorate
breaker 4 cask, wave 6 comber 7 crusher 8
  boat cask 9 destroyer
break faith with 6 betray 7 do wrong 9 play
  false 11 double-cross 12 be unfaithful 13
  be treacherous 16 sell down the river
Breakfast at Tiffany's
  author: 12 Truman Capote
  director: 12 Blake Edwards
  cast: 10 Buddy Ebsen 12 Mickey
  Rooney, Patricia Neal 13 Audrey
  Hepburn (Holly Golightly), George
  Peppard
  score: 12 Henry Mancini
  song: 9 Moon River
Breakfast Club, The
  director: 10 John Hughes
  cast: 10 Ally Sheedy 13 Emilio Estevez,
  Molly Ringwald 18 Anthony Michael Hall
Breakfast of Champions
  author: 12 Kurt Vonnegut
break free 4 bolt, flee, skip 6 escape 7 get
  away, make off, run away 9 cut and run 10
  fly the coop 12 make a getaway
breakfront 5 hutch 7 cabinet 8 bookcase,
  cupboard 12 china cabinet
break in 5 train 7 intrude 8 accustom, initiate 9 acclimate, interrupt 10 burglarize 12
  indoctrinate
break-in 5 theft 7 robbery 8 burglary, stealing 12 burglarizing 13 housebreaking 19
  breaking and entering
Breaking Away
  director: 10 Peter Yates
  screenplay: 11 Steve Tesich
  cast: 10 Paul Dooley 11 Daniel Stern,
  Dennis Quaid 13 Barbara Barrie 16
  Jackie Earle Haley 17 Dennis Christopher
  setting: 7 Indiana 11 Bloomington
break loose 4 bolt, flee, skip 6 escape 7
  get away, make off 9 cut and run 10 fly the
  coop 12 make a getaway
breakneck 4 rash 5 risky 8 reckless, very
  fast 9 dangerous, daredevil 12 death-
  defying
break of day 4 dawn 5 sunup 7 dawning,
  sunrise 8 daybreak 11 crack of dawn

break off 3 end 4 halt 5 cease 6 recess 7 adjourn, snap off, suspend 8 conclude, shut down 11 discontinue

breakout 6 escape, flight 7 getaway 10 decampment

break out 4 bolt, skip 5 begin, erupt 6 escape 7 bust out, get away 10 burst forth, fly the coop 12 make a getaway

Break the Bank
   host: 9 Bert Parks 10 Bud Collyer

break the habit 4 kick, quit, stop 6 eschew, give up 8 renounce, withdraw 14 quit cold turkey

breakthrough 7 advance 11 advancement, improvement, penetration, step forward

breakup 5 split 7 crackup 9 dispersal, splitting 10 separation 14 disintegration

break with 5 leave 8 be untrue, part from 10 be disloyal 11 divorce from 12 fall away from, separate from

breast 4 bust, core 5 bosom, chest, heart 10 very marrow
   Italian: 5 petto

breastwork 7 bastion, rampart 8 barbette 9 earthwork 13 fortification

breath 4 wind 6 spirit 9 animation, breathing, lifeblood, life force 10 exhalation, inhalation, vital spark 11 divine spark, respiration, vital spirit 12 vitalization

breathe 4 gasp, huff, pant, puff 5 utter 6 impart, murmur 7 respire, whisper 9 draw in air 10 draw breath 15 inhale and exhale

breathe in 6 inhale 7 inspire, respire

breathe out 4 huff, pant, puff 6 exhale, expire 7 respire

breathing 4 live 5 alive 6 living 7 animate 11 respiratory 13 drawing breath

Breathless
   director: 14 Jean-Luc Goddard
   written by: 16 Francois Truffaut
   cast: 10 Jean Seberg 16 Jean-Paul Belmondo
   setting: 5 Paris

breathtaking 7 amazing, awesome 8 exciting 9 startling 10 surprising 11 astonishing

Brecht, Bertolt
   author of: 13 Mother Courage 15 Drums in the Night 18 The Threepenny Opera 21 St Joan of the Stockyards 23 The Caucasian Chalk Circle 27 The Resistable Rise of Arturo Ui 29 The Private Life of the Master Race

Breck, Alan
   character in: 9 Kidnapped
   author: 9 Stevenson

breech 4 rump, seat 6 behind 8 buttocks, haunches, hind part 9 fundament, posterior 12 hindquarters

breeches 5 pants 8 trousers

breed 4 bear, grow, kind, race, sire, sort, type 5 beget, cause, order, raise, spawn, stock 6 family, father, foster, lead to, mother, strain 7 develop, nurture, produce, promote, species, variety 8 generate, multiply, occasion 9 cultivate, give forth, procreate, propagate, reproduce 10

bring forth, give rise to 11 proliferate 16 produce offspring

breeding 4 line 5 grace 6 mating, polish 7 bearing, descent, growing, lineage, manners, raising, rearing 8 ancestry, courtesy, hatching, heredity, pedigree, spawning, training 9 begetting, bloodline, genealogy, gentility, parentage, producing 10 background, extraction, family tree, generation, politeness, production, refinement, upbringing 11 cultivation, germination, multiplying, procreation, propagation 12 reproduction

breeze 4 flit, pass, sail, waft 5 coast, float, glide, sweep 6 zephyr 9 light gust, light wind 10 gentle wind, puff of wind

breezy 3 gay 4 airy, pert, spry 5 blowy, brisk, fresh, gusty, light, merry, peppy, sunny, windy 6 bouncy, casual, frisky, jaunty, lively 7 buoyant, squally 8 animated, blustery, carefree, cheerful, debonair, spirited 9 energetic, resilient, sprightly, vivacious, windswept 10 blithesome 11 free and easy

Brennan, Walter
   born: 12 Swampscott MA
   roles: 8 Kentucky 12 Come and Get It, The Westerner 13 The Real McCoys 16 To Have and Have Not

Brent, George
   real name: 18 George Brendan Nolan
   wife: 11 Ann Sheridan 14 Ruth Chatterton
   born: 7 Ireland 14 Shannonsbridge
   roles: 7 Jezebel 11 Dark Victory, The Great Lie 17 Forty-Second Street

Bres
   origin: 5 Irish
   king of: 7 Ireland

Breton, Andre
   author of: 5 Nadja 21 Manifesto of Surrealism

Breuer, Marcel
   architect of: 17 IBM Research Center (La Gaude France) 18 UNESCO headquarters (Paris) 25 St John's Abbey and University (Collegeville MN) 26 Whitney Museum of American Art (NYC)

brevity 9 briefness, pithiness, quickness, shortness, terseness 10 transience 11 conciseness 12 ephemerality, impermanence, succinctness

brew 3 ale 4 beer, boil, cook, form, make, plan, plot, soak 5 begin, drink, hatch, ripen, start, steep, stout 6 cook up, devise, foment, gather, porter, scheme, seethe 7 arrange, concoct, ferment, mixture, prepare, produce, think up 8 beverage, contrive, initiate 9 formulate, germinate, originate 10 concoction, malt liquor

brewery
   German: 8 Brauhaus

Brian de Bois, Sir
   character in: 7 Ivanhoe
   author: 5 Scott

Briareus
  also: 7 Aegaeon
  member of: 13 Hecatonchires
bribe 5 graft 6 buy off, grease, pay off, payola, suborn 9 hush money 10 inducement 11 illegal gift 15 grease the hand of, grease the palm of
  French: 7 douceur
bric-a-brac 7 baubles, gewgaws 8 bibelots, trinkets 9 gimcracks, kickshaws, ornaments 11 knickknacks
Brick
  character in: 16 Cat on a Hot Tin Roof
  author: 8 Williams
Bricks
  god of: 5 Kulla
bridal 7 nuptial, wedding 8 marriage 11 matrimonial
Bridehead, Sue
  character in: 14 Jude the Obscure
  author: 5 Hardy
Bride of Lammermoor, The
  author: 8 Sir Walter Scott
  character: 10 Lady Ashton, Lucy Ashton, Ravenswood 14 Laird of Bucklaw 16 Sir William Ashton
Brideshead Revisited
  author: 11 Evelyn Waugh
  character: 5 Celia, Julia 8 Cordelia 9 Sebastian 10 Brideshead (Bridey), Rex Mottram 12 Boy Mulcaster, Charles Ryder 13 Lady Marchmain, Lord Marchmain 14 Anthony Blanche
bridge 3 tie 4 band, bind, bond, link, span 5 cross, unify, union 6 go over 7 catwalk, connect, liaison, viaduct 8 alliance, overpass, traverse 9 cross over 10 connection, passageway 11 association, reach across 12 extend across
bridge
  derived from: 5 whist
  variation: 14 contract bridge
  partnership: 9 East/West 11 North/South
  cards/hand: 8 thirteen
  no cards of a suit: 4 void
  one card of a suit: 9 singleton
  two cards of a suit: 9 doubleton
  rule book by: 5 Goren
Bridge of San Luis Rey, The
  author: 14 Thornton Wilder
  character: 5 Clara, Jaime 6 Manuel, Pepita 7 Esteban, Viceroy 8 Uncle Pio 11 La Perichole 14 Brother Juniper 20 Marquesa de Montemayor
Bridge on the River Kwai, The
  director: 9 David Lean
  based on story by: 12 Pierre Boulle
  cast: 11 Jack Hawkins 12 Alec Guinness 13 William Holden 14 Sessue Hayakawa
  Oscar for: 5 actor (Guinness) 7 picture
Bridges, Beau
  real name: 21 Lloyd Vernet Bridges III
  father: 5 Lloyd
  brother: 4 Jeff
  born: 12 Los Angeles CA
  roles: 5 Space 8 Norma Rae 11 The

Landlord 25 The Other Side of the Mountain
Bridges, Jeff
  father: 5 Lloyd
  brother: 4 Beau
  born: 12 Los Angeles CA
  roles: 4 Tron 7 Starman 8 King Kong 10 Jagged Edge 13 Kiss Me Goodbye 14 Against All Odds 18 The Last Picture Show
Bridges, Lloyd
  son: 4 Beau, Jeff
  born: 12 San Leandro CA
  roles: 7 Sea Hunt 8 Airplane, High Noon
Bridges at Toko-ri, The
  author: 13 James Michener
Bridget
  character in: 19 Every Man in His Humour
  author: 6 Jonson
Bridge Too Far, A
  author: 13 Cornelius Ryan
Bridgetown
  capital of: 8 Barbados
bridle 3 gag 4 curb, rule 5 check 6 arrest, direct, draw up, flinch, hinder, manage, master, muzzle, rear up, recoil 7 control, harness, inhibit, repress 8 draw back, restrain, restrict, suppress 9 constrain, restraint 11 bit and brace, head harness
brief 4 case 5 hasty, pithy, quick, short, swift, terse 6 advise, inform, precis, resume 7 capsule, compact, concise, defense, limited, prepare, summary 8 abridged, abstract, argument, fill in on, fleeting, instruct, succinct 9 condensed, curtailed, momentary, shortened, temporary, thumbnail, transient 10 abridgment, compressed, contention, describe to, short-lived, summarized, transitory 11 abbreviated 12 legal summary
brief account 6 precis, sketch 7 outline, summary 8 anecdote
brier, briar 4 Rosa 5 Rubus, thorn 6 Smilax 7 bramble
  varieties: 3 Cat, Dog, Hag, Saw 4 Bull 5 Green, Horse, Sweet 7 Jackson 8 Austrian 9 Sensitive 14 Austrian copper
brigade 4 crew, team, unit 5 corps, force, group, squad 6 legion, outfit 7 company 9 regiments, squadrons 10 army groups, battalions, contingent, detachment
Brigadoon
  director: 16 Vincente Minnelli
  based on Broadway hit by: 14 Lerner and Loewe
  cast: 9 Gene Kelly 10 Van Johnson 11 Cyd Charisse
brigand 5 thief 6 bandit, gunman, looter, outlaw, pirate, robber, vandal 7 corsair, hoodlum, ruffian, rustler, spoiler 8 marauder, pilferer, pillager 9 buccaneer, cutthroat, desperado, despoiler, plunderer, privateer 10 highwayman
bright 3 gay 4 glad, good, keen, rosy, sage, warm, wise 5 acute, alert, aware, grand, great, happy, jolly, merry, quick, sharp,

smart, sunny, vivid 6 astute, blithe, brainy, clever, gifted, joyful, joyous, lively, shrewd 7 beaming, blazing, capable, glowing, healthy, hopeful, intense, lambent, radiant, shining 8 cheerful, dazzling, exciting, gleaming, luminous, lustrous, profound, splendid, talented 9 brilliant, competent, effulgent, excellent, favorable, ingenious, inventive, masterful, promising, sagacious, sparkling, wide-awake 10 auspicious, discerning, glittering, optimistic, perceptive, proficient, propitious, prosperous, remarkable, shimmering, successful 11 clearheaded, illuminated, illustrious, intelligent, light-filled, magnificent, outstanding, quickwitted, resourceful, resplendent 12 exhilarating

brighten 4 lift **5** boost, cheer, light **6** buoy up, lift up, perk up **7** animate, enliven, gladden, lighten **9** make happy, stimulate **10** illuminate

bright-eyed 5 alert, awake **9** wide-awake **12** on the qui vive

Bright Flows the River
　　author: **14** Taylor Caldwell

brightness 4 glow **5** glare, gleam, shine **6** dazzle, luster **7** glitter, sparkle **8** radiance **9** lightness **10** brilliance, luminosity **12** intelligence

bright spot 3 joy **6** solace **7** comfort **8** pleasure **13** consolidation

Brigit
　　origin: **5** Welsh
　　goddess of: **4** fire **6** wisdom **9** fertility, household **11** agriculture

Brigitte Bardot & the Lolita Syndrome
　　author: **16** Simone de Beauvoir

Brill Among the Ruins
　　author: **14** Vance Bourjaily

brilliance, brilliancy 4 gift, glow **5** blaze, gleam, sheen, shine **6** acuity, dazzle, genius, luster, talent, wisdom **7** glitter, shimmer, sparkle **8** grandeur, keenness, radiance, sagacity, splendor **9** alertness, awareness, greatness, ingenuity, intensity, quickness, sharpness, smartness, vividness **10** braininess, brightness, capability, cleverness, competence, effulgence, excellence, luminosity, perception, profundity, shrewdness **11** discernment, distinction, proficiency **12** intelligence, magnificence, resplendence **13** inventiveness, masterfulness **15** clearheadedness, illustriousness, resourcefulness

brilliant see **6** bright

brim 3 fill, lip, rim **5** brink, flood, ledge, verge **6** border, fill up, margin, well up **8** overflow

brimless hat 3 cap **5** beret **6** beanie **11** stocking cap, tam o'shanter

brimming 4 full **7** flooded, teeming **8** overfull, swarming **11** overflowing

Brimo
　　origin: **5** Greek
　　form: **7** goddess
　　corresponds to: **6** Hecate **7** Demeter **10** Persephone

brine 6 the sea **8** sea water **9** salt water **12** salt solution **14** saline solution **16** pickling solution

bring 4 bear, make, take, tote **5** begin, carry, cause, fetch, force, start **6** compel, convey, create, effect, induce **7** deliver, produce, sell for, usher in **8** convince, engender, generate, initiate, persuade, result in **9** accompany, institute, originate, transport **10** bring about

bring about 2 do **4** form, open **5** begin, cause, found, set up, start **6** attain, create, effect, lead to **7** achieve, execute, produce **8** carry out, generate, initiate, organize **9** establish, institute, succeed at **10** accomplish, effectuate, inaugurate **11** bring to pass, precipitate **18** bring into existence

bring back 6 return **7** restore **8** recreate **9** surrender **10** return with

bring down a peg 5 abase **6** humble **7** mortify **9** humiliate **13** cut down to size

bring down to earth 10 disenchant **11** disenthrall, disillusion, open the eyes **13** break the spell **14** burst the bubble **20** shatter one's illusions

bring forth 4 bear **5** breed, elicit, evoke, hatch, spawn, whelp **7** deliver, produce **9** reproduce **10** make appear **11** give birth to

bring home to 7 blame on, clarify **11** attribute to **15** place emphasis on

bringing together 7 joining, wedding **8** amassing **9** combining, gathering, including **10** assembling, collecting **12** accumulating **13** incorporating

Bringing Up Baby
　　director: **11** Howard Hawks
　　cast: **9** Cary Grant **14** Charlie Ruggles **16** Katharine Hepburn

Bringing Up Father
　　creator: **13** George McManus
　　character: **5** Jiggs **6** Maggie
　　daughter: **5** Rosie
　　brother-in-law: **5** Bimmy
　　place: **11** Dinty Moore's
　　favorite dish: **20** corned beef and cabbage

bring into being 4 bear, form, make **5** erect, hatch, spawn, whelp **6** create, design, devise, invent, render **7** concoct, deliver, develop, fashion, produce **8** contrive, generate **9** construct, fabricate, formulate, originate **10** bring forth **11** give birth to

bring into existence 4 form **5** begin, set up, start **6** create **8** organize **9** establish, institute **10** bring about, inaugurate

bring into line 5 adapt **6** adjust **7** conform, shape up **9** harmonize, reconcile **10** discipline **11** accommodate **13** whip into shape

bring into question 11 cast doubt on **18** throw suspicion upon

bring into relief 6 accent, stress **7** dwell on, feature, point up **9** emphasize, press home, underline **10** accentuate, underscore

bring low 5 abase, shame **6** humble **8** cast down **9** denigrate, humiliate

bring off 4 gain 6 attain, effect, secure 7 achieve 10 accomplish

bring to an end 5 cease 6 finish 8 break off, conclude 9 call a halt, terminate 11 discontinue

bring to a standstill 3 end 4 halt, stay, stop 5 block, check 6 arrest 12 bring to a halt

bring to bay 4 trap, tree 6 corner 8 confront, hunt down

bring to bear 5 apply 6 employ 7 utilize 9 implement

bring together 5 amass 6 gather, muster 7 collect, marshal, round up 8 assemble 10 accumulate

bring to light 6 expose, reveal, unveil 7 clarify, divulge, explain, uncover 8 disclose 9 explicate, make known, make plain 10 illuminate, make public

bring to one's senses 3 jar 5 alarm, alert, shock 9 make aware

bring to pass 5 cause 6 create, effect 8 carry out 10 bring about, effectuate

bring to terms 6 settle 7 mediate 9 arbitrate, reconcile

bring to view 5 dig up 6 reveal 7 exhibit, uncover, unearth 8 disclose, retrieve 10 come up with

bring word 4 tell 6 advise, convey, inform, notify, relate, reveal 7 divulge, publish 8 announce, disclose, proclaim 9 apprise of, broadcast, make known, publicize 11 communicate

brink 3 rim 4 bank, brim, edge 5 point, shore, skirt, verge 6 border, margin 9 threshold

briny 4 salt 5 salty 6 saline

brio, con
   music: 9 with vigor 10 with spirit

Briseis
   origin: 5 Greek
   mentioned in: 5 Iliad
   father: 18 Briseus of Lyrnessus
   husband: 5 Mynes
   captured by: 8 Achilles
   caused: 7 quarrel
   between: 8 Achilles 9 Agamemnon

Briseus
   origin: 5 Greek
   mentioned in: 5 Iliad
   daughter: 7 Briseis
   death by: 7 suicide

Brisingamen 8 necklace
   origin: 12 Scandinavian
   trait: 5 magic
   owned by: 5 Freia, Freya

brisk 4 busy, spry 5 alert, fresh, peppy, quick, swift 6 active, breezy, lively, snappy 7 bracing, chipper, dynamic, rousing 8 animated, bustling, spirited, stirring, vigorous 9 energetic, sprightly, vivacious, vivifying 10 refreshing 11 stimulating 12 exhilarating, invigorating

briskness 3 pep 5 vigor 6 energy 8 alacrity, spryness 9 quickness, swiftness 13 sprightliness

bristle 4 hair 5 quill 7 stiffen, whisker

bristles 5 barbs 6 quills 7 stubble 8 prickles, whiskers

bristletail
   variety: 7 jumping 8 firebrat 9 primitive 10 nicoletiid, silverfish

bristly 5 rough 6 barbed, coarse 7 prickly, stubbly 8 unshaven 9 whiskered 11 bewhiskered

Britannia *see* 7 England

British 6 Breton, Briton 7 English 8 Brittany

British Columbia
   bordered by: 5 Idaho, Yukon 6 Alaska 7 Montana 10 Washington 12 Pacific Ocean, United States 20 Northwest Territories
   country: 6 Canada
   Indian: 5 Haida 6 Nootka, Salish 8 Kwakiutl 9 Tsimshian 10 Bella Coola
   island: 9 Vancouver 14 Queen Charlotte
   mountain: 5 Coast, Rocky 7 Cascade 8 Columbia 11 Cordilleran 14 Cassiar Omineca
   nickname: 2 BC
   park: 7 Glacier
   rank in size: 5 sixth
   river: 6 Fraser
   section: 8 province

British Guiana *see* 6 Guyana

British Honduras *see* 6 Belize

British Mythology
   god of rebirth/afterlife: 4 Gwyn
   chief of gods: 5 Woden
   island of paradise: 6 Avalon

Britomart
   character in: 15 The Faerie Queene
   author: 7 Spenser

Britomartis
   origin: 6 Cretan
   goddess of: 7 hunters, sailors 9 fishermen
   father: 4 Zeus
   mother: 5 Carme
   corresponds to: 7 Artemis 8 Dictynna

Briton 4 Celt 6 Celtic 7 British

Brittany
   coast: 5 Armor
   country: 6 France
   inhabitant: 5 Celts 6 French, Romans
   interior: 6 Argoat
   land form: 9 peninsula
   language: 6 Breton
   other name: 5 Breiz 6 Breton 8 Bretagne

Britten, (Edward) Benjamin
   born: 7 England 9 Lowestoft
   composer of: 8 Gloriana 9 Billy Budd 10 Paul Bunyan, War Requiem 11 Curlew River, Peter Grimes, Winter Words 12 Owen Wingrave, The Poet's Echo 13 Albert Herring, Death in Venice 14 The Prodigal Son, Turn of the Screw 15 Phantasy Quartet 17 A Ceremony of Carols, A Charm of Lullabies, Sinfonia da Requiem, The Rape of Lucretia 18 Holderlin Fragments 20 Cantata Misericordium 21 A Midsummer Night's Dream, Sonnets of

Michelangelo 22 The Burning Fiery Furnace

brittle 7 crumbly, fragile, friable 9 breakable, frangible

Brize
form: 6 gadfly
sent by: 4 Hera
sent to annoy: 2 Io

Brizo
origin: 5 Greek
goddess of: 7 sailors
prophesied through: 6 dreams

broach 4 pose 6 launch, open up, submit 7 advance, bring up, mention, propose, suggest, touch on 9 institute, introduce

broad 4 full, open, wide 5 ample, clear, large, plain, rangy, roomy, thick 7 general, immense, obvious, sizable 8 extended, spacious, sweeping 9 capacious, expansive, extensive, inclusive, outspread, universal, unlimited 10 undetailed 11 far-reaching, nonspecific, wide-ranging 12 all-embracing, encyclopedic 13 comprehensive

broadcast 4 beam, show, talk 5 cable, radio, relay 7 program, send out 8 televise, transmit 9 statement 10 distribute 11 disseminate, put on the air 12 announcement

broaden 5 boost, raise, swell, widen 6 dilate, expand, extend 7 advance, amplify, augment, build up, develop, distend, enlarge, improve, stretch 8 increase 9 intensify, reinforce, spread out 10 strengthen, supplement

broadened 7 dilated, swelled, swollen, widened 8 enlarged, expanded, extended 9 distended, spread out

broad-minded 7 liberal 8 amenable, catholic, flexible, tolerant, unbiased 9 receptive, unbigoted 10 charitable, open-minded, undogmatic 11 magnanimous 12 unprejudiced, unprovincial

Broadway Joe
nickname of: 9 Joe Namath

Brobdingnag
fictional land in: 16 Gulliver's Travels
author: 5 Swift

Brobdingnagian 4 huge 5 giant 7 immense, mammoth 8 colossal, enormous, gigantic 10 gargantuan, tremendous 11 elephantine

broccoli 9 vegetable 12 Brassica rapa 16 Brassica oleracea (Botyris Group) 17 Brassica septiceps
variety: 6 Turnip 7 Italian 9 Asparagus, Sprouting

brochure 5 flier 6 folder 7 booklet, leaflet 8 circular, handbill, pamphlet 9 throwaway

Brockton Blockbuster
nickname of: 13 Rocky Marciano

Broglie, Louis Victor de
field: 7 physics
nationality: 6 French
developed: 13 wave mechanics
awarded: 10 Nobel Prize

broil 3 fry 4 bake, burn, cook, sear 5 parch, roast, toast 6 scorch 7 blister

broiler 3 hot, pan 4 rack 5 grill 6 cooker 8 scorcher 12 young chicken

broke 8 bankrupt, strapped, wiped out 9 insolvent, penniless 10 down and out 12 impoverished, on one's uppers, without funds 16 strapped for funds

broken 4 torn 5 rough, split, tamed 6 ruined, uneven 7 crushed, damaged 8 bankrupt, in pieces, ruptured 9 fractured, separated, shattered 10 incomplete 11 fragmentary, interrupted

Broken Commandment, The
author: 14 Toson Shimazaki

broken-down 6 beat-up, ruined 7 rickety, worn-out 8 battered, decrepit 10 ramshackle 11 dilapidated 12 deteriorated

broken-hearted 3 sad 6 gloomy, woeful 7 crushed, doleful, forlorn, unhappy 8 dejected, desolate, downcast, mournful, wretched 9 depressed, long-faced, miserable, sorrowful, woebegone 10 despairing, despondent, melancholy 11 heartbroken 12 disconsolate, inconsolable

Brom Bones
also: 12 Brom Van Brunt
character in: 23 The Legend of Sleepy Hollow
author: 6 Irving

Brome
form: 5 nymph
cared for: 8 Dionysus

Bromfield, Louis
author of: 11 Early Autumn, Malabar Farm 12 The Rains Came 13 Mrs Parkington, Night in Bombay 14 Wild Is the River 15 The Green Bay Tree 31 The Strange Case of Miss Annie Spragg

bromide 6 cliche 8 banality 9 platitude 10 stereotype 11 trite phrase 19 hackneyed expression

bromidic 4 dull 5 banal, corny, stale, tired, trite, vapid 6 jejune 7 humdrum, insipid 8 ordinary 9 hackneyed 10 pedestrian, unexciting, unoriginal 13 platitudinous, unimaginative

bromine
chemical symbol: 2 Br

Bromius
epithet of: 8 Dionysus
means: 7 thunder

Bronson, Charles
real name: 16 Charles Buchinsky
wife: 11 Jill Ireland
born: 11 Ehrenfeld PA
roles: 9 Death Wish 13 The Dirty Dozen 14 The Great Escape 16 Battle of the Bulge, The Valachi Papers 19 The Magnificent Seven

Bronte, Anne
author of: 9 Agnes Grey 23 The Tenant of Wildfell Hall

Bronte, Charlotte
author of: 7 Shirley 8 Jane Eyre, Villette 12 The Professor

Bronte, Emily
author of: 16 Wuthering Heights

Brontes
member of: 8 Cyclopes
brontophobia
fear of: 7 thunder
Brontosaurus
also: 11 Apatosaurus
type: 8 dinosaur, sauropod
period: 8 Jurassic
Bronx Bull
nickname of: 11 Jake La Motta
bronze 3 tan 5 metal 8 brownish, chestnut
10 reddish-tan 12 reddish-brown 13
copper-colored
brooch 3 pin 5 clasp
brood 4 chew, fret, mope, mull, sulk 5
cover, dwell, hatch, spawn, worry, young 6
chicks, family, litter 7 agonize, sit upon 8
children, incubate 9 offspring 10 hatchlings
brook 3 run 4 bear, rill, take 5 abide, allow,
creek, stand 6 accept, endure, stream,
suffer 7 rivulet, stomach 8 tolerate 9 put up
with, streamlet
Brooks, Gwendolyn
author of: 4 Riot 10 Annie Allen 14 Family Pictures
Brooks, James L
director of: 17 Terms of Endearment
(Oscar)
Brooks, Mel
real name: 14 Melvin Kaminsky
wife: 12 Anne Bancroft
born: 10 Brooklyn NY
director of/roles: 11 High Anxiety, Silent
Movie 12 The Producers 14 Blazing Saddles 17 Young Frankenstein 20 The History of the World
Brooks, Richard
director of: 11 Elmer Gantry, In Cold
Blood 16 Cat on a Hot Tin Roof, Sweet
Bird of Youth 19 The Blackboard Jungle
broom 4 bush 5 besom, brush, whisk 7
sweeper
Broteas
father: 8 Tantalus
devotee of: 6 Cybele
denied divinity of: 7 Artemis
broth 5 stock 8 bouillon, consomme 9 clear
soup
brothel 4 stew 5 house 6 bagnio, bordel 8
bordello, cathouse 10 bawdy house, fancy
house, whorehouse 11 maison close 13
maison de passe, sporting house 14
house of ill fame 16 house of ill repute 19
house of prostitution
brother 3 pal 4 chum, monk, peer 5 buddy,
friar 6 cleric 7 comrade, kinsman, partner, sibling 8 confrere, landsman, monastic, relative, relation 9 associate, colleague, companion, fellowman 10 countryman 11 male sibling 12 fellow member 13
fellow citizen
French: 5 frere
brotherhood 4 club 5 amity, lodge 10 fellowship, fraternity, friendship 11 association

Brother Juniper
character in: 21 The Bridge of San Luis
Rey
author: 6 Wilder
Brothers Karamazov, The
author: 10 Dostoevsky 17 Fyodor
Dostoyevsky
character: 4 Ivan 6 Dmitri 7 Alyosha
(Alexey), Zossima 8 Katerina 9 Grushenka 10 Smerdyakov 15 Fyodor
Karamazov
brougham 3 car 8 carriage 10 automobile
brought 6 caused 7 carried, fetched, sold
for 8 conveyed 9 conducted, convinced,
persuaded
brow 3 rim 4 brim, edge, side 5 brink, verge
6 border, margin 8 boundary, forehead 9
periphery
browbeat 3 cow 5 abash, bully, cower 6
badger, harass, hector 7 henpeck 8 bulldoze, domineer, frighten, threaten 9 terrorize, tyrannize 10 intimidate
browbeater 5 bully 6 despot 7 coercer 9
oppressor, tormenter, tormentor 11 intimidator, petty tyrant
browbeating 8 bullying 11 threatening, tyrannizing 12 intimidation
brown 3 bay, dun, fry, tan 4 buff, cook,
drab, fawn, puce, roan, rust 5 beige,
camel, cocoa, hazel, khaki, saute, tawny, toast, umber 6 auburn, bronze, brunet,
coffee, copper, ginger, russet, sorrel, walnut 8 brunette, chestnut, cinnamon, mahogany 9 chocolate, olive drab 10 terra-
cotta 11 dirt-colored, sand-colored 12
liver-colored
Brown, Angeline
real name of: 14 Angie Dickinson
Brown, Berenice Sadie
character in: 19 A Member of the Wedding
author: 9 McCullers
Brown, Charles Brockden
author of: 6 Ormond 7 Wieland 11 Edgar
Huntly 12 Arthur Mervyn
Brown, Claude
author of: 16 The Children of Ham 25
Manchild in the Promised Land
Brown, Dee
author of: 15 Creek Mary's Blood 24
Bury My Heart at Wounded Knee
Brown, Helen Gurley
author of: 19 Sex and the Single Girl
editor of: 12 Cosmopolitan
Brown, Helen Hayes
real name of: 10 Helen Hayes
Brown, Jim (Jimmy)
sport: 8 football
position: 8 fullback
team: 15 Cleveland Browns
actor in: 10 Dirty Dozen
Brown, Robert
field: 6 botany
nationality: 8 Scottish
established: 16 Brownian movement
Brown Bomber
nickname of: 8 Joe Louis

Browne, Dik
  creator/artist of: 9 Hi and Lois **12** Beetle
  Bailey **16** Hagar the Horrible
Browne, Sir Thomas
  author of: 9 Urn Burial **12** Hydriotaphia
  13 Religio Medici **16** The Garden of Cy-
  rus
brownie 3 elf **4** cake, puck **5** fairy, pixie **6**
sprite **10** leprechaun
Browning, Elizabeth Barrett
  author of: 11 Aurora Leigh **14** How Do I
  Love Thee **16** Casa Guidi Windows **24**
  Sonnets from the Portuguese
Browning, Robert
  author of: 8 Sordello **10** Paracelsus **11**
  Pippa Passes **13** Fra Lippo Lippi, My Last
  Duchess **14** Andrea del Sarto **17** The
  Ring and the Book **20** The Pied Piper of
  Hamlin **29** Soliloquy of the Spanish Cloister **30** Childe Roland to the Dark Tower
  Came
brownish 3 tan **5** taupe **6** bronze **8** chestnut **13** copper-colored
Brownlow, Mr
  character in: 11 Oliver Twist
  author: 7 Dickens
Brownmiller, Susan
  author of: 14 Against Our Will
Brown's Descent
  author: 11 Robert Frost
browse 3 eat **4** feed, scan, skim **5** graze **6**
nibble, peruse, survey **7** dip into, pasture **8**
look over **9** check over **11** look through **13**
glance through
Bruckner, Anton
  born: 7 Austria **9** Ansfelden
  composer of: 6 Te Deum **7** Psalm CL **11**
  Grosse Messe **16** Romantic Symphony
  26 Intermezzo for String Quartet
Brueghel, Pieter (the Elder)
  born: 5 Breda **8** Flanders
  nickname: 14 Peasant Bruegel
  son: 11 Jan Brueghel
  artwork: 9 Blue Cloak, The Months **10**
  Dulle Griet (Mad Meg) **12** Fall of Icarus,
  Peasant Dance, Tower of Babel **14** Children's Games, The Misanthrope **15** Return of the Herd **16** Hunters in the Snow
  17 The Triumph of Death **19** Peasant
  Wedding Dance **21** Peasant Wedding
  Banquet, The Magpie on the Gallows **22**
  Massacre of the Innocents **23** The Blind
  Leading the Blind, The Fall of the Rebel
  Angels
Brueghel, Jan
  born: 8 Brussels, Flanders
  nickname: 6 Velvet
  father: 13 Pieter Bruegel
  artwork: 12 Four Elements **13** Village
  Street **15** The Garden of Eden (with Rubens) **17** The Battle of Arbela
Brueghel, Pieter (the Younger)
  born: 8 Brussels, Flanders
  nickname: 12 Hell Brueghel **19** The Infernal Brueghel
  father: 13 Pieter Bruegel (the Elder)

artwork: 11 Village Fair **14** The Crucifixion **16** The Burning of Troy
Brugh, Spangler Arlington
  real name of: 12 Robert Taylor
bruise 3 mar **4** hurt, mark **5** abuse, wound
  6 damage, injure, injury, offend **7** blacken,
  blemish **8** discolor **9** black mark, contusion
  13 discoloration
bruit 3 din **5** noise, rumor **6** clamor, hubbub, racket, report, uproar **7** clangor **10**
  clattering, noise about **11** voice abroad
Brunei
  capital/largest city: 17 Bandar Seri
  Begawan
  others: 4 Labi **5** Badas, Danau, Muara,
  Seria **6** Bangar, Tutong **7** Kampong **10**
  Kuala Abang, Kuala Balai **11** Kuala Belait
  head of state/government: 6 sultan
  island: 6 Borneo **8** Sipitang
  mountain: 6 Teraja **9** Ulu Tutong
  highest point: 10 Pagon Priok
  river: 6 Belait, Brunei, Tutong **9** Tem-
  burong
  sea: 10 South China
  physical feature:
  bay: 6 Brunei
  people: 4 Iban **5** Dayak, Malay **7** Chinese, Kadazan
  language: 4 Iban **5** Malay **7** Chinese, English
  religion: 5 Islam **6** Taoism **7** animism **8**
  Buddhism **12** Christianity
  feature: 3 oil
Brunelleschi, Filippo
  architect of: 10 San Lorenzo **11** Pazzi
  Chapel (Santa Croce), Pitti Palace **12**
  Santo Spirito **14** Badia Fiesolana **15**
  Duomo of Florence **16** Palazzo Quaratesi
  21 Santa Maria degli Angeli **22** Ospedale
  degli Innocenti **23** Dome of Florence Cathedral
brunet, brunette 4 dark **5** black **9** brown-
  eyed, dark brown **10** dark-haired **11**
  brown-haired, dark-skinned **12** olive-
  skinned **16** dark-complexioned
Brunhild
  origin: 8 Germanic
  Scandinavian: 8 Brynhild
  character in: 14 Nibelungenlied
  queen of: 8 Isenland
  husband: 7 Gunther
  won by: 9 Siegfried
brunt 5 force **6** impact, stress, thrust **8** violence **9** full force, main shock
brush 4 bush, dust, fern, wash **5** clean,
  copse, flick, graze, groom, paint, run-in,
  scrub, sedge, set-to, shine, sweep, touch,
  whisk **6** battle, bushes, caress, duster, forest, fracas, polish, shrubs, stroke **7**
  bracken, cleanse, dusting, grazing,
  meeting, scuffle, thicket, varnish **8** skirmish, woodland **9** encounter, shrubbery,
  woodlands **10** engagement, underbrush,
  whiskbroom **11** bush country, undergrowth
  12 bristled tool **13** confrontation
  type: 4 hair, nail, shoe, wash **5** paint,
  scrub, tooth **7** clothes

brush aside 6 slight 7 neglect 8 pass over
9 disregard
brush-off 3 cut 4 snub 5 brush 6 rebuff,
slight 7 put-down, squeich 9 disregard, rejection 11 repudiation 12 cold shoulder
brusque 4 curt, rude, tart 5 bluff, blunt,
gruff, harsh, rough, short 6 abrupt, crusty 7
bearish 8 impolite, ungentle 10 ungracious
12 discourteous 13 unceremonious
Brussels
  canal: 9 Charleroi 10 Willebroek
  capital of: 7 Belgium
  cathedral: 26 Saint Michel and Sainte
  Gudule
  early name: 10 Bruoc-sella
  means: 16 marshy settlement
  Flemish: 7 Brussel
  French: 9 Bruxelles
  headquarters of: 3 EEC 4 NATO 12
  Common Market 25 European Economic
  Community
  landmark: 11 Royal Palace 15 Palace of
  Justice 17 Palace of the Nation
  province: 7 Brabant
  river: 5 Senne, Zenne
  square: 11 Grande Place
brutal 5 crude, cruel, harsh 6 bloody,
coarse, fierce, savage 7 brutish, hellish,
inhuman, vicious 8 barbaric, pitiless, ruthless 9 atrocious, barbarous, heartless,
merciless, unfeeling 10 demoniacal 11
hardhearted, remorseless 12 bloodthirsty
brutality 7 cruelty 8 ferocity, savagery 9
barbarity, harshness 10 inhumanity,
savageness 11 brutishness, viciousness
12 ruthlessness
brute 5 beast, demon, devil, fiend, swine 6
animal, savage 7 monster 9 barbarian 10
wild animal 11 cruel person 12 dumb creature
brutish 5 cruel, feral 6 bloody, brutal,
fierce, savage 7 inhuman 8 barbaric 9 barbarous, ferocious, unfeeling 11 remorseless
brutishness 8 ferocity, savagery 9 barbarity, brutality 10 bestiality, coarseness, inhumanity, savageness 11 viciousness 15 re-
morselessness
Brutus
  also: 12 Marcus Brutus
  character in: 12 Julius Caesar
  author: 11 Shakespeare
Bruxelles *see* 8 Brussels
Bryan, C D B
  author of: 12 Friendly Fire 24 Ugly
  Scenes Beautiful Women
Bryant, Bear (Paul)
  sport: 8 football
  position: 5 coach
  team: 7 Alabama 11 Crimson Tide
Brynhild
  origin: 12 Scandinavian
  Germanic: 8 Brunhild
  husband: 6 Gunnar
  won by: 6 Sigurd
  position: 8 Valkyrie

Brynhildr Sigrdrifa *see* 9 Sigrdrifa
Brynner, Yul
  real name: 10 Taidje Khan
  born: 14 Sakhalin Island
  roles: 9 Anastasia, West World 11 The
  King and I (Oscar) 18 The Ten Commandments 19 The Magnificent Seven
  20 The Brothers Karamazov 23 Invitation
  to a Gunfighter
Brythonic
  language family: 12 Indo-European
  group: 5 Welsh 6 Breton 7 Cornish, Pic-
  tish
Bschliessmayer, Oskar Josef
  real name of: 11 Oskar Werner
Bubba Smith
  nickname of: 17 Charles Aaron Smith
bubble, bubbles 4 bleb, boil, fizz, foam 5
froth 6 burble, fizzle, gurgle, seethe 7 air
ball, blister, droplet, globule, sparkle 9 percolate 10 effervesce 13 effervescence
bubbliness 9 fizziness, foaminess 10 ebullience, enthusiasm, frothiness, liveliness
11 high spirits 13 effervescence
bubbling 5 fizzy, foamy 6 frothy 7 fizzing,
foaming 9 sparkling 12 effervescent
bubbly 5 fizzy, foamy 6 frothy, lively 7
fizzing, foaming 9 champagne, sparkling
12 effervescent, high-spirited
Bubona
  origin: 5 Roman
  protectress of: 4 cows, oxen
buccaneer 6 pirate 7 corsair 9 privateer 10
freebooter
Buchan, John (Baron Tweedsmuir)
  author of: 10 John Macnab 11 Greenmantle, Pilgrim's Way 17 John Burnet of
  Barns 18 The Thirty-Nine Steps
Buchanan, Daisy
  character in: 14 The Great Gatsby
  author: 10 Fitzgerald
Buchanan, Edgar
  born: 13 Humansville MO
  roles: 5 Shane, Texas 7 Arizona 8 Cimarron 9 McLintock 13 Penny Serenade 17
  Petticoat Junction 18 Ride the High
  Country
Buchanan, James
  nickname: 7 Old Buck
  presidential rank: 9 fifteenth
  party: 8 Democrat
  state represented: 2 PA
  defeated: 7 (John Charles) Fremont 8
  (Millard) Fillmore
  vice president: 12 (John Cabell)
  Breckinridge
  cabinet:
    state: 4 (Lewis) Cass 5 (Jeremiah
    Sullivan) Black
    treasury: 3 (John Adams) Dix 4 (Howell)
    Cobb 6 (Philip Francis) Thomas
    war: 4 (Joseph) Holt 5 (John Buchanan)
    Floyd
    attorney general: 5 (Jeremiah Sullivan)
    Black 7 (Edwin McMasters) Stanton
    navy: 6 (Isaac) Toucey

postmaster general: 4 (Horatio) King, (Joseph) Holt 5 (Aaron Venable) Brown
interior: 8 (Jacob) Thompson
born: 11 Cove Gap PA (near Mercersburg)
died/buried: 11 Lancaster PA
education:
Academy: 8 Old Stone
College: 9 Dickinson
studied: 3 law
religion: 12 Presbyterian
political career: 13 state assembly 24 US House of Representatives
secretary of: 5 State
minister: 6 Russia 12 Great Britain
civilian career: 6 lawyer
notable events of lifetime/term: 5 Panic (of 1857) 11 English Bill, Pony Express
raid by: 9 John Brown
raid on: 12 Harper's Ferry
Supreme Court case: 9 Dred Scott
father: 5 James
mother: 9 Elizabeth (Speer)
siblings: 4 Jane, John, Mary 5 Maria, Sarah 7 Harriet 9 Elizabeth 11 Edward Young 12 William Speer 16 George Washington
wife: 4 none
children: 4 none

Bucharest
capital of: 7 Romania, Rumania
founder: 5 Bucur
landmark: 8 Scinteia 13 Village Museum
river: 9 Dimbovita
Rumanian: 9 Bucuresti

Buchinsky, Charles
real name of: 14 Charles Bronson

buck 3 man 4 beau, deer, dude, kick, male 5 dandy 6 dollar, oppose 7 coxcomb 8 cavalier, gay blade 9 go against 10 young blood

Buck
character in: 16 The Call of the Wild
author: 6 London

Buck, Pearl S
author of: 8 The Exile 9 Other Gods 10 Dragon Seed 12 The Good Earth 13 A House Divided

bucket 3 can, hod, tub 4 cask, pail 5 scoop 6 vessel 7 pailful, pitcher, scuttle 9 container 10 receptacle

Buckeye State
nickname of: 4 Ohio

buckle 3 sag 4 bend, clip, curl, hasp, hook, warp 5 bulge, catch, clasp 6 cave in, couple, fasten, secure 7 contort, crinkle, crumple, distort, wrinkle 8 belly out, collapse, fastener

buckle down 8 attend 12 apply oneself

Buckley, William F Jr
author of: 11 Who's on First? 15 God and Man at Yale, God Save the Queen

Buck Rogers
creator: 14 Richard Calkins
character: 5 Alura, Buddy, Dercu, Kayla, Wilma 6 Ardala 10 Killer Kane

bucolic 4 idyl, poem 5 idyll, rural 6 poetic, rustic 7 eclogue, idyllic, peasant 8 pastoral, shepherd

Bucolion
father: 8 Laomedon
son: 7 Aesepus
wife: 9 Abarbarea

bud 4 open 5 shoot 6 flower, sprout 7 blossom, burgeon, develop

Bud, Rosa
character in: 22 The Mystery of Edwin Drood
author: 7 Dickens

Budapest
area: 4 Buda, Pest 5 Obuda
capital of: 7 Hungary
cathedral: 13 Saint Matthias
hill: 10 Castle Hill
island: 6 Csepel
river: 6 Danube
Roman town: 8 Aquincum

Buddenbrooks
author: 10 Thomas Mann

Buddha
also called: 5 Butsu
born: 11 Kapilavastu
father: 11 Suddhodhana
founded: 8 Buddhism
means: 15 enlightened one
message: 6 dharma
name for: 17 Siddhartha Gautama
son: 6 Rahula
tree: 2 bo 5 bodhi
wife: 9 Yasodhara

Buddhism
action: 5 karma
branch: 8 Mahayana 9 Theravada 12 Great Vehicle 14 way of the elders
doctrine: 6 duhkha 7 nirvana 9 suffering 13 eightfold path 15 four noble truths 17 pratityasamutpada
founded by: 6 Buddha 17 Siddhartha Gautama
monk: 7 bhikshu
nun: 9 bhikshuni
rebirth: 7 samsara
religious community: 6 sangha

buddy 3 pal 4 chum, mate 5 amigo, crony 6 cohort, fellow, friend 7 brother, comrade, partner 8 confrere, intimate, playmate, sidekick 9 associate, colleague, companion, confidant 10 playfellow 11 confederate

buddy-buddy 5 close, palsy 6 chummy 8 friendly, intimate 10 palsy-walsy

budge 4 move, push, roll, stir, sway 5 shift, slide 6 change 8 convince, dislodge, persuade 9 dislocate, influence

budget 4 cost, plan 5 funds, means 6 moneys, ration 7 arrange 8 allocate, schedule 9 allotment, allowance, apportion, resources 10 allocation, portion out 12 spending plan 13 financial plan

budgetary 6 fiscal 8 economic, monetary 9 financial, pecuniary

buenas noches 9 good night

bueno 4 good

Buenos Aires
   capital of: 9 Argentina
   landmark: 11 Teatro Colon 16 Saavedra
   Monument, San Martin Theater 17 Wilde-
   stein Gallery, Witcomb Art Gallery 18
   Church of El Salvador 27 Christopher
   Columbus Monument
   park: 7 Palermo
   people: 8 portenos
   means: 15 people of the port
   river: 12 Rio de la Plata

buff 3 bug, fan, nut, rub, tan 4 swab 5
   freak, hound, mavin, sandy, straw, tawny 6
   addict, dauber, polish, smooth, the raw 7
   admirer, burnish, devotee, leather 8 bare
   skin, follower, polisher 9 nakedness, yellowish 10 aficionado, enthusiast 11 buffalo
   hide, connoisseur 14 yellowish-brown

buffalo 5 bison 6 puzzle 7 mystify 10 intimidate
   kind: 7 African 10 Asian water
   African: 14 syncerus caffer
   Asian water: 14 bubalus bubalis

Buffalo
   football team: 5 Bills
   hockey team: 6 Sabres

buffer 6 bumper, fender, shield 7 cushion 9
   protector

buffet 3 box, hit, jab, rap 4 bang, beat,
   bump, cuff, meal, push, slap 5 baste,
   knock, pound, shove, thump 6 pummel, strike, supper, thrash, thwack, wallop
   7 cabinet, counter 8 credenza 9 cafeteria,
   sideboard 11 smorgasbord

Buffone, Carlo
   character in: 22 Every Man out of His
   Humour
   author: 6 Jonson

buffoon 3 wag 4 fool, zany 5 clown, comic,
   joker, mimic, Punch 6 jester, madcap 7
   Pierrot 8 comedian, funnyman 9 harlequin,
   pantaloon, prankster, trickster 10 Scaramouch, silly-billy 11 merry-andrew, punchinello, Scaramouche

buffoonery 6 antics, comedy 7 foolery,
   inanity 8 zaniness 9 asininity, horseplay,
   silliness, slapstick 10 tomfoolery 11 foolishness, loutishness 12 clownishness,
   monkeyshines, prankishness 14 clowning
   around, playing the fool

bug 3 nag 4 flaw, germ 5 annoy, fault, virus
   6 badger, bother, defect, insect, pester 7
   wiretap 8 drawback, listen in, weakness 9
   eavesdrop, Hemiptera 11 Heteroptera
   variety: 3 bat, bed, red 4 gnat, lace,
   leaf, seed, toad 5 negro, plant, shore,
   stilt, stink, water 6 ambush, damsel, fungus, pirate, ripple 7 boatman, stainer 8
   assassin, burrower, creeping 9 royal palm
   10 leaf footed 11 ashgray leaf, backswim-
   mer, broadheaded, jumping tree, velvet
   water 12 velvety shore, water strider, water treader 13 jumping ground, water
   measurer, water scorpion 14 scentless
   plant 17 terrestrial turtle

bugaboo 5 scare 6 fright 7 anxiety

bugbear 4 ogre 5 bogey 6 goblin 7 bugaboo 8 bogeyman 9 bete noire

buggy 4 cart 5 wagon 7 vehicle 8 carriage
   10 conveyance

bugle 4 horn 10 instrument

Bugs Bunny
   creator: 15 Leon Schlesinger
   character: 9 Elmer Fudd
   voice of: 8 Mel Blanc
   saying: 10 what's up doc

build 4 body, form, make, mold, open 5 begin, brace, erect, forge, found, put up,
   raise, renew, set up, shape, start, steel 6
   create, extend, figure, harden, launch 7
   amplify, augment, develop, enhance, enlarge, fashion, greaten, improve, produce
   8 embark on, increase, initiate, multiply,
   physique 9 construct, establish, fabricate, institute, intensify, originate, rein
   force, structure, undertake 10 inaugurate,
   strengthen, supplement 11 manufac
   ture, put together 12 construction

building 7 edifice 9 structure 12 construction

building front 6 facade 8 frontage

build up 5 amass 7 develop, promote 8 increase 10 accumulate

Bujold, Genevieve
   born: 6 Canada 8 Montreal
   roles: 4 Coma 9 Monsignor, Obsession
   12 King of Hearts 21 Anne of the Thousand Days

Bujumbura
   capital of: 7 Burundi

Bul 17 eighth Hebrew month

bulb 3 bud 4 corm, seed 5 plant, tuber 8
   swelling

Bulfinch, Charles
   architect of: 7 Capitol (Washington DC)
   16 Hartford City Hall (CT) 23 Massachusetts State House (Boston)
   style: 7 Federal

Bulgakov, Mikhail
   author of: 9 Black Snow 13 The White
   Guard 14 The Heart of a Dog 19 The
   Days of the Turbins 21 The Master and
   Margarita

Bulgaria
   capital/largest city: 5 Sofia
   others: 3 Lom 4 Rila, Ruse 5 Aytos,
   Butan, Byclu, Elena, Iskra, Stara, Varna 6
   Bleven, Burgas, Devnia, Dulovo, Levsky,
   Pernik, Pleuna, Pleven, Plevna, Shumen,
   Shumla, Sliven, Slivno, Widden, Yambol,
   Zagora 7 Gabrovo, Karlovo, Plovdiv,
   Sistova, Timova 8 Khaskovo, Rustchuk,
   Svishtov 9 Ruse Vidin, Silistria 11
   Kolorovgrad 12 Dimitrovgrad
   school: 5 Sofia 7 Plovdiv 13 Veliko
   Turnovo
   measure: 3 oka, oke 5 krine, lekhe, likhe
   monetary unit: 3 lev 8 stotinki
   weight: 3 oka, oke 5 tovar
   mountain: 3 Kom 5 Botev, Pirin, Sapka 6
   Balkan, Sredna 7 Vikhren 11 Rila-
   Rhodope

highest point: 6 Musala 8 Musallah

river: 3 Lom, Vit 4 Arda, Osma 5 Isker, Iskur, Mesta 6 Danube, Marica, Ogosta, Struma, Yantra 7 Maritsa, Stryama, Tundzha

sea: 5 Black

physical feature:

cape: 5 Emine, Sabla 7 Kuratan

gulf: 5 Burga

plateau: 6 Danube

resort: 9 Pyassatzi 13 Slunchev Bryay

valley: 7 Maritsa

people: 4 Slav, Turk 5 Gypsy, Pomak, Tatar 6 Bulgar, Slavic 7 Chuvash 9 Cheremiss 10 Macedonian

language: 9 Bulgarian

religion: 5 Islam 24 Bulgarian Eastern Orthodox

place:

church: 9 St Nedelja

monastery: 4 Rila 6 Rilski

monument: 7 Red Army

mosque: 10 Banya Bashi

museum: 21 Revolutionary Movement

square: 5 Lenin

valley of roses: 8 Kazanluk

feature:

dance: 4 horo

holiday: 12 St Georges Day

newspaper: 17 Rabot Nichesko Delo

food:

stew: 8 giuvetch

bulge 3 bag, sag 4 bump, lump 5 curve, swell 6 excess 7 distend, project, puff out, sagging 8 protrude, stand out, stick out, swelling, swell out 9 bagginess 10 projection, prominence, protrusion 12 protuberance

bulk 4 body, mass, most, size 6 extent, volume, weight 7 bigness, measure 8 enormity, hugeness, main part, majority, quantity 9 amplitude, greatness, largeness, magnitude, major part, plurality, substance 10 better part, dimensions, lion's share 11 greater part, massiveness, proportions 13 preponderance

bulky 3 big 4 huge 5 large 6 clumsy 7 awkward, hulking, immense, lumpish, massive, sizable, unhandy 8 enormous, ungainly, unwieldy 9 capacious, extensive 10 cumbersome, voluminous 12 unmanageable

bull 2 ox 4 male

male of the: 3 elk 4 seal 5 moose, whale 6 bovine 8 elephant

constellation of: 6 Taurus

Spanish: 4 toro

bulldoze 3 cow 4 bump, fell, push, rage, raze 5 abash, bully, drive, force, level, press, shove 6 coerce, hector, jostle, propel, subdue, thrust 7 buffalo, dragoon, flatten 8 bludgeon, browbeat, domineer, shoulder 9 push about, tyrannize 10 intimidate

Bullen, Frank T

author of: 19 Told in the Dry Watches 22 The Cruise of the Cachalot

bullet 4 ball, lead, shot, slug 7 missile 8 buckshot

bulletin 4 note 6 report 7 account, message, release 8 dispatch 9 statement 10 communique, news report 12 notification 13 communication

Bullet Park

author: 11 John Cheever

bull fighter 6 torero 7 matador, picador 8 toreador 10 El Cordobes 15 Miguel Dominguin

Bullion State

nickname of: 8 Missouri

Bullitt

director: 10 Peter Yates

cast: 9 Don Gordon 12 Robert Duvall, Robert Vaughn, Steve McQueen 16 Jacqueline Bisset

setting: 12 San Francisco

bullock 2 ox 4 beef, bull 5 steer

bullocks 4 kine, oxen 5 beefs, bulls 6 beeves, cattle, steers

bull session 3 rap 4 talk 7 gabfest, palaver 8 dialogue 9 discourse 10 discussion 12 conversation 13 confabulation

bull's-eye 5 black 6 center 7 exactly 8 on target 9 dead center, precisely

bully 3 cow 4 good 5 annoy, swell, tough 6 cheers, coerce, despot, harass, hurrah, hurray 7 coercer, right on, ruffian, tread on 8 browbeat, bulldoze, domineer, frighten, ride over, well done 9 oppressor, terrorize, tormentor, tyrannize 10 browbeater, intimidate 11 intimidator

bullying 7 torment 8 coercion 9 despotism 10 harassment, tormenting 11 browbeating, domineering, tyrannizing 12 intimidation

bulrush 5 plant, sedge 7 cattail, papyrus

bulwark 4 guard 7 barrier, parapet, rampart, support, defense 8 mainstay 9 earthwork 10 embankment

Bulwer-Lytton, Edward

author of: 6 Harold, Pelham, Rienzi 9 Richelieu 13 The Coming Race 16 Kenelm Chillingly 18 The Last of the Barons 20 The Last Days of Pompeii

bum 3 beg 4 grub, hobo 5 cadge, idler, mooch, tramp 6 borrow, loafer, sponge 7 drifter, vagrant 8 derelict, vagabond

bumble 6 bungle 7 blunder, stagger, stumble 8 flounder

Bumble

character in: 11 Oliver Twist

author: 7 Dickens

bumcombe, bunkum 3 rot 4 bosh, bunk 6 drivel 7 twaddle 8 nonsense, tommyrot 10 balderdash 16 stuff-and-nonsense

bump 3 hit, jar, rap 4 bang, blow, butt, hump, jolt, knob, knot, lump, node, poke, slam, slap, sock 5 bulge, clash, crack, crash, gnarl, knock, punch, shake, smack, smash, thump, whack 6 bounce, buffet, impact, jostle, jounce, nodule, rattle, strike, wallop 7 collide, run into 8 swelling 9 collision, crash into, smash into 11 excrescence 12 protuberance

bump into 4 meet 7 collide, run into 9 encounter

bumpkin 3 oaf 4 boor, lout 5 churl, yokel 8 ship beam 10 clodhopper

bump off 4 do in, kill, slay 6 murder, rub out 7 execute, gun down 8 dispatch 11 assassinate 12 take for a ride

bumptious 4 bold 5 cocky, pushy 6 brazen 7 forward, haughty 8 arrogant, boastful, cocksure, impudent, insolent 9 bodacious, conceited, obtrusive 10 aggressive, swaggering 11 impertinent, overbearing 12 presumptuous 13 overconfident, self-assertive

bumptiousness 4 gall 5 cheek 8 audacity, boldness 9 impudence 11 forwardness, presumption 12 impertinence 13 obtrusiveness 17 self-assertiveness

bumpy 5 lumpy, rocky, rough 6 uneven 10 undulating

bun 4 coil, knot, roll 8 soft roll 9 sweet roll

Bunaea
  epithet of: 4 Hera
  refers to: 6 temple

bunch 3 lot, mob 4 band, bevy, gang, heap, herd, host, knot, mass, pack, pile, team 5 array, batch, clump, crowd, flock, group, shock, stack, tribe, troop 6 amount, bundle, gather, huddle, number, string 7 cluster, collect, company 8 assemble, assembly, quantity 9 gathering, multitude 10 assortment, collection, congregate 12 accumulation

bundle 4 lot 4 bale, bind, heap, mass, pack, pile, wrap 5 array, batch, bunch, group, sheaf, stack, truss 6 amount, packet, parcel 7 package 8 quantity 9 multitude 10 assortment, collection 11 tie together 12 accumulation

Bundren family
  characters in: 11 As I Lay Dying
  member: 4 Anse, Cash, Darl 5 Addie, Jewel 9 Dewey Dell
  author: 8 Faulkner

bungalow 5 cabin, house, lodge 7 cottage

bungle 3 mar 4 flub, goof, miff, ruin 5 botch, spoil 6 foul up, mess up, muddle 7 blunder, butcher, do badly, louse up, screw up 8 misjudge 9 mismanage, misreckon 10 miscompute 11 make a mess of, misestimate 12 miscalculate

Bunin, Ivan Alekseyevich
  author of: 10 The Village 15 The Elagin Affair 17 The Life of Arseniev 28 The Gentleman from San Francisco

bunk 3 bed, cot, rot 4 bull 5 berth, hokum, hooey, stuff 6 bunkum, hot air, humbug, pallet 7 baloney, blather, bombast, hogwash, inanity, malarky, spinach 8 claptrap, nonsense, tommyrot 9 poppycock 10 applesauce, balderdash 11 foolishness 16 stuff and nonsense

Bunsen, Robert Wilhelm
  nationality: 6 German
  inventor of: 9 gas burner 10 photo meter 12 Bunsen burner, spectroscope 24 electromechanical battery

Bunshaft, Gordon
  architect of: 10 Lever House (NY) 23 Beinecke Rare Book Library (Yale) 33 Hirshhorn Museum and Sculpture Garden (Washington DC) 34 Lyndon Baines Johnson Memorial Library (Austin TX)

Bunus
  father: 6 Hermes
  mother: 9 Aleidamea
  raised temple honoring: 4 Hera
  location of temple: 7 Corinth

Bunyan, John
  author of: 10 The Holy War 16 Pilgrim's Progress 25 The Life and Death of Mr Badman 33 Grace Abounding to the Chief of Sinners

buona notte 9 good night

buona sera 11 good evening

buon giorno 7 good day 11 good morning

Buono, Victor
  born: 10 San Diego CA
  roles: 11 The Stranger 12 Four for Texas 22 Hush Hush Sweet Charlotte 26 Whatever Happened to Baby Jane

buoy 4 bell, lift 5 boost, cheer, float, raise 6 beacon, uplift 7 cheer up, elevate, gladden, lighten 8 brighten 10 keep afloat 14 floating marker

buoyancy, buoyance 4 glee 6 gaiety 7 jollity 8 gladness, vivacity 9 animation, good humor, joviality, lightness, sunniness 10 brightness, cheeriness, enthusiasm, floatiness, joyousness 11 good spirits 12 cheerfulness, exhilaration, floatability 14 weightlessness 16 lightheartedness

buoyant 3 gay 4 glad 5 happy, jolly, light, merry, peppy, sunny 6 afloat, breezy, bright, elated, joyful, joyous, lively 7 hopeful 8 animated, carefree, cheerful, floating, sportive 9 energetic, floatable, sprightly, vivacious 10 blithesome, optimistic, weightless 11 exhilarated, free and easy 12 enthusiastic, lighthearted

buoyed 6 elated 7 exalted, pleased 8 elevated 9 confident, heartened, reassured 10 inspirited

buoy up 4 warm 6 assure, uplift 7 comfort, hearten, inspire 8 inspirit, reassure 9 encourage

Buphagus
  father: 7 Iapetus
  slain by: 7 Artemis
  epithet of: 8 Hercules
  means: 7 ox-eater

Burbank, Luther
  field: 7 biology
  developed: 13 plant breeding

burble 6 babble, bubble, gurgle, murmur 8 babbling

Burce, Suzanne
  real name of: 10 Jane Powell

Burchill, Mr
  character in: 19 The Vicar of Wakefield
  author: 9 Goldsmith

burden 3 tax, try, vex 4 care, load, onus, pack 5 cargo 6 hamper, hinder, strain, stress, weight 7 afflict, anxiety, freight, oppress, trouble 8 encumber, handicap, hardship, load with, obligate, overload 9 press down, weigh down 10 saddle with 11 encumbrance 14 responsibility

Burden, Jack
character in: 14 All the King's Men
author: 6 Warren

burden of proof
Latin: 12 onus probandi

burdensome 4 hard 5 heavy 6 tiring 7 arduous, onerous 8 wearying 9 Herculean, laborious 10 exhausting

bureau 6 agency, branch, office 7 cabinet, commode, dresser, service, station 8 division 10 chiffonier, department 14 administration, chest of drawers

bureaucrat 8 mandarin, official, politico 9 penpusher 10 politician 11 apparatchik, functionary, rubber stamp 12 civil servant, officeholder 13 public servant

burgee 4 flag 6 banner, colors, ensign 7 pennant

burgeon 3 wax 4 blow, grow, open 5 bloom 6 expand, flower, spread, thrive 7 augment, blossom, develop, enlarge, prosper, shoot up, succeed 8 escalate, flourish, fructify, increase, mushroom, spring up 9 bear fruit 10 effloresce 11 proliferate

Burgess, Anthony
author of: 2 MF 13 Man of Nazareth, Time for a Tiger 14 Enderby Outside, The Wanting Seed 16 A Clockwork Orange, Beard's Roman Women 17 Nothing Like the Sun 20 The End of the World News

burgher 7 citizen 9 bourgeois 11 townsperson

burglar 3 cat 4 yegg 5 thief 6 robber 7 prowler 8 pilferer 9 cracksman, purloiner 12 housebreaker 14 second-story man

burglary 5 theft 6 felony 7 break-in, larceny, robbery 8 filching, stealing 9 pilfering 10 purloining 13 housebreaking 19 breaking and entering

burgundy 3 red 4 wine 5 color 13 reddish-purple

Burgundy
ancient city: 5 Autun
city: 5 Dijon
district: 5 Youne 6 Nievre 7 Cote d' Or 12 Saone-et-Loire
French: 9 Bourgogne
location: 6 France
river: 5 Rhone, Saone
tribe: 9 Burgundii

Buri
origin: 12 Scandinavian
first: 3 god
revealed by: 8 Audhumla 9 Audhumbla

burial 5 rites 7 funeral 9 interment, obsequies 10 entombment, inhumation

burial ground 7 ossuary 8 boneyard, Boot Hill, catacomb, cemetery 9 graveyard 10 churchyard, necropolis 12 potter's field

buried 4 laid, sunk 6 hidden 7 covered, inhumed, immured 9 concealed, deep sixed 10 laid to rest 11 underground

Burke, Francis
character in: 21 The Master of Ballantrae
author: 9 Stevenson

Burkina Faso see Upper Volta

burlap 3 bag 4 hemp, jute 5 cloth 6 fabric 8 material

burlesque 5 farce, spoof 6 comedy, parody, satire 7 mockery, takeoff 8 ridicule, travesty 10 buffoonery, caricature 15 slapstick comedy

burly 3 big 5 beefy, bulky, hefty, large 6 brawny, stocky, strong, sturdy 7 hulking, sizable 8 thickset 9 ponderous, strapping

Burma see 7 Myanmar

burn 3 nip, tan 4 bite, char, fire, glow, hurt, pain, sear, skin 5 be hot, blaze, brown, chafe, flame, flare, flash, parch, prick, scald, singe, smart, smoke, sting 6 abrade, bronze, flames, ignite, kindle, nettle, scorch, scrape, suntan, tingle, wither 7 blister, consume, cremate, flicker, oxidize, prickle, shrivel, smolder, sunburn, swelter 8 abrasion, be ablaze, be on fire, charring, irritate, kindling 9 be flushed, reddening, set fire to, set on fire, use as fuel 10 be feverish, be in flames, blistering, incandesce, incinerate, irritation, smoldering 12 incineration 13 reduce to ashes

burnable 9 flammable, ignitable 10 combustive 11 combustible, inflammable 13 conflagrative

Burne-Jones, Sir Edward Coley
born: 7 England 10 Birmingham
artwork: 11 Laus Veneris 15 The Golden Stairs 16 The Mirror of Venus 18 The Star of Bethlehem 28 King Cophetua and the Beggar Maid

burner, gas
invented by: 6 Bunsen

Burnett, Carol
born: 12 San Antonio TX
roles: 14 The Four Seasons 19 The Carol Burnett Show

Burnett, Frances H
author of: 20 Little Lord Fauntleroy

Burney, Fanny
author of: 7 Camilla, Diaries, Evelina

Burnham, Daniel Hudson
partner: 16 John Wellborn Root
architect of: 7 Rookery 12 Union Station (Washington DC) 15 Calumet Building 16 Flatiron Building (NYC), Reliance Building 17 Monadnock Building 25 World's Columbian Exposition

burning 3 hot 5 acrid, afire, aglow, eager, fiery, sharp 6 aflame, ardent, biting, fervid, heated, raging, red-hot 7 blazing, boiling, caustic, earnest, fanatic, fervent, flaming, flaring, frantic, glowing, ignited, intense, kindled, painful, pungent, sincere, smoking, zealous 8 flashing, frenzied, piercing, resolute, sizzling, smarting, stinging, tingling 9 corroding, prickling 10 astringent, compelling, flickering, irritating, passionate, smoldering 11 impassioned 12 all-consuming

burnish 3 wax 4 buff 5 rub up, shine 6 polish, smooth

burnished 5 shiny 6 bright, buffed, shined 8 lustrous, polished, smoothed

burnoose 4 cape, robe 5 cloak 6 mantle 7 pelisse

burn out 3 pop 4 blow 7 exhaust 10 exhaustion, extinguish

Burns, George
real name: 14 Nathan Birnbaum
wife: 11 Gracie Allen
born: 9 New York NY
roles: 5 Oh God 12 Going in Style 15 The Sunshine Boys 17 Burns and Allen Show

Burns, Robert
author of: 8 To a Louse, To a Mouse 11 A Red Red Rose, Tam O'Shanter 12 Auld Lang Syne 16 Address to the Deil, Coming Thro the Rye 17 Holy Willie's Prayer 20 Flow Gently Sweet Afton 22 My Heart's in the Highlands 23 The Cotter's Saturday Night 32 Poems Chiefly in the Scottish Dialect

Burnt Norton
author: 7 T S Eliot

burp 5 belch, eruct 10 eructation

burr 4 buhr, rock 5 notch, stone 9 whetstone 13 pronunciation

Burr
author: 9 Gore Vidal

Burr, Raymond
born: 6 Canada 14 New Westminster 15 British Columbia
roles: 8 Ironside 10 Perry Mason, Rear Window

burro 3 ass 4 mule 6 donkey, onager 7 jackass

Burroughs, Edgar Rice
author of: 15 Tarzan of the Apes

Burroughs, William S
author of: 5 Queer 6 Junkie 13 The Naked Lunch

Burroughs, William Seward
nationality: 8 American
inventor of: 13 adding machine
grandson: 17 William S Burroughs (author)

burrow 3 den, dig 4 cave, hole, lair 6 covert, dugout, furrow, tunnel 8 excavate, scoop out 9 hollow out

Burrows, Abe
author of: 41 How to Succeed in Business without Really Trying

bursa 3 bag, sac 5 pouch, purse 6 cavity

bursar 6 purser 7 cashier 9 paymaster, treasurer 10 cashkeeper

burst 3 fly, pop, run 4 bang, bust, rend, rush 5 barge, blast, break, crack, erupt, split, spout 6 blow up, detach, divide, sunder 7 disjoin, explode, rupture, shatter, torrent 8 breaking, break out, cracking, crashing, detonate, eruption, fly apart, fracture, fragment, outbreak, separate, splinter 9 break open, discharge, explosion, gush forth, pull apart, splitting, tear apart 10 detonation, disconnect, outpour-

ing, shattering 11 spring forth 12 disintegrate

burst forth 5 arise, begin, erupt, start 6 arrive, emerge 8 break out, commence

Burstyn, Ellen
real name: 14 Edna Rae Gillooly
born: 9 Detroit MI
roles: 11 The Exorcist 16 Same Time Next Year 18 The Last Picture Show 26 Alice Doesn't Live Here Anymore (Oscar)

Burton, Richard
real name: 22 Richard Walter Jenkins Jr
wife: 15 Elizabeth Taylor
born: 5 Wales 11 Pontrhydfen Wales
roles: 6 Becket, Hamlet 7 Camelot, The Robe 9 Cleopatra 14 My Cousin Rachel 19 The Night of the Iguana, The Taming of the Shrew 21 Anne of the Thousand Days 25 Who's Afraid of Virginia Woolf 26 The Spy Who Came in from the Cold

Burton, Robert
author of: 22 The Anatomy of Melancholy

Burundi
capital/largest city: 9 Bujumbura
others: 5 Ngozi 6 Bururi, Gitega, Kitega, Rutana, Ruyigi 7 Kibumbu, Muyinga
monetary unit: 5 franc 7 centime
lake: 7 Rugwero 8 Tshohoha 10 Tanganyika
mountain: 9 Nyamisana
highest point: 8 Nyarwana
river: 6 Akanya, Ruvuvu, Ruzizi 8 Rukagera 10 Malagarasi
people: 3 Twa 4 Hutu 5 Bantu, Batwa, Pygmy, Tutsi 6 Bahutu, Watusi 7 Barundi
language: 6 French 7 Kirundi, Swahili
religion: 5 Islam 7 animism 10 Protestant 13 Roman Catholic
feature:
king: 4 mwam
food:
coffee: 7 Arabica

Burushaski
language spoken in: 7 Kashmir

bury 4 hide 5 cache, cover, inter 6 encase, engulf, entomb, inhume 7 conceal, cover up, enclose, immerse, secrete 8 submerge, submerse 13 lay in the grave 17 consign to the grave

Bury My Heart at Wounded Knee
author: 8 Dee Brown

bush 4 veld 5 brush, hedge, plant, shrub, woods 6 forest, jungle 7 barrens 9 shrubbery, woodlands

Bush, George Herbert Walker
presidential rank: 10 forty-first
party: 10 Republican
state represented: 2 TX 5 Texas
defeated: 7 (Michael) Dukakis
defeated by: 7 (Bill) Clinton
vice president: 6 (James Danforth) Quayle
born: 8 Milton MA
education: 4 Yale 7 Andover
religion: 12 Episcopalian

vacation spot: 5 Maine 13 Kennebunkport

political career: 13 vice president 14 representative 21 Ways and Means Committee

ambassador to: 2 UN 13 United Nations

chairman of: 27 Republican National Committee

head of: 3 CIA

liaison with: 5 China

civilian career: 3 oil 14 Zapata Offshore

military career: 5 pilot 6 US Navy

vice president under: 12 Ronald Reagan

notable events of lifetime/term: 7 Gulf War 14 Persian Gulf War 20 Operation Desert Storm

Supreme Court appointments: 11 David Souter 14 Clarence Thomas

invasion of: 6 Panama

father: 15 Prescott Sheldon

mother: 13 Dorothy Walker

wife: 13 Barbara Pierce

children: 4 John, Neil 5 Robin (died 1953) 6 George, Marvin 7 Dorothy

bush country 5 scrub, wilds 7 outback 10 wilderness

bushed 4 beat 5 all in, spent, tired, weary 6 done it, pooped 7 drained, wearied, worn out 8 dog tired, fatigued, tired out 9 dead tired, exhausted, played out

bushel

abbreviation: 2 bu 4 bush

bushes 5 brush 6 shrubs 9 brushwood, shrubbery 10 underbrush 11 undergrowth

bushy 5 hairy 6 fluffy, shaggy 7 hirsute 9 overgrown

business 3 job 4 case, duty, firm, line, shop, task, work 5 chore, field, place, point, store, topic, trade 6 affair, career, living, matter, office, racket 7 affairs, calling, company, concern, dealing, factory, mission, problem, pursuit, subject, venture 8 activity, commerce, function, industry, position, province, question, vocation 9 procedure, situation, specialty 10 assignment, bargaining, employment, enterprise, livelihood, occupation, profession, walk of life 11 corporation, negotiation, partnership, transaction, undertaking 13 establishment, manufacturing, merchandising 14 bread and butter, responsibility

businesslike 7 careful, correct, orderly, regular, serious 8 diligent, sedulous, thorough 9 assiduous, efficient, organized, practical 10 methodical, systematic 11 industrious, painstaking 12 professional

Busiris

king of: 5 Egypt

father: 8 Poseidon

mother: 10 Lysianassa

Busoni, Ferruccio

born: 5 Italy 6 Empoli

composer of: 8 Turandot 10 Arlecchino 11 Doctor Faust, Doktor Faust 12 Die Brautwahl 14 Comedy Overture 25 Fantasia Contrappuntistica

bus station 5 depot 8 terminal, terminus

Bus Stop

director: 11 Joshua Logan

cast: 9 Don Murray 10 Betty Field 13 Eileen Heckart, Marilyn Monroe 14 Arthur O'Connell

bust 3 nab 4 head, raid 5 bosom, chest, seize 6 arrest, breast, collar 7 capture 9 apprehend, sculpture 12 take prisoner 15 take into custody

Buster Brown

creator: 10 RF Outcault

bulldog: 4 Tige

trademark: 9 sailor hat 10 wide collar

bustle 3 ado, fly 4 dash, flit, fuss, rush, stir, tear, to-do 5 hurry 6 bestir, flurry, hustle, pother, scurry, tumult 7 be quick, fluster, flutter, press on, scamper, scuttle 8 activity, be active, scramble 9 agitation, commotion, make haste 10 excitement, hurly-burly

busy 4 full 6 active, employ, engage, intent, occupy, on duty, work at 7 engaged, labor at, slaving, toiling, working 8 absorbed, bustling, employed, laboring, occupied 9 engrossed, in harness, strenuous 10 hard at work 11 industrious 12 be absorbed in, keep occupied 13 be engrossed in

busybody 3 pry 5 snoop 6 gossip 7 blabber, meddler, Paul Pry 8 telltale 10 chatterbox, newsmonger, talebearer, tattletale 12 blabbermouth 13 scandalmonger

busy place 4 hive 6 warren 7 anthill, beehive

but 3 yet 4 save, than that 5 if not, still 6 except, saving, unless 7 however, outside, that not 9 excepting, other than, otherwise 10 except that 14 on the other hand

Butch Cassidy and the Sundance Kid

director: 13 George Roy Hill

cast: 10 Paul Newman (Butch) 13 Katharine Ross (Etta Place), Robert Redford (The Kid)

score: 13 Burt Bacharach

Oscar for: 5 score

song: 27 Raindrops Keep Fallin' on My Head

butcher 4 goof, kill, muff, ruin, slay 5 botch, purge, spoil 6 boggle, bungle, fumble, hack up, hit man, killer, mess up, murder 7 louse up, screw up 8 assassin, decimate, homicide, massacre, murderer 9 liquidate, manhandle, mishandle, slaughter 10 annihilate, hatchet man, liquidator 11 assassinate, exterminate, make a mess of, slaughterer 12 exterminator, massmurderer 15 homicidal maniac

butchery 4 flop, mess 5 botch 8 massacre 9 slaughter

Butes

father: 6 Boreas 7 Pandion

mother: 8 Zeuxippe

brother: 8 Lycurgus 10 Erechtheus

sister: 6 Procne 9 Philomela

son: 4 Eryx

priest of: 6 Athena 8 Poseidon

member of: 9 Argonauts

stricken with: 8 insanity
enticed by: 6 Sirens
leaped into: 3 sea
rescued by: 9 Aphrodite

Butkus, Dick (Richard Marvin)
sport: 8 football
position: 10 linebacker
team: 12 Chicago Bears

Butler, Rhett
character in: 15 Gone With the Wind
author: 8 Mitchell

Butler, Samuel
author of: 7 Erewhon 8 Hudibras 16 The
Way of All Flesh 20 The Elephant in the
Moon

butt 3 end, hit, jab, ram, rap 4 buck, bump,
bunt, dupe, goat, mark, push, slap, stub 5
knock, shank, shove, smack, stump,
thump 6 bottom, buffet, jostle, object,
strike, target, thrust, thwack, victim 8 blunt
end 13 laughingstock

buttercup 10 Ranunculus
variety: 4 Tall 5 Early 6 Common 7 Bermuda, Bulbous, Persian 8 Colombia,
Creeping 11 Yellow water

butterfingered 5 inept 6 clumsy 7 awkward
8 bungling 9 maladroit 10 ungraceful

butterfly
pupa: 9 chrysalis 10 chrysalids 11 chry-
salides
variety: 4 blue 5 giant, nymph, satyr,
snout, tiger, zebra 6 alpine, apollo, arctic,
kalima 7 alfalfa, budwing, dogface, monarch, peacock, viceroy 9 Baltimore,
bathwhite, brimstone, christmas, metal-
mark, orange tip, wood nymph 10 Par-
nassian 11 painted lady, spring azure 12
blue mountain, cabbage white, clouded
white, silver stripe, white admiral 13
chalkhill blue, mourning cloak, pearl crescent 14 American copper, gulf fritillary,
tailed birdwing 15 longtail skipper, regal
fritillary 16 black swallowtail, black veined
white, camberwell beauty, green veined
white, Leonardus skipper, red-spotted
purple 18 orchard swallowtail 19 European swallowtail 20 spicebush swallowtail, variegated fritillary 21 great purple
hairstreak, questionmark anglewing,
white admiral wood nymph

butter up 4 coax 6 cajole 7 flatter, wheedle
8 soft-soap

buttocks 4 buns, butt, rear, rump, seat 5
fanny, nates 6 behind, bottom 7 keister,
rear end 8 backside, derriere, haunches 9
fundament, posterior 12 hindquarters

buttonhole 4 halt, slit, stop 6 accost, waylay 7 solicit 8 approach, confront

button one's lip 7 keep mum 10 keep silent 16 keep one's trap shut 18 keep one's
lips sealed

Buttons, Red
real name: 11 Aaron Chwatt
born: 9 New York NY
roles: 8 Sayonara 13 The Longest Day
20 The Poseidon Adventure 23 They
Shoot Horses Don't They

buttress 4 arch, prop, stay 5 boost, brace,
shore, steel 6 prop up 7 bolster, shore
up, support 8 abutment, shoulder 9 reinforce, stanchion 10 strengthen

buxom 5 plump 6 bosomy, chesty, robust,
zaftig 9 strapping 10 voluptuous 13 large-
breasted, well-developed

buy 3 get 4 deal, gain 5 bribe 6 buy off, obtain, pay for, suborn 7 acquire, bargain,
corrupt, procure 8 invest in, purchase 9 influence

buy and sell 4 deal 5 trade 6 market

buy off 5 bribe 6 pay off 13 grease the
palm

Buzi
son: 7 Ezekiel

Buz Sawyer
creator: 8 Roy Crane
sidekick: 7 Sweeney

Buzuhov, Pierre
character in: 11 War and Peace
author: 7 Tolstoy

buzz 3 hum 4 whir 5 drone 6 murmur 7
whisper

by 4 near, over, past 5 along 6 beside, beyond, during, toward 7 through 9 alongside
10 concerning, on or before 11 according
to, no later than

by air
French: 8 par avion

Byam, Roger
character in: 17 Mutiny on the Bounty
authors: 4 Hall 8 Nordhoff

Byblis
father: 7 Miletus
mother: 6 Cyanea
twin brother: 6 Caunus
loved: 6 Caunus
changed into: 8 fountain

by few words
Latin: 12 paucis verbis

bygone 4 past 5 olden 6 former, gone by,
of yore 7 ancient, earlier 8 departed, obsolete, previous 10 antiquated

by horse
French: 7 a cheval

Byington, Spring
born: 17 Colorado Springs CO
roles: 7 Jezebel 11 Little Women 13 December Bride, Heaven Can Wait 17 Mutiny on the Bounty 20 The Devil and Miss
Jones, You Can't Take It with You 26 The
Charge of the Light Brigade

by itself 4 solo 5 alone, aloof, apart 8 isolated 13 unaccompanied

Byng, Admiral
character in: 7 Candide
author: 8 Voltaire

by oneself 4 solo 5 alone, aloof 8 isolated
10 solitarily 13 unaccompanied
Latin: 4 sola 5 solus

by operation of law
Latin: 8 ipso jure

bypass 4 go by 5 avert, avoid, dodge 8 go
around 10 circumvent 12 detour around

bypath 3 way 4 lane 5 alley, byway, track, trail 6 bypass 7 footway, pathway, towpath, walkway 8 back road, dirt road, footpath, shortcut, side road 10 beaten path, bridle path, garden path

by-product 8 offshoot 9 aftermath 16 incidental result

by right
  Latin: 6 de jure

Byron, Lord (George Gordon)
  author of: 7 Don Juan, Manfred 10 The Corsair 19 The Vision of Judgment 20 The Prisoner of Chillon 23 Childe Harold's Pilgrimage

byrrh
  type: 8 aperitif
  origin: 6 France
  flavor: 6 orange 7 quinine

bystander 6 viewer 7 watcher, witness 8 attender, beholder, looker-on, observer, onlooker, passerby 9 spectator

by the book 9 by the rule 13 authoritarian 16 according to Hoyle

by the fact itself
  Latin: 9 ipso facto

by the grace of God
  Latin: 9 Dei gratia

by the law itself
  Latin: 8 ipso jure

by the month
  Latin: 9 per mensem

by the rule 9 by the book 11 as specified 13 authoritarian

by the skin of one's teeth 6 barely, hardly 8 only just, scarcely 11 by an eyelash

by the very nature of the deed
  Latin: 9 ipso facto

by the way
  French: 9 en passant

by virtue and arms
  Latin: 13 virtute et armis
  motto of: 11 Mississippi

byway 4 lane 5 alley 6 detour, street 8 shunpike

by what right?
  Latin: 7 quo jure

byword 3 law, saw 4 rule 5 adage, axiom, maxim, motto, truth 6 dictum, saying, slogan 7 precept, proverb 8 aphorism, apothegm 9 catchword, pet phrase, principle, watchword 10 shibboleth

Byzantine 6 complex 8 scheming 9 expedient, intricate 13 Machiavellian

Byzas
  founder of: 9 Byzantium
  father: 8 Poseidon

C

Caan, James
  born: 9 New York NY
  roles: 9 Funny Lady 10 Brian's Song,
    Rollerball 12 Brian Piccolo, The God-
    father 13 Sonny Corleone 17 Cinderella
    Liberty

Caanthus
  father: 7 Oceanus
  sister: 5 Melia
  killed by: 6 Apollo

cab 4 hack, taxi 7 taxi cab

Cab 15 Biblical measure

cabal 4 band, plan, plot, ring 5 junta 6 de-
    sign, league, scheme 7 faction 8 intrigue
    10 connivance, conspiracy 11 combina-
    tion, machination

cabalistic 6 arcane, mystic, occult, secret 7
    cryptic, obscure, strange 8 abstruse, eso-
    teric, mystical 10 mysterious, unknowable
    11 inscrutable 12 impenetrable, supernatu-
    ral, unfathomable 16 incomprehensible

cabaret 4 cafe, club 6 bistro 9 nightclub 10
    supper club
  French: 5 boite 11 boite de nuit

Cabaret
  director: 8 Bob Fosse
  based on stories by: 20 Christopher
    Isherwood
  cast: 8 Joel Grey 11 Fritz Wepper,
    Helmut Griem, Michael York 12 Liza
    Minnelli (Sally Bowles) 14 Marisa
    Berenson
  Oscar for: 7 actress (Minnelli) 8 director
    15 supporting actor (Grey)
  song: 12 The Money Song

cabbage 16 Brassica oleracea (Capitata
    Group)
  varieties: 3 Cow 4 Deer, Head, Wild 5
    John's, Savoy, Skunk 6 Celery 7 Chinese
    9 Flowering, Tronchuda 10 Portuguese
    11 Yellow skunk 12 Western skunk

Cabecar
  language family: 10 Talamancan
  location: 9 Costa Rica 12 Sixaola River
    14 Central America, Talamanca Plain
  intermixed with: 6 Bribri

Cabell, James Branch
  author of: 6 Jurgen 12 The High Place
    14 Figures of Earth 17 The Cream of the
    Jest

cabin 3 hut 4 room 5 hutch, lodge, shack 6
    shanty 7 cottage 8 bungalow, log cabin,
    quarters 9 stateroom 11 compartment

cabinet 3 box 4 case, file 5 chest 6 bureau
    7 council 8 advisors, cupboard, ministry 10
    breakfront, counselors, receptacle 11
    china closet 13 advisory board 14 chest of
    drawers

cable 4 cord, line, rope, wire 5 chain, wires
    6 hawser 7 mooring 8 wire line, wire rope
    12 electric wire 16 overseas telegram

Cable, George W
  author of: 8 Dr Sevier 13 Old Creole
    Days 15 The Grandissimes

cablegram 4 wire 5 cable 7 message 8
    wireless 16 overseas telegram

Cabot, Ephraim
  character in: 18 Desire Under the Elms
  author: 6 O'Neill

Caca
  origin: 5 Roman
  goddess of: 6 hearth
  corresponds to: 5 Vesta

Cacambo
  character in: 7 Candide
  author: 8 Voltaire

cache 4 heap 5 hoard, stock, store 8 hide-
    away 9 stockpile 11 hiding place, secret
    place

cachet 4 mark, seal 5 stamp, wafer 6 de-
    sign, slogan 7 capsule

cackle 7 chatter 10 harsh laugh 11 shrill
    laugh
  sound made by: 3 hen 4 chicken

cacophonous 5 harsh 6 off-key 7 grating,
    jarring, raucous 8 off-pitch, screechy, stri-
    dent 9 dissonant, out of tune, unmusical
    10 discordant 11 unmelodious 12 inharmo-
    nious, nonmelodious 13 disharmonious

cacophony 7 discord 9 harshness 10 dis-
    harmony, dissonance

cactus
  varieties: 3 Cob, Sun 4 Ball, Cane, Chin,
    Claw, Club, Comb, Crab, Hook, Lace,
    Leaf, Moon, Rose, Star, Toad, Vine, Yoke
    5 Agave, Apple, Brain, Chain, Coral,
    Crown, Devil, False, Giant, Leafy, Melon,
    Paper, Plain, Prism, Snake, Spice, Torch
    6 Barrel, Button, Cholla, Dagger, Dollar,
    Easter, Hatpin, Hot-dog, Myrtle, Nipple,
    Old-man, Orchid, Peanut, Pencil, Ribbon,
    Spider 7 Cushion, Eve's pin, Feather,
    Hatchet, Hat-rack, Jumping, Old-lady,
    Popcorn, Rainbow, Rattail, Redbird, Ser-
    pent, Thimble, Whisker 8 Cinnamon,
    Dumpling, Fishbone, Fishhook, Flapjack,
    Gold lace, Golf-ball, Hedgehog, Old-
    woman, Polka-dot, Pond-lily, Snowball,
    Snowdrop, Starfish, Tortoise, Turk's-cap
    9 Bird's nest, Chain-link, Christmas, Cow-
    tongue, Electrode, Fire-crown, Hairbrush,
    Lamb's-tail, Mistletoe, New old-man,
    Organ-pipe, Porcupine, Red orchid, Sea-
    urchin, Spineless, Teddy-bear, Toothpick,
    Totem-pole, Turk's-head, White chin 10
    Bluebarrel, Candelabra, Cotton-pole,

Easter-lily, Golden ball, Golden-star, Living-rock, Powder-puff, Silver ball, Strawberry, Unguentine, White torch, Wickerware **11** Frilled lace, Grizzly-bear, Joseph's coat, Large barrel, Scarlet ball, Woolly torch **12** Dancing-bones, Golden barrel, Mule-crippler, Scarlet crown, Thanksgiving **13** Colombian ball, Creeping-devil, Dutchman's pipe, Peruvian apple, Peruvian torch, Silver cluster **15** Golden bird's nest **16** Mexican dwarf tree **17** Burbank's spineless **18** Fishhook pincushion

Cacus
form: **5** giant
father: **6** Vulcan
eats: **3** men
killed by: **8** Hercules

cad 3 cur, rat **4** heel, lout **5** churl, knave, louse, rogue **6** rascal, rotter **7** bounder, caitiff, dastard, villain **9** scoundrel

cadaver 4 body **5** stiff **6** corpse **7** remains **8** dead body, deceased

cadaverous 4 pale **5** ashen, gaunt **6** chalky, pallid **7** deathly, ghastly **8** blanched **9** bloodless, deathlike **10** corpselike

caddisfly
variety: **5** micro **8** northern **9** fingernet, primitive, snailcase **10** longhorned, trumpetnet, tubemaking **11** netspinning

Caddoan
tribe: **6** Pawnee **14** Chahiksichhiks

caddy 3 box, can, tin **5** chest **6** coffer

cadence 4 beat, lilt **5** meter, pulse, swing, tempo, throb **6** accent, rhythm **7** measure

Caderousse
character in: **21** The Count of Monte Cristo
author: **5** Dumas (pere)

cadet 5 plebe **7** recruit, student **11** youngest son **14** military student

cadge 3 beg, bum **5** mooch **6** hustle, peddle, sponge **7** solicit, scrounge **9** panhandle

cadmium
chemical symbol: **2** Cd

Cadmus
form: **6** prince
realm: **9** Phoenicia
father: **6** Agenor
mother: **10** Telephassa
brother: **5** Cilix **7** Phoenix
sister: **6** Europa
wife: **8** Harmonia
son: **8** Illyrius **9** Polydorus
daughter: **3** Ino **5** Agave **6** Semele **7** Autonoe
introduced to the Greeks: **7** writing
founded: **6** Thebes
planted: **12** dragons teeth

Caduceus
staff of: **7** Mercury

Caeneus
also: **6** Caenis
member of: **9** Argonauts
gift: **15** invulnerability
former identity: **6** Caenis

Caenis
also: **7** Caeneus
father: **6** Elatus
violated by: **8** Poseidon
changed into: **3** man
subsequent identity: **7** Caeneus

caesar, Caesar 5 ruler **6** despot, tyrant **7** emperor **8** autocrat, dictator

Caesar, Julius
adopted son: **8** Octavian **14** Caesar Augustus
author of: **13** On the Civil War **14** On the Gallic War
battle: **4** Zela **5** Munda **7** Durazzo, Thapsus **8** Mytilene **9** Pharsalus **11** Dyrrhachium
conquered: **4** Gaul
crossed: **7** Rubicon (river)
defeated: **6** Pompey
lover: **9** Cleopatra
member of: **16** First Triumvirate
murdered by: **5** Casca **6** Brutus **7** Cassius
murdered on: **11** Ides of March
other triumvirs: **6** Pompey **7** Crassus
saying: **9** Et tu Brute? (Even you Brutus?) **12** Veni vidi vici (I came I saw I conquered)
wife: **7** Pompeia **8** Cornelia **9** Calpurnia

Caesar, Sid
partner: **11** Imogene Coca
born: **9** Yonkers NY
roles: **15** Your Show of Shows

Caesar and Cleopatra
author: **17** George Bernard Shaw

Caesar or Nothing
author: **9** Pio Baroja

caesura 5 break, pause **6** hiatus **12** interruption

cafe 3 bar, inn **5** diner **6** bistro, eatery, nitery, tavern **7** automat, beanery, cabaret **9** cafeteria, chophouse, hash house, lunchroom, nightclub **10** restaurant, supper club **11** bar and grill, coffeehouse, discotheque **12** luncheonette
French: **9** estaminet

cafe au lait 10 light brown **14** coffee with milk

cafe noir 11 black coffee

cage 3 pen **4** coop **5** pen in **6** coop up, encage, lock up, shut in **7** confine, impound **8** imprison, restrain, restrict **9** enclosure

cagey 3 sly **4** foxy, keen, wary, wily **5** alert, chary, leery, sharp **6** artful, crafty, shifty, shrewd **7** careful, cunning, heedful, prudent **8** cautious, discreet, watchful

Cagliari
capital of: **8** Sardinia

Cagney, James
nickname: **5** Jimmy
born: **9** New York NY
roles: **7** Ragtime **14** The Public Enemy **17** Yankee Doodle Dandy (Oscar) **19** Man of a Thousand Faces

Cagney and Lacey
cast: **8** Tyne Daly **11** Sharon Gless

Cahita
  tribe: 5 Yaqui
Cain
  father: 4 Adam
  mother: 3 Eve
  brother: 4 Abel, Seth
  home: 4 Eden
  son: 5 Enoch
  killed: 4 Abel
  traveled to: 3 Nod
Caine, Michael
  real name: 24 Maurice Joseph Micklewhite
  born: 6 London 7 England
  roles: 4 Zulu 5 Alfie 6 Sleuth 9 Deathtrap 13 Educating Rita 14 The Ipcress File
Caine Mutiny, The
  author: 10 Herman Wouk
  director: 13 Edward Dmytryk
  cast: 7 May Wynn 9 Lee Marvin 10 E G Marshall, Jose Ferrer, Van Johnson 13 Fred MacMurray, Robert Francis 14 Humphrey Bogart (Captain Queeg)
Caingua see 7 Guarani
Cairo
  Arab camp: 8 al-Fustat
  Arabic: 9 al-Qahirah
  capital of: 5 Egypt
  island: 5 Rodah 7 Zamalik
  landmark:
    mosque: 7 al-Azhar 11 Muhammed Ali
    statue: 8 Ramses II
    museum: 8 Egyptian
    river: 4 Nile
    Roman fortress: 7 Babylon
  rulers: 5 Turks 7 British, Saladin 8 Fatimids 9 Mamelukes 11 Ismail Pasha, Muhammed Ali 12 Ottoman Turks
  university: 7 Al-Azhar 8 Ain Shams, American
Cairo, Joel
  character in: 16 The Maltese Falcon
  author: 7 Hammett
caitiff 3 cad, cur, rat 4 heel 5 churl, knave, louse, rogue 6 rascal, rotter 7 bounder, dastard, villain 9 scoundrel 10 blackguard
cajole 4 coax 7 beguile, deceive, flatter, wheedle 8 blandish, inveigle, persuade
cajolery 7 blarney, coaxing, fawning 8 flattery, promises, soft soap 9 adulation, sweet talk, wheedling 10 enticement, inveigling, persuasion 11 beguilement 12 blandishment
cake 3 bar, bun, dry 4 lump, mass 5 block, crust, tort 6 cookie, eclair, gateau, harden, pastry, 7 congeal, cupcake, thicken 8 compress, solidify 9 coagulate, sweet roll 11 consolidate
Cakes and Ale
  author: 16 W Somerset Maugham
cakewalk 5 cinch, dance 9 promenade 12 dance contest
calaboose 3 pen 4 jail, stir 6 prison 7 slammer 8 hoosegow
Calah
  founder: 6 Nimrod

Calais
  origin: 5 Greek
  member of: 9 Argonauts
  father: 6 Boreas
  mother: 8 Orithyia
  twin brother: 5 Zetes
calamitous 5 fatal 6 tragic, woeful 7 adverse, baleful, harmful, ruinous, unlucky 8 dreadful 9 blighting 10 disastrous, pernicious 11 cataclysmic, deleterious, destructive, detrimental, distressful, unfortunate 12 catastrophic
calamity 3 ill, woe 4 blow, ruin 5 trial 6 misery, mishap 7 bad luck, failure, ill wind, reverse, scourge, tragedy, trouble, undoing 8 disaster, distress, downfall, hardship 9 adversity, cataclysm, mischance 10 affliction, ill fortune, misfortune 11 catastrophe, tribulation 13 sea of troubles 15 stroke of ill luck
calando
  music: 22 getting weaker and slower
Calchas
  vocation: 10 soothsayer
  father: 7 Thestor
  burial place: 6 Notium
calcium
  chemical symbol: 2 Ca
calculate 4 mean, plan 5 add up, aim at, count, judge, sum up 6 design, devise, figure, intend, reckon 7 compute, measure, predict, project, surmise, work out 8 estimate 9 ascertain, determine 10 conjecture
calculated 7 planned 10 deliberate, purposeful, thought out 11 intentional, prearranged 12 premeditated
calculating 3 sly 4 foxy, wily 6 artful, crafty, shrewd, tricky 7 cunning, devious 8 plotting, scheming 9 designing 10 contriving, intriguing 12 manipulative 13 Machiavellian
calculating machine
  invented by: 7 Babbage
calculation 6 answer, result 8 figuring, judgment 9 reckoning 10 estimation 11 computation
calculator 6 abacus 7 counter, thinker 8 computer, reckoner
Calcutta
  captured by: 5 Clive
  founded by: 23 British East India Company
  landmark: 10 Jain Temple 12 Howrah Bridge, Indian Museum 16 Botanical Gardens, Victoria Memorial 17 Zoological Gardens 18 Dakshineswar Temple
  opposite city: 6 Howrah
  river: 7 Hooghly
  state: 10 West Bengal
Calder, Alexander
  born: 14 Philadelphia PA
  sculptures also called: 7 mobiles
  artwork: 3 Man 5 Whale 6 Spiral 10 Teodelapio 12 Ticket Window 13 La Grande Voile 14 The Brass Family 23 Lobster Traps and Fish Tail

Calderon de la Barca, Pedro
　author of: 12 Life Is a Dream
caldron, cauldron 3 pot 6 boiler, kettle
Caldwell, Erskine
　author of: 10 Georgia Boy 11 Tobacco
　　Road 14 God's Little Acre
Caldwell, Taylor
　author of: 12 Answer as a Man 13 A Pillar of Iron 14 Great Lion of God 17 Testimony of Two Men, The Devil's Advocate 19 Bright Flows the River 20 Glory and the Lightning 22 The Captains and the Kings 24 Dear and Glorious Physician
Caleb
　father: 8 Jepunneh
　brother: 5 Kenaz
　daughter: 6 Achash
　nephew: 7 Othniel
　descendant: 8 Calebite
Caleb Williams
　author: 13 William Godwin
Caledonia see 8 Scotland
calendar 4 list 5 chart, diary, table 6 agenda, docket 7 day book, program 8 register, schedule
Caletor
　origin: 5 Greek
　mentioned in: 5 Iliad
　cousin: 6 Hector
　killed by: 14 Telamonian Ajax
calf 4 veal 5 dogie 6 weaner 7 leg part
　young of: 3 cow 4 bull, seal 5 whale 8 elephant
Calgary
　hockey team: 6 Flames
Calhern, Louis
　real name: 13 Carl Henry Vogt
　born: 10 Brooklyn NY
　roles: 8 King Lear 12 Julius Caesar 15 Annie Get Your Gun 16 The Asphalt Jungle 20 The Magnificent Yankee
Calhoun, Rory
　real name: 20 Francis Timothy Durgin
　born: 12 Los Angeles CA
　roles: 8 The Texan 21 Treasure of Pancho Villa 22 How to Marry a Millionaire, Requiem for a Heavyweight
Caliban
　character in: 10 The Tempest
　author: 11 Shakespeare
caliber 4 bore, rank 5 gifts, merit, place, power, scope, skill, worth 6 repute, talent 7 ability, quality, stature 8 capacity, diameter, eminence, position, prestige 10 capability, competence, estimation, excellence, importance, prominence, reputation 11 achievement, distinction
California
　abbreviation: 2 CA 3 Cal 5 Calif
　nickname: 6 Golden 8 Eldorado 12 Promised Land
　capital: 10 Sacramento
　largest city: 10 Los Angeles
　others: 4 Lodi 5 Azusa, Chico, Chino, Indio 6 Blythe, Carmel, Covina, Eureka, Fresno, Lompoc, Merced, Oxnard, Pomona, Sonoma, Tulare 7 Alameda, Ana-
heim, Burbank, Gardena, Needles, Oakland, Salinas, Vallejo, Visalia 8 Altadena, Berkeley, Palo Alto, Pasadena, Redlands, San Diego, Stockton 9 Cucamonga, Long Beach 11 Palm Springs, Santa Monica 12 Beverly Hills, San Francisco, Santa Barbara
　college: 3 USC 4 UCLA 5 Mills 6 Pitzer, Pomona 7 Caltech, Chapman, Scripps 8 Stanford, Whittier 10 Occidental, Pepperdine
　explorer: 6 Cortez
　feature:
　amusement park: 10 Disneyland 15 Knotts Berry Farm
　area: 9 Hollywood 15 Fishermans Wharf
　dam: 6 Hoover, Shasta 7 Boulder
　island prison: 8 Alcatraz
　mill: 7 Sutters
　national park: 7 Redwood, Sequoia 8 Yosemite 11 Kings Canyon 14 Channel Islands, Lassen Volcanic
　parade: 4 Rose
　prison: 6 Folsom 10 San Quentin
　tribe: 4 Hupa, Pomo, Yana, Yuki 5 Karok, Maidu, Miwok, Wappo, Wiyot, Yurok 6 Patwin, Shasta, Tolowa, Yokuts 7 Chumash, Luiseno, Salinan, Serrano 8 Dieguено
　people: 6 Sutter 10 Earl Warren 11 Robert Frost 13 George S Patton, John Steinbeck 14 William Saroyan
　island: 4 Goat, Mare 7 Anacapo, Channel 8 Alcatraz, Catalina, Coronado 9 Farallone
　lake: 4 Mono, Soda 5 Clear, Eagle, Owens, Tahoe 6 Salton, Tulare 7 Almanor 8 Elsinore 9 Berryessa
　land rank: 5 third
　mountain: 4 Muir 5 Coast 6 Lassen, Shasta, Wilson 7 Cascade, Klamath, Palomar, Whitney 10 Peninsular, Transverse 12 Sierra Nevada
　highest point: 7 Whitney
　physical feature:
　bay: 8 Monterey, San Diego 12 San Francisco
　cape: 9 Mendocino
　desert: 6 Mohave, Mojave 8 Colorado
　fault: 10 San Andreas
　glacier: 8 Palisade
　sea: 6 Cortez 7 Pacific
　tree: 7 redwood
　valley: 5 Death
　volcano: 6 Lassen
　wind: 7 Collada 8 Santa Ana
　president: 13 Richard M Nixon, Ronald W Reagan
　river: 3 Eel, Mad, Pit 4 Kern 5 Kings, Owens, Putah, Smith, Stony 6 Little, Merced, Salmon 7 Feather, Klamath, Rubicon, Russian, Salinas, Trinity, Truckee 10 Sacramento, San Jacinto, San Joaquin, Stanislaus
　state admission: 11 thirty-first
　state bird: 21 California Valley quail
　state fish: 21 California golden trout

state flower: 11 golden poppy
state motto: 6 Eureka (I have found it)
state song: 18 I Love You California
state symbol: 11 grizzly bear
state tree: 17 California redwood
baseball team: 6 Angels, Giants, Padres 7 Dodgers
basketball team: 6 Lakers 8 Clippers 19 Golden State Warriors
football team: 4 Rams 7 Raiders 8 Chargers 11 Forty-Niners

Calinieff, Martin
real name of: 13 Michael Callan

Calinky State
nickname of: 13 South Carolina

calisay
type: 7 liqueur
origin: 5 Spain 9 Catalonia
flavor: 5 herbs 7 quinine

Calkins, Richard
creator/artist of: 10 Buck Rogers

call 3 ask, bid, cry, dub, tag 4 bawl, buzz, hail, name, need, plea, ring, roar, stop, term, yell 5 cause, claim, label, order, phone, rally, right, shout, style, title, visit 6 appeal, ask for, bellow, charge, clamor, cry out, decree, demand, direct, drop in, excuse, gather, halloo, holler, invite, invoke, know as, muster, notice, outcry, pray to, reason, scream, stop by, summon 7 collect, command, contact, convene, convoke, declare, entitle, entreat, grounds, refer to, request, require, specify, stop off, summons, warrant 8 announce, appeal to, assemble, christen, entreaty, identify, instruct, look in on, occasion, petition, proclaim 9 crying out, designate, direction, pay a visit, telephone 10 describe as, invitation, supplicate 11 declaration, instruction 12 announcement, call together, characterize, proclamation, supplication 13 justification

Callan, Michael
real name: 15 Martin Calinieff
born: 14 Philadelphia PA
roles: 9 Cat Ballou 10 The Interns 18 Gidget Goes Hawaiian, The Flying Fontaines 23 The Magnificent Seven Ride

call for 4 need 6 demand, pick up 7 request, require

call forth 4 spur 5 evoke, raise 6 arouse, awaken, excite, incite, invoke, kindle, stir up 7 command, conjure, provoke 8 summon up 9 make aware, stimulate 10 make appear

Callidice
form: 5 queen
realm: 10 Thesprotia
husband: 8 Odysseus
son: 10 Polypoetes

calling 3 job 4 line, work 5 craft, field, forte, trade 6 career, crying, living, metier, outcry 7 hailing, mission, passion, yelling 8 activity, business, devotion, function, province, shouting, vocation 9 bellowing, crying out, first love, hallooing, life's work, screaming, specialty 10 assignment, attachment, dedication, employment, enthusiasm, livelihood, occupation, profession, walk of life 14 bread and butter, means of support, specialization

calling off 6 ending 7 halting 8 giving up 11 termination 12 backing out of, cancellation

calling oneself thus
French: 9 soi-disant

Calliope
member of: 5 Muses
presided over: 10 epic poetry
father: 4 Zeus
mother: 9 Mnemosyne
son: 7 Orpheus

Callipolis
father: 9 Alcathous

Callirrhoe, Callirhoe
father: 6 Oeneus 8 Achelous
husband: 4 Tros 8 Alcmaeon
son: 4 Ilus 8 Ganymede 10 Amphoterus
ended plague in: 7 Calydon
death by: 9 sacrifice

Calliste
epithet of: 7 Artemis
means: 7 fairest

Callisto
form: 5 nymph
attended: 7 Artemis
loved: 4 Zeus
changed into: 4 bear
killed by: 7 Artemis

call off 3 end 4 halt 5 abort 6 cancel, give up 8 postpone 9 back out of, terminate 10 summon away 12 dispense with

Call of the Wild, The
author: 10 Jack London
dog: 4 Buck
master: 12 John Thornton

callous 4 cold, hard 5 cruel, horny, tough 6 inured 8 hardened, uncaring 9 apathetic, heartless, unfeeling 11 hard-hearted, indifferent, insensitive 12 thick-skinned, unresponsive 13 dispassionate, unsympathetic 14 pachydermatous

call out 3 cry 4 bawl, hail, yell 5 shout 6 bellow, cry out, holler, summon 9 challenge

callow 3 raw 5 crude, green, naive 7 artless, awkward, puerile, shallow, untried 8 childish, ignorant, immature, juvenile 9 infantile 10 sophomoric, uninformed, unschooled, unseasoned 11 hard-nosed, uninitiated 13 inexperienced 15 unsophisticated

call to 4 hail 5 greet 6 accost, salute 7 address, shout at

call to account 5 chide, scold 6 accuse, charge, rebuke 7 arraign, bawl out, censure, chasten, reprove, upbraid 8 admonish, denounce, reproach 9 criticize, dress down, reprimand 10 take to task 11 remonstrate

call to arms 6 war cry 9 battle cry 11 rallying cry

call to order 4 open 6 muster 7 convene, convoke

call upon 3 ask, bid 4 urge 5 visit 6 charge, enjoin, exhort, invite, invoke 7 beseech, entreat, request, require 8 appeal to, petition, summon up 9 encourage 11 acknowledge

callused 4 hard 5 horny, tough 8 hardened 12 thick-skinned 14 pachydermatous

calm 4 cool, ease, mild 5 allay, balmy, bland, quell, quiet, still 6 becalm, gentle, lessen, pacify, placid, reduce, repose, sedate, serene, smooth, soothe, subdue 7 assuage, collect, compose, cool off, halcyon, mollify, pacific, placate, relaxed, relieve 8 composed, coolness, diminish, mitigate, moderate, peaceful, serenity, tranquil, unshaken 9 alleviate, collected, composure, impassive, placidity, quietness, stillness, unexcited, unruffled 10 cool-headed, motionless, simmer down, smoothness, unagitated, untroubled 11 impassivity, passionless, restfulness, self-control, tranquility, tranquilize, undisturbed, unflappable, unperturbed 12 peacefulness, tranquility, windlessness 13 imperturbable, self-possessed, stormlessness 14 self-possession 16 imperturbability

calmness 5 poise 6 aplomb 8 coolness, serenity 9 composure, placidity, sangfroid, stillness 10 equanimity, steadiness 11 self-control, tranquility 12 peacefulness, tranquility 14 presence of mind, self-possession 16 imperturbability

Calpurnia
   character in: 12 Julius Caesar
   author: 11 Shakespeare

calumnious 8 libelous 9 maligning, vilifying 10 defamatory, derogatory, slanderous 11 disparaging

calumny 4 barb, slur 5 libel, smear 6 malice 7 slander 8 innuendo 9 aspersion 10 backbiting, defamation, derogation, revilement 11 denigration, deprecation, insinuation 12 backstabbing, calumniation, depreciation, vilification 13 animadversion, disparagement, malicious lies

calvados
   type: 6 brandy
   origin: 6 France 8 Normandy
   flavor: 5 apple
   aged in: 3 oak

Calvary 8 Golgotha
   means: 10 skull place

Calyce
   father: 6 Aeolus
   mother: 7 Enarete
   son: 8 Endymion

Calydonian boar
   sent by: 5 Diana
   killed by: 8 Meleager

Calydonian hunt
   pursuit of: 4 boar

Calypso
   form: 5 nymph
   home: 6 Ogygia
   father: 10 Titan Atlas
   detained by: 8 Odysseus
   for: 10 seven years

calyx 4 husk 5 sepal

cam 3 cog 4 disk 8 cylinder 10 projection
   located on: 5 shaft, wheel
   motion: 7 rocking 8 circular 12 back and forth

camaraderie 7 jollity 8 bonhomie, good will 10 affability, clubbiness, fellowship, friendship 11 brotherhood, comradeship, sociability 12 congeniality, conviviality, friendliness 13 companionship, esprit de corps 14 good-fellowship

Camarasaurus
   type: 8 dinosaur, sauropod
   location: 12 United States
   period: 8 Jurassic

Cambodia
   other name: 7 Camboja 8 Cambodge 9 Kampuchea
   capital/largest city: 8 Pnom-Penh
   others: 3 Som 4 Ream 5 Takeo 6 Kampot, Kratie, Pursat 7 Kohnieh, Kompong, Kracheh, Rovieng, Samrong 8 Siem Reap, Sisophon 10 Battambang, Stung Treng 11 Kompong Cham 12 Krungkoh Kong 13 Sihanoukville
   head of state: 4 King
   monetary unit: 3 sen 4 quan, riel 6 puttan 7 piaster
   weight: 4 mace, tael
   island: 4 Kong, Rong
   lake: 8 Tonle Sap
   mountain: 3 Pan 7 Dangrek, Dong Rek 8 Cardamom, Elephant
   highest point: 10 Phnom Aoral, Phnom Aural
   river: 3 San, Sen 5 Sreng 6 Bassae, Chinit, Mekong, Porong, Pursat, Srepok 7 Kamlong, Sekhong 8 Tonle Sap
   physical feature:
     bay: 10 Kompongsom
     cape: 5 Samit
     gulf: 4 Siam 8 Thailand
   people: 4 Cham, Thai 5 Khmer 7 Chinese 10 Vietnamese
     leader: 6 Pol Pot 8 Sihanouk
   language: 5 Khmer 6 French 9 Cambodian 10 Vietnamese
   religion: 7 animism 8 Buddhism 12 Christianity
   places:
     ruins/temple: 6 Angkor 9 Angkor Wat
   feature:
     Communist group: 10 Khmer Rouge

Cambria *see* 5 Wales

cambric 5 cloth, linen 6 cotton, fabric 8 material

camel
   called: 13 beast of burden 15 ship of the desert
   chews: 3 cud
   group: 4 herd
   habitat: 4 Asia 6 Africa, desert
   kind: 7 Arabian 8 Bactrian 9 dromedary
   number of humps: 3 one, two
   species: 6 mammal
   type of: 8 ruminant
   young: 4 calf

camellia
varieties: 5 Silky 6 Common 8 Mountain, Sasanqua
Camenae
means: 11 foretellers
form: 6 nymphs 7 deities
gift: 8 prophecy
names: 6 Egeria 8 Carmenta 9 Antevorta, Postvorta
habitat: 8 fountain
correspond to: 5 Muses
camera
invented by:
Kodak: 6 Walker 7 Eastman
Polaroid: 4 Land
photography: 6 Niepce, Talbot 8 Daguerre
film, celluloid: 6 Edison 11 Reichenbach
film, transparent: 7 Eastman, Goodwin
color photo: 4 Ives
Cameroon
capital: 7 Yaounde
largest city: 6 Douala
others: 3 Wum 4 Bali, Buea, Edea, Tiko 5 Kumba, Lomie, Mamfe 6 Garona, Maroua 7 Batouri, Dschang, Ebolowa, Foumban 8 Victoria 10 N'Gaoundere, N'Kongsamba
monetary unit: 5 franc 7 centime
island: 5 Nanny 8 Fernando
lake: 4 Chad
mountain: 5 Mbabo 7 Bambuto, Kapsiki, Mandara 8 Batandji 9 Atlantika
highest point: 8 Cameroon
river: 3 Dja, Lom 4 Faro, Mbam, Vina 5 Benue, Campo, Cross, Kadei, Mbere, Nyong, N'Goko, Sanga, Shari 6 Djerem, Ivindo, Logone, Sanaga
sea: 8 Atlantic
physical feature:
cape: 10 Debundscha
gulf: 6 Guinea
plateau: 7 Adamawa 8 Mambilla
people: 3 Abo, Edo, Ibo 4 Beti, Bulu, Ekoi, Ijaw, Sara 5 Bantu, Bassa, Kirdi, Pygmy, Tikar 6 Bamoun, Donala, Ewondo, Fulani, Ibibio 7 Bakweri 8 Bamileke
Fulani chief: 7 Lamidos
language: 4 Bulu 5 Bantu, Bassa, Hausa 6 Douala, Ewondo, French, Fulani 7 English 8 Bamileke, Fulfulde
religion: 5 Islam 7 animism 12 Christianity
places:
home of prime minister: 7 Schloss
Camilla
form: 5 woman
occupation: 7 warrior
father: 7 Metabus
mother: 7 Casmila
fought with: 6 Turnus
fought against: 6 Aeneas
Camille
also: 17 La Dame aux camelias
author: 14 Alexander Dumas (fils)

character: 6 Nanine 11 Armand Duval 17 Marguerite Gautier (Camille)
director: 11 George Cukor
cast: 10 Greta Garbo (Camille) 12 Henry Daniell, Robert Taylor (Armand) 14 Elizabeth Allan, Laura Hope Crews 15 Lionel Barrymore
Camillo
character in: 14 The Winter's Tale
author: 11 Shakespeare
Camirus
origin: 5 Greek
grandfather: 6 Helios, Helius
camisole 3 top 4 slip 6 jacket 10 underwaist
camouflage 4 hide, mask, veil 5 blind, cloak, cover, front 6 screen, shroud 7 conceal, cover up 8 disguise 10 masquerade, subterfuge 11 concealment
camouflaged 6 hidden, masked 7 cloaked 8 shrouded 9 concealed, disguised
camp 4 tent 5 tents 7 bivouac, lodging, rough it 8 army base, barracks, quarters 10 pitch a tent
campaign 3 run 4 push 5 drive, stump 6 action, effort 7 crusade 8 endeavor, movement 9 offensive, operation 11 electioneer, whistle-stop 12 battle series, beat the drums, solicit votes
campanile 6 belfry 9 bell tower
campari
type: 7 bitters 8 aperitif
origin: 5 Italy
Campe
form: 8 old woman
occupation: 6 jailer
place: 8 Tartarus
campground 7 bivouac 8 tent city 16 temporary shelter
Campin, Robert
born: 8 Flanders
also known as/identified with: 14 Master of Merode 16 Master of Flemalle
artwork: 10 St Veronica, The Trinity 13 The Entombment 16 Merode Altarpiece (Merode Triptych) 17 The Virgin and Child 18 The Thief on the Cross
Camptosaurus
type: 8 dinosaur 10 ornithopod
location: 12 North America
period: 8 Jurassic
characteristic: 10 duck-billed
Camus, Albert
author of: 4 L'ete 6 Summer 7 The Fall 8 Caligula, The Rebel 9 The Plague 11 A Happy Death, The Stranger 12 Cross Purpose 17 The Myth of Sisyphus
can 3 tin 4 buns, fire, rump, seat 5 fanny, put up 6 bottom 8 backside, buttocks, preserve 9 container, fundament, give the ax
Canaan
father: 3 Ham
brother: 4 Cush
grandfather: 4 Noah
known as: 12 promised land
see also 6 Israel

Canace
  father: 6 Aeolus
  brother: 8 Macareus
  death by: 7 suicide
Canada
  capital: 6 Ottawa
  largest city: 8 Montreal
  others: 4 Hull 5 Banff, Laval 6 Dawson, Guelph, London, Oshawa, Quebec, Regina, Sarnia, Val d'or 7 Calgary, Halifax, Moncton, Nanaimo, Sudbury, Toronto, Welland, Windsor 8 Edmonton, Hamilton, Kingston, Moose Jaw, Victoria, Winnipeg 9 Saskatoon, Vancouver 10 Port Arthur, Sherbrooke 11 Fredericton 12 Niagara Falls, Peterborough, Prince Albert, Prince George 13 Charlottetown 21 St Catherines Stratford
  school: 3 UBC 5 Laval 6 McGill, Queens 7 Toronto 8 McMaster, Montreal 9 Concordia, Dalhousie 11 Simon Fraser
  division: 5 Yukon 6 Quebec 7 Alberta, Ontario 8 Manitoba 10 Nova Scotia 12 Newfoundland, New Brunswick, Saskatchewan 15 British Columbia 18 Prince Edward Island 20 Northwest Territories
  New division: 7 Nunavut
  head of state: 14 British monarch 15 governor general
  measure: 3 ton 5 minot, perch, point 6 arpent 7 chainon
  island: 4 Read 5 Banks, Bylot, Coats, Devon, Grand, Manan, Parry, Sable 6 Baffin, Breton, Mansel, Middle 7 Belcher 8 Bathurst, Magdalen, Victoria 9 Anticosti, Ellesmere, Vancouver 10 Campobello, Manitoulin 11 Southampton 14 Queen Charlotte
  lake: 4 Cree, Erie, Gras, Seul 5 Garry, Huron, Rainy 6 Louise, St John 7 Abitibi, Dubawnt, Nipigon, Ontario, Testlin 8 Kootenay, Manitoba, Okanagan, Reindeer, Superior, Winnipeg 9 Athabaska, Great Bear, Nipissing 10 Great Slave, Mistassini 12 Winnipegosis
  mountain: 5 Coast, Royal 6 Robson, Skeena 7 Cariboo, Cascade, Purcell, Rockies, Selkirk, St Elias 8 Columbia, Hazelton, Monashee 9 Mackenzie, Notre Dame, Tremblant 10 Laurentian, Richardson, Shickshock 14 Jacques Cartier
  highest point: 5 Logan
  river: 3 Hay, Red 4 Peel 5 Liard, Peace, Slave, Yukon 6 Albany, Fraser, Nelson, Nicola, Ottawa, Skeena, St John, Thames, Thelon 7 St Marys 8 Columbia, Gatineau, Kootenay, Petawawa, Saguenay 9 Athabasca, Athapaska, Churchill, Mackenzie, Richelieu 10 Coppermine, St Lawrence 11 Assiniboine, 12 Saskatchewan
  sea: 6 Arctic 7 Pacific 8 Atlantic, Labrador
  physical features:
  bay: 5 Basin, Fundy, Hecla, James, Minas 6 Baffin, Griper, Hudson, Ungava 8 Georgian
  canal: 3 Soo 7 Welland 10 Wellington
  cape: 5 Canso
  falls: 7 Niagara 9 Horseshoe
  gulf: 10 St Lawrence
  pass: 8 Chilkoot
  peninsula: 5 Gaspe 7 Boothia 8 Labrador, Melville
  plain: 11 Barren lands
  port: 6 Quebec 7 St Johns 8 Hamilton, Victoria 9 Churchill
  strait: 5 Cabot, Davis, Dease 6 Hecate, Hudson 7 Georgia 9 Belle Isle 10 Juan de Fuca
  people: 5 Inuit 6 Canuck, Eskimo, French 7 English
  explorer: 5 Cabot 6 Fraser, Joliet 7 Cartier, LaSalle, Selkirk 8 Thompson 9 Champlain, MacKenzie, Marquette
  leader: 4 King, Riel 5 Clark 6 Borden 7 Laurier, Trudeau 8 Campbell, Chretien, Mulroney 9 Macdonald, St Laurent 11 Diefenbaker
  language: 6 Eskimo, French 7 English
  religion: 8 Anglican 13 Roman Catholic 20 United Church of Canada
  places:
  battlefield: 15 Plains of Abraham
  national park: 4 Yoho 5 Banff 6 Jasper 7 Glacier 8 Kootenay 9 Elk Island 10 La Maurice, Revelstoke 11 Wood Buffalo 12 Prince Albert 13 Waterton Lakes
  resort: 5 Banff 10 Lake Louise
  feature:
  airport: 6 Gander
  emblem: 9 maple leaf
  fish: 5 charr, trout
  flower: 10 Juneflower
  police: 8 Mounties 12 Royal Mounted
  food:
  soup: 7 rubaboo
canaille 6 proles, rabble 8 riffraff 9 commoners, hoi polloi 11 proletariat 13 great unwashed
canal 4 duct, tube 7 channel, conduit, passage 8 aqueduct
Canaletto
  real name: 20 Giovanni Antonio Canal
  born: 5 Italy 6 Venice
  artwork: 18 The Stonemason's Yard
canard 4 hoax 5 rumor 7 slander 9 falsehood 12 exaggeration
canasta
  number of players: 4 four
  cards/hand: 6 eleven
  meld: 12 three of a kind
  wild card: 5 deuce, joker
Canberra
  capital of: 9 Australia
  territory: 13 New South Wales 26 Australian Capital Territory
  lake: 13 Burley Griffin
cancel 4 void 5 annul, erase, quash 6 delete, offset, recall, recant, repeal, revoke 7 abolish, call off, nullify, rescind, retract, vitiate 8 abrogate, call back, set aside 9 re-

pudiate **10** balance out, blue-pencil, do away with, invalidate, neutralize **11** countermand **12** dispense with **13** compensate for **14** counterbalance **18** declare null and void

cancellation 6 repeal **9** abolition **10** abrogation, effacement, rescinding, revocation **11** abolishment, eradication, repudiation, termination

cancer 3 rot **6** plague **7** sarcoma, scourge **8** neoplasm, sickness **9** carcinoma **10** malignancy **14** malignant tumor **15** malignant growth

Cancer
  symbol: 4 crab
  planet: 4 Moon
  rules: 4 home **6** family
  born: 4 July, June

Cancer Ward, The
  author: 21 Aleksandr Solzhenitsyn

candelabrum 7 menorah **8** dikerion **9** girandole, trikerion **11** candlestick **12** candleholder

Candia *see* **5** Crete

candid 4 fair, free, just, open **5** blunt, frank, plain **6** direct, honest **7** genuine, natural, relaxed, sincere, unposed **8** informal, outright, truthful **9** downright, impromptu, outspoken **10** forthright **11** plain spoken, spontaneous, unvarnished **14** extemporaneous **15** straightforward

Candida
  author: 17 George Bernard Shaw

candidate 7 hopeful, nominee **8** aspirant, eligible **9** applicant, contender, job seeker **10** competitor, contestant **11** possibility **12** office seeker

Candid Camera
  host: 9 Allen Funt
  co-host: 11 Bess Myerson **12** Durward Kirby **13** Arthur Godfrey

Candide
  author: 8 Voltaire
  character: 6 Martin **7** Cacambo **8** Pangloss **9** Cunegonde **11** Admiral Byng **17** Thunder-ten-Tronckh

candidness 6 candor **7** honesty, openess **9** frankness, sincerity **10** directness **12** truthfulness **13** guilelessness

candle 3 dip, wax **5** light, taper **6** bougie, cierge, tallow **9** rush light

candleholder, candlestick 6 sconce **7** menorah **8** dikerion **9** girandole, trikerion **10** chandelier **11** candelabrum

candor 7 honesty **8** fairness, justness, openness **9** bluntness, frankness, sincerity **10** directness **11** artlessness **12** impartiality, truthfulness **14** forthrightness **15** plainspokenness **19** straightforwardness

candy 3 bar **4** kiss **5** cream, fudge, jelly, sweet, taffy **6** bonbon, comfit, dainty, nougat, sweets, toffee **7** brittle, caramel, fondant, gumdrop, praline **8** lollipop **9** chocolate, jellybean, sweetmeat **10** confection **12** all-day sucker **13** confectionery, peanut brittle

cane 3 hit, rap, rod, tan **4** beat, drub, flog, lash, whip **5** baste, flail, smite, staff, stick, whack **6** strike, switch, thrash, wallop **7** trounce **12** walking stick

cane 11 Arundinaria
  varieties: 4 Dumb, Wild **5** Arrow, Sugar **6** Rattan, Switch, Tobago, Tonkin **7** Tsingli **8** Southern **11** Spotted dumb **12** Chinese sweet **14** Yellow-leaf dumb

Canea
  capital of: 5 Crete

Canens
  father: 5 Janus
  mother: 7 Venilia
  betrothed to: 5 Picus
  cried over: 5 Picus
  death by: 6 crying

Canephora
  form: 7 maidens
  carried: 7 baskets

Canetti, Elias
  author of: 8 Auto da Fe **12** Tower of Babel **14** Crowds and Power **15** The Torch in My Ear **16** Kafka's Other Trial, The Tongue Set Free

Caniff, Milton
  creator/artist of: 10 Dickie Dare **11** Steve Canyon **14** The Gay Thirties **18** Terry and the Pirates

canine 3 cur, dog, fox, pup **4** mutt, wolf **5** hound, hyena, puppy **6** coyote, cuspid, jackal **7** mongrel **8** eyetooth

canker 4 sore **5** ulcer **6** blight, cancer, lesion **9** mouth sore **12** inflammation

Cannibal Galaxy, The
  author: 12 Cynthia Ozick

cannon 3 bit, gun **4** bone **5** carom **6** mortar **7** battery **8** field gun, howitzer, ordnance **9** artillery **10** field piece, mounted gun, pickpocket

Cannon
  character: 11 Frank Cannon
  cast: 13 William Conrad

Cannon, Dyan
  real name: 19 Samille Diane Friesen
  husband: 9 Cary Grant
  born: 8 Tacoma WA
  roles: 6 Shamus **9** Deathtrap **13** Heaven Can Wait **15** Such Good Friends **19** Bob & Carol & Ted & Alice **23** Revenge of the Pink Panther

cannonade 5 burst, salvo **6** volley **7** barrage, battery **8** shelling **9** fusillade **11** bombardment

canny 4 foxy, wary, wily, wise **5** cagey, sharp **6** artful, astute, clever, crafty, shrewd, subtle **7** careful, cunning, knowing **8** skillful **9** judicious, sagacious **10** convincing **11** circumspect, intelligent **13** perspicacious

Cano, Alonso
  born: 5 Spain **7** Granada
  artwork: 16 Granada Cathedral (facade) **18** Madonna of the Rosary **20** Immaculate Conception **23** The Seven Joys of the Virgin

canoe 4 boat 5 bungo, kayak 6 dugout 7 pirogue

canoeing
  athlete: 11 Marcia Smoke

canon 3 law 4 code, rule 5 dogma, edict, model, order 6 decree 7 pattern, precept, statute 8 doctrine, standard 9 bench mark, criterion, ordinance, principle, yardstick 10 regulation, touchstone

canonical 6 proper 8 accepted, approved, official orthodox 9 authentic, customary 10 authorized, legitimate, recognized, sanctioned 12 conventional 13 authoritative

Canonization, The
  author: 9 John Donne

canopy 4 hood 5 cover 6 awning, tester 8 covering

Canova, Antonio
  born: 5 Italy 8 Possagno
  artwork: 7 Perseus 12 Venus Victrix (Pauline Bonaparte Borghese) 14 Cupid and Psyche 16 Letizia Bonaparte 17 Daedalus and Icarus

Cansino, Margarita Carmen
  real name of: 12 Rita Hayworth

cant 4 sham, talk 5 argot, lingo, slang 6 humbug, jargon 8 parlance, pretense 9 hypocrisy 10 lip service, vernacular 11 insincerity 15 pretentiousness 17 sanctimoniousness

cantabile
  music: 7 flowing, singing 8 songlike

cantaloupe 5 fruit, melon 9 muskmelon

cantankerous 4 mean 5 cross, huffy, short, sulky, surly, testy 6 cranky, crusty, grumpy, morose, sullen, touchy 7 bearish, crabbed, fretful, grouchy, peevish, waspish 8 choleric, churlish, contrary, snappish 9 irascible, irritable, splenetic 10 ill-humored, ill-natured 11 contentious, ill-tempered, quarrelsome 12 disagreeable 13 argumentative

cantatrice 6 singer 9 chanteuse 10 songstress 18 professional singer

canteen 2 PX 4 club 5 flask 6 bottle 10 commissary 11 pocket flask 12 post exchange

canter 4 gait, lope, trot 6 gallop, singer, whiner

Canterbury Tales, The
  author: 15 Geoffrey Chaucer
  starting point: 9 Southwark, Tabard Inn
  goal:
    tomb of: 6 Becket
  character/tale: 3 Nun 4 Cook, Dyer, Monk 5 Canon, Friar, Reeve, Webbe 6 Knight, Miller, Parson, Squire, Yeoman 7 Shipman, Tapicer 8 Franklin, Manciple, Merchant, Pardoner, Pricress, Summoner 9 Carpenter, Ploughman 10 Wife of Bath 11 Haberdasher 13 Clerk of Oxford, Sergeant of Law 14 Doctor of Physic

Canthus
  member of: 9 Argonauts

Cantor, Eddie
  real name: 21 B Edward Israel Iskowitz
  nickname: 9 Banjo Eyes
  wife: 9 Ida Tobias
  born: 9 New York NY
  roles: 7 Whoopee 8 Kid Boots 9 Banjo Eyes

cantor of a synagogue
  Hebrew: 5 hazan

Cantos
  author: 9 Ezra Pound

can't stand 4 hate 5 abhor 6 detest, eschew, loathe 7 despise 8 execrate 9 abominate, can't abide 11 can't stomach 14 hate the sight of

can't stomach 4 hate 5 abhor 6 detest, loathe 7 despise 8 execrate 9 abominate, can't abide, can't stand 10 shrink from 13 find repulsive

canvas 4 duck 7 painting 8 painting 9 sailcloth, tarpaulin, tent cloth

canvass 4 poll, scan, sift 5 study, tally 6 survey 7 analyze, discuss, examine, explore, inquiry, inquire, inspect, solicit 8 analysis, campaign, scrutiny 10 evaluation, scrutinize 11 enumeration, exploration, inquire into, investigate, take stock of 13 give thought to, investigation

canyon 3 col, cut, gap 4 draw, pass, wadi, wash 5 break, chasm, cleft, crack, gorge, gulch, gully, notch 6 arroyo, coulee, defile, divide, ravine, valley 7 fissure, opening 8 corridor, crevasse, water gap

cap 3 lid, top 4 seal 5 cover, outdo 6 better, exceed, top off 7 surpass 8 headgear, outstrip 9 headdress 10 visored hat

capability 3 art 4 gift 5 flair, knack, power, skill 6 talent 7 ability, faculty, know-how 8 capacity, efficacy, facility 9 potential 10 attainment, competence, competency 11 proficiency 12 potentiality 13 qualification

capable 3 apt 4 able, deft 5 adept 6 adroit, artful, clever, expert, gifted 7 skilled 8 masterly, skillful, talented 9 competent, effective, ingenious 10 proficient 11 efficacious, intelligent 12 accomplished

capable of assuming legal responsibility
  Latin: 8 sui juris

Capable of Honor
  author: 10 Allan Drury

capable of managing one's own affairs
  Latin: 8 sui juris

capacious 3 big 4 huge, vast, wide 5 ample, broad, large, roomy 7 mammoth, massive 8 gigantic, spacious 9 expansive, extensive 10 commodious, expandable, tremendous, voluminous 13 amplitudinous

capaciousness 9 amplitude, roominess 12 spaciousness 14 commodiousness

capacitate 5 allow 6 enable, permit 7 empower, qualify 8 make able

capacity 4 mind, role, room, size 5 gifts, limit, might, power, range, scope, space 6 extent, talent, volume 7 ability, faculty 8 aptitude, facility, function, judgment, position, sagacity, strength 9 amplitude, endowment, intellect, potential 10 brain power, capability 11 discernment 12 intelligence, perspicacity 15 maximum contents

Capaneus
  member of: 18 Seven against Thebes
  father: 9 Hipponous
  mother: 8 Astynome
  wife: 6 Evadne
  son: 9 Sthenelus
  crime: 9 blasphemy
  destroyed by: 4 Zeus

caparison 5 adorn, equip 6 bedeck 9 equipment, trappings

cape 4 spit 5 cloak, manta, point, shawl 6 mantle, poncho, serape, tabard, tongue 7 pelisse 8 headland 9 peninsula 10 promontory

Capek, Karel
  author of: 3 R U R 8 Hordubal, Krakatit 9 The Mother 13 Power and Glory 18 The War with the Newts

caper 3 hop 4 jape, jump, lark, leap, romp, skip 5 antic, bound, fling, frisk, prank, spree, stunt, trick 6 bounce, cavort, frolic, gambol, prance 7 caprice 8 escapade 9 adventure, high jinks 10 carrying on 11 shenanigans 14 monkey business

Canary Islands
  other name: 14 Fortunate Isles 15 Isles of the Blest
  named for: 3 dog 5 canis 6 canine
  capital: 9 Las Palmas 19 Santa Cruz de Tenerife
  largest city: 9 Las Palmas
  others: 4 Icod 6 Laguna 7 Orotava 8 Arrecife, Valverde 12 San Sebastian
  government: 16 overseas province
  of: 5 Spain
  measure: 8 fanegada
  monetary unit: 6 peseta
  island: 4 Roca 5 Clara, Ferro, Lobos, Rocca 6 Gomera, Hierro 7 Inferno, La Palma 8 Graciosa, Tenerife 9 Lanzarote 10 Lanzarotte 11 Gran Canaria 13 Fuerteventura
  mountain: 6 La Cruz 8 El Cumbre, Tenerife
  highest point: 5 Teide, Teyde
  sea: 8 Atlantic
  people: 7 Spanish
  language: 7 Spanish
  religion: 13 Roman Catholic

capital 4 cash, fine 5 great, money, super 6 center, riches, superb, wealth 7 supreme 9 excellent, financing, first-rate, majuscule, matchless, principal, resources 10 cash on hand, first-class 11 large letter, wherewithal 12 headquarters 13 working assets 14 available means 15 investment funds, upper-case letter

capital city (of countries)
  of Afghanistan: 5 Kabul
  of Albania: 6 Tirana, Tirane
  of Algeria: 7 Algiers
  of Andorra: 14 Andorra-la-Vella
  of Angola: 6 Luanda
  of Antigua and Barbuda: 7 St John's
  of Argentina: 11 Buenos Aires
  of Armenia: 6 Erivan 7 Yerevan
  of Australia: 8 Canberra
  of Austria: 6 Vienna
  of Azerbaijan: 4 Baku
  of the Bahamas: 6 Nassau
  of Bahrain: 6 Manama
  of Bangladesh: 5 Dacca
  of Barbados: 10 Bridgetown
  of Belarus: 5 Minsk
  of Belgium: 8 Brussels 9 Bruxelles
  of Belize: 8 Belmopan
  of Benin: 9 Porto-Novo
  of Bermuda: 8 Hamilton
  of Bhutan: 6 Thimbu 7 Thimphu
  of Bolivia: 5 Sucre
  of Bosnia-Herzegovina: 8 Sarajevo
  of Botswana: 8 Gaborone 9 Gaberones
  of Brazil: 8 Brasilia 12 Rio de Janeiro
  of Brunei: 17 Bandar Seri Begawan
  of Bulgaria: 5 Sofia
  of Burkina Faso: 11 Ouagadougou
  of Burundi: 9 Bujumbura
  of Cambodia: 8 Pnom-Penh
  of Cameroon: 7 Yaounde
  of Canada: 6 Ottawa
  of the Canary Islands: 9 Las Palmas 19 Santa Cruz de Tenerife
  of Cape Verde: 5 Praia
  of the Central African Republic: 6 Bangui
  of Chad: 8 Fort-Lamy, N'Djamena
  of Chile: 8 Santiago
  of China: 6 Peking
  of Colombia: 6 Bogota
  of Comoros: 6 Moroni
  of the Congo: 11 Brazzaville
  of Costa Rica: 7 San Jose
  of Crete: 5 Canea 8 Iraklion
  of Croatia: 6 Zagreb
  of Cuba: 6 Havana 8 La Habana
  of Cyprus: 7 Nicosia
  of Czechoslovakia/ Czech Republic: 6 Prague
  of Denmark: 10 Copenhagen
  of Djibouti: 8 Djibouti
  of the Dominican Republic: 12 Santo Domingo 14 Ciudad Trujillo
  of Ecuador: 5 Quito
  of Egypt: 5 Cairo
  of El Salvador: 11 San Salvador
  of England: 6 London
  of Equatorial Guinea: 6 Malabo
  of Eritrea: 6 Asmara
  of Estonia: 7 Tallinn
  of Ethiopia: 10 Addis Ababa
  of Fiji: 4 Suva
  of Finland: 8 Helsinki 11 Helsingfors
  of France: 5 Paris
  of the Gabon Republic: 10 Libreville
  of The Gambia: 6 Banjul 8 Bathurst
  of Georgia: 7 Tbilisi
  of Germany (East): 10 East Berlin
  of Germany (West): 4 Bonn
  of Ghana: 5 Accra, Akkra
  of Greece: 6 Athens
  of Greenland: 3 Nuk 8 Godthaab, The Point

of Grenada: 9 St Georges
of Guatemala: 13 Guatemala City
of Guinea: 7 Conakry
of Guinea-Bissau: 6 Bissau
of Guyana: 10 Georgetown
of Haiti: 12 Port-au-Prince
of Honduras: 11 Tegucigalpa
of Hong Kong: 8 Victoria
of Hungary: 8 Budapest
of Iceland: 9 Reykjavik
of India: 8 New Delhi
of Indonesia: 7 Jakarta 8 Djakarta
of Iran: 6 Tehran 7 Teheran
of Iraq: 7 Baghdad
of Ireland: 6 Dublin
of Israel: 9 Jerusalem
of Italy: 4 Roma, Rome
of the Ivory Coast: 7 Abidjan
of Jamaica: 8 Kingston
of Japan: 3 Edo 5 Tokyo
of Java: 7 Jakarta 8 Djakarta
of Jordan: 5 Amman
of Kazakhstan: 7 Alma-Ata
of Kenya: 7 Nairobi
of Kiribati: 6 Tarawa
of Korea (North): 9 Pyongyang
of Korea (South): 5 Seoul
of Kuwait: 10 Kuwait City
of Kyrgyzstan: 7 Bishkek (Frunze)
of Laos: 9 Viengchan, Vientiane
of Latvia: 4 Riga
of Lebanon: 6 Beirut 8 Beyrouth
of Lesotho: 6 Maseru
of Liberia: 8 Monrovia
of Libya: 7 Tripoli
of Liechtenstein: 5 Vaduz
of Lithuania: 5 Vilna 6 Kausas 7 Vilnius
of Luxembourg: 10 Luxembourg
of Macedonia: 6 Skopje
of Madagascar: 10 Tananarive 12 Antananarivo
of Malawi: 8 Lilongwe
of Malaysia: 11 Kuala Lumpur
of Maldives: 4 Male
of Mali: 6 Bamako
of Malta: 8 Valletta
of Mauritania: 10 Nouakchott
of Mauritius: 9 Port Louis
of Mexico: 10 Mexico City
of Moldova: 16 Chisinau, Kishinev
of Monaco: 11 Monaco-Ville
of Mongolia: 9 Ulan Bator
of Montenegro: 7 Cetinje 8 Titograd 9
Podgorica
of Morocco: 5 Rabat 6 Rabbat
of Mozambique: 6 Maputo 15 Lourenco
Marques
of Myanmar: 6 Yangon 7 Rangoon
of Namibia: 8 Windhoek
of Nauru: 13 Yaren District
of Nepal: 8 Katmandu 9 Kathmandu
of Netherlands: 8 The Hague 9 Amsterdam
of New Guinea: 11 Port Moresby
of New Zealand: 10 Wellington
of Nicaragua: 7 Managua
of Niger: 6 Niamey

of Nigeria: 5 Abuja, Lagos
of Norway: 4 Oslo 11 Christiania
of Oman: 6 Masqat, Muscat
of Pakistan: 9 Islamabad
of Panama: 10 Panama City
of Paraguay: 8 Asuncion
of Peru: 4 Lima
of the Philippines: 6 Manila
of Poland: 6 Warsaw
of Portugal: 6 Lisbon
of Puerto Rico: 7 San Juan
of Qatar: 4 Doha 7 al-Dawha
of Romania: 9 Bucharest
of Russia: 6 Moscow
of Rwanda: 6 Kigali
of Samoa (American): 8 Pago Pago
of Samoa (Western): 4 Apia
of San Marino: 9 San Marino
of Sao Tome and Principe: 7 Sao Tome
of Sardinia: 8 Cagliari
of Saudi Arabia: 6 Riyadh
of Scotland: 9 Edinburgh
of Senegal: 5 Dakar
of Seychelles: 8 Victoria
of Sicily: 7 Palermo
of Sierra Leone: 8 Freetown
of Sikkim: 7 Gangtok
of Singapore: 9 Singapore
of Slovakia: 10 Bratislava
of Slovenia: 9 Ljubljana
of the Solomon Islands: 7 Honiara
of Somalia: 9 Mogadishu 10 Mogadiscio
of South Africa: 8 Cape Town, Pretoria
12 Bloemfontein
of Spain: 6 Madrid
of Sri Lanka: 7 Colombo
of the Sudan: 8 Khartoum
of Suriname: 10 Paramaribo
of Swaziland: 7 Mbabane
of Sweden: 9 Stockholm
of Switzerland: 4 Bern
of Syria: 8 Damascus
of Taiwan: 6 Taipei
of Tajikistan: 8 Dushanbe
of Tanzania: 11 Dar es Salaam
of Thailand: 6 Bankok 7 Bangkok 8
Thonburi 9 Ayutthaya
of Tibet: 5 Lassa, Lhasa
of Togo: 4 Lome
of Tongo: 9 Nukualofa
of Trinidad and Tobago: 11 Port of
Spain
of Tunisia: 5 Tunis
of Turkey: 6 Ankara
of Turkmenistan: 9 Ashkhabad
of Tuvalu: 8 Funafuti
of Uganda: 7 Kampala
of Ukraine: 4 Kiev
of United Arab Emirates: 8 Abu Dhabi
of United States: 12 Washington DC
of Uruguay: 10 Montevideo
of Uzbekistan: 8 Tashkent
of Vanuatu: 4 Vila
of Venezuela: 7 Caracas
of Vietnam: 5 Hanoi 6 Saigon
of Wales: 7 Cardiff
of Western Sahara: 6 Al Aiun 7 El Aaiun

of Western Samoa: 4 Apia
of Yemen: 4 Sana, Aden 5 Sanaa
of Yugoslavia: 7 Beograd 8 Belgrade
of Zaire: 8 Kinshasa
of Zambia: 6 Lusaka
of Zimbabwe: 6 Harare 9 Salisbury
capital city (of states) see 13 state capitals
capitalism 14 free enterprise
capitalist 5 mogul 6 tycoon 8 investor 9 financier, plutocrat 14 businessperson
capitalize 4 back, fund 5 stake 7 exploit, finance, support, trade on, utilize 8 bankroll, cash in on, profit by 9 subsidize 11 foot the bill 13 make the most of 17 turn an honest penny 23 strike while the iron is hot 24 make hay while the sun shines
capitalize on 7 exploit, utilize 8 profit by 13 turn to account 14 use to advantage
capitol 10 statehouse 11 legislature 15 government house
capitulate 5 yield 6 accede, give in, give up, relent, submit 7 succumb 8 cry quits 9 acquiesce, surrender 11 come to terms, sue for peace 15 lay down one's arms 17 acknowledge defeat, hoist the white flag
capitulation 8 giving in, giving up, quitting, yielding 9 surrender 10 submission
Capote, Truman
  author of: 11 In Cold Blood 12 A Tree of Night 19 Breakfast at Tiffany's
  character: 14 Holly Golightly
Capp, Al
  real name: 18 Alfred George Caplin
  creator/artist of: 8 Li'l Abner
Cappotas
  epithet of: 4 Zeus
  means: 8 reliever
Capra, Frank
  director of: 11 Lady for a Day, Lost Horizon 13 State of the Union 17 Arsenic and Old Lace, It's a Wonderful Life, Mr Deeds Goes to Town (Oscar) 18 It Happened One Night (Oscar) 20 You Can't Take It with You (Oscar) 23 Mr Smith Goes to Washington
caprice 3 fad 4 lark, whim 5 antic, caper, craze, fancy, fling, prank, quirk, spree, stunt 6 notion, oddity, vagary 7 impulse 8 crotchet, escapade 10 erraticism 11 peculiarity 12 eccentricity, idiosyncrasy
capricious 6 fickle, fitful, quirky, uneven 7 erratic, faddish, flighty 8 fanciful, skittish, unstable, unsteady, variable, wavering 9 eccentric, impulsive, mercurial, uncertain, undecided 10 changeable, indecisive, irresolute 11 vacillating 12 inconsistent 13 irresponsible 15 shilly-shallying
capriciousness 7 caprice 10 fickleness 11 instability 12 irresolution 13 impulsiveness, inconsistency 15 shilly-shallying
Capricorn
  symbol: 4 goat
  planet: 6 Saturn
  rules: 6 career
  born: 7 January 8 December

capsicum peppers
  origin: 15 tropical America
  color: 3 red 5 green, white 6 violet, yellow
  variety: 7 cayenne, paprika 9 red pepper 11 chili pepper, chili powder, curry powder, sweet pepper
  flavor: 3 hot
  use: 5 chili, curry, pizza 8 barbecue 9 paprikash
capsize 5 upset 6 invert 7 tip over 8 flip over, keel over, overturn, turn over 10 turn turtle
capsule 4 case, pill 6 ampule 7 cockpit 8 covering 9 spore case 12 condensation
captain 4 boss, head 5 chief, pilot 6 leader, master, old man 7 headman, skipper 9 chieftain, commander 10 commandant 12 chief officer 16 company commander 17 commanding officer
Captain Blood
  director: 13 Michael Curtiz
  cast: 10 Errol Flynn 12 Lionel Atwill 13 Basil Rathbone 17 Olivia de Havilland
Captain Carpenter
  author: 15 John Crowe Ransom
Captain Craig
  author: 22 Edwin Arlington Robinson
Captain Hook
  character in: 8 Peter Pan
  author: 6 Barrie
Captain Horatio Hornblower
  author: 10 C S Forester
Captains Courageous
  author: 14 Rudyard Kipling
  director: 13 Victor Fleming
  cast: 12 Mickey Rooney, Spencer Tracy 13 John Carradine, Melvyn Douglas 15 Lionel Barrymore 18 Freddie Bartholomew
  Oscar for: 5 actor (Tracy)
Captain's Daughter, The
  author: 16 Alexander Pushkin
Captain Video and His Video Rangers
  character: 7 Dr Pauli 9 The Ranger 12 Captain Video
  cast: 7 Al Hodge 10 Hal Conklin 11 Don Hastings 13 Richard Coogan
  slogan: 29 Guardian of the Safety of the World
  villain: 4 Atar 7 Nargola 8 Dahoumie, Kul of Eos 9 Dr Clysmok 12 Heng Foo Seeng 14 Mook the Moon Man
  gimmick: 5 Tobor 9 Discatron 11 Atomic Rifle 16 Barrier of Silence, Radio Scillograph 17 Cosmic Ray Vibrator 18 Opticon Scillometer 19 Cloak of Invisibility, Trisonic Compensator
  spaceship: 6 Galaxy
caption 5 title 6 legend 7 heading, subhead 8 headline, subtitle 11 explanation
captious 4 mean 5 picky, testy 6 ornery 7 carping, cutting, peevish 8 caviling, contrary, niggling, perverse, petulant, picayune, snappish 9 fractious, querulous 10 belittling, censorious, nitpicking 11 depre-

cating 12 cantankerous, faultfinding 13 hypercritical

captivate 4 lure 5 charm 6 dazzle, enamor, seduce 7 attract, bewitch, delight, enchant, win over 8 enthrall 9 carry away, enrapture, fascinate, hypnotize, infatuate, mesmerize, transport 13 turn the head of 14 take the fancy of

captivated 7 charmed, pleased 9 delighted, enchanted 10 enraptured, enthralled, spellbound

captivating 7 winning, winsome 8 adorable, charming, dazzling, engaging, fetching, magnetic 9 appealing, beguiling, disarming 10 attractive, bewitching, delightful, enchanting, entrancing 11 enthralling, fascinating, mesmerizing 12 ingratiating, irresistible

captive 5 caged 6 penned 7 hostage 8 confined, enslaved, interned, locked up, prisoner 9 oppressed 10 imprisoned, subjugated 12 incarcerated

captivity 7 bondage, holding, slavery 9 servitude 10 detainment 12 imprisonment

capture 3 bag, nab 4 bust, grab, snag, take, trap 5 catch, grasp, pinch, seize, snare 6 arrest, collar, taking 7 bagging, ensnare, procure, seizure, snaring 8 catching, trapping 9 apprehend, collaring, ensnaring, lay hold of 12 apprehension, laying hold of, take prisoner 14 taking prisoner 15 take into custody

Capulet family
  characters in: 14 Romeo and Juliet
  author: 11 Shakespeare

Capys
  father: 9 Assaracus
  son: 7 Laocoon 8 Anchises
  grandson: 6 Aeneas
  founded: 5 Capua
  warned against: 11 Trojan horse

car 4 auto, heap 5 buggy, coach, diner, motor 6 boxcar, hot rod, jalopy, wheels 7 flivver, machine, sleeper, vehicle 8 carriage 9 tin lizzie 10 automobile 12 motor vehicle
  kind: 4 coal 5 cable, horse, motor 6 cattle, dining, parlor, street 7 baggage, freight, Pullman, railway 8 sleeping

Car
  father: 9 Phoroneus
  mother: 5 Cerdo
  founder of: 6 Megara

carabiniere 9 policeman

Caracas
  birthplace of: 12 Simon Bolivar
  capital of: 9 Venezuela
  founder: 13 Diego de Losada
  museum: 7 Bolivar 8 Criolan 11 Colonial Art, Raul Santana
  river: 6 Guaire

carafe 5 flask 6 bottle, vessel 9 container

carapax 4 case 5 shell 6 lorica, shield 7 carapace 8 calipash, covering 11 turtle shell

Caravaggio, Michelangelo Merisi da
  born: 5 Italy 10 Caravaggio
  artwork: 12 Young Bacchus 14 Burial of St Lucy 16 Raising of Lazarus 17 The Supper at Emmaus 18 Calling of St Matthew, The Life of St Matthew 20 St Matthew and the Angel 21 The Conversion of St Paul 23 The Crucifixion of St Peter 30 The Beheading of St John the Baptist

caravan 4 band, file, line 5 queue, train, troop 6 coffle, column, convoy, parade, string 7 company, cortege, retinue 9 cavalcade, chain gang, entourage, motorcade 10 procession, wagon train

caravansary 3 inn 5 hotel 8 hostelry

caraway
  botanical name: 10 Carum carvi
  origin: 6 Europe 9 Asia Minor 14 the Netherlands
  liqueur: 6 Kummel
  candy-covered caraway seeds: 6 comfit 12 whisky-killer
  use: 4 pork, soup, stew 8 rye bread

carbohydrate
  consists of: 5 water 6 carbon, oxygen 8 hydrogen 13 carbon dioxide
  kinds: 5 sugar 6 simple, starch, xylose 7 complex, glucose, lactose, maltose, sucrose 8 dextrose, fructose 9 cellulose

carbon 4 coal, coke, copy 8 charcoal 9 lampblack
  chemical symbol: 1 C

carbon copy 5 clone 7 replica 9 duplicate, facsimile 12 reproduction

carbonize 4 burn, char, sear 5 singe 6 scorch 10 incinerate

carbuncle 4 boil, sore 11 excrescence 12 inflammation

carcass 4 body, bouk, husk, wall 5 shell, stiff, trunk 6 corpse 7 cadaver, carrion, remains 8 dead body, fireball, skeleton 9 framework

carcinoma 5 tumor 6 cancer 8 neoplasm 10 malignancy 15 malignant growth

card 4 bill 6 ticket 7 program 8 postcard
  kind: 7 calling, get-well, playing 8 birthday, business, greeting 9 Christmas, Valentine

cardamon
  botanical name: 19 Elettaria cardamomum
  origin: 4 Asia 5 India 13 southeast Asia
  related to: 6 ginger
  color: 5 black
  use: 5 curry 7 dessert 12 Danish pastry

Cardea
  origin: 5 Roman
  goddess of: 6 family 10 door hinges

Cardew, Cecily
  character in: 27 The Importance of Being Earnest
  author: 5 Wilde

card game 3 loo, war 4 brag, fish, skat, vint 5 ombre, poker, rummy, whist 6 boston, bridge, casino, chemmy, ecarte, euchre, go fish, hearts, memory, piquet, pocher 7 bezique, canasta, cooncan, Old Maid, plafond, primero 8 baccarat, conquian, cribbage, gin rummy, napoleon, patience, pinochle, slapjack 9 blackjack, pelmanism, solitaire, spoil five, twenty-one 11 chemin

de fer, crazy eights 13 concentration 14
contract bridge 16 beggar-my-neighbor,
trente et quarante
   card names: 3 ace 4 fool, jack, king, trey
   5 joker, queen
   combination of cards: 4 meld
   one hand or round: 5 trick
   rulebook by: 5 Hoyle
   suits: 4 club 5 heart, spade 7 diamond
   French: 5 coeur, pique 6 trefle 7 carreau
   German: 4 grun, herz, piks 5 karos, treff
   6 eichel 7 schelle
   Italian: 5 coppa, cuori, fiori, spada 6
   denaro, picchi, quadri 7 bastone
   Spanish: 3 oro 4 copa 5 basto 6 espada
Cardiff
   capital of: 5 Wales
cardigan 5 corgi 6 jacket, wampus 7
sweater 10 Welsh corgi
cardinal 3 key, top 4 head, main 5 basic,
chief, first, prime, vital 6 cherry, claret 7
carmine, central, deep-red, highest, leading, primary, scarlet 8 blood-red, dominant,
foremost, greatest 9 essential, intrinsic,
necessary, paramount, principal, uppermost 10 elementary, preeminent, underlying 11 fundamental, outstanding, predominant, wine-colored 13 indispensable, most
important
care 4 heed, load, mind, want, wish 5 grief,
pains, worry 6 bother, charge, desire, effort, misery, regard, sorrow, strain, stress 7
anguish, anxiety, caution, concern, control,
custody, keeping, sadness, thought, trouble 8 distress, hardship, nuisance, pressure, vexation 9 annoyance, attention, be
worried, diligence, exactness, heartache,
vigilance 10 affliction, management, precaution, protection, solicitude 11 application, be concerned, bother about, carefulness, supervision, tribulation, unhappiness
12 ministration, trouble about, watchfulness 13 attentiveness, consideration 14 be
interested in, circumspection, discrimination, fastidiousness, meticulousness, responsibility, scrupulousness 17 conscientiousness
Careas 6 eunuch
careen 3 tip, yaw 4 lean, list, sway, tilt, veer
5 heave, slant, slope 7 capsize 8 lean
over, overturn
career 3 job 4 line, work 7 calling, pursuit 8
activity, business, lifework, vocation 10
employment, livelihood, occupation, profession, walk of life
care for 4 like, mind, tend 5 fancy 7 oversee 8 attend to, wait upon 9 look after,
watch over 10 minister to, provide for
carefree 3 gay 4 glad 5 happy, jolly, sunny
6 breezy, elated, jaunty, joyous 7 buoyant,
gleeful, radiant, relaxed, smiling 8 careless, cheerful, jubilant, laughing 9 easygoing 10 full of life, optimistic, untroubled 11
free-and-easy 12 happy-go-lucky, lighthearted, without worry 13 in high spirits 23
without a worry in the world
   French: 9 sans souci

careful 4 fine, nice, wary 5 alert, chary, exact, fussy 7 correct, guarded, heedful,
mindful, on guard, precise, prudent, tactful
8 accurate, cautious, diligent, discreet, vigilant, watchful 9 attentive, concerned, judicious, observant, regardful 10 fastidious,
meticulous, particular, scrupulous, solicitous, thoughtful 11 circumspect, painstaking, punctilious 13 conscientious
carefulness 7 caution 10 steadiness 12 deliberation 14 circumspection
careless 3 lax 4 rash 5 messy, slack 6 casual, sloppy, untidy 7 inexact, offhand 8
heedless, mindless, slapdash, slipshod,
slovenly 9 forgetful, imprecise, incorrect,
negligent, unmindful 10 disorderly, inaccurate, neglectful, nonchalant, unthinking,
untroubled 11 indifferent, thoughtless,
unconcerned 12 absent-minded, devil-
may-care 13 inconsiderate, lackadaisical
carelessness 6 laxity 7 neglect 9 messiness, slackness 10 inaccuracy, negligence, sloppiness, untidiness 11 imprecision, inexactness 12 heedlessness,
indiscretion, slovenliness 13 unmindfulness 14 disorderliness 15 thoughtlessness
16 absentmindedness, irresponsibility
Care of Time, The
   author: 10 Eric Ambler
caress 3 hug, pat, pet 5 clasp, touch 6 cuddle, fondle, stroke 7 embrace, petting, toy
with 8 fondling, stroking 11 gentle touch
caretaker 6 keeper, porter, warden 7 curator, janitor, steward 8 overseer, watchman
9 concierge, custodian 10 gatekeeper 14
superintendent
careworn 7 haggard, worried 8 fatigued,
troubled 11 pessimistic
cargo 4 load 5 goods 6 burden, lading 7
freight 8 shipment 11 consignment, merchandise
Carib
   language family: 7 Cariban
   location: 7 Guianas 9 Caribbean, Venezuela 12 South America
   custom: 11 cannibalism
Cariban
   tribe: 5 Carib 6 Acawai, Akawai
Caribbean 3 sea
   channel: 7 Yucatan
   city: 6 Havana 7 San Juan 8 Santiago 10
   Guantanamo 12 Port au Prince 13 Santo
   Domingo 15 Charlotte Amalie
   Indian: 5 Carib 6 Arawak
   island: 4 Cuba 5 Aruba, Haiti, Nevis 6
   Cayman, Nassau, Tobago, Virgin 7
   Antigua, Bahamas, Barbuda, Curacao,
   Grenada, Jamaica, Leeward 8 Anguilla,
   Dominica, Trinidad, Windward 9 Saint
   John 10 Guadeloupe, Hispaniola, Marti-
   nique, Montserrat, Puerto Rico, Saint
   Kitts, Saint Lucia 11 Saint Thomas 12
   Saint Vincent 14 Lesser Antilles 15
   Greater Antilles 19 Dominican Republic,
   Netherlands Antilles
   language: 6 gullah 10 papiamento

product: 3 rum 5 fruit, spice, sugar 6 coffee

caricature 4 mock 6 parody, satire 7 lampoon, mockery, takeoff 8 satirize, travesty 9 absurdity, burlesque 10 distortion 12 exaggeration

Carker
  character in: 12 Dombey and Son
  author: 7 Dickens

Carlisle, Kitty
  real name: 13 Katherine Conn
  husband: 8 Moss Hart
  born: 12 New Orleans LA
  roles: 13 She Loves Me Not 14 To Tell the Truth 16 A Night at the Opera 19 Murder at the Vanities

Carlton, Steve (Steven Norman)
  nickname: 5 Lefty
  sport: 8 baseball
  position: 7 pitcher
  team: 20 Philadelphia Phillies

Carlyle, Thomas
  author of: 8 Cromwell 14 Sartor Resartus 17 Frederick the Great 19 The French Revolution 20 Heroes and Hero-Worship

Carmanor
  king of: 5 Crete
  purified: 6 Apollo 7 Artemis

Carme
  daughter: 11 Britomartis

Carmen
  author: 14 Prosper Merimee
  opera by: 5 Bizet
  setting: 7 Seville
  character: 7 Don Jose 9 Escamillo, Frasquita

Carmen Jones
  director: 13 Otto Preminger
  based on opera by: 5 Bizet (Carmen)
  adaptation by: 18 Oscar Hammerstein II
  cast: 11 Pearl Bailey 14 Harry Belafonte 16 Dorothy Dandridge

Carmenta
  origin: 5 Roman
  member of: 7 Camanae
  protectress of: 10 childbirth
  husband: 7 Evander
  son: 7 Evander

carmine 3 red 6 cherry 7 crimson, deep red, scarlet 8 blood red 9 bright red

carnage 4 butchery, massacre 9 blood bath, slaughter

carnal 4 lewd 6 erotic, impure, sexual, sinful, wanton 7 fleshly, immoral, lustful, sensual 8 prurient, sensuous, unchaste, venereal 9 lecherous, salacious 10 lascivious, libidinous, voluptuous

Carnegie, Dale
  author of: 33 How To Win Friends and Influence People

carnelian
  species: 6 quartz

Carnera, Primo
  nickname: 13 the Ambling Alp
  sport: 6 boxing
  class: 11 heavyweight

Carneus
  epithet of: 6 Apollo
  alludes to: 11 cornel trees

Carney, Art
  real name: 26 Arthur William Matthew Carney
  partner: 13 Jackie Gleason
  born: 12 Mount Vernon NY
  roles: 8 Ed Norton 13 Harry and Tonto (Oscar) 15 The Honeymooners

carnival 4 fair, fete, gala 6 circus 7 holiday, jubilee 8 festival, jamboree, sideshow 9 Mardi Gras 11 celebration

carnivore 3 cat, dog, fox 4 bear, lion, lynx, mink, puma, wolf 5 civet, dingo, fossa, hyena, otter, panda, skunk, tayra, tiger 6 badger, bobcat, coyote, ferret, grison, hyaena, jackal, jaguar, marten, olingo, weasel 7 polecat, raccoon, suricat 8 aardwolf, kinkajou, mongoose 9 meat eater, wolverine 10 cacomistle, coatimundi, flesh eater

carnivorous 9 predatory 10 meat-eating, predaceous 11 flesh-eating

Carnus
  occupation: 4 seer
  seer of: 6 Apollo
  killed by: 10 Heraclidae

carol 4 hymn, noel, sing 5 paean 6 warble 8 canticle 9 song of joy 12 song of praise

Caroline Islands
  district: 3 Yap 4 Truk 5 Palau 6 Ponape
  inhabitant: 10 Polynesian 11 Micronesian
  island: 3 Yap 6 Ponape, Ulithi 8 Nukuroro 10 Babelthuap 14 Kapinamarangi
  language: 7 English 10 Polynesian 11 Micronesian
  ocean: 7 Pacific

carom 6 bounce, strike 7 collide, rebound, 8 billiard, ricochet 9 bounce off

Caron, Leslie
  born: 6 France 19 Boulogne-Billancourt
  roles: 4 Gaby, Gigi, Lili 5 Fanny 11 Father Goose 13 Daddy Longlegs 14 The L-Shaped Room 17 An American in Paris

Carothers, Wallace Hume
  field: 9 chemistry
  discovered: 5 nylon

carousal 4 orgy 5 binge, drunk, spree 7 debauch 9 bacchanal 10 debauchery, saturnalia

carouse 5 drink, party, quaff, revel 6 guzzle, imbibe, tipple 7 roister, wassail 8 live it up 9 make merry 10 go on a binge 11 make whoopee

Carousel
  director: 9 Henry King
  based on: 6 Liliom
  adaptation by: 21 Rodgers and Hammerstein
  cast: 12 Gordon MacRae (Billy Bigelow), Shirley Jones 15 Cameron Mitchell
  song: 9 Soliloquy 11 If I Loved You 19 You'll Never Walk Alone

carp 3 nag 5 cavil, chide, decry, knock 6 deride, impugn, jibe at, pick on 7 censure, condemn 8 belittle, complain, reproach 9 criticize, deprecate, disparage, fault-find, find fault 10 disapprove

Carpaccio, Vittore
 born: 5 Italy 6 Venice
 artwork: 13 Two Courtesans 18 The Dream of St Ursula 19 The Legend of St Ursula 21 St Augustine in his Study 24 St George Killing the Dragon 28 St Augustine's Vision of St Jerome 29 The Arrival of St Ursula at Cologne

carpal
 bone of: 5 wrist

carpe diem 11 seize the day 15 enjoy the present

carpenter 6 fitter, joiner 7 builder 8 repairer 10 woodworker 12 cabinetmaker
 ant: 10 camponotus
 bee: 8 xylocopa
 bird: 10 woodpecker
 fish: 10 hammerhead
 moth: 10 prinoxysus

Carpenter, Harlean
 real name of: 10 Jean Harlow

carper 6 critic 7 caviler 9 nit-picker 11 fault-finder

carpet 3 mat, rug 5 cover, layer, sheet 7 blanket, matting 8 covering

Carpetbaggers, The
 author: 13 Harold Robbins

Carpo
 origin: 5 Greek
 member of: 5 Horae
 goddess of: 11 summer fruit

Carpophorus
 epithet of: 7 Demeter 10 Persephone
 means: 11 fruit bearer

Carr, Emily
 born: 6 Canada 8 Victoria 15 British Columbia
 artwork: 3 Sky 8 Big Raven 14 Blunden Harbour, Kispiax Village 15 Woods and Blue Sky 17 Forest Landscape II 36 Cape Mudge An Indian Family with Totem Pole

Carra, Carlo
 born: 5 Italy 9 Quargneto
 artwork: 13 Lot's Daughters 16 Metaphysical Muse 20 Patriotic Celebration 29 The Funeral of the Anarchist Galli

Carradine, David
 father: 4 John
 half-brothers: 5 Keith 6 Robert
 born: 11 Hollywood CA
 roles: 6 Kung Fu 13 Bound for Glory 14 The Serpent's Egg

Carradine, John
 real name: 21 Richmond Reed Carradine
 son: 5 David, Keith 6 Robert
 born: 16 Greenwich Village NY
 roles: 9 Cleopatra, Kidnapped 10 Stagecoach 14 Count Dracula 15 The Invisible Man 18 Captains Courageous, The Three Musketeers

Carradine, Keith
 father: 4 John
 brother: 6 Robert
 half-brother: 5 David
 born: 10 San Mateo CA
 roles: 9 Nashville 10 Pretty Baby

Carraway, Nick
 character in: 14 The Great Gatsby
 author: 10 Fitzgerald

Carrere, John Merven
 partner: 14 Thomas Hastings
 architect of: 19 House Office Building (Washington DC) 20 New York Public Library, Senate Office Building (Washington DC) 21 Henry Clay Frick mansion (now Frick Collection NYC)
 style: 18 French neo-classical, Spanish Renaissance

carriage 3 air, rig 4 mien 5 buggy, coach, poise, wagon 6 aspect, manner 7 bearing, posture, vehicle 8 attitude, behavior, demeanor, presence 10 appearance, conveyance, deportment 11 comportment

Carrie
 author: 11 Stephen King

carried away 7 excited, frantic, seduced 8 ecstatic, frenzied, overcome 9 delirious 10 fascinated, infatuated 11 transported

carrier 3 bus, car 4 rack, wave 5 agent, barge, plane, coach, drain, ferry, train, truck, wagon 6 bearer, boxcar, pigeon, porter 7 airline, channel, mailman, postman, trucker, vehicle 8 airplane, aircraft, carriage, catalyst, railroad 9 messenger 11 transmitter, wheelbarrow

carrion 5 bones, offal, waste 6 corpse, refuse 7 cadaver, carcass, garbage, remains, wastage 8 crowbait, dead body, leavings

Carroll, Leo G
 born: 6 Weedon 7 England
 roles: 6 Topper 7 Rebecca 9 Suspicion 10 Spellbound 11 Cosmo Topper 15 A Christmas Carol, The Man from UNCLE, The Paradine Case 16 Father of the Bride, North by Northwest

Carroll, Lewis
 real name: 22 Charles Lutwidge Dodgson
 author of: 11 Jabberwocky 22 Through the Looking Glass 28 Alice's Adventures in Wonderland

carrousel 4 ride, tray 8 conveyor 9 quadrille, whirligig 10 tournament 12 merry-go-round

carry 3 lug, run 4 bear, cart, haul, lift, move, prop, ship, take, tote 5 brace, bring, fetch, offer, print, shift, stock 6 convey, hold up, supply, uphold 7 conduct, deliver, display, publish, release, support, sustain 8 displace, maintain, shoulder, transfer, transmit 9 broadcast, transport 10 keep on hand 11 communicate, disseminate

carry away 4 lure 6 abduct, kidnap, seduce 7 attract 9 captivate, fascinate, infatuate, transport

carry off 5 seize, steal 6 abduct, kidnap 7 bear off 9 succeed at 11 get away with

carry out 2 do **6** effect, wind up **7** achieve, execute, fulfill, perform, realize **8** complete, conclude, dispatch **9** discharge, dispose of, succeed at **10** accomplish, bring about **11** bring to pass

carry through 6 effect, finish **7** achieve, develop, execute, fulfill, perform, realize **8** complete, consummate, effectuate, perpetuate **13** put into effect

Carson, Rachel Louise
  field: 7 biology
  studied: 9 pollution
  author of: 12 Silent Spring **14** The Sea Around Us **15** The Edge of the Sea

Carstone, Richard
  character in: 10 Bleak House
  author: 7 Dickens

cart 3 gig, lug **4** bear, dray, haul, move, take, tote, trap **5** bring, carry, fetch, truck, wagon **6** barrow, convey **7** schlepp, tumbrel **8** curricle, transfer, transmit **9** transport **10** handbarrow, transplant, two-wheeler **11** wheelbarrow
  kind: 2 go **3** dog, tip **4** dump, hand, push

carte blanche 7 license **9** a free hand, free reign **10** blank check **12** open sanction **13** full authority **18** unconditional power

cartel 4 pool **5** chain, trust **7** combine **8** monopoly **9** syndicate **10** consortium, federation **11** corporation

Carter, Charles
  real name of: 14 Charlton Heston

Carter, James Earl, Jr
  nickname: 3 Hot **5** Jimmy **7** Hotshot
  presidential rank: 11 thirty-ninth
  party: 10 Democratic
  state represented: 2 GA **7** Georgia
  defeated: 4 (Gerald R) Ford **8** (Eugene) McCarthy
  vice president: 7 (Walter Frederick "Fritz") Mondale
  cabinet:
    state: **5** (Cyrus R) Vance **6** (Edmund S) Muskie
    treasury: **6** (G William) Miller **10** (W Michael) Blumenthal
    defense: **5** (Harold) Brown
    attorney general: **4** (Griffin B) Bell **9** (Benjamin R) Civiletti
    interior: **6** (Cecil D) Andrus
    agriculture: **8** (Robert S) Bergland
    commerce: **5** (Juanita Morris) Kreps **9** (Philip M) Klutznick
    labor: **8** (F Ray) Marshall
    HEW: **6** (Patricia Roberts) Harris **8** (Joseph A) Califano (Jr)
    HUD: **6** (Patricia Roberts) Harris **8** (Moon) Landrieu
    transportation: **5** (Brockman) Adams **11** (Neil E) Goldschmidt
    education: **10** (Shirley) Hufstedler
  born: 2 GA **6** Plains
  education: 14 US Naval Academy **26** Georgia Southwestern College **28** Georgia Institute of Technology
  religion: 15 Southern Baptist

  interests: 5 track **6** tennis **7** fishing, hunting **8** football, softball **10** basketball **12** cross couhtry **13** square dancing **17** collecting bottles
  music: **8** folk rock **9** classical
  author: 13 Why Not the Best?
  political career: 12 state senator
  governor of: **7** Georgia
  civilian career: 12 peanut farmer
  military service: 6 US Navy
  notable events of lifetime/term: 6 SALT II **9** Love Canal, recession **18** Habitat for Humanity
  deaths at: **9** Jonestown
  eruption of: **13** Mount St Helens
  first baby from: **8** test tube
  hostages taken in: **4** Iran
  nuclear accident: **15** Three Mile Island
  pipeline: **4** Alcan
  scandal/investigation: **6** Abscam **9** Bert Lance, Koreagate **11** Billy Carter
  Supreme Court case: **5** Bakke
  treaty: **11** Panama Canal **16** Camp David Accords
  father: 11 James Earl Sr
  mother: 7 Lillian (Gordy)
  nickname: 11 Miss Lillian
  siblings: 6 Gloria **17** William "Billy" Alton **19** Ruth Carter Stapleton
  wife: 8 Rosalynn (Smith)
  children: 7 Amy Lynn **11** John William (Jack) **12** James Earl III (Chip) **13** Donnel Jeffrey (Jeff)
  first lady: 36 Presidential Commission on Mental Health
  author: **19** First Lady from Plains

Carthage *see* **7** Tunisia

carton 3 box **4** case **5** crate **9** container **11** packing case **12** cardboard box, packing crate **18** cardboard container

Carton, Sydney
  character in: 16 A Tale of Two Cities
  author: 7 Dickens

cartoon 5 comic **6** design, satire, sketch **7** drawing, funnies, picture **8** animated **10** caricature, comicstrip

cartoonist 6 artist, drawer **7** gagster **12** caricaturist
  famous: 6 Al Capp, C C Beck, Ted Key **8** Herblock (Herbert L. Block), Jim Davis, Roy Crane **9** Bud Fisher, Chic Young, Dik Browne, Frank King, Hal Foster, Ham Fisher, Walt Kelly **10** Bob Montana, Harold Gray, Johnny Hart, Mort Walker, Paul Conrad, Thomas Nast, Walt Disney **11** Alex Raymond, Bill Mauldin, Dale Messick, David Levine, Ding Darling, Elzie C. Segar, Hank Ketcham, Max Beerbohm, Rollin Kirby **12** Brad Anderson, Chester Gould, Garry Trudeau, James Thurber, Jeff MacNelly, Jules Feiffer, Milton Caniff, Rube Goldberg, Rudolph Dirks, Virgil Partch **13** Charles Addams, Charles Schulz, George McManus, Honore Daumier, Joseph Keppler, Saul Steinberg **14** Homer Davenport, William Hogarth **15** Ernie

Bushmiller, Patrick Oliphant, Richard Outcault 16 Benjamin Franklin, George Cruikshank

cartridge 3 dud 4 case, tape 5 blank, shell 6 holder 7 capsule, package 8 cassette, cylinder 9 container

Cartwright, Edmund
nationality: 7 English
inventor of: 9 power loom 18 wool-combing machine

carve 3 hew, saw 4 etch, form, hack, mold, rend, turn, work 5 allot, cleve, cut up, model, shape, slash, slice, split 6 chisel, divide, incise, sculpt 7 engrave, fashion, pattern, quarter 8 block out, dissever 9 apportion, sculpture

Carver, George Washington
field: 9 chemistry
worked in: 11 agriculture
studied: 6 peanut 7 soybean 11 sweet potato

carving 5 cameo 8 intaglio, triptych 9 sculpture

Carya
origin: 8 Laconian
form: 6 maiden
home: 7 Laconia
changed into: 10 walnut tree
changed by: 8 Dionysus

Caryatis
epithet of: 7 Artemis
means: 15 of the walnut tree

Casablanca
director: 13 Michael Curtiz
cast: 10 Peter Lorre 11 Claude Rains (Louis), Conrad Veidt, Paul Henreid (Victor Laslo) 12 Dooley Wilson (Sam), 13 Ingrid Bergman (Ilsa Lund) 14 Humphrey Bogart (Rick) 17 Sydney Greenstreet
Oscar for: 7 picture
song: 12 As Time Goes By

Casanova 3 cad, rip 4 beau, lech, roue, wolf 5 lover, Romeo, swain, wooer 6 chaser, lecher, suitor 7 admirer, bounder, Don Juan, gallant, rounder 8 cavalier, Lothario, lover boy, paramour 9 ladies' man, libertine, womanizer 10 lady-killer, profligate 11 philanderer

Casby
character in: 12 Little Dorrit
author: 7 Dickens

cascade 4 fall, gush, pour, rush 5 chute, falls, surge 6 plunge, rapids, tumble 7 Niagara 8 cataract 9 waterfall

case 3 bin, box 4 plea, suit, tray 5 cause, chest, cover, crate, event 6 action, affair, appeal, carton, debate, injury, jacket, matter, sheath, victim 7 cabinet, concern, disease, dispute, episode, example, hearing, housing, inquiry, invalid, lawsuit, overlay, patient, wrapper 8 argument, business, covering, envelope, incident, instance, sufferer 9 condition, container, happening, incidence, sheathing, situation 10 litigation, occurrence, proceeding, protection, receptacle, sick person 11 controversy 12 circumstance, illustration

case in point 7 example 8 instance 12 illustration

Case of Sergeant Grischa, The
author: 11 Arnold Zweig

Casey
nickname of: 20 Charles Dillon Stengel

cash 5 bills, bread, coins, dough, money 6 change, redeem 8 currency, exchange 9 bank notes 10 paper money 11 legal tender 13 turn into money 14 coin of the realm

cashier 6 banker, bursar, purser, teller 9 treasurer 10 bank teller

cash register
invented by: 5 Ritty

casing 4 skin 5 frame 9 sheathing

Casino Royale
author: 10 Ian Fleming

cask 3 keg, tub, tun, vat 4 butt, pipe 6 barrel 8 hogshead

casket 4 case, pall 5 chest 6 coffer, coffin 8 jewel box 11 sarcophagus

Cask of Amontillado, The
author: 13 Edgar Allan Poe
character: 9 Fortunato, Montresor

Cassandra
also: 9 Alexandra
father: 5 Priam
mother: 6 Hecuba
brother: 5 Paris
concubine of: 9 Agamemnon
son: 6 Pelops 9 Teledamus
cursed by: 6 Apollo
violated by: 4 Ajax
killed by: 12 Clytemnestra

Cassatt, Mary
born: 15 Allegheny City PA
artwork: 6 La Loge 7 The Bath 11 The Cup of Tea 12 After the Bath, Woman Bathing 14 Gathering Fruit 15 Reading Le Figaro 20 Girl Arranging Her Hair, Woman and Child Drawing

Cassavetes, John
wife: 12 Gena Rowlands
born: 9 New York NY
roles/films: 8 Husbands 10 The Tempest 13 Rosemary's Baby, The Dirty Dozen 23 A Woman Under the Influence

casserole 4 dish, food, mold 6 tureen, vessel 8 saucepan

Cassio
character in: 7 Othello
author: 11 Shakespeare

Cassiopeia
husband: 7 Cepheus
daughter: 9 Andromeda
offended: 7 Nereids

Cassius
also: 12 Caius Cassius
character in: 12 Julius Caesar
author: 11 Shakespeare

Cass Timberlane
author: 13 Sinclair Lewis
character: 11 Bradd Criley 24 Jinny Marshland Timberlane

cast 3 set, sow 4 fire, form, hurl, look, mien, mint, mold, pick, shed, toss 5 fling, heave, model, pitch, shape, shoot, sling, stamp, throw 6 actors, assign, casing, choose, direct, launch, let fly, propel, sculpt, spread, troupe 7 appoint, company, deposit, diffuse, pattern, players, project, scatter 8 catapult, disperse 9 broadcast, circulate, discharge, launching, semblance 10 appearance, distribute, impression, performers, propulsion 11 disseminate, give parts to 16 dramatis personae

Castalia
origin: 5 Greek
sacred: 6 spring
location: 14 Mount Parnassus
sacred to: 5 Muses 6 Apollo
source of: 11 inspiration

Castalides see 5 Muses

cast aside 4 junk, shed 6 desert, reject 7 abandon, discard, forsake, neglect 8 get rid of, renounce, throw out 9 repudiate, throw away 11 discontinue

cast a spell on 5 charm 7 bewitch, conjure, enchant 8 entrance 11 work magic on

cast aspersions on 5 knock, scorn 6 deride, malign 7 disdain, put down, run down, sneer at 8 belittle, pooh-pooh 9 criticize, disparage 13 find fault with

castaway 3 bum 4 hobo, waif 5 exile, leper, nomad, rover, stray 6 outlaw, pariah 7 Ishmael, outcast, vagrant 8 deportee, derelict, renegade, unperson, vagabond, wanderer 9 foundling, nonperson 10 expatriate 11 beachcomber, offscouring, untouchable 12 down-and-outer 13 knight-of-the-road

cast away 4 junk 6 launch, propel, reject 7 abandon, discard, toss out 8 get rid of, pitch out, throw out 9 throw away

cast down 5 abase, droop, lower 6 abased, deject, droopy, humble, sadden 7 depress, humbled, lowered 8 bring low, dejected, disgrace, saddened 9 depressed, disgraced, humiliate 10 brought low, dishearten, humiliated 11 crestfallen 12 disheartened

caste 4 rank 6 status 7 lineage, station 8 position 9 condition
Hindu: 5 sudra, varna 6 vaisya 7 brahman 9 kshatriya

castigate 5 chide, scold 6 berate, punish, rebuke 7 bawl out, censure, chasten, chew out, correct, reprove, upbraid 8 admonish, chastise, penalize, reproach 9 criticize, dress down, reprimand 10 discipline, take to task 15 call on the carpet 16 haul over the coals

castigation 9 reprimand 10 chastening, correction, discipline, penalizing, punishment 12 chastisement

Castiglione, Baldassare
author of: 20 The Book of the Courtier

castle 4 hall, keep 5 manor, tower, villa 6 palace 7 chateau, citadel, mansion 8 fortress 10 stronghold

Castle, The
author: 10 Franz Kafka
character: 1 K

Castle of Otranto, The
author: 13 Horace Walpole
character: 6 Conrad 7 Alfonso, Manfred, Matilda 8 Isabella, Theodore 12 Father Jerome

Castle Rackrent
author: 14 Maria Edgeworth

cast off 4 shed 6 reject 7 discard, set sail, toss out 8 throw off, throw out 9 repudiate, throw away 11 weigh anchor

Castor and Pollux
also: 8 Dioscuri 10 Polydeuces, Tyndaridae
form: 8 twin sons
mother: 4 Leda
father: 4 Zeus
sister: 5 Helen 12 Clytemnestra
members of: 9 Argonauts
protectors of: 6 seamen

cast out 4 oust 5 eject, evict, exile, expel 6 banish, reject 7 discard, dismiss, turn out 8 drive out, send away, throw out

cast up 4 spew 5 eject, expel, vomit 6 spew up 7 cough up, throw up 8 disgorge

casual 3 cool, so-so 5 blase, vague 6 chance, random, sporty 7 offhand, passing, relaxed 8 informal 9 easygoing, haphazard, non-dressy, unplanned 10 accidental, fortuitous, incidental, nonchalant, unarranged, undesigned, undirected, unexpected, unforeseen 11 half-hearted, indifferent, unlooked for 13 lackadaisical, serendipitous, unintentional 14 indiscriminate, unpremeditated

Casuals of the Sea
author: 12 William McFee

casualty 6 injury, victim 7 injured 8 fatality

casuistry 5 guile 6 deceit 7 fallacy, sophism 8 subtlety 9 Jesuitism, quibbling, sophistry 10 nitpicking 12 equivocation, pettifoggery, speciousness 13 deceptiveness, hair-splitting 14 sophistication

casus belli 10 cause of war

Casy, Jim
character in: 16 The Grapes of Wrath
author: 9 Steinbeck

cat 3 pet 4 puss, whip 5 kitty, pussy, tabby 6 feline, kitten, mouser, tomcat
anatomy: 3 paw 4 loin, nape, rump, tail 5 break, flank, shank 6 feeler 7 dewclaw, leather, whisker 8 vibrissa 10 metatarsus
breed/kind: 3 tom 4 coon, Eyra, lion, lynx, Manx, puma 5 alley, civet, hyena, kitty, Korat, tabby, tiger 6 Angola, angora, bobcat, cougar, jaguar, ocelot, serval 7 Burmese, caracal, cheetah, leopard, linsang, Maltese, panther, Persian, polecat, Siamese, Turkish, wildcat 8 Balinese, Cheshire, Egyptian, ringtail 9 Himalayan, shorthair 10 Abyssinian, chinchilla 11 Russian blue 13 tortoise-shell
combining form: 5 aelur, ailur, felin 6 aeluro, ailuro, felino

Egyptian goddess of: 4 Bast

extinct: 10 saber-tooth
family: 7 Felidae
famous: 6 Morris 8 Cheshire, Garfield, Kilkenny 9 Mehitabel 10 Heathcliff
fastest: 7 cheetah
fear of: 12 aelurophobia, ailurophobia
female: 5 queen 7 lioness, tigress 8 wheencat 9 grimalkin
genus: 5 Felis
grinning: 8 Cheshire
group: 7 clowder, clutter
group of kittens: 6 kendle, kindle
lover: 11 aelurophile, ailurophile
male: 3 gib, tom 6 tomcat
ring-tailed: 6 serval 10 cacomistle
tailless: 4 Manx
young: 6 kitten
cataclysm 4 blow 7 debacle 8 calamity, disaster, upheaval 11 catastrophe, devastation
cataclysmic 4 dire 6 tragic 7 ruinous 10 calamitous, disastrous 12 catastrophic, earth-shaking
catacomb 4 tomb 7 ossuary 8 cemetery 10 passageway 12 burial ground
Cataebates
epithet of: 4 Zeus
means: 9 descender
catafalque 3 box 4 pall 6 casket, coffin
catalog, catalogue 4 file, list, post, roll 5 index 6 record, roster 7 listing 8 classify, register, syllabus, tabulate 9 directory, enumerate, inventory
Catamitus see 8 Ganymede
Cat and Mouse
author: 11 Gunter Grass
catapult 4 cast, hurl, toss 5 fling, heave, pitch, shoot, sling, throw 6 hurtle, propel 9 slingshot 13 hurling engine
cataract 5 falls, flood 6 deluge, rapids 7 cascade, torrent 8 downpour 9 waterfall 10 inundation
catastrophe 4 blow 5 havoc 6 mishap, ravage 7 debacle, scourge, tragedy 8 calamity, disaster 9 cataclysm 10 affliction, misfortune 11 devastation
catastrophic 6 tragic 7 ruinous 10 calamitous, disastrous 11 cataclysmic
catcall 3 boo 4 gibe, hiss, hoot, jeer 7 whistle 8 heckling 9 raspberry 10 Bronx cheer
catch 3 bag, bat, get, hit, nab 4 bait, bang, belt, bump, bust, dupe, feel, find, fool, grab, hasp, haul, hoax, hook, lock, lure, make, snag, snap, spot, take, trap 5 booty, break, charm, clasp, crack, get to, grasp, hitch, latch, prize, reach, seize, sense, smack, smite, snare, trick, whack, yield 6 allure, arrest, betray, buffet, collar, corner, corral, dazzle, deceit, delude, descry, detect, expose, fasten, fathom, kicker, snatch, strike, take in, turn on, unmask 7 attract, bewitch, capture, closure, deceive, delight, discern, enchant, ensnare, find out, gimmick, mislead, rasping, seizure 8 catching, come upon, contract, coupling, discover, drawback, enthrall, hoodwink, overtake, perceive, pickings, surprise 9 apprehend, bamboozle, captivate, carry away, enrapture, fastening, intercept, lay hold of, play false, recognize, transport 10 comprehend, understand 11 take captive 12 break out with, come down with, disadvantage, seize and hold, take off guard 14 stumbling block 15 take into custody 18 become infected with
catch-as-catch-can 7 cursory 9 haphazard, hit-or-miss, unplanned 10 disorderly, incomplete 11 superficial, unorganized 12 disorganized, unsystematic
Catcher in the Rye, The
author: 10 J D Salinger
character: 15 Holden Caulfield
catching 10 contagious, infectious 12 communicable 13 transmittable
catch on to 3 get 5 grasp, savvy 6 absorb, digest, fathom, pick up 10 assimilate, comprehend, get the idea, understand
catch sight of 3 see 4 espy 6 behold, descry, detect, notice 7 discern, make out, observe, pick out 8 perceive
Catch-22
author: 12 Joseph Heller
character: 9 Yossarian
catchword 5 motto 6 byword, cliche, slogan, war cry 8 password 9 battle cry, guide word, pet phrase, watchword 10 shibboleth
categorical 4 flat, sure 7 certain, express 8 absolute, definite, emphatic, explicit 10 pronounced, unreserved 11 unequivocal, unqualified 12 unmistakable 13 unconditional
categorically 10 absolutely, definitely, positively 12 conclusively
categorization 5 order 11 arrangement 14 classification
category 5 class, group 8 division, grouping 14 classification
cater 5 humor 6 pamper, pander, please 7 gratify, indulge, satisfy
caterpillar 4 moth, worm 5 larva 7 cutworm, tractor, webworm 8 hangworm, silkworm, wortworm 9 butterfly, woolybear 10 astragalus
caterwaul 3 cry 4 bawl, howl, wail, yelp 5 whine 6 clamor, scream, shriek, squawk, squeal 7 screech 10 rend the air
catfish 4 barb 5 banjo 6 dorado, madtom, mudcat, sucker 7 ariidae, bluecat 8 bagridae, bullhead, claridae, electric, flathead 9 siluridae 10 channel cat, cuttlefish, mochocidae, plotosidae, spotted cat 11 ictaluridae, pimelodidae, schilbeidae 12 aspredinidae, ostariophysi 14 malapteruridae 16 trichomycteridae
Catfish
nickname of: 9 Jim Hunter
catharsis 7 purging, release, venting 9 cleansing 12 purification
Catharsius
epithet of: 4 Zeus
means: 8 purifier

cathartic 5 purge 6 physic 8 aperient, evacuant, laxative 9 castor oil, purgative, purifying

cathedral 3 see 6 church, temple 7 lateran 8 basilica, official 9 authority 10 pontifical
Italian: 5 duomo

Cather, Willa
author of: 9 A Lost Lady, My Antonia, One of Ours, O Pioneers! 13 My Mortal Enemy 16 Shadows on the Rock, The Song of the Lark 18 The Professor's House 23 Sapphira and the Slave Girl 26 Death Comes for the Archbishop

cathode ray tube
abbreviation: 3 CRT
invented by: 7 Crookes

catholic, Catholic 5 broad 7 liberal 9 universal, worldwide 12 all-embracing, all-inclusive 13 comprehensive

cathouse 4 stew 5 house 6 bagnio, bordel 7 brothel 8 bordello 10 bawdy house, fancy house, whorehouse 13 sporting house 14 house of ill fame 16 house of ill repute 19 house of prostitution

Cat Jumps, The
author: 14 Elizabeth Bowen

catlike 5 catty, lithe 7 sinuous 8 stealthy 14 light on the feet

Catlin, George
born: 13 Wilkes-Barre PA
artwork: 16 Gallery of Indians

catnap 3 nap 4 doze 6 siesta, snooze 10 forty winks, light sleep

Cato
author: 13 Joseph Addison

Cat on a Hot Tin Roof
author: 17 Tennessee Williams
director: 13 Richard Brooks
cast: 8 Burl Ives (Big Daddy) 10 Jack Carson, Paul Newman (Brick) 14 Judith Anderson 15 Elizabeth Taylor (Maggie)

Catreus
king of: 5 Crete
father: 5 Minos
mother: 8 Pasiphae
son: 11 Althaemenes
daughter: 6 Aerope 7 Clymene 9 Apemosyne
grandson: 8 Menelaus

cats-eye
species: 11 chrysoberyl
source: 8 Sri Lanka

cat's paw 4 dupe, pawn, tool 5 patsy 7 fall guy

cattle 4 cows, kine, oxen 5 beefs, bulls, stock 6 beeves, calves, dogies, steers 8 bullocks, milk cows 9 livestock
family: 7 Bovidae
group of: 5 drove
kind: 2 ox 3 yak 4 Zebu 5 Angus 6 Ankole, Jersey 7 Brahman 8 Ayrshire, Guernsey, Hereford, Highland, Holstein 9 Charolais 12 water buffalo 13 Texas Longhorn 16 English Shorthorn, Holstein-Friesian
young: 4 calf 6 heifer 8 yearling

Catton, Bruce
author of: 22 A Stillness at Appomattox

catty 4 mean 7 catlike 8 spiteful 9 malicious, malignant 10 malevolent

catwalk 6 bridge 7 walkway 10 passageway

Caucasian
language branch: 5 Ubykh 9 Daghestan 10 Circassian 11 Khartvelian

Caucon
brought mysteries to: 8 Messenia

caucus 6 parley, powwow 7 council, meeting, session 8 assembly, conclave 10 conference

caudal 4 back, tail 7 tail-end

cauldron see 7 caldron

Caulfield, Holden
character in: 18 The Catcher in the Rye
author: 8 Salinger

Caulfield, Joan
real name: 21 Beatrice Joan Caulfield
born: 8 Orange NJ
roles: 8 Dear Ruth 17 My Favorite Husband

Caunus
brother: 6 Byblis

causation 4 root 5 cause 6 author, origin, reason, source 7 creator, genesis 8 etiology, inventor, stimulus 9 generator, invention 10 antecedent, conception, mainspring, originator 11 determinant, inspiration, origination

cause 4 goal, make, root, side 5 ideal, impel, tenet 6 belief, create, effect, incite, lead to, motive, object, origin, reason, source, spring, stir up 7 genesis, grounds, incline, inspire, produce, provoke, purpose 8 etiology, generate, motivate, occasion, stimulus 9 inducement, principle, stimulate 10 aspiration, bring about, conviction, foundation, give rise to, inducement, initiation, mainspring, motivation, persuasion, prime mover 11 bring to pass, inspiration, instigation, precipitate, provocation

cause of war
Latin: 10 casus belli

cause to appear 6 expose, reveal 7 uncover 8 disclose 12 bring to light 13 bring into view

caustic 4 tart 5 acrid, harsh, sharp 6 biting, bitter 7 burning, cutting, erosive, gnawing 8 scathing, stinging 9 corroding, corrosive, sarcastic 10 astringent 11 acrimonious

caution 4 care, heed, warn 5 alarm, alert 6 advise, caveat, exhort, notify, regard, tip-off 7 concern, thought, warning 8 admonish, forewarn, prudence, wariness 9 alertness, restraint, vigilance 10 admonition, discretion, precaution 11 carefulness, forewarning, guardedness, heedfulness, mindfulness 12 deliberation, watchfulness 14 circumspection, put on one's guard

cautionary 7 warning 8 advisory 10 admonitory 11 admonishing

cautious 4 wary 5 alert, cagey 7 careful, guarded, prudent 8 discreet, vigilant, watchful 9 attentive, judicious 11 circumspect

cavalcade 5 troop 6 column, parade 7 caravan, retinue 10 procession

Cavalcade
  director: 10 Frank Lloyd
  based on play by: 10 Noel Coward
  cast: 10 Clive Brook 11 Ursula Jeans 12 Diana Wynyard 13 Herbert Mundin 15 Margaret Lindsay
  Oscar for: 7 picture

cavalier 3 fop 4 beau 5 blade, cocky, dandy, swell 6 hussar, lancer 7 cursory, dragoon, gallant, haughty, offhand, playboy 8 arrogant, courtier, gay blade, horseman, uncaring 9 easygoing 10 cavalryman, disdainful, nonchalant 11 indifferent, thoughtless

cavalry 7 hussars, lancers 8 dragoons 10 mounted men 11 horse troops 13 horse soldiers, mounted troops

cavalryman 6 hussar, lancer 7 dragoon 8 cavalier, horseman 12 horse soldier, horse trooper 14 mounted soldier

cave 3 den 4 lair, sink 6 burrow, cavern, cavity, dugout, grotto, hollow
  growth: 10 stalactite, stalagmite
  explorer: 9 spelunker

caveat 5 alarm, alert, aviso 6 tip-off 7 caution, red flag, warning 8 high sign, red light 10 admonition, danger sign, yellow jack 11 forewarning 12 admonishment, flea in the ear 13 word to the wise 20 handwriting on the wall

caveat emptor 17 let the buyer beware

cave canem 14 beware of the dog

cave in 6 buckle, fall in, give up, submit 7 crumple, give way, implode 8 collapse 10 capitulate 12 fall to pieces

Cavendish, Henry
  field: 7 physics 9 chemistry
  nationality: 7 British
  discovered: 8 hydrogen
  determined composition of: 3 air 5 water 10 nitric acid
  method: 19 Cavendish experiment

cavernous 4 huge, vast 5 roomy 6 gaping 7 chasmal, immense, yawning 8 cavelike, enormous, spacious 10 tremendous

cavil 6 deride 7 nitpick, quibble 8 belittle, complain 9 criticize, deprecate, discredit, disparage, faultfind, find fault 12 pick to pieces

cavity 3 dip, pit 4 bore, dent, hole, sink 5 basin, niche 6 burrow, crater, hollow, pocket, tunnel 7 opening, orifice, vacuity 8 aperture 9 concavity 10 depression, excavation

cavort 4 play, romp 5 bound, caper, frisk 6 frolic, gambol, prance

Cawdor
  author: 15 Robinson Jeffers

Caxtons, The
  author: 12 Bulwer Lytton

Cayster
  river in: 5 Lydia

Cayuga
  language family: 9 Iroquoian
  location: 4 Ohio 6 Canada 7 New York 8 Oklahoma 9 Wisconsin
  branch of: 10 Six Nations 19 Iroquois Confederacy, League of the Iroquois

cease 3 end 4 halt, pass, quit, stop 5 abate, pause 6 desist, finish 7 adjourn, die away, forbear, suspend 8 break off, conclude, leave off 9 terminate 11 abstain from, discontinue, refrain from 12 bring to an end

cease-fire 5 truce 9 armistice

ceaseless 7 endless, eternal 8 constant, enduring, unending 9 continual, incessant, permanent, perpetual, unceasing 10 continuous, protracted 11 everlasting, neverending, unremitting 12 interminable 13 uninterrupted

cease to be 3 die, end 6 die out, expire, vanish 9 disappear, evaporate 13 become extinct

Cebriones
  father: 5 Priam
  brother: 6 Hector
  charioteer for: 6 Hector

Cecilia (Memoirs of an Heiress)
  author: 11 Fanny Burney

Cecrops
  also: 8 Cecropia
  form: 3 man 6 dragon
  founder of: 6 Attica
  king of: 6 Attica
  father: 14 King Erechtheus
  brother: 6 Metion, Orneus
  wife: 8 Aglaurus
  son: 11 Erysichthon
  daughter: 5 Herse 8 Aglaurus 9 Pandrasos
  renamed Attica: 8 Cecropia

Cedalion
  occupation: 5 smith
  forge owner: 10 Hephaestus
  served as guide for: 5 Orion

cedar 6 Cedrus
  varieties: 3 red 4 pink, salt 5 Atlas, giant, white 6 Alaska, Cyprus, ground, Mlanje 7 Bermuda, incense, Russian, Spanish 8 Barbados, cigar-box, creeping, Japanese, stinking 10 Ozark white, Port Orford, swamp white, western red, West Indian, Willowmore 11 Clanwilliam, Colorado red, southern red 13 Atlantic white, southern white 14 Chilean incense, Formosa incense 17 California incense

cede 4 give 5 grant, leave, yield 6 tender 7 abandon, deliver, release 8 hand over, transfer 9 deliver up, surrender 10 relinquish

cedez
  music: 8 slow down

Cedreatis
  epithet of: 7 Artemis
  means: 14 of the cedar tree

Cedric the Saxon
   character in: 7 Ivanhoe
   author: 5 Scott

ceiling 3 top 4 roof 5 cover, limit 6 canopy, cupola, lining 7 maximum 8 altitude 10 upperlimit

Celaeno
   member of: 7 Harpies 8 Pleiades

Celebes
   also: 8 Sulawesi
   bordered by: 6 Borneo 8 Moluccas 10 Celebes Sea, Kalimantan 12 Flores Strait 14 Makassar Strait
   city: 4 Poso 6 Manado 7 Kendari, Madjene 8 Bonthain, Donggala, Makassar 9 Gorontalo
   location: 9 Indonesia
   people: 4 Bugi, Laki, Mori, Muna, Napu, Palu, Peso, Seko, Wana 5 Besoa, Buton, Toala 6 Bungku, Butung, Parigi, Sadang, Sangir, Toland 7 Banggai, Bolaang, Kabaena, Loinang, Toradja 8 Balantak, Buginese, Mongondu, Rongkong, Sanghike 9 Gorontalo 11 Makassarese
   province: 13 North Sulawesi, South Sulawesi 15 Central Sulawesi 17 Southeast Sulawesi

celebrate 4 laud 5 bless, cheer, exalt, extol, honor 6 hallow, praise, revere 7 acclaim, applaud, commend, glorify, observe 8 proclaim, sanctify, venerate 9 broadcast, ritualize, solemnize 10 consecrate 11 commemorate 13 ceremonialize

celebrated 5 famed, noted 6 famous, prized 7 eminent, honored, notable, revered 8 lionized, renowned 9 acclaimed, important, prominent, respected, treasured, venerable, well-known 11 illustrious, outstanding 13 distinguished

Celebrated Jumping Frog of Calaveras County, The
   author: 9 Mark Twain

celebration 4 fete, gala 5 feast, party 6 ritual 7 jubilee, revelry 8 carnival, ceremony, festival 9 festivity, hallowing 10 ceremonial, observance 13 commemoration, solemnization 14 sanctification 15 memorialization

celebrity 3 VIP 4 fame, name, note, star 5 glory, wheel 6 bigwig, renown 7 big shot, notable, stardom 8 eminence, luminary 9 dignitary, notoriety, personage 10 notability, popularity, prominence 11 distinction, personality 12 famous person, person of note

celerity 5 haste, hurry, speed 6 hustle 8 alacrity, dispatch, fast clip, fastness, legerity, rapidity 9 briskness, quickness, swiftness 10 expedition, snappiness, speediness 12 precipitation 14 lightning speed 15 expeditiousness

celery seed
   also called: 8 smallage
   origin: 13 Mediterranean
   use: 4 soup 5 salad, sauce 6 pickle 10 vegetables

celestial 3 sky 5 solar 6 astral, divine 7 angelic, elysian, stellar, sublime 8 beatific, blissful, empyrean, ethereal, hallowed, heavenly, seraphic 9 planetary, unearthly 12 astronomical, otherworldly, paradisiacal

celestial being 3 god 5 angel, deity 7 goddess 8 divinity 11 divine being

Celestial City
   place in: 16 Pilgrim's Progress
   author: 6 Bunyan

Celia (Aliena)
   character in: 11 As You Like It
   author: 11 Shakespeare

celibacy 8 chastity 9 virginity 10 abstinence, continence 12 bachelorhood, spinsterhood

celibate 4 pure 5 unwed 6 chaste, single 8 bachelor, spinster, virginal 9 abstinent, continent, unmarried

Celine, Louis-Ferdinand
   author of: 12 Guignol's Band 25 Death on the Installment Plan, Journey to the End of the Night

cell
   part: 7 nucleus 8 membrane 9 cytoplasm
   made of: 3 fat 4 salt 5 water 7 protein 9 compounds 12 carbohydrate
   theory of: 7 (Rudolf) Virchow, (Theodor) Schwann

cellar 3 den 4 cave 6 dugout 8 basement 10 downstairs

Cellini, Benvenuto
   born: 5 Italy 8 Florence
   artwork: 7 Cosimo I, Perseus 13 Bindo Altoviti 18 The Crucified Christ 20 Nymph of Fontainebleau
   autobiography: 22 Life of Benvenuto Cellini

Celsius
   abbreviation of: 1 C

Celt 4 Gaul, Kelt, Manx, Scot 5 Irish, Welsh 6 Breton, Briton, chisel 8 Scottish 10 Highlander

Celtic
   language group: 6 Gaelic 9 Brythonic
   family: 12 Indo-European
   language of: 5 Gauls

cement 3 fix, set 4 bind, fuse, glue, join, seal, weld 5 paste, stick, unite 6 mortar, secure 8 concrete

cemetery 7 ossuary 8 boneyard, Boot Hill, catacomb 9 graveyard 10 churchyard, necropolis 12 burial ground, memorial park, potter's field 13 burying ground

Cenaean see 4 Zeus

Cenchrias
   father: 8 Poseidon
   mother: 6 Pirene
   killed by: 7 Artemis

Cenci, The
   author: 18 Percy Bysshe Shelley

cenobite 4 monk 7 ascetic 8 celibate 9 religious

censor 4 blip, edit 5 amend, judge, purge 6 critic, delete, excise 7 amender, clean up 8 black out, examiner, reviewer, suppress 9 expurgate, inspector 10 blue-pencil, bowd-

lerize, expurgator, suppressor **11**
bowdlerizer, faultfinder, scrutinizer **12** investigator **17** custodian of morals **25**
guardian of the public morals
censorious 5 picky **7** abusive, carping **8**
critical **10** defamatory **12** faultfinding
censurable 8 blamable **10** deplorable, punishable, reprovable **11** blameworthy **12** reproachable **13** reprehensible
censure 3 pan, rap **5** chide, scold **6** berate,
rebuke **7** bawl out, chew out, chiding, condemn, reproof, reprove, upbraid **8** admonish, denounce, reproach, scolding **9** castigate, complaint, criticism, criticize,
reprehend, reprimand **10** admonition,
bawling-out, chewing-out, disapprove, upbraiding **11** castigation, disapproval, reprobation **12** condemnation, dressing-down,
remonstrance **13** tongue-lashing **14**
disapprobation **16** rap on the knuckles,
take over the coals
god of: 5 Momos, Momus
census 3 tax **4** data, list, poll **5** count **6**
amount, number **11** enumeration **12** registration
Centaur
  form: 3 man **5** horse **7** monster **16** half-
  man half-horse
  constellation of: 9 Centaurus
  famous: 6 Chiron
  represents: 11 Sagittarius
Centaurus
  father: 5 Ixion
  mother: 7 Nephele
  father of: 8 Centaurs
Centennial
  author: 13 James Michener
Centennial State
  nickname of: 8 Colorado
center, centre 3 fix, hub, mid **4** axis, core,
crux **5** focus, heart, pivot, point **6** direct,
gather, middle **7** address, essence, nucleus **8** converge, interior **9** middle **10** focal point **11** concentrate
centered 4 even, true **5** right **7** focused **8**
straight **10** pinpointed **12** concentrated
centigrade 5 scale **6** degree **7** celcius **11**
thermometer
centigram
  abbreviation of: 2 cg
centiliter
  abbreviation of: 2 cl
Centimani *see* **13** Hecatonchires
centimeter
  abbreviation of: 2 cm
centipede 4 boat **5** shrub **6** earwig, insect **8**
chilopod, multiped **9** arthropod **13** mueh-
lenbeckia
central 3 key **4** main **5** basic, chief, focal,
inner, major, prime **6** inmost, middle **7**
leading, midmost, pivotal, primary **8** dominant, foremost, interior **9** essential, paramount, principal **10** middlemost **11** fundamental, predominant **13** most important

Central African Republic
  other name: 11 Ubangi-Chari **20** Central
  African Empire
  capital/largest city: 6 Bangui
  others: 3 Obo **4** Bria, Ippy **5** Birao,
  Bouar, Kembe, Ndele, Ngoto, Paoua,
  Rafai, Zemio **6** Baboua, Bakala, Bozoum,
  Mbaiki **7** Bambari, Grimari, Zemongo **9**
  Bangassou, Berberati, Bossangoa, Fort-
  Sibut
  monetary unit: 5 franc **7** centime
  lake: 4 Chad
  mountain: 5 Karre, Tinga **6** Mongos **9**
  Dar Challa
  highest point: 11 Kayagangiri
  river: 4 Bomu, Nana **5** Chari, Kotto,
  Mbari, Mpoko, Ouaka **6** Chinko, Lobaye,
  Mbomou, Ubangi **11** Upper Sangha
  people: 4 Baya, Sara **5** Banda, Bwaka,
  Sango **6** Azande, Yakoma **7** Banziri,
  Mandjia, Nzakara
  language: 5 Sango, Zande **6** French
  religion: 5 Islam **7** animism **12** Christianity **13** Roman Catholic
  place:
  plaza: **13** Edouard Renard
  food:
  tapioca: **6** manioc **7** cassava
Central America
  land form: 7 isthmus
  countries: 6 Belize, Panama **8** Honduras
  9 Costa Rica, Guatemala, Nicaragua **10**
  El Salvador
  bordered by: 6 Mexico, **8** Colombia **12**
  Caribbean Sea, North America, Pacific
  Ocean, South America
  capital city: 7 Managua, San Jose **8**
  Belmopan **10** Panama City **11** San Salvador, Tegucigalpa **13** Guatemala City
  river: 3 New **4** Axul, Coco, Sico, Tuma,
  Ulua, Wawa **5** Aguan, Chepo, Hondo,
  Lempa, Wauks **6** Chixoy, Grande,
  Pasion, Patuca, Sulaco, Waspuk **7**
  Motagua, Paulaya, San Juan, Sarstun,
  Segovia **8** Kukalaya **9** Choluteca,
  Escondido **10** Chucunaque **11**
  Prinzapolca
  lake: 5 Gatun, Guija, Yojoa **7** Atitlan, Ma-
  nagua **9** Nicaragua, Peten Itza
  mountain: 4 Maya, Pija **5** Colon, Huapi,
  Minas, Pando **6** Blanco **7** Dipilto,
  Gongora, San Blas **8** Brewster, Dariense,
  Isabelia, San Pablo, Santa Ana **9**
  Esperanza **14** Chirripo Grande
  people: 3 Mam **5** Zambo **6** Indian, Ladi-
  no, Quiche **7** mestizo **8** Miskitas **10** Black
  Carib, Cakchiquel
  animal: 5 tapir **6** agouti **7** opossum, peccary **8** anteater, kinkajou, marmoset **9** armadillo, porcupine, tree sloth **12** howler
  monkey, spider monkey **14** capuchin
  monkey
Central Amerind
  language branch: 9 Oto-Mangue **10**
  Uto-Aztecan **11** Kiowa-Tanoan

central city 8 core city, downtown 9 inner city, urban area 10 metropolis 16 business district, metropolitan area

central idea 3 nut 4 core, crux, gist, meat 5 heart, theme 6 kernel 7 essence 9 main point

centralization 5 focus 11 convergence 13 concentration, consolidation

centralize 5 focus, unify 6 center, gather 7 collect, compact 8 center on, coalesce, converge, pinpoint 9 integrate 10 congregate 11 concentrate, consolidate

central part 4 core, crux, gist, pith 5 heart 6 center, kernel 7 nucleus

century
abbreviation of: 4 cent
French: 6 siecle

cephalopod 5 squid 7 mollusk, octopus 8 nautilus 10 cuttlefish

Cephalus
father: 6 Hermes
mother: 5 Herse
brother: 5 Ceryx
wife: 7 Clymene, Procris

Cephas see 5 Peter

Cepheus
king of: 8 Ethiopia
wife: 10 Cassiopeia
daughter: 9 Andromeda

Cerambus
form: 6 beetle

ceramic ware 5 china, glass 7 pottery 8 crockery 9 chinaware, glassware, porcelain, stoneware 10 enamelware 11 earthenware

ceratopsid
type of: 8 dinosaur
member: 10 Torosaurus 11 Monoclonius, Triceratops 13 Protoceratops, Styracosaurus 14 Psittacosaurus

Ceratosaurus
type: 8 dinosaur
period: 8 Jurassic

Cerberus
form: 3 dog
father: 6 Typhon
mother: 7 Echidna
sibling: 5 Hydra 7 Orthrus 8 Chimaera 10 Nemean lion 12 Theban Sphinx
number of heads: 5 three
guarded: 10 Underworld

Cercopes
race of: 6 Gnomes

Cercyon
king of: 7 Arcadia
daughter: 5 Alope

cereal 4 corn, oats, rice, seed 5 grain, grass, gruel, plant, wheat 6 barley, pablum 7 oatmeal, pabulum 8 porridge

cerebellum
part of: 5 brain
controls: 7 balance 8 movement

cerebrum
part of: 5 brain
controls: 6 seeing 7 hearing, tasting 8 deciding, feelings, learning, smelling,

thinking, touching 9 awareness 11 remembering

ceremonial 4 rite 6 formal, ritual 7 liturgy, service 8 ceremony 9 formality, sacrament 10 liturgical, observance 11 celebration, ritualistic

ceremonialize 7 observe 9 celebrate, ritualize 11 commemorate

ceremonious 5 exact, fussy, rigid, stiff 6 formal, proper, solemn 7 careful, correct, pompous, precise 8 starched 9 dignified 10 methodical, meticulous 11 punctilious

ceremony 4 rite 6 custom, nicety, ritual 7 amenity, decorum, pageant, service 8 function, protocol 9 etiquette, formality, propriety 10 observance, politeness 11 celebration, formalities 13 commemoration

Cerenkov, Pavel Alekseevich
field: 7 physics
nationality: 7 Russian
discovered: 12 cause of light 14 Cerenkov effect

Ceres
origin: 5 Roman
goddess of: 11 agriculture
corresponds to: 7 Demeter

certain 4 sure 5 valid 6 secure 7 assured, express, settled, special 8 absolute, cocksure, definite, positive, reliable, specific 9 confident, convinced, satisfied 10 conclusive, individual, inevitable, particular, undeniable, undisputed, undoubtful, undoubting, unshakable 11 indubitable, inescapable, irrefutable, unalterable, unequivocal, unqualified 12 indisputable, unchangeable, unmistakable, well-grounded 13 bound to happen, incontestable 14 unquestionable 16 incontrovertible

certainly 5 truly 6 indeed, surely 7 for sure 8 of course 9 decidedly 10 absolutely, definitely, positively 11 indubitably, undoubtedly 13 unequivocally, without a doubt 14 unquestionably 21 beyond a shadow of a doubt

Certain Smile, A
author: 14 Francoise Sagan

certainty 4 fact 5 faith, trust 6 belief, surety 7 reality, sure bet 8 sureness 9 actuality, assurance, certitude, sure thing 10 confidence, conviction 11 presumption 12 positiveness 13 inevitability 14 conclusiveness, inescapability 17 authoritativeness

certificate 4 deed 6 permit 7 diploma, license, voucher 8 document, warranty 9 affidavit 10 credential 11 testimonial 13 authorization 14 authentication

certification 7 voucher 8 approval 10 validation 11 endorsement 12 confirmation, ratification, verification 13 authorization, corroboration 14 authentication, substantiation

certify 4 aver 5 swear, vouch 6 assure, attest, ratify, second, verify 7 confirm, declare, endorse, support, warrant, witness 8 notarize, sanction, validate 9 authorize, guarantee, testify to 10 underwrite 11 corroborate 12 authenticate, give one's word, substantiate

certitude 5 faith, trust 6 belief, surety 8 reliance, sureness 9 assurance, certainty 10 confidence 12 positiveness 14 conclusiveness

cerulean 4 blue 5 azure 6 cobalt 7 sky blue 9 clear blue

Cervantes Saavedra, Miguel de
   author of: 20 Don Quixote de la Mancha

Cerynean stag
   also: 12 Arcadian stag
   home: 7 Arcadia
   captured by: 8 Hercules

Ceryx
   herald of: 4 gods
   father: 6 Hermes
   mother: 5 Herse
   brother: 8 Cephalus

Cesar Birotteau
   author: 14 Honore de Balzac

cessation 3 end 4 halt, stay, stop 5 pause 6 ending, recess 7 ceasing, halting, respite 8 quitting, stopping, surcease 9 desisting 10 concluding, leaving off, suspension 11 adjournment, breaking off, termination 12 interruption 13 coming to a halt, discontinuing 14 discontinuance

c'est la vie 9 that's life 10 such is life

Cestrinus
   father: 7 Helenus
   mother: 10 Andromache

Cestus
   girdle of: 5 Venus

cetacean 4 apod 5 whale 6 beluga, mammal 7 cetacea, dolphin, dowfish, grampus, narwhal 8 porpoise, sturgeon 9 blue whale 11 baleen whale, killer whale

Cetinje
   capital of: 10 Montenegro

Ceto
   father: 6 Pontus
   mother: 4 Gaea
   brother: 7 Phorcys
   husband: 7 Phorcys
   mother of: 6 Graeae 7 Gorgons
   children called: 8 Phorcids

Ceylon see 8 Sri Lanka

Ceyx
   father: 9 Eosphorus
   wife: 7 Alcyone

Cezanne, Paul
   born: 6 France 13 Aix-en-Provence
   artwork: 7 Bathers 11 Card Players 13 The Black Clock, The Railway Out 14 Uncle Dominique 15 La Maison du Pendu 16 The Suicide's House 17 Grandes Baigneuses 19 Woman with a Coffee Pot 36 Mont-Sainte-Victoire with Large Pine Trees

Chabrier, (Alexis) Emmanuel
   born: 6 Ambert, France
   composer of: 6 Espana 7 L'Etoile 10 Gwendoline 13 Marche Joyeuse 14 Le Roi Malgre Lui 18 King Despite Himself 19 Une Education Manquee

Chad
   other name: 5 Tchad
   capital/largest city: 8 Fort-Lamy, N'Djamena
   others: 3 Ati, Bol, Lai, Mao 4 Fada, Faya, Sarh 5 Mongo 6 Abeche, Bongor 7 Largeau, Moundou 8 Moussoro
   monetary unit: 5 franc 7 centime
   lake: 4 Chad
   mountain: 7 Tibesti, Touside
   highest point: 9 Emi Koussi
   river: 5 Chari 6 Logone 8 Bahraouk
   physical feature:
      plateau: 6 Ennedi
   people: 4 Arab, Daza, Maba, Sara, Teda, Tubu 5 Barma, Hakka, Kreda, Massa 6 Fulani, Kotoko, Toubou, Wadaii 7 Kamadja, Kanembu, Moundan
   language: 4 Sara 5 Turku 6 Arabic, French
   religion: 5 Islam 7 animism 12 Christianity

Chadband
   character in: 10 Bleak House
   author: 7 Dickens

Chadic
   language family: 11 Afroasiatic 13 Hamito-Semitic
   includes: 5 Hausa
   spoken in: 6 Africa 8 Lake Chad

Chadwick, James
   field: 7 physics
   nationality: 7 British
   discovered: 7 neutron
   awarded: 10 Nobel Prize

chafe 3 rub 4 boil, burn, foam, fume, rage, rasp 6 abrade, rankle, scrape, seethe 7 scratch 9 be annoyed 11 be irritated

chaff 3 bug, kid, rag, rib 4 josh, junk, pods, razz, ride, slag, twit 5 dross, hulls, husks, jolly, trash, waste 6 banter, debris, litter, refuse, rubble, shells, shoddy, shucks 7 kidding, ragging, remnant, residue, ribbing, rubbish, waggery 8 badinage, chaffing, leavings, raillery, ridicule 9 sweepings 9 give and take

chaffing 6 banter 7 jesting, joshing, kidding, ragging, ribbing, waggery 8 badinage, raillery

chafing 5 harsh 6 fuming 7 rasping, rubbing. 8 abrading, abrasive 10 irritating

Chagall, Marc
   born: 6 Liosno, Liozno, Russia
   artwork: 8 Birthday, Cockcrow 9 The Circus, The Red Sun 10 The Juggler 11 Over Vitebsk 12 The Violinist 14 Double Portrait, I and the Village 16 The Jewish Wedding 17 Lovers with Rooster 20 Paris Through My Window

chagrin 5 shame 6 dismay 8 distress 11 humiliation 13 embarrassment, mortification

chagrined 7 abashed, ashamed 9 mortified 10 humiliated 11 embarrassed

Chahiksichhiks *see* 6 Pawnee

chain 3 fob 5 cable, links 7 shackle 8 necklace 10 metal links 11 linked cable
   abbreviation: 2 ch

Chain, Ernst Boris
   field: 12 biochemistry
   nationality: 7 British
   discovered: 10 penicillin
   worked with: 6 Florey 7 Fleming
   awarded: 10 Nobel Prize

Chained Lady
   constellation of: 9 Andromeda

chains 3 tie 4 bind, lash, moor 5 bonds, irons, tie up, train 6 fasten, fetter, secure, series, string, tether 7 bondage, fetters, manacle, serfdom, shackle, slavery 8 leg irons, manacles, sequence, shackles 9 handcuffs, servitude, thralldom 10 put in irons, succession 11 enslavement, subjugation

chair 4 seat 5 bench, couch, sedan stool 6 chaise, lounge, rocker, settee, throne 7 conduct, ottoman 11 preside over 16 presiding officer

chairman 4 head 5 chair, emcee 6 leader 7 manager, speaker 8 director 9 chairlady, executive, moderator 10 chairwoman, supervisor 11 chairperson, toastmaster 13 administrator 16 presiding officer 18 master of ceremonies

Chair of Forgetfulness
   form: 4 seat
   made of: 5 stone
   location: 10 Underworld

chaise 3 gig 4 shay 5 chair 6 daybed, lounge 7 calesin 8 carriage, duchesse

chalcedony 3 gem 4 onyx, opal, sard 5 agate, prase 6 jasper, plasma, quartz, silica 7 catseye, mineral, opaline, sardius 8 hematite, sardonyx 9 carnelian 10 bloodstone, heliotrope 11 chrysoprase 12 semiprecious 14 silicon dioxide

Chalcis
   father: 6 Asopus
   mother: 6 Metope

Chaldean 4 seer 5 magic 6 Syriac 7 Aramaic, semitic 8 magician 9 astrology, enchanter, Nabonidus 10 astrologer, Babylonian, soothsayer 12 Nabopolassar 14 Nebuchadnezzar

chalice 3 cup 5 grail 6 goblet, vessel

Chalinitis
   epithet of: 6 Athena
   means: 7 bridler

chalk 4 draw 6 crayon, pastel, sketch 9 limestone

chalk up 4 earn 5 score 6 attain, charge, credit 7 achieve, ascribe

chalky 3 wan 4 pale 5 ashen, white 6 pallid 7 powdery 8 blanched 9 bloodless

challenge 3 bid, tax, try 4 dare, defy, gage, test 5 doubt, trial 6 demand, impute, summon 7 defiant, dispute, summons 8 question 15 take exception to 20 fling down the gauntlet

chamber 4 diet, hall, room 5 board, court, house, salon 6 office, parlor 7 bedroom, boudoir, council 8 assembly, congress 9 apartment

Chamberlain, Owen
   field: 7 physics
   developed: 8 atom bomb
   awarded: 10 Nobel Prize

Chamberlain, Richard
   real name: 24 George Richard Chamberlain
   born: 12 Los Angeles CA
   roles: 6 Shogun 9 Dr Kildare 10 Wallenberg 13 The Thorn Birds 17 The Bourne Identity 21 The Count of Monte Cristo

Chamberlain, Wilt (Wilton Norman)
   nickname: 6 Dipper 12 Wilt the Stilt
   sport: 10 basketball
   position: 5 coach 6 center
   team: 16 Los Angeles Lakers 17 Philadelphia 76ers 20 Philadelphia Warriors, San Francisco Warriors 21 San Diego Conquistadors

chambermaid
   French: 14 femme de chambre

chambord
   type: 7 liqueur
   origin: 6 France
   flavor: 9 raspberry

chameleon 4 newt 6 lizard 8 renegade, turncoat 10 fickleness 14 changeableness

champ 4 bite, chew, gnaw 5 chomp, crush, grind, munch 6 crunch 8 champion

champagne
   type: 4 wine
   drink: 7 the Pope
   with white wine: 8 Cold Duck
   with orange juice: 6 Mimosa
   measure: 6 magnum 8 jeroboam, rehoboam 9 balthazar 10 methuselah, salmanazar 14 Nebuchadnezzar

Champaigne, Philippe de
   born: 7 Belgium 8 Brussels
   artwork: 6 Ex Voto 17 Cardinal Richelieu 26 The Adoration of the Shepherds

champion 3 aid 4 abet, back 6 backer, defend, master, uphold, victor, winner 7 espouse, paragon, promote, support 8 advocate, defender, fight for, laureate, promoter, speak for, upholder 9 battle for, conqueror, protector, supporter 10 stand up for, vanquisher 11 protagonist, title holder

Champion
   constellation of: 7 Perseus

championship 3 cup 5 crown, title 7 backing, defense, support, winning 8 advocacy, espousal

Chamyne
   epithet of: 7 Demeter

chance 3 try 4 fall, fate, luck, risk 5 lucky, occur 6 befall, danger, gamble, happen, hazard, random 7 attempt, destiny, fortune, turn out, venture 8 accident, jeopardy, occasion 9 come about, fortunate, unplanned 10 accidental, fortuitous, likelihood, likeliness, providence, undesigned, unexpected, unforeseen 11 opportunity, possibility, probability, speculation, unlooked for 12 happenstance 13 unintentional 14 unpremeditated

chance upon 4 find, meet 7 learn of, run into 8 come upon, discover 9 encounter, light upon 10 happen upon 11 stumble upon

chancy 4 iffy 5 dicey, risky 6 touchy, tricky 7 dubious, erratic, unsound 8 doubtful 9 hazardous, uncertain, whimsical 10 capricious, precarious 11 speculative, venturesome 13 problematical, unpredictable

chandelier 11 hanging lamp 12 candleholder 15 lighting fixture

Chandler, Jeff
  real name: 10 Ira Grossel
  born: 10 Brooklyn NY
  roles: 7 Cochise 11 Broken Arrow 17 Merrill's Marauders

Chandler, Raymond
  author of: 11 The Big Sleep 14 The Long Goodbye 16 Farewell My Lovely
  character: 13 Philip Marlowe
  screenplay: 13 The Blue Dahlia 15 Double Indemnity 17 Strangers on a Train

Chaney, Lon
  real name: 12 Alonso Chaney
  son: 9 Creighton (Lon Chaney Jr)
  nickname: 19 Man of a Thousand Faces
  born: 17 Colorado Springs CO
  roles: 14 The Unholy Three 18 Tell It to the Marines 20 Hunchback of Notre Dame, The Phantom of the Opera

Chaney, Lon Jr
  real name: 9 Creighton
  father: 3 Lon
  born: 14 Oklahoma City OK
  roles: 6 Lennie 8 The Mummy 10 The Wolf Man 12 Of Mice and Men, Son of Dracula 20 Frankenstein's Monster

change 4 swap, turn, vary 5 alter, coins, shift, trade 6 modify, mutate, recast, reform, silver, switch 7 convert, novelty, remodel, replace, restyle, shuffle, variety, veering 8 pin money, swapping, transfer 9 deviation, diversion, exception, restyling, transform, transmute, turn about, variation 10 alteration, conversion, difference, remodeling, reorganize, revolution, small coins, substitute 11 fluctuation, pocket money, reformation 12 metamorphose, modification, substitution 13 make different, metamorphosis, revolutionize, transmutation, transposition 14 reorganization, transformation 15 transfiguration

changeable 6 fickle, fitful 7 erratic, flighty, mutable, varying 8 unstable, unsteady, variable, volatile 9 deviating, irregular, mercurial, uncertain 10 capricious, inconstant, modifiable, reversible 11 alternating, convertible, fluctuating, vacillating 13 transformable

change in plan
  French: 8 demarche

changeless 4 fast 5 fixed 6 stable 7 abiding, certain, durable, eternal, lasting 8 constant, enduring 9 immutable, steadfast, unvarying 10 unshakable 11 everlasting, unalterable 12 indissoluble

changelessness 9 certainty, constancy, stability 10 durability, permanence 12 immutability 13 steadfastness

change of heart 10 conversion 16 change of attitude

changeover 10 conversion

channel 3 cut 4 gash, lead, send 5 guide, route, steer 6 convey, course, direct, furrow, groove, gutter, strait, trough 7 narrows, passage 11 watercourse 21 avenue of communication

Channing, Carol
  born: 9 Seattle WA
  roles: 10 Hello Dolly 22 Gentlemen Prefer Blondes, Thoroughly Modern Millie

chanson 4 song

Chanson de Roland
  also: 12 Song of Roland
  author: 7 unknown
  character: 4 Aude 6 Turpin 7 Ganelon, Marsile, Olivier 11 Charlemagne, Twelve Peers
  foe: 8 Saracens

chant 3 ode 4 hymn, lied, sing, song 5 carol, croon, dirge, elegy, psalm, theme, trill, troll 6 chorus, intone, melody, monody, strain 7 chanson, chorale, descant 8 canticle, doxology, threnody, vocalize 9 homophony, monophony, offertory, plainsong 11 Gloria Patri 14 Gregorian chant

chanteuse 6 singer (female)

Chants de Maldoror, Les
  author: 18 Comte de Lautreamont

Chaon
  father: 5 Priam
  mother: 6 Hecuba
  brother: 5 Paris 6 Hector 7 Helenus
  sister: 8 Polyxena 9 Cassandra

chaos 4 mess 5 furor 6 bedlam, jumble, muddle, tumult, uproar 7 turmoil 8 disarray, disorder, upheaval 9 agitation, commotion, confusion 10 turbulence 11 pandemonium 12 discomposure 14 disarrangement 15 disorganization

Chaos
  origin: 5 Greek
  personifies: 9 confusion

chaotic 7 jumbled, mixed-up, muddled, tangled 8 confused 9 confusing, illogical, turbulent 10 disjointed, incoherent, in disarray 11 unorganized 12 disorganized 13 disharmonious

chap 3 boy, dry, guy, jaw, lad, man, rap 4 chop, gent 5 bloke, buyer, crack, knock, split 6 fellow, redden, split, stroke 7 fissure, roughen 8 customer 9 purchaser

chapbook 7 garland 8 treasury 9 anthology 10 collection 11 florilegium

chapeau 3 hat

chapel 6 church, shrine 7 oratory 9 sanctuary 10 house of God, tabernacle 14 place of worship

chaperon, chaperone 5 guard, watch 6 duenna, escort 7 oversee 8 guardian, shepherd 9 accompany, attendant, custodian, protector, safeguard 11 keep an eye on

chaperoned 7 oversaw 8 attended, escorted 10 supervised 11 accompanied

chapfallen 6 droopy 8 cast down, dejected 9 depressed

chaplain 4 abbe 5 padre, rabbi, vicar 6 cleric, curate, father, parson, pastor, priest, rector 7 Holy Joe 8 minister, preacher, reverend, sky pilot 9 churchman, clergyman 12 ecclesiastic

chaplet 4 band 6 fillet, wreath 7 circlet, coronet

Chaplin, Charlie
  real name: 24 Sir Charles Spencer Chaplin
  nickname: 14 the Little Tramp
  wife: 10 Oona O'Neill 15 Paulette Goddard
  daughter: 9 Geraldine
  born: 6 London 7 England
  director of/roles: 6 The Kid 8 The Tramp 9 Limelight 10 City Lights 11 Modern Times, The Gold Rush 15 Monsieur Verdoux 16 The Great Dictator

Chaplin, Geraldine
  father: 14 Charlie Chaplin
  mother: 17 Oona O'Neill Chaplin
  born: 13 Santa Monica CA
  roles: 12 The Hawaiians 13 Doctor Zhivago

chapter 3 era 4 body, part, span, unit 5 group, phase 6 branch, clause, period 7 episode, portion, section 8 division 9 affiliate 11 subdivision

Chapters of Erie
  author: 10 Henry Adams

char 4 burn, sear 5 singe 6 scorch 9 carbonize 10 incinerate

character 4 part, role, self 5 being, honor 6 makeup, nature, person, traits, weirdo 7 honesty, oddball, persona 8 goodness, morality, original, specimen 9 eccentric, integrity, odd person, qualities, rectitude 10 attributes, individual, one-of-a-kind 11 personality, uprightness 13 individuality, moral strength 15 distinctiveness 16 dramatis personae

characteristic 4 mark 5 trait 6 aspect 7 earmark, feature, quality, typical 8 property, symbolic 9 attribute, mannerism, specialty, trademark 10 emblematic, indicative 11 distinctive, peculiarity 14 distinguishing, representative

characterization 8 portrait 9 depiction, picturing, portrayal 11 delineation, description 12 representing 14 representation

characterize 4 mark 5 class 6 define, depict, typify 7 earmark, portray 8 classify, describe, indicate 9 designate, represent 11 distinguish

characterless 4 weak 5 vague 6 anemic 11 nondescript 13 indeterminate 14 expressionless

Characters of Shakespeare's Plays, The
  author: 14 William Hazlitt

Charcot, Jean Martin
  nationality: 6 French
  father of: 9 neurology

Chardin, Jean Baptiste Simeon
  born: 5 Paris 6 France
  artwork: 7 The Kiss 8 The Grace 14 Young Governess 16 The Copper Cistern 17 Attributes of Music 19 Attributes of the Arts 28 Rayfish Cat and Kitchen Utensils

charge 3 ask, bid, fee 4 care, cost, duty, fill, heap, lade, levy, load, pack, pile, rate, rush, toll 5 beset, blame, debit, exact, onset, order, price, stack, storm, stuff 6 accuse, advice, amount, assail, assess, assign, attack, come at, demand, direct, enjoin, impute, indict, sortie, summon 7 ascribe, assault, bidding, command, control, custody, dictate, expense, keeping, payment, require 8 call upon, instruct, storming 9 attribute, complaint, direction, enjoining, onslaught 10 accusation, allegation, assessment, indictment, injunction, management, protection 11 arraignment, incriminate, instruction, safekeeping, supervision 12 delay payment, guardianship, jurisdiction 14 administration, lay the blame for, request payment 15 superintendence 16 put on one's account

chargeable 6 liable 10 answerable 11 responsible

charged 5 taxed, tense 6 blamed, filled, levied, loaded, priced 7 accused, ordered, uptight 8 assessed, attacked, exhorted, mandated, prepared 9 commanded, entrusted 10 accusation, allegation, indictment

Charge of the Light Brigade, The
  author: 18 Alfred Lord Tennyson
  director: 13 Michael Curtiz
  cast: 10 David Niven, Errol Flynn, Nigel Bruce 11 Donald Crisp 13 Patric Knowles 15 Henry Stephenson 17 Olivia de Havilland
  setting: 6 Russia

charger 5 horse, mount, steed 6 vessel 7 accuser, platter 8 warhorse

charge with 5 trust 6 assign, commit 7 consign, entrust 8 delegate, hand over, turn over 9 authorize

Chariclo
  husband: 6 Chiron
  son: 8 Tiresias
  companion of: 6 Athena

chariot 3 car 5 buggy 7 phaeton, vehicle 8 carriage

Charioteer
  constellation of: 6 Auriga

Chariots of Fire
  director: 10 Hugh Hudson
  cast: 7 Ian Holm 8 Ben Cross (Harold Abrahams) 11 John Gielgud, Nigel Havers 12 Ian Charleson (Eric Liddell)
  Oscar for: 5 score (Vangelis) 6 script 7 picture

Charis
member of: 6 Graces
husband: 10 Hephaestus

charisma 5 charm 6 allure, appeal 7 glamour 8 presence, witchery 9 magnetism, sex appeal 10 bewitchery 11 enchantment, fascination 14 attractiveness

charitable 4 kind 6 giving, kindly 7 lenient, liberal 8 generous, gracious, tolerant 9 bounteous, bountiful, forgiving, indulgent 10 almsgiving, benevolent, munificent, open-handed 11 considerate, kindhearted, magnanimous, sympathetic, warmhearted 12 eleemosynary, sympathizing 13 philanthropic, understanding

charitableness 10 liberality 11 benevolence, generousity 12 philanthropy 13 bountifulness 14 openhandedness 15 humanitarianism

Charites see 6 Graces

charity 3 aid 4 alms, fund, gift, help, love 6 bounty, giving 7 handout 8 altruism, donating, good will, goodness, humanity, kindness, offering, sympathy 9 benignity, donations, endowment, tolerance 10 alms-giving, assistance, compassion, generosity 11 benefaction, benevolence, fundraising, munificence 12 graciousness, philanthropy 13 contributions, financial help, love of mankind 14 open-handedness

charlatan 4 fake 5 cheat, fraud, quack 7 cozener 8 deceiver, imposter, impostor, swindler 9 trickster 10 mountebank 16 confidence artist

Charles, Nick and Nora
characters in: 10 The Thin Man
author: 7 Hammett

Charles O'Malley
author: 12 Charles Lever

Charleston 5 dance 13 ballroom dance
capital of: 9 W Virginia

Charlie's Angels
character: 10 Jill Monroe, John Bosley, Kris Munroe 12 Kelly Garrett 13 Sabrina Duncan 15 Charlie Townsend
cast: 10 Cheryl Ladd, David Doyle 11 Jaclyn Smith, Kate Jackson 18 Farah Fawcett-Majors
voice of Charlie: 12 John Forsythe

Charlotte's Web
author: 7 E B White

Charly
director: 11 Ralph Nelson
based on story by: 11 Daniel Keyes (Flowers for Algernon)
cast: 10 Leon Janney, Lilia Skala 11 Claire Bloom 13 Dick van Patten 14 Cliff Robertson
Oscar for: 5 actor (Robertson)

charm 4 draw, grip, lure, take 5 magic, spell 6 allure, amulet, bauble, cajole, engage, please, seduce, turn on 7 attract, beguile, bewitch, conjure, delight, enchant, gratify, sorcery, trinket, win over 8 charisma, enthrall, entrance, ornament, talis-

man 9 captivate, enrapture, fascinate, magnetism 10 allurement, attraction, cast a spell, lucky piece 11 conjuration, enchantment, fascination, incantation, work magic on

charmer 4 vamp 5 belle, siren 9 enchanter, temptress 11 enchantress, femme fatale, spellbinder

charming 6 lovely 7 likable, winning, winsome 8 alluring, engaging, enticing, fetching, graceful, magnetic, pleasing 9 agreeable 10 attractive, bewitching, delightful, enchanting, entrancing 11 captivating, charismatic, enthralling, fascinating 12 irresistible

charmless 4 dull 5 blunt 6 dreary 9 repulsive, unlikable, unlovable 10 unpleasant 12 disagreeable, unattractive

Charon
father: 6 Erebus
mother: 3 Nyx
occupation: 8 ferryman
river: 4 Styx

Charops
epithet of: 8 Hercules
means: 14 with bright eyes

Charpentier, Gustave
born: 6 Dieuze, France
composer of: 6 Julien, Louise 18 Impressions of Italy

chart 3 map 4 plan, plot 5 draft, graph, table 6 design, draw up, lay out, map out, scheme, sketch 7 diagram, outline 8 tabulate 9 blueprint, delineate 10 tabulation

charter 3 let 4 deed, hire, rent 5 grant, lease 6 employ, engage, permit 7 compact, license 8 contract, covenant, sanction 9 agreement, authority, authorize, franchise 10 commission, concession

Charterhouse of Parma, The
author: 23 Marie Henri Beyle Stendhal
character: 8 Marietta 10 Count Mosca 11 Clelia Conti 14 Gina Pietranera 16 Fabrizio del Dongo

chartreuse
type: 7 liqueur
origin: 6 France 15 Carthusian monks
flavor: 4 herb
color: 5 green 6 yellow
with apricot brandy: 13 Golden Slipper
with gin: 5 Bijou 9 Green Lady

chary 3 shy 4 wary 5 alert, cagey, leery 7 careful, guarded, heedful, prudent, sparing 8 cautious, hesitant, vigilant, watchful 10 economical, suspicious 11 circumspect, distrustful

Charybdis
form: 7 monster
father: 8 Poseidon
mother: 4 Gaea
identified with: 9 whirlpool

chase 3 dog 4 hunt, oust, rout, shoo, tail 5 drive, evict, hound, quest, stalk, track, trail 6 dispel, follow, pursue, shadow 7 cast out, go after, hunting, pursuit, repulse, scatter 8 pursuing, run after, send away, stalking, tracking 9 drive away, following 11 put to flight, send packing

Chase, Chevy
real name: 19 Cornelius Crane Chase
born: 9 New York NY
roles: 8 Foul Play, Vacation 10 Caddyshack 17 Saturday Night Live

chasm 3 gap, pit 4 gulf, hold, rift 5 abyss, break, cleft, crack, gorge, gulch, split 6 breach, cavity, crater, divide, ravine 7 fissure 8 crevasse

chasseur 6 hunter

chaste 4 pure 5 clean 6 decent, modest, severe, strict 7 austere, classic, precise, sinless 8 virginal, virtuous 9 continent, righteous, unadorned, unsullied, untainted, wholesome 10 immaculate, restrained 11 clean-living, uncorrupted 12 unornamented 13 unembellished

chasten 5 chide, scold 6 berate, punish, rebuke 7 censure, reprove, upbraid 8 admonish, chastise, reproach 9 reprimand 10 discipline, take to task

chastened 7 humbled 8 contrite, penitent 9 repentant 10 remorseful 18 conscience-stricken

chastise 4 beat, flog, whip 5 chide, roast, scold, spank, strap 6 berate, punish, rebuke, thrash 7 censure, chasten, correct, reprove, scourge, upbraid 8 admonish, call down, penalize, reproach 9 castigate, criticize, reprimand 10 discipline, take to task, tongue-lash 15 call on the carpet 16 fulminate against, haul over the coals

chastisement 10 correction, discipline, punishment 11 castigation 12 reprimanding

chastity 6 purity 8 celibacy 9 innocence, virginity 10 abstinence, continence, singleness 12 bachelorhood, spinsterhood 14 abstemiousness
goddess of: 5 Diana, Fauna 7 Artemis, Bona Dea

chasuble 6 casual 7 garment 8 vestment

Chasuble, Reverend Canon
character in: 27 The Importance of Being Earnest
author: 5 Wilde

chat 3 gab, rap 4 talk 5 prate 7 chatter, palaver, prattle 8 chitchat, converse 10 chew the fat, chew the rag, rap session 11 talk session 12 conversation 13 confabulation 16 heart-to-heart talk

chateau 4 wine 6 castle, estate 7 mansion 8 chatelet 12 country house

Chateaubriand, Francois Rene
author of: 4 Rene 5 Atala 10 Los Natchez, The Martyrs 19 Memoires d'Outre-tombe 24 Memoirs from Beyond the Tomb

Chateau d'If
prison in: 21 The Count of Monte Cristo
author: 5 Dumas (pere)

Chateaupers, Phoebus de
character in: 23 The Hunchback of Notre Dame
author: 4 Hugo

chattel 4 gear 6 things 7 effects 8 movables 9 trappings 10 belongings 13 accoutrements, paraphernalia 15 personal effects 19 personal possessions

chatter 3 gas 4 blab, talk 5 clank, click, prate 6 babble, gabble, gibber, gossip, jabber, patter 7 blabber, blather, clatter, palaver, prattle, talking, twaddle 8 blabbing, chitchat, idle talk, talk idly 11 confabulate 14 chitterchatter

chatterbox 6 gabber, gasbag, gossip, talker 7 babbler, tattler, windbag 8 jabberer, prattler, tell tale 9 chatterer 10 talebearer, tattle tale 12 blabbermouth, blatherskite, hot-air artist 13 chatterbasket

chatty 5 gabby, gassy, gushy, talky, windy 7 gossipy, gushing, prating, verbose, voluble 8 babbling, chatting, effusive 9 garrulous, jabbering, talkative 10 blabbering, longwinded, loquacious 11 loose-lipped 12 loose-tongued 13 tongue-wagging

Chaucer, Geoffrey
author of: 18 The Canterbury Tales, Troilus and Criseyde 19 The Book of the Duchess 20 The Legend of Good Women, The Parlement of Fowles

Chauchoin, Claudette Lily
real name of: 16 Claudette Colbert

chauffeur 6 driver

chaussure 4 boot, shoe 8 footwear

chauvinism 8 jingoism 10 flag-waving, militarism, patriotism 11 nationalism 15 ethnocentricity, superpatriotism

cheap 4 base, easy, mean, poor 5 close, gaudy, petty, tacky, tight 6 common, flashy, meager, paltry, shabby, shoddy, sordid, stingy, tawdry, trashy, two-bit, vulgar 7 ignoble, immoral, miserly 8 costless, gimcrack, indecent, inferior, wretched 9 inelegant, low-priced, penurious, worthless 10 despicable, economical, effortless, in bad taste, reasonable, second-rate 11 inexpensive, tightfisted 12 contemptible

Cheaper by the Dozen
author: 14 Frank B Gilbreth (with Ernestine Gilbreth Carey)

cheat 3 con, gyp 4 bilk, dupe, fake, foil, fool, gull, hoax, rook, take 5 cozen, crook, fraud, quack, shark, trick 6 baffle, betray, defeat, delude, dodger, escape, fleece, humbug, outwit, thwart 7 deceive, defraud, mislead, swindle 8 chiseler, deceiver, hoodwink, imposter, impostor, swindler 9 bamboozle, charlatan, con artist, frustrate, trickster, victimize 10 circumvent, mountebank 11 short-change 13 break the rules, double-crosser

check 3 bar, end, fit, gag 4 curb, halt, hold, jibe, mesh, rein, slow, stay, stop, test 5 agree, block, brake, chime, choke, limit, probe, stall, study, tally 6 arrest, bridle, impede, look at, muzzle, peruse, rein in, retard, review, search, survey, thwart 7 barrier, conform, control, examine, explore, harness, inhibit, inspect, perusal, prevent, smother 8 hold back, look into, look over, obstacle, obstruct, restrain, scrutiny, stoppage, suppress 9 cessation, constrain, frustrate, harmonize, hindrance, restraint 10 circumvent, constraint, correspond, impediment, inspection, limitation, prevention, repression, scrutinize 11 examination, exploration, investigate, obstruction, prohibition, restriction, take stock of 13 investigation 18 bring to a standstill

checkered 4 pied 6 fitful, motley, seesaw, uneven, varied 7 checked, dappled, mottled, piebald 9 irregular, up-and-down 10 inconstant, variegated 11 fluctuating, vacillating 12 parti-colored

checkmate 4 rout, stop 6 corner, defeat, outwit, stymie, thwart 8 deadlock 9 frustrate, overthrow 11 countermove

cheder, heder 12 Jewish school

cheek 4 jowl 5 brass, nerve 8 audacity, boldness, temerity 9 arrogance, brashness, impudence, insolence 10 brazenness, effrontery 11 forwardness 12 impertinence

cheep 4 peep 5 chirp, tweet 7 chirrup, chitter, twitter

cheer 3 cry, fun, joy 4 glee, hail, hope, root, warm, yell 5 bravo, shout 6 assure, buoy up, gaiety, hooray, hurrah, huzzah, shriek, uplift 7 acclaim, animate, comfort, delight, enliven, fortify, gladden, hearten, inspire, revelry 8 brighten, buoyance, buoyancy, gladness, optimism, pleasure, reassure, vivacity 9 animation, assurance, encourage, festivity, geniality, joviality, merriment, rejoicing 10 joyfulness, jubilation, liveliness 11 acclamation, high spirits, hopefulness, merrymaking, reassurance 13 encouragement

cheerful 3 gay 4 airy, glad 5 happy, jolly, merry, sunny 6 blithe, breezy, bright, cheery, elated, jaunty, jovial, joyful, joyous, lively 7 buoyant, gleeful 8 gladsome, pleasant 9 agreeable, sparkling, sprightly 10 optimistic 11 in high humor 12 highspirited, lighthearted

cheerfulness 5 gaity 7 jollity 8 buoyancy, optimism 9 joviality, merriment 10 brightness, cheeriness 11 high spirits 16 lightheartedness

cheerless 3 sad 4 dull, glum, gray, grim 5 bleak 6 dismal, dreary, gloomy, morose, rueful, solemn, somber, sullen, woeful 7 austere, doleful, forlorn, joyless, sunless, unhappy 8 dejected, desolate, dolorous, downcast, funereal, mournful 9 miserable, saturnine, woebegone 10 depressing, despondent, dispirited, lugubrious, melan-

choly, spiritless, uninviting 11 comfortless, downhearted 12 disconsolate, heavyhearted

Cheers
    location: 3 bar 6 Boston
    character: 4 Norm 5 Cliff, Coach, Woody 5 Lilith 7 Rebecca 9 Sam Malone 13 Carla Tortelli, Diane Chambers
    cast: 9 Ted Danson 11 George Wendt, Rhea Perlman, Shelley Long 12 Kirstie Alley 13 Kelsey Grammer 14 Woody Harrelson 16 John Ratzenberger

cheer up 5 pep up 6 buoy up 7 comfort, enliven, hearten 8 brighten, inspirit 9 bolster up, encourage 18 bolster one's spirits

cheery 3 gay 5 happy, jolly, merry, sunny 6 bright, joyful 9 sprightly 12 lighthearted

Cheeryble Brothers
    nephew: 5 Frank
    characters in: 16 Nicholas Nickleby
    author: 7 Dickens

cheese
    French: 7 fromage
    kind: 4 bleu, blue, brie, edam, feta, jack 5 brick, colby, cream, gouda, Swiss 6 romano, samsoe 7 cheddar, cottage, fontina, gjetost, gruyere, limburg, munster, ricotta, sapsago, stilton 8 American, bel paese, cheshire, emmental, muenster, parmesan, port wine, raclette 9 camembert, jarlsberg, limburger, port salut, provolone, roquefort 10 caerphilly, Danish blue, Gloucester, gorgonzola, mozzarella, neufchatel 11 emmenthaler, liederkranz, petit suisse, port du salut, wensleydale 12 monterey jack

Cheever, John
    author of: 8 Falconer 10 Bullet Park 16 The Enormous Radio, The World of Apples 17 The Wapshot Scandal 19 The Wapshot Chronicle 20 The Way Some People Live 22 Oh What a Paradise It Seems

Chekhov, Anton
    author of: 6 Ivanov 10 The Sea Gull, Uncle Vanya 15 The Three Sisters 16 The Cherry Orchard

Chelciope
    father: 6 Aeetes
    mother: 5 Idyia
    sister: 5 Medea
    husband: 7 Phrixus
    son: 5 Argus, Melas 8 Phrontis 9 Thessalus 10 Cytissorus

Chelidon
    sister: 5 Aedon
    brother-in-law: 11 Polytechnus
    changed into: 7 swallow
    changed by: 7 Artemis

chemical symbols
    actinium: 2 Ac
    aluminum: 2 Al

antimony: 2 Sb
argon: 2 Ar
arsenic: 2 As
barium: 2 Ba
boron: 1 B
bromine: 2 Br
cadmium: 2 Cd
calcium: 2 Ca
carbon: 1 C
chlorine: 2 Cl
chromium: 2 Cr
cobalt: 2 Co
columbium: 2 Cb
copper: 2 Cu
fluorine: 1 F
gold: 2 Au
hafnium: 2 Hf
helium: 2 He
hydrogen: 1 H
iodine: 2 I
iron: 2 Fe
krypton: 2 Kr
lead: 2 Pb
lithium: 2 Li
magnesium: 2 Mg
manganese: 2 Mn
mercury: 2 Hg
molybdenum: 2 Mo
neon: 2 Ne
nickel: 2 Ni
nitrogen: 1 N
oxygen: 1 O
phosphorus: 1 P
platinum: 2 Pt
plutonium: 2 Pu
potassium: 1 K
radium: 2 Ra
radon: 2 Rn
rhodium: 2 Rh
rubidium: 2 Rb
silicon: 2 Si
silver: 2 Ag
sodium: 2 Na
sulfur: 1 S
thorium: 2 Th
tin: 2 Sn
titanium: 2 Ti
tungsten: 1 W
uranium: 1 U
xenon: 2 Xe
zinc: 2 Zn
zirconium: 2 Zr
chemise 4 slip 5 dress, shift, shirt, smock 6
blouse 7 garment 8 camisole, lingerie, un-
belted 12 undergarment
chemist
American: 4 Urey 5 Tatum 6 Carver 7
Axelrod, Lipmann, Pauling 8 Kornberg,
Langmuir, McMillan 9 Carothers 10
Baekleland
British: 4 Davy 5 Boyle, Chain, Soddy 6
Dalton, Ramsay 7 Faraday 8 Smithson 9
Cavendish, Priestley, Wollaston
Dutch: 4 Hoff
French: 5 Curie, Le Bel 6 Cuvier, Dulong
7 Pasteur 9 Gay-Lussac, Lavoisier 10
Berthollet 11 Joliot-Curie

German: 4 Hahn 5 Krebs 6 Baeyer,
Wohler 7 Glauber, Ostwald
Italian: 8 Avogadro
Russian: 9 Mendeleev 10 Mendeleyev
Scottish: 5 Dewar
Swedish: 7 Scheele 9 Arrhenius,
Berzelius
Swiss: 6 Muller
Chemosh 10 Moabite god
Chennault, Claire L
served in: 4 WWII 15 Sino-Japanese
War
commander of: 12 Flying Tigers
general in: 12 Army Air Force
air advisor to: 13 Chiang Kai-shek
cherchez la femme 15 look for the woman
cherie 4 dear 10 sweetheart
cherish 4 love 5 honor, nurse, prize, value
6 dote on, esteem, revere, succor 7 care
for, idolize, nourish, nurture, shelter, sustain 8 hold dear, treasure, venerate 10 appreciate, take care of
cherished 4 dear 5 loved 7 beloved, darling, dearest 8 favorite, held dear, precious
9 treasured
Cherokee
language family: 9 Iroquoian
location: 7 Alabama, Georgia 8 Oklahoma, Virginia 9 Tennessee 13 North
Carolina, South Carolina
associated with: 12 Trail of Tears
scholar: 7 Sequoya
cherry
varieties: 3 pie, pin, rum 4 bing, bird,
duke, fire, sand, sour, wild 5 black, brush,
choke, dwarf, Higan, Naden, sweet 6 bitter, Brazil, ground, Indian, Madden, Oregon, Taiwan, winter 7 bastard, Cayenne,
Morello, Nanking, Potomac, prairie, rose-
bud, sargent, Spanish, St Lucie, wild red,
Windsor, Yoshino 8 Barbados, Catalina,
oriental, perfumed, Suriname 9 christmas, cornelian, evergreen, Jerusalem,
wild black 10 west indian 11 downy
ground, Hansen's bush, holly-leaved,
western sand 12 clammy ground, European bird, Japanese bush, purple ground
13 European dwarf 14 European ground,
false Jerusalem, purple-leaf sand 15
Australian brush 17 Japanese cornelian, Japanese flowering, north Japanese
hill
drink: 6 kirsch
cherry brandy 6 kirsch 12 Peter Heering
Cherry Orchard, The
author: 12 Anton Chekhov
character: 4 Anya, Gaev 5 Fiers, Varya,
Yasha 7 Pischin 8 Dunyasha, Lopakhin,
Trofimov 9 Charlotta 16 Madame
Ranevskaya
cherub 4 amor 5 angel, child, cupid, youth
6 moppet 8 cherubim 13 heavenly being
cherubic 7 angelic 8 innocent 9 spiritual

Cherubin
  character in: **19** The Marriage of Figaro
  author: **12** Beaumarchais
chervil
  botanical name: **20** Anthriscus cerefolium
  origin: **6** Europe, Russia
  use: **4** soup **5** salad **11** fines herbes, potato salad
Chesapeake
  author: **13** James Michener
Cheshire Cat
  character in: **28** Alice's Adventures in Wonderland
  author: **7** Carroll
chess
  also called: **9** Royal Game
  chess champion: **4** Euwe, Fine, Tahl **6** Karpov, Lasker **7** Fischer, Kashdan, Smyslov, Spassky **8** Alekhine, Kasparov, Philador, Steinitz **9** Anderssen, Botvinnik, Petrosian, Reshevsky **10** Capablanca
  French: **6** echecs
  German: **11** schachspiel
  horizontal rows: **4** rank
  international chess federation: **4** FIDE
  patron goddess/muse: **6** Caissa
  piece: **4** king, pawn, rook **5** queen **6** bishop, castle, knight **8** chessman, material
  Russian: **8** shakhmat
  Spanish: **7** Ajedrez
  term: **3** pin **4** fork, hole **5** check, tempo **6** center **7** isolani, outpost **8** castling, majority, open file, queening, zugzwang **9** checkmate, en passant, promotion **10** fianchetto **11** zwischenzug
  tied game: **4** draw **9** stalemate
  vertical rows: **4** file
chest
  Italian: **5** petto
Chester, Edward
  character in: **12** Barnaby Rudge
  author: **7** Dickens
chesterfield 4 coat, sofa **5** couch **8** overcoat **9** davenport
Chesterton, G K (Gilbert Keith)
  author of: **20** The Man Who Was Thursday **24** The Napoleon of Notting Hill **25** The Innocence of Father Brown
chestnut 8 Castanea
  varieties: **4** Cape, Wild **5** Horse, Water **6** Guiana, Marron **7** Chinese, Spanish **8** American, Eurasian, European, Japanese, Red horse **10** Dwarf horse, Moreton Bay **11** Common horse **12** Chinese water **13** European horse, Japanese horse **15** California horse
chestnut-colored 6 auburn, russet, sienna **8** cinnamon, nut-brown **11** golden-brown, rust-colored **12** reddish-brown
chest of drawers 5 chest **6** bureau, lowboy **7** cabinet, commode, dresser, highboy, tallboy **10** chiffonier
cheval 5 horse
chevalier 4 lord **5** cadet, noble **6** knight **7** gallant **8** cavalier

Chevalier, Maurice
  born: **5** Paris **6** France
  roles: **4** Gigi **5** Fanny **6** Can-Can **13** The Love Parade, The Merry Widow **18** Love in the Afternoon
chew 4 gnaw **5** champ, crush, grind, munch **6** crunch, nibble **8** ruminate **9** masticate
Chew
  character in: **21** The Master of Ballantrae
  author: **9** Stevenson
chewing-out 6 rebuke **7** censure, chiding, reproof **8** reproach, scolding **9** reprimand **10** bawling-out, upbraiding **11** castigation, reprobation **12** dressing-down, remonstrance **13** tongue-lashing
chew noisily 4 gnaw **5** chomp, gnash, grind, munch **6** crunch
chew out 5 scold **6** berate, rail at, rebuke **7** bawl out, reprove, upbraid **8** reproach **9** castigate, reprimand **10** take to task, tongue-lash **14** read the riot act
chew the fat 3 gab, gas **4** blab, chat, talk **5** prate **6** gossip, patter **7** blather, chatter, palaver, prattle, twaddle **8** chitchat, converse, talk idly **10** chew the rag **11** confabulate **14** chitterchatter
chew the rag 3 gab, gas, jaw, rap **4** chat, chin, talk **5** prate **7** chatter, palaver, prattle **8** chitchat, converse **10** chew the fat **11** confabulate
Cheyenne
  language family: **9** Algonkian **10** Algonquian
  location: **6** Platte **7** Montana, Wyoming **8** Oklahoma, Red River **9** Minnesota **11** South Dakota
  allied with: **7** Arapaho
Cheyenne
  character: **6** Smitty **13** Cheyenne Bodie
  cast: **7** L Q Jones **11** Clint Walker
chez 4 with **6** at home
Chiang Kai-shek
  leader of: **5** China **6** Taiwan
  ally: **9** Sun Yat-sen
  party: **10** Kuomintang **11** Nationalist
  defeated by: **10** Communists
  wife: **12** Soong Mei-ling
Chibcha (Muisca)
  location: **6** Bogota, Panama **8** Colombia **12** South America
  associated with: **8** El Dorado
Chibchan
  language family: **13** Macro-Chibchan
  group: **4** Cuna, Paya, Rama **5** Lenca, Xinca **7** Chibcha
chic 5 natty, ritzy, smart, swank **6** classy, modish, snazzy, swanky **7** elegant, stylish, voguish **11** fashionable
Chicago
  author: **12** Carl Sandburg

Chicago

airport: 5 O'Hare 6 Midway
baseball team: 4 Cubs 8 White Sox
basketball team: 5 Bulls
downtown area: 4 Loop
football team: 5 Bears
fort: 8 Dearborn
hockey team: 10 Black Hawks
lake: 4 Wolf 7 Calumet 8 Michigan
landmark: 10 Meigs Field, Sears Tower 12 Board of Trade, Comiskey Park, Humboldt Park, Soldier Field, Wrigley Field 13 Shedd Aquarium 15 Lincoln Monument, Merchandise Mart, Newberry Library, Wrigley Building 16 Adler Planetarium 17 Holy Name Cathedral, John Hancock Center 18 Mercantile Exchange, Prudential Building 20 Midwest Stock Exchange 21 Art Institute of Chicago 23 Museum of Contemporary Art 26 Museum of Science and Industry 27 Field Museum of Natural History:
mayor: 5 Byrne, Daley 10 Washington
nickname: 9 Windy City
river: 7 Chicago 10 Des Plaines
street: 11 Wacker Drive 13 Chicago Skyway 14 Lake Shore Drive
university: 6 DePaul, Loyola 9 Roosevelt 12 Northwestern 29 Illinois Institute of Technology

chicanery 4 ruse, wile 5 craft, fraud, guile 6 deceit, duping 7 cunning, gulling, knavery, roguery 8 artifice, cozenage, trickery, villainy 9 deception, duplicity, rascality, sophistry 10 craftiness, hocus-pocus, humbuggery, subterfuge 11 hoodwinking 12 pettifoggery 13 double-dealing

chichi 4 arty 5 fussy, showy 6 flashy, frilly, garish, prissy, vulgar 7 finical, pompous, splashy 8 affected, gimcrack, overnice, precious, sissyish 9 arty-tarty, grandiose, nasty-nice 10 flamboyant 11 overrefined, pretentious 12 artsy-craftsy, ostentatious

chick
group of: 5 brood 6 clutch

Chickasaw

language family: 10 Muskhogean
location: 8 Oklahoma 9 Tennessee 11 Mississippi
related to: 7 Choctaw
member of: 19 Five Civilized Tribes

chicken, chickenhearted 3 hen 4 cock, fowl 5 layer, timid 6 afraid, coward, craven, pullet, scared, yellow 7 caitiff, dastard, fearful, gutless, rooster 8 cowardly, poltroon, timorous 9 flinching, fraidy-cat, shrinking 11 lily-livered, yellow-belly 12 fainthearted 13 pusillanimous, yellow-bellied 22 showing the white feather

chickenheartedness 8 timidity 9 cowardice 10 yellowness 11 fearfulness, poltroonery 12 timorousness 13 pusillanimity 16 faintheartedness

chide 5 scold 6 berate, rebuke 7 censure, chasten, reprove, upbraid 8 admonish, denounce, reproach 9 criticize, find fault, reprimand 10 take to task

chief 3 key 4 boss, head, lord, main 5 first, major, prime, ruler 6 leader, master, ruling 7 captain, highest, leading, monarch, primary, supreme 8 cardinal, chairman, crowning, director, dominant, foremost, greatest, overlord, overseer 9 chieftain, commander, governing, number-one, paramount, potentate, principal, sovereign, uppermost 10 prevailing, ringleader, supervisor 11 outstanding, predominant 12 preponderant 13 administrator

chief good
Latin: 11 summum bonum

chiefly 5 first 6 mainly, mostly 8 above all 9 expressly, in the main, most of all, primarily 10 especially 11 principally 12 particularly 13 predominantly

chieftain 4 boss, head 6 leader 7 captain, head man

chiffonier 6 bureau 7 dresser 8 cupboard 14 chest of drawers

chignon 3 bun 4 knot, roll 6 hairdo 9 hairpiece, hairstyle

child 3 boy, kid, lad, son, tad, tot 4 baby, girl, lass, tyke 5 youth 6 infant, moppet 7 toddler 8 daughter, juvenile 9 little one, offspring, youngster

childbearing 5 birth 11 parturition

childbirth 8 delivery 11 confinement, parturition
French: 12 accouchement
goddess of: 4 Upis 5 Parca 6 Lucina, Matuta 7 Artemis 8 Ilithyia 10 Eileithyia

Childe Harold's Pilgrimage
author: 21 George Gordon Lord Byron

Childe Roland to the Dark Tower Came
author: 14 Robert Browning

childhood 5 youth 7 boyhood 8 girlhood 10 school days 11 adolescence, nursery days

childish 5 naive, silly 6 callow, simple 7 asinine, babyish, foolish, puerile 8 immature, juvenile 9 infantile 10 adolescent

childlike 8 childish, immature, innocent 9 ingenuous

child prodigy
German: 10 Wunderkind

children 4 boys, kids, sons, tads, tots 5 girls, issue, young 6 babies, result, youth 7 infants, product, progeny 9 daughters, juveniles 11 descendants

Children of God
author: 12 Vardis Fisher

Children of Paradise
director: 11 Marcel Carne
cast: 7 Arletty 11 Albert Remay 14 Pierre Brasseur 17 Jean-Louis Barrault

Child's Garden of Verses, A
author: 20 Robert Louis Stevenson

Chile

other name: 6 Tchile
name means: 21 deepest part of the Earth
capital/largest city: 8 Santiago
others: 4 Boco, Cuya, Lebu, Lota, Ocoa, Tome 5 Angol, Arica, Cobya, Talca 6 Arauco, Calama, Curico, Gatico, Osorno, Ovalle, Serena, Temuco, Vicuna, Yumbel,

Yungay **7** Caldera, Chillan, Copiapo, Iquique, Valdiva **8** Coquimbo, Rancagua, Santiago, Vallenar **9** Cauquenes **10** Concepcion, Coquembana, Valparaiso, Vina del Mar **11** Antofagasta, Puerto Montt, Punta Arenas, San Bernardo

measure: 4 vara **5** legua, linea **6** cuadra, fanega

monetary unit: 4 peso **5** libra **6** condor, escudo

weight: 5 grano, libra **7** quintal

island: 3 Luz **4** Prat **5** Byron, Guafo, Hoste, Mocha, Nueva, Nunez, Vidal **6** Chiloe, Chonos, Dawson, Easter, Lennox, Piazzi, Picton, Quilan, Riesco, Stosch, Talcan **7** Angamos, Campana, Hanover, Hermite, Pajaros, Refugio, Tranqui **8** Chauques, Clarence, Huamblin, Nalcayec, Navarino, Traiguen **13** Juan Fernandez **14** Tierra del Fuego

lake: 5 Ranco **6** Yelcho **7** Puyehue, Rupanco **8** Cochrane **10** General Paz, Llanquihue **11** Buenos Aires

mountain: 4 Maca, Toro **5** Chato, Maipo, Maipu, Paine, Potro, Pular, Torre, Yogan **6** Apiwan, Burney, Conico, Jervis, Poquis, Rincon **7** Chaltel, Copiapo, Fitzroy, Palpana, Velluda **8** Cochrane, Tronador, Yanteles **9** Tupungato

highest point: 13 Ojos del Salado

river: 3 Loa **4** Laja, Yali **5** Alhue, Azapa, Bravo, Bueno, Elqui, Lauca, Lluta, Maipo, Maule, Puelo, Rahue, Rapel, Stata, Vitor **6** Biobio, Camina, Choapa, Choros, Cisnes, Colina, Huasco, Limari, Morado, Palena, Poscua, Tolten **7** Copiapo **8** Valdivia

sea: 7 Pacific

physical features:

bay: 4 Cook, Eyre, Nena, Tarn **5** Lomas, Otway, Sarco **6** Darwin, Inutil, Moreno, Stokes, Tongoy **7** Dyneley, Inglesa, Skyring **8** Desolate

cape: 4 Dyer, Horn **6** Choros, Falsos, Hornos, Quilan, Tablas **7** Deseado **10** Tres Montes

channel: 5 Ancho, Cheap **6** Beagle **8** Cockburn, Moraleda

desert: 7 Atacama

gulf: 5 Ancud, Guafo, Penas **6** Arauco

isthmus: 5 Ofqui

peninsula: 5 Hardy, Lacuy **6** Taitao, Tumbes

point: 4 Toro **5** Gallo, Liles, Lobos, Loros, Morro, Talca, Tetas, Vieja **6** Cachos, Galera, Molles **7** Angamos, Lavapie

strait: 6 Nelson **8** Magellan

volcano: 5 Lanin, Maipo **6** Antuco, Llaima, Oyahue, Tacora **7** Peteroa, Socomap

people: 3 Ona **4** Auca, Inca, Onan **6** Arauca, Chango, Yahgan **7** Mapuche, mestizo, Moluche, Pampean, Patagon, Puegian, Ranquel **8** Alikuluf, Picunche, Tsonecan

author: 5 Bello **6** Donoso, Neruda **7** Mistral

conqueror: 7 Valdiva

explorer: 8 Magellan

leader: 7 Allende **8** O'Higgins, Pinochet **9** San Martin **10** Alessandri

language: 7 Spanish

religion: 13 Roman Catholic

places:

copper mine: 12 Chuquicamata

resort: 8 Portillo **10** Vina del Mar

possession: 12 Easter Island **20** Juan Fernandez Islands

feature:

cowboy: 5 huaso

dance: 5 cueca **6** pequen **9** resbalosa

shrub: 5 litre

slum: 9 callempas

tree: 5 rauli

wind instrument: 4 sicu

food:

drink: 5 pisco **6** chicha

hot red pepper: 3 aji

meat pie: 8 empanada

soup: 7 cazuela **8** caldillo

chill, chilly 3 icy, nip, raw **4** bite, cold, cool, keen **5** aloof, brisk, crisp, fever, harsh, nippy, sharp, stiff, stony **6** arctic, biting, bitter, frigid, frosty, frozen, wintry **7** callous, coolish, cutting, glacial, hostile, iciness, rawness, shivery **8** coolness, uncaring **9** crispness, frigidity, sharpness, unfeeling **10** forbidding, frostiness, unfriendly **11** indifferent, passionless, penetrating **12** unresponsive

chilled 4 cold, iced **6** cooled, frozen **7** frosted **8** hardened **10** dispirited **11** discouraged **12** refrigerated

chilling 3 icy, raw **5** nippy, on ice **6** frigid **7** bracing, cooling **10** unfriendly

Chillingworth, Roger

character in: 16 The Scarlet Letter

author: 9 Hawthorne

chime 4 gong, peal, ring, toll **5** knell, sound **6** jingle, tinkle **7** pealing, ringing **8** carillon, ding-dong, tinkling, tollings **10** set of bells **14** tintinnabulate **16** tintinnabulation

Chimene

character in: 6 The Cid

author: 9 Corneille

chimera 5 dream, fancy **6** bubble, mirage **7** fantasy, monster, phantom **8** daydream, delusion, idle whim, illusion **9** pipe dream **10** self-deceit, she-monster **12** will-o'-the-wisp **13** castle in Spain, fool's paradise, hallucination, self-deception **14** castle in the air **24** figment of one's imagination

Chimera

form: 7 monster

father: 6 Typhon

mother: 7 Echidna

breathes: 4 fire

Chimera

author: 9 John Barth

chimerical 6 absurd, unreal **7** utopian **8** delusive, ethereal, fabulous, fanciful, illusory, mythical quixotic **9** fantastic, imaginary, visionary 10 impossible, phantasmal, 11 nonexistent

chimney 4 flue, tube, vent 5 cleft, gully, spout, stack 6 funnel, hearth 7 opening 9 stovepipe 10 smokestack

chimpanzee 3 ape 6 animal, baboon, monkey

chin 3 gab, jaw, rap 4 chat, talk 7 chatter, palaver 8 chitchat, converse 10 chew the fat, chew the rag 11 confabulate

china 6 dishes, plates 7 pottery 8 crockery 9 chinaware, porcelain, stoneware, tableware 11 ceramicware, earthenware 14 cups and saucers

China

other name: 3 PRC 13 Middle Kingdom 14 Flowery Kingdom 22 People's Republic of China

capital: 6 Peking 7 Beijing

largest city: 8 Shanghai

others: 3 Bai, Noh 4 Ahpa, Amoy, Fuyu, Guma, Hami, Huma, Ipin, Kian, Kisi, Lini, Loho, Luta, Moho, Moyu, Niya, Noho, Omin, Rima, Saka, Sian, Taku, Tali, Tayu, Wuhu, Yaan 5 Chiai, Fusin, Kirin, Koklu, Linyu, Macao, Penki, Shasi, Soche, Taian, Talai, Tihwa, Tuyun, Wuhan, Wusih, Yenan, Yenki, Yulin, Yumen 6 Anshan, Antung, Canton, Dairen, Fuchau, Fuchow, Fushun, Hankow, Harbin, Ilhasa, Kalgan, Loyang, Lushun, Mukden, Nanhai, Ningpo, Singan, Sining, Taipei, Tsinan, Yangku, Yunnan 7 Fuskhih, Hanyang, Kunming, Lanchow, Lioyang, Mengtze, Nanking, Nanning, Paoshan, Peiping, Soochow, Taiyuan, Tatshan, Urumchi, Urumsti, Waichow, Wuchang, Yenping 8 Chinchow, Fengkiek, Fengtien, Hangchow, Kingchow, Nanchang, Shanghai, Shenyang, Siangtan, Tientsin, Tungchow, Wanchuan, Wanhsien 9 Chungking, Kiangling, Tsingyuan 10 Chiangling, Port Arthur

school: 5 Futan 6 Peking 7 Nanking 8 Hangchow 9 Sun Yat-sen 16 Cheng-tu Technical

division:

province: 5 Honan, Hunan, Hupei, Kansu 6 Anhwei, Fukien, Shansi, Shensi, Yunnan 7 Kiangsi, Kiangsu 8 Chekiang, Kweichow, Shantung, Szechwan, Tientsin, Tsinghai 9 Kwangtung, Manchuria

measure: 3 cho, fan, fen, pau, tou, tun, yan, yin 4 chek, chih, fang, kish, papa, quei, shih, teke, tsan, tsun 5 catty, chang, ching, sheng, shing 6 chupak, gungli, kungho, kungmu, tching 7 kungfen, kungyin 8 kungchih, kungshih, 9 kungching

monetary unit: 4 cash, cent, fyng, mace, tael, tiao, yuan 5 sycee 12 jen nin piao pu

weight: 3 fan, fen, hao, kin, ssu, tan, yin 4 chee, chin, dong, shih, tael, tsin 5 catty, chien, picul, tchin, tsien 6 kungli 7 haikwan, kungfen, kungssu, kungtun 8 kungchin 9 candareen 10 kupingtael

island: 4 Amoy 5 Macao, Matsu, Namki,

Taipa 6 Chusan, Hainan, Pratas, Quemoy, Taiwan, Tinian, Yuhwan 7 Coloane, Formosa, Hungtow, Tungsha 8 Ching Hai, Chouchan, Kulangsu

lake: 3 Tai 4 Chao, Na-mu 5 Kaoyu, Oling, Telli 6 Bamtso, Bornor, Ebinor, Erhhai, Khanka, Lopnor, Namtso, Poyang 7 Chaling, Hungtse, Karanor, Kokonor 8 Hulunnor, Montcalm, Taroktso, Tellinor, Tienchih, Tsinghai, Tungting

sea: 6 Yellow 9 East China 10 South China

physical features:

bay: 7 Laichow 8 Hangchow

cape: 7 Olwanpi

channel: 5 Bashi

desert: 4 Gobi 5 Ordos, Shamo 7 Alashan 10 Takla Makan

dry lake: 6 Lopnor

gulf: 5 Pohai 6 Chihli, Tonkin 7 Pechili 8 Liaotung

peninsula: 6 Leichu 7 Luichow 8 Liaotung

plateau: 5 Loess 7 Tibetan

port: 4 Amoy, Wuhu 5 Aigun, Shasi 6 Antung, Canton, Chefoo, Dairen, Ichang, Ningpo, Pakhoi, Swatow, Wuchow 7 Foochow, Hunchun, Luichow, Nanking, Samshui, Santuao, Soochow, Wenchow, Yinkkow, Yungkia 8 Changsha, Hangchow, Kiukiang, Kongmoon, Shanghai, Tengyueh, Tientsin, Tsingtao, Wanhsien 9 Kwangchow, Weihaiwei 10 Tsingkiang

strait: 6 Hainan, Taiwan 7 Formosa

people: 3 Han, Yis 4 Huis, Lolo, Miao, Pu-is 5 Hakka, Hoklo, Seres, Sinic 6 Cataia, Chuang, Johnny, Korean, Manchu, Mongol, Serian, Uighun 7 Sinaean, Tibetan

leader: 9 Sun Yat-sen, Zhou Enlai 10 Kublai Khan, Mao Tse-tung 11 Genghis Khan 12 Deng Xiaoping 13 Chiang Kai-shek

philosopher: 6 Lao-tzu 9 Confucius

language: 7 Chinese 8 Mandarin, Shanghai 9 Cantonese

religion: 5 Islam 6 Taoism 8 Buddhism 12 Christianity, Confucianism

place:

palace: 6 Summer 8 Imperial 13 Forbidden City

ruins: 9 Ming Tombs

square: 9 Tiananmen

wonder: 9 Great Wall

feature:

boat: 4 junk

conspirators: 10 Gang of Four

dynasty: 3 Han, Sui 4 Chou, Ch'in, Ming, Sung, T'ang 5 Ch'ing, Shang 6 Manchu

military academy: 7 whompoa

watercolor: 8 shan shiu

China Syndrome, The

director: 12 James Bridges

cast: 9 Jane Fonda 10 Jack Lemmon, Scott Brady 14 Michael Douglas

setting: 17 nuclear power plant

Chinatown
 director: **13** Roman Polanski
 cast: **10** John Huston **11** Faye Dunaway **13** Jack Nicholson
 Oscar for: **5** story **10** screenplay
chinaware 6 dishes, plates **7** pottery **8** crockery **9** porcelain, stoneware, tableware **11** ceramicware, earthenware **14** cups and saucers
chine 5 spine **6** dorsum **8** backbone
Chinese book of divination 6 I Ching
Chingachgook
 character in: **13** The Pathfinder **20** The Last of the Mohicans
 author: **6** Cooper
chink 3 cut, gap **4** gash, hole, rent, rift, ring, slit **5** break, clank, cleft, clink, crack, fault, split **6** breach, jangle, jingle, rattle, tinkle **7** crevice, fissure, opening **8** aperture
Chinook (Flathead)
 language family: **9** Chinookan
 location: **7** Pacific **10** Washington
 ritual: **15** head deformation
Chinookan
 tribe: **7** Chinook **8** Flathead
chintzy 5 cheap, close, dowdy, tacky, tatty, tight **6** frowzy, frumpy, shabby, sleazy, stingy **7** miserly **8** grudging, schlocky, stinting **9** niggardly, penurious **11** closefisted **12** parsimonious **13** penny-pinching
Chione
 father: **6** Boreas **9** Daedalion
 mother: **8** Orithyia
 son: **9** Autolycus, Philammon
chip 3 bit, cut, hew **4** chop, gash, hack, nick **5** chunk, crumb, flake, scrap, shred, slice, split, wafer **6** chisel, morsel, paring, sliver **7** cutting, shaving, whittle **8** fragment, splinter
chipmunk 6 chippy, gopher, rodent **8** chipmuck, squirrel **14** ground squirrel **16** chipping squirrel
chipper 3 gay **4** pert, spry **5** alive, brisk, peppy **6** frisky, jaunty, lively **8** animated, carefree, cheerful, spirited **9** easygoing, energetic, sprightly, vivacious **12** high-spirited, light-hearted
Chippewa (Ojibwa, Ojibway)
 language family: **9** Algonkian **10** Algonquian
 tribe: **4** Cree **6** Ottawa **8** Chippewa **10** Missisauga
 location: **6** Canada **9** Lake Huron **11** North Dakota **12** Lake Superior, Niagara Falls
 leader: **7** Pontiac
CHiPs
 character: **8** (Officer) Jon Baker **10** (Sgt) Joe Getraer **16** (Officer) Frank (Ponch) Poncherello
 cast: **10** Robert Pine **11** Erik Estrada, Larry Wilcox
Chirico, Giorgio de
 born: **5** Volos **6** Greece
 artwork: **15** Enigma of the Hour **19** Enigma of an Afternoon **21** Enigma of an Au-

tumn Night **22** Nostalgia of the Infinite **32** The Melancholy and Mystery of a Street
Chiron
 also: **7** Cheiron
 form: **7** centaur
 father: **6** Cronos, Cronus, Kronos
 mother: **7** Philyra
 wife: **8** Chariclo
 daughter: **6** Endeis
 grandson: **6** Peleus
 occupation: **7** teacher
chirp 4 peep, sing **5** cheep, chirr, tweet **7** chirrup, chitter, peeping, twitter **8** cheeping
chirrup 4 peep **5** cheep, chirp, tweet **7** chitter, twitter
chisel 3 cut, gyp **4** gull, hoax, rook, tool **5** blade, cheat, slice **6** incise
 type: **4** cape, cold, wood **7** v-shaped
Chisel
 constellation of: **6** Caelum
chiseler 4 fake **5** cheat, fraud, quack **7** cheater **8** swindler
Chislev 16 ninth Hebrew month
chit 3 IOU, tab **4** note **5** check **7** voucher
chitchat 3 gab **4** chat **5** prate **6** drivel, gossip **7** chatter, palaver, prattle **8** converse **9** small talk **10** chew the fat, chew the rag **11** confabulate **13** confabulation
Chitimacha
 language family: **6** Tunica
 location: **9** Louisiana
 noted for: **8** basketry
chitter 4 peep **5** cheep, chirp, tweet **7** chatter, chirrup, twitter
chitter-chatter 3 gab **4** blab **6** babble, drivel, gabble, jabber **7** blabber, prattle, twaddle **8** chitchat **9** jabbering **16** idle conversation
chivalrous 6 polite **7** courtly, gallant **8** mannerly
chivalry 8 courtesy **9** gallantry **10** knighthood, politeness **11** courtliness
Chivery, Young John
 character in: **12** Little Dorrit
 author: **7** Dickens
chivy 3 nag **4** hunt, race **5** annoy, chase, chevy, hound, trail, worry **6** badger, bother, harass, pursue **7** scamper, torment
Chldanope
 form: **5** Naiad
Chloe
 epithet of: **7** Demeter
 means: **5** green
chloride 7 muriate **8** chemical, compound
chlorine
 chemical symbol: **2** Cl
Chloris
 father: **7** Amphion
 mother: **5** Niobe
 daughter: **4** Pero
chocolate 5 brown, candy, cacao, cocoa, drink **6** bon bon **10** confection
Choctaw
 language family: **10** Muskhogean
 location: **7** Alabama **11** Mississippi
 related to: **9** Chickasaw

Choephoroe
   author: 9 Aeschylus
   character: 6 Furies 7 Electra, Orestes, Pylades 9 Aegisthus 12 Clytemnestra
choice 3 say 4 A-one, best, fine, pick, vote 5 array, elite, prime, prize, stock, store, voice 6 better, opting, option, select, supply, tip-top 7 display, special, variety 8 choosing, deciding, decision, superior 9 excellent, exclusive, first-rate, preferred, selection, top drawer 10 assemblage, assortment, collection, consummate, discretion, first-class, preferable, preference, well-chosen 11 alternative, appointment, exceptional, superlative 13 determination, extraordinary
choice food 5 treat 8 delicacy
choicest part
   French: 14 creme de la creme
choir 4 band 5 quire 6 angels, chorus 7 chorale, singers 10 choristers
Choirboys, The
   author: 14 Joseph Wambaugh
choke 3 dam, gag 4 clog, plug 5 block, check, dam up, stuff 6 arrest, bridle, hamper, hinder, impede, plug up, retard, stifle, stop up 7 congest, garrote, inhibit, repress, smother 8 blockade, hold back, obstruct, restrain, strangle, suppress, throttle 9 constrain, constrict, suffocate 10 asphyxiate
choler 3 ire 4 fury, rage 5 anger, wrath 6 spleen, temper
choleric 3 mad 5 angry, irate, testy, vexed 6 cranky, grumpy, shirty, touchy 7 enraged, furious, grouchy, peevish, waspish 8 snappish, wrathful 9 dyspeptic, indignant, irritable, irascible, splenetic 10 infuriated, short-fused 11 contentious, hot-tempered, ill-tempered, thin-skinned 12 cantankerous, sour-tempered 13 quick-tempered, short-tempered
choose 3 opt 4 like, pick, take, wish 5 adopt, elect 6 decide, desire, intend, opt for, prefer, see fit, select 7 call out, embrace, espouse, extract, fix upon, pick out, resolve 8 decide on, settle on 9 determine, single out 10 be inclined 13 commit oneself 14 make up one's mind
choosy 5 fussy, picky 7 finicky 9 selective 10 fastidious, particular 14 discriminating
chop 3 cut, hew, hit, lop 4 blow, chip, crop, cube, dice, fell, gash, hack 5 cut up, mince, slash, slice, split, swipe, whack 6 cleave, cutlet, stroke, sunder 8 fragment, rib slice 9 cotelette, pulverize
Chopin, Frederic Francois
   born: 6 Poland 12 Zelazowawola
   companion: 10 George Sand
   composer of: 5 Etude 7 Ballade 8 Berceuse, Cat Valse, Dog Valse, Fantasie 9 Ecossaise 10 Barcarolle 11 Minute Valse 15 Andante Spianato, Heroic Polonaise (No 6), Raindrop Prelude, Winter Wind Etude 16 Shepherd Boy Etude 17 Impromptu Fantasie, Rondo a la Krakowiak 18 Revolutionary Etude 20 Butterfly's Wings Etude

choral ode
   Greek: 7 parodos 8 stasimon
chord 4 cord, line, note, tone 5 music, triad 6 accord, string, tendon 7 cadence, emotion, feeling, harmony 9 harmonize
chore 3 job 4 duty, task, work 5 stint 6 burden, errand, strain 8 farm task, small job 10 assignment 13 household task 14 responsibility
choreography 5 dance 12 stage dancing 16 dance composition
chorister 6 singer 7 changer 8 choirboy
chortle 5 laugh 7 chuckle
chorus 5 choir, unity 6 accord, unison 7 concert, concord, refrain 8 glee club, one voice, response 9 antiphony, consensus, unanimity 11 concordance 12 singing group
chosen 5 elite 6 picked, sorted 7 elected 8 selected 9 picked out
Chosen, The
   author: 10 Chaim Potok
Choson see 5 Korea
Chouans, The
   author: 14 Honore de Balzac
chough
   group of: 10 chattering
Chowbok
   character in: 7 Erewhon
   author: 6 Butler
Christ, the see 5 Jesus
christen 3 dip, dub 4 name 6 launch 7 baptize, immerse 8 dedicate, sprinkle 9 designate
Christian
   character in: 16 Pilgrim's Progress
   author: 6 Bunyan
Christian, Fletcher
   character in: 17 Mutiny on the Bounty
   authors: 4 Hall 8 Nordhoff
Christian, Linda
   real name: 16 Blanca Rosa Welter
   husband: 11 Tyrone Power 12 Edmund Purdom
   born: 6 Mexico 7 Tampico
   roles: 6 Athena 15 Slaves of Babylon 18 Green Dolphin Street
Christiania
   capital of: 6 Norway
Christie, (Dame) Agatha
   author of: 7 Curtain 12 The Mousetrap 14 Death on the Nile 15 The Mirror Crack'd 16 Ten Little Indians 19 Murder at the Vicarage 20 And Then There Were None 22 What Mrs McGillicuddy Saw! 23 The Murder of Roger Ackroyd 24 Murder on the Orient Express, Witness for the Prosecution 27 The Mysterious Affair at Styles
   character: 10 Jane Marple 13 Hercule Poirot
Christie, Julie
   born: 5 Assam, India 6 Chukua
   roles: 7 Darling (Oscar), Shampoo 9 Billy Liar 11 Heat and Dust 13 Doctor Zhivago, Fahrenheit 451, Heaven Can Wait 18 Mc-

Cabe and Mrs Miller 22 Far From the
Madding Crowd

Christine
 author: 11 Stephen King

Christmas
 also: 4 Noel, Yule 8 Yuletide
 feature/symbol: 4 bell, star, tree 5 angel,
 gifts, holly 6 candle, carols, creche, manger, sleigh, wreath 7 Yule log 8 presents
 9 evergreen, mistletoe, snowflake, stockings 10 Santa Claus

Christmas, Joe
 character in: 13 Light in August
 author: 8 Faulkner

Christmas Carol, A
 author: 14 Charles Dickens
 character: 7 Tiny Tim 8 Fezziwig 11 Bob
 Cratchit 12 Marley's Ghost 15 Ebenezer
 Scrooge
 ghosts of: 13 Christmas Past 15 Christmas Future 16 Christmas Present
 director: 17 Brian Desmond Hurst
 cast: 10 Jack Warner 11 Alastair Sim
 (Ebenezer Scrooge), Mervyn Johns 14
 Michael Hordern 16 Kathleen Harrison

Chrome Yellow
 author: 12 Aldous Huxley

chromium
 chemical symbol: 2 Cr

chronic 7 abiding, lasting 8 constant, enduring, habitual, periodic 9 confirmed,
 continual, ingrained, perennial, recurrent,
 recurring 10 continuous, deep-rooted,
 deep-seated, inveterate, persistent, persisting 12 intermittent, longstanding

chronicle 3 log 4 epic, list, note, post, saga
 5 diary, enter, story 6 annals, docket, record, relate, report 7 account, history, journal, narrate, recount, set down 8 archives
 9 narrative 10 chronology

**Chronicles of England, Scotland, and
Ireland**
 author: 16 Raphael Holinshed

chronological 5 dated 6 serial 7 ordered,
 sequent 10 sequential, succeeding, successive 11 consecutive, progressive, time-
 ordered 12 chronometric, chronoscopic 13
 chronographic

chronology 6 annals, record 7 history 9
 chronicle 13 order of events

chronometer 5 clock 8 horologe 9 timepiece

chrysanthemum
 varieties: 3 Max 4 Corn 5 Daisy, Tansy 6
 Nippon 7 Garland 8 Florist's, Tricolor 10
 Portuguese

Chrysaor
 father: 8 Poseidon
 mother: 6 Medusa
 brother: 7 Pegasus

Chryseis
 father: 7 Chryses
 concubine of: 9 Agamemnon

Chryses
 priest of: 6 Apollo
 daughter: 8 Chryseis

Chrysippus
 father: 6 Pelops
 abducted by: 5 Laius
 half-brother: 6 Atreus 8 Thyestes

chrysoberyl
 variety: 7 cat's-eye 11 alexandrite

chrysolite 4 iron, lava 5 beryl, green, stone
 6 yellow 7 mineral, olivine, peridot 8 sili-
 cate 9 magnesium 10 aquamarine

chrysoprase
 species: 6 quartz
 color: 5 green

Chrysothemis
 father: 9 Agamemnon
 mother: 12 Clytemnestra
 brother: 7 Orestes
 sister: 7 Electra 9 Iphigenia
 daughter: 5 Rhoeo

Chthonian
 form: 5 deity 6 spirit
 habitat: 10 underworld

Chthonius
 member of: 6 Sparti
 epithet of: 4 Zeus
 means: 15 of the underworld

Chuang-tzu, Chwang-tse
 author: 9 Chuang-tzu

chubby 3 fat 5 buxom, plump, podgy,
 pudgy, stout, tubby 6 chunky, flabby,
 fleshy, portly, rotund, stocky, zaftig 7
 paunchy 8 heavyset, roly-poly, thickset 9
 corpulent 10 overweight 15 pleasingly
 plump

chuck 3 pat, pet, tap 4 cast, toss 5 fling,
 heave, pitch, sling, throw 6 tickle

chuckle 5 cluck, laugh 6 clumsy 7 cackle,
 chortle, snicker

chum 3 pal 5 buddy, crony 6 cohort, friend
 7 comrade 8 intimate, playmate, sidekick 9
 companion, confidant 10 bosom buddy,
 playfellow 11 close friend

chummy 5 close, palsy 7 devoted 8 familiar, friendly, intimate 9 congenial 10 buddy-
 buddy, palsy-walsy 12 affectionate

chump 4 dolt, dupe, fool, goof, goon, head
 5 champ, munch 6 sucker 9 blockhead

chunk 3 gob, wad 4 clod, hunk, lump, mass
 5 batch, block, piece 6 nugget, square

chunky 5 beefy, dumpy, lumpy, pudgy,
 squat, stout, thick 6 chubby, portly, stocky,
 stodgy, stubby 7 squabby 8 heavyset,
 thickset 11 thick-bodied

church 4 cult, sect 5 faith 6 belief, chapel,
 mosque, temple 7 service 8 basilica, religion 9 cathedral, devotions, synagogue 10
 house of God, Lord's house, persuasion,
 tabernacle 11 affiliation 12 denomination
 13 divine worship 14 house of worship

Church, Frederick Edwin
 born: 10 Hartford CT
 artwork: 14 Andes of Ecuador, Falls of
 Niagara (Niagara Falls) 18 The Heart of
 the Andes 19 Morning in the Tropics

Churchill, Frank
 character in: 4 Emma
 author: 6 Austen

Churchill, Sarah
father: 19 Sir Winston Churchill
born: 6 London 7 England
roles: 12 Royal Wedding

Churchill, Winston Spencer
born: 14 England 14 Blenheim Palace
father: 8 Randolph
mother: 12 Jennie Jerome
wife: 16 Clementine Hosier
daughter: 5 Sarah
school: 6 Harrow 9 Sandhurst
captured by: 5 Boers
position: 13 prime minister
author of: 11 Marlborough, My Early Life
14 The World Crisis 17 The Second
World War 35 A History of the English-
Speaking Peoples

churchly 8 clerical, pastoral, priestly 9 parochial 11 ministerial 14 ecclesiastical

churchman 5 vicar 6 bishop, cleric, curate,
deacon, parson, pastor, priest, rector 7
prelate 8 chaplain, minister, preacher 9
clergyman 12 ecclesiastic

church official 5 elder 6 beadle, deacon 9
presbyter

churchyard 8 cemetery 9 graveyard 12
burial ground 13 burying ground

churl 3 cad, oaf 4 boor, lout 7 bounder

churlish 4 rude, sour, tart 5 crude, surly,
testy 6 crusty, sullen 7 bearish, bilious,
boorish, brusque, crabbed, grouchy, ill-
bred, uncivil, uncouth, waspish 8 arrogant,
captious, choleric, impolite, impudent, insolent, petulant 9 dastardly, insulting, irascible, irritable, obnoxious, rancorous, splenetic 10 unmannerly 11 ill-mannered,
ill-tempered, quarrelsome 12 contemptible,
discourteous

churn 4 beat, foam, rage, roil, roll, toss,
whip 5 heave, shake, swirl, whisk 6 stir up
7 agitate, disturb, pulsate, shake up, vibrate 8 convulse 9 palpitate

chute 5 rapid, slide, slope 7 incline, passage 9 parachute

chutzpa, chutzpah 4 gall 5 brass, cheek,
nerve 8 audacity, boldness, temerity 9
brashness, impudence 10 brazenness, effrontery 11 forwardness, presumption

Chwatt, Aaron
real name of: 10 Red Buttons

ciao hi 5 hello 6 so long 7 goodbye 11
see you later

Cicero, Marcus Tullius
lived in: 11 ancient Rome
noted as: 6 author, lawyer, orator 9
statesman 11 philosopher 12 letter writer
position: 6 aedile, consul 7 praetor
author of: 9 De finibus, De oratore 10
De amicitia, De officiis 11 De republica,
De senectute, In Catilinam 14 De natura
deorum, Pro lege Manilia 23 Tusculanae
Disputationes

cicerone 5 guide, pilot 8 conductor 9 explainer

cicisbeo 5 lover

Cid, The
also: 11 Poema del Cid
author: 7 unknown 15 Pierre Corneille
character: 7 Chimene 8 Rodrigue
Cid also called: 14 el Cid Campeador 18
Rodrigo Diaz de Bivar
horse: 7 Babieca

ci-devant 6 former 7 retired 10 heretofore

cierge 3 dip, wax 5 light, taper 6 bougie,
candle, tallow

cigar 4 toby 5 claro 6 corona, havana, ma-
duro, stogie 7 cheroot 8 panatela, pane-
tela, perfecto 9 cigarillo, panatella
ingredient: 11 tobacco leaf
part: 6 binder, filler 7 wrapper
made in: 4 Cuba 6 Havana
kept in: 7 humidor

cigarette, cigaret 3 cig, fag 4 biri 5 smoke
6 gasper, reefer 10 coffin nail
ingredient: 3 tar 7 menthol, tobacco 8
nicotine

Cilissa
nurse of: 7 Orestes

Cilix
father: 6 Agenor
sister: 6 Europa
searched for: 6 Europa

Cilla
brother: 5 Priam
killed by: 5 Priam

Cillus
charioteer of: 6 Pelops

Cimabue
real name: 11 Cenni di Pepi
born: 5 Italy 8 Florence
artwork attributed: 18 The S Trinita Madonna 29 Madonna Enthroned with St
Francis 45 Madonna and Child Enthroned with Angels and Prophets

Cimarron
author: 10 Edna Ferber
director: 13 Wesley Ruggles
cast: 10 Irene Dunne, Richard Dix 13
Estelle Taylor
Oscar for: 7 picture 10 screenplay

Cimarron Strip
character: 8 (US Marshal) Jim Crown 9
Mac Gregor 12 Francis Wilde 17 Dulcey
Coopersmith
cast: 10 Randy Boone 12 Jill Townsend,
Percy Herbert 13 Stuart Whitman

Cimino, Michael
director of: 11 Heaven's Gate 13 The
Deer Hunter (Oscar)

Cimmerian
mentioned by: 5 Homer
form: 10 Westerners
live in: 8 darkness

cinch 4 band, snap 5 girth 6 clinch, ensure,
girdle, shoo-in 8 lead-pipe 9 pull tight, sure
thing 11 piece of cake

Cincinnati
baseball team: 4 Reds
football team: 7 Bengals

cincture 4 band, belt, cord, sash 6 girdle

cinder 3 ash 4 slag 5 ashes, dross, ember 6 embers, scoria 8 clinkers, iron slag 10 burned coal, burned wood

Cinderella
  author: 7 unknown
  source: 8 Perrault
  character: 14 Fairy Godmother, Handsome Prince 15 Ugly Stepsisters 16 Wicked Stepmother
  coach: 7 pumpkin
  horses: 9 white mice
  footman: 4 frog
  loses: 12 glass slipper

cinema 5 films 6 flicks, movies 7 theater 14 motion pictures, moving pictures

cinnamon 5 spice
  botanical name: 20 Cinnamomum zeylanicum
  variety: 6 cassia, Ceylon 10 zeylanicum
  color: 4 buff 5 tawny 6 auburn 8 nut-brown 11 golden-brown, yellow-brown 12 reddish-brown 13 chestnut-brown 14 yellowish-brown
  origin: 5 China 7 Vietnam 9 Indonesia 10 East Indies

Cinyras
  king of: 6 Cyprus
  son: 5 Melus
  daughter: 6 Myrrha
  introduced worship of: 9 Aphrodite
  crime: 6 incest
  death by: 7 suicide

cipher 3 nil, zip 4 code, zero 5 aught 6 naught, nobody 7 anagram, nothing, nullity 8 acrostic, goose egg 9 nonentity, obscurity 10 cryptogram 11 cryptograph

Cipus
  origin: 5 Roman
  occupation: 7 praetor

Circe
  form: 11 enchantress
  father: 6 Helios
  mother: 5 Perse
  brother: 6 Aeetes
  son: 6 Agrius 7 Latinus 9 Telegonus
  home: 5 Aeaea
  turned men into: 4 pigs 5 swine

circle 3 orb, set 4 belt, curl, gird, girt, halo, hoop, knot, loop, reel, ring, turn 5 arena, bound, cabal, crowd, curve, cycle, field, girth, group, hem in, orbit, pivot, range, reach, realm, round, sweep, swing 6 border, bounds, clique, cordon, corona, course, domain, girdle, region, sphere 7 circlet, circuit, company, compass, coterie, enclose, envelop, hedge in, revolve, ringlet, society, theater 8 dominion, encircle, province, sequence, surround 9 bailiwick, encompass, territory, wind about 10 move around, revolution, ring around 11 curve around, progression 12 circumrotate, circumscribe 13 revolve around 14 circumnavigate

Circle 6 gilgal

circlet 4 band, halo, ring 5 tiara 6 diadem, fillet, wreath 7 chaplet, coronet, ringlet

circuit 3 lap, run 4 area, beat, edge, tour, trek, walk 5 jaunt, limit, round, route 6 border, bounds, course, margin, sphere 7 compass, confine, journey 8 circling, frontier, orbiting, pivoting 9 excursion, extremity, perimeter, revolving, territory 10 revolution 13 circumference 14 distance around

circuitous 7 devious, turning, winding 8 circular, indirect, rambling, tortuous, twisting 10 meandering, roundabout, serpentine 12 labyrinthine 14 circumlocutory

circular 4 bill 5 flier, round 6 curved, notice, rotary 7 coiling, curling, leaflet, rocking, rolling, rounded, turning, winding 8 bulletin, gyrating, handbill, pivoting, spinning, twirling 9 revolving, spiraling, swiveling, throwaway 10 circuitous, ring-shaped 12 announcement 13 advertisement

circulate 4 flow 5 issue, strew 6 circle, course, spread, travel 7 give out, go forth, journey, publish, radiate, scatter 8 announce, disperse, go around, put about 9 broadcast, get abroad, make known, move about, publicize 10 distribute, make public, move around, pass around, put forward 11 disseminate, pass through, visit around 13 make the rounds

circulation 4 flow 6 motion 7 flowing 8 circling, rotation 9 diffusion, radiation 10 dispersion 11 propagation 12 distribution, promulgation, transmission 13 dissemination

circulatory system
  part: 4 vein 5 heart 6 artery 9 capillary 15 lymphatic vessel
  carries: 6 plasma 9 platelets 13 red blood cells 15 white blood cells

circumcision
  Hebrew: 4 Bris 5 Berit, Brith 6 Berith

circumference 3 rim 4 edge 5 girth 6 border, bounds, fringe, girdle, limits, margin 7 circuit, compass, outline 8 boundary 9 extremity, perimeter, periphery 14 distance around

circumlocution 8 rambling, verbiage 9 garrulity, verbosity, wordiness 10 digression, meandering 14 discursiveness, long-windedness, roundaboutness

circumlocutory 5 wordy 7 diffuse, verbose 8 rambling 9 wandering 10 digressive, discursive, maundering, roundabout

circumnavigate 5 skirt 6 bypass, circle 8 encircle, go around 10 circumvent

circumnavigation 8 circling, skirting 9 bypassing 11 going around 12 encirclement 13 circumvention

circumscribe 3 fix 4 curb 5 check, hem in, limit 6 bridle, circle, corset, define, impede 7 confine, enclose, outline 8 encircle, restrain, restrict, surround 9 constrain, delineate, encompass, proscribe

circumscribed 6 narrow 7 limited 10 restricted

circumscription 5 limit 7 outline 9 hemming in, restraint 10 constraint 11 confinement 12 encirclement 14 restrictedness

circumspect 4 sage, wary 5 alert 7 careful, guarded, prudent 8 cautious, discreet, vigilant, watchful 9 judicious, sagacious, wide-awake 10 deliberate, discerning, particular, thoughtful 13 contemplative, perspicacious 14 discriminating

circumspection 4 care, heed .7 caution 8 prudence 10 discretion, precaution, steadiness 11 carefulness, heedfulness, mindfulness 12 deliberation

circumstance 4 fact, item 5 event, point, thing 6 detail, factor, matter, ritual 7 element 8 ceremony, incident, splendor 9 condition, formality, happening, pageantry 10 brilliance, occurrence, particular, phenomenon 11 vicissitude 12 happenstance, magnificence, resplendence 14 state of affairs

circumstances 5 state 9 situation 11 environment 16 living conditions

circumstantial 4 full 6 minute 7 deduced, hearsay, implied, precise 8 accurate, complete, detailed, explicit, inferred, presumed, thorough 9 secondary 10 blow-by-blow, evidential, exhaustive, extraneous, incidental, particular, unabridged 11 conjectural, inferential, provisional 12 nonessential

circumvent 4 miss, shun 5 avoid, dodge, elude, evade, skirt 6 bypass, circle, escape, outwit, thwart 8 go around 9 frustrate 12 keep away from 14 circumnavigate

circumvention 7 dodging, ducking, eluding, evasion 9 avoidance, bypassing 11 frustration 12 sidestepping

circus 4 ring 5 arena 6 big top, circle, uproar 8 carnival, coliseum 9 spectacle 10 exhibition, hippodrome 11 amphitheater 12 intersection
    act: 5 clown, flyer 7 acrobat, juggler, trapeze 8 side show 9 lion tamer, menagerie 10 equestrian 13 flying trapeze
    famous: 6 Astley 12 Cirque d'Hiver 15 Barnum and Bailey 16 Ringling Brothers

Cissaea
    epithet of: 6 Athena
    means: 10 ivy goddess

Cist
    form: 9 sacred box
    used for: 8 utensils

cistern 3 box, tub, vat 4 tank, well 6 cavity, vessel 8 aqueduct 9 reservoir

citadel 4 fort 7 bastion, rampart 8 fortress 10 stronghold 13 fortification

citation 4 cite 5 award, honor, kudos, medal, quote 7 example, excerpt, extract, passage 8 instance 9 quotation 12 commendation, illustration 14 official praise

cite 4 name, note 5 honor, quote 6 praise 7 advance, commend, mention, present, refer to, specify 8 allude to, document, indicate 9 enumerate, exemplify 12 bring forward 13 give as example

Cithaeron
    brother: 7 Helicon
    crime: 6 murder
    changed into: 8 mountain

Cithaeronian see 4 Zeus

citified 5 urban 6 urbane 12 cosmopolitan 13 sophisticated

citizen 6 native 7 denizen, subject 8 national, resident 10 inhabitant
    French: 7 citoyen

Citizen Kane
    director: 11 Orson Welles
    script: 11 Orson Welles 17 Herman J Mankiewicz
    cast: 11 Orson Welles 12 Joseph Cotten 13 Everett Sloane 14 Agnes Moorehead
    score: 15 Bernard Herrmann
    sled: 7 Rosebud

citizenry 4 folk 6 people, public 7 society 8 populace 9 community 10 population

citoyen 7 citizen

citrine
    species: 6 quartz
    color: 6 yellow

citron 3 rue 4 lime, rind 5 lemon 6 cedrat, orange, yellow 8 Rutaceae 9 tangerine 10 watermelon 12 citrus medica
    Jewish: 6 ethrog

city 4 burg, town 7 big town 8 denizens, township 9 residents 10 metropolis 11 inhabitants, megalopolis, townspeople 12 municipality 16 incorporated town, metropolitan area

city hall
    French: 12 hotel de ville

City Life
    author: 15 Donald Barthelme

City Lights
    director: 14 Charles Chaplin
    cast: 8 Hank Mann 10 Harry Myers 14 Charlie Chaplin 16 Virginia Cherrill

City of God, The (De Civitate Dei)
    author: 11 St Augustine

City of the Lion see 9 Singapore

city slicker 4 dude 8 urbanite 11 cosmopolite 12 sophisticate

City Without Walls and Other Poems
    author: 7 W H Auden

Ciudad Trujillo
    capital of: 17 Dominican Republic

civic 5 local 6 public 8 citizen's, communal 9 community

civil 3 lay 4 city 5 civic, state 6 genial, polite, public 7 affable, amiable, citizen, cordial, secular 8 citizen's, communal, decorous, gracious, mannerly, obliging 9 civilized, community, courteous, municipal 10 individual, neighborly, respectful 11 gentlemanly, nonmilitary 12 conciliatory, well-mannered

Civil Disobedience
    author: 17 Henry David Thoreau

civilian 9 lay person 14 private citizen 17 nonmilitary person 18 nonuniformed person

civility 4 tact 7 manners, respect 8 courtesy 10 affability, amiability, cordiality, good temper, politeness 11 good manners 12 graciousness, pleasantness 13 agreeableness, courteousness 14 respectfulness

civilization 7 culture, society 10 refinement 11 cultivation, worldliness 13 enlightenment 14 sophistication

civilize 5 edify, teach, train 6 inform, polish, refine 7 culture, develop, educate, elevate 8 humanize, instruct 9 cultivate, enlighten 11 acculturate 12 sophisticate

civil law
  Latin: 9 jus civile

clad 6 garbed 7 arrayed, attired, clothed, dressed 9 outfitted

Claggart
  character in: 9 Billy Budd
  author: 8 Melville

claim 3 ask 4 avow, call, plea, take 5 exact, right, title 6 access, affirm, allege, assert, avowal, charge, demand, pick up 7 call for, collect, command, declare, profess, request 8 exaction, insist on, maintain, proclaim 9 assertion, ownership, seek as due, statement 10 allegation, lay claim to, pretension, profession 11 affirmation, declaration, postulation, requirement 12 proclamation, protestation

claimant 6 suitor 9 applicant, pretender 10 petitioner

clairvoyant 7 psychic 8 divining, oracular 9 prescient, prophetic 10 telepathic 11 foreknowing, telekinetic 12 extrasensory, precognitive, psychometric 13 psychokinetic, second-sighted

clam 4 vise 5 clamp, clasp 6 dollar, marine 7 bivalve, mollusk
  kind: 5 pismo, razor 6 butter, quahog 7 geoduck, steamer 10 little neck 11 cherrystone
  part: 4 foot, palp 5 gills, shell, valve 6 mantle, siphon 7 sinuses 8 ligament
  habitat: 3 mud 4 sand
  relative: 6 mussel, oyster

clamber up 5 climb, mount, scale 10 scramble up, struggle up

clamminess 4 damp 7 wetness 8 dampness, dankness 10 stickiness, sweatiness

clammy 3 wet 4 damp 5 pasty, slimy 6 sticky, sweaty 10 perspiring 11 cold and damp

clamor 3 cry, din 4 call, howl, yell 5 blast, chaos, noise, shout, storm 6 bedlam, bellow, cry out, hubbub, jangle, outcry, racket, rumpus, tumult, uproar 7 bluster, call out, clangor, thunder 8 brouhaha, shouting 9 commotion, hue and cry 10 hullabaloo, vociferate, wild chorus

clamorous 4 loud 5 noisy 10 boisterous, uproarious

clamp 4 clip, grip, vise 5 brace, clasp 6 clench, clinch, fasten, secure 7 bracket 8 fastener

clan 4 gang, knot, line, ring 5 breed, cabal, crowd, group, guild, house, party, stock 6 circle, league, strain 7 company, dynasty,

lineage, society 8 alliance, pedigree 10 fraternity 11 affiliation, association, brotherhood, family group, lineal group 12 tribal family

clandestine 6 covert, hidden, masked, secret, veiled 7 cloaked, furtive, private 8 secluded, sneaking, stealthy 9 concealed, secretive, underhand 10 undercover, unrevealed 11 underground, underhanded, undisclosed 12 confidential 13 surreptitious

clang 3 din 4 bong, gong, peal, toll 5 chime, clank, clash, knell 6 jangle 7 clangor, resound, ringing, tolling 8 clashing 10 resounding, ring loudly

clangor 3 din 5 noise 6 clamor, hubbub, jangle, racket, uproar

clank 5 chink, clang, clash, clink 6 jangle, rattle 7 clangor, clatter 8 clashing

clannish 4 cold 5 aloof 6 narrow 7 distant, insular 8 cliquish, snobbish 9 exclusive, parochial, sectarian 10 provincial, restricted, unfriendly 11 unreceptive

Clan of the Cave Bear, The
  author: 9 Jean M Auel

clap 3 bat, hit, rap, tap 4 bang, bump, cast, cuff, dash, hurl, peal, push, roar, rush, slam, slap, swat, toss 5 burst, clack, crack, drive, fling, force, pitch, shove, smack, smite, thump, whack 6 buffet, plunge, propel, strike, thrust, thwack, wallop 7 applaud, clatter 9 explosion 11 set suddenly

claptrap 3 rot 4 bosh, bull, bunk, sham, 5 bilge, hokum, hooey, stuff, trash, tripe 6 bunkum, drivel, hot air, humbug, tinsel 7 baloney, blarney, fustian, hogwash, spinach, twaddle 8 buncombe, nonsense, quackery, tommyrot 9 gaudiness, poppycock, staginess 10 applesauce, flapdoodle, tawdriness, tomfoolery 11 foolishness 15 pretentiousness 16 stuff and nonsense

claque 10 sycophants 15 cheering section

Clare, Ada
  character in: 10 Bleak House
  author: 7 Dickens

claret 3 red 7 carmine, deep red, red wine 8 blood-red, Bordeaux, cardinal 11 purplish red, wine-colored

clarification 10 commentary 11 elucidation, explanation, explication 14 further comment
  French: 15 eclaircissement

clarify 5 clear, purge, solve 6 purify, refine 7 clear up, explain, lay open, resolve 9 elucidate, explicate, make clear, make plain 10 illuminate 11 disentangle, shed light on 12 bring to light 18 make understandable

clarinet 4 wind 8 woodwind 11 transposing
  mouthpiece: 4 reed
  ancestor: 9 chalumeau
  musician: 12 Benny Goodman

clarion 5 acute, clear, sharp 6 shrill 7 blaring, ringing 8 distinct, piercing, resonant, sonorous, stirring 10 commanding, compelling, imperative 11 high-pitched

Clarissa Harlowe
  author: 16 Samuel Richardson
  character: 8 Miss Howe 11 John Belford
  14 Robert Lovelace 20 Colonel William
  Morden
clarity 6 purity 8 lucidity, radiance 9 clearness, exactness, plainness, precision 10
  brightness, brilliance, directness, effulgence, glassiness, luminosity, simplicity
  12 explicitness, translucence, transparency 15 intelligibility 17 comprehensi-
  bility
Clark, Mark W
  served in: 3 WWI 4 WWII 9 Korean War
  rank: 22 allied commander in Italy 24
  commander of forces in Korea 30 chief of
  staff of army ground forces 42 commander of Allied occupation forces in
  Austria
  president of: 7 Citadel
Clark, Walter Van Tilburg
  author of: 16 The Ox-Bow Incident
Clarke, Arthur C
  author of: 10 (2010) Odyssey Two 13
  (2001) A Space Odyssey, Childhood's
  End
clash 4 bang, boil, feud, fray, tiff 5 argue,
  clang, clank, crash, fight, set-to 6 battle,
  combat, fracas, jangle, rattle, tussle 7
  clangor, clatter, contend, contest, discord,
  dispute, grapple, jarring, quarrel, wrangle
  8 conflict, crashing, friction, skirmish,
  squabble, struggle 9 altercate, encounter,
  lock horns 10 antagonism, difference, disharmony, dissidence, opposition 11 cross
  swords 12 disagreement 13 exchange
  blows
clash of arms 5 fight 6 battle, combat 8
  conflict, skirmish, struggle 9 encounter 10
  engagement
clash with 9 fight with 12 do battle with 14
  contend against 15 cross swords with
clasp 3 hug 4 bolt, clip, grip, hasp, hold,
  hook, link, lock, snap 5 catch, clamp,
  grasp, latch, press 6 buckle, clinch, clutch,
  couple, fasten, secure 7 coupler, embrace,
  grapple, squeeze 8 fastener 9 fastening
clasp in the arms 3 hug 4 hold 6 enfold 7
  embrace
class 3 set 4 form, kind, rank, rate, size,
  sort, type 5 brand, breed, caste, genre, genus, grade, group, index, label, order,
  state 6 circle, clique, codify, course, lesson, number, sphere, status 7 arrange,
  catalog, section, session, species, station,
  variety 8 category, classify, division, pedigree, position 9 condition, designate 10
  categorize, pigeonhole, social rank 11 set
  of pupils 13 social stratum 14 classification
  15 departmentalize, graduating group
classic, classical 4 epic 5 model 6 heroic
  7 ageless, paragon 8 absolute, accepted,
  enduring, masterly 9 archetype, excellent,
  exemplary, first-rate, prototype 10 archetypal, consummate, definitive, first-class,
  Greco-Roman, prototypal 11 masterpiece,
  outstanding, traditional 12 ancient Greek,

ancient Roman, standard work 13 authoritative, distinguished 14 distinguishing 17
  first-class example
classification 4 kind, rank, sort, type 5
  class, genus, group, order 6 family, series
  7 section, species 8 category, classing, division, grouping, labeling, ordering, taxonomy 9 arranging, gradation 10 assortment,
  organizing 11 arrangement, designation,
  disposition 12 categorizing, codification,
  organization 14 categorization 15 systematization
classified 5 secret 6 sorted 7 classed 8 assorted 10 restricted 11 categorized 12 confidential
classify 3 tag 4 list, rank, rate, size, type 5
  brand, class, grade, group, index, label,
  order, range 6 assort, codify, number,
  ticket 7 arrange, catalog 8 organize 9 segregate 10 categorize, pigeonhole 11 distinguish
classy 4 chic, posh, tony 5 nifty, nobby,
  ritzy, smart, swank, swell 6 dressy, modish, spiffy, swanky 7 elegant, genteel, opulent, refined, stylish 8 cultured, polished,
  tasteful 9 high-class 10 ultrasmart 11 fashionable, in good taste 12 aristocratic, well-
  mannered
clatter 4 bang 5 clack, clang, clank, clash,
  clink, clump, crash 6 clamor, jangle,
  racket, rattle 7 chatter 8 crashing, rattling
clattering 3 din 6 clamor, hubbub, racket,
  uproar 7 clangor
Claude
  real name: 12 Claude Gellee
  also called: 14 Claude Lorraine
  born: 6 France 9 Champagne
  artwork: 7 The Mill 16 Hagar and the Angel 18 Ascanius and the Stag, The Enchanted Castle 27 The Rest on the Flight
  into Egypt 31 The Embarkation of the
  Queen of Sheba
Claudel, Paul
  author of: 6 L'Otage 10 The Hostage 13
  Partage de Midi 15 The Satin Slipper 20
  Tidings Brought to Mary
Claudia Quinta
  freed: 12 grounded ship
  feat proved: 8 chastity
Claudio
  character in: 17 Measure for Measure
  19 Much Ado About Nothing
  author: 11 Shakespeare
Claudius
  character in: 6 Hamlet
  author: 11 Shakespeare
Claudius the God
  author: 12 Robert Graves
clause 4 term 7 article, proviso 8 covenant
  9 condition, provision 11 proposition, stipulation 13 specification 14 simple sentence
claustrophobia
  fear of: 12 closed spaces 14 confined
  spaces
Clavell, James
  author of: 6 Shogun, Tai-Pan 7 King Rat
  9 Whirlwind 10 Noble House

clavicle
bone of: 10 collarbone
claw 3 paw 4 foot, grip, maul, tear 5 seize, slash, talon 6 clutch, pincer, scrape 7 scratch 8 lacerate 10 animal nail
Clay, Cassius
former name of: 11 Muhammad Ali
Clayburgh, Jill
born: 9 New York NY
roles: 9 Semi-Tough 12 Starting Over 16 An Unmarried Woman, North Dallas Forty 21 I'm Dancing as Fast as I Can
Clayhanger Trilogy, The
author: 13 Arnold Bennett
clean 3 mop 4 dust, fine, neat, pure, tidy, trim, wash 5 bathe, clear, fresh, moral, order, scour, scrub, sweep 6 bathed, chaste, decent, neaten, tidy up, vacuum, washed 7 cleaned, cleanse, healthy, launder, orderly, perfect, scoured, shampoo, upright 8 cleansed, decorous, flawless, innocent, sanitary, scrubbed, spotless, unsoiled, virtuous, well-made 9 exemplary, faultless, honorable, laundered, stainless, undefiled, unspotted, unstained, unsullied, untainted, wholesome 10 immaculate, uninfected, unpolluted 11 unblemished 13 unadulterated 14 uncontaminated
cleaner, cleanser 4 soap 5 borax 6 washer 7 ammonia, janitor 8 purifier, scrubber 9 detergent 14 scouring powder
cleaning 7 bathing, washing 8 scouring 9 cleansing, going-over, scrubbing, tidying up 10 laundering
cleanse 3 rid 4 free, wash 5 bathe, clean, clear, erase, flush, scour, scrub 7 absolve, deliver, expunge, launder, release, shampoo 8 sweep out, unburden 9 expurgate
clean-shaven 5 smooth 9 unbearded 11 unwhiskered 12 smooth-shaven
cleansing 7 bathing, healing, purging, washing 8 flushing, scouring 9 expunging, purifying, scrubbing 10 absolution
cleanup 4 gain 6 profit 8 windfall
baseball: 12 fourth batter
clear 3 rid 4 fair, free, keen, make, open 5 alert, clean, empty, gauzy, lucid, plain, sharp, sunny 6 acquit, bright, patent, remove, serene, unstop, wholly 7 absolve, audible, audibly, certain, clearly, evident, express, fly over, glowing, halcyon, hop over, lighten, obvious, plainly, radiant, unblock 8 apparent, brighten, clear-cut, dazzling, definite, distinct, entirely, explicit, gleaming, leap over, luminous, manifest, pass over, pellucid, positive, skip over, unhidden 9 all the way, bound over, brilliant, cloudless, exculpate, exonerate, sparkling, unblocked, unclouded, unimpeded, unmuddled, vindicate, wide-awake 10 articulate, become fair, completely, diaphanous, discerning, distinctly, glistening, pronounced, unconfused, undeniable, unobscured 11 crystalline, inescapable, self-evident, translucent, transparent, unambiguous, unconcealed, undisguised, unequivocal, unqualified 12

articulately, intelligible, recognizable, unencumbered, unmistakable, unobstructed 14 comprehensible 15 distinguishable, straightforward
clearance 4 room, sale 6 margin, permit 7 removal 8 clearing 10 offsetting 11 elimination 13 authorization, certification
clear as day 5 plain 7 obvious 8 apparent, clear-cut, manifest 11 self-evident
clear-cut 4 open 5 exact, lucid, plain 6 patent 7 evident, express, obvious, precise 8 definite, detailed, distinct, explicit, manifest 10 clear as day, unconfused, undeniable 11 appreciable, conspicuous, self-evident, substantial, unambiguous, undisguised, unequivocal, well-defined 12 crystal-clear, unmistakable 14 comprehensible, understandable 15 straightforward
clearheaded 5 acute, alert, awake, aware, sharp 6 astute 8 rational, sensible 9 on the ball, practical, realistic, wide-awake 10 discerning, insightful, on one's toes, on the stick, perceptive 13 perspicacious
clearheadedness 7 insight 8 sagacity 9 alertness, sharpness 10 perception 11 discernment 12 perspicacity
clearing 5 glade
clearly 6 surely 7 plainly 8 markedly, palpably, patently 9 assuredly, certainly, decidedly, evidently, obviously 10 distinctly, manifestly, noticeably, observably, undeniably 11 beyond doubt, indubitably, perceptibly, undoubtedly 12 recognizably, unmistakably 13 unequivocally 14 beyond question, unquestionably
clearly expressed 8 coherent 10 articulate 11 unambiguous 12 intelligible
clearness 7 clarity 10 brightness, brilliance 12 explicitness 15 unmistakability
clear-sighted 4 sage, wise 5 acute, sharp 6 astute, shrewd 8 piercing 9 judicious, sagacious, sensitive 10 discerning, perceptive 11 intelligent, keen-sighted, penetrating 12 sharp-sighted 13 perspicacious
clear up 6 settle 7 clarify, unsnarl 8 untangle 11 disentangle 12 uncomplicate 13 straighten out
Cleary, Beverly
author of: 6 Ramona 7 Fifteen 12 Henry Huggins 13 Jean and Johnny 15 Beezus and Ramona 16 Sister of the Bride
cleat 5 block, chock, spike, wedge 6 batten 7 bollard
cleavage 3 gap 4 rent, rift, slit 5 cleft, crack, notch, split 6 furrow, trench, trough 7 crevice, fissure, opening 9 crevasse
cleave 3 cut, hew 4 chop, fuse, hack, hold, open, part, plow, rend, rive, slit, tear 5 cling, crack, halve, sever, slash, slice, split, stick, unite 6 adhere, be true, bisect, cut off, detach, divide, furrow, sunder, uphold 7 abide by, chop off, disjoin, lay open, stand by 8 be joined, break off, hold fast, separate 9 disengage, dismember

cleaver 3 axe 4 tool 5 knife ridge
cleft 3 gap 4 rent, rift, slit 5 break, crack, notch, split 6 breach, cloven, cranny, divide, forked, furrow, trench, trough 7 crevice, divided, fissure, notched, opening, slotted 8 aperture, bisected, branched, cleavage, crevasse, division 10 separation 11 indentation
clemency 5 mercy 7 charity 8 humanity, kindness, leniency, mildness, softness, sympathy 9 tolerance 10 compassion, indulgence, moderation, temperance 11 benevolence, forbearance, magnanimity 12 mercifulness, pleasantness 13 forgivingness
clement 4 kind, mild, warm 5 balmy 6 benign, gentle, humane 7 lenient 8 merciful, tolerant 9 not severe, not strict 10 benevolent 13 compassionate
clench 3 set 4 grip 5 clasp, tense 6 clinch, clutch 7 stiffen, tighten 8 fasten on, hold fast 11 grasp firmly, strain tight 12 close tightly
Clennam, Arthur
  character in: 12 Little Dorrit
  author: 7 Dickens
Cleobis
  mother: 7 Cydippe
  brother: 5 Biton
Cleodaeus
  father: 6 Hyllus
  mother: 4 Iole
  grandfather: 8 Hercules
Cleone
  father: 6 Asopus
Cleopas see 4 Mary
Cleopatra
  queen of: 5 Egypt
  father: 7 Ptolemy
  brother/husband: 7 Ptolemy
  lover: 10 Mark Antony 12 Julius Caesar
  son: 9 Caesarion 15 Alexander Helios 19 Ptolemy Philadelphos
  daughter: 15 Cleopatra Selene
  death by: 3 asp 7 suicide
Cleopatra
  director:
    1934 version: 13 Cecil B DeMille
    1963 version: 17 Joseph L Mankiewicz
  cast:
    1934 version: 13 Henry Wilcoxon, Warren William 16 Claudette Colbert
    1963 version: 11 Rex Harrison 13 Richard Burton, Roddy McDowall 15 Elizabeth Taylor
Cleothera
  father: 9 Pandareus
clergy 6 rabbis 7 clerics, pastors, priests 8 ministry, prelates, the cloth 9 churchmen, clergymen, clericals, ministers, pastorate, preachers, rabbinate, the church, the pulpit 10 priesthood 14 the first estate
clergyman 5 padre, rabbi 6 cleric, father, parson, pastor, priest 7 prelate 8 chaplain, minister, preacher, reverend, sky pilot 9 churchman 13 man of the cloth

cleric 6 parson, pastor 8 chaplain, preacher 9 churchman, clergyman 13 man of the cloth
clerical 6 cleric, filing, office, typing 7 clerkly 8 churchly, of clerks, pastoral, priestly 10 accounting, rabbinical 11 bookkeeping, ministerial 13 record-keeping 14 ecclesiastical
clerical worker 5 clerk 6 typist 9 file clerk 10 bookkeeper, keypuncher 12 office worker 13 data processor
clerk 6 typist 8 salesman 9 file clerk 10 bookkeeper, salesclerk, saleswoman 11 salesperson 12 office worker
Cleta
  member of: 6 Graces
  worshipped at: 6 Sparta
Cleveland
  baseball team: 7 Indians
  basketball team: 9 Cavaliers
  football team: 6 Browns
Cleveland, Grover
  name at birth: 22 Stephen Grover Cleveland
  nickname: 5 Grove
  presidential rank: 12 twenty-fourth, twenty-second
  party: 8 Democrat
  state represented: 2 NY
  defeated: 4 (Simon) Wing 6 (Benjamin Franklin) Butler, (James Baird) Weaver, (James Gillespie) Blaine, (John Pierce) St John 7 (John) Bidwell 8 (Belva Ann Bennett) Lockwood, (Benjamin) Harrison
  vice president: 9 (Adlai Ewing) Stevenson, (Thomas Andrews) Hendricks
  cabinet:
    state: 5 (Richard) Olney 6 (Thomas Francis) Bayard 7 (Walter Quinton) Gresham
    treasury: 7 (Daniel) Manning 8 (John Griffin) Carlisle 9 (Charles Stebbins) Fairchild
    war: 6 (David Scott) Lamont 8 (William Crowninshield) Endicott
    attorney general: 5 (Richard) Olney 6 (Judson) Harmon 7 (Augustus Hill) Garland
    interior: 5 (Hoke) Smith, (Lucius Quintus Cincinnatus) Lamar, (William Freeman) Vilas 7 (David Rowland) Francis
  born: 2 NJ 8 Caldwell
  died/buried: 2 NJ 9 Princeton
  education:
    high school: 16 Liberal Institute
  religion: 12 Presbyterian
  interests: 7 fishing 8 shooting 13 gun collecting
  political career:
    mayor of: 7 Buffalo
    governor of: 7 New York
  civilian career: 6 lawyer
  notable events of lifetime/term: 5 Panic (of 1893) 10 gold crisis (of 1895)
  Act: 6 Tariff 14 Dawes Severalty 18 Interstate Commerce
  strike: 7 Pullman

father: 13 Richard Falley
mother: 4 Anne (Neal)
siblings: 7 Ann Neal 9 Mary Allen 11 Susan Sophia, William Neal 12 Richard Cecil 13 Rose Elizabeth 14 Lewis Frederick 20 Margaret Louise Falley
wife: 7 Frances (Folsom)
children: 4 Ruth 6 Esther, Marion 13 Francis Grover, Richard Folsom

clever 4 able, cute, deft, keen 5 acute, quick, sharp, smart, witty 6 adroit, artful, astute, bright, crafty, expert, shrewd 8 creative, humorous, original 9 ingenious, inventive 11 imaginative, intelligent, quickwitted, resourceful

cleverly 6 deftly 7 sharply, smartly, wittily 8 adroitly, artfully, craftily, expertly 10 creatively, humorously 11 ingeniously, inventively 13 imaginatively, intelligently

cleverness 3 wit 6 acumen 8 ableness, deftness, keenness 9 expertise, ingenuity, quickness, sharpness, smartness 10 adroitness, artfulness, astuteness, brightness, craftiness 12 intelligence, skillfulness 13 inventiveness 15 imaginativeness, quick-wittedness

clew *see* 4 clue

Clew
  thread in: 9 Labyrinth
  showed way to: 7 Theseus
  given by: 7 Ariadne

cliche 3 saw 6 old saw 7 bromide 8 banality, old story 9 platitude 10 stereotype 11 trite phrase

cliche-ridden 5 corny, stale, tired, trite, vapid 6 jejune 8 bromidic 9 hackneyed 10 unoriginal 13 platitudinous, unimaginative

click 3 tap 4 clap, snap 5 clack, clink, crack 6 rattle 7 crackle

Clide
  form: 5 nymph
  habitat: 5 Naxos

client 5 buyer 6 patron 7 advisee, shopper 8 customer 9 purchaser 17 person represented

cliff 3 tor 4 crag 5 bluff, ledge 8 palisade 9 precipice 10 promontory

Cliff Dwellers *see* 6 Pueblo

Clift, Montgomery
  real name: 21 Edward Montgomery Clift
  nickname: 5 Monty
  born: 7 Omaha NE
  roles: 9 The Search 10 The Heiress, The Misfits 14 A Place in the Sun 18 From Here to Eternity, Suddenly Last Summer

climactic 7 crucial 8 critical, dramatic 11 sensational, suspenseful

climate 3 air 4 mood, tone 5 pulse 6 spirit, temper 7 quality, weather 8 ambience, attitude 9 character, condition 10 atmosphere 11 disposition, frame of mind, weather zone 12 usual weather 13 weather region 14 general feeling, weather pattern

climax 4 acme, apex, peak 5 crown 6 crisis, height, summit 8 best part, pinnacle 9 high point 10 denouement 11 culmination 12 highest point, turning point 13 critical

point, crowning point, decisive point, supreme moment 18 moment of revelation

climb 4 go up, rise 5 mount, scale 6 ascend, ascent, come up 8 climbing 9 clamber up 10 scramble up

climb down 6 go down 7 descend 8 back down, come down

clinch 3 cap, fix, win 4 bind, bolt, grip, nail 5 cinch, clamp, clasp, close, crown, grasp, screw 6 assure, clutch, couple, decide, fasten, obtain, secure, settle, verify, wind up 7 confirm, grapple 8 complete, conclude, make fast, make sure 9 culminate, establish, finish off 10 grab hold of, hold firmly 12 seize and hold 13 ensure victory

cling 3 hug 4 fuse, grip, hold 5 clasp, grasp, stick 6 adhere, be true, cleave, clutch 7 stand by 8 hang on to, hold fast, hold on to, maintain 9 stay close 10 be constant, be faithful, grab hold of

clinging 6 sticky 7 holding 8 adherent, adhering, adhesive, clasping, cleaving, grasping, gripping, sticking 9 hanging on, holding on 11 holding fast 12 grabbing, hold

clinic 9 infirmary 10 polyclinic 13 medical center 15 outpatients' ward

Clinis
  form: 3 man
  home: 11 Mesopotamia
  loved by: 6 Apollo 7 Artemis

clink 4 ting 5 clack, clank, click 6 jangle, jingle, rattle, tinkle 11 ring sharply

clinkers 4 duds, slag 5 dross, flops 6 cinder, scoria 8 failures

Clinton, William Jefferson
  original last name: 6 Blythe
  nickname: 4 Bill
  presidential rank: 11 forty-second
  party: 10 Democratic
  state represented: 2 AR 8 Arkansas
  defeated: 4 (George) Bush
  vice president: 4 (Albert) Gore
  cabinet:
    state: 11 (Warren) Christopher
    treasury: 7 (Lloyd) Bentsen
    attorney general: 4 (Janet) Reno
    interior: 7 (Bruce) Babbitt
    labor: 5 (Robert) Reich
    HUD: 8 (Henry) Cisneros
  born: 2 AR 4 Hope
  education: 6 Oxford 7 Yale Law 10 Georgetown
  honor: 13 Rhodes Scholar
  political career:
    governor of: 7 Arkansas
    attorney general of: 7 Arkansas
  notable events of lifetime/term: 5 NAFTA 10 Whitewater 13 Anticrime Bill, Rhodes Scholar, 15 Branch Davidians 17 Health Security Act
  Supreme Court appointments: 13 Stephen Breyer 17 Ruth Bader Ginsburg
  father: 13 William Blythe
  mother: 12 Virginia Cassidy Blythe
  stepfather: 12 Roger Clinton
  sibling: 12 Roger Clinton

wife: 13 Hillary Rodham
children: 7 Chelsea

Clio
  muse of: 7 history

clip 3 bob, cut, fix 4 crop, grip, hook, snip, trim 5 clamp, clasp, shear 6 attach, buckle, clinch, couple, cut off, cut out, fasten, paring, secure, staple 7 cutting, shorten 8 clipping, cropping, cut short, fastener, shearing, snipping

clipper 4 boat, ship 6 cutter, shears 8 aircraft, airplane, sailboat, scissors 9 racehorse

clipping 7 cutting, pruning, snippet 8 trimming

clique 3 set 4 clan, gang 5 crowd, group 6 circle 7 coterie, faction

cliquish 4 cold 5 aloof 7 distant 8 clannish, snobbish 9 exclusive 10 unfriendly 11 unreceptive

Clite
  father: 6 Merops
  husband: 7 Cyzicus
  killed by: 7 hanging, suicide

cloak 4 cape, hide, mask, robe, veil, wrap 5 cover, tunic 6 mantle, screen, shield, shroud 7 conceal, curtain, pelisse, secrete 8 burnoose, disguise 10 camouflage 11 concealment

cloaked 7 covered, muffled, wrapped 9 disguised

cloaking 7 masking, veiling 8 covering 9 obscuring 10 disguising

cloakroom 8 anteroom, coatroom

clobber 3 hit 4 beat, belt, drub, lick, maul, rout, slug, sock, trim, whip 5 clout, pound, punch, smash, smear, whack 6 batter, beat up, strike, subdue, thrash, wallop 7 conquer, shellac, trounce 8 beat up on, lambaste

clock 5 watch 8 horologe 9 timepiece 11 chronometer

Clockwork Orange, A
  author: 14 Anthony Burgess
  director: 14 Stanley Kubrick
  cast: 12 Patrick Magee 13 Adrienne Corri 15 Malcolm McDowell

clod 3 oaf, wad 4 boor, dolt, dope, glob, hunk, lout, lump, rube 5 chunk, clown, clump, dummy, dunce, moron, yokel 7 bumpkin, fathead 8 imbecile, numskull 9 blockhead, ignoramus, simpleton

clodhopper 3 oaf 4 boot, clod, hick, lout, rube, slob 5 booby, clown, yokel 6 galoot, lubber, lummox, rustic 7 bumpkin, hayseed, peasant, plowboy, redneck 8 clodpole, lunkhead 9 heavy shoe, hillbilly 10 provincial

clog 4 stop 5 block, check, choke, close, dam up 6 stop up 7 barrier, congest 8 blockage, obstacle, obstruct, stoppage 9 restraint 10 impediment 11 obstruction

clogged 6 choked, halted, jammed 7 clotted, impeded 8 choked up, filled up, hampered, hindered, restrained 10 encumbered, obstructed, overloaded

cloister 4 stoa, walk 5 abbey, aisle 6 arcade, closet, coop up, friary, hole up, immure, shut up, wall up 7 conceal, confine, convent, embower, gallery, nunnery, passage, portico, seclude, walkway 8 shut away 9 colonnade, courtyard, monastery, promenade, sequester 10 ambulatory, passageway

cloistered 5 alone, aloof, apart 6 hidden 7 immured, recluse 8 closeted, confined, detached, isolated, secluded, secreted, separate, solitary 9 concealed, insulated, sheltered, withdrawn 11 dissociated, sequestered

clone 4 copy 5 robot 6 double 7 android, replica 9 automaton, duplicate, replicate 10 carbon copy 12 doppelganger 13 identical copy

close 3 end, hot, pen 4 akin, clog, fast, fill, firm, fuse, halt, join, keen, link, near, neat, nigh, plug, shut, stop, trim, warm 5 alert, block, cease, dense, fixed, humid, muggy, pen in, sharp, short, solid, stuff, tight, unite 6 allied, at hand, clog up, coop up, couple, ending, fill in, fill up, finale, finish, hard by, intent, jammed, loving, narrow, nearby, next to, plug up, recess, secure, shut in, shut up, smooth, stingy, stop up, stuffy, windup 7 adjourn, careful, close up, closing, compact, confine, connect, cramped, crowded, devoted, dismiss, enclose, intense, miserly, pinched, seal off, shut off, similar, stuffed, suspend, teeming 8 attached, blockade, break off, conclude, confined, familiar, friendly, grudging, imminent, intimate, leave off, obstruct, populous, shut down, squeezed, stagnant, stifling, stinting, swarming, thorough, vigilant, watchful 9 attentive, congested, impending, niggardly, penurious, scrimping, terminating 10 almost like, completion, compressed, conclusion, nearly even, nip-and-tuck, resembling, restricted, sweltering, ungenerous 11 almost alike, approaching, approximate, close-fisted, discontinue, forthcoming, impermeable, in proximity, inseparable, nearly equal, neighboring, suffocating, termination, tight-fisted, well-matched 12 bring to an end, impenetrable, parsimonious, unventilated 13 bring together, near to the skin, penny-pinching, uncomfortable 14 thick as thieves

closed 6 secret 7 private 9 exclusive

closed-minded 5 rigid 7 adamant, uptight 8 obdurate, stubborn 9 hidebound, obstinate, pig-headed, unbending 10 inflexible, unyielding 12 intransigent 14 uncompromising

Close Encounters of the Third Kind
  director: 15 Steven Spielberg
  cast: 8 Teri Garr 13 Melinda Dillon 15 Richard Dreyfuss 16 Francois Truffaut
  score: 12 John Williams

closefisted 4 mean 5 cheap, close, mingy, tight 6 stingy 7 miserly 8 grudging 9 niggardly, penurious 10 economical, ungenerous 11 close-handed, tightfisted 12 parsimonious 13 penny-pinching

close-fitting 4 snug 5 tight 9 skintight 11 constricted, form-fitting 12 constricting, tight-fitting 15 like a second skin

close friend 3 pal 4 chum, mate 5 buddy, crony 6 cohort 7 best pal 8 alter ego, intimate 9 companion, confidant 10 bosom buddy 17 intimate confidant

close loudly 4 bang, clap, slam

closely 6 keenly 7 alertly, sharply 8 intently 9 carefully, heedfully, intensely 10 diligently, vigilantly, vigorously, watchfully 11 attentively

close-mouthed 3 shy 4 cool 5 terse 7 bashful, distant 8 reserved, reticent, retiring, taciturn 9 diffident, secretive, withdrawn 11 tight-lipped 15 uncommunicative

closeness 8 meanness, nearness 10 stinginess 11 familiarity, miserliness 15 tightfistedness

close of day 3 eve 4 dusk, even 6 sunset 7 evening, sundown 8 eventide, gloaming, twilight 9 nightfall

closet 2 WC 4 eury, safe 5 ambry, cuddy 6 covert, hidden, locker pantry, secret, toilet 7 cabinet, private 8 coatroom, cupboard, imprison, secluded 9 cloakroom, storeroom, visionary 11 speculative, theoretical, unpractical, water closet

close tightly 3 set 4 seal, slam 5 latch 6 clench, secure 13 press together

close to 4 near 6 almost, around 9 just about 12 on the point of 13 approximately

closure 3 lid, tap 4 bung, cork, plug, stop 5 cover 6 ending, faucet, finish, spigot 7 barring, bolting, closing, cloture, locking, sealing, stopper 8 securing, shutting, stoppage 9 cessation 10 conclusion, stoppering 11 termination 14 discontinuance 15 discontinuation

clot 3 gob 4 lump, mass 7 congeal, thicken 8 embolism, solidify, thrombus 9 coagulate, occlusion 11 coagulation

Cloten
    character in: 9 Cymbeline
    author: 11 Shakespeare

cloth 5 goods 6 fabric 7 textile 8 dry goods, material 9 yard goods 10 piece goods

clothe 3 don 4 case, coat, deck, garb, robe, veil, wrap 5 array, cloak, cloud, cover, drape, dress 6 attire, bedeck, encase, enwrap, outfit, rig out, screen, shroud 7 bedizen, costume, deck out, envelop, sheathe, swaddle 8 accouter

clothed 4 clad 5 robed 6 draped 7 cloaked, couched, covered, dressed, mantled, wearing 8 equipped, provided 9 expressed, furnished

clothes 4 duds, garb, rags, togs, wear 5 dress 6 attire, finery 7 apparel, costume, raiment, regalia 8 clothing, ensemble, garments, wardrobe 11 habiliments

clotheshorse 3 fop 5 dandy, model 12 Beau Brummell, fashion plate, man of fashion, sharp dresser 14 woman of fashion

clothing see 7 clothes

Clotho
    member of: 5 Fates
    spinner of: 12 thread of life

cloud 3 dim, mar 4 blur, hide, veil 5 blind, cloak, cover, muddy, shade, sully, upset 6 darken, impair, muddle, screen, shadow, shroud 7 conceal, confuse, curtain, distort, disturb, eclipse, obscure, tarnish 8 overcast 9 discredit, make vague 10 overshadow 11 cast doubt on 14 call to question 19 place under suspicion

cloudburst 6 deluge 8 downpour, rainfall 9 rainstorm

clouded 3 dim 5 dusky, murky 7 blurred, obscure, sullied, tainted, unclear 8 confused, darkened, obscured 10 ill-defined, indistinct

cloudless 4 fair 5 clear, sunny 6 bright 7 halcyon 8 sunshiny 9 unclouded 10 unobscured

Clouds
    goddess of: 3 Fri 5 Frigg, Frija 6 Frigga

Clouds, The (Nephelai)
    author: 12 Aristophanes
    character: 8 Just Plea, Socrates 10 Unjust Plea 11 Strepsiades 12 Pheidippides

cloudy 4 dark, gray, hazy 5 murky, vague 6 dreary, gloomy, leaden, veiled 7 clouded, obscure, sunless, unclear 8 confused, nebulous, overcast 9 confusing, undefined 10 indefinite, mysterious 11 overclouded

Clouet, Jean
    born: 8 Flanders
    artwork attributed: 13 Guillaume Bude 16 Madame de Canaples, Man with Gold Coins 17 The Count of Brissac, The Dauphin Francis 22 Man with a Book by Petrarch

clout 3 box, hit, jab 4 bash, belt, blow, pull, sock 5 crack, knock, punch, smack, thump, whack 6 wallop 9 influence 10 importance

clove
    botanical name: 16 Eugenia aromatica 18 Syzygium aromaticum
    origin: 5 Pemba 7 Far East 8 Moluccas, Zanzibar 9 Mauritius 10 Madagascar
    use: 3 ham 8 pickling, pomander 16 yellow vegetables

cloven 5 cleft, split 7 divided, notched, slotted 8 bisected

clover 9 Trifolium
    varieties: 3 bur, elk, hop, low, pin, red 4 bush, holy, Kura, musk, owl's, tick 5 Alyce, Hubam, lucky, sweet, water, white 6 Alsike, cow hop, indoor, Korean, Ladino, yellow 7 Bukhara, crimson, Italian, mammoth, Mexican, Persian, prairie 8 Japanese, large hop, reversed, small hop, stinking 9 Hungarian 10 strawberry, toothed bur, white Dutch, white sweet 11 yellow sweet 12 silky prairie, subterranean, white prairie 13 European water 16 strawberry-headed

clown 3 wag, wit 4 card, fool, jest, joke, mime, zany 5 comic, cut up, joker 6 jester, madcap 7 buffoon 8 comedian, humorist 9 harlequin, kid around 10 comedienne, fool around 11 funny person, merry-andrew

Clown, The
  author: 12 Heinrich Boll

clownishness 6 antics 10 buffoonery, tom-foolery 12 monkeyshines 14 playing the fool

Clowns of God, The
  author: 11 Morris L West

cloy 3 gag 4 bore, glut, pall, sate, tire 5 choke, weary 6 benumb, overdo 7 ex-haust, satiate, surfeit 8 nauseate, saturate

cloying 5 sweet 6 sugary 9 excessive, sa-tiating 10 saccharine

club 3 bat, hit 4 bash, beat, flog, slug 5 billy, flail, group, guild, lay on, lodge, stick, union 6 batter, buffet, cudgel, league, pommel, pummel, strike 7 society 8 alli-ance, bludgeon, sorority 9 billyclub, club-house, truncheon 10 fraternity, shillelagh, sisterhood 11 affiliation, association, broth-erhood, country club

clubhouse 4 club, hall 5 lodge 11 locker rooms 12 meeting house

clue 3 cue, key 4 clew, hint, mark, sign 5 guide, scent, trace 7 glimmer, inkling, pointer 8 evidence 9 indicator, inference 10 indication, intimation, suggestion 11 in-sinuation

clump 4 bulb, bump, knob, knot, lump, mass, plod, thud 5 batch, bunch, clomp, clunk, copse, group, grove, plunk, shock, stamp, stomp, thump, tramp 6 lumber 7 cluster, thicket 9 aggregate 10 assem-blage, collection

clumsiness 9 gawkiness 10 ineptitude 11 awkwardness 12 carelessness, ungainli-ness 13 gracelessness, maladroitness

clumsy 5 bulky, crude, gawky, inept, rough 6 klutzy 7 awkward, unhandy 8 bungling, careless, ungainly, unwieldy 9 graceless, makeshift, maladroit, unskilled 10 blunder-ing, cumbersome, ungraceful 11 heavy-handed 12 ill-contrived, unmanageable 14 butterfingered 21 like a bull in a china shop

cluster 4 band, bevy, heap, herd, knot, mass, pack, pile 5 amass, batch, block, bunch, clump, crowd, flock, group, sheaf, shock, swarm 6 gather, muster, throng 7 collect, company 8 assemble, converge 9 aggregate 10 accumulate, assemblage, collection, congregate 12 accumulation, congregation 13 agglomeration 14 con-glomeration

cluster around 6 gather 7 collect 10 con-gregate 12 herd together 13 flock together

clutch 3 hug 4 grip, hold 5 clasp, grasp 6 clench 7 cling to, embrace, squeeze 8 hang on to

clutter 4 fill, heap, mess, pile 5 chaos, strew 6 jumble, litter, tangle 7 scatter 8 dis-array, disorder 9 confusion 10 hodge-podge

cluttered 5 messy 7 chaotic, crowded, jum-bled, muddled 8 confused, littered 9 scat-tered 10 disordered, disorderly

Clymene
  origin: 5 Greek
  mentioned in: 5 Iliad
  form: 5 nymph
  habitat: 5 ocean
  father: 6 Mimyas, Minyas 7 Catreus, Oceanus
  mother: 6 Tethys
  husband: 7 Iapetus 8 Cephalus, Phae-thon, Phylacus
  son: 4 Oeax 5 Atlas 8 Iphiclus, Phaethon 9 Palamedes 10 Epimetheus, Nausi-medon, Prometheus
  daughter: 8 Alcimede
  attended: 11 Helen of Troy
  sold to: 8 Nauplius
  beloved of: 3 Sun

Clymenus
  king of: 10 Orchomenus
  grandfather: 7 Phrixus
  son: 7 Erginus
  daughter: 9 Harpalyce
  violated: 9 Harpalyce
  home: 7 Arcadia

Clytemnestra
  father: 9 Tyndareus
  mother: 4 Leda
  brother: 6 Castor, Pollux
  sister: 5 Helen 8 Timandra
  cousin: 7 Perilaus
  husband: 9 Agamemnon
  son: 7 Orestes
  daughter: 7 Electra, Erigone 9 Iphigenia 12 Chrysothemis
  lover: 9 Aegisthus
  killed: 9 Agamemnon
  killed by: 7 Orestes

Clytie
  form: 5 nymph
  habitat: 5 water
  loved: 6 Apollo
  changed into: 10 heliotrope

Clytius
  member of: 8 Gigantes
  father: 8 Laomedon
  brother: 5 Priam
  companion of: 5 Jason
  killed by: 8 Hercules

coach 3 bus 5 drill, guide, sedan, stage, teach, train, tutor 6 advise, direct, mentor 7 omnibus, trainer 8 carriage, instruct 9 limousine, preceptor 10 automobile, in-hand, motor coach, stagecoach 11 four-wheeler, second class 12 economy class 14 private teacher 16 athletic director

coachman 3 fly 4 jehu, whip 5 pilot 6 driver 10 charioteer

Coactrice 14 poisonous snake

coagulate 3 gel, set 4 clot, jell 6 curdle, harden 7 congeal, jellify, thicken 8 solidify

coagulation 3 gob 4 clot, mass 8 clotting, curdling, thrombus 10 thickening

coal 4 ash, bass, char, coke, coom, culm, dust, fuel, slag, smut, swad 5 ember 6 cannel, cinder 7 lignite, clinker 8 charcoal 10 fossil fuel 11 charred wood

  box: 3 hod 7 scuttle

  made from: 6 carbon

  type: 4 hard, soft 7 lignite 10 anthracite, bituminous

  mining method: 4 deep 8 opencast 10 strip auger 11 underground

  mine: 5 drift, shaft, slope, strip

  size: 3 egg, nut, pea 5 stove

coal-black 3 jet 4 dark, inky 5 black, ebony, raven, sable 9 pitch-dark

coalesce 3 mix 4 ally, form, fuse, join, meld 5 blend, merge, unify, unite 6 cohere 7 combine 9 become one, integrate 10 amalgamate, join forces 11 agglutinate, consolidate 12 band together, come together 14 form an alliance

coalition 5 union 6 fusion, league 7 society 8 alliance 9 syndicate 10 federation 11 affiliation, association, combination, confederacy, partnership 12 amalgamation 13 agglomeration, consolidation 14 conglomeration

Coal Miner's Daughter

  director: 12 Michael Apted

  cast: 9 Levon Helm 11 Sissy Spacek (Loretta Lynn) 13 Tommy Lee Jones 14 Beverly D'Angelo

  Oscar for: 7 actress (Spacek)

  screenplay: 10 Tom Rickman

Coaluitecan

  tribe: 6 Payaya

coarse 4 lewd, rude, vile 5 crass, crude, dirty, gross, harsh, rough 6 common, nubbly, odious, ribald, shaggy, sordid, vulgar 7 boorish, bristly, brutish, ill-bred, loutish, obscene, prickly, uncouth 8 impolite, improper, indecent, scratchy 9 bristling, inelegant, offensive, repulsive, revolting, sandpaper, unrefined 10 disgusting, indecorous, indelicate, lascivious, licentious, scurrilous, unladylike, unpolished 11 foulmouthed, ill-mannered 12 lacking taste 13 rough-textured, ungentlemanly

coarse-grained 5 crude, harsh, nubby, rough 6 coarse, grainy, shaggy 7 bristly 8 scratchy 9 unrefined 13 rough-textured

coarseness 9 crudeness, grossness, roughness, vulgarity 10 indelicacy, inelegance 11 boorishness 16 lack of refinement

coast 4 skim, slip, waft 5 drift, float, glide, shore, slide, sweep 6 strand 7 seaside 8 glissade, littoral, seaboard, seacoast, seashore 9 shoreline

coaster 3 mat 4 ship, sled, tray 5 wagon 6 cradle, glider, slider 8 toboggan 9 tray stand 13 decanter stand, roller coaster

coat 3 fur 4 hair, hide, pelt, wrap 5 cover, glaze, layer, paint, smear 6 blazer, enamel, encase, jacket, spread 7 coating, encrust, envelop, lacquer, overlay, plaster, slicker, topcoat 8 covering, laminate,

mackinaw, overcoat, raincoat 9 whitewash 10 mackintosh, sports coat

coating 4 coat, film, skin 5 layer, sheet 6 veneer 7 overlay 8 covering, envelope

coat of arms 4 arms 5 crest 6 creast 8 insignia 9 blaconwry 10 escutcheon 14 heraldic emblem 16 armorial bearings

coat of mail 4 mail 5 armor 9 chain mail 11 suit of armor

Coat of Varnish, A

  author: 6 C P Snow

coax 6 cajole 7 wheedle 8 butter up, inveigle, soft-soap, talk into 9 sweet-talk

cobalt 4 blue 5 azure 7 element, sky blue 10 bright blue 12 greenish blue

  chemical symbol: 2 Co

Cobb, Lee J

  born: 9 New York NY

  roles: 10 Willy Loman 12 The Virginian 14 Twelve Angry Men 15 On the Waterfront 16 Death of a Salesman

Cobb, Ty (Tyrus Raymond)

  nickname: 12 Georgia Peach

  sport: 8 baseball

  position: 8 outfield

  team: 13 Detroit Tigers

cobbler 3 pie 9 bootmaker, shoemaker 12 shoe repairer 16 deepdish fruit pie

cobra

  also: 3 asp 5 mamba 11 hooded snake

  native to: 4 Asia 6 Africa

  kind: 4 king 6 hooded, Indian 8 Egyptian

  enemy: 8 mongoose

Coburn, Charles

  born: 10 Savannah GA

  roles: 9 Boss Tweed 17 The More the Merrier

Coburn, James

  born: 8 Laurel NE

  roles: 11 In Like Flint, Our Man Flint 14 The Great Escape 19 The Magnificent Seven

Coca, Imogene

  partner: 9 Sid Caesar

  born: 14 Philadelphia PA

  roles: 15 Your Show of Shows

Cocalus

  king of: 6 Sicily

Coccygius

  epithet of: 4 Zeus

  means: 6 cuckoo

cock 3 tip 4 knob 5 raise, valve 6 faucet, handle, perk up 7 rooster, stand up 8 cockerel, male bird, set erect 9 bristle up 11 chanticleer 13 turn to one side 16 raise the hammer of 17 draw back the hammer

cockade 4 knot 5 badge 6 ribbon 7 rosette 8 ornament 10 party badge

Cockade State

  nickname of: 8 Maryland

cock-and-bull story 3 fib, lie 4 myth, yarn 5 fable 7 fiction, untruth, whopper 9 fairy tale, falsehood, fish story, invention, tall story 11 fabrication 13 prevarication

Cockcroft, John Douglas

  field: 7 physics

  nationality: 7 British

developed: 24 Cockcroft-Walton generator

worked with: 6 Walton

awarded: 10 Nobel Prize

cockeyed 3 mad **4** awry, wild **5** askew, crazy, goofy, inane, nutty, weird **6** absurd, aslant, insane, tilted **7** crooked, foolish, twisted **8** lopsided, sideways **9** irregular, off-center, senseless **10** cockamamie, out of whack, ridiculous, unbalanced **11** nonsensical **12** asymmetrical, preposterous

Cockpit of Europe see **7** Belgium

cockscomb 4 comb **5** crest **7** celosia, coxcomb **8** amaranth, caruncle

cocksure 4 pert, smug, vain **5** brash, cocky, pushy **6** cheeky, snooty **8** arrogant, positive **9** assertive, audacious, bumptious, conceited **10** aggressive, swaggering **11** overbearing, self-assured, swellheaded **13** overconfident, self-confident

cocktail 5 drink, fruit, horse **6** shrimp **10** docked tail, semi-formal

type: 4 grog **6** brandy, gibson, gimlet, mai tai, rob roy, zombie **7** gin fizz, martini, sidecar, stinger **8** daiquiri, highball, hot toddy, pink lady **9** cuba libre, hurricane, gin rickey, manhattan, margarita, mint julep, rusty nail **10** bloody mary, tom collins **11** boilermaker, gin and tonic, grasshopper, screwdriver, sloe gin fizz **12** black russian, old-fashioned, tom and jerry, whiskey sour **13** planter's punch **15** brandy alexander

mixer: 4 soda **5** tonic, water **7** bitters, seltzer **9** ginger ale

garnish: 4 lime **5** lemon, olive, orange, twist **16** maraschino cherry

cocktail lounge 3 bar **6** saloon, tavern **7** gin mill, taproom

cocky 5 brash, saucy **6** jaunty **8** arrogant, cocksure, impudent **9** conceited, egotistic **10** swaggering

Cocles see **8** Horatius

Coco, James

born: 9 New York NY

roles: 11 Sancho Panza **13** Man of La Mancha **21** Last of the Red Hot Lovers

cocoa 5 brown, cacao **9** chocolate **12** hot chocolate

cocoon

covering for: 5 larva

stage: 5 pupal

made of: 4 silk

Cocteau, Jean

author of: 7 Orpheus **8** Antigone **12** Blood of a Poet **18** The Infernal Machine **19** Les Enfants Terribles, Les Parents Terribles **20** The Beauty and the Beast

Cocytus

river in: 5 Hades

coddle 3 pat, pet **4** baby **5** humor, spoil **6** caress, cuddle, dote on, fondle, pamper **7** indulge **11** mollycoddle

code 4 laws **5** rules **6** cipher **7** statute **8** precepts **9** ordinance, standards **10** cryptogram, guidelines, principles **11** cryp-

tograph, proprieties, regulations **13** secret writing **14** secret language

codger 5 crank, miser **6** oddity, old man **9** eccentric, odd person

codicil 5 rider **8** addendum, addition, appendix **9** extension, subscript **10** postscript, supplement **11** added clause

codify 4 rank, rate **5** grade, group, index, order **7** arrange, catalog **8** classify, organize, tabulate **9** methodize **10** categorize, coordinate, regularize **11** systematize

coelenterate 5 coral, hydra, polyp **6** Medusa **7** acaleph, radiate **8** acalephe **9** jellyfish **10** sea anemone

habitat: 5 ocean **9** salt water

Coelophysis

type: 8 dinosaur, therapod

location: 7 Arizona

period: 8 Triassic

coequal 5 equal **10** coordinate **16** equally important

coequality 6 parity **8** equality, evenness, sameness **10** uniformity **11** equivalency **14** correspondence

coerce 3 cow **4** make **5** bully, drive, force **6** compel, oblige **7** dragoon **8** browbeat, bulldoze, pressure, threaten **9** constrain, strong-arm **10** intimidate

coercer 5 bully **9** oppressor, tormenter, tormentor **10** browbeater **11** intimidator, petty tyrant

coercion 5 force **6** duress **7** threats **8** bullying, pressure **10** compulsion, constraint **11** browbeating **12** intimidation

coercive 8 enforced, forcible **10** compulsory, obligatory **11** threatening

Coeus

form: 5 Titan

father: 6 Uranus

mother: 4 Gaea

daughter: 4 Leto **7** Asteria

coexist with 12 go hand in hand, go side by side, live together **13** go hand in glove

coffee 6 Coffea **13** Coffea arabica

varieties: 4 Java, Kona, Wild **5** Irish, Mocha **6** Almond, Common **7** Arabian, Arabica, Robusta, Vanilla **8** Liberian, Liberica, Zanzibar **9** Colombian **11** French Roast, Wild robusta **13** Decaffeinated **20** Jamaican Blue Mountain

beverage: 6 kahlua **8** espresso **10** cafe au lait, cappuccino

small cup: 9 demitasse

coffee (black)

French: 8 cafe noir **10** cafe nature

coffee brandy 6 Kahlua **8** Tia Maria

coffee with milk

French: 10 cafe au lait

coffer 3 box **4** case **5** chest **9** strongbox **10** depository, repository **13** treasure chest

coffers 5 safes **6** vaults **8** treasury **9** cash boxes **11** money supply

coffin 3 box **4** pall **6** casket **10** catafalque **11** sarcophagus

cog 3 cam, lie **4** gear **5** cheat, cozen, tenon, tooth, wedge, wheel **8** small boat **10** projection

cogent 5 sound, valid 6 potent 7 weighty 8 forceful, powerful 9 effective, trenchant 10 compelling, convincing, persuasive, undeniable 11 meritorious, well-founded 12 well-grounded 16 incontrovertible

cogitate 5 study, think, weigh 6 ponder 7 reflect 8 meditate, mull over, ruminate 9 think over 10 deliberate, think about 11 contemplate, reflect upon 18 consider thoroughly

cogito ergo sum 18 I think therefore I am
   said by: 9 Descartes

cognac
   type: 6 brandy 7 liqueur
   origin: 6 France
   brand: 7 Bisquit, Martell 8 Hennessy 10 Remy Martin 11 Courvoisier
   label: 2 VO (very old), VS (very special), XO (extra old) 3 XXO (extra extra old) 4 VSOP (very superior old pale) 8 Napoleon (5 year premium)
   drink: 9 Andalusia
   with Cointreau: 10 Rolls Royce
   with Triple Sec: 7 Chicago 10 Rolls Royce
   with vodka: 7 Cossack

cognate 4 akin, like 5 alike, close 7 kindred, related, similar 8 familial, parallel, relative 9 affiliate 10 derivative 11 consanguine

cognition 7 knowing 9 awareness, knowledge 11 familiarity 13 comprehension, understanding

cognizance 4 heed, note 5 grasp 6 notice, regard 8 scrutiny 9 attention, awareness, cognition, knowledge 10 perception 11 familiarity, observation, recognition, sensibility 12 apprehension 13 comprehension, consciousness, understanding

cognizant 5 aware 6 posted 7 knowing, mindful 8 familiar, informed, versed in 9 conscious 10 acquainted, conversant, instructed 11 enlightened 13 knowledgeable, understanding

cognomen 4 name 6 handle 7 epithet, moniker, surname 11 appellation, designation

cognoscenti 6 judges 7 experts 8 insiders 11 authorities 12 connoisseurs 14 those in the know

cohere 3 fit, set 4 bind, fuse, glue, hold, jibe, join 5 agree, cling, match, stick, tally, unite 6 cement, concur, square 7 combine, conform, congeal 8 coalesce, coincide, dovetail, solidify 9 coagulate, harmonize 10 correspond 11 consolidate, synchronize 12 hold together 13 stick together

coherence 5 logic, unity 7 clarity, concord, harmony 8 cohesion 9 congruity 10 accordance, conformity, consonance 11 consistency, rationality 12 organization

coherent 5 clear, lucid 7 logical, orderly 8 cohesive, rational 9 congruous, connected, in keeping, organized 10 articulate, consistent, harmonious, meaningful, systematic 11 in agreement 12 intelligible

13 corresponding 14 comprehensible, understandable

cohesion 4 bond 5 union, unity 7 bonding 8 adhesion 10 attraction, solidarity

cohesive 3 set 5 solid 6 sticky 7 viscous 8 cemented, coherent, cohering, sticking 9 connected 11 indivisible, inseparable 12 consolidated 13 agglutinative

Cohn, Ferdinand Julius
   field: 6 botany
   nationality: 6 German
   founded: 12 bacteriology

Cohn, Robert
   character in: 15 The Sun Also Rises
   author: 9 Hemingway

cohort 3 pal 4 chum 5 buddy, crony 6 fellow, friend 7 comrade 8 follower, myrmidon 9 associate, companion 10 accomplice

coif 3 cap 4 hood, veil 6 beggin, burlet, hairdo 8 biggonet, coiffure, skull cap 9 head-dress

coiffed 6 capped, styled 7 dressed 8 arranged

coiffeur 7 stylist 11 hairdresser 15 male hairdresser

coiffure 2 DA, GI 3 bob, bun 4 Afro, coif, perm, shag, trim, wave 6 hairdo 7 beehive, blowcut, comb-out, flattop, haircut, pageboy, upsweep 8 cold wave, cornrows, ducktail 9 hairstyle, permanent, pompadour

coil 4 curl, loop, ring, roll, wind 5 braid, twine, twist 6 circle, spiral, writhe 7 entwine 8 encircle

coin 4 mint 5 hatch, money, piece 6 change, create, devise, invent, make up, silver, strike 7 concoct, dream up, think up 8 conceive 9 fabricate, originate

coin/currency
   of Afghanistan: 3 pul 5 abaze, riyal, rupee 6 abbasi, amania 7 afghani
   of Albania: 3 lek 5 franc 6 qintar 7 quintar
   of Algeria: 5 dinar 7 centime
   of Andorra: 5 franc 6 peseta
   of Angola: 6 escudo, kwanza, macuta, macute 7 angolar, centavo
   of Argentina: 4 peso 7 centavo 9 argentino
   of Armenia: 5 ruble
   of Australia: 4 dump, tray, zack 5 pound 6 dollar 8 shilling
   of Austria: 4 lira 5 crown, ducat, krone 6 florin, gulden, heller, zehner 8 albertin, groschen, kreutzer 9 schilling
   of Azerbaijan: 5 manat
   of Bahrain: 5 dinar
   of Bangladesh: 4 taka 5 paisa
   of Belarus: 5 ruble
   of Belgium: 5 belga, franc 7 brabant, centime, crocard
   of Benin: 5 franc 7 centime
   of Bhutan: 5 paisa, rupee 7 chetrum 8 ngultrum
   of Bolivia: 4 peso 7 centavo 9 boliviano
   of Bosnia-Herzegovina: 5 dinar
   of Botswana: 4 pula, rand

of Brazil: 3 joe 4 reis 5 dobra 7 centara, halfjoe, milreis 8 cruzeiro
of Bulgaria: 3 lev 8 stotinki
of Burkina Faso: 5 franc 7 centime
of Burundi: 5 franc 7 centime
of Cambodia: 3 sen 4 quan, riel 6 puttan 7 piaster
of Cameroon: 5 franc 7 centime
of Canary Islands: 6 peseta
of Cape Verde: 6 escudo 7 centavo
of Central African Republic: 5 franc 7 centime
of Chad: 5 franc 7 centime
of Chile: 4 peso 5 libra 6 condor, escudo
of China: 4 cash, cent, fyng, mace, tael, tiao, yuan 5 sycee 12 jen nin piao pu
of Colombia: 4 peso, real 6 condor, peseta 7 centavo
of Comoros: 5 franc 7 centime
of Congo: 5 franc 7 centime
of Costa Rica: 5 colon 6 colone 7 centimo
of Crete: 7 drachma
of Croatia: 5 dinar
of Cuba: 4 peso 7 centavo 8 cuarenta
of Cyprus: 4 para 5 pound
of Czechoslovakia/ Czech Republic: 5 crown, ducat 6 heller, koruna
of Denmark: 3 one, ora, ore 4 fyrk 5 krone 8 frederik, skilling 9 rigsdaler
of Djibouti: 5 franc 7 centime
of Dominican Republic: 3 oro 4 peso 6 franco
of Ecuador: 5 sucre 7 centavo
of Egypt: 4 fils, kees, para 5 asper, dinar, fodda, gersh, girsh, medin, pound, riyal 6 ahmadi, dirham, foddah, guinea, junayh, maidin, medine, medino 7 piaster, piastre, tallard 8 bedidlik, millieme
of El Salvador: 4 peso 5 colon 7 centavo
of England: 3 ora 4 rial 5 achey, crown, groat, noble, pence, penny, pound 6 bawbee, florin, guinea 7 angelet, hapenny 8 farthing, shilling, sixpence, tuppence, tuppenny 13 pound sterling
of Equatorial Guinea: 6 ekuele, peseta 7 centimo
of Estonia: 3 lat 4 sent 5 kroon 7 estmark
of Ethiopia: 4 besa, birr, harf 5 amole, girsh 6 dollar, kharaf, levant, pataca, talari 7 ashrafi, menelik, plaster, tallero 12 maria theresa
of Fiji: 6 dollar
of Finland: 4 mark 5 penni 6 markka 7 markkaa
of France: 5 franc 7 centime 8 napoleon
of Gabon Republic: 5 franc 7 centime
of the Gambia: 5 pound 6 butbut, dalasi
of Georgia: 5 ruble
of Germany: 4 mark 7 Ostmark, pfennig 12 Deutsche mark
of Ghana: 4 cedi, cidi 5 ackey
of Greece: 5 lepta 7 drachma
of Greenland: 3 ore 5 krone
of Guatemala: 4 peso 7 centavo, quetzal
of Guinea: 4 iliy, syli 5 franc 6 cauris

of Guinea-Bissau: 4 peso 6 escudo 7 centavo
of Haiti: 6 gourde 7 centime
of Honduras: 4 peso 7 centavo, lempira
of Hungary: 4 gara 5 balas, krone, pengo 6 filler, forint, gulden, korona, ongara, ungara
of Iceland: 5 aurar, eyrir, krona 6 kronur
of India: 3 lac, pie 4 anna, fels, lakh, pice, tara 5 abidi, crore, paisa, rupee
of Indonesia: 3 sen 6 rupiah
of Iran: 3 pul 4 asar, gran, lari, rial 5 bisti, daric, dinar, larin, shahi, toman 6 stater 7 ashrafi, kasbeke, pahlavi
of Iraq: 4 fils 5 dinar
of Ireland: 3 rap 4 real 5 pence, pound 6 turney 8 shilling
of Israel: 3 mil 5 agora, agura, pound, pruta 6 agorot, shekel
of Italy: 4 lira, lire, tara 5 grano, paoli, paolo, scudo, soldo 6 danaro, denaro, ducato, sequin 7 testone 8 zecchino 9 centesini
of Ivory Coast: 5 franc 7 centime
of Jamaica: 7 quattie
of Japan: 2 bu 3 mon, rin, rio, sen, shu, yen 4 cash, mibu, oban 5 koban, obang, tempo 6 cobang, ichebu, ichibu, itzebu, kogang 7 itzeboo, itziboo
of Jordan: 4 fils 5 dinar
of Kazakhstan: 5 ruble
of Kenya: 4 cent 5 pound 8 shilling
of Kiribati: 4 cent 6 dollar
of Korea: 3 woh, won 4 chun, hwan, kwan
of Kuwait: 4 fils 5 dinar
of Kyrgyzstan: 3 som
of Laos: 2 at 3 att, kip
of Latvia: 3 lat 4 latu 6 rublis, santim 7 kapeika, santima
of Lebanon: 5 livre, pound 7 piastre
of Lesotho: 4 cent, rand 6 maloti
of Liberia: 4 cent 6 dollar
of Libya: 5 dinar
of Liechtenstein: 5 franc 6 rappen 7 franken
of Lithuania: 3 lit 5 litas, marka 6 centas, fennig 7 ostmark, skatiku 8 auksinas, skatikas
of Luxembourg: 5 franc 7 centime
of Macao: 3 avo 6 pataca, pataco
of Macedonia: 5 denar
of Madagascar: 5 franc 7 centime
of Malawi: 6 kwacha 7 tambala
of Malaysia: 3 sen, tra 4 taro, trah 7 ringgit, tampang
of Maldives: 5 laree, rupee 7 rufiyaa
of Mali: 5 franc 7 centime
of Malta: 4 cent 5 grain, grano, pound
of Mauritania: 5 khoum 7 ouguiya
of Mauritius: 4 cent 5 rupee
of Mexico: 4 onza, peso 5 adobe, claco, tlaco 6 azteca, cuarto, dinero 7 centavo, piaster
of Moldova: 5 ruble
of Monaco: 5 franc 7 centime

of **Mongolia:** 5 mongo, mungo 6 tugrik 7 tughrik

of **Montenegro:** 4 para 6 florin 7 perpera

of **Morocco:** 4 flue, okia, rial 5 floos, franc, okieh, ounce 6 dirham, miskal 8 mouzouna

of **Mozambique:** 6 escudo 7 centavo, metical

of **Myanmar:** 3 pya 4 kyat

of **Namibia:** 4 cent, rand

of **Nauru:** 4 cent 6 dollar

of **Nepal:** 4 anna, pice 5 mohar, rupee

of **the Netherlands:** 4 doit, oord, raps 5 crown, daler, rider, ryder 6 florin, gulden, stiver, suskin 7 daalder, ducaton, escalan, escalin, guilder, stooter, stuiver 8 albertin, ducatoon 9 dubbeltje 12 rijksdaalder 13 albertustaler

of **New Guinea:** 4 kina, toea

of **New Zealand:** 4 cent 6 dollar

of **Nicaragua:** 4 peso 7 centavo, cordoba

of **Niger:** 5 franc 7 centime

of **Nigeria:** 4 kobo 5 naira

of **Norway:** 3 ore 5 krone 6 kroner

of **Oman:** 3 gaj, gaz 4 rial 5 baiza, ghazi 7 mahmudi

of **Pakistan:** 4 anna, pice 5 paisa, rupee

of **Panama:** 4 cent 6 balboa 9 centesimo

of **Paraguay:** 4 peso 7 centimo, guarani

of **Peru:** 3 sol 5 libra 6 dinero, reseta 7 centavo

of **the Philippines:** 4 peso 6 conant, peseta 7 centavo

of **Poland:** 4 abia 5 dalar, ducat, grosz, marka, zloty 6 fening, groszy, gulden, halerz, korona 8 groschen

of **Portugal:** 3 avo, joe 4 peca, real 5 conto, crown, dobra, indio, justo, rupia 6 escudo, macuta, octave, pataca, testad, tostao, vintem 7 angalar, centavo, crusado, miereis, moidore, testone 8 equipaga, johannes

of **Qatar:** 5 riyal 6 dirham

of **Rumania:** 3 ban, lei, leu, lev, ley 4 bani 5 uncia 6 triens

of **Russia:** 5 altin, bisti, copec, genga, grosh, kopek, ruble, shaur 6 abassi, copeck, grivna, kopeck, piatak, rouble 7 poltina, valiuta 8 auksinas, deneshka, imperial, polushka 9 poltinnik 10 altininink, chervonets

of **Rwanda:** 3 franc 7 centime

of **San Marino:** 4 lira, lire 9 centesimi

of **Samoa:** 4 tala

of **Sao Tome and Principe:** 5 dobra 6 escudo 7 centavo

of **Sardinia:** 7 carline

of **Saudi Arabia:** 5 girsh, gursh, pound, riyal

of **Scotland:** 3 ecu 4 demy, doit, lion, mark, rial, ryal 5 bodle, broad, groat, plack, rider, turne 6 bawbee, folles 7 unicorn 8 atchison, hardhead 9 halfpenny 11 bonnetpiece

of **Senegal:** 5 franc 7 centime

of **Sicily:** 5 litra, oncia, uncia 6 carlin 7 carline, oncetta

of **Sierra Leone:** 4 cent 5 leone

of **Singapore:** 4 cent 6 dollar

of **Slovakia:** 6 koruna

of **Slovenia:** 5 tolar

of **Solomon Islands:** 4 cent 6 dollar

of **Somalia:** 4 besa 6 somalo 8 shilling 9 centesimi

of **South Africa:** 4 cent, pond, rand 5 pound 6 florin 7 daalder 9 krugerand

of **Spain:** 3 cob 4 duro, peso, real 5 dobla 6 cuarto, dinero, doblon, escudo, peseta 7 alfonso, centimo, pistole, realdor 8 doubloon

of **Sri Lanka:** 4 cent 5 rupee

of **Sudan:** 5 pound 7 piastre

of **Suriname:** 4 cent 7 guilder

of **Swaziland:** 4 rand 9 lilangeni

of **Sweden:** 3 ore 5 krona, krone 7 carolin 8 skilling 9 rigsdaler

of **Switzerland:** 5 franc, rappe 6 hallar, rappen 7 angster, centime, duplone 8 baetzner, blaffert

of **Syria:** 4 lira 5 pound 6 talent 7 piaster

of **Taiwan:** 4 yuan 6 dollar

of **Tajikistan:** 5 ruble

of **Tanzania:** 4 cent 8 shilling

of **Thailand:** 2 at 3 att 4 baht 5 cutty, fuang, tical 6 pynung, salung, satang 11 bullet money

of **Tibet:** 5 tanga

of **Togo:** 5 franc 7 centime

of **Tonga:** 6 paanga, seniti

of **Trinidad and Tobago:** 4 cent 6 dollar

of **Tunisia:** 5 dinar 6 dollar 7 millime

of **Turkey:** 4 lira, para 5 akcha, asper, attun, kurus, pound, rebia 6 akcheh, sequin, zequin 7 aetilik, beshlik, pataque piaster 8 medjidie, zecchino

of **Turkmenistan:** 5 ruble

of **Tuvalu:** 4 cent 6 dollar

of **Uganda:** 4 cent 8 shilling

of **Ukraine:** 6 grivna 10 karbovanet

of **United Arab Emirates:** 3 fil 6 dirham

of **Uruguay:** 4 peso 9 centesimo, centisimo

of **Uzbekistan:** 5 ruble

of **Vanuatu:** 5 franc 6 dollar

of **Venezuela:** 4 peso, real 5 medio 6 fuerte 7 bolivar, centimo 8 morocota 10 venezolano

of **Vietnam:** 2 xu 4 dong 7 piaster

of **Western Samoa:** 4 sene, tala

of **Yemen:** 4 fils, rial 5 dinar, riyal

of **Yugoslavia:** 4 para 5 dinar

of **Zaire:** 5 zaire 6 makuta

of **Zambia:** 5 ngwee 6 kwacha

of **Zimbabwe:** 4 cent 6 dollar

coincide 3 fit 4 jibe, meet 5 agree, cross, match, tally 6 accord, concur, square 7 conform 8 converge, dovetail 9 harmonize 10 correspond 11 synchronize 12 be concurrent, come together 19 occur simultaneously

coincidence 4 fate, luck 6 chance 8 accident 11 concurrence, synchronism 12 happenstance 22 simultaneous occurrence

coincident 10 coexistent, concurrent 12 contemporary, simultaneous 15 contemporaneous

coincidental 6 chance 9 unplanned 10 accidental, contiguous, synchronal 11 concomitant, synchronous 12 happenstance, simultaneous

cointreau
type: 7 liqueur
variety: 7 curacao 9 triple sec
origin: 6 France
flavor: 6 orange
drink: 8 Applecar
with bourbon: 10 Temptation
with brandy: 7 Sidecar
with cognac: 10 Rolls Royce
with gin: 7 Florida 9 White Lady 13 Sweet Patootie 14 Flying Dutchman
with rum: 8 Acapulco 10 Casa Blanca 11 Beachcomber 12 Blue Hawaiian
with rye: 10 Temptation
with tequila: 9 Margarita
with whiskey: 16 Canadian Cocktail

Colavito, Rocky (Rocco Domenico)
sport: 8 baseball
team: 16 Cleveland Indians

Colbert, Claudette
real name: 22 Claudette Lily Chauchoin
born: 5 Paris 6 France
roles: 8 Tovarich 9 Cleopatra 14 Palm Beach Story 18 It Happened One Night (Oscar)

cold 3 icy, old 4 cool, dead, flat, hard 5 aloof, brisk, chill, crisp, cruel, faded, faint, gelid, harsh, nippy, polar, sharp, stale, stiff, stony 6 arctic, biting, bitter, chilly, cooled, frigid, frosty, frozen, inured, numbed, remote, severe, snappy, steely, wintry 7 callous, chilled, cutting, distant, frosted, glacial, haughty, nipping, passive, unmoved 8 chilling, coolness, detached, freezing, hardened, piercing, reserved, reticent, stinging, uncaring, unheated, unloving, unwarmed 9 apathetic, heartless, impassive, insensate, unfeeling, unstirred 10 disdainful, forbidding, impervious, insensible, phlegmatic, unfriendly 11 frozen stiff, indifferent, passionless, penetrating, unconcerned, unconscious, unemotional, unexcitable 12 antipathetic, bone-chilling, inaccessible, supercilious, uninterested, unresponsive 13 uninteresting, unsympathetic 14 marrow-chilling, unapproachable 15 teeth-chattering, uncommunicative, undemonstrative 16 chilled to the bone, unimpressionable 18 chilled to the marrow

cold-blooded 4 evil, hard 5 cruel, harsh, stiff, stony 6 brutal, flinty, formal, frigid, inured, savage, steely 7 callous, demonic, inhuman, passive, satanic, unmoved 8 detached, fiendish, hardened, inhumane, pitiless, reserved, ruthless, uncaring 9 barbarous, heartless, impassive, merciless, unfeeling, unpitying, unstirred 10 deliberate, diabolical, disdainful, impervious, implacable, unfriendly, unmerciful, villainous 11 calculating, hard-hearted, indiffer-

ent, insensitive, passionless, unconcerned, unemotional, unexcitable 12 bloodthirsty, contemptuous, uninterested, unresponsive 13 disinterested, unimpassioned, unimpressible, unsympathetic 16 unimpressionable

cold-hearted 5 cruel 9 heartless, unfeeling 11 hard-hearted 13 unsympathetic

coldness 5 chill 7 iciness 9 aloofness 10 chilliness, frostiness 12 indifference 13 unfeelingness 14 unfriendliness 15 hardheartedness

Cole, Janet
real name of: 9 Kim Hunter

Cole, Thomas
born: 7 England 13 Bolton-le-Moors
artwork: 8 The Ox-Bow 15 The Voyage of Life 17 The Course of Empire

coleoptera
class: 8 hexopoda
phylum: 10 arthropoda
group: 6 beetle, weevil

Coleridge, Samuel
author of: 9 Kubla Khan 10 Christabel 14 Dejection An Ode, Lyrical Ballads (with Wordsworth) 19 Biographia Literaria 26 The Rime of the Ancient Mariner

Colette (Sidonie)
author of: 4 Gigi, Sido 5 Cheri 8 Claudine 11 La Vagabonde 14 The Evening Star

coliseum 4 bowl 5 arena 6 circus 7 stadium, theater 10 hippodrome 12 amphitheater 14 exhibition hall

collaborate 4 join 5 unite 6 assist, team up 7 collude 9 cooperate 10 join forces 12 work together 14 work side by side

collaborationist 6 puppet 7 traitor 8 quisling

collaborator 4 ally 6 puppet 7 traitor 8 coworker, quisling, teammate 9 associate, colleague, co-partner 11 confederate

collapse 4 coma, fail, fall, flop, fold 5 faint, swoon 6 attack, buckle, cave-in, fizzle 7 break up, crack-up, crumple, failure, give way, seizure 8 be in vain, buckling, downfall, flounder, keel over, take sick 9 become ill, break down 10 be stricken, break apart, run aground 11 fall through 12 disintegrate, falling apart, fall helpless, fall to pieces 13 come to nothing, sudden illness 14 disintegration 17 become unconscious

collapsed 4 limp 7 caved in, compact 8 deflated, fallen in, folded up 13 disintegrated

Collapse of the Third Republic, The
author: 14 William L Shirer

collapsible 7 folding 8 foldable 10 deflatable

collar 3 nab 4 eton, grab 5 catch, fichu, pinch, seize 6 arrest, bertha 7 capture 9 apprehend, neckpiece 12 take prisoner 15 take into custody

collate 5 order 6 bestow, verify 7 compare 8 assemble, organize 9 integrate 11 put together

collateral 4 bond 5 extra 6 pledge, surety 7 warrant 8 parallel, security, warranty 9 accessory, ancillary, auxiliary, guarantee, insurance, secondary 10 additional, incidental, supporting, supportive 11 endorsement, subordinate 12 contributory 13 supplementary

collation 3 tea 4 meal 5 lunch 6 brunch, repast, sermon 7 address, reading 8 hotchpot, luncheon, treatise 10 comparison 11 description

colleague 4 mate 6 fellow 7 partner 8 confrere, co-worker, teammate 9 associate, co-partner 11 confederate 12 collaborator, fellow worker

collect 3 get 4 calm, meet 5 amass, raise, rally 6 gather, heap up, muster, obtain, pick up, pile up, summon 7 call for, compile, compose, control, convene, marshal, prepare, receive, solicit 8 assemble, gather up, scrape up 9 aggregate, get hold of 10 accumulate, congregate 11 concentrate, get together

collectanea 8 analects, treasury 9 anthology, gleanings 10 collection, miscellany, selections 11 miscellanea

collected 4 calm, cool 5 quiet 6 placid, poised, serene, steady 8 composed, peaceful, tranquil 9 confident, unruffled 10 cool-headed, restrained 11 level-headed, self-assured, undisturbed, unemotional, unflappable, unperturbed 12 even-tempered 13 self-possessed 14 self-controlled

collection 3 mob 4 bevy, body, gift, heap, mass, pack, pile 5 array, bunch, clump, crowd, drove, flock, group, hoard, store, swarm 6 corpus, jumble, muster, throng 7 cluster, clutter, variety 8 amassing, assembly, oblation, treasury 9 anthology, gathering, offertory, receiving 10 assemblage, assortment, hodgepodge, miscellany, soliciting 11 aggregation, compilation 12 accumulating, accumulation

Collection of Ten Thousand Leaves (Manyoshu)
author: 7 unknown

collective 5 joint 6 common, mutual, united 7 unified 8 combined, gathered 9 aggregate, composite 10 cumulative, integrated 11 accumulated, cooperative

collector 6 grouper 7 dustman 8 antiquer, compiler, composer, gatherer, zamindar 9 assembler 10 garbageman 11 anthologist

Collector, The
author: 10 John Fowles

college 7 academy 8 seminary 9 institute 10 university 11 institution

college-preparatory 4 prep 8 academic 11 liberal-arts 12 nontechnical 13 nonvocational

collegiate 8 academic 10 scholastic, university 11 educational

collembola
class: 8 hexopoda
phylum: 10 arthropoda
group: 10 springtail

collide 3 hit 4 meet 5 clash, crash, smash 7 crack up, diverge, run into 8 bump into, conflict, disagree 9 knock into 10 meet head on 11 beat against 13 hurtle against, strike against

Collier, Lucille Ann
real name of: 9 Ann Miller

Collins, Mary Catherine
real name of: 7 Bo Derek

Collins, Mr
character in: 17 Pride and Prejudice
author: 6 Austen

Collins, Wilkie
author of: 6 No Name 12 The Moonstone 15 The Woman in White

collision 4 bump 5 clash, crash, fight, smash 6 battle, combat, impact 7 smash-up 8 accident, conflict, skirmish, struggle 9 encounter 10 engagement 11 clash of arms

colloquial 5 homey, plain 6 casual, chatty, common, folksy 8 everyday, familiar, homespun, informal, ordinary, workaday 9 idiomatic 10 vernacular 14 conversational 15 unsophisticated

colloquy 4 chat, talk 6 caucus, parley 7 council, palaver, seminar 8 commerce, congress, converse, dialogue 9 communion, discourse 10 conference, discussion, rap session 11 interchange, intercourse 12 conversation 13 confabulation

collude 4 plot 7 connive 8 conspire, intrigue 9 cooperate 11 collaborate

collusion 5 fraud 7 treason 8 intrigue 10 complicity, connivance, conspiracy 13 collaboration 15 secret agreement 17 guilty association

Colman, Ronald
born: 7 England 8 Richmond
roles: 9 Beau Geste 10 Arrowsmith 11 A Double Life (Oscar), Lost Horizon 16 A Tale of Two Cities

cologne 5 scent 7 essence, perfume 9 fragrance 11 toilet water

Colomba
author: 14 Prosper Merimee

Colombia
other name: 6 Darien 10 New Granada
capital/largest city: 6 Bogota
others: 3 Ten 4 Amza, Buga, Cali, Mitu, Muzo, Paez, Sipi, Tado, Tolu, Yari 5 Bello, Chinu, Guapi, Neiva, Pasto, Tulua, Tunja 6 Cucuta, Ibaque, Lorica, Quibdo, Sangil, Tumaco 7 Cartago, Ipiates, Leticia, Palmira, Pereira, Popayan 8 Girardot, Maganque, Medellin, Monteria 9 Cartagena, Manizales 10 Santa Marta 11 Bucaramanga 12 Barranquilla, Buenaventura
school: 5 Andes, Valle 20 Instituto Caro y Cuervo 21 Industrial de Santander
measure: 4 vara 7 azumbre, celemin
monetary unit: 4 peso, real 6 condor, peseta 7 centavo
weight: 3 bag 4 saco 5 libra 7 quintal
island: 4 Baru 5 Naipo 6 Fuerte 7

Gorgona, Malpelo 8 Cusachon 9 San Andres 11 Providencia
lake: 4 Tota
mountain: 5 Abibe, Andes, Baudo, Chita, Cocuy, Huila, Pasto 6 Ayapel, Perija, Purace, Tolima, Tunahi 7 Chamusa, del Ruiz 8 Oriengal 10 Santa Marta 17 Central Cordillera, Eastern Cordillera, Western Cordillera
highest point: 14 Cristobal Colon
river: 3 Uva 4 Bita, Meta, Muco, Sinu, Tomo, Yari 5 Cauca, Cesar, Isana, Mesai, Nechi, Pauto, Sucio 6 Amazon, Arauca, Ariari, Atrato, Atroto, Caguan, Pattia, Yapura 7 Apapois, Caqueta, Guainia, Inirida, Truando, Vichada 8 Casanare, Guaviara, Putumayo 9 Magdalena
sea: 7 Pacific 9 Caribbean
physical feature:
cape: 4 Vela 5 Aguja, Marzo, Punta 7 Augusta 8 Gallinas
falls: 10 Tequendama
gulf: 5 Uraba 6 Cupica, Darien, Tibuga 8 Tortugas
inlet: 6 Tumaco
plains: 6 llanos
point: 6 Cruces, Lacruz, Solano 8 Caribana, Gallinas
people: 4 Boro, Cuna, Duit, Hoka, Macu, Muso, Muzo, Paez, Tama, Tapa 5 Carib, Catio, Choco, Cofan, Cogui, Cubeo, Guane, Haida, Mocoa, Paeze, Pijao, Seona, Yagua 6 Arawak, Betoya, Calima, Colima, Ingano, Mirana, Saliva, Tahami, Ticuna, Tucano, Tunebo, Witoto, Yahuna 7 Achagua, Andaqui, Chibcha, Chimila, Churoya, Guahibo, Guajiro, Panches, Puinave, Puitoto, Quechua, Shuswap, Tairona, Telembi 8 Coconuco, Guarauno, mestizos, Motilone, Puinavis, Quimbaya, Sinsigas 9 Cocanucos, Coconucan, mulattoes, Panaquita 10 Bellacoola
leader: 7 Bolivar
language: 7 Spanish
religion: 13 Roman Catholic
place:
museum: 4 Gold 8 Colonial
palace: 11 Inquisition
feature:
dance: 7 bambuco 8 merengue
game: 4 tejo
guitar: 5 tiple
poncho: 5 ruana
shoes: 10 alpargatas
shoulder bag: 7 carriel
tree: 8 arboloco
woven hat: 5 jipas
Colombo
capital of: 8 Sri Lanka
colon 4 coin 6 farmer, vitals 7 pioneer, planter, settler, viscera 9 hemistich, intestine 15 plantation owner, punctuation mark
colonize 6 found, plant 6 gather, settle 7 migrate 8 establish 10 infiltrate
colonnade 3 row 4 stoa 5 porch 6 arcade, piazza 7 portico, terrace 8 cloister 9 peristyle

colony 3 set 4 band, body 5 flock, group, swarm 7 mandate 8 dominion, province 9 community, territory 10 dependency, possession, settlement 12 protectorate 14 satellite state
colophon 6 design, device, emblem 7 insigne 8 insignia 11 inscription
color 3 dye, hue 4 bias, burn, cast, glow, mood, tint, tone, warp, wash 5 bloom, blush, chalk, drift, flame, flush, force, paint, sense, shade, slant, stain, taint, tinge, twist 6 affect, aspect, crayon, effect, import, intent, redden, spirit, stress 7 distort, feeling, meaning, pervert, pigment, redness, skin hue 8 dyestuff, rosiness 9 go crimson, influence, intention, prejudice 10 intimation 11 connotation, implication, insinuation 12 become florid, pigmentation, significance 17 natural complexion
Colorado
abbreviation: 2 CO 4 Colo
nickname: 10 Centennial
capital/largest city: 6 Denver
others: 4 Vail 5 Aspen, Delta, Lamar, Ouray 6 Arvada, Aurora, Denver, Golden, Pueblo, Salida 7 Alamosa, Boulder, Durango, Greeley, Manassa, Manitou 8 Gunnison, Loveland, Trinidad 9 Purgatory, Silverton, Telluride 11 Central City 12 Cripple Creek 13 Grand Junction 15 Colorado Springs
college: 5 Regis 6 Denver 7 Boulder 17 US Air Force Academy
feature: 11 Four Corners 15 Garden of the Gods 17 Continental Divide
national monument: 8 Dinosaur 14 Great Sand Dunes
national park: 5 Estes 9 Mesa Verde 13 Rocky Mountain
tribe: 3 Ute 7 Arapaho 8 Cheyenne
people: 11 Jack Dempsey 12 Ralph Edwards 14 Scott Carpenter 18 Douglas Fairbanks Sr
lake: 6 Frozen
land rank: 6 eighth
mountains: 5 Longs, Rocky 7 San Juan 9 Pikes Peak 14 Sangre de Cristo
highest point: 6 Elbert
physical feature:
canyon: 5 Black
gorge: 5 Royal
plains: 5 Great
wind: 7 Chinook
river: 4 Gila 5 Yampa 6 Platte 7 Dolores 8 Apishapa, Arikaree, Arkansas, Gunnison 9 Rio Grande 10 Purgatoire
state admission: 12 thirty-eighth
state bird: 11 lark bunting
state flower: 22 Rocky Mountain columbine
state motto: 24 Nothing Without Providence
state song: 22 Where the Columbines Grow
state tree: 18 Colorado blue spruce

colored 4 dyed, hued 5 dusky 6 biased, shaded, tinged, tinted 7 blushed, excused, flushed, glossed, labeled, painted, stained 8 affected, labelled, reddened 9 chromatic, distorted, pigmented 10 influenced, prejudiced 12 complexioned 13 characterized 14 misrepresented

colorful 3 gay 4 loud 5 showy, vivid 6 bright, florid, unique 7 dynamic, graphic, unusual, vibrant, zestful 8 animated, forceful, spirited, vigorous 9 brilliant, full-toned, vivacious 10 compelling, variegated 11 distinctive, interesting, many-colored, picturesque 12 multicolored, particolored

coloring 3 dye 4 tint 5 color, shade, stain 10 coloration, complexion

colorless 3 wan 4 ashy, drab, dull, flat, pale 5 ashen, dingy, faded, pasty, vapid, white 6 anemic, boring, dreary, grayed, pallid, sallow, sickly, undyed 7 ghastly, ghostly, insipid, natural, neutral, prosaic 8 blanched, bleached, lifeless, ordinary, whitened 9 bloodless, washed out 10 cadaverous, lackluster, monotonous, spiritless, unanimated, unexciting, uninspired 11 commonplace 13 uninteresting

Color Purple, The
    author: 11 Alice Walker
    director: 15 Steven Spielberg
    cast: 11 Danny Glover 12 Adolph Caesar, Oprah Winfrey 13 Margaret Avery 14 Whoopi Goldberg

colors 4 flag, jack 6 banner, ensign, pennon 7 pennant 8 standard

colossal 4 huge, vast 5 giant, grand, great 6 mighty 7 extreme, immense, mammoth, massive, titanic 8 enormous, gigantic, imposing 9 exceeding, excessive 10 incredible, inordinate, monumental, prodigious, tremendous 11 extravagant, spectacular 12 awe-inspiring, overwhelming

Colossus of Rhodes
    statue of: 6 Apollo

colt 4 foal 5 horse 6 novice 8 equuleus, yearling 9 fledgling, youngster
    constellation of: 8 Equuleus

columbium
    chemical symbol: 2 Cb

Columbo
    character: 9 Lt Columbo
    cast: 9 Peter Falk

column 3 row 4 file, line, post 5 pylon, queue, shaft, train 6 parade, pillar, string 7 caravan, phalanx, support, upright 8 pilaster 9 cavalcade, formation 10 procession 11 vertical row 12 vertical list

columnist 6 writer 7 analyst
    famous: 7 Heloise 8 Dear Abby, Herb Caen 9 HL Mencken, Jack Smith 10 Ann Landers 11 Miss Manners 15 Abigail van Buren

coma 6 stupor, torpor 8 collapse 15 unconsciousness

Comaetho
    form: 9 priestess
    father: 9 Pterelaus
    loved: 10 Amphitryon

    lover: 10 Melanippus
    killed by: 10 Amphitryon

Comanche
    language family: 10 Shoshonean
    location: 5 Texas 6 Kansas, Mexico 8 Oklahoma
    noted as: 8 horsemen

comatose 3 lax 4 dull, idle, lazy 5 inert 6 leaden, torpid 7 drugged, languid, passive 8 inactive, indolent, lifeless, listless, slothful, sluggish 9 apathetic, catatonic, lethargic, stuporous 10 cataleptic, insensible, narcotized, phlegmatic, spiritless 11 indifferent, unconcerned, unconscious 12 unresponsive

comb 4 card, tuft 5 curry, dress, groom, plume, scour, style 6 search 7 arrange, explore, panache, ransack, topknot 8 head tuft, hunt over, untangle 9 cast about, cockscomb, currycomb 11 look through 14 rummage through

combat 5 clash, fight 6 action, attack, battle, oppose, resist 7 contest, go to war, wage war 8 conflict, fighting, skirmish, struggle 9 encounter 10 contention, engagement, war against 11 come to blows, grapple with, make warfare, work against 12 do battle with, march against 13 confrontation 14 military action

Combat
    character: 4 Caje (Caddy Cadron) 5 Kirby 8 (Pvt) Braddock 9 Doc Walton, (Lt) Gil Hanley 12 (Sgt) Chip Saunders
    cast: 9 Jack Hogan, Rick Jason, Vic Morrow 12 Shecky Greene, Steven Rogers 13 Pierre Jalbert

combatant 7 fighter, soldier, warrior 9 man-at-arms 10 serviceman 11 fighting man

combating 8 battling, clashing, fighting, opposing 9 waging war 10 contention, contesting, opposition, struggling 11 doing battle 13 grappling with 17 coming to blows with

combative 6 bantam 8 militant 9 agonistic, bellicose 10 aggressive, pugnacious 11 belligerent, contentious 12 antagonistic

combativeness 9 hostility, pugnacity 10 antagonism 12 belligerence 14 aggressiveness 15 contentiousness

combination 3 mix 5 alloy, blend, union 6 fusion, league, medley, merger, mixing 7 amalgam, joining, mixture, pooling, variety 8 alliance, blending, compound 9 coalition, composite, synthesis 10 assortment, coalescing, federation 11 association, composition, confederacy 12 amalgamation 13 confederation

combine 3 mix 4 fuse, join, pool 5 blend, merge, unify, unite 6 couple, league, mingle 8 compound 9 commingle 10 amalgamate, synthesize 11 consolidate, incorporate

combo 4 band 5 group 11 aggregation, combination

comb out 4 curl 5 dress 7 arrange, unsnarl 8 untangle

combustible 8 burnable 9 flammable, ignitable 10 combustive, incendiary 11 inflammable 13 conflagrative

combustion 6 firing 7 burning, flaming 8 ignition, kindling 12 incineration 13 conflagration

combustive 8 burnable 9 flammable, ignitable 11 combustible, inflammable 13 conflagrative

come 2 be, go 3 bud 4 fall, loom, rise 5 arise, issue, occur, range, reach 6 appear, arrive, be made, drop in, emerge, extend, follow, happen, impend, show up, spread, spring, turn up 7 advance, descend, emanate, stretch 8 approach, draw near, go toward, grow to be 9 be a native, germinate, take place 10 be imminent, move toward 11 be a resident, be in the wind, materialize, originate in, spring forth

come about 5 occur 6 chance, happen 7 turn out 10 come to pass

come afterward 5 ensue 6 derive, follow, result 7 succeed

come apart 6 detach 7 disjoin, unstick 9 separate

come back 5 rally 6 answer, retort, return 7 rebound 8 recovery

Come Back Little Sheba
  director: 10 Daniel Mann
  based on play by: 11 William Inge
  cast: 10 Terry Moore 12 Shirley Booth 13 Burt Lancaster
  Oscar for: 7 actress (Booth)

come clean 4 sing 5 own up 7 confess 14 unbosom oneself 18 make a clean breast of

come close to 7 verge on 8 approach, border on 11 approximate, nearly equal

comedian 3 wag 4 fool, zany 5 clown, comic, cutup, joker 6 jester, madcap 7 buffoon 8 humorist, jokester 9 prankster 10 comedienne, comic actor 14 practical joker

comedown 4 drop 8 lowering 10 anticlimax

come down 4 dive, drop, fall, sink 6 plunge, tumble 7 descend, plummet 8 decrease

come down a peg 5 deign, stoop 6 unbend 7 descend 10 condescend 12 lower oneself 13 humble oneself

comedy 3 fun, wit 5 farce, humor 6 banter, joking, pranks, satire 7 foolery, jesting 8 drollery, raillery, travesty 9 burlesque, cutting up, horseplay, silliness 10 buffoonery, pleasantry, tomfoolery 13 fooling around

Comedy of Errors, The
  author: 18 William Shakespeare
  character: 6 Aegeon, Dromio 7 Adriana, Aemilia, Luciana, Solinus 10 Antipholus

come face to face with 4 meet 8 confront 9 encounter

come first 7 precede, predate 8 antecede, antedate, go before 10 anticipate

come into being 4 dawn, show 5 arise, begin, occur, set in, start 6 appear, be born, crop up, emerge, sprout 8 commence, spring up 9 germinate, originate 11 come to light

come into port 4 dock 5 berth

come into view 4 show 6 appear, come up, emerge, show up 7 surface 11 come to light 13 become visible

come loose 5 let go 6 detach, loosen 7 slip off 8 break off, separate, unfasten 9 break away 10 come undone, come untied, disconnect 11 come unglued, come unstuck

comely 4 fair, nice 5 bonny 6 pretty, proper, seemly, simple 7 correct, fitting, natural, sightly, winning, winsome 8 becoming, blooming, charming, decorous, engaging, fetching, pleasant, pleasing, suitable, tasteful 9 agreeable, appealing, wholesome 10 attractive, unaffected 11 well-favored

come near 4 loom, near 6 appear 8 approach 9 draw close 10 move toward

come-on 4 bait, hook, lure, trap 5 decoy, snare 6 magnet 9 seduction 10 allurement, attraction, bewitchery, enticement, inducement, seducement, temptation 12 inveiglement

comestibles 5 foods 7 edibles 8 victuals 10 foodstuffs, provisions

Cometes
  lover of: 8 Aegialia

come to a decision 6 decide, settle 7 resolve 8 conclude 9 determine

come to an understanding 5 agree 6 settle 11 come to terms 12 agree to marry 16 reach an agreement

come to a standstill 4 halt, quit, stop 5 abate, cease 7 die away 8 quit cold

come to blows 5 fight 7 contest 8 do battle 9 square off 12 start to fight

come together 4 meet 5 flock, group, rally 6 gather 7 collect, convene 8 assemble 10 congregate 11 get together

come to light 4 dawn 5 arise 6 appear, crop up, emerge, evolve, show up, turn up, unfold 7 develop, surface, turn out

come to nothing 4 fail, flop, fold 6 fizzle 8 be in vain, collapse 9 break down 11 fall through 12 come to naught 17 fail to materialize

come to pass 5 ensue, occur 6 arrive, befall, follow, happen 9 take place

come to terms 5 agree, yield 6 give up, settle 7 succumb 8 contract, cry quits 9 make a deal, negotiate, surrender 10 capitulate, compromise 11 come to grips, meet halfway, sue for peace 13 resign oneself 14 strike a bargain 15 lay down one's arms 16 reach an agreement 17 acknowledge defeat, hoist the white flag 18 split the difference

come unglued 6 detach, loosen 8 separate 9 fall apart 11 come unstuck

come unstuck 4 lift 6 detach, loosen 8 break off, unfasten 9 break away, come apart, come loose, fall apart 11 come unglued

come up 4 rise 5 arise 7 quicken, sharpen 8 heighten, increase 9 intensify 10 accelerate, strengthen 12 be referred to

come upon 4 find, meet **7** learn of, run into **8** discover **9** encounter

comfit 5 candy, sweet **9** sweetmeat **10** confection, sugar candy **13** confectionery

comfort 4 calm, ease, help **5** cheer, peace, quiet **6** luxury, relief, solace, soothe, succor, warmth **7** cheer up, compose, console, hearten **8** coziness, opulence, pleasure, reassure, serenity, snugness **9** bolster up, comforter, composure, encourage, well-being **10** cheering up, relaxation **11** consolation, contentment, reassurance **12** satisfaction **13** encouragement, gratification **14** quiet one's fears **16** source of serenity **17** lighten one's burden **18** bolster one's spirits

Comfort, Alex
    author of: **11** The Joy of Sex **12** More Joy of Sex

comfortable 4 cozy, easy **6** at ease, at home, serene **7** relaxed **8** adequate, pleasant, suitable **9** agreeable, congenial, contented **10** giving ease, gratifying, untroubled **11** pleasurable, undisturbed **12** satisfactory **16** free from distress

comforter 4 balm, puff **5** quilt, scarf **6** afghan, solace **7** anodyne, blanket, comfort, soother **8** coverlet **10** palliative

comic, comical 4 rich **5** droll, funny, merry, silly, witty **6** absurd, jocose, jovial **7** amusing, jocular, risible **8** farcical, humorous, mirthful **9** facetious, laughable, ludicrous, whimsical **10** ridiculous **11** nonsensical **12** nimble-witted

coming 4 next **6** advent, future, in view, to come **7** arrival, nearing **8** approach, arriving, imminent, on the way **9** advancing, emergence, imminence, impending, in the wind, proximity **10** appearance, occurrence, subsequent **11** approaching, forthcoming, prospective **12** on the horizon **13** materializing

Coming Home
    director: **8** Hal Ashby
    cast: **9** Bruce Dern, Jane Fonda, Jon Voight **15** Robert Carradine
    Oscar for: **5** actor (Voight) **7** actress (Fonda) **10** screenplay

Coming into the Country
    author: **10** John McPhee

Coming of Age, The
    author: **16** Simone de Beauvoir

Coming of Age in Samoa
    author: **12** Margaret Mead

Coming Race, The
    author: **18** Edward Bulwer-Lytton

command 3 bid, get **4** boss, call, draw, fiat, grip, head, hold, lead, rule **5** edict, evoke, grasp, guide, order, power **6** adjure, behest, charge, compel, decree, demand, direct, elicit, enjoin, govern, incite, induce, kindle, manage, ordain, prompt, summon **7** call for, conduct, control, deserve, extract, inspire, mastery, provoke, receive, require, summons **8** call upon, instruct, motivate **9** authority, call forth, direction, directive, governing, knowledge, ordinance, super-

vise, ultimatum **10** administer, be master of, domination, injunction, leadership, management **11** familiarity, instruction, superintend, supervision **12** have charge of **13** comprehension, understanding **14** administration **17** have authority over

commandant 7 captain **9** commander **12** chief officer

commandeer 4 take **5** seize, usurp **8** shanghai **11** appropriate, expropriate

commander 4 boss, head **5** chief, ruler **6** leader **7** manager **8** director **9** conductor

commanding 4 head **5** chief, grand, lofty **6** ruling, senior, strong **7** dynamic, leading, ranking, stately **8** forceful, gripping, imposing, powerful, striking, towering **9** arresting, directing, governing, important, prominent **10** compelling, dominating, impressive **11** controlling, significant **13** authoritative, distinguished, overshadowing

commandment
    Hebrew: **7** mitsvah, mitzvah

comme il faut 6 proper **7** fitting **12** as it should be

commemorate 4 hail, mark **5** extol, honor **6** hallow, revere, salute **7** acclaim, glorify, observe **8** venerate **9** celebrate, solemnize **11** acknowledge, memorialize, pay homage to **12** pay tribute to

commence 5 begin, start **8** get going, initiate **10** get started, inaugurate, originated

commencement 4 dawn **5** birth, onset, start **6** outset **7** genesis, morning **9** beginning, first step, inception **10** graduation, initiation **11** origination **12** inauguration **13** graduation day **20** graduation ceremonies

commend 2 OK **4** back, give, laud **5** extol **6** commit, confer, convey, praise **7** acclaim, approve, consign, endorse, entrust, stand by, support **8** delegate, give over, hand over, pass over, relegate, transfer **13** speak highly of

commendable 6 worthy **7** notable **8** laudable **9** admirable, deserving, estimable, exemplary, honorable **10** creditable **11** meritorious **12** praiseworthy

commendation 5 honor **6** praise **7** support **8** approval **10** acceptance **11** acclamation, approbation

commendatory 8 admiring, praising **9** laudatory, praiseful **10** plauditory **13** complimentary **14** congratulatory

commensurate, commensurable 4 even, meet **5** equal **6** square **7** fitting **8** balanced, in accord, parallel, relative, suitable **10** comparable, compatible, consistent, equivalent **11** appropriate, in agreement **13** corresponding, proportionate **14** on a proper scale

comment 4 note, word **6** remark **7** clarify, discuss, explain, expound **8** expand on **9** assertion, criticism, elucidate, shed light, statement, talk about, touch upon, utterance **10** annotation, expression, reflection **11** elucidation, explanation, explication, observation 13 clarification 15 exemplification

commentary 6 review 8 critique, scholium, treatise 9 criticism 10 exposition 11 explanation, explication 12 dissertation 14 interpretation 16 explanatory essay

commentator 6 critic, writer 7 speaker 8 panelist, reporter, reviewer 9 columnist, explainer 10 newscaster 11 interpreter, news analyst

comment upon 7 clarify, clear up, explain 8 spell out 9 delineate, elucidate, explicate, interpret, make plain 10 illuminate, illustrate 14 throw light upon

commerce 5 trade 6 barter 7 trading, traffic 8 business, exchange, industry 12 mercantilism 16 buying and selling

god of: 6 Hermes 7 Mercury

commercial 2 ad 5 sales, trade 8 business 10 mercantile, sales pitch 12 profit-making 13 advertisement 16 buying-and-selling

commingle 3 mix 4 fuse 5 blend, merge, unify 7 combine 10 amalgamate

commiserate 7 feel for 8 show pity 10 grieve with, lament with 13 express sorrow 14 sympathize with 15 share one's sorrow 17 have compassion for

commiseration 4 pity 8 sympathy 10 compassion, tenderness 13 fellow feeling

commission 3 act, bid, cut, fee 4 duty, hire, name, rank, role, task 5 board, doing, order, piece, power, proxy, trust 6 agency, assign, charge, direct, employ, engage, office 7 appoint, certify, charter, conduct, council, empower, license, mandate, mission, portion, rake-off, stipend, warrant 8 capacity, contract, delegate, dividend, document, exercise, function, position 9 acting out, allotment, allowance, authority, authorize, committal, committee 10 assignment, commitment, committing, delegation, deputation, entrusting, percentage, performing 11 appointment, carrying out, certificate, performance, transacting 12 officer's rank, perpetration 13 authorization, written orders 14 give the go-ahead 15 representatives 16 piece of the action 17 appointment papers, grant officer's rank

commissioner 5 envoy, trier 7 officer, pristaw 8 delegate, official 9 authority, commissar

commissioning 10 assignment, delegation 11 appointment, designation, entrustment 13 authorization

commit 2 do 3 act, put 4 bind, pull 5 enact, place 6 assign, decide, effect, engage, intern, pursue 7 confine, consign, deliver, deposit, entrust, execute, perform, pull off, resolve 8 carry out, give over, obligate, practice, transact, transfer 9 determine 10 make liable, perpetrate 13 participate in 16 institutionalize

commitment 3 vow 4 bond, word 5 stand 6 pledge 7 promise 8 decision, delivery, transfer, warranty 9 assurance, detention, guarantee, liability, restraint 10 assignment, giving over, internment, obligation,

resolution 11 confinement, consignment, dispatching 12 imprisonment 13 determination, incarceration 14 responsibility 18 institutionalizing

commit oneself 3 act 7 resolve 8 dedicate, obligate 9 determine

committed 6 active, liable 8 confined, detained, interned 9 concerned, delivered, entrusted, obligated 10 interested, responsive 11 responsible 17 institutionalized

committee 4 body, jury 5 bench, board, group, junta, table 6 bureau, soviet 7 cabinet, council 9 gathering, syndicate 10 assemblage 12 organization

commode 6 bureau 7 cabinet, dresser 9 washstand 14 chest of drawers

commodious 5 ample, large, roomy 8 spacious 9 capacious, uncramped 11 unconfining

commodity 4 ware 5 asset, goods, stock 6 staple 7 chattel, holding, product 8 property 9 advantage, belonging to 10 possession 11 convenience, merchandise 14 article of trade 17 article of commerce

common 3 bad, low 4 base, lewd, mean, rude, vile 5 brash, cheap, crass, crude, gross, joint, lowly, minor, plain, stock 6 brazen, brutal, coarse, lesser, normal, old-hat, public, ribald, shared, simple, smutty, tawdry, vulgar 7 average, boorish, callous, general, ignoble, ill-bred, loutish, low-bred, obscene, obscure, popular, prosaic, regular, routine, settled, uncouth, unknown, worn-out 8 communal, everyday, familiar, frequent, homespun, impolite, informal, mediocre, middling, nameless, ordinary, plebeian, shameful, standard, workaday, worn thin 9 bourgeois, customary, deficient, household, low-minded, moth-eaten, obnoxious, offensive, pervasive, shameless, tasteless, unexalted, universal, unnoticed, unrefined, well-known 10 collective, colloquial, despicable, dime-a-dozen, inglorious, threadbare, unblushing, uncultured, unpolished, widespread 11 disgraceful, established, ill-mannered, insensitive, middle-class, oft-repeated, subordinate, traditional, unimportant, widely known, without rank 12 contemptible, conventional, disagreeable 13 garden-variety, insignificant 15 undistinguished

commoners 5 plebs 6 masses 8 plebians

common law

Latin: 13 lex non scripta

commonly 5 often 6 widely 7 as a rule, usually 8 normally, of course 9 generally, in general, most often, popularly, regularly, routinely 10 by and large, familiarly, frequently, habitually, informally, ordinarily, repeatedly 11 customarily 13 traditionally 14 by force of habit, conventionally, for the most part 15 in most instances 17 generally speaking

common people 5 demos, plebs 6 masses 8 populace 9 hoi polloi, plebeians 11 bourgeoisie

commonplace 3 old 4 dull 5 adage, banal, stale, trite, usual 6 cliche, old-hat, truism 7 bromide, general, humdrum, regular, routine, worn-out 8 banality, everyday, familiar, ordinary, standard, worn thin 9 customary, hackneyed, moth-eaten, platitude 10 pedestrian, threadbare, un original, widespread 11 oft-repeated, stereotyped, traditional 12 received idea, run-of-the-mill 13 unimaginative, uninteresting

commonplace book 9 anthology, gleanings, scrapbook

Common Sense
    author: 11 Thomas Paine

common-sense 5 sound 8 everyday, sensible 9 mother wit, practical, pragmatic, realistic 10 no-nonsense 11 down-to-earth, levelheaded, serviceable, utilitarian 12 matter-of-fact

commonwealth 5 state 6 nation 8 republic
    Latin: 10 res publica

commotion 3 ado 4 fuss, stir, to-do 5 furor 6 bustle, racket, ruckus, tumult, uproar 7 clatter, turmoil 9 agitation 10 excitement, hullabaloo 11 disturbance 12 perturbation

communal 5 joint 6 common, mutual, public, shared 9 community 10 collective

commune 3 gab, rap, yak 4 chat, chin, talk 5 visit 6 babble, confer, gossip, parley, powwow 7 chatter, palaver, prattle 8 converse, schmooze 9 discourse 10 chew the fat, chew the rag 11 communicate, confabulate 14 shoot the breeze

communicable 8 catching 10 contagious, infectious 12 transferable 13 transmissible, transmittable

communicate 3 say 4 give, show, talk, tell 5 state, write 6 advise, convey, impart, notify, pass on, relate, reveal 7 declare, divulge, exhibit, mention, publish, signify 8 announce, converse, disclose, inform of, proclaim, transmit 9 apprise of, bring word, broadcast, make known, publicize 10 correspond

communication 4 news, note, wire 5 cable 6 letter, missal, report 7 liaison, message, missive, notices, rapport, writing 8 bulletin, dispatch, document, speaking, telegram 9 broadcast, cablegram, directive, statement 10 communique 11 declaration, information 12 conversation, intelligence, proclamation, radio message 13 telephone call 14 correspondence

communicative 4 open 5 frank 6 candid, chatty 7 voluble 8 friendly, outgoing, sociable 9 revealing, talkative 10 expressive, forthright, free-spoken, loquacious, revelatory, unreserved 11 informative

communion, Communion 6 accord 7 concord, harmony, rapport, sharing 8 affinity, sympathy 9 agreement 12 the Eucharist 13 communication, contemplation

communique 4 note, wire 5 aviso, cable, flash 6 report, letter 7 epistle, message, missive, release, telegram 8 bulletin, dispatch 9 directive, statement 10 memo-

randum 12 announcement, intelligence, notification 13 communication

Communist 3 red 6 soviet 7 comrade, marxist 8 Leninist 9 bolshevik, socialist 10 bolshevist 12 totalitarian

Communist Manifesto
    author: 8 Karl Marx 15 Friedrich Engels

community 4 area, folk, town 5 arena, field, group, range, realm, scope 6 locale, people, public, sphere, suburb 7 quarter, society 8 affinity, district, environs, likeness, populace, province, sameness, vicinity 9 agreement, citizenry 10 population, similarity 11 environment, social group 12 commonwealth, neighborhood, surroundings

commute 4 ride, trip 5 alter 6 adjust, change, redeem, soften, switch, travel 7 convert, journey, replace, reverse 8 diminish, exchange, mitigate 9 alleviate, supersede, transform, transmute, transpose 10 substitute 11 transfigure 12 metamorphose, transmogrify

comodo
    music: 9 leisurely

Comoros
    other name: 26 lost pearls of the Indian Ocean
    capital/largest city: 6 Moroni
    others: 6 Bambao 7 Fomboni 8 Dzaoudzi 9 Mutsamudu 11 Mitsamiouli
    monetary unit: 5 franc 7 centime
    island: 6 Moheli 7 Anjouan, Mayotte 12 Grande Comoro
    highest point: 7 Kartala 8 Karthala
    sea: 6 Indian
    physical feature:
    channel: 10 Mozambique
    people: 4 Arab 5 Bantu, Malay 7 African 8 Malagasy
    language: 6 Arabic, French 7 Swahili 8 Malagasy
    religion: 5 Islam 13 Roman Catholic

compact 4 bond, cram, deal, pack, pact, snug, tidy 5 close, dense, press, small, stuff 6 little, treaty 7 bargain, crammed, pressed, squeeze, stuffed 8 alliance, compress, contract, covenant 9 agreement, clustered, concordat 10 compressed 11 arrangement, pack closely 12 concentrated 13 tightly packed, understanding

compactness 7 density 8 snugness 9 smallness 10 littleness 11 compression 13 concentration

companion 3 pal 4 chum, mate 5 buddy, crony 6 escort, friend, helper 7 comrade 9 assistant, associate, attendant

companionable 6 social 7 amiable, cordial 8 friendly, sociable 9 agreeable, congenial, convivial

companionate 4 warm 6 genial 7 cordial 8 amicable, friendly, platonic, suitable 9 accordant, agreeable, consonant, easygoing, nonsexual, spiritual, unfleshly 10 compatible, concordant, harmonious 11 nonphysical, passionless, warm-hearted 12 affectionate 13 companionable

companionship 4 pals 5 chums 7 buddies, company, friends 8 comrades 10 associates, companions, fellowship, friendship 11 camaraderie, comradeship, familiarity, sociability 17 close acquaintance, friendly relations

company 3 mob 4 band, firm, gang 5 bunch, group, guest, party 6 guests, outfit, people, throng 7 callers, concern, friends, society, visitor 8 assembly, comrades, presence, visitors 9 gathering, multitude, syndicate 10 assemblage, companions, fellowship, friendship 11 camaraderie, comradeship, corporation, sociability 12 conglomerate, congregation 13 companionship, establishment 15 business concern

comparable 4 like, up to 5 close, equal 6 akin to 7 similar 8 as good as, parallel 9 a match for, analogous 10 equivalent, on a par with, tantamount 11 approaching, approximate 12 commensurate, in a class with 13 commensurable

comparative 4 near 8 relative 11 approximate

compare 5 equal, liken, match 6 be up to, equate, relate 7 vie with 8 approach, contrast 9 correlate 11 compete with 12 be on a par with 13 hold a candle to 14 be in a class with 20 draw a parallel between

compare notes 6 confer 7 consult 8 talk over 13 exchange views

comparison 7 analogy, kinship 8 contrast, equality, likeness, parallel, relation 10 connection, similarity 11 correlation, resemblance 13 comparability

compartment 3 box, pew 4 brig, cell, crib, hold, hole, nook, room 5 berth, booth, cabin, crypt, niche, stall, vault 6 alcove, bunker, closet 7 chamber, cubicle, section 8 anteroom, roomette 9 cubbyhole 10 pigeonhole 11 antechamber

compass 5 bound, range, reach, scope, sweep 6 domain, extent 8 boundary, province 13 circumference

Compass, Mariner's Compass
constellation of: 5 Pyxis

Compasses, Pair
constellation of: 8 Circinus

compassion 4 pity 5 heart 7 empathy, feeling 8 humanity, sympathy 10 tenderness 13 commiseration, fellow feeling 17 tender-heartedness
Latin: 12 misericordia

compassionate 4 kind 6 humane 7 pitying 8 merciful 10 benevolent, charitable 11 kindhearted, sympathetic 13 tender-hearted

compatibility 6 accord 7 concord, harmony, rapport 8 affinity 9 agreement, unanimity 12 congeniality 14 like-mindedness

compatible 3 apt, fit 6 seemly 7 fitting 8 in accord, suitable 9 congenial, in harmony, in keeping 10 like-minded 11 appropriate

compel 4 make 5 drive, force 6 oblige 7 require 11 necessitate

compelled 4 must 5 bound, urged 6 driven, forced 7 coerced, obliged, pressed 8 commanded, dragooned, enforced, impelled, obsessed, pressured, required 11 constrained, overpowered

compelling 7 driving, dynamic 8 forceful 10 commanding 12 overwhelming

compel obedience to 5 force 6 coerce 7 enforce 8 carry out, insist on 10 administer

compendium 4 list 5 brief 6 apercu, digest, precis, survey 7 abstract, capsule, catalog, epitome, summary 8 syllabus, synopsis 9 catalogue 11 abridgement, compilation 12 condensation

compensate 3 pay 5 cover, repay 6 make up, offset, redeem, square 7 balance, pay back, redress 9 indemnify, reimburse 10 make amends, recompense, remunerate 14 counterbalance 15 make restitution

compensation 3 fee, pay 4 gain 5 wages 6 income, profit, return, reward, salary 7 payment, redress 8 benefits, earnings, gratuity 9 indemnity, repayment 10 recompense, settlement 11 restitution 12 remuneration, satisfaction 13 consideration, reimbursement

compete 3 vie 5 fight 6 battle, combat, oppose 7 contend, contest 8 be rivals 9 lock horns, match wits

competence 5 skill 7 ability, know-how, mastery 8 ableness 9 expertise 10 capability, competency, expertness 11 proficiency

competent 3 fit 6 expert, versed 7 skilled, trained 8 skillful 9 efficient, practiced, qualified 10 dependable, proficient 11 experienced, responsible, trustworthy

competition 4 game 5 event, match, rival 7 contest, rivalry, tourney 8 conflict, opponent, struggle 9 contender 10 contention, opposition, tournament

competitive 8 fighting, opposing, striving 9 combative 10 aggressive, contending

competitor 5 rival 7 fighter 8 opponent 9 adversary, contender 10 contestant, opposition

compilation 4 body 5 group 9 collating, garnering, gathering, mustering 10 assemblage, assembling, assortment, collecting, collection, compendium, marshaling 11 aggregating, aggregation, marshalling 12 accumulating, accumulation

compile 5 amass 6 garner, gather, heap up, muster 7 collate, collect, marshal 8 assemble 10 accumulate

complacent 4 smug 6 at ease 7 content 9 contented 10 self-secure, unbothered, untroubled 13 self-satisfied

complain 3 nag 4 beef, carp, kick, moan, pick 5 cavil, gripe, whine 6 grouch, grouse, squawk 7 grumble 9 bellyache, criticize, find fault 15 state a grievance

complaint 4 beef, kick 5 gripe 6 malady, squawk, tirade 7 ailment, illness, protest 8 debility, disorder, sickness 9 criticism, grievance, infirmity, objection 10 impairment 12 faultfinding 15 dissatisfaction

complaisance 7 pliancy **8** docility **10** affability, amiability, compliance **12** acquiescence

complaisant 4 warm **7** affable, amiable, cordial **8** friendly, gracious, obliging, pleasant, pleasing **9** agreeable, compliant, congenial, easygoing **10** solicitous **11** good-humored, good-natured

Compleat Angler, The
 author: **11** Izaak Walton

complement 3 cap **5** crown, match, total, whole **7** balance, perfect **8** ensemble, entirety, parallel, round out **9** aggregate, companion **10** completion, consummate, full amount, full number, supplement **11** counterpart, rounding-out **12** consummation **14** required number

complementary 7 matched **8** integral, opposite **9** companion **10** additional, compatible, completing **11** correlative **12** interrelated, supplemental **13** correspondent, corresponding

complete 3 cap, end **4** full **5** crown, total, utter, whole **6** entire, finish, intact, settle, wrap up **7** achieve, execute, fulfill, perfect, perform, plenary, settled **8** absolute, achieved, carry out, conclude, executed, round out, thorough, unbroken **9** discharge, make whole, performed, polish off, terminate, undivided **10** accomplish, carried out, complement, conclusive, consummate, unabridged **11** consummated **12** accomplished

completed 4 done **5** ended, whole **6** closed, entire, filled **7** matured, through **8** achieved, finished, realized **9** concluded, executed, fulfilled, perfected **10** terminated, wrapped up **11** consummated **12** accomplished

completeness 8 fullness, richness **9** wholeness **10** perfection **12** thoroughness

completion 3 end **5** close **6** ending, finish, windup **7** closing **9** finishing **10** concluding, conclusion, expiration **11** fulfillment, terminating, termination **12** consummation

complex 4 maze **5** mixed **6** knotty, system **7** network, tangled **8** compound, involved, manifold, multiple, puzzling **9** aggregate, composite, difficult, enigmatic, fixed idea, intricate, obsession **10** perplexing, variegated **11** bewildering, complicated **12** conglomerate, labyrinthian, labyrinthine, multifarious **13** preoccupation

complexion 3 hue **4** look, tone **5** color, guise, image, slant **6** aspect **7** outlook **8** coloring **9** character **10** appearance, coloration, impression **11** countenance, skin texture **12** pigmentation, skin coloring

complexity 6 puzzle **9** intricacy, obscurity **10** bafflement, involution, perplexity **11** crabbedness, elaboration, involvement **12** complication, entanglement **15** inextricability **17** unintelligibility **19** incomprehensibility

compliance 6 assent **7** pliancy **8** docility, giving in, meekness, yielding **9** deference, obedience, passivity **10** conforming, conformity, submission **12** acquiescence, complaisance **13** nonresistance

compliant 8 flexible, yielding **9** agreeable **10** submissive

complicate 4 knot **5** ravel, snarl **6** muddle, tangle **7** confuse, involve **8** confound, entangle **11** make complex **13** make difficult, make intricate

complicated 7 complex **8** involved **9** elaborate, intricate

complication 4 snag **5** hitch **7** dilemma, problem **8** drawback, handicap, obstacle, quandary **9** hindrance **10** difficulty, impediment, perplexity **11** aggravation, obstruction, predicament **12** disadvantage **14** stumbling block

complicity 8 abetment, intrigue, plotting, schemery, scheming **9** collusion, finagling **10** connivance, conspiracy **11** confederacy, contrivance, implication, involvement **12** entanglement

compliment 5 honor, kudos **6** homage, praise **7** tribute **8** flattery **9** adulation, laudation **11** acclamation **12** commendation **14** congratulation

complimentary 4 free **6** gratis **8** admiring, praising **9** adulatory, extolling, laudatory, panegyric, praiseful **10** flattering, gratuitous, plauditory **12** appreciative, commendatory **13** without charge **14** congratulatory

compliments 4 best, laud **5** exalt, extol, toast **6** homage, praise, salute **7** applaud, commend, regards **8** respects **9** greetings **10** best wishes, good wishes **11** salutations **13** felicitations **15** congratulations

comply 3 bow **4** bend, mind, obey **5** defer, yield **6** accede, adhere, follow, give in, submit **7** abide by, conform, consent, fulfill, observe, satisfy **9** acquiesce, surrender

component 4 item, part **5** piece **6** detail, member, module **7** element, modular, segment **8** material **9** composing, elemental, essential, intrinsic **10** elementary, ingredient, particular **11** constituent, fundamental **13** component part

component part 4 item, part **5** piece **6** detail, member **7** element **10** ingredient, particular **11** constituent, fundamental

comport 3 act **4** bear **5** carry **6** acquit, behave, deport **7** conduct

comportment 7 bearing, conduct **8** attitude, behavior, carriage, demeanor, presence **9** acquittal **10** appearance, deportment

comport oneself 3 act **6** behave **13** acquit oneself **14** conduct oneself

compose 4 calm, form, lull, make **5** frame, quell, quiet, relax, shape, write **6** create, devise, make up, pacify, settle, soothe **7** collect, fashion, placate **8** be part of, belong to, comprise, conceive, modulate **9** formulate **10** constitute

composed 4 calm, cool **5** quiet **6** at ease, placid, poised, sedate, serene, steady **8** peaceful, tranquil **9** collected, quiescent, unexcited, unruffled **10** controlled, coolheaded, restrained, unagitated, untroubled 11 level-headed, undisturbed, unemotional, unflappable, unperturbed 12 eventempered 13 dispassionate, imperturbable 15 undemonstrative

composer 4 bard, poet 6 author, writer 7 creator 8 musician, producer 10 compositor, typesetter

composite 6 mosaic 7 blended 8 combined, compound 10 compounded

composition 4 form, opus, work 5 essay, etude, piece 6 design, layout, make-up, making 7 forming, framing, product, shaping 8 creating, creation, devising, exercise 9 framework, structure 10 concoction, fashioning, organizing, production 11 arrangement, combination, compilation, formulation, preparation 12 constitution, organization 13 configuration

compos mentis 4 sane 13 mentally sound

composure 4 calm, cool, ease 5 poise 6 aplomb 7 control, dignity 8 calmness, coolness, patience, serenity 9 sangfroid 10 equanimity 11 self-control 13 self-assurance, self-restraint 14 coolheadedness, self-possession, unexcitability, unflappability 15 levelheadedness 16 even-temperedness, imperturbability

compound 3 mix 4 fuse, make 5 add to, alloy, blend, boost, mixed, union, unite 6 devise, fusion, mingle 7 amalgam, amplify, augment, blended, combine, complex, concoct, enlarge, magnify, mixture, prepare 8 combined, heighten, increase 9 composite, fabricate, formulate, reinforce 10 synthesize 11 combination, complicated, composition, incorporate, put together 12 conglomerate 14 conglomeration

comprehend 3 dig, get 5 catch, grasp, savvy 6 absorb, digest, fathom 7 make out 8 conceive, perceive 9 penetrate 10 appreciate, assimilate, understand

comprehensible 5 clear, plain 7 evident 8 apparent 11 unambiguous 12 intelligible

comprehension 5 grasp 7 insight 9 awareness 10 conception, perception 11 realization 12 acquaintance, appreciation, apprehension 13 consciousness, understanding

comprehensive 4 full 5 broad 7 copious, general, overall 8 complete, sweeping, thorough 9 expansive, extensive, universal 10 exhaustive, widespread 11 compendious 12 all-embracing, all-inclusive

compress 4 cram, pack 5 press 6 reduce, shrink 7 abridge, bandage, compact, curtail, plaster, shorten, squeeze 8 condense, dressing 10 abbreviate

compressed 5 dense 6 jammed, packed 7 crowded 8 squashed, squeezed 9 compacted 12 concentrated

compressed form 6 digest 7 summary 8 cake form, synopsis 10 shortening 11 abridgement, contraction, curtailment 12 abbreviation, condensation

compression 9 narrowing, squeezing, stricture, tightness 10 compaction, constraint 12 constriction

compressor 4 pump 7 presser, reducer 8 squeezer 9 compactor, condenser

comprise 4 form 6 make up 7 compose, contain, include 8 be made of 9 consist of 10 constitute 12 be composed of

compromise 4 risk 5 agree, truce 6 settle 7 balance, compact, imperil 8 endanger, undercut 9 agreement, discredit, embarrass, implicate, make a deal, prejudice 10 adjustment, jeopardize, settlement 11 arrangement, come to terms, happy medium, make suspect, meet halfway 12 conciliation 13 accommodation, rapprochement 14 make vulnerable, strike a bargain 16 mutual concession 18 split the difference 21 come to an understanding
  German: 9 Ausgleich

compromising 7 risking 8 settling 9 adjusting 10 bargaining 11 give and take, making a deal 12 embarrassing, jeopardizing 13 accommodating, coming to terms 14 meeting halfway

Compsognathus
  type: 8 dinosaur, theropod
  characteristic: 8 smallest
  location: 6 Europe 7 Bavaria
  period: 8 Jurassic

Compson, Quentin
  character in: 14 Absalom Absalom 18 The Sound and the Fury
  author: 8 Faulkner

Compson family
  characters in: 18 The Sound and the Fury
  member: 5 Benjy, Caddy, Jason 7 Candace, Quentin 8 Benjamin
  author: 8 Faulkner

compte rendu 6 record, report, review 7 account 15 account rendered

comptroller 7 auditor 9 treasurer 10 accountant, bookkeeper, controller

compulsion 5 force 6 demand, duress, urging 8 coercion, pressure 9 necessity 10 obligation 11 domineering, requirement

compulsive 6 driven, hooked 7 driving, fanatic 8 addicted, habitual 9 compelled, obsessive 10 compelling 14 unable to resist, uncontrollable

compulsory 7 binding 8 coercive, demanded, enforced, forcible, required 9 mandatory, requisite 10 compulsive, imperative, obligatory 11 unavoidable 12 prescriptive

compunction 5 demur, qualm, shame 6 regret, unease 7 anxiety, concern, remorse, scruple 9 misgiving 10 contrition 16 pang of conscience

computation 5 tally, total 8 figuring 9 numbering, reckoning 10 numeration 11 calculation, enumeration

compute 3 add 5 add up, sum up, tally, total 6 figure, reckon 7 count up, work out 9 ascertain, calculate, figure out

computer 5 adder 9 processor 10 calculator

language: 3 ADA 4 LOGO 5 ALGOL, BASIC, COBOL 6 PASCAL 7 FORTRAN

term: 2 PC 3 bit, CAD, CAM, CPU, RAM, ROM 4 boot, byte, chip, hack 5 drive, input, modem, pixel, queue 6 analog, glitch, hacker, memory, online, output 7 digital, network, offline, program 8 database, hardware, lightpen, printout, software, terminal 9 interface, mainframe 10 binary code, floppy disk 12 minicomputer 13 microcomputer, word processor 14 microprocessor

comrade 3 pal 4 ally, chum 5 buddy, crony 6 friend 7 partner 8 confrere, co-worker, helpmate, intimate 9 associate, colleague, companion, confidant 10 bosom buddy 11 confederate 12 collaborator 13 boon companion

Russian: 8 tovarich

comradeship 8 alliance 10 fellowship, friendship 11 association, camaraderie 13 companionship

comte 5 count

Comte Ory, Le
also: 8 Count Ory
opera by: 7 Rossini
character: 13 Countess Adele

Comus
author: 10 John Milton

Comus
origin: 5 Roman
god of: 7 revelry 8 drinking

con 3 gyp 4 anti, bilk, coax, fool, gull, hoax, lure, rook 5 cheat, cozen, felon, trick 6 delude 7 against, beguile, convict, defraud, mislead, swindle 8 hoodwink, jailbird, prisoner, yardbird 9 bamboozle

Conakry
capital of: 6 Guinea

concatenation 4 link 5 union 6 hookup 7 joining, linking, reunion 8 coupling, junction 10 bracketing, confluence, connection 11 conjunction 12 interlinking 15 interconnection 16 interassociation 18 intercommunication

concave 6 hollow, sunken 8 indented 9 depressed 13 curving inward

conceal 4 hide, mask 5 cloak, cover 6 screen, shield 7 cover up, obscure, secrete 8 disguise 10 camouflage, keep secret

concealed 5 blind, doggo 6 covert, hidden, latent, masked, perdue, secret, veiled 7 cloaked, covered, obscure, unknown, wrapped 8 abstruse, shrouded, ulterior 9 disguised, incognito 11 clandestine

concealment 5 cover 6 hiding 7 hideout, masking 8 covering, hideaway 9 screening, secreting, secretion 10 covering up, under cover

concede 3 own 4 cede 5 admit, agree, allow, grant, yield 6 accept, give up, resign, tender 7 abandon, confess, deliver 8 hand over 9 acquiesce, recognize, surrender,

vouchsafe 10 relinquish 11 acknowledge, be persuaded

conceit 5 pride 6 vanity 7 ego trip, egotism 8 bragging, self-love 9 vainglory 10 self-esteem 12 boastfulness 14 self-importance

conceited 4 smug, vain 7 stuck-up 8 arrogant, boasting, bragging, puffed up 9 bombastic, overproud, strutting 11 egotistical, swellheaded 12 vainglorious 13 self-important

conceivable 8 credible, knowable, possible 9 thinkable 10 believable, imaginable, supposable 11 perceivable

conceive 4 form 5 frame, hatch, start 6 create, invent 7 concoct, dream up, imagine, produce, think of, think up 8 consider, contrive, envisage, envision, initiate 9 originate 10 comprehend, understand

concentrate 4 mass 5 amass, bunch, focus, hem in 6 center, gather, heap up, reduce 7 close in, cluster, pay heed, thicken 8 assemble, attend to, condense, converge, fasten on 10 accumulate, congregate 11 bring to bear 12 direct toward

concentrated 7 dense 7 crowded, focused, thought 8 centered 10 compressed

concentration 4 mass 5 focus 7 cluster 9 diligence, gathering, reduction 10 absorption, assemblage, collection, intentness, thickening 11 aggregation, boiling down, convergence, deep thought, engrossment 12 accumulation 13 concentrating, consolidation 14 centralization

concept 4 idea, view 5 image 6 belief, notion, theory 7 opinion, surmise, thought 9 postulate 10 conviction, hypothesis, impression 11 supposition

conception 4 idea 5 birth, image, start 6 notion 7 forming, genesis, inkling, picture 8 creating, devising, hatching 9 beginning, formation, imagining, inception, invention, launching 10 conceiving, concocting, initiation, perception 11 envisioning, formulation, originating 12 apprehension 13 fertilization, understanding 16 becoming pregnant

conceptual 8 abstract 9 visionary 11 conjectural, ideological, speculative, theoretical 12 experimental, hypothetical 15 impressionistic

concern 3 job 4 care, duty, firm, heed 5 chore, house, store, touch, worry 6 affair, affect, charge, matter, occupy, regard 7 anxiety, apply to, company, disturb, involve, mission, trouble 8 bear upon, business, distress, interest, relate to 9 attention, pertain to 10 disconcert, enterprise, solicitude 11 appertain to, corporation, disturbance, involvement, undertaking 12 apprehension 13 consideration, establishment 14 thoughtfulness

concerned 5 upset 6 active, caring, uneasy 7 alarmed, anxious, engaged, fearful, worried 8 involved, troubled 9 attentive, committed, disturbed 10 disquieted, distressed, interested, solicitous 12 apprehensive 13 participating

concerning 2 of, on, re 3 for 4 as to, over, upon 5 about, anent 7 apropos 8 engaging, touching, worrying 9 affecting, involving, mattering, regarding 10 relating to, respecting

concert 5 union, unity 6 accord, settle 7 concord, harmony 8 teamwork 9 agreement, congruity, unanimity 10 accordance, complicity 11 association, cooperation 13 collaboration 14 correspondence 18 musical performance

concerted 5 joint 6 united 7 planned 8 by assent 10 agreed upon 11 cooperative, prearranged 12 premeditated 13 predetermined

concert hall 9 music hall 10 auditorium 12 symphony hall

concession 5 lease 6 assent 8 giving in, yielding 9 admission, franchise, privilege 10 adjustment, compromise, indulgence 12 acquiescence, modification 14 acknowledgment

Conch
  form: 7 trumpet
  made of: 5 shell
  owned by: 7 Tritons

Conchobar
  origin: 5 Irish
  king of: 6 Ulster
  nephew: 10 Cuchulainn

concierge 7 janitor 9 custodian 10 doorkeeper

conciliate 6 pacify 7 appease, placate 9 make peace, reconcile 11 accommodate

conciliation 11 appeasement, peacemaking 12 propitiation 13 accommodation 14 reconciliation

conciliatory 8 friendly 9 appeasing, pacifying, placatory 10 mollifying, reassuring 11 peacemaking, reconciling 13 accommodative

concise 5 brief, pithy, short, terse 7 compact 8 succinct 9 condensed 10 to the point 11 abbreviated

conciseness 7 brevity 9 terseness 11 compactness 12 condensation, succinctness

conclave 6 parley, powwow 7 council, meeting, session 8 assembly 10 conference, convention 11 convocation 13 secret council

conclude 3 end 4 halt, stop 5 close, infer, judge 6 decide, deduce, effect, finish, gather, reason, settle 7 arrange, resolve, surmise 8 break off, carry out, complete 9 determine, terminate 10 accomplish 11 bring to pass, discontinue 12 draw to a close

concluded 5 bound, ended, guess 6 closed, judged 7 decided, deduced, expired, settled, wound up 9 completed 10 culminated, determined, restrained, terminated

conclusion 3 end 5 close 6 finale, finish, result, upshot, windup 7 finding, outcome 8 decision, judgment 9 agreement, deduc-

tion, final part, inference, summation 10 completion, denouement, resolution, settlement, working out 11 arrangement, presumption, termination 13 determination

conclusive 5 clear 6 patent 7 certain, obvious 8 absolute, decisive, definite, manifest, palpable 9 clinching 10 compelling, convincing, undeniable 11 categorical, determining, inescapable, irrefutable 12 demonstrable, unanswerable 13 incontestable, unimpeachable 14 unquestionable 16 incontrovertible

concoct 3 mix 4 brew 5 frame, hatch 6 cook up, create, devise, invent, make up 7 think up 8 compound, contrive 9 fabricate, formulate

concoction 4 brew 5 blend 6 jumble, medley 7 mixture 8 compound, creation 9 invention, potpourri 11 contrivance, fabrication 14 conglomeration

concomitant 7 related 9 accessory, attendant, connected, corollary, secondary 10 additional 12 accompanying, contributing, supplemental 13 complementary

concord 5 amity, peace 6 accord 7 harmony 8 goodwill 9 agreement 10 friendship 11 amicability, cooperation 16 cordial relations 19 mutual understanding

concordance 5 index 6 accord 7 concord 9 agreement, consensus, unanimity 17 meeting of the minds

concordant 6 unison 7 calming 8 agreeing, unifying 9 assenting, consonant 10 concurrent, harmonious

concordat 4 pact 8 covenant 9 agreement

Concordia
  origin: 5 Roman
  goddess of: 5 peace 7 harmony

concourse 7 conflux, joining, linkage, meeting 8 junction 9 amassment 10 assembling, concursion, confluence 11 aggregation, association, convergence 12 congregation, focalization 13 concentration 14 conglomeration 15 flowing together 16 flocking together

concrete 4 real 5 solid 6 cement 7 express, factual, precise 8 definite, distinct, explicit, material, specific, tangible 10 particular 11 fused stones, substantial 12 alloyed rocks

concupiscence 4 itch, lust 6 desire 7 craving, lechery, longing, passion 8 appetite, hot pants, lewdness, satyrism 9 horniness, lubricity, prurience, randiness 10 wantonness 11 goatishness, libertinism, lustfulness 12 sexual desire 13 lecherousness 14 lasciviousness, libidinousness

concur 5 agree, match, tally 6 square 7 conform 8 coincide, hold with 9 be uniform 10 be in accord, correspond 11 go along with 12 go hand in hand

concur in 7 approve 9 agree with 11 go along with

concurrence, concurrency 6 accord 7 concord, consent, harmony 8 approval 9 agreement, consensus, unanimity 10 acceptance, conformity 11 affirmation, coexistence, coincidence, conjuncture, cooperation, synchronism 12 acquiescence 13 collaboration, mutual consent 14 correspondence 15 working together 17 meeting of the minds 22 simultaneous occurrence

concurrent 5 at one 6 allied 7 aligned 8 agreeing, matching 9 congenial, congruous, consonant 10 coexisting, coincident, coinciding, compatible, harmonious 11 in agreement, sympathetic, synchronous 12 commensurate, contemporary, in accordance, simultaneous 13 correspondent, of the same mind 15 contemporaneous

concurring 8 agreeing 10 consenting 11 affirmative, in agreement, synchronous 12 coincidental, simultaneous 13 corresponding

concussion 3 jar 4 blow, bump 5 clash, shock 6 buffet, impact 7 shaking 8 pounding 9 agitation, collision 11 brain injury

condemn 4 damn, doom 5 decry 6 rebuke 7 censure, denounce, sentence 9 criticize, proscribe, reprehend 10 disapprove

condemnation 6 rebuke 7 censure, reproof 8 judgment, reproach, sentence 9 criticism 10 conviction, punishment 11 disapproval 12 denunciation, reprehension 14 disapprobation 20 pronouncement of guilt

condensation 6 digest 9 reduction 10 abridgment 13 shortened form 16 condensed version

condense 3 cut 4 trim 6 digest, reduce 7 abridge, compact, liquefy, shorten, thicken 8 boil down, compress, contract, pare down 10 abbreviate, blue-pencil 11 concentrate, consolidate, precipitate

condensed form 6 digest 7 summary 8 synopsis 10 shortening 11 abridgement, compression, contraction, curtailment 12 abbreviation

condescend 5 deign, stoop 6 submit, unbend 7 descend, disdain 9 patronize 10 look down on, talk down to 12 come down a peg, lower oneself 13 humble oneself

condescending 7 high-hat 8 superior 10 disdainful 11 overbearing, patronizing

condescension 6 airs 7 disdain, hauteur, modesty 8 humility 9 deference, loftiness 10 humbleness 11 haughtiness 12 graciousness 13 self-abasement 14 self-effacement 19 patronizing attitude 20 assumption of equality 21 high-and-mighty attitude

condign 3 due 4 fair, just, meet 5 right 6 earned, proper, worthy 7 fitting, merited 8 deserved, suitable 9 warranted 11 appropriate

condiment 4 herb 5 sauce, spice 8 dressing, flavorer, seasoner 9 seasoning
kind: 3 bay 4 dill, mace, mint, sage, salt 5 caper, clove, curry, onion, thyme 6 catsup, garlic, ginger, nutmeg, pepper, pickle, relish 7 caraway, chutney, ketchup, mustard, parsley, oregano, paprika, pimento, tabasco, vinegar 8 cardamon, marjoram, turmeric 9 pimpernel 10 bell pepper, mayonnaise

condition 3 fit 4 term 5 adapt, equip, ready, shape, state, train 6 demand, fettle, malady, status, tone up 7 ailment, prepare, problem, proviso 8 accustom, position, standing 9 agreement, complaint, provision, requisite, situation 10 limitation, make used to, put in shape 11 arrangement, contingency, malfunction, reservation, restriction, stipulation 12 prerequisite 13 circumstances, qualification, state of health 14 state of affairs 15 physical fitness

conditional 7 limited 9 dependent, qualified, tentative 10 contingent, restricted 11 provisional, stipulative 16 with reservations

condolence 4 pity 6 solace 7 comfort 8 sympathy 10 compassion 11 consolation 13 commiseration

Condon, Richard
  author of: 11 Winter Kills 18 Death of a Politician 22 The Manchurian Candidate

condonation 11 forgiveness, overlooking 12 disregarding 13 putting up with

condone 6 excuse, forget, ignore, pardon, wink at 7 absolve, forgive, justify, let pass 8 overlook 9 disregard, put up with

conduce 3 aid 4 help, lead, tend 5 bring, favor, guide 6 effect 7 advance, forward, further, promote 10 contribute

conducive 7 helpful 8 salutary 9 favorable, promotive 10 beneficial 11 expeditious 12 contributive, contributory, instrumental 19 calculated to produce 22 helpful in bringing about

conduct 3 act 4 bear, lead, rule, ways 5 carry, chair, deeds, enact, guide, pilot, steer, usher 6 action, attend, behave, convey, convoy, direct, escort, govern, manage, manner 7 carry on, comport, control, execute, marshal, operate, perform 8 behavior, carry out, dispatch, guidance, regulate, transact 9 accompany, direction, discharge, look after, supervise 10 administer, deportment, government, leadership, management 11 comportment, generalship, preside over, superintend, supervision 14 administration

conduct oneself 3 act 6 behave 13 acquit oneself 14 comport oneself

conductor 3 cad 5 guide 6 carman, escort, leader 7 cathode, channel, maestro, manager 8 aqueduct, batonist, cicerone, conveyor, director, operator, stickman, trainman 9 collector, drum major 10 impresario, supervisor 11 choirmaster, transmitter 13 concert master

conduit 4 duct, main, pipe, tube 5 canal, drain, flume, sewer 6 gutter, trough 7 channel, passage 8 aqueduct 11 watercourse

cone 5 bevel, shape, spire 6 bobbin, conoid, funnel 7 pyramid, volcano 8 pyramid
  kind: 3 fir 4 pine 5 larch 7 conifer, retinal 8 ice cream

confabulate 4 chat, talk 6 confer, patter 7 chatter, discuss 8 chitchat, converse, talk idly confabulation 4 chat, talk 8 chitchat 10 conference, discussion 12 conversation

confection 3 jam 5 candy 6 pastry 7 dessert 8 conserve, delicacy 9 preserves, sweetmeat 10 sugar candy

confectionery 5 candy 6 sweets 7 goodies, pasties 10 sugar candy, sweetmeats

confederacy, Confederacy 3 CSA 4 band, bloc 5 guild, union 6 fusion, league 7 combine, society 8 alliance, the South 9 coalition, syndicate 10 federation 11 association 13 confederation 14 Southern states 18 secessionist states 26 Confederate States of America

confederate 4 ally 5 merge, unite 6 cohort, helper 7 abettor, comrade, partner 8 coalesce, coworker 9 accessory, affiliate, associate, colleague, companion 10 accomplice, cooperator, join forces 11 consolidate, helping hand 12 band together, collaborator, right hand man 17 fellow conspirator

Confederates
  author: 14 Thomas Keneally

confederation 4 band 5 guild, union 6 fusion, league 7 combine, society 8 alliance 9 coalition, syndicate 10 federation 11 association, confederacy

confer 4 give 5 award 6 accord, parley 7 consult, discuss, palaver 8 converse 9 present to 10 bestow upon 12 compare notes, talk together 15 hold a conference 18 deliberate together

conference 4 talk 6 parley 7 council, meeting, seminar 8 conclave 9 symposium 10 convention, discussion 12 consultation, deliberation

conferment 4 gift 5 award 8 bestowal 12 presentation

confess 4 avow, sing 5 admit, own up 6 expose, reveal 7 declare, divulge, lay bare 8 blurt out, disclose 9 come clean, make known 11 acknowledge 12 bring to light 14 unbosom oneself 18 make a clean breast of

confessed 6 avowed 8 admitted 9 professed 12 self-declared 14 self-proclaimed

confession 6 avowal, shrift 9 admission 10 disclosure, divulgence, revelation 11 declaration 12 confessional 14 acknowledgment

Confessions of an English Opium Eater
  author: 15 Thomas DeQuincey

Confessions of Nat Turner, The
  author: 13 William Styron

confidant, confidante 5 crony 6 friend 8 intimate 10 bosom buddy 15 trusty companion

confide 6 impart, reveal 7 confess, divulge, lay bare, let in on, let know 8 disclose 9 make known 10 tell secretly 13 tell privately 14 unbosom oneself

confidence 4 grit, guts 5 faith, nerve, pluck, spunk, trust 6 belief, daring, mettle, secret, spirit 7 courage 8 audacity, boldness, credence, intimacy, reliance 9 certainty, certitude 10 conviction 11 intrepidity 12 self-reliance 13 private matter, self-assurance 14 faith in oneself 17 inside information

confidence man 4 cheat 5 con man 8 swindler 9 charlatan, trickster 10 mountebank

confident 4 bold, sure 5 cocky 6 daring, secure 7 assured, certain 8 cocksure, intrepid, positive 9 convinced, dauntless, expectant 10 optimistic 11 self-assured, self-reliant 13 sure of oneself

confidential 5 privy 6 secret 7 private 8 hush-hush 9 top-secret 10 classified 11 undisclosed 12 off-the-record 16 not to be disclosed

confidentially 7 sub rosa 8 in secret, secretly 9 privately 16 between ourselves 17 behind closed doors
  French: 9 entre nous

confiding 6 trusty 7 reliant 8 trustful, trusting 9 confident 11 trustworthy

configuration 4 form 6 design, makeup 11 arrangement, composition

confine 3 pen, tie 4 bind, cage, hold, jail, keep 5 limit 6 coop up, govern, keep in, lock up, shut in, shut up 7 fence in, impound 8 imprison, regulate, restrain, restrict 9 sequester 11 incarcerate 13 hold in custody

confined 5 close, tight 6 jailed, narrow 7 cramped 8 locked up 10 imprisoned, restricted

confinement 7 custody, lying in 9 cooping up, detention, restraint 10 childbirth, constraint, limitation, shutting in 11 parturition, restriction 12 accouchement, imprisonment 13 incarceration 15 circumscription

confines 4 edge 6 border, bounds, limits 7 margins 8 precinct 10 boundaries 13 circumference

confirm 5 prove 6 accept, clinch, ratify, uphold, verify 7 agree to, approve, bear out, certify, sustain 8 make firm, validate 9 authorize, establish 11 acknowledge, corroborate, make binding, make certain 12 authenticate, substantiate

confirmation 5 proof 6 assent 8 approval, sanction 9 agreement 10 acceptance, validation 11 affirmation, endorsement 12 ratification, verification 13 corroboration 14 authentication, substantiation

confirmed 3 set 5 fixed 7 chronic 8 hardened, verified 9 ingrained, validated 10 deep-rooted, deep-seated, inveterate, proven true 11 established 12 corroborated 13 authenticated, dyed-in-the-wool, substantiated

confiscate 4 take 5 seize 7 impound, possess, preempt 8 take over 9 sequester 10 commandeer 11 appropriate, expropriate

confiscation 7 seizure 10 impounding, preemption 13 appropriation, commandeering, expropriation

conflagration 4 fire 5 blaze 7 bonfire, inferno 8 conflict, fighting, wildfire 9 brush fire, firestorm, holocaust 10 forest fire, raging fire, wall of fire 11 sea of flames 12 sheet of flame

conflagrative 8 burnable 9 flammable, ignitable 10 combustive, incendiary 11 combustible, inflammable

conflict 4 fray 5 clash, fight, melee, set-to 6 action, battle, combat, fracas, oppose, strife, tussle 7 collide, discord, dissent, scuffle, warfare 8 disagree, division, friction, skirmish, struggle, variance 9 encounter, hostility 10 antagonism, be contrary, difference, dissension, engagement 12 disagreement 13 confrontation 14 be inharmonious 15 be contradictory
  Spanish: 9 mano a mano

conflicting 7 warring 8 clashing, opposing 10 ambivalent 13 contradictory

confluence 5 union 7 conflux, joining, linkage, meeting 8 junction, juncture 9 concourse, gathering 10 assembling, concursion 11 association, convergence 13 concentration 14 coming together 15 flowing together

conform 4 fit 4 obey 5 adapt 6 adjust, follow 8 adhere to, jibe with, submit to 9 agree with, reconcile, tally with 10 be guided by, comply with, fall in with, square with 11 acquiesce in 12 correspond to

conformable 8 amenable 9 agreeable, malleable 10 submissive 12 in compliance

conformance 7 harmony 9 agreement 10 accordance, compliance, conformity 13 compatibility

conformation 4 form 5 build, shape 6 figure 7 anatomy 9 formation, framework, structure 11 arrangement 13 configuration

conformist 12 well-adjusted 13 unadventurous

conformity 6 accord, assent 7 harmony 8 likeness 9 agreement, obedience 10 compliance, observance, similarity, submission, uniformity 11 resemblance 12 acquiescence 14 correspondence 15 conventionality

confound 4 amaze, mix up 6 baffle, puzzle, rattle 7 astound, confuse, fluster, mystify, nonplus, perplex, startle 8 astonish, bewilder, dumfound, surprise, unsettle 10 disconcert 11 flabbergast 16 strike with wonder, throw off the scent

confounded 8 confused 10 bewildered, nonplussed 11 dumbfounded 12 disconcerted

confraternity 4 body 5 guild, union 7 society 8 sodality 9 confrairy 11 association, brotherhood

confrere 3 pal 4 ally, chum 5 buddy 6 friend 7 brother, comrade, partner 9 associate, colleague

confront 4 dare, defy, face, meet 5 brave 8 cope with, face up to 9 challenge, encounter, withstand

confrontation 5 clash, run-in, set-to 6 battle, combat, debate 7 contest, dispute, face-off 8 conflict, showdown, skirmish 9 encounter 10 engagement, opposition 11 controversy 17 face-to-face meeting
  Spanish: 9 mano a mano

Confucius
  author of: 10 Book of Odes 11 The Analects

confuse 5 addle, befog, mix up, stump 6 baffle, muddle, puzzle, rattle 7 fluster, mistake, mystify, nonplus, perplex 8 befuddle, bewilder, confound, unsettle 10 discompose, disconcert 11 make unclear 12 make baffling 14 make perplexing 17 throw into disorder

confused 5 fazed 6 addled 7 abashed, baffled, chaotic, jumbled, mixed-up, muddled, tangled 8 rambling 9 befuddled, illogical, perplexed, unsettled 10 bewildered, disjointed, distracted, incoherent, nonplussed 11 dumbfounded 12 disconcerted, disorganized 13 disharmonious, heterogeneous

confusing 7 addling 8 baffling, blinding, blurring, dizzying, jumbling, mixing up, muddling 9 deranging, mistaking 10 befuddling, disorderly, flustering, mystifying, perplexing, stupefying 11 bewildering, confounding 13 disconcerting, unintelligible

confusion 4 mess, riot 5 chaos, snarl 6 bedlam, hubbub, jumble, muddle, tangle, tumult, uproar 7 clutter, ferment, turmoil 8 disarray, disorder, madhouse, shambles, upheaval 9 abashment, commotion 10 bafflement, hodgepodge, hullabaloo, perplexity, puzzlement, untidiness 11 disturbance, pandemonium 12 bewilderment, discomposure, stupefaction 13 mystification 14 disarrangement, disconcertment 15 disorganization
  French: 14 bouleversement

confutation 6 denial 7 counter 8 negation, rebuttal 10 refutation 13 contradiction

confute 4 deny 5 rebut 6 impugn, oppose, refute 7 counter, gainsay 10 contradict, controvert 12 be contrary to

congeal 3 set 4 clot, jell 6 curdle, freeze, harden 7 stiffen, thicken 8 solidify 9 coagulate 10 gelatinize

congenial 4 like 6 genial, social 7 affable, cordial, kindred, related, similar 8 agreeing, amenable, gracious, pleasant, pleasing, sociable 9 agreeable, convivial 10 compatible, consistent, harmonious, well-suited 11 sympathetic 13 companionable, corresponding
  French: 9 en rapport
  German: 9 gemutlich

congeniality 7 harmony, rapport 8 affinity 11 sociability 12 conviviality, friendliness, pleasantness 13 compatibility 14 like-mindedness

congenital 6 inborn, inbred, innate, native 7 natural 8 inherent 9 ingrained, inherited, intrinsic 10 hereditary

congested 6 filled, gorged, jammed, packed 7 crowded 9 saturated 11 overcrowded

congestion 3 jam, mob 4 mass 5 snarl 6 pile-up 8 crowding 10 bottleneck 11 obstruction 12 overcrowding

conglomerate 4 heap, mass, pile **5** amass, blend, stack **7** mixture **8** assemble **9** aggregate **10** accumulate, assemblage **12** accumulation **16** large corporation

conglomeration 6 jumble, medley **7** mixture **8** mishmash **9** aggregate, potpourri **10** assortment, collection, hodgepodge **11** aggregation, combination **13** agglomeration

Congo

other name: 10 Moyen Congo **11** Middle Congo

capital/largest city: 11 Brazzaville

others: 3 Ewo **4** Boko **5** Epena, Kayes, Kelle, Okoyo, Sembe **6** Dongou, Komono, Makoua, Matadi, M'Binda, M'Vouti, Ouesso, Sibiti, Zanaga **7** Cabinda, Dolisie, Etoumbi, Gamboma, Kinkala, Loubomo, Loudima, Madingo, Mossaka, Souanke **8** Djambala, Impfondo, Kibangou, Madingou, Mindouli **9** Mossendjo **11** Fort-Rousset, Pointe-Noire **17** Mayombe Escarpment

school: 13 Marien Ngoubai

monetary unit: 5 franc **7** centime

lake: 5 Mweru, Tumba **6** Albert, Nyanza, Upemba **7** Leopold **11** Stanley Pool

highest point: 6 Leketi

river: 3 Dja **4** Uele **5** Alima, Congo, Kasal, Kwilu, Lulua, Ngoko, Niari, Sanga, Swilu, Wamba, Zahir, Zaire **6** Kwango, Kwenge, Loange, Lobaye, Lomami, Ogooue, Ubangi **7** Aruwimu, Kouilou, Lualaba, Luapula, N'Gounie **8** Itimbiri, Likouala, Lubilash

sea: 8 Atlantic

physical feature:

plateau: 6 Bateke

people: 3 Rua **4** Akka, Susa, Teke, Vili **5** Amadi, Bantu, Figot, Kongo, Mantu, Pygmy, Sanga, Warua, Zambi **6** Ababua, Bafyot, Bateke, Mbochi, Nzambi, Wabuma **7** Bacongo, Bakongo, Bangala, Batetla, Manyema **10** Binga Pygmy

discoverer: 3 Cam

language: 4 Susu **5** Bantu, Fiote **6** French, Kituba **7** Bangala, Lingala

religion: 5 Islam **7** animism **10** Protestant **13** Roman Catholic

place:

church: 9 Saint Anne

stadium: 5 Eboue

feature:

tree: 5 limba

congratulate 4 hail **6** salute **10** compliment, felicitate, wish one joy **11** rejoice with **18** give one's best wishes **28** wish many happy returns of the day

congratulations 6 salute **9** blessings, greetings **10** best wishes, good wishes **11** well-wishing **13** felicitations **24** many happy returns of the day

congregate 4 mass **5** amass, flock, swarm **6** gather, throng **7** cluster, collect **8** assemble **12** come together **13** crowd together

congregation 5 crowd, flock, group, horde, laity **6** parish, throng **8** assembly, audience, brethren **9** gathering, multitude **12** parishioners **16** church membership **17** religious assembly

congress, Congress 4 diet **6** caucus **7** council **8** assembly **9** delegates, gathering **10** conference, convention, parliament **11** legislature **14** federal council **15** discussion group, legislative body, national council, representatives **17** chamber of deputies

Congreve, William

author of: 11 Love for Love **15** The Double-Dealer **16** The Mourning Bride, The Way of the World

congruity 7 harmony **9** agreement, coherence **10** consonance **11** consistency **12** congeniality **13** compatibility **14** correspondence **15** appropriateness

congruous 4 meet **6** seemly **7** apropos **8** becoming, relevant, suitable **9** congenial, consonant, in keeping **10** harmonious **11** appropriate, in agreement **13** corresponding

conifer

means: 11 cone bearing

order: 11 coniferales

class: 10 gymnosperm

kind: 3 fir, yew **4** pine **5** cedar, larch, pinal **6** ginkgo, pinale, spruce, torrey **7** cypress, hemlock, juniper, redwood, sequoia **8** softwood **9** evergreen

Coningsby

author: 16 Benjamin Disraeli

conjectural 7 reputed **8** abstract, academic, doubtful, putative, supposed, surmised **11** inferential, speculative, theoretical **12** hypothetical **13** suppositional **14** supposititious

conjecture 4 idea, view **5** fancy, guess, infer, judge, think **6** augury, notion, reckon, theory **7** imagine, opinion, presume, suppose, surmise **8** estimate, forecast, judgment, theorize **9** calculate, deduction, guesswork, inference, speculate, suspicion **10** assumption, guestimate, hypothesis, presuppose **11** guesstimate, hypothesize, speculation, supposition **13** shot in the dark

conjoin 4 join, knit, link **5** touch, unite **7** combine, connect, overlap **8** together **9** associate

conjoined 6 joined, linked, united **7** knitted, meeting **8** combined, touching **9** connected **10** associated **11** overlapping **14** joined together

conjugal 6 wedded **7** marital, married, nuptial, spousal **9** connubial **11** matrimonial

conjugate 4 join, pair, yoke **5** mated, unite, yoked **6** couple, joined, paired, united **7** connect, coupled, related **9** connected **10** paronymous

conjunction 5 union **7** joining, meeting **11** association, coincidence, combination, concurrence

conjuration 5 charm, spell, trick **11** incantation

conjure 5 allay, charm, raise 6 invoke, summon 7 bewitch, command, enchant 8 call away, call upon 9 call forth 10 cast a spell, make appear 13 make disappear 15 practice sorcery

conjurer 6 wizard 8 magician

conk 3 die, hit 4 bean, blow, fail, head 5 decay, faint, sleep, stall 6 fungus, strike 7 bracket 8 knock out 9 break down 10 straighten

Conn, Katherine
  real name of: 13 Kitty Carlisle

connect 3 tie 4 join 5 hinge, merge, unite 6 attach, couple, relate 7 combine, compare 9 associate, correlate 14 fasten together

connected 4 tied 6 joined, merged, united 7 coupled 8 abutting, adjacent, attached, combined, touching 9 bordering, proximate 10 connecting, contiguous, juxtaposed 12 conterminous 16 fastened together

connected group 5 cycle 6 series 8 sequence 11 progression

Connecticut
  abbreviation: 2 CT 4 Conn
  nickname: 6 Nutmeg 7 Blue Law 9 Freestone 12 Constitution 18 Land of Steady Habits
  capital/largest city: 8 Hartford
  others: 4 Avon 6 Bethel, Canaan, Cos Cob, Darien, Hamden, Mystic, Sharon, Storrs 7 Ansonia, Bristol, Danbury, Enfield, Madison, Meriden, Milford, Niantic, Norwalk, Norwich, Shelton, Tolland, Windsor 8 Guilford, New Haven, Simsbury, Stamford, Westport 9 Greenwich, Naugatuck, New London, Stratford, Waterbury 10 Bridgeport, Manchester, New Britain, Torrington 11 Wallingford
  college: 4 Yale 7 Trinity 8 Hartford, St Joseph, Wesleyan 9 Fairfield 10 Bridgeport, Quinnipiac 11 Sacred Heart 12 U S Coast Guard
  feature: 10 Charter Oak
  museum: 8 PT Barnum
  seaport: 6 Mystic
  theater: 27 American Shakespeare Festival
  tribe: 6 Pequot 7 Mohegan, Niantic 10 Quinnipiac
  people: 8 PT Barnum 9 John Brown 10 Nathan Hale 11 Noah Webster 12 Thomas Hooker 19 Harriet Beecher Stowe
  lake: 10 Candlewood
  land rank: 11 forty-eighth
  mountain: 4 Bear 7 Taconic
  hills: 10 Berkshires
  highest point: 8 Frissell
  physical feature: 15 Long Island Sound
  river: 6 Thames 9 Naugatuck 10 Housatonic 11 Connecticut
  state admission: 5 fifth
  state bird: 5 robin
  state flower: 14 mountain laurel
  state motto: 30 He Who Transplanted Still Sustains
  state song: 12 Yankee Doodle
  state tree: 8 white oak

Connecticut Yankee in King Arthur's Court, A
  author: 9 Mark Twain
  character: 5 Sandy 6 Merlin 8 Alisande, Clarence 11 Morgan le Fay 12 Hello-Central 18 Sir Kay the Seneschal

connection 3 kin, tie 4 bond, link 5 nexus 6 family, friend 7 contact, coupler, kinfolk, kinsman, linkage 8 affinity, alliance, coupling, junction, kinsfolk, relation, relative 9 associate, connector, fastening 10 attachment, kith and kin 11 association, correlation 12 acquaintance, relationship 13 flesh and blood, interrelation

Connelly, Marc
  author of: 16 The Green Pastures
  with Frank Elser: 19 The Farmer Takes a Wife
  with George S Kaufman: 5 Dulcy 11 To the Ladies 17 Beggar on Horseback, Merton of the Movies

Connery, Sean
  real name: 13 Thomas Connery
  born: 8 Scotland 9 Edinburgh
  roles: 6 Marnie 14 Robin and Marian 15 The Untouchables 16 The Molly Maguires 20 The Man Who Would Be King 28 Darby O'Gill and the Little People
  James Bond: 4 Dr No 10 Goldfinger 11 Thunderball 16 You Only Live Twice 18 Diamonds Are Forever, From Russia with Love, Never Say Never Again

connivance 4 plot 5 cabal 6 design, scheme 8 intrigue 9 collusion 10 complicity, conspiracy 11 machination

connive 3 aid 4 abet, plan, plot 5 allow 6 wink at 7 collude 8 conspire 10 be a party to 13 be accessory to, lend oneself to 14 shut one's eyes to 17 be in collusion with, cooperate secretly

conniving 4 wily 6 artful, crafty 7 cunning 8 plotting, scheming 9 designing 10 intriguing 11 calculating

connoisseur 5 judge, maven, mavin 6 expert 7 epicure, gourmet 9 authority 11 cognoscente 17 person of good taste

Connolly, Maureen
  nickname: 8 Little Mo
  sport: 6 tennis

Connor, Dale
  creator/artist of: 9 Mary Worth

connotation 5 drift 6 import, spirit 8 coloring 9 evocation, undertone 10 intimation, suggestion 11 implication, insinuation 12 significance

connote 5 imply 6 hint at 7 suggest 8 intimate 9 insinuate 11 bring to mind

connubial 6 wedded 7 marital, married, nuptial 8 conjugal 11 matrimonial

conquer 4 beat, best, drub, lick, rout, rule, trim, whip 5 floor, quell 6 defeat, humble, master, occupy, subdue, thrash 7 possess, win over 8 overcome, surmount, vanquish 9 overpower, rise above, subjugate 11 prevail over, triumph over 14 get the better of

conqueror 6 victor, winner 7 subduer 8 champion 10 subjugator, vanquisher 12 conquistador

conquest 3 fan 4 sway 5 lover 6 adorer, defeat 7 captive, mastery, triumph, victory, winning 8 adherent, follower, whip hand 9 upper hand 10 ascendancy, conquering, domination, overcoming 11 acquisition, subjugation 12 vanquishment 17 captured territory

Conrad, Joseph
    real name: 29 Josef Teodor Konrad Korzeniowski
    author of: 6 Chance 7 Lord Jim, Typhoon, Victory 8 Nostromo 13 Almayer's Folly 14 The Secret Agent 15 Heart of Darkness 16 Under Western Eyes 21 An Outcast of the Islands 23 The Nigger of the Narcissus

consanguine 4 akin 7 cognate, kindred, related 8 relative

consanguineous 3 kin 4 akin 7 kindred, related 9 connected 21 having a common ancestor

conscience 8 scruples 10 moral sense, principles 15 ethical feelings 20 sense of right and wrong

conscience-stricken 6 guilty 7 ashamed 8 contrite, penitent 9 chastened, regretful, repentant 10 remorseful 13 guilt-stricken

conscientious 5 exact 6 honest 7 careful, dutiful, ethical, upright 10 fastidious, meticulous, particular, scrupulous 11 painstaking, responsible, trustworthy 12 conscionable 14 high-principled

conscious 7 aware 7 alert to, alive to, awake to, studied 8 noticing, sensible, sentient 9 cognizant, in the know, observing 10 calculated, deliberate, discerning, perceiving 12 apperceptive, premeditated 13 knowledgeable

consciousness 4 mind 6 senses 8 feelings, thoughts 9 awareness 10 cognizance, perception 11 discernment, sensibility

conscript 3 PFC 4 boot, hire, levy 5 draft 6 call up, employ, engage, enlist, enroll, induct, muster, rookie, seaman, select, take on 7 draftee, impress, private, recruit 8 enlistee, inductee, mobilize, register, selectee, shanghai 9 conscribe 11 buck private

consecrate 5 bless 6 hallow 7 glorify 8 sanctify 10 make sacred 11 immortalize 13 declare sacred

consecrated 4 holy 7 blessed 8 hallowed 10 sanctified

consecutive 6 in turn, serial 8 unbroken 10 continuous, sequential, successive 11 progressive 13 uninterrupted 19 following one another

consensus 6 accord 7 concord 9 unanimity 11 concurrence 13 common consent 14 general opinion 15 majority opinion 16 general agreement

consent 5 agree, allow, yield 6 accede, accept, accord, assent, concur, permit, ratify, submit 7 approve, concede, concord, confirm, endorse 8 approval, sanction 9 acquiesce, agreement 10 acceptance, fall in with, permission 11 concurrence, endorsement, willingness 12 acquiescence, confirmation, ratification

Consenting Adults
    author: 12 Peter DeVries

consent to 2 OK 4 okay 6 permit 7 approve 8 accede to 10 concur with 11 acquiesce to, go along with 14 give the go-ahead

consequence 3 end 4 note 5 avail, fruit, issue, value, worth 6 import, moment, result, sequel, upshot 7 account, gravity, outcome 9 aftermath, influence, magnitude, outgrowth 10 importance, notability, prominence, usefulness 11 development, distinction, seriousness 12 significance

consequent 7 ensuing 8 eventual 9 following, resulting

consequential 7 crucial, epochal 8 historic 9 important, momentous 10 meaningful 11 significant

consequently 2 so 4 ergo, then 5 and so, hence, later 9 as a result, therefore 11 accordingly 12 subsequently

conservation 4 care 6 upkeep 9 husbandry 10 careful use, protection 11 maintenance, safekeeping 12 preservation

conservative 5 quiet 6 square 7 old-line 8 cautious, moderate, undaring 9 right-wing 10 nonliberal, unchanging 11 reactionary, right-winger, traditional 13 unprogressive 15 middle-of-the-road 16 opponent of change 17 middle-of-the-roader 22 champion of the status quo

conservatoire 11 music school 12 conservatory, music academy

conservatory 7 nursery 8 hothouse 9 arboretum 10 glasshouse, greenhouse 11 music school 12 music academy 13 conservatoire

conserve 4 save 5 guard 7 care for, cut back, husband, use less 8 maintain, not waste, preserve 9 safeguard 12 use sparingly

consider 4 deem, hold, note 5 gauge, honor, judge, opine, study, think, weigh 6 ponder, regard, review 7 believe, examine, pay heed, respect 8 appraise, envision, hold to be, mull over 9 be aware of, reflect on 10 bear in mind, cogitate on, think about 11 contemplate 12 deliberate on 17 make allowances for 18 turn over in one's mind

considerable 4 tidy 5 ample, great, large 6 goodly 7 notable, sizable 8 not small 9 estimable, important 10 impressive, noteworthy, noticeable, of some size, remarkable 11 a good deal of, significant, substantial

considerably 5 amply 7 greatly, largely, notably, sizably 9 estimably 10 abundantly, noticeably, remarkably 13 significantly, substantially

considerate 4 kind 6 kindly 7 mindful 8 obliging 9 attentive, concerned 10 solicitous, thoughtful

consideration 4 heed, tact 5 cause, honor, point, study 6 factor, ground, motive, notice, reason, regard, review 7 concern, respect, thought 8 interest, judgment 9 attention 10 advisement, cogitation, inducement, kindliness, meditation, reflection, solicitude 11 examination 12 deliberation 13 contemplation 14 thoughtfulness 15 considerateness

consider closely 7 pay heed 11 concentrate 12 pay attention 13 put one's mind to 21 give one's full attention

considered 5 mused 6 deemed, heeded, judged, mulled 7 advised, express, honored, noticed, studied, thought, weighed, willful 8 believed, esteemed, looked on, pondered, regarded, supposed 9 reflected, respected, ruminated 10 deliberate, looked upon, thought out 11 deliberated, entertained, intentional 12 contemplated, premeditated, thought about

consign 5 remit 6 assign, commit, convey, remand 7 deliver, entrust 8 delegate, hand over, relegate, transfer 9 commend to 11 deposit with

consignment 8 delivery, shipment, transfer 10 assignment, committing, consigning, delegation, depositing, entrusting, relegation 11 handing over 12 goods for sale, goods shipped 19 goods sent on approval

consist 3 lie 6 reside 7 contain, include 10 be made up of 11 to be found in 13 be comprised of 14 to be composed of

consistency, consistence 4 body 5 unity 6 makeup 7 density, harmony, texture 8 firmness 9 agreement, coherence, congruity, stiffness, structure, thickness, viscosity 10 accordance, conformity, connection, uniformity 11 compactness, composition, persistence 12 construction, faithfulness, steady effort 13 compatibility, steadfastness 14 correspondence 16 uniform standards 19 constant performance, undeviating behavior

consistent 4 meet 6 steady 7 regular, unified 8 agreeing, constant, of a piece, suitable 9 congenial, congruous, consonant 10 compatible, harmonious, persistent, unchanging 11 in agreement, undeviating 13 correspondent 16 conforming to type

consolation 4 help 5 cheer 6 relief, solace, succor 7 comfort, support 8 easement, soothing, sympathy 10 condolence 11 alleviation, assuagement 13 encouragement

Consolation of Philosophy (De Consolatione Philosophiae)
   author: 31 Anicius Manlius Severinus Boethius

console 4 calm, ease 5 cheer 6 soothe, succor 7 comfort, support, sustain 10 lament with, sympathize 11 condole with 13 express sorrow 15 commiserate with 18 express sympathy for

consolidate 4 fuse, join 5 merge, unify, unite 6 league 7 combine, fortify 8 coalesce, compress, condense, federate, make firm, make sure, solidify 9 integrate, make solid 10 amalgamate, centralize, strengthen 11 concentrate, incorporate 12 band together 13 bring together

consolidation 5 union 6 fusion, merger 8 alliance 9 coalition 11 unification 12 amalgamation 13 agglomeration 14 conglomeration

consommé 4 soup 5 broth 9 madrilene

consonance 5 amity, unity 6 accord, unison 7 concord, harmony, oneness 9 agreement, coherence, congruity, unanimity 10 accordance, conformity, congruence, consonancy 11 concordance, consistency, homogeneity 13 compatibility 14 correspondence, like-mindedness

consonant 8 in accord 9 agreeable, congruous, in harmony 10 concordant, consistent 11 in agreement

consort 3 mix 4 club, mate, wife 6 mingle, spouse 7 hang out, husband, pair off, partner 8 go around, sidekick 9 accompany, associate, companion, other half, pal around, rub elbows 10 fraternize 11 keep company

conspicuous 5 clear, great, plain 6 famous, patent 7 eminent, evident, glaring, notable, obvious 8 distinct, flagrant, glorious, manifest, renowned, splendid, striking 9 arresting, brilliant, memorable, notorious, prominent, well-known 10 celebrated, easily seen, remarkable 11 illustrious, outstanding, standing out 13 distinguished, easily noticed, highly visible

conspicuousness 9 celebrity, flagrance, notoriety 10 prominence, visibility 11 obviousness 13 noticeability

conspiracy 4 plot 7 treason 8 intrigue, sedition 9 collusion, treachery 10 connivance, secret plan 11 machination 12 criminal plan 14 treasonous plan

conspirator 7 plotter, schemer, traitor 8 conniver 9 intriguer 10 subversive

conspire 5 unite 6 concur, scheme 7 collude, combine, connive 8 intrigue 9 cooperate, machinate 11 plot treason 12 work together

Constable, John
   born: 7 England 12 East Bergholt
   artwork: 10 The Haywain 12 Cloud Studies 14 Hadleigh Castle 39 Salisbury Cathedral from the Bishop's Grounds

constancy 6 fealty 7 loyalty 8 devotion 9 fixedness, stability 10 allegiance, permanence 12 faithfulness, immutability 13 dependability, invariability, steadfastness 15 trustworthiness 16 unchangeableness

constant 4 even, true 5 fixed, loyal 6 stable, steady, trusty 7 abiding, devoted, endless, eternal, regular, staunch, uniform 8 diligent, enduring, faithful, resolute, stalwart, unbroken, unvaried 9 ceaseless, continual, immutable, incessant, permanent, perpetual, steadfast, sustained, unceasing, unfailing **10** dependable, invariable, persistent, unchanging, unflagging, unswerving, unwavering **11** everlasting, never-ending, trustworthy, unalterable, undeviating, unrelenting **12** interminable, tried-and-true **13** uninterrupted

Constant Nymph, The
    director: **14** Edmund Goulding
    cast: **11** Alexis Smith **12** Charles Boyer, Joan Fontaine **14** Brenda Marshall

constellation 4 host **5** group, rally **6** circle, galaxy, nebula, spiral, throng **7** cluster, company, pattern **9** gathering **10** assemblage, collection **12** spiral nebula **13** configuration **14** island universe
    name: **3** Ara, Leo **4** Apus, Crux, Grus, Lynx, Lyra, Pavo, Vela **5** Aries, Cetus, Draco, Hydra, Indus, Lepus, Libra, Lupus, Mensa, Musca, Norma, Orion, Pyxis, Virgo **6** Antlia, Aquila, Auriga, Bootes, Caelum, Cancer, Carina, Corvus, Crater, Cygnus, Dorado, Fornax, Gemini, Hydrus, Octans, Pictor, Pisces, Puppis, Scutum, Taurus, Tucana, Volans **7** Cepheus, Columba, Lacerta, Pegasus, Perseus, Phoenix, Sagitta, Serpens, Sextans **8** Aquarius, Circinus, Equuleus, Eridanus, Hercules, Leo Minor, Scorpius, Sculptor **9** Andromeda, Centaurus, Delphinus, Monoceros, Ophiuchus, Reticulum, Ursa Major, Ursa Minor, Vulpecula **10** Canis Major, Canis Minor, Cassiopeia, Chamaeleon, Horologium, Triangulum **11** Capricornus, Sagittarius, Telescopium **12** Microscopium **13** Canes Venatici, Coma Berenices **14** Camelopardalis, Corona Borealis **15** Corona Australis, Piscis Austrinus **18** Triangulum Australe

consternation 5 alarm, panic, shock **6** dismay, fright, horror, terror **11** trepidation **12** apprehension

constituent 4 atom, part **5** piece, voter **6** factor, member **7** elective, element, essence **8** electing, integral, making up **9** component, formative, principal, supporter **10** appointing, ingredient

constitute 4 form, make, name **5** found, set up **6** create, invest, make up **7** appoint, compose, empower, produce **8** compound, delegate **9** authorize, establish, institute **10** commission

constitution 6 figure, health, make-up, mettle **7** charter, stamina, texture **8** physique, strength, vitality **9** basic laws, formation, structure **10** figuration **11** composition **12** construction **13** configuration **16** governing charter **17** physical condition **21** fundamental principles

constitutional 4 turn, walk **5** basic **6** inborn, ramble, stroll, vested **7** natural, organic **8** inherent, internal, physical **9** chartered, intrinsic **10** congenital **11** fundamental

Constitution State
    nickname of: **11** Connecticut

constrain 4 curb, urge **5** check, crush, drive, force, quash **6** coerce, compel, oblige, subdue **7** confine, enforce, put down, repress, squelch **8** hold back, pressure, restrain, restrict, suppress **9** fight down, necessity, strong-arm **14** put the screws on

constrained 3 shy **5** timid **6** forced **7** bashful **8** reserved, reticent **9** compelled, diffident **10** restricted **11** embarrassed

constraint 5 force **6** duress **7** reserve **8** coercion, pressure **9** restraint **10** compulsion, diffidence, inhibition, obligation **11** enforcement **13** necessitation

constrict 4 bind **5** choke, cramp, pinch **6** shrink **7** squeeze **8** compress, contract, strangle **11** strangulate

constriction 7 binding, choking **8** cramping, pinching **9** narrowing, shrinking, squeezing, stricture, tightness **10** constraint, strangling **11** compression, contraction

construct 4 form, make **5** build, erect, frame, set up, shape **6** create, design, devise **7** arrange, fashion **8** organize **9** fabricate, formulate

construction 4 form, make **5** build, style **6** format **7** edifice, raising, reading, rearing, version **8** building, creation, erecting **9** rendition, structure **10** fashioning, production **11** composition, elucidation, explanation, explication, fabrication, manufacture **12** conformation, constructing **13** configuration **14** interpretation **15** putting together

constructive 5 handy **6** useful **7** helpful **8** valuable **9** practical **10** beneficial, productive **12** advantageous

construe 4 read, take **7** explain, make out **8** decipher **9** elucidate, figure out, interpret, translate **10** comprehend, understand

Consuelo
    author: **10** George Sand

consul 5 envoy **8** emissary, minister **14** foreign officer, representative **15** diplomatic agent

Consul, The
    opera by: **7** Menotti
    character: **10** Magda Sorel

consult 6 confer, parley, regard **7** refer to **8** consider, talk over **9** inquire of **11** ask advice of, have an eye to **12** compare notes **13** exchange views **15** discuss together, seek counsel from, take into account **16** seek the opinion of **18** deliberate together

consultant 6 expert **7** adviser, advisor, counsel **9** discusser

consultation 7 council, hearing, meeting, palaver **9** interview **10** conference, discussion **12** deliberation

consumable 6 edible **7** eatable **10** comestible

consume 3 eat **4** gulp **5** drain, eat up, spend, use up, waste **6** absorb, devour, expend, guzzle, ravage **7** deplete, destroy, drink up, engross, exhaust **8** demolish, lay waste, squander **9** devastate, dissipate, swallow up **10** annihilate

consumed 4 used 5 burnt, drank, drunk, eaten, spent 6 used up, wasted 7 drained, outworn 8 absorbed, burned up, expended, perished 9 destroyed, engrossed, exhausted, swallowed 10 squandered 11 annihilated

consume greedily 6 devour 7 stuff in 8 bolt down, gobble up, gulp down, wolf down 12 swallow whole 13 eat ravenously 14 eat voraciously

consumer 4 user 5 buyer, drain 6 client, patron, waster 7 spender 8 customer 9 purchaser 10 dissipater, squanderer

consummate 2 do 5 sheer, total, utter 6 effect, finish 7 achieve, execute, fulfill, perfect, perform, realize, supreme 8 absolute, carry out, complete, finished, thorough 9 faultless 10 accomplish, bring about, undisputed 11 unmitigated 12 accomplished, unquestioned 13 unconditional 17 through-and-through

consummation 3 end 5 close 6 finish 9 execution 10 attainment, completion, conclusion 11 achievement, culmination, fulfillment, realization 14 accomplishment

consumption 2 TB 3 use 7 using up 9 consuming, depletion 10 exhaustion 11 expenditure, utilization 12 exploitation, tuberculosis

Consus

origin: 5 Roman

god of: 11 good counsel, horse racing

protector of: 5 grain

corresponds to: 3 Ops

contact 4 join, meet 5 reach, touch, union 7 connect, meeting 8 abutment, junction, touching 9 adjacency, get hold of 10 connection 11 association 13 communication 14 get in touch with 15 communicate with

contagion 7 disease 8 epidemic, outbreak 9 infection, spreading 13 contamination

contagious 8 catching 9 spreading 10 infectious, spreadable 12 communicable 13 transmittable

contain 4 curb, hold 5 check 6 embody, hold in 7 control, embrace, enclose, include, inhibit, involve, repress 8 hold back, keep back, restrain, suppress 11 accommodate, incorporate 12 keep the lid on 16 keep within bounds

container 3 bag, box, can, jar, vat 4 pail 6 barrel, bottle, bucket, carton, holder, vessel 10 receptacle

containment 7 control 9 restraint, retention

contaminate 4 foul, soil 5 dirty, spoil, taint 6 befoul, blight, debase, defile, infect, poison 7 corrupt, pollute 8 besmirch 10 adulterate, make impure

contamination 5 filth 7 fouling, soiling 8 dirtying, foulness, impurity, spoiling 9 dirtiness, poisoning, polluting, pollution, putridity 10 defilement 11 uncleanness 12 adulteration

Conte, Richard

real name: 18 Nicholas Peter Conte

born: 12 Jersey City NJ

roles: 8 Barabbas 13 A Bell for Adano 24 The Greatest Story Ever Told

contemplate 4 note, plan, scan 5 weigh 6 expect, gaze at, intend, ponder, regard, survey 7 examine, imagine, inspect, observe, project, stare at, think of 8 aspire to, envision, mull over, ruminate 9 muse about 10 anticipate, cogitate on, have in view, meditate on, think about 11 reflect upon 12 deliberate on 13 consider fully, look at fixedly, look forward to 14 speculate about 15 view attentively

contemplation 5 study 6 gazing, musing, seeing, survey 7 looking, reverie, thought, viewing 8 scanning, thinking 9 pondering 10 cogitation, inspection, meditation, reflection, rumination 11 examination, observation 12 deliberation 13 consideration

contemplative 6 musing 7 pensive 8 studious 9 engrossed 10 cogitative, meditative, reflective, ruminating, thoughtful 11 speculative 13 introspective, lost in thought

contemporaneous 6 coeval 10 coexistent, coincident, concurrent 11 synchronous 12 contemporary, simultaneous

contemporary 3 new 4 late 6 modern, recent, with-it 7 current 8 advanced, brand-new, up-to-date 10 coexistent, coincident, concurrent, newfangled, present-day 11 ultra-modern 12 simultaneous 13 of the same time, up-to-the-minute 15 contemporaneous

contempt 4 hate 5 scorn, shame 6 hatred 7 disdain, disgust 8 aversion, derision, disfavor, disgrace, dishonor, distaste, ignominy, loathing, ridicule 9 antipathy, disregard, disrepute, revulsion 10 abhorrence, repugnance 11 detestation, humiliation

contemptible 3 low 4 base, mean, vile 5 cheap 6 abject, paltry, shabby 8 shameful, unworthy, wretched 9 miserable, repugnant, revolting 10 despicable, detestable, disgusting 11 ignominious

contemptuous 6 lordly 7 haughty, pompous 8 arrogant, derisive, insolent, scornful, snobbish 10 disdainful 12 supercilious 13 condescending, disrespectful

contemptuousness 5 scorn 7 disdain 8 contempt, rudeness 9 arrogance, insolence

contend 3 vie, war 4 aver, avow, hold, spar 5 argue, claim, clash, fight 6 allege, assert, battle, combat, debate, insist, jostle, strive, tussle 7 compete, contest, declare, dispute, grapple, quarrel, wrestle 8 be a rival, maintain, propound, skirmish, struggle 10 put forward

content 4 area, core, gist, load, size, text 5 cheer, happy, heart, ideas, peace 6 at ease, at rest, matter, please, serene, thesis, volume 7 appease, comfort, essence, gratify, insides, meaning, pleased, satisfy, suffice, unmoved 8 capacity, make easy, pleasure, serenity, thoughts 9 contented, gratified, happiness, satisfied, set at ease, substance 10 complacent, untroubled 11 comfortable, contentment, peace of mind, unconcerned 12 satisfaction 13 gratification

contented 5 happy 6 at ease, serene 7 at peace, content, pleased 9 gratified, satisfied 11 comfortable

contentedness 4 ease 5 peace 7 comfort, content 8 pleasure, serenity 9 happiness 11 contentment 12 satisfaction 13 gratification

contention 5 clash, fight 6 battle, combat, strife 7 contest, discord, dispute, rivalry 8 argument, conflict, disunity, fighting, friction, skirmish, struggle, variance 9 assertion, encounter, wrangling 10 dissension, quarreling 11 competition, discordance 12 disagreement 13 confrontation

contentious 5 angry, cross 7 bateful, scrappy 8 captious 9 bellicose 10 pugnacious 11 belligerent, competitive, quarrelsome 12 cantankerous, disputatious 13 argumentative, controversial

contentment 4 ease 5 peace 7 comfort, content 8 pleasure, serenity 9 happiness 12 satisfaction 13 contentedness, gratification

conterminous 8 abutting, adjacent, touching 9 bordering 11 right beside 14 contiguous with

contest 3 war 4 bout, game 5 fight, match 6 battle, combat, debate, oppose, vie for 7 dispute, rivalry, tourney 8 conflict, fight for, object to, struggle 9 battle for, challenge, combat for, encounter 10 compete for, contend for, controvert, engagement, tournament 11 competition, struggle for 12 argue against 14 call in question

contestant 5 rival 6 player 7 entrant, fighter 8 competer, prospect 9 combatant, contender 10 challenger, competitor

context 6 milieu 7 climate, meaning, setting 8 ambience 9 framework, precincts, situation 10 atmosphere, background, conditions, connection 11 environment 12 relationship, surroundings 13 circumstances 16 frame of reference

contiguous 5 close, handy 6 nearby 7 close-by, tangent 8 abutting, adjacent, next-door, touching 9 adjoining, bordering, in contact 10 juxtaposed 11 neighboring 12 conterminous

continence 6 purity 8 chastity, sobriety 10 abstinence, moderation, temperance 11 forbearance 13 self-restraint

continent 4 Asia, pure 6 Africa, chaste, Europe 8 celibate, land mass, mainland, virginal 9 abstinent, Australia, temperate 10 abstemious, Antarctica 12 North America, South America

contingency 7 urgency 8 accident 9 emergency, extremity 10 likelihood 11 possibility, predicament 15 unforeseen event

contingent 9 dependent, subject to 11 conditioned 12 controlled by

continual 7 endless, eternal 8 constant, frequent, habitual, unbroken, unending 9 ceaseless, incessant, perennial, perpetual, recurring, unceasing 10 continuous, per-

sistent 11 everlasting, never-ending, oft-repeated, unremitting 12 interminable 13 uninterrupted

continually 3 aye 4 ever 6 always, steady 7 endless, eternal, forever, on and on 8 steadily 9 recurring 10 constantly, frequently, repeatedly

continuance 4 stay, term 6 extent, period 7 lasting 8 duration 9 extension 10 continuing, permanence 11 adjournment, persistence, protraction 12 continuation, perseverance, prolongation

continuation 6 sequel 8 addition, sequence 9 extension 10 continuing, supplement 11 continuance, protraction 12 prolongation

continue 4 go on, last, stay 5 abide 6 drag on, endure, extend, keep on, keep up, remain, resume, stay on 7 carry on, persist, proceed 9 persevere

continued 6 kept on, kept up, lasted, went on 7 endured 8 extended 9 carried on, persisted, proceeded, prolonged 10 persevered, protracted

continuing 6 steady 7 abiding, eternal, ongoing 8 constant, enduring, extended, unbroken, unending 9 ceaseless, incessant, perpetual, prolonged 10 dragged out, persistent, protracted 11 persevering, unremitting 12 interminable 13 uninterrupted

continuity 4 flow 5 chain 9 continuum 10 succession 11 continuance, progression 12 continuation

continuous 6 linked, steady 7 endless, eternal, lasting 8 constant, enduring, unbroken 9 ceaseless, connected, continual, extensive, incessant, perpetual, prolonged, unceasing 10 continuing, persistent, protracted, successive 11 consecutive, everlasting, persevering, progressive, unremitting 12 interminable 13 uninterrupted

continuum 4 flow 5 chain 8 sequence 10 continuity, succession 11 continuance, progression 12 continuation

contort 4 bend, warp 5 twist 6 deform 7 distort 11 be misshapen

contorted 4 bent 7 crooked, twisted 8 deformed 9 distorted

contortion 7 bending 8 twisting 10 distortion 11 crookedness

contour 4 form 5 lines, shape 6 figure 7 outline, profile 10 silhouette 11 physiognomy

contraband 11 bootlegging 13 smuggled goods 14 illegal exports, illegal imports 15 unlicensed goods 17 black-marketeering 18 prohibited articles 19 unlawful trafficking

contract 3 get 4 pact, take 5 agree, incur 6 absorb, assume, narrow, pledge, reduce, shrink, treaty 7 acquire, compact, develop, dwindle, promise, shorten, tighten 8 compress, condense, covenant, engender 9 constrict, enter into, negotiate, undertake 11 arrangement, come to terms 12 draw together, make a bargain 13 become smaller, legal document **15** sign an agreement **16** written agreement

contracted form 6 digest **7** summary **8** synopsis **9** short form **11** abridgement, compression **12** abbreviation, condensation

contraction 8 decrease **9** drawing in, lessening, narrowing, reduction, shrinkage **10** shortening, shriveling, tightening **11** compression **12** abbreviation, condensation, constriction

contradict 4 deny **5** belie, rebut **6** impugn, oppose, refute **7** confute, counter, dispute, gainsay **8** disprove **10** controvert **12** be contrary to, disagree with

contradiction 6 denial **7** counter **8** negation, rebuttal **10** refutation **11** confutation **12** disagreement

contradictory 8 contrary, opposing **10** discrepant, dissenting, refutatory **11** conflicting, disagreeing **12** antithetical, inconsistent **14** countervailing, irreconcilable

contradistinction 8 contrast **10** difference **13** dissimilarity

contraption 6 device, gadget **9** apparatus, invention **11** contrivance

contrariety 9 deviation **10** difference, divergence **13** contradiction

contrary 5 balky **7** adverse, counter, froward, hostile, opposed, wayward, willful **8** converse, inimical, opposite, stubborn, untoward **9** disparate, obstinate, unfitting **10** at variance, discordant, headstrong, refractory, unsuitable **11** conflicting, disagreeing, intractable, unfavorable **12** antagonistic, antithetical, disagreeable, inauspicious, incompatible, recalcitrant, unpropitious **13** contradictory **15** at cross purposes, unaccommodating

contrast 6 depart, differ **7** deviate, diverge **8** variance **9** disparity **10** comparison, difference, divergence, unlikeness **11** distinction **12** disagree with **13** differentiate, dissimilarity **15** differentiation, set in opposition

contrasting 8 clashing, dividing, opposing **9** comparing, differing **10** discordant, juxtaposed **14** distinguishing **15** differentiating

contravene 4 deny **5** annul, fight, spurn **6** abjure, breach, combat, disown, negate, offend, oppose, reject, resist **7** disobey, exclude, gainsay, infract, nullify, violate **8** abrogate, disclaim, overstep **9** overreach, repudiate **10** act against, contradict, infringe on, transgress **12** encroach upon **15** trespass against

contretemps 4 spat **5** clash, set-to **7** dispute, quarrel **8** argument, squabble **10** difference, falling out **12** disagreement **18** embarrassing mishap

contribute 4 give **5** endow, grant **6** bestow, confer, donate, lead to **7** advance, forward, hand out, present **9** bear a part, influence **11** have a hand in **13** be conducive to **14** help bring about

contribution 4 alms, gift **5** grant **7** charity, subsidy **8** bestowal, donation, offering **9** endowment **11** benefaction **12** dispensation

contributive 8 valuable **9** favorable **10** beneficial

contributory 9 accessory, ancillary, auxiliary **13** supplementary

contrite 6 rueful **7** humbled **8** penitent **9** chastened, regretful, repentant, sorrowful **10** apologetic, remorseful **18** conscience-stricken

contrition 6 regret **7** penance, remorse **9** atonement, penitence **10** repentance **11** compunction **12** self-reproach **18** qualms of conscience

contrivance 4 plan, plot, tool **5** gizmo, trick **6** design, device, doodad, gadget **7** machine, measure **8** artifice, intrigue **9** apparatus, implement, invention, mechanism, stratagem **10** instrument **11** contraption, machination, thingamajig

contrive 4 plan, plot **6** create, design, devise, invent, manage, scheme **7** concoct **8** maneuver **9** improvise **11** devise a plan **17** effect by stratagem

contrived 7 labored, studied **8** mannered **9** unnatural **10** artificial

contriver 7 creator, deviser **8** designer, inventor **9** architect

control 4 curb, rule, sway **5** brake, steer **6** bridle, charge, govern, manage, master, subdue **7** command, contain, mastery, repress **8** dominate, dominion, regulate, restrain, restrict **9** authority, direction, reign over, restraint, supervise **10** domination, management, manipulate, regulation **11** superintend, supervision, suppressant **12** have charge of, jurisdiction

controlled 5 ruled **6** curbed, steady, swayed **7** checked, managed, powered, servile, subdued **8** directed, governed, held back, kept down, reserved, verified **9** commanded, contained, dominated, moderated, regulated, repressed **10** authorized, regimented, restrained, supervised **11** manipulated

controlling 6 ruling **8** dominant **9** governing **10** commanding **11** influencing, predominant **13** predominating

controversial 7 at issue **8** arguable **9** debatable, polemical **10** disputable **12** questionable **13** causing debate **15** widely discussed **16** open to discussion

controversy 6 debate **7** dispute, quarrel, wrangle **8** argument, squabble **10** contention, discussion, dissension **11** altercation **12** disagreement

controvert 4 deny **5** belie, rebut **6** negate, oppose, refute **7** confute, dispute, gainsay, protest **8** confound, disprove, question **9** challenge, disaffirm **10** contradict, contravene, invalidate **12** give the lie to

contumacious 6 unruly **7** froward **8** contrary, factious, insolent, mutinous, perverse **9** fractious, seditious **10** headstrong, rebellious, refractory **11** disobedient, intractable

12 ungovernable, unmanageable **13** disrespectful, insubordinate

contumely 5 abuse, insult, scorn **7** disdain, obloquy **8** contempt, diatribe, reproach, rudeness **9** arrogance, insolence, invective, pomposity **10** opprobrium, scurrility **11** brusqueness, haughtiness **12** billingsgate, vituperation **15** overbearingness

contusion 4 hurt, mark, sore **5** mouse **6** bruise, injury, shiner **7** blemish **8** abrasion, black eye **9** black mark **13** discoloration **16** black-and-blue mark

conundrum 5 poser, rebus **6** enigma, puzzle, riddle **7** arcanum, mystery, paradox, problem, puzzler, stopper, stumper **11** brain-teaser **13** Chinese puzzle

convalesce 4 mend **5** rally **6** revive **7** improve, recover, restore **8** progress **9** get better **10** recuperate

convalescence 7 recruit **8** recovery **11** restoration **12** recuperation **14** return to health

convene 6 gather, muster, summon **7** collect, convoke, round up **8** assemble **12** call together, come together, hold a session **13** bring together

convenience 3 use **4** ease **6** chance **7** benefit, comfort, service, utility **8** facility, pleasure **9** appliance, enjoyment, handiness, work saver **10** usefulness **11** opportunity **12** availability, satisfaction, suitable time **13** accessibility, accommodation

convenient 5 handy **6** at hand, nearby, suited, useful **7** adapted, helpful **8** suitable **9** easy to use **10** beneficial **11** serviceable **12** advantageous **16** easily accessible

convent 7 nunnery **8** cloister **13** society of nuns

convention 4 code **6** caucus, custom **7** meeting, precept **8** assembly, conclave, congress, practice, propriety, protocol, standard **9** formality, gathering **10** conference, social rule **11** convocation

conventional 5 usual **6** common, normal, proper **7** regular, routine **8** accepted, orthodox, standard **9** customary **11** traditional

converge 4 meet **5** focus **8** approach **11** concentrate **12** come together **13** bring together

convergence 6 accord **8** junction **9** congruity **10** confluence **12** meeting place **14** correspondence

conversant 4 up on **5** aware **6** au fait **7** erudite, privy to, skilled, tutored **8** familiar, informed, sensible, sentient **9** au courant, cognizant, practiced **10** acquainted, proficient **12** well-informed **13** knowledgeable

conversation 3 rap **4** chat, talk **7** gabfest, palaver **8** chit-chat, dialogue **9** discourse, tete-a-tete **11** bull session **13** confabulation

Italian: **13** conversazione

Conversation, The
director: **18** Francis Ford Coppola
cast: **10** John Cazale **11** Gene Hackman **13** Allen Garfield

conversational 6 casual, chatty **8** everyday, informal **9** idiomatic **10** colloquial, vernacular

conversazione 12 conversation

converse 3 gab, jaw, rap **4** chat, chin, talk **7** palaver, reverse **8** chitchat, contrary, opposite **10** antithesis, chew the fat, chew the rag **11** confabulate **13** speak together **14** shoot the breeze

conversely 12 contrariwise **14** antithetically, on the other hand

conversion 6 change **10** changeover **12** modification **13** change of heart, metamorphosis, transmutation **14** transformation **15** change in beliefs, transfiguration **16** change of religion

convert 4 turn **6** change, modify, novice **8** neophyte **9** proselyte, transform **11** proselytize

convex 7 bulging, rounded **11** protuberant **13** curved outward

convey 4 bear, cede, deed, give, move, tell, will **5** bring, carry, grant, leave **6** impart, relate, reveal **7** conduct, consign, deliver, divulge **8** bequeath, disclose, dispatch, transfer, transmit **9** confide to, make known, transport **11** communicate

conveyance 3 bus, car, rig, van **4** cart **5** buggy, truck, wagon **7** vehicle **8** carriage, carrying, movement, transfer **9** conveying, transport **12** transmission **14** transportation

convict 3 con **4** doom **5** felon **7** condemn **8** jailbird, prisoner, yardbird **10** find guilty **11** prove guilty **13** declare guilty

conviction 4 view, zeal **5** ardor, creed, dogma, faith, fever, tenet **6** belief, fervor **7** opinion **8** doctrine, judgment, position **9** assurance, certainty, certitude, intensity, principle, viewpoint **10** persuasion **11** earnestness **13** steadfastness

convince 4 sway **6** assure **7** satisfy, win over **8** persuade **9** influence **11** bring around, prevail upon

convincing 5 sound, valid **6** cogent, potent **7** evident **8** assuring, forceful, powerful **9** plausible **10** persuading, persuasive, satisfying

convivial 5 merry **6** genial, jovial **7** affable, festive **8** friendly, sociable **9** agreeable, fun-loving **10** gregarious **13** companionable

convocation 6 caucus, muster, roster **7** council, meeting, roundup **8** assembly, conclave, congress **9** gathering **10** conference, convention **11** ingathering

convoke 4 meet, open **6** gather, muster **8** assemble, converse **11** call to order **12** call together

convolute 4 coil, wave, wavy, wind **5** twirl, twist **6** coiled, rolled, spiral, tangle **7** contort, sinuous, twisted **8** involved, spiraled **9** intricate **11** complicated **12** turn and twist

convolution 4 coil, maze **5** twist **7** coiling, winding **8** twisting **9** labyrinth, sinuosity **10** contortion, undulation **11** sinuousness **12** tortuousness

convoy 5 fleet, usher 6 column, escort 7 conduct 9 accompany, formation, safeguard 10 armed guard, protection
convulse 4 rock, stir 5 laugh, shake, spasm, wring 6 excite 7 agitate, disturb, perturb, trouble 8 double up
convulsion 3 fit 5 spasm 6 tumult 7 seizure 8 outburst, paroxysm 9 agitation, commotion 10 contortion 11 disturbance
convulsive 6 fitful 7 hurtful, rending, shaking 8 exciting, stirring 9 agitating, epileptic, spasmodic, troubling 10 disturbing
Conway, Tim
   real name: 18 Thomas Daniel Conway
   born: 12 Willoughby OH
   roles: 11 McHale's Navy 16 Carol Burnett Show 17 The Steve Allen Show
coo 6 babble, gurgle, murmur 20 whisper sweet nothings
Coogan, Jackie
   real name: 16 Jack Leslie Coogan
   wife: 11 Betty Grable
   born: 12 Los Angeles CA
   roles: 6 The Kid 9 Tom Sawyer 11 Oliver Twist, Peck's Bad Boy 15 Huckleberry Finn
cook 3 fix 4 chef, fire, heat, make 5 occur 6 cookie, doctor, happen, seethe 7 concoct, falsify, prepare, process 8 work well 9 improvise
   method: 3 fry 4 bake, boil, brew, sear, stew 5 baste, broil, grill, poach, roast, saute, scald, shirr, steam 6 braise, coddle, simmer 7 parboil 8 barbecue 9 fricassee
Cooke, Alistair
   author of: 14 One Man's America 18 A Generation on Trial 26 Around the World in Fifty Years
   TV host of: 18 Masterpiece Theatre
cooked sufficiently 4 done 5 ready 7 al dente 11 done to a turn
cookie 3 bar, gal, gul 4 cake, cook 5 wafer 6 person 7 biscuit, brownie 10 shortbread
   type: 4 oreo 5 sugar 7 oatmeal 8 macaroon, molasses 9 girl scout, tollhouse 10 gingersnap, lorna doone 12 peanut butter 13 chocolate chip
cooking, fine/gourmet
   French: 12 haute cuisine
cooking term 3 a la, cut, dot, fry 4 bake, beat, boil, chop, coat, cube, dice, dust, flan, fold, lard, roux, sear, snip, stew, toss, whip 5 aspic, au jus, baste, blend, bread, broil, brush, candy, cream, crepe, devil, dough, flake, glace, glaze, grate, grill, knead, plank, puree, roast, saute, scald, score, shirr, steep, stock, torte 6 au lait, blanch, braise, coddle, devein, dredge, fillet, flambe, fondue, render, simmer, skewer, sliver 7 a la mode, compote, crouton, garnish, goulash, liquefy, parboil, precook, preheat, rissole, scallop, stir-fry 8 aperitif, au gratin, barbecue, conserve, consomme, julienne, marinate, pot roast 9 brochette, demitasse, drippings, force-

meat, fricassee, lyonnaise, macedoine 10 caramelize, cracklings
   boneless strips of meat/ fish: 6 fillet
   clear soup: 8 bouillon, consomme
   cubed toasted bread: 7 crouton
   food cooked and served in foil or paper: 11 en papillote
   fruit preserve with nuts/raisins: 8 conserve
   fruits in syrup: 7 compote
   in the fashion: 7 a la mode
   remove veins: 6 devein
   skewered meat: 5 kebab 9 brochette
   small cup of black coffee: 9 demitasse
   thin strips: 6 sliver 8 julienne
   with cheese: 8 au gratin
   with ice cream: 7 a la mode
   with juice/with its own juices: 5 au jus
   with milk: 6 au lait
cook up 3 mix 4 brew 5 hatch 6 create, devise, invent, make up 7 concoct, think up 8 compound, contrive 9 fabricate, formulate
cool 3 icy 4 calm, cold 5 aloof, chill 6 chilly, frosty, offish, serene 7 distant, not warm 8 composed, lose heat, make cool, reserved 9 collected, impassive, uncordial, unexcited 10 become cool, cool-headed, deliberate, nonchalant, unfriendly, unsociable, untroubled 11 indifferent, stand-offish, undisturbed, unemotional, unflappable 12 slightly cold, somewhat cold, unresponsive 13 dispassionate, imperturbable, self-possessed
cooler 3 ade, can, fan, jug 4 coop, icer, jail 5 drink, icier 6 calmer, icebox, lockup, prison 11 refrigerant 12 refrigerator 14 air conditioner
Cool Hand Luke
   director: 15 Stuart Rosenberg
   cast: 8 J D Cannon 10 Jo Van Fleet, Lou Antonio, Paul Newman 12 Anthony Zerbe, Dennis Hopper 13 George Kennedy 14 Strother Martin
   Oscar for: 15 supporting actor (Kennedy)
Coolidge, Calvin
   name at birth: 18 John Calvin Coolidge
   nickname: 9 Silent Cal
   presidential rank: 9 thirtieth
   party: 10 Republican
   state represented: 2 MA
   succeeded: 7 Harding
   defeated: 5 (Frank Thomas) Johns, (Herman P) Faris, (John William) Davis 6 (William Zebulon) Foster 7 (Gilbert O) Nations, (William James) Wallace 10 (Robert Marion) La Follette
   vice president: 4 none (first term) 5 (Charles Gates) Dawes
   cabinet:
    state: 6 (Charles Evans) Hughes 7 (Frank Billings) Kellogg
    treasury: 6 (Andrew William) Mellon
    war: 5 (Dwight Filley) Davis, (John Wingate) Weeks
    attorney general: 5 (Harlan Fiske) Stone

6 (Charles B) Warren **7** (John Garibaldi) Sargent **9** (Harry Micajah) Daugherty
navy: **5** (Edwin) Denby **6** (Curtis Dwight) Wilbur
postmaster general: **3** (Harry Stewart) New
interior: **4** (Hubert) Work, (Roy Owen) West
agriculture: **4** (Howard Mason) Gore **7** (Henry Cantwell) Wallace, (William Marion) Jardine
commerce: **6** (Herbert Clark) Hoover **7** (William Fairfield) Whiting
labor: **5** (James John) Davis
born: **2** VT **13** Plymouth Notch
died: **2** MA **11** Northampton
buried: **2** VT **8** Plymouth
education:
College: **7** Amherst
later studied: **3** law
religion: **17** Congregationalist
vacation spot: **10** Black Hills
author: **32** The Autobiography of Calvin Coolidge
political career: **13** vice president
state senator/lieutenant governor/ governor of: **2** Ma **13** Massachusetts
civilian career: **6** lawyer **17** bank vice president **18** newspaper columnist
notable events of lifetime/term: **22** Pennsylvania coal strike
Act: **8** Volstead **10** Boulder Dam **11** Immigration **17** Japanese Exclusion
bribery case: **8** Elks Hill
conference: **11** Geneva Naval
flight by: **16** Charles Lindbergh
Lindbergh's plane: **15** Spirit of St Louis
Pact: **13** Kellogg-Briand
trial: **6** Scopes **12** Scopes monkey
quote: **35** (After all) the chief business of America is business **43** Spend less than you make and make more than you spend
father: **10** John Calvin
mother: **8** Victoria (Josephine Moor)
stepmother: **8** Caroline (Brown)
sibling: **13** Abigail Gratia
wife: **5** Grace (Anna Goodhue)
children: **4** John **6** Calvin
coolness 5 chill **7** dislike **8** distance **9** aloofness, composure, sangfroid **10** chilliness, detachment, frostiness **11** impassivity **12** indifference **13** lack of emotion, lack of feeling **14** unfriendliness **15** emotionlessness, standoffishness **16** imperturbability, unresponsiveness
coop 3 car, mew, pen, sty **4** auto, cage, cote **5** cramp, hutch **6** encase, prison **7** confine **8** imprison **9** enclosure **11** cooperation, cooperative
Cooper, Gary
real name: **16** Frank James Cooper
born: **8** Helena MT
roles: **8** High Noon (Oscar) **9** Beau Geste **12** Sergeant York (Oscar), The Virginian **15** A Farewell to Arms **17** Mr Deeds Goes to Town **19** For Whom the Bell Tolls, The Cowboy and the Lady **20** The Pride of the Yankees **22** North West Mounted Police

Cooper, James Fenimore
author of: **6** The Spy **8** The Bravo, The Pilot **9** Wyandotte **10** The Prairie **11** The Pioneers, The Red Rover **13** The Deerslayer, The Pathfinder, The Water-Witch **20** Leatherstocking Tales, The Last of the Mohicans
character: **4** Cora **5** Alice, Magua, Uncas **7** Hawkeye **11** Natty Bumppo **12** Chingachgook
cooperate 4 join **5** unite **7** go along, pitch in, share in **8** take part **9** join hands **10** act jointly, bear part in, join forces **11** collaborate, participate **12** pull together, work together **14** work side by side
cooperation 7 concert, detente **8** teamwork **9** agreement **10** accordance **11** concurrence, cooperating, give and take, joint action **13** collaboration, participation **15** pulling together, working together
coop up 3 pen **4** cage **5** pen in **6** closet, encage, shut in **7** confine, impound **8** restrain, restrict
coordinate 4 mesh **5** equal, match, order **6** relate **7** arrange, coequal **8** organize, parallel **9** correlate, harmonize **11** correlative, systematize **16** equally important
coordination 4 bond **5** skill **6** accord **7** harmony, liaison **10** adaptation, adjustment **12** equalization, organization **15** synchronization
cop 3 bag, nab, rob, win **4** bull, grab, take **5** bobby, catch, filch, pinch, snare, steal, swipe **6** peeler, pilfer, snatch **7** capture **8** gendarme, purchase **9** policeman **11** acquisition, policewoman **13** police officer
cope 4 face, spar **6** hurdle, manage, strive, tussle **7** contend, wrestle **8** struggle **11** hold one's own
copious 4 full **5** ample **6** lavish **7** liberal, profuse **8** abundant, generous **9** bountiful, extensive, plenteous, plentiful
copiousness 6 bounty, plenty, wealth **7** surfeit **8** fullness, plethora **9** abundance, ampleness, plenitude, profusion **10** lavishness, oversupply
Copland, Aaron
born: **10** Brooklyn NY
composer of: **5** Rodeo **9** Quiet City **10** Statements **11** Billy the Kid **12** Connotations **13** Dance Symphony, El Salon Mexico, The Tender Land **15** Outdoor Overture **17** Appalachian Spring **18** Music for a Great City, Music for the Theater
Copley, John Singleton
born: **8** Boston MA
artwork: **11** Samuel Adams **19** The Siege of Gibraltar **21** The Boy with the Squirrel **22** Brook Watson and the Shark, The Death of Major Pierson **26** The Death of the Earl of Chatham
copper
chemical symbol: **2** Cu

copper-colored 5 henna 6 auburn, russet 11 golden-brown, rust-colored 12 reddish-brown

coppice 4 bosk, wood 5 bluff, copse, firth, grove 6 forest, growth 7 boscage, thicket

Coppola, Francis Ford
  director of: 12 The Godfather (Part I) (Part II, Oscar) 13 Apocalypse Now, The Cotton Club 15 The Conversation

Copreus
  father: 6 Pelops
  son: 10 Periphetes
  herald of: 14 King Eurystheus

copse 5 brush, clump, grove 6 forest 7 coppice, thicket 8 woodland

copy 3 ape 4 fake, sham, text 5 clone, mimic, story, Xerox 6 follow, mirror, parody, repeat 7 emulate, forgery, imitate, replica 8 likeness 9 duplicate, facsimile, imitation, photostat, reportage, reproduce 10 carbon copy, manuscript 11 counterfeit, make a copy of 12 reproduction 14 representation 15 written material

coquette 4 vamp 5 flirt, tease 12 heartbreaker

coquettish 3 coy 9 kittenish 11 flirtatious

Cor 15 Biblical measure

Cora *see* 10 Persephone

coral 3 red 4 fire, pink, rose 5 horny, polyp, snake 6 orange, sea fan 8 acropora, hydrozoa, staghorn 9 gorgonian 10 sea feather 12 coelenterata

coram populo 8 publicly 15 before the public

corban 8 offering

Corbett, James (John)
  nickname: 12 Gentleman Jim
  sport: 6 boxing
  class: 11 heavyweight

cord 5 braid, twine 8 thin rope 11 heavy string
  abbreviation: 2 cd

Cordelia
  character in: 8 King Lear
  author: 11 Shakespeare

cordial 4 warm 6 genial, hearty 7 affable, amiable, sincere 8 friendly, gracious 9 heartfelt 11 good-natured 12 affectionate, wholehearted

cordiality 6 warmth 8 goodwill 9 affection, geniality, sincerity 10 affability, amiability, heartiness 11 amicability, earnestness 12 friendliness, graciousness, pleasantness 13 agreeableness

cordial relations 5 amity 6 accord 7 concord, harmony 8 goodwill 9 agreement 10 friendship 11 amicability 15 entente cordiale

cordon 4 cord, ring, rope 6 circle 8 encircle

cordon bleu 4 bird 5 finch 7 waxbill 10 red cheeked 11 estrildidae
  school for: 5 chefs 7 cooking
  where: 5 Paris 6 France

  founded by: 13 Marthe Distell
  means: 10 blue ribbon

core 3 nub 4 crux, gist, guts, meat, pith 5 heart 6 center, kernel 7 essence, nucleus 9 substance 10 brass tacks 11 central part, nitty-gritty 13 essential part, innermost part 15 sum and substance

Corelli, Arcangelo
  born: 5 Imola, Italy
  composer of: 7 La Folia (sonata No 12) 14 Concerti Grossi

Coresus
  form: 6 priest
  father: 6 Asopus
  loved: 10 Callirrhoe
  rejected by: 10 Callirrhoe

coriander
  botanical name: 17 Coriandrum sativum
  origin: 13 Mediterranean
  color: 5 brown, white 6 yellow
  flavor: 4 sage 5 cumin 7 caraway 9 lemon peel
  candy: 6 comfit

Corinth, Lovis
  born: 6 Tapiau 7 Prussia
  artwork: 6 Salome 8 Ecce Homo 10 Apocalypse 29 The Walchensee with a Yellow Field

Corinthus
  founder of: 7 Corinth
  possible father: 4 Zeus 8 Marathon

Coriolanus
  author: 18 William Shakespeare
  character: 8 Cominius, Virgilia, Volumnia 12 Junius Brutus, Titus Lartius 14 Tullus Aufidius 15 Menenius Agrippa, Sicinius Velutus 22 Caius Marcius Coriolanus

cork 3 bob, oak 4 bark, bung, plug, seal, stop 5 check, close, float 7 confine, filling stopper, stopple 8 restrain, suppress 10 insulation

corker 3 ace 4 whiz 7 stopper 8 clencher, striking, top notch 9 excellent, humdinger 10 remarkable 11 astonishing

corkscrew 4 coil, curl 5 twist 6 spiral 7 winding 10 serpentine 12 bottle opener

Corleone family
  characters in: 12 The Godfather
  author: 4 Puzo
  member: 5 Sonny 7 Don Vito, Freddie, Michael

corn 4 cure 5 grain 6 callus 7 Zea Mays 8 preserve, schmaltz 9 vegetable
  varieties: 3 Pod 4 Crow, Dent, Rice, Sand 5 Broom, Flint, Kafir, maize, Sugar, Sweet 6 Indian, Turkey 8 Egyptian, Squirrel
  bread/cake: 4 pone 7 hoecake 8 tortilla 9 hushpuppy 10 johnnycake
  beverage: 7 bourbon, whiskey

Corncracker State
  nickname of: 8 Kentucky

Corneille, Pierre
  author of: 5 Cinna, Le Cid, Medea, Medee 6 Horace, The Cid 8 Nicomede 9 Polyeucte

Cornelius, Peter von (van)
 born: 7 Germany 10 Dusseldorf
 artwork: 12 Last Judgment 24 The Wise
  and Foolish Virgins 30 The Four Horsemen of the Apocalypse

Cornell, Katharine
 nickname: 21 first lady of the theater
 born: 6 Berlin 7 Germany
 roles: 8 Dear Liar 9 Saint Joan 18 Antony and Cleopatra 26 The Barretts of
  Wimpole Street

corner 3 fix, jam, nab 4 bend, grab, hole,
 nail, nook, spot, trap 5 angle, seize 6 collar, pickle, plight, scrape 7 dead end, dilemma, impasse 10 blind alley, pigeonhole
 11 predicament

cornerstone 4 base 5 basis 9 principle 10
 foundation 11 fundamental

cornet 4 cone, horn 7 trumpet 9 corno-
 pean

Cornhuskers, The
 author: 12 Carl Sandburg

Cornhusker State
 nickname of: 8 Nebraska

cornice 4 drip 5 ancon, crown 7 molding,
 valance 8 astragal

Cornopian see 8 Hercules

Cornwallis, Charles
 also: 10 second Earl 13 first Marquess
 nationality: 7 British
 served in: 5 India 7 Ireland 18 American
  Revolution
 battle: 8 Yorktown 10 Brandywine
 captured: 10 Charleston 12 Philadelphia
 surrendered at: 8 Yorktown

Cornwell, David
 real name of: 11 John Le Carre

corny 5 banal, hokey, inane, stale, tired,
 trite, vapid 6 jejune, square 7 fatuous, insipid 8 bromidic, ordinary, shopworn 9
 hackneyed 10 threadbare, unoriginal
 11 commonplace, stereotyped 12
 cliche-ridden, old-fashioned 13 platitudinous, unimaginative 15 unsophisticated

Coroebus
 form: 4 hero
 home: 5 Argos
 father: 6 Mygdon
 built: 6 temple
 temple honored: 6 Apollo
 killed: 5 Poena
 killed by: 8 Diomedes

corona 4 halo, ring 5 cigar 6 circle, nimbus

coronet 5 tiara 6 diadem 7 chaplet, circlet
 10 small crown

Coronis
 form: 5 nymph 8 princess
 father: 9 Phylegyas
 husband: 6 Ischys
 son: 9 Asclepius
 cared for: 8 Dionysus
 killed by: 6 Apollo

Coronus
 king of: 7 Lapiths
 father: 7 Caeneus

 son: 8 Leonteus
 daughter: 10 Anaxirrhoe
 companion: 5 Jason

Corot, Jean-Baptiste-Camille
 born: 5 Paris 6 France
 artwork: 9 Pastorale 11 Ville d'Avray,
  Woman in Blue 15 Woman with a Pearl
  16 The Farnese Garden, Woman in the
  Studio 21 Memory of Mortefontaine 23
  Souvenir de Mortefontaine

corporal 6 bodily 8 physical 9 corporeal

corporation 7 combine, company 9 syndicate 11 association 14 conglomeration

corporeal 6 bodily, mortal 7 worldly 8 material, physical 11 perceptible 12 nonspiritual

corps 4 band, crew, team 5 force, party,
 squad, troop 6 outfit

corpse 4 body 5 stiff 7 cadaver, remains 8
 dead body

corpselike 4 pale 5 ashen 6 pallid 9 bloodless, deathlike 10 cadaverous

corpulent 3 fat 5 dumpy, hefty, obese,
 plump, pudgy, stout 6 chubby, chunky,
 fleshy, portly, rotund 7 lumpish, well-fed 8
 roly-poly 10 overweight, well-padded

corral 4 herd 5 pen 6 shut in 7 enclose,
 fence in, round up

correct 3 fit, fix 4 true 5 alter, amend,
 chide, exact, right, scold 6 adjust, berate,
 change, modify, proper, punish, rebuke,
 remedy, repair, revamp, revise, rework,
 seemly 7 censure, chasten, factual, fitting,
 improve, lecture, perfect, precise, rectify,
 reprove 8 accurate, admonish, becoming,
 chastise, flawless, regulate, suitable, unerring 9 castigate, dress down, faultless,
 make right, reprimand 10 acceptable, discipline, take to task 11 appropriate 12 conventional 16 haul over the coals, read the
 riot act to

correction 6 change 8 revision 10 adjustment, alteration, discipline, emendation,
 punishment 11 castigation, improvement,
 reformation 12 chastisement, modification
 13 rectification

corrective 7 counter 8 remedial 9 improving 10 palliative, rectifying 11 reformatory,
 restorative, therapeutic 12 ameliorative,
 compensatory 13 counteractive 16 coun-
 terbalancing

correctness 8 accuracy 9 exactness, precision, propriety, rightness 10 exactitude,
 seemliness 11 suitability 12 becomingness, flawlessness 13 acceptability

Correggio
 real name: 14 Antonio Allegri
 born: 5 Italy 6 Emilia 9 Correggio
 artwork: 5 Danae 12 Jupiter and Io 14
  Leda and the Swan 17 The Rape of
  Ganymede 21 The Madonna of St
  Francis 23 Adoration of the Shepherds
  28 Mystic Marriages of St Catherine

correlate 7 compare, connect 8 parallel 10 correspond

correlation 8 parallel 10 comparison, connection 14 correspondence

correlative 4 akin 7 related 8 agreeing, parallel 9 analogous 10 comparable, connecting, equivalent 13 corresponding

correspond 3 fit 4 jibe, suit 5 agree, match, tally 6 accord, be like, concur, equate, square 7 conform 8 coincide, dovetail, parallel 9 harmonize 11 communicate, drop a line to, keep in touch

correspondence 4 mail 7 analogy, letters 8 epistles, missives, relation 9 bulletins 10 dispatches, similarity 11 association, communiques, resemblance

corresponding 4 akin 5 alike, equal 7 similar 8 agreeing, matching, tallying 9 according 10 equivalent 11 correlative 12 proportional

corridor 3 way 4 hall, road 5 aisle 6 artery 7 hallway, passage 8 approach 10 passageway

Corridors of Power
    author: 6 C P Snow

corroborate 4 back 5 prove 6 affirm, back up, uphold, verify 7 bear out, certify, confirm, endorse, support, sustain 8 validate 9 vindicate 12 authenticate, substantiate

corroborated 6 backed, proved, proven, upheld 7 factual 8 affirmed, backed up, borne out, verified 9 certified, confirmed, supported, sustained, validated 10 vindicated 11 well-founded 12 well-grounded 13 authenticated, substantiated

corroboration 5 proof 7 support 8 evidence 10 validation 11 affirmation, endorsement, vindication 12 confirmation, verification 13 certification, documentation 14 authentication, substantiation

corroborative 7 proving 9 affirming, backing up, upholding, verifying 10 bearing out, concurring, confirming, supporting, validating 11 affirmative 12 confirmative 14 substantiating

corrode 4 rust 7 oxidize 12 disintegrate

corrosive 4 acid 7 burning, caustic, erosive, mordant 8 abrasive 9 corroding 11 destructive

corrugated 6 fluted, ridged 7 creased, grooved, pleated 8 crinkled, furrowed, puckered, wrinkled 10 crenulated

corrupt 3 low 4 base, evil, mean 5 shady 6 debase, poison, seduce, sinful, wicked 7 crooked, debased, debauch, deprave, immoral, pervert, subvert 9 depraved 9 dishonest, unethical 10 fraudulent, iniquitous 11 contaminate 12 dishonorable, unprincipled, unscrupulous

corruption 4 vice 5 fraud, graft 7 bribery 8 iniquity 9 decadence, depravity, looseness, turpitude 10 debauchery, degeneracy, dishonesty, immorality, perversion, sinfulness, wickedness, wrongdoing 11 malfeasance

corsair 6 pirate, sea dog, Viking 7 brigand, sea wolf 8 marauder, picaroon, sea rover 9 buccaneer, plunderer, privateer, sea looter, sea robber 10 Blackbeard, freebooter 11 Captain Kidd 14 Long John Silver

corset 5 laces 6 girdle 8 corselet 17 foundation garment

Corsica 6 island
    located in: 16 Mediterranean Sea
    capital: 7 Ajaccio
    colony of: 4 Rome
    purchased by: 6 France
    birthplace of: 8 Napoleon
    industry: 7 tourism 10 wine making 12 sheep raising, cheese making

Corsican Brothers, The
    author: 14 Alexandre Dumas (pere)

Cortazar, Julio
    author of: 7 Rayuela 9 A Model Kit, Bestiario, Hopscotch 10 The Winners 12 Book of Manuel, End of the Game 15 All Fires the Fire 18 We Love Glenda So Much

cortege 4 line 5 court, staff, suite, train 6 column, escort, parade, string 7 caravan, company, retinue 9 cavalcade, entourage, following, motorcade 10 attendants, procession 17 funeral procession

corundum
    variety: 4 ruby 8 sapphire, star ruby 12 star sapphire

coruscate 4 beam 5 flash, gleam 7 glimmer, glitter, shimmer, sparkle

Corybant
    attendant of: 6 Cybele

Corycia
    form: 5 nymph
    bore son to: 6 Apollo

Corynetes
    also: 8 Pelasgus
    epithet of: 10 Periphetes
    means: 12 cudgel bearer

Coryphaeus
    epithet of: 4 Zeus
    means: 7 highest

Corythosaurus
    type: 8 dinosaur 10 ornithopod
    period: 10 Cretaceous
    characteristic: 10 duck-billed

Corythus
    father: 5 Priam
    mother: 6 Oenone
    adopted son: 8 Telephus
    loved: 5 Helen
    killed by: 5 Priam
    birthplace of: 8 Dardanus

Cosby, Bill
    born: 14 Philadelphia PA
    roles: 4 I Spy 12 The Cosby Show 19 Mother Juggs and Speed, Uptown Saturday Night

Cosby Show, The
    character: 4 Rudy, Theo 6 Denise, Sondra 7 Vanessa 13 Clair Huxtable, (Dr) Cliff (Heathcliff) Huxtable
    cast: 9 Bill Cosby, Lisa Bonet 14 Sabrina LeBeauf 15 Tempestt Bledsoe 18

Malcolm Jamal-Warner 19 Keshia Knight Pulliam, Phylicia Ayers-Rashad

Cosi fan tutte
also: 11 So Do They All 16 Women Are Like That
opera by: 6 Mozart
character: 7 Despina 8 Ferrando 9 Dorabella, Guglielmo 10 Don Alfonso, Fiordiligi

Cosmetas
epithet of: 4 Zeus
means: 7 orderer

cosmetic 5 paint, rouge 6 powder 7 mascara, surface 8 artifice, eyeliner, lipstick 9 cold cream, eye shadow 10 foundation, nail polish 11 beautifying 13 eyebrow pencil

cosmic 4 vast 7 immense 8 colossal, enormous, infinite 9 grandiose, universal 10 stupendous, widespread 12 interstellar 14 interplanetary 16 extraterrestrial

cosmopolitan 6 urbane 7 worldly 8 traveler 11 broad-minded, worldly-wise 12 globetrotter, sophisticate 13 international, sophisticated

cosmos 5 stars 8 universe 9 macrocosm 10 starry host 13 vault of heaven

Cossack 7 czarist, Russian, trooper 8 horseman 10 cavalry man

cosset 3 pet 6 caress, coddle, fondle, pamper

cost 3 fee, run, tab 4 bill, harm, hurt, loss, pain, take, toll 5 fetch, go for, price, value, worth 6 amount, burden, charge, come to, damage, injure, injury, outlay 7 bring in, expense, penalty, sell for, set back 8 amount to, distress 9 face value, sacrifice, suffering, valuation, weigh down 11 expenditure, market price

Costa-Gavras, Constantine
director of: 7 Missing

Costard
character in: 16 Love's Labour's Lost
author: 11 Shakespeare

Costa Rica
name means: 9 rich coast
other name: 19 Land of Eternal Spring
capital/largest city: 7 San Jose
others: 5 Canas, Limon, Vesta 6 Boruca, Nicoya 7 Cartago, Golfito, Heredia, Liberia, Negrita 8 Alajuela, Colorado, Guapiles 9 Turrialba 10 Puntarenas
measure: 4 vara 5 cafiz, cahiz 6 fanega, tercia 7 cajuela, cantaro, manzana 10 caballeria
monetary unit: 5 colon 7 centimo
weight: 3 bag 4 caja 5 libra
island: 4 Cano, Coco
lake: 6 Arenal
mountain: 4 Poas 5 Barba, Irazu 6 Blanco 7 Central, Gongora 9 Talamanca, Turrialba 10 Guanacaste
highest point: 14 Chirripo Grande
river: 4 Poas 5 Irazu 6 Matina 7 San Juan, Sixaola, Tenoria 8 Tarcoles
sea: 7 Pacific 9 Caribbean

physical feature:
bay: 7 Salinas 8 Coronada
cape: 5 Velas 6 Blanco 8 Matapalo 10 Santa Elena
crater: 4 Poas
gulf: 5 Dulce 6 Nicoya 8 Papagayo
hot springs spa: 12 Agua Caliente
peninsula: 3 Osa 6 Nicoya
point: 5 Judas 6 Blanca, Burica, Quepos 7 Cahuito, Galonos, Guionos, Llerena
valley: 8 Tarcoles 10 Reventazon
people: 4 Voto 6 Boruca, Bribri, Guaymi 7 Guatuso, mestizo, Spanish
explorer: 8 Columbus, Coronado
language: 7 Spanish
religion: 13 Roman Catholic
place:
shrine: 18 Our Lady of the Angels
theater: 14 Teatro Nacional
feature:
barbecue: 5 asado
dance: 6 torito 9 botijuela, zapateado 11 baile suelto 17 punto guanacasteco
drum: 8 quijonga
gourd: 4 caro
outdoor concerts: 7 retreta
plantation: 5 finca
wind instrument: 8 chirimia
food:
hearts of palm salad: 7 palmito
pudding: 10 tamal asado

Costello, Lou
real name: 21 Louis Francis Cristillo
partner: 9 Bud Abbott
born: 10 Paterson NJ
roles: 11 Who's on First

costly 4 dear 5 steep, stiff 7 harmful 8 damaging, precious 9 expensive 10 disastrous, exorbitant, high-priced 11 deleterious, extravagant 12 catastrophic

Costner, Kevin
born: 2 CA 10 Los Angeles
films: 3 JFK 9 Silverado 10 Bull Durham 12 The Bodyguard 13 Field of Dreams, A Perfect World 15 The Untouchables 16 Dances With Wolves 24 Robin Hood: Prince of Thieves

costume 4 garb 5 dress 6 attire, livery, outfit 7 apparel, clothes, raiment, uniform 8 clothing, garments

costuming 8 disguise 10 masquerade

cot 3 bed, hut, pen 4 coop, crib 5 cover, stall 7 cottage

cotelette 3 cut 4 chop 5 slice 6 cutlet

coterie 3 set 4 band, camp, clan, club, crew, gang 5 crowd, group 6 circle, clique 7 faction

cottage 3 cot, hut 5 lodge, shack 6 chalet 8 bungalow

Cotten, Joseph
born: 12 Petersburg VA
roles: 8 Gaslight 11 Citizen Kane, The Third Man 12 Duel in the Sun 14 Shadow of a Doubt 15 Journey into Fear 16 Portrait of Jennie 23 The Magnificent Ambersons

cotton 9 Gossypium
  varieties: 3 bog 4 tree, wild 6 kidney, levant, upland 8 lavender 9 sea island 11 Arizona wild
  fabric: 4 duck, jean, lawn, pima 5 baize, chino, denim, drill, khaki, lisle, pique, scrim, terry, twill 6 burlap, calico, canvas, chintz, dimity, madras, muslin, nankin, oxford, poplin, sateen 7 batiste, buckram, cambric, flannel, fustian, gingham, holland, jaconet, oilskin, organdy, percale, ticking 8 chambray, cretonne, sheeting 9 crinoline, sailcloth 10 broadcloth, hopsacking, printcloth, seersucker, terrycloth 11 cheesecloth, dotted Swiss
Cotton Club, The
  director: 18 Francis Ford Coppola
  cast: 9 Diane Lane 11 Richard Gere 12 Gregory Hines
cotton gin
  invented by: 7 Whitney
Cotton State
  nickname of: 7 Alabama
cottonwood 7 Populus 16 Populus deltoides
  varieties: 5 black, Jack's, swamp 7 Fremont 9 Rio Grande 10 Wislizenus 11 Great Plains
Cottus
  member of: 13 Hecatonchires
Cotyleus
  epithet of: 9 Asclepius
  means: 13 of the hip joint
Cotys, Cotytto
  origin: 8 Thracian
  form: 7 goddess
  corresponds to: 6 Cybele 11 Great Mother
couch 3 put 4 sofa, word 5 divan, draft, frame, state, utter, voice 6 daybed, draw up, lounge, phrase, settee 7 express 8 love seat, set forth 9 davenport 12 chesterfield
cougar 3 cat 4 lion, puma 7 panther 9 catamount 12 mountain lion
cough 4 hack 6 tussis 9 pertussis
cough up 3 pay 5 eject, expel 7 deliver 8 disgorge, hand over 9 surrender 11 regurgitate
Coulomb, Charles Augustin de
  field: 7 physics
  nationality: 6 French
  invented: 14 torsion balance
  discovered: 16 inverse square law
council 5 board, panel, synod 7 cabinet, chamber 8 assembly, colloquy, conclave, congress, ministry 9 committee, gathering, sanhedrin 10 conference, convention 11 convocation 12 congregation 15 representatives
counsel 4 urge, warn 6 advice, advise, charge, lawyer, prompt 7 call for, caution, opinion, suggest 8 admonish, advocate, attorney, guidance, instruct 9 barrister, counselor, recommend, solicitor 10 advisement, suggestion 12 consultation 14 recommendation

counsel house
  German: 7 Rathaus
Counsellor-at-Law
  director: 12 William Wyler
  based on play by: 9 Elmer Rice
  cast: 11 Bebe Daniels, Doris Kenyon 12 Isabel Jewell 13 John Barrymore, Melvyn Douglas, Onslow Stevens
counselor, counsellor 5 tutor 6 lawyer, mentor 7 adviser 8 advocate, attorney, minister 9 barrister, solicitor 10 instructor
counselor-at-law 6 lawyer 8 advocate, attorney 9 barrister, solicitor 10 mouthpiece
count 4 deem, hold, lord, rate, tell 5 add up, judge, noble, tally, total 6 impute, look on, matter, number, reckon, regard 7 ascribe, include, tick off 8 consider, estimate, look upon, numerate 9 attribute, enumerate, numbering, reckoning 10 numeration 11 calculation, computation, enumeration
  German: 4 Graf
  French: 5 comte
  Italian: 5 conte
countenance 3 aid, air 4 back, face, help, look, mien 5 build, favor 6 aspect, permit, traits, uphold, visage 7 advance, approve, condone, endorse, forward, further, profile, promote, support, work for 8 advocacy, advocate, approval, auspices, champion, contours, features, presence, sanction 9 promotion 10 appearance, assistance, expression, silhouette 11 approbation, physiognomy 12 championship, moral support 13 encouragement
counter 3 bar, man 4 defy, disk 5 piece, stand, table 6 buffet, contra, offset, oppose, resist 7 against, get even, hit back, opposed, pay back, reverse 8 contrary, fountain, opposite 9 fight back, retaliate 11 conflicting 13 contradictory
counteract 4 curb, undo 5 check, fight 6 defeat, hinder, negate, offset, oppose, resist, thwart 7 assuage, nullify, repress 8 overcome, restrain 9 alleviate, frustrate, overpower 10 annihilate, contravene, neutralize
counteraction 8 negation 10 offsetting, opposition 13 contravention, nullification 14 neutralization
counteractive 7 adverse 8 inimical 10 corrective 11 unfavorable 12 antagonistic, neutralizing
counteractor 7 negator 9 nullifier, offsetter 11 neutralizer
counteragent 8 antidote 9 antitoxin 10 antipoison 11 double agent
counterbalance 5 amend, check 6 cancel, offset, redeem, set off 7 correct, rectify 8 atone for, equalize, make good, outweigh 9 make up for 10 balance out, neutralize, outbalance, recompense 12 compensation
counterfeit 4 copy, fake, sham 5 bogus, fraud, phony 6 ersatz, forged 7 feigned, forgery 8 spurious 9 facsimile, imitation, simulated 10 artificial, fraudulent, substitute 11 make-believe

Counterfeiters, The
  author: 9 Andre Gide
countermand 4 void 5 annul, quash 6 cancel, recall, repeal, revoke 7 abolish, nullify, rescind, retract, reverse 8 abrogate, call back, disenact, override, overrule, set aside, withdraw, write off 12 disestablish
counterpart 4 copy, mate, twin 5 equal, match 6 double, fellow 8 parallel 9 duplicate 11 correlative 12 doppelganger 13 correspondent, spitting image
counterpoise 7 balance 9 stability 11 equilibrium
countersign 4 sign 7 certify, confirm, endorse 8 validate 9 authorize 11 corroborate 12 authenticate
countess
  French: 8 comtesse
  Italian: 8 contessa
countless 6 myriad, untold 7 endless 8 infinite 9 limitless, unlimited 10 numberless, unnumbered 11 innumerable, measureless 12 immeasurable, incalculable 13 multitudinous
Count of Monte Cristo, The
  author: 14 Alexandre Dumas (pere)
  character: 6 Albert, Haydee, Morrel 7 Fernand (Comte de Morcerf) 8 Danglars, Mercedes 9 Abbe Faria, Valentine, Villefort 10 Caderousse, Maximilian 12 Edmond Dantes
  prison: 10 Chateau d'If
count on 6 expect 7 hope for 10 anticipate
countrified 5 rural 6 rustic 9 backwoods 15 unsophisticated
country 4 area, farm, land 5 realm, rural, state 6 nation, people, public, region, rustic, simple, sticks 7 boonies, farming, kingdom, natives, scenery, terrain 8 citizens, district, homeland, populace 9 backwoods, boondocks, community, landscape, territory 10 fatherland, native land, native soil, population, provincial, rural areas 11 farming area, hinterlands, inhabitants, nationality 12 commonwealth 15 unsophisticated
Country Cousin
  author: 16 Louis Auchincloss
Country Girl, The
  director: 12 George Seaton
  based on play by: 13 Clifford Odets
  cast: 10 Bing Crosby, Grace Kelly 11 Anthony Ross 13 William Holden
  Oscar for: 7 actress (Kelly)
countryman 4 hick, rube 5 yokel 6 farmer, rustic 7 bumpkin, hayseed, peasant 8 landsman 10 clodhopper, compatriot, provincial
Country of the Pointed Firs, The
  author: 15 Sarah Orne Jewett
country place 4 farm 5 manor 6 estate
countryside 6 sticks 7 boonies 9 backwater, backwoods, boondocks, rural area 10 hinterland
count up 3 add 5 tally, total 6 reckon 7 compute 9 calculate
count upon 6 expect 7 foresee 10 anticipate

coup 3 act 4 blow, deed, feat 6 stroke 12 master stroke
coup de grace 9 deathblow 11 mercy stroke 12 decisive blow 15 finishing stroke
  literally: 11 blow of mercy
coup de main 14 surprise attack 17 sudden development
  literally: 15 blow from the hand
coup d'etat 6 mutiny 8 uprising 9 overthrow, rebellion 10 revolution, subversion
coup de theatre 15 theatrical trick
coup d'oeil 11 quick glance
  literally: 14 stroke of the eye
Couperin, Francois (Le Grand)
  born: 5 Paris 6 France
  composer of: 9 La Sultane, Les Fastes (de la grande et ancienne) 13 Concert Royaux 16 Apotheose de Lulli, Pieces de Clavecin 17 Lecons des Tenebres 20 Les Follies Francoises 31 Le Parnasse on l'Apotheose de Corelli
couple 3 duo, tie 4 bind, join, link, pair, yoke 5 hitch 6 fasten 7 connect, doublet, twosome 10 man and wife 11 man and woman 14 husband and wife
coupler 4 link, lock 5 clasp, hitch 6 buckle 8 fastener 9 fastening
Couples
  author: 10 John Updike
coupling 5 clasp, hatch 6 hookup, yoking 7 joining, pairing 8 hitching 9 attaching, fastening 10 attachment, connecting, connection
courage 4 grit, guts, sand 5 nerve, pluck, spunk, valor 6 daring, mettle 7 bravery 8 boldness 9 derring-do, fortitude 11 intrepidity 12 fearlessness 13 dauntlessness 16 stout-heartedness
courageous 4 bold 5 brave, manly 6 dogged, heroic 7 dashing, doughty, gallant, valiant 8 fearless, intrepid, resolute, stalwart, unafraid, valorous 9 dauntless 10 chivalrous 11 indomitable 12 bold-spirited 13 stronghearted
Courbet, Jean Desire Gustave
  born: 6 France, Ornans
  artwork: 16 The Artist's Studio, The Stonebreakers 17 The Burial at Ornans 19 The Peasants of Flagey 25 Self-Portrait with a Black Dog
courier 4 mule 5 envoy 6 herald, legate, runner 7 Gabriel, mailman, Mercury, postman 8 emissary 9 go-between, harbinger, messenger, postrider 11 herald angel, internuncio
course 3 run, way 4 flow, gush, mode, path, pour, race, road 5 march, orbit, round, route, surge, track 6 action, circle, method, policy, stream 7 channel, circuit, classes, conduct, lessons, passage, subject 8 behavior, lectures, sequence 9 direction, procedure, unfolding 10 curriculum, racecourse, trajectory 11 development, progression
court 3 bar, woo 4 hall, quad, seek, suit, yard 5 bench, manor, plaza, staff, train 6 atrium, castle, homage, induce, invite, pal-

ace, pursue, wooing 7 address, attract, chateau, cortege, council, flatter, hearing, meeting, provoke, retinue, session 8 advisers, assembly, audience, blandish, fawn upon, pander to, respects, run after 9 entourage, following 10 attendants, quadrangle 13 solicitations

Courtenay, Tom
  born: 4 Hull 7 England
  roles: 9 Billy Liar 10 The Dresser 36 The Loneliness of the Long Distance Runner

courteous 4 kind, mild 5 civil 6 polite 7 refined, tactful 8 gracious, mannerly, well-bred 10 diplomatic, respectful, soft-spoken 11 considerate, well-behaved 12 well-mannered

courtesy 5 favor 7 manners, regards, respect 8 civility, kindness, respects 9 deference, gallantry, gentility 10 indulgence, politeness, refinement 11 cultivation 12 graciousness 13 consideration

courtier 4 beau 7 gallant 8 cavalier 9 attendant 18 gentleman-in-waiting

Courtier, The
  author: 21 Baldassare Castiglione

Court Jester
  director: 11 Melvin Frank 12 Norman Panama
  cast: 9 Danny Kaye 11 Glynis Johns 13 Basil Rathbone 14 Angela Lansbury

courtly 5 suave 6 polite 7 elegant, gallant, genteel, refined, stately 8 debonair, decorous, highbred, ladylike, mannerly, polished 9 civilized, courteous, dignified 10 chivalrous 11 blue-blooded, gentlemanly 12 aristocratic 14 silk-stockinged

courtship 4 suit 6 wooing 14 keeping company

Courtship of Eddie's Father, The
  character: 4 Tina 10 Tom Corbett 12 Eddie Corbett, Norman Tinker 13 Mrs Livingston
  cast: 9 Bill Bixby 11 Brandon Cruz, James Komack 12 Miyoshi Umeki 15 Kristina Holland

Courtship of Miles Standish, The
  author: 24 Henry Wadsworth Longfellow
  character: 9 John Alden, Priscilla

courtyard 4 area, quad 9 curtilage, enclosure 10 quadrangle

cousin 7 kinsman 8 relation, relative 9 kinswoman

Cousin Bette
  author: 14 Honore de Balzac
  character: 6 Crevel 7 Adeline 10 Baron Hulot 11 Mme Marneffe 13 Hortense Hulot, Marechal Hulot 14 Lisbeth Fischer 23 Count Wenceslas Steinbock

Cousin Pons
  author: 14 Honore de Balzac

Cousy, Bob
  nickname: 12 Mr Basketball
  sport: 10 basketball
  position: 5 guard
  team: 13 Boston Celtics

couturier, couturiere 8 designer 9 midinette 10 dressmaker, seamstress

cove 3 bay 5 inlet 6 lagoon 7 estuary

covenant 3 vow 4 bond, oath, pact 6 pledge, treaty 7 bargain, promise 8 contract 9 agreement 15 solemn agreement
  Hebrew: 4 Brit 5 Berit, Brith 6 Berith

Covenant, The
  author: 13 James Michener

cover 3 cap, lid, top 4 case, hide, hood, mask, veil, wrap 5 cloak, cross, guard, lay on, put on, quilt 6 asylum, clothe, defend, embody, enwrap, jacket, refuge, report, screen, sheath, shield, shroud, take in, tell of 7 binding, blanket, conceal, contain, defense, embrace, envelop, include, involve, obscure, overlay, protect, put over, secrete, sheathe, shelter, wrapper, write up 8 comprise, deal with, describe, disguise, envelope, pass over, traverse 9 chronicle, comforter, eiderdown, encompass, sanctuary 10 camouflage, comprehend, encasement, protection 11 concealment, hiding place

coverage 7 payment 8 analysis 9 indemnity, reporting 10 protection, publishing 11 description 12 broadcasting 13 reimbursement

covered 4 clad 6 hidden 7 aimed at, cloaked, guarded, insured 8 included, overlaid, screened 9 blanketed, concealed, protected, sheltered, traversed 10 overspread

covering 6 casing, sheath 7 wrapper 8 envelope, wrapping 11 descriptive, explanatory 12 introductory

coverlet 5 quilt, throw 6 afghan, spread 7 blanket 9 bedspread, comforter

Coverly, Sir Roger de
  character in: 12 The Spectator
  authors: 6 Steele 7 Addison

covert 6 hidden, secret, veiled 7 sub rosa, unknown 9 concealed, disguised 11 clandestine 13 surreptitious

cover up 4 hide, mask, veil 6 hush up 7 conceal 8 disguise, keep back, suppress, withhold 9 gloss over, whitewash

cover-up 4 mask 5 blind 6 screen 8 disguise 9 whitewash 11 concealment

covet 4 want 5 crave, fancy 6 desire 7 long for

covetous 6 greedy 7 craving, envious, jealous, lustful, selfish 8 desirous, grasping, yearning 9 mercenary, rapacious 10 avaricious

covetousness 4 envy 5 greed 7 avarice 8 jealousy, rapacity 10 greediness 12 graspingness 13 mercenariness

covey 4 bevy 5 flock, group 6 family

cow 4 beef 5 abash, bossy, bully, deter, scare 6 bovine, cattle, dismay 7 terrify 8 browbeat, bulldoze, frighten, threaten 9 terrorize 10 discourage, dishearten, intimidate, make cringe
  young: 4 calf 6 heifer

coward 3 cad 5 sissy 6 craven 7 caitiff, chicken, dastard, milksop 8 poltroon 11 Milquetoast, mollycoddle, yellow-belly

Coward, Sir Noel
  author of: 8 Hay Fever **9** Cavalcade **10** Sigh No More **12** Blithe Spirit, Private Lives **14** In Which We Serve, Nude with Violin **15** Design for Living
cowardliness 8 timidity **10** yellowness **12** irresolution **13** pusillanimity, spinelessness **18** chicken-heartedness
cowardly 5 shaky, timid **6** afraid, craven, yellow **7** anxious, fearful, gutless, nervous **8** timorous **9** dastardly, tremulous **10** frightened **11** lily-livered **12** apprehensive, faint-hearted, uncourageous **13** pusillanimous, yellow-bellied **14** chicken-hearted
Cowardly Lion
  character in: 13 The Wizard of Oz
  author: 4 Baum
cowboy 6 drover, gaucho **7** vaquero **8** buckaroo **10** roughrider **12** broncobuster, cattle-herder
cowed 6 fazed **7** abashed, crushed, subdued **8** dismayed **11** intimidated **12** disconcerted **14** under one's thumb
cower 5 crawl, quail, toady **6** cringe, flinch, grovel, recoil, shrink **7** tremble, truckle **8** bootlick, draw back
cowl 4 cope, hood **5** cloak
Cowley, Malcolm
  author of: 12 Exile's Return **16** A Second Flowering **27** And I Worked at the Writer's Trade **28** The Dream of the Golden Mountains
coworker 7 partner **8** teammate **9** associate, colleague **10** accomplice **11** confederate **12** collaborator
Cowper, William
  author of: 7 The Task **11** The Cast-Away
Cowperwood, Frank
  character in: 8 The Titan **12** The Financier
  author: 7 Dreiser
coxcomb 3 fop **4** beau **5** dandy **8** popinjay
coy 3 shy **5** timid **6** demure, modest **7** bashful, prudish **8** blushing, sheepish, skittish, timorous **9** diffident, kittenish, shrinking **10** coquettish, overmodest
Coyote State
  nickname of: 11 South Dakota
cozen 3 con, gyp **4** bilk, coax, dupe, gull, rook **5** cheat, trick **6** fleece **7** deceive, defraud, swindle, wheedle **9** bamboozle, victimize
cozener 4 fake **5** cheat, fraud, quack **6** con man **8** deceiver, swindler **9** charlatan, trickster **10** mountebank **13** confidence man
coziness 6 warmth **7** comfort **8** intimacy, snugness **11** contentment
cozy 4 easy, snug **5** comfy, homey **7** restful **8** homelike, relaxing **9** gemutlich, simpatico **11** comfortable **16** snug as a bug in a rug
  French: 6 intime
Cozzens, James Gould
  author of: 12 Guard of Honor **15** By Love Possessed
CPA 7 auditor **10** accountant, bookkeeper **25** certified public accountant

crab 4 carp **5** crank, gripe, grump **6** grouch, grouse **8** complain, sourball **9** shellfish **10** crustacean, curmudgeon
  constellation of: 6 Cancer
Crabbe, Buster
  real name: 20 Clarence Linden Crabbe
  nickname: 16 King of the Serials
  born: 9 Oakland CA
  roles: 6 Tarzan **10** Buck Rogers **11** Flash Gordon **15** King of the Jungle
crabbed 4 mean, sour **6** cranky, morose **7** grouchy, peevish, pinched **8** churlish, spiteful **9** irascible, irritable, rancorous
crabby 5 cross, testy **6** cranky, touchy **7** grouchy, peevish **8** petulant, snappish **9** irritable **10** ill-humored, out of sorts **11** ill-tempered **12** cantankerous
crack 3 gag, jab, pop **4** chip, clap, gash, gibe, jest, joke, quip, rent, rift, slit, snap **5** break, burst, cleft, split, taunt **6** cleave, insult, report **7** crackle, crevice, fissure, give way, rupture, thunder **8** fracture, splinter **9** break down, wisecrack, witticism **10** go to pieces
cracked 3 mad **4** daft, nuts **5** crazy, nutty **6** crazed, insane **8** demented, deranged, unhinged **10** unbalanced **12** mad as a hatter **13** off one's rocker, out of one's head **14** off one's trolley **15** mad as a March hare
cracker 5 snack, wafer **7** biscuit, redneck **10** party favor **11** backsettler **12** backwoodsman
crackerjack 2 A-1 **3** ace **4** a-one, fine **5** super **6** superb, tip-top **8** splendid, terrific **9** excellent, fantastic, first-rate, wonderful **10** first-class
Cracker State
  nickname of: 7 Georgia
crackle 4 snap **5** craze, crink **9** crepitate
crackpot 3 nut, odd **4** fool, kook **5** balmy, crank, flake, freak, kinky, kooky, loony, nutty, wacko **6** freaky, insane, looney, madman, maniac, weirdo **7** dingbat, foolish, lunatic, oddball **9** character, eccentric, screwball **11** impractical
cracksman 4 yegg **7** burglar **10** cat burglar **14** second-story man
crackup 5 crash, smash, split, wreck **6** mishap, pileup **7** breakup, debacle, smashup **8** accident, calamity, collapse, disaster **9** breakdown, collision, splitting **10** exhaustion, shellshock **11** catastrophe, prostration **14** disintegration
cradle 3 hug **4** crib, font, rock **6** cuddle, enfold, origin, source, spring **7** nursery, snuggle **8** bassinet, fountain **10** birthplace, wellspring **12** fountainhead
craft 3 art **4** boat, ruse, ship, wile **5** guile, knack, plane, skill, trade **6** deceit, vessel **7** ability, calling, cunning, know-how, mastery, perfidy, pursuit **8** airplane, artifice, business, commerce, deftness, fineness, industry, intrigue, trickery, vocation **9** adeptness, chicanery, deception, duplicity, expertise, technique **10** adroitness, artfulness, competency, craftiness, employ-

ment, expertness, handicraft, occupation 11 proficiency

craftiness 4 ruse, wile 5 guile 7 cunning, slyness 8 artifice, foxiness, scheming, trickery, wiliness 9 chicanery 10 artfulness 11 machination

craftsman 4 hand 5 smith 6 worker, wright 7 artisan 8 mechanic

crafty 3 sly 4 foxy, wily 5 canny, sharp 6 artful, astute, shifty, shrewd, tricky 7 cunning, devious 8 guileful, plotting, scheming 9 deceitful, deceptive, designing, dishonest, underhand, unethical 10 intriguing, perfidious, suspicious 11 calculating

crag 3 tor 4 rock 5 bluff, cliff 9 precipice

craggy 5 rocky, rough, sheer, steep, stony 6 abrupt, jagged, ragged, rugged, snaggy 7 scraggy 8 bouldery 9 rockbound 10 rock-ribbed 11 precipitous

Crain, Jeanne
born: 9 Barstow CA
roles: 5 Pinky 6 Margie 9 State Fair 17 Cheaper by the Dozen 19 A Letter to Three Wives

cram 3 jam 4 fill, pack 5 crowd, force, grind, press, stuff 7 congest, squeeze 8 compress 9 overcrowd, study hard

Cram, Ralph
architect of: 17 US Military Academy (West Point) 29 Cathedral of Saint John the Divine (NYC)
style: 13 Gothic Revival

crammed 4 full 6 filled, packed 7 studied, stuffed 9 jam-packed 11 overflowing, well-stocked

cramp 4 pang 5 block, check, crick, limit, spasm 6 hamper, hinder, stitch, stymie, thwart 7 prevent, seizure 8 handicap, obstruct, restrain, restrict 9 frustrate 12 charley horse

cramped 5 close, tight 6 narrow 7 compact, pinched 8 confined 10 compressed, restrained, restricted ·

Cranach, Lucas (Lukas) (the Elder)
born: 7 Kronach, Germany
artwork: 6 Luther 10 Adam and Eve 11 Crucifixion 14 Apollo and Diana 15 Rest on the Flight 18 The Judgment of Paris 22 Duke and Duchess of Saxony

Cranaus
king of: 6 Athens, Attica
wife: 6 Pedias
daughter: 6 Atthis, Cranae
renamed Athens: 6 Attica

cranberry 9 Vaccinium 19 Vaccinium vitis-idaea 20 Vaccinium macrocarpon
varieties: 3 bog 4 rock, tree 5 large, small 8 American, European, highbush, mountain 10 Australian

crane 4 bird, boom 5 davit, heron 7 derrick 10 wading bird
group of: 5 sedge, siege
constellation of: 4 Grus

Crane, Bob
born: 11 Waterbury CT
roles: 12 Colonel Hogan, Hogan's Heroes

Crane, Hart
author of: 9 The Bridge 14 White Buildings

Crane, Ichabod
character in: 23 The Legend of Sleepy Hollow
author: 6 Irving

Crane, Roy
creator/artist of: 9 Buz Sawyer, Wash Tubbs 11 Captain Easy

Crane, Stephen
author of: 11 The Open Boat 20 The Red Badge of Courage 23 Maggie: A Girl of the Streets 24 The Bride Comes to Yellow Sky

Cranford
author: 10 Mrs Gaskell

cranium 4 head 5 skull 6 noggin 8 brain box, brainpan 9 brain case

crank 4 turn, whim 5 brace, winch 6 grouch, handle 7 fanatic 8 crotchet 9 eccentric

cranky 5 cross, testy 6 crabby, touchy 7 bearish, grouchy, peevish, waspish 8 captious, petulant 9 crotchety, irascible, splenetic 10 ill-humored, out of sorts 11 ill-tempered 12 cantankerous

cranny 3 gap 4 nook, slit 5 break, chink, cleft, crack, notch, split 7 crevice, fissure 8 cleavage

crash 3 din 4 bang, boom, bump, dash, ruin 5 crack, slump, smash, wreck 6 hurtle, invade, pileup, plunge, racket, slip in, topple, tumble 7 bumping, clangor, clatter, collide, crackup, decline, failure, hitting, intrude, setback, shatter, smashup, sneak in 8 accident, smashing, toppling, tumbling 9 collision, recession 10 bankruptcy, depression, shattering

crass 4 crude, cruel, gross 6 coarse, oafish, vulgar 7 boorish 8 uncaring 9 inelegant, unfeeling, unrefined 10 unpolished 11 hardhearted, insensitive 13 unsympathetic

crassness 9 crudeness, grossness, vulgarity 10 coarseness, inelegance, oafishness 11 boorishness 13 insensitivity

Crataeis
daughter: 6 Scylia

Cratchit, Bob
character in: 15 A Christmas Carol
author: 7 Dickens

crate 3 box, car 4 auto, case, pack 5 plane 6 jalopy, pallet 8 airplane 9 container

crater 3 pit 4 hole 6 cavity 10 depression

Cratus
origin: 5 Greek
personifies: 8 strength

cravat 3 tie 5 ascot, scarf, stock 7 necktie 11 neckerchief

crave 4 need, want 5 covet 6 desire 7 hope for, long for, pine for, require, sigh for, wish for 8 yearn for 9 hunger for, lust after, thirst for 11 hanker after, have a yen for 13 have a fancy for

craven 3 low 4 base 5 timid 6 scared, yellow 7 fearful, lowdown 8 cowardly, timorous 9 dastardly 10 frightened 11 lily-livered 12 mean-spirited 13 pusillanimous 14 chicken-hearted

craving 3 yen 4 need 6 desire, hunger, thirst 7 longing 9 hankering

Crawford, Broderick
  real name: 24 William Broderick Crawford
  wife: 11 Jan Sterling
  born: 14 Philadelphia PA
  roles: 6 The Mob 10 The Interns 12 Of Mice and Men 13 Born Yesterday, Highway Patrol 14 All the King's Men (Oscar)

Crawford, Henry
  character in: 13 Mansfield Park
  author: 6 Austen

Crawford, Joan
  real name: 17 Lucille Fay Le Sueur
  husband: 12 Franchot Tone 18 Douglas Fairbanks Jr
  daughter: 6 Cheryl 9 Christina
  born: 12 San Antonio TX
  biography: 13 Mommie Dearest
  roles: 8 The Women 10 Grand Hotel 13 Mildred Pierce (Oscar) 26 What Ever Happened to Baby Jane

crawl 3 drag, inch, poke, worm 5 creep, mosey 6 squirm, wiggle, writhe 7 slither, wriggle

Crawley, Rawdon
  character in: 10 Vanity Fair
  author: 9 Thackeray

crayon 3 chalk, draft 6 pastel, pencil, sketch 7 drawing 8 charcoal

craze 3 fad 4 rage 5 furor, mania 6 dement 7 derange, passion, unhinge 11 infatuation

crazed 3 mad 6 insane 7 cracked, lunatic 8 demented, deranged

crazy 3 mad, odd 4 avid, daft, gaga, keen, nuts, wild 5 nutty, rabid, silly, weird 6 absurd, far-out, insane, stupid, unwise 7 berserk, bizarre, cracked, excited, foolish, frantic, idiotic, strange, touched, unusual, zealous 8 demented, deranged, maniacal, peculiar, uncommon, unhinged 9 fanatical, foolhardy, imprudent, laughable, senseless 10 hysterical, infatuated, outrageous, passionate, ridiculous, unbalanced 11 smitten with 12 enthusiastic, mad as a hatter 13 out of one's head 15 mad as a March hare

creak 4 rasp 5 grate, grind 6 scrape, screak, squeak 7 screech

Creakle
  character in: 16 David Copperfield
  author: 7 Dickens

cream 3 top 4 beat, best, drub 5 elite 6 choice, flower 7 the pick, trounce 8 greatest, off-white 14 creme de la creme

Cream, Arnold Raymond
  real name of: 10 Joe Walcott

cream of the cream
  French: 14 creme de la creme

Cream of the Jest, The
  author: 17 James Branch Cabell

creamy 5 thick, foamy 6 smooth, yellow 8 emulsive

crease 4 fold 5 crimp, pleat, ridge 6 furrow, pucker, ruffle, rumple 7 crimple, crinkle, wrinkle 9 corrugate 11 corrugation

create 4 form, make, mold 5 cause, erect, found, set up 6 design, devise, invent 7 appoint, concoct, develop, fashion 8 conceive, contrive, organize 9 construct, establish, fabricate, formulate, institute, originate

creation 5 world 6 making, nature 8 building, devising, erection, founding 9 all things, formation, handiwork, invention 10 brainchild, conception, concoction, fashioning, production 11 development, fabrication, institution, origination 12 construction 13 establishment

Creation
  author: 9 Gore Vidal

creative 8 fanciful, original 9 ingenious, inventive 11 imaginative, resourceful

creator 5 maker 6 author, father, framer 7 founder 8 begetter, designer, inventor, producer 9 architect, generator, initiator 10 originator

creature 3 man 4 bird, fish 5 beast, human 6 animal, insect, mammal, mortal, person 7 critter, reptile 9 earthling, quadruped 10 individual, vertebrate 12 invertebrate

credence 5 faith, trust 6 belief, credit 8 reliance 9 certainty, certitude 10 confidence 11 reliability 13 believability 14 acceptableness, dependableness 15 trustworthiness

credentials 6 permit 7 diploma, license, voucher 9 reference 11 certificate, testimonial 13 authorization

credenza 5 shelf, table 6 buffet 8 bookcase 9 sideboard

credible 6 likely 7 tenable 8 possible, probable, reliable 9 plausible, thinkable 10 believable, dependable, imaginable, reasonable 11 conceivable, trustworthy

credit 3 buy 4 time 5 glory, honor, trust 6 accept, assign, esteem, rely on 7 acclaim, ascribe, believe, fall for, swallow 9 allowance, attribute, recognize 10 prepayment 11 acknowledge, recognition 12 commendation 14 acknowledgment

creditable 6 worthy 8 laudable 9 admirable, estimable, reputable 11 commendable, meritorious, respectable 12 praiseworthy

credo 4 code, rule 5 maxim, motto, tenet 8 doctrine 10 philosophy

credulous 5 naive 8 gullible, trusting 9 believing 12 overtrustful, unsuspecting, unsuspicious 13 unquestioning 15 unsophisticated

Cree
  language family: 9 Algonkian 10 Algonquian
  tribe: 10 Plains Cree 13 Woodlands Cree
  location: 6 Canada 8 Manitoba
  related to: 8 Chippewa

creed 5 dogma 6 belief, canons, gospel 8 doctrine

creek 3 run 4 rill 5 brook 6 branch, spring, stream 7 freshet, rivulet 10 millstream, small river

Creek
language family: 10 Muskhogean
location: 7 Alabama, Florida, Georgia 11 Mississippi
leader: 8 Red Eagle 15 William McIntosh 20 Alexander McGillivray

Creek Mary's Blood
author: 8 Dee Brown

creep 4 inch, worm 5 crawl, sneak, steal 6 dawdle, squirm, writhe 7 slither, wriggle

creeper 3 ivy 4 bird, iron, vine, worm 5 snake 7 climber, crawler, grapnel, trailer

creepy 4 eery 5 eerie, scary 6 crawly, spooky, uneasy 12 apprehensive

cremate 4 burn, char, fire, sear 5 roast 6 ignite, kindle, scorch 8 enkindle 10 incinerate 11 conflagrate 17 consume with flames

creme de banane
type: 7 liqueur
flavor: 7 banana
color: 6 yellow

creme de cacao
type: 6 brandy 7 liqueur
origin: 6 France
flavor: 9 chocolate
color: 5 brown, white
drink: 11 Fifth Avenue
with rum: 6 Panama
with tequila: 8 Toreador
with vodka: 9 Ninotchka 11 Russian Bear 12 Velvet Hammer, White Russian

creme de cassis
type: 7 liqueur
origin: 6 France 8 Burgundy
flavor: 12 black currant
with gin: 8 Parisian

creme de fraise
type: 7 liqueur
flavor: 10 strawberry

creme de framboise
type: 7 liqueur
flavor: 9 raspberry

creme de la creme 3 top 4 best 5 cream, elite 6 choice, flower 8 choicest, very best 12 choicest part 15 cream of the cream

creme de menthe
type: 7 liqueur
flavor: 4 mint
color: 5 green, white
with brandy: 7 Stinger
with cream: 11 Grasshopper
with gin: 6 Caruso, Virgin

creme de noyau
type: 7 liqueur
flavor: 6 almond

creme de violette
type: 7 liqueur
flavor: 7 violets
color: 8 lavender

creme Yvette
type: 7 liqueur
origin: 12 United States
flavor: 7 violets
with gin: 9 Union Jack

Crenna, Richard
born: 12 Los Angeles CA
roles: 9 Death Ship 13 Our Miss Brooks, The Real McCoys

Creole 6 patois 7 criollo, dialect, Haitian 10 West Indian

Creole State
nickname of: 9 Louisiana

Creon
king of: 6 Thebes 7 Corinth
father: 9 Lycaethus, Menoeceus
sister: 7 Jocasta
daughter: 6 Creusa, Glauce
nephew: 7 Oedipus 8 Eteocles 9 Polynices
niece: 6 Ismene 8 Antigone
defeated: 18 Seven against Thebes

crescendo
music: 22 gradually getting louder
abbreviation: 5 cresc

crescent 3 arc, bow 4 arch 5 curve 8 half-moon

crescit eundo 15 it grows as it goes
motto of: 9 New Mexico

Cresius
epithet of: 8 Dionysus
means: 6 Cretan

Cresphontes
member of: 8 Heraclid
father: 12 Aristomachus
brother: 7 Temenus 11 Polyphontes
wife: 6 Merope
father-in-law: 8 Cypselus
son: 7 Aepytus
controlled: 8 Messenia
invaded: 12 Peloponnesus

Cressida
also: 8 Criseyde 9 Crisseyde
based on characters of: 7 Bryseis 8 Chryseis
setting: 9 Trojan War
loved: 7 Troilus
deserted Troilus for: 8 Diomedes

crest 3 tip, top 4 apex, arms, comb, peak, tuft 5 crown, plume 6 emblem, height, summit 7 topknot 8 pinnacle 10 coat of arms, escutcheon

crestfallen 8 dejected, downcast 9 depressed, woebegone 10 despondent, dispirited 11 discouraged, downhearted, low-spirited 12 disappointed, disheartened

Creta
daughter: 8 Pasiphae

Cretaceous period
dinosaur from: 9 Euhelopus, Iguanodon 10 Allosaurus, Antrodemus 11 Anatosaurus, Ankylsaurus, Deinonychus, Gorgosaurus, Triceratops 12 Lambeosaurus, Ornithomimus 13 Albertosaurus, Corythosaurus, Hypselosaurus, Hypsilophodon, Palaeoscincus, Protoceratops, Struthiomimus, Styracosaurus, Tyrannosaurus 14 Psittacosaurus, Thescelosaurus 15 Parasaurolophus, Procheneosaurus

Cretan bull
also: 15 Marathonian bull
form: 4 bull
son: 8 Minotaur
captured on: 5 Crete
captured by: 8 Hercules
roamed: 8 Marathon
recaptured by: 7 Theseus
Cretan Mythology
goddess of fishermen/hunters/sailors:
11 Britomartis
corresponds to Greek: 7 Artemis
goddess of the sea: 8 Dictynna
maze: 9 labyrinth
monster: 8 Minotaur
Crete
other name: 5 Kriti 6 Candia
capital/largest city: 5 Canea 8 Iraklion
others: 3 Hag 4 Lato 5 Khora, Sitia,
Zakro 6 Anoyia, Candia, Khania, Lisamo,
Mallia, Meleme, Retimo 7 Malerni 8
Kastelli, Nikolaos, Sphakion 9 Heraclion,
Heraklion, Rethymnon, Tympakion 11
Palaiophora
government: division of: 6 Greece
monetary unit: 7 drachma
mountain: 3 Ida 5 Dikte, Phino 6 Juktas
7 Lasithi, Madaras 8 Leuka Ori, Theodore, Thriphte 9 Psiloriti
highest point: 3 Ida
sea: 5 Crete 6 Aegean 13 Mediterranean
physical feature:
bay: 4 Suda 5 Kanca 6 Kisamo, Mesara
cape: 4 Buza 5 Liano 6 Salome, Sidero,
Spatha 7 Stavros 8 Lithinon, Sidheros
gulf: 6 Khania 9 Merabello
people: 7 Candiot, Cretans, Minoans 9
Caphtorim, Sphakiots 11 Philistines
artist: 7 El Greco
author: 11 Kazantzakis
conqueror: 8 Metellus
king: 5 Minos
language: 5 Greek 6 Minoan 7 Linear A,
Linear B
religion: 14 Greek Orthodoxy
place:
ruins: 15 Palace at Knossos
Cretheis
husband: 7 Acastus
killed by: 6 Peleus
Cretheus
founder of: 6 Iolcus
father: 6 Aeolus
mother: 7 Enarete
brother: 9 Salmoneus
wife: 4 Tyro
son: 4 Aeson 6 Pheres 8 Amythaon
companion: 6 Aeneas
Creusa
also: 6 Glauce
father: 5 Creon, Priam 8 Cychreus 10
Erechtheus
mother: 6 Hecuba
husband: 6 Aeneas 7 Telamon
son: 3 Ion 8 Ascanius
bride of: 5 Jason
killed by: 5 magic, Medea

crevasse 3 gap 4 rift 5 abyss, break,
chasm, cleft, gorge, gulch, gully, split 6
breach, divide 7 fissure
crevice 4 rent, rift, slit 5 chasm, cleft, crack,
split 6 breach 7 fissure 8 crevasse, fracture
crew 3 mob 4 band, body, herd, mass,
pack, team 5 corps, force, group, hands,
horde, party, squad, troop 6 seamen,
throng 7 company, sailors 8 mariners 9
multitude, seafarers 10 assemblage, complement
crib 3 bed, bin, cot, hut, key 4 pony 5
cheat, shack, stall, steal 6 creche, manger
7 purloin 8 bassinet 10 plagiarize
cribbage
score kept on: 5 board
points/game: 8 sixty-one
third hand: 4 crib
Crich, Gerald
character in: 11 Women in Love
author: 8 Lawrence
Crichton, Michael
author of: 5 Congo 6 Sphere 9 Rising
Sun 10 Disclosure 12 Jurassic Park 14
The Terminal Man 18 The Andromeda
Strain 20 The Great Train Robbery
cricket
players/team: 6 eleven
equipment: 3 bat 4 bail, ball 5 stump 6
wicket
position: 5 gully, mid on, slops 6 bowler,
long on, mid off 7 batsman, fine leg, long
off 8 third man 9 mid wicket, square leg
10 cover point, extra cover, silly mid on
11 silly mid off 12 wicket keeper 13 deep
mid wicket 16 backward short leg
lines: 7 creases
period of play: 4 over 7 innings
championship game: 9 test match
England/Australia match: 8 the Ashes
cricket
variety: 4 bush, cave, sand, tree 5
camel, field, house 6 ground 9 Jerusalem, pygmy mole
Cries and Whispers
director: 12 Ingmar Bergman
cast: 10 Liv Ullmann 12 Ingrid Thulin 16
Harriet Andersson
crime 3 sin 4 tort 5 wrong 6 felony 7 misdeed, offense, outrage 8 foul play, iniquity,
villainy 10 misconduct, wrongdoing 11
abomination, lawbreaking, malfeasance,
misdemeanor 13 transgression
Crime and Punishment
author: 16 Fyodor Dostoevsky
character: 5 Sonya 6 Dounia 7 Porfiry 9
Razumihin 11 Raskolnikov
criminal 4 hood 5 crook, felon, wrong 6
guilty, outlaw 7 crooked, culprit, illegal, illicit, lawless 8 culpable, offender, unlawful,
wasteful 9 felonious, senseless, wrongdoer 10 abominable, delinquent, indictable, lawbreaker, malefactor, outrageous,
villainous 11 blameworthy, disgraceful,
lawbreaking 12 transgressor

crimp 4 curl, fold, kink, wave 5 clamp, flute, frill, frizz 7 crinkle, frizzle, wrinkle 8 obstacle

crimple 4 curl 6 pucker 7 crinkle, crumple, wrinkle 9 corrugate

crimson 3 red 5 blush, flush 6 redden 7 carmine, scarlet

cringe 4 duck 5 cower, dodge, quail, toady 6 blench, flinch, grovel, recoil, shrink 7 truckle

cringing 6 abject 7 fawning, ignoble, servile, wincing 8 cowering, toadying 9 flinching, groveling, shrinking, sniveling

crinkle 5 crush 6 rumple, rustle 7 crumple, wrinkle

crinkly 4 wavy 5 curly, kinky 6 crimpy, frizzy 7 cockled, crimped, crimply, puckery, ruffled, rumpled, twisted, wrinkly 8 crimpled, frizzled, puckered, wrinkled 9 shriveled

crinoline 4 hoop 5 skirt 9 hoopskirt, petticoat 10 underskirt

Criophorus
  epithet of: 6 Hermes
  means: 9 ram bearer

cripple 4 gimp, halt, harm, maim, stop 6 damage, impair 7 disable 8 make lame, paralyze 9 hamstring 10 debilitate, inactivate 12 incapacitate

crisis 6 climax 9 emergency

crisp 5 brisk, fresh, nippy, sharp, terse, witty 6 candid, chilly, crispy, lively, snappy 7 bracing, brittle, crunchy, pointed 8 incisive 9 energetic, sparkling, vivacious 10 refreshing 12 invigorating

crisscross 4 awry 5 cross 8 confused, traverse

Crisseyde *see* 8 Cressida

Cristillo, Louis Francis
  real name of: 11 Lou Costello

criterion 3 law 4 norm, rule 5 gauge, model 7 example, measure 8 standard 9 guidepost, precedent, principle, yardstick 10 touchstone

critic 5 judge, mavin, scold 6 carper, censor, expert, rapper 7 analyst, arbiter, knocker, reviler 8 attacker, vilifier, virtuoso 9 authority, backbiter, detractor, evaluator 10 antagonist, criticizer 11 cognoscente, commentator, connoisseur, faultfinder

critical 5 fussy, grave, hairy, picky, risky, vital 6 urgent 7 carping, crucial, finicky, judging, nagging, serious 8 caviling, decisive, perilous, pressing 9 dangerous, harrowing, hazardous, judicious, momentous, sensitive 10 analytical, censorious, derogatory, diagnostic, nitpicking, precarious 11 disparaging 12 disapproving, faultfinding

critical situation 3 jam 4 mess 6 crisis, pickle 7 straits, trouble 8 hot water 9 deep water 10 difficulty 11 predicament

critical stage 6 climax, crisis 9 emergency

critical success
  French: 13 succes d'estime

criticism 4 fire, flak, slam 5 blame, knock 6 review 7 censure, comment 8 analysis, critique, judgment 9 aspersion, stricture 10 commentary, evaluation 12 faultfinding

criticize 4 carp, fuss, pick 5 cavil, nag at 7 censure, nitpick, reprove 8 denounce, reproach 9 disparage

critique 6 review 8 analysis

Crna Gora *see* 10 Montenegro

croak 3 caw, die 4 kill, moan, roup 7 grumble, kick off 8 complain, harsh cry 13 kick the bucket

Croatia
  capital/largest city: 5 Zagreb
  others: 4 Knin 5 Split, Zadar 6 Osijek, Rijeka (Fiume) 7 Vukovar, Sibenik 8 Karlovac, Varazdin, Vinkovci 9 Dubrovnik 10 Kostajnica
  head of state: 9 president
  government: 9 democracy
  monetary unit: 5 dinar
  mountain: 10 Julian Alps 11 Styrian Alps
  sea: 8 Adriatic
  people: 5 Serbs 6 Croats 7 Muslims 9 Yugoslavs
  language: 8 Croatian 10 Serbo Croat
  religion: 17 Catholic Christian, Orthodox Christian

Crocetti, Dino Paul
  real name of: 10 Dean Martin

crocodile 4 croc 6 cayman, gavial, lizard 7 reptile, asurian

crock 3 jar, pot 9 container

crockery 5 china 6 dishes, plates 7 pottery 8 clayware 9 chinaware, tableware 11 ceramic ware, earthenware 14 cups and saucers

Crock of Gold
  author: 13 James Stephens

crocus
  varieties: 4 fall, wild 5 dutch 6 autumn, scotch 7 Chilean, saffron 8 tropical 9 celandine 12 iris-flowered

Crocus
  form: 5 youth
  changed into: 12 saffron plant

Crome Yellow
  author: 12 Aldous Huxley

Crommyonian sow
  also: 5 Phaea
  killed by: 7 Theseus

Cromwell, Oliver
  also: 13 Lord Protector
  served in: 15 English Civil War
  fought against: 8 Charles I 9 Cavaliers
  fought for: 10 Parliament, Roundheads
  regiment: 9 Ironsides
  battle: 6 Naseby, Oxford 7 Preston 11 Marston Moor

crone 3 hag 5 witch 6 beldam 7 beldame, old wife

Cronia
  festival in: 6 Athens

Cronus
  also: 6 Cronos, Kronos
  form: 5 Titan
  father: 6 Uranus
  mother: 4 Gaea
  sister: 4 Rhea
  wife: 4 Rhea
  son: 4 Zeus 5 Hades 8 Poseidon

daughter: 4 Hera 6 Hestia 7 Demeter
corresponds to: 6 Saturn

crony 3 pal 4 ally, chum, mate 5 buddy 6 bunkie, cohort, friend 7 comrade 8 bunkmate, intimate, shipmate, sidekick 9 accessory, associate, companion, old friend 10 accomplice, bosom buddy 11 confederate 12 acquaintance, collaborator 13 co-conspirator

Cronyn, Hume
wife: 12 Jessica Tandy
born: 6 London 7 Canada, Ontario
roles: 13 The Fourposter 17 Phantom of the Opera 19 Sunrise at Campobello

crook 3 arc, bow 4 bend, hook, thug, turn 5 angle, cheat, curve, knave, thief, twist 6 bandit, outlaw, robber 7 burglar 8 criminal, swindler 9 curvature, embezzler

crooked 4 awry, bent, wily 5 askew, bowed, shady 6 crafty, curved, hooked, shifty, sneaky, spiral, warped, zigzag 7 corrupt, sinuous, twisted, winding 8 criminal, deformed, tortuous, twisting, unlawful 9 deceitful, deceptive, dishonest, distorted, nefarious, unethical 10 fraudulent, meandering, perfidious, serpentine 11 underhanded 12 dishonorable, unscrupulous

crookedness 10 dishonesty 11 deviousness 13 deceitfulness, double-dealing

Crookes, William
nationality: 7 British
invented: 8 thallium 10 radiometer 11 Crookes tube

croon 3 hum 4 sing 6 murmur, warble

crop 3 bob, cut, lop 4 clip, snip, trim 5 prune, shear, yield 6 growth 7 harvest, reaping 8 cut short, gleaning 9 gathering 10 production

crop-raising 7 farming, tillage 11 agriculture 12 agribusiness, truck farming 15 market gardening

crop up 5 arise, ensue, occur 6 appear 7 develop, surface 11 come to light

croquet
equipment: 4 hoop 6 mallet, wicket
variation: 5 roque
term: 5 rover

Crosby, Bing
real name: 17 Harry Lillis Crosby
partner: 7 Bob Hope 10 Hedy Lamarr 13 Dorothy Lamour
nickname: 8 Der Bingle
wife: 8 Dixie Lee 12 Kathryn Grant
born: 8 Tacoma WA
roles: 10 Going My Way (Oscar), Holiday Inn 11 High Society 14 The Country Girl, White Christmas 17 The Bells of St Mary's 22 Christmas in Connecticut
Road to: 3 Rio 4 Bali 7 Morocco 8 Hong Kong, Zanzibar 9 Singapore

cross 3 mad, mix 4 crux, ford, meet, rood 5 angry, blend, erase, gruff, surly, testy, trial 6 burden, cancel, cranky, delete, go over, hybrid, ordeal, shirty, touchy 7 amalgam, annoyed, athwart, grouchy, oblique, peevish, trouble, waspish 8 captious, choleric, churlish, contrary, crucifix, distress, inter-

mix, pass over, petulant, snappish, traverse 9 adversity, crotchety, half-breed, hybridize, intersect, irascible, irritable, querulous, splenetic, strike out, suffering 10 affliction, difficulty, ill-humored, interbreed, misfortune, obliterate, out of sorts, transverse 11 combination, ill-tempered, intractable, tribulation 12 cantankerous, disagreeable, intersecting

crossbar 3 bar 4 spar 5 sprit 6 stripe

crossbreed 3 mix 8 intermix 9 hybridize 10 interbreed

cross-fertilize 9 hybridize

crossing 4 pass 7 mixture, passage 8 blocking, opposing, traverse 9 thwarting 10 traversing 11 hybridizing, intersection 13 hybridization

cross over 4 span 5 cross 6 bridge 8 traverse

crosspiece 3 bar 4 spar 5 sprit

cross-pollinate 9 hybridize

crossroad 12 intersection, turning point

cross swords 5 clash, fight 6 battle, combat, tussle 7 contend, contest 8 skirmish

crossways 7 athwart 12 transversely

crosswise 6 across 7 athwart 8 sideways, traverse 10 transverse

crotchet 4 bent, whim 5 habit, quirk, trait 6 foible, hang-up, oddity, vagary, whimsy 7 caprice 8 quiddity 9 mannerism 10 erraticism 11 peculiarity 12 eccentricity, idiosyncrasy, irregularity 14 characteristic

crotchety 3 odd 5 fussy 6 cranky 7 erratic, grouchy 8 contrary, peculiar 9 eccentric

Crotopus
king of: 5 Argos
daughter: 8 Psamathe
killed: 8 Psamathe

Crotus
father: 3 Pan
skilled in: 7 archery
companion of: 5 Muses

crouch 4 bend, duck 5 cower, squat, stoop 6 cringe, recoil, shrink 9 hunch over 10 hunker down 11 scrooch down, scrunch down

crow 3 daw, jay, kae 4 blow, brag, rook 5 boast, crake, exult, gloat, raven, strut, vaunt 6 cackle, chough, corbie, magpie 7 corvine, jackdaw, rejoice, swagger, triumph, trumpet 8 jubilate 14 cock-a-doodle-doo
group of: 6 murder

Crow
constellation of: 6 Corvus

Crow
language family: 6 Siouan
tribe: 9 River Crow 12 Mountain Crow
location: 7 Montana, Wyoming
related to: 7 Hidatsa

crowbar 3 bar, pry 5 jimmy, lever

crowd 3 jam, mob, set 4 cram, gang, herd, host, mass, push 5 crush, flock, group, horde, press, shove, surge, swarm 6 circle, claque, clique, gather, huddle, legion, throng 7 cluster, coterie, elbow in, squeeze 8 assemble 9 gathering, multitude 10 assemblage, congregate 11 concentrate 12 congregation

Crowd, The
director: 9 King Vidor
cast: 9 Bert Roach 11 James Murray 15 Eleanor Boardman

crowded 4 full 6 filled, jammed, mobbed, packed 7 crammed, teeming 8 swarming, thronged 9 congested, jampacked 11 overflowing

crowd out 8 displace 9 overwhelm

crown 3 cap, top 4 acme, apex, head, pate, peak 5 crest, tiara 6 climax, diadem, noggin, noodle, summit, top off, wreath, zenith 7 chaplet, circlet, coronet, fulfill, garland, perfect, royalty 8 complete, monarchy, pinnacle, round out 11 sovereignty

Crowne, Lenina character in: 13 Brave New World
author: 6 Huxley

crowning point 3 cap, tip 4 apex, peak 6 summit, vertex, zenith 8 pinnacle

crown of thorns 4 bane 5 cross 6 burden, ordeal 7 torment 8 vexation 10 affliction 11 tribulation

crow over 5 gloat 9 brag about 10 boast about

crucial 5 grave 6 knotty, urgent 7 serious, weighty 8 critical, decisive, pressing 9 essential, important, momentous 11 determining, significant

Crucible, The
author: 12 Arthur Miller

crude 3 raw 5 crass, gross, rough 6 coarse, vulgar 7 obscene, sketchy, uncouth 9 imperfect, tasteless, unrefined 10 incomplete, unfinished, unpolished, unprepared 11 uncompleted, undeveloped, unprocessed

crudeness 7 rawness 8 bad taste 9 crassness, grossness, obscenity, vulgarity 10 coarseness, indelicacy 13 tastelessness

cruel 6 brutal, savage 7 inhuman, vicious 8 inhumane, pitiless, ruthless, sadistic 9 heartless, merciless, unfeeling 10 unmerciful 11 cold-blooded, hardhearted, remorseless 15 uncompassionate

cruelty 6 sadism 8 ferocity, savagery 9 barbarity, brutality 10 bestiality, inhumanity 11 viciousness 12 ruthlessness 13 heartlessness

cruet 3 jar, jug 6 bottle 7 urceole 9 dispenser

cruise 4 sail, scud, skim 5 coast, drift, float, glide, sweep 6 stream, voyage 7 seafare 8 navigate

Cruise, Tom
original name: 21 Thomas Cruise Mapother
born: 2 NY 8 Syracuse
wife: 10 Mimi Rogers 12 Nicole Kidman
films: 4 Taps 6 Top Gun 7 The Firm, Rain Man 8 Cocktail 10 Far and Away 11 Endless Love, A Few Good Men 12 The Outsiders 13 Risky Business 15 The Color of Money 16 All the Right Moves 21 Born on the Fourth of July

crumb 3 bit 5 grain, scrap, shred, speck 6 morsel, sliver 8 fragment, particle

crumble 5 crush, decay, grate, grind 6 powder 8 fragment, splinter 9 decompose, pulverize 12 disintegrate

crumbly 7 brittle, friable 9 breakable

Crummles, Vincent
character in: 16 Nicholas Nickleby
author: 7 Dickens

crummy 5 awful, lousy 6 rotten 8 terrible

crumple 4 fall 5 crush 6 cave in, crease, pucker, rumple 7 crimple, crinkle, wrinkle 8 collapse 9 corrugate

crunch 4 chew, gnaw 5 chomp, gnash, grind, munch 9 masticate

Cruncher, Jerry
character in: 16 A Tale of Two Cities
author: 7 Dickens

crunchy 3 dry 5 crisp 6 crispy 7 crackly

crusade, Crusade 5 drive, rally 8 movement

crusader, Crusader 6 knight, zealot 7 pilgrim, Templar 8 champion 11 Hospitaller

crush 4 mash 5 break, press, quash, quell, smash 6 enfold, quench, squash, subdue 7 crumble, crumple, embrace, put down, shatter, squeeze, squelch 8 compress, overcome, suppress 9 granulate, overpower, overwhelm, pulverize 10 extinguish

crushed 3 sad 5 cowed 6 broken, mashed, woeful 7 abashed, doleful, forlorn, pressed, put down, quashed, quelled, smashed, subdued 8 crumbled, crumpled, dejected, desolate, overcame, overcome, quenched, squashed, squeezed, wretched 9 flattened, miserable, squelched, woebegone 10 compressed, despondent, pulverized, suppressed 11 overpowered, overwhelmed 12 disconsolate, extinguished, inconsolable 13 broken-hearted

crushing 7 mashing 8 decisive, quelling, smashing 10 shattering 11 humiliating, putting down, stamping out, suppression 12 obliterating, overwhelming 13 pulverization

crust 4 coat, gall, hull, rind, scab 5 brass, nerve, shell 6 harden 7 coating 8 chutzpah, covering, pie shell 9 impudence 11 pastry shell

crustacean 4 crab, flea 5 louse, prawn 6 isopod, shrimp 7 lobster 8 barnacle, crawfish, crayfish 9 shellfish, water flea

crusty 4 curt 5 blunt, gruff, rough, short, stern, surly, testy 6 abrupt, crabby, cranky, shirty, snippy, sullen 7 brusque, peevish, waspish 8 choleric, snappish, snippety 9 irascible, splenetic 10 ill-natured 11 ill-tempered 13 short-tempered

crux 3 nub 4 core, gist 5 basis, heart 7 essence 9 essential 10 brass tacks 11 nitty-gritty

cry 3 beg, sob, sue 4 bawl, call, hawk, howl, keen, moan, plea, roar, wail, weep, yell, yelp 5 blare, cheer, groan, mourn, plead, shout, utter, whoop 6 appeal, bellow, blazon, boohoo, clamor, hurrah, huzzah, lament, outcry, prayer, scream, shriek, snivel 7 blubber, call out, exclaim, implore, request, screech, trumpet, whimper 8 entreaty, petition, proclaim 9 advertise, importune 10 adjuration, promulgate 11 exclamation 12 solicitation, supplication

Cry, the Beloved Country
 author: 9 Alan Paton
 locale: 11 South Africa

cry out 4 bark, bawl, call, howl, roar, yell 5 shout 6 bellow, clamor, holler 7 exclaim 8 proclaim 9 ejaculate

cry over 5 mourn 6 bemoan, bewail, lament

crypt 4 tomb 5 vault 8 catacomb 9 mausoleum, sepulcher

cryptic 4 dark 5 vague 6 arcane, hidden, occult, secret 7 obscure, strange 8 esoteric, mystical, puzzling 9 ambiguous 10 cabalistic, mysterious, perplexing 11 enigmatical

cryptogram 4 code 6 cipher

cryptograph 4 code 6 cipher, encode

crystal 3 ice 5 clear, flake, glass, lucid 8 quartz 7 diamond 8 stemware 9 glassware, snowflake, watch part 10 rhinestone 11 transparent

crystallize 3 fix, gel 4 firm, jell 5 candy 6 harden 8 solidify 9 granulate

Csonka, Larry (Lawrence Richard)
 nickname: 9 Lawnmower
 sport: 8 football
 position: 8 fullback
 team: 13 Miami Dolphins, New York Giants

Cteatus
 origin: 5 Greek
 mentioned in: 5 Iliad
 father: 5 Actor
 mother: 7 Molione

Ctesippus
 father: 8 Hercules
 suitor of: 8 Penelope

Ctesius
 epithet of: 4 Zeus
 means: 9 god of gain

cub 3 boy, pup 4 bear, lion 5 scout, whelp 6 novice 8 reporter 9 youngling, youngster 10 apprentice

Cuba
 other name: 18 pearl of the Antilles
 capital/largest city: 6 Havana 8 Le Habana
 others: 5 Bauta, Colon, Duabi, Guane, Manes 6 Baines, Bayamo, Gibara, Guines, Mayari 7 Antilla, Baracoa, Fomento, Holguin, Holquin, Jiguani, Niquero, Palmira, Sanhuis 8 Artemisa, Camaguey, Cardenas, Guaimaro, Guayabal, Marianao, Matanzas, Nuevitas, Varadero, Yaguajay 9 Cabaiguan, Camajuani, Cienfuego 10 Cienfuegos, Guanabacoa, Guantanamo, Manzanillo, Santa Clara 11 Campechuela, Pinar del Rio, Puerto Padre 12 Ciego de Avila 13 Sagua de Tanamo 14 Sancti Spiritus, Santiago de Cuba 17

Aguada de Pasajeros, Consolacion del Sur
 measure: 4 vara 5 bocoy, cocoy, tarea 6 cordel, fanega 10 caballeria
 monetary unit: 4 peso 7 centavo 8 cuarenta
 weight: 5 libra 6 tercio
 island: 5 Pines, Pinos 6 Sabana 8 Camaguey, Juventud 9 Canarreos 17 Jardines de la Reina
 cay: 4 Coco 5 Largo 6 Romano 7 Guajaba, Rosareo, Sabinal 8 Cantiles 9 San Felipe 10 Santa Maria
 mountain: 6 Copper 7 Cristal, Maestra, Organos 8 Camaguey, Trinidad 9 Las Villas 11 Pinar del rio 12 Guaniguanico 14 Sancti-Spiritus
 highest point: 8 Turquino
 river: 4 Zaza 5 Cauto 8 San Pedro
 sea: 8 Atlantic 9 Caribbean
 physical feature:
 bay: 4 Nipe, Pigs 6 Jiguey 8 Cochinos 10 Buena Vista, Guantznamo
 cape: 4 Cruz 5 Maisi 8 Lucrecia 10 Corrientes, San Antonio
 channel: 8 Nicholas 9 Old Bahama
 falls: 3 Toa 7 Agabama, Caburni
 gulf: 6 Mexico 7 Cazones 8 Anamaria, Batabano 12 Guancanayabo
 inlet: 4 Broa 10 Corrientes
 peninsula: 6 Zapata
 point: 7 Guarico
 swamp: 6 Zapata
 people: 5 Carib, Negro, Taino, white 6 Arawak 7 Ciboney, mestizo 8 Ciboneye
 conqueror: 9 Velazquez
 explorer: 8 Columbus
 leader: 6 Castro 7 Batista 10 Che Guevara
 language: 7 Spanish
 religion: 13 Roman Catholic
 cult: 6 Chango, Yemaya
 places:
 castle: 5 Morro
 cathedral: 8 Santiago
 feature:
 dance: 5 conga, rumba 6 danzon, rhumba 8 guaracha, pachanga
 harvest: 5 zafra
 peasant: 7 guajiro
 tree: 5 jique, jiqui
 witch doctor: 7 nanigos
 food:
 dish: 6 paella
 drink: 4 pina

cubbyhole 4 nook 5 niche 6 cranny 10 pigeonhole 11 compartment

cube of deep-fried pork
 American Spanish: 10 cuchifrito

cubic centimeter
 abbreviation: 4 cu cm

cubic dekameter
 abbreviation: 5 cu dkm

cubic foot
 abbreviation: 4 cu ft

cubic inch
 abbreviation: 4 cu in

cubicle 3 bay 4 cell, nook 5 booth, niche 6 alcove, recess

cubic meter
abbreviation: 3 cu m

cubic millimeter
abbreviation: 4 cu mm

cubic yard
abbreviation: 4 cu yd

cubit 15 Biblical measure

cuchifrito 19 cube of deep-fried pork

Cuchulainn
origin: 5 Irish
hero of: 6 Ulster
uncle: 9 Conchobar
guarded house of: 10 Smith Culan
killed by: 6 Lugaid

cuckoo 3 ani 4 bats, bird, fool, gaga, nuts 5 balmy, batty, crazy, daffy, dotty, goofy, loony, nutty, silly, wacky 6 screwy 7 idiotic 9 screwball 12 crackbrained 13 off one's rocker 14 off one's trolley

cucumber 14 Cucumis sativus
varieties: 3 bur 4 mock, star, wild 6 bitter 7 prickly, serpent 9 squirting 13 African horned

cuddle 3 pet 5 clasp 6 caress, curl up, fondle, huddle, nestle, nuzzle 7 cling to, embrace, lie snug, snuggle

Cuddly Dudley
nickname of: 11 Dudley Moore

cudgel 4 club 5 baton, staff, stick 8 bludgeon 9 billy club, blackjack, truncheon 10 shillelagh 12 quarterstaff

cue 3 key, tip 4 clue, hint, sign 6 signal 7 inkling 10 intimation, suggestion 11 insinuation

cuff 3 box, hit, rap 4 blow 5 clout, smack, thump, whack 6 thwack, wallop

cui bono 10 for what use, of what good 15 for whose benefit

cuisine 4 fare, food, menu 5 table 6 viands 7 cookery, cooking, edibles 8 victuals, vittles 11 comestibles

Cukor, George
director of: 7 Camille 8 Adam's Rib, Gaslight, The Women 10 My Fair Lady (Oscar) 11 A Double Life, A Star Is Born, Little Women 13 Born Yesterday, Dinner at Eight 14 Romeo and Juliet 16 David Copperfield 18 A Bill of Divorcement 20 The Philadelphia Story

cul-de-sac 6 pocket 7 dead-end, impasse 10 blind alley

cull 4 junk, pick, sift, take 5 dross, glean, scrap, trash 6 choose, divide, garner, gather, jetsam, reject, second, select, winnow 7 castoff, collect, discard, excerpt, extract, leaving 8 abstract, scouring, separate 9 segregate

culminate 3 cap, end, top 5 crown, end up 6 climax, finish, result, top off, wind up 8 complete, conclude 9 terminate 10 consummate

culmination 4 acme, apex, peak 6 apogee, climax, height, zenith 7 epitome 8 pinnacle 10 conclusion 11 fulfillment, realization 12 consummation

Culp, Robert
born: 10 Berkeley CA
roles: 4 I Spy 20 Greatest American Hero

culpability 4 onus 5 blame, fault, guilt 9 liability 14 accountability, responsibility

culpable 6 guilty, liable 7 at fault, to blame 8 blamable 10 censurable 11 blameworthy

culprit 5 felon 6 sinner 8 criminal, evildoer, offender 9 miscreant, wrongdoer 10 lawbreaker, malefactor 12 transgressor

cult 4 sect 7 faction, zealots 8 admirers, devotees, devotion 9 disciples, followers 10 admiration

cultivable 6 arable 7 fertile, friable 8 farmable, plowable, tillable

cultivate 3 dig, hoe, sow 4 farm, grow, plow, seek, till, weed 5 court, plant, spade 6 enrich, garden 7 acquire, advance, develop, elevate, enhance, improve

cultivated 3 dug 4 fine, grew, hoed 6 farmed, forked, sought, spaded, tilled, weeded 7 courted, planted 8 advanced, cultured, elevated, enhanced, enriched, finished, improved, polished 9 developed

cultivation 5 grace 6 polish, sowing 7 farming, manners, tilling 8 agronomy, planting 9 elevation, gardening, gentility, good taste, husbandry 10 refinement 11 agriculture

culture 3 art 5 music 7 the arts 8 learning 9 erudition, knowledge 10 enrichment, literature, refinement 12 civilization 13 enlightenment 15 accomplishments

Culture and Anarchy
author: 13 Matthew Arnold

cultured 7 elegant, erudite, genteel, learned, refined 8 polished, well-bred, well-read 11 enlightened 12 accomplished, well-educated 13 sophisticated

culvert 5 ditch, drain, sewer 6 trench 7 channel, conduit, fox-hole

Cumaean sibyl
prophetess of: 5 Cumae
guided: 6 Aeneas

cumbersome 5 bulky, hefty 6 clumsy 7 awkward 8 cumbrous, ungainly, unwieldy 9 ponderous 12 unmanageable

cum grano salis 15 not too seriously 16 with a grain of salt

cumin
botanical name: 14 Cuminum cyminum
other name: 6 comino, jiraka, kummel
origin: 5 Egypt
family: 7 parsley
symbol of: 5 greed
guards against straying: 7 pigeons 8 chickens, husbands
use: 4 fish, meat, rice, soup, stew 5 bread, curry 6 cheese 7 pickles, sausage 8 potatoes 11 chili powder

cum laude 10 with praise

cummings, e e (Edward Estlin)
author of: 12 in just spring 15 The Enormous Room 17 Tulips and Chimneys 18 Chansons Innocentes

Cummings, Robert
  real name: 29 Clarence Robert Orville Cummings
  born: 8 Joplin MO
  roles: 8 King's Row 14 Dial M for Murder 18 The Bob Cummings Show
cumulate 5 amass 6 gather, heap up, pile up 10 accumulate
cumulative 7 amassed, piled up 8 additive, heaped up 9 aggregate 10 collective 12 accumulative, conglomerate
Cunegonde
  character in: 7 Candide
  author: 8 Voltaire
Cunina
  origin: 5 Roman
  goddess of: 15 sleeping infants
cunning 3 art, sly 4 foxy, wily 5 canny, craft, guile, knack, skill 6 artful, crafty, deceit, genius, shifty, shrewd, talent, tricky 7 ability, devious, finesse, slyness 8 aptitude, artifice, deftness, foxiness, guileful, subtlety, trickery, wiliness 9 chicanery, deceitful, deception, deceptive, dexterity, duplicity, ingenious, underhand 10 adroitness, artfulness, cleverness, craftiness, expertness, shrewdness 11 deviousness 13 Machiavellian
  god of: 6 Hermes
Cunning Little Vixen, The
  opera by: 7 Janacek
cup 3 cup 5 glass, grail, stein 6 beaker, goblet, vessel 7 chalice, tankard 8 schooner
  abbreviation: 1 c
Cup
  constellation of: 6 Crater
Cupava
  companion of: 6 Aeneas
cupbearer of gods 8 Ganymede
cupboard 6 buffet, bureau, closet 7 armoire, cabinet 9 sideboard, storeroom 10 chiffonier 11 china closet 12 clothespress
Cupid
  also: 4 Amor
  origin: 5 Roman
  god of: 4 love
  mother: 5 Venus
  corresponds to: 4 Eros
cupidity 5 greed 7 avarice, avidity 8 rapacity 10 greediness 11 selfishness 12 covetousness, graspingness 13 concupiscence, insatiability, rapaciousness 14 avariciousness 15 acquisitiveness
cupola 4 dome, roof 5 tower, vault 6 belfry, turret 7 ceiling
cur 3 cad 4 mutt 5 rogue 6 rascal, varlet, wretch 7 mongrel, varmint, villain 9 scoundrel 10 blackguard
curacao
  type: 7 liqueur
  origin: 19 Netherlands Antilles
  flavor: 6 orange
  with gin: 8 Blue Moon, Napoleon 9 Blue Devil 14 Flying Dutchman
  with rum: 6 Mai-Tai 8 Blue Lady 12 Blue Hawaiian

  with vodka: 8 Aqueduct
curate 5 vicar 6 cleric, deacon, parson, pastor, priest, rector 8 minister, preacher 9 churchman, clergyman 12 ecclesiastic
curative 4 balm 7 healing 11 restorative
curator 5 doyen 6 keeper 8 director, overseer 9 caretaker, custodian
curb 3 rim 4 edge, rein 5 brink, check, ledge, limit 6 border, bridle, halter, retard, slow up 7 control, harness, inhibit, repress, slacken 8 hold back, moderate, restrain, restrict, slow down, suppress 9 curbstone, hindrance, restraint 10 decelerate, limitation 11 restriction, retardation
curdle 3 rot 4 clot, curd, sour, turn 5 decay, go bad, go off, spoil 7 clabber, congeal, ferment, putrefy, thicken 8 putresce, solidify 9 coagulate 11 deteriorate
cure 3 dry 4 heal, salt 5 smoke 6 remedy 8 antidote, make well, preserve 10 corrective
cure-all 4 balm 6 elixir, remedy 7 panacea 10 catholicon
cured 5 dried 6 healed, mended, smoked 8 made well, remedied 9 preserved, recovered
Curetes
  form: 8 demigods
  attendants of: 4 Zeus
Curiatii see 7 Horatii
Curie, Marie Sklodowska and Pierre
  field: 7 physics 9 chemistry
  discovered: 6 radium 8 polonium 13 radioactivity
  awarded: 10 Nobel Prize
curio 7 bibelot, trinket 9 bric-a-brac, objet d'art
curiosity 5 freak, sight 6 marvel, oddity, prying, rarity, wonder 7 novelty 8 interest, nosiness 10 phenomenon, rare object 11 questioning 15 inquisitiveness
curious 3 odd 4 nosy, rare 5 funny, novel, queer, weird 6 prying, quaint, unique 7 bizarre, strange, unusual 8 peculiar, singular, snooping, uncommon 9 inquiring, searching 11 inquisitive, questioning
Curitis
  epithet of: 4 Juno
  means: 10 of the spear
curl 4 coil, lock, wave, wind 5 crimp, frizz, swirl, twirl, twist 6 spiral 7 frizzle, ringlet, scallop 8 curlicue 9 corkscrew
curled 3 set 5 kinky, waved, wound 6 coiled, frizzy spiral 7 crimped, frizzed, twisted 8 crinkled, scrolled 9 curlicued
curlicue 4 coil 5 twist 6 spiral 8 flourish
curly 4 wavy 5 kinky 6 frizzy 7 rippled 8 crinkled 9 ringleted
curmudgeon 4 crab 5 crank, grump 6 grouch 8 grumbler, sourball
currant 5 Ribes
  varieties: 3 red 5 black, fetid, skunk, squaw, stink 6 alpine, cherry, common, garden, Indian, Sierra 7 Buffalo 8 Missouri, mountain, swamp red 9 chaparral, wild black 11 northern red 12 bristly black 13 American black, European black,

northern black, white-flowered 15 California black

currency 4 cash, coin 5 bills, money, vogue 7 coinage 9 bank notes 10 acceptance, popularity, prevalence 12 predominance, universality

current 3 now 4 flow, flux, mood, tide 5 draft, drift, trend 6 modern, spirit, stream, with-it 7 feeling, in style, in vogue, popular, present 8 existing, tendency, up-to-date 9 prevalent, zeitgeist 10 atmosphere, present-day, prevailing 11 inclination 12 contemporary, undercurrent

current of air 4 wind 5 draft 6 breeze, zephyr

curricle 3 gig 4 cart, trap 6 chaise 8 carriage

curry powder
origin: 5 India
ingredient: 5 cumin 6 cloves 8 capsicum, turmeric 9 coriander, fenugreek, red pepper 13 cayenne pepper
use: 5 kebab, kebob, kofta, malai 6 kormas 7 curries, pea soup 8 meat loaf, vindaloo, zucchini 11 potato salad

curse 3 vex 4 bane, cuss, damn, oath 5 blast, cross, swear, trial 6 burden, ordeal, plague, whammy 7 afflict, condemn, evil eye, scourge, swear at, torment, trouble 8 anathema, denounce, execrate, swearing, vexation 9 annoyance, blasphemy, damnation, evil spell, expletive, obscenity, profanity 10 affliction, execration, misfortune 11 imprecation, malediction, tribulation 12 anathematize, denunciation

cursory 5 brief, hasty, quick, swift 6 casual, random 7 hurried, offhand, passing 8 careless 9 desultory, haphazard 11 inattentive, perfunctory, superficial

curt 4 rude 5 bluff, blunt, gruff, short, terse 6 abrupt, crusty, snappy 7 brusque, summary 8 petulant 10 peremptory

curtail 3 cut 4 clip, trim 6 reduce 7 abridge, shorten 8 condense, contract, cut short, decrease, diminish, pare down 10 abbreviate

curtailed 3 cut 7 checked, concise, cut back, reduced, slashed 8 abridged, cut short 9 shortened 10 retrenched

curtailment 7 cutback, cutting, halting, pruning 8 clipping, decrease, trimming 9 lessening, reduction, restraint 10 limitation, shortening 11 abridgement, contraction 12 abbreviation, condensation

curtain 3 end 4 mask, veil 5 blind, cover, drape, shade, sheet 6 screen, shroud 7 conceal, drapery, hanging 8 portiere

Curtis, Tony
real name: 15 Bernard Schwartz
wife: 10 Janet Leigh
daughter: 8 Jamie Lee
born: 9 New York NY
roles: 7 Houdini, Trapeze 12 The Great Race 13 Some Like It Hot 14 The Defiant Ones 16 The Great Imposter 18 The Boston Strangler 22 The Sweet Smell of Success

Curtius
also: 6 Marcus
volunteered as: 17 sacrificial victim

Curtiz, Michael
director of: 10 Casablanca (Oscar), The Sea Hawk 12 Captain Blood 13 Mildred Pierce 14 Life with Father 17 Yankee Doodle Dandy 24 The Adventures of Robin Hood (with William Keighley) 26 The Charge of the Light Brigade 34 The Private Lives of Elizabeth and Essex

curtsy, curtsey 3 bob, bow, dip 5 honor 6 homage 9 obeisance, reverence 11 bend the knee

curvature 3 arc 4 arch, bend 5 crook 6 bowing

curve 3 arc, bow 4 arch, bend, coil, hook, loop, turn, wind 5 crook, twist 6 spiral, swerve

curved 4 bent 5 bowed 6 arched, looped, turned

curved span 3 bow 4 arch, dome 5 vault 6 bridge

Curve of Binding Energy, The
author: 10 John McPhee

curving 4 bent 5 bowed 6 arched 7 bending, looping, turning, winding 8 twisting

curving inward 6 hollow, sunken 7 concave 8 hollowed 9 depressed

curving outward 5 bowed 6 convex 7 bulging, rounded 8 bellying 11 protuberant

Cuscatlan see 10 El Salvador

Cush
father: 3 Ham
grandfather: 4 Noah
brother: 6 Canaan
son: 6 Nimrod
Hebrew for: 8 Ethiopia

cushion 3 mat, pad 4 damp 5 quiet 6 dampen, deaden, muffle, pillow, soften, stifle 7 bolster 8 suppress

Cushitic
language family: 11 AfroAsiatic 13 Hamito-Semitic
branch: 6 Somali 8 Gallinya
spoken in: 7 Somalia 8 Ethiopia, Tanzania

cusp 4 apex, barb, horn, peak 5 angle, point, tooth 6 corner

custard 4 flan, fool 5 creme 6 junket 7 dessert, pudding 8 flummery 10 blanc-mange, zabaglione

Custer, George A
served in: 8 Civil War 10 Indian Wars
side: 5 Union
battle: 13 Little Big Horn
defeated: 11 Black Kettle
defeated by: 10 Crazy Horse

custodian 6 duenna, keeper, warden 7 janitor 8 chaperon, guardian, watchman 9 attendant, caretaker, chaperone, concierge 14 superintendent

custody 4 care 5 watch 6 charge 9 detention 10 possession, protection 11 confinement, safekeeping, trusteeship 12 conservation, guardianship, preservation

custom 4 form, mode 5 habit, usage 7 fashion 10 convention

customarily 7 as a rule, usually 8 commonly, normally 9 generally, regularly 10 frequently, habitually, ordinarily 13 traditionally

customary 5 usual 6 common, normal, wonted 7 general, regular, routine, typical 8 everyday, habitual, ordinary 10 accustomed 11 traditional 12 conventional

customer 5 buyer 6 client, patron 7 habitue, shopper 9 purchaser

customs 4 duty, levy, toll 6 excise, tariff 9 import tax 10 assessment

cut 3 mow, saw 4 chop, clip, crop, cube, dice, fall, gash, hack, move, nick, pare, part, rent, rive, slit, snip, snub, trim 5 carve, cross, lance, mince, piece, prune, sever, share, shave, shear, slash, slice, split, wound 6 bisect, course, delete, divide, furrow, hollow, ignore, incise, pierce, reduce, sunder, trench 7 abridge, channel, curtail, decline, dissect, opening, passage, portion, section, segment 8 condense, contract, decrease, diminish, incision, lacerate 9 abatement, intersect, lessening, reduction, shrinkage 10 abbreviate, diminution, excavation, shortening 11 contraction, curtailment, indentation

cut and run 4 bolt, flee, skip 6 escape 7 abscond, get away, make off, run away 8 slip away 9 break free 10 break loose, fly the coop 12 make a getaway

cut apart 7 dissect 9 anatomize

cutback 4 decrease, trimming 9 reduction 11 abridgement, curtailment

cut back 4 trim 5 prune 6 reduce 7 abridge, curtail 8 decrease

cut costs 4 save 5 skimp, stint 6 scrimp 7 husband 8 conserve 9 economize 15 tighten one's belt

cut down 4 kill, trim 5 limit 6 lessen, reduce 7 abridge, curtail, destroy, disable, remodel, shorten 8 condense, decrease, diminish, restrict 10 abbreviate

cut-down form 6 digest, precis 7 summary 8 synopsis, trimming 10 shortening 11 abridgement, contraction, curtailment 12 abbreviation, condensation

cut down to size 6 abase 6 humble 7 mortify 8 belittle, bring low, disgrace 9 humiliate 13 bring down a peg

cute 5 sweet 6 dainty, pretty 7 darling, lovable 8 adorable, handsome, precious 9 beautiful 10 attractive

cut expenses 4 save 5 skimp, stint 6 scrimp 8 conserve 9 economize 12 pinch pennies 15 tighten one's belt

cut in half 5 halve 6 bisect

cut in two 5 halve, sever 6 bisect

cutlet 3 cut 4 chop 5 slice 9 cotelette, croquette

cut off 4 dock, trim 5 apart, sever 6 detach, remove 7 chop off, divorce, isolate 8 amputate, divorced, isolated, separate 10 disconnect

cut out 2 go 4 blow, exit 5 be off, erase, leave, scram, split 6 beat it, delete, depart, escape, excise, go away, remove, set out 7 abolish 8 designed, get rid of, set forth 9 eliminate 10 do away with, hit the road, make tracks 11 exterminate, take a powder

cut short 4 clip, crop, dock, trim 7 abridge, shorten 8 truncate 10 abbreviate

cutter 4 boat 5 blade, hewer, knife 6 sledge, sleigh, tailor 11 cutting edge

cutthroat 5 cruel 6 outlaw 7 brigand, hoodlum, ruffian 8 ruthless 9 merciless

cutting 3 raw 4 acid, cold 5 harsh, nasty, sharp 6 biting, bitter 7 acerbic, caustic, nipping, pruning, searing 8 clipping, derisive, piercing, scathing, smarting, snubbing, stinging, trimming 9 reduction, sarcastic, stringent 11 abridgement, acrimonious, compression, contraction, curtailment, disparaging, penetrating 12 abbreviation, condensation

cutting edge 5 blade 8 vanguard 9 forefront

cutting off 8 severing 9 severance 10 detachment, separation 13 disconnection, disengagement

cutting remark 3 dig 4 gibe, jeer 5 taunt

Cuttle
  character in: 12 Dombey and Son
  author: 7 Dickens

cut up 4 chop, hack, maim, rend 5 caper, carve, halve, mince, slash, slice, split 6 cleave, deface, deform, divide 7 portion, quarter 8 dissever, mutilate 9 apportion, kid around 10 fool around 11 clown around, play the fool

Cuvier, Georges
  field: 7 geology, zoology
  nationality: 6 French
  founded: 12 paleontology 18 comparative anatomy

Cyane
  form: 5 nymph 8 princess
  violated by: 6 father

Cyaxares see 9 Ahasuerus

Cybele
  also: 9 Dindymene 10 Berecyntia, Magna Mater 11 Great Mother 12 Mater Turrita 17 Great Idaean Mother
  origin: 8 Phrygian 9 Asia Minor
  goddess of: 6 nature
  priest: 5 Galli 10 Corybantes
  corresponds to: 3 Ops 4 Rhea
  epithet: 6 Antaea

Cychreus
  king of: 7 Salamis
  father: 8 Poseidon
  mother: 7 Salamis
  daughter: 6 Glauce

Cyclades 3 Dos, Zea 4 Keos, Nios, Sira, Syra 5 Delos, Melos, Naxos, Paros, Siros, Syros, Tenos, Tinos 6 Andros 7 Amorgos, islands, Kythnos 13 Aegean islands

cycle 3 run 6 series 8 sequence 10 succession 11 progression 14 connected group

cyclone 4 gale, gust, wind 5 storm 7 tornado, twister, typhoon 9 whirlwind, windstorm
  Australian: 10 willy-nilly

Cyclone (Cy)
  nickname of: 15 Denton True Young

Cyclops, Cyclopes
  form: 5 giant
  number of eyes: 3 one
  father: 6 Uranus
  mother: 2 Ge
  blinded by: 8 Odysseus

Cycnus
  father: 4 Ares
  killed in: 4 duel
  killed by: 8 Hercules
  changed into: 4 swan

Cydippe
  priestess of: 4 Hera
  location: 5 Argos
  father: 7 Ochimus
  son: 5 Biton 7 Cleobis

cylinder 3 can, tin 4 drum, pipe, roll, tube 5 spool 6 barrel, column, pillar, piston, platen, roller 13 piston chamber

cylindrical 5 round 6 tarete 7 tubular 8 columnar

Cyllene
  form: 5 nymph
  nursed: 6 Hermes

Cyllenian
  pertains to: 6 Hermes 12 Mount Cellene

Cymbeline
  author: 18 William Shakespeare
  character: 6 Cloten, Imogen 7 Iachimo, Pisanio 9 Bellarius 17 Leonatus Posthumus

Cymodoce
  mentioned in: 6 Aeneid
  form: 4 ship
  fleet of: 6 Aeneas
  changed by: 6 Cybele
  changed into: 8 sea nymph

Cymru see 5 Wales

cynic 7 scoffer, skeptic 9 pessimist 10 misogynist 11 faultfinder, misanthrope

cynical 8 derisive, sardonic, scoffing, scornful, sneering 9 misogynic, sarcastic, skeptical 12 misanthropic

Cynortes
  father: 7 Amyclas
  mother: 7 Diomede

Cynosura
  nurse of: 4 Zeus

Cynthia see 7 Artemis

Cynurus
  father: 7 Perseus

Cyparissia
  epithet of: 6 Athena
  means: 14 cypress goddess

Cyparissus
  killed: 4 stag
  changed into: 11 cypress tree

cypress 8 Taxodium 9 Cupressus
  varieties: 3 toy 4 bald, berg, pond 5 false, Gowen, Modoc, Piute 6 Bhutan, Hinoki, Lawson, MacNab, Nootka, Sawara, summer, Tecate 7 African, Arizona, Italian, Mexican, Sargent 8 Cuyamaca, golfball, Monterey, mourning, Siskiyou, standing 9 Guadalupe, Mendocino, Montezuma, red summer, Santa Cruz 10 Portuguese, tennis-ball 12 Chinese swamp 18 rough-barked Arizona 19 smoothbarked Arizona

Cyprian see 9 Aphrodite

Cyprus
  biblical name: 6 Kittim
  capital/largest city: 7 Nicosia
  city: 6 Paphos 7 Kyrenia, Larnaca 8 Limassol 9 Famagusta
  monetary unit: 4 para 5 pound
  mountain: 7 Kyrenia, Troodos
  highest point: 7 Olympus
  river: 6 Pedias
  sea: 13 Mediterranean
  physical feature:
    bay: 8 Episkopi
    cape: 4 Gata 5 Greco 7 Andreas, Arnauti 9 Kormakiti
    peninsula: 6 Karpas
    plain: 8 Mesaoria 9 Messaoria
  people: 5 Greek, Turks 9 Cypriotes
  ruler: 5 Turks 6 Greeks, Romans 7 British 9 Egyptians, Lusignans, Venetians 10 Byzantines 11 Phoenicians
  language: 5 Greek 7 Turkish
  religion: 5 Islam 6 Muslim 13 Greek Orthodox 16 Eastern Orthodoxy

Cypselus
  king of: 7 Arcadia
  father: 7 Aepytus
  daughter: 6 Merope
  son-in-law: 11 Cresphontes
  grandson: 7 Aepytus

Cyrano de Bergerac
  director: 13 Michael Gordon
  author: 13 Edmond Rostand
  cast: 10 Jose Ferrer (Cyrano), Mala Powers 13 William Powers
  character: 6 Roxane 22 Christian de Neuvillette
  setting: 5 Paris
  Oscar for: 9 best actor (Ferrer)

Cyrano de Bergerac, Savinien
  author of: 25 Voyages to the Moon and the Sun
  play based on his life by: 13 Edmond Rostand

Cyrene
  father: 7 Hypseus
  mother: 6 Creusa
  lover: 6 Apollo
  son: 5 Idmon 9 Aristaeus

Cytherea see 9 Aphrodite

Cytissorus
  father: 7 Phrixus
  mother: 9 Chalciope
  brother: 5 Argus, Melas 8 Phrontis

cytology
  study of: 5 cells
czar, tsar 4 king 5 ruler 6 caesar, despot, tyrant 7 emperor, monarch 8 dictator, overlord 9 potentate, sovereign
czarina 7 empress
czaristic 10 autocratic 11 all-powerful, dictatorial, monarchical
Czechoslovakia/Czech Republic see 8 Slovakia
  capital/largest city: 5 Praha 6 Prague
  others: 2 As 4 Asch, Brno, Cheb, Most 5 Brunn, Nitra, Opava, Plzen, Tabor, 6 Aussig, Bilina, Kladno, Kosice, Pilsen, Presov, Sadowa, Trnava, Vsetin 7 Budweis, Jihlava, Liberec, Olomouc, Ostrava, Teplitz 8 Carlsbad, Jachymov, Karlsbad 9 Pressburg 10 Austerlitz, Bratislava, Koniggratz 11 Reichenberg
  university: 7 Charles
  division: 7 Bohemia, Moravia, Silesia 8 Ruthenia, Slovakia
  measure: 3 Lan 4 Mira 5 Korec, Liket, Stopa 6 Merice, Strych
  monetary unit: 5 crown, ducat 6 heller, Koruna
  mountain: 3 Erz, Ore 5 Giant, Tatra 6 Sumava 7 Sudeten, Sudetes 8 Krkonose 10 Carpathian
  highest point: 7 Gerlach 11 Gerlachovka
  river: 2 Uh, 3 Mze, Vag, Vah 4 Dyje, Eger, Elbe, Gran, Hron, Ipel, Iser, Labe, Nisa, Oder, Odra, Ohre, Olse, Waag 5 Becva, Dunaj, March, Nitra, Slana, Tisza 6 Danube, Moldau, Morava, Ondava, Sazava, Torysa, Vltava 7 Laborec, Luznice 8 Berounka
  physical feature:
  plateau: 8 Bohemian 11 Sudetenland
  people: 4 Slav 5 Czech 6 Slovak 8 Bohemian, Moravian
  author: 5 Capek, Hasek, Havel 7 Kundera, Seifert
  composer: 6 Dvorak 7 Janacek, Martinu, Smetana
  director: 11 Milos Forman
  philosopher/reformer: 8 Comenius, John Huss
  language: 5 Czech 6 German, Magyar, Slovak 7 Russian 9 Hungarian
  religion: 6 Uniate 8 Lutheran 9 Orthodoxy 13 Roman Catholic
  place:
  castle: 8 Hradcany
  cathedral: 7 St Vitus 10 St Nicholas
  resort/spa: 8 Carlsbad, Piestany 9 Marienbad 10 Luhacovice 11 Karlovy Vary 14 Marianske Lazne
  square: 9 Wenceslas
  feature:
  dance: 5 polka 6 redowa, talian 7 furiant
  gymnastics festival: 11 spartakiada
  song: 7 Mà Vlast
  food:
  beer: 6 pilsen
  sausage: 5 parky 6 vursty

D

dab 3 bit, pat, tap 6 stroke 7 smidgen, soupcon

dabble 5 slosh 6 fiddle, putter, splash 7 spatter, toy with 8 sprinkle

dabbler 7 amateur, trifler 10 dilettante 12 experimenter 15 nonprofessional

da capo
music: 22 repeat from the beginning
abbreviation: 2 D C

Dacca
capital of: 10 Bangladesh

d'accord 2 OK 6 agreed 7 granted

Dactyls
also: 7 Daktyls
dwellers of: 8 Mount Ida

dad 2 da, pa 3 pop 4 papa, pops, sire 5 daddy, pappy, pater 6 father, parent 11 the old man

Daedala
festival in: 7 Boeotia

Daedalion
father: 9 Eosphorus
mother: 10 Phosphorus
daughter: 6 Chione
leaped off: 9 Parnassus
changed into: 4 hawk

Daedalus
occupation: 9 architect
father: 6 Metion
son: 5 Iapyx 6 Icarus
nephew: 5 Talos 6 Perdix
killed: 5 Talos
built: 9 labyrinth
for: 5 Minos
made: 5 wings

daffodil 9 Narcissus 24 Narcissus pseudo-narcissus
varieties: 3 sea 6 winter 8 Peruvian 9 petticoat 13 hoop-petticoat

daft 3 mad 4 loco 5 balmy, batty, crazy, daffy, dizzy, goofy, loony, nutty, silly, wacky 6 cuckoo, insane, screwy 7 foolish, lunatic, witless

Dagan
origin: 12 Mesopotamian
god of: 5 earth 11 agriculture
corresponds to: 5 Dagon

dagger 4 dirk, snee 5 blade, knife 6 weapon 7 poniard 8 stiletto

Dagon
origin: 10 Philistine, Phoenician
god of: 5 earth 11 agriculture
corresponds to: 5 Dagan

Daguerre, Louis J M
nationality: 6 French
inventor of: 11 photography 13 daguerreotype

dahlia
varieties: 3 sea 4 tree 6 common, garden 7 bedding 8 bell tree 10 candelabra

Dahomey, Republic of *see* 5 Benin

daily 7 diurnal, per diem 9 circadian, quotidian

Daimler, Gottlieb
nationality: 6 German
inventor of: 10 carburetor, motorcycle 14 gasoline engine 18 gasoline automobile 25 compression ignition engine

daimyo 4 lord 10 feudal lord

dainty 4 fine 5 fussy, tasty 6 choice, choosy, lovely, pretty, savory 7 choosey, elegant, refined 8 delicate, pleasing 9 beautiful, delicious, exquisite 10 attractive, fastidious, particular

Daira
father: 7 Oceanus

dais 5 stage 6 podium 7 rostrum 8 platform

daisy 6 Bellis 23 Chrysanthemum frutescens 25 Chrysanthemum leucanthemum
varieties: 4 blue, cape, high, lazy 5 crown, giant, globe, oxeye, Paris, veldt, white 6 butter, Easter, Nippon, shasta, sleepy, Tahoka 7 African, English, painted, seaside, turfing 8 Dahlberg, mountain, panamint 9 Barberton, Englemann, Swan River, Transvaal 10 Kingfisher, Michaelmas, Portuguese 11 Clanwilliam, Livingstone, Namaqualand 12 Boston yellow, double orange 15 blue-eyed African

Daisy Miller
author: 10 Henry James
character: 10 Giovanelli 12 Winterbourne

Dakar
capital of: 7 Senegal

Dakota (Sioux)
language family: 6 Siouan
tribe: 5 Teton 6 Lakota, Nakota, Santee 7 Yankton 8 Sisseton, Wahpeton, Wiciyela 9 Wahpekute, Yanktonai 11 Mdewakanton
location: 7 Montana 9 Minnesota 11 North Dakota, South Dakota
leader: 4 Gall 10 Crazy Horse 11 Sitting Bull 13 Jashunca-Uiteo
noted for: 15 military prowess
deity: 10 Wakan Tanka

Daktyls *see* 7 Dactyls

dale 4 dell, dene, glen, vale 6 dingle, hollow, valley

D'Alembert
author of: 12 Encyclopedia

Dali, Salvador
 born: 5 Spain 7 Figuras
 artwork: 10 Last Supper 17 Atomic Leda
 and Swan 19 Persistence of Memory 22
 Accommodations of Desire 24 Christ of
 St John of the Cross

Dalibor
 opera by: 7 Smetana
 character: 6 Milada

Dallas
 airport: 23 Dallas-Fort Worth Regional
 basketball team: 4 Mavs 9 Mavericks
 football team: 7 Cowboys
 landmark: 15 Turtle Creek Park 16 Museum of Fine Arts 19 Dallas Theater
 Center 25 Margo Jones Memorial Theater
 river: 7 Trinity
 stadium: 10 Cotton Bowl
 university: 3 SMU 13 Bishop College 17
 Southern Methodist

Dallas
 character: 7 JR Ewing 9 Jack Ewing,
 Jenna Wade, Jock Ewing, Miss Ellie, Ray
 Krebbs 10 Bobby Ewing 11 Christopher,
 Cliff Barnes, Mandy Winger, Mark Grai-
 son 12 Digger Barnes 13 Clayton Farlow,
 John Ross Ewing, Sue Ellen Ewing 16
 Donna Culver Krebs 17 Pamela Barnes
 Ewing 22 Eleanor Southworth Ewing
 cast: 8 John Beck 9 Dack Rambo, Linda
 Gray 10 Howard Keel 11 Larry Hagman,
 Steve Kanaly, Susan Howard 12 Ken
 Kercheval, Patrick Duffy 16 Barbara Bel
 Geddes, Priscilla Presley 17 Victoria
 Principal
 ranch: 9 Southfork
 business: 3 oil 8 Ewing Oil

dalliance 6 affair, toying 7 romance 8 fid-
 dling, trifling 10 flirtation, lovemaking

dally 3 toy 4 play 5 flirt 6 dawdle, loiter, trifle

Dalmatia see 10 Yugoslavia

Dalton, John
 field: 7 physics 9 chemistry
 nationality: 7 British
 formulated: 12 atomic theory
 first: 18 atomic weights table
 described: 14 color blindness

dam 3 bar, cow 4 clog, mare, plug, stop,
 wall 5 bitch, block, check 6 bridle, hinder,
 hold in, impede, plug up, stanch, stop up 7
 barrier, block up, confine, congest, inhibit,
 repress, stopper, stuff up 8 blockade, hold
 back, obstruct, restrain 9 barricade, hindrance 11 obstruction

damage, damages 3 mar 4 cost, harm,
 hurt, loss 6 impair, injure, injury, ravage 10
 impairment, reparation, settlement 11 destruction 12 compensation, despoliation

damaging 7 harmful, hurtful, ruinous 9 injurious 11 destructive, detrimental

Damascus
 ancient kingdom: 8 Aramaean
 Arabic: 7 Dimashq
 capital of: 5 Syria
 monastery: 22 Suleiman the Magnificent

 mosque: 5 Great 7 Umayyad
 mount: 6 Qasyun
 museum: 8 National 9 Qasr al-Azm
 river: 4 Awaj 6 Barada
 rulers: 5 Arabs, Timur 6 Romans 7 Mongols, Saladin 8 Assyrian 9 Caliphate, Seleucids 12 Ottoman Turks 15 Byzantine
 Empire 17 Alexander the Great
 tomb: 7 Saladin

Damastes see 10 Procrustes

Dame Pliant
 character in: 12 The Alchemist
 author: 6 Jonson

Damia
 spirit of: 9 fertility

damn 4 doom 5 blast 6 rail at 7 censure,
 condemn 8 denounce 9 criticize, disparage

damned 4 lost 6 cursed, darned, doomed,
 fallen 7 doggone, dratted, godless 8 accursed, doggoned 9 condemned, exe-
 crated, reprobate 12 unregenerate

Damocles
 offended: 9 Dionysius
 seated under: 14 suspended sword

Damon
 friend: 7 Pythias

damp 3 wet 4 curb, dank, dash, dewy, dull,
 mist 5 check, foggy, humid, misty, moist,
 muggy, rainy, soggy, spoil 6 clammy, dead-
 en, hamper, hinder, reduce, soaked, sodden 7 depress, drizzly, inhibit, sopping,
 wettish 8 dankness, diminish, dripping, humidity, moisture, restrain 9 mugginess, restraint 10 clamminess, discourage 14 discouragement

dampen 3 wet 7 moisten, wet down

dampen one's spirits 5 daunt, unman 6
 deject 7 depress 10 discourage, dishearten

damper 4 curb 8 obstacle 9 hindrance, restraint 10 constraint, impediment, wet
 blanket 14 discouragement

damsel 4 girl, lass 6 maiden 9 young lady

damselfly
 varieties: 8 forktail 10 civilbluet 11 black-
 winged, broad-winged 12 narrow-winged,
 spread-winged, violet dancer

dam up 4 clog, plug 5 block, choke 6 plug
 up, stop up 7 congest 8 obstruct

Damysus
 member of: 8 Gigantes

Dan
 means: 5 judge
 father: 5 Jacob
 mother: 6 Bilhah
 brother: 3 Gad 4 Levi 5 Asher, Judah 6
 Joseph, Reuben, Simeon 7 Zebulun 8
 Benjamin, Issachar, Naphtali
 sister: 5 Dinah
 descendant of: 6 Danite

Dana see 4 Danu

Dana, Richard Henry
 author of: 21 Two Years Before the Mast

Danae
  form: 6 maiden
  father: 8 Acrisius
  mother: 8 Eurydice
  imprisoned by: 8 Acrisius
  lover: 4 Zeus
  son: 7 Perseus

Danai
  members of: 6 Greeks 7 Argives

Danaides
  daughters of: 6 Danaus
  number of daughters: 5 fifty

Dan August
  character: 9 (Sgt) Joe Rivera 14 (Sgt) Charles Wilentz 16 (Chief) George Untermeyer
  cast: 9 Ned Romero 10 Norman Fell 12 Burt Reynolds 15 Richard Anderson

Danaus
  ruler of: 5 Argos
  father: 5 Belus
  twin brother: 8 Aegyptus
  daughters called: 8 Danaides
  number of daughters: 5 fifty

dance 3 hop 4 ball, jump, leap, prom, reel, skip 5 lindy, party, polka, twist 6 bounce, cavort, frolic, gambol, prance, square 7 fox-trot, perform 8 cakewalk 9 jitterbug 10 Charleston 11 Boston waltz 12 choreography, Virginia reel 15 hesitation waltz
  Renaissance/17th century: 3 jig 5 galop, gigue 6 branle, pavane, redowa 7 bourree, gavotte, lancers, lavolta, mazurka 8 canaries, chaconne, courante, galliard, rigadoon, rigaudon, tourdion 9 allemande, passepied, polonaise, sarabande 10 danse basse, danse haute
  18th century: 6 minuet 9 cotillion 11 contre danse 12 country dance
  19th century: 5 waltz 9 quadrille
  early 1900's: 7 foxtrot, one-step, two-step 8 bunny hug 10 turkey trot 11 grizzly bear
  1920's: 5 tango 6 shimmy, toddle 10 Charleston 11 black bottom
  1930's: 4 shag 5 conga, rumba, samba, Suzy-Q 7 pecking 8 big apple, lindy hop, trucking 9 jitterbug
  1940's: 5 mambo 6 cha-cha
  1950's and 1960's: 4 frug, go-go 5 twist 6 monkey 9 rock-'n'-roll
  1970's: 5 disco
  Argentine: 5 tango
  Austrian: 13 schuhplattler
  Balinese: 6 legong
  Brazilian: 5 samba 6 maxixe
  Cuban: 5 conga, rumba 6 cha-cha
  Czech: 5 polka
  Dominican: 8 marengue, merengue
  folk: 6 Morris 7 maypole
  French: 6 can-can 8 galliard 9 ecossaise
  German: 11 schottische
  Indian: 6 kathak 8 manipuri 9 kathakali 13 bharata nat yam
  Japanese: 6 bugaku 7 dengaku 8 sarugaku
  dance/theater: 2 no 3 noh 6 kabuki

  Mexican: 3 hat
  Polish: 7 mazurka 9 krakoviak, polonaise 11 varsovienne
  Scottish: 5 sword
  Siamese: 10 wayang wong
  Spanish: 4 jota 6 bolero 8 flamenco 9 sevillana 10 seguidilla
  modern dancer/choreographer: 4 Juba 8 Ted Shawn 9 Eliot Feld, Gene Kelly, Ray Bolger 10 Mary Wigman, Paul Draper, Twyla Tharp 11 Anna Sokolow, Antony Tudor, Eric Hawkins, Fred Astaire, Irene Castle, Ruth St Denis 12 Bill Robinson, Ginger Rogers, Martha Graham, Vernon Castle 13 Alwin Nikolais, Doris Humphrey, Isadora Duncan 14 Charles Weidman 15 Merce Cunningham
  see also: 6 ballet

dance of death
  French: 12 danse macabre

Dandelion Wine
  author: 11 Ray Bradbury

dander 5 anger, Irish 6 temper

Dandie Dinmont terrier 24 soft-coated wheaten terrier, Staffordshire bull terrier, West Highland white terrier

dandy 3 fop 4 beau, dude, fine 5 beaut, great, super, swell 6 beauty, superb 7 coxcomb, peacock 8 terrific 9 excellent 12 clotheshorse

danger 4 risk 5 peril 6 hazard, menace, threat 8 jeopardy 12 endangerment

dangerous 5 hairy, risky 6 chancy, unsafe 8 menacing, perilous 9 hazardous 10 precarious 11 threatening, treacherous

danger signal 5 alarm, alert 7 red flag, warning

dangle 3 sag 4 drag, hang, sway 5 droop, swing, trail 6 depend 7 draggle, hang out, suspend 8 hang down, hang over 9 oscillate

Daniel
  Babylonian name: 12 Belteshazzar
  companion: 7 Meshach 8 Abednego, Shadrach

Daniel Boone
  character: 5 Mingo 6 Yadkin 11 Cincinnatus, Israel Boone, Jemima Boone 12 Rebecca Boone
  cast: 6 Ed Ames 10 Fess Parker 11 Albert Salmi, Dal McKennon, Darby Hinton 13 Patricia Blair 18 Veronica Cartwright

Danielovitch, Issur
  real name of: 11 Kirk Douglas

dank 3 wet 4 cold, damp 5 humid, moist, muggy, soggy 6 chilly, clammy, sodden, sticky

danke 8 thank you

danke schon 16 thank you very much

dankness 4 damp 7 wetness 8 dampness, humidity 9 humidness, moistness, mugginess 10 clamminess

Danner, Blythe
  born: 14 Philadelphia PA
  roles: 8 Betrayal 15 The Great Santini 16 Man Woman and Child

Danny Deever
  story in: 18 Barrack-Room Ballads
  author: 14 Rudyard Kipling
Danny Thomas Show, The
  character: 6 Clancy 12 Uncle Tonoose
  13 Danny Williams, Linda Williams, Rusty
  Williams, Terry Williams 16 Mrs Kathy
  Williams 18 Uncle Charley Halper
  cast: 9 Sid Melton 10 Rusty Hamer 11
  Hans Conried 12 Marjorie Lord, Penney
  Parker 13 Sherry Jackson 16 Angela
  Cartwright
danse macabre 12 dance of death
Dante (Alighieri)
  author of: 9 Vita Nuova 15 The Divine
  Comedy
  Divine Comedy Part I: 10 The Inferno
  Divine Comedy Part II: 9 Purgatory
  Divine Comedy Part III: 8 Paradise
  heroine: 8 Beatrice
Dantes, Edmond
  character in: 21 The Count of Monte
  Cristo
  author: 5 Dumas (pere)
Danton, Ray
  born: 9 New York NY
  roles: 14 I'll Cry Tomorrow 18 The
  George Raft Story 27 The Rise and Fall
  of Legs Diamond
Danu
  also: 4 Dana
  origin: 5 Irish
  mother of: 14 Tuatha De Danann
Danvers, Mrs
  character in: 7 Rebecca
  author: 9 Du Maurier
Daphnaea
  epithet of: 7 Artemis
  means: 11 of the laurel
Daphne
  form: 5 nymph
  father: 5 Ladon 6 Peneus
  pursued by: 6 Apollo 9 Leucippus
  changed into: 7 bay tree
Daphnephoria
  festival of: 6 Apollo
Daphnis
  occupation: 7 cowherd 8 shepherd
  father: 6 Hermes
  originated in: 14 pastoral poetry
  blinded by: 5 Nomia
Daphnis and Chloe
  characters in: 12 Greek romance
  author: 6 Longus
Daphnis et Chloe
  ballet by: 5 Ravel
  choreographer: 12 Michel Fokine
dapper 4 neat, trim 5 natty, smart 6 jaunty,
  modish, spiffy, sporty, spruce 7 stylish
dapple 3 dab, dot 4 spot 6 mottle
dappled 7 flecked, mottled, spotted 10 variegated
Darcy, Fitzwilliam
  character in: 17 Pride and Prejudice
  author: 6 Austen

Dardanus
  father: 4 Zeus
  mother: 7 Electra
  twin brother: 6 Iasion
  wife: 6 Myrina
  son: 12 Erechthonius
  ancestor of: 7 Trojans
dare 3 bet 4 defy 5 taunt 7 venture 9 challenge 11 provocation
daredevil 4 bold, rash 5 risky 8 heedless,
  reckless 9 audacious, breakneck, risk-
  taker 11 adventurous 12 death-defying,
  devil-may-care 13 adventuresome
daredevilry 6 daring 8 rashness 9-
  derring-do 10 imprudence 12 carelessness, heedlessness, recklessness 13 foolhardiness
Dares
  companion of: 6 Aeneas
  noted for: 6 boxing
Dares Phrygius
  priest of: 10 Hephaestus
Dar es Salaam
  former capital of: 8 Tanzania
Darien *see* 8 Colombia
daring 4 bold, game 5 brave 6 plucky 7
  bravery, courage, gallant, valiant 8 audacity, boldness, intrepid 9 audacious, dauntless, undaunted 10 courageous 11 adventurous, venturesome 13 audaciousness 15
  adventurousness
daring deed 4 feat 7 exploit 11 achievement
dark 3 dim 4 deep, evil, inky 5 angry, black,
  bleak, dingy, dusky, murky, night, shady 6
  dismal, dreary, gloomy, hidden, opaque,
  secret, somber, sullen, wicked 7 evening,
  joyless, obscure, ominous, shadowy, sunless 8 eventide, frowning, hopeless, overcast, sinister, twilight 9 concealed, nightfall, nighttime, sorrowful 10 forbidding 11
  threatening 12 discouraging 13 disheartening
darken 3 dim, dye 4 tint 5 cloud, color 6
  sadden 7 blacken, obscure 8 dispirit
darkened 3 dim 5 dusky, unlit 6 cloudy,
  gloomy 7 clouded 9 blackened, tenebrous,
  unlighted 10 blacked out 13 unilluminated
darkening 7 eclipse, shading 8 clouding,
  lowering 9 obscuring, shadowing 10 black-
  ening 12 clouding over
Dark Frontier, The
  author: 10 Eric Ambler
dark-hued 5 black, dusky, ebony, raven 6
  somber 7 swarthy
Dark Is Light Enough, The
  author: 14 Christopher Fry
Dark Lady, The
  author: 16 Louis Auchincloss
Dark Laughter
  author: 16 Sherwood Anderson
darkness 4 dusk 5 night, shade 7 dimness,
  evening 8 eventide, twilight 9 blackness,
  nightfall, nighttime
Darkness at Noon
  author: 14 Arthur Koestler

Darkness Visible
  author: 14 William Golding
Dark Victory
  director: 14 Edmund Goulding
  cast: 10 Bette Davis 11 George Brent 12 Ronald Reagan 14 Humphrey Bogart 19 Geraldine Fitzgerald
  remade as: 11 Stolen Hours
darling 4 cute, dear, love 5 loved, sweet 6 adored, lovely 7 beloved, dearest, lovable 8 adorable, charming, precious 9 cherished 10 attractive, enchanting, sweetheart 11 captivating
Darling
  director: 15 John Schlesinger
  cast: 11 Dirk Bogarde 13 Julie Christie 14 Laurence Harvey
  Oscar for: 6 script 7 actress (Christie)
Darling, Wendy
  character in: 8 Peter Pan
  author: 6 Barrie
darn 4 damn, dang, dash, drat, mend 5 blast, patch, sew up 6 hang it, stitch 7 consarn, doggone, goldang 8 confound 10 confound it
Darnay, Charles
  character in: 16 A Tale of Two Cities
  author: 7 Dickens
darnel 12 Biblical weed
Darnell, Linda
  real name: 20 Monetta Eloyse Darnell
  born: 8 Dallas TX
  roles: 12 Blood and Sand, Forever Amber 14 The Mark of Zorro 17 Unfaithfully Yours
Darren, James
  real name: 13 James Ercolani
  born: 14 Philadelphia PA
  roles: 6 Gidget 13 The Time Tunnel
dart 3 run 4 bolt, dash, flit, jump, leap, race, rush, tear 5 bound, fling, hurry, spear, spurt 6 hasten, spring, sprint 7 javelin, missile 10 projectile
D'Artagnan
  character in: 18 The Three Musketeers
  author: 5 Dumas (pere)
Dartle, Rosa
  character in: 16 David Copperfield
  author: 7 Dickens
Darwin, Charles
  author of: 15 The Descent of Man 18 The Origin of Species 20 The Voyage of the Beagle
  studied: 16 Galapagos Islands
  field: 6 nature 7 biology
  nationality: 7 British
  theory of: 9 evolution 16 natural selection
  ship: 6 Beagle
Dascylus
  member of: 9 Argonauts
  father: 5 Lycus
dash 3 bit, run, zip 4 bolt, dart, drop, elan, foil, hurl, race, ruin, rush, slam, tear, zeal 5 bound, crash, flair, fling, hurry, oomph, pinch, smash, speed, spoil, throw, touch, verve, vigor 6 dampen, energy, hasten, pi-

zazz, spirit, splash, sprint, thrust, thwart 7 a little, panache, shatter, soupcon, spatter 8 splatter, splinter, vivacity 9 animation, frustrate 10 disappoint, discourage
dashing 4 bold 5 brave 6 daring, plucky 7 gallant 8 fearless, spirited, unafraid 9 audacious, impetuous 10 courageous 13 swashbuckling
dash one's hopes 5 daunt, unman 6 deject 7 depress 8 dispirit 10 discourage, dishearten
Dashwood, Elinor and Marianne
  characters in: 19 Sense and Sensibility
  author: 6 Austen
DaSilva, Howard
  real name: 17 Harold Silverblatt
  born: 11 Cleveland OH
  roles: 8 Oklahoma 12 Sergeant York 14 The Great Gatsby 20 Abe Lincoln in Illinois
Dass, Secundra
  character in: 21 The Master of Ballantrae
  author: 9 Stevenson
dastard 3 cad 6 coward, craven 7 bounder, caitiff, chicken 8 poltroon 11 yellow-belly
dastardly 3 low 4 base, mean, vile 6 sneaky 8 cowardly, shameful 9 atrocious 10 despicable
data 4 dope, info 5 facts 7 dossier, figures 8 evidence 9 documents 11 information
Datchery, Mr
  character in: 22 The Mystery of Edwin Drood
  author: 7 Dickens
date 3 age, era 5 court, epoch, stage 6 escort, period 7 partner, take out 9 companion, originate 10 engagement, rendezvous 11 appointment
date 18 Phoenix dactylifera
  varieties: 5 cliff 6 Ceylon 7 Chinese 9 Jerusalem 12 Canary Island
dated 5 passe 6 old hat 8 obsolete, outmoded 9 out-of-date 10 antiquated 12 old-fashioned 13 unfashionable
daub 4 blot, coat, soil, spot 5 cover, dirty, paint, smear, stain 6 blotch, smirch, smudge 7 splotch
Daudet, Alphonse
  author of: 6 Sappho 15 The Woman of Arles 17 Letters from My Mill 18 Tartarin of Tarascon
Daughter of the Regiment, The
  opera by: 9 Donizetti
Daumier, Honore
  born: 6 France 10 Marseilles
  artwork: 7 Bathers 9 Gargantua 12 Men of Justice 13 Bluestockings 14 The Washerwoman 16 The Good Bourgeois 18 The Legislative Body 19 Professors and Pupils 20 Stories from Antiquity 21 The Third-Class Carriage
daunt 3 cow 4 dash, faze 5 abash, alarm, scare 6 deject, dismay, menace, subdue 7 depress, unnerve 8 affright, browbeat, frighten, threaten 10 discourage, dishearten, intimidate

dauntless 4 bold **5** brave, gutsy **6** daring, heroic **7** gallant, valiant **8** fearless, resolute, unafraid, valorous **10** courageous **12** stouthearted

dauntlessness 4 grit, guts, sand **5** nerve, pluck, spunk, valor **6** daring, mettle **7** bravery, courage, resolve **8** boldness **9** fortitude **10** resolution **12** fearlessness, resoluteness **16** stout-heartedness

Davers, Lady
  character in: 6 Pamela
  author: 10 Richardson

David
  king of: 6 Israel
  father: 5 Jesse
  wife: 6 Maacah, Michal **7** Abigail, Ahinoam, Haggith **9** Bathsheba
  son: 5 Amnon **7** Absalom, Chileab, Solomon **8** Adonijah
  daughter: 5 Tamar
  brother: 5 Eliab **7** Shammah **8** Abinadab
  sister: 7 Abigail
  friend: 5 Abner **8** Jonathan
  nephew: 5 Amasa
  city of: 9 Bethlehem, Jerusalem
  anointed by: 6 Samuel
  killed: 7 Goliath
  wrote: 6 Psalms
  comforter: 7 Abishag
  conspirators against: 4 Joab **8** Abiathar, Adonijah
  pertaining to: 7 Davidic

David, Jacques-Louis
  born: 5 Paris **6** France
  artwork: 13 Mme de Verninac **15** The Death of Marat **19** The Oath of the Horatii **23** The Coronation of Napoleon **26** View of the Luxembourg Gardens **31** The Intervention of the Sabine Women

David Copperfield
  author: 14 Charles Dickens
  character: 3 Ham **6** Barkis, Mr Dick **7** Creakle **8** Traddles **9** Mr Spenlow, Uriah Heep **10** Aunt Betsey, Little Em'ly, Mr Micawber, Rosa Dartle, Steerforth **11** Dora Spenlow, Little Emily, Mr Murdstone, Mr Wickfield, Mrs Gummidge **13** Clara Peggotty **14** Agnes Wickfield, Betsey Trotwood
  director: 11 George Cukor
  cast: 8 W C Fields **10** Madge Evans **11** Frank Lawton, Roland Young **13** Basil Rathbone, Edna May Oliver **15** Lionel Barrymore **16** Maureen O'Sullivan **18** Freddie Bartholomew

David Harum
  author: 19 Edward Noyes Westcott

Davies, Arthur Bowen
  born: 7 Utica NY
  artwork: 5 Dream **8** Unicorns **9** Crescendo **13** Every Saturday **15** Dancing Children, Sacramental Tree **17** Along the Erie Canal **18** Leda and the Dioscuri

Davies, Marion
  real name: 19 Marion Cecilia Douras
  lover: 21 William Randolph Hearst
  born: 10 Brooklyn NY

roles: 12 Cain and Mable **13** Runaway Romany **15** Tillie the Toiler

Davis, Bette
  real name: 18 Ruth Elizabeth Davis
  husband: 11 Gary Merrill
  born: 8 Lowell MA
  roles: 7 Jezebel (Oscar) **9** Dangerous (Oscar), The Letter **10** Now Voyager, The Old Maid **11** All About Eve, Dark Victory **14** Of Human Bondage, The Little Foxes **18** The Petrified Forest **22** Hush Hush Sweet Charlotte **26** What Ever Happened to Baby Jane?

Davis, H L
  author of: 14 Honey in the Horn

Davis, Ossie
  wife: 7 Ruby Dee
  born: 9 Cogdell GA
  author: 16 Purlie Victorious
  roles/films: 7 Jamaica **15** A Raisin in the Sun **18** No Time for Sergeants **19** Cotton Comes to Harlem

Davis, Sammy Jr
  wife: 8 May Britt
  group: 14 Will Master Trio
  born: 9 New York NY
  autobiography: 7 Yes I Can
  roles: 11 Mr Wonderful **12** Porgy and Bess **20** The Benny Goodman Story

Davis, Stuart
  born: 14 Philadelphia PA
  artwork: 4 Visa **9** Eggbeater **11** Lucky Strike, Ready to Wear **11** Owh! In Sao Pao **12** The Mellow Pad **14** Colonial Cubism **15** Cigarette Papers

Davy, Humphrey
  field: 9 chemistry
  nationality: 7 British
  isolated: 5 boron **6** barium, sodium **7** calcium **8** chlorine **9** magnesium, potassium, strontium
  invented: 8 Davy lamp **10** miner's lamp

dawdle 4 idle, loaf **5** dally, delay **6** loiter **10** dillydally **12** putter around **13** procrastinate

dawdler
  French: 7 flaneur

dawdling
  French: 8 flanerie

dawn 4 rise **5** begin, birth, occur, start, sunup **6** advent, appear, Aurora, emerge, origin, strike, unfold **7** develop, sunrise **8** commence, daybreak, daylight **9** beginning, emergence, inception, unfolding **12** commencement
  god of: 8 Heimdall
  goddess of: 3 Eos **6** Aurore, Matuta

dawning 5 sunup **7** morning, sunrise **8** daybreak, daylight

Dawn Patrol, The
  director: 14 Edmund Goulding
  cast: 10 David Niven, Errol Flynn **11** Donald Crisp **13** Basil Rathbone **14** Melville Cooper **15** Barry Fitzgerald

day 3 age **4** date, time **5** epoch **6** period

Day, Clarence (Jr)
  author of: 14 God and My Father, Life with Father, Life with Mother

Day, Doris
    real name: 18 Doris von Kappelhoff
    born: 12 Cincinnati OH
    autobiography: 19 Doris Day Her Own
    Story
    roles: 10 Pillow Talk 12 Calamity Jane 13
    The Pajama Game 15 Move Over Dar-
    ling, The Doris Day Show 23 Please
    Don't Eat the Daisies
daybed 5 couch 6 lounge 12 chaise longue
day book 5 diary 6 agenda 7 journal 8 cal-
    endar, schedule
daybreak 4 dawn 5 sunup 7 sunrise
daydream 4 muse 5 fancy 7 fantasy, imag-
    ine, reverie 9 fantasize 10 wool-gather 14
    castle in the air
Day for Night
    director: 16 Francois Truffaut
    cast: 15 Jean-Pierre Leaud 16 Francois
    Truffaut, Jacqueline Bisset, Jean-Pierre
    Aumont
    Oscar for: 11 foreign film
daylight 4 dawn 5 sunup 7 morning, sun-
    rise 8 full view, openness, sunlight, sun-
    shine
Days and Nights
    author: 17 Konstantin Simonov
day's end 3 eve 4 dusk, even 6 sunset 7
    evening, sundown 8 gleaming, twilight 9
    nightfall
Days of Heaven
    director: 14 Terrence Malick
    cast: 9 Linda Manz 10 Sam Shepard 11
    Brooke Adams, Richard Gere
    Oscar for: 14 cinematography
Days of Wine and Roses
    director: 12 Blake Edwards
    cast: 9 Lee Remick 10 Jack Lemmon 11
    Jack Klugman 15 Charles Bickford
    score: 12 Henry Mancini
daze 4 numb, stun 5 amaze, shock 6 be-
    numb, dazzle, excite, muddle, stupor 7 as-
    tound, confuse, stagger, startle, stupefy 8
    astonish, bewilder, surprise 9 disorient,
    electrify 11 flabbergast 12 astonishment,
    bewilderment, blow one's mind 14 discom-
    bobulate
dazed 5 woozy 6 groggy 7 confused, daz-
    zled, stunned 9 befuddled, stupefied 10
    bewildered, punch-drunk
dazzle 3 awe 4 blur, daze 5 blind 6 excite 7
    confuse, overawe 9 electrify, overpower,
    overwhelm
dazzling 7 radiant 8 blinding 9 sparkling 10
    impressive, staggering 11 coruscating 12
    breathtaking, electrifying, overwhelming 14
    flabbergasting
deacon 6 cleric 9 churchman, clergyman
    12 ecclesiastic
deactivate 6 defuse 9 switch off 10 neutral-
    ize
dead, the dead 4 beat, cold, dull, flat 5
    depth, exact, midst, quiet, spent, tired, to-
    tal, utter, vapid 6 entire, middle, unused 7
    defunct, expired, extinct, insipid, precise,
    useless, utterly, worn-out 8 abruptly, abso-
    lute, complete, deceased, entirely, inac-

tive, lifeless, obsolete, perished, stagnant,
suddenly, thorough, unerring 9 exhausted,
inanimate, inorganic 10 absolutely, completely, lackluster, unemployed, unexciting
11 ineffectual, inoperative 12 unproductive,
unprofitable
    Latin: 8 ad patres
    god of: 6 Osiris 7 Veiovis
dead body 5 stiff 6 corpse 7 cadaver, re-
    mains
deaden 4 dope, drug, dull, mute, numb 5
    abate, blunt 6 lessen, muffle, soothe, sub-
    due, weaken 7 assuage, smother 8 dimin-
    ish, mitigate, moderate 9 alleviate 11
    anesthetize
deadened 5 muted 6 dulled, numbed 7
    muffled, subdued
Dead Father, The
    author: 15 Donald Barthelme
Dea Dia
    origin: 5 Roman
    goddess of: 11 agriculture
    corresponds to: 13 Acca Laurentia
deadlock 7 impasse 8 standoff 9 stalemate
    10 standstill
deadly 3 wan 4 dull 5 ashen, awful, fatal,
    fully, undue 6 boring, lethal, mortal, pallid 7
    awfully, baneful, destroy, extreme, ghostly,
    tedious, totally 8 dreadful, entirely, horri-
    bly, terrible, terribly, tiresome 9 excessive,
    malignant, wearisome 10 cadaverous,
    completely, implacable, inordinate, relent-
    less, thoroughly 11 destructive, unrelenting
deadpan 5 sober 8 detached 9 impassive
    11 unemotional 13 straight-faced
dead ringer 4 copy, mate, twin 6 double 9
    duplicate 11 counterpart 13 spitting image
Dead Souls
    author: 12 Nikolai Gogol
dead to the world 6 asleep 7 out cold 9
    konked out 10 fast asleep, slumbering 11
    sound asleep
dead weight 7 ballast 9 inert mass
Dead Zone, The
    author: 11 Stephen King
deal 3 act 4 give, hand 5 round, see to,
    trade, treat 6 behave, handle, market 7
    bargain, concern, deliver, dole out, give
    out, mete out, oversee 8 consider, dis-
    pense 9 agreement, apportion 10 ad-
    minister, distribute, 11 arrangement 12 dis-
    tribution 13 apportionment
dealer 5 agent 6 monger, trader, vendor 8
    merchant 10 trafficker 11 distributor
dealing, dealings 5 trade 7 traffic 8 busi-
    ness, practice 9 relations, treatment 12
    transactions
dealing out 8 dividing 9 allotting, bestowing
    10 conferring, consigning, dispensing 12
    apportioning, distributing
Dea Marica *see* 6 Marica
Dean, Dizzy (Jay Hanna)
    sport: 8 baseball
    position: 7 pitcher
    team: 16 St Louis Cardinals
    part of: 12 Gashouse Gang
    brother: 4 Paul

Dean, James (Jimmy)
  real name: 14 James Byron Dean
  born: 8 Marion IN
  roles: 5 Giant 10 East of Eden 18 Rebel
    Without a Cause
Deane, Seneca
  character in: 7 Babbitt
  author: 5 Lewis
Dean's December
  author: 10 Saul Bellow
dear 4 love 5 angel, loved 6 costly 7 beloved, darling 8 esteemed, favorite, precious 9 cherished, expensive, respected
  10 sweetheart
    French: 5 cheri 6 cerie
Dear Antoine
  author: 11 Jean Anouilh
Dear Brutus
  author: 12 James M Barrie
dearest 7 beloved, darling
dearth 4 lack 7 paucity 8 scarcity, shortage
  10 deficiency
death, Death 5 dying 6 demise 7 decease,
  passing 9 departure 10 expiration, grim
  reaper
    goddess of: 3 Hel 7 Berchta, Perchta 10
      Ereshkigal
Death Be Not Proud
  author: 9 John Donne
death blow
  French: 11 coup de grace
Death Comes for the Archbishop
  author: 11 Willa Cather
  character: 7 Jacinto 9 Kit Carson 16
    Bishop Jean Latour 20 Father Joseph
    Vaillant
death-dealing 5 fatal 6 lethal, mortal 7 killing 11 destructive
death-defying 4 bold, rash 5 risky 6 daring
  8 reckless 9 audacious, breakneck, daredevil
Death in the Family, A
  author: 9 James Agee
Death in Venice
  director: 15 Luchino Visconti
  author: 10 Thomas Mann
  cast: 9 Mark Burns 11 Dirk Bogarde 14
    Marisa Berenson
deathless 7 eternal 8 immortal 9 perpetual
  11 everlasting
deathlike 3 wan 4 pale 5 ashen 6 pallid 7
  ghastly 9 bloodless 10 cadaverous,
  corpselike
deathly 4 very 7 extreme, intense 8 terrible
  9 extremely 12 overwhelming 15 resembling death
Death of a Salesman
  director: 12 Laslo Benedek
  author: 12 Arthur Miller
  character: 4 Biff 5 Happy, Linda 7
    Bernard, Charley 8 Uncle Ben 10 Willy
    Loman
  cast: 13 Frederic March, Kevin McCarthy
    14 Mildred Dunnock 15 Cameron Mitchell
Death of Ivan Ilyich, The
  author: 10 Leo Tolstoy

Death of the Gods, The
  author: 17 Dmitri Merejkowski
Death of the Heart
  author: 14 Elizabeth Bowen
Death on the Nile
  author: 14 Agatha Christie
Death Takes a Holiday
  director: 14 Mitchell Leisen
  cast: 11 Guy Standing 13 Evelyn
    Venable, Frederic March (Death)
Death Valley Days
  host: 12 Robert Taylor, Ronald Reagan
    13 Dale Robertson 14 Stanley Andrews
debacle 4 rout, ruin 5 havoc, wreck 8 collapse, disaster, downfall 9 breakdown,
  cataclysm, overthrow, ruination 10 bankruptcy 11 catastrophe, devastation, dissolution 12 vanquishment 14 disintegration
debar 3 ban 6 reject 7 exclude, keep out 8
  preclude, prohibit 9 blackball, blacklist
debark 4 land
debarment 7 removal 8 omission 9 exception, exclusion, exemption, rejection 11
  elimination, prohibition 12 nonadmission
debase 5 lower 6 befoul, defile 7 corrupt,
  degrade 8 disgrace, dishonor 9 desecrate
  10 adulterate 11 deteriorate 16 impair the
  worth of 18 reduce the quality of
debased 4 vile 6 impure 7 corrupt, defiled,
  lowered 8 degraded, depraved 9 debauched, disgraced, dissolute, perverted
  10 degenerate, dissipated 11 adulterated
debasement 9 decadence, depravity 10
  corruption, debauchery, degeneracy, immorality, perversion 13 dissoluteness
debatable 4 iffy 6 arguable 7 dubious 8 arguable, doubtful 9 uncertain, undecided 10
  disputable 12 questionable 13 problematical
debate 5 argue 6 ponder 7 discuss, dispute, reflect 8 argument, cogitate, consider, hash over 10 cogitation, deliberate,
  discussion, meditation, reflection, think
  about 12 deliberation, meditate upon 13
  consideration
debauch 4 orgy 5 revel, spree 6 debase 7
  carouse, corrupt, deprave, revelry, subvert
  8 carousal 9 bacchanal 10 lead astray,
  saturnalia
debauched 4 lewd 6 wanton 7 corrupt, debased, immoral 8 degraded, depraved,
  perverse, vitiated 9 abandoned, corrupted,
  dissolute, lecherous, led astray, perverted, reprobate, shameless 10 degenerate,
  dissipated, lascivious, libidinous, licentious, profligate 12 disreputable
debauchery 6 excess 11 dissipation 12
  immoderation, intemperance 14 self-
  indulgence
DeBeck, Billy
  creator/artist of: 12 Barney Google 20
    Parlor Bedroom and Sink
debilitate 6 weaken 7 wear out 8 enervate
  10 devitalize, make feeble 17 deprive of
  strength

debilitated 5 frail 6 feeble, infirm 7 worn out 8 delicate, weakened 9 enervated 11 devitalized

debilitation 8 handicap, weakness 9 infirmity 10 affliction, disability, impairment, inadequacy 11 disablement

debility 7 fatigue, frailty 8 asthenia, handicap, senility, weakness 9 infirmity, lassitude, weakening 10 affliction, enervation, exhaustion, feebleness, impairment, invalidism, sickliness 11 decrepitude, prostration

Debir
conqueror: 7 Othniel

debit 4 debt 6 red ink 7 account, payable 9 liability 10 balance due, obligation 11 ledger entry, shortcoming

debonair 5 suave 6 dapper, jaunty, urbane 7 buoyant, elegant, genteel, refined 8 carefree, charming, gracious, well-bred 9 sprightly 11 free and easy 12 lighthearted 13 sophisticated

Deborah 11 Hebrew judge
companion: 7 Rebekah
summoned: 5 Barak

debouch 5 drain 6 emerge, let out 7 flow out 9 discharge

debris 4 crap, junk 5 dreck, dregs, dross, ruins, scrap, trash, waste 6 litter, rubble, shards 7 clutter, garbage, rubbish 8 detritus, wreckage 9 fragments

debt 4 bill 5 debit 7 arrears 9 liability 10 obligation 15 deferred payment, that which is owed

debunk 4 bare 5 strip 6 expose, send up, show up, unmask 7 deflate, lampoon, take off, uncloak, uncover 8 ridicule, satirize 9 burlesque, demystify, disparage 13 demythologize

Debussy, Claude Achille
born: 6 France 15 St Germain-en-Laye
composer of: 5 La Mer 6 Gigues, Iberia, Images 8 Estampes 9 Nocturnes, Printemps 11 Clair de Lune 13 En Blanc et Noir 15 Children's Corner, L'Enfant prodigue 16 La Demoiselle Elue, Suite Bergamasque 17 Rondes de Printemps, The Blessed Damozel 18 Pelleas et Melisande 24 The Girl with the Flaxen Hair 26 Prelude a l'apres-midi d'un faune 28 Prelude to the Afternoon of a Faun

debut 9 coming out 12 presentation

decadence 5 decay 7 decline 10 corruption, debasement, degeneracy, immorality 12 degeneration 13 deterioration

decadent 7 corrupt, debased, immoral 8 decaying, depraved, perverse 9 debauched, dissolute, perverted 10 degenerate
French: 11 fin de siecle

Decalogue 15 Ten Commandments

Decameron, The
author: 17 Giovanni Boccaccio

decamp 7 move off, run away, take off 8 march off, sneak off

decampment 6 escape, flight 7 getaway

decant 4 pour 7 draw off, pour out

decanter 6 bottle, carafe, vessel

decathlon winner 11 Bruce Jenner

Decatur, Stephen
served in: 11 Algerine War, Barbary Wars 13 Tripolitan War 19 War of Eighteen Twelve
commander of ship: 12 United States
defeated ship: 10 Macedonian (British)
saying: 22 "Our country right or wrong"

decay 3 rot 5 spoil 7 corrode, putrefy, rotting 8 spoiling 9 decompose 12 disintegrate, putrefaction 13 decomposition
goddess of: 4 Hour 5 Horae

decayed 3 bad 6 putrid, rotted, rotten, ruined 7 corrupt, gone bad, spoiled 10 decomposed 12 deteriorated 13 disintegrated

deceased see 4 dead

deceit 5 fraud 8 cheating, trickery 9 duplicity 10 dishonesty, trickiness 11 fraudulence 13 double-dealing 15 underhandedness 17 misrepresentation

deceitful 5 false 6 crafty, sneaky, tricky 7 cunning 9 dishonest, insincere 11 duplicitous, treacherous, underhanded 12 hypocritical 13 double-dealing, untrustworthy

deceitfulness 5 fraud 7 cunning, slyness 9 falseness, hypocrisy, treachery 10 craftiness, dishonesty, sneakiness, trickiness 11 insincerity 15 underhandedness 17 untrustworthiness

deceive 3 con 4 fool 5 cheat, put on, trick 6 delude 7 defraud, mislead, swindle

deceiver 4 fake 5 cheat, fraud, quack 6 con man 7 cozener 8 impostor, swindler 9 charlatan, trickster 10 mountebank 13 confidence man

decelerate 5 brake 8 slow down

deceleration 7 braking, slowing

December
event: 11 Pearl Harbor (7), Winter solstice (21, 22)
flower: 5 holly 9 narcissus
French: 8 Decembre
gem: 4 ruby 6 zircon 9 turquoise
German: 8 Dezember
holiday: 8 Hanukkah 9 Boxing Day (26), Christmas (25) 16 Saint Nicholas Day (6)
Italian: 8 Dicembre
number of days: 9 thirty-one
origin of name: 5 decem (Latin meaning ten)
place in year:
Gregorian: 7 twelfth
Roman: 5 tenth
Julian: 7 twelfth
Spanish: 9 Diciembre
Zodiac sign: 9 Capricorn 11 Sagittarius

decency 7 decorum, modesty 9 propriety 14 respectability 15 appropriateness

decent 4 fair, nice 5 ample 6 proper, seemly 7 correct, fitting 8 adequate, gracious, obliging, passable, suitable 9 courteous 10 acceptable, sufficient 11 appropriate 12 satisfactory 13 accommodating

deception 5 fraud, trick 7 cunning 8 artifice, illusion, trickery 9 duplicity, treachery 10 trickiness 11 fraudulence, insincerity 13 double-dealing

deceptive 5 phony 9 dishonest 10 fraudulent, misleading

deceptiveness 5 fraud 11 fraudulence

decibel
   abbreviation: 2 dB

decide 4 rule 5 elect, judge 6 choose, decree, select, settle 7 resolve 10 determine

decided 4 firm 7 certain 8 clear-cut, definite, emphatic, resolute 9 assertive 10 deliberate, determined, unwavering 12 indisputable, strong-willed, unhesitating, unmistakable 14 unquestionable

decidedly 9 certainly 10 absolutely 11 indubitably, undoubtedly 12 indisputably, unmistakably 13 unequivocally 14 unquestionably

decidedness 7 purpose, resolve 10 resolution 12 resoluteness 13 determination 14 purposefulness

decide on 5 adopt, elect 6 choose, opt for, select, settle 7 appoint, arrange, embrace, espouse, pick out 8 settle on 9 determine, establish, single out

decigram
   abbreviation: 2 dg

deciliter
   abbreviation: 2 dL

decimate 6 reduce 7 destroy 8 massacre 9 slaughter 13 greatly reduce

decimeter
   abbreviation: 2 dm

decipher 5 solve 6 decode, deduce, render 7 decrypt, dope out, explain, make out, unravel 8 construe, untangle 9 interpret, translate 12 cryptanalyze

decision 6 decree, ruling 7 finding, outcome, purpose, resolve, verdict 8 judgment 10 conclusion, resolution 12 resoluteness 13 determination 14 purposefulness

decisive 4 firm 5 final 8 absolute, definite, positive, resolute 10 conclusive, convincing, definitive, determined, undeniable 12 indisputable

decisive blow 9 deathblow 11 coup de grace

decisiveness 7 purpose, resolve 10 resolution 12 resoluteness 14 purposefulness

decisive point 3 nut 4 core, crux, gist 5 basis, heart 6 kernel 7 essence 9 essential

deck 4 garb, trim 5 adorn, array, dress, prank 6 clothe, doll up, enrich, outfit, tog out 7 apparel, bedizen, festoon, furbish, garnish, gussy up 8 accouter, beautify, ornament, spruce up 9 embellish

Decker, Mary
   sport: 7 running
   married name: 6 Slaney

deck out 5 adorn, array, dress 6 attire, clothe, fit out, outfit, rig out 7 costume

declaim 4 rail 5 orate 6 recite 7 inveigh 9 sermonize 11 pontificate

declaration 6 avowal, notice 8 document 9 assertion, statement, testimony 10 deposition 11 affirmation, attestation, publication 12 announcement, notification, proclamation 14 acknowledgment

declare 4 show 6 affirm, reveal 7 express 8 announce, proclaim 9 pronounce

declare null and void 6 cancel, repeal, revoke 7 abolish, rescind, retract 8 abrogate, set aside 9 repudiate 10 invalidate 11 countermand

declare untrue 4 deny 9 repudiate 10 contradict

decline 3 ebb 4 drop, fail, flag, sink, wane 5 decay, slump, spurn 6 balk at, eschew, lessen, refuse, reject, weaken, worsen 7 dwindle 8 decrease, diminish, downfall 9 downgrade, downswing 11 deteriorate 13 deterioration

Decline and Fall
   author: 11 Evelyn Waugh

Decline and Fall of the Roman Empire, The
   author: 12 Edward Gibbon

declivity 4 drop 5 slant, slope 6 plunge 7 descent

decompose 3 rot 5 decay, spoil 7 putrefy 8 separate 10 go to pieces 12 disintegrate

decomposed 6 putrid, rotted, rotten 7 decayed, spoiled 9 putrefied 13 disintegrated

decontaminate 6 purify 9 disinfect, sterilize

decor 6 ornamentation

decorate 4 trim 5 adorn, array, honor 7 festoon, garnish 8 beautify, ornament 9 embellish

decorated 5 fancy 6 decked, ornate 7 adorned, trimmed 8 bedecked 9 bemedaled, bedizened, garnished 10 ornamented 11 embellished

decoration 4 trim 5 award, badge, medal 6 emblem, ribbon 7 garnish 8 ornament, trimming 9 adornment 13 embellishment, ornamentation 14 beautification

decorous 3 fit 6 decent, polite, proper, seemly 7 correct 8 becoming, mannerly, suitable 9 dignified 10 respectful 11 appropriate

decorum 4 tact 5 taste 7 dignity 8 good form 9 gentility, propriety 10 politeness 14 respectability

decoy 4 bait, lure 5 plant, snare 6 allure, come-on, entice 10 enticement, inducement 11 smoke screen

decrease 4 drop, ease, loss 5 abate, taper 6 lessen, reduce 7 cutback, decline, dwindle, fall-off, slacken, subside 8 diminish 9 abatement, dwindling, lessening, reduction 10 de-escalate, diminution 12 de-escalation

decree 3 law 5 edict, order 6 dictum, ruling 7 command, mandate, statute 8 proclaim 9 authorize 12 proclamation

decrepit 7 rickety 8 battered 10 broken-down 11 dilapidated

decrescendo
  music: 22 gradually getting softer
  abbreviation: 4 decr
decry 7 censure, condemn 8 denounce 9 criticize, deprecate, disparage
Dedalus, Stephen
  character in: 7 Ulysses 30 Portrait of the Artist as a Young Man
  author: 5 Joyce
dedicate 6 commit, devote, launch, pledge 7 address, present 8 inscribe
dedication 8 devotion 10 commitment 11 devotedness 16 prefatory address 20 prefatory inscription
Dedlock, Sir Leicester and Lady
  characters in: 10 Bleak House
  author: 7 Dickens
deduce 5 infer 6 gather, reason 8 conclude 10 comprehend, understand
deduct 4 take 6 remove 8 subtract, take from, withdraw 10 decrease by
deduction 5 guess 6 belief, credit, rebate 7 removal 8 analysis, decrease, discount, judgment, markdown, rollback 9 abatement, allowance, exemption, gathering, inference, lessening, reasoning, reduction 10 assumption, concession, conclusion, diminuition, hypothesis, reflection, taking away, withdrawal 11 calculation, presumption, speculation, subtraction, supposition 13 comprehension, consideration, understanding 14 interpretation
Dee, Ruby
  real name: 14 Ruby Ann Wallace
  husband: 10 Ossie Davis
  born: 11 Cleveland OH
  roles: 15 A Raisin in the Sun 16 Purlie Victorious
Dee, Sandra
  real name: 13 Alexandra Zuck
  husband: 10 Bobby Darin
  born: 9 Bayonne NJ
  roles: 6 Gidget 12 A Summer Place 15 Tammy Tell Me True
deed 3 act 4 feat 5 title 6 action, effort 11 achievement 14 accomplishment
deeds are manly, words are womanish
  Italian: 24 fatti maschii parole femine
  motto of: 8 Maryland
deem 4 hold, view 5 judge, think 6 regard 7 believe 8 consider
de-emphasize 8 play down 9 underplay
deep 3 far, sea 4 dark, late, lost, rich, wise 5 far in, midst, ocean, vivid 6 astute, strong 7 extreme, intense, learned 8 absorbed, immersed, involved, profound, resonant, sonorous 9 engrossed, sagacious 10 discerning 11 intelligent 13 philosophical
Deep, The
  author: 13 Peter Benchley
deeply 6 richly 7 acutely, gravely, greatly, vividly 8 entirely 9 intensely, seriously 10 completely, profoundly, resonantly, sonorously, thoroughly 12 passionately

deeply felt 6 ardent, fervid 7 earnest, fervent, intense, sincere, zealous 9 heartfelt 10 passionate 11 impassioned 12 wholehearted
deepness 10 profundity
deep-rooted 7 abiding, lasting 8 enduring 9 confirmed, ingrained
deep-seated 7 abiding, lasting 8 enduring 9 confirmed, ingrained
deep thought 10 absorption, brown study, intentness 11 engrossment 13 concentration
deep water 3 jam 4 mess 5 ocean 6 pickle 7 trouble 8 distress 10 difficulty 11 dire straits, predicament 12 over one's head
deer
  young: 4 fawn
  female: 3 doe
Deer Hunter, The
  director: 13 Michael Cimino
  cast: 10 John Cazale, John Savage 11 Meryl Streep 12 Robert De Niro 17 Christopher Walken
  Oscar for: 7 picture 8 director 15 supporting actor (Walken)
Deerslayer, The
  author: 19 James Fenimore Cooper
  first of: 20 Leatherstocking Tales
  character: 4 Hist 5 Hetty 6 Judith 10 Hurry Harry 11 Natty Bumppo (Deerslayer) 12 Chingachgook, Thomas Hutter
de-escalate 5 limit 6 lessen, narrow 8 contract, minimize
deface 3 mar 4 mark, scar 5 spoil 6 bruise, damage, impair, injure 9 disfigure
de facto 4 real 6 actual, really 8 actually
defalcate 8 embezzle 14 misappropriate
defamation 5 libel 7 calumny, slander 12 vilification 13 disparagement
defamatory 8 libelous 9 vilifying 10 calumnious, derogatory, slanderous 11 disparaging
defame 5 libel 6 malign, vilify 7 degrade, slander 8 derogate 9 denigrate, discredit, disparage 10 calumniate
Defarge, Madame
  character in: 16 A Tale of Two Cities
  author: 7 Dickens
default 10 nonpayment
defeat 4 foil, loss, rout 5 cream, crush, elude, quell 6 baffle, thwart 7 conquer, setback, shellac, trounce 8 confound, overcome, vanquish 9 frustrate, overpower, overthrow, overwhelm, thwarting 11 frustration 14 disappointment
defeated 4 beat 5 upset 6 beaten, bested, licked, routed 7 outdone, whipped, worsted 8 overcame 9 conquered, overthrew, put to rout 10 frustrated, overthrown 11 overpowered, overwhelmed 12 hors de combat
defect 4 flaw, scar, spot 5 break, crack, fault, stain 6 blotch, foible 7 blemish, default, failing, frailty 8 omission, weakness 10 deficiency 11 shortcoming 12 imperfection 14 incompleteness

defective 6 broken, faulty, flawed 7 lacking, wanting 8 abnormal, impaired 9 deficient, imperfect, subnormal 10 inadequate, out of order 11 inoperative 12 insufficient

Defence of Poetry
author: 18 Percy Bysshe Shelley

defend 5 guard 6 secure, shield, uphold 7 endorse, protect, shelter, stand by, support, sustain 8 advocate, champion, maintain, preserve 9 safeguard

defender 8 advocate, champion, guardian, upholder 9 protector, supporter

Defender of the Faith
Latin: 13 Fidei Defensor
title of: 17 English sovereigns

Defenders, The
character: 10 Joan Miller 14 Helen Donaldson, Kenneth Preston 15 Lawrence Preston
cast: 10 E G Marshall, Robert Reed 11 Joan Hackett, Polly Rowles

defense 4 care 5 guard 7 custody, support 8 advocacy, security 9 barricade, safeguard, upholding 10 protection, stronghold 11 maintenance, safekeeping 12 preservation 13 fortification, justification

defenseless 7 unarmed 8 helpless 10 on one's back, vulnerable, weaponless 11 unprotected, unresisting

defensible 3 fit 5 valid 6 proper 7 tenable 8 sensible, suitable 9 allowable, excusable 10 admissible, condonable, forgivable, pardonable, vindicable 11 justifiable, permissible, supportable 12 warrantable

defer 4 obey 5 delay, table, yield 6 accede, give in, put off, shelve, submit 7 respect, suspend 8 postpone 10 capitulate

deference 5 honor 6 esteem, regard 7 respect 9 obedience, reverence 12 capitulation 13 consideration

deferential 6 civil 6 polite 7 dutiful 8 obedient, reverent 9 courteous, regardful 10 respectful, submissive 11 acquiescent, considerate, reverential

deferment 4 stay 5 delay 9 extension 12 postponement

deferral 5 pause 6 hiatus, recess 8 abeyance 10 suspension 12 postponement 14 discontinuance

defiance 9 hostility, obstinacy, rebellion 12 disobedience 14 rebelliousness

defiant 4 bold 6 truculent 10 aggressive, rebellious 11 disobedient, provocative

Defiant Ones, The
director: 13 Stanley Kramer
cast: 10 Tony Curtis 11 Lon Chaney Jr 12 Cara Williams 13 Charles McGraw, Sidney Poitier, Theodore Bikel
Oscar for: 10 screenplay

deficiency 4 flaw 6 defect 7 failing, frailty 8 shortage, weakness 10 inadequacy 11 shortcoming 12 imperfection 13 insufficiency

deficient 4 weak 6 flawed 7 lacking, short on 8 inferior 9 defective 10 inadequate 11 substandard 12 insufficient 14 unsatisfactory

deficit 8 shortage 9 shortfall 10 deficiency
de fide 10 of the faith

defile 4 soil 5 dirty, smear, spoil, stain, taint 6 befoul, debase 7 degrade, profane, tarnish 8 besmirch, disgrace, dishonor 9 desecrate

defiled 5 dirty 6 fouled, impure, soiled 7 debased, dirtied, stained, sullied, tainted, unclean 8 befouled, polluted, ravished, smirched, violated 9 blackened, corrupted, tarnished 10 besmirched 12 contaminated

define 5 state 7 clarify, explain, specify 8 describe, spell out 9 delineate, designate

definite 3 set 4 sure 5 exact, fixed 7 certain, precise 8 clear-cut, positive

definitely 5 truly 6 indeed, surely 7 for sure, no doubt 9 assuredly, certainly, decidedly, doubtless, expressly 10 absolutely, decisively, explicitly, positively, undeniably 11 indubitably, inescapably, unavoidably, undoubtedly 12 unmistakably 13 categorically, unequivocally 14 unquestionably 16 incontrovertibly

definiteness 8 sureness 9 certainty, precision 10 exactitude 11 unambiguity

definition 6 limits 7 clarity, purpose 11 description 15 distinctiveness

definitive 5 exact 7 decided, perfect 8 complete, decisive, reliable 10 conclusive, consummate

deflate 6 reduce 7 flatten 8 contract 9 devaluate

deflect 6 divert, swerve

Defoe, Daniel
author of: 6 Roxana 11 Colonel Jack 12 Moll Flanders 14 Robinson Crusoe 23 A Journal of the Plague Year

DeForest, Lee
invented/worked on: 10 audion tube, television 13 sound pictures

deform 3 mar 4 maim 5 twist 6 mangle 7 contort, distort 9 disfigure

deformation 9 deformity 10 distortion 12 malformation 13 disfigurement

deformed 6 marred, warped 7 defaced, mangled, spoiled, twisted 8 crippled 9 misshapen, monstrous 10 disfigured

deformity 12 malformation

defraud 3 con 5 bilk, rook 5 cheat 6 fleece, rip off 7 swindle

defray 3 pay 5 cover 11 foot the bill

deft 3 apt 4 able, sure 5 quick 6 adroit, expert 8 skillful 9 dexterous

deftness 5 knack, skill 7 ability 8 facility 9 adeptness, dexterity, handiness 10 adroitness, competency 11 proficiency 12 skillfulness

defunct 4 dead 7 extinct

defy 5 spurn 6 oppose, resist 7 disdain 8 confront 9 challenge, disregard, withstand

degage 4 easy 8 detached 10 disengaged 13 unconstrained

Degas, (Hilaire Germain) Edgar
born: 5 Paris 6 France
artwork: 14 The Ballet Class, The Morning Bath 15 Ballet Rehearsal 16 The Mil-

linery Shop **17** The Glass of Absinth **23**
Woman with Chrysanthemums **30** The
Little Fourteen-Year-Old Dancer

degeneracy 9 decadence, depravity **10** debasement, debauchery, immorality, perversion **11** dissolution

degenerate 3 rot **4** base, sink, vile **5** decay **6** revert, wanton, wicked, worsen **7** corrupt, debased, decline, go to pot, immoral, pervert, vicious **8** decadent, degraded, depraved **9** abandoned, backslide, debauched, dissolute, perverted **10** dissipated, go downhill, profligate, retrograde, retrogress **11** deteriorate, hit the skids **12** disintegrate

degeneration 7 decline **9** depravity **10** corruption, debasement, immorality, perversion **11** degradation, dissolution, viciousness **13** deterioration

degradation 8 disgrace **11** humiliation

Degradation of the Democratic Dogma, The
  author: 10 Henry Adams

degrade 5 lower, shame **6** debase, demote **7** corrupt **8** disgrace, dishonor

degraded 4 vile **6** wicked **7** corrupt, debased, lowered **8** depraved, shameful, unworthy **9** debauched, perverted, reprobate **10** degenerate **11** undignified **12** unregenerate

degrading 3 low **6** menial **8** shameful **11** humiliating

degree 4 mark, step, unit **5** grade, level, order, phase, point, stage **8** division, interval
  abbreviation: 3 deg

De Guiche, Lillian
  real name of: 11 Lillian Gish

de gustibus non est disputandum 29
there is no disputing about tastes

De Havilland, Joan de Beauvoir
  real name of: 12 Joan Fontaine

De Havilland, Olivia
  sister: 12 Joan Fontaine
  born: 5 Japan, Tokyo
  roles: 7 Melanie **10** The Heiress (Oscar) **11** The Snake Pit **12** Captain Blood, To Each His Own (Oscar) **14** Anthony Adverse, My Cousin Rachel **15** Gone With the Wind, Hold Back the Dawn **16** Light in the Piazza **22** Hush Hush Sweet Charlotte **24** The Adventures of Robin Hood

dehydrate 3 dry **5** parch **6** dry out

dehydrated 3 dry **7** parched, thirsty **8** dried-out **9** shriveled **10** desiccated

Deianira
  father: 6 Oeneus
  mother: 7 Althaea
  brother: 8 Meleager
  husband: 8 Heracles
  killed: 8 Heracles

Deicoon
  father: 8 Hercules
  mother: 6 Megara
  killed by: 8 Hercules

Deidamia
  father: 9 Lycomedes
  lover: 8 Achilles
  son: 11 Neoptolemus

deification 7 worship **8** idolatry **10** exaltation **13** glorification

deify 5 exalt **7** glorify, idolize, worship

Deighton, Len
  author of: 4 SS-GB **14** The Ipcress File **15** Funeral in Berlin **16** Catch a Falling Spy

deign 4 deem **5** stoop **6** see fit **7** consent **8** think fit **10** condescend

Dei gratia 15 by the grace of God

Deimos
  origin: 5 Greek
  father: 4 Ares
  mother: 9 Aphrodite
  brother: 6 Phobus
  personifies: 4 fear

Deino
  member of: 6 Graeae, Graiae

Deinonychus
  type: 8 dinosaur
  period: 10 Cretaceous

Deiope
  father: 11 Triptolemus

Deiphobe
  form: 5 sibyl
  father: 7 Glaucus

Deiphobus
  father: 5 Priam
  mother: 6 Hecuba
  brother: 6 Hector
  wife: 5 Helen
  killed by: 8 Menelaus

Deipyle
  father: 8 Adrastus
  husband: 6 Tydeus
  son: 8 Diomedes

Deipylus
  grandfather: 5 Priam

Deirdre
  origin: 5 Irish
  husband: 6 Naoise
  father-in-law: 6 Usnach
  uncle: 9 Conchobar

Deirdre of the Sorrows
  author: 19 John Millington Synge

deity, the Deity 3 god **4** idol **7** goddess, godhead, Jehovah **8** Almighty, divinity, immortal, Olympian

deja vu 11 already seen

dejected 3 low, sad **4** blue, down **7** doleful, unhappy **8** desolate **9** depressed, sorrowful **10** despondent, dispirited, spiritless **11** discouraged, downhearted, low-spirited **12** disconsolate, disheartened

dejection 5 gloom **7** sadness **10** depression, low spirits, melancholy **11** despondency **15** dispiritedness, downheartedness

dejeuner 5 lunch

de jure 7 by right **14** according to law

dekagram
  abbreviation: 3 dkg

dekaliter
  abbreviation: 3 dkL

dekameter, decameter
  abbreviation: 3 dkm
Dekker, Thomas
  author of: 11 Westward Ho! (with John
  Webster) 20 The Shoemaker's Holiday
de Kooning, Willem
  born: 9 Rotterdam 14 The Netherlands
  artwork: 5 Woman 8 Painting 15 Woman
  and Bicycle
Delacroix, Eugene
  born: 6 France 18 Charenton-St Maurice
  artwork: 8 Paganini 14 Women of Algiers 15 Massacre at Chios 16 The
  Barque of Dante 19 Chopin and George
  Sand 20 Dante and Virgil in Hell 22 Liberty at the Barricades, The Death of
  Sardanapalus
Delaroche, Paul
  born: 5 Paris 6 France
  artwork: 24 The Death of Queen Elizabeth, The Death of the Duke of Guise, 26
  The Execution of Lady Jane Grey 36
  Children of Edward Imprisoned in the
  Tower
Delaunay, Robert
  born: 5 Paris 6 France
  artwork: 5 Disks 6 Cities, Rhythm 7 Run-
  ners, Windows 10 Cathedrals 11 City of
  Paris, Eiffel Tower 14 The Cardiff Team
  19 Cosmic Circular Forms 28 Simultaneous Prismatic Windows
Delaware
  abbreviation: 2 DE 3 Del
  nickname: 5 First 7 Blue Hen, Diamond
  capital: 5 Dover
  largest city: 10 Wilmington
  others: 5 Acoma, Lewes 6 Easton, Newark, Smyrna 7 Briston, Elsmere, Milford 8
  Claymont 9 New Castle 10 Georgetown
  college: 6 Wesley 10 Brandywine, Wilmington 12 Goldey Beacom
  feature: 10 Winterthur 15 Old Swedes
  Church 17 E I du Pont de Nemours
  tribe: 4 Leni 5 Lenni 6 Lenape, Munsee
  people: 10 Howard Pyle
  island: 7 Fenwick
  land rank: 10 forty-ninth
  physical feature:
  bay: 8 Delaware, Rehoboth
  sea: 8 Atlantic
  river: 8 Delaware 9 Christina, Nanticoke
  10 Brandywine
  state admission: 5 first
  state bird: 14 blue hen chicken
  state flower: 12 peach blossom
  state motto: 22 Liberty and Independence
  state song: 11 Our Delaware
  state tree: 13 American holly
Delaware (Lenni-Lenape)
  language family: 9 Algonkian 10 Algonquian
  tribe: 5 Munsi, Unami 6 Munsee 11 Una-
  lachtigo
  location: 7 New York 8 Delaware 9 Manhattan, New Jersey 10 Long Island 12
  Pennsylvania, Staten Island

  leader: 7 Tamanen, Tammany
  deity: 11 Kitanitowet
delay 4 slow, stay 5 check, table, tarry 6
  dawdle, detain, hamper, hinder, hold up,
  impede, linger, put off, retard, shelve 7 inhibit, slowing, suspend 8 dawdling, obstruct, postpone, reprieve, stoppage, tarrying 9 deferment, lingering, loitering 10
  suspension 12 postponement, prolongation 13 procrastinate
delayed 4 late 6 put off, slowed 7 held up,
  stalled, tarried 8 arrested, deferred, detained, retarded 9 postponed, slackened
  12 dillydallied 14 procrastinated 15
  dragged one's feet
Delbruck, Max
  field: 7 biology 17 molecular genetics
  researched: 20 genetic recombination
  awarded: 10 Nobel Prize
delectable 8 pleasant 9 agreeable, delicious, enjoyable 10 delightful, gratifying 11
  pleasurable
delegate 4 give, name 5 agent, envoy,
  proxy 6 assign, charge, deputy 7 entrust 8
  give over, transfer 9 authorize, designate
  10 commission 14 representative
delegation 11 designation, entrustment 13
  authorization, commissioning
delete 3 cut 4 omit 5 erase 6 cancel, remove
deleterious 7 harmful, hurtful, ruinous 9
  dangerous, injurious 11 destructive, detrimental
Delia
  festival of: 6 Apollo
deliberate 4 easy, slow, wary 5 weigh 6
  confer, debate 7 careful, discuss, examine,
  express, planned, prudent, willful 8 cautious, cogitate, consider, measured, meditate, mull over 9 leisurely, unhurried 10
  calculated, considered, purposeful,
  thoughtful 11 circumspect, contemplate,
  intentional, prearranged 12 premeditated
deliberate together 6 confer 7 consult, discuss
deliberation 4 care 6 debate 10 conference, discussion, steadiness 11 calculation, carefulness, forethought 13 premeditation 14 circumspection
Delibes, C P (Clement Philibert) Leo
  born: 6 France 14 St Germain-du-Val
  composer of: 5 Lakme 6 Sylvia 8
  Coppelia 10 Le Roi l'a dit
delicacy 4 tact 5 taste 7 frailty 8 accuracy,
  elegance, fineness, softness, weakness 9
  fragility, frailness, lightness, precision 10
  perfection, smoothness 11 savoir-faire,
  sensibility, sensitivity, unsoundness 13
  consideration, exquisiteness, sensitiveness 14 discrimination
delicate 4 fine, soft 5 frail, muted 6 ailing,
  dainty, feeble, flimsy, infirm, minute, savory, sickly, touchy, unwell 7 careful, elegant, fragile, refined, subdued, tactful 8
  detailed, luscious, tasteful, ticklish, weakened 9 breakable, delicious, difficult, exquisite, palatable, sensitive, toothsome 10

appetizing, diplomatic, fastidious, perishable, precarious, scrupulous 11 debilitated

Delicate Balance, A
author: 11 Edward Albee

delicious 5 tasty 6 joyful, savory 8 charming, luscious, pleasant 9 palatable 10 appetizing, delectable, delightful 11 pleasurable 13 mouth-watering

delight 3 joy 5 amuse, charm, cheer, revel 6 please 7 enchant, gratify, rapture 8 pleasure 9 enjoyment, fascinate, happiness 13 gratification

delighted 6 elated 7 pleased 8 ecstatic 9 enchanted 10 captivated, enraptured, enthralled

delightful 6 peachy 7 amiable, amusing 8 charming, engaging, pleasing 9 agreeable, congenial, enjoyable 10 enchanting 11 pleasurable 12 entertaining

delight in 4 love 5 adore, eat up, enjoy, fancy, savor 6 dote on, relish 7 cherish 8 treasure 10 appreciate

Delilah
lover: 6 Samson
betrayed: 6 Samson

delineate 4 draw 5 draft 6 define, depict, design, lay out, sketch 7 outline, portray 8 describe 9 represent 12 characterize

delineation 9 depiction, portrayal 11 description 12 illustration 14 representation 16 characterization

delineavit 6 he drew (this) 7 she drew (this)

delinquency 7 misdeed 10 misconduct, negligence 11 dereliction, misbehavior 19 neglect of obligation

delinquent 3 due 4 late 6 remiss 7 hoodlum, misdoer, overdue 8 derelict 9 in arrears, miscreant, negligent, wrongdoer 10 neglectful

delirious 6 raving 7 excited, frantic 8 ecstatic, frenzied 10 incoherent 11 carried away 13 hallucinating

delirium 5 fever 6 frenzy, raving 7 madness, ranting 8 insanity 10 brain fever

Deliro
character in: 22 Every Man Out of His Humour
author: 6 Jonson

Delisle, Guillaume
field: 9 geography
nationality: 6 French
founder of: 15 modern geography

Delius, Frederick
born: 7 England 8 Bradford
composer of: 5 Paris 6 Koanga 7 Eventyr, Irmelin 8 Sea-Drift 9 Brigg Fair 10 Appalachia 11 A Mass of Life, Sur les Cimes 17 Fennimore and Gerda 20 North Country Sketches 22 A Village Romeo and Juliet, Over the Hills and Far Away

deliver 3 aim, say 4 bear, deal, free, give, save 5 bring, carry, throw, utter 6 convey, direct, launch, rescue, strike 7 release, set free 8 give over, hand over, liberate, proclaim, turn over 9 surrender 10 emancipate

deliverance 6 rescue 7 release 9 salvation 10 liberation 12 emancipation

Deliverance
director: 11 John Boorman
author: 11 James Dickey
cast: 8 Ronny Cox 9 Jon Voight, Ned Beatty 12 Burt Reynolds
song: 13 Dueling Banjos

deliver up 4 cede, give 5 grant, yield 8 fork over, hand over, transfer 9 surrender 10 relinquish

delivery 8 transfer 11 transferral, transmittal 12 transmission

dell 4 dale, dene, glen, vale 5 glade 6 dingle, hollow, valley

Della Robbia, Luca
born: 5 Italy 8 Florence
artwork: 8 Cantoria (Singing Gallery) 12 The Ascension 13 Altman Madonna 15 Madonna and Child, The Resurrection

Dello Joio, Norman
born: 9 New York NY
composer of: 7 The Ruby 12 Psalm of David 15 New York Profiles, The Trial at Rouen, Triumph of St Joan 20 Proud Music of the Storm, The Lamentation of Saul

Delon, Alain
born: 6 France, Sceaux
roles: 10 Purple Noon, The Leopard 13 The Black Tulip 14 Is Paris Burning? 19 Rocco and His Brothers

Delphic
pertains to: 6 Apollo, Delphi

Delphic oracle
oracle of: 6 Apollo
located at: 6 Delphi
priestess: 6 Pythia

Delphinia
festival of: 6 Apollo

Delphinius
epithet of: 6 Apollo
means: 7 dolphin

Delphinus
function: 12 intermediary
persuaded Amphitrite to marry: 8 Poseidon

Delphus
father: 8 Poseidon
mother: 8 Melantho

Delphyne
also: 6 Python
form: 7 monster
guarded: 4 Zeus 5 chasm
location: 6 Delphi
killed by: 6 Apollo

Del Rio, Dolores
real name: 21 Lolita Dolores Negrette
born: 6 Mexico 7 Durango
roles: 11 The Fugitive 13 Madame duBarry 15 Flying Down to Rio, Journey into Fear, Maria Candelaria

Delta Wedding
author: 11 Eudora Welty

delude 3 con 4 dupe, fool 5 put on, trick 7 deceive, mislead

deluge 4 bury, glut 5 drown, flood, spate, swamp 6 engulf 7 barrage, torrent 8 inundate, overflow, submerge 10 inundation

DeLuise, Dom
born: 10 Brooklyn NY
roles: 5 Fatso 6 The End 11 Silent Movie 14 Blazing Saddles

delusion 8 illusion 9 misbelief 10 aberration 11 derangement 13 hallucination, irrationality, misconception, self-deception

Delusions, Etc. of John Berryman
author: 12 John Berryman

deluxe 4 fine, posh 5 grand 6 choice, classy 7 elegant 8 splendid 9 luxurious

delve 5 probe 6 search 7 examine, explore 8 look into

demagogue 6 ranter 7 hothead, spouter 8 agitator, fomenter, inflamer 9 firebrand, haranguer 10 incendiary, malcontent, tubthumper 12 rabble-rouser, troublemaker

demand 4 call, need, want 5 exact, order 7 command, require 11 requirement

demanding 4 hard 5 harsh, rigid 6 strict 8 exacting 9 difficult

demantoid
species: 6 garnet

demarche 4 gait, plan

demean 5 lower, shame 6 debase, humble 7 degrade 8 disgrace 9 humiliate

demeanor 6 manner 7 bearing, conduct 8 behavior, presence 10 appearance, deportment 11 comportment

demented 3 mad 4 nuts 5 crazy 6 crazed, cuckoo, insane 7 lunatic 8 deranged

dementia praecox 13 schizophrenia

dementophobia
fear of: 8 insanity

demesne 4 land 5 realm 6 domain, estate 8 property

Demeter
origin: 5 Greek
goddess of: 8 earth 9 fertility
protectress of: 8 marriage 11 social order
father: 6 Cronus
mother: 4 Rhea
daughter: 10 Persephone
corresponds to: 5 Brimo, Ceres 8 Despoena
epithet: 5 Chloe, Lusia, Mysia 6 Antaea, Erinys, Stiria 7 Chamyne, Thesmia 8 Stiritis 9 Anesidora, Thermasia 11 Carpophorus 13 Thesimophorus

Demetrius
character in: 21 A Midsummer Night's Dream
author: 11 Shakespeare

DeMille, Cecil B
director of: 9 Cleopatra 18 The Ten Commandments 22 The Greatest Show on Earth

Demiphon
form: 4 king
sacrificed: 7 maidens
to prevent: 6 plague

demise 3 end 4 fall, ruin 5 death 7 decease, passing 8 collapse 10 expiration

demobilization 7 release 9 discharge 10 disbanding

demobilize 7 disband, release 9 discharge

Democoon
father: 5 Priam
birth: 12 illegitimate
killed by: 8 Odysseus

democracy 8 equality, fairness

Democracy
author: 10 Henry Adams

Democracy in America
author: 19 Alexis de Tocqueville

Democratic Party
symbol: 6 donkey
president belonging to: 4 Polk 6 Carter, Pierce, Truman, Wilson 7 (Lyndon Baines) Johnson, Jackson, Kennedy, Clinton 8 Buchanan, Van Buren 9 Cleveland, (Franklin D) Roosevelt

Democratic Republican Party
president belonging to: 5 (John Quincy) Adams 6 Monroe 7 Madison 9 Jefferson

demode 8 outmoded 13 unfashionable

Demodocus
minstrel of: 8 Alcinous

Demogorgon
object of: 3 awe 4 fear

demoiselle 4 girl

demolish 4 raze, ruin 5 level, total, wreck 7 destroy 9 devastate

demolition 6 razing 8 leveling, wrecking 11 destruction

demon 5 devil, fiend 7 monster 8 go-getter

Demonassa
father: 10 Amphiaraus
mother: 8 Eriphyle
husband: 10 Thersander
son: 9 Tisamenus

demonic, demoniacal 6 hectic 7 frantic, hellish 8 devilish, fiendish, frenzied

demonstrable 7 evident 8 apparent, manifest, palpable 11 supportable

demonstrate 4 show 5 march, prove, teach 6 parade, picket, reveal 7 display, exhibit, explain 8 describe, manifest 9 establish 10 illustrate

demonstration 5 march, rally 6 parade 7 display 9 picketing 10 exhibition, exposition, expression 12 illustration, presentation 13 manifestation

demonstrative 7 gushing 8 effusive 12 affectionate

demonstrativeness 9 gushiness 12 effusiveness, emotionalism

Demophon
father: 7 Theseus
mother: 7 Phaedra
brother: 6 Acamas
wife: 7 Phyllis

Demophoon
father: 6 Celeus
mother: 8 Metanira
nursed by: 7 Demeter

demoralize 8 dispirit 9 undermine 10 disconcert, discourage, dishearten 11 disorganize

de mortuis nil nisi bonum 26 of the dead say nothing but good

demos 5 plebs 6 masses 7 commons 8 populace 9 commoners

demote 4 bust 7 degrade

Dempsey, Jack (William Harrison)
nickname: 13 Manassa Mauler
sport: 6 boxing
class: 11 heavyweight

demur 5 qualm 6 object 7 protest, scruple 8 disagree 9 misgiving, objection 10 hesitation 11 compunction

demure 3 shy 4 prim 6 modest 7 bashful 8 reserved

demurrer 5 doubt, qualm 7 dissent, protest, scruple 8 objector, question, rebuttal 9 challenge, exception, misgiving, objection, protester, protestor, stricture 11 compunction 12 remonstrance

den 4 lair 5 haunt, study 6 hotbed 7 hangout, library, retreat, shelter 9 sanctuary

denial 7 refusal 9 disavowal, disowning, rejection 10 disclaimer

denigrate 4 soil 5 abuse, smear, sully 6 defame, dump on, malign, revile, vilify 7 asperse, blacken, degrade, run down, slander, traduce 8 backbite, badmouth, belittle, besmirch, tear down 9 call names, discredit, disparage, downgrade 10 calumniate, stigmatize

De Niro, Robert
born: 9 New York NY
roles: 10 Raging Bull (Oscar), Taxi Driver 11 Mean Streets 13 The Deer Hunter 14 New York New York, The Godfather II 15 The King of Comedy, True Confessions 17 Bang the Drum Slowly

denizen 7 dweller 8 resident 10 inhabitant

Denmark
other name: 17 Kongeriget Danmark
capital/largest city: 9 Kobenhavn 10 Copenhagen
others: 3 Hov 4 Hals, Koge, Nibe, Ribe, Soro 5 Arhus, Kosor, Vejle 6 Aarhus, Abenra, Alborg, Dorsor, Dragor, Nyberg, Odense, Skagen, Struer, Viborg 7 Aalborg, Esbjerg, Horsens, Kolding, Morsens, Randers 8 Ballerup, Elsinore, Gentofte, Glostrup, Hillerod, Naestred, Roskilde, Slagelse 9 Haderslev, Helsingor, Svendborg 10 Fredericia 13 Frederikshavn
school:
university institute of: 18 Theoretical Physics
folk high school: 14 folkehojskoler
continuation school: 11 efterskoler
division: 3 Fyn 7 Jutland, Lolland 9 Schleswig, Sjaelland
measure: 3 ell, fod, mil, pot 4 alen, favn, last, rode 5 album, anker, kande, linje, paegl, tomme 6 achtel, paegel, skeppe 7 landmil, oltonde, ortonde, skieppe, viertel 8 fjerding 9 ottingkar 10 komtonmde
monetary unit: 3 one, ora, ore 4 fyrk 5 krone 8 frederik, skilling 9 rigsdaler
weight: 2 es 3 lod, ort, vog 4 last, mark, pund, unze 5 carat, kvint, pound, quint, tonde 6 toende 7 centner, lispund, quintin 8 lispound, skippund 9 skibslast, skippound 10 bismerpund
island: 2 Oe 3 Als, Fyn, Mon, Rum, Thy 4 Aaro, Aero, Fano, Fohr, Moen, Mors, Romo 5 Baago, Faero, Faroe, Funen, Laeso, Samso, Sando 6 Amager, Sandoy, Sejero, Sudero 7 Faeroes, Falster, Hesselo, Laaland, Lolland, Seeland, Zealand 8 Bornholm, Eysturoy, Sudhuroy 9 Greenland, Langeland, Sjaelland 10 Vendsyssel
lake: 6 Arreso
hill: 12 Ejer Bavnehoj 14 Himmelbjaerget
highest point: 12 Yding Skovhoj
river: 3 Asa 4 Holm, Omme, Stor 5 Skive, Susaa, Varde 6 Gelsaa, Gudena, Vorgod 7 Gudenaa, Lilleaa, Lonborg
sea: 5 North 6 Baltic 7 Oresund 8 Atlantic, Kattegat 9 Skagerrak
physical feature:
fjord: 3 Ise 4 Isse 5 Lamme
inlet: 3 Ise 5 Fjord, Vejle 6 Nissum, Odense 7 Horsens, Logstor 8 Limfjord, Mariager
peninsula: 7 Jutland
strait: 7 Otesund 8 Kattegat 9 Skagerrak
people: 4 Dane, Jute 5 Angle 6 Cimbri, Eskimo, German, Ostmen, Teuton, Viking 12 Scandinavian
astronomer: 10 Tycho Brahe
author: 11 Isak Dinesen 21 Hans Christian Andersen
founder: 4 Axel 7 Absalon
king: 4 Hans, Knud 6 Canute 8 Frederik 9 Christian 10 Gorm the Old 15 Harold Bluetooth
philosopher: 11 Kierkegaard
physicist: 9 Niels Bohr
queen: 9 Margrethe 12 Thyra Danebod
sculptor: 11 Thorvaldsen
teacher: 4 Kold
language: 4 Odan 6 Danish, German 8 Faeroese 11 Greenlander
religion: 19 Evangelical Lutheran
place:
airport: 7 Kastrup
castle: 7 Egeskov 8 Kronborg 13 Frederiksborg
museum: 6 Rebild 9 Glyptotek 11 Thorvaldsen 15 Rosenborg Castle
park: 10 Langelinie 13 Tivoli Gardens
royal palace: 11 Amalienborg
statue: 13 Little Mermaid
stock exchange: 5 Borse 6 Borsen
feature:
dance: 6 sextur
drink: 5 glogg 7 aquavit
beer: 6 Tuborg 9 Carlsberg
food:
cheese: 3 Ost 4 Blue, Tybo 5 Esrom, Samso 6 Samsoe 7 Havarti, Mycella
meat patty: 11 frikadeller
pudding: 15 rodgrod med flode

Dennis, Patrick
author of: 10 Auntie Mame

Dennis, Sandy
  real name: 16 Sandra Dale Dennis
  born: 10 Hastings NE
  roles: 12 Any Wednesday 15 A Thousand Clowns 18 Up the Down Staircase 25 Who's Afraid of Virginia Woolf?

Dennis the Hangman
  character in: 12 Barnaby Rudge
  author: 7 Dickens

Dennis the Menace
  creator: 11 Hank Ketcham
  character: 9 Mrs Elkins 10 John Wilson 12 Eloise Wilson, George Wilson, Joey McDonald, Martha Wilson 13 Alice Mitchell, Henry Mitchell, Tommy Anderson 14 Dennis Mitchell
  dog: 4 Ruff
  cast: 8 Gil Smith, Jay North 10 Billy Booth, Gale Gordon, Sara Seeger 11 Gloria Henry, Irene Tedrow, Sylvia Field 12 Joseph Kearns 15 Herbert Anderson

denomination 4 name, sect, size 5 class, value 8 category, grouping 10 persuasion 11 designation

denotation 4 mark, name, sign 6 symbol 7 meaning 9 indication

denote 4 mark, mean, name 6 signal 7 signify 8 indicate

denouement 3 end 6 finale, upshot 7 outcome 8 solution 10 conclusion 11 termination

denounce 6 accuse, vilify 7 censure, condemn 9 criticize

denouncement 7 censure 12 condemnation, denunciation

de novo 4 anew 5 again 6 afresh 16 from the beginning

dense 4 dull, dumb, slow 5 close, heavy, thick 6 stupid 7 compact, crowded, intense 8 ignorant 9 dimwitted 10 compressed 11 thickheaded 12 concentrated, impenetrable

Densher, Merton
  character in: 17 The Wings of the Dove
  author: 5 James

density 4 mass 6 weight 7 opacity 8 dullness, solidity 9 stupidity, thickness 10 obtuseness, opaqueness 11 compactness

dent 3 pit 4 nick 6 hollow 10 depression 11 indentation

denude 4 bare 5 strip 6 divest 7 lay bare 8 unclothe

denuded 4 bare 5 naked 6 barren 8 stripped 9 unclothed, uncovered

denunciation 7 censure 12 condemnation, denouncement 13 attack against

Denver
  basketball team: 7 Nuggets
  football team: 4 Gold 7 Broncos

deny 6 refuse, refute 7 disavow 8 disallow, disclaim 9 disaffirm 10 contradict

deny oneself 5 avoid, forgo 6 eschew, give up, refuse 7 abstain, forbear 8 renounce 9 sacrifice

deny responsibility 7 disavow

Deo gratias 13 thanks be to God

Deo volente 10 God willing

DePalma, Brian
  director of: 6 Carrie 13 Dressed to Kill

depart 2 go 4 exit 5 leave 7 deviate, digress

departed 4 dead, gone, late, left, past, went 6 at rest, bygone 7 gone off 8 gone away 10 passed away 11 gone to glory 12 late-lamented 20 gone the way of all flesh

depart for 8 leave for 9 adjourn to, set off for, set out for 10 head toward, move toward

depart hastily 3 fly 4 flee 6 decamp, escape 7 abscond 9 skedaddle

department 4 unit 6 branch, bureau, sector 7 section 8 district, division, province

departure 4 exit 5 going 6 exodus 7 leaving 9 deviation 10 digression, divergence

depend 4 rely, rest 5 count, hinge 6 hang on

dependable 4 sure, true 5 loyal 6 steady, trusty 7 trusted 8 faithful, reliable 9 steadfast, unfailing 11 trustworthy

dependence 5 trust 8 reliance 10 confidence, dependency

dependency 10 dependence

dependent 7 reliant

depict 4 draw, limn 5 carve, chart, draft, paint 6 define, detail, map·out, recite, record, relate, sculpt, sketch 7 diagram, narrate, picture, portray, recount 8 describe 9 chronicle, delineate, dramatize, represent, verbalize 10 illustrate 12 characterize

depiction 6 sketch 7 drawing, picture 8 portrait 9 picturing, portrayal 11 delineation 12 illustration 14 representation 16 characterization

deplete 5 drain, use up 6 lessen, reduce 7 consume, exhaust 8 decrease 10 impoverish

depleted 5 empty, spent, waste 6 barren, used up 7 drained, emptied, reduced, worn out 8 bankrupt, consumed, expended, lessened 9 exhausted, infertile 10 unfruitful

depletion 5 drain 7 using up 8 decrease 9 lessening, reduction 10 exhaustion 11 consumption

deplorable 5 awful 8 wretched 9 miserable 11 blameworthy 13 reprehensible 17 deserving reproach

deplore 5 mourn 6 bemoan, bewail, lament 7 censure, condemn 9 grieve for 12 disapprove of

deport 3 act 4 oust 5 carry, exile, expel 6 banish, behave 7 cast out 10 expatriate 14 conduct oneself

deported person 2 DP 5 exile 8 deportee 10 expatriate 14 banished person

deportment 7 conduct 8 behavior, demeanor 11 comportment

depose 4 oust 6 unseat 8 dethrone 16 remove from office

deposit 3 put 4 pile 5 place 7 put down, set down 8 sediment 10 accumulate 11 down payment, give in trust, installment 12 accumulation 14 partial payment

deposition 7 deposit 9 statement, testimony 11 declaration 12 accumulation

depository 4 bank, safe 5 vault 6 museum 7 library 8 archives 10 storehouse

depot 4 dump 8 terminal, terminus 10 bus station 15 railroad station 20 military storage place

depraved 4 vile 6 wicked 7 corrupt, debased 8 degraded 9 debauched, perverted 10 degenerate

depravity 8 vileness 9 decadence 10 corruption, debasement, debauchery, degeneracy, immorality, perversion, wickedness 11 degradation, dissolution

deprecate 7 condemn, protest 8 belittle, object to, play down 10 depreciate 15 take exception to

deprecated 7 defamed, put down 8 despised 9 belittled, derogated, disdained

deprecation 4 slur 5 abuse 7 protest, put-down 9 aspersion 10 aspersions, belittling, defamation, derogation 11 disapproval 12 condemnation 13 disparagement

deprecatory 8 critical 9 maligning, vilifying 10 belittling, defamatory, derogatory, slanderous 11 disparaging 12 disapproving

depreciate 5 scorn 7 run down 8 belittle, diminish 9 denigrate, disparage, downgrade, lose value 13 reduce in value, lower the value

depreciation 5 scorn 7 disdain 8 contempt 9 criticism, deflation 10 belittling, disrespect 11 devaluation 13 disparagement

depredation 4 sack 6 rapine, ravage 7 looting, pillage, plunder, robbery, sacking 8 spoiling 9 marauding 10 brigandage, ravishment, spoliation 11 desecration, devastation, freebooting, laying waste

depress 5 lower 6 deject, lessen, reduce, sadden, weaken 7 cut back 8 diminish, dispirit 9 press down 10 dishearten 14 lower in spirits

depressed 3 sad 4 blue 7 unhappy 8 dejected, downcast 10 despondent, dispirited, melancholy 11 low-spirited 12 disconsolate, inconsolable

depressing 3 sad 6 gloomy 8 lowering 9 dejecting, saddening 10 oppressing 11 casting down, dispiriting, melancholic, pushing down 12 discouraging, pressing down, weighing down 14 causing sadness

depression 5 gloom 6 dimple, hollow 7 sadness 9 dejection, recession 10 desolation, melancholy 11 despondency, indentation, melancholia 14 discouragement 15 downheartedness, economic decline

deprive 5 strip 6 divest 8 take from 10 confiscate, dispossess

deprived 8 divested, stripped 11 handicapped 12 dispossessed, impoverished 13 disadvantaged 15 underprivileged

deprive of honor 5 abase, shame, sully 6 defame 7 blacken, tarnish 8 disgrace, dishonor 9 discredit 10 stigmatize

deprive of strength 6 hinder, weaken 7 disable, wear out 8 enervate, enfeeble, handicap 10 debilitate, devitalize

de profundis 13 from the depths

depth 6 timbre 8 deepness 10 profundity 19 downward measurement 24 perpendicular measurement

depths 4 deep 6 bowels 8 interior, recesses

deputation 9 committee 10 commission, delegation 15 representatives

deputize 6 assign 7 appoint 8 delegate 10 commission

deputy 4 aide 5 agent, envoy, proxy 6 second 8 delegate, emissary, minister 9 alternate, assistant, go-between, messenger, middleman, surrogate 10 ambassador, substitute 11 pinch hitter 12 spokesperson 14 representative 15 second-in-command

DeQuincey, Thomas
 author of: 19 The English Mail-Coach 31 On the Knocking at the Gate in Macbeth 32 Confessions of an English Opium-Eater

derail 3 bar 4 balk, foil 5 block, check, spike 6 hinder, impede, thwart 7 inhibit, prevent 8 obstruct 14 throw off course

deranged 5 crazy 6 insane 8 demented 10 irrational, unbalanced

derangement 6 lunacy 7 madness 8 insanity 9 craziness 11 peculiarity 13 irrationality, mental illness 14 mental disorder

Der Bingle
 nickname of: 10 Bing Crosby

Derek, Bo
 husband: 4 John
 roles: 3 Ten (10) 6 Bolero, Tarzan

derelict 3 bum 4 hobo 5 tramp 6 remiss 7 outcast, vagrant 8 careless, deserted 9 abandoned, negligent 10 delinquent, neglectful

dereliction 7 failure, neglect 9 disregard 10 negligence 11 delinquency 13 noncompliance, nonobservance

De rerum natura
 author: 9 Lucretius

deride 4 mock 5 scoff, scorn 7 sneer at 8 ridicule

de rigueur 11 fashionable 16 strictly required

derision 5 scorn 7 disdain, mockery 8 ridicule, sneering

derivation 5 stock 6 origin, source 7 descent, getting, lineage 8 ancestry, deriving, heritage 9 acquiring, etymology, parentage 10 background, beginnings, extraction 21 historical development

derive 4 gain 5 arise, enjoy, glean 6 obtain 7 descend 8 stem from 9 originate

dermaptera
 class: 8 hexapoda
 phylum: 10 arthropoda
 group: 6 earwig

dermatitis 4 rash 6 eczema 9 psoriasis 12 inflammation

Dern, Bruce
born: 9 Chicago IL
roles: 6 Marnie, Tattoo 10 Coming Home, Family Plot 11 Black Sunday 13 The Wild Angels 14 The Great Gatsby 22 The King of Marvin Gardens

dernier 4 last 5 final 8 ultimate

dernier cri 9 latest cry 10 latest word 13 latest fashion

derogate 4 blot 5 taint 6 smirch 8 disgrace 9 disparage

derogation 4 blot 5 odium, stain 7 blemish 8 contempt, disfavor, disgrace, ignominy 9 disesteem, disrepute 10 disrespect 11 humiliation 13 disparagement

derogatory 9 injurious 10 belittling 11 disparaging, unfavorable 12 unflattering 15 uncomplimentary

derrick 3 rig 5 crane, hoist, tower 9 framework
kind: 3 oil 6 sheers 7 gin-pole
part: 3 gin, leg 4 boom, mast 6 pulley 7 guy line

derring-do 6 daring 8 audacity, boldness 11 daredevilry 12 daredeviltry, recklessness 15 venturesomeness

dervish 5 fakir 6 Muslim 7 ascetic

De Sapientia Veterum
author: 12 Francis Bacon

Descartes, Rene
author of: 17 Discourse on Method
field: 11 mathemathics
nationality: 6 French
developed: 18 analytical geometry
quote: 13 Cogito ergo sum 18 I think therefore I am

descend 3 dip 4 drop, pass 5 slant, slope, swoop 6 go down, invade 7 incline 8 come down, inherited 11 come in force 12 be handed down, move downward

descendant 5 issue 7 progeny 9 offspring

descend upon 6 assail, attack, charge 7 assault, set upon 12 bear down upon

descent 4 drop, fall, raid 5 slant, slope 6 origin 7 assault, decline, lineage 8 ancestry 9 declivity, incursion 10 coming down 11 sneak attack, sudden visit

describe 4 draw 5 trace 6 depict, detail, recite, relate 7 explain, mark out, narrate, outline, portray, recount, speak of 9 delineate 10 illustrate 12 characterize

description 3 ilk 4 kind, sort, type 5 brand, class, genus 6 manner, nature 7 account, species, variety 9 depiction, narration, portrayal 12 illustration 16 characterization

descry 3 see 4 spot 6 behold, notice 7 discern, observe, pick out 8 discover 12 catch sight of

Desdemona
character in: 7 Othello
author: 11 Shakespeare

desecrate 6 defile 7 profane, violate 8 dishonor

desecration 8 dishonor 9 violation 10 defilement 11 profanation

desert 3 dry 4 arid, wild 5 leave, waste 6 barren 7 abandon, forsake 8 desolate, untilled 9 infertile, wasteland 10 arid region 11 run away from, uninhabited 12 uncultivated 16 barren wilderness

deserted 4 AWOL, left 5 empty 6 lonely, vacant 7 cast off, forlorn, reneged 8 defected, desolate, forsaken, marooned 9 abandoned, absconded 12 quit one's post 14 left in the lurch

desertedness 9 emptiness 10 desolation 13 uncrowdedness

Deserted Village, The
author: 15 Oliver Goldsmith

desertion 8 quitting 9 forsaking 11 abandonment 14 relinquishment

desertlike 3 dry 4 arid 5 sandy 6 barren 7 dried up, parched 9 waterless

deserts 5 due 5 worth 6 reward 7 payment

deserve 4 rate 5 merit 7 warrant 9 earn as due 10 be worthy of, qualify for 12 be entitled to 13 be deserving of

deserving 6 worthy 9 qualified

deserving reproach 8 blamable 10 deplorable, punishable, reprovable 11 blameworthy 12 reproachable 13 reprehensible

De Sica, Vittorio
director of: 15 The Bicycle Thief 27 The Garden of the Finzi-Continis

desiccate 5 dry up, parch 6 wither 7 shrivel 9 dehydrate

design 3 aim, end 4 draw, form, goal, plan, plot 5 draft, motif, set up 6 devise, intend, scheme, sketch, target 7 destine, diagram, drawing, fashion, outline, pattern, project, purpose 8 conceive, intrigue 9 blueprint, intention, objective 11 arrangement 14 draw up plans for

designate 4 call, name, term 5 elect, label 6 assign, choose, select 7 appoint, signify, specify 8 identify, indicate, nominate, pinpoint

designation 5 label 6 naming 10 delegation 11 appointment 13 specification 14 identification

designer 7 creator, deviser, planner 9 contriver 10 originator

designing 4 wily 6 artful, crafty 7 cunning 8 plotting, scheming 9 conniving

desirable 4 fine 8 in demand, pleasing 9 advisable 10 beneficial 11 worth having 12 advantageous

desire 4 need, urge, want, wish 5 crave 6 ask for, hunger, thirst 7 craving, longing, long for, request 8 yearning, yearn for 9 hunger for, thirst for

Desire Under the Elms
author: 12 Eugene O'Neill
character: 4 Eben 5 Peter 6 Simeon 11 Abbie Putnam 12 Ephraim Cabot

desirous 4 avid, keen 5 eager 7 hopeful, longing, wishful 8 yearning

desist 4 stop 5 cease 6 lay off 7 suspend 8 leave off 11 discontinue, refrain from

Desk Set
director: 10 Walter Lang
cast: 8 Gig Young 11 Dina Merrill 12

Joan Blondell, Spencer Tracy **16** Katharine Hepburn

Desmontes
foster son: 4 Arne

desolate 3 sad **4** bare, ruin **5** bleak, empty **6** barren, grieve, ravage, sadden **7** depress, destroy, forlorn **8** dejected, demolish, deserted, distress, downcast, forsaken, lay waste, wretched **9** abandoned, depressed, devastate, miserable, sorrowful **10** despondent, discourage, dishearten, melancholy **11** downhearted, uninhabited

desolating 6 tragic **7** ruinous **8** dreadful, grievous, terrible **10** calamitous, horrendous **11** devastating **12** catastrophic

desolation 4 ruin **6** misery, sorrow **7** sadness **8** bareness, distress, solitude **9** bleakness, dejection, emptiness, seclusion **10** barrenness, depression, dreariness, loneliness, melancholy, wilderness **11** destruction, devastation, unhappiness **12** solitariness

despair 5 gloom, trial **6** burden, ordeal **9** lose heart **10** depression, have no hope **11** despondency, lose faith in **12** hopelessness **13** discouragement

despair of 5 doubt **8** give up on **10** have no hope

desperado 4 thug **5** rowdy **6** bandit, gunman, outlaw **7** brigand, convict, hoodlum, ruffian **8** criminal, fugitive, hooligan **9** terrorist **10** lawbreaker

desperate 4 dire, rash, wild **5** grave, great **6** daring, urgent **7** extreme, frantic, serious **8** critical, hopeless, reckless, wretched **9** dangerous, incurable **10** beyond hope, despairing, despondent

Desperate Hours, The
director: 12 William Wyler
cast: 8 Gig Young **11** Dewey Martin, Martha Scott **13** Arthur Kennedy, Frederic March **14** Humphrey Bogart

Desperately Seeking Susan
director: 14 Susan Seidelman
cast: 7 Madonna **15** Rosanna Arquette

desperation 7 despair **12** hopelessness, recklessness

despicable 4 base, mean, vile **10** detestable, outrageous **11** disgraceful **12** contemptible **13** reprehensible

despise 5 abhor, scorn **6** detest, loathe **7** contemn, disdain, dislike **10** look down on

Despoena
origin: 5 Greek
father: 8 Poseidon
mother: 7 Demeter
corresponds to: 10 Persephone

despoil 3 rob **4** loot **6** ravage **7** pillage, plunder

despoiler 6 looter, robber, vandal **7** brigand **8** pillager **9** plunderer

despondency 5 gloom **6** dismay **7** despair, sadness **9** dejection, pessimism **10** depression, desolation, low spirits, melancholy **11** melancholia **12** hopelessness **14** discouragement **15** downheartedness

despondent 3 low **4** blue, down **8** dejected, downcast, hopeless **9** depressed **11** discouraged, downhearted **12** disconsolate, disheartened

despot 6 tyrant **8** autocrat, dictator **9** oppressor

despotic 9 imperious **10** autocratic, tyrannical **11** dictatorial **13** authoritarian

despotism 7 tyranny **9** autocracy **10** absolutism

dessert 3 pie **4** cake, nuts, tart **5** fruit, sweet **8** ice cream **11** final course

destination 3 aim, end **4** goal, plan **6** object, target **7** purpose **8** ambition **9** objective **11** journey's end

destiny 3 lot **4** fate **5** karma, moira **6** future, kismet **7** fortune **9** necessity
goddess of: 5 Fates, Morae, Parca **6** Moerae, Moirai, Parcae

destitute 4 poor **5** broke, needy **6** busted **8** indigent **9** penniless **15** poverty-stricken

destitution 4 lack, want **6** penury **7** beggary, poverty **9** indigence, privation **11** extreme want **13** pennilessness **14** impoverishment

destroy 4 ruin **5** waste, wreck **6** ravage **8** demolish **9** devastate

destroy completely 3 end **7** abolish, wipe out **8** lay waste **9** eradicate, extirpate, liquidate **10** annihilate, obliterate **11** exterminate

destroyer 4 bane **6** blight, killer **7** gunboat, warship **10** affliction **11** anniihilator

destruct 3 gut **4** raze, ruin **5** wreck **7** despoil, destroy, wipe out **8** decimate, demolish, desolate, pull down, tear down **9** devastate **10** lay in ruins

destruction 4 ruin **5** havoc **6** wreckage, wrecking **10** demolition **11** devastation

destructive 7 harmful, hurtful, ruinous **8** damaging **9** injurious **11** detrimental, devastating **15** not constructive

Destry Rides Again
director: 14 George Marshall
based on a story by: 8 Max Brand
cast: 12 Brian Donlevy, James Stewart **15** Marlene Dietrich **16** Charles Winninger
song: 35 See What the Boys in the Back Room Will Have

desultory 6 casual, chance, fitful, random **7** aimless, cursory **9** haphazard **10** without aim **11** unconnected

detach 3 sever **6** loosen **7** unhitch **8** separate, unfasten **9** disengage **10** disconnect **11** disentangle

detached 4 fair **5** aloof **7** distant, neutral, severed **8** reserved, unbiased **9** impartial, objective, separated, uncoupled, unhitched **10** disengaged, fair-minded, unfastened **11** indifferent, unconnected **12** disconnected, unprejudiced **13** disinterested, dispassionate
French: 6 degage

detachment 4 unit **5** force **8** coolness, fairness, severing **9** aloofness, isolation, severance **10** cutting off, neutrality, separation 11 objectivity 12 impartiality, indifference 13 disconnection, disengagement, preoccupation 16 special task force

detail 4 fact, iota, item 6 aspect, relate 7 appoint, feature, itemize, recount, respect, specify 9 component, delineate, designate, enumerate 10 detachment, particular 11 special duty 13 assign to a task, particularize 14 special service 20 particular assignment

detailed 6 minute 8 itemized, thorough 10 item by item 12 point by point

detailed list 9 breakdown 11 itemization 14 categorization

detain 4 hold, slow, stop 5 delay 6 arrest, hinder, retard, slow up 7 confine 8 slow down 13 keep in custody

detainment 7 custody, holding 9 detention 11 confinement 12 imprisonment 13 incarceration

detect 3 see 4 espy, note, spot 5 catch 6 notice 7 observe, uncover 8 discover, perceive

detectable 10 noticeable 11 appreciable, discernible, perceivable, perceptible 13 ascertainable

detective 2 Pl 6 shamus, sleuth 7 gumshoe 10 private eye 12 investigator 19 special investigator

detention 7 custody, holding 9 keeping in 10 detainment 11 confinement, holding back 12 imprisonment 13 incarceration

deter 4 stop 5 daunt 6 divert, hinder, impede 7 prevent 8 dissuade 10 discourage

deteriorate 3 ebb 4 fade, wane 5 decay, lapse 6 worsen 7 crumble, decline, fall off 10 degenerate 12 disintegrate

deteriorated 6 shabby 7 rickety 8 decaying, worsened 9 crumbling 10 broken-down, tumble-down 11 dilapidated, in disrepair 13 disintegrated

deterioration 5 decay, lapse 6 fading, waning 7 decline 9 crumbling, decadence, worsening 12 degeneration, dilapidation 14 disintegration

determination 4 grit 5 pluck, power, spunk 6 fixing 7 finding, resolve, verdict 8 boldness, decision, judgment, settling, solution, tenacity 9 reasoning, resolving 10 conclusion, resolution 11 determining, persistence 12 perseverance, resoluteness 13 act of deciding, steadfastness 16 stick-to-it-iveness

determine 5 learn 6 affect, decide, detect, settle 7 control, find out, resolve 8 conclude, discover, regulate 9 ascertain, establish, figure out, influence 15 come to a decision, give direction to

determined 7 dead set, decided, settled 8 found out, obdurate, resolute, stubborn 9 obstinate, tenacious 10 figured out 11 ascertained, established 15 come to a decision

deterrent 4 curb 5 check 9 hindrance, restraint 14 discouragement

detest 4 hate 5 abhor 6 loathe 7 despise 10 recoil from 16 dislike intensely

detestable 4 vile 6 odious 7 hateful 9 abhorrent, loathsome, obnoxious, offensive, repulsive, revolting 10 disgusting, unpleasant 12 disagreeable

detestation 4 hate 6 hatred 7 disgust, dislike 8 aversion, distaste, loathing 9 antipathy, repulsion, revulsion 10 abhorrence, repugnance

dethrone 4 oust 6 depose, unseat

detonate 4 fire 5 blast, burst, erupt, go off, shoot 6 blow up, ignite, report, set off 7 explode 8 touch off 9 discharge, fulminate

detonation 5 blast, burst 6 report 9 discharge, explosion

detour 5 skirt 6 bypass, byroad, divert 7 digress 9 deviation, diversion 10 digression

detract 5 lower 6 lessen, reduce 8 diminish 12 subtract from, take away from

detraction 4 flaw 11 shortcoming 12 disadvantage

detractor 5 enemy 6 critic 8 opponent 9 adversary, belittler, slanderer 10 antagonist, bad mouther, disparager

detriment 4 harm, loss 6 damage, injury 10 impairment 12 disadvantage

detrimental 7 adverse, harmful 8 damaging 9 injurious 10 pernicious 11 deleterious, destructive, unfavorable 15 disadvantageous

Detroit
  baseball team: 6 Tigers
  basketball team: 7 Pistons
  football team: 5 Lions
  hockey team: 8 Redwings

de trop 7 too many, too much 8 in the way 9 not wanted

Deucalion
  father: 10 Prometheus
  mother: 7 Pronoia
  wife: 6 Pyrrha
  son: 6 Hellen
  founded: 9 human race
  after: 6 deluge

deus ex machina 15 god from a machine 18 improbable solution

Deus vobiscum 12 God be with you

Deus vult 8 God wills (it)
  cry of: 9 Crusaders

devaluate 6 lessen, reduce 7 deflate, degrade 10 depreciate

devaluation 4 drop 7 decline 12 depreciation

devalue 5 lower, taint 6 debase, defile, infect 7 cheapen, corrupt, degrade, pervert, pollute, revalue 8 mark down 9 devaluate, underrate, write down 10 adulterate, degenerate, demonetize, depreciate, remonetize 11 contaminate

devastate 4 ruin 5 level, spoil, waste, wreck 6 ravage 7 despoil, destroy 8 demolish, desolate, lay waste

devastating 7 ruinous 8 damaging 9 injurious 10 calamitous, disastrous 11 cataclysmic, destructive, detrimental 12 catastrophic

devastation 4 ruin 9 ruination 10 demolition 11 destruction

develop 4 grow 5 print, ripen 6 evolve, expand, finish, flower, mature, pick up, unfold 7 acquire, advance, amplify, augment, broaden, build up, convert, enlarge, improve, process, turn out 8 contract, energize 9 cultivate 10 come to have 11 come to light, elaborate on

development 5 event 6 growth, result 7 advance, history 8 progress 9 evolution

deviant 4 warp 5 shift 7 deviate, pervert 8 aberrant, abnormal 9 deflected, divergent

deviate 4 part, vary, veer 5 stray 6 depart, swerve, wander 8 go astray 9 sidetrack, turn aside

deviation 6 change 7 veering 8 rambling, straying 9 wandering 10 aberration, digression, divergence 11 abnormality, fluctuation

device 4 plan, plot, ploy, ruse, wile 5 angle, trick 6 design, gadget, scheme 7 gimmick 8 artifice, strategy 9 apparatus, invention, mechanism, stratagem 11 contraption, contrivance

devil, the Devil 3 guy 5 rogue, Satan, thing 6 Azazel, fellow, wretch 7 hellion, Lucifer, ruffian, serpent, villain 8 creature 9 Archfiend, Beelzebub, scoundrel 11 unfortunate 12 spirit of evil 13 mischief-maker 16 prince of darkness

Devil and Daniel Webster, The
  author: 19 Stephen Vincent Benet
  director: 15 William Dieterle
  character: 5 Devil 7 Webster 9 Mr Scratch
  cast: 10 James Craig 11 Anne Shirley 12 Edward Arnold, Walter Huston
  score: 15 Bernard Herrmann
  Oscar for: 5 score
  also titled: 18 All That Money Can Buy

devilish 4 evil 6 wicked 7 demonic, heinous, impious, satanic, vicious 8 demoniac, fiendish 9 nefarious 10 demoniacal, diabolical, villainous

devil-may-care 4 bold, rash, wild 5 risky 6 daring, rakish 8 heedless, reckless 9 audacious, daredevil

devil's advocate
  Latin: 16 advocatus diaboli

Devil's Advocate
  author: 14 Taylor Caldwell

Devil's Disciple, The
  author: 17 George Bernard Shaw

Devine, Andy
  real name: 16 Jeremiah Schwartz
  born: 11 Flagstaff AZ
  roles: 7 Jingles 9 Andy's Gang 14 Wild Bill Hickok

devious 3 sly 4 wily 6 sneaky, tricky 7 crooked 9 deceitful, dishonest 11 treacherous 12 dishonorable 13 double-dealing

devise 4 plot 5 forge, frame 6 design, invent, map out 7 concoct, prepare, think up 8 block out, conceive, contrive 9 construct, formulate

deviser 6 author, framer 7 creator, planner 8 inventor 9 architect, contriver 10 originator

devitalize 4 kill 6 deaden, weaken 8 enervate 10 debilitate

devoid 5 empty 6 barren 7 lacking, wanting, without 8 bereft of 9 destitute 11 unblest with

devote 5 apply 6 direct 7 address, utilize 8 dedicate 10 consecrate, give over to 11 concentrate 15 give oneself up to 22 center one's attentions on

devoted 4 fond, true 5 loyal 6 ardent, loving 7 earnest, staunch, zealous 8 adhering, faithful 9 dedicated, steadfast 10 passionate, unwavering 17 strongly committed

devotedness 8 devotion 10 commitment, dedication 13 attentiveness 17 earnest attachment

devoted to luxury 9 sybaritic 10 hedonistic, voluptuous

devotee 3 fan 6 rooter 7 booster 8 adherent, advocate, champion, disciple, follower 10 aficionado, enthusiast 11 afficionado

devotion, devotions 4 love, zeal 5 ardor, piety 6 fealty, regard 7 loyalty 8 fondness, holiness 9 adherence, godliness, reverence 10 allegiance, commitment, concern for, dedication, devoutness, meditation 11 religiosity 12 faithfulness, spirituality 13 attentiveness, prayer service 15 religious fervor 17 earnest attachment 19 religious observance

De Voto, Bernard A
  author of: 21 Across the Wide Missouri

devour 7 stuff in 8 bolt down, gobble up, gulp down, knock off, wolf down 9 go through 10 read widely 14 eat voraciously 15 absorb oneself in, consume greedily 16 read compulsively, take in ravenously 17 become engrossed in

devout 5 pious 6 ardent 7 earnest, fervent, intense, serious, zealous 8 orthodox, reverent 9 religious 10 passionate, worshipful

devoutness 5 piety 8 devotion, holiness 9 godliness, reverence 12 spirituality 15 religious fervor

DeVries, Hugo
  field: 6 botany
  nationality: 5 Dutch
  researched: 8 heredity, mutation

DeVries, Peter
  author of: 16 Consenting Adults 24 Slouching Toward Kalamazoo

dew 8 moisture 12 condensation 18 droplets of moisture

Dewar, James
  field: 7 physics 9 chemistry
  nationality: 8 Scottish
  liquified: 8 hydrogen
  solidified: 8 hydrogen
  developed: 7 cordite 10 Dewar flask 12 liquid oxygen

Dewey, George
  served in: 18 Spanish-American War
  battle: 9 Manila Bay
  destroyed: 12 Spanish fleet

Dewhurst, Colleen
  husband: 12 George C Scott
  born: 6 Canada 8 Montreal

roles: 12 The Nun's Story **18** Desire
Under the Elms **22** A Moon for the Misbegotten
De Wilde, Brandon
 born: 10 Brooklyn NY
 roles: 3 Hud **5** Shane **11** All Fall Down
dewy 4 damp **5** moist **7** bedewed
Dexamenus
 form: 7 centaur
 king of: 6 Olenus
dexterity 8 deftness, facility **9** handiness **10**
adroitness, nimbleness **11** manual skill,
proficiency
dexterous 4 able, deft **5** agile, quick **6** active, adroit, gifted, nimble **8** skillful **9** efficient, ingenious **11** resourceful
Dhegiha
 tribe: 5 Omaha
Dia
 father: 7 Eioneus
 husband: 5 Ixion
 son: 9 Pirithous
diabolic, diabolical 4 evil, foul **6** wicked **7**
baleful, demonic, heinous, impious, sa-
tanic, vicious **8** devilish, fiendish **9** monstrous, nefarious **10** malevolent, villainous
diadem 4 halo **5** crown **7** circlet, coronet **8**
headband
diagnosis 5 study **8** analysis, scrutiny **11**
examination **13** investigation, medical report **16** scientific report **22** conclusion from
symptoms, specification of illness
diagonal line 4 bias **5** angle, slant
diagram 3 map **4** plan **5** chart **6** sketch **7**
drawing, outline **9** breakdown **11** line drawing **12** illustration **14** representation **15**
rough projection
dialect 5 argot, idiom, lingo **6** jargon, patois
8 localism **10** vernacular **11** regionalism **13**
colloquialism, provincialism **15** language
variety
Dial M for Murder
 director: 15 Alfred Hitchcock
 based on play by: 14 Frederick Knott
 cast: 10 Grace Kelly, Ray Milland **14**
Robert Cummings
dialogue, dialog 4 talk **5** lines **6** parley,
speech **8** conclave **10** conference **12** conversation **14** verbal exchange **15** personal
meeting **16** formal discussion
diamond
 characteristic: 7 hardest
 color: 4 blue, pink **9** blue-white **12** canary yellow
 element: 6 carbon
 famous: 4 Hope **6** Jonker **8** Cullinan,
Idol's Eye, Koh-i-Noor **9** Excelsior **12** Star
of Africa **13** Star of the East **17** Star of Sierra Leone
 quality: 3 cut **4** fire **5** color **7** clarity **10**
brilliance
 source: 5 Congo, India **6** Africa, Borneo,
Brazil, Guyana **8** Tanzania **9** Australia,
Venezuela **11** South Africa, Soviet Union
12 South America **15** South West Africa
 weight: 5 carat, point

Diamond State
 nickname of: 8 Delaware
Diana
 origin: 5 Roman
 goddess of: 4 moon **6** slaves **7** hunting
 protectress of: 5 women
 corresponds to: 6 Phoebe **7** Artemis
 epithet: 10 Nemorensis
 means: **10** of the grove
Diana of the Crossways
 author: 14 George Meredith
 character: 9 Mr Warwick **11** Diana Mer-
ion, Percy Dacier **12** Lady Dunstane **14**
Thomas Redworth **15** Lord Dannisburgh
diaphanous 5 filmy, gauzy, lucid, sheer **6**
flimsy, limpid **8** gossamer, pellucid **11**
translucent, transparent
diary 3 log **7** daybook, journal **9** chronicle
12 daily journal **14** day-to-day record
Diary of Anne Frank, The
 author: 9 Anne Frank
 director: 13 George Stevens
 cast: 6 Ed Wynn **9** Lou Jacobi **10** Diane
Baker **13** Millie Perkins, Richard Beymer
14 Shelley Winters (Mrs Van Daan) **17**
Joseph Schildkraut (Father Frank)
 Oscar for: 17 supporting actress (Winters)
Diasia
 festival of: 4 Zeus
diatribe 6 tirade **9** contumely, invective **11**
castigation **12** vituperation **13** stream of
abuse **14** bitter harangue **18** accusatory
language **19** violent denunciation
dice 4 chop, cube **5** bones, cubes, cut up,
mince
 singular: 3 die
Dice
 also: 4 Dike
 origin: 5 Greek
 member of: 5 Horae
 goddess of: 7 justice
 father: 4 Zeus
 mother: 6 Themis
Dick, Mr
 character in: 16 David Copperfield
 author: 7 Dickens
Dickens, Charles
 author of: 9 Hard Times **10** Bleak House
11 Oliver Twist **12** Barnaby Rudge,
Dombey and Son, Little Dorrit **14** Pickwick Papers **15** A Christmas Carol, Our
Mutual Friend **16** A Tale of Two Cities,
David Copperfield, Martin Chuzzlewit,
Nicholas Nickleby **17** Great Expectations
19 The Old Curiosity Shop **22** The Mystery of Edwin Drood
dicker 4 deal **6** haggle, higgle, outbid **7** bargain, chaffer, quibble, wrangle **8** beat
down, talk down, underbid **9** negotiate **17**
drive a hard bargain
Dickey, James
 author of: 9 The Zodiac **11** Deliverance
16 Strength of Fields **17** Buckdancer's
Choice

Dickinson, Angie
    real name: 13 Angeline Brown
    husband: 13 Burt Bacharach
    born: 6 Kulm ND
    roles: 8 Rio Bravo 11 Police Woman 13 Dressed to Kill 19 The Sins of Rachel Cade

Dick Tracy
    creator: 12 Chester Gould
    character: 8 BO Plenty, Moonmaid 12 Gravel Gertie 13 Sparkle Plenty 16 Jeremiah Truehart
    wife: 12 Tess Truehart
    daughter: 11 Bonny Braids
    assistant: 9 Pat Patton
    protege: 6 Junior
    villain: 5 Itchy 6 B-B Eyes 7 Flattop, Flyface, Measles, Mumbles, The Brow, The Mole 8 The Blank 9 Pruneface, The Midget, The Rodent
    equipment: 16 two-way wristradio

Dick Van Dyke Show, The
    character: 9 Alan Brady, Rob Petrie 11 Jerry Helper, Laura Petrie, Sally Rogers 12 Buddy Sorrell, Melvin Cooley, Millie Helper 13 Ritchie Petrie
    cast: 9 Rose Marie 10 Carl Reiner, Jerry Paris 13 Larry Matthews, Richard Deacon 14 Mary Tyler Moore, Morey Amsterdam 17 Ann Morgan Guilbert

dictate 4 rule 5 edict, order 6 decree, dictum, direct, enjoin, impose, ordain, ruling, urging 7 bidding, counsel, lay down, mandate 8 set forth 9 determine, ordinance, prescribe, prompting, pronounce, stricture 11 exhortation; inclination, requirement

dictator 4 czar, duce 6 caesar, despot, fuhrer, kaiser, tyrant 7 emperor 8 autocrat 13 absolute ruler
    Argentinian: 5 Peron
    German: 6 Hitler
    Italian: 9 Mussolini
    Russian: 5 Lenin 6 Stalin
    Spanish: 6 Franco

dictatorial 6 lordly 7 haughty, willful 8 absolute, arrogant, despotic 9 arbitrary, imperious, unlimited 10 autocratic, peremptory, tyrannical 11 categorical, domineering, magisterial, overbearing 12 supercilious, unrestricted 13 authoritative 17 inclined to command

diction 7 wording 8 delivery, rhetoric, verbiage 9 elocution 10 intonation, use of idiom, vocabulary 11 enunciation, phraseology, verbal style 12 articulation 13 choice of words, pronunciation 16 turn of expression 17 command of language 18 manner of expression

dictum 3 saw 4 fiat 5 adage, axiom, edict, maxim, order 6 decree, saying, truism 7 dictate, precept, proverb 11 commandment 13 pronouncement 15 dogmatic bidding 22 authoritative statement

Dictynna
    origin: 6 Cretan
    goddess of: 3 sea
    corresponds to: 11 Britomartis

Dictys
    occupation: 9 fisherman
    found: 5 chest
    containing: 5 Danae 7 Perseus

didactic 7 donnish, preachy 8 academic, edifying, pedantic, tutorial 9 doctrinal, homiletic, pedagogic 10 expository, moralizing 11 educational, instructive, lecture-like, overbearing 12 prescriptive 17 inclined to lecture

didactics 8 teaching 9 education, teachings 10 pedagogics 11 instruction

Diderot, Denis
    author of: 12 Encyclopedia 13 Rameau's Nephew

Didion, Joan
    author of: 8 Salvador 10 White Album 14 Play It as It Lays 19 A Book of Common Prayer 24 Slouching Toward Bethlehem

Dido
    queen of: 8 Carthage
    father: 5 Mutto
    brother: 9 Pygmalion
    sister: 4 Anna
    husband: 8 Sychaeus
    lover: 6 Aeneas
    corresponds to: 6 Elissa

Dido and Aeneas
    opera by: 7 Purcell
    character: 4 Dido (Queen of Carthage) 6 Aeneas

Didymaea
    festival of: 4 Zeus 6 Apollo

Didymus *see* 6 Thomas

die 3 ebb, rot 4 ache, fade, fail, long, pass, stop, wane 5 croak, yearn 6 depart, expire, go flat, pass on, perish, recede, run out, wither 7 be eager, decline, die away, go stale, run down, subside 8 fade away, melt away, pass away, pass over, wear away 9 be anxious, break down, lose force, lose power, meet death 10 degenerate, want keenly 11 come to an end, suffer death 12 wish ardently 13 come to one's end, desire greatly, go to one's glory, kick the bucket 14 leave this world, pine with desire, become inactive 15 slowly disappear 17 become inoperative
    plural: 4 dice

die away 4 fade 5 abate, cease 8 diminish

die down 5 abate 7 subside 8 diminish, slack off

die out 6 vanish 9 cease to be, disappear 13 become extinct

Diesel, Rudolf
    field: 11 engineering
    invented: 12 Diesel engine

diet 5 board, synod 7 edibles, nurture 8 congress, victuals 9 nutriment, nutrition 10 assemblage, convention, parliament, provisions, sustenance 11 comestibles, convocation, legislature, nourishment, subsistence 12 eating habits, eat sparingly 13 eating regimen, lawmaking body 14 eat judiciously 15 eat abstemiously, eat restrictedly, general assembly 16 limitation of fare, regulate one's food 17 bicameral assembly **18** nutritional regimen, representative body, restrict one's intake

Dietrich, Marlene
  real name: 22 Maria Magdalene Dietrich
  born: 7 Germany
  roles: 8 Lola Lola **11** Blonde Venus **12** The Blue Angel **15** Rancho Notorious **16** Destry Rides Again, The Garden of Allah **17** The Scarlet Empress **24** Witness for the Prosecution

Dietrich von Bern
  origin: 8 Germanic
  king of: 10 Ostrogoths
  Latin name: 9 Theodoric

Diety 3 Bel, God **4** Baal **6** Marduk, Molech, Moloch, Yahweh **7** Chemosh, Jehovah **10** Anammelech **11** Adrammelech

Dieu et mon droit 13 God and my right
  motto of: 18 royal arms of England

differ 5 demur **7** dispute, dissent **8** be unlike, contrast, disagree **9** take issue **10** be distinct, depart from, stand apart **11** be disparate, deviate from, diverge from **12** be at variance, be dissimilar, stand opposed

difference 4 spat **5** clash, set-to **7** dispute, quarrel **8** argument, contrast, squabble **9** deviation, disparity, variation **10** divergence, falling out, unlikeness **11** contrariety, contretemps, discrepancy, distinction **12** disagreement **13** contradiction, dissimilarity, dissimilitude **17** contradistinction, lack of resemblance

different 4 rare **6** divers, sundry, unique, unlike **7** bizarre, diverse, foreign, several, strange, unusual, various **8** aberrant, atypical, distinct, manifold, not alike, peculiar, separate, singular, uncommon **9** anomalous, disparate, divergent, other than, unrelated **10** dissimilar, individual, variegated **11** contrasting, distinctive, diversified, not ordinary **12** not identical **13** miscellaneous **14** unconventional

differential 8 contrast **11** distinction

differentiate 6 set off **8** contrast, separate, set apart **11** distinguish, draw the line **12** discriminate **13** make different

differentiation 8 contrast **10** comparison, separation **11** discernment, distinction

differing 6 unlike **7** variant **8** distinct, opposing **9** deviating, disparate, dissident, divergent **10** dissenting, dissimilar **11** contrasting, disagreeing

difficult 4 grim, hard **5** hairy, rough, tough **6** knotty, thorny, trying, unruly, uphill **7** arduous, complex, forward, not easy, onerous, tedious, willful **8** critical, exacting, perverse, stubborn, ticklish, toilsome **9** demanding, enigmatic, fractious, Herculean, intricate, laborious, obstinate, Sisyphean, strenuous, wearisome **10** burdensome, exhausting, fastidious, formidable, inflexible, perplexing, unyielding **11** bewildering, complicated, hard to solve, intractable, troublesome **12** hard to manage, hard to please, obstreperous, rambunctious, recalcitrant, unmanageable **13** hard to satisfy,

problematical, unpredictable **14** hard to deal with **15** unaccommodating

difficulty 3 jam **4** mess, snag **5** trial **6** crisis, muddle, pickle, puzzle **7** barrier, dilemma, problem, straits, trouble **8** hot water, obstacle, quandary, tough job **9** deep water, hindrance, intricacy **10** impediment, perplexity, rough going, uphill work **11** arduousness, obstruction, predicament **12** hard sledding **13** laboriousness **14** stumbling block **15** troublesomeness **17** critical situation

diffidence 7 reserve, shyness **8** meekness, timidity **9** hesitancy, timidness **10** constraint, humbleness, insecurity, reluctance **11** bashfulness **12** introversion, sheepishness, timorousness **14** extreme modesty **15** unassertiveness **19** lack of self-assurance, retiring disposition

diffident 3 shy **6** modest **7** anxious, bashful **8** doubtful, hesitant, reserved, reticent, retiring **11** distrustful, unassertive **12** apprehensive

diffuse 5 wordy **7** verbose **8** rambling **9** desultory, dispersed, scattered, spread out, wandering **10** digressive, discursive, disjointed, long-winded, maundering, meandering, roundabout **14** circumlocutory, extended widely, unconcentrated, vaguely defined **15** not concentrated **18** lacking conciseness

diffuseness 8 rambling **9** prolixity, verbosity, wandering, wordiness **10** dispersion **11** indirection **14** circumlocution, long-windedness

diffusion 6 spread **8** rambling, verbiage **9** dispersal, prolixity, verbosity, wordiness **10** maundering, scattering **11** indirection, profuseness **14** circumlocution, discursiveness, disjointedness, roundaboutness

dig 3 jab **4** gibe, jeer, poke, prod, slur **5** aside, drive, gouge, punch, taunt **6** exhume, thrust **7** put-down, salvage, unearth **8** disinter, excavate, pinpoint, retrieve, scoop out **9** extricate, find among, hollow out **10** come up with, excavation, wry comment **11** bring to view **12** verbal thrust **13** cutting remark, search and find

digest 3 dig **5** grasp **6** absorb, fathom, precis, resume **7** realize, summary **8** abstract, dissolve, synopsis **10** abridgment, appreciate, assimilate, comprehend, understand **12** condensation, take in wholly **14** take in mentally

digestive system
  component: 5 liver, mouth, teeth **6** tongue **7** stomach **8** appendix, pancreas **9** esophagus, intestine **11** gall bladder **13** salivary gland

dig in 4 root **5** embed, imbed, plant **6** anchor **7** pitch in **8** entrench, go to work **10** begin to eat **12** apply oneself

digit 3 one, six, two, toe **4** five, four, nine, unit, zero **5** light, seven, three **6** cipher, figure, finger, number **7** integer, numeral

dignified 5 proud 6 august, proper 7 upright 8 decorous, reserved 9 honorable 10 upstanding 11 circumspect 13 distinguished 14 self-respecting

dignify 5 raise 6 uplift 7 elevate, inflate, promote

dignitary 3 VIP 7 notable 8 luminary 9 personage 12 person of note

dignity 5 honor 7 decorum, majesty, station 9 loftiness, solemnity 10 augustness, importance 11 comportment, stateliness 12 high position, lofty bearing 13 proud demeanor 14 self-possession

digress 5 stray 6 back up, wander 7 deviate 8 divagate 9 turn aside 15 go off on a tangent 17 depart from subject

digression 6 detour 8 straying 9 departure, deviation, diversion, wandering 10 divagation, divergence, side remark 12 obiter dictum

digressive 7 diffuse 9 wandering 10 disjointed, maundering, roundabout 11 off the point 14 circumlocutory

dig up 6 locate 7 find out, root out, uncover, unearth 8 discover 9 ferret out 12 bring to light

dike 4 bank 5 levee, ridge 10 embankment

Dike *see* 4 Dice

dikerion 11 candelabrum, candlestick 12 candleholder

dilapidated 4 shot 6 beat-up, ruined, shabby 7 rickety, run-down, worn-out 8 battered, decaying, decrepit 10 broken-down, ramshackle, tumble-down 11 in disrepair 12 deteriorated, falling apart 15 falling to pieces

dilate 5 swell, widen 6 expand, extend 7 broaden, distend, enlarge, inflate, puff out 9 make wider

dilation 8 swelling, widening 9 expansion 10 broadening, distension, distention

dilatory 4 lazy, slow 5 tardy 6 remiss 8 dawdling, indolent, slothful, sluggish 9 negligent, reluctant 10 phlegmatic 13 lackadaisical 15 inclined to delay, procrastinating

dilemma 4 bind 6 crunch, plight 7 impasse, problem 8 deadlock, quandary 9 stalemate 11 predicament 13 Hobson's choice 15 difficult choice

dilettante 7 amateur, dabbler, trifler 12 experimenter 16 cultured hobbyist

diligence 4 zeal 8 industry 10 commitment, dedication 11 persistence 12 perseverance

diligent 6 active 7 careful, earnest, patient, zealous 8 plodding, sedulous, studious, thorough, untiring 9 assiduous, concerted 10 persistent 11 hardworking, industrious, painstaking, persevering 12 pertinacious 15 well-intentioned

dill
    botanical name: 17 Anethum graveolens
    origin: 9 Asia Minor 13 Mediterranean
    family: 7 parsley
    guards against: 7 Evil Eye 10 witchcraft
    use: 6 sauces 7 pickles 10 vegetables

Dillon, Matt
    roles: 3 Tex 10 Rumblefish 12 The Outsiders

dillydally 3 lag 4 idle, loaf 5 dally, delay 6 dawdle, loiter 8 kill time 9 waste time 10 fool around 13 procrastinate

Dilsey
    character in: 18 The Sound and the Fury
    author: 8 Faulkner

dilute 4 thin, weak 6 reduce, temper, watery, weaken 7 diffuse, diluted, thin out 8 decrease, diminish, make weak, mitigate, weakened 9 attenuate, liquidify, water down 10 add water to, adulterate, thinned out 11 adulterated, make thinner, watered down

diluted 4 weak 6 dilute, watery 8 weakened 10 thinned out 11 adulterated, watered down

dilution 8 thinning 9 weakening 12 watering down

dim 3 low 4 hazy, soft, weak 5 dusky, faint, foggy, murky, muted, vague 6 blurry, feeble, gloomy, remote 7 blurred, clouded, muffled, shadowy 8 darkened, nebulous, obscured 9 not bright, tenebrous 10 adumbrated, ill-defined, indefinite, indistinct, intangible 13 unilluminated

DiMaggio, Joe
    nickname: 9 Joltin Joe
    sport: 8 baseball
    position: 8 outfield
    team: 14 New York Yankees
    wife: 13 Marilyn Monroe

dime-a-dozen 6 common 7 humdrum 8 ordinary, workaday 9 plentiful 10 ubiquitous 11 commonplace 12 easy to come by 13 garden-variety 15 undistinguished

dimension, dimensions 4 bulk, mass, size 5 range, scope, width 6 extent, height, length, volume, weight 7 measure 9 amplitude, greatness, magnitude, thickness 10 importance, proportion 11 massiveness 12 measurements 14 physical extent

diminish 3 ebb 4 wane 5 abate, lower 6 lessen, narrow, reduce, shrink 7 decline, dwindle, fall off, shorten, shrivel 8 decrease, peter out 9 be reduced 11 make smaller 13 become smaller

diminuendo
    music: 22 gradually getting softer
    abbreviation: 3 dim

diminution 6 ebbing, waning 7 decline 8 decrease, lowering 9 dwindling, lessening, reduction, shrinkage 10 falling off, shortening, shriveling, subsidence 11 petering out, slacking off

diminutive 3 wee 4 tiny 5 elfin, short, small, teeny 6 little, minute, petite, slight 7 pet name, stunted 8 dwarfish, half-pint, nickname 9 miniature, short form 10 pocket-size, undersized, vest-pocket 11 liliputian, small-scale, unimportant 13 insignificant 14 inconsiderable

Dimmesdale, Arthur
    character in: 16 The Scarlet Letter
    author: 9 Hawthorne

dimness 4 dusk 5 gloom, shade 8 darkness 14 indistinctness

dimwit 4 fool 5 dummy, dunce, idiot, moron 6 cretin, nitwit 7 dingbat, dullard, dumbell, pinhead 8 dumbbell, dummkopf, imbecile, meathead, numskull 9 birdbrain, blockhead, ding-a-ling, lamebrain, numbskull, simpleton 11 chowderhead, knucklehead

dim-witted 4 dull, dumb 5 dense 6 stupid 7 foolish, idiotic, moronic, witless 8 retarded 9 cretinous, imbecilic

din 4 stir, to-do 5 bruit 6 babble, clamor, hubbub, racket, ruckus, tumult, uproar 7 clangor 9 commotion 10 clattering, hullabaloo

Dinah
  father: 5 Jacob
  mother: 4 Leah
  brother: 3 Dan, Gad 4 Levi 5 Asher, Judah 6 Joseph, Reuben, Simeon 7 Zebulun 8 Benjamin, Issachar, Naphtali
  violated by: 7 Shechem

Dindymene *see* 6 Cybele

dine 3 eat, sup 4 feed 5 feast, lunch 6 fall to, supper 7 banquet, partake 9 breakfast, eat dinner 10 break bread, gluttonize, have dinner 11 gourmandize 14 take sustenance

Dine *see* 6 Navajo

Dinesen, Isak
  real name: 18 Karen Blixen-Finecke
  author of: 9 Last Tales 11 Out of Africa 12 Winter's Tales 16 Seven Gothic Tales

dinghy 5 skiff 7 rowboat 8 sailboat 9 small boat

dingy 4 dull 5 dusty, grimy, murky, tacky 6 dismal, dreary, gloomy, shabby 12 dirty and drab

dining room
  French: 12 salle a manger

dinner 4 food, meal 5 beano, feast 6 repast, supper 7 banquet
  French: 8 dejeuner 10 table d'hote

Dinner at Eight
  director: 11 George Cukor
  author: 10 Edna Ferber 14 George S Kaufman
  cast: 8 Lee Tracy 10 Jean Harlow 11 Billie Burke 12 Wallace Beery 13 John Barrymore, Marie Dressler 15 Lionel Barrymore

dinosaur
  means: 14 fearfully great, terrible lizard
  subclass: 11 Archosauria
  characteristic: 7 diapsid 14 teeth in sockets, two-arched skull 18 three-element pelvis
  group: 11 Saurischian 13 Ornithischian
  flesh-eating biped: 8 therapod
  plant-eating quadruped: 8 sauropod
  plant-eating biped: 10 ornithopod
  armored: 10 ceratopsid
  of Africa: 9 Iguanodon 13 Brachiosaurus 17 Heterodontosaurus
  of Asia: 13 Hypselosaurus, Protoceratops

  of Europe: 9 Iguanodon 12 Plateosaurus 13 Compsognathus, Hypselosaurus, Hypsilophodon
  of North America: 10 Diplodocus, Edmontonia, Nodosaurus 11 Anatosaurus, Anchisaurus, Gorgosaurus, Monoclonius, Saurolophus, Scolosaurus, Stegosaurus, Triceratops 12 Ankylosaurus, Camarasaurus, Camptosaurus, Coelophysics, Lambeosaurus, Paleoscincus 13 Brachiosaurus, Styracosaurus, Tyrannosaurus 14 Thescelosaurus 15 Parasaurolophus, Procheneosaurus
  of South America: 12 Pisanosaurus
  fictional: 4 Puff 6 Barney 12 Jurassic Park

dint 4 push, will 5 drive, force, labor, might, power 6 charge, effort, energy, strain, stress 8 endeavor, exertion, strength, struggle 10 insistence 12 forcefulness 13 determination 14 relentlessness

diocese 3 see 7 eparchy 9 bishopric 14 church district
  jurisdiction of: 6 bishop

Diomedes
  king of: 6 Thrace
  father: 4 Ares 6 Tydeus
  mother: 6 Cyrene 7 Deipyle
  member of: 7 Epigoni
  kept: 9 wild mares
  fed mares on: 10 human flesh
  death planned by: 8 Hercules

Dione
  consort of: 4 Zeus

Dionysia
  festival of: 8 Dionysus

Dionysus *see* 7 Bacchus

Diores
  father: 10 Amarynceus
  fought against: 7 Trojans

Dioscuri *see* 15 Castor and Pollux

dip 4 bail, dish, dunk, sink, skim, soak 5 droop, ladle, scoop, slope, spoon 6 dabble, dish up, peruse, shovel 7 decline, descend, dish out, run over 8 drop down, glance at, submerge, turn down 13 study slightly 14 immerse briefly, lift by scooping, try tentatively 15 incline downward

dip into 4 scan, skim 5 ladle 6 browse, peruse 7 deplete 8 look over 13 glance through, make inroads in

Diplodocus
  type: 8 dinosaur, sauropod
  period: 8 Jurassic
  location: 12 North America

diplomacy 4 tact 5 craft, skill 7 finesse 8 delicacy, prudence, subtlety 10 artfulness, discretion 11 maneuvering, savoir-faire 13 statesmanship 14 foreign affairs 16 artful management 18 foreign negotiation 21 international politics

diplomat 5 envoy 6 consul 7 attache 8 emissary, minister 9 statesman 10 ambassador, negotiator 12 interlocutor 13 tactful person
  acceptable: 12 persona grata
  unacceptable: 15 persona non grata

diplomatic 5 adept, suave **6** artful, urbane **7** attuned, politic, prudent, tactful **8** discreet **9** sensitive, strategic **13** ambassadorial **14** foreign-service **15** state-department

Dipolia
 festival of: 4 Zeus
 location: 6 Athens
 slaughter of: 2 ox

Dipper
 nickname of: 15 Wilt Chamberlain

Dipsas
 form: 7 serpent

dipsomaniac 3 sot **4** lush, soak, wino **5** drunk, rummy, souse, toper **6** barfly, boozer **7** tippler **8** drunkard **9** alcoholic, inebriate

diptera
 class: 8 hexapoda
 phylum: 10 arthropoda
 group: 7 true fly

Dirae see **6** Furies

dire 4 grim **5** awful, grave **6** dismal, urgent, woeful **7** crucial, extreme, fearful, ominous, ruinous **8** critical, dreadful, horrible, terrible **9** appalling, desperate, harrowing, illboding, ill-omened **10** calamitous, disastrous, portentous **11** apocalyptic, cataclysmic **12** catastrophic, inauspicious

direct 3 aim **4** head, lead, urge **5** blunt, clear, focus, frank, guide, order, pilot, usher **6** advise, candid, charge, enjoin, handle, head-on, honest, manage **7** address, command, conduct, control, earmark, forward, level at, oversee, pointed, sincere, train at **8** explicit, indicate, instruct, navigate, personal **9** conduct to, designate, firsthand, intend for, supervise **10** administer, face-to-face, forthright, point-blank, show the way, unmediated **11** plain-spoken, point the way, point toward, preside over, superintend **15** straightforward

direction 3 aim, way **4** bent, care, path **5** drift, order, route, track, trend **6** charge, course, recipe **7** bearing, command, control, current **8** guidance, headship, tendency **9** alignment **10** guidelines, leadership, management, regulation **11** inclination, instruction, line of march, supervision **12** line of action, prescription, surveillance **13** line of thought **14** administration, point of compass **15** superintendence

directive 3 ukase **8** bulletin **9** statement **11** communique **11** declaration **12** instructions, proclamation **13** communication

directly 4 soon **6** at once, openly **7** exactly, frankly **8** candidly, honestly, in person, promptly, straight **9** forthwith, precisely, presently, right away **10** face-to-face, in a beeline, personally **11** immediately, momentarily **12** in plain terms, not obliquely, unswervingly **13** unambiguously, unequivocally **14** as the crow flies **15** in a straight line **16** as soon as possible **17** on a straight course, straightforwardly

directness 6 candor **9** bluntness, frankness **10** candidness **14** forthrightness **19** straightforwardness

direct opposite 7 reverse **8** converse **10** antithesis

director 4 boss, head **5** chief **6** leader, master **7** curator, foreman, manager **8** chairman, governor, overseer **9** commander, conductor, organizer **10** controller, supervisor **13** administrator **14** superintendent

dirge 6 lament **7** requiem **8** threnody **9** death song **10** burial hymn, death march **11** funeral song **13** mournful sound **19** mournful composition

dirigo 7 I direct
 motto of: 5 Maine

dirk 3 sny **4** snee, stab **5** knife, skean **6** dagger, skiver **7** poniard
 origin: 8 Scotland

Dirks, Rudolph
 creator/artist of: 12 Hans and Fritz **17** Captain and the Kids **19** The Katzenjammer Kids

dirt 3 mud **4** dust, loam, mire, muck, scum, slop, smut, soil, soot **5** dross, earth, filth, grime, humus, offal, rumor, slime, trash **6** gossip, ground, refuse, sludge, smudge **7** garbage, rubbish, scandal, slander **8** impurity, leavings, vileness **9** excrement, indecency, obscenity, profanity, sweepings **10** foul matter, moral filth, scurrility **11** pornography, scuttlebutt, squalidness **12** scabrousness **13** salaciousness **14** defamatory talk **15** filthy substance, unclean language **17** sensational expose

dirt-cheap 6 a steal **7** bargain **11** inexpensive **14** very reasonable **15** bargain-basement

dirty 4 base, foul, hard, lewd, mean, soil, spot, vile **5** grimy, messy, muddy, nasty, smear, stain, sully **6** coarse, filthy, grubby, mess up, muck up, risque, rotten, shabby, slop up, smudge, smudgy, smutty, soiled, sordid, untidy, vulgar **7** begrime, besmear, blacken, corrupt, crooked, devious, illegal, illicit, immoral, low-down, muddied, obscene, pollute, squalid, sullied, tarnish, unclean **8** befouled, begrimed, indecent, off-color, polluted, prurient, scabrous, unwashed **9** besmeared, deceitful, difficult, dishonest, tarnished, unsterile **10** despicable, fraudulent, licentious, perfidious, unpleasant, villainous **11** distasteful, treacherous **12** contemptible, disagreeable, dishonorable, pornographic, unscrupulous **14** morally unclean

Dirty Dozen, The
 director: 13 Robert Aldrich
 cast: 8 Jim Brown **9** Lee Marvin **10** Robert Ryan, Trini Lopez **11** Clint Walker **13** George Kennedy **14** Charles Bronson, Ernest Borgnine, John Cassavetes, Richard Jaeckel **16** Donald Sutherland

Dis
    also: 8 Dis Pater
    means: 5 Hades
    god of: 10 underworld
    corresponds to: 5 Orcus, Pluto
disability 5 minus 6 defect 8 handicap, weakness, 9 infirmity, unfitness 10 affliction, impairment, impediment, inadequacy 11 shortcoming 12 debilitation, disadvantage 16 disqualification
disable 6 damage, hinder, impair, weaken 7 cripple 8 handicap 12 incapacitate
disabled
    French: 12 hors de combat
disabuse 8 set right 9 relieve of 10 disenchant 11 disillusion, set straight
disaccord 7 discord 10 disharmony 12 disagreement 15 incompatibility
disacknowledge 4 deny 6 disown 7 disavow 8 disallow, disclaim 9 repudiate
disadvantage 4 flaw 6 burden 7 trouble 8 drawback, handicap, hardship, nuisance, weakness 9 detriment, hindrance, in arrears, weak point 10 impediment 12 weak position 13 inconvenience 16 fly in the ointment
disadvantaged 8 deprived, emergent, emerging, troubled 10 struggling 11 handicapped 12 impoverished 14 underdeveloped 15 underprivileged
disadvantageous 7 harmful 9 injurious 11 detrimental, inadvisable, inexpedient, undesirable, unfavorable, unfortunate
disaffect 4 wean 8 alienate, estrange 10 drive apart
disaffected 5 upset 7 hostile 8 agitated, inimical 9 alienated, disturbed, estranged, withdrawn 10 unfriendly 11 belligerent, discomposed, disgruntled, quarrelsome 12 antipathetic, discontented, dissatisfied 14 irreconcilable
disaffection 7 dislike 8 aversion, distaste 9 antipathy 10 alienation, discontent, disloyalty 12 estrangement
disaffirm 4 deny 5 annul 6 disown 7 decline, disavow 8 abnegate, disclaim, forswear, renounce 9 repudiate 15 wash one's hands of
disaffirmation 6 denial 9 annulment, disavowal 10 abnegation, disclaimer 11 repudiation 12 renunciation 13 contradiction
disagree 4 vary 5 clash, upset 6 depart, differ 7 deviate, diverge, make ill 8 be unlike, conflict, distress 9 discomfit 10 disconcert, stand apart 11 be injurious, fail to agree, not coincide 12 be at variance, be discordant, be dissimilar 13 cause problems 14 be unreconciled 15 be at loggerheads, differ in opinion 16 oppose one another, think differently
disagreeable 5 cross, harsh, nasty, surly, testy 7 grating, grouchy, peevish 8 churlish, petulant 9 difficult, irascible, irritable, obnoxious, offensive, repellent, repugnant, repulsive, unamiable, unwelcome 10 disgusting, ill-natured, uninviting, unpleasant 11 acrimonious, bad-tempered, displeas-

ing, distasteful, ill-tempered, uncongenial, unpalatable 13 uncomfortable
disagreeing 6 at odds 7 deviant, varying 8 clashing 9 deviating, differing, disputing 10 quarreling 11 conflicting 13 at loggerheads
disagreement 5 clash, fight 7 discord, dispute, quarrel 8 argument, squabble, variance 9 deviation, disaccord, disparity, diversity 10 difference, divergence, falling-out, unlikeness 11 discrepancy, incongruity 13 dissimilarity, dissimilitude, lack of harmony 15 incompatibility 16 misunderstanding
disallow 4 deny, veto 6 abjure, forbid, refuse, reject 8 prohibit 9 repudiate
disallowance 4 veto 6 denial 7 refusal 9 rejection 11 prohibition, repudiation
disallowed 6 vetoed 7 abjured, refused 8 rejected 9 forbidden 10 repudiated 12 inadmissible, unacceptable
disappear 2 go 3 end 4 exit, fade, flee 5 leave 6 be gone, depart, die out, retire, vanish 8 be no more, fade away, melt away, withdraw 9 evaporate 12 be lost to view, cease to exist, leave no trace 13 cease to appear, cease to be seen 14 become obscured, cease to be known, pass out of sight 15 vanish from sight
disappearance 7 vanishing 11 evanescence 16 passing from sight
disappoint 4 foil 6 hinder, sadden, thwart 7 chagrin, let down, mislead 9 frustrate 10 dishearten 11 disillusion
disappointing 11 frustrating 12 unfulfilling 13 dissatisfying 14 unsatisfactory
disappointment 3 dud 4 bomb, loss 6 defeat, fiasco, fizzle 7 failure, letdown, setback, washout 8 disaster 9 the knocks 11 frustration 12 unfulfillment, unrealization 15 disillusionment, dissatisfaction
disapprobation 7 censure 8 disfavor 9 criticism, disesteem, objection 11 disapproval, displeasure 12 condemnation 15 dissatisfaction
disapprove 4 veto 5 decry 6 refuse, reject 7 censure, condemn, deplore, dislike 8 denounce, disallow, object to, turn down 9 criticize, deprecate, disparage, frown upon 10 think ill of 13 look askance at, regard as wrong 14 discountenance, refuse assent to 15 take exception to 16 find unacceptable, view with disfavor
disapprove of 7 censure, condemn, deplore 8 object to
disarm 4 move, sway 5 charm 6 entice 7 attract, bewitch, enchant, win over 8 convince, persuade 9 captivate, fascinate, influence, prevail on
disarming 7 melting, winning, winsome 8 charming, magnetic 9 appealing, beguiling, ingenuous, seductive 10 bewitching, entrancing 11 captivating 12 ingratiating, irresistible
disarrange 5 mix up, upset 6 jumble, mess up, muddle, ruffle, rumple 7 confuse, scatter 8 disarray, dishevel, disorder, displace,

put askew, scramble 11 disorganize 13 put out of order 14 turn topsy-turvy

disarranged 5 messy 6 mussed, sloppy, untidy 7 jumbled, ruffled, rumpled, tousled, unkempt 8 uncombed 9 cluttered 10 disarrayed, disheveled, disordered, disorderly, in disorder 11 in a shambles

disarrangement 4 mess 5 chaos, mix-up, upset 6 jumble, mixing, muddle 7 clutter 8 disarray, disorder, scramble, shambles 9 confusion, messiness, messing up 10 disharmony, disruption, sloppiness, untidiness 12 dishevelment 14 disorderliness 15 disorganization, heaping together

disarray 5 chaos, mix-up, upset 6 jumble 7 clutter 8 disorder, scramble, shambles 9 confusion, messiness 10 disharmony, sloppiness, untidiness 12 dishevelment 14 disarrangement 15 disorganization

disarrayed 5 messy 6 mussed, sloppy, untidy 7 chaotic, jumbled, mixed up 10 disheveled, disordered, disorderly, in disorder 11 disarranged

disarticulate 6 detach 7 unhinge 8 disjoint, disunite, separate 9 disengage, dislocate 10 disconnect 13 put out of joint

disarticulated 5 apart 7 divided 8 unhinged 9 disunited, separated 10 disengaged, disjointed, dislocated, unattached 11 unconnected 12 disconnected 13 helter-skelter

disassemble 7 disband, scatter 8 disperse 9 knock down, take apart

disassociate 7 divorce 8 separate 10 disconnect 12 disaffiliate

disassociation 5 break, split 6 schism 7 divorce 8 division 10 separation

disaster 4 harm 5 wreck 6 blight, fiasco 7 scourge, tragedy, trouble 8 accident, calamity 9 adversity, cataclysm, ruination 10 misfortune 11 catastrophe, great mishap 12 misadventure

disastrous 4 dire 5 fatal 6 tragic 7 adverse, hapless, harmful, ruinous 8 dreadful, grievous, ill-fated, terrible 9 harrowing 10 calamitous, desolating, horrendous, illstarred 11 destructive, devastating, unfortunate 12 catastrophic, inauspicious

disavow 4 deny 6 abjure, disown, recant, reject 7 gainsay, retract 8 denounce 9 repudiate 10 contradict

disavowal 6 denial 8 demurrer 9 rejection 10 abjuration, disclaimer, refutation 11 repudiation 13 contradiction

disband 7 adjourn, dismiss, scatter 8 disperse, dissolve 11 disassemble

disbelief 5 doubt 7 dubiety 8 distrust, mistrust, unbelief 10 skepticism 11 incredulity 12 doubtfulness 14 lack of credence

disbelieve 5 doubt 6 refuse, reject 7 suspect 8 discount, distrust 9 discredit, unbelieve 10 misbelieve

disbeliever 7 atheist, skeptic 8 apostate

disbursable 7 payable 9 available, spendable 10 expendable

disburse 6 lay out, pay out 7 fork out 8 allocate, shell out 10 distribute

disbursement 6 outlay 7 payment 8 spending 9 paying out 10 dispensing 11 expenditure 12 dispensation, distribution

discard 4 drop, dump, junk, shed 5 scrap 6 remove, shelve 7 abandon, weed out 8 get rid of, jettison, throw out 9 cast aside, dispose of, eliminate, throw away 10 relinquish 11 thrust aside 12 dispense with, have done with 14 throw overboard

discarded 6 dumped, junked 7 cast off, dropped 8 deserted, forsaken, rejected, scrapped 9 abandoned, cast aside, tossed out 10 jettisoned, left behind, thrown away

discern 3 see 4 espy 6 behold, descry, detect, notice 7 make out, observe, pick out 8 perceive 9 ascertain 12 catch sight of

discernible 7 visible 8 apparent 10 detectable, noticeable 11 perceivable, perceptible

discerning 4 sage, wise 5 acute, sharp 6 astute, shrewd 8 piercing 9 judicious, sagacious, sensitive 10 perceptive 11 intelligent, keen-sighted, penetrating 12 clearsighted, sharp-sighted 13 perspicacious 14 discriminating

discernment 6 acumen, senses 7 insight 8 feelings, sagacity, thoughts 10 cognizance, discretion, perception 11 distinction 13 consciousness, judiciousness 14 discrimination 15 differentiation

discharge 3 axe, can 4 emit, fire, flow, free, gush, ooze, oust, sack, shot 5 blast, burst, eject, expel, exude, issue, let go, shoot 6 bounce, firing, launch, lay off, let fly, propel, report, set off 7 cashier, dismiss, explode, fire off, project, release, seepage, set free, trigger 8 activate, detonate, drainage, emission, get rid of, liberate, throw off, touch off 9 allow to go, exploding, explosion, firing off, fusillade, give forth, pour forth, secretion, send forth, terminate 10 activating, detonating, detonation, triggering 11 send packing, suppuration 13 give the gate to, walking papers 14 demobilization 15 release document 16 remove from office

disciple 3 nut 5 freak, pupil 7 admirer, convert, devotee, pursuer, student 8 adherent, believer, follower, neophyte, partisan 9 proselyte, supporter 10 aficionado 11 afficionado

Disciple, The
author: 11 Paul Bourget

disciplinarian 8 martinet 13 authoritarian 16 stickler for rules, strict taskmaster

disciplinary 8 punitive 9 punishing 10 corrective 13 authoritarian

discipline 5 drill, prime, rigor, train 6 method, punish 7 break in, chasten, regimen 8 chastise, drilling, instruct, practice, training 9 schooling 11 preparation 14 indoctrination 15 prescribed habit, teach by exercise 16 course of exercise

disclaim 4 deny 6 disown 7 decline, disavow 8 abnegate, forswear, renounce 9 disaffirm, repudiate

disclaimer 6 denial 8 demurrer 9 disavowal 10 abnegation 11 repudiation 12 renunciation

disclose 4 bare, leak, show, tell 6 expose, impart, reveal, unveil 7 divulge, lay bare, publish, uncover 9 broadcast, make known 10 make public 11 communicate 12 bring to light 13 allow to be seen, bring into view, cause to appear

discolor 4 spot 5 stain, tinge 6 bleach, streak 7 tarnish

discoloration 4 blot, mark, spot 5 smear, stain 6 blotch, bruise, smudge 7 blemish 9 contusion

discolored 4 doty 5 dingy, dirty, faded, livid 6 soiled, tinged 7 bruised, stained 9 tarnished

discomfit 5 upset 6 thwart 7 chagrin 8 confound, distress 9 embarrass, frustrate 10 disconcert

discomfited 5 upset 6 uneasy 7 ashamed 8 thwarted 9 chagrined, ill at ease 10 distressed 11 embarrassed 12 disconcerted

discomfiture 7 anxiety 9 agitation, confusion 10 uneasiness 11 disquietude, distraction, nervousness 12 discomposure, perturbation 13 embarrassment

discomfort 3 try 4 ache, hurt, pain 5 trial 6 misery 7 malaise, trouble 8 disquiet, distress, hardship, nuisance, soreness, vexation 9 annoyance, discomfit, embarrass 10 affliction, discompose, irritation, make uneasy 11 disquietude

discompose 5 abash, upset 6 rattle 7 agitate, confuse, disturb, fluster, nonplus, perturb, trouble, unnerve 8 disquiet, distract, distress, unsettle 9 discomfit, embarrass 10 disconcert

discomposed 5 upset 6 jolted, rocked, shaken, uneasy 7 anxious, nervous, worried 8 agitated, confused, troubled 9 disturbed, flustered, perturbed 10 disquieted, distracted 11 discomfited, uncollected

discomposure 6 flurry 7 anxiety 8 disquiet 9 agitation, confusion 10 discomfort, uneasiness 11 awkwardness, disquietude, distraction, nervousness 12 discomfiture, perturbation 13 embarrassment 17 self-consciousness

disconcert 5 abash, annoy, upset 6 raffle, ruffle 7 agitate, confuse, disturb, nonplus, perturb, trouble 8 unsettle 10 discompose

disconcerted 5 fazed, upset 7 annoyed, rattled, ruffled 8 agitated, confused, troubled 9 disturbed, perturbed, thrown off, unsettled 10 distracted, nonplussed

disconcertment 8 rattling 9 abashment, agitation, confusion 11 disturbance 12 discomposure

disconnect 6 detach 8 separate, uncouple 9 disengage

disconnected 5 split 6 cut off 7 jumbled, mixed-up, severed 8 confused, detached, rambling 9 illogical, separated, uncoupled 10 disengaged, disjointed, incoherent, irrational, unattached, unfastened 12 disorganized

disconnection 8 severing 9 severance 10 cutting off, detachment, separation 13 disengagement

disconsolate 3 sad 4 blue, down 6 woeful 7 crushed, doleful, forlorn, unhappy 8 dejected, desolate, downcast, wretched 9 depressed, miserable, sorrowful, woebegone 10 despondent, dispirited, melancholy 11 discouraged, low-spirited, pessimistic 12 heavyhearted, inconsolable 13 brokenhearted 14 down in the dumps, down in the mouth

discontent 9 displease 10 discomfort, disgruntle 11 displeasure, unhappiness 15 dissatisfaction

discontented 6 bored 7 fretful, unhappy 9 miserable, regretful 10 displeased, malcontent 11 disgruntled 12 dissatisfied

discontinuance 3 end 4 halt, stop 6 ending, recess 7 ceasing, halting 8 abeyance, giving up, quitting, stoppage, stopping, surcease 9 cessation, desisting 10 concluding, leaving off, suspension 11 abandonment, breaking off, termination

discontinue 3 end 4 drop, quit, stop 5 cease 6 desist, give up 7 abandon, abstain, suspend 8 break off, leave off 9 interrupt, terminate 10 put an end to

discontinuous 3 discrete, episodic, sporadic 9 segmented, spasmodic 10 occasional 11 interrupted 12 disconnected, intermittent

discord 6 strife 7 dispute 8 clashing, conflict, disunity, division, friction 9 cacophony, harshness, wrangling 10 contention, disharmony, dissension, dissonance, quarreling 11 being at odds, differences, discordance 12 disagreement, grating noise 13 lack of concord 15 incompatibility 16 unpleasant sounds
    goddess of: 4 Eris 9 Discordia

discordance 6 strife 7 discord, dispute 8 clashing, conflict, disunity, division, friction 9 wrangling 10 contention, disharmony, dissension, quarreling 12 disagreement 15 incompatibility

discordant 6 at odds 9 disparate, dissonant 10 at variance, discrepant 11 conflicting, disagreeing 12 unharmonious

Discordia
    origin: 5 Roman
    goddess of: 7 discord
    corresponds to: 4 Eris

discount 3 cut 5 break 6 rebate 7 cut rate 9 abatement, allowance, deduction, exemption, reduction 10 concession 11 subtraction

discountenance 7 condemn, despise, disdain, dislike 8 object to 9 frown upon 10 disapprove, think ill of 12 look down upon 13 look askance at, regard as wrong 14 hold in contempt 15 take exception to

discourage 4 do in 5 daunt, deter, unman 6 deject, dismay 7 depress, unnerve 8 decimate, dispirit, dissuade, keep back, restrain 9 disparage, prostrate 10 dishearten, disincline, divert from 13 advise against, dash one's hopes **17** dampen one's spirits

discouraged 3 low **7** daunted **8** dejected, downcast, hopeless **9** depressed **10** despondent, dispirited **11** downhearted, pessimistic **12** disconsolate, disheartened

discouragement 4 curb **5** gloom, worry **6** damper, dismay **7** despair **8** obstacle **9** dejection, hindrance, pessimism, restraint **11** constraint, depression, impediment, low spirits, melancholy, moroseness **11** despondency **12** hopelessness, lack of spirit **13** consternation **15** downheartedness

discourse 3 gab **4** chat, talk **5** essay **6** confer, sermon, speech **7** address, discuss, lecture, oration **8** colloquy, converse, dialogue, diatribe, harangue, treatise **10** discussion **11** intercourse **12** conversation, dissertation, talk together **16** formal discussion

Discourse on Method
    author: 13 Rene Descartes

discourteous 4 rude **5** fresh, surly **6** cheeky **7** boorish, ill-bred, uncivil, uncouth **8** impolite, impudent, insolent **9** uncourtly, ungallant **10** ill-behaved, ungracious, unladylike, unmannerly **11** ill-mannered, impertinent **13** disrespectful, ungentlemanly

discourtesy 8 rudeness **9** impudence, insolence **10** incivility **11** boorishness **12** impoliteness

discover 3 see **4** find, spot **5** dig up **6** detect, locate, notice **7** discern, find out, learn of, realize, root out, uncover, unearth **8** come upon, perceive **9** ascertain, determine, ferret out, light upon, recognize **10** chance upon **11** gain sight of, stumble upon **12** bring to light

discredit 4 deny, slur **5** abuse, smear, sully, taint **6** debase, defame, demean, reject, smirch, vilify **7** degrade, dispute, tarnish, vitiate **8** disallow, disgrace, dishonor, disprove, question **9** challenge, disparage, undermine **10** prove false, stigmatize **16** shake one's faith in **17** drag through the mud

discreditable 8 shameful, shocking **9** appalling **10** outrageous, scandalous **11** disgraceful, ignominious **12** dishonorable, disreputable

discreet 6 polite **7** careful, politic, prudent, tactful **8** cautious **9** judicious, sensitive **10** diplomatic, thoughtful **11** circumspect

Discreet Charm of the Bourgeoisie, The
    director: 10 Luis Bunuel
    cast: 11 Fernando Rey **14** Delphine Seyrig, Stephane Audran
    Oscar for: 11 foreign film

discrepancy 3 gap **8** variance **9** disparity **10** difference, divergence **11** discordance, incongruity **12** disagreement **13** dissimilarity, inconsistency

discrepant 6 at odds **8** contrary, opposing **9** disparate **10** at variance, discordant, dissimilar, refutatory **11** conflicting, contrasting, disagreeing **12** antithetical, incon-

sistent **13** contradictory **14** countervailing, irreconcilable

discrete 7 several, various **8** detached, distinct, separate **9** different **10** unattached **11** disjunctive, independent **12** disconnected, unassociated **13** discontinuous

discretion 4 tact **6** acumen, option **8** judgment, prudence, sagacity, volition **9** good sense **10** preference **11** discernment, inclination **12** good judgment, predilection **13** judiciousness, sound judgment **14** discrimination **15** power of choosing **16** individual choice

discretionary 8 optional **9** voluntary **10** nonbinding **11** nonrequired, unnecessary **12** nonrequisite, unimperative **13** nonobligatory

discriminate 7 disdain **8** separate **11** distinguish **12** disfranchise **13** differentiate

discriminating 5 acute **6** astute, biased, shrewd **7** bigoted, refined **9** judicious, sensitive **10** cultivated, discerning, fastidious **11** intelligent, prejudicial **13** perspicacious **15** differentiating

discrimination 4 bias **5** taste **6** acumen **7** bigotry **8** inequity, judgment, keenness, sagacity **9** prejudice **10** astuteness, discretion, favoritism, refinement, shrewdness **11** discernment, distinction **12** perspicacity **21** differential treatment

discursive 7 diffuse **8** rambling **9** wandering **10** circuitous, digressive, long-winded, meandering, roundabout

discursiveness 8 rambling **10** digression, meandering **14** circumlocution

discuss 6 debate, parley, review **7** dissect, examine, speak of **8** consider, talk over **9** talk about **13** converse about, exchange views **14** discourse about

discussion 3 rap **4** talk **6** debate, parley, powwow, review **7** inquiry **8** analysis, argument, colloquy, dialogue, scrutiny **9** discourse **10** hashing-out **11** disputation **12** deliberation **13** consideration, investigation

disdain 4 snub **5** abhor, scorn, spurn **6** deride, detest, loathe **7** despise, dislike **8** contempt, distaste **9** frown upon **10** abhorrence, brush aside, disrespect **11** intolerance **12** icy aloofness, look down upon **14** deem unbecoming, discountenance

disdained 7 derided, scorned, spurned **8** abhorred, despised **10** deprecated, disparaged **14** held in contempt

disdainful 4 cold **5** aloof **7** haughty, high-hat **8** derisive, scornful, superior **11** overbearing, patronizing **12** contemptuous, supercilious **13** condescending

disease 6 malady **7** ailment, illness **8** sickness **9** ill health, infirmity **10** affliction **15** morbid condition **16** physical disorder

disembark 4 land **7** deplane, detrain, pile out **10** leave a ship **11** get off a ship

disenchant 6 put off **7** turn off **8** alienate, disabuse, turn away **9** undeceive **11** disenthrall, disillusion **12** open one's eyes **13** break the spell **15** burst one's bubble **16** bring down to earth

disencumber 8 unburden 9 disburden, extricate 11 disentangle

disengage 5 sever 6 detach 7 disjoin. 8 separate 9 extricate 10 disconnect

disengaged 7 unmoved 8 detached 9 apathetic, disjoined, separated 11 indifferent, uncommitted, unconcerned 12 disconnected, unresponsive
French: 6 degage

disengagement 6 apathy 8 severing 9 severance, unconcern 10 detachment, separation 12 indifference 13 disconnection 16 unresponsiveness

disentangle 4 free 6 detach, loosen, remove 7 unravel 9 extricate

disenthrall 9 undeceive 10 disenchant 11 disillusion 12 open one's eyes 13 break the spell 15 burst one's bubble 16 bring down to earth

disesteem 7 dislike 8 disfavor 9 disrepute 11 disapproval, displeasure 14 disapprobation

disfavor 5 odium 7 dislike, ill turn 8 disgrace, ignominy 9 disesteem, disregard 10 disrespect, disservice, harmful act 11 disapproval, discourtesy, displeasure 14 disapprobation 15 dissatisfaction 16 unacceptableness

disfigure 3 mar 4 maim, scar 5 cut up 6 damage, deface, deform, impair 7 blemish, scarify 8 make ugly, mutilate

disfigurement 4 blot, flaw, mark, scar, spot 6 blotch, defect 7 blemish 12 imperfection

disfranchise, disenfranchise 15 deprive of a right 19 discriminate against

disgorge 4 spew 5 eject, expel, spout, vomit 6 cast up, spew up 7 cough up, throw up 8 dislodge 9 discharge 10 vomit forth 11 regurgitate

disgrace 4 blot 5 abase, shame, stain, taint 6 debase, smirch 7 blemish, degrade, eyesore, scandal, tarnish 8 contempt, derogate, disfavor, dishonor, ill favor, reproach 9 discredit, disparage, disrepute, embarrass, humiliate 13 embarrassment, in the doghouse 14 bring shame upon

disgraceful 3 low 4 base, mean, vile 6 odious 8 infamous, shameful, shocking, unseemly, unworthy 9 appalling, degrading, obnoxious 10 despicable, detestable, inglorious, outrageous, scandalous, unbecoming 11 ignominious, opprobrious 12 dishonorable, disreputable 13 discreditable, reprehensible

disgruntled 5 sulky, testy, vexed 6 grumpy, shirty, sullen 7 grouchy, peevish 8 petulant 9 irritated 10 displeased, malcontent 12 discontented, dissatisfied

disguise 4 garb, hide, mask, pose, sham, veil 5 blind, cloak, cover, feign, getup, guise 6 facade, muffle, screen, shroud, veneer 7 conceal, cover-up, dress up, falsify 8 pretense, simulate 9 costuming, dissemble, gloss over 10 camouflage, false front, masquerade 11 concealment, counterfeit 12 misrepresent 13 false identity 15 false appearance

disguised 6 masked, veiled 7 cloaked 9 dressed up, incognito 10 undercover 11 camouflaged 14 unrecognizable

disgust 5 repel 6 appall, hatred, offend, put off, revolt, sicken 7 dislike 8 aversion, contempt, distaste, loathing, nauseate 9 antipathy, disrelish, repulsion, revulsion 10 abhorrence, repugnance 11 detestation, displeasure 12 disaffection 13 be repulsive to, cause aversion 15 turn one's stomach

disgusting 4 vile 5 hasty 6 horrid, odious 7 hateful 9 abhorrent, appalling, loathsome, offensive, repellent, repugnant, repulsive, revolting, sickening 10 abominable, despicable, nauseating 13 reprehensible

dish 4 dole, fare, food 5 ladle, place, plate, scoop, serve, spoon 6 recipe, saucer, vessel 7 bowlful, dishful, edibles, helping, platter, portion, serving 8 dispense, plateful, transfer, victuals 10 comestible 11 shallow bowl

dishabille 7 undress 8 bathrobe, disarray, disorder, informal, negligee 9 housecoat

disharmonious 7 chaotic 8 clashing, confused 9 dissonant, illogical 10 discordant, incoherent 11 conflicting, contentious 12 incompatible 13 heterogeneous

disharmony 5 chaos 6 strife 7 discord 8 clashing, conflict, disarray, disunity, division, friction 9 cacophony, confusion, disaccord, harshness 10 contention, dissension, dissonance 11 discordance 12 disagreement, grating noise 15 disorganization, incompatibility

dishearten 4 dash, faze 5 abash, crush, daunt 6 deject, dismay, sadden 7 depress 8 dispirit 10 discourage

disheartened 3 low 6 dismal 8 dejected, desolate, downcast 9 depressed 10 despondent, dispirited 11 discouraged 12 disconsolate

disheartening 4 dark 7 adverse 8 hopeless 11 dispiriting 12 discouraging, inauspicious

disheveled 5 messy 6 blowsy, frowzy, mussed, sloppy, untidy 7 ruffled, rumpled, tousled, unkempt 8 uncombed 10 bedraggled, disarrayed, disorderly, in disorder 11 disarranged

dishevelment 5 chaos, mix-up, upset 6 jumble 7 clutter 8 disarray, disorder, scramble, shambles 9 messiness 10 sloppiness, untidiness 14 disarrangement 15 disorganization

dishonest 5 false 7 corrupt, crooked 8 cheating, specious, spurious, two-faced 9 deceitful, deceptive, faithless, insincere, not honest 10 fraudulent, mendacious, misleading, perfidious, untruthful 11 underhanded 12 disingenuous, false-hearted, unprincipled, unscrupulous 13 untrustworthy

dishonesty 8 cheating 9 duplicity, falseness, mendacity 10 corruption 11 crookedness 12 speciousness 14 untruthfulness

dishonor 4 blot 5 abase, odium, shame, stain, sully 6 debase, defame, infamy, insult, slight, stigma 7 affront, blacken, blemish, degrade, offense, scandal, tarnish 8 disfavor, disgrace, ignominy 9 discredit, disparage, disrepute, humiliate, ill repute 10 derogation, stigmatize 11 discourtesy, humiliation 12 bring shame on 14 public disgrace

dishonorable 4 base 7 debased, ignoble 8 shameful 10 despicable 12 contemptible, disreputable 13 reprehensible

dishonorableness 4 blot 5 odium, shame, stain 6 stigma 7 blemish 8 disfavor, disgrace, ignominy 9 discredit, disrepute, ill repute 10 derogation 11 humiliation

dishonoring 8 disgrace 10 debasement 11 degradation, humiliation

dish up 3 dip 5 ladle, serve, spoon 7 dish out, serve up

disillusion 6 clue in 8 disabuse 9 undeceive 10 disenchant 11 disenthrall 13 break the spell, open the eyes of 14 burst the bubble 16 bring down to earth

disinclination 8 aversion 9 hesitancy 10 reluctance 13 indisposition, unwillingness

disincline 5 deter 8 dissuade, keep back, restrain 10 discourage, divert from 13 advise against 16 attempt to prevent

disinclined 5 loath 6 averse 8 hesitant 9 reluctant, unwilling 10 indisposed

disinfect 6 purify 7 cleanse 8 sanitize 9 kill germs, sterilize 13 decontaminate 15 destroy bacteria

disinfectant 9 germicide 10 antiseptic, germ killer 11 bactericide

disinherit 6 cut off, disown 15 deprive of rights

disintegrate 7 break up, crumble, shatter 8 splinter 9 fall apart 10 break apart, go to pieces

disintegration 4 ruin 5 decay 7 breakup, erosion 8 biolysis 9 crumbling 10 dispersion, dissolving, separation 11 decomposing 12 falling apart 13 decomposition, deterioration, pulverization

disinter 5 dig up 6 exhume 7 unearth

disinterest 6 apathy 9 disregard, unconcern 12 indifference

disinterested 7 neutral, outside 8 unbiased 9 impartial 10 impersonal, uninvolved 11 free from bias, unprejudiced 13 dispassionate

disinterment 9 digging up 10 exhumation, unearthing

disjecta membra 15 disjointed parts 16 scattered members

disjoin 4 part, undo 5 break, sever 6 detach, divide 8 disunite, separate 9 disengage

disjoint 6 detach 7 unhinge 8 disunite, separate 9 dislocate 10 disconnect 13 disarticulate

disjointed 5 apart, split 7 chaotic, divided, jumbled, mixed-up, tangled 8 confused, detached, rambling 9 illogical, spasmodic 10 incoherent, irrational, unattached 11 unconnected 12 disconnected, disorganized 13 discontinuous, disharmonious,

helter-skelter, heterogeneous 14 disarticulated

disjointedness 8 rambling 11 indirection 14 discursiveness 16 disconnectedness

disjointed parts
    Latin: 14 disjecta membra

disk, disc 3 cam 4 aten, coin, dial, face, plow, puck 5 plate, wafer, wheel 6 harrow, record, sequin 7 discuss 8 diskette 9 cultivate, videodisc 11 discotheque
    type: 4 hard 5 fixed 6 floppy 8 magnetic 10 Winchester

dislike 4 hate 5 abhor, scorn 6 animus, detest, enmity, hatred, loathe, malice, rancor 7 despise, disdain, disgust, not like 8 aversion, distaste, loathing, object to 9 abominate, animosity, antipathy, hostility, repulsion, revulsion 10 abhorrence, antagonism, repugnance 11 abomination, detestation 12 disaffection

disliked 5 hated 7 loathed, unloved 8 abhorred, despised, detested 10 abominated

dislike intensely 4 hate 5 abhor 6 detest, loathe 7 despise 9 abominate 10 recoil from

dislocate 6 uproot 7 unhinge 8 disjoint, disunite, separate 9 disengage 10 disconnect 13 disarticulate, put out of joint

dislodge 4 oust 5 eject, expel 6 dig out, dispel, remove, uproot 7 disturb 8 displace, force out 9 extricate 11 disentangle

disloyal 6 untrue 8 recreant 9 faithless, seditious, undutiful 10 inconstant, perfidious, subversive, traitorous, unfaithful 11 treacherous, treasonable 12 dishonorable

disloyalty 7 falsity, perfidy, treason 8 apostasy, betrayal, sedition 9 falseness, rebellion, recreancy, treachery 10 infidelity, subversion 11 inconstancy 12 insurrection 13 breach of trust, deceitfulness, doubledealing, faithlessness 14 lack of fidelity, perfidiousness, unfaithfulness 15 betrayal of trust, breaking of faith 18 subversive activity

dismal 3 sad 4 drab, grim, poor 5 awful, bleak 6 dreary, gloomy, morbid, rueful, somber, woeful 7 abysmal, doleful, forlorn, joyless, unhappy, very bad, visaged 8 dejected, desolate, dolorous, downcast, dreadful, hopeless, horrible, mournful, terrible 9 cheerless, depressed, long-faced, sorrowful, woebegone 10 abominable, despondent, in the dumps, lugubrious, melancholy 11 pessimistic 12 disconsolate, disheartened, heavy-hearted 13 unmentionable 14 down-in-the-mouth

dismantle 5 strip 6 denude, divest 9 take apart

dismay 3 cow 5 abash, alarm, daunt, dread, panic, scare 6 appall, fright, horror, put off, terror 7 anxiety, concern, horrify, unnerve 8 affright, distress, frighten 10 disappoint, discourage, dishearten, intimidate 11 disillusion, trepidation 12 apprehension, exasperation, intimidation, perturbation 13 consternation 14 disappointment, discouragement 15 disillusionment

dismayed 7 abashed, daunted 8 appalled 10 confounded, nonplussed 12 disconcerted

dismember 4 limb 6 hack up 8 disjoint 16 tear limb from limb

dismiss 3 can 4 fire, free, oust, sack 5 let go 6 bounce, excuse, reject 7 adjourn, cashier, disband, discard, release 8 disclaim, disperse, dissolve, lay aside, liberate, pink-slip, set aside 9 disregard, eliminate, repudiate, send forth, terminate 10 permit to go 11 send packing 12 allow to leave, put out of a job, put out of mind 14 give the heave-ho 17 remove from service, give walking papers 19 discharge from office

dismissal 6 firing 7 release 9 discharge, dispersal, disregard 10 disclaimer 11 adjournment, repudiation

Disney, Walt
  creator/artist of: 10 Donald Duck 11 Mickey Mouse

disobedience 8 defiance 9 rebellion 10 resistance 13 noncompliance, nonconformity 14 rebelliousness

disobedient 6 unruly 7 defiant, froward, haughty, wayward 8 contrary, mutinous, perverse, stubborn 9 fractious, insurgent, obstinate, seditious, undutiful 10 disorderly, rebellious, refractory, unyielding 11 intractable 12 noncompliant, recalcitrant, ungovernable, unmanageable, unsubmissive 13 insubordinate

disobey 4 defy 5 break 6 ignore, resist 7 violate 8 overstep 9 disregard 10 infringe on, transgress 11 go counter to 12 rebel against

disoblige 5 annoy 6 bother 7 trouble 13 inconvenience

disobliging 4 rude 8 churlish 9 unhelpful 13 inconsiderate

disorder 4 mess, riot 5 chaos 6 fracas, jumble, malady, muddle, ruckus, uproar 7 ailment, clutter, disease, illness, turmoil 8 disarray, sickness 9 commotion, complaint, confusion 10 affliction, disruption, dissension 11 disturbance 13 indisposition, minor uprising 14 disarrangement 15 disorganization

disordered 7 jumbled 8 confused, messed up 9 haphazard 11 disarranged 12 disorganized

disorderliness 4 mess 5 chaos 6 muddle 8 disarray 9 confusion 10 disruption 14 disarrangement 15 disorganization

disorderly 3 bad 4 wild 5 messy, noisy, rowdy 6 sloppy, unruly, untidy 7 chaotic, jumbled, lawless, riotous, unkempt, wayward 8 careless, confused, improper, pellmell, rowdyish, slipshod, slovenly, unlawful, unsorted 10 boisterous, disheveled, disordered, disruptive, rebellious, straggling, topsy-turvy 11 disarranged 12 disorganized, disreputable, obstreperous, unrestrained, unsystematic 13 helter-skelter,

undisciplined 14 rough-and-tumble, unsystematized

disorganization 4 mess 5 chaos, upset 6 jumble, muddle 7 clutter 8 disarray, disorder, shambles 9 confusion, messiness 10 disharmony, disruption, sloppiness, untidiness 12 dishevelment 14 disarrangement, disorderliness

disorganize 5 mix up, upset 6 jumble, mess up, muddle 7 confuse, scatter 8 disarray, disorder, put askew, scramble 10 disarrange 13 put out of order 14 turn topsy-turvy

disorganized 5 messy, upset 7 chaotic, jumbled, mixed-up, muddled 8 confused, rambling 9 haphazard, illogical 10 disordered, disorderly, incoherent, in disarray, irrational 12 unsystematic 16 at sixes and sevens

disoriented 7 mixed-up 8 confused, unstable 10 distracted, out of joint, out of touch 11 not adjusted

disown 6 reject 7 cast off, disavow, forsake 8 denounce, disclaim, renounce 9 repudiate 10 disinherit 17 refuse to recognize 19 refuse to acknowledge

disparage 4 mock 6 demean, slight 7 put down, run down 8 belittle, derogate, ridicule 9 denigrate, discredit, underrate 10 depreciate, undervalue 11 detract from

disparaged 7 ran down 9 belittled, ridiculed 10 denigrated, deprecated 11 depreciated

disparagement 5 abuse, libel 7 slander 8 ridicule 9 criticism 10 belittling, defamation, derogation, detraction 11 denigration, putting down 12 vilification 17 defamatory remarks

disparaging 5 snide 10 belittling, derogatory 11 unfavorable 15 uncomplimentary

disparate 6 at odds, unlike 9 different 10 at variance, discordant, discrepant, dissimilar 11 contrasting

disparity 3 gap 8 contrast, imparity, variance 10 difference, divergence, inequality, unlikeness 11 discrepancy, incongruity 12 disagreement, dissemblance 13 contradiction, disproportion, dissimilarity, dissimilitude, inconsistency

dispassion 6 apathy 8 coolness 10 detachment 12 indifference

dispassionate 4 calm, cool, fair 6 serene 7 neutral, unmoved 8 composed, detached, unbiased 9 collected, impartial, unexcited, unruffled 10 impersonal, uninvolved 11 levelheaded, undisturbed, unemotional 12 unprejudiced 13 disinterested, imperturbable

dispatch 4 item, kill, post, slay 5 flash, haste, piece, speed, story 6 finish, letter, murder, report, settle, wind up 7 bump off, execute, forward, message, missive, send off 8 alacrity, bulletin, carry out, celerity, complete, conclude, expedite, massacre, rapidity 9 finish off, quickness, slaughter, swiftness 10 communique, expedition, promptness, put an end to, put to death 11 assassinate, news account 12 send on the way 14 execute quickly, summarily shoot, swift execution 15 make short work of, transmit rapidly 16 carry out speedily, dispose of rapidly 18 telegraphic message 21 official communication

Dis Pater *see* 3 Dis

dispel 4 rout 5 allay, expel, repel 6 banish, remove 7 diffuse, dismiss, resolve, expendable 8 drive off 9 dissipate, drive away, eliminate 10 put an end to 11 disseminate 13 make disappear

dispensable 8 nonvital 9 accessory, extrinsic, secondary 10 disposable, expendable, extraneous 11 superfluous, unessential, unimportant, unnecessary 12 nonessential

dispensation 6 decree 8 approval, bestowal, division 9 allotment, diffusion, exemption, meting out 10 allocation, conferment, credential, dealing out, dispensing, permission, reparation 11 consignment, designation 12 apportioning, distribution, remuneration 13 authorization, dissemination

dispense 6 confer 7 dole out, mete out 8 allocate 9 apportion 10 administer, distribute

dispense with 4 drop, dump, junk, shed 5 scrap 6 shelve 7 abandon, discard 9 dispose of

dispensing 9 bestowing, doling out, meting out 10 allocating, conferring 12 distributing

dispersal 7 breakup, parting 9 dismissal 10 breaking up, scattering 12 distributing, distribution

disperse 4 rout 6 dispel 7 diffuse, disband, scatter, send off 8 drive off 9 dissipate 10 distribute 11 disseminate 13 send scurrying 16 spread throughout

dispersed 7 diffuse 9 scattered, spread out 10 dissipated 11 distributed 14 extended widely, unconcentrated

dispersion 9 dispersal 10 disbanding, scattering 11 dissipation 12 distribution

dispirit 5 cloud 6 darken, deject, sadden 7 depress 10 demoralize, dishearten

dispirited 3 sad 4 blue, down, glum 5 moody 6 morose 7 forlorn, unhappy 8 dejected, downcast, listless 9 cheerless, depressed 10 melancholy 11 crestfallen, demoralized, discouraged, downhearted, pessimistic 12 disconsolate, disheartened 14 down in the dumps, down in the mouth, unenthusiastic

dispiriting 4 cold, dark 6 chilly, dismal, gloomy 9 dampening 10 depressing 12 discouraging 13 disheartening

displace 4 bump, move, oust 5 shift 6 unseat 7 replace 8 crowd out, dislodge, force out, supplant 9 dislocate, supersede

displaced person 2 DP 5 exile 6 emigre 7 refugee 8 expellee 10 expatriate

display 4 show 6 reveal 7 exhibit 8 manifest 10 exhibition 11 demonstrate, make visible 12 presentation 13 bring into view, demonstration, manifestation 15 put in plain sight

display case 7 cabinet, vitrine 8 showcase

displease 3 irk 5 annoy, pique 6 offend 7 disturb, incense, provoke 8 irritate

displeasing 8 annoying 9 loathsome, offensive, repellent, repugnant 10 irritating 11 distasteful, distressing 12 disagreeable

displeasure 5 wrath 7 dislike 8 vexation 9 annoyance 10 irritation 11 disapproval, indignation 15 dissatisfaction

disport 3 act 4 play, romp 5 amuse, caper, sport 6 divert, frolic, gambol 7 display, pastime 9 amusement, entertain 10 recreation 13 entertainment

disposal 5 array, order, power 7 command, control, dumping, junking, pattern, ridding 8 grouping, riddance 9 authority, clearance, direction, placement 10 discarding, government, management, regulation, settlement 11 arrangement, destruction, disposition, supervision 12 distribution, organization, throwing away 13 authorization, configuration, juxtaposition 14 administration

dispose 4 rank 5 array, order, place 7 arrange, deal out, incline 8 classify, get rid of, motivate, organize 9 be willing 10 distribute

dispose of 4 dump 5 scrap 6 unload 7 discard 8 get rid of, throw out 9 cast aside, throw away

disposition 6 nature, spirit 7 control 8 bestowal, grouping, tendency 9 placement 11 arrangement, inclination, temperament 12 distribution, organization 14 predisposition 15 final settlement

dispossess 4 oust 5 evict, expel 8 take away, take back 9 deprive of

disproportionate 7 unequal 9 disparate 10 dissimilar, unbalanced

disprove 6 refute 9 discredit 10 controvert

disputable 7 dubious 8 doubtful 9 debatable, uncertain 12 questionable 14 controvertible

disputant 5 rival 7 opposer 8 opponent 9 adversary 10 antagonist, competitor, contestant

disputation 6 debate, review 8 argument, dialogue 10 discussion

dispute 4 feud 5 argue, clash, doubt 6 debate, impugn 7 quarrel, wrangle 8 argument, question, squabble 9 bickering, challenge 10 contradict 11 altercation, controversy 12 disagreement

disputed 6 argued 8 wrangled 9 debatable, in dispute, quarreled 10 in question, unverified 12 questionable 13 controversial 15 unsubstantiated

disqualification 5 minus 8 handicap 10 disability 11 shortcoming 13 ineligibility

disqualify 7 disable 9 make unfit 17 declare ineligible, deny participation

disquiet, disquietude 3 awe 6 unease 7 anxiety 8 distress 9 agitation 10 uneasiness 11 fretfulness, trepidation 12 apprehension, discomposure, perturbation 13 consternation

disquieted 6 uneasy 7 anxious, worried 9 concerned 10 distressed 12 apprehensive

disquieting 6 vexing 8 annoying 9 troubling, upsetting 10 bothersome, disturbing, irritating, perturbing, unsettling 11 distressing 13 disconcerting

disquisition 8 tractate, treatise 9 discourse, monograph 12 dissertation

disregard 6 ignore 8 overlook 11 pay no heed to 13 lack of respect 14 take no notice of 15 lack of attention 16 willful oversight

disregardful 8 careless, heedless 9 unmindful 11 insensitive, thoughtless 13 inconsiderate

disreputable 5 shady 8 infamous, shameful, shocking 9 notorious 10 scandalous 11 disgraceful 12 dishonorable, unprincipled 14 not respectable, of bad character

disrespect 8 contempt, dishonor, rudeness 9 disregard 11 discourtesy, irreverence 12 impoliteness

disrespectful 4 rude 8 impolite 11 impertinent 12 contemptuous, discourteous

disrobe 5 strip 7 undress 16 divest of clothing

disrupt 5 upset 9 interrupt 13 interfere with 17 throw into disorder

disruption 5 upset 8 disorder 9 confusion 11 disturbance 12 interference, interruption 14 disarrangement 15 disorganization

dissatisfaction 4 veto 7 protest 9 rejection 10 discontent 11 disapproval, displeasure, unhappiness

dissatisfied 7 unhappy 10 displeased 12 discontented

dissect 5 study 7 analyze, lay open 8 cut apart, separate 9 anatomize, break down

dissemble 4 hide, mask 5 feign 7 conceal 8 disguise 10 camouflage 11 dissimulate

disseminate 6 spread 7 diffuse, scatter 8 disperse 9 broadcast, circulate

dissemination 9 diffusion, dispersal, spreading 10 scattering 12 broadcasting, distribution

dissension 7 discord, dispute 8 conflict, disunity, division 9 rebellion 10 contention, disharmony, quarreling 11 discordance 12 disagreement 14 rebelliousness

dissent 6 object, oppose 7 discord, protest 8 disagree 10 difference, dissension, opposition 12 disagreement 14 withhold assent 16 withhold approval

dissenter 5 rebel 9 dissident, protester 13 nonconformist

dissenting 9 differing, dissident 11 disagreeing

dissertation 6 memoir, thesis 8 tractate, treatise 9 discourse, monograph 12 disquisition

disservice 4 harm, hurt 5 wrong 6 injury 7 bad turn 9 injustice

dissever 3 saw 4 hack, rend 5 carve, sever, slash, slice, split 6 cleave, divide 8 disunite, separate

dissident 5 rebel 8 agitator, opposing 9 differing, dissenter 10 dissenting 11 disagreeing

dissimilar 6 unlike 8 distinct 9 different, disparate

dissimilarity 8 contrast, variance 9 disparity 10 difference, dissonance, divergence, inequality, unlikeness 11 discrepancy 12 disagreement 13 inconsistency 17 lack of resemblance

dissimilitude 8 variance 9 disparity 10 difference, unlikeness 11 incongruity 12 disagreement 17 lack of resemblance

dissimulate 4 hide, mask 7 conceal 8 disguise 9 dissemble 10 camouflage

dissipate 5 waste 6 dispel 7 carouse, deplete, scatter 8 disperse, misspend, squander 11 fritter away, overindulge 13 be intemperate 14 spend foolishly

dissipated 6 wasted 8 misspent 9 abandoned, debauched, dispelled, dispersed, dissolute, scattered 10 squandered 11 intemperate 12 disreputable 13 frittered away

dissipater 5 waste 7 wastrel 8 prodigal 10 profligate, squanderer 11 spendthrift

dissipation 8 excess 7 wasting 9 dispersal 10 debauchery, dispelling, scattering 11 dissolution, loose living 12 immoderation, intemperance 14 disintegration, frittering away, self-indulgence

dissociate 8 separate 10 disconnect 12 break off with

dissociation 7 breakup 10 separation

dissolute 5 loose 7 corrupt, immoral 9 abandoned, debauched 10 dissipated 12 unrestrained

dissolution 9 annulment 10 separation 11 termination 14 disintegration

dissolve 3 end, run 4 fade, melt, thaw, void 5 annul, sever 6 finish, render, soften, vanish 7 break up, disband, liquefy, thaw out 8 abrogate, conclude, evanesce 9 disappear, dissipate, terminate 10 deliquesce 12 disintegrate 13 dematerialize

dissonance 5 clash 7 discord 9 cacophony, harshness 10 difference, disharmony 11 discordance 12 disagreement 13 dissimilarity

dissonant 5 harsh 7 grating, hostile, jarring, raucous, warring 8 clashing, jangling 10 discordant, discrepant 11 cacophonous, disagreeing, incongruent, incongruous, unmelodious 12 incompatible, inconsistent, inharmonious 13 contradictory 14 irreconcilable

dissuade 9 urge not to 10 discourage 13 advise against, persuade not to

distance 3 gap 4 span 7 reserve, stretch 8 coldness, coolness, interval 9 aloofness, formality, restraint, stiffness 11 reservation 16 intervening space

distant 3 far 4 cold, cool 5 aloof 6 far-off, remote 7 faraway 8 detached, reserved 10 far-removed, restrained, unfriendly 11 standoffish 17 not closely related

Distant Mirror, A
  author: 15 Barbara W Tuchman

distaste 7 disgust, dislike 8 aversion 9 antipathy 10 repugnance 11 displeasure

distasteful 9 loathsome, repugnant 10 disgusting, unpleasant 11 displeasing 12 disagreeable

distastefulness 13 offensiveness 14 unpleasantness 16 disagreeableness

distasteful work 8 drudgery 11 menial labor

distend 5 bloat, bulge, swell 6 billow, expand 7 inflate, puff out 8 swell out

distended 4 full, taut 5 puffy, tumid 7 blown up, bloated, dilated, swelled, swollen enlarged, expanded, extended, inflated, patulant 9 edematous, stretched

distill 7 draw out, extract 8 condense, vaporize 9 draw forth, evaporate

distillate 7 essence, extract 11 concentrate 13 concentration

distilled 9 condensed, extracted, vaporized 10 evaporated

distinct 5 clear, lucid, plain 7 diverse, supreme 8 clear-cut, definite, explicit, separate 9 different 10 dissimilar, individual 11 unmitigated, well-defined 12 not identical, unmistakable 13 extraordinary 14 unquestionable

distinction 6 renown 8 contrast, eminence 9 greatness 10 difference, excellence, importance, notability, prominence, separation 11 discernment, preeminence, superiority 12 differential 14 discrimination 15 differentiation

distinctive 6 unique 7 special 8 atypical, original, singular, uncommon 9 different 10 individual 13 extraordinary 14 characteristic

distinctiveness 7 clarity 9 character 10 definition, uniqueness 11 personality 13 individuality

distingue 13 distinguished

distinguish 6 decide, define 7 discern 8 set apart 9 single out 10 make famous 12 characterize, discriminate 13 differentiate, make prominent, make well known 14 make celebrated 15 make distinctive, note differences

distinguished 5 grand, great 6 famous, superb 7 elegant, eminent, notable, refined 8 renowned, splendid 9 acclaimed, dignified, distingue, prominent 10 celebrated 11 illustrious, magnificent
  French: 9 distingue

distort 6 deform 7 contort 8 misshape 9 disfigure 11 misconstrue 12 misrepresent 15 twist out of shape, twist the meaning

distorted 4 awry 5 askew 6 belied, loaded, warped 7 altered, colored, crooked, twisted 8 cockeyed, deformed, wrenched 9 contorted, falsified, grotesque, irregular, misshapen, misstated, perverted 13 unsymmetrical 14 misrepresented 15 misproportioned

distortion 7 skewing 8 twisting 10 aberration, caricature 11 crookedness, deformation 12 malformation 17 misrepresentation

distract 5 amuse, craze, worry 6 divert, madden 7 agitate, confuse, disturb, perplex, torment, trouble 8 bewilder, disorder 9 entertain

distracted 3 mad 4 wild 6 amused, crazed, insane, raving 7 frantic, pleased, puzzled 8 agitated, confused, deranged, diverted, frenzied, harassed, heedless, occupied 9 disturbed, stirred up 10 bewildered, distraught, irrational 11 entertained, turned aside

distraction 5 fazed, upset 6 frenzy 7 frantic, madness, pastime, rattled, ruffled 8 agitated, confused 9 amusement, diversion, unsettled 10 distraught, distressed, nonplussed, recreation 11 desperation 12 disconcerted 13 entertainment 14 mental distress

distractive 9 confusing 10 disturbing, unsettling 11 distressing, troublesome

distraught 3 mad 7 anxious, frantic 8 agitated, frenzied, seething 10 distracted, distressed 13 beside oneself

distress 4 need, pain, want 5 agony, upset 6 danger, grieve 7 anguish, disturb, torment, torture, trouble 14 acute suffering

distressed 5 upset 7 anxious, fearful, frantic, grieved, unhappy, worried 8 agitated, troubled 9 anguished, concerned, disturbed, tormented 10 distracted, distraught

distressing 5 acute 7 nagging, painful 8 grievous 9 agonizing, upsetting 10 disturbing, tormenting, unpleasant 11 displeasing, troublesome, unfortunate 13 uncomfortable

distribute 5 allot, class 6 divide, parcel 7 arrange, catalog, deliver, dole out, give out, scatter 8 classify, dispense, disperse, separate, tabulate 9 apportion, circulate, methodize, spread out 11 disseminate, systematize

distribution 7 sorting 8 division, grouping 9 allotment, spreading 10 allocation, dispersion, scattering 11 arrangement, circulation, disposition 12 organization 13 apportionment, dissemination

distribution center
  French: 8 entrepot

district 4 area, ward 6 parish, region 8 precinct 12 neighborhood

distrust 5 doubt 7 suspect 8 question 9 misgiving, suspicion 11 lack of faith

distrustful 3 shy 4 wary 5 leery 7 dubious, jealous 8 cautious, doubtful, doubting 9 diffident 10 suspicious, untrusting 11 incredulous, mistrustful 12 disbelieving

disturb 5 annoy, upset, worry 6 bother 7 disrupt, perturb, trouble 8 distress, unsettle 9 dislocate, interrupt, intrude on 10 disarrange 11 disorganize

disturbance 5 upset, worry 6 bother, hubbub, ruckus, tumult, uproar 7 rioting, turmoil 8 disorder, distress, outbreak 9 annoyance 11 distraction 12 interruption, perturbation

disturbance of peace 4 riot 6 fracas, ruckus, uproar 7 turmoil 8 disorder 9 commotion 13 breach of order

disturbed 5 upset 6 uneasy 7 annoyed, anxious, nervous, rattled 8 agitated, confused, troubled 9 perturbed 10 disquieted 11 discomfited 12 disconcerted

disunion 7 divorce 8 division 9 secession 10 separation 14 disintegration

disunite 4 part 6 divide 7 divorce 8 separate 9 disengage 10 disconnect 12 disintegrate 13 disarticulate

disunited 6 parted 8 diverged, divorced, unallied 9 came apart, dispersed, separated 10 uncombined 13 disassociated

disunity 6 strife 7 discord 8 clashing, conflict, division, friction 9 wrangling 10 contention, dissension, separation 11 being at odds, discordance 12 disagreement 15 incompatibility

ditat Deus 11 God enriches
   motto of: 7 Arizona

ditch 3 pit 4 junk 5 scrap 6 hollow, trench 7 abandon, discard 8 get rid of 10 excavation

dither 4 flap, fuss 5 tizzy, waver, whirl 6 bother, flurry, lather, quiver, shiver, thrill 7 fluster, tremble, twitter 8 hesitate 9 agitation, commotion, confusion, vacillate, vibration 10 excitement

Dithyrambus
   epithet of: 8 Dionysus
   means: 20 child of the double door

ditty 3 lay 4 song, tune 6 ballad 7 refrain

Dius Fidius
   origin: 5 Roman
   god of: 5 oaths 11 hospitality 20 international affairs
   corresponds to: 6 Sancus 10 Semo Sancus

divagation 8 straying 9 wandering 10 digression, divergence

divan 4 book, hall, poem, room, salon, seat, sofa 5 couch, court 6 canape, daybed, leewan, lounge, settee 7 chamber, council, ottoman, davenport

dive 4 dash, fall, jump, leap 5 lunge 6 plunge 7 gin mill 9 honky-tonk, shabby bar 15 sleazy nightclub

Diver, Dick and Nicole
   characters in: 16 Tender Is the Night
   author: 10 Fitzgerald

diverge 6 differ, swerve 7 deflect, deviate 8 be at odds, conflict, disagree, separate, split off

divergence 7 parting 8 conflict, rambling, straying, variance 9 deviation, disparity, wandering 10 difference 11 discrepancy, incongruity 13 dissimilarity, inconsistency

divergent 8 separate 9 different 11 conflicting, disagreeing 12 drawing apart, splitting off

diverse 6 sundry, varied 8 eclectic, far-flung, opposite 9 different, differing, disparate 10 dissimilar 11 conflicting, of many kinds 13 contradictory

diversified 6 divers 7 various 8 manifold 9 different, unrelated 13 miscellaneous

diversify 4 vary 7 diffuse 8 divide up 9 spread out, variegate

diversion 5 hobby 7 pastime 9 amusement, avocation 10 deflection 11 distraction, drawing away 12 turning aside
   French: 14 divertissement

diversity 7 variety 8 variance 10 assortment, difference 13 heterogeneity

divert 5 amuse 7 deflect 8 distract 9 entertain, sidetrack, turn aside

diverting 7 amusing 10 deflecting 11 distracting 12 entertaining, sidetracking

divertissement 9 diversion 13 entertainment

divest 3 rid 4 free 5 strip 7 deprive, disrobe, peel off, take off 8 get out of 10 dispossess 14 remove clothing

divest oneself of 6 give up 7 take off 8 get rid of, give over, hand over, put aside, strip off 9 surrender 10 relinquish

divide 4 part, sort 5 share, split 7 arrange, deal out, divvy up 8 allocate, classify, disunite, separate 9 apportion, partition 10 distribute, put in order

divide and rule
   Latin: 14 divide et impera
   maxim of: 11 Machiavelli

divided 5 apart, split 6 parted 8 meted out 9 disunited, separated 10 unattached 11 apportioned 12 disconnected, portioned out

divide et impera 13 divide and rule
   maxim of: 11 Machiavelli

divide in two 5 halve, split 6 bisect 8 cut in two, separate 9 cut in half 10 break in two 11 split in half 18 split down the middle

dividing line 4 edge 5 brink, verge 6 border, margin 8 boundary 9 threshold

divination 5 guess 6 augury 8 prophecy 10 conjecture, foreboding, prediction, prescience 11 premonition, soothsaying 15 prognostication

divine 4 holy 5 guess 6 fathom, sacred 7 predict, surmise, suspect 8 forecast, foretell, heavenly, prophesy 9 admirable, celestial, excellent, marvelous, wonderful

divine being 3 god 5 deity 7 goddess 8 divinity 14 celestial being

Divine Comedy
   author: 14 Dante Alighieri
   part: 7 Inferno 8 Paradiso 10 Purgatorio
   guide: 6 Virgil 8 Beatrice

diviner 4 seer 5 augur 10 soothsayer 14 prognosticator

Divine retribution
   goddess of: 7 Nemesis 8 Adrastea

Divine Sarah
   nickname of: 14 Sarah Bernhardt

divinity 3 god 5 deity 7 goddess 8 holiness, religion, theology 9 theosophy 12 science of God 14 celestial being

division 4 part, unit, wing 5 split 6 branch 7 discord, divider, section 8 disunion, variance 9 partition 10 department, difference, divergence, separation 11 splitting up 12 disagreement

divorce 4 rift 5 split 6 breach, divide 7 rupture 8 disunite, separate 9 segregate 10 dissociate, separation

divulge 4 tell 6 impart, relate, reveal 8 disclose 9 make known 11 communicate

divulgence 7 telling 8 exposure 9 imparting 10 disclosure, giving away, laying open, revelation 13 communication 15 bringing to light 17 bring out in the open

divulge to 4 tell 6 advise, inform, notify, reveal 7 apprise 8 acquaint, disclose 9 enlighten, make aware 11 familiarize 13 spill the beans 20 let the cat out of the bag

Dix, Otto
  born: 7 Germany 11 Unterhausen
  artwork: 6 The War 7 The City 12 The Procuress 16 Sylvia von Harden 18 Parents of the Artist 39 Prague Street—Dedicated to My Contemporaries

Dixie Dugan
  creator: 8 J P McEvoy 13 John H Striebel

dizzy 5 fleet, giddy, quick, rapid, shaky, swift 6 whirly 7 confuse, reeling 8 bewilder, unsteady 9 make giddy 11 lightheaded, vertiginous 12 make unsteady

Djawa see 4 Java

Djebel al-Tarik see 9 Gibraltar

Djibouti
  other name: 16 French Somaliland 39 The French Territory of the Afars and the Issas
  capital/largest city: 8 Djibouti
  others: 5 Obock 6 Dikhil 8 Tadjoura 9 Ali-Sabieh
  monetary unit: 5 franc 7 centime
  lake: 4 Abbe 5 Assal
  mountain: 5 Gouda
  highest point: 9 Moussa Ali
  sea: 3 Red
  physical feature:
  gulf: 4 Aden 8 Tadjoura
  strait: 11 Bab el-Mandeb
  people: 4 Afar, Arab 5 Issas 6 French 8 European
  language: 4 Afar 6 Arabic, French, Somali
  religion: 5 Islam

do 3 act 4 fare 5 clean, cover, get on, serve, visit 6 behave, finish, look at, stop in 7 achieve, arrange, carry on, conduct, execute, fulfill, make out, perform, prepare, proceed, suffice 8 be enough, carry out, complete, conclude, organize 10 accomplish, administer, bring about, put in order 13 travel through 14 be satisfactory, comport oneself, conduct oneself

do a favor 4 help 6 assist, oblige 7 help out 11 accommodate, do a kindness

do away with 3 end 4 junk, kill, void 5 erase, quash 6 banish, cancel, cut out, give up, remove, repeal, revoke, rub out 7 abolish, blot out, nullify, rescind, weed out, wipe out 8 abrogate, stamp out, throw out 9 eliminate, eradicate, terminate 10 annihilate, put an end to 11 exterminate

Dobbin, Captain William
  character in: 10 Vanity Fair
  author: 9 Thackeray

Dobie Gillis, The Many Loves of
  character: 11 Zelda Gilroy 13 Maynard G Krebs 14 Herbert T Gillis, Milton Armitage, Winifred (Winnie) Gillis 15 Thalia Menninger 19 Chatsworth Osborne Jr
  cast: 9 Bob Denver 11 Frank Faylen, Sheila James, Tuesday Weld 12 Warren Beatty 13 Dwayne Hickman 14 Florida Friebus, Stephen Franken
  Dobie imitated pose of: 7 Thinker

do business 4 deal 5 trade 10 buy and sell

docile 4 tame 7 willing 8 obedient, obliging 9 agreeable, compliant, tractable 10 manageable 11 complaisant

docility 7 pliancy 8 meekness 9 passivity 10 placidness 12 acquiescence, complaisance 13 nonresistance

dock 4 crop, join, pier, quay 5 berth, wharf 6 couple, cut off, deduct, hook up, link up 7 landing 8 cut short 10 waterfront 12 come into port 13 subject to loss 14 fasten together

dock 5 Rumux
  varieties: 3 Bur 4 Sour 5 Green 6 Golden 7 Prairie, Spinach, Tanner's, Western 8 Patience 9 Purple-wen 10 Giant water

docket 4 bill, card, list 5 slate 6 agenda, lineup, roster 7 program 8 calendar, schedule 9 timetable 14 things to be done 15 order of business

doctor 2 GP, MD 3 PhD 5 alter, treat 6 change 7 dentist, falsify, surgeon 9 internist, osteopath, physician 10 podiatrist, tamper with 11 pathologist 12 gynecologist, obstetrician, pediatrician, psychiatrist, veterinarian 15 ophthalmologist 17 apply medication to 19 general practitioner, medical practitioner

Doctor Brodie's Report
  author: 15 Jorge Luis Borges

Doctor Faustus
  author: 10 Thomas Mann 18 Christopher Marlowe

Doctor Grimshaw's Secret
  author: 18 Nathaniel Hawthorne

Doctor J
  nickname of: 12 Julius Erving

Doctorow, E L
  author of: 7 Ragtime 15 The Book of Daniel

Doctor's Dilemma, The
  author: 17 George Bernard Shaw

Doctor Zhivago
  director: 9 David Lean
  author: 14 Boris Pasternak
  cast: 10 Omar Sharif (Zhivago), Rod Steiger 12 Alec Guinness, Tom Courtenay 13 Julie Christie (Lara) 14 Rita

Tushingham 15 Ralph Richardson 16 Geraldine Chaplin

doctrinaire 5 rigid 6 mulish 8 absolute, dogmatic, stubborn 9 arbitrary, imperious, pigheaded 10 bullheaded, inflexible, pontifical 11 dictatorial, opinionated, overbearing, stiff-necked 12 narrow-minded 13 authoritarian 14 disciplinarian

doctrinal 8 didactic, dogmatic, edifying, tutorial 11 educational, instructive 12 prescriptive

doctrine 5 dogma, tenet 6 belief, gospel 7 precept 8 teaching 9 principle 10 conviction, philosophy

document 6 back up, record, verify 7 certify, support 9 legal form 10 instrument 12 give weight to, substantiate 13 official paper

documentation 5 proof 7 support 8 evidence 12 verification 13 corroboration 14 substantiation

doddering 4 weak 6 feeble, senile 7 shaking 8 decrepit 9 tottering, trembling

dodge 4 duck, wile 5 avoid, elude, evade, hedge, trick 6 device, swerve 7 fend off 8 sidestep 9 jump aside, stratagem, turn aside 10 equivocate 11 machination

dodging 7 ducking, eluding, evading 8 shunning 12 sidestepping 13 circumventing

Dodgson, Charles Lutwidge
　real name of: 12 Lewis Carroll

Dodoma
　capital of: 8 Tanzania

Dodonian
　epithet of: 4 Zeus

Dodsworth
　director: 12 William Wyler
　author: 13 Sinclair Lewis
　character: 4 Fran 12 Arnold Israel 14 Edith Cortright, Renee de Penable 15 Samuel Dodsworth 16 Kurt von Obersdorf 17 Major Clyde Lockert
　cast: 9 Mary Astor, Paul Lukas 10 David Niven 12 Walter Huston 14 Ruth Chatterton

doer 6 dynamo 7 hustler 8 activist, go-getter 12 active person

doff 4 bare, drop, junk, shed 5 scrap, strip 6 put off, remove 7 abandon, cast off, discard, disrobe, take off, toss off, undress 8 throw off, throw out 9 eliminate, step out of 10 do away with

dog 3 cur, pup 4 heel, mutt 5 beast, puppy 6 canine 7 mongrel, villain 9 scoundrel 10 blackguard
　Alaskan: 5 husky 6 malamute, malemute
　anatomy: 3 hip, lip, pad, paw, toe 4 arch, back, hock, loin, rump, stop 5 cheek, crest, croup, flews, skull 6 carpus, dewlap, muzzle, stifle, tarsus 7 brisket, cushion, knuckle, occiput, pastern, withers 8 heelknob, shoulder 10 metacarpus, metatarsus
　Australian: 5 dingo 8 warragal
　barkless: 7 basenji
　breed:

herding group: 5 pulik 6 briard, collie 13 bearded collie 14 German Shepherd 15 Belgian malinois, Belgian sheepdog, Belgian tervuren 16 Shetland sheepdog 18 Cardigan Welsh corgi, Old English sheepdog, Pembroke Welsh corgi 19 Australian cattle dog, Bouviers des Flandres

hound group: 6 beagle, borzoi, saluki 7 basenji, harrier, whippet 9 dachshund, greyhound 10 bloodhound, otter hound 11 Afghan hound, basset hound, Ibizan hound 12 pharaoh hound 14 Irish wolfhound 15 English foxhound 16 American foxhound 17 Norwegian elkhound, Scottish deerhound 18 Rhodesian ridgeback 20 black and tan coonhound

nonsporting group: 6 poodle 7 bulldog 8 chow chow, keeshond 9 dalmatian, lhasa apso 10 keeshonden, schipperke 11 Bichon frise 13 Boston terrier, French bulldog 14 Tibetan spaniel, Tibetan terrier

sporting group: 6 vizsla 7 pointer 8 Brittany 10 weimaraner 11 Irish setter 12 field spaniel, Gordon setter 13 cocker spaniel, English setter, Sussex spaniel 14 Clumber spaniel 15 golden retriever 17 Irish water spaniel, Labrador retriever 19 flat-coated retriever 20 American water spaniel, curly-coated retriever, English cocker spaniel, Welsh springer spaniel 22 Chesapeake Bay retriever, English springer spaniel 23 German wirehaired pointer 24 German shorthaired pointer 25 wirehaired pointing griffon

terrier group: 10 fox terrier 11 bull terrier, Skye terrier 12 Cairn terrier, Irish terrier, Welsh terrier 13 border terrier 14 Norfolk terrier, Norwich terrier, wire fox terrier 15 Airedale terrier, Lakeland terrier, Scottish terrier, Sealyham terrier 16 Kerry blue terrier, smooth fox terrier 17 Australian terrier, Bedlington terrier, Manchester terrier 18 miniature schnauzer 20 Dandie Dinmont terrier 24 soft-coated wheaten terrier, Staffordshire bull terrier, West Highland white terrier 28 American Staffordshire terrier

toy group: 3 pug 7 Maltese, shih tzu 8 papillon 9 chihuahua, pekingese, toy poodle 10 pomeranian 12 Japanese chin, silky terrier 13 affenpinscher 15 Brussels griffon 16 Italian greyhound, Yorkshire terrier 17 English toy spaniel, Manchester terrier, miniature pinscher

working group: 5 akita, boxer 7 mastiff, samoyed 8 kuvaszok 9 great Dane, St Bernard 10 komondorok, rottweiler 11 bullmastiff 12 Newfoundland 13 great Pyrenees, Siberian husky 14 giant schnauzer 15 Alaskan malamute 16 doberman pinscher 17 standard schnauzer 18 Bernese mountain dog, Portuguese water dog
　Buster Brown's: 4 Tige
　Chinese: 7 shih tzu
　coach: 9 dalmatian
　combining form: 3 cyn 4 cani, cyno

constellation: 12 Canis Majoris
Dorothy's: 4 Toto
family: 7 Canidae
FDR's: 4 Fala **5** Falla
female: 3 dam, gip, gyp **4** slut **5** bitch, brach **7** brachet
genus: 5 Canis
group: 4 pack **5** leash **6** kennel
"His Master's Voice": 6 Nipper
Hungarian: 4 puli **6** kuvasz, vizsla
Indian: 5 dhole
Japanese: 5 akita
Little Orphan Annie's: 5 Sandy
male: 3 dog
movie/TV: 4 Asta, Lady **5** Benji, Tramp **6** Lassie **9** Old Yeller, Rin Tin Tin
mythical: 8 Cerberus
Nixon's: 8 Checkers
Punch and Judy's: 4 Toby
Russian: 6 borzoi **7** samoyed
star: 6 Sirius **8** Canicula
Welsh: 5 corgi
wild: 5 adjag, dhole, dingo, guara, rabid **6** jackal **7** agouara **8** cimarron
young: 3 pup **5** puppy, whelp

Dogberry
character in: 19 Much Ado About Nothing
author: 11 Shakespeare

Dog Day Afternoon
director: 11 Sidney Lumet
cast: 8 Al Pacino **10** John Cazale **14** Charles Durning

dogged 8 stubborn **9** tenacious **10** determined, persistent **11** unremitting
dogie 4 calf **14** motherless calf
dogies 6 calves, cattle **16** motherless calves
dogma 5 credo, tenet **7** beliefs **8** doctrine **9** teachings **10** philosophy, principles **11** convictions
dogmatic 6 biased **8** stubborn **9** arbitrary, doctrinal, imperious, obstinate **10** prejudiced **11** dictatorial, domineering, opinionated

Dog Star
constellation of:
Hunting Dogs: **13** Canes Venatici
Larger Dog: **10** Canis Major
Smaller Dog: **10** Canis Minor

dogwood 6 Cornus
varieties: 5 Brown, Creek, False, Giant, Silky, Stiff **6** Pagoda, Poison **7** Chinese **8** American, Jamaican, Mountain, Panicled, Redosier, Siberian, Tatarian **9** Blood-twig, Flowering, Tartarian **10** Golden-twig, West Indian **11** Round-leaved **13** White Mountain

Doha, al-Dawha
capital of: 5 Qatar

do in 4 kill **6** murder **7** destroy, exhaust, tire out

Doktor Faust
opera by: 6 Busoni
character: 5 Faust **14** Duchess of Parma **14** Mephistopheles

dolce
music: 7 sweetly
dolce far niente 18 pleasing inactivity **20** it is sweet to do nothing
dolce vita 9 sweet life

Dol Common
character in: 12 The Alchemist
author: 6 Jonson

doldrums 5 blues, dumps, gloom **10** depression, melancholy
dole 4 deal, give **5** share **6** parcel **7** charity, handout, welfare **9** allotment **10** allocation **13** apportionment
doleful 3 sad **6** dismal, dreary, gloomy, woeful **7** joyless, unhappy **9** sorrowful

dolente
music: 9 sorrowful
dole out 4 give, mete **5** allot **6** parcel **7** portion **8** allocate, dispense **9** apportion **10** distribute
doling out 7 dealing **9** allotment, parceling **10** allocation, assignment **12** distribution **13** apportionment

Dolius
epithet of: 6 Hermes
means: 6 crafty
form: 5 slave
given to: 8 Penelope

doll 5 dolly, dummy, honey **6** beauty, puppet **7** darling, rag doll **8** baby doll, figurine, golliwog **9** teddy bear **10** marionette, sweetheart **11** pretty child
dollar 3 one **4** bean, bill, buck, coin, note, skin, yuan **5** money, tater, token **6** single **7** ironman, smacker **8** cartwheel, simolean

Dollar A Second
host: 9 Jan Murray

Dollar Bill
nickname of: 11 Bill Bradley
dollop 3 dab **4** blob, dash, lump **11** small amount

Doll's House, A
author: 11 Henrik Ibsen
character: 8 Krogstad **10** Nora Helmer **13** Torvald Helmer

dolly 3 toy **4** cart, doll **9** plaything **15** wheeled platform

Dolon
mentioned in: 5 Iliad
father: 7 Eumedes
killed by: 8 Diomedes, Odysseus

dolor 5 grief **6** sorrow **7** anguish, sadness
dolorous 3 sad **6** rueful, woeful **7** doleful, tearful, unhappy **8** dejected, downcast, grievous, mournful, pathetic, pitiable, wretched **9** anguished, cheerless, harrowing, miserable, sorrowful, woebegone **10** calamitous, despondent, lamentable, melancholy **11** distressing **12** disconsolate, heavy-hearted **13** grief-stricken

Dolphin
constellation of: 9 Delphinus

Dolphin, The
author: 12 Robert Lowell

dolt 4 clod, fool, jerk **5** idiot, moron **6** nitwit **7** half-wit, jackass **8** bonehead, imbecile, numskull **9** blockhead

doltish 4 dumb, slow 5 thick 6 simple, stupid 7 asinine, foolish, idiotic, moronic, witless 8 ignorant, retarded 9 brainless, imbecilic 10 half-witted, slow-witted 12 dunderheaded, muddleheaded, simple-minded 13 rattlebrained 14 featherbrained

domain 4 area, fief, land 5 field 6 empire, estate, region, sphere 7 kingdom 8 dominion, property, province 9 bailiwick, territory

Dombey and Son
  author: 14 Charles Dickens
  character: 4 Paul 5 Toots 6 Carker, Cuttle 8 Florence, Mr Dombey 9 Dr Blimber, Walter Gay 11 Joe Bagstock, Susan Nipper 12 Cousin Feenix, Edith Granger, Solomon Gills

dome
  Italian: 5 duomo

Domenichino
  real name: 16 Domenico Zampieri
  born: 5 Italy 7 Bologna
  artwork: 11 Hunt of Diana 16 Monsignor Agucchi 18 The Four Evangelists, The Life of St Cecilia 23 Last Communion of St Jerome 30 Landscape with Tobias and the Angel

domestic 4 cook, maid, tame 6 butler, native 7 endemic, servant 8 homemade, houseboy 9 attendant, home-grown 10 indigenous, not foreign 11 housebroken, native-grown, not imported 12 domesticated, hearth-loving 13 household help

domesticated 4 tame 11 housebroken

domicile 4 home 5 house 8 dwelling 9 residence 14 legal residence

dominance 4 edge 8 hegemony 9 advantage, authority, upper hand 10 precedence 11 preeminence, superiority

dominant 5 chief, major 6 ruling 8 superior 9 principal 10 commanding 11 controlling, outstanding 13 authoritative, most important, most prominent

dominate 4 rule 5 dwarf 6 direct, govern 7 command, control 8 domineer 9 tower over 11 preside over

dominating 6 lordly, ruling 7 topmost 8 dominant 9 directing, governing, principal, prominent 10 commanding 11 controlling, domineering, outstanding 12 advantageous 13 authoritative, most important 15 most outstanding

domination 4 rule 5 power 7 command, control, mastery 9 authority 11 superiority

domineer 7 control 8 dominate, lord over 9 dictate to, tyrannize

Dominican Republic
  capital/largest city: 12 Santo Domingo 14 Ciudad Trujillo
  others: 4 Azua, Bani, Moca, Pena, Polo 5 Bonao, Cotui, Nagua, Neiba, Nizao, Sosua 6 Higuey, La Vega, Oviedo 7 Sanchez 8 Barahona, Santiago 11 Puerto Plata 17 San Pedro de Macoris 21 San Francisco de Macoris
  measure: 3 ona 5 tarea 6 fanega
  monetary unit: 3 oro 4 peso 6 franco

  island: 5 Beata, Saona 8 Altovelo, Catalina 10 Hispaniola
  lake: 10 Enriquillo
  mountain: 4 Tina 5 Gallo, Neiba 7 Baoruco, Central 8 Bahoruco, Oriental 13 Sententrional
  highest point: 6 Duarte
  river: 4 Yuna 5 Ozama 11 Yaque del Sur 13 Yaque del Norte
  sea: 8 Atlantic 9 Caribbean
  physical feature:
  bay: 4 Ocoa, Yuma 5 Neiba 6 Rincon, Samana 7 Isabela 8 Calderas, Escocesa
  cape: 5 Beata, Falso 6 Cabron, Engano 7 Caucedo, Isabela, Macoris
  valley: 4 Real 5 Neyba
  people: 5 Negro, Taino 6 Indian 7 mulatto, Spanish 9 Caucasian
  discoverer: 8 Columbus
  language: 6 French 7 English, Spanish
  religion: 13 Roman Catholic
  feature:
  dance: 8 merengue
  religious pilgrimage: 8 romerias
  food:
  dessert: 8 pinonate
  fish/meat pastry: 10 pastelitos
  stew: 8 sancocho

domineering 8 arrogant, despotic, dogmatic 9 imperious 10 commanding, oppressive, tyrannical 11 dictatorial, overbearing 13 authoritative

dominion 4 land, rule 5 realm 6 domain, empire, region 7 command, mastery 9 authority, supremacy, territory 11 sovereignty 12 jurisdiction
  Hindu: 3 raj

Dominus 3 God 4 Lord

Dominus vobiscum 16 the Lord be with you

don 4 wear 5 put on 6 pull on 7 dress in, get into

Don
  origin: 5 Welsh
  form: 7 goddess
  son: 7 Gwydion
  daughter: 8 Arianrod

dona 4 lady 5 madam

Dona Flor and Her Two Husbands
  author: 10 Jorge Amado

Donalbain
  father: 6 Duncan
  brother: 7 Malcom

Donald Duck
  creator: 10 Walt Disney
  character:
  girlfriend: 5 Daisy
  nephew: 4 Huey 5 Dewey, Louie
  uncle: 7 Scrooge

Donar
  origin: 8 Germanic
  god of: 7 thunder

donate 4 give 6 bestow 7 present 8 bequeath 10 contribute 11 make a gift of

Donatello
  real name: 15 Donato di Niccolo
  born: 5 Italy 9 Florence

artwork: 5 David 6 St Mark 7 Zuccone 8 Jeremiah, St George 11 Gattamelata 12 Mary Magdalen 19 Judith and Holofernes, St John the Evangelist 22 Cavalcanti Annunciation

donation 4 gift 7 present 12 contribution

Don Careless
author: 8 Rex Beach

Don Carlos
author: 14 Johann Schiller
opera by: 5 Verdi
character: 7 Rodrigo 8 Philip II 9 Don Carlos 13 Princess Eboli 15 Grand Inquisitor 17 Elizabeth de Valois

Dondi
creator: 8 Gus Edson 10 Irwin Hasen
dog: 7 Queenie

done 5 ready 8 finished, prepared 9 completed 12 cooked enough 18 cooked sufficiently

done for 4 dead, gone, over, sunk 5 all up, ended, kaput, spent 6 beaten, doomed, ruined 7 all over, damaged, through 8 finished 9 exhausted

done in 4 beat 5 all in, slain, spent, tired, weary 6 bushed, killed, pooped 7 drained, wearied, worn out 8 dog tired, fatigued, murdered, tired out 9 bone weary, dead tired, played out 10 knocked off

Don Giovanni
also: 7 Don Juan 15 The Rake Punished
opera by: 6 Mozart
setting: 7 Seville
character: 7 Masetto, Zerlina 9 Donna Anna, Leporello 10 Don Ottavio 11 Donna Elvira 15 The Commendatore

Donizetti, Gaetano
born: 5 Italy 7 Bergamo
composer of: 10 Anna Bolena, La Favorita 11 Don Pasquale 12 Elixir of Love, Maria Stuarda 13 L'elisir d'amore, Marino Faliero, Torquato Tasso 14 Lucrezia Borgia 15 Roberto Devereux 16 Linda di Chamounix 17 Lucia di Lammermoor 21 Daughter of the Regiment

Don Juan 3 man 4 beau, wolf 5 Romeo, swain, wooer 6 fellow, squire, steady, suitor 7 admirer, courter, gallant, pursuer 8 Casanova, lothario, lover boy, paramour, young man 9 boyfriend, Lochinvar 10 ladykiller 15 gentleman caller

Don Juan
author: 21 George Gordon Lord Byron
character: 6 Haidee 9 Donna Inez 10 Donna Julia

donkey 3 ass 4 fool, mule 5 burro, idiot 7 jackass

Donlevy, Brian
wife: 12 Marjorie Lane
born: 7 Ireland 9 Portadown
roles: 9 Beau Geste 15 The Great McGinty 21 Two Years Before the Mast

Donn, Arabella
character in: 14 Jude the Obscure
author: 5 Hardy

donna 4 lady 5 madam

Donna Reed Show, The
character: 9 Jeff Stone, Mary Stone 10 Donna Stone 11 Dr Alex Stone, Midge Kelsey, Trisha Stone 12 Dr Dave Kelsey
cast: 8 Bob Crane, Carl Betz 9 Ann McCrea, Donna Reed 12 Paul Peterson 13 Patty Peterson 14 Shelley Fabares

Donne, John
author of: 7 Sermons 10 The Ecstasy, The Extasie 11 Holy Sonnets 15 Death Be Not Proud, Songs and Sonnets, The Canonization 20 Paradoxes and Problems 30 A Valediction Forbidding Mourning

donnish 7 preachy 8 academic, didactic, pedantic 9 pedagogic

Donnithorne, Arthur
character in: 8 Adam Bede
author: 5 Eliot

donnybrook 3 row 4 fray 5 brawl, fight, melee, set-to 6 affray, dustup, fracas, ruckus, rumpus 7 ruction, scuffle 8 skirmish 10 free-for-all 19 knock-down-and-drag-out

donor 5 giver 10 benefactor 11 contributor 12 humanitarian 14 philanthropist

do-nothing 5 idler 6 loafer 14 good-for-nothing

do not prosecute
Latin: 13 nolle prosequi

do not repeat
Latin: 12 non repetatur

Don Pasquale
opera by: 9 Donizetti
character: 6 Norina 7 Ernesto 11 Dr Malatesta

Don Quixote de la Mancha
also: 38 El ingenioso hidalgo Don Quijote de la Mancha
author: 17 Miguel de Cervantes (Saavedra)
character: 10 Pedro Perez 11 Sancho Panza 17 Dulcinea del Toboso
horse: 9 Rosinante
musical: 13 Man of La Mancha

doodad 5 gizmo 6 device, gadget 8 ornament 9 doohickey 10 decoration 11 contraption, contrivance, thingamabob, thingamajig 15 whatchamacallit

doohickey 5 gizmo, thing 6 device, dingus, gadget, object, widget 7 dojiggy, whatsis 8 dojigger 9 thingummy 11 thingamabob, thingamajig 14 thingamadoodle 15 whatchamacallit

Dooley, Thomas Anthony
founded: 6 MEDICO 31 Medical International Corporation
worked in: 13 Southeast Asia

Doolittle, Eliza
character in: 9 Pygmalion 10 My Fair Lady
author: 4 Shaw

doom 3 end, lot 4 fate, ruin 5 death, judge 7 condemn, convict, destiny, portion, verdict 8 judgment 10 Armageddon 11 destruction, Judgment Day 13 consign to

ruin, end of the world, pronouncement 15
resurrection day, the Last Judgment 17
mark for demolition

doomed 5 fated 6 damned, ruined 8 ill-
fated 9 condemned

doomsday 11 Judgment Day 13 Day of
Judgment, end of the world 15 the Last
Judgment

do one's best 3 try 6 strive 7 attempt 8 endeavor, go all out 9 take pains 12 make an
effort 13 give all one has 15 knock oneself
out

Doonesbury
   creator: 12 Garry Trudeau
   character: 2 B D 5 Honey, Rufus 6
   Calvin 7 Boopsie 9 Uncle Duke 12 Joanie
   Caucus 14 Mark Slackmeyer 18 Michael
   J Doonesbury

door 4 exit 5 entry 6 egress, portal 7 hallway, ingress 8 entrance 11 entranceway

Door hinges
   goddess of: 6 Cardea

doorway 5 entry 7 ingress, opening 8 entrance

Doorways
   god of: 5 Janus

dope 3 tip 4 drip, drug, fool, jerk, nerd,
news 5 creep, drugs, dummy, klutz, scoop
6 sedate, uppers 7 downers, opiates 8 additive 9 narcotics, narcotize, substance 10
antiseptic, astringent, medication 11 anesthetize, preparation 12 disinfectant 17 inside information

dope fiend 4 head, user 5 doper, freak 6
addict, junkie 7 hophead 8 cokehead 10
dope addict, drug abuser, drug addict

do penance 5 atone 7 expiate 10 make
amends

dopey 4 dumb 6 leaden, stupid, torpid 7 asinine, idiotic, witless 8 comatose, mindless, sluggish 9 brainless, lethargic 10
dull-witted, slow-witted, slumberous 11
block-headed, thickheaded 12 simple-
minded

Doppelganger 6 double 13 ghostly double
   literally: 12 double-walker

Doppler, Christian Johann
   field: 7 physics
   nationality: 8 Austrian
   discovered: 13 Doppler Effect

Dorcas
   also called: 7 Tabitha
   revived by: 5 Peter
   hometown: 5 Joppa

Doris
   father: 7 Oceanus
   mother: 6 Tethys
   husband: 6 Nereus
   mother of: 7 Nereids

Doritis
   epithet of: 9 Aphrodite
   means: 9 bountiful

dormancy 7 latency 8 inaction 10 inactivity,
quiescence, somnolence 11 hibernation

dormant 4 idle 8 inactive, sleeping 9 quiescent, somnolent 11 hibernating

Dorothy
   character in: 13 The Wizard of Oz
   author: 4 Baum

Dorset, Bertha and George
   characters in: 15 The House of Mirth
   author: 7 Wharton

dorsum 5 chine, spine 8 backbone

Dorus
   father: 6 Apollo, Hellen
   mother: 6 Orseis, Phthia
   killed by: 7 Aetolus

dose 2 OD 3 cut, nip 4 dram, pill, shot, slug
5 quota, share, slice 6 amount, needle, ration, tablet 7 capsule, measure, portion,
section, segment 8 division, overdose,
quantity 9 allotment, allowance, daily
dose, injection 10 percentage

Dos Passos, John
   author of: 3 U S A 11 The Big Money 13
   Three Soldiers 16 Nineteen Nineteen 17
   Manhattan Transfer 22 The Forty-Second
   Parallel

dossier 4 file 5 brief 6 record 9 portfolio 14
detailed report

Dostoevsky, Fyodor Mikhailovich
   author of: 8 The Idiot 9 The Double 10
   The Gambler 12 The Possessed 18
   Crime and Punishment 20 The Brothers
   Karamazov 23 Notes from the Under-
   ground

dot 3 dab 4 mark, spot 5 fleck, point, speck
6 dapple, period 9 small spot

dotage 8 senility 15 second childhood 16
feeblemindedness

dote 8 be senile, fuss over

dote on 5 adore, prize, spoil, value 6 pamper 7 cherish, indulge 8 fuss over, treasure
15 lavish affection

doting 4 fond 6 loving 9 indulgent, pampering 12 affectionate

double 4 dual, twin 5 clone 6 paired 7 replica, two-part 8 two-sided 9 ambiguous,
duplicate 10 dead ringer 11 again as
much, counterpart, meant for two, twice as
much 12 twice as great 13 multiply by two,
spitting image 15 increase twofold
   German: 12 Doppelganger

Double, The
   author: 16 Fyodor Dostoevsky

double-cross 5 rat on 6 betray, do dirt, tell
on, turn in 7 abandon, deceive, let down,
sell out, two-time 8 denounce, inform on,
run out on, snitch on 9 play Judas 10 be
disloyal 13 be treacherous, inform against,
play false with 14 break faith with 16 blow
the whistle on, sell down the river

double-crosser 5 cheat 7 traitor 8 betrayer,
deceiver, informer

Double-Dealer, The
   author: 15 William Congreve

double-dealing 5 false 6 deceit, sneaky,
tricky 7 crooked, devious, perfidy 8 bad
faith, betrayal, disloyal 9 deceitful, duplicity, falseness, treachery, two-timing 10
disloyalty, perfidious, sneakiness 11 crookedness, double-cross, duplicitous, treach-

erous 12 dishonorable 13 breach of faith, faithlessness

double entendre 12 off-color joke, risque remark 18 ambiguous statement

double entente 9 ambiguity

Double Indemnity
    director: 11 Billy Wilder
    cast: 13 Fred MacMurray 15 Barbara Stanwyck, Edward G Robinson
    script: 9 James Cain 15 Raymond Chandler

Double Life, A
    director: 11 George Cukor
    cast: 10 Signe Hasso 12 Edmond O'Brien, Ronald Colman 14 Shelley Winters
    Oscar for: 5 actor (Colman)
    script: 10 Ruth Gordon 11 Garson Kanin

double meaning 9 ambiguity
    French: 13 double entente 14 double entendre

doublet 4 pair 5 tunic 6 couple, jacket 10 two of a kind

double-talk 4 bunk, jazz 5 hokum 6 bunkum, drivel, gabble, jabber 7 baloney, blather, palaver, prattle, twaddle 8 flimflam, flummery, nonsense 9 gibberish 10 balderdash, hocus-pocus, mumbo jumbo 11 obfuscation 12 gobbledygook

double-walker
    German: 12 Doppelganger

Double X
    nickname of: 9 Jimmy Foxx

doubt 5 qualm 6 wonder 7 suspect 8 distrust, mistrust, question 9 misgiving, skeptical, suspicion 10 be doubtful, indecision 11 uncertainty 12 apprehension 13 feel uncertain 14 waver in opinion 15 have doubts about 16 lack confidence in, lack of conviction

Doubter see 6 Thomas

doubtful 5 vague 7 dubious, obscure, suspect, unclear 9 tentative, uncertain, undecided, unsettled 10 hesitating, irresolute, suspicious 11 unconvinced 12 inconclusive, questionable

doubtfulness 5 doubt 7 dubiety 8 distrust, mistrust, unbelief 9 disbelief, suspicion 10 skepticism 11 incredulity 14 lack of credence

Doubting see 6 Thomas

doucement
    music: 6 gently

douceur 3 tip 5 bribe 8 gratuity 9 sweetness

dough 4 cash, duff, spud 5 bread, crust, money, paster 6 batter, change, leaven, noodle 8 doughboy 11 infantryman

doughnut 4 cake, tire 5 bagel, torus 6 cymbal, dunker, sinker 7 beignet, cruller, twister

doughty 4 bold 5 brave 6 strong 8 fearless, intrepid, unafraid 9 confident, dauntless 10 courageous, determined 12 stout-hearted

Douglas, Archibald
    character in: 7 Marmion
    author: 5 Scott

Douglas, Kirk
    real name: 17 Issur Danielovitch
    son: 7 Michael
    born: 11 Amsterdam NY
    roles: 8 Champion 9 Spartacus 10 The Vikings 11 Lust for Life 14 Detective Story, Seven Days in May 17 The Glass Menagerie, Young Man with a Horn 18 Letter to Three Wives 22 Mourning Becomes Electra

Douglas, Lloyd C
    author of: 7 The Robe 23 The Magnificent Obsession

Douglas, Melvyn
    real name: 23 Melvyn Edouard Hesselberg
    wife: 12 Helen Gahagan
    born: 7 Macon GA
    roles: 3 Hud 9 Ninotchka 10 Being There

Douglas, Michael
    father: 4 Kirk
    roles: 4 Coma 10 Wall Street 11 Star Chamber 14 Jewel of the Nile 15 Fatal Attraction (Oscar) 16 The China Syndrome 17 Romancing the Stone

dour 4 sour 6 gloomy, morose, solemn, sullen 9 cheerless 10 forbidding, unfriendly

Douras, Marion Cecilia
    real name of: 12 Marion Davies

douse 4 soak 5 souse 6 drench 7 immerse 8 saturate, submerge 15 plunge into water

Dove, Noah's
    constellation of: 7 Columba

Dover Beach
    author: 13 Matthew Arnold

dovetail 4 jibe, join 5 match, tally, unite 8 coincide 9 harmonize 11 fit together 12 interlocking

dowager 5 widow 6 relict 7 elderly

dowdy 4 drab 5 tacky 6 frumpy, shabby, sloppy 8 slovenly 12 unattractive

dowel 3 peg, pin, rod 4 pole 5 stick 7 spindle

down 3 ill 4 blue, deck, drop, fell, gulp, sick 5 drink, floor 6 ailing 7 put away, swallow 8 dejected, downcast, feathers 9 depressed 10 dispirited 12 disheartened

down-and-out 4 sick 5 broke 9 penniless 12 impoverished, on one's uppers 13 incapacitated 15 under the weather

downcast 3 low, sad 4 blue 7 unhappy 8 dejected 9 cheerless, depressed 11 discouraged 12 disconsolate, disheartened

downfall 4 fall, ruin 6 shower 8 collapse, downpour 9 rainstorm, ruination 10 rain shower 11 destruction

downgrade 4 drop 5 lower 6 debase 7 decline, descent, way down 8 belittle, minimize 9 declivity, denigrate, devaluate 10 depreciate

downhearted 3 sad 7 unhappy 8 dejected, downcast 9 depressed, sorrowful 10 dispirited 11 discouraged 12 disheartened

downheartedness 5 gloom 6 dismay 7 despair, sadness 9 dejection, pessimism 10 depression, low spirits, melancholy 11 despondency 12 hopelessness 14 discouragement

down in the dumps 4 blue, glum 6 gloomy 7 in a funk 9 depressed 10 despondent 13 in the doldrums

down in the mouth 3 sad 6 dismal, woeful 7 joyless, unhappy 8 dejected, downcast 9 depressed, sorrowful, woebegone 10 lugubrious 12 disconsolate

downpayment 6 binder 7 advance, deposit 9 money down

downpour 6 shower 9 rainstorm 10 cloudburst, rain shower

downright 4 open 5 blunt, frank, total, utter 6 candid, direct, honest, really 7 in truth, plainly, sincere, utterly 8 absolute, actually, complete 9 out-and-out 10 aboveboard, completely, thoroughly 12 unmistakably 13 thoroughgoing, unequivocally 15 straightforward

Downright
  character in: 19 Every Man in His Humour
  author: 6 Jonson

downstairs 5 below 6 cellar 8 basement 10 first floor 11 ground floor

down the drain 4 gone, lost 9 up in smoke 12 out the window

down-to-earth 5 crass, plain, sober, solid 6 casual, coarse, earthy, simple 7 relaxed 8 informal, sensible 9 practical, pragmatic, realistic 10 hardheaded, hard-boiled, nononsense 11 plain-spoken, substantial 12 matter-of-fact, unidealistic 13 unsentimental

downtown 9 inner city, urban area 10 center city, metropolis 16 business district, metropolitan area

downtrodden 9 exploited, oppressed 10 tyrannized 11 subservient 12 harshly ruled

downturn 3 dip, sag 4 drop, fall, skid, slip 5 slide, slump 6 plunge, waning 7 decline, reverse, setback 8 decrease 9 downslide, downswing, downtrend, dwindling, recession 10 depression, diminution 12 degeneration 13 deterioration

Down Under see 9 Australia

down with
  French: 4 a bas

downy 4 soft 5 fuzzy, nappy, plumy, quiet 6 fleecy, fluffy 7 cunning, knowing 8 feathery 9 featherbed

do wrong 3 err, sin 8 go astray 9 misbehave 10 transgress

Doyle, Sir Arthur Conan
  author of: 13 The Sign of Four 15 A Study in Scarlet, The White Company 25 The Hound of the Baskervilles 26 Adventures of Sherlock Holmes
  character: 12 Dr John Watson 13 Mycroft Holmes 14 Sherlock Holmes 17 Inspector Lestrade, Professor Moriarty

doze 3 nap 6 catnap, siesta, snooze 10 forty winks, light sleep 12 sleep lightly

dozy 4 lazy 6 drowsy, sleepy 7 languid 9 lethargic, somnolent

D P 5 exile 6 emigre 7 outcast, refugee 8 deportee 10 expatriate 14 banished person, deported person 15 displaced person 16 political refugee

drab 4 dull, gray 5 dingy 6 dismal, dreary, gloomy, somber 9 cheerless, dull brown 10 lackluster

drabness 8 dullness 9 dinginess 10 dreariness, gloominess 13 colorlessness

Dracula
  author: 10 Bram Stoker
  character: 8 Dr Seward 10 Mina Murray 12 Count Dracula, Dr Van Hesling, Lucy Westenra 14 Arthur Holmwood, Jonathan Harker

draft 4 drag, gulp, haul, pull, wind 5 drink 6 breeze, induct, sketch 7 diagram, outline, swallow 9 conscript, induction 10 money order 11 postal order, rough sketch 12 conscription, current of air 15 military service 16 drawing from a cask 18 preliminary version 22 call for military service

drafty 6 breezy, chilly

drag 3 lug 4 bore, haul, pull 5 bring, crawl, trail 6 dredge 7 be drawn 9 inch along 10 creep along, move slowly, spoilsport, wet blanket 11 party-pooper

Dragnet
  character: 8 (Sgt) Ed Jacobs 9 (Sgt) Ben Romero, (Sgt) Joe Friday 10 (Officer) Bill Gannon, (Officer) Frank Smith
  cast: 8 Jack Webb 9 Herb Ellis 11 Harry Morgan 12 Ben Alexander 14 Barney Phillips 16 Barton Yarborough
  setting: 10 Los Angeles

Dragon 14 Leviathan
  constellation of: 5 Draco

drag on 4 last 6 endure, keep on, keep up 7 persist 8 continue 9 persevere

drag one's feet 5 crawl, creep 6 dawdle 9 waste time 10 move slowly 13 procrastinate

dragonfly
  varieties: 5 biddy 6 darner 7 skimmer 8 clubtail, grayback 9 amberwing 12 elisa skimmer

Dragon Seed
  author: 10 Pearl S Buck

Dragon's teeth
  sown by: 6 Cadmus
  location: 6 Thebes
  grew into: 8 warriors

dragoon 5 bully, force 6 coerce, compel 7 trooper 8 browbeat, bulldoze, cavalier, horseman, pressure 9 strong-arm 10 cavalryman 12 horse soldier, horse trooper 14 mounted soldier

drag through the mud 5 smear, sully, taint 6 debase, defame, smirch, vilify 7 degrade, tarnish, vitiate 8 disgrace, dishonor 9 discredit, disparage 10 stigmatize

drain 3 sap 4 drag, pipe, tube 5 empty, sewer, use up 6 outlet, strain 7 channel, conduit, debouch, deplete, flow out, pump off 8 empty out 9 depletion, discharge, dissipate 10 impoverish

drainage 4 flow 9 discharge

drained 4 beat 5 all in, empty, spent, tired, weary 6 bushed, done in, pooped, used up 7 emptied, wearied, worn out 8 consumed, depleted, dog tired, expended, fatigued, finished, tired out 9 dead tired, enervated, exhausted, played out

Drake, Stan
    creator/artist of: 21 The Heart of Juliet Jones

Drake, Temple
    character in: 9 Sanctuary
    author: 8 Faulkner

dram
    abbreviation: 2 dr

drama 4 play 6 acting 8 the stage 9 direction, vividness 10 excitement, the theater 11 mise-en-scene 15 dramatic quality, intense interest, theatrical piece
    god of: 7 Bacchus

dramatic 8 striking 9 climactic, emotional 10 theatrical 11 suspenseful 12 melodramatic 13 for the theater

dramatics 6 acting 7 emoting 9 theatrics 10 dramaturgy, stagecraft 11 hamming it up, histrionics, thespianism

dramatis personae 4 cast 6 actors 7 players 10 performers 16 cast of characters, list of performers

dramaturgy 5 drama 7 theater 10 stagecraft 11 dramatic art

Drambuie
    type: 7 liqueur
    origin: 8 Scotland
    flavor: 5 herbs, honey
    with scotch: 9 Rusty Nail

Drances
    enemy of: 6 Turnus

drape 4 deck, garb, veil, wrap 5 adorn, array, cloak, cover, dress 6 attire, bedeck, enrobe, enwrap, shroud, swathe, wrap up 7 apparel, bedight, envelop, festoon, sheathe, swaddle 8 enshroud, enswathe

drastic 4 dire, rash 7 bizarre, extreme, radical 8 dreadful 9 dangerous 10 outlandish 11 deleterious

Dravidian
    language group: 3 Kui 5 Ghond, Tamil 6 Teluga 8 Kanarese 9 Malayalam
    spoken in: 5 India 6 Ceylon 8 Sri Lanka

draw 3 get, tie, tow 4 drag, etch, haul, limn, lure, pick, pull, take 5 charm, draft, drain, evoke, infer, write 6 allure, come-on, deduce, elicit, entice, extend, make up, siphon, sketch 7 attract, distort, draw out, extract, make out, pick out, pull out, pump out, stretch, suck dry, take out, wrinkle 8 contract, deadlock, elongate, protract 9 attenuate, pull along, stalemate 10 attraction, bring forth, enticement, inducement, make appear 14 make a picture of

draw away 2 go 5 leave 6 go back, shrink 7 retreat 8 withdraw

drawback 8 handicap, obstacle 9 detriment, hindrance 10 impediment 12 disadvantage 14 stumbling block

draw back 6 flinch, recoil 7 back off, retreat 8 move away, withdraw

draw close 3 hug 4 come, near 6 arrive, enfold 7 embrace 8 approach, come nigh, gain upon 10 move toward

drawers 5 pants 6 shorts 7 panties 8 bloomers, calzoons, trousers 9 pantalets, underwear 10 underpants

draw forth 5 evoke 6 elicit 7 distill, extract

drawing 5 study 6 sketch 7 lottery, picture 9 depiction, selection 11 delineation 12 illustration

drawing apart 8 dividing 9 diverging 10 separating 12 splitting off

drawing out 9 expansion, extension 10 elongation, stretching 11 attenuation, lengthening, protraction 12 prolongation

drawing power 4 pull 6 allure, appeal 9 magnetism 10 attraction, enticement 11 fascination

drawing room 5 salon 6 parlor 10 living room 11 sitting room 13 reception room

drawn out 4 long 7 lengthy 8 extended 9 elongated, prolonged 10 lengthened, protracted

draw out 5 educe, evoke 6 elicit, expand, extend, extort 7 distill, enlarge, extract, prolong, spin out, stretch 8 elongate, lengthen, protract 9 attenuate, call forth 10 stretch out

draw the line 5 limit 8 contrast, separate 12 fix a boundary 13 differentiate

draw to a close 3 end 6 finish 8 conclude 11 come to an end

draw together 4 herd, mass, pack 5 bunch, crowd, flock, group 6 gather, huddle 7 cluster, collect, tighten 8 assemble, compress, contract 9 constrict 10 congregate

draw up 3 map 5 draft 6 make up, map out 7 charter, diagram, outline 9 blueprint

draw up plans 5 draft 6 design, sketch 7 outline

dray 4 cart 5 wagon 7 tipcart, tumbrel 8 dumpcart

dread 4 fear 5 awful 6 fright, terror 7 anguish, anxiety, cower at, fearful 8 alarming, cringe at 10 be afraid of, horrifying, shrink from, terrifying 11 fearfulness, frightening, trepidation 12 apprehension 20 anticipate with horror

dreaded object
    French: 9 bete noire

dreadful 5 awful 6 tragic 7 fearful 8 alarming, horrible, shocking, terrible 9 frightful 11 distressing

dream 3 joy 4 goal, hope, muse, wish 5 think 6 desire, vision 7 delight, fantasy, hope for, incubus, reverie, think up 8 consider, pleasure, prospect 9 nightmare 11 expectation, have as a goal 13 look forward to, lost in thought

Dream Merchants, The
    author: 13 Harold Robbins

Dream of the Golden Mountains, The
    author: 13 Malcolm Cowley

Dreams

god of: 6 Icelus, Oniros 7 Oneiros 8 Morpheus 9 Phantasus

Dream Songs, The

author: 12 John Berryman

dream up 5 frame, hatch 6 create, invent 7 concoct 8 conceive, contrive

dreamy 4 airy 5 blank, empty, vague 6 absent, musing, unreal 8 ethereal, fanciful, illusory, soothing 9 fantastic, wonderful 10 delightful 11 preoccupied, unrealistic 13 unsubstantial 14 out of this world

dreariness 9 bleakness 10 desolation, dismalness, gloominess, melancholy 13 cheerlessness

dreary 3 sad 4 drab 5 bleak 6 dismal, gloomy 7 forlorn 8 mournful 9 cheerless 10 depressing, melancholy

dregs 6 rabble 7 deposit, grounds, residue 8 canaille, riffraff, sediment 9 settlings, worst part 11 lower depths

Dreiser, Theodore

author of: 8 The Titan 12 Sister Carrie, The Financier 17 An American Tragedy

drench 3 wet 4 soak 5 douse 8 saturate

dress 4 curl, deck, do up, garb, gown, robe, trim 5 adorn, frock, groom, treat 6 attire 7 apparel, arrange, bandage, cleanse, clothes, comb out, costume, garnish 8 clothing, decorate, ornament 9 disinfect, embellish 12 put on clothes 13 clothe oneself

Dressed to Kill

director: 12 Brian De Palma

cast: 10 Nancy Allen 11 Keith Gordon 12 Michael Caine 14 Angie Dickinson

dressed up 7 adorned, duded up 8 costumed, dolled up, tarted up 9 decorated, disguised, in costume 10 ornamented 11 embellished

dresser 6 bureau 7 cabinet, commode 8 cupboard 10 chiffonier 14 chest of drawers

dressing-down 6 rebuke 7 censure, chiding, reproof 8 reproach, scolding 9 reprimand 10 bawling-out, chewing-out, upbraiding 11 castigation, reprobation 12 remonstrance 13 tongue-lashing

dressing-gown

French: 13 robe-de-chambre

dressmaker 9 couturier, midinette 10 couturiere, seamstress

dress up 5 adorn 6 doll up 7 enhance, improve 8 beautify, ornament, spruce up 9 embellish, embroider, smarten up 10 exaggerate

Dreyfuss, Richard

born: 10 Brooklyn NY

roles: 4 Jaws 6 Tin Men 8 Stakeout 14 The Goodbye Girl (Oscar) 15 Moon Over Parador 16 American Graffiti 24 Down and Out in Beverly Hills 29 Close Encounters of the Third Kind 31 The Apprenticeship of Duddy Kravitz

dribble 4 drip, kick 6 bounce 7 drizzle, trickle 11 fall in drops, run bit by bit

driblet 4 drip, drop, tear 7 droplet, globule

dried up 4 arid 7 drained, parched 9 prunelike, shriveled 10 dehydrated, desiccated

drift 3 aim 4 flow, gist, heap, mass, pile 5 amass, amble, sense 6 course, gather, object, pile up, ramble, stream, wander 7 current, meander, meaning, purpose, scatter 8 movement 9 direction, intention, objective 10 accumulate 11 implication, peregrinate 12 accumulation, be borne along

drifter 3 bum 4 hobo 5 idler, tramp 6 loafer 8 derelict, vagabond 16 ne'er-do-well

drill 4 bore 5 punch, train 6 pierce 8 exercise, practice, puncture, training, work with 10 boring tool, repetition 11 instruction 17 repeated exercises

type: 4 hand 5 twist 8 electric

drilling 4 rote 6 boring 8 practice, training 9 schooling 10 discipline 11 preparation

drink 3 sip 4 gulp, swig 5 booze, taste, toast 6 absorb, imbibe, ingest, salute, take in 7 alcohol, swallow 8 beverage, libation 9 partake of, the bottle 10 alcoholism 11 drunkenness 15 alcoholic liquor 17 liquid refreshment

type of: 3 cup, fix 4 fizz, flip, mull, puff, sour 5 daisy, julep, punch, shrub, sling, smash 6 cooler, frappe, rickey 7 cobbler, stinger 8 highball

drinker 3 sot 4 lush, wino 5 dipso, drunk, rummy, souse 6 bibber, boozer, sponge 7 guzzler, imbiber, tippler, waterer 8 drunkard 9 alcoholic, inebriate

drink in 6 absorb, digest, soak up, take in 10 assimilate 14 immerse oneself

Drinking

god of: 5 Comus

drinking spree 4 orgy, toot 5 binge, drunk 6 bender 8 beer-bust, carousal 9 bacchanal

drink up 4 gulp 5 quaff 6 absorb, guzzle, soak up 7 consume, swallow

drip 3 ass 4 bore, jerk, nerd 5 creep, dummy, klutz 6 splash 7 dribble, drizzle, trickle 8 sprinkle

dripping 3 wet 4 damp 5 soggy 6 soaked, sodden 10 soaking wet

drive 4 goad, lead, mean, move, prod, push, ride, rush, spur, urge 5 force, guide, impel, motor, press, steer, surge 6 coerce, compel, incite, intend, outing 7 advance, conduct, go by car, impulse, operate, suggest 8 ambition, campaign, motivate 9 excursion, insinuate, trip by car, urge along 10 motivation

drive apart 8 alienate, estrange 9 disaffect

drive away 4 rout, shoo 5 chase, deter, repel 6 rebuff 7 repulse 8 alienate 11 put to flight, send packing

drive home 7 impress 8 hammer at

drivel 5 drool 6 babble, ramble, slaver 7 dribble, slobber 8 babbling, nonsense, rambling 9 gibberish 12 talk nonsense 13 senseless talk, talk foolishly

drive out 4 fire 5 chase, depel, eject, evict, exile, expel, force, roust 6 compel, remove 7 dismiss, repulse 8 discharge, exorcise

driver 6 cowboy, drover 8 herdsman 9 chauffeur

drizzle 3 fog 4 mist, rain 7 dribble 8 sprinkle

drizzly 3 wet 4 damp 5 foggy, misty, rainy

Dr Jekyll and Mr Hyde
   author: 20 Robert Louis Stevenson
   character: 5 Poole 10 Mr Utterson 13 Dr Henry Jekyll 14 Dr Hastie Lanyon

Dr Kildare
   character: 14 Dr James Kildare 18 Dr Leonard Gillespie
   cast: 13 Raymond Massey 18 Richard Chamberlain
   hospital: 12 Blair General

Dr No
   author: 10 Ian Fleming

Dr Strangelove or How I Learned to Stop Worrying and Love the Bomb
   director: 14 Stanley Kubrick
   cast: 9 Peter Bull 10 Keenan Wynn 11 Slim Pickens 12 George C Scott, Peter Sellers 14 James Earl Jones, Sterling Hayden

Dr Zhivago
   author: 14 Boris Pasternak
   character: 4 Lara
   setting: 17 Russian Revolution

droll 5 funny 7 offbeat, strange 8 humorous 9 eccentric, laughable, whimsical 12 oddly amusing

drollery 3 wit 5 humor 6 banter, comedy, whimsy 7 jesting

Dromio
   character in: 17 The Comedy of Errors
   author: 11 Shakespeare

drone 3 hum 4 buzz, whir 5 idler 6 loafer 7 vibrate 8 parasite 9 murmuring, vibration 10 lazy person

drool 6 drivel, slaver 7 dribble, slobber 8 salivate 15 water at the mouth

droop 3 dim, sag 4 flag, sink 5 lower 6 weaken, wither 8 diminish, hang down 9 lose vigor 14 hang listlessly 15 incline downward

droopy 4 bent, blue, down, limp 5 baggy, bowed, slack 6 dashed, pining 7 doleful, sagging, subdued 8 cast down, dangling, dejected, downcast 9 depressed 10 despairing, despondent, dispirited, spiritless, world-weary 11 downhearted, hanging down, languishing 14 down in the mouth

drop 3 can, dab 4 bead, dash, deck, dive, drip, fall, fell, fire, omit, sack, sink, tear 5 abyss, floor, leave, lower, pinch, slide, slope, smack, trace 6 give up, lessen, plunge 7 abandon, decline, descend, descent, dismiss, dribble, driblet, dwindle, forsake, globule, plummet, slacken, smidgen, soupcon, trickle 8 decrease, diminish, leave out, lowering 9 declivity, discharge, knock down, precipice, terminate 10 sprinkling 12 bring to an end 13 fail to include 15 cease to consider, fail to pronounce

drop anchor 4 dock, moor 5 tie up

drop in 4 call, come 5 visit 6 appear, come by, look in, show up, stop by, turn up 7 stop off 9 pay a visit

droplet 4 bead, drip, tear 7 driblet, globule 8 spherule

droplets of moisture 3 dew, fog 4 mist 5 sweat 12 condensation

drop out 4 quit 5 leave 6 resign, retire

dross 4 scum, slag 5 waste 6 cinder, scoria 8 clinkers, impurity

drought, drouth 4 lack, need, want 6 dearth 7 aridity, paucity 8 scarcity, shortage 10 deficiency, dry weather, lack of rain 13 insufficiency

drover 6 cowboy, driver 7 cowpoke 8 herdsman, shepherd 10 cowpuncher

drown 4 soak 5 flood 6 deluge, drench, engulf 7 immerse 8 inundate, overcome, submerge 9 overpower, overwhelm, suffocate, swallow up 10 asphyxiate

drowse 3 nap, nod 4 doze, laze 5 dover, drone, sleep 6 snooze 7 slumber 8 languish 10 sleepiness

drowsy 4 dozy, lazy, slow 5 tired 6 sleepy 7 languid 8 hypnotic, listless, sluggish, soothing 9 lethargic, somnolent, soporific

drub 3 hit 4 beat, cane, flog, whip 5 whale 6 thrash 9 bastinado

drubbing 6 caning 7 beating, licking, tanning 9 trouncing 11 shellacking

drudge 4 grub, hack, plod, toil 5 labor, slave 6 lackey, menial, toiler 7 grubber 8 inferior, struggle 9 underling 11 subordinate

drudgery 4 toil 5 grind 7 travail 8 hack work 11 menial labor 15 distasteful work

Druk-Yul *see* 6 Bhutan

drum 3 din, keg, rap, tap, tub 4 beat, cask, roar, roll 5 expel, force 6 barrel, harp on, rumble, tattoo 7 dismiss, pulsate 8 drive out, hammer at 9 discharge, drive home, reiterate 11 beat a tattoo, din in the ear, reverberate

Drums
   author: 9 James Boyd

Drums Along the Mohawk
   author: 14 Walter D Edmonds
   character: 4 Lana 9 Blue Black, John Wolff 11 Joseph Brant, Mark Demooth 12 Mrs McKlennan 13 Gilbert Martin 20 Magdelena Borst Martin

drunk 3 sot 4 bast, lush, soak 5 binge, rummy, souse, tipsy, toper 6 barfly, bender, looped, sodden, soused, stewed, zapped, zonked 7 smashed 8 beer-bust, besotted, carousal 9 alcoholic, plastered 10 inebriated 11 dipsomaniac, intoxicated 13 drinking spree, under the influence

drunkard 3 sot 4 lush, soak, wino 5 rummy, souse, toper 6 barfly 9 alcoholic 11 dipsomaniac

drunkenness 10 alcoholism 11 inebriation 12 intoxication

Drury, Allen
   author of: 14 Capable of Honor, Return to Thebes 15 The Promise of Joy 16 Ad-

vise and Consent 19 Come Nineveh
Come Tyre

dry 4 arid, blot, dull, wipe 5 droll 6 boring,
low-key 7 deadpan, parched, tedious,
thirsty 8 rainless 9 dehydrate, desiccate, shrivel up, wearisome 10 dehydrated, monotonous 13 uninteresting

Dryad
  form: 5 deity, nymph
  location: 5 woods

Dryas
  father: 8 Lycurgus
  killed by: 8 Lycurgus

dry as dust 4 arid, dull, sere 7 parched 8
pedantic, withered 9 shriveled 13 unimaginative

Dryden, John
  author of: 10 All for Love 11 Mac
  Flecknoe 14 Annus Mirabilis 15 Alexander's Feast, Marriage-a-la-Mode 20
  Absalom and Achitophel, Essay on Dramatic Poesy, The Hind and the Panther
  22 Fables Ancient and Modern

dry goods 5 cloth, goods 6 fabric 8 material 9 yard goods 10 piece goods

dryness 7 aridity, drought 8 aridness 11 de-
hydration

Dryope
  form: 5 nymph
  changed into: 6 poplar

Dry Salvages
  author: 7 T S Eliot

dry up 6 wither 7 shrivel 9 dehydrate, desiccate, evaporate

dual 6 double 7 twofold, two-part

dub 4 call, name 5 label 6 knight 7 baptize
8 christen, nickname 9 designate

dublety 5 doubt 8 unbelief 9 disbelief 10
skepticism 11 incredulity 12 doubtfulness
14 lack of credence

Dubin's Lives
  author: 14 Bernard Malamud

dubious 5 shady 6 unsure 7 suspect 8
doubtful 9 skeptical, uncertain 10 suspicious, unreliable 11 unconvinced 12 questionable, undependable 13 untrustworthy

Dublin
  brewery: 8 Guinness
  capital of: 7 Ireland
  Irish: 8 Dubh Linn (black pool) 15 Baile
  Atha Cliath (town of the Hurdle Ford)
  landmark: 10 Four Courts 11 Custom
  House 12 Abbey Theater, Christ Church,
  Dublin Castle 13 Leinster House 18
  Kilmainham 19 St Patrick's Cathedral
  mountain: 7 Wicklow
  museum: 8 National 10 James Joyce
  park: 7 Phoenix
  river: 6 Liffey
  rulers: 7 English, Vikings
  scene of: 12 Easter Rising (1916)
  university: 14 Trinity College

Dubliners
  author: 10 James Joyce

DuBois, Blanche
  character in: 21 A Streetcar Named Desire
  author: 8 Williams

Du Bois, W E B
  founded: 5 NAACP
  author of: 19 The Souls of Black Folk

Dubonnet
  type: 8 aperitif
  origin: 6 France
  ingredient: 7 quinine, red wine
  with gin: 3 BVD 8 Napoleon
  with rum: 10 Bushranger

duc 4 duke

Duccio di Buoninsegna
  born: 5 Italy 6 Sienna
  artwork: 6 Maesta 18 The Rucellai Madonna (attributed)

duce, il duce 6 despot, tyrant 8 dictator 9
Mussolini

Duchamp, Marcel
  born: 6 France 8 Normandy 10 Blainville
  artwork: 5 LHOOQ 9 Given That 11
  Etant Donnes 12 Bicycle Wheel 13 The
  Large Glass (The Bride Stripped Bare by
  Her Bachelors Even) 24 Nude Descend-
  ing a Staircase 37 The King and Queen
  Surrounded by Swift Nudes

Duchess of Malfi, The
  author: 11 John Webster
  character: 6 Bosola 7 Antonio 8
  Giovanna 9 Ferdinand 11 The Cardinal

duck 4 clee, coot, lory, smew, teal, veer 5
avoid, dodge, drake, eider, elude, evade,
goose, ruddy, shirk, stoop 6 canard, canvas, crouch, gannet, Peking, scoter,
swerve 7 gadwall, mallard, Muscovy, pintail, pochard 8 baldpate, freckled, redshank, shelduck, shoveler, sidestep, submerge 9 merganser, whistling 10 bufflehead, canvasback 11 wood steamer 13
give the slip to
  male: 5 drake
  group of: 5 brace

Duck Soup
  director: 10 Leo McCarey
  cast: 5 Chico, Harpo, Zeppo 7 Groucho
  (Rufus T Firefly) 12 Louis Calhern,
  Raquel Torres 14 Margaret Dumont
  setting: 9 Freedonia

duct 4 pipe, tube 6 vessel 7 channel, conduit

ductile 6 docile, pliant, supple 7 elastic,
plastic, pliable, tensile 8 amenable, bendable, flexible, formable, moldable, shapable, swayable 9 adaptable, compliant,
malleable, tractable 10 extensible, manageable, submissive 11 complaisant, ma-
nipulable, stretchable, susceptible

dud 3 dog 4 bomb, bust, flop, hash 5 botch,
lemon, loser 6 bummer, fiasco, fizzle 7
clinker, debacle, failure, washout 11 lead
balloon, miscarriage 14 disappointment

dude 3 fop 4 beau 5 dandy 7 peacock 11
city dweller, city slicker 12 Beau Brummel

Dudevant, Aurore
  real name of: 10 George Sand

duds 4 togs 5 flops 6 attire 7 apparel, clothes, fizzles, threads 8 clothing, failures, garments

due 4 owed 5 ample, owing 6 enough, proper, unpaid 7 fitting, merited 8 adequate, becoming, deserved, expected, plenty of, rightful, suitable 9 in arrears, scheduled 10 sufficient 11 appropriate, outstanding

duel
  French: 15 affaire d'honneur

Duel, The
  author: 15 Alexander Kuprin

duenna 8 guardian 9 attendant, chaperone, custodian, protector

dues 4 fees 7 charges 10 assessment

Duessa
  character in: 15 The Faerie Queene
  author: 7 Spenser

duet 3 duo, two 4 pair 6 couple 7 twosome

Dufy, Raoul
  born: 6 France 7 Le Havre
  artwork: 7 The Palm 15 Riders in the Wood 16 Chateau and Horses 18 Deauville Racetrack, Posters at Trouville

dugout 3 den 4 cave 5 canoe 6 cavity, hollow 7 shelter

Duino Elegies
  author: 16 Rainer Maria Rilke

Dukas, Paul
  born: 5 Paris 6 France
  composer of: 6 La Peri 18 Ariane et Barbe-Bleue 19 Ariadne and Bluebeard 22 The Sorcerer's Apprentice

duke
  French: 3 duc

Duke
  nickname of: 9 John Wayne

Duke, Patty (Patty Duke Astin)
  real name: 13 Anna Marie Duke
  husband: 9 John Astin
  born: 10 Elmhurst NY
  roles: 11 Helen Keller 16 The Miracle Worker, The Patty Duke Show, Valley of the Dolls

Dukenfield, William Claude
  real name of: 8 W C Fields

Duke Snider
  nickname of: 11 Edwin Snider

dulcet 7 lyrical, musical, tuneful 8 pleasing, sonorous 9 melodious 11 mellifluous

Dulcinea del Toboso
  character in: 10 Don Quixote
  author: 9 Cervantes

dull 4 slow 5 blunt, dense, muted, quiet, thick, trite, vapid 6 boring, obtuse, stupid 7 muffled, not keen, prosaic, subdued, vacuous 8 deadened, inactive, not brisk, not sharp 9 dimwitted 10 indistinct, lackluster, uneventful 13 unimaginative, uninteresting

Dull
  character in: 16 Love's Labour's Lost
  author: 11 Shakespeare

dullard 4 dolt 5 dummy, dunce 6 nitwit 7 halfwit 8 dumbbell, imbecile

Dullea, Keir
  born: 11 Cleveland OH
  roles: 12 David and Lisa 18 Butterflies Are Free 27 Two Thousand One: A Space Odyssey

dullness 6 idiocy, tedium 8 dumbness, lethargy, monotony, slowness 9 bluntness, ignorance, stupidity, vapidness 10 boringness, imbecility, obtuseness 11 tediousness 13 dim-wittedness 15 thickheadedness

dull-witted 5 dazed, fuzzy 7 bemused, muddled, stunned 8 confused 9 stupefied

Dulong, Pierre-Louis
  field: 7 physics 9 chemistry
  nationality: 6 French
  discovered: 19 nitrogen trichloride
  studied: 4 heat 13 atomic weights

duly 6 on time 8 properly, suitably 9 correctly 10 deservedly, punctually, rightfully 13 appropriately 15 at the proper time

Dumaine
  character in: 16 Love's Labour's Lost
  author: 11 Shakespeare

Dumas, Alexandre (fils)
  author of: 7 Camille 11 Le Demi-Monde 17 La Dame aux Camelias 21 The Lady of the Camellias
  Camille inspired: 10 La Traviata
  opera by: 5 Verdi

Dumas, Alexandre (pere)
  author of: 17 The Queen's Necklace 18 The Three Musketeers 19 The Man in the Iron Mask 21 The Count of Monte Cristo 22 The Vicomte de Bragelonne

Du Maurier, Daphne
  author of: 7 Rebecca 10 Jamaica Inn 11 Don't Look Now 14 My Cousin Rachel 15 Frenchman's Creek 19 The House on the Strand

Du Maurier, George
  author of: 6 Trilby 10 The Martian 13 Peter Ibbetson

dumb 3 mum 4 dull, mute 5 dense, dopey 6 silent, stupid 7 foolish, aphasic 8 aphasiac 9 dim-witted 13 unintelligent 17 incapable of speech

dumbbell 3 oaf 4 clod, dolt, dope, fool 5 booby, clown, dummy, dunce, idiot, moron 6 dimwit, nitwit 7 dullard, halfwit 8 dumb-dumb, dummkopf, imbecile, lunkhead, meathead, numskull 9 birdbrain, blockhead, ignoramus, lamebrain, numbskull, simpleton 10 noodlehead

dumb-dumb 3 ass 4 dope, fool 5 booby, dunce, idiot, moron, ninny 6 dimwit, nitwit 7 halfwit 8 bonehead, imbecile, lunkhead, numskull 9 blockhead, lamebrain, numbskull 10 nincompoop

dumbfound, dumfound 4 stun 5 amaze 7 startle 8 astonish 11 flabbergast

dumbfounded 5 agape 6 amazed 7 stunned 9 astounded, stupefied 10 astonished, speechless 11 open-mouthed 13 flabbergasted

dumbness 6 idiocy 8 dullness 9 asininity, stupidity, thickness 10 imbecility 11 witlessness 12 wordlessness 14 speechlessness 15 thickheadedness

dumbstruck 5 agape 6 amazed, gaping 7 riveted 9 awestruck, stupefied 10 speechless 11 electrified, open-mouthed 13 flabbergasted

dummy 3 oaf 4 dolt, form 5 clown, idiot, klutz, model 6 figure 9 blockhead, mannequin, simpleton 10 dunderhead 11 chowderhead, knucklehead

dump 3 hut 4 hole, toss 5 empty, hovel, shack 6 shanty, unload 8 get rid of, junkyard 9 dispose of 10 refuse pile 11 rubbish heap

dumpy 5 squat 7 lumpish 13 short and stout

Dumuzi
   origin: 8 Sumerian
   god of: 8 pastures 10 vegetation
   consort of: 6 Inanna

Dunaway, Faye
   real name: 18 Dorothy Faye Dunaway
   born: 8 Bascom FL
   roles: 6 Barfly, Milady 7 Network (Oscar) 8 The Champ 9 Chinatown 13 Mommie Dearest 14 Bonnie and Clyde 15 Towering Inferno 17 The Four Musketeers 18 The Three Musketeers

Duncan
   character in: 7 Macbeth
   author: 11 Shakespeare

Duncan, Sandy
   born: 11 Henderson TX
   roles: 8 Peter Pan 9 Funny Face 12 The Boyfriend

dunce 4 fool 5 dummy, idiot, moron 6 dimwit, nitwit 8 imbecile, numskull 9 blockhead, numbskull, simpleton

Dunciad, The
   author: 13 Alexander Pope

dunderhead 3 ass 4 dolt, fool 5 booby, dunce, idiot, moron, ninny 6 dimwit, nitwit 7 dullard, fathead, halfwit 8 bonehead, dumb-dumb, imbecile, lunkhead, numskull 9 blockhead, dumb bunny, lamebrain, numbskull 10 nincompoop 11 chowderhead

dune 4 bank 5 mound 8 sandbank, sandpile

dunk 3 dip, sop 4 duck, soak 5 bathe, douse, drown, slosh, souse, steep 6 deluge, drench, engulf, plunge 7 baptize, immerse 8 inundate, saturate, submerge

Dunne, John Gregory
   author of: 11 Dutch Shea Jr 18 Quintana and Friends

Dunnock, Mildred
   born: 11 Baltimore MD
   roles: 9 Baby Doll 12 The Nun's Story 14 The Corn Is Green 16 Butterfield Eight, Cat on a Hot Tin Roof, Death of a Salesman

duo 4 pair 5 combo 6 couple 7 twosome 11 combination

duomo 4 dome 9 cathedral

dupe 4 fool, pawn 5 patsy, trick 6 humbug, sucker 7 cat's paw, deceive, fall guy, mislead 8 hoodwink 9 bamboozle

duplicate 4 copy 5 clone, match 6 repeat 7 replica 8 parallel 9 facsimile, imitation, make again, photocopy, photostat 10 carbon copy 12 reproduction

duplicity 5 fraud, guile 6 deceit 7 cunning 9 deception, falseness 10 dishonesty 13 deceitfulness

Du Pont Labs
   founder: 17 E I du Pont de Nemours
   inventor of: 5 nylon

Duquesnoy, Francois
   born: 8 Brussels, Flanders
   nickname: 11 Il Fiammingo
   artwork: 8 St Andrew 9 St Susanna

dur
   musical term: 5 major 8 major key

durability 7 stamina 8 strength 9 endurance, toughness 10 sturdiness

durable 5 sound, tough 6 strong, sturdy 7 lasting 8 enduring 11 long-wearing, substantial

Durand, Asher Brown
   born: 18 Jefferson Village NJ
   artwork: 14 Kindred Spirits

Durant, Will and Ariel
   authors of: 20 The Story of Philosophy 21 Rousseau and Revolution 22 The Story of Civilization

Durante, Jimmy
   real name: 19 James Francis Durante
   nickname: 10 Schnozzola 15 Inka Dinka Doo Man
   born: 9 New York NY
   roles: 5 Jumbo 21 It's a Mad Mad Mad Mad World

duration 4 term 6 extent, period 11 continuance 12 continuation

Durdles
   character in: 22 The Mystery of Edwin Drood
   author: 7 Dickens

Durer, Albrecht
   born: 7 Germany 9 Nuremberg
   artwork: 10 Adam and Eve, Apocalypse, The Triumph 11 Wehlsch Pirg 12 Four Apostles, Large Passion, Melancholia I 13 Castle of Trent 15 Life of the Virgin 18 St Jerome in his Study 19 Virgin with the Siskin 21 Christ Among the Doctors 22 Knight Death and the Devil 24 Crowned Death on a Thin Horse 25 The Feast of the Rose Garlands 28 The Festival of the Rose Garlands

duress 5 force 6 threat 8 coercion, pressure 10 compulsion, constraint

Durgin, Francis Timothy
   real name of: 11 Rory Calhoun

during litigation
   Latin: 12 pendente lite

Durocher, Leo
   nickname: 9 Leo the Lip
   sport: 8 baseball
   position: 7 manager

team: 11 Chicago Cubs 13 New York Giants 15 Brooklyn Dodgers
saying: 18 Nice guys finish last

Durrenmatt, Friedrich
author of: 5 Traps 8 The Visit 9 The Pledge, The Quarry 13 The Physicists 21 The Judge and His Hangman 27 The Marriage of the Mississippi

Durrie, James and Henry
character in: 21 The Master of Ballantrae
author: 9 Stevenson

dusk 6 sunset 7 sundown 8 twilight 9 nightfall

dusky 3 dim 4 dark 5 murky 6 cloudy, gloomy, veiled 7 swarthy 8 dark-hued

dust 4 dirt, lint 5 brush, motes 8 sprinkle

duster 3 rag 4 coat, robe 5 brush, cloth, whisk 9 housecoat 10 whisk broom

Dutch Guiana see 8 Suriname

Dutch Shea, Jr
author: 16 John Gregory Dunne

dutiful 5 loyal 8 diligent, faithful, obedient 9 compliant 13 conscientious

duty 3 tax 4 levy, onus, task 6 charge, excise, tariff 7 customs 8 business, function, province 10 assignment, obligation 14 responsibility

Duval, Armand
character in: 7 Camille
author: 5 Dumas (fils)

Duvall, Robert
born: 10 San Diego CA
roles: 4 MASH 11 Godfather II 12 The Godfather 13 Apocalypse Now, Tender Mercies (Oscar) 15 The Great Santini, True Confessions 18 To Kill a Mockingbird

Duvall, Shelley
born: 9 Houston TX
roles: 6 Popeye 9 Nashville 10 The Shining, Three Women 15 Brewster McCloud

Dvorak, Antonin
born: 11 Nelahozeves 14 Czechoslovakia
composer of: 5 Dumky 6 Hymnus, Te Deum 8 Carnival (overture) 10 St Ludmilla 11 Stabat Mater 15 American Quartet, From the New World (Symphony in E Minor) 16 The Specter's Bride 17 The Bells of Zlonice

dwarf 3 dim, elf, imp 4 baby, tiny 5 fairy, gnome, pixie, pygmy, small, troll 6 bantam, goblin, petite, sprite 8 diminish 9 miniature 10 diminutive, leprechaun, overshadow

dwarfish 3 wee 4 tiny 5 pygmy, short, small 6 bantam, little, midget 7 compact, squatty 10 diminutive, undersized 13 foreshortened

dwell 4 live 5 abide 6 harp on, reside 7 inhabit 10 linger over

dwelling 4 home 5 abode, house 8 domicile 9 residence 10 habitation

dwelling place 4 home 5 abode, house 7 habitat, lodging 8 domicile 9 residence 10 habitation 14 living quarters

dwell on 6 accent, stress 7 feature, iterate 9 emphasize, press home

dwindle 4 fade, wane 6 lessen, shrink 7 decline 8 decrease, diminish 13 become smaller

dye 4 tint 5 color, shade, stain 8 coloring 10 coloration

dyed-in-the-wool 9 confirmed, ingrained 10 deep-rooted, inveterate 11 established

dyestuff 14 coloring matter

Dymas
home: 4 Troy
fought with: 6 Aeneas
fought against: 6 Greeks

dynamic 5 vital 6 active 7 driving 8 forceful, powerful, vigorous 9 energetic

dynamism 3 pep 4 life 5 verve, vigor 6 energy, spirit 8 vitality, vivacity 9 animation 10 liveliness

dynamite 4 raze, ruin 5 blast, trash, wreck 6 blow up, charge 7 destroy, shatter, wipe out 8 decimate, demolish 9 devastate, dismantle, eradicate, explosive 10 annihilate, extinguish, obliterate 11 exterminate

dynamo 4 doer 7 hustler 8 activist, gogetter 9 generator 12 active person 14 bundle of energy, mover and shaker

Dynasts, The
author: 11 Thomas Hardy
subject: 17 Napoleon Bonaparte

dynasty 4 line 5 crown, reign 6 regime 7 lineage, regency 8 dominion, hegemony, kingship, monarchy, regnancy 9 authority 10 government, suzerainty 11 ruling house 12 jurisdiction 14 administration

Dynasty
character: 9 Dex Dexter, Jeff Colby 12 Alexis (Morel Carrington Colby) Dexter 14 Adam Carrington 15 Blake Carrington 16 Amanda Carrington, Steven Carrington 17 Krystle Carrington 18 Dominique Devereaux, Krystina Carrington 21 Fallon Carrington Colby
cast: 9 John James 10 Linda Evans 11 Joan Collins 12 John Forsythe
setting: 6 Denver 8 Colorado
hotel: 8 La Mirage

dyspeptic 4 mean 6 crabby, grumpy, ornery, shirty, touchy 7 grouchy, waspish 8 choleric 9 crotchety, fractious, irascible, irritable 10 ill-humored, ill-natured 11 bad-tempered, contentious, hot-tempered 12 cantankerous, sour-tempered 13 short-tempered

E

Ea
  origin: 8 Akkadian
  god of: 6 wisdom
  father: 4 Apsu
  son: 6 Marduk 8 Merodach 12 Baal
    Merodach
  corresponds to: 4 Enki
each 5 every 6 apiece 7 that one, this one
  8 everyone, separate 12 respectively
Eagels, Jeanne
  born: 12 Kansas City MO
  roles: 4 Rain 8 Jealousy 9 The Letter 13
    Sadie Thompson 14 Man Woman and
    Sin
eager 4 agog, avid, keen 6 ardent, fervid,
  intent, raring 7 athirst, earnest, excited,
  fervent, intense, longing, zealous 8 desirous, diligent, resolute, spirited, yearning 9
  ambitious, hungering, impatient, thirsting
  10 aggressive, passionate 11 hardworking,
  impassioned, industrious, persevering 12
  enterprising, enthusiastic
eagerly 6 avidly, keenly 8 ardently, desiring,
  fervidly, intently 9 anxiously, earnestly, fervently, zealously 16 enthusiastically
eagerness 4 zeal, zest 5 ardor 6 fervor 7
  avidity 9 readiness 10 enthusiasm 11 willingness
eagle
  young: 6 eaglet
Eagle
  constellation of: 6 Aquila
Eakins, Thomas
  born: 14 Philadelphia PA
  artwork: 11 Agnew Clinic 13 Mrs Edith
    Mahon 14 The Gross Clinic 24 Max
    Schmitt in a Single Scull
ear
  section: 5 inner, outer 6 middle
  part: 4 drum 5 anvil, canal 6 hammer 7
    cochlea, stirrup 8 hair cell 14 eustachian
    tube
earl 4 lord, peer 5 noble 8 nobleman
  wife: 8 countess
earlier 6 before, in time, sooner 9 before
  now, in advance 10 beforehand 11 ahead
  of time 13 before the fact
earliest 5 first 6 oldest, primal 7 ancient,
  initial, primary, soonest 8 original, primeval
  9 beginning, primitive 10 aboriginal, indigenous 11 fundamental
Earl of Baltimore
  nickname of: 10 Earl Weaver
Earl the Pearl
  nickname of: 10 Earl Monroe
early 5 first 6 primal 7 ancient, archaic, betimes, initial, too soon, very old 8 primeval
  9 in advance, premature, primitive 10 be-

forehand, in good time, primordial 11
  ahead of time, prehistoric, prematurely
Early Autumn
  author: 14 Louis Bromfield
early man 6 Peking 9 Cro-Magnon, Stein-
  heim 11 Neanderthal 18 Trobriand Islanders 24 Australopithecus robustus 25 Australopithecus africanus
earmark 3 tag 4 band, hold, sign 5 allot, label, stamp, token, trait 6 aspect, assign 7
  feature, put away, quality, reserve 8 allocate, property, set aside 9 attribute, designate 11 peculiarity, singularity 14 characteristic
earn 3 get, net 4 draw, gain, make, rate,
  reap 5 clear, merit 6 attain, pick up, secure
  7 achieve, collect, deserve, realize, receive, warrant 9 bring home 12 be entitled to
earn as due 4 rate 5 merit 7 deserve 10
  be worthy of 12 be entitled to 13 be deserving of
earnest 4 firm 5 eager, fixed, grave, sober,
  staid 6 ardent, fervid, honest, intent, sedate, solemn, stable, steady, urgent 7 devoted, fervent, intense, serious, sincere,
  zealous 8 constant, diligent, resolute, spirited, vehement 9 ambitious, assiduous,
  heartfelt, insistent 10 deeply felt, determined, passionate, purposeful, thoughtful
  11 hard-working, impassioned, industrious,
  persevering 12 enthusiastic, wholehearted
earnest attachment 4 love 6 regard 7 concern 8 devotion, fondness 9 reverence 10
  commitment, dedication 11 devotedness
  13 attentiveness
earnest request 4 plea 6 appeal 8 entreaty,
  petition 11 importunity 12 supplication
earnings 3 pay 5 wages 6 income, salary 7
  payment, profits 8 proceeds, receipts 12
  compensation
Earnshaw, Catherine
  character in: 16 Wuthering Heights
  author: 6 Bronte
ear-splitting 7 blaring 8 piercing 9 clamorous, deafening 10 thunderous
earth 3 sod 4 clay, dirt, dust, land, loam,
  soil, turf 6 ground 7 topsoil
  god of: 3 Geb, Keb 5 Dagan, Dagon 10
    Trophonius
  goddess of: 2 Ge 4 Gaea, Gaia 6 Hec-
    ate, Hekate, Tellus
earthen pot
  Spanish: 4 olla
earthenware 5 china 7 pottery 8 clayware,
  crockery 11 ceramic ware

earthly 6 bodily 7 mundane, secular, ungodly, worldly 8 feasible, material, physical, possible, temporal 9 corporeal, practical 10 imaginable 11 conceivable, terrestrial 12 nonspiritual 13 materialistic

earthquake 5 quake, seism, shock 6 tremor 8 temblor, upheaval 11 earth tremor

earth tremor 5 quake, seism, shock 6 tremor 8 temblor, upheaval 10 earthquake

earthy 5 bawdy, crude, dirty, funky, gross, lusty, rough 6 coarse, filthy, ribald, robust, smutty, vulgar 7 obscene, peasant, raunchy 8 indecent 9 primitive, unrefined 10 unblushing, uncultured 12 uncultivated

Earwicker family
    characters in: 13 Finnegans Wake
    author: 5 Joyce

earwig
    variety: 5 black 6 little 10 long horned

ease 4 calm, rest, slip 5 abate, allay, poise, quiet, slide, still 6 aplomb, lessen, luxury, pacify, plenty, relief, repose, solace, soothe 7 assuage, comfort, console, leisure, lighten, mollify, relieve 8 diminish, easement, easiness, facility, maneuver, mitigate, palliate, security, serenity 9 abundance, affluence, alleviate, composure, disburden, readiness 10 confidence, prosperity, relaxation 11 assuagement, naturalness, peace of mind, restfulness 12 tranquillity, unconstraint 13 luxuriousness, move carefully, relaxed manner 14 effortlessness, handle with care, unaffectedness

easement 4 ease 6 relief, solace, succor 7 comfort 8 soothing 10 right of way 11 assuagement

easily 5 by far 6 freely, surely 7 clearly, handily, lightly, plainly, readily 8 facilely, smoothly, with ease 9 certainly 10 far and away, undeniably 11 beyond doubt, undoubtedly 12 effortlessly, with facility 13 without a hitch 14 beyond question, without trouble 17 without difficulty 23 beyond the shadow of a doubt

easily embarrassed 3 shy 5 timid 7 bashful 8 blushing, skittish, timorous 9 diffident, shrinking 11 constrained, unconfident

easily noticed 5 clear, plain 6 patent 7 evident, glaring, obvious, visible 8 flagrant, striking 9 arresting, prominent 10 noticeable 11 conspicuous, outstanding

easily ruffled 9 emotional, excitable 11 hot-tempered 13 quick-tempered

easiness 4 ease 10 equanimity, simplicity 11 naturalness 12 indifference 13 impassiveness

East, the 4 Asia 9 the Orient 10 the Far East 11 the Near East 17 Eastern Hemisphere

East Bengal see 10 Bangladesh

East Berlin
    capital of: 11 East Germany

East Coker
    author: 7 T S Eliot

Eastern Slavic
    language family: 12 Indo-European
    group: 11 Balto-Slavic
    branch: 6 Slavic
    language: 7 Russian 9 Ukrainian 12 White Russian

Easter Parade
    director: 14 Charles Walters
    based on musical by: 12 Irving Berlin
    cast: 9 Ann Miller 11 Fred Astaire, Judy Garland 12 Peter Lawford

East Germany see Germany, East

Eastman, George
    nationality: 8 American
    founder of: 14 Eastman Kodak Co
    inventor of: 9 Kodak film 11 Kodak camera 20 transparent photo film

East of Eden
    author: 13 John Steinbeck
    director: 9 Elia Kazan
    cast: 8 Burl Ives 9 James Dean 10 Jo Van Fleet 11 Julie Harris 13 Raymond Massey
    Oscar for: 17 supporting actress (Van Fleet)

East wind
    associated with: 5 Eurus 9 Volturnus

Eastwood, Clint
    born: 14 San Francisco CA
    roles: 7 Firefox, Rawhide 10 Dirty Harry, Hang Em High, Unforgiven 11 Magnum Force, The Dead Pool 12 Coogan's Bluff, Kelly's Heroes, Sudden Impact 13 A Perfect World 14 Play Misty for Me 15 In The Line of Fire, Where Eagles Dare 17 A Fistful of Dollars, Any Which Way You Can, High Plains Drifter 18 Escape from Alcatraz, For a Few Dollars More 21 Two Mules for Sister Sara 23 The Good the Bad and the Ugly
    mayor of: 6 Carmel

easy 4 calm, mild, open, soft 5 cushy, frank, light, naive 6 benign, calmly, candid, docile, easily, gentle, secure, serene, simple 7 lenient, natural, not hard, relaxed, restful, wealthy 8 affluent, carefree, composed, friendly, gracious, gullible, informal, outgoing, painless, peaceful, pleasant, scarcely, serenely, tranquil, unforced, well-to-do, yielding 9 compliant, indulgent, leisurely, luxurious, tractable, unworried 10 effortless, peacefully, permissive, unaffected, untroubled 11 comfortable, comfortably 12 not difficult, unsuspicious 13 accommodating, unconstrained

easygoing 4 calm 6 casual 7 offhand, patient, relaxed 8 carefree 9 unruffled, unworried 10 insouciant, nonchalant 11 unconcerned, unexcitable 12 even-tempered, happy-go-lucky, mild-tempered

Easy Rider
    director: 12 Dennis Hopper
    cast: 10 Karen Black, Peter Fonda 11 Luana Anders 12 Dennis Hopper, Robert Walker 13 Jack Nicholson

easy to use 7 adapted, helpful 9 adaptable 10 convenient 11 serviceable 12 advantageous

eat 3 sup 4 bolt, dine, feed, gulp, rust, take 5 feast, lunch 6 devour, gobble, ingest, nibble 7 consume, corrode 8 dispatch, dissolve, wear away, wolf down 9 breakfast, take a meal, waste away 10 break bread, gormandize 14 take sustenance 15 take nourishment

eatable 4 food 6 edible 8 fit to eat 10 comestible, consumable

eat away 4 rust 5 erode 7 corrode, oxidize

eating habits 4 diet 13 eating regimen

eating regimen 4 diet 12 eating habits

eat into 4 bite 5 erode 6 nibble 7 consume, corrode 8 wear away 9 swallow up

eat one's fill 5 feast, gorge 6 pig out 7 banquet 12 stuff oneself

eat rapidly 4 bolt, gulp, wolf 5 scarf 6 gobble 12 swallow whole

eat up 5 enjoy, savor 6 devour, relish 7 consume, swallow 9 delight in, rejoice in 13 be pleased with, get a kick out of 14 take pleasure in

eat voraciously 6 cram in, devour, gobble 7 stuff in 8 bolt down, gulp down, wolf down 10 gormandize 12 swallow whole

eau, eaux 5 water

eau de vie 5 brandy 11 water of life

eavesdrop 3 bug, pry, spy, tap 5 snoop 6 attend, harken 7 monitor, wiretap 8 listen in, overhear 9 bend an ear 11 cock one's ear 14 strain one's ears 15 prick up one's ears

ebb 5 abate, go out 6 go down, lessen, recede, shrink, weaken 7 decline, dwindle, retreat, slacken, subside 8 decrease, diminish, fade away, fall away, flow away, flow back, move back, withdraw 9 waste away 10 degenerate 11 deteriorate

ebony 3 jet 4 dark, inky 5 black, raven, sable 8 hardwood 9 coal-black 15 Diospyros Ebenum

   varieties: 5 Green, Texas 8 Macassar, Mountain 10 East Indian, Queensland

Ebsen, Buddy

   real name: 23 Christian Rudolph Ebsen Jr

   born: 12 Belleville IL

   roles: 12 Barnaby Jones, Davy Crockett 21 The Beverly Hillbillies

ebullience 3 zip 7 elation 8 buoyancy 9 animation 10 enthusiasm, exuberance, joyousness, liveliness 11 high spirits 12 exhilaration 13 effervescence

ebullient 6 elated, joyful, joyous 9 exuberant 11 exhilarated 12 effervescent, enthusiastic, high-spirited

ecce homo 12 behold the man

   said by: 13 Pontius Pilate

   spoken of: 6 Christ

eccentric 3 nut, odd 4 kook, rash, sick 5 curio, flake, funny, kooky, nutty, queer, weird 6 freaky, insane, quaint, unique, weirdo 7 bizarre, curious, erratic, oddball, offbeat, strange, unusual, weirdie 8 aber-

rant, abnormal, crackpot, freakish, peculiar, quixotic, singular, uncommon 9 character, irregular, odd person, off center, parabolic, psychotic, screwball, unnatural, whimsical 10 capricious, elliptical, outlandish, unorthodox 13 extraordinary 14 unconventional

eccentricity 6 oddity, whimsy 7 caprice 9 deviation, queerness 10 aberration 11 abnormality, peculiarity, strangeness 12 idiosyncrasy, irregularity

ecclesiastic, ecclesiastical 5 rabbi, vicar 6 cleric, curate, deacon, parson, pastor, priest, rector 7 prelate 8 chaplain, churchly, clerical, minister, pastoral, preacher 9 churchman, clergyman, episcopal, parochial, religious

Echecles

   father: 5 Actor

   wife: 8 Polymela

   raised child of Polymela and: 6 Hermes

echelon 4 file, line, rank, rung, tier 5 grade, level 6 office 8 position 9 authority, hierarchy

Echemus

   king of: 7 Arcadia

   father: 7 Cepheus

   wife: 8 Timandra

   son: 8 Laodocus

   delayed: 18 Heraclidan invasion

   killed: 6 Hyllus

Echetus

   king of: 6 Epirus

   daughter: 8 Amphissa

   blinded: 8 Amphissa

Echidna

   form: 7 monster

   mother of: 5 Hydra 6 Sphinx 7 Chimera 8 Cerberus

   slain by: 5 Argus

echinoderm 9 sea animal

   characteristic: 10 spiny shell

   form: 6 radial

   kind: 6 cystid 7 crinoid 8 starfish 9 sea urchin 10 basket star 11 sea cucumber

Echion

   member: 6 Sparti

   wife: 5 Agave

   son: 8 Pentheus

echo 3 ape 4 copy, ring 5 match 6 follow, mirror, parrot, repeat 7 imitate, reflect, resound 8 parallel, simulate 9 duplicate, reproduce, take after 11 reverberate 13 reverberation

Echo

   form: 5 nymph

   location: 8 mountain

   loved: 9 Narcissus

   loved by: 3 Pan

   changed into: 4 echo

eclair 6 pastry 7 dessert 9 creampuff

eclaircissement 11 explanation 13 clarification, (the) Enlightenment

eclipse 3 dim 4 hide, loss, mask 5 cloak, cover, excel, outdo 6 darken, exceed 7 blot out, conceal, erasing, masking, obscure, surpass, veiling, wipe out 8 cloaking, clouding, covering, outrival, outshine 9 darkening, shadowing, transcend 10 obliterate, overshadow, tower above 11 blotting out, diminishing, eradicating, obscuration 12 annihilation, obliteration 13 overshadowing

eclogue 4 idyl, poem 5 idyll 7 bucolic 8 dialogue, pastoral

Eclogues
   author: 6 Vergil, Virgil

ecole 6 school

economic 6 fiscal 8 material, monetary 9 budgetary, financial, pecuniary 10 productive 12 distributive

economical 5 chary, cheap 6 frugal, modest, saving 7 careful, prudent, sparing, spartan, thrifty 8 economic 9 low-priced, niggardly, penurious, scrimping 10 reasonable 11 closefisted, tightfisted 12 parsimonious

economic decline 8 downturn 9 recession 10 depression

economics
   term: 3 GNP 5 labor 7 capital, Marxism, surplus 8 property 9 commodity, Communism, inflation, Keynesian, recession 10 capitalism, monetarist, supply-side 11 bourgeoisie, central bank, competition, consumption, marketplace, proletariat, stagflation 12 distribution, econometrics, fiscal policy, interest rate, laissez-faire, mercantilism 14 federal deficit, macroeconomics, microeconomics, monetary policy 17 trickle-down theory 20 gross national product

economist
   American: 6 George, Hansen, Sumner, Veblen 7 Commons 8 Friedman, Laughlin 10 Schumpeter
   British: 4 Mill 5 Smith 6 Keynes 7 Malthus, Ricardo 8 Marshall
   French: 3 Say 7 Quesnay
   German: 4 Marx 7 Schacht
   Italian: 6 Pareto
   Scottish: 5 Smith

economize 4 save 5 pinch, skimp, stint 6 scrimp 7 husband 8 be frugal, conserve, cut costs 9 be prudent 10 avoid waste 11 cut expenses 12 be economical, use sparingly 14 be parsimonious 15 practice economy, tighten one's belt

economizing 10 conserving 11 cutting down 13 penny-pinching 14 belt-tightening 15 pinching pennies 18 tightening one's belt

economy 6 thrift 8 prudence 9 frugality 10 providence 11 thriftiness 15 financial status, productive power

ecstasy 3 joy 5 bliss 6 frenzy, thrill, trance 7 delight, emotion, madness, rapture 8 delirium, gladness, pleasure 9 happiness, transport 10 enthusiasm, exultation

ecstatic 4 glad, rapt 5 happy 6 elated, joyful, joyous 7 exalted, excited 8 blissful 9 delighted, delirious, ebullient, entranced, overjoyed, rapturous 10 enraptured 11

transported 12 enthusiastic 13 beside oneself

Ecuador
   name means: 7 equator
   other name: 5 Quito
   capital: 5 Quito
   largest city: 9 Guayaquil
   others: 4 Jama, Loja, Napo, Puyo, Tena 5 Guano, Manta, Pajan, Pinas, Piura, Pojan, Yaupi 6 Ambato, Cuenca, Ibarra, Tulcan, Zaruma 7 Azogues, Cayambe, Guamote, Guapulo, Machala, Pelileo, Pillaro, Salinas 8 Riobamba 10 Esmeraldas, Portoviejo
   division: 5 Costa 6 Sierra 7 Oriente
   measure: 5 libra 6 cuadra, fanega
   monetary unit: 5 sucre 7 centavo
   weight: 5 libra
   island: 4 Puna, Wolf 5 Colon, Mocha, Pinta 6 Baltra, Chaves, Darwin, Pinzon, Rabida, Wenman 7 Isabela, La Plata, Sante Fe, Tortuga 8 Espanola, Floreana, Genovesa, Marchena, Santiago 9 Culpepper, Galapagos, Santa Cruz 10 Fernandina, Santa Maria 11 San Salvador 12 San Cristobal
   mountain: 5 Andes 6 Condor, Sangay 7 Cayambe 8 Antisana, Cotopaxi 9 Cotacachi, Pichincha
   highest point: 10 Chimborazo
   river: 4 Coca, Mira, Napo 5 Cocoa, Daule, Paute, Pindo, Tigre 6 Blanco, Guayas, Tumbes, Zamora 7 Conambo, Curaray, Jubones, Pastaza, Puyango 8 Aguarico, Bobonaza, Cononaco, Naranjal, Putumayo 9 San Miguel 10 Esmeraldas, Nangaritza 12 Guaillabamba
   sea: 7 Pacific
   physical feature:
   bay: 5 Manta 7 Isabela 9 Elizabeth 11 Santa Elenas 15 Ancon de Sardinas
   cape: 4 Rosa 6 Pasado 8 Marshall, Puntilla 10 San Lorenzo
   channel: 7 Jambeli
   gulf: 9 Guayaquil, Pichincha
   peninsula: 10 Santa Elena
   point: 4 Jama 5 Essex 6 Galera 9 Albemarle 10 Christobal
   people: 4 Cara, Cixo, Inca 5 Ardan, Aucas, Macoa, Maina, Palta, Quitu, Yumbo 6 Canelo, Jibaro, Jivaro, Puruha 7 Cayapas, Jivaros, mestizo, mulatto 8 Barbacoa, Colorado, Montuvio, Serranos 9 Montubios
   artist: 4 Egas 8 Santiago 9 Caspicara 10 Guayasamin
   author: 6 Espejo 14 Carrera Andrade
   conqueror: 7 Pizarro 10 Benalcazar 11 Huayna-Capac
   god: 5 umina
   leader: 6 Alfaro, Flores 10 Plaza Lasso, Rocafuerte 12 Garcia Moreno 13 Velasco Ibarra
   language: 6 Jibaro 7 Quechua, Spanish
   religion: 13 Roman Catholic
   feature:
   animal: 6 vicuna

dictator: 8 caudillo
estate: 8 hacienda
festival: 5 Yamor
hat: 6 Panama 8 jipijapa, toquilla
tree: 5 balsa
food:
baked guinea pig: 3 cuy
corn tamale: 6 humita
drink: 6 chicha
marinated raw shrimp/fish: 7 ceviche, seviche
potato/cheese patty: 11 llapingacho
potato soup: 5 locro

ecumenical 6 global 7 general 8 catholic 9 communist, planetary, universal, worldwide 10 heavenwide 11 communalist 12 all-embracing, all-including, all-inclusive, all-pervading, collectivist, cosmopolitan 13 communitarian, comprehensive, international

eczema 4 rash 8 eruption 10 dermatitis 12 inflammation

eddy 6 vortex 9 maelstrom, whirlpool 14 countercurrent

Eddy, Nelson
partner: 17 Jeanette MacDonald
born: 12 Providence RI
roles: 9 Rose Marie 15 Naughty Marietta 16 Northwest Outpost

Eden 8 Paradise
see also: 4 Adam

edentate 5 manis, sloth 7 antbear 8 aardvark, anteater 9 armadillo, toothless

Edgar Huntly
author: 20 Charles Brockden Brown

edge 3 hem, rim 4 bind, inch, line, side, trim 5 bound, brink, creep, limit, sidle, slink, sneak, steal, verge 6 border, fringe, margin 7 contour, outline 9 extremity, periphery, threshold 12 boundary line, dividing line, move sideways

Edgeworth, Maria
author of: 7 Belinda 11 The Absentee 14 Castle Rackrent

edging 3 hem 4 trim 5 limit 6 border, fringe, margin, ruffle 7 binding, curbing, salvage 8 boundary, fringing, trimming

edgy 5 sharp, testy 7 anxious, nervous 8 snappish 9 excitable, impatient, irascible, irritable 10 highstrung

edible 7 eatable 10 comestible, consumable, digestible 12 fit to be eaten, nonpoisonous 13 safe for eating

edict 3 law 4 bull, fiat 5 order, ukase 6 decree, dictum, ruling 7 command, dictate, mandate, statute 9 enactment, manifesto, ordinance, prescript 10 injunction, regulation 12 proclamation, public notice 13 pronouncement 14 pronunciamento

edification 8 guidance, teaching 9 direction, education, elevation, uplifting 11 advancement, information, instruction 13 enlightenment 14 indoctrination

edifice 8 building 9 structure 12 construction

edify 5 teach 6 inform 7 educate, improve 8 instruct 9 enlighten

edifying 8 didactic, tutorial 11 educational, instructive 12 enlightening

Edinburgh
bay: 12 Firth of Forth
capital of: 8 Scotland
Celtic: 11 Dune-eideann (Eidin's Fort)
church: 7 St Giles
landmark: 14 Holyrood Palace 15 Edinburgh Castle
port: 5 Leith
rocks: 10 Castle Rock 11 Arthur's Seat

Edison, Thomas Alva
nickname: 17 Wizard of Menlo Park
inventor of: 6 (wax cylinder) record 9 light bulb, (quadruplex) telegraph 10 phonograph 11 kinetoscope, stock ticker 14 movie projector 16 incandescent lamp 18 automatic telegraph (transmitter and receiver) 21 flexible celluloid film 22 alkaline storage battery

edit 5 adapt, amend 6 censor, polish, redact, revise 7 abridge, clean up, correct, expunge, rewrite, touch up 8 annotate, condense, copy-edit, rephrase 9 expurgate 10 blue-pencil, bowdlerize

edition 4 book, copy, kind 5 issue 6 number 7 imprint, version 8 printing 9 redaction

editor 2 ed 6 writer 7 newsman, reviser 8 compiler, redactor 10 journalist

Edmonds, Walter D
author of: 8 Rome Haul 19 Drums Along the Mohawk

Edmonton
hockey team: 6 Oilers

Edmontonia
type: 8 dinosaur 10 ornithopod
location: 12 North America

Edmund Campion
author: 11 Evelyn Waugh

Edom
name given: 4 Esau
descendants: 8 Edomites

Edson, Gus
creator/artist of: 5 Dondi 8 The Gumps

Ed Sullivan Show, The
regular cast: 17 June Taylor Dancers 23 Ray Bloch and His Orchestra
noted appearances: 7 Beatles, Bob Hope 10 Walt Disney 12 Elvis Presley 14 Martin and Lewis

educate 5 coach, edify, teach, train, tutor 6 inform, school 7 develop 8 civilize, instruct 9 enlighten

education 5 study 7 culture 8 learning, pedagogy, teaching, training, tutelage 9 didactics, erudition, knowledge, schooling 10 pedagogics 11 cultivation, edification, information, instruction, scholarship 13 enlightenment

Education of Henry Adams, The
author: 10 Henry Adams

educe 5 evoke 6 elicit, extort 7 draw out, extract 8 bring out 9 draw forth 12 bring to light

Edward II
author: 18 Christopher Marlowe

Edwards, Blake
   director of: 3 SOB, Ten 14 The Pink Panther, Victor Victoria 18 Days of Wine and Roses 19 Breakfast at Tiffany's

Edwards, Vince
   real name: 18 Vincent Edward Zoimo
   roles: 8 Ben Casey 13 Devil's Brigade 14 The Desperadoes 15 Three Faces of Eve

Edwin Drood, The Mystery of
   author: 14 Charles Dickens
   character: 7 Durdles, Mr Tatar, Rosa Bud 8 Mr Sapsea 10 John Jasper, Mr Datchery 11 Mr Grewgious 12 Mr Crisparkle 13 Deputy Bazzard 14 Helena Landless, Miss Twinkleton, Mr Honeythunder 15 Neville Landless

eel
   young: 5 elver

eerie 3 odd 5 queer, weird 6 creepy, spooky, uneasy 7 bizarre, fearful, ghostly, ominous, strange, uncanny 10 mysterious, portentous 11 frightening 12 apprehensive

Eetion
   king of: 6 Thebes 7 Cilicia
   daughter: 10 Andromache

Eeyore
   character in: 13 Winnie-the-Pooh
   author: 5 Milne

efface 4 raze 5 erase 6 cancel, delete, excise, rub out 7 blot out, destroy, expunge, wipe out 9 eradicate, extirpate 10 annihilate, obliterate

effect, effects 4 fact, gist, make 5 cause, drift, force, goods, power, tenor, truth 6 action, assets, attain, create, impact, import, intent, result, sequel, things, upshot, weight 7 achieve, essence, execute, meaning, outcome, perform, produce, purport, reality, realize 8 carry out, chattels, efficacy, function, holdings, movables, validity 9 actuality, aftermath, execution, furniture, influence, intention, operation, outgrowth, trappings 10 accomplish, bring about, impression 11 commodities, consequence, development, enforcement, general idea, implication, possessions 12 significance 14 accomplishment

effective 4 real 6 active, actual, cogent, moving, potent, strong, useful 7 capable, current, dynamic, telling 8 a reality, eloquent, forceful, forcible, incisive, powerful, striking 9 activated, competent, effectual, efficient, operative 10 compelling, convincing, impressive, persuasive, productive, successful 11 efficacious, influential, in operation, serviceable

effectiveness 5 power 6 effect, impact 7 potency 8 efficacy, strength 9 influence 10 efficiency, usefulness 14 serviceability

effectual 6 acting, active, useful 7 working 8 adequate 9 effective, efficient, operative 11 efficacious, functioning

effectuate 6 effect 7 achieve, execute, realize 8 carry out, complete 9 discharge 10 accomplish, consummate, perpetrate 12 carry through 13 put into effect

effeminate 7 unmanly 8 sissyish, womanish 9 sissified

effervesce 4 fizz, foam 5 froth 6 bubble, fizzle 7 sparkle

effervescence 3 zip 4 dash, fizz, life 5 froth, vigor 6 fizzle, gaiety, spirit 7 foaming 8 bubbling, buoyancy, vitality, vivacity 9 animation, fizziness 10 bubbliness, bubbling up, ebullience, enthusiasm, liveliness

effervescent 3 gay 5 fizzy, merry 6 bubbly, lively 7 fizzing, foaming 8 animated, bubbling 9 ebullient, exuberant, sparkling, vivacious 13 irrepressible

effete 5 spent 6 barren, wasted 7 sterile, worn-out 8 decadent, depraved 9 enervated, exhausted 10 degenerate, unprolific 12 unproductive

efficacious 9 effective, effectual, efficient

efficacy 6 impact 10 efficiency 13 effectiveness

efficiency 5 skill 6 energy 8 efficacy, facility 9 apartment 10 competence 11 proficiency 13 effectiveness

efficient 3 apt 7 capable 8 skillful 9 competent, effective, effectual 10 productive, proficient, timesaving, unwasteful, worksaving 11 crackerjack, efficacious, workmanlike 12 businesslike

effigy 4 doll 5 dummy, image 6 puppet, statue 8 likeness, straw man 9 mannequin, scarecrow 10 marionette 14 representation

effluence 6 efflux 7 outflow, outpour 8 effluent 9 discharge

effluent 5 waste 6 efflux, sewage 7 outflow 9 effluence

effluvium 4 aura, odor, ooze, reek 5 vapor 6 efflux, flatus 8 outgoing

efflux 7 outflow 8 effluent, emission 9 discharge, effluence

effort 3 try 4 toil, work 5 force, labor, pains, power 6 energy, strain, stress 7 attempt, travail, trouble 8 endeavor, exertion, industry, struggle 11 elbow grease

effortless 4 easy 6 facile, simple, smooth 8 graceful, painless 12 not difficult 13 uncomplicated

effortlessness 4 ease 8 easiness, facility 9 readiness 12 painlessness

effrontery 4 gall 5 brass, cheek, nerve 8 audacity, temerity 9 arrogance, brashness, impudence, insolence 10 brazenness 11 presumption 12 impertinence 13 shamelessness
   Yiddish: 7 chutzpa 8 chutzpah

effulgence 6 dazzle 8 radiance, splendor 10 brilliance 12 resplendence

effulgent 6 bright 7 radiant 8 dazzling, splendid 9 brilliant 11 resplendent

effusive 5 gushy 6 lavish 7 copious, gushing, profuse 9 ebullient, expansive, exuberant 10 unreserved 11 extravagant, free-flowing, overflowing 12 unrestrained

eft 4 newt 5 again 6 lizard 9 afterward

egalitarian 10 democratic 11 equal-rights 14 constitutional

egalite 8 equality

Egeria
also: 7 Aegeria
member of: 7 Camenae
husband: 13 Numa Pompilius
instructed: 13 Numa Pompilius

Egesta
also: 7 Aegesta
home: 4 Troy
position: 5 slave
sold by: 8 Laomedon
rescued by: 9 Aphrodite

egg 3 ova, roe 4 bomb, goad, mine, oval, ovum, seed, spur 6 embryo, fellow, incite, person 7 albumen 9 instigate, stimulate

Eggar, Samantha
born: 6 London 7 England
roles: 12 The Collector, Walking Stick 15 Doctor Doolittle, The Lady in the Car 16 The Molly Maguires

egghead 8 highbrow 13 intellectual

Eggleston, Edward
author of: 15 The Circuit Rider 19 The Hoosier Schoolboy 22 The Hoosier Schoolmaster

egg on 4 abet, back, goad, spur 6 exhort, incite 8 talk into 9 encourage

egg-shaped 4 oval 5 ovoid 7 oviform 10 elliptical

Egmont
author: 12 Johann Goethe

egocentric 8 egoistic 11 egomaniacal, egotistical, on an ego trip, self-seeking, self-serving 12 narcissistic, self-absorbed, self-centered, self-involved, self-obsessed 13 self-concerned 14 megalomaniacal, stuck on oneself 18 wrapped up in oneself

egoism 6 vanity 8 self-love 10 narcissism 14 self-absorption, self-importance 16 overweening pride, self-centeredness

egoist 10 narcissist, selfish one 13 selfish person 18 self-centered person

Egoist, The
author: 14 George Meredith

egoistic 7 selfish 12 narcissistic, self-centered

egotism 6 vanity 7 conceit 8 bragging, smugness 9 arrogance, immodesty, vainglory 10 self-praise 11 braggadocio 12 boastfulness

egotist 6 gascon 7 boaster, peacock 8 blowhard, braggart 9 swaggerer 11 braggadocio

egotistic 4 vain 10 egocentric 12 self-centered 13 self-important

egregious 5 gross 7 extreme, glaring, heinous 8 flagrant, grievous, shocking 9 monstrous, notorious 10 outrageous 11 intolerable 12 insufferable

egress 4 exit, vent 5 issue 6 escape, outlet, way out 7 leakage, outflow, seepage 8 aperture 9 departure, discharge 10 passage out, withdrawal

Egypt
other name: 3 UAR 5 Kemet 6 To-meri 11 The Two Lands 12 The Black Land
capital/largest city: 5 Cairo

others: 3 Tor 4 Edfu, Gaza, Giza, Idfu, Said, Suez 5 Altur, Aswan, Tanta 6 Boolak, Dumyat, Faiyum, Quseir, Safaga, Sallum 7 Alemein, Memphis, Raschid, Rosetta, Zagazig 8 Damietta, Hurghada, Ismailia, Mansurah 10 Alexandria
school: 5 Cairo 7 Al-Azhar 8 American
division: 5 Lower, Nubia, Upper
measure: 3 apt, dra, hen, rob 4 arab, dira, draa, khet, nief, ocha, roub, theb, wudu 5 abdat, ardab, cubit, farde, fedan, keleh, kerat, kilah, sahme 6 artaba, aurure, baladi, kantar, keddah, robhah, schene 7 choryos, daribah, malouah, roubouh, toumnah 8 kassabah, kharouba 10 diramimari, diribaladi
monetary unit: 4 fils, kees, para 5 asper, dinar, fodda, gersh, girsh, medin, pound, riyal 6 ahmadi, dirham, foddah, guinea, junayh, maidin, medine, medino 7 piaster, piastre, tallard 8 bedidlik, millieme
weight: 3 kat, ket, oka, oke 4 dera, heml, khar, okia, rotl 5 artal, artel, deben, kerat, minae, minas, okieh, pound, ratel, uckia 6 hamlah, kantar 7 drachma, quintal
island: 4 Roda 6 Philae 7 Shadwan 11 Elephantine
lake: 4 Edku, Idku 5 Qarun 6 Maryut, Moeris, Nasser 7 Manzala 8 Burullus, Mareotis
mountain: 5 Sinai, Uekia 6 Gharib 13 Shayib al-Banat
highest point: 8 Katerina 9 Katherina
river: 4 Bahr, Nile
Nile branch: 7 Rosetta 8 Damietta
sea: 3 Red 13 Mediterranean
physical feature:
cape: 4 Sudr 5 Banas 8 Rasbanas
desert: 3 Tih 5 Dakla, Scete, Sinai, Skete 6 Libyan, Nubian, Sahara 7 Arabian
gulf: 4 Suez 5 Aqaba
isthmus: 4 Suez
oasis: 4 Siwa 6 Dakhel, Dakhla, Kharga 7 Farafra, Khargeh 8 Bahariya 9 Bahariyeh 12 Wahel-Khargeh
peninsula: 5 Sinai 6 Pharos
plain: 7 Asaseff
plateau: 3 Tih
people: 3 Kem 4 Arab, Copt, Misr, Wafd 5 Gippy, Gyppy, Gypsy, Nilot 6 Ababda, Berber, Hyksos, Nubian, Tasian 7 Mizraim, Pharian 8 Badarian, Bisharin, Memphian
leader: 5 Jawar, Sadat 6 Nasser 7 Mubarak, Saladin 10 King Farouk 11 Ismail Pasha, Mohammed Ali, Tawfiq Pasha
pharaoh: 5 Khufu, Menes, Zoser 6 Khafre, Ptulol, Ramses 8 Horemheb, Menkaure 9 Akhenaten, Amenemhet, Amenhotep 10 Mentuhotep 11 Tutankhamen
queen: 9 Cleopatra, Nefertari, Nefertiti 10 Hatshepsut, Hetepheres
language: 6 Arabic, French 7 English
for liturgy: 6 Coptic
religion: 5 Islam 18 Coptic Christianity

ancient god: 2 Ra 3 Geb, Nut, Shu 4
Aton, Atum, Isis, Ptah, Seth 5 Horus,
Thoth 6 Anubis, Hathor, Osiris, Tefnut 8
Nephthys
place:
dam: 4 Sadd, Sudd 5 Aswan 6 Assuan
mosque: 5 Rifai 9 Alabaster 11 Sultan
Hasan
palace: 6 Kubbeh
pyramids: 4 Giza 5 Khufu 6 Cheops 7
Saqqara
ruins: 5 Miroe 6 Abydos, Sphinx, Thebes
7 Memphis 8 Berenice 9 Abu Simbel 13
Valley of Kings, Valley of Tombs
temple: 4 Idfu 5 Edoon, Luxor, Thoth 6
Abydos, Karnak, Osiris 7 Dendera
feature:
dynasty: 5 Saite 7 Ayyubid, Fatimid 8
Mameluke 9 Ptolemaic
long robe: 10 gallabiyea
peasant: 6 fellah 8 fellahin 9 fellaheen
sacred bird: 4 benu, ibis 5 bennu
sailboat: 7 felucca
statue: 6 Sphinx 15 Colossi of Memnon
food:
bean: 5 lotus
beer: 6 zythum
bread: 6 herisa
dish: 3 ful
drink: 4 bosa, boza 5 bozah
Egyptian
language family: 11 Afro-Asiatic 13
Hamito-Semitic
later form: 6 Coptic
Egyptian cross 4 ankh
Egyptian Mythology
deities: 6 Ennead
eight gods: 3 Heh 6 Ogdoad
goddess of evil: 7 Sekhmet
goddess of fertility: 2 Io 4 Isis
goddess of law/righteousness: 4 Maat
goddess of love/joy/music/dance: 6
Hathor
goddess of sky: 3 Nut
goddess personifying sky: 6 Hathor
god of bricks: 5 Kulla
god of creation: 4 Ptah
god of dead/Nile: 6 Osiris
god of earth: 3 Geb, Keb
god of ocean: 3 Nun 4 Nunu
god of sun: 2 Ra, Re 5 Horus
corresponds to Greek: 10 Harcorates
god of tombs/embalming: 6 Anubis
god of wisdom/magic/learning: 5 Thoth
corresponds to Greek: 6 Hermes
immortal spirit: 2 Ka
judge of dead: 6 Osiris
king of dead: 6 Osiris
king of gods: 4 Amen, Amon 5 Ammon
6 Amen Ra, Amon Ra
corresponds to Greek: 4 Zeus
corresponds to Roman: 4 Jove 7 Jupiter
personification of femininity: 5 Neith
corresponds to Greek: 6 Athena
ram god: 5 Khnum
vulture: 7 Nekhbet

Ehrlich, Paul
field: 12 bacteriology
nationality: 6 German
studied: 6 toxins 8 immunity 10 antitox-
ins
discovered: 9 salvarsan
coined term: 12 chemotherapy
awarded: 10 Nobel Prize
Ehud 11 Hebrew judge
Eichenor
mentioned in: 5 Iliad
father: 8 Polyidus
fought with: 6 Greeks
slain by: 5 Paris
Eichmann in Jerusalem
author: 12 Hannah Arendt
eiderdown 4 puff 5 cover, quilt 8 coverlet 9
comforter 10 featherbed
Eight and a half, 8 1/2
director: 15 Federico Fellini
cast: 10 Anouk Aimee 16 Claudia Cardi-
nale 19 Marcello Mastroianni
Eighteen Seventy-Six, 1876
author: 9 Gore Vidal
Eijkman, Christiaan
nationality: 5 Dutch
discovered: 19 antineuritic vitamin
researched: 8 beriberi
awarded: 10 Nobel Prize
Eileithyia
also: 8 Ilithyia
origin: 5 Greek
goddess of: 10 childbirth
father: 4 Zeus
mother: 4 Hera
corresponds to: 6 Lucina
Einstein, Albert
field: 7 physics
theory of: 10 relativity 14 uranium fission
awarded: 10 Nobel Prize
Eioneus
son: 6 Rhesus
daughter: 3 Dia
Eire *see* 7 Ireland
Eisenhower, Dwight David
nickname: 3 Ike
changed name from: 21 David Dwight
Eisenhower
presidential rank: 12 thirty-fourth
party: 10 Republican
state represented: 2 NY
defeated: 4 (Eric) Hass, (Harry Flood)
Byrd 5 (Farrell) Dobbs 6 (Darlington)
Hoopes, (William Ezra) Jenner 7 (Stuart)
Hamblen, (Thomas Coleman) Andrews 8
(Enoch Arden) Holtwick, (Vincent William)
Hallinan 9 (Adlai Ewing) Stevenson
vice president: 5 (Richard Milhous)
Nixon
cabinet:
state: 6 (Christian Archibald) Herter,
(John Foster) Dulles
treasury: 8 (George Magoffin)
Humphrey, (Robert Bernard) Anderson
defense: 5 (Thomas Sovereign) Gates
(Jr) 6 (Charles Erwin) Wilson 7 (Neil
Hesler) McElroy

attorney general: 6 (William Pierce) Rogers 8 (Herbert) Brownell (Jr)
postmaster general: 11 (Arthur Ellsworth) Summerfield
interior: 5 (Douglas) McKay 6 (Frederick Andrew) Seaton
agriculture: 6 (Ezra Taft) Benson
commerce: 5 (Sinclair) Weeks 7 (Frederick Henry) Mueller, (Lewis Lichtenstein) Strauss
labor: 6 (Martin Patrick) Durkin 8 (James Paul) Mitchell
HEW: 5 (Oveta Culp) Hobby 6 (Marion Bayard) Folsom 8 (Arthur Sherwood) Flemming
born: 9 Denison TX
died: 12 Washington DC
buried: 9 Abilene KS
education: 9 West Point 17 US Military Academy
religion: 12 Presbyterian
interest: 4 golf 6 flying 7 fishing, hunting 8 football, painting
vacation spot: 2 CA 11 Palm Springs
author: 11 Waging Peace 15 Crusade in Europe 16 Mandate for Change 27 At Ease: Stories I Tell to Friends
political career: 4 none (prior to presidency)
civilian career:
president of: 18 Columbia University
military service: 7 general 9 World War I 10 World War II 16 Army Chief of Staff
supreme commander of: 6 Allies 15 European Defense (NATO) 18 US occupation forces (Europe)
head of: 18 Joint Chiefs of Staff
notable events of lifetime/term: 4 D-Day, NATO
Acts: 11 Civil Rights
battle of the: 5 Bulge
conference: 7 Big Four 10 NATO Summit 11 Paris Summit
Cuba taken over by: 11 Fidel Castro
invasion: 9 Normandy
trial/execution of: 14 Ethel Rosenberg 15 Julius Rosenberg
USSR shot down: 9 U-Two plane
father: 10 David Jacob
mother: 3 Ida (Elizabeth Stover)
siblings: 3 Roy 4 Earl, Paul 5 Edgar 6 Arthur, Milton
wife: 5 Marie (Geneva Doud)
nickname: 5 Mamie
children: 10 Doud Dwight 15 John Sheldon Doud

ejaculate 4 howl, yell, yelp 5 shout 6 bellow, cry out 7 exclaim 10 vociferate
ejaculation 3 cry 4 howl, yell, yelp 5 shout 6 bellow, outcry, shriek, squeal 7 screech 11 exclamation 12 vociferation
eject 4 emit, oust, spew 5 evict, exile, expel, exude, spout 6 banish, bounce, deport, remove 7 cast out, kick out, spit out, turn out 8 disgorge, drive out, force out, throw out 9 discharge 10 dispossess

ejection 4 gush 5 spurt 6 ouster 7 issuing, removal 8 emission, eruption, eviction 9 dismissal, expelling, expulsion 10 banishment 11 throwing out
Ekdal, Hjalmar
  character in: 11 The Wild Duck
  author: 5 Ibsen
eke 3 add 4 also 7 augment, enlarge, stretch 8 increase, lengthen, likewise, moreover 10 in addition, supplement
elaborate 5 fancy, gaudy, showy 6 expand, flashy, garish, ornate 7 clarify, complex, elegant, labored, specify 8 involved, overdone 9 embellish, intricate 10 add details 11 complicated, painstaking 12 ostentatious 13 particularize
elaborate on 6 expand 7 amplify, develop 9 embellish 10 supplement 11 expatiate on
elaboration 11 added detail, rounding out 12 augmentation 13 amplification, embellishment
Elaine
  character in: 16 Arthurian romance
Elais
  father: 5 Anius
  mother: 7 Dorippe
  changed things into: 3 oil
elan 4 dash, zeal 5 flair, verve, vigor 6 energy, spirit 8 vivacity 9 animation 10 enthusiasm
eland 3 elk 8 antelope 11 taurotragus
elapse 4 go by, pass 5 lapse 6 pass by, roll by, slip by 7 glide by, slide by 8 slip away 9 intervene
Elara
  mother of: 6 Tityus
elastic 6 pliant, supple 7 pliable, rubbery, springy 8 flexible, tolerant, yielding 9 adaptable, recoiling, resilient 10 rebounding, responsive 11 complaisant, stretchable 12 recuperative 13 accommodating
elate 5 cheer, exalt 6 excite, lift up, please 7 animate, delight, elevate, enliven, gladden, gratify, inspire 10 exhilarate
elated 4 glad 5 happy, proud 6 joyful, joyous 7 exalted, excited, gleeful, pleased 8 animated, blissful, ecstatic, jubilant 9 overjoyed, rejoicing 10 delightful 11 exhilarated 13 in high spirits 18 flushed with success
elation 3 joy 4 glee 5 pride 7 triumph 8 gladness 9 happiness 10 excitement, exultation, jubilation 12 cheerfulness
Elatus
  father: 5 Arcas
  son: 6 Pereus 10 Polyphemus
elbow grease 4 work 5 force, labor 6 effort, energy, muscle 8 exertion, hard work 11 application
elbow in 4 push 5 force, press, shove 6 horn in 7 crowd in
El Cordobes (Manuel Benitez Perez)
  sport: 12 bullfighting
elder 4 head 5 older 6 senior 8 old-timer 9 firstborn, patriarch, presbyter 14 church official 15 church dignitary
  French: 4 aine

elder, elderberry 8 Sambucus
 varieties: 3 Box **4** Blue **5** Dwarf, Sweet **6** Ground, Poison, Yellow **8** American, European, Stinking **10** Red-berried **11** American red, European red **15** Pacific Coast red
elderly 3 old **4** aged **9** venerable **11** over the hill **13** past one's prime
Eldorado
 nickname of: 10 California
Eleanor and Franklin
 author: 11 Joseph P Lash
Eleazar
 father: 4 Dodo **5** Aaron, Elind, Mahli **6** Parosh **7** Phineas **8** Abinadab
 mother: 8 Elisheba
 brother: 5 Abihu, Nadab **7** Ithamar
 succeeded: 5 Aaron
elect 4 pick **5** adopt **6** choose, opt for, select, take up **7** embrace, espouse, fix upon, pick out **8** decide on, settle on **9** single out
election 4 poll, vote **6** choice, option, voting **7** resolve **8** decision **9** balloting, selection **10** resolution **11** alternative **13** determination
electioneer 3 run **5** stump **8** campaign **11** whistle-stop **12** beat the drums, solicit votes
elective 8 optional **9** selective, voluntary **11** not required **12** open to choice, passed by vote **13** discretionary, not obligatory
Electra
 author: 9 Euripides, Sophocles
 character: 7 Orestes, Pylades **8** Dioscuri **9** Aegisthus **12** Clytemnestra
 father: 9 Agamemnon
 mother: 12 Clytemnestra
 brother: 7 Orestes
 sister: 9 Iphigenia **12** Chrysothemis
 husband: 7 Pylades
 son: 5 Medon **9** Strophius
electric 7 dynamic, rousing **8** exalting, exciting, spirited, stirring **9** inspiring, thrilling **10** full of fire **11** galvanizing, power-driven, stimulating **12** electrifying, soul-stirring
electric battery
 invented by: 5 Volta
electricity measure 3 ohm **4** volt, watt **5** joule **6** ampere **10** horsepower
Electric Kool-Aid Acid Test, The
 author: 8 Tom Wolfe
Electrides
 form: 7 islands
 color: 5 amber
electrify 4 daze, stir, stun **5** amaze, rouse **6** dazzle, excite, fire up, thrill **7** animate, astound, quicken, startle **8** astonish, surprise **9** fascinate, galvanize, stimulate **18** take one's breath away
electrifying 8 dazzling, shocking, stunning **10** astounding, stupefying **11** astonishing
electromagnet
 invented by: 8 Sturgeon

Electryon
 king of: 7 Mycenae
 father: 7 Perseus
 mother: 9 Andromeda
 brother: 6 Mestor **9** Sthenelus
 wife: 5 Anaxo
 son: 9 Licymnius
 daughter: 7 Alcmene
 grandson: 8 Hercules
eleemosynary 10 altruistic, beneficent, benevolent, charitable **13** philanthropic **15** non-profitmaking
elegance 5 class, grace, taste **6** purity **7** balance **8** delicacy, grandeur, richness, symmetry **10** refinement **12** gracefulness **13** exquisiteness, luxuriousness, sumptuousness
elegant 4 fine, rich **5** grand **6** classy, dapper, lovely, ornate, polite, urbane **7** classic, courtly, genteel, refined, stylish **8** artistic, charming, debonair, delicate, graceful, gracious, handsome, polished, tasteful, well-bred **9** beautiful, dignified, exquisite, luxurious, sumptuous **10** attractive, cultivated **11** fashionable, symmetrical **16** well-proportioned
elegiac 3 sad **8** funereal, mournful **10** melancholy
elegy 7 requiem, sad poem **11** funeral song **14** melancholy poem **16** lament for the dead **17** poem of lamentation, song of lamentation **22** melancholy piece of music
Elegy Written in a Country Churchyard
 author: 10 Thomas Gray
Elektra see **7** Electra
element, elements 3 air **4** fire **5** earth, water **6** basics, member, milieu **7** essence, factors, origins **8** original **9** basic part, basic unit, component, rudiments **10** basic ideas, ingredient, principles, simple body **11** constituent, environment, foundations, native state, subdivision **13** building block, component part, natural medium **14** natural habitat
elemental 5 basal, basic **10** elementary **11** fundamental, rudimentary
elementary 4 easy **5** basal, basic, crude, first, plain **6** simple **7** primary **8** original **9** elemental, primitive **11** fundamental, rudimentary, undeveloped **13** uncomplicated
elephant
 group of: 4 herd
elephantine 4 huge **7** immense, mammoth, titanic **8** colossal, enormous, gigantic **9** ponderous **10** gargantuan, tremendous **14** Brobdingnagian
Elephant Man, The
 director: 10 David Lynch
 cast: 8 John Hurt **11** John Gielgud, Wendy Hiller **12** Anne Bancroft **14** Anthony Hopkins
Eleusinia
 origin: 5 Greek
 form: 8 festival

Eleusinian mysteries
   in memory of: 10 Persephone
   in honor of: 7 Bacchus, Demeter
   celebrated at: 6 Athens 7 Eleusis
   founded by: 8 Eumolpus
   god of: 7 Bacchus

Eleutherius
   epithet of: 4 Zeus
   means: 12 god of freedom

elevate 4 lift 5 boost, cheer, elate, heave, hoist, raise 6 better, excite, lift up, move up, perk up, refine, uplift 7 advance, animate, dignify, enhance, ennoble, improve, inspire, promote, upraise 8 heighten 9 place high 10 exhilarate, raise aloft

elevated 4 high 5 lofty 6 raised 7 exalted 8 improved, uplifted 9 prominent 10 heightened

elevation 4 hill, lift, rise 5 boost 6 ascent, height 8 altitude, mountain 9 acclivity, bettering, high place, promotion 10 prominence, refinement 11 advancement, cultivation, improvement

elevator 4 cage, lift, silo, wing 5 hoist 7 granary 10 dumbwaiter

elevator brake
   invented by: 4 Otis

elf 4 puck 5 fairy, gnome, pixie, troll 6 goblin, sprite 7 brownie, gremlin 9 hobgoblin 10 leprechaun

elfin 3 wee 4 tiny 7 pixyish 9 fairylike 10 diminutive

Elgar, Sir Edward William
   born: 7 England 10 Broadheath
   composer of: 8 Falstaff 9 Cockaigne, Froissart 10 Caractacus, The Kingdom 11 The Apostles 14 The Black Knight, The Light of Life 16 Enigma Variations 19 Pomp and Circumstance, The Banner of St George, The Dream of Gerontius 30 Scenes from the Bavarian Highlands

Eli
   son: 6 Hophni 7 Phineas
   home: 6 Shiloh

Eli, Eli, Lama sabachthani
   means: 31 My God My God why hast thou forsaken me?

elicit 5 cause, educe, evoke, exact, fetch, wrest 6 derive, extort 7 draw out, extract 9 call forth, draw forth 10 bring forth 12 bring to light

Elicius
   origin: 5 Roman
   epithet of: 7 Jupiter

elide 4 omit, slur 5 annul 6 delete 7 neglect 8 slur over, suppress 9 eliminate, strikeout 10 abbreviate

Eliezar
   father: 5 Moses
   mother: 8 Zipporah
   brother: 7 Gershom

eligible 6 proper 7 fitting 8 suitable 9 desirable, qualified 10 acceptable, applicable, authorized, worthwhile 11 appropriate

Elihu
   brother: 5 David
   friend: 3 Job 6 Bildad, Zophar 7 Eliphaz

Elijah
   opposed: 4 Ahab, Baal 7 Jezebel
   successor: 6 Elisha

Elimelech
   wife: 5 Naomi

eliminate 4 drop, omit, oust 5 eject, erase, exile, expel 6 banish, cut out, delete, except, reject, remove, rub out 7 abolish, cast out, dismiss, exclude, weed out 8 get rid of, leave out, stamp out, throw out 9 eradicate 10 annihilate, do away with 11 exterminate

Eliot, George
   real name: 13 Mary Anne Evans
   author of: 6 Romola 8 Adam Bede 11 Middlemarch, Silas Marner 17 The Mill on the Floss

Eliot, John
   author of: 12 Bay Psalm Book

Eliot, T S
   author of: 9 East Coker, Gerontion, Hollow Men 11 Burnt Norton, Dry Salvages 12 Ash Wednesday, Four Quartets, The Waste Land 13 Little Gidding, The Sacred Wood 16 The Family Reunion 20 Murder in the Cathedral 27 Sweeney Among the Nightingales 28 The Love Song of J Alfred Prufrock

Eliphaz
   father: 4 Adah, Esau
   friend: 3 Job 5 Elihu 6 Bildad, Zophar

Elisabeth see 9 Elizabeth

Elisha
   home: 11 Abelmeholah
   succeeded: 6 Elijah

Elissa
   origin: 10 Phoenician
   corresponds to: 4 Dido

elite 3 top 4 best 5 cream 6 choice, flower 7 bigwigs, society, the pick, wealthy 8 big shots, personages, select body, upper class 11 aristocracy, celebrities, high society 14 creme-de-la-creme

elixir 7 essence, extract, spirits 8 tincture 11 concentrate 17 alcoholic solution

Eliza
   character in: 14 Uncle Tom's Cabin
   author: 5 Stowe

Elizabeth
   husband: 9 Zacharias, Zechariah
   son: 14 John the Baptist

Elizabeth I
   queen of: 7 England
   father: 10 Henry Tudor 14 Henry the Eighth
   mother: 10 Anne Boleyn
   sister: 4 Mary 10 Bloody Mary
   brother: 14 Edward the Sixth
   advisor: 5 Cecil 8 Burghley 10 Walsingham
   suitor: 5 Essex 6 Dudley 9 Leicester
   victory over: 13 Spanish Armada

Elizabeth II
   father: 14 George the Sixth
   mother: 9 Elizabeth
   husband: 17 Philip Mountbatten

son: 6 Andrew, Edward 7 Charles
daughter: 4 Anne
Elizabeth the Queen
author: 15 Maxwell Anderson
elk
group of: 4 gang
Ellas see 6 Greece
Elli
origin: 12 Scandinavian
personifies: 5 aging
defeated: 4 Thor
sport: 9 wrestling
Ellice Islands see 6 Tuvalu
Ellington, Duke
real name: 22 Edward Kennedy Ellington
born: 12 Washington DC
composer of: 10 Mood Indigo 14 Creole Love Call, Creole Rhapsody, Hot and Bothered 17 Concerto for Cootie 18 Black and Tan Fantasy
Elliot family
characters in: 10 Persuasion
member: 4 Anne 7 William 9 Elizabeth, Sir Walter
author: 6 Austen
Ellison, Harlan
author of: 7 Paingod 10 Spider Kiss 13 A Boy and His Dog 16 Deathbird Stories 19 Approaching Oblivion 20 Alone Against Tomorrow
Ellison, Ralph
author of: 12 Invisible Man
elm 5 Ulmus
varieties: 3 red 4 bush, cork, rock, vase, wych 5 cedar, Dutch, dwarf, globe, wahoo, water, white 6 Exeter, horned, Jersey, moline, Scotch, willow, winged 7 Belgian, Chinese, Cornish, English, Holland 8 American, fern-leaf, Guernsey, Japanese, Siberian, slippery, tabletop, wheatley 9 September 10 camperdown, Chichester, Huntingdon, smooth-leaf 11 small-leaved 13 European white
Elmer Gantry
author: 13 Sinclair Lewis
director: 13 Richard Brooks
cast: 10 Dean Jagger 11 Jean Simmons 12 Shirley Jones 13 Arthur Kennedy, Burt Lancaster
Oscar for: 5 actor (Lancaster) 17 supporting actress (Jones)
elocution 6 speech 7 diction, oratory 10 intonation 11 enunciation 12 articulation 13 pronunciation 14 public speaking
Elohim 3 God
Eloisa to Abelard
author: 13 Alexander Pope
Elon 11 Hebrew judge
elongate 6 extend 7 draw out, prolong 8 lengthen, protract 10 stretch out
elongated 4 long 8 drawn out, extended 9 prolonged 10 attenuated, lengthened, protracted 12 stretched out
eloquence 5 force, grace 7 fluency, oratory 8 rhetoric 9 elocution, speakwell, vividness 10 expression 12 silver tongue
god of: 4 Ogma 6 Ogmios 7 Mercury

eloquent 5 vivid 6 moving, poetic 8 emphatic, forceful, spirited, stirring, striking 10 articulate, passionate, persuasive 11 impassioned
Elpenor
companion of: 7 Ulysses 8 Odysseus
El Salvador
other name: 9 Cuscatlan
capital/largest city: 11 San Salvador
others: 6 Cutuco, Izalco 7 Corinto, Metapan 8 Acajutla, Libertad, Santa Ana, Usulutan 9 San Miguel, Sonsonate 10 San Vicente, Santa Tecla 11 Union-Cutuco 12 Chalatenango
school: 15 Jose Simeon Canas 16 Alberto Masferrer
measure: 4 vara 5 cafiz, cahiz 6 fanega 7 batella, botella, cantara, manzana
monetary unit: 4 peso 5 colon 7 centavo
weight: 3 bag 4 caja 5 libra
lake: 5 Guiha, Guija 8 Ilopango 10 Coatepeque
mountain: 6 Izalco
highest point: 8 Santa Ana
river: 5 Jiboa, Lempa, Lopaz 6 Torola 7 de la Paz 9 Goasoaran 17 Grande de San Miguel
sea: 7 Pacific
physical feature:
bay: 10 Jiquilisco
coast: 6 Balsam
gulf: 7 Fonseca
point: 7 Amapala 8 Remedios
valley: 7 Hamacas
people: 5 Lenca, Pipil 6 Indian, Mangue 7 mestizo, Spanish 9 Matagalpa
artist: 8 Salarrue 10 Mejia Vides
author: 8 Salarrue 14 Antonio Gavidia
conqueror: 8 Alvarado
leader: 6 Osorio 8 Jose Arce 13 Matias Delgado 15 Manuel Rodriguez 17 Hernandez Martinez
philosopher/journalist: 9 Masferrer
language: 7 Spanish
religion: 13 Roman Catholic
place:
ruins: 7 Tazumal
feature:
blouse: 9 volcanena
dance: 7 pasillo 15 los historiantes
drum: 8 huehuetl
estate: 5 finca
musical instrument: 7 caramba
food:
bread: 10 quesadilla
cheese pancake: 6 pupusa
Elscheimer, Adam
born: 7 Germany 15 Frankfurt am Main
artwork: 17 Tobias and the Angel 21 The Stoning of St Stephen 24 Rest on the Flight into Egypt
else 3 and, too 4 also, more 5 if not, other 7 besides, instead 9 different, otherwise 10 additional, contrarily, in addition
elsewhere 4 away 6 except 7 absence, not here

Elsinore
   castle in: 6 Hamlet
   author: 11 Shakespeare

Elton, Mr
   character in: 4 Emma
   author: 6 Austen

elucidate 6 detail 7 clarify, clear up, explain, expound 8 describe, spell out 9 delineate, explicate, interpret, make plain 10 illuminate, illustrate 11 comment upon 14 throw light upon

elucidation 7 account 10 commentary 11 description, explanation, explication 13 clarification 14 interpretation 15 exemplification

elude 4 shun 5 avoid, dodge, evade 6 escape, slip by 10 circumvent, fight shy of 11 get away from, keep clear of

eluding 7 dodging, ducking, evading, evasion 8 avoiding 9 avoidance 12 escaping from, sidestepping 13 circumventing 15 getting away from

Elul 16 sixth Hebrew month

elusive 4 foxy, wily 6 crafty, shifty, tricky 7 evasive 8 baffling, puzzling, slippery 11 hard to catch, hard to grasp

elusory 4 wily 6 shifty 7 devious, dodging, elusive, evasive, hedging 8 slippery 9 ambiguous, deceitful, deceptive, equivocal 10 misleading 12 equivocating

Elvsted, Thea
   character in: 11 Hedda Gabler
   author: 5 Ibsen

elysian 7 sublime 8 blissful, empyreal, empyrean, ethereal, heavenly 9 celestial, unearthly 12 otherworldly, paradisiacal

Elysium
   also: 17 islands of the blest
   afterworld of the: 7 blessed

Elytis, Odysseus
   real name: 19 Odysseus Alepoudelis
   author of: 10 Seemly It Is 20 Heroic and Elegiac Song

emaciated 4 lank, lean, thin 5 gaunt 6 sickly, skinny, wasted 7 haggard, scrawny, wizened 8 skeletal, starving, underfed 10 cadaverous 14 undernourished

emanate 4 flow, rise, stem, well 5 exude, issue 6 spring 7 give off, proceed 8 come from 9 come forth, originate, send forth

emanation 6 coming 7 arising, flowing, issuing 8 effusion 9 effluence, radiation, springing 10 exhalation 11 coming forth

emancipate 4 free 7 manumit, release, set free, unchain 8 liberate, unfetter 9 unshackle 12 set at liberty

emancipation 7 freedom, liberty 10 liberation 11 manumission 12 independence

emasculate 4 geld 5 alter 6 soften, weaken 8 castrate 9 undermine 10 devitalize

Emathion
   father: 8 Tithonus
   mother: 3 Eos
   brother: 7 Memnon

Emaux et Camees
   author: 16 Theophile Gautier

Embalming
   god of: 6 Anubis

embankment 4 bank, dike, wall 5 levee

embargo 3 ban 8 shutdown, stoppage 10 impediment, inhibition, injunction, quarantine, standstill 11 prohibition, restriction 12 interdiction, proscription 16 restraint of trade

embark 5 begin, board, start 6 launch, set out 7 enplane, entrain 8 commence, go aboard 9 board ship, enter upon

embark on 5 begin, start 8 approach, commence, initiate, set about 9 enter upon, undertake

embarras de richesses 13 overabundance 21 embarrassment of riches

embarrass 4 faze 5 abash, shame, upset 6 rattle 7 agitate, chagrin, confuse, fluster, mortify, nonplus 8 distress 9 discomfit 10 discompose, disconcert 13 make ill at ease 14 discountenance 17 make self-conscious

embarrassed 7 abashed 8 red-faced 9 chagrined, mortified 10 nonplussed 11 discomfited 13 self-conscious

embarrassing 7 awkward 8 confused, crushing 9 bothering 10 disturbing, mortifying, unpleasant 12 demoralizing, discomfiting 13 discomforting, disconcerting, uncomfortable

embarrassment 4 blot 5 stain 6 smirch 7 blemish, scandal, tarnish 8 disgrace 9 discredit 19 financial difficulty

embarrassment of riches
   French: 19 embarras de richesses

embattled 8 fighting 9 embroiled, fortified 11 battle-ready, hard-pressed

embed 3 fix, set 4 bond 5 plant 6 fasten 8 ensconce 9 establish

embedded 3 set 5 fixed 6 bonded 7 engaged, planted 8 immersed, inserted 9 ensconced 11 established

embellish 4 gild 5 adorn, color 6 set off 7 dress up, enhance, fancy up, garnish, gussy up 8 beautify, decorate, ornament 9 elaborate, embroider 10 exaggerate

embellished 6 ornate 7 adorned, flowery 8 brocaded 9 decorated 10 beautified, elaborated, ornamented, rhetorical 11 embroidered

embellishment 5 frill 6 accent 7 garnish 8 furbelow, ornament, trimming 9 adornment 10 decoration, embroidery 11 elaboration 14 beautification 15 fuss and feathers

ember 3 ash 4 slag 6 cinder 7 clinker 8 live coal

embezzle 4 bilk, rook 5 cheat, filch 6 fleece 7 defraud, swindle 9 defalcate 14 misappropriate

embezzler 5 cheat, crook, thief 8 swindler

Embezzler, The
   author: 16 Louis Auchincloss

embitter 4 sour 6 rankle 7 envenom 10 make bitter 11 make cynical 13 make rancorous, make resentful 15 make pessimistic

embittered 6 soured 7 cynical 9 rancorous, resentful 11 acrimonious

Embla
origin: 12 Scandinavian
first: 5 woman
made by: 4 gods
made from: 4 tree

emblem 4 sign 5 badge 6 design, device, symbol 7 insignia 8 colophon, hallmark

emblematic 7 typical 8 symbolic 10 indicative 11 distinctive 14 characteristic, representative

embodiment 7 epitome, essence 14 representation 15 exemplification, personification

embody 4 fuse 5 blend, merge 6 typify 7 collect, contain, embrace, express, include, realize 8 manifest, organize 9 exemplify, personify, represent, symbolize 10 assimilate 11 consolidate, incorporate 12 substantiate

embolden 7 fortify, hearten, inspire 8 inspirit 9 encourage

emboldened 6 poised 7 assured, unfazed 9 confident, heartened, unabashed 10 courageous, encouraged, inspirited

embonpoint 9 plumpness, stoutness 15 in good condition

emboss 4 knob, knot, stud 5 adorn, chase 6 indent 7 engrave, exhaust 8 decorate

embossed 4 bold 6 raised 7 adorned, antique, knotted 8 engraved, indented 9 decorated, exhausted

embrace 3 hug 5 adopt, clasp, cover, grasp 6 accept, embody 7 contain, espouse, include, involve 8 comprise 9 encompass 10 comprehend 11 consolidate, incorporate

embroider 5 color 7 dress up 9 elaborate, embellish, fabricate 10 exaggerate 11 romanticize

embroidery 8 tapestry 9 adornment, gros point 10 crewelwork, decoration, needlework, petit point 11 imagination 12 exaggeration 13 ornamentation

embroil 4 trap 6 enmesh 7 ensnare, involve 8 entangle 10 complicate

embroiled 6 enmeshed 9 embattled, entangled 11 hard-pressed

embroilment 3 row 4 fray, tilt 5 brawl, brush, clash, melee 6 fracas, ruckus, rumpus, uproar 7 scuffle 8 conflict, disorder, struggle 9 confusion, imbroglio 10 contention 11 altercation 12 entanglement

embryo 3 bud, egg 4 germ 5 fetus, larva, ovule 6 budding, source 8 immature, rudiment 9 beginning 11 rudimentary, undeveloped

embryonic 5 rough 6 unborn 7 nascent 8 immature, inchoate 9 beginning, imperfect, incipient 10 incomplete, unfinished 11 rudimentary, undeveloped

emend 6 change, revise 7 correct, improve, rectify

emendation 8 revision 10 alteration, correction 11 improvement

emerald
species: 5 beryl
source: 4 Muzo 5 Egypt, India 6 Chivor 8 Colombia, Rhodesia, Zimbabwe 11 South Africa, Soviet Union 13 Ural Mountains
color: 5 green

Emerald City
setting in: 13 The Wizard of Oz
author: 4 Baum

Emerald Isle see 7 Ireland

emerge 3 run 4 dawn, emit, flow, gush, loom, pour, rise 5 arise, issue 6 appear, come up, crop up, escape, stream, turn up 7 develop, surface 9 come forth, discharge 11 come to light 12 come into view 13 become visible 14 become apparent, become manifest

emergence 4 dawn 7 dawning 10 appearance 11 development 13 coming to light, manifestation 15 materialization

emergency 5 pinch 6 crisis 7 urgency 8 exigency 11 contingency, predicament 16 unforeseen danger

Emergency
character: 8 (Dr) Joe Early, (Paramedic) John Gage 9 (Paramedic) Roy DeSoto 11 (Nurse) Dixie McCall 13 (Dr) Kelly Brackett
cast: 10 Bobby Troup, Kevin Tighe 11 Julie London 12 Robert Fuller 16 Randolph Mantooth

Emerson, Ralph Waldo
nickname: 13 Sage of Concord
author of: 4 Fate 6 Brahma, Nature 10 Friendship, The Rhodora 12 Compensation, Self-Reliance 14 The Concord Hymn 18 The American Scholar
philosophy: 17 Transcendentalism

emeute 4 riot

emigrant 6 emigre 8 wanderer, wayfarer 10 expatriate

Emigrants, The
author: 10 Johan Bojer

emigrate 4 move, quit 5 leave 6 depart, remove 7 migrate

emigration 5 exile 6 exodus 12 expatriation

emigre 2 DP 5 alien, exile 7 evacuee, refugee 8 defector, emigrant, expellee, fugitive 9 immigrant 10 expatriate 15 displaced person 16 political refugee

Emile
author: 19 Jean Jacques Rousseau
treatise on: 9 education

Emilia
character in: 7 Othello
author: 11 Shakespeare

eminence 4 fame, hill, note, peak, rise 5 bluff, cliff, glory, knoll, ridge 6 height, repute, summit, upland 7 hillock, hummock 8 mountain, standing 9 celebrity, elevation, greatness, high place, high point 10 excellence, importance, notability, prominence, promontory, reputation 11 distinction, preeminence 12 elevated rank, high position, public esteem 15 conspicuousness

eminence grise 15 unofficial power
literally: 12 gray eminence

eminent 3 top 5 grand, great, noted 6 famous, signal, utmost 7 exalted, notable, unusual 8 elevated, esteemed, glorious, imposing, laureate, renowned 9 important, memorable, paramount, prominent, well-known 10 celebrated, noteworthy, preeminent, remarkable 11 high-ranking, illustrious, outstanding 13 distinguished, extraordinary

emir 4 amir, Arab, Turk 5 chief, emeer, ruler 6 leader, prince 9 chieftain, commander, dignitary

emissary 5 agent, envoy 6 deputy, herald, legate 7 courier 8 delegate 9 go-between, messenger 10 ambassador 14 representative

emission 5 fumes, smoke, waste 8 ejection, emitting, impurity, issuance, voidance 9 discharge, emanation, excretion, expulsion, extrusion, pollutant 10 sending out 11 throwing out 12 transmission

emit 4 beam, give, shed, vent 5 expel, issue 7 cast out, excrete, secrete, send out 8 dispatch, throw out, transmit 9 discharge, give forth, pour forth

Emma
author: 10 Jane Austen
character: 7 Mr Elton 9 Miss Bates, Mrs Weston 11 Jane Fairfax 12 Harriet Smith, Robert Martin 13 Emma Woodhouse 14 Frank Churchill 15 George Knightley

Emmanuel 7 Messiah 11 Jesus Christ
means: 9 God with us

emollient 3 oil 4 balm 5 balmy, cream, salve 6 lotion 7 calming, easeful, healing, unguent 8 allaying, lenitive, ointment, relaxing, soothing 9 assuasive, lubricant, relieving 10 palliative 11 alleviative, restorative

emolument 3 fee, pay 4 gain, wage 6 income, profit, salary 7 benefit, stipend 9 advantage 10 honorarium 12 compensation, remuneration

emotion 4 fear, hate, heat, love, zeal 5 anger, ardor, pride 6 fervor, sorrow, warmth 7 concern, despair, passion, sadness 8 jealousy 9 agitation, happiness, sentiment, vehemence 10 excitement 12 satisfaction

emotional 4 warm 5 fiery 6 ardent, moving 7 fervent, zealous 8 stirring, touching 9 excitable, impetuous, thrilling, wrought-up 10 high-strung, hysterical, passionate, responsive, vulnerable 11 impassioned, sentimental, tear-jerking 12 enthusiastic, heartwarming, heart-rending, soul-stirring 13 demonstrative, temperamental 14 hypersensitive

emotionalism 8 hysteria 9 gushiness, hysterics, melodrama, theatrics 11 mawkishness 13 melodramatics, show of emotion 14 sentimentality 17 demonstrativeness

emotionless 6 stolid 7 unmoved 9 apathetic, impassive, unfeeling 11 passionless, unemotional

emperor, empress 4 czar, king, shah 5 queen, ruler 6 caesar, kaiser, mikado, sultan 7 czarina, monarch, sultana 9 sovereign 14 dowager empress

Emperor Jones, The
author: 12 Eugene O'Neill
character: 4 Jeff 8 Smithers 11 Brutus Jones

Emperor's New Clothes, The
author: 21 Hans Christian Andersen

emphasis 6 accent, stress, weight 7 feature 10 focal point 12 accentuation, underscoring

emphasize 6 accent, stress 7 dwell on, feature, iterate, point up 9 press home, punctuate, underline 10 accentuate, underscore

emphatic 4 flat 6 marked, strong 7 certain, decided, express, telling 8 absolute, decisive, definite, distinct, forceful, striking, vigorous 9 assertive, insistent, momentous 10 pronounced, undeniable, unwavering, unyielding 11 categorical, conspicuous, significant, unequivocal, unqualified 12 unmistakable

empire 4 rule 5 realm 6 domain 8 dominion, imperium 11 sovereignty 12 commonwealth

Empire State
nickname of: 7 New York

Empire State of the South
nickname of: 7 Georgia

Empire Strikes Back, The
director: 13 Irvin Kershner
cast: 10 Kenny Baker, Mark Hamill (Luke Skywalker) 11 David Prowse, Peter Mayhew 12 Alec Guinness, Carrie Fisher (Princess Leia), Harrison Ford (Han Solo) 14 Anthony Daniels (C3PO) 16 Billy Dee Williams (Lando Calrissian)
sequel to: 8 Star Wars
sequel: 15 Return of the Jedi

empirical 9 firsthand, practical, pragmatic 12 experiential, experimental

employ 3 use 4 hire 5 apply 6 devote, engage, occupy, retain, take on 7 service, utilize 8 exercise, keep busy, put to use 9 make use of 10 commission, employment 12 retainership

employee 6 member, worker 8 hireling 9 job holder, underling 10 wage earner

employer 4 boss, firm 6 outfit 7 company 8 business 10 proprietor 12 organization 13 establishment

employment 3 job, use 4 line, task, work 5 chore, field, trade, using 6 employ 7 calling, pursuit, service 8 business, exercise, exertion, vocation 9 employing 10 engagement, occupation, profession 11 application, utilization 13 preoccupation

emporium 5 store 6 bazaar, market 9 warehouse 10 large store 12 general store 15 department store

empower 4 vest 5 allow, endow 6 enable, invest, permit 7 license 8 delegate, sanction 9 authorize 10 commission

empress 5 queen, ruler 7 czarina, monarch, sultana 9 sovereign

emprise 7 venture 9 adventure 10 enterprise 11 undertaking

emptied 6 used up 7 drained, vacated 8 consumed, depleted, finished 9 evacuated, exhausted

emptiness 4 void 6 vacuum 7 vacancy 8 bareness 10 barrenness, desolation, hollowness

empty 4 bare, dump, flow, idle, void 5 banal, drain, inane 6 futile, hollow, vacant 7 aimless, debouch, insipid, pour out, shallow, trivial, vacuous 8 evacuate 9 discharge, frivolous, worthless 10 unoccupied 11 meaningless, purposeless, unfulfilled, uninhabited 13 insignificant

empty space 3 gap 4 void 5 blank 6 cavity, lacuna, vacuum 7 vacancy

Empusae
    form: 7 monster
    eats: 3 man

empyrean 7 elysian, sublime 8 blissful, heavenly 9 celestial 12 paradisiacal

emu
    also: 4 emeu
    form: 4 bird
    characteristic: 9 nonflying, three toed

emulate 3 ape 4 copy 5 mimic, rival 6 follow 7 imitate

emulative 5 model 9 exemplary

enable 3 aid 5 allow 6 assist, permit 7 benefit, empower, qualify, support 8 make able 10 capacitate, facilitate 15 make possible for

enact 4 pass 6 decree, ratify 7 approve 8 proclaim, sanction 9 authorize, institute, legislate 11 pass into law 12 vote to accept

enactment 3 law 4 bill 5 canon, edict, ukase 6 decree 7 statute 9 ordinance, prescript 11 legislation 12 proclamation, ratification

Enalus
    loved: 7 Phineis
    saved by: 7 dolphin

enamel 4 coat 5 paint 7 coating 12 glossy finish, tooth coating

enamor 5 charm 6 allure, attach, draw to, excite 7 bewitch, enchant 8 enthrall, entrance 9 captivate, enrapture, fascinate, infatuate 12 take a fancy to

enamored 6 in love 7 amorous 8 lovesick 10 infatuated .

en arriere 8 backward

en avant 6 onward 7 forward

en bloc 8 as a whole

encage 3 pen 4 cage 5 pen in 6 coop up, lock up, shut in 7 confine 8 restrain 11 incarcerate

encamp 4 camp 7 bivouac 9 set up camp 10 pitch a tent

encampment 4 camp 5 tents 7 bivouac 8 tent city

encase 4 wrap 5 cover 6 enfold, enwrap 7 enclose, envelop, sheathe

enceinte 8 pregnant

Enceladus
    form: 5 giant
    hit by: 5 stone
    stone flung by: 6 Athena
    location: 6 Sicily
    buried under: 9 Mount Etna

enchain 7 enslave, shackle 8 enthrall 11 put in chains 13 hold in bondage

enchant 5 charm 7 bewitch, delight 8 enthrall, entrance 9 captivate, enrapture, fascinate, hypnotize, mesmerize, transport 14 cast a spell over 16 place under a spell

enchanted 7 charmed, pleased 9 bewitched, delighted, entranced 10 captivated, enraptured, enthralled, spellbound 11 under a spell

enchanting 8 charming, pleasant 9 agreeable, wonderful 10 bewitching, delightful, entrancing 11 captivating, enthralling, fascinating, hypnotizing 12 spellbinding 15 casting a spell on 17 casting a spell over

enchantment 5 spell 6 allure, appeal 9 magnetism 10 attraction 11 captivation, fascination

enchantress 4 vamp 5 siren, witch 7 charmer, vampire 9 sorceress, temptress 10 seductress 11 femme fatale

Enchiridion
    author: 11 St Augustine

encircle 4 gird, ring, wall 5 fence, hem in 6 circle, girdle 7 enclose, wreathe 8 surround 9 encompass 12 circumscribe

enclose, inclose 4 ring 6 circle, girdle, insert, wall in 7 close in, fence in, include 8 encircle, surround 9 encompass, send along 12 circumscribe

enclosed area 4 quad 5 court, patio 6 atrium 9 courtyard 10 quadrangle

enclosure 3 sty 4 cage, coop, jail, wall 5 fence, hedge, stall 6 corral, kennel, pigsty 7 paddock, wrapper 8 envelope, stockade 9 cartridge, inclosure 10 receptacle

encomium 5 paean 6 eulogy 7 plaudit, tribute 8 citation 9 laudation, panegyric 11 acclamation

encompass 4 hold, ring 5 cover, hem in 6 circle, embody, girdle, take in, wall in 7 contain, embrace, enclose, fence in, include, involve, touch on 8 comprise, encircle, surround 11 incorporate 12 circumscribe

encounter 4 bout, face, meet 5 brush, clash, fight 6 affray, battle, combat, endure, fracas, suffer 7 run into, sustain, undergo 8 come upon, confront, meet with, skirmish 9 clash with 10 chance upon, engagement, experience 11 grapple with 12 do battle with, meet and fight, skirmish with 13 confrontation 14 contend against, engage in combat, hostile meeting 18 come face to face with

Encounters with the Archdruid
    author: 10 John McPhee

encourage 3 aid 4 help, spur, sway 5 boost, cheer, egg on, favor, impel, rally 6 assist, exhort, foster, induce, prompt 7 advance, forward, further, hearten, inspire, promote 8 embolden, inspirit, reassure 10 give hope to

encouragement 4 lift 5 boost 6 praise 7 backing, support 11 approbation, encouraging, reassurance 12 shot in the arm 13 reinforcement

encroach 6 invade 7 impinge, intrude, overrun, violate 8 infringe, overstep, trespass 9 break into, interfere 10 transgress 11 make inroads

encumber 3 tax 4 lade, load 6 burden, hinder, impede, saddle 8 handicap, load down, obstruct, slow down 9 weigh down 13 inconvenience

encumbrance 4 load, onus 6 burden 9 hindrance 10 impediment 11 obstruction 13 inconvenience

Encyclopedia
    author: 9 D'Alembert 12 Denis Diderot

encyclopedic 5 broad 7 erudite 9 scholarly, universal 10 exhaustive 11 wide-ranging 13 comprehensive 15 all-encompassing

end 3 aim 4 edge, goal, halt, kill, ruin, stop 5 cease, close, death, issue, limit, scrap 6 border, demise, design, effect, ending, finale, finish, object, result, run out, upshot, windup 7 destroy, outcome, purpose, remnant 8 boundary, conclude, fragment, leave off, leftover, terminus 9 cessation, eradicate, extremity, finish off, intention, objective, terminate 10 annihilate, completion, conclusion, denouement, expiration, extinction, extinguish, put an end to, settlement 11 consequence, culmination, destruction, exterminate, fulfillment, termination 12 annihilation, consummation, draw to a close 13 extermination 19 bring down the curtain

endanger 4 risk 6 expose, hazard 7 imperil 8 threaten 10 compromise, jeopardize 11 put in danger

endear 8 make dear 10 ingratiate 11 make beloved

endearment 7 pet name 9 sweet talk 10 loving word 12 sweet nothing 13 fond utterance

endeavor 3 aim, job, try 4 seek, work 5 essay, labor 6 aspire, career, effort, strive, work at 7 attempt 8 exertion, interest, striving, struggle, vocation 9 take pains, undertake 10 do one's best, enterprise, occupation 11 undertaking 12 make an effort 13 preoccupation

ended 4 done, over 6 ceased, closed, halted, runout 7 expired, stopped, wound up 8 finished, over with, resulted 9 completed, concluded, destroyed 10 terminated 11 annihilated 12 discontinued, exterminated

Endeis
    father: 6 Sciron
    husband: 6 Aeacus
    son: 6 Peleus 7 Telamon
    stepson: 6 Phocus

Enderby
    author: 14 Anthony Burgess

end from which
    Latin: 12 terminus a quo

ending 3 end 5 close 6 finale, finish, windup 9 cessation 10 completion, conclusion, expiration 11 culmination, termination 12 consummation

ending point
    Latin: 14 terminus ad quem

Ending Up
    author: 12 Kingsley Amis

endless 7 eternal 8 constant, infinite, unbroken, unending 9 boundless, continual, perpetual, unlimited 10 continuous, persistent, without end 11 everlasting, measureless, never-ending 12 interminable 13 uninterrupted

endlessly 7 forever 10 constantly 11 ceaselessly, continually, perpetually 12 continuously
    Latin: 11 ad infinitum

endocrine system
    component: 5 ovary 6 testes, thymus 7 adrenal, thyroid 9 pituitary 11 parathyroid

endocuticle
    consists of: 6 chitin

end of the century
    French: 11 fin de siecle

End of the Road, The
    author: 9 John Barth

end of the world 8 doomsday 10 Armageddon 11 Judgment Day 13 Day of Judgment 15 the Last Judgment

End of the World News, The
    author: 14 Anthony Burgess

endorse, indorse 2 OK 4 back, sign 6 affirm, ratify, second 7 approve, certify, support 8 advocate, champion, sanction, validate, vouch for 9 authorize, recommend 11 countersign, stand behind, subscribe to 14 lend one's name to

endorsement 2 OK 7 support 8 approval 9 signature 10 acceptance 12 commendation, ratification 14 seal of approval 16 official sanction

endow 4 will 5 award, bless, equip, favor, grace, grant, leave 6 accord, bestow, confer, invest, supply 7 furnish, provide 8 bequeath, settle on

endowed 6 graced 7 blessed, favored 8 bestowed, enriched, provided 10 bequeathed

endowment 4 gift 5 award, flair, grant 6 legacy, talent 7 ability, bequest, faculty 8 aptitude, donation 9 attribute 10 capability 11 benefaction, natural gift

end to which
    Latin: 14 terminus ad quem

endue 5 dress, endow, equip, indue, put on 6 bestow, clothe, outfit, supply 7 furnish

endurable 8 bearable 9 tolerable 11 sustainable

endurance 7 stamina 8 strength, tenacity 9 fortitude, hardihood, stability 10 durability, permanence, resolution 11 durableness, persistence 12 immutability, perseverance, staying power 13 tenaciousness 14 changelessness 16 stick-to-itiveness

endure 4 bear, last, live 5 brave, brook, stand 6 live on, remain, suffer 7 persist, prevail, sustain, undergo, weather 8 continue, cope with, tolerate 9 go through, withstand 10 experience 11 bear up under, countenance

enduring 7 abiding, durable, eternal, lasting 8 constant, unending 9 immutable, permanent, steadfast 10 changeless, continuing, unchanging 11 everlasting, longlasting 12 indissoluble

Endymion
   author: 9 John Keats
   form: 5 youth
   father: 8 Aethlios
   mother: 6 Calyce
   loved by: 4 Moon 6 Selene
   son: 5 Epeus, Paeon 7 Aetolus
   number of daughters: 5 fifty
   granddaughter: 7 Hyrmina

enemy 3 foe 5 rival 7 nemesis 8 armed foe, attacker, opponent 9 adversary, assailant, detractor 10 antagonist, competitor

Enemy of the People, An
   author: 11 Henrik Ibsen

energetic 5 alert, brisk, peppy, zippy 6 active, lively, robust 7 dynamic 8 animated, forceful, restless, spirited, vigorous 9 go-getting 11 hard-working, high-powered, industrious, quick-witted 12 enthusiastic

energize 7 animate, enliven, quicken 8 vitalize 9 galvanize, stimulate 10 invigorate, strengthen

energy 2 go 3 pep, vim, zip 4 elan, zeal, zest 5 drive, force, power, verve, vigor 6 hustle 8 dynamism, vitality, vivacity 9 animation 10 enterprise, liveliness

enervate 3 fag 4 bush, tire 5 weary 6 tucker, weaken 7 deplete, disable, exhaust, fatigue, wash out 8 enfeeble 9 prostrate 10 debilitate, devitalize 13 sap one's energy

enervated 5 spent 6 effete, wasted 7 languid, worn-out 8 fatigued, listless, sluggish, unmanned, unnerved, weakened 9 enfeebled, exhausted, lethargic, washed out 11 debilitated, devitalized, emasculated

enervation 7 fatigue 9 tiredness, weariness 10 exhaustion

en famille 11 in the family

Enfants Terribles, Les
   author: 11 Jean Cocteau

enfant terrible 16 indiscreet person 17 incorrigible child 19 irresponsible person

enfeeble 3 sap 6 impair, weaken 8 enervate 10 debilitate

enfin 7 finally 8 in the end 12 in conclusion

enfold 4 veil, wrap 5 cloak, cover 6 encase, enwrap, shroud 7 blanket, contain, embrace, enclose, envelop, sheathe 8 surround

enforce 5 apply, exact 6 defend, impose 7 execute, support 8 carry out, insist on 9 implement 10 administer

enforcement 5 force 6 duress 7 defense, support 8 coercion, pressure 9 execution 10 compulsion, constraint, imposition, obligation 11 carrying out 13 necessitation, strengthening 14 implementation

engage 4 hire 6 absorb, combat, employ, occupy, pledge, retain, secure, take on 7 betroth, engross, involve, partake, promise, war with 8 affiance, embark on, set about, takepart 9 enter into, fight with, undertake 10 commission 11 busy oneself, participate 12 give battle to 15 take into service

engaged 5 hired, in use 6 active, took on 7 partook, pledged, secured 8 absorbed, employed, involved, occupied, promised, retained, took part 9 affianced, betrothed, engrossed, undertook 10 embarked on 11 entered into, particpated 15 took into service

engagement 3 gig, job 4 bout, date, duty, fray, post 5 banns, berth, brush, fight, troth 6 action, battle, billet, combat 7 contest, meeting, scuffle 8 conflict, position, skirmish 9 betrothal, encounter, situation 10 affiancing, commitment, employment, obligation 11 appointment, arrangement

engage pleasantly 5 amuse, charm 6 divert, please 7 beguile, delight 8 enthrall, interest 9 entertain

engaging 7 likable, lovable, winning, winsome 8 charming, fetching, pleasing 9 agreeable, appealing, disarming 10 attractive, enchanting 11 captivating 12 ingratiating

Engels, Friedrich
   author of: 18 Communist Manifesto (with Karl Marx)

engender 5 beget, breed, cause 7 produce 8 generate, occasion 10 bring about, give rise to 11 precipitate

engine
   inventor:
     of compression ignition: 7 Daimler
     of electric ignition: 4 Benz
     of gas (compound): 10 Eickemeyer
     of gasoline: 7 Brayton, Daimler
     of piston steam: 4 Watt 8 Newcomen

engineer 5 pilot 6 driver, hogger 7 builder, hoghead, planner 8 maneuver, motorman, operator 10 accomplish

England
   other name: 6 Albion 7 Britain 9 Britannia 12 Great Britain
   capital/largest city: 6 London
   others: 3 Ely 4 Bath, Deal, Hull, Ryde, Ware, York 5 Blyth, Brent, Derby, Dover, Erith, Flint, Leeds, Ripon, Truro, Wigan 6 Barnet, Bolton, Bootle, Camden, Durham, Ealing, Exeter, Henley, Jarrow, Leyton, Oldham, Oxford, Yeovil 7 Bristol, Bromley, Burnley, Chelsea, Croydon, Enfield, Grimsby, Halifax, Hornsey, Ipswich, Lambeth, Newport, Norwich, Preston, Salford, 8 Bradford, Brighton, Cornwall, Coventry, Dewsbury, Hastings, Plymouth 9 Greenwich, Liverpool, Newcastle, Sheffield 10 Birmingham, Manchester 15 Stratford-on-Avon
   school: 4 Eton 5 Leeds, Rugby 6 Har-

row, London, Oxford **9** Cambridge, Sandhurst **23** London School of Economics

division: 4 Avon, Kent **5** Devon, Essex, **6** Dorset, Durham, Surrey, Sussex **7** Norfolk, Suffolk **8** Cheshire, Cornwall, Somerset **9** Hampshire, Wiltshire, Yorkshire **10** Derbyshire, East Sussex, Humberside, Lancashire, Merseyside, Shropshire, West Sussex **11** Oxfordshire, Tyne and Wear **12** Bedfordshire, Lincolnshire, Warwickshire, West Midlands **13** Hertfordshire, Staffordshire, West Yorkshire **14** Cambridgeshire, Leicestershire, Northumberland, North Yorkshire, South Yorkshire **15** Buckinghamshire, Gloucestershire, Nottinghamshire **16** Northamptonshire **20** Hereford and Worcester

head of state: 4 king **5** queen **7** monarch

measure: 3 cut, lea, pin, rod, ton, tun, vat **4** acre, bind, butt, comb, coom, foot, gill, goad, hand, hank, heer, hide, inch, last, line, mile, nail, pace, palm, peck, pint, pipe, pole, pool, rood, rope, sack, seam, span, trug, typp, wist, yard, yoke **5** bodge, chain, coomb, cubit, digit, float, floor, fluid, hutch, jugum, minim, ounce, perch, point, prime, quart, skein, stack, truss **6** barrel, bovate, bushel, cranne, fathom, firkin, gallon, hobbet, hobbit, league, manent, oxgang, pottle, runlet, square, strike, sulung, thread, tierce **7** auchlet, furlong, kenning, quarter, rundlet, seamile, spindle, tertian, virgate **8** carucate, chaldron, hogshead, landyard, puncheon, quadrant, standard

monetary unit: 3 ora **4** rial **5** ackey, crown, groat, noble, pence, penny, pound, sprat, unite **6** bawbee, florin, guinea, seskin **7** angelet, hapenny **8** farthing, shilling, sixpence, tuppence

weight: 3 bag, kip, tod, ton **4** keel, last, mast, maun **5** barge, fagot, grain, pound, score, stone, truss **6** bushel, cental, fangot, fother, fotmal, pocket **7** quarter, sarpler

island: 3 Man **4** Holy **5** Farne, Lundy, Wight **6** Coquet, Mersea, Scilly, Thanet, Tresco, Walney **7** Bardsey, Channel, Hayling, Ireland, Sheppey **8** Anglesea, Anglesey, Foulness, Holyhead

lake: 8 Grasmere **9** Ennerdale, Ullswater, Wastwater **10** Buttermere, Windermere **12** Derwentwater **13** Coniston Water

mountain: 5 Black **7** Pennine, Snowdon **8** Cambrian, Cumbrian

hill: 6 Formby, Lizard, Mendip **7** Brendon, Cemmaes, Trevose

highest point: 11 Scafell Pike

river: 3 Cam, Dee, Don, Esk, Exe, Lea, Nen, Ure, Wye **4** Aire, Avon, Eden, Lune, Nene, Nidd, Ouse, Penk, Tame, Tees, Till, Tyne, Wear, Yare **5** Anker, Colne, Deben, Stour, Swale, Tamar, Tawar, Trent, Tweed **6** Humber, Kennet, Mersey, Rother, Severn, Thames, Wharfe,

Witham **7** Derwent, Parrett, Waveney, Welland **8** Torridge **9** Yorkshire **12** Wensum Ribble

sea: 5 Irish, North **6** Celtic **8** Atlantic

physical feature:

bay: 3 Tor **4** Lyme, Wash **5** Start **6** Mounts **7** Bigbury **8** Bideford, Cardigan, Falmouth, Tremadoc, Weymouth

chalk cliffs: 5 Dover

channel: 6 Solent **7** Bristol, English **8** Spithead

firth: 6 Solway

forest: 5 Arden **6** Exmoor **8** Dartmoor, Sherwood

point: 4 Naze **5** Lynas, Morte, Sales **6** Dodman, Lizard, Prawle **8** Hartland, Landsend

region: 5 Weald **8** Midlands **10** West Riding **11** North Riding **12** Lake District

valley: 4 Coom, Eden, Tees, Tyne **5** Combe, Coomb **6** Coquet

people: 4 Celt, Pict **5** Jutes, Norse, Saxon **6** Angles, Briton, Norman, Viking

artist: 6 Romney, Turner **7** Hogarth **8** Reynolds, Rossetti **9** Constable **12** Gainsborough

author: 3 Kyd **4** Bede, Hume, Pope, Shaw **5** Auden, Bacon, Blake, Burke, Byron, Defoe, Donne, Eliot, Hardy, Joyce, Keats, Scott, Swift, Waugh, Wilde, Woolf **6** Austen, Bronte, Bunyan, Conrad, Dryden, Gibbon, Jonson, Milton, Newton, Ruskin, Sterne, Thomas **7** Boswell, Chaucer, Dickens, Kipling, Marlowe, Shelley, Spenser, Walpole **8** Browning, Fielding, Lawrence, Sheridan, Smollett, Tennyson, Trollope **9** Churchill, Coleridge, Stevenson, Thackeray **10** Galsworthy, Richardson, Thomas More, Wordsworth **11** Shakespeare

king: 3 Hal **4** Cnut, John, Lear **5** Henry, James **6** Alfred, Arthur, Canute, Edmund, Edward, Egbert, George, Harold **7** Charles, Richard, Stephen, William **9** Cymbeline **18** Richard Coeur de Lion **19** Richard the Lionheart

leader: 4 Eden, Grey, Lamb, Peel, Pitt **5** Heath, Major **6** Attlee, Wilson **7** Baldwin, Balfour, Canning, Fitzroy, Spencer, Stanley, Walpole **8** Disraeli, Stanhope, Thatcher **9** Cavendish, Churchill, Gladstone, Grenville, MacDonald, Macmillan **10** Palmerston, Wellington **11** Chamberlain, Douglas-Home, Lloyd George

queen: 3 Mab **4** Anne, Bess, Jane, Mary **7** Eleanor **8** Boadicea, Victoria **9** Catherine, Charlotte, Elizabeth, Guinevere **10** Bloody Mary **11** Jane Seymour

language: 7 English

religion: 6 Jewish **8** Anglican **9** Methodist, Unitarian **13** Roman Catholic **15** Church of England

place:

bridge: 5 Tower **6** London **11** Westminster

cathedral: 4 York **6** Exeter **7** St Pauls **8**

St Albans **9** Salisbury **10** Canterbury, Winchester **16** Westminster Abbey
clock: **6** Big Ben
fortification: **12** Hadrian's Wall
museum: **4** Tate **7** British **9** Ashmolean **17** Madame Tussauds Wax
palace: **7** St James, Windsor **10** Buckingham **12** Hampton Court
racetrack: **5** Ascot
ruins: **10** Stonehenge
street: **5** Fleet **12** Threadneedle **16** Piccadilly Circus
tower: **6** London
feature:
dance: **6** morris
food:
bacon: **6** gammon, rasher **7** streaky
beer: **5** grout, stout
cookie: **7** biscuit
dessert: **6** trifle **11** plum pudding
dish: **12** fish and chips **14** Cornish pasties **15** bubble and squeak **16** Yorkshire pudding
drink: **3** ale, tea **6** squash
English, Julian
character in: 20 Appointment in Samarra
author: 5 O'Hara
English Mail-Coach, The
author: 15 Thomas DeQuincey
engrave 3 cut **4** etch **5** carve, stamp **6** chisel **7** decorate, stipple
engraving 3 cut, die **5** print, stamp **7** etching, gravure **9** woodblock **11** copperplate, lithography **12** photogravure
engross 4 hold **6** absorb, arrest, engage, occupy, take up **7** immerse, involve **9** preoccupy
engrossed 4 busy, deep **6** intent **7** engaged **8** absorbed, immersed, involved, occupied **11** preoccupied
engrossing 8 engaging, exciting **9** absorbing, arresting, thrilling **10** intriguing **11** captivating, fascinating, interesting
engrossment 9 immersion **10** absorption, intentness **11** involvement **13** concentration, preoccupation
engulf 4 bury **5** swamp **6** deluge **7** envelop, immerse, overrun **8** inundate, submerge **9** swallow up
enhance 4 lift **5** add to, boost, raise **7** augment, elevate, magnify **8** heighten, redouble **9** embellish, intensify **10** complement
enhancement 11 heightening, improvement **15** intensification
Enid
character in: 12 The Mabinogion **15** Idylls of the King **16** Arthurian romance
author: 3 Tennyson
enigma 6 puzzle, riddle, secret **7** mystery **8** question **9** conundrum **10** perplexity
enigmatic, enigmatical 7 cryptic, elusive **8** baffling, puzzling **9** ambiguous, equivocal, secretive **10** mysterious, perplexing **11** inscrutable, paradoxical **12** unfathomable **14** indecipherable

Eniopeus
mentioned in: 5 Iliad
charioteer of: 6 Hector
slain by: 8 Diomedes
enjoin 3 ask, ban, bar, beg, bid **4** urge, warn **6** advise, charge, direct, forbid **7** command, counsel, entreat **8** admonish, call upon, instruct, prohibit, restrain, restrict **9** interdict, proscribe
enjoy 3 own **4** have, like **5** eat up, fancy, savor **6** admire, relish **7** possess **9** delight in, rejoice in **10** appreciate **11** think well of **13** be blessed with, be pleased with, get a kick out of **14** take pleasure in **16** have the benefit of
enjoyable 8 pleasant, pleasing **9** agreeable, fun-filled, rewarding **10** delightful, gratifying, satisfying **11** pleasurable
enjoyment 3 fun, joy **4** zest **5** gusto, right **6** relish **7** benefit, delight **8** blessing, exercise, good time, pleasure **9** advantage, amusement, diversion, happiness, privilege **10** possession, recreation **11** prerogative **12** satisfaction **13** entertainment, gratification
Enki
origin: 8 Sumerian
god of: 6 wisdom
habitat: 5 water
corresponds to: 2 Ea
Enkidu
origin: 8 Sumerian
servant of: 9 Gilgamesh
friend of: 9 Gilgamesh
enlarge 4 grow **5** add to, swell, widen **6** expand, extend **7** amplify, augment, broaden, develop, expound, inflate, magnify **8** elongate, increase, lengthen, multiply **9** discourse, elaborate, expatiate
enlarged 7 swollen, widened **8** expanded, extended, inflated **9** amplified, broadened, distended, elongated, magnified
enlargement 6 growth **8** addition, increase, swelling, widening **9** expansion, extension, inflation **10** broadening, elongation **11** development, elaboration, expatiation, lengthening **12** augmentation **13** amplification, magnification **14** multiplication
enlighten 5 edify **6** advise, inform, wise up **7** apprise, clarify, educate **8** civilize, instruct **9** make aware **10** illuminate **12** sophisticate
enlightenment 8 learning **9** erudition, knowledge **11** edification, instruction
French: 15 Eclaircissement
German: 10 Aufklarung
Enlil
origin: 8 Sumerian
king of: 4 gods
god of: 3 air
son: 5 Ninib **7** Ninurta
enlist 4 join **6** engage, enroll, join up, obtain, secure, sign up **7** procure, recruit **8** register **9** volunteer **19** gain the assistance of
enlistment 9 signing up **10** admittance, enrollment, recruiting

enliven 4 fire 5 pep up, renew 6 excite, vivify, wake up 7 animate, cheer up, quicken 8 brighten, vitalize 10 make lively, rejuvenate

enlivened 7 revived 8 animated, vivified 9 refreshed 11 invigorated

en masse 7 in a body 8 as a group, as a whole, in a group, together 11 all together

enmesh 4 trap 5 catch, snare, snarl 6 tangle 7 embroil, ensnare, entwine, involve 8 entangle

enmity 6 animus, hatred, malice, rancor, strife 7 ill will 8 acrimony, bad blood 9 animosity, antipathy, hostility 10 bitterness

Ennead 7 dieties
  origin: 8 Egyptian
  number: 4 nine

ennoble 5 raise 6 refine 7 dignify, elevate

Ennomus
  vocation: 6 angler
  joined: 7 Trojans

Ennosigaeus
  epithet of: 8 Poseidon
  means: 11 earth shaker

ennui 6 apathy, tedium 7 boredom, languor 9 lassitude, weariness 12 indifference, listlessness
  Latin: 12 taedium vitae

Enoch
  father: 4 Cain 5 Jared
  son: 10 Methuselah
  grandfather: 4 Adam

Enoch Arden
  author: 18 Alfred Lord Tennyson
  character: 8 Annie Lee 9 Philip Ray 10 Miriam Lane

enormity 8 baseness, evilness, hugeness, vastness, vileness, villainy 9 depravity, immensity, largeness, malignity 10 wickedness 11 heinousness, viciousness 12 enormousness 13 atrociousness, monstrousness, offensiveness 14 outrageousness

enormous 4 huge, vast 7 immense, mammoth, massive, titanic 8 colossal, gigantic 10 gargantuan, prodigious, tremendous 11 elephantine 14 Brobdingnagian

enormousness 8 enormity, hugeness, vastness 9 amplitude, immensity, largeness 11 massiveness

Enormous Room, The
  author: 10 e e cummings

Enos
  father: 4 Seth
  grandfather: 4 Adam

enough 5 ample, amply 6 plenty 7 copious 8 abundant, adequate, passably 9 tolerably 10 abundantly, adequately, competence, plentitude, reasonably, sufficient 11 ample supply, full measure, sufficiency 12 sufficiently 14 satisfactorily

enounce 8 set forth 9 enunciate 10 articulate

en passant 8 by the way 9 in passing

enrage 5 anger 6 madden 7 incense, inflame 9 aggravate, infuriate 11 make furious 13 make one see red 14 throw into a rage 17 make one's blood boil

enraged 3 mad 5 angry, irate 7 angered, furious, violent 8 incensed, inflamed, maddened, provoked 9 irritated 10 aggravated, infuriated 11 exasperated

en rapport 8 in accord 9 congenial 10 in sympathy 11 in agreement

enrapture 5 charm 6 thrill 7 beguile, bewitch, delight, enchant 8 enthrall, entrance, hold rapt 9 captivate, transport

enraptured 4 rapt 8 beatific, blissful, ecstatic 9 delighted, enchanted 10 enthralled 11 transported

enravel 5 snare, snarl, twist 6 enmesh, tangle 7 ensnare, ensnarl, entwine 8 entangle 10 intertwine

enrich 5 adorn, endow 6 refine 7 elevate, enhance, fortify, improve, upgrade 8 make rich 9 embellish 10 ameliorate 11 make wealthy 15 feather one's nest

enroll 4 join 5 admit, enter 6 accept, engage, enlist, join up, sign up, take on 7 recruit 8 register

enrollment 6 roster 9 enrolling, signing up 10 admittance, enlistment, recruiting 12 registration 13 matriculation

en route 8 on the way 9 in transit, on the road

ensconce 4 bury, hide, seat 5 lodge 6 settle 7 conceal, secrete, shelter 9 establish

ensemble 5 getup 6 attire, outfit, troupe 7 company, costume 8 assembly, entirety, grouping, totality 9 aggregate

ensign 4 flag, jack, mark, sign 5 badge 6 banner, colors, emblem, pennon, symbol 7 pennant 8 insignia, standard

enslave 6 addict, subdue 7 capture, control, enchain, shackle 8 dominate, enthrall 9 indenture, subjugate 13 hold in bondage, put in shackles

enslavement 4 yoke 6 chains, thrall 7 bondage, serfdom, slavery 9 captivity, servitude, thralldom, vassalage 11 subjugation

ensnare 4 trap 5 catch 6 enmesh, entrap, tangle 7 enravel 8 entangle

Ensor, James
  born: 6 Ostend 7 Belgium
  artwork: 8 Intrigue 19 Bourgeois Living Room 25 Entry of Christ into Brussels 26 The Tribulations of St Anthony 29 Self-Portrait Surrounded by Masks

enstatite
  source: 5 Burma, Mogok

ensue 6 derive, follow, result 7 succeed 10 come to pass 13 come afterward

ensuing 8 eventual 9 following, resulting 10 consequent, succeeding

en suite 6 in a set 9 in a series 12 in succession

ensure, insure 5 guard 6 assure, clinch, secure 7 protect, warrant 8 be sure of, make safe, make sure 9 guarantee, safeguard 13 make certain of

entail 6 demand 7 call for, include, involve, require 8 occasion 11 incorporate, necessitate

entangle 4 trap **5** catch, mix up, snare, snarl **6** enmesh, foul up, muddle, tangle **7** confuse, embroil, enravel, ensnare, involve **8** encumber **9** embarrass, implicate **10** complicate, compromise, intertwine

entanglement 5 mixup, snarl **6** foul-up, muddle **7** problem **9** confusion, imbroglio **10** difficulty, entrapment **11** embroilment **12** complication

Entellus
vocation: **5** boxer
home: **6** Sicily
defeated: **5** Dares

entente 4 pact **6** accord, treaty **7** compact **8** alliance, covenant **9** agreement, consensus, unanimity **10** consortium **12** conciliation **13** rapprochement, understanding **14** likemindedness

entente cordiale 21 friendly understanding

enter 4 go in, join, list, post **6** arrive, come in, record **8** enlist in, enroll in, inscribe, pass into, set out on, trespass **9** penetrate, sign up for **10** embark upon, take part in

enterprise 4 push, task, zeal **5** drive, vigor **6** daring, effort, energy, spirit **7** attempt, program, project, venture **8** ambition, boldness, campaign, endeavor, industry **9** alertness, eagerness, ingenuity, operation **10** enthusiasm, initiative **11** undertaking, willingness **14** aggressiveness **15** adventurousness

enterprising 4 bold, keen **5** alert, eager **6** active **7** earnest, zealous **8** intrepid **9** ambitious, energetic, inventive, wide-awake **10** aggressive **11** hardworking, industrious, self-reliant, up-and-coming, venturesome **12** enthusiastic

entertain 4 heed **5** admit, amuse, charm **6** absorb, divert, foster, harbor, please, ponder, regale **7** beguile, delight, dwell on, engross, imagine, nurture, support **8** consider, enthrall, interest, muse over, play host **10** cogitate on, give a party, have guests, keep in mind, think about **11** contemplate **13** keep open house

entertainer 4 host **5** actor **6** amuser, artist, dancer, singer **7** hostess **8** magician, musician **9** performer

entertaining 3 fun **7** amusing, hosting **8** charming, pleasing **9** beguiling, diverting, enjoyable **10** delightful, hostessing **11** playing host **12** having guests **14** having people in

entertainment 3 fun **4** play **7** novelty, pastime **8** good time, pleasure **9** amusement, diversion, enjoyment **10** recreation **11** distraction **12** satisfaction
French: **14** divertissement

enter upon 5 begin **6** assume **9** undertake

enthrall, enthral 5 charm, rivet **6** seduce, thrill **7** beguile, bewitch, enchant, enslave **8** entrance, intrigue, transfix **9** captivate, enrapture, fascinate, hypnotize, overpower, spellbind, subjugate, transport **13** keep in bondage **14** put into slavery

enthralled 4 rapt **8** beguiled, enslaved **9** bewitched, enchanted, entranced, in bondage, intrigued **10** captivated, enraptured, fascinated, hypnotized, spellbound, subjugated

enthusiasm 4 love, rage, zeal, zest **5** ardor, craze, hobby, mania **6** fervor, relish **7** elation, passion **8** devotion, interest, keenness **9** diversion, eagerness **10** excitement, exuberance, hobbyhorse **11** distraction, pet activity **12** anticipation

enthusiast 3 bug, fan, nut **4** buff **5** freak **6** addict **7** devotee, fanatic **10** aficionado

enthusiastic 5 eager **6** ardent, fervid **7** fervent, zealous **8** spirited **9** exuberant **10** passionate, unstinting **11** unqualified **12** wholehearted

entice 4 coax, lure **5** tempt **6** allure, incite, induce, seduce **7** attract, beguile, wheedle **8** inveigle, persuade

enticement 4 bait, draw, lure **6** allure **9** seduction, siren song **10** attraction, temptation

entire 4 full **5** gross, total, whole **6** in toto, intact **8** absolute, complete, thorough, unbroken **9** undamaged **10** unimpaired **12** all-inclusive

entirely 5 fully **6** wholly **7** totally, utterly **10** absolutely, altogether, completely, thoroughly **12** unreservedly **13** unqualifiedly
French: **9** tout a fait

entitle 4 dub, tag **4** call, name **5** allow, label, style, title **6** enable, permit **7** qualify **9** authorize, designate **12** make eligible

entity 4 body **5** being, thing **6** matter, object **7** article **8** creature, presence, quantity **9** real thing, structure, substance **10** individual

entomb 4 bury **5** inter **7** confine

entombment 6 burial **9** interment **10** inhumation

Entommeures, Frere Jean des
character in: **22** Gargantua and Pantagruel
author: **8** Rabelais

entourage 5 court, staff, suite, train **6** convoy, escort **7** cortege, retinue **9** followers, following **10** associates, attendants, companions

entrails 4 guts **5** offal **6** bowels **7** innards, insides, viscera **10** intestines

entrance 4 door, gate **5** charm, entry, way in **6** access, entree, portal **7** beguile, bewitch, delight, doorway, gateway, gladden, ingress, opening **8** approach, coming in, enthrall **9** captivate, enrapture, fascinate, hypnotize, mesmerize, spellbind, transport **10** admittance, appearance, passageway **12** introduction

entranced 4 rapt **7** charmed **8** beguiled **9** entralled, rapturous **10** enraptured, fascinated, spellbound **11** carried away, transported

entranceway 5 entry, foyer, way in **7** doorway, ingress **8** entryway **9** front hall, vestibule

entrancing 6 lovely 8 adorable, charming 9 appealing, beautiful, beguiling, disarming 10 bewitching, delightful 11 captivating, fascinating 12 irresistible

entrap 3 bag, nab 4 hook, land, nail 5 catch, snare, tempt 6 allure, collar, drag in, draw in, entice, rope in, seduce, suck in 7 beguile, capture, ensnare 8 inveigle

entreat 3 beg 6 adjure, enjoin, exhort 7 beseech, implore, request 8 appeal to, petition 9 importune, plead with 10 supplicate

entreaty 4 plea 6 appeal, prayer 8 petition 11 importunity 12 supplication

entree 4 pull 5 entry 6 access 7 ingress 8 entrance, main dish 9 admission 10 acceptance, admittance, main course

entremets 8 side dish

entrench, intrench 3 fix, set 4 root 5 dig in, embed, plant 6 anchor 7 implant, ingrain, install, solidly 8 ensconce 12 establish

entrenched leaders 11 ruling class 12 powers that be 13 Establishment 14 power structure

entre nous 9 between us, privately 14 confidentially 15 between you and me 16 between me and thee, between ourselves 18 in strict confidence

entrepot 5 depot 9 warehouse 18 distribution center

entrepreneur 7 manager 8 director 9 organizer 10 impresario 11 coordinator

entrust, intrust 5 trust 6 assign, commit 7 consign 8 delegate, hand over, turn over 9 authorize 10 charge with

entrustment 10 delegation 13 authorization, commissioning

entry 3 way 4 door, gate, item, memo, note 5 foyer, way in 6 access, entree, minute, portal, record 7 account, doorway, gateway, ingress, jotting 8 approach, entrance 9 admission, vestibule 10 admittance, appearance, competitor, contestant, memorandum, passageway 11 entranceway 12 entrance hall, introduction, registration

entwine, intwine 4 fold, lace, wind 5 braid, plait, twine, twist, weave 9 interlace 10 interweave

enumerable 6 finite 7 limited 11 denumerable

enumerate 3 add 4 cite, list 5 add up, count, sum up, tally, total 6 detail, number, relate 7 count up, recount, specify, tick off 8 numerate, spell out, tabulate

enumeration 4 list 5 tally 7 account, listing 8 adding up, addition, citation, tallying, totaling 9 checklist, detailing, numbering, reckoning, summing up 10 counting up, recounting, tabulation, ticking off 11 tabling out

enunciate 5 sound, speak, voice 8 vocalize 10 articulate 15 utter distinctly 16 pronounce clearly

enunciation 6 accent, speech 7 diction 9 utterance 12 articulation 13 pronunciation

envelop 4 hide, veil, wrap 5 cloak, cover 6 encase, enfold, engulf, enwrap, shroud, swathe 7 blanket, conceal, contain, enclose, obscure, sheathe, swaddle 8 encircle, surround 9 encompass

envelope 5 cover 6 jacket 8 covering, wrapping

envenom 4 sour 6 rankle 8 embitter 13 make poisonous

enviable 5 lucky 8 salutary 9 agreeable, covetable, desirable, excellent, fortunate 10 beneficial 12 advantageous

envious 5 green 7 jealous 8 covetous, grudging, spiteful 9 jaundiced, resentful

enviousness 4 envy 8 jealousy 10 resentment 12 covetousness 13 resentfulness 19 the green-eyed monster

environment 5 scene 6 locale, medium, milieu 7 climate, element, habitat, setting 8 ambience 9 situation 10 atmosphere, background 12 surroundings 13 circumstances

    French: 11 mise en scene

environs 6 exurbs 7 suburbs 8 vicinity 9 outskirts, precincts 11 outer limits 12 outlying area 15 surrounding area

envisage 5 fancy 7 dream of, dream up, imagine, picture 8 conceive, envision 9 conjure up, visualize 11 contemplate 13 conceptualize 14 have a picture of 16 picture to oneself

envoy 5 agent 6 deputy, legate 7 attache, courier 8 delegate, emissary, minister 9 messenger, middleman 10 ambassador 12 intermediary 14 representative

envy 5 greed, spite 6 resent 8 begrudge, grudging, jealousy 10 resentment 11 be jealous of, enviousness, malevolence 12 covetousness 13 resentfulness 16 be spiteful toward 19 the green-eyed monster

enwrap 6 absorb, engage, enrobe 7 engross, envelop 9 preoccupy

Enyalius

    epithet of: 4 Ares

    means: 14 slayer of heroes

Enyeus

    king of: 6 Scyrus

Enyo

    origin: 5 Greek

    goddess of: 3 war

    companion of: 4 Ares

    member of: 6 Graeae, Graiae

    corresponds to: 7 Bellona

enzyme 7 protein 8 molecule 13 macromolecule

    function: 8 catalyst

    acts on: 9 substrate

    kind: 5 amino, malic 6 lactic, lipase, pepsin, rennin, urease 7 amylase, glucose, trypsin 8 aldehyde, glutamic, glycolic, lipozyme, thrombin, xanthine 9 cellulase 12 ribonuclease

eon 3 age, era 8 eternity, long time 9 many years 15 one billion years

Eos

    origin: 5 Greek

    goddess of: 4 dawn

    father: 8 Hyperion

    mother: 5 Theia

    brother: 6 Helios

sister: 6 Selene
husband: 8 Astraeus, Tithonus 10 Eosophorus
son: 6 Memnon 8 Phaethon, Zephyrus 10 Eosophorus
horse: 6 Lampos 8 Phaethon
mother of: 5 stars, winds
corresponds to: 6 Aurore 7 Hermera

Epaphus
king of: 5 Egypt
father: 4 Zeus
mother: 2 Io
wife: 7 Memphis
daughter: 5 Lybia 10 Lysianassa

Epeans see 5 Epeus

Epeus
king of: 12 Peloponnesus
father: 8 Endymion, Panopeus
brother: 5 Paeon 7 Aetolus
wife: 10 Anaxirrhoe
noted for: 9 cowardice
built: 11 Trojan horse
helped by: 6 Athena
descendants: 6 Epeans

Epheh 15 Biblical measure

ephemeral 5 brief 7 passing 8 fleeting, flitting, fugitive, temporal 9 fugacious, momentary, temporary, transient 10 evanescent, fly-by-night, inconstant, nondurable, short-lived, transitory, unenduring 11 impermanent 21 here today gone tomorrow

ephemeroptera
class: 8 hexapoda
phylum: 10 arthropoda
group: 6 mayfly

Ephialtes
form: 5 giant
member of: 7 Aloidae
father: 8 Poseidon
mother: 9 Iphimedia
brother: 5 Oteus

Ephraim
father: 6 Joseph
mother: 7 Asenath
brother: 8 Manasseh
blessed by: 5 Jacob
descendant of: 10 Ephraimite

Ephraimi 16 Greek unical codex

Epibaterius
epithet of: 6 Apollo
means: 9 seafaring

epic 4 saga 5 drama, great, noble 6 fabled, heroic 7 exalted, storied 8 fabulous, imposing, majestic 9 legendary 10 heroic poem, superhuman

Epicaste see 7 Jocasta

epicure 7 glutton, gourmet 8 gourmand, hedonist, sybarite 9 bon vivant 10 gastronome

epicurean 4 rich 6 lavish 7 gourmet, sensual 8 hedonist, Lucullan, sybarite 9 libertine, luxurious, sybaritic 10 hedonistic, sensualist, voluptuary, voluptuous 11 intemperate 13 self-indulgent

epidemic 4 rife 6 plague 7 rampant, scourge 8 catching, outbreak, pandemic 9 contagion, infection, pervasive, prevalent 10 infectious, pestilence, prevailing, widespread 11 far-reaching

Epigoni
sons of: 18 Seven against Thebes

epigram 4 quip 5 adage, maxim 6 bon mot 8 aphorism, apothegm 9 witticism

epilogue 4 coda 5 rider 7 codicil 8 addendum 9 afterword 10 supplement 12 final section

Epimetheus
father: 7 Iapetus
brother: 5 Atals 9 Menoetius 10 Prometheus
wife: 7 Pandora
daughter: 6 Pyrrha

Epione
husband: 9 Asclepius

episcopal 8 churchly, diocesan, pastoral 12 ecclesiastic(al)

episode 4 part 5 event, scene 6 affair, period 7 chapter, passage, section 8 incident 9 adventure, happening, milestone 10 experience, occurrence 11 installment

Episode of Sparrows, An
author: 11 Rumer Godden

episodic 7 halting 8 rambling 9 segmented, wandering 10 digressive, discursive, meandering 13 discontinuous

epistle 6 letter 7 message, missive 10 encyclical

Epistle to a Godson and Other Poems
author: 7 W H Auden

Epistle to Dr Arbuthnot
author: 13 Alexander Pope

Epithalamion
author: 13 Edmund Spenser

epithet 5 curse 6 insult 8 nickname 9 blasphemy, expletive, obscenity, sobriquet 10 ascription 11 appellation, designation

Epithet
of Aphrodite: 6 Acraea, Scotia 7 Doritis, Erycina, Limenia 8 Melaenis, Nymphaea, Pandemos 9 Migonitis 11 Aphrogeneia, Apostrophia
of Apollo: 6 Loxias 7 Acesius, Agraeus, Agyieus, Carneus, Phyteus, Spodius 8 Grynaeus 9 Parnopius, Smintheus 10 Alexicacus, Archegetes, Boedromius, Delphinius 11 Argyrotoxus, Epibaterius 12 Platanistius
of Ares: 8 Enyalius 14 Gynaecothoenas
of Argus: 8 Panoptes
of Artemis: 6 Orthia 7 Eurippa, Laphria, Limnaea, Pyronia 8 Aeginaea, Agrotera, Calliste, Caryatis, Daphnaea 9 Hemerasia, Lygodesma 10 Polymastus 11 Leucophryne
of Asclepius: 8 Cotyleus
of Athena: 4 Alea 5 Meter, Xenia 6 Ergane, Itonia, Polias 7 Agoraea, Cissaea, Paeonia, Pronaus, Pronoea 8 Anemotis, Poliates, Zosteria 9 Oxyderces, Parthenia, Poliuchus, Promachus 10

Axiopoenus, Chalinitis, Cyparissia 11 Promachorma

of Cybele: 6 Antaea

of Demeter: 5 Chloe, Lusia, Mysia 6 Antaea, Erinys, Stiria 7 Chamyne, Thesmia 8 Stiritis 9 Anesidora, Thermasia 11 Carpophorus 12 Thesmophorus

of Dionysus: 6 Lyaeus 7 Bromius, Cresius 8 Thyoneus, Triambus 9 Pyrigenes 11 Dithyrambus, Mitrephorus

of Hera: 6 Anthea, Bunaea 8 Henioche 9 Prodromia

of Hercules: 7 Charops 8 Buphagus 9 Ipoctonus

of Hermes: 6 Dolius 8 Agoraeus 9 Spelaites 10 Criophorus 11 Argiphontes 12 Argeiphontes, Psychopompus

of Icelus: 8 Phobetor

of Juno: 6 Moneta 7 Curitis, Pronuba, Sospita

of Jupiter: 5 Ultor 7 Elicius, Pluvius

of Mopsus: 9 Ampycides

of Nestor: 7 Nelides

of Odin: 7 Alfader, Alfadir

of Odysseus: 10 Laertiades

of Persephone: 11 Carpophorus

of Pheriphetes: 9 Corynetes

of Poseidon: 11 Ennosigaeus, Hippocurius 12 Prosclystius

of Rhea: 6 Antaea

of Sinis: 12 Pityocamptes

of Vulcan: 8 Mulciber

of Zeus: 5 Areus, Soter 6 Aqueus, Areius, Nemean, Philus 7 Alastor, Apemius, Ctesius, Lycaeus, Polieus, Stenius 8 Agoraeus, Aphesius, Apomyius, Cappotas, Cosmetas, Dodonian, Herceius, Leucaeus, Tropaean 9 Aegiochus, Chthonius, Coccygius, Hecaleius, Lecheates, Mechaneus 10 Cataebates, Catharsius, Coryphaeus, Homagyrius, Laphystius, Meilichius 11 Eleutherius 12 Panhellenius

epitome 4 peak 5 ideal, model 6 height 7 essence, summary 9 summation 10 embodiment 12 typification 14 representation 15 exemplification, sum and substance

e pluribus unum 12 out of many one

motto of: 12 United States

epoch 3 age, era 4 time 6 period 8 interval

epochal 7 weighty 8 historic 9 important, momentous 11 significant 13 consequential

Eppie

character in: 11 Silas Marner

author: 5 Eliot

Epstein, Sir Jacob

born: 9 New York NY

artwork: 4 Adam 7 Genesis 8 Ecce Homo, Einstein 9 Rock Drill 10 Visitation 11 Night and Day, Paul Robeson 12 Behold the Man, Joseph Conrad 13 Haile Selassie 14 Consummatum Est 19 Social Consciousness 20 Monument to Oscar Wilde, St Michael and his (the) Devil

equable 4 calm, even 5 sunny 6 placid, serene, stable, steady 7 regular, uniform 8 constant, pleasant, tranquil, unvaried 9 agreeable, easygoing, unruffled 10 consistent, dependable, unchanging 11 goodnatured, predictable, unexcitable, unflappable 12 even-tempered 13 imperturbable

equably

Latin: 9 pari passu

equal 4 even, like, peer 5 match 7 matched, the same, uniform 8 balanced, be even to, equalize, jibe with, of a piece, parallel 9 agree with, identical, tally with 10 accord with, comparable, equate with, equivalent, square with, tantamount 11 balance with, be the same as, correlative, counterpart, symmetrical 12 commensurate, correspond to, proportional 13 be identical to, corresponding, evenly matched, one and the same

equality 6 parity 7 balance, justice 8 evenness, fair play, fairness, sameness 10 similarity, uniformity 11 equivalency 12 impartiality 13 fair treatment 14 correspondence

French: 7 egalite

Equality

author: 13 Edward Bellamy

Equality State

nickname of: 7 Wyoming

equalization 7 balance 9 stability 11 equilibrium 14 counterbalance

German: 9 Ausgleich

equalize 7 balance 9 make equal 11 make uniform 13 compensate for

equal to 3 fit 4 able, up to 5 adept 7 capable 8 adequate, master of 9 competent, qualified

equanimity 4 cool 5 poise 6 aplomb 8 calmness, coolness 9 composure, sangfroid 10 steadiness 11 self-control, tranquility 12 tranquillity 14 presence of mind, self-possession 16 imperturbability

equate 5 liken, match 7 average, balance, compare, even out 8 equalize, equal out 9 think of as 10 consider as 14 be commensurate, be equivalent to 17 be proportionate to

Equatorial

language family: 16 Andean-Equatorial

group: 8 Arawakan 11 Tupi-Guarani

Equatorial Guinea

other name: 13 Spanish Guinea

capital/largest city: 6 Malabo

others: 4 Bata 9 Rio Benito

division: 5 Bioko 7 Rio Muni

monetary unit: 6 ekuele, peseta 7 centimo

island: 5 Bioko 6 Pagalu 7 Corisco 11 Chico Elobey 12 Grande Elobey

mountain: 5 Mitra

highest point: 11 Santa Isabel

river: 5 Mbini

physical feature:

gulf: 6 Guinea

people: 4 Bubi, Fang 5 Benge, Combe 6 Bujeba 10 Fernandino
explorer: 2 Po
leader: 12 Nguema Biyogo
language: 4 Bubi, Fang 7 Spanish 13 pidgin English
religion: 7 animism 10 Protestant 13 Roman Catholic

equilibrium 7 balance 8 symmetry 9 equipoise, stability 14 sense of balance

equip 3 rig 5 stock 6 fit out, outfit, supply 7 appoint, furnish, prepare, provide 8 accoutre 9 caparison, provision

equipage 4 gear 6 outfit 8 carriage 9 equipment 13 accoutrements

equipment 4 gear 5 stuff 6 tackle 8 equipage, material, materiel, supplies 9 apparatus 11 furnishings, outfittings 13 accoutrements, paraphernalia

equipoise 7 balance 9 stability 11 equilibrium

equitable 3 due 4 fair, just 6 proper 8 unbiased 9 impartial 10 evenhanded, reasonable 12 unprejudiced

equity 4 cash 5 value 6 assets, profit 7 justice 8 fairness, justness 9 cash value 10 investment 12 fair dealings, impartiality 14 evenhandedness, fairmindedness, reasonableness

equivalency 6 parity 7 balance 8 equality 10 coequality, uniformity 14 correspondence

equivalent 4 even, peer 5 equal, match 8 of a piece, parallel 9 the same as 10 comparable, tantamount 11 correlative, counterpart, equal amount

equivocal 4 hazy 5 vague 7 dubious 8 doubtful 9 ambiguous, enigmatic, imprecise, qualified, uncertain, undecided 10 ambivalent, indefinite, suspicious 11 nonspecific 12 undetermined 13 indeterminate

equivocate 5 dodge, evade, fudge, hedge, stall 9 pussyfoot 10 mince words 11 be ambiguous, prevaricate 13 avoid the issue 16 straddle the fence 17 beat around the bush

equivocating 6 shifty 7 devious, dodging, elusive, elusory, evasive, hedging 8 stalling 9 ambiguous, deceptive, equivocal 11 dissembling

era 3 age 4 time 5 epoch 6 period 8 interval

eradicate 5 erase 6 remove 7 abolish, blot out, destroy, expunge, wipe out 8 get rid of 9 eliminate, extirpate, liquidate 10 annihilate, do away with, extinguish, obliterate 11 exterminate

eradication 7 erasure, removal 9 abolition 11 blotting out, destruction, elimination 12 obliteration

erase 6 delete, remove, rub out 7 expunge, scratch 8 wipe away 9 eliminate, eradicate, strike out

Erasistratus
  field: 10 physiology
  nationality: 5 Greek
  described: 5 brain, heart

Erasmus, Desiderius
  author of: 14 Encomium Moriae 16 The Praise of Folly

Erato
  muse of: 10 love poetry

Ercolani, James
  real name of: 11 James Darren

Erebus
  location: 10 underworld
  means: 8 darkness

Erechtheus
  king of: 6 Athens
  father: 7 Pandion
  wife: 9 Praxithea
  son: 6 Metion, Orneus, Sicyon 7 Cecrops 8 Pandorus, Thespius 9 Eupalamus
  daughter: 6 Creusa 7 Otionia, Procris 8 Chthonia, Orithyir 10 Protogonia

erect 5 build, put up, raise, rigid, stiff 6 unbent 7 stand up, upright 8 straight, vertical 9 construct, unstooped 12 place upright

erection 7 raising 8 building 9 putting up 11 fabrication 12 construction

eremite 4 monk 6 hermit 7 ascetic, recluse 9 anchorite, religious

Ereshkigal
  origin: 8 Akkadian, Sumerian
  goddess of: 5 death
  consort of: 6 Nergal

Ereuthalion
  mentioned in: 5 Iliad
  vocation: 7 warrior
  home: 7 Arcadia
  dueled with: 6 Nestor

Erewhon
  author: 12 Samuel Butler
  title anagram of: 7 nowhere
  character: 5 Higgs 6 Strong 7 Chowbok 8 Arowhena

Ergane
  epithet of: 6 Athena
  means: 6 worker

ergo 4 work 6 hence 7 because 9 therefore 11 accordingly

Eriboea
  husband: 6 Aloeus

Erigone
  father: 7 Icarius 9 Aegisthus
  mother: 12 Clytemnestra
  brother: 6 Aletes
  death by: 7 suicide

Eriking
  origin: 8 Germanic 12 Scandinavian
  form: 6 spirit
  personifies: 6 nature
  works: 8 mischief

Erin *see* 7 Ireland

Erin go bragh 14 Ireland forever

Erinys
  also: 6 Furies
  epithet of: 7 Demeter
  means: 4 fury

Eris
  origin: 5 Greek
  goddess of: 7 discord
  brother: 4 Ares
  threw: 14 apple of discord

corresponds to: 9 Discordia

Eritrea
capital/largest city: 6 Asmara
others: 5 Assab, Keren 6 Ghinda 7 Massawa
formerly division of: 8 Ethiopia
river: 5 Mareb
highest point: 5 Soira
strait: 11 Bab el Mandeb
sea: 3 Red
language: 7 Amharic
religion: 5 Islam 6 Coptic, Muslim

ermine 3 fur 4 duty, rank 6 weasel 7 ermal-in 8 position

Ernani
opera by: 5 Verdi
setting: 6 Aragon
character: 6 Ernani 11 Donna Elvira

Ernst, Max
born: 5 Bruhl 7 Germany
co-founder of: 7 Dadaism 10 Surrealism
artwork: 7 Moon Man 8 Lady Bird 11 A Little Calm, Femme Oiseau 12 The Whole City 13 The Table Is Set, Totem and Taboo 14 Lunar Asparagus

erode 5 spoil, waste 6 ravage 7 corrode, despoil, eat away 8 wear away 12 disintegrate

Eros
origin: 5 Greek
god of: 4 love
mother: 9 Aphrodite
corresponds to: 4 Amor 5 Cupid

erosion 8 abrasion, ravaging 9 corrosion 10 eating away 11 wearing away, wearing down

erosive 7 burning, caustic 9 corrosive

erotic 3 hot 4 lewd, sexy 5 bawdy, lusty 6 ardent, carnal, impure, ribald, risque, sexual, wanton 7 amatory, amorous, obscene, raunchy 8 immodest, indecent, unchaste 9 salacious 10 lascivious, passionate, suggestive

err 3 sin 6 mess up, slip up 7 blunder, do wrong 8 go astray 9 be in error, misbehave 10 transgress 12 make a mistake, miscalculate 13 slip from grace

errand 4 duty, task 6 office 7 mission 10 assignment

errant 5 wrong 6 arrant, astray, erring, roving 7 erratic, wayward 8 mistaken, straying 9 incorrect, wandering, wayfaring 11 adventurous

errare humanum est 12 to err is human

erratic 3 odd 5 queer 6 fitful 7 strange, unusual, wayward 8 aberrant, abnormal, peculiar, shifting, unstable, variable 9 eccentric, unnatural 10 capricious, changeable 11 vacillating 12 inconsistent 13 unpredictable

erroneous 5 false, wrong 6 all wet, faulty, untrue 7 off base, unsound 8 mistaken, spurious 9 incorrect, unfounded 10 fallacious, inaccurate 12 full of hot air 13 unsupportable

error 4 flaw 5 boner, botch, fault 6 boo-boo, bungle, howler 7 blooper, fallacy, mistake 9 oversight 10 inaccuracy 13 misconception 14 miscalculation 15 misapprehension 16 misunderstanding 17 misinterpretation

ersatz 4 fake, sham 5 bogus, phony 9 imitation, pretended, synthetic 10 artificial, not genuine 11 counterfeit

Erse 4 Celt, Gael, Scot 5 Irish 6 Celtic, Gaelic 7 Ireland 8 Scottish 10 Highlander

erstwhile 2 ex 4 past 6 bygone, former 8 previous

eruct 4 burp 5 belch

eructation 4 burp 5 belch

erudite 4 wise 7 learned, sapient 8 cultured, literate, well-read 9 scholarly 10 cultivated, thoughtful, well-versed 11 intelligent 12 well-educated, well-informed, well-reasoned

erudition 5 skill 7 culture 8 learning, literacy 9 education, expertise, knowledge, schooling 10 refinement 11 cultivation, learnedness, scholarship 12 book learning 13 enlightenment

Erulus
king of: 5 Italy
mother: 7 Feronia
gift: 10 three lives

erupt 4 emit, gush, vent 5 eruct 6 blow up 7 explode 8 break out, throw off 9 be ejected, discharge, flow forth, pour forth 10 belch forth, burst forth

eruption 4 rash 6 eczema 7 flare-up, gushing, venting 8 ejection, emission, outbreak, outburst 9 blowing up, discharge, explosion, festering 10 dermatitis, outpouring 11 breaking out 12 flowing forth, inflammation, pouring forth 13 belching forth, bursting forth

Erving, Julius
nickname: 7 Doctor J
sport: 10 basketball
position: 7 forward
team: 11 New York Nets 15 Virginia Squires 25 Philadelphia Seventy-Sixers

Erycina
epithet of: 9 Aphrodite

Erymanthian boar
form: 4 boar
plagued: 7 Arcadia
captured by: 8 Hercules

Erysichthon
cut sacred tree of: 7 Demeter

Erytheis
member: 10 Hesperides
changed into: 3 elm

erythrophobia
fear of: 8 blushing

Eryx
vocation: 5 boxer
challenged: 8 Hercules
killed by: 8 Hercules

Esau
also called: 4 Edom
father: 5 Isaac
mother: 7 Rebekah
twin brother: 5 Jacob

wife: 6 Judith 8 Makalath
son: 7 Eliphaz
birthright sold to: 5 Jacob

escadrille 6 armada 8 flotilla, squadron

escalate 4 rise 5 boost, mount, swell 6 ascend, expand, extend, step up 7 advance, amplify, broaden, elevate, enlarge, magnify 8 increase 9 intensify 10 accelerate, aggrandize

Escalus
character in: 17 Measure for Measure
author: 11 Shakespeare .

escapade 4 lark 5 antic, caper, fling, prank, revel, spree, trick 7 caprice 8 mischief 9 adventure 11 high old time

escape 4 bolt, exit, flee, flow, gush, leak, seep, shun, skip 5 avert, avoid, dodge, elude, issue, skirt 6 efflux, egress, emerge, eschew, exodus, flight, stream 7 abscond, emanate, getaway, leakage, make off, outflow, outpour, run away, seepage 8 breakout, emission, outburst, slip away, steal off 9 be emitted, break free, cut and run, discharge, diversion, effluence, pour forth 10 break loose, decampment, fly the coop 11 avoid danger, deliverance, distraction, extrication, safe getaway 12 make a getaway

escargot 5 snail

escarpment 4 bank, crag 5 bluff, cliff, ridge, slope 8 headland, palisade 9 precipice 10 promontory

eschew 4 shun 5 avoid, forgo 6 give up 7 forbear 9 keep shy of 11 abstain from 12 steer clear of

eschewal 7 refusal 8 forgoing, shunning 9 avoidance 10 abnegation, abstention, self-denial 11 forbearance 13 nonindulgence 16 nonparticipation

escort 4 date, take 5 guard, guide, train, usher 6 squire 7 company, conduct, cortege, retinue 8 chaperon 9 companion, conductor, entourage 10 attendants, lead the way

escritoire 4 desk 5 table 9 secretary 10 secretaire 11 writing desk

escutcheon 4 arms 5 crest 6 shield 10 coat of arms 16 armorial bearings

Eskimo (Eskimantsic, Askkimey, Inuit, Yuit)
tribe: 5 Aleut
location: 6 Alaska, Arctic, Canada 9 Greenland
noted for: 7 fishing 9 mechanics

Eskimo-Aleut
language branch: 5 Aleut, Yupik
spoken in: 6 Alaska 7 Siberia 15 Aleutian Islands

Esmeralda
character in: 23 The Hunchback of Notre Dame
author: 4 Hugo

esoteric 6 arcane, covert, hidden, occult, secret, veiled 7 cloaked, cryptic, obscure, private 8 abstruse, mystical 9 concealed, enigmatic, recondite 10 inviolable, mysteri-

ous 11 inscrutable, undisclosed 12 confidential 16 incomprehensible

espanol 7 Spanish 13 Spanish person 15 Spanish language

especial see 7 special

especially 6 really 7 notably 9 expressly, intensely, primarily, unusually 10 singularly, uncommonly 11 exclusively, principally 12 particularly, specifically 13 exceptionally, outstandingly 15 extraordinarily

espiegle 7 playful, roguish

espieglerie 12 playful trick

esplanade 4 mall, path, walk 5 drive 9 boardwalk 10 quadrangle

espousal 7 backing, support, wedding 8 adoption, advocacy, marriage, taking up 9 betrothal, promotion 10 supporting 12 championship

espouse 3 wed 4 back, tout 5 adopt, boost, marry 6 take up 7 embrace, further, promote, support 8 advocate, champion, side with 10 stand up for

espressivo
music: 12 expressively
abbreviation: 4 espr

esprit de corps 10 fellowship, group pride, group unity, high morale, solidarity, team spirit 11 camaraderie

espy 3 see, spy 4 spot, view 6 behold, descry, detect, locate, notice 7 discern

essay 3 try 5 paper, theme, tract 6 effort, take on 7 article, attempt, venture 8 critique, endeavor, treatise 9 editorial, undertake 10 commentary, experiment 11 make a stab at, undertaking 12 dissertation, take a crack at, take a fling at 14 make an effort at 16 short composition

Essay on Criticism, An
author: 13 Alexander Pope

Essay on Man, An
author: 13 Alexander Pope

Essays
author: 12 Francis Bacon

Essays in Criticism
author: 13 Matthew Arnold

esse 5 being 9 existence

essence 4 core, germ, gist, pith, soul 5 heart, point, scent 6 elixir, nature, spirit 7 cologne, extract, meaning, perfume, spirits 8 tincture 9 fragrance, lifeblood, principle, substance 11 concentrate, toilet water 12 basic quality, quintessence, significance 15 sum and substance

essential, essentials 3 key 4 main 5 basic, vital 6 basics, needed 7 crucial, leading 8 cardinal, inherent 9 basic need, important, ingrained, intrinsic, necessary, necessity, principal, requisite, rudiments, vital part 10 key element, principles 11 fundamental, nitty-gritty 12 fundamentals 13 indispensable

essential ingredient 9 necessity 10 sine qua non 22 indispensable component

establish 3 fix 4 form, open, show 5 begin, found, prove, set up, start 6 create, settle, uphold, verify 7 confirm, implant, install, justify, situate, sustain, warrant 8 initiate, organize, validate 9 institute 10 bring about, inaugurate, make secure 11 corroborate, demonstrate 12 authenticate 16 win acceptance for 18 bring into existence

established 6 common 7 regular 8 accepted, familiar 9 customary 10 recognized

establishment, Establishment 4 firm 5 plant 6 office, outfit, system 7 company, concern, factory 8 building, business, creation, founding 9 formation, setting up 10 foundation 11 corporation, development, instituting, institution, ruling class 12 organization, powers that be 13 bringing about

estaminet 4 cafe 6 bistro

estate 4 rank, will 5 class, grade, manor, money, order, state 6 assets, legacy, status, wealth 7 bequest, fortune, station 8 compound, holdings, property 9 condition, situation 10 belongings, plantation 11 inheritance 12 country place

esteem 4 deem, hold 5 honor, judge, prize, think, value 6 admire, reckon, regard, revere 7 believe, cherish, respect 8 approval, consider, estimate, look up to, treasure, venerate 9 calculate, reverence 10 admiration, set store by, veneration 12 appreciation 13 think highly of 16 favorable opinion, hold in high regard 18 attach importance to

esteemed 5 great, noted 6 prized, valued, worthy 7 admired, eminent, honored, notable, revered 9 admirable, important, respected 10 looked up to, preeminent 11 illustrious 13 distinguished, well thought of 14 highly regarded

Estella
character in: 17 Great Expectations
author: 7 Dickens

Estevez, Ramon
real name of: 11 Martin Sheen

Esther
author: 10 Henry Adams

Esther
Persian name of: 8 Hadassah
father: 7 Abihail
grandfather: 6 Shimei
cousin: 8 Mordecai
husband: 9 Ahasuerus
displaced: 6 Vashti
enemy: 5 Haman

Esther Waters
author: 11 George Moore

esthetic 7 refined 8 artistic 9 sensitive 10 cultivated, fastidious 12 aesthetic 14 discriminating

estimable 4 good 6 prized 7 admired, revered 8 laudable 9 admirable, honorable, important, reputable, respected, treasured 10 worthwhile 11 commendable 12 praiseworthy 14 highly regarded

estimate 4 view 5 assay, guess, judge, opine, think, value 6 assess, belief, figure, reckon 7 believe, opinion, surmise 8 appraise, conclude, consider, evaluate, judgment, thinking 9 appraisal, calculate,

reckoning 10 assessment, conjecture, evaluation 11 calculation

estimation 4 view 6 belief, esteem, regard 7 opinion, respect 8 approval, judgment 9 appraisal, reckoning 10 admiration, evaluation 13 consideration

estimator 7 analyst 8 assessor 9 appraiser, evaluator 10 calculator

Estonia
capital/largest city: 7 Tallinn
others: 5 Narva, Paide, Parnu, Tartu, Valga 6 Dorpat 7 Petseri 8 Paldiski 11 Kohtla-Jarve
government: 8 republic
measure: 3 tun 4 elle, liin, sund, toll, toop 5 verst 6 sagene, versta 7 kulimet 8 tonnland
monetary unit: 3 lat 4 sent 5 kroon 7 estmark
weight: 4 lood, nael, puud
island: 4 Dago, Muhu 5 Kihnu, Oesel, Saare 6 Sarema, Vormsi 7 Hiiumaa 8 Saaremaa
lake: 5 Pskov 6 Peipus 9 Vortsjarv
highest point: 8 Munamagi
river: 3 Ema 5 Narva, Parnu
sea: 6 Baltic
physical feature:
gulf: 4 Riga 5 Parnu 7 Finland
strait: 4 Irbe
people: 4 Esth, Finn 5 Aesti 6 Jewish 8 Estonian 9 Ukrainian 11 Belorussian
language: 5 Tartu 10 Finno-Ugric
religion: 8 Lutheran

estop 3 bar 4 fill, plug, stop 7 prevent 8 obstruct

esto perpetua 17 may she live forever
motto of: 5 Idaho

Estragon
character in: 15 Waiting for Godot
author: 7 Beckett

estrange 4 part 8 alienate 9 disaffect 10 antagonize, dissociate, drive apart

estranged 5 aloof 6 cut off 7 distant 8 detached, divorced 9 alienated, separated 10 unfriendly

estrangement 8 coolness 10 alienation 12 disaffection

estuary 5 firth, inlet 10 river mouth, tidal basin

etagere 7 whatnot 11 open shelves

etc (&c) 4 et al 7 and so on, whatnot 8 et cetera, whatever 9 and others 10 and so forth, and the rest

etch 3 cut, fix 5 carve, stamp 7 corrode, engrave, impress, scratch

Eteocles
father: 7 Oedipus
mother: 7 Jocasta 10 Euryganeia
uncle: 5 Creon
brother: 9 Polynices
sister: 6 Ismene 8 Antigone
son: 8 Laodamas
slain by: 9 Polynices

eternal 7 abiding, endless 8 constant, immortal, infinite, timeless, unending 9 ceaseless, continual, perpetual 10 persistent, relentless, without end 11 everlasting, never-ending 12 interminable 13 uninterrupted

eternity 4 Zion 6 Heaven 7 forever, nirvana 8 infinity, paradise 11 ages and ages, endlessness, eons and eons, immortality 12 New Jerusalem, the hereafter, the next world 13 the afterworld 14 the world to come, time without end 15 everlasting life

Ethan Frome
    author: 12 Edith Wharton
    character: 5 Zeena 7 Zenobia 12 Mattie Silver

Ethanim 18 seventh Hebrew month

ether 5 ester, ethyl, ozone, vapor 7 diethyl, solvent 10 anesthetic 11 refrigerant

ethereal 4 airy, rare 6 aerial 7 elusive, refined, sublime 8 delicate, rarefied 9 celestial, exquisite, unearthly, unworldly

ethical 4 fair, just 5 moral, right 6 decent, kosher, proper 7 correct, fitting, upright 8 virtuous 9 honorable 10 aboveboard, scrupulous 15 straightforward 17 open and aboveboard

ethical feelings 9 integrity 10 conscience, moral sense 16 incorruptibility

ethics, ethic 8 morality 9 integrity, moral code 10 conscience, principles 11 moral values, sense of duty 14 moral standards, rules of conduct

Ethics of Ambiguity
    author: 16 Simone de Beauvoir

Ethiopia
    Biblical name: 4 Cush
    other name: 9 Abyssinia
    capital/largest city: 10 Addis Ababa
    others: 3 Edd 4 Axum, Bako, Dori, Goba, Gore, Thio 5 Adola, Adowa, Aduwa, Aksum, Assab, Awash, Dimtu, Elfud, Harar, Jidda, Jimma, Kecha, Meroe, Mojjo 6 Antalo, Asmara, Dessye, Dunkur, Gondar, Harrar, Makale, Napata 7 Ankober, Gambela, Gardula, Magdala, Massawa, Nakamti 8 Dire Dawa, Lalibala, Mustahil
    school: 13 Haile Selassie
    division: 5 Tigre 6 Amhara, Ogaden
    former division: 7 Eritrea
    measure: 3 tat 4 cubi, kuba 5 derah, messe 6 cabaho, sinjer, sinzer, tanica 7 entelam, farsakh, farsang, ghebeta
    monetary unit: 4 besa, birr, harf 5 amole, girsh 6 dollar, kharaf, levant, pataca, talari 7 ashrafi, menelik, plaster, tallero 12 maria theresa
    weight: 3 pek 4 kasm, natr, oket, rotl 5 alada, artal, mocha, neter, ratel, wakea 6 wogiet 8 farasula 9 mutagalla
    island: 6 Dahlak
    lake: 3 Abe 4 Tana 5 Abaya, Shola, Tanna, Tsana, Tzana, Zeway 6 Dambea, Dembea 7 Rudolph 8 Stefanie 11 The Blue Nile
    mountain: 4 Amba, Batu, Guge, Guna, Talo 5 Ahmar, Choke 9 Rasdashan
    highest point: 9 Ras Deshen
    river: 3 Omo 4 Baro, Dawa, Gibe, Gila,

Juba 5 Abbai, Akoho, Albai, Awash, Fafan, Mareb, Mofer, Rahad, Webbe 6 Tekeze 7 Tacazze, Takkaze 8 Gashgash, Shebante 11 The Blue Nile
    sea: 3 Red
    physical feature:
    desert: 17 Danákil Depression
    falls: 7 Tisisat 8 Blue Nile
    valley: 4 Rift
    people: 4 Afar, Agau, Beja, Doko, Kafa, Kala, Saho, Shoa 5 Afara, Agows, Galas, Galla, Negro, Tigre 6 Abigar, Amhara, Annuak, Gondar, Hamite, Harari, Sidama, Sidamo, Somali, Tigrai, Wolamo 7 Cushite, Danakil, Donakus, Falasha, Somalis 8 Assamite, Blemmyes 10 Abyssinian, Troglodyte
    leader: 7 Menelik 8 Mengistu 13 Haile Selassie
    language: 3 Giz 4 Afar, Agow, Geez, Saho 5 Geeze, Ghese, Smali, Tigre 6 Arabic, Harari 7 Amharic, English, Italian, Russian 8 Gallinya, Irob-Saho, Tigrinya
    religion: 5 Islam 7 Falasha, Judaism 18 Ethiopian Orthodoxy
    place:
    cathedral: 8 St George
    hall: 6 Africa
    palace: 7 Jubilee 9 Menelik II
    park: 4 Lion
    feature:
    flower: 7 brayera
    game: 5 dulla 8 shum-shir
    garment: 4 toga 5 kamis 6 barnos, chamma, netela, shamma
    tree: 4 koho, koso 5 cusso
    food:
    banana: 4 musa 6 ensete
    beer: 5 talla
    bread dish: 6 injera
    cereal: 4 teff
    honey liquor: 3 tej
    spicy sauce: 3 wat

ethnic 6 native, racial, unique 8 cultural, national, original 10 indigenous

ethnic group
    of Afghanistan: 5 Aimak, Aymak, Kafir, Nuris 6 Baloch, Baluch, Chahar, Durani, Hasara, Hazara, Kaffir, Kirgiz, Pathan, Tajiks, Uzbeks 7 Beluchi, Belucki, Ghilzai, Pakhton, Pakhtun, Pashtun, Pukhtun, Pushtun, Sistani, Taimani, Taimuri 8 Jamshidi, Siah Push 9 Firuzkuhi, Safed Push, Safid Push
    of Albania: 3 Geg 4 Cham, Gheg, Gueg, Tost 6 Arnaut, Arnout 8 Illyrian, Skipetar
    of Algeria: 4 Arab 6 Berber, Kabyle, Shawai, Tuareg 7 Haratin
    of Andorra: 7 Catalan
    of Angola: 5 Bantu, Kongo, Lundu 6 Chokwe, Herero, Mbundi, Ovambo 7 Bakongo, Kangela, Kikongo 8 Kimbundu, Kwangare 9 Ovinbundu 12 Nyaneka-Humbi
    of Antigua and Barbuda: 7 African, British 8 Lebanese 10 Portuguese
    of Argentina: 3 Api 4 Lule 5 Vejoz 6 Abi-

pon, Vilela 7 Guarani, Puelche, Ranquel, Taluhet 8 Querandi, Querendy

of Armenia: 5 Armen, Ermyn, Gomer, Hadji

of Australia: 3 Abo 4 Koko, Mara, Wong 5 Anzac, Bieri, Binge, Maori, Myall 6 Aranda, Arunta, Aussie, Binghi, Digger, Kipper, Papuan 7 Arawong, Billjim, Ilpirra 8 Antipode, Barkinji, Euahlayi, Warragal, Warrigal 9 Aborigine 10 Austroloid, Melanesian, Sandgroper 12 Jindyworobak

of Austria: 4 Pole 5 Croat, Czech, Gypsy 6 German 7 Slovene 9 Hungarian

of Azerbaijan: 5 Azeri 11 Azerbaijani

of the Bahamas: 5 black 7 Haitian

of Bahrain: 4 Arab 6 Indian 7 Persian 8 European 9 Pakistani

of Bangladesh: 7 Bengali

of Barbados: 5 Bajan 9 Barbadian

of Belarus: 12 Byelorussian

of Belgium: 4 Remi 6 Nervii 7 Belgian, Fleming, Flemish, Walloon 9 Bellovaci

of Benin: 3 Fon, Pla 4 Adja, Aizo, Mina, Peul 5 Pedah, Peuhl, Somba 6 Bariba, Fulani, Yoruba 8 Pilapila 9 Dahomeyan

of Bhutan: 5 Monpa 6 Bhutia 7 Tibetan 8 Assamese, Nepalese

of Bolivia: 6 Aymara 7 mestizo, Quechua

of Borneo: 4 Iban 5 Bukat, Dajak, Dayak, Dusan, Malay, Punan 6 Illano 7 Bakatan, Chinese, Illanun

of Bosnia-Herzegovina: 4 Serb 5 Croat 8 Yugoslav

of Botswana: 5 Bantu 6 Tswana 7 Bakatla, Bakwena, Bushman 8 Bamalete, Baralong, Batawana, Batlokwa, Botswana 10 Bamangwato 11 Bangwaketse

of Brazil: 2 Ge 4 Anta 5 Acroa, Arara, Araua, Bravo, Carib, Guana, Negro 6 Arawak, Caraja 7 Carayan, Javahai, mulatto, Tariana 8 Botocudo, Chambioa, mameluco 9 Caucasian 10 Portuguese 11 Tupi-Guarani

of Brunei: 4 Iban 5 Dayak, Malay 7 Chinese, Kadazan

of Bulgaria: 4 Slav, Turk 5 Gypsy, Pomak, Tatar 6 Bulgar, Slavic 7 Chuvash 9 Cheremiss 10 Macedonian

of Burkina Faso: 4 Bobo, Lobi, Samo 5 Bella, Bissa, Dyula, Fulbe, Hausa, Mande, Marka, Mossi, Puchl 6 Fulani, Senufo, Tuareg 7 Grunshi, Voltaic, Yatenga 8 Mandingo 9 Gourounsi 15 Bunsansi Gambaga

of Burundi: 3 Twa 4 Hutu 5 Bantu, Batwa, Pygmy, Tutsi 6 Bahutu, Watusi 7 Barundi

of Cambodia: 4 Cham, Thai 5 Khmer 7 Chinese 10 Vietnamese

of Cameroon: 3 Abo, Edo, Ibo 4 Beti, Bulu, Ekoi, Ijaw, Sara 5 Bantu, Bassa, Kirdi, Pygmy, Tikar 6 Bamoun, Donala, Ewondo, Fulani, Ibibio 7 Bakweri 8 Bamileke

of Canada: 6 Canuck, Eskimo, French, Innuit 7 English

of the Canary Islands: 7 Spanish

of Cape Verde: 6 Creole 7 African, mulatto 8 European 10 Portuguese

of Central African Republic: 4 Baya, Sara 5 Banda, Bwaki, Sango 6 Azande, Yakoma 7 Banziri, Mandjia, Nzakara

of Chad: 4 Arab, Daza, Maba, Sara, Teda, Tubu 5 Barma, Hakka, Kroda, Massa 6 Fulani, Kotoko, Toubou, Wadaii 7 Kamadja, Kanembu 8 Moundang

of Chile: 3 Ona,4 Auca, Inca, Onan 6 Arauca, Chango, Yahgan 7 Mapuche, mestizo, Moluche, Pampean, Patagon, Puegian, Ranquel 8 Alikuluf, Picunche, Tsonecan

of China: 3 Han, Yis 4 Huis, Lolo, Miao, Pu-is 5 Hakka, Hoklo, Seres, Sinic 6 Cataia, Chuang, Johnny, Korean, Manchu, Mongol, Serian, Uighun 7 Sinaean, Tibetan

of Colombia: 4 Boro, Cuna, Duit, Hoka, Macu, Muso, Muzo, Paez, Tama, Tapa 5 Carib, Catio, Choco, Cofan, Cogui, Cubeo, Guane, Haida, Mocoa, Paeze, Pijao, Seona, Yagua 6 Arawak, Betoya, Calima, Colima, Ingano, Mirana, Saliva, Tahami, Ticunu, Tucano, Tunebo, Witoto, Yahuna 7 Achagua, Andaqui, Chibcha, Chimila, Churoya, Guahibo, Guajiro, mestizo, mulatto, Panches, Puinave, Pultoto, Quechua, Shuswap, Tairona, Telembi 8 Coconuco, Guarauno, Motilone, Puinavis, Quimbaya, Sinsigas 9 Cocanucos, Coconucan, Panaquita 10 Bellacoola

of Comoros: 4 Arab 5 Bantu, Malay 7 African 8 Malagasy

of the Congo: 3 Rua 4 Akka, Susa, Teke, Vili 5 Amadi, Bantu, Figót, Kongo, Mantu, Pygmy, Sanga, Warua, Zambi 6 Ababua, Bafyot, Bateke, Mbochi, Nzambi, Wabuma 7 Bacongo, Bakongo, Bangala, Batetla, Manyema 10 Binga Pygmy

of Costa Rica: 4 Voto 6 Boruca, Bribri, Guaymi 7 Guatuso, mestizo, Spanish

of Crete: 6 Cretan, Minoan 7 Candiot 8 Sphakiot 9 Caphtorim 10 Philistine

of Croatia: 4 Serb 5 Croat 8 Yugoslav

of Cuba: 5 Carib, Negro, Taino 6 Arawak 7 Ciboney, mestizo 8 Ciboneye 9 Caucasian

of Czechoslovakia/Czech Republic: 4 Slav 5 Czech 6 Slovak 8 Bohemian, Moravian

of Denmark: 4 Dane, Jute 5 Angle 6 Cimbri, Eskimo, German, Ostmen, Teuton, Viking 12 Scandinavian

of Djibouti: 4 Afar, Arab 5 Issas 6 French 8 European

of Dominican Republic: 5 Negro, Taino 6 Indian 7 mulatto, Spanish 9 Caucasian

of Ecuador: 4 Cara, Cixo, Inca 5 Ardan, Aucas, Macoa, Maina, Palta, Quitu, Yumbo 6 Canelo, Jibaro, Jivaro, Puruha 7 Cayapas, Jivaros, mestizo, mulatto 8

Barbacoa, Colorado, Montuvio, Serranos 10 Montubious

of Egypt: 3 Kem 4 Arab, Copt, Misr, Wafd 5 Gippy, Gyppy, Gypsy, Nilot 6 Ababda, Berber, Hyksos, Nubian, Tasian 7 Mizraim, Pharian 8 Badarian, Bisharin, Memphian

of El Salvador: 5 Lenca, Pipil 6 Indian, Mangue 7 mestizo, Spanish 9 Matagalpa

of England: 4 Celt, Jute, Pict 5 Norse, Saxon 6 Angles, Briton, Norman, Viking

of Equatorial Guinea: 4 Bubi, Fang 5 Benge, Combe 6 Bujeba 10 Fernandino

of Estonia: 4 Esth, Finn 5 Aesti 6 Jewish 8 Estonian 9 Ukrainian 11 Belorussian

of Ethiopia: 4 Afar, Agau, Beja, Doko, Kafa, Kala, Saho, Shoa 5 Afara, Agows, Galas, Galla, Negro, Tigre 6 Abigar, Amhara, Annuak, Gondar, Hamite, Harari, Sidama, Sidamo, Somali, Tigrai, Wolamo 7 Cushite, Danakil, Donakus, Falasha 8 Assamite, Blemmyes 10 Abyssinian, Troglodyte

of Fiji: 6 Fijian, Indian 7 Chinese 10 Melanesian, Polynesian 11 Micronesian

of Finland: 3 Jew, Vod, Vot, Yak 4 Avar, Finn, Hame, Lapp, Turk, Veps 5 Fioun, Gypsy, Ijore, Inger, Suomi, Vepse, Zyrin 6 Magyar, Ostiak, Ostyak, Tarast, Tavast, Ugrian 7 Lappish, Mordvin, Permiak, Samoyed, Uralian 8 Cheremis, Estonian, Karelian, Livonian, Swekoman 9 Tavastian 11 Karjalaiset, Suomalaiset

of France: 5 Frank

of the Gabon Republic: 4 Fang 6 Adouma, Bakota, Bateke, Echira, Okande, Omyene 7 Eshiras 8 Bandjabi, Bapounou

of The Gambia: 4 Fula, Jola 5 Foula, Wolof 6 Fulani 8 Mandingo, Serahuli 9 Seranuleh

of Georgia: 5 Azeri 7 Russian 8 Armenian, Georgian, Ossetian

of Germany: 3 Hun 4 Slav, Sorb, Wend 5 Saxon

of Ghana: 2 Ga 3 Ewe 4 Akan, Akim, Akra, Aksa 5 Ahafo, Brong, Inkra 7 Akwapim, Ashanti, Dagomba, Maprusi 11 Mole-Dagbani

of Gibraltar: 6 Jewish 7 British, Italian, Maltese, Spanish 10 Portuguese

of Greece: 5 Greek 6 Achean, Dorian, Ionian 7 Aeolian, Hellene

of Greenland: 3 Ita 6 Eskimo 8 European

of Grenada: 5 Negro 6 Indian

of Guatemala: 3 Mam 4 Chol, Itza, Ixil, Maya 5 Xinca 6 Caribe, Quiche 7 ladinos, mestizo, Pocomam 13 Guatemaltecos

of Guinea: 4 Koma, Loma, Nalu, Susu, Toma 5 Kissi, Manon 6 Fulani, Guerzi 7 Landoma, Malinke 8 Kouranke, Landuman 11 Kissi-Sherbo 12 Guerze-Kpelle

of Guinea-Bissau: 6 Fulani 7 Balanta, Balante, mulatto 8 Mandingo, Mandyako

of Guyana: 6 Akawai, Arawak, Creole,

Taruma 7 African, Chinese, mulatto 10 Portuguese

of Haiti: 5 Taino 7 African, mulatto

of Honduras: 4 Maya, Paya, Sumo, Ulva 5 Carib, Lenoa, Pipil 6 Tauira 7 Jicaque, mestizo, Miskito 8 Mosquito

of Hong Kong: 5 Hakka, Haklo, Punti, Tanka 7 British, Chinese 8 American, Japanese 9 Cantonese 10 Portuguese

of Hungary: 3 Hun 4 Serb 5 Croat, Gypsy 6 Cigany, Magyar, Slovak, Ugrian

of Iceland: 6 Celtic, Viking 8 Norseman 9 Norwegian

of India: 2 Ao 3 Gor 4 Bhil 5 Aryan 6 Badaga, Pathan 7 Sherani 9 Dravidian 10 Andamanese

of Indonesia: 4 Dyak 5 Batak, Dayak, Malay 6 Battak, Papuan, Toraja 7 Chinese, Igorots 8 Acehnese, Achinese, Balinese, Javanese, Madurese, Sudanese 11 Minang Kabau

of Iran: 3 Lur, Tat 4 Arab, Kurd, Turk 5 Medes 6 Galcha, Gilani, Jewish, Shugni 7 Baluchi, Persian 8 Armenian, Bactrian, Bartangi, Parthian, Scythian 9 Bakhtiari 11 Azerbaijani, Mazandarani

of Iraq: 4 Arab, Kurd 7 Bedouin

of Ireland: 4 Celt, Erse, Gael 5 Irish 6 Celtic 9 Hibernian

of Israel: 3 Jew 4 Arab 5 Druze 10 Circassian

of Italy: 5 Latin 6 Sabine 7 Italian, Lombard 8 Etruscan

of Ivory Coast: 3 Abe, Dan, Kru, Kwa 4 Akan, Bete, Dida, Guro, Koua, Lobi, Wobe 5 Abron, Abure, Attie, Baule, Guere, Mande, Mossi 6 Baoule, Lagoon, Senufo, Senufu 7 Kroumen, Malinke, Voltaic 8 Dan-Gouro 10 Anyi-Baoule 11 Lobi-Kulango 12 Agnis-Ashanti

of Jamaica: 7 African, Chinese 10 East Indian

of Japan: 3 Eta 6 Korean 8 Japanese, Okinawan 10 Buramkumin

of Java: 5 Krama, Kromo 6 Kalang 8 Javanese, Madurese, Sudanese

of Jordan: 4 Arab, Kurd 7 Bedouin, Checher 8 Armenian, Assyrian 10 Circassian 11 Palestinian

of Kazakhstan: 6 Kazakh

of Kenya: 3 Luo 4 Arab, Meru 5 Bantu, Elgey, Galla, Kamba, Kisii, Luhya, Masai, Nandi, Tugen 6 Kikuyu, Ogaden, Somali 7 Baluyha, Hamitic, Hilotic, Kipsigi, Swahili, Turkana 8 Kalenjin, Marakwet

of Kiribati: 8 Banabans 10 Polynesian 11 Micronesian

of Korea: 6 Korean

of Kuwait: 4 Arab 5 Iraqi, Saudi 6 Indian 7 Bedouin 8 Egyptian 9 Pakistani 11 Palestinian

of Kyrgyzstan: 5 Uzbek 6 Kyrgyz 7 Kirghiz

of Laos: 2 Lu 3 Kha, Lao, Man, Meo, Tai, Yao, Yun 4 Miao, Thai 5 Hmong 8 Lao Teung 10 Phoutheung of **Latvia:** 3 Kur, Liv 4 Balt, Cour, Lett 7 Latgale, Latvian, Russian, Zemgale

of **Lebanon:** 4 Arab 9 Canaanite 10 Phoenician 11 Palestinian

of **Lesotho:** 4 Zulu 5 Bantu, Tembu 6 Basuto 7 Basotho

of **Liberia:** 2 Gi 3 Gio, Kra, Kru, Kwa, Vai, Vei 4 Gola, Kroo, Krou, Loma, Mano, Toma 5 Bassa, Gibbi, Gissi, Grebo 6 Gbande, Kpelle, Kpuesi, Krooby, Kruman 7 Krooboy, Krooman 8 Mandingo 15 Americo-Liberian

of **Libya:** 4 Arab, Tebu 6 Berber, Tuareg 7 Gaetuli 8 Getulans, Harratin

of **Liechtenstein:** 8 Alamanni, Alemanni

of **Lithuania:** 4 Balt, Lett, Pole 5 Zhmud 6 Jewish, Litvak 7 Aistian, Russian, Yatvyag 10 Lithuanian, Samogitian 11 Belorussian

of **Luxembourg:** 6 French, German 12 Luxembourger

of **Macao:** 6 Macaon 7 Chinese 10 Portuguese

of **Macedonia:** 4 Turk 8 Albanian 10 Macedonian

of **Madagascar:** 4 Arab, Bara, Hova 5 Malay 6 Merina, Tanala 7 African 8 Betsileo, Mahafaly, Malagasy, Sakalava 9 Antaimoro, Antaisaka, Antandroy, Tsimihety 10 Indonesian, Polynesian 13 Betsimisaraka

of **Malawi:** 3 Yao 4 Sena 5 Bantu, Lomwe, Ngoni 6 Cheiva, Maravi, Ngonde, Nyanja 7 Tumbuka

of **Malaysia:** 4 Iban 5 Dayak, Malay 6 Indian 7 Chinese, Kadazan 9 Pakistani, Sri Lankan 10 Bangladesh, Indonesian

of **Maldives:** 4 Arab 6 Indian 9 Sinhalese 10 Singhalese

of **Mali:** 3 Bwa 4 Fula, Kyan, Moor, Peul 5 Dogon, Dyula, Fulbe, Marka 6 Berber, Dognon, Fulani, Senufo, Tuareg 7 Bembara, Fellata, Malinke, Miniaka, Songhai, Soninke 8 Khasonke, Mandingo, Senoulfo

of **Malta:** 7 Maltese

of **Mauritania:** 4 Arab, Fula, Moor 5 Black, Fulbe, Wolof 6 Bafour, Berber, Fulani 7 African, Soninke, Tukulor 8 Sarakole 9 Sarakolle 10 Toucouleur 12 Halphoolaren

of **Mauritius:** 6 Creole, French, Indian 7 African, Chinese 8 European 13 Indo-Mauritian

of **Mexico:** 3 Ixe, Mam, Mie, Ser 4 Chol, Cora, Jova, Meco, Mixe, Pame, Pima, Roto, Seri, Teca, Teco, Texo, Xova 5 Aztec, Chizo, Chora, Mayan, Nahua, Opata, Otomi, Zoque 6 Eudeve, Indian, Mixtec, Pueblo, Toltec, Zotzil 7 Chincha, mestizo, Nahuatl, Nayarit, Spanish, Tehueco, Tepanec, Totonac, Zacatec, Zapotec 8 Lagunero, Mazateca, Tezcucan, Totonaco, Tzapotec, Yucateco, Zacateco, Zapoteca 9 Tlascalan 10 Coahuiltec, Cuitlateco, Tarahumara

of **Moldova:** 7 Gagauzi 8 Moldovan 9 Moldovian

of **Monaco:** 6 French 7 Italian 10 Monegasque

of **Mongolia:** 5 Oirat, Tungu 6 Buryat, Darbet, Khoton, Mongol 7 Kazakhs, Khalkha 8 Tuvinian 9 Dariganga

of **Montenegro:** 4 Serb, Slav 11 Montenegrin

of **Morocco:** 4 Arab, Moor 6 Berber, French 7 Spanish

of **Mozambique:** 3 Yao 5 Bantu, Chopi, Lomue, Lomwe, Macua, Makua, Ngoni, Nguni, Shona 6 Maravi, Thouga 7 Maconde, Makonde 10 Portuguese

of **Myanmar:** 4 Shan 7 Burmese, Siamese

of **Namibia:** 4 Nama 5 Bantu 6 Damara, Herero, Ovambo, Tswara 7 Bushman, Colored 8 Okavango 9 Hottentot

of **Nauru:** 7 Chinese 10 Melanesian, Polynesian 11 Micronesian

of **Nepal:** 3 Rai 4 Aoul 5 Limbu, Magar, Murmi, Newar, Tharu 6 Gurkha, Gurung, Nepali, Sherpa, Tamang 7 Bhutias, Kiranti 8 Gorkhali, Nepalese

of **the Netherlands:** 5 Dutch 7 Frisian 9 Hollander 10 Surinamese 12 Netherlander 13 South Moluccan

of **New Guinea:** 5 Pygmy 6 Papuan 7 Negrito 10 Melanesian

of **New Zealand:** 3 Ati 5 Arawa, Dutch, Maori 7 British, Ringatu 10 Polynesian

of **Nicaragua:** 4 Mico, Mixe, Rama, Smoo, Ulva 5 Cukra, Diria, Lenca, Sambo, Toaca 6 Mangue 7 mestizo, Miskito 8 Mosquito 9 Matagalpa

of **Niger:** 4 Daza, Idjo, Idyo, Idzo, Peul, Teda 5 Hausa, Warri 6 Djerma, Fulani, Kanuri, Songha, Toubou, Tuareg 13 Djerma-Songhai

of **Nigeria:** 3 Abo, Aro, Djo, Ebo, Edo, Ibo, Ijo, Tiv, Vai 4 Beni, Bini, Eboe, Efik, Egba, Ejam, Ekoi, Idyo, Igbo, Ijaw, Nupe 5 Angas, Benin, Gwari, Hausa 6 Chamba, Fulani, Ibibio, Kanuri, Yoruba 11 Hausa-Fulani

of **Norway:** 4 Lapp 5 Samme 6 Nordic, Viking

of **Oman:** 4 Arab

of **Pakistan:** 5 Sindi, Wazir 6 Afridi, Bengal, Mahsud, Pathan, Puktun, Sindhi 7 Baluchi, Brahuis, Punjabi, Pushtun, Sherani 8 Khattack, Shinwari, Yusefazi 11 Mohammedzai

of **Panama:** 4 Cuna 5 Choco 6 Guaymi 7 mestizo

of **Qatar:** 4 Arab 6 Pushtu, Yemeni 7 Baluchi, Iranian 9 Pakistani

of **Romania:** 6 Dacian 8 Romanian, Rumanian

of **Russia:** 4 Slav 5 Kulak 6 Jewish, Soviet, Velika 7 Chukchi, Latvian, Russian, Turkmen 8 Armenian, Estonian, Georgian, Siberian, Ukrainian 10 Lithuanian 11 Belorussian

of Rwanda: 3 Twa 4 Hutu 5 Batwa, Pygmy, Tutsi 6 Bahutu, Watusi 7 Batutsi

of Samoa: 6 Samoan 10 Polynesian

of San Marino: 7 Italian 11 San Marinese

of Sao Tome and Principe: 7 African 10 Portuguese 11 Cape Verdean

of Saudi Arabia: 4 Arab 7 Bedouin

of Scotland: 4 Gael, Pict, Scot 5 Norse

of Senegal: 4 Lebu, Peul, Soce 5 Diola, Dyola, Foula, Laobe, Peulh, Serer, Wolof 6 Fulani, Serere 7 Bambara, Malinke, Tukuler, Tukulor 8 Mandingo

of Seychelles: 5 Asian 6 Creole, French, Indian 7 African, Chinese

of Sicily: 5 Elymi, Sican, Sicel 6 Sicani, Siculi

of Sierra Leone: 3 Vai 4 Kono, Loko, Susu 5 Bulom, Kissi, Limba, Mande, Mendi, Temne 6 Creole, Fulani, Syrian 7 Gallina, Koranko, Kuranko, Sherbro, Yalunka 8 Lebanese, Mandingo

of Sikkim: 4 Rong 5 Bhote 6 Bhotia, Bhutia, Indian, Lepcha 7 Tibetan 8 Nepalese 9 Mongoloid

of Singapore: 5 Malay 6 Indian 7 Chinese 9 Malaysian, Pakistani, Sri Lankan

of Slovakia: 5 Czech 6 Slavic, Slovak 9 Hungarian

of Slovenia: 7 Slovene

of the Solomon Islands: 7 Chinese 8 European 10 Melanesian, Polynesian

of Somalia: 3 Sab 4 Asha 5 Galla 6 Hawiya, Isbaak, Somali 7 Danakil, Hamitic, Marehan, Samaale, Shuhali 8 Rahanwin

of South Africa: 4 Boer, Yosa, Zulu 5 Asian, Bantu, Namas, Nguni, Pondo, Sotho, Swazi, Tembu, Venda 6 Damara, Kaffir 7 African, British, Bushmen, English, Swahili 8 Bechuana, Coloured, Khoikhoi, San Xhosa 9 Afrikaner, Hottentot

of Spain: 4 Pict 5 Diego, Gente, Latin 6 Basque, Espana 7 Catalan, Espanol, Iberian 8 Galician, Gallegos, Maragato

of Sri Lanka: 5 Malay, Tamil, Vedda 6 Veddah, Weddah 7 Burgher, Mahinda, Malabar 8 Eurasian 9 Cingalese, Dravidian, Sinhalese 10 Ginghalese 12 Bandaranaike

of the Sudan: 3 Bor, Dor, Fur 4 Arab, Bari, Beri, Bobo, Daza, Egba, Fula, Golo, Nuba, Nuer, Poul, Sere 5 Anuak, Bongo, Dinka, Fulah, Hausa, Joluo, Junje, Mosgu, Mossi, Negro, Tibbu, Volta 6 Acholi, Azande, Gurusi, Hamite, Lotuho, Makari, Nilote, Nubian, Senufo, Surhai, Taureg 7 Balante, Baqqara, Gubayna, Jaaliin, Nilotes, Shilluk, Songhai, Songhay, Songhoi, Sourhai 8 Kababish, Mandingo, Menkiera 9 Sarakille 10 Gurmantshi, Shaiquiyya

of Suriname: 4 Boni, Bush, Trio 5 Djuka, Dutch 6 Creole, Wayana 7 African, Chinese 10 Amerindian, Boschneger, West Indian 11 Asian Indian

of Swaziland: 5 Asian, Bantu, Swazi 10 Eurafrican

of Sweden: 4 Lapp 5 Norse, Swede 6 Viking

of Switzerland: 5 Swiss, 6 Franks 8 Alamanni, Alemanni, Italians 12 Rhaeto-Romans

of Syria: 4 Arab, Kurd, Turk 5 Alawi, Aptal, Druse, Druze 6 Afshar, Aissor, Aushar, Avshar, Awshar 7 Amorite, Ansarie, Bedouin, Nosaris, Saracen, Shemite 8 Ansarieh, Armenian 9 Ansariyah 10 Circassian 12 Khachaturian

of Taiwan: 4 Yami 5 Hakka, Hoklo 7 Chinese, Malayan 9 Fukienese, Taiwanese 10 Indonesian, Polynesian 12 Kwangtungese

of Tajikistan: 5 Tajik, Uzbek 7 Tadzhik

of Tanzania: 2 Ha 4 Arab, Gogo, Goma, Haya, Hehe 5 Asian, Bantu, Masai 6 Arusha, Chagga, Sukuma, Wagogo, Wagoma 7 African, Makonde, Sambara, Sandawe, Shirazi, Swahili, Wabunga, Zongora 8 Nyakyusa, Nyamwezi

of Thailand: 3 Lao, Mon 4 Lawa, Shan, Thai 5 Malay 6 Indian, Khymer 7 Chinese, Siamese 9 Cambodian 10 Vietnamese

of Tibet: 5 Asian, Balti, Bodpa, Drupa 6 Bhotia, Champa, Drokpa, Khamba, Khambu, Mongol, Panaka, Sherpa, Tangut 7 Bhotiya, Bhutani, Gyarung, Taghlik, Tibetan

of Togo: 3 Ana, Ewe, Twi 4 Mina 5 Hausa 6 Akposa, Kabrai 7 Bassari, Cabrais, Kabrais, Ouatchi 8 Konkomba, Kotokoli, Lotokoli

of Tonga: 10 Polynesian

of Trinidad and Tobago: 5 Irish 6 French, Syrian 7 African, Chinese, English, Spanish 8 European, Lebanese 10 East Indian, Portuguese, Venezuelan 11 Asian Indian 13 Latin American

of Tunisia: 4 Arab 6 Berber, Jewish

of Turkey: 4 Arab, Kurd, Turk 6 Seljuk

of Turkmenistan: 7 Turkmen 10 Turkmenian

of Tuvalu: 6 Samoan 10 Polynesian

of Uganda: 4 Alur, Gisu, Soga, Teso 5 Ateso, Bantu, Chiga, Ganda, Langi, Lango, Nkole, Pygmy 6 Acholi, Ankole, Bagisu, Bakega, Basoga, Batoro 7 Baganda, Banyoro, Bunyoro, Hamitic, Lugbara, Nilotic, Sudanic 9 Nyoro-Toro 10 Banyankole, Karamojong

of Ukraine: 7 Russian 9 Ukrainian

of United Arab Emirates: 4 Arab 6 Indian 7 African, Iranian 9 Pakistani 10 South Asian

of Uruguay: 4 Yaro 5 Swiss 6 Indian 7 Italian, mestizo, Russian, Spanish 8 Charruas

of Uzbekistan: 5 Uzbek

of Vanuatu: 8 European 10 Melanesian, Polynesian 11 Micronesian

of Venezuela: 4 Bare, Pume 5 Bello, Carib, pardo, zambo 6 Arawak, Creole,

Timote 7 Charoya, Guahibo, Kaliana, mestizo, mulatto, Otomaca, Timotex 8 Caquetio, Guarauno, Matilone 11 Maquiritare

of Vietnam: 3 Hoa, Man, Meo, Tai, Tay 4 Cham, Kinh, Nung, Thai 5 Khmer, Malay, Muong 7 Chinese 8 Annamese, Annamite 9 Cambodian 10 montagnard, Vietnamese

of Wales: 4 Celt, Kelt 5 Cymry, Kymry, Welsh 7 Brython, Silures, Taffies 8 Awabokal, Cambrian 9 Siluridan

of Western Sahara: 4 Arab 6 Berber

of Western Samoa: 6 Samoan 10 Melanesian, Polynesian

of Yemen: 4 Arab 5 Zaidi 6 Shafai, Yemeni 8 Yemenite

of Yugoslavia: 4 Serb, Slav 5 Croat 7 Bosnian, Slovene 8 Albanian, Croatian 9 Hungarian 10 Macedonian 11 Montenegrin 13 Herzegovinian

of Zaire: 4 Kuba, Luba, Yaka 5 Bantu, Bashi, Bemba, Kongo, Lulue, Lunda, Mongo, Pygmy 6 Azande, Baluba, Watusi 7 Bakongo, Nilotes, Tshokwe 8 European, Mangbetu, Sudanese

of Zambia: 4 Lozi 5 Bantu, Bemba, Ngoni, Tonga

of Zimbabwe: 3 Ila 4 Sena 5 Asian, Bantu, Bemba, Sotho, Tongo, white 6 Indian 7 Barotse, Chinese, English, Mashoma, Mashona, Ndebele 8 Coloured, Japanese, Matabele 9 Afrikaner 10 Balakwakwa

etiquette 5 usage 7 decorum, manners 8 behavior, courtesy, good form, protocol 9 amenities, gentility, good taste 10 civilities, politeness 11 conventions, proprieties 15 rules of behavior

etoile 4 star

Ettarre
    character in: 16 Arthurian romance

ET The Extra-Terrestrial
    director: 15 Steven Spielberg
    cast: 10 Dee Wallace 11 Henry Thomas, Peter Coyote 13 Drew Barrymore 17 Robert MacNaughton

et tu, Brute 13 and thou Brutus
    spoken by: 12 Julius Caesar

etymology 7 history 10 derivation

Etzel
    origin: 8 Germanic
    mentioned in: 14 Nibelungenlied
    represents: 6 Attila
    wife: 9 Kriemhild

Euaechme
    parent: 8 Megareus
    husband: 9 Alcathous

Euboean see 7 Abantes

Eubuleus
    father: 9 Trochilus
    helped: 7 Demeter

Eucharist 8 viaticum 9 Communion, sacrament 13 Holy Communion

euchre
    number of players: 3 two 4 four 5 three
    derived from: 8 triomphe
    five tricks won: 5 march
    jack of trump: 10 right bower
    second highest trump: 9 left bower

Euclid
    field: 11 mathematics
    nationality: 5 Greek
    founder of: 8 geometry
    author of: 8 Elements

Eugene Onegin
    author: 16 Alexander Pushkin
    opera by: 11 Tchaikovsky
    character: 4 Olga 6 Lensky, Onegin 7 Tatyana 12 Prince Gremin, Tatyana Larin 14 Vladimir Lensky

Eugenie Grandet
    author: 14 Honore de Balzac
    character: 5 Nanon 7 Charles, Eugenie 11 Mme d'Aubrion

Euhelopus
    type: 8 dinosaur, sauropod
    period: 10 Cretaceous

Euhemerism
    theory of: 9 Euhemerus
    reduced deification of: 4 gods

Euippe
    origin: 5 Roman
    form: 6 maiden
    parent: 6 Daunus
    husband: 8 Diomedes
    changed into: 5 horse

Euler, Leonhard
    field: 7 physics 11 mathematics
    nationality: 5 Swiss
    first: 12 calculus book

eulogize 4 hail, laud, tout 5 boost, exalt, extol 7 acclaim, commend, glorify, magnify 9 celebrate 10 compliment, panegyrize 12 pay tribute to, praise highly

eulogy 5 paean 6 homage 7 hosanna, plaudit, tribute 8 citation, encomium 9 laudation, panegyric 10 high praise 11 acclamation

Eumedes
    father: 5 Dolon
    companion of: 6 Aeneas
    vocation: 6 herald

Eumelus
    member of: 7 Trojans
    commander of: 13 Thessalonians
    lost race to: 8 Diomedes
    wife: 8 Iphthime
    companion: 6 Aeneas

Eumenides
    author: 9 Aeschylus
    character: 6 Apollo, Athene, Furies 7 Orestes see 6 Furies

Eumolpus
    king of: 6 Thrace
    father: 8 Poseidon
    mother: 6 Chione
    son: 7 Ismarus
    founded: 19 Eleusinian mysteries
    supported accusations of: 9 Phylonome

Euneus
    father: 5 Jason
    mother: 9 Hypsipyle
Eunice
    son: 7 Timothy
Eunomia
    member of: 5 Horae
    personifies: 5 order
Eunomus
    father: 10 Architeles
    cup bearer of: 6 Oeneus
    slain by: 8 Hercules
Eunuch 6 Biztha, Careas, Zethar 7 Abagtha, Harbona, Mehuman
Eunuch, The
    author: 7 Terence
euphemism 11 prudishness, refined term 12 delicate term, overdelicacy 13 prudish phrase 14 mild expression, overrefinement
Euphemus
    father: 8 Poseidon
    mother: 6 Europa
    aided: 9 Argonauts
Euphorbus
    father: 8 Panthous
    brother: 9 Hyperenor, Polydemas
    fought with: 7 Trojans
euphoria 7 ecstasy, elation, rapture 9 wellbeing
Euphorion
    father: 8 Achilles
    mother: 5 Helen
Euphrosyne
    member of: 6 Graces
Euphues
    character in: 20 Euphues and His England 22 Euphues The Anatomy of Wit
    author: 4 Lyly
Euripides
    author of: 3 Ion 5 Medea 6 Hecuba 7 Electra, Orestes 8 Alcestis, Heracles 10 Andromache, Heraclidae, Hippolytus, Phoenissae, The Bacchae 13 The Suppliants 14 The Trojan Women 16 Iphigenia in Aulis 17 Iphigenia in Tauris 21 The Children of Heracles
Eurippa
    epithet of: 7 Artemis
    means: 18 delighting in horses
Europa
    also: 6 Europe
    father: 8 Agenor
    mother: 10 Telephassa
    brother: 5 Cilix 6 Cadmus 7 Phoenix
    son: 5 Minos 8 Sarpedon 12 Rhadamanthus
    daughter: 5 Crete
    abducted by: 4 Zeus
Europe see 6 Europa
Europe
    country: 5 Italy, Malta, Spain, Wales 6 France, Greece, Latvia, Monaco, Norway, Poland, Russia, Sweden 7 Albania, Andorra, Armenia, Austria, Belarus, Belgium, Croatia, Denmark, England, Estonia, Georgia, Germany, Hungary, Iceland, Ireland, Romania, Ukraine 8 Bulgaria,

Portugal, Scotland, Slovakia, Slovenia 9 Lithuania, Macedonia, San Marino 10 Azerbaijan, Luxembourg, Yugoslavia 11 Byelorussia, Netherlands, Switzerland, Vatican City 13 Czech Republic, Liechtenstein 14 Czechoslovakia 17 Bosnia Herzegovina
    city: 4 Bern, Bonn, Oslo, Rome 5 Paris, Sofia, Vaduz 6 Athens, Dublin, Lisbon, London, Madrid, Monaco, Moscow, Prague, Tirana, Vienna, Warsaw 7 Cardiff 8 Belgrade, Brussels, Budapest, Helsinki, Valletta 9 Amsterdam, Bucharest, Edinburgh, Reykjavik, San Marino, Stockholm 10 Bratislava, Copenhagen, Luxembourg 14 Andorra la Vella
    river: 3 Don 4 Ebro, Elbe, Oder 5 Loire, Neman, Rhine, Rhone, Seine, Tagus, Volga 6 Danube, Thames 7 Dnieper, Pechora, Vistula 8 Dniester
    island: 3 Man 4 Skye 5 Crete, Malta 6 Faeroe, Sicily 7 Corsica, Iceland, Ireland 8 Balearic, Sardinia 12 British Isles
    mountain/mountain range: 4 Alps 7 Balkans 8 Caucasus, Pyrenees 9 Apennines 11 Carpathians 12 Sierra Nevada
    highest point: 11 Mount Elbrus
    lowest point: 10 Caspian Sea
    sea: 4 Aral, Azov, Kara 5 Black, North, White 6 Aegean, Baltic 7 Caspian, Marmara 8 Adriatic 13 Mediterranean
    people: 3 Hun 4 Gael, Pict, Serb 5 Celts, Croat, Danes, Dutch, Jutes, Kymry, Marur, Poles, Scots, Slavs, Tatar, Welsh 6 Czechs, Franks 7 Basques, Britons, Gypsies, Iberian, Magyars, Slovaks, Slovene 8 Alamanni, Cossacks, Tyrolean, Walloons
    language: 5 Czech 6 Danish, German, French, Polish, Slovak 7 English, Italian, Romance, Russian, Spanish, Swedish 8 Germanic 9 Bulgarian, Portugese 11 Balto-slavic
    religion: 5 Islam 6 Jewish, Muslim 8 Anglican, Lutheran 9 Methodist 10 Protestant 12 Presbyterian 13 Dutch Reformed, Greek Orthodox, Roman Catholic 15 Church of England, Eastern Orthodox
    holiday: 11 Bastille Day, National Day 12 Guy Fawkes Day 13 Liberation Day, St Patricks Day 14 Queens Birthday 15 Independence Day 19 Heroes of the Republic
Eurotes
    father: 5 Myles
Eurus
    origin: 5 Greek
    personifies: 8 east wind 13 southeast wind
Euryale
    member of: 7 Gorgons
Euryanthe
    opera by: 5 Weber
    character: 6 Adolar 7 Lysiart 9 Eglantine
Eurybates
    companion of: 8 Odysseus

Eurybia
  father: 6 Pontus
  mother: 4 Gaea
  mated with: 5 Crius

Euryclea
  nurse of: 10 Telemachus

Eurydamas
  member of: 9 Argonauts

Eurydice
  also: 7 Agriope
  form: 5 dryad
  husband: 7 Orpheus
  daughter: 8 Themiste
  pursued by: 9 Aristaeus

Euryganeia
  son: 8 Eteocles 9 Polynices

Eurylochus
  companion of: 8 Odysseus

Eurynome
  father: 7 Oceanus
  mother: 6 Tethys
  sister: 6 Thetis
  daughters: 6 Graces

Eurypylus
  origin: 5 Greek
  occupation: 7 warrior
  father: 8 Poseidon, Telephus
  mother: 8 Astyoche
  uncle: 5 Priam
  killed by: 8 Hercules 11 Neoptolemus

Eurysaces
  father: 14 Telamonian Ajax
  mother: 8 Tecmessa
  inherited: 6 shield

Eurysthenes
  origin: 7 Spartan
  father: 11 Aristodemus
  twin brother: 7 Procles
  shared: 6 throne
  shared throne with: 7 Procles

Eurystheus
  king of: 6 Tiryns 7 Mycenae
  father: 9 Sthenelus
  mother: 7 Nicippe
  cousin: 8 Hercules
  son: 9 Perimedes
  imposed: 6 labors
  number of labors: 6 twelve
  imposed on: 8 Hercules

Eurytion
  form: 7 centaur
  father: 4 Ares 5 Actor
  companion of: 6 Aeneus
  guarded cattle of: 6 Geryon
  killed by: 6 Peleus 8 Hercules

Eurytus
  form: 5 giant
  father: 5 Actor 7 Auglaus 8 Melaneus
  twin brother: 7 Cteatus
  noted for: 7 archery
  slain by: 8 Hercules

Euterpe
  member of: 5 Muses
  muse of: 5 music 11 lyric poetry

evacuate 4 quit 5 leave 6 desert, remove, vacate 7 abandon, forsake, move out, take out 8 order out 12 withdraw from

evade 4 duck, shun 5 avoid, dodge, elude, hedge, parry 6 escape, eschew 7 fend off 8 sidestep 10 circumvent, equivocate 12 steer clear of

Evadne
  father: 6 Pelias 8 Poseidon
  mother: 6 Pitana
  sister: 9 Amphinome
  husband: 8 Capaneus

evaluate 4 rate 5 assay, gauge, judge, value, weigh 6 assess, size up 8 appraise, estimate

evaluation 4 test 8 analysis, judgment 9 appraisal 10 assessment, estimation

evaluator 5 judge 6 critic, tester 7 analyst, arbiter 8 assessor, reviewer 9 appraiser, estimator

Evander
  father: 6 Hermes 9 Carmentis
  mother: 6 Themis
  daughter: 4 Roma
  allied with: 6 Aeneas

evanesce 6 vanish 8 fade away, pass away 9 disappear, dissipate, evaporate

evanescence 9 vanishing 10 fading away 12 ephemerality 13 disappearance 14 transitoriness

evanescent 8 fleeting 9 ephemeral, transient 10 short-lived, transitory

Evangeline
  author: 24 Henry Wadsworth Longfellow
  character: 17 Gabriel Lajeunesse 23 Evangeline Bellefontaine

evangelist 4 John, Luke, Mark 7 apostle, Matthew 8 disciple, minister, preacher, reformer 9 apostolic, missioner, soul-saver 10 missionary, revivalist 12 Bible Thumper, propagandist, proselytizer 17 religious crusader

Evan Harrington
  author: 14 George Meredith
  character: 6 Louisa 10 Jack Raikes 11 Rose Jocelyn 12 Tom Cogglesby 13 Count de Saldar, Juliana Bonner 14 Caroline Strike 15 Andrew Cogglesby, Ferdinand Laxley, Melville Jocelyn 16 Countess de Saldar, Harriet Cogglesby 21 Melchisedek Harrington

Evans, Dame Edith
  born: 6 London 7 England
  roles: 8 Tom Jones 11 A Doll's House 13 The Whisperers 14 The Chalk Garden 27 The Importance of Being Earnest

Evans, Mary Anne
  real name of: 11 George Eliot

Evans, Maurice
  born: 6 Dorset 7 England 10 Dorchester
  roles: 9 Saint Joan 13 Rosemary's Baby 14 Man and Superman, Romeo and Juliet 15 Heartbreak House, Planet of the Apes 17 The Devil's Disciple 18 Gilbert and Sullivan 19 Androcles and the Lion

evaporate 5 dry up 6 dispel, vanish 7 scatter 8 dissolve, evanesce, fade away, melt away, vaporize 9 dehydrate, desiccate, disappear, dissipate

evasion 7 dodging, ducking, eluding 8 shunning 9 avoidance 12 sidestepping 13 circumventing, shrinking from 15 attempt to escape

evasive 6 shifty 7 devious, dodging, elusive, elusory, hedging 9 ambiguous, deceitful, deceptive, equivocal 10 misleading 11 dissembling 12 equivocating

Eva Trout
author: 14 Elizabeth Bowen

eve 4 dusk 6 female, sunset 7 evening, sunset 8 eventide 9 day before

Eve
husband: 4 Adam
son: 4 Abel, Cain, Seth
home: 4 Eden

Evelina
author: 11 Fanny Burney

even 4 calm, fair, flat, just, true 5 equal, flush, level, plane, plumb 6 placid, smooth, square, steady 7 balance, equable, flatten, regular, the same, uniform 8 balanced, constant, equalize, matching, parallel, straight, unbiased 9 equitable, identical, impartial, make flush, unruffled, unvarying 10 straighten, unwavering 11 make uniform, unexcitable 12 eventempered, make parallel 13 dispassionate

evening 3 eve 4 dusk, even 6 sunset 7 day's end, sundown 8 eventide, gloaming, twilight 9 nightfall 10 close of day

evenly matched 5 equal 8 of a piece 9 identical 10 well suited 13 one and the same

evenness 7 balance 8 calmness, equality, fairness, flatness, sameness 9 placidity 10 regularity, smoothness, steadiness, uniformity 11 equivalency

event 4 bout, game 7 contest, episode 8 incident, occasion 9 happening, milestone 10 experience, occurrence, tournament 11 competition

even-tempered 4 calm 6 serene 7 equable, patient 11 good-natured, unflappable 12 mild-tempered, well-adjusted

eventful 7 crucial, epochal, fateful, notable, weighty 8 critical, exciting, historic 9 important, memorable, momentous, thrilling 10 noteworthy 11 significant 13 consequential, unforgettable

eventide 4 dusk 6 sunset 7 evening, sundown 8 gloaming, twilight 9 nightfall

eventual 5 final, later 6 coming, future 7 ensuing 8 imminent, ultimate, upcoming 9 following, impending, resulting 10 consequent, subsequent 11 prospective

eventually 6 one day 7 finally 8 in the end, sometime 10 ultimately 12 in the long run 13 sooner or later 17 in the course of time 20 when all is said and done

Eventus see 12 Bonus Eventus

even up 3 tie 5 align 8 make even 10 straighten

Evenus
father: 4 Ares
mother: 8 Demonice
daughter: 8 Marpessa

Eve of St Agnes, The
author: 9 John Keats

ever 5 at all 6 always 7 forever 9 at any time, eternally, in any case 10 at all times, constantly 11 incessantly, perpetually 12 continuously

Everdene, Bathsheba
character in: 22 Far From the Madding Crowd
author: 5 Hardy

Everes
son: 8 Tiresias

Everglade State
nickname of: 7 Florida

evergreen 3 fir, yew 4 pine 5 heath, holly 6 jujube, laurel, myrtle, needle, privet 7 arbutus, casiope, conifer, jasmine, juniper 8 camellia, hawthorn, oleander, rosemary 9 mistletoe, sugarbush 11 conebearing 12 rhododendrum

Evergreen State
nickname of: 10 Washington

everlasting 7 durable, endless, eternal, lasting, tedious, undying 8 constant, immortal, infinite, timeless, tiresome 9 ceaseless, continual, incessant, perpetual, unceasing, wearisome 10 continuous, ever-living 11 long-lasting, never-ending 12 imperishable, interminable 14 indestructible

evermore 6 always 7 forever 9 eternally 10 for all time 13 everlastingly

ever upward
Latin: 9 excelsior
motto of: 7 New York (state)

everybody
French: 11 tout le monde

everyday 4 dull 5 daily, stock, trite, usual 6 common, square 7 mundane, regular, routine 8 familiar, ordinary, workaday 9 customary, hackneyed, quotidian 11 commonplace, day after day, established, stereotyped 12 conventional, run-of-the-mill 13 unimaginative

Everyman
author: 7 unknown
character: 3 God 5 Death, Goods 6 Beauty 7 Kindred 8 Strength 9 Good Deeds, Knowledge, Messenger 10 Fellowship

every man for himself
French: 12 sauve qui peut

Every Man in His Humour
author: 9 Ben Jonson
character: 6 Kitely 7 Bridget 8 Bobadill, Wellbred 9 Brainworm, Downright 13 Edward Knowell 14 Justice Clement

Every Man out of His Humour
author: 9 Ben Jonson
character: 6 Deliro 7 Fungoso, Sordido 9 Macilente, Sogliardo 10 Puntarvolo 12 Carlo Buffone 15 Fastidious Brisk

everyone
French: 11 tout le monde

everywhere 7 all over 10 every place, far and near, far and wide, throughout 11 extensively, in all places, universally 12 the world over, ubiquitously **14** to the four winds

evict 4 oust **5** eject, expel **6** remove **7** kick out, turn out **8** dislodge, get rid of, throw out **10** dispossess

evidence 4 fact, sign **5** proof, token **7** exhibit, grounds **9** testimony **10** indication **11** affirmation **12** confirmation, illustration **13** corroboration, documentation, material proof **14** authentication, substantiation **15** exemplification

evident 5 clear, plain **6** patent **7** certain, obvious, visible **8** apparent, manifest, tangible **10** noticeable, undeniable **11** conspicuous, perceptible **12** demonstrable, unmistakable **14** unquestionable **24** plain as the nose on your face

evidently 7 clearly, plainly **9** assumedly, certainly, doubtless, obviously **10** apparently, undeniably **11** doubtlessly **12** unmistakably **14** unquestionably **16** to all appearances

evil 3 bad, sin **4** base, vice, vile **5** venal **6** sinful, wicked **7** heinous, immoral, vicious **8** baseness, iniquity, sinister **9** depravity, malicious, malignant, nefarious, turpitude **10** corruption, immorality, iniquitous, malevolent, pernicious, villainous, wickedness, wrongdoing **12** black-hearted, unprincipled, unscrupulous

    goddess of: 7 Sekhmet

evildoer 6 sinner **7** culprit, villain **9** miscreant, wrongdoer **10** malefactor **12** transgressor

evil-minded 4 base **5** nasty **6** wicked **7** ignoble, immoral **8** depraved **10** despicable, iniquitous, villainous **12** dishonorable, unprincipled

evilness 6 malice **7** cruelty **8** villainy **9** barbarity, malignity **10** sinfulness, wickedness

evince 4 show **6** convey, reveal **7** display, exhibit, express **11** communicate, demonstrate **12** give evidence

Evius *see* **7** Bacchus

Evnissyen

    origin: 5 Welsh

    brother: 4 Bran **10** Manawyddan

    sister: 7 Branwen

    caused: 3 war

    between: **5** Irish **7** British

    killed: 6 nephew

evoke 4 stir **5** rouse, waken **6** arouse, awaken, call up, elicit, excite, induce, invite, invoke, summon **7** produce, provoke, suggest **9** call forth, conjure up, stimulate **10** bring forth

evolution 4 rise **6** change, growth **8** fruition, increase **9** expansion, unfolding **10** maturation **11** development, enlargement, progression **13** metamorphosis

    founder of theory: 13 Charles Darwin

    forerunner of theory: 12 Charles Lyell **18** Chevalier de Lamarck

evolve 4 grow **5** ripen **6** expand, mature, unfold, unroll **7** develop, enlarge **8** increase

Ewell, Tom

    real name: 14 Yewell Tompkins

    born: 11 Owensboro KY

    roles: 8 Adam's Rib **9** State Fair **14** The Great Gatsby **16** Tender Is the Night, The Seven Year Itch

ewer 3 jug, urn **5** basin **6** vessel **7** pitcher

Ewing, Patrick

    sport: 10 basketball

    team: 13 New York Knicks **15** Georgetown Hoyas

exacerbate 3 irk **5** anger **6** deepen, worsen **7** inflame, magnify, provoke, sharpen **8** heighten, increase, irritate **9** aggravate, intensify **10** exaggerate **12** fan the flames **16** pour oil on the fire **17** add insult to injury **18** add fuel to the flames **19** rub salt into the wound

exact 4 take, true **5** claim, force, mulct, right, wrest **6** compel, demand, extort, strict **7** careful, correct, extract, literal, precise, require, squeeze **8** accurate, clearcut, exacting, explicit, specific **9** on the head, on the nose **10** methodical, meticulous, scrupulous, systematic **11** painstaking, punctilious, to the letter, unequivocal

exacting 4 hard **5** harsh, rigid, stern, tough **6** severe, strict, trying **7** arduous **8** critical **9** demanding, difficult, hard-nosed, strenuous, unbending, unsparing **10** hardheaded, meticulous, no-nonsense

exactly 4 just **5** fully, quite, truly **6** indeed, just so, wholly **7** quite so **8** entirely, of course, strictly **9** assuredly, certainly, correctly, literally, precisely **10** absolutely, accurately, definitely, explicitly, that's right **12** specifically

exactness 8 accuracy **9** precision **10** exactitude **12** accurateness

exact satisfaction 6 avenge, punish **7** get back, get even, revenge **9** retaliate **14** get one's own back

exaggerate 5 boast **6** overdo **7** amplify, lay it on, magnify, stretch **9** embellish, embroider, enlarge on, overstate **11** hyperbolize

exaggerated 7 extreme, intense **10** inordinate, overstated **14** overemphasized

exalt 4 laud **5** cheer, elate, extol, honor **6** praise, uplift **7** acclaim, applaud, commend, elevate, ennoble, glorify, inspire, magnify, worship **8** venerate **9** celebrate, stimulate **10** exhilarate, make much of **12** pay tribute to

exaltation 4 high **5** bliss, glory, honor **6** praise **7** dignity, ecstasy, elation, rapture, tribute, worship **8** grandeur, nobility, praising **9** happiness, panegyric, transport **10** eulogizing, exultation, veneration **11** celebration, deification **12** exhilaration

exalted 2 up **5** grand, happy, lofty, noble **6** august, elated, lordly **7** excited, notable **8** blissful, ecstatic, elevated, glorious, inspired, uplifted **9** dignified, honorable, rapturous, venerable **10** heightened **11** highranking, illustrious, magnificent

exaltedness 5 bliss **6** height **7** ecstasy, elation, heights, rapture **8** highness, nobility **9** elevation, loftiness, transport

examination 4 exam, quiz, test **5** assay, audit, final, orals, probe, study **6** review, survey **7** midterm, perusal **8** analysis, scrutiny **10** inspection **11** looking over **13** investigation **15** physical checkup

examine 4 pump, quiz, scan, test, view **5** audit, grill, probe, query, study **6** peruse, ponder, review, survey **7** explore, inspect, observe **8** consider, look into, look over, question **10** scrutinize **11** inquire into, interrogate, investigate, take stock of

examiner 6 tester **8** inquirer, reviewer, surveyor **12** interrogator, investigator

example 5 ideal, model **6** sample **7** paragon, pattern **8** exemplar, specimen, standard **9** archetype, prototype **11** case in point **12** illustration **14** representation **15** exemplification

exasperate 3 bug, irk, vex **4** rile **5** anger, annoy, chafe, pique **6** bother, enrage, harass, madden, offend, rankle, ruffle **7** incense, provoke, turn off **8** irritate **9** aggravate, infuriate **15** try one's patience

exasperating 7 irksome **8** annoying **9** vexatious **10** irritating **11** infuriating

ex cathedra 12 from the chair **13** with authority **22** from the seat of authority

excavate 3 dig **4** mine **5** dig up, gouge **6** burrow, cut out, dig out, furrow, groove, quarry, tunnel **7** uncover, unearth **8** scoop out **9** hollow out **11** make a hole in

excavation 3 dig, pit **4** hole, mine, sump **5** ditch, grave, shaft, space **6** cavity, dugout, trench, trough **7** digging, opening

exceed 4 pass **5** excel **6** go over, outrun, overdo **7** outpace, outrank, surpass **8** go beyond, outreach, outrival, outstrip, surmount **9** come first, overshoot, transcend **10** be superior **11** predominate

exceedingly 4 very **6** vastly **7** greatly, notably **9** amazingly, eminently, extremely, supremely, unusually **10** enormously, especially, unwontedly, very highly **11** excessively **12** immeasurably, impressively, inordinately, preeminently, surpassingly **13** astonishingly, outstandingly, superlatively **15** extraordinarily

excel 5 outdo **6** exceed **7** prevail, surpass **8** outrival, outstrip **9** rank first **10** tower above **11** predominate, take the cake **20** walk off with the honors

excellence 5 merit **7** quality **8** eminence **9** greatness **10** perfection **11** distinction, high quality, preeminence, superiority **13** transcendence

excellent 4 aces, A-one, fine, tops **5** great, nifty, prime, super, swell **6** bang-up, choice, grade A, superb **7** capital, classic, notable **8** peerless, sterling, superior, terrific, top-notch **9** admirable, exemplary, first-rate, matchless, superfine, wonderful **10** first-class, preeminent, tremendous **11** exceptional, outstanding, superlative

excelsior 10 ever upward
 motto of: 7 New York (state)

Excelsior State
 nickname of: 7 New York

except 3 ban, bar, but **4** omit, save **6** enjoin, excuse, exempt, reject, remove, saving **7** barring, besides, exclude, shut out **8** count out, disallow, pass over **9** eliminate, excepting, excluding, other than **11** exclusive of

excepted 6 exempt **7** excused **8** excluded **11** not included

exception 6 oddity, rarity **7** anomaly, removal **8** omission **9** debarment, deviation, exclusion, exemption, isolation, rejection, seclusion **10** difference, leaving out, separation **11** elimination, peculiarity, repudiation, segregation, shutting out, special case **12** disallowment, irregularity, renunciation **13** inconsistency

exceptional 3 odd **4** rare **5** great, queer **6** unique **7** special, strange, unusual **8** aberrant, abnormal, atypical, freakish, peculiar, singular, superior, terrific, uncommon, unwonted **9** anomalous, excellent, irregular, marvelous, unheard of, unnatural, wonderful **10** first-class, inimitable, noteworthy, out-of-sight, phenomenal, remarkable **11** outstanding **12** incomparable **13** extraordinary, unprecedented **17** better than average

exception to the rule 7 anomaly **11** abnormality **12** irregularity

excerpt 4 part **5** piece **7** extract, portion, section **8** abstract, fragment **9** quotation, selection **13** quoted passage

excess 4 glut **5** extra, flood, spare **7** residue, surfeit, surplus, too much **8** fullness, overflow, plethora **9** avalanche, excessive, profusion, remainder, repletion **10** inundation, lavishness, oversupply **11** undue amount **13** overabundance **14** superabundance

excessive 5 undue **6** excess **7** extreme, profuse, too much **8** needless **9** senseless **10** immoderate, inordinate **11** exaggerated, extravagant, superfluous, unnecessary **12** overabundant, unreasonable **16** disproportionate

excessively 5 enorm **7** greatly **9** extremely, intensely **11** exceedingly, fanatically **12** boisterously, exorbitantly, inordinately **14** overabundantly

exchange 4 swap **5** trade **6** barter, switch **8** bandying, trade off **9** tit for tat **10** quid pro quo **11** convert into, give-and-take, interchange, reciprocate, reciprocity

exchange blows 3 box **5** clash, fight **6** battle, combat, tussle **7** contend, contest, grapple **8** skirmish **11** cross swords

exchange of viewpoints 6 debate, parley **8** dialogue **10** conference, discussion

exchange views 6 confer, debate **7** consult, discuss **8** consider, talk over **12** compare notes

excise 3 tax 4 duty 6 cut off, cut out, impost, remove 7 extract 8 pluck out 9 eradicate, surcharge

excitable 4 edgy 5 jumpy 7 jittery, nervous 8 feverish, frenzied, skittish 9 flappable, hotheaded 10 highstrung, passionate 11 combustible, inflammable

excite 4 fire, move, whet 5 evoke, pique, rouse, waken 6 arouse, awaken, elicit, foment, incite, kindle, spur on, stir up, thrill 7 agitate, animate, inflame, provoke 8 energize 9 electrify, galvanize, instigate, stimulate, titillate 13 get a kick out of

excited 4 daft 5 afire, astir 6 ablaze 7 aroused 8 agitated, ecstatic, frenzied, inflamed, turned on 9 disturbed, stirred up 10 magnetized 11 electrified

excitement 5 ado 4 flap, stir, to-do 5 furor, kicks 6 action, flurry, frenzy, hoopla, thrill, tumult 7 elation, ferment, flutter, turmoil 8 activity, brouhaha, interest 9 adventure, agitation, animation, commotion, fireworks 10 enthusiasm 11 stimulation

exciting 5 spicy 6 moving, risque 7 rousing, zestful 8 dazzling, stirring 9 affecting, impelling, inspiring, thrilling 11 hair-raising, provocative, sensational, stimulating, titillating 12 breathtaking, electrifying 13 spine-tingling

exclaim 4 howl, yell 5 shout 6 bellow, cry out 7 call out 8 proclaim 9 ejaculate 10 vociferate

exclamation 3 cry 4 howl, yell, yelp 5 shout 6 bellow, outcry, shriek, squeal 7 screech 9 expletive 11 ejaculation 12 interjection, vociferation

exclude 4 ban, bar 4 omit, oust 5 eject, evict, expel 6 banish, except, forbid, refuse, reject, remove 7 boycott, keep out, rule out, shut out 8 disallow, leave out, prohibit, set aside, throw out 9 blackball, repudiate 13 shut the door on

excluding 3 but 4 save 6 except, saving 7 banning, barring, besides 9 excepting, other than 10 keeping out

exclusion 6 ouster 7 barring, refusal, removal 8 ejection, eviction 9 debarment, dismissal, expelling, expulsion, rejection, restraint 10 banishment, keeping out, preclusion, prevention 11 prohibition, throwing out 12 nonadmission

exclusive 4 full, posh, sole 5 aloof, total 6 closed, entire, single 7 private 8 absolute, clannish, cliquish, complete, snobbish, unshared 9 undivided, selective 10 restricted 11 restrictive

exclusive of 3 but 4 save 6 except, saving 7 barring, besides 9 excepting, excluding, other than

excommunicate 3 ban 4 oust 5 eject, expel 6 banish, remove 8 unchurch 12 anathematize

excommunication 3 ban 6 ouster 8 anathema 10 banishment 12 proscription

excoriate 4 flay 5 curse 6 berate, revile 7 censure 8 denounce, execrate 9 skin alive

excrescence 4 bump, hump, knob, knot, lump 5 bulge, gnarl 6 nodule 8 swelling 10 protrusion 12 protuberance

excrete 4 void 5 expel 8 evacuate 9 discharge, eliminate

excruciating 5 acute 6 fierce, severe 7 cutting, extreme, intense, racking, violent 9 agonizing, exquisite, torturous 10 lacerating, tormenting, unbearable 11 unendurable 12 insufferable

exculpate 5 clear 6 acquit, excuse, pardon 7 absolve 9 exonerate, let one off, vindicate

excursion 4 hike, ride, tour, trek, trip, walk 5 drive, jaunt, sally, tramp 6 cruise, flight, junket, outing, ramble, sortie, stroll, voyage 10 expedition 12 pleasure trip

excusatory 9 defensive 10 apologetic 11 extenuatory, vindicatory 13 justificatory

excuse 4 free 5 alibi, clear, spare 6 acquit, defend, exempt, let off, pardon, reason 7 absolve, condone, defense, explain, forgive, indulge, justify, release 8 argument, bear with, mitigate, overlook, palliate, pass over 9 disregard, exculpate, exemption, exonerate, extenuate, gloss over, let one off, relieve of, vindicate, whitewash 10 absolution 11 exoneration, vindication 12 apologize for 13 justification 16 make allowance for 17 accept one's apology

execrable 4 vile 5 awful 8 dreadful, terrible 9 atrocious, revolting 10 abominable

execrate 4 hate 5 abhor 6 detest, loathe 7 despise 9 abominate, can't stand, excoriate 10 shrink from 11 can't stomach 12 be revolted by 13 be nauseated by, find repulsive 15 be disgusted with 20 regard with repugnance

execration 4 hate 6 hating 7 disgust 8 loathing 9 despising, repulsion, revulsion 10 repugnance 11 abomination, detestation

execute 2 do 3 act 4 kill, play, slay 5 enact 6 effect, murder, render 7 achieve, enforce, fulfill, perform, realize, sustain 8 carry out, complete, massacre 9 discharge 10 accomplish, administer, consummate, effectuate, perpetrate, put to death 11 assassinate 12 carry through 13 put into effect

execution 5 doing 7 killing, slaying 9 discharge, effecting, rendition 10 completion 11 achievement, carrying out, fulfillment, performance, realization, transaction 14 accomplishment, administration, implementation, interpretation, putting to death

executioner 6 hit man, killer, slayer 7 butcher, hangman 8 assassin, murderer

Executioner's Song, The
   author: 12 Norman Mailer

executive 7 manager 8 chairman, director, overseer 9 president 10 leadership, managerial, supervisor 11 directorial, supervisory 13 administrator 14 administrative, superintendent

executives 7 leaders 8 managers, officers 9 directors 13 governing body 14 administration

executor 4 doer 5 agent 9 performer 13 administrator

exegesis 10 exposition 11 explanation 14 interpretation 18 explication de texte

exemplar 5 ideal, model 7 example, pattern 8 original, standard 9 archetype, prototype

exemplary 5 ideal, model 6 sample 7 typical 8 laudable, sterling 9 admirable, emulative, estimable, nonpareil 10 noteworthy 11 commendable, meritorious 12 illustrative, praiseworthy 14 characteristic, representative

exemplification 7 epitome, essence, example 8 citation, evidence 10 embodiment 11 case in point 12 illustration 13 documentation 14 representation 15 personification

exemplify 6 depict, embody, typify 8 instance 9 epitomize, personify, represent 10 illustrate 11 demonstrate 12 characterize

exempli gratia 6 such as 10 for example 19 for the sake of example
   abbreviation: 2 eg

exempt 4 free 5 clear, freed, spare 6 except, excuse, immune, pardon, spared 7 absolve, cleared, excused, release, relieve 8 absolved, excepted, relieved 9 not liable, privilege 10 privileged

exemption 6 excuse 7 expense, freedom, release 8 immunity 9 allowance, deduction, exception 10 absolution 12 dispensation

exercise 3 use 4 show 5 apply, drill, exert, teach, train, tutor, wield 6 employ, school, warm-up 7 break in, develop, display, execute, exhibit, perform, prepare, program, utilize, workout 8 accustom, aerobics, carry out, ceremony, movement, practice, training 9 discharge, inculcate, schooling 10 daily dozen, discipline, employment, gymnastics, isometrics 11 application, demonstrate, give lessons, performance, utilization 12 calisthenics 14 do calisthenics

exert 3 use 5 apply, wield 6 employ, expend 7 utilize 8 exercise, put forth, resort to 9 discharge, make use of 11 put in action, set in motion

exertion 4 toil, work 5 labor, pains 6 effort, energy 7 travail, trouble 8 activity, endeavor, industry, strength, struggle 11 application, elbow grease

ex facie 6 on the face 10 apparently 11 from the face

ex facto 8 actually 15 according to fact

exhalation 4 puff 6 breath, wheeze, whoosh 10 expiration 12 breathing out

exhale 4 huff, pant, puff 6 expire 7 breathe, respire 10 breathe out

exhaust 3 fag, tax 4 bush, poop, tire 5 drain, empty, spend, use up 6 expend, finish, strain, weaken 7 consume, deplete, disable, draw off, draw out, fatigue, wear

out 8 enervate, overtire 9 dissipate 10 debilitate, devitalize, run through 13 sap one's energy

exhausted 4 beat, gone 5 all in, spent 6 bushed, done in, pooped, used up 7 drained, emptied, wearied, worn out 8 bankrupt, consumed, depleted, expended, fatigued, finished, tired out 9 dead tired, enervated, played out 11 devitalized 12 impoverished

exhausting 5 tough 6 tiring, uphill 7 arduous 8 toilsome 9 difficult, fatiguing, Herculean, laborious, Sisyphean, wearisome 10 burdensome

exhaustion 7 fatigue, using up 8 draining, spending 9 depletion, tiredness, weariness 10 enervation 11 consumption

exhaustive 6 all-out 7 in-depth 8 complete, profound, sweeping, thorough 9 intensive 12 all-embracing, all-inclusive 13 comprehensive

exhibit 3 air 4 show 6 flaunt, parade, reveal, unveil 7 display 8 brandish 9 put on view 10 exhibition, exposition, make public 11 demonstrate 12 bring to light 13 public showing

exhibition 4 show 5 array 7 display, exhibit, showing 9 unveiling 10 exposition 13 demonstration, public showing

exhibitionist 7 flasher, show-off 15 attention-seeker

exhilarate 4 lift 5 cheer, elate 6 excite, perk up 7 animate, delight, enliven, gladden, hearten, quicken 9 stimulate 10 invigorate

exhilaration 6 gaiety 7 delight, elation 8 gladness, vivacity 9 animation 10 exaltation, excitement, joyousness, liveliness 11 high spirits 16 lightheartedness

exhort 3 bid 4 goad, prod, spur, urge 5 egg on, press 6 advise, enjoin 7 beseech, implore 8 admonish, advocate, appeal to, persuade 9 encourage, plead with, recommend 14 give a pep talk to

exhortation 6 sermon, urging 7 bidding, lecture, pep talk 8 dictates, harangue, prodding 9 prompting

exhumation 9 digging up 12 disinterment 13 disentombment

exhume 5 dig up 8 disinter

exigency 3 fix, jam 5 needs, pinch 6 crisis, pickle, plight, scrape, strait 7 demands 8 hardship, quandary 9 emergency, extremity, urgencies 10 difficulty 11 constraints, contingency, necessities, predicament 12 circumstance, requirements

exigent 5 vital 6 urgent 8 critical, exacting, pressing 9 demanding, difficult, necessary

exile 2 DP 4 oust 5 eject, expel 6 banish, deport, emigre, pariah 7 outcast, refugee 8 drive out, expellee 9 expulsion 10 banishment, expatriate

Exile, The
   author: 9 Pearl Buck

exiled person 5 exile 6 emigre 7 outcast 8 expellee 10 expatriate

Exile's Return
   author: 13 Malcolm Cowley

exist 4 last, live, stay **5** abide, ensue, occur **6** endure, happen, obtain, remain **7** breathe, prevail, survive

existence 4 life **5** being **7** reality **8** presence, survival **9** actuality, animation, endurance **11** continuance, materiality, subsistence, tangibility

existent 4 real **5** alive **6** actual, extant, living **7** present **8** existing, tangible **9** surviving, to be found **11** in existence

existing 4 real **5** being **6** actual, extant, living **7** ongoing, present **9** existence, surviving, to be found **10** continuing, prevailing **11** established, in existence **12** accomplished

exit 4 blow **5** go out, leave, split **6** cut out, depart, egress, escape, exodus, way out **7** retreat **8** withdraw **9** departure **10** withdrawal **11** take a powder

ex libris 15 out of the books of **16** from the library of

ex nihilo nihil fit 25 out of nothing nothing is made **27** nothing is created from nothing

exocuticle
consists of: **9** sclerotin

exodus 4 exit **5** exile **6** flight, hegira **9** departure, migration **10** emigration, going forth

Exodus
author: **8** Leon Uris
story of founding of: **6** Israel

exonerate 4 free **5** clear **6** acquit **7** absolve, forgive **9** exculpate, vindicate **12** find innocent

exoneration 8 clearing **10** absolution **11** exculpation, vindication

exorbitant 4 dear **5** undue **6** costly **7** extreme **8** enormous **9** egregious, excessive, expensive, out-of-line **10** high-priced, inordinate, oppressive, outrageous, overpriced **11** extravagant **12** extortionate, preposterous, unreasonable

exorcise 5 expel **7** cast out **8** get rid of

Exorcist, The
author: **18** William Peter Blatty
director: **15** William Friedkin
cast: **8** Lee J Cobb **10** Linda Blair **11** Jason Miller, Max von Sydow **12** Ellen Burstyn
Oscar for: **10** screenplay

exoskeleton
of insect: **5** shell **8** body wall
part: **10** epicuticle, exocuticle **11** endocuticle

exoteric 4 open **6** public, simple **7** popular **8** exterior, external, outsider

exotic 5 alien **6** quaint, unique **7** foreign, strange, unusual **8** colorful, peculiar, striking **9** different, not native **10** from abroad, intriguing, outlandish, unfamiliar **11** exceptional **13** not indigenous

expand 4 grow, open **5** swell, widen **6** dilate, evolve, extend, fatten, spread, unfold, unfurl, unroll **7** amplify, augment, develop, distend, enlarge, inflate, magnify, stretch, unravel **8** heighten, increase, multiply **9** outspread, spread out **10** aggrandize

expanded 4 grew **5** grown **7** dilated, swelled, swollen, widened **8** enlarged, extended, unfolded, unfurled, unrolled **9** augmented, broadened, increased, outspread, spread out, stretched **10** heightened **11** aggrandized

expanse 4 area **5** field, range, reach, space, sweep **6** extent **7** breadth, compass, stretch **9** magnitude

expansion 6 growth **8** dilation, increase, swelling, widening **9** enlarging, extension, spreading **10** amplifying, distention, magnifying, stretching **11** development, enlargement, lengthening, multiplying **12** augmentation **13** amplification

expansive 4 free, open, vast, wide **5** broad **6** genial **7** affable, amiable, general, liberal **8** effusive, generous, outgoing **9** bounteous, bountiful, capacious, extensive, exuberant **10** voluminous **11** extroverted, far-reaching, uninhibited, unrepressed, wide-ranging **12** unrestrained **13** comprehensive

expatiate 6 expand **7** amplify, enlarge, expound **9** discourse, elaborate

expatriate 2 DP **5** exile **6** emigre, pariah **7** outcast, refugee **15** displaced person

expatriation 5 exile **9** expulsion **10** banishment

expect 5 guess, trust **6** assume, demand, plan on, reckon **7** believe, count on, foresee, hope for, imagine, look for, presume, require, suppose, surmise **8** envision, reckon on, rely upon **9** calculate **10** anticipate, bargain for, conjecture, reckon upon **11** contemplate **13** look forward to

expectancy 11 expectation **12** anticipation

expectant 4 agog **5** eager, ready **7** anxious, hopeful, waiting **9** expecting **10** looking for, optimistic **12** anticipating, apprehensive

expectation 4 hope **5** trust **6** belief, chance **8** prospect, reliance **9** assurance **10** confidence, expectancy, likelihood **11** presumption **12** anticipation **13** contemplation

expedient 4 help, wise **5** means **6** resort, tactic, useful **7** benefit, measure, politic, selfish, stopgap **9** advantage, advisable, conniving, desirable, effective, judicious, makeshift, opportune, practical, strategem **10** beneficial, instrument, profitable, worthwhile **11** calculating, self-seeking, self-serving **12** advantageous **14** self-interested

expedite 4 rush **5** hurry **6** hasten **7** advance, forward, further, promote, quicken, speed up **8** dispatch **10** accelerate, facilitate **11** precipitate, push through

expedition 4 trek **6** voyage **7** journey, mission **8** campaign, voyagers **9** explorers, travelers, wayfarers **10** enterprise **11** adventurers, exploration

expeditious 4 fast **5** alert, awake, hasty, quick, rapid, ready, swift **6** prompt, snappy, speedy **7** instant **8** punctual **9** effective, immediate **10** bright-eyed **11** efficacious

expel 4 fire, oust, sack, spew, void **5** eject, evict, exile **6** banish, bounce, remove **7** cashier, cast out, dismiss, drum out, excrete **8** dislodge, drive out, evacuate, force out, throw out **9** discharge, eliminate

expellee 2 DP **5** exile **14** banished person **15** displaced person

expend 3 pay **4** give **5** drain, empty, spend, use up **6** donate, lay out, pay out **7** consume, exhaust, fork out, wear out **8** disburse, dispense, shell out, squander **9** dissipate, go through **10** contribute

expendable 7 payable **9** available, forgoable, spendable **10** consumable, extraneous **11** disbursable, dispensable, replaceable, superfluous **12** nonessential **14** relinquishable

expended 5 spent **6** used up **7** drained, emptied, paid out **8** consumed **9** disbursed, exhausted **10** dissipated

expenditure 3 use **4** cost **5** price **6** charge, outlay, output **7** payment **8** exertion, expenses, spending **9** expending, paying out **10** employment, money spent **11** application, consumption **12** disbursement

expense 4 cost, rate **5** drain, price **6** amount, charge, figure, outlay **9** depletion, quotation

expensive 4 dear **6** costly **9** excessive **10** exorbitant, high-priced, immoderate, overpriced **11** extravagant **12** uneconomical, unreasonable **15** beyond one's means

experience 3 see **4** bear, feel, know, meet, view **5** doing, event, sense **6** affair, behold, endure, suffer **7** episode, observe, sustain, undergo **8** exposure, incident, perceive, practice, training **9** adventure, encounter, go through, happening, seasoning, withstand **10** occurrence **11** familiarity, live through, observation **17** personal knowledge **18** firsthand knowledge

experienced 4 able, wise **6** expert, master **7** capable, knowing, skilled, trained, veteran **8** seasoned **9** competent, efficient, practical, qualified **10** well-versed **11** worldly-wise **12** accomplished **13** sophisticated

experiential 9 empirical, firsthand, practical

experiment 4 test **5** assay, flier, trial **6** feeler, try out **7** analyze, examine, explore, venture **8** analysis, research **11** examination, investigate **12** seek proof for, verification **13** investigation **14** mess around with

experimental 3 new **4** test **5** fresh, rough, trial **7** radical **9** tentative **10** conceptual, first-draft **11** conjectural, speculative **13** developmental, trial-and-error

experimentation 7 testing **8** analysis, research **10** experiment **11** examination, exploration **13** investigation, trial and error

experimenter 6 tester **10** researcher **15** experimentalist

expert 3 ace, apt, pro, wiz **4** able, deft, whiz **5** adept, crack, doyen, maven, mavin, shark **6** adroit, artist, facile, master, wizard **7** artiste, capable, perfect, skilled, trained, veteran **8** masterly, skillful, virtuoso **9** authority, competent, masterful, practiced, qualified **10** first-class, past-master, proficient, specialist **11** connoisseur, crackerjack, experienced **12** accomplished, professional **13** knowledgeable

French: **6** au fait

expertise 5 savvy, skill **7** know-how **10** expertness **12** special skill **14** specialization **15** professionalism

expertness 5 savvy, skill **7** ability, know how **8** training **9** expertise **10** capability, competence, experience **11** proficiency **12** special skill **13** qualification **14** accomplishment, specialization **15** professionalism

expiate 7 appease **8** atone for **13** make amends for **16** pay the penalty for

expiation 6 amends, shrift **7** penance **9** atonement **11** appeasement **16** paying the penalty

expiration 3 end **5** death, dying **6** demise, ending, finish **7** passing, closing **8** decrease, exhaling **10** conclusion **11** termination **12** breathing out

expire 3 die, end **5** cease, lapse **6** finish, perish, run out **7** decease, kick off, succumb **8** conclude, pass away **9** terminate **11** come to an end, discontinue **13** kick the bucket **14** give up the ghost

expired 4 dead, died **6** lapsed, ran out, run out **7** defunct, laspsed **8** deceased, lifeless, perished **10** passed away **11** came to an end, come to an end **14** gave up the ghost

explain 6 fathom **7** clarify, clear up, justify, resolve **8** describe, spell out **9** elucidate, explicate, interpret, make clear, make plain **10** account for, illuminate, illustrate **11** demonstrate, rationalize **14** give a reason for **20** give an explanation for

explainer 6 critic **7** analyst **8** reviewer **10** translator **11** commentator, interpreter

explanation
French: **15** eclaircissement

explicate 7 analyze, clarify, develop, explain **8** annotate **9** elucidate, interpret **10** elucidated, illuminate, illustrate

explication 8 analysis **10** commentary **11** elucidation, explanation **12** illumination **13** clarification **14** interpretation

explication de texte 8 exegesis **11** explanation **14** interpretation **17** literary criticism

explicit 5 blunt, clear, exact, frank, plain **6** candid, direct **7** certain, express, pointed, precise **8** absolute, definite, distinct, specific **9** outspoken **10** unreserved **11** categorical, unequivocal, unqualified **15** straightforward **16** clearly expressed

explicitness 7 clarity **9** clearness, precision **11** unambiguity

explode 5 belie, blast, burst, erupt, go off 6 blow up, expose, refute, set off 7 destroy 8 detonate, disprove 9 discredit, repudiate 10 invalidate, prove false, prove wrong 11 burst loudly 12 utter noisily 14 burst violently, express noisily 18 discharge violently 19 burst out emotionally

exploit 4 feat 5 abuse 6 misuse 7 utilize 8 profit, put to use 9 adventure, brave deed, heroic act, make use of 10 daring deed 11 achievement 12 capitalize on 14 accomplishment, use to advantage 15 take advantage of 16 make selfish use of 21 take unfair advantage of 22 turn to practical account

exploited 6 abused 7 ill used, misused 11 downtrodden 15 took advantage of 16 taken advantage of

exploration 5 probe 7 inquiry 8 scrutiny 9 discovery 10 expedition, experiment 11 examination 12 scouting trip 13 investigation

explore 3 try 5 plumb, probe, scout 6 survey, try out 7 analyze, examine, feel out, pry into 8 look into, research, traverse 9 delve into, penetrate, range over 10 scrutinize, search into, travel over 11 inquire into, investigate, reconnoiter 14 experiment with

explorer

American: 4 Byrd, Pike 5 Boone, Clark, Lewis, Peary, Perry
Australian: 4 Hume 5 Sturt 6 Stuart 8 Mitchell
British: 4 Bell, Cook, Park 5 Baker, Bligh, Bruce, Cabot, Davis, Drake, Grant, Puget, Scott, Smith, Speke 6 Baffin, Burton, Hudson, Lander 7 Raleigh, Stanley 8 Franklin 9 Frobisher, MacKenzie, Vancouver 11 Livingstone
Danish: 6 Bering 7 Niebuhr
Dutch: 6 Tasman 7 Barents, Le Maire 8 Schouten 10 Linschoten
French: 6 Joliet 7 Cartier, Jolliet, La Salle 9 Champlain, Marquette 12 Bougainville
Italian: 8 Columbus 9 Marco Polo, Verrazano 15 Amerigo Vespucci
Moslem: 10 Ibn Battuta
Norwegian: 8 Amundsen
Portuguese: 3 Cam, Cao 4 Dias, Diaz 5 Cabral, Da Gama 7 Almeida 8 Covilhao, Magellan 11 Albuquerque 23 Prince Henry the Navigator
Russian: 10 Middendorf 11 Przhevalsky
Spanish: 5 Balboa, Cortes, De Soto 7 Pizarro 8 Coronado, Orellana, Valdivia 11 Ponce de Leon
Swedish: 12 Nordenskjold
Viking: 10 Eric the Red 11 Leif Ericson

explosion 3 fit 4 clap 5 blast, burst, crack 6 report 7 tantrum 8 eruption, outbreak, outburst, paroxysm 9 blowing up, discharge 10 detonation 11 fulmination

explosive 5 shaky, tense 6 touchy 7 keyed up 8 critical, perilous, strained, ticklish, unstable, volatile 9 dangerous, emotional 10 ammunition, precarious 12 pyrotechnics

exponent 6 backer 8 advocate, champion, defender, promoter 9 expounder, proponent, spokesman, supporter 12 propagandist

export 7 send out 8 dispatch 10 sell abroad 11 foreign sale 12 ship overseas

expose 4 bare, risk, show 5 brand, offer, strip 6 betray, denude, divest, hazard, let out, reveal, submit 7 display, divulge, exhibit, imperil, let slip, subject, uncover, unearth 8 denounce, disclose, endanger 10 jeopardize, reveal to be 12 acquaint with, bring to light 16 leave unprotected

exposé 6 baring 8 exposure 10 divulgence, revelation

exposed 4 open 5 bared 6 divulged, laid open, revealed, unmasked 9 denounced, disclosed, displayed, uncovered, unearthed 11 unprotected, unsheltered

exposition 4 expo, fair, mart, show 6 bazaar, market 7 account, display, exhibit, picture 8 exegesis 9 trade fair, trade show 10 commentary, exhibition, world's fair 11 description, elucidation, explanation, explication 12 illustration, presentation 13 clarification, demonstration 14 interpretation

expostulate 5 argue 6 enjoin, exhort, object, reason 7 caution, counsel, protest 8 forewarn 9 plead with 11 remonstrate 13 cry out against, reason against 14 inveigh against

exposure 4 view 5 vista 6 expose 7 outlook 8 frontage, prospect 9 divulging, unmasking 10 disclosure, divulgence, laying bare, laying open, revelation, subjection, submission, uncovering 11 perspective 12 public notice 15 bringing to light

expound 6 defend, uphold 7 explain 8 describe 9 elucidate, explicate, hold forth, make clear

express 3 say 4 fast, show, word 5 clear, couch, exact, lucid, plain, quick, rapid, speak, state, swift, utter, vivid, voice 6 convey, direct, evince, phrase, relate, reveal 7 certain, declare, divulge, exhibit, nonstop, precise 8 definite, describe, disclose, evidence, explicit, forceful, specific, vocalize 9 high-speed, make known, verbalize 10 articulate, particular 11 categorical, communicate, unequivocal 12 put into words

expression 4 look, mien, term, tone, word 5 idiom, style 6 airing, aspect, phrase, saying 7 emotion, meaning, stating, telling, venting, voicing, wording 8 language, locution, phrasing, relating, speaking, uttering 9 assertion, eloquence 10 appearance, modulation 11 countenance, declaration, enunciation, phraseology 12 articulation, setting forth, turn of phrase 13 communication

expressionless 5 blank, empty 6 vacant 7 deadpan 12 inexpressive

expressive 5 vivid 6 moving 7 telling 8 eloquent, forceful, poignant, powerful, striking 9 effective 10 compelling, indicative, meaningful, thoughtful 11 significant 14 characteristic

expressly 7 clearly, plainly **9** decidedly, pointedly, precisely, specially **10** definitely, distinctly, explicitly **12** particularly, specifically **13** categorically, unequivocally **18** in no uncertain terms

express sorrow 3 cry **4** weep **6** grieve, lament **7** condole, console **10** sympathize **11** commiserate

expropriate 4 take **5** seize **8** take over **10** commandeer, confiscate **11** appropriate

expropriation 7 seizure **10** arrogation, taking over **12** confiscation **13** commandeering

expulsion 5 exile **6** ouster **7** ousting, removal **8** ejection, eviction **9** debarment, discharge, dismissal, exclusion, expelling **10** banishment **11** elimination, prohibition, throwing out **12** proscription

expunge 5 erase **6** delete, efface, rub out **7** blot out, destroy, wipe out **9** eradicate, strike out **10** obliterate

expurgate 3 cut **4** blip, edit **5** purge **6** censor, cut out, delete, excise, remove **8** bleep out **10** blue-pencil, bowdlerize

exquisite 4 fine **5** dainty **6** choice, lovely, superb **7** elegant, perfect **8** delicate, flawless, peerless, precious, splendid **9** admirable, excellent, faultless, matchless **10** consummate, fastidious, impeccable, meticulous **11** superlative **12** incomparable **14** discriminating

exquisiteness 6 beauty **8** delicacy, elegance, fineness **10** loveliness, perfection **12** flawlessness

extant 6 living **7** present **8** existent, existing **9** surviving, to be found **11** in existence

Extasie, The
   author: 9 John Donne

extemporaneous 5 ad-lib **7** offhand **9** extempore, impromptu **10** improvised, off the cuff, unprepared **11** extemporary, spontaneous, unrehearsed **12** without notes **13** without notice **14** unpremeditated **15** spur-of-the-moment **19** off the top of one's head

extemporary 5 ad-lib **9** extempore, impromptu **10** improvised, off the cuff, unprepared **14** extemporaneous **19** off the top of one's head

extempore 5 ad-lib **7** offhand **9** impromptu **10** improvised, off the cuff, unprepared **11** extemporary, unrehearsed **12** without notes **14** extemporaneous, unpremeditated **15** spur-of-the-moment **19** off the top of one's head

extemporize 5 ad-lib **6** make up **9** improvise **14** speak impromptu **15** speak off the cuff

extend 4 give **5** grant, offer, widen **6** bestow, expand, impart, put out, spread, submit **7** advance, amplify, augment, broaden, draw out, enlarge, hold out, proffer, prolong, stretch **8** continue, elongate, increase, lengthen, protract, reach out **10** make longer, stretch out **12** stretch forth

extended 4 long **7** widened **8** drawn out, enlarged, expanded, thorough, unfolded, unfurled **9** broadened, continued, extensive, prolonged, spread out **10** lengthened, protracted, widespread **12** stretched out **13** comprehensive

extending 8 full form **9** expansion **10** drawing out, elongation, proffering, stretching **11** enlargement, lengthening **12** putting forth

extension 3 arm **4** wing **5** annex, delay **6** branch, length, outlay **7** adjunct **8** addition, appendix, increase **9** appendage, expansion, outgrowth **10** drawing out, proffering **11** enlargement, lengthening **12** continuation, postponement, prolongation

extensive 4 huge, long, vast, wide **5** broad, great, large **7** lengthy **8** enormous, extended, far-flung, thorough **9** capacious, universal **10** protracted, voluminous **12** all-inclusive, considerable **13** comprehensive

extensiveness 4 span **5** range, reach, scope **6** extent, spread **7** breadth, compass, expanse, stretch

extent 4 area, size, time **5** range, reach, scope, sweep **6** amount, degree, length **7** breadth, compass, expanse, stretch **8** duration **9** amplitude, magnitude **10** dimensions

extenuate 6 excuse, temper **7** explain, justify, qualify **8** mitigate, moderate

extenuating 9 lessening, tempering **10** mitigating, moderating, qualifying **11** attenuating, diminishing, explanatory, justifiable

exterior 4 face, skin **5** alien, outer, shell **6** exotic, facade, finish, manner **7** bearing, coating, foreign, outside, outward, surface **8** covering, demeanor, external **9** extrinsic, outer side, outermost **10** extraneous **11** superficial

exterminate 3 zap **4** kill **5** erase, waste **7** abolish, destroy, expunge, root out, wipe out **8** demolish, massacre **9** eliminate, eradicate, slaughter **10** annihilate, extinguish

external 5 alien, outer **7** foreign, outside, outward, surface **8** exterior **9** extrinsic, outermost **10** extraneous **11** superficial

extinct 4 dead, gone, lost **5** put out **7** defunct, died out, gone out **8** quenched, vanished **12** extinguished

extinction 5 death **7** eclipse **9** wiping out **11** destruction, eradication **13** disappearance

extinguish 3 end, zap **4** dash, do in, kill **5** crush, douse, quash **6** cancel, dispel, put out, quench, stifle **7** abolish, blow out, destroy, smother, wipe out **8** demolish, snuff out **9** eliminate, eradicate, suffocate

extinguished 6 put out **7** gone out **8** quenched **15** no longer burning

extirpate 5 erase **7** abolish, destroy, extract, pull out, root out, wipe out **8** demolish **9** eradicate **10** annihilate, extinguish, obliterate **11** exterminate

extol 4 laud **6** praise **7** acclaim, applaud, commend, glorify **8** eulogize **9** celebrate **10** compliment **16** sing the praises of

extort 5 educe, exact **6** coerce, elicit **7** extract **9** shake down

extortion 5 force, graft 6 payola, ransom 7 threats, tribute 8 coercion 9 blackmail, hush money, shakedown 14 forced payments

extortionate 5 undue 7 extreme 9 excessive, out-of-line 10 exorbitant, inordinate 12 unreasonable

extra 4 more 5 spare 7 adjunct, further, surplus 9 accessory, auxiliary, redundant, unusually 10 additional, attachment, complement, especially, remarkably, uncommonly 11 superfluous, unnecessary 12 additionally, appurtenance, particularly, supplemental 13 exceptionally 15 extraordinarily

extract 3 get 4 cite, cull 5 educe, evoke, exact, gleen, juice, quote, wrest 6 choose, deduce, derive, elicit, obtain, pry out, remove, select 7 copy out, distill, draw out, essence, excerpt, passage, pull out, root out, take out 8 abstract, bring out, citation, pluck out, press out, separate 9 extirpate, extricate, quotation, selection 10 distillate, squeeze out 11 concentrate

extraction 5 stock 7 descent, removal 8 ancestry 10 derivation, drawing out, pulling out

extraneous 5 alien 6 exotic 7 foreign, strange 9 extrinsic, unrelated 10 immaterial, incidental, irrelevant, not germane 11 superfluous 12 adventitious, inadmissible, nonessential, not pertinent 13 inappropriate

extraordinary 3 odd 4 rare 5 queer 6 unique 7 amazing, notable, strange, unusual 8 uncommon 9 fantastic, monstrous, unheard of 10 incredible, phenomenal, remarkable 11 exceptional 12 unbelievable 13 inconceivable

extraterrestrial 6 cosmic 10 outer-space 12 interstellar, otherworldly 14 interplanetary

extravagance 5 folly, waste 6 excess 7 caprice 9 absurdity 10 profligacy 11 prodigality, squandering, unrestraint 12 immoderation, improvidence, overspending, recklessness, wastefulness 13 excessiveness 14 capriciousness 16 inordinate outlay, unreasonableness

extravagant 4 wild 6 absurd, costly, unreal 7 foolish 8 fabulous, lavishly, prodigal, spending, wasteful 9 excessive, expensive, fantastic, high-flown, imprudent 10 exorbitant, high-priced, immoderate, inordinate, openhanded, outlandish, outrageous, overpriced, profligate 11 improvident, spendthrift, squandering 12 overspending, preposterous, unreasonable, unrestrained

extravaganza 4 fair 5 opera 6 ballet 7 pageant 8 carnival, operetta 9 spectacle, stage show 10 exposition, vaudeville 11 opera bouffe, spectacular 12 Broadway show, opera comique, son et lumiere, wild west show 14 phantasmagoria 17 sound and light show

extreme 3 end 5 depth 6 excess, height, severe 7 intense, radical, unusual 8 advanced, boundary, farthest, uncommon 9 excessive, extremity, nth degree, outermost, very great 10 avant-garde, immoderate, inordinate, outrageous 11 exaggerated, extravagant, most distant 13 extraordinary

extremely 4 very 5 quite 7 awfully 8 terribly 9 curiously, intensely, unusually 10 abnormally, especially, freakishly, peculiarly, remarkably, singularly, uncommonly 11 exceedingly, excessively, unnaturally 12 immoderately, surprisingly 13 exceptionally 15 extraordinarily

extremely painful 7 racking 9 agonizing, torturous 10 tormenting, unbearable 11 intolerable, unendurable 12 excruciating, insufferable

extremity 3 arm, end, leg, tip, toe 4 edge, foot, hand, limb 5 bound, brink, limit, reach 6 border, finger, margin 7 confine, extreme 8 boundary, terminus 9 outer edge, periphery

extricate 4 free 5 loose 6 get out, rescue 7 deliver, release 8 liberate, untangle 9 disengage 11 disencumber, disentangle 12 wriggle out of

extrication 6 escape 7 loosing, release 10 liberation 11 deliverance 13 disengagement 15 disentanglement

extrinsic 5 alien 7 foreign 9 accessory 10 accidental, extraneous, incidental 11 dispensable 12 nonessential

extrovert 7 show-off 13 exhibitionist 14 life of the party 17 hail-fellow-well-met

extroverted 8 outgoing, sociable 9 expansive 10 gregarious 12 unrestrained

extrude 4 spew 5 eject, expel 7 project, push out 8 force out, protrude, stickout 9 thrust out

exuberance 3 zip 4 elan, life, zeal 5 vigor 6 energy, spirit 8 buoyancy, vitality, vivacity 9 animation, eagerness 10 enthusiasm, excitement, liveliness 13 effervescence, sprightliness

exuberant 4 lush, rich 5 eager 6 lavish, lively 7 copious, excited, profuse, zealous 8 abundant, animated, spirited, vigorous 9 bounteous, energetic, luxuriant, plenteous, plentiful, sprightly 12 enthusiastic 13 superabundant

exudation 3 sap, tar 4 ooze 5 pitch, sweat 7 leakage, seepage 8 bleeding, drainage 9 discharge, excretion

exude 4 drip, emit, ooze 5 sweat 7 secrete 9 discharge

exult 4 crow 5 gloat, glory 7 rejoice 8 be elated 10 be jubilant, jump for joy 11 be delighted 13 be exhilarated 15 be in high spirits

exultant 5 happy 6 elated, joyful 7 crowing 8 boasting, ecstatic, euphoric, gloating, jubilant 9 rapturous, rejoicing 10 triumphant

exultation 3 joy 7 elation, ovation, rapture, triumph 9 rejoicing 10 jubilation

Eyck, Jan van
born: 8 Flanders, Maaseyck 10 Maastricht
artwork: 9 Timotheos 15 Ghent Altarpiece 18 Adoration of the Lamb, The Man in a Red Turban, The Virgin in a Church 20 The Arnolfini Marriage 24 Arnolfini Wedding Portrait 29 The Madonna with Chancellor Rolin 30 The Madonna with Canon van der Paele

eye 3 orb 4 scan, view 5 sight, study, taste, watch 6 behold, gaze at, look at, peeper, regard, survey, take in, vision 7 inspect, observe, stare at 8 eyesight, glance at 10 perception, scrutinize 14 discrimination
part: 4 iris, lens, rods 5 cones, nerve, pupil 6 cornea, muscle, retina 11 blood vessel

eyeful 4 doll 5 beaut, peach, Venus 6 beauty 7 stunner 8 knockout 10 goodlooker 13 beautiful girl 14 beautiful woman
eyeglass, eyeglasses 4 lens 5 specs 6 eyecup, lenses 7 goggles, monocle 8 cheaters, contacts, pincenez 9 lorgnette 10 spectacles
Eye of the Needle
author: 10 Ken Follett
eyesight 4 eyes 5 sight 6 vision
eyewitness 5 gaper, gazer 6 gawker, viewer 7 witness 8 attester, attestor, beholder, informer, looker-on, observer, onlooker, passerby 9 bystander, spectator, testifier 10 rubberneck
Ezekiel
father: 4 Buzi
Ezra
father: 7 Seraiah

F

Fabares, Ruby Bernadette Nanette
   real name of: 13 Nanette Fabray

fable 3 fib, lie 4 hoax, myth, tale, yarn 6 legend 7 fiction, leg-pull, parable, romance, untruth, whopper 8 allegory 9 fairy tale, falsehood, invention, tall story 11 fabrication

fabled 6 unreal 7 storied 8 fabulous, fanciful, mythical 9 imaginary, legendary 10 fictitious 12 mythological

Fables
   author: 16 Jean de La Fontaine

Fabray, Nanette
   real name: 28 Ruby Bernadette Nanette Fabares
   partner: 9 Sid Caesar
   born: 10 San Diego CA
   roles: 7 Baby Nan 12 The Band Wagon 13 Sid Caesar Hour 15 High Button Shoes, Our Gang comedies

fabric 5 cloth, frame, stuff 6 makeup 7 textile, texture 8 dry goods, material 9 framework, structure, substance, yard goods 10 foundation 12 organization, substructure 14 infrastructure, superstructure
   cotton: 4 duck 5 denim, drill, scrim, terry 6 burlap, calico, canvas, chintz, dimity, madras, muslin, oxford, poplin 7 batiste, buckram, flannel, gingham, organdy, percale, ticking 8 chambray 9 crinoline, sailcloth 10 broadcloth, printcloth, seersucker 11 cheesecloth, dotted Swiss
   linen: 6 canvas, damask 7 butcher, cambric 8 birds-eye 9 huckaback
   natural: 4 jute, silk, wool 5 linen 6 cotton 8 asbestos
   silk: 3 raw 4 tram 7 organza 8 organzie 9 organzine
   synthetic: 5 nylon, orlon, rayon 6 olefin 7 acetate, acrylic 9 polyester
   type: 4 felt, lace, lame 5 crepe, gauze, moire, serge, voile 6 damask, faille, jersey, melton, velour, velvet 7 brocade, chiffon, flannel, foulard, gingham, taffeta 8 chenille, corduroy, tapestry 9 gabardine, velveteen
   wool: 4 felt 5 crepe, serge, tweed, twill 6 boucle, covert, faille, melton, woolen 7 challis, doeskin, Donegal, worsted 8 homespun, Shetland 9 Astrakhan, gabardine, sharkskin 10 hopsacking 11 Harris tweed, herringbone
   from goats: 8 cashmere
   sheep: 5 Iraqi 6 Hirrik, merino, Romney, Somali 7 Lincoln 8 Cotswold, Tatarian 9 Hampshire, Southdown 10 Corriedale, Dorset Down, Dorset Horn, Shropshire, Sikkim Bera 13 Hampshire Down

   other wool-bearing animals: 5 camel, llama 6 alpaca, vicuna

fabricate 4 fake, form 5 build, erect, feign, forge, frame, hatch, shape 6 design, devise, invent, make up 7 compose, concoct, falsify, fashion, produce, trump up 8 assemble, contrive, simulate 9 construct, embroider, formulate 11 counterfeit, manufacture

fabrication 3 fib, lie 4 myth, yarn 5 fable 6 makeup 7 fiction, forgery, untruth 8 building, creation, erection 9 fairy tale, falsehood, invention 10 assemblage, concoction, fashioning, production 11 composition, manufacture 12 constructing, construction 13 prevarication 16 cock-and-bull story

Fabritius, Carel
   real name: 13 Carel Pietersz
   born: 14 Midden-Beemster, The Netherlands
   artwork: 11 View of Delft 12 The Goldfinch 19 The Raising of Lazarus

fabulous 5 great 6 fabled, superb 7 amazing, storied 8 fanciful, invented, mythical, smashing 9 fantastic, imaginary, legendary, marvelous, wonderful 10 apocryphal, astounding, fictitious, incredible, stupendous 11 astonishing, spectacular 12 mythological, unbelievable 13 extraordinary

facade 4 face, mask 6 veneer 8 frontage, pretense 9 front view 10 false front 13 building front

face 3 air, mug, pan 4 coat, gall, grit, look, pout, puss, sand 5 brass, cheek, cover, front, image, nerve, pluck, spunk 6 aspect, daring, facade, kisser, mettle, repute, visage 7 bravado, dignity, front on, grimace, obverse, overlay; surface 8 boldness, confront, features, forepart, frontage, good name, overlook, prestige 9 encounter, hardihood, impudence, semblance 10 appearance, confidence, effrontery, expression, give toward, look toward, reputation, turn toward 11 countenance, physiognomy, self-respect

Face
   character in: 12 The Alchemist
   author: 6 Jonson

facet 3 cut 4 part, side 5 angle, phase, plane 6 aspect 7 surface

facetious 5 comic, droll, funny, witty 6 clever, jocose, joking, jovial 7 amusing, comical, jesting, jocular, playful 8 humorous 12 wisecracking

face-to-face 6 direct 8 personal 9 firsthand

facile 3 apt 4 glib 5 adept, handy, quick, slick 6 adroit, artful, casual, clever, fluent, smooth 7 cursory, shallow 8 careless, skillful 10 effortless, proficient 11 superficial

facilitate 3 aid 4 ease 6 foster, help in, smooth 7 advance, forward, further, lighten, promote, speed up 8 expedite, simplify 10 accelerate, make easier

facility 3 aid 4 bent, ease 5 knack, means, skill 7 aptness, fluency 8 deftness, easiness, resource 9 advantage, appliance, dexterity, readiness 10 adroitness, capability, competence, efficiency, expertness, smoothness 11 convenience, proficiency 14 effortlessness, practicability

facsimile 4 copy 5 clone 7 replica, reprint 8 likeness 9 duplicate, imitation, photostat 10 transcript 12 reproduction

fact 3 act 4 deed 5 event, truth 6 verity 7 reality 8 incident, specific 9 actuality, certainty, happening, thing done 10 occurrence, particular 12 circumstance

faction 3 set 4 bloc, gang, ring, sect, side, unit 5 cabal, clash, group, split 6 breach, circle, clique, schism, strife 7 combine, coterie, discord, rupture, section 8 conflict, division, minority, sedition 9 rebellion 10 contention, disruption, dissension, dissidence, insurgency, quarreling 11 subdivision 12 disagreement 13 splinter group 15 incompatibility

factious 7 warring 8 divisive, fighting, mutinous 9 alienated, bickering, combative, estranged 10 contending, rebellious 11 belligerent, contentious, disaffected, disagreeing, dissentious, quarrelsome 12 disputatious 13 at loggerheads, insubordinate 15 insurrectional 16 at sixes and sevens

factitious 4 sham 5 phony 9 pretended, synthetic, unnatural 10 artificial 12 manufactured

factor 4 part 5 cause 6 reason 7 element 9 component, influence 11 constituent 12 circumstance 13 consideration

factory 4 mill, shop 5 plant, works 8 workshop 10 manufactory

factotum 8 handyman 9 gal Friday, guy Friday, man Friday 10 girl Friday 12 right-hand man 15 jack-of-all-trades

factual 4 real, true 5 exact, plain 6 actual 7 certain, correct, genuine, literal 8 accurate, concrete, definite, faithful 9 authentic, unadorned 10 scrupulous, verifiable

faculty, faculties 4 bent, gift, wits 5 flair, knack, power, skill 6 genius, reason, talent 7 quality 8 aptitude, capacity, function, penchant, teachers 9 adeptness, endowment 10 capability, professors 12 mental powers, skillfulness 13 teaching staff

fad 4 mode, rage, whim 5 craze, fancy, mania, vogue 6 whimsy 7 fashion 10 dernier cri, latest word 11 latest thing

faddish 2 in 6 trendy 10 innovative 11 fashionable

fade 3 die, dim, ebb 4 blur, dull, fail, flag, pale, wane 5 droop, taper 6 bleach, lessen, recede, whiten, wither 7 crumble, decline, dwindle, fall off, grow dim, shrivel 8 diminish, dissolve, evanesce, languish; make pale, melt away, pass away 9 disappear dissipate, evaporate, lose color

fade away 3 die, ebb 6 recede 7 subside 8 diminish

faded 4 drab, dull, pale 5 dingy 6 grayed 7 died out 8 bleached, dwindled, whitened, withered 9 colorless, shriveled, washed out

Faerie Queene, The
    author: 13 Edmund Spenser
    character: 3 Una 5 Guyon 6 Duessa 8 Artegall, Gloriana (the Faerie Queen) 9 Archimago, Britomart 12 Prince Arthur 14 Red Cross Knight

Fafnir
    origin: 12 Scandinavian
    form: 6 dragon
    father: 8 Hreidmar
    brother: 5 Otter, Regin
    killed: 8 Hreidmar
    killed by: 6 Sigurd

fag 4 bush, butt, poop, tire, weed 5 weary 6 tucker 7 exhaust 9 cigarette

Fagin
    character in: 11 Oliver Twist
    author: 7 Dickens

Fahrenheit
    abbreviation: 1 F

Fahrenheit 451
    author: 11 Ray Bradbury

Fahrenheit, Gabriel Daniel
    field: 7 physics
    nationality: 6 German
    invented: 16 thermometer scale 18 alcohol thermometer, mercury thermometer

fail 3 die, ebb 4 bomb, flag, flop, fold, wane 5 abort, crash, droop, flunk 6 desert, slip up 7 decline, dwindle, forsake, founder, give out, go under, let down, misfire 8 be in vain, collapse, fade away, languish, lay an egg, miscarry 9 disappear, fall short, fizzle out 10 end in smoke, go bankrupt, not succeed, run aground 11 be stillborn, come to grief, deteriorate, fall through, go up in smoke, miss the mark 12 come to naught, turn out badly 13 come to nothing 15 go out of business 16 meet one's Waterloo, meet with disaster

fail at 11 fall short of 12 be defeated in, not succeed at 16 be unsuccessful at

failed
    French: 6 manque

failing 4 weak 5 shaky 6 defect, ebbing, waning 7 folding, frailty 8 drooping, flagging, giving up, slipping, weakness 9 deficient, dwindling, giving out, weakening, weak point 10 deficiency, going under 11 shortcoming 12 unsuccessful 13 insufficiency

fail to include 4 drop, omit 8 leave out

failure 3 dud 4 bomb, flop, mess, ruin 5 botch, crash, loser 6 fizzle, mishap, muddle 7 decline, default, failing, folding, misfire, washout 8 collapse, downfall 9 breakdown, ruination 10 bankruptcy, ne'er-do-well

Fainall, Mrs
   character in: 16 The Way of the World
   author: 8 Congreve

faint 3 dim, low 4 pale, soft, thin, weak 5 dizzy, faded, frail, giddy, muted, small, swoon, timid 6 dulcet, feeble, little, meager, remote, slight, subtle, torpid 7 fearful, fragile, languid, muffled, obscure, pass out, worn out 8 black out, collapse, cowardly, delicate, drooping, fatigued, timorous 9 exhausted, inaudible, lethargic, whispered 10 indistinct 11 lightheaded, lily-livered, vertiginous 13 inconspicuous 17 lose consciousness

fainthearted 4 weak 5 timid 6 feeble 8 cowardly 10 irresolute 11 halfhearted, indifferent, lily-livered

faintheartedness 9 cowardice 12 cowardliness, yellow streak 13 pusillanimity, yellow feather 17 pusillanimousness 18 chicken-heartedness

fair 4 fine, just, pale, so-so 5 blond, bonny, sunny 6 bright, comely, creamy, decent, honest, justly, kosher, lovely, medium, pretty, proper, square 7 average, legally, not dark, upright 8 adequate, candidly, carnival, honestly, mediocre, middling, moderate, ordinary, passable, pleasant, rainless, squarely, sunshiny, unbiased 9 beautiful, cloudless, equitable, ethically, honorable, honorably, impartial, justified, objective, tolerable, unclouded 10 aboveboard, attractive, evenhanded, exhibition, legitimate, pretty good, reasonable, truthfully 11 indifferent, respectable 12 forthrightly, light-colored, light-skinned, on the up-and-up, run-of-the-mill, satisfactory, unprejudiced 13 disinterested, dispassionate 19 according to the rules

Fair, A A
   pseudonym of: 18 Erle Stanley Gardner

Fairbanks, Douglas
   real name: 17 Douglas Elton Ulman
   wife: 12 Mary Pickford
   son: 18 Douglas Fairbanks Jr
   born: 8 Denver CO
   roles: 9 Robin Hood 11 The Iron Mask 14 The Black Pirate, The Mark of Zorro 16 The Thief of Bagdad 18 The Three Musketeers 23 The Private Life of Don Juan

Fairbanks, Douglas Jr
   father: 16 Douglas Fairbanks
   wife: 12 Joan Crawford
   born: 9 New York NY
   roles: 8 Gunga Din 12 Little Caesar 15 Sinbad the Sailor 16 That Lady in Ermine 17 Catherine the Great 18 The Prisoner of Zenda 19 The Corsican Brothers

fair dealing 7 honesty 8 fairness 15 trustworthiness

Fairfax, Gwendolen
   character in: 27 The Importance of Being Earnest
   author: 5 Wilde

Fairfax, Jane
   character in: 4 Emma
   author: 6 Austen

Fairfax, Mrs
   character in: 8 Jane Eyre
   author: 6 Bronte

Fair Land, Fair Land
   author: 11 A B Guthrie Jr

fairly 5 fully 6 justly, rather, really 7 rightly 8 actually, honestly, passably, properly, somewhat, squarely 9 equitably, honorably, so to speak, tolerably 10 absolutely, completely, moderately, positively, reasonably 11 impartially, objectively 12 evenhandedly, legitimately 15 dispassionately 19 in a manner of speaking
   Latin: 9 pari passu

fairness 7 balance, honesty, justice 8 equality, fair play 11 objectivity 12 impartiality 14 even-handedness 16 equal opportunity

fair play 7 justice 8 equality, fairness 12 impartiality 16 equal opportunity

fair-skinned 4 pale 5 blond, light 6 blonde 17 light-complexioned

fairy 3 elf 5 pixie 6 sprite 10 leprechaun

fairy tale 3 fib 4 myth 5 fable 6 legend 7 fantasy, fiction 8 tall tale 9 invention 11 fabrication 16 cock-and-bull story
   German: 7 Marchen

fait accompli 16 accomplished fact, thing already done

faith 4 sect 5 creed, trust 6 belief, church, fealty 7 loyalty, promise 8 credence, fidelity, reliance, religion, security 9 assurance, certainty, certitude, constancy 10 confidence, conviction, obligation, persuasion

faithful 4 true 5 close, exact, loyal, tried 6 honest, strict, trusty 7 devoted, factual, precise, similar, staunch, upright 8 accurate, constant, lifelike, reliable, resolute, truthful 9 steadfast 10 dependable, scrupulous, true-to-life, unswerving, unwavering, verifiable 11 trustworthy 13 conscientious, incorruptible

faithfulness 6 fealty 7 loyalty 8 devotion, fidelity 9 constancy 10 allegiance 11 reliability 13 steadfastness

faithless 5 false 6 fickle 8 disloyal 10 inconstant, perfidious, unreliable 11 treacherous 13 untrustworthy

faithlessness 5 doubt 7 perfidy 9 disbelief, falseness, treachery 10 disloyalty, fickleness, infidelity, skepticism 11 inconstancy 13 unreliability 14 perfidiousness, unfaithfulness

fake 4 hoax, ruse, sham 5 bogus, dodge, dummy, faker, false, feign, forge, fraud, phony, put-on, quack, trick 6 deceit, forged, humbug, poseur, pseudo 7 falsify, forgery, not real, pretend, trump up 8 artifice, contrive, deceiver, delusion, imposter, invented, simulate, specious, spurious 9 charlatan, concocted, contrived, deception, dissemble, fabricate, imitation, imposture, pretender, simulated 10 artificial, fabricated, fictitious 11 contrivance, counterfeit, dissimulate, fabrication, make-believe

faker 5 fraud, phony 6 humbug 8 imposter 9 charlatan, pretender

fakir 5 Hindu 6 Muslim 7 ascetic, dervish

falcon 5 hobby, saker 6 desert, lanner, merlin 7 goshawk, kestrel, prairie, shaheen, tiercel 8 caracara, falconet 9 gyrfalcon, peregrine

Falcon and the Snowman, The
   author: 13 Robert Lindsey
   director: 15 John Schlesinger
   cast: 8 Sean Penn (Andrew Daulton Lee, the Snowman) 13 Timothy Hutton (Christopher John Boyce, the Falcon)

Falconer
   author: 11 John Cheever

Falconet, Etienne-Maurice
   born: 5 Paris 6 France
   artwork: 9 The Bather 12 Bathing Nymph 13 Milo of Crotona, Peter the Great 19 Pygmalion and Galatea

falconry 7 hawking
   equipment: 4 lure 5 cadge 6 jesses 7 creance

Falk, Lee
   creator/artist of: 10 The Phantom 19 Mandrake the Magician

Falk, Peter
   born: 9 New York NY
   roles: 7 Columbo 9 Murder Inc 12 The Great Race 13 Murder by Death 17 The Cheap Detective 19 Pocketful of Miracles 21 It's a Mad Mad Mad Mad World, Robin and the Seven Hoods

fall, falls 3 die, ebb, err, sin 4 drop, plop, ruin, slip, wane 5 droop, lapse, occur, slope, slump, spill 6 autumn, crop up, defeat, happen, perish, plunge, topple, tumble 7 be slain, be taken, capture, cascade, cheapen, come off, crumple, decline, descend, descent, falling, plummet, sinking, succumb 8 cataract, collapse, come down, decrease, diminish, disgrace, downfall, drop down, dropping, go astray, hang down, lowering 9 crash down, overthrow, reduction, surrender, take place, waterfall 10 capitulate, come to pass, corruption, debasement, depreciate, diminution, subsidence, subversion, transgress 11 be destroyed, harvest time 12 capitulation, depreciation, Indian summer 15 loss of innocence

Fall, The
   author: 11 Albert Camus

Falla, Manuel de
   born: 5 Cadiz, Spain
   composer of: 11 El Amor Brujo, La Atlantida, La Vida Breve, Life Is Short 14 Fantasia Betica 15 Love the Magician 19 The Three-Cornered Hat 21 El sombrero

de tres picos 25 Nights in the Gardens of Spain

fallacious 5 false, wrong 6 faulty, flawed, untrue 8 delusive, mistaken 9 deceptive, erroneous, illogical, incorrect 10 inaccurate, misleading, untruthful

fallacy 4 flaw 5 catch, error, fault 7 mistake, pitfall 8 delusion, illusion 9 misbelief 10 faultiness 11 false belief, false notion 13 inconsistency, misconception 15 misapprehension

fall apart 5 decay 7 break up, crumble, shatter 8 fragment, splinter 10 go to pieces 11 fragmentize 12 disintegrate

fall away 4 fade, wane 5 abate 7 drop off, slacken, subside 8 diminish, taper off

fall back 6 recede 7 back off, retreat

fallen 4 dead 5 loose, slain 6 ousted, ruined, sinful 7 debased, deposed, dropped, immoral, spilled, toppled, tumbled 8 sprawled 9 butchered, disgraced, massacred, turned out 10 discharged, overthrown 11 slaughtered

fallen short
   French: 6 manque

fall for 7 believe, swallow

fall guy 4 dupe, pawn, tool 5 patsy 7 cat's-paw

fallible 5 frail, human 6 faulty, mortal, unsure 9 imperfect 10 unreliable

fall in drops 4 drip, rain 7 dribble, drizzle 8 sprinkle

falling apart 6 ruined, shabby 7 rickety, run-down 8 decaying, decrepit 9 crumbling 10 broken-down, collapsing, ramshackle, tumbledown 11 dilapidated 13 deteriorating

Falling in Place
   author: 10 Ann Beattie

falling into decay 6 ruined, shabby 7 rotting, run-down 8 decrepit 9 crumbling, moldering 10 broken-down, tumbledown 11 dilapidated, in disrepair 13 deteriorating

falling off 3 ebb 4 fall, wane 7 decline 8 decrease 9 dwindling, lessening, reduction 10 diminution 13 deterioration

falling out 4 spat 7 dispute, quarrel 8 argument, squabble 10 difference 12 disagreement

fall in with 6 concur 7 conform 8 accede to 9 acquiesce 11 go along with

fall off 4 drop, wane 6 lessen, plunge, reduce, topple 7 decline, drop off, plummet, slacken, subside 8 decrease, diminish, moderate, peter out

Fall of the House of Usher, The
   author: 13 Edgar Allan Poe
   character: 8 Narrator 13 Madeline Usher, Roderick Usher

fallow 4 arid, idle 5 inert 6 barren, unused 7 dormant, unsowed, worn out 8 depleted, inactive, untilled 9 exhausted, unplanted 10 unfruitful 12 uncultivated, unproductive

fall short 6 be less, fail at, give up 9 be lacking, lag behind 10 have too few 11 fail to reach, miss the mark 12 be inadequate 14 be insufficient

fall to one's lot 4 fall 5 occur 6 befall, chance, happen 7 turn out 9 come about 10 come to pass

fall upon 5 fly at 6 assail, attack, dive at 7 embrace, lunge at, set upon 8 thrust at, tuck into

false 4 fake, sham 5 bogus, phony, wrong 6 ersatz, faulty, forged, pseudo, tricky, unreal, untrue 7 devious, feigned, inexact, invalid, unsound 8 delusive, disloyal, mistaken, spurious, two-faced 9 deceitful, deceiving, deceptive, dishonest, erroneous, faithless, imitation, incorrect, unfounded 10 apocryphal, artificial, factitious, fallacious, inaccurate, inconstant, misleading, not correct, perfidious, traitorous, unfaithful, untruthful 11 counterfeit, make-believe, treacherous 12 hypocritical 13 double-dealing

false front 4 mask, sham, show 6 facade, screen, veneer 8 pretense

false-hearted 8 two-faced 9 deceitful, deceiving, faithless 10 perfidious 13 double-dealing, untrustworthy

falsehood 3 fib, lie 5 lying, story 6 canard, deceit 7 fiction, figment, perfidy, perjury, untruth, whopper 8 bad faith, white lie 9 deception, duplicity, hypocrisy, invention, mendacity 10 dishonesty, distortion, inaccuracy 11 dissembling, fabrication, insincerity 12 misstatement, two-facedness 13 deceptiveness, dissimulation, double-dealing, falsification 17 misrepresentation

falseness 5 fraud 6 deceit 7 perfidy 9 duplicity, treachery 10 dishonesty 12 spuriousness 13 deceitfulness, double-dealing, faithlessness 14 untruthfulness

falsified 5 false, phony 6 forged, made-up 7 assumed 10 fictitious

falsify 4 fake 5 belie, rebut 6 doctor, misuse, refute 7 confute, distort, pervert 8 disprove 10 tamper with 12 misrepresent

Falstaff
  opera by: 5 Verdi
  character: 4 Anne 6 Fenton, Pistol 7 Dr Caius 8 Bardolph 11 Dame Quickly 12 Mistress Ford, Mistress Page 15 Mistress Quickly, Sir John Falstaff

Falstaff, Sir John
  character in: 22 The Merry Wives of Windsor
  author: 11 Shakespeare

falter 3 lag 4 halt, reel 5 demur, waver 6 dodder, mumble, shrink, teeter, totter 7 shamble, shuffle, stagger, stammer, stumble, stutter 8 hesitate 9 fluctuate, vacillate 10 dillydally 11 be undecided 12 be irresolute, show weakness 14 blow hot and cold

fame 4 note 5 glory 6 renown, repute 7 laurels 8 eminence, prestige 9 celebrity, notoriety 10 notability, popularity, prominence, reputation 11 distinction, preeminence 15 illustriousness

famed 5 noted 6 famous 7 notable 8 renowned 9 prominent, well-known 10 celebrated

familiar 3 pal 4 bold, chum, cozy, free, snug 5 buddy, close, crony, known, stock, usual 6 chummy, common, friend 7 forward, general 8 accepted, amicable, at home in, everyday, frequent, friendly, habitual, informal, intimate, ordinary, seasoned, versed in 9 abreast of, brotherly, confidant, customary, fraternal, gemutlich, intrusive, simpatico, skilled in, well-known 10 accessible, accustomed, acquainted, apprised of, conversant, proverbial, unreserved 11 cognizant of, commonplace, impertinent, traditional 12 confidential, conventional, hand and glove, no stranger to, proficient at 13 boon companion, companionable, disrespectful 15 taking liberties

familiarity 4 ease 5 amity, skill 7 know-how, mastery 8 coziness, intimacy 9 closeness, impudence, indecorum, knowledge, unreserve 10 casualness, chumminess, cognizance, disrespect, experience, fellowship, fraternity, friendship 11 association, brotherhood, conversance, forwardness, impropriety, informality, naturalness, presumption, proficiency 12 acquaintance, impertinence, unconstraint, undue liberty, unseemliness 13 brotherliness, comprehension, intrusiveness, understanding, undue intimacy 16 acquaintanceship

familiarize 5 edify, teach, tutor 6 inform, school, season 7 educate 8 accustom, acquaint, instruct 9 enlighten, habituate, inculcate 11 acclimatize

family 3 kin, set 4 clan, kind, line, race 5 blood, breed, brood, class, group, house, issue, order, stock, tribe 7 dynasty, kinfolk, kinsmen, lineage, progeny 8 ancestry, category, division, kinsfolk 9 forebears, genealogy, offspring, parentage, relations, relatives 10 extraction, kith and kin 11 forefathers 14 classification
  goddess of: 6 Cardea

Family Affair
  character: 4 Jody 5 Buffy, Cissy 8 Mr (Giles) French 9 Bill Davis
  cast: 10 Brian Keith 11 Anissa Jones, Kathy Garver 14 Sebastian Cabot 15 Johnnie Whitaker

family line 7 lineage 8 ancestry 9 blood line, genealogy, parentage

Family Moskat, The
  author: 19 Isaac Bashevis Singer

Family Reunion, The
  author: 7 T S Eliot

Family Ties
  character: 4 Nick 5 Ellen 6 Skippy 10 Alex Keaton 11 Elyse Keaton 12 Andrew Keaton, Steven Keaton 13 Mallory Keaton 14 Jennifer Keaton
  cast: 9 Marc Price 11 Michael J Fox, Tina Yothers 12 Michael Gross 14 Justine Bateman 20 Meredith Baxter-Birney

family tree 7 lineage 8 ancestry, pedigree 9 blood line, genealogy

famine 4 lack, want **6** dearth **7** paucity, poverty **8** scarcity **9** depletion **10** deficiency, exhaustion, famishment, meagerness, scantiness, starvation **11** destitution, half rations, short supply **13** acute shortage, extreme hunger, insufficiency

famish 6 hunger, starve

famous 5 noted **7** eminent, notable **8** far-famed, renowned, well-known **9** notorious, prominent **10** celebrated **11** conspicuous, illustrious **13** distinguished

famous person 4 name, star **7** notable **8** luminary, somebody **9** celebrity, personage, superstar **11** personality

fan 3 bug, nut **4** buff **5** fiend, freak **6** addict, rooter, zealot **7** booster, fanatic **8** follower, partisan

fanatic 5 crazy **6** maniac, zealot **7** hothead, radical **8** activist, militant **9** extremist **10** enthusiast **24** member of the lunatic fringe

fanaticism 6 fervor **8** activism, zealotry **9** dogmatism, extremism, monomania, obsession **10** enthusiasm, radicalism **11** extreme zeal, militantism **12** intemperance **13** ruling passion **15** opinionatedness

fancied 5 liked **6** dreamt, took to, unreal **7** assumed, desired, dreamed, thought **8** imagined, supposed **9** conceived, imaginary, preferred

fanciful 3 odd **6** unreal **7** bizarre, curious, flighty, unusual **8** fabulous, humorous, illusory, mythical, quixotic, romantic **9** eccentric, fantastic, imaginary, invective, legendary, visionary, whimsical **10** apocryphal, capricious, chimerical, fictitious **11** imaginative

fanciful talk 7 blarney **9** hyperbole, tall tales **11** fish stories **12** exaggeration

fancy 3 yen **4** fine, idea, like, want **5** crave, dream, enjoy, favor, opine, showy, taste, think **6** assume, custom, deluxe, desire, florid, liking, notion, ornate, relish, rococo, take it, take to, vagary, vision, whimsy **7** baroque, caprice, conceit, dream of, elegant, fantasy, figment, gourmet, imagine, leaning, longing, long for, picture, presume, reverie, special, suppose, surmise, suspect, unusual **8** be fond of, crotchet, daydream, fondness, illusion, not plain, penchant, superior, weakness, yearn for **9** elaborate, epicurean, expensive, hankering, superfine **10** be bent upon, conceive of, conjecture, decorative, high-priced, ornamental, partiality **11** distinctive, exceptional, extravagant, gingerbread, hanker after, have a mind to, imagination, inclination **12** have an eye for, predilection **13** be pleased with, take a liking to

fancy house 4 stew **5** house **6** bagnio **7** brothel **8** bordello, cathouse **10** bawdy house, whorehouse **13** sporting house **14** house of ill fame **16** house of ill repute **19** house of prostitution

fang 4 claw, nail, root, take, tang, tusk **5** prong, seize, tooth **6** obtain **7** capture, procure **8** eyetooth **9** chelicera

fanny 4 buns, rump, seat **6** behind, bottom **8** backside, buttocks **9** fundament

Fanny
  author: 9 Erica Jong

Fanny
  character in: 13 Joseph Andrews
  author: 8 Fielding

fan out 7 scatter **8** disperse **9** spread out

fantasize 5 dream, fancy **7** imagine **8** daydream

fantastic 3 mad, odd **4** huge, wild **5** antic, crazy, great, queer, weird **6** absurd, superb **7** amazing, bizarre, extreme, strange **8** enormous, fabulous, fanciful, freakish, illusory, quixotic, romantic, terrific **9** grotesque, imaginary, marvelous, visionary, wonderful **10** chimerical, far-fetched, incredible, irrational, outlandish, ridiculous, tremendous **11** extravagant, implausible, sensational **12** preposterous, unbelievable

fantasy 4 mind **5** dream, fancy **6** mirage, notion, vision, whimsy **7** caprice, chimera, fiction, figment, phantom, reverie **8** daydream, illusion, phantasm **9** imagining, invention, nightmare, unreality **10** apparition **11** fabrication, imagination, make-believe, supposition **13** hallucination, realm of dreams, visionary idea

Fantasy Island
  character: 6 Tattoo **8** Mr Roarke
  cast: 16 Herve Villechaize, Ricardo Montalban

far 4 afar, much **6** deeply, remote, way-off, yonder **7** distant, greatly **11** beyond range, out-of-the-way **12** considerably, immeasurably, incomparably

Faraday, Michael
  field: 7 physics **9** chemistry
  worked in: 11 electricity
  developed: 9 generator **12** electrolysis
  liquified: 8 chlorine
  discovered: 6 carbon **7** benzene **24** electromagnetic induction
  named for him: 5 farad

far and near 10 every place, everywhere, far and wide **11** in all places

far and wide 10 every place, everywhere, far and near **11** in all places

Far Away and Long Ago
  author: 8 W H Hudson

farce 4 sham **6** parody **7** mockery **8** drollery, nonsense, pretense, travesty **9** absurdity, burlesque, horseplay, low comedy **10** buffoonery, tomfoolery **11** broad comedy, make-believe **12** harlequinade **14** ridiculousness

farceur 3 wag **5** joker

farcical 5 droll, funny, silly **6** absurd, stupid **7** asinine, comical, foolish **8** humorous **9** laughable, ludicrous, senseless **10** irrational, ridiculous

fare 2 do **3** fee **4** diet, food, menu **5** board, get on, rider, table **6** charge, client, manage **7** make out, perform, regimen, turn out **8** customer, get along, victuals **10** provisions **11** comestibles, ticket price **12** food and drink, passage money 15 paying passenger 20 cost of transportation

farewell 6 so long 7 good-bye, parting 8 Godspeed 9 departing, departure 11 leave-taking, parting wish, valediction 17 parting compliment
   French: 5 adieu 8 au revoir
   German: 14 auf Wiedersehen
   Hawaiian: 5 aloha
   Italian: 4 ciao 5 addio 11 arrivederci
   Japanese: 8 sayonara
   Latin: 4 vale
   Spanish: 5 adios

Farewell to Arms, A
   author: 15 Ernest Hemingway
   character: 13 Frederic Henry 16 Catherine Barkley

far-fetched 7 dubious 8 doubtful, strained, unlikely 10 cockamamie, improbable 11 implausible 12 preposterous, unconvincing

Far From the Madding Crowd
   author: 11 Thomas Hardy
   character: 10 Fanny Robin, Gabriel Oak 12 Sergeant Troy 14 Farmer Boldwood 17 Bathsheba Everdene
   setting: 6 Wessex

farina 4 meal, mush 5 flour 6 cereal, pollen, starch 8 semolina

farm 3 sow 4 plow, reap 5 plant, ranch, tract 6 grange, spread 7 harvest 9 cultivate 10 plantation 11 till the soil 12 country place

farmable 6 arable 7 friable 8 plowable, tillable 10 cultivable

farm animal 2 ox 3 cow, ewe, hen, hog, pig, ram, sow 4 bull, goat 5 beast, brute, horse, sheep 7 chicken, rooster

farm boundaries
   god of: 8 Silvanus, Sylvanus

farmer 6 grower, raiser, reaper 7 granger, planter, rancher 8 agrarian 9 harvester 10 agronomist, husbandman 12 sharecropper 13 agriculturist, truck gardener 15 tiller of the soil

farming
   god of: 4 Thor

far-off 6 remote 7 distant, far-away 11 unreachable 12 inaccessible 13 unforeseeable

farouche 3 shy 6 fierce, sullen 10 unsociable

far-out 3 mad 4 wild 5 crazy, weird 7 bizarre, strange 10 outlandish 14 fantastic

Far Pavilions, The
   author: 6 M M Kaye

Farragut, David
   served in: 8 Civil War 10 Mexican War 19 War of Eighteen Twelve
   captured: 9 Mobile Bay 10 New Orleans
   saying: 30 Damn the torpedoes full speed ahead

far-reaching 4 wide 5 broad 8 sweeping 9 expansive, extensive, universal, unlimited 11 wide-ranging

Farrell, James T
   author of: 11 Judgment Day 12 Studs Lonigan, Young Lonigan 29 The Young Manhood of Studs Lonigan

far-removed 6 far-off, remote 7 distant, far-away

farrow 6 barren 7 piglets, sterile 9 infertile 10 unpregnant

Farrow, Mia
   real name: 27 Maria de Lourdes Villier Farrow
   father: 10 John Farrow
   mother: 16 Maureen O'Sullivan
   husband: 11 Andre Previn 12 Frank Sinatra
   born: 12 Los Angeles CA
   roles: 5 Zelig 11 John and Mary, Peyton Place 12 The Hurricane 13 Rosemary's Baby 14 The Great Gatsby 16 Allison MacKenzie 19 Hannah and Her Sisters 20 The Purple Rose of Cairo

Far side 4 back 7 reverse 8 back side

Far Side, The
   creator/artist: 10 Gary Larson

farsighted 4 wise 5 acute 6 shrewd 7 prudent 9 farseeing, hyperopic, judicious, prescient, provident 10 forehanded, foreseeing 11 clairvoyant, levelheaded

farther 6 beyond, deeper, longer 7 further, remoter 9 lengthier 10 more remote 11 more distant, more removed

farthermost 7 extreme 8 farthest, furthest 11 furthermost, most distant

farthest 3 end 4 most 7 extreme, longest 8 furthest, remotest, ultimate 9 uttermost 11 farthermost, furthermost

fascia 4 band, sash 5 board, strip 6 fillet, girdle, ribbon, tissue 7 bandage 8 membrane 9 dashboard

fascinate 5 charm, rivet 6 absorb, allure 7 beguile, bewitch, delight, enchant, engross 8 enravish, enthrall, entrance, transfix 9 captivate, enrapture, overpower, spellbind 14 hold spellbound

fascinating 8 alluring, charming, gripping, riveting 9 absorbing, beguiling 10 bewitching, delightful, enchanting, engrossing, entrancing 11 captivating, enthralling, interesting 12 overpowering, spellbinding

fascination 4 draw, lure 5 charm 6 allure 9 magnetism 10 attraction 11 captivation

fascism 6 Nazism 9 autocracy, oligarchy 10 plutocracy 11 corporatism, police state 13 corporativism 14 corporate state 15 totalitarianism 17 national socialism 21 right-wing dictatorship

fascist 9 right-wing 10 repressive, tyrannical 11 dictatorial, doctrinaire

fashion 3 air, fad, hew, way 4 form, make, mode, mold, rage 5 carve, craze, forge, frame, habit, shape, style, tenor, trend, usage, vogue 6 create, custom, design, devise, manner 7 compose, pattern, produce 8 attitude, behavior, contrive, demeanor 9 construct, fabricate 10 convention 11 manufacture

fashionable 2 in **3** hip **4** chic **5** smart **6** modish, with-it **7** current, in style, in vogue, popular, stylish, voguish **9** in fashion **10** all the rage, prevailing
French: **9** de rigueur

fashionable world
French: **10** grand monde

fashion designer 4 (Christian) Dior **5** Kenzo, (Jean) Patou **6** Adolfo, Lanvin, Poiret, (Coco) Chanel **7** Galanos, Halston, Missoni, (Pierre) Balmain **8** Givenchy **9** Courreges, Mary Quant, Valentino **10** Balenciaga, Mainbocher, Perry Ellis **11** Calvin Klein, Emilio Pucci, Ralph Lauren **12** Liz Claiborne, Lucien Lelong, Norman Norell, Pierre Cardin, Schiaparelli **13** Karl Lagerfeld, Rudi Gernreich **14** Pauline Trigere **15** Claire McCardell **16** Gloria Vanderbilt, Yves Saint-Laurent
Empress Eugenie's: 5 (Charles Frederick) Worth
Marie Antoinette's: 10 Rose Bertin
Empress Josephine's: 19 Louis Hippolyte Leroy

fashioned 4 made **5** built **6** formed, framed, molded, shaped, styled **7** adapted, crafted, created, devised, managed, modeled **9** contrived, patterned **11** constructed **12** accommodated

fashion plate 4 dude **5** dandy **12** Beau Brummell, clotheshorse, man of fashion, sharp dresser **14** woman of fashion

fast 4 firm, taut, true, wild **5** ahead, brisk, fleet, fully, hasty, loose, loyal, quick, rapid, rigid, swift, tight **6** famish, firmly, flying, rakish, secure, speedy, stable, starve, steady, wanton, winged **7** abiding, devoted, durable, fasting, fast day, fixedly, hastily, hurried, immoral, lasting, lustful, quickly, rapidly, solidly, soundly, staunch, swiftly, tightly **8** constant, enduring, faithful, fastened, go hungry, immodest, reckless, resolute, securely, speedily, unfading **9** debauched, dissolute, hurriedly, immovable, immovably, in advance, permanent, resistant, steadfast **10** completely, dissipated, firmly tied, lascivious, licentious, profligate, starvation, stationary, unswerving, unwavering **11** accelerated, expeditious, extravagant, intemperate, pleasure-mad, tenaciously **12** hunger strike, ineradicable, lickety-split

Fast, Howard
author of: **9** Spartacus **11** Freedom Road **13** The Immigrants **15** Citizen Tom Paine

fasten 3 bar, fix, pin, tie, wed **4** bind, bolt, clip, fuse, hold, hook, join, lash, link, lock, moor, snap, weld, yoke **5** affix, clamp, clasp, dowel, focus, hitch, close, latch, rivet, screw, stick, truss, unite **6** adhere, anchor, attach, button, cement, couple, direct, pinion, secure, solder, tether **7** connect **8** dovetail **11** put together

fastener 3 peg, pin, tie **4** clip, glue, grip, hook, line, nail, snap, tack **5** catch, clamp, clasp, cleat, latch, screw, strap, truss **6**

buckle, button, cement, staple, thread, zipper **7** bracket **8** barrette **9** fastening, safety pin, thumbtack **10** clothespin, connection, hook and eye

fastening 4 snap **5** clasp **8** coupling **9** attaching **10** attachment, connection

fasten together 3 tie **4** dock, join **6** couple, hook up, link up

fastidious 5 fussy, picky **6** choosy, dainty, proper, queasy **7** finicky **8** exacting, precious **9** difficult, squeamish **10** meticulous, particular **11** overprecise, overrefined, persnickety **12** hard to please, overdelicate **13** hypercritical

Fastidious Brisk
character in: **22** Every Man out of His Humour
author: **6** Jonson

fastidious connoisseur 7 epicure, gourmet **9** bon vivant **10** gastronome

fastidiousness 4 care **12** exactingness **14** discrimination **15** persnicketiness

fat 4 full, oily **5** beefy, fatty, flush, heavy, obese, palmy, plump, pudgy, stout, suety **6** chubby, fleshy, grease, greasy, portly, rotund **7** copious, fertile, lumpish, paunchy, replete, stuffed **8** abundant, blubbery, chockful, fruitful, thickset, unctuous **9** animal fat, corpulent, fortunate, lucrative, plenteous, plentiful, rewarding **10** overweight, potbellied, productive **11** wellstocked **12** remunerative

fatal 6 deadly, lethal, mortal **7** ruinous **8** terminal, virulent **10** calamitous, disastrous **11** destructive **12** catastrophic, causing death

fatalism 8 stoicism **11** resignation **12** acquiescence, helplessness **13** powerlessness **14** predestination

fatality 5 death **8** casualty **9** lethality, mortality **10** deadliness, malignancy **11** banefulness

fatal woman
French: **11** femme fatale

fate 3 lot **4** doom **5** karma, moira **6** effect, future, kismet, upshot **7** chances, destiny, fortune, outcome, portion **8** prospect **10** providence **11** consequence **12** will of heaven **14** predestination

fated 4 sure **5** bound, meant **6** doomed **7** certain **8** destined

fateful 6 fatal **7** crucial, ominous **8** critical, decisive **9** momentous **10** disastrous, portentous **11** significant

Fates
also: **5** Morae **6** Moerae, Moirai, Parcae
named: **6** Clotho **7** Atropos **8** Lachesis
goddesses of: **7** destiny
number of goddesses: **5** three
called: **12** weird sisters
parents: **4** Zeus **5** Night **6** Themis

father 3 dad, pop **4** abbe, cure, papa, sire **5** beget, begin, daddy, found, hatch, maker, padre, pater **6** author, create, design, old man, parson, pastor, priest **7** creator, founder **8** ancestor, begetter, designer, engender, forebear, inventor, preacher **9** ar-

chitect, confessor, originate, procreate 10
forefather, male parent, originator, progenitor

French: 4 pere

Father 4 Abba

Father, The
  author: 16 August Strindberg

Father Knows Best
  character: 11 Jim Anderson 13 Betty
Anderson (Princess), Kathy Anderson
(Kitten) 15 James Anderson Jr (Bud) 16
Margaret Anderson
  cast: 9 Billy Gray, Jane Wyatt 11 Robert
Young 12 Lauren Chapin 13 Elinor Donahue

fatherland 6 Heimat, patria, patrie 8 homeland 10 birthplace, motherland, native
land, native soil 13 mother country, native
country

fatherly 6 benign, kindly, tender 8 parental,
paternal 9 indulgent 10 beneficent, benevolent

father of his country
  Latin: 12 Pater Patriae

father of stars/wind 8 Astraeus

Father of the Bride
  director: 16 Vincente Minnelli
  cast: 11 Billie Burke, Joan Bennett,
Leo G Carroll 12 Spencer Tracy 15 Elizabeth Taylor
  sequel: 21 Father's Little Dividend

father of the family
  Latin: 13 paterfamilias

Father of the Rivers see 4 Nile

Fathers and Sons
  author: 12 Ivan Turgenev
  character: 5 Katya, Pavel 6 Arkady,
Vasily 8 Bazaroff, Fenichka 9 Kirsanoff 15
Madame Odintzoff

fathom 5 probe 6 divine, follow 7 hunt out,
root out, uncover, unravel 8 discover 9 ferret out, figure out, penetrate 10 comprehend, understand 16 get to the bottom of

fathom
  abbreviation: 4 fath

fatigue 3 fag 4 bush, tire 5 drain, weary 6
tedium, tucker, weaken 7 exhaust, languor,
wear out 8 enervate, overtire 9 heaviness,
lassitude, tiredness, weariness 10 debilitate, drowsiness, enervation, exhaustion
12 debilitation, listlessness 13 overtiredness

fatigued 4 beat 5 all in, jaded, spent, tired,
weary 6 bushed, done in, fagged, pooped
7 worn out 8 dog-tired, weakened 9 dead
tired, enervated, exhausted, overtaxed 10
overworked 11 debilitated, tuckered out

fatiguing 6 tiring 7 arduous, tedious 8 tiresome 9 wearisome 10 exhausting

Fatima
  character in: 9 Bluebeard

fatti maschii, parole femine 29 deeds are
manly words are womanish
  motto of: 8 Maryland

fatty 4 oily 5 lardy, suety 6 greasy 7 buttery
8 blubbery 9 shortened

fatuous 5 inane, silly, vapid 6 obtuse, simple, stupid 7 asinine, foolish, idiotic, moronic, puerile, vacuous, witless 8 besotted,
imbecile 9 brainless, senseless 10 ridiculous

faucet 3 tap 4 cock 5 spout, valve 6 nozzle,
outlet, spigot 7 bibcock

Faulkland
  character in: 9 The Rivals
  author: 8 Sheridan

Faulkner, William
  author of: 7 The Bear 8 Sartoris 9 Sanctuary, The Hamlet 10 The Reivers 11 As
I Lay Dying 13 Light in August 15 Absalom Absalom! 17 Intruder in the Dust
18 The Sound and the Fury
  fictional county: 13 Yoknapatawpha

fault 3 bug, sin 4 flaw, slip, snag 5 blame,
crime, error, guilt, stain, taint, wrong 6
defect, foible, glitch, impugn 7 blemish,
blunder, censure, failing, frailty, misdeed,
mistake, offense, reprove 8 drawback,
weakness 9 criticize, infirmity, oversight,
weak point 10 deficiency, impediment,
negligence, peccadillo, wrongdoing 11 culpability, dereliction, misdemeanor, shortcoming 12 imperfection, indiscretion 13
answerability, transgression 14 accountability, responsibility

faultfind 3 nag 4 beef, carp, kick 5 cavil,
gripe, knock 6 deride, squawk 7 nitpick 8
complain 9 criticize

faultfinder 3 nag 4 bear, crab 5 crank 6
carper, censor, critic, grouch 7 caviler,
grouser 8 quibbler, sorehead 9 derogator,
detractor, Mrs Grundy, nitpicker 10 bellyacher, complainer, curmudgeon, fuddyduddy, fussbudget

faultfinding 4 beef, kick 5 gripe 6 squawk 7
beefing, carping, griping, kicking, nagging
9 complaint, criticism, squawking 10
nitpicking 11 complaining, criticizing

faultless 5 ideal 7 correct, perfect 8 accurate, flawless 9 exemplary 10 immaculate,
impeccable 11 unblemished 13 unimpeachable 14 irreproachable, without
blemish

faulty 3 bad 4 awry 5 amiss, false, wrong 7
injured, unsound 8 impaired, inferior, mistaken 9 defective, deficient, erroneous, imperfect, incorrect 10 inadequate, out of order, unreliable 14 unsatisfactory

faun
  form: 5 deity
  location: 5 rural

Fauna see 7 Bona Dea

Faunus
  origin: 5 Roman
  form: 5 deity
  location: 5 woods
  also called: 5 Inuus 6 Fatuus
  king of: 6 Latium
  father: 5 Picus
  son: 7 Latinus
  corresponds to: 3 Pan

Faure, Gabriel Urbain
born: 6 France 7 Pamiers
composer of: 5 Dolly 6 Pavane 7 Ballade, Mirages, Requiem, Shylock 8 Penelope 9 Fantaisie, Promethee 12 Le Jardin Clos 13 La Chanson d'Eve 14 La Bonne Chanson 18 L'Horizon Chimerique, Pelleas et Melisande 21 Masques et Bergamasques

Faust
author: 12 Johann Goethe
character: 6 Wagner 8 Gretchen 10 Homunculus 11 Helen of Troy 14 Mephistopheles

Faust
opera by: 6 Gounod
character: 9 Valentine 10 Marguerite 14 Mephistopheles

Faustulus
vocation: 8 herdsman, shepherd
raised: 5 Remus 7 Romulus

faute de mieux 24 for lack of something better

faux pas 4 goof 5 boner, error, gaffe, lapse 6 boo-boo, howler, slip-up 7 blooper, blunder, mistake 9 false step 11 impropriety 12 indiscretion

favela 4 slum 10 shanty town

Favell, Jack
character in: 7 Rebecca
author: 9 Du Maurier

Favonius
origin: 5 Roman
personifies: 8 west wind

favor 3 aid 4 abet, back, gift, help, like 5 be for, fancy, humor 6 assist, esteem, foster, oblige, pamper, prefer, succor, uphold 7 approve, commend, endorse, go in for, indulge, kind act, memento, present, service, support 8 advocacy, approval, courtesy, espousal, good deed, good turn, goodwill, largesse, look like, resemble, sanction, side with, souvenir 9 encourage, patronage, patronize, smile upon, take after, use gently 10 act of grace, use lightly 11 accommodate, approbation, be partial to, benefaction, countenance, good opinion 12 be the image of, championship, commendation, dispensation, kindly regard 13 accommodation, goodwill token

favorable 4 fair, good, kind 6 benign, timely 7 helpful, hopeful 8 amicable, friendly, salutary 9 approving, conducive, opportune, promising 10 auspicious, beneficial, convenient, propitious 11 predisposed, serviceable, sympathetic 12 advantageous, commendatory, well-disposed

favorable opinion 6 esteem, regard 7 respect 8 approval 10 admiration 12 appreciation

favorably disposed 7 willing 8 amenable, inclined, obliging 9 agreeable 11 sympathetic

favorite 3 pet 5 fancy, jewel 6 choice 7 darling, special 9 best-liked, preferred 11 front-runner, most popular 13 fair-haired one 14 apple of one's eye

favoritism 4 bias 10 partiality 12 one-sidedness, partisanship

Fawley, Jude and Drusilla
characters in: 14 Jude the Obscure
author: 5 Hardy

fawn 5 toady 6 pander 7 flatter, truckle 8 pay court 9 be servile, seek favor 12 be obsequious, bow and scrape

fawning 7 servile 8 flattery, toadying 9 adulating, adulation, truckling 10 flattering, obsequious 11 sycophantic 12 ingratiating 14 obsequiousness

faze 4 fret 5 abash, daunt, upset, worry 6 bother, flurry, rattle 7 disturb, fluster, perturb 8 confound 9 discomfit, embarrass 10 discompose, disconcert

fazed 5 upset 7 abashed, ruffled 8 agitated, bothered, confused 9 chagrined, unsettled 10 confounded, distracted, nonplussed 11 embarrassed 12 disconcerted

FBI, The
character: 10 Arthur Ward 21 Inspector Lewis Erskine
cast: 12 Philip Abbott 16 Efrem Zimbalist Jr

fealty 7 loyalty 8 devotion, fidelity 9 adherence, constancy 10 allegiance, attachment 12 faithfulness

fear 3 awe 4 care 5 alarm, bogey, dread, panic, qualm, worry 6 dismay, esteem, fright, horror, phobia, revere, terror, threat, wonder 7 anxiety, bugaboo, bugbear, concern, quaking, specter 8 affright, venerate 9 cowardice, nightmare, reverence, shudder at, tremble at 10 be afraid of, be scared of, feel awe for, foreboding, take fright, veneration 11 trepidation 12 apprehension, perturbation 13 consternation 14 be frightened of

fearful 4 dire 5 awful, dread, eerie, lurid, timid 6 afraid, aghast, horrid, scared, uneasy 7 alarmed, anxious, ghastly, macabre, nervous, ominous, panicky, worried 8 alarming, dreadful, horrible, shocking, sinister, skittish, terrible, timorous 9 appalling, concerned, diffident, frightful, tremulous 10 formidable, frightened, portentous, terrifying 11 distressing, frightening, intimidated 12 apprehensive, fainthearted 13 panic-stricken 14 chicken-hearted

fearfulness fear 5 alarm, dread, panic 6 fright, terror 7 anguish, anxiety 8 timidity 11 trepidation 12 apprehension

fearless 4 bold 5 brave 6 daring, gritty, heroic, plucky 7 doughty, gallant, valiant 8 intrepid, unafraid, valorous 9 audacious, confident, dauntless, unabashed, undaunted 10 courageous, undismayed 11 adventurous, indomitable, lionhearted, unflinching, unshrinking, venturesome, without fear 12 stout-hearted

fearlessness 4 grit 5 pluck, valor 7 bravery, courage 8 boldness 10 confidence 13 dauntlessness

Fear of Flying
author: 9 Erica Jong

feasible 6 viable 7 fitting, politic 8 possible, suitable, workable 9 advisable, desirable 10 achievable, attainable, reasonable 11 appropriate, conceivable, practicable

feast 4 dine, fete 5 festa, gorge 6 bounty 7 banquet, holiday, jubilee, surplus 8 feast day, festival 9 bacchanal, saint's day 10 gluttonize, gormandize, have a feast, rich supply 11 celebration, eat one's fill, elegant meal, wine and dine

feat 3 act 4 deed, task 6 action, stroke 7 exploit, triumph 8 maneuver 9 adventure 10 attainment, enterprise 11 achievement, performance, tour de force 14 accomplishment

feather 4 down, kind, sort 5 adorn, eider, plume, quill 7 bristle, plumage, variety 9 character, turn an oar

featherbrained 4 dumb 5 silly 6 simple, stupid 7 foolish, witless 9 brainless 12 muddleheaded, simple-minded 13 rattlebrained 14 scatterbrained

feather in one's cap 5 honor 6 credit 11 distinction

feather one's nest 6 enrich 15 fill one's pockets

feature, features 3 see 4 mark, star 5 fancy, trait 6 aspect, play up, visage 7 display, earmark, imagine, picture, present, quality 8 envision, hallmark, headline, main item, property 9 attribute, character, highlight, specialty, spotlight 10 conceive of, lineaments 14 characteristic

February
  event: 4 Lent 5 Purim 8 Leap year 9 Mardi Gras 12 Ash Wednesday, Groundhog Day (2)
  flower: 6 violet 8 primrose
  French: 7 Fevrier
  gem: 8 amethyst
  German: 7 Februar
  holiday: 9 Candlemas (2) 13 Valentine's Day (14) 14 Chinese New Year 16 Lincoln's Birthday (12) 19 Washington's Birthday (22)
  Italian: 8 Febbraio
  Latin: 6 Februa
  number of days: 10 twenty-nine (every 4 years) 11 twenty-eight
  origin of name: 7 Februus
  Roman god of: 12 purification
  place in year:
  Gregorian: 6 second
  Roman: 7 twelfth
  Spanish: 7 Febrero
  Zodiac signs: 6 Pisces 8 Aquarius

Fechner, Gustav Theodore
  nationality: 6 German
  founder of: 22 experimental psychology

fecit 6 he made (it) 7 she made (it)

feckless 3 lax 5 slack 6 remiss 8 careless, heedless 9 negligent, worthless 10 neglectful 11 thoughtless 13 irresponsible

Fecundity
  goddess of: 5 Freia, Freya

Federalist Party
  president belonging to: 5 Adams 10 Washington

federate 5 unite 7 combine 12 join together

federation 5 union 6 league 7 combine 8 alliance 9 coalition, syndicate 10 sisterhood 11 association, brotherhood, confederacy 12 amalgamation 13 confederation

fee 4 fare, hire, toll, wage 5 price 6 charge, salary, tariff 7 payment, stipend 9 emolument 10 commission, honorarium 12 compensation, remuneration 13 consideration

feeble 4 flat, lame, poor, puny, tame, thin, weak 5 faint, frail, vapid 6 ailing, flabby, flimsy, infirm, meager, paltry, senile, sickly, slight 7 fragile, insipid 8 decrepit, delicate, disabled, impotent, weakened 9 colorless, declining, doddering, enervated, enfeebled, forceless, not strong, powerless 10 inadequate, spiritless, wishywashy 11 debilitated, ineffective, ineffectual

feeble-minded 4 dull 6 senile, stupid 7 moronic 8 backward, childish, retarded 9 imbecilic, senseless, subnormal 10 halfwitted, weak-minded 12 mentally slow

feeble-mindedness 6 dotage, idiocy 8 dullness, senility, slowness 9 denseness, stupidity 11 retardation

feed 3 eat 4 fare, fuel, mash 5 cater, feast, graze 6 devour, fodder, forage, foster, viands 7 augment, bolster, consume, gratify, nourish, nurture, pasture, satisfy, support, sustain 8 maintain, take food, victuals 9 encourage, foodstuff, provender 10 minister to, provisions, strengthen 11 comestibles, nourishment, wine and dine

feeder 6 branch 7 channel 9 tributary

feel 3 paw, see 4 know 5 grope, press, probe, reach, sense, think, touch 6 finger, fumble, handle, makeup, notice 7 believe, discern, feeling, observe, palpate, texture 8 perceive 9 be aware of, be moved by, character, sensation 10 comprehend, experience, manipulate, suffer from, understand 11 be convinced, be stirred by, be touched by, composition

feel aversion toward 4 hate 5 abhor 6 detest 7 despise 9 abominate, can't abide, can't stand 11 can't stomach 12 be revolted by 13 find repugnant, find repulsive 14 view with horror

feeler 7 antenna 8 proposal, tentacle 10 experiment 12 trial balloon

feel indebted 6 appreciate, be beholden, be grateful 13 feel obligated

feeling 4 aura, pity, view, zeal 5 ardor, gusto, sense, verve 6 fervor, spirit, thrill, warmth 7 concern, emotion, opinion, passion 8 attitude, instinct, reaction, response, sympathy 9 affection, awareness, intuition, sensation, sentiment, vehemence 10 atmosphere, compassion, enthusiasm, impression 11 earnestness, inclination, point of view, sensibility, sensitivity

feeling life is wearisome
  Latin: 12 taedium vitae

feelings 3 ego 5 pride 8 emotions, passions 10 self-esteem 13 sensibilities, sensitivities 16 susceptibilities

feel pain 4 ache, hurt 5 smart 6 suffer 7 agonize 9 be in agony 11 be tormented 12 be in distress

Feenix, Cousin
   character in: 12 Dombey and Son
   author: 7 Dickens

feet 4 dogs, pads, paws 5 hoofs 6 hooves 8 gunboats, tootsies

feign 4 fake, sham 5 forge, put on 6 affect, assume, cook up, invent, make up 7 concoct, pretend 8 simulate 9 fabricate 11 counterfeit, make a show of, make believe

feigned 4 fake, sham 5 bogus, phony 6 ersatz 8 spurious 9 imitation, insincere, pretended, simulated 10 artificial 11 counterfeit, make-believe

feint 4 hoax, mask, move, pass, ploy, ruse, wile 5 bluff, dodge, trick 6 gambit 7 pretext 8 artifice, maneuver, pretense 9 stratagem 10 subterfuge 13 feigned attack

Feldman, Marty
   born: 6 London 7 England
   roles: 11 Silent Movie 17 Young Frankenstein 24 The Last Remake of Beau Geste

feldspar
   varieties: 8 sunstone 9 amazonite, moonstone

felicitate 4 hail 6 salute 10 wish one joy 11 rejoice with 12 congratulate 18 give one's best wishes 28 wish many happy returns of the day

felicitations 3 joy 6 cheers 9 blessings, greetings 10 best wishes, good wishes 11 compliments, salutations 12 pat on the back 15 congratulations 24 many happy returns of the day

felicitous 3 apt 5 happy 6 joyful, joyous 7 fitting, germane, well-put 8 inspired, pleasing, relevant, suitable, well-said 9 effective, fortunate, pertinent 10 propitious, well-chosen 11 appropriate

felicity 5 bliss, charm, grace, knack, skill 6 heaven, nicety 7 aptness, delight, ecstasy, fitness 8 paradise 9 beatitude, happiness 12 blissfulness 13 effectiveness 15 appropriateness

Felix the Cat
   creator: 11 Pat Sullivan

fell 4 raze 5 level 7 cut down, destroy, hew down 8 demolish 9 knock down, prostrate

Feller, Bob (Robert)
   nickname: 11 Rapid Robert
   sport: 8 baseball
   position: 7 pitcher
   team: 16 Cleveland Indians

Fellini, Federico
   director of: 8 Amarcord, Casanova, La Strada 11 La Dolce Vita 15 Nights of Cabiria 18 Juliet of the Spirits

fellow 3 boy, guy, man, pal 4 chap, chum, dude, mate, peer 5 equal 6 friend 7 comrade, consort 8 coworker 9 associate, colleague, companion 10 compatriot

fellow-conspirator 4 ally 6 cohort 7 abettor 8 henchman 9 accessory 11 confederate 12 collaborator

fellow creature 6 mortal, person 10 individual

fellow feeling 6 regard 7 kinship 8 affinity, fondness 10 attraction, partiality

fellowship 5 amity 7 society 8 intimacy 10 affability, cordiality, fraternity, friendship 11 amicability, association, brotherhood, comradeship, familiarity, sociability 12 friendliness 13 companionship

felon 5 crook, cruel, thief 6 fierce, outlaw, wicked 7 convict, illegal, villain, whitlow 8 criminal, gangster, jailbird, murderer 10 law-breaker, malefactor 11 public enemy 12 inflammation

felony 5 arson, crime 6 murder 7 assault, misdeed, offense, robbery 8 burglary 9 blackmail 10 kidnapping, wrongdoing 12 capital offense

female 3 cow, dam, hen, sow 4 girl, mare 5 bitch, tabby, woman 6 heifer 7 distaff, womanly 8 feminine, ladylike 9 womanlike

feminine 4 soft 5 woman 6 dainty, female, gentle 7 distaff, girlish, womanly 8 delicate, ladylike 10 femalelike, like a woman 14 of the female sex

femininity 8 softness 10 femaleness, gentleness 11 girlishness, womanliness 12 feminineness 13 female quality

femme 4 wife 5 woman

femme de chambre 9 lady's maid 11 chambermaid

femme fatale 4 vamp 5 siren 7 charmer 10 fatal woman, seductress 11 enchantress

femur
   bone of: 5 thigh 8 upper leg

fen 3 bog 4 moor, sump 5 marsh, swale, swamp 6 bottom, morass, slough 7 lowland, wetland 8 quagmire

fence 3 pen 4 coop, duel, gird, rail 5 hedge, hem in 6 corral, secure, wall in 7 barrier, confine, palings 8 encircle, palisade, stockade, surround 9 barricade, encompass 11 cross swords

fencing
   equipment: 4 epee, foil, mask 5 saber, sword 8 plastron
   part of weapon: 5 blade, forte, guard 6 foible, handle, medium, pommel
   term: 3 hit 5 prime, sixte, touch 6 octave, quarte, quinte, tierce 7 on guard, seconde, septime
   deceptive move: 5 feint
   movement: 4 beat 5 lunge, parry 6 double, fleche, thrust 7 advance, cutover, recover, retreat, riposte 9 disengage 11 froissement

fend 2 do 5 avert, avoid, parry, repel, shift 6 manage 7 keep off, make out, provide, repulse, support, survive, ward off 8 push away

fender 3 pad 4 curb 5 guard 6 buffer, bumper, shield, sluice 7 cushion, railing 9 fireguard, protector 10 cowcatcher, fire screen, protection, wheel guard

fend off 5 avert, dodge, evade, parry, repel 6 escape 7 ward off 8 sidestep, stave off

fennel
 botanical name: 17 Foeniculum vulgare
 family: 7 parsley
 varieties: 3 dog 4 wild 5 giant 8 Florence 9 common dog 11 common giant
 mythical aid to: 9 fortifier 11 aphrodisiac, slenderizer 12 rejuvenation, stops hiccups 16 restores eyesight
 use: 4 duck, fish 5 bread, rolls 7 chicken 8 apple pie 16 seafood casserole

Fenrir
 also: 6 Fenris
 origin: 12 Scandinavian
 form: 4 wolf 7 monster
 father: 4 Loki
 mother: 9 Angerboda, Angrbodha, Angurboda
 sister: 3 Hel
 brother: 11 Iormungandr, Jormungandr 14 Midgard Serpent
 ate: 4 Odin 5 Othin
 killed by: 5 Vidar

Fenris see 6 Fenrir

Fenton
 character in: 22 The Merry Wives of Windsor
 author: 11 Shakespeare

feral 4 wild 6 brutal, deadly, ferine, fierce, savage 7 bestial, untamed, vicious 9 ferocious 12 uncultivated 14 undomesticated

Ferber, Edna
 author of: 5 Giant, So Big 8 Cimarron, Show Boat 9 Ice Palace, Stage Door (with George S Kaufman) 13 Dinner at Eight (with George S Kaufman), Saratoga Trunk 14 The Royal Family (with George S Kaufman)

Ferdinand
 character in: 10 The Tempest
 author: 11 Shakespeare

Ferdinand
 character in: 16 Love's Labour's Lost
 author: 11 Shakespeare

Ferd'nand
 creator: 3 Mik 13 Dahl Mikkelsen

Feria
 origin: 5 Roman
 form: 7 holiday

Fermat, Pierre de
 field: 11 mathematics
 nationality: 6 French
 discovered: 16 analytic geometry

ferment 4 foam, mold, sour, turn 5 froth, yeast 6 enzyme, fester, leaven, seethe, tumult, unrest, uproar 7 agitate, inflame, smolder, turmoil 8 bubble up, disquiet 9 agitation, commotion, leavening 10 disruption, effervesce, turbulence 11 be turbulent, fomentation

fermented 6 soured, worked 7 seethed 8 agitated

Fermi, Enrico
 field: 7 physics
 nationality: 7 Italian
 developed: 10 atomic bomb 20 uranium fission theory
 awarded: 10 Nobel Prize

fern
 varieties: 3 air, cup, lip, man, oak, saw 4 ball, blue, claw, deer, dish, felt, fire, gold, hand, iron, king, lace, lady, male, moss, nest, pine, sago, tara, tree, wall, wart, wood 5 beard, beech, chain, cloak, fancy, glade, glory, grape, grass, hedge, holly, marsh, plume, royal, strap, swamp, sweet, sword, table, water, whisk 6 adder's, bamboo, basket, Boston, button, carrot, coffee, cotton, cuplet, dagger, ladder, meadow, mother, ribbon, shield, silver, tongue, turnip, winter 7 bladder, boulder, brittle, bulblet, crested, emerald, feather, Fee's lip, fragile, Goldie's, hacksaw, Halberd, hammock, leather, New York, ostrich, parsley, peacock, rainbow, walking 8 bear-foot, bear's-paw, cinnamon, climbing, elk's-horn, fishtail, floating, florist's, fragrant, hairy lip, Hartford, licorice, mosquito, Nebraska, Savannah, snuffbox, soft tree, staghorn 9 asparagus, bird's-nest, black tree, blond tree, Christmas, common cup, deer's-foot, downy wood, flowering, glossy cup, hare's foot, long beech, sensitive, vegetable, Venus hair, viscid lip, wavy cloak, woolly lip 10 Alabama lip, Boott's wood, broad beech, deer-tongue, Duff's sword, erect sword, five-finger, hay-scented, lady ground, maidenhair, scented oak, shoestring, silver tree, silver-back, silver-lace, silver-leaf, slender lip, strawberry, upside-down, woolly tree 11 Braun's holly, coastal wood, Coville's lip, crested felt, crested wood, dwarf Boston, elephant-ear, Fendler's lip, hart's-tongue, interrupted, Jamaica gold, leatherleaf, leatherwood, narrow beech, netted chain, Northern oak, Parry's cloak, Pursh's holly, rabbit's-foot, rattlesnake, Sierra water, walking leaf 12 Adder's-tongue, American wall, berry bladder, Clinton's wood, Dudley's holly, Eaton's shield, English hedge, Hawaiian tree, Java staghorn, limestone oak, mountain wood, Northern lady, resurrection, Southern lady, squirrel-foot, toothed sword, Western holly, Western sword 13 California lip, Cleveland's lip, Dudley's shield, European chain, fan maidenhair, Fendler's cloak, Florida ribbon, leathery grape, Malay climbing, mountain holly, Northern holly, prickly shield, Prince-of-Wales, spinulose wood, Tasmanian tree, triangle water, Virginia chain, wild bird's nest 14 Anderson's holly, Australian tree, bulblet bladder, California gold, common staghorn, dissected grape, dwarf asparagus, hen-and-chickens, imbricate sword, silver-king tree, West Indian tree 15 American parsley, California cloak, California holly, Delta maidenhair, East Indian holly, European parsley, mountain bladder, moun-

tain parsley **16** black-stemmed tree, daisy-leaved grape, Farley maidenhair, Tassel maidenhair, Tracy's maidenhair **17** Bermuda maidenhair, brittle maidenhair, climbing bird's nest, walking maidenhair **18** Aleutian maidenhair, American maidenhair, Barbados maidenhair, Northern maidenhair, Trailing maidenhair, Triangular staghorn **20** Australian maidenhair, California maidenhair

fernet-branca
   type: 8 aperitif
   origin: 5 Italy
   flavor: 4 herb

Fern Hill
   author: 11 Dylan Thomas

ferocious 6 brutal, deadly, fierce, savage **7** bestial, brutish, enraged, violent **8** fiendish, maddened, ravening, ruthless **9** atrocious, barbarous, merciless, murderous, predatory, rapacious **10** relentless **11** cold-blooded **12** bloodthirsty

ferocity 7 cruelty **8** savagery **9** barbarity, brutality, harshness **10** fierceness, inhumanity, savageness **11** brutishness, viciousness **12** ruthlessness

Ferrer, Jose
   real name: 33 Jose Vincente Ferrer de Otero y Cintron
   wife: 8 Uta Hagen **15** Rosemary Clooney
   born: 8 Santurce **10** Puerto Rico
   roles: 7 I Accuse **9** Joan of Arc **11** Moulin Rouge, Ship of Fools **14** The Caine Mutiny **16** Cyrano de Bergerac (Oscar), Lawrence of Arabia **24** The Greatest Story Ever Told

ferret out 5 dig up **6** detect **7** find out, root out, uncover, unearth **8** discover **9** ascertain

fertile 4 rich **5** loamy **6** fecund **8** creative, fruitful, original, prolific **9** fructuous, ingenious, inventive, luxuriant, plenteous **10** fecundated, fertilized, fructified, generative, productive, vegetative **11** imaginative, resourceful **12** reproductive

Fertility
   god of: 7 Bacchus, Mutinus **8** Lupercus, Picumnus
   goddess of: 4 Isis **5** Fauna **6** Athena, Athene, Brigit, Libera, Pallas, Saitis, Tellus **7** Astarte, Berchta, Bona Dea, Demeter, Perchta **11** Tritogeneia **12** Pallas Athena **16** Alalcomean Athena

fertilize 6 enrich, manure **8** fructify **9** fecundate, pollinate **10** impregnate, inseminate

fertilizer 4 dung, muck **5** guano **6** manure, potash **7** compost **8** bonemeal, dressing **10** enrichener **14** superphosphate

fervent 4 keen **5** eager, fiery **6** ardent, devout, fervid, fierce, hearty, heated **7** burning, earnest, intense, zealous **8** spirited, vehement **9** heartfelt **10** passionate **11** impassioned, warmhearted **12** enthusiastic, wholehearted

fervid 5 eager **6** ardent, raging **7** burning, earnest, fanatic, fervent, intense, zealous **8** spirited **10** passionate **11** impassioned **12** all-consuming

fervor 4 fire, zeal, zest **5** ardor, gusto, piety, verve **6** warmth **7** passion **9** animation, eagerness, intensity, vehemence **10** devoutness, enthusiasm, heartiness **11** earnestness, seriousness **14** purposefulness

Feste
   character in: 12 Twelfth Night
   author: 11 Shakespeare

fester 3 rot, vex **4** fret, gall, grow, rile **5** chafe, pique **6** nettle, plague, rankle **7** blister, form pus, inflame, putrefy, smolder, torment **8** irritate, ulcerate **9** intensify, suppurate

festering 6 putrid **7** rotting **8** infected, inflamed, rankling **10** putrefying **11** suppurating

festina lente 15 make haste slowly

festival 4 fete, gala **5** feast **6** fiesta **7** gala day, holiday, jubilee **8** carnival, jamboree **11** celebration, festivities

Festival of
   Adonis: 6 Adonia
   Apollo: 5 Delia **8** Didymaea **9** Delphinia **12** Daphnephoria
   Athena: 6 Lenaea **8** Diipolia **9** Pyanepsia **11** Oschophoria
   Attica: 13 Rural Dionysia **14** Lesser Dionysia
   Bacchus: 11 Bacchanalia
   Boeotians: 7 Daedala **13** Little Doedala
   Demeter: 5 Haloa
   Dionysus: 5 Haloa **8** Dionysia
   flowers: 11 Anthesteria
   Greeks: 6 Heraea **9** Pyanepsia **11** Scirophoria, Skirophoria **13** Thesmorphoria
   Persephone: 5 Haloa
   Roman: 8 Floralia, Matralia **9** Lemuralia, Liberalia **10** Larentalia, Lupercalia, Matronalia, Parentalia, Saturnalia
   spring: 11 Anthesteria
   wine: 11 Anthesteria
   Zeus: 6 Diasia **8** Didymaea

festive 3 gay **4** gala **5** jolly, merry **6** festal, joyous **7** larkish, playful **8** sportive **9** convivial **10** frolicsome **11** celebratory **12** lighthearted

festivity 3 joy **4** fete, gala **5** feast, mirth **6** fiesta, gaiety, levity **7** fanfare, jollity, jubilee, revelry **8** festival, jamboree **9** merriment, rejoicing **11** celebration, merrymaking

festoon 3 lei **4** swag **5** chain, curve **6** wreath **7** garland, hanging **8** decorate

fetch 3 get **4** cost **5** bring, go for, yield **6** afford, obtain **7** procure, realize, sell for **8** amount to, retrieve

fetching 6 divine, lovely **8** adorable, becoming, charming, engaging, pleasing **9** appealing **10** attractive, delightful **11** captivating

fete 4 gala 5 feast, party, treat 6 regale 7 banquet, holiday 8 carnival, festival 9 bal masque 11 celebration, garden party, wine and dine 13 fete champetre

fete champetre 11 garden party 15 outdoor festival

fetid 4 foul, gamy, rank 5 fusty, moldy, musty, nasty 6 putrid, rancid, rotten 7 noisome, stenchy, tainted 8 mephitic, stifling, stinking 9 stenchful 10 malodorous 11 illsmelling, suffocating

fetish 4 idol, joss 5 charm, craze, image, mania, totem 6 amulet, scarab 7 passion 8 idee fixe, talisman 9 obsession 10 golden calf, phylactery 11 magic object 12 superstition 13 preoccupation

fetter 4 bind, bond, cage, curb, yoke 5 chain, tie up 6 duress, hamper, hinder, hobble, impede, shut in, tether 7 confine, durance, manacle, pin down, shackle, tie down, trammel, truss up 8 bracelet, encumber, handcuff, hold back, restrain 9 hindrance, restraint 13 put into bilbos 15 bind hand and foot

feud 3 row 4 fuss, spat, tiff 5 argue, brawl, clash, set-to 6 affray, bicker, breach, enmity, fracas, schism, strife 7 discord, dispute, faction, ill will, quarrel, rupture, wrangle 8 argument, bad blood, be at odds, clashing, conflict, disagree, squabble, vendetta 9 animosity, bickering, hostility 10 falling out 11 altercation, controversy 12 disagreement, hard feelings

Feud, The
    author: 12 Thomas Berger

feudal lord
    Japanese: 6 daimyo

Feuerbach, Anselm
    born: 6 Speyer 7 Germany
    artwork: 9 Iphigenia 15 Judgment of Paris, Plato's Symposium 18 The Fall of the Titans

fever 4 fire, heat 5 ardor, craze, flush, furor 6 desire, frenzy, warmth 7 ferment, illness, pyrexia 8 delirium, sickness 9 agitation 10 enthusiasm, excitement 11 temperature 12 restlessness

feverish 3 hot 5 fiery 6 ardent, red-hot 7 burning, excited, fanatic, febrile, fervent, fevered, flushed, parched, pyretic, zealous 8 frenzied, inflamed, restless 9 impatient, overeager, wrought-up 10 high-strung, passionate 11 impassioned

few 4 rare, some, thin 5 scant 6 meager, paltry, scanty, scarce, skimpy, sparse, unique 7 handful, limited, not many, several, unusual 8 exiguous, piddling, sporadic, uncommon 9 hardly any 10 infrequent, occasional 11 scarcely any, small number 13 infinitesimal, insignificant 14 inconsiderable

Fezziwig
    character in: 15 A Christmas Carol
    author: 7 Dickens

fiance, fiancee 6 future 7 engaged, pledge 8 intended, promised 9 affianced, betrothed, bride-to-be, groom-to-be 10 bride-elect, groom-elect

fiasco 4 bomb, flop 5 botch 6 fizzle 7 debacle, washout 8 disaster 10 nonsuccess

fiat 3 act, law 4 rule 5 edict, order, ukase 6 decree, dictum, ruling 7 command, mandate 11 commandment

fiat lux 15 let there be light

fib 3 lie 5 hedge 7 fiction, untruth 8 white lie 9 half-truth, invention 10 equivocate 11 fabrication, harmless lie, prevaricate 13 falsification, prevarication, tell a white lie 15 stretch the truth 17 misrepresentation

fiber 4 hemp, jute, silk 5 fibre, linen, nylon, rayon, shred, sinew, sisal 6 cotton, dacron, manila, nature, strand, thread 7 quality, texture 8 filament 9 character, polyester, structure

fibrolite
    source: 5 Burma, Mogok

fibula
    bone of: 8 lower leg

fickle 5 giddy 6 fitful 7 erratic, flighty 8 shifting, unstable, unsteady, variable, volatile, wavering 9 frivolous, mercurial, spasmodic, whimsical 10 capricious, changeable, inconstant, irresolute, unreliable 11 fluctuating, light-headed, vacillating 12 inconsistent 13 feather-headed, unpredictable, untrustworthy 14 feather-brained

fiction 3 fib, lie 4 play, tale, yarn 5 fable, novel 7 fantasy, forgery, novella, romance, whopper 8 tall tale 9 falsehood, invention, narrative 10 concoction, short novel, short story 11 fabrication, imagination, made-up story 12 storytelling 13 prevarication 16 cock-and-bull story

fictional 6 made-up 8 invented, literary, mythical 9 storybook 10 fictitious 11 theoretical 12 hypothetical

fictitious 4 fake, sham 5 bogus, false, phony 6 forged, made-up, unreal, untrue 7 assumed, feigned 8 fanciful, invented, mythical, spurious 9 imaginary, legendary, simulated, trumped-up, unfounded 10 apocryphal, artificial, fabricated, fraudulent, not genuine 11 counterfeit 14 supposititious

fiddle 3 bow, saw, toy 4 fool 5 cheat, dally, fraud 6 dawdle, monkey, potter, putter, tamper, trifle, violin 7 falsify, finagle, fritter, swindle 9 deception 10 fool around, mess around 12 monkey around

Fidei Defensor 18 Defender of the Faith
    title of: 17 English sovereigns

Fidelio
    opera by: 9 Beethoven
    character: 5 Rocco 7 Leonora (Fidelio), Pizarro 8 Fernando 9 Florestan

fidelity 5 honor 6 fealty 7 honesty, loyalty, probity 8 accuracy, devotion 9 adherence, closeness, constancy, exactness, good faith, integrity, precision, sincerity 10 allegiance, exactitude 11 earnestness, reliability, staunchness 12 faithfulness, truthfulness **14** correspondence **15** true-heartedness, trustworthiness

Fides
origin: 5 Roman
personifies: 9 good faith

fidget 4 fret, fuss, jerk, stew, toss **5** chafe, worry **6** jiggle, squirm, twitch, wiggle, writhe **7** twiddle, wriggle

fidgety 5 antsy, fussy, jerky, jumpy **6** uneasy **7** jittery, nervous, restive, squirmy, twitchy, unquiet **8** restless **9** impatient, irritable, tremulous **12** apprehensive

fief 4 land **6** domain, estate **9** territory

field 3 lea **4** area, grab, lawn, line, mead, turf, yard **5** arena, catch, court, front, glove, green, heath, lists, orbit, range, reach, realm, scope, sward, sweep **6** circle, common, course, domain, extent, meadow, pick up, region, sphere **7** acreage, calling, diamond, expanse, pasture, run down, stretch **8** clearing, province, retrieve, spectrum **9** bailiwick, grassland, territory **10** department, occupation, profession **12** battleground

Field, Sally
born: 10 Pasadena CA
roles: 5 Sybil **6** Gidget **8** Norma Rae (Oscar) **9** Punchline, Surrender **12** The Flying Nun **14** Murphy's Romance **15** Absence of Malice **16** Places in the Heart (Oscar) **18** Smokey and the Bandit

Fielding, Cecil
character in: 15 A Passage to India
author: 7 Forster

Fielding, Henry
author of: 6 Amelia **7** Shamela **8** Tom Jones, Tom Thumb **12** Jonathan Wild **13** Joseph Andrews

Field of Blood 8 Aceldama

Fields, W C
real name: 23 William Claude Dukenfield
born: 14 Philadelphia PA
roles: 5 Poppy **8** Micawber **11** The Bank Dick **14** David Copperfield **17** My Little Chickadee **27** Never Give a Sucker an Even Break

Fields of Mourning
location: 10 underworld
inhabited by: 14 shades of lovers
lovers who died by: **7** suicide

Fields of Visions, The
author: 12 Wright Morris

fiend 5 beast, brute, demon, devil, Satan **6** dybbuk **7** incubus, monster, villain **8** succubus **9** barbarian, hellhound, scoundrel **10** evil spirit **12** wicked person **14** devil incarnate **16** prince of darkness

fiendish 4 evil, foul **5** cruel **6** wicked **7** demonic, heinous, impious, satanic, vicious **8** barbaric, demoniac, devilish **9** monstrous, nefarious **10** demoniacal, diabolical, villainous

fierce 4 fell, wild **5** cruel, feral, fiery **6** brutal, fervid, raging, savage, strong **7** enraged, extreme, fearful, fervent, furious, intense, leonine, untamed, violent **8** horrible, menacing, powerful, ravening, ravenous, terrible, tigerish, uncurbed, vehement **9** barbarous, bellicose, ferocious, impetuous, merciless, truculent, unbridled, voracious **10** immoderate, inordinate, passionate **11** threatening **12** bloodthirsty, overpowering, overwhelming, unrestrained
French: 8 farouche

fierceness 4 zeal **7** passion **8** ferocity, wildness **9** pugnacity, vehemence **10** savageness

fiery 5 afire, angry, irate **6** ablaze, alight, ardent, fervid, fierce, red-hot, torrid **7** blazing, burning, febrile, fervent, fevered, flaming, glaring, glowing, peppery, pyretic, violent, zealous **8** choleric, feverish, flashing, headlong, inflamed, spirited, vehement, wrathful **9** excitable, hotheaded, impetuous, impulsive, irascible, irritable **10** full of fire, high-strung, mettlesome, passionate, sweltering **11** hot-tempered, impassioned, precipitate **12** enthusiastic

fiesta 4 fete, gala **5** feast, party **6** picnic **7** funfair **8** carnival, feast day, festival, jamboree **9** saint's day **10** block party, observance, street fair **11** celebration **13** commemoration **15** festive occasion

fig 5 Ficus
varieties: 3 keg, sea **4** bush, cape, Java, Zulu **5** cedar, clown, Congo, rusty **6** common, Devil's, exotic, golden, Indian, Kaffir, Mysore, sacred **7** Barbary, cluster, oak-leaf, spotted, weeping **8** climbing, creeping, Dracaena, mulberry, sycamore **9** Hottentot, mistletoe, strangler **10** East Indian, fiddle-leaf, glossy-leaf, little-leaf, Moreton Bay, Philippine **11** Port Jackson **16** West Indian laurel

Figaro
character in: 18 The Barber of Seville **19** The Marriage of Figaro
author: 12 Beaumarchais

fight 3 box, row, war **4** bout, duel, feud, fray, grit, spar, spat, tiff, tilt, wage **5** argue, brawl, brush, clash, event, joust, match, melee, pluck, round, scrap, set-to **6** battle, bicker, combat, engage, fracas, mettle, oppose, resist, spirit, strife, tussle **7** carry on, conduct, contend, contest, discord, dispute, go to war, quarrel, repulse, scuffle, tourney, wage war, wrangle **8** confront, dogfight, gameness, skirmish, squabble, struggle **9** bickering, encounter, pugnacity, scrimmage, toughness, wrangling **10** contention, difference, dissension, prizefight, strive with, tournament **11** altercation, armed action, battle royal, bellicosity, clash of arms, controversy **12** belligerency, do battle with, rise up in arms, struggle with **13** armed conflict, combativeness, confrontation, exchange blows, pitched battle

fight back 7 counter, get even, hit back, pay back **9** retaliate **10** strike back **13** counterattack

fighter 5 boxer 7 soldier, sparrer, warrior 8 pugilist, scrapper 9 combatant 10 militarist 11 belligerent

fighting 3 war 4 fray 5 brawl, melee 6 action, battle, bicker, combat, rumpus, tumult, tussle 7 contest, dispute, quarrel, warfare 8 battling, brawling, conflict, skirmish, squabble 9 bickering, disputing 10 engagement, quarreling, squabbling 11 clash of arms, controversy, hostilities

Fighting Marine
  nickname of: 10 Gene Tunney

fighting men 4 army 6 legion, troops 7 legions, militia 8 military, soldiers, soldiery 13 military force 15 military machine

fighting spirit 9 animosity, hostility, pugnacity 10 antagonism 11 bellicosity 12 belligerence 14 aggressiveness

fight shy of 5 avoid, dodge, elude, evade, skirt 6 escape 8 sidestep

figment 5 fable, fancy, story 6 canard 7 fantasy, fiction, product 8 creation 9 falsehood, invention 10 concoction 11 fabrication

figuration 4 form 7 outline 9 formation, structure 12 constitution

figurative 6 florid, ironic, ornate 7 flowery 8 humorous, symbolic 9 satirical 10 not literal 11 allegorical 12 hyperbolical, metaphorical

figure, figures 3 cut, man, sum 4 body, cast, cost, foot, form, mark, plan, rate, sign, sums 5 add up, adorn, build, count, digit, force, frame, guess, judge, motif, price, shape, think, total, tot up, value, woman 6 amount, appear, assess, cipher, design, device, emblem, factor, leader, number, person, reckon, schema, symbol 7 anatomy, believe, compute, contour, count up, diagram, drawing, imagine, notable, numeral, outline, pattern, presume, suppose 8 appraise, be placed, eminence, estimate, ornament, physique, presence 9 calculate, character, diversify, embellish, have a part, personage, play a part, quotation, variegate 10 arithmetic, conjecture, shine forth, silhouette 11 be mentioned, be prominent 12 calculations, computations, illustration

figurehead 4 tool 5 dummy, front, token 6 cipher, puppet 8 ornament 9 nonentity

figure out 6 reckon 7 compute, find out, work out 8 discover 9 ascertain, calculate, determine

figure roughly 5 guess 6 reckon 8 estimate 11 approximate, make a stab at

figure up 3 add 5 add up, total, tot up 6 reckon 7 compute, count up 9 calculate

figurine 7 bibelot 8 ornament 9 statuette

Fiji
  capital/largest city: 4 Suva
  others: 3 Mba 4 Mbua 5 Navua 6 Labasa 7 Lautoka, Nausori, Vaileka, Vunisea 8 Korolevu, Savusavu 9 Singatoka
  school: 12 South Pacific
  head of state: 14 British monarch 15 governor general

monetary unit: 6 dollar
  island: 4 Ngau 6 Ovalau, Rotuma, Yasawa 7 Kandavu, Taveuni 8 Viti Levu 9 Vanua Levu
  highest point: 8 Victoria 9 Tomaniivi
  river: 4 Rewa 8 Ndreketi
  sea: 4 Koro 7 Pacific
  people: 6 Fijian, Indian 7 Chinese 10 Melanesian, Polynesian 11 Micronesian
  language: 5 Hindi 6 Fijian 7 English
  religion: 5 Hindu, Islam 9 Methodist 13 Roman Catholic
  feature:
    cluster houses: 5 mbure

filament 4 hair, line, wire 5 fiber, fibre 6 cilium, ribbon, strand, string, thread

filbert 7 Corylus
  varieties: 3 red 4 cork, Momi, plum 5 azure, China, giant, Greek, joint, Nikko, noble, white 6 alpine, balsam, Fraser, Korean, needle, Scotch, silver, summer 7 cascade, Douglas, lowland, Spanish 8 Algerian, Japanese, Sakhalin, Southern 9 Himalayan, Shasta Red 10 dwarf Nikko, Santa Lucia 11 bristle-cone 13 Pacific silver 14 Southern balsam

filch 3 cop, rob 4 copy, crib, hook, lift 5 boost, heist, steal, swipe 6 pilfer, pirate 7 purloin 8 arrogate 10 plagiarize 11 appropriate, expropriate

file 3 row 4 data, line, list, rank, tier 5 apply, chain, index, put in, queue, store 6 drawer, folder, record, stacks, string 7 catalog, dossier, put away, records, request 8 archives, classify, petition 9 catalogue, chronicle
  type: 4 mill, nail, rasp, wood 5 round 9 half-round 13 three-cornered

filial 7 dutiful, sonlike 10 daughterly, respectful

fill 3 act 4 cram, glut, lade, load, meet, pack, puff, sate 5 crowd, gorge, lay by, lay in, serve, stock, store 6 answer, assign, blow up, charge, dilate, do duty, expand, infuse, make up, occupy, outfit, supply, take up 7 distend, execute, furnish, inflate, pervade, preside, provide, satiate, satisfy, suffuse, surfeit 8 carry out, function, permeate, saturate 9 discharge, provision, replenish 10 full amount, impregnate, overspread

filled in 7 stood in 9 completed, 11 substituted

filled out 6 marked 7 matured 9 completed

fillet 4 band 5 slice, strip 6 ribbon 7 bandeau, circlet

fillip 3 tap 4 flip, snap, toss 5 flick, tonic 6 buffet 8 stimulus

Fillmore, Millard
  presidential rank: 10 thirteenth
  party: 4 Whig
  state represented: 2 NY
  defeated: 5 no one
  succeeded upon death of: 6 Taylor
  vice president: 4 none
  cabinet:

State: 7 (Daniel) Webster, (Edward) Everett

Treasury: 6 (Thomas) Corwin

War: 6 (Charles Magill) Conrad

Attorney General: 10 (John Jordan) Crittenden

Navy: 6 (William Alexander) Graham 7 (John Pendleton) Kennedy

Postmaster General: 4 (Nathan Kelsey) Hall 7 (Samuel Dickinson) Hubbard

Interior: 6 (Alexander Hugh Holmes) Stuart

born: 7 Locke NY

died/buried: 9 Buffalo NY

education:

college: 4 none

studied: 3 law

religion: 9 Unitarian

interests: 5 civic

first chancellor of University of: 7 Buffalo

founder: 22 Buffalo General Hospital 24 Buffalo Historical Society

author: 21 Millard Fillmore Papers

political career: 13 state assembly, Vice President 24 US House of Representatives

civilian career: 6 lawyer (New York Supreme Court) 7 teacher 10 wool carder 12 cloth dresser

notable events of lifetime/term: 25 Compromise of Eighteen-Fifty

act: 13 Fugitive Slave

father: 9 Nathaniel

mother: 6 Phoebe (Millard)

siblings: 5 Cyrus, Julia 11 Phoebe Maria 12 Almon Hopkins, Calvin Turner 13 Charles DeWitt 14 Darius Ingraham, Olive Armstrong

wife: 7 Abigail (Powers) 8 Caroline (Carmichael McIntosh)

children: 11 Mary Abigail 13 Millard Powers

fill with air 5 bloat 6 billow, blow up, expand 7 balloon, distend, inflate, puff out 8 swell out

fill with dread 5 alarm, panic 6 dismay 7 perturb, terrify, unnerve 8 disquiet, frighten

fill with gloom 6 darken, sadden 8 dispirit

fill with wonder 3 awe 5 amaze 7 astound 8 astonish 9 fascinate

film, films 4 coat, haze, mist, skin, veil 5 cloud, flick, movie, sheet, shoot 6 cinema, flicks, movies, screen 7 coating 8 membrane

filmy 3 dim 4 fine, hazy, thin 5 gauzy, misty, sheer, wispy 8 cobwebby, finespun, gossamer 10 diaphanous

fils 3 son

filter 4 leak, ooze, seep 5 drain, exude, sieve 6 effuse, purify, refine, screen, strain 7 clarify, cleanse, dribble, trickle, well out 8 filtrate, strainer

filth 3 mud 4 dirt, dung, mire, muck, slop, smut 5 feces, offal, slime, slush, trash 6 manure, ordure, refuse, sewage, sludge 7 carrion, excreta, garbage, squalor 8 impurity, lewdness, ribaldry, vileness 9 excrement, grossness, indecency, nastiness, obscenity, pollution 10 corruption, defilement, immorality, indelicacy, putridness 11 pornography, squalidness 13 contamination 14 suggestiveness

filthy 4 foul, vile 5 black, dirty, grimy, gross, messy, nasty 6 grubby, impure, odious, soiled 7 defiled, dirtied, obscene, smirchy, squalid, unclean 8 befouled, slovenly, unwashed 9 repulsive 10 besmirched, disgusting 12 contaminated

finagle 3 con, gyp 4 plot, rook 5 cheat, mulct, trick 6 chisel, fleece, scheme, wangle 7 defraud, swindle 8 engineer, intrigue, maneuver

final 4 last, rear 6 ending, latest 7 closing, extreme 8 complete, decisive, finished, hindmost, rearmost, terminal, thorough, ultimate 10 concluding, conclusive, definitive, exhaustive, hindermost 11 irrevocable, terminating 12 unappealable, unchangeable 13 determinative

French: 7 dernier

finale 3 end 5 close, finis 6 finish, windup 7 curtain 8 epilogue, last part, swan song 10 conclusion 11 culmination, termination

final limit

Latin: 14 terminus ad quem

finally 6 lastly 10 eventually, inexorably, ultimately 11 inescapably 12 conclusively, definitively, in conclusion 16 incontrovertibly

French: 5 enfin

Latin: 10 ad extremum

final section 4 coda 5 rider 6 ending 7 last act 8 addendum, epilogue 9 afterword 10 conclusion

final settlement 8 solution 11 disposition

finance 6 pay for 7 banking 8 accounts 9 economics 10 underwrite

financial backer 5 angel 6 patron 7 sponsor 9 supporter 10 benefactor

financial support 7 backing, subsidy 10 assistance 12 contribution

financier 5 angel 6 backer, banker, broker 7 rich man 10 capitalist 11 millionaire, underwriter

Financier, The

author: 15 Theodore Dreiser

character: 12 Aileen Butler, Edward Butler 15 Henry Cowperwood 16 Frank A Cowperwood 23 Lillian Semple Cowperwood

Finch, Peter

real name: 15 Peter Ingle-Finch

born: 6 London 7 England

roles: 7 Network (Oscar) 11 Lost Horizon 12 The Nun's Story 15 The Pumpkin Eater 18 Sunday Bloody Sunday

Finchley, Sondra

character in: 17 An American Tragedy

author: 7 Dreiser

find 3 get, see, win 4 earn, espy, gain, meet, rule, spot 5 award, catch, dig up, judge, learn 6 attain, come by, decide, decree, detect, expose, locate, regain 7 achieve, acquire, adjudge, bargain, bonanza, discern, get back, godsend, good buy, hit upon, procure, recover, uncover, unearth 8 bump into, come upon, discover, disinter, lucky hit, meet with, retrieve, windfall 9 ascertain, determine, discovery, encounter, pronounce, repossess 10 adjudicate 11 acquisition

fin de siecle 8 decadent 15 end of the century

find fault 3 nag 4 beef, carp 5 blame, cavil, gribe 6 grouse, squawk 7 nitpick 8 complain 9 bellyache, criticize, disparage 10 disapprove

find guilty 5 blame 6 indict 7 condemn, convict 8 sentence 9 implicate

finding 6 decree, ruling 7 verdict 8 decision

find innocent 5 clear 6 acquit 9 exonerate

find out 5 learn 6 detect, locate 7 uncover, unearth 8 discover 9 ascertain, determine, establish

find repulsive 4 hate 5 abhor 6 detest, loathe 7 despise 8 execrate, recoil at 9 abominate

fine 4 airy, chic, fair, keen, neat, nice, rare, thin 5 bonny, clear, dandy, gauzy, mulct, nifty, sharp, sheer, silky, small, smart, sunny, swell 6 assess, bonnie, bright, charge, choice, comely, dainty, flimsy, ground, lovely, minute, modish, pretty, silken, slight, spiffy, subtle, superb 7 damages, elegant, forfeit, fragile, penalty, perfect, powdery, precise, refined, slender, stylish, tenuous 8 cobwebby, delicate, ethereal, flawless, gossamer, handsome, penalize, pleasant, polished, powdered, rainless, skillful, splendid, superior, tasteful 9 admirable, beautiful, brilliant, cloudless, excellent, exquisite 10 assessment, attractive, consummate, diaphanous, fastidious, pulverized, swimmingly 11 excellently, exceptional, lightweight, magnificent, transparent, well-favored 12 accomplished 13 hairsplitting, unsubstantial
music: 3 end

fine clothes 5 glad rags 10 Sunday best 16 best bib and tucker

fine-looking 4 fair 5 bonny 6 bonnie, comely, lovely, pretty, seemly 8 gorgeous, handsome 9 beauteous, beautiful, exquisite, ravishing 10 attractive 11 resplendent 15 pulchritudinous

fineness 6 beauty 8 delicacy, elegance, thinness 10 perfection, smoothness 12 flawlessness 13 exquisiteness

fine points 3 art 7 finesse, nuances 8 niceties 10 subtleties 11 refinements 12 distinctions

finer 6 better 8 superior

finery 6 frills, tinsel 7 baubles, gaudery, gewgaws 8 frippery, spangles, trinkets 9 trappings, trimmings 13 paraphernalia

finesse 4 ruse, tact, wile 5 craft, dodge, guile, savvy 7 cunning 8 artifice, delicacy, intrigue, trickery 9 deception, stratagem 10 artfulness, discretion, subterfuge
French: 11 savoir-faire

fine workmanship 8 delicacy 9 precision 13 craftsmanship

finger 3 paw 4 feel, poke 5 digit, punch, thumb, touch 6 caress, feeler, handle 7 pointer, squeeze, toy with, twiddle 8 play with 10 manipulate

finicky 5 fussy, picky 6 choosy 8 niggling 10 fastidious, meticulous, nitpicking, overprecise, particular, pernickety 11 persnickety 14 discriminating, overparticular

finish 3 end 4 coat, face, gild, goal, kill, last, seal, stop 5 cease, close, glaze, use up 6 clinch, defeat, devour, ending, finale, settle, veneer, wind up 7 achieve, coating, consume, curtain, destroy, fulfill, get done, lacquer, realize, surface, varnish 8 carry out, complete, conclude, dispatch, epilogue, exterior, get rid of, knock off, make good 9 discharge, eradicate, objective, polishing, terminate 10 accomplish, completion, consummate, consummate, denouement 11 discontinue, exterminate, termination

finished 4 full 5 ended, final, ideal, whole 6 entire, urbane 7 classic, elegant, perfect, refined, shapely, skilled, trained, well-set 8 complete, flawless, polished, well-bred 9 beautiful, completed, concluded, exquisite, faultless 10 consummate, cultivated, impeccable 11 consummated 12 accomplished

finishing stroke 9 death blow
French: 11 coup de grace

finish off 4 kill, slay 7 destroy, execute, wipe out 8 complete, dispatch 9 eradicate, polish off 10 annihilate 11 exterminate

finite 7 bounded, limited 8 confined, temporal 9 countable 10 measurable, restricted, short-lived, terminable 13 circumscribed

Finland
other name: 5 Suomi 15 Suomen Tasavalta
capital/largest city: 8 Helsinki 11 Helsingfors
others: 3 Aba, Abo, Kem 4 Kemi, Ouli, Oulu, Ouou, Pori, Vasa 5 Enare, Espoo, Kotka, Lahti, Rauma, Turku, Vaasa 6 Imatra, Kuopio 7 Joensuu, Kajaani, Kokkola, Mikkeli, Tampere, Tapiola 9 Jyvaskyla, Mariehamn, Rovaniemi 12 Lappeenranta
measure: 5 kannu, verst 6 fathom, kannor 8 otlinger, skalpund, tunnland
monetary unit: 4 mark 5 penni 6 markka
island: 5 Aland, Karlo 6 Aaland 7 Hailuto 9 Vallgrund 10 Ahvenanmaa
lake: 3 Juo, Muo 4 Kemi, Kiui, Nasi, Oulu, Puru, Pyha, Simo 5 Enara, Enare, Hauki, Inari, Kalla, Lappa, Lesti, Puula, Saima 6 Ladoya, Lentua, Saimaa, Sounne, Syvari 7 Koitere, Nilakka, Pielien 9 Kallavesi, Pielavesi
mountain: 7 Laltiva 10 Saari Selka
highest point: 6 Haltia 11 Haldetsokka
river: 4 Kala, Kemi, Kymi, Oulu, Pats, Simo, Teno 5 Ivalo, Lotta, Ounas, Siika,

Torne **6** Iijoki, Lapuan, Muonio, Pasvik, Tornoi, Vuoski **7** Kitinen **8** Kokemaki
sea: 6 Baltic **8** Atlantic
physical feature:
  gulf: **7** Bothnia, Finland
  isthmus: **7** Karelia
  peninsula: **13** Fennoscandian
people: 3 Jew, Vod, Vot, Yak **4** Avar, Finn, Hame, Lapp, Turk, Veps **5** Fioun, Gypsy, Ijore, Inger, Suomi, Vepse **6** Magyar, Ostiak, Ostyak, Tarast, Tavast, Ugrian, Zyrian **7** Lappish, Mordvin, Permiak, Samoyed, Uralian **8** Cheremis, Estonian, Karelian, Livonian, Swekoman **9** Tavastian **11** Karjalaiset, Suomalaiset
  athlete: **10** Paavo Nurmi
  composer: **8** Sibelius
  designer: **9** Marimekko
language: 4 Avar, Lapp **5** Karel, Ugric, Vogul **6** Magyar, Ostyak, Tarast **7** Finnish, Olonets, Samoyed, Swedish **8** Estonian **10** Olonetsian
religion: 19 Evangelical Lutheran
place:
  canal: **6** Saimaa
  castle: **10** Saint Olaf's **11** Olavinlinna
  fortress: **8** Sveaborg **11** Suomenlinna
  memorial: **8** Sibelius
  pine ridge: **10** Punkaharju
feature:
  game: **9** pesapallo
food:
  dish: **11** Karelian pie
  fruit: **16** yellow cloudberry
  liqueur: **9** Mesimarja
Finn
  also: 5 Fionn **13** Fionn MacCumal
  origin: 5 Irish
  king of: 4 gods **14** Tuatha De Danann
  son: 6 Ossian
  father: 5 Cumal **6** Comhal
Finnegan's Wake
  author: 10 James Joyce
  family: 9 Earwicker
Finney, Albert
  wife: 10 Anouk Aimee
  born: 7 England, Salford
  roles: 5 Annie **7** Scrooge **8** Tom Jones **10** The Dresser **12** Shoot the Moon **13** Two for the Road **17** Under the Volcano **29** Saturday Night and Sunday Morning
Finnish Mythology *see* **21** Scandinavian Mythology
Finno-Ugric
  language family: 6 Uralic
  Finnic group: 4 Lapp **6** Votyak, Zyrian **7** Finnish, Mordvin, Permian **8** Estonian **9** Cheremiss
  Ugric group: 5 Vogul **6** Ostyak **7** Ob-Ugric **9** Hungarian
Fionn, Fionn MacCumal *see* **4** Finn
fiord, fjord 5 firth, inlet **7** estuary
fir 4 pine **5** cedar, larch **6** alpine, balsam, linden, spruce **7** conifer, cypress, douglas **9** evergreen

Firbolg
  origin: 5 Greek, Irish
  defeated by: 9 Fomorians
  ousted by: 4 gods **14** Tuatha De Danann
fire 3 can, vim **4** bake, boot, burn, cook, dash, dump, elan, hurl, oust, sack, stir **5** ardor, blaze, eject, flame, flare, flash, force, gusto, let go, light, power, punch, rouse, salvo, shell, shoot, spark, verve, vigor **6** arouse, bounce, depose, excite, fervor, foment, genius, ignite, incite, kindle, luster, spirit, stir up, vivify, volley **7** animate, bombard, bonfire, cashier, dismiss, inferno, inflame, inspire, project, quicken, sniping, trigger **8** enfilade, fervency, inspirit, radiance, splendor, vivacity **9** broadside, cannonade, discharge, eagerness, fusillade, galvanize, holocaust, instigate, intensity, stimulate, vehemence **10** brilliance, effulgence, enthusiasm **11** bombardment, earnestness, inspiration **13** conflagration, sharpshooting **15** imaginativeness
  god of: 4 Loki **5** Ishum **6** Vulcan **10** Hephaestus, Hephaistos
  goddess of: 6 Brigit
Fire and Ice
  author: 11 Robert Frost
firearm 3 gun, rod **5** piece, rifle **6** pistol **7** shotgun **8** revolver **10** machine gun **12** shooting iron **13** submachine gun **20** Saturday-night special
firefight 5 clash **6** battle, combat **8** skirmish
firefly 8 glowworm, lampyrid **9** candlefly **12** lightning bug
Fire Next Time, The
  author: 12 James Baldwin
fire off 5 eject, shoot **6** launch **8** detonate **9** discharge
Fireside Theatre
  host: 9 Jane Wyman **11** Frank Wisbar, Gene Raymond
Firestarter
  author: 11 Stephen King
fire up 4 fuel, rile **5** anger, light, rouse **6** arouse, excite, ignite, incite, kindle **7** animate, enthuse, inspire **8** activate, energize, irritate, vitalize **9** galvanize, stimulate
firm 4 bent, fast, grim, hard, taut **5** close, dense, fixed, house, rigid, rocky, solid, stiff, stony, tight, tough **6** dogged, flinty, intent, moored, rooted, secure, stable, steady, steely **7** compact, company, dead set, decided, earnest, serious, settled, staunch **8** anchored, business, constant, definite, fearless, obdurate, resolute, resolved, unshaken **9** confirmed, hard-nosed, immovable, obstinate, steadfast, tenacious, unbending **10** adamantine, compressed, determined, inexorable, inflexible, invincible, persistent, unwavering, unyielding **11** corporation, established, partnership, unalterable, unfaltering, unflinching **12** conglomerate, indissoluble, organization **13** establishment

firmament 3 air, sky 5 ether, space, vault 6 canopy, welkin 7 heavens, the blue, the void 10 outer space

firmness 8 tenacity 9 obstinacy 10 resolution 11 persistence, staunchness 12 resoluteness 13 determination, inflexibility, steadfastness

first 4 head, main 5 basic, prime, start, vital 6 before, eldest, maiden, outset, primal, rather, sooner 7 highest, leading, premier, primary, ranking, supreme 8 earliest, foremost, original, primeval, superior 9 beginning, essential, inception, initially, paramount, primitive, principal 10 aboriginal, elementary, preeminent, preferably, primordial 11 fundamental, rudimentary 12 commencement, introduction, introductory

first among equals
  Latin: 16 primus inter pares

first appearance 4 dawn 5 debut 9 beginning 12 introduction

firstborn 5 elder, older 6 eldest, oldest

Firstborn, The
  author: 14 Christopher Fry

First Circle
  author: 23 Aleksandr Solzhenitsyn Jr

first god see 8 god, first

firsthand 6 direct 8 personal 9 empirical 10 unmediated 12 experimental

First Lady of the Theater
  nickname of: 10 Helen Hayes 16 Katharine Cornell

first-line 4 main 5 chief 7 primary 8 foremost

first moving thing
  Latin: 12 primum mobile

first-rate 3 ace 4 A-one, best, fine, tops 5 crack, elite, great, prime 6 choice, finest, select 7 top-hole 8 splendid, superior, topnotch, very good 9 admirable, estimable, excellent, exclusive, nonpareil, top drawer, topflight, wonderful 10 noteworthy, stupendous 11 commendable, outstanding 12 above-average, incomparable 13 distinguished

First State
  nickname of: 8 Delaware

first step 5 start 9 beginning 12 commencement

firth 5 fjord, inlet 7 estuary

fiscal 8 economic, monetary 9 budgetary, financial, pecuniary

fish 3 net 4 cast, hook, hunt 5 angle, grope, seine, trawl, troll 6 ferret, search 7 rummage

fish
  class: 7 Agnatha 12 Osteichthyes 14 Chondrichthyes
  fin: 4 anal, tail 6 caudal, dorsal, median, paired, pelvic 7 adipose, ventral 8 pectoral
  kind: 3 cod, eel, gar, ray 4 bass, carp, hake, opah, pike, tuna 5 brill, blenny, perch, shark, skate, sword, trout 6 bichir, blenny, marlin, minnow, mullet, salmon, tarpon 7 anchovy, catfish, dogfish, dolphin, hagfish, herring, lamprey, piranha, sunfish 8

bluefish, cavefish, crayfish, flounder, goldfish, lungfish, mackerel, menhaden, moray eel, pilchard, sea horse, squirrel, sturgeon 9 killifish, pygmy goby, swordfish 10 coelacanth, flying fish, paddlefish, rabbit fish, rocksucker, whale shark 11 anemonefish, electric eel, electric ray, lanternfish, long-nose gar 13 butterflyfish 14 largemouth bass
  part: 3 fin 4 gill 5 scale 6 cirrhi 10 gas bladder 11 swim bladder 12 rete mirabile
  shellfish:
  crustacean: 4 crab 6 shrimp 7 lobster 8 blue crab, king crab, snow crab 9 langouste 11 langoustine 13 Dungeness crab, horseshoe crab
  mollusk: 4 clam 6 mussel, oyster, quahog 8 surf clam 9 horse clam, razor clam 11 geoduck clam
  young: 3 fry 10 fingerling

Fisher, Bud
  creator/artist of: 11 Mutt and Jeff

Fisher, Carrie
  father: 11 Eddie Fisher
  mother: 13 Debbie Reynolds
  role: 12 Princess Leia
  films: 7 Shampoo 8 Star Wars 12 This Is My Life 16 The Blues Brothers 17 When Harry Met Sally 18 The Return of the Jedi 19 The Empire Strikes Back, Hannah and Her Sisters
  author: 20 Postcards from the Edge

Fisher, Ham
  creator/artist of: 10 Joe Palooka

Fisher, Vardis
  author of: 10 The Mothers 13 Children of God 17 The Testament of Man

fisherman 5 eeler 6 angler, caster, jacker, netter, seiner 7 trawler, troller 8 piscator 9 flycaster, Waltonian 17 the compleat angler

Fishermen
  goddess of: 11 Britomartis

Fishes
  constellation of: 6 Pisces

fish story 3 fib, lie 7 fiction, whopper 9 falsehood, tall story 16 cock-and-bull story

fishy 3 odd 4 dull 5 blank, queer, shady, weird 6 vacant 7 dubious, strange, suspect 8 doubtful, peculiar, slippery 9 dishonest 10 farfetched, glassy-eyed, improbable, suspicious, unreliable 11 exaggerated, extravagant 12 questionable, unscrupulous 14 expressionless

fission 7 atomize 8 breaking, cleavage, scission 9 severance, splitting 10 breaking up, sunderance 12 disseverance, reproduction

fissure 3 gap 4 rift, slit 5 chink, cleft, crack, gully, split 6 breach, cranny, groove, hiatus 8 aperture, cleavage

fit 4 able, good, hale, meet, ripe, suit, well, whim 5 adapt, agree, alter, burst, equal, equip, hardy, match, ready, right, shape, sound, spasm, spell, train 6 access, accord, adjust, become, concur, enable, in trim, mature, primed, proper, robust, seemly, strong, timely, worthy **7** adapted, apropos, capable, caprice, conform, correct, empower, fashion, healthy, prepare, qualify, rectify, seizure, toned up, trained **8** apposite, becoming, coincide, crotchet, decorous, eligible, graduate, grand mal, outbreak, outburst, paroxysm, petit mal, prepared, relevant, suitable **9** calibrate, competent, consonant, deserving, efficient, explosion, harmonize, initiated, opportune, pertinent, qualified **10** acceptable, applicable, capacitate, convenient, convulsion, correspond, seasonable **11** appropriate, capacitated

fitful 4 weak **6** broken, random, uneven **7** erratic **8** listless, off-and-on, periodic, sporadic, unsteady, variable **9** irregular, spasmodic **10** capricious, changeable, convulsive **11** fluctuating **12** disconnected, intermittent

fitness
   Hebrew: **7** kashrut **8** kashruth

fit out 4 robe **5** array, dress, equip **6** attire, clothe, supply **7** appoint, prepare

fitting 3 apt **4** meet **6** proper, seemly **8** decorous, suitable **9** congruous **11** appropriate
   French: **11** comme il faut

fit to be eaten 6 edible **9** palatable **10** comestible, consumable, digestible

fit together 4 join **5** hinge, unite **6** hook up **7** connect **8** dovetail **9** interlock **10** articulate

Fitzgerald, Barry
   real name: **20** William Joseph Shields
   born: **6** Dublin **7** Ireland
   roles: **10** Going My Way **11** The Quiet Man **19** How Green Was My Valley

FitzGerald, Edward
   author of: **24** The Rubaiyat of Omar Khayyam (translation)

Fitzgerald, F Scott
   wife: **10** Zelda Sayre
   author of: **10** The Crack-Up **13** The Last Tycoon **14** The Great Gatsby **16** Tender Is the Night **18** This Side of Paradise **24** The Beautiful and the Damned

Fitzgerald, George Francis
   field: **7** physics
   nationality: **5** Irish
   theory of: **24** electromagnetic radiation

Fitzgerald, Geraldine
   born: **6** Dublin **7** Ireland
   roles: **11** Dark Victory **12** Ah Wilderness, Rachel Rachel **15** Watch on the Rhine **16** Wuthering Heights **24** Long Day's Journey Into Night

Fitzsimmons, Bob (Robert Prometheus)
   sport: **6** boxing

FitzSimons, Maureen
   real name of: **12** Maureen O'Hara

Five, The
   group of: **16** Russian composers
   member: **3** Cui **7** Borodin **9** Balakirev **10** Mussorgsky **14** Rimsky-Korsakov

Five Easy Pieces
   director: **11** Bob Rafelson
   cast: **10** Karen Black **11** Fannie Flagg **12** Susan Anspach **13** Jack Nicholson **14** Billy Breen Bush, Sally Struthers

Five Men and Pompey
   author: **19** Stephen Vincent Benet

five-o'clock shadow 5 beard **7** stubble **8** bristles, whiskers

fix 3 jam, put, set **4** bind, make, mend, mess, moor, spot **5** place, rivet **6** adjust, anchor, attach, decide, fasten, harden, impose, muddle, pickle, plight, repair, scrape, secure, settle **7** congeal, connect, correct, dilemma, impasse, implant, patch up, prepare, rebuild **8** assemble, hot water, make fast, make firm, quandary, regulate, renovate, set right, solidify **9** establish, prescribe, retaliate, stabilize **10** difficulty **11** consolidate, involvement, predicament **12** entanglement

fixation 5 quirk **6** fetish **7** complex **8** crotchet, delusion **9** monomania, obsession **13** preoccupation

fixed 3 set **4** fast, firm **5** rigid, still **6** intent, rooted, stable, steady **8** constant, fastened, resolute, unpliant **9** immovable, unbending **10** determined, inflexible, motionless, persistent, stationary, unwavering

fixed idea 4 bias **5** slant **9** obsession **13** preconception
   French: **8** idee fixe

fixedness 8 firmness **9** constancy, stability **10** immobility **12** immutability **16** unchangeableness

fixed regard 7 staring **9** diligence **10** absorption, intentness **11** engrossment **13** concentration

Fixer, The
   author: **14** Bernard Malamud

fixing 6 repair **7** mending, mooring, placing, putting, setting **8** deciding, imposing, righting, riveting, settling, trimming **9** adjusting, anchoring, attaching, fastening, hardening, preparing, repairing **10** adjustment, assembling, congealing, connecting, correcting, implanting, rectifying, regulating, regulation **11** determining, prescribing, solidifying, stabilizing **12** establishing **13** consolidating

fixture 6 addict **7** devotee, habitue, regular **8** equipage **9** apparatus, appendage, appliance, equipment **10** attachment **11** appointment **12** appurtenance **13** paraphernalia

fix up 4 plan **6** design, devise **7** arrange, prepare **8** renovate, schedule

fix upon 4 pick **6** choose, opt for, select **7** call out, extract, pick out

fizz 4 foam **5** froth **7** bubbles **11** carbonation **13** effervescence

fizziness 9 foaminess **10** bubbliness, frothiness **13** effervescence

fizzing 6 bubbly **7** foaming **8** bubbling **9** sparkling **12** effervescent, effervescing

fizzle 3 dog, dud **4** bomb, fail, flop, hiss, mess **5** abort, botch **6** bubble, fiasco, gurgle, muddle, turkey **7** failure, founder, misfire, sputter, washout **8** collapse, disaster, miscarry

fizzy 6 bubbly 8 bubbling 9 sparkling 12 effervescent

flabbergast 4 stun 5 amaze, shock 6 puzzle 7 astound, stagger, stupefy 8 astonish, bewilder, bowl over, confound, overcome 9 dumbfound

flabbergasted 5 agape 6 amazed, gaping 9 awestruck, stupefied 10 astonished, dumbstruck, spellbound 11 dumbfounded 12 hornswoggled 13 thunderstruck

flabby 4 lame, limp, soft, weak 5 baggy, slack 6 doughy, effete, feeble, flimsy, floppy, spongy 7 flaccid 8 impotent, listless, yielding 9 enervated, inelastic 10 spiritless 11 adulterated, emasculated

flag 3 ebb, sag 4 fade, fail, pall, sink, tire, wane, warn, wave, wilt 5 abate, faint, slump 6 banner, colors, dodder, emblem, ensign, signal, totter 7 decline, give way, languish, Old Glory, standard, streamer 9 grow weary, Union Jack 12 Stars and Bars 15 Stars and Stripes

flagellant 7 ascetic 8 penitent 13 self-mortifier

flagon 3 gun, jug, mug 4 ewer 5 flask, stein 6 bottle, carafe, vessel 7 canteen 8 schooner

flagrant 5 gross, sheer 6 arrant, brazen, crying 7 blatant, glaring, heinous, obvious 8 immodest 9 audacious, barefaced, flaunting, monstrous, notorious, shameless 10 outrageous, scandalous 11 conspicuous

Flaherty, Margaret (Pegeen)
character in: 24 Playboy of the Western World
author: 5 Synge

flail 4 beat, lash, whip 5 swing 6 thresh 7 scourge

flair 4 bent, dash, feel, gift 5 knack, style, taste, touch, verve 6 genius, talent 7 faculty, feeling, panache 8 aptitude, capacity 9 ingenuity 11 discernment

flake 3 bit 4 chip, peel 5 fleck, layer, patch, scale, sheet, strip 7 chip off, crumble, peel off, shaving 8 scale off

flaky 4 bats, gaga, nuts 5 balmy, batty, crisp, daffy, dotty, goofy, loony, nutty, scaly, short, wacky 6 scabby, screwy, scurfy 8 scabious, squamous 9 eccentric 10 flocculent

flamboyant 4 wild 5 gaudy, jazzy, showy 6 flashy, florid, garish, ornate, rococo 7 baroque, dashing 8 colorful, exciting 10 theatrical 11 sensational 12 ostentatious

flame 4 beau, fire, glow 5 ardor, blaze, blush, flare, flash, flush, glare, gleam, light, lover, spark, swain 6 fervor, ignite, kindle, redden, warmth 7 passion 8 fervency 9 affection, boyfriend, intensity 10 enthusiasm, excitement, girlfriend, sweetheart 13 conflagration

flaming 5 afire, fiery 6 ablaze, alight, ardent, bright, fervid, stormy 7 blazing, burning, fervent, glaring, glowing, igneous, intense, shining, violent 8 flagrant,

vehement 9 brilliant, egregious 10 passionate, smoldering 11 conspicuous, inflammable

flammable 7 igneous 10 combustive, incendiary 11 combustible, inflammable

flan 3 pie 4 gust, puff, tart 6 expand, pastry 7 custard, dessert 12 creme caramel

flanerie 8 dawdling, idleness

flaneur 5 idler 6 loafer 7 dawdler

flank 3 hip 4 edge, line, loin, side, wing 5 cover, skirt 6 border, fringe, haunch, screen, shield

Flannagan, John Bernard
born: 7 Fargo ND
artwork: 6 New One, Not Yet 9 Beginning 11 Dragon Motif 15 Triumph of the Egg 16 Jonah and the Whale

flap 3 bat, fly, tab 4 bang, beat, flop 5 apron, shake, skirt 6 lappet 7 agitate, banging, flutter, vibrate 9 oscillate

flare 4 burn, glow 5 blaze, erupt, flame, flash, glare, gleam, taper, torch, widen 6 blow up, dilate, expand, ignite, signal, spread 7 bell out, broaden, distend, explode, stretch 8 boil over, break out 9 coruscate 10 incandesce

flash 4 glow, wink 5 blaze, blink, burst, flame, flare, glare, gleam, jiffy, shake, shine, spark, touch, trice 6 minute, moment, second, streak 7 flicker, glimmer, glisten, glitter, instant, sparkle 8 instance, outburst, radiance 9 coruscate 10 occurrence 11 coruscation, fulmination, scintillate 13 incandescence

Flash Gordon
creator: 8 Dan Berry 11 Alex Raymond 12 Austin Briggs
character:
companion: 4 Dale

flashy 4 loud 5 gaudy, jazzy, showy, smart 6 garish, sporty, tawdry, tinsel, vulgar 7 raffish 8 dazzling 9 bedizened 10 flamboyant, tricked out 11 pretentious 12 ostentatious

flask 6 bottle 7 canteen 9 container

flat, flats 3 low 4 dead, dull 5 clear, equal, flush, level, marsh, plain, plane, prone, shoal, shoes, stale, total, vapid 6 direct, planar, smooth, supine 7 blowout, exactly, insipid, laid low, leveled, levelly, loafers, prairie, regular, shallow 8 absolute, complete, definite, lowlands, positive, puncture, thorough, unbroken 9 apartment, downright, precisely, prostrate, reclining, recumbent, tasteless 10 flavorless, horizontal, peremptory 11 unequivocal, unpalatable, unqualified 12 deflated tire, horizontally, unmistakable

flatfish 3 ray 4 sole 5 brill, fluke 6 turbot 7 halibut, sand dab, sunfish, teleost 8 flounder

Flathead *see* 5 Salis 7 Chinook

flatness 8 dullness 9 levelness, staleness 10 insipidity 13 tastelessness 14 flavorlessness

flatten 4 deck, even, fell 5 crush, floor, level, plane 6 defeat, ground, smooth 7 deflate 8 compress, overcome 9 overwhelm, prostrate

flatter 4 fool, laud 5 court, extol, honor, toady 6 become, cajole, delude 7 adulate, beguile, deceive, mislead, wheedle 8 blandish, bootlick, butter up, eulogize, softsoap 9 brown-nose, sweet-talk, truckle 10 compliment,overpraise, panegyrize

flatterer 5 toady 6 fawner, yes man 8 eulogist, truckler, wheedler 9 sycophant 10 bootlicker 11 lickspittle 13 apple-polisher

flattering 7 lauding 8 praising 9 extolling, favorable, laudatory 10 gratifying 13 complimentary

flattering attention 5 court 7 fawning

flattery 6 eulogy 7 blarney, fawning, snow job 8 cajolery, encomium, jollying, soft soap, toadying, toadyism 9 adulation, panegyric, servility, truckling, wheedling 10 sycophancy 12 blandishment 14 obsequiousness

Flaubert, Gustave
   author of: 8 Salammbo 12 Madame Bovary 21 A Sentimental Education 24 The Temptation of St Anthony

flaunt 3 air 4 brag, wave 5 boast, sport, strut, vaunt 6 blazon, dangle, parade 7 exhibit, show off 8 brandish, flourish 9 advertise, broadcast

flavor 4 aura, lace, soul, tang, tone 5 gusto, imbue, savor, spice, style, tenor 6 aspect, infuse, lacing, relish, season, spirit 7 essence, instill 8 ambience, piquancy 9 attribute, seasoning

flavorful 4 rich 5 nutty, sapid, spicy, tangy, tasty, zesty 6 savory 7 peppery, piquant 8 aromatic 9 palatable, toothsome 10 appetizing

flavoring 4 herb, salt 5 spice 6 pepper 7 essence, extract, vanilla 8 additive, seasoner 9 chocolate, condiment, seasoning

flavorless 4 dull, flat, thin, weak 5 bland, stale, vapid 6 watery 7 insipid 9 tasteless

flaw 3 mar 4 blot, harm, spot, vice 5 error, fault, speck, stain 6 blotch, deface, defect, foible, impair, injure, injury, smudge, weaken 7 blemish, failing, fallacy, frailty, mistake 8 weak spot, weakness 9 deformity, disfigure 10 compromise, defacement 11 shortcoming 12 imperfection 13 disfigurement

flawed 6 faulty 8 impaired 9 defective, imperfect

flawless 5 sound 7 perfect 9 errorless, faultless 10 immaculate, impeccable

flawlessness 8 accuracy 10 perfection 11 correctness 14 immaculateness

flay 4 bark, pare, peel, skin 5 scalp, scold, strip 6 assail, fleece, punish, rebuke 7 plunder, upbraid 9 castigate, excoriate 11 decorticate

flea
   varieties: 3 bat, dog, rat 5 mouse 6 rodent 9 carnivore 10 sticktight

fleck 3 dot, jot 4 drop, mark, mole, spot 5 flake, speck 6 bespot, dapple, mottle, streak, tittle 7 blemish, freckle, spatter, speckle, stipple 8 particle, small bit 9 bespeckle 10 besprinkle

Fledermaus, Die
   also: 6 The Bat
   operetta by: 7 (Johann) Strauss
   character: 5 Adele, Falke, Frank 6 Alfred 9 Rosalinda 14 Prince Orlofsky 18 Baron von Eisenstein

fledgling 4 tyro 6 novice 8 beginner, freshman 9 greenhorn 10 apprentice, tenderfoot

flee 4 shun, skip 5 avoid, dodge, elude, evade, split 6 decamp, desert, vanish 7 abscond, fly away, make off 8 speed off 9 cut and run, disappear 10 fly the coop

fleece 3 gyp 4 bilk, dupe, gull, rook, wool 5 cheat, cozen, trick 7 deceive, defraud, swindle 9 bamboozle, victimize

fleet 3 run 4 band, fade, fast, flow, navy, skim, spry, swim, unit 5 agile, array, brief, creek, drift, float, hasty, inlet, light, quick, rapid, shift, ships, short, swift 6 abound, active, armada, nimble, number, speedy, sudden, vanish 7 caravan, cursory, hurried 8 flotilla, squadron 9 disappear, momentary, transient 10 evanescent, transitory 11 expeditious 13 instantaneous

fleeting 5 brief, quick 7 passing 8 flitting, fugitive, temporal 9 ephemeral, fugacious, momentary, temporary, transient 10 evanescent, perishable, transitory 11 impermanent, precarious, unenduring

Fleming, Alexander
   field: 12 bacteriology
   nationality: 7 British
   discovered: 10 penicillin
   awarded: 10 Nobel Prize

Fleming, Henry
   character in: 20 The Red Badge of Courage
   author: 5 Crane

Fleming, Ian
   author of: 4 Dr No 9 Moonraker 10 Goldfinger 11 Thunderball 12 Casino Royale 13 Live and Let Die 15 For Your Eyes Only 16 The Spy Who Loved Me, You Only Live Twice 18 From Russia with Love
   character: 1 M, Q 6 Oddjob 7 SPECTRE (organization) 9 James Bond 14 Miss Moneypenny 15 Auric Goldfinger

Fleming, Victor
   director of: 13 The Wizard of Oz 14 Treasure Island 15 Gone With the Wind (Oscar) 18 Captains Courageous

flesh 3 fat, man 4 body, meat, pulp 5 brawn, power, vigor 6 embody, fatten, people 7 fatness, fill out, mankind, realize 8 humanity, physique, strength 9 carnality, substance 10 sensuality 11 materiality 13 individualize, particularize

flesh and blood 3 kin 4 real 5 a body, child
6 family 7 kindred 8 children 9 corporeal,
offspring, relations, relatives 10 kith and
kin 11 substantial

flesh-eating 9 predatory 10 predaceous 11
carnivorous

fleshy 3 fat 5 beefy, obese, plump, stout,
tubby 6 chubby, portly, rotund, stocky 7
paunchy 8 roly-poly, thickset 9 corpulent,
succulent 10 overweight, potbellied

Fletcher, Louise
   born: 12 Birmingham AL
   roles: 17 The Cheap Detective 25 One
   Flew Over the Cuckoo's Nest (Oscar)

Fletcher, Susannah Yolande
   real name of: 12 Susannah York

flex 4 bend 5 curve

flexible 4 mild, soft 5 lithe 6 docile, genial,
gentle, limber, pliant, supple 7 amiable,
ductile, elastic, plastic, pliable, springy 8
bendable, yielding 9 adaptable, compliant,
malleable, resilient, tractable 10 changeable, extensible, manageable, responsive,
submissive 11 complaisant

Flibbertigibbet
   character in: 10 Kenilworth
   author: 5 Scott

flick 4 film 5 brush, graze, movie, sweep,
whisk

flicker 4 flit, glow, sway 5 blaze, flame,
flare, flash, gleam, glint, shake, spark,
throb, trace, waver 6 quaver, quiver, waggle 7 flutter, glimmer, glisten, glitter, modicum, pulsate, shimmer, sparkle, tremble,
vestige, vibrate, wriggle 8 undulate 9 coruscate, fluctuate, oscillate, scintilla, vacillate

Flickertail State
   nickname of: 11 North Dakota

flicks 5 films 6 cinema, grazes, movies,
sweeps, whisks 7 brushes

flier 4 bill 5 pilot 6 notice 7 aviator, leaflet,
venture 8 brochure, bulletin, circular, handbill 10 experiment 12 announcement 13
advertisement

flight 4 rout, rush, wing 5 flock 6 escape,
exodus, flying, hegira 7 fleeing, retreat,
soaring, winging 8 squadron 10 withdrawal
11 aeronautics

flighty 5 dizzy, giddy 6 fickle 8 quixotic,
reckless, unstable, volatile 9 frivolous,
mercurial, whimsical ,10 capricious,
changeable, inconstant, indecisive, irresolute 11 harebrained, impractical, light-
headed, thoughtless 13 irresponsible 14
scatterbrained

flimsy 4 poor, thin, weak 5 cheap, filmy,
frail, gauzy, petty, sheer 6 feeble, shabby, shoddy, sleazy, slight, trashy 7 foolish,
fragile, ill-made, shallow, trivial 8 cobwebby, delicate, gossamer, trifling 9 frivolous, worthless 10 diaphanous, inadequate, jerry-built, ramshackle 11 dilapidated, superficial 13 unsubstantial

flinch 3 fly, shy 4 jerk 5 cower, quail, quake,
start, wince 6 blench, cringe, falter, quaver,
quiver, recoil, shiver, shrink 7 contort, grimace, retreat, shudder

fling 2 go 3 try 4 ball, bash, cast, dash,
emit, hurl, lark, toss 5 eject, expel, heave,
pitch, sling, spree, trial 6 let fly, propel 7 attempt 8 bit of fun 11 precipitate

Flintstones, The
   character: 7 Pebbles 8 Bamm Bamm 11
   Betty Rubble 12 Barney Rubble 14 Fred
   Flintstone 15 Dino the Dinosaur, Wilma
   Flintstone
   voice: 8 Alan Reed, Mel Blanc 10 Don
   Messick 12 Bea Benaderet, Gerry Johnson 13 Jean Vander Pyl
   city: 7 Bedrock
   creator: 12 Hanna-Barbera

Flintwinch
   character in: 12 Little Dorrit
   author: 7 Dickens

flinty 4 cold, hard 5 cruel, harsh, stern,
stony 6 inured, steely 7 callous 8 hardened 10 unyielding 11 hardhearted, insensitive

flip 3 tap 4 bold, pert, spin, toss, turn 5
brash, fresh, fresh, throw, thumb 6 cheeky,
fillip 8 impudent, insolent, turn over 9 unabashed

flippant 4 glib, pert, rude 5 brash, lippy,
saucy 6 cheeky, nimble 7 voluble 8 impudent, insolent, trifling 9 bumptious, frivolous, talkative 11 impertinent 12 presumptuous 13 disrespectful

Flipper
   character: 8 Bud Ricks 10 Sandy Ricks
   11 Porter Ricks
   cast: 10 Brian Kelly, Luke Halpin 11 Tommy Norden

Flipper played by: 4 Suzy

flirt 3 toy 4 play, vamp 5 dally, tease 6 trifle
8 coquette 12 heartbreaker

flit 4 dart, scud, skim, wing 5 speed 6 hasten, scurry 7 flicker, flutter

Flitch of Bacon, The
   author: 16 William Ainsworth

Flite, Miss
   character in: 10 Bleak House
   author: 7 Dickens

flivver 3 car 4 auto, heap 5 motor 6 jalopy,
wheels 7 machine, vehicle 8 motorcar 9 tin
lizzie 10 automobile

float 3 bob 4 waft 5 drift, hover, slide 6 bear
up, buoy up, hold up, launch 8 levitate

floating 4 free 5 awash, loose 6 adrift,
afloat, errant 7 buoyant, wafting 8 drifting 9
fluctuant, wandering 10 unattached

flock 2 go 3 mob, run 4 band, bevy, gang,
herd, mass, pack, rush 5 bunch, crowd,
crush, drove, group, surge, troop 6 clique,
gather, huddle, muster, stream, throng 7
cluster, company, coterie 8 converge 9
gathering, multitude 10 assemblage, collection, congregate 11 aggregation 12 congregation
   of fish: 6 school
   of game birds: 5 covey

of **geese:** 6 gaggle
of **insects:** 5 swarm
of **lions:** 5 pride
of **seals or whales:** 3 pod
of **young birds:** 5 brood
flocks
  god of: 3 Pan
flock together 6 gather, mingle 7 convene
  8 assemble 9 associate 10 congregate
flog 4 beat, cane, club, cuff, drub, hide,
  lash, maul, whip 5 birch, flail, smite, strap
  6 cudgel, paddle, strike, switch, thrash 7
  scourge 8 lambaste 9 horsewhip 10 flagellate
flood 4 flow, glut, gush, tide 6 deluge,
  drench, shower, stream 7 cascade, current, torrent 8 downpour, flow over, inundate, overflow, saturate, submerge, wash
  over 9 overwhelm 10 cloudburst, inundation, outpouring, oversupply
  period before: 12 antediluvian
Flood
  author: 16 Robert Penn Warren
flooded 6 flowed, surged 7 deluged, glutted, overran, swamped 8 drenched, en-
  gulfed 9 inundated, outpoured, washed out
  10 downpoured, overflowed
floor 4 base, deck, fell, tier 5 level, stage,
  story 6 bottom, ground 7 minimum, parquet 8 base rate, flooring, pavement 9
  prostrate
flop 4 bomb, bust, drop, fail, fold, plop 5
  close 6 fiasco, fizzle, topple, tumble, turkey 7 failure, go under, shutter, washout 8
  disaster, lay an egg 14 disappointment
Flora
  origin: 5 Roman
  goddess of: 7 flowers
floral 6 bloomy 7 verdant 8 blossomy 9 botanical 10 herbaceous
Floralia
  origin: 5 Roman
  form: 8 festival
Florence
  artist: 6 Giotto 7 Cimabue 8 Ghiberti 9
    Donatello 10 Michelozzi 11 della Robbia
    12 Brunelleschi, Michelangelo
  capital of: 7 Tuscany 15 Firenze prov-
    ince
  cathedral/church: 10 San Lorenzo, San
    Miniato, Santa Croce 18 Santa Maria del
    Fiore
  Italian: 7 Firenze
  landmark: 5 Pieta 6 Uffizi 8 Bargello 11
    Pitti Palace 12 Ponte Vecchio 13 Boboli
    Gardens 14 Loggia dei Lanzi, Palazzo
    Vecchio 19 Piazza della Signoria 22 Bap-
    tistry of San Giovanni, Ospedale degli
    Innocenti
  mountain: 9 Apennines
  religious reformer: 10 Savonarola
  river: 4 Arno
  ruler: 5 Goths 6 Medici, Romans 8 Lom-
    bards 9 Etruscans 15 Byzantine Empire
  tomb of: 7 Galileo, Rossini 11
    Machiavelli 15 Lorenzo
    de Medici

florescence 5 bloom 9 flowerage 10 blossoming
florid 4 rosy 5 gaudy, ruddy, showy 6
  blowsy, hectic, ornate, rococo 7 baroque,
  flowery, flushed, reddish 8 inflamed, red-
  faced, rubicund, sanguine 9 elaborate 10
  flamboyant, ornamented 12 ostentatious
  13 grandiloquent
Florida
  abbreviation: 2 FL 3 Fla
  nickname: 6 Flower 8 Sunshine 10 Pe-
    ninsular
  capital: 11 Tallahassee
  largest city: 12 Jacksonville
  others: 4 Tice 5 Cocoa, Miami, Ocala,
    Tampa 7 Hialeah, Orlando, Palatka,
    Sebring 8 Sarasota 9 Bradenton, Palm
    Beach, Pensacola 10 Clearwater 11
    Brooksville, Coral Gables, Gainesville, St
    Augustine 12 Daytona Beach, Ft Lau-
    derdale, St Petersburg
  college: 4 Nova 5 Barry, Miami, Tampa 6
    Eckerd 7 Rollins, Stetson
  explorer: 11 Ponce de Leon
  feature:
    amusement park: 5   Epcot   10
      Marineland 11 Disney World
    canal: 5 Miami 7 Tamiami
    museum: 8 Ringling
    national park: 10 Everglades
  tribe: 3 Ais 5 Ocale, Utina 6 Calusa,
    Chatot, Potano 7 Timucua 8 Seminole
  people: 5 conch 7 cracker, Osceola
  island: 7 Bahamas, Sanibel 8 Biscayne
  key: 4 Long, Vaca, West 5 Largo 7 Big
    Pine 8 Biscayne 9 Sugarloaf
  lake: 4 Dora 5 Apopka, Harney, Jessup,
    Newnan 7 Ledwith 8 Arbuckle 9
    Kissimmee 10 Okeechobee
  land rank: 12 twenty-second
  physical feature:
    bay: 8 Biscayne 9 Apalachee 10
      Waccasassa
    cape: 5 Sable 7 Kennedy 9 Canaveral
    gulf: 6 Mexico
    sea: 8 Atlantic
    springs: 6 Silver 7 Rainbow
    swamp: 10 Everglades, Okefenokee
  river: 6 Banana, Indian 7 Aucilla, Mana-
    tee, Scambia, St Johns, Suwanee 9
    Ochlawaha 12 Apalachicola
  state admission: 13 twenty-seventh
  state bird: 11 mockingbird
  state fish: 16 Atlantic sailfish
  state mammal: 7 dolphin
  state flower: 13 orange blossom
  state motto: 12 In God We Trust
  state song: 11 Swanee River 14 Old
    Folks at Home
  state tree: 13 sabal palmetto 15 cabbage
    palmetto
florilegium 7 garland 8 chapbook, treasury
  9 anthology
Florizel
  character in: 14 The Winter's Tale
  author: 11 Shakespeare

floruit 12 he flourished 13 she flourished

flotilla 5 fleet 6 armada

Flotow, Friedrich von
born: 7 Germany 11 Mecklenburg
composer of: 6 Martha 11 Die Matrosen
19 Alessandro Stradella

flotsam 4 junk 6 debris, refuse 7 garbage 8 castoffs

flounce 3 hem 4 edge, leap, skip, trim, trip 5 bound, caper, frill, stamp, stomp, storm, strut 6 bounce, edging, fringe, gambol, prance, ruffle, sashay, spring 7 valance 8 furbelow, ornament, skirting, trimming

flounder 4 fish, flop, halt, limp 5 lurch, waver 6 falter, hobble, muddle, totter, tumble, wallow, welter 7 blunder, shamble, stagger, stumble 8 flatfish, hesitate, struggle

Flounder, The
author: 11 Gunter Grass

flourish 4 curl, dash, grow, pomp, rant, show, turn 5 bloom, bluff, get on, shake, strut, sweep, swing, swish, twirl, twist, wield 6 flaunt, flower, hot air, parade, splash, thrive, waving 7 blossom, bravado, burgeon, cadenza, fanfare, fustian, glitter, prosper, shaking, succeed, swagger 8 boasting, brandish, curlicue, fare well, get ahead, swinging, vaunting, wielding 9 agitation, grace note, thrashing 10 decoration 11 braggadocio, brandishing, fanfaronade, ostentation 12 appoggiatura 13 embellishment, magniloquence, swashbuckling 14 grandiloquence

flourishing 8 swinging, swishing, thriving, wielding 9 flaunting 10 prospering, successful 11 brandishing

flout 3 rag 4 defy, mock, twit 5 chaff, scorn, spurn, taunt 6 gibe at, insult

flow 3 jet, run 4 flux, gush, pass, pour, rush, seep, tide 5 drain, drift, float, flood, glide, issue, spout, spurt, surge, sweep, swirl, train 6 abound, course, deluge, efflux, effuse, filter, plenty, rapids, stream 7 cascade, current, debouch, torrent, well out 8 effusion, millrace, plethora, sequence 9 abundance, discharge, effluence, emanation 10 outpouring, succession 11 debouchment, progression

flower 3 bud 4 best, blow, open, pick, posy 5 bloom, cream, elite, ripen 6 mature 7 blossom, bouquet, burgeon, develop, nosegay, prosper 8 flourish 11 aristocracy

flower arranging, art of
Japanese: 7 ikebana

Flower Fables
author: 15 Louisa May Alcott

flowering 4 peak 5 bloom 6 height, heyday 8 blooming, maturing 10 blossoming, developing, prospering 11 flourishing

Flowering Judas
author: 19 Katherine Anne Porter

flowers
goddess of: 5 Flora

Flowers of Evil
author: 17 Charles Baudelaire

Flower State
nickname of: 7 Florida

flowery 5 fancy 6 floral, florid, ornate 8 blooming 10 blossoming, burgeoning, euphuistic, figurative, florescent, ornamental, rhetorical 11 embellished 12 efflorescent, magniloquent 13 grandiloquent

Flowery Kingdom see 5 China

flowing 4 flux 5 fluid 6 ebbing, fluent, smooth 7 current, copious, gliding, running 8 abundant 9 liquefied, plentiful 10 continuity, pouring out, proceeding

fluctuate 4 sway, vary, veer 5 shift, swing, waver 6 dawdle, falter, wobble 8 hesitate, undulate 9 alternate, oscillate, vacillate 10 dillydally

fluctuation 5 shift 6 change 7 veering 8 shifting, swinging 9 deviation, variation 11 alternation, oscillation, vacillation

flue 3 net 4 barb, down, pipe, tube, vent 5 fluff, fluke, shaft 6 funnel 7 channel, chimney, passage 9 smokejack

fluent 4 glib 5 vocal 6 facile 7 voluble 8 effusive, eloquent 9 garrulous, talkative 10 articulate, effortless

fluff 3 err, nap 4 down, flub, fuzz, lint, miss, puff, slip, soft 5 botch, floss, froth, primp 6 forget 7 blunder 8 feathers

fluffy 5 downy, fuzzy, nappy, wooly 6 fleecy, woolly 8 feathery

fluid 6 liquid, watery 7 unfixed 8 flexible, floating, shifting, solution, unsettled 9 adaptable, liquefied, unsettled 10 adjustable, changeable, indefinite

fluid ounce
abbreviation: 4 fl oz

fluke 3 hap 5 freak 6 chance 7 miracle 8 accident, windfall 9 mischance 11 vicissitude 12 stroke of luck

flummery 7 dessert, pudding 9 gibberish 10 doubletalk, mumbo jumbo 11 obfuscation

flunky 6 lackey, menial, minion 7 servant 9 attendant, underling

fluorine
chemical symbol: 1 F

flurry 3 ado 4 fuss, gust, heat, puff, stir 5 alarm, fever, flush, haste, panic 6 breeze, bustle, pother, rattle, shower, squall, tumult 7 agitate, confuse, disturb, fidgets, fluster, flutter, perturb 8 confound, disquiet 9 agitation, commotion, confusion 10 discompose, disconcert, turbulence 11 disturbance, hurry-scurry, trepidation 12 discomposure, perturbation, restlessness

flush 4 even, glow, swab, tint, wash 5 bloom, blush, color, elate, flood, level, rinse, scour, scrub, shock, spray 6 access, dampen, deluge, douche, drench, excite, puff up, quiver, redden, sponge, thrill, tremor 7 animate, flutter, glowing, impulse, moisten, redness, wash out 8 rosiness, rosy glow, squarely, strength 9 freshness, make proud, ruddiness 10 exultation, jubilation

flushed 3 hot, red 4 rosy, ruby 5 aglow, 6 florid, torrid 7 crimson, excited, scarlet 8 blushing, feverish 10 prosperous

flushed with success 5 proud 6 elated

fluster 4 daze 5 shake, upset 6 dither, flurry, hubbub, muddle, ruffle 7 agitate, confuse, disturb, flutter, perplex, perturb, startle, turmoil 8 befuddle, bewilder 9 agitation, commotion, confusion, discomfit 10 discompose, disconcert 12 bewilderment, discomfiture, discomposure 14 discombobulate

flute 4 fife, fold, pipe, roll, tube, wind 5 crimp 6 furrow, groove 7 piccolo, whistle 8 recorder 9 wine glass 14 champagne glass

flutter 3 bob 4 flap, flit, soar, stir, wave, wing 5 hurry, shake, throb 6 flurry, quiver, ripple, thrill, tremor, wobble 7 beating, flitter, fluster, pulsate, tremble, twitter 8 flapping, tingling 9 agitation, commotion, confusion, palpitate, sensation, vibration 12 perturbation

fluvial 7 aquatic

fluviatile 7 aquatic

flux 4 flow, tide 5 flood 6 course, motion, stream, unrest 7 current 8 mutation, shifting 10 alteration, transition 11 fluctuation 12 modification 14 transformation

fly 4 flap, flee, sail, skip, soar, wave, wing 5 coast, float, glide, hover, hurry, split, swoop 6 hasten, hustle 7 flutter, run away, take off, vibrate 8 take wing, undulate

fly
   varieties: 3 bat, bot 4 blow, deer, dung, gnat, horn, moth, rust, sand 5 beach, black, crane, dance, drone, flesh, fruit, horse, house, march, marsh, midge, mydas, punky 6 bee fly, cactus, maggot, pomace, robber, stable, tsetse, warble, window 7 chalcid, seaweed, skipper, soldier, tachina 8 lousefly, mosquito, stiletto 9 leaf miner 10 flat-footed, fungus gnat, humpbacked 11 thickheaded 14 black scavenger

fly apart 5 burst 6 blow up 7 explode, shatter 8 detonate, fragment

fly at 6 assail, attack

fly-by-night 5 shady 6 shifty 7 crooked 8 unstable, untrusty 9 dishonest 10 unreliable 12 disreputable, undependable 13 irresponsible, untrustworthy

Flying Dutchman, The
   opera by: 6 Wagner
   character: 4 Erik 5 Senta 6 Daland 11 The Dutchman

Flying Fish
   constellation of: 6 Volans

Flying Nun, The
   character: 9 Sister Ana 11 Sister Sixto 13 Carlos Ramirez 14 Mother Superior 15 Sister Bertrille 16 Sister Jacqueline
   cast: 10 Sally Field 12 Alejandro Rey, Linda Dangcil, Marge Redmond 14 Shelly Morrison 17 Madeleine Sherwood

fly in the ointment 5 hitch 7 problem, trouble 8 drawback, nuisance 9 hindrance 10 impediment 12 disadvantage

Flynn, Errol
   real name: 17 Leslie Thomas Flynn
   born: 6 Hobart 8 Tasmania
   roles: 10 The Sea Hawk 12 Captain Blood 14 Too Much Too Soon 15 The Sun Also Rises 24 The Adventures of Robin Hood 26 The Charge of the Light Brigade

fly off the handle 6 see red

fly the coop 4 bolt, flee 6 escape, run off 7 abscond, get away, make off, run away, skip out, take off

foal 4 cade, colt 5 filly, young 9 fledgling

foam 4 fizz, head, scum, suds 5 froth, spume 6 lather 7 sparkle 8 bubbling 13 effervescence

foaming 5 sudsy 6 bubbly, frothy 7 lathery 8 bubbling, frothing

foamy 5 fizzy 6 frothy 7 lathery 8 bubbling 9 sparkling 12 effervescent

fob 5 chain, medal, strap 6 ribbon 8 ornament 9 medallion

focal 3 key 4 main 5 chief 7 central, pivotal 8 foremost 9 principal

Foch, Ferdinand
   served in: 3 WWI
   nationality: 6 French
   rank: 7 marshal 16 commander-in-chief
   battle: 5 Marne, Somme

Foch, Nina
   real name: 20 Nina Consuelo Maud Fock
   born: 6 Leyden 11 Netherlands
   roles: 9 Spartacus 14 Executive Suite, Song to Remember 17 An American in Paris, My Name Is Julia Ross 18 The Ten Commandments

Fock, Nina Consuelo Maud
   real name of: 8 Nina Foch

focus 3 aim, fix, hub 4 core 5 haunt, heart 6 adjust, center, direct, middle, resort 7 nucleus, retreat 8 converge 9 limelight, spotlight 10 rendezvous 11 concentrate 12 headquarters

focusing 6 aiming 9 adjusting, centering, directing 10 adjustment, converging 11 pinpointing 13 concentrating

fodder 4 feed, food 6 forage, silage 7 rations 9 provender

foe 5 enemy, rival 8 attacker, opponent 9 adversary, assailant, combatant, contender, disputant 10 antagonist, competitor

fog 3 dim 4 daze, haze, smog, soup 5 brume, cloud 6 darken, muddle, stupor, trance 7 confuse, obscure, pea soup, perplex 8 bewilder 9 murkiness 10 cloudiness 12 bewilderment

Fogg, Phileas
   character in: 26 Around the World in Eighty Days
   author: 10 Jules Verne

foggy 3 dim 4 dark, hazy 5 dusky, filmy, fuzzy, misty, murky, musty, soupy, vague 6 cloudy, smoggy, spacey 7 brumous, clouded, obscure, shadowy, unclear 8 confused, nebulous, overcast, vaporous 9 beclouded 10 indistinct

foible 4 kink 5 quirk 6 defect, whimsy 7 failing, frailty 8 crotchet, weak side, weakness 9 infirmity 10 deficiency 11 shortcoming 12 imperfection

Foible
  character in: 16 The Way of the World
  author: 8 Congreve

foil 3 nip 4 balk, film, leaf 5 check, flake, match, sheet, wafer 6 hinder, lamina, set off, thwart 7 enhance, prevent 8 backdrop, contrast 9 frustrate 10 antithesis, complement, supplement 11 correlative, counterpart

foist 6 impose, unload 7 palm off, pass off

fold 3 hug, lap, pen, sty 4 bend, curl, sect, tuck, wrap, yard 5 clasp, close, crimp, flock, group, layer, pleat 6 corral, crease, dog-ear, double, encase, enfold, furrow, gather, parish, pucker, ruffle, rumple, wrap up 7 crinkle, crumple, embosom, embrace, entwine, envelop, flounce, overlap, wrinkle 8 barnyard, compound, doubling, stockade 9 community, corrugate, enclosure 12 congregation

folder 7 booklet, leaflet 8 brochure, circular, pamphlet 9 portfolio

foliage 6 leaves 7 leafage, verdure

folklore 5 myths 6 fables 7 legends 10 traditions

folks 3 kin 6 family, people 7 kinsmen, parents 8 everyone 9 relatives 10 kith and kin

folksy 6 casual, chatty 8 familiar, friendly, homespun, informal, sociable 10 neighborly 14 conversational 15 unsophisticated

folk tale
  German: 7 Marchen

Follett, Ken
  author of: 14 Eye of the Needle 15 On Wings of Eagles, The Key to Rebecca 22 The Man from St Petersburg

follow 3 dog 4 copy, heed, hunt, mind, note, obey, tail 5 aim at, chase, grasp, hound, stalk, trace, track, trail, watch 6 attend, notice, pursue, regard, shadow, take up 7 cherish, emulate, imitate, observe, replace, succeed 8 practice, supplant 9 accompany, cultivate, prosecute 10 comprehend, understand

follower 3 fan 4 tail 5 pupil, toady 6 chaser, hunter, shadow, stooge 7 admirer, apostle, convert, devotee, protege, pursuer, servant, stalker 8 adherent, advocate, disciple, hanger-on, henchman, parasite, partisan, retainer, servitor 9 accessory, attendant, dependent, proselyte, satellite, supporter, sycophant

following 4 next 5 below, suite, train 6 public 7 ensuing, retinue 8 audience 9 adherents, clientele, entourage, partisans, patronage 10 attendance, consequent, sequential, subsequent, succeeding, successive 11 consecutive

Follow the Fleet
  director: 12 Mark Sandrich
  cast: 11 Fred Astaire 12 Ginger Rogers 13 Randolph Scott 21 Harriet Hilliard Nelson

song: 11 We Saw the Sea 13 Let Yourself Go 24 Let's Face the Music and Dance

follow-up 7 ensuing 8 sequence 9 aftermath 10 subsequent

folly 6 idiocy, levity 7 inanity, mistake 8 nonsense, trifling 9 absurdity, asininity, frivolity, giddiness, silliness 10 imbecility, imprudence, tomfoolery 11 doltishness, fatuousness, foolishness 12 indiscretion 13 brainlessness, irrationality, senselessness

foment 4 goad, spur, urge 5 rouse 6 arouse, excite, foster, incite, kindle, stir up 7 agitate, inflame, promote, provoke, quicken 8 irritate 9 aggravate, galvanize, instigate, stimulate 10 exacerbate

Fomorian
  origin: 5 Irish
  form: 5 demon 6 pirate
  habitat: 3 sea
  raided: 7 Ireland
  personifies: 13 hostile nature

fond 5 naive 6 ardent, doting, loving, tender 7 amorous, devoted 8 desirous, enamored, harbored, held dear 9 cherished, indulgent, preserved, sustained 10 infatuated, passionate 11 impassioned, sentimental 12 affectionate 16 overaffectionate

Fonda, Henry
  wife: 16 Margaret Sullavan
  son: 5 Peter
  daughter: 4 Jane
  born: 13 Grand Island NE
  roles: 7 Jezebel, Warlock 8 Fail Safe 10 Fort Apache, In Harm's Way, The Best Man, The Lady Eve 12 On Golden Pond (Oscar) 13 Mister Roberts, Ox-Bow Incident, The Longest Day 14 Twelve Angry Men, Young Mr Lincoln 16 Advise and Consent, Battle of the Bulge, How the West Was Won, The Grapes of Wrath 18 The Boston Strangler 19 My Darling Clementine, The Immortal Sergeant 21 Sometimes a Great Notion

Fonda, Jane
  father: 5 Henry
  brother: 5 Peter
  husband: 9 Ted Turner, Tom Hayden 10 Roger Vadim
  born: 9 New York NY
  roles: 5 Julia, Klute (Oscar) 10 Barbarella, Coming Home (Oscar) 11 A Doll's House 12 Any Wednesday, On Golden Pond 13 China Syndrome 17 Barefoot in the Park 23 They Shoot Horses Don't They?

Fonda, Peter
  father: 5 Henry
  sister: 4 Jane
  born: 9 New York NY
  roles: 7 The Trip 9 Easy Rider 13 The Wild Angels

fondle 3 hug, pet 5 spoon 6 caress, cuddle, nestle, nuzzle, smooch, stroke 7 embrace, make out 10 bill and coo

fondness 4 bent, care, love 5 ardor, fancy 6 desire, liking 7 passion 8 devotion, penchant, weakness 9 affection 10 attachment, partiality, preference, propensity, tenderness 11 amorousness, inclination 12 predilection 14 susceptibility

fond utterance 9 sweet talk 10 endearment 12 sweet nothing

Fons
  origin: 5 Roman
  god of: 7 springs

fons et origo 15 source and origin

Fontaine, Joan
  real name: 25 Joan de Beauvoir de Havilland
  sister: 17 Olivia de Havilland
  husband: 11 Brian Aherne
  born: 5 Japan, Tokyo
  roles: 3 Ivy 7 Ivanhoe, Rebecca 8 Casanova, Gunga Din, Jane Eyre, The Women 9 Suspicion (Oscar) 12 The Devil's Own 15 Frenchman's Creek, September Affair 16 Tender Is the Night, The Constant Nymph

Fontanne, Lynn
  husband: 10 Alfred Lunt
  born: 6 London 7 England
  roles: 8 The Visit 9 Quadrille, The Pirate 10 The Sea Gull 13 O Mistress Mine 15 Design for Living 18 The Great Sebastians 19 The Taming of the Shrew

food 4 chow, feed, grub 5 board 6 fodder, forage, silage, viands 7 edibles, nurture, pasture, rations 8 eatables, victuals 9 nutrition, pasturage, provender 10 provisions, sustenance 11 comestibles, nourishment, subsistence

food, miraculous 5 manna

fool 3 ass, con, oaf 4 bilk, clod, dolt, dupe, gull, hoax, jest, joke 5 cheat, chump, clown, cozen, cut up, dummy, dunce, feign, goose, idiot, klutz, moron, ninny, tease, trick 6 diddle, fleece, frolic, humbug, jester, nitwit, rip off, stooge 7 beguile, buffoon, deceive, defraud, half-wit, Pierrot, pretend 8 bonehead, dummkopf, flimflam, hoodwink, imbecile, lunkhead, meathead, numskull 9 bamboozle, blockhead, harlequin, ignoramus, numbskull, simpleton 10 dunderhead, nincompoop, scaramouch 11 Punchinello

fool around 3 toy 4 idle 5 clown, dally 6 dawdle, loiter, trifle

foolhardy 4 rash 5 brash, hasty 6 madcap 8 careless, heedless, reckless 9 daredevil, hotheaded, impetuous, imprudent, impulsive 10 headstrong, incautious 11 harebrained, thoughtless

foolish 5 inane, silly 6 absurd, stupid, unwise 7 asinine, fatuous, idiotic, moronic, witless 9 brainless, imbecilic, imprudent, ludicrous, senseless 10 boneheaded, incautious, indiscreet, ridiculous 12 preposterous 13 irresponsible, unintelligent

foolishness 5 folly 6 idiocy, lunacy 8 unwisdom 9 absurdity, asininity, puerility, silliness, stupidity 10 imbecility, imprudence

11 fatuousness, witlessness 12 childishness, extravagance, indiscretion 13 brainlessness, senselessness 14 ridiculousness 15 injudiciousness 16 irresponsibility, preposterousness

Fool of Quality, The
  author: 11 Henry Brooke

foot 3 dog, pad, paw 4 base, hoof 6 bottom, tootsy 7 trotter 8 infantry 10 foundation
  abbreviation: 2 ft

football
  term: 3 end 4 bomb, down, draw, flat, punt, sack 5 blitz, guard, zebra 6 center, fumble, option, pocket, safety, tackle 7 audible, bootleg, flanker, holding, kickoff, lateral, offside, platoon, reverse, rollout, shotgun 8 clipping, gridiron, halfback, turnover 9 crackback, field goal, nose guard, scrimmage, touchback 10 conversion, cornerback, linebacker, nose tackle 11 quarterback 12 encroachment

Hall of Fame:
  1963: 4 Bell (Bert), Carr (Joe), Hein (Mel), Mara (Tim) 5 Baugh (Sammy), Clark (Dutch), Halas (George), Henry (Pete) 6 Hutson (Don), Nevers (Ernie), Thorpe (Jim) 7 Hubbard (Cal), Lambeau (Curly), McNally (John Blood) 8 Nagurski (Bronko), Marshall (George P)
  1964: 5 Lyman (Link) 6 Healey (Ed), Hinkle (Clarke), Rooney (Art) 7 Trafton (George) 9 Conzelman (Jimmy), Michalske (Mike)
  1965: 6 Graham (Otto), Grange (Red) 7 Luckman (Sid) 8 Driscoll (Paddy), Fortmann (Daniel J), Van Buren (Steve) 10 Chamberlin (Guy), Waterfield (Bob)
  1966: 3 Ray (Hugh "Shorty") 5 Guyon (Joe), Owens (Steve) 6 Dudley (Bill), Herber (Arnie), McAfee (George), Turner (Clyde "Bulldog") 8 Kiesling (Walt)
  1967: 5 Brown (Paul E), Layne (Bobby) 6 Reeves (Dan), Strong (Ken) 7 Bidwill (Charles W), Tunnell (Emlen) 8 Bednarik (Chuck), Stydahar (Joe)
  1968: 6 Hirsch (Elroy), Motley (Marion), Trippi (Charley) 7 Battles (Cliff), Donovan (Art), Millner (Wayne) 13 Wojciechowicz (Alex)
  1969: 5 Neale (Earle "Greasy"), Perry (Joe) 7 Edwards (Albert Glen "Turk") 8 Stautner (Ernie) 9 Nomellini (Leo)
  1970: 5 Fears (Tom), Pihos (Pete) 9 McElhenny (Hugh) 12 Christiansen (Jack)
  1971: 5 Brown (Jim) 6 Hewitt (Bill), Kinard (Frank "Bruiser"), Tittle (Y A) 8 Lombardi (Vince) 10 Robustelli (Andy) 11 Van Brocklin (Norm)
  1972: 4 Hunt (Lamar) 6 Matson (Ollie), Parker (Ace) 9 Marchetti (Gino)
  1973: 5 Berry (Raymond) 6 Parker (Jim) 7 Schmidt (Joe)
  1974: 4 Lane (Dick "Night Train") 5 Groza (Lou "The Toe") 6 George (Bill) 7 Canadeo (Tony)

1975: 5 Brown (Roosevelt), Moore (Lenny) 6 Connor (George) 7 Lavelli (Dante)
1976: 4 Ford (Len) 6 Taylor (Jim) 8 Flaherty (Ray)
1977: 5 Gregg (Forrest), Starr (Bart) 6 Sayers (Gale), Willis (Bill) 7 Gifford (Frank)
1978: 6 Ewbank (Weeb), Wilson (Larry) 7 Alworth (Lance), Leemans (Tuffy) 8 Nitschke (Ray)
1979: 3 Mix (Ron) 4 Lary (Yale) 6 Butkus (Dick), Unitas (Johnny)
1980: 4 Otto (Jim) 5 Jones (David "Deacon"), Lilly (Bob) 8 Adderley (Herb)
1981: 5 Davis (Willie), Ringo (Jim) 6 Badgro (Morris "Red"), Blanda (George)
1982: 4 Huff (Sam) 5 Musso (George), Olsen (Merlin) 6 Atkins (Doug)
1983: 4 Bell (Bobby) 6 Gilman (Sid) 8 Mitchell (Bobby), Warfield (Paul) 9 Jurgensen (Sonny)
1984: 5 Brown (Willie) 6 Taylor (Charley) 9 McCormack (Mike) 11 Weinmeister (Arnie)
1985: 6 Gatski (Frank), Namath (Joe) 7 Rozelle (Pete), Simpson (OJ) 8 Staubach (Roger)
1986: 6 Lanier (Willie), Walker (Doak) 7 Hornung (Paul), Houston (Ken) 9 Tarkenton (Fran)
1987: 6 Csonka (Larry), Dawson (Len), Greene (Joe), Langer (Jim), Upshaw (Gene) 7 Johnson (John Henry), Maynard (Don)
1988: 3 Ham (Jack) 4 Page (Alan) 5 Ditka (Mike) 11 Biletnikoff (Fred)
1989: 4 Wood (Willie) 5 Shell (Art) 6 Blount (Mel) 8 Bradshaw (Terry)
1990: 6 Griese (Bob), Harris (Franco), Landry (Tom) 7 Lambert (Jack), St Clair (Bob) 8 Buchanan (Buck) 9 Hendricks (Ted)
1991: 5 Jones (Stan) 6 Hannah (John) 7 Schramm (Tex) 8 Campbell (Earl), Stenerud (Jan)
1992: 5 Davis (Al) 6 Barney (Lem), Mackey (John) 7 Riggins (John)
1993: 6 Noll (Chuck) 5 Fouts (Dan), Walsh (Bill) 6 Little (Larry), Payton (Walter)
1994: 5 Grant (Bud), Kelly (Leroy), Smith (Jackie), White (Randy) 7 Dorsett (Tony), Johnson (Jimmy)
other player/coach: 8 Don Shula, Kyle Rote 9 Amos Stagg, Dan Marino, Earl Blaik, Jerry Rice, Lou Little, 10 Bear Bryant, Bruce Smith, Bubba Smith, Joe Montana, Joe Paterno, Ken Stabler, Larry Brown, Troy Aikman, Walter Camp 11 Ahmad Rashad, Craig Morton, Deion Sanders, Earl Morrall, Floyd Little, Jim Plunkett, Knute Rockne, Reggie White 12 Bud Wilkinson, Joe Thiesmann, Ozzie Newsome, Roman Gabriel, William Perry 13 Ara Parseghian, Eric Dickerson, 14 Lawrence Taylor, Lydell Mitchell

football bowl games 3 Sun 4 Rose 5 Aloha, Gator, Peach, Sugar, Super 6 Citrus, Copper, Cotton, Fiesta, Orange 7 Holiday, Liberty 10 Bluebonnet, California 12 Independence

football leagues
National Football League (NFL): 11 New York Jets 12 Buffalo Bills, Chicago Bears, Detroit Lions 13 Dallas Cowboys, Denver Broncos, Houston Oilers, Miami Dolphins, New York Giants 14 Atlanta Falcons, Los Angeles Rams 15 Cleveland Browns, Green Bay Packers, Seattle Seahawks 16 Kansas City Chiefs, Minnesota Vikings, New Orleans Saints, Phoenix Cardinals (formerly St Louis), San Diego Chargers 17 Cincinnati Bengals, Indianapolis Colts (formerly Baltimore), Los Angeles Raiders (formerly Oakland) 18 New England Patriots, Philadelphia Eagles, Pittsburgh Steelers, Tampa Bay Buccaneers, Washington Redskins 23 San Francisco Forty-Niners

United States Football League (USFL): 10 Denver Gold 12 Chicago Blitz 14 Baltimore Stars, Boston Breakers 15 Houston Gamblers, Oakland Invaders, Oklahoma Outlaws, Tampa Bay Bandits 16 Arizona Wranglers, Memphis Showboats, Michigan Panthers, Orlando Renegades, Portland Breakers 17 Jacksonville Bulls, Los Angeles Express, New Jersey Generals, Philadelphia Stars 18 Washington Federals 19 Birmingham Stallions 21 San Antonio Gunslingers

football team (NFC)
Atlanta: 7 Falcons
stadium: 11 Georgia Dome
Chicago: 5 Bears
stadium: 12 Soldier Field
Dallas: 7 Cowboys
stadium: 5 Texas
Detroit: 5 Lions
stadium: 17 Pontiac Silverdome
Green Bay: 7 Packers
stadium: 9 Milwaukee 12 Lambeau Field
Los Angeles: 4 Rams
stadium: 7 Anaheim
Minnesota: 7 Vikings
stadium: 9 Metrodome
New Orleans: 6 Saints
stadium: 18 Louisiana Superdome
New York: 6 Giants
stadium: 6 Giants
Philadelphia: 6 Eagles
stadium: 8 Veterans
Phoenix: 9 Cardinals
stadium: 8 Sun Devil
formerly in: 7 St Louis
San Francisco: 11 Forty-Niners
stadium: 15 Candlestick Park
Tampa Bay: 10 Buccaneers
stadium: 5 Tampa
Washington: 8 Redskins
stadium: 14 Robert F Kennedy

football team (AFC)
Buffalo: 5 Bills
stadium: 4 Rich
Cincinnati: 7 Bengals
stadium: 10 Riverfront
Cleveland: 6 Browns
stadium: 9 Cleveland
Denver: 7 Broncos
stadium: 8 Mile High
Houston: 6 Oilers
stadium: 9 Astrodome
Indianapolis: 5 Colts
stadium: 11 Hoosier Dome
formerly in: 9 Baltimore
Kansas City: 6 Chiefs
stadium: 9 Arrowhead
Los Angeles: 7 Raiders
stadium: 16 Memorial Coliseum
formerly in: 7 Oakland
Miami: 8 Dolphins
stadium: 9 Joe Robbie
New England: 8 Patriots
stadium: 7 Foxboro
New York: 4 Jets
stadium: 6 Giants
Pittsburgh: 8 Steelers
stadium: 11 Three Rivers
San Diego: 8 Chargers
stadium: 8 San Diego
Seattle: 8 Seahawks
stadium: 8 Kingdome

footfall 3 pad 4 pace, step 5 tread 8 footstep

foothold 4 grip, hold 7 support 8 purchase

footloose 4 free 8 carefree 9 fancy-free 10 unattached 11 uncommitted 12 unencumbered

footnote 5 gloss 9 reference 10 annotation 11 explanation 12 afterthought

footpad 5 thief 6 bandit, mugger, outlaw, robber 10 highwayman

footpath 4 lane, ramp 5 jetty, trail 8 sidewalk

foot soldiers 8 infantry 10 fusilliers, musketeers

footstool 6 buffet 7 hassock, ottoman 8 footrest

footwear
French: 9 chaussure

fop 4 beau, dude 5 dandy, swell 7 coxcomb 8 popinjay 9 prettyboy 11 Beau Brummel

foppish 4 vain 5 gaudy, showy 6 ornate 7 finical 8 affected, dandyish 9 dandified 12 ostentatious 13 overelaborate

forage 4 feed, food, hunt, raid, seek 6 fodder, ravage, search, silage 7 despoil, explore, pasture, plunder, rummage 8 scavenge, scrounge 9 pasturage, provender 10 provisions

foray 4 raid 5 sally 6 attack, inroad, invade, ravage, thrust 7 pillage, plunder, venture 8 invasion 9 incursion 10 expedition 11 depredation

forbear 4 quit, stop 5 cease, forgo 6 desist, endure, eschew, forego, give up, suffer 7 abstain, refrain 8 abnegate, renounce, tolerate

forbearance 4 pity 5 mercy 6 pardon 8 clemency, eschewal, leniency, meekness, mildness, patience 9 endurance, tolerance 10 abstention, abstinence, continence, indulgence, moderation, submission, temperance 11 longanimity, resignation 12 mercifulness

forbearing 6 denial 7 lenient, refusal 8 eschewal, tolerant 9 indulgent 10 abnegation, abstention, abstinence, permissive, refraining 13 nonindulgence 16 nonparticipation

forbid 3 ban, bar 4 veto 5 taboo 6 enjoin, hinder, impede, oppose, refuse, reject 7 exclude, gainsay, inhibit, obviate, prevent 8 disallow, obstruct, preclude, prohibit, restrain 9 interdict, proscribe

forbiddance 3 ban 5 taboo 7 barring, embargo 9 exclusion, interdict 11 prohibition 12 interdiction, proscription

forbidden 5 taboo 6 banned 8 debarred 10 prohibited, proscribed
German: 8 verboten

forbidden fruit
type: 6 brandy 7 liqueur
origin: 7 America
flavor: 5 honey 6 orange 10 grapefruit

forbidden marriage
goddess of: 4 Lofn

forbidding 4 dour, grim, ugly 6 odious 7 hideous, ominous 8 horrible, sinister 9 abhorrent, offensive, repellent, repulsive 10 unfriendly, unpleasant 11 prohibitive, prohibitory, threatening 12 disagreeable, inhospitable 14 unapproachable

force 3 pry, vim 4 army, body, coax, crew, drag, gang, make, pull, push, team, unit, urge 5 break, clout, corps, drive, group, impel, might, power, press, squad, value, vigor, wrest 6 coerce, compel, duress, effect, elicit, energy, enjoin, extort, impact, import, impose, induce, oblige, propel, stress, thrust, weight, wrench 7 cogency, intrude, meaning, obtrude, potency, require, squeeze, stamina 8 charisma, coercion, division, efficacy, emphasis, momentum, persuade, pressure, squadron, strength, validity, violence, vitality 9 animation, battalion, constrain, magnetism, overpower, puissance 10 attraction, compulsion, constraint, detachment 11 necessitate, weightiness 12 significance 13 effectiveness
Latin: 3 vis

forced 5 slave 7 binding, coerced, labored, obliged 8 affected, enslaved, grudging, mannered, required, strained 9 compelled, impressed, insincere, mandatory, unwilling 10 artificial, compulsory, obligatory 11 constrained, involuntary

forceful 5 pithy, valid, vivid **6** cogent, potent, robust, strong, virile **7** dynamic, intense **8** emphatic, powerful, puissant, vigorous **9** effective, energetic **10** impressive

forceless 4 weak **8** impotent

force measurement 4 dyne **6** newton **7** poundal

Force of Circumstance
　author: **16** Simone de Beauvoir

Force of Destiny, The
　also: **17** La Forza del Destino
　opera by: **5** Verdi
　character: **7** Leonora **8** Don Carlo **9** Don Alvaro

forcible 8 coercive **10** compulsory

ford 3 car **4** span, wade **5** cross, edsel, shoal **6** bridge, model T, stream **7** passage **8** crossing, tin lizzy

Ford, Gerald Rudolph
　born: **17** Leslie Lynch King Jr
　adopted by/named after: **10** stepfather
　nickname: **5** Jerry **7** Mr Clean
　presidential rank: **12** thirty-eighth
　party: **10** Republican
　state represented: **2** MI
　defeated: **5** no one
　elected to neither: **10** presidency **14** vice presidency
　vice president: **11** (Nelson A) Rockefeller
　cabinet:
　　state: **9** (Henry A) Kissinger
　　treasury: **5** (William E) Simon
　　defense: **8** (Donald H) Rumsfeld **11** (James) Schlesinger
　　attorney general: **4** (Edward H) Levi **5** (William B) Saxbe
　　interior: **6** (Rogers Clark Ballard) Morton, (Thomas S) Kleppe **8** (Stanley K) Hathaway
　　agriculture: **4** (Earl Lauer) Butz **6** (John A) Knebel
　　commerce: **4** (Frederick B) Dent **6** (Rogers Clark Ballard) Morton **10** (Elliot L) Richardson
　　labor: **5** (W J) Usery (Jr) **6** (John T) Dunlop **7** (Peter J) Brennan
　　HEW: **7** (F David) Mathews **10** (Caspar W) Weinberger
　　HUD: **4** (James T) Lynn **5** (Carla Anderson) Hills
　　transportation: **7** (William T) Coleman (Jr) **8** (Claude S) Brinegar
　born: **7** Omaha NE
　education:
　　University: **8** Michigan
　　Law School: **4** Yale
　religion: **12** Episcopalian
　interests: **4** golf **6** boxing, skiing **8** football, swimming
　vacation spot: **2** CO **4** Vail
　author: **21** Portrait of the Assassin (with John R Stiles) **27** A Time To Heal: An Autobiography
　political career: **13** vice president **19** House minority leader **24** US House of Representatives

　civilian career: **6** lawyer
　assistant football coach at: **4** Yale
　military service: **6** US Navy **10** lieutenant, World War II
　notable events of lifetime/term: **9** recession **12** Bicentennial
　assassination attempts on: **4** Ford
　clemency for: **12** draft dodgers, draft evaders
　kidnapping/trial/conviction of: **11** Patty Hearst
　scandal: **8** Lockheed **10** Hays Affair
　talks: **4** SALT
　quotes: **19** I am a Ford not a Lincoln **41** Indebted to no man—the president of all the people **50** Our long national nightmare is over Our constitution works
　father:
　　natural: **15** Leslie Lynch King
　　adoptive: **17** Gerald Rudolph Ford
　mother: **7** Dorothy (Gardner King Ford)
　siblings:
　　half-brothers: **12** James Francis **13** Thomas Gardner **14** Richard Addison
　wife: **9** Elizabeth (Bloomer Warren)
　　nickname: **5** Betty
　children: **4** John **5** Susan **6** Steven **7** Michael

Ford, Glenn
　real name: **11** Gwyllyn Ford
　wife: **13** Eleanor Powell
　born: **6** Canada, Quebec
　roles: **4** Rage **5** Gilda, Jubal **6** Santee **8** Cimarron **11** The Rounders **14** Is Paris Burning? **17** Interrupted Melody **18** Don't Go Near the Water **19** The Blackboard Jungle **23** Teahouse of the August Moon

Ford, Harrison
　born: **9** Chicago IL
　roles: **7** Frantic, Witness **8** Star Wars **11** Blade Runner **15** Return of the Jedi **16** American Graffiti **19** Raiders of the Lost Ark **20** The Empire Strikes Back **30** Indiana Jones and the Temple of Doom

Ford, John
　author of: **13** Perkin Warbeck **17** 'Tis Pity She's a Whore **19** The Lover's Melancholy

Ford, John
　director of: **10** Stagecoach **11** The Informer (Oscar), The Quiet Man (Oscar) **12** The Hurricane, The Searchers **13** Grapes of Wrath (Oscar), Mister Roberts (with Mervyn LeRoy), The Lost Patrol **17** The Long Voyage Home **19** How Green Was My Valley (Oscar), My Darling Clementine **27** The Man Who Shot Liberty Valence

Ford, Thelma Booth
　real name of: **12** Shirley Booth

Ford and Mistress Ford
　characters in: **22** The Merry Wives of Windsor
　author: **11** Shakespeare

fore 5 front 7 frontal 8 anterior, headmost

forearm 4 ulna 5 prime, ready 7 prepare

forebear 6 ancestor, begetter 10 antecedent, procreator, progenitor

foreboding 4 omen 5 dread 6 augury, boding 7 portent 9 intuition, misgiving 10 prescience, prognostic 11 premonition 12 apprehension, presentiment

forecast 5 augur 6 augury, divine, expect 7 outlook, portend, predict, presage, project 8 envisage, envision, prophesy 9 calculate, prevision, prognosis 10 anticipate, conjecture, prediction, prescience, projection 11 extrapolate 12 anticipation, precognition, presentiment 13 prognosticate 15 prognostication

forefather 6 author 8 ancestor, begetter 9 patriarch, precursor 10 antecedent, originator, procreator, progenitor 12 primogenitor

forefront 4 fame, head, lead 8 vanguard 9 celebrity

foreign 5 alien 6 exotic, remote 7 distant, strange, unknown, unusual 8 imported 9 barbarous, extrinsic, irregular, unrelated 10 extraneous, heathenish, introduced, irrelevant, outlandish, unfamiliar 11 incongruous, inconsonant, unconnected 12 antipathetic, inadmissible, inapplicable, incompatible, inconsistent 13 inappropriate 16 uncharacteristic

Foreign Correspondent
   director: 15 Alfred Hitchcock
   cast: 10 Joel McCrea, Laraine Day 13 George Sanders 14 Robert Benchley 15 Albert Basserman, Herbert Marshall

foreigner 5 alien, pagan 6 emigre 8 newcomer, outsider, stranger 9 barbarian, immigrant, nonnative, outlander
   German: 9 Auslander

foreign officer 6 consul 8 diplomat, minister 10 ambassador 14 representative 15 charge d'affaires

foreknowledge 9 intuition, prevision 10 prescience 11 premonition 12 anticipation, apprehension, clairvoyance, precognition, presentiment

foreman 4 boss 7 manager 8 chairman, overseer 9 president, spokesman 10 supervisor 11 coordinator 14 superintendent

foremost 4 head, main 5 chief, vital 7 capital, leading, supreme 8 cardinal 9 essential, paramount, principal 10 preeminent

forerunner 4 omen, sign 5 token 6 augury, herald 7 portent, presage 8 ancestor 9 harbinger, precursor, prototype 10 progenitor, prognostic 11 predecessor, premonition

foresee 5 augur 6 divine, expect 7 predict, presage 8 envision, prophesy 10 anticipate 13 prognosticate

foreshadow 5 augur 7 presage, promise 9 prefigure

foresight 6 wisdom 8 planning, prudence, sagacity 9 prevision 10 discretion, precaution, prescience, providence, shrewdness

12 anticipation, clairvoyance, perspicacity, precognition, preparedness 13 premeditation 14 farsightedness

forest 4 bush, wood 5 copse, grove, stand, woods 6 jungle 7 thicket 8 wildwood, woodland 10 timberland, wilderness

forestall 5 avert, avoid, block, deter 6 thwart 7 head off, obviate, prevent, ward off 8 preclude 10 anticipate, circumvent, counteract

Forester, C S (Cecil Scott)
   author of: 6 The Gun 14 A Ship of the Line 15 Payment Deferred, The African Queen 24 Captain Horatio Hornblower

forests
   god of: 3 Pan 7 Silenus, Virbius

foretell 5 augur 6 divine 7 portend, predict, presage 8 prophesy, soothsay 9 apprehend 13 prognosticate

forethought 4 heed 7 caution 8 prudence, sagacity, wariness 10 discretion, precaution, providence, shrewdness 11 carefulness 12 anticipation, deliberation 13 consideration, premeditation 14 circumspection, farsightedness

forever 6 always 9 eternally, undyingly 10 constantly 11 ceaselessly, continually, incessantly, perpetually, unceasingly 12 interminably 13 everlastingly, unremittingly
   Latin: 11 in perpetuum

forewarn 4 bode 5 alert 6 advise, notify, signal, tip off 7 caution, portend, presage, prewarn 8 cry havoc

foreword 7 preface, prelude 8 preamble, prologue 12 introduction

Forewords and Afterwords
   author: 7 W H Auden

for example
   Latin: 2 eg 13 exempli gratia

forfeit 4 fine, miss 5 waive, waste, yield 6 waiver 7 damages, default, let slip, penalty 8 squander 9 surrender 10 assessment

Forfeit
   author: 11 Dick Francis

forge 4 copy, form, make 5 clone, shape 6 devise, hearth, smithy 7 falsify, fashion, furnace, imitate, produce, turn out 8 contrive, simulate 9 fabricate, ironworks 11 counterfeit, manufacture

forgery 4 copy, fake, hoax, sham 5 clone, fraud 7 cloning 9 deception, imitation 11 counterfeit, fraudulence 13 falsification 14 counterfeiting 17 misrepresentation

forget 6 slight 7 neglect 8 overlook, pass over 9 disregard

forgetful 6 remiss 7 out of it 8 amnesiac, careless, heedless, mindless 9 negligent, oblivious, unmindful 10 neglectful 11 inattentive

forget-me-not 8 Myosotis
   varieties: 5 white 6 alpine, garden 7 Chinese 8 creeping

forgive 5 clear 6 acquit, excuse, pardon 7 absolve, condone, release, set free 8 overlook, reprieve 9 discharge, exculpate, exonerate

forgiveness 6 pardon 7 amnesty 9 remission 10 absolution

forgiving 6 benign, kindly 8 excusing 9 benignant, pardoning 11 kindhearted

forgo, forego 4 skip 5 waive, yield 6 eschew, give up 8 abnegate, renounce 9 sacrifice, surrender 10 relinquish

fork 4 bend, stab 5 angle, elbow, split 6 branch, crotch, divide, impale, pierce, ramify, skewer 7 diverge, trident 8 division 9 bifurcate, pitchfork 10 divergence, separation 11 bifurcation 12 intersection

forked 5 cleft 6 horned, zigzag 7 angular, divided, pronged 8 branched 9 ambiguous, deceitful, equivocal 10 bifurcated

For Kicks
　author: 11 Dick Francis

fork out 5 spend 6 expend 8 disburse, dispense

for lack of something better
　French: 12 faute de mieux

forlorn 4 lone 6 abject, bereft, dismal, dreary, lonely 7 unhappy 8 bereaved, dejected, deserted, desolate, forsaken, helpless, hopeless, lonesome, pathetic, pitiable, solitary, wretched 9 abandoned, depressed, desperate, destitute, forgotten, miserable, woebegone 10 despairing, despondent, dispirited, friendless 11 comfortless 12 disconsolate, inconsolable 13 brokenhearted

form 3 cut, hew, way 4 body, cast, kind, make, mode, mold, plan, rite, rule, sort, trim, type 5 being, brand, build, carve, class, forge, found, frame, genre, genus, guise, habit, image, model, order, phase, set up, shape, stamp, style, usage 6 aspect, chisel, create, custom, design, devise, fettle, figure, manner, matrix, person, ritual, sculpt, system 7 acquire, anatomy, compose, conduct, contour, decorum, develop, fashion, fitness, harmony, liturgy, manners, outline, pattern, produce, species, variety 8 ceremony, comprise, contract, likeness, practice, presence, rough-hew, symmetry 9 character, construct, establish, etiquette, fabricate, framework, propriety, sculpture, semblance, structure 10 appearance, constitute, deportment, figuration, proceeding, proportion, regularity 11 arrangement, description, incarnation, manufacture, orderliness, shapeliness 12 denomination 13 configuration, manifestation 15 conventionality

formal 4 cool, prim 5 aloof, fancy, fixed, grand, legal, rigid, smart, stiff 6 dressy, lawful, proper, solemn, strict 7 distant, outward, pompous, prudish, regular, settled, stilted, stylish 8 decorous, definite, explicit, external, official, positive, reserved, starched 9 customary 10 ceremonial, inflexible, prescribed 11 ceremonious, highfalutin, perfunctory, punctilious, ritualistic, standoffish, straitlaced 12 conventional 13 authoritative 14 uncompromising

formal discussion 6 debate, parley 8 dialogue 10 conference

formality 4 rite 6 custom, motion, ritual 7 decorum, reserve 8 ceremony, coolness 9 etiquette, propriety, punctilio 10 ceremonial, convention 15 conventionality

Forman, Milos
　director of: 7 Amadeus (Oscar), Ragtime 25 One Flew Over the Cuckoo's Nest (Oscar)

formation 3 set 6 makeup 7 genesis 8 building, creation 9 structure 10 generation, production 11 arrangement, composition, development, fabrication, manufacture 12 organization 13 configuration, constellation, establishment

formative 7 plastic, shaping 9 sensitive 10 accessible 11 susceptible 13 determinative 14 impressionable

former 2 ex 4 gone, past 5 olden, prior 6 bygone, gone by, lapsed, of yore, whilom 7 ancient, earlier, elapsed, old-time, quondam 8 anterior, previous 9 aforesaid, erstwhile, preceding 10 antecedent, first-named 14 aforementioned
　French: 8 ci-devant

formerly 4 once 5 of old 6 ere now, lately, of yore, whilom 7 long ago 8 hitherto 9 anciently 10 originally, previously

former student 6 alumna 7 alumnus, dropout 8 graduate

formidable 6 taxing 7 awesome, fearful, mammoth, onerous 8 alarming, dreadful, imposing, menacing, terrific 9 dangerous, demanding, difficult 10 forbidding, impressive, portentous, terrifying 11 threatening 12 overpowering, overwhelming

formless 5 vague 9 amorphous, shapeless

Formosa see 6 Taiwan

formula 4 cant, plan, rule 5 chant 6 cliche, recipe, saying, slogan 7 precept 9 blueprint, guideline, platitude, principle, rigmarole 10 pleasantry 11 incantation 12 prescription

formulate 5 draft, frame, state 6 define, devise, invent 7 compose, itemize, specify 11 systematize 13 particularize

Fornax
　origin: 5 Roman
　goddess of: 6 baking

fornication 8 adultery

for one's country
　Latin: 9 pro patria

Forrest, Nathan Bedford
　served in: 8 Civil War
　side: 11 Confederate
　known for: 12 cavalry raids

forsake 4 deny, drop, flee, quit 5 leave, spurn, waive, yield 6 abjure, depart, desert, give up, reject, resign, vacate 7 abandon, cast off, disavow, discard, lay down 8 abdicate, disclaim, go back on, jettison, part with, renounce 9 repudiate, surrender 10 relinquish

forsaken 4 bare 5 empty 8 deserted, desolate, rejected 9 abandoned, discarded, neglected 11 uninhabited

Forsete *see* 7 Forseti
Forseti
  also: 7 Forsete
  origin: 12 Scandinavian
  god of: 7 justice
  father: 5 Baldr 6 Balder, Baldur
  mother: 5 Nanna
  dwelling place: 7 Glitnir
Forster, E M (Edward Morgan)
  author of: 7 Maurice 10 Howard's End
  14 A Room with a View 15 A Passage to
  India 17 The Longest Journey 22 Where
  Angels Fear to Tread
  member of: 15 Bloomsbury Group
forswear, foreswear 4 deny 5 spurn 6 abjure, disown, eschew, give up, recant, reject, revoke 7 disavow, gainsay, retract 8 abdicate, disclaim, renounce, take back 9 disaffirm, repudiate 10 contravene
Forsyte Saga, The
  author: 14 John Galsworthy
  trilogy including: 5 To Let 10 In Chancery 16 The Man of Property
  character: 3 Jon 4 June 5 Fleur 6 Dartie 7 Annette 8 Winifred 9 Old Jolyon 11 Young Jolyon 12 Irene Forsyte 13 Soames Forsyte 14 Philip Bosinney
Forsythe, John
  real name: 17 John Lincoln Freund
  born: 12 Penn's Grove NJ
  roles: 5 Topaz 7 Dynasty, Madame X 11 In Cold Blood 14 Bachelor Father, Charlie's Angels 15 Blake Carrington 16 And Justice for All 19 The Trouble with Harry 23 Teahouse of the August Moon
fort 4 base, camp 6 castle 7 bastion, bulwark, citadel, station 8 fastness, garrison 10 stronghold
forte 4 bent 5 knack, skill 8 strength 9 specialty 11 proficiency
  music: 4 loud
  abbreviation: 1 f
forth 5 ahead 6 onward 7 outward
forthcoming 5 handy, on tap 6 at hand 7 helpful 8 imminent 9 available, impending 10 accessible, obtainable, openhanded 11 approaching, cooperative, prospective
for the greater glory of God
  Latin: 19 ad majorem Dei gloriam
for the public good
  Latin: 14 pro bono publico
for the time being
  Latin: 10 pro tempore
For the Time Being
  author: 7 W H Auden
for this purpose only
  Latin: 5 ad hoc
forthright 4 open 5 blunt, frank 6 candid, direct, openly 7 bluntly, frankly, up-front 8 candidly, directly, straight 9 outspoken 10 truthfully 11 outspokenly, plain-spoken 15 straightforward 17 straightforwardly
forthrightness 6 candor 7 honesty 8 openness 9 frankness, sincerity 19 straightforwardness

forthwith 6 at once, pronto 7 quickly 8 directly, in a jiffy, promptly, right off 9 instantly 11 immediately 12 straightaway
fortification 5 tower 7 bastion, bulwark, citadel, rampart 8 fortress, garrison 9 earthwork 10 breastwork, stronghold
fortify 4 lace 5 boost, brace, cheer 6 buoy up, enrich, harden, secure, shield, urge on 7 build up, bulwark, hearten, protect, shore up, stiffen, support, sustain 8 buttress, embolden, garrison, reassure 9 encourage, reinforce, stimulate 10 invigorate, strengthen
fortissimo
  music: 8 very loud
  abbreviation: 2 ff
fortitude 4 dash, grit, guts, sand 5 nerve, pluck, spunk, valor 6 daring, mettle, spirit 7 bravery, courage, heroism, prowess 8 backbone, boldness, firmness, tenacity 9 endurance, hardihood 10 resolution 11 intrepidity 12 fearlessness, resoluteness 13 dauntlessness, determination
Fortitude
  author: 11 Hugh Walpole
Fort-Lamy
  capital of: 4 Chad
fortress 7 bastion, bulwark, citadel, rampart 8 buttress 9 acropolis 10 stronghold
Fortress, The
  author: 11 Hugh Walpole
fortuitous 5 happy, lucky, stray 6 casual, chance, random 9 haphazard, hit-or-miss 10 accidental, incidental, undesigned, unexpected, unintended, unpurposed 11 inadvertent 12 adventitious 13 serendipitous, unintentional 14 unpremeditated
fortuity 6 chance 8 accident 12 happenstance
Fortuna
  origin: 5 Roman
  goddess of: 7 fortune
  corresponds to: 5 Tyche
fortunate 4 fair, rich, rosy 5 happy, lucky, palmy 6 benign, bright, timely 7 blessed, booming, favored, halcyon, well-off 8 well-to-do 9 favorable, opportune, promising 10 auspicious, convenient, felicitous, profitable, propitious, prosperous, successful 11 encouraging, flourishing 12 advantageous, providential
Fortunate Isles *see* 13 Canary Islands
Fortunato
  character in: 20 The Cask of Amontillado
  author: 3 Poe
fortune, fortunes 3 lot 4 doom, fate, luck, mint, pile, star 5 means 6 chance, estate, income, kismet, riches, wealth 7 bonanza, capital, destiny, godsend, portion, revenue 8 accident, fatality, gold mine, good luck, lady luck, opulence, property, treasure, windfall 9 affluence, haphazard, substance 10 prosperity, providence 12 circumstance 13 circumstances
  goddess of: 5 Tyche 7 Fortuna

Fortunes of Nigel, The
  author: 14 Sir Walter Scott
fortuneteller 4 seer 5 augur, Gypsy, sibyl 6 medium, oracle 7 palmist, prophet 8 magician 10 soothsayer 11 chiromancer, clairvoyant 12 crystal gazer
for two
  French: 5 a deux
Forty Days of Musa Dagh, The
  author: 11 Franz Werfel
42nd Parallel, The
  author: 13 John Dos Passos
Forty-Second Street
  director: 10 Lloyd Bacon
  cast: 9 Guy Kibbee, Una Merkel 10 Dick Powell, Ruby Keeler 11 Bebe Daniels, George Brent 12 Ginger Rogers, Warner Baxter
  choreographer: 13 Busby Berkeley
  song: 15 Young and Healthy 17 Forty-second Street 19 Shuffle Off to Buffalo 28 You're Getting to Be a Habit with Me
Forty Thieves, The
  author: 7 unknown
  character: 7 Ali Baba
  code word: 10 Open Sesame
forty winks 3 nap 4 doze 6 catnap, snooze
forum 6 medium, outlet 7 rostrum, seminar 8 platform 9 symposium 10 colloquium
forward, forwards 3 out 4 back, bold 5 ahead, brash, fresh, relay, sassy 6 assist, brazen, cheeky, hasten, onward, pass on, send on, spread 7 advance, frontal, further, go-ahead, promote, quicken, re-route 8 anterior, champion, immodest, impudent, insolent, up-to-date 9 advancing, barefaced, intrusive, offensive, presuming, re-address, shameless 10 accelerate, unmannerly 11 impertinent, progressive 13 enterprising, presumptuous 13 overconfident
  French: 7 en avant
forwardness 4 gall 5 brass, cheek 8 audacity, boldness 10 brazenness, effrontery 11 presumption 13 bumptiousness, obtrusiveness
for what use
  Latin: 7 cui bono
For Whom the Bell Tolls
  author: 15 Ernest Hemingway
  director: 7 Sam Wood
  character: 5 Maria, Pablo, Pilar 6 Andres, Rafael 7 Anselmo, El Sordo 8 Augustin, Fernando 12 Robert Jordan
  cast: 10 Gary Cooper 12 Akim Tamiroff 13 Ingrid Bergman, Joseph Calleia, Katina Paxinou 15 Arturo de Cordova
  score: 11 Victor Young
  Oscar for: 17 supporting actress (Paxinou)
for whose benefit
  Latin: 7 cui bono
For Your Eyes Only
  author: 10 Ian Fleming
Fosse, Bob
  director of: 5 Lenny 7 Cabaret (Oscar) 11 All That Jazz

fossil 4 fogy, rock 5 fogey, oldie, relic, stone 7 imprint, antique 9 remainder 13 petrification
foster 3 aid 4 back, feed, rear, tend 5 favor, nurse, raise 6 foment, harbor, mother, rear up, take in 7 advance, bring up, care for, cherish, forward, further, nourish, nurture, promote, protect, support, sustain 8 advocate, befriend, hold dear, sanction, side with, treasure 9 encourage, patronize, stimulate 11 accommodate, countenance
Foster, Alicia Christian
  real name of: 11 Jodie Foster
Foster, Harold
  creator/artist of: 6 Tarzan 13 Prince Valiant
Foster, Jodie
  real name: 21 Alicia Christian Foster
  born: 7 Bronx NY
  roles: 9 Tom Sawyer 10 Taxi Driver 11 Bugsy Malone
Foster, Stephen Collins
  born: 15 Lawrenceville PA
  composer of: 11 Swanee River 13 Camptown Races 16 Beautiful Dreamer 17 My Old Kentucky Home, The Old Folks at Home 27 Jeanie with the Light Brown Hair
Foucault, Jean Bernard Leon
  field: 7 physics
  nationality: 6 French
  proved: 19 Earth spins on its axis
  measured: 15 velocity of light
  named for him: 16 Foucault currents
foul 3 wet 4 base, clog, evil, lewd, soil, vile 5 dirty, foggy, grimy, gross, gusty, misty, muddy, murky, nasty, rainy, sully, taint 6 choked, cloudy, coarse, defile, filthy, grubby, odious, putrid, risque, scurvy, smelly, smutty, soiled, sordid, stormy, tangle, turbid, vulgar, wicked 7 abusive, begrime, drizzly, ensnare, hateful, heinous, impeded, obscene, pollute, profane, smeared, squalid, squally, stained, sullied, tangled, unclean 8 begrimed, besmirch, blustery, ensnared, entangle, immodest, indecent, infamous, stinking, unseemly 9 atrocious, besmeared, entangled, insulting, loathsome, monstrous, nefarious, notorious, obnoxious, repulsive, revolting 10 abominable, bedraggled, detestable, disgusting, encumbered, flagitious, indelicate, malodorous, putrescent, scurrilous, villainous 11 blasphemous, disgraceful 12 contemptible
foul-mouthed 4 lewd, rude, vile 5 dirty, gross 6 coarse, filthy, vulgar 7 abusive, obscene, profane 9 offensive 10 indelicate
foul play 5 crime 6 murder 8 violence 9 treachery
foul-smelling 4 rank 5 acrid, fetid, musty 6 putrid, smelly 7 noisome, reeking 8 stinking 10 malodorous
foul up 3 mar 4 goof, muff, ruin 5 botch, mix up, spoil 6 bungle, mess up, muddle 7 blunder, butcher, confuse, louse up, screw up 9 mismanage

found 4 base, rear, rest 5 build, erect, raise, set up, start 6 create, ground, locate, settle 7 develop, sustain 8 colonize, organize 9 construct, establish, institute, originate

foundation 3 bed 4 base, foot, fund, rock, root 5 basis, cause 6 bottom, cellar, ground, motive, origin, reason, source 7 charity, premise, purpose, support 8 basement, creation, pedestal 9 endowment, rationale 10 assumption, groundwork, settlement 11 benefaction, institution 12 commencement, installation, philanthropy, substructure, underpinning 13 establishment, justification 14 infrastructure, understructure

foundational 3 key 4 base, core 5 basic, prime 7 primary 9 essential 10 elementary

foundation garment 6 corset, girdle 8 corselet

founder 4 fall, limp, reel, sink, trip 5 abort, drown, lurch, swamp 6 author, father, go down, go lame, hobble, perish, plunge, sprawl, topple, tumble 7 break up, builder, capsize, creator, go under, planner, stagger, stumble, succumb 8 collapse, miscarry 9 architect, organizer, shipwreck 10 originator, strategist 12 disintegrate

foundered 4 sank 6 failed 7 beached, swamped 8 capsized, went down 9 collapsed

founding 5 birth 8 creation, settling 9 beginning 11 institution, origination 12 introduction, organization 13 establishment

found on 6 base on 7 model on 8 stem from 10 derive from 11 establish on

fountain 3 jet 4 flow, gush, well 5 birth, cause, spout 6 cradle, feeder, origin, reason, source, spring 7 genesis 8 purveyor, supplier 9 beginning, reservoir, upswelling 10 derivation, wellspring

fountainhead 4 font 6 origin, source, spring 9 beginning 10 wellspring

Fountainhead, The
  author: 7 Ayn Rand

fourgon 3 van 7 tumbril

Four Horsemen of the Apocalypse, The
  author: 19 Vicente Blasco Ibanez
  based on: 10 Revelation

400 Blows, The
  director: 16 Francois Truffaut
  cast: 10 Albert Remy 13 Claire Maurier 14 Patrick Auffray 15 Jean-Pierre Leaud

Four Quartets
  author: 7 T S Eliot

Four-Season Recreation State
  nickname of: 7 Vermont

fowl 3 hen 4 cock, duck, game 5 banty, capon, chick, goose, quail 6 bantam, grouse, pigeon, turkey 7 chicken, cornish, leghorn, poultry 8 duckling

Fowles, John
  author of: 8 Mantissa, The Magus 10 The Aristos 12 Daniel Martin, The Collector 13 The Ebony Tower 25 The French Lieutenant's Woman

fox 9 scavenger
  young: 3 kit, pup
  group of: 5 leash, skulk

Fox (Mesquakie, Red Earth People)
  language family: 9 Algonkian 10 Algonquian
  location: 4 Iowa 9 Wisconsin
  allied with: 4 Sauk 8 Kickapoo

Fox, Fontaine
  creator/artist of: 16 Toonerville Folks 18 Toonerville Trolley

foxglove 9 digitalis
  varieties: 5 false, rusty 6 common, yellow 7 Grecian, Mexican 10 downy false 12 willow-leaved

foxiness 5 guile 7 cunning, slyness 8 artifice, trickery, wiliness 10 craftiness, shrewdness

fox-trot 5 dance 13 ballroom dance

Foxx, Jimmy (James Emory)
  nickname: 7 Double X
  sport: 8 baseball
  team: 12 Boston Red Sox 21 Philadelphia Athletics

Foxx, Redd
  real name: 16 John Elroy Sanford
  born: 9 St Louis MO
  roles: 13 Sanford and Son 19 Cotton Comes to Harlem

foxy 3 sly 4 wily 5 canny, sharp, slick 6 artful, astute, clever, crafty, shifty, shrewd, sneaky, tricky 7 cunning, devious, oblique 8 guileful, scheming, stealthy 9 conniving, deceitful, deceptive, designing, insidious, underhand 10 intriguing

foyer 4 hall 5 lobby 6 loggia 8 anteroom 9 vestibule 11 antechamber

fracas 3 row 4 fray, to-do 5 brawl, broil, clash, fight, melee, scrap 6 battle, ruckus, rumpus, strife, uproar 7 scuffle 9 imbroglio 10 donnybrook, free-for-all 11 altercation, embroilment

fraction 3 bit, few 4 chip 5 crumb, piece, ratio, scrap 6 morsel, trifle 7 cutting, portion, section, segment, shaving 8 fragment, particle, quotient 10 proportion 11 subdivision

fractious 5 cross, huffy 6 shirty, touchy, unruly 7 fretful, grouchy, peevish, pettish, waspish, wayward, willful 8 contrary, perverse, petulant, shrewish, snappish 9 irascible, irritable, querulous 10 rebellious, refractory 11 quarrelsome 12 disputatious, recalcitrant, unmanageable

fracture 4 rend, rift 5 break, crack, fault, sever, split 6 breach, cleave 7 disrupt, rupture, shatter 8 cleavage, division 9 severance 10 separation

Fra Diavolo, ou L'Hotellerie de Terracine
  also: 31 Brother Devil or The Inn at Terracina
  comic opera by: 5 Auber
  character: 7 Lorenzo, Zerlina 11 Lady Allcash, Lord Allcash 17 Marquis di San Marco

fragile 4 soft, weak 5 crisp, frail 6 dainty, feeble, flimsy, infirm, sleazy, slight, tender 7 brittle, crumbly, friable, rickety, shivery 8 decrepit, delicate 9 breakable, ephemeral, frangible, splintery 10 evanescent, tumbledown 11 dilapidated 13 unsubstantial

fragility 7 frailty 8 delicacy, weakness 9 frailness 10 feebleness 11 brittleness 12 frangibility

fragment 3 bit 4 chip, snip 5 crumb, cut up, piece, scrap, shard, shred, trace 6 chop up, divide, morsel 7 break up, crumble, portion, remnant, section, segment, shatter, vestige 8 disunite, fraction, separate, splinter, survival 12 disintegrate

fragmentary 6 broken, choppy 7 scrappy 8 detached 9 piecemeal, scattered, segmented 10 disjointed, fractional, incomplete, unfinished 12 disconnected

Fragonard, Jean-Honore
  born: 6 France, Grasse
  artwork: 8 The Swing 10 Stolen Kiss, The Bathers, The Warrior 12 Le Billet Doux 14 Progress of Love 16 La Chemise Enlevee 18 Storming the Citadel 40 Coresus Sacrificing Himself to Save Callirhoe

fragrance 4 aura, balm 5 aroma, scent 7 bouquet, incense, perfume 9 redolence, sweetness

fragrant 5 balmy, spicy 7 odorous 8 aromatic, perfumed, redolent 11 odoriferous

Fragrant Harbor see 8 Hong Kong

frail 4 puny, weak 6 feeble, flimsy, infirm, sleazy, slight, weakly 7 brittle, crumbly, fragile, rickety, shivery 8 decrepit, delicate, fallible 9 breakable, frangible, splintery 10 perishable, vulnerable 11 dilapidated 13 unsubstantial

frailness 8 delicacy, weakness 9 fragility 11 unsoundness

frailty 3 sin 4 flaw, vice 5 fault 6 defect, foible 7 blemish, failing 11 fallibility 12 imperfection 14 susceptibility

Fra Lippo Lippi
  author: 14 Robert Browning

frame 3 rim, set 4 body, case, cast, form, make, mold, mood, plan 5 build, draft, hatch, humor, set up, shape, state 6 border, casing, design, devise, edging, figure, indite, invent, map out, nature, scheme, sketch, system, temper 7 anatomy, backing, chassis, concoct, contour, housing, outline, setting 8 attitude, conceive, contrive, mounting, organize, physique, skeleton 9 formulate, structure 11 disposition, scaffolding, systematize, temperament 12 constitution, construction

frame of mind 4 mood 7 climate 8 attitude 10 atmosphere 11 disposition

framer 6 author, shaper 7 creator, planner 10 formulator

framework 5 shell, truss 7 carcass 8 skeleton, template 9 structure 10 foundation 11 scaffolding 14 infrastructure

Framley Parsonage
  author: 15 Anthony Trollope

France
  other name: 4 Gaul
  anthem: 14 La Marseillaise
  capital/largest city: 5 Paris
  others: 4 Nice 5 Brest, Lille, Lyons, Rouen, Vichy 6 Amiens, Calais, Cannes, Carnac, Cognac, Dieppe, Grasse, Nantes, Prades, Rheims 7 Antibes, Avignon, Bayonne, Dunkirk, Le Havre, Les Baux 8 Bordeaux, Boulogne, Chartres, Grenoble, Poitiers, Toulouse 9 Cherbourg, Roquefort 10 La Rochelle, Marseilles, Saint-Denis, Strasbourg 12 Saint-Nazaire 13 Aix-en-Provence, Fontainebleau
  school: 8 Grenoble, Saint Cyr, Sorbonne 10 Montpelier
  division: 5 Anjou, Bearn, Berry, Maine, Savoy 6 Alsace, Artois, Marche, Poitou 7 Gascony, Guienne, Picardy 8 Auvergne, Bordeaux, Brittany, Burgundy, Dauphine, Flanders, Lorraine, Lyonnais, Normandy, Provence, Touraine 9 Aquitaine, Champagne, Languedoc 11 Ile de France 12 Bourbonnaise, Franche-Comte
  measure: 3 pot, sac 4 aune, mine, muid, pied, velt 5 arpen, carat, ligne, minot, pinte, point, pouce, velte 6 arpent, hemine, league, quarte, setier
  monetary unit: 5 franc 7 centime
  weight: 3 sol 4 gros, kilo, once 5 carat, livre, pound, tonne 6 gramme 7 tonneau 8 esterlin 9 esterling
  island: 2 Re 3 Yeu 4 Cite 5 Groix, Hyere 6 Comoro, Oleron, Tahiti, Ushant 7 Corsica, Leeward, Reunion 8 Windward 10 Guadeloupe, Martinique 12 New Caledonia
  lake: 6 Annecy, Cazaux, Geneva
  mountain: 4 Jura 5 Pelat 6 Vosges 8 Ardennes, Pyrenees 10 French Alps 11 Pic Montcalm
  highest point: 5 Blanc 9 Mont Blanc
  river: 3 Lys 4 Yser 5 Aisne, Eiser, Isere, Loire, Meuse, Rhine, Rhone, Saone, Seine 7 Garonne, Gironde
  sea: 5 North 8 Atlantic 13 Mediterranean
  physical feature:
  bay: 6 Biscay 7 Arachon
  beach: 5 Omaha
  cape: 5 Hague, Talma
  channel: 7 English 8 La Manche
  gulf: 4 Lion
  people: 6 Franks
  artist: 5 Corot, David, Degas, Manet, Monet 6 Braque, Ingres, Millet, Renoir, Seurat 7 Cezanne, Daumier, Gauguin, Matisse, Utrillo 8 Pissarro 9 Delacroix, Fragonard, Gericault
  author: 4 Gide, Hugo, Zola 5 Camus, Dumas 6 France, Proust, Racine, Sartre, Villon 7 Moliere 8 Rabelais, Rousseau, Voltaire 9 Corneille, Descartes, Giraudoux, Montaigne 10 Baudelaire
  composer: 5 Bizet, Ravel, Satie 6 Franck, Gounod 7 Berlioz, Debussy, Poulenc
  king: 5 Henri, Louis 6 Clovis, Philip 7

Charles 9 Hugh Capet 11 Charlemagne
13 Louis Philippe 14 Henry of Navarre
leader: 6 Danton, Petain 7 Colbert, Mazarin 8 de Gaulle, D'Estaing, Pompidou 9
Joan of Arc, Richelieu 10 Mitterrand 11
Robespierre 17 Napoleon Bonaparte
queen: 7 Eugenie 9 Josephine 13 Marie
de Medici 15 Marie Antoinette
language: 6 French
religion: 5 Islam 7 Judaism 8 Huguenot
10 Protestant 13 Roman Catholic
place:
cathedral: 6 Rheims 8 Chartres 9 Madeleine, Notre Dame 10 Sacre-Coeur 14
Sainte-Chapelle 15 Mont-Saint-Michel
chapel: 8 Ronchamp
gardens: 9 Tuileries
hall of mirrors: 16 Galerie des Glaces
museum: 6 Louvre
palace: 6 Elysee 10 Luxembourg,
Versailles 12 Grand Trianon, Petit Trianon, 13 Fontainebleau
prison: 8 Bastille
racetrack: 6 Le Mans 7 Auteuil 10
Longchamps
resort: 3 Pau 5 Vichy 6 Cannes, Menton
7 Antibes, Mentone, Riviera 8 Biarritz,
Chamonix, Grenoble 9 Cote d'Azur 11
Aix-les-Bains
section of Paris: 8 Left Bank 9 Right
Bank 10 Montmartre, Rive Droite, Rive
Gauche 12 Latin Quarter
street: 13 Champs-Elysees 17 Place de
la Concorde
woods: 14 Bois de Boulogne 15 Bois de
Vincennes
possession: 12 French Guiana
island: 6 Futuna, Hoorne, Wallis 7 Reunion 8 Miquelon 10 Guadeloupe, Martinique 11 Saint Pierre 12 New Caledonia
15 French Polynesia
feature:
airport: 4 Orly 9 Le Bourget 15 Charles
de Gaulle
bicycle race: 12 Tour de France
dance: 5 gavot 6 branle, canary, cancan
7 boutade, gavotte
fortification: 11 Maginot Line
holiday: 11 Bastille Day
monument: 13 Arc de Triomphe 14
Tomb of Napoleon
national theater: 16 Comedie Francaise
sightseeing boat: 12 bateau mouche
tower: 6 Eiffel
food:
cheese: 4 bleu, Brie 6 bonbel 7 boursin 8
Muenster 9 camembert, marcillat, portsalut, Roquefort 11 coulommiers
dessert: 6 mousse
dish: 4 pate 5 crepe 6 canape, quiche 7
souffle 8 escargot, piperade, pot au feu 9
cassoulet, tournedos 14 pate de foie gras
drink: 6 cognac 8 bordeaux, burgundy 9
champagne
french fries: 12 pommes frites
pastry: 7 brioche 8 napoleon 9 croissant
soup: 8 a l'oignon 13 bouillabaisse

steak: 7 bifteck
France, Anatole
  real name: 30 Jacques Anatole Francois
  Thibault
  author of: 5 Thais 12 Golden Verses 13
  My Friend's Book, Penguin Island 17 The
  Gods Are Athirst 20 The Revolt of the Angels 25 Le Crime de Sylvestre Bonnard
  27 At the Sign of the Reine Pedauque
franchise 5 grant, right 6 ballot 7 charter,
freedom, license 8 immunity, suffrage 9
privilege 10 permission 11 prerogative 13
authorization
Franciosa, Anthony
  real name: 14 Anthony Papaleo
  born: 9 New York NY
  wife: 14 Shelley Winters
  roles: 12 The Naked Maja 13 A Hatful of
  Rain, Long Hot Summer, Name of the
  Game, Wild Is the Wind 15 Assault on a
  Queen
Francis, Dick
  author of: 4 Bolt, Risk 5 Nerve, Proof 6
  Banker, Reflex 7 Break In, Enquiry, Forfeit, Rat Race 8 Dead Cert, For Kicks,
  Slayride, Trial Run, Twice Shy, Whip
  Hand 9 Bonecrack, The Danger, Knockdown 10 Blood Sport, High Stakes, In the
  Frame 11 Smokescreen 12 Flying Finish
Franck, Cesar
  born: 5 Liege 7 Belgium
  composer of: 4 Ruth 5 Hulda 6 Psyche
  7 Rebecca 8 Ghiselle 9 Les Djinns 10
  Les Eolides, Redemption 13 La Tour de
  Babel, Les Beatitudes, The Beatitudes 16
  Le Chasseur Maudit 17 The Accursed
  Hunter
Franglais 13 French-English 14 French-American
frank 4 bold, free, open 5 clear, plain,
round 6 candid, direct, honest, patent 7
artless, evident, genuine, natural, sincere,
up-front 8 apparent, distinct, explicit, manifest 9 downright, ingenuous, outspoken
10 aboveboard, forthright, unreserved 11
plain-spoken, transparent, unambiguous,
undisguised, unequivocal 12 unmistakable
15 straightforward
Frank, Anne
  author of: 19 The Diary of Anne Frank
Frankenstein
  author: 17 Mary Godwin Shelley
  character: 7 Clerval, Justine, William 9
  Elizabeth 10 The Monster 12 Robert Walton 18 Victor Frankenstein
Franklin, Benjamin
  author of: 20 Poor Richard's Almanack
  inventor of: 12 lightning rod 13 bifocal
  lenses, Franklin stove
frankness 6 candor 7 honesty 8 openness
9 bluntness, sincerity 10 directness 11
artlessness 13 guilelessness 14 forthrightness 19 straightforwardness
frantic 3 mad 4 wild 5 crazy, rabid 6 hectic,
insane, raging, raving 7 berserk, excited,
furious, nervous, violent 8 agitated, deranged, frenetic, frenzied 9 delirious 10

distracted, distraught, infuriated 11 impassioned, overwrought 12 ungovernable

fraternal 6 hearty, loving, social 7 devoted, kindred, related 8 amicable, friendly 9 brotherly 11 warmhearted 12 affectionate 14 consanguineous

fraternity 4 clan, club 5 union 6 circle, clique, league 7 company, coterie, kinship, society 8 alliance 9 coalition 10 federation 11 association, brotherhood, confederacy, propinquity 13 brotherliness, consanguinity, interrelation

Fraternity
  author: 14 John Galsworthy

fraternize 3 mix 5 unite 6 concur, hobnob, mingle 7 combine, consort 8 coalesce 9 associate, cooperate, harmonize, pal around, socialize 10 sympathize 11 confederate

Fratres Arvales see 5 Arval

frau 4 lady, wife 12 married woman

fraud 4 fake, hoax, hype, ruse, sham 5 cheat, craft, guile, knave, quack, rogue, trick 6 deceit, humbug, rascal 7 swindle 8 artifice, cheating, cozenage, impostor, swindler, trickery 9 charlatan, chicanery, con artist, deception, duplicity, imposture, pretender, stratagem, swindling, treachery 10 dishonesty, mountebank, subterfuge 11 counterfeit, four-flusher, machination 13 dissimulation

fraudulence 6 deceit 8 trickery 9 deception 13 deceitfulness, deceptiveness 17 misrepresentation

fraudulent 4 sham, wily 5 bogus, false 6 crafty, tricky 7 crooked, cunning, knavish 8 cheating, guileful, spurious 9 deceitful, deceptive, dishonest 11 counterfeit, treacherous, underhanded 12 dishonorable, unprincipled

fraught 4 full 5 heavy, laden 6 filled, loaded 7 charged, replete, teeming 8 attended, pregnant 9 abounding 11 accompanied

fraulein 9 young lady 14 unmarried woman

Fraunhofer, Joseph von
  field: 7 physics
  nationality: 6 German
  established: 12 spectroscopy

fray 3 rub 4 fret, fuss, riot, spat, tiff 5 brawl, chafe, fight, melee, ravel, set-to 6 battle, combat, fracas, rumble, rumpus, strain, tatter, tumult, tussle 7 contest, dispute, frazzle, quarrel, scuffle, warfare, wear out, wrangle 8 conflict, skirmish, squabble 9 bickering, commotion 10 contention, dissension, engagement 11 altercation, controversy 12 disagreement

Frazer, Sir James G
  author of: 14 The Golden Bough

freak 3 fad, odd 4 kink, turn, whim 5 craze, fancy, humor, queer, quirk, sport, twist 6 marvel, oddity, vagary, whimsy, wonder 7 anomaly, bizarre, caprice, erratic, monster, strange, unusual 8 crotchet, mutation, peculiar 9 curiosity, deviation 10 aberration 11 abnormality, monstrosity 12 irregularity

freakish 3 odd 5 queer, weird 7 bizarre, strange, unusual 8 peculiar, singular, uncommon 9 eccentric, fantastic 10 outlandish 13 extraordinary

Frederick
  character in: 11 As You Like It
  author: 11 Shakespeare

Frederick I
  nickname: 10 Barbarossa
  position: 16 Holy Roman Emperor
  dynasty: 12 Hohenstaufen
  wife: 7 Beatrix
  battle: 7 Legnano

Frederick II
  position: 12 king of Sicily 13 king of Germany 16 Holy Roman Emperor
  battle: 8 Bouvines

Frederick the Great
  nickname: 8 Old Fritz
  position: 13 King of Prussia
  invaded: 7 Silesia
  war: 13 Seven Years' War 18 Austrian Succession

free 3 big, lax 4 able, bold, easy, idle, idly, open, save 5 clear, extra, let go, loose, rid of, spare 6 daring, devoid, exempt, giving, gratis, lavish, parole, ransom, redeem, unbond, uncage, wanton 7 allowed, assured, forward, liberal, loosely, manumit, release, unchain, unleash 8 at no cost, careless, costless, devoid of, familiar, fearless, generous, handsome, immune to, informal, let loose, liberate, prodigal, released, unfasten 9 abandoned, audacious, available, boundless, bounteous, bountiful, confident, delivered, discharge, disengage, dissolute, expansive, extricate, footloose, lacking in, leisurely, liberated, permitted, unblocked, unbridled, unchained, unclogged, unimpeded, unmuzzled, unshackle 10 autonomous, bighearted, carelessly, chargeless, emancipate, gratuitous, licentious, manumitted, munificent, openhanded, unattached, unconfined, unfettered, unhampered, unoccupied, unreserved, unshackled 11 emancipated, enfranchise, independent, uncluttered, uncommitted, uninhibited, unrepressed 12 enfranchised, overfamiliar, uncontrolled, unencumbered, unobstructed, unrestrained 13 complimentary, unceremonious, unconstrained

free-and-easy 6 breezy, casual, jaunty 7 buoyant, relaxed 8 debonair, informal 12 lighthearted, presumptuous, unrestrained 13 unconstrained

freed 6 exempt, loosed, spared 7 cleared, excused 8 absolved, let loose, released, relieved 11 emancipated

freedom 4 play 5 range, scope, sweep, swing 6 candor, margin 7 abandon, license, release 8 autonomy, boldness, latitude, openness, rudeness 9 bluntness, frankness, impudence, indecorum 10 directness, disrespect, liberation 11 abandonment, forwardness, impropriety, inormality, manumission, naturalness, sovereignty, unrestraint **12** emancipation, impertinence, unconstraint **13** downrightness **14** unreservedness **15** enfranchisement

Freedom of the Poet, The
  author: **12** John Berryman
free-flowing 7 copious, gushing, profuse **8** effusive
free-for-all 3 row **4** fray **5** brawl, fight, melee, scrap **6** affray, fracas, ruckus, tussle **7** rhubarb, ruction, wrangle **9** brannigan **10** donnybrook
free from bias 7 neutral **9** impartial, unbigoted **12** unprejudiced **13** disinterested
free from moisture 3 dry **4** arid, sere **5** parch **6** dry out **7** parched **8** dried out, rainless **9** dehydrate **10** dehydrated, desertlike, desiccated
free hand 12 carte blanche, open sanction **13** full authority
free rein 12 carte blanche, open sanction **13** full authority
free-spoken 6 chatty **7** voluble **9** talkative **10** loquacious, unreserved **13** communicative
Free State
  nickname of: **8** Maryland
Freestone State
  nickname of: **11** Connecticut
Free to Choose
  author: **14** Milton Friedman (with Rose Friedman)
Freetown
  capital of: **11** Sierra Leone
freeze 3 nip **4** bite, cool, halt, stop **5** chill, frost, sting **6** arrest, benumb, harden, pierce **7** ceiling, congeal, terrify **8** glaciate, solidify **11** anesthetize, refrigerate, restriction
freezing 3 icy **6** arctic, frigid **7** glacial
Frege, Gottlieb
  field: **11** mathematics
  nationality: **6** German
  founded: **13** symbolic logic
Freia see **5** Freya
freight 4 haul, lade, load, ship **5** cargo, carry, goods **6** burden, charge, convey, lading **7** baggage, cartage, luggage, portage **8** transmit, truckage **9** transport **10** conveyance **13** transshipment
Freischutz, Der
  also: **11** The Marksman
  opera by: **5** Weber
  character: **3** Max **6** Agathe, Caspar, Samiel
Freki
  origin: **12** Scandinavian
  form: **4** wolf
  owner: **4** Odin **5** Othin
  received: **4** food
  exception: **4** meat
  fellow wolf: **4** Geri
French, Daniel Chester
  born: **8** Exeter NH
  artwork: **7** (seated) Lincoln (at Lincoln Memorial) **21** The Minute Man of Concord

French-American
  French: **9** Franglais
French civil code 12 Code Napoleon
French Connection, The
  director: **15** William Friedkin
  cast: **11** Fernando Rey, Gene Hackman (Popeye Doyle), Roy Scheider
  Oscar for: **5** actor (Hackman) **7** editing, picture **8** director **10** screenplay
  sequel: **21** The French Connection II
French-English
  French: **9** Franglais
French Guinea see **6** Guinea
French Indonesia see **7** Vietnam
French is spoken here
  French: **18** ici on parle francais
French Lieutenant's Woman, The
  director: **10** Karel Reisz
  author: **10** John Fowles
  cast: **9** Leo McKern **11** Hilton McRae, Jeremy Irons, Meryl Streep
  script: **12** Harold Pinter
French national anthem 12 Marseillaise
French national theater 16 Comedie Francaise
French parliament
  formal sessions: **12** lit de justice
French Somaliland see **8** Djibouti
French Sudan, Soudan see **4** Mali
French Togoland see **4** Togo
frenzied 3 mad **4** wild **7** excited, frantic, furious **8** agitated, ecstatic **9** delirious
frenzy 3 fit **4** fury **5** craze, furor, mania, state **6** access **7** mad rush, madness, seizure, turmoil **8** delirium, hysteria, outburst **9** obsession, transport **11** distraction
Frenzy
  director: **15** Alfred Hitchcock
  cast: **8** Jon Finch **10** Anna Massey **11** Barry Foster **16** Barbara Leigh-Hunt
frequency 9 iteration **10** recurrence, regularity, repetition **11** persistence, reiteration
frequent 5 daily, haunt, usual **6** common, wonted **7** regular **8** constant, everyday, familiar, habitual, numerous, ordinary, resort to **9** continual, customary, incessant, perpetual, recurrent **10** accustomed **11** reiterative
frequently 5 often **7** usually **8** ofttimes **9** generally **10** constantly, habitually, ordinarily, repeatedly **11** continually, customarily, incessantly, perpetually, recurrently
frere 4 monk **5** friar **7** brother
Frescobaldi, Girolamo
  born: **5** Italy **7** Ferrara
  composer of: **13** Fiori Musicali **14** Musical Flowers
fresh 3 fit, hot, new **4** bold, cool, fair, keen, late, pert, pure, rare, rosy, rude **5** alert, brisk, chill, clear, green, nervy, novel, ready, ruddy, sassy, saucy, stiff, sweet **6** active, biting, brassy, brazen, bright, cheeky, lively, modern, recent, rested, snotty, unique, unused, unworn **7** bracing, cutting, forward, glowing, just out, nipping, strange, uncured, undried, unfaded, untried, unusual **8** assuming, blooming,

brand-new, creative, flippant, gleaming, impudent, insolent, original, stinging, unabated, undimmed, unsalted, unsmoked, unwilted, up-to-date 9 energetic, inventive, obtrusive, refreshed, sparkling, undecayed, unpickled, unspoiled, unwearied, wholesome 10 meddlesome, new-fangled, refreshing, unfamiliar, unimpaired, unwithered 11 flourishing, invigorated, modernistic, smart-alecky, untarnished 12 presumptuous, unaccustomed

freshen 4 wash 5 brace, calve, clean, groom, renew 6 air out, breeze, desalt, revive 7 cool off, sweeten 8 renovate, spruce up 9 deodorize

freshet 5 crest, flood 11 overflowing

Freshman, The
   director: 9 Sam Taylor 12 Fred Newmeyer
   cast: 11 Harold Lloyd 13 Jobyna Ralston 14 Brooks Benedict

Fresnel, Augustin Jean
   field: 7 physics
   nationality: 6 French
   worked in: 6 optics

fret 3 eat, rub, vex 4 fray, fume, gall, gnaw, mope, pine, pout, stew, sulk 5 brood, chafe, erode, sulks, worry 6 abrade, lament, ruffle, tatter 7 agonize, corrode, fidgets 8 disquiet, distress, irritate, vexation, wear away 9 annoyance, excoriate 10 irritation 11 displeasure, peevishness 12 discomposure

fretful 5 cross, huffy, sulky, tense 6 cranky, shirty, touchy 7 grouchy, nervous, peevish, pettish, waspish 8 contrary, petulant, snappish 9 crotchety, irritable, querulous 11 complaining 12 cantankerous

fretfulness 6 worry 6 unease 7 anxiety 10 crankiness 11 peevishness 12 irritability

Freud, Sigmund
   lived in: 6 Vienna
   collaborator: 6 Breuer
   disciple: 4 Jung 5 Adler
   daughter: 4 Anna
   method: 15 free association 19 dream interpretation
   coined: 2 id 8 superego 14 psychoanalysis
   author of: 13 Totem and Taboo 22 Interpretation of Dreams 37 Group Psychology and the Analysis of the Ego, Jokes and Their Relation to the Unconscious

Freund, John Lincoln
   real name of: 12 John Forsythe

Frey
   also: 5 Freyr
   origin: 12 Scandinavian
   god of: 5 peace 8 marriage 10 prosperity
   race: 5 Vanir
   father: 5 Niord, Njord
   home: 7 Alfheim

Freya
   also: 5 Freia
   origin: 8 Teutonic
   goddess of: 4 love 6 beauty 9 fecundity
   race: 5 Vanir
   leader of: 9 Valkyries
   father: 5 Niord, Njord

Fri see 5 Frigg

friable 7 crumbly 9 breakable, frangible

friar
   French: 5 frere

Friar Lawrence
   character in: 14 Romeo and Juliet
   author: 11 Shakespeare

Friar Tuck
   character in: 9 Robin Hood

friary 5 abbey 6 priory 8 cloister 9 hermitage, monastery

friction 6 strife 7 chafing, discord, grating, quarrel, rubbing 8 abrasion, bad blood, conflict, fretting 9 animosity, attrition, hostility 10 antagonism, contention, dissension, dissidence, opposition, resentment, resistance 12 disagreement 13 counteraction

Friday
   character in: 14 Robinson Crusoe
   author: 5 Defoe

Friday
   from: 5 Freya, Frigg
   heavenly body: 5 Venus
   French: 8 vendredi
   Italian: 7 venerdi
   Spanish: 7 viernes
   German: 7 freitag

Friedan, Betty
   author of: 19 The Feminine Mystique
   co-founder of: 3 NOW 28 National Organization for Women

Friedkin, William
   director of: 11 The Exorcist 19 The French Connection (Oscar)

Friedman, Milton
   author of: 12 Free to Choose (with Rose Friedman) 20 Capitalism and Freedom

Friedrich, Caspar David
   born: 7 Germany 10 Greifswald
   artwork: 22 The Cross on the Mountains 26 Man and Woman Gazing at the Moon, The Ruined Monastery of Eldena, Two Men Contemplating the Moon

friend 3 ally, beau, chum, date, mate 5 amigo, buddy, crony, lover 6 backer, cohort, escort, fellow, intime, minion, patron 7 brother, comrade, consort, partner 8 adherent, advocate, confrere, co-worker, defender, favorite, follower, henchman, intimate, mistress, myrmidon, paramour, partisan, playmate, retainer, sidekick, soul mate 9 associate, bedfellow, colleague, companion, confidant, copartner, supporter 10 benefactor, encourager, playfellow, well-wisher 12 acquaintance
   French: 3 ami 4 amie 9 bonne amie
   Spanish: 5 amiga, amigo

friendliness 5 amity 8 bonhomie, good will 9 geniality 10 affability, amiability, cordiality, fraternity 11 amicability, camaraderie, sociability 14 neighborliness 16 companionability

friendly 4 kind 6 allied, ardent, benign, chummy, clubby, genial, kindly, loving, social 7 affable, amiable, cordial, devoted, helpful 8 amicable, familiar, generous, gracious, intimate, salutary 9 brotherly, convivial, favorable, fortunate, fraternal, opportune 10 accessible, auspicious, beneficial, hospitable, neighborly, not hostile, propitious 11 kindhearted, sympathetic, warmhearted 12 advantageous, affectionate 13 companionable

Friendly Fire
  author: 8 C D B Bryan
Friendly Islands *see* 5 Tongo
Friendly Persuasion
  director: 12 William Wyler
  author: 12 Jessamyn West
  cast: 10 Gary Cooper 11 Richard Eyer 12 Marjorie Main 14 Anthony Perkins, Dorothy McGuire
  score: 14 Dimitri Tiomkin
friendly understanding
  French: 15 entente cordiale
friend of the court
  Latin: 12 amicus curiae
friendship 5 amity 6 accord, comity 7 concord, harmony 8 close tie, goodwill, intimacy, sympathy 10 consonance, cordiality, fellowship, fraternity 11 brotherhood, comradeship, familiarity 12 amicableness 13 companionship, understanding 14 neighborliness 16 acquaintanceship

Friesen, Samille Diane
  real name of: 10 Dyan Cannon
Frigg
  also: 3 Fri 5 Frija 6 Frigga
  origin: 8 Teutonic
  goddess of: 3 sky 6 clouds 8 marriage
  husband: 4 Odin 5 Othin
  race: 4 Asar 5 Aesir
Frigga *see* 5 Frigg
fright 4 fear, funk 5 alarm, dread, panic, scare 6 dismay, horror, terror, tremor 7 anxiety, concern, flutter, quaking 8 cold feet 9 misgiving, quivering, the creeps 10 the jitters, the willies 11 disquietude, palpitation, trepidation 12 apprehension, intimidation, perturbation 13 consternation

frighten 5 alarm, daunt, scare, shock 6 affray, excite 7 agitate, horrify, petrify, startle, terrify 8 disquiet 9 terrorize 10 intimidate

frightened 6 afraid, scared 7 alarmed, panicky 9 horrified, petrified, terrified 10 terrorized

frightening 5 awful, dread 7 fearful 8 alarming, dreadful 10 horrifying, terrifying 11 hair-raising

frightful 5 awful, lurid, nasty 6 grisly, horrid 7 baleful, extreme, fearful, ghastly, hideous, macabre, ogreish 8 alarming, dreadful, fearsome, freakish, gruesome, horrible, horrific, shocking, sinister, terrible, terrific 9 appalling, loathsome, monstrous, offensive, repellent, repulsive, revolting 10 abominable, detestable, disgusting, horrendous 12 insufferable

frigid 3 icy, raw 4 cold, cool, prim 5 aloof, bleak, gelid, stiff 6 biting, bitter, chilly, formal, frosty 7 austere, cutting, distant, glacial, nipping 8 freezing, piercing 10 forbidding 11 straitlaced 12 unresponsive

frigidity 7 iciness 8 coldness 9 aloofness 10 frostiness 16 unresponsiveness

Frija *see* 5 Frigg

frill 3 air 6 edging, fringe, ruffle 7 flounce 8 falderal, frippery, furbelow, ornament 9 gathering, mannerism 10 decoration 11 affectation, superfluity 13 embellishment

fringe 3 hem, rim 4 edge, mane 5 limit, skirt 6 border, edging, margin, tassel 7 enclose, outline, selvage 8 decorate, frontier, skirting, surround, trimming 9 embellish, periphery

frisk 3 hop 4 jump, lark, leap, romp, skip, trip 5 bound, caper, cut up, dance, sport 6 bounce, cavort, frolic, gambol, prance, search, spring 7 disport, examine, inspect, ransack 8 look over

frisky 4 spry 5 agile, peppy 6 active, lively, nimble 7 jocular, playful, waggish 8 animated, mirthful, prankish, spirited, sportive 9 vivacious 10 frolicsome, rollicking

fritter 4 blow 5 use up, waste 7 deplete 8 fool away, idle away, squander 9 dissipate

fritter away 4 blow 5 waste 6 misuse 8 misspend, squander 9 dissipate

fritter away time 4 idle 6 dawdle 10 dillydally

Fritzi Ritz
  also named: 5 Nancy
  creator: 15 Ernie Bushmiller 16 Larry Whittington
  character: 4 Phil 5 Nancy 6 Sluggo

frivolity 3 fun 4 jest, play 5 folly, sport 6 levity, whimsy 7 abandon 8 airiness, dallying, frippery 9 emptiness, flippancy, giddiness, lightness 10 fickleness, triviality, wantonness 11 flightiness 15 thoughtlessness

frivolous 4 airy, vain 5 barmy, dizzy, empty, inane, light, minor, petty, silly 6 flimsy, frothy, paltry, slight, stupid 7 fatuous, flighty, foolish, trivial, witless 8 careless, flippant, heedless, niggling, piddling, trifling 9 brainless, imprudent, pointless, senseless, unserious, worthless 10 insouciant 11 extravagant, harebrained, impractical, improvident, nonsensical, superficial, unimportant 13 insignificant, rattlebrained 14 shallowbrained

frizzle 4 curl 5 crimp

frock 4 coat, gown, robe, suit 5 cloak, dress, smock 6 blouse 7 cassock, soutane 8 chasuble, surplice, vestment 9 clericals 10 canonicals

frog 3 pad, pod 4 knot, wood 5 frosh, hitch, track 6 holder, peeper, toggle 7 crawler, croaker, cushion, leopard, tadpole 8 bullfrog, fastener, pickerel, pollywog 9 amphibian, plow frame 12 flower holder

Frogs, The
  author: 12 Aristophanes
  character: 5 Pluto 6 Charon 7 Bacchus 8

Dionysus, Hercules, Xanthias 9 Aeschylus, Euripides

Froissart, Jean
   author of: 8 Meliador 10 Chronicles

frolic 3 fun 4 lark, play, romp, skip 5 act up, antic, caper, frisk, mirth, prank, sport, spree 6 cavort, gaiety, gambol 7 disport, jollity, make hay 8 escapade 9 amusement, festivity, joviality, merriment 10 buffoonery, pleasantry, recreation, skylarking, tomfoolery 11 merrymaking 13 entertainment

frolicsome 5 antic, jolly, merry 6 cheery, jaunty, lively 7 playful 8 cheerful, mirthful, prankish 9 sprightly 12 lighthearted

Frollo, Claude
   character in: 23 The Hunchback of Notre Dame
   author: 4 Hugo

from 2 de, ex, of 3 for, fro 5 off of, out of 7 against 8 starting 9 beginning

from abroad 5 alien 6 exotic 7 foreign 8 imported

fromage 6 cheese

from behind
   Latin: 6 a tergo

From Here to Eternity
   director: 13 Fred Zinnemann
   author: 10 James Jones
   cast: 9 Donna Reed 11 Deborah Kerr 12 Frank Sinatra, George Reeves 13 Burt Lancaster 14 Ernest Borgnine 15 Montgomery Clift
   setting: 11 Pearl Harbor
   Oscar for: 7 picture 8 director 12 screenwriter 15 supporting actor (Sinatra) 17 supporting actress (Reed)

from inside
   Latin: 7 ab intra

from outside
   Latin: 7 ab extra

From Russia With Love
   author: 10 Ian Fleming

from scratch 4 anew 14 from ground zero 16 from the beginning 20 from fresh ingredients

from side to side 4 over, sway 5 cross 7 athwart, swaying, zigzag 12 back and forth

from the beginning
   Latin: 5 ab ovo 6 de novo 8 ab initio

from the chair
   Latin: 10 ex cathedra

from the depths
   Latin: 11 de profundis

from the face
   Latin: 7 ex facie

from the fact
   Latin: 7 de facto

from the founding of the city
   Latin: 13 ab urbe condita

from the library of
   Latin: 8 ex libris

from the seat of authority
   Latin: 10 ex cathedra

front 3 air, top 4 face, fore, head, lead, mask, mien 5 first 6 facade, give on, regard 7 bearing, initial, look out 8 anterior,

carriage, demeanor, presence, pretense, trenches, vanguard 9 beginning, semblance

Front, The
   director: 10 Martin Ritt
   cast: 10 Lloyd Gough, Woody Allen, Zero Mostel 13 Joshua Shelley, Michael Murphy 16 Herschel Bernardi

frontage 7 outlook 8 exposure, prospect

frontier 4 edge 5 march, verge 6 border, limits 7 extreme, marches 8 boundary, confines, outposts 9 backlands, backwoods, outskirts, perimeter 10 hinterland 11 territories

front matter 8 foreword 9 title page 12 introduction 15 table of contents 20 introductory material

Front Page, The
   author: 8 Ben Hecht 16 Charles MacArthur
   director: 11 Billy Wilder 14 Lewis Milestone
   actor: 9 Mae Clarke, Mary Brian, Pat O'Brien 10 Jack Lemmon, David Wayne 12 George E Stone, Carol Burnett 13 Adolphe Menjou, Allen Garfield, Susan Sarandon, Walter Catlett, Walter Matthau 14 Charles Durning 15 Andrew Pendleton, Vincent Gardenia 19 Edward Everett Horton
   character: 4 Earl 5 Burns, Grant, Hildy, Peggy 6 Walter 7 Hartman, Johnson 8 Williams

frost 4 rime 5 chill 7 iciness 8 coolness, distance 9 aloofness, cold spell, frigidity 10 chilliness, glaciality 13 inhospitality 14 unfriendliness

Frost, Robert
   author of: 7 Birches 10 Fire and Ice, Home Burial 11 Mending Wall 13 Brown's Descent 15 The Road Not Taken 17 After Apple-Picking 21 The Death of the Hired Man 30 Stopping by Woods on a Snowy Evening

frostiness 3 nip 4 bite 5 chill 7 iciness 8 coldness, coolness 9 crispness, frigidity, hoariness, sharpness 10 chilliness, wintriness

frosting 3 mat 4 trim 5 glass, icing 7 cooling, topping 8 chilling, divinity, freezing, trimming 13 embellishment, ornamentation

frosty 3 icy 4 cold, cool 5 bleak, chill, hoary 6 frigid, wintry 8 freezing

froth 4 bosh, fizz, foam, fume, head, scum, suds, surf 5 spume, trash, yeast 6 lather, trivia 7 bubbles, rubbish 8 flummery, frippery, nonsense, trumpery, whitecap 9 frivolity 10 balderdash, triviality 12 fiddlefaddle

frothy 5 fizzy, foamy, light 6 bubbly 7 trivial 9 frivolous 15 inconsequential

froward 5 balky 6 unruly 7 wayward, willful 8 contrary, perverse, stubborn 9 difficult, fractious, obstinate 10 headstrong, refractory 11 disagreeing, intractable 12 recalcitrant 13 contradictory 15 unaccommodating

frown 4 fret, mope, muse, pout, sulk 5 glare, scowl 6 glower, ponder 14 discountenance

frowning 4 dark 5 angry 6 gloomy, somber, sullen 8 scowling 9 glowering

frown upon 7 condemn, dislike 8 object to 14 discountenance

frowsy, frowzy 5 fusty, musty, stale 6 sloppy, untidy 7 tousled, unkempt 8 slovenly

frozen 3 icy 4 cold, iced, numb 5 chill, gelid, polar 6 arctic, chilly, cooled, wintry 7 chilled, clogged, glacial, stymied 8 benumbed, hibernal, icebound 10 obstructed, stalemated 11 frostbitten, immobilized 12 refrigerated

fructify 5 bloom 6 sprout, thrive 7 blossom, prosper, succeed 8 flourish

frugal 4 slim 5 scant, tight 6 skimpy, stingy 7 ascetic, sparing, thrifty 9 niggardly, penny-wise 10 abstemious, economical, unwasteful 12 parsimonious

frugality 6 thrift 7 economy 8 prudence, stinting 9 parsimony 10 scantiness, stinginess 11 thriftiness 12 cheeseparing 13 niggardliness, penny-pinching 16 parsimoniousness

fruit 4 crop 5 award, issue, yield, young 6 effect, profit, result, return, reward, upshot 7 benefit, harvest, outcome, produce, product, progeny, revenue 8 earnings 9 advantage, emolument, offspring, outgrowth 10 production 11 consequence 12 remuneration

fruitful 6 fecund 7 fertile 8 blooming, prolific, yielding 9 effective 10 productive, profitable, successful 11 efficacious 12 advantageous, fructiferous

fruition 8 maturity, ripeness 10 attainment 11 achievement, fulfillment, realization 12 consummation, satisfaction 13 actualization, gratification 15 materialization

fruitless 4 arid, vain 5 empty, inept 6 barren, futile, hollow 7 sterile, useless 8 abortive, bootless, nugatory 9 infertile, pointless, worthless 10 profitless, unavailing, unprolific 11 incompetent, ineffective, ineffectual, inoperative, purposeless, unrewarding 12 unproductive, unprofitable, unsuccessful 13 inefficacious

fruit trees
 goddess of: 6 Pomona

frumpy 4 drab 5 dowdy 8 slovenly 10 slatternly 12 unattractive

frustrate 3 bar 4 balk, foil 5 block, check, upset 6 baffle, cancel, defeat, hinder, impede, thwart 7 counter, cripple, fluster, inhibit, nullify, prevent 8 dispirit, obstruct, prohibit, suppress 9 forestall, hamstring, undermine 10 circumvent, disappoint, disconcert, discourage, dishearten

frustration 6 defeat 7 balking, chagrin, failure, foiling, letdown 8 futility 9 hindrance, thwarting 10 bafflement, inhibition, nonsuccess 11 obstruction 13 discomfiture, interference 13 contravention, counteraction 14 disappointment, nonfulfillment 15 dissatisfaction

fry 4 cook 5 brown, grill, saute 7 frizzle 9 fricassee

Fry, Christopher
 author of: 9 Yard of Sun 12 The Firstborn 13 Venus Observed 20 The Dark Is Light Enough 21 The Lady's Not for Burning

frying pan 3 wok 6 frypan 7 browner, griddle, skillet

fuchsia
 varieties: 4 cape, tree 5 hardy 10 California 11 honeysuckle

fuddled 5 bosky, dopey, drunk, tipsy 6 boozed, groggy 7 maudlin, muddled, sozzled, tippled 8 confused 9 stupefied 10 inebriated 11 intoxicated

fudge 3 lie 4 bosh, fake 5 candy, cheat, evade, hedge, hunch, patch, welch 7 falsify, penuche 8 divinity

fuel 3 fan, gas, oil 4 coal, feed, fire, wood 5 light, means, stoke 6 charge, fill up, fodder, ignite, incite, kindle 7 impetus, inflame, sustain 8 activate, energize, gasoline, material, recharge, stimulus 9 petroleum, stimulate 10 ammunition, motivation, sustenance 11 inspiration, wherewithal

fugitive 4 hobo 5 brief, exile, hasty, nomad, rover, short, tramp 6 errant, fading, flying, loafer, outlaw 7 cursory, elusive, erratic, escaped, escapee, fleeing, hurried, passing, refugee, runaway, summary, vagrant 8 apostate, deserter, escaping, fleeting, flitting, renegade, shifting, unstable, vagabond, volatile, wanderer 9 ephemeral, fugacious, itinerant, momentary, straggler, temporary, transient, uncertain 10 evanescent, expatriate, short-lived, transitory 11 impermanent

Fugitive, The
 character: 9 Donna Taft 11 Fred Johnson (one-armed man) 12 (Lt) Philip Gerard 13 (Dr) Richard Kimble
 cast: 10 Barry Morse, Bill Raisch 12 David Janssen 15 Jacqueline Scott

fuhrer, Fuhrer, der fuhrer 4 Nazi 6 Hitler, leader, tyrant 8 dictator 11 Adolf Hitler

fulfill 2 do 4 heed, keep, meet, obey, suit 6 answer, effect, follow, redeem 7 achieve, execute, observe, perfect, perform, realize, satisfy 9 discharge, establish, implement 10 accomplish, consummate, effectuate

fulfillment, fulfilment 7 delight 8 crowning, pinnacle, pleasure 9 execution, happiness 10 attainment, completion 11 achievement, contentment, culmination, realization 12 effectuation, satisfaction 13 contentedness, establishment, gratification 14 accomplishment, implementation

Fulks, Sarah Jane
 real name of: 9 Jane Wyman

full 3 big 4 rich, very, wide 5 ample, broad, flush, laden, large, plump, quite, round, sated, total, whole 6 entire, gorged, intact, loaded, mature, packed, rotund 7 brimful, crammed, exactly, fraught, glutted, heaping, maximum, perfect, plenary, replete, shapely, stuffed, teeming 8 brimming, bursting, complete, resonant, swarming, thorough 9 abounding, capacious, perfectly, precisely, saturated, surfeited 10 unabridged, voluminous

full amount 3 all, sum 5 total, whole 8 entirety, totality 9 aggregate 10 complement

full-bodied 3 fat 4 rich 5 ample, lofty 6 hearty, mature, robust 9 flavorful 10 meaningful

Fuller, R Buckminster
   architect of: 10 US Pavilion (Expo '67 Montreal) 13 Dymaxion House
   form: 12 geodesic dome

full-fledged 5 adept 6 expert, mature 7 skilled, trained 8 complete, masterly, schooled 9 qualified, topflight 10 proficient 11 experienced 13 authoritative

full form 9 extension 10 elongation 11 enlargement 12 augmentation 13 amplification

full-grown 4 ripe 5 adult, manly, of age, matured, womanly 9 developed

full measure 6 enough, plenty 9 abundance, plenitude 10 competence 11 sufficiency

Full Moon
   author: 11 P G Wodehouse

fullness 7 satiety 8 richness 9 amplitude, roundness, satiation 12 completeness 14 voluminousness

full of fire 7 rousing 8 electric, exciting, spirited 9 thrilling 11 galvanizing, stimulating 12 electrifying, soul-stirring

full of life 5 vital 8 animated, spirited, vigorous 9 ebullient, energetic, exuberant, vivacious

full of pep 5 vital 6 lively 8 animated

full of vim and vigor 5 peppy 6 lively 11 invigorated

full view 7 the open 8 daylight, openness

fully 5 amply, quite 6 richly, wholly 7 totally, utterly 8 entirely 9 copiously, perfectly 10 abundantly, altogether, completely, positively, throughout 11 plentifully 12 sufficiently 13 substantially

fully realized 7 perfect 8 achieved, complete, executed, finished 9 completed, perfected, performed 11 consummated 12 accomplished

fulminate 4 boil, rage, rant 7 explode 8 denounce

fulminate against 5 roast 6 berate 7 scourge 8 call down, chastise 9 castigate

fulmination 7 violent 8 bursting, eruption 9 discharge, explosion

fulsome 3 fat 4 foul 5 suave 6 lavish, odious 7 cloying, lustful, noisome, obscene 8 overdone, unctuous 9 excessive, obnoxious, offensive, repulsive, tasteless 10 disgusting, obsequious

Fulton, Robert
   nationality: 8 American
   inventor of: 9 steamboat (Clermont), submarine 13 marine torpedo

fumble 3 err, mar 4 blow, muff 5 grope, spoil 6 bobble, boggle, bollix, bungle, goof up, mess up, muddle 7 butcher, louse up, screw up 9 mishandle

fume 3 gas 4 boil, burn, emit, foam, haze, puff, rage, rant, rave, reek, waft 5 exude, scent, smell, smoke, stink, vapor 6 billow, exhale, miasma, seethe, stench 7 carry on, explode, flame up, flare up, smolder 10 exhalation

fun 3 gas 4 ball, game, jest, lark, play, romp, trip 5 antic, blast, cheer, mirth, prank, sport, spree 6 frolic, gaiety, joking 7 jollity, revelry, whoopee 8 escapade, good time, pleasure 9 amusement, diversion, enjoyment, horseplay, joviality, merriment 10 buffoonery, recreation, relaxation, skylarking, tomfoolery 11 distraction, playfulness, waggishness 13 entertainment

Funafuti
   capital of: 6 Tuvalu

function 3 act, job 4 duty, fete, gala, help, role, task, work 5 feast, field, niche, party, place, power, range, scope, serve 6 affair, behave, do duty, office, soiree, sphere 7 banquet, benefit, concern, faculty, operate, perform, purpose 8 activity, business, capacity, ceremony, occasion, province 9 festivity, objective, operation, reception 13 entertainment

functional 6 useful 7 working 8 operable 9 operative, practical 11 serviceable, utilitarian

functionary 7 employee, official 10 bureaucrat 13 administrator

functioning 5 in use 6 active, at work, usable 7 working 9 effectual, operating, operative

fund 3 pot 4 bank, foot, lode, mine, pool, vein, well 5 endow, float, fount, hoard, kitty, stock, store 6 pay for, spring, supply 7 finance, nest egg, reserve, savings, support 8 treasure 9 endowment, patronize, reservoir 10 foundation, investment, repository, storehouse, underwrite 12 accumulation

fundament 3 can 4 buns, rump, seat 5 fanny 6 behind, bottom 8 backside, buttocks, haunches 9 posterior 12 hindquarters

fundamental 3 key 4 ABC's, base, main 5 axiom, basic, basis, chief, first, major, vital 7 central, crucial, element, primary 8 cardinal, integral 9 component, essential, necessary, principal, principle, requisite 10 elementary, foundation, groundwork, underlying 11 cornerstone 13 indispensable

funds 4 cash, jack, pelf 5 bread, dough, lucre, means, money, moola 6 assets, income, wampum, wealth 7 capital, scratch 8 finances, property 9 resources 11 wherewithal

funeral 4 wake 5 rites 6 burial 7 requiem 9 cremation, interment, obsequies 10 entombment, inhumation

funeral song 5 dirge, elegy 6 lament 7 requiem 8 threnody 11 lamentation

funereal 3 sad 4 grim 5 weepy 6 dismal, dreary, gloomy, solemn, somber, woeful 7 doleful 8 desolate, dirgeful, grieving, mournful 9 cheerless, woebegone 10 depressing, lachrymose, lugubrious 13 brokenhearted

fun-filled 5 happy 6 joyful, joyous 8 pleasant, pleasing 9 enjoyable 10 delightful 11 pleasurable

Fungoso
   character in: 22 Every Man Out of His Humour
   author: 6 Jonson

fungus, fungi 4 mold, myco, rust, smut 5 ergot, yeast 6 mildew 7 truffle 8 mushroom 9 toadstool 11 thallophyte

fun-loving 3 jolly, merry 6 genial, jovial 7 affable 8 sociable 9 convivial 10 gregarious

funnel 4 cone, duct, flue, pipe, pour 5 focus, shaft 6 direct, filter, siphon 7 channel, chimney, conduit 9 stovepipe 10 smokestack, ventilator 11 concentrate

funny 3 odd 5 antic, comic, droll, merry, queer, weird, witty 6 absurd, jocose 7 amusing, bizarre, comical, curious, jesting, jocular, offbeat, strange, unusual, waggish 8 farcical, humorous, mirthful, peculiar, sporting, uncommon 9 diverting, facetious, hilarious, laughable, ludicrous 10 outlandish, ridiculous

Funny Girl
   director: 12 William Wyler
   cast: 8 Lee Allen 10 Kay Medford, Omar Sharif 11 Anne Francis 13 Walter Pidgeon 15 Barbra Streisand (Fanny Brice)
   score: 9 Jule Styne 10 Bob Merrill
   sequel: 9 Funny Lady
   song: 6 People 18 Don't Rain on My Parade

funnyman 3 wag, wit 4 card, fool, mime, zany 5 clown, comic, joker 6 jester, madcap 7 buffoon 8 comedian, humorist, jokester 9 harlequin

fuoco, con
   music: 8 with fire

fur 3 fox 4 down, hair, lamb, mink, pelt, seal 5 coney, lapin, otter, sable 6 beaver, fleece, jaguar, kit fox, nutria, rabbit, red fox 7 blue fox, cheetah, leopard, muskrat, opossum, raccoon 8 black fox, cross fox, squirrel, white fox 9 silver fox 10 animal skin, chinchilla 11 karakul lamb, Persian lamb 13 broadtail lamb 14 mouton-dyed lamb

furbelow 5 frill 6 fringe 7 falbala, flounce 8 trimming

furbish 4 buff 5 renew, shine 6 polish 7 burnish 8 renovate

Furiae *see* 6 Furies

Furies
   also: 5 Dirae 6 Erinys, Furiae, Semnai 7 Allecto, Erinyes, Megaera 9 Eumenides, Tisiphone
   corresponds to: 3 Ker

furious 3 mad 4 wild 5 angry, fiery, irate, rabid 6 enrage, fierce, fuming, raging, savage, stormy 7 intense, rampant, violent 9 frenetic, frenzied, heedless, maddened, provoked, reckless, up in arms, vehement, wrathful 9 fanatical, irascible, turbulent 10 infuriated, passionate, tumultuous, unbalanced 11 tempestuous 12 ungovernable, unrestrained

furl 4 coil, curl, fold, roll, wrap 5 truss 6 curl up, fold up, furdle, roll up, spiral

furlong
   abbreviation: 3 fur

furnace 4 kiln, oven 5 forge, stove 6 boiler, heater 11 incinerator

Furnace
   constellation of: 6 Fornax

furnish 3 arm, rig 4 gird, give, vest 5 array, dress, endow, equip, favor, fit up, grant, stock 6 fit out, outfit, purvey, render, supply 7 appoint, indulge, prepare, provide 8 accoutre, bestow on 9 provision 11 accommodate

furnishings 9 equipment 11 accessories 12 haberdashery

furnish room for 5 lodge, put up 6 billet 7 shelter 11 accommodate

furniture 7 effects 8 chattels, movables, property 11 possessions 12 appointments

furor 3 fad 4 flap, rage, to-do, word 5 craze, mania, noise, thing, vogue 6 fervor, frenzy, hoopla, lunacy, raving, uproar 7 fashion, madness, passion 8 brouhaha, insanity, reaction 9 agitation, commotion, obsession, transport 10 dernier cri, enthusiasm, excitement, fanaticism

furrow 3 cut, dig, rut 4 knit, line, plow, rift, seam 5 cleft, crack, ditch, ridge, track 6 crease, groove, pucker, trench, trough 7 channel, crevice, fissure, wrinkle 10 depression 11 corrugation

furry 4 soft 5 downy, hairy, scary 6 cuddly, fleecy, pelted, shaggy 8 fearsome, horrible 11 hair-raising

further 3 aid, new, too, yet 4 also, back, help, more 5 again, extra, favor, fresh, other, spare, speed 6 abroad, assist, back up, beyond, foster, hasten, oblige, to boot, yonder 7 advance, afar off, besides, farther, forward, promote, quicken, stand by, work for 8 champion, expedite, likewise, moreover 9 accessory, ancillary, auxiliary, encourage, propagate 10 accelerate, additional, strengthen 11 accommodate 12 additionally, contributory, supplemental 13 supplementary

furtherance 3 aid 4 help, lift 5 favor 6 succor 7 advance, defense, support 8 advocacy, interest 9 patronage, promotion 10 assistance 11 advancement, cooperation, countenance 12 championship

furthering 3 aid 6 aiding, growth 8 abetting, advocacy, espousal 9 assisting, fostering, promoting, promotion 10 assistance, supporting 11 advancement, encouraging, propagating, propagation 12 accelerating, acceleration, encouragement 13 strengthening

furthermore 3 too 4 also 6 as well, to boot 7 besides 8 likewise, moreover 10 in addition 12 additionally

furthermost 7 extreme 8 farthest 11 farthermost

furtive 3 sly 4 wily 5 shady 6 covert, crafty, hidden, masked, secret, shifty, sneaky, unseen, veiled 7 cloaked, elusive, evasive, private 8 secluded, shrouded, skulking, sneaking, stealthy 9 collusive, secretive, underhand 10 mysterious, undercover, unrevealed 11 clandestine 12 confidential 13 surreptitious 14 conspiratorial

fury 3 fit, hag, ire, pet 4 gall, huff, rage, snit 5 force, might, shrew, vixen, wrath 6 attack, choler, frenzy, spleen, virago 7 assault, bluster, dudgeon, hellcat, tantrum 8 acerbity, acrimony, ferocity, outburst, severity, she-devil, spitfire, violence 9 intensity, termagant, vehemence, virulence 10 excitement, fierceness, turbulence 11 impetuosity

Fury
  form: 8 divinity
  sex: 6 female
  mother: 4 Gaea
  father: 6 Uranus
  born of the blood of: 6 Uranus
  Greek name: 6 Erinys 7 Erinyes 9 Eumenides
  Roman name: 5 Dirae 6 Furiae

fuse 4 join, link, meld, melt, weld, wick 5 blend, merge, smelt, torch 6 league, mingle, solder 7 combine 8 coalesce, federate, ignition, solidify 9 associate, detonator 10 amalgamate, assimilate 11 confederate, consolidate, incorporate, intermingler

fusillade 4 hail, rain 5 salvo, spray 6 volley 7 barrage, battery 8 drumfire, enfilade 9 broadside, cannonade 11 bombardment

fusion 5 blend, union 6 league 7 combine, melding, melting, merging 8 alliance, blending, compound, smelting 9 coalition, synthesis 10 commixture, dissolving, federation 11 association, coalescence, combination, commingling, confederacy, unification 12 amalgamation, intermixture, liquefaction 13 agglomeration, confederation

fuss 3 ado, nag 4 carp, fool, fret, fume, pomp, spat, stew, stir, tiff, to-do 5 annoy, cavil, labor, set-to, worry 6 bother, bustle, excite, fidget, flurry, hubbub, hustle, niggle, pester, pother, potter, putter, rattle, scurry, tinker 7 agitate, confuse, dispute, fluster, flutter, nitpick, quarrel, quibble, perturb, trouble, turmoil 8 ceremony 9 agitation, commotion, confusion 10 disconcert, hurly-burly, turbulence 11 disturbance, superfluity 12 perturbation 15 ceremoniousness
  Yiddish: 7 tzimmes

fuss over 6 dote on

fussy 4 busy 6 ornate 7 finical, finicky, nervous 8 bustling, critical, exacting 9 assiduous, cluttered, crotchety, demanding, squeamish 10 compulsive, fastidious, meticulous, nitpicking, old-maidish, particular, scrupulous 11 painstaking, persnickety

fusty 5 moldy, musty, stale 6 foisty, rancid, stuffy 8 obsolete 9 out of date 10 malodorous 12 old fashioned

Futabatei, Shimei
  author of: 16 The Drifting (Floating) Cloud

futile 4 idle, vain 5 empty, petty 7 trivial, useless 8 abortive, bootless, nugatory, trifling 9 frivolous, fruitless, valueless, worthless 10 profitless, unavailing 11 ineffective, ineffectual, unimportant 12 unprofitable, unsuccessful 13 insignificant

future 4 hope 5 after, later 6 coming, latter, morrow, offing, to come 7 by-and-by, ensuing, outlook 8 eventual, prospect, tomorrow, ultimate 9 following, hereafter, impending, projected 10 in prospect, subsequent, succeeding 11 anticipated, expectation, opportunity, prospective 12 anticipation
  Spanish: 6 manana

Future Shock
  author: 12 Alvin Toffler

fuzz 4 down, lint 5 fluff

fuzzy 3 dim 4 hazy 5 downy, foggy, linty, misty, murky, vague, wooly 6 fluffy, frizzy, woolly 7 blurred, obscure, shadowy, unclear 8 confused 9 pubescent 10 indefinite, indistinct

G

gab 3 jaw, rap 4 blab, chat 5 prate 6 babble, gibber, gossip, jabber, patter 7 baloney, blarney, blather, chatter, prattle 8 chitchat, idle talk, talk idly 10 balderdash 12 conversation

gabble 3 rap 4 blab 5 prate 6 babble, drivel, gossip, jabber 7 blather, chatter, prattle, twaddle 8 babbling, chitchat, idle talk 9 gibbering, jabbering 10 blathering, chattering 14 chitterchatter

gabfest 3 rap 4 chat, talk 7 palaver 8 chitchat 10 discussion 12 conversation 13 confabulation

gable 4 edge, peak, roof, wall 6 detail, dormer, pinion 7 aileron 8 pediment, triangle

Gable, Clark
  real name: 17 William Clark Gable
  wife: 13 Carole Lombard
  nickname: 7 The King
  born: 7 Cadiz OH
  roles: 7 Red Dust 8 Saratoga 10 The Misfits 11 Rhett Butler 15 Gone With the Wind 18 It Happened One Night (Oscar)

Gabo, Naum
  real name: 17 Naum Neemia Pevsner
  born: 6 Russia 7 Brainsk
  founder: 14 Constructivism
  artwork: 6 Column 11 Spiral Theme 16 Sculptural Models 19 Kinetic Construction 24 Variations of Spheric Theme

Gabon Republic
  capital/largest city: 10 Libreville
  others: 4 Oyem 5 Bongo, Kango 6 Mitzic, Moanda, Mouila, Omvane 7 Makokou, Mounana 9 Lambarene 10 Port-Gentil 11 Franceville
  monetary unit: 5 franc 7 centime
  lake: 7 Anengue, Azinguo
  mountain: 5 Mpele 7 Chaillu, Cristal, Mikongo 8 Balaquri, Birougou
  highest point: 8 Iboundji
  river: 4 Como 6 Abanga, Ivindo, Ogooue 7 Ngounie
  sea: 8 Atlantic
  physical feature:
  cape: 5 Lopez
  people: 4 Fang 6 Adouma, Bakota, Bateke, Echira, Okande, Omyene 7 Eshiras 8 Bandjabi, Bapounou
  leader: 3 Mba 5 Bongo
  philanthropist: 16 Albert Schweitzer
  language: 6 French
  religion: 5 Islam 7 animism 10 Protestant 13 Roman Catholic
  feature:
  tree: 6 okoume
  food: 6 manioc 9 Dika bread

Gabor, Eva
  mother: 5 Jolie
  sister: 5 Magda 6 Zsa Zsa
  born: 7 Hungary 8 Budapest
  roles: 4 Gigi 10 Green Acres 12 My Man Godfrey 13 A Royal Scandal, Forced Landing 15 Youngblood Hawke 18 The Truth About Women 20 The Last Time I Saw Paris

Gabor, Sari
  real name of: 11 Zsa Zsa Gabor

Gabor, Zsa Zsa
  real name: 9 Sari Gabor
  mother: 5 Jolie
  sister: 3 Eva 5 Magda
  husband: 10 Nick Hilton 13 George Sanders
  born: 7 Hungary 8 Budapest
  roles: 4 Lili 11 Moulin Rouge 14 Lovely To Look At 20 The Story of Three Loves

Gaboriau, Emile
  author of: 9 File No 113

Gaborone, Gaberones
  capital of: 8 Botswana

Gabriel 9 archangel
  means: 8 man of God 11 God is strong
  spoke to: 4 Mary 9 Zacharias, Zechariah

Gad
  father: 5 Jacob
  mother: 6 Zilpah
  brother: 3 Dan 4 Levi 5 Asher, Judah 6 Joseph, Reuben, Simeon 7 Zebulun 8 Benjamin, Issachar, Naphtali
  sister: 5 Dinah
  descendant of: 6 Gadite

gadget 4 tool 6 device, doodad, jigger 7 gimmick, novelty 9 accessory, doohickey 10 attachment 11 contraption, contrivance, thingamabob, thingamajig

Gaea
  also: 2 Ge 4 Gaia
  origin: 5 Greek
  goddess of: 5 earth
  husband: 6 Uranus
  children: 6 Pontus, Titans, Uranus 7 Cyclops, Erinyes 9 mountains 13 Hecatonchires
  son: 6 Nereus 7 Iapetus, Oceanus
  daughter: 4 Rhea 5 Theia 6 Phoebe, Tethys, Themis 9 Mnemosyne
  corresponds to: 6 Tellus

Gaelic
  language family: 12 Indo-European
  branch: 6 Celtic
  subgroup: 4 Manx 5 Irish 8 Scottish

gaffe 4 goof 5 boner 6 boo-boo 7 blunder 11 impropriety 12 indiscretion
  French: 7 faux pas 9 gaucherie

gag 4 hoax, hush, jest, joke, stop 5 block, choke, heave, retch 6 muffle, muzzle, stifle 7 cloture, foolery, silence, smother 8 stoppage, suppress 9 horseplay, restraint 13 facetiousness

Gaia see 4 Gaea

gaiety, gayety 3 fun 4 show 5 mirth 6 frolic, tinsel 7 elation, glitter, jollity, spirits 8 airiness, frippery, trumpery, vivacity 9 amusement, animation, brummagem, gaudiness, merriment, showiness 10 brightness, brilliance, garishness, jauntiness, joyousness, liveliness 11 celebration, merrymaking 12 cheerfulness, colorfulness, exhilaration, sportiveness 13 effervescence, sprightliness

gain, gains 3 add, bag, get, hit, net, win 4 jump, leap, plus, reap 5 bloom, bonus, fetch, glean, put on, reach, wages, yield 6 attain, come to, gather, income, obtain, pick up, profit, return, salary, secure, thrive 7 achieve, acquire, blossom, capture, collect, improve, procure, produce, prosper, recover, revenue 8 addition, arrive at, black ink, dividend, earnings, flourish, increase, overtake, proceeds, winnings 9 accretion, advantage, increment 10 attainment 11 improvement 12 accumulation, compensation, remuneration

Gaines, Ernest J
author of: 33 The Autobiography of Miss Jane Pittman

gainful 4 rich 6 paying 9 lucrative 10 productive, profitable 12 remunerative

gainfully 8 usefully 10 profitably 11 lucratively 12 productively 14 remuneratively

gain recognition 9 establish

gainsay 4 deny 6 abjure, oppose, refute 7 disavow, dispute 9 repudiate 10 contradict, controvert

Gainsborough, Thomas
born: 7 England, Sudbury
artwork: 10 The Blue Boy 14 The Morning Walk 15 Mr and Mrs Andrews, The Hon Mrs Graham 16 Viscount Ligonier 26 Peasant Girl Gathering Sticks

gait 4 pace, step, walk 5 tread 6 stride 7 bearing 8 carriage 10 deportment
French: 8 demarche

gaiter 4 boot, shoe, spat, vamp 5 chaps, strad 6 gaskin, hugger, puttee 7 legging 8 cuttikin, overshoe

gala 3 gay 5 grand, party 7 benefit, festive, opulent 8 material, majestic, splendid 9 festivity, glamorous, sumptuous 10 ceremonial, fancy-dress, glittering 11 celebration, celebratory, magnificent, spectacular, star-studded
French: 4 fete

Galahad
character in: 16 Arthurian romance

Galatea
form: 6 maiden, statue 8 sea nymph
father: 6 Nereus
mother: 5 Doris
courted by: 10 Polyphemus
lover: 4 Acis

killed: 4 Acis
statue carved by: 9 Pygmalion
brought to life by: 9 Aphrodite
son: 6 Paphos

gale 3 fit 4 blow, gust, stir 6 flurry, squall, tumult, uproar 7 cyclone, tempest 8 eruption, outbreak, outburst 9 agitation, commotion, windstorm

Galeus
form: 6 lizard
father: 6 Apollo

Galileo Galilei
nationality: 7 Italian
inventor of: 6 sector 11 thermometer
studied: 6 motion 8 pendulum
discovered: 18 Jupiter's satellites
constructed: 9 telescope
formulated: 18 law of falling bodies
author of: 8 Dialogue 10 Discourses 18 The Starry Messenger

Galinthias
handmaiden of: 7 Alcmene

gall 3 bug, irk, vex 4 bile, flay, fret, miff, rile 5 anger, annoy, brass, chafe, cheek, gripe, nerve, score, sting, venom 6 abrade, bruise, enrage, harass, injure, nettle, offend, rancor, ruffle, spleen 7 affront, incense, provoke, rub sore 8 acrimony, audacity, boldness, irritate, rudeness, temerity 9 animosity, assurance, displease, excoriate, impudence, insolence, malignity, sauciness, virulence 10 bitterness, brazenness, effrontery, exacerbate, exasperate 11 presumption

gallant 3 fop 4 bold, dude, game, stud 5 blood, brave, dandy, gutsy, noble, suave, swell 6 daring, heroic, kindly, plucky, polite, urbane 7 courtly, dashing, valiant 8 cavalier, fearless, gay blade, intrepid, mannerly, obliging, resolute, stalwart, valorous, well-bred 9 attentive, courteous, dauntless 10 chivalrous, courageous, thoughtful 11 considerate, gentlemanly, lionhearted 12 stouthearted

gallantries 10 attentions 11 compliments 12 pleasantries

gallantry 4 grit, sand 5 nerve, pluck, valor 6 daring, mettle, spirit 7 bravery, courage, dashing, heroism, prowess, suavity 8 chivalry, courtesy, urbanity 9 derring-do, fortitude, gentility 10 politeness 11 courtliness, intrepidity 12 fearlessness, resoluteness 13 attentiveness, dauntlessness, determination 14 courageousness

gallery 4 stoa 5 salon 6 arcade, loggia, piazza 7 balcony, passage, portico 8 cloister, corridor 9 bleachers, colonnade, mezzanine, triforium 10 ambulatory, grandstand, passageway

Gallia Belgica see 7 Belgium

galliano
type: 7 liqueur
origin: 5 Italy
flavor: 5 herbs, spice
color: 6 yellow
with creme de cacao: 14 Golden Cadillac

with rum: 9 Bossa Nova
with vodka: 16 Harvey Wallbanger

gallinule 3 hen 4 coot, fowl, rail, sora 7 moorhen 8 dabchick, hyacinth, rallidae, ricebird, swamphen

Gallipoli
director: 9 Peter Weir
cast: 7 Mark Lee 8 Bill Kerr 9 Mel Gibson 11 Robert Grubb

gallivant, galavant 3 gad 4 kite, roam, rove 5 jaunt, range, stray 6 ramble, travel, wander 7 gallant, meander, traipse, 8 gad about 9 philander

gallon
abbreviation: 3 gal

gallop 3 fly, hie, jog, run 4 bolt, dart, dash, flit, race, rush, scud, skim, trot, whiz 5 bound, hurry, scoot, shoot, speed, whisk 6 hasten, scurry, spring, sprint 7 mad dash, scamper, scuttle, tear off 8 fast clip, fast gait 9 skedaddle

Galloping Ghost
nickname of: 9 Red Grange

gallows 4 rope 5 noose 6 gibbet, halter 8 scaffold

galore 7 aplenty, to spare

galosh, galoche 4 boot, clog, shoe 6 arctic, patten, rubber 8 overshoe

Galsworthy, John
author of: 5 To Let 6 Strife 7 Justice 9 Loyalties 10 In Chancery 11 The Skin Game 13 A Modern Comedy 14 The Forsyte Saga 15 End of the Chapter 16 The Man of Property 22 Indian Summer of a Forsyte

Galt, John
character in: 13 Atlas Shrugged
author: 4 Rand

galvanize 4 fire, move, stir, wake 5 rally, rouse, treat 6 arouse, awaken, charge, excite, foment, spur on, thrill 7 inspire, provoke, quicken 8 activate, energize, vitalize 9 electrify, stimulate

galvanizing 7 rousing 8 electric, exciting, spirited 9 inspiring, thrilling 11 stimulating 12 electrifying, soul-stirring

Galveston Giant
nickname of: 11 Jack Johnson

Gamaliel
father: 6 Simeon 8 Pedahzur
grandfather: 6 Hillel
taught: 4 Paul

Gambia, The
capital/largest city: 6 Banjul 8 Bathurst
others: 5 Bakau, Basse, Mansa 7 Bintang, Brikama, Kuntaur 10 Georgetown
monetary unit: 5 butut, pound 6 dalasi
island: 7 Ft James, St Mary's 8 Elephant
river: 3 Bao 6 Gambia 7 Bintang, Nianija 9 Sandougou
sea: 8 Atlantic
people: 4 Fula, Jola 5 Foula, Wolof 6 Fulani 8 Mandingo, Serahuli 9 Seranuleh
language: 4 Fula 5 Wolof 6 Fulani 7 English, Malinke 8 Mandingo

religion: 5 Islam 10 Protestant 13 Roman Catholic

gambit 4 ploy, ruse 5 feint, trick 6 scheme 8 artifice, maneuver 9 stratagem

gamble 3 bet 4 back, risk 5 flyer, wager 6 chance, hazard, toss-up 7 trust in, venture 9 speculate 11 speculation, uncertainty

gambler 5 dicer, shark, sharp, sport 6 banker, bettor, bookie, dealer, player 7 hustler 8 gamester, hazarder 10 speculator

Gambler, The
author: 16 Fyodor Dostoevsky
character: 6 Astley, Polina 10 The General 11 Mlle Blanche 15 Marquis de Grieux 16 Alexey Ivanovitch 22 Antonida Tarasyevitchev

gambol 3 hop 4 leap 5 bound, caper, frisk, sport, vault 6 bounce, cavort, frolic, prance, spring 7 disport, rollick

game 3 bad, fun 4 golf, halt, lame, lark, play, polo, pool, prey, romp 5 antic, brave, cocky, darts, gimpy, jacks, match, rugby, sport, spree 6 boccie, boxing, daring, frolic, gaiety, gambol, heroic, plucky, quarry, soccer, spunky, squash, tennis 7 archery, bowling, contest, crooked, croquet, curling, fencing, frisbee, gallant, hawking, hunting, hurling, jai alai, limping, pastime, tourney, valiant, willing 8 baseball, crippled, deformed, disabled, fearless, football, handball, hobbling, intrepid, lacrosse, ping pong, resolute, skittles, spirited, valorous, wild fowl 9 amusement, badminton, billiards, dauntless, diversion, festivity, merriment, wrestling 10 basketball, courageous, determined, horseshoes, ice-skating, lawn tennis, recreation, tournament, volleyball 11 competition, distraction, merrymaking, racquetball, table tennis, unflinching 12 shuffleboard 13 entertainment, incapacitated, roller-skating
board game: 4 Clue, Life, ludo 5 chess 7 Othello 8 checkers, cribbage, dominoes, draughts, fanorona, Monopoly, Scrabble 10 backgammon 14 Trivial Pursuit
Chinese: 6 Ma-jong, wei-ch'i 7 mahjong 8 Mah-jongg
Egyptian: 5 Senat
Indian: 7 pachisi 8 parchesi, shatranj 9 ashtapada, parcheesi 10 shaturanga
Japanese: 2 Go 3 I-go 5 Sho-gi
Korean: 5 Nyout, Pa-tok
Swedish: 6 tablut
card game: 3 loo, war 4 brag, fish, skat, vint 5 ombre, poker, rummy, tarot, whist 6 boston, bridge, casino, chemmy, ecarte, euchre, go fish, hearts, memory, piquet, pocher 7 bezique, canasta, cooncan, old maid, plafond, primero 8 baccarat, conquian, cribbage, gin rummy, napoleon, patience, pinochle, slapjack 9 blackjack, pelmanism, solitaire, spoil five, twenty-one 11 chemin de fer, crazy eights 13 concentration 14 contract bridge 16 beggar-my-neighbor, trente et quarante

gamete 3 egg 4 ovum 5 sperm 6 oocyte, zygote 8 germ cell, oosphere 12 spermatozoan, spermatozoon

Gamow, George
field: 7 physics 9 cosmology
proponent of: 13 big bang theory
deciphered: 11 genetic code
proposed: 17 quantum theory
established: 17 Gamow-Teller theory

Gamp, Sarah
character in: 16 Martin Chuzzlewit
author: 7 Dickens

gamut 3 ken 5 reach, scope, sweep 6 extent 7 compass, purview

Gandhi
director: 19 Richard Attenborough
cast: 11 Ben Kingsley 13 Candice Bergen
Oscar for: 5 actor (Kingsley) 7 picture

gang 3 mob 4 band, body, crew, pack, pals, ring, team 5 chums, crowd, flock, group, party, relay, shift, squad, troop 6 clique, outfit 7 buddies, company, coterie, cronies, friends, phalanx 8 comrades 9 coworkers, neighbors 10 associates, classmates, companions, contingent, detachment 11 schoolmates

gangster 4 goon, hood, thug 5 crook, felon, tough 6 bandit, gunman 7 hoodlum, mafioso, mobster, ruffian 8 criminal, hooligan 9 racketeer

Gant, Eugene
character in: 17 Look Homeward Angel, Of Time and the River
author: 5 Wolfe

Ganymede
also: 9 Catamitus
cupbearer of: 4 gods

gap 3 cut 4 gash, hole, rent, rift, slit, slot, void 5 abyss, break, chasm, chink, cleft, crack, gulch, gully, notch, pause 6 breach, canyon, cavity, divide, hiatus, lacuna, ravine, recess, vacuum, valley 7 crevice, fissure, interim, opening 8 aperture, crevasse, fracture, interval, puncture 9 disparity, interlude 10 difference, divergence 12 intermission, interruption

gape 4 gasp, gawk, gaze, ogle, part, peer, yawn 5 split, stare 6 cleave, expand 7 fly open 8 wide open, separate 10 rubberneck

gaping 6 astare 7 gawking, staring, yawning 13 rubbernecking

Garamas see 11 Amphithemis

garb 3 rig 4 gear, gown, robe, suit, togs 5 dress, getup, habit 6 attire, finery, livery, outfit 7 apparel, clothes, costume, raiment, uniform, vesture 8 clothing, garments, vestment, wardrobe 9 trappings 11 habiliments

garbage 4 dirt, junk 5 offal, swill, trash, waste 6 debris, litter, refuse 7 carrion, rubbish 9 sweepings

garble 5 mix up 6 jumble 7 confuse, distort 8 fragment

Garbo, Greta
real name: 21 Greta Louisa Gustaffson
born: 6 Sweden 9 Stockholm
roles: 4 Love 7 Camille 8 Conquest, Mata Hari 9 Ninotchka 10 Grand Hotel 12 Anna Christie, Anna Karenina 13 Queen Cristina, Two-Faced Woman 14 The Painted Veil 16 Flesh and the Devil

Garcia Lorca, Federico
author of: 5 Yerma 12 Blood Wedding, Gypsy Ballads 19 House of Bernarda Alba

Garcia Marquez, Gabriel
author of: 9 Leaf Storm 23 The Autumn of the Patriarch 25 One Hundred Years of Solitude

garcon 3 boy 6 waiter 7 servant

garden 4 Eden, lawn, plot, yard 7 Arcadia 8 paradise 10 Gethsemane
type: 4 herb, rock, rose 5 truck 6 flower, formal 7 kitchen 9 botanical, vegetable

gardenia
varieties: 5 crape 9 butterfly

Garden of Cypress, The
author: 15 Sir Thomas Browne

Garden of the Finzi-Continis, The
director: 14 Vittorio De Sica
author: 11 Rumer Godden
cast: 10 Fabio Testi 11 Romolo Valli 12 Helmut Berger 14 Dominique Sanda 15 Lino Capolicchio
Oscar: 11 foreign film

Garden of the West
nickname of: 6 Kansas

garden party
French: 13 fete champetre

gardens
god of: 9 Vertumnus
goddess of: 5 Venus

Garden State
nickname of: 9 New Jersey

garden variety 5 plain 6 common, simple 7 regular 8 everyday, familiar, ordinary 11 commonplace

Gardner, Ava
husband: 9 Artie Shaw 12 Frank Sinatra, Mickey Rooney
born: 12 Smithfield NC
roles: 7 Mogambo 8 Show Boat 9 Mayerling, Naked Maja 10 On the Beach 15 The Sun Also Rises 18 Snows of Kilimanjaro 19 The Barefoot Contessa, The Night of the Iguana

Gardner, Erle Stanley
character: 9 Paul Drake 10 Perry Mason 11 Della Street 14 Hamilton Burger
also wrote as: 6 A A Fair

Gardner, John
author of: 7 Grendel 12 October Light 14 Nickel Mountain, The Art of Living, The King's Indian 17 Michelsson's Ghosts 20 The Sunlight Dialogues, The Wreckage of Agathon

Gareth
character in: 16 Arthurian romance

Garfield, James Abram
  presidential rank: 9 twentieth
  party: 10 Republican
  state represented: 2 OH
  defeated: 3 (Neal) Dow 6 (James Baird)
  Weaver, (John Wolcott) Phelps 7
  (Winfield Scott) Hancock
  vice president: 6 (Chester Alan) Arthur
  cabinet:
  state: 6 (James Gillespie) Blaine
  treasury: 6 (William) Windom
  war: 7 (Robert Todd) Lincoln
  attorney general: 8 (Isaac Wayne)
  MacVeagh
  navy: 4 (William Henry) Hunt
  postmaster general: 5 (Thomas
  Lemuel) James
  interior: 8 (Samuel Jordan) Kirkwood
  born: 2 OH 6 Orange 8 log cabin
  died: 9 Elberon NJ
  died by: 13 assassination
  buried: 11 Cleveland OH
  education:
  seminary: 6 Geauga
  college: 5 Hiram (Eclectic Institute) 8
  Williams
  studied: 3 law
  religion: 17 Disciples of Christ
  political career: 8 US Senate (declined
  seat) 11 state Senate 24 US House of
  Representatives
  civilian career: 6 lawyer 7 teacher 11 lay
  preacher
  military service: 6 US Army 8 Civil War
  12 major general
  notable events of lifetime/term:
  exposure of: 15 Star Route frauds
  father: 7 Abraham
  mother: 8 Eliza (Ballou)
  siblings: 4 Mary 5 James 6 Thomas 9
  Mehitabel
  wife: 8 Lucretia (Rudolph)
  nickname: 5 Crete
  children: 4 Mary 5 Abram, Eliza 6
  Edward 12 James Rudolph 13 Harry Augustus, Irvin McDowell
Garfield, John
  real name: 15 Julius Garfinkle
  born: 9 New York NY
  roles: 6 Juarez 10 Humoresque 11 Body
  and Soul 26 The Postman Always Rings
  Twice
Garfinkle, Julius
  real name of: 12 John Garfield
Gargamelle
  character in: 22 Gargantua and Pantagruel
  author: 8 Rabelais
Gargantua and Pantagruel
  author: 16 Francois Rabelais
  character: 7 Panurge 10 Gargamelle,
  Grangosier, Picrochole 23 Frere Jean
  des Entommeures
gargantuan 4 huge, vast 5 great 7 hulking,
  immense, mammoth, massive, titanic 8 colossal, enormous, gigantic, lubberly, towering 9 herculean, monstrous, overgrown 10

prodigious, stupendous, tremendous 11 elephantine 13 amplitudinous
Gargaphia
  death place of: 7 Actaeon
Gargery, Joe
  character in: 17 Great Expectations
  author: 7 Dickens
garish 4 loud 5 cheap, gaudy, showy 6
  brassy, bright, flashy, tawdry, tinsel, vulgar
  7 blatant, glaring 9 flaunting, obtrusive 11
  pretentious 12 ostentatious 13 overelaborate
garland 3 bay, lei 4 halo 5 crown 6 corona,
  diadem, fillet, laurel, wreath 7 chaplet, circlet, coronet, festoon 8 chapbook, headband, treasury 9 anthology 10 collection
  11 florilegium
Garland, Hamlin
  author of: 18 Main-Travelled Roads 20
  Rose of Dutcher's Coolly
Garland, Judy
  real name: 11 Frances Gumm
  husband: 7 Sid Luft 16 Vincente Minnelli
  daughter: 9 Lorna Luft 12 Liza Minnelli
  costar: 12 Mickey Rooney
  born: 13 Grand Rapids MN
  roles: 7 Dorothy 11 A Star Is Born,
  Babes in Arms 12 Easter Parade 13 The
  Wizard of Oz 14 The Harvey Girls 15 A
  Child Is Waiting, Meet Me in St Louis
garlic
  botanical name: 13 Allium sativum
  origin: 4 Asia 13 Mediterranean
  charm against: 7 poverty, witches 13
  whooping cough
  use: 4 fish, fowl, meat 5 salad 10 vegetables 13 Italian dishes, salad dressing
  varieties: 4 crow, hog's, wild 5 bear's,
  false, field, giant, grace, mouse, stag's,
  sweet 6 levant 7 serpent, society, Spanish, striped 8 daffodil, oriental 11 great-
  headed, round-headed 16 fragrant-
  flowered
Garm
  origin: 12 Scandinavian
  form: 8 watchdog
  watches over: 3 Hel
  location: 8 Niflheim
garment, garments 4 garb, gear, togs 5
  dress, habit 6 attire, outfit 7 apparel,
  clothes, costume, raiment 8 clothing, vestment 10 habiliment
garner 4 reap 5 amass, hoard 6 gather,
  heap up 7 acquire, collect 8 assemble 10
  accumulate
Garner, James
  real name: 15 James Baumgarner
  born: 8 Norman OK
  roles: 8 Maverick, Sayonara 11 Jim
  Rockford 12 Bret Maverick, Hour of the
  Gun 13 Darby's Rangers, Rockford Files
  14 Murphy's Romance, Victor Victoria 23
  Support Your Local Sheriff 25 The Americanization of Emily

garnet
 varieties: 6 syrope 9 almandite, demantoid, hessonite, rhodolite 12 grossularite
 month: 7 January
Garnett, David
 author of: 11 Lady into Fox
garnish 4 deck, gild, trim 5 adorn, array 6
 bedeck, doll up, set off 7 festoon, furbish,
 smarten 8 beautify, decorate, emblazon,
 ornament, spruce up, trimming 9 adornment, embellish, embroider 10 decoration
 13 embellishment
garret 4 loft 5 attic
garrison 4 fort 5 guard 6 patrol, secure 7
 battery, bivouac, brigade, platoon, station
 8 division, regiment, squadron 10 detachment, escadrille 13 fortification
garrulity 8 verbiage 9 loquacity, prosiness,
 verbosity, wordiness 13 talkativeness
garrulous 5 gabby, windy, wordy 6 chatty 7
 gossipy, prating, verbose, voluble 8 babbling, chattery, effusive 9 prattling, talkative 10 loquacious
Garry Moore Show, The
 cast: 9 Allen Funt, Denise Lor, John
 Byner, Ken Carson 11 Chuck McCann,
 Marion Lorne 12 Carol Burnett, Durward
 Kirby, Jackie Vernon, Pete Barbutti 13
 Dorothy Loudon
Garson, Greer
 born: 7 Ireland 10 County Down
 roles: 10 Mrs Miniver (Oscar) 11 Madame Curie 12 Her Twelve Men 13 Mrs
 Parkington, Random Harvest 14
 Goodbye Mr Chips 16 That Forsyte
 Woman 17 Pride and Prejudice 19 Sunrise at Campobello
gas 4 fuel, fume 5 vapor 6 petrol 7 essence
gascon 7 boaster, bragger, egotist 8 blowhard, braggart 9 swaggerer 11 braggadocio
gasconade 4 brag, crow 5 boast 7 bravado
 8 boasting 11 braggadocio
gash 4 hack, rend, rent, slit, tear 5 carve,
 cleft, crack, lance, slash, slice, split,
 wound 6 cleave, incise, pierce 7 dissect, fissure, quarter 8 incision, lacerate
Gaskell, Elizabeth
 author of: 4 Ruth 8 Cranford 10 Mary
 Barton 13 North and South 24 The Life of
 Charlotte Bronte
Gaslight
 director: 11 George Cukor
 cast: 10 Terry Moore 12 Charles Boyer
 13 Dame May Whitty, Ingrid Bergman 14
 Angela Lansbury 15 Halliwell Hobbes
Gasoline Alley
 creator: 9 Bill Perry, Frank King 10 Dick
 Moores
 character: 3 Eve 4 Adam, Hope 6 Clovia,
 Gideon, Nubbin 7 Chipper, Gabriel 10
 Walt Wallet
 wife: 14 Phyllis Blossom
 children: 4 Judy 5 Corky 7 Skeezix
 daughter-in-law: 9 Nina Clock
 dog: 5 Punky

gasp 4 gulp, pant, puff 5 blurt 6 suck in,
 wheeze 10 vociferate
Gasterocheires
 companions of: 7 Proteus
gastronome 7 epicure, gourmet 9 bon vivant
gastronomy 9 epicurism
gastropod, gasteropod 4 slug 5 cowry,
 snail, whelk 6 cowrie, limpet, nerite 7 abalone, mollusk 8 univalve
gate 3 tap 5 crowd, house, valve 6 portal, sluice, spigot 7 doorway 8 audience,
 hatchway 9 turnstile 10 attendance
gateau 4 cake 7 dessert
gatekeeper 5 guard 6 porter 8 watchman
Gates, Horatio
 served in: 16 Revolutionary War 18
 French and Indian War
 battle: 6 Camden 8 Saratoga
 defeated: 8 Burgoyne
 defeated by: 10 Cornwallis
gateway 4 adit 5 entry 6 access, portal 7
 doorway, opening 8 entrance, entryway 10
 passageway
Gath 14 Philistine city
gather 4 fold, mass 5 amass, group, infer,
 learn, pleat, shirr, stack 6 assume, deduce, heap up, muster, pile up, pucker, ruffle 7 cluster, collect, convene, marshal, observe 8 assemble, conclude 9 stockpile 10
 accumulate, congregate, understand 11
 concentrate
gathering 3 mob 4 gang, pack 5 bunch,
 crowd, crush, drove, flock, horde, party,
 press 6 throng 7 company, meeting,
 roundup, turnout 8 assembly, conclave 9
 concourse, multitude 10 assemblage, collection, conference, convention 11 aggregation, convergence, convocation 12
 accumulation, congregation 13 concentration
gather together 4 herd 5 amass, hoard,
 rally 6 muster 7 collate, collect, compile,
 marshal, round up, sweep up 8 assemble, shepherd 9 aggregate, stockpile 10
 accumulate, congregate
Gatling, Richard Jordan
 nationality: 8 American
 inventor of: 10 machine gun 16 steam-
 powered plow
gatophobia
 fear of: 4 cats
gauche 5 inept 6 clumsy, oafish 7 awkward,
 boorish, ill-bred, uncouth 8 bungling, plebeian, tactless 9 inelegant, maladroit,
 tasteless, unrefined 10 blundering, uncultured, ungraceful, unmannerly, unpolished
 11 proletarian 13 ungentlemanly
gaucherie 5 gaffe 7 blunder, faux pas 11
 impropriety 12 indiscretion
Gaudeamus igitur 22 Let us therefore be
 joyful
gaudy 4 loud, sham 5 cheap, showy, vivid
 6 flashy, flimsy, garish, tawdry, tinsel, vulgar 7 glaring, intense 8 colorful, dazzling,
 lustrous, striking 9 brilliant, sparkling,

tasteless, worthless 10 bespangled, glittering 11 pretentious 12 ostentatious

gauge, gage 4 rate, size 5 guess, judge, meter 6 assess 7 adjudge, measure 8 appraise, estimate, evaluate, standard 9 ascertain, calculate, criterion, yardstick 11 measurement

    type: 4 ring 5 bevel

Gauguin, Paul Eugene Henri
    born: 5 Paris 6 France
    artwork: 9 Nevermore 12 The Tahitians 13 The White Horse 15 The Yellow Christ 18 Horsemen on the Beach 23 The Vision after the Sermon (Jacob Wrestling with the Angel) 25 Be in Love and You Will Be Happy 26 The Spirit of the Dead Watching 36 Where Do We Come From? Who Are We? Where Do We Go?
    book: 6 Noa Noa

Gaul see 6 France

gaunt 4 bony, grim, lank, lean, slim, thin 5 bleak, lanky, spare 6 barren, meager, skinny, wasted 7 haggard, pinched, scraggy, scrawny, slender, spindly, starved 8 deserted, desolate, forsaken, rawboned, skeletal, withered 9 emaciated, shriveled 10 cadaverous, forbidding 14 spindle-shanked

Gauss, Carl Friedrich
    field: 7 physics 9 astronomy 11 mathematics
    nationality: 6 German
    worked in: 9 magnetism 11 electricity 12 number theory
    named for him: 9 Gauss's Law

Gautier, Marguerite
    character in: 7 Camille
    author: 5 Dumas (fils)

Gautier, Theophile
    author of: 6 La Peri 7 Giselle 8 Albertus 11 Young France 13 Emaux et Camees 16 Enamels and Cameos 20 Mademoiselle de Maupin, The Romance of the Mummy
    doctrine: 14 Art for art's sake

gauzy 5 filmy, sheer 6 flimsy, sleazy 10 diaphanous 11 translucent, transparent

gave up 4 quit 5 ceded 7 dropped, forsook, yielded 8 forswore, resigned 9 abandoned, abdicated, forfeited, renounced 11 surrendered 12 discontinued, relinquished

Gawain
    character in: 16 Arthurian romance

gawk 4 gape, gaze, peer 10 rubberneck

gawky 4 clumsy, klutzy 7 awkward, lumpish 8 bungling, fumbling, lubberly, ungainly, unwieldy 9 all thumbs, graceless, hamfisted, ham-handed, maladroit 10 blundering, ungraceful

gay 3 fun 4 airy, glad 5 happy, jolly, merry, showy, sunny, vivid 6 blithe, bright, cheery, elated, frisky, genial, jaunty, jocose, jovial, joyful, joyous, lively, social 7 buoyant, chipper, coltish, dashing, festive, gleeful, glowing, intense, jocular, playful, smiling, waggish 8 animated, cheerful, colorful, exultant, gladsome, humorous, jubilant, lustrous, skittish, spirited, splendid, sportive, volatile 9 brilliant, convivial, frivolous, hilarious, rejoicing, sparkling, sprightly, sumptuous, vivacious 10 flamboyant, frolicsome, glittering, insouciant, theatrical, variegated 12 effervescent, lighthearted, multicolored

Gay, John
    author of dialogue/lyrics for: 15 The Beggar's Opera

Gay, Walter
    character in: 12 Dombey and Son
    author: 7 Dickens

gay blade 3 fop 4 beau 5 blade, dandy 7 playboy 8 cavalier 9 ladies' man 12 boulevardier, man-about-town

Gay Divorcee, The
    director: 12 Mark Sandrich
    cast: 10 Alice Brady, Erik Rhodes 11 Betty Grable, Fred Astaire 12 Ginger Rogers 19 Edward Everett Horton
    song: 11 Continental, Night and Day

Gay-Lussac, Joseph
    field: 7 physics 9 chemistry
    nationality: 6 French
    discovered: 24 law of combining gas volumes
    invented: 10 hydrometer

Gaynor, Mitzi
    real name: 20 Franceska Mitzi Gerber
    husband: 8 Jack Bean
    born: 9 Chicago IL
    roles: 8 Les Girls 10 Golden Girl 12 Anything Goes, South Pacific 14 The Joker Is Wild 32 There's No Business Like Show Business

gaze 3 eye 4 gape, ogle, peek, peer, scan 5 glare, lower, stare, study, watch 6 behold, glance, glower, peruse, regard, survey 7 examine, inspect, observe, witness 8 look long, pore over, scrutiny 10 rubberneck, scrutinize 11 contemplate

gaze at 4 view 5 watch 6 behold, look at 7 stare at 8 look upon 11 contemplate

Gazza Ladra, La
    also: 17 The Thieving Magpie
    opera by: 7 Rossini

Ge see 4 Gaea

gear 3 cam, rig 4 duds, garb, togs 5 dress, tools 6 attire, outfit, tackle, things 7 apparel, clothes, rigging 8 clothing, cogwheel, flywheel, garments, material, property 9 apparatus, equipment, trappings 10 belongings, implements 11 accessories, instruments 12 contrivances 13 accoutrements, paraphernalia

Geb
    also: 3 Keb
    origin: 8 Egyptian
    god of: 5 earth
    daughter: 4 Isis
    son: 6 Osiris
    sister: 3 Nut

Gedaliah
    means: 14 Jehovah is great
    father: 6 Ahikam, Pashur 8 Jeduthun
    descendant: 9 Zephaniah

Geer, Will
born: 11 Frankfort IN
roles: 7 Grandpa 10 The Waltons 11 In Cold Blood

Gehenna 4 hell

Gehrig, Lou (Henry Louis)
nickname: 9 Iron Horse
sport: 8 baseball
position: 9 first base
team: 14 New York Yankees

Geisman, Ella
real name of: 11 June Allyson

Geist 4 mind 6 spirit

gelatin 3 agar, glue 5 aspic, gelee, jelly 6 glutin, pectin 7 protein, sericin

gelatinize 3 set 4 jell 7 congeal, stiffen, thicken 9 coagulate

gelatinous 7 colloid, viscous 8 muculent 9 jelly-like

geld 5 alter 8 castrate 10 emasculate

gelid 3 icy 6 frigid, frozen 8 freezing

Gelonus
father: 8 Hercules

gem 4 dear, doll, rock 5 beaut, bijou, jewel, peach, prize 6 marvel, wonder 8 treasure
type: 4 jade, opal, ruby, sard 5 agate, amber, beryl, coral, pearl, topaz 6 garnet, pyrope, quartz, spinel, zircon 7 apatite, cat's-eye, citrine, diamond, emerald, jadeite, kunzite, olivine, peridot 8 amethyst, corundum, feldspar, hematite, lazurite, nephrite, sapphire, steatite, sunstone 9 almandite, amazonite, carnelian, demantoid, enstatite, fibrolite, malachite, moonstone, morganite, rhodolite, scapolite, spodumene, tiger's-eye, turquoise 10 aquamarine, bloodstone, chalcedony, hessionite, rose quartz, tourmaline 11 alexandrite, chrysoberyl, chrysocolla, chrysoprase, lapis lazuli, rock crystal, topaz quartz 12 grossularite

Gemini
symbol: 5 twins
planet: 7 Mercury
rules: 14 communications
born: 3 May 4 June

Gemini Contenders, The
author: 12 Robert Ludlum

Gem State
nickname of: 5 Idaho

gemutlich 4 easy 9 agreeable, congenial, simpatico 11 comfortable

gendarme 9 policeman

gender 3 sex 4 kind, male, sort, type 5 class 6 female, neuter 8 feminine 9 masculine

Gendre, Louis
real name of: 12 Louis Jourdan

genealogy 4 line 5 birth, house, stock 7 lineage 8 ancestry, pedigree 9 parentage 10 derivation, extraction

Gene Autry Show, The
cast: 10 Pat Buttram
horse: 8 Champion
theme song: 20 Back in the Saddle Again

general 5 basic, broad, usual, vague 6 common, normal, public, wonted 7 blanket, current, generic, inexact, natural, overall, popular, regular, typical 8 everyday, frequent, habitual, ordinary, pandemic, sweeping 9 customary, extensive, imprecise, panoramic, prevalent, universal, worldwide 10 accustomed, collective, ecumenical, prevailing, widespread 11 unspecified 12 conventional, nonexclusive, nontechnical 13 comprehensive, miscellaneous

General Electric Theater
host: 12 Ronald Reagan

general idea 4 gist 5 drift, tenor 6 effect, import 7 purport 10 impression 11 implication

generality 6 cliche, truism 9 platitude 12 universality 14 collectiveness 17 miscellaneousness 18 indiscriminateness

generalization 3 law 5 axiom 7 bromide 9 inference, statement

generalize 5 infer, judge 8 conclude

generally 5 often 6 always, mainly, mostly 7 as a rule, chiefly, largely, usually 9 currently, typically 10 frequently, habitually, ordinarily, repeatedly 11 extensively, principally, universally

general/military leader
American:
Revolutionary War: 3 (Light Horse Harry) Lee 5 Allen, Barry, Gates, Jones, Wayne 6 Arnold, Greene, Marion, Morgan 10 Washington
War of 1812: 4 Hull 5 Perry, Scott 7 Decatur
Mexican War: 5 Scott 6 Kearny
Civil War: 3 Lee 5 Early, Grant, Meade 6 Thomas, (JEB) Stuart 7 Forrest, Pickett, Sherman, (Stonewall) Jackson 8 Farragut, Sheridan 9 McClellan 10 Beauregard, Longstreet
Indian Wars: 6 Custer 7 Houston 10 Crazy Horse
WWI: 4 Sims 8 Mitchell, Pershing
WWII: 4 King 5 Clark 6 Arnold, Halsey, Nimitz, Patton 7 Bradley, Merrill 8 Marshall, Stilwell 9 Chennault, Doolittle, MacArthur 10 Eisenhower, Wainwright
Korean War: 5 Clark 9 MacArthur
Vietnam War: 6 Abrams 12 Westmoreland
Gulf War: 11 Schwarzkopf
British: 4 Byng, Haig, Howe, Slim 5 Wolfe 6 French, Gordon, Harris, Nelson, Wavell 7 Allenby, Clinton, Dowding, Wingate 8 Braddock, Burgoyne, Cromwell, Jellicoe, Lawrence 9 Alexander, Kitchener 10 Cornwallis, Montgomery, Wellington 11 Marlborough, Mountbatten
Carthagenian: 8 Hannibal 13 Hamilcar Barca
French: 3 Ney 4 Foch 5 Murat 6 Giraud, Joffre, Petain, Roland 7 Nivelle 8 De Gaulle, Montcalm, Napoleon 9 Lafayette 10 Bernadotte

German: 5 Kluck 6 Moltke, Paulus, Rommel, Scheer 7 Blucher, Goering, Tirpitz 8 Bismarck, Goebbels, Guderian 9 Rundstedt 10 Falkenhayn, Hindenburg, Kesselring, Ludendorff, Schlieffen 17 Frederick the Great

Israeli: 5 Dayan

Japanese: 10 Tojo Hideki 15 Yamamoto Isoroku

Macedonian: 7 Ptolemy 8 Philip II 9 Alexander (the Great)

Norman: 7 William (the Conqueror)

Roman: 5 Sulla 6 Brutus, Pompey, Seneca, Trajan 7 Crassus, Hadrian, Lepidus 8 Gracchus, Octavian (Caesar Augustus), Tiberius 9 Vespasian 10 Flaminius, Mark Antony 11 Gaius Marius 12 Julius Caesar 15 Cassius Longinus, Scipio Africanus 18 Tarquinius Superbus

Russian: 6 Zhukov 7 Kutuzov, Voronov 8 Brusilov, Kerensky, Kornilov, Samsonov 9 Bagration 10 Timoshenko, Vasilevsky

generate 4 bear, coin, form, make, sire 5 beget, breed, cause, frame, spawn, yield 6 create, evolve, father, induce, invent 7 develop, fashion, produce 8 contrive, engender, fructify, occasion 9 construct, fabricate, fecundate, fertilize, institute, originate, procreate, propagate, reproduce 10 effectuate, impregnate 11 proliferate

generation 3 kin 4 clan, line, race 5 breed, house, issue, stock, tribe 6 family, growth, strain 7 genesis, lineage, progeny 8 breeding, creation 9 begetting, causation, evolution, formation, offspring 10 production 11 development, engendering, origination, procreation, propagation 12 impregnation, reproduction 13 fertilization, proliferation

generic 6 common 7 general 8 sweeping 9 universal 10 collective 11 generalized, unspecified 12 nonexclusive 13 comprehensive 14 nonrestrictive

generosity 6 bounty 7 charity 8 altruism, courtesy, kindness, largesse 9 abundance, nobleness 10 liberality 11 benevolence, hospitality, magnanimity

generous 5 ample, large, lofty, noble 6 humane, lavish 7 copious, liberal 8 abundant, effusive, obliging, princely, prodigal 9 bounteous, bountiful, honorable, plenteous, plentiful, plethoric, unselfish, unstinted 10 altruistic, beneficent, benevolent, bighearted, charitable, freehanded, free-giving, high-minded, hospitable, munificent, openhanded, ungrudging, unstinting 11 considerate, extravagant, magnanimous, overflowing 12 humanitarian, largehearted, unrestricted 13 accommodating, philanthropic

genesis 4 rise, root 5 birth 6 origin 8 creation 9 begetting, beginning, inception 10 generation 11 engendering 12 commencement

geneticist
  American: 5 Temin 6 Morgan, Muller

genetics
  science of: 8 heredity
  researcher: 6 Mendel

Genetyllis
  origin: 5 Greek
  protectress of: 6 births

Genghis Khan
  also: 11 Jenghiz Khan
  name means: 14 universal ruler
  position: 13 Mongol emperor
  defeated: 6 Russia 10 Chin empire
  occupied: 6 Peking

genial 3 gay 4 glad, kind, warm 5 civil, happy, jolly, merry, sunny 6 bright, cheery, hearty, jaunty, jocund, jovial, joyful, joyous, kindly, lively, social 7 affable, amiable, chipper, cordial, festive 8 cheerful, friendly, gracious, mirthful, pleasant, sociable 9 agreeable, congenial, convivial, courteous, expansive, sparkling, vivacious 10 neighborly 12 lighthearted 13 companionable

geniality 10 affability, cordiality 11 sociability 12 conviviality, friendliness 13 expansiveness

genius 3 ace, wit 4 bent, gift, mind, whiz 5 brain, flair, knack 6 expert, master, wisdom 7 faculty, insight, prodigy 8 aptitude, judgment, penchant, sagacity, wizardry 9 ingenuity, intuition, invention 10 mastermind, perception, proclivity, propensity 11 imagination, percipience 12 intelligence, predilection 13 understanding

Genius, The
  author: 15 Theodore Dreiser

genius loci 16 guardian of a place

genre 4 kind, sort, type 5 breed, class, genus, group, order, style 6 school 7 fashion, species, variety 8 category, division 11 description 14 classification

genteel 4 tony 5 civil, elite, ritzy, swank, swell 6 modish, poised, polite, urbane 7 courtly, elegant, high-hat, refined, stylish 8 cultured, decorous, ladylike, mannerly, polished, well-bred 9 courteous, high-class, high-toned, patrician 10 cultivated, well-spoken 11 fashionable, gentlemanly, high-falutin, over-refined, pretentious 12 aristocratic, silk-stocking, thoroughbred

gentian 8 Gentiana
  varieties: 5 blind, green, horse 6 alpine, bottle, closed, Sierra, yellow 7 crested, fringed, prairie, spurred 8 Catesby's, soapwort, stemless 9 Mendocino 10 pine barren

gentil 4 kind 5 noble 6 gentle

gentile
  Yiddish: 3 goy
  man: 7 shegetz
  woman: 6 shiksa

gentility 6 polish 7 decorum, suavity 8 breeding, chivalry, civility, courtesy, urbanity 9 gallantry, propriety, punctilio 10 refinement 11 cultivation, savoir-faire 12 mannerliness

gentle 3 low 4 calm, easy, kind, meek, mild, soft, tame 5 balmy, bland, light, quiet 6 benign, broken, docile, kindly, placid, serene,

slight, smooth, tender 7 lenient, pacific, subdued 8 harmless, merciful, moderate, peaceful, tolerant, tranquil 9 indulgent, temperate, tractable 10 manageable, thoughtful, untroubled 11 considerate, sympathetic 12 domesticated 13 compassionate, tenderhearted
  French: 6 gentil
gentleman 3 don, guy, man, one 4 chap, gent 5 swell 6 fellow, person, squire 7 esquire, hidalgo 8 cavalier 9 caballero, chevalier, patrician 10 aristocrat, individual
Gentleman Jim
  nickname of: 12 James Corbett
gentlemanly 6 polite 7 courtly, gallant, refined 8 cultured, decorous, mannerly, polished, well-bred 9 courteous, dignified 10 cultivated
Gentleman's Agreement
  director: 9 Elia Kazan
  based on novel by: 12 Laura Z Hobson
  cast: 10 Anne Revere 11 Celeste Holm, Gregory Peck 12 John Garfield 14 Dorothy McGuire
  Oscar for: 7 picture 17 supporting actress (Holm)
Gentlemen Prefer Blondes
  author: 9 Anita Loos
gentleness 8 calmness, docility, mildness, serenity, tameness 10 compassion, tenderness 12 mercifulness, peacefulness, tractability
gentle wind 4 waft 6 breath, breeze, zephyr
gently 6 easily, kindly, meekly, mildly, softly, tamely 7 amiably, lightly 8 benignly, placidly, smoothly, tenderly 9 gradually 10 delicately, moderately, pleasantly, soothingly 15 compassionately, sympathetically
gentry 5 elite 7 society 8 nobility 10 blue bloods, gentlefolk 11 aristocracy, aristocrats
genuflect 4 bend 6 kowtow
genuine 4 open, pure, real, true 5 frank, naive, plain, solid 6 actual, candid, honest, proven, simple 7 artless, earnest, natural, sincere 8 bona fide, sterling, true-blue 9 authentic, guileless, heartfelt, ingenuous, simon-pure, unalloyed, veritable 10 legitimate, unaffected 13 unadulterated 15 straightforward, unsophisticated
genuineness 7 honesty 9 frankness, sincerity 10 candidness, simplicity 11 artlessness 13 guilelessness 14 unaffectedness 19 straightforwardness
genus 4 kind, sort, type 5 class, group 7 variety 8 category, division 14 classification
geologist
  British: 4 Hall
  German: 6 Werner
  Scottish: 6 Hutton
geoponics 7 tillage 8 agronomy 9 husbandry 10 agronomics 11 agriculture, cultivation

George Burns and Gracie Allen Show, The
  character: 9 Mr Beasley (Mailman) 11 Harry Morton 13 Blanche Morton
  theme song: 8 Love Nest
Georgetown
  capital of: 6 Guyana
Georgia (Russia)
  capital/largest city: 7 Tbilisi
  others: 6 Batumi 7 Kutaisi, Rustavi, Sukhumi
  division: 7 Ossetia 8 Abkhazia, Adzharia
  head of state: 9 president
  government: 8 republic
  monetary unit: 5 ruble
  mountain: 8 Caucasus
  river: 4 Kura 5 Rioni
  sea: 5 Black
  people: 5 Azeri 7 Russian 8 Armenian, Georgian, Ossetian 9 Abkhazian
  language: 8 Georgian
  religion 14 Georgian Church 15 Russian Orthodox
Georgia (US)
  abbreviation: 2 GA
  nickname: 5 Peach 7 Cracker 21 Empire State of the South
  capital/largest city: 7 Atlanta
  others: 4 Rome 5 Jesup, Macon 6 Albany, Athens, Dalton, Plains, Sparta 7 Augusta, Conyers, Cordele, Decatur, Griffen, Vidalia 8 Columbus, LaGrange, Marietta, Moultrie, Savannah, Valdosta, Waycross 9 Brunswick 11 College Park, Gainesville, Thomasville 13 Andersonville
  college: 4 Tift 5 Clark, Emory, Paine 6 Mercer 7 Atlanta, Spelman 8 Wesleyan 9 Morehouse 10 Agnes Scott 11 Georgia Tech
  explorer: 15 James Oglethorpe
  feature: 16 Little White House
  amusement park: 19 Six Flags Over Georgia
  national cemetery: 13 Andersonville
  national monument: 8 Ocmulgee 11 Fort Pulaski 13 Fort Frederica
  tribe: 5 Creek, Guale, Yuchi 6 Chiaha, Oconee, Uchean 7 Yamasee 8 Hitchiti
  people: 6 Ty Cobb 7 cracker 10 Bobby Jones 11 Juliette Low 15 Erskine Caldwell 16 Margaret Mitchell 18 Joel Chandler Harris
  island: 3 Sea 6 Jekyll, Sapelo 7 Ossabaw 10 Cumberland
  lake: 6 Lanier, Martin 7 Harding, Nottely 8 Bankhead, Hartwell, Sinclair
  land rank: 11 twenty-first
  mountain: 5 Stone 7 Lookout 8 Kennesaw 9 Blue Ridge 11 Alleghenies 13 High Point Peak
  highest point: 17 Brasstown Bald Peak
  physical feature:
  sea: 8 Atlantic
  springs: 4 Warm
  swamp: 10 Okefenokee
  president: 11 Jimmy Carter
  river: 3 Pea 5 Flint 6 Etowah, Oconee,

Pigeon 7 Conecuh, Satilla, St Mary's, Tugaloo 8 Altamaha, Ocmulgee, Ogeechee, Savannah, Suwannee 9 Chattooga 13 Chattahoochie

state admission: 6 fourth

state bird: 13 brown thrasher

state fish: 14 largemouth bass

state flower: 12 Cherokee rose

state motto: 6 Wisdom 20 Justice and Moderation

state song: 7 Georgia

state tree: 7 live oak

Georgia Peach
  nickname of: 6 Ty Cobb

Georgics, The
  author: 6 Vergil, Virgil
  called: 17 agricultural poems

Ge-Pano-Carib
  language branch: 7 Macro-Ge 10 Macro-Carib 11 Macro-Panoan

gephyrophobia
  fear of: 7 bridges

Geraint
  character in: 16 Arthurian romance

geranium 11 Pelargonium
  varieties: 3 ivy 4 fish, lime, mint, pine, rock, rose, show, wild 5 apple, fancy, house, lemon, regal, zonal 6 almond, alpine, cactus, jungle, nutmeg, orange 7 apricot, bedding, coconut, feather, hanging, knotted, polecat 8 crowfoot, fern-leaf, horsehoe 9 beefsteak, oak-leaved 10 California, gooseberry, peppermint, strawberry, sweetheart, village-oak 11 grape-leaved, herb-scented, maple-leaved, rose-scented 12 silver-leaved, southernwood, sweet-scented 13 black-flowered, pansy-flowered, pheasant's-foot 14 Lady Washington, little-leaf rose 15 mint-scented rose 16 Martha Washington 17 English finger-bowl

Gerber, Franceska Mitzi
  real name of: 11 Mitzi Gaynor

Gerd, Gerda
  origin: 12 Scandinavian
  husband: 4 Frey 5 Freyr

Gere, Richard
  roles: 5 Yanks 10 Breathless, Cotton Club 12 Days of Heaven 14 American Gigolo 19 Looking for Mr Goodbar 22 An Officer and a Gentleman

Geri
  origin: 12 Scandinavian
  form: 4 wolf
  owner: 4 Odin 5 Othin
  received: 4 food
  exception: 4 meat
  fellow wolf: 5 Freki

germ 3 bud, bug, egg 4 ovum, root, seed 5 ovule, spark, spore, virus 6 embryo, origin, source, sprout 7 microbe, nucleus, seed bud 8 bacillus, offshoot, rudiment 9 bacterium, beginning 12 fountainhead 13 microorganism

German 3 Hun 4 balt, Goth 5 boche, heine, jerry, kraut, Saxon 6 Teuton 7 tedesco 8 Prussian, Teutonic 9 deutscher

article: 3 das, dem, den, der, des, die, ein 4 eine

empire: 5 reich

man: 4 herr

storm and stress: 13 sturm und drang

thank you: 5 danke 10 danke schon

toast: 6 prosit

woman: 4 frau 8 fraulein

German-Dutch
  language family: 12 Indo-European
  branch: 8 Germanic
  group: 15 Western Germanic
  language: 9 Low German 10 High German

germane 3 apt, fit 6 native, proper 7 apropos, fitting, related 8 material, relative, relevant, suitable 9 connected, intrinsic, pertinent 10 applicable 11 appropriate 12 appertaining

germaneness 9 relevance 10 pertinence 13 applicability 15 appropriateness

Germanic
  language family: 12 Indo-European
  group: 6 Gothic 15 Western Germanic

Germanic Mythology
  chief of gods: 5 Wotan
  corresponds to Scandinavian: 4 Odin
  dwarf: 15 Rumpelstiltskin
  dwarves: 8 Niblungs 9 Nibelungs
  emperor: 15 Dietrich von Bern
  epic: 14 Nibelungenlied
  goddess of clouds/sky/ marriage: 3 Fri 5 Frigg, Frija 6 Frigga
  goddess of death/fertility: 7 Berchta, Perchta
  goddess of love/ beauty/fecundity: 5 Freya
  goddess of moon/ witch: 5 Holle
  god of thunder: 5 Donar
  god of winter sports: 4 Ullr 5 Uller
  hero: 6 Sigurd 9 Siegfried
  heroine: 6 Gudrun, Kudrun 7 Guthrun 8 Brunhild 9 Kriemhild
  king: 7 Siggeir
  king of dwarves: 8 Alberich
  knight of the holy grail: 9 Lohengrin
  magic cloak: 9 Tarnkappe
  maidens: 9 Valkyries
  nature spirit: 7 Eriking
  nymph: 7 Lorelei, Lurelei
  water spirit: 3 Nix

German is spoken here
  German: 25 hier wird Deutsch gesprochen

German literary movement (18th cent) 13 sturm und drang

Germany
  capital: 6 Berlin
  government leader: 10 chancellor, Helmut Kohl
  monetary unit: 12 Deutsche mark
  people: 3 Hun 4 Slav, Sorb, Wend 5 Saxon
  artist: 4 Marc 5 Durer 7 Barlach, Cranach, Gropius, Holbein 9 Grunewald 14 Mies van der Rohe
  author: 4 Mann, Marx 5 Grass 6 Brecht,

Elsner, Goethe 7 Johnson, Lessing 8 Hochhuth

composer: 4 Bach 5 Weill 6 Brahms, Handel, Wagner 7 Strauss 8 Schumann 9 Beethoven, Hindemith 11 Mendelssohn
conductor: 5 Henze 6 Walter 9 Klemperer 11 Furtwangler, Stockhausen
historical leader: 6 Hitler, Kaiser 8 Bismarck 10 Barbarossa
Prussian noble: 6 Junker
religious leader: 6 Luther
language: 6 German 10 High German 11 Hochdeutsch
religion: 8 Lutheran 10 Protestant 13 Roman Catholic 17 Evangelical Church
food:
bread: 12 pumpernickel
dish: 9 lebkuchen 15 wiener schnitzel
dumpling: 6 knodel
frankfurter: 15 wiener wurstchen
fruit bread: 7 stollen
ham: 11 Westphalian
potato salad: 14 kartoffelsalat
pot roast: 11 sauerbraten
sausage: 5 wurst 9 blutwurst, bratwurst 10 brockwurst, knackwurst, leberwurst
sole: 8 seezunge

Germany, East

capital/largest city: 10 East Berlin
others: 4 Jena 5 Halle, Waren 6 Erfurt, Weimar 7 Cottbus, Dresden, Leipzig, Meissen, Potsdam, Rostock, Schwedt, Wannsee, Zwickau 9 Frankfurt, Magdeburg 10 Angermunde, Warnemunde, Wittenberg 11 Neustrelitz 13 Karl-Marx-Stadt (Chemnitz)
school: 8 Humboldt
division: 6 Saxony 9 Thuringia 11 Brandenburg, Mecklenburg 12 Saxony-Anhalt
government: 11 Volkskammer (Peoples' Chamber)
monetary unit: 4 mark 7 Ostmark, pfennig
lake: 6 Muritz
mountain: 3 Ore 4 Harz 10 Erzgebirge
highest point: 11 Fichtelberg
river: 4 Elbe, Oder 5 Havel, Saale, Spree 6 Neisse, Warnow
sea: 6 Baltic
physical feature:
forest: 10 Thuringian
place: 10 Berlin Wall 17 Checkpoint Charlie
castle: 9 Sans Souci
church: 8 St Thomas 12 Thomaskirche
city center: 13 Karl Marx Platz 14 Alexanderplatz, Neubrandenberg
comic opera: 12 Komische Oper
gate: 11 Brandenburg
museum: 7 Zwinger 8 Pergamon 10 Goethe Haus
opera house: 18 Deutsche Staatsoper
feature:
china: 7 Dresden
fair: 7 Leipzig
theater company: 16 Berliner Ensemble

Germany, West

capital: 4 Bonn
largest city: 10 West Berlin
others: 4 Kiel 5 Essen, Mainz, Trier 6 Aachen, Bochum, Bremen, Kassel, Lubeck, Minden, Munden, Munich 7 Cologne, Hamburg, Hanover, Krefeld, Munster 8 Augsburg, Biberach, Dortmund, Duisberg, Duisburg, Freiburg, Mannheim, Solingen 9 Darmstadt, Karlsruhe, Nuremberg, Oldenburg, Stuttgart, Wiesbaden, Wuppertal 10 Dusseldorf, Heidelberg, Steingaden 11 Saarbrucken 12 Oberammergau 13 Gelsenkirchen 15 Frankfurt am Main 16 Mulheim an der Ruhr
school: 4 Bonn 7 Hamburg 10 Heidelberg 16 Ludwig-Maximilian
division: 4 Saar 5 Baden, Hesse 6 Bremen 7 Bavaria 9 Rhineland 10 Palatinate, Westphalia 11 Lower Saxony, Wurttemberg 17 Schleswig-Holstein
head of government: 10 chancellor
monetary unit: 4 mark 7 pfennig 12 Deutsche mark
island: 11 East Frisian 12 North Frisian
lake: 9 Constance 11 Inner Alster, Outer Alster
mountain: 4 Harz 8 Feldberg 11 Black Forest 12 Bavarian Alps
highest point: 9 Zugspitze
river: 3 Ems 4 Elbe, Main, Nahe, Ruhr, Saar, Wese 5 Rhine, Weser 6 Danube, Neckar 7 Moselle, Pegnitz
sea: 5 North 6 Baltic
physical feature:
canal: 4 Kiel 10 Mittelland
forest: 5 Black 7 Bohemia 9 Teu Toburg
place: 17 Checkpoint Charlie
botanical garden: 18 Pflanzen und Blumen
boulevard: 14 Kurfurstendamm
church: 12 Frauenkirche (Cathedral of Our Lady) 13 Kaiser Wilhelm 16 Gadachtniskirche
city center: 11 Marienplatz
fortress: 9 Marksburg
fountain: 14 Schoner Brunnen
garden: 10 Englischer
hall: 9 Beethoven
museum: 8 Residenz 9 Durer Haus 12 Schatzkammer 14 Alte Pinakothek
opera house: 18 Deutsches Opern Haus
park/zoo: 18 Hagenbecks Tierpark
residential district: 11 Hansa Vierte 12 Hanse Viertel
resort (on Baltic): 10 Travemunde
theater: 9 Cuvillies
feature:
beer cellar: 11 bierkellern
beer garden: 10 biergarten
beer hall: 10 bierhallen
beer room: 10 bierstuben
cars: 3 BMW 7 Porsche 10 Volkswagen 12 Mercedes-Benz
children: 6 kinder
city hall: 5 Romer 7 Rathaus

festival: 11 Oktoberfest
folk songs: 11 volkslieder
kitchen: 5 kuche
old city: 8 Altstadt
pre-Lent carnival: 8 Fasching
secondary school: 9 gymnasium
states: 6 lander
wine street: 11 Weinstrasse
germicide 11 bactericide 12 disinfectant
Germinal author: 9 Emile Zola
germinate 3 bud 4 blow, open 5 bloom, shoot 6 flower, push up, sprout 7 blossom, burgeon, develop 8 generate, spring up, vegetate
germination 9 sprouting 11 propagation
Gershom
    means: 13 stranger there
    father: 5 Moses
    mother: 8 Zipporah
    brother: 12 Eliezar
Gershwin, George
    born: 10 Brooklyn NY
    partner/lyricist: 11 Ira Gershwin
    composer of: 9 Funny Face 11 Of Thee I Sing 12 Porgy and Bess 13 Cuban Overture 14 Rhapsody in Blue 15 Strike Up the Band 17 An American in Paris
Gertrude
    character in: 6 Hamlet
    author: 11 Shakespeare
Gervin, George
    nickname: 6 Iceman
    sport: 10 basketball
    team: 15 San Antonio Spurs
Geryon
    form: 7 monster
    father: 8 Chrysaor
    mother: 10 Callirrhoe
    home: 7 Erythea
    possessed: 6 cattle
    color of cattle: 3 red
    herdsman: 8 Eurytion
    dog: 7 Orthrus
    killed by: 8 Heracles
    cattle stolen by: 8 Heracles
Gesta Romanorum
    author: 7 unknown
gestation 9 evolution, pregnancy 10 epigenesis, generation, incubation, maturation 11 development, propagation
gesticulate 3 nod 4 wink 5 nudge, shrug 6 beckon, motion, signal 8 indicate 9 pantomime
gesture 3 nod 4 sign, wave, wink 5 nudge, shrug, touch 6 beckon, motion, signal 8 courtesy, dumb show, flourish, high sign 9 formality, pantomime 13 demonstration
get 3 bag, fix, net, wax, win 4 beat, coax, earn, gain, grab, grip, grow, have, hear, move, reap, sway, take, turn 5 annoy, catch, fetch, glean, grasp, learn, reach, seize, sense, upset 6 arrive, attain, baffle, become, collar, come by, come to, enlist, entrap, fathom, follow, induce, obtain, pick up, pocket, prompt, puzzle, secure, snatch, suborn, take in, turn to 7 achieve, acquire, capture, confuse, contact, dis-

pose, ensnare, go after, incline, inherit, mystify, perplex, prepare, procure, realize; receive, wheedle, win over 8 bewilder, confound, contract, irritate, perceive, persuade 9 influence, transport 10 comprehend, disconcert, predispose, understand
get a kick out of 4 like 5 eat up, enjoy, fancy, savor 6 relish 10 appreciate
getaway 6 escape, exodus, flight 10 decampment
get done 2 do 6 finish 8 complete 10 accomplish
get even 6 avenge 7 counter, hit back, pay back, revenge 9 retaliate
Gethsemane 6 garden
get into 3 don 5 enter, put on
get in touch with 5 reach 7 contact
get lost 4 scat, shoo 5 be off, leave, scram 6 beat it, begone, depart, go away 7 vamoose
get one's dander up 4 gall, rile 5 anger 6 enrage, madden, nettle, ruffle 7 incense, inflame, outrage 9 infuriate
get out of bed 4 rise 5 arise 12 rise and shine
get rid of 4 drop, dump, junk, shed 5 ditch, scrap 6 banish, cut out, delete, remove, unload 7 abolish, discard, weed out 8 jettison, stamp out, throw out 9 eliminate, eradicate 10 annihilate 11 exterminate
Get Smart
    character: 5 Hymie (CONTROL robot) 7 Agent 99, Carlson, Starker 8 Larrabee, The Chief (Thaddeus) 12 Maxwell Smart (Agent 86) 15 Conrad Siegfried
    cast: 8 Don Adams 9 King Moody 10 Stacy Keach 11 Dave Ketchum, Dick Gautier, Edward Platt 12 Bernie Kopell 13 Barbara Feldon 14 Robert Karvelas
    Max worked for: 7 CONTROL
    foe: 4 KAOS
get the better of 4 foil, rout 5 crush, quell 6 baffle, defeat, thwart 7 conquer 8 confound, overcome 9 frustrate, overthrow
get the upper hand of 5 quell 6 master 7 conquer 8 dominate, overcome, surmount
get the worst of 4 fail, fall, lose
Getting Even
    author: 10 Woody Allen
get to 5 reach 8 approach
get-together 2 do 3 bee 4 meet 5 agree, party, visit 6 affair, gather, hobnob 7 meeting 8 assemble, assembly 9 gathering
getup 3 rig 6 attire, outfit 7 costume 8 disguise, ensemble
get up 4 find, rise 5 arise, rouse, stand 8 assemble
get used to 5 adapt, inure 6 adjust 8 accustom 9 acclimate, habituate
gewgaws 7 baubles, doodads, trifles 8 trinkets 9 bric-a-brac, gimcracks, kickshaws, ornaments 11 knickknacks
Ghana
    other name: 9 Gold Coast
    capital/largest city: 5 Accra, Akkra
    others: 3 Oda 4 Axim, Fian, Keta, Tala,

Tema 5 Bawku, Enchi, Lawra, Legon, Sampa, Yapei 6 Dunkwa, Karaga, Kpandu, Kumasi, Nsawam, Obuasi, Swedru, Tamale, Tarkwa, Wasipe 7 Antubia, Damongo, Mampong, Prestea, Sekondi, Sunyani, Winneba 8 Akosombo, Kintampo, Takoradi 9 Cape Coast 15 Sekondi-Takoradi

school: 6 Kumasi 9 Cape Coast

monetary unit: 4 cedi 5 ackey

lake: 5 Volta 8 Bosumtwi

mountain: 12 Akwapim Hills

highest point: 8 Afadjato

river: 3 Oti, Pra 4 Daka, Tano 5 Afram, Volta 7 Ankobra, Kulpawn 10 Black Volta, White Volta

sea: 8 Atlantic

physical feature:

gulf: 6 Guinea

people: 2 Ga 3 Ewe 4 Akan, Akim, Akra, Aksa 5 Ahafo, Brong, Inkra 7 Akwapim, Ashanti, Dagomba 8 Mamprusi 11 Mole-Dagbani

language: 2 Ga 3 Ewe, Gur, Kwa, Twi 5 Fanti, Hausa 7 Dagomba, English

religion: 5 Islam 7 animism 13 Roman Catholic

feature:

castle: 14 Christiansborg

dam: 8 Akosombo

national dress: 5 kente

ghastly 3 wan 4 grim, ugly 5 ashen, pasty, weird 6 dismal, glassy, grisly, horrid, odious, pallid 7 fearful, ghostly, haggard, hideous, uncanny 8 blanched, dreadful, gruesome, horrible, shocking, spectral, terrible 9 appalling, colorless, deathlike, frightful, ghostlike, loathsome, repellent, repulsive, revolting 10 cadaverous, corpselike, forbidding, horrendous, lackluster, terrifying

Ghiberti, Lorenzo

born: 5 Italy 8 Florence

artwork: 9 St Matthew, St Stephen 15 Gates of Paradise (baptistry doors) 16 St John the Baptist 19 The Sacrifice of Isaac

ghost 4 hint 5 demon, shade, spook, trace 6 goblin, shadow, sprite, wraith 7 banshee, chimera, phantom, specter 8 phantasm 9 hobgoblin, phantasma, semblance 10 apparition, suggestion 12 Doppelganger 13 manifestation 15 materialization

Ghost and Mrs Muir, The

character: 11 Candice Muir, Martha Grant 12 Jonathan Muir 13 Claymore Gregg 14 Mrs Carolyn Muir 18 Captain Daniel Gregg

TV cast: 8 Reta Shaw 9 Hope Lange 13 Edward Mulhare 14 Harlen Carraher, Kellie Flanagan 19 Charles Nelson Reilly

setting: 11 Gull Cottage

director: 17 Joseph L Mankiewicz

movie cast: 8 Edna Best 11 Gene Tierney, Rex Harrison 13 George Sanders

Ghostbusters

director: 11 Ivan Reitman

screenplay: 10 Dan Ackroyd 11 Harold Ramis

cast: 10 Bill Murray, Dan Ackroyd 11 Harold Ramis 15 Sigourney Weaver

ghostly 4 pale 5 eerie, weird 6 spooky, unreal 7 ghastly, phantom, shadowy, uncanny 8 illusive, spectral 9 unearthly 10 phantasmal, wraithlike 11 phantomlike 12 supernatural

ghostly double

German: 12 Doppelganger

Ghosts

author: 11 Henrik Ibsen

character: 7 Manders 12 Oswald Alving 14 Jacob Engstrand, Mrs Helen Alving 15 Regina Engstrand

ghoulish 5 eerie, scary, weird 7 demonic, hellish, macabre, ogreish, satanic 8 diabolic, fiendish, gruesome, infernal, sinister 9 monstrous 10 horrifying, zombielike 11 hair-raising, necrophilic

Giacometti, Alberto

born: 11 Switzerland 12 Stampa-Tessin

artwork: 3 Dog 7 The Cage 8 Caroline 10 City Square 11 Head of Diego, Man Pointing 14 Reclining Woman 17 The Palace at Four Am 19 Hands Holding the Void

Gianni Schicchi

opera by: 7 Puccini

character: 11 Buoso Donati

giant 3 big 4 huge 5 titan 7 Goliath, spanker, thumper, whopper 8 behemoth, colossus, strapper 9 Gargantua 14 Brobdingnagian

Giant

director: 13 George Stevens

author: 10 Edna Ferber

cast: 9 James Dean 10 Chill Wills, Rock Hudson 11 Jane Withers 12 Carroll Baker 15 Elizabeth Taylor

setting: 5 Texas

Oscar for: 8 director

Giant see 8 Gigantes

giant people 6 Anakim

Giants in the Earth

author: 9 O E Rolvaag

character: 3 Ole 5 Beret 8 Per Hansa 9 Anna Marie 12 Hans Kristian 15 Peder Victorious

gibber 3 gab 4 blab 5 prate 6 babble, gabble, jabber 7 blabber, blather, chatter, prattle 8 chitchat

gibberish 4 blab, bosh 6 babble, drivel, gabble 7 blather, twaddle 8 nonsense 10 balderdash, double-talk, flapdoodle, hocus-pocus, mumbo-jumbo 12 gobbledegook

Gibbon, Edward

author of: 33 The (History of the) Decline and Fall of the Roman Empire

gibbous 6 convex, curved, humped 7 bulging, rounded, swollen 8 swelling 10 humpbacked, protuberant

Gibbs family
  characters in: 7 Our Town
  member: 6 George 7 Rebecca
  author: 6 Wilder
gibe, jibe 3 rag 4 jeer, mock, quip, razz, twit 5 chaff, flout, knock, toast, scoff, sneer, taunt 6 deride, needle, rail at 7 mockery, poke fun, sarcasm 8 brickbat, derision, ridicule, taunting 9 criticism, wisecrack
Gibraltar
  other name: 11 rock of Tarik 13 Djebel al-Tarik 15 rock of Gibraltar
  largest city: 9 Gibraltar
  government: 18 British crown colony
  head of government: 15 governor general
  mountain: 6 Misery
  sea: 13 Mediterranean
  physical feature:
    bay: 5 Ceuta, Rosia, Sandy 6 Catlan 9 Algeciras
    cliffs: 17 Pillars of Hercules
    people: 6 Jewish 7 British, Maltese, Spanish 8 Italians 10 Portuguese
    language: 7 English, Spanish
    feature: 12 King's Bastion
    gardens: 7 Alameda
Gibson, Mel
  roles: 6 Mad Max 9 Gallipoli, The Bounty 12 Lethal Weapon 14 The Road Warrior 26 The Year of Living Dangerously
Giddens, Regina
  character in: 14 The Little Foxes
  author: 7 Hellman
giddy 5 dizzy, faint, silly 6 fickle, fitful 7 awesome, erratic, flighty, muddled, reeling 8 careless, dizzying, fainting, fanciful, reckless, swimming, unsteady, volatile, whirling 9 befuddled, frivolous, impulsive, mercurial, whimsical 10 capricious, changeable, inconstant 11 hare-brained, harum-scarum, lightheaded, thoughtless, vacillating, vertiginous 12 inconsistent, overpowering 13 irresponsible, rattlebrained
Gide, Andre
  author of: 13 The Immoralist 15 Strait Is the Gate 17 The Counterfeiters 18 Lafcadio's Adventure (The Vatican Swindle) 19 The Pastoral Symphony
Gideon 11 Hebrew judge
  father: 5 Joash, Ophra
  son: 9 Abimelech
  also called: 9 Jerubbaal
Gidget
  character: 5 Larue 10 Anne Cooper, John Cooper 16 Francine (Gidget) Lawrence 21 Professor Russ Lawrence
  cast: 9 Don Porter 10 Peter Deuel, Sally Field 11 Betty Conner 13 Lynette Winter
Gielgud, Sir John
  born: 6 London 7 England
  roles: 6 Arthur, Becket, Hamlet 7 Macbeth 9 Saint Joan 26 The Barretts of Wimpole Street 27 The Importance of Being Earnest

gift 3 aid, dot, fee, sop, tip 4 alms, bent, boon, dole, help, turn 5 award, bonus, bribe, craft, dower, dowry, favor, flair, forte, graft, grant, knack, power, prize, skill 6 genius, legacy, talent, virtue 7 aptness, bequest, faculty, handout, largess, premium, present, quality, tribute 8 aptitude, capacity, donation, facility, gratuity, offering, property 9 attribute, endowment, expertise, ingenuity 10 adroitness, capability, competency 11 benefaction, proficiency 12 contribution 13 consideration, qualification
gifted 4 able, deft 5 adept, crack, handy, quick, slick 6 adroit, bright, clever, expert, facile, master, wizard 7 capable, skilled 8 finished, masterly, polished, superior, talented 9 brilliant, ingenious, inventive, practiced, qualified 10 proficient 11 crackerjack, experienced, resourceful 12 accomplished
Gift From the Sea, The
  author: 19 Anne Morrow Lindbergh
gig 3 job 4 trap 5 stint 6 chaise 7 dogcart 8 carriage, curricle 10 engagement
Gigantes
  single member: 5 giant
  father: 6 Uranus
  mother: 4 Gaea
  heads of: 3 men
  bodies of: 8 serpents
  attacked: 4 gods
gigantic 4 huge, vast 5 bulky, jumbo 6 mighty 7 hulking, immense, lumpish, mammoth, massive, titanic 8 colossal, enormous, lubberly, towering, unwieldy 9 herculean, monstrous, ponderous, strapping 10 gargantuan, prodigious, stupendous, tremendous, voluminous 11 elephantine
Gigantomachia
  war of: 6 giants
giggle 6 cackle, hee-hee, simper, tee-hee, titter 7 chuckle, snicker, snigger, twitter
Gigi
  director: 16 Vincente Minnelli
  based on story by: 7 Colette
  cast: 8 Eva Gabor 11 Leslie Caron 12 Louis Jourdan 15 Hermione Gingold, Jacques Bergerac 16 Maurice Chevalier
  score: 14 Lerner and Loewe
  Oscar for: 7 picture 8 director
  song: 4 Gigi 15 I Remember It Well 25 Thank Heaven for Little Girls 29 The Night They Invented Champagne
Gilbert, Cass
  architect of: 14 US Customs House (NYC) 17 Woolworth Building (NYC) 20 Supreme Court Building (Washington DC) 21 Minnesota State Capitol (St Paul) 22 George Washington Bridge
Gilbert, John
  real name: 11 John Pringle
  wife: 9 Ina Claire 11 Leatrice Joy 13 Virginia Bruce
  born: 7 Logan UT
  roles: 4 Love 12 The Big Parade 13 The Merry Widow 15 A Woman of Affairs 16 Flesh and the Devil

Gilbert, William
  field: 7 physics
  nationality: 7 British
  father of: 11 electricity
  named for him: 27 CGS unit of magnetomotive force

Gilbert, W S, and Sullivan, Arthur Seymour
  composers of: 7 Ivanhoe 8 Iolanthe, Patience 9 Ruddigore, The Mikado 11 H M S Pinafore, Princess Ida, The Sorcerer, Trial by Jury 12 The Grand Duke 13 The Gondoliers, Utopia Limited 19 The Yeoman of the Guard 20 The Pirates of Penzance 24 Thespis or The Gods Grown Old

Gilbert Islands see 8 Kiribati

Gil Blas (of Santillane)
  author: 11 Alain LeSage
  character: 6 Scipio 11 Don Alphonso

Gilbreth, Frank B, Jr
  author of: 17 Cheaper by the Dozen (with Ernestine Gilbreth Carey)

gild 4 bend 5 slant, twist 7 cover up, stretch, touch up 10 exaggerate

Gilded Age, The
  authors: 9 Mark Twain 19 Charles Dudley Warner

gilded youth
  French: 13 jeunesse doree

Gileadite password 10 Shibboleth

Giles Goat-Boy
  author: 9 John Barth

Gilgal 5 wheel 6 circle

Gilgamesh
  origin: 8 Sumerian
  king of: 4 Uruk 5 Erech
  servant: 6 Enkidu

gill
  abbreviation: 2 gi

Gilligan's Island
  character: 7 Skipper (Jonas Grumby) 8 Gilligan 9 Mrs Howell (Lovey), Professor (Roy Hinkley) 11 Ginger Grant 14 Mary Ann Summers 17 Thurston Howell III
  cast: 9 Bob Denver, Dawn Wells, Jim Backus 10 Alan Hale Jr, Tina Louise 14 Natalie Schafer, Russell Johnson
  ship: 6 Minnow

Gillooly, Edna Rae
  real name of: 12 Ellen Burstyn

Gills, Solomon
  character in: 12 Dombey and Son
  author: 7 Dickens

Gilyak
  language spoken in: 4 Amur 8 Sakhalin

gimcrack 5 bijou, curio 6 bauble, gewgaw, trifle 7 trinket, whatnot 8 kickshaw, ornament 9 bagatelle, plaything 10 knickknack 11 contrivance, thingamabob, thingamajig

gimmick 4 plan, ploy, ruse, wile 5 angle, dodge, stunt 6 design, device, gadget, scheme 7 wrinkle 9 stratagem 10 subterfuge 11 contrivance

gin
  origin: 11 Netherlands
  ingredient: 6 grains 12 juniper berry
  type: 6 Geneva 8 Plymouth 9 London dry
  drink: 5 Allen 6 Gibson, gimlet 7 Belmont, Bennett, gin Fizz, swizzle 8 Pink Lady 9 Gin Rickey 10 Tom Collins 11 Alabama Fizz, gin and tonic 12 Grand Passion 14 Casino Cocktail
  with anisette: 8 Snowball 11 Bachio Punch
  with apricot brandy: 14 Boston Cocktail
  with brandy: 15 Bermuda Highball
  with Chartreuse: 5 Bijou 9 Green Lady
  with cherry brandy: 14 Singapore Sling
  with Cointreau: 7 Florida 9 White Lady 13 Sweet Patootie 14 Flying Dutchman
  with creme de cacao: 9 Alexander
  with creme de cassis: 8 Parisian
  with creme de menthe: 6 Caruso, Virgin
  with creme Yvette: 9 Union Jack
  with Curacao: 8 Blue Moon, Napoleon 9 Blue Devil 14 Flying Dutchman
  with Dubonnet: 3 BVD 8 Napoleon
  with Grand Marnier: 7 Red Lion
  with grapefruit juice: 8 Salty Dog
  with kirsch, kirschwasser: 7 Florida 11 Lady Finger
  with onions: 6 Gibson
  with orange juice: 5 Abbey 13 Orange Blossom
  with Pernod: 7 Dubarry
  with rum: 3 BVD
  with scotch: 12 Barbary Coast
  with sherry: 11 Renaissance
  with strawberries: 10 Bloodhound
  with Swedish Punch: 5 Biffy
  with vermouth: 5 Bijou, Bronx, Tango 6 Caruso 7 Bermuda, Cabaret, Martini 10 Bloodhound
  with vodka: 15 Russian Cocktail

ginger 3 pep, tan 5 brown, spice 6 energy
  varieties: 3 red 4 wild 5 crape, crepe, shell, torch, white 6 canton, common, Kahili, orchid, spiral, yellow 9 butterfly 10 small shell, variegated
  botanical name: 8 Zingiber 12 Z officinales
  Sanskrit: 9 singabera
  origin: 4 Asia 5 China, India 7 Jamaica
  use: 6 tongue 7 vinegar 9 beef stock 11 baked dishes, gingerbread 12 chicken stock

gingerly 6 warily 7 charily, timidly 8 daintily 9 carefully, finically, guardedly, heedfully, mincingly, prudently 10 cautiously, delicately, discreetly, hesitantly, vigilantly, watchfully 11 squeamishly 12 fastidiously, suspiciously 13 circumspectly

gingham 5 cloth 6 cotton, fabric, striped 8 chambray 9 checkered

gin mill 4 dive 9 honky-tonk, roadhouse

Ginnungagap
  origin: 12 Scandinavian
  void filled with: 4 mist
  between: 9 Nifelheim 10 Muspelheim

Ginsberg, Allen
author of: 4 Howl 7 Kaddish 10 Planet News 11 Mind Breaths 16 The Fall of America 20 Reality and Sandwiches

Giono, Jean
author of: 6 Regain 7 Colline, Harvest 13 Hill of Destiny 18 The Hussar on the Roof

Giordano, Umberto
born: 5 Italy 6 Foggia
composer of: 6 Fedora 8 Mala Vita 13 Andrea Chenier 14 Madame Sans-Gene

Giorgione da Castelfranco
born: 5 Italy 12 Castelfranco
artwork: 10 The Tempest 13 Ordeal of Moses, Sleeping Venus 17 Judgment of Solomon 19 The Concert Champetre (disputed) 20 The Three Philosophers 23 Adoration of the Shepherds

Giotto di Bondone
born: 5 Italy 8 (near) Florence
artwork attributed: 17 Ognissanti Madonna 31 Presentation of Christ in the Temple 32 St Francis Surrounded by his Brothers

Giovanelli
character in: 11 Daisy Miller
author: 5 James

Giovanni's Room
author: 12 James Baldwin

Giraffe
constellation of: 14 Camelopardalis

girandole 11 candelabrum, candlestick 12 candleholder

Girardon, Francois
born: 6 France, Troyes
artwork: 13 Bathing Nymphs 14 Galley of Apollo, Virgin of Troyes 16 Rape of Persephone 17 (tomb for) Cardinal Richelieu 23 Apollo Tended by the Nymphs

Giraudoux, Jean
author of: 5 Bella 6 Judith, Ondine, Racine 7 Electra 12 Amphitryon 38 15 Tiger at the Gates 18 Madwoman of Chaillot 20 My Friend from Limousin

gird 3 pen, tie 4 belt, girt, loop, ring 5 brace, hem in, hitch, steel, strap, truss 6 circle, fasten, girdle, harden, secure, wall in 7 besiege, confine, enclose, fortify, hedge in, prepare, stiffen, sustain, tighten 8 blockade, buttress, encircle, lay siege, surround 9 encompass 10 strengthen 12 circumscribe

girder 4 beam 5 brace, truss 6 binder, rafter 7 support, tie-beam

girdle 3 hem 4 band, belt, ring, sash 5 girth, hedge, stays 6 bodice, circle, corset 7 baldric, circlet, contour 8 boundary, cincture, corselet 9 surcingle, waistband 10 cummerbund 12 waist cincher 17 foundation garment

girl 4 bird, cook, help, lass, maid, minx, miss 5 angel, chick, nymph, wench 6 damsel, kitten, lassie, maiden, pigeon, virgin 7 baggage, colleen, darling, fiancee, ingenue, nymphet 8 daughter, domestic, handmaid, lady love, mistress, scullion 9 affianced, betrothed, inamorata, lady's maid, soubrette 10 sweetheart 11 maidservant
French: 10 demoiselle, jeune fille

girl Friday 4 aide 6 helper 9 assistant, secretary 10 amanuensis 12 office worker 23 administrative assistant

girlfriend 6 steady 7 beloved, sweetie 8 best girl 10 one and only, sweetheart

Girl in a Swing
author: 12 Richard Adams

girlish 8 girl-like, maidenly, youthful 10 maidenlike

Girl of the Golden West, The
opera by: 7 Puccini
setting: 8 Gold Rush 10 California
character: 6 Minnie 7 Johnson, Sheriff

girt 4 belt, bind, gird, ring 5 bound, girth 6 belted, circle, girdle, ringed 7 circled, girdled 9 encircled

girth 5 cinch 9 perimeter 10 saddle band 13 circumference

Giselle
ballet by: 4 (Adolphe Charles) Adam

Gish, Lillian
real name: 12 Lillian Gishi 15 Lillian de Guiche
born: 13 Springfield OH
roles: 8 La Boheme 10 Enoch Arden 11 Annie Laurie, Intolerance, Way Down East 12 Duel in the Sun 13 Scarlet Letter 14 Broken Blossoms 16 Portrait of Jennie 17 Orphans of the Storm, The Birth of a Nation

Gissing, George
author of: 5 Demos 13 New Grub Street 14 The Nether World

gist 4 core, crux, meat, pith 5 drift, force, heart, sense, tenor, theme 6 burden, center, effect, import, kernel, marrow, spirit 7 essence, purport 8 main idea 9 main point, substance 11 implication 12 significance

Giuki
also: 5 Gjuki
origin: 12 Scandinavian
mentioned in: 8 Volsunga
form: 4 king
wife: 8 Grimhild
daughter: 6 Gudrun, Kudrun 7 Guthrun
son: 6 Gunnar

Glukung
also: 7 Gjukung
origin: 12 Scandinavian
family member of: 5 Giuki, Gjuki

Giullo Romano
architect of: 12 Palazzo del Te
style: 9 Mannerist

give 3 buy, pay, tip 4 bend, ease, emit, hire, lend, show, sink 5 admit, allot, allow, apply, award, bribe, deign, endow, grant, issue, leave, offer, relax, utter, voice, yield 6 accord, addict, afford, assign, attach, bestow, bounce, commit, confer, convey, devote, donate, enable, enrich, hand to, impart, loosen, notify, open on, permit, recede, relent, render, shrink, supply, tender, unbend, vest in 7 concede, consign, deliver, entrust, fork out, furnish, hand out, let know, present, proffer, provide, requite, retreat, slacken 8 announce, bequeath, collapse, dispense, exchange, fork over, hand over, lead on to, make over, move back, put forth, shell out 9 apportion, break down, dispose of, equip with, favor with, look out on, present to, pronounce, subscribe, surrender, vouchsafe 10 articulate, become soft, compensate, contribute, deliquesce, distribute, recompense, remunerate, resilience, supply with 11 communicate, flexibility, provide with, springiness

give aid to 4 help 6 assist, succor 7 help out 8 befriend 9 look after 10 minister to

give a leg up 3 aid 4 help, lift 5 boost, hoist, raise 6 assist 7 elevate

give and take 8 exchange 10 compromise 11 interchange, reciprocity

give a pep talk to 4 goad, prod, spur 5 press 6 exhort 9 encourage

give a reason for 7 clarify, clear up, explain, justify 8 elucidate 10 account for

give as security 4 pawn 6 pledge 7 deposit, pay down, put down

give away 6 bestow, betray, donate, reveal 7 hand out

give birth 4 bear 5 hatch 6 create, invent 7 deliver, develop 9 originate 10 bring forth

give confidence to 7 inspire 8 embolden, inspirit 9 encourage

give courage 6 brace 6 buck up 7 hearten 8 inspirit, motivate

give energy to 6 animate, enliven 8 activate, energize, vitalize 9 stimulate 10 invigorate

give enjoyment 5 amuse, charm 6 divert, please 7 beguile, delight 8 enthrall 9 entertain

give forth 4 emit, gush 5 exude, issue 7 send out 8 throw off, transmit 9 discharge

give full attention 7 pay heed 8 fasten on 11 concentrate

give in 5 defer, yield 6 accede, cave in, submit 7 succumb 9 surrender 10 capitulate 12 knuckle under

give in to 7 yield to 9 indulge in, partake of 16 abandon oneself to

give leave 3 let 5 allow 6 permit 8 sanction 9 authorize 14 give permission

give moral support to 3 aid 4 abet, back, help 6 assist, uphold 7 support, sustain 8 sanction 9 encourage

given 3 apt 4 wont 5 prone 6 likely, wonted 7 awarded, donated, granted, offered 8 accorded, bestowed 9 committed, conferred, entrusted, presented 10 accustomed, handed over, in the habit 11 contributed 13 furnished with, made a donation, presented with 17 made a contribution

give new life to 3 fan 4 fire 6 awaken, revive 8 revivify 10 rejuvenate 11 reincarnate

give oneself to 8 dedicate 10 buckle down, consecrate

give one's word 3 vow 5 swear 6 assure, pledge 7 certify, promise, warrant 9 guarantee

give one walking papers 3 axe, can 4 fire, oust, sack 5 let go 6 bounce, lay off 7 cashier, dismiss, release 8 get rid of 9 discharge, terminate 11 give the gate, send packing

give out 4 quit, tell, tire 6 assign, inform, reveal, run out 7 divulge, dole out, mete out 8 allocate, announce, disclose, dispense, proclaim 9 apportion, broadcast, parcel out 10 distribute, make public, portion out 11 disseminate

give over 4 cede 5 yield 9 surrender 10 relinquish

give permission 3 let 5 allow 6 accede, permit 7 approve 8 sanction 9 acquiesce, authorize, give leave

give rise to 4 sire 5 breed, cause 6 lead to 7 produce 8 engender, generate, occasion 9 call forth 10 bring about

give support to 3 aid 4 abet 5 serve 6 defend, prop up, second 7 bolster, comfort, sustain 8 buttress, champion 10 contribute, minister to, provide for, stick up for

give the go-ahead 4 okay 5 order 6 direct 7 appoint, charter, empower 8 contract 9 authorize 10 commission

give the lie to 5 belie 8 disprove 9 repudiate 10 contradict, controvert

give the raspberry 3 boo, pan 4 razz 6 deride, hoot at 8 ridicule 11 give the bird 17 give the Bronx cheer

give the right to 5 allow 6 permit 7 entitle, qualify 9 authorize

give the slip 4 duck 5 avoid, dodge, elude, evade

give up 4 cede, drop, lose, quit, skip 5 forgo, let go, waive, yield 6 eschew, resign 7 abandon, forfeit, forsake 8 abdicate, forswear, renounce 9 sacrifice, surrender 10 relinquish 11 discontinue

give up the ghost 3 die 6 expire, pass on, perish 7 decease 8 pass away 15 breathe one's last

give vent 4 free 5 let go 7 release 8 let loose, liberate 12 give free rein

give way 4 fall 6 buckle, cave in 7 crumple 8 collapse 10 break apart

giving birth 7 bearing 8 creating, creation, delivery, hatching 9 inventing, invention 10 childbirth, delivering 11 originating, origination, parturition

giving up 7 refusal 8 dropping, quitting, yielding 9 resigning 10 abandoning, abdicating, abdication, abstinence, continence, forbearing, forfeiting, forfeiture, self-denial 11 abandonment, forswearing, resignation 12 renunciation, surrendering 14 relinquishment

gizmo 4 tool 6 device, doodad, gadget 9 apparatus, implement, invention, mechanism 10 instrument 11 contraption, contrivance, thingamabob, thingamajig

Gjuki see 5 Giuki

Gjukung see 7 Giukung

glacial 3 icy, raw 4 cold 5 chill, gelid, polar 6 arctic, biting, bitter, frigid, frosty, frozen, wintry 7 hostile 8 freezing, inimical, piercing 9 congealed 10 disdainful, unfriendly 12 antagonistic, bone-chilling, contemptuous

Glackens, William James
  born: 14 Philadelphia PA
  artwork: 9 Promenade 11 Chez Mouquin 15 Nude with an Apple 16 Washington Square (A Holiday in the Park) 17 Luxembourg Gardens

glad 5 happy 6 elated, joyful, joyous 7 elating, gleeful, pleased, tickled 8 blissful, cheerful, cheering, pleasing, rejoiced 9 contented, delighted, joy-giving 10 delightful, entrancing, gratifying 11 exhilarated, tickled pink 12 exhilarating

gladden 5 cheer, elate 6 please 7 animate, cheer up, delight, enliven, gratify, hearten, rejoice 8 inspirit, pleasure 9 make happy 10 exhilarate

gladdened 5 happy 6 joyful, joyous 8 cheerful

glade 4 dell, glen, lawn, vale, wood 5 grove, marsh, vista 6 canada, hollow, valley 7 opening 8 clearing

gladness 3 joy 4 glee 5 bliss, cheer, mirth 7 delight, gaiety, jollity 8 pleasure 9 happiness 10 joyfulness 11 contentment 12 cheerfulness

glad rags 5 array 6 attire, finery 10 Sunday best

Gladsheim
  origin: 12 Scandinavian
  palace of: 4 Odin 5 Othin
  location: 8 Valhalla

gladsome 3 gay 5 happy, merry 6 cheery, joyful, joyous 8 cheerful 12 lighthearted

glamor, glamour 5 charm, magic 6 allure 7 glitter, romance 8 illusion 9 adventure, challenge, magnetism 10 excitement 11 enchantment, fascination 14 attractiveness

glamorous, glamourous 8 alluring, charming, dazzling, exciting, magnetic 10 attractive, bewitching, enchanting 11 captivating, charismatic, fascinating

glance 4 kiss, peek, peep, scan, skim, slip 5 brush, graze, shave, touch 6 bounce, careen, squint 7 glimpse, rebound 8 ricochet 9 brief look, quick look, quick view
  French: 6 apercu

glance through 4 scan, skim 6 browse, peruse 7 dip into 8 look over 9 check over

gland
  part of: 15 endocrine system
  type: 4 duct 8 ductless
  kind: 3 oil 5 sweat 7 adrenal, thyroid 8 pancreas 9 pituitary 11 parathyroid
  ductless gland secretes: 8 hormones

glare 4 glow 5 blaze, flame, flare, flash, gleam, glint, gloss, lower, scowl, sheen 6 dazzle, glower 7 flicker, glimmer, glisten, glitter, radiate, shimmer, sparkle, twinkle 8 radiance 9 angry look, black look, dirty look 10 brightness, harsh light, luminosity 12 resplendence

glaring 4 rank 5 gross, harsh, vivid 6 arrant, bright, strong 7 blatant, flaring, intense, obvious 8 blinding, dazzling, fla-

grant, piercing 9 audacious, brilliant, egregious 10 glittering, outrageous, shimmering 11 conspicuous, penetrating, resplendent, unconcealed, undisguised 12 unmistakable

Glasgow, Ellen
  author of: 10 Vein of Iron 12 Barren Ground 13 In this Our Life, Sheltered Life 18 They Stooped to Folly 20 The Romantic Comedians

glass 6 beaker, goblet 7 chalice, tumbler 10 tumblerful
  type of: 4 fizz, sour 5 flute, tulip 6 jigger, sherry 7 balloon, collins, cordial, red wine, snifter 8 cocktail, highball 9 champagne, white wine 10 hollow-stem, pousse cafe 12 old-fashioned

glasshouse 7 nursery 8 hothouse 10 greenhouse 12 conservatory

glassiness 7 clarity 8 dullness, flatness 9 shininess 10 brilliance, luminosity 12 lifelessness, transparency

Glass Key, The
  author: 15 Dashiell Hammett
  character: 9 Shad O'Rory 10 Janet Henry, Opal Madvig, Paul Madvig 11 Ned Beaumont 12 Senator Henry 13 Bernie Despain

Glass Menagerie, The
  director: 12 Irving Rapper
  author: 17 Tennessee Williams
  character: 5 Laura 6 Amanda 12 Tom Wingfield
  cast: 9 Jane Wyman 11 Kirk Douglas 13 Arthur Kennedy 16 Gertrude Lawrence

glassware 5 agata 6 aurene 7 crystal, favrile, steuben, vitrics 8 amerina, stemware
  worker: 7 glazier

glassy 4 dull 5 clear, shiny 6 glazed, smooth 8 lifeless 10 glittering 11 transparent

Glauber, Johann Rudolf
  field: 9 chemistry
  nationality: 6 German
  prepared: 12 tartar emetic 13 sodium sulfate (Glauber's salt) 16 hydrochloric acid

Glauce see 6 Creusa

Glaucus
  god of: 3 sea
  father: 5 Minos
  ally of: 7 Trojans
  loved by: 5 Circe 6 Scylla 10 Amphitrite

glaze 4 blur 5 gloss 6 enamel, finish 7 grow dim, varnish 8 film over 9 glass over

glazed 4 iced 5 filmy 6 coated, glassy, shined, smooth 7 glossed, sugared 8 enameled, lustrous, polished 9 burnished, varnished

Glazunoff, Alex K (Glazunov, Alexander Konstantinovich)
  born: 6 Russia 12 St Petersburg
  composer of: 10 Chopiniana, The Seasons 11 Stenka Razin 13 Hymn to Pushkin 15 Memorial Cantata

gleam 3 bit, jot, ray 4 beam, drop, glow, hint, iota 5 blink, flare, flash, glare, glint, gloss, grain, sheen, shine, spark, speck, trace 6 luster, streak 7 flicker, glimmer, glimpse, glisten, glitter, inkling, shimmer, sparkle, tiny bit, twinkle 8 least bit, radiance 9 coruscate 10 brightness, brilliance, effulgence 11 coruscation, scintillate

gleaming 5 clear, shiny 6 bright, flashy, glossy 7 shining, radiant 8 dazzling, glinting, luminous, lustrous, polished, splendid 9 brilliant, burnished, sparkling 10 glistening

glean 4 cull 5 amass 6 gather, pick up 7 harvest 10 accumulate 13 piece together 14 scrape together

gleanings 8 analects, extracts 10 miscellany, selections 11 collectanea, miscellanea 15 commonplace book

Gleason, Jackie
  real name: 18 Herbert John Gleason
  nickname: 15 Mr Saturday Night
  born: 10 Brooklyn NY
  roles: 5 Gigot 6 The Toy 10 The Hustler 11 Life of Riley, The Poor Soul 12 Ralph Kramden 15 Joe the Bartender, The Honeymooners 17 Don't Drink the Water, Jackie Gleason Show, The Time of Your Life 22 Requiem for a Heavyweight 24 Reggie Van Gleason the Third

glebe 3 sod 4 clod, land, plot, soil 5 earth, field 6 termon 8 kirktown 10 church land

glee 3 joy 5 mirth, verve 6 gaiety 7 delight, ecstasy, jollity, rapture 8 gladness, hilarity, laughter 9 joviality, merriment 10 exultation, jocularity, joyfulness, joyousness, liveliness 11 playfulness 12 cheerfulness, exhilaration, sportiveness 13 jollification, sprightliness

glee club 6 chorus 12 singing group 13 choral society

gleeful 3 gay 4 glad 5 happy, jolly, merry 6 elated, jocund, jovial, joyful, joyous, lively 7 festive 8 blissful, cheerful, exultant, mirthful 9 delighted 11 exhilarated 12 lighthearted

Gleipnir
  origin: 12 Scandinavian
  chain that bound: 6 Fenrir, Fenris

glen 4 dale, dell, vale 6 bottom, hollow

Glencaire Cycle
  author: 12 Eugene O'Neill

glib 4 oily 5 gabby, quick, ready, suave 6 facile, fluent, smooth 7 devious, voluble 8 flippant, slippery, unctuous 9 insincere, talkative

glide 3 run 4 flow, roll, sail, skim, slip, soar 5 coast, drift, float, issue, skate, slide, steal 6 elapse, stream 7 proceed 8 glissade

glider 5 swing 7 aviator 9 sailplane 10 hydroplane

glimmer 3 bit, ray 4 beam, drop, glow, hint 5 blink, flare, flash, glare, gleam, grain, shine, speck, trace 7 flicker, glimpse, glisten, glitter, shimmer, sparkle, twinkle 9

coruscate, scintilla 10 flickering, intimation 11 scintillate

glimpse 3 see, spy 4 espy, peek, peep, spot 6 glance, peek at, peep at, squint 9 brief look, quick look, quick view 12 catch sight of, fleeting look
  French: 6 apercu

Glinka, Mikhail Ivanovich
  born: 6 Russia 8 Smolensk
  composer of: 12 Ivan Sussanin, Karaminskaya 13 Jota Aragonesa 18 Russlan and Ludmilla

glint 4 gaze, look, peep 5 flash, gleam, sheen, shine, stare 6 glance 7 appear, glimmer, glimpse, glisten, glitter, shimmer, sparkle, twinkle 9 coruscate 11 scintillate

glissade 5 coast, glide, slide

glissando
  music: 7 sliding

glisten 4 glow 5 flash, gleam, glint, shine 7 flicker, glimmer, glister, glitter, radiate, shimmer, sparkle, twinkle 9 coruscate 11 scintillate

glitter 4 fire, glow, pomp, show 5 flare, flash, gleam, glint, sheen, shine 6 luster, thrill, tinsel 7 beaming, display, glamour, glimmer, glisten, radiate, sparkle, twinkle 8 grandeur, radiance, splendor 9 pageantry, showiness 10 brilliance, excitement, refulgence 11 electricity

glittering 6 bright 7 radiant, shining 8 luminous, lustrous 9 brilliant, sparkling 11 coruscating

gloaming 4 dusk 7 evening 8 twilight

gloat 4 bask, brag 5 exult, strut, vaunt 7 revel in, swagger, triumph 8 crow over 9 glory over

global 5 world 6 all-out 7 general 9 planetary, unbounded, universal, unlimited, worldwide 10 widespread 13 comprehensive, international 16 intercontinental

globe 3 orb 4 ball 5 Earth, world 6 planet, sphere 7 globule 8 spheroid, spherule 9 biosphere

globule 4 ball, bead, bleb, blob, drop 5 globe 6 bubble, pellet, sphere 7 blister, droplet 8 particle, spheroid

glogg
  type: 5 punch
  origin: 6 Sweden

gloom 3 woe 4 dark, dusk, murk 5 blues, dolor, grief, shade 6 misery, sorrow 7 despair, dimness, sadness, shadows 8 darkness, distress, doldrums 9 blackness, dejection, dinginess, duskiness, murkiness, obscurity 10 cloudiness, depression, gloominess, low spirits, melancholy, mopishness, moroseness, oppression 11 despondency, forlornness, unhappiness 12 hopelessness 13 cheerlessness 16 disconsolateness, heavy-heartedness

gloomy 3 dim, sad 4 dark, dour, down, dull, glum, grim, mopy, sour 5 dusky, moody, mopey, murky, shady 6 cloudy, dismal, dreary, morbid, morose, shaded, somber 7 doleful, forlorn, shadowy, sunless, unhappy 8 dejected, desolate, downcast, frowning, funereal, overcast 9 cheerless, depressed, heartsick, miserable, sorrowful, woebegone 10 chapfallen, despondent, dispirited, ill-humored, melancholy 11 comfortless, crestfallen, discouraged, downhearted, low-spirited, pessimistic 12 disconsolate, disheartened, heavy-hearted 13 in the doldrums 14 down in the dumps, down in the mouth

Gloria in Excelsis Deo 22 Glory in the highest to God

Gloriana
character in: 15 The Faerie Queene
author: 7 Spenser

Gloriana
opera by: 7 Britten
character: 10 Elizabeth I 11 Earl of Essex

glorification 7 worship 8 devotion 9 adoration, adulation 10 exaltation, veneration 13 magnification

glorify 4 laud 5 adore, deify, exalt, extol, honor 6 praise, revere 7 beatify, dignify, elevate, ennoble, idolize, worship 8 canonize, enshrine, sanctify, venerate 9 celebrate, glamorize 10 consecrate 11 apotheosize, immortalize, romanticize

glorious 4 fine 5 grand, great, noble, noted 6 august, divine, famous, superb 7 eminent, glowing, honored, notable, radiant, shining, stately, sublime, supreme 8 dazzling, gorgeous, imposing, lustrous, majestic, renowned, splendid 9 beautiful, brilliant, dignified, excellent, marvelous, sparkling, wonderful 10 celebrated, delightful, impressive, preeminent 11 illustrious, magnificent, resplendent 12 praiseworthy 13 distinguished

glory 4 fame, mark, name 5 boast, honor, revel, vaunt 6 esteem, homage, praise, renown, repute 7 dignity, majesty, worship 8 blessing, eminence, grandeur, nobility, prestige, splendor 9 adoration, celebrity, gratitude, solemnity, sublimity 10 admiration, excellence, notability, veneration 11 benediction, distinction, preeminence, stateliness 12 magnificence, resplendence, thanksgiving 14 impressiveness 15 illustriousness

Glory in the highest to God
Latin: 19 Gloria in Excelsis Deo

gloss 4 glow, mask, veil 5 cloak, color, glaze, gleam, japan, sheen, shine 6 enamel, excuse, luster, polish, veneer 7 cover up, lacquer, shimmer, varnish 8 annotate, disguise, mitigate, radiance 9 whitewash 10 annotation, brightness, brilliance, commentary, smooth over 11 explain away, explanation, rationalize 12 luminousness, treat lightly 14 interpretation

gloss over 4 hide, mask, veil 7 conceal, cover up 9 dissemble, whitewash 12 misrepresent

glossy 5 photo, shiny, showy, silky, sleek, slick 6 bright, satiny, smooth 7 picture, shining 8 gleaming, lustrous, magazine, polished 9 burnished

glove 3 kid 4 cuff, mitt 5 catch, thumb 6 gusset, mitten, muffle 7 chevron 8 gauntlet

glow 4 fill, heat 5 ardor, bloom, blush, color, flush, gleam, gusto, shine 6 fervor, thrill, tingle, warmth 7 flicker, glimmer, glisten, glitter, radiate, shimmer, smolder, twinkle 8 radiance 9 eagerness, intensity, radiation, reddening, vividness 10 brightness, enthusiasm 11 earnestness

glower 4 pout, sulk 5 frown, glare, lower, scowl, stare

glowing 3 hot, red 4 rave 5 ruddy, vivid 6 ardent, bright, florid, raving 7 fervent, flaming, flushed 8 ecstatic, exciting 9 rhapsodic, thrilling 10 passionate 11 luminescent, sensational, stimulating 12 enthusiastic

Glubbdubdrib
fictional land in: 16 Gulliver's Travels
author: 5 Swift

Gluck, Christoph Willibald (von)
born: 7 Bavaria 8 Neumarkt
composer of: 5 Orfeo 6 Armide 7 Alceste 13 Paride ed Elena 14 Echo et Narcisse 17 Iphigenie en Aulide 18 Iphigenie en Tauride

glue 3 fix, gum 5 affix, epoxy, paste, putty, stick 6 adhere, cement, fasten, mortar 7 plaster, stickum 8 adherent, adhesive, concrete, fixative, mucilage 11 agglutinate

gluey 5 gooey, gummy, mucid, ropey, slimy, tacky, thick, 6 sticky, viscid 7 stringy, viscous 8 adhesive 12 mucilaginous

glum 6 gloomy, morose 8 dejected 9 cheerless 10 melancholy 14 down in the mouth

glut 4 bolt, clog, cram, drug, fill, gulp, jade, load, sate 5 choke, flood, gorge, stuff 6 burden, deluge, devour, excess, gobble 7 congest, overeat, satiate, surfeit, surplus 8 gobble up, obstruct, overdose, overfeed, overload, plethora, saturate 10 gormandize, oversupply, saturation 11 obstruction, superfluity 13 overabundance, supersaturate 14 superabundance 15 supersaturation

glutinous 5 gluey, bummy, mucid, ropey, slimy, tacky, thick 6 sticky, viscid 7 viscous 8 adhesive 10 gelatinous 12 musilaginous

glutton 3 hog, pig 6 gorger 7 stuffer 8 gourmand 9 chowhound, overeater 10 bellyslave 11 gormandizer, trencherman

gluttonous 6 greedy 7 hoggish, piggish, swinish 8 edacious, grasping, ravening, ravenous 9 excessive, voracious 10 insatiable, omnivorous 11 intemperate

gluttony 8 rapacity, voracity 10 overeating 11 gourmandism, hoggishness, piggishness 12 gormandizing, intemperance, ravenousness 13 voraciousness

gnarled 6 knotty, rugged, snaggy 7 crooked, knotted, nodular, twisted 8 leathery, wrinkled 9 contorted, distorted 11 full of knots 13 weather-beaten

gnash 4 gnaw 5 chomp

gnat 7 no-see-um

group of: 5 cloud, horde

gnaw 4 bite, chew, fret, gall 5 chafe, chomp, eat at, grate, graze, munch, worry 6 browse, crunch, harrow, nibble, rankle 7 torment, trouble 8 distress, nibble at, ruminate 9 eat away at, masticate

gnome 4 elf 4 pixy 5 dwarf, troll 6 goblin, sprite 10 leprechaun

gnostic 4 sage, wise 6 clever, shrewd 7 knowing 8 mandaean, simonian 10 insightful

gnothi seauton 11 know thyself

gnu 7 brindle 8 antelope 10 wildebeest

type: 5 C gnou 9 C taurinus 12 Connochaetes

go 3 act, end, fit, fly, pep, run, try, vim 4 blow, dash, elan, fare, flee, flow, jibe, lead, life, pass, quit, stir, turn, wend, work 5 agree, begin, be off, blend, drive, force, get on, lapse, leave, reach, scram, slide, split, steam, tally, trial, verve, vigor, whirl 6 accord, beat it, be used, belong, chance, decamp, depart, effort, elapse, energy, expire, extend, mettle, pass by, repair, result, retire, spirit 7 advance, attempt, be given, be known, comport, fall out, glide by, move out, operate, perform, proceed, slip off, take off, turn out, vamoose, work out 8 ambition, endeavor, function, move away, progress, slip away, sneak off, spread to, start for, steal off, vitality, vivacity, withdraw 9 animation, harmonize, terminate, transpire 10 enterprise, experiment, initiative

goad 4 move, prod, push, spur, urge, whet 5 drive, egg on, impel, press, prick, set on 6 arouse, exhort, fillip, incite, motive, propel, stir up 8 pressure, stimulus 9 constrain, incentive, stimulant, stimulate 10 cattle prod, inducement, motivation 11 instigation

goal 3 aim, end 4 home, mark, wire 5 point, score, tally 6 design, intent, object, target 7 end line, purpose 8 ambition, goal line, terminus 9 intention, objective 10 finish line

go along with 5 usher 6 assent, convoy, escort 8 accede to, shepherd 9 accompany, agree with, chaperone, consent to 10 comply with

go ashore 4 land 6 debark 9 disembark

go astray 3 err, sin 6 wander 7 deviate, do wrong 8 misbehave 10 transgress 13 fall from grace

goat 3 kid 4 buck, butt 5 billy, nanny 6 victim 7 fall guy 9 scapegoat 11 whipping boy 13 laughingstock

breed: 6 Angora, Chamal, Nubian, Saanen 7 Granada 8 La Mancha 10 Toggenburg 11 Anglo-Nubian 12 French Alpine 13 British Alpine

combining form: 4 aego 5 capri

family: 7 Bovidae

female: 3 doe 5 capra, nanny 7 doeling

genus: 5 Capra

goat-boy: 5 Giles

goat-milk cheese: 7 chevret

goat-man: 5 satyr

god: 3 Pan 5 satyr 7 Aegipan

group of: 4 herd 5 tribe

hair: 5 kasha, tibet

hair of Angora goat: 6 mohair

male: 4 buck 5 billy

meat: 7 cabrito

star: 7 capella

young: 3 kid

Goat, Horned Goat

constellation of: 11 Capricornus

goat god 3 Pan 5 satyr

go away 3 ebb 4 fade, scat, wane 5 abate, leave, scram 6 depart, lessen, retire 8 withdraw 9 disappear

gob 3 dab, tar 4 clot, glob, lump, mass 6 sailor 7 Jack Tar

go back 6 return 7 retreat

gobble 3 caw 4 bolt, gulp, wolf 5 raven, stuff 6 cackle, devour, gabble, gaggle 8 bolt down, cram down, gulp down

gobbledygook 4 bosh, bunk, cant, tosh 6 jargon 7 rubbish, twaddle 8 buncombe, nonsense, tommyrot 9 gibberish, moonshine 10 balderdash, double-talk, hocuspocus, mumbo jumbo 11 foolishness 12 fiddle-faddle

gobble up 6 devour 8 bolt down, gulp down, wolf down

go before 7 precede, predate 8 antecede, antedate 9 come first, go ahead of 10 anticipate

go-between 5 agent, envoy, fixer, proxy 6 deputy, second 7 arbiter 8 delegate, emissary, mediator 9 messenger, middleman, moderator 10 arbitrator, interceder, negotiator 12 intermediary 13 intermediator 14 representative

goblet 3 cup 5 glass 6 vessel 7 chalice

goblin 4 ogre 5 bogey, demon, troll 7 gremlin 8 bogeyman

Gobseck

author: 14 Honore de Balzac

go by 4 pass 6 elapse, pass by, roll by, rush by, slip by 7 glide by, slide by 8 slip away

go by car 4 ride 5 drive, motor

go-cart 4 cart 5 buggy 6 barrow 8 carriage, handcart, pushcart, stroller 11 wheelbarrow

go crimson 4 burn, glow 5 blush, color, flame, flush 6 redden

God, god 4 Lord 5 Allah, deity, Jeveh 6 Elohim, Yahweh 7 Holy One, Jehovah, Skaddai 8 divinity, the Deity 9 Our Father 10 the Creator, the Godhead 11 divine being, God Almighty, the Almighty 13 the Omnipotent, the Omniscient 14 the All-Merciful, the Man Upstairs 15 the Supreme Being

Hebrew: 6 Adonai

Latin: 7 Dominus

god, first

origin: 12 Scandinavian

known as: 7 Forsete, Forseti

God and Man at Yale
　author: **17** William F Buckley Jr
God and my right
　French: **14** Dieu et mon droit
　motto of: **18** royal arms of England
God be with us
　German: **10** Gott mit uns
God be with you
　Latin: **12** Deus vobiscum
Godbole, Professor
　character in: **15** A Passage to India
　author: **7** Forster
Goddard, Jean-Luc
　director of: **10** Breathless
Goddard, Paulette
　real name: **10** Marion Levy
　husband: **14** Charlie Chaplin **15** Burgess
　Meredith **18** Erich Maria Remarque
　born: **11** Great Neck NY
　roles: **11** Modern Times, Unconquered
　15 So Proudly We Hail **16** Standing
　Room Only, The Great Dictator **19** Diary
　of a Chambermaid
Goddard, Robert Hutchings
　nationality: **8** American
　inventor of: **12** rocket engine **22** liquid
　propellant rocket
Godden, Rumer
　author of: **8** The River **14** Black Narcis-
　sus, Kitchen Madonna **16** The Peacock
　Spring **18** In This House of Brede, The
　Greengage Summer **19** An Episode of
　Sparrows **23** The Battle of Villa Fiorita
God enriches
　Latin: **9** ditat Deus
　motto of: **7** Arizona
Godfather, The
　author: **9** Mario Puzo
　family: **8** Corleone
　director: **18** Francis Ford Coppola
　cast: **8** Al Pacino (Michael) **9** James
　Caan (Sonny) **10** John Marley **11** Diane
　Keaton **12** Marlon Brando (Don Vito
　Corleone), Richard Conte, Robert Duvall
　14 Sterling Hayden **17** Richard Caste-
　llano
　Oscar for: **5** actor (Brando) **7** picture **10**
　screenplay
　sequel: **18** The Godfather Part II
Godfather, The, Part II
　director: **18** Francis Ford Coppola
　cast: **8** Al Pacino **10** John Cazale, Talia
　Shire **11** Diane Keaton **12** Lee Strasberg,
　Robert DeNiro, Robert Duvall
　Oscar for: **7** picture **10** screenplay **15**
　supporting actor (DeNiro)
　sequel to: **12** The Godfather
godforsaken 5 bleak **6** lonely, remote **8** de-
　serted, desolate, wretched **9** abandoned,
　neglected
god from a machine
　Latin: **13** deux ex machina
God is with us
　German: **10** Gott mit uns
godless 4 evil **6** wicked **7** heathen, im-
　pious, profane, ungodly **8** agnostic,
　depraved **9** atheistic **10** unhallowed **11**
blasphemous, irreligious, unrepentant, un-
　righteous **12** sacrilegious, unsanctified
godlessness 7 atheism **8** apostasy, unbe-
　lief **9** disbelief **10** irreligion
godlike 4 holy **5** godly, pious **6** deific, di-
　vine, sacred **8** immortal, olympian
godliness 5 piety **8** devotion, holiness **9**
　reverence **10** devoutness **12** spirituality
godly 4 good, holy **5** moral, pious **6** devout,
　divine, sacred **7** devoted, saintly **8** faithful,
　hallowed, reverent **9** believing, God-loving,
　pietistic, religious, righteous, spiritual **10**
　God-fearing, sanctified **11** consecrated,
　pure in heart, reverential
God of Vengeance, The
　author: **10** Sholem Asch
go down 3 ebb **4** drop, fade, wane **5** abate,
　lower, slide **6** lessen, plunge, reduce,
　weaken **7** descend, plummet, slacken,
　subside **8** decrease, diminish, moderate
God Save the Queen
　author: **17** William F Buckley Jr
God's Grace
　author: **14** Bernard Malamud
God's Little Acre
　author: **15** Erskine Caldwell
Godthaab
　capital of: **9** Greenland
God willing
　Latin: **10** Deo volente
God wills it
　Latin: **8** Deus vult
　cry of: **9** Crusaders
Godwin, William
　author of: **13** Caleb Williams **35** An En-
　quiry Concerning Political Justice
Goes, Hugo van der
　born: **5** Ghent **8** Flanders
　artwork: **7** The Fall **14** The Lamentation
　19 The Death of the Virgin **21** The Adora-
　tion of the Magi **22** The Adoration of the
　Child **26** The Adoration of the Shepherds
Goethe, Johann
　author of: **5** Faust **6** Egmont **24** The Sor-
　rows of Young Werther **29** Wilhelm Meis-
　ter's Apprenticeship
go-getter 4 doer **7** hustler **8** achiever, live
　wire
go-getting 7 driving, dynamic **8** forceful,
　hustling **9** ambitious, assertive, energetic
　10 aggressive **11** hard-driving, hard-
　working, industrious
Gogol, Nikolai
　author of: **7** The Nose **9** Dead Souls **10**
　Taras Bulba **11** The Overcoat **19** The
　Inspector-General
go hand in hand 5 match, tally **6** concur,
　square **7** coexist **9** accompany
go hungry 4 fast **6** famish, starve **7** abstain
Going My Way
　director: **10** Leo McCarey
　cast: **10** Bing Crosby (Father O'Malley)
　12 Gene Lockhart **15** Barry Fitzgerald
　Oscar for: **4** song **5** actor (Crosby) **7** pic-
　ture **8** director **15** supporting actor (Fitz-
　gerald)
　song: **15** Swinging on a Star

gold 3 bar 4 gilt 5 aurum, ingot 6 beauty, nugget, purity, yellow 7 bullion 8 goodness, goodwill, humanity, kindness 11 beneficence
   chemical symbol: 2 Au
gold and silver
   Spanish: 9 oro y plata
   motto of: 7 Montana
Gold Bug, The
   author: 13 Edgar Allan Poe
Gold Coast *see* 5 Ghana 11 Sierra Leone
golden 4 best, gilt, rosy 5 blest, blond, great, happy, palmy 6 bright, gilded, joyous, timely 7 aureate, halcyon, richest, shining 8 beatific, glorious, happiest, splendid 9 favorable, opportune, priceless, promising 10 auspicious, delightful, propitious, seasonable 11 exceptional, flourishing, resplendent 12 advantageous, bright-yellow 13 extraordinary
Golden Age
   first age of: 3 man
   world ruled by: 6 Cronus, Saturn
Golden Ass, The
   author: 14 Lucius Apuleius
   character: 4 Milo 5 Fotis 6 Lucius 8 Charites, Pamphile 9 Lepolemus 10 Thrasillus
Goldenberg, Emmanuel
   real name of: 15 Edward G Robinson
Golden Bough, The
   branch of: 9 mistletoe
   sacred to: 10 Proserpina
   used by: 6 Aeneas
   at shrine of: 5 Diana 7 Virbius
   author: 15 Sir James G Frazer
Golden Bowl, The
   author: 10 Henry James
   character: 8 Mr Verver 12 Maggie Verver, Mrs Assingham 13 Prince Amerigo 14 Charlotte Stant
Golden Boy
   nickname of: 11 Paul Hornung
golden brown 3 tan 5 tawny, toast 6 sienna 7 tobacco 8 chestnut
Golden Cockerel, The
   also: 8 Le Coq d'Or 15 Zolotoy Petushok
   opera by: 14 Rimsky-Korsakov
   character: 9 King Dodon 14 Queen of Shemaka
golden egg-layer
   form: 5 goose
   made of: 4 gold
Golden Fleece
   made of: 4 gold
   kept at: 7 Colchis
   kept by: 10 King Aeetes
   stolen by: 5 Jason 9 Argonauts
   accomplice: 5 Medea
Golden Legend
   author: 13 William Caxton
goldenrod 8 Solidago
   varieties: 5 sweet, white 6 Wreath 7 seaside 8 blue-stem, European 10 California
Golden State
   nickname of: 10 California

golden youth
   French: 13 jeunesse doree
goldfinch
   group of: 5 charm
Goldfinger
   director: 11 Guy Hamilton
   author: 10 Ian Fleming
   cast: 9 Gert Frobe (Auric Goldfinger) 10 Bernard Lee (M) 11 Lois Maxwell (Miss Moneypenny) 12 Harold Sakata (Oddjob), Shirley Eaton 13 Honor Blackman (Pussy Galore), Sean Connery (James Bond, 007)
Golding, William
   author of: 8 Free Fall 13 A Moving Target 14 Lord of the Flies, Rites of Passage 15 Darkness Visible
gold mine 7 bonanza 10 mother lode
Gold Rush, The
   director: 14 Charlie Chaplin
   cast: 9 Mack Swain, Tom Murray 11 Georgia Hale 14 Charlie Chaplin (Little Tramp)
   setting: 5 Yukon
Goldsmith, Oliver
   author of: 18 She Stoops to Conquer, The Deserted Village 19 The Vicar of Wakefield
Goldstein, Elliott
   real name of: 12 Elliott Gould
goldwasser
   form: 7 liquor
   origin: 6 France 7 Germany
   flavor: 4 herb 5 spice 7 caraway
   flecked with: 8 gold leaf
golf
   average number strokes to reach a hole: 3 par
   ball in another's path: 6 stymie
   championship: 6 US Open 9 Grand Slam 11 British Open 17 Masters' Tournament
   club: 4 iron, wood 6 driver, putter 7 brassie 8 long iron 9 sand wedge, short iron 10 middle iron 13 pitching wedge
   club carrier: 6 caddie
   course also called: 5 links
   golf ball formerly called: 6 guttie 8 feathery
   hole scored in one stroke: 3 ace 9 hole-in-one
   one stroke less than par: 6 birdie
   one stroke more than par: 5 bogey
   part of the course: 3 cup, tee 4 hole 5 apron, green, rough 6 bunker, hazard 7 fairway 8 sand trap
   position: 3 lie
   stance: 4 open 6 closed, square 7 address
   two strokes less than par: 5 eagle
   type of competition: 5 match 6 stroke
   uprooted turf: 5 divot
   warning cry: 4 fore
golfer 8 Ben Hogan, Lee Elder, Sam Snead 9 Carol Mann, Hale Irwin, Patty Berg, Tom Watson 10 Betsy Rawls, Bobby Jones, Deane Beman, Gary Player, Hubie Green,

Jim Demaret, Judy Rankin, Lee Trevino, Nancy Lopez 11 Ben Crenshaw, Billy Casper, Byron Nelson, Calvin Peete, Donna Caponi, Gene Sarazen, Julius Boros, Tom Weiskopf, Walter Hagen 12 Arnold Palmer, Jack Nicklaus, Joanne Carner, Johnny Miller, Mickey Wright, Sandra Haynie 14 Cary Middlecoff, Kathy Whitworth 16 Roberto DeVicenzo 19 Susie Maxwell Berning 20 Severiano Ballesteros 21 Babe Didrikson Zaharias

Golgotha 7 Calvary
  means: 10 skull place

Goliath
  killed by: 5 David

golliwogg 3 toy **4** doll **9** plaything

Gomer
  father: 7 Diblaim
  husband: 5 Hosea

Gomer Pyle USMC
  character: 5 Bunny **7** Frankie **9** Corp Boyle **11** Duke Slayter, (Sgt) Vince Carter
  cast: 9 Jim Nabors, Roy Stuart **10** Ted Bessell **11** Frank Sutton **12** Ronnie Schell **13** Barbara Stuart

Gomorrah
  destroyed with: 5 Sodom **6** Zeboim **10** Admah

Gondoliers, The
  operetta by: 18 Gilbert and Sullivan
  character: 4 Luiz **5** Tessa **7** Casilda **8** Gianetta **13** Marco Palmieri **15** Duke of Plaza-Toro **16** Giuseppe Palmieri

gone 3 ago, out **4** away, dead, left, lost, past **6** absent, ruined, used up **7** defunct, died out, extinct, missing **9** departed, finished, hopeless, vanished **11** disappeared

Goneril
  character in: 8 King Lear
  author: 11 Shakespeare

Gone With the Wind
  author: 16 Margaret Mitchell
  character: 5 Mammy **6** Big Sam, Prissy **7** Dr Meade **10** Ellen (Robillard) O'Hara **11** Gerald O'Hara, Honey Wilkes, India Wilkes **12** Ashley Wilkes, Aunt Pittypat, Belle Watling **13** Scarlett O'Hara, Tarleton twins **15** Mrs Merriweather **21** Melanie Hamilton Wilkes
  Scarlett's husband: 11 Rhett Butler **12** Frank Kennedy **15** Charles Hamilton
  Scarlett's children: 4 Emma, Wade **6** Bonnie
  Scarlett's sister: 7 Carreen, Suellen
  director: 13 Victor Fleming
  cast: 9 Ona Munson **10** Clark Gable (Rhett Butler) **11** Evelyn Keyes, Vivien Leigh (Scarlett O'Hara) **12** Leslie Howard (Ashley Wilkes) **13** Ann Rutherford **14** Hattie McDaniel (Mammy), Thomas Mitchell (Gerald O'Hara) **16** Butterfly McQueen (Prissy) **17** Olivia de Havilland (Melanie Hamilton Wilkes)
  score: 10 Max Steiner
  Oscar for: 7 actress (Leigh), picture **8** director **12** screenwriter **17** supporting actress (McDaniel)

producer: 14 David O Selznick

good 3 ace, fit, new **4** best, boon, fine, full, gain, kind, pure, real **5** ample, crack, favor, great, large, merit, moral, pious, prize, right, solid, sound, sunny, valid, value, worth **6** adroit, choice, devout, entire, genial, honest, humane, kindly, lively, newest, profit, proper, seemly, select, tiptop, useful, virtue, wealth, worthy **7** adapted, benefit, capable, capital, dutiful, fitting, genuine, godsend, healthy, orderly, service, sizable, skilled, success, upright, welfare **8** adequate, becoming, blessing, bonafide, cheerful, complete, decorous, gracious, innocent, interest, kindness, obedient, obliging, pleasant, precious, reliable, salutary, skillful, smartest, sociable, splendid, suitable, thorough, topnotch, valuable, virtuous, windfall **9** admirable, advantage, agreeable, authentic, convivial, deserving, efficient, enjoyable, enjoyment, excellent, exemplary, expensive, favorable, first-rate, happiness, healthful, honorable, priceless, qualified, religious, righteous, unsullied, untainted, wholesome, wonderful **10** altruistic, beneficent, beneficial, benevolent, excellence, first-class, legitimate, proficient, prosperity, sufficient, worthwhile **11** appropriate, commendable, considerate, improvement, kindhearted, substantial, sympathetic, well-behaved **12** advantageous, considerable, praiseworthy, satisfactory **13** companionable, conscientious, righteousness
  French: 3 bon **4** bien
  Spanish: 5 bueno
  German: 3 gut

Good as Gold
  author: 12 Joseph Heller

Good Book 5 Bible

good breeding 5 grace **6** polish **7** manners **9** gentility **10** refinement **11** cultivation

good buy 4 deal **5** steal **7** bargain

good-by, good-bye 3 bye **6** bye-bye, bye now, so long **7** parting, send-off **8** farewell, Godspeed **9** departure **10** separation **11** be seeing you, leave-taking, see you later **12** God be with you **15** till we meet again
  French: 5 adieu **8** au revoir
  German: 14 auf Wiedersehen
  Hawaiian: 5 aloha
  Italian: 4 ciao **5** addio **11** arrivederci
  Japanese: 8 sayonara
  Latin: 4 vale
  Spanish: 5 adios **12** hasta la vista

Goodbye, Darkness
  author: 17 William Manchester

Goodbye, Mr Chips
  director: 7 Sam Wood
  author: 11 James Hilton
  cast: 11 Greer Garson, Paul Henreid (von Henreid), Robert Donat
  Oscar for: 5 actor (Donat)
  character: 7 Mr Chips **10** Mrs Wickett **12** Kathy Bridges
  school: 10 Brookfield

Goodbye Girl, The
director: 11 Herbert Ross
based on play by: 9 Neil Simon
cast: 11 Marsha Mason 13 Quinn
Cummings 15 Richard Dreyfuss
Oscar for: 5 actor (Dreyfuss)

Good Companions, The
author: 11 J B Priestley

good counsel
god of: 6 Consus

good day
French: 7 bonjour
German: 8 guten tag
Spanish: 10 buenos dias
Italian: 10 buon giorno

good deal 3 buy 5 steal 7 bargain

good deed 8 kindness 11 benefaction 12
philanthropy
Hebrew: 7 mitsvah, mitzvah

Good Earth, The
author: 10 Pearl S Buck
character: 4 O-Lan 6 Nung En 7 Nung
Wen, The Fool 8 Wang Lung 11 Pear
Blossom 12 Lotus Blossom
director: 14 Sidney Franklin
cast: 8 Keye Luke, Paul Muni 10 Tilly
Losch 11 Jessie Ralph, Luise Rainer 14
Walter Connolly 15 Charley Grapewin
Oscar for: 7 actress (Rainer)

good feelings 8 good will 11 benevolence
12 friendliness

good form 9 etiquette, good taste 10 politeness 11 good manners

good-for-nothing 5 idler 6 loafer 7 useless
9 no-account, shiftless, worthless

good fortune 4 luck 7 bonanza 8 fortuity,
lady luck, windfall 9 blessings 10 lucky
break

good friend
French: 6 bon ami 9 bonne amie

good health 5 vigor 7 fitness 8 vitality 10
robustness

Goodhue, Bertram Grosvenor
architect of: 13 St Bartholomew (NYC)
14 St Thomas Church (NYC) 25 Chapel
at US Military Academy (West Point), National Academy of Sciences (Washington
DC) 28 Nebraska State Capitol Building
(Lincoln)
style: 13 Gothic Revival 15 Spanish Colonial

good humor 10 affability, amiability, cheeriness, kindliness, mellowness 12 cheerfulness, complaisance, pleasantness 15
kindheartedness

good-humored 4 mild, warm 6 cheery, genial, gentle, kindly, mellow 7 affable, amiable 8 cheerful, pleasant 9 congenial,
easygoing 11 complaisant

good-looker 3 fox 4 doll, hunk 5 beaut, Venus 6 Adonis, beauty, eyeful 7 stunner 8
knockout 11 handsome Dan

good-looking 4 fair, foxy, sexy 5 bonny 6
comely, lovely, pretty 8 alluring, clean-cut,
gorgeous, handsome, stunning 9 beauteous, beautiful, exquisite, ravishing 10 attractive, bewitching, enchanting 11 capti-

vating, eye-catching, well-favored 15
pulchritudinous

good looks 6 beauty 10 comeliness, loveliness 11 pulchritude 12 handsomeness 14
attractiveness

good luck
Yiddish: 8 mazel tov

goodly 4 tidy 5 ample, large 7 sizable 11
substantial 12 considerable

Goodman, Theodosia
real name of: 9 Theda Bara

good manners 8 courtesy 9 amenities, etiquette, gentility 10 politeness, refinement

good name 4 face 5 image 10 reputation
11 self-respect

good nature 6 warmth 9 geniality, good humor 10 affability, amiability, cordiality,
likability 12 complaisance, pleasantness
13 agreeableness

good-natured 4 warm 5 sunny 6 genial,
kindly 7 affable, amiable 8 cheerful,
friendly, obliging, pleasant 9 agreeable,
congenial, easygoing 11 complaisant,
good-humored, warm-hearted 13 accommodating

goodness 3 boy, gee, hey, say, wow 5 favor, honor, mercy, merit, piety, value,
worth, wowee 6 profit, purity, virtue 7 benefit, decorum, gee whiz, heavens, honesty,
probity, service 8 boy-oh-boy, devotion,
gracious, kindness, morality 9 advantage, innocence, integrity, land alive,
landsakes, nutrition, propriety, rectitude 10
generosity, kindliness, sakes alive, usefulness 11 benevolence, nourishment 12
virtuousness 13 righteousness, wholesomeness 14 heavens to Betsy

good night
French: 7 bon soir 9 bonne nuit
German: 9 gute nacht
Spanish: 12 buenas noches
Italian: 10 buona notte

good opinion 6 esteem, regard 7 respect 8
approval 10 admiration

good person 4 dear, love 5 angel 7 darling
10 sweetheart

goods 4 gear 5 cloth, stock, wares 6 fabric,
things 7 effects, fabrics 8 chattels, material, movables, property, textiles 9 inventory, trappings 11 commodities, furnishings, merchandise, possessions 13
appurtenances, paraphernalia

good sense 6 brains, wisdom 8 judgment
12 intelligence

good taste 10 refinement 11 cultivation,
discernment 14 discrimination

good-tempered 5 sunny 7 amiable, smiling
8 cheerful 12 sweet-natured

good time 3 fun 9 amusement, diversion,
enjoyment 13 entertainment

good times 4 boom 8 fat years

good turn 5 favor 7 service 8 good deed

goodwill 5 amity 8 kindness 9 benignity 10
cordiality, kindliness 11 amicability,
benevolence 12 friendliness 15 kindheartedness

good wishes 4 best 5 favor 6 regard 7 consent, regards 8 approval, blessing, respects, sanction 11 compliments

Goodwood, Caspar
   character in: 18 The Portrait of a Lady
   author: 5 James

good word of 5 praise 10 compliment 11 approbation 12 commendation 14 congratulation

Goodyear, Charles
   nationality: 8 American
   developed: 16 vulcanized rubber

goof 3 err 4 boob, flub, fool, mess 5 botch, error, gum up 6 bollix, boo-boo, bungle, fumble, slip up 7 blunder, mistake 9 oversight

Goolagong Cawley, Evonne
   sport: 6 tennis
   heritage: 19 Australian Aborigine

go on all fours 5 crawl, creep

goose
   young: 7 gosling
   group of: 5 flock, skein 6 gaggle

goose egg 3 nil, zip 4 zero 5 aught 6 cipher, naught 7 nothing 11 horse collar

go over 5 audit, check 6 review 7 examine, inspect 10 scrutinize 11 investigate

Gopher State
   nickname of: 9 Minnesota

Gorbachev, Mikhail Sergeyevich
   party: 9 Communist
   country: 4 USSR 6 Russia 31 Union of Soviet Socialist Republics
   born: 9 Stavropol 10 Privolnoye 16 Krasnogvardeisky
   education: 21 Moscow State University
   political career: 9 Politburo 16 General Secretary 20 Agriculture Secretary 23 Stavropol Communist Party 35 Deputy Supreme Soviet Central Committee
   policy: 8 glasnost 11 perestroika
   distinguishing characteristic: 19 strawberry birthmark (head)
   wife: 15 Raisa Maksimovna
   occupation: 7 teacher
   daughter: 5 Irisa
   occupation: 6 doctor 9 physician
   grandchild: 6 Oksana

Gorcey, Leo
   born: 9 New York NY
   roles: 4 Spit 10 Bowery Boys 11 Dead End Kids

Gordimer, Nadine
   author of: 11 July's People 12 The Lying Days 13 A Guest of Honor 15 Burger's Daughter 16 A Soldier's Embrace 21 The Late Bourgeois World
   award: 10 Nobel Prize

Gordon, Ruth
   real name: 15 Ruth Gordon Jones
   husband: 11 Garson Kanin
   born: 11 Wollaston MA
   roles: 11 Where's Poppa? 13 Rosemary's Baby 14 Harold and Maude 17 Inside Daisy Clover 20 Abe Lincoln in Illinois

gore 5 blood 7 carnage 8 butchery 9 bloodshed, slaughter

Gore, Albert
   born: 10 Washington (DC)
   wife: 6 Tipper 13 Mary Elizabeth
   children: 5 Sarah 6 Albert 7 Karenna, Kristin
   education: 7 Harvard 10 Vanderbilt
   profession: 10 journalist
   author of: 17 Earth in the Balance
   political career: 6 Senate 13 vice president 22 House of Representatives

Gorgas, William Crawford
   field: 8 medicine
   position: 18 army surgeon general
   conquered: 7 malaria 11 yellow fever
   location: 11 Panama Canal

gorge 3 gap, ire 4 bolt, cram, craw, dale, dell, fill, glen, glut, gulp, pass, sate, vale 5 abyss, anger, blood, chasm, cleft, gulch, gully, mouth, stuff, wrath 6 canyon, defile, devour, gobble, gullet, hatred, hollow, muzzle, nausea, ravine, throat 7 disgust, indulge, overeat, satiate 8 crevasse 9 animosity, esophagus, repulsion, revulsion 10 gluttonize, gormandize, repugnance 11 overindulge

gorgeous 4 fine, rich 5 grand 6 bright, costly, lovely 7 elegant, opulent, shining 8 dazzling, glorious, imposing, splendid, stunning 9 beautiful, brilliant, exquisite, luxurious, ravishing, sumptuous 10 attractive, glittering, impressive 11 goodlooking, magnificent, resplendent, splendorous 13 splendiferous

Gorgons
   form: 7 maidens 8 monsters
   names: 6 Medusa, Stheno 7 Euryale, Sthenno
   father: 7 Phorcys
   mother: 4 Ceto
   protectress: 6 Graeae, Graiae
   hair of: 6 snakes
   hands of: 5 brass
   turned viewers to: 5 stone

Gorgophone
   father: 7 Perseus
   mother: 9 Andromeda
   husband: 7 Oebalus 8 Perieres
   son: 9 Leucippus

Gorgosaurus
   type: 8 dinosaur, theropod
   location: 7 Alberta 12 North America
   period: 10 Cretaceous

Gorgythion
   mentioned in: 5 Iliad
   father: 5 Priam
   killed by: 6 Teucer

gorilla
   group of: 4 band

Gorky, Arshile
   real name: 21 Vosdanig Manoog Adokian
   born: 7 Armenia 11 Khorkomvari
   artwork: 5 Agony 15 Diary of a Seducer 17 Making the Calendar 21 The Artist

and his Mother, Water of the Flowery Hill **22** The Liver is the Cock's Comb

Gorky, Maxim (Maksim)
  real name: 25 Alekseimaksimovich Peshkov
  author of: 7 V I Lenin **11** My Childhood **14** The Lower Depths **18** The Small Town Okurov **20** City of the Yellow Devil, Twenty-six Men and a Girl **27** The Life of Matthew Kozhemyakin

gormandize 5 feast, raven **6** devour

Gortys
  father: 10 Stymphalus **12** Rhadamanthys

gory 5 scary **6** bloody, creepy **9** murderous **10** horrifying, sanguinary, terrifying **11** bloodsoaked, ensanguined, frightening **12** bloodstained, bloodthirsty **13** bloodcurdling

gospel, Gospel 5 credo, creed **8** doctrine **11** the good news, the last word **12** the final word **13** the whole truth, ultimate truth
  the first four books of the New Testament: 4 Luke, John, Mark **7** Matthew

Gospel writers 4 John, Luke, Mark **7** Matthew **9** synoptist

gospodin 2 Mr **6** Mister

gossamer 5 filmy, gauzy, sheer **8** cobwebby **10** diaphanous **13** insubstantial

gossip 4 news **5** babble, report, tattle **7** comment, hearsay, prattle, scandal, twaddle **8** idle talk **10** backbiting **12** tittle-tattle **13** newsmongering

gossiper 3 pry **4** blab **5** prate, snoop, yenta **6** gabble, magpie, meddle, tattle **7** babbler, meddler, prattle, snooper, tattler **8** busybody **9** chatterer **10** chatterbox, newsmonger, talebearer, tattletale **11** rumormonger **12** blabbermouth, gossipmonger **13** scandalmonger

go stale 3 die

Go Tell It on the Mountain
  author: 12 James Baldwin

Gothic
  language family: 12 Indo-European

go through 4 bear **6** endure, suffer **7** sustain, undergo **9** encounter, withstand **10** experience

go to 3 see **5** visit **6** attend **8** appear at, frequent

go to bed 6 retire, turn in **7** lie down, sack out **8** flake out **9** hit the hay **10** call it a day, hit the sack **11** catch some z's

go to pieces 5 break, crack **7** break up, crack up, crumble, give way, shatter **8** splinter **9** break down, fall apart **11** lose control **12** disintegrate

go to work on 6 attack, tackle **8** set about **9** undertake

go to wrack and ruin 5 decay **7** crumble **9** fall apart **12** disintegrate

Gotterdammerung 17 Twilight of the Gods
  see: 8 Ragnarok

Gott mit uns 11 God be with us, God is with us

gouge 5 carve, drill, scoop **6** chisel, extort **10** overcharge

gouge out 5 drill **6** hollow **8** carve out, scoop out **9** chisel out, hollow out **10** whittle out

Gould, Chester
  creator/artist of: 9 Dick Tracy

Gould, Elliott
  real name: 16 Elliott Goldstein
  wife: 15 Barbra Streisand
  born: 10 Brooklyn NY
  roles: 4 MASH **13** Little Murders **14** The Long Goodbye **15** California Split, Getting Straight **19** Bob & Carol & Ted & Alice

Goulding, Edmund
  director of: 10 Grand Hotel **11** Dark Victory **13** The Dawn Patrol

go under 4 fail, fall, sink **9** go belly up **10** go bankrupt

Gounod, Charles Francois
  born: 5 Paris **6** France
  composer of: 5 Faust **6** Gallia, Sappho, Te Deum **8** Cinq-Mars, Mireille **9** La Colombe, Polyeucte **10** Mors 'et Vita **11** Marie Stuart, Stabat Mater **13** La Reine de Saba **14** Romeo and Juliet **16** La Nonne Sanglante, Philemon et Baucis **17** La Tribute de Zamora **18** Le Medecin Malgre Lui

gourd 9 Cucurbita **13** Cucurbita pepo
  varieties: 3 ash, ivy, rag, wax **4** club **5** snake, white **6** bitter, bottle, dipper, sponge, teasel, viper's **7** fig-leaf, Malabar, serpent, trumpet **8** calabash, hedgehog, Missouri **9** dishcloth **10** goareberry, gooseberry, knob-kerrie, silverseed **11** sugar-trough **12** Hercules'-club **14** scarlet-fruited

gourmand 7 glutton **8** big eater **9** bon vivant, chowhound **11** gormandizer, trencherman

gourmet 7 epicure **9** bon vivant **10** gastronome **11** connoisseur, gastronomer **12** gastronomist

gourmet cooking
  French: 12 haute cuisine

Gourmont, Remy de
  author of: 18 A Night in Luxembourg

gout 5 style, taste **10** preference

govern 3 run **4** boss, curb, form, head, lead, rule, sway, tame **5** check, guide, pilot, steer **6** bridle, direct, manage **7** command, control, incline, inhibit, oversee **8** dominate, restrain **9** influence, supervise **10** administer, discipline, hold in hand **11** hold in check, superintend **13** be at the helm of **14** pull the strings **16** keep under control **17** exercise authority **18** be in the driver's seat

governed 3 led **5** ruled **6** guided **7** steered, subject **8** directed **9** dependent **10** controlled, supervised **12** administered **13** superintended

governing 6 ruling **7** curbing, guiding, heading, leading, swaying **8** bridling, checking, managing, piloting, reigning, steering **9** directing, inclining **10** inhibiting, management, overseeing **11** controlling, influencing, restraining, supervision

13 administering **14** administrating, administration, superintending

governing body 10 government, management, parliament **12** powers that be **14** administration **16** board of directors, board of governors **18** executive committee

government 3 law **4** rule **5** state **6** regime **7** command, control **8** dominion, guidance **9** authority, direction **10** domination, management, regulation **11** supervision **13** governing body, statesmanship **14** administration

governor

    Turkish: 3 beg, bey

Gowan

    character in: 12 Little Dorrit

    author: 7 Dickens

go with 6 convey, convoy, escort **7** conduct **9** accompany

gown 4 robe **5** dress, frock **10** nightdress

goy 6 non-Jew **7** Gentile

Goya (y Lucientes, Francisco Jose de)

    born: 5 Spain **13** Fuente de todos

    artwork: 8 Proverbs **10** Disparates **11** Tauromaquia **12** Los Caprichos, The Naked Maja **15** Majas on a Balcony **17** The Disasters of War **21** Charles IV and his Family

grab 3 bag, nab **4** grip, hold, pass **5** catch, clasp, grasp, lunge, pluck, seize **6** clutch, collar, snatch **7** capture

grace 4 deck, love, tact, trim **5** adorn, charm, endow, exalt, favor, honor, mercy, merit, piety, skill, taste **6** beauty, bedeck, enrich, pardon, polish, set off, virtue **7** charity, culture, decorum, dignify, dress up, elevate, enhance, garnish, glorify, manners, smarten, suavity **8** beautify, clemency, decorate, elegance, felicity, fluidity, God's love, holiness, lenience, ornament, reprieve, sanctity, spruce up, urbanity **9** embellish, endowment, etiquette, exemption, extra time, God's favor, good looks, propriety **10** aggrandize, comeliness, devoutness, excellence, indulgence, refinement **11** cultivation, forgiveness, lissomeness, pulchritude, saintliness, willowiness **12** dispensation, gracefulness, mannerliness, mercifulness **14** accomplishment, divine goodness

    French: 11 savoir faire

graceful 5 lithe **6** comely, limber, lovely **7** elegant, lissome, shapely, sinuous, willowy **8** delicate **9** beautiful, lithesome, sylphlike **10** attractive **11** light-footed

gracefulness 8 delicacy, fluidity **10** suppleness **11** lissomeness

graceless 5 gawky, inept **6** clumsy **7** awkward **10** ungraceful **11** heavy-handed

Graces

    also: 7 Gratiae **9** Charities

    goddesses of: 6 beauty

    father: 4 Zeus

    mother: 8 Eurynome

    names: 4 Auxo **5** Cleta **6** Aglaia, Thalia **7** Phaenna **8** Hegemone **10** Euphrosyne

gracious 2 my **3** boy, gee, wow **4** kind **5** civil, mercy, oh boy **6** benign, humane, kindly, polite, tender, ye gods **7** affable, amiable, clement, cordial, courtly, gee whiz, lenient, my stars **8** friendly, goodness, merciful, obliging, pleasant **9** benignant, courteous, landsakes **10** benevolent, charitable, chivalrous, hospitable **11** good heavens, good natured, kindhearted **13** compassionate **14** heavens to Betsy

gradation 4 step **5** stage **6** degree **7** shading **8** grouping, ordering **9** arranging **11** arrangement **12** organization **14** classification

grade 4 bank, even, hill, mark, ramp, rank, rate, sort, step **5** brand, caste, class, level, order, pitch, place, slope, stage, value **6** degree, estate, rating, smooth, sphere, status **7** flatten, incline, quality, station **8** classify, gradient, position, standing **9** acclivity, condition, declivity, intensity

grade-A 2 A-1 **4** aces, a-one, fine, tops **5** grade, great, prime, super **6** choice, superb, tip-top **7** capital **8** peerless, sterling, superior, top-notch **9** excellent, first-rate, matchless, superfine **10** first-class, preeminent, tremendous **11** outstanding, superlative

Gradgrind, Thomas and Louisa

    characters in: 9 Hard Times

    author: 7 Dickens

gradient 4 ramp, tilt **5** pitch, slant, slope **6** ascent **7** incline, leaning **9** steepness **11** inclination

gradual 4 slow **6** gentle, steady **7** regular **8** measured **9** graduated, piecemeal **10** continuous, deliberate, drop-by-drop, inch-by-inch, step-by-step, successive **11** incremental, progressive **13** imperceptible, slow-but-steady **14** little-by-little

graduate 5 grade **6** alumna **7** alumnus, mark off **9** calibrate **10** measure out **14** grant a degree to, receive a degree

Graduate, The

    director: 11 Mike Nichols

    cast: 12 Anne Bancroft (Mrs Robinson) **13** Dustin Hoffman, Katharine Ross **14** Murray Hamilton, William Daniels

    score: 17 Simon and Garfunkel

    Oscar for: 8 director

Graeae

    also: 6 Graiae

    goddesses of: 3 sea

    number: 5 three

    names: 4 Enyo **5** Deino **9** Pemphredo

    father: 7 Phorcys

    mother: 4 Ceto

    sisters: 7 Gorgons

    protectresses of: 7 Gorgons

    personifed: 6 old age

    three shared: 6 one eye **8** one tooth

    eye stolen by: 7 Perseus

    corresponds to: 4 Enyo

Graeme, Alison

    character in: 21 The Master of Ballantrae

    author: 9 Stevenson

Graf 5 count
graft 3 bud 4 join, last, slip, swag 5 booty, infix, inset, plant, scion 6 bribes, payola, splice, spoils, sprout 7 bribery, implant, ingraft, payoffs, plunder, rake-off 8 kickback 9 hush money 10 corruption, transplant 12 implantation 13 inserted shoot
Graham, Bruce
  architect of: 17 John Hancock Center (Chicago)
Grahame, Kenneth
  author of: 19 The Wind in the Willows
Graiae see 6 Graeae
grain 3 bit, dot, jot, rye 4 atom, corn, dash, iota, mite, oats, seed, whit 5 crumb, grist, maize, ovule, pinch, spark, speck, touch, trace, wheat 6 barley, cereal, kernel, millet, morsel, pellet, tittle, trifle 7 granule, modicum 8 fragment, molecule, particle 9 scintilla
  abbreviation: 2 gr
  god of: 7 Robigus
  goddess of: 6 Ribigo
Grain Coast see 11 Sierra Leone
Grainger, Percy Aldridge
  born: 9 Australia, Melbourne
  composer of: 14 Country Gardens 17 Handel in the Strand 19 Rosenkavalier Ramble
gram
  abbreviation of: 1 g
Gram
  origin: 12 Scandinavian
  mentioned in: 8 Volsunga
  form: 5 sword
  owned by: 7 Sigmund
  used by: 6 Sigurd
  killed: 6 Fafnir
grand 2 A-1 3 big 4 fine, full, good, head, huge, keen, main 5 chief, fancy, great, large, lofty, noble, regal, royal, showy, super, swell 6 august, choice, groovy, kingly, lordly, superb 7 dashing, elegant, exalted, haughty, mammoth, opulent, pompous, queenly, stately, sublime, supreme 8 arrogant, complete, elevated, fabulous, glorious, imperial, imposing, majestic, palatial, princely, real cool, real gone, smashing, splendid, striking, terrific 9 admirable, dignified, excellent, first-rate, grandiose, luxurious, marvelous, principal, sumptuous, wonderful 10 impressive, monumental, out-of-sight 11 highfalutin, magnificent, pretentious, sensational 12 ostentatious 13 comprehensive, distinguished
Grand Canyon State
  nickname of: 7 Arizona
grande dame 9 great lady
grandee 5 noble 8 nobleman 9 blue blood 10 aristocrat
Grandees
  author: 17 Stephen Birmingham
grandeur 4 fame, pomp 5 glory, state 6 luster 7 dignity, majesty 8 eminence, nobility, splendor 9 celebrity, loftiness, solemnity, sublimity 10 augustness, excellence, importance 11 distinction, stateliness 12

magnificence, resplendence 14 impressiveness
Grand Hotel
  author: 9 Vicki Baum
  character: 9 Miss Flamm 12 Baron Gaigern 14 Dr Otternschlag, Otto Kringelein 27 Herr Generaldirektor Preysing 32 Elisaveta Alexandrovna Grusinskaya
  director: 14 Edmund Goulding
  cast: 10 Greta Garbo 12 Joan Crawford, Wallace Beery 13 John Barrymore 15 Lionel Barrymore
  setting: 6 Berlin
Grand Illusion
  director: 10 Jean Renoir
  cast: 5 Dalio 7 Carette 9 Dita Parlo, Jean Gabin 13 Pierre Fresnay 16 Erich von Stroheim
grandiloquent 5 lofty 6 florid, turgid 7 flowery, pompous, stilted, swollen 8 inflated 9 bombastic, grandiose, high-flown 10 rhetorical 11 highfalutin, pretentious 12 high-sounding, magniloquent
grandiose 5 grand 7 pompous, splashy 8 affected 9 high-flown 10 flamboyant, theatrical 11 extravagant, highfalutin, pretentious
Grand Marnier
  type: 6 brandy, cognac 7 liqueur
  origin: 6 France
  flavor: 6 orange
  with gin: 7 Red Lion
grand monde 10 great world 11 best society 16 fashionable world
grand prix 10 grand prize
grand prize
  French: 9 grand prix
Grange, Red (Harold)
  nickname: 14 Galloping Ghost
  sport: 8 football
  team: 11 U of Illinois 12 Chicago Bears
Granger, Edith
  character in: 12 Dombey and Son
  author: 7 Dickens
Grangosier
  character in: 22 Gargantua and Pantagruel
  author: 8 Rabelais
Granite State
  nickname of: 12 New Hampshire
grant 4 boon, cede, gift, give 5 admit, allot, allow, award, endow, favor, yield 6 accord, assign, bestow, confer, donate, permit 7 agree to, bequest, concede, consent, deal out, largess, present, subsidy, tribute 8 accede to, allocate, bestowal, dispense, donation, gratuity, offering 9 allotment, allowance, apportion, consent to, endowment, vouchsafe 10 assignment, concession, indulgence 11 benefaction 12 contribution, presentation 13 appropriation
Grant, Cary
  real name: 23 Archibald Alexander Leach
  wife: 10 Dyan Cannon 13 Barbara Hutton
  born: 7 England 8 Bristol

roles: 6 Topper 9 Dream Wife, Houseboat 10 Indiscreet 11 Blonde Venus, Father Goose 13 To Catch a Thief 14 Bringing Up Baby, Monkey Business, The Bishop's Wife 15 She Done Him Wrong 16 North by Northwest 17 Arsenic and Old Lace, I Was a Male War Bride 18 Operation Petticoat 20 The Philadelphia Story 21 None But the Lonely Heart

Grant, Lee
real name: 21 Lyova Haskell Rosenthal
born: 9 New York NY
roles: 7 Shampoo 10 Plaza Suite 11 Peyton Place, The Landlord 14 Detective Story 19 In the Heat of the Night 20 Divorce American Style

Grant, Ulysses Simpson
real name: 17 Hiram Ulysses Grant
nickname: 3 Sam 4 Lyss 27 Unconditional Surrender Grant
presidential rank: 10 eighteenth
party: 10 Republican
state represented: 2 IL
defeated: 5 (David) Davis, (James) Black 6 (Charles) O'Conor 7 (Horace) Greeley, (Horatio) Seymour 9 (William Slocomb) Groesbeck
vice president: 5 (Thomas W) Ferry (acting) 6 (Henry) Wilson (died in office 1875), (Schuyler) Colfax
cabinet:
state: 4 (Hamilton) Fish 9 (Elihu Benjamin) Washburne
treasury: 7 (Alexander Turney) Stewart, (Benjamin Helm) Bristow, (Lot Myrick) Morrill 8 (George Sewall) Boutwell 10 (William Adams) Richardson
war: 4 (Alphonso) Taft 7 (James Donald) Cameron, (John Aaron) Rawlins, (William Worth) Belknap
attorney general: 4 (Alphonso) Taft, (Ebenezer Rockwood) Hoar 7 (Amos Tappan) Akerman 8 (George Henry) Williams 10 (Edwards) Pierrepont
navy: 5 (Adolph Edward) Borie 7 (George Maxwell) Robeson
postmaster general: 5 (James Noble) Tyner 6 (Marshall) Jewell 8 (James William) Marshall, (John Angel James) Creswell
interior: 3 (Jacob Dolson) Cox 6 (Columbus) Delano 8 (Zachariah) Chandler
born: 15 Point Pleasant OH
died: 15 Mount McGregor NY
buried: 9 New York NY
education: 9 West Point 17 US Military Academy
religion: 9 Methodist
author: 24 Personal Memoirs of US Grant 30 Around the World with General Grant
political career:
secretary of: 3 War (interim appointment)
civilian career: 6 farmer
military service: 6 US Army 8 Civil War 10 Mexican War 18 Illinois Volunteers 20 Commander of Union Army
notable events of lifetime/career: 5 Panic (of 1873) 11 Black Friday (gold panic) 16 Custer's Last Stand
Act: 10 Salary Grab
conspiracy: 11 Whiskey Ring
scandal: 14 Credit Mobilier
quote: 60 "No terms except unconditional and immediate surrender can be accepted"
father: 9 Jesse Root
mother: 6 Hannah (Simpson)
siblings: 5 Clare 10 Orvil Lynch 11 Mary Frances 13 Samuel Simpson, Virginia Paine
wife: 5 Julia (Boggs Dent)
children: 5 Ellen 9 Jesse Root 13 Frederick Dent 14 Ulysses Simpson

granted
French: 7 d'accord

grantee 8 receiver 9 recipient 11 beneficiary

grant immunity to 4 free 5 clear, spare 6 except, excuse, exempt 7 absolve, release, relieve 9 privilege

grantor 5 giver 8 bestower 10 benefactor

granulate 5 crush 6 powder 9 pulverize 11 crystallize

granulated 6 ground 7 crushed 8 powdered 10 pulverized 12 crystallized

granule 5 grain 7 crystal 8 particle

grape 5 Vitis 13 Vitis vinifera
varieties: 3 cat, red, sea 4 amur, blue, bush, cape, rock, sand, tail 5 bear's, bunch, frost, Javan, sugar, veldt 6 canyon, Damson, Miller, Oregon, pigeon, possum, summer, winter 7 African, Bullace, catbird, chicken, Concord, Spanish 8 European, mountain 9 evergreen, panhandle, river-bank 10 silver-leaf 11 southern fox 13 sweet mountain
wine: 5 Gamay 6 Cayuga, Duriff, Merlot, Muscat, Shiraz 7 Barbera, Catawba 8 Baco Noir, Dolcetto, Labrusca, Nebbiolo, Verduzzo 9 Aglianico, Fume Blanc, Huxelrebe, Pinot Noir, Primitivo, Trebbiano, Zinfandel 10 Chardonnay, Sangiovese 11 Chenin Blanc, Petite Sirah, Pinot Bianco, Seyval Blanc 13 Cabernet Franc, Montepulciano 14 Sauvignon Blanc 15 Gewurztraminer 17 Cabernet Sauvignon 20 Johannisberg Riesling

Grapes of Wrath, The
author: 13 John Steinbeck
character: 4 Noah 6 Connie, Ma Joad, Pa Joad 7 Jim Casy, Tom Joad 12 Rose of Sharon
director: 8 John Ford
cast: 10 Henry Fonda 11 Jane Darwell 12 Dorris Bowden 13 John Carradine 15 Charley Grapewin
Oscar for: 17 supporting actress (Darwell)

graphic 4 seen 5 clear, drawn, lucid, vivid 6 visual 7 painted, printed, visible, written 8 distinct, explicit, forcible, lifelike, pictured,

striking 9 pictorial, realistic, trenchant 10
expressive 11 descriptive, picturesque 12
illustrative

grappa
   type: 6 brandy 7 liqueur
   origin: 5 Italy
   made from: 9 grape pulp

grapple 4 face, grip, hold, meet 5 catch,
clasp, fight, grasp, seize 6 breast, clutch,
combat, engage, fasten, tackle, take on 7
contend, grapnel, wrestle 8 confront, deal
with, do battle, make fast, struggle 9 encounter, large hook, lay hold of 11 hold
tightly

grasp 3 get, ken 4 grab, grip, hold, sway,
take 5 catch, clasp, infer, power, range,
reach, savvy, scope, seize, sense, skill,
sweep 6 clinch, clutch, deduce, fathom,
follow, master, snatch, take in, talent 7
catch at, compass, control, embrace, grapple, mastery, seizing, seizure 8 clutches,
gripping, perceive 9 handclasp, knowledge, seize upon 10 comprehend, perception, understand 13 comprehension, understanding

grasping 6 venal 6 greedy 7 hoggish, miserly, selfish, wolfish 8 covetous 9 mercenary, predatory, rapacious 10 avaricious 11
acquisitive

graspingness 5 greed 7 avarice 8 rapacity,
venality 10 greediness 12 covetousness

grass
   varieties: 3 cup, cut, dog, eel, elk, mat,
   nut, oat, oil, pin, rib, rye, Uva 4 barn,
   bear, bent, blue, chee, cord, crab, deer,
   fish, hair, lace, love, Lyme, moor, Nard,
   palm, Para, rice, rush, silk, star, tape,
   worm, yard 5 arrow, Bahia, beach, beard,
   Brome, Carib, China, cloud, curly, Ditch,
   fever, goose, lemon, Means, Melic,
   Mondo, natal, quack, sedge, shave,
   shore, Smilo, spike, squaw, Sudan,
   sword, Vasey, wheat, white, witch, zebra
   6 Aleppo, alkali, basket, Bengal, Buffel,
   Canary, carpet, Dallis, Dudder, finger, gal-
   low, Guinea, Indian, Korean, Manila, Napier, orange, orchid, Pampas, Rescue,
   Rhodes, ribbon, ripple, scurvy, signal,
   starry, switch, Tobosa, velvet, vernal, viper's, Zoysia 7 Bermuda, Brahman, Bristle, Buffalo, Esparto, Harding, Johnson,
   Kleberg, Pangola, poverty, pudding,
   quaking, Ravenna, sea lyme, serpent, tall
   oat, Wallaby, Widgeon 8 Angleton, blue-
   eyed, blue love, Boer love, elephant,
   fountain, hairy cup, lazy-man's, molasses, Ree wheat, sand love, scorpion, tuber oat 9 blue conch, centipede, common
   rye, hairy crab, hare's-tail, Hungarian,
   Malojilla, Mascarene, Oregon rye, ran-
   cheria, tall wheat, water star, yellow nut
   10 Amur silver, beavertail, big quaking,
   blue finger, citronella, English rye, false
   wheat, golden-eyed, Indian rice, Italian
   rye, Korean lawn, Kuma bamboo, purple-
   eyed, rabbit-foot, rabbit-tail, reed canary,
   tufted hair, Washington, western rye, yel-

low-eyed 11 annual beard, branched cup,
desert wheat, domestic rye, dwarf
meadow, feather love, giant finger, green
needle, Lehmann love, Nepal silver,
Pentz finger, prairie cord, ringed beard,
St Augustine, sweet vernal, Texas needle, Texas winter, weeping love 12 Common carpet, crested wheat, crinkled hair,
European dune, Indian basket, Japanese
lawn, Japanese love, Korean velvet, perennial rye, slender wheat, squirreltail,
western wheat 13 American beach, Australian rye, billion-dollar, European beach,
Himalaya fairy, Japanese sedge, little
quaking, Paraguay Bahia, plains bristle,
Siberian wheat 14 African Bermuda,
bluebunch wheat, Japanese carpet, Pensacola Bahia, perennial veldt, pubescent
wheat, Saint Augustine, stiff-hair wheat
15 European feather, Wilmington Bahia
16 creeping windmill, Pacey's English rye
17 Australian feather, intermediate wheat,
Mediterranean salt, Transvaal dog-tooth
18 Australian windmill, California blue-
eyed, Mexican everlasting 19 Fairway
crested wheat 20 standard crested wheat

Grass, Gunter
   author of: 6 Floods 8 Dog Years 10 The
   Tin Drum 11 Cat and Mouse, The Flounder 16 Local Anaesthetic 18 The Meeting
   at Telgte 20 From the Diary of a Snail 33
   Headbirths or The Germans Are Dying
   Out

grasshopper
   variety: 5 pygmy 6 meadow, monkey 7
   katydid 10 band winged, cone headed,
   long-horned, slant-faced 11 bush katydid,
   leaf-rolling, short-horned 12 shield-
   backed, spur-throated

grassland 3 lea 4 farm, vale, veld 5 field,
pampa, plain, range, veldt 6 meadow 7
pasture, prairie, savanna 8 farmland, flat-
land, savannah 10 plantation

grate 3 irk, jar, rub, vex 4 bars, burr, buzz,
gall, rasp 5 annoy, chafe, clack, grill, grind,
mince, shred 6 abrade, gnaw at, hearth,
jangle, rankle, scrape, scream, screen 7
firebed, firebox, grating, lattice, scratch,
screech 8 irritate 9 fireplace, pulverize 10
exasperate, firebasket 11 latticework

grateful 7 obliged 8 beholden, indebted,
thankful 9 gratified, obligated 12 appreciative

gratefulness 6 thanks 9 gratitude 12 appreciation, thankfulness

Gratiae see 6 Graces

Gratiano
   character in: 19 The Merchant of Venice
   author: 11 Shakespeare

gratification 3 joy 4 glee, kick 5 bliss 6 relish, solace, thrill 7 comfort, delight, ecstasy, elation, rapture 8 gladness, humoring, pleasing, pleasure, soothing 9 enjoyment, happiness, transport 10 indulgence,
jubilation, satisfying 11 contentment, enchantment 12 exhilaration, satisfaction

gratified 5 happy **7** content, pleased **9** satisfied **11** comfortable

gratify 4 suit **5** amuse, favor, humor **6** coddle, divert, pamper, please, regale, soothe, thrill, tickle **7** appease, delight, enchant, flatter, gladden, indulge, refresh, satisfy **8** enthrall, entrance, interest, recreate **9** enrapture, entertain, transport **10** compliment, exhilarate

gratifying 8 humoring, pleasant, pleasing, soothing **9** agreeable, enjoyable, indulging, pampering, rewarding **10** delightful, satisfying **11** pleasurable

grating 4 bars, fret, grid **5** grate, harsh, raspy **6** creaky, grille, shrill **7** jarring, lattice, rasping, raucous, squeaky, tracery, trellis **8** abrasive, annoying, filigree, fretwork, gridiron, jangling, piercing, scraping, strident **9** offensive, vexatious **10** discordant, gate of bard, irritating, unpleasant **11** cacophonous, displeasing, high-pitched **12** disagreeable, exacerbating, exasperating

grating noise 7 discord, rasping **8** grinding **9** cacophony, harshness **10** disharmony, dissonance

gratis 4 free **10** gratuitous, on the house **13** complimentary, without charge

gratitude 6 thanks **10** obligation **11** recognition **12** appreciation, beholdenness, gratefulness, thankfulness, thanksgiving **14** acknowledgment

gratuitous 4 free **6** gratis, wanton **7** donated, willing **8** baseless, unproven **9** unfounded, voluntary **10** free of cost, groundless, irrelevant, unasked for, unprovoked **11** conjectural, impertinent, presumptive, spontaneous, uncalled for, unjustified, unwarranted **13** complimentary, unrecompensed

gratuity 3 tip **4** gift **8** donation
   French: 7 douceur **9** pourboire

Graustark
   author: 20 George Barr McCutcheon

grave 4 dour, sage, tomb **5** acute, crypt, mound, quiet, sober, staid, vault, vital **6** gloomy, sedate, solemn, somber, urgent **7** crucial, earnest, ossuary, serious, subdued, weighty **8** catacomb, cenotaph, critical, frowning, pressing **9** dignified, important, long-faced, mausoleum, momentous, sepulcher **10** thoughtful **11** burial ground, grim visaged, significant **13** consequential, philosophical **16** last resting place, place of interment
   music: 6 solemn **7** serious

Graves, Robert
   author of: 9 I Claudius, King Jesus **14** Claudius the God **15** The White Goddess **16** Goodbye to All That

graveyard 7 charnel, ossuary **8** boneyard, boot hill, cemetery **10** churchyard, necropolis **12** memorial park, potter's field **13** burying ground

gravitate 4 fall, head, move, sink, tend **6** settle **7** be drawn, descend, incline **8** converge, zero in on **9** be prone to **10** lean toward

gravity 4 pull **6** danger, import, moment **7** concern, dignity, urgency **8** calmness, enormity, grimness, serenity, sobriety **9** emergency, magnitude, solemnity, staidness **10** attraction, gloominess, importance, sedateness, solemnness, somberness **11** consequence, earnestness, gravitation, seriousness **12** significance, tranquillity **13** consideration, crucial nature **14** critical nature, pull of the earth, thoughtfulness **16** mutual attraction

gray, grey 3 dun **4** ashy, dark, drab, pale **5** ashen, foggy, hoary, misty, murky, slate **6** cloudy, dismal, gloomy, silver, somber **7** clouded, grayish, grizzly, neutral, silvery, sunless **8** overcast **9** cheerless, pearl-gray **10** depressing, gray-haired, gray-headed **11** dove-colored, hoary-headed **12** mousecolored, silver-haired **13** salt and pepper

Gray, Harold
   creator/artist of: 17 Little Orphan Annie

Gray, Thomas
   author of: 32 Elegy Written in a Country Churchyard

grayness 4 murk **6** pallor **8** drabness **9** bleakness **10** somberness

Grayson, Kathryn
   real name: 19 Zelma Kathryn Hedrick
   born: 14 Winston-Salem NC
   roles: 8 Show Boat **10** Kiss Me Kate **13** Anchors Aweigh, The Desert Song **15** The Vagabond King

graze 3 rub **4** crop, rasp, skim, skin **5** brush, grind, swipe **6** abrade, browse, bruise, glance, scrape **7** pasture, scratch **8** abrasion, eat grass **16** turn out to pasture

grease 3 fat, oil **4** balm, lard **5** salve **6** anoint, tallow **7** unguent **8** ointment **9** drippings, lubricant, lubricate

grease the palm 3 tip **5** bribe **6** buy off, pay off

greasy 3 fat **4** oily, waxy **5** fatty, lardy, slick **7** buttery **8** slippery, slithery **10** lardaceous, oleaginous

great 3 apt, big **4** able, a-one, fine, good, high, huge, kind, many, vast, well **5** chief, crack, grand, grave, gross, heavy, large, noble, noted, super, swell **6** adroit, choice, expert, famous, groovy, humane, loving, strong, superb **7** crucial, decided, eminent, extreme, grandly, immense, leading, mammoth, notable, serious, titanic, weighty **8** abundant, colossal, critical, enormous, esteemed, fabulous, generous, gigantic, glorious, gracious, manifold, renowned, skillful, smashing, splendid, superbly, superior, terrific, very well **9** boundless, countless, cyclopean, excellent, fantastic, first-rate, important, marvelous, momentous, monstrous, prominent, unlimited, wonderful **10** altruistic, celebrated, gargantuan, highminded, inordinate, out-of-sight, prodigious, proficient, pronounced, remarkable, splendidly, stupendous, tremendous, voluminous **11** crackerjack, excellently, extravagant, illustrious, magnanimous, magnificent, outstanding, sensational, significant, superlative, wonderfully **12** considerable **13** consequential, distinguished, inexhaustible, magnificently, multitudinous **14** out of this world

Great Ajax
origin: **5** Greek
hero of: **9** Trojan War

greater 4 more **5** finer **6** better, bigger, larger **8** superior

Great Escape, The
director: **11** John Sturges
cast: **11** James Coburn, James Garner **12** Steve McQueen **13** David McCallum **14** Charles Bronson **15** Donald Pleasance **19** Richard Attenborough
setting: **7** Germany, POW camp

greatest 4 best, most **5** ultra **6** picked, select, utmost **7** extreme, highest, maximal, maximum, noblest, supreme **8** champion **9** first-rate **11** superlative, unsurpassed

Greatest Show on Earth, The
director: **13** Cecil B DeMille
cast: **11** Betty Hutton, Cornel Wilde **12** James Stewart **13** Dorothy Lamour, Gloria Grahame **14** Charlton Heston
Oscar for: **7** picture

Great Expectations
author: **14** Charles Dickens
character: **3** Pip **7** Estella **9** Compeyson, Mr Jaggers **10** Joe Gargery **12** Abel Magwitch, Miss Havisham **13** Herbert Pocket
director: **9** David Lean
cast: **9** John Mills **11** Martita Hunt **12** Alec Guinness, Bernard Mills **13** Valerie Hobson **16** Francis L Sullivan

Great Gatsby, The
author: **16** F Scott Fitzgerald
character: **9** Jay Gatsby **11** Tom Buchanan **12** Myrtle Wilson, Nick Carraway **13** Daisy Buchanan

Great God Brown, The
author: **12** Eugene O'Neill

Great Idean Mother *see* **6** Cybele

great lady
French: **10** grande dame

Great Lake 4 Erie **5** Huron **7** Ontario **8** Michigan, Superior

Great Land
nickname of: **6** Alaska

greatly 6 vastly **7** largely, notably **8** markedly, mightily, very much **9** immensely **10** abundantly, enormously, infinitely, powerfully, remarkably **12** considerably, immeasurably, tremendously

great mishap 5 wreck **6** blight, fiasco **7** tragedy **8** calamity, disaster **9** cataclysm, ruination **11** catastrophe

greatness 8 eminence, nobility **9** loftiness **10** excellence, importance, notability, prominence **11** preeminence, superiority **12** magnificence **15** illustriousness

Great Profile
nickname of: **13** John Barrymore

Great Railway Bazaar, The
author: **11** Paul Theroux

great world
French: **10** grand monde

Great Ziegfeld, The
director: **14** Robert Z Leonard
cast: **8** Myrna Loy **10** Fanny Brice **11** Frank Morgan, Luise Rainer (Anna Held) **13** Virginia Bruce, William Powell
Oscar for: **7** actress (Rainer), picture

grebe 4 bird, fowl, loon **5** diver **6** dipper **7** henbill **8** dabchick **9** hell-diver **10** water witch

Grecco, Al
character in: **20** Appointment in Samarra
author: **5** O'Hara

Greco, El Greco
real name: **23** Domenikos Theotokopoulos
born: **5** Crete **6** Candia
artwork: **7** Espolio (Disrobing of Christ), Laocoon **12** View of Toledo **19** Cleaning of the Temple **20** Healing of the Blind Man **21** Burial of the Count Orgaz **27** Christ Stripped of his Garments **28** San Ildefonso at his Writing Desk **29** Cardinal Fernando Nino de Guevara **42** Christ Driving the Money-Changers from the Temple

Greece
other name: **5** Ellas **16** Hellenic Republic
capital/largest city: **6** Athens
others: **4** Enor **5** Canea, Corfu, Pylos, Volos **6** Delphi, Patras, Sparta **7** Chalcis, Corinth, Olympia, Piraeus **8** Salonika, Thessaly **9** Epidaurus, Gallipoli **10** Herakleion **11** Hermoupolis
school: **5** Crete **6** Athens, Patras, Thrace **8** Ioannina, Salonika
division: **6** Attica, Epirus, Thrace **7** Boeotia **8** Thessaly **9** Macedonia
measure: **3** pik **4** bema, piki, pous **5** baril, chous, cubit, diote, doron, maris, pekhe, podos, pygon, xylon **6** acaena, bacile, barile, cotula, dichas, gramme, hemina, koilon, lichas, milion, orgyia, palame, pechys, schene, xestes **7** amphora, bacvhel, chenica, choenix, cyathos, diaulos, metreta, stadium, stremma **8** condylos, daktylos, dekapode, dolichos, medimnos, medimnus, metretes, palaiste, plethron, plethrum, stathmos **9** hemiekton, oxybaphon
monetary unit: **5** lepta **7** drachma
weight: **3** mna, oke **4** mina, obol **5** livre, pound **6** diobol, kantar, obolos, obolus, talent **7** chalcon, drachma **8** diobolon
island: **3** Ios **5** Chios, Corfu, Crete, Delos, Melos, Naxos, Paros, Samos, Syros, Tenos, Thera, Zante **8** Andros, Euboea, Ionian, Ithaca, Lemnos, Lesbos, Patmos, Rhodes, Skyros, Thasos **7** Mykonos **8** Cyclades, Mytilene, Skiathos, Skopelos **9** Alonnisos **10** Cephalonia, Dodecanese, Samothrace **16** Northern Sporades
lake: **5** Karla, Volve **6** Copais, Kopais, Prespa, Voweis **8** Ioannina, Koroneia, Vistonis **9** Trichonis, Vegoritis

mountain: 3 Ida 4 Idhi, Oeta, Oite, Ossa 5 Athos 6 Ithome, Peleon, Pelion, Pindus 7 Grammos, Helicon, Rhodope 8 Hymettos, Smolikas, Taygetos, Taygetus 9 Parnassus 10 Hagion Oros, Lycabettus, Pentelicus

highest point: 7 Olympus

river: 4 Arta 6 Peneus, Struma, Vardar 7 Hellada, Maritsa 8 Achelous, Aliakmon

sea: 5 Crete 6 Aegean, Ionian 7 Mirtoon 13 Mediterranean

physical feature:

gulf: 7 Corinth, Saronic

peninsula: 6 Balkan 10 Chalcidice 12 Peloponnesus

plain: 7 Boeotia 8 Thessaly

plateau: 7 Arcadia

valley: 5 Nemea

people: 5 Greek 6 Achean, Dorian, Ionian 7 Aeolian, Hellene

artist: 7 El Greco

author: 6 Homer 6 Hesiod, Pindar 8 Menander 9 Aeschylus, Euripides, Sophocles 11 Kazantzakis 12 Aristophanes

god: 4 Ares, Hera, Leto, Zeus 5 Cupid 6 Apollo, Cronus, Hermes, Hestia 7 Artemis, Demeter 8 Dionysus, Poseidon 9 Aphrodite 10 Hephaestus, Persephone 12 Pallas Athena 13 Phoebus Apollo

historian: 9 Herodotus 10 Thucydides

king: 11 Constantine

lawmaker: 5 Draco, Solon 8 Lycurgus, Pericles

leader: 10 Papandreou

mathematician: 6 Euclid 10 Archimedes, Pythagoras

mythological: 5 Atlas, Helen, Jason, Medea, Paris 6 Hector, Medusa 7 Ariadne, Chimera, Pandora, Pegasus, Perseus, Theseus 8 Achilles, Heracles, Minotaur, Odysseus 9 Agamemnon, Andromeda, Iphigenia, King Minos 10 Prometheus 11 Bellerophon

orator: 11 Demosthenes

philosopher: 5 Plato 8 Socrates 9 Aristotle

physician: 11 Hippocrates

sculptor: 5 Myron 7 Phidias 10 Praxiteles

tycoon: 7 Onassis

language: 5 Greek

religion: 14 Greek Orthodoxy

place:

ruins: 5 Delos, Pella, Pylos, Samos 6 Delphi, Sparta, Thebes, Tiryns 7 Corinth, Eleusis, Elevsis, Knossos, Mycenae, Olympia 9 Acropolis, Epidaurus, Parthenon 13 Palace of Minos

feature:

coffeeshop: 7 kaphene

marketplace: 5 agora

port 7 Piraeus

presidential guard: 7 Evzones

village square: 7 plateia

food:

dish: 7 mousaka 8 moussaka, souvlaka, dolmades, souvlakia 10 shish kabob

liquor: 4 ouzo

wine: 7 retsina

greed 7 avarice, avidity, craving 8 cupidity, rapacity 11 itching palm, money-hunger, piggishness, selfishness 12 covetousness 13 rapaciousness 14 avariciousness

greediness 7 avarice 8 gluttony, rapacity, voracity 12 covetousness, graspingness 15 acquisitiveness

greedy 4 avid 5 eager 6 ardent, hungry 7 anxious, burning, craving, fervent, hoggish, piggish, selfish, swinish, wolfish 8 covetous, famished, grasping, ravenous 9 devouring, impatient, mercenary, predatory, rapacious, thirsting, voracious 10 avaricious, gluttonous, insatiable 11 acquisitive, money-hungry 12 gormandizing

Greek

language family: 12 Indo-European

ancient branch: 5 Doric, Ionic 6 Aeolic

Greek alphabet

a: 5 alpha

b: 4 beta

ch/kh: 3 chi

d: 5 delta

e: 3 eta 7 epsilon

g: 5 gamma

i: 4 iota

k: 5 kappa

l: 6 lambda

m: 2 mu

n: 2 nu

o: 5 omega 7 omicron

p: 2 pi

ph: 3 phi

ps: 3 psi

r: 3 rho

s: 5 sigma

t: 3 tau

th: 5 theta

x: 2 xi

y: 7 upsilon

z: 4 zeta

Greek Anthology, The

author: 8 Cephalas, Meleager

Greek measure 4 mina 5 cubit 6 obolos, talent 7 drachma, stadion

Greek Mythology

afterworld of the blessed: 7 Elysium

amber islands: 10 Electrides

architect of labyrinth: 8 Daedalus

blood-sucking monster: 5 Lamia

cupbearer to the gods: 8 Ganymede 9 Catamitus

dragon: 8 basilisk

drink of the gods: 6 nectar

eagle/lion monster: 7 griffin, griffon, gryphon

enchantress: 5 Circe

female warrior: 6 Amazon

fire-breathing monster: 7 Chimera

first man: 12 Alalcomeneus

food/drink/perfume of the gods: 8 ambrosia

the Furies: 5 Dirae 6 Erinys, Furiae, Semnai 7 Erinyes 9 Eumenides
names: 7 Allecto, Megaera 9 Tisiphone
goat god: 7 Aegipan
goddess of beauty: 6 Graces 7 Gratiae 9 Charities
names: 4 Auxo 5 Cleta 6 Aglaia, Thalia 7 Phaenna 8 Hegemone 10 Euphrosyne
goddess of childbirth: 8 Ilithyia 10 Eileithyia
corresponds to Roman: 6 Lucina
goddess of the dawn: 3 Eos
corresponds to Roman: 6 Aurora
goddesses of destiny: 5 Fates, Morae 6 Moerae, Moirai
names: 5 Moira 6 Clotho 8 Lachesis
corresponds to Roman: 6 Parcae
goddess of discord: 4 Eris
corresponds to Roman: 9 Discordia
goddess of divine punishment/recklessness: 3 Ate
goddess of divine retribution: 8 Adrastea
goddess of the earth: 2 Ge 4 Gaea, Gaia
corresponds to Roman: 6 Tellus
goddess of earth/fertility: 7 Demeter
corresponds to Roman: 5 Ceres
goddess of earth/Hades: 5 Brimo 6 Hecate, Hekate
goddess of fortune: 5 Tyche
corresponds to Roman: 7 Fortuna
goddess of healing: 4 Iaso
goddess of health: 6 Hygeia
corresponds to Roman: 5 Salus
goddess of the hearth: 6 Hestia
corresponds to Roman: 5 Vesta
goddess of justice: 4 Dice, Dike 6 Astrea 7 Astraea
goddesses of literature/the arts: 5 Muses 7 the Nine 8 Pierides 10 Castalides
names: 4 Clio 5 Aoede, Erato, Mneme 6 Melete, Thalia, Urania 7 Euterpe 8 Calliope 9 Melpomene 10 Polyhymnia 11 Terpsichore
corresponds to Roman: 7 Camenae
muse of astronomy: 6 Urania
muse of dancing/choral song: 11 Terpsichore
muse of history: 4 Clio
muse of idyllic poetry/comedy: 6 Thalia
muse of love poetry: 5 Erato
muse of meditation: 6 Melete
muse of memory: 5 Mneme
muse of music/lyric poetry: 7 Euterpe
muse of poetry/epic: 8 Calliope
muse of sacred music/dance: 10 Polyhymnia
muse of song: 5 Aoede
muse of tragedy: 9 Melpomene
goddess of love/beauty: 6 Urania 7 Cyprian, Paphian 8 Cytherea 9 Aphrodite 10 Anadyomene
corresponds to Roman: 5 Venus
goddess of memory: 9 Mnemosyne

goddess of the night: 3 Nox, Nyx
goddess of peace: 5 Irene
corresponds to Roman: 3 Pax
goddess of the rainbow: 4 Iris
goddess of sailors: 5 Brizo
goddess of the sea: 10 Amphitrite
goddesses of the sea: 6 Graeae, Graiae
names: 4 Enyo 5 Deino 9 Pemphredo
goddesses of seasons/growth/decay/social order: 4 Hour 5 Horae
names: 4 Dice, Dike 5 Carpo, Irene 6 Thallo 7 Eunomia
goddess of spring flowers: 6 Thallo
goddess of summer fruit: 5 Carpo
goddess of victory: 4 Nike
corresponds to Roman: 6 Athena 8 Victoria
goddess of war: 4 Enyo
corresponds to Roman: 7 Bellona
goddess of wisdom/fertility/arts/warfare: 6 Athena, Athene, Pallas, Saitis 11 Tritogeneia 12 Pallas Athena 18 Alalcomenean Athena
corresponds to Roman: 7 Minerva
goddess of youth/spring: 4 Hebe
god of beekeeping/winemaking/husbandry: 9 Aristaeus
god of censure/ridicule: 5 Momos, Momus
god of dreams: 6 Icelus, Oniros 7 Oneiros 8 Morpheus
god of earth: 10 Trophonius
god of Eleusinian mysteries: 7 Bacchus
god of erotic desire: 7 Himeros
god of fire/metalworking/handicrafts: 10 Hephaestus, Hephaistos
corresponds to Roman: 6 Vulcan
god of the heavens: 4 Zeus
corresponds to Roman: 4 Jove 7 Jupiter
corresponds to Egyptian: 4 Amen, Amon 5 Ammon 6 Amen Ra, Amon Ra
god of light/healing/music/poetry/prophecy/beauty: 6 Apollo
god of love: 4 Eros
corresponds to Roman: 4 Amor 5 Cupid
god of male power/procreation: 7 Priapus
corresponds to Roman: 7 Mutinus
god of marriage: 5 Hymen 9 Hymenaeus
corresponds to Roman: 8 Talassio
god of medicine/healing: 9 Asclepius
corresponds to Roman: 11 Aesculapius
god of oaths: 6 Horcus
god of recovery from illness: 11 Telesphorus
god of sea/caused earthquakes: 8 Poseidon
corresponds to Roman: 7 Neptune
god of shepherds/flocks/pastures/forests: 3 Pan 7 Sinoeis
god of sleep: 6 Hypnos, Hypnus
corresponds to Roman: 6 Somnus

god of the sun: 6 Helios 8 Hyperion
corresponds to Roman: 3 Sol
god of the underworld: 6 Infiri
god of war: 4 Ares 8 Theritas
corresponds to Roman: 4 Mars
god of wine/fertility/drama: 5 Evius 7 Bacchus 8 Dionysus
Gorgon monster: 6 Medusa
hundred-headed monster: 5 Ladon 8 Typhoeus
islands of the blessed: 10 Hesperides
man/horse monster: 7 centaur
messenger of gods/god of roads/ commerce/invention/ cunning/thieves: 6 Hermes
corresponds to Roman: 7 Mercury
monster that asked riddles: 6 Sphinx
monsters that turn people to stone: 7 Gorgons
moon goddess/huntress/virgin: 6 Phoebe, Selene 7 Artemis
corresponds to Roman: 5 Diana
corresponds to Cretan: 11 Britomartis
nine-headed water serpent: 5 Hydra
nymph: 7 Calypso
one-eyed giant: 7 Cyclops
oracle of Apollo: 13 Delphic oracle
personification of death: 4 Mors 8 Thanatos
personification of punishment/ revenge: 5 Poena, Poine
personification of soul: 6 Psyche
physician to gods of Olympia: 5 Paeon
prophetess: 9 Alexandra, Cassandra
queen of heaven: 4 Hera, Here
corresponds to Roman: 4 Juno
race of gods: 6 Titans
names: 4 Rhea, Thia 5 Coeus, Crius 6 Cronus, Phoebe, Tethys, Themis 7 Iapetus, Oceanus 8 Hyperion 9 Mnemosyne
river god: 6 Asopus, Peneus, Simois 7 Inachus, Pelegon 8 Achelous
river in Hades: 4 Styx 5 Lethe 7 Acheron, Cocytus
ferryman: 6 Charon
river of forgetfulness: 5 Lethe
ruler of the winds: 6 Aeolus
satyr/god of the forest: 7 Silenus
sea god: 6 Nereus, Triton 7 Glaucus, Phorcys, Proteus
sea monster: 6 Scylla
seer: 6 Mopsus 8 Tiresias
serpent: 6 dipsas
serpent of darkness: 5 Apepi 7 Apophis
seven against Thebes: 6 Tydeus 8 Adrastus, Capaneus 9 Polynices 10 Amphiaraus, Hippomedon 13 Parthenopaeus
seven sisters: 8 Pleiades
names: 4 Maia 6 Merope 7 Alcyone, Celaeno, Electra, Sterope, Taygete
sorceress: 5 Medea
spirits of disease/evil/old age/death: 5 Keres
three-headed dog that guards underworld: 8 Cerberus

twins: 8 Dioscuri 15 Castor and Pollux
two-headed serpent: 11 Amphisbaena
underworld: 5 Hades, Pluto
corresponds to Roman: 3 Dis 5 Orcus 8 Dis Pater
underworld darkness: 6 Erebus
underworld spirit: 9 Chthonian
virgin huntress: 8 Atalanta, Atalante
whirlpool: 9 Charybdis
winged horse: 5 Arion 7 Pegasus
woman/beast monster: 6 Python 8 Delphyne
woman/bird monster: 5 Harpy
woman/serpent monster: 7 Echidna
wood nymph: 5 dryad

Greek uncial codex 4 Syri 6 Regius 8 Ephraemi 9 Laudianus, Vaticanus 10 Sinaiticus 11 Basiliensis 12 Alexandrinus, Sangallensis 13 Koridethianus

green 3 raw 4 jade, lawn, lime, turf 5 crude, heath, olive, rough, sward, young 6 callow, campus, common, tender, unripe 7 awkward, emerald, verdant, verdure 8 greenish, gullible, ignorant, immature, inexpert, not cured, not dried, pea-green, sea-green, unsmoked, untanned, unversed 9 blue-green, credulous, grassplot, lime-green, unfledged, unskilled, untrained 10 aquamarine, chartreuse, golf course, grass-green, greensward, kelly-green, olive green, uninformed, unmellowed, unpolished, unseasoned 11 cobalt green, forest green, undeveloped, yellow-green 12 easily fooled, green-colored, not fully aged, putting green, village green 13 inexperienced, undisciplined 14 underdeveloped 15 unsophisticated

Green Acres
character: 7 Mr Haney 8 Eb Dawson 10 Fred Ziffel, Sam Drucker 11 Doris Ziffel, Hank Kimball, Lisa Douglas 20 Oliver Wendell Douglas
cast: 8 Eva Gabor, Fran Ryan 9 Alvy Moore, Frank Cady, Tom Lester 10 Pat Buttram 11 Eddie Albert 13 Barbara Pepper, Hank Patterson
pig: 6 Arnold
town: 11 Hooterville

green at the gills 6 queasy, sickly 7 bilious 8 nauseous 9 nauseated, sickening

greenback 4 bill 8 banknote 12 treasury note 15 legal-tender note 17 silver certificate

Green Bay
football team: 7 Packers

Green Bay Tree, The
author: 14 Louis Bromfield

Greene, Graham
author of: 11 The Third Man 12 Brighton Rock, Ways of Escape 14 The Human Factor 16 Monsignor Quixote, 17 The End of the Affair, The Ministry of Fear, Travels with My Aunt 19 The Heart of the Matter, The Power and the Glory

Greene, Joe
nickname: 7 Mean Joe
sport: 8 football
position: 7 lineman
team: 18 Pittsburgh Steelers
Greene, Lorne
born: 6 Canada, Ottawa 7 Ontario
roles: 5 Adama 7 Bonanza 11 Peyton
Place 12 Autumn Leaves, The Buccaneer
13 Ben Cartwright 16 The Silver Chalice
19 Battlestar Galactica
Greene, Nathanael
served in: 16 Revolutionary War
rank: 16 brigadier general 20 quarter-
master general
battle: 7 Cowpens, Trenton 12 Eutaw
Springs, Hobkirk's Hill 18 Guilford Court
House
green-eyed monster 4 envy 8 jealousy 12
covetousness
Green for Danger
director: 13 Sidney Gilliat
cast: 7 Leo Genn 9 Sally Gray 11
Alastair Sim 12 Rosamund John, Trevor
Howard
greenhorn 4 rube, tyro 6 novice, rookie 7
learner 8 beginner, neophyte, newcomer 9
fledgling 10 apprentice, tenderfoot 14
babe in the woods
Green Hornet, The
character: 4 Kato 9 Britt Reid (The
Green Hornet)
cast: 8 Bruce Lee 11 Van Williams
car: 11 Black Beauty
creator: 11 Bert Whitman
sidekick: 4 Kato
Green House, The
author: 16 Mario Vargas Llosa
Greening of America, The
author: 12 Charles Reich
greenish 6 sickly 7 bilious
Greenland
alternate name: 14 Kalaallit Nunaat
capital/largest city: 3 Nuk 8 Godthaab,
The Point
others: 4 Etah, Nord 5 Thule 6 Ivigut,
Umanak 7 Godhavn, Ivigtut 10 Nanortalik
11 Julianehaab 12 Angmagssalik, Suk-
kertoppen 14 Christianshaab
government: 20 home rule under Denmark
monetary unit: 3 ore 5 krone
island: 5 Disko
mountain: 5 Forel, Payer 7 Khardyu 8
Peterman 15 Petermannsbjerg
highest point: 9 Gunnbjorn 16 Gunnbjornsfjaeld
sea: 6 Arctic 9 Greenland
physical feature: 9 Inland Ice
bay: 5 Disko 6 Baffin 8 Melville
cape: 4 Jaal 6 Grivel, Walker 8 Bismarck,
Brewster, Farewell, Lowenorn 11 Morris
Jesup
glacier: 10 Jacobshavn
strait: 5 Davis 7 Denmark
people: 3 Ita 6 Eskimo 8 European
explorer: 10 Eric the Red

language: 6 Danish, Eskimo 11 Greenlandic
religion: 19 Evangelical Lutheran
feature:
airbase: 4 Etah 5 Thule
animal: 7 caribou
Green Mansions
author: 8 W H Hudson
character: 4 Rima 5 Nuflo 6 Mr Abel
Greenmantle
author: 10 John Buchan
Green Mountain State
nickname: 7 Vermont
Greenough, Horatio born: 8 Boston MA
artwork: 16 George Washington 18 The
Chanting Cherubs
Green Pastures, The
author: 12 Marc Connelly
Greenstreet, Sydney
born: 7 England 8 Sandwich
roles: 9 The Fat Man 10 Casablanca 16
The Maltese Falcon 19 Passage to Marseilles
green with envy 7 envious, jealous 8 covetous
greet 4 hail, meet 5 admit 6 accept, accost,
salute 7 receive, speak to, welcome 9
smile upon, recognize 10 bid welcome
greeting 6 salute 7 welcome 8 saluting 9
reception, welcoming 10 salutation 12
introduction, presentation
greetings 4 best 5 hello 7 regards 8 respects 10 best wishes, good wishes,
salutation 11 compliments, remembrance,
well-wishing 13 felicitations
Latin: 5 salve
gregarious 6 genial, lively, social 7 affable
8 friendly, outgoing, sociable 9 convivial,
talkative, vivacious 11 extroverted 13 companionable
gremlin 3 imp 5 demon, gnome 6 goblin
Grenada
other name: 11 Isle of Spice
capital/largest city: 9 St Georges
others: 8 Sauteurs
head of state: 14 British monarch 15
governor general
island: 8 Windward 9 Carriacou 10 Grenadines
lake: 10 Grand Etang
highest point: 11 St Catherine
sea: 9 Caribbean
physical feature:
bay: 9 St Georges'
people: 5 Black, Negro 6 Indian
discoverer: 8 Columbus
language: 7 English
religion: 8 Anglican 10 Protestant 13 Roman Catholic
food:
spice: 4 mace 6 nutmeg
grenade 7 missile 9 pineapple
Grendel
character in: 7 Beowulf
author: 7 unknown

Grewgious, Mr
   character in: 22 The Mystery of Edwin Drood
   author: 7 Dickens

Grey, Joel
   real name: 8 Joel Katz
   born: 13 Cleveland Ohio
   roles: 7 Cabaret, George M 13 Come September 23 The Seven Percent Solution

Grey, Zane
   author of: 18 Valley of Wild Horses 20 The Spirit of the Border 21 Riders of the Purple Sage, The Last of the Plainsmen

greyhound
   group of: 5 leash

Greystoke, Lord
   real identity of: 6 Tarzan

griddle cake 6 blintz, waffle 7 crumpet, hot cake, pancake 8 corncake, flapcake, flapjack 10 battercake 11 flannel cake 13 buckwheat cake
   French: 5 crepe 12 crepe suzette
   German: 11 pfannkuchen
   Hungarian: 10 palacsinta
   Indian: 8 chapatty

Gride, Arthur
   character in: 16 Nicholas Nickleby
   author: 7 Dickens

grief 3 woe 4 care 5 agony, worry 6 burden, misery, ordeal, sorrow 7 anguish, anxiety, concern, despair, remorse, sadness, trouble 8 distress, grieving, hardship, nuisance, vexation 9 grievance, heartache, suffering 10 affliction, desolation, discomfort, heartbreak 11 despondency, tribulation 12 wretchedness 13 inconvenience

griefstricken 7 joyless, unhappy 8 saddened, wretched 9 sorrowful 13 brokenhearted

Grieg, Edvard Hagerup
   born: 6 Bergen, Norway
   composer of: 5 I Host 8 Bergljot, In Autumn, Peer Gynt 11 Lyric Pieces 12 Landjaenning 14 Fra Holbergs Tid, Lyriske Stykker 15 Sigurd Jorsalfar 16 From Holberg's Time 17 Recognition of Land 18 Foran Sydens Kloster 22 At a Southern Convent Gate

grievance 4 beef, hurt 5 wrong 6 injury 7 outrage 8 hardship, iniquity 9 complaint, injustice 10 affliction, bone to pick, disservice

grieve 3 cry, rue, sob 4 moan, pain, wail, weep 5 be sad, mourn 6 bemoan, deject, harass, lament, sadden, sorrow 7 afflict, agonize, depress, oppress, torture 8 disquiet, distress 10 discomfort 11 be anguished

grieve over 5 mourn 6 bemoan, bewail, lament 7 cry over 8 moan over, weep over

grievous 3 sad 5 acute, grave, harsh, heavy 6 severe, tragic, woeful 7 crucial, glaring, harmful, heinous, painful, serious, very bad 8 critical, shameful, shocking 9 agonizing, appalling, atrocious, monstrous, nefarious, sorrowful 10 burdensome, calamitous, deplorable, iniquitous, lamentable, outrageous, unbearable 11 destructive, distressing, intolerable, significant 12 insufferable 13 heartbreaking

griffin
   also: 7 griffon, gryphon
   form: 7 monster
   head of: 5 eagle
   wings of: 5 eagle
   body of: 4 lion
   guards of: 4 gold
   location: 7 Scythia

Griffith, Andy
   real name: 20 Andrew Samuel Griffith
   born: 8 Mt Airy NC
   roles: 7 Matlock 13 Will Stockdale 15 A Face in the Crowd, Angel in My Pocket 18 No Time for Sergeants 19 The Andy Griffith Show

Griffith, D W
   director of: 11 Intolerance 14 Broken Blossoms 17 Orphans of the Storm, The Birth of a Nation

Griffith, Hugh
   born: 5 Wales 8 Anglesey 10 Marian Glas
   roles: 6 Ben-Hur 8 Lucky Jim, Tom Jones

griffon see 7 griffin

grill 3 fry 4 cook, grid, pump, quiz, sear 5 broil, query 7 broiler, grating, griddle 8 gridiron, question 9 crossbars 11 interrogate 12 cross-examine

grim 4 foul, hard, ugly 5 cruel, harsh, lurid, stern, sulky 6 brutal, fierce, gloomy, grisly, grumpy, horrid, morose, odious, severe, somber, sullen 7 austere, ghastly, hideous, inhuman, macabre, squalid, vicious 8 dreadful, fiendish, gruesome, horrible, resolute, scowling, shocking, sinister 9 appalling, ferocious, frightful, heartless, loathsome, merciless, obstinate, repellent, repugnant, repulsive, revolting 10 determined, forbidding, implacable, inexorable, relentless, unyielding

grimace 4 face 5 scowl, smirk, sneer 6 glower 7 wry face
   French: 4 moue

grime 4 dirt, dust, smut, soil, soot 5 filth 6 smudge

Grimhild
   origin: 12 Scandinavian
   mentioned in: 8 Volsunga
   form: 9 sorceress
   husband: 5 Gluki, Gjuki
   daughter: 6 Gudrun, Kudrun 7 Guthrun
   son: 6 Gunnar
   tricked Sigurd to marry: 6 Gudrun, Kudrun 7 Guthrun

Grimm Brothers (Jakob and Wilhelm)
   editors of: 15 Hansel and Gretel 16 Grimm's Fairy Tales

grim reaper 5 death 12 angel of death

grim-visaged 8 frowning, scowling 9 longfaced 10 stern-faced

grin 4 beam 5 smile, smirk 6 rictus, simper 11 crack a smile

grind 4 file, grit, mill, rasp, whet 5 chore, crush, gnash, grate 6 abrade, drudge, polish, powder, scrape 7 crammer, hard job, plodder, sharpen, slavery 8 bookworm, drudgery 9 granulate, pulverize, triturate

Gringoire
  character in: 23 The Hunchback of Notre Dame
  author: 4 Hugo

grip 3 bag 4 grab, hilt, hold 5 clasp, grasp, rivet, seize 6 clench, clutch, handle, retain, snatch, valise 7 attract, control, impress, mastery, satchel 8 clutches, hold fast, suitcase 9 gladstone, handclasp, handshake, retention, spellbind 10 domination, perception

gripe, gripes 4 beef, carp, fret, kick, pain, pang, rail 5 cavil, colic, spasm, whine 6 cramps, grouch, grouse, kvetch, mutter, squawk, twinge, twitch 7 grumble, protest, whining 8 complain, distress, grousing, bellyache, complaint, find fault, grievance, grumbling 10 affliction

Grisham, ~~John~~
  author of: 7 The Firm 9 The Client 10 The Chamber 11 A Time to Kill 15 The Pelican Brief
  movie:
    7 The Firm
  actors: 9 Tom Cruise 11 Gene Hackman 9 The Client
  actors 13 Tommy Lee Jones, Susan Sarandon
  movie:
    15 The Pelican Brief
  actors: 12 Julia Roberts 16 Denzel Washington

grisly 4 foul, gory, grim 5 lurid 6 horrid, odious 7 ghastly, hideous, macabre 8 dreadful, gruesome, horrible, shocking, sinister 9 abhorrent, appalling, frightful, loathsome, repellent, repugnant, repulsive, revolting 10 abominable, forbidding, horrendous

grit 3 rub 4 dirt, dust, guts, muck, rasp, sand, soot 5 filth, gnash, grate, nerve, pluck, spunk 6 crunch, mettle, scrape 7 courage, stamina 8 backbone, tenacity 9 fortitude 10 doggedness, resolution 12 perseverance 13 determination, grind together

Grizzly Bear State 10 California

groan 4 howl, moan, roar, wail 5 bleat, crack, creak, whine 6 bellow, bemoan, lament, murmur, squeak 7 grumble, screech, whimper 8 complain

grocery store
  Spanish: 6 bodega

groggy 5 dazed, dizzy, dopey, shaky, woozy 6 addled, punchy 7 muddled, reeling, stunned 8 confused, sluggish, unsteady 9 befuddled, lethargic, perplexed, stupefied 10 bewildered, punch-drunk, staggering

groom 4 comb, wash 5 boots, brush, curry, dress, drill, preen, prime, primp, train, valet 6 flunky, lackey, spouse 7 clean up, consort, develop, educate, footman, freshen,

hostler, husband, prepare, refresh, rub down, servant 8 exercise, initiate, make neat, make tidy, practice, spruce up 9 currycomb, make ready, stableboy 10 bridegroom, manservant 12 indoctrinate 13 livery servant

groove 3 cut, rut, use 4 rule 5 flute, habit, score, usage 6 custom, furrow, gutter, hollow, trench 7 channel, cutting, scoring 8 practice 9 procedure 10 beaten path, convention 11 corrugation 12 fixed routine, second nature

grope 3 paw 5 probe 6 finger, fumble 7 fish for, venture 9 feel about 11 feel one's way, move blindly, try one's luck 13 search blindly

Gropius, Walter
  architect of: 5 Fagus (factory) 7 Bauhaus (Dessau) 13 Pan Am Building (NYC) 31 Harvard University Graduate Center

gross 3 bag, big, fat 4 bulk, earn, huge, lewd, mass, rank, reap, vast 5 bulky, crude, great, heavy, large, obese, plain, sheer, total, utter, whole 6 carnal, coarse, earthy, entire, pick up, ribald, smutty, sordid, take in, vulgar 7 glaring, heinous, immense, lump sum, massive, obscene, obvious, titanic, uncouth 8 colossal, complete, enormous, flagrant, gigantic, improper, indecent, manifest, unseemly, unwieldy 9 aggregate, downright, egregious, lecherous, monstrous, offensive, unrefined 10 gargantuan, indelicate, lascivious, licentious, outrageous, overweight, prodigious, stupendous 11 unequivocal, unmitigated, unqualified

Grossel, Ira
  real name of: 12 Jeff Chandler

grossness 7 obesity 8 hugeness, lewdness, ribaldry 9 crudeness, heaviness, indecency, obscenity, roughness, vulgarity 10 coarseness, indelicacy, inelegance 14 lasciviousness

grossularite
  species: 6 garnet

Gros Ventre *see* 7 Hidatsa

grotesque 3 odd 4 wild 5 antic, weird 6 absurd, exotic, far-out, rococo, way-out 7 baroque, bizarre, strange 8 deformed, fanciful, peculiar 9 contorted, distorted, eccentric, fantastic, misshapen, odd-shaped, unnatural 10 outlandish 11 extravagant, incongruous 12 preposterous

grotto 4 cave 6 burrow, cavern, hollow, recess, tunnel 8 catacomb

grouch 3 cry 4 beef, carp, crab, fret, kick, mope, pout, rail, sulk 5 cavil, crank, gripe, growl, moper, whine 6 grouse, mutter, pouter 7 grumble, killjoy, protest 8 complain, grumbler 9 bellyache, find fault 10 complainer, curmudgeon, spoilsport, wet blanket

grouchy 5 cross, testy 6 crabby, cranky, grumpy, touchy 8 snappish 10 ill-humored, out of sorts 11 ill-tempered 12 cantankerous 13 short-tempered

grubby

ground, grounds 3 set, sod **4** area, base, call, dirt, farm, land, loam, soil, turf, yard **5** acres, basis, beach, cause, dregs, drill, earth, field, found, lawns, realm, teach, train **6** campus, domain, estate, excuse, inform, motive, object, reason, region, secure, settle, sphere, strand **7** account, confirm, deposit, dry land, educate, founder, gardens, habitat, prepare, purpose, support, terrain **8** district, exercise, firm land, initiate, instruct, occasion, organize, practice, premises, property, province, sediment, the earth **9** arguments, bailiwick, establish, fix firmly, institute, principle, rationale, settlings, territory **10** discipline, inducement, real estate, terra firma **11** pros and cons **12** indoctrinate **14** considerations

grounded 5 based **6** kept in, taught **7** aground, beached, bounded, drilled, founded, secured, trained **8** informed, prepared, stranded **9** foundered, initiated **10** kept at home, instructed, restricted **11** disciplined, established **12** washed ashore **13** indoctrinated

grounding 8 training **9** education **10** background, experience **11** preparation **14** indoctrination **15** familiarization

groundless 4 idle **5** empty, false **6** faulty, flimsy, unreal, untrue **8** baseless, needless, unproved **9** erroneous, illogical, imaginary, unfounded **10** chimerical, fallacious, gratuitous **11** uncalled for, unjustified, unsupported, unwarranted **13** unjustifiable, without reason

groundwork 4 base, root **5** basis **6** cradle, ground, origin, source, spring **7** bedrock, footing, grounds, taproot **8** keystone, learning, planning, practice, training **9** spadework **10** foundation **11** cornerstone, fundamental, preparation **12** fundamentals, underpinning **14** apprenticeship, indoctrination

group 3 set **4** band, clan, file, gang, herd, pack, sift, size, sort **5** align, bunch, class, crowd, flock, grade, hoard, index, party, place, range, swarm, tribe, troop **6** assign, branch, circle, clique, family, hobnob, league, line up, mingle, throng **7** arrange, catalog, cluster, combine, company, consort, coterie, faction, marshal, section, species, variety **8** classify, division, graduate, organize, register **9** associate, gathering **10** assemblage, collection, coordinate, detachment, fraternity, fraternize **11** aggregation, alphabetize, association, brotherhood, subdivision **12** congregation **14** classification, representation

Group, The
    author: 12 Mary McCarthy

grouping 7 sorting **8** arraying, ordering **10** assemblage, assortment **11** arrangement, disposition **12** distribution, organization

group of performers 6 troupe **7** company **8** ensemble

Group Portrait of a Lady
    author: 12 Heinrich Boll

grouse 4 beef, crab, fret, fume, fuss, kick **5** gripe **6** grouch, mutter, squawk, take on **7** carry on, grumble **8** complain, gamebird **9** bellyache

grove 4 bosk **5** brake, copse **6** forest, pinery, timber **7** coppice, orchard, thicket, wood lot **8** wildwood, woodland **9** shrubbery **10** plantation

grovel 4 fawn **5** cower, crawl, stoop, toady **6** cringe, kowtow, snivel **7** flatter, truckle **12** bow and scrape **13** demean oneself, humble oneself **14** lick the boots of

groveling 6 abject **7** fawning, servile **8** cowering, crawling, cringing, toadying **9** kowtowing, truckling **11** bootlicking **17** bowing and scraping

grow 3 bud, sow, wax **4** boom, farm, rise, till **5** bloom, breed, plant, raise, ripen, surge, swell, widen **6** become, expand, extend, flower, garden, mature, spread, sprout, thrive **7** advance, amplify, blossom, develop, enlarge, fill out, get to be, improve, magnify, produce, prosper, shoot up, stretch, succeed **8** come to be, flourish, fructify, increase, mushroom, progress, spring up, vegetate **9** cultivate, germinate, propagate, skyrocket **10** aggrandize

Growing Up in New Guinea
    author: 12 Margaret Mead

growl 4 fret, snap **5** croak, grind, gripe, groan, grunt, snarl, whine **6** grouse, murmur, mutter, rumble **7** grumble **8** complain, talk back

grown-up 3 big, man **4** lady, ripe **5** adult, of age, woman **6** mature, senior **7** worldly **9** full-blown, full-grown, gentleman **11** full-fledged **13** sophisticated

growth 4 crop, hump, lump, rise **5** gnarl, prime, surge, swell, tumor **6** sowing, spread **7** advance, harvest, produce, success **8** increase, maturity, planting, progress **9** expansion, extension, flowering, increment **10** burgeoning, matureness, production, prospering **11** advancement, cultivation, development, enlargement, excrescence, flourishing, improvement, propagation **12** augmentation, mass of tissue **13** amplification

goddess of: 4 Hour **5** Horae

Groza, Lou
    nickname: 6 The Toe
    sport: 8 football
    team: 15 Cleveland Browns

grub 3 bum, dig **4** food, toil, worm **5** cadge, dig up, larva, mooch, slave **6** drudge, sponge **7** rummage

grubber 5 slave **6** drudge, toiler **7** laborer

grubby 4 foul **5** dirty, grimy, messy, muddy, nasty, seedy, tacky **6** beat-up, filthy, frowzy, frumpy, shabby, shoddy, sloppy, smudgy, soiled, sordid **7** squalid, unclean, unkempt **8** begrimed, slovenly, unwashed **9** besmeared **10** bedraggled

grudge 4 envy 5 pique, spite 6 animus, hatred, malice, rancor, resent 7 dislike, ill will 8 aversion, begrudge 9 animosity 10 resentment 11 malevolence 12 hard-feelings

grudging 7 envious 8 hesitant, spiteful 9 reluctant, resentful, unwilling 10 ungenerous 13 penny-pinching

grueling 4 hard 6 brutal, tiring 7 racking 9 fatiguing, punishing, torturous 10 exhausting

gruesome 4 gory, grim 5 awful 6 grisly, horrid 7 fearful, ghastly, hideous, macabre 8 horrible, shocking, terrible 9 frightful, loathsome, repellent, repulsive, revolting 10 forbidding, horrendous, horrifying 13 bloodcurdling, spine-chilling

gruff 4 curt, rude, sour, tart 5 bluff, blunt, harsh, husky, raspy, rough, sharp, short, stern, sulky, surly 6 abrupt, croaky, crusty, grumpy, hoarse, ragged, sullen 7 bearish, brusque, caustic, crabbed, cracked, grouchy, peevish, throaty, uncivil, waspish 8 churlish, guttural, impolite, snarling, strident 9 bristling, insulting 10 ill-humored, ill-natured, ungracious 11 ill-tempered 12 discourteous

grumble 4 fret 5 chafe, gripe, growl 6 grouch, grouse, mutter 8 complain 9 find-fault

grump 4 crab 5 crank 6 grouch 8 grumbler, sourball 10 curmudgeon

grumpy 4 sour 5 moody, sulky, surly, testy 6 crabby, cranky, crusty, sullen 7 grouchy, peevish, pettish 8 churlish 9 irritable, splenetic 10 ill-humored, out of humor, out of sorts 11 disgruntled, ill-disposed, ill-tempered 12 cantankerous

grunt 3 cry 4 bark, call, gasp, howl 5 burro, croak, groan, snort, utter 6 bellow, grouch, mumble, murmur, mutter, shriek 7 howling, whisper 8 complain 9 ululation 11 foot soldier, infantryman

Grunwald, Matthais (Grunewald, Mathis)
  real name: 23 Mathis Gothardt Neithardt
  born: 7 Germany 8 Wurzburg
  artwork: 14 The Crucifixion 15 The Resurrection 20 Altarpiece at Isenheim

Grushenka
  character in: 20 The Brothers Karamazov
  author: 11 Dostoyevsky

Gryce, Percy
  character in: 15 The House of Mirth
  author: 7 Wharton

Grynaeus
  epithet of: 6 Apollo

gryphon see 7 griffin

Guam
  capital: 5 Agana
  largest city: 8 Tamuning
  others: 4 Agat, Apra, Toto, Yigo 5 Magua 6 Dededo, Merizo 8 Inarajan, Mangilao, Mongmong, Sinajana, Talofofo, Tamuning 9 Barrigada, Finegayan, Santa Rita
  member of: 7 Mariana (islands)
  mountain: 5 Tenjo
  highest point: 6 Lamlam

  sea: 7 Pacific 10 Philippine
  people: 7 Spanish 8 American, Chamorro, Filipino 11 Micronesian
  explorer: 8 Magellan
  ruler: 5 Japan, Spain 12 United States
  language: 7 English 8 Chamorro
  religion: 16 Roman Catholicism
  feature: 7 typhoon 9 coral reef
  Air Force base: 8 Andersen
  product: 5 copra 6 banana, papaya

Guarani (Caingua)
  language family: 7 Guarani
  location: 6 Brazil 8 Paraguay 9 Argentina 12 South America
  allied to: 4 Tupi

guarantee, guaranty 4 avow, bail, bond, pawn, word 5 swear 6 affirm, allege, assure, attest, avowal, insure, pledge, surety 7 deposit, endorse, promise, sponsor, testify, voucher, warrant 8 contract, covenant, security, vouch for, warranty 9 agreement, answer for, assurance, insurance, testimony 10 collateral, underwrite 11 affirmation, endorsement, word of honor 12 give one's word

guard 4 mind, save, tend 5 watch 6 attend, convoy, defend, escort, patrol, picket, screen, secure, sentry, shield, warder 7 conduct, defense, protect, shelter 8 defender, garrison, guardian, keep safe, preserve, security, sentinel, watchdog, watchman 9 bodyguard, concierge, custodian, guardsman, protector, safeguard, watch over 10 doorkeeper, gatekeeper, protection 12 preservation 13 keep watch over

guard against 6 beware 10 look out for 11 take warning, watch out for

guarded 4 wary 5 cagey, chary, leery 7 careful, heedful, mindful, prudent 8 cautious, discreet, hesitant 9 in custody, protected, tentative 10 restrained, suspicious, under guard 11 circumspect, on one's guard

guardian 5 guard 6 convoy, escort, keeper, patrol, patron, picket, sentry, warden, warder 7 curator, trustee 8 advocate, champion, defender, sentinel, shepherd, wardsman, watchdog 9 attendant, bodyguard, caretaker, conductor, custodian, preserver, protector, safeguard, vigilante 10 benefactor 11 conservator 13 friend at court, guardian angel 14 legal custodian

guardian of a place
  Latin: 10 genius loci

guardianship 4 care 6 charge 7 custody, keeping 10 protection 11 safekeeping, supervision, trusteeship

Guatemala
  capital/largest city: 13 Guatemala City
  others: 4 Ocos 5 Coban, Vieja 6 Chahal, Chisec, Cuiloo, Flores, Iztapa, Jalapa, Salama, Solola, Tacana, Tecpan, Yaloch, Zacapa 7 Antigua, Cuilapa, Jutiapa, San Jose 8 Progreso 9 Escuintla, Tiquisate 10 Livingston 11 Totonicapan 13 Puerto Barrios, Quezaltenango 14 San Pedro Carcha 16 Chichicastenango

school: 9 San Carlos
measure: 4 vara 6 cuarta, tercia 7 cajuela, manzana 10 caballeria
monetary unit: 4 peso 7 centavo, quetzal
weight: 4 caja 5 libra
lake: 5 Dulce, Guija, Peten 6 Izabal 7 Atitlan 9 Amatitlan, Peten Itza
mountain: 4 Agua, Mico 5 Fuego, Madre 6 Pacaya, Tacana 7 Atitlan, Toliman 8 La Candon, Las Minas 10 Acatenango, Santa Maria 12 Cuchumatanes
highest point: 8 Tajumuko 9 Tajamulco
river: 4 Azul 5 Bravo, Dulce, Lapaz 6 Belize, Chixoy, Negino, Pasion, Samala 7 Chiapas, Motagua, Sarstun, Sastoon 8 Polochic, Rio Dulce, Sarstoon 10 Usumacinta
sea: 7 Pacific 8 Atlantic 9 Caribbean
physical feature:
  bay: 8 Amatique
  gulf: 8 Honduras
people: 3 Mam 4 Chol, Itza, Ixil, Maya 5 Xinca 6 Caribe, Quiche 7 ladinos, mestizo, Pocomam 13 Guatemaltecos
language: 6 Quiche 7 Spanish
religion: 13 Roman Catholic
place:
  church: 10 Santo Tomas
  ruins: 5 Mayan, Tikal 8 Uaxactun
feature:
  bird: 7 quetzal
  clarinet: 8 chirimta
  dance: 5 elson 8 guarimba
  flute: 3 xul
  military dictator: 8 Caudillo
food:
  dish: 6 pepian 10 enchiladas 13 gallo en chicha
  fruit: 4 anay
guava 7 Psidium 16 Psidium guineense
  varieties: 5 apple 6 common, purple, yellow 7 Cattley, Chilean 9 pineapple 10 Costa Rican, strawberry 13 yellow cattley 16 purple strawberry, yellow strawberry
Gubitosi, Michael James Vijencio
  real name of: 11 Robert Blake
Gudrun
  also: 6 Kudrun 7 Guthrun
  origin: 12 Scandinavian
  mentioned in: 8 Volsunga
  father: 5 Giuki, Gjuki 6 Hertel
  mother: 8 Grimhild
  brother: 6 Gunnar
  husband: 4 Atli 6 Herwig, Sigurd
  killed: 4 Atli
  corresponds to: 9 Kriemhild
Guerrillas
  author: 9 V S Naipaul
guess 4 deem, view 5 fancy, judge, opine, think 6 assume, belief, deduce, divine, gather, reckon, regard, theory 7 believe, daresay, feeling, imagine, opinion, predict, suppose, surmise, suspect, venture 8 conclude, estimate, theorize 9 postulate, speculate, suspicion 10 assumption, conjecture, divination, hypothesis, predic-

tion 11 hypothesize, make a stab at, postulation, presumption, speculation, supposition
guesswork 7 surmise 10 conjecture, hypothesis 11 supposition 13 shot in the dark
guest 5 diner 6 caller, client, friend, inmate, lodger, patron, roomer 7 boarder, company, habitue, invitee, patient, visitor 8 customer 9 sojourner 10 frequenter 14 paying customer
Guest, Edgar A
  author of: 12 A Heap of Livin'
Guest, Judith
  author of: 14 Ordinary People
guffaw 4 howl 6 scream 10 belly laugh, horse laugh
Guglielmi, Rodolfo
  real name of: 16 Rudolph Valentino
Guicciardini, Francesco
  author of: 13 Storia d'Italia
guidance 3 tip 4 clue, help, hint, lead 6 advice, escort 7 conduct, counsel, pointer 8 auspices 9 direction 10 leadership, management, protection, suggestion 11 information, instruction, supervision 12 intelligence 13 enlightenment
guide 4 lead, rule 5 model, pilot, steer, usher 6 beacon, convoy, direct, escort, govern, handle, leader, manage, marker, master, mentor 7 adviser, command, conduct, control, example, marshal, monitor, oversee, pattern, steerer, teacher 8 chaperon, cicerone, director, engineer, helmsman, landmark, lodestar, maneuver, polestar, regulate, shepherd, signpost 9 accompany, attendant, conductor, counselor 10 manipulate
guidebook 5 bible 6 manual 8 Baedeker, handbook 13 reference book
Guidry, Ron (Ronald Ames)
  nickname: 18 Louisiana Lightning
  sport: 8 baseball
  position: 7 pitcher
  team: 14 New York Yankees
guild 5 order, union 6 league 7 company, society 8 alliance 9 coalition 10 craft union, federation, fraternity, labor union, sisterhood, trade union 11 association, brotherhood, confederacy, corporation
Guildenstern
  character in: 6 Hamlet
  author: 11 Shakespeare
guile 5 craft, fraud 6 deceit, tricks 7 cunning, slyness 8 artifice, strategy, trickery, wiliness 9 chicanery, deception, duplicity, treachery 10 artfulness, craftiness, dishonesty, hanky-panky, stratagems, trickiness 11 fraudulence 13 sharp practice
guileless 4 open 5 frank, naive 6 candid, honest, simple 7 artless, natural, sincere 8 harmless, innocent, truthful 9 ingenuous, innocuous 10 aboveboard, unaffected 11 undesigning, unoffending 15 straightforward, unselfconscious, unsophisticated
guilelessness 6 candor 9 innocence, sincerity 10 candidness, directness 11 artlessness 13 ingenuousness

guilt 3 sin 4 blot, vice 5 shame, wrong 6 infamy, stigma 7 misdeed 8 disgrace, dishonor, misdoing, trespass 9 black mark, turpitude 10 guiltiness, misconduct, sinfulness, wrongdoing 11 criminality, culpability, degradation, delinquency, dereliction, humiliation, misbehavior, self-disgust 13 transgression

guiltless 4 good, pure 5 clean 6 chaste 7 angelic, sinless 8 innocent, unfallen, virtuous 9 blameless, childlike, faultless 10 immaculate, inculpable, unblamable 11 uncorrupted

French: 12 sans reproche

guilt-stricken 7 ashamed 18 conscience-stricken

guilty 5 sorry, wrong 6 erring, sinful 7 ashamed, corrupt, hangdog, immoral 8 blamable, contrite, criminal, culpable, penitent, sheepish 9 offensive, regretful, repentant 11 blameworthy 18 conscience-stricken

Guilty Pleasures
　author: 15 Donald Barthelme

Guinea
　other name: 12 French Guinea 13 Rivieres du Sud
　capital/largest city: 7 Conakry
　others: 4 Boke, Fria, Labe 5 Beyla 6 Dabola, Kankan, Kindia 7 Dubreka, Siguiri 8 Kerouane 9 Kouroussa, Nzerekore
　measure: 7 jacktan
　monetary unit: 4 iliy, syli 5 franc 6 cauris
　weight: 4 akey, piso, uzan 5 benda, seron 6 quinto 8 aguirage
　island: 3 Los 5 Tombo 7 Tristao
　mountain: 4 Loma 6 Tamgue 11 Fouta Djalon
　highest point: 5 Nimba
　river: 4 Milo 5 Kogon, Niger 6 Bafing, Faleme, Gambia 7 Kolente, Senegal 8 Konkoure, Tinkisso 13 Great Scarcies
　sea: 8 Atlantic
　physical feature:
　cape: 5 Verga
　people: 4 Koma, Loma, Nalu, Susu, Toma 5 Kissi, Manon 6 Fulani, Guerzi 7 Landoma, Malinke 8 Kouranke, Landuman 11 Kissi-Sherbo 12 Guerze-Kpelle
　language: 4 Fulbe, Mande 6 Arabic, French, Fulani 7 English
　religion: 5 Islam 7 animism
　feature:
　plant: 11 globeflower
　tree: 4 akee 5 dalli

Guinea-Bissau
　other name: 16 Portuguese Guinea
　capital/largest city: 6 Bissau
　others: 4 Buba 5 Catio, Farim 6 Bafata, Bolama, Cacheu, Cacine, Dandum, Mansoa 7 Bissora, Bubaque, San Joav 9 Fulacunda 10 Nova Lamego 11 Madina do Boe, Madine do Boe, Sao Domingos
　monetary unit: 4 peso 6 escudo 8 centavos
　island: 4 Roxa 6 Orango 7 Bijagos, Formosa
　river: 4 Geba 6 Cacheu, Mansoa 7 Corubal
　sea: 8 Atlantic
　people: 6 Fulani 7 Balanta, Balante, mulatto 8 Mandingo, Mandyako
　language: 5 Fulah 7 Balante, Crioulo 8 Mandingo 10 Portuguese 21 Cape Verde-Guinea Creole
　religion: 5 Islam 7 animism 12 Christianity

Guinevere
　character in: 16 Arthurian romance
　husband: 6 Arthur
　lover: 8 Lancelot

Guinness, Sir Alec
　born: 6 London 7 England
　roles: 8 Star Wars 11 Oliver Twist 13 Doctor Zhivago 14 Our Man in Havana, The Ladykillers 15 A Passage to India, Ben Obi Wan Kenobi, Lavender Hill Mob 16 Lawrence of Arabia 17 Great Expectations 21 Kind Hearts and Coronets 22 Tinker Tailor Soldier Spy 23 The Bridge on the River Kwai (Oscar)

guise 4 garb, mode 5 dress, habit 6 attire 7 apparel, clothes, costume, fashion 8 clothing, disguise, pretense 10 masquerade

Gujarati
　language family: 12 Indo-European
　branch: 11 Indo-Iranian
　group: 5 Indic
　spoken in: 5 (northern) India

Gulag Archipelago, The
　author: 23 Aleksandr Solzhenitsyn Jr

gulch 3 gap 4 rift 5 abyss, chasm, cleft, crack, gorge, gully, split 6 arroyo, breach, divide, ravine 8 crevasse

gulf 4 cove, rent, rift 5 abyss, chasm, cleft, firth, fjord, gully, inlet, split 6 canyon, lagoon 7 estuary, opening 8 crevasse 10 separation

gull 3 gyp 4 dupe, rook 5 cozen, trick 7 deceive, defraud, sea gull, sea bird, swindle 9 bamboozle, victimize

gullet 3 maw 4 craw, crop 5 belly, gorge, tummy 6 dewlap, throat 7 abdomen, channel, stomach, weasand 9 beer belly, esophagus

gullible 5 green, naive 6 simple 8 innocent, trustful, trusting 9 credulous 11 easily duped 12 easily fooled, overtrusting, unsuspicious 13 easily cheated, inexperienced 14 easily deceived 15 unsophisticated

Gulliver's Travels
　author: 13 Jonathan Swift
　character: 14 Lemuel Gulliver
　visited: 6 Laputa, Yahoos 8 Blefuscu, Lilliput, Luggnagg 9 Balnibari 10 Houyhnhnms 11 Brobdingnag 12 Glubbdubdrib

gully 3 gap 5 ditch, gorge, gulch 6 defile, furrow, gutter, ravine, trench 7 channel 11 small canyon, small valley, watercourse 13 drainage ditch

gulp 4 bolt, swig, wolf 5 quaff, swill 6 devour, guzzle 7 swallow, toss off 8 mouthful

gulp down 4 bolt 6 devour, gobble 7 swallow 8 gobble up, wolf down

gum 3 wax 5 latex, resin 6 chicle 8 mucilage 10 Eucalyptus

  varieties: 3 cup, red 4 blue, cape, gray, rose, snow, sour 5 apple, black, cider, coral, giant, gully, Karri, Manna, sugar, swamp, sweet 6 cotton, Deane's, desert, gimlet, salmon, snappy, Tupelo 7 Barbary, cabbage, Fuchsia, maiden's, Morocco, scarlet, spotted 8 Formosan, Lehmann's, mountain, scribbly, spinning 9 forest red, Murray red, steedman's 10 Australian, candle-bark, red-spotted, Sydney blue, Timor white, tumble-down, urnfruited 11 Blakely's red, blue weeping, salmon white, small-leaved, strickland's 12 lemon-scented, red-flowering, silverdollar 13 American sweet, Oriental sweet, Tasmanian blue, Tasmanian snow 14 yellow-flowered 15 Omeo round-leaved, round-leaved snow 16 rough-barked manna, scarlet-flowering 17 heart-leaved silver 20 silver-leaved mountain

Gumm, Frances

  real name of: 11 Judy Garland

gummed 5 glued, gummy, stuck 6 sticky 8 adhering, adhesive

Gummidge, Mrs

  character in: 16 David Copperfield

  author: 7 Dickens

gummy 5 gluey, gooey, gunky 6 gloppy, sticky, viscid 7 rubbery, viscous 8 adhesive 10 gelatinous 12 mucilaginous

gumption 3 zip 4 dash, push 5 drive, spunk, verve 6 energy, hustle, pizazz, spirit 7 courage 10 enterprise, get-up-and-go, initiative 12 forcefulness 14 aggressiveness 15 resourcefulness

gumshoe 4 dick 6 shamus 9 detective 10 private eye 12 investigator

gun 3 aim, gat, rod, try 4 Colt, hunt, iron 5 piece, rifle, shoot 6 cannon, Magnum, mortar, musket, pistol 7 attempt, carbine, firearm, Gatling, go after, Long Tom, shotgun 8 howitzer, ordnance, revolver 9 automatic, Big Bertha, derringer, equalizer, flintlock, forty-five, twenty-two, Remington 10 fieldpiece, machine gun, six-shooter, three-fifty, Walther PPK, Winchester 11 blunderbuss, thirty-eight, trusty-rusty 12 fowling piece, muzzle loader, shooting iron 13 Kentucky rifle 14 artillery piece, Smith and Wesson

  invented by:

    breechloader: 8 Thornton

    magazine: 9 Hotchkiss

    silencer: 5 Maxim

Gunga Din

  story in: 18 Barrack-Room Ballads

  author: 14 Rudyard Kipling

  director: 13 George Stevens

  cast: 8 Sam Jaffe 9 Cary Grant 12 Joan Fontaine 14 Victor McLaglen 18 Douglas Fairbanks Jr

  setting: 5 India

  remade as: 13 Soldiers Three 14 Sergeants Three

gunman 6 bandit, outlaw, robber, sniper 7 hoodlum 9 assailant, desperado, holdup man

Gunn, Ben

  character in: 14 Treasure Island

  author: 9 Stevenson

Gunnar

  origin: 12 Scandinavian

  father: 5 Giuki, Gjuki

  mother: 8 Grimhild

  sister: 6 Gudrun, Kudrun 7 Guthrun

  wife: 8 Brynhild

  Brynhild won by: 6 Sigurd

Gunsmoke

  character: 3 Sam (the bartender) 8 Doc (Dr Galen) Adams 10 Quint Asper 11 Newly O'Brien 12 Chester Goode, Festus Haggen, Kitty Russell (Miss Kitty) 18 Marshall Matt Dillon 24 Clayton Thaddeus (Thad) Greenwood

  cast: 9 Ken Curtis 10 Buck Taylor, Roger Ewing 11 Amanda Blake, James Arness 12 Burt Reynolds, Dennis Weaver, Glenn Strange, Milburn Stone

  setting: 9 Dodge City

  saloon: 10 Longbranch

Guns of August, The

  author: 15 Barbara W Tuchman

Guns of Navarone, The

  director: 12 J Lee Thompson

  based on novel by: 15 Alistair MacLean

  cast: 10 David Niven 11 Gregory Peck, James Darren 12 Anthony Quinn, Stanley Baker 13 Anthony Quayle

Gunther

  origin: 8 Germanic

  mentioned in: 14 Nibelungenlied

  king of: 8 Burgundy

  wife: 8 Brunhild

  sister: 9 Kriemhild

  killed by: 9 Kriemhild

Guppy

  character in: 10 Bleak House

  author: 7 Dickens

Gurdin, Natasha

  real name of: 11 Natalie Wood

gurgle 5 plash 6 bubble, burble, murmur, ripple 7 sputter 8 bubbling, gurgling

guru 5 guide 6 leader, master 7 teacher 9 preceptor 10 instructor

gush 3 gab, gas, jet, run 4 blab, bull, rush, well 5 issue, prate, spout, spurt 6 babble, burble, drivel, hot air, splash, squirt, stream 7 baloney, blabber, blather, chatter, pour out, prattle, rubbish, torrent, twaddle 8 nonsense, outburst, rattle on 10 outpouring 11 mawkishness 12 emotionalism 14 sentimentalism, talk effusively 16 run off at the mouth

gushiness 12 effusiveness, emotionalism 17 demonstrativeness

gushing 6 lavish 7 pouring, profuse 8 effusive, spurting 10 flattering 11 free-flowing 12 demonstrative, unrestrained 16 overenthusiastic

gushy 8 effusive 12 unrestrained 13 demonstrative 16 overenthusiastic

gussy up 5 adorn 7 dress up, enhance 8 beautify, decorate, ornament 9 embellish

gust 3 fit 4 blow, puff, wind 5 blast, burst, draft 6 breeze, flurry, squall, zephyr 8 outbreak, outburst, paroxysm 9 explosion

Gustaffson, Greta Louisa
　real name of: 10 Greta Garbo

Guster
　character in: 10 Bleak House
　author: 7 Dickens

gusto 3 joy 4 zeal, zest 5 savor 6 fervor, relish 7 delight 8 appetite, pleasure 10 enthusiasm 12 appreciation, exhilaration, satisfaction

gusto, con
　music: 9 with style, with taste

gusty 5 blowy, windy 6 breezy 7 squally 8 blustery

gut 4 raze 5 belly, clean, level, tummy 6 bowels, paunch, ravage 7 abdomen, consume, midriff, stomach, viscera 8 entrails, lay waste 9 bay window, beer belly, spare tire 10 disembowel, eviscerate, intestines, midsection 11 breadbasket

guten abend 11 good evening

Gutenberg
　nationality: 6 German
　inventor of: 11 movable type
　printer of: 14 Gutenberg Bible

guten morgen 11 good morning

guten tag 7 good day

Guthrie, A B Jr
　author of: 6 Arfive 9 The Big Sky 10 The Way West 13 The Last Valley 16 Fair Land Fair Land, The Blue Hen's Chick, The Thousand Hills

Guthrun see 6 Gudrun

Gutman, Casper
　character in: 16 The Maltese Falcon
　author: 7 Hammett

guts 4 dash, grit 5 nerve, pluck, spunk 6 bowels, daring, mettle, spirit, vitals 7 bravado, bravery, courage, gizzard, innards, insides, viscera 8 audacity, backbone, boldness 9 fortitude 10 intestines 11 intrepidity

gutsy 4 game 5 brave 6 heroic, plucky 7 doughty, valiant 8 fearless, intrepid, stalwart, unafraid, valorous 9 dauntless, undaunted 10 courageous 11 lionhearted, unflinching 12 stouthearted

guttural 3 low 4 deep 5 gruff, harsh, husky, raspy, thick 6 hoarse 7 throaty 8 croaking 12 inarticulate

guy 3 boy, joe, kid, man 4 body, chap, dude, gent, rope 5 bloke, human, joker 6 fellow, hombre, person 8 blighter, upholder 9 supporter 10 individual

Guyana
　name means: 12 land of waters
　other name: 13 British Guiana
　capital/largest city: 10 Georgetown
　others: 7 Charity 8 Hyde Park, Rosignol 9 Jonestown, Mackenzie
　island: 6 Leguan 8 Wakenaam
　mountain: 5 Amuku, Ariwa, Kamoa 6 Akarai, Kanuku 7 Caburai 9 Pacaraima
　highest point: 7 Roraima
　river: 5 Waini 6 Barama 7 Amakura, Baruima, Berbice 8 Demerara, Mazaruni, Rupununi 9 Essequibo 10 Burro-Burro
　sea: 8 Atlantic
　physical feature:
　　falls: 5 Great, Tiger 7 Kamaria 8 Kaieteur 9 Serikoeng 10 Surwakwima 15 Fredrik Willem IV
　people: 6 Akawai, Arawak, Creole, Taruma 7 African, Chinese, mulatto 10 Portuguese
　language: 5 Hindi 7 English
　religion: 5 Hindu, Islam 8 Anglican 13 Roman Catholic

Guy Fawkes
　author: 16 William Ainsworth

Guy Mannering
　author: 14 Sir Walter Scott

Guyon
　character in: 15 The Faerie Queene
　author: 7 Spenser

Guys and Dolls
　director: 17 Joseph L Mankiewicz
　based on story by: 11 Damon Runyon
　cast: 10 Stubby Kaye 11 Jean Simmons 12 Frank Sinatra, Marlon Brando, Vivian Blaine
　setting: 11 New York City
　score: 12 Frank Loesser
　song: 11 Luck Be a Lady 12 Guys and Dolls 26 Sit Down You're Rocking the Boat

guzzle 4 bolt, swig 5 quaff, swill 6 devour, imbibe, tipple 7 toss off 8 gulp down

guzzler 5 drunk 6 boozer 7 imbiber, tippler 8 devourer, drunkard 9 alcoholic

Gwawl
　origin: 5 Welsh
　mentioned in: 10 Mabinogion
　rival of: 5 Pwyll
　sought hand of: 8 Rhiannon

Gwydion
　origin: 5 Welsh
　son: 14 Llew Llaw Gyffes
　sister: 9 Arianhrod
　lover: 9 Arianhrod

Gwyn
　origin: 7 British
　god of: 7 rebirth 9 afterlife

Gyas
　companion of: 6 Aeneas

Gyes see 5 Gyges

Gygaea, Gyge
　form: 5 nymph
　location: 4 lake

Gyges
  also: 4 Gyes
  member of: 13 Hecatonchires
gymnasium 5 arena 6 circus 7 stadium 10
  hippodrome
gymnast 10 Olga Korbut 13 Mary Lou
  Retton, Nadia Comaneci
gymnastics 9 exercises 10 acrobatics 11
  contortions 16 physical training
Gynaecothoenas
  epithet of: 4 Ares
  means: 17 feasted by the women
gynophobia
  fear of: 5 women
gyp 3 con 4 bilk, burn, fake, hoax, rook,
  scam, soak 5 cheat, cozen, fraud, phony,
  trick 6 diddle, fleece, humbug, ripoff 7 con
  game, defraud, swindle 8 flimflam, hoodwink 9 bamboozle, deception
gypsy
  Italian: 7 zingara, zingaro
gyrate 5 swirl, twirl, wheel, whirl 6 circle, rotate, spiral 7 revolve 9 pirouette 10 spin
  around

H

habeas corpus 11 have the body **23** produce the person in court
    legal writ guards against: 19 illegal imprisonment

habiliments 4 garb, wear **5** dress **6** attire, outfit **7** clothes, costume, raiment, regalia **8** clothing, wardrobe **9** vestments

habit 3 rut, way **4** garb, gear, robe, rule, wont **5** dress, trait **6** attire, custom, groove, livery, manner, outfit **7** apparel, clothes, costume, garment, leaning, raiment, routine, uniform, vesture **8** clothing, fondness, habitude, practice **9** mannerism, trappings **10** beaten path, convention, observance, partiality, proclivity, propensity **11** habiliments, inclination, peculiarity **12** predilection, second nature **13** accoutrements, fixed practice **14** matter of course, predisposition **15** behavior pattern

habitat 3 pad **4** digs, home, spot, zone **5** abode, haunt, place, range, realm, roost **6** domain, locale, milieu, region **7** housing, lodging, setting, terrain **8** domicile, dwelling, home base, lodgment, precinct, quarters **9** territory **10** habitation **11** environment, natural home **12** place of abode **13** dwelling place **14** stamping ground **15** natural locality **17** native environment

habitation 3 pad **4** digs, home **5** abode, haunt, house, roost **6** colony **7** habitat, housing, lodging, shelter, tenancy **8** domicile, dwelling, lodgment, quarters **9** community, occupancy, residence **10** occupation, settlement **12** place of abode **13** dwelling place, temporary stay **16** place of residence

Habit of Being, The
    author: 15 Flannery O'Connor

habitual 5 fixed, usual **6** common, normal, wonted **7** chronic, natural, regular, routine, typical **8** addicted, constant, expected, familiar, frequent, periodic, repeated **9** confirmed, continual, customary, incessant, ingrained, perpetual, recurrent **10** accustomed, deep-rooted, deep-seated, inveterate, methodical, systematic **11** established, traditional **12** conventional, second nature **14** by force of habit

habitual practice 4 wont **5** habit **6** custom

habituate 5 adapt, drill, imbue, inure, train **6** harden, school, season **7** break in, instill **8** accustom, initiate **9** inculcate **10** discipline, make used to **12** indoctrinate

habitue 7 regular **10** frequenter **13** regular patron **15** frequent visitor **16** constant customer

hack 3 cab, cut, hew, nag **4** bark, chip, chop, gash, plug, rasp, slit, taxi **5** coach, cut up, notch, slash, slice, whack **6** cleave, mangle **7** hackney, taxicab **8** lacerate, mutilate **9** cart horse, dray horse, scribbler, workhorse **10** cough drily, cut roughly, draft horse, hired horse, shaft horse **11** common horse, penny-a-liner **12** hackney coach, worn-out horse **13** carriage horse **16** grubstreet writer **18** horse-drawn carriage

hackle 3 peg **4** card, comb, hack, hook, ruff **5** curry, plume, quill **6** heckle, mangle **7** bristle, feather, plumage

Hackman, Gene
    born: 15 San Bernardino CA
    roles: 8 Superman **11** Popeye Doyle **14** Bonnie and Clyde **15** The Conversation **19** The French Connection (Oscar) **20** The Poseidon Adventure

hackneyed 4 dull, worn **5** banal, inane, stale, stock, trite, vapid **6** common, jejune **7** cliched, humdrum, insipid, routine, worn-out **8** bromidic, ordinary, shopworn, well-eaten **9** moth-eaten **10** pedestrian, threadbare, uninspired **11** commonplace, stereotyped **12** conventional **13** platitudinous, unimaginative

Hadassah 6 Esther

Hades 4 hell
    also: 5 Pluto **10** lower world, Underworld
    corresponds to: 5 Orcus
    god of: 5 Orcus, Pluto
    goddess of: 6 Hecate, Hekate

Haemon
    father: 5 Creon
    loved: 8 Antigone
    died at tomb of: 8 Antigone
    death by: 7 suicide

Haenigsen, Harry
    creator/artist of: 5 Penny **7** Our Bill

hafnium
    chemical symbol: 2 Hf

hag 3 bat, nag **4** drab, fury **5** biddy, crone, frump, harpy, shrew, vixen, witch **6** beldam, gorgon, ogress, virago **7** hellcat **8** battle-ax, harridan **9** termagant

Hagar
    servant of: 5 Sarah
    husband: 7 Abraham
    son: 7 Ishmael

Hagar the Horrible
    creator: 9 Dik Browne

Hagen
    origin: 8 Germanic
    mentioned in: 14 Nibelungenlied
    killed by: 9 Kriemhild
    killed: 9 Siegfried

haggard 4 beat, wild, worn **5** gaunt, spent, tired, upset, weary **6** bushed, fagged, pooped, raging, wasted **7** ranting **8** careworn, drooping, fatigued, flagging, frenzied, harassed, harrowed, overcome, toilworn, wild-eyed **9** exhausted, woebegone **10** hollow-eyed **11** debilitated, overwearied, overwrought, tuckered out, wildlooking **12** tired-looking

Haggard, H Rider
  author of: 3 She **17** King Solomon's Mines

haggle 6 barter, bicker, dicker, higgle **7** bargain, dispute, quarrel, quibble, wrangle **8** beat down, squabble

Hagiographa
  Hebrew: 7 Ketubim

hagiographer 19 writer of saints' lives

Hagman, Larry
  mother: 10 Mary Martin
  born: 13 Weatherford TX
  roles: 6 Dallas **7** J R Ewing **15** I Dream of Jeannie

Hagno
  origin: 8 Arcadian
  form: 5 nymph
  location: 6 spring

Hahn, Otto
  field: 9 chemistry
  nationality: 6 German
  discovered: 13 protoactinium **14** nuclear isomers
  awarded: 10 Nobel Prize

Haida
  language family: 6 Masset, Na-Dene **10** Skidegatta
  tribe: 7 Kaigani
  location: 6 Alaska **15** British Columbia **21** Queen Charlotte Islands
  related to: 7 Tlingit **9** Tsimshian
  associated with: 9 totem pole **13** wood sculpture

hail 4 call **5** cheer, exalt, extol, greet, hello, honor, shout **6** accost, call to, esteem, salute **7** acclaim, address, applaud, commend, glorify, receive, shout at, usher in, welcome **8** cry out to, eulogize, greeting **9** accosting **10** calling out, compliment, panegyrize, salutation **11** make welcome
  German: 4 heil
  Latin: 5 salve

Halley, Arthur
  author of: 5 Hotel **6** Wheels **7** Airport **12** In High Places **14** Final Diagnosis **16** The Moneychangers

hail-fellow-well-met 8 familiar, friendly, intimate, outgoing, sociable **9** extrovert **10** gregarious

Hail Mary
  Latin: 8 Ave Maria

Hail the Conquering Hero
  director: 14 Preston Sturges
  cast: 10 Ella Raines **12** Eddie Bracken **14** Raymond Walburn **15** William Demarest **17** Franklin Pangborn

hail to victory
  German: 8 Sieg Heil

hair 3 fur, mop **4** coat, down, iota, mane, pelt, wool **5** bangs, curls, locks **6** fleece **7** tresses **8** ringlets **12** narrow margin

haircut, hairdo 3 bob, bun, cut **4** Afro, clip, crop, perm, shag, trim **5** bangs, braid, butch, swirl **6** boogie, mohawk **7** beehive, chignon, cornrow, crewcut, flattop, fuzz cut, natural, pachuco, page boy, pigtail, shingle, tonsure **8** bouffant, brushcut, coiffure, ducktail, ponytail, razorcut **9** barbering, hairstyle, permanent, pompadour **10** feathercut, french knot

haircutter 6 barber **11** hairdresser, hair stylist

hairdresser 8 coiffeur **9** coiffeuse **10** beautician, haircutter **11** beauty salon **12** beauty parlor
  French: 8 coiffeur

hair-raising 8 exciting **9** thrilling **10** terrifying **11** astonishing **12** breathtaking, electrifying

hairsplitting 4 fine **6** minute, subtle **7** carping **8** caviling, delicate, hairline, niggling **9** minuscule, quibbling **10** nitpicking, unapparent **12** faultfinding, overcritical **13** imperceptible, inappreciable, infinitesimal **15** inconsequential

hairy 5 bushy, furry, wooly **6** fleecy, pilose, shaggy, woolly **7** hirsute

Hairy Ape, The
  author: 12 Eugene O'Neill

Haiti
  name means: 15 mountainous land
  other name: 12 Santo Domingo
  capital/largest city: 12 Port-au-Prince
  others: 5 Aquin, Furcy, Limbe **6** Hinche, Jacmel, St Marc **7** Jeremie, Leogane, Saltrou **8** Gonaives, Kenscoff, Les Cayes **10** Cap-Haitien
  monetary unit: 6 gourde **8** centimes
  island: 5 Vache **6** Gonave, Tortue **7** Navassa, Tortuga **8** Caymites **10** Hispaniola **14** Grande Cayemite **15** Greater Antilles
  lake: 8 Saumatre
  mountain: 4 Nord **5** Cahos **6** Macaya, Noires **7** Lahotte **8** Troudeau
  highest point: 7 La Selle, Laselle
  river: 9 Guayamoul **10** Artibonite
  sea: 8 Atlantic **9** Caribbean
  physical feature:
  gulf: 6 Gonave
  passage: 8 Windward
  people: 5 Taino **7** African, mulatto
  discoverer: 8 Columbus
  liberator: 19 Toussaint Louverture
  ruler: 8 Duvalier
  language: 6 Creole, French, patois
  religion: 6 voodoo **13** Roman Catholic
  feature:
  dance: 5 mambo
  festival: 9 Mardi Gras
  fortress: 10 La Ferriere **24** Citadelle du Roi Christophe
  security force: 8 bogeymen **15** Tontons Macoutes
  food:

sweet potato: 6 batata

Hakenkreuz 11 hooked cross 12 Nazi swastika

Hakluyt, Richard
author of: 7 Voyages 15 Hakluyt's Voyages

HAL
character in: 14 Two Thousand One (2001)
author: 6 Clarke

Halas, George
nickname: 8 Papa Bear
sport: 8 football
position: 5 coach
team: 12 Chicago Bears

halcyon 4 calm, fair 5 happy, quiet, sunny 6 blithe, golden, hushed, joyous, placid, serene 7 pacific 8 carefree, cheerful, peaceful, tranquil 9 cloudless, contented, reposeful, unclouded, unruffled 10 unagitated, untroubled

Halcyon see 7 Alcyone

hale 3 fit 4 well 5 hardy, sound 6 hearty, robust, rugged, sturdy 7 healthy, in shape 8 vigorous 9 energetic, in the pink, strapping 10 able-bodied, robustious 12 in fine fettle

Hale, Edward Everett
author of: 21 The Man Without a Country

Hale, George Ellery
field: 9 astronomy
initiated: 20 Mt Palomar Observatory
invented: 17 spectroheliograph

Halevy, Ludovic
author of: 17 The Abbe Constantin

Haley, Alex
author of: 5 Roots

Haley, Jack
born: 8 Boston MA
roles: 6 Tin Man 13 The Wizard of Oz

half 4 part, some 6 all but, barely, fairly, feebly, halved, in part, meager, partly, rather, scanty, skimpy, slight, weakly 7 divided, faintly, limited, partial, portion, section 8 fraction, middling, moderate, passable, passably, slightly 9 deficient, imperfect, partially, tolerable, tolerably 10 fractional, inadequate, incomplete, moderately, relatively 12 fifty percent, inadequately, insufficient, pretty nearly 13 after a fashion, comparatively 14 insufficiently

half-asleep 6 drowsy, groggy, unwary 7 out-of-it, unaware 8 sluggish 9 not-with-it, oblivious

half-hearted 4 cold, cool, tame 5 blase, faint 7 languid, passive 8 listless, lukewarm 9 apathetic, lethargic 10 ambivalent, irresolute, lackluster, phlegmatic, spiritless, unaspiring 11 indifferent, perfunctory 13 lackadaisical 14 unenthusiastic

half homer 15 Biblical measure

half-moon 3 arc, bow 4 arch 5 curve 8 crescent

halfway 6 almost, in part, medial, medium, middle, midway, nearly, partly, rather 7 midmost 8 somewhat 9 partially, to a degree 10 middlemost, moderately 11 equi-distant, in the middle 12 intermediate, pretty nearly, to some extent 13 in some measure 18 between two extremes

half-wit 4 dolt, dope, fool 5 dummy, dunce, idiot, moron, ninny 6 dimwit, nitwit 7 dullard 8 dumb-dumb, imbecile, numskull 9 blockhead, numbskull, simpleton 10 nincompoop 15 mental defective, mental deficient

half-witted 4 dumb 5 silly 6 stupid 7 asinine, foolish, idiotic, moronic 9 dimwitted, imbecilic, senseless 11 lamebrained 12 feeble-minded, simple-minded

Halirrhothius
father: 8 Poseidon
mother: 6 Euryte
raped: 7 Alcippe
killed by: 4 Ares

Halitherses
origin: 6 Ithaca
form: 4 seer

hall 5 entry, foyer, lobby 6 arcade 7 chamber, gallery, hallway, passage 8 anteroom, club room, corridor, entrance 9 vestibule 10 auditorium, dining hall, passageway 11 antechamber, banquet hall, concert hall, waiting room 12 amphitheater, assembly room, meeting place 13 reception room

Hall, Diane
real name of: 11 Diane Keaton

Hall, James
field: 7 geology 9 chemistry
nationality: 7 British
founded: 12 geochemistry 19 experimental geology

Hall, James Norman
author of: 17 Mutiny on the Bounty
co-author: 15 Charles Nordhoff

Hallel 6 praise 16 liturgical prayer

Haller, Albrecht von
field: 7 biology
nationality: 5 Swiss
founded: 15 modern neurology

Haller, Harry
character in: 11 Steppenwolf
author: 5 Hesse

Halley, Edmund
field: 9 astronomy
nationality: 7 British
discovered: 12 Halley's Comet

hallmark 4 sign 5 badge, stamp 6 device, emblem, symbol 14 characteristic

halloo 3 cry 4 call, hail, yell 5 shout 6 cry out, holler

hallow 5 bless 7 respect 8 dedicate, sanctify, venerate 10 consecrate

hallowed 4 holy 6 sacred 7 blessed, honored 9 beatified, dedicated 10 sacrosanct, sanctified 11 consecrated

hallucination 5 dream 6 mirage, vision 7 chimera, fantasy, figment 8 delusion, illusion 9 nightmare 10 aberration, apparition 14 phantasmagoria

hallway 4 hall 7 passage 8 corridor, entryway 10 passageway

halo 6 aurora, corona, luster, nimbus 7 aureole, dignity, majesty 8 grandeur, holiness, radiance, sanctity, splendor 9 solemnity, sublimity 11 ring of light 12 chromosphere, luminousness, magnificence, resplendence 13 spiritual aura 15 illustriousness

Haloa
  event: 8 festival
  origin: 5 Greek
  honoring: 7 Demeter 8 Dionysus 10 Persephone

Hals, Franz
  born: 7 Antwerp, Holland
  artwork: 9 Gypsy Girl 10 Hille Bobbe (The Witch of Haarlem) 13 The Jolly Toper 14 Jacobus Zaffius 15 The Merry Company 19 The Laughing Cavalier 22 Portrait of a Standing Man 24 The Regents of the Almshouse 26 Yonker Ramp and his Sweetheart 28 The Regentesses of the Almshouse 33 The Banquet of the St George Civic Guard

Halsey, William F
  served in: 3 WWI 4 WWII
  rank: 12 fleet admiral
  battle: 9 Leyte Gulf 11 Philippines 14 Solomon Islands

halt 3 end 4 balk, curb, foil, quit, rest, rout, stay, stem, stop, wait 5 abate, block, brake, break, cease, check, close, crush, delay, pause, quash, quell, stall, tarry 6 bridle, cut off, defeat, draw up, hamper, hinder, impede, linger, pull up, recess, rein in, scotch, subdue, thwart, wind up 7 heave to, inhibit, prevent, put down, repress, respite, squelch, suspend, time out 8 break off, breather, choke off, don't move, hang fire, interval, knock off, leave off, overturn, prohibit, restrain, restrict, shut down, suppress, vanquish 9 cessation, frustrate, interlude, interrupt, overthrow, terminate 10 call it a day, extinguish, shut up shop, standstill, suspension 11 come to a halt, come to a stop, discontinue, hold in check, termination 12 intermission, interruption, throttle down 13 spike one's guns 14 breathing spell, discontinuance

halting 6 ending 7 curbing 8 episodic, hesitant, stopping 9 faltering, stumbling 10 calling off, discursive, suspending 11 restraining, terminating 13 discontinuous 14 calling a halt to, putting a stop to

halting place
  Spanish: 6 posada

halutz 7 pioneer 26 person who emigrates to Israel

halve 6 bisect 9 cut in half 10 split in two 13 divide equally

Ham
  character in: 16 David Copperfield
  author: 7 Dickens

Ham
  father: 4 Noah
  brother: 4 Shem 7 Japheth
  son: 3 Put 4 Cush 6 Canaan 7 Misraim
  descendant of: 6 Hamite

Hamadryad
  form: 5 dryad
  spirit of: 4 tree

Haman
  served: 9 Ahasuerus

Hamill, Mark
  born: 9 Oakland CA
  roles: 8 Star Wars 13 Luke Skywalker 15 Return of the Jedi 20 The Empire Strikes Back

Hamilton
  capital of: 7 Bermuda

Hamilton, Charles
  character in: 15 Gone With the Wind
  author: 8 Mitchell

Hamilton, Iain
  composer of: 6 Aurora 7 Alastor 8 Sinfonia 9 Pharsalia 11 The Bermudas 18 Threnos In Time of War 20 The Royal Hunt of the Sun 21 The Catiline Conspiracy

Hamilton, Margaret
  real name: 23 Margaret Hamilton Meserve
  born: 11 Cleveland OH
  roles: 4 Cora 13 The Wizard of Oz 23 The Wicked Witch of the West

Hamito-Semitic
  language also known as: 11 Afro-Asiatic
  branch: 6 Berber, Chadic 7 Semitic 8 Cushitic, Egyptian

hamlet 4 burg 7 village 8 hick town, tank town 10 crossroads 11 whistle stop 12 one-horse town, small village 13 jerkwater town

Hamlet
  author: 18 William Shakespeare
  character: 7 Horatio, Laertes, Ophelia 8 Claudius, Gertrude, Polonius, The Ghost 11 Rosencrantz 12 Guildenstern
  skull: 6 Yorick
  castle: 8 Elsinore
  setting: 7 Denmark
  director: 15 Laurence Olivier
  cast: 11 Basil Sydney, Felix Aylmer, Jean Simmons 12 Eileen Herlie 15 Laurence Olivier
  Oscar for: 5 actor (Olivier) 7 picture

Hamlet, The
  author: 15 William Faulkner
  character: 4 Eula, Jody 6 Labove 8 Ab Snopes 9 V K Ratliff 10 Flem Snopes, Mink Snopes, Will Varner 11 Isaac Snopes 12 Henry Armstid

Hamlin, Vincent T
  creator/artist of: 8 Alley Oop

hammer 3 hit, tap 4 bang, form, make, nail 5 drive, forge, knock, pound, punch, shape, whack 6 pummel, rammer, strike 7 beat out, fashion
  type: 4 claw, jack, tack 5 gavel, steam 6 mallet, sledge 8 ballpeen 10 pile driver 12 upholsterers

Hammer, Mike
  detective created by: 14 Mickey Spillane

hammered 6 banged, beaten, shaped 7 knocked, pounded, whipped, wrought 8 battered, repeated 10 terrorized

Hammett, Dashiell
  author of: 10 Red Harvest, The Thin Man 11 The Glass Key 12 The Dain Curse 16 The Maltese Falcon
  character: 8 Sam Spade 11 Miles Archer, Nick Charles, Nora Charles 13 Continental Op

hamper 3 gag 4 balk, curb, stem 5 block, check, stall 6 fetter, hinder, hog-tie, hold up, impede, muzzle, retard, thwart 7 inhibit, prevent, shackle 8 encumber, handicap, obstruct, restrain, restrict 9 frustrate 13 interfere with

Hampton, Hope
  nickname: 22 The Duchess of Park Avenue
  born: 14 Philadelphia PA
  roles: 8 Star Dust 13 Lawful Larceny, The Road to Reno 16 The Price of a Party

hamstring 6 impair, muscle, tendon 7 cripple, disable 8 handicap 10 debilitate

Hamsun, Knut
  author of: 3 Pan 6 August, Hunger 8 Victoria 9 Mysteries, Vagabonds 16 Children of the Age 18 The Growth of the Soil

Hananiah see 8 Shadrach

hand, hands 3 aid, man, paw 4 care, fist, give, help, hold, lift, mitt, palm, pass 5 guide, power, reach 6 assist, charge, convey, helper, menial, script, worker 7 command, control, custody, deliver, keeping, laborer, ovation, present, support, workman 8 auspices, dominion, employee, guidance, handyman, hired man, longhand, meat-hook 9 assistant, associate, authority, hired hand 10 assistance, domination, management, minister to, penmanship, possession, turn over to, workingman 11 calligraphy, furnish with, handwriting, supervision 12 jurisdiction 13 member of a crew 15 burst of applause, manual extremity; round of applause

handbag 3 bag 4 grip 5 purse 6 clutch, valise 7 satchel 8 moneybag, reticule 10 pocketbook, portmanteau

handbill 5 flier 6 notice 7 leaflet 8 bulletin, circular 12 announcement 13 advertisement

handbook 5 bible 6 manual 9 guidebook 13 reference book

hand by hand
  Spanish: 9 mano a mano

handcart 4 cart 6 barrow 8 pushcart 10 handbarrow 11 wheelbarrow

handcuffs 5 cuffs, irons 6 chains 7 fetters 8 manacles, shackles 9 bracelets

hand down 4 will 5 leave 6 hand on, pass on 8 bequeath

Handel, George Frederick (Georg Friedrich)
  born: 5 Halle 7 Germany
  composer of: 4 Nero, Saul 5 Serse, Silla, Siroe, Teseo 6 Admeto, Alcina, Almira, Esther, Flavio, Jeptha, Joseph, Ottone, Samson, Semele, Xerxes 7 Amadigi, Athalia, Deborah, Lotario, Messiah, Rinaldo, Rodrigo, Solomon, Tolomeo 8 Atalanta, Berenice, Hercules, Scipione, Theodora 9 Agrippina, Radamisto, Rodelinda, Tamerlano 10 Alessandro, Belshazzar, Floridante, Water Music 12 Giulio Cesare, Il Pastor Fido, Muzio Scevola 13 Israel in Egypt, Riccardo Primo 14 Acis and Galatea, Fireworks Music 15 Alexander's Feast, Judas Maccabaeus 16 Hornpipe Concerto 19 Julius Caesar in Egypt, Ode for St Cecilia's Day 22 The Royal Fireworks Music 23 Hallelujah Organ Concerto, The Harmonious Blacksmith 24 The Triumph of Time and Truth

handful 7 minimum, modicum 10 scattering, smattering, sprinkling, thimbleful, tiny amount 11 scant amount, small number 13 small quantity

Handful of Dust, A
  author: 11 Evelyn Waugh

handgun 3 rod 5 piece, rifle 6 pistol, weapon 7 firearm, shotgun 8 revolver 9 automatic, twenty-two 12 shooting iron 20 Saturday night special

handicap 4 curb 5 limit 6 burden, defect, hamper, hinder, impede, retard, thwart 7 barrier, inhibit, repress, shackle 8 deafness, drawback, encumber, hold back, lameness, obstacle, restrain, restrict, suppress 9 blindness, detriment 10 difficulty, impediment, inhibition, limitation 11 encumbrance, restriction, shortcoming 12 disadvantage 13 inconvenience 14 stumbling block

handicapped 7 limited 8 burdened, disabled, held back, hindered, impaired, retarded 10 encumbered, restrained, restricted 13 disadvantaged

handicrafts
  god of: 10 Hephaestus, Hephaistos

handicraftsman 7 artisan 10 handworker 12 handicrafter

handiness 7 utility 8 deftness 9 dexterity 10 adroitness, usefulness 11 convenience 12 availability 13 accessibility

hand in glove 5 as one 10 side by side 13 close together

handle 3 paw, ply, run, tag, use 4 feel, grip, hilt, hold, knob, name, poke, pull, sell, work 5 carry, grasp, guide, knead, pilot, pinch, shaft, shank, steer, swing, touch, treat 6 caress, deal in, employ, finger, fondle, manage, market, pick up, stroke 7 care for, command, conduct, control, massage, moniker, operate, paw over, trade in, utilize 8 cognomen, deal with, maneuver 9 traffic in 10 manipulate, take care of 11 appellation, merchandise **12** offer for sale **13** bring into play

Handley Cross
   author: **18** Robert Smith Surtees

handout 4 alms, dole **7** freebie **19** something for nothing

hand out 4 give **5** grant **6** bestow, confer, donate **7** dole out, mete out, present **8** dispense **9** apportion **10** contribute, distribute

hand over 4 cede **5** grant, yield **6** give up, tender **7** abandon, release **8** transfer **9** deliver up, surrender **10** relinquish

handsome 4 fair **5** ample, bonny, noble **6** benign, comely, lovely, pretty **7** elegant, liberal, sightly, sizable, stately **8** abundant, generous, gracious, imposing, merciful, princely, splendid, stunning, tasteful **9** beauteous, beautiful, bountiful, exquisite, unselfish **10** attractive, benevolent, bighearted, impressive, sufficient, well-formed **11** fine-looking, good-looking, magnanimous **12** considerable, easy to look at, humanitarian **13** compassionate, easy on the eyes **16** well-proportioned

handy 4 deft, near, nigh **5** adept, on tap **6** adroit, at hand, clever, expert, on call, on hand, useful, wieldy **7** capable, helpful, skilled **8** skillful **9** available, competent, dexterous, easy to use, efficient, practical **10** accessible, convenient, manageable, obtainable, proficient **11** at one's elbow, close at hand, in readiness, ready to hand, serviceable **12** accomplished **14** nimble-fingered **15** within easy reach **16** easily accessible **17** at one's beck and call

hang 3 bow, sag **4** drop, gist, rest **5** affix, hinge, knack, lie in, lower, lynch, point, trail **6** append, attach, dangle, depend **7** incline, meaning, suspend, thought **8** lean over, let droop, repose in, string up, turn upon **9** be pendant, be pendent **11** be dependent, be subject to, bend forward, swing freely **12** be contingent, bend downward **13** revolve around **15** die on the gallows, fasten from above **16** execute by hanging, send to the gallows

hangdog 6 abject **7** ashamed **8** defeated, degraded, hopeless, resigned, wretched **9** miserable **10** browbeaten, chapfallen, humiliated, shamefaced **11** crestfallen, embarrassed, intimidated **13** guilty-looking

hang down 3 sag **5** droop

hanger-on 7 admirer, groupie **8** follower **9** sycophant

hanging object
   Japanese: **8** kakemono

hang loosely 3 bag, sag **5** droop

hangout 3 den **5** haunt

hang out 3 mix **4** live **5** dwell **6** hobnob, loiter, mingle, reside **7** consort **9** associate, be friends, pal around, run around **10** fraternize, hang around **11** keep company

hanker after 4 want **5** covet, crave, fancy **6** desire **7** long for, pine for **8** aspire to, yearn for **9** lust after **11** have a yen for, have an eye on, hunger after, thirst after

hankering 3 yen **4** itch, urge **6** aching, desire, hunger, pining, thirst **7** craving, longing **8** yearning

Hanna-Barbera
   creators of: **8** Yogi Bear **14** The Flintstones

Hannah
   husband: **7** Elkanah
   son: **6** Samuel

Hanoi
   capital of: **7** Vietnam **12** North Vietnam
   river: **3** Red **4** Yuan **7** Song Koi
   delta: **6** Tonkin
   airport: **6** Gia Lam

Hans Brinker
   author: **5** (Mary Elizabeth Mapes) Dodge
   character: **4** Raff **5** Gleck, Hilda **6** Gretel **7** Boekman, Mevrouw

Hansel and Gretel
   author: **13** Grimm Brothers (Jakob and Wilhelm)
   opera by: **11** Humperdinck
   character: **5** Witch

Hans Kristian
   character in: **16** Giants of the Earth
   author: **7** Rolvaag

Hanson, Howard
   born: **7** Wahoo NE
   composer of: **5** Sacra (symphony No 5) **6** Nordic (symphony No 1) **7** Requiem (symphony No 4) **8** Romantic (symphony No 2) **10** Merry-Mount

Hap see **4** Apis

haphazard 6 casual, chance, fitful, random **7** aimless, chaotic **8** careless, on-and-off, slapdash, sporadic **9** arbitrary, hit-or-miss **10** accidental, disordered, disorderly, fortuitous, undesigned, undirected, unthinking **11** purposeless, unorganized **12** disorganized, unmethodical, unsystematic **14** indiscriminate, unpremeditated **15** catch-as-catch-can

Hapi see **4** Apis, Nile

hapless 5 lousy **6** cursed, jinxed, no-good, rotten, woeful **7** forlorn, unhappy, unlucky **8** accursed, hopeless, ill-fated, luckless, wretched **9** miserable **10** ill-starred **11** star-crossed, unfortunate

happen 5 arise, ensue, occur **6** appear, befall, betide, crop up, result **7** turn out **8** become of, spring up **9** be borne by, be the case, come about, eventuate, take place, transpire **10** be one's fate, come to pass **11** be endured by **12** be suffered by **13** be one's fortune, fall to one's lot, present itself

happening 4 case **5** event **6** advent, affair, matter **7** episode **8** accident, incident, occasion **9** adventure, incidence **10** experience, occurrence, proceeding **11** vicissitude **12** circumstance, happenstance **20** just one of those things

happenstance 4 luck **6** chance **8** accident, fortuity

happiness 3 joy **4** glee **5** bliss, cheer, mirth **6** gaiety **7** comfort, content, delight, ecstasy, elation, jollity, rapture **8** blessing, felicity, gladness, pleasure **9** beatitude, enjoyment, merriment, rejoicing, transport 10 cheeriness, exuberance, exultation, jubilation 11 blessedness, contentment, high spirits 12 cheerfulness, satisfaction 13 gratification 16 lightheartedness, sense of well-being

happy 3 fit, gay 4 glad, meet 5 lucky 6 elated, joyful, joyous, timely 7 content, fitting, gleeful, pleased, tickled 8 blissful, cheerful, cheering, ecstatic, exultant, jubilant, pleasant, pleasing 9 agreeable, contented, delighted, exuberant, favorable, fortunate, gratified, opportune, overjoyed, rapturous, rhapsodic 10 auspicious, convenient, delightful, felicitous, gratifying, propitious, seasonable 11 exhilarated, tickled pink, transported 12 advantageous 13 in high spirits 15 in seventh heaven

Happy Days
character: 6 Arnold, Fonzie 10 Ralph Malph 11 Potsie Weber 12 Chachi Arcola 14 Pinky Tuscadero 15 Chuck Cunningham 16 Alfred Delvecchio, Arthur Fonzarelli, Howard Cunningham, Joanie Cunningham, Leather Tuscadero, Marion Cunningham, Richie Cunningham
cast: 8 Roz Kelly 9 Donny Most, Erin Moran, Pat Morita, Ron Howard, Scott Baio, Tom Bosley 10 Al Molinaro, Marion Ross, Suzi Quatro 12 Henry Winkler 13 Anson Williams, Gavan O'Herlihy 15 Randolph Roberts

happy-go-lucky 6 blithe 7 buoyant, flighty, relaxed 8 carefree, careless, feckless, heedless, skittish 9 easygoing, unworried 10 insouciant, nonchalant, optimistic, untroubled 11 free-and-easy, unconcerned 12 devil-may-care, light-hearted 13 irresponsible 14 scatterbrained 23 without a worry in the world

harangue 6 speech, tirade 7 lecture, oration 8 diatribe, scolding 9 contumely, sermonize 12 denunciation, vituperation

Harare
capital of: 8 Zimbabwe

harass 3 cow, irk, vex 4 bait, ride 5 annoy, beset, bully, harry, hound, tease, worry 6 attack, badger, bother, heckle, hector, pester, plague 7 assault, bedevil, besiege, disturb, torment 8 browbeat, distress, irritate 9 persecute 10 discommode, exasperate, intimidate 14 raid frequently

harbinger 4 clue, omen 5 token 6 herald, symbol 7 portent 8 signaler 9 announcer, first sign, precursor 10 forerunner, indication, proclaimer

Harbonna 6 eunuch

harbor 3 bay 4 cove, dock, feel, goal, hide, hold, keep, pier, port, quay 5 basin, haven, house, inlet, lodge, wharf 6 asylum, billet, foster, lagoon, refuge, retain, shield, take in 7 care for, cling to, conceal, nurture, protect, quarter, retreat, shelter 8 hideaway, keep safe, maintain, muse over, terminus 9 brood over, sanctuary 11 concealment, destination, hiding place 12 give

refuge to 13 bear in the mind, terminal point 18 protected anchorage

harbors
god of: 8 Portunus
goddess of: 6 Matutu

Harcorates *see* 5 Horus

hard 3 sad 4 cold, firm, mean, ugly 5 cruel, eager, harsh, heavy, rigid, rough, solid, stern, stiff, stony, tight, tough 6 bitter, brutal, fierce, firmly, keenly, knotty, severe, steely, strict, strong, sullen, thorny, unkind 7 angrily, arduous, callous, closely, complex, cryptic, eagerly, earnest, harmful, heavily, hostile, hurtful, inhuman, intense, onerous, sharply, solidly, tightly, to heart, vicious, violent, willing, zealous 8 animated, baffling, critical, diligent, exacting, fiercely, forceful, forcibly, hardened, intently, involved, pitiless, powerful, puzzling, rocklike, ruthless, severely, spirited, spiteful, steadily, strongly, stubborn, untiring, venomous, vigorous 9 arduously, assiduous, bellicose, confusing, difficult, earnestly, energetic, furiously, Herculean, insulting, intensely, intricate, laborious, malicious, merciless, painfully, rancorous, seriously, strenuous, stringent, unbending, unpliable, unsparing, violently, wearisome 10 burdensome, diligently, forcefully, formidable, impervious, implacable, inexorable, inflexible, lamentable, melancholy, oppressive, perplexing, persistent, powerfully, relentless, resolutely, rigorously, tormenting, unbearable, unflagging, unfriendly, unpleasant, untiringly, unyielding, vigorously, vindictive 11 acrimonious, agonizingly, assiduously, belligerent, bewildering, complicated, distressing, emotionally, hardhearted, industrious, insensitive, intolerable, laboriously, persevering, troublesome, unceasingly, unmalleable, unrelenting, unremitting, unsparingly 12 antagonistic, cantankerous, determinedly, disagreeable, enterprising, impenetrable, persistently, relentlessly, thick-skinned, unfathomable, unflaggingly 13 conscientious, disheartening, distressfully, energetically, indefatigable, industriously, with much anger 14 uncompromising, with much sorrow 15 conscientiously 16 with all one's might 18 with strong feelings

hard-and-fast 3 set 6 strict 7 binding 8 exacting, rigorous 9 mandatory, unbending 10 compelling, compulsory, inflexible, obligatory, undeniable, unyielding 11 irrevocable, unalterable, unremitting 12 indisputable 13 incontestable 14 uncompromising

Hardcastle family
characters in: 18 She Stoops to Conquer
author: 9 Goldsmith

hard drinker 3 sot 4 lush, soak, wino 5 drunk, rummy, souse, toper 6 barfly, boozer 7 guzzler, imbiber, tippler 8 drunkard 9 alcoholic 11 dipsomaniac 14 problem drinker 16 two-fisted drinker

harden 3 dry, gel, set 4 cake, fire, firm 5 adapt, adjust, blunt, enure, inure, steel 6 anneal, freeze, season, temper 7 calcify, callous, congeal, fortify, petrify, stiffen, thicken, toughen 8 accustom, solidify 9 fossilize, make tough, reinforce 10 discipline, invigorate, strengthen 11 crystallize, turn to stone 12 restrengthen 13 make unfeeling

hard feelings 5 anger 6 grudge, hatred, rancor 7 ill will 8 acrimony 9 animosity, hostility 10 antagonism, bitterness spitefulness

hardheaded 4 cool 5 balky 6 astute, mulish, poised, shrewd 7 willful 8 contrary, sensible, stubborn 9 immovable, objective, obstinate, pigheaded, practical, pragmatic, realistic, unbending, unfeeling 10 coolheaded, impersonal, inflexible, refractory, self-willed, unyielding 11 down-to-earth, intractable, tough-minded, unemotional, unflappable 14 self-controlled

hardhearted 4 cold, hard, mean 5 cruel, stony 6 brutal 7 callous, inhuman 8 pitiless, ruthless, uncaring 9 heartless, merciless, unfeeling, unpitying, unsparing 11 coldblooded, indifferent, insensitive, remorseless, unforgiving 12 cruelhearted, thick-skinned 13 unsympathetic

hardihood 4 grit 5 pluck, spunk 6 mettle 7 courage 8 strength 9 endurance, fortitude 10 resolution 12 resoluteness

Harding, Warren Gamaliel
  presidential rank: 11 twenty-ninth
  party: 10 Republican
  state represented: 2 OH
  defeated: 3 (James Middleton) Cox, (William Wesley) Cox 4 (Eugene Victor) Debs 7 (Aaron Sherman) Watkins 8 (Robert Charles) Macauley 11 (Parley Parker) Christensen
  vice president: 8 (Calvin) Coolidge
  cabinet:
    state: 6 (Charles Evans) Hughes
    treasury: 6 (Andrew William) Mellon
    war: 5 (John Wingate) Weeks
    attorney general: 9 (Harry Micajah) Daugherty
    navy: 5 (Edwin) Denby
    postmaster general: 3 (Harry Stewart) New 4 (Hubert) Work, (William Harrison) Hays
    interior: 4 (Albert Bacon) Fall, (Hubert) Work
    agriculture: 7 (Henry Cantwell) Wallace
    commerce: 6 (Herbert Clark) Hoover
    labor: 5 (James John) Davis
  born: 9 Corsica OH (now Blooming Grove)
  died: 2 CA (while in office) 12 San Francisco
  buried: 8 Marion OH
  education:
    College: 11 Ohio Central
  religion: 7 Baptist
  interests: 5 poker

  played musical instrument: 6 cornet 7 helicon
  political career: 8 US Senate 15 Ohio State Senate
  lieutenant governor of: 4 Ohio
  civilian career: 9 publisher 13 schoolteacher 15 newspaper editor 17 insurance salesman
  notable events of lifetime/term:
    Act: 21 Fordney-McCumber Tariff
    peace treaty with: 7 Austria, Germany, Hungary
    scandal: 10 Teapot Dome (oil)
    Treaty: 9 Five-Power, Nine-Power 16 Four-Power Pacific
  father: 11 George Tryon
  mother: 6 Phoebe (Elizabeth Dickerson)
  stepmother: 4 Mary (Alice Severns) 6 Eudora (Kelley Luvisi)
  siblings: 11 George Tryon 12 Mary Clarissa 14 Charity Malvina, Phoebe Caroline 15 Abigail Victoria 16 Charles Alexander, Eleanor Priscilla
  wife: 8 Florence (Kling DeWolfe)
  children:
    illegitimate daughter: 21 Elizabeth Ann Christian (by mistress Nan Britton)

hardly 4 just, only 6 barely, rarely 7 faintly, in no way 8 not often, not quite, scarcely 9 almost not, by no means 10 in no manner, uncommonly 12 certainly not, infrequently 13 not by any means 15 not by a great deal

hardnosed 4 hard 5 harsh, rigid, stern, tough 6 severe, shrewd, strict 8 critical, hard-line, exacting, stubborn 9 demanding, unbending, unsparing 10 hardheaded, inflexible, no-nonsense, unyielding 11 calculating, intractable 12 unsentimental 14 uncompromising

Hardouin-Mansart, Jules
  architect of: 8 Orangery (Versailles) 12 Chateau du Val (St Germain-en-Laye), Grand Trianon (Versailles), Place Vendome (Paris) 15 Chateau de Clagny (Versailles) 16 Galerie des Glaces (Hall of Mirrors at Versailles), Les Invalides (Church of the Dome, Paris)

hard-pressed 7 harried, put-upon 9 embattled 10 overworked

hardship 3 woe 4 load 5 agony, grief 6 burden, misery, ordeal, sorrow 7 problem, travail, trouble 8 handicap 9 adversity, privation, suffering 10 affliction, difficulty, misfortune 11 cross to bear, encumbrance, tribulation, unhappiness 12 wretchedness

hard sledding 8 tough job 10 difficulty, tough going, uphill work 11 arduousness 13 laboriousness

hard times 4 bust 5 slump 8 bad times 9 recession 10 depression

Hard Times
  author: 11 Studs Terkel

Hard Times
  author: 14 Charles Dickens
  character: 9 Sissy Jupe 10 Mrs Sparsit 11 Mr Bounderby 12 Tom Gradgrind 14

James Harthouse 15 Louisa Gradgrind, Thomas Gradgrind 16 Stephen Blackpool

hard to catch 4 foxy, wily 6 crafty, shifty, tricky 7 elusive, evasive 8 slippery

hard to grasp 7 elusive 8 baffling, puzzling, slippery 9 difficult 10 perplexing 16 incomprehensible

hard to manage 6 unruly 7 froward, willful 8 perverse, stubborn 9 difficult, fractious, obstinate 10 inflexible, refractory, unyielding 11 intractable 12 obstreperous, unmanageable

hard to please 5 fussy, picky 7 exigent, finicky 8 critical 10 fastidious, meticulous, particular

hard to understand 7 complex 9 difficult, intricate 10 perplexing 11 bewildering, complicated

Hardwick, Elizabeth
  author of: 11 Simple Truth 12 A View of My Own 15 Sleepless Nights 20 Seduction and Betrayal

Hardwicke, Sir Cedric
  born: 3 Lye 7 England
  roles: 14 On Borrowed Time 21 Livingstone and Stanley 36 A Connecticut Yankee in King Arthur's Court

hardwood 4 wood 8 leadwood
  kind: 3 ash, elm, oak 4 teak 5 beech, birch, maple 6 cherry, linden, walnut 7 hickory 8 mahogany, rosewood, sycamore

hardworking 8 diligent, sedulous 9 assiduous 11 industrious, persevering 12 enterprising 13 conscientious

hardy 3 fit 4 hale 5 tough 6 hearty, mighty, robust, rugged, strong, sturdy 7 healthy 8 stalwart, vigorous 9 strapping 10 ablebodied 12 in fine fettle 13 physically fit 15 in good condition

Hardy, Oliver
  partner: 10 Stan Laurel
  born: 8 Harlem GA
  roles: 8 Pardon Us 9 Saps at Sea 10 Way Out West

Hardy, Thomas
  author of: 10 The Dynasts 14 Jude the Obscure 20 The Return of the Native 21 Tess of the D'Urbervilles 22 Far from the Madding Crowd, The Mayor of Casterbridge
  mythical county: 6 Wessex

hare
  constellation of: 5 Lepus
  group of: 4 down, husk

harebrained 5 silly, wacko, wacky 7 asinine, flighty, foolish 8 skittish 9 dimwitted, senseless 10 half-witted 11 empty-headed 12 simple-minded 13 rattlebrained 14 featherbrained, scatterbrained

Haredale, Reuben
  character in: 12 Barnaby Rudge
  author: 7 Dickens

harem 5 serai 6 purdah, serail, senana, zenana 8 love nest, seraglio

Hargreaves, James
  nationality: 7 English
  inventor of: 13 spinning jenny

Harker, Jonathan
  character in: 7 Dracula
  author: 6 Stoker

harlot 3 pro 4 bawd, doxy, jade, pros, slut, tart 5 whore 6 chippy, wanton 7 jezebel, trollop 8 call girl, mistress, strumpet 9 courtesan, kept woman 10 prostitute 11 fallen woman 12 painted woman, scarlet woman, streetwalker

Harlow, Jean
  real name: 16 Harlean Carpenter
  nickname: 15 Blonde Bombshell
  born: 12 Kansas City MO
  roles: 7 Red Dust 8 Riffraff, Saratoga 9 Bombshell, China Seas 11 Hell's Angels, Libeled Lady 13 Dinner at Eight

harm 3 ill, mar, sin 4 evil, hurt, maim, pain, ruin, vice 5 abuse, agony, havoc, spoil, wound, wrong 6 damage, debase, deface, ill-use, impair, injure, injury, malice, misuse, trauma 7 blemish, cripple, degrade, scourge 8 aggrieve, calamity, hardship, iniquity, maltreat, mischief, villainy 9 adversity, detriment, disfigure, suffering, undermine 10 defacement, immorality, impairment, misfortune, sinfulness, wickedness 11 destruction, devastation, malevolence 12 do violence to 13 deterioration, maliciousness

harmful 3 bad 7 adverse, baneful, hurtful, ruinous 8 damaging 9 dangerous, injurious, unhealthy 10 pernicious 11 deleterious, destructive, detrimental, unhealthful, unwholesome 17 counterproductive

harmless 4 mild, safe 6 benign, gentle 7 sinless 8 innocent, nontoxic 9 blameless, guiltless, incorrupt, innocuous, peaceable 10 not hurtful 11 inoffensive 12 not dangerous 15 unobjectionable

harmlessness 6 safety 9 innocence 10 gentleness 11 nontoxicity 12 nonvirulence 13 innocuousness 15 inoffensiveness

Harmon, Young John
  character in: 15 Our Mutual Friend
  author: 7 Dickens

Harmonia
  father: 4 Ares
  mother: 9 Aphrodite
  husband: 6 Cadmus
  daughter: 3 Ino

Harmonides see 9 Phereclus

harmonious 5 sweet 6 dulcet 7 amiable, cordial, unified 8 amicable, friendly, in accord, matching 9 agreeable, congenial, in harmony, melodious 10 compatible, consistent, euphonious, likeminded 11 coordinated, harmonizing, in agreement, mellifluous, sympathetic 12 synchronized 13 sweet-sounding 17 agreeably combined

harmonize 3 fit 4 jibe, mesh 5 agree, blend, chime, tally 6 accord, adjust, attune 7 conform 8 be in tune 9 reconcile 10 complement, correspond, go together 13 sing in harmony

harmony 5 amity, order, peace, unity 6 accord 7 balance, concord 8 matching, symmetry, sympathy 9 agreement, unanimity 10 conformity, fellowship, friendship, proportion 11 amicability, cooperation, correlation, parallelism 12 congeniality, coordination, mutual regard 13 compatibility, mutual fitness 14 like-mindedness 15 organic totality 17 good understanding 19 harmonious relations, pleasing consistency 21 concurrence in opinions

Harmony
goddess of: 9 Concordia

harness 4 curb, rein, tugs, yoke 5 lines, reins, rig up 6 bridle, collar, employ, halter, muzzle, straps, tackle, traces 7 exploit, hitch up, utilize 8 restrain 9 caparison, trappings 12 put in harness, render useful 13 control and use, turn to account 14 make productive 22 direct to a useful purpose

Harold
author: 18 Edward Bulwer-Lytton

Harper, Joe
character in: 9 Tom Sawyer
author: 5 Twain

Harphlyce
father: 8 Clymenus
husband: 7 Alastor
vocation: 8 huntress
violated by: 8 Clymenus
killed by: 8 Clymenus 9 shepherds

Harpina
father: 6 Asopus
son: 8 Oenomaus

harp on 7 dwell on 9 reiterate 18 repeat persistently

Harpy
form: 7 monster
head of: 5 woman
body of: 4 bird
father: 7 Thaumas
mother: 7 Electra
names: 5 Aello 7 Celaeno, Ocypete, Podarge

harridan 3 hag 5 crone, shrew, witch 6 virago 8 battle-ax, old crone 12 mean old woman

harried 5 upset 7 worried 8 harassed, troubled 10 distraught

Harris, Joel Chandler
author of: 10 Uncle Remus (His Songs and Sayings)

Harris, Julie
real name: 14 Julia Ann Harris
born: 18 Grosse Pointe Park MI
roles: 6 Harper 10 East of Eden, I Am a Camera 11 The Haunting 14 A Shot in the Dark, The Hiding Place 19 The Last of Mrs Lincoln 21 The Member of the Wedding 22 Requiem for a Heavyweight 27 And Miss Reardon Drinks a Little

Harris, Richard
born: 7 Ireland 8 Limerick
roles: 7 Camelot 8 Cromwell 15 A Man Called Horse 16 The Molly Maguires, This Sporting Life 17 Mutiny on the Bounty, The Guns of Navarone 20 The Cassandra Crossing 26 The Return of a Man Called Horse

Harris, Roy
composer of: 16 Folksong Symphony 17 American Portraits 27 When Johnny Comes Marching Home (overture)

Harrison, Benjamin
nickname: 3 Ben 9 Little Ben
presidential rank: 11 twenty-third
party: 10 Republican
state represented: 2 IN
defeated: 4 (Clinton Bowen) Fisk 6 (James Langdon) Curtis 7 (Robert Hall) Cowdrey 8 (Albert) Redstone, (Alson Jenness) Streeter, (Belva Ann Bennett) Lockwood 9 (Grover) Cleveland
vice president: 6 (Levi Parsons) Morton
cabinet:
state: 6 (James Gillespie) Blaine, (John Watson) Foster
treasury: 6 (Charles) Foster, (William) Windom
war: 6 (Stephen Benton) Elkins 7 (Redfield) Proctor
attorney general: 6 (William Henry Harrison) Miller
navy: 5 (Benjamin Franklin) Tracy
postmaster general: 9 (John) Wanamaker
interior: 5 (John Willock) Noble
agriculture: 4 (Jeremiah McLain) Rusk
born: 11 North Bend OH
died/buried: 14 Indianapolis IN
education:
prep school: 14 Farmer's College
University: 21 Miami University of Ohio
later studied: 3 law
religion: 12 Presbyterian
interests: 7 fishing, hunting 8 swimming
author: 17 This Country of Ours 20 Views of An Ex-President
political career: 8 US Senate
city attorney: 12 Indianapolis
reporter of: 19 Indiana supreme court
secretary of: 31 Republican state central committee
civilian career: 6 lawyer 12 law professor
military service: 8 Civil War 16 brigadier general
notable events of lifetime/term:
Act: 16 Dependent Pension, Sherman Anti-Trust 21 Sherman Silver Purchase
Tariff: 8 McKinley
father: 9 John Scott
mother: 9 Elizabeth (Ramsey Irwin)
siblings: 8 Mary Jane 9 John Irwin, John Scott 10 Anna Symmes, James Irwin 12 James Findlay 13 Carter Bassett 14 Archibald Irwin
half sisters: 9 Elizabeth 13 Sarah Lucretia
wife: 4 Mary (Scott Lord Dimmick) 8 Caroline (Lavinia Scott)
children: 9 Elizabeth, Mary Scott 15 Russell Benjamin

Harrison, Lou
  born: 10 Portland OR
  composer of: 8 Rapunzel, Solstice 13
  Changing World 15 Four Strict Songs,
  Johnny Appleseed 17 The Perilous
  Chapel 19 Almanac of the Seasons 22 At
  the Tomb of Charles Ives
Harrison, Peter
  architect of: 11 Brick Market (Newport
  RI), King's Chapel (Boston) 14 Redwood
  Library (Newport RI), Touro Synagogue
  (Newport RI)
Harrison, Rex
  real name: 21 Reginald Carey Harrison
  nickname: 8 Sexy Rexy
  wife: 10 Kay Kendall 11 Lilli Palmer 13
  Rachel Roberts
  born: 6 Huyton 7 England
  roles: 9 Cleopatra 10 My Fair Lady (Os-
  car) 12 Blithe Spirit 14 Doctor Dolittle 16
  The Foxes of Harrow 17 Unfaithfully
  Yours 18 The Ghost and Mrs Muir 20
  Anna and the King of Siam
Harrison, Wallace K
  architect of: 13 Lincoln Center (NYC) 14
  Socony Building (NYC) 17 Rockefeller
  Center (NYC) 22 Metropolitan Opera
  House (NYC) 25 United Nations Headquarters (NYC) 34 Nelson A Rockefeller
  Empire State Plaza (Albany NY), ALCOA
  Building (Pittsburgh, with Max Abramovitz)
Harrison, William Henry
  nickname: 6 Old Tip 22 The Washington
  of the West
  presidential rank: 5 ninth
  party: 4 Whig
  state represented: 2 OH
  defeated: 6 (James G) Birney 8 (Martin)
  Van Buren
  vice president: 5 (John) Tyler
  cabinet:
    state: 7 (Daniel) Webster
    treasury: 5 (Thomas) Ewing
    war: 4 (John) Bell
    attorney general: 10 (John Jordan)
    Crittenden
    navy: 6 (George Edmund) Badger
    postmaster general: 7 (Francis)
    Granger
  born: 2 VA 17 Charles City County 18
  Berkeley plantation
  died: 12 Washington DC
  buried: 11 North Bend OH
  education: 16 privately tutored (at home)
  College: 13 Hampden-Sydney (did not
  graduate)
  later studied: 8 medicine
  religion: 12 Episcopalian
  political career: 8 US Senate 11 state
  Senate 24 US House of Representatives
  governor of: 16 Indiana Territory
  minister: 8 Columbia
  civilian career: 6 farmer 7 soldier
  military service: 6 US Army 12 major
  general 19 War of Eighteen Twelve

  battle: 6 (the) Thames 8 Lake Erie 10
  Tippecanoe
  notable events of lifetime/term: 24
  Land Act of Eighteen Hundred
  campaign slogan: 21 Tippecanoe and
  Tyler too
  treaty of: 10 Greenville
  father: 8 Benjamin
  mother: 9 Elizabeth (Bassett)
  siblings: 3 Ann 4 Lucy 5 Sarah 8 Benjamin 9 Elizabeth 13 Carter Bassett
  wife: 4 Anna (Tuthill Symmes)
  children: 8 Benjamin 9 John Scott 10
  Mary Symmes 11 Anna Tuthill 12 James
  Findlay, William Henry 13 Carter Bassett,
  Lucy Singleton 16 Elizabeth Bassett,
  John Cleves Symmes
harrowing 7 fearful, painful 8 alarming,
chilling 9 traumatic, upsetting 10 disturbing, terrifying, tormenting 11 distressing,
frightening 13 bloodcurdling
harry 3 irk, vex 4 bait, gall, raid, ride, sack
5 annoy, beset, bully, haunt, hound, tease,
worry 6 badger, bother, harass, heckle,
hector, pester, plague 7 disturb, pillage,
plunder, torment, trouble 8 distract, distress, irritate 9 terrorize 10 exasperate, intimidate 16 attack repeatedly
harsh 4 hard, mean 5 cruel, raspy, rough,
sharp, stern 6 bitter, brutal, hoarse, severe, shrill, unkind 7 abusive, caustic, glaring, grating, jarring, rasping, raucous,
squawky 8 piercing, pitiless, ruthless,
scratchy, strident, ungentle 9 Draconian,
heartless, merciless, too bright, unmusical,
unsparing 10 discordant, overbright, unpleasant, vindictive 11 cacophonous, hardhearted 12 uncharitable, unharmonious
harshness 5 rigor 7 cruelty, discord 9 brutality, cacophony, raspiness, roughness,
sternness, stridency 10 dissonance, shrill-
ness, unkindness 12 ungentleness 13
heartlessness 14 unpleasantness 15 hardheartedness
Hart, Johnny
  creator/artist of: 2 B C 13 The Wizard of
  Id
Hart, Moss
  author of: 15 Once in a Lifetime 20 You
  Can't Take It with You (with George S
  Kaufman) 21 The Man Who Came to Dinner (with George S Kaufman)
Harte, Bret
  author of: 20 The Luck of Roaring Camp
  22 The Outcasts of Poker Flat
Hartford
  hockey team: 7 Whalers
Harthouse, James
  character in: 9 Hard Times
  author: 7 Dickens
Hartley, Vivian Mary
  real name of: 11 Vivien Leigh
harum-scarum 5 giddy 6 wildly 7 erratic,
flighty, foolish 8 careless, confused 9 aimlessly, haphazard, impetuous, impulsive,
unplanned, unsettled 10 bewildered, recklessly, unreliable 11 haphazardly, hare-

brained, impulsively **12** absent-minded, capriciously, disorganized, inconsistent, undependable **13** rattlebrained **14** feather-brained, scatterbrained

harvest 3 cut, mow **4** crop, gain, pick, reap **5** amass, fruit, pluck, yield **6** gather, haying, mowing, output, result, return, reward **7** benefit, collect, cutting, picking, produce, product, reaping **8** fruition, gleaning, proceeds **9** aftermath, amassment, gathering, outgrowth **10** accumulate, collection, harvesting **12** accumulation **13** season's growth

harvest time 4 fall **6** autumn **8** maturity **12** Indian summer

Harvey
   director: 11 Henry Koster
   based on play by: 9 Mary Chase
   cast: 8 Peggy Dow **12** James Stewart (Elwood P Dowd) **13** Cecil Kellaway, Josephine Hull
   Oscar for: 17 supporting actress (Hull)

Harvey, Laurence
   real name: 19 Larushka Misch Skikne
   wife: 16 Margaret Leighton
   born: 9 Lithuania, Yomishkis
   roles: 7 Darling **12** Life at the Top, Room at the Top **14** Of Human Bondage, Summer and Smoke **16** Butterfield Eight **17** Walk on the Wild Side

Harvey, William
   field: 7 anatomy
   nationality: 7 British
   discovered: 18 circulation of blood

Hasen, Irwin
   creator/artist of: 5 Dondi **9** Goldbergs **11** Wonder Woman **12** Green Lantern

hash out 6 review **7** discuss **8** consider, talk over

hasp 4 lock **5** catch, clasp, latch **7** closure **8** fastener

Hassam, (Frederick) Childe
   born: 12 Dorchester MA
   artwork: 13 Southwest Wind **14** Summer Sunlight, Washington Arch **15** Against the Light **23** Boston Commons at Twilight

hassle 3 bug, row, vex **5** annoy, fight, harry, hound, scrap, set-to **6** badger, battle, bother, harass, tussle **7** contest, dispute, quarrel **8** argument, conflict, squabble, struggle **9** persecute

hassock 4 boss, pess, seat, tuft, weed **5** bunch, chair, group, trush **6** buffet, plants, tuffet **7** ottoman, tussock **9** footstool, vegetable

hasta la vista 6 good-by, so long **7** goodbye **12** until I see you **16** until we meet again

hasta manana 13 until tomorrow **14** see you tomorrow

haste 4 rush **5** hurry, speed **8** celerity, dispatch, rapidity, rashness **9** fleetness, quickness, swiftness **10** expedition, speediness, undue speed **11** hurriedness **12** recklessness **13** careless hurry, impetuousness, impulsiveness, precipitation

hasten 3 fly, run **4** bolt, dart, dash, flit, jump, race, rush **5** egg on, hurry, impel, speed, whisk **6** hustle, incite, scurry, sprint, urge on **7** advance, drive on, hurry on, hurry up, promote, quicken, scamper, scuttle, speed up **8** expedite, make time **10** accelerate, lose no time **11** go full blast, precipitate, push forward **12** step on the gas **13** go on the double **14** step right along **15** go like lightning, make short work of, work against time **20** go hell-bent for leather

hastily 4 fast **5** apace **6** pronto, rashly **7** quickly **8** promptly, speedily **9** hurriedly, like a shot, posthaste, summarily **10** carelessly, heedlessly, recklessly, too quickly **11** impetuously, impulsively, on the double **12** lickety-split, straightaway **13** precipitately, thoughtlessly **18** hell-bent for leather **20** like greased lightning, on the spur of the moment

Hastings, Thomas see **17** Carrere, John Merven

hasty 4 fast, rash **5** brief, fleet, quick, rapid, swift **6** abrupt, prompt, rushed, speedy **7** cursory, hurried, passing **8** fleeting, headlong, heedless, reckless **9** impetuous, impulsive, momentary **10** breathless **11** precipitate, superficial, unduly quick **12** quick as a wink **19** without deliberation

hat
   French: 7 chapeau

hatch 4 plan, plot **5** frame **6** cook up, create, design, devise, evolve, invent, make up **7** concoct, dream up, fashion, produce, think up **8** conceive, contrive **9** construct, fabricate, formulate, improvise, originate **10** bring forth **11** give birth to, manufacture

hatchlings 5 brood, young **6** chicks **9** offspring

hate 5 abhor, dread, venom **6** animus, detest, enmity, hatred, loathe, malice, rancor **7** be sorry, despise, dislike, wince at **8** acrimony, aversion, be sick of, distaste, execrate, loathing **9** abominate, animosity, antipathy, be tired of, disliking, hostility, not care to **10** abhorrence, be averse to, feel sick at, recoil from, repugnance, resentment, shrink from **11** abomination, be hostile to, be reluctant, be unwilling, detestation, malevolence, wish to avoid **12** be repelled by **14** have no taste for, hold in contempt, revengefulness, vindictiveness **16** bear malice toward, have no stomach for **17** feel disinclined to, not have the heart to **19** regard as distasteful

hateful 4 evil, foul, mean, ugly, vile **5** nasty **6** odious, sinful, wicked **7** heinous **8** infamous, scornful **9** abhorrent, atrocious, loathsome, monstrous, obnoxious, offensive, repellent, repugnant, revolting, sickening **10** abominable, deplorable, despicable, detestable, disdainful, disgusting, forbidding, full of hate, irritating, unbearable, unpleasant, villainous **11** distasteful, intolerable, unendurable **12** contemptible, contemptuous, insufferable **13** objectionable

Hathor
  origin: 8 Egyptian
  goddess of: 3 joy 4 love
  symbol: 4 ears, head 5 horns
  patron of: 5 dance, music
  personifies: 3 sky
Hat on the Bed, The
  author: 9 John O'Hara
hatred 4 hate 5 venom 6 animus, enmity, malice, rancor 7 disgust, dislike, ill will 8 acrimony, aversion, bad blood, distaste, loathing 9 animosity, antipathy, hostility, revulsion 10 abhorrence, antagonism, bitterness, repugnance, resentment 11 abomination, detestation, malevolence 12 revengefulness, vindictiveness
haughtiness 4 airs 5 pride 7 conceit, hauteur 8 snobbery 9 arrogance 10 snootiness 13 condescension 14 disdainfulness, high-handedness 16 superciliousness
haughty 5 aloof 6 lordly, snooty, uppish, uppity 7 high-hat, stuck-up 8 arrogant, scornful, snobbish 9 conceited, officious 10 disdainful, high-handed, hoity-toity 11 highfalutin, overbearing, overly proud, patronizing, swell-headed 12 contemptuous 13 condescending, high and mighty
haul 3 bag, lug, tow, tug 4 cart, drag, draw, gain, jerk, move, pull, swag, take, tote, yank 5 booty, bring, carry, catch, fetch, heave, truck, yield 6 convey, profit, remove, reward, spoils, wrench 7 capture, takings 9 transport
haunches 4 buns, rear, rump, seat 5 nates 7 rear end 8 buttocks 9 fundament, posterior 12 hindquarters
haunt 3 vex 4 beset, worry 6 live in, obsess, plague, prey on 7 disturb, terrify, torment, trouble, weigh on 8 distress, frequent, frighten 9 hang out at, preoccupy, terrorize 10 hang around, hover about, loiter near, visit often 11 beat a path to 12 linger around
haunts 3 den 4 cave, hole, lair, nest 6 burrow 7 hangout 8 hideaway 9 waterhole 10 rendezvous 12 meeting place 14 gathering place 15 stamping grounds
Hauptmann, Gerhart
  author of: 10 Before Dawn, The Weavers
haute couture 11 high fashion
haute cuisine 11 fine cooking 14 gourmet cooking
hauteur 5 swank 7 conceit, disdain 8 snobbery 9 arrogance, loftiness 10 snootiness 11 haughtiness 12 affectedness, snobbishness 13 condescension 14 disdainfulness, high-handedness 16 superciliousness 19 patronizing attitude
haut monde 5 elite 10 blue bloods, upper class, upper crust 11 aristocracy, high society 14 creme de la creme
Havana
  capital of: 4 Cuba
  gulf: 6 Mexico
  landmark: 15 Cabaret Parisien 16 Castillo del Morro 17 Castillode la Punta,

Jose Marti Monument 18 Castillo de la Atares, Castillo de la Fuerza, Garcia Lorca Theater 19 Maximo Gomez Monument 21 Latinamericano Stadium 22 Academy of Science of Cuba
  river: 10 (Rio) Almendares
  Spanish: 8 La Habana
Havasupai, Supai
  location: 7 Arizona 11 Grand Canyon
  related to: 7 Yavapai 8 Hualapai
have 3 buy, eat, get, own, use 4 bear, fool, gain, gull, hold, host, keep, make, must 5 beget, carry, cheat, drink, enjoy, force, grasp, ought, smoke, trick 6 accept, affirm, compel, harbor, obtain, outwit, permit, retain, suffer 7 achieve, acquire, defraud, exhibit, possess, realize, receive, swindle 8 comprise, maintain, manifest, outsmart, perceive, tolerate 9 encompass, encounter, partake of, recognize, victimize 10 comprehend, experience, understand
have a fancy for 4 want 5 covet, crave 6 desire 7 long for, wish for 8 yearn for 11 hanker after, have a yen for
have a go at 3 try 6 hazard, tackle 7 attempt 8 give a try 9 undertake 10 give a whirl 12 take a crack at, take a whack at
have a good opinion of 5 favor 6 admire, revere 7 approve, respect 9 believe in 10 appreciate
have a hand in 7 advance, forward 9 influence 10 take part in 12 contribute to 13 be conducive to, participate in 14 help bring about
have an eye on 4 want 5 covet, crave, fancy 6 desire 7 long for, pine for 8 aspire to, yearn for 9 lust after 11 have a yen for
have a yen for 4 want 5 covet, crave 6 desire 7 long for, wish for 8 yearn for 9 lust after 11 hanker after 13 have a fancy for
have bearing on 5 apply, refer 6 relate 7 concern, pertain 9 appertain, touch upon 13 be pertinent to, have respect to
have done with 4 drop, junk, shed 7 abandon, discard 9 dispose of 10 relinquish 12 dispense with
have faith in 5 trust 6 rely on 9 believe in 16 have confidence in
have guests 8 play host 9 entertain 10 give a party 13 keep open house 16 offer hospitality
Have Gun Will Travel
  character: 6 Hey Boy 7 Hey Girl, Paladin
  cast: 6 Lisa Lu 7 Kam Tong 12 Richard Boone
  setting: 12 San Francisco 13 Hotel Carleton
have in mind 4 mean, want, wish 6 desire, intend 10 think about
haven 4 port 5 cover 6 asylum, harbor, refuge 7 hideout, retreat, shelter 8 hideaway 9 sanctuary
have no hope 6 give up 7 despair 11 be desperate

have plenty 6 abound, be rich **8** flourish, overflow **10** be numerous, have enough **11** be plentiful **14** be well supplied **18** have more than enough
have the body
  Latin: 12 habeas corpus
  legal writ guards against: 19 illegal imprisonment
have too few 4 lack, want **7** be scant **9** fall short **13** be deficient in, have a dearth of **14** have a paucity of **15** be in short supply, have a scarcity of, not have enough of
having life 5 alive, vital **6** living, viable **7** animate
having the means 3 fit **4** able **6** fitted **7** capable, equal to **8** adequate **9** qualified **12** being solvent **20** having the wherewithal
Havisham, Miss
  character in: 17 Great Expectations
  author: 7 Dickens
havoc 4 ruin **5** chaos **8** calamity, disaster, disorder, upheaval **9** cataclysm, ruination **11** catastrophe, destruction, devastation **12** wrack and ruin **16** widespread damage
Hawaii
  abbreviation: 2 HI
  nickname: 5 Aloha **15** Sandwich Islands **20** Paradise of the Pacific
  capital/largest city: 8 Honolulu
  others: 3 Ewa **4** Aiea, Hana, Hilo, Laie, Paia **5** Kapaa, Kapaa, Lihue, Maili **6** Kailua, Kekaha **7** Kahului, Kaneohe, Lanikae, Wahiawa, Waianae, Wailuku
  college: 9 Chaminade, Hawaii Loa **12** Brigham Young **13** Hawaii Pacific
  explorer: 4 Cook **5** Gaetano
  feature:
  district: 7 Lahaina
  national park: 9 Haleakala **15** Hawaii Volcanoes
  people: 9 Hiram Fong **10** Polynesian **11** Sanford Dole **12** Daniel Inouye
  island name: 4 Kure **9** Kahoolawe
  big isle: 6 Hawaii
  friendly isle: 7 Molokai
  garden isle: 5 Kauai
  gathering place: 4 Oahu
  house of the sun: 9 Haleakala
  mystery isle: 6 Niihau
  pineapple isle: 5 Lanai
  valley isle: 4 Maui
  lake: 5 Waiau
  land rank: 12 forty-seventh
  mountain: 3 Kea, Loa **5** Kaala **6** Kohala, Kohala, Koolau **7** Kamakou, Waianae **8** Maunaloa **9** Lanaihale
  highest point: 8 Maunakea
  physical feature:
  bay: 5 Pohue **6** Halawa, Kiholo, Mamala **7** Kamohio, Kaneohe, Waiagua **8** Kawaihae, Maunalua
  beach: 7 Waikiki
  canyon: 6 Waimea
  channel: 3 Aua **5** Kaiwi **6** Kalohi **7** Pailolo
  crater: 7 Kilauea **9** Punchbowl
  desert: 3 Kau

harbor: 5 Pearl
promontory: 11 Diamond Head
valley: 3 Iao **5** Manoa
volcano: 7 Kilauea **8** Maunakea, Maunaloa **9** Haleakala
state admission: 8 Fiftieth
state bird: 4 nene **13** Hawaiian goose
state flower: 5 lehua **11** red hibiscus **15** scarlet hibiscus
state motto: 44 The Life of the Land is Perpetuated in Righteousness
state song: 11 Hawaii Ponoi **12** Our Own Hawaii
state tree: 5 kukui **9** candlenut
Hawaii
  author: 13 James Michener
Hawaiian swimmer 14 Duke Kahanamoku
Hawaii Five-O
  character: 4 Kono **5** Wo Fat **8** Ben Kokua **11** Chin Ho Kelly **13** Danny Williams **14** Steve McGarrett
  cast: 4 Zulu **7** Kam Fong **8** Jack Lord **11** Khigh Dhiegh **12** Al Harrington **14** James MacArthur
hawk 4 bird, sell, vend **6** falcon, peddle **8** militant **9** accipiter, warmonger
  young: 4 eyas
  group of: 4 cast
Hawk, Sir Mulberry
  character in: 16 Nicholas Nickleby
  author: 7 Dickens
Hawkes, John
  author of: 10 Second Skin **11** The Cannibal, The Lime Twig **12** The Beetle Leg **15** The Blood Oranges
Hawkeye State
  nickname of: 4 Iowa
Hawkins, Jim
  character in: 14 Treasure Island
  author: 9 Stevenson
Hawkline Monster, The
  author: 16 Richard Brautigan
Hawks, Howard
  director of: 8 Red River, Rio Bravo, Scarface **11** The Big Sleep **12** Sergeant York **13** His Girl Friday **14** Bringing Up Baby **16** To Have and Have Not, Twentieth Century
Hawn, Goldie
  husband: 12 Gus Trinkonis
  born: 12 Washington DC
  roles: 7 Laugh-In, Shampoo **8** Foul Play **12** Cactus Flower **15** Private Benjamin **18** Butterflies Are Free
hawser 4 line, rope **5** cable **7** mooring
hawthorn 9 Crataegus
  varieties: 5 water, yeddo **6** Indian **7** English
Hawthorne, Nathaniel
  author of: 13 The Marble Faun **14** Twice-told Tales **16** The Scarlet Letter **20** Mosses from an Old Manse **24** The House of the Seven Gables
Haydee
  character in: 21 The Count of Monte Cristo
  author: 5 Dumas (pere)

Haydn, Franz Joseph
  born: 6 Rohrau 7 Austria
  composer of: 7 The Bird, The Joke 10
  Gypsy Rondo, The Seasons 11 The Creation 12 Emperor's Hymn, Wild Band
  Mass 13 The Apothecary 14 Lord Nelson
  Mass, Theresienmesse 15 Mass in Time
  of War 16 Il Mondo della Luna, Mariazel-
  lermesse 17 The World of the Moon 38
  The Seven Last Words of Our Savior on
  the Cross
  quartet: 3 Sun 4 Bird, Frog, Lark, Tost 5
  Dream, Razor, Witch 6 Fifths, Maiden 7
  Emperor, Erdoedy, Russian, Sunrise, The
  Bell, The Hunt 8 Farmyard, Horseman,
  The Jokes 9 The Donkey 14 The House
  on Fire, The Row in Vienna
  symphony: 4 Fire 5 Paris 6 Le Midi, Le
  Soir, Loudon, Merkur, Oxford, The Hen 7
  Evening, Le Matin, Mercury, Morning,
  Salomon, The Bear, The Hunt 8 Ab-
  schied, Alleluia, Drum Roll, Farewell, Mil-
  itary, Mourning, Surprise, The Clock, The
  Queen, The Storm 9 Children's, Christ-
  mas 10 La Passione, La Tempesta, The
  Miracle, The Passion 11 The Imperial 12
  Der Philosoph, Maria Theresa, The Af-
  ternoon 13 Auf dem Anstand 14 The
  Philosopher 15 The Schoolmaster,
  Trauersymphonie, With the Horn Call 17
  At the Hunting Place 18 Mit dem
  Hornersignal

Hayes, Elvin
  nickname: 4 Big E
  sport: 10 basketball
  team: 8 San Diego 14 Houston Rockets

Hayes, Helen
  real name: 15 Helen Hayes Brown
  nickname: 29 First Lady of the American
  Theater
  son: 14 James MacArthur
  roles: 7 Airport 9 Anastasia 22 The Sin
  of Madelon Claudet (Oscar)

Hayes, Rutherford B (Birchard)
  nickname: 8 Rud Hayes
  presidential rank: 10 nineteenth
  party: 10 Republican
  state represented: 2 OH
  defeated: 5 (Green Clay) Smith 6
  (James B) Walker, (Peter) Cooper, (Samuel Jones) Tilden
  vice president: 7 (William Almon)
  Wheeler
  cabinet:
  state: 6 (William Maxwell) Evarts
  treasury: 7 (John) Sherman
  war: 6 (Alexander) Ramsey 7 (George
  Washington) McCrary
  attorney general: 6 (Charles) Devens
  navy: 4 (Nathan) Goff (Jr) 8 (Richard
  Wigginton) Thompson
  postmaster general: 3 (David McKen-
  dree) Key 7 (Horace) Maynard
  interior: 6 (Carl) Schurz
  born: 10 Delaware OH
  died/buried: 9 Fremont OH
  education:

preparatory school: 4 Webb
College: 6 Kenyon
Law School: 7 Harvard
religion: 9 Methodist
political career: 24 US House of Representatives
city solicitor of: 10 Cincinnati
governor of: 4 Ohio
civilian career: 6 farmer, lawyer
military service: 6 US Army 8 Civil War
12 Ohio infantry 18 brevet major general
notable events of lifetime/term: 10 Depression (of 1873) 15 railroad strikes (of
1877) 18 civil service reform 24 specie
payments resumption
Act: 26 Bland-Allison Silver Purchase
father: 10 Rutherford
mother: 6 Sophia (Birchard)
siblings: 7 Lorenzo 11 Sarah Sophia 13
Fanny Arabella
wife: 4 Lucy (Ware Webb)
children: 5 Fanny 9 James Webb (renamed Webb Cook) 11 George Crook 12
Manning Force, Scott Russell 14 Joseph
Thompson, Sardis Birchard (renamed
Birchard Austin) 15 Rutherford Platt

hayseed 4 hick, rube 5 yokel 6 rustic 7
bumpkin, peasant 10 clodhopper

Hayward, Susan
  real name: 14 Edythe Marrener
  husband: 10 Jess Barker
  born: 10 Brooklyn NY
  roles: 11 I Want to Live (Oscar) 14 I'll
  Cry Tomorrow, My Foolish Heart 18 With
  a Song in My Heart 23 Smash Up The
  Story of a Woman

Hayworth, Rita
  real name: 22 Margarita Carmen
  Cansino
  husband: 7 Aly Khan 10 Dick Haymes
  11 Orson Welles
  born: 10 Brooklyn NY
  roles: 5 Gilda 9 Cover Girl 14 Separate
  Tables 17 Miss Sadie Thompson, You'll
  Never Get Rich

hazan 18 cantor of a synagogue

hazard 3 bet 4 dare, luck, risk 5 fluke,
guess, offer, peril, stake, wager 6 chance,
danger, expose, gamble, menace, mishap,
submit, threat 7 advance, daresay, imperil,
pitfall, presume, proffer, suppose, venture
8 accident, chance it, endanger, jeopardy,
theorize, threaten, throw out 9 mischance,
speculate, tempt fate, volunteer 10 conjecture, jeopardize, misfortune 11 coincidence, hypothesize, imperilment, take a
chance, trust to luck 12 endangerment,
happenstance, stroke of luck

Hazard of New Fortunes, A
  author: 18 William Dean Howells

hazardous 4 iffy 5 risky, shaky 6 chancy,
unsafe, unsure 7 dubious, unsound 8
doubtful, insecure, perilous, unstable 9
dangerous, uncertain 10 precarious, unreliable 11 speculative, threatening 13 untrustworthy

haze 3 fog **4** daze, film, mist, pall, veil **5** cloak, cloud, smoke, vapor **6** mantle, muddle, screen **9** fogginess **12** befuddlement, bewilderment **16** state of confusion

hazel 3 nut **4** tree **5** brown, shrub, tawny **8** brownish **14** yellowish-brown
   varieties: 4 tree **5** Chile, witch **6** winter **7** Chinese, Turkish **8** American, European, Japanese **11** spike winter **12** Chinese witch **13** Japanese witch **15** buttercup winter

Hazel
   character: 12 George Baxter, Harold Baxter **13** Dorothy Baxter
   cast: 9 Don DeFore **12** Shirley Booth, Whitney Blake **13** Bobby Buntrock
   creator: 6 Ted Key

hazelnut 7 Corylus
   varieties: 6 beaked **7** Chinese, Turkish **8** American, European, Japanese

Hazlitt, William
   author of: 17 The Spirit of the Age **32** The Characters of Shakespeare's Plays

hazy 3 dim **5** dusky, faint, filmy, foggy, misty, murky, smoky, vague **6** bleary, blurry, cloudy, smoggy, veiled **7** bleared, general, muddled, obscure, unclear **8** confused, nebulous, overcast **9** ambiguous, uncertain **10** ill-defined, indefinite

head 2 go, IQ **3** aim, CEO, end, hie, tip, top **4** acme, apex, bent, boss, czar, font, fore, gift, king, lead, main, mind, peak, rise, rule, turn, well **5** begin, brain, chief, crest, crown, drive, first, front, guide, pilot, prime, queen, ruler, start, steer **6** climax, crisis, direct, genius, govern, launch, leader, manage, origin, ruling, source, spring, summit, talent, vertex, zenith **7** ability, admiral, captain, command, conduct, control, foreman, general, go first, highest, leading, make for, manager, marshal, monarch, precede, premier, primary, proceed, ranking, supreme, topmost **8** aptitude, be head of, big wheel, capacity, chairman, dictator, director, dominant, foremost, fountain, fruition, headmost, initiate, judgment, managing, pinnacle, start off, superior, suzerain, upper end **9** acuteness, beginning, commander, commodore, extremity, forefront, front rank, governing, intellect, introduce, mentality, paramount, potentate, president, principal, sovereign, supervise, uppermost **10** administer, be master of, birthplace, cleverness, commandant, commanding, conclusion, first place, gray matter, inaugurate, lead the way, move toward, perception, preeminent, supervisor, wellspring **11** be at the helm, controlling, culmination, discernment, forward part, highest rank, officiate at, preside over, superintend, take the lead, termination **12** apprehension, field marshal, fountainhead, guiding light, place of honor, take charge of, take the reins, turning point, utmost extent **13** administrator, go at the head of, most prominent, prime minister, understanding **14** chief executive, highest ranking, superin-

tendent **15** be in the vanguard, make a beeline for, quickness of mind **16** commander-in-chief, direct one's course, inevitable result **17** commanding general, have authority over **18** be in the driver's seat, chairman of the board, go in the direction of **21** chief executive officer

head
   contains: 4 eyes **5** brain, mouth, skull **9** braincase **10** optic nerve **12** ocular muscle **13** cranial cavity, lacrimal organ, orbital cavity **14** buccaval cavity

headache 5 trial **6** strain, stress **7** problem, trouble **8** migraine, nuisance **10** affliction, difficulty **13** inconvenience, pain in the neck

headdress 3 cap, hat **6** bonnet **7** chapeau **12** headcovering

headland 4 bank, crag **5** bluff, cliff **8** palisade **9** precipice **10** promontory

headlong 6 abrupt **8** abruptly, heedless, pell-mell, reckless **9** headfirst, impetuous **10** heedlessly, recklessly **11** impetuously, precipitate, precipitous **13** head over heels, precipitously

Headlong Hall
   author: 17 Thomas Love Peacock

headman 5 chief **6** leader **7** foreman **8** alderman, princeps **9** commander **10** councilman, supervisor **14** public official, superintendent

head-on 6 direct **7** frontal **10** face-to-face

headshrinker 6 shrink **7** analyst **12** psychiatrist **13** psychoanalyst

headstrong 4 rash **6** dogged, mulish, unruly **7** defiant, froward, willful **8** contrary, obdurate, reckless, stubborn **9** hotheaded, imprudent, impulsive, obstinate, pigheaded **10** bullheaded, incautious, refractory **11** intractable **12** incorrigible, recalcitrant, ungovernable, unmanageable **14** uncontrollable **22** bent on having one's own way

heady 4 hard **6** potent, strong **8** alluring, exciting, inviting, stirring, tempting **9** seductive, thrilling **10** high-octane **11** high-voltage, tantalizing **12** exhilarating, intoxicating

heal 4 cure, knit, mend **5** right, salve, treat **6** heal up, remedy, settle, soothe **7** compose, get well, improve, recover, rectify, relieve **8** heal over, make well **9** alleviate, make whole, reconcile **10** conciliate, convalesce, recuperate **11** set to rights **14** make harmonious, return to health **20** restore good relations

healed 4 knit **5** cured **6** mended **7** got well **8** relieved

healing 6 curing **7** mending **8** knitting, soothing **9** emollient, improving, restoring **10** making well **11** restorative **13** strengthening
   god of: 6 Apollo **7** Phoebus, Pythius **9** Asclepius, Musagetes **11** Aesculapius
   goddess of: 4 Iaso

health 5 vigor 7 fitness, stamina 8 strength, vitality 9 hardihood, hardiness, well-being 10 robustness 16 general condition 17 physical condition

goddess of: 6 Hygeia

healthful 7 healthy 8 hygienic, salutary 9 wholesome 10 beneficial, nourishing, nutritious, salubrious 12 healthgiving, invigorating

healthiness 6 health 9 good shape, soundness 10 good health, robustness 12 salutariness 13 good condition, healthfulness, wholesomeness 14 salubriousness

healthy 3 fit 4 hale 5 hardy, sound 6 hearty, robust, strong, sturdy 8 vigorous 9 in the pink 10 able-bodied 12 in fine fettle 18 sound of mind and limb

heap 3 gob, lot 4 fill, gobs, hunk, load, lots, lump, mass, mess, pack, pile, slew 5 amass, award, batch, bunch, flood, group, mound, ocean, slews, stack, store, world 6 accord, assign, bundle, deluge, engulf, gather, jumble, load up, oceans, oodles, pile up, plenty, worlds 7 barrels, cluster, collect, mete out, present 8 good deal, inundate, pour upon 9 abundance, gathering, great deal, multitude, profusion 10 assemblage, collection, shower upon 11 aggregation, concentrate 12 accumulation 13 agglomeration

heap up 5 amass 6 pile up 7 stack up 10 accumulate

hear 4 heed 5 admit, favor, grant, judge, learn 6 attend, be told, gather, look on 7 approve, concede, examine, find out, receive, witness 8 accede to, appear at, discover, hear tell, hold with, listen to 9 acquiesce, ascertain, hearken to 10 understand 11 acknowledge

hear!
French: 4 oyez
cry used by: 10 court crier
preceded: 12 proclamation

hearing 5 probe, sound 6 review 7 council, earshot, inquiry 8 audience 9 interview 10 conference 11 examination, questioning 12 consultation 13 interrogation, investigation

hearken to 4 heed, mark, mind 6 attend 8 listen to 11 take to heart 14 pay attention to

Hearns, Thomas
nickname: 6 Hitman
sport: 6 boxing
class: 12 middleweight, welterweight

hearsay 4 talk 5 rumor 6 gossip, report 8 idle talk 9 grapevine 11 scuttlebutt

heart 3 hub, nub 4 base, core, crux, guts, love, meat, mood, pith, root, soul 5 humor, pluck, spunk, valor 6 center, daring, desire, kernel, middle, nature, source, spirit 7 bravery, charity, courage, emotion, essence, nucleus, stomach 8 audacity, backbone, boldness, clemency, feelings, firmness, fondness, gameness, interior, main part, sympathy 9 affection, fortitude, gallantry, inner part, rudiments, sentiment, tolerance 10 brass tacks, compassion, enthusiasm, essentials, foundation, gentleness, indulgence, manfulness, principles, resolution, tenderness, true nature 11 busiest part, central part, disposition, forgiveness, nitty-gritty, temperament 12 fearlessness, fundamentals, quintessence, resoluteness 13 audaciousness

part: 5 aorta, valve 6 atrium 7 chamber 9 ventricle
pumps: 5 blood

heartache 3 woe 4 pain 5 grief 6 misery, sorrow 7 anguish, sadness, torment, trouble 8 distress 9 suffering 11 tribulation, unhappiness

heartbreaker 4 vamp 5 flirt, tease 8 coquette

Heartbreak House
author: 17 George Bernard Shaw

hearten 4 abet 5 cheer 6 assure, solace 7 animate, cheer up, comfort, console, enliven, gladden 8 brighten, embolden, energize, inspirit, reassure 9 encourage 10 invigorate

heartening 7 hopeful 9 favorable 10 auspicious, reassuring 11 encouraging

heartfelt 4 deep, full 5 total 6 ardent, devout, entire, honest 7 earnest, fervent, genuine, intense, sincere 8 complete, profound, thorough 10 keenly felt 12 all-inclusive, wholehearted

hearth 4 home 5 abode, house 8 fireside 9 fireplace, household 10 family life 12 family circle 13 chimney corner
goddess of: 4 Caca 5 Salus, Vesta 6 Hestia

Heart Is a Lonely Hunter, The
author: 15 Carson McCullers
character: 8 Mr Singer 9 Mick Kelly 10 Dr Copeland, Jake Blount 11 Biff Brannon

heartless 4 cold, mean 5 cruel 6 brutal, savage, unkind 7 callous, inhuman, unmoved 8 pitiless, ruthless, uncaring 9 unfeeling, unpitying, unstirred 10 unmerciful 11 coldhearted, cold-blooded, hardhearted, insensitive 12 cruelhearted, unresponsive 13 unsympathetic

Heart of Darkness
author: 12 Joseph Conrad
character: 5 Kurtz 7 Marlowe

Heart of Dixie
nickname of: 7 Alabama

Heart of Juliet Jones, The
creator: 9 Stan Drake
character: 3 Eve

Heart of Midlothian, The
author: 14 Sir Walter Scott

Heart of the Matter, The
author: 12 Graham Greene
character: 5 Yusef 6 Wilson 7 Mrs Rolt 9 Mrs Scobie 11 Major Scobie

heart-stopper 5 belle 6 beauty 7 charmer, stunner 8 knockout 10 good-looker 13 beautiful girl 14 beautiful woman

hearty 4 hale, warm, well 5 ample, hardy, sound 6 lively, robust, strong 7 cordial, genuine, healthy, profuse, sincere, zestful 8 complete, effusive, generous, thorough, vigorous 9 heartfelt, unbounded 10 unreserved 12 enthusiastic, unrestrained, wholehearted 13 physically fit

hearty appetite
    French: 10 bon appetit

Heaslop, Ronald
    character in: 15 A Passage to India
    author: 7 Forster

heat 3 fry 4 bake, boil, cook, sear, stew, warm, zeal 5 ardor, broil, roast, steam 6 braise, climax, fervor, height, simmer, stress, thrill, warmth, warm up 7 hotness, make hot, passion, rapture, swelter 8 fervency, hot spell, warmness 9 eagerness, intensity, transport 10 enthusiasm, excitement 12 bring to a boil

heated 3 hot 5 angry, fiery, irate 6 bitter, fierce, raging, stormy 7 excited, fervent, furious, intense, violent 8 frenzied, inflamed, vehement 9 emotional 10 infuriated, passionate 11 impassioned, tempestuous

heated discussion 7 dispute 8 argument 10 war of words 11 controversy 12 disagreement

heath 5 Erica
    varieties: 4 Tree 5 Berry, Besom, Irish, Otago, Spike 6 Dorset, Scotch, Spring 7 Cornish, Fringed, Spanish, Twisted 9 Cranberry 11 Cross-leaved

Heathcliff
    character in: 16 Wuthering Heights
    author: 6 Bronte

heathen 3 goy 4 boor 5 pagan 6 savage 7 atheist, gentile, infidel 8 agnostic, idolator 9 barbarian, ignoramus 10 polytheist, troglodyte, unbeliever 11 non-believer 17 uncivilized native

heather 7 Calluna
    varieties: 3 Bog, Red 4 Bell, Snow 5 Beach, False, White 6 French, Golden, Scotch 8 Corsican, Mountain 9 Christmas 11 White winter 13 Mediterranean 18 Everblooming French

Heat of the Day, The
    author: 14 Elizabeth Bowen

heat up 3 fan 4 goad, warm, whet 6 arouse 7 enhance, sharpen 8 increase 9 aggravate, intensify 10 strengthen

heave 3 peg, pry, sob 4 arch, blow, cast, emit, fire, hurl, lift, moan, pant, puff, puke, toss 5 boost, bulge, chuck, eject, fling, groan, hoist, lever, pitch, raise, retch, sling, surge, swell, throw, vomit 6 dilate, drag up, draw up, exhale, expand, haul up, launch, let fly, propel, pull up, tilt up, yank up 7 elevate 8 thrust up 9 discharge, palpitate 11 regurgitate

heaven, Heaven, the Heavens 3 wow 4 Zion 5 bliss, glory, mercy, space 6 my oh my, utopia 7 delight, ecstasy, Elysium, my stars, nirvana, Olympus, rapture 8 boy oh boy, goodness, land sake, paradise, Valhalla 9 afterlife, dreamland, next world, Shangri-la 10 afterworld, Beulah Land, life beyond, outer space, perfection, sheer bliss 11 enchantment, the Holy City, world beyond, world to come 12 eternal bliss, good gracious, New Jerusalem, the City of God, the firmament 13 Abraham's bosom, Elysian fields, seventh heaven 14 heavens to Betsy, our eternal home 15 life everlasting, our Father's house, the heavenly city 16 goodness gracious, Isle of the Blessed, supreme happiness, the abode of saints, the Celestial City, the vault of heaven 17 complete happiness, the wild blue yonder 18 Island of the Blessed, the celestial sphere, the heavenly kingdom, the kingdom of Heaven 19 the celestial expanse 21 the happy hunting ground
    god of: 2 An 3 Anu 4 Jove, Zeus 7 Jupiter

Heaven Can Wait (1943)
    director: 13 Ernst Lubitsch
    cast: 9 Don Ameche 11 Gene Tierney 12 Marjorie Main 13 Charles Coburn

Heaven Can Wait (1978)
    director: 9 Buck Henry 12 Warren Beatty
    cast: 10 Dyan Cannon, Jack Warden 12 Warren Beatty 13 Julie Christie
    remake of: 17 Here Comes Mr Jordan

heavenly 6 divine 7 angelic, blessed, saintly, sublime 8 beatific, blissful

Heavens and Earth
    author: 19 Stephen Vincent Benet

Heaven's My Destination
    author: 14 Thornton Wilder

heavy 3 big, fat, sad 4 deep, dull, full, hard, lazy, slow 5 broad, bulky, dense, grave, gross, harsh, hefty, large, obese, plump, rough, stout, thick 6 clumsy, coarse, deadly, dreary, fierce, gloomy, leaden, pained, portly, raging, rugged, savage, solemn, strong, sturdy, torpid, woeful 7 awesome, complex, copious, doleful, forlorn, furious, intense, joyless, languid, lumpish, massive, notable, onerous, profuse, roaring, ruinous, serious, tearful, tedious, violent, weighty 8 abundant, agonized, burdened, crushing, cumbrous, damaging, dejected, desolate, downcast, forceful, grieving, grievous, imposing, lifeless, listless, mournful, pedantic, profound, seething, sluggish, stricken, tiresome, unwieldy 9 apathetic, cheerless, corpulent, depressed, difficult, excessive, extensive, harrowing, important, injurious, laborious, lethargic, lumbering, miserable, momentous, ponderous, rampaging, sorrowful, turbulent, wearisome 10 burdensome, calamitous, cumbersome, distressed, full of care, immoderate, impressive, inordinate, melancholy, monotonous, noteworthy, oppressive, overweight, pernicious, phlegmatic, unbearable, unstinting 11 crestfallen, deleterious, destructive, detrimental, distressing, extravagant, intemperate, intolerable, significant, tempestuous, unendurable, unrelenting, unremitting **12** considerable, disconsolate, hard to endure, overwhelming, unrestrained **13** consequential, grief-stricken, of great import **16** laden with sorrows **18** of great consequence

heavy-handed 5 harsh **6** clumsy **7** awkward **8** bungling **9** graceless, maladroit **10** blundering, oppressive, ungraceful

heavyhearted 3 sad **4** glum **6** dismal, gloomy, morose **7** doleful, forlorn, joyless, unhappy **8** dejected, downcast **9** cheerless, depressed, sorrowful **10** despondent, melancholy **11** downhearted **14** down in the dumps, down in the mouth

Hebe
  goddess of: 5 youth **6** spring
  father: 4 Zeus
  mother: 4 Hera
  brother: 4 Ares
  husband: 8 Hercules
  handmaiden to: 4 gods
  corresponds to: 8 Juventas

Heber
  wife: 4 Jael

Hebrew alphabet
  or: 5 aleph
  b/v: 4 beth
  g: 5 gimel
  d: 6 daleth
  h: 2 he **5** cheth
  v/w: 3 vav
  z: 5 zayin
  y/j/î: 3 yod
  k/kh: 4 kaph
  l: 5 lamed
  m: 3 men
  n: 3 nun
  ': 4 ayin
  p/f: 2 pe
  k: 4 koph
  r: 4 resh
  sh/s: 4 shin
  s: 3 sin **4** sadi **6** samekh
  t: 3 tav **4** teth

Hebrew Judge 4 Ehud, Elon, Jair, Tola **5** Abdon, Ibzan **6** Gideon, Samson, Samuel **7** Deborah, Othniel, Shamgar **8** Jephthah

Hebrew months
  first: 4 Ahib, Nisn **6** Ehanim, Tishri
  second: 3 Bul, Civ **4** Iyar **7** Heshvan
  third: 5 Sivan **6** Kislev
  fourth: 5 Tebet **6** Tammuz, Tebeth
  fifth: 2 Ab **7** Shelbat
  sixth: 4 Adar, Elul **6** Veadar
  seventh: 4 Abib **5** Nisan **6** Tishri **7** Ethanim
  eighth: 3 Zif **4** Iyer **11** Marcheshvan
  ninth: 5 Sivan **7** Chislev
  tenth: 6 Tabeth, Tammuz
  eleventh: 2 Ab **6** Shebat
  twelfth: 4 Adar, Elul

Hecabe *see* **6** Hecuba

Hecaleius
  epithet of: 4 Zeus

he carved it
  Latin: 8 sculpsit

Hecate
  also: 6 Hekate
  goddess of: 5 earth, Hades
  associated with: 6 hounds **7** sorcery **10** crossroads
  corresponds to: 5 Brimo

Hecatonchires
  also: 9 Centimani
  form: 5 giant
  names: 5 Gyges **6** Cottus **8** Briareus
  father: 6 Uranus
  mother: 4 Gaea
  number of heads: 5 fifty
  number of arms: 10 one hundred

heckle 3 boo **4** bait, hiss, hoot, mock, ride, twit **5** annoy, bully, chivy, harry, hound, taunt **6** badger, harass, harrow, hector, jeer at, molest, needle **7** provoke **9** shout down

hectare
  abbreviation of: 2 ha

hectic 3 mad **4** wild **6** stormy **7** chaotic, frantic, furious **8** feverish, frenetic, frenzied, headlong **9** breakneck, turbulent **10** tumultuous

hectoliter
  abbreviation of: 2 hl

hectometer
  abbreviation of: 2 hm

hector 4 bait, ride **5** bully, harry, hound, tease, worry **6** badger, harass, needle, plague **7** torment

Hector
  father: 5 Priam
  mother: 6 Hecuba
  brother: 5 Paris
  sister: 9 Cassandra
  wife: 10 Andromache
  son: 8 Astyanax
  hero of: 9 Trojan War
  killed by: 8 Achilles

Hecuba
  also: 5 Maera **6** Hecabe
  father: 5 Atlas
  husband: 5 Priam **8** Tegeates
  son: 5 Paris **6** Hector **7** Helenus, Polites, Troilus **9** Deiphobus, Polydorus
  daughter: 6 Creusa **7** Laodice **8** Polyxena **9** Cassandra
  changed into: 3 dog **5** bitch
  hound of: 7 Icarius

Hecuba
  author: 9 Euripides
  character: 8 Odysseus, Polyxena **9** Agamemnon, Polydorus **10** Polymestor

Hedda Gabler
  author: 11 Henrik Ibsen
  character: 10 Judge Brack **11** Hedda Tesman, Thea Elvsted **12** George Tesman **13** Eilert Lovberg **17** Miss Juliana Tesman

heder 12 Jewish school

hedge 3 hem **4** duck, edge, ring, wall **5** bound, dodge, evade, fence, guard, hem in, limit **6** border, margin, shut in, waffle **7** barrier, enclose, mark off, outline **8** encircle, hedgerow, surround **9** be evasive, delineate, demarcate, insurance, pussyfoot, temporize 10 equivocate, protection 11 delineation, row of bushes 12 compensation 13 circumference, fence of shrubs 14 beg the question, counterbalance 17 beat around the bush

he died
Latin: 5 obiit

he does not pursue
Latin: 14 non prosequitur

hedonist 8 Sybarite 9 debauchee, libertine 10 dissipater, profligate, sensualist, voluptuary 14 pleasure seeker

hedonistic 7 sensual 9 epicurean, libertine, sybaritic 10 voluptuous 11 intemperate 13 self-indulgent 15 pleasure-seeking

he drew this
Latin: 10 delineavit

Hedrick, Zelma Kathryn
real name of: 14 Kathryn Grayson

heed 4 care, mind, obey 5 bow to, pains, study 6 concur, follow, hold to, notice, regard 7 defer to, observe, perusal, respect, yield to 8 accede to, consider, listen to, prudence, scrutiny, submit to 9 attention, be ruled by, give ear to 10 bear in mind comply with, precaution, take note of 11 carefulness, examination, heedfulness, mindfulness, observation, take to heart 12 take notice of 13 attentiveness 14 fastidiousness, meticulousness, pay attention to, scrupulousness 17 conscientiousness

heedful 4 wary 5 alert, aware, cagey, chary 7 alive to, careful, mindful, prudent 8 cautious, discreet, vigilant, watchful 9 attentive, concerned, conscious

heedless 3 lax 4 rash 5 slack 6 remiss, unwary 7 foolish, unaware, witless 8 careless, mindless, reckless, uncaring 9 foolhardy, frivolous, impetuous, imprudent, negligent, oblivious, unheeding, unmindful 10 incautious, neglectful, unthinking, unwatchful 11 harebrained, improvident, inattentive, thoughtless, unconcerned, unobservant, unobserving 12 happy-go-lucky 14 scatterbrained

heedlessly 5 blind 6 rashly 8 headlong 9 foolishly, witlessly 10 carelessly, mindlessly, recklessly 11 frivolously, impetuously, impulsively, negligently, unmindfully 12 neglectfully, unthinkingly 13 inattentively, thoughtlessly, unconcernedly 15 inconsiderately, uncooperatively

heedlessness 8 rashness 9 unconcern 10 negligence 11 inattention, unawareness 12 carelessness, indiscretion, mindlessness, recklessness 13 unmindfulness 15 thoughtlessness 16 irresponsibility

heel 3 cad, cur, end, rat 4 list, rind, tilt 5 churl, crust, louse 6 rotter 7 bounder, caitiff, dastard

he engraved it
Latin: 8 sculpsit

Heep, Uriah
character in: 16 David Copperfield
author: 7 Dickens

he flourished
Latin: 7 floruit

hefty 3 big 5 beefy, bulky, burly, heavy, husky, large, stout 6 brawny, hearty, mighty, robust, rugged, strong, sturdy 7 hulking, massive, sizable, weighty, well-fed 8 muscular, powerful, stalwart, thickset 9 corpulent, strapping 11 substantial

Hegeleos
father: 8 Tyrsenus

Hegemone
origin: 8 Athenian
member of: 6 Graces

hegemony 7 control 9 authority, dominance, influence, supremacy

Heggen, Thomas
author of: 9 Mr Roberts

hegira 6 exodus, flight 7 journey

Heh see 6 Ogdoad

he himself said it
Latin: 9 ipse dixit

Heidrun
origin: 12 Scandinavian
form: 4 goat
yields: 4 mead
feeds warriors in: 8 Valhalla

height 4 acme, apex, hill, peak, rise 5 bluff, cliff, crest, knoll, limit, mound, tower 6 apogee, heyday, summit, zenith 7 hilltop, maximum, plateau 8 altitude, eminence, highland, highness, mountain, palisade, pinnacle, tallness, ultimate 9 elevation, extremity, flowering, high point, loftiness, supremacy 10 perfection, promontory 11 culmination 12 consummation, upward extent, utmost degree, vantage point

heighten 5 raise 7 elevate 8 increase 9 aggravate, intensify

heil 4 hail

Heimberger, Eddie Albert
real name of: 11 Eddie Albert

Heimdall
origin: 12 Scandinavian
god of: 4 dawn 5 light
number of mothers: 4 nine
guards: 7 bifrost 13 rainbow bridge
killed by: 4 Loki
noted for: 7 hearing 8 eyesight

Heine, Heinrich
author of: 9 Atta Troll 11 Book of Songs 19 Germany A Winter's Tale

Heinlein, Robert
author of: 10 Double Star 16 Starship Troopers 20 The Green Hills of Earth 22 Stranger in a Strange Land 23 The Moon Is a Harsh Mistress

heinous 4 evil, foul, vile 5 gross, nasty 6 grisly, horrid, odious, sinful, wicked 7 beastly, ghastly, hideous, inhuman, vicious 8 infamous, shocking, terrible 9 abhorrent, atrocious, loathsome, monstrous, nefarious, offensive, repugnant, repulsive, revolting, sickening 10 abominable, deplorable, despicable, detestable, disgusting, iniquitous, outrageous, scandalous, villainous 11 disgraceful, distasteful 12 contemptible 13 objectionable, reprehensible

heinousness 4 evil 7 outrage 8 atrocity, baseness, enormity, foulness, savagery, vileness, villainy 9 barbarity, depravity, malignity 10 inhumanity 13 loathsomeness, monstrousness 14 outrageousness

heir, heiress 7 legatee 9 inheritor 10 inheritrix 11 beneficiary, inheritress 12 heir apparent 15 heir presumptive

Heiress, The
director: 12 William Wyler
based on novel by: 10 Henry James
  entitled: 16 Washington Square
cast: 13 Miriam Hopkins 15 Montgomery Clift, Ralph Richardson 17 Olivia de Havilland
score: 12 Aaron Copland
Oscar for: 7 actress (de Havilland)

Hekate see 6 Hecate

Hel
origin: 12 Scandinavian
goddess of: 5 death
rules: 8 Niflheim
father: 4 Loki
mother: 9 Angerboda, Angrbodha, Angurboda
brother: 6 Fenrir, Fenris 11 Iormungandr, Jormungandr 14 Midgard Serpent
color of body: 4 blue 5 flesh
home of: 4 dead

Helen
father: 4 Zeus
mother: 4 Leda
brother: 6 Castor, Pollux
sister: 8 Timandra 12 Clytemnestra
husband: 8 Menelaus
abducted by: 5 Paris
carried off to: 4 Troy
abduction caused: 9 Trojan War

Helena
character in: 20 All's Well That Ends Well 21 A Midsummer Night's Dream
author: 11 Shakespeare

Helenor
mentioned in: 6 Aeneid
position: 6 prince
home: 5 Lydia
accompanied: 6 Aeneas

Heliadae
sons of: 6 Helius, Rhodes

helicopter
invented by: 8 Sikorsky

Heliopolis
city of: 2 On

Helios
origin: 5 Greek
god of: 3 sun
father: 8 Hyperion
mother: 4 Thia
children: 5 Circe 6 Aeetes 8 Phaethon
corresponds to: 3 Sol

heliotrope 12 Heliotropium
varieties: 6 garden, winter, yellow 7 seaside

helium
chemical symbol: 2 He

hell, Hell 5 agony, grief, Hades 6 misery, the pit 7 Abaddon, anguish, despair, Gehenna, inferno, remorse, torment 8 Appolyons, hell fire, the abyss 9 martyrdom, perdition, suffering 10 lake of fire 12 hopelessness, wretchedness 13 bottomless pit, Satan's kingdom, the lower world, the underworld 14 place of the lost, the Devil's house, the nether world, the shades below 15 everlasting fire, home of lost souls, infernal regions 16 abode of the damned

Helle
father: 7 Athamas
mother: 7 Nephele
stepmother: 3 Ino
brother: 7 Phrixus
death by: 8 drowning

Hellen
king of: 8 Thessaly
father: 9 Deucalion
mother: 6 Pyrrha
wife: 6 Orseis
son: 5 Dorus 6 Aeolus, Xuthus
ancestor of: 8 Hellenes

Hellenic Republic see 6 Greece

Heller, Joseph
author of: 10 Good as Gold 14 Catch-Twenty-Two 17 Something Happened

hellion 5 devil, rogue, scamp 9 scoundrel 13 mischief-maker

hellish 4 foul, vile 5 awful 6 brutal 7 hateful 8 accursed, damnable, dreadful, horrible, infernal 9 atrocious, revolting 10 abominable, disgusting

Hellman, Lillian
author of: 5 Maybe 10 Pentimento 13 Scoundrel Time 14 The Little Foxes, Toys in the Attic 15 Watch on the Rhine 16 The Children's Hour 17 An Unfinished Woman 22 Another Part of the Forest

hello
French: 7 bonjour
German: 8 guten tag
Spanish: 10 buenos dias
Italian: 4 ciao 10 buon giorno
Latin: 5 salve

Hello-Central
character in: 36 A Connecticut Yankee in King Arthur's Court
author: 5 Twain

help 3 aid 4 back, balm, calm, care, crew, cure, ease, gift, lift, save 5 allay, emend, force, guide, hands, salve, serve, staff 6 advice, advise, assist, give to, menial, relief, remedy, rescue, soothe, succor, uphold 7 advance, backing, console, correct, endorse, further, helpers, improve, nurture, promote, rectify, relieve, servant, service, stand by, support, welfare, workers, workmen 8 advocate, befriend, champion, domestic, factotum, farmhand, guidance, laborers, maintain, mitigate, retainer, retrieve, side with 9 alleviate, chip in for, employees, encourage, extricate, lend a hand, make whole, promotion, put at ease, underling, workhands, work force 10 ameliorate, apprentice, assistance, assistants, bring round, corrective, friendship, go to bat for, hired hands, kind regard, minister to, preventive, protection, stick up for 11 advancement, benevolence, cooperation, endorsement, furtherance, good offices, helping hand, make healthy, restorative 12 bring through, contribute to, contribution, hired helpers, intercede for 13 collaboration, cooperate with, encouragement, take the part of

helper 3 aid 4 aide 5 angel 6 backer, deputy, patron, second 7 adjunct, partner, servant 8 adjutant, advocate, champion, confrere, co-worker, employee, retainer 9 assistant, associate, auxiliary, colleague, man Friday, right hand, supporter 10 accomplice, aide-de-camp, apprentice, benefactor, girl Friday 11 confederate, helping hand, subordinate 12 collaborator, right-hand man 13 good samaritan 14 fairy godmother

helpful 4 fine, good, kind, nice 6 usable, useful 8 obliging, splendid, valuable 9 excellent, favorable, practical 10 beneficial, profitable, supportive 11 considerate, cooperative, serviceable 12 advantageous, constructive 13 accommodating

helping hand 3 aid 4 aide, hand 5 boost 6 assist, hand up, helper, succor 7 abettor, support 9 assistant 10 assistance

helplessness 8 weakness 9 impotence, inability, infirmity 10 dependence, feebleness, ineptitude 12 incapability, incompetence, inefficiency 13 powerlessness, vulnerability

Helsinki
  capital of: 7 Finland

hem 3 box, rim 4 bind, brim, edge, welt 5 bound, brink, skirt, verge 6 border, edging, fringe, impede, margin, turn up 7 confine, enclose, stammer, stutter, turning 8 compress, encircle, restrain, surround

he made it
  Latin: 5 fecit

Hemera
  father: 6 Erebus
  mother: 3 Nyx
  corresponds to: 3 Eos

Hemerasia
  epithet of: 7 Artemis
  means: 13 she who soothes

hem in 4 best 5 fence 7 besiege, confine, enclose 8 encircle, surround

Hemingway, Ernest
  author of: 9 In Our Time 14 A Moveable Feast 15 A Farewell to Arms, The Sun Also Rises 16 To Have and Have Not 18 Islands in the Stream, The Old Man and the Sea 19 For Whom the Bell Tolls 21 The Snows of Kilimanjaro 34 The Short Happy Life of Francis Macomber

hemiptera
  class: 8 hexapoda
  phylum: 10 arthropoda
  group: 3 bug

Hemithea
  father: 6 Cycnus
  mother: 7 Proclea
  sister: 5 Tenes
  pursued by: 8 Achilles
  swallowed up by: 5 earth

hemlock 5 Tsuga 15 Conium maculatum
  varieties: 5 Dwarf, Water 6 Canada, Ground, Poison 7 Siebold, Spotted, Western 8 Carolina, Japanese, Mountain

hemp 14 Cannabis sativa
  varieties: 3 Bog 5 Cuban, Sisal 6 Deccan, Indian, Manila 7 African 8 Deckaner 9 Bowstring, Mauritius 10 New Zealand 13 Colorado River 15 Ceylon bowstring, Indian bowstring 16 African bowstring

hen
  young: 6 pullet

Henchard, Michael
  character in: 22 The Mayor of Casterbridge
  author: 5 Hardy

henchman 4 goon, thug 6 flunky, lackey, minion, stooge, yes-man 7 gorilla 8 hanger-on, hireling, retainer 9 attendant, bodyguard 10 hatchet man, lieutenant 12 right-hand man, strong-arm man

Henderson, Marge
  creator/artist of: 10 Little Lulu

Henioche
  epithet of: 4 Hera
  means: 10 charioteer

henna 3 dye 5 rinse 6 auburn, russet 8 cinnamon 11 rust-colored 12 reddish-brown 13 copper-colored

henpecked 4 meek 5 timid 6 docile 8 obedient 10 browbeaten, submissive, wife-ridden 11 unassertive

Henry, Frederic
  character in: 15 A Farewell to Arms
  author: 9 Hemingway

Henry Esmond
  author: 16 William Thackeray
  character: 5 Frank 7 Beatrix 9 Lord Mohun 10 Father Holt 11 James Stuart 12 Rachel Esmond 13 Francis Esmond

Henry IV
  author: 18 William Shakespeare
  character: 7 Hotspur 11 Prince Henry, Thomas Percy 14 Edmund Mortimer, Sir Walter Blunt 15 John of Lancaster, Mistress Quickly, Sir John Falstaff 18 Earl of Westmoreland, King Henry the Fourth

Henry V
  author: 18 William Shakespeare
  character: 7 Dauphin, Montjoy 15 Charles the Sixth (King of France) 17 Princess Katharine
  director: 15 Laurence Olivier
  cast: 11 Leslie Banks 12 Robert Newton 13 Renee Asherson 15 Laurence Olivier

Henry VI
  author: 18 William Shakespeare
  character: 6 Edward (Prince of Wales) 7 Charles (Dauphin of France), Eleanor, Louis XI (King of France) 8 Lady Bona, Lady Grey 9 Joan of Arc 10 Lord Talbot 11 Bolingbroke 12 John Beaufort, Lord Clifford, Lord Hastings 13 Henry Beaufort, Joan La Pucelle 15 Margaret of Anjou, Margery Jourdain 16 Bastard of Orleans, Cardinal Beaufort
  duke: 4 York (Richard Plantagenet) 7 Bedford, Suffolk 8 Somerset 10 Gloucester
  earl: 7 Suffolk, Warwick 9 Salisbury
  Richard Plantagenet's son: 6 Edmund, Edward, George 7 Richard

Henry VIII
  author: 18 William Shakespeare
  character: 7 Cranmer 8 Gardiner 10 Anne Boleyn 12 Thomas Wolsey 14 Queen Katharine, Thomas Cromwell 16 Cardinal Campeius
  duke: 7 Norfolk, Suffolk 10 Buckingham

Henze, Hans Werner
  born: 7 Germany 10 Westphalia
  composer of: 6 Ariosi, Ondine 8 King Stag 10 El Cimarron 11 Konig Hirsch 12 The Bassarids, The Young Lord 14 Being Beauteous 15 The Runaway Slave 17 Boulevard Solitude 18 Der Prinz von Homburg, The Raft of the Medusa 19 Elegy for Young Lovers 48 The Long and Weary Journey to the Flat of Natasha Ungeheur

Heorot
  great hall in: 7 Beowulf
  author: 7 unknown

he painted it
  Latin: 6 pinxit

Hepburn, Audrey
  real name: 19 Audrey Hepburn-Ruston
  husband: 9 Mel Ferrer
  born: 7 Belgium 8 Brussels
  roles: 6 Ondine 7 Charade, Sabrina 9 Bloodline, Funny Face 10 My Fair Lady 11 War and Peace 12 Roman Holiday (Oscar), The Nun's Story 13 Green Mansions, Wait Until Dark 18 Love in the Afternoon 19 Breakfast at Tiffany's

Hepburn, Katharine
  co-star: 12 Spencer Tracy
  born: 10 Hartford CT
  roles: 7 Desk Set, Holiday 8 Adam's Rib 10 Alice Adams, Pat and Mike, Summertime 12 Morning Glory (Oscar), On Golden Pond (Oscar), The Rainmaker 14 Woman of the Year 15 The African Queen, The Lion in Winter (Oscar) 18 Suddenly Last Summer 20 The Philadelphia Story 23 Guess Who's Coming to Dinner (Oscar) 24 Long Day's Journey into Night

Hephaestus
  also: 10 Hephaistos
  father: 4 Zeus
  mother: 4 Hera

  god of: 4 fire 11 handicrafts 12 metalworking
  vocation: 5 smith
  wife: 9 Aphrodite
  corresponds to: 6 Vulcan

Hephaistos *see* 10 Hephaestus

Hephzibah
  husband: 8 Hezekiah
  son: 8 Manasseh

Hepzibah *see* 9 Hephzibah

Hera
  also: 4 Here
  origin: 5 Greek
  queen of: 6 Heaven
  father: 6 Cronos, Cronus, Kronos
  mother: 4 Rhea
  brother: 4 Zeus
  husband: 4 Zeus
  son: 4 Ares
  daughter: 9 Eilithyia 10 Hephaestus
  birthplace: 5 Samos
  festival: 7 Daedala
  counterfeit: 7 Nephele
  corresponds to: 4 Juno
  epithet: 6 Anthea, Bunaea 8 Henioche 9 Prodromia

Heracles *see* 8 Hercules

Heracles, Children of
  author: 9 Euripides
  character: 6 Hyllus, Iolaus 7 Alcmene, Macaria 8 Demophon 10 Eurystheus

Heracles, Madness of
  author: 9 Euripides
  character: 4 Hera 5 Lycus 6 Megara 7 Theseus 8 Heracles 10 Amphitryon

Heraclid
  descendant of: 8 Hercules

Heraclidae
  children of: 8 Hercules

Heraea
  origin: 5 Greek
  form: 8 festival

Herakles *see* 8 Hercules

herald 4 clue, omen, sign 5 crier, envoy, token, usher 6 augury, inform, report, reveal, symbol 7 courier, divulge, portent, presage, publish, usher in, warning 8 announce, forecast, foregoer, foretell, proclaim 9 advertise, harbinger, indicator, make known, messenger, precursor, prefigure, publicize 10 forerunner, indication, proclaimer 11 bruit abroad, communicate, give voice to, predecessor 13 give tidings of

heraldic emblem 4 arms 5 crest 8 blazonry, insignia 10 coat of arms

heraldry
  also called: 4 arms 10 coat of arms
  black: 5 sable
  blue: 5 azure
  bottom: 5 base
  center: 5 fesse
  coat of arms of cities/countries/colleges: 14 impersonal arms
  coat of arms on shield/crest/helmet/motto: 19 armorial achievement
  colors: 8 tincture

concerns family's: 8 heritage 9 genealogy

described as: 9 blazoning

divided diagonally: 7 per bend

divided vertically and horizontally: 9 quartered

for holding shield: 10 supporters

fur: 4 vair 6 ermine

gold/yellow: 2 or

green: 4 vert

helmet top: 5 crest

horizontal band: 4 fess

intrafamily distinctions: 12 differencing

daughter: 7 lozenge

eldest son: 5 label

younger son: 7 cadency

left part: 8 sinister

main figure: 6 charge 8 ordinary 14 heraldic device

metal: 2 or 6 argent

motto in: 6 scroll

orange: 5 tenne

placed on lord's: 6 banner, shield 8 garments 14 horse trappings

portrayed as: 6 emblem, symbol

purple: 7 purpure

red: 5 gules

red-purple: 8 sanguine

right part: 6 dexter

shield: 10 escutcheon

sunshade: 8 mantling

held by: 6 wreath

made of: 4 silk

surface/background: 5 field

top: 5 chief

two or more colors: 16 lines of partition

vertical band: 4 pale

when worn by followers: 5 badge 6 livery

white/silver: 6 argent

herb 4 drug 5 plant, spice 6 annual, physic 7 herbage, perfume 8 aromatic, biennial, medicine 9 flavoring, perennial, seasoning, succulent

kind: 3 bay, rue 4 corn, dill, hemp, mint, rose, sage 5 anise, basil, curry, chili, grass, onion, peony, thyme, wheat 6 catnip, celery, chives, clover, fennel, garlic, pepper, sesame 7 boneset, caraway, ginseng, lavender, mustard, oregano, parsley 8 camomile, licorice, rosemary, tarragon 9 buttercup, marijuana, spearmint 10 peppermint 11 wintergreen

Herbert, George

author of: 9 The Temple

Herbert, Victor

born: 6 Dublin 7 Ireland

composer of: 14 Babes in Toyland, Hero and Leander 15 Naughty Marietta

herbivorous 10 vegetarian 11 plant-eating 14 noncarnivorous

Herceius

epithet of: 4 Zeus

means: 14 of the courtyard

herculean, Herculean 4 hard 5 burly, hefty, tough 6 brawny, mighty, robust, rugged, strong, sturdy 7 arduous, onerous 8 muscular, powerful, toilsome, wearying 9 difficult, fatiguing, laborious, strapping, strenuous 10 burdensome, exhausting, formidable, prodigious 12 backbreaking

Hercules

also: 7 Alcides 8 Heracles, Herakles 9 Carnopian

father: 4 Zeus

mother: 7 Alcmene

cousin: 10 Eurystheus

wife: 4 Hebe 6 Megara 8 Deianira

son: 5 Lamus 6 Hyllus 8 Telephus 11 Therimachus

daughter: 7 Macaria

teacher: 6 Chiron

gift: 8 strength

performed: 6 labors

number of labors: 6 twelve

epithet: 7 Charops 8 Buphagus 9 Ipoctonus

corresponds to: 6 Sancus 10 Semo Sancus

Hercyna

form: 5 nymph

location: 8 fountain

playmate: 10 Persephone

herd 3 lot, mob 4 army, band, body, gang, goad, host, lead, mass, pack, spur 5 array, bunch, crowd, drive, drove, flock, force, group, guide, horde, party, press, rally, swarm, tribe, troop 6 gather, huddle, legion, muster, number, throng 7 cluster, collect, company, convene, round up 8 assemble, assembly, conclave 9 gathering, multitude 10 assemblage, collection 11 convocation 12 congregation

Herds

god of: 8 Silvanus, Sylvanus

herdsman 6 cowboy, driver, drover 7 cowpoke 8 shepherd

Herdsman

constellation of: 6 Bootes

herd together 5 flock, group 6 gather 7 cluster, collect 10 congregate 12 band together

Here *see* 4 Hera

hereafter 5 limbo 6 heaven 8 paradise 9 afterlife, from now on, next world, Purgatory 10 afterworld, future life, henceforth, life beyond, ultimately 11 in the future, world to come 12 at a later date, at a later time, henceforward, subsequently 14 life after death 15 heavenly kingdom

here and there 6 around 11 at intervals 18 in this place and that

Latin: 6 passim

Here Comes Mr Jordan

director: 13 Alexander Hall

cast: 11 Claude Rains, Evelyn Keyes, Rita Johnson 16 Robert Montgomery

remade as: 13 Heaven Can Wait

hereditary 6 inborn, inbred 7 genetic 9 ancestral, heritable, inherited 10 congenital, handed-down 11 established, inheritable, traditional

here lies

Latin: 8 hic jacet

heresy 7 dissent, fallacy 8 apostasy 10 dissension, heterodoxy, iconoclasm, irreligion 11 unorthodoxy 13 nonconformity 15 unsound doctrine

heretic 7 skeptic 8 apostate, recreant, recusant, renegade 9 dissenter 10 backslider 11 freethinker, misbeliever 12 deviationist 13 nonconformist

heretical 7 radical 9 dissident 10 unorthodox 12 iconoclastic 13 nonconforming, nonconformist 14 unconventional

heretofore
  French: 8 ci-devant

Hereward the Wake
  author: 15 Charles Kingsley

Hergesheimer, Joseph
  author of: 8 Java Head 19 The Three Black Pennys

heritage 6 estate, legacy 7 portion 9 patrimony, tradition 10 birthright 11 inheritance 16 family possession

Hermaphroditus
  father: 6 Hermes
  mother: 9 Aphrodite
  loved by: 8 Salmacis
  joined with: 8 Salmacis
  became: 8 bisexual

Hermes
  origin: 5 Greek
  occupation: 6 herald
  messenger of: 4 gods
  father: 4 Zeus
  mother: 4 Maia
  son: 3 Pan 6 Prylis 7 Daphnis 14 Hermaphroditus
  birthplace: 7 Arcadia
  god of: 4 luck 5 roads, sleep 6 dreams, wealth 7 cunning, thieves 8 commerce 9 fertility, invention, merchants
  invented: 4 lyre
  sandals had: 5 wings
  epithet: 6 Dolius 8 Agoraeus 9 Spelaites 10 Criophorus 11 Argiphontes 12 Argeiphontes, Psychopompus
  corresponds to: 5 Thoth 7 Mercury

hermetic 6 mystic, occult 7 obscure 8 abstruse, airtight, esoteric, mystical 9 recondite

Hermia
  character in: 21 A Midsummer Night's Dream
  author: 11 Shakespeare

hermine, L'
  author: 11 Jean Anouilh

Hermione
  character in: 14 The Winter's Tale
  author: 11 Shakespeare

Hermione
  father: 8 Menelaus
  mother: 5 Helen
  husband: 7 Orestes
  son: 9 Tisamenus

hermit 7 eremite, recluse 8 cenobite, monastic, solitary 9 anchorite 11 desert saint 14 solitudinarian 16 religious recluse

hermitage 5 abbey 6 friary, priory 7 convent, retreat 8 cloister 9 monastery

Hermod
  origin: 12 Scandinavian
  father: 4 Odin 5 Othin
  race: 4 Asar 5 Aesir
  negotiates return of: 5 Baldr 6 Balder, Baldur

hero, heroine 4 idol, star 7 gallant 8 brave man, champion, great man, male lead, male star, noble man 9 daredevil, daring man, main actor 10 adventurer, leading man 11 protagonist, valorous man 12 man of courage, man of the hour 13 chivalrous man, popular figure 15 fearless fighter, idealized person, intrepid warrior, legendary person

Hero
  character in: 19 Much Ado About Nothing
  author: 11 Shakespeare

Hero
  vocation: 9 priestess
  priestess of: 9 Aphrodite
  lover: 7 Leander
  death by: 7 suicide 8 drowning

Herod Antipas
  father: 13 Herod the great
  mother: 8 Malthace
  grandfather: 9 Antipater
  wife: 8 Herodias
  half brother: 6 Philip
  beheaded: 14 John the Baptist

Herodias
  husband: 6 Philip 12 Herod Antipas
  daughter: 6 Salome

Herodotus
  called: 15 Father of History
  wrote history of: 11 Persian Wars

Herod Philip
  daughter: 6 Salome

heroic 4 bold, epic 5 brave, grand, noble 6 daring 7 classic, exalted, gallant, Homeric, valiant 8 elevated, fearless, highbrow, inflated, intrepid, mythical, resolute, valorous 9 bombastic, dauntless, dignified, grandiose, high-flown, legendary, undaunted 10 chivalrous, courageous 11 exaggerated, extravagant, lionhearted, pretentious, unflinching 12 mythological, ostentatious, stouthearted

heroic act 4 feat 7 exploit 9 brave deed

heroism 5 valor 6 daring 7 bravery, courage, prowess 8 boldness, chivalry, nobility 9 fortitude, gallantry 11 intrepidity 12 fearlessness 13 dauntlessness 14 courageousness 15 lionheartedness

Herophilus
  field: 7 anatomy
  nationality: 5 Greek
  experimented with: 15 post-mortem exams

Heros
  author: 8 Menander

herpetophobia
  fear of: 8 reptiles

Herrenvolk 10 master race
Herrick, Robert
   author of: 10 Hesperides 20 Corinna's
   Going A Maying 26 Gather ye rosebuds
   while ye may
Herriman, George
   creator/artist of: 8 Krazy Kat
Herschel, William
   field: 9 astronomy
   nationality: 7 British
   discovered: 6 Uranus
Herse
   father: 7 Cecrops
   sister: 8 Aglauros, Aglaurus, Agraulos
   lover: 6 Hermes
   son: 5 Ceryx 8 Cephalus
Hersey, John
   author of: 7 The Wall 9 Hiroshima 13 A
   Bell for Adano, The Conspiracy 22 My
   Petition for More Space
Hertz, Heinrich
   field: 7 physics
   nationality: 6 German
   discovered: 13 electric waves 18 wireless telegraphy
   named for him: 13 hertzian waves
Herzog
   author: 10 Saul Bellow
he sculptured it
   Latin: 8 sculpsit
Hesiod
   author of: 8 Theogony 12 Works and
   Days
Hesione
   father: 8 Laomedon
   husband: 7 Telamon
   son: 6 Teucer
   rescued by: 8 Hercules
hesitancy 10 indecision, reluctance, unsureness 11 uncertainty, vacillation 12 irresolution
hesitant 5 loath 6 unsure 7 halting 8 doubtful, wavering 9 diffident, faltering, reluctant, tentative, uncertain, undecided 10
hesitating, indecisive, irresolute 11 halfhearted, hanging back, vacillating 15
shilly-shallying 17 lacking confidence, sitting on the fence
hesitate 4 balk, halt 5 delay, pause, shy at,
waver 6 falter 7 scruple, stick at 8 be unsure, hang back 9 stickle at, vacillate 10
dillydally, shrink from, think twice 11 be reluctant, be uncertain, be undecided, be unwilling, stop briefly 12 be irresolute, shilly-
shally 16 straddle the fence
hesitating 8 doubtful, hesitant 10 indecisive, irresolute, on the fence
he speaks
   Latin: 8 loquitur
Hesperia
   also: 5 Italy 16 Iberian Peninsula
Hesperides
   author: 13 Robert Herrick
Hesperides
   form: 6 nymphs
   guarded: 12 golden apples
   guarded with: 5 Ladon 6 dragon

   names: 5 Aegle 6 Hestia 7 Erythea,
   Hespera 8 Arethusa 9 Hespereia, Hes-
   perusa
   islands of the: 7 blessed
   form of: 6 heaven
Hesperis
   mother: 8 Hesperus
   mother of: 10 Hesperides
Hess, Victor Francis
   field: 7 physics
   discovered: 10 cosmic rays
   awarded: 10 Nobel Prize
Hesse, Hermann
   author of: 6 Demian 9 Rosshalde 10
   Siddhartha 11 Steppenwolf 12 Magister
   Ludi 14 Peter Camenzind 15 Beneath the
   Wheel 16 Death and the Lover, Journey
   to the East, The Glass Bead Game
Hesselberg, Melvyn Edouard
   real name of: 13 Melvyn Douglas
hessionite
   species: 6 garnet
Hestia
   origin: 5 Greek
   goddess of the: 6 hearth
   father: 6 Cronos, Cronus, Kronos
   mother: 4 Rhea
   corresponds to: 5 Vesta
Heston, Charlton
   real name: 13 Charles Carter
   born: 10 Evanston IL
   roles: 5 El Cid, Moses 6 Ben-Hur (Oscar)
   15 Planet of the Apes 18 The Ten
   Commandments 21 The Agony and the
   Ecstasy 22 The Greatest Show on Earth
Heterodontosaurus
   type: 8 dinosaur 10 ornithopod
   location: 6 Africa
   period: 8 Triassic
heterogeneous 5 mixed 6 motley, unlike,
varied 7 diverse, jumbled 8 assorted 9
composite, disparate, divergent, unrelated
10 dissimilar, variegated 11 diversified 13
miscellaneous
hew 2 ax 3 cut, lop 4 chop, form, hack,
mold 5 carve, model, prune, sever, shape
6 chisel, cut out, devise 7 cut down, fashion, whittle 8 chop down 9 sculpture
He Who Gets Slapped
   author: 14 Leonid Andreyev
he wrote it
   Latin: 8 scripsit
hex 4 harm, jinx, sign 5 curse, spell, witch
6 hoodoo, voodoo, whammy 7 bewitch,
evil eye, ill wind, possess 8 sorcerer 9 sorceress 11 malediction
Hexateuch 27 first six books of Old Testament
   see also: 7 Books of 12 Old Testament
heyday 4 acme 5 bloom, crest, flush,
prime, vigor 6 zenith 9 flowering, salad
days
Heyerdahl, Thor
   author of: 7 Kon-Tiki 16 The Ra Expedi-
tions

Hezekiah
  father: 4 Ahaz
  wife: 9 Hephzibah
  means: 18 Jehovah strengthens
Hi and Lois
  creator: 9 Dik Browne 10 Mort Walker
  character:
    brother: 12 Beetle Bailey
    children: 3 Dot 4 Chip 5 Ditto 6 Trixie
    dog: 4 Dawg
    friend: 7 Thirsty
hiatus 3 gap 4 void 5 blank, break, lapse,
  space 6 lacuna, vacuum 7 interim 8 interval 10 disruption 12 interruption
Hiawatha, The Song of
  author: 24 Henry Wadsworth Longfellow
  character: 5 Nahma 7 Kwasind,
    Nokomis, Wenonah 8 Mondamin 9
    Chibiabos, Minnehaha 11 Mudjekeewis
    12 Pau-Puk-Keewis, Pearl-Feather
hibernate 5 sleep 6 retire 8 withdraw 13
  become dormant
hibernating 6 asleep 7 dormant 8 inactive,
  sleeping 9 quiescent
Hibernia see 7 Ireland
hibiscus
  varieties: 7 Chinese 8 Hawaiian, Japa-
    nese
Hicetaon
  father: 8 Laomedon
  brother: 5 Priam
hic jacet 8 here lies
hickory 5 Carya
  varieties: 4 Pale, Sand 5 Broom,
    Swamp, Water 6 Pignut 7 Chinese 8
    Mountain, Shagbark 9 Mockernut, Shell-
    bark 10 White-heart 12 Small-fruited
Hicks, Edward
  born: 11 Attleboro PA
  artwork: 19 The Peaceable Kingdom
Hidatsa (Minitari, Gros Ventre)
  language family: 6 Siouan
  location: 7 Montana 11 North Dakota
  related to: 6 Mandan 7 Arikara
hidden away 6 buried, cached 7 stashed 8
  closeted, pocketed, secluded, secreted 9
  concealed 10 out of sight 11 stashed away
  12 inaccessible, undiscovered
hidden meaning 6 enigma, puzzle, riddle,
  secret 7 mystery
hidden motive
  French: 13 arriere pensee
hide 4 mask, pelt, skin, veil 5 cache, cloak,
  cloud, cover 6 lie low, screen, shroud 7
  conceal, curtain, leather, obscure, repress,
  seclude, secrete 8 disguise, suppress
hideaway 7 hideout, retreat 11 hiding
  place, secret place
hideous 4 grim, ugly, vile 5 awful 6 horrid,
  odious 7 ghastly, macabre 8 dreadful,
  gruesome, horrible, shocking 9 abhorrent,
  appalling, frightful, grotesque, loathsome,
  monstrous, repellent, repugnant, repulsive,
  revolting, sickening 10 abominable, detestable, disgusting, horrendous
hiding place 5 cache 8 hideaway 9 hidey
  hole 10 repository 11 secret place

Hieronimo
  character in: 17 The Spanish Tragedy
  author: 3 Kyd
hier wird Deutsch gesprochen 18 German is spoken here
Higgins, Henry
  character in: 9 Pygmalion 10 My Fair
    Lady
  author: 4 Shaw
Higgs
  character in: 7 Erewhon
  author: 6 Butler
high 3 gay, top 4 main, tall 5 aloft, chief, far
  up, grand, great, jolly, lofty, merry, noble,
  prime, sharp, undue, way up 6 alpine, august, elated, jovial, joyful, joyous, shrill 7
  capital, eminent, exalted, excited, extreme,
  gleeful, leading, notable, playful, primary,
  serious, soaring, soprano 8 cheerful, elevated, exultant, foremost, imposing, jubilant, mirthful, peerless, piercing, strident,
  superior, towering, uncurbed 9 ascendant,
  excellent, excessive, exuberant, important,
  overjoyed, principal, prominent, unbridled,
  uppermost 10 exorbitant, immoderate, inordinate, preeminent 11 cloud-capped, exaggerated, exhilarated, extravagant, high-
  pitched, illustrious, intemperate, predominant, significant, sky-scraping 12 earsplitting, high-reaching, lighthearted, unreasonable, unrestrained 13 consequential,
  distinguished
high-and-mighty 5 lofty 6 lordly 7 haughty
  8 arrogant 9 imperious 11 overbearing
highborn 5 noble 8 highbred, wellborn 9
  patrician 10 of high rank, upper-class 12
  aristocratic, of high degree, silk-stocking
  13 of gentle blood
highbred 5 noble, regal 6 lordly 7 refined 8
  highborn, wellborn 9 patrician 11 aristocracy, blue-blooded
highbrow 4 snob 5 brain 7 bookish, Brahmin, egghead, elitist, erudite, scholar,
  thinker 8 cultured, mandarin, snobbish 9
  scholarly 10 cultivated, double-dome,
  mastermind 12 intellectual 13 knowledgeable
highest good
  Latin: 11 summum bonum
highest point
  Latin: 11 ne plus ultra
high fashion
  French: 12 haute couture
high-flown 4 wild 5 lofty, proud 6 absurd,
  florid, lordly, turgid, unreal 7 flowery, orotund, pompous 8 elevated, fabulous, inflated 9 bombastic, excessive, fantastic,
  grandiose 10 flamboyant, immoderate, inordinate, outrageous 11 exaggerated, extravagant, highfalutin, pretentious, sententious 12 magniloquent, preposterous,
  presumptuous, unreasonable, unrestrained 13 grandiloquent, self-important
High-German
  language family: 12 Indo-European
  branch: 8 Germanic
  group: 15 Western Germanic

subgroup: 11 German-Dutch
division: 6 German 7 Yiddish
high-hat 5 aloof 6 formal, la-di-da, snooty 7 haughty 8 snobbish 12 supercilious
highjinks, hijinks 6 antics, capers, pranks, stunts 11 shenanigans 12 monkeyshines
highland, Highlands 4 rise 7 heights, plateau, uplands 8 headland 9 tableland 10 promontory 11 hill country 17 mountainous region
refers especially to: 8 Scotland
highlight 4 peak 6 accent, climax, stress 7 feature, point up 9 emphasize, high point, underline 10 accentuate, focal point, make bright
highly qualified 3 fit 4 able 7 trained 8 eligible, prepared, skillful 9 practiced 10 proficient 11 experienced 12 accomplished
highly regarded 6 prized 7 admired, revered 8 esteemed 9 respected, treasured 13 well thought of
highly valued 4 dear 5 loved 6 adored 7 beloved, revered 8 esteemed, precious 9 cherished, treasured
highly visible 7 glaring, obvious 8 distinct 9 prominent 11 conspicuous, outstanding
high-minded 4 fair, just 5 lofty, moral, noble 6 honest, worthy 7 ethical, sincere, upright 8 truthful, virtuous 9 exemplary, honorable, reputable, righteous, uncorrupt 10 chivalrous, idealistic, principled, scrupulous 13 conscientious, square-dealing

High Noon
director: 13 Fred Zinnemann
cast: 10 Gary Cooper (Will Kane), Grace Kelly 12 Lloyd Bridges 14 Thomas Mitchell
score: 14 Dimitri Tiomkin
Oscar for: 5 actor (Cooper)
high old time 4 ball, lark 5 fling, revel, spree 8 escapade
high-pitched 5 acute, sharp 6 shrill 7 clarion, squeaky 8 piercing
high place 4 hill, peak, rise 5 bluff, cliff, knoll, ridge 6 height, summit, upland 7 hillock, hummock, plateau 8 eminence, mountain 9 elevation 10 prominence, promontory
high point, highest point 3 cap, top4 acme, apex, peak 5 crest, crown 6 apogee, climax, height, heyday, summit, tiptop, vertex, zenith 8 eminence, pinnacle 9 flowering 10 prominence 11 culmination
high position 4 note 8 eminence, high rank, standing 9 supremacy 10 ascendancy, importance, notability, prominence 11 distinction, preeminence
high-powered 7 driving, dynamic 8 forceful 9 ambitious, assertive, energetic, go-getting 10 aggressive 11 hard-driving
high praise 5 kudos, paean 6 eulogy 7 hosanna, plaudit 8 encomium 9 laudation, panegyric 11 acclamation
high-priced 4 dear, high 6 costly, pricey 9 expensive 10 exorbitant, overpriced 11 extravagant

high-principled 5 moral, noble 6 chaste, honest, worthy 7 ethical, upright 9 honorable, reputable 10 idealistic 11 responsible, trustworthy 13 conscientious
high quality 5 merit 7 quality 9 greatness 10 excellence, perfection 11 distinction, superiority
high-ranking 3 top 5 grand, great, lofty, regal, royal 6 august 7 eminent, exalted, supreme 8 elevated, esteemed, imposing 9 important, paramount, venerable 10 preeminent 11 illustrious 13 distinguished

High Sierra
director: 10 Raoul Walsh
cast: 9 Ida Lupino 10 Alan Curtis, Joan Leslie 13 Arthur Kennedy 14 Humphrey Bogart (Mad Dog Earle)
remade as: 17 Colorado Territory 19 I Died a Thousand Times
high society 5 elite 9 haut monde, top drawer 11 aristocracy 14 creme de la creme
French: 9 haut monde

High Society
director: 14 Charles Walters
cast: 10 Bing Crosby, Grace Kelly 11 Celeste Holm 12 Frank Sinatra, Louis Calhern 14 Louis Armstrong
score: 10 Cole Porter
remake of: 20 The Philadelphia Story
song: 8 True Love 10 Did You Evah? 16 You're Sensational
high-speed 4 fast 5 quick, rapid, swift 6 speedy 7 express
high-spirited 5 vital 6 lively 8 animated 9 exuberant, vivacious 12 effervescent, enthusiastic
high spirits 5 vigor 6 gaiety 7 delight, elation 8 gladness, vitality, vivacity 9 animation 10 enthusiasm, exaltation, excitement, joyousness, liveliness 12 exhilaration 16 lightheartedness
high-strung 4 edgy 5 jumpy, moody, tense 6 uneasy 7 jittery, nervous, uptight 8 neurotic, restless, skittish 9 emotional, excitable, impatient, wrought-up 10 hysterical 13 oversensitive, temperamental 14 easily agitated, hypersensitive

High Tor
author: 15 Maxwell Anderson
highway 7 freeway, parkway, thruway 8 hard road, highroad, main road, speedway, turnpike 9 paved road 10 expressway, interstate, main artery 12 four-lane road, thoroughfare
British: 9 coach road, royal road 12 King's highway 13 Queen's highway
highwayman 5 crook, thief 6 bandit, outlaw, robber 7 brigand, footpad
hike 4 rise, roam, rove, trek, walk 5 leg it, march, raise, tramp 6 draw up, hoof it, jerk up, pull up, ramble, trudge, wander 7 hitch up, raise up 8 addition, increase 9 expansion 10 escalation 12 augmentation 13 journey on foot 14 go by shank's mare

Hilaira
vocation: 9 priestess
priestess of: 7 Artemis
father: 9 Leucippus
abducted by: 6 Castor

hilarious 3 gay 5 jolly, merry, noisy 6 jocund, jovial, joyful, joyous, lively 7 comical, gleeful, riotous 8 jubilant, mirthful 9 exuberant, laughable, very funny 10 boisterous, hysterical, rollicking, uproarious, vociferous 11 exhilarated 12 high-spirited 13 highly amusing 14 laugh-provoking

hilarity 3 fun, gig, joy 4 glee, riot 5 laugh, mirth, noisy 6 comedy, gaiety, giggle, levity 7 chortle, chuckle, jollity 8 hysteria, laughter 9 amusement, funniness, joviality, jubilance, merriment 10 exuberance 12 exhilaration, humorousness 14 uproariousness

Hilbert, David
field: 8 geometry 11 mathematics
nationality: 6 German
formulated: 12 modern axioms

Hilda Lessways
author: 13 Arnold Bennett

hill 4 bank, dune, heap, pile, ramp, rise 5 bluff, butte, cliff, climb, grade, knoll, mound, mount, slope 6 height 7 hillock, hilltop, hummock, incline, upgrade 8 eminence, foothill, highland, hillside 9 acclivity, declivity, downgrade, elevation 10 prominence, promontory

Hill, Arthur
born: 6 Canada 7 Melfort 12 Saskatchewan
roles: 13 All the Way Home 15 The Ugly American 17 Look Homeward Angel 25 Who's Afraid of Virginia Woolf?

Hill, George Roy
director of: 8 The Sting (Oscar) 23 The World According to Garp 29 Butch Cassidy and the Sundance Kid

Hiller, Arthur
director of: 25 The Americanization of Emily

hillock 4 hill, rise 5 knoll, mound 7 hummock 8 eminence

Hill Street Blues
character: 5 LaRue, Renko 9 Bobby Hill, Jablonski, Joe Coffey, Lucy Bates 10 Fay Furillo, Mick Belker, Washington 11 (Lt) Norman Buntz 12 Howard Hunter, (Captain) Frank Furillo 13 Henry Goldblum 14 Joyce Davenport
cast: 8 Joe Spano 10 Bruce Weitz, Ed Marinaro, Kiel Martin 11 Betty Thomas, Charles Haid, Dennis Franz 12 Robert Prosky 13 James B Sikking, Michael Warren, Veronica Hamel 14 Taurean Blacque 15 Daniel J Travanti

Hilton, James
author of: 11 Lost Horizon 14 Good-Bye Mr Chips

Himeros
origin: 5 Greek
god of: 12 erotic desire
associated with: 4 Eros

Hind see 5 India

Hind and the Panther, The
author: 10 John Dryden

Hindarfjall see 8 Hindfell

Hindemith, Paul
born: 5 Hanau 7 Germany
composer of: 8 The Demon 9 Cardillac 10 Heriodiade 12 Ludus Tonalis, Neues vom Tage, News of the Day 13 Sancta Susanna 14 Cupid and Psyche, Mathis Der Maler 15 In Praise of Music 17 Murder Hope of Women 18 Die Harmonie der Welt, Nobilissima Visione 19 The Four Temperaments 23 Morder Hoffnung der Frauen

hinder 3 bar 4 curb, foil, stay, stop 5 block, check, defay, deter, spike, stall 6 arrest, detain, fetter, hamper, hobble, hog-tie, hold up, impede, retard, stifle, stymie, thwart 7 inhibit 8 encumber, handicap, hold back, obstruct, restrain, slow down 9 frustrate, hamstring 13 interfere with

Hindfell
also: 11 Hindarfjall
origin: 12 Scandinavian
mountain slept on by: 8 Brynhild

Hindi
language family: 12 Indo-European
branch: 11 Indo-Iranian
group: 5 Indic
official language of: 5 India

hindmost 4 last, rear 7 tail end 12 farthest back

hindpart 4 tail 6 far end 7 rear end 8 backside, buttocks, haunches 9 afterpart, posterior

hindquarters 4 rear, rump 7 rear end, tail end 8 back legs, backside, buttocks, haunches 9 posterior

hindrance 3 bar 4 clog, curb, snag 5 catch 6 fetter 7 barrier, shackle 8 blockade, blockage, handicap, obstacle 9 barricade, restraint, retardant 10 constraint, difficulty, impediment, limitation 11 encumbrance, obstruction, restriction 12 interference 14 stumbling block

hinge 4 hang, rest, turn 5 pivot, swing 6 depend 7 be due to 9 arise from 10 result from 11 be subject to, emanate from 13 revolve around

hint 3 bit, jot, tip 4 clue, idea, iota 5 grain, imply, pinch, tinge, touch, trace, whiff 6 little, notion, tip off 7 inkling, pointer, signify, soupcon, suggest, whisper 8 allusion, indicate, innuendo, intimate 9 insinuate, suspicion 10 impression, indication, intimation, smattering, suggestion 11 implication, indirection, insinuation 12 flea in the ear, slight amount 13 word to the wise

hinted 7 implied, oblique 8 implicit, indirect 9 suggested

hinterland 6 sticks 7 boonies, country 8 interior, midlands 9 backwater, backwoods, boondocks, rural area 11 countryside

Hiordis
  also: 7 Hjordis
  origin: 12 Scandinavian
  mentioned in: 8 Volsunga
  husband: 7 Sigmund
  son: 6 Sigurd

Hippalectryon
  form: 7 monster
  head and forelegs of: 5 horse
  legs, tail and body of: 4 cock

Hippocampus
  form: 7 monster
  body of: 5 horse
  tail of: 4 fish

Hippocrene
  form: 6 spring
  location: 12 Mount Helicon

Hippocurius
  epithet of: 8 Poseidon
  means: 12 horse tending

Hippodamas
  daugher: 8 Perimele
  drowned: 8 Perimele

hippodrome 5 arena 6 circus 7 stadium 8 coliseum

Hippogriff
  form: 7 monster
  combined: 5 horse 7 griffin

Hippolochus
  father: 11 Bellerophon
  son: 7 Glaucus

Hippolyta see 9 Hippolyte

Hippolyte
  also: 7 Antiope 9 Hippolyta
  queen of: 7 Amazons
  husband: 7 Theseus
  son: 10 Hippolytus
  Hercules stole her: 6 girdle

Hippolytus
  author: 9 Euripides
  character: 7 Artemis, Phaedra, Theseus 9 Aphrodite

Hippolytus
  father: 7 Theseus
  mother: 9 Hippolyta
  stepmother: 7 Phaedra
  loved by: 7 Phaedra
  killed by: 8 Poseidon

Hippomedon
  member of: 18 Seven against Thebes

Hippomenes
  suitor of: 8 Atalanta
  son: 13 Parthenopaeus

Hipponous
  vocation: 7 warrior
  home: 4 Troy
  daughter: 8 Periboea
  killed by: 8 Achilles

Hippothous
  king of: 7 Arcadia
  father: 8 Poseidon
  mother: 5 Alope

hire 3 fee, get, let, pay 4 cost, gain, rent 5 lease, wages 6 charge, employ, engage, income, obtain, profit, retain, reward, salary, secure, take on 7 appoint, charter, payment, procure, stipend 8 earnings, re-

ceipts 9 emolument 10 recompense 12 compensation, remuneration

hireling 4 goon, thug 6 flunky, lackey, menial, minion, stooge 7 gorilla 8 henchman, retainer 9 strong-arm 10 hatchet man

Hiroshima
  author: 10 John Hersey

hirsute 5 bushy, downy, hairy, nappy, wooly 6 shaggy, woolly 7 bearded, bristly, prickly, unshorn 8 bristled, unshaven 9 whiskered 11 bewhiskered

His Girl Friday
  director: 11 Howard Hawks
  cast: 9 Cary Grant 12 Gene Lockhart, Ralph Bellamy 15 Rosalind Russell
  remake of: 12 The Front Page

Hispania see 5 Spain

hiss 3 boo 4 mock, razz 6 deride, heckle, hoot at, jeer at, revile 7 catcall, scoff at, sneer at 9 shout down 10 Bronx cheer 16 give the raspberry

histology
  study of: 6 tissue

historian
  American: 4 Webb 5 Adams 6 Brooks, De Voto, Durant, Fisher, Miller, Nevins, Sparks, Turner 7 Morison, Parkman, Taussig 8 Bancroft, Channing, Prescott, Robinson 10 Hofstadter
  British: 4 Bede (the Venerable) 6 Gibbon, Turner 7 Toynbee 8 Macaulay 9 Trevelyan
  Chinese: 10 Ssu-ma Ch'ien, Ssu-Ma Kuang
  French: 5 Bayle, Blanc, Bloch, Taine 7 Braudel 8 Mabillon, Michelet, Voltaire 11 Tocqueville
  German: 5 Ranke 7 Mommsen 8 Spengler 10 Burckhardt, Treitschke
  Greek: 8 Polybius 9 Herodotus 10 Thucydides
  Islamic: 8 al Tabari 10 Ibn Khaldun
  Italian: 4 Polo, Vico 5 Croce 11 Machiavelli 12 Guicciardini
  Latin: 4 Livy 7 Sallust, Tacitus
  Scottish: 7 Carlyle

historic 5 famed 7 notable 8 renowned 9 memorable, well-known 10 celebrated 11 outstanding

historical 4 past, real, true 6 actual, bygone, former 7 ancient, factual 8 attested, recorded 9 authentic 10 chronicled, documented

historical period 3 age, era 4 date, time 5 epoch, stage

history 4 epic, saga, tale 5 story 6 annals, change, growth, record, resume, review 7 account, the past 8 old times 9 chronicle, days of old, narration, narrative, portrayal, tradition, yesterday 10 bygone days, days of yore, olden times, the old days, yester-year 11 bygone times, development, former times, local events, major events, world events 12 actual events 13 an unusual past, human progress 14 military action, national events, recapitulation 15 political change

History of Colonel Jacque, The
   author: 11 Daniel Defoe
History of Henry VII
   author: 12 Francis Bacon
History of Mr Polly, The
   author: 7 H G Wells
   character: 6 Miriam 8 Uncle Jim 13 The
   Plump Woman
History of the English-Speaking Peoples, A
   author: 17 Winston S Churchill
His Toy, His Dream, His Rest
   author: 12 John Berryman
histrionics 4 fuss 6 acting, tirade 7 bluster,
bombast 8 outburst 9 dramatics, hammi-
ness, staginess, theatrics 10 dramaturgy,
playacting 11 performance, rodomontade
13 melodramatics, temper tantrum, theatricality 16 ranting and raving
hit 3 bat, jab, lob, rap, tap 4 bang, bash,
beat, belt, blow, boon, bump, butt, clip,
club, coup, cuff, damn, drub, find, flog,
hurt, move, pelt, poke, slam, slap, slug,
sock, stir, swat 5 abash, baste, clout,
crack, crush, flail, knock, paste, pound,
punch, reach, rouse, smack, smash,
smite, thump, touch, upset, whack 6 affect,
arouse, assail, attack, attain, batter, cudgel, effect, impact, incite, pommel, revile,
strike, thrash, thwack, wallop, winner 7
achieve, assault, censure, clobber, condemn, execute, godsend, impress, inflame, provoke, quicken, realize, shatter,
success, triumph, trounce, victory 8 arrive
at, bang into, blessing, bring off, denounce, lambaste, overcome, reproach 9
criticize, deal a blow, devastate, lash out
at, overwhelm, sensation, smash into 11
collide with, connect with, deal a stroke,
strike out at 12 go straight to 13 make a
bull's-eye, send to the mark 14 popular
success, strike together 16 mount an offensive
hit back 7 counter, get even, pay back 9
fight back, retaliate 10 strike back
hitch 3 tie, tug 4 curb, draw, halt, haul,
hike, jerk, knot, loop, pull, snag, stop,
yank, yoke 5 catch, check, clamp, delay,
raise, tying 6 attach, couple, fasten, mishap, secure, tether 7 bracket, connect,
harness, joining, mistake, problem, trouble
8 coupling, handicap, make fast, obstacle
9 attaching, fastening, hindrance, mischance, restraint 10 connection, difficulty,
impediment, limitation 11 restriction 12
complication, interruption, loop together,
put in harness 14 stumbling block
Hitchcock, Alfred
   director of: 6 Frenzy, Marnie, Psycho 7
   Rebecca, Vertigo 8 Lifeboat, The Birds 9
   Notorious, Suspicion 10 Family Plot,
   Rear Window, Spellbound 13 To Catch a
   Thief 14 Dial M for Murder, Shadow of a
   Doubt 15 The Lady Vanishes 16 North by
   Northwest 17 Strangers on a Train 18
   The Thirty-Nine Steps 19 The Trouble
   with Harry 20 Foreign Correspondent

hither 2 on 4 here, near 5 close 6 closer,
nearby, nearer, onward 7 close by, forward
8 over here 11 to this place 12 to the
speaker
hitherto 6 ere now, hereto 7 thus far, till
now, up to now 8 until now 10 before this,
heretofore
Hitler, Adolf
   author of: 9 Mein Kampf
hit man 6 killer, slayer 8 assassin, hired
gun, murderer 11 executioner 12 exterminator
Hitman
   nickname of: 12 Thomas Hearns
hit-or-miss 3 lax 6 casual, fitful 7 aimless,
cursory 8 slapdash 9 haphazard 10 incomplete 11 purposeless, superficial, unorganized 12 unsystematic 15 catch-as-catch-
can
hive 3 hub 5 heart 6 center, colony 7 cluster 9 busy place 11 swarm of bees
Hjordis see 7 Hiordis
Hliod see 4 Liod
H M S Pinafore
   subtitle: 23 The Lass That Loved a
   Sailor
   operetta by: 18 Gilbert and Sullivan
   character: 11 Dick Deadeye 14 Ralph
   Rackstraw 15 Captain Corcoran, Little
   Buttercup, Sir Joseph Porter 17 Josephine Corcoran
Hoagland, Edward
   author of: 15 African Calliope 17 The
   Tugman's Passage
hoar 3 old 4 aged, rime 5 frost, moldy,
mushy, passe, stale, white 6 old hat 7 ancient, antique, elderly, grayish 8 grizzled 9
out of date
hoard 4 fund, heap, mass, pile 5 amass,
buy up, cache, lay up, store 6 save up,
supply 7 acquire, collect, lay away, reserve
8 quantity 9 amassment, gathering, stockpile, store away 10 accumulate, collection
12 accumulation
hoarse 5 gruff, harsh, husky, raspy, rough 6
croaky 7 cracked, rasping, raucous,
throaty 8 gravelly, guttural, scratchy
hoary 3 old 4 aged, gray, hoar 5 dated,
passe, white 6 grayed, old hat 7 ancient,
antique, grizzly 8 grizzled, whitened 9 out-
of-date 11 gray with age 12 white with age
hoax 4 gyp 4 bilk, dupe, fake, fool, gull,
yarn 5 bluff, cheat, cozen, fraud, prank,
spoof, trick 6 canard, delude, humbug,
take in 7 deceive, defraud, fiction, mislead,
swindle 8 hoodwink 9 bamboozle, chicanery, deception, fish story, victimize 10
hocus-pocus
Hoban, James
   architect of: 13 The White House, Great
   Hotel (Washington, DC)
Hobbes, Thomas
   author of: 9 Leviathan
Hobbit, The
   part of: 14 Lord of the Rings
   author: 10 J R R Tolkien

hobble 4 bind, gimp, halt, limp 5 block, check, cramp 6 fetter, hamper, hinder, hog-tie, impede, lumber, stymie, thwart, toddle 7 inhibit, manacle, shackle, shamble, shuffle, stagger, stumble 8 encumber, handicap, hold back, lame gait, obstruct, restrain, restrict 9 constrain, frustrate, hamstring 10 uneven gait, walk lamely 13 interfere with

hobby 7 pastime, pursuit 8 sideline 9 amusement, avocation, diversion 10 relaxation 13 entertainment 14 divertissement

hobbyhorse 5 hobby 7 pastime 8 interest, toy horse 9 diversion 10 enthusiasm 11 distraction 12 rocking horse

hobgoblin 3 imp 5 bogey 6 goblin 7 bugaboo

hobnob 3 mix 4 club 6 mingle 7 consort, hang out 9 associate, rub elbows 10 fraternize

hobo 3 beg, bum 5 stiff, tramp 6 beggar, cadger, loafer 7 drifter, migrant, moocher, vagrant 8 derelict, vagabond, wanderer 9 scrounger 11 beachcomber

hoc est 6 this is

Ho Chi Minh City
 formerly: 6 Saigon
 river: 6 Saigon
 delta: 6 Mekong
 former capital of: 9 Indochina 11 Cochin China 12 South Vietnam

hockey
 athlete: 8 Bobby Orr, Brad Park 9 Bobby Hull, Ken Dryden, Mike Bossy 10 Doug Harvey, Eddie Shore, Ed Giacomin, Gordie Howe, Guy Lafleur, Ray Bourque, Rod Gilbert, Stan Mikita 11 Bobby Clarke, Brian Leetch, Denis Potvin, Eric Lindros, Jean Ratelle, Mark Messier 12 Emile Francis, Jean Beliveau, Marcel Dionne, Mario Lemieux, Phil Esposito, Wayne Gretzky 13 Bernard Parent, Jacques Plante, Larry Robinson, Pat La Fontaine 14 Alex Delvecchio, Maurice Richard 15 Bernie Geoffrion 18 Yvan Serge Courneyer

hockey team
 Anaheim: 11 Mighty Ducks
 Boston: 6 Bruins
 Buffalo: 6 Sabres
 Calgary: 6 Flames
 Chicago: 10 Black Hawks
 Dallas: 5 Stars
 Detroit: 8 Red Wings
 Edmonton: 6 Oilers
 Florida: 8 Panthers
 Hartford: 7 Whalers
 Los Angeles: 5 Kings
 Montreal: 9 Canadiens
 New Jersey: 6 Devils
 New York: 7 Rangers 9 Islanders
 Ottawa: 8 Senators
 Philadelphia: 6 Flyers
 Pittsburgh: 8 Penguins
 Quebec: 9 Nordiques
 St Louis: 5 Blues
 San Jose: 6 Sharks

Tampa Bay: 9 Lightning
 Toronto: 10 Maple Leafs
 Vancouver: 7 Canucks
 Washington: 8 Capitals
 Winnipeg: 4 Jets

hocus-pocus 4 bosh, bull, hoax, sham 5 chant, charm, cheat, magic, spell 6 bunkum, deceit, fakery, humbug 7 con game, hogwash, rubbish, swindle 8 delusion, flimflam, tommyrot, trickery 9 deception, moonshine, poppycock 10 dishonesty, flapdoodle, hanky-panky, magic spell, magic words, mumbo jumbo, subterfuge 11 bewitchment, incantation, legerdemain, magic tricks 12 fiddle-faddle, magic formula 13 sleight of hand

Hoder
 also: 5 Hodur
 origin: 12 Scandinavian
 brother: 5 Baldr 6 Balder, Baldur
 father: 4 Odin 5 Othin
 killed: 5 Baldr 6 Balder, Baldur

hodgepodge, hotchpotch 3 mix 4 hash, mess 6 jumble, medley, muddle 7 melange, mixture 8 mishmash 9 composite, confusion, patchwork, potpourri 10 miscellany

Hodur *see* 5 Hoder

Hoenir
 origin: 12 Scandinavian
 race: 5 Vanir
 created: 3 Ask 5 Embla

Hoff, Jacobus Hendricus van't
 field: 9 chemistry
 nationality: 5 Dutch
 researched: 7 gas laws 10 carbon atom 14 thermodynamics
 awarded: 10 Nobel Prize

Hoffman, Dustin
 born: 12 Los Angeles CA
 roles: 5 Lenny 6 Ishtar 7 Tootsie 8 Papillon 10 Ratso Rizzo 11 The Graduate 12 Little Big Man 14 Kramer vs Kramer (Oscar), Midnight Cowboy 19 All the President's Men

Hofmann, Hans
 born: 7 Germany 11 Weissenberg
 artwork: 6 Spring 7 The Gate 13 Effervescence 14 Fantasia in Blue, Magenta and Blue 16 Sanctum Sanctorum

Hofstadter, Richard
 author of: 14 The Age of Reform

hog 3 pig, sow 4 arch, boar, trim 5 broom, sheep, swine 6 gorger, porker 7 baconer, glutton, take all 9 razorback 10 locomotive

Hogan, Paul
 country: 9 Australia
 roles: 10 Mick Dundee 15 Crocodile Dundee

Hogan's Heroes
 character: 7 (Peter) Newkirk 8 Lt Carter 10 Sgt (Hans) Schultz 11 Louis LeBeau 14 Col Robert Hogan 15 Col Wilhelm Klink
 cast: 8 Bob Crane 10 John Banner, Larry Hovis 11 Robert Clary 13 Richard Dawson 15 Werner Klemperer

Hogarth, William
  born: 6 London 7 England
  artwork: 12 Captain Coram 14 A Rake's Progress 15 Marriage a la Mode, The Beggar's Opera 16 A Harlot's Progress 19 Garrick as Richard III
hogshead 3 keg, tun, vat 4 butt, cask, drum 6 barrel
hogwash 3 rot 4 bull, bunk 5 hokum, hooey, stuff 6 bunkum, drivel, hot air, humbug 7 baloney, blather, spinach, twaddle 8 claptrap, nonsense, tommyrot 9 poppycock 10 applesauce 11 foolishness 13 horsefeathers 16 stuff and nonsense
hoi polloi 6 rabble, the mob 7 the herd 8 canaille, populace, riffraff, the crowd, the plebs 9 the masses, the proles, the vulgar 10 commonalty 12 the multitude 14 the lower orders, the proletariat, the rank and file 15 the common people, the lower classes, the working class
hoist 4 lift 5 heave, raise, run up 6 bear up, pull up, take up, uplift 7 elevate, raise up, upraise 9 bear aloft
Hokan
  language family: 17 Hokan-Coahuiltecan
  subgroup: 4 Pomo, Seri, Yana 5 Karok, Washo, Yuman 7 Chontal, Chumash, Esselen, Jicaque 8 Subtiaba 9 Chimariko 14 Shasta-Achomawi
  tribe: 8 Achomawi
Hokan-Coahuiltecan
  language branch: 5 Hokan 12 Coahuiltecan 17 Subtiaba-Tlappanec
Hokusai, Katsushika
  born: 3 Edo 5 Japan, Tokyo
  artwork: 5 Crabs, Manga 10 Waterfalls 11 Chushingura 25 Thirty-six Views of Mount Fuji
Holabird, William
  partner: 11 Martin Roche
  architect of: 12 Gage Building 13 Cable Building, Crerar Library (City Hall, Chicago) 14 Tacoma Building 15 McClurg Building 17 Marquette Building
Holbein, Hans (the Elder)
  born: 7 Germany 8 Augsburg
  son: 11 Hans Holbein (the Younger)
  artwork: 11 St Sebastian 14 Fountain of Life 18 Kaisheim Altarpiece 31 Presentation of Christ in the Temple
Holbein, Hans (the Younger)
  born: 7 Germany 8 Augsburg
  father: 11 Hans Holbein (the Elder)
  artwork: 7 Erasmus 9 Henry VIII 11 Jane Seymour 12 Dance of Death 13 The Dead Christ
hold 4 bear, bind, bond, curb, deem, grip, halt, have, hilt, keep, knob, lock, prop, rule, stay, sway, take, urge 5 brace, carry, check, clasp, cling, count, defer, grasp, guard, limit, offer, power, shaft, shore, stall, stand, stick, strap, think, unite, watch 6 adhere, affirm, assert, assume, cleave, clinch, clutch, deduct, detain, direct, enfold, handle, hinder, hold up, join in, manage, occupy, reckon, regard, retain,

submit, take in, tender, thwart, uphold 7 advance, believe, carry on, command, conduct, confine, contain, control, declare, embrace, enclose, enforce, execute, hold off, include, inhibit, mastery, possess, present, presume, prevent, profess, propose, protect, repress, reserve, support, suppose, surmise, suspend, toehold, venture 8 advocate, conceive, conclude, consider, engage in, foothold, handhold, hold back, hold down, leverage, maintain, obligate, postpone, purchase, put forth, restrain, restrict, set aside, suppress, withhold 9 advantage, anchorage, authority, be in force, dominance, forestall, frustrate, influence, keep valid, ownership, stay fixed, stick fast 10 ascendancy, attachment, desist from, domination, possession, put forward, understand 11 accommodate, preside over
hold a candle to 5 equal, match 6 be up to 7 compare 8 approach 10 be as good as 11 come close to, compete with 12 be comparable 14 bear comparison
hold against 6 resent 8 begrudge
hold back 3 lag 4 curb, deny, keep, slow 5 check, dally, limit, stall 6 arrest, bridle, falter, refuse 7 contain, inhibit, keep out, reserve, retrain 8 hesitate, keep back, maintain, restrain, withhold 9 constrain
hold close 3 hug 5 clasp 6 cuddle, harbor 7 cherish, embrace, snuggle
Holden, William
  real name: 23 William Franklin Beedle Jr
  nickname: 4 Bill
  born: 9 O'Fallon IL
  roles: 6 Picnic 7 Network, Sabrina 9 Golden Boy 13 Born Yesterday 14 The Country Girl 15 Stalag Seventeen (Oscar), Sunset Boulevard 23 The Bridge on the River Kwai
hold fast 4 fuse, hold 5 cling, stick 6 adhere
hold firmly 4 grip 5 clasp, grasp 6 clench, clinch, clutch 10 grab hold of
hold forth 7 expound 9 discourse, expatiate
hold in abeyance 5 table 6 recess, shelve 7 suspend 8 lay aside, postpone
hold in bondage 7 control, enchain, enslave, entrall 8 dominate 9 subjugate 12 make a slave of
holdings 6 assets 8 property 10 securities 11 commodities
hold in high regard 5 honor, prize, value 6 admire, esteem, revere 7 cherish, respect 8 look up to, treasure, venerate 10 rate highly, set store by 13 think highly of 18 attach importance to
hold one's own 4 cope 6 manage 7 contend 11 be a match for 20 maintain one's position 22 keep one's head above water
hold rapt 5 charm 7 beguile, bewitch, enchant 8 enthrall, entrance 9 captivate, enrapture, fascinate, spellbind, transport

hold to 3 bind 8 obligate

hold together 4 bind, fuse, glue, hold, join 5 cling, stick, unite 6 cement, cohere 7 combine 11 consolidate

holdup 3 rob 4 bear, halt, stay, stop 5 delay, heist, steal, theft 6 hijack, retain, uphold 7 robbery, stickup, support, sustain 8 stoppage 9 hindrance 12 interruption

hold up 4 prop, slow 5 block, brace, check, delay 6 bear up, detain, endure, hinder, impede, manage 7 bolster, present, stand up, support, sustain 8 keep back, obstruct 13 rob at gunpoint

hold up under 4 bear 6 endure, manage 8 tolerate

hold warmly 3 hug 5 clasp 6 cuddle 7 embrace, snuggle

hole 3 den, gap, pit 4 brig, cage, cave, flaw, keep, lair, rent, slit, slot 5 break, crack, fault, shaft 6 breach, burrow, cavern, cavity, crater, defect, dugout, lockup, pocket, prison, tunnel 7 dungeon, fallacy, opening, orifice, slammer 8 aperture, dark cell, puncture 9 concavity, open space 10 depression, excavation 11 discrepancy, hollow place, indentation, perforation 13 inconsistency

Holgrave, Mr
    character in: 24 The House of the Seven Gables
    author: 9 Hawthorne

holiday 3 gay 4 fete, gala 6 cheery, fiesta, joyful, joyous, junket, outing 7 festive, holy day, jubilee 8 cheerful, feast day, festival, vacation 11 celebrating, celebration, merrymaking
    American: 6 Easter 8 Arbor Day, Labor Day 9 Christmas (Dec 25), Halloween (Oct 31) 10 Father's Day, Good Friday, Mother's Day 11 Columbus Day, Election Day, Memorial Day, New Year's Day (Jan 1), Veterans' Day (Nov 11) 12 Children's Day, Thanksgiving 15 Independence Day (July 4), St Valentine's Day (Feb 14) 23 National Grandparents' Day
    birthday: 8 Lincoln's 11 Robert E Lee's (Jan 19), Washington's 17 Martin Luther King's (Jan 15)
    Hawaiian: 13 Kamehameha Day (June 11)
    British: 8 Hogmanay (Dec 31) 9 Boxing Day (Dec 26) 11 Harvest Home 12 Guy Fawkes Day (Nov 5), Twelfth Night (Jan 5) 14 Queen's Birthday (June) 15 Commonwealth Day (May 24), Mothering Sunday 19 Feast of Saint Swithin (July 15)
    Canadian: 11 Victoria Day 14 Queen's Birthday, Remembrance Day
    Chinese: 7 New Year 15 Lantern Festival 17 Confucius' Birthday (Sept 28) 18 Dragon Boat Festival
    French: 11 Bastille Day (May 14)
    German: 11 Oktoberfest
    Greek: 7 Genesia 11 Feast of Pots
    Indian: 4 Holi 6 Basant, Diwali (New

Year) 17 Hindu fire festival 22 Mahatma Gandhi's Birthday (Oct 2)
    Irish: 16 Saint Patrick's Day (March 17)
    Italian: 13 Liberation Day (April 25)
    Japanese: 11 Hina-Matsuri 12 Children's Day (May 5), Feast of Dolls (March 3) 15 Constitution Day (May 3) 17 Girls' Doll Festival
    Jewish: 5 Purim 6 Sukkot 7 Shavuot, Sukkoth 8 Hanukkah, Passover 9 Yom Kippur 12 Rosh Hashanah 20 Hamishah Assar B'Shevat, The New Year of the Trees 21 Feast of the Tabernacles
    Korean: 6 Ch'usok
    Latin American: 12 Day of the Race
    Moslem: 7 Mouloud 8 Id-al-Adha, Id-al-Fitr 12 Maulid-an-Nabi 14 month of Ramadan
    religious: 6 Advent 7 Lady Day (Mar 25) 8 Epiphany, Shabuoth 9 Candlemas, Mardi Gras, Martinmas (Nov 11), Pentecost 10 Whitsunday 11 All Souls' Day (Nov 2) 12 Ascension Day, Ash Wednesday, Feast of Weeks 13 Shrove Tuesday, Trinity Sunday 15 Annunciation Day (Mar 25) 16 Feast of All Saints 20 Feast of Corpus Christi 23 Day of Our Lady of Guadalupe (Dec 12) 27 Purification of the Virgin Mary 30 Feast of the Immaculate Conception (Dec 8)
    Roman: 7 Feralia 10 Saturnalia
    Scottish: 8 Hogmanay 12 Candlemas Day 19 Festival of the Virgin
    South American: 21 Simon Bolivar's Birthday (July 24)
    Sri Lankan: 5 Wesak
    Soviet Union: 6 May Day (May 1) 14 Lenin's Birthday (April 22) 39 Day of the Great October Socialist Revolution (Nov 7)
    Swedish: 13 Santa Lucia Day (Dec 13)
    Thailand: 11 Visakha Puja

holiness 8 sanctity 9 godliness 10 sacredness 11 blessedness, saintliness

Holland *see* 11 Netherlands

Holie
    origin: 8 Germanic
    goddess of: 4 moon
    corresponds to: 7 Berchta, Perchta
    form: 5 witch

holler 4 bark, roar, yell 5 gripe, shout 6 bellow, cry out, grouse 8 complain 9 hue and cry

Holliday, Judy
    real name: 11 Judith Tuvim
    born: 9 New York NY
    roles: 8 Adam's Rib 13 Born Yesterday (Oscar) 15 Bells Are Ringing

Hollinshed, Raphael
    author of: 37 Chronicles of England Scotland and Ireland

hollow 3 dip, low, rut 4 cave, dale, deep, dell, dent, dull, glen, hole, sink, vain, vale, void 5 ditch, empty, false, muted 6 cavern, cavity, crater, dig out, dimple, furrow, futile, groove, pocket, sunken, vacant, vacuum, valley 7 channel, concave, useless 8 crevasse, empty out, excavate, gouge out, indented, not solid, nugatory, rumbling, scoop out, specious, unfilled 9 cavernous, concavity, deceptive, depressed, fruitless, pointless, valueless, worthless 10 depression, profitless, sepulchral, unavailing, unresonant 11 indentation, meaningless, nonresonant 12 unprofitable 13 curving inward, disappointing, reverberating 14 expressionless, unsatisfactory 15 inconsequential

Holloway, Stanley
   born: 6 London 7 England
   roles: 10 My Fair Lady 15 Alfred Doolittle 18 The Lavender Hill Mob

Hollow Men
   author: 7 T S Eliot

hollowness 4 void 6 vacuum 7 vacancy 9 emptiness

hollow out 4 bore 5 drill 6 dig out 8 carve out, gouge out, scoop out 9 chisel out 13 tunnel through

holly 4 ilex
   varieties: 3 box, sea 4 dune 5 Cuban, Dutch, dwarf, false, Furin, Kashi, swamp, Tsuru 6 desert, horned, Oregon, Sarvis, Soyogo, summer 7 African, Chinese, English, Georgia, Madeira 8 American, European, hedgehog, Japanese, Kurogane, mountain 9 box-leaved, Highclere, miniature, moonlight, porcupine, Singapore 10 Costa Rican, luster-leaf, West Indian 11 large-leaved, Puerto Rican, screw-leaved 12 Canary Island, gold hedgehog, myrtle-leaved, smooth-leaved 14 silver hedgehog

hollyhock 6 mallow 7 Antwerp, figleaf 8 biennial 9 ficifolia, Malvaceae 10 alcea rosea

Hollywood's Mermaid
   nickname of: 14 Esther Williams

Hollywood Squares
   host: 12 John Davidson 13 Peter Marshall
   regular: 8 Wally Cox 10 Joan Rivers 13 Charley Weaver, Shadoe Stevens

Holmes, Oliver Wendell
   author of: 12 Old Ironsides 30 The Autocrat of the Breakfast Table

Holmes, Sherlock
   address: 11 (221B) Baker Street
   appears in: 13 The Sign of Four 14 The Naval Treaty 15 A Study in Scarlet, The Speckled Band 16 Scandal in Bohemia, The Blue Carbuncle, The Copper Beeches 18 The Red-Headed League, The Solitary Cyclist 22 Hound of the Baskervilles
   assistants: 21 Baker Street Irregulars
   author: 16 (Sir) Arthur Conan Doyle
   brother: 7 Mycroft
   foe: 17 Professor Moriarty
   hat: 11 deerstalker
   hobby: 6 violin
   housekeeper/landlady: 9 Mrs Hudson
   keeps tobacco in: 7 slipper 14 Turkish slipper

   police: 17 Inspector Lestrade
   sidekick: 12 Dr John Watson
   vice: 7 cocaine 17 hypodermic syringe 20 seven-per-cent solution

Holmwood, Arthur
   character in: 7 Dracula
   author: 6 Stoker

holocaust 4 ruin 5 havoc 6 ravage 7 bonfire, carnage, inferno, killing 8 butchery, genocide, massacre 10 deadly fire, mass murder 11 devastation 12 annihilation 13 conflagration

Holofernes
   character in: 16 Love's Labour's Lost
   author: 11 Shakespeare

Holofernes
   general of: 14 Nebuchadnezzar
   killed by: 6 Judith

Holst, Gustav Theodore
   born: 7 England 10 Cheltenham
   composer of: 7 Savitri 10 Egdon Heath, Ode to Death, The Planets 11 Hammersmith 12 St Paul's Suite 13 Fugal Concerto 14 The Hymn of Jesus, The Perfect Fool 16 Somerset Rhapsody 17 The Cloud Messenger 19 Hymns from the Rig-Veda

holy 4 pure 5 godly, moral, pious 6 adored, devout, divine, sacred, solemn 7 angelic, blessed, from God, revered, saintly, sinless 8 faithful, hallowed, heavenly, reverent, virtuous 9 from above, guileless, religious, righteous, spiritual, undefiled, unspotted, unstained, unworldly, venerated, worshiped 10 heaven-sent, immaculate, inviolable, sacrosanct, sanctified, worshipped 11 consecrated, pure in heart, uncorrupted
   Latin: 7 sanctus

Holy Ark
   Hebrew: 10 Aron Kodesh

holy of holies
   Latin: 16 sanctum sanctorum

Holy one see see Jesus

Holy Spirit, Holy Ghost 9 Paraclete 13 presence of God 23 third person of the Trinity
   Latin: 15 Spiritus Sanctus
   Greek: 12 Hagion Pneuma

holy war
   Arabic: 5 jehad, jihad

Holy Willie's Prayer
   author: 11 Robert Burns

Homadus
   form: 7 centaur
   killed by: 8 Hercules

homage 5 honor 6 esteem, praise, regard 7 respect, tribute, worship 8 devotion 9 adoration, adulation, deference, obeisance, reverence 10 exaltation, veneration 13 glorification

Homagyrius
   epithet of: 4 Zeus
   means: 9 assembler

hombre 3 man
home 5 abode, haunt, haven, house **6** asylum, cradle, refuge **7** habitat, hangout **8** domicile, dwelling, hospital **9** orphanage, poorhouse, residence **10** habitation, native land, sanatorium **11** institution **12** fountainhead **13** dwelling place, home sweet home **14** stamping ground **16** place of residence **18** natural environment **25** place where one hangs one's hat
Home Burial
  author: **11** Robert Frost
homegrown 5 local **6** native **8** domestic **10** indigenous
Home Is the Sailor
  author: **10** Jorge Amado
homelike 4 cozy **5** comfy, homey **6** simple **8** cheerful, domestic, familiar, informal, inviting **11** comfortable
homely 4 cozy, drab, snug **5** comfy, homey, plain **6** modest, rustic, simple **7** artless, natural **8** everyday, familiar, homelike, homespun, ordinary, uncomely **9** graceless **10** ill-favored, provincial, unaffected, unassuming, ungraceful, unhandsome **11** comfortable **12** plain-looking, unattractive **13** unpretentious
homer 15 Biblical measure
Homer
  author of: **5** Iliad **7** Odyssey
Homer, Winslow
  born: **8** Boston MA
  artwork: **9** High Cliff **10** Breezing Up, Eight Bells **11** Marine Coast, Northeaster, The Life Line **13** The Fog Warning, The Gulf Stream **21** Inside the Bar Tynemouth, Prisoners from the Front
home rule 8 autonomy **11** sovereignty **12** independence **14** self-government
homespun 5 plain **6** folksy, homely, modest, native, simple **7** artless, natural **8** down-home, homemade **9** hand-woven **10** hand-loomed, unaffected **11** hand-crafted, hand-wrought **13** unpretentious
homey 4 cozy **6** casual, folksy **8** down-home, homelike, homespun, informal **15** unsophisticated
homicide 6 killer, murder, slayer **7** slaying **8** foul play, murderer, regicide, vaticide **9** bloodshed, man killer, manslayer, matricide, parricide, patricide, uxoricide **10** fratricide **11** infanticide **12** manslaughter
homiletic 7 preachy **8** didactic **10** moralizing
homily 6 sermon **7** lecture **10** preachment **11** exhortation
homogeneous 4 akin, pure **7** kindred, similar, uniform, unmixed **8** all alike, constant, of a piece **9** identical, unvarying **10** consistent **13** of the same kind, unadulterated
homology 7 analogy **8** likeness, relation **10** similarity **12** relationship **14** correspondence
Honduras
  name means: **6** depths
  capital/largest city: **11** Tegucigalpa
  others: **4** Tela, Yoro **5** Copan, Danli,

Lapaz **6** Roatan **7** Gracias, La Ceiba **8** Trujillo, Yuscaran **9** Choluteca, Juticalpa **10** El Progreso **11** Comayaguela **12** Puerto Cortes, San Pedro Sula
  measure: **4** vara **5** milla **6** mecate **7** cajuela
  monetary unit: **4** peso **7** centavo, lempira
  island: **3** Bay **5** Bahia, Utila **6** Roatan **7** Bonacca, Guanaja
  lake: **5** Criba, Yojoa **6** Brewer
  mountain: **4** Pija **6** Agalta **7** Celaque **9** Esperanza
  highest point: **8** Las Minas
  river: **4** Coco, Sico, Ulua **5** Aguan, Lempa, Negro, Tinto, Wanks **6** Patuca, Sulaco **7** Olancho, Paulaya, Segovia **8** Guiavope, Santiago **9** Choluteca **10** Chamelecon
  sea: **7** Pacific **8** Atlantic **9** Caribbean
  physical feature:
  coast: **5** North **8** Mosquito **10** Costa Norte
  gulf: **7** Fonseca **8** Honduras
  port: **7** Laceiba **8** Trujillo
  people: **4** Maya, Paya, Sumo, Ulva **5** Carib, Lenca, Pipil **6** Tauira **7** Jicaque, mestizo, Miskito **8** Mosquito
  discoverer: **8** Columbus
  farmer: **9** campesino
  language: **7** English, Spanish
  religion: **13** Roman Catholic
  place:
  ruins: **5** Copan **8** Tenampua
  feature:
  bird: **9** zenzontle
  dance: **5** sique **7** mascaro
  estate: **10** latifundia
  farm: **6** milpas **10** minifundia
  musical instrument: **7** caramba, marimba
  tree: **8** cockspur
  food:
  beans: **8** frijoles
  beef dish: **6** tapado
  corn: **5** maize
  stuffed corn cake: **10** naca tamale
  tripe stew: **8** mondongo
hone 4 long, moan, pine, tool, whet **5** stroke, strope, whine, yearn **6** hanker, grumble, mutter, sharpen **9** whetstone
Honegger, Arthur
  born: **5** Havre **6** France
  nationality: **5** Swiss
  member of: **6** Les Six, The Six
  composer of: **5** Rugby **6** Judith **7** L'Aiglon **8** Antigone **9** The Eaglet **10** Le Roi David **13** Pastorale d'ete **18** Jeanne d'Arc au Bucher, Liturgical Symphony **19** Pacific Two-Thirty-One
honest 4 fair, just, open, real, true **5** blunt, frank, legal, plain, solid, valid **6** candid, decent, lawful, proper, square **7** artless, ethical, genuine, sincere, upright **8** bona fide, clear-cut, faithful, innocent, reliable, straight, true-blue, truthful, virtuous **9** authentic, blameless, guileless, honorable,

ingenuous, reputable, righteous 10 above-board, dependable, forthright, law-abiding, legitimate, on the level, principled, reasonable, scrupulous, unaffected, unreserved 11 plainspoken, trustworthy, undisguised 12 on the up-and-up, tried and true 13 conscientious, fair and square 15 straightforward, unsophisticated 16 as good as one's word, straight-shooting 17 open and aboveboard

honesty 4 word 5 honor 7 probity 8 fairness, good name, morality, scruples, veracity 9 innocence, integrity, rectitude, sincerity 10 principles 11 just dealing, uprightness 12 faithfulness, reputability, truthfulness 13 guiltlessness, square dealing 15 trustworthiness 16 incorruptibility, straight shooting

honeybee
  classification: 6 social
  live in: 4 hive 6 colony
  headed by: 5 queen
  male: 5 drone
  laborer: 6 worker
  food-gatherer: 7 forager
  gather: 6 nectar, pollen
  produce: 5 honey
  queen's food: 10 royal jelly

honeyed 4 kind 5 sweet 6 sugary 7 cloying, fawning 10 flattering, saccharine 12 ingratiating 13 complimentary

honeyed words 4 line 7 blarney 8 cajolery, flattery, soft soap 9 sweet talk

Honey in the Horn
  author: 7 H L Davis

Honeymooners, The
  character: 8 Ed Norton 12 Alice Kramden, Ralph Kramden, Trixie Norton
  cast: 9 Jane Kean 12 Art Carney 12 Sheila MacRae 13 Audrey Meadows, Jackie Gleason, Joyce Randolph
  Ralph's job: 9 bus driver
  Ed's job: 5 sewer
  lodge: 8 Raccoons

honeysuckle 8 Lonicera 19 Aquilegia canadensis, Justicia californica 24 Rhododendron prinophyllum
  varieties: 3 fly 4 bush, cape 5 coral, giant, grape, hairy, swamp 6 desert, French, purple, yellow 7 Arizona, Jamaica, trumpet 8 Himalaya, Japanese, swamp fly, Tatarian 9 chaparral, Tatarian 10 yellow cape 11 European fly 12 giant Burmese, long-flowered, South African 13 Hall's Japanese

Honeythunder, Mr
  character in: 22 The Mystery of Edwin Drood
  author: 7 Dickens

Hong Kong
  name means: 13 incense harbor 14 fragrant harbor
  capital: 8 Victoria
  largest city:
  section: 7 Kowloon 8 Hong Kong, Victoria
  others: 4 Tai O 5 Tai Po 8 Aberdeen,

Pingshan, Yuenlong 9 Shataukok 10 Sheungshui
  division: 7 Kowloon 8 Hong Kong 14 New Territories
  government: 18 British crown colony
  head of state: 14 British monarch 15 governor general
  island: 5 Lamma 6 Lan Tao, Lantau, Middle, Poi Toi 8 Hong Kong 9 Ap Lei Chau 11 Stonecutter
  mountain: 6 Castle 8 Victoria
  highest point: 9 Tai Mo Shan
  river: 5 Pearl 6 Canton 8 Sham Chun
  sea: 10 South China
  physical feature:
  bay: 4 Mirs 6 Quarry 7 Kowloon, Repulse 9 Deep Water
  harbor: 4 Tolo 8 Aberdeen, Hong Kong, Victoria
  peak: 8 Victoria
  peninsula: 7 Kowloon
  people: 5 Hakka, Haklo, Punti, Tanka 7 British, Chinese 8 American, Japanese 9 Cantonese 10 Portuguese
  language: 7 Chinese, English 9 Cantonese
  religion: 5 Hindu, Islam 6 Taoism 8 Buddhism 12 Christianity
  feature:
  airport: 6 Kai Tak
  clothing: 6 samfoo 9 cheongsam
  houseboat: 6 sampan
  rock: 5 Amahs 6 Sha Tin
  temple: 18 Ten Thousand Buddhas

Honiara
  capital of: 14 Solomon Islands

honi soit qui mal y pense 31 shamed be the one who thinks evil of it
  motto of: 16 Order of the Garter

honk 4 toot 5 blare, blast 7 trumpet

honky-tonk 4 dive 7 gin mill 9 roadhouse, nightclub

honor 3 pay 4 cash, fame, laud, note, take 5 adore, exalt, extol, favor, glory, grant, leave, power, right, truth, value 6 accept, admire, credit, esteem, homage, praise, redeem, regard, renown, repute, revere, virtue 7 acclaim, commend, decency, dignify, glorify, honesty, liberty, probity, respect, tribute, worship 8 eminence, fairness, good name, goodness, justness, look up to, make good, pleasure, prestige, sanction, venerate, veracity 9 adoration, celebrity, constancy, deference, greatness, integrity, principle, privilege, rectitude, reverence, sincerity 10 admiration, compliment, exaltation, good report, importance, notability, permission, prominence, veneration 11 acknowledge, approbation, distinction, pay homage to, recognition, think much of, uprightness 12 commendation, faithfulness, high standing, pay tribute to, truthfulness 13 authorization, bow down before, glorification, have regard for, honorableness, make payment on 14 high-mindedness, scrupulousness 15 illustriousness, trustworthiness 17 a feather in one's cap, conscientiousness

honorable 4 good 5 noble, title 6 decent, honest, lordly, square 7 upright 9 elevated, reputable, respected 10 creditable 11 distinctive, illustrious, respectable, trustworthy 12 considerable 13 distinguished

hood 4 cowl, lout, punk 5 bully, rowdy, scarf, tough 6 vandal 7 hoodlum, ruffian 8 hooligan 9 barbarian, roughneck 10 delinquent 12 headcovering

Hood, Raymond
architect of: 11 RCA Building (Rockefeller Center) 17 Daily News Building (NYC) 18 McGraw-Hill Building (NYC) 22 Chicago Tribune Building 24 American Radiator Building
style: 13 International

hoodlum 4 hood, punk, thug 5 crook, rowdy, tough 6 gunman 7 bruiser, gorilla, mobster, ruffian 8 criminal, gangster, hooligan, plug-ugly 9 desperado, strong arm 10 delinquent

hoodwink 3 gyp 4 dupe, fool, gull, hoax, rook 5 cheat, cozen, trick 7 deceive, defraud, mislead, swindle 8 inveigle 9 bamboozle, victimize

hook 3 arc, bag, bow, nab, net 4 arch, bend, bill, curl, gaff, grab, loop, take, trap, wind 5 angle, catch, crook, curve, elbow, fluke, hitch, latch, seize, snare 6 buckle, collar, fasten, peavey, secure 7 capture, crampon, ensnare, grapnel, grapple, pothook 8 crescent, make fast 9 horseshoe

Hooke, Robert
field: 7 physics 9 astronomy
nationality: 7 British
discovered: 9 Orion star 15 Jupiter rotation 20 moon's center of gravity 21 earth's center of gravity
invented: 10 microscope
named for him: 15 law of elasticity

hooked 8 addicted 9 compelled, obsessive 10 compulsive, habituated 14 uncontrollable

hooked cross
German: 10 Hakenkreuz

hook up 4 ally, dock, join 5 hinge 6 couple, link up 7 connect 8 assemble 10 articulate 11 fit together 14 fasten together

hooligan 4 hood, lout, punk 5 bully, rowdy, tough 6 vandal 7 hoodlum, ruffian 9 barbarian, roughneck 10 delinquent

hoopla 4 hype 5 ballyhoo 9 promotion, publicity 10 hullabaloo, propaganda 11 advertising 15 public relations

Hoosier Schoolmaster, The
author: 15 Edward Eggleston

Hoosier State
nickname of: 7 Indiana

hoot 3 boo, din 4 bawl, blow, hiss, honk, howl, jeer, moan, mock, razz, roar, wail, yelp, yowl 5 shout, sneer, taunt, whoop 6 bellow, chorus, cry out, deride, outcry, racket, scream, shriek, shrill, tumult, uproar 7 catcall, cry down, scoff at, screech, sing out, sneer at, snicker, ululate, wailing,

whistle 8 proclaim, shouting 9 caterwaul, commotion, raspberry, screaming, snicker at 10 Bronx cheer, screeching

Hoover, Herbert Clark
nickname: 13 Great Engineer 14 Great Secretary 17 Great Humanitarian 18 Great Public Servant
presidential rank: 11 thirty-first
party: 10 Republican
state represented: 2 CA
defeated: 5 (Alfred Emanuel) Smith 6 (George William) Norris, (Norman) Thomas, (William Frederick) Varney, (William Zebulon) Foster 8 (Verne L) Reynolds
vice president: 6 (Charles) Curtis
cabinet:
state: 7 (Henry Lewis) Stimson
treasury: 5 (Ogden Livingston) Mills 6 (Andrew William) Mellon
war: 4 (James William) Good 6 (Patrick Jay) Hurley
attorney general: 8 (William DeWitt) Mitchell
navy: 5 (Charles Francis) Adams
postmaster general: 5 (Walter Folger) Brown
interior: 6 (Ray Lyman) Wilbur
agriculture: 4 (Arthur Mastick) Hyde
commerce: 6 (Robert Patterson) Lamont, (Roy Dikeman) Chapin
labor: 4 (William Nuckles) Doak 5 (James John) Davis
born: 12 West Branch IA
died: 13 New York City NY
buried: 12 West Branch IA
education:
University: 8 Stanford
religion: 5 Quaker 16 Society of Friends
interests: 7 fishing
vacation spot: 10 Camp Hoover 11 Rapidan Camp 22 Shenandoah National Park
author: 7 Memoirs 11 On Growing Up 14 An American Epic 16 Years of Adventure 18 Principles of Mining, The Great Depression 20 America's First Crusade 21 American Individualism, The Challenge to Liberty 24 The Ordeal of Woodrow Wilson 25 The Problems of Lasting Peace 26 The Cabinet and the Presidency 28 Addresses Upon the American Road 51 The State Papers and Other Public Writings of Herbert Hoover
political career: 19 US Food Administrator
head of: 23 American Relief Committee 28 Commission for Relief in Belgium
director: 38 General Relief and Reconstruction of Europe
member/chairman: 22 Supreme Economic Council
secretary of: 8 Commerce
chairman of: 17 Hoover Commissions
civilian career: 6 author 14 mining engineer 18 consulting engineer

notable events of lifetime/term: 15 Great Depression
conference: 11 London Naval
crash of: 11 stock market
independence for: 11 Philippines
Tariff: 11 Hawley-Smoot
father: 10 Jesse Clark
mother: 6 Huldah (Randall Minthorn)
siblings: 3 May 13 Theodore Jesse
wife: 3 Lou (Henry)
children: 10 Allan Henry 12 Herbert Clark
first lady:
vice president of: 10 Girl Scouts

hop 3 bob 4 ball, jump, leap, prom, romp, skip, step, trip 5 bound, caper, dance, frisk, mixer, vault 6 bounce, gambol, prance, soiree, spring 7 Humulus
varieties: 4 Wild 5 False 6 Common 8 European, Japanese

hope 3 yen 4 help, wish 5 crave, dream, faith, fancy, trust 6 aspire, belief, chance, desire, expect, hunger, rescue, yen for 7 believe, count on, craving, dream of, longing, long for 8 ambition, daydream, feel sure, optimism, prospect, reckon on, reliance, yearn for, yearning 9 assurance, hankering, have faith, hunger for, salvation, take heart 10 anticipate, aspiration, assumption, be bent upon, confidence, conviction, expectancy 11 be confident, contemplate, expectation, have an eye to, possibility, presumption, reassurance, saving grace 12 anticipation, be optimistic, heart's desire 13 encouragement, have a fancy for, look forward to 14 have a hankering 17 great expectations 18 have one's heart set on 19 look on the bright side

Hope, Anthony
real name: 21 Sir Anthony Hope Hawkins
author of: 15 Rupert of Hentzau 18 The Prisoner of Zenda

Hope, Bob
real name: 16 Leslie Townes Hope
co-star: 10 Bing Crosby 13 Dorothy Lamour
born: 6 Eltham 7 England
roles:
Road to: 3 Rio 4 Bali 6 Utopia 7 Morocco 8 Hong Kong, Zanzibar 9 Singapore

hopeful 7 assured, in hopes 8 cheering, sanguine, trusting 9 confident, expectant, favorable, fortunate, promising 10 auspicious, heartening, of good omen, optimistic, propitious, reassuring 11 encouraging 12 anticipative

hopeless 3 sad 4 lost, vain 6 abject, futile 7 forlorn, useless 8 dejected, downcast 9 depressed, incurable, pointless 10 beyond help, despairing, despondent, impossible, melancholy, past remedy 11 downhearted, heartbroken, irreparable, irrevocable, pessimistic, sick at heart 12 beyond recall, disconsolate, heavyhearted, irredeemable,

irreversible 13 grief-stricken, irretrievable 14 down in the mouth, sorrow-stricken
hopelessness 7 despair 8 futility 9 pessimism 11 uselessness

Hopi (Hopitu, Moki)
language family: 10 Shoshonean
location: 7 Arizona
adapted culture of: 6 Pueblo
ceremony: 10 snake dance

Hopkins, Anthony
born: 5 Wales 10 Port Talbot
roles: 10 Audrey Rose 11 A Doll's House 12 Young Winston 14 The Elephant Man 15 The Lion in Winter

Hoples
father: 3 Ion

Hopper, Edward
born: 7 Nyack NY
artwork: 10 Nighthawks 18 Early Sunday Morning, House by the Railroad 19 Second Story Sunlight 20 Sunlight in a Cafeteria 21 Lighthouse at Two Lights

Horae
also: 4 Hour
goddesses of: 5 decay 6 growth 7 seasons 11 social order
names: 4 Dice, Dike 5 Irene 7 Eunomia

Horatii
form: 7 triplets 8 brothers
sister: Horatia
champions of: 4 Rome
fought: 8 Curiatii

Horatio
character in: 6 Hamlet
author: 11 Shakespeare

Horatio
character in: 17 The Spanish Tragedy
author: 3 Kyd

Horatius
origin: 5 Roman
defended: 6 bridge
over: 5 Tiber
against: 9 Etruscans

Horcus
origin: 5 Greek
god of: 5 oaths

horde 3 mob 4 band, gang, host, pack 5 bunch, crowd, crush, drove, party, swarm, tribe, troop 6 legion, throng 7 company 8 assembly 9 gathering, multitude 10 assemblage 12 congregation

Horgan, Paul
author of: 10 Whitewater 13 Lamy of Santa Fe 18 The Thin Mountain Air

horizon 4 area 5 field, range, realm, scope, vista, world 6 bounds, domain, sphere 7 compass, expanse, outlook, purview, stretch 8 frontier, prospect 11 perspective

horizontal 4 even, flat 5 flush, level, plane, plumb, prone 6 supine 8 parallel (to something) 9 lying down, prostrate, reclining, recumbent 14 flat on one's back

horizontal support 3 tie 4 beam 5 brace, joist 6 girder, header, lintel 8 crossbar

hormone 5 auxin **6** cortin **7** estrone, insulin, steroid **8** endocrin, estrogen, galactin, lactogen, secretin **9** adrenalin, cortisone **12** progesterone, testosterone

horn 4 tusk **5** cornu, point, spike **6** antler **11** excrescence

    brass instrument: 4 oboe, tuba **5** bugle **6** cornet **7** bassoon, trumpet **8** alto horn, baritone, clarinet, trombone **9** euphonium, saxophone **10** French horn, mellophone, sousaphone **11** English horn

Horn of Africa *see* **7** Somalia

Hornung, Paul
    nickname: 9 Golden Boy
    sport: 8 football
    position: 6 runner **11** placekicker
    team: 15 Green Bay Packers

horny 4 hard **5** tough **7** callous **8** calloused, hardened **12** thick-skinned **14** pachydermatous

horologe 5 clock **9** timepiece **11** chronometer

horrendous 4 gory **5** awful **6** horrid **7** ghastly, hideous **8** dreadful, horrible, shocking, terrible **9** appalling, frightful, repellent, repulsive, revolting **10** horrifying

horrible 3 bad **4** foul, rank, vile **5** awful, nasty **6** grisly, horrid, odious **7** ghastly, hideous **8** dreadful, gruesome, shocking, terrible, unsavory **9** abhorrent, appalling, atrocious, frightful, harrowing, loathsome, monstrous, obnoxious, repellent, repulsive, revolting, sickening **10** abominable, despicable, detestable, disgusting, forbidding, nauseating, unbearable, unpleasant **11** disquieting, distasteful, unspeakable **12** disagreeable, insufferable

horrid 3 bad **4** foul, grim, ugly **5** awful, nasty, rough **6** bratty, horror, shaggy, wicked **7** fearful, hideous **8** dreadful, gruesome, horrible, shocking, terrible **9** bristling, frightful, offensive, revolting, vexatious **10** abominable, detestable, unpleasant **11** troublesome **12** disagreeable

horrific 4 dire **5** awful **7** fearful, ghastly **8** dreadful, horrible, shocking, terrible **9** appalling

horrified 6 aghast **8** appalled **9** petrified, terrified **10** frightened **13** thunderstruck **14** terror-stricken

horrify 5 daunt, repel, shock **6** appall, dismay, revolt, sicken **7** disgust, petrify, terrify **8** affright, disquiet, frighten, nauseate **10** disconcert, dishearten **11** make one sick **15** make one turn pale **18** make one's flesh creep **22** make one's hair stand on end

horrifying 5 awful, dread **8** alarming, dreadful **10** terrifying **11** frightening, hair-raising

horror 3 woe **4** fear **5** alarm, crime, dread, panic **6** dismay, hatred, misery, terror **7** anguish, cruelty, disgust, dislike, outrage, torment **8** atrocity, aversion, distaste, distress, hardship, loathing **9** antipathy, awfulness, privation, repulsion, revulsion,

suffering **10** abhorrence, affliction, discomfort, inhumanity, repugnance **11** abomination, detestation, hideousness, trepidation **12** apprehension, terribleness, wretchedness

horror-struck 6 aghast **7** fearful **8** appalled **9** horrified, terrified **10** frightened **13** scared to death

hors de combat 8 disabled **13** out of the fight

hors d'oeuvre 3 dip **6** canape, relish, tidbit **9** antipasto, appetizer **10** finger food

horse 4 colt, foal, hack, jade, mare, plug, pony, sire, stud **5** bronc, filly, mount, pacer, pinto, steed **6** bronco, dobbin, equine **7** cavalry, charger, cow pony, gelding, hackney, hussars, lancers, mustang, palfrey, trotter **8** cossacks, dragoons, galloper, stallion, troopers, yearling **9** broodmare, racehorse **10** cavalrymen, draft horse **12** horse cavalry, horse marines, quarter horse, thoroughbred **13** horse soldiers, mounted troops **15** mounted troopers, mounted warriors

    Achilles': 7 Xanthus
    Alexander the Great's: 10 Bucephalus
    anatomy: 4 hock, hoof, loin, mane, tail **5** croup, flank, shank **6** cannon, gaskin, haunch, stifle **7** coronet, crupper, fetlock, gambrel, nostril, pastern, withers **11** throatlatch
    Australian: 5 dingo, myall **8** warragal, warrigal, yarraman
    breed: 6 Morgan, Nubian, Tarpan **7** Arabian, Belgian, mustang **8** Galloway, Shetland **9** Appaloosa, Percheron **10** Clydesdale, Lippizaner **12** Narragansett, Standardbred, Thoroughbred **15** Tennessee-Walker
    Caligula's: 9 Incitatus (made a senator)
    castrated: 7 gelding
    color: 3 bay, dun **4** gray, pied, roan, zain **5** morel, pinto **6** calico, dapple, sorrel **7** piebald **8** chestnut, palomino, schimmel (gray)
    combining form: 4 eque, equi **5** hippo
    Dick Turpin's: 9 Black Bess
    Don Quixote's: 9 Rosinante
    family: 7 Equidae **9** Miohippus, Orohippus
    female: 3 dam **4** mare **5** filly
    French: 6 cheval
    gear: 3 bit **4** rein, tack **6** saddle **7** blinder, harness, snaffle **9** surcingle **11** saddlecloth
    Gen Custer's: 8 Comanche
    Gen Grant's: 10 Cincinnati
    Gen Robert E Lee's: 9 Traveller
    Gen Sherman's: 6 Rienzi
    genus: 7 equus
    Gulliver's Travels: 9 Houyhnhnm
    kind: 3 cob **4** race **6** bronco, hunter, jumper **7** charger, mustang, palfrey, quarter, trotter **8** destrier
    legendary: 6 Trojan
    Lone Ranger's: 6 Silver
    male: 4 colt **8** stallion

measure: 4 hand
Mohammed's: 7 Alborak
movie/story: 6 Flicka 8 Champion 11 Black Beauty 14 National Velvet 16 The Black Stallion
Napoleon's: 7 Morengo
Orlando's: 11 Vegliantino
pace: 4 lope, trot 5 amble 6 canter, gallop
pair of: 4 span, team 6 tandem
race: 5 derby, plate 6 exacta 7 pick six 8 claiming, handicap 9 allowance 11 daily double, sweepstakes 12 steeplechase, weight-for-age
Triple Crown: 7 Belmont 9 Preakness 13 Kentucky Derby
riding show: 8 gymkhana
Rinaldo's: 6 Bayard
Roy Rogers': 7 Trigger
Sigurd's: 5 Grani
small: 4 pony
Stonewall Jackson's: 12 Little Sorrel
Tom Mix's: 4 Tony
three: 6 randem, troika 7 unicorn
Wellington's (at Waterloo): 10 Copenhagen
wild: 5 fuzzy 6 bramby, kumrah, outlaw, tarpan 7 jughead 8 bangtail, fuzztail, warragal, warrigal
Will Rogers': 8 Soapsuds 10 Bootlegger
winged: 7 Pegasus
young: 4 colt, foal 5 filly 8 yearling

horseback riding
athlete: 11 Frank Chapot 17 William Steinkraus

horse collar 3 zip 4 zero 5 aught, zilch 6 cipher, naught 8 goose egg
Horse Knows the Way, The
author: 9 John O'Hara
horseman 5 groom, rider 6 hussar, jockey, lancer, ostler 7 cossack, dragoon, hostler, trainer, trooper 9 postilion, stableboy, stableman 10 cavalryman, equestrian, roughrider 11 horse marine, stable owner 12 equestrienne, horse breeder, horse soldier, stable keeper 14 cavalry soldier, horseback rider, mounted trooper
horseplay 6 pranks 7 foolery 9 cutting up 10 buffoonery, tomfoolery 13 fooling around, horsing around
horse racing
jockey: 8 Del Insko 11 Bill Hartack, Eddie Arcaro 12 Angel Cordero, Bill Haughton, Laffit Pincay, Steve Cauthen 13 Johnny Longden, Stanley Dancer 15 Willie Shoemaker
god of: 6 Consus
Horseshoe Robinson
author: 12 John P Kennedy
horse soldier 6 hussar, lancer 7 dragoon, trooper 8 cavalier, horseman 10 cavalryman
horse trooper 6 hussar, lancer 7 dragoon, Mountie 8 cavalier, horseman 10 cavalryman 12 horse soldier 14 mounted soldier 16 mounted policeman

Horton, Edward Everett
sidekick of: 11 Fred Astaire
born: 10 Brooklyn NY
roles: 15 Cinderella Jones, Her Primitive Man 18 Springtime for Henry
Horus
origin: 8 Egyptian
god of: 3 sun
Greek name: 10 Harcorates
symbol: 6 falcon
mother: 4 Isis
father: 6 Osiris
enemy: 3 Set 4 Seth
hosannas 4 yeas 5 kudos 6 bravos, cheers, paeans 7 acclaim, hurrahs, huzzahs, yippees 8 applause 10 hallelujas 11 halleluiahs
hose 5 socks 7 hosiery 9 stockings
Hosea
father: 5 Beeri
hosiery 3 sox 4 hose 5 socks 6 nylons, tights 7 leotard 9 stockings
hospitable 4 open, warm 6 genial 7 cordial 8 amenable, amicable, friendly, gracious, sociable, tolerant 9 agreeable, convivial, receptive, welcoming 10 accessible, gregarious, neighborly, openhanded, openminded, responsive 12 approachable
hospital 4 home 6 asylum, clinic 7 sick bay 8 pavilion, rest home 9 infirmary 10 polyclinic, sanatorium 11 nursing home 13 medical center
French: 9 hotel Dieu
hospital, private
French: 13 maison de sante
hospitality 5 cheer 6 warmth 7 welcome 8 openness 9 geniality 10 cordiality, heartiness, kindliness 11 amicability, sociability 12 congeniality, conviviality, friendliness 13 Gemutlichkeit 14 hospitableness, neighborliness 15 warmheartedness
god of: 6 Sancus 10 Dius Fidius, Semo Sancus
host, hostess 3 lot, mob 4 army, band, body, crew, gang, mess 5 array, crowd, drove, group, horde, party, swarm, troop 6 legion, throng 7 company, maitre d', meeting 8 conclave, congress, hosteler, hotelier, landlord, welcomer 9 gathering, innkeeper, multitude 10 confluence, convention, headwaiter, party giver, proprietor 11 convocation, hotel keeper 12 congregation, head waitress, hotel manager, proprietress, receptionist 17 restaurant manager 18 master of ceremonies 20 mistress of ceremonies
hostage 7 captive 8 prisoner
Hostage, The
author: 12 Brendan Behan
hostel 3 inn 4 hall 5 hotel, lodge 7 hospice, lodging, shelter 8 hospital, hostelry
hostile 3 icy 4 cold, mean, ugly 5 angry, at war, enemy, testy 6 at odds, at outs, bitter, chilly, cranky, malign, touchy, unkind 7 opposed, vicious, warring 8 battling, clashing, contrary, fighting, opposing, snappish, spiteful, venomous 9 bellicose, bristling,

dissident, malicious, malignant, truculent 10 contending, ill-natured, malevolent, on bad terms, unfriendly 11 belligerent, contentious, disagreeing, ill-disposed, quarrelsome 12 antagonistic, cantankerous, disagreeable, disputatious, incompatible 13 argumentative, at loggerheads, unsympathetic

hostile act 4 raid 6 strike, threat 7 assault, offense 8 act of war, invasion 9 hostility, incursion 10 aggression

hostile nation 5 enemy 7 invader

hostility 3 war 4 duel, feud, fray, hate 5 anger, clash, fight, venom 6 battle, combat, enmity, fracas, hatred, malice, rancor, spleen 7 contest, dispute, ill will, scuffle, warfare, warring 8 act of war, argument, battling, conflict, fighting 9 animosity, antipathy, bickering 10 antagonism, bitterness, contention, dissidence, opposition, state of war 11 altercation, malevolence, viciousness 12 belligerence, contrariness, disagreement 14 unfriendliness, vindictiveness

hot 3 new, top 4 good, late, live, near, warm 5 fiery, fresh, nippy, sharp 6 ardent, baking, biting, fervid, fierce, heated, hectic, latest, molten, raging, recent, red-hot, stormy, sultry, torrid 7 boiling, burning, earnest, excited, furious, intense, melting, peppery, piquant, popular, pungent, searing, violent 8 agitated, animated, broiling, feverish, frenzied, roasting, scalding, sizzling, steaming, vehement, very warm 9 emotional, excellent, scorching, simmering, very close, wrought-up 10 attractive, blistering, passionate, smoldering, successful, sweltering 11 electrified, fastselling, most popular, radioactive, sought after, tempestuous 12 incandescent 14 fast and furious, highly seasoned, in close pursuit

hot air 7 bombast 8 rhetoric 9 hyperbole 12 exaggeration 14 overstatement

hotel 3 inn 5 lodge, motel 6 hostel 7 hospice, lodging 8 hostelry, motor inn

Hotel, The
  author: 14 Elizabeth Bowen

hotel de ville 9 a city hall
  literally: 16 mansion of the city

hotel Dieu 9 a hospital 12 mansion of God

Hotel New Hampshire, The
  author: 10 John Irving

hothouse 6 tender 7 fragile, nursery 8 delicate 10 glasshouse, greenhouse 12 conservatory 13 over-protected

hot temper 4 fire 5 anger 6 pepper 8 acrimony 9 short fuse

hot-tempered 7 peppery 9 emotional, excitable 13 easily ruffled, quick-tempered

hot water 3 jam 4 mess 6 pickle 7 trouble 10 difficulty 11 predicament

Houghston, Walter
  real name of: 12 Walter Huston

hound 3 dog, fan, nag, nut, pup 4 bait, buff, hunt, mutt, tail 5 annoy, chase, doggy, freak, harry, lover, pooch, puppy, stalk, track, trail, whelp, worry 6 addict, badger, canine, follow, harass, hector, keep at, needle, pester, pursue 7 bedevil, poochie 9 keep after 10 aficionado, hunting dog 11 aficionado

  dog breed: 6 beagle, borzoi, saluki 7 basenji, harrier, whippet 9 dachshund, greyhound 10 bloodhound, otter hound 11 Afghan hound, basset hound, Ibizan hound 12 pharaoh hound 14 Irish wolfhound 15 English foxhound 16 American foxhound 17 Norwegian elkhound, Scottish deerhound 18 Rhodesian ridgeback 20 black and tan coonhound

  group of: 3 cry 4 mute, pack

Hound of the Baskervilles, The
  author: 19 Sir Arthur Conan Doyle
  character: 8 Dr Watson 14 Sherlock Holmes 19 Sir Henry Baskerville

hour 3 day 4 span, time 5 space 6 period 8 interval
  abbreviation: 2 hr

Hour see 5 Horae

house, House 4 clan, firm, hall, home, keep, line, shop 5 abode, board, lodge, put up, store 6 billet, church, family, garage, harbor, strain, temple 7 Commons, company, concern, contain, council, descent, dynasty, lineage, quarter, shelter, theater 8 ancestry, assembly, audience, building, business, congress, domicile, dwelling 9 ancestors, household, residence 10 auditorium, family tree, habitation, hippodrome, opera house, spectators 11 accommodate, concert hall, corporation, legislature, noble family, partnership, royal family 12 business firm, lower chamber, meeting place, organization 13 dwelling place, establishment

  god of: 8 Silvanus, Sylvanus

housebreaker 5 thief 6 robber 7 burglar 8 pilferer 9 purloiner 10 cat burglar 14 second-story man

housebreaking 5 theft 7 break-in, robbery 8 burglary, stealing 12 burglarizing 19 breaking and entering

House Divided, A
  author: 9 Pearl Buck

House for Mr Biswas, A
  author: 9 V S Naipaul

household 4 home 5 house 6 family, hearth 8 of a house 9 for a house 10 for a family, for home use 12 family circle
  goddess of: 6 Brigit

household help 4 cook, maid 7 footman, steward 8 domestic, gardener, handyman, houseboy 9 charwoman, chauffeur, domestics, majordomo, nursemaid 11 housekeeper

household of three
  French: 12 menage a trois

House in Paris, The
  author: 14 Elizabeth Bowen

House Made of Dawn
  author: 13 N Scott Momaday

House of Atreus, The
  author: 9 Aeschylus
  character: 7 Electra, Orestes 9 Aegisthus, Agamemnon, Cassandra 12 Clytemnestra

house of health
  French: 13 maison de sante

House of Mirth, The
  author: 12 Edith Wharton
  character: 8 Lily Bart, Mr Selden 9 Gus Trenor 10 Judy Trenor, Mr Rosedale, Percy Gryce 12 Bertha Dorset, George Dorset

House of the Seven Gables, The
  author: 18 Nathaniel Hawthorne
  character: 10 Mr Holgrave 14 Phoebe Pyncheon 16 Clifford Pyncheon 20 Judge Jaffrey Pyncheon, Miss Hepzibah Pyncheon

house of worship 6 chapel, church, mosque, temple 8 basilica 9 cathedral, synagogue 10 house of God, Lord's house, tabernacle

housewife 4 wife 9 homemaker 11 housekeeper

housing 4 case, home 5 abode, house 6 casing, jacket, sheath, shield 7 lodging, shelter 8 covering, domicile, dwelling, envelope, lodgment, quarters 9 enclosure, residence 10 habitation 14 accommodations

Housman, A E
  author of: 14 A Shropshire Lad

Houston
  baseball team: 6 Astros
  basketball team: 7 Rockets
  canal: 11 Houston Ship
  channel: 12 Buffalo Bayou
  football team: 6 Oilers 8 Gamblers
  landmark: 4 NASA 12 Alley Theater 14 Jesse James Hall 22 Manned Spacecraft Center 29 San Jacinto Battlefield Monument
  battleship: 5 Texas
  named after: 10 Sam Houston
  planned by: 7 A C Allen, J K Allen
  stadium: 9 Astrodome
  street: 15 Old Spanish Trail
  university: 4 Rice 12 Texas Medical 13 Texas Southern

Houston, Sam
  position: 9 US Senator
  governor of: 5 Texas 9 Tennessee
  president of: 15 Republic of Texas
  served in: 9 Creek Wars 15 Texas Revolution
  battle: 10 San Jacinto
  defeated: 9 Santa Anna

Houyhnhnms
  fictional people in: 16 Gulliver's Travels
  author: 5 Swift

hovel 3 hut 4 dump, hole 5 cabin, shack 6 shanty

hover 4 flit, hang 5 float, haunt, pause, poise, waver 6 attend, falter, seesaw 7 flitter, flutter 9 fluctuate, hang about, vacillate

Hovhaness, Alan
  born: 12 Somerville MA
  composer of: 10 Magnificat

how
  Latin: 7 quo modo

Howard, Ron
  born: 2 OK 6 Duncan
  roles: 4 Opie 9 Happy Days 16 American Graffiti, Richie Cunningham 19 The Andy Griffith Show
  director of: 6 Cocoon, Gung Ho, Splash, Willow

Howard, Sidney
  author of: 13 The Silver Cord 22 They Knew What They Wanted

Howard, Trevor
  born: 7 England 12 Cliftonville
  roles: 6 The Key 13 Ryan's Daughter, Sons and Lovers 14 Brief Encounter 23 The Invincible Mr Disraeli

Howard's End
  author: 9 E M Forster
  character: 9 Jacky Bast 10 Paul Wilcox, Ruth Wilcox 11 Henry Wilcox, Leonard Bast 13 Charles Wilcox, Helen Schlegel 16 Margaret Schlegel, Theobald Schlegel

how are you
  German: 8 wie geht's 9 wie geht es

Howe, Elias
  nationality: 8 American
  invented: 13 sewing machine

Howells, William Dean
  author of: 12 Indian Summer 15 A Modern Instance 20 A Hazard of New Fortunes, The Rise of Silas Lapham

How Green Was My Valley
  author: 16 Richard Llewellyn
  director: 8 John Ford
  character: 6 Marged 7 Bronwen 10 Beth Morgan 11 Iestyn Evans 12 Gwilym Morgan
  Morgan children: 4 Davy, Huur, Ivor, Owen 5 Ianto 6 Gwilym 8 Angharad
  cast: 7 Anna Lee 9 John Loder 11 Donald Crisp 12 Maureen O'Hara 13 Roddy McDowall, Walter Pidgeon
  Oscar for: 7 picture 8 director 15 supporting actor (Crisp)

howl 3 bay, cry 4 bark, hoot, roar, wail, yell, yelp, yowl 5 groan, shout, whine 6 bellow, clamor, cry out, outcry, scream, shriek, uproar 7 ululate

howler 4 goof 5 error 6 boo-boo 7 blooper, blunder, mistake

How To Win Friends and Influence People
  author: 12 Dale Carnegie

hoyden 3 imp 4 brat, chit 6 tomboy

Hoyle, Fred
  field: 9 astronomy
  nationality: 7 British
  developed: 17 steady-state theory

Hoyt, Rosemary
  character in: 16 Tender Is the Night
  author: 10 Fitzgerald

Hreidmar
origin: 12 Scandinavian
mentioned in: 8 Volsunga
son: 5 Otter, Regin 6 Fafnir
killed by: 6 Fafnir

Hsitsang see 5 Tibet

Hualapai
language family: 5 Yuman
location: 7 Arizona
related to: 7 Yavapai 9 Havasupai

hub 3 nub 4 axis, core 5 focus, heart, pivot 6 center, middle 10 focal point

Hubble, Edwin Powell
field: 9 astronomy
studied: 15 galactic nebulae
named for him: 14 Hubble constant

hubbub 3 din 4 fuss, stir, to-do 5 noise 6 babble, bedlam, bustle, clamor, pother, racket, ruckus, tumult, uproar 7 ferment, turmoil 8 disorder 9 agitation, commotion, confusion, hue and cry 10 hullabaloo, hurly-burly 11 disturbance, pandemonium 12 perturbation

Hubert
creator: 11 Dick Wingert

huckleberry 9 Vaccinium 11 Gaylussacia
varieties: 2 He 3 Box, Red 4 Blue, Shot 5 Black, Dwarf, Hairy, Squaw, Sugar 6 Garden 8 Thin-leaf 9 Evergreen 10 California, Little-leaf

Huckleberry Finn (The Adventures of)
author: 9 Mark Twain
character: 3 Jim 9 Tom Sawyer 12 Widow Douglas 13 Judge Thatcher

huckster 5 adman 6 badger, hawker, kidder, seller, vendor 7 haggler, peddler

Hud
director: 10 Martin Ritt
cast: 10 John Ashley, Paul Newman 12 Patricia Neal 13 Melvyn Douglas 14 Brandon de Wilde
Oscar for: 7 actress (Neal) 15 supporting actor (Douglas)

huddle 4 heap, herd, mass, mess 5 bunch, crowd, group 6 cuddle, curl up, jumble, medley, muddle, nestle, throng 7 cluster, collect, meeting, snuggle 8 converge, disarray, disorder 9 confusion, gathering 10 conference, discussion, hodge-podge 12 think session

Hudibras
author: 12 Samuel Butler
character: 6 Ralpho 8 Crowders 9 Sidrophel

Hudson, Rock
real name: 12 Roy Scherer Jr
co-star: 8 Doris Day
born: 10 Winnetka IL
roles: 5 Giant 10 Pillow Talk 15 A Farewell to Arms, McMillan and Wife 20 Magnificent Obsession

Hudson, W H
author of: 13 Green Mansions, The Purple Land 17 Far Away and Long Ago

hue 4 cast, tint, tone 5 color, shade, tinge 8 tincture 10 coloration

hue and cry 4 call, howl, roar, yell, yowl 5 alarm, alert, shout, storm 6 bellow, clamor, hubbub, outcry, shriek, uproar 7 thunder 10 cry of alarm, hullabaloo

huff 3 pet 4 fury, rage, snit 7 bad mood, dudgeon, outrage 8 ill humor, vexation 9 annoyance, petulance 10 fit of anger, fit of pique, resentment

huffy 4 curt, hurt 5 angry, cross, irate, moody, sulky, surly, testy 6 cranky, grumpy, moping, morose, shirty, sullen, touchy 7 in a snit, peevish, waspish, wounded 8 churlish, offended, petulant, snappish 9 glowering, in a lather, in a pucker, irritable, querulous, rancorous, resentful, sensitive 10 ill-humored, out of sorts 11 disgruntled, quarrelsome, thin-skinned 12 discontented 14 easily offended, hard to live with, hypersensitive

hug 4 hold 5 clasp 6 clutch, cuddle, nestle 7 cling to, embrace, snuggle, squeeze 9 hold close, hover near 11 keep close to 13 cling together, follow closely 15 parallel closely, press to the bosom

huge 4 vast 5 giant, great, jumbo 6 mighty 7 immense, mammoth, massive, titanic 8 colossal, enormous, gigantic, imposing 9 cyclopean, extensive, herculean, leviathan, monstrous 10 gargantuan, monumental, prodigious, staggering, stupendous 11 elephantine, extravagant, spectacular 12 overwhelming 14 Brobdingnagian

hugeness 4 bulk 8 enormity, vastness 9 great size, immensity, largeness, magnitude 11 massiveness

Huggins, Charles Brenton
field: 10 physiology
researched: 6 cancer 12 chemotherapy
awarded: 10 Nobel Prize

Hughes, Langston
author of: 9 The Big Sea 12 One-Way Ticket 13 The Weary Blues 19 Shakespeare in Harlem 20 The Panther and the Lash

Hughes, Richard
author of: 18 A High Wind in Jamaica

Hughes, Thomas
author of: 19 Tom Brown's Schooldays

Hugh the Drover
opera by: 15 Vaughan Williams
character: 4 Mary 12 The Constable 14 John the Butcher

Hugin
origin: 12 Scandinavian
form: 5 raven
owned by: 4 Odin 5 Othin
personifies: 7 thought
duty: 10 newsbearer
other raven: 5 Munin

Hugo, Victor
author of: 13 Les Miserables 16 Notre Dame de Paris 23 The Hunchback of Notre Dame
character: 9 Esmeralda, Quasimodo

hulk 4 ship 5 giant, wreck 8 behemoth

hulking 3 big 5 bulky, heavy, husky 7 massive 8 powerful, unwieldy 9 oversized, ponderous 10 cumbersome

hull 3 pod 4 case, husk, peel, rind, skin 5 shell, shuck 7 coating 8 carapace 9 epidermis, tegmentum 10 integument

Hull, Isaac
  served in: 19 War of Eighteen-Twelve
  sunk ship: 9 Guerriere (British)
  commander of ship: 12 Constitution

hullabaloo 3 din 4 stir 5 babel 6 bedlam, clamor, hubbub, ruckus, tumult, uproar 9 confusion 11 pandemonium
  Yiddish: 7 tzimmes

hum 4 buzz, purr, whir 5 croon, drone, thrum 6 be busy, bustle, intone, murmur, thrive 7 buzzing, droning, purring, vibrate 8 be active, whirring 9 vibration 10 faint sound 13 be in full swing

human 3 man 5 of man, of men 6 gentle, humane, kindly, mortal, person 7 hominid, like man, manlike 8 merciful, personal 10 anthropoid, individual 11 Homo sapiens, sympathetic

Human Comedy, The
  author: 14 Honore de Balzac, William Saroyan

Human Condition, The
  author: 12 Hannah Arendt

humane 4 kind 5 human 6 kindly, tender 7 pitying 8 merciful 9 unselfish 10 benevolent, bighearted, charitable, good-willed 11 magnanimous, sympathetic, warmhearted 12 humanitarian 13 compassionate, philanthropic

humaneness 8 kindness, sympathy 10 compassion, gentleness, kindliness 11 benevolence 12 mercifulness 15 warmheartedness

Human Factor, The
  author: 12 Graham Greene

humanitarian 4 kind 6 humane 8 generous 10 altruistic, benevolent, charitable 11 kind-hearted 12 large-hearted 13 compassionate, philanthropic 14 philanthropist

humanity 3 man 4 love 5 mercy 6 people 7 charity, mankind, mortals 8 goodwill, kindness, sympathy 9 humankind, humanness, mortality 10 compassion, gentleness, humaneness, kindliness, tenderness 11 benevolence, Homo sapiens, human beings, human nature, magnanimity 12 the human race 13 brotherly love, fellow feeling 15 warmheartedness 16 fraternal feeling

humanum est errare 12 to err is human

Humbert Humbert
  character in: 6 Lolita
  author: 7 Nabokov

humble 3 low 4 meek, poor 5 abase, abash, crush, lower, lowly, plain, shame 6 common, debase, demean, demure, gentle, modest, shabby, simple, subdue 7 chasten, conquer, degrade, mortify, obscure, put down 8 bring low, derogate, disgrace, dishonor, inferior, ordinary, plebeian, pull down, wretched 9 bring down,

embarrass, humiliate, make lowly, miserable 10 inglorious, low-ranking, make humble, obsequious, put to shame, respectful, unassuming 11 deferential, subservient, unimportant, unpresuming 12 self-effacing, take down a peg 13 insignificant, unpretentious 14 unostentatious 15 inconsequential, undistinguished

humbled 5 cowed 7 abashed, debased, subdued 9 conquered, disgraced 10 brought low, humiliated

Humboldt, Alexander von
  nationality: 6 German
  originator of: 7 ecology 10 geophysics

Humboldt's Gift
  author: 10 Saul Bellow

humbug 3 fib, gyp, lie 4 bull, bunk, dupe, fake, fool, gull, hoax, liar, lies, sham 5 cheat, cozen, dodge, faker, fraud, hokum, lying, quack, spoof, trick 6 bunkum, con man, deceit, fibber, phooey, take in 7 beguile, blather, cheater, deceive, falsify, fiction, forgery, mislead, rubbish, sharper, swindle 8 artifice, claptrap, flimflam, flummery, hoodwink, impostor, nonsense, perjurer, pretense, swindler, trickery 9 bamboozle, charlatan, deception, fabricate, falsehood, hypocrisy, hypocrite, imposture, mendacity, poppycock, trickster 10 balderdash, hocus-pocus, mountebank, pretension 11 counterfeit, make-believe 12 equivocation, misrepresent 13 confidence man, double-dealing, falsification 15 pretentiousness

humdinger 4 lulu 5 dandy, doozy 6 beauty, hummer, marvel 8 Jim dandy, superior 10 ripsnorter 12 lollapalooza 13 extraordinary

humdrum 4 blah, dull, dumb, flat 5 banal, trite 6 boring, common, dreary 7 insipid, mundane, routine, tedious, trivial 8 everyday, lifeless, mediocre, ordinary, tiresome, wearying 9 hackneyed, unvarying, wearisome 10 monotonous, pedestrian, uneventful, unexciting, uninspired 11 commonplace, indifferent, uninspiring 12 conventional, run-of-the-mill 13 unexceptional, uninteresting

humerus
  bone of: 8 upper arm

humid 4 damp, dank 5 moist, muggy, soppy 6 clammy, steamy, sticky, sultry

humidity 4 smog 8 dampness, moisture 9 mugginess 10 stickiness

humiliate 5 abash, crush, shame 6 debase, humble, subdue 7 chagrin, chasten, degrade, mortify, put down 8 belittle, bring low, disgrace, dishonor 9 discomfit, embarrass 11 make ashamed 13 bring down a peg

humiliated 7 abashed, crushed, debased, humbled 8 degraded 9 chagrined, disgraced, mortified

humiliation 5 shame 7 chagrin 8 disgrace, dishonor 9 abasement 10 debasement 11 degradation 12 discomfiture 13 embarrassment, mortification

humility 7 modesty, shyness **8** meekness, timidity **9** lowliness **10** demureness, diffidence, humbleness **11** bashfulness **13** self-abasement **17** unpretentiousness

hummock 4 hill, rise **5** knoll, mound **7** hillock, tussock

Humologumena 17 New Testament books

humor 3 wit **4** baby, gags, mood, puns **5** farce, jests, jokes, spoil **6** cajole, comedy, joking, pamper, parody, satire, soothe, suffer, temper, whimsy **7** appease, flatter, foolery, fooling, indulge, jesting, mollify, placate, spirits, waggery **8** drollery, give in to, jocosity, low humor, nonsense, raillery, ridicule, tolerate, travesty, wordplay **9** burlesque, funniness, low comedy, put up with, slapstick, wittiness **10** buffoonery, caricature, comicality, comply with, high comedy, jocoseness, jocularity, tomfoolery, wisecracks, witticisms **11** broad comedy, disposition, foolishness, frame of mind, go along with **12** monkeyshines **13** ludicrousness **14** ridiculousness

humorist 3 wag, wit **4** card **5** comic **8** comedian

humorous 5 comic, droll, funny, witty **6** jocose **7** amusing, comical, jocular, waggish **8** farcical, mirthful, sportive **9** facetious, laughable, ludicrous, satirical, whimsical **10** ridiculous **11** nonsensical, rib-tickling **13** sidesplitting

hump 4 arch, bend, bump, knob, lift, lump, rise **5** bulge, hunch, knurl, mound, put up, tense **8** swelling **9** convexity **10** projection, prominence **11** excrescence

Humperdinck, Engelbert
　born: 4 Bonn **7** Germany
　composer of: 10 The Miracle **15** Hansel and Gretel

Humphry Clinker
　author: 19 Tobias George Smollet
　character: 10 Mr Dennison **12** Jerry Melford, Lydia Melford **14** George Dennison, Matthew Bramble **15** Winifred Jenkins **18** Miss Tabitha Bramble **26** Lieutenant Obadiah Lismahago

Humpty Dumpty
　character in: 22 Through the Looking Glass
　author: 7 Carroll

hunch 4 arch, bend, clue, hump, idea **5** tense **7** feeling, glimmer, inkling **8** good idea **9** intuition, suspicion **10** foreboding **11** premonition **12** presentiment

Hunchback of Notre Dame, The
　author: 10 Victor Hugo
　character: 9 Esmeralda, Gringoire, Quasimodo **12** Claude Frollo **20** Phoebus de Chateaupers

hunched 4 bent **7** crooked, slumped, stooped **9** contorted

hundredweight
　abbreviation: 3 cwt

Hungary
　capital/largest city: 8 Budapest
　others: 4 Gyor, Pecs **5** Harta **6** Mohacs, Sopron, Szeged **7** Komarom, Miskolc,

Szentes **8** Dubrecen, Kaposuar, Szegedin **9** Kecskemet **10** Albertirsa **11** Nagykanizsa, Szombathely
　measure: 3 ako **4** hold, yoke **5** itcze, marok, metze **7** huvelyk
　monetary unit: 4 gara **5** balas, krone, pengo **6** filler, forint, gulden, korona, ongara, ungara
　weight: 7 vamfont **8** vammazsa
　island: 8 Margaret
　lake: 5 Ferto **7** Balaton, Velence **9** Blatensee **10** Neusiedler, Plattensee
　mountain: 4 Alps, Bukk **5** Matra, Tatra **6** Bakony, Mecsek, Vertes **7** Cserhat, Gerecse **8** Borzsony, Zempleni **9** Korishegy **10** Carpathian
　highest point: 5 Kekes
　river: 3 Mur, Sio **4** Duna, Raab, Raba, Sajo, Zala **5** Bodva, Drava, Drave, Ipoly, Kapos, Koros, Maros, Tarna, Tisza **6** Danube, Henrad, Poprad, Szamos, Theiss, Zagyva **7** Vistula **8** Berretyo
　physical feature:
　　canal: 3 Sio **6** Sarviz
　　forest: 6 Bakony
　　plain: 6 Puszta
　　port: 5 Fiume
　people: 3 Hun **4** Serb **5** Croat, Gypsy **6** Cigany, Magyar, Slovak, Ugrian
　composer: 5 Lehar, Liszt **6** Bartok, Kodaly
　national hero: 5 Arpad
　playwright: 6 Molnar
　language: 6 German, Magyar, Slovak **8** Croatian **9** Hungarian **10** Finno-Ugric
　religion: 8 Lutheran **9** Calvinism **13** Roman Catholic **16** Eastern Orthodoxy
　place:
　　church: 32 Gothic Coronation Church of Matthias
　　ruins: 8 Aquincum
　　square: 6 Heroes
　　tomb: 14 Turbe of Gul Baba **16** Father of the Roses
　feature:
　　dance: 3 kos **7** czardas **10** varsoviana
　　dog: 4 puli
　　musical instrument: 8 taragata **9** czimbalom
　food:
　　dish: 6 gulyas **7** goulash **15** chicken paprikas
　　pastry: 4 rete **5** torte
　　wine: 5 Tokay **10** Bulls Blood

hunger 3 yen **4** itch, love, lust, want, wish **5** crave, greed **6** desire, famine, hanker, liking, relish, thirst **7** burn for, craving, itch for, long for, pant for **8** appetite, fondness, voracity, yearn for, yearning **9** hankering, lust after **10** greediness, starvation **11** have a yen for, thirst after **12** malnutrition, ravenousness

hungry 5 eager **6** greedy **7** starved **8** ravenous, starving **9** voracious

hunk 3 gob, wad **4** clod, glob, lump, mass **5** block, chunk, piece **6** gobbet **7** portion **8** quantity

hunt 4 seek 5 chase, probe, shoot, stalk, trace, track, trail 6 course, follow, pursue 7 explore, go after, look for 8 coursing, drive out 9 ferret out, search for, try to find 11 go in quest of, inquire into 14 riding to hounds 20 leave no stone unturned

Hunt, Richard Morris
architect of: 8 Biltmore (Asheville NC) 11 Marble House (Newport RI), The Breakers (Newport RI) 12 Lenox Library (NYC) 14 Studio Building (NYC) 19 National Observatory (Washington DC) 22 William Vanderbilt House (NYC) 23 Metropolitan Museum of Art (NYC)

hunter
constellation of: 5 Orion
French: 8 chasseur

Hunter, Jim
nickname: 7 Catfish
sport: 8 baseball
position: 7 pitcher
team: 14 New York Yankees 16 Oakland Athletics

Hunter, Kim
real name: 8 Jane Cole
born: 9 Detroit MI
roles: 16 Stairway to Heaven, The Seventh Victim 21 A Streetcar Named Desire

Hunters
goddess of: 11 Britomartis

Hunting
god of: 7 Verbius
goddess of: 5 Diana 7 Artemis

Hunting Dogs
constellation of: 13 Canes Venatici

hurdle 4 jump, leap, snag, wall 5 bound, clear, fence, hedge, vault 6 hazard 7 barrier 8 obstacle, surmount 9 hindrance, roadblock 10 difficulty, impediment, spring over 11 obstruction 12 interference 14 stumbling block

hurl 4 cast, toss 5 chuck, fling, heave, pitch, sling, throw 6 launch, let fly, propel 7 fire off, project 9 discharge

hurly-burly 4 stir 5 furor 6 action, bustle, hubbub, hustle, uproar 8 activity 9 commotion 10 hullabaloo

hurrah, hurray 4 fine, good 5 bravo, cheer, great, huzza 6 huzzah, salute 7 acclaim, hosanna 9 excellent, halleluia, wonderful 10 exaltation, hallelujah

hurricane 7 cyclone, monsoon, tempest, typhoon 9 windstorm

Hurricane, The
director: 8 John Ford
cast: 7 Jon Hall 9 Mary Astor 12 C Aubrey Smith 13 Dorothy Lamour, Raymond Massey
setting: 9 Manikoora

hurried 4 fast 5 hasty 6 hectic, rushed, speedy 7 cursory, frantic 8 careless, feverish, frenetic, headlong, slapdash, slipshod 9 breakneck, haphazard, impulsive 11 precipitate, superficial

hurry 3 ado, zip 4 bolt, dart, dash, fuss, goad, prod, rush, stew, whiz 5 egg on, haste, speed 6 flurry, hasten, hustle, push

on, scurry, tumult, urge on 7 drive on, flutter, press on, scuttle, speed up, turmoil 8 make time, move fast, pressure, scramble, step on it 9 commotion, go quickly, make haste, step along 10 accelerate, get a move on, get hopping, lose no time, make tracks 11 come quickly, get cracking, go like a shot, go like sixty 12 step on the gas 13 go like the wind 14 cover the ground 15 hustle and bustle

hurt 3 cut, mar 4 ache, balk, burn, foil, harm, lame, maim, mark, maul, pain, pang, scar 5 agony, block, check, grief, limit, lower, pique, smart, spike, sting, stung 6 aching, bruise, damage, deface, dismay, grieve, hamper, hinder, impair, impede, injure, lessen, mangle, marked, miffed, misery, morose, narrow, offend, oppose, pained, piqued, reduce, retard, thwart, weaken 7 agonize, bruised, chagrin, cripple, crushed, damaged, disable, exclude, inhibit, injured, mangled, painful, scarred, scratch, torment, torture, trouble, wounded 8 aggrieve, crippled, decrease, dejected, diminish, disabled, dismayed, distress, encumber, hold back, minimize, mutilate, obstruct, offended, preclude, restrain, smarting, soreness, wretched 9 aggrieved, annoyance, chagrined, dejection, disfigure, forestall, frustrate, heartsick, indignant, miserable, mortified, mutilated, resentful, scratched, suffering 10 discomfort, distressed, heartbreak, melancholy, resentment 11 aggravation, crestfallen, heartbroken 12 disheartened, wretchedness 13 cut to the quick, embarrassment, mortification

Hurt, John
born: 7 England 22 Chesterfield Derbyshire
roles: 5 Allen 8 Partners 14 The Elephant Man 15 Midnight Express

Hurt, William
roles: 8 Body Heat 9 Gorky Park 10 Eyewitness 11 The Big Chill 13 Broadcast News 20 Kiss of the Spider Woman, Children of a Lesser God

hurtful 5 cruel 6 deadly 7 abusive, baleful, harmful 8 crushing, improper, stinging, wounding 9 injurious

hurtle 3 fly, hie, run, zip 4 bolt, dart, dash, race, rush, tear, whiz 5 bound, lunge, scoot, shoot, speed, spurt, whisk 6 charge, gallop, plunge, scurry 7 scamper, scuttle 11 go like a shot 13 go like the wind 14 go lickety-split

husband 3 man 4 keep, mate, save 5 amass, groom, hoard, hubby, store 6 old man, retain, save up, spouse 7 consort 8 conserve, maintain, preserve, set aside 10 accumulate, bridegroom, married man

husbandry 7 farming 9 geoponics 11 agriculture, crop-raising 12 conservation
god of: 9 Aristaeus

hush 4 calm 5 quell, quiet, shush, still 6 shut up, soothe 7 be quiet, be still, keep mum, mollify, silence 8 be silent, pipe down, quietude 9 quiet down, quietness, stillness 10 knock it off 11 tranquility 12 peacefulness, tranquillity

hushed 4 calm 5 quiet, still 6 calmed, gentle, lulled, silent 7 allayed, quieted, soothed, stifled 8 pacified, silenced, tranquil 12 tranquilized 13 tranquillized

hush money 5 bribe 6 payoff, payola 7 tribute 9 blackmail, extortion

huskiness 5 brawn 9 beefiness 10 hoarseness, robustness, ruggedness, sturdiness 11 muscularity

husky 3 big 5 beefy, burly, gruff, harsh, hefty, plump, rough, solid, stout, thick 6 brawny, coarse, hoarse, robust, stocky, strong, sturdy 7 cracked, grating, rasping, raucous, throaty 8 athletic, croaking, guttural, muscular, powerful, thickset 9 strapping 10 overweight 12 strong as an ox 15 broad-shouldered

hussar 8 cavalier, horseman 10 cavalryman 12 horse soldier, horse trooper 14 mounted soldier

hussy 4 bawd, jade, minx, tart 5 wench, whore 6 harlot, wanton 7 baggage, trollop 8 strumpet 9 brash girl, lewd woman, saucy miss 10 adulteress, loose woman, prostitute 11 brazen woman, fallen woman 12 scarlet woman 17 woman of easy virtue

hustle 3 ado, fly 4 bolt, dart, dash, fuss, prod, push, rush, stir, toss 5 elbow, hurry, nudge, scoot, shove, throw 6 bounce, bustle, flurry, hasten, hubbub, jostle, scurry, tumult 7 flutter, scuttle, speed up, turmoil 8 make time, scramble, shoulder, step on it 9 commotion, make haste, step along 10 lose no time 11 hurry-scurry, move quickly 12 be aggressive

hustler 4 doer 6 con man, dynamo, hooker 8 go-getter, live-wire, swindler 10 prostitute 12 streetwalker

Hustler, The
   director: 12 Robert Rossen
   cast: 10 Paul Newman 11 Piper Laurie 12 George C Scott 13 Jackie Gleason (Minnesota Fats)

Huston, John
   director of: 8 Key Largo 10 The Misfits 11 Moulin Rouge 12 Prizzi's Honor 13 Asphalt Jungle 15 The African Queen 16 The Maltese Falcon 19 The Night of the Iguana 27 The Treasure of the Sierra Madre (Oscar)
   father: 12 Walter Huston
   wife: 11 Evelyn Keyes
   born: 8 Nevada MO
   roles: 9 Chinatown 11 Winter Kills

Huston, Walter
   real name: 15 Walter Houghston
   son: 10 John Huston
   born: 6 Canada 7 Toronto
   roles: 9 Dodsworth 18 All That Money Can Buy 27 The Treasure of the Sierra Madre

hut 4 shed 5 cabin, hutch, shack 6 lean-to, shanty 7 cottage, shelter

hutch 3 pen, sty 4 cage, coop, cote, crib, shed 5 stall 9 enclosure

Hutchinson, A S M
   author of: 13 If Winter Comes

Hutton, Betty
   real name: 18 Betty June Thornburg
   born: 13 Battle Creek MI
   roles: 15 Annie Get Your Gun 19 Greatest Show on Earth

Hutton, James
   field: 7 geology
   nationality: 8 Scottish
   founder of: 7 geology

Hutton, Timothy
   father: 9 Jim Hutton
   roles: 4 Taps 6 Daniel 14 Ordinary People 22 The Falcon and the Snowman

Huxley, Aldous
   author of: 11 Crome Yellow 13 Brave New World 17 Point Counter Point

Huxley, Julian
   field: 7 biology
   nationality: 7 British
   promoted theory of: 9 evolution

Huygens, Christiaan
   nationality: 5 Dutch
   invented: 13 pendulum clock
   discovered: 12 Saturn's rings
   formulated: 17 wave theory of light

hyacinth 10 Hyacinthus 20 Hyacinthus orientalis
   varieties: 4 musk, pine, star, wild, wood 5 Dutch, grape, Roman, water 6 common, garden, meadow, nutmeg, starry, summer, Tassel 7 feather, peacock 11 common grape

Hyacinthus
   father: 7 Amyclas
   daughter: 7 Orthaea
   loved by: 6 Apollo 8 Zephyrus
   killed by: 5 quoit 6 discus
   from his blood sprang: 6 flower
   petals marked: 4 AI-AI
   means: 4 alas

Hyades
   also: 5 Hyads 10 Palilicium
   form: 6 nymphs
   father: 5 Atlas 7 Oceanus
   mother: 6 Tethys 7 Pleione
   sisters: 8 Pleiades
   nurtured: 8 Dionysus
   placed among: 5 stars

Hyads *see* 6 Hyades

hybrid 5 cross 7 amalgam, mixture 9 composite, half-breed 10 crossbreed

hybridize 5 cross 14 cross-fertilize, cross-pollinate

Hydra
   form: 12 water serpent
   number of heads: 4 nine
   killed by: 8 Hercules

hydrangea
   varieties: 4 Wild 6 French, Peegee 8 Climbing

hydrogen
   chemical symbol: 1 H

hydrophobia 6 rabies
  fear of: 5 water
Hygeia
  father: 9 Asclepius
  goddess of: 6 health
  corresponds to: 5 Salus
hygienic 4 pure 5 clean 7 aseptic, healthy, sterile 8 germ-free, harmless, salutary, sanitary 9 healthful, wholesome 10 salubrious, unpolluted 11 disease-free, disinfected, uninjurious 12 prophylactic 14 uncontaminated
Hylaeus
  form: 7 centaur
  born on: 5 cloud
Hylas
  father: 9 Thiodamas
  mother: 8 Menodice
  companion of: 8 Hercules
Hyllus
  father: 8 Hercules
  mother: 6 Melite 8 Deianira
  wife: 4 Iole
  son: 9 Cleodaeus
  grandson: 7 Temenus
  built: 11 funeral pyre
  for: 8 Hercules
Hymen
  also: 9 Hymenaeus
  god of: 8 marriage
  holds: 5 torch
  corresponds to: 8 Talassio
Hymenaeus see 5 Hymen
hymenoptera
  class: 8 hexapoda
  phylum: 10 arthropoda
  group: 3 ant, bee 4 wasp 6 chacid, sawfly 12 ichneumon fly
hymn 5 paean, psalm 6 anthem 12 song of praise 14 devotional song 17 song in praise of God
Hymn to Proserpine
  author: 24 Algernon Charles Swinburne
Hypatia
  author: 15 Charles Kingsley
hyperbole 8 metaphor 11 enlargement 12 exaggeration 13 magnification, overstatement 14 figure of speech
hyperbolize 6 overdo 7 amplify, magnify, stretch 8 embroider, overstate 10 exaggerate
hyperborean 6 arctic 8 freezing, northern 13 septentrional
Hyperborean
  inhabitant of: 8 Paradise
Hyperenor
  mentioned in: 5 Iliad
  brother: 9 Euphorbus, Polydamas
  member of: 6 Sparti
  killed by: 8 Menelaus
Hyperion
  also: 6 Helios
  form: 5 Titan
  father: 6 Uranus
  mother: 4 Gaea
  sister: 5 Theia
  son: 6 Helios

  daughter: 3 Eos 6 Selene
  corresponds to: 6 Apollo
Hyperion
  author: 9 John Keats 24 Henry Wadsworth Longfellow
Hypermnestra
  member of: 8 Danaides
  husband: 7 Lynceus
  son: 4 Abas
hypersensitive 6 touchy 9 emotional 13 temperamental
Hypnos
  also: 6 Hypnus
  god of: 5 sleep
  father: 6 Erebus
  mother: 3 Nyx
  brother: 8 Thanatos
  corresponds to: 6 Somnus
hypnotic 9 soporific 11 mesmerizing 12 spellbinding
hypnotize 7 control 9 mesmerize, spellbind
Hypnus see 6 Hypnos
hypocrisy 6 deceit, fakery 7 falsity 9 duplicity, mendacity, phoniness 10 dishonesty 11 dissembling, insincerity 12 two-facedness
hypocrite 5 phony 8 deceiver 9 pretender 10 dissembler
Hypocrite 15 whited sepulcher
hypocritical 5 false, phony 7 feigned 8 feigning, two-faced 9 deceitful, deceptive, dishonest, insincere, truthless 11 counterfeit
hyporchema
  form: 9 choral ode
  origin: 5 Greek
  honored: 6 Apollo 8 Dionysus
hypothalamus
  regulates: 15 body temperature
  located in: 5 brain
hypothesis 6 theory, thesis 7 premise, theorem 8 proposal 9 assertion, postulate 10 assumption, conclusion, conjecture 11 explanation, guesstimate, presumption, proposition, speculation, supposition
hypothesize 5 infer 6 assume 7 imagine, presume, suppose 8 theorize 9 postulate, speculate 10 conjecture
hypothetical 7 assumed, dubious 8 possible, supposed 9 imaginary, uncertain 10 contingent, postulated 11 conditional, conjectural, presumptive, speculative, theoretical 12 questionable 13 suppositional
Hypselosaurus
  type: 8 dinosaur, sauropod
  location: 6 France 8 Mongolia
  period: 10 Cretaceous
Hypseus
  king of: 7 Lapiths
  father: 6 Peneus
  mother: 6 Creusa
  daughter: 6 Cyrene 8 Themisto 9 Astyagyia
Hypsilophodon
  type: 8 dinosaur 10 ornithopod
  location: 7 England
  period: 10 Cretaceous

Hyrie
   transformed into: 4 swan
Hyrmina
   grandfather: 8 Endymion
   son: 5 Actor
Hyrnetho
   father: 7 Temenus
   grandfather: 12 Aristomachus
   husband: 10 Deiphontes
Hyrtius
   allied with: 7 Trojans
hyssop 8 Hyssopus **18** Hyssopus officialis
   varieties: 5 anise, giant, water **9** blue giant **10** nettle-leaf **11** fennel giant, purple
   giant, yellow giant **12** Mexican giant **13**
   fragrant giant, wrinkled giant
Hyssop 13 Biblical plant
hysteria 3 fit **5** panic **6** frenzy **8** delirium
hysterical 5 crazy, droll **6** absurd, crazed,
   raving **7** amusing, comical **8** farcical, frenzied, worked-up **9** laughable, ludicrous,
   wrought-up **10** distracted, distraught, ridiculous, uproarious **11** carried away, overwrought, wildly funny **13** beside oneself,
   out of one's wits **14** uncontrollable
hysterics 3 fit **12** emotionalism

I

I, Claudius
author: 12 Robert Graves
story of: 36 Tiberius Claudius Drusus Nero Germanicus (Emperor of Rome)

I, the Jury
author: 14 Mickey Spillane

Iache
form: 5 nymph
companion of: 10 Persephone

I Am a Fugitive from a Chain Gang
director: 11 Mervyn LeRoy
cast: 8 Paul Muni 11 Helen Vinson 13 Glenda Farrell, Preston Foster

Iambe
occupation: 11 storyteller
storyteller for: 7 Demeter

I am unwilling to contend
Latin: 14 nolo contendere

Iamus
father: 6 Apollo
mother: 6 Evadne
became: 7 prophet

Ianthe
husband: 5 Iphis

Iapetus
member of: 6 Titans
father: 6 Uranus
mother: 4 Gaea
wife: 6 Themis
son: 5 Atlas 9 Menoetius 10 Epimetheus, Prometheus

Iapyx
father: 8 Daedalus

Iardanus
king of: 5 Lydia
daughter: 7 Omphale

Iasion
founder of: 7 Trojans
twin brother: 8 Dardanus

Iaso
goddess of: 7 healing
father: 9 Asclepius

Iasus
father: 8 Lycurgus
daughter: 8 Atalanta
abandoned: 8 Atalanta

Ibanez, Vicente Blasco
author of: 30 The Four Horsemen of the Apocalypse

Iberian Peninsula
also: 8 Hesperia

Ibsen, Henrik
author of: 6 Ghosts 8 Peer Gynt 11 A Doll's House, Hedda Gabler, Rosmersholm, The Wild Duck 16 The Master Builder 18 An Enemy of the People, John Gabriel Borkman

Ibzan 11 Hebrew judge

I came, I saw, I conquered
Latin: 12 veni vidi vici
author: 12 Julius Caesar

Icarius
son: 8 Perilaus
daughter: 7 Erigone 8 Penelope
hospitable to: 8 Dionysus
hound dog: 5 Maera

Icarus
father: 8 Daedalus
built: 5 wings
flew too near: 3 sun
death by: 8 drowning

ice 3 gem 4 berg, floe, gems, rime 5 chill, frost, glace 6 freeze, icicle, jewels 7 crystal, dessert, glacier, jewelry, sherbet 8 diamonds 11 refrigerant, refrigerate

ice-cold 3 icy 4 cold 5 gelid, polar 6 arctic, bitter, frigid, frosty, wintry 7 chilled, frosted, glacial, subzero 8 chilling, freezing, Siberian, unheated, unwarmed 9 stone-cold, supercold 11 hyperborean, supercooled 12 bone-chilling

ice cream 7 dessert, sherbet

Iceland
other name: 15 Lydveldid Island
capital/largest city: 9 Reykjavik
others: 3 Hof 6 Geysir 7 Akranes, Husavik 8 Akureyri, Keflavik, Kopasker 9 Kopavogur 10 Hveragerdi, Isafjordur 12 Siglufjordur 13 Hafnarfjordur, Neskaupstadur, Seydisfjordur
government:
general assembly: 7 Althing
measure: 3 set 4 alin 5 almud 6 almenn, ferfet, pattur 7 fathmur, fermila, oltunna
monetary unit: 5 aurar, eyrir, krona
weight: 4 pund 5 pound, tunna 6 smjors
island: 7 Heimaey, Surtsey, Westman
lake: 6 Myvatn 10 Thorisvatn 14 Thingvallavatn
mountain: 5 Jokul 10 Orafajokul
volcano: 4 Laki 5 Askja, Hekla, Katla 7 Surtsey
highest point: 17 Hvannadalshnjukur
river: 5 Hvita 7 Fnjoska, Thjorsa 15 Jokulsa a Fjollum
sea: 9 Greenland 13 North Atlantic
physical feature:
fjord: 4 Eyja
geyser: 5 gryla 6 geysir 11 Great Gusher
glacier: 6 Jokull 11 Orafajokull, Vatnajokull
plain: 15 Skeidharasandur
waterfall: 8 Godafoss, Gullfoss 9 Dettifoss

people: 6 Celtic, Viking 8 Norseman 9 Norwegian
first settler: 8 Arnarson
hero: 4 Bele, Eric, Leif 10 Sigurdsson
language: 5 Norse 9 Icelandic
religion: 19 Evangelical Lutheran
place:
national shrine: 11 Thingvellir
feature:
airport: 9 Kopavogur
bird: 4 gull 6 falcon 9 gyrfalcon
literary genre: 4 saga
wrestling: 5 glima
food:
dish: 4 skyr, svio 7 bloomor 8 harofisk

Icelus
origin: 5 Greek
god of: 6 dreams
assumed shapes of: 7 animals
epithet: 8 Phobetor
corresponds to: 8 Morpheus

Iceman
nickname of: 12 George Gervin

Iceman Cometh, The
author: 12 Eugene O'Neill

Ice Palace
author: 10 Edna Ferber

ice skating
athlete: 9 Janet Lynn, John Curry 10 Carol Heiss, Dick Button, Eric Heiden, Sonja Henie 11 Sheila Young 12 Peggy Fleming 13 Dorothy Harhill, Scott Hamilton 14 Linda Fratianne

ich dien 6 I serve
motto of: 13 Prince of Wales

I Ching 30 ancient Chinese book of divination

ichor
form: 5 fluid
in veins of: 4 gods

Ichthyocentaur
form: 8 creature
location: 3 sea
head/torso: 5 human
legs: 5 horse
tail: 4 fish

iciness 4 cold 5 chill 9 frigidity 10 chilliness, frostiness, wintriness 12 slipperiness

ici on parle francais 18 French is spoken here 19 here one speaks French

icky 5 gluey, gooey, gross, gucky, gummy, mushy, nasty, tacky, weepy 6 sticky, syrupy, viscid 7 maudlin, viscous 8 bathetic 9 glutinous, offensive, repulsive, revolting 10 disgusting 12 mucilaginous

icon, ikon 4 idol 5 image 6 effigy, figure, statue 7 picture 8 likeness 11 sacred image

iconoclast 5 rebel 7 radical, upstart 9 dissenter 13 nonconformist, revolutionary

icy 3 raw 4 cold, cool 5 aloof, gelid 6 arctic, chilly, frigid, frosty, frozen, glazed, sleety, wintry 7 distant, glacial, haughty, hostile 8 chilling, freezing, slippery 9 impassive 10 forbidding, unfriendly 11 coldhearted, unemotional

Ida
form: 5 nymph
watched over: 4 Zeus

Idaea
form: 5 nymph
domain: 8 Mount Ida
husband: 7 Phineus 9 Scamander
son: 6 Teucer

Idaho
abbreviation: 2 ID 3 Ida
nickname: 3 Gem
capital/largest city: 5 Boise
others: 4 Buhl 5 Malad, Nampa 6 Moscow 7 Orofino, Rexburg 8 Caldwell, Lewiston 9 Pocatello, Twin Falls 10 Idaho Falls 11 Coeur d'Alene
college: 17 Northwest Nazarene
explorer: 13 Lewis and Clark
feature: 9 Sun Valley 17 Continental Divide
dam: 5 Oxbow 8 Brownlee
national monument: 16 Craters of the Moon
tribe: 5 Banak, Shake 6 Cayuse, Paiute, Spokan 7 Bannock, Kutenai, Spokane 8 Kalispel, Nez Perce, Sahaptin, Shoshone, Shoshoni 9 Shoshonee 11 Coeur d'Alene
people: 9 Ezra Pound, Sacagawea 11 Chief Joseph 17 William Edgar Borah
lake: 4 Bear 5 Grey's 6 Priest 11 Coeur d'Alene, Pend Oreille 22 American Falls Reservoir
land rank: 10 thirteenth
mountain: 4 Ryan 5 Rocky 6 Rhodes, Taylor, Tetons 7 Cabinet 8 Bannocks, Big Baldy, Bluenose, Sawtooth 9 Wasatches 10 Clearwater 11 Beaverheads, Bitterroots 13 Selkirk Ranges
highest point: 5 Borah
physical feature:
falls: 5 Moyie 8 Shoshone 9 Upper Mesa
springs: 4 Soda 6 Hooper 7 Lavahot
river: 4 Bear 5 Boise, Snake, St Joe 6 Locksa, Salmon 7 Payette, Spokane 8 Kootenai 11 Coeur d'Alene, Pend Oreille
state admission: 10 forty-third
state bird: 16 mountain bluebird
state flower: 7 syringa
state motto: 13 It Is Perpetual 16 Let It Be Perpetual
state song: 15 Here We Have Idaho
state tree: 16 western white pine

Idas
father: 8 Aphareus
mother: 5 Arene
brother: 7 Lynceus
wife: 8 Marpessa
daughter: 9 Cleopatra

idea 4 clue, hint, view 6 belief, notion 7 concept, feeling, inkling, insight, opinion, outlook, thought 8 approach, proposal, solution 9 sentiment 10 conception, conclusion, conviction, impression, indication, intimation, suggestion 12 apperception, appreciation 13 approximation, mental picture, understanding 14 interpretation, recommendation

ideal 3 aim 4 hero, idol 5 dream, model 7 epitome, optimal, pattern, perfect 8 exemplar, last word, paradigm, standard, ultimate 9 archetype, criterion, excellent, exemplary, faultless, matchless, objective 10 impeccable 11 inspiration

idealism 8 optimism 9 meliorism 10 utopianism 11 romanticism

idealist 7 dreamer, utopian 8 romantic 9 Pollyanna, stargazer, visionary 11 romanticist 13 perfectionist

idealized 6 dreamy 7 utopian, wishful 8 fanciful, illusory, romantic 10 optimistic 11 pie-in-the-sky, unrealistic 13 insubstantial

idea man 7 advisor 8 inventor 9 innovator 10 consultant 12 entrepreneur

idee fixe 9 fixed idea
　　music: 14 recurring motif

idem 24 the same as previously given 28 the same as previously mentioned

identical 4 twin 7 uniform 8 self-same, very same 9 duplicate 15 interchangeable 17 indistinguishable

identification 5 badge, label 8 passport 9 detection 10 connection, revelation 11 affiliation, association, credentials, pinpointing, recognition 12 confirmation, verification 13 ascertainment

identify 4 know 5 place 6 verify 7 combine, pick out, specify 9 associate, designate, determine, recognize, single out 11 distinguish

identifying device 4 logo, mark, sign 5 badge 6 emblem, ensign, symbol 8 insignia, logotype

identity 4 name, self 6 accord 7 harmony, oneness, rapport 9 unanimity 11 delineation, duplication, personality 13 individuality 15 differentiation, distinctiveness

ideology 5 dogma, ethos 6 ideals, theory 7 program 8 doctrine 9 rationale 10 principles

Ides of March, The
　　author: 14 Thornton Wilder

id est 6 that is
　　abbreviation: 2 ie

idiocy 5 folly 6 lunacy 7 fatuity, inanity, madness, suicide 8 insanity 9 absurdity, asininity, cretinism, mongolism, stupidity 11 foolishness 13 foolhardiness, senselessness

idiom 5 argot, lingo, slang 6 brogue, jargon, patois, phrase, speech 7 dialect 8 language, localism, parlance 10 vernacular 13 colloquialism

idiomatic 6 common 8 informal, ordinary 10 vernacular 14 conversational

idiosyncrasy 5 quirk 6 oddity 7 anomaly 9 mannerism 11 distinction, peculiarity 12 eccentricity

idiot 3 ass 4 boob, dolt, dope, fool, jerk 5 cluck, dummy, dunce, moron, ninny 6 cretin, dimwit, nitwit 7 halfwit 8 dumbbell, numskull 9 blockhead, numbskull, simpleton 10 nincompoop

Idiot, The
　　author: 16 Fyodor Dostoevsky
　　character: 7 Myshkin 11 Mme Epanchin 14 Aglaya Epanchin, Parfen Rogozhin 16 Natasya Filipovna 19 Ganya Ardalionovitch 22 Prince Lef Nicolaievitch

idiotic 5 crazy, dopey, nutty 6 absurd, addled, stupid 7 asinine, doltish, foolish, moronic 9 foolhardy, imbecilic, senseless 10 half-witted, irrational, ridiculous 12 feebleminded 13 rattlebrained

I direct
　　Latin: 6 dirigo
　　motto of: 5 Maine

idle 4 laze, lazy, loaf, vain 5 empty, inert, petty, vapid, waste, while 6 drowsy, fallow, futile, otiose, putter, torpid, unused 7 aimless, fritter, jobless, languid, trivial, useless, wait out 8 baseless, bootless, fool away, inactive, indolent, listless, slothful, sluggish, trifling 9 at leisure, enervated, fruitless, lethargic, out of work, pointless, somnolent, valueless, worthless 10 not working, unemployed, unoccupied 11 unimportant 12 unproductive 15 unsubstantiated

idleness 5 sloth 7 inertia 8 laziness, lethargy 9 indolence 10 inactivity 11 joblessness, languidness 12 sluggishness, unemployment

idler 3 bum 6 loafer 7 drifter, vagrant 10 ne'er-do-well
　　French: 7 flaneur

idol 4 hero, icon 5 relic 6 effigy, statue 7 darling 8 artifact 10 simulacrum, golden calf 11 graven image, inspiration

idolatry 5 mania 7 madness, passion, worship 8 devotion 9 adoration, obsession 10 veneration 11 idolization, infatuation 12 image worship 13 preoccupation

idolization 7 worship 9 adulation, reverence 10 exaltation, veneration

idolize 5 adore, deify, honor, prize 6 admire, revere 7 worship 8 treasure, venerate 9 reverence 11 apotheosize

Idomeneo, re di Creta
　　also: 20 Idomeneus King of Crete
　　opera by: 6 Mozart
　　character: 4 Ilia 7 Electra 8 Idamante, Poseidon

Idomeneus
　　king of: 5 Crete
　　father: 9 Deucalion

I don't know what
　　French: 12 je ne sais quoi

Idothea
　　form: 5 nymph
　　father: 7 Proteus

I Dream of Jeannie
　　character: 7 Jeannie 9 Dr Bellows 10 (Captain) Tony Nelson 11 Gen Peterson, (Captain) Roger Healey 13 Amanda Bellows
　　cast: 9 Bill Daily 11 Barbara Eden, Hayden Rorke, Larry Hagman 13 Barton MacLane, Emmaline Henry

Tony's job: 9 astronaut

Idun, Iduna
also: 5 Ithun 6 Ithunn
origin: 12 Scandinavian
goddess of: 6 spring
husband: 5 Brage, Bragi
kept: 11 youth apples

idyllic 6 rustic, sylvan 7 bucolic 8 arcadian, pastoral, peaceful, romantic 9 unspoiled

Idylls of the King, The
author: 8 Alfred Lord Tennyson
based on story of: 10 King Arthur

Ierne see 7 Ireland

if 2 an 6 though 7 whether 8 although, provided 9 condition, supposing 10 even though 11 stipulation, supposition

iffy 4 moot 5 risky 6 chancy, unsure 7 dubious, erratic 8 arguable, doubtful 9 debatable, uncertain, undecided, unsettled, whimsical 10 capricious, disputable, unresolved 11 conjectural, speculative 12 questionable 13 problematical, unpredictable

Ifriqiyah see 7 Tunisia

If Winter Comes
author: 13 A S M Hutchinson

if you please
French: 12 s'il vous plaît

Iggdrasil see 9 Yggdrasil

ignitable 8 burnable 9 flammable 10 combustive, incendiary 11 combustible, inflammable 13 conflagrative

ignite 4 burn, fire 5 blaze, flame, light 6 blow up, kindle 7 explode, inflame 8 take fire, touch off 9 catch fire, set fire to, set on fire 11 catch on fire

ignoble 3 low 4 base, foul, mean, vile 6 craven 7 debased, heinous 8 cowardly, degraded, depraved, indecent, infamous, inferior, shameful, unworthy 9 dastardly, nefarious 10 degenerate, despicable 11 disgraceful 12 contemptible, dishonorable 13 discreditable, pusillanimous 14 unconscionable

ignominious 3 low 5 sorry 6 abject 8 grievous, shameful, wretched 9 degrading 10 despicable, inglorious, unbearable 11 disgraceful, humiliating 12 dishonorable, disreputable 13 discreditable

ignominy 5 shame 6 infamy 8 contempt, disgrace, dishonor 11 degradation, humiliation

ignoramus 4 fool 5 dunce 6 nitwit 7 lowbrow 8 numskull 9 numbskull, simpleton 10 illiterate 11 know-nothing

ignorance 9 confusion 10 illiteracy 11 unawareness 12 backwardness 13 obliviousness, unfamiliarity 15 unenlightenment

ignorant 4 dumb 5 naive 6 stupid 7 asinine, blind to, fatuous, shallow, unaware 8 innocent, untaught 9 in the dark, unknowing, unlearned, untrained, untutored, unworldly 10 illiterate, uneducated, uninformed, unlettered, unschooled 11 insensitive, uncognizant 12 unperceptive 13 irresponsible, unenlightened, unintelligent 15 unknowledgeable

ignore 4 omit, skip, snub 5 scorn 6 eschew, slight 7 neglect 8 overlook, pass over 9 disregard

Igraine
character in: 16 Arthurian romance
son: 6 Arthur

Iguanodon
type: 8 dinosaur 10 ornithopod
means: 11 iguana tooth
found by: 13 Gideon Mantell
location: 6 Africa, Europe, Sussex 7 Belgium, England
period: 10 Cretaceous
characteristic: 10 duck-billed

ikebana
Japanese: 21 art of arranging flowers

Ile de France see 9 Mauritius

Ilha Formosa see 6 Taiwan

Iliad, The
author: 5 Homer
character: 5 Paris, Priam 6 Hector 8 Achilles, Menelaus 9 Agamemnon, Patroclus 11 Helen of Troy
subject: 9 Trojan War

Iliniwek see 8 Illinois

Ilion
Greek name for: 11 ancient Troy

Ilione
father: 5 Priam
mother: 6 Hecuba
husband: 11 Polymnestor
son: 8 Deipylus
raised: 9 Polydorus

Ilioneus
mentioned in: 6 Aeneid
home: 4 Troy
vocation: 7 warrior
fled: 4 Troy
fled with: 6 Aeneas
killed by: 8 Peneleus

Ilithyia see 10 Eileithyia

Ilium
Latin name for: 11 ancient Troy

ill, ills 3 woe 4 evil, foul, harm, sick, vile 5 abuse, cross, no way, surly, trial 6 ailing, damage, hardly, injury, laid up, malady, malice, nowise, plague, poorly, sickly, sorrow, unkind, unwell, wicked 7 ailment, cruelty, disease, failing, harmful, invalid, not well, ominous, outrage, peevish, trouble, unlucky, unsound 8 diseased, mischief, scarcely, sinister, vengeful 9 afflicted, complaint, infirmity, malicious, unhealthy 10 affliction, disturbing, foreboding, indisposed, misfortune, wickedness 11 abomination, acrimonious, malefaction, threatening, unfavorable 12 inauspicious, unpropitious 15 under the weather

ill-advised 4 dumb, rash 5 hasty, silly 6 myopic, stupid, unwise 7 foolish 8 foolhardy, ill-judged, impolitic, imprudent, misguided, senseless 10 indiscreet, unthinking 11 injudicious 12 shortsighted 13 ill-considered, irresponsible

ill-at-ease 3 shy 4 edgy 6 on edge, uneasy 7 abashed, fidgety, nervous 8 bothered, troubled 9 disturbed, nonplused, perturbed

10 disquieted, nonplussed **11** discomfited, discomposed, embarrassed **12** disconcerted **13** self-conscious, uncomfortable **15** discountenanced

ill-boding 4 dire **7** ominous **9** ill-omened **11** apocalyptic **12** inauspicious

ill-bred 4 rude **5** crude **7** boorish, uncivil, uncouth **8** churlish, impolite **10** unmannerly **11** ill-mannered **12** discourteous

ill-defined 3 dim **4** hazy **5** faint, murky **6** blurry **7** blurred, clouded, shadowy **8** nebulous, obscured **10** indistinct

illegal 5 wrong **6** banned **7** illicit **8** criminal, not legal, outlawed, unlawful **9** felonious, forbidden **10** actionable, prohibited, proscribed **12** illegitimate, unauthorized, unsanctioned **13** against the law

illegible 7 unclear **8** obscured **9** scribbled **10** unreadable **14** indecipherable, undecipherable, unintelligible

illegitimate 7 bastard, illegal, illicit, lawless, natural **8** baseborn, improper, unlawful **10** prohibited **11** misbegotten, unwarranted **12** unauthorized, unsanctioned

ill-fated 4 doomed, jinxed **7** hapless, unlucky **8** blighted, luckless **9** ill-omened **10** ill-starred

ill-favored 4 ugly **5** plain **6** homely **8** unlovely **9** repulsive, unsightly **12** disagreeable, unattractive

ill-fortune 6 mishap **7** bad luck **8** calamity, disaster, hardship **9** adversity **10** misfortune **11** catastrophe

ill health 6 malady **7** ailment, disease, illness **8** sickness **9** infirmity

ill-humored 5 sulky, testy **6** crabby, grumpy, sullen **7** grouchy **10** in a bad mood, unfriendly, unsociable

illiberal 5 petty, small **6** biased, narrow **7** bigoted **9** hidebound **10** brassbound, intolerant, prejudiced, ungenerous **11** opinionated, small-minded **12** narrow-minded, short-sighted

illicit 7 illegal, lawless **8** criminal, improper, not legal, unlawful **9** felonious **10** prohibited **11** black-market, clandestine **12** illegitimate, not permitted, unauthorized **13** against the law, impermissible **15** under-the-counter

Illinois
abbreviation: 2 IL **3** Ill
nickname: 4 Tall **6** Sucker **7** Prairie **13** Land of Lincoln
capital: 11 Springfield
largest city: 7 Chicago
others: 4 Pana **5** Alton, Cairo, Elgin, Flora, Olney, Pekin **6** Albion, Berwyn, Canton, Herrin, Joliet, Peoria, Skokie **7** Batavia, Decatur, Genesco, Mendota, Nokomis **8** Evanston, Rockford, Waukegan **9** Centralia **10** Barrington **11** Bloomington
college: 4 Knox **5** Barat **6** Aurora, DePaul, Eureka, Loyola, Olivet, Quincy, Shimer **7** Bradley, Chicago, Wheaton **8** Millikin **9** Augustana **12** Northwestern **16**

Illinois Wesleyan **23** Illinois Institute of Tech
explorer: 6 Joliet **7** Jolliet **9** Marquette
feature: 10 stockyards
airport: **5** O'Hare
museum: **18** Science and Industry
seaway: **10** St Lawrence
trail: **7** Lincoln
tribe: 3 Fox **4** Sauk **9** Kaskaskia
people: 9 Black Hawk, Jack Benny **10** Jane Addams, Walt Disney **12** Carl Sandburg **15** Ernest Hemingway **18** Engineer Casey Jones **20** William Jennings Bryan
lake: 3 Fox **5** Grass **7** Calumet **8** Michigan, Pistakee
land rank: 12 twenty-fourth
mountain: 6 Ozarks
highest point: **12** Charles Mound
physical feature:
hills: **7** Shawnee
president: 14 Abraham Lincoln
river: 4 Ohio, Rock **5** Spoon **6** Wabash **7** Chicago, Elkhorn **8** Big Muddy, Illinois, Mackinaw, Sangamon **9** Kaskaskia **10** Des Plaines **11** Mississippi
state admission: 11 twenty-first
state bird: 8 cardinal
state flower: 6 violet
state motto: 29 State Sovereignty—National Union
state song: 8 Illinois
state tree: 7 burl oak **8** white oak

Illinois (Iliniwek)
language family: 9 Algonkian **10** Algonquian
tribe: 6 Peoria **7** Cahokia, Tamaroa **9** Kaskaskia, Moingwena **10** Michigamea
location: 4 Iowa, Ohio **7** Indiana **8** Illinois, Michigan, Missouri **9** Wisconsin
built: 12 Cahokia Mound
murdered: 7 Pontiac
related to: 5 Miami **6** Ojibwa **7** Ojibway

illiterate 7 witless **8** childish, ignorant, unversed **9** unlearned, untutored **10** amateurish, incoherent, uneducated, uninformed, unlettered, unreliable, unschooled **11** not educated, uninitiated, unscholarly **12** uninstructed **13** unenlightened, ungrammatical **15** unknowledgeable

ill-made 6 shoddy **7** awkward **8** deformed, inferior **9** makeshift, malformed **10** jerry-built, jury-rigged **15** misproportioned

ill-mannered 4 rude **5** crude **6** coarse **7** boorish, ill-bred, loutish, uncivil **8** impolite **9** offensive, ungallant **10** ill-behaved, ungracious **12** discourteous **13** disrespectful

ill-natured 4 sour **5** cross, nasty, surly **6** bitter, cranky, malign **7** caustic, grouchy, peevish **8** captious, churlish, spiteful, venomous **9** crotchety, irascible, irritable, malignant, rancorous, splenetic **10** ill-humored, unfriendly **11** acrimonious, contentious, quarrelsome **12** antagonistic, cantankerous

illness 6 malady 7 ailment, disease 8 disorder, sickness 9 complaint, ill health, infirmity 10 affliction, disability, poor health 11 malfunction 13 indisposition

illness recovery
 god of: 11 Telesphorus

illogical 4 wild 5 crazy, dopey, nutty, silly, wacky 6 absurd, far-out, screwy 7 asinine, offbeat, unsound 9 erroneous, senseless 10 fallacious, irrational, off-the-wall, ridiculous 11 incongruent, incongruous, nonsensical, unreasoning 12 inconsistent, preposterous, unreasonable 13 contradictory

ill-omened 4 dire 7 adverse, ominous 9 ill-boding 11 apocalyptic, unfavorable 12 inauspicious, unpropitious

ill-smelling 4 foul, high, olid, rank 5 fetid, fusty 6 putrid, rancid, smelly, stinky, strong 7 reeking 8 stinking 10 malodorous

ill-starred 4 dire 5 fatal 6 tragic 7 adverse 8 ill-fated 10 calamitous, disastrous 11 unfortunate 12 catastrophic, inauspicious

ill-suited 4 inapt 8 mismated, unsuited 9 misjoined, unfitting 10 ill-adapted, ill-matched, malapropos, mismatched, unbecoming, unsuitable 11 incongruous, unbefitting, uncongenial 12 incompatible, inconsistent 13 inappropriate

ill-tempered 4 mean, rude, sour 5 angry, cross, harsh, nasty, testy 6 bitter, cranky, shirty 7 acerbic, furious, grouchy, peevish, waspish 8 choleric, churlish, petulant 9 crotchety, irascible, irritable 10 bad-natured, ill-humored, ill-natured, in a bad mood, unpleasant 11 acrimonious 12 cantankerous

ill-treatment 4 harm 5 abuse 6 ill-use, injury, misuse 7 cruelty 13 mortification

illuminate 5 edify, light 7 clarify, enhance, explain, light up 8 brighten, illumine, instruct, spell out 9 elucidate, enlighten, exemplify, irradiate, make clear 12 throw light on 13 cast light upon

illuminated 3 lit 5 lit up 6 bright 7 lighted 9 clarified, decorated, illumined 10 brightened, elucidated, irradiated

illumination 6 lights, wisdom 7 insight 8 lighting 9 education, knowledge 10 illumining, lighting up, perception, revelation 11 edification, information, instruction, irradiation 13 comprehension, enlightenment

Illuminations, Les
 author: 13 Arthur Rimbaud

illumined 3 lit 7 lighted 8 luminous 11 illuminated

ill-use 4 harm, hurt 5 abuse 6 injure, misuse 7 assault, cruelty, harming 8 maltreat, mistreat 10 bodily harm 12 maltreatment, mistreatment

illusion 5 error, fancy 6 mirage, vagary, vision 7 caprice, chimera, fallacy 8 delusion, phantasm 9 deception, false idea, misbelief, semblance, unreality 10 apparition, false image, hocus-pocus, humbuggery, impression 11 false belief 13 hallucination, misconception, misimpression 15 misapprehension

illusive 5 false 6 unreal 7 phantom, seeming 8 apparent, chimeric, fanciful, fantastic, illusory 9 deceptive 10 ostensible 11 illusionary

illusory 4 sham 5 false 6 unreal 7 seeming 8 apparent, delusive, fanciful, illusive, spurious 9 deceptive, erroneous, imaginary 10 fallacious, misleading, ostensible 11 counterfeit, unrealistic 13 hallucinatory

illustrate 4 show 6 define 7 clarify, explain, picture, point up, portray 8 decorate, ornament 9 bring home, delineate, elucidate, emphasize, make clear, represent 10 illuminate 11 demonstrate 12 pictorialize, throw light on 16 make intelligible

illustration 5 image, plate 6 figure 7 drawing, example, picture 8 instance, specimen 9 portrayal 10 photograph 14 representation 15 exemplification

illustrious 5 famed, great 6 famous 7 eminent, honored 8 glorious, lustrous, peerless, renowned, splendid 9 acclaimed, brilliant, exemplary, matchless, prominent 10 celebrated 11 magnificent 13 distinguished

illustriousness 8 grandeur 9 greatness 11 distinction 12 magnificence

ill will 4 gall 5 anger, spite 6 animus, enmity, hatred, malice, rancor, spleen 7 dislike 8 acrimony, aversion, bad blood, loathing 9 animosity, antipathy, hostility 10 abhorrence, antagonism, bitterness, contention 11 malevolence 12 hard feelings, spitefulness

ill wind 7 bad luck 8 bad break, hard luck 9 adversity, mischance 10 misfortune

Illyrius
 father: 6 Cadmus

Ilmarinen
 origin: 7 Finnish
 form: 10 blacksmith
 hero in: 8 Kalevala
 forged: 5 Sampo
 Sampo's owner: 5 Louhi

I Love Lucy
 character: 9 Fred Mertz 10 Ethel Mertz 11 Little Ricky, Lucy Ricardo 12 Ricky Ricardo
 cast: 9 Desi Arnaz 11 Lucille Ball, Vivian Vance 14 William Frawley
 Ricky's club: 7 Babaloo 9 Tropicana

Il Penseroso
 author: 10 John Milton
 companion piece: 8 L'Allegro

image 4 copy, icon, idea, idol 6 double, effigy, fetish, figure, memory, simile, statue, symbol, visage 7 concept, picture, replica 8 likeness, metaphor, portrait 9 depiction, duplicate, facsimile, mirroring, semblance 10 photograph, reflection, simulacrum 11 countenance, delineation, incarnation 12 recollection, reproduction 13 mental picture 14 figure of speech, representation

imaginable 8 feasible 9 thinkable 11 conceivable

imaginary 4 sham 5 fancy, phony 6 made-up, unreal 7 fancied, fiction, figment 8 delusion, fabulous, fanciful, illusion, illusory, invented, mythical, romantic 9 fantastic, figmental, legendary 10 factitious, fictitious 11 counterfeit, make-believe

imagination 5 fancy 7 cunning, thought 9 ingenuity, invention 10 astuteness, creativity, enterprise 12 creativeness 13 inventiveness 14 thoughtfulness 15 creative thought, resourcefulness

imaginative 6 clever 7 unusual 8 creative, inspired, original 9 ingenious, inventive 10 innovative 11 resourceful 12 enterprising 16 off the beaten path, out of the ordinary

imagine 5 fancy, guess, infer, judge 6 assume, gather 7 believe, dream up, picture, presume, pretend, project, suppose, surmise, suspect 8 conceive, envisage, envision 9 fantasize, visualize 10 conjecture

imbecile 3 ass 4 dolt, dope, fool, jerk 5 dummy, dunce, idiot, moron, ninny 6 nitwit 7 dingbat 8 dumbbell 9 blockhead, simpleton 10 nincompoop

imbecilic 4 dumb 5 inane, silly 6 absurd, stupid 7 asinine, foolish 8 careless, mindless 11 thoughtless

imbecility 6 idiocy 8 dullness, dumbness 9 asininity, stupidity, thickness 16 simplemindedness

imbibe 4 swig, tope 5 drink, quaff 6 guzzle, ingest, tipple 7 consume, partake, swallow 8 chugalug, toss down, wash down

imbiber 4 wino 5 drunk, toper 7 drinker, tippler 8 consumer, drunkard, ingester

Imbrius
   mentioned in: 5 Iliad
   father: 6 Mentor
   killed by: 6 Teucer

imbroglio 3 row 4 fray 5 brawl, broil, clash, fight, melee, scrap 6 fracas, ruckus, rumpus, uproar 7 scuffle 8 argument 9 confusion 11 altercation, embroilment 12 entanglement 13 embarrassment

imbue 4 fill, fire, tint 5 bathe, color, endow, steep, tinge 6 arouse, infuse 7 animate, impress, ingrain, inspire, instill, pervade, suffuse 8 permeate, tincture 9 inculcate

Imhotep
   father: 4 Ptah
   mother: 7 Sekhmet
   position: 6 scribe, vizier, writer 9 architect, physician
   architect of pyramid: 8 Sakkarah

imitate 3 ape 4 copy, mime 5 mimic 6 mirror, parody, parrot 7 emulate, pass for 8 look like, simulate 9 duplicate, represent 10 caricature 11 counterfeit, impersonate

imitation 4 fake, mock, sham 5 aping, phony 6 ersatz, parody 7 man-made, mimicry, takeoff 8 travesty 9 burlesque, facsimile, semblance, simulated, synthetic 10 adaptation, artificial, caricature, impression, similarity, simulation 11 counterfeit, duplication, make-believe 12 reproduction 13 impersonation 14 representation

Imitation of Christ, The
   author: 13 Thomas a Kempis

immaculate 4 pure 5 clean, ideal 6 chaste, intact, virgin 7 perfect, saintly, sinless 8 flawless, innocent, spotless, unsoiled, virginal, virtuous 9 faultless, guiltless, shipshape, stainless, unstained, unsullied 11 spic and span, untarnished 13 above reproach, unimpeachable 14 irreproachable 15 unexceptionable

immanent 6 inborn, inbred, innate 7 natural 8 inherent 9 ingrained, intrinsic 10 congenital, deep-rooted, deep-seated, indigenous, indwelling 11 instinctive, instinctual

Immanuel 7 Messiah 11 Jesus Christ
   means: 9 God with us

immaterial 7 ghostly, shadowy, trivial 8 bodiless, ethereal, mystical, noumenal, spectral, trifling, unbodied 9 spiritual, unearthly 10 evanescent, extraneous, impalpable, intangible, irrelevant, of no moment 11 disembodied, incorporeal, not relevant, unimportant 12 extramundane, extrasensory 13 insignificant, insubstantial, unsubstantial 14 of no importance 15 inconsequential, of little account

immature 5 green, young 6 callow, unripe 7 babyish, kiddish, puerile 8 childish, juvenile, unformed, youthful 9 embryonic, half-grown, infantile, not mature, pubescent 10 unfinished, unmellowed 11 out of season, rudimentary, undeveloped 16 wet behind the ears

immeasurable 7 endless, immense 8 infinite 9 boundless, limitless, unbounded, unlimited 10 fathomless 11 illimitable, inestimable, measureless, never-ending 12 incalculable, interminable, unfathomable 13 inexhaustible

immediate 4 near, next, nigh 5 close, hasty, local, swift 6 abrupt, nearby, prompt, recent, speedy, sudden 7 express, instant, nearest 8 adjacent, punctual 9 proximate, undelayed 10 contiguous 13 instantaneous

immediately 3 now 9 instantly, right away 10 this minute 12 without delay
   French: 11 tout de suite

immemorial 5 olden 7 ageless, ancient 8 dateless, hallowed, timeless 9 ancestral, legendary, venerable 11 time-honored 12 long-standing, mythological 15 long-established

immense 4 huge, vast 5 great 7 mammoth, massive 8 colossal, enormous, gigantic 9 extensive, monstrous 10 prodigious, stupendous, tremendous 11 measureless 14 Brobdingnagian

immensity 8 enormity, hugeness, vastness 9 largeness 12 enormousness

immerse 3 dip 4 duck, dunk, sink, soak 5 bathe, douse, lower, steep 6 absorb, drench, engage, occupy, plunge 7 engross 8 submerge

immerse briefly 3 dip 4 dunk

immersion 7 bathing, dunking 8 drowning 10 absorption, submersion 11 engrossment, involvement, submergence 13 concentration, preoccupation

immigrant 5 alien **7** migrant, settler **8** colonist, newcomer **9** foreigner, nonnative

immigrate 6 move to, settle **7** migrate **8** colonize

imminent 4 near **7** looming **8** menacing, perilous **9** immediate, impending **10** near at hand **11** approaching, close at hand, threatening

immobile 4 fast **5** fixed, quiet, rigid, stiff, still **6** at rest, laid up, rooted, secure, stable, static **7** riveted **9** immovable, not moving, quiescent, steadfast **10** motionless, stationary, stock-still **11** unbudgeable **13** incapacitated

immobilize 3 fix, set **4** stud **6** disarm, freeze, splint **7** disable **8** paralyze, transfix **12** incapacitate

immoderate 5 undue **7** extreme **8** whopping **9** excessive, unbridled **10** exorbitant, gargantuan, inordinate, prodigious **11** extravagant, intemperate, uncalled-for **12** unreasonable, unrestrained **14** unconscionable

immoderation 6 excess **10** debauchery **11** dissipation, prodigality, unrestraint **12** extravagance, intemperance, recklessness **13** excessiveness **14** prodigiousness

immodest 6 lewd, vain **5** gross, loose **6** brazen, coarse, risque, wanton **7** pompous **8** boastful, braggart, indecent, inflated, unchaste **9** bombastic, conceited, shameless **10** indecorous, indelicate, peacockish, suggestive **11** exaggerated, pretentious **12** self-centered

immoral 4 evil, lewd **5** dirty, wrong **6** sinful, wicked **7** corrupt, heinous, obscene, raunchy, vicious **8** depraved, indecent, infamous, prurient **9** debauched, dissolute, nefarious, salacious, unethical **10** dissipated, iniquitous, licentious, profligate **12** pornographic, unprincipled

Immoralist, The
   author: **9** Andre Gide

immorality 3 sin **4** evil **9** decadence, depravity, indecency, obscenity, prurience **10** corruption, debasement, degeneracy, sinfulness **13** salaciousness

immortal 3 god **6** divine **7** abiding, eternal, undying **8** enduring **9** deathless **11** everlasting **12** imperishable

Immortals 6 giants, greats, titans **7** the gods **8** demigods **13** all-time greats
   Greek/Roman: 8 pantheon

immovable 3 icy, set **4** cold, fast **5** fixed **6** dogged, secure, steely, stolid **7** adamant, settled **8** detached, fastened, immobile, obdurate, resolute, stubborn **9** heartless, impassive, unfeeling **10** inexorable, inflexible, stationary, unbendable **11** coldhearted, unbudgeable **12** unchangeable **13** unimpressible, unsympathetic **16** unimpressionable

immune 4 free, safe **5** clear **6** exempt **9** protected, resistant **12** invulnerable **13** unsusceptible

immunity 7 freedom **9** exemption **10** resistance **16** unsusceptibility

immure 3 hem, pen **4** cage, coop, jail, wall **6** entomb, intern, wall in, wall up **7** confine, enclose, seclude **8** cloister, imprison **11** incarcerate

immutability 9 endurance, stability **14** changelessness

immutable 4 firm **5** fixed, solid **6** stable **7** lasting **8** constant, enduring **9** permanent, unaltered, unvarying **10** changeless, inflexible, unchanging **11** unalterable **12** unchangeable, unmodifiable **14** intransmutable **16** incontrovertible

Imogen
   character in: **9** Cymbeline
   author: **11** Shakespeare

imp 3 elf **4** brat **5** demon, devil, gnome, pixie, scamp **6** goblin, hoyden, rascal, sprite, urchin **7** upstart **9** hobgoblin **10** evil spirit, leprechaun

impact 4 jolt **5** brunt, crash, force, shock, smash **6** burden, effect, thrust **7** contact **9** collision, influence **10** concussion **11** implication **12** repercussion

impair 3 mar **4** harm, hurt **6** damage, hinder, injure, lessen, reduce, weaken, worsen **7** cripple, subvert, vitiate **8** decrease, enervate, enfeeble, undercut **10** debilitate **11** detract from

impaired 6 broken, faulty, flawed **7** damaged **9** defective, deficient, imperfect

impairment 4 flaw, harm **5** fault **6** damage, defect, injury, malady **7** ailment, illness **8** debility, disorder, handicap, sickness, weakness **9** detriment, hindrance, infirmity **10** disability, impediment, inadequacy **12** debilitation

impale 3 fix, pin **4** tack **5** affix, stick **8** transfix **10** run through

impart 4 give, lend, tell **5** grant, offer, share **6** accord, afford, pass on, relate, render, report, reveal **7** confide, consign, deliver, divulge, mention **8** bestow on, confer on, disclose, dispense **9** make known **10** contribute **11** communicate

impartial 4 fair, just **7** neutral **8** detached, unbiased **9** equitable, objective **10** evenhanded, fair-minded, open-minded **11** nonpartisan **12** unprejudiced **13** disinterested, dispassionate

impartiality 7 justice **8** equality, fair play, fairness **10** detachment, neutrality **11** objectivity

impasse 4 snag **7** dead end, dilemma **8** cul-de-sac, deadlock, quandary, standoff **9** stalemate **10** blind alley, bottleneck, standstill **11** predicament

impassioned 5 eager, fiery **6** ardent, heated **7** earnest, excited, fervent, intense, rousing, zealous **8** animated, forceful, inspired, stirring

impassive 4 calm, cool **5** aloof, stony **6** sedate, stolid **7** stoical, unmoved **8** reserved **9** apathetic, untouched **10** impervious, insensible, phlegmatic **11** emotionless, indifferent, inscrutable, unemotional, unperturbed **13** dispassionate, imperturbable, unimpressible **16** unimpressionable

impassiveness 8 coldness 9 aloofness, stolidity 12 indifference 15 emotionlessness

impassivity 6 apathy 8 coolness, stoicism 9 aloofness, stolidity 10 dispassion 15 emotionlessness 16 imperturbability

impatient 4 edgy 5 fussy, hasty, itchy, rabid, tense, testy 6 ardent, touchy 7 annoyed, anxious, brusque, hurried, nervous, peevish, restive 8 agitated, feverish, restless 9 excitable, irascible, irritable, irritated 10 high-strung, intolerant, passionate 12 enthusiastic

impeach 4 slur 6 accuse, assail, attack, charge, impugn, indict 7 arraign, slander 8 badmouth, belittle, question 9 challenge, discredit, disparage, inculpate 11 incriminate 16 call into question

impeccable 7 perfect 8 flawless 9 blameless, excellent, faultless 10 immaculate 11 unblemished 12 irreprovable, unassailable 13 unimpeachable 14 irreproachable 15 unexceptionable

impecunious 4 poor 5 broke, needy 6 hard-up 7 pinched 8 bankrupt, indigent 9 destitute, insolvent, penniless 10 down-and-out, straitened 12 impoverished 15 poverty-stricken

impede 5 block, check, delay, deter, stall 6 arrest, halter, hamper, hinder, retard, stymie, thwart 7 disrupt, inhibit 8 hold back, obstruct, slow down 9 frustrate, interrupt, sidetrack 13 interfere with

impediment 4 flaw 5 block, delay 6 defect 7 barrier 8 blockage, drawback, handicap, obstacle 9 deformity, hindrance 10 detraction 11 obstruction 12 interference 14 stumbling block

impedimenta 4 gear 7 baggage 9 equipment 13 accoutrements, paraphernalia

impel 4 goad, prod, push, spur, urge 5 drive, force 6 compel, incite, induce, prompt 7 require 8 motivate 9 constrain, stimulate 11 necessitate

impend 4 brew, hang, loom 5 hover, lower 6 menace 8 approach, draw near, overhang, threaten

impending 4 near 6 coming 7 brewing, looming 8 imminent, menacing, oncoming 9 immediate 11 approaching, forthcoming, threatening

impenetrable 5 dense, solid, thick 6 sealed 7 elusive, obscure 8 puzzling 9 insoluble 10 impassable, impervious, insensible, intangible, inviolable, mysterious, unpalpable 11 inscrutable, unenterable 12 inaccessible, inexplicable, invulnerable, unfathomable 16 incomprehensible

impenitent 4 lost 6 inured 7 callous, defiant 8 hardened, obdurate 9 unashamed 10 uncontrite 11 remorseless, unrepentant, unrepenting 12 incorrigible, unapologetic 13 irreclaimable

imperative 6 urgent 7 crucial, needful 8 critical, pressing 9 essential, mandatory, necessary, requisite 10 compulsory, obligatory 11 unavoidable

imperceptible 5 minor, scant, small 6 hidden, minute, slight, subtle 7 minimal 8 academic 10 indistinct 12 undetectable, unnoticeable 13 infinitesimal, insignificant, unappreciable, unperceivable 14 inconsiderable

imperceptive 5 blind 9 unfeeling 11 insensitive, unobservant 12 inpercipient, unperceptive 13 unsympathetic

imperfect 6 faulty, flawed 8 deformed, fallible, impaired 9 blemished, defective

imperfection 4 flaw 5 fault 6 defect 7 blemish 8 weakness 9 deformity 10 faultiness, impairment, inadequacy 11 fallibility, shortcoming 13 insufficiency 14 incompleteness

imperial 5 bossy 6 feudal, lordly 8 despotic 9 arbitrary, imperious 10 autocratic, highhanded, peremptory, repressive, tyrannical 11 dictatorial, domineering, magisterial, overbearing 13 authoritarian

Imperial Presidency, The
author: 20 Arthur M Schlesinger Jr

imperil 4 risk 6 chance, expose, gamble, hazard 8 endanger 10 compromise, jeopardize 13 put in jeopardy

imperious 5 bossy, lofty 6 lordly 7 haughty 8 arrogant, despotic, imperial 10 autocratic, commanding, peremptory, tyrannical 11 dictatorial, domineering, overbearing 13 high-and-mighty

imperiousness 9 arrogance, loftiness 11 haughtiness

imperishable 6 stable 7 durable, lasting 14 indestructible

imperium 4 rule 5 realm 6 domain, empire 8 dominion 11 sovereignty

impermanent 7 passing 8 fleeting, fugitive, not fixed, unstable 9 ephemeral, temporary, transient 10 evanescent, transitory, unenduring

impermeable 5 dense, solid, tight 6 opaque 9 nonporous 10 impervious, waterproof

impersonal 4 dead 6 remote 7 general, inhuman, neutral 8 detached, lifeless, soulless 9 impartial, impassive, inanimate, inorganic, objective 10 spiritless 11 perfunctory 13 disinterested, dispassionate

impersonate 3 ape 4 copy, mime 5 mimic 6 pose as 7 imitate, portray 9 personify, represent 11 pretend to be 12 masquerade as

impertinence 4 sass 5 cheek, sauce 7 affront 8 audacity, boldness, rudeness 9 freshness, impudence, insolence, sauciness 10 cheekiness, disrespect, effrontery, incivility 11 irrelevance 17 disrespectfulness, inappropriateness

impertinent 4 rude 5 fresh, surly 6 brassy, brazen, smarty 7 uncivil 8 arrogant, impudent, insolent 9 extrinsic, insulting, unrelated 10 extraneous, immaterial, irrelevant, not germane, peremptory, unmannerly 11 unimportant 12 discourteous, presumptuous 13 disrespectful, inappropriate 14 beside the point

imperturbability 5 poise 6 aplomb 8 calmness, coolness 9 composure, sangfroid 10 equanimity, steadiness 11 self-control, tranquility 12 tranquillity 14 presence of mind, self-possession

imperturbable 4 calm, cool 6 sedate, serene 8 composed 9 collected, impassive, unanxious, unfazable, unruffled 10 impervious 11 levelheaded, undisturbed, unexcitable, unflappable, unflustered 13 dispassionate, unsusceptible

impervious 6 closed 8 immune to 11 impermeable 12 impenetrable, inaccessible, invulnerable 14 unapproachable

impetuosity 8 rashness 11 spontaneity, unrestraint 12 recklessness 13 impulsiveness 14 capriciousness

impetuous 4 rash 5 hasty 6 abrupt, stormy 7 rampant, violent 8 forcible, headlong, vehement 9 impulsive 10 capricious, inexorable, relentless, unexpected 11 precipitate 14 unpremeditated

impetus 4 prod, push, spur 5 boost, drive, force, start 6 motive 7 impulse 8 momentum, stimulus 9 impulsion, incentive 10 motivation, propulsion 11 moving force, stimulation

impiety 9 blasphemy, sacrilege 10 disrespect, irreligion 11 irreverence, ungodliness

impinge 7 intrude, obtrude, violate 8 encroach, infringe, trespass 10 transgress

impious 7 godless, immoral, profane, ungodly 8 apostate, renegade 9 perverted 10 iniquitous, irreverent 11 blasphemous, irreligious 12 iconoclastic, sacrilegious 13 disrespectful

impiousness 7 impiety 9 blasphemy, sacrilege 10 disrespect 11 irreverence, ungodliness

impish 5 elfin 7 implike, puckish, roguish 8 prankish, rascally, sportive 11 mischievous

implacable 10 inexorable, inflexible, relentless, unamenable 11 intractable, unrelenting 12 unappeasable, unpacifiable 14 irreconcilable, uncompromising

implant 3 fix, set, sow 4 root 5 embed, graft, imbed, inlay, teach 6 infuse, insert 7 impress, instill 8 entrench 9 establish, inculcate 10 impregnate

implausible 8 doubtful, unlikely 9 illogical, senseless 10 far-fetched, improbable, incredible, outrageous, ridiculous 12 preposterous, unbelievable, unreasonable 13 inconceivable

implement 4 tool 5 begin, enact, piece, start 6 device 7 achieve, article, fulfill, realize, utensil 8 activate, carry out 9 apparatus, appliance, equipment, materials 10 accomplish, bring about, instrument 11 set in motion 13 put into effect

implicate 7 connect, embroil, ensnare, involve 8 entangle 9 associate, inculpate 11 incriminate

implication 6 effect 7 outcome 8 innuendo, overtone 9 inference 10 connection, intimation, suggestion 11 association, connotation, consequence, insinuation, involvement 12 entanglement, ramification, significance

implicit 5 total 6 hinted, innate 7 certain, implied, staunch 8 absolute, complete, inferred, inherent, profound, resolute 9 deducible, steadfast, suggested 10 understood, unreserved, unshakable 13 unquestioning

implied 5 tacit 7 oblique 8 indirect 9 implicity, indicated

implode 11 burst inward 17 compress violently

implore 3 beg 4 urge 6 obtest 7 beseech, entreat 9 importune, plead with 10 supplicate

imply 4 hint, mean 6 denote 7 bespeak, betoken, connote, presume, signify, suggest 8 evidence, indicate, intimate 9 insinuate 10 presuppose

impolite 4 rude 7 ill-bred, uncivil 9 impolitic, unfitting, ungenteel, unrefined 10 undecorous, unmannerly 12 discourteous 13 disrespectful, inconsiderate

impoliteness 8 rudeness 10 bad manners, incivility 11 boorishness, discourtesy

import 6 burden, moment, thrust 7 meaning 9 overtones 10 importance 11 connotation, implication 12 ramification, significance

importance 4 rank 5 value, worth 6 esteem, import, moment, repute, weight 7 stature 8 eminence, position 9 influence, relevance 11 consequence, seriousness, weightiness 12 significance 13 essentialness, momentousness

Importance of Being Earnest, The
    author: 10 Oscar Wilde
    character: 12 Cecily Cardew, Jack Worthing, Letitia Prism 16 Gwendolen Fairfax 17 Algernon Moncrieff (Algy) 20 Lady Augusta Bracknell 21 Reverend Canon Chasuble

important 5 great, major 7 leading, notable, seminal, serious, weighty 8 creative, esteemed, foremost, original 9 momentous, prominent 10 imperative, meaningful, preeminent, remarkable 11 distinctive, influential, significant 13 consequential

imported 5 alien 6 exotic 7 foreign 9 not native

importunate 7 begging 8 pleading 9 imploring 10 entreating, persistent 11 troublesome 12 supplicating

importune 3 beg, sue 4 pray 5 plead 6 adjure, exhort 7 beseech, entreat, implore 8 appeal to, petition 10 supplicate

importunity 4 plea 6 appeal 7 request 8 entreaty, petition 12 supplication

impose 3 set 4 levy 5 apply, enact, foist, force, lay on 6 peddle, slap on 7 command, dictate, inflict, palm off, place on 9 establish, institute, introduce, prescribe 10 thrust upon

impose upon 5 annoy 6 bother, ill-use 8 illtreat, maltreat, mistreat 15 take advantage of

imposing 5 grand, lofty 7 massive, stately 8 majestic, striking, towering 10 commanding, impressive, monumental 11 outstanding 12 awe-inspiring

imposition 5 abuse 6 burden, ill use 8 foisting 10 obligation 15 taking advantage

impossible 8 stubborn 9 insoluble 10 unbearable, unsolvable, unyielding 11 intolerable, intractable, not possible 12 insufferable, intransigent, unachievable, unanswerable, unattainable, unimaginable, unmanageable 13 inconceivable 16 out of the question

impost 3 fee, tax 4 duty, fine, toll 6 charge, excise, tariff 10 assessment

impostor 4 sham 5 cheat, duper, fraud, phony, quack 6 con man 7 bluffer, shammer 8 deceiver 9 charlatan, defrauder, pretender, trickster 10 dissembler, mountebank 11 counterfeit, flimflam man, masquerader, pettifogger 12 impersonator

imposture 4 fake, hoax, play, ruse, sham 5 cheat, fraud, trick 6 deceit, humbug 7 forgery, swindle 8 artifice, delusion, pretense, quackery 9 deception, falsehood, imitation 10 pretension 11 charlatanry, counterfeit, fraudulence 12 charlatanism 13 impersonation, mountebankery

impotence 8 weakness 9 paralysis 10 disability, incapacity, inefficacy 12 helplessness 13 powerlessness 14 ineffectuality 15 ineffectiveness

impotent 4 weak 5 frail 6 feeble 7 hapless 8 disabled, feckless, helpless 9 paralyzed, powerless 11 ineffective

impound 3 pen 4 cage 5 pen in, seize 6 coop up, encage, lock up, shut in 7 confine 13 hold in custody

impoverish 4 bust, ruin 5 break, drain 6 beggar, drench, pauper, reduce 7 deplete, exhaust 8 bankrupt, make poor 9 pauperize 11 send to the poorhouse

impoverished 4 poor 6 abject, barren, bereft, effete, used up 7 drained, sterile, wanting, worn out 8 depleted, indigent, wiped out 9 destitute, exhausted 10 downand-out, pauperized 11 impecunious 12 unproductive, without means

impractical 6 sloppy, unwise 8 careless, quixotic, romantic 10 loose-ended, starryeyed 11 unrealistic 12 disorganized 13 helter-skelter, unintelligent

imprecation 5 curse 8 anathema 11 malediction

impregnable 6 mighty, potent, strong, sturdy 8 powerful 10 invincible 12 invulnerable, unassailable, unattackable 13 unconquerable

impregnate 3 wet 4 soak 5 steep 6 dampen, drench, imbrue, infuse 7 moisten, suffuse 8 fructify, inundate, permeate, saturate 9 fecundate, fertilize 10 inseminate

impresario 7 manager, sponsor 8 director 9 conductor, organizer 12 entrepreneur

impress 4 grab, move, stir, sway 5 reach, touch 6 affect, excite, sink in, strike 8 bedazzle 9 electrify, influence, overpower, overwhelm

impression 4 idea, mark, mold, view 5 hunch, stamp, trace, track 6 belief, effect, impact, notion 7 contour, feeling, impress, imprint, opinion, outline, surmise 9 influence, reception, sensation 10 conviction 11 indentation 13 understanding

impressionable 8 gullible, passible, sentient 9 affective, receptive 10 vulnerable 11 suggestible

impressive 5 grand 6 august, moving 8 exciting, imposing, majestic, striking 9 memorable, thrilling 11 magnificent, outstanding 12 awe-inspiring, overpowering, soul-stirring 13 unforgettable

imprimis 15 in the first place

imprint 3 fix 4 etch, mark, sign 5 infix, press, stamp, title 6 indent 7 engrave, impress 8 inscribe 9 engraving 10 depression, impression 11 indentation

imprison 3 pen 4 jail 6 coop up, engage, entomb, immure, lock up 7 confine, fence in, impound, shackle 8 restrain 9 constrain 11 hold captive, incarcerate

improbable 8 doubtful, unlikely 9 illogical 11 implausible 12 unreasonable 13 unforeseeable

improbable solution in a play's plot
  Latin: 13 deus ex machina

impromptu 6 sudden 7 offhand 9 impulsive, makeshift, on the spot 10 improvised, off the cuff, unexpected, unprepared 11 spontaneous, unrehearsed 14 extemporaneous, unpremeditated, without warning 15 spur-of-the-moment 16 extemporaneously, on a moment's notice 19 off the top of one's head

improper 4 lewd 5 inapt, unfit 8 indecent, off-color, unseemly 9 ill-suited, irregular 10 indecorous, malapropos, out of place, suggestive, unbecoming, unsuitable 12 inharmonious 13 inappropriate, unconformable

  French: 5 outre

impropriety 5 gaffe 7 blunder, faux pas 9 gaucherie, indecorum, vulgarity 10 bad manners 11 boorishness 12 impoliteness, indiscretion

improve 4 help 5 rally 6 better, enrich, repair 7 correct, develop, enhance 9 cultivate 10 ameliorate, recuperate

improvement 4 gain 6 reform, repair 7 advance, upswing 8 additive, progress 9 amendment 10 betterment, emendation, refinement 11 advancement, enhancement, reclamation 12 amelioration 14 reconstruction

improvidence 10 imprudence 11 prodigality 12 extravagance, wastefulness 13 shiftlessness 16 shortsightedness

improvident 6 lavish 8 prodigal, reckless, wasteful 9 imprudent, negligent, unthrifty 10 thriftless 11 extravagant, spendthrift 12 shortsighted 14 unparsimonious

improvise 5 ad-lib 6 make up, wing it 11 extemporize

improvised 5 ad-lib 7 devised, offhand 8 invented 9 concocted, contrived, dreamed-up, extempore, hatched-up, impromptu, makeshift 10 off-the-cuff, originated, unprepared 11 extemporary, spontaneous, unrehearsed 12 extemporized 14 extemporaneous, unpremeditated 15 improvisational, spur-of-the-moment

imprudent 4 rash 5 crazy, dopey 6 unwise 7 foolish 8 heedless, mindless, untoward 9 foolhardy 10 ill-advised, incautious, indiscreet, unthinking 11 inadvisable, injudicious, thoughtless 13 ill-considered

impudence
    Yiddish: 7 chutzpa 8 chutzpah

impudent 4 bold, rude 5 brash, fresh, nervy, saucy 6 brazen, cheeky 7 forward, upstart 8 impolite, insolent 9 bumptious, shameless 11 impertinent, smart-alecky, wiseacreish 12 discourteous 13 disrespectful

impugn 4 deny 5 knock, libel 6 assail, attack, berate, negate, oppose 7 asperse, slander 8 denounce, question 9 challenge, criticize 10 contradict 14 call in question, cast aspersions 16 call into question

impugnment 7 slander 10 aspersions

impulse 4 bent, goad, push, spur, urge, whim 5 drive, fancy, force 6 desire, motive, notion, thrust, whimsy 7 caprice, impetus, whimsey 8 instinct, momentum, movement, stimulus, stirring 9 incentive 10 incitement, motivation 11 inclination, inspiration, instigation

impulsive 4 rash 7 driving, offhand 8 forceful, forcible, notional 9 impelling, impetuous, impromptu, unplanned, whimsical 10 capricious, incautious, propellant, propelling 11 involuntary, spontaneous 12 devil-may-care 13 unpredictable 14 extemporaneous, unpremeditated 15 spur-of-the-moment

impulsiveness 8 rashness 11 impetuosity, spontaneity, unrestraint 12 recklessness, whimsicality 14 capriciousness

impunity 8 immunity 9 clearance, exemption, privilege 10 absolution 11 prerogative 12 dispensation

impure 4 foul, lewd 5 dirty 6 coarse, filthy, smutty 7 debased, defiled, immoral, lustful, noisome, noxious, obscene, sullied, tainted, unclean 8 degraded, devalued, immodest, improper, indecent, polluted, prurient, unchaste, vitiated 9 lecherous, salacious, unrefined 10 indecorous, indelicate, libidinous, licentious 11 adulterated, depreciated, unwholesome 12 contaminated

impurity 5 alloy, dross, filth, taint 8 foulness 9 dirtiness, pollutant, pollution 10 adulterant, corruption, defilement 11 contaminant, taintedness, uncleanness 12 adulteration 13 contamination, foreign matter 15 unwholesomeness

imputation 6 charge 10 accusation, allegation, ascription 11 attribution

impute 5 refer 6 assign, charge, credit, relate 7 ascribe 9 attribute

inability 10 inaptitude, incapacity, ineptitude 12 helplessness, incapability, incompetence 13 maladroitness, powerlessness

in absence
    Latin: 10 in absentia

in absentia 9 in absence

inaccessible 9 not at hand 11 unreachable 12 unattainable, unobtainable 14 unapproachable

in accord 9 agreeable, approving, in harmony, of one mind 10 concurring, consenting 11 in agreement
    French: 9 en rapport

inaccuracy 4 goof, slip 5 error, fault, wrong 6 boo-boo 7 blunder, erratum, fallacy, mistake 9 unclarity 10 faultiness 11 imprecision, inexactness 13 incorrectness, unreliability 14 fallaciousness

inaccurate 3 off 5 false, wrong 6 faulty 7 inexact 8 mistaken 9 erroneous, imprecise, incorrect, off target 10 fallacious, unreliable 11 not on target, off the track 13 wide of the mark

Inachus
    god of: 6 rivers
    king of: 5 Argos
    father: 7 Oceanus
    mother: 6 Tethys
    wife: 5 Melia
    son: 9 Aegialeus, Phoroneus
    daughter: 2 Io

inaction 8 abeyance, deferral, dormancy, dullness, idleness 9 cessation, indolence 10 inactivity, quiescence, somnolence, suspension 11 complacency

inactive 4 dull, idle, lazy 5 inert, quiet, still 6 low-key, otiose, static, torpid, unused 7 dormant, languid 8 indolent, slothful, sluggish 9 do-nothing, easygoing, leisurely, sedentary, somnolent 10 on the shelf 11 inoperative 12 out of service

inactivity 4 rest 5 quiet 6 disuse 7 inertia 8 dormancy, idleness, inaction 9 stillness 10 quiescence

in actuality
    Latin: 6 in esse

in addition 3 and, too 4 also, more, plus, then 5 above, added, again, extra 6 as well, beyond 7 besides, further 8 moreover 10 additional 12 additionally, supplemental

inadequacy 4 lack 7 failing 10 deficiency, impairment 11 shortcoming 13 insufficiency

inadequate 5 inept, short, unfit 6 meager, scanty, too raw 7 lacking, not up to, wanting 8 below par, unfitted 9 deficient, imperfect, incapable 11 incompetent, unqualified 12 insufficient

inadmissible 10 disallowed, extraneous 11 intolerable 12 not permitted, unacceptable 14 nonpermissible

in advance 6 before, in time, sooner 7 earlier 9 before now 10 beforehand 11 ahead of time 13 before the fact

inadvertent 7 unmeant 10 accidental, fortuitous, unintended, unthinking 11 involuntary 13 unintentional 14 unpremeditated

inadvisable 5 risky 6 chancy, unwise 9 impolitic, imprudent 10 ill-advised 11 inexpedient, injudicious, inopportune

in aeternum 7 forever

in agreement
French: 7 en rapport

inalienable 6 sacred 8 absolute, defended, inherent 9 protected 10 inviolable, sacrosanct 12 unassailable 13 unforfeitable, unimpeachable

in all
Latin: 6 in toto

in all places 10 every place, everywhere, far and near, far and wide

in a low voice
Latin: 9 sotto voce

inamorata 4 lady, love 5 lover 7 beloved, darling 8 ladylove, mistress, paramour, truelove 10 sweetheart

inane 4 dumb 5 dopey, empty, silly, vapid 6 absurd, jejune, stupid 7 asinine, fatuous, foolish, idiotic, insipid, shallow, vacuous 9 pointless, senseless 10 ridiculous, unthinking 11 meaningless, nonsensical 13 unintelligent

inanimate 4 cold, dead, dull 5 inert 6 asleep, stolid 8 lifeless, soulless 9 inorganic, insensate, nonliving, senseless, unfeeling 10 insensible, insentient 11 unconscious

inanity 6 drivel 7 hogwash, vacuity 8 nonsense, vapidity 9 absurdity, asininity, silliness 11 foolishness 13 pointlessness, senselessness 14 ridiculousness

Inanna
origin: 8 Sumerian
goddess of: 3 war 4 love
sister: 10 Ereshkigal
realm: 6 heaven
corresponds to: 6 Ishtar 7 Astarte, Mylitta 9 Ashtoreth

in any case 6 anyhow, anyway 9 at any rate 10 in any event

in any event 6 anyhow, anyway 9 at any rate, in any case

inapplicable 5 unfit 6 not apt 8 unsuited 10 inapposite, irrelevant, not germane, unsuitable 12 incompatible, not pertinent 13 inappropriate

inappropriate 5 inapt 8 ill-timed, improper, unsuited 9 unfitting 10 indecorous, in bad taste, out of place, unbecoming, unsuitable 11 incongruous 12 incompatible, infelicitous
French: 10 mal a propos

inapt 8 improper, unseemly, unsuited 9 ill-suited, incorrect, unfitting 11 incongruous 13 inappropriate

inaptness 7 inability, ineptness 10 clumsiness, inaptitude, ineptitude 12 incompetence 13 maladroitness 14 unskillfulness

in arrears 4 late 7 overdue 10 delinquent

inarticulate 4 dumb, mute 7 babbled, blurred, garbled, mumbled 8 confused, wordless 9 paralyzed 10 incoherent, indistinct, speechless, tongue-tied 12 inexpressive 14 unintelligible 15 uncommunicative

inartistic 9 graceless, inelegant, tasteless 10 ungraceful 11 unaesthetic 12 unattractive

in a series
French: 7 en suite

in a set
French: 7 en suite

in attendance 4 here 7 present, serving 9 appearing, caring for, on the spot, waiting on 12 accompanying, looking after, taking care of

inattention 6 apathy 10 negligence 12 carelessness 14 lack of interest 16 absentmindedness, unresponsiveness

inattentive 7 unaware 8 careless, heedless 9 forgetful, negligent, unmindful 10 distracted 11 daydreaming, thoughtless, unobservant 12 absentminded

inaugurate 5 set up, start 6 induct, launch 7 instate, kick off, usher in 8 initiate 9 institute, undertake 10 embark upon 11 set in action

inauguration 5 start 9 beginning, induction 10 dedication 11 origination 12 commencement

inaugurator 6 author, father 7 creator, founder, starter 9 initiator, organizer 10 originator, prime mover

inauspicious 7 unlucky 9 ill-chosen, ill-omened 10 badly timed, disastrous 11 unfavorable, unfortunate, unpromising 12 infelicitous, unpropitious

in a vacuum
Latin: 7 in vacuo

in bad faith
Latin: 8 mala fide

in being
Latin: 6 in esse

in blazing crime
Latin: 18 in flagrante delicto

inborn 5 basic 6 inbred, innate, native 7 natural 8 inherent 9 inherited, intrinsic, intuitive 10 congenital 11 fundamental, instinctive 14 constitutional

inbred 6 inborn, innate, primal 7 natural 8 inherent 9 ingrained, inherited, intrinsic, intuitive 10 congenital, deep-rooted, deep-seated, hereditary, indwelling 11 instinctive, instinctual 12 deeply rooted 14 constitutional

Inca
language family: 7 Quechua
location: 4 Peru 5 Chili 7 Bolivia, Ecuador 9 Argentina 12 South America
leader: 7 Huascar 8 Topa Inca 9 Atahualpa, Pachacuti 10 Manco Capac 11 Huayna Capac
conquered by: 7 Pizarro
ruins: 11 Machu Picchu, Sacsahuaman, Tambo Machay

incalculable 7 dubious 8 infinite 9 countless, uncertain 11 inestimable, innumerable, measureless, uncountable 12 immeasurable, incomputable 13 unforeseeable, unpredictable

incandesce 4 burn, glow 5 flare, flash

incandescent 7 dynamic, glowing, radiant 8 electric, galvanic, magnetic, white-hot 9 brilliant 11 high-powered 12 electrifying 13 scintillating

incantation 3 hex 4 jinx 5 chant, charm, magic, spell 6 voodoo 7 sorcery 8 wizardry 10 black magic, hocus-pocus, invocation, mumbo-jumbo, necromancy, witchcraft 11 abracadabra, conjuration

incapable 5 inept, unfit 6 unable 8 helpless, impotent, inferior 9 powerless, unskilled, untrained 10 inadequate 11 incompetent, ineffective, inefficient, unqualified

incapacitate 4 maim, undo 5 lay up 7 cripple, disable 8 enfeeble, handicap, paralyze, sideline 9 make unfit 10 disqualify 13 make powerless 14 put out of action 15 render incapable

incapacitated 6 laid up 8 crippled, disabled, disarmed, helpless, stricken 9 hamstrung, paralyzed, sidelined 10 on the shelf, prostrated 11 immobilized, out of action 12 hors de combat 14 flat on one's back

incapacity 7 illness 8 sickness 9 crippling 10 deficiency, disability 12 incapability

incarcerate 3 pen 4 jail 5 commit, coop up, immure, intern, lock up 7 confine, impound 8 imprison, restrain

incarceration 9 detention 10 commitment, internment 11 confinement, durance vile 12 imprisonment 18 institutionalizing

incarnate 8 embodied, manifest 9 personify 10 actualized, in the flesh 11 objectified, personified

Incarnations
    author: 16 Robert Penn Warren

incautious 4 rash 5 brash 6 unwary 8 careless, heedless, reckless 9 hotheaded, impetuous, imprudent, impulsive, overhasty 10 headstrong, indiscreet, unthinking 11 injudicious, thoughtless

incendiary 8 agitator, arsonist 12 inflammatory

incense 5 anger 6 burn up, enrage, madden 7 inflame, provoke 9 infuriate, make angry 13 make indignant
    spice: 6 stacte

incensed 3 mad 5 angry, irate 6 fuming, raging 7 enraged, furious 8 burned up, inflamed, outraged, provoked 9 affronted, indignant 10 infuriated

incentive 4 lure, spur 5 come-on, motive 8 stimulus 9 enticement, inducement, motivation 11 inspiration 13 encouragement

inception 5 birth, debut, onset, start 6 origin, outset 7 arrival 9 beginning 12 commencement, inauguration

incessant 8 constant, unbroken, unending 9 ceaseless, continual, perpetual, unceasing 10 continuous, persistent 11 everlasting, unrelenting, unremitting 12 interminable 13 uninterrupted

inch
    abbreviation: 2 in

In Chancery
    author: 14 John Galsworthy
    part of trilogy: 11 Forsyte Saga

inchoate 7 budding, nascent 8 formless, unformed, unshaped 9 amorphous, beginning, embryonic, incipient, shapeless 10 commencing, disjointed, uncohesive 11 unorganized 12 disconnected

incidence 4 rate 5 range, scope 6 extent 8 occasion 9 frequency, happening 10 commonness, occurrence, phenomenon 11 routineness

incident 5 clash, event, scene 6 affair 7 episode, related 8 occasion 9 happening 10 incidental, occurrence 11 contretemps, disturbance

incidental 5 minor 9 accessory, secondary 10 extraneous, unexpected 11 subordinate, unlooked-for

incidentally 7 apropos, by the by 8 by the way 9 in passing 14 speaking of that 15 parenthetically 21 while we're on the subject

incidentals 6 extras 8 minutiae 10 minor items 11 accessories, odds and ends 13 appurtenances

incinerate 4 burn 7 consume, cremate 9 carbonize 13 reduce to ashes

incineration 6 firing 7 burning, flaming 8 ignition, kindling 9 cremation 10 combustion 13 carbonization

incinerator 4 oven 6 burner 7 furnace

incipient 7 budding, nascent 8 inchoate 9 beginning, embryonic, fledgling, promising 10 developing, half-formed 11 rudimentary

in circulation 4 rife 6 abroad, around 7 at large 9 all around 11 going around 12 spread around 14 around and about 15 making the rounds

incise 4 etch 5 carve 7 cut into, engrave

incision 3 cut 4 scar, gash, nick, slit 5 cleft, notch, score, slash, slice, wound 6 furrow

incisive 4 curt, keen 5 acute, brisk, crisp, sharp 6 biting, shrewd 7 cutting, express, mordant, precise, probing, summary 8 analytic, piercing 9 trenchant, well-aimed 10 perceptive 11 intelligent, penetrating

incite 4 goad, prod, stir 5 drive, egg on, impel, rouse 6 arouse, excite, fire up, foment, induce, prompt, stir up, urge on 7 actuate, agitate, inflame, provoke 8 activate 9 instigate, stimulate

incitement 6 urging 7 arousal, driving, goading 8 egging on, exciting, firing up, stirring 9 agitating, fomenting, inflaming, prompting, provoking 10 activation, stirring up 11 provocation, stimulation

incivility 8 rudeness 9 barbarism, impudence, indecorum, surliness, vulgarity 10 bad manners, coarseness, disrespect 11 boorishness, discourtesy, misbehavior, uncouthness 12 impoliteness, tactlessness 14 unpleasantness

inclement 3 raw 4 foul 5 harsh, nasty, rough 6 bitter, severe, stormy 7 violent 11 tempestuous

inclination 3 bow, dip, nod 4 bend, bent, hill, rake, rise 5 grade, pitch, slant, slope 6 liking 7 bending, leaning, sloping 8 fondness, lowering, penchant, tendency 9 acclivity, inclining, proneness 10 preference, proclivity, propensity 11 disposition 12 predilection 14 predisposition

incline 3 bow 4 bend, cant, hill, lean, like, rake, seem, tend, tilt, wont 5 be apt, enjoy, pitch, slant, slope 6 prefer 7 decline 8 be likely, gradient 9 acclivity 10 lean toward 11 bend forward, have a mind to

inclined 3 apt 5 prove 6 liable, likely 7 given to 10 disposed to 11 predisposed

incline downward 3 dip, sag 4 sink 5 droop, slant, slope

inclined to delay 4 slow 5 tardy 6 remiss 8 dawdling, dilatory, sluggish 9 reluctant 12 foot-dragging 13 dillydallying 15 procrastinating

include 5 cover 6 enfold, entail, take in 7 contain, embrace, involve, subsume 8 comprise 9 encompass 10 comprehend 11 incorporate

inclusive 7 general, overall 8 sweeping, taking in 9 embracing, including 10 comprising, encircling 11 surrounding 12 encyclopedic 13 comprehending, comprehensive, incorporating 15 all-encompassing

incognito 7 unknown, unnamed 8 nameless 9 concealed, disguised, protected 10 in disguise, uncredited, undercover, unrevealed 11 undisclosed 12 unidentified 14 unacknowledged, unrecognizable

incognizant 7 obtuse 7 unaware 8 ignorant, unseeing 9 unknowing 13 unconscious of 15 uncomprehending

incoherent 7 muddled, unclear 8 confused, rambling 9 illogical 10 disjointed, irrational 11 bewildering, nonsensical 12 inconsistent 14 unintelligible

In Cold Blood
   author: 12 Truman Capote
   director: 13 Richard Brooks
   cast: 11 Paul Stewart, Robert Blake, Scott Wilson 12 John Forsythe

income 5 means, wages 6 salary 7 revenue 8 earnings 9 emolument 10 livelihood

income, annual
   French: 5 rente

incomparable 8 peerless 9 matchless, unequaled, unrivaled 10 inimitable 11 superlative 12 transcendent 13 beyond compare 14 unapproachable

incompatible 6 at odds 7 jarring 8 clashing, contrary, unsuited 10 at variance, discordant, mismatched 11 disagreeing, incongruous, uncongenial 12 antagonistic, inconsistent, inharmonious 13 contradictory, inappropriate

incompatibility 6 strife 7 discord 8 friction, variance 9 disaccord, wrangling 10 antagonism 11 being at odds, discordance 13 lack of harmony

incompetency 9 inability, unfitness 10 ineptitude 11 lack of skill 12 inefficiency 15 ineffectiveness

incompetent 5 inept, unfit 8 inexpert 9 incapable, unskilled, untrained 11 ineffective, ineffectual, inefficient, unqualified 14 lacking ability

incomplete 6 broken 7 partial, wanting 9 defective, deficient 10 unfinished 11 fragmentary

incompleteness 8 omission 10 deficiency 11 shortcoming 15 unfinished state

incomprehensible 7 obscure 8 abstruse, baffling 9 confusing 10 befuddling 11 bewildering, inscrutable, ungraspable 12 impenetrable, unfathomable 14 unintelligible 19 beyond comprehension, beyond understanding

incomprehension 10 bafflement, puzzlement 12 bewilderment 19 failure to understand

inconceivable 7 strange 8 unlikely 10 improbable, incredible 11 unthinkable 12 beyond belief, unbelievable, unimaginable 14 highly unlikely

in conclusion
   French: 5 enfin

inconclusive 4 open 9 unsettled 10 indecisive, indefinite, unresolved, up in the air 11 not definite 12 unconvincing, undetermined 13 indeterminate

incongruity 8 variance 9 disparity 10 aberration, disharmony, divergence 11 abnormality, discrepancy 13 dissimilarity, inconsistency, unsuitability 17 inappropriateness

incongruous 3 odd 6 far-out 8 contrary 10 at variance, discrepant, out of place, outlandish, unsuitable 11 conflicting, disagreeing 12 incompatible, inconsistent, out of keeping 13 contradictory, inappropriate 14 irreconcilable

inconsequential 5 petty 6 slight 7 trivial 8 nugatory, picayune, piddling, trifling 9 valueless 10 negligible, of no moment 11 meaningless, unimportant 13 insignificant 15 of no consequence

inconsiderable 5 light, minor, petty, small 6 little, modest, paltry, slight 7 minimal, trivial 8 picayune, trifling 9 no big deal 10 negligible 11 unimportant 13 insignificant, no great shakes 15 inconsequential

inconsiderate 4 rash, rude 6 remiss, unkind 7 uncivil 8 careless, impolite, tactless, uncaring 9 negligent 10 ungracious, unthinking 11 insensitive, thoughtless 12 disregardful, uncharitable

inconsistency 8 variance 9 disparity 10 difference, divergence 11 discrepancy, incongruity 12 disagreement 13 dissimilarity

inconsistent 6 fickle 7 erratic, wayward 8 contrary, notional, unstable, variable 9 changeful, dissonant 10 changeable, discrepant, inconstant, irresolute 11 inaccordant, incongruous, inconsonant, vacillating 12 incompatible, inharmonious 13 contradictory, unpredictable 14 irreconcilable

inconsolable 7 crushed 8 dejected, desolate, wretched 9 unnoticed 10 despondent 12 disconsolate 13 broken-hearted

inconsonant 10 discordant 12 out of keeping, unharmonious

inconspicuous 3 dim 5 faint, muted 6 modest 9 unnoticed 10 unapparent, unassuming 11 unobtrusive 12 not egregious, unnoticeable 14 unostentatious

inconstancy 10 fickleness, infidelity 11 instability 14 capriciousness, changeableness, unfaithfulness

inconstant 6 fickle, untrue 7 erratic 8 cavalier, disloyal, unstable 9 mercurial 10 capricious, changeable, unfaithful 11 interrupted, uncommitted, undedicated, unsteadfast

incontinence 8 rashness 12 recklessness 13 lack of control 16 irresponsibility

incontinent 8 unchaste 12 unrestrained

incontrovertibility 8 sureness 9 certainty 12 absoluteness, definiteness 13 undeniability 14 irrefutability, conclusiveness 15 indisputability 16 incontestability 17 unquestionability

incontrovertible 9 apodictic 10 unarguable, undeniable 11 established, irrefutable 12 indisputable 14 beyond question, unquestionable

inconvenience 6 bother, put out 7 trouble 8 hardship, headache, nuisance 9 annoyance, disoblige, put one out 10 discomfort 13 be a nuisance to, pain in the neck

inconvenient 7 awkward, unhandy 8 annoying, tiresome, untimely 10 bothersome, burdensome 11 distressing, inopportune, troublesome

Incoronazione di Poppea, L'
also: 22 The Coronation of Poppaea
opera by: 10 Monteverdi
character: 4 Nero 6 Ottone 7 Ottavia

incorporate 4 fuse 5 embody, work in 7 include 10 amalgamate, assimilate 11 consolidate

incorporated 6 united 8 embodied, included 11 amalgamated, assimilated 12 consolidated

incorporeal 6 occult, unreal 7 ghostly, phantom 8 bodiless 9 spiritual, unearthly, unfleshly, unworldly 10 immaterial, intangible 11 disembodied 12 supernatural 13 insubstantial

incorrect 5 false, wrong 6 untrue 7 inexact 8 mistaken 9 erroneous 10 fallacious, inaccurate

incorrectness 5 error 9 wrongness 10 inaccuracy 12 carelessness, slovenliness

incorrigible 6 unruly 8 hardened, hardcore, hopeless 10 beyond help, delinquent 11 intractable 12 beyond saving, past changing, unmanageable 14 uncontrollable

incorrigible child
French: 14 enfant terrible

incorruptible 4 pure 6 honest 7 upright 8 reliable 9 faultless, righteous 10 unbribable 11 trustworthy 14 irreproachable

increase 3 wax 4 grow 5 add to, swell 6 enrich, expand 7 advance, augment, burgeon, enhance, enlarge 8 multiply 12 become larger

increasing 7 growing 9 enlarging, expansion, extending, extension 10 drawing out 11 enlargement 12 augmentation

incredible 6 absurd 7 amazing, awesome 10 astounding, farfetched, remarkable 11 astonishing 12 preposterous, unbelievable, unimaginable 13 extraordinary, inconceivable

Incredible Hulk, The
character: 9 Jack McGee 11 David Banner
cast: 9 Bill Bixby 10 Jack Colvin 11 Lou Ferrigno

incredulous 7 dubious 8 doubtful 9 skeptical 10 suspicious 11 distrustful 12 disbelieving

increment 4 gain, rise 5 raise 6 growth, profit 7 benefit 8 addition, increase 9 accretion 10 supplement 11 enlargement 12 accumulation, appreciation, augmentation 13 proliferation

incriminate 5 blame 6 accuse, charge, indict

incrimination 5 blame 7 charges 10 accusation, indictment

incubate 3 set, sit 4 plot 5 breed, brood, clock, cover, hatch 6 scheme 7 develop, gestate, sit upon 8 generate

incubus 5 demon 8 bad dream 9 nightmare

inculcate 5 drill, imbue, infix, teach, train 6 impart, infuse 7 implant, impress, instill 8 instruct 9 brainwash, condition, enlighten 12 indoctrinate

inculpable 5 clear 8 innocent 9 blameless, guiltless, not guilty 10 not at fault, unblamable 14 not responsible

incur 6 arouse, assume, incite, stir up 7 acquire, bring on, involve, provoke 8 bring out, contract, fall into

incurable 8 cureless, hopeless 9 ceaseless 10 beyond cure, inveterate, relentless, unflagging 12 incorrigible, irremediable 13 dyed-in-the-wool, uncorrectable

incursion 4 push, raid 5 foray 6 attack, inroad, sortie 7 assault 8 invasion 11 advance into, impingement 12 encroachment, infiltration

indebted 5 bound 7 bounden 8 beholden, grateful, thankful 9 obligated 10 chargeable 11 accountable 15 under obligation

indebtedness 4 debt 5 debit 7 arrears 9 liability 10 balance due, obligation 11 liabilities

indecency 10 immorality 12 unseemliness 13 offensiveness, salaciousness 14 indecorousness

indecent 4 blue, lewd, rude 5 bawdy, dirty 6 filthy, smutty, vulgar 7 ignoble, ill-bred, immoral, obscene, uncivil 8 immodest, improper, prurient, unseemly 9 offensive, salacious 10 in bad taste, indecorous, indiscreet, licentious, unbecoming 11 unwholesome 12 pornographic

Indecent Obsession, An
   author: 17 Colleen McCullough

indecipherable 7 cryptic 9 enigmatic, illegible 10 unreadable 11 inscrutable

indecision 5 doubt 6 acrisy 7 dilemma, swither 8 wavering 10 hesitation 11 fluctuation, vacillating, vacillation, uncertainty 12 irresolution

indecisive 4 weak 7 dubious, unclear 8 doubtful, hesitant, wavering 9 confusing, debatable, mercurial, uncertain, unsettled 10 disputable, hesitating, irresolute, wishywashy 11 halfhearted, vacillating 12 inconclusive 13 indeterminate 17 blowing hot and cold

indecorous 5 gross 6 sinful, wicked 7 illbred 8 immodest, improper, low-class, unseemly 9 unfitting 10 unbecoming, unsuitable 11 blameworthy 13 inappropriate, reprehensible

indecorum 8 bad taste 9 immodesty, indecency, vulgarity 11 impropriety 12 impoliteness, unseemliness

indeed 5 truly 6 in fact, really 7 for sure, in truth 8 actually, to be sure 9 certainly, in reality, veritably 10 positively, to be honest, undeniably 11 joking apart 13 in point of fact, with certainty 14 to tell the truth 15 as a matter of fact, without question 16 strictly speaking

indefatigable 6 dogged 7 staunch 8 diligent, sedulous, tireless, untiring 9 energetic 10 persistent, unflagging, unwearying 11 persevering, unfaltering 13 inexhaustible

indefensible 8 improper, vincible 9 pregnable, untenable 10 vulnerable 11 defenseless, inexcusable, unprotected, unspeakable 12 open to attack, unpardonable 13 unjustifiable

indefinite 3 dim 5 vague 6 unsure 7 inexact, obscure, unknown 8 doubtful 9 ambiguous, amorphous, limitless, tentative, uncertain, unsettled 10 ill-defined, indecisive, indistinct, inexplicit 11 illimitable, measureless, unspecified 12 undetermined 13 indeterminate

indefiniteness 6 vagary 9 ambiguity, vagueness 10 indecision 11 uncertainty 12 equivocation

indelible 4 fast 5 fixed, vivid 7 lasting 8 deep-dyed 9 ingrained, memorable, permanent 10 unerasable 11 unremovable 12 ineradicable 13 unforgettable

indelicate 4 lewd, rude 5 broad, crude, gross 6 clumsy, coarse, risque, vulgar 7 awkward, obscene 8 immodest, improper, indecent, off-color, unseemly 9 offensive, unrefined 10 indecorous, indiscreet, suggestive, unbecoming

in demand 7 popular 9 desirable 11 sought after

indemnification 7 payment 10 recompense, reparation 12 compensation

indemnify 3 pay 5 atone, cover, repay 6 insure, secure 7 pay back, protect, rectify, requite, satisfy 8 make good 9 make right, make up for, reimburse 10 compensate, make amends, recompense, remunerate 15 make restitution

indemnity 7 redress 8 coverage, security 9 insurance, repayment 10 protection 11 restitution 12 compensation 15 indemnification

indent 5 notch, set in 6 recess 7 set back

indentation 3 bay, cut, pit 4 dent, nick 5 gouge, inset, niche, notch, score 6 cavity, furrow, pocket, recess 8 incision 9 concavity 10 depression

indented 6 hollow, sunken, zigzag 7 concave, notched 9 depressed

indenture 4 bind 8 contract 10 apprentice

indentured 5 bound 10 contracted 11 apprenticed

independence 7 freedom, liberty 8 autonomy 10 liberation 11 sovereignty 12 emancipation, self-reliance 14 self-government 17 self-determination

independent 4 free 7 solvent, well-off 8 affluent, separate, unallied, well-to-do 9 apart from, exclusive, on one's own, sovereign, uncoerced, well-fixed 10 autonomous, well-heeled 11 self-reliant, unconnected 12 unassociated, uncontrolled 13 self-directing, self-governing, unconstrained 15 individualistic, self-determining

indescribable 9 ineffable 11 beyond words, indefinable, unutterable 12 overwhelming 13 inexpressible 17 beyond description 20 beggaring description

indestructible 8 enduring 9 permanent 11 everlasting, infrangible, unbreakable 12 imperishable

indeterminate 5 vague 7 obscure, unclear 8 not clear 9 ambiguous, uncertain, undefined 10 indefinite, perplexing, unresolved 11 problematic, unspecified 12 undetermined, unstipulated

index 4 clue, mark, sign 5 proof, token 7 catalog, symptom 8 evidence, glossary, register 9 catalogue, indicator 10 indication 13 manifestation 16 alphabetical list

Index Librorum Prohibitorum 22 index of prohibited books

index of prohibited books
   Latin: 25 Index Librorum Prohibitorum

India
   other name: 4 Hind 6 Bharat 12 Bharat Varsha
   capital: 8 New Delhi
   largest city: 8 Calcutta
   others: 4 Agra, Gaya, Pune 5 Dacca, Poona, Surat 6 Bombay, Jaipur, Kanpur, Lahore, Madras, Madura, Mysore, Nagpur 7 Banaras 8 Kolhapur, Mandalay, Mirzapur, Shahpura, Srinagar 9 Ahmedabad, Bangalore, Hyderabad 10 Darjeeling
   division: 3 Goa 5 Assam, Bihar, Jammu 6 Kerala, Orissa, Punjab, Sikkim 7 Gujarat, Haryana, Kashmir, Manipur,

Tripura **8** Nagaland **9** Karnataka, Meghalaya, Rajasthan, Tamil Nadu **10** West Bengal **11** Daman and Diu, Maharashtra, Pondicherry **12** Uttar Pradesh **13** Andhra Pradesh, Madhya Pradesh **15** Himachal Pradesh

measure: 3 ady, gaz, gez, jow, lan **4** byee, coss, depa, doph, hath, koss, kunk, raik, rati, seit, taun, tola **5** bigha, covid, crosa, denda, depoh, drona, erosa, garce, hasta, krosa, parah, ratti, salay, yojan **6** adhaka, amunam, covido, cudava, dumbha, geerah, moolum, mushti, ouroub, palgat, parran, prasha, ropani, tipree, unglee, yojana **7** dhanush, gavyuti, khahoon, niranga, prastha **8** okthabah

monetary unit: 3 lac, pie **4** lakh, pice **5** abidi, rupee

weight: 3 mod, pai, vis **4** drum, hoen, kona, pala, pank, pice, ruay, tael, tali, tola, wang, yava **5** adpad, candy, hubba, maund, tical **6** karsha **8** mangelin

island: 6 Agatti, Chilka **7** Andaman, Minicoy, Nicobar **8** Amindivi **9** Laccadive **11** Lakshadweep

lake: 5 Jheel, Lonar, Wular **6** Chilka, Colair, Dhebar, Kolair **7** Kolleru, Pulicat, Pushkar, Sambahr

mountain: 8 Aravalli **9** Broad Peak, Distaghil, Himalayas, Karakoram, Nanda Devi, Rakaposhi **10** Gasherbrum, Masherbrum **11** Nanga Parbat **12** Eastern Ghats, Kanchenjunga, Western Ghats

hills: 4 Chin, Naga **5** Khasi **6** Lushai **7** Nilgiri

highest point: 12 Godwin Austen

river: 3 Son **4** Beas, Kosi, Tapi **5** Gogra, Indus, Jumna, Tapti **6** Gandak, Ganges, Jhelum, Kaveri, Kistna, Sutlej, Yamuna **7** Cauveri, Cauvery, Chambal, Damodar, Hooghly, Krishna, Narbada, Narmada **8** Godavari, Mahanadi **10** Bhagirathi **11** Brahmaputra

sea: 6 Indian **7** Arabian

physical feature:

bay: **6** Bengal

cape: **7** Comorin

desert: **4** Thar **9** Rajasthan

forest: **3** Gir

gulf: **5** Kutch **6** Cambay, Mannar

pass: **9** Karakoram

plain: **12** Indo-Gangetic

plateau: **6** Deccan **7** Shillon **11** Chota Nagpur

rains: **7** monsoon

strait: **4** Palk

swamp: **9** Sundarban **11** Rann of Kutch

valley: **13** Vale of Kashmir

people: 2 Ao **3** Gor **4** Bhil **5** Aryan **6** Badaga, Pathan **7** Sherani **9** Dravidian **10** Andamanese

caste: 3 Jat **5** Sudra **6** Rajput, Shudra **7** Brahman, Brahmin, Harijan, Maratha, Vaishya **9** Kshatriya **11** Untouchable

dynasty: **5** Gupta, Mogul **6** Maurya, Rajput **8** Marathas **14** Delhi Sultanate

god: **4** Kali, Rama, Siva **5** Durga, Laxmi, Shiva **6** Brahma, Kumara, Vishnu **7** Ganesha, Hanuman, Krishna, Lakshmi **9** Kartikeya **10** Subramanya

ruler: **5** Akbar, Asoka, Babur, Timur **7** Humayun **8** Hyder Ali, Jahangir **9** Aurangzeb, Shah Jahan **11** Rajiv Gandhi, Tippu Sultan **12** Indira Gandhi **13** Queen Victoria **15** Jawaharlal Nehru, Mohandas K (Mahatma) Gandhi **18** Chandragupta Maurya

language: **4** Urdu **5** Hindi, Oriya, Tamil **6** Sindhi, Telugu **7** Bengali, English, Kannada, Malayam, Marathi, Punjabi **8** Assamese, Gujarati, Kashmiri, Sanskrit **9** Malayalam

religion: **4** Sikh **5** Hindu, Islam, Parsi **7** Jainist, Judaism **8** Buddhism **11** Zoroastrian **12** Christianity

place:

cathedral: **10** Saint Thome

fortress: **3** Red **11** Saint George

mausoleum: **8** Taj Mahal

minaret: **9** Qutb Minar

mosque: **10** Jama Masjid

park: **6** Maidan

president's residence: **17** Rashtrapati Bhavan

railway station: **8** Victoria

shrine: **7** Raj Ghat

street: **7** Raj Path **11** Chowringhee, Marine Drive **12** Chandni Chauk **14** Connaught Place

temple: **5** Birla **6** Ellora, Golden **7** Kailasa **10** Ajanta Cave

feature:

dance: **6** nautch **7** cantico

religious text: **7** Rig Veda

shrine: **5** stupa

food:

beer: **5** apong

bread: **7** chapati

liquor: **4** soma, sura **5** shrab

tea: **5** assam

Indian

constellation: 5 Indus

Indiana

abbreviation: 2 IN **3** Ind

nickname: 7 Hoosier

capital/largest city: 12 Indianapolis

others: 4 Gary, Peru **6** Brazil, Goshen, Hobart, Jasper, Kokomo, Marion, Muncie, Wabash **7** Elkhart, Ft Wayne, Hammond, LaPorte, Whiting **8** Columbus, Richmond **9** Lafayette, Mishawaka, South Bend, Vincennes **10** Evansville, Huntington, Logansport, Terre Haute **11** Bloomington, East Chicago **12** Connorsville, Michigan City

college: 4 Ball **6** Bethel, Butler, DePauw, Goshen, Marion, Purdue, Wabash **9** Notre Dame **10** Evansville, Valparaiso

explorer: 7 La Salle

feature: 10 New Harmony **12** Indian mounds

national memorial: 14 Lincoln boyhood
tribe: 3 Wea 5 Miami 7 Shawnee
people: 7 Hoosier 10 Cole Porter, Eugene Debs, Gus Grissom, Red Skelton 12 Wilbur Wright 15 Booth Tarkington, Theodore Dreiser 18 James Whitcomb Riley
lake: 5 Clear, James 6 Monroe 7 Manitou, Wawasee 8 Michigan 9 Mansfield 11 Maxinkuckee
land rank: 12 thirty-eighth
mountain: 13 Greensfort Top
physical feature:
cave: 9 Wyandotte
river: 4 Ohio 5 White 6 Maumee, Wabash 8 Kankakee 10 Tippecanoe, Whitewater
state admission: 10 nineteenth
state bird: 8 cardinal
state flower: 5 peony 6 zinnia
state motto: 19 Crossroads of America
state song: 28 On the Banks of the Wabash Far Away
state tree: 5 tulip 11 tulip poplar

Indiana
basketball team: 6 Pacers

Indiana
author: 10 George Sand
character: 4 Noun 7 Delmare 13 Rodolphe Brown 15 Raymon de Ramiere

Indianapolis
football team: 5 Colts

Indic
language family: 12 Indo-European
branch: 11 Indo-Iranian
subgroup: 5 Hindi, Oriya 6 Nepali, Sindhi 7 Bengali, Marathi, Pakrits, Panjabi 8 Assamese, Gujarati, Kashmiri 9 Sinhalese

indicate 4 mean, show, tell 5 imply 6 denote, evince, record, reveal 7 bespeak, point to, signify, specify, suggest 8 point out, register, stand for 9 be a sign of, designate, establish, make known, represent, symbolize

indication 4 clue, hint, mark, omen, sign 5 token 6 augury, boding, signal 7 gesture, mention, portent, presage, showing, symptom, telling, warning 8 evidence, pointing 9 foretoken 10 foreboding, indicating, intimation, signifying, suggestion 11 designation, premonition 13 demonstration, manifestation

indicative 8 symbolic 10 denotative, emblematic, evidential, expressive, indicatory, suggestive 11 connotative, designative, significant, symptomatic 13 symptomatical 14 characteristic, representative

indicator 4 clue 5 guide 7 pointer 10 indication

indict 4 cite 6 accuse, charge, have up, impute, pull up 7 arraign, bring up, impeach 9 criminate, inculpate, prosecute 11 incriminate 13 prefer charges

indifference 6 apathy 7 disdain, neglect 8 coldness, no import 9 aloofness, unconcern 10 negligence, paltriness, triviality 11

disinterest, impassivity, inattention, insouciance, nonchalance 12 carelessness, unimportance 13 impassiveness, insensibility, insensitivity 14 insignificance, lack of interest

indifferent 4 cool, fair, rote, so-so 5 aloof 6 medium, modest 7 average, unmoved 8 detached, mediocre, middling, moderate, ordinary, passable 9 apathetic, impassive, not caring, unmindful 10 impervious, insensible, insouciant, nonchalant, secondrate, uninspired 11 commonplace, perfunctory, unconcerned 12 uninterested 13 insusceptible 15 undistinguished 17 betwixt and between, neither good nor bad

indigence 4 need, want 6 penury 7 beggary, poverty 9 pauperism, privation 11 destitution, dire straits 13 pennilessness

indigenous 6 native 7 endemic 8 domestic, homebred 9 home-grown 10 aboriginal 13 autochthonous, originating in

indigent 4 poor 5 needy 6 hard-up, in need, in want 7 pinched 8 badly off 9 destitute, moneyless, penniless 12 impoverished 15 poverty-stricken

indiges
title in: 4 Rome
suggests: 11 deification
for service to: 7 country

indigestible 4 rich 13 unassimilable

indignant 3 mad 4 sore 5 angry, huffy, irate, riled 6 fuming, miffed, peeved, piqued, put off, put out 8 incensed, offended, provoked, steaming, worked up, wrathful 9 resentful, wrought up 10 displeased, infuriated 15 on one's high horse

indignation 3 ire 4 fury, huff, rage 5 pique, wrath 6 animus, choler, dismay, uproar 7 umbrage 8 vexation 9 annoyance 10 irritation, resentment 11 displeasure

indignity 4 slur 5 abuse 6 insult, slight 7 affront, offense, outrage 8 dishonor, rudeness 9 injustice 11 discourtesy, humiliation 12 mistreatment 13 slap in the face

indigo 3 dye 4 blue 8 dark blue, deep blue, navy blue 10 Indigofera
varieties: 4 wild 5 false 7 bastard 8 wild blue 9 blue false 10 plains wild, white false 12 prairie false 13 fragrant false

indirect 5 vague 6 remote, zigzag 7 crooked, devious, distant, evasive, hedging, oblique, winding 8 rambling, tortuous 9 ancillary, secondary 10 circuitous, derivative, digressive, discursive, incidental, meandering, roundabout, unintended 13 unintentional

indirection 8 rambling 10 digression, meandering, zigzagging 14 circuitousness, circumlocution, roundaboutness

indiscernible 6 hidden 9 invisible 10 indistinct 12 undetectable, unnoticeable 13 imperceptible

indiscreet 6 unwise 7 foolish 8 careless, tactless, unseemly 9 foolhardy, ill-judged, impolitic, imprudent, tasteless, untactful 10 incautious 11 improvident, injudicious, thoughtless, unbefitting, uncalled-for 12 undiplomatic 13 inconsiderate, uncircumspect

indiscretion 8 rashness 10 imprudence 12 carelessness, heedlessness, recklessness, tactlessness 13 foolhardiness, insensitivity 15 thoughtlessness 16 irresponsibility

indiscriminate 6 motley, random 7 aimless, chaotic, jumbled, mongrel 8 confused, slapdash, unchoosy 9 haphazard, hit-or-miss 10 hodgepodge 11 promiscuous, unselective 12 disorganized, unsystematic 16 higgledy-piggledy, undistinguishing

in disorder 5 messy 6 blowsy, frowsy, mussed, sloppy, untidy 7 ruffled, rumpled, tousled, unkempt 8 uncombed 10 disarrayed, disheveled, disordered, disorderly 11 disarranged

indispensable 5 basic, vital 6 needed 7 crucial, needful 8 required 9 essential, mandatory, necessary, requisite 10 compulsory, imperative, obligatory 11 fundamental

indispensable condition
  Latin: 10 sine qua non

indispensable element 9 basic need, essential, necessity, requisite 10 sine qua non 11 requirement

indisposed 3 ill 5 loath 6 ailing, averse, laid up, sickly, unwell 7 opposed 8 hesitant, taken ill 9 bedridden, reluctant, unwilling 10 not oneself 11 disinclined 15 under the weather

indisposition 5 upset 6 malady 7 ailment, illness 8 sickness 9 complaint, ill health

indisputable 4 sure 7 assured, certain, decided, evident, obvious 8 absolute, apparent, clear-cut, definite, positive 10 conclusive, unarguable, undeniable 11 indubitable, irrefutable 12 unassailable, unmistakable 13 incontestable 14 unquestionable 16 incontrovertible 20 beyond a shadow of doubt

indissoluble 5 fixed 7 abiding, lasting 8 constant, enduring 9 immutable, indelible, permanent, perpetual 11 everlasting 12 imperishable, ineradicable

indistinct 3 dim 4 weak 5 faint, muddy, murky, vague 6 cloudy, hidden 7 blurred, clouded, muffled, obscure, shadowy, unclear 8 confused, nebulous, puzzling 9 ambiguous, enigmatic, illegible, inaudible, uncertain 10 ill-defined, incoherent, indefinite, mysterious, out of focus 11 not distinct 13 indeterminate 14 indecipherable, unintelligible 16 incomprehensible

indistinguishable 7 obscure, unclear 9 invisible 10 indistinct, unapparent 12 unnoticeable, unobservable 13 a carbon copy of, identical with, imperceptible, inconspicuous, indiscernible

individual 6 person, unique 7 one's own, private, special, unusual 8 distinct, especial, original, personal, separate, singular, somebody, specific, uncommon 9 different, exclusive 10 particular 11 distinctive, independent 12 personalized 14 characteristic, unconventional

individuality 6 cachet 10 uniqueness 11 distinction, singularity, specialness 13 particularity 15 distinctiveness

individually 4 each 5 apart 6 apiece, singly 8 a la carte, uniquely 10 one at a time, peculiarly, personally, separately 12 respectively 13 distinctively 18 characteristically

indoctrinate 5 brief, drill, teach, train, tutor 6 infuse, school 7 educate, implant, instill 8 initiate 9 brainwash, inculcate 12 propagandize

indoctrination 5 drill 8 drilling, teaching, training 9 education, schooling 10 initiation, instilling 11 inculcation, instruction

Indo-European
  language branch: 5 Greek 6 Celtic, Italic 7 Romance 8 Albanian, Armenian, Germanic 9 Anatolian, Tocharian 11 Balto-Slavic, Indo-Iranian

Indo-Iranian
  language family: 12 Indo-European
  ancient: 7 Avestan 8 Sanskrit 10 Old Persian
  modern Iranian: 5 Indic, Tajik 6 Pashto 7 Baluchi, Kurdish, Persian
  modern Indic: 4 Pali 5 Hindi, Oriya 6 Nepali, Sindhi 7 Bengali, Marathi, Panjabi 8 Assamese, Gujarati, Kashmiri 9 Sinhalese

indolence 5 sloth 7 inertia, languor, laxness 8 idleness, laziness 10 inactivity

indolent 4 lazy 5 inert, slack 7 lumpish 8 dawdling, dilatory, inactive, listless, slothful, sluggish 9 do-nothing, easygoing, lethargic, shiftless 13 lackadaisical

indomitable 6 dogged 7 doughty, staunch, valiant 8 cast-iron, fearless, intrepid, resolute, stalwart, stubborn 9 dauntless, steadfast, undaunted 10 courageous, formidable, invincible, unwavering, unyielding 11 insuperable, persevering, unflinching, unshrinking 12 invulnerable, unassailable 13 indefatigable, irrepressible, unconquerable

Indonesia
  other name: 9 Nusantara 12 Tanah Airkita 21 Netherlands East Indies
  capital/largest city: 7 Jakarta 8 Djakarta
  others: 5 Bogor, Medan 6 Malang, Manado 7 Bandung 8 Macassar, Semarang, Surabaya 9 Hollandia, Palembang, Surakarta 10 Jogjakarta, Yogyakarta 11 Banjarmasin
  measure: 5 depah, depoh
  monetary unit: 3 sen 6 rupiah
  weight: 5 catty, ounce, thail 6 soekoe
  island: 3 Aru 4 Bali, Buru, Java 5 Ambon, Ceram, Seram, Spice, Sumba, Timor 6 Bangka, Borneo, Flores, Lombok, Madura, Tidore 7 Belawan, Celebes, Morotai, Sumatra, Sumbawa, Ternate 8 Belitung, Moluccas, Sulawesi 9 Halmahera, New Guinea 10 Kalimantan 11 Lesser Sunda 12 Greater Sunda
  lake: 4 Toba 5 Ranau 6 Towuti

river: 4 Hari, Musi, Solo 5 Rokan 6 Asahan, Barito, Kampar 7 Brantas, Kaptuas 9 Indrogiri, Mamberamo, Martapura

sea: 4 Java, Savu 5 Banda, Ceram, Timor 6 Flores, Indian 7 Arafura, Celebes, Molucca, Pacific 10 Philippine, South China

physical feature:

strait: 5 Sunda 7 Makasar, Malacca 8 Makassar

volcano: 6 Slamet 8 Krakatoa

people: 5 Batak, Dayak, Dyaks, Malay 6 Papuan, Toraja 7 Battaks, Chinese, Igorots 8 Acehnese, Achinese, Balinese, Javanese, Madurese, Sudanese 11 Minang Kabau

leader: 7 Suharto, Sukarno

language: 5 Tetum 6 Bahasa, Igorot 7 English, Gyarung, Malayan 8 Balinese, Chamorro, Javanese, Madurese, Sudanese 10 Indonesian, Polynesian

religion: 5 Hindu, Islam 7 animism 8 Buddhism 12 Christianity, Confucianism

place:

palace: 6 Kraton

pyramid: 5 Stupa 9 Borobudur

shrine: 6 Dagoba, Kraton

feature:

cap: 5 pitji

cloth: 5 batik

jacket: 6 kebaja

lizard: 12 Komodo dragon

scarf: 9 selendang

shadow play: 6 wajang, wayang

skirt: 4 kain 6 sarong

tree: 4 supa

food:

ceremonial dinner: 9 selamatan

indoors 6 at home, inside, shut in, shut up, within 10 in the house 11 sequestered

Indo-Pacific

language subgroup: 4 Kate 5 Kiwai 7 Andaman, Merauke 8 Highland, Tasmania 9 Ekari-Moni, Hollandia, Timor-Alor 10 New Britain 12 Astrolabe Bay, Bougainville 14 Vogelkop-Kamoro 16 Eastern New Guinea, Northern Salomons 17 Northern Halmahera

indorse *see* 7 endorse

In Dubious Battle

author: 13 John Steinbeck

indubitable 4 sure 7 certain 9 undoubted 10 conclusive 11 irrefutable, unequivocal 12 indisputable, unmistakable 14 unquestionable 16 incontrovertible

indubitably 6 surely 7 for sure 8 of course 9 certainly, doubtless 10 for certain 11 undoubtedly 12 without doubt 14 unquestionably, with no question

induce 3 get 4 coax, spur, sway 5 cause, impel 6 arouse, effect, incite, lead to, prompt 7 actuate, bring on, dispose, incline, inspire, produce, provoke, win over 8 activate, motivate, occasion, persuade 9 encourage, influence, instigate, prevail on

10 bring about, bring round, give rise to 11 prevail upon, set in motion

inducement 4 bait, goad, spur 5 cause 6 ground, motive, reason 8 stimulus 9 incentive 10 allurement, attraction, enticement, incitement, persuasion, temptation 11 inspiration, instigation, provocation

induct 5 crown, draft, frock 6 enlist, invest, lead in, ordain, sign up 7 bring in, install, instate, usher in 8 enthrone, initiate, register 9 conscript, establish, introduce 10 consecrate, inaugurate

in due course 4 then 6 thence 10 eventually 11 accordingly 15 at the proper time 19 in the fullness of time

indulge 4 baby 5 favor, humor, serve, spoil, treat 6 coddle, cosset, oblige 7 appease, cater to, gratify, yield to 8 pander to 9 give way to 11 accommodate, go along with, mollycoddle

indulgence 6 excess, luxury 8 kindness, lenience, patience 9 allowance, benignity, tolerance 10 compassion, debauchery, profligacy, sufferance 11 dissipation, forbearance, forgiveness 12 extravagance, graciousness, immoderation, intemperance 13 understanding 14 permissiveness

indulgent 4 kind 6 benign, tender 7 clement, lenient, patient, sparing 8 humoring, obliging, tolerant, yielding 9 easygoing, forgiving, pampering 10 forbearing, permissive 11 complaisant, forebearing 12 conciliatory 13 understanding

industrious 4 busy 6 active 7 zealous 8 diligent, occupied, sedulous, tireless 9 assiduous, energetic 10 productive, purposeful, unflagging 11 hardworking, painstaking, persevering, unremitting 12 businesslike, enterprising 13 indefatigable

industry 2 go 4 toil, zeal 5 field, labor, trade 6 bustle, energy, hustle 8 activity, business, commerce, hard work 9 assiduity, diligence 10 enterprise 11 application, manufacture 12 perseverance, sedulousness 13 assiduousness 15 industriousness 16 indefatigability

inebriate 3 sot 4 lush, soak, wino 5 drunk, rummy, souse, toper 6 barfly, boozer 7 tippler 8 drunkard 9 alcoholic 11 dipsomaniac

inebriated 4 high 5 drunk, oiled, tight, tipsy 6 bombed, loaded, potted, stoned, tanked, zonked 7 drunken, smashed, sozzled, wrecked 8 besotted 9 befuddled, plastered 10 in one's cups 11 intoxicated 12 drunk as a lord 17 under the influence 20 three sheets to the wind

ineffable 5 ideal 6 divine, sacred 9 spiritual 10 indefinite, untellable 11 indefinable, unspeakable, unutterable 12 transcendent 13 indescribable, inexpressible 14 incommunicable, transcendental

in effect 6 active 8 a reality 9 activated, effective, operative 11 in operation

ineffective 4 vain, weak 6 futile 7 useless 8 impotent 9 fruitless, incapable, powerless, worthless 10 inadequate 11 inefficient, inoperative, not much good, of little use **12** unproductive

ineffectual 4 lame, vain, weak **5** inept **6** feeble, futile **7** hapless, useless **8** impotent **10** inadequate, not up to par, profitless, unavailing **11** incompetent, ineffective, inefficient **12** unproductive, unprofitable, unsuccessful **13** inefficacious **14** unsatisfactory

inefficient 5 inept, slack **6** futile **8** slipshod **9** pointless, unskilled **10** inadequate **11** incompetent, indifferent, ineffective, ineffectual **12** not efficient, unproductive **13** inefficacious **14** good-for-nothing

inelegance 9 crudeness, grossness, roughness, vulgarity **10** coarseness **13** tastelessness

inelegant 4 ugly **6** coarse, common **8** inferior **9** tasteless, unrefined **10** ungraceful

ineligible 5 unfit **10** unentitled, unsuitable **11** not eligible, unqualified **12** disqualified, unacceptable

ineluctable 4 sure **5** fated **7** certain **10** ineludible, inevasible, inevitable, inexorable, sure as fate, unevadable **11** inescapable, irrevocable, unavoidable, unstoppable **13** unpreventable

inept 5 empty, inane, silly, unapt **6** clumsy **7** asinine, awkward, fatuous, foolish **8** bungling **9** maladroit, pointless, senseless, unfitting, unskilled, untrained **10** out of place, unsuitable **11** incompetent, ineffective, ineffectual, inefficient, nonsensical, unqualified **13** inappropriate, inefficacious

ineptitude 9 inability **10** clumsiness, inadequacy **11** awkwardness **12** incompetence **14** ineffectuality **15** ineffectiveness

inequality 8 imparity, inequity **9** disparity, diversity, prejudice **10** difference, divergence, favoritism, unfairness, unlikeness **11** inconstancy, unequalness **12** irregularity, variableness **13** disproportion, dissimilarity, dissimilitude

inequity 4 bias **9** injustice, prejudice **10** favoritism, inequality, unfairness **14** discrimination

ineradicable 7 lasting **9** indelible, permanent **10** inerasable **12** ineffaceable **14** indestructible

inert 4 dull, numb **5** black, still **6** leaden, static, supine, torpid **7** languid, passive **8** immobile, inactive, listless, sluggish **9** impassive, inanimate, quiescent **10** motionless, phlegmatic, stationary

inertia 6 apathy, stupor, torpor **7** languor **8** dullness, inaction, laziness, lethargy **9** indolence, inertness, lassitude, passivity, torpidity, weariness **10** inactivity, supineness **11** passiveness **12** listlessness, sluggishness

inertness 6 apathy **8** lethargy **9** passivity **10** quiescence **12** sluggishness **14** motionlessness

inescapable 4 sure **7** certain, evident **8** manifest, positive **10** inevitable **11** ineluctable, predestined, unavoidable

in esse 7 in being **11** in actuality **16** actually existing

inestimable 7 sumless **8** precious **9** priceless **10** invaluable **11** beyond price, measureless **12** immeasurable, incalculable, unmeasurable

inevitable 4 sure **5** fated **7** certain **8** destined **10** ineludible **11** ineluctable, inescapable, predestined, unavoidable **13** predetermined, unpreventable

inexact 3 off **6** faulty, sloppy **8** careless, slovenly **9** defective, imperfect, imprecise **10** inaccurate, unspecific **11** approximate

in exactly the same words
   Latin: 19 verbatim et literatim

inexcusable 10 unbearable **11** intolerable, unallowable **12** indefensible, unforgivable, unpardonable **13** unjustifiable

inexhaustible 7 endless **8** infinite, tireless, unending **9** boundless **13** indefatigable **15** measurelessness

in existence 5 alive **6** extant, living **8** existent, existing **9** surviving, to be found

inexorable 4 firm **5** cruel, stiff **6** dogged **7** adamant **8** obdurate, pitiless, ruthless **9** immovable, merciless, unbending **10** adamantine, determined, inflexible, relentless, unyielding **11** inescapable, intractable **12** irresistible **14** uncompromising

inexpedient 6 futile, unwise **7** useless **11** detrimental, impractical, inadvisable, injudicious, undesirable **13** not worthwhile **15** disadvantageous

inexpensive 5 cheap **8** moderate **9** low-priced **10** economical, reasonable **13** nominal-priced, popular-priced

inexpensive table wine
   French: 12 vin ordinaire

inexperienced 5 fresh, green, naive **6** callow **7** untried **8** inexpert, unversed **9** unfledged, unskilled, untrained, untutored **10** unfamiliar, unschooled, unseasoned **11** uninitiated, unpracticed **12** unaccustomed, unacquainted, unconversant **15** unsophisticated

inexpert 5 inept **6** clumsy, gauche **7** awkward **8** bungling **9** incapable, maladroit **10** amateurish, unpolished, unskillful **11** incompetent, ineffective, inefficient, unqualified **14** unaccomplished

inexplicable 8 abstruse, baffling, puzzling **9** insoluble, insolvable, mysterious, mystifying, perplexing **11** enigmatical, inscrutable **12** unfathomable **13** unaccountable, unexplainable **14** undecipherable **16** incomprehensible

inexpressive 5 blank, empty **6** vacant **14** expressionless

in extenso 12 at full length

in extremis 9 near death **11** in extremity **15** on the outer edges **19** at the uttermost limit

in extremity
   Latin: 10 in extremis

in fact
   Latin: 7 de facto

infallible 4 sure 7 assured, certain, perfect 8 flawless, inerrant, positive, reliable, sure-fire, unerring 9 apodictic, faultless, fool-proof, unfailing 10 dependable, impeccable 11 irrefutable 13 unimpeachable 16 incontrovertible

infamous 3 low 4 base, evil, foul, vile 6 odious, sinful, sordid, wicked 7 corrupt, heinous, ignoble, immoral, knavish 8 damnable, recreant, shameful 9 abhorrent, monstrous, nefarious, notorious 10 abominable, detestable, iniquitous, of evil fame, outrageous, perfidious, profligate, scandalous, scurrilous, villainous 11 disgraceful, of ill repute, opprobrious, treacherous 12 dishonorable, disreputable

infamy 4 evil 5 odium, shame 7 scandal 8 contempt, disgrace, dishonor, ignominy, villainy 9 discredit, disesteem, disrepute, notoriety 10 corruption, opprobrium, wickedness 11 abomination 13 despicability, notoriousness

infancy 4 cradle, nonage 8 babyhood, minority 9 beginning, childhood, inception 10 immaturity

infant 3 kid 4 babe, baby 5 child 7 neonate, newborn, toddler 8 nursling, suckling

infantile 7 babyish 8 childish, juvenile 9 childlike, infantine 10 infantlike, sophomoric

infantryman 6 Zouave 7 dogface, dragoon 8 chasseur, doughboy, sorefoot 11 foot soldier

infatuated 7 charmed, smitten 8 beguiled, enamored, inflamed, obsessed 9 bewitched, enchanted, entranced 10 captivated, enraptured, enthralled, spellbound 11 carried away, intoxicated 12 having a crush

infatuation 4 rave 5 craze, crush, folly, mania 6 desire 7 passion 9 obsession, puppy love 10 enthusiasm 11 fascination, foolishness 12 passing fancy

infect 4 ruin 5 spoil, taint, touch 6 blight, damage, poison 7 afflict, corrupt 9 indispose, influence 11 contaminate

infected 6 impure, morbid, septic 7 corrupt, tainted 8 cankered, diseased, poisoned 12 contaminated

infection 6 blight 7 disease 9 contagion, virulence 11 suppuration

infectious 8 catching, epidemic, virulent 9 catchable, infective, spreading 10 compelling, contagious, inoculable 11 captivating 12 communicable, irresistible

infecund 6 barren, farrow 7 sterile 9 infertile 12 unproductive

infer 4 deem 5 glean, guess, judge, opine 6 deduce, gather, reason, reckon 7 presume, suppose, surmise 8 conclude 9 speculate 10 conjecture

inference 4 clue 10 intimation, suggestion 11 insinuation

inferior 4 poor 6 junior 8 low-grade, mediocre 9 secondary 10 low-quality, second-rate, subsidiary 11 indifferent, subordinate, subservient, substandard 12 not up to snuff

infernal 4 vile 5 awful, black, lower 6 cursed, Hadean, nether 7 heinous, hellish, Stygian, vicious 8 accursed, damnable, devilish, fiendish, horrible, terrible 9 atrocious, execrable, malicious, monstrous, nefarious, Plutonian 10 abominable, demoniacal, diabolical, flagitious, horrendous, iniquitous

    also: 9 Tartarean

    refers to: 10 underworld

inferno 4 hell, oven 5 abyss, Hades 6 hotbox, the pit, Tophet 7 furnace, roaster, sizzler 8 hellfire, hellhole, scorcher 9 perdition 10 lower world, underworld 11 netherworld 12 fiery furnace 13 nether regions 15 infernal regions 16 fire and brimstone, the bottomless pit

Inferno

    part I of: 12 Divine Comedy

    author: 14 Dante Alighieri

infertile 4 arid, bare 6 barren, effete, fallow 7 drained, sterile 8 depleted, desolate, impotent, infecund 9 exhausted, fruitless 10 unfruitful, unprolific 12 unproductive 13 nonproductive

infest 4 team 5 beset, crawl, creep, swarm 6 abound, infect, plague, ravage 7 overrun, torment 9 crawl with, swarm with

infestation 6 plague, ravage 9 lousiness, pervasion 11 overrunning 12 overswarming

in few words

    Latin: 12 paucis verbis

infidel 5 pagan 6 savage 7 atheist, heathen, heretic, skeptic 8 agnostic, apostate, idolater 9 barbarian 10 unbeliever 11 nonbeliever

infidelity 6 breach 7 falsity, perfidy 8 adultery, betrayal 9 disregard, violation 10 disloyalty, infraction 12 nonadherence 13 nonobservance, transgression 14 unfaithfulness

infiltrate 4 leak, seep 5 imbue, steep 6 absorb, seep in 7 pervade 8 colonize, permeate 9 insinuate, penetrate

infinite 4 vast 5 great 7 endless, immense 8 enormous 9 boundless, limitless, unbounded, unlimited 10 tremendous, without end 11 illimitable, measureless 12 immeasurable, incalculable, interminable 13 inexhaustible 15 uncircumscribed

infinitesimal 3 wee 4 puny, tiny 6 minute 10 diminutive, negligible 11 microscopic 13 imperceptible, inappreciable, insignificant, undiscernible 14 extremely small, inconsiderable

infinity 7 forever 8 eternity 10 infinitude, perpetuity 11 endlessness, eternal time 12 sempiternity 13 boundlessness, limitlessness 14 illimitability 15 everlastingness, immeasurability, incalculability, measurelessness 16 inexhaustibility 19 incomprehensibility

Infiri

    gods of: 10 underworld

infirm 3 ill 4 weak, worn 5 anile, frail, shaky 6 ailing, feeble, poorly, sickly 7 failing, fragile, unsound 8 decrepit, disabled, helpless, unstable, weakened 9 doddering, emaciated, enervated, enfeebled, powerless 11 debilitated 12 strengthless

infirmary 6 clinic 7 sick bay 8 hospital

infirmity 4 flaw 5 fault 6 defect, malady 7 ailment, failing, frailty, illness 8 debility, disorder, handicap, sickness 9 fragility, frailness 10 deficiency, disability, infirmness 11 instability 12 debilitation, imperfection, unstableness 13 indisposition, vulnerability

in flagrante delicto 14 in blazing crime 22 in the heat of the evil deed

inflame 4 fire, rile 5 craze, rouse 6 arouse, enrage, excite, heat up, ignite, incite, kindle, madden, stir up, work up 7 agitate, incense, provoke 8 enkindle 9 electrify, stimulate 10 intoxicate

inflamed 3 mad 5 angry, irate, riled 6 crazed, fuming, roused 7 aroused, enraged, excited, fired up, furious, incited 8 agitated, incensed, provoked, reddened 9 steamed up, stirred up 10 infuriated 11 intensified

inflame with love 6 enamor 9 enrapture, impassion, infatuate

inflammable 5 fiery 8 choleric, volatile 9 excitable, flammable, ignitable, impetuous, overhasty, sensitive 10 high-strung, incendiary 11 combustible, precipitate 12 inflammatory

inflammation 4 acne, fire, gout, sore 6 canker, firing 7 arousal, chafing 8 bursitis, ignition, kindling, soreness, sore spot, swelling 9 agitation 10 incitement, irritation 13 conflagration, rabblerousing
    suffix: 4 itis

inflammatory 5 fiery, rabid 8 arousing, enraging, inciting, mutinous, volcanic 9 demagogic, explosive, insurgent 10 incendiary, rebellious 11 combustible, fulminating, inflammable, intemperate, provocative 13 rabble-rousing, revolutionary

inflate 5 bloat, swell 6 blow up, dilate, expand, fill up, pump up 7 distend, improve, puff out 10 appreciate 11 rise in value

inflated 5 blown, gassy, tumid, wordy 6 blew up, turgid 7 bloated, blown up, dilated, flowery, pompous, swollen, verbose 8 boastful, enlarged, expanded 9 bombastic, distended, overblown, swelled up 10 rhetorical, swelled out 11 exaggerated, pretentious

inflection 4 tone 5 tenor 8 accent 10 modulation 11 enunciation, tone of voice 12 articulation 13 pronunciation

inflexible 4 firm, hard, taut 5 fixed, rigid, solid, stiff 6 dogged, mulish 7 adamant 8 obdurate, resolute, stubborn 9 hidebound, immovable, immutable, ironbound, obstinate, pigheaded, stringent, tenacious, unbending, unplastic 10 adamantine, determined, headstrong, impervious, implacable, inexorable, unwavering, unyielding 11 hard and fast, intractable, not flexible,

unmalleable 12 unchangeable 14 uncompromising

inflict 4 dump 5 lay on, wreak 6 impose, unload 7 put upon 9 visit upon 10 administer, perpetrate 11 bring to bear

inflorescence 5 bloom 6 flower 7 blossom, cluster 8 blooming 9 flowering 10 blossoming
    type: 4 cyme 5 spike, umbel 6 corymb, raceme, spadix 7 panicle 9 capitulum 14 verticillaster

influence 4 hold, move, pull, stir, sway 5 clout, guide, impel, power 6 arouse, effect, incite, induce, prompt, weight 7 act upon, actuate, control, dispose, incline, inspire, mastery, potency, provoke 8 dominion, leverage, persuade, pressure, prestige 9 advantage, authority 10 ascendancy, domination, predispose

influential 6 moving, potent, strong 7 leading, weighty 8 forceful, powerful, puissant 9 effective, effectual, important, inspiring, momentous 10 activating 11 efficacious, significant 12 instrumental 13 consequential

influx 5 entry 6 inflow 7 arrival, indraft, ingress 9 flowing in, incursion, inpouring 10 converging, inundation 12 infiltration

in force 6 extant 7 en masse 8 in effect 9 effective, operative 11 in existence, in operation, operational 14 in large numbers

inform 3 rat 4 fink, tell 5 edify 6 advise, clue in, notify, snitch, squeal, tattle, tell on, tip off 7 apprise, let know 8 acquaint, denounce, forewarn, report to 9 declare to, enlighten 11 communicate, familiarize, serve notice 14 blow the whistle

inform against 5 rat on 6 betray, fink on, tell on 7 sell out 8 denounce, squeal on 11 double-cross 16 blow the whistle on

informal 4 easy 6 casual, simple 7 natural, offhand 8 familiar 9 easygoing, not formal 10 unofficial 11 spontaneous 12 come-as-you-are 13 unceremonious, unconstrained 14 unconventional

informal preliminary conference
    French: 10 pourparler

informant 6 source 7 adviser, tipster 8 appriser, informer, notifier, reporter 9 announcer, spokesman 10 respondent 11 enlightener, horse's mouth, spokeswoman

information 4 data, news 5 facts, notes 6 notice, papers, report 7 account, tidings 8 briefing, bulletin, evidence, material 9 documents, knowledge, materials 10 communique 11 fact-finding 12 announcement, intelligence, notification 13 enlightenment

informed 4 told, up on, wise 5 aware, posted, talked, taught, warned 7 abreast, advised, knowing, learned, tattled 8 apprised, betrayed, educated, notified, reported, snitched, up to date 9 au courant, permeated 10 acquainted, instructed 11 enlightened, intelligent 13 knowledgeable

informer 3 rat 4 fink 5 Judas 6 canary 7 blabber, stoolie, tattler, traitor 8 betrayer, mouchard, snitcher, squealer 11 stool pigeon

Informer, The
author: 13 Liam O'Flaherty
director: 8 John Ford
cast: 10 Una O'Connor 11 Wallace Ford 12 Heather Angel 13 Margot Grahame, Preston Foster 14 Victor McLaglen
score: 10 Max Steiner
remade as: 7 Up Tight

infraction 6 breach 8 trespass 9 violation 10 peccadillo 11 lawbreaking 12 disobedience, encroachment, infringement, unobservance 13 nonobservance, transgression

infrastructure 4 base, root 5 basis 6 bottom, fabric, ground 7 bedrock, footing, support 9 framework, substrate 10 foundation, groundwork, substratum 12 substructure, underpinning 14 understructure

infrequent 3 few 4 rare 6 fitful, seldom, unique 7 unusual 8 sporadic, uncommon 9 spasmodic 10 occasional 16 few and far between

infringe 5 break 6 butt in, invade 7 disobey, impinge, infract, intrude, violate 8 encroach, overstep, trespass 10 contravene, transgress

in front 5 ahead, first 6 before 7 forward

in full possession of one's faculties
Latin: 12 compos mentis

infuriate 3 vex 4 gall, rile 5 anger, chafe 6 enrage, madden, offend 7 incense, inflame, outrage, provoke 8 irritate 9 aggravate, burn one up, make angry 10 exasperate 15 raise one's dander

infuriating 7 irksome 8 annoying, enraging 9 maddening, provoking 10 irritating 11 aggravating 12 exasperating, inflammatory

infuse 5 imbue 7 fortify, implant, inspire, instill 8 impart to, pour into 9 inculcate, insinuate, introject

in futuro 11 in the future

Inge, William
author of: 6 Picnic 7 Bus Stop 19 Come Back Little Sheba 26 The Dark at the Top of the Stairs

in general 7 as a rule, usually 10 by and large, on the whole

ingenious 4 deft 6 adroit, artful, clever, crafty, expert, shrewd 7 cunning 8 masterly, original, skillful, stunning 9 brilliant, dexterous, inventive, masterful 11 resourceful

ingenuity 5 flair, skill 7 cunning, know-how, mastery 8 aptitude, deftness, facility 9 adeptness, dexterity, expertise, sharpness 10 adroitness, astuteness, brilliance, cleverness, shrewdness 11 imagination 12 good thinking, skillfulness 13 ingeniousness, inventiveness 15 imaginativeness, quick-wittedness, resourcefulness

ingenuous 4 open 5 frank, naive 6 direct, honest 7 artless, genuine, natural, up front 8 trusting 9 guileless 10 unaffected 11 openhearted 13 simplehearted 15 straightforward, unsophisticated 16 straightshooting

ingenuousness 7 naivete 8 openness 9 frankness 11 artlessness

ingest 3 eat 4 gulp, take 5 drink 6 absorb, devour, imbibe, take in 7 consume, swallow 8 gulp down

inglorious 3 low 4 base, evil, mean, vile 6 odious 7 corrupt, heinous, ignoble 8 depraved, flagrant, infamous, shameful, shocking 9 atrocious, degrading, nefarious 10 despicable, detestable, outrageous, scandalous 11 disgraceful, ignominious, opprobrious 12 contemptible, dishonorable

in good condition
French: 10 embonpoint

in good health 2 OK 4 fine, hale, well 6 hearty, robust, tiptop 7 healthy 8 all right, blooming, vigorous 9 full of pep, in the pink 17 full of vim and vigor

in good time 5 early 7 betimes 11 ahead of time

ingot 3 bar 5 block

ingrained 4 deep, firm 5 fixed 6 inborn, inbred, innate, rooted 8 inherent, thorough 9 confirmed, implanted, indelible, intrinsic 10 deep-rooted, deep-seated, inveterate 14 constitutional

Ingram, Blanche
character in: 8 Jane Eyre
author: 6 Bronte

ingratiating 4 oily 5 sweet 6 genial, smarmy 7 affable, amiable, cordial, fulsome, gushing, likable, lovable, winning, winsome 8 charming, engaging, friendly, gracious, magnetic, pleasing, unctuous 9 appealing, congenial 10 attractive, enchanting, obsequious, oleaginous, personable, persuasive 11 captivating, goodhumored, self-serving 12 presumptuous

ingratiation 7 blarney 8 flattery 9 sweet talk 12 inveiglement 13 blandishments

ingratitude 14 ungratefulness 18 lack of appreciation

ingredient 4 part 6 aspect, factor 7 element, feature 9 component, essential, principle 11 constituent, contributor 12 integral part

Ingres, Jean-Auguste-Dominique
born: 6 France 9 Montauban
artwork: 9 Odalisque, The Source 13 Mme Moitessier 14 The Turkish Bath 15 Valpincon Bather 16 Roger and Angelica 17 The Vow of Louis XIII 21 Comtesse d'Haussonville 25 The Ambassadors of Agamemnon 26 The Vow of Louis the Thirteenth

ingress 5 entry, way in 6 access 8 entrance

inhabit 5 lodge 6 live in, occupy, people, settle, tenant 7 dwell in 8 populate, reside in

inhabitant 6 inmate, lessee, lodger, native, renter, tenant 7 boarder, citizen, denizen, dweller, settler 8 occupant, occupier, resident, villager 9 inhabiter

inhalation 4 gasp 5 sniff 6 breath 11 breathing in

inhale 5 sniff, snuff 6 suck in 7 inspire, respire 9 breathe in, inbreathe

inherent 6 inborn, inbred, innate, native 7 natural 9 essential, ingrained, intrinsic 10 deep-rooted, hereditary, inveterate 11 inalienable, inseparable 14 constitutional

inherit 3 get 6 be left, come by 7 acquire 8 come into 9 come in for 10 fall heir to

inheritance 6 devise, estate, legacy 7 bequest 8 bestowal, heritage 9 endowment, patrimony 10 bequeathal, birthright

inherited 8 came into, heirloom, unearned 10 handed down

inheritor 4 heir 7 legatee 11 beneficiary

Inherit the Wind
  director: 13 Stanley Kramer
  based on play by: 10 Robert E Lee 14 Jerome Lawrence
  cast: 8 Dick York 9 Gene Kelly 11 Elliot Reid 11 Harry Morgan 12 Spencer Tracy (Clarence Darrow) 13 Frederic March (William Jennings Bryan) 16 Florence Eldridge

inhibit 3 bar, gag 4 curb, stop 5 block, check 6 arrest, enjoin, forbid, hinder, impede, muzzle 7 control, harness, prevent, repress, smother 8 hold back, obstruct, prohibit, restrain, restrict, suppress 9 constrain 11 hold in leash

inhibited 4 cold 6 barred, curbed, frigid 7 bridled, checked, guarded 8 hindered, reserved 9 repressed 10 controlled, obstructed, restrained 11 constrained, discouraged, held in check 12 unresponsive 14 under restraint

inhibition, inhibitions 5 check 7 reserve 8 blockage 9 misgiving, restraint, stricture 10 constraint, impediment 11 guardedness, mental block, obstruction, restriction 12 constriction 17 self-consciousness

in high spirits 2 up 3 gay 5 happy, merry 6 elated, jaunty, joyful, joyous 7 buoyant 8 carefree, ecstatic, exultant, jubilant 9 overjoyed 11 exhilarated, on cloud nine 13 up in the clouds 15 on top of the world

in hoc signo vinces 26 in this sign shalt thou conquer
  motto of: 19 Constantine the Great
  from vision of: 5 cross

inhospitable 4 cold, cool, rude 5 aloof 6 unkind 7 distant, hostile 8 impolite 10 unfriendly, ungracious, unobliging, unsociable 11 standoffish, uncongenial, unreceptive, unwelcoming 12 discourteous, unneighborly 13 inconsiderate 14 unapproachable 15 unaccommodating

inhuman 5 cruel 6 brutal, savage 7 brutish, satanic, vicious 8 barbaric, demoniac, fiendish, pitiless, ruthless, venomous 9 barbarous, heartless, malignant, merciless, monstrous, unfeeling 10 diabolical, malevolent 11 coldhearted, cold-blood, hardhearted

inhumane 6 brutal, savage 7 inhuman 8 fiendish, pitiless, ruthless 9 barbarous, heartless, merciless, unfeeling, unpitying 10 unmerciful 11 cold-blooded, hardhearted 12 bloodthirsty 13 unsympathetic

inhumanity 6 sadism 7 cruelty 8 atrocity, savagery 9 barbarism, barbarity, brutality 11 brutishness, heinousness, malevolence, viciousness 12 fiendishness, ruthlessness 13 heartlessness, mercilessness 15 cold-bloodedness 16 bloodthirstiness

inhumation 6 burial 9 interment 10 entombment

inimical 5 toxic 6 at odds 7 harmful, hateful, hostile, hurtful, ruinous 8 venomous, virulent 9 dangerous, ill-willed, injurious, on the outs, poisonous, rancorous 10 unfriendly 11 acrimonious, deleterious, destructive, detrimental, ill-disposed 12 antagonistic, antipathetic, disputatious 13 at loggerheads, at sword's point

inimitable 4 rare 6 unique 7 supreme 8 peerless 9 matchless, nonpareil, unequaled, unmatched, unrivaled 10 consummate, preeminent, unexcelled 11 superlative, unsurpassed 12 incomparable, unparalleled 13 beyond compare

iniquitous 4 base, evil, vile 6 sinful, wicked 7 corrupt, debased, immoral, vicious 8 depraved, infamous 9 nefarious 10 evilminded 12 blackhearted 13 reprehensible

iniquity 3 sin 4 evil, vice 5 wrong 6 infamy 7 knavery, outrage, roguery 8 inequity, villainy 9 depravity, evildoing, flagrancy, turpitude 10 corruption, dishonesty, immorality, miscreancy, profligacy, sinfulness, unfairness, unjustness, wickedness, wrongdoing 11 abomination 13 transgression 14 gross injustice 15 unrighteousness

in isolation
  Latin: 7 in vacuo

initial 5 first 6 maiden, primal 7 opening, primary 8 germinal, original, starting 9 beginning, inaugural, incipient 10 commencing, initiatory 12 introductory

initiate 4 haze, open 5 begin, found, set up, start 6 induct, invest, launch, take in 7 bring in, install, kick off, receive, usher in 8 be opened, commence, get going, set afoot, set going 9 enter upon, establish, institute, introduce, originate 10 inaugurate, lead the way 11 break ground, get under way, take the lead 12 acquaint with 13 blaze the trail 15 familiarize with 16 lay the first stone, lay the foundation 19 start the ball rolling

initiation 5 onset, start 6 outset 7 genesis, opening 8 entrance, guidance, outbreak, starting 9 beginning, inception, induction 10 admittance, initiating, ushering in 11 inculcation 12 commencement, inauguration, introduction 14 indoctrination 15 formal admission

initiative 4 lead 8 dynamism 9 first move, first step 10 creativity, enterprise, get-up-and-go, leadership 11 originality 12 forcefulness 14 aggressiveness

in its original place
Latin: 6 in situ

inject 3 put 4 pump 5 force, imbue, infix 6 infuse, insert 7 instill, throw in 8 intromit 9 interject, introduce 11 interpolate

injection 4 hypo, shot 7 booster, vaccine 9 antitoxin, insertion 10 hypodermic 11 inoculation, vaccination 12 shot in the arm

injudicious 4 dumb, wild 5 crazy 6 stupid, unwise 7 foolish, unsound 8 heedless, reckless 9 audacious, foolhardy, hot-headed, imprudent, senseless 10 self-willed, unsuitable 11 inadvisable

injunction 4 writ 5 edict, order 7 command 10 admonition, court order

Injun Joe
character in: 9 Tom Sawyer
author: 9 Mark Twain

injure 3 mar 4 harm, hurt, lame, maim 5 abuse, spoil, stain, sting, sully, wound, wrong 6 bruise, damage, debase, deface, deform, impair, malign, mangle, misuse, offend, scathe 7 afflict, affront, blemish, violate, vitiate 8 do harm to, ill-treat, lacerate, maltreat, mutilate 9 disfigure

injured 4 hurt, lame 6 abused, harmed, maimed, marred, piqued 7 bruised, damaged, defaced, grieved, scathed, wounded, wronged 8 crippled, deformed, impaired, insulted, offended 9 afflicted, affronted, aggrieved 10 disfigured

injurious 7 abusive, adverse, harmful, hurtful, noxious, ruinous 8 damaging, inimical 9 corrosive 10 calamitous, disastrous, pernicious 11 deleterious, destructive, detrimental

injury 4 cut 4 blow, gash, harm, hurt, stab 5 abuse, wound 6 bruise, damage, lesion 7 affront, outrage, scratch 9 aspersion, contusion, indignity, injustice 10 affliction, defamation, detraction, disservice, impairment, laceration, mutilation 12 vilification

injustice 3 sin 4 bias, evil 5 wrong 6 injury 7 bigotry, offense, tyranny 8 foul play, inequity, iniquity 9 prejudice, unjust act 10 disservice, favoritism, inequality, infraction, partiality, unfairness, unjustness, wrongdoing 11 malpractice, persecution 12 encroachment, infringement, partisanship 13 transgression

in keeping 6 normal 7 natural 8 becoming 9 congruous, consonant 10 consistent 11 appropriate, in agreement 12 in compliance, in conformity

inkling 3 cue, tip 4 clue, hint, idea 6 notion 7 glimmer, whisper 8 innuendo 9 suspicion, vague idea 10 conception, glimmering, indication, intimation, suggestion 11 insinuation, supposition

inky 3 jet 4 dark 5 black, raven, sable 7 stygian 9 coal-black

inlet 3 bay 4 cove, gulf 5 bight, fiord, firth, fjord 6 harbor, strait 7 estuary, narrows 8 waterway

in line 4 even 6 in a row 7 aligned, in order 8 queued up, straight 12 under control

in loco 7 in place 16 in the proper place

in loco parentis 16 replacing a parent 19 in the place of a parent

inmate 3 con 5 felon 6 lodger, tenant 7 convict, denizen 8 prisoner, resident 10 inhabitant

in medias res 19 in the middle of things 21 in the middle of the story

in memoriam 10 in memory of 13 as a memorial to, to the memory of

In Memoriam A H H
author: 18 Alfred Lord Tennyson

in memory of
Latin: 10 in memoriam

In Memory of W B Yeats
author: 7 W H Auden

inmost 5 inner 6 inside 7 central 8 interior 9 innermost

in motion 5 afoot, astir 6 active, moving 7 on the go, working 8 under way 9 on the move, operating, operative 10 responsive

In My Father's Court
author: 19 Isaac Bashevis Singer

inn 5 hotel, lodge, motel 6 hostel, tavern 7 hospice, pension 8 hostelry 9 roadhouse 11 caravansary, public house
French: 7 auberge
Spanish: 6 posada

innards 4 guts 6 bowels, vitals 7 gizzard, insides, viscera 10 intestines 14 liver and lights

innate 6 inborn, inbred, native 7 natural 8 inherent 9 essential, ingrained, inherited, intrinsic, intuitive 10 congenital, hereditary, indigenous 11 instinctive 14 constitutional

inner 6 hidden, inside, inward, mental, middle 7 central, private, psychic 8 esoteric, interior, internal 9 concealed, emotional, spiritual, unobvious 10 more secret 12 more intimate 13 psychological

inner circle 4 core 5 bosom, heart 6 center 7 nucleus

inner city 8 core city, downtown 9 urban area 10 city limits, metropolis 11 central city 16 metropolitan area

Inner Mongolia
other name: 9 Neimenggu, Neimengku
capital: 6 Hohhot 7 Huhehot
desert: 4 Gobi
tent: 4 yurt

innermost 6 inmost, secret 7 deepest 10 deep-rooted, deep-seated 11 most private 12 most intimate, most personal

innermost part 4 core, crux, pith, soul 6 center, kernel 7 essence, nucleus

Inness, George
born: 10 Newburgh NY
artwork: 7 The Monk 14 Home of the Heron, Peace and Plenty 16 Delaware Water Gap 17 The Delaware Valley 19 The Lackawanna Valley

Innisfail see 7 Ireland

innkeeper 4 host 6 tapper, venter 7 padrone 8 boniface, hosteler, hotelier, landlord, publican 10 proprietor 12 maitre d'hotel, restaurateur

innocence 6 purity 7 naivete 8 chastity 9 freshness 10 clean hands, simplicity 11 artlessness, sinlessness 12 incorruption, spotlessness 13 blamelessness, guilelessness, guiltlessness, impeccability, inculpability, ingenuousness, stainlessness 14 immaculateness

innocent 3 tot 4 baby, naif, open, pure, tyro 5 clean, naive 6 chaste, honest, novice, simple 7 artless, ingenue, sinless, upright 8 harmless, pristine, spotless, virginal, virtuous 9 blameless, childlike, faultless, greenhorn, guileless, guiltless, ingenuous, innocuous, little one, stainless, uncorrupt, undefiled, unstained, unsullied, unworldly, well-meant 10 artless one, immaculate, impeccable, inculpable, tenderfoot, young child 11 inoffensive, unblemished, uncorrupted, unmalicious, unoffending 12 unsuspicious 13 meaning no harm, unimpeachable 14 above suspicion, irreproachable 15 unsophisticated
   Latin: 12 integer vitae

Innocents, The
   director: 11 Jack Clayton
   based on story by: 10 Henry James (The Turn of the Screw)
   cast: 11 Deborah Kerr, Megs Jenkins 13 Peter Wyngarde 15 Michael Redgrave
   script: 12 Truman Capote 16 William Archibald

Innocents Abroad, The
   author: 9 Mark Twain (Samuel Clemens)

innocuous 4 dull, mild 5 banal, empty, trite, vapid 6 barren 7 insipid 8 harmless, innocent, painless 9 pointless 11 commonplace, inoffensive, meaningless

innocuousness 6 safety 9 blandness, innocence 12 harmlessness 15 inoffensiveness

in no uncertain terms 7 clearly, plainly 9 expressly 10 definitely, distinctly 13 categorically, unequivocally

innovation 5 shift 7 novelty 8 updating 10 alteration, dernier cri, new measure, remodeling, renovation 11 institution, latest thing 12 commencement, inauguration, introduction, streamlining 13 modernization

innovator 7 deviser, planner 9 contriver 10 instigator, originator 11 inaugurator

Innu see 17 Montagnais-Naskapi

innuendo 4 hint 7 whisper 9 overtone 9 inference 10 imputation, intimation 11 implication, insinuation

innumerable 6 myriad 8 numerous 9 countless 10 numberless, unnumbered 12 incalculable 13 multitudinous

Ino
   also: 9 Leucothea
   goddess of: 3 sea
   father: 6 Cadmus
   mother: 8 Harmonia
   sister: 5 Hgave 6 Semele 7 Autonoe
   husband: 7 Athamas
   son: 8 Learchus 10 Melicertes
   stepson: 7 Phrixus
   stepdaughter: 5 Helle

saved: 8 Odysseus
   cared for infant: 8 Dionysus
   changed into: 10 sea goddess

inoculate 5 imbue, shoot 6 infuse, inject, insert 7 implant, instill 8 immunize 9 inculcate, vaccinate

inoculation 4 shot 6 needle 7 booster 9 injection 10 hypodermic 11 vaccination 12 immunization

inoffensive 4 mild, safe 5 bland 7 neutral 8 harmless, innocent 9 endurable, innocuous, tolerable 10 sufferable 11 unoffending 15 unobjectionable

inoffensiveness 6 safety 9 innocence 10 neutrality 12 harmlessness 13 innocuousness

in one's debt 7 obliged 8 beholden, indebted 9 obligated 15 under obligation

in one's own person
   Latin: 16 in propria persona

in one's own place
   Latin: 7 suo loco

in one's own right
   Latin: 7 suo jure

in one's rightful place
   Latin: 7 suo loco

inoperable 6 broken 10 broken down, unworkable 11 ineffective

in operation 5 in use 7 in force, working 8 in effect 9 operating, operative

inoperative 4 dead, down 8 inactive 10 not working, out of order

inopportune 7 awkward 8 ill-timed, untimely 10 badly timed, ill-advised, unsuitable 11 troublesome, undesirable, unfavorable, unfortunate 12 inauspicious, incommodious, inconvenient, unpropitious, unseasonable 13 inappropriate 15 disadvantageous

in order 2 OK 4 neat, tidy 6 proper 7 correct, perfect 8 all right

inordinate 5 undue 6 lavish, wanton 7 extreme, profuse, surplus 8 needless, overmuch, shocking 9 excessive 10 deplorable, exorbitant, immoderate, irrational, outrageous, scandalous 11 disgraceful, extravagant, intemperate, overflowing, superfluous, uncalled-for, unnecessary 12 unreasonable, unrestrained 13 superabundant 14 super-saturated, unconscionable 16 disproportionate

inordinately 6 overly, unduly 9 extremely 11 excessively 12 immoderately, outrageously, prodigiously 13 extravagantly, intemperately, superfluously, unnecessarily

inorganic 4 dead 7 mineral 8 lifeless 9 inanimate, nonliving 10 artificial

in passing
   French: 9 en passant

in perpetuum 7 forever

in petto 11 in the breast 12 not disclosed

in pieces 6 broken 7 asunder, smashed 8 in shreds, sundered 9 torn apart 13 in smithereens

in place
   Latin: 6 in loco, in situ

in plain sight 7 exposed, obvious 10 in full view, noticeable 12 out in the open 17 in front of one's nose

in posse 11 potentially 13 in possibility

in possibility
Latin: 7 in posse

In Praise of Darkness
author: 15 Jorge Luis Borges

in propria persona 15 in one's own person

inquest 5 probe 7 autopsy, delving, hearing, inquiry, probing 8 necropsy 10 postmortem 11 inquisition 13 investigation

inquire 3 ask 5 probe, query, study 6 search 7 examine, explore, inspect 8 check out, look into, look over, question 9 track down 10 look deeper, scrutinize 11 investigate

inquirer 5 asker, snoop 6 seeker 7 auditor, querier, quizzer, student 8 pollster, searcher 9 catechist 10 inquisitor, questioner 12 interlocutor, interrogator, investigator

inquiry, enquiry 4 hunt, quiz 5 probe, query, quest, study 6 search, survey 7 inquest 8 analysis, question, research, scrutiny 9 interview 10 inspection 11 examination, exploration, inquisition, questioning 13 interrogation, investigation

inquisitive 4 nosy 6 prying, snoopy 8 meddling, snooping 9 inquiring, intrusive, searching 10 meddlesome, too curious 11 interfering, overcurious, questioning

in re 13 in the matter of

in reality
Latin: 7 de facto

in rem 15 against the thing
of a legal proceeding: 18 against the property

in rerum natura 19 in the nature of things

in retreat 10 backing off, retreating 11 withdrawing, backing away

in reverse 8 backward 9 backing up 22 in the opposite direction

insalubrious 7 harmful, noisome, noxious 8 inimical, virulent 9 injurious, unhealthy 10 pernicious 11 deleterious, detrimental, unhealthful, unwholesome

insane 3 mad 4 bats, daft, dumb, loco, nuts, wild, zany 5 balmy, batty, crazy, loony, manic, nutty, potty 6 absurd, crazed, raving 7 berserk, bizarre, bonkers, cracked, foolish, idiotic, lunatic, tetched, touched, unsound 8 demented, frenzied, maniacal, unhinged 9 eccentric, imbecilic, imprudent, insensate, paranoiac, psychotic, senseless 10 ridiculous, unbalanced 11 injudicious 12 mad as a hatter, off one's chump, round the bend, unreasonable 13 off one's rocker, out of one's head, out of one's mind, out of one's wits, schizophrenic 15 bats in the belfry, mad as a March hare, stark staring mad 17 nutty as a fruitcake

insanity 5 folly, mania 6 idiocy, lunacy, raving 7 madness 8 dementia, paranoia 9 aberrance, absurdity, craziness, monomania, psychosis, stupidity 10 aberration 11 derangement, foolishness, unsoundness 12 loss of reason 13 hallucination, mental illness, schizophrenia, senselessness

insatiable 8 ravenous 9 insatiate, limitless, voracious 10 bottomless, gluttonous, implacable, omnivorous 12 unappeasable, unquenchable

inscribe 3 pen 4 etch, mark, seal, sign 5 blaze, brand, carve, write 6 chisel, incise, letter, scrawl 7 engrave, impress, imprint 8 scribble 9 autograph

inscription 5 motto, title 6 legend, rubric 7 address, caption, epigram, epitaph, heading, titulus, writing 8 colophon, epigraph, graffiti 9 engraving, lettering 10 dedication

inscrutable 6 arcane, hidden, masked, veiled 7 deadpan, elusive 8 baffling, puzzling 9 concealed, enigmatic 10 mysterious, mystifying, perplexing, poker-faced, unknowable, unreadable, unrevealed 12 inexplicable, unfathomable, unsearchable 14 indecipherable, unintelligible 16 incomprehensible

In Search of Identity
author: 12 Anwar el-Sadat

insect 3 ant, bee, bug, fly 4 flea, gnat, moth, pest, wasp 5 aphid, imago 6 bedbug, beetle, cicada, earwig, hornet, mantis, mayfly, vermin 7 chigger, cricket, firefly, katydid, ladybug, termite 8 horsefly, housefly, lacewing, mosquito 9 arthropod, butterfly, cockroach, dragonfly 10 silverfish 11 grasshopper

study of: 10 entomology
young: 4 grub, pupa 5 larva, nymph 6 larvae, maggot 9 chrysalis 11 caterpillar
anatomy: 4 palp 5 cerci, notum 6 cercus, feeler, labium, labrum, ocelli, thorax 7 antenna, maxilla, ocellus 8 antennae, mandible, maxillae 9 proboscis, spiracles 10 ovipositor 11 exoskeleton

insectivore 4 mole 5 shrew 6 desman, tenrec 7 moon rat 8 alamiqui, anteater, hedgehog 9 solenodon

insecure 4 weak 5 frail, risky, shaky 6 infirm, unsafe, unsure, wobbly 7 dubious, exposed, not firm, not sure, rickety, unsound 8 critical, doubtful, in danger, perilous, unstable, unsteady 9 dangerous, diffident, hazardous, in a bad way, tottering, unassured, uncertain, under fire 10 endangered, precarious, ramshackle, unreliable, unshielded, vulnerable 11 defenseless, dilapidated, unprotected, unsheltered

insecurities 4 risk 5 peril 6 danger, hazard 7 pitfall 8 jeopardy 11 contingency

insecurity 5 doubt 9 self-doubt, shakiness 10 diffidence, unsafeness 11 dubiousness, incertitude, instability, uncertainty 12 doubtfulness, endangerment, insecureness, unsteadiness 13 vulnerability 14 precariousness 15 defenselessness, lack of assurance 16 apprehensiveness

insensate 4 cold 5 cruel 6 brutal 8 inhumane 9 heartless, unfeeling 11 unconscious

insensibility 4 coma 5 swoon 6 apathy, torpor, trance 8 blackout, dullness, lethargy, numbness, obduracy, oblivion, stoicism 9 analgesia, catalepsy 10 anesthesia, obtuseness 12 incognizance, indifference, mindlessness 13 insensitivity, unfeelingness 15 unconsciousness

insensible 4 cold 9 insensate, senseless 11 unconscious

insensitive 4 cold, dead, numb 5 blasé 7 callous 8 hardened 9 apathetic, impassive, insensate, unaware of, unfeeling 10 impervious, insensible 11 indifferent, unconcerned 12 thick-skinned 15 uncompassionate

insensitiveness 8 rudeness 10 coarseness, indelicacy 12 tactlessness 13 insensibility, insensitivity 17 inconsiderateness

inseparable 8 attached 11 indivisible, unseverable 12 indissoluble

insert 3 add 5 embed, enter, imbed, infix, inlay, inset, pop in, put in, set in 6 infuse, inject, push in, tuck in 7 drive in, implant, intrude, place in, press in, slide in, stick in, stuff in, wedge in 8 thrust in 9 interject, interlard, interpose, introduce 10 put between 11 interpolate, intersperse

insertion 2 ad 5 entry, graft, inlay, inset 7 implant 11 insinuation, parenthesis 12 interjection 13 advertisement

inset 4 gore 5 embed, godet, imbed, inlay, panel 6 insert 9 insertion

in seventh heaven 6 elated, joyful, joyous 8 ecstatic, euphoric 9 exuberant, rapturous 11 on cloud nine 13 up in the clouds

inside 2 in 5 inner 6 inmost, inward, secret 7 private 8 cliquish, esoteric, interior, internal, intimate 9 inner part, inner side, innermost 12 confidential

inside information 3 tip 10 inside dope

inside out 9 backwards 10 in disorder, topsy turvy 11 wrong side to

insides 4 guts 6 bowels, vitals 7 gizzard, innards, viscera 10 intestines

insidious 3 sly 4 foxy, wily 5 shady 6 artful, covert, crafty, sneaky, subtle, tricky 7 crooked, cunning, devious, furtive 8 guileful, slippery, sneaking, stealthy 9 concealed, deceitful, designing, disguised, secretive, underhand 10 contriving, perfidious, pernicious, undercover, undetected 11 clandestine, deleterious, treacherous, underhanded 12 disingenuous, falsehearted 13 Machiavellian, surreptitious

insight 6 acumen 9 intuition 10 perception 11 discernment, penetration 12 apprehension, perceptivity, perspicacity 13 comprehension, intuitiveness 14 perceptiveness
    French: 6 apercu

insignia 3 bar 4 mark, sign, star 5 badge, medal, patch 6 emblem, stripe, symbol 7 chevron, epaulet, oak leaf 10 decoration 13 badge of office

insignificance 8 puniness 9 pettiness, smallness 10 meagerness, triviality 11 irrelevance 12 unimportance

insignificant 4 puny 5 petty, small 6 flimsy, meager, minute, paltry 7 trivial 8 niggling, not vital, nugatory, picayune, piddling, trifling 9 minuscule, worthless 10 immaterial, irrelevant, negligible, of no moment, second-rate 11 indifferent, meaningless, unimportant 12 nonessential 13 small potatoes 14 inconsiderable 15 inconsequential, of little account, of no consequence 18 not worth mentioning

insincere 5 false, lying 6 untrue 7 devious, evasive 8 guileful, two-faced, uncandid 9 deceitful, dishonest, equivocal 10 fraudulent, perfidious, untruthful 11 dissembling 12 disingenuous, hypocritical, mealymouthed 13 dissimulating, double-dealing

insincerity 4 sham 6 deceit 8 pretense, uncandor 9 deception, falseness, hypocrisy, mendacity 11 affectation, shallowness, unfrankness 12 uncandidness 13 artificiality 16 disingenuousness

insinuate 5 imply 6 inject, insert 7 asperse, let fall, suggest, wheedle, whisper 8 intimate 10 ingratiate 11 worm one's way

insinuation 4 hint 8 allusion, infusion, innuendo 9 aspersion, insertion, intrusion 10 allegation, imputation, intimation, suggestion 11 implication, penetration 12 ingratiation, interjection

insipid 4 arid, blah, drab, dull, flat, lean 5 banal, bland, empty, inane, stale, trite, vapid 6 barren, boring, jejune, stupid 7 prosaic 8 lifeless, zestless 9 pointless, savorless, tasteless, wearisome 10 monotonous, namby-pamby, wishy-washy 11 commonplace 12 unappetizing 13 characterless, uninteresting

insist 4 aver, hold, urge, warn 5 claim, vouch 6 assert, demand, exhort, repeat, stress 7 caution, command, contend, persist, protest, require 8 admonish, maintain 9 reiterate 10 asseverate 13 lay down the law 14 take a firm stand 15 stand one's ground

insistence 6 demand, urging 7 urgency 8 exigency, pressure 9 clamoring 11 persistence 12 perseverance 14 imperativeness

insistent 4 firm 7 adamant 8 emphatic, repeated, stubborn 9 assertive, demanding 10 determined, unyielding 11 unrelenting

in situ 7 in place 18 in its original place

insolence 4 gall 7 disdain, hauteur 8 audacity 9 arrogance, impudence 10 brazenness, disrespect, effrontery, incivility, lordliness 11 haughtiness, presumption 12 disobedience, impertinence, impoliteness 13 bumptiousness, imperiousness 14 unmannerliness 16 superciliousness

insolent 4 rude 5 fresh, nervy 6 brazen, cheeky 7 defiant, galling, haughty 8 arrogant, impolite, impudent 9 audacious, bumptious, insulting 10 disdainful, outrageous, unmannerly 11 impertinent, overbearing 12 contemptuous, discourteous, presumptuous, supercilious 13 disrespectful

insoluble 12 inexplicable, unanswerable 13 undissolvable, unexplainable 14 undecipherable 16 incomprehensible

insolvent 5 broke 6 ruined 8 bankrupt, wiped out 9 destitute, moneyless, penniless 10 down-and-out, out of money 11 impecunious 12 impoverished, overextended

insomnia 11 nuit blanche, pervigilium, wakefulness 12 insomnolence 13 sleeplessness

insouciant 4 airy 5 perky 6 breezy, casual, jaunty 7 buoyant, offhand 8 carefree, debonair, flippant 9 easygoing, mercurial, unruffled, sans souci, whimsical 10 capricious, nonchalant, untroubled 11 free and easy, indifferent, unconcerned 12 devil-may-care, happy-go-lucky, lighthearted

inspect 3 eye 4 scan 5 probe, study 6 peer at, peruse, review, survey 7 examine, explore, observe 8 pore over 10 scrutinize 11 contemplate, investigate, reconnoiter

inspection 4 scan 5 audit, check, probe, study 6 review, survey 7 perusal 8 checking, scrutiny 9 appraisal, oversight 11 examination

inspector 7 analyst, auditor 8 analyzer, examiner, overseer, reviewer 9 appraiser, detective 11 scrutinizer 12 investigator

Inspector-General, The
  author: 12 Nikolai Gogol
  character: 4 Anna, Osip 5 Maria 26 Ivan Alexandrovich Hlestakov 35 Anton Antonovich Skvoznik-Dmukhanovsky

inspiration 4 idea, spur 5 fancy, flash 6 motive 7 impulse 8 afflatus, stimulus 9 incentive, influence, prompting 10 compulsion, incitement, motivation, revelation 13 encouragement

inspire 4 fire, stir 5 cause, exalt, impel, rouse 6 arouse, excite, induce, prompt, vivify 7 animate, enliven, hearten, produce, promote, provoke, quicken 8 embolden, engender, enkindle, illumine, inspirit, motivate, occasion 9 encourage, galvanize, influence, stimulate 10 give rise to, illuminate

inspired 3 apt 5 fired, moved 6 elated 7 elegant, exalted, excited, incited, touched, well-put 8 creative, original, prompted 9 impressed, ingenious, inventive, motivated 10 encouraged, felicitous, influenced, stimulated, well-chosen 11 exhilarated, imaginative 13 well-expressed

inspiring 5 grand 6 moving 7 awesome 8 eloquent, stirring 9 affecting, brilliant 10 impressive 11 encouraging, magnificent, stimulating

inspirit 5 boost, cheer, rouse 6 buoy up, uplift 7 animate, comfort, enliven, hearten, inspire 9 encourage, give a lift

in spite of himself
  French: 9 malgre lui

instability 8 wavering, weakness 9 hesitancy 10 fitfulness, hesitation, indecision, insecurity 11 flightiness, fluctuation, inconstancy, vacillation 12 irresolution, unstableness, unsteadiness 13 changeability,

inconsistency, mercurialness, vulnerability 14 capriciousness, changeableness

install, instal 3 lay 4 seat 5 crown, embed, imbed, lodge, plant 6 induct, invest, locate, move in, ordain 7 arrange, emplace, instate, receive, situate, station, usher in 8 coronate, initiate, position 9 establish 10 inaugurate, set in place

installation 5 plant 6 agency 8 facility 9 formation, induction 10 foundation, initiation, ordination 11 appointment, institution, investiture 12 inauguration, military base, organization 13 establishment

installment 4 part, unit 5 issue 6 laying 7 chapter, payment, section, segment 8 division, fragment, locating

instance 4 case, time 6 sample 7 example 8 occasion, specimen 9 precedent, prototype 10 antecedent 11 case in point 12 circumstance, illustration

instant 5 flash, jiffy, quick, trice 6 abrupt, minute, moment, prompt, second, sudden 8 premixed 9 immediate, on the spot, precooked, twinkling 10 ready-to-use 11 split second 12 unhesitating

instantaneous 5 rapid, swift 6 abrupt, direct, prompt, speedy, sudden 9 immediate 13 quick as a flash

instantaneously 6 at once 7 quickly, rapidly 8 in a flash, in no time, instanter, right now 9 on the spot, right away 11 immediately 21 in the twinkling of an eye

instantly 6 at once 7 quickly 8 directly, in a flash, promptly, right now 9 instanter, on the spot 10 here and now 11 immediately 12 quick as a wink, without delay 15 instantaneously 17 without hesitation

instar
  insect period between: 5 molts 7 molting

in statu quo 17 in the state in which (something is or was)

Instauratio Magna
  author: 12 Francis Bacon

instead 6 in lieu, rather 10 in its place

instigate 4 goad, spur, urge 5 begin, rouse, start 6 foment, incite, kindle, prompt, stir up 7 provoke 8 initiate 9 stimulate 10 bring about 11 set in motion

instigator 6 shaper 7 inciter 9 architect, innovator 10 prime mover, ringleader

instill, instil 4 pour 5 mix in, teach 6 impart, induce 7 implant, inspire 8 engender 9 inculcate

instinct 4 gift 5 knack 6 genius, nature 7 faculty 8 aptitude, capacity, tendency 9 intuition, mother wit 10 proclivity

instinctive 6 inborn, inbred, innate, native 7 natural 8 inherent, inspired 9 automatic, impulsive, intuitive, unlearned 10 deepseated, unacquired 11 instinctual, involuntary, spontaneous

institute 4 pass 5 begin, enact, found, set up, start 6 ordain, school 7 academy, college, society 8 commence, get going, initiate, organize 9 establish, introduce, originate, prescribe, undertake 10 constitute, foundation, inaugurate 11 association, get under way 13 put into effect 14 bring into being

institution 4 rite 5 habit, usage 6 custom, prison, ritual, school 7 academy, college, company, fixture 8 bughouse, madhouse, nuthouse, seminary 9 institute 10 convention, crazy house, foundation, university 11 association 12 organization 13 establishment

institutionalize 6 commit, detain 7 confine, put away 8 imprison 11 incarcerate

in strict confidence 7 sub rosa 9 between us, entre nous, privately 14 confidentially 15 between you and me 16 between me and thee, between ourselves

instruct 3 bid 5 brief, coach, drill, guide, order, teach, train, tutor 6 advise, direct, inform, notify, school 7 apprise, command, educate 8 acquaint 9 catechize, enlighten 12 indoctrinate

instruction 8 coaching, guidance, pedagogy, teaching, training, tutelage, tutoring 9 education 11 instructing 14 indoctrination

instructions 4 rule 5 maxim, moral, motto 6 advice, homily, lesson 7 precept 9 direction, guideline 11 explanation, information 12 prescription 13 specification 14 recommendation

instructive 8 didactic, edifying 11 educational 12 enlightening

instructor 3 don 4 guru 5 coach, guide, tutor 6 mentor 7 counsel, maestro, teacher, trainer 8 educator, lecturer 9 governess, pedagogue, preceptor, professor 10 schoolmarm 12 schoolmaster 13 schoolteacher 14 schoolmistress

instrument 4 deed, tool 5 agent, grant, means, paper 6 agency, device, gadget, medium 7 charter, machine, utensil, vehicle 8 contract 9 apparatus, appliance, equipment, expedient, implement, mechanism 11 contrivance

Instrument, The
   author: 9 John O'Hara

instrumental 5 vital 6 active, useful 7 crucial, helpful 8 a means to, decisive, valuable 9 assisting, conducive, effective, effectual, essential 10 functional 12 contributory

instrumentality 5 force, means 6 agency, charge 9 influence, mediation 12 intervention

insubordinate 6 unruly 7 defiant 8 insolent, mutinous 9 fractious 10 disorderly, rebellious, refractory 11 disobedient, intractable, uncompliant 12 recalcitrant, ungovernable, unsubmissive

insubordination 6 mutiny, revolt 7 anarchy 8 sedition 9 rebellion 10 dissention, insurgence, unruliness 12 disobedience, insurrection 13 noncompliance 14 refractoriness

insubstantial 4 airy, weak 5 frail, shaky, small 6 flimsy, modest, paltry, slight, unreal 7 fragile, trivial, unsound 8 baseless, bodiless, delicate, ethereal, gossamer, pidding, trifling, unstable 9 imaginary, visionary 10 groundless, immaterial, impalpable, intangible 12 apparitional 14 inconsiderable

in succession
   French: 7 en suite

insufferable 7 hateful 8 dreadful 10 abominable, detestable, disgusting, outrageous, unbearable 11 intolerable, unendurable, unspeakable 13 insupportable

insufficiency 4 lack, need, want 6 dearth 7 drought, paucity 8 scarcity, shortage 10 deficiency, inadequacy, meagerness, scantiness 11 undersupply

insufficient 6 scanty, skimpy, sparse 7 lacking, wanting 8 impotent 9 deficient, not enough 10 inadequate 11 incompetent 14 unsatisfactory

insular 5 petty 6 biased, narrow 7 bigoted, limited 8 isolated 9 illiberal, insulated, parochial 10 intolerant, prejudiced, provincial 12 narrow-minded

insulate 5 cover 6 cut off, detach, enisle, shield 7 cushion, isolate, protect, seclude 8 separate 9 segregate, sequester 10 disconnect

insult 3 cut 4 slap 5 abuse, cheek, scorn 6 deride, offend, slight 7 affront, offense, outrage 8 be rude to, belittle, rudeness 9 disparage, impudence, indignity 11 discourtesy, lese majesty

insulting 4 rude 5 nasty 7 abusive, uncivil, vicious 8 impolite, insolent 9 invidious, offensive 10 defamatory, derogatory 11 disparaging 12 discourteous 13 disrespectful

insuperable 8 crushing 9 defeating 10 impassable, impossible, invincible, unbeatable, unyielding 12 inexpugnable, overpowering, overwhelming 13 overmastering, unconquerable 14 insurmountable

insurance 6 policy 8 coverage, security, warranty 9 assurance, guarantee, indemnity

insure 6 secure 10 underwrite

insurgent 5 rebel 7 lawless 8 mutineer, mutinous, partisan, renegade, resister, revolter 9 breakaway, dissident, guerrilla 10 disorderly, rebellious 11 disobedient 13 insubordinate, revolutionary, revolutionist 15 insurrectionist

insurmountable 8 hopeless, too great 10 unbeatable 11 beyond reach, insuperable 13 unconquerable

insurrection 4 riot 6 mutiny, revolt, rising 8 outbreak, uprising 9 rebellion 10 insurgence, revolution

intact 4 safe 5 sound, whole 6 unhurt 7 perfect 8 complete, integral, unbroken, unharmed 9 undamaged, uninjured, untouched 10 in one piece, unimpaired 11 in good shape 15 without a scratch

intangible 5 vague 7 elusive, shadowy 8 abstract, ethereal, fleeting, fugitive 9 transient 10 accidental, evanescent, immaterial, impalpable 11 abstraction, untouchable 12 imponderable 13 imperceptible, insubstantial

integer 5 digit, whole 6 entity, figure, number 7 numeral 11 whole number

integer vitae 8 innocent 15 blameless in life

integral 4 full 5 basic, total, whole 6 entire, intact 7 perfect, rounded 8 complete, finished, inherent 9 component, essential, fulfilled, necessary, requisite 10 fulfilling 11 constituent, well-rounded 13 indispensable

integrate 3 mix 4 fuse 5 blend, merge, unify, unite 6 mingle 7 combine 8 intermix 10 amalgamate 11 desegregate 13 bring together

integrated 6 entire, joined, linked, united 7 blended, merged, unified, unitary 8 combined 9 composite, undivided 10 harmonized, reconciled 11 coordinated, synthesized 12 desegregated, unsegregated

integration 5 union 6 fusion, mixing 8 blending 9 combining, synthesis 11 combination 12 assimilation 13 desegregation

integrity 5 unity 6 purity, virtue 7 decency, honesty, probity 8 cohesion, morality, strength 9 character, coherence, principle, rectitude, wholeness 11 reliability, self-respect, uprightness 12 completeness

integument 4 coat, hide, husk, rind, skin 5 shell, 7 coating, cuticle, epiderm, exoderm 8 covering, envelope, membrane

integumentary system
  component: 4 hair, skin 5 nails

intellect 3 wit 4 mind 5 brain, sense 6 brains, wisdom 7 thinker 9 cognition, mentality 10 perception 11 mental power, rationality 12 intellectual, intelligence 13 consciousness, understanding

intellectual 4 sage 5 brain 6 brainy, mental, pundit, savant 7 bookish, egghead, scholar, thinker 8 abstract, academic, cerebral, highbrow, longhair, mandarin, rational, studious 9 intellect, of the mind, reasoning, scholarly 10 thoughtful 11 intelligent
  French: 9 bel-esprit

intelligence 4 dope, news 6 acumen, advice, brains, notice, report, wisdom 7 tidings 8 sagacity 9 intellect, knowledge 10 advisement, shrewdness 11 information 12 notification, perspicacity 13 comprehension, understanding

intelligent 4 keen, sage, wise 5 alert, canny, quick, sharp, smart 6 astute, brainy, bright, clever, shrewd 7 knowing, prudent 8 informed, sensible, thinking 9 brilliant, sagacious 10 perceptive, thoughtful 11 clearheaded, quick-witted, sharp-witted 12 well-informed 13 perspicacious

intelligentsia 7 academe 8 thinkers 10 ivory tower 13 intellectuals

intelligible 5 clear, lucid 7 evident, obvious 8 apparent, clear-cut, coherent, definite, distinct 11 unambiguous, well-defined 12 unmistakable 14 comprehensible, understandable

intemperance 10 alcoholism, insobriety 11 dissipation, drunkenness, inebriation 12 immoderation, recklessness 13 excessiveness 16 irresponsibility

intemperate 5 harsh 6 brutal, rugged, severe 7 extreme, violent 8 bibulous, uncurbed 9 dissolute, excessive, inclement 10 dissipated, gluttonous, immoderate, inordinate 11 extravagant, inabstinent, incontinent 12 unrestrained 13 overindulgent

intend 3 aim 4 mean, plan, wish 6 aspire, design, expect 7 project, propose, resolve 9 calculate, determine 10 have in mind 11 contemplate

intended 5 meant 6 fiance, future 7 engaged, fiancee, implied, willful 8 proposed, purposed 9 affianced, betrothed, bride-to-be, groom-to-be, voluntary 10 calculated, deliberate 11 intentional

intense 4 deep, keen 5 acute, sharp 6 ardent, potent, strong 7 burning, earnest, extreme, fervent, violent 8 emphatic, forceful, forcible, powerful, vehement 10 passionate 12 concentrated, considerable

intensely 4 very 5 hotly 6 deeply, keenly 7 acutely, eagerly, vividly 8 ardently, heatedly, terribly 9 extremely, fervently, seriously, violently, zealously 10 forcefully, powerfully, profoundly, vehemently, vigorously 11 excessively, exquisitely, strenuously 12 considerably, passionately 13 energetically

intensify 5 boost 6 deepen, worsen 7 magnify, quicken, sharpen 8 escalate, heighten, increase, redouble 9 aggravate, reinforce 10 accelerate, strengthen

intensifying 9 worsening 10 increasing, magnifying, redoubling, sharpening 11 aggravating, heightening, reinforcing 12 exacerbating 13 strengthening

intensity 4 zeal 5 ardor, depth, force, power, vigor 6 energy, fervor 7 emotion, passion, potency 8 severity, strength 9 magnitude, vehemence 11 earnestness 12 forcefulness

intensive 6 all-out 7 growing, radical 8 complete, sweeping, thorough 10 exhaustive, increasing 11 comprehensive 12 concentrated 13 thoroughgoing

intent 3 aim, end, set 4 bent, gist, plan 5 drift, fixed 6 burden, design, import, steady 7 earnest, intense, meaning, purport, purpose 8 absorbed, piercing, resolved 9 engrossed, insistent, intention, steadfast, substance, tenacious, unbending 10 determined, unwavering 11 preoccupied 12 concentrated, significance, undistracted 13 determination, premeditation

intention 3 aim, end 4 goal, plan 6 design, intent, object, target 7 purpose, resolve 9 objective 10 resolution 13 determination

intentional 6 willed 7 planned 8 designed, intended 9 voluntary 10 calculated, deliberate, purposeful 12 contemplated, premeditated 13 done on purpose

intently 6 deeply, raptly 9 fervently, zealously 10 absorbedly 11 attentively 12 passionately 18 without distraction 22 with undivided attention

intentness 10 absorption 11 engrossment 13 concentration

inter 4 bury 5 inurn 6 entomb, inhume 7 inearth, lay away 9 lay to rest 11 ensepulcher

interact 4 join, mesh 5 coact, unite 6 engage 7 combine, conjoin 8 dovetail 9 cooperate, interlace, intermesh, interplay, interwork 10 coordinate, interreact

inter alia 16 among other things

inter alios 17 among other persons

interbreed 3 mix 5 cross 8 intermix 10 crossbreed

intercede 5 plead 6 step in 7 mediate, speak up 9 arbitrate, interpose, intervene, offer help 12 offer support 14 put in a good word 16 lend a helping hand

intercept 3 nab 4 grab, stay, stop, take 5 catch, seize 6 ambush, arrest, cut off, detain 7 deflect, reroute

intercessor 5 agent 6 bishop, broker 8 advocate, mediator 9 go-between, middleman 12 intermediary, spokesperson

interchange 5 shift 6 switch 7 trading 8 exchange, junction, swapping, transfer 9 alternate, crossover 10 substitute 11 give and take, reciprocity

interchangeable 8 parallel, tradable 9 analogous 10 equivalent, switchable, synonymous 12 exchangeable, transposable 13 corresponding

interconnected 8 adjacent 10 contiguous, juxtaposed 12 conterminous, labyrinthine

intercourse 4 talk 5 trade 6 coitus, parley 7 pairing, traffic 8 colloquy, commerce, congress, coupling, dealings, exchange 9 communion, discourse, relations 10 connection, copulation 12 conversation 14 communications, correspondence

interdict 3 ban, bar 5 taboo 6 enjoin, forbid 7 barring, censure 8 prohibit, restrain, restrict 9 proscribe 11 forbiddance, prohibition 12 proscription

interdiction 3 ban 7 barring 11 forbiddance, prohibition 12 proscription

interest, interests 4 gain, good, part, weal 5 bonus, hobby, share, stake, touch, yield 6 absorb, affect, behalf, divert, engage, notice, profit, regard 7 attract, benefit, concern, holding, involve, pastime, portion, pursuit, service 8 dividend 9 advantage, attention, avocation, curiosity, preoccupy, suspicion 10 absorption, investment 11 engrossment 13 preoccupation

interested 6 active 7 engaged 8 diverted 9 committed, concerned 10 fascinated, responsive

interesting 7 curious 8 engaging, magnetic, pleasing, riveting, striking 9 absorbing, appealing, arresting 10 attractive, suspicious 11 fascinating, stimulating 12 entertaining

interfere 3 jar, mix 6 butt in, horn in, meddle, rush in, step in 7 counter, intrude 8 conflict 9 frustrate, intercede, interpose, intervene 11 get in the way 14 be a hindrance to, be an obstacle to, be inconsistent, stick in one's oar

interference 3 bar 6 static 8 clashing, conflict, friction, invasion, meddling 9 collision, hindrance, intrusion 12 interception, interruption, intervention

interfere with 6 hinder, impede, thwart 7 disrupt 9 interrupt

interim 7 stopgap 8 interval, meantime, temporal 9 interlude, temporary, tentative 10 pro tempore 11 provisional

interior 4 bush 5 inner 6 inmost, inside, inward 8 internal 9 backwoods, heartland, innermost, upcountry 10 hinterland

Interiors
  director: 10 Woody Allen
  cast: 10 E G Marshall 11 Diane Keaton 12 Marybeth Hurt 13 Geraldine Page 15 Kristin Griffith 16 Maureen Stapleton
  screenplay: 10 Woody Allen

interject 5 put in 6 inject, insert, slip in 7 force in, sneak in, throw in 9 interpose, introduce 11 interpolate

interjection 2 ah, er, lo, oh, ow, um 3 aha, cry, fie, hey, huh, ugh, wow 4 ahem, alas, darn, dear, drat, egad, gosh, heck, jeez, oops, ouch, phew, rats 5 aside, golly, zowie 6 eureka, hooray, hurrah, hurray 7 gee-whiz, jeepers 9 insertion 11 ejaculation, exclamation 13 interpolation, interposition

interlace 3 mix 4 knit, link 5 braid, plait, twine, twist, weave 7 wreathe 9 alternate 10 intertwine, interweave 11 intersperse

interlaced 5 woven 6 linked, twined 7 braided, knitted, plaited, twisted 8 entwined, latticed, wreathed 9 interknit 10 interwoven 11 intertwined 12 interspersed

interlocutor 8 minstrel 9 converser, dialogist 12 interrogator 14 man in the middle

interlope 6 invade, meddle 7 intrude, obtrude 8 encroach, infringe, trespass 9 interfere

interloper 7 invader, meddler 8 intruder, outsider 10 interferer, trespasser 11 gatecrasher 15 persona non grata

interlude 5 break, event, letup, pause 6 recess 7 episode, respite 8 incident, interval 12 intermission 14 breathing spell

intermediary 6 midway, umpire 7 referee 8 bridging, mediator 9 go-between, inbetween, mediating, middleman 10 arbitrator 11 adjudicator, arbitrating

intermediate 3 mid 4 fair, mean, so-so 6 median, medium, middle, midway 7 average, halfway, mediate, midmost 8 mediocre, middling, moderate 11 intervening

interment 6 burial 7 funeral 10 entombment, inhumation

Intermezzo
  director: 13 Gregory Ratoff
  cast: 8 Edna Best 12 Leslie Howard 13 Cecil Kellaway, Ingrid Bergman

interminable 6 prolix 7 endless 8 infinite, unending 9 boundless, ceaseless, incessant, limitless, perpetual, unlimited 10 continuous, long-winded 11 illimitable 12 long-drawn-out

intermingle 3 mix 4 fuse 5 blend, merge, mix up, unite 6 commix 7 combine 8 emulsify, intermix 9 commingle, interfuse, interlace 10 amalgamate, homogenize, interblend 12 conglomerate

intermission 3 gap 4 halt, rest, stop 5 break, pause 6 hiatus, recess 7 interim 8 interval, stoppage 9 interlude 10 suspension

intermittent 6 fitful 8 on and off, periodic, sporadic 9 irregular, recurrent, spasmodic 10 occasional 13 discontinuous 15 on-again-off-again

intermix 3 mix 5 blend, cross, mix in 6 mingle 10 crossbreed, interbreed 11 intermingle, intersperse

intern 6 commit, detain 7 confine, impound 8 imprison, restrain

internal 5 inner, state 6 inmost 8 domestic, interior 9 executive, political, sovereign 12 governmental 14 administrative

international 9 worldwide 12 cosmopolitan

international affairs
  god of: 6 Sancus 10 Dius Fidius, Semo Sancus

internment 9 detention 10 commitment, impounding 11 confinement 12 imprisonment

inter nos 16 between ourselves

interpolate 3 add 5 put in 6 inject, insert, work in 7 implant, intrude, stick in, throw in, wedge in 8 sandwich 9 insinuate, interject, interlard, interline, intervene, introduce 11 intercalate, intersperse

interpose 6 butt in, impose, inject, insert, meddle, step in 7 intrude, mediate, obtrude 9 arbitrate, insinuate, intercede, interfere, interject, interrupt, intervene, negotiate 11 come between, interpolate

interpret 3 see 4 read, take 6 accept, define, render, reword 7 clarify, explain, make out, restate, unravel 8 construe, decipher 9 elucidate, explicate, figure out, make clear, puzzle out, translate 10 account for, paraphrase, understand

interpretation 7 reading, version 8 analysis 9 rendition 10 commentary 11 explanation 12 construction

interpreter 7 analyst 9 explainer 10 translator 11 commentator

interrelated 9 companion, connected 10 compatible, correlated 13 complementary, correspondent, corresponding

interrelation 10 connection 11 association, correlation 12 relationship

interrogate 3 ask 4 test 5 grill, probe, query 7 examine 8 question 9 catechize 11 investigate 12 cross-examine 18 give the third degree

interrogation 4 quiz 5 probe, query 7 inquiry 8 grilling, querying, question, quizzing 9 catechism, inquiring 11 examination, inquisition, questioning

interrupt 4 stop 5 sever 7 cut in on, disjoin, disturb 8 break off 9 break in on, intersect, punctuate 10 disconnect 11 discontinue 13 interfere with

interrupted 6 broken, cut off, halted 7 checked, stalled, stopped 8 arrested, broke off, deferred 9 broken off, disturbed, suspended 11 broke in upon, intercepted 12 discontinued

interruption 3 gap 4 halt, rift, stop 5 break, pause 6 hiatus, lacuna 9 hindrance, interlude 11 obstruction 12 interference, intermission 13 disconnection, discontinuity

inter se 15 among themselves 17 between themselves

intersect 4 meet 5 cross 6 bisect, divide 7 overlap 8 crosscut, transect, traverse 9 cut across 10 crisscross

intersection 6 corner 7 crossing, junction 10 crossroads 11 interchange

intersperse 3 dot, mix 5 strew 6 mingle, pepper 7 bestrew, scatter, wedge in 8 disperse, intermix, sprinkle 9 broadcast, interfuse, interject, interlard, interpose 11 intercalate, interpolate

interstice 4 slit, slot 5 crack, space 7 opening, orifice 8 aperture, interval

intertwine 4 lace 5 braid, plait, twine, twist, weave 7 entwine 8 entangle 9 interlace

interval 3 gap 4 gulf, rest, rift 5 break, cleft, pause, space, spell 6 breach, hiatus, recess, season 7 interim, opening 9 interlude 10 interspace, separation 12 intermission, interruption

intervene 4 pass 6 befall, butt in, step in 7 break in, intrude, mediate 9 arbitrate, intercede, interfere, interpose, interrupt, take place 10 come to pass 11 come between

intervention 9 butting in, intrusion, mediation 10 breaking in, stepping in 11 arbitration 12 intercession, interference 13 interposition 14 intermediation

interview 4 chat, talk 6 parley 7 meeting 8 audience 10 conference, evaluation, round table 11 questioning 12 consultation, conversation

interweave 3 mix 4 fuse, join, knit, lace, link 5 blend, braid, plait, twine, twist 6 splice 7 wreathe 9 interlace, interknit 10 intertwine 11 intersperse

intestinal 5 inner 7 enteric 8 internal, visceral

intestines 4 guts 6 bowels 7 insides, viscera 8 entrails

in the air 2 up 5 above, aloft 7 skyward 8 all about, in the sky, overhead 10 everywhere 11 in the clouds

in the doghouse 9 in bad odor 10 in disfavor, in disgrace, in ill favor 11 in disrepute

in the end 6 one day 7 finally 8 sometime 10 eventually, ultimately 13 sooner or later 17 in the course of time
  French: 5 enfin

in the family
  French: 9 en famille

in the first place
  Latin: 8 imprimis

in the future
Latin: 8 in futuro
Spanish: 6 manana
In the Heat of the Night
director: 13 Norman Jewison
cast: 8 Lee Grant 10 Rod Steiger 11 Warren Oates 13 Sidney Poitier (Virgil Tibbs)
score: 11 Quincy Jones
Oscar for: 5 actor (Steiger) 7 picture 10 screenplay
in the know 9 cognizant 11 on the inside 13 fully informed, knowledgeable 23 having inside information
in the manner of
French: 3 a la 7 a la mode
in the matter of
Latin: 4 in re
in the meantime
Latin: 9 ad interim
in the middle of things
Latin: 11 in medias res
in the midst of 5 among 7 amongst 12 surrounded by 13 in the middle of
in the nature of things
Latin: 13 in rerum natura
In the neighborhood of 6 almost, around, nearly 7 close to 9 generally, just about 10 more or less, not far from 13 approximately 15 in the vicinity of
in the place cited
Latin: 6 loc cit 10 loco citato
in the place of a parent
Latin: 14 in loco parentis
in the same manner that
Latin: 7 quo modo
in the same place
Latin: 4 ibid 6 ibidem
in the state in which
Latin: 10 in statu quo
in the style of
French: 7 a la mode
in the very act of committing the crime
Latin: 18 in flagrante delicto
in the vicinity of 4 near 6 almost, around, nearly 7 close to 9 just about 10 more or less, not far from 13 approximately 19 in the neighborhood of
in the way
French: 6 de trop
in the whole
Latin: 6 in toto
In the work cited
Latin: 5 op cit 11 opere citato
in the year of the reign
Latin: 9 anno regni
in the year of the world
Latin: 9 anno mundi
In This House of Brede
author: 11 Rumer Godden
in this sign shalt thou conquer
Latin: 16 in hoc signo vinces
motto of: 19 Constantine the Great
from vision of: 5 cross
Intimacy 5 amity 6 caring, warmth 8 dearness, fondness 9 affection, closeness 10 chumminess, endearment, fraternity, love-

making, tenderness 11 brotherhood, camaraderie, familiarity 12 friendliness
intimate 3 pal 4 chum, dear, deep, hint 5 bosom, buddy, close, crony, imply, rumor 6 allude, direct 7 guarded, private, special, suggest 8 detailed, familiar, indicate, personal, profound, thorough 9 cherished, confidant, first-hand, innermost, insinuate 12 confidential
French: 6 intime
intimately 7 closely 8 secretly, very well 9 privately 10 familiarly, personally 11 essentially 13 intrinsically 14 confidentially
intimation 4 clue, hint, sign 5 rumor 7 inkling, portent 8 allusion, innuendo 10 indication, suggestion 11 insinuation 13 veiled comment
Intimations of Immortality
author: 17 William Wordsworth
Intime 4 cozy 8 intimate
in time 6 before, sooner 7 earlier 9 before now, in advance 10 beforehand, eventually 11 ahead of time 13 before the fact, sooner or later
intimidate 3 cow 5 alarm, bully, daunt, scare 6 coerce, menace, subdue 7 buffalo, terrify 8 browbeat, frighten 9 terrorize
intimidated 5 cowed, fazed 6 scared 7 crushed, daunted, subdued 10 browbeaten, frightened, terrorized
intimidation 7 tyranny 8 bullying, coercion 9 despotism 11 browbeating, terrorizing, tyrannizing 12 scare tactics
intimidator 5 bully 6 despot 7 coercer 9 oppressor, tormenter, tormentor 10 browbeater
into 2 in, to 5 among 6 inside, toward, within 7 against
Intolerable 7 hateful, racking 9 abhorrent, agonizing, excessive, loathsome, torturous 10 abominable, outrageous, unbearable 11 unendurable 12 excruciating, insufferable, unreasonable 13 insupportable
intolerance 4 bias 5 racism 7 bigotry 8 weak spot 9 no stomach, prejudice 10 chauvinism, xenophobia 12 low tolerance 16 hypersensitivity, narrow-mindedness
Intolerance
director: 10 D W Griffith
cast: 8 Mae Marsh 11 Lillian Gish 12 Robert Harron 17 Constance Talmadge
Intolerant 7 bigoted, hostile, jealous 9 fanatical, parochial, resentful, sectarian 10 prejudiced, xenophobic 11 mistrustful 12 chauvinistic, closed-minded, narrowminded
intonation 4 tone 5 pitch 6 accent 8 chanting 10 modulation, inflection
intone 3 hum, say 4 song 5 chant, croon, drawl, mouth, speak, utter, voice 6 murmur, recite 8 intonate, modulate, singsong, vocalize 9 enunciate, pronounce 10 articulate
in toto 5 in all, uncut 6 entire, wholly 7 totally 8 as a whole, entirely, outright 10 completely, in the whole, unabridged 11 all together, uncondensed

intoxicant 3 gin, rum 4 beer, grog, wine 5 booze, drink 6 liquor, tipple, whisky 7 alcohol, spirits, whiskey 8 cocktail, highball 9 inebriant

intoxicated 4 high, rapt 5 drunk, oiled, tight, tipsy 6 bombed, elated, loaded, stewed, stinko, stoned, zonked 7 drunken, exalted, smashed, wrecked 9 delighted, enchanted, entranced, plastered 10 enthralled, inebriated, infatuated, in one's cups 11 exhilarated, transported

intoxicating 4 hard 5 heady 6 potent 7 elating 9 alcoholic, spiritous 11 inebriating 12 exhilarating

intoxication 3 joy 5 bliss 7 elation, rapture 8 euphoria 9 poisoning, tipsiness 10 excitement, insobriety 11 drunkenness, inebriation 12 befuddlement, stupefaction

intractable 6 mulish, ornery, unruly 7 froward, willful 8 obdurate, perverse, stubborn 9 fractious, obstinate 10 headstrong, inflexible, refractory 11 unmalleable 12 contumacious, incorrigible, ungovernable, unmanageable 14 hard to cope with, uncontrollable

intransigent 7 diehard 8 obdurate, stubborn 9 steadfast, unmovable 10 inflexible, iron-willed, unyielding 11 intractable, unbudgeable 14 uncompromising

intrepid 4 bold 5 brave 6 daring, heroic 7 doughty, valiant 8 fearless, resolute, valorous 9 audacious, dauntless 10 courageous, undismayed 11 adventurous

intrepidity 4 guts 5 spunk, valor 6 mettle 7 bravery, courage 8 backbone 9 fortitude, sangfroid 12 fearlessness 13 dauntlessness

intricacy 10 complexity 11 involvement 12 complication, entanglement 15 complicatedness

intricate 6 knotty, tricky 7 complex, devious, tangled 8 involved 9 entangled 11 complicated

intrigue 3 spy 4 fire, plot 5 amour 6 absorb, arrest, scheme 7 attract, collude, knavery, romance 8 conspire, enthrall, scheming 9 fascinate, machinate, titillate 10 conspiracy, love affair 11 machination 13 double-dealing 15 interest greatly, tickle one's fancy

intriguer 7 cheater, plotter, schemer 8 conniver, finagler 9 trickster 10 machinator, wirepuller 11 conspirator, Machiavelli, manipulator

intriguing 8 engaging, exciting 9 absorbing, beguiling 11 captivating, enthralling, fascinating, interesting

intrinsic 5 basic, per se 6 inborn, inbred, innate, native 7 natural 8 inherent 9 essential, ingrained 10 indigenous, underlying 11 fundamental

introduce 3 add 4 show, urge 5 begin, offer, put in, start 6 create, expose, import, inform, infuse, insert 7 advance, bring in, kick off, lead off, present, propose, sponsor, throw in 8 acquaint, initiate, lead into 9 establish, institute, interject, interpose,

make known, originate, recommend 10 put forward 11 familiarize, interpolate

introduction 6 change 7 novelty, opening, preface, prelude 8 foreword, preamble, prologue 9 insertion, precursor 10 bringing in, conducting, innovation, ushering in 11 instituting, institution

introductory 7 initial 9 beginning, prefatory 10 initiatory, precursory 11 acquainting, preliminary 13 get-acquainted

introspection 8 brooding 10 meditation, reflection, rumination 12 deliberation, self-analysis, self-scrutiny 13 contemplation, soul-searching 15 self-examination, self-observation, self-questioning

introspective 7 pensive 10 reflective 13 contemplative, private person

introversion 7 reserve 8 brooding 10 constraint, diffidence, withdrawal 13 introspection

introvert 5 loner 7 brooder, thinker 13 contemplative, private person

introverted 3 shy 5 stiff 8 reserved 9 inhibited, repressed, withdrawn 10 antisocial, restrained 13 inner-directed, introspective

intrude 4 push 6 butt in, impose, meddle, thrust 7 obtrude 8 encroach, trespass 9 interfere, interlope, interpose, intervene

intruder 10 encroacher, interferer, interloper, intervener, trespasser 11 gatecrasher

Intruder in the Dust
  author: 15 William Faulkner

intrusive 4 nosy 5 pushy 6 prying, snoopy 8 in the way, invasive 9 hindering, obtrusive, officious, unwelcome 10 meddlesome 11 impertinent, interfering, interruptive

intuition 5 flash, hunch 7 insight, surmise 8 instinct 9 guesswork, telepathy 10 sixth sense 11 second sight 12 clairvoyance, precognition

intuitive 6 inborn, inbred, innate, native 7 natural, psychic 10 telepathic 11 clairvoyant, instinctive, intuitional, nonrational 12 extrasensory

Inuit see 6 Eskimo

inundate 4 glut 5 drown, flood, swamp 6 deluge, drench, engulf 8 load down, overcome, overflow, saturate, submerge 9 overwhelm 10 overburden, overspread

inundation 4 glut 5 flood 6 deluge 9 avalanche

in unison 5 as one 8 in chorus 9 all at once 11 all together

inure 5 adapt, steel, train 6 adjust, custom, harden, season, temper 7 toughen 8 accustom 9 acclimate, get used to, habituate 10 discipline, naturalize, strengthen 11 acclimatize, desensitize, familiarize 12 become used to 15 learn to live with 16 become hardened to

in use 8 employed 9 operating 11 functioning, operational

in vacuo 9 in a vacuum 11 in isolation

invade 5 flood, limit 6 assail, attack, engulf, infect, infest 7 assault, overrun, violate 8 permeate, restrict, strike at, trespass 9 intrude on, march into, penetrate

invader 6 raider 8 attacker, intruder, marauder 9 aggressor, assailant 10 trespasser

invalid 4 null, sick, void, weak 5 false 6 ailing, infirm, sickly, unwell 7 amputee, cripple, unsound, useless 8 disabled, not valid, nugatory, weakened 9 enfeebled, forceless, illogical, paralytic, powerless, worthless 10 dead letter, fallacious, paraplegic 11 debilitated, ineffective, inoperative, unsupported 12 unconvincing 13 incapacitated, unsupportable 14 good-for-nothing, valetudinarian

invalidate 5 annul 6 cancel, refute, repeal, weaken 7 nullify, vitiate 8 abrogate, make void, undercut 9 discredit, undermine 11 countermand

invalidation 7 voiding 9 annulment 10 abrogation 12 cancellation 13 nullification

invaluable 4 rare 6 choice 9 priceless 11 beyond price, inestimable

invariable 7 uniform 8 constant 9 immutable, unfailing, unvarying 10 changeless, consistent, unchanging, unwavering 11 unalterable, undeviating 12 unchangeable

invariably 4 ever 6 always 7 forever 9 every time, uniformly 10 all the time, constantly 11 perpetually, universally 15 in every instance 16 without exception

invasion 4 raid 5 foray 6 attack, breach, inroad, sortie 7 assault 8 trespass 9 incursion, intrusion, onslaught 10 aggression, juggernaut, usurpation 11 penetration 12 encroachment, infiltration, infringement, overstepping

Invasion of the Body Snatchers
director:
  1956 version: 9 Don Siegel
  1978 version: 13 Philip Kaufman
cast:
  1956 version: 10 Dana Wynter, Larry Gates 11 King Donovan 13 Kevin McCarthy
  1978 version: 11 Brooke Adams 12 Jeff Goldblum, Leonard Nimoy 16 Donald Sutherland

invective 4 rant 5 venom 6 insult 7 censure, railing, sarcasm 8 diatribe 9 contumely 10 execration, harsh words, revilement 11 verbal abuse 12 billingsgate, denunciation, vilification, vituperation

inveigh 4 rail, slam 5 abuse, knock, scold 6 rebuke, revile 7 censure, put down, run down, upbraid 8 belittle, denounce, harangue, reproach 9 castigate, criticize, dress down 10 vituperate

inveigh against 5 abuse 6 defame, rail at, revile 7 protest 8 denounce 9 castigate

inveigle 4 coax, lure 5 tempt, trick 6 allure, cajole, entice, rope in, seduce, suck in 7 beguile, ensnare, flatter, mislead, wheedle 8 persuade, soft-soap 9 bamboozle, sweet-talk

inveiglement 7 coaxing 8 cajolery, flattery 9 wheedling 10 enticement, persuasion 13 blandishments

invent 4 coin 6 cook up, create, devise, make up 7 concoct, develop, fashion, think up, trump up 8 conceive, contrive 9 conjure up, fabricate, formulate, originate 10 come up with 11 put together

invented 6 fabled, made up 8 fabulous, fanciful, mythical 9 fantastic, imaginary, legendary 10 apocryphal, fictitious

Inventing America
author: 10 Garry Wills

invention 3 lie 4 fake, sham 6 design, device, gadget 7 fiction, forgery, machine 8 creation, trumpery 9 apparatus, discovery, fertility, implement, ingenuity, inventing 10 concoction, creativity, production 11 contraption, contrivance, development, fabrication, imagination, originality, origination 13 dissimulation, inventiveness, prevarication 15 resourcefulness

invention
god of: 6 Hermes

inventive 6 bright, clever 9 ingenious 11 resourceful

inventiveness 9 ingenuity 10 cleverness, creativity 11 imagination, orgininality 15 imaginativeness

inventor 5 maker 6 author 7 creator, deviser 8 engineer, producer, tinkerer 9 architect, generator, innovator 10 discoverer, originator
  of air brake: 12 Westinghouse
  of automobile: 7 Daimler
  of barometer: 10 Torricelli
  of camera: 7 Eastman
  of cotton gin: 7 Whitney
  of cylinder lock: 4 Yale
  of dynamite: 5 Nobel
  of elevator: 4 Otis
  of gyrocompass: 6 Sperry
  of helicopter: 8 Sikorsky
  of linotype: 12 Mergenthaler
  of machine gun: 7 Gatling
  of movable type: 9 Gutenberg
  of phonograph, incandescent lamp, mimeograph, dictating machine, fluoroscope: 6 Edison
  of photography: 6 Niepce, Talbot 8 Daguerre
  of reaper: 9 McCormick
  of radio: 7 Marconi
  of revolver: 4 Colt
  of rocket engine: 7 Goddard
  of sewing machine: 4 Howe
  of sleeping car: 7 Pullman
  of steamboat: 6 Fulton
  of steam engine: 4 Watt
  of steam locomotive: 10 Stephenson
  of telegraph: 5 Morse
  of telephone: 4 Bell
  of wireless telegraph: 7 Marconi
  of vulcanized rubber: 8 Goodyear

inventory 4 roll 5 goods, index, stock 6 roster, supply 7 catalog 8 register, schedule 9 stock list 10 accounting 11 merchandise, stock-taking

inverse 8 backward, contrary, converse, indirect, inverted, opposite, reversed 11 back to front, bottom-to-top, right-to-left

inversion 7 turning 8 reversal 9 ectropion, turnabout 10 transposal 12 resupination 13 transposition

inverted 7 inverse 8 bottom up 10 upside-down

invest 4 fill, garb, give 5 adorn, allot, array, color, cover, dress, endow, imbue 6 clothe, devote, enable, enrich, infuse, supply 7 appoint, license 8 set aside 9 apportion

investigate 4 sift 5 probe, query, study 6 survey 7 analyze, dissect, explore, inspect 8 ask about, look into, pore over, question, research 9 anatomize, delve into 10 scrutinize

investigation 5 probe, study 6 review, search, survey 7 anatomy, inquiry 8 analysis, research, scrutiny 10 dissection, inspection 11 fact-finding

investigator 6 shamus 7 analyst, gumshoe 8 examiner, inquirer, observer 9 detective 10 private eye, researcher

investment 4 ante, risk 5 share, stake 7 venture 8 offering

inveterate 6 inured 7 adamant, chronic, diehard 8 constant, habitual, hardened 9 confirmed, incurable, ingrained, recurrent, steadfast 10 continuous, deep-rooted, deep-seated 11 established 12 longstanding, unregenerate 15 unreconstructed

invidious 7 vicious 8 spiteful 9 insulting, malicious, offensive, rancorous, resentful, slighting 10 malevolent

invigorate 4 stir 5 brace, cheer, liven, pep up, renew, rouse, zip up 6 jazz up, vivify 7 animate, enliven, fortify, refresh, restore 8 energize, vitalize 9 stimulate 10 exhilarate, rejuvenate, strengthen

invigorated 6 braced 7 revived 8 animated, restored, vivified 9 energized, full of pep, quickened, refreshed 10 stimulated 11 rejuvenated 12 strengthened 17 full of vim and vigor

invigorating 7 bracing 9 animating, healthful 10 energizing, enlivening, quickening, refreshing, vitalizing 11 restorative, stimulating 12 rejuvenating 13 strengthening

invincible 10 unbeatable 11 impregnable, indomitable, insuperable 12 invulnerable, undefeatable 13 irrepressible, unconquerable 14 insurmountable

in vino veritas 18 in wine there is truth

inviolable 4 holy, pure 6 chaste, divine, sacred, secret 7 blessed 8 hallowed 9 dedicated, inviolate, undefiled 10 sacrosanct 11 consecrated, impregnable, trustworthy 12 impenetrable, invulnerable, unassailable 13 incorruptible

inviolate 4 pure 6 intact, sacred, secret 8 hallowed 9 unaltered, unchanged, undefiled, unstained 10 inviolable, sacrosanct

invisible 6 covert, hidden, unseen, veiled 7 obscure 9 concealed, unseeable 10 unapparent 13 imperceptible, undiscernible

Invisible Man
　author: 12 Ralph Ellison

Invisible Man, The
　author: 7 H G Wells
　character: 4 Hall 6 Dr Kemp, Marvel 7 Griffin 11 Colonel Ayde

invitation 3 bid 4 call, lure 5 offer 7 bidding, summons 8 open door 9 challenge 10 allurement, enticement, inducement, temptation 12 solicitation

invite 3 bid 4 call, lure, urge 5 tempt 6 entice, induce 7 attract, solicit, welcome 9 encourage

inviting 4 warm 8 alluring, charming, engaging, enticing, magnetic, tempting 9 appealing, welcoming 10 attractive, intriguing

invocation 4 plea 6 appeal, orison, prayer 8 petition 9 summoning 12 supplication

in vogue 2 in 6 modish 7 a la mode, current, in style, stylish 9 in fashion 11 fashionable 12 le dernier cri

invoke 3 beg, use 5 apply 6 ask for, employ 7 beseech, conjure, entreat, implore, pray for 8 call upon, petition, resort to 9 appeal for, call forth, implement, importune, introduce 10 supplicate

involuntary 6 forced, reflex 7 coerced 8 unchosen, unwilled 9 automatic, reluctant, unwilling 10 compulsory 11 inadvertent, instinctive, spontaneous, unconscious 13 unintentional 15 against one's will

involve 5 imply, mix up 6 commit, engage, entail, wrap up 7 contain, embroil, include 8 comprise, depend on, entangle 9 implicate, preoccupy

involved 7 complex, engaged, mixed up, wound up 8 absorbed, immersed 9 committed, elaborate, embroiled, engrossed, entangled, intricate, wrapped up 10 implicated 11 complicated, preoccupied

involve deeply 5 mix up 6 absorb, commit, wrap up 7 embroil, engross, immerse 8 entangle 9 implicate, preoccupy

invulnerable 10 formidable, invincible, unbeatable 11 impregnable, indomitable, insuperable 12 imperishable, inexpugnable, unassailable, undefeatable 13 unconquerable, undestroyable

inward, inwards 5 inner 6 mental, toward 7 going in, ingoing 8 incoming, interior, inwardly, personal 9 spiritual, the inside 10 interiorly

in what way
　Latin: 7 quo modo

in which case 4 then, when 6 thence 9 whereupon 11 accordingly 12 at which point

In Which We Serve
　director: 9 David Lean 10 Noel Coward
　script: 10 Noel Coward

cast: 9 John Mills 10 Noel Coward 12 Bernard Miles, Celia Johnson

in wine there is truth
  Latin: 13 in vino veritas

Io
  father: 7 Inachus
  husband: 9 Telegonus
  loved by: 4 Zeus
  son: 7 Epaphus
  changed into: 6 heifer
  color of heifer: 5 white
  guarded by: 5 Argus
  persecuted by: 6 gadfly
  sent by: 4 Hera
  corresponds to: 4 Isis

Iobates
  king of: 5 Lycia
  son-in-law: 7 Proteus
  commissioned to kill: 11 Bellerophon

Iodama
  priestess of: 6 Athena

iodine
  chemical symbol: 1 I

Iolanthe
  author: 9 W S Gilbert

Iolaus
  father: 8 Iphicles
  mother: 10 Automedusa
  uncle: 8 Hercules
  companion: 8 Hercules
  charioteer of: 8 Hercules

Iole
  father: 7 Eurytus
  loved by: 8 Heracles
  husband: 6 Hyllus

Ion
  author: 9 Euripides
  character: 6 Apollo, Athene, Crensa, Xuthus

Iormungandr *see* 11 Jormungandr

iota 3 bit, jot 4 atom, spot, whit 5 shred, spark, speck 7 smidgin 8 particle 9 scintilla 11 faint degree, small amount 15 tiniest quantity

IOU 4 chit, debt, note 10 obligation 12 promise to pay 14 promissory note

Iowa
  abbreviation: 2 IA
  nickname: 7 Hawkeye
  capital/largest city: 9 Des Moines
  others: 4 Ames 5 Amana, Mason, Perry 6 Algona, Keokuk, Le Mars, Marion, Newton 7 Anamosa, Clinton, Dubuque, Ft Dodge, Ottumwa 8 Waterloo 9 Davenport, Ft Madison, Marquette, Mason City, Sioux City 10 Burlington, Cedar Falls, West Branch 11 Cedar Rapids 12 Marshalltown 13 Council Bluffs
  college: 3 Coe 5 Corot, Drake, Loras 7 Cornell, Parsons 8 Grinnell, Wartburg 12 Iowa Wesleyan
  explorer: 6 Joliet 7 Jolliet 9 Marquette 13 Lewis and Clark
  feature: 13 Amana Colonies 17 first apple orchard
  church: 11 Little Brown

national historical site: 13 Herbert Hoover

national monument: 12 Effigy Mounds

state fair: 4 Iowa

tribe: 3 Fox 4 Sauc 5 Ioway, Omaha 9 Muscoutin, Winnebago

people: 7 Hawkeye 9 Grant Wood 10 John L Lewis 11 Billy Sunday 15 Buffalo Bill Cody, Charles Ringling

lake: 5 Clear, Storm 6 Spirit 7 Rathbun 11 East Okoboji, West Okoboji

land rank: 11 twenty-fifth

president: 13 Herbert Hoover

river: 4 Iowa 5 Cedar, Floyd, Skunk 8 Big Sioux, Missouri 9 Des Moines 11 Mississippi, Nishnabotna 12 Wapsipinicon

state admission: 11 twenty-ninth

state bird: 16 eastern goldfinch

state flower: 8 wild rose

state motto: 45 Our Liberties We Prize and Our Rights We Will Maintain

state song: 13 The Song of Iowa

state tree: 3 oak

Iowa, Ioway
  language family: 6 Siouan
  location: 4 Iowa
  related to: 3 Oto 8 Missouri

Ioxus
  father: 10 Melanippus
  grandfather: 7 Theseus
  grandmother: 8 Perigune

Iphicles
  father: 10 Amphitryon
  mother: 7 Alcmene
  half-brother: 8 Hercules
  son: 6 Iolaus

Iphidamas
  father: 7 Antenor
  mother: 6 Theano
  killed by: 9 Agamemnon

Iphigenia
  father: 9 Agamemnon
  mother: 12 Clytemnestra
  brother: 7 Orestes
  sister: 7 Electra 12 Chrysothemis
  saved by: 7 Artemis

Iphigenia in Aulis
  author: 9 Euripides
  character: 8 Achilles, Menelaus 9 Agamemnon 12 Clytemnestra

Iphigenia in Tauris
  author: 9 Euripides
  character: 5 Thoas 6 Athena 7 Orestes, Pylades

Iphigenie en Aulide
  also: 16 Iphigenia in Aulis
  opera by: 5 Gluck
  character: 7 Artemis, Calchas 8 Achilles 9 Agamemnon 12 Clytemnestra

Iphigenie en Tauride
  also: 17 Iphigenia in Tauris
  opera by: 5 Gluck
  character: 5 Diana, Thoas (King of Scythia) 7 Orestes, Pylades 9 the Furies

Iphitus
  father: 7 Eurytus
  sister: 4 Iole

Ipoctonus
epithet of: 8 Hercules
means: 10 worm-killer

ipse dixit 15 he himself said it 21 assertion without proof

ipsissima verba 8 verbatim 12 the very words

ipso facto 15 by the fact itself 24 by the very nature of the deed

ipso jure 14 by the law itself 16 by operation of law

Iraklion
capital of: 5 Crete

Iran
name means: 15 land of the Aryans
other name: 6 Persia
capital/largest city: 6 Tehran 7 Teheran
others: 3 Qum 4 Shah 5 Ahwaz, Urmia 6 Abadan, Bandar, Kashan, Meshed, Shiraz, Tabriz 7 Birjand, Hamadan, Isfahan, Mashhad, Zahidan 11 Bandar Abbas
supreme head of state: 5 faghi 17 religious guardian
measure: 3 gaz, zar, zer 4 cane 5 gareh, kafiz, makuk, qasab 6 charac, chebel, ghalva 7 capicha, chenica, farsakh, mansion, mishara 8 parasang, piamaneh, stathmos
monetary unit: 3 pul 4 asar, gran, rial 5 bisti, daric, dinar, larin, shahi, toman 6 stater 7 ashrafi, pahlavi
weight: 3 ser 4 dung, rotl, seer 5 abbas, artel, pinar, ratel 6 batman, dirhem, karwar, miscal, nimman 7 abbassi 8 tcheirek
lake: 5 Niris, Tasht, Tuzlu, Urmia 6 Sahweh, Sistan 7 Maharlu 8 Nemekser, Urumiyeh
mountain: 6 Elburz, Zagros
highest point: 8 Demavend
river: 4 Aras 5 Araks, Atrak, Atrek, Karun, Safid, Sefid 6 Gargan
sea: 7 Arabian, Caspian
physical feature:
desert: 9 Dasht-i-Lut 11 Dasht-i-Kavir
gulf: 4 Oman 7 Persian
strait: 6 Hormuz
people: 3 Lur, Tat 4 Arab, Kurd, Turk 5 Medes 6 Galcha, Gilani, Jewish, Shugni 7 Baluchi, Persian 8 Armenian, Bactrian, Bartangi, Parthian, Scythian 9 Bakhtiari 11 Azerbaijani, Mazandarani
dynasty: 5 Qajar 7 Arsacid, Pahlavi, Safavid 8 Parthian, Seleucid 9 Sassanian 10 Achaemenid
poet: 11 Omar Khayyam
ruler: 5 Abbas, Cyrus 6 Darius, Xerxes 10 Rafsanjani 23 Shah Mohammed Reza (Riza) Pahlavi 25 Ayatollah Ruhollah Khomeini
language: 4 Luri, Zend 5 Farsi, Turki 6 Arabic 7 Baluchi, Kurdish, Persian 8 Armenian 11 Azerbaijani
religion: 5 Baha'i, Islam 7 Judaism 9 Shia Islam 11 Zoroastrian 12 Christianity
place:
dam: 5 Karaj

mosque: 4 Shad 5 Royal 12 Masjidi-i-Shah 18 Madreseh Chahar Bagh
ruins: 4 Susa 10 Persepolis
feature: 13 Peacock Throne
head cloth: 6 chador 7 chawdar
parliament: 6 majlis
underground water channel: 5 qanat
food: 5 kabob
soured milk: 4 mast
stuffed vegetables/leaves: 5 dolma 6 dolmeh

Iraq
capital/largest city: 7 Baghdad
others: 2 Ur 3 Kut 5 Al Faw, Amara, Ashur, Basra, Erbil, Mosul, Najaf, Qurna 6 Hillah, Kirkuk, Tikrit 7 Karbala, Mandali, Samarra, Umm Qasr 8 Al Zubair
division:
ancient: 5 Akkad, Sumer 7 Assyria 9 Babylonia 11 Mesopotamia
monetary unit: 4 fils 5 dinar
lake: 6 al-Milh 7 Sanniya 8 al-Hammar
mountain: 6 Qalate, Zagros 7 Qaarade 9 Kurdistan
highest point: 7 Halgurd
river: 6 Diyala, Hawran, Tigris 8 Great Zab 9 al-Ubayyid, Euphrates, Little Zab 11 Shatt-al-Arab
physical feature:
desert: 6 Syrian 8 al-Hajava
gulf: 7 Persian
people: 4 Arab, Kurd 7 Bedouin
leader: 6 Faisal, Sargon 7 Abbasid, Hussein, Ottoman 9 Hammurabi 13 Harun al-Rashid, Saddam Hussein 14 Nebuchadnezzar 16 Abbasid Caliphate
language: 5 Farsi 6 Arabic 7 Kurdish, Persian, Turkish
religion: 5 Islam 12 Christianity
place:
ancient: 14 Hanging Gardens
arch: 9 Ctesiphon
mosque: 5 Great 9 Kadhimain
ruins: 2 Ur 7 Babylon, Nineveh, Samarra
Sumerian temple tower: 8 Ziggurat
feature:
marketplace: 4 souk
war: 4 Gulf 11 Desert Storm 12 Desert Shield

irascibility 8 acerbity 9 bad temper, crossness, testiness 10 crabbiness, crankiness 11 peevishness, waspishness 12 irritability 16 cantankerousness

irascible 5 cross, testy 6 cranky, grumpy, ornery, touchy 7 grouchy, peevish, waspish 8 choleric 9 irritable, splenetic 10 ill-humored 11 bad-tempered, hot-tempered, intractable 12 cantankerous

irate 3 mad 5 angry, livid, rabid, riled, vexed 6 galled 7 angered, annoyed, enraged, furious 8 burned up 9 indignant, irritated 10 infuriated

ire 4 fury, rage 5 anger, wrath 6 choler 7 outrage, umbrage 8 vexation 10 resentment 11 indignation

Ireland
  other name: 4 Eire, Erin 5 Ierne 8
  Hibernia 9 Innisfail 11 Emerald Isle
  capital/largest city: 6 Dublin
  others: 4 Cobh, Cork, Erne, Suir, Tara 5
  Adare, Ennis, Sligo 6 Bangor, Galway,
  Lurgan, Mallow, Tralee, Ulster 7 Athlone,
  Belfast, Donegal, Dundalk, Kildare, Wex-
  ford 8 Drogheda, Kilkenny, Limerick 9
  Craigavon, Tipperary, Waterford 10
  Queenstown 11 Londonderry
  school: 7 Trinity
  division: 4 Cork, Down, Mayo 5 Clare,
  Kerry, Meath 6 Antrim, Armagh, Galway,
  Tyrone, Ulster 7 Donegal, Kildare, Wex-
  ford, Wicklow 8 Kilkenny, Limerick 9 Fer-
  managh, Killarney, Tipperary, Waterford
  11 Londonderry
  ancient: 6 Ulster 7 Munster 8 Connacht,
  Leinster
  head of government: 9 taoiseach (prime
  minister)
  measure: 4 mile 6 bandle 8 crannock
  monetary unit: 3 rap 4 real 5 pence,
  pound 6 turney 8 shilling
  island: 3 Man 4 Aran, Bear, Holy, Tory 5
  Clare, Clear, Magee 6 Achill, Saltee,
  Whiddy 7 Blasket, Gorumna, Rathlin 8
  Aranmore, Inisheer 9 Inishmore 10
  Inishbofin
  lake: 3 Doo, Key, Ree, Tay 4 Conn, Derg,
  Erne, Mask 5 Allen, Barra, Capra,
  Gowna, Leane, Lough, Neagh 6 Boderg,
  Cooter, Corrib, Ennell 7 Dromore,
  Gougane, Oughter, Sheelin 9 Killarney
  mountain: 5 Galty 6 Croagh, Mourne 7
  Errigal, Muckish, Patrick, Wicklow 8
  Comeragh 10 Benna Beola, Twelve
  Bens, Twelve Pins 13 Knockmealdown
  19 Macgillycuddy's Reeks
  highest point: 13 Carrantuohill
  river: 3 Lee, May 4 Bann, Deel, Erne,
  Nore, Suir 5 Boyne, Clare, Feale, Flesk,
  Foyle, Laune 6 Bandon, Barrow, Corrib,
  Liffey, Slaney 7 Kenmare, Munster,
  Shannon 10 Blackwater
  sea: 5 Irish 8 Atlantic
  physical feature:
  bay: 4 Clew 5 Sligo 6 Bantry, Dingle, Galway, Tralee 7 Donegal, Dundalk
  cape: 5 Clear
  channel: 5 North 9 St George's
  cliffs: 5 Moher
  point: 6 Cahore 8 Carnsore
  people: 4 Celt, Erse, Gael 6 Celtic 9 Hibernian
  author: 4 Shaw 5 Behan, Burke, Joyce,
  Swift, Synge, Wilde, Yeats 6 O'Casey,
  Steele 7 Beckett, O'Connor 8 O'Faolain,
  Sheridan, Stephens 9 Goldsmith,
  O'Flaherty 13 St John Gogarty
  leader: 4 Tone 6 Devlin, Valera 7
  Grattan, Parnell, Redmond 8 O'Connell 9
  Brian Boru 12 Saint Patrick
  legend: 9 Cuchulain 11 Finn MacCool
  language: 5 Irish 6 Gaelic 7 English
  religion: 8 Anglican 13 Roman Catholic

  feature:
  airport: 7 Shannon
  castle: 4 Tara 7 Blarney
  crystal: 9 Waterford
  dance: 3 jig 4 reel
  game: 7 hurling
  lottery: 16 Irish Sweepstakes
  manuscript: 11 Book of Kells
  museum: 10 James Joyce
  political movement: 8 Sinn Fein
  race: 10 Irish Derby
  relic: 13 Ardagh Chalice
  revolutionary society: 6 Fenian
  stone: 7 Blarney
  street: 8 O'Connell
  theater: 5 Abbey
  food:
  beer: 5 stout
Ireland forever
  Gaelic: 11 Erin go bragh
I Remember Mama
  director: 13 George Stevens
  based on play by: 13 John Van Druten
  cast: 10 Ellen Corby, Irene Dunne, Philip
  Dorn 12 Oscar Homolka 16 Barbara Bel
  Geddes
  setting: 12 San Francisco
Irene
  member of: 5 Horae
  personifies: 5 peace
  corresponds to: 3 Pax
iridescence 7 glitter 11 opalescence, pearl-
  iness 12 nacreousness, play of colors
iridescent 5 shiny 7 glowing 8 colorful, na-
  creous 9 prismatic 10 changeable, opalescent 11 rainbowlike
iris
  varieties: 3 fan, red 4 roof, wall, wild 5
  Dutch, dwarf, house 6 copper, German,
  orchid, Sierra, Spuria, violet, yellow 7 African, bearded, crested, English, Evansia,
  Lamance, peacock, Persian, Prairie,
  Spanish, walking 8 Japanese, mourning, Siberian, stinking 9 beachhead,
  beardless, butterfly, Palestine 10 snake's-
  head
Iris
  goddess of: 7 rainbow
  messenger of: 4 gods
  father: 7 Thaumas
  mother: 7 Electra
  sisters: 7 Harpies
  husband: 8 Zephyrus
Irish 4 Erse 4 Celtic, dander, Gaelic, temper
  accent: 6 brogue
  death spirit: 7 banshee
  flower: 8 shamrock
  girl: 7 colleen
  king: 9 Brian Boru
  legislature: 4 Dail
  saint: 7 Patrick
  society: 8 Sinn Fein
  theater: 5 Abbey

Irish gods 14 Tuatha De Danann
Irishman 4 Celt, Gael, Kelt, Mick 5 Paddy 7 Irisher 9 Hibernian, orangeman 10 bogtrotter
Irish Mist
  origin: 7 Ireland
  ingredient: 5 cream 12 Irish whiskey
Irish Mythology
  cats: 8 Kilkenny
  fairies: 4 Side
  god of love/beauty/youth: 7 Angus Og
  god of poetry/eloquence: 4 Ogma
  god of sea: 8 Manannan
  gods: 14 Tuatha De Danann
  hero: 10 Cuchulainn
  invaders/ancestors: 9 Milesians
  king: 4 Bres 5 Ronan 9 Conchobar 10 Matholwych
  king of gods: 4 Finn 5 Fionn
  pirate/demon: 8 Fomorian
  sea goddess: 3 Ler, Lir
  spirit: 4 Puca 5 Pooka
  corresponds to British: 4 Puck
irk 3 bug, vex 4 gall 5 annoy 6 bother, pester, ruffle 7 provoke 8 irritate
irksome 5 pesky 6 plaguy, vexing 7 plaguey, tedious 8 annoying, tiresome, wearying 9 difficult, provoking, vexatious, wearisome 10 bothersome, irritating, nettlesome 11 troublesome
iron
  chemical symbol: 2 Fe
Iron Age
  period of: 4 time
  followed age of: 6 Bronze
ironclad 5 fixed 6 strict 9 immutable, permanent 10 inexorable, inflexible, rigoristic, unchanging 11 irrevocable, unalterable 12 irreversible, unchangeable, unmodifiable
Iron Horse
  nickname of: 9 Lou Gehrig
ironic, ironical 3 odd 5 funny, weird 6 biting 7 abusive, caustic, curious, cutting, mocking, strange 8 derisive, sardonic, sneering, stinging 9 facetious, insincere, pretended, sarcastic 10 surprising, unexpected 11 implausible, incongruous 12 inconsistent 13 contradictory
irons 5 bonds 6 chains 7 fetters, presses, smooths 8 manacles, shackles 9 golf clubs, handcuffs 10 restraints
Ironside
  character: 7 (Det Sgt) Ed Brown 10 Mark Sanger 11 Fran Belding 12 Eve Whitfield 14 Robert Ironside
  cast: 11 Don Galloway, Don Mitchell, Raymond Burr 13 Elizabeth Baur 15 Barbara Anderson
irony 7 mockery, sarcasm 9 absurdity 11 incongruity, indirection 12 contrariness 13 facetiousness 14 implausibility
Iroquoian
  tribe: 6 Cayuga, Mohawk, Oneida, Seneca 8 Cherokee, Iroquois, Onandaga 9 Tuscarora 12 Kaniengehaga

Iroquois
  language family: 9 Iroquoian
  tribe: 6 Cayuga, Mohawk, Oneida, Seneca 8 Onondaga 9 Tuscarora
  location: 6 Canada 7 New York 11 Connecticut 13 Massachusetts
  leader: 11 Cornplanter, Joseph Brant
  formed: 10 Six Nations 19 League of the Iroquois
  supernatural force: 6 Orenda
  prophet: 10 Ganiodaiyo
irra
  origin: 8 Akkadian
  god of: 10 pestilence
irrational 6 absurd 7 foolish, unsound 8 baseless 9 illogical, unfounded 10 ill-advised, unthinking 11 nonsensical, unreasoning 12 unreasonable
irreclaimable 4 lost 6 wicked 7 corrupt, debased 9 abandoned, reprobate 12 disreputable, irredeemable, irreformable 16 beyond redemption
irreconcilable 7 opposed 12 incompatible, inconsistent, intransigent, unadjustable, unappeasable, unbridgeable
irreformable 6 wicked 7 corrupt 9 abandoned, reprobate, shameless 11 unrepentant 12 disreputable 13 irreclaimable
irrefutable 10 undeniable 13 indisputable, not refutable 13 proof positive 14 unquestionable 16 incontrovertible
irrefutably 6 surely 10 definitely, positively, undeniably 12 conclusively, indisputably 13 incontestably 14 unquestionably 16 incontrovertibly
irregular 3 odd 5 bumpy, queer, rough 6 broken, uneven 7 crooked, unusual 8 aberrant, abnormal, improper, peculiar, singular 9 anomalous, desultory, eccentric, haphazard, not smooth, out of line, unaligned, unfitting 10 indecorous, unexpected, unsuitable 12 asymmetrical, unmethodical, unsystematic 13 inappropriate, nonconforming 14 unconventional 16 uncharacteristic
irregularity 7 anomaly 9 asymmetry, deviation 10 aberration, divergence, unevenness 11 abnormality, peculiarity 12 constipation, eccentricity
irrelevant 5 inapt 7 foreign, off base 9 unfitting, unrelated 10 extraneous, immaterial, malapropos, not apropos, not germane 11 impertinent, unconnected 12 nonpertinent 14 beside the point
irreligion 7 atheism 8 apostasy, unbelief 9 disbelief 11 godlessness
irreligious 6 unholy 7 godless, impious, profane, ungodly 8 agnostic 9 atheistic 10 irreverent 11 unbelieving 12 not religious, sacrilegious
irremediable 8 hopeless 9 incurable 11 irreparable 12 beyond remedy
irreparable 9 unfixable 10 remediless 12 irremediable, irreversible 13 beyond redress, uncompensable, uncorrectable
irreplaceable 6 unique 9 essential 13 indispensable

irrepressible 7 vibrant **8** bubbling, galvanic, undamped **9** ebullient **10** boisterous, full of life **11** tempestuous **12** unquenchable **13** unsquelchable **14** uncontrollable, unrestrainable

irreproachable 8 flawless **9** blameless, faultless, stainless, unspotted **10** impeccable, inculpable **11** unblemished **12** above reproof, without fault **13** unimpeachable

irresistible 8 alluring, enticing **9** beckoning, seductive **10** enchanting, superhuman **11** tantalizing **12** overpowering, overwhelming

irresolute 4 weak **6** fickle, unsure **8** doubtful, hesitant, unsteady, wavering **9** faltering, uncertain, undecided, unsettled **10** changeable, hesitating, indecisive, unresolved **11** vacillating

irresolution 5 doubt **9** hesitancy **10** hesitation, indecision

irresponsibility 8 rashness **10** immaturity, imprudence **11** foolishness **12** carelessness, heedlessness, indifference, indiscretion, recklessness **13** unreliability **15** thoughtlessness, undependability **17** untrustworthiness

irresponsible 4 rash **7** foolish **8** careless, immature, reckless **9** imprudent, overhasty **10** capricious, incautious, unreliable **11** harebrained, indifferent, injudicious, thoughtless **12** undependable **13** illconsidered, untrustworthy **14** not responsible, scatterbrained

irresponsible person
French: 14 enfant terrible

irreverence 7 impiety **9** blasphemy, sacrilege **10** irreligion

irreverent 5 saucy **6** brazen **7** impious, profane **8** critical, impudent, sneering **9** debunking, shameless, skeptical, slighting **11** blasphemous, disparaging, irreligious **12** nose-thumbing **13** disrespectful

irrevocable 5 final **10** conclusive **11** unalterable **12** irreversible, unchangeable

irritability 6 spleen **8** acerbity, edginess **9** crossness, huffiness, petulance, testiness **10** crabbiness, crankiness, impatience **11** fretfulness, peevishness, short temper, waspishness **12** irascibility

irritable 5 testy **6** grumpy, touchy **7** fretful, grouchy, peevish, pettish, waspish **8** snappish **9** impatient, irascible **10** ill-humored **11** easily vexed, ill-tempered

irritate 3 irk, vex **5** anger, annoy, chafe, peeve **6** nettle, worsen **7** inflame, provoke **8** make sore **9** aggravate, make angry **10** exasperate

irritated 3 mad, raw **4** sore **5** cross, irked, irate, testy, vexed **6** chafed, crabby, galled, miffed, peeved, piqued, put out **7** annoyed, burning, nettled, peevish **8** burned up, choleric, incensed, inflamed, provoked **9** impatient, irascible **10** aggravated **11** exasperated

irritating 5 acrid, harsh, rough **7** caustic, chafing, galling, irksome, rasping **8** abrasive, annoying **9** provoking, vexatious **10**

bothersome **11** infuriating, troublesome **12** exasperating

irritation 6 bother **7** chafing **8** distress, vexation **9** annoyance **10** discomfort **11** irksomeness

irruption 4 raid **5** break, foray **6** inroad **7** upsurge **8** bursting, invasion **9** incursion, intrusion

Irus *see* **7** Arnaeus

Irving, John
author of: **20** The Hotel New Hampshire **23** The World According to Garp

Irving, Washington
author of: **10** Salmagundi **12** Rip Van Winkle **13** The Sketch Book **23** The Legend of Sleepy Hollow

Isaac
father: **7** Abraham
mother: **5** Sarah
brother: **7** Ishmael
wife: **7** Rebekah
son: **4** Esau **5** Jacob
birthplace: **5** Gerar
burial place: **9** Machpelah
blessed: **5** Jacob
sacrificed at: **6** Moriah

Isaac of York
character in: **7** Ivanhoe
author: **5** Scott

Isabella
character in: **17** Measure for Measure
author: **11** Shakespeare

Isaiah
means: **12** Jehovah saves
father: **4** Amoz
son: **11** Shearzashub **18** Maharshalalhashbaz

Iscariot *see* **5** Judas

Ischepolis
father: **9** Alcathous

Ischys
killed because of: **10** infidelity
loved: **7** Coronis
Coronis loved by: **6** Apollo

Isenstein
origin: **12** Scandinavian
home of: **8** Brunhild
location: **8** Isenland

I serve
German: **7** ich dien
motto of: **13** Prince of Wales

Iseult, Isolde
character in: **16** Arthurian romance

I shall rise again
Latin: **8** resurgam

Ishbosheth
father: **4** Saul
killed by: **6** Baanah, Rechab
burial place: **6** Hebron

Isherwood, Christopher
author of: **13** Berlin Stories **17** Down There on a Visit
character: **11** Sally Bowles

Ishmael
character in: **8** Moby Dick
author: **8** Melville

Ishmael
father: 7 Abraham
mother: 5 Hagar
means: 11 God will hear
brother: 5 Isaac
son: 5 Kedar 7 Kedemah
descendant of: 10 Ishmaelite

Ishtar
also: 7 Mylitta
origin: 8 Assyrian 10 Babylonian
goddess of: 3 war 4 love
queen of: 6 heaven
corresponds to: 6 Inanna 7 Astarte 9 Ashtoreth

Ishum
origin: 8 Akkadian
god of: 4 fire
companion: 4 Irra

Isis
origin: 8 Egyptian
goddess of: 9 fertility
hieroglyphic symbol: 6 throne
husband: 6 Osiris
brother: 6 Osiris
son: 5 Horus
father: 3 Geb, Keb
mother: 3 Nut
horns of: 3 cow
headdress: 9 solar disk
corresponds to: 2 Io

Iskowitz, B Edward Israel
real name of: 11 Eddie Cantor

Islam
adherent: 4 Sufi 5 Shiah 6 Moslem, Muslim, Shiite, Wahabi 7 Sunnite 8 Islamite 9 Mussulman 10 Mohammedan
crusade: 5 Jahad, Jihad
deity: 5 Allah
flight from Mecca: 6 hegira
founder/prophet: 8 Mohammed, Muhammad
holy city: 5 Mecca 6 Medina
other names: 9 Moslemism 13 Mohammedanism
pilgrimage to Mecca: 4 hadj
priest: 4 imam
scripture: 5 Koran

Islamabad
capital of: 8 Pakistan

Islamic 6 Moslem, Muslim 10 Mohammedan

island 4 isle 5 atoll, haven, islet, oasis 6 refuge 7 enclave, retreat, shelter 9 sanctuary

Islands of the Blessed see 10 Hesperides

isle, islet 3 ait, cay, key 4 holm 5 islet 6 island

Isle of Cloves see 8 Tanzania

Isle of Spice see 7 Grenada

Isleta (Tuei)
language family: 6 Pueblo, Tanoan
location: 9 New Mexico, Rio Grande

Ismene
father: 7 Oedipus
mother: 7 Jocasta
uncle: 5 Creon
sister: 8 Antigone

brother: 9 Polynices

isn't that so?
French: 9 n'est-ce pas?
German: 9 nicht wahr?

isolate 6 banish, detach 7 seclude 8 insulate, separate, set apart 9 segregate, sequester 10 disconnect, place apart, quarantine

isolated 4 lone, solo 5 alone, apart 6 cut off, lonely, remote, unique 7 insular, removed 8 detached, secluded, set apart, solitary 9 separated, unrelated 10 segregated 11 out-of-the-way, quarantined, sequestered

isolation 7 privacy 8 solitude 9 aloneness, apartness, hermitism, seclusion 10 desolation, detachment, insularity, insulation, quarantine, separation 11 confinement, segregation 12 separateness

Isoptera
class: 8 hexapoda
phylum: 10 arthropoda
group: 7 termite 8 white ant

Ispahan
also: 7 Isfahan 8 Aspadana
location: 4 Iran
capital of: 6 Persia
river: 8 Zayandeh

I Speak for Thaddeus Stevens
author: 15 Elsie Singmaster

I Spy
character: 13 Kelly Robinson 14 Alexander Scott
cast: 9 Bill Cosby 10 Robert Culp
Kelly's cover: 9 tennis pro

Israel
former name: 5 Jacob
means: 12 soldier of God
wrestled with: 5 angel

Israel
other name: 4 Zion 6 Canaan, Yishuv 9 Palestine 12 Promised Land
capital: 9 Jerusalem
largest city: 12 Tel Aviv-Jaffa
others: 4 Acre, Elat, Gaza 5 Eilat, Elath, Haifa, Holon, Jaffa, Jenin 6 Ashdod, Bat Yam, Dimona, Hebron, Nablus 7 Netanya, Rehovot, Tel Aviv 8 Nazareth, Ramallah, Ramat Gan 9 Beersheba, Bene Beraq, Bethlehem
school: 6 Hebrew 14 Technion-Israel 26 Weizmann Institute of Science
division: 5 Judea, Negev, Sinai 7 Galilee 8 West Bank 9 Gaza Strip 12 Golan Heights
government:
legislature: 7 Knesset
political parties: 5 Labor, Likud, Mapam
measure: 3 cab, car, hin, kab, kor 4 bath, ezba, omer, reed 5 cubit, donum, dunam, ephah, ganeh, homer, kaneh
monetary unit: 3 mil 5 agora, agura, pound, pruta 6 agorot, shekel
lake: 5 Huleh 7 Dead Sea 8 Kinneret, Tiberias 12 Sea of Galilee
mountain: 4 Nafh, Sagi 5 Harif, Ramon, Tabor 6 Atzmon, Carmel, Hatira

highest point: 5 Meron **6** Meiron
river: 4 Qarn **5** Faria, Malik, Sareq **6** Hadera, Jordan, Kishon, Qishon, Sarida, Yarkon, Yarmuk **7** Lakhish
sea: 3 Red **4** Dead **7** Galilee **13** Mediterranean
physical feature:
bay: 5 Haifa
desert: **5** Negev, Sinai
gulf: **5** Aqaba
plain: 5 Judea **6** Sharon **7** Zebulun **9** Esdraelon
people: 3 Jew **4** Arab **5** Druze **10** Circassian
ancient: **6** Hebrew
immigrant: **4** olim
Jew born in Israel: **5** sabra
leader: 4 Eban, Meir **5** Begin, Dayan, Herzl, Peres, Rabin **6** Ben-Zvi, Eshkol **7** Sharett **8** Weizmann **9** Ben-Gurion
language: 6 Arabic, French, Hebrew **7** English, Yiddish
religion: 5 Baha'i, Islam **7** Judaism **12** Christianity
place:
church: **13** Holy Sepulcher
gates to Old Jerusalem: **3** New **4** Dung, Zion **5** Jaffa **6** Herod's **8** Damascus **10** St Stephen's
mosque: **13** Dome of the Rock
mount: **4** Zion **6** Olives, Scopus
shrine: **3** Bab **4** Book **11** Wailing Wall, Western Wall **18** Garden of Gethsemane
tomb: **9** Sanhedrin **10** King David's
way of sorrows: **11** Via Dolorosa
feature: 14 Dead Sea Scrolls
collective village: 7 kibbutz **9** kibbutzim
cooperative village: **6** moshav **8** moshavim
dance: **4** hora
movement: **7** Zionism
Palestinian uprising: **8** intifada
peace agreement: **16** Camp David Accords
tree: **5** judas
wave of immigration: **5** aliya **6** aliyot
food:
dish: **4** pita **6** hummus **7** falafel
Israel, tribes of 3 Dan, Gad **4** Levi **5** Asher, Judah **6** Joseph, Reuben, Simeon **7** Zebulun **8** Benjamin, Issachar, Naphtali
Israel-born
Hebrew: 5 sabra
Israelite 3 Jew **6** Hebrew, Jewish, Semite **7** Judaist **8** Hebraist
descended from: 5 Jacob
king: 4 Ahab, Elah, Jehu, Omri, Saul **5** David, Hosea, Nadab, Zimri
Issachar
father: 5 Jacob
mother: 5 Leah
brother: 3 Dan, Gad **4** Levi **5** Asher, Judah **6** Joseph, Reuben, Simeon **7** Zebulun **8** Benjamin, Naphtali
sister: 5 Dinah
descendant of: 11 Issacharite

Is Sex Necessary?
author: 7 E B White **12** James Thurber
issuance 8 emission **9** allotment, discharge, emanation **12** dispensation, distribution
issue 4 gush, rise, stem **5** allot, arise, ensue, erupt, go out, heirs, spout, yield **6** emerge, follow, number, result, spring **7** dispute, emanate, flow out, give out, outcome, outflow, pass out, problem, proceed, product, progeny **8** children, dispense, drainage, eruption, granting, heritors, issuance, question **9** circulate, discharge, effluence, grow out of, offspring, posterity, pour forth **10** distribute, outpouring **11** consequence, descendants, publication **12** dispensation, distributing
Istanbul
area: 7 Beyoglu **8** Stamboul
capital of: 6 Turkey
formerly: 9 Byzantium **14** Constantinople
landmark: 10 Hippodrome **11** Hagia Sophia **12** Galata Bridge **14** Bosporus Bridge **26** Palais de la Culture d'Istanbul
mosque: 3 New **8** Mihrimah **9** Yeni Camli **11** Suleymaniye
museum: 13 Topkapi Palace **14** Archaeological **20** Turkish and Islamic Art
rulers: 4 Rome **6** Athens, Darius, Rhodes, Sparta **8** Persians, Suleiman **9** Macedonia **11** Latin Empire **12** Ottoman Turks **15** Byzantine Empire, Turkish Republic **19** Constantine the Great
sea: 5 Black **7** Marmara **8** Bosporus **10** Golden Horn
isthmus 4 neck, spit **5** point, strip **6** narrow, strait, tongue **7** narrows
name: 4 Suez **6** Panama **7** Corinth
Isus
father: 5 Priam
killed by: 9 Agamemnon
I sustain the wings
Latin: 12 sustineo alas
motto of: 10 US Air Force
Italiano, Anna Maria Louise
real name of: 12 Anne Bancroft
Italic
language family: 12 Indo-European
branch: 5 Latin, Oscan **7** Umbrian
Italy
also: 8 Hesperia
capital/largest city: 4 Roma, Rome
others: 4 Pisa **5** Genoa, Milan, Padua, Turin, Udine **6** Amalfi, Ancona, Assisi, Naples, Rimini, Savona, Venice, Verona **7** Bologna, Bolzano, Brescia, Catania, Messina, Palermo, Ravenna, Taranto, Trieste **8** Florence
division: 6 Apulia, Latium, Marche, Molise, Umbria, Veneto **7** Abruzzi, Liguria, Tuscany **8** Calabria, Campania, Lombardy, Piedmont **10** Basilicata **12** Valle d'Agosta **13** Emilia-Romagna **17** Trentino-Alto Adige **19** Friuli-Venezia Giulia
independent enclave: **9** San Marino **11** Vatican City

measure: 3 pie 4 orna 5 palma, palmo, punto, salma, stero 6 barile, miglie, moggio, rubbio, tomolo 7 braccio, secchio 8 giornata, quadrato

monetary unit: 4 lira, lire, tara 5 grano, paolo, soldo 6 danaro, denaro, ducato 7 testone 8 zecchino 9 centesini

weight: 5 carat, libra, oncia, pound 6 denaro, libbra

island: 4 Elba 5 Capri, Egadi, Eolie 6 Ischia, Istria, Linosa, Lipari, Sicily, Ustica 7 Aeolian, Trieste, Vulcano 8 Lampione, Sardinia 9 Borromean, Lampedusa, Stromboli 10 Isola Bella 11 Pantelleria

lake: 4 Como, Iseo, Nemi 5 Garda 6 Albano, Lesina, Lugano, Varano 7 Bolsena, Perugia 8 Maggiore 9 Bracciano, Trasimeno

mountain: 4 Alps, Etna, Visa 5 Amaro, Blanc, Corno, Somma 6 Cimone, Ortles 9 Apennines, Dolomites, Maritimes 11 Gennargentu 12 Gran Paradiso 16 Abruzzi Apennines

Alps: 6 Apuane, Carnic, Julian, Otztal 7 Bernina 8 Ligurian 9 Lepontine

volcano: 7 Vulcano 8 Vesuvius 9 Stromboli

highest point: 4 Rosa

river: 2 Po 4 Adda, Agri, Arno, Liri, Nera, Reno, Sele, Taro 5 Adige, Crati, Mannu, Oglio, Parma, Piave, Salso, Stura, Tiber, Tirso 6 Aniene, Belice, Isonzo, Mincio, Ofanto, Panaro, Rapido, Sangro, Simeto, Tanaro, Tevere, Ticino 7 Biferno, Bradano, Chienti, Metauro, Montone, Ombrone, Pescara, Rubicon, Secchia, Trebbia 8 Volturno

sea: 6 Ionian 8 Adriatic, Ligurian 10 Tyrrhenian 13 Mediterranean

physical feature:

bay: 6 Naples

channel: 5 Malta

grotto: 4 Blue

gulf: 5 Gaeta, Genoa 6 Venice 7 Salerno, Taranto 11 Manfredonia

hills of Rome: 7 Caelian, Viminal 8 Aventine, Palatine, Quirinal 9 Esquiline 10 Capitoline

lagoon: 6 Venice

pass: 5 Resia 6 Maloja 7 Bernina, Brenner, Simplon 9 Mont Cenis 13 Saint Gotthard 17 Great Saint Bernard

resort: 14 Italian Riviera

strait: 6 Sicily 7 Messina, Otranto 9 Bonifacio

people: 7 Italian

ancient: 5 Latin, Remus 6 Sabine 7 Lombard, plebian, Romulus 8 Etruscan 9 patrician

architect: 5 Nervi, Ponti, Salvi 6 Vasari 7 Alberti, Guarini, Juvarra, Vignola 8 Ammanati, Bramante, Palladio 9 Borromini, De Sanctis 12 Brunelleschi, Michelangelo

artist: 5 Balla, Carra 6 Batoni, Gaulli, Guardi, Titian 7 Bellini, Chirico, Cimabue, Cortona, Da Vinci, Raphael, Tiepolo, Uccello 8 Carracci, Mantegna, Masaccio, Severini 9 Benvenuti, Canoletto, Giorgione 10 Botticelli, Caravaggio, Modigliani, Tintoretto 11 Buoninsegna, Fra Angelico 12 Michelangelo 13 Giotto Bondone 14 della Francesca

composer: 5 Verdi 7 Bellini, Cavalli, Corelli, Puccini, Rossini, Vivaldi 8 Mascagni, Piccinni 9 Donizetti, Scarlatti 10 Monteverdi, Palestrina 11 Leoncavallo

emperor: 4 Nero, Otho 5 Galba, Nerva, Titus 6 Trajan 7 Hadrian 8 Caligula, Claudius, Commodus, Domitian, Octavian, Tiberius 9 Caracalla, Vespasian, Vitellius 10 Diocletian 11 Constantine 13 Antoninus Dius 14 Caesar Augustus, Marcus Aurelius

film director: 6 de Sica 7 Fellini 8 Visconti 9 Antonioni 10 Bertolucci, Rossellini, Wertmuller, Zeffirelli

god: 4 Juno, Mars 5 Ceres, Diana, Janus, Lares, Venus 6 Apollo, Vulcan 7 Bacchus, Jupiter, Minerva, Neptune, Penates 8 Quirinus

Italian author: 4 Levi 5 Bembo, Bruno, Pulci, Tasso 6 Artino, Vasari 7 Ariosto, Bassani, Deledda, Moravia 8 Bandello, Petrarch 9 Boccaccio, D'Annunzio, Sannazaro 10 Cavalcanti, Guinicelli, Metastasio, Pirandello, Straparola 11 Castiglione, Machiavelli 12 Guicciardini, Michelangelo 14 Dante Alighieri

Latin author: 4 Cato, Livy, Ovid 5 Pliny, Varro 6 Cicero, Gallus, Horace, Seneca, Vergil, Virgil 7 Donatus, Juvenal, Martial, Plautus, Sallust, Tacitus, Terence 8 Boethius, Catullus, Lucilius, St Jerome 9 St Ambrose, Suetonius 11 St Augustine

ruler: 4 Moro 5 Cavour, Enrico 7 Mazzini 9 Mussolini 10 Berlinguer 14 Victor Emmanuel 15 Alcide de Gasperi

ruler/military leader: 5 Sulla 6 Brutus, Pompey, Seneca 7 Crassus, Lepidus 8 Gracchus 10 Mark Antony 12 Gaius Marious, Julius Caesar 15 Cassius Longinus, Scipio Africanus 18 Tarquinius Superbus

ruling family of city-state: 4 Este 6 Medici, Sforza 8 Visconti

sculptor: 6 Canova, Marini, Pisano 7 Bernini, Bologna, Cellini 8 Antelami, Boccioni, Ghiberti 9 Donatello, Sansovino 10 Giacometti, Pollaiuolo, Verrocchio 11 Della Robbia 12 Michelangelo

wife: 7 Poppaea 9 Agrippina, Messalina 13 Livia Drusilla

language: 5 Ladin, Latin 6 French, German 7 Italian, Slovene 8 Friulian 9 Sardinian

religion: 13 Roman Catholic

place:

arch: 11 Constantine

baths: 9 Caracalla

bridge: 5 Sighs 12 Ponte Vecchio

cathedral/church: 5 Siena 7 St Mark's, Vatican 8 San Marco, St Peter's 13 Sistine Chapel *fountain:* 5 Trevi

museum: 5 Duomo 6 Uffizi 8 Bargello, National 10 Capitoline 11 Pitti Palace, Villa Giulia 16 Galterio Borghese

opera house: 7 La Scala

palace: 5 Doges

road: 9 Appian Way

ruins: 5 Forum 7 Capitol, Pompeii 8 Pantheon 9 Catacombs, Colosseum 11 Herculaneum 13 Circus Maximus

steps: 7 Spanish

tower: 18 Leaning Tower of Pisa

feature:

unification movement: 12 Risorgimento

food:

cheese: 6 romano 7 fontina, ricotta 8 parmesan

dish: 5 pizza 6 scampi 7 gnocchi, lasagna, lasagne, polenta, ravioli, risotto 9 antipasti, antipasto 17 chicken cacciatora, cacciatore

ice cream: 6 gelato 7 spumoni

meat: 6 salami 9 pepperoni 10 mortadella, prosciutto

soup: 8 caciucco 10 minestrone

wine: 7 Chianti

itch 3 yen 4 ache, long, pine 5 crave, crawl, creep, yearn 6 desire, hanker, hunger, thirst, tickle 7 craving, prickle 8 appetite, have a yen, pruritis, tingling, yearning 9 hankering

it does not follow

Latin: 11 non sequitur

item 4 unit 5 entry, piece, point, story, thing 6 detail, matter, notice, report 7 account, article, feature, subject 8 dispatch, notation 9 paragraph 10 particular 11 news article

itemization 4 list 7 listing 11 enumeration

itemize 6 detail 7 specify 8 spell out 9 enumerate

items of business 4 list 6 agenda, docket 7 program 8 schedule

iterate 6 repeat 7 restate 9 reiterate

It Girl

nickname of: 8 Clara Bow

it grows as it goes

Latin: 12 crescit eundo

motto of: 9 New Mexico

It Happened One Night

director: 10 Frank Capra

cast: 8 Alan Hale, Ward Bond 10 Clark Gable 11 Roscoe Karns 14 Walter Connolly 16 Claudette Colbert

Oscar for: 5 actor (Gable) 7 actress (Colbert), picture 8 director

remade as: 16 Eve Knew Her Apples 20 You Can't Run Away from It

I think therefore I am

Latin: 13 cogito ergo sum

said by: 9 Descartes

Ithomatas *see* 4 Zeus

Ithun, Ithunn *see* 4 Idun

itinerant 5 nomad, rover 6 roamer, roving 7 migrant, nomadic, roaming, vagrant 8 vagabond, wanderer, wayfarer 9 footloose, transient, traveling, wandering, wayfaring 11 peripatetic

itinerary 3 log 5 diary, route 6 course 7 account, circuit, day book, journal 8 schedule 9 timetable 10 travel plan

it is not clear; it is not evident

Latin: 9 non liquet

it is not lawful; it is not permitted

Latin: 8 non licet

it is sweet to do nothing

Italian: 14 dolce far niente

Itonia

epithet of: 6 Athena

It's a Gift

director: 13 Norman Z McLeod

cast: 8 W C Fields 9 Baby LeRoy, Tommy Bupp 10 T Roy Barnes 13 Charles Sellon, Morgan Wallace 14 Kathleen Howard

remake of: 17 It's the Old Army Game

It's a Wonderful Life

director: 10 Frank Capra

cast: 9 Donna Reed 11 Beulah Bondi 12 Henry Travers, James Stewart 13 Gloria Grahame 15 Lionel Barrymore

remade as: 22 It Happened One Christmas

itsy-bitsy 3 wee 4 tiny 5 dwarf, pygmy, small, teeny 6 bantam, little, minute, petite 9 miniature, miniscule 10 diminutive, teeny-weeny 11 microscopic, pocket-sized

It Takes a Thief

character: 8 Noah Bain 12 Alister Mundy, Wallie Powers 14 Alexander Mundy

cast: 11 Edward Binns, Fred Astaire 12 Robert Wagner 13 Malachi Throne

Itylus

father: 6 Zethus

mother: 5 Aedon

killed by: 5 Aedon

Itys

father: 6 Tereus

mother: 6 Procne

killed by: 6 Procne

to revenge: 9 Philomela

Itza

language family: 6 Toltec

location: 6 Mexico 7 Chichen, Yucatan 14 Central America

Iulus *see* 8 Ascanius

Ivanhoe

author: 14 Sir Walter Scott

character: 7 Rebecca 8 Guilbert 9 Robin Hood 10 Lady Rowena 11 Isaac of York 12 King Richard I 14 Cedric the Saxon, Sir Brian de Bois 16 Wilfred of Ivanhoe 19 King Richard the First

Ivanhoe, Burle Icle

real name of: 8 Burl Ives

I've Got a Secret

host: 10 Bill Cullen, Garry Moore, Steve Allen

Ives, Burl

real name: 16 Burle Icle Ivanhoe

nickname: 17 Wayfaring Stranger

born: 6 Hunt IL

roles: 8 Big Daddy **10** East of Eden **13** The Big Country **14** Our Man in Havana **16** Cat on a Hot Tin Roof **18** Desire Under the Elms

Ives, Charles

born: 9 Danbury CT

composer of: 11 Putnam's Camp **13** Concord Sonata **19** Washington's Birthday **20** Central Park in the Dark **21** The Unanswered Question **23** Three Places in New England

Ivory Coast

capital/largest city: 7 Abidjan

new capital: **12** Yamoussoukro

others: 3 Man **4** Divo **5** Daloa, Tabou **6** Adzobe, Bonoua, Bouake, Danane, Gagnoa **7** Korhogo, Odienne, Seguela **8** Dimbokro **9** Agboville, Bondoukou, Sassandra **10** Abengourou **11** Grand Bassam **14** Ferkessedougou

monetary unit: 5 franc **7** centime

highest point: 5 Nimba

river: 3 Bia **5** Comoe, Komoe **7** Bandama, Cavally **9** Sassandra

ocean: 8 Atlantic

physical feature:

cape: **6** Palmas

gulf: **6** Guinea

lagoon: **3** Aby **5** Ebrie

wind: **9** harmattan

people: 4 Abe, Dan, Kru, Kwa **4** Akan, Bete, Dida, Guro, Koua, Lobi, Wobe **5** Abron, Abure, Attie, Baule, Guere, Mande, Mossi **6** Baoule, Lagoon, Senufo, Senufu **7** Dan Guro, Kroumen, Malinke, Voltaic **10** Anyi-Baoule **11** Lobi-Kulango **12** Agnis-Ashanti

language: 4 Akan **6** Dioula, French

religion: 5 Islam **7** animism **13** Roman Catholic

place:

canal: **5** Vridi

dam: **7** Bandama

game reserve: **9** Sassandra

feature: **7** kola nut

Ivory Coast *see* **11** Sierra Leone

ivory-towered 6 remote **8** academic, romantic **11** conjectural, impractical, theoretical, unrealistic **12** hypothetical

ivy 6 Cissus, Hedera **15** Kalmia latifolia

varieties: 3 fan, red **4** baby, tree **5** grape, Irish, Nepal, water **6** aralia, Baltic, Boston, canary, devil's, German, ground, marine, parlor, poison, spider, switch **7** colchis, English, Italian, Madeira, Mexican, parsley, Persian, Swedish **8** Algerian, American, coliseum, fragrant, Japanese, red-flame **9** bird's-foot, ghost-tree, heart-leaf **10** five-leaved, Kenilworth, variegated **12** Hagenburger's **13** Solomon Island **14** miniature grape **15** Gloire-de-Marengo

Ivy League colleges 4 Yale **5** Brown **7** Cornell, Harvard **8** Columbia **9** Dartmouth, Princeton **12** Pennsylvania (Penn)

I Want to Live!

director: 10 Robert Wise

cast: 12 Simon Oakland, Susan Hayward (Barbara Graham) **13** Theodore Bikel **15** Virginia Vincent

score: 12 Johnny Mandel

Oscar for: 7 actress (Hayward)

I will defend

Latin: 6 tuebor

IWW 8 Wobblies **10** labor union **27** Industrial Workers of the World

leader: 4 Debs **6** DeLeon **7** Haywood

members: 6 miners **9** lumbermen **16** migratory workers

Ixion

king of: 8 Lapithae

wife: 3 Dia

son: 9 Pirithous

children: 8 centaurs

loved: 4 Hera

punished by: 4 Zeus

bound to: 5 wheel

Iyar 17 second Hebrew month

Iynx

father: 3 Pan

mother: 4 Echo

Izmir

formerly: 6 Smyrna

location: 6 Turkey **9** Aegean Sea **11** Gulf of Izmir

settle by: 7 Ionians **8** Aeolians

ruled by: 13 Ottoman Empire

J

ja 3 yes
jab 3 cut, dig, hit, rap, tap 4 belt, blow, bump, clip, goad, lick, pelt, plug, poke, poke, prod, sock, stab, swat 5 elbow, nudge, paste, swing 6 strike, stroke

Jabal
  father: 6 Lamech
  mother: 4 Adah
  brother: 5 Jubal

jabber 3 gab, gas 4 blab 5 clack, prate 6 babble, cackle, drivel, gibber, gossip, hot air, patter, ramble, rattle, raving 7 blabber, blather, chatter, gushing, maunder, palaver, prating, prattle, ranting, twaddle, twattle 8 chitchat, idle talk, nonsense, talk idly 9 gibberish 10 maundering 14 chitterchatter

jack 4 flag 5 knave 6 ensign
jackass 3 ass 4 fool, mule 5 burro, dummy, idiot 6 donkey

Jack Benny Show, The
  cast: 8 Mel Blanc 9 Dennis Day, Don Wilson 11 Frank Nelson 13 Artie Auerbach, Eddie (Rochester) Anderson 14 Mary Livingston
  Jack's car: 7 Maxwell
  Jack played: 6 violin

jacket 4 case, coat 5 cover 6 blazer, casing, folder, sheath 7 wrapper 8 envelope, mackinaw, wrapping 9 container, enclosure, short coat, sport coat 10 dinner coat 11 windbreaker

Jack Sheppard
  author: 16 William Ainsworth

Jackson, Andrew
  nickname: 10 Old Hickory
  presidential rank: 7 seventh
  party: 10 Democratic
  state represented: 2 TN 9 Tennessee
  defeated: 4 (Henry) Clay 5 (John Quincy) Adams
  vice president: 7 (John Caldwell) Calhoun 8 (Martin) Van Buren
  cabinet:
  state: 6 (Louis) McLane 7 (John) Forsyth 8 (Martin) Van Buren 10 (Edward) Livingston
  treasury: 5 (William John) Duane 6 (Louis) McLane, (Samuel Dulucenna) Ingham 8 (Levi) Woodbury
  war: 4 (Lewis) Cass 5 (John Henry) Eaton
  attorney general: 5 (Roger Brooke) Taney 6 (Benjamin Franklin) Butler 7 (John McPherson) Berrien
  navy: 6 (John) Branch 8 (Levi) Woodbury 9 (Mahlon) Dickerson
  postmaster general: 5 (William Taylor) Barry 7 (Amos) Kendall
  born: 8 Waxhaw SC
  died/buried: 11 Nashville TN
  education:
  college: 4 none
  studied: 3 law
  admitted to: 3 bar
  religion: 12 Presbyterian
  political career: 8 US Senate 24 US House of Representatives
  judge: 22 Tennessee Superior Court
  civilian career: 6 lawyer
  military service: 12 major general 16 brigadier general
  defeated: 6 Creeks 9 Cherokees
  captured: 9 Pensacola
  military governor of: 7 Florida
  notable events of lifetime/term:
  battle: 5 Alamo 10 New Orleans
  fought: 5 duels
  scandal/wife suspected of: 6 bigamy
  war: 8 Creek War 13 Revolutionary 16 First Seminole War 19 War of Eighteen Twelve
  father: 6 Andrew
  mother: 9 Elizabeth (Hutchinson)
  siblings: 4 Hugh 6 Robert
  wife: 6 Rachel (Donelson Robards)
  children:
  adopted: 11 wife's nephew 15 Andrew Jackson Jr

Jackson, Anne
  husband: 10 Eli Wallach
  born: 10 Millvale PA
  roles: 3 Luv 10 The Typists

Jackson, Charles
  author of: 14 The Lost Weekend

Jackson, Glenda
  born: 7 England 10 Birkenhead
  roles: 10 Elizabeth R 11 Women in Love (Oscar) 13 A Touch of Class (Oscar) 14 The Music Lovers 16 Mary Queen of Scots 18 Sunday Bloody Sunday
  politics: 11 Labour Party 18 Member of Parliament

Jackson, Jesse Louis
  party: 10 Democratic
  born: 12 Greenville SC
  education: 20 University of Illinois 26 Chicago Theological Seminary 49 North Carolina Agricultural and Technical State College
  religion: 7 Baptist
  political career: 17 Democratic primary
  civilian career: 4 SCLC 9 PUSH Excel

13 Operation PUSH 20 Operation Breadbasket 24 National Rainbow Coalition 37 Southern Christian Leadership Conference

Jackson, Michael
born: 2 IN 4 Gary
father: 6 Joseph
mother: 9 Katherine
siblings: 4 Tito 5 Janet, Randy 6 Jackie, La Toya, Marlon 7 Maureen 8 Jermaine
wife: 16 Lisa Marie Presley
trademark: 5 glove
recordings: 3 Bad 7 Triumph, Victory 8 Thriller 9 Dangerous 10 Off the Wall
film: 6 The Wiz
group: 8 Jacksons 11 Jackson Five

Jackson, Reggie
nickname: 13 Mister October
sport: 8 baseball
position: 8 outfield
known for: 7 hitting
team: 9 Oakland A's 14 New York Yankees 16 California Angels

Jackson, Shirley
author of: 10 The Lottery 28 We Have Always Lived in the Castle

Jackson, Stonewall (Thomas)
served in: 8 Civil War 10 Mexican War
side: 11 Confederate
battle: 7 Bull Run 8 Antietam, Richmond 9 Seven Days 14 Fredericksburg 16 Chancellorsville, Shenandoah Valley

Jacksonville
football team: 5 Bulls 7 Jaguars

Jacob
father: 5 Isaac
mother: 7 Rebekah
brother: 4 Esau
wives: 4 Leah 6 Rachel
concubines: 5 Bilah 6 Zilpah
son: 3 Dan, Gad 4 Levi 5 Asher, Judah 6 Joseph, Reuben, Simeon 7 Zebulun 8 Benjamin, Issachar, Naphtali
daughter: 5 Dinah
dream of: 6 ladder
wrestled with: 5 angel
name changed to: 6 Israel
burial place: 9 Machpelah

Jacob, Francois
field: 7 biology
nationality: 6 French
discovered: 3 RNA
awarded: 10 Nobel Prize

Jacobs, Amos Muzyad
real name of: 11 Danny Thomas

jade
species: 7 jadeite 8 nephrite
source: 5 Burma, China 6 Mexico 7 Mogaung 10 New Zealand 12 United States

jaded 5 blase, bored, sated, spent, stale, tired, weary 6 cloyed, dulled, fagged 7 glutted, satiate, spoiled, wearied, worn-out 8 dog-tired, fatigued, overused, satiated, shopworn, tired out 9 exhausted, played out, surfeited 11 overwearied 12 overindulged

jadeite
variety: 4 jade

Jael
husband: 5 Heber
killed: 11 Sisera

jagged 5 jaggy, rough, spiny 6 barbed, broken, craggy, nicked, ridged, rugged, snaggy, spiked, thorny, uneven, zigzag 7 angular, bristly, cragged, notched, pointed, spinous, studded 8 indented, serrated 9 irregular, knifelike 10 crenulated, sawtoothed 12 sharp-toothed

Jaggers, Mr
character in: 17 Great Expectations
author: 7 Dickens

jaguar 3 cat 5 tiger 6 feline 7 panther 8 uturuncu

jail 3 bag, can, jug, nab, pen 4 book, brig, bust, cell, keep, stir 5 clink, pinch, pound, run in, seize 6 arrest, collar, cooler, lockup, prison, take in 7 arraign, bring in, capture, confine, dungeon, slammer 8 bastille, big house, hoosegow, imprison, stockade 9 apprehend, black hole, calaboose, guardroom, workhouse 10 guardhouse 11 incarcerate, reformatory 12 halfway house, penitentiary, reform school, station house 13 hold in custody, police station 14 detention house 16 penal institution 17 house of correction

jailbird 3 con 5 felon 7 convict 8 prisoner

jailer 5 guard, screw 6 gaoler, keeper, warden 7 turnkey 9 custodian

Jair 11 Hebrew judge

Jakarta, Djakarta
capital of: 9 Indonesia

Jake's Thing
author: 12 Kingsley Amis

jalopy 3 car 4 auto, heap 5 motor 6 wheels 7 flivver, machine, vehicle 8 motorcar 9 tin lizzie 10 automobile

jam 3 fix, mob, ram, sea 4 army, cram, herd, host, mess, pack, push, stop 5 block, cease, crowd, crush, drove, flock, horde, pinch, press, shove, stall, stick, stuff, swarm, tie-up, wedge 6 arrest, edge in, pickle, plight, scrape, strait, throng, thrust, work in, worm in 7 congest, dilemma, foist in, force in, squeeze, suspend, trouble 8 hot water, obstruct, quandary, sandwich 9 interrupt, multitude, overcrowd 11 malfunction, predicament 13 agglomeration

Jamaica
name means: 18 land of wood and water
capital/largest city: 8 Kingston
others: 6 May Pen 8 Ocho Rios 9 Morant Bay, Port Maria, Port Royal 10 Mandeville, Montego Bay 11 Port Antonio, Spanish Town 12 Saint Ann's Bay, Savanna-la-Mar
head of state: 14 British monarch 15 governor general
monetary unit: 7 quattie
island: 4 Navy 15 Greater Antilles
mountain: 8 Sir John's
highest point: 4 Blue

river: 5 Black, Cobre, Great, Minho, White 9 Rio Grande

sea: 8 Atlantic 9 Caribbean

physical feature: 13 Portland Bight

area: 14 Cockpit Country

bay: 4 Buff, Hope, Long 6 Morant 9 Discovery 10 Black River, Bluefield's, Old Harbour

point: 6 Galina 8 Portland 9 North East, North West, South East 11 North Negril, South Negril

people: 7 African, Chinese 10 East Indian

ancient: 6 Arawak 7 Ciboney

discoverer: 8 Columbus

leader: 5 Seaga 6 Garvey, Manley 10 Bustamente

language: 6 Creole 7 English

religion: 7 Baptist 8 Anglican 9 Methodist 11 Church of God, Rastafarian 13 Roman Catholic

place:

beach: 11 Doctor's Cave

botanical garden: 4 Hope

racetrack: 12 Caymanas Park

feature:

evil spirits: 7 duppies

guerrilla fighters: 7 Maroons

tree: 4 poui 5 cedar, ceiba, mahoe, saman 6 cassia, guango 7 logwood 8 mahogany 9 casuarina, poinciana 10 silkcotton 11 lignum vitae

witch doctor: 8 obeah man

food:

coffee: 12 Blue Mountain

drink: 3 rum 4 jake 8 tia maria

fruit: 5 guava, mango 6 pawpaw

spicy soup: 9 pepper pot

jamboree 2 do 4 bash, gala 5 party, revel, spree 6 fiesta, frolic 7 blowout, jubilee, shindig 8 carnival, carousal, festival 9 festivity 11 celebration

French: 4 fete 13 fete champetre

James 7 apostle

also called: 12 James the Less

father: 7 Zebedee 8 Alphaeus

brother: 4 John, Levi 5 Judas

disciple of: 5 Jesus

killed by: 12 Herod Agrippa

with John called: 13 sons of thunder

James, Henry

author of: 11 Daisy Miller, The American 13 The Bostonians, The Golden Bowl 14 Roderick Hudson, The Ambassadors 15 The Aspern Papers 16 Washington Square 17 The Turn of the Screw, The Wings of the Dove 18 The Portrait of a Lady 19 Princess Casamassima

James, P D

author of: 12 Cover Her Face 13 Innocent Blood 15 Unnatural Causes 21 Shroud for a Nightingale 22 Death of an Expert Witness

character: 13 Adam Dalgliesh

James the Less see 5 James

jammed 4 full 5 stuck 6 filled, loaded, massed, packed, rammed, wedged 7 blocked, crammed, crowded, crushed, pressed, stuffed 8 overfull, squeezed 10 obstructed, sandwiched 11 overcrowded

Janacek, Leos

born: 8 Hukvaldy 14 Czechoslovakia

composer of: 5 Mladi, Youth 6 Jenufa 9 In the Mist 10 Taras Bulba 13 Katya Kabanova 14 Glagolitic Mass 17 On an Overgrown Path 18 The Makropoulus Case 21 From the House of the Dead, The Cunning Little Vixen 24 The Diary of One Who Vanished, The Excursions of Mr Broucek

Jane

character in: 6 Tarzan

author: 9 Burroughs

Jane Eyre

author: 15 Charlotte Bronte

character: 5 Mason 7 Mrs Reed 10 Grace Poole, Mary Rivers, Mrs Fairfax 11 Adele Varens, Bertha Mason, Diana Rivers 12 Bessie Leaven, St John Rivers 13 Blanche Ingram 15 Edward Rochester

school: 6 Lowood

house: 10 Thornfield

director: 15 Robert Stevenson

cast: 11 Orson Welles 12 Joan Fontaine 14 Margaret O'Brien

jangle 3 din, jar 4 ring 5 annoy, chime, clang, clank, clash, crash, upset 6 jingle, racket, rattle 7 clangor, clatter, grate on 8 irritate 9 cacophony 11 reverberate 13 reverberation 14 tintinnabulate

janitor 5 super 6 porter 8 handyman 9 caretaker, custodian, janitress 11 cleaning man 12 cleaning lady 13 cleaning woman 14 maintenance man, superintendent

Janssen, David

real name: 16 David Harold Meyer

born: 9 Naponee NE

roles: 6 Harry O 11 The Fugitive 14 Richard Diamond 15 Dr Richard Kimble

January

event: 15 Inauguration Day (every 4 years)

flower: 8 snowdrop 9 carnation

French: 7 Janvier

gem: 6 garnet

German: 6 Januar

holiday: 8 Epiphany (6) 11 New Year's Day (1) 12 Twelfth Night (5)

Italian: 7 Gennaio

number of days: 9 thirty-one

origin of name: 5 Janus

Roman god of: 5 doors 8 doorways 10 beginnings

place in year:

Gregorian: 5 first

Julian/Roman: 8 eleventh

Spanish: 5 Enero

Zodiac sign: 8 Aquarius 9 Capricorn

Janus

Janus

origin: 5 Roman
god of: 8 doorways 9 rising sun 10 beginnings, setting sun

Japan

other name: 5 Nihon 6 Nippon
name means: 18 Land of the Rising Sun
capital/largest city: 3 Edo 5 Tokyo
others: 4 Kobe, Naha 5 Kyoto, Osaka 6 Nagoya, Sendai 7 Fukuoka, Niigata, Sapporo 8 Kanazawa, Kawasaki, Nagasaki, Yokohama 9 Hiroshima, Kagoshima 10 Kitakyushu
school: 4 Chuo, Keio 5 Hosei, Kyoto, Nihon, Tokyo 6 Sophia, Waseda 7 Fukuoka 8 Doshisha
head of state: 7 emperor
measure: 2 go 3 boo, cho, djo, fun, inc, ken, kin, kon, rin, shi, sho, sun, tan 4 hiro, isse, kati, koku, niyo, shoo 5 carat, catty, issho, ittan, momme, picul, shaku 6 kwamme 8 hiyak-kin 9 hiyak-hiro 11 komma-ichida, kujira-shaku
monetary unit: 2 bu 3 mon, rin, rio, sen, shu, yen 4 cash, mibu, oban 5 koban, obang, tempo 6 cobang, ichebu, ichibu, itzebu, kobang 7 itzeboo, itziboo
weight: 2 mo 3 fun, kon, rin 4 kati, kwan 5 carat, catty, momme 8 hiyakkin
island: 3 Iki, Izu, Oki, Tsu 4 Oita, Sado, Yaku 5 Amami, Awaji, Bonin, Hondo, Kuril, Rebun, Sikok 6 Honshu, Kiushu, Kyushu, Loochu, Marcus, Riukiu, Tanega, Tyukyu 7 Cipango, Hachijo, Iwo Jima, Okinawa, Rishiri, Shikoko, Shikoku, Volcano 8 Hokkaido, Miyajima, Okigunto, Okushiri, Tsushima, Yakujima
lake: 4 Biwa, Suwa, Toya 6 Towada 8 Kutchawa, Shikotsu
mountain: 3 Uso, Zao 5 Asahi, Asama, Hondo, Yesso 6 Asosan, Enasan, Hiuchi, Kiusiu, Yariga 7 Hakusan, Kujusan, Tokachi 8 Fujiyama 9 Japan Alps
highest point: 4 Fuji 7 Fujisan
river: 4 Tone, Yalu 8 Ishikari, Tonegawa 11 Shinano-gawa
sea: 3 Suo 5 Japan 6 Inland 7 Amakusa, Okhotsk, Pacific 8 Tsushima
physical feature:
bay: 3 Ise 4 Miku, Tosa, Yedo 5 Amort, Mutsu, Osaka, Otaru, Tokyo 6 Ariake, Atsumi, Sendai, Suruga, Toyama, Wakasa 7 Uchiura
cape: 2 Iro, Oki, Oma, Toi 4 Daio, Esan, Jizo, Mela, Mino, Noma, Nomo, Sada, Sawa, Shio, Soya, Suzu 5 Erimo, Kyoga, Rurui 6 Todoga 7 Shiriya 8 Ashizuri, Shakotan 12 Muroto Nojima
channel: 3 Kii 5 Bungo
current: 5 Japan 7 Okhotsk 8 Kuro Shio
divine wind: 8 kamikaze
gulf: 6 Sagami
plain: 4 Nobi 5 Kanto
strait: 4 Soya 5 Korea, Osumi 6 Nemuro, Tanega, Tokara 7 Tsugaru 8 Tsushima 9 La Perouse

people: 3 Eta 6 Korean 8 Japanese, Okinawan 10 Buramkumin
ancient: 4 Ainu 5 Jomon, Yayoi
artist: 4 Okyo 5 Buson, Jocho, Korin, Taiga, Unkei 6 Buncho, Eitoku, Kenzan, Koetsu, Reisai, Sesshu, Sesson, Shubun 7 Baiitsu, Choshun, Foujita, Gyokudo, Hokusai, Josetsu, Sanraku, Sharaku, Sotatsu, Utamaro 8 Harunobu, Kiyonaga, Motonobu 9 Hiroshige, Mitsunobu
author: 5 Basho 7 Abe Kobo 8 Mori Ogai 11 Ueda Akinari 12 Ihara Saikaku, Mishima Yukio, Sakyo Komatsu 13 Natsume Soseki, Zeami Motokiyo 14 Shimazaki Toson, Tsubouchi Shoyo 15 Motoori Norinaga, Murasaki Shikibu 16 Fujiwara Nokisaki, Kawabata Yasunari 17 Tanizaki Junichiro 19 Chikamatsu Monzaemon
dynasty: 5 Meiji, Taira 6 Yamato 8 Fujiwara, Minamoto
leader: 4 Hojo 5 Kammu, Meiji 6 Go-Toba, Ieyasu 7 Akihito, Go-Daigo 8 Hirohito, Nobunaga, Yoritomo 9 Hideyoshi, Yoshimasa 10 Tojo Hideki, Yoshimitsu 11 Hara Takashi, Ito Hirobumi 12 Tanaka Kakuei 13 Konoe Fumimaro, Shotoku Taishi 14 Yoshida Shigeru 15 Ashikaga Takauji 18 Matsukata Mayayoshi
legendary ruler: 5 Jimmu, Jingo 7 Izanagi
shogunate: 8 Ashikaga, Kamakura, Tokugawa
language: 8 Japanese
alphabet/characters: 4 kana 5 kanji 8 hiragana, katakana
dialect: 5 Kanto
religion: 6 Tendai 7 Shingon 8 Buddhism 9 Shintoism 12 Confucianism
place:
castle: 4 Nijo
hall: 5 Hoodo 7 Phoenix 12 Golden Buddha
mausoleum: 4 Ojin 7 Nintoku
palace: 7 Akasaka, Katsura
shrine: 5 Heian 11 Itsukushima 16 Grand Shrine of Ise
temple: 6 Kotoku 7 Byodoin, Horyuji, Ryoanji, Senso-ji, Todaiji 8 Enkakuji, Kenchoji, Kofukuji 9 Kinkakuji 13 Asakusa Kannon
feature:
abacus: 7 soroban
bed: 5 futon
clothing: 6 kimono
festival: 13 Cherry Blossom
firm: 4 Sony 5 Honda 6 Mitsui, Nissan, Toyota, Yasuda 7 Iwasaki 8 Sumitomo 10 Mitsubishi
flower arranging: 7 ikebana
painting style: 4 kano, tosa 5 nanga, nisee, onnae, rarae, rimpa, shijo 6 chinso, otokoe, sesshu, uklyoe 7 konpeki, nihonga, yamatoe
paper folding art: 7 origami
poem: 4 waka 5 haiku, tanka

puppet theater: 7 bunraku
rush floor covering: 6 tatami
sport: 4 judo 6 karate 13 sumo wrestling
statue: 8 Daibutsu 11 Great Buddha
tea ceremony: 7 chanoyu
theater: 2 no 3 noh 6 kabuki
the way of the warrior/code of honor: 7 bushido
tree: 6 bonsai
wood block print: 6 ukiyoe
food:
  beverage: 4 sake 8 green tea
  dish: 5 sushi 7 sashimi, tempura 8 sukiyaki, teriyaki, yakitori
  noodle: 4 soba

Japanese
  independent language of: 5 Japan 13 Ryukyu Islands

jape 4 gibe, joke 5 antic, caper, prank 7 mockery

Japheth
  father: 4 Noah
  brother: 3 Ham 4 Shem

Jaques
  character in: 11 As You Like It
  author: 11 Shakespeare

jar 3 din, jug, pot, urn 4 bong, bray, buzz, daze, faze, jolt, rock, stir, stun 5 blare, blast, brawl, clang, clank, crash, crock, flask, floor, quake, shake, shock, throw, upset 6 beaker, bottle, impact, jangle, jiggle, joggle, racket, rattle, vessel 7 agitate, astound, clangor, clatter, confuse, disturb, fluster, perturb, shake up, startle, stupefy, trouble, upheave, vibrate 8 befuddle, bewilder, bleating, canister, clashing, convulse, decanter, demijohn, disquiet, distract, unsettle 9 agitation, cacophony, container 10 concussion, discompose, disconcert, receptacle 11 discordance
  Spanish: 4 olla

jargon 4 bosh, bull, bunk, cant 5 argot, fudge, hooey, idiom, lingo, prate, usage 6 babble, brogue, drivel, patois, pidgin, piffle 7 baloney, blabber, blather, dialect, fustian, hogwash, prattle, rubbish, twaddle 8 folderol, malarkey, nonsense, parlance, tommyrot, verbiage 9 gibberish, moonshine, poppycock, rigmarole 10 balderdash, flapdoodle, hocus-pocus, rigamarole, vernacular, vocabulary 11 abracadabra, jabberwocky, phraseology, shibboleths 12 gobbledygook, lingua franca 14 grandiloquence

Jarley, Mrs
  character in: 19 The Old Curiosity Shop
  author: 7 Dickens

Jarndyce, John
  character in: 10 Bleak House
  author: 7 Dickens

jarring 4 rude 5 harsh, rough 6 jangly 7 grating, jolting, rasping, shaking 8 clashing, grinding, jangling, rattling, strident 9 dissonant, wrenching 10 discordant 12 nerve-racking 13 nerve-wracking

Jarry, Alfred
  author of: 7 King Ubu 11 Ubu in Chains 13 Ubu the Cuckold

jasmine 8 Jasminum
  varieties: 4 blue, cape, rock, star 5 crape, night, royal 6 orange, yellow 7 Arabian, Chilean, Italian, Spanish 8 Carolina, cinnamon, Japanese, Paraguay, pinwheel, primrose, windmill 9 angel-wing 10 Catalonian, Madagascar 11 Confederate

Jason
  leader of: 9 Argonauts
  father: 5 Aeson
  mother: 8 Alcimede, Polymede
  half-brother: 6 Pelias
  son: 5 Thoas 6 Euneus, Pheres 7 Medeius 8 Mermerus, Tisander 9 Alcimenes, Thessalus
  daughter: 7 Eriopis
  teacher: 6 Chiron 7 centaur, Cheiron
  retrieved: 12 Golden Fleece
  ship: 4 Argo
  loved by: 5 Medea
  loved: 6 Glauce

Jasper, John
  character in: 22 The Mystery of Edwin Drood
  author: 7 Dickens

jaundiced 5 blase, bored 6 bitter 7 cynical, envious, hostile, jealous 8 covetous, doubting, satiated 9 green-eyed, resentful, skeptical 10 embittered, suspicious 11 mistrustful

jaunt 4 spin, tour, trip 6 airing, flight, junket, outing, ramble, stroll 9 adventure, excursion, promenade, short trip 10 expedition

jaunty 4 airy, neat, trim 5 natty, perky 6 blithe, bouncy, breezy, dapper, lively, sporty, spruce 7 buoyant 8 carefree, debonair 9 sprightly, vivacious 12 lighthearted, high-stepping, high-spirited

Java
  other name: 5 Djawa
  capital/largest city: 7 Jakarta 8 Djakarta
  others: 5 Bogor, Dessa 6 Kediri, Malang 7 Bandung, Batavia 8 Semarang, Surabaja, Surabaya 9 Surakarta 11 Djokjakarta 13 Pelabuhanratu
  government: 17 island of Indonesia
  measure: 3 kan 4 paal, rand 5 palen
  weight: 4 amat, pond, tali 5 pound 6 soekel
  island: 4 Bali 5 Sunda 6 Lombok, Madura
  mountain: 4 Amat, Gede 5 Lawoe, Murjo, Prahu 6 Raoeng, Slamet 8 Soembing
  highest point: 6 Semuru 7 Semeroe
  river: 4 Solo 7 Brantas
  sea: 4 Java 6 Indian 7 Pacific
  physical feature:
    plateau: 4 Ijen
    strait: 5 Sunda
  people: 5 Krama, Kromo 6 Kalang 8 Javanese, Madurese 9 Sundanese

dynasty: 7 Mataram 9 Majapahit, Srivijaya

language: 4 Kavi, Kawi 5 Malay 6 Sassak 8 Balinese, Madurese, Sudanese 16 Bahasa Indonesian

religion: 5 Hindu, Islam 7 animism 8 Buddhism

place:

temple: 6 Chandi, Thandi 9 Borobudur, Prambanan

feature:

cloth: 3 kat 5 batik, kapok

dance: 7 seri mpi

dancer: 6 bedoyo

fishing boat: 4 prau

ornamental dagger: 4 kris

puppet play: 6 wajang, wayang

food:

fruit: 6 durian, lomboy, nangca 7 gondang

javelin 4 dart 5 lance, shaft, spear 10 projectile

jaw 3 gab, rap 4 chat, chin, talk 7 jawbone, palaver 8 chitchat, converse, mandible 10 chew the fat, chew the rag 11 confabulate

Jaws

author: 13 Peter Benchley

director: 15 Steven Spielberg

cast: 10 Robert Shaw 11 Roy Scheider 12 Lorraine Gary 15 Richard Dreyfuss

score: 12 John Williams

Oscar for: 5 score

Jayhawker State

nickname of: 6 Kansas

jazz musician 8 Art Tatum 10 Miles Davis 11 Lester Young 12 Benny Goodman, John Coltrane 13 Charlie Parker, Duke Ellington 14 Dizzy Gillespie, Louis Armstrong, Ornette Coleman

jealous 4 wary 7 anxious, envious, mindful 8 covetous, grudging, watchful 9 concerned, green-eyed, regardful, resentful 10 possessive, protective, suspicious 11 mistrustful, mistrusting 12 apprehensive

jealousy 4 envy 8 distrust, jaundice, mistrust 9 suspicion 10 resentment 12 covetousness 14 possessiveness 16 greeneyed monster

color: 5 green

Jebus

city captured by: 5 David

renamed: 9 Jerusalem

inhabitant: 8 Jebusite

jeer 3 boo, bug, dig, rap 4 barb, hiss, hoot, mock, razz, slam, slur 5 abuse, flout, hound, knock, scoff, scorn, sneer, taunt, whoop 6 deride, harass, heckle, hector, insult, revile 7 catcall, laugh at, mockery, obloquy 8 derision, ridicule, scoffing 9 aspersion, contumely, poke fun at, whistle at

Jeffers, Robinson

author of: 5 Medea, Tamar 6 Cawdor 8 Solstice 9 Dear Judas 12 Roan Stallion 14 Thurso's Landing 18 The Women at Point Sur 21 The Tower Beyond Tragedy

Jefferson, Arthur Stanley

real name of: 10 Stan Laurel

Jefferson, Thomas

nickname: 16 Sage of Monticello

presidential rank: 5 third

party: 20 Democratic-Republican

state represented: 2 VA

defeated: 5 (John) Adams 8 (Charles Cotesworth) Pinckney

vice president: 4 (Aaron) Burr 7 (George) Clinton

cabinet:

state: 7 (James) Madison

treasury: 6 (Samuel) Dexter 8 (Albert) Gallatin

war: 8 (Henry) Dearborn

attorney general: 6 (Caesar Augustus) Rodney 7 (Levi) Lincoln 12 (John) Breckenridge

navy: 5 (Robert) Smith

born: 2 VA 14 Shadwell estate 15 Goochland (Albemarle) County

died/buried: 10 Monticello

education: 14 William and Mary

interests: 6 violin 7 writing 11 agriculture 12 architecture

favorite foods: 10 French food 11 French wines

vacation: 12 Poplar Forest

author: 25 Declaration of Independence, Notes on the State of Virginia 39 A Summary View of the Rights of British America

political career: 8 governor 16 House of Burgesses 19 Virginia legislature 25 Declaration of Independence, Second Continental Congress

secretary of: 5 state

minister to: 6 France

civilian career: 6 farmer, lawyer

notable events of lifetime/term:

expedition: 13 Lewis and Clark

prohibition of: 19 importation of slaves

purchase: 9 Louisiana

father: 5 Peter

mother: 4 Jane (Randolph)

siblings: 4 Jane, Lucy, Mary 6 Martha 8 Randolph 9 Anna Scott, Elizabeth 10 Peter Field

wife: 6 Martha (Wayles Skelton)

children: 4 Mary 6 Martha

Jeffersons, The

character: 8 Florence 9 Tom Willis 11 Helen Willis 12 Harry Bentley 15 George Jefferson, Lionel Jefferson, Louise Jefferson, Ralph the Doorman 20 Jenny Willis Jefferson

cast: 9 Mike Evans 10 Damon Evans, Marla Gibbs, Roxie Roker 11 Ned Wertimer 12 Paul Benedict 13 Franklin Cover, Isabel Sanford 14 Sherman Hemsley 15 Berlinda Tolbert

George's business: 11 dry cleaning

spinoff from: 14 All in the Family

Jeffreys, Harold

field: 7 physics 9 astronomy

nationality: 7 British

explained: 7 weather

studied: 10 Earth's core 11 solar system

Jeffries, James Jackson
   nickname: 14 The Boilermaker
   sport: 6 boxing
   class: 11 heavyweight

jehad, jihad 6 strife 7 holy war 8 struggle

Jehloada
   father: 7 Paseach
   son: 7 Benaiah
   means: 12 Jehovah knows

Jehoshaphat
   father: 3 Asa 6 Ahitub, Nimshi, Parnah
   mother: 8 Jehorani
   means: 13 Jehovah judges

Jehova 3 god 5 diety

Jehu
   father: 6 Hanani 11 Jehoshaphat

jejune 4 dull 5 banal, inane, stale, trite,
   vapid 7 humdrum, insipid, puerile 8 ordinary 9 hackneyed 10 pedestrian, unexciting, unoriginal, wishy-washy 11 commonplace 12 conventional 13 uninteresting

jell 3 gel, jam, set 4 clot, firm 5 jelly 7 congeal, thicken 9 coagulate 10 gelatinize

Jellyby, Mrs
   character in: 10 Bleak House
   author: 7 Dickens

jellyfish 5 hydra, polyp, softy 6 coward,
   medusa, nettle 7 sunfish 8 weakling 10
   ctenophore, pantywaist 11 milquetoast,
   mollycoddle 12 coelenterate, invertebrate,
   siphonophore 18 Portuguese man-of-war

je ne sais quoi 13 I don't know what 18 indefinable quality

Jenkins, Richard Walter, Jr
   real name of: 13 Richard Burton

Jenner, Bruce
   sport: 13 track and field
   known for: 9 decathlon
   won: 8 Olympics

Jenner, Edward
   nationality: 7 British
   discovered: 11 vaccination 19 smallpox
   inoculation

Jenney, William Le Baron
   architect of: 21 Home Insurance Building (Chicago)

jeopardize 4 risk 6 expose, hazard 7 imperil 8 endanger 10 compromise 11 put
   into danger

jeopardy 4 risk 5 peril 6 danger, hazard 8
   exposure, unsafety 9 liability 10 insecurity
   11 imperilment 12 endangerment 13 vulnerability 14 precariousness

Jephthah 11 Hebrew judge
   father: 6 Gilead

Jeremiah
   father: 7 Hilkiah 10 Habazaniah
   daughter: 7 Mamutal
   grandson: 7 Jehohaz
   friend, scribe: 6 Baruch

jerk 3 ass, tic, tug 4 dope, dupe, fool, pull,
   snap, yank 5 dummy, dunce, idiot, klutz,
   pluck, shake, spasm, start, twist 6 quiver,
   reflex, thrust, twitch, wrench 7 tremble 8
   convulse 9 trembling

jerky 4 beef, meat 5 jolty, jumpy 6 choppy,
   elboic, jouncy 7 biltong, charqui, fidgety,
   twitchy 9 dried beef, spasmodic, twitching

Jeroboam
   father: 5 Joash, Nebat
   successor: 9 Zachariah

jerry-built 4 weak 5 frail, run-up, shaky,
   tacky 6 faulty, flimsy, shoddy, sleazy 7 rickety, unsound 8 gimcrack, slipshod,
   thrown-up, unstable 9 cheap-jack, defective 10 ramshackle 13 unsubstantial 14
   thrown-together

jersey 3 cow 5 maillot, shirt 6 tricot 7
   sweater 8 camisole, guernsey, pullover 10
   undershirt

Jersey Joe
   nickname of: 10 Joe Walcott

Jerubbaal see 6 Gideon

Jerusalem
   author: 12 William Blake

Jerusalem
   former name: 5 Jebus
   pool of: 6 Siloam 8 Bethesda

Jerusalem
   Arabic: 14 Bayt al-Muqaddas
   capital of: 6 Israel
   Hebrew: 12 Yerushalayim
   hills: 7 Judaean
   landmark: 6 al-Aqsa 11 Wailing Wall,
   Western Wall 12 Israel Museum 13 Dome
   of the Rock 14 Dead Sea Scrolls 15
   Shrine of the Book 17 Rockefeller Museum 24 Church of the Holy Sepulcher
   mount: 6 Olives, Scopus
   river: 6 Kidron
   ruler: 5 Arabs, David, Herod 6 Persia,
   Romans 7 British, Saladin, Seljuks, Solomon 8 Ayyubids, Fatimids, Ptolemy I 9
   Crusaders, Maccabees, Mamelukes 10
   Canaanites 12 Antiochus III 13 Pontius
   Pilate 15 Byzantine Empire 17 Alexander
   the Great, Antiochus the Third
   street: 11 Via Dolorosa

Jerusalem Delivered
   author: 13 Torquato Tasso

Jervis, Mrs
   character in: 6 Pamela
   author: 10 Richardson

jessamine 8 Jasminum

Jesse •
   father: 4 Obed
   grandfather: 4 Boaz
   grandmother: 4 Ruth
   great-grandfather: 5 Rahab
   son: 5 David, Eliab 7 Shammah 8
   Abinadab

jest 3 gag, pun 4 fool, game, gibe, jape,
   joke, josh, quip 5 act up, crack, laugh,
   prank, tease, trick 6 banter, bon mot 9
   wisecrack, witticism 10 crack jokes, pleasantry 11 horse around

jester 3 wag, wit 4 card, fool, mime, zany 5
   clown, comic, joker, mimer, mimic 6 madcap, mummer 7 buffoon 8 comedian, fun-

nyman, humorist, quipster 9 harlequin 10 motley fool 11 merry-andrew, pantomimist, punchinello

jesting 6 joking 7 teasing 8 sportive 9 bantering, unserious 12 wisecracking

Jesus
  also called: 7 Holy One, Messiah 8 Nazarene, Son of God 9 the Christ 12 Man of Sorrows 13 Prince of Peace 14 Savior Anointed
  mother: 4 Mary
  stepfather: 6 Joseph
  birthplace: 9 Bethlehem
  lived in: 8 Nazareth
  death place: 9 Jerusalem
  buried by: 17 Joseph of Arimathea
  disciples: 4 John, Jude 5 James, Peter, Simon 6 Andrew, Philip, Thomas 7 Matthew 12 James the Less 13 Judas Iscariot 20 Bartholomew Nathanael
  secret follower: 9 Nicodemus
  famous discourse: 16 Sermon on the Mount

jet 4 gush 5 flush, issue, shoot, spout, spray, spurt, surge, swash 6 effuse, nozzle, rush up, squirt, stream 7 sparger, sprayer, Spritze, syringe 8 atomizer, fountain, shoot out, Spritzer 9 discharge, sprinkler

Jethro
  daughter: 8 Zipporah
  son-in-law: 5 Moses

Jetsons, The
  character: 5 Astro 10 Jane Jetson, Judy Jetson 11 Elroy Jetson 12 George Jetson 13 Cosmo G Spacely
  voices: 8 Mel Blanc 10 Daws Butler, Don Messick, Janet Waldo 13 George O'Hanlon 14 Penny Singleton

jettison 4 dump 5 eject, scrap 6 unload 7 cast off, discard 8 throw out 9 discharge, eliminate, pitch over, throw over 13 toss overboard

jetty 4 dike, dock, mole, pier, quay, slip 5 black, ebony, groin, levee, raven, sable, wharf 6 bridge 7 sea wall 8 buttress 10 breakwater

jeu de mots 3 pun 11 play on words

jeu d'esprit 9 witticism 17 witty literary work
  literally: 12 play of spirit

jeune fille 4 girl 9 young girl 13 unmarried girl

jeunesse doree 11 gilded youth, golden youth

Jeven 3 God

Jew 6 Essene, Hebrew, Judean, Semite 7 Edomite, Judaist, Moabite 8 Hebraist, Sephardi 9 Israelite

jewel 3 ace, gem, pip 4 bead, dear, find, ring, whiz 5 honey, pearl, prize, stone, tiara 6 bangle, bauble, brooch, locket, winner 7 earring, pendant, trinket 8 bracelet, knockout, necklace, ornament, pure gold, treasure 9 humdinger, lavaliere 10 topnotcher 11 crackerjack, masterpiece

jewelry 4 gems, gold 6 silver 7 bangles, gewgaws, regalia 8 trinkets 10 adornments 14 precious stones

Jewett, Sarah Orne
  author of: 26 The Country of the Pointed Firs

Jewish 6 Hebrew, Judaic 7 Hebraic, Semitic
  bread: 5 matzo 6 matzoh 7 challah
  candelabrum: 7 menorah
  ceremonial robe: 5 kitel
  color: 5 white
  coming of age: 10 bar mitzvah, bat mitzvah
  dietary laws: 7 kashrut 8 kashruth
  group: 8 Hadassah 9 B'nai B'rith
  holy day/festival: 5 Purim, seder 6 Sukkot 7 Shavuot 8 Chanukah, Hanukkah, Passover 9 Yom Kippur 12 Rosh Hashanah
  law/scripture: 5 Torah 6 Gemara, Talmud, Tanach 7 Mishnah
  liturgical prayer: 6 Yigdal 8 Kol Nidre
  recited on eve of: 9 Yom Kippur
  marriage canopy: 6 chupah
  prayerbook: 6 mahzor, siddur 7 machzor
  quarter: 6 ghetto, mellah
  school: 5 heder 6 cheder
  skullcap: 5 kipah 8 yarmulka
  service to commemorate the dead: 6 Yizkor
  synagogue: 4 shul 5 schul
  toast: 8 mazel tov

Jewkes, Mrs
  character in: 6 Pamela
  author: 10 Richardson

Jew of Malta, The
  author: 18 Christopher Marlowe
  character: 7 Abigail, Barabas 8 Ithamore 15 Governor of Malta

Jezebel
  director: 12 William Wyler
  cast: 10 Bette Davis, Fay Bainter, Henry Fonda 11 Donald Crisp, George Brent 15 Margaret Lindsay
  Oscar for: 7 actress (Davis) 17 supporting actress (Bainter)

Jezebel
  father: 7 Ethbaal
  husband: 4 Ahab
  daughter: 8 Athaliah
  opposed: 6 Elijah
  killed: 6 Naboth
  father-in-law: 4 Omri

jib 3 arm, shy 4 balk, boom, sail, tack 5 demur, gigue, stick 6 recoil 7 scruple

Jibaro see 6 Jivaro

jibe 2 go 3 fit 4 mesh, tack 5 agree, fit in, match, shift, tally 6 accord, concur, square 7 conform 8 coincide, dovetail 9 harmonize 10 correspond, go together 11 fit together

jiffy 4 jiff 5 flash, shake, trice 6 minute, moment, second 7 half a mo, instant 9 twinkling 10 nanosecond 11 microsecond, millisecond, split second

jigger 4 dram, shot 5 glass 6 device, doo-dad, gadget, object 7 bicycle, gimmick, measure 9 doohickey, shot glass 10 bone-shaker 11 contraption, thingumabob

jiggle 4 jerk 5 shake 6 bounce, fidget, jog-gle, jostle, twitch, wiggle 7 agitate, wriggle

jihad see 5 jehad

jilt 5 leave 6 betray, desert 7 forsake, let down 12 break off with 17 break an en-gagement

Jim
character in: 15 (The Adventures of) Huckleberry Finn
author: 5 Twain

jimmy 3 bar, pry 5 force, lever 7 crowbar

jingle 4 ring 5 clang, clank, clink, ditty 6 jangle, tinkle 7 clatter, ringing 8 doggerel, facetiae, limerick 10 catchy poem, catchy song 12 product theme 13 reverberation 14 commercial tune 16 tintinnabulation

Jingle, Alfred
character in: 14 Pickwick Papers
author: 7 Dickens

jingoism 10 chauvinism, flag-waving, patri-otics 11 nationalism 14 overpatriotism, spread-eagleism 15 superpatriotism 16 ul-tranationalism

jinn 3 imp 5 afrit, demon, genie, jinni 6 afreet, spirit 8 jinniyeh

jinx 3 hex 5 curse 6 plague, whammy 7 bugaboo, bugbear, evil eye, ill wind, nem-esis 9 evil spell
French: 5 bete noire

jitterbug 5 dance, lindy 8 lindy hop 12 boogie-woogie

jitters 6 shakes 7 anxiety, fidgets, jim-jams, shivers, willies 9 jumpiness, quivering, shakiness, tenseness, the creeps, whim-whams 10 uneasiness 11 butterflies, fid-getiness, nervousness 12 skittishness 13 heebie-jeebies 16 screaming-meemies

jittery 5 jumpy 6 uneasy 7 anxious, nervous

Jivaro, Shuara, Jibaro
tribe: 6 Achual, Antipa 8 Aguaruna, Huambiza
location: 4 Peru 7 Ecuador 12 South America
noted for: 7 tsantsa (shrunken heads)

Joab
mother: 7 Zeruiah
brother: 6 Asahel 7 Abishai
commanded: 10 David's army
killed: 5 Abner, Amasa 7 Absalom
killed by: 7 Benaiah
conspired to overthrow: 5 David

Joad family
characters in: 16 The Grapes of Wrath
members: 2 Ma, Pa 3 Tom 4 Noah 6 Connie 12 Rose of Sharon
author: 9 Steinbeck

Joakim
wife: 7 Susanna

Joash
means: 15 Jehovah is strong
father: 4 Ahab 7 Ahaziah, Jehohaz
son: 6 Gideon, Shelah 7 Amaziah
succeeded: 8 Athaliah

job 3 lot 4 care, duty, part, role, spot, task, work 5 chore, craft, field, place, quota, share, stint, trade, trust 6 affair, career, charge, errand, living, metier, office, output 7 calling, concern, mission, opening, por-tion, product, pursuit 8 activity, business, capacity, contract, exercise, function, posi-tion, province, vocation 9 allotment, piece-work, situation 10 assignment, commis-sion, engagement, enterprise, livelihood, occupation, profession 11 achievement, appointment, performance, undertaking 14 accomplishment, responsibility

Job
father: 8 Issachar
friend: 5 Elihu 6 Bildad, Zophar 7 Eliphaz

job holder 6 worker 8 employee, hireling

job seeker 7 hopeful 8 aspirant 9 applicant, candidate

Jocasta
also: 8 Epicaste
queen of: 6 Thebes
father: 9 Menoeceus
brother: 5 Creon
husband: 5 Laius 7 Oedipus
son: 7 Oedipus 8 Eteocles 9 Polynices
daughter: 6 Ismene 8 Antigone
death by: 7 hanging, suicide

Jochebed
father: 4 Levi
husband: 5 Amram
nephew: 5 Amram
son: 5 Aaron, Moses

jockey 5 Baeza, Krone 6 Arcaro, Pincay 7 Cauthen, Cordero, Cruguet, Hartack 8 McCarron, McHargue, Turcotte 9 Shoe-maker, Velasquez

jocose 3 fun 4 arch 5 comic, droll, funny, jolly, merry, witty 6 joking, jovial 7 amusing, comical, jesting, jocular, playful, roguish, teasing, waggish 8 humorous, mirthful, prankish, sportive 9 facetious

jocular 3 gay 5 droll, funny, jolly, merry, witty 6 jocose, jocund, joking, jovial 7 amusing, jesting, playful, roguish, rompish, waggish 8 humorous, mirthful, prankish, sportive 9 facetious 10 frolicsome 12 en-tertaining, lighthearted

jocund 5 jolly, merry 6 breezy, cheery, elated, jovial, lively 8 cheerful, debonair, pleasant 9 easygoing 10 untroubled 12 happy-go-lucky, lighthearted

Joel
means: 12 Jehovah is God
father: 4 Nebo 6 Samuel 7 Azariah, Pedaiah, Pethuel
brother: 6 Nathan

Joe Palooka
creator: 9 Ham Fisher 11 Tony DiPreta
character:
children: 3 Joe 5 Buddy 7 Joannie
friend: 9 Little Max 10 Jerry Leemy
manager: 11 Knobby Walsh
valet: 6 Smokey
wife: 8 Anne Howe
profession: 5 boxer

jog 3 bob, jar, tug 4 jerk, pull, rock, stir, trot, yank 5 nudge, shake, twist 6 bounce, jiggle, jostle, jounce, prompt, twitch, wrench 7 actuate, animate 8 activate, energize 9 stimulate

jogger 4 memo 6 layboy, runner 7 trotter 8 reminder 10 memorandum

Johannesburg
airport: 8 Jan Smuts
area: 4 Rand 9 Transvaal
capital of: 11 South Africa
landmark: 13 Carlton Centre 14 Africana Museum 16 Union Observatory 17 Zoological Gardens 20 Melrose Bird Sanctuary
township: 6 Soweto 7 Lenasia 10 Nancefield
university: 13 Rand Afrikaans, Witwatersrand

John
father: 7 Zebedee
brother: 5 James
son: 5 Peter
called, with brother: 9 Boanerges 13 sons of thunder
pertaining to John or his writings: 9 Johannine

John Brown's Body
author: 19 Stephen Vincent Benet

John Gabriel Borkman
author: 11 Henrik Ibsen

John Mark *see* 4 Mark

Johnny Belinda
director: 13 Jean Negulesco
cast: 8 Lew Ayres 9 Jane Wyman 15 Charles Bickford
Oscar for: 7 actress (Wyman)

Johnny Cash Show, The
cast: 9 Jim Varney 10 Howard Mann 11 Carl Perkins, Steve Martin 14 June Carter Cash, Tennessee Three 15 Statler Brothers 32 Mother Maybelle and the Carter Family

Johnny-come-lately 8 newcomer 9 latecomer 10 new arrival 11 late arrival

Johnny U
nickname of: 12 Johnny Unitas

Johns, Glynis
born: 8 Pretoria 11 South Africa
roles: 11 Mary Poppins 13 The Sundowners 17 A Little Night Music 26 Around the World in Eighty Days

Johns, Jasper
born: 9 Augusta GA
artwork: 4 Flag 6 Studio, Target 8 Watchman 10 Fool's House 12 Device Circle 13 Painted Bronze (Beer Cans) 14 The Barber's Tree 19 Target with Four Faces 22 Target with Plaster Casts

Johnson, Andrew
presidential rank: 11 seventeenth
party: 8 Democrat
state represented: 2 TN
defeated: 5 no one
succeeded upon death of: 7 Lincoln
vice president: 4 none
cabinet:

state: 6 (William Henry) Seward
treasury: 9 (Hugh) McCulloch
war: 7 (Edwin McMasters) Stanton 9 (John McAllister) Schofield
attorney general: 5 (James) Speed 6 (William Maxwell) Evarts 8 (Henry) Stanbery
navy: 6 (Gideon) Welles
postmaster general: 7 (Alexander Williams) Randall 8 (William) Dennison
interior: 5 (John Palmer) Usher 6 (James) Harlan 8 (Orville Hickman) Browning
born: 9 Raleigh NC
died: 16 Carter's Station TN
buried: 13 Greeneville TN
education: 9 no college 12 self-educated
political career: 8 US Senate 13 vice president 22 House of Representatives
only president to be: 9 impeached (1868)
found: 9 not guilty
mayor of: 11 Greeneville (TN)
governor of: 9 Tennessee
civilian career: 6 tailor
military service: 8 Civil War 12 US Volunteers 16 brigadier general
military governor of: 9 Tennessee
notable events of lifetime/term: 14 Reconstruction
Purchase: 6 Alaska
father: 5 Jacob
mother: 4 Mary (McDonough)
stepfather: 15 Turner Dougherty
sibling: 7 William
wife: 5 Eliza (McCardle)
children: 4 Mary 6 Andrew, Martha, Robert 7 Charles

Johnson, Earvin
nickname: 5 Magic
sport: 10 basketball
position: 5 guard
team: 16 Los Angeles Lakers

Johnson, Jack (John Arthur)
nickname: 11 Little Artha 14 Galveston Giant
sport: 6 boxing
class: 11 heavyweight

Johnson, Lyndon Baines
nickname: 3 LBJ 15 Landslide Lyndon
presidential rank: 11 thirty-sixth
party: 10 Democratic
state represented: 2 TX
succeeded upon death of: 7 Kennedy
defeated: 4 (Earle Harold) Munn, (Eric) Hass 6 (John) Kasper 7 (Clifton) DeBerry 9 (Barry Morris) Goldwater
vice president: 4 none (first term) 8 (Hubert Horatio) Humphrey
cabinet:
state: 4 (David Dean) Rusk
treasury: 4 (Joseph William) Barr 6 (Clarence Douglas) Dillon, (Henry Hamill) Fowler
defense: 8 (Clark McAdams) Clifford, (Robert Strange) McNamara
attorney general: 5 (William Ramsey)

Clark **7** (Robert Francis) Kennedy **10** (Nicholas deBelleville) Katzenbach
postmaster general: **6** (Lawrence Francis) O'Brien, (William Marvin) Watson **9** (John Austin) Gronouski
interior: **5** (Stewart Lee) Udall
agriculture: **7** (Orville Lothrop) Freeman
commerce: **5** (Cyrus Rowlett) Smith **6** (John Thomas) Connor, (Luther Hartwell) Hodges **10** (Alexander Buel) Trowbridge
labor: **5** (William Willard) Wirtz
HEW: **5** (Wilbur Joseph) Cohen **7** (John William) Gardner **10** (Anthony Joseph) Celebrezze
HUD: **4** (Robert Colwell) Wood **6** (Robert Clifton) Weaver
transportation: **4** (Alan Stevenson) Boyd
born: **11** (near) Stonewall TX
died/buried: **13** (near) Johnson City TX
education:
teachers' college: **19** Southwest Texas State
law school: **10** Georgetown
religion: **17** Disciples of Christ
vacation spot: **8** LBJ Ranch
author: **15** The Vantage Point
political career: **8** US Senate **13** vice president **24** US House of Representatives
civilian career: **7** teacher
military service: **6** US Navy **10** World War II **11** World War Two
notable events of lifetime/term: **9** race riots **12** Great Society
act: **11** Civil Rights **12** Voting Rights **19** Economic Opportunity
assassination of: **14** Robert F Kennedy **18** Martin Luther King Jr
capture of: **6** Pueblo
Pueblo captured by: **10** North Korea
treaty: **23** Nuclear Non-Proliferation
war: **7** Vietnam **11** Arab-Israeli
father: **7** Sam Ealy
mother: **7** Rebekah (Baines)
siblings: **10** Sam Houston **12** Lucia Huffman **13** Josefa Hermine, Rebekah Luruth
wife: **7** Claudia (Alta Taylor)
nickname: **8** Lady Bird
children: **9** Lynda Bird **10** Luci Baines
First Lady:
responsible for: **24** Highway Beautification Act
author: **16** A White House Diary
Johnson, Philip Cortelyou
    architect of: **10** Glass House (New Canaan CT), Wiley House (New Canaan CT) **12** Hodgson House (New Canaan CT) **13** Pennzoil Place (Houston TX) **14** Boissonas House (New Canaan CT) **16** Amon Carter Museum (Ft Worth TX) **17** Sheldon Art Gallery (Lincoln NE) **18** A T and T Headquarters (NYC), Kline Science Center (Yale) **19** New York State Theater (Lincoln Center)

Johnson, Samuel
    author of: **8** Rasselas, The Idler **18** The Lives of the Poets **22** The Vanity of Human Wishes **30** Dictionary of the English Language
Johnson, Walter
    nickname: **8** Big Train
    sport: **8** baseball
    position: **7** pitcher
    team: **18** Washington Senators
John the Baptist
    father: **9** Zechariah
    mother: **9** Elizabeth
    descendant of: **5** Aaron
    precursor of: **5** Jesus **10** the Messiah
joie de vivre 11 joy of living **19** delight in being alive
join 3 hug, mix **4** abut, ally, band, bind, fuse, glue, link, meet, pool **5** affix, brush, chain, enter, graze, marry, merge, paste, reach, skirt, stick, touch, unify, unite **6** adjoin, attach, bridge, cement, cohere, couple, fasten, scrape, solder, splice **7** combine, connect, verge on **8** border on, enlist in, enroll in, federate, hold fast **9** associate, cooperate, syndicate **10** amalgamate, fraternize **11** confederate, consolidate **12** conglomerate
joined 3 met, wed **4** tied **5** bound, fused, glued, mated, yoked **6** allied, bonded, linked, merged, paired, seamed, united, welded **7** coupled, married, related, spliced **8** attached, cemented, combined, enlisted, fastened **9** bracketed, connected **10** associated, hand-in-hand, integrated **11** hand-in-glove
join forces 4 ally **5** merge, unite **6** league, team up **7** combine **8** coalesce **9** affiliate, cooperate **11** consolidate **12** band together
joint 4 hock, knee, knot, link **5** elbow, hinge, nexus **6** allied, common, mutual, shared, united **7** knuckle, unified **8** combined, communal, coupling, junction, juncture **9** associate, community, conjoined, corporate, unanimous **10** associated, collective, connection, hand-in-hand, like-minded **11** coalitional, conjunctive, cooperative **12** articulation, consolidated **13** collaborative
    kind:
    ball and socket: **3** hip **8** shoulder
    fused: **5** skull **11** base of spine
    hinged: **4** knee **5** elbow
    unfused: **3** hip, jaw **4** knee **5** elbow **8** shoulder
joint action 7 concert **8** teamwork **11** cooperating, cooperation, give-and-take **13** collaboration, participation
joint effort 7 concert **8** teamwork **11** cooperation **13** collaboration
jointly 8 arm in arm, in common, in unison, mutually, together, unitedly **10** conjointly, hand-in-hand, side by side **12** collectively **13** in association, in conjunction
join together 3 wed **4** fuse, weld **5** marry, unify, unite **6** solder **9** integrate **10** amalgamate **11** consolidate, incorporate

join up 6 enlist, enroll, sign up 9 volunteer

joist 4 beam 5 brace 6 timber 7 support

joke 3 gag, pun, wit 4 butt, dupe, fool, gibe, goof, gull, jape, jest, josh, lark, mock, quip 5 antic, caper, cinch, clown, farce, prank, put-on, roast, tease, trick 6 banter, bon mot, deride, frolic, gambol, gibe at, jeer at, parody, satire, take in, target, trifle, whimsy 7 buffoon, bumpkin, chortle, lampoon, laugh at, nothing, scoff at, smile at, snicker 8 anecdote, badinage, pooh-bah, push-over, repartee, ridicule, town fool, travesty 9 burlesque, diversion, horseplay, simpleton, wisecrack, witticism 10 pleasantry 11 horse around, monkeyshine 13 facetiousness, laughingstock

joker 3 wag, wit 4 snag, trap, zany 5 catch, clown, hitch, mimic, rider, snare, trick 6 jester, madcap 7 codicil, pitfall, punster 8 addendum, comedian, funnyman, humorist 10 subterfuge, supplement 11 wisecracker
   French: 7 farceur

jokester 3 wag 5 comic, cutup, joker 8 comedian 9 prankster

Joliba see 5 Niger

Joliot-Curie, Frederic
   field: 9 chemistry
   nationality: 6 French
   discovered: 23 artificial radioisotopes
   awarded: 10 Nobel Prize
   wife: 16 Irene Joliot-Curie

Joliot-Curie, Irene
   field: 7 physics
   nationality: 6 French
   discovered: 23 artificial radioisotopes
   awarded: 10 Nobel Prize
   husband: 14 Frederic Joliot
   father: 11 Pierre Curie
   mother: 10 Marie Curie

jollity 3 fun 4 glee, play, romp 5 cheer, mirth, revel, sport 6 frolic, gaiety 7 revelry, whoopee 8 hilarity 9 amusement, festivity, jocundity, joviality, merriment, pleasure 10 jocularity 11 merrymaking 12 conviviality

jolly 3 gay 5 droll, funny, happy, merry 6 jocund, jovial 7 gleeful, jocular, playful 8 cheerful, mirthful, sportive 9 fun-loving 10 delightful, rollicking 12 high-spirited

jolt 3 bob, jar, jog 4 bump, jerk, jump, stun 5 lurch, quake, shake, shock, start, throw, upset 6 bobble, bounce, jiggle, joggle, jostle, jounce, quiver, trauma, twitch 7 disturb, perturb, setback, shake up, shaking, startle 8 convulse, reversal 9 agitation, take aback 11 thunderbolt

Joltin' Joe
   nickname of: 11 Joe DiMaggio

Jonah
   father: 7 Amittai
   swallowed by: 9 large fish
   preached in: 7 Nineveh
   hometown: 10 Gathhepher

Jonathan
   means: 11 Jehovah gave
   father: 4 Jada, Saul 6 Joiada, Kereah 8 Abiathar
   friend: 5 David

son: 9 Meribkaal 12 Mephibosheth

Jonathan Livingston Seagull
   author: 11 Richard Bach

Jonathan Wild
   author: 13 Henry Fielding

Jones, Carolyn
   born: 10 Amarillo TX
   roles: 8 Morticia 15 The Addams Family

Jones, Inigo
   architect of: 11 Queen's House (Greenwich) 14 Banqueting Hall (Whitehall Palace, London)
   restoration: 16 St Paul's Cathedral

Jones, James
   author of: 7 Whistle 14 The Thin Red Line 15 Some Came Running 18 From Here to Eternity

Jones, James Earl
   born: 11 Arkabutla MS
   roles: 6 The Man 7 Othello 8 Star Wars 15 The Emperor Jones 17 The Great White Hope
   voice of: 10 Darth Vader

Jones, John Paul
   served in: 11 Russian navy 16 Revolutionary War 21 British merchant marine
   commander of ship: 6 Ranger 10 Providence 15 Bonhomme Richard
   defeated ship: 7 Serapis
   saying: 23 "I have not yet begun to fight"

Jones, Shirley
   husband: 11 Jack Cassidy, Marty Ingels
   born: 10 Smithton PA
   roles: 8 Carousel, Oklahoma 11 Elmer Gantry, The Music Man 18 The Partridge Family

Jong, Erica
   author of: 5 Fanny 12 Fear of Flying 18 At the Edge of the Body 20 How to Save Your Own Life

jonquil 4 bulb, lily 8 daffodil 9 narcissus

Jonson, Ben
   author of: 6 The Fox 7 Sejanus, Volpone 11 A Tale of a Tub 12 The Alchemist 15 Bartholomew Fair 18 Every Man in His Humo(u)r 21 Every Man out of His Humo(u)r 23 Epicene or the Silent Woman

Jordan
   other name: 24 Hashemite Kingdom of Jordan
   capital/largest city: 5 Amman
   ancient name: 12 Philadelphia
   others: 4 Krak, Ma'an, Salt 5 Agaba, Ariha, Irbid, Jenin, Karak, Kerak, Sarga, Zarga, Zerke 6 Bethel, Hebron, Jarash, Jerash, Madaba, Nablus, Ramtha 7 Al-Agaba, Bethany, El-Kerak, El Zerga, Jericho, Kirmoab, Nabulus, Samaria 8 Al-Khalii, Ram Allah 9 Bethlehem, Jerusalem
   school: 7 yarmouk
   division: 8 East Bank, West Bank 11 Transjordan
   ancient state: 4 Edom, Moab 5 Ammon, Judah 6 Gilead
   head of state: 4 king

monetary unit: 4 fils 5 dinar
mountain: 3 Hor 4 Nebo 5 Bukka, Dabab 6 Ataiba, Gilead, Mubrak
highest point: 9 Jabal Ramm, Jebel Ramm
river: 6 Jordan, Yarmuk 11 Nahr-az-Zarga
sea: 3 Red 4 Dead 7 Galilee 13 Mediterranean
physical feature:
desert: 6 Syria
gulf: 5 Aqaba
plateau: 11 Transjordan
valley: 4 Ghor 9 Great Rift
wind: 7 Khamsin
people: 4 Arab, Kurd 7 Bedouin, Checher 8 Armenian, Assyrian 10 Circassian 11 Palestinian
ancient: 8 Armonite 9 Nabataean
ruler: 5 Talal 6 Faisal, Greeks, Romans 7 Hussein 8 Abdullah, Selucidas 9 Crusaders 10 Ibn Hussein, Nabataeans 12 Ottoman Turks 18 Abdullah Ibn Hussein
tribe: 5 Qaysi 6 Yamani
language: 6 Arabic
religion: 5 Islam 13 Greek Orthodox
place:
canal: 8 East Gher
ruins: 5 Ajlun, Petra 6 Jarash 7 Al Karak
feature:
headdress: 8 kaffiyeh
village headman: 7 mukhtar
village square: 5 sahah
food:
dessert: 7 baklava
pastry: 7 katayif
Jordan, Robert
  character in: 19 For Whom the Bell Tolls
  author: 9 Hemingway
Jormungandr
  also: 10 Jormungand 11 Iormungandr 14 Midgard Serpent
  origin: 12 Scandinavian
  form: 7 serpent
  father: 4 Loki
  mother: 9 Angerboda, Angrbodha, Angurboda
  brother: 6 Fenrir, Fenris
  sister: 3 Hel
  wrapped around: 5 world
  killed by: 4 Thor
  death place: 6 Vigrid
  killed: 4 Thor
Jo's Boys
  author: 15 Louisa May Alcott
Joseph
  father: 4 Bani 5 Aseph, Jacob 10 Mattathias
  mother: 6 Rachel
  brother: 3 Dan, Gad 4 Levi 5 Asher, Judah 6 Reuben, Simeon 7 Zebulun 8 Benjamin, Issachar, Naphtali
  wife: 4 Mary 7 Asenath
  stepson: 5 Jesus
  also called: 20 Barsabbas of Arimathea 21 Barsabbas of Arimathaea
  buried: 5 Jesus

slave of: 8 Potiphar
Joseph Andrews
  author: 13 Henry Fielding
  character: 5 Fanny 9 Lady Booby 11 Mrs Slipslop, Parson Adams, Peter Pounce 13 Pamela Andrews
josh 3 guy, kid, rag, rib 4 dish, haze, jape, jest, jive, joke, quiz, razz, ride, twit 5 chaff, jolly, put on, roast, tease 6 banter, needle 8 ridicule
Joshua
  means: 18 Jehovah is salvation
  father: 3 Nun
  succeeded: 5 Moses
  captured: 7 Jericho, Lachish
  hid spies: 5 Rahab
Josiah
  means: 12 Jehovah heals
  father: 9 Zephaniah
  succeeded: 4 Amon
jostle 3 jab 4 bump, butt, poke, prod, push 5 crowd, elbow, shove 7 collide 8 shoulder 10 hit against, run against 12 knock against
jot 3 bit, dot 4 list, mite, note, snip, whit 5 enter, speck, trace 6 record, trifle 7 modicum, one iota, put down, set down, smidgen, snippet 8 flyspeck, particle, register, scribble, take down 9 scintilla
Jotham
  son: 4 Ahaz
Jo the crossing sweeper
  character in: 10 Bleak House
  author: 7 Dickens
jotting 4 memo, note 6 doodle 8 scribble 10 memorandum, scribbling
Jotun
  origin: 12 Scandinavian
  form: 5 giant
  conflicts with: 4 gods
  enemy: 4 Asar 5 Aesir
Jotunheim
  origin: 12 Scandinavian
  realm of: 6 giants
Joukahainen
  origin: 7 Finnish
  form: 8 magician
  location: 7 Lapland
  tried to kill: 11 Vainamoinen
Joule, James Prescott
  field: 7 physics
  nationality: 7 British
  established law of: 20 conservation of energy
  named for him: 10 unit of work
jounce 3 bob 6 bounce 7 rebound 8 ricochet
Jourdain, Monsieur
  character in: 21 The Bourgeois Gentleman 22 Le Bourgeois Gentilhomme
  author: 7 Moliere
Jourdan, Louis
  real name: 11 Louis Gendre
  born: 6 France 9 Marseille
  roles: 4 Gigi 6 Can Can 9 Octopussy 15 The Paradine Case 23 Three Coins in the

Fountain **24** Letter from an Unknown Woman

journal 3 log **5** album, daily, diary, paper, sheet **6** annual, ledger, memoir, record, weekly **7** almanac, daybook, gazette, history, logbook, monthly, tabloid **8** calendar, magazine, notebook, register, yearbook **9** chronicle, newspaper, quarterly, scrapbook **10** chronology, confession, memorandum, memory book, periodical, record book **11** account book, daily record, publication **13** autobiography

journalist 6 author, editor, writer **7** byliner, diarist, newsman **8** reporter **9** columnist, newswoman **12** newspaperman **13** correspondent **14** newspaperwoman

Journal of the Plague Year, A
    author: **11** Daniel Defoe

journey 3 fly, way **4** roam, rove, sail, tour, trek, trip, wend **5** jaunt, quest, route, tramp **6** course, cruise, flight, junket, outing, ramble, roving, travel, voyage, wander **7** circuit, meander, odyssey, passage, transit **8** divagate, navigate, sightsee, vagabond **9** excursion, itinerary, take a trip, wandering **10** divagation, expedition, pilgrimage **11** peregrinate **13** peregrination

Journey Into Fear
    author: **10** Eric Ambler

journey's end 4 goal **9** objective **11** destination

Journey to the End of the Night
    author: **20** Louis-Ferdinand Celine

joust 4 tilt **5** combat, jostle **7** contend, contest, tourney **8** run a tilt **10** contention, tournament

Jove see **7** Jupiter

jovial 3 gay **5** jolly, merry, sunny **6** blithe, cheery, hearty, jocose, jocund **7** buoyant, gleeful, jocular, playful, zestful **8** cheerful, humorous, laughing, mirthful, sportive **9** convivial, fun-loving, hilarious **10** delightful, frolicsome, rollicking

joviality 3 fun **4** glee **5** cheer, gaity, mirth **7** delight, jollity, revelry **8** buoyancy **9** jocundity, merriment **10** joyfulness, liveliness **11** high spirits

jowl 3 jaw **5** cheek, chops **6** muzzle **8** mandible

joy 3 gem **4** glee **5** jewel, pride, prize **6** gaiety **7** delight, ecstasy, elation, rapture **8** gladness, pleasure, treasure **9** enjoyment, happiness **10** excitement, exultation, jubilation **11** contentment, delectation **12** cheerfulness, exhilaration, satisfaction
    goddess of: **6** Hathor

Joyce, James
    author of: **7** Ulysses **9** Dubliners **13** Finnegan's Wake **31** A Portrait of the Artist as a Young Man

joyful 4 glad, rosy **5** happy **6** bright, elated **7** blessed, pleased **8** cheerful, ecstatic, exultant, gladsome, jubilant, pleasing **9** delighted, full of joy, overjoyed **10** delightful, enraptured, gratifying, heartening **11** pleasurable, transported **12** heartwarming

joyless 3 sad **4** glum, grim **5** black **6** dismal, gloomy, morbid, woeful **7** doleful, forlorn, unhappy **8** dejected, desolate, dolorous, downcast, mournful **9** cheerless, depressed, sorrowful, woebegone **10** despondent, in the dumps, lugubrious, melancholy **11** downhearted, pessimistic **12** disconsolate, heavyhearted **14** down in the mouth

joy of living
    French: **11** joie de vivre

Joy of Sex, The
    author: **11** Alex Comfort

joyous 3 gay **4** glad **5** happy, merry **7** festive, gleeful **8** cheerful, gladsome, mirthful **9** rapturous, wonderful **10** delightful, gratifying, heartening **11** pleasurable **12** heartwarming, lighthearted

joyousness 4 glee **8** gladness **9** happiness, merriment **10** blitheness, exuberance **11** high spirits **16** lightheartedness

Jubal
    father: **6** Lamech
    mother: **4** Adah
    brother: **5** Jabal

jubilant 3 gay **4** glad **5** happy, jolly, merry **6** blithe, cheery, elated, enrapt, joyful, joyous **7** buoyant, charmed, gleeful, pleased, radiant, smiling **8** cheerful, ecstatic, exultant, gladsome, laughing, mirthful **9** delighted, delirious, exuberant, gladdened, gratified, overjoyed, rapturous, rejoicing, rhapsodic **10** blithesome, captivated, enraptured **11** exhilarated, intoxicated, tickled pink **12** happy as a lark, lighthearted **13** in high spirits

jubilation 5 bliss **9** rejoicing **11** celebration **12** exhilaration

jubilee 2 do **4** bash, fete, gala **5** blast, party **6** frolic, revels **7** blowout, holiday, revelry, shindig **8** festival, wingding **9** festivity **10** jubilation, observance **11** anniversary, celebration, merrymaking **12** conviviality **13** commemoration

Juda
    father: **6** Joanna, Joseph **8** Haneniah

Judah
    father: **5** Jacob
    mother: **4** Leah
    brother: **3** Dan, Gad **4** Levi **5** Asher, Judah **6** Joseph, Reuben, Simeon **8** Benjamin, Issachar, Naphtali
    sister: **5** Dinah
    wife: **5** Shuah
    son: **2** Er **4** Onan **5** Perez, Zerah **6** Baruch, Shelah
    daughter-in-law: **5** Tamar
    last king of: **8** Zedekiah
    descendant of: **8** Judahite

Judah, tribes of see **14** Israel, tribes of

Judas
    brother: **5** James
    also called: **8** Thaddeus
    disciple of: **5** Jesus

Judas Iscariot 8 betrayer
  disciple of: 5 Jesus
  betrayed: 5 Jesus
  replaced by: 8 Matthias
Jude 7 apostle
  brother: 5 James
Jude the Obscure
  author: 11 Thomas Hardy
  character: 10 Jude Fawley 12 Arabella
  Donn, Sue Bridehead 14 Drusilla Fawley
  16 Little Father Time 17 Richard
  Phillotson
judge 3 try 4 deem, find, hear, rank, rate 5
  fancy, gauge, guess, infer, juror, value,
  weigh 6 assess, assume, censor, critic,
  decide, deduce, expert, reckon, regard, review, rule on, settle, size up, umpire 7 adjudge, analyze, arbiter, believe, conduct,
  discern, imagine, justice, referee, resolve,
  suppose, surmise 8 appraise, assessor,
  conclude, consider, estimate, official, reviewer 9 appraiser, arbitrate, ascertain, authority, determine, evaluator, moderator 10
  adjudicate, arbitrator, conjecture, magistrate 11 adjudicator, connoisseur, distinguish 12 pass sentence
judgment, judgement 4 view 5 sense,
  taste 6 acumen, belief, decree, ruling 7
  finding, opinion, verdict 8 decision, estimate, sentence 9 appraisal, deduction,
  valuation 10 assessment, conclusion, conviction, discretion, perception, persuasion,
  shrewdness 11 arbitration, discernment,
  percipience 14 discrimination, perceptiveness
Judgment at Nuremberg
  director: 13 Stanley Kramer
  cast: 11 Judy Garland 12 Spencer Tracy
  13 Burt Lancaster 14 Richard Widmark,
  William Shatner 15 Marlene Dietrich,
  Montgomery Clift 16 Maximilian Schell
  Oscar for: 5 actor (Schell)
Judgment Day 8 doomsday 13 end of the
  world 14 day of reckoning 15 the Last
  Judgment
Judgment Day
  author: 13 James T Farrell
Judgment of Paris see 5 Paris
judicial 5 legal 8 imposing, juristic, majestic, official 9 magistral 11 magisterial 13
  distinguished
judiciary 5 bench, court 11 court system
judicious 4 just, sage, wise 5 acute, sober,
  sound 6 astute, shrewd 7 knowing, politic,
  prudent, tactful 8 sensible 9 sagacious 10
  diplomatic, discerning, percipient, reasonable, reflective, thoughtful 11 levelheaded
  13 perspicacious 14 discriminating
judiciousness 4 tact 6 acumen, wisdom 8
  prudence, sagacity 9 good sense 10 discretion 11 discernment, percipience 12
  perspicacity 14 discrimination
Judique, Mrs Tanis
  character in: 7 Babbitt
  author: 5 Lewis

Judith
  husband: 4 Esau
  killed: 10 Holofernes
Judith Paris
  author: 11 Hugh Walpole
jug 3 jar, urn 4 ewer 5 crock, stein 6 bottle,
  carafe, flagon, vessel 7 pitcher, tankard 8
  decanter, demijohn 9 container
juggle 4 redo 5 alter 6 modify 7 falsify 8
  disguise, fool with 9 keep aloft 10 manipulate, meddle with, reorganize, tamper with,
  tinker with 12 misrepresent
juggler 5 cheat 6 jester 8 conjuror, deceiver, jongleur, magician, shuffler 15
  prestidigitator
Juice
  nickname of: 9 O J Simpson
juicy 3 wet 4 lush, racy 5 fluid, lurid, moist,
  pulpy, runny, sappy, spicy, vivid 6 fluent,
  liquid, risque, watery 7 flowing, graphic 8
  colorful, dripping, exciting, luscious 9 succulent, thrilling 10 intriguing 11 captivating,
  fascinating, picturesque, provocative, sensational, tantalizing
Jules and Jim
  director: 16 Francois Truffaut
  cast: 10 Henri Serre 11 Marie Dubois,
  Oskar Werner 12 Jeanne Moreau
Julia
  character in: 20 Two Gentlemen of Verona
  author: 11 Shakespeare
Julia
  character: 10 Corey Baker, Eddie
  Edson, Julia Baker 11 Hannah Yarby 14
  Earl J Waggedorn, Marie Waggedorn 15
  Dr Morton Chegley
  cast: 10 Lloyd Nolan, Marc Copage 11
  Betty Beaird, Michael Link 12 Eddie
  Quillan, Lurene Tuttle, Paul Winfield 14
  Diahann Carroll
Julia
  director: 13 Fred Zinnemann
  based on story by: 14 Lillian Hellman
  (Pentimento)
  cast: 9 Jane Fonda (Lillian Hellman) 11
  Hal Holbrook 12 Jason Robards (Dashiell
  Hammett) 15 Vanessa Redgrave (Julia)
  16 Maximilian Schell
  Oscar for: 12 screenwriter 15 supporting
  actor (Robards) 17 supporting actress
  (Redgrave)
Julius Caesar
  author: 18 William Shakespeare
  character: 6 Brutus (Marcus Brutus),
  Portia 7 Cassius (Gaius Cassius) 9
  Calpurnia 10 Mark Antony (Marcus
  Antonius)
  director: 17 Joseph L Mankiewicz
  cast: 10 James Mason 11 Deborah Kerr,
  Greer Garson, John Gielgud 12 Edmond
  O'Brien, Louis Calhern, Marlon Brando
July
  flower: 8 larkspur 9 water lily
  French: 7 Juillet
  holiday: 11 Bastille Day (14), Dominion

Day (1) 15 Independence Day (4) 16
Saint Swithin's Day (15)
gem: 4 ruby
German: 4 Juli
Italian: 6 Luglio
number of days: 9 thirty-one
origin of name: 12 Julius Caesar
place in year:
Gregorian: 7 seventh
Roman: 5 fifth
Spanish: 5 Julio
Zodiac sign: 3 Leo 6 Cancer

jumble 3 mix 4 heap, mess, olio, stew 5
bunch, chaos, mix up, pitch, snarl 6 ball
up, medley, muddle, pile up, tangle, tumble
7 clutter, farrago, melange, mixture, scatter 8 disarray, mishmash 9 aggregate,
confusion, patchwork, potpourri 10 hodgepodge, miscellany, salmagundi 11 gallimaufry 12 accumulation 14 conglomeration

jumbled 5 messy 7 chaotic, mixed up,
snarled, tangled 8 confused 9 cluttered,
illogical 10 disjointed, incoherent 11 disarranged 12 disconnected, disorganized

jumbo 4 huge, vast 5 giant 6 mighty 7 immense, mammoth, titanic 8 colossal, enormous, gigantic, towering 9 cyclopean,
monstrous, oversized 10 monumental,
stupendous 11 elephantine, mountainous

jump 3 hop 4 buck, leap, pass, skip 5
boost, bound, pitch, start, surge, vault,
wince 6 ambush, attack, blench, bounce,
flinch, gambol, go over, hurdle, prance, recoil, spring, switch, upturn, zoom up 7 advance, barrier, digress, maunder, overrun,
upsurge 8 fall upon, obstacle 9 barricade,
increment, skyrocket 10 impediment 11
obstruction 12 augmentation

jumper 4 frog, sled, toad 5 dress, horse,
shirt, smock 6 blouse, hopper, jacket,
leaper 7 overall 8 coverall, kangaroo

jump for joy 5 exult 7 rejoice

jumpy 5 nervy, shaky 6 goosey, uneasy 7
alarmed, anxious, fidgety, fretful, jittery,
nervous, panicky, twitchy, uptight 8 aflutter,
agitated, fluttery, skittish 9 trembling,
twitching 10 frightened 12 apprehensive

junction 6 linkup 7 conflux, joining 10 confluence, crossroads 11 concurrence,
convergence, interchange 12 intersection

juncture 4 pass, seam 5 joint 6 crisis,
linkup, moment 7 closure, joining, meeting
8 interval, occasion 10 confluence, connection 11 convergence, point in time 12
intersection 13 critical point

June
characteristic: 8 weddings
event: 12 Midsummer Day (24), Midsummer Eve (23) 14 summer solstice (21)
flower: 4 rose
French: 4 Juin
gem: 5 pearl 9 moonstone 11 alexandrite
German: 4 Juni
holiday: 7 Flag Day (14) 10 Father's Day
(third Sunday) 13 Kamehameha Day (11)
22 Jefferson Davis' birthday (3)

Italian: 6 Giugno
number of days: 6 thirty
origin of name: 4 Juno (Roman goddess) 6 Junius (Roman clan) 8 juniores
(youths)
place in year:
Gregorian: 5 sixth
Roman: 6 fourth
saying: 24 What is so rare as a day in
June
Spanish: 5 Junio
Zodiac sign: 6 Cancer, Gemini

jungle 4 bush, wild 5 woods 10 rain forest,
wilderness 11 undergrowth 12 swampy
forest, virgin forest

Jungle, The
author: 13 Upton Sinclair
character: 3 Ona 5 Jonas 6 Marija 8
Elzbieta 12 Jurgis Rudkus 13 Antanas
Rudkus
criticism of: 19 meat-packing industry

Jungle Books, The
author: 14 Rudyard Kipling
character: 3 Kaa 5 Akela, Baloo, Hathi 6
Buldeo, Messua, Mowgli 8 Bagheera 9
Shere Khan 11 Gray Brother

Jungle Jim
creator: 11 Alex Raymond
character: 4 Joan, Kolu

junior 5 later, lower, minor, newer 6 lesser
7 younger 8 inferior 9 secondary 11 subordinate

juniper 9 Juniperus
varieties: 4 ashe, plum 5 Greek, Irish,
shore 6 common, ground, needle, Polish,
Sierra, Syrian 7 African, incense, prickly,
Sargent 8 creeping, drooping, mountain,
red-berry, Waukegan 9 alligator, blue-
spire, Himalayan, prostrate 10 California
11 cherrystone 12 Canary Island, sweet-
fruited 13 Rocky Mountain

junk 4 dump 5 scrap, trash, waste 6 debris,
litter, refuse 7 clutter, discard, garbage,
rubbish, rummage 8 castoffs, oddments,
throw out 9 dispose of, throw away 11
odds and ends

junket 4 tour, trip 7 journey 9 excursion

Juno
origin: 5 Roman
queen of: 6 heaven
father: 6 Saturn
brother: 7 Jupiter
husband: 7 Jupiter
son: 4 Mars
protectress of: 5 women 8 marriage
epithet: 6 Lucina, Moneta 7 Curitis,
Pronuba, Sospita
festival: 10 Matronalia
corresponds to: 4 Hera, Here

Juno and the Paycock
author: 10 Sean O'Casey

junta 5 cabal 7 council 9 committee 18 military government

Jupe, Sissy
character in: 9 Hard Times
author: 7 Dickens

Jupiter
 also: 4 Jove
 god of: 5 light 7 heavens, weather 9 lightning 11 thunderbolt
 epithet: 5 Ultor 7 Elicius, Pluvius
 corresponds to: 4 Zeus

Jupiter
 position: 5 fifth
 satellite: 2 Io 6 Europa 8 Amalthea, Callisto, Ganymede
 characteristic: 7 red spot

Jurassic period
 dinosaur from: 10 Diplodocus 11 Apatosaurus, Stegosaurus 12 Brontosaurus, Camarasaurus, Camptosaurus, Ceratosaurus, Megalosaurus 13 Brachiosaurus, Compsognathus, Ornitholestes

Jurgen
 author: 17 James Branch Cabell

Jurgens, Curt
 also: 11 Curd Jurgens
 born: 6 Munich 7 Germany
 roles: 12 The Blue Angel 16 The Spy Who Loved Me

jurisdiction 3 say 4 area, beat, rule, sway, zone 5 field, range, reach, scope 6 bounds, domain, sphere 7 circuit, command, compass, control, quarter 8 district, dominion, hegemony, latitude, precinct, province 9 authority, bailiwick 10 legal right 11 prerogative

jurist 5 judge 6 lawyer 7 counsel, justice 8 advocate, attorney 9 barrister, counselor, solicitor 10 magistrate 12 legal adviser 13 attorney-at-law

jury 5 panel, peers 6 assize, twelve 9 committee, makeshift, veniremen

jury-rigged 9 improvised, makeshift, temporary

jus 3 law 5 right
jus civile 8 civil law
jus gentium 12 law of nations
jus naturale 11 law of nature
jus sanguinis 12 right of blood
 (law) citizenship of child is same as: 7 parents

jus soli 11 right of land, right of soil
 (law) citizenship of child based on place of: 5 birth

just 3 but, due 4 fair, firm, good, only, sane 5 fully, moral, quite, solid, sound 6 at most, barely, decent, hardly, honest, lately, merely, proper, simply, strong, worthy 7 condign, ethical, exactly, fitting, logical, merited, only now, upright 8 adequate, balanced, deserved, entirely, narrowly, recently, scarcely, sensible, suitable, unbiased 9 befitting, blameless, equitable, honorable, impartial, justified, objective, perfectly, precisely, reputable, righteous, unbigoted, uncorrupt 10 aboveboard, absolutely, acceptable, completely, evenhanded, fair-minded, high-minded, no more than, nothing but, not long ago, principled, reasonable, scrupulous, upstanding 11 appropriate, justifiable, trustworthy, well-founded 12 conscionable, open to reason, unprejudiced, well-grounded 13 conscientious, disinterested, dispassionate

just about 6 almost, around, barely, nearly 7 close to 10 not far from 12 on the point of 13 approximately

Just Above My Head
 author: 12 James Baldwin

just a moment ago
 French: 11 tout a l'heure

justice 5 honor, right, truth 6 amends, equity, the law, virtue 7 honesty, payment, penalty, probity, redress 8 fair play, fairness, goodness, legality 9 atonement, integrity, rightness 10 correction, lawfulness, legitimacy, reparation 11 just desserts, proper cause, uprightness 12 chastisement, compensation, equitability, remuneration, satisfaction 13 due punishment, equitableness, justification, righteousness 17 constitutionality
 god of: 7 Forsete, Forseti
 goddess of: 4 Dice, Dike 6 Astrea 7 Astraea

Justice
 author: 14 John Galsworthy

Justice Clement
 character in: 19 Every Man in His Humour
 author: 6 Jonson

justice to all
 Latin: 15 justitia omnibus
 motto of: 18 District of Columbia

justifiable 9 excusable 10 defensible 11 explanatory, extenuating, supportable

justification 5 alibi 6 excuse 7 apology, defense, pretext, support 8 sanction 10 accounting, adjustment, validation 11 explanation, vindication 12 confirmation 13 rectification 14 reconciliation

justification for existence
 French: 11 raison d'etre

justify 6 back up, defend, excuse, uphold 7 bear out, confirm, explain, support, sustain, warrant 8 sanction, validate 9 vindicate 10 account for, prove right

justitia omnibus 12 justice to all
 motto of: 18 District of Columbia

just now
 French: 11 tout a l'heure

just the same 6 anyhow, anyway 12 nevertheless

just the thing 7 apropos 8 suitable 11 appropriate 12 exactly right

Justus see 5 Titus

jut 5 bulge 6 beetle, extend 7 poke out, project 8 overhang, protrude, shoot out, stand out, stick out 13 thrust forward

jute 19 Corchorus capsularis
 varieties: 5 Bimli, China, Tossa, white 7 bastard 10 Bimlipatum

Juturna
 form: 5 nymph
 goddess of: 5 lakes 7 streams
 father: 6 Daunus
 brother: 6 Turnus
 loved by: 7 Jupiter

juvenile 5 child, minor, young, youth **6** boyish, callow, infant, junior **7** girlish **8** childish, immature, teenager, youthful **9** childlike, pubescent, stripling, youngster **10** adolescent, sophomoric **15** unsophisticated

Juventas

protectress of: 14 military age men

juxtaposed 6 next to **8** adjacent, touching **9** proximate **10** contiguous, side by side **12** conterminous

juxtaposition 5 touch **7** balance, contact **8** contrast, nearness **9** adjacency, proximity **10** apposition, contiguity

K

K
  character in: 9 The Castle
  author: 5 Kafka
Ka
  origin: 8 Egyptian
  form: 6 spirit
  trait: 11 immortality
kabob 5 cabab, cabob, kabab, kebab, kebob 7 shaslik 8 shashlik 9 shashlick
Kabul
  capital of: 11 Afghanistan
Kafka, Franz
  author of: 7 Amerika 8 The Trial 9 The
  Castle 16 The Metamorphosis
kahlua
  type: 6 brandy
  origin: 6 Mexico
  flavor: 6 coffee
  with rum: 10 Black Maria
  with tequila: 9 Brave Bull
  with vodka: 12 Black Russian
Kahn, Albert
  architect of: 15 River Rouge Plant 17
  Highland Park Plant 20 Athletic Club
  Building (Detroit) 21 General Motors
  Building (Detroit)
Kahn, Louis Isadore
  architect of: 16 Kimbell Art Museum (Ft
  Worth TX) 23 Yale Center for British Art
  24 Yale University Art Gallery 28 Phillips
  Exeter Academy Library (NH) 31 Richards Medical Research Building (U of PA)
  33 Salk Institute for Biological Studies (La
  Jolla CA)
Kahn, Madeline
  born: 8 Boston MA
  roles: 9 Paper Moon 10 What's Up Doc?
  14 Blazing Saddles 17 Young Frankenstein
kaiser 5 ruler 7 emperor, Wilhelm 8 autocrat
kakemono 6 scroll 13 hanging object
kale 16 Brassica oleracea (Acephala
  Group)
    varieties: 3 sea 4 Ruvo, tall, tree 6 In-
    dian, Scotch 7 cabbage, Chinese, Italian,
    kitchen 8 Siberian 9 flowering, Tronchuda
    10 decorative, ornamental, Portuguese
    13 dwarf Siberian 16 ornamental-leaved
kaleidoscopic 6 mobile, motley 7 protean
  8 shifting, unstable, variable 9 checkered
  10 changeable, variegated 11 fluctuating,
  many colored, rainbowlike, vacillating 12
  ever-changing
Kaleva 8 folk hero
  origin: 7 Finnish 8 Estonian

Kalevala
  origin: 7 Finnish
  form: 4 epic
Kali
  also: 3 Uma 5 Durga 7 Parvati
  husband: 4 Siva 5 Shiva
  festival: 6 dewali
  goddess of: 5 death 7 disease
Kalidasa
  author of: 9 MeghadutaSakuntala 10
  Shakuntala 14 Cloud Messenger
Kalimantan see 6 Borneo
Kalki
  author: 9 Gore Vidal
Kampala
  capital of: 6 Uganda
Kampuchea see 8 Cambodia
Kandinsky, Wassily (Vasily)
  born: 6 Moscow, Russia
  artwork: 7 Striped 8 Twilight 10 Black
  Lines 11 Impressions 12 Blue Mountain
  (no 84), Compositions, Violet Orange 13
  Black Relation 14 Improvisations 15 Capricious Forms 17 Bavarian Mountains,
  The Street in Murnau 23 Painting with
  White Border
Kanga
  character in: 13 Winnie the Pooh
  author: 5 Milne
kangaroo
  young: 4 joey
  group of: 3 mob 5 troop
Kaniengehaga see 6 Mohawk
Kansas
  abbreviation: 2 KS 4 Kans
  nickname: 5 Wheat 9 Jayhawker, Sunflower 15 Garden of the West
  capital: 6 Topeka
  largest city: 7 Wichita
  others: 4 Hays, Iola 5 Colby, Dodge 6
  Salina 7 Abilene, Chanute, Emporia, Liberal 8 Atchison, Lawrence 9 Great Bend
  10 Belleville, Hutchinson, Kansas City 11
  Coffeeville, Leavenworth 12 Junction City
  college: 5 Baker, Tabor 7 Bethany 8
  Sterling, Washburn
  explorer: 8 Coronado
  feature: 16 Eisenhower Center
  fort: 5 Riley, Scott
  Indian training school: 16 Haskell Institute
  penitentiary: 11 Leavenworth
  reservoir: 11 Tuttle Creek
  tribe: 3 Kaw 4 Pani 5 Kansa, Kiowa,
  Osage 6 Pawnee 7 Arapaho, Wichita 8
  Cheyenne, Comanche, Kickapoo
  people: 7 Jayhawk 11 Damon Runyon

13 Amelia Earhart, Karl Menninger 14 Walter Chrysler 15 Edgar Lee Masters
lake: 6 Cheney, Kerwin, Neosho 7 Milford
land rank: 10 fourteenth
mountain:
highest point: 9 Sunflower
physical feature:
plains: 5 Great, Osage
president: 17 Dwight D Eisenhower
river: 3 Kaw 6 Kansas 8 Arkansas, Cimarron, Missouri 9 Smoky Hill 10 Republican
state admission: 12 thirty-fourth
state bird: 17 western meadowlark
state flower: 9 sunflower
state motto: 29 To the Stars Through Difficulties
state song: 14 Home on the Range
state tree: 10 cottonwood

Kansas City
baseball team: 6 Royals
football team: 6 Chiefs
landmark: 12 Union Station 22 Nelson-Atkins Art Gallery
river: 6 Kansas 8 Missouri

Kant, Immanuel
author of: 20 Critique of Pure Reason

Kantor, MacKinlay
author of: 13 Andersonville

Karloff, Boris
real name: 17 William Henry Pratt
born: 7 Dulwich, England
roles: 12 Frankenstein

karma 3 act 4 aura, deed, duty, fate, rite 5 force, power 6 action, kismet, spirit 7 destiny 9 vibration

Kasdan, Lawrence
director of: 11 The Big Chill

Kashmiri
language family: 12 Indo-European
branch: 11 Indo-Iranian
group: 5 Indic
spoken in: 5 (northern) India

kashruth, kashrut 7 fitness 17 Jewish dietary laws

Katharina
character in: 19 The Taming of the Shrew
author: 11 Shakespeare

Katmandu, Kathmandu
capital of: 5 Nepal

Katzenjammer Kids
also: 17 Captain and the Kids
creator: 12 Rudolph Dirks
character: 4 Hans 5 Fritz, Momma 10 der Captain 12 der Inspector

Kaufman, George S
author of:
with Edna Ferber: 9 Stage Door 13 Dinner at Eight 14 The Royal Family
with Moss Hart: 15 Once in a Lifetime 20 You Can't Take It with You 21 The Man Who Came to Dinner

Kay (Sir Kay)
character in: 16 Arthurian romance
foster brother: 6 Arthur

Kaye, Danny
real name: 19 David Daniel Kaminski
born: 10 Brooklyn NY
roles: 19 The Inspector General 21 Hans Christian Andersen 26 The Secret Life of Walter Mitty

Kaye, M M
author of: 9 Trade Wind 12 Death in Kenya 15 Death in Zanzibar, Shadow of the Moon, The Far Pavilions

Kazakhstan
capital/largest city: 7 Alma-Ata
others: 9 Karaganda 13 Petropavlovsk, Semipalatinsk
head of state: 9 president
government: 8 republic
monetary unit: 5 ruble
sea: 4 Aral 7 Caspian
physical feature: 7 steppes 12 Lake Balkhash
people: 6 Kazakh
language: 6 Kazakh

Kazan, Elia
director of: 10 East of Eden, Viva Zapata 15 On the Waterfront (Oscar) 18 Splendor in the Grass 19 Gentleman's Agreement (Oscar) 20 A Tree Grows in Brooklyn 21 A Streetcar Named Desire

Kazantzakis, Nikos
author of: 13 Zorba the Greek 14 Freedom or Death, The Greek Passion 25 The Last Temptation of Christ

kazoo 5 bazoo, zarah 6 hewgag 11 eunuch flute
French: 8 mirliton

Keach, Stacy
real name: 18 Walter Stacy Keach Jr
born: 10 Savannah GA
roles: 3 Doc 6 Luther 10 Mike Hammer 24 Twinkle Twinkle Killer Kane

Kearny, Stephen Watts
served in: 10 California, Mexican War
commander of: 13 Army of the West
occupied: 9 New Mexico
battle: 10 San Gabriel, San Pasqual

Keaton, Buster
real name: 19 Joseph Francis Keaton
born: 7 Piqua KS
roles: 6 Go West 7 College 10 The General 12 The Cameraman

Keaton, Diane
real name: 9 Diane Hall
born: 12 Los Angeles CA
roles: 4 Reds 7 Sleeper 8 Baby Boom 9 Annie Hall (Oscar) 12 Shoot the Moon, The Godfather 13 The Good Mother 14 Play It Again Sam 19 Looking for Mr Goodbar 20 The Little Drummer Girl

Keats, John
author of: 5 Lamia 8 Endymion, Hyperion, Isabella 11 Ode to Autumn, Ode to Psyche 14 Ode on Indolence 15 Ode on Melancholy, The Eve of St Agnes 16 Ode on a Grecian Urn 17 Ode to a Nightingale 20 La Belle Dame Sans Merci 31 On First Looking into Chapman's Homer

Kedemah
  also called: 5 Kedar
  father: 7 Ishmael
  mother: 5 Hagar
  descendant of: 8 Kedarite
Keel (of Argo)
  constellation of: 6 Carina
Keel, Howard
  real name: 17 Harry Clifford Leek
  costar: 14 Kathryn Grayson
  born: 11 Gillespie IL
  roles: 6 Dallas, Kismet 8 Showboat 10
  Kiss Me Kate 13 Clayton Farlow 15 Annie
  Get Your Gun 27 Seven Brides for Seven
  Brothers
Keeler, Ruby
  husband: 8 Al Jolson
  costar: 10 Dick Powell
  born: 6 Canada 7 Halifax
  roles: 15 Footlight Parade 17 Forty-
  Second Street 32 Gold Diggers of Nineteen Thirty Three
keel over 5 faint, swoon, upset 7 capsize,
  tip over 8 collapse, fall down, fall flat, flip
  over, overturn, turn over 10 turn turtle
keen 4 avid, fine 5 acute, alert, eager,
  sharp 6 ardent, astute, clever, fervid,
  fierce, shrewd 7 earnest, excited, fervent,
  intense, zealous 8 incisive 9 impatient, paper thin, razorlike 10 discerning 11 finely
  honed, impassioned, penetrating, quick-
  witted 12 enthusiastic 13 perspicacious 14
  discriminating
keen-eyed 5 alert 8 vigilant, watchful 9 attentive, eagle-eyed, observant, sharp-
  eyed, wide-awake
keen-minded 5 acute, sharp, smart 6 astute, clever, shrewd 10 perceptive 11 penetrating
keenness 4 zeal, zest 5 ardor 6 acumen,
  fervor 8 passion 9 acuteness, eagerness,
  sharpness 10 astuteness, cleverness, enthusiasm, excitement, shrewdness 11 discernment 12 anticipation, intelligence, perspicacity
keen-sighted 4 sage, wise 5 acute, sharp 6
  astute, shrewd 8 piercing 9 eagle-eyed, judicious, sagacious, sharp-eyed 10 discerning 11 intelligent, penetrating 12 clear-
  sighted, sharp-sighted 13 perspicacious
keep 3 bar 4 clog, fort, have, heap, hold,
  mind, pile, stay 5 abide, block, carry,
  cramp, delay, deter, guard, honor, lay in,
  place, stack, stall, stand, stick, stock,
  store, tie up, tower 6 arrest, castle, detain,
  donjon, endure, hamper, hinder, hobble,
  hold up, impede, living, pay for, remain, retain, retard 7 care for, carry on, citadel, deposit, furnish, inhibit, observe, possess,
  prevent, shackle, support, sustain 8 conserve, continue, encumber, fortress, hang
  on to, hold back, maintain, obstruct, preserve, restrain 9 celebrate, constrain,
  hamstring, persevere, persist in, ritualize,
  safeguard, solemnize, watch over 10 accumulate, daily bread, livelihood, provide
  for, stronghold, sustenance 11 commem-

orate, maintenance, memorialize, subsistence 12 room and board 13 fortification
keep an eye on 5 watch 7 oversee 9 chaperone, look after, watch over
keep apart 7 isolate 8 separate 9 segregate
keep at bay 7 beat off, fend off, ward off 8
  stave off
keep back 5 check, delay 6 detain, hold up,
  retain 8 withhold
keep busy 3 use 6 employ, engage, occupy 7 utilize
keep clear of 4 shun 5 avoid, dodge,
  elude, evade, skirt 6 escape
keep company 4 date 5 court 7 consort,
  hang out 8 go around, go steady 9 accompany, associate 10 fraternize, go together
keeper 5 guard, nurse 6 duenna, escort,
  jailer, sentry, warden 7 curator 8 chaperon,
  guardian, retainer, sentinel, wet nurse 9
  attendant, bodyguard, caretaker, chaperone, custodian, governess, nursemaid,
  protecter, protector 11 conservator, nur-
  serymaid 13 guardian angel
keep in mind 8 consider, remember 10
  think about
keep mum 13 button one's lip
keep off 7 fend off, stay off, ward off 8
  stave off
keep one's counsel 12 remain silent 13
  button one's lip
keep open 8 hold open 16 leave unsched-
  uled
keep out 6 reject 8 prohibit 9 blackball,
  blacklist
keep out of sight 4 hide 5 cover 6 lay low,
  lie low 7 conceal, cover up, secrete 10
  camouflage
keep private 4 hide 7 conceal, reserve 8
  withhold
keepsake 5 relic, token 6 emblem, memory, symbol 7 memento 8 memorial, reminder, souvenir 11 remembrance 18 token of remembrance
keep secret 4 hide 6 hush up 7 conceal,
  cover up 8 suppress, withhold
keep silent 10 remain dumb 15 not breathe
  a word
keep steady 5 poise 7 balance 9 stabilize
keep to 5 cling, stick 6 adhere, be true,
  cleave, hold to 7 be loyal, stand by 8 maintain
keg 3 tub, tun, vat 4 butt, cask, drum, tank
  6 barrel 7 rundlet 8 hogshead, puncheon 9
  container, kilderkin
Kellerman, Sally
  born: 11 Long Beach CA
  roles: 4 MASH 15 Hot Lips Houlihan
Kelly, Gene
  real name: 17 Eugene Curran Kelly
  born: 12 Pittsburgh PA
  roles: 7 Pal Joey 9 Brigadoon, On the
  Town 13 Anchors Aweigh 15 Singin' in
  the Rain 17 An American in Paris 18 The
  Three Musketeers

Kelly, Grace
husband: 21 Prince Rainier Grimaldi
nickname: 11 Ice Princess
born: 14 Philadelphia PA
roles: 7 Mogambo 8 High Noon 10 Rear Window 11 High Society 13 To Catch a Thief 14 Dial M for Murder, The Country Girl (Oscar)

Kelly, Walt
creator/artist of: 4 Pogo

kelp 3 ash 4 agar, alga, leag 5 varec, varic, wrack 7 seaweed
source of: 4 soda 6 iodine 9 potassium

Kelpie
origin: 8 Scottish
form: 5 horse 6 spirit
habitat: 4 lake 5 river
causes: 8 drowning
warns of: 8 drowning

Kelvin
abbreviation: 1 K

Kelvin, William Thomson
field: 7 physics 11 mathematics
nationality: 7 British
worked on: 4 heat 11 electricity
invented: 12 electrometer, galvanometer 13 tide predictor
named for him: 22 Kelvin temperature scale

Kempis, Thomas a
author of: 20 The Imitation of Christ

Kenaz
father: 7 Eliphaz
son: 5 Caleb 7 Othniel

Keneally, Thomas
author of: 12 Confederates 14 Schindler's List

Kenilworth
author: 14 Sir Walter Scott
character: 6 Alasco, Dudley (Earl of Leicester) 10 Amy Robsart 12 Wayland Smith 13 Richard Varney 14 Queen Elizabeth 15 Flibbertigibbet 16 Edmund Tressilian

Kennedy, Arthur
real name: 17 John Arthur Kennedy
born: 11 Worcester MA
roles: 8 Becket 9 All My Sons 11 Peyton Place 12 Blind Victory 16 Death of a Salesman

Kennedy, Frank
character in: 15 Gone With the Wind
author: 8 Mitchell

Kennedy, John Fitzgerald
nickname: 3 JFK 4 Jack
presidential rank: 11 thirty-fifth
party: 10 Democratic
state represented: 2 MA
defeated: 5 (Richard Milhous) Nixon
vice president: 7 (Lyndon Baines) Johnson
cabinet:
state: 4 (David Dean) Rusk
treasury: 6 (Clarence Douglas) Dillon
defense: 8 (Robert Strange) McNamara
attorney general: 7 (Robert Francis) Kennedy

postmaster general: 3 (James Edward) Day 9 (John Austin) Gronouski
interior: 5 (Stewart Lee) Udall
agriculture: 7 (Orville Lothrop) Freeman
commerce: 6 (Luther Hartwell) Hodges
labor: 5 (William Willard) Wirtz 8 (Arthur J) Goldberg
HEW: 8 (Abraham Alexander) Ribicoff 10 (Anthony Joseph) Celebrezze
born: 11 Brookline MA
died: 8 Dallas TX
died by: 13 assassination
assassinated by: 6 (Lee Harvey) Oswald
buried: 25 Arlington National Cemetery
education:
prep school: 6 Choate
University: 7 Harvard 9 Princeton 23 London School of Economics
religion: 13 Roman Catholic
interests: 7 sailing 8 football 13 touch football
vacation spot: 9 Cape Cod MA 13 Hyannis Port MA
author: 15 Strategy of Peace, Why England Slept 17 Profiles in Courage (Pulitzer Prize)
political career: 9 US Senator 24 US House of Representatives
civilian career: 17 newspaper reporter
military service: 6 US Navy 10 lieutenant 11 World War Two
commander of: 6 PT boat
notable events of lifetime/term: 9 Bay of Pigs 10 Berlin Wall, Peace Corps 18 Cuban missile crisis
march: 11 Civil Rights
treaty: 14 Nuclear Test-Ban
quote: 17 Ich bin ein Berliner (I am a Berliner) 35 We stand today on the edge of a New Frontier 61 Ask not what your country can do for you ask what you can do for your country
father: 13 Joseph Patrick
mother: 4 Rose (Fitzgerald)
siblings: 4 Jean 6 Eunice, Joseph 8 Kathleen, Patricia, Rosemary 11 Edward Moore 13 Robert Francis
wife: 10 Jacqueline (Lee Bouvier)
nickname: 6 Jackie
second marriage to: 7 Onassis
children: 14 John Fitzgerald, Patrick Bouvier (died in infancy) 15 Caroline Bouvier

Kennicott, Dr Will and Carol
characters in: 10 Main Street
author: 5 Lewis

Kentucky
abbreviation: 2 KY
nickname: 9 Bluegrass 11 Corncracker
capital: 9 Frankfort
largest city: 10 Louisville
others: 5 Berea 6 Corbin, Hazard 7 Ashland, Glasgow, Newport, Paducah, Shively 8 Danville 9 Covington, Henderson, Lexington, Owensboro 12 Bowling Green, Hopkinsville, Madisonville

college: 5 Berea 6 Centre 7 Ashbury, Brescia 8 Ursuline 12 Transylvania
explorer: 11 Daniel Boone
feature: 7 Obelisk
birthplace: 14 Abraham Lincoln
fort: 4 Knox
national park: 11 Mammoth Cave
race: 13 Kentucky Derby
racetrack: 14 Churchill Downs
trail: 10 Wilderness
tribe: 7 Shawnee 8 Cherokee, Iroquois
people: 11 corncracker, John M Harlan 13 Louis Brandeis 16 Frederick M Vinson, Robert Penn Warren
lake: 8 Kentucky 10 Cumberland
land rank: 13 thirty-seventh
mountain: 4 Pine 10 Cumberland
highest point: 5 Black 8 Big Black
physical feature:
basin: 9 Bluegrass
cave: 7 Mammoth
gap: 10 Cumberland
plain: 7 Coastal
plateau: 10 Cumberland
president: 14 Abraham Lincoln
Confederate president: 14 Jefferson Davis
river: 3 Dix 4 Ohio, Salt 5 Green 6 Barren 7 Licking 8 Big Sandy, Kentucky 9 Tennessee 10 Cumberland 11 Mississippi
state admission: 9 fifteenth
state bird: 8 cardinal
state flower: 9 goldenrod
state motto: 26 United We Stand Divided We Fall
state song: 17 My Old Kentucky Home
state tree: 10 coffee tree 11 tulip poplar 12 yellow poplar

Kenya
capital/largest city: 7 Nairobi
others: 5 Nyeri, Thika, Wajir 6 Kisumu, Kitale, Lodwar, Moyale, Nakuru, Webuye 7 Eldoret, Kericho, Malindi, Mandera, Mombasa, Nanyuki 9 Lokitaung
measure: 4 wari
monetary unit: 4 cent 5 pound 8 shilling
island: 5 Manda, Patta
lake: 6 Magadi, Nakuru, Natron, Rudolf 7 Turkana 8 Naivasha, Victoria
mountain: 5 Elgon, Kulai, Nyira, Nyiru 6 Matian 7 Logonot 8 Aberdare
highest point: 5 Kenya 6 Kinyaa 9 Kirinyaga
river: 3 Lak 4 Athi, Dawa, Kuja, Tana 5 Nzoia 6 Galana 8 Turkwell
sea: 6 Indian
physical feature:
bay: 7 Formosa
desert: 6 Chalbi
escarpment: 3 Mau
gulf: 9 Kavirondo
highlands: 5 Kenya, Kisii, Luyla 7 Kericho
plain: 4 Kano
plateau: 5 Nandi, Yatta 6 Elgeyo
valley: 9 Great Rift
people: 3 Luo 4 Arab, Meru 5 Bantu,

Elgey, Galla, Kamba, Kisii, Luhya, Masai, Nandi, Tugen 6 Kikuyu, Ogaden, Somali 7 Baluhya, Hamitic, Hilotic, Kipsigi, Swahili, Turkana 8 Kalenjin, Marakwet
god: 4 Ngai
leader: 5 Mboya 12 Jomo Kenyatta 13 Daniel Arap Moi
language: 3 Luo 5 Bantu, Luhya, Masai 6 Kikuyu 7 English, Swahili 8 Guyerati 10 Hindustani
religion: 5 Islam 7 animism 8 Anglican 13 Roman Catholic
place:
archeological excavation: 11 Gamble's Cave
mosque: 5 Khoja
museum: 9 Fort Jesus
national park/wildlife preserve: 4 Meru 5 Nyeri, Tsavo 6 Arusha 7 Manyara, Nairobi, Samburu 8 Aberdare, Amboseli 10 Lake Nakuru, Mount Kenya, Rift Valley
ruins: 4 Gedi
feature:
garment: 5 kanga 7 kitenge
round house: 6 shamba
secret organization: 6 Mau Mau
tree: 6 ayieke, baobab
food:
fish: 7 tilapia
wine: 5 tembo

Kepler, Johannes
nationality: 6 German
invented: 14 convex eyepiece 21 astronomical telescope
formulated:
three laws of planetary motion (Kepler's Laws): 10 law of areas 11 harmonic law 24 elliptical orbit of planets
author of: 14 Astronomia nova, Harmonice mundi 16 Rudolphine Tables 23 Mysterium cosmographicum 30 Epitome astronomiae Copernicanae

Ker
form: 6 spirit
associated with: 5 death
corresponds to: 6 Furies

kerchief 5 cloth, scarf 7 muffler 8 babushka, neckwear 9 headpiece, neckcloth 11 neckerchief 12 handkerchief

Keres
origin: 5 Greek
spirits of: 4 evil 5 death 6 old age 7 disease

Keres-Siouan
language branch: 5 Keres 7 Caddoan 9 Iroquoian 11 Siouan-Yuchi

kernel 3 nub, nut, pip, pit 4 core, germ, gist, pith, seed 5 grain, stone 6 center, marrow 7 nucleus 12 quintessence

Kerouac, Jack
author of: 6 Big Sur 9 On the Road 13 The Dharma Bums 16 Lonesome Traveler

Kerr, Deborah
real name: 22 Deborah Jane Kerr-Trimmer
born: 8 Scotland 11 Helensburgh

roles: 11 Edward My Son, The King and I 12 The Hucksters 13 The Sundowners 14 Separate Tables, The Chalk Garden 18 From Here to Eternity 19 The Night of the Iguana 20 Heaven Knows Mr Allison

Kesey, Ken
author of: 21 Sometimes a Great Notion 25 One Flew Over the Cuckoo's Nest

Ketcham, Hank
creator/artist of: 15 Dennis the Menace

kettle 3 pan, pot, tub, vat 6 boiler, teapot, tureen 8 cauldron, crucible, saucepan

Ketubim 8 writings 11 Hagiographa

Keturah
husband: 7 Abraham

key 3 cue, fit 4 clue, gear, mode, suit 5 adapt, light, point, scale 6 adjust, answer, direct, opener 7 address, finding, meaning, pointer 8 indicant, solution, tonality 9 indicator 10 exposition, indication, resolution 11 elucidation, explanation, explication, translation 14 interpretation

Key, Ted
creator/artist of: 5 Hazel

keyboard instrument 5 organ, piano 6 spinet 8 psaltery, virginal 9 harmonium 10 clavichord, pianoforte 11 harpsichord

keyed up 5 tense 7 excited, nervous 8 volatile 9 emotional, explosive

key element 9 essential, vital part 18 primary constituent 20 indispensable element

Key Largo
director: 10 John Huston
based on story by: 15 Maxwell Anderson
cast: 12 Claire Trevor, Lauren Bacall 14 Humphrey Bogart 15 Edward G Robinson, Lionel Barrymore
Oscar for: 17 supporting actress (Trevor)

Keynes, John Maynard
author of: 44 The General Theory of Employment Interest and Money

keynote 3 nub 4 core, gist, pith 5 heart, theme 6 marrow 7 essence, nucleus, pattern 8 main idea, quiddity 9 substance 11 nitty-gritty, salient idea 12 central point

keystone 4 base, crux, root 5 basis 8 gravamen, linchpin 9 principle 10 foundation, mainspring

Keystone State
nickname of: 12 Pennsylvania

Key to Rebecca, The
author: 10 Ken Follett

Khachaturian, Aram Ilich
born: 6 Tiflis 7 (Soviet) Georgia
composer of: 6 Gayane 9 Spartacus 12 Song of Stalin

khaki 5 cloth 6 fabric 7 uniform 9 olive-drab 14 yellowish-brown

khan, kahn 3 inn 4 lord 5 chief, ruler 6 prince 7 emperor 9 chieftain, sovereign 11 caravansary
famous: 4 Yuan 6 Kublai 7 Genghis 8 Ghenghis

Khartoum
capital of: 5 Sudan

Khartvelian
language family: 9 Caucasian
includes: 8 Georgian

Khayyam, Omar
author of: 11 The Rubaiyat

Khnum
origin: 8 Egyptian
form: 3 ram
created: 6 humans
used: 4 clay

Khoisan
language spoken by: 3 San 7 Bushmen 9 Khoikhoin 10 Hottentots
includes: 5 Hatsa 7 Sandawe
distinguishing sound: 5 click

kibitzer 3 pry 5 prier, snoop 6 butt-in 7 meddler, snooper, watcher 8 busybody 9 buttinsky

kick 3 fun, hit, out, pep, vim 4 beef, boot, dash, fret, fume, fuss, life, punt, snap, tang, zest 5 eject, force, gripe, growl, power, punch, verve, vigor 6 flavor, grouch, grouse, object, recoil, remove, return, strike, stroke, thrill 7 boot out, cast out, grumble, fly back, protest, rebound, sparkle, turn out 8 backlash, complain, jump back, piquancy, pleasure, pungency, reaction, throw out, vitality 9 amusement, animation, complaint, enjoyment, find fault, grievance, intensity, make a fuss, objection 10 excitement, spring back 11 give the gate, remonstrate, send packing, show the door 12 protestation 13 gratification, remonstration

Kickapoo
language family: 9 Algonkian 10 Algonquian
location: 5 Texas 6 Kansas, Mexico 9 Chihuahua, Wisconsin
related to: 3 Fox, Sac 4 Sauk

kickback 3 cut 5 bribe, graft, share 6 boodle, payoff, payola 9 hush money 10 commission, percentage, protection, recompense 12 compensation, remuneration 15 protection money

kick downstairs 4 bust 6 demote 7 degrade

kickoff 5 start 7 opening 9 beginning, inception, launching 12 inauguration

kick out 4 oust 5 eject, evict, expel 8 throw out 9 discharge

kicks 3 fun 7 thrills 8 pleasure 10 excitement 11 stimulation

kick upstairs 5 boost 7 advance, elevate, promote

Kicva
origin: 5 Welsh
husband: 7 Pryderi

kid 3 rag, rib, tot 4 baby, fool, gull, jest, joke, josh, mock, ride, tyke 5 bluff, child, cozen, harry, put on, tease, trick, youth 6 delude, infant, moppet, plague, shaver, squirt 7 beguile, deceive, laugh at, mislead 8 goat hide, goatskin, hoodwink, juvenile, ridicule, teenager, yearling 9 bamboozle, billy goat, little one, make fun of, nanny goat, offspring, young goat, youngster 10 adolescent 11 goat leather, young person 12 little shaver

Kid, The
   nickname of: 11 Ted Williams

kid around 5 clown, cut up 10 fool around, play around 11 clown around

Kidder, Margot
   born: 6 Canada 11 Yellow Knife
   roles: 7 Sisters 8 Lois Lane, Superman 14 Some Kind of Hero 19 The Amityville Horror

Kiddush 6 prayer 8 blessing 14 sanctification

kidnap 5 seize, steal 6 abduct, hijack, snatch 7 bear off, capture, impress, skyjack 8 bear away, carry off, shanghai 10 run off with 11 make off with 13 hold for ransom

Kidnapped
   author: 20 Robert Louis Stevenson
   character: 9 Alan Breck 10 Rankeillor 12 David Balfour 15 Ebenezer Balfour

Kigali
   capital of: 6 Rwanda

Kiley, Richard
   born: 9 Chicago IL
   roles: 13 Redhead 13 Man of La Mancha 16 Advise and Consent

Kilkenny Cats
   origin: 5 Irish
   form: 4 cats
   number: 3 two
   left after fight: 5 tails

kill 4 beat, do in, halt, hang, ruin, slay, stay 5 break, check, drown, erase, lynch, quell, shoot, waste 6 behead, defeat, murder, poison, rub out, stifle 7 bump off, butcher, cut down, destroy, execute, garrote, silence, smother, squelch, wipe out 8 blow away, dispatch, get rid of, knock off, massacre, strangle, string up 9 dismember, finish off, shoot down, slaughter, suffocate 10 asphyxiate, decapitate, disembowel, extinguish, guillotine, put a stop to, put an end to, put to death 11 assassinate, burn to death, electrocute, exterminate 13 mortally wound

killer 6 hit man, slayer 7 butcher 8 assassin, murderer 11 executioner 12 exterminator

Killers, The
   director: 13 Robert Siodmak
   based on story by: 15 Ernest Hemingway
   cast: 10 Ava Gardner 12 Edmond O'Brien 13 Burt Lancaster

killer whale 4 orca 7 grampus 11 Orcinus orca

killing 4 coup 5 fatal 6 big hit, deadly, lethal, mortal, murder 7 bonanza, cleanup, deathly, hanging, slaying, success, suicide 8 butchery, fatality, homicide, lynching, massacre, regicide, shooting, smash hit, stabbing, windfall 9 bloodshed, execution, garroting, martyrdom, matricide, murderous, patricide, poisoning, slaughter, uxoricide 10 cleaning up, decimation, fratricide,

immolation, impalement, sororicide, strangling 11 crucifixion, devastating, elimination, infanticide 12 annihilation, deathdealing, decapitation, excruciating, guillotining, manslaughter, master stroke, stroke of luck, violent death 13 electrocution, extermination, strangulation 17 capital punishment

Killing Fields
   director: 11 Roland Joffe
   based on article by: 15 Sydney Schanberg (The Death and Life of Dith Pran)
   cast: 10 Haing S Ngor 12 Sam Waterston
   Oscar for: 15 supporting actor (Ngor)

Killing Time
   author: 12 Thomas Berger

killjoy 6 grouch 8 grumbler, sourball, sourpuss 9 Cassandra, gloomy Gus, worrywart 10 complainer, malcontent, spoilsport, wet blanket 11 crapehanger, party-pooper

kill time 4 idle 6 dawdle 9 waste time 10 fool around

Kilmer, Joyce
   author of: 5 Trees

kiln 3 ost 4 bake, burn, fire, oast, oven 5 drier, glaze, stove, tiler 7 furnace 8 calciner, limekiln 9 oasthouse

kiloliter
   abbreviation: 2 kL

kilometer
   abbreviation: 2 km

Kilwich
   origin: 5 Welsh
   form: 6 prince
   performed: 6 labors
   number of labors: 4 five
   married: 5 Olwen

Kim
   author: 14 Rudyard Kipling
   character: 9 Mahbub Ali 11 Tibetan Lama 12 Kimball O'Hara 16 Colonel Creighton 22 Hurree Chunder Mookerjee

kin 4 akin, clan, kith, race 5 folks, tribe 6 family, people 7 kinfolk, kinsmen, related 8 clansmen, kinfolks 9 next of kin, relations, relatives, tribesmen 10 kith and kin 11 connections, consanguine, distaff side, spindle side 13 flesh and blood 14 kissing cousins

kind 3 ilk 4 cast, make, mold, sort, type 5 brand, breed, caste, civil, class, genre, genus, style 6 benign, gentle, kidney, kindly, nature, polite, strain, tender 7 amiable, cordial, variety 8 amicable, friendly, generous, gracious, merciful, obliging 9 courteous 10 bighearted, charitable, neighborly, thoughtful 11 considerate, description, designation, good-hearted, good-humored, good-natured, softhearted, sympathetic, warmhearted, well-meaning 12 affectionate, well-disposed 13 accommodating, compassionate, tenderhearted, understanding

   French: 6 gentil

kindhearted 4 good, warm 6 benign, gentle, humane, kindly, loving 7 helpful 8 amicable, generous, gracious, merciful 10 altruistic, charitable, thoughtful 11 considerate, good-hearted, good-natured, softhearted, sympathetic, warmhearted, well-meaning 12 affectionate, humanitarian 13 accommodating, compassionate, philanthropic, tenderhearted, understanding

kindheartedness 5 mercy 8 altruism, goodness, goodwill, humanity, sympathy 10 compassion, humaneness, tenderness 11 benefaction, benevolence, magnanimity 12 graciousness, philanthropy 13 consideration, understanding, unselfishness 14 charitableness 15 humanitarianism

kindle 4 fire, goad, prod, stir, urge, whet 5 awake, light, rouse, waken 6 arouse, excite, foment, ignite, incite, induce, stir up 7 agitate, animate, inflame, inspire, provoke, quicken, sharpen 8 enkindle 9 call forth, intensify, set fire to, set on fire, stimulate 10 invigorate

kindling 4 fuel 5 brush, paper, twigs 6 firing, tinder 7 burning, flaming 8 firewood, igniting, ignition, lighting, shavings 9 brushwood 10 combustion, enkindling

kindly 4 good, warm 6 benign, gentle, gently, humane, tender, warmly 7 amiable, amiably, civilly, cordial, devoted, patient 8 amicable, amicably, benignly, friendly, generous, gracious, humanely, merciful, tenderly 9 cordially, courteous 10 benevolent, bighearted, charitable, charitably, generously, graciously, mercifully, neighborly 11 considerate, good-humored, good-natured, magnanimous, softhearted, sympathetic, warmhearted, well-meaning 12 affectionate, benevolently, bigheartedly, humanitarian 13 compassionate, considerately, good-humoredly, good-naturedly, magnanimously, philanthropic, softheartedly, tenderhearted, understanding, warmheartedly, well-meaningly 14 affectionately, well-manneredly 15 compassionately, sympathetically, tenderheartedly, understandingly 17 philanthropically

kindness 3 aid 4 gift, help 5 favor, grace, mercy 6 bounty 7 charity 8 good deed, good turn, goodness, goodwill, humanity, patience, sympathy 9 tolerance 10 act of grace, assistance, compassion, generosity, humaneness, kind office, toleration 11 benefaction, beneficence, benevolence, magnanimity 12 act of charity, graciousness, philanthropy 13 consideration, understanding, unselfishness 14 charitableness 15 humanitarianism

Kind of Anger, A
  author: 10 Eric Ambler

kindred 4 akin, like 5 alike 6 allied, united 7 related, similar 8 agreeing, familial, matching 9 accordant, analogous, congenial, simpatico 10 harmonious, resembling 11 consanguine, sympathetic 13 corresponding

kine 4 cows, oxen 6 cattle 9 livestock

kinfolk 3 kin 6 family 7 kinsmen 9 relations, relatives 10 kith and kin

king 3 HRH 5 liege, ruler 7 monarch 8 suzerain 9 potentate, protector, sovereign 10 His Majesty 11 crowned head, royal person, the anointed 18 defender of the faith
  Latin: 3 rex

king/emperor/dynasty
  of Afghanistan: 8 Barakzai
  of Albania: 3 Zog 9 Ahmet Zogu
  of Algeria: 3 bey, dey 6 disawa 8 Jugurtha 9 bevlerbay, Masinissa
  of Austria: 7 Charles, Francis 9 Ferdinand, Habsburgs 10 Franz Josef
  of Bahrain: 9 al-Khalifa
  of Belgium: 7 Leopold 8 Baudouin
  of China: 3 Han, Sui 4 Chou, Ch'in, Ming, Sung, T'ang 5 Ch'ing, Shang 6 Manchu
  of Crete: 5 Minos
  of Denmark 4 Hans, Knud 6 Canute 8 Frederik 9 Christian 10 Gorm the Old 15 Harold Bluetooth
  of Egypt: 5 Khufu, Menes, Zoser 6 Farouk, Khafre, Ptulol, Ramses 7 Saladin 8 Horemheb, Menkaure 9 Akhenaten, Amenemhet, Amenhotep 10 Mentuhotep 11 Tutankhamen
  of England: 3 Hal 4 Cnut, John, Lear 5 Henry, James 6 Alfred, Arthur, Canute, Edmund, Edward, Egbert, George, Harold 7 Charles, Richard, Stephen, William 9 Cymbeline 18 Richard Coeur de Lion 19 Richard the Lionheart 21 Richard the Lionhearted
  of France: 5 Henri, Louis 6 Clovis, Philip 7 Charles 8 Napoleon 9 Hugh Capet 11 Charlemagne 21 Richard the Lionhearted 13 Louis Philippe 14 Henry of Navarre
  of Germany: 6 Kaiser 7 Wilhelm 9 Frederick 10 Barbarossa
  of Greece: 5 Creon 6 Atreus 7 Theseus 8 Menelaus 10 Agammemnon 11 Constantine
  of India: 5 Akbar, Asoka, Babur, Gupta, Mogul, Timur 6 Maurya, Rajput 7 Humayun 8 Hyder Ali, Jahangir, Marathas 9 Aurangzeb, Shah Jahan 11 Tippu Sultan 14 Delhi Sultanate 18 Chandragupta Maurya
  of Iran: 5 Abbas, Cyrus, Qajar 6 Darius, Xerxes 7 Arsacid, Pahlavi, Safavid 8 Parthian, Seleucid 9 Sassanian 10 Achaemenid 15 Shah Reza Pahlavi
  of Iraq: 6 Faisal, Sargon 7 Hussein 9 Hammurabi 13 Harun al-Rashid 14 Nebuchadnezzar
  of Ireland: 9 Brian Boru
  of Italy/Rome: 4 Nero, Otho 5 Galba, Nerva, Titus 6 Trajan 7 Hadrian 8 Caligula, Claudius, Commodus, Domitian, Octavian, Tiberius 9 Caracalla, Vespasian, Vitellius 10 Diocletian 11 Constantine 13 Antoninus Dius 14 Caesar Augustus, Marcus Aurelius, Victor Emmanuel

of Japan: 5 Jimmu, Jingo, Meiji, Taira 6 Yamato 7 Akihito, Izanagi 8 Ashikaga, Fujiwara, Hirohito, Kamakura, Minamoto, Tokugawa

of Java: 7 Mataram 9 Majapahit, Srivijaya

of Jordan: 5 Talal 6 Faisal 7 Hussein 8 Abdullah, Selucidas 10 Ibn Hussein, Nabataeans

of Korea: 2 Yi 4 Choe 5 Ki-tse, Koryo 6 Chi-tsi, Chi-tzu, Tangun

of Kuwait: 5 Ahmad, Sabah, Salem 7 Mubarak 12 Jaber al-Ahmed, Sabah al-Salim 15 Abdullah al-Salim

of Liechtenstein: 7 Florian 13 Francis Joseph 16 von Liechtenstein

of Luxembourg: 8 Sigefroi, Wencelas 12 Jean l'Aveugle 21 House of Nassau-Weilburg

of Madagascar: 6 Merina

of Malawi: 6 Maravi

of Maldives: 4 Didi

of Mexico: 10 Maximilian

of Monaco: 5 Louis 6 Albert, Honore 7 Antoine, Charles, Rainier 9 Florestan

of Mongolia: 8 Jahangir, Jehangir 10 Kublai Khan, Tsendenbal 11 Genghis Khan

of Morocco: 7 Alawite, Almohad 9 Almoravid

of Nepal: 8 Mahendra 9 Tribhuwan 10 Birenda Bir 12 Bikram Sha Dev 17 Prithwi Narayan Sha

of the Netherlands: 7 William

of Nigeria: 3 Ife, Nok, Oyo 5 Benin 6 Fulani 10 Kanem-Borno

of Norway: 4 Olaf, Olav 5 Olave, Oscar 6 Haakon, Harold, Magnus, Sverre

of Peru: 7 Huascar 9 Atahualpa 10 Manco Capac

of Poland: 5 Piast 7 Casimir, Jagello 8 Augustus

of Portugal: 6 Manuel, Philip, Sancho 7 Alfonso 9 Ferdinand, Sebastian 23 Prince Henry the Navigator

of Qatar: 18 Ahmad bin Ali al-Thani 22 Khalifa bin Hamad al-Thani

of Rumania: 5 Carol 7 Michael

of Russia: 4 Ivan, Paul 5 Peter 6 Alexis 7 Michael 8 Nicholas 9 Alexander 12 Boris Godunov

of Sardinia: 12 Charles Felix 13 Charles Albert 14 Victor Emmanuel

of Saudi Arabia: 4 Fahd, Saud 6 Faisal, Khalid 7 Ibn Saud 9 Abdul Aziz

of Scotland: 5 David, James 6 Duncan 7 Kenneth, Macbeth, Malcolm, Stuarts, William 9 Alexander 14 Robert the Bruce 19 Bonnie Prince Charlie

of Sicily: 4 Eryx 5 Bomba, Henry, Peter, Roger 7 Charles, Cocalus, Leontes 9 Ferdinand, Frederick

of Spain: 6 Pelayo, Philip, Ramiro, Sancho, Witiza 7 Alfonso, Almohad, Charles, Umayyad 8 al-Mansur, Reccared, Roderick 9 Almoravid, Ferdinand,

Leovigild 10 Juan Carlos 11 Abd al-Rahman, Reccosvinth

of Swaziland: 3 Kbe 5 Nyama 6 Mswati, Sozisa 7 Sobhuza

of Sweden: 4 Vosa, Wasa 5 Oscar 6 Gustav 8 Gustavus 10 Carl Gustav 12 Gustav Adolph 13 Charles Gustav 22 Jean Baptiste Bernadotte

of Syria: 5 Rezin 6 Faisal, Hazael 8 Benhadad 9 Antiochus

of Thailand: 4 Rama 7 Chakkri, Mongkut 10 Chao Phraya 12 Prahjadhipok 13 Chulalongkorn 17 Bhumibol Adulyadej

of Tongo: 11 George Tupou 14 Taufaahau Tupou

of Tunisia: 6 Hafsid 7 Fatimid 8 Aghlabid, Almohade 10 Husseinite

of Turkey: 8 Mausolus

of Uganda: 6 Mutesa, Mwanga 8 Kabarega

of Upper Volta: 4 Naba 5 Mogho

of Zimbabwe: 9 Lobengula, Mzilikaze

King, Frank
   creator/artist of: 13 Gasoline Alley

King, Stephen
   author of: 2 It 4 Cujo 6 Carrie, Misery 9 Christine, Salem's Lot, The Stand 10 Night Shift, The Shining 11 Firestarter, Pet Sematary, The Dead Zone 12 Skeleton Crew, The Dark Tower 16 Different Seasons, The Tommyknockers

King and I, The
   director: 10 Walter Lang
   cast: 10 Rita Moreno, Yul Brynner 11 Deborah Kerr 12 Martin Benson
   score: 21 Rodgers and Hammerstein
   remake of: 20 Anna and the King of Siam
   song: 12 Shall We Dance? 16 Getting to Know You, Hello Young Lovers 18 Something Wonderful

King Arthur
   opera by: 7 Purcell
   character: 6 Merlin, Osmond, Oswald 8 Emmeline, Philadel 14 Duke of Cornwall

kingdom 4 land 5 duchy, field, realm, state 6 domain, empire, nation, sphere 7 country, dukedom 8 dominion, monarchy 9 territory 12 principality

King John
   author: 18 William Shakespeare
   character: 6 Elinor 9 Constance 11 Prince Henry 13 Hubert de Burgh 15 Blanch of Castile, Lewis the Dauphin 16 Arthur of Bretagne Cardinal Pandulph, William Longsword, William Mareshall 19 Philip Faulconbridge, Robert Faulconbridge

King Kong
   director: 13 Merian C Cooper 17 Ernest B Schoedsack
   cast: 7 Fay Wray 10 Bruce Cabot 11 James Flavin 12 Noble Johnson 15 Robert Armstrong
   setting (final scene): 19 Empire State Building
   score: 10 Max Steiner

King Lear
 author: 18 William Shakespeare
 character: 5 Edgar, Regan 6 Edmund 7 Goneril 8 Cordelia 10 Earl of Kent 12 Duke of Albany, King of France 14 Duke of Cornwall 16 Earl of Gloucester
kingly 5 grand, noble, regal, royal 6 august, lordly, mighty 7 queenly, stately 8 absolute, despotic, glorious, kinglike, imperial, majestic, princely, splendid 9 imperious, monarchal, patrician, sovereign 10 autocratic, commanding, tyrannical 11 magnificent 12 awe-inspiring

Kingman, Dave
 nickname: 4 Kong
 sport: 8 baseball
 position: 8 outfield 9 first base
 team: 11 Chicago Cubs, New York Mets 14 New York Yankees, San Diego Padres 16 California Angels 18 San Francisco Giants

king of gods 4 Amen, Amon, Finn, Zeus 5 Ammon, Enlil, Fionn, Wotan 6 Marduk 8 Merodach 12 Baal Merodach 13 Fionn MacCumal

King of Hearts
 character in: 28 Alice's Adventures in Wonderland
 author: 7 Carroll

King of Righteousness 11 Melchizedek

Kingsley, Ben
 roles: 6 Gandhi (Oscar) 8 Betrayal

Kingsley, Charles
 author of: 7 Hypatia 10 Alton Locke 11 Westward Ho! 14 The Water Babies 15 Hereward the Wake

King Solomon's Mines
 author: 13 H Rider Haggard
 character: 5 Twala 6 Gagool, Umbopa 14 Sir Henry Curtis 15 Allan Quatermain, Captain John Good

King's Row
 author: 14 Henry Bellamann
 director: 7 Sam Wood
 cast: 10 Betty Field 11 Ann Sheridan, Claude Rains 12 Ronald Reagan 13 Charles Coburn 14 Judith Anderson, Robert Cummings
 score: 21 Erich Wolfgard Korngold
 character: 11 Drake McHugh, Elise Sandor 13 Randy Monaghan 14 Cassandra Tower, Parris Mitchell

Kingston
 capital of: 7 Jamaica

Kingu
 origin: 8 Akkadian
 father: 4 Apsu
 mother: 6 Tiamet
 blood used by: 2 Ea 6 Marduk 8 Merodach 12 Baal Merodach
 blood used for: 8 creation

kink 4 coil, flaw, knot, pang 5 cramp, crick, crimp, frizz, gnarl, hitch, quirk, snarl, spasm, twist 6 defect, foible, glitch, oddity, tangle, twinge, vagary 7 crinkle, frizzle 8 crotchet 9 queerness, stiffness, weirdness 10 difficulty 11 peculiarity, singularity 12 charley horse, complication, eccentricity, freakishness, idiosyncrasy, imperfection

kinky 3 odd 4 sick, wiry 5 kooky, queer 6 frizzy, matted, quirky, twisty 7 bizarre, deviant, frizzly, knotted, strange, tangled, twisted, unusual 8 aberrant, abnormal, crinkled, freakish, frizzled, peculiar, perverse 9 eccentric, unnatural 10 unorthodox 13 idiosyncratic

Kinshasa
 capital of: 5 Zaire

kinsman 3 sib, son 4 aunt, heir 5 child, uncle 6 cousin, father, mother, parent, sister 7 brother 8 daughter, landsman, relation, relative 9 offspring 10 countryman 11 grandfather, grandmother 13 blood relation, blood relative

Kiowa
 language family: 6 Tanoan
 location: 6 Plains 7 Montana 8 Colorado, Oklahoma
 allied with: 7 Arapaho 8 Comanche 11 Kiowa Apache
 deity: 5 Taime

Kiowa Apache
 language family: 12 Shapwailutan
 location: 6 Plains

Kipling, Rudyard
 author of: 3 Kim 8 Gunga Din, Mandalay 11 Danny Deaver 12 The Seven Seas 13 Just So Stories, The Jungle Book 18 Barrack-Room Ballads, Captains Courageous

Kipps
 author: 7 H G Wells

Kirchhoff, Gustav Robert
 field: 7 physics
 nationality: 6 German
 discovered: 6 cesium 8 rubidium
 developed: 12 spectroscope
 named for him: 19 electric circuit laws

Kirchner, Ernst Ludwig
 born: 7 Germany 13 Aschaffenburg
 artwork: 11 Street Scene 12 Street Berlin 13 Moonlit Winter 21 Self-portrait with Model

Kiribati
 other name: 14 Gilbert Islands
 capital/largest city: 6 Tarawa
 others: 5 Betio 7 Bairiki, Bonriki 9 Bikenibeu
 school: 12 South Pacific
 monetary unit: 4 cent 6 dollar
 island: 5 Flint, Ocean 6 Banaba, Canton, Malden, Tarawa 7 Abemama, Fanning, Gilbert, Marakei, Nonouti, Phoenix, Vostock 8 Caroline, Starbuck 9 Christmas, Enderbury, Tabiteuea 10 Butaritari, Equatorial, Washington 12 Northern Line, Southern Line
 sea: 7 Pacific
 people: 8 Banabans 10 Polynesian 11 Micronesian
 language: 6 Samoan 7 English 10 Gilbertese
 religion: 5 Baha'i 8 Anglican 9 Methodist

11 Church of God 13 Roman Catholic 19
Seventh Day Adventist

kirsch, kirschwasser
 type: 6 brandy 7 liqueur
 origin: 6 France 7 Germany 11 Switzerland
 flavor: 6 cherry
 with gin: 7 Florida 10 Lady Finger
 with vodka: 12 Volga Boatman

kismet 3 end, lot 4 doom, fate 5 moira 7
destiny, fortune, portion 8 God's will 10
Providence 11 will of Allah 12 circumstance 13 inevitability 14 predestination

kiss 4 buss, neck 6 smooch, salute 8 osculate

Kiss for Cinderella, A
 author: 12 James M Barrie

kit 3 rig 4 gear 5 tools 6 outfit, tackle, things
7 devices 8 supplies, utensils 9 equipment, trappings 10 implements, provisions
11 furnishings, impediments, instruments,
necessaries 13 accoutrements, paraphernalia

Kitasato, Shibasaburo
 field: 12 bacteriology
 nationality: 8 Japanese
 isolated: 7 anthrax, tetanus 9 dysentery
 13 bubonic plague
 developed: 19 diphtheria antitoxin

kitchen 6 bakery, cocina, galley 7 cuisine 8
cookroom, scullery 9 bakehouse, cookhouse

Kitchener, Horatio Herbert
 also: 18 first Earl Kitchener
 nationality: 7 British
 served in: 7 Boer War 15 South African
 War
 battle: 8 Khartoum, Omdurman
 governor of: 8 the Sudan
 commander in chief of: 5 India 12
 Egyptian army
 consul general of: 5 Egypt

kitel 20 Jewish ceremonial robe
 color: 5 white

Kitely
 character in: 19 Every Man in His
 Humour
 author: 6 Jonson

kittenish 3 coy 7 playful 10 coquettish

Klamath
 language family: 8 Penutian
 location: 6 Oregon 10 California
 related to: 5 Modoc 6 Cayuse, Molala

Klee, Paul
 born: 11 Switzerland 14 Munchenbuchsee
 artwork: 9 Locksmith 11 Ad Parnassum
 18 Barbarian Sacrifice, Demon above the
 Ships 20 The Twittering Machine 22 Revolution of the Viaduct 23 Dance-Play of
 the Red Skirts 24 Dance Monster to my
 Soft Song 35 The Vocal Fabric of the
 Singer Rosa Silber

Kleist, Heinrich von
 author of: 11 Penthesilea 14 The Marquise of O 16 The Broken Pitcher 18 The
 Prince of Homburg

Kline, Kevin
 roles: 11 The Big Chill 13 Sophie's
 Choice 17 Pirates of Penzance

Klugman, Jack
 born: 14 Philadelphia PA
 roles: 6 Quincy 12 Oscar Madison, The
 Odd Couple

klutz 5 dummy 9 blockhead 11 satchelfoot
13 fumblefingers

klutzy 4 dumb 6 clumsy, stupid 7 awkward
9 graceless

knack 4 bent, gift, turn 5 flair, forte, skill 6
genius, talent 7 ability, faculty, finesse 8
aptitude, capacity, facility 9 dexterity, expertise, ingenuity, quickness, readiness 10
adroitness, capability, cleverness, competence, efficiency, propensity 11 inclination,
proficiency 13 dexterousness

knave 3 cad, cur, dog, rat 5 phony, rogue,
scamp 6 con man, rascal, rotter, varlet,
wretch 7 bounder, culprit 8 scalawag,
swindler 9 charlatan, con artist, reprobate,
scoundrel 10 blackguard 11 rapscallion 14
good for nothing

knee breeches 8 breeches, jodhpurs,
knickers 9 plus fours

kneel 3 bow 6 curtsy, kowtow, salaam 7
bow down 9 genuflect 13 make obeisance
16 prostrate oneself

knell 4 peal, ring, toll 5 chime, sound 6
stroke 7 pealing, ringing, tolling

Knickerbocker Holiday
 author: 15 Maxwell Anderson

knickknack, nicknack 3 toy 6 bauble,
gewgaw, trifle 7 bibelot, trinket 8 frippery,
gimcrack 9 bagatelle, bric-a-brac, plaything 11 thingamajig

knife 3 cut 4 dirk, shiv, stab 5 blade, slash,
wound 6 cutter, pierce 7 cut down, cutlery
8 cut apart, lacerate, mutilate
 type: 3 pen 4 jack 5 bowie, bread, putty,
 table 6 dagger, paring, pocket 7 butcher,
 carving, hunting, machete, palette, pruning, scalpel 8 skinning, stiletto, surgical
 11 switchblade

knight 4 hero 7 fighter, gallant, paladin, soldier, Templar, warrior 8 cavalier, champion,
defender, guardian, horseman, Lancelot 9
gentleman, man-at-arms, protecter, protector 10 equestrian, vindicator

Knight
 character in: 18 The Canterbury Tales
 author: 7 Chaucer

Knightley, George
 character in: 4 Emma
 author: 6 Austen

Knights, The
 author: 12 Aristophanes
 character: 5 Demus 6 Nicias 11
 Demosthenes 20 Cleon the Paphlagonian

knit 3 tat 4 ally, bind, draw, join, knot, link 5
braid, plait, twist, unify, unite, weave 6 attach, crease, fasten, furrow, stitch 7 connect, crochet, wrinkle 10 intertwine, interweave 12 draw together

knob 3 nub 4 bulb, bump, grip, hold, hump, knot, knur, lump, node, snag 5 bulge, gnarl, knurl, latch, lever, swell 6 handle, nubbin 8 handhold, swelling, tubercle 9 convexity 10 projection, prominence, protrusion 12 protuberance, protuberancy

knock 3 bat, hit, pat, rap, tap 4 bang, beat, belt, blow, bomb, bump, clip, cuff, dash, kick, lick, push, slam, slap, sock, swat, thud 5 abuse, cavil, clout, crack, crash, decry, pound, punch, smack, smash, smite, thump, whack 6 batter, carp at, defeat, hammer, jostle, murder, peck at, pummel, strike, stroke, thwack, wallop 7 censure, condemn, failure, setback 8 belittle, lambaste 9 criticism, criticize, deprecate, disparage, reprehend 12 condemnation, faultfinding, reprehension

knock down 4 deck, down, drop, fell 5 floor 7 flatten 8 bowl over, discount 9 take apart 11 disassemble

knock off balance 6 rattle 7 shake up 8 unsettle 9 take aback 11 disorganize

knockout 2 KO 4 doll 5 beaut, Venus 6 beauty, eyeful 7 stunner

knock out of shape 4 maul 5 crush 6 batter, beat up, mangle

knoll 4 hill, rise 5 mound

knot 3 bun 4 bump, frog, heap, hump, loop, lump, mass, pack, pile, star, tuft 5 braid, bunch, clump, group, hitch, knurl, plait, twist 6 bundle, circle 7 cat's-paw, chignon, cluster, epaulet, rosette 8 ornament 9 gathering 10 assemblage, collection, intertwist 13 interlacement

  type: 3 bow, top 4 flat, slip 5 slide 6 double, single, square 7 running 8 hangman's, overhand, shoulder, surgeon's 9 half-hitch 11 figure-eight, midshipman's

Knots Landing

  character: 9 Abby Ewing, Gary Ewing 10 Greg Sumner 11 Valene Ewing 12 Mac Mackenzie 14 Karen Mackenzie, Paige Forrester

  cast: 10 Donna Mills, Joan Van Ark 11 Julie Harris, Kevin Dobson, Michelle Lee 13 William Devane 14 Douglas Sheehan, Ted Shackelford 17 Nicolette Sheridan

knotty 4 hard 5 bumpy, rough, tough 6 coarse, flawed, knobby, knurly, rugged, snaggy, thorny, tricky, uneven 7 complex, gnarled, knurled, nodular 8 baffling, involved, puzzling, ticklish, unsmooth 9 blemished, difficult, intricate 10 perplexing 11 complicated, troublesome 12 roughgrained 13 coarse-grained, problematical

know 3 see 6 be sure, be wise, notice 7 be smart, discern, make out, realize 8 identify, perceive 9 apprehend, be assured, be aware of, be certain, be close to, get wise to, recognize 10 be informed, be positive, understand 11 be confident, be sagacious, be thick with, distinguish, feel certain, have down pat, have no doubt 12 discriminate, have down cold, have the ear of 13 be cognizant of, be intelligent, have knowledge, rub elbows with 14 be familiar with

knowable 9 thinkable 11 conceivable, discernible, perceivable 14 understandable

Knowell, Edward

  character in: 19 Every Man in His Humour

  author: 6 Jonson

know for sure 9 be certain 10 be positive

know-how 3 art 4 bent, gift 5 craft, flair, knack, savvy, skill 6 talent 7 ability, mastery 8 aptitude, capacity, deftness 9 adeptness, expertise, knowledge, technique 10 adroitness, capability, competence, experience, expertness 11 proficiency 12 skillfulness 15 professionalism

  French: 11 savoir-faire

knowing 4 deep, wise 5 aware, canny, sharp, smart, sound 6 astute, brainy, bright, clever, shrewd 7 erudite, fraught, learned, sapient 8 academic, educated, eloquent, highbrow, literary, profound, schooled, sensible 9 conscious, judicious, revealing, sagacious 10 discerning, expressive, meaningful, perceptive, percipient, scholastic, widely read 11 enlightened, intelligent, significant 12 intellectual, well-informed 13 comprehending, knowledgeable, perspicacious, philosophical, sophisticated, understanding

knowing how to live

  French: 11 savoir-vivre

knowing just what to do

  French: 11 savoir-faire

know-it-all 5 brash 13 overconfident

knowledge 3 ken, tip 4 data, hint, news 5 sense 6 memory, notice, report, wisdom 7 inkling, mention, tidings 8 learning 9 awareness, education, erudition, schooling, statement 10 cognizance, intimation, perception 11 cultivation, declaration, familiarity, information, realization, recognition, revelation, scholarship 12 announcement, book learning, intelligence, notification 13 communication, comprehension, consciousness, enlightenment, pronouncement

  god of: 4 Odin 5 Othin

knowledgeable 3 hip 8 at home in, versed in 12 familiar with, well-informed 14 acquainted with, conversant with

  French: 9 au courant

knowledge of the world

  French: 11 savoir-vivre

known 5 noted, plain 6 common, famous, patent 7 evident, obvious, popular 8 apparent, definite, distinct, familiar, manifest, palpable 9 notorious, prominent 10 celebrated, recognized 11 self-evident

know thyself

  Greek: 13 gnothi seauton

knuckle under 5 yield 6 give in, submit 7 bow down 9 surrender 10 capitulate

knurled 5 bumpy, lumpy 6 gnarly, knobby, knotty, knurly, nubbly, ridged 7 bulging, gnarled, knotted, nodular

Koch, Robert
field: 12 bacteriology
nationality: 6 German
isolated: 2 TB 12 tuberculosis
awarded: 10 Nobel Prize

Kodaly, Zoltan
born: 7 Hungary 9 Kecskemet
composer of: 9 Hary Janos 11 Czinka Panna, Missa Brevis, Szekely Fono 14 Budavari Te Deum 15 Dances of Galanta 17 Dances of Marosszek, Peacock Variations, Psalmus Hungaricus 28 The Spinning Room of the Szekelys

Koestler, Arthur
author of: 14 Darkness at Noon 15 The Sleepwalkers

Kojak
character: 5 (Det) Rizzo 7 (Det) Stavros 9 (Lt) Theo Kojak 10 (Det) Saperstein 11 Frank McNeil 12 (Lt) Bobby Crocker
cast: 9 Dan Frazer 10 Vince Conti 11 Kevin Dobson, Mark Russell 12 Telly Savalas 13 George Savalas (Demosthenes)
trademark: 8 lollipop
phrase: 17 Who loves ya baby?

Kollwitz, Kathe
real name: 12 Kathe Schmidt
born: 10 Konigsberg 11 East Prussia
artwork: 3 War 5 Death, Pieta 11 Proletariat 13 Weavers' Revolt (Weaver's Rebellion) 14 Mother and Child, The Peasants' War 18 Death Seizing a Woman

Kol Nidre vows 4 vows 8 promises 22 Jewish liturgical prayer
recited on eve of: 9 Yom Kippur

Kong
nickname of: 11 Dave Kingman

Kon-Tiki
author: 13 Thor Heyerdahl

kook 3 nut 5 crazy, flake, loony, wacko 6 cuckoo, weirdo 7 dingbat 8 crackpot 9 ding-a-ling, eccentric, fruitcake, harebrain, screwball 10 crackbrain

Korah
father: 4 Esau 6 Hebron 7 Eliphaz
conspired with: 5 Abiram, Dathan
rebelled against: 5 Aaron, Moses

Korea
other name: 6 Choson 17 land of morning calm
capital:
North Korea: 9 Pyongyang
South Korea: 5 Seoul
largest city: 5 Seoul
others: 5 Masan, Mokpo, Pusan, Sinpo, Suwon, Taegu, Wonju 6 Chonju, Inchon, Kangso, Kunsan, Taejon, Wonsan 7 Hanyang, Hungnam, Kaesong, Kangson, Kwangju 8 Chongjin, Chunchon, Kimchaek
school: 5 Busan 6 Yonsei 7 Hanyang 8 Kim Chaek, Kyung Hee 9 Kim Il Sung
division:
ancient: 5 Silla 6 Choson 7 Koguryo, Paekche

monetary unit: 3 woh, won 4 chun, hwan, kwan
weight: 3 won
island: 4 Chin, Koje 5 Cheju, Sinmi 6 Anmyon, Huksan, Namhae 7 Tokchok 8 Quelpart 10 Paengnyong
mountain: 4 Wang 5 Chiri, Halla 6 Kwanmo, Sobaek 7 Diamond, Kyebang, Nangnim, Taebaek 8 Chang-pai, Hamgyong, Myohyang 9 Paektu-san 10 Kumgang-san
highest point: 6 Paektu 9 Paektu-san
river: 3 Han, Kin, Kum, Kun, Nam 4 Lobk, Yalu 5 Amnok, Imjin, Tumen 6 Namhan, Pukhan, Somjin, Soyang, Yesong 7 Naktong, Taedong 8 Changjin, Youngsan 9 Chongchon
sea: 5 Japan 6 Yellow 9 East China
physical feature:
bay: 5 Korea 6 Yongil 7 Kanghwa, Kyonggi 9 Tongjoson
cape: 4 Musu
point: 7 Changgi 8 Changsan
strait: 5 Korea
valley: 7 Naktong
people: 6 Korean
artist: 8 Chong Son 10 Kimtlong-do
dynasty: 2 Yi 4 Choe 5 Koryo
leader: 6 Sejong 8 Yi Sung-gy 9 Kim Il Sung 11 Chun Doo Hwan, Syngman Rhee 12 Park Chung Hee
legendary leader: 5 Ki-tse 6 Chi-tse, Chi-tzu, Tangun
poet: 10 Hwang Chini
language: 6 Korean
alphabet: 6 hangul
religion: 6 Taoism 7 animism 8 Buddhism 9 Chondogyo 12 Christianity, Confucianism
place:
palace: 8 Kyongbok
temple: 7 Haein-sa 17 Hall of Eternal Life
tomb: 14 Dancing Figures
feature:
clothing: 5 chima
game: 3 yut 5 akoan 6 ho-hpai 7 kol-ye-si 9 ryong-hpai, sang-ryouk 10 ke-pouk-hpai, sin-syo-tyen 12 tjak-ma-tchi-ki 15 kko-ri-pouk-tchi-ki
martial art: 9 tae-kwon-do
musical instrument: 6 chaing 7 kaya-gum, komungo
porcelain: 7 Celadon
porch: 4 maru
pottery: 8 pun-chong
food:
bean curd: 4 tubu
hot pickle: 6 kimchi
meat-filled dumpling: 5 mandu
noodle: 5 kuksu

Koridethianus 16 Greek unical codex

Korman, Harvey
born: 9 Chicago IL
roles: 11 High Anxiety 13 Danny Kaye Show 14 Blazing Saddles 16 Carol Burnett Show

Kornberg, Arthur
field: 12 biochemistry
sythesized: 3 DNA, RNA 15 ribonucleic acid 20 deoxyribonucleic acid
awarded: 10 Nobel Prize

kosher 5 right 6 proper 7 ethical 10 aboveboard 12 on the up and up

Kosinski, Jerzy
author of: 5 Steps 7 Cockpit 9 Blind Date 10 Being There 11 Passion Play 12 The Devil Tree 14 The Painted Bird

Kowalski, Stanley
character in: 21 A Streetcar Named Desire
author: 8 Williams

kowtow 4 bend, fawn 5 cower, stoop, toady 6 bow low, cringe, curtsy, grovel, salaam 7 truckle 8 bootlick, butter up, softsoap 9 genuflect 11 apple-polish 12 bow and scrape 16 prostrate oneself

kowtowing 7 fawning, servile 8 toadying 9 groveling 10 obsequious

Kraken
origin: 9 Norwegian
form: 7 monster
habitat: 3 sea
caused: 10 whirlpools

Kramer, Stanley
director of: 10 On the Beach 11 Ship of Fools 14 Inherit the Wind, The Defiant Ones 19 Judgment at Nuremberg

Kramer vs Kramer
director: 12 Robert Benton
based on novel by: 11 Avery Corman
cast: 10 Howard Duff 11 Justin Henry, Meryl Streep 13 Dustin Hoffman, Jane Alexander
Oscar for: 5 actor (Hoffman) 7 picture 8 director 10 screenplay 17 supporting actress (Streep)

Krantz, Judith
author of: 8 Scruples 13 Princess Daisy 16 I'll Take Manhattan, Mistral's Daughter

Krazy Kat
creator: 14 George Herriman
character:
cop: 12 Offissa B Pupp
mouse: 6 Ignatz
prop: 5 brick
place: 4 jail 14 Coconino County 24 Kelly's Exclusive Brick Yard

Krebs, Hans Adolf
field: 9 chemistry
nationality: 6 German
discovered: 15 citric acid cycle
awarded: 10 Nobel Prize

Kreisler, Fritz
born: 6 Vienna 7 Austria
composer of: 7 Allegro 10 Praeludium 15 Caprice Viennois 16 Tambourin Chinois

Kreutzer, Rodolphe
born: 6 France 10 Versailles
composer of: 16 Etudes ou Caprices

Kreutzer Sonata, The
author: 10 Leo Tolstoy
character: 13 Mme Pozdnishef, Trukhashevsky 16 Vasyla Pozdnishef

Krieg 3 war

Kriemhild
origin: 8 Germanic
mentioned in: 14 Nibelungenlied
brother: 7 Gunther
husband: 9 Siegfried
slew: 5 Hagan 7 Gunther
avenged: 6 murder 9 Siegfried
corresponds to: 6 Gudrun, Kudrun 7 Guthrun

Kristin Lavransdatter
author: 12 Sigrid Undset

Krook
character in: 10 Bleak House
author: 7 Dickens

Kropp, Albert
character in: 25 All Quiet on the Western Front
author: 8 Remarque

krypton
chemical symbol: 2 Kr

Kuala Lumpur
capital of: 8 Malaysia

Kubla Khan
author: 15 Samuel Coleridge

Kubrick, Stanley
director of: 6 Lolita 9 Spartacus 11 Barry Lyndon 12 Paths of Glory, 13 Dr Strangelove (or How I Learned to Stop Worrying and Love the Bomb) 16 A Clockwork Orange 30 Two Thousand and One A Space Odyssey

kudo, kudos 4 fame 5 award, glory, honor, prize 6 esteem, praise, renown, repute 7 acclaim, plaudit 8 citation, prestige 9 celebrity, laudation 10 admiration, decoration 12 commendation 14 celebratedness

Kudrun see 6 Gudrun

Kukla, Fran & Ollie
hostess: 11 Fran Allison
puppet: 5 Kukla, Ollie (Oliver J Dragon) 8 Mercedes 9 Cecil Bill 10 Col Crackie 11 Beulah Witch 12 Olivia Dragon 13 Delores Dragon 14 Fletcher Rabbit 18 Mme Ophelia Oglepuss

Kulla
origin: 8 Egyptian, Sumerian
world of: 4 dead
god of: 6 bricks

Kullervo
origin: 7 Finnish
mentioned in: 8 Kalevala
form: 5 slave
death: 7 suicide

kummel
origin: 7 Germany
flavor: 7 caraway

kumquat 10 Fortunella
varieties: 4 oval 5 round 6 Marumi, Nagami 16 Australian desert

Kung Fu
  character: 8 Master Po 9 Master Kan 14 Kwai Chang Caine
  cast: 8 Keye Luke 9 Philip Ahn 11 Radames Pera 14 David Carradine
  Caine raised in: 13 Shaolin Temple

kunzite
  species: 9 spodumene

Kupka, Frank (Frantisek)
  born: 6 Opocno 7 Bohemia 14 Czechoslovakia
  artwork: 12 Black Accents, The Cathedral 16 Etude pour la Fugue 17 Fugue in Red and Blue 23 Fugue in Two Colors Amorpha 25 Philosophical Architecture

Kuprin, Aleksandr
  author of: 7 The Duel 10 Yama the Pit

Kurosawa, Akira
  director of: 3 Ran 8 Rashomon 12 Seven Samurai

Kurtz
  character in: 15 Heart of Darkness
  author: 6 Conrad

Kuwait
  name means: 9 small fort
  capital/largest city: 10 Kuwait City
  others: 6 Ahmadi 7 Hawalli 8 Abdullah, al-Jahrah, Fahaheel, Shuwaykh 9 al-Shuayba 12 Mena al-Ahmadi, Mina Abd Allah, Mina al-Ahmadi
  head of state: 4 emir
  monetary unit: 4 fils 5 dinar
  island: 5 Warba 7 Bubiyan, Failaka
  physical feature:
  bay: 6 Kuwait 12 Khor Abdullah
  duststorm: 4 kaus
  gulf: 7 Persian
  oasis: 6 Jahrah
  people: 4 Arab 5 Iraqi, Saudi 6 Indian 7 Bedouin 8 Egyptian 9 Pakistani 11 Palestinian
  ruling family: 5 Sabah
  sheikh (Sabah family): 5 Ahmad, Salem 7 Mubarak 12 Jaber al-Ahmed, Sabah al-Salim 15 Abdullah al-Salim
  religion: 5 Islam
  war: 4 Gulf 11 Desert Storm, Persian Gulf 12 Desert Shield
  enemy: 4 Iraq 13 Saddam Hussein

Kwa
  language family: 16 Niger-Kordofanian
  group: 10 Niger-Congo
  includes: 3 Ewe, Ibo, Twi 4 Bini, Nupe, Togo 6 Yoruba 7 Dahomey

Kwakiutl
  language family: 8 Wakashan
  location: 6 Canada 15 British Columbia, Vancouver Island 20 Queen Charlotte Island
  related to: 6 Nootka 10 Bellabella
  noted for: 10 totem poles 15 Cannibal Society, wooden sculpture
  called: 14 potlatch people

Kyd, Thomas
  author of: 17 The Spanish Tragedy

Kyrgyzstan
  other name: 9 Kirghizia
  capital/largest city: 6 Frunze 7 Bishkek
  head of state: 9 president
  government: 8 republic
  monetary unit: 3 som
  mountain: 8 Tian Shan
  people: 5 Uzbek 6 Kyrgyz 7 Kirghiz
  language: 6 Turkic 7 Kirghiz
  religion: 6 Muslim 10 Sunni Islam

Kyrie eleison 13 Lord have mercy

L

Laban
father: 7 Bethuel
grandfather: 5 Nahor
daughter: 4 Leah 6 Rachel
sister: 7 Rebekah
son-in-law: 5 Jacob

Labdacus
king of: 6 Thebes
father: 9 Polydorus
mother: 7 Nycteis
grandfather: 7 Nycteus
brother: 5 Lycus
son: 5 Laius
grandson: 7 Oedipus

label 3 tag 4 mark, name, note, seal, sign, slip 5 brand, stamp, tally, title 6 define, docket, ticket 7 earmark, mark off, sticker 8 classify, describe 9 designate 10 denominate, put a mark on 11 appellation, designation, inscription 12 characterize 13 specification 14 classification, identification 16 characterization

labor, labour 4 plod, toil, work 5 slave, sweat 6 drudge, effort, suffer 7 agonize, travail, workers, workmen 8 drudgery, exertion, laborers, manpower, plodding, plug away, struggle 9 employees, grind away, work force 10 birth pangs, childbirth, menial work, smart under 11 birth throes, manual labor, parturition 12 accouchement, be affected by, be burdened by, be troubled by 13 be the victim of 14 employ one's time, work like a slave

labored 5 heavy, stiff 6 clumsy, forced, wooden 7 awkward, cramped, halting, studied 8 drawnout, overdone, strained 9 contrived, difficult, laborious, maladroit, ponderous, unnatural 13 self-conscious, unspontaneous

laborer 4 hand 6 coolie, drudge, menial, toiler, worker 7 plodder, workman 8 handyman, hired man, hireling, workhand 9 hired hand 10 roustabout, wage earner, workingman 11 proletarian 12 manual worker 16 blue-collar worker

laborious 4 hard 6 brutal, severe, uphill 7 arduous, irksome, labored, onerous, wearing 8 rigorous, tiresome, toilsome, wearying 9 demanding, difficult, effortful, fatiguing, herculean, strenuous, wearisome 10 burdensome, oppressive, struggling 11 troublesome

laboriously 4 hard 9 arduously 14 with difficulty 15 with great effort

laboriousness 5 trial 8 tough job 10 difficulty, rough going, uphill work 11 arduousness 12 hard sledding 15 troublesomeness

labor omnia vincit 15 work conquers all
motto of: 8 Oklahoma

Labors of Hercules *see* 8 Hercules

labyrinth 3 web 4 knot, maze 5 snarl 6 jungle, morass, riddle, tangle 7 complex, network 9 intricacy, mare's nest 10 complexity, perplexity, wilderness 11 convolution

Labyrinth
form: 4 maze
location: 5 Crete
built by: 8 Daedalus
housed: 8 Minotaur

Lacaille, Nicholas Louis de
field: 9 astronomy
nationality: 6 French
mapped: 14 constellations

lace 3 tie 4 beat, bind, cane, dope, lash, whip 5 braid, cinch, close, flail, spank, spike, strap, tie up, truss 6 dope up, fasten, flavor, infuse, punish, secure, switch, tether, thrash 7 fortify, spice up, suffuse, tighten 8 chastise, make fast, make taut 10 strengthen 11 add liquor to 12 add spirits to, draw together, give a beating

Lacedaemon
father: 4 Zeus
mother: 8 Taygete
wife: 6 Sparta
son: 7 Amyclas
daughter: 8 Eurydice
founder of: 6 Sparta

lacerate 3 cut, rip 4 gash, hurt, pain, scar, stab, tear 5 lance, sever, slash, slice, wound 6 deface 7 agonize, scratch, torment, torture 8 distress, give pain, puncture 10 excruciate 11 inflict pain

lacerating 5 acute 6 fierce, severe 7 cutting, extreme, intense, violent 12 excruciating

laceration 3 cut, rip 4 tear 5 wound 10 mutilation

Lachaise, Gaston
born: 5 Paris 6 France
artwork: 12 Standing Nude 13 Standing Woman 14 Floating Figure

Lachesis
form: 4 Fate
holds: 12 thread of life
determines: 6 length 7 destiny

lachrymose 3 sad 5 teary, weepy 6 crying 7 maudlin, tearful, weeping 8 mournful 10 melancholy

lack 4 miss, need, want 6 dearth 7 absence 8 omission, scarcity, shortage 9 be missing, be short of, depletion, neediness, privation, scantness 10 deficiency, exhaustion 11 deprivation, fall short of 12 be inadequate 13 be caught short, be deficient in **14** be found wanting, be insufficient

lackadaisical 4 idle **7** languid, loafing **8** lifeless, listless, mindless **9** apathetic, lethargic, unexcited **10** inanimated, phlegmatic, spiritless, unaspiring, uninspired **11** indifferent, languishing, unambitious, unconcerned, unexcitable, unmotivated **12** uninterested **13** dillydallying

lackey 4 page **5** slave, toady, usher, valet **6** butler, flunky, helper, menial, minion, squire, waiter **7** servant, steward **8** employee, follower, hanger-on, hireling, inferior, retainer **9** assistant, attendant, cupbearer, mercenary, underling

lacking 7 needing, wanting **9** deficient **10** inadequate **12** falling short, insufficient
   French: **6** manque

lackluster 4 blah, dead, drab, dull **5** bland, muted **6** boring, dreary, leaden, pallid, somber **7** humdrum, nothing, prosaic, subdued **8** lifeless, mediocre, ordinary **9** colorless **10** lusterless **11** commonplace **12** run-of-the-mill **13** uninteresting

lack of conviction 5 doubt **8** question **9** misgiving **10** hesitation, indecision **11** uncertainty

lack of faith 5 doubt **7** atheism **8** distrust, mistrust **9** disbelief, suspicion

lack of feeling 6 apathy **8** coldness, numbness **11** impassivity **15** emotionlessness, hardheartedness, passionlessness

lack of interest 5 ennui **6** apathy **7** boredom **9** unconcern **12** indifference

lack of respect 8 contempt, rudeness **9** disregard **10** disrespect **11** discourtesy, irreverence **12** impoliteness

lack of skill 9 inability **10** clumsiness, ineptitude **11** awkwardness **12** incompetency

Laclos, Pierre Choderlos de
   author of: **22** Les Liaisons Dangereuses

Lacombe, Lucien
   director: **10** Louis Malle
   cast: **12** Pierre Blaise **13** Aurore Clement **16** Holger Lowenadler

laconic 4 curt **5** blunt, brief, pithy, short, terse **7** compact, concise, pointed, summary **8** succinct **9** condensed **10** to the point **12** concentrated **14** sparing of words

lacquer 4 coat **5** glaze **7** coating, shellac, varnish

lacrimoso
   music: **7** tearful

lacrosse
   Indian name: **9** bagataway
   circle around goal: **6** crease
   players/team: **3** ten
   position: **6** goalie **9** attackman **10** defenseman, midfielder
   term: **6** riding **8** clearing

lacuna 3 gap, pit **4** gulf, hole, void **5** blank, break, crack, ditch, pause, space **6** breach, cavity, hiatus **7** caesura, fissure, interim, opening, vacancy **8** interval, omission **10** interstice, suspension **12** interruption **13** discontinuity

lacustrine 7 aquatic **11** lake-growing **12** lake-dwelling

lacy 4 fine **5** filmy, gauzy, meshy, netty, sheer, webby **6** barred, frilly, netted, porous, webbed **7** gridded, netlike **8** cobwebby, delicate, filigree, gossamer, lacelike, retiform **9** filigreed **10** diaphanous, reticulate **11** latticelike, transparent

lad 3 boy, kid **5** sprig, youth **6** shaver, sprout **8** juvenile, young man **9** schoolboy, stripling, young chap, youngster **11** young fellow

Ladd, Alan
   son: **5** David **6** Alan Jr
   co-star: **12** Veronica Lake
   born: **12** Hot Springs AR
   roles: **5** Shane **13** The Blue Dahlia **14** The Great Gatsby, This Gun for Hire

ladies' man 4 beau, stud **5** spark **7** playboy **8** cavalier, gay blade

La Dolce Vita
   director: **15** Federico Fellini
   cast: **9** Lex Barker, Nadia Gray **10** Anouk Aimee **11** Anita Ekberg **19** Marcello Mastroianni

Ladon
   form: **6** dragon
   father: **6** Typhon
   mother: **7** Echidna
   number of heads: **7** hundred
   guarded: **6** garden
   garden owned by: **10** Hesperides
   killed by: **8** Hercules

ladrone 5 thief **6** bandit, outlaw

lady 4 wife **5** woman **6** female, matron, spouse **7** duchess, peeress **8** baroness, countess **10** aristocrat, noblewoman **11** gentlewoman, marchioness, viscountess, woman of rank **13** well-bred woman
   German: **4** frau
   Italian: **5** donna
   Spanish/Portuguese: **4** dona

Lady Chatterley's Lover
   author: **10** D H Lawrence
   character: **7** Mellors **19** Constance Chatterley

Lady Eve, The
   director: **14** Preston Sturges
   cast: **10** Henry Fonda **13** Charles Coburn **14** Eugene Pallette **15** Barbara Stanwyck, William Demarest

Lady for a Day
   director: **10** Frank Capra
   based on story by: **11** Damon Runyon
   cast: **9** Guy Kibbee, May Robson **13** Warren William
   remade as: **19** Pocketful of Miracles

Lady from Dubuque, The
   author: **11** Edward Albee

Lady from the Sea, The
   author: **11** Henrik Ibsen

Lady in Chair
   constellation of: **10** Cassiopeia

ladylike 5 civil **6** modest, polite, proper **7** courtly, elegant, genteel, refined **8** cultured, decorous, mannerly, polished, wellbred **9** courteous, dignified **10** cultivated

11 respectable 12 well mannered 13 well brought up

Lady of the Camellias, The see 7 Camille

Lady of the Lake, The
  author: 14 Sir Walter Scott
  character: 9 Allan Bane 11 Roderick Dhu 12 Ellen Douglas 13 Malcolm Graeme 14 James Fitz-James, James of Douglas

Lady Oracle
  author: 14 Margaret Atwood

lady's maid
  French: 14 femme de chambre

Lady's Not for Burning, The
  author: 14 Christopher Fry

lady's-slipper, Lady-slipper 11 Cypripedium 13 Paphiopedilum, Phragmipedium
  varieties: 4 pink 5 showy 8 mountain, ram's-head 9 two-leaved 10 small white 11 large yellow, small yellow

Lady Vanishes, The
  director: 15 Alfred Hitchcock
  cast: 9 Paul Lukas 13 Dame May Whitty 15 Michael Redgrave 16 Margaret Lockwood

Lady Windermere's Fan
  author: 10 Oscar Wilde
  character: 10 Mrs Erlynne 14 Lord Darlington, Lord Windermere 18 Lord Augustus Lorton

Laelaps
  form: 5 hound
  borrowed from: 8 Cephalus
  borrowed by: 10 Amphitryon

Laertes
  son: 8 Odysseus

Laertes
  character in: 6 Hamlet
  author: 11 Shakespeare

Laertiades
  epithet of: 8 Odysseus
  means: 12 son of Laertes

Laestrygones
  form: 6 giants
  characteristic: 9 cannibals

La Farge, John
  born: 9 New York NY
  artwork: 14 Maua Our Boatman 17 The Muse of Painting 18 Red and White Peonies

La Fayette, Comtesse de
  author of: 19 La Princesse de Cleves

Lafayette, Marquis de
  also: 38 Marie Joseph Paul Yves Roch Gilbert du Motier
  nationality: 6 French
  served in: 14 July Revolution 16 French Revolution 18 American Revolution
  battle: 8 Yorktown 10 Brandywine

Lafcadio's Adventures (The Vatican Swindle)
  author: 9 Andre Gide

La Fontaine, Jean de
  author of: 6 Fables

lag 4 drag, halt, inch, limp, snag 5 dally, delay, hitch, tarry, trail 6 be idle, be late, be slow, dawdle, falter, hold up, linger, loiter, trudge 7 be tardy, setback, slacken, stag-

ger 8 be behind, hang back, slowdown 9 be overdue, inch along 10 drag behind, slackening 11 slowing down 12 bide one's time, take one's time 13 falling behind, procrastinate

laggard 4 mope, poke, slow, slug 5 idler, snail, tardy 6 loafer, remiss 7 dallier, dawdler, lounger 8 lingerer, loiterer, potterer, putterer, slowfoot, slowpoke, sluggard, sluggish 9 do-nothing, straggler 12 dilly-dallier 13 stick-in-the-mud

lagniappe, lagnappe 3 tip 4 gift, perk 5 bonus, favor, prize 7 largess, memento, present 8 gratuity, largesse 9 pourboire

Lagos
  former capital of: 7 Nigeria

Lahr, Bert
  real name: 14 Irving Lahrheim
  born: 9 New York NY
  roles: 12 Cowardly Lion 13 The Wizard of Oz

laic 3 lay 5 civil 6 laical 7 amateur, popular, profane, secular, worldly 8 temporal 11 nonclerical, nonpastoral 12 secularistic 13 inexperienced 15 nonprofessional 17 nonecclesiastical

lair 3 den, lie, mew 4 hole, nest 5 cover, haunt 6 burrow, cavern, covert 7 hideout, retreat 8 hideaway 9 sanctuary 12 resting place

laissez-faire, laisser-faire 8 hands off 9 let them be, unconcern 12 indifference 14 let-alone policy, live and let live 15 noninterference, nonintervention

laissez-passer 4 pass 6 permit 11 allow to pass

Laius
  king of: 6 Thebes
  father: 8 Labdacus
  great-grandfather: 6 Cadmus
  wife: 7 Jocasta
  son: 7 Oedipus
  killed by: 7 Oedipus

Lajeunesse, Gabriel
  character in: 10 Evangeline
  author: 10 Longfellow

lake
  of Afghanistan: 7 Helmand 13 Hamud-i-Helmand
  of Albania: 4 Ulze 5 Matia, Ohrid 6 Prespa 7 Ochrida, Scutari, Shkoder 8 Ohridsko
  of Algeria: 5 Hodna 6 Sabkha 7 Cherqui, Fedjadj, Meirhir 10 Azzel Matti, Meherrhane
  of Andorra: 11 Engolasters
  of Argentina: 6 Viedma 7 Cardiel, Fagnano, Musters 11 Buenos Aires, Mar Chiquita, Nahuel Huapi
  of Armenia: 3 Van 5 Sevan, Urmia 8 Urumiyah
  of Australia: 4 Eyre 5 Carey, Cowan, Frome, Moore, Wells 6 Austin, Barlee, Bulloo, Dundas, Harris, Mackay 7 Amadeus, Blanche, Everard, Torrens 8 Carnegie, Gairdner 9 MacDonald 10 Yammayamma 14 Disappointment

of Austria: 6 Almsee 7 Fertoto, Mondsee 8 Bodensee, Traunsee 9 Constance 10 Neusiedler

of Benin: 5 Aheme 6 Nokoue

of Bolivia: 5 Poopo 7 Allagas, Coipasa, Rogagua 8 Titicaca 10 Desaguader

of Botswana: 3 Dow, Xau 5 Ngami

of Brazil: 4 Aima, Feia 5 Mirim 13 Logo dos Platos

of Burundi: 7 Rugwero 8 Tshohoha 10 Tanganyika

of Cambodia/Kampuchea: 8 Tonle Sap

of Cameroon: 4 Chad

of Canada: 4 Cree, Erie, Gras, Seul 5 Garry, Huron, Rainy 6 Louise, St John 7 Abitibi, Dubawnt, Nipigon, Ontario, Testlin 8 Kootenay, Manitoba, Okanagan, Reindeer, Superior, Winnipeg 9 Athabaska, Great Bear, Nipissing 10 Great Slave, Mistassini 12 Winnipegosis

of Central African Republic: 4 Assa

of Chad: 4 Chad

of Chile: 5 Ranco 6 Yelcho 7 Puyehue, Rupanco 8 Cochrane 10 General Paz, Llanquihue 11 Buenos Aires

of China: 3 Tai 4 Chao, Na-mu 5 Kaoyu, Oling, Telli 6 Bamtso, Bornor, Ebinor, Erhhai, Khanka, Lopnor, Namtso, Poyang 7 Chaling, Hungtse, Karanor, Kokonor 8 Hulunnor, Montcalm, Taroktso, Tellinor, Tienchih, Tsinghai, Tungting

of Colombia: 4 Tota

of the Congo: 5 Mweru, Tumba 6 Albert, Nyanza, Upemba 7 Leopold 11 Stanley Pool

of Costa Rica: 6 Arenal

of Denmark 6 Arreso

of Djibouti: 4 Abbe 5 Assal

of Dominican Republic: 10 Enriquillo

of Egypt: 4 Edku, Idku 5 Qarun 6 Maryut, Moeris, Nasser 7 Manzala 8 Burullus, Mareotis

of El Salvador: 5 Guiha, Guija 8 Ilopango 10 Coatepeque

of England: 8 Grasmere 9 Ennerdale, Ullswater, Wastwater 10 Buttermere, Windermere 12 Derwentwater 13 Coniston Water

of Estonia: 5 Pskov 6 Peipus 9 Vortsjarv

of Ethiopia: 3 Abe 4 Tana 5 Abaya, Shola, Tanna, Tsana, Tzana, Zeway 6 Dambea, Dembea, Rudolf 8 Blue Nile, Stefanie

of Finland: 3 Juo, Muo 4 Kemi, Kiui, Nasi, Oulu, Puru, Pyha, Simo 5 Enara, Enare, Hauki, Inari, Kalla, Lappa, Lesti, Puula, Saima 6 Ladoya, Lentua, Saimaa, Sounne, Syvari 7 Koitere, Nilakka 8 Pielinen 9 Kallavesi, Pielavesi

of France: 6 Annecy, Cazaux, Geneva

of Gabon Republic: 7 Anengue, Azinguo

of Germany, East: 6 Muritz

of Germany, West: 9 Constance 11 Inner Alster, Outer Alster

of Ghana: 5 Volta 8 Bosumtwi

of Greece: 5 Karla, Volve 6 Copais, Kopais, Prespa, Voweis 8 Ioannina, Koroneia, Vistonis 9 Trichonis, Vegoritis

of Grenada: 10 Grand Etang

of Guatemala: 5 Dulce, Guija, Peten 6 Izabal 7 Atitlan 9 Amatitlan, Peten Itza

of Haiti: 8 Saumatre

of Honduras: 5 Criba, Yojoa 6 Brewer

of Hungary: 5 Ferto 7 Balaton, Velence 9 Blatensee 10 Neusiedler, Plattensee

of Iceland: 6 Myvatn 10 Thorisvatn 14 Thingvallavatn

of India: 5 Jheel, Lonar, Wular 6 Chilka, Colair, Dhebar, Kolair 7 Kolleru, Pulicat, Pushkar, Sambahr

of Indonesia: 4 Toba 5 Ranau 6 Towuti 8 Sahweh, Sistan 7 Maharlu 8 Nemekser, Urumiyeh

of Iran: 5 Niris, Tasht, Tuzlu, Urmia 6 Sahweh, Sistan 7 Maharlu 8 Nemekser, Urumiyeh

of Iraq: 6 al-Milh 7 Sanniya 8 al-Hammar

of Ireland: 3 Doo, Key, Ree, Tay 4 Conn, Derg, Erne, Mask 5 Allen, Barra, Carra, Gowna, Leane, Lough, Neagh 6 Boderg, Cooter, Corrib, Ennell 7 Dromore, Gougane, Oughter, Sheelin 9 Killarney

of Israel: 5 Huleh 7 Dead Sea 8 Kinneret, Tiberias 12 Sea of Galilee

of Italy: 4 Como, Iseo, Nemi 5 Garda 6 Albano, Lesina, Lugano, Varano 7 Bolsena, Perugia 8 Maggiore 9 Bracciano, Trasimeno

of Japan: 4 Biwa, Suwa, Toya 6 Towada 8 Kutchawa, Shikotsu

of Kazakhstan: 8 Balkhash

of Kenya: 6 Magadi, Nakuru, Natron, Rudolf 7 Turkana 8 Naivasha, Victoria

of Lebanon: 5 Quran 6 Qirawn

of Lithuania: 5 Dysna

of Luxembourg: 8 Haut Sure

of Macedonia: 5 Ohrid 6 Prespa 7 Ochrida

of Madagascar: 5 Itasy 7 Alaotra, Kinkony

of Malawi: 5 Nyasa 6 Chilwa, Malawi

of Mali: 2 Do 4 Debo 5 Garou 7 Korarou 9 Faguibine

of Mexico: 7 Chapala, Texcoco 9 Patzcuaro

of Mongolia: 3 Uvs 5 Har Us 6 Bor Nor 7 Ghirgis, Ubsa Nor 8 Airik Nor, Durga Nor, Hobsogol, Khara Usu 9 Khubsugul, Khukhu-Nur 10 Khirgis Nor

of Montenegro: 7 Scutari, Shkoder

of Mozambique: 5 Nyasa 6 Chuali, Nyassa 8 Nhavarre

of Myanmar: 4 Inle

of Nauru: 11 Buada Lagoon

of the Netherlands: 7 Haarlem 10 Ijsselmeer 11 Grevelingen, Hazinguliet

of New Zealand: 3 Ada 4 Gunn, Ohau 5 Hawea, Taupo 6 Pukaki, Pupuke, Te Anau, Tekapo, Wanaka 7 Brunner, Diamond, Kanieri, Okareka, Rotorua 8 Okataina, Paradise, Rotoaira, Wakatipi 9 Manapouri

of Nicaragua: 7 Managua 9 Nicaragua

of Niger: 4 Chad

of Nigeria: 4 Chad

of the Nile: 4 Tana 5 Kyoga, Tsana 6 Albert, Edward, Nasser 8 Victoria

of Norway: 4 Alte 5 Ister, Mjosa, Snasa 6 Femund 7 Rostavn, Tunnsjo

of Panama: 5 Gatun

of Paraguay: 4 Vera, Ypoa 8 Ypacarai

of Peru: 8 Titicaca

of Poland: 5 Goplo, Mamry 8 Niegocin, Sniardwy 13 Stettin Lagoon

of Puerto Rico: 5 Loiza 6 Carite 8 Dos Bocas 9 Caonillas, Guatajaca

of Romania: 5 Sinoe 6 Snagov

of Russia: 3 Seg 4 Azov, Kola, Neva 5 Byelo, Chany, Elton, Erara, Ilmen, Lacha, Onega, Vozhe 6 Baikal, Ladoga 10 Caspian Sea

of Rwanda: 4 Kivu 5 Ihema 6 Bufera, Bulera, Mohasi 7 Rugwero, Ruhnodo 8 Mugesera, Tshohoha

of Sardinia: 6 Omodeo

of Scotland: 3 Awe, Dee, Lin, Tay 4 Earn, Fyne, Gair, Gare, Linn, Ness, Oich, Ryan, Sloy 5 Duich, Leven, Lochy, Lough, Morar, Maree, Nevis 6 Laggan, Linnhe, Lomond 7 Katrine, Rannoch, St Marys

of Senegal: 6 Guiers

of Sicily: 7 Pergusa 8 Camarina

of Slovenia: 4 Bled

of Spain: 4 Lago 8 Albrifera

of the Sudan: 2 No 4 Chad, Toad 6 Nasser

of Sweden: 4 Ster 5 Asnen, Malar, Silja, Vaner 6 Vanern, Vatter, Wennen 7 Hielmar, Malaren, Vattern 8 Dalalven 9 Hjalmaren

of Switzerland: 3 Uri, Zug 4 Biel, Thon, Thun 5 Ageri, Leman, Morat 6 Bienne, Brienz, Geneva, Lugano, Sarnen, Wallen, Zurich 7 Hallwil, Lucerne, Lungern 8 Maggiore, Vierwald 9 Bielersee, Constance, Neuchatel, Sarnersee, Thunersee

of Syria: 5 Merom 7 Djeboid 8 Tiberias

of Tanzania: 5 Eyasi, Nyasa, Rukwa 6 Malawi, Natron, Nyassa 7 Manyara 8 Victoria 10 Tanganyika

of Thailand: 9 Nong Lahan

of Tibet: 3 Aru, Bam, Bum, Nam 4 Mema, Tosu 5 Jagok, Tabia 6 Dagtse, Garhur, Kashun, Nam Iso, Seling, Tangra, Yamdok 7 Kyaring, Terinam, Tsaring, Zilling 8 Jiggitai 9 Tengrinor 11 Manasarowar

of Tunisia: 6 Achkel, Djerid 7 Bizerte

of Turkey: 3 Tuz, Van 7 Egridir 8 Beysehir

of Uganda: 5 Kioga, Kyoga 6 Albert, Edward, George 8 Victoria

of the United States: 4 Erie, Mead 5 Huron, Tahoe 6 Cayuga, Finger, George, Itasca, Oneida, Seneca 7 Iliamma, Ontario 8 Michigan, Superior 9 Champlain, Great Salt, Salton Sea, Teshekpuk, Winnebago 10 Okeechobee 11 Yellowstone 13 Pontchartrain, Wallenpaupack, Winnipesaukee 14 Lake of the Woods

of Uruguay: 5 Merin, Mirim 18 Embalse del Rio Negro

of Venezuela: 9 Maracaibo, Tacarigua

of Wales: 4 Bala 6 Vyrnwy

of Yugoslavia: 4 Bled 5 Ohrid 6 Prespa 7 Ochrida, Scutari

of Zaire: 4 Kivu 5 Mweru, Tumba 6 Albert, Edward, Upemba 9 Mai-Ndombe 10 Tanganyika

of Zambia: 5 Mweru 6 Kariba 9 Bangweulu 10 Tanganyika

of Zimbabwe: 4 Kyle 6 Kariba

Lake, Harriette
  real name of: 10 Ann Sothern

Lake, Veronica
  real name: 29 Constance Frances Marie Ockelman
  co-star: 8 Alan Ladd
  born: 10 Brooklyn NY
  roles: 13 The Blue Dahlia 14 I Married a Witch, This Gun for Hire 16 Sullivan's Travels

Lake Isle of Innisfree, The
  author: 7 W B Yeats

Lakes
  goddess of: 7 Juturna

L'Allegro
  author: 10 John Milton
  companion piece: 11 Il Penseroso

Lalo, (Victor Antoine) Edouard
  born: 5 Lille 6 France
  composer of: 7 Namouna 8 Le Roi d'Ys 11 The King of Ys 15 Spanish Symphony 18 Symphonie Espagnole

Lamar, Ruby
  character in: 9 Sanctuary
  author: 8 Faulkner

Lamarck, Jean B
  field: 7 biology
  forerunner of theory of: 9 evolution
  author of: 21 Philosophie Zoologique

La Mare, Walter de
  author of: 16 Memoirs of a Midget

Lamarr, Hedy
  real name: 21 Hedwig Eva Maria Kiesler
  born: 6 Vienna 7 Austria
  roles: 7 Ecstasy 16 Samson and Delilah

Lamas, Fernando
  wife: 10 Arlene Dahl 14 Esther Williams
  born: 9 Argentina 11 Buenos Aires
  roles: 13 The Merry Widow 16 Dangerous When Wet 23 The Girl Who Had Everything

Lamb, Charles
  author of: 12 Essays of Elia 13 Dream Children 25 A Dissertation upon Roast Pig 31 Specimens of English Dramatic Poets

lambaste 4 beat, drub, lick, pelt, whip 5 scold, smear 6 berate, defeat, pummel, rebuke, subdue, thrash, wallop 7 bawl out, censure, chew out, clobber, cuss out, shellac, trounce 8 bludgeon, denounce, vanquish 9 castigate, dress down, light into, overwhelm, reprimand

lambent 6 bright 7 radiant, shining 8 luminous, lustrous 10 flickering, shimmering

Lambeosaurus
   type: 8 dinosaur 10 ornithopod
   location: 6 Canada
   period: 10 Cretaceous

Lambert, Constant
   born: 6 London 7 England
   composer of: 9 Horoscope, Rio Grande 14 Romeo and Juliet 17 Music for Orchestra 27 Summer's Last Will and Testament

lame 4 game, halt, weak 5 sorry 6 clumsy, feeble, flimsy, infirm, maimed 7 failing, halting, hobbled, limping, unsound, wanting 8 crippled, deformed, disabled 9 deficient, faltering 10 inadequate 11 ineffectual 12 insufficient, unconvincing, unpersuasive 14 unsatisfactory

lamebrain 3 ass, sap 4 fool 5 booby, dunce, idiot, moron, ninny 6 dimwit, nitwit 7 fathead, half-wit 8 bonehead, dumb-dumb, imbecile, lunkhead, numskull 9 blockhead, numbskull 10 dunderhead, nincompoop 11 chowderhead

lamebrained 4 dumb 6 stupid 7 asinine, foolish, idiotic, moronic 8 crackpot 9 dimwitted, imbecilic 10 half-witted 12 feeble-minded, simple-minded

Lamech
   father: 9 Methusael 10 Methuselah
   wives: 4 Adah 6 Zillah
   son: 5 Jabal, Jubal 9 Tubalcain
   daughter: 6 Naamah

lament 3 cry, sob 4 moan, wail, weep 5 dirge, mourn 6 bewail, outcry, plaint, regret 7 deplore, keening, requiem, whimper 9 mourning 9 death song 11 condole with, lamentation 12 funeral music 13 complain about 14 express pity for, show concern for, sympathize with 15 commiserate with

lamentable 4 dire 6 woeful 7 piteous 8 dreadful, grievous, pathetic, pitiable, shameful, terrible, wretched 9 miserable 10 deplorable 11 distressing, regrettable, unfortunate 13 disheartening, heartbreaking

Lamia
   author: 9 John Keats

Lamia
   form: 7 monster
   characteristic: 12 blood-sucking

La Motta, Jake (Jacob)
   nickname: 9 Bronx Bull
   sport: 6 boxing
   class: 12 middleweight
   movie biography: 10 Raging Bull

Lamour, Dorothy
   real name: 23 Mary Leta Dorothy Kaumeyer
   trademark: 6 sarong
   co-star: 7 Bob Hope 10 Bing Crosby
   born: 12 New Orleans LA
   roles:
   Road to: 3 Rio 4 Bali 6 Utopia 7 Morocco 8 Hong Kong, Zanzibar 9 Singapore

L'Amour, Louis
   author of: 5 Hondo, Lando 7 Sackett, Shalako 8 Conagher 10 Key-Lock Man, Rivers West 14 The Californios, The Daybreakers 15 Westward the Tide 16 How the West Was Won, Over on the Dry Side 21 The Man from Broken Hills, To the Far Blue Mountains

lamp 4 bulb 5 light, torch 6 beacon 7 blinker, lantern 9 headlight, spotlight 10 chandelier, floodlight, Kleig light, night light 11 searchlight 12 ceiling light, reading light 14 ceiling fixture
   invented by:
   arc: 6 Staite
   incandescent: 6 Edison
   incandescent frosted: 6 Pipkin
   incandescent gas: 8 Langmuir
   Kleig: 7 Kleigel
   mercury vapor: 6 Hewitt
   miner's safety: 4 Davy
   neon: 6 Claude

Lampedusa, Giuseppe di
   author of: 10 The Leopard

Lampetia
   father: 6 Helius
   mother: 6 Neaera

lampoon 5 farce, put-on, spoof, squib 6 parody, satire, send up 7 mockery, takeoff 8 diatribe, ridicule, satirize, travesty 9 broadside, burlesque 10 caricature, pasquinade 11 make light of

Lamus
   father: 8 Hercules
   mother: 7 Omphale
   attacked: 5 ships

Lamy of Santa Fe
   author: 10 Paul Horgan

lanai 7 veranda

Lancaster, Burt
   real name: 22 Burton Stephen Lancaster
   born: 9 New York NY
   roles: 5 Moses 9 All My Sons, Local Hero 11 Elmer Gantry (Oscar) 12 Atlantic City, The Rainmaker 13 The Rose Tattoo 14 Seven Days in May 16 Sorry Wrong Number 17 Birdman of Alcatraz 18 From Here to Eternity 19 Come Back Little Sheba, Sweet Smell of Success

lance 4 gaff, pike 5 shaft, spear 7 assegai, halberd, harpoon, javelin

Lancelot, Launcelot
   character in: 16 Arthurian romance
   lover: 9 Guinevere
   home: 10 Joyous Gard

lancer 6 cavalier, horseman 10 cavalryman 12 horse soldier, horse trooper 14 mounted soldier

Lanchester, Elsa
   real name: 17 Elizabeth Sullivan
   husband: 15 Charles Laughton
   born: 7 England 8 Lewisham
   roles: 15 Come to the Stable 22 The Bride of Frankenstein 24 Witness for the Prosecution 25 The Private Life of Henry VIII 31 The Private Life of Henry the Eighth

land 3 get, lea, nab, net **4** area, dirt, dock, gain, grab, lawn, loam, moor, park, soil, take, ward, zone **5** acres, catch, earth, grass, green, humus, light, put in, realm, seize, shire, snare, state, tie up, tract **6** alight, anchor, canton, clinch, colony, county, debark, domain, empire, fields, ground, meadow, nation, parish, realty, region, secure **7** acreage, capture, country, descend, dry land, grounds, kingdom, pasture, section, set down, subsoil, terrain, win over **8** come down, district, dominion, farmland, homeland, location, mainland, make land, make port, precinct, property, province, republic, vicinity **9** cornfield, disembark, grassland, lay anchor, lay hold of, lead one to, reach land, territory **10** bring one to, carry one to, come to land, drop anchor, fatherland, motherland, native land, native soil, real estate, settle down, settlement, terra firma, wheat field **11** countryside, put into port **12** commonwealth, put into shore, real property, village green **13** the old country

Landau, Lev Davidovitch
  field: **7** physics
  nationality: **7** Russian
  discovered: **12** liquid helium **14** ferromagnetism
  awarded: **10** Nobel Prize

landed property 5 manor **6** estate **8** compound **12** countryplace

land force 4 army **6** legion, troops **7** legions **8** infantry, soldiers, soldiery **9** artillery

Landless, Neville and Helena
  characters in: **22** The Mystery of Edwin Drood
  author: **7** Dickens

landlord 5 owner **6** holder, squire **8** landlady **9** landowner, possessor **10** freeholder, landholder, proprietor **13** property owner **14** lord of the manor

landmark 8 keystone, monument, signpost **9** benchmark, guidepost, highlight, high point, milestone, watershed **11** cornerstone **12** turning point **16** historic building

Landmarks
  god of: **8** Terminus

Land of Enchantment
  nickname of: **9** New Mexico

Land of Lincoln
  nickname of: **8** Illinois

Land of Opportunity
  nickname of: **8** Arkansas

Land of Sky-blue Waters
  nickname of: **9** Minnesota

Land of Steady Habits
  nickname of: **11** Connecticut

Land of Ten Thousand Lakes
  nickname of: **9** Minnesota

Land of the Dakotas
  nickname of: **11** North Dakota

Land of the Midnight Sun
  nickname of: **6** Alaska

Landon, Michael
  real name: **20** Eugene Maurice Orowitz
  born: **13** Forest Hills NY
  roles: **7** Bonanza **15** Highway to Heaven **19** Little Joe Cartwright **20** I Was a Teenage Werewolf **23** Little House on the Prairie

landscape 4 view **5** scene, sight, vista **6** aspect **7** scenery **8** panorama, prospect **9** spectacle **10** rural scene, scenic view **14** natural scenery

landscape architect 7 Le Notre, Olmsted

landsman 10 countryman **13** fellow citizen

Landsteiner, Karl
  field: **8** medicine **9** pathology
  distinguished: **10** blood types
  identified: **8** RH factor
  awarded: **10** Nobel Prize

lane 3 way **4** pass, path, road **5** alley, byway, drive, route, track, trail **6** access, avenue, bypath, course **7** passage, roadway **8** alleyway, approach, footpath **10** passageway

Lang, Walter
  director of: **7** Desk Set **11** The King and I

Lange, Jessica
  born: **9** Cloquet MN
  roles: **7** Country, Frances, Tootsie **8** King Kong **11** All That Jazz **16** Crimes of the Heart **26** The Postman Always Rings Twice

Langella, Frank
  born: **9** Bayonne NJ
  roles: **7** Dracula **23** The Diary of a Mad Housewife

Langhanke, Lucille Vasconcellos
  real name of: **9** Mary Astor

Langland, William
  author of: **12** Piers Plowman

Langmuir, Irving
  field: **9** chemistry
  invented: **15** atomic blowtorch **17** gas-tungsten lights
  awarded: **10** Nobel Prize

language 4 cant, jive **5** argot, idiom, lingo, prose, slang, words **6** jargon, patois, speech, tongue **7** cursing, cussing, dialect, diction, wording **8** parlance, rhetoric, swearing, verbiage **9** discourse, elocution, profanity **10** expression, use of words, vernacular, vocabulary **11** imprecation, phraseology, profane talk **12** mother tongue, native tongue **13** colloquialism **14** public speaking, self-expression **16** manner of speaking, mode of expression **17** oral communication, reading and writing, verbal intercourse
  of Afghanistan: **4** Dari **5** Farsi **6** Afghan, Pashto, Pushtu **7** Balochi, Baluchi, Persian
  of Albania: **3** Geg **4** Cham, Gheg, Hish, Tosk **5** Greek **8** Albanian
  of Algeria: **6** Arabic, Berber, French, Zenata **7** Senhaja
  of Andorra: **6** French **7** Catalan, Spanish

of **Angola:** 5 Bantu 8 Kimbundu, Oumbundu 9 Ovimbundu 10 Portuguese
of **Antigua and Barbuda:** 7 English
of **Argentina:** 7 Spanish
of **Armenia:** 7 Russian 8 Armenian
of **Australia:** 6 Yabber 7 English 9 aborigine (dialects)
of **Austria:** 5 Czech 6 German, Magyar 8 Croatian 9 Slovenian
of **Azerbaijan:** 6 Turkic
of the **Bahamas:** 6 Creole 7 English
of **Bahrain:** 4 Urdu 5 Farsi 6 Arabic 7 English, Persian
of **Bangladesh:** 6 Bihari 7 Bengali, English
of **Barbados:** 7 English
of **Belgium:** 5 Dutch 6 French, German 7 Flemish
of **Benin:** 3 Fon 5 Dendi 6 Bariba, French, Fulani, Yoruba
of **Bermuda:** 7 English
of **Bhutan:** 5 Hindi, Lhoke 7 Tibetan 8 Dzongkha, Nepalese
of **Bolivia:** 6 Aymara 7 Quechua, Spanish
of **Borneo:** 5 Malay 7 Chinese, English
of **Bosnia-Herzegovina:** 13 Serbo Croatian
of **Botswana:** 5 Bantu, Click 6 Tswana 7 English, Khoisan 8 Setswana
of **Brazil:** 10 Portuguese
of **Brunei:** 4 Iban 5 Malay 7 Chinese, English
of **Bulgaria:** 9 Bulgarian
of **Burkina Faso:** 4 Bobo, Lobi, More, Samo 5 Dyula, Mande, Mossi 6 French
of **Burundi:** 6 French 7 Kirundi, Swahili
of **Cambodia/Kampuchea:** 5 Khmer 6 French
of **Cameroon:** 4 Bulu 5 Bantu, Bassa, Hausa 6 Douala, Ewondo, French, Fulani 7 English 8 Bamileke, Fulfulde
of **Canada:** 6 Eskimo, French 7 English
of **Canary Islands:** 7 Spanish
of **Cape Verde:** 7 Crioulo 10 Portuguese 13 Verdean Creole
of **Central African Republic:** 5 Sango, Zande 6 French
of **Chad:** 4 Sara 5 Turku 6 Arabic, French
of **Chile:** 7 Spanish
of **China:** 7 Chinese 8 Mandarin, Shanghai 9 Cantonese
of **Colombia:** 7 Spanish
of **Comoros:** 6 Arabic, French 7 Swahili 8 Malagasy
of **Congo:** 4 Susu 5 Bantu, Fiote 6 French, Kituba 7 Bangala, Lingala
of **Costa Rica:** 7 Spanish
of **Crete:** 5 Greek 6 Minoan 7 Linear A, Linear B
of **Croatia:** 8 Croatian 10 Serbo Croat
of **Cuba:** 7 Spanish
of **Cyprus:** 5 Greek 7 Turkish 8 Armenian
of **Czechoslovakia/Czech Republic:** 5

Czech 6 German, Magyar, Slovak 7 Russian 9 Hungarian
of **Denmark:** 4 Odan 6 Danish 8 Faeroese 11 Greenlander
of **Djibouti:** 4 Afar 6 Arabic, French, Somali
of **Dominican Republic:** 6 French 7 English, Spanish
of **Ecuador:** 6 Jibaro 7 Quechua, Spanish
of **Egypt:** 6 Arabic, Coptic, French 7 English
of **El Salvador:** 7 Spanish
of **England:** 7 English
of **Equatorial Guinea:** 4 Bubi, Fang 6 pidgin 7 Spanish
of **Eritrea:** 7 Amharic
of **Estonia:** 5 Tartu 10 Finno-Ugric
of **Ethiopia:** 3 Giz 4 Afar, Agow, Geez, Saho 5 Geeze, Ghese, Smali, Tigre 6 Arabic, Harari 7 Amharic, English, Italian, Russian 8 Gallinya, Irob-Saho, Tigrinya
of **Fiji:** 5 Hindi 6 Fijian 7 English
of **Finland:** 4 Avar, Lapp 5 Karen, Ugric, Vogul 6 Magyar, Ostyak, Tarast 7 Finnish, Olonets, Samoyed, Swedish 8 Estonian 10 Olenetsian
of **France:** 6 French
of **Gabon Republic:** 6 French
of **The Gambia:** 4 Fula 5 Wolof 6 Fulani 7 English, Malinke 8 Mandingo
of **Georgia:** 8 Georgian
of **Germany:** 6 German 10 High German 11 Hochdeutsch
of **Ghana:** 2 Ga 3 Ewe, Gur, Kwa, Twi 5 Fanti, Hausa 7 Dagomba, English
of **Gibraltar:** 7 English, Spanish
of **Greece:** 5 Greek
of **Greenland:** 6 Danish, Eskimo 11 Greenlandic
of **Grenada:** 7 English
of **Guatemala:** 6 Quiche 7 Spanish
of **Guinea:** 5 Fulbe, Mande 6 Arabic, French, Fulani 7 English
of **Guinea-Bissau:** 5 Fulah 7 Balante, Crioulo 8 Mandingo 10 Portuguese 21 Cape Verde–Guinea Creole
of **Guyana:** 5 Hindi 7 English
of **Haiti:** 6 Creole, French, patois
of **Honduras:** 7 English, Spanish
of **Hong Kong:** 7 Chinese, English 9 Cantonese
of **Hungary:** 6 German, Magyar, Slovak 8 Croatian 9 Hungarian 10 Finno-Ugric
of **Iceland:** 5 Norse 9 Icelandic
of **India:** 4 Urdu 5 Hindi, Oriya, Tamil 6 Sindhi, Telugu 7 Bengali, English, Kannada, Malayam, Marathi, Punjabi 8 Assamese, Gujarati, Kashmiri, Sanskrit 9 Malayalam
of **Indonesia:** 5 Tetum 6 Bahasa, Igorot 7 English, Gyarung, Malayan 8 Balinese, Chamorro, Javanese, Madurese, Sudanese 10 Indonesian, Polynesian
of **Iran:** 4 Luri, Zend 5 Farsi, Turki 6 Arabic 7 Baluchi, Kurdish, Persian 8 Armenian 11 Azerbaijani

of Iraq: 5 Farsi 6 Arabic 7 Kurdish, Persian, Turkish

of Ireland: 5 Irish 6 Gaelic 7 English

of Israel: 6 Arabic, French, Hebrew 7 English

of Italy: 5 Ladin, Latin 6 French, German 7 Italian, Slovene 8 Friulian 9 Sardinian

of Ivory Coast: 4 Akan 6 Dioula, French

of Jamaica: 6 Creole 7 English

of Japan: 5 Kanto 8 Japanese

of Java: 4 Kavi, Kawi 5 Malay 6 Sassak 8 Balinese, Madurese, Sudanese 16 Bahasa Indonesian

of Jordan: 6 Arabic

of Kazakhstan: 6 Kazakh

of Kenya: 3 Luo 5 Bantu, Luhya, Masai 6 Kikuyu 7 English, Swahili 8 Buyerati 10 Hindustani

of Kiribati: 6 Samoan 7 English 10 Gilbertese

of Korea: 6 Korean

of Kuwait: 6 Arabic

of Kyrgyzstan: 6 Turkic 7 Kirghiz

of Laos: 3 Lao, Man, Meo 6 French 7 English

of Latvia: 7 Lettish

of Lebanon: 6 Arabic, French, Syriac 7 English, Turkish 8 Armenian

of Lesotho: 5 Sotho 7 English, Sesotho

of Liberia: 3 Kru, Kwa 5 Mande 7 English

of Libya: 6 Arabic, Berber 7 English, Italian

of Liechtenstein: 6 German 10 Alemannish

of Lithuania: 5 Zmudz 6 Baltic 10 Lithuanian

of Luxembourg: 6 French, German 7 English 13 Letzeburgesch

of Macao: 7 Chinese, English 9 Cantonese 10 Portuguese

of Macedonia: 10 Macedonian

of Madagascar/Malagasy Republic: 6 French 8 Malagasy, Malgache

of Malawi: 3 Yao 4 Cewa 5 Bantu, Ngoni, Tonga 6 Nyanja 7 English, Tumbuka 8 Chichewa 10 Chitumbuka

of Malaysia: 4 Bugi, Dyak 5 Malay, Tamil 6 Battok, Rejang 7 Chinese, English, Lampong, Niasese 8 Achinese, Javanese, Makassar 14 Bahasa Malaysia

of Maldives: 6 Arabic, Divehi

of Mali: 5 Dogon, Dyula, Feulh, Mande, Marka 6 Berber, French, Fulani 7 Bambara, Malinke, Senoufo, Songhai

of Malta: 7 English, Italian, Maltese

of Mauritania: 4 Fula 5 Wolof 6 Arabic, French 7 Phoolor, Tukulor 8 Fulfulde, Mandingo 9 Sarakolle 10 Hassaniyya

of Mauritius: 4 Urdu 5 Hindi, Tamil 6 Creole, French 7 English

of Mexico: 5 Mayan, Otomi 6 Mixtec 7 Mazahua, Mazatec, Nahuatl, Spanish, Totonac, Zapotec 8 Tarascan

of Moldova: 8 Romanian 9 Moldovian

of Monaco: 6 French 7 English, Italian 10 Monegasque

of Mongolia: 6 Kazakh 16 Khalkha Mongolian

of Montenegro: 13 Serbo-Croatian

of Morocco: 6 Arabic, Berber, French 7 Spanish

of Mozambique: 3 Yao 5 Makua 6 Nyanji, Thonga 7 Swahili 10 Portuguese

of Myanmar: 3 Lai 4 Chin, Kuki, Pegu, Shan 5 Karen 6 Kachin 7 Burmese

of Namibia: 5 Bantu 6 German 7 English, Khoisan 9 Afrikaans

of Nauru: 7 English, Nauruan

of Nepal: 6 Nepali, Newari 7 English

of the Netherlands: 5 Dutch 7 English, Frisian

of New Guinea: 4 Motu 7 English 16 Melanesian Pidgin

of New Zealand: 5 Maori 7 English

of Nicaragua: 7 English, Spanish

of Niger: 5 Hausa, Mande 6 Djerma, French, Fulani, Tuareg 8 Mandingo, Tamashek

of Nigeria: 3 Ibo 4 Efik, Igbo 5 Hausa 6 Yoruba 7 English

of Norway: 4 Lapp 5 Norse 6 Bokmal 7 Nynorsk, Riksmal 8 Landsmal, Samnorsk 9 Landsmaal, Norwegian

of Oman: 4 Urdu 5 Hindi 6 Arabic 7 Baluchi

of Pakistan: 4 Urdu 6 Pushtu, Sindhi 7 Baluchi, Bengali, English, Punjabi

of Panama: 7 English, Spanish

of Paraguay: 6 German 7 Guarani, Spanish

of Peru: 6 Aymara 7 English, Quechua, Spanish

of the Philippines: 4 Moro 5 Bicol, Bikol 6 Ibanag 7 Cebuano, English, Ilocano, Spanish, Tagalog, Visayan 8 Filipino 9 Pampangan, Philipino 10 Samar-Leyte 13 Bamboo-English 14 Panay-Hiligayon

of Poland: 6 Kaszub, Polish 10 Pomeranian

of Polynesia: 4 Niue, Uvea 5 Maori 6 Samoan, Tongan 7 Austral, Tagalog, Tokelau 8 Hawaiian, Tahitian 9 Marquesan, Tuamatuan 10 Mangarevan

of Portugal: 10 Portuguese

of Qatar: 6 Arabic

of Romania: 6 French, Magyar 7 Russian 8 Romanian, Rumanian 9 Hungarian

of Russia: 5 Evenk 6 Buriat, Kalmyk 7 Finnish, Russian 8 Ossetian

of Rwanda: 6 French 7 Swahili 11 Kinyarwanda

of Samoa: 6 Samoan 7 English

of San Marino: 7 Italian

of Sao Tome and Principe: 10 Portuguese

of Sardinia: 7 Italian

of Saudi Arabia: 6 Arabic

of Scotland: 4 Erse 6 Celtic, Gaelic, Keltic, Lallan 7 English, Lalland

of Senegal: 5 Wolof 6 French

of the Seychelles: 6 Creole, French 7 English

of Sierra Leone: 4 Krio 5 Limba, Mende, Mendi, Temne 6 Creole 7 English

of Singapore: 5 Malay, Tamil 7 Chinese, English 8 Mandarin

of Slovakia: 6 Slovik Slovak

of Slovenia: 7 Slovene

of the Solomon Islands: 7 English 13 Pidgin English 16 Melanesian Pidgin

of Somalia: 6 Arabic, Somali 7 English, Italian

of South Africa: 4 Taal, Zulu 5 Bantu, Hindi, Nguni, Sotho, Swazi, Tamil, Venda, Xhosa 6 Telegu, Thonga 7 English, Khoisan, Ndebele, Sesotho 8 Bujarati, Fanakalo 9 Afrikaans 13 Kitchen-Kaffir

of Spain: 6 Basque 7 Catalan, Spanish 8 Balearic, Galician 9 Castilian, Valencian

of Sri Lanka: 4 Pali 5 Tamil 7 English 9 Sinhalese

of Sudan: 2 Ga 3 Efe, Ewe, Ibo, Kru, Vak, Vei 4 Efik, Mole, Tshi 6 Arabic, Nubian, Yoruba 7 English 8 Mandango, Mandingo 9 Ta Bedawie

of Suriname: 5 Carib, Dutch, Hindi 6 Arawak 7 English 8 Javanese, Taki-Taki 10 Hindustani 11 Sranan Tongo 12 Sranag Tongo

of Swaziland: 5 Ngumi 7 English, Siswati 9 Afrikaans 10 Portuguese

of Sweden: 5 Lapp 7 Swedish

of Switzerland: 5 Ladin 6 French, German 7 Italian 8 Romansch 14 Switzerdeutsch

of Syria: 6 Arabic, French, Syriac 7 Aramaic, English, Kurdish, Turkish 8 Armenian

of Taiwan: 4 Amon, Amoy 5 Hakka, Kuo Yu 6 Minnan 9 Taiwanese 15 Mandarin Chinese

of Tajikistan: 5 Tajik 7 Tadzhik

of Tanzania: 5 Bantu 6 Arabic 7 English, Khoisan, Nilotic, Swahili 8 Cushitic, Gujarati

of Thailand: 3 Lao, Tai 4 Ahom, Shan, Thai 5 Kadai 7 Bangkok, English 9 Krung Thep 12 Chinese Malay

of Tibet: 5 Balti 6 Ladkhi 7 Bhutani, Bodskad 8 Sanskrit 9 Bhutanese

of Togo: 3 Ana, Ewe, Twi 4 Mina 5 Hausa 6 French, Kabrai, Kabrie 7 Bassari, Dagomba, Quatchi 8 Kotokoli, Lotocoli

of Tonga: 6 Tongan 7 English

of Trinidad and Tobago: 6 French 7 Chinese, English, Spanish 10 Portuguese 12 French Patois

of Tunisia: 6 Arabic, Berber, French

of Turkey: 6 Arabic 7 Kurdish, Turkish

of Turkmenistan: 6 Turkic 10 West Turkic

of Tuvalu: 6 Samoan 7 English 8 Tuvaluan 10 Polynesian

of Uganda: 5 Ateso, Ganda 7 English, Luganda, Swahili

of Ukraine: 9 Ukrainian

of United Arab Emirates: 5 Farsi 6 Arabic 7 English, Persian

of Uruguay: 7 Italian, Spanish

of Uzbekistan: 5 Uzbek

of Vanuatu: 6 French 7 Bislama, English 16 Melanesian Pidgin

of Venezuela: 4 Pume 7 Spanish

of Vietnam: 3 Yue 4 Cham 5 Khmer, Rhade 6 French 7 Chinese, English 9 Cantonese 10 Vietnamese

of Wales: 5 Welsh 6 Celtic, Cymric, Keltic, Kymric 7 Cymraeg, English

of Western Sahara: 16 Hassaniyya Arabic

of Western Samoa: 6 Samoan 7 English

of Yemen: 6 Arabic

of Yugoslavia: 7 Bosnian, Slovene 8 Albanian, Croatian 9 Hungarian, Slovenian 10 Macedonian 11 Montenegrin 13 Herzegovinian, Serbo-Croatian

of Zaire: 5 Bantu 6 French 7 Chiluba, Kikongo, Lingala, Swahili 8 Sudanese, Tshiluba

of Zambia: 4 Lozi 5 Bemba, Lunda, Tonga 6 Luvale, Nyanja 7 English 9 Afrikaans

of Zimbabwe: 3 Ila 5 Bantu, Shona 7 English, Ndebele

language, artificial
  of James Cooke Brown: 6 Loglan
  of Hans Freudenthal: 6 Lincos 13 Lingua Cosmica
  of Alexander Gode: 11 Interlingua
  of C K Ogden: 12 Basic English
  of J M Schleyer: 7 Volapuk
  of Jean Francois Sudre: 8 Solresol
  of L L Zamehof: 9 Esperanto

language, extinct 6 Dacian, Hattic, Lycian, Lydian, Palaic 7 Cornish, Elamite, Hittite, Hurrian 8 Etruscan, Illyrian, Phrygian, Sumerian, Thracian, Urartian 9 Dalmatian 15 Cuneiform Luwian 18 Hieroglyphic Luwian

languid 4 dull, slow, weak 5 faint, heavy, inert, shaky, spent, weary 6 feeble, infirm, leaden, sickly, supine, torpid 7 rickety, unsound, worn-out 8 drooping, fatigued, inactive, lifeless, listless, sluggish, unstable 9 apathetic, declining, doddering, enervated, exhausted, inanimate, lethargic, trembling, unhealthy 10 indisposed, spiritless 11 debilitated 12 on the decline 13 lackadaisical

languidness 6 apathy, torpor 7 inertia 8 lethargy 12 listlessness, sluggishness 13 indisposition

languish 3 ebb 4 fade, fail, flag, wane, wilt 5 covet, droop, faint 6 desire, hunger, sicken, thirst, wither 7 dwindle, long for, pine for, sigh for 8 diminish, give away, take sick, yearn for 9 become ill, break down, hanker for, hunger for, thirst for, waste away 10 go downhill 11 deteriorate, have a yen for, hunger after 12 be desirous of 13 go into decline

Languish, Lydia
  character in: 9 The Rivals
  author: 8 Sheridan

languor 5 ennui 6 torpor 7 inertia 8 dullness, hebetude, lethargy 9 indolence, lassitude, torpidity, weariness 10 dispassion, dreaminess 11 languidness, leisureness 12 lifelessness, listlessness, sluggishness

lank 4 bony, lean, limp, thin 5 gaunt, spare 6 skinny, slight 7 angular, scrawny 8 straight

lanky 4 bony, lean 5 gaunt, gawky, rangy, spare, weedy 6 skinny 7 angular, scrawny 8 gangling, rawboned 11 tall and thin

La Nouvelle Heloise
  author: 10 J J.Rousseau

Lansbury, Angela
  born: 6 London 7 England
  roles: 4 Mame 8 Gaslight 10 JB Fletcher 11 Sweeney Todd 14 Murder She Wrote 15 Jessica Fletcher 22 The Manchurian Candidate

Laocoon
  vocation: 6 priest
  father: 5 Capys
  brother: 8 Anchises
  son: 10 Thymbraeus
  warned: 7 Trojans
  warned of: 11 Trojan horse
  killed by: 8 serpents

Laodamas
  father: 8 Eteocles
  defended: 6 Thebes
  killed: 9 Aegialeus
  killed by: 8 Alcmaeon

Laodamia
  father: 7 Acastus 11 Bellerophon
  mother: 9 Astydamia
  husband: 11 Protesilaus
  lover: 4 Zeus
  son: 8 Sarpedon

Laodice
  father: 5 Priam
  mother: 6 Hecuba
  husband: 8 Helicaon
  son: 6 Pereus 7 Munitus

Laodocus
  father: 6 Apollo
  mother: 6 Phthia
  killed by: 7 Aetolus

Laomedon
  king of: 4 Troy
  father: 4 Ilus
  wife: 6 Strymo
  son: 5 Priam 6 Lampus 7 Clytius 8 Hicetaon, Tithonus
  daughter: 7 Hesione 8 Themiste

Laos
  other name: 7 Lan Xang 23 land of a million elephants
  capital/largest city: 9 Viengchan, Vientiane
  others: 4 Nape 5 Pakse, Xieng 6 Paklay 7 Thakhek 11 Savannakhet, Xiang Khoang 12 Luang Prabang 14 Louangphrabang
  school: 12 Sisavangvong
  measure: 3 bak
  monetary unit: 2 at 3 att, kip
  mountain: 3 Lai, Loi, San 4 Copi, Khat 5

Atwat 6 Khoung, Tiubia 15 Annam Cordillera
  highest point: 3 Bia 7 Phou Bia
  river: 3 Noi 4 Done 5 Khong 6 Mekong, Sebang
  physical feature:
  plain: 4 Jars
  plateau: 8 Bolovens
  people: 2 Lu 3 Kha, Lao, Man, Meo, Tai, Yao, Yun 4 Miao, Thai 5 Hmong 8 Lao Teung 10 Phoutheung
  leader: 2 Fa Ngoun 13 Souphanouvong 14 Souligna Vongsa, Souvanna Phouma
  language: 3 Lao, Man, Meo 6 French 7 English
  religion: 7 animism 8 Buddhism 17 Theravada Buddhism
  feature:
  Buddhist priest: 5 bonze
  Communist guerrilla group: 9 Pathet Lao
  musical instrument: 5 khene
  temple: 3 wat
  trail: 9 Ho Chi Minh

Laothoe
  concubine of: 5 Priam
  son: 6 Lycaon 9 Polydorus

Lao-tzu
  author of: 10 Tao Te Ching

lap 3 sip 4 lick, wash 5 awash, drink, plash, slosh 6 babble, bubble, gurgle, lick up, murmur, ripple, splash, tongue

La Paz
  administrative capital of: 7 Bolivia

Laphria
  epithet of: 7 Artemis

Laphystius
  epithet of: 4 Zeus

lapis lazuli
  species: 8 lazurite
  source: 10 Badakhshan 11 Afghanistan

Laplace, Pierre S
  field: 7 physics 9 astronomy
  nationality: 6 French
  hypothesis of: 18 nebular solar system

lapse 3 gap, sag 4 drop, fall, flaw, go by, loss, sink, slip, stop, wane 5 boner, break, cease, droop, error, fault, pause, slump 6 breach, elapse, expire, hiatus, laxity, pass by, period, recede, recess, run out, slip by, wither, worsen 7 blunder, decline, descent, failing, failure, faux pas, interim, passage, relapse, respite, subside 8 collapse, downfall, elapsing, interval, omission, slip away 9 backslide, disregard, interlude, oversight, slump down, terminate 10 degenerate, falling off, forfeiture, infraction, negligence, peccadillo, regression 11 backsliding, delinquency, dereliction, deteriorate, shortcoming 12 degeneration, intermission, interruption, lose validity 13 deterioration, process of time, slight mistake 14 become obsolete, fall into disuse

lapsus linguae 16 a slip of the tongue

Laputa
  fictional land in: 16 Gulliver's Travels
  author: 5 Swift

lar *see* 5 lares

Lara
character in: 9 Dr Zhivago
author: 9 Pasternak

Laraia, Carol Marla
real name of: 13 Carol Lawrence

Laramie
character: 6 Jonesy 9 Mort Corey 10
Jess Harper 11 Andy Sherman, Daisy
Cooper, Slim Sherman 12 Mike Williams
cast: 9 John Smith 12 Dennis Holmes,
Robert Fuller 13 Stuart Randall 14 Spring
Byington 15 Bobby Crawford Jr, Hoagy
Carmichael

larceny 5 fraud, theft 7 bilking, forgery,
looting, robbery, sacking 8 burglary, cheating, fleecing, stealing 9 extortion, pilferage,
pilfering, swindling 10 absconding, pecula-
tion, plagiarism, purloining 11 defalcation,
depredation 12 embezzlement, grand larceny, petit larceny, petty larceny, safe-
cracking 13 appropriation, housebreaking
16 misappropriation

larder 5 cuddy 6 pantry, spence 7 buttery 8
food room 9 stillroom, storeroom 10 supply
room 11 storage room

Lardner, Ring
author of: 11 The Love Nest, You Know
Me Al 12 Treat Em Rough 16 Gullible's
Travels

Larentalia
origin: 5 Roman
event: 8 festival

lares
form: 7 spirits
watched over: 5 house 6 hearth 9 community 10 crossroads
single member: 3 lar
companions: 7 penates
correspond to: 8 Dioscuri

large 3 big, fat 4 high, huge, vast, wide 5
ample, broad, grand, great, heavy, hulky,
obese, plump, roomy 6 goodly, mighty,
portly, rotund 7 copious, immense, liberal, massive, sizable 8 colossal, enormous,
gigantic, imposing, man-sized, outsized,
spacious, sweeping, towering 9 boundless, capacious, expansive, extensive, gi-
antlike, kingsized, limitless, monstrous,
overgrown, ponderous, strapping, unlimited, unstinted 10 exorbitant, gargantuan,
stupendous 11 extravagant, far-reaching,
magnificent, substantial 12 considerable
13 comprehensive 14 Brobdingnagian

large-hearted 8 generous 10 altruistic, benevolent, charitable 12 humanitarian 13
philanthropic

largely 6 mainly, mostly, widely 7 chiefly,
greatly 9 generally, primarily 10 on the
whole 11 extensively, principally 12 considerably 13 predominantly, substantially
14 for the most part, to a great extent

largeness 7 bigness 8 enormity, hugeness
9 amplitude, greatness, immensity 11
massiveness 12 enormousness

large-scale 3 big 4 huge, vast, wide 5
broad, great 6 all-out, mighty 8 colossal,
far-flung, gigantic 9 extensive, monstrous
10 gargantuan, stupendous, tremendous
11 far-reaching, wide-ranging 15 all-
encompassing

largess, largesse 3 aid 4 boon, gift, help 5
favor, mercy 6 bounty, reward 7 charity,
payment 8 bestowal, donation, gratuity,
kindness, offering 9 benignity 10 assistance, generosity 11 benefaction, benevolence 12 philanthropy, remuneration

large store 8 emporium 11 supermarket 15
department store

largo
music: 4 slow 14 dignified tempo

lark 3 gag 4 game, jape, romp, whim 5 antic, caper, fling, prank, spree, trick 6 frolic,
gambol 7 caprice 8 escapade 11 high old
time 12 sportiveness
group of: 10 exaltation

larkspur 9 Consolida 10 Delphinium
varieties: 4 Tall 5 Dwarf 6 Rocket

La Rochefoucauld, Francois
author of: 6 Maxims 7 Maximes

larva
insect stage after: 3 egg
insect stage before: 4 pupa
legless: 6 maggot

larvae
form: 6 ghosts
characteristic: 9 malignant

lascivious 4 foul, lewd 5 bawdy, dirty,
gross, lurid 6 coarse, filthy, impure, ribald, sordid, vulgar, wanton 7 immoral, lustful, obscene, ruttish, squalid 8 depraved,
immodest, improper, indecent, prurient 9
lecherous, salacious, shameless 10 indelicate, licentious, unblushing 11 dirty-
minded, unwholesome

lash 3 fix, hit, tie 4 beat, bind, blow,
flog, moor, rope, whip 5 brace, curse, flail,
hitch, knock, leash, pound, scold, smack,
strap, thong, tie up, truss 6 attach, berate, buffet, fasten, hammer, pinion, revile,
secure, strike, stroke, tether, thrash, whip
up 7 lecture, scourge, upbraid 8 lambaste,
make fast 9 castigate, horsewhip 10 take
to task, tongue-lash 11 rail against 13 cat-
o'-nine-tails

Lash, Joseph P
author of: 18 Eleanor and Franklin

lashed together 4 tied 5 bound 6 tied up 7
secured, trussed 8 fastened

lash out at 5 fly at 6 assail, attack, strike 8
fall upon

Las Palmas
capital of: 13 Canary Islands

lass 4 girl, maid, miss 5 wench 6 damsel,
female, lassie, lovely, maiden, pretty, virgin
7 colleen 10 schoolgirl, young woman

Lasser, Louise
father: 8 S J Lasser
husband: 10 Woody Allen
born: 9 New York NY
roles: 22 Mary Hartman Mary Hartman

lassie 4 girl, lass, maid 6 maiden 7 colleen 10 young woman

Lassie
character: 5 Timmy 9 Doc Weaver 10 Jeff Miller, Paul Martin, Ruth Martin 11 Corey Stuart, Ellen Miller 12 Gramps Miller 17 Sylvester (Porky) Brockway
cast: 10 Jan Clayton, Jon Provost, Jon Shepodd, Robert Bray 11 Arthur Space, Tommy Rettig 12 Donald Keeler, June Lockhart 14 Cloris Leachman, George Chandler 15 George Cleveland

lassitude 5 ennui 6 apathy, torpor 7 boredom, fatigue, inertia, languor, malaise 8 debility, doldrums, dullness, lethargy, weakness 9 faintness, indolence, tiredness, torpidity, weariness 10 droopiness, drowsiness, enervation, exhaustion, feebleness, supineness 11 languidness, prostration 12 indifference, lack of energy, listlessness, sluggishness

lasso 4 lash, rope 5 catch, noose, reata, riata, thong 6 lariat

last 3 end 4 go on, keep, live, stay, wear 5 abide, after, exist, final, stand 6 behind, ending, endure, extend, finale, finish, hold on, hold up, remain, utmost 7 carry on, closing, extreme, finally, hold out, outlive, outwear, persist, stand up, subsist, survive, tailing 8 at the end, continue, doomsday, farthest, final one, furthest, hindmost, hold good, in back of, maintain, rearmost, terminal, terminus, trailing, ultimate 9 in the rear, persevere 10 Armageddon, concluding, conclusion, conclusive, eventually, terminally, ultimately 11 crack of doom, crucial time 12 in conclusion, tagging along 13 Day of Judgment
French: 7 dernier

Last Analysis, The
author: 10 Saul Bellow

Last Days of Pompeii, The
author: 18 Edward Bulwer-Lytton
character: 4 Ione 5 Nydia 7 Arbaces, Glaucus 9 Apaecides

Last Frontier
nickname of: 6 Alaska

lasting 4 firm 5 fixed, solid 7 abiding, chronic, durable, eternal 8 constant, enduring, immortal, lifelong, long-term 9 incessant, lingering, long-lived, permanent, perpetual, steadfast, unceasing 10 continuing, deep-rooted, deep-seated, perdurable, persistent, protracted 11 established, never-ending 12 indissoluble 14 indestructible, of long duration 17 firmly established

Last Lion, The
author: 17 William Manchester

lastly 6 at last 7 finally, to sum up 8 after all, in the end 10 on the whole 12 in conclusion 19 all things considered 33 taking everything into consideration

Last of the Barons, The
author: 18 Edward Bulwer-Lytton

Last of the Mohicans, The
author: 19 James Fenimore Cooper
character: 5 Magua, Uncas 9 Cora Munro 10 Alice Munro 11 Natty Bumppo 12 Chingachgook 18 Major Duncan Heyward

last part 3 end 6 ending, finale, finish 8 third act 10 denouement 12 final chapter

Last Picture Show, The
director: 16 Peter Bogdanovich
based on story by: 13 Larry McMurtry
cast: 10 Ben Johnson 11 Jeff Bridges 12 Ellen Burstyn 13 Eileen Brennan 14 Cloris Leachman, Cybill Shepherd, Timothy Bottoms
Oscar for: 15 supporting actor (Johnson) 17 supporting actress (Leachman)

Last Puritan, The
author: 15 George Santayana

La Strada
director: 15 Federico Fellini
cast: 11 Aldo Silvana 12 Anthony Quinn 15 Giulietta Masina, Richard Basehart
score: 8 Nino Rota
Oscar for: 11 foreign film

last resort
French: 8 pis aller

last resource
French: 8 pis aller

Last Tango in Paris
director: 18 Bernardo Bertolucci
cast: 12 Marlon Brando 14 Maria Schneider

Last Things
author: 6 C P Snow

Last Valley, The
author: 11 A B Guthrie Jr

Last Waltz, The
director: 14 Martin Scorsese
cast: 7 The Band 8 Bob Dylan 9 Neil Young 10 The Staples 11 Eric Clapton, Muddy Waters, Neil Diamond, Van Morrison 12 Joni Mitchell 13 Emmylou Harris

latch 3 bar 4 bolt, clip, hasp, hook, lock, loop, shut, snap 5 catch, clamp, close 6 buckle, button, clinch, fasten, secure 8 make fast 9 fastening

late 3 new 4 dead, gone, slow 5 fresh, tardy 6 held up, put off, recent 7 delayed, newborn, overdue, tardily 8 departed, detained, dilatory, passed on 9 after time, postponed 10 behindhand, behind time, dilatorily, unpunctual 16 recently deceased

late arrival 7 laggard 8 lateness, newcomer 9 immigrant, latecomer, tardiness 16 Johnny-come-lately

Late George Apley, The
author: 10 J P Marquand

lately 6 of late 7 just now 8 latterly, recently, right now 9 currently, presently, yesterday 10 not long ago 13 a short time ago

Late Mattia Pascal, The
author: 15 Luigi Pirandello

latency 8 abeyance, deferral, dormancy, inaction 10 quiescence, suspension

Late Night with David Letterman
    feature: 11 Ask Mr Melman 15 Stupid
    Pet Tricks 18 Brush with Greatness, Stu-
    pid People Tricks
    bandleader: 10 Paul Shafer
    city: 7 New York

latent 6 covert, hidden 7 abeyant, dormant,
    lurking, passive 8 inactive, sleeping 9 con-
    cealed, potential, quiescent, suspended,
    unaroused, unexposed 10 in abeyance,
    intangible, unapparent, unrealized 11 not
    manifest, undeveloped, unexpressed 13
    inconspicuous

later 4 next 5 since 6 behind, in time, ma-
    ture 7 ensuing, tardily 8 in a while, in se-
    quel 9 afterward, following, presently,
    thereupon 10 consequent, more re-
    cent, most recent, subsequent, succeed-
    ing, successive, thereafter 11 after a while,
    consecutive 12 subsequently, succes-
    sively, toward the end

lateral 4 side 5 sided 7 flanked, oblique,
    sloping 8 edgeways, edgewise, flank-
    ing, sidelong, sideward, sideways, side-
    wise, skirting, slanting

latest cry
    French: 10 dernier cri

latest fashion
    French: 10 dernier cri

latest word
    French: 10 dernier cri

lather 4 foam, head, scum, soap, suds 5
    froth, spume, sweat 6 soap up 8 make
    foam, soapsuds 9 make froth 11 shaving
    foam

Latin
    language family: 12 Indo-European
    branch: 6 Italic
    group: 8 Romance
    subgroup: 6 French 7 Catalan, Italian,
    Romansh, Spanish 8 Romanian 9 Pro-
    vencal 10 Portuguese 13 Rhaeto-
    Romanic

Latinus
    king of: 6 Latium
    father: 6 Faunus
    mother: 6 Marica
    wife: 5 Amata
    daughter: 7 Lavinia

latitude 5 range, scope, sweep 6 leeway,
    margin 7 license 8 free play 9 amplitude,
    elbowroom, full swing 10 indulgence, liber-
    ality 11 opportunity, unrestraint 12 inde-
    pendence 15 freedom of action, freedom
    of choice 16 unrestrictedness

Latona see 4 Leto

La Tour, Georges de
    born: 3 Vic 6 France 8 Lorraine
    artwork: 7 Peasant 10 The New Born 12
    Peasant's Wife, The Card Cheat 15 St
    Peter Penitent 16 The Fortune Teller 18
    The Denial of St Peter 23 The Education
    of the Virgin 31 St Sebastian Tended by
    the Holy Women

Latrobe, Benjamin Henry
    architect of: 9 US Capitol 15 Sedgeley
    Mansion (PA) 18 Baltimore Cathedral 22
    Philadelphia Waterworks
    style: 12 Greek Revival, Neoclassical 13
    Gothic Revival

latter 3 end 4 last 5 final, later 6 ending,
    latest, modern 7 ensuing 8 terminal 10
    most recent, subsequent, succeeding,
    successive 13 last-mentioned 15 second-
    mentioned

lattice 4 fret, grid 5 frame, grate 6 grille,
    screen 7 framing, grating, network, trellis,
    webwork 8 fretwork, openwork 9 frame-
    work, reticulum 11 trelliswork 12 reticula-
    tion

Latvia
    former name: 30 Latvian Soviet Socialist
    Republic
    capital/largest city: 4 Riga
    others: 5 Cesis, Libau 6 Dvinsk, Libava,
    Tukums 7 Jelgava, Jurmala, Liepaja,
    Rezekne 8 Dunaberg, Dunaburg, Val-
    miera 9 Ventspils 10 Daugavpils
    government: 8 republic
    measure: 3 let 4 stof 5 stoff, verst 6 ar-
    shin, kulmet 7 verchoc, verchok 8
    krouchka, pourvete 9 deciatine, lofstelle,
    pourvette 10 tonnseteel
    monetary unit: 3 lat 4 latu 6 rublis,
    santim 7 kapeika, santima
    weight: 9 liespfund
    lake: 7 Aluksne
    river: 4 Ogre 5 Gauja, Venta 6 Salaca 7
    Daugava, Lielupe 12 Western Dvina
    sea: 6 Baltic
    physical feature:
        cape: 8 Domesnes
        gulf: 4 Riga
        strait: 4 Irbe
    people: 3 Kur, Liv 4 Balt, Cour, Lett 7
    Latgale, Latvian, Russian, Zemgale
    former ruler: 15 Teutonic Knights
    language: 7 Lettish
    religion: 8 Lutheran 13 Roman Catholic

laud 5 extol, honor 6 praise 7 acclaim, com-
    mend, glorify

laudable 5 model, noble 8 sterling 9 admi-
    rable, estimable, excellent, exemplary 10
    creditable 11 commendable, meritorious
    12 praiseworthy 13 unimpeachable 17
    deserving of esteem 18 worthy of admira-
    tion

laudation 6 praise 7 acclaim 8 applause,
    approval 11 approbation 12 commendation

laudatory 8 admiring, honoring, praising 9
    adulatory, approving, extolling, favorable
    10 eulogistic, eulogizing, flattering, glorify-
    ing 11 acclamatory, approbatory, celebra-
    tory, encomiastic, panegyrical 12 commen-
    datory 13 complimentary

Laudianus 16 Greek unical codex

laugh 4 glee, ha-ha, ho-ho, howl, roar 5
    mirth 6 cackle, giggle, guffaw, titter 7 break
    up, chortle, chuckle, snicker, snigger 10
    bellylaugh, horselaugh 12 express mirth
    14 roll in the aisle, split one's sides

laughable 5 comic, dopey, droll, funny, inane, merry, silly, witty 6 absurd, stupid 7 amusing, asinine, comical, foolish, risible 8 farcical, tickling 9 diverting, grotesque, hilarious, ludicrous 10 outlandish, outrageous, ridiculous 11 rib-tickling 12 preposterous 13 sidesplitting

Laugh-In, Rowan & Martin's
regular: 8 Dan Rowan 9 Gary Owens, Judy Carne, Ruth Buzzi 10 Dick Martin, Goldie Hawn, Larry Hovis, Lily Tomlin 11 Arte Johnson, Henry Gibson 12 Jo Anne Worley 13 Eileen Brennan
saying: 10 Sock it to me 15 Here come de judge, You bet your bippy 24 Beautiful downtown Burbank 33 Look that up in your Funk and Wagnalls

laughingstock 3 ass 4 butt, dupe, fool, joke 8 fair game 11 figure of fun

laugh off 6 deride 7 dismiss, put down 8 belittle, ridicule 9 disparage

laughter 3 joy 4 glee 5 mirth 6 gaiety 7 jollity, revelry 8 hilarity 9 joviality, merriment 11 merrymaking 12 conviviality, exhilaration

Laughton, Charles
wife: 14 Elsa Lanchester
born: 7 England 11 Scarborough
roles: 9 Rembrandt 10 Jamaica Inn 13 Les Miserables 15 Ruggles of Red Gap, The Paradine Case 16 Advise and Consent 17 Mutiny on the Bounty 23 Barretts of Wimpole Street, The Hunchback of Notre Dame 24 Witness for the Prosecution 25 The Private Life of Henry VIII (Oscar)

launch 4 fire, hurl 5 begin, eject, float, found, impel, shoot, start, throw 6 let fly, propel, unveil 7 fire off, project, send off 8 catapult, initiate, premiere, put to sea 9 cast forth, discharge, establish, institute, introduce, set afloat 10 embark upon, inaugurate, set forth on 11 set in motion, venture upon 13 thrust forward 15 set into the water

launder 4 soak, wash 5 clean, rinse, scour, scrub 7 cleanse, wash out 11 wash and iron

Launfal
knight of: 10 roundtable

Laura
director: 13 Otto Preminger
cast: 11 Clifton Webb, Dana Andrews, Gene Tierney 12 Vincent Price 14 Judith Anderson

laurel 6 Kalmia, Laurus 13 Laurus nobilis 14 Ficus benjamina 15 Cordia alliodora
varieties: 3 bog, pig 4 pale 5 black, dwarf, great, sheep 6 Alpine, cherry, ground, Indian, purple, Sierra, spurge, tropic 7 Chinese, English, redtwig, weeping, western 8 American, drooping, Himalaya, Japanese, mountain, Portugal 9 Tasmanian 10 Australian, California, variegated 11 Alexandrian

Laurel, Stan
real name: 22 Arthur Stanley Jefferson
partner: 11 Oliver Hardy
born: 7 England 9 Ulverston
roles: 8 Pardon Us 9 Saps at Sea 10 Way Out West

laurels 4 fame 5 award, glory, honor, kudos, prize 6 credit, praise, renown, reward 7 acclaim, tribute 8 accolade, applause, citation 9 celebrity 10 decoration, popularity 11 acclamation, distinction, recognition 12 commendation 15 illustriousness

Laurie
also: 16 Theodore Laurence
character in: 11 Little Women
author: 6 Alcott

laus Deo 11 praise to God 13 praise be to God

Lautreamont, Comte de
author of: 19 Les Chants de Maldoror

lavation 7 bathing, washing 8 ablution, cleaning 9 cleansing

lavender 4 herb, mint 5 aspic, behen, lilac, spick, spike 6 purple 7 inkroot 8 amethyst, stichado 9 lavendula
represents: 6 purity
uses: 6 sachet 7 perfume 8 medicine 9 cosmetics

laver 11 footed basin

Laverne and Shirley
character: 12 Frank De Fazio 13 Carmine Ragusa, Lenny Kolowski, Mrs Edna Babish, Shirley Feeney 14 Laverne De Fazio 15 Andrew (Squiggy) Squiggman
cast: 10 Eddie Mekka, Phil Foster 12 Betty Garrett, David L Lander 13 Cindy Williams, Michael McKean, Penny Marshall
girls worked in: 12 Shotz Brewery
theme song: 23 Making Our Dreams Come True
spinoff from: 9 Happy Days

Lavinia
father: 7 Latinus
mother: 5 Amata
husband: 6 Aeneas

lavish 4 free, lush, wild 5 plush, waste 6 shower 7 copious, opulent, pour out, profuse 8 abundant, effusive, generous, prodigal, squander 9 bounteous, bountiful, dissipate, excessive, exuberant, impetuous, luxuriant, plenteous, plentiful, sumptuous, unsparing 10 immoderate, munificent, profligate, unstinting 11 extravagant, fritter away, intemperate, overindulge, overliberal, spend freely 12 give overmuch, greathearted, overwhelming, unrestrained, without limit

lavishness 6 bounty 8 lushness, opulence 9 profusion 10 luxuriance 11 munificence, prodigality 12 extravagance, immoderation 13 bountifulness, plenteousness, sumptuousness

Lavoisier, Antoine
field: 9 chemistry
nationality: 6 French
founder: 15 modern chemistry

named: 6 oxygen 8 hydrogen

law 3 act 4 bill, code, fuzz, rule, writ 5 axiom, bylaw, canon, dogma, edict, model, truth 6 decree, police 7 justice, mandate, precept, statute, theorem 8 absolute, legality, standard 9 criterion, enactment, gendarmes, legal form, ordinance, postulate, principle 10 civil peace, convention, due process, invariable, regulation 11 commandment, formulation, fundamental, orderliness, working rule 13 jurisprudence, standing order 14 generalization, rules of conduct 15 legal profession
   Latin: 3 jus
   goddess of: 4 Maat

law-abiding 6 honest 7 upright 9 honorable 10 aboveboard, principled

lawbreaker 4 con 5 crook, thug 5 crook, felon 6 outlaw 7 convict, culprit 8 criminal, jailbird, offender, scofflaw 9 miscreant, wrongdoer 10 delinquent, malefactor, recidivist 11 perpetrator 12 transgressor

lawful 3 due 5 legal, licit 6 proper, titled 7 allowed, granted 8 rightful 9 legalized, statutory, warranted 10 authorized, legitimate, prescribed 11 legitimized, permissible 15 legally entitled 16 legally permitted

lawless 6 unruly, wanton 7 chaotic, defiant, illegal, riotous, wayward 8 anarchic, mutinous, unlawful, wide open 9 insurgent, out of hand, unbridled 10 disorderly, licentious, rebellious, refractory, ungoverned 11 disobedient, lawbreaking, terroristic 12 disorganized, freewheeling, illegitimate, noncompliant, unrestrained 13 insubordinate, transgressive 14 uncontrollable

lawlessness 5 chaos 7 anarchy 8 disorder

lawn 4 park, turf, yard 5 glade, grass, sward 7 grounds, terrace 10 grassy plot, green field, greensward, meadowland 12 grassy ground

law of a place
   Latin: 7 lex loci

Law of Moses 5 Torah 10 Pentateuch 15 Ten Commandments

law of nations
   Latin: 10 jus gentium

law of nature
   Latin: 11 jus naturale

Lawrence, Carol
   real name: 16 Carol Maria Laraia
   husband: 12 Robert Goulet
   born: 13 Melrose Park IL
   roles: 5 Maria 13 West Side Story

Lawrence, D H
   author of: 10 The Rainbow 11 Women in Love 13 Sons and Lovers 20 Lady Chatterley's Lover

Lawrence, Ernest Orlando
   field: 7 physics
   invented: 9 cyclotron
   awarded: 10 Nobel Prize

Lawrence, Gertrude
   real name: 29 Alexandra Dagmar Lawrence Klasen
   born: 6 London 7 England

   roles: 9 Pygmalion 11 The King and I 17 The Glass Menagerie

Lawrence, T E
   also: 16 Lawrence of Arabia
   served in: 3 WWI 10 Arab Revolt
   advisor to: 6 Faisal 12 Husayn Ibn Ali
   fought against: 5 Turks 8 Ottomans
   author of: 20 Seven Pillars of Wisdom

Lawrence of Arabia
   director: 9 David Lean
   cast: 10 Jose Ferrer, Omar Sharif 11 Claude Rains, Jack Hawkins, Peter O'Toole (T E Lawrence) 12 Alec Guinness, Anthony Quinn 13 Anthony Quayle
   Oscar for: 7 picture 8 director 14 cinematography

Lawrence Welk Show, The
   champagne lady: 8 Alice Lon 11 Norma Zimmer
   cast: 7 Aladdin 11 Larry Hooper, Myron Floren 12 Bobby Burgess 13 Barbara Boylan, Lennon Sisters
   Welk played: 9 accordion

lawyer 6 jurist, legist 7 counsel, shyster 8 advocate, attorney 9 barrister, counselor, solicitor 10 mouthpiece, prosecutor 11 pettifogger 12 legal advisor 14 special pleader 15 ambulance chaser

lax 4 hazy, limp, weak 5 agape, loose, slack, vague 6 casual, flabby, floppy, remiss 7 cryptic, flaccid, inexact, lenient, not firm, relaxed 8 careless, derelict, drooping, heedless, nebulous, slipshod, uncaring, yielding 9 confusing, imprecise, negligent, oblivious, undutiful, unheeding, unmindful 10 ill-defined, incoherent, neglectful, permissive 11 hanging open, indifferent, thoughtless, unconcerned 12 loose-muscled, unstructured 13 irresponsible 15 unconscientious

laxness 7 neglect 9 looseness, slackness 10 negligence 11 imprecision 12 carelessness, indifference

Laxness, Halldor Kiljan
   author of: 12 Iceland's Bell 14 The Atom Station 17 Independent People 25 The Great Weaver from Kashmir

lay 3 air, bet, put, set 4 bear, fell, fine, form, give, laic, lend, levy, make, plan, poem, raze, rest, seat, song, tune 5 align, allot, apply, ditty, exact, floor, hatch, level, offer, place, stage, wager 6 assess, assign, ballad, charge, demand, depict, devise, gamble, ground, hazard, impose, impute, laical, layout, locate, melody, repose, strain 7 amateur, arrange, concoct, contour, deposit, dispose, forward, present, produce, profane, proffer, refrain, secular, set down, situate, station 8 allocate, assemble, beat down, give odds, inexpert, organize, oviposit, position 9 attribute, elucidate, enunciate, formulate, knock down, knock over, prostrate, roundelay, situation 10 cause to lie, topography 11 arrangement, disposition, nonclerical, orientation, put together 12 conformation 13 configuration, inexperienced, nonspecialist 14 partly informed, unprofessional 15 nonprofessional 17 nonecclesiastical

lay at the door of 6 assign 7 ascribe 8 charge to 9 attribute

lay bare 4 bare, show 6 expose, reveal, unmask, unveil, unwrap 7 divulge, exhibit, publish, uncover 8 disclose 9 broadcast, make known 10 make public 11 communicate

lay down arms 5 yield 6 give up 7 succumb 8 cry quits 9 surrender 10 capitulate 11 come to terms, sue for peace 13 declare a truce 17 acknowledge defeat

layer 3 bed, lap, ply 4 coat, fold, leaf, seam, slab, tier, zone 5 level, plate, scale, sheet, stage, story 6 lamina 7 stratum 9 thickness

layman 4 laic 6 sister 7 amateur, brother 8 outsider 9 churchman 10 catechumen 11 churchwoman, communicant, parishioner 15 nonprofessional 16 member of the flock

layoff 4 fire 6 firing, idling, ouster, the axe 7 dismiss, release, sacking, the boot, the gate, the sack 8 pink slip, shutdown 9 closedown, discharge, dismissal, hard times, the bounce 10 cashiering, depression, the heave-ho 11 furloughing, termination 12 unemployment 13 disemployment, walking papers 20 discharge temporarily

lay off 7 dismiss, forfeit, release, set free 8 get rid of, liberate 9 discharge, terminate 11 give the gate, send packing

Lay of the Last Minstrel, The
    author: 14 Sir Walter Scott
    character: 8 Margaret, The Dwarf 13 Lady Buccleuch, Lord Cranstoun 17 Master of Buccleuch 19 Ghost of Michael Scott 21 Sir William of Deloraine

lay on 6 bestow, confer, supply 7 present, provide

lay open 4 open 6 expose, open up 7 clarify 9 make plain 18 make understandable

layout 4 form, plan 5 chart, draft, dummy, model, motif, spend 6 design, expend, pay out, sketch, spread 7 diagram, drawing, fork out, outline, pattern 8 disburse, shell out 9 blueprint, delineate, placement, spread out, structure 11 arrangement, composition

lay waste 4 ruin 5 level, wreck 6 ravage 7 despoil, destroy, wipe out 8 demolish, desolate 9 devastate, eradicate 10 annihilate, obliterate

Lazarus 6 beggar
    means: 8 God helps
    sister: 4 Mary 6 Martha
    hometown: 7 Bethany
    resurrected by: 5 Jesus

Lazarus
    author: 14 Leonid Andreyev

Lazarus, Mell
    creator/artist: 5 Momma 9 Miss Peach

lazurite
    variety: 11 lapis lazuli

lazy 3 lax 4 idle, slow 5 inert, slack 6 drowsy, sleepy, torpid 7 laggard, languid 8 inactive, indolent, listless, slothful, sluggish 9 apathetic, easygoing, lethargic, shiftless 10 languorous, slow-moving 13 unindustrious 15 unwilling to work

lazy person 5 drone, idler 6 loafer 14 good-for-nothing

Leach, Archibald Alexander
    real name of: 9 Cary Grant

Leachman, Cloris
    born: 11 Des Moines IA
    roles: 7 Phyllis 11 High Anxiety 12 Kiss Me Deadly 17 Young Frankenstein 18 Mary Tyler Moore Show, The Last Picture Show

lead 2 go 3 aim, top 4 clue, draw, edge, have, head, hero, hint, live, lure, pass 5 charm, excel, guide, model, outdo, pilot, steer, tempt 6 allure, convey, direct, entice, extend, induce, manage, margin, pursue, seduce 7 advance, attract, bring on, command, conduct, control, example, go first, incline, issue in, marshal, pioneer, precede, proceed, produce, stretch, surpass, undergo 8 domineer, go before, guidance, moderate, outstrip, persuade, priority, result in, shepherd, star part 9 advantage, come first, direction, go through, headliner, influence, plurality, rank first 10 branch into, experience, first place, indication, precedence, precedency, set the pace, show the way, tend toward 11 antecedence, be in advance, leading role, preside over, protagonist

lead
    chemical symbol: 2 Pb

lead astray 4 dupe, lure 6 delude 7 beguile, deceive, ensnare, mislead 19 lead up the garden path

leaden 4 dark, dull, glum, gray 5 inert, murky 6 dreary, gloomy, numbed, somber, torpid 7 grayish, languid 8 burdened, careworn, darkened, deadened, listless, sluggish, unwieldy 9 depressed, inanimate 10 cumbersome, hard to move

leader 4 boss, guru, head 5 chief, guide, mogul 6 bigwig, honcho, master, mentor, tycoon 7 captain, foreman, kingpin, magnate, manager, pioneer, prophet 8 director, superior 9 chieftain, commander, conductor, godfather, pacemaker, patriarch 10 forerunner, pacesetter, pathfinder, supervisor 11 frontrunner, torchbearer, trailblazer

leadership 4 helm, lead, sway 5 reins, wheel 7 command, primacy 8 charisma, guidance, headship, hegemony 9 captaincy, supremacy 10 domination, mastership 11 managership, preeminence, stewardship 12 directorship, governorship, guardianship, self-reliance 13 ability to lead, self-assurance 14 administration 15 managerial skill, superintendency 17 authoritativeness

leading 3 top 4 head, main 5 basic, chief, first, great, prime 6 ruling 7 advance, guiding, initial, leadoff, notable, primary, ranking, stellar, supreme, topmost 8 advanced, dominant, foremost 9 directing, essential, governing, nonpareil, paramount, principal, prominent, sovereign, unrivaled 10 motivating, preeminent, underlying 11 controlling, outstanding, pacesetting 12 unchallenged, unparalleled 13 most important 14 quintessential 15 most influential, most significant

lead on 4 goad 5 egg on 6 entice 7 mislead, support 9 encourage 19 lead up the garden path

lead the way 4 lead, show, take 5 guide 6 escort 7 conduct

leaf 4 flip, foil, page, skim 5 blade, bract, folio, frond, green, inset, petal, sheet, thumb 6 browse, glance, insert, needle 7 foliole, lamella, leaflet 9 cotyledon, extension, turn green 10 lamination 12 sheet of metal

leaflet 2 ad 4 bill 5 flier, flyer, tract 6 folder, notice 7 booklet, handout 8 brochure, bulletin, circular, handbill, pamphlet 9 broadside, throwaway 10 broadsheet 12 announcement 13 advertisement

league 4 ally, band 5 cabal, group, guild, merge, union 6 cartel 7 combine, compact, company, network, society 8 alliance 9 coalition 11 conspiracy, federation, fraternity, join forces 11 association, confederacy, confederate, consolidate, cooperative, partnership 13 collaboration, confederation, confraternity

Leah
  means: 7 wild cow
  father: 5 Laban
  husband: 5 Jacob
  sister: 6 Rachel
  slave: 6 Zilpah
  son: 4 Levi 5 Judah 6 Reuben, Simeon 7 Zebulun 8 Issachar
  daughter: 5 Dinah
  burial place: 9 Machpelah

leak 3 ebb, rip 4 blab, gash, hole, ooze, rent, rift, seep, vent 5 break, chink, cleft, crack, drain, exude, fault, spill 6 breach, efflux, escape, filter, let out, reveal, take in 7 confide, crevice, divulge, dribble, fissure, let slip, opening, outflow, rupture, seepage 8 aperture, disclose, draining, give away, puncture 9 discharge, percolate 10 interstice, make public 11 be permeable, perforation 12 admit leakage 16 let enter or escape

leakage 5 issue 7 outflow, seepage 9 discharge

Leakey, Louis S Bazett
  field: 12 anthropology
  discovered: 8 early man
  worked at: 8 Tanzania 12 Olduvai Gorge
  wife: 4 Mary
  son: 7 Richard

lean 3 aim, bow, tip 4 bend, cant, lank, list, poor, rely, rest, slim, tend, thin, tilt 5 gaunt, lanky, lurch, scant, slant, slope, small, spare, weedy 6 barren, depend, meager, modest, nonfat, prefer, scanty, skinny, sparse, svelte 7 angular, count on, incline, recline, scraggy, scrawny, slender, spindly, trust in, willowy 8 exiguous, rawboned, resort to, skeletal 9 emaciated 10

inadequate, set store by 11 be partial to, have faith in, prop oneself 12 insufficient, seek solace in 14 rest one's weight, support oneself

Lean, David
  director of: 10 Summertime 11 Oliver Twist 13 Doctor Zhivago, Ryan's Daughter 15 A Passage to India 16 Lawrence of Arabia (Oscar) 17 Great Expectations 23 The Bridge on the River Kwai (Oscar)

Leander
  loved: 4 Hero
  swam nightly: 10 Hellespont
  death by: 8 drowning

leaning 4 bent, turn 5 slant 7 relying 8 affinity, tendency 9 proneness 10 dependence, partiality, preference, proclivity, propensity 11 inclination 14 predisposition

leap 3 hop 4 jete, jump, romp, rush, skip 5 bound, caper, frisk, vault 6 bounce, cavort, frolic, gambol, hasten, hurtle, prance, spring 7 hop over 8 jump over 9 bound over, saltation 10 hurtle over, jump across, spring over

Learchus
  father: 7 Athamas
  mother: 3 Ino
  killed by: 7 Athamas

learn 3 con 4 hear 6 detect, master, pick up 7 find out, uncover, unearth 8 discover, memorize 9 ascertain, determine, ferret out 10 become able 12 find out about

learned 4 deep, wise 7 erudite 8 cultured, educated, informed, lettered, literate, profound, schooled, well-read 9 scholarly 10 cultivated 12 accomplished, intellectual, well-educated 13 knowledgeable

Learned, Michael
  roles: 5 Nurse 10 The Waltons

learner 4 tyro 5 pupil 6 novice, rookie 7 draftee, recruit, scholar, student, trainee 8 beginner, disciple, enlistee, follower, freshman, neophyte 9 fledgling, greenhorn, novitiate, proselyte, schoolboy 10 apprentice, schoolgirl, tenderfoot 11 schoolchild

learning 5 study 6 wisdom 7 culture 8 teaching 9 education, erudition, knowledge, schooling 11 cultivation, edification, information, instruction, scholarship 13 comprehension, enlightenment, understanding

Learning
  god of: 5 Thoth

leash 4 curb, lead, line, rein, ruin 5 strap, thong 6 bridle, choker, fasten, hold in, stifle, string, tether 7 contain, control, harness 8 restrain, suppress

Leather-Stocking Tales
  author: 19 James Fenimore Cooper
  includes: 10 The Prairie 11 The Pioneers 13 The Deerslayer, The Pathfinder 20 The Last of the Mohicans
  hero of: 7 Hawkeye 10 Pathfinder, The Trapper 11 Natty Bumppo 13 The Deerslayer 15 Leather-stocking 16 Le Longue Carabine

leave 2 go 3 fly 4 cede, exit, flee, keep, quit, will 5 allot, be off, cause, endow, forgo, going, split, waive, yield 6 assign, bug out, commit, decamp, depart, desert, eschew, forego, give up, legate, move on, recess, resign, retain, set out 7 abandon, abscond, bequest, consent, consign, deposit, entrust, forsake, holiday, let stay, liberty, parting, produce, push off, release, respite, retreat, sustain, take off, time off 8 approval, bequeath, farewell, furlough, generate, give over, maintain, result in, sanction, shove off, vacation 9 allowance, apportion, departure, hotfoot it, let remain, surrender, tolerance 10 concession, depart from, embark from, go away from, indulgence, permission, relinquish, retire from, sabbatical, sufferance, withdrawal 11 bid farewell, endorsement 13 absent oneself, understanding

leave a ship 4 land 6 debark 8 go ashore 9 disembark 11 abandon ship

leave behind 6 desert, vacate 7 abandon, discard, forsake 8 evacuate 9 cast aside 10 relinquish 11 outdistance

leave cold 4 bore 12 leave unmoved 15 leave unaffected

Leave It To Beaver
  character: 11 June Cleaver, Ward Cleaver 12 Eddie Haskell, Wally Cleaver 13 Beaver (Theodore) Cleaver
  cast: 7 Tony Dow 9 Ken Osmond 12 Hugh Beaumont, Jerry Mathers 18 Barbara Billingsley

leave off 3 end 4 halt, quit, stop 5 cease 6 desist, finish 7 suspend 8 conclude 11 discontinue, refrain from

leave out 4 drop, omit 6 except, reject 7 exclude

Leaves of Grass
  author: 11 Walt Whitman

leave suddenly 3 fly 4 flee 6 cut out, decamp, run off 7 abscond, make off, run away, rush off, take off 11 take a powder 15 be off and running

leave-taking 4 exit 5 adieu 7 good-bye, leaving, parting, send-off 8 au revoir, farewell 9 departure 10 withdrawal

leave undone 4 quit 6 give up 7 abandon, forsake, neglect 8 give up on

Lebanon
  ancient name: 9 Phoenicia
  capital/largest city: 6 Beirut 8 Beyrouth
  others: 3 Sur 4 Arca, Tyre 5 Ehden, Halba, Hamat, Sahle, Saida, Sayda, Sidon, Sofar, Zahla, Zahle 6 Byblos, Ghazir, Juniye, Tibnin 7 Baalbek, Batroun, Bsherri, Rachaya, Tripoli, Zgharta 8 Djezzine, El Hermel, Hasbaiya, Merjuyun 9 Broummana, Marjayoun 10 Beited Dine, Heliopolis
  ancient city: 8 Carthage
  school: 4 Arab 8 American, Lebanese 11 Saint Joseph
  division:
  ancient: 4 Tyre 5 Arwad, Sidon 6 Byblos, Jubayl
  monetary unit: 5 livre, pound 7 piastre
  lake: 5 Quran 6 Qirawn
  mountain: 4 Mzar 5 Aruba 6 Hermon 7 Lebanon, Sannine 8 Kadischa, Kenisseh 9 Kennisseh 10 al-Mukammal 11 Anti-Lebanon
  highest point: 7 es Sauda 13 Qurnat al-Sawda
  river: 3 Dog, Joz 5 Barid, Kebir, Lycos 6 Auwali, Barada, Damour, Litani 7 Hasbani, Leontes, Orontes 8 Kasemieh
  sea: 13 Mediterranean
  physical feature:
  cape: 10 Pigeon Rock 11 Ras esh Shiqa 12 Qadisha Gorge
  plain: 4 Bika 5 Bekaa
  valley: 5 Beqaa 6 al-Biqa 9 Great Rift
  wind: 7 khamsin
  people: 4 Arab 11 Palestinian
  ancient: 9 Canaanite 10 Phoenician
  leader: 6 Bashir, Sarkis 7 Chamoun 8 Franjieh 9 al-Din Maan 11 Amin Gemayel 13 Bashir Gemayel
  poet: 11 Kahlil Gibran
  rulers: 5 Arabs 6 French, Greeks, Romans 8 Hittites, Ottomans, Persians 9 Assyrians, Crusaders, Egyptians, Mamelukes 11 Babylonians
  language: 6 Arabic, French, Syriac 7 English, Turkish 8 Armenian
  religion: 5 Druse, Druze, Islam 8 Maronite, Melchite 10 Protestant 11 Monophysite 12 Christianity 13 Greek Catholic 14 Greek Orthodoxy 17 Armenian Orthodoxy
  place:
  dam: 5 Qarun
  ruins: 7 Baalbek 15 Temple of Bacchus, Temple of Jupiter
  feature:
  Christian group: 10 Phalangist
  dance: 6 dabkeh, dabkey
  tree: 5 cedar
  food:
  dish: 6 kibbeh 8 tabouleh
  drink: 4 arak 6 arrack

Le Bel, Joseph Achille
  field: 9 chemistry
  nationality: 6 French
  founded: 15 stereochemistry

Le Bourgeois Gentilhomme
  author: 7 Moliere
  character: 7 Cleonte, Dorante 9 M Jourdain 16 Monsieur Jourdain

Le Carre, John
  real name: 13 David Cornwell
  author of: 11 A Perfect Spy 13 Smiley's People 18 The Looking Glass War 19 A Small Town in Germany 20 The Little Drummer Girl 21 The Honorable Schoolboy 22 Tinker Tailor Soldier Spy 26 The Spy Who Came in from the Cold

lechayim, lehayim 6 to life

Lecheates
  epithet of: 4 Zeus
  means: 10 in childbed

lecherous 4 lewd 5 randy 6 carnal 7 goatish, lustful, ruttish 8 prurient 9 salacious, satyrlike 10 lascivious, libidinous, licentious, lubricious

lechery 4 lust 8 lewdness 9 carnality, prurience 10 satyriasis 11 lustfulness, nymphomania 13 salaciousness 14 lasciviousness

Le Cid
    author: 9 Corneille
    composer:
    Leconte dehisle, Charles 13 Jules Massenet

Le Corbusier
    real name: 23 Charles Edouard Jeanneret
    architect of: 10 La Tourette (monastery) 15 Notre Dame du Haut (Ronchamp France) 16 Unite d'Habitation (Marseilles)
    planned city of: 10 Chandi garh (capital of the Punjab)
    style: 6 Purism 12 New Brutalism

lecture 4 talk 5 chide, scold, speak 6 homily, preach, rail at, rebuke, sermon, speech 7 address, censure, chiding, expound, oration, reading, re proof, reprove, upbraid, warning 8 admonish, call down, harangue, moralize, reproach 9 discourse, hold forth, reprimand, sermonize, talking-to 10 preachment, take to task 12 chastisement, disquisition, remonstrance

lecture hall 9 classroom 10 auditorium 12 amphitheater, assembly hall

lecturelike 7 donnish, preachy 8 academic, didactic, pedantic 9 homiletic 10 moralizing

Leda
    father: 8 Thestius
    husband: 9 Tyndareus
    lover: 4 swan, Zeus
    son: 6 Castor, Pollux 8 Dioscuri 10 Polydeuces
    daughter: 5 Helen 6 Phoebe 8 Philonoe, Timandra 12 Clytemnestra

Leda and the Swan
    author: 7 W B Yeats

ledge 4 sill, step 5 ridge, shelf 6 mantel, offset 8 foothold, shoulder 10 projection 11 mantelpiece, mantelshelf, outcropping

Lee, Henry
    nickname: 15 Light Horse Harry
    served in: 16 Revolutionary War
    member of: 10 US Congress 19 Continental Congress
    governor of: 8 Virginia
    suppressed: 16 Whiskey Rebellion
    son: 7 Robert E

Lee, Robert E
    father: 5 Henry 15 Light Horse Harry
    born: 11 Stratford VA 18 Westmoreland County
    wife: 21 Mary Ann Randolph Custis
    served in: 8 Civil War 10 Mexican War
    commander of: 22 Army of Northern Virginia
    suppressed raid: 9 John Brown 12 Harper's Ferry

battle: 7 Bull Run 8 Antie tam 10 Gettysburg 14 Fredericksburg 16 Chancellorsville, Seven Days' Battles
    surrendered at: 20 Appomattox Court House
    president of: 17 Washington College

Lee, Spike
    original name: 17 Sheldon Jackson Lee
    born: 2 GA 7 Atlanta
    wife: 17 Tonya Linette Lewis
    films: 8 Malcolm X 10 School Daze 11 Jungle Fever 15 Do the Right Thing, She's Gotta Have It 31 Joe's Bed-Stuy Barbership We Cut Heads
    company: 18 Forty Acres and A Mule
    ads for: 4 Nike

leek 18 Allium ampeloprasum
    varieties: 4 lily, rose, sand, wild 5 lady's 6 meadow

leer 4 ogle 5 fleer, smirk 6 goggle

leery 4 wary 5 cagey, chary 6 unsure 7 guarded 8 cautious, doubtful, hesitant 9 skeptical, undecided 10 suspicious 11 circumspect, distrustful, mistrustful

Leeuwenhoek, Anton van
    field: 10 microscopy
    father of: 12 microbiology
    discovered: 13 red blood cells

leeway 4 play 5 scope, slack 6 margin 7 cushion, headway, reserve 8 headroom, latitude 9 allowance, clearance, elbow room, extra time, tolerance 11 flexibility 13 room for choice 14 margin for error 15 maneuverability

left behind 7 vacated 8 deserted, forsaken, forsook 9 abandoned, discarded, evacuated 12 relinquished

leftover 6 excess, legacy, unused 7 overage, residue, surplus, uneaten 8 leavings, oddments, residual, survivor 9 carry-over, remainder, remaining

left-wing 7 leftist, liberal, radical 9 socialist 11 progressive

left-winger 7 leftist, liberal, radical 9 socialist 11 progressive

Lefty
    nickname of: 5 Gomez 12 Steve Carlton

leg 3 gam, lap, pin 4 limb, part, post, prop 5 brace, femur, shank, stage, stump, tibia 6 column, fibula, member, pillar 7 portion, section, segment, stretch, support, upright

legacy 4 gift 6 devise, estate 7 bequest, vestige 8 heirloom, heritage, leftover, survivor 9 carry-over, throwback, tradition 10 birthright, hand-me-down 11 inheritance

legal 4 fair 5 licit, of law, valid 6 kosher, lawful 7 cricket 8 forensic, judicial, juristic, rightful 9 courtroom, juridical 10 legitimate, sanctioned 11 permissible

legal advisor 6 lawyer 7 counsel 8 advocate, attorney 9 barrister, counselor, solicitor 13 attorney-at-law 14 counselor-at-law

legal form 4 writ 8 document 10 instrument

legality 8 validity 9 licitness 10 lawfulness, legitimacy 17 constitutionality

legalization 8 sanction 9 enactment 10 permission, validation 13 authorization 14 legitimization

legalize 5 enact 6 permit 8 sanction, validate 9 authorize 10 legitimize

legal residence 4 home 8 domicile, dwelling

legal tender 4 cash 5 money 8 currency

legate 5 agent, envoy 6 deputy 8 emissary 14 representative

legatee 4 heir 9 inheritor 11 beneficiary

legation 7 embassy, mission 8 ministry 9 consulate 10 delegation 11 chancellery

legend 3 key 4 edda, lore, myth, saga, tale 5 fable, motto, story, title 7 caption, fiction, proverb 8 folklore 11 inscription

legendary 5 famed 6 fabled, famous, mythic 7 storied 8 fabulous, fanciful, mythical 9 imaginary 10 apocryphal, celebrated, fictitious, proverbial

Legend of Good Women, The
  author: 15 Geoffrey Chaucer
  character: 4 Dido 5 Medea 6 Thisbe 7 Alceste, Ariadne, Lucrece, Phyllis 9 Cleopatra, Hypsipyle, Philomela 12 Hypermnestra

Legend of Sleepy Hollow, The
  author: 16 Washington Irving
  character: 12 Brom Van Brunt (Brom Bones), Ichabod Crane 16 Katrina Van Tassel

Leger, Fernand
  born: 6 France 8 Argentan
  artwork: 8 Bargeman 10 Adam and Eve, The Wedding, Three Women 11 The Builders, The Cyclists, The Mechanic, The Stairway 14 The Great Parade 15 Le Grand Dejeuner 16 Contrasting Forms, Nudes in the Forest 21 Butterflies and Flowers

legerdemain 7 cunning 8 deftness, jugglery, juggling, trickery 9 deception 10 adroitness, artfulness 11 maneuvering 13 sleight of hand 16 prestidigitation

legible 4 neat 5 clear, plain 7 visible 8 clear-cut, distinct, readable 12 decipherable 14 comprehensible, understandable

legion 3 mob, sea 4 army, host, mass 5 corps, drove, horde, spate, swarm 6 myriad, throng, troops 7 brigade 8 division 9 multitude

leg irons 5 bonds, irons 6 chains 7 fetters 8 shackles

legislation 3 act 4 bill 6 ruling 7 measure, statute 9 amendment, enactment, law making, ordinance

legislator 7 senator 8 alder man, delegate, lawgiver, lawmaker 10 councilman 11 assemblyman, congressman 13 congresswoman 14 representative 15 parliamentarian

legislature 4 diet 5 house 6 senate 7 chamber, council 8 assembly, congress 10 parliament

legitimacy 8 legality, validity 10 lawfulness 11 correctness, genuineness 12 authenticity, rightfulness 15 appropriateness

legitimate 4 fair, just, true 5 legal, licit, sound, valid 6 lawful, proper 7 correct, genuine, logical, tenable 8 rightful 9 authentic, justified, plausible 10 believable, reasonable 11 appropriate, well-founded

leg-pull 4 hoax 9 deception 13 practical joke

Legree, Simon
  character in: 14 Uncle Tom's Cabin
  author: 5 Stowe

LeGuin, Ursula K
  author of: 13 Lathe of Heaven 14 Rocannon's World 15 The Dispossessed 16 Always Coming Home 21 The Left Hand of Darkness

Lehar, Franz (Ferencz)
  born: 7 Komarno (then Hungary, now Czechoslovakia)
  composer of: 9 Gipsy Love 13 The Merry Widow 20 The Count of Luxembourg

Lehmbruck, Wilhelm
  born: 7 Germany 9 Meiderich
  artwork: 11 Rising Youth 12 Man Flung Down, Praying Woman, Seating Youth 13 Kneeling Woman, Standing Woman, Standing Youth

Leigh, Janet
  husband: 10 Tony Curtis
  daughter: 14 Jamie Lee Curtis
  born: 8 Merced CA
  roles: 6 Psycho, The Fog 10 The Vikings 11 Little Women, Touch of Evil

Leigh, Vivien
  real name: 17 Vivian Mary Hartley
  husband: 15 Laurence Olivier
  born: 5 India 10 Darjeeling
  roles: 11 Ship of Fools 12 Anna Karenina 13 Blanche du Bois, Scarlett O'Hara 14 Waterloo Bridge 15 Gone With the Wind (Oscar) 17 That Hamilton Woman 21 A Streetcar Named Desire (Oscar), Roman Spring of Mrs Stone

Leighton, Margaret
  husband: 12 Max Reinhardt 14 Laurence Harvey, Michael Wilding
  born: 7 England 10 Barnt Green 14 Worcestershire
  roles: 12 The Go-Between 13 The Winslow Boy 14 Separate Tables 19 The Night of the Iguana

leisure 4 ease, rest 6 recess, repose 7 holiday, respite, time off 8 free time, vacation 9 diversion, idle hours, spare time 10 recreation, relaxation

leisurely 4 idle, slow 6 casual, slowly 7 languid, relaxed, restful 9 unhurried 10 slowmoving 11 lingeringly, unhurriedly 12 without haste 13 lackadaisical

Lemminkainen
  origin: 7 Finnish
  mentioned in: 8 Kalevala
  role: 4 hero

Lemmon, Jack
  real name: 18 Jack Uhler Lemmon III
  wife: 11 Felicia Farr
  born: 8 Boston MA

roles: 7 Missing 10 April Fools 12 Save the Tiger (Oscar), The Apartment, The Great Race, The Odd Couple 13 China Syndrome, Mister Roberts, Some Like It Hot 18 Days of Wine and Roses, Under the Yum-Yum Tree 19 How to Murder Your Wife

lemon 11 Citrus limon
   varieties: 4 wild 5 dwarf, giant, Meyer, water 6 garden, wonder 9 wild water 12 Chinese dwarf 14 American wonder

Lemuralia
   origin: 5 Roman
   event: 8 festival
   to exorcise: 6 ghosts

lemures
   form: 6 ghosts
   characteristic: 10 maleficent 11 troublesome

Lenaea
   origin: 8 Athenian
   event: 8 festival

lend 4 give, loan 6 impart, in vest, supply 7 advance, furnish 10 contribute

lend a hand 3 aid 6 assist 7 help out

lend assistance 3 aid 4 abet, help 6 succor 7 relieve 16 give a helping hand

lend one's name to 7 endorse, support 9 recommend

length 3 run 4 span, term, time 5 piece, range, reach 6 extent, period 7 compass, measure, portion, section, segment, stretch 8 distance, duration, end to end 9 longitude, magnitude 11 elapsed time, measurement

lengthen 3 pad 5 add to 6 expand, extend, let out, pad out 7 augment, drag out, draw out, fill out, prolong, spin out, stretch 8 elongate, flesh out, increase, protract 9 attenuate, string out

lengthened 8 drawn out, extended 9 augmented, elon gated, prolonged, stretched 10 attenuated, grew longer

lengthening 8 full form 9 extending, extension 10 elongation, stretching 11 extenuation, protraction 12 prolongation

lengthy 5 windy, wordy 6 padded, prolix 7 endless 8 drawn out, extended, overlong, rambling 9 elongated, extensive, garrulous, long-drawn, prolonged 10 digressive, discursive, long-winded, protracted 12 interminable

leniency 5 mercy 7 charity 8 clemency 9 tolerance 10 compassion 11 forbearance, magnanimity 12 mercifulness 13 forgivingness

lenient 4 kind, mild, soft 6 gentle 7 clement, liberal, patient, sparing 8 merciful, moderate, tolerant 9 easygoing, forgiving, indulgent 10 benevolent, charitable, forbearing, permissive 11 kindhearted, softhearted, sympathetic 13 compassionate, tenderhearted

Lenni-Lenape see 8 Delaware

Lenny
   director: 8 Bob Fosse
   cast: 8 Jan Miner 11 Stanley Beck 13 Dustin Hoffman (Lenny Bruce) 14 Valerie Perrine (Honey Harlowe)

Le Notre, Andre
   landscape architect of: 6 Clagny 9 Tuileries 10 Ver sailles 12 Saint Germain 13 Fontainebleau 22 Chateau de Vaux-le-Vicomte

lens
   invented by:
      achromatic: 7 Dollond
      bifocal: 8 Franklin
      fused bifocal: 6 Borsch

Lenya, Lotte
   real name: 16 Karoline Blamauer
   husband: 9 Kurt Weill
   born: 7 Austria, Hitzing
   roles: 5 Jenny 18 From Russia with Love, The Seven Deadly Sins, The Three-penny Opera

Leo
   symbol: 4 lion
   planet: 3 Sun
   rules: 7 romance 10 creativity
   born: 4 July 6 August

Leonard, Elmore
   author of: 4 Swag 5 Glitz, Stick 6 Hombre 7 La Brava 9 Cat Chaser, Gold Coast, Gunsights, The Hunted 10 Mr Majestyk 12 The Big Bounce 14 Fifty-Two Pick-Up, Valdez Is Coming 16 Double Dutch Treat, The Bounty Hunters 18 Forty Lashes Less One

Leonardo da Vinci
   born: 5 Italy, Vinci
   artwork: 8 Mona Lisa 13 The Last Supper 15 The Annunciation 19 The Battle of Anghiari 21 The Adoration of the Magi

Leonato
   character in: 19 Much Ado About Nothing
   author: 11 Shakespeare

Leoncavallo, Ruggiero
   born: 5 Italy 6 Naples
   composer of: 8 Serafita 9 Pagliacci

Leontes
   character in: 14 The Winter's Tale
   author: 11 Shakespeare

Leonteus
   leader of: 6 Greeks
   leader at: 4 Troy
   suitor of: 5 Helen

leopard 3 cat 7 panther 10 spotted cat
   group of: 4 leap

Leos
   occupation: 6 herald
   father: 7 Orpheus
   sacrificed: 9 daughters

Leo the Lip
   nickname of: 11 Leo Durocher

lepidoptera
   class: 8 hexapoda
   phylum: 10 arthropoda
   group: 4 moth 9 butterfly

leprechaun 3 elf, imp 5 dwarf, gnome 6 sprite 12 little person

Ler

also: 3 Lir

origin: 5 Irish

personifies: 3 sea

son: 8 Manannan

corresponds to: 4 Llyr

Lesage, Alain

author of: 7 Gil Blas 8 Turcaret

Lescaze, William

architect of: 18 Borg-Warner Building (Chicago) 38 Philadelphia Savings Fund Society Building

Lescot, Pierre

architect of: 10 Cour Carree 20 Fontaine des Innocents

rebuilding of: 6 Louvre

Lesotho

other name: 10 Basutoland

capital/largest city: 6 Maseru

others: 4 Roma 5 Joels 6 Leribe, Morija 7 Quthing, Sekakes 8 Mafeteng, Matsieng 9 Marakabei, Qachas Nek, Semonkong 10 Butha Buthe, Mokhotlong, Thaba Bosiu 11 Mohales Hoek 12 Sehlabathebe, Teyateyaneng

head of state: 4 king

monetary unit: 4 cent, rand

mountain: 6 Maloti, Maluti 7 Central 8 Injasuti, Machache 10 Ben Macdhui 11 Drakensberg, Thaba Putsoa

highest point: 16 Thabana Ntlenyana

river: 5 Senqu 6 Orange, Tugela 7 Caledon 9 Makhaleng

physical feature:

gorge: 5 Oxbow

people: 4 Zulu 5 Bantu, Tembu 6 Basuto 7 Basotho

leader: 7 Moshesh 9 Mosheshwe 10 Moshoeshoe 14 Leabua Jonathan

language: 5 Sotho 7 English, Sesotho

religion: 7 animism 13 Roman Catholic 18 Lesotho Evangelical

feature:

blanket: 4 kobo

house: 8 rondavel

water project: 11 Malibamatso

less 6 barely, little 7 smaller 8 meagerly, slighter 10 not as great 11 more limited

lessen 3 ebb 4 ease, sink, thin, wane 5 abate, lower 6 dilute, reduce, shrink 7 abridge, decline, dwindle, lighten, slacken, subside 8 contract, decrease, diminish, mitigate, wind down 9 alleviate 10 depreciate

lessening 6 waning 8 decrease, dilution 9 abatement, deduction, dwindling, reduction, shrinkage 10 diminution, lightening, mitigation, shortening, slackening 11 abridgement, alleviation, contraction, diminishing, slacking off 12 abbreviation, condensation, depreciation

lesser 4 less 5 minor 7 humbler, smaller 8 inferior, slighter 9 secondary 11 secondarily

Lesser Dionysia

also: 13 Rural Dionysia

event: 8 festival

origin: 6 Attica

Lessing, Doris

author of: 8 Shikasta 16 The Four-Gated City 17 The Golden Notebook 20 The Sirian Experiments 21 The Children of Violence 37 Marriages Between Zones Three Four and Five 42 The Making of the Representative for Planet Eight

lesson 5 class, drill, guide, model, moral, study 6 caveat, notice, rebuke 7 caution, example, message, reading, segment, warning 8 exemplar, exercise, homework 9 deterrent 10 admonition, advisement, assignment, punishment, recitation, Scriptures 11 instruction 12 remonstrance

Lestrade, Inspector

character in: 14 (The Adventures of) Sherlock Holmes

author: 10 Conan Doyle

Le Sueur, Lucille Fay

real name of: 12 Joan Crawford

let 4 make, rent 5 admit, allow, cause, grant, lease, leave 6 enable, permit, sublet, suffer 7 approve, charter, concede, empower, endorse, hire out, license, warrant 8 sanction, sublease, tolerate 9 authorize

let down 4 drop 5 lower 6 betray 8 push down 10 disappoint 11 disillusion

letdown 3 rue 4 balk, blow 6 fizzle, regret 7 chagrin, set back 8 comedown 10 anticlimax, bafflement, bitter pill, dashed hope, discontent 11 frustration 12 blighted hope, discomfiture 13 mortification 14 disappointment, disenchantment, disgruntlement 15 disillusionment, dissatisfaction

let fall 4 drop 5 let go 7 release

let fly 4 cast, hurl 5 eject, fling, heave, sling, throw 6 launch, propel

let go 3 axe, can 4 fire, free, lose, oust, sack 6 bounce, give up

lethal 5 fatal, toxic 6 deadly, mortal 7 baneful, killing 8 venomous, virulent 9 dangerous, malignant, poisonous 11 destructive 13 mortally toxic

lethargic 4 dull, idle, lazy 5 inert 6 drowsy, sleepy, torpid 7 languid, passive 8 comatose, indolent, listless, slothful, sluggish 9 apathetic, enervated, somnolent, soporific 10 dispirited, lackluster, unspirited 11 debilitated, indifferent

lethargy 5 sloth 6 apathy, stupor, torpor 7 inertia, languor 8 dullness, laziness 9 indolence, lassitude, torpidity 10 drowsiness, inactivity 12 indifference, listlessness, slothfulness, sluggishness

Lethe

form: 5 river

location: 5 Hades

caused: 13 forgetfulness

let in 5 admit 7 receive 12 allow to enter

let loose 4 free 5 let go 6 let fly 7 release, set free, unleash 8 give vent, liberate 12 give free rein

Leto
  also: 6 Latona
  form: 7 goddess
  father: 5 Coeus
  mother: 6 Phoebe
  son: 6 Apollo
  daughter: 7 Artemis

let off 5 let go 6 acquit, excuse, exempt 7 release, set free 8 liberate 9 discharge

let slip 6 betray, expose, reveal 7 divulge, uncover 8 blurt out, disclose, give away

Let's Make a Deal
  host: 9 Monty Hall
  announcer: 10 Jay Stewart

letter 4 note 7 epistle, message, missive 8 dispatch, document 9 substance 10 billet-doux

Letter, The
  director: 12 William Wyler
  based on story by: 15 Somerset Maugham
  cast: 10 Bette Davis 14 Frieda Inescort 15 Gale Sondergaard, Herbert Marshall, James Stephenson
  setting: 6 Malaya

letter ordering imprisonment
  French: 14 lettre de cachet
  carried seal of: 4 king 9 sovereign

letters 8 learning 9 erudition 10 literature 13 belles lettres

Letters from the Underground
  author: 16 Fyodor Dostoevsky

Letter to Three Wives, A
  director: 17 Joseph L Mankiewicz
  cast: 10 Ann Sothern 11 Jeanne Crain, Jeffrey Lynn, Kirk Douglas, Paul Douglas 12 Linda Darnell, Thelma Ritter
  Oscar for: 6 script 8 director

let the buyer beware
  Latin: 12 caveat emptor

let the people rule
  Latin: 13 regnat populus
  motto of: 8 Arkansas

let there be light
  Latin: 7 fiat lux

lettre de cachet 26 letter ordering imprisonment 28 letter under the sovereign's seal

lettuce 7 Lactuca
  varieties: 3 cos 5 chalk, frog's, lamb's, water 6 Boston, garden, miner's 7 iceberg, prickly, romaine 8 escarole 9 asparagus 11 common lamb's

letup 4 lull 5 pause 6 relief 7 respite 8 decrease, interval, slowdown, stopping, surcease, vacation 9 abatement, cessation, interlude, lessening, remission 10 slackening 11 retardation

Let Us Now Praise Famous Men
  author: 9 James Agee

Let us therefore be joyful
  Latin: 15 Gaudeamus igitur

Leucaeus
  epithet of: 4 Zeus
  means: 16 of the white poplar

Leuce
  form: 5 nymph
  changed into: 6 poplar
  color of poplar: 5 white

Leucippe
  father: 6 Minyas 7 Thestor
  mother: 10 Orchomenus
  son: 8 Teuthras

Leucippides
  refers to: 6 Phoebe 7 Hilaira

Leucippus
  father: 8 Perieres
  mother: 10 Gorgophone
  brother: 8 Aphareus
  fathered: 11 Leucippides
  daughter: 6 Phoebe 7 Arsinoe, Hilaira
  pursued: 6 Daphne
  disguised as: 4 girl
  killed by: 6 nymphs

Leucophryne
  epithet of: 7 Artemis

Leucothea *see* 3 Ino

Leucus
  mentioned in: 5 Iliad
  companion of: 8 Odysseus
  usurped throne of: 9 Idomeneus
  killed by: 8 Antiphus

Le Vau, Louis
  architect of: 6 Louvre 10 Versailles 12 Hotel Lambert 22 Chateau de Vaux-le-Vicomte 24 College des Quatres Nations

levee 3 dam 4 bank, dike, pier, quay, wall 5 ditch, jetty, ridge, wharf 6 durbar 9 reception 10 embankment

level 3 aim, bed 4 even, flat, rank, raze, tied, vein, zone 5 align, floor, flush, grade, layer, plane, point, stage, story, wreck 6 direct, height, lay low, reduce, smooth, topple 7 aligned, even out, flatten, landing, on a line, station, stratum, uniform 8 equalize, make even, position, tear down, together 9 devastate, elevation, knock down 10 consistent, horizontal, on a par with, unwrinkled 11 achievement, neck and neck 12 on an even keel

level-headed 4 sage 5 sound 6 poised, stable, steady 7 prudent 8 balanced, cautious, composed, sensible 9 collected, judicious, practical, unruffled 10 coolheaded, dependable, thoughtful 11 circumspect 12 even-tempered 13 dispassionate 14 self-controlled

levelheadedness 6 aplomb 9 good sense, soundness, stability 10 equanimity 11 common sense 13 judiciousness

Levene, Sam
  real name: 12 Samuel Levine
  born: 6 Russia
  roles: 12 Guys and Dolls 13 Nathan Detroit 15 The Sunshine Boys

lever 3 bar, pry 5 jimmy, raise 7 crowbar

Lever, Charles
  author of: 14 Charles O'Malley

Leverrier, Urbain Jean Joseph
  field: 9 astronomy
  nationality: 6 French
  co-discovered: 7 Neptune
  worked with: 14 John Couch Adams

Levi
  father: 5 Jacob 6 Melchi, Symeon
  mother: 4 Leah
  son: 6 Kohath, Merari 7 Gershom
  brother: 3 Dan, Gad 5 Asher, Judah 6
    Joseph, Reuben, Simeon 7 Zebulun 8
    Benjamin, Issachar, Naphtali
  sister: 5 Dinah
  violated: 5 Dinah
  also called: 7 Matthew
  descendant of: 6 Levite

Leviathan 6 dragon 10 sea monster
  means: 13 spirally bound
  represents: 14 terrible powers

Leviathan
  author: 12 Thomas Hobbes

Levin, Ira
  author of: 13 Rosemary's Baby

Levin, Konstantin
  character in: 12 Anna Karenina
  author: 7 Tolstoy

Levi-Strauss, Claude
  method: 13 structuralism
  author of: 13 Mythologiques, The Sav-
    age Mind 16 Tristes Tropiques 22 Struc-
    tural Anthropology 29 Elementary Struc-
    tures of Kinship

Levitch, Joseph
  real name of: 10 Jerry Lewis

levity 3 fun 5 mirth 6 joking, whimsy 8 hilarity, trifling 9 flippancy, frivolity, lightness,
  silliness 10 jocularity, pleasantry, triviality
  11 flightiness, foolishness 16 lightheartedness

levy 3 fee, tax 4 duty, make, toll, wage 5
  draft, exact, start 6 assess, call up,
  charge, demand, enlist, excise, impose,
  muster, pursue, tariff 7 carry on, collect 9
  calling up, conscript, prosecute 10 assessment, imposition 12 conscription

Levy, Marion
  real name of: 15 Paulette Goddard

Lew Archer, Private Detective
  author: 13 Ross MacDonald

lewd 5 bawdy 6 ribald, risque, vulgar, wanton 7 goatish, immoral, lustful, obscene 8
  indecent, prurient 9 lecherous, libertine,
  salacious 10 lascivious, libidinous, licentious, lubricious 11 Rabelaisian 12 pornographic

Lewis, C S
  author of: 10 Perelandra 13 Prince Cas-
    pian, The Last Battle 14 Surprised by
    Joy, The Silver Chair, Til We Have Faces
    17 The Horse and His Boy 18 The Magi-
    cian's Nephew 19 The Screwtape Letters
    20 Out of the Silent Planet 21 The
    Chronicles of Narnia 25 The Voyage of
    the Dawn Treader 29 The Lion the Witch
    and the Wardrobe

Lewis, Jerry
  real name: 13 Joseph Levitch
  partner: 10 Dean Martin
  born: 8 Newark NJ
  roles: 8 The Caddy 10 The Bellboy, The
    Sad Sack 11 Cinderfella 12 The Geisha
    Boy 16 Artists and Models 17 The Nutty
    Professor 20 The Disorderly Orderly

Lewis, Sinclair
  author of: 7 Babbitt 9 Dodsworth 10
    Arrowsmith, Main Street 11 Elmer Gantry
    14 Cass Timberlane

lexicon 5 gloss, index 8 code book, glossary, synonymy, wordbook, wordlist 9 thesaurus, wordstock 10 dictionary, vocabulary 11 concordance, onomasticon

lex loci 11 law of a place

lex non scripta 9 common law 12 unwritten law

lex scripta 10 statute law, written law

Leyden, Lucas (Lukas) van
  born: 6 Leiden, Leyden 14 The Nether-
    lands
  artwork: 12 Last Judgment 14 The Card
    Players, The Game of Chess 26 Moham-
    med and the Murdered Monk

Lhasa, Lassa
  capital of: 5 Tibet

liability 4 debt, drag, duty, onus 5 debit, minus 6 arrear, burden 7 drawback, handicap, obstacle 9 hindrance 10 impediment,
  obligation 11 encumbrance, shortcoming
  12 disadvantage, indebtedness 13 inconvenience 14 responsibility, stumbling block

liable 3 apt 4 open 5 prone 6 likely 7 exposed, ripe for, subject 8 disposed, inclined 9 obligated, sensitive 10 answerable, chargeable, vulnerable 11 accountable, responsible, susceptible

liaison 4 bond, link 5 amour, union 7 contact 8 alliance, intrigue, mediator 9 adventure, dalliance, go-between 10 connection, flirtation, love affair 11 association,
  cooperation, interchange 12 coordination,
  entanglement 13 communication

liar 6 fibber 8 perjurer 9 falsifier 10 fabrica-
  tor 11 story teller 12 prevaricator

libation 4 wine 5 drink, water 6 liquid 8 ambrosia, beverage, offering, potation 9 sacrifice

Libation Bearers, The see 10 Choephoroe

libel 4 slur 5 smear 6 defame, malign, revile, vilify 7 asperse, blacken, calumny, obloquy, slander 8 derogate 9 aspersion,
  discredit, disparage 10 calumniate, defamation 12 vilification

Libeled Lady
  director: 10 Jack Conway
  cast: 8 Myrna Loy 11 Jean Harlow 12
    Spencer Tracy 13 William Powell 14 Wal-
    ter Connolly
  remade as: 9 Easy to Wed

Libera
  origin: 7 Italian
  goddess of: 4 wine 9 fertility, vineyards
  husband: 5 Liber
  corresponds to: 10 Persephone

liberal 5 ample, broad 6 casual, lavish 7 leftist, lenient 8 abundant, advanced, flexible, generous, handsome, left-wing, prodigal, reformer, tolerant, unbiased 9 bounteous, bountiful, impartial, not strict, plenteous, reformist, unbigoted, unsparing 10 fair-minded, forbearing, left-winger, munificent, not literal, openhanded, open-minded, unrigorous, unstinting 11 broad-minded, enlightened, extravagant, libertarian, magnanimous, progressive 12 freethinking, humanitarian, open to reason, unprejudiced 14 latitudinarian

Liberalia
   origin: 5 Roman
   event: 8 festival

liberality 10 generosity 11 benevolence, munificence 12 philanthropy 13 bountifulness 14 openhandedness

liberate 5 let go 6 let out, redeem, rescue, spring 7 absolve, deliver, manumit, release, set free 8 let loose 9 discharge, disengage, extricate, unshackle 10 emancipate 11 disencumber

liberated 5 freed, let go 7 rescued, set free 8 let loose, released 10 discharged, extricated 11 emancipated

liberation 6 escape, rescue 7 freedom, freeing, release 8 delivery 9 letting go, releasing 11 manumission 12 emancipation

Liberia
   capital/largest city: 8 Monrovia
   others: 4 Sino 5 Gribo, Rebbo 6 Bopora, Gbanga, Harper, Kakata 7 Bgarnga, Kolahun, Nanakru, Tappita, Vonjama 8 Buchanan, Garraway, Marshall, Nanakaru, Sass Town 9 Grand Cess, River Cess, Roysville 10 Careysburg, Green ville, Sanoquelli 11 Robertsport 12 Sanniquellie
   school: 7 Liberia 10 Cuttington 15 Our Lady of Fatima 16 Booker Washington
   religious school/secret society: 4 poro 5 sande
   measure: 4 kuba
   monetary unit: 4 cent 6 dollar
   mountain: 3 Uni 4 Bong, Putu 5 Niete, Nimba 9 Bomi Hills
   highest point: 6 Wutivi
   river: 4 Cess, Lofa, Mano 5 Duobe, Lotta, Manna, Morro, Sinoe 6 Cestos, Douobe 7 Cavalla, Cavally 8 San Pedro 9 Saint John, Saint Paul, Sehnkwehn
   sea: 8 Atlantic
   physical feature:
      wind: 9 harmattan
   people: 2 Gi 3 Gio, Kra, Kru, Kwa, Vai, Vei 4 Gola, Kroo, Krou, Loma, Mano, Toma 5 Bassa, Gibbi, Gissi, Grebo 6 Gbande, Kpelle, Kpuesi, Krooby, Kruman 7 Krooboy, Krooman 8 Mandingo 15 Americo-Liberian
   leader: 3 Doe 6 Tubman 7 Roberts, Tolbert
   language: 3 Kru, Kwa 5 Mande 7 English
   religion: 5 Islam 7 animism 10 Protestant 12 Christianity

feature:
   clothing: 5 lappa
   rubber plantation: 9 Firestone

Libertas
   origin: 5 Roman
   personifies: 7 liberty

liberte egalite fraternite 25 liberty equality fraternity
   motto of: 16 French Revolution

liberties 6 misuse 7 license 9 violation 10 distortion 11 familiarity, impropriety 13 falsification

libertine 4 goat, lewd, rake, roue 5 loose, satyr 6 lecher, wanton 7 immoral, lustful, seducer 8 unchaste 9 debauchee, dissolute, lecherous, reprobate, womanizer 10 immoralist, lascivious, libidinous, licentious, profligate, sensualist, voluptuary

liberty 5 leave, right 7 freedom, license 8 autonomy, delivery, free time, furlough, sanction, vacation 9 privilege 10 liberation, permission, shore leave 11 citizenship, manumission 12 carte blanche, dispensation, emancipation, independence 15 enfranchisement 17 self-determination

liberty equality fraternity
   French: 24 liberte egalite fraternite
   motto of: 16 French Revolution

Libra
   symbol: 6 scales 7 balance
   planet: 5 Venus
   rules: 8 marriage
   born: 7 October 9 September

Libreville
   capital of: 13 Gabon Republic

Libya
   capital/largest city: 7 Tripoli
   summer capital: 8 Benghazi
   others: 4 Homs, Marj, Surt 5 Beida, Darna, Derna, Khums, Kufra, Sebha, Sidri, Zawia 6 Garian, Murzuq, Tobruk 7 Es Sidar, Gharyan, Misrata 8 Ajdabiya, Misurata, Rashanuf 12 Marsa el Brega
   school: 7 Alfateh 9 Garyounis
   division: 6 Fezzan 9 Cyrenaica 12 Tripolitania
   measure: 3 dra, pik, saa 4 kele 5 bozze, donum, jabia, teman, uckia 6 barile, gorraf, misura 7 mattaro, termino 8 kharouba
   weight: 4 kele 6 gorraf 8 kharouba
   monetary unit: 5 dinar
   mountain: 5 Green 13 Jabal al Akhdar, Tibesti Massif
   highest point: 9 Bette Peak
   sea: 13 Mediterranean
   physical feature:
      desert: 6 Libyan, Sahara 9 Calanscio
      gulf: 5 Bomba, Sidra, Sirte
      oasis: 4 Ghat 5 Kufra, Sebha 7 Tazerbo 8 Al-Kufrah, Ghudamis
      plain: 6 al Marj, Gefara 7 Jaffara
      plateau: 12 Gebel Nefuisa, Jabal Nafusah
      wind: 6 ghibli

people: 4 Arab, Tebu 6 Berber, Tuareg 7 Gaetuli 8 Getu Ians, Harratin
leader: 6 Battus 7 Jalloud, Qadhafi 8 Aegyptus 9 al-Qaddafi, Karamanli 13 Idris al-Senusi
religious leader: 8 al-Senusi
ruler: 4 Rome 5 Italy 6 Greece 9 Phoenicia 12 Ottoman Turks
language: 6 Arabic, Berber 7 English, Italian
alphabet: 8 tifinagh
religion: 5 Islam
feature: 14 Tropic of Cancer
clothing: 5 Ianaf 9 barracano
festival: 3 Mez 7 Fantasi
Islamic law: 6 sharia
leader: 6 sheikh
ruins: 11 Leptis Magna
food:
dish: 5 bazin 8 couscous
red pepper: 6 filfil

lice
variety: 4 bird, crab 5 human, pubic, spiny 7 chewing, sucking 8 barklice, booklice 9 guinea pig 13 mammal chewing

license 3 let 4 pass, visa 5 allow, grant, leave, right 6 enable, laxity, permit 7 anarchy, approve, certify, charter, empower, endorse, freedom, liberty, warrant 8 accredit, audacity, disorder, latitude, passport, sanction, temerity 9 admission, allowance, authorize, franchise, looseness, privilege, slackness 10 brazenness, commission, debauchery, unruliness 11 certificate, free passage, lawlessness, libertinism, presumption, safe-conduct 12 carte blanche, dispensation, recklessness

licentious 4 lewd 5 dirty, loose 6 amoral, sleazy, wanton 7 brutish, goatish, immoral, lawless, lustful, raunchy, ruttish 8 depraved, prodigal 9 abandoned, debauched, dissolute, excessive, lecherous, libertine, salacious 10 dissipated, lascivious, libidinous, lubricious, profligate, ungoverned 11 promiscuous 12 unprincipled, unrestrained, unscrupulous 13 irresponsible, unconstrained

licentiousness 7 abandon 8 lewdness 10 immorality, wantonness

licit 5 legal, legit, valid 6 kosher, lawful 9 allowable, statutory 10 acceptable, admissible, authorized, legitimate, sanctioned 11 permissible 12 authorizable, sanctionable 14 constitutional

lick 3 bit, dab, hit, jot, lap 4 beat, blow, drub, fire, hint, iota, rout, slap, snip, sock, suck, whip 5 crack, punch, sally, shred, spank, speck, taste, touch, trace 6 defeat, ignite, kindle, master, sample, stroke, subdue, thrash, tongue, wallop 7 clobber, conquer, modicum, smidgen, trounce 8 outmatch, overcome, particle, vanquish 9 overpower, overthrow, scintilla, subjugate 10 smattering 12 denunciation

Licymnius
father: 9 Electryon
mother: 5 Midea
wife: 8 Perimede
son: 5 Melas 6 Oeonus 7 Argeius
nephew: 8 Hercules

lid 3 cap, top 4 cork, curb, plug 5 cover, limit 7 ceiling, maximum, stopper, stopple 9 operculum, restraint

lie 3 fib 4 loll, rest, stay 5 abide, exist, range, story 6 belong, deceit, extend, inhere, lounge, obtain, remain, repose, sprawl 7 falsify, fiction, perjury, recline, romance, untruth 8 misstate, tall tale 9 deception, embellish, embroider, fabricate, falsehood, invention 10 equivocate 11 fabrication, prevaricate 12 equivocation 13 falsification, prevarication 17 misrepresentation

Liechtenstein
capital/largest city: 5 Vaduz
others: 4 Haag 6 Balzer, Eschen, Iradug, Schaan 7 Balzers, Bendern, Nendeln, Planken, Triesen 12 Schellenberg
division:
ancient province: 6 Rhaeti 7 Rhaetia
government:
legislature: 7 Landtag
monetary unit: 6 rappen 7 franken
mountain: 4 Alps 8 Naafkopf, Rhatikon 12 Three Sisters
highest point: 15 Vorder-Grauspitz
river: 5 Rhine
physical feature:
valley: 6 Lavena, Samina
people: 8 Alemanni
leader: 7 Florian 15 Francis Joseph II 16 von Liechtenstein
language: 6 German 10 Alemannish
religion: 13 Roman Catholic
place:
castle: 9 Gutemburg, Gutenberg
feature:
legendary dwarf: 10 wildmannli
wine: 7 Vaduzer

lie down 6 retire 7 go to bed, recline 8 take a nap 11 take a snooze 15 catch forty winks

life 4 path, soul, zest 5 being, human, plant, story, verve, vigor 6 animal, career, course, energy, memoir, person, spirit 8 creature, duration, life span, lifetime, lifework, organism, survival, vitality, vivacity 9 animation, biography, existence, life story, longevity 11 subsistence 13 autobiography
French: 3 vie

Life at the Dakota
author: 17 Stephen Birmingham

Life Before Man
author: 14 Margaret Atwood

Lifeboat
director: 15 Alfred Hitchcock
cast: 10 John Hodiak 12 Mary Anderson 13 William Bendix 16 Tallulah Bankhead

life-giving 5 vital 9 vivifying 12 invigorating
lifeless 4 dead, dull, flat, late 5 inert, stiff, vapid 6 boring, hollow, static, torpid, wooden 7 defunct 8 deceased, departed, inactive, lifeless, sluggish 9 colorless, inanimate 10 lackluster, spiritless
lifelessness 5 death 7 inertia 8 dullness, limpness, vapidity 9 blandness 10 flaccidity, inactivity 13 colorlessness
Life of Dante
   author: 17 Giovanni Boccaccio
Life of Emile Zola
   director: 15 William Dieterle
   cast: 8 Paul Muni 11 Donald Crisp 12 Gloria Holden 15 Gale Sondergaard 17 Joseph Schildkraut (Dreyfus)
   Oscar for: 7 picture
Life of Man, The
   author: 14 Leonid Andreyev
Life of Riley, The
   character: 4 Babs 6 Dangle, Junior 8 Peg Riley 9 Jim Gillis 10 Cunningham, Digby (Digger) O'Dell 11 Waldo Binney 13 Chester A Riley 14 Honeybee Gillis
   cast: 9 John Brown, Lanny Rees, Sid Tomack 10 Tom D'Andrea 12 Emory Parnell, Wesley Morgan 13 Gloria Winters, Jackie Gleason, Lugene Sanders, Robert Sweeney, William Bendix 14 Gloria Blondell, Rosemary DeCamp 16 Douglas Dumbrille, Marjorie Reynolds, Sterling Holloway
Life of Samuel Johnson, The
   author: 12 James Boswell
life of the party 7 show-off 9 extrovert 13 exhibitionist 17 hail-fellow-well-met
Life on the Mississippi
   author: 9 Mark Twain
life span 4 life 8 lifetime 14 life expectancy
Life Studies
   author: 12 Robert Lowell
Life With Father
   author: 13 Clarence Day Jr
   director: 13 Michael Curtiz
   cast: 9 ZaSu Pitts 10 Irene Dunne 11 Edmund Gwenn 13 William Powell 15 Elizabeth Taylor
   setting: 11 New York City
lifework 6 career 7 calling 8 vocation 10 livelihood, occupation, profession
lift 4 high, palm, pick, rear, rise, soar, take 5 boost, climb, exalt, filch, heave, hoist, pinch, raise, steal, swipe 6 ascend, ascent, banish, cancel, pilfer, pirate, pocket, remove, revoke, snatch, thieve, uplift, vanish 7 elation, elevate, purloin, raise up, raising, rescind, scatter, upraise 8 disperse 9 disappear, dissipate, float away 10 ascendance, move upward, plagiarize, put an end to 11 appropriate, countermand, inspiration, make off with, reassurance 12 give a boost to, shot in the arm 13 encouragement, enheartenment
ligament
   holds: 5 bones

Ligeia
   author: 13 Edgar Allan Poe
   character: 19 Lady Rowena Trevanion
Ligeti, Gyorgy
   composer of: 7 Lontano 11 Atmospheres 13 Ramifications
light 3 gay 4 airy, beam, easy, fair, fall, find, fire, glow, lamp, land, pale, puny, side, soft, stop 5 aglow, angle, blaze, blond, faint, flame, funny, glare, guide, happy, jolly, match, model, perch, petty, put on, roost, shine, slant, small, spare, spark, sunny, torch 6 alight, aspect, beacon, blithe, bright, candle, chance, frugal, gentle, get off, ignite, jaunty, kindle, luster, meager, paltry, scanty, settle, simple, slight, turn on 7 amusing, buoyant, chipper, clarify, come off, descend, get down, gleeful, insight, lantern, lighten, lighter, lucifer, not dark, not rich, paragon, radiant, radiate, sparkle, sunbeam, trivial 8 approach, attitude, bleached, blondish, brighten, carefree, cheerful, come upon, discover, dismount, ethereal, exemplar, gossamer, graceful, illumine, jubilant, luminous, meet with, moderate, moonbeam, not heavy, paradigm, radiance, sportive, step down, switch on, trifling, untaxing 9 brilliant, catch fire, direction, encounter, frivolous, irradiate, light-hued, set fire to, sprightly, stumble on, sylphlike, viewpoint 10 abstemious, brightness, brilliance, burdenless, come across, come to rest, effortless, effulgence, floodlight, happen upon, illuminate, light-toned, luminosity, manageable, restricted, set burning, weightless 11 conflagrate, elucidation, illuminated, information, make radiant, superficial, undemanding, underweight 15 inconsequential
   god of: 6 Apollo 7 Mithras, Phoebus, Pythius 8 Heimdall 9 Musagetes
   Latin: 3 lux
   measurement: 7 candela 11 candlepower
light-colored 4 pale 5 beige, blond 6 blonde, flaxen, pastel 7 neutral, whitish 9 yellowish
light-complexioned 4 fair, pale 12 white-skinned
lighten 4 buoy, ease, lift 5 abate, allay, blaze, elate, flare, flash, gleam, shine 6 buoy up, lessen, reduce, revive, temper, unload, uplift 7 assuage, enliven, gladden, inspire, light up, relieve 8 brighten, mitigate, moderate, unburden 9 alleviate, coruscate, disburden, irradiate 10 illuminate, make bright 11 become light, disencumber, make lighter, scintillate
light-filled 5 sunny 6 bright 7 well-lit 11 illuminated
lighthearted 3 gay 4 airy, glad 5 jolly, merry, sunny 6 blithe, cheery, joyful, joyous, lively 7 buoyant, cheered, chipper 8 carefree, cheerful, sanguine 9 sprightly 10 insouciant, untroubled 11 free and easy 12 effervescent

lightheartedness 3 joy 4 glee 5 mirth 8 gladness 9 happiness, merriment 10 blitheness, exuberance, joyfulness, joyousness 11 high spirits

Light in August
author: 15 William Faulkner
character: 8 Doc Hines, Joe Brown 9 Lena Grove, McEachern 10 Byron Bunch 12 Joanna Burden, Joe Christmas

lightless 4 dark 5 black, murky 7 stygian 9 unlighted 13 unilluminated

lightly 6 airily, easily, gently, nimbly, softly, thinly, weakly 7 blandly, faintly, quickly, readily, swiftly, timidly 8 blithely, facilely, gingerly, meagerly, slightly, sparsely 9 buoyantly, sparingly 10 carelessly, flippantly, hesitantly, moderately 11 frivolously, slightingly 13 indifferently, thoughtlessly, unconcernedly, without effort 14 without concern

lightness 8 airiness, radiance 10 brightness, fluffiness, luminosity 12 illumination, luminousness

lightning rod
invented by: 8 Franklin

light of day 8 daylight, sunlight, sunshine

light sleep 3 nap 4 doze 6 catnap, snooze 10 forty winks

light wind 4 waft 6 breeze, zephyr 10 gentle wind 11 breath of air

Lightwood, Mortimer
character in: 15 Our Mutual Friend
author: 8 Dickens

lignum vitae 10 wood of life
tree species: 8 Guaiacum

Ligure 8 gemstone

likable, likeable 4 nice 6 genial 7 amiable, lovable, winsome 8 charming, engaging, loveable, pleasant, pleasing 9 agreeable, appealing, simpatico 10 attractive 11 complaisant, sympathetic

like 4 akin, care, dote, same, wish 5 enjoy, equal, fancy, favor, savor 6 admire, allied, choose, esteem, relish 7 approve, cognate, endorse, matched, related, similar, support, uniform 8 be fond of, parallel, selfsame, think fit 9 analogous, congruent, have a mind, identical 10 comparable, equivalent, homologous, resembling 11 be partial to, much the same 12 feel in clined, have a crush on, take a shine to 13 corresponding, find agreeable 14 take pleasure in

Like a Bulwark
author: 13 Marianne Moore

likelihood 8 prospect 10 good chance 11 possibility, probability 12 potentiality

likely 3 apt, fit 4 able 6 liable, proper 8 credible, destined, inclined, probable, probably, rational, reliable, suitable 9 befitting, plausible, promising, qualified 10 believable, presumably, reasonable 11 appropriate, verisimilar 16 in all probability

like-mindedness 6 accord 7 concord, harmony, rapport 8 affinity 9 agreement 12 congeniality 13 compatibility

likeness 5 image, model, study 6 effigy 7 analogy, picture, replica 8 affinity, portrait 9 agreement, depiction, facsimile, portrayal, rendition, semblance 10 similarity, similitude 11 delineation, resemblance 14 correspondence, representation

likes 9 favorites 10 prejudices 11 preferences 12 inclinations, partialities

likewise 3 and, eke, too 4 also 5 ditto 6 as well 7 be sides, equally, the same 8 moreover 9 similarity 10 in addition

liking 4 bent 5 fancy, taste 7 leaning 8 affinity, appetite, fondness, penchant, soft spot, weakness 9 affection 10 partiality, preference, proclivity, propensity 11 inclination 12 predilection

Li'l Abner
creator: 6 Al Capp
character: 5 Pappy 7 Wolf Gal 10 Joe Btfsplk, Mammy Yokum, Marryin' Sam 11 Adam Lazonga, Hairless Joe 12 Tobacco Rhoda 13 Joanie Phoanie 14 Daisy Mae Scragg, Evil-Eye Flee gle, Stupefyin' Jones 15 Fearless Fosdick, Henry Cabbage Cod, Lonesome Polecat, Moonbeam McSwine 16 General Bullmoose, Sir Cecil Cesspool 17 Sen Jack S Phogbound 18 J Roaringham Fatback 21 Appassionata von Climax
brewery: 23 Big Barnsmell's Skonk Works
event: 15 Sadie Hawkins Day
juice: 16 Kickapoo Joy Juice
kingdom: 14 Lower Slobbovia
mountain: 11 Onnecessary
people: 7 Schmoos 8 Kingmies
place: 8 Dogpatch
railroad: 11 West Po'k Chop
ruler: 14 King Nogoodnick

lilac 7 Syringa
varieties: 4 late, vine, wild 6 common, Indian, summer 7 Chinese, cut-leaf, Persian 9 Himalayan, Hungarian 12 Japanese tree 16 Catalina mountain

Lili
director: 14 Charles Walters
cast: 9 Mel Ferrer 11 Leslie Caron, Zsa Zsa Gabor 16 Jean-Pierre Aumont

Lilies of the Field
director: 11 Ralph Nelson
cast: 8 Lisa Mann 10 Lilia Skala 13 Sidney Poitier
Oscar for: 5 actor (Poitier)

Liliom
author: 12 Ferenc Molnar

lillet
type: 8 aperitif
origin: 6 France
flavor: 6 orange
color: 3 red 5 white

Lilliput
fictional land in: 16 Gulliver's Travels
author: 5 Swift

lilliputian 3 wee 4 tiny 5 dwarf, short, small, teeny, weeny 6 little, midget, minute, petite 9 miniature 10 diminutive, teeny-weeny 11 pocket-sized

Lilongwe
  capital of: 6 Malawi
lily 6 Lilium
  varieties: 3 Alp, cow, day, pig 4 Arum,
bell, boat, corn, fawn, fire, flax, herb,
palm, pine, pond, rain, roan, rock, sand,
Sego, star, toad, wood 5 adobe, Aztec,
blood, bugle, calla, coast, cobra, crane,
Cuban, fairy, globe, glory, Gray's, Ifafa,
lemon, magic, natal, queen, regal, royal,
showy, snake, spear, swamp, sword, tiger, torch, trout, water, wheel 6 Alpine,
Amazon, Canada, Crinum, desert,
Easter, eureka, ginger, hidden, Kaffir,
Marhan, meadow, one-day, orange, Oregon, shasta, Sierra, spider, sunset, tartar,
turban, voodoo, yellow, Zephyr 7 African,
Bermuda, chamise, checker, garland,
leopard, madonna, Nankeen, panther,
redwood, thimble, toad-cup, triplet,
trumpet, western 8 Atamasco, Barbados,
bluebead, Carolina, climbing, Columbia,
flamingo, gloriosa, Guernsey, Humboldt,
Jacobean, Japanese, long's red, Mari-
posa, Martagon, Michigan, mountain,
paradise, Peruvian, plan tain, Siberian,
Solomon's, St Bruno's, St James's, turk's
cap 9 alligator, avalanche, butterfly,
caucasian, celestial, chaparral, checkered, Eucharist, Kamchatka, naked-lady,
orange-cup, pineapple, pinewoods, pot-
of-gold, red ginger, red spider, St Joseph's 10 belladonna, blackberry, blue
funnel, fairy water, giant water, globe
spear, gold-banded, Josephine's, orange-
bell, pink Easter, pygmy water, royal water, small tiger, St Bernard's, Washington,
white water, wild yellow, yellow-bell, yellow pond 11 African corn, Amazon water,
blue African, candlestick, dwarf ginger,
golden-rayed, milk-and-wine, Palmer
spear, Scarborough, southern red, yellow
water 12 African blood, Chinese white,
golden spider, prickly water, resurrection,
speckled wood, white trumpet 13 Bermuda Easter, cape blue water, Chinese
sacred, Egyptian water, fragrant water,
India red water, lavender globe, magnolia
water, minor Turk's-cap, per fumed fairy,
pink porcelain, scarlet ginger, showy Japanese, tuberous water, wild orange-red
14 Chinese-lantern, lesser Turk's cap, little Turk's-cap, Santa Cruz water, yellow
Turk's-cap 15 Australian water, back-
house hybrid, golden hurricane, scarlet
Turk's-cap 16 American Turk's cap,
Bellingham hybrid, Cape Cod pink water,
fragrant plantain, Japanese Turk's-cap,
western orange-cup 17 midsummer plantain 18 European white water, seer
sucker plantain 20 narrow-leaved plantain
lily-livered 6 afraid, craven, scared, yellow
7 chicken, fearful, gutless 8 cowardly 9
dastardly 12 fainthearted 13 pusillanimous, yellow-bellied 14 chicken-hearted,

chicken-livered 22 showing the white
feather
lily-white 4 good, pure 6 biased, decent,
proper, racist 7 bigoted, upright 8 all-white,
innocent, virtuous 9 blameless, exclusive,
exemplary, faultless, guiltless, honorable,
righteous 10 impeccable, inculpable, prejudiced, segregated, upstanding 11 uncorrupted 12 unintegrated 13 unimpeachable
14 discriminatory, irreproachable
Lima
  capital of: 4 Peru
  foothills of: 5 Andes
  founder: 7 Pizarro
  nickname: 11 city of kings
  ocean: 7 Pacific
  port: 6 Callao
  river: 5 Rimac
  square: 12 Plaza de Armas
limb 3 arm, gam, leg, pin 4 part, spur, twig,
wing 5 bough, shoot, sprig 6 branch, member 9 appendage, extension, outgrowth 10
projection, prosthesis
limber 5 agile, lithe, relax 6 loosen, pliant,
supple 7 bending, elastic, loose, pliable
8 flexible 9 lithesome, malleable
lime 18 Citrus aurantifolia
  varieties: 3 key 4 wild 7 Mexican, Persian, Rangpur, Spanish 8 Mandarin 10
West Indian 14 Australian wild 15 Australian round 16 Australian desert, Australian finger
Limenia
  epithet of: 9 Aphrodite
  means: 11 of the harbor
limit 3 end 4 curb 6 boundary, end point,
restrain, ultimate 13 breaking point
limitation 4 curb 5 quota 6 boundary, decrease 9 lessening, reduction, restraint 10
shortening 11 abridgement, restriction,
shortcoming 13 qualification, specification
limited 5 fixed 6 finite, narrow 7 bounded,
cramped, defined, minimal, special 8 confined 9 delimited, specified 10 controlled,
restrained, restricted 13 circumscribed
limitless 7 endless, eternal, unbound 8 infinite, unending 9 boundless, unlimited 11
measureless 12 immeasurable
limits 3 rim, top 4 curb, edge 5 bound,
check, quota 6 border, define, fringe, margin, narrow 7 ceiling, confine, delimit, inhibit, maximum, qualify 8 confines, frontier,
restrain, restrict 9 perimeter, periphery,
prescribe, restraint 10 boundaries 11 limi-
tations 12 restrictions
limn 4 draw 6 sketch 7 picture 9 delineate
Limnaea
  epithet of: 7 Artemis
  means: 9 of the lake
Limnoria
  member of: 7 Nereids
Limon
  father: 8 Tegeates
  mother: 5 Maera
  brother: 8 Scephrus
  killed: 8 Scephrus

limp 3 lax 4 gimp, halt, soft, weak 5 crawl, loose, skulk, slack 6 droopy, falter, flabby, floppy, hobble 7 flaccid 8 drooping, lameness, yielding 9 dead tired, enervated, exhausted

limpid 4 pure 5 clear, lucid 8 clear-cut, pellucid, vitreous 11 crystalline, perspicuous, translucent, transparent, unambiguous 15 straightforward

Lincoln, Abraham
  nickname: 9 Honest Abe 20 Illinois Rail Splitter
  presidential rank: 9 sixteenth
  party: 4 Whig 10 Republican
  state represented: 2 IL
  defeated: 4 (John) Bell 7 (John Charles) Fremont, (Stephen Arnold) Douglas 9 (George Brinton) McClellan 12 (John Cabell) Breckinridge
  vice president: 6 (Hannibal) Hamlin 7 (Andrew) Johnson
  cabinet:
  state: 6 (William Henry) Seward
  treasury: 5 (Salmon Portland) Chase 9 (Hugh) McCulloch, (William Pitt) Fessenden
  war: 7 (Edwin McMasters) Stanton, (Simon) Cameron
  attorney general: 5 (Edward) Bates, (James) Speed
  navy: 6 (Gideon) Welles
  postmaster general: 5 (Montgomery) Blair 8 (William) Dennison
  interior: 5 (Caleb Blood) Smith, (John Palmer) Usher
  born: 2 KY 8 log cabin 11 Larue County 17 Sinking Spring farm
  died: 12 Washington DC, Fords Theater
  died by: 13 assassination
  assassinated by: 15 John Wilkes Booth
  buried: 13 Springfield IL
  education:
  educated by: 4 self
  studied: 3 law
  interests: 7 theater
  received patent for: 25 adjustable buoyant chambers (for lifting boats)
  political career: 16 state legislature 24 US House of Representatives
  civilian career: 6 lawyer 8 surveyor 10 postmaster
  military service:
  War: 9 Black Hawk
  US Army: 7 private
  captain of company of: 10 volunteers
  notable events of lifetime/term: 8 Civil War 24 Emanci pation Proclamation
  Act: 9 Homestead, Income Tax, Judiciary 12 Conscription
  debates: 14 Lincoln-Douglas
  speech: 17 Gettysburg Address
  father: 6 Thomas
  mother: 5 Nancy (Hanks)
  stepmother: 5 Sarah (Bush Johnston)
  siblings: 5 Sarah 6 Thomas
  stepbrother: 4 John
  stepsister: 7 Matilda 9 Elizabeth

  wife: 4 Mary (Ann Todd)
  children: 6 Thomas 10 Robert Todd 11 Edward Baker 14 William Wallace

Lind, James
  field: 8 medicine
  nationality: 8 Scottish
  eliminated: 6 scurvy

Lindbergh, Anne Morrow
  author of: 14 Gift from the Sea 15 Bring Me a Unicorn 16 North to the Orient 19 War Within and Without

linden 5 Tilia
  varieties: 6 Indoor 7 Crimean 8 American, Japanese 9 Mongolian 10 Manchurian 11 Large-leaved 13 Pendent silver 19 Small-leaved European

lindy 5 dance 8 lindy hop 9 jitterbug

line, lines 4 card, cord, dash, draw, file, idea, mark, note, part, race, rank, rope, rule, tier, word 5 align, array, breed, cable, craft, front, house, model, queue, range, score, slash, stock, trade 6 belief, border, column, crease, family, furrow, letter, method, metier, policy, report, scheme, series, stance, strain, strand, streak, stripe, system, thread 7 calling, circuit, conduit, contour, cordage, example, lineage, marshal, outline, pattern, purpose, pursuit, queue up, routine, towline, wrinkle 8 ancestry, business, dialogue, doctrine, fishline, ideology, inscribe, position, postcard, trenches, vanguard, vocation 9 conductor, crow's foot, direction, frontline, genealogy, intention, principle 10 barricades, convention, firing line, livelihood, long stroke, occupation, procession, profession, underscore 11 demarcation

lineage 4 line 5 blood, stock 7 descent 8 ancestry, heredity, pedigree 9 genealogy, parentage 10 derivation, extraction

linen
  fabric: 6 canvas, damask 7 butcher, cambric 8 birds-eye 9 huckaback
  plant: 4 flax
  finest from: 7 Belgium, Ireland
  processing term: 6 shives, sliver 7 carding, hackled, retting 8 beetling, breaking, rippling, spinning 9 scutching

line of march 4 path 5 route, track 11 parade route

line of reasoning 4 case 7 premise 8 argument 10 hypothesis

line up 4 book 5 align 6 engage, even up 7 arrange, procure, program, queue up 8 schedule 9 form a line, put in a row 10 arrange for

line-up 5 slate 6 roster 8 schedule

linger 3 lag 4 idle, last, stay, wait 5 daily, delay, tarry, trail 6 dawdle, hang on, loiter, remain 7 persist, survive 9 die slowly 10 dillydally, hang around

lingering 4 slow 7 abiding, chronic, delayed, lagging, lasting, staying, waiting 8 dawdling, delaying, dragging, drawn out, dwelling, enduring, hovering, tarrying 9 loitering, remaining 10 protracted, sauntering 15 procrastinating

lingo 4 cant, talk 5 argot, idiom, slang 6 jargon, patois, tongue 7 dialect 8 language, parlance 10 vernacular

linguist 8 polyglot 10 grammarian, translator 11 etymologist, interpreter, philologist, phonetician, phonologist, semanticist 12 morphologist 13 lexicographer

liniment 4 balm 5 salve 7 unguent 8 ointment 9 emollient

link 3 tie 4 bind, bond, fuse, loop, ring 5 group, joint, tie in, unite 6 couple, relate, splice 7 bracket, combine, con join, connect, involve, liaison 8 junction, relation 9 associate, implicate 10 connection, connective 11 association 12 interconnect, relationship

linkage 3 tie 4 bond 6 hookup 10 connection 11 affiliation, association, correlation

link up 4 dock, join 6 couple, hook up 7 connect 9 affiliate 14 fasten together

Linnaeus, Carolus
  field: 6 botany
  nationality: 7 Swedish
  developed: 8 taxonomy 18 nomenclature system

linotype
  invented by: 12 Mergenthaler

Linton, Edgar
  character in: 16 Wuthering Heights
  author: 6 Bronte

Linus
  vocation: 4 poet 8 musician
  father: 6 Apollo
  mother: 8 Psamathe
  inventor of: 6 melody, rhythm
  identified with: 5 crops 9 withering 10 harvesting
  student: 8 Hercules
  killed by: 8 Hercules

Liod
  also: 4 Ljod 5 Hliod
  origin: 12 Scandinavian
  mentioned in: 8 Volsunga
  husband: 7 Volsung
  daughter: 5 Signy
  son: 7 Sigmund

lion 3 cat 6 cougar 7 wildcat 9 celebrity 12 man of the hour 15 king of the jungle
  group of: 5 pride
  constellation of: 3 Leo

lionhearted 4 bold 5 brave 6 heroic 7 valiant 8 fearless, intrepid, stalwart, unafraid, valorous 9 audacious, dauntless 10 courageous 11 indomitable 12 stouthearted

Lion in Winter, The
  director: 13 Anthony Harvey
  cast: 10 Jane Merrow 11 Peter O'Toole (Henry II) 13 Timothy Dalton 14 Anthony Hopkins 16 Katharine Hepburn (Eleanor of Aquitaine)
  Oscar for: 7 actress (Hepburn)

lionize 5 deify, exalt 6 admire, praise, revere 7 acclaim, adulate, ennoble, flatter, glorify 8 enshrine, eulogize 9 celebrate, glamorize 10 aggrandize 11 immortalize

lion's share 4 bulk, most 8 majority 9 major part 11 greater part 13 preponderance

lip 3 lap, rim 4 brim, edge, kiss, lick, wash 5 apron, mouth, spout, utter 6 labial, labium, margin 8 backtalk, labellum 9 insincere 10 embouchure, mouthpiece 11 superficial

Lipchitz, Jacques
  real name: 17 Chaim Yakob Lipchiz
  born: 9 Lithuania 11 Druskieniki 12 Druskininkai
  artwork: 4 Head 6 Bather, Figure 7 Harpist 9 Sacrifice 10 Prometheus 11 Benediction, Joie de Vivre 12 Peace on Earth 14 Man with a Guitar 15 Acrobats on a Ball, Man with Mandolin, Song of the Vowels 17 Notre Dame de Liesse, Sailor with a Guitar 19 Pierrot with Clarinet, Return of the Prodigal 24 Virgin of the Inverted Heart

Lipmann, Fritz Albert
  field: 12 biochemistry
  discovered: 9 Coenzyme A
  awarded: 10 Nobel Prize

Lippi, Filippino
  born: 5 Italy, Prato
  father: 15 Fra Filippo Lippi
  artwork: 20 The Vision of St Bernard 24 The Life of St Thomas Aquinas 26 The Lives of Sts Philip and John

Lippi, Fra Filippo
  born: 5 Italy 8 Florence
  son: 9 Filippino
  artwork: 15 Madonna and Child, The Feast of Herod 19 The Tarquinia Madonna 21 Coronation of the Virgin 25 The Madonna Adoring Her Child

liqueur 3 ale 4 beer, grog 5 booze, drink, hooch 7 alcohol, potable, spirits 8 beverage, potation 9 aqua vitae, drinkable, inebriant, moonshine 10 intoxicant
  almond: 8 amaretto
  anise: 8 absinthe
  apple: 8 calvados
  apricot: 10 abricotine
  caraway: 6 kummel 7 aquavit
  chocolate: 12 creme de cacao
  citrus: 10 goldwasser, liquor d'or
  coffee: 6 Kahlua
  grape: 6 Metaxa
  herb: 6 pernod 7 raspail 10 vielle cure 11 fiori alpini
  honey: 8 Drambuie
  medicinal: 11 Benedictine
  mint: 13 creme de menthe
  orange: 6 strega 7 curacao 9 cointreau 12 Grand Marnier
  raspberry: 9 framboise

liquid 5 drink, fluid 6 melted, molten, thawed 7 potable 8 beverage, solution

liquidate 3 hit, pay 4 kill 5 clear, erase, waste 6 cancel, murder, pay off, rub out, settle, wind up 7 abolish, break up, destroy, wipe out 8 close out, conclude, demolish 9 discharge, dispose of, eradicate, put to rest, terminate 10 account for, do away with 11 assassinate

liquor 3 gin, rum, rye **5** booze, broth, hooch, juice, sauce, vodka **6** brandy, liquid, Scotch **7** bourbon, extract, spirits, whiskey **9** drippings **10** inebriants **11** intoxicants

    measure: 4 pint, pony, shot **5** fifth, quart **6** jigger, magnum

Lir see **3** Ler

Lisbon
    capital of: 8 Portugal
    landmark:
        castle: **11** Saint George
        monastery: **9** Jeronimos
        square: **10** Black Horse
        tower: **5** Belem
    Moorish name: 7 Lixbuna
    ocean: 8 Atlantic
    Portuguese: 6 Lisboa
    river: 5 Tagus
    Roman name: 14 Felicitas Julia
    rulers: 5 Moors **6** French, Romans **7** British, Germans, Spanish **11** Phoenicians

Leconte de Lisle, Charles
    author of: 14 Poemes Antiques, Poemes Barbares

lissome 5 agile, lithe, quick **6** limber, lively, nimble, pliant, supple **7** slender **8** delicate, graceful **9** lithesome, sprightly **11** light-footed

list 3 tip **4** bend, heel, lean, roll, tilt **5** index, slant, slate, slope, table **6** careen, muster, record, roster **7** catalog, in cline, leaning **8** register, schedule, tabulate **9** catalogue, inventory

listen 4 hark, hear, heed, list **6** attend **7** give ear, hearken **8** give heed, listen in, overhear **9** be all ears, bend an ear, eavesdrop **10** take notice **12** pay attention

listener 3 ear **6** hearer **7** auditor **10** overhearer **12** eavesdropper

Lister, Joseph
    field: 7 surgeon **8** medicine
    nationality: 7 British
    pioneer of: 17 antiseptic surgery

listless 4 down, dull, lazy **6** dreamy, drowsy, leaden, mopish, torpid **7** languid **8** in active, indolent, lifeless, sluggish **9** apathetic, enervated, lethargic, soporific **10** phlegmatic, spiritless **11** indifferent, unconcerned **12** uninterested **13** lackadaisical

Liston, Charles
    nickname: 5 Sonny
    sport: 6 boxing
    class: 11 heavyweight

Liszt, Franz (Ferencz)
    born: 7 Hungary, Raiding
    composer of: 5 Dante (symphony), Faust (symphony) **8** Christus **9** Psalm XIII **10** Nuages gris **13** Psalm Thirteen **17** Years of Pilgrimage **18** Annees de Pelerinage **19** Hungarian Rhapsodies **22** The Legend of St Elizabeth

Litae
    daughters of: 4 Zeus
    personify: 6 prayer

litany 4 list **7** account, catalog, recital **9** catalogue, narration, rendition **10** recitation, repetition **11** description, enumeration

lit de justice 32 formal sessions of French parliament
    literally: 12 bed of justice

literacy 7 culture **8** learning **9** erudition **11** edification, refinement, learnedness, scholarship **12** intelligence **13** enlightenment

literal 4 real, true **5** exact **6** actual, direct, honest, strict **7** correct, factual, precise, prosaic **8** accurate, faithful, reliable, truthful, verbatim **9** authentic **10** adlitteram, dependable, meticulous, scrupulous, undisputed **11** trustworthy, undeviating, word-for-word **12** matter-of-fact **13** authoritative, conscientious, unimaginative, unimpeachable

literary 6 poetic **7** bookish, of books **8** artistic, lettered, literate **12** intellectual

literate 7 learned **8** cultured, educated, lettered, literary, schooled, well-read **12** well-informed **13** knowledgeable

literati 9 highbrows **12** connoisseurs **13** intellectuals **14** intelligentsia

literature 4 lore **5** books, works **6** papers, theses **7** letters **8** classics, writings **9** treatises **11** scholarship **12** publications **13** belles lettres, dissertations

lithe 5 agile **6** limber, nimble, pliant, supple **7** lissome, pliable **8** bendable, flexible, graceful

Lithgow, John
    roles: 9 Footloose **17** Terms of Endearment **21** Harry and the Hendersons **23** The World According to Garp

lithium
    chemical symbol: 2 Li

Lithuania
    other/former name: 5 Litva **7** Lietuva **33** Lithuanian Soviet Socialist Republic
    capital/largest city: 5 Vilna **6** Kaunas **7** Vilnius
    others: 4 Balt, Lett **5** Aesti, Kouno, Memel **6** Kovnac **7** Jel gava, Palanga, Telsiai **8** Ignalina, Kapsukas, Klaipeda, Siauliai **9** Panevezys **10** Elektrenai
    government: 8 republic
    monetary unit: 3 lit **5** marka **6** centas **7** ostmark, skatiku **8** auksinas
    lake: 5 Dysna
    mountain: 15 Samogitian Hills
    highest point: 9 Juozapine
    river: 5 Neman, Neris, Rusne **6** Dubysa, Nieman, Viliya **7** Nemunas, Nevezis, Nevezys **8** Pregolya
    sea: 6 Baltic
    physical feature:
        lagoon: **8** Courland, Kuronian
    people: 4 Balt, Lett **5** Zhmud **6** Jewish, Litvak, Polish **7** Aistian, Russian, Yatvyag **10** Lithuanian, Samogitian **11** Belorussian
    language: 5 Zmudz **6** Baltic **10** Lithuanian
    religion: 8 Lutheran **13** Roman Catholic

litigation 4 suit 7 contest, dispute, lawsuit
10 contention, day in court 11 controversy,
disputation, legal action, prosecution

litter 3 bed 4 heap, junk, lair, mess, nest,
pile 5 issue, strew, trash, young 6 debris, jumble, pallet, refuse 7 bedding, clutter, kittens, progeny, puppies, rubbish,
scatter 8 leavings 9 offspring, stretcher

little 3 bit, dot, jot, wee 4 dash, drop, hint,
iota, mean, mild, tiny, whit 5 brief, crumb,
elfin, faint, fleet, hasty, never, petty,
pinch, pygmy, quick, scant, short, small,
speck, trace 6 bantam, hardly, meager,
minute, narrow, paltry, petite, rarely, seldom, skimpy, slight, trifle 7 minimum, modicum, not much, passing, stunted, trivial 8
dwarfish, fragment, inferior, mediocre, not
at all, not often, particle, piddling, pittance,
scarcely, slightly, some what, trifling, unworthy 9 by no means, deficient, hardly
any, itsy-bitsy, itty-bitty, miniature, momentary, pint-sized, third-rate, worthless 10 diminutive, inflexible, negligible, short-lived,
suggestion, undersized 11 commonplace,
Lilliputian, microscopic, of no account,
opinionated, pocket-sized, scarcely any,
small amount, unimportant 12 insufficient,
run-of-the-mill, short-sighted 13 infinitesimal, insignificant, next to nothing

Little Annie Rooney
  creator: 14 Darrell McClure

Little Artha
  nickname of: 11 Jack Johnson

Little Big Man
  author: 12 Thomas Berger
  director: 10 Arthur Penn
  cast: 11 Faye Dunaway 12 Martin Balsam 13 Dustin Hoffman (Jack Crabb) 14
  Chief Dan George 15 Richard Mulligan

little by little
  French: 7 peu a peu
  Spanish: 9 poco a poco

Little Caesar
  director: 11 Mervyn LeRoy
  cast: 13 Glenda Farrell 15 Edward G
  Robinson (Caesar Enrico Bandello) 18
  Douglas Fairbanks Jr

Little Daedala
  origin: 7 Boeotia
  event: 8 festival
  honoring: 4 Hera, Zeus

Little Dorrit
  author: 14 Charles Dickens
  character: 3 Amy (Little Dorrit), Tip 4
  Rugg 5 Casby, Fanny, Flora, Gowan 6 Affery, Merdle, Pancks, Rigaud (Blandois) 7
  Meagles 8 Mr F's Aunt 9 Mrs Merdle 10
  Flintwinch 13 Arthur Clennam, William
  Dorrit 16 Monsieur Blandois, Young John
  Chivery

Little Drummer Girl, The
  author: 11 John Le Carre

Little Emily, Little Em'ly
  character in: 16 David Copperfield
  author: 7 Dickens

Little Fox
  constellation of: 9 Vulpecula

Little Foxes, The
  author: 14 Lillian Hellman
  character: 13 Regina Giddens
  director: 12 William Wyler
  cast: 10 Bette Davis (Regina) 12 Teresa
  Wright 14 Richard Carlson 15 Herbert
  Marshall
  prequel: 22 Another Part of the Forest

Little Gidding
  author: 7 T S Eliot

Little Girls
  author: 14 Elizabeth Bowen

Little House on the Prairie
  author: 18 Laura Ingalls Wilder
  character: 6 Albert 7 Dr Baker 8 Rev
  Alden 9 Mr Edwards 10 Andy Garvey,
  Lars Hanson, Nels Oleson 11 Adam
  Kendall, Alice Garvey, Mary Ingalls 12
  Grace Ingalls, Laura Ingalls, Nellie
  Oleson, Willie Oleson 13 Carrie Ingalls,
  Harriet Oleson 14 Charles Ingalls, Eva
  Beadle Simms, Jonathan Garvey 15 Caroline Ingalls
  cast: 10 Dabbs Greer, Kevin Hagen 11
  Karl Swenson, Merlin Olsen, Richard Bull
  12 Hersha Parady, Karen Grassle, Victor
  French 13 Alison Arngrim, Linwood
  Boomer, Michael Landon 14 Melissa Gilbert 15 Jonathon Gilbert, Sidney Greenbush, Wendy Turnbeaugh 16 Brenda
  Turnbeaugh, Charlotte Gilbert, Lindsay
  Greenbush 17 Katherine McGregor, Matthew Laborteaux, Patrick Laborteaux 18
  Melissa Sue Anderson
  setting: 6 Winoka 9 Minnesota, Plum
  Creek 11 Walnut Grove

Little John
  character in: 9 Robin Hood

Little King, The
  creator: 10 Otto Soglow
  technique: 9 pantomine

little-known 6 unsung 7 obscure, unnoted
10 unrenowned

Little Learning, A
  author: 11 Evelyn Waugh

Little Lord Fauntleroy
  author: 15 Frances H Burnett

Little Lulu
  creator: 14 Marge Henderson

Little Match Girl, The
  author: 21 Hans Christian Andersen

Little Men
  author: 15 Louisa May Alcott

Little Mermaid, The
  author: 21 Hans Christian Andersen

Little Minister, The
  author: 12 James M Barrie

Little Mo
  nickname of: 15 Maureen Connolly

Little Nemo in Slumberland
  creator: 11 Winsor McCay
  character: 6 Dr Pill 8 cannibal, princess
  clown: 4 Flip
  dog: 6 Blutch

little one 3 tot **4** babe, baby, tyke **5** child **6** infant, wee one **7** toddler

Little Orphan Annie
   creator: **10** Harold Gray
   character:
     foster father: **13** Daddy Warbucks
     dog: **5** Sandy
     saying: **13** Leapin' Lizards

Little Prince, The
   author: **21** Antoine de Saint-Exupery

Little Rhody
   nickname of: **11** Rhode Island

Little Tramp
   nickname of: **14** Charlie Chaplin

Little Women
   author: **15** Louisa May Alcott
   character: **6** Laurie (Theodore Laurence), Marmee **10** John Brooke **14** Professor Bhaer
   March sisters: **2** Jo **3** Amy, Meg **4** Beth
   director:
     1933 version: **11** George Cukor
     1949 version: **11** Mervyn LeRoy
   cast (1933): **9** Paul Lukas **10** Frances Dee, Jean Parker **11** Joan Bennett **16** Katharine Hepburn (Jo)
   cast (1949): **9** Mary Astor **10** Janet Leigh **11** June Allyson **12** Peter Lawford **14** Margaret O'Brien **15** Elizabeth Taylor

liturgical 6 ritual **10** ceremonial **11** ceremonious, sacramental

liturgy 4 mass, rite **6** ritual **7** service, worship **8** ceremony, services **9** communion, sacrament

lituus
   form: **5** staff
   shape: **7** crooked

Lityerses
   father: **9** King Midas
   held: **15** reaping contests
   killed: **6** losers

livable, liveable 4 cozy, snug **5** comfy, homey **8** bearable, passable, pleasant, suitable **9** agreeable, endurable, enjoyable, habitable, tolerable **10** acceptable, convenient, gratifying, satisfying, worthwhile **11** comfortable

live 2 be **3** hot **4** bunk, feed, stay **5** abide, afire, aglow, alive, dwell, exist, fiery, lodge, quick, stand, vital **6** ablaze, active, aflame, alight, at hand, billet, bodily, endure, hold on, living, obtain, occupy, redhot, remain, reside, settle, thrive **7** animate, at issue, be alive, blazing, breathe, burning, current, flaming, fleshly, going on, ignited, persist, prevail, subsist, survive **8** existent, flourish, get ahead, get along, have life, increase, multiply, physical, pressing, take root, up-to-date, white-hot **9** breathing, corporeal **10** draw breath

live and keep well
   Latin: **11** vive valeque

Live and Let Die
   author: **10** Ian Fleming

live dissolutely 7 carouse, debauch **9** dissipate **11** overindulge

livelihood 3 job **5** trade **6** career, living, metier **7** calling, support, venture **8** business, position, vocation **9** situation **10** enterprise, line of work, occupation, profession, sustenance **11** maintenance, subsistence, undertaking

liveliness 3 pep, zip **5** vigor **7** agility **8** alacrity, vitality, vivacity **9** animation, briskness, eagerness **10** ebullience, nimbleness **13** sprightliness

lively 5 alert, brisk, eager, peppy, perky, vivid **6** active, ardent, bouncy **7** buoyant, excited, fervent, intense **8** animated, spirited, vigorous **9** energetic, excitable, sprightly, vivacious **12** enthusiastic

liven 4 buoy **5** cheer, elate, pep up **6** perk up, vivify **7** animate, delight, enliven, fortify, gladden, hearten, punch up, quicken **8** brighten, embolden, energize, inspirit **10** exhilarate, invigorate, strengthen

liver
   stores: **8** glycogen
   color: **3** red **5** brown
   produces: **4** bile **10** blood cells

Livermore Larruper
   nickname of: **7** Max Baer

livery 4 garb, suit **5** dress **6** attire **7** costume, raiment, regalia, uniform **8** clothing **9** vestments

Lives of a Bengal Lancer
   director: **13** Henry Hathaway
   cast: **10** Gary Cooper **12** Franchot Tone **14** Sir Guy Standing **15** Richard Cromwell

Lives of the Poets, The
   author: **13** Samuel Johnson

live through 4 know **7** survive, undergo **9** go through **10** experience

livid 3 mad **5** angry, irate, riled, vexed **6** fuming, galled, purple, raging **7** bruised, enraged, furious **8** contused, incensed, inflamed, outraged, provoked, wrathful **10** indignant, steamed up, ticked off **10** discolored, infuriated **11** exasperated

living 3 job **4** life, live, work **5** alive, being, quick, trade **6** active, bodily, career, extant, income **7** animate, calling, fleshly, going on, organic, venture **8** business, embodied, enduring, existent, existing, material, up-to-date, vocation **9** animation, breathing, corporeal, existence, incarnate, lifestyle, operative, permanent, remaining, surviving, way of life **10** employment, enterprise, having life, in the flesh, line of work, livelihood, occupation, persisting, prevailing, profession, subsisting, sustenance **11** maintenance, subsistence **13** drawing breath

living being 8 creature, organism

living conditions 10 atmosphere **11** environment **13** circumstances

living picture
   French: **13** tableau vivant

living quarters 4 home **5** abode, house **6** billet **7** housing, lodging, shelter **8** domicile, dwelling, quarters **9** apartment, residence **10** habitation **13** dwelling place

Livy
also: 11 Titus Livius
author of: 13 Ab urbe condita 26 From the Foundation of the City

lizard 3 dab, eft, uma 4 adda, gila, newt, seps, tegu 5 agama, anole, anoli, gecko, idler, shrink 6 aguana, dragon, iguana, komodo, moloch 7 lounger, monitor, reptile, saurian 8 dinosaur, lacerata, scorpion 9 alligator, blind worm, chameleon, crocodile, galliwasp 10 chuckwalla, glass snake, horned toad, salamander 11 gila monster 12 Komodo dragon
characteristic: 6 scales 7 molting 9 oviparous 11 cold-blooded 12 regeneration
constellation of: 7 Lacerta

Ljod see 4 Liod

llama 6 alpaca, kechua, mammal, vicuna 7 guanaco 8 ungulate 13 Peruvian sheep

Llewellyn, Richard
author of: 19 How Green Was My Valley

Llew Llaw Gyffes
origin: 5 Welsh
father: 7 Gwydion
mother: 9 Arianhrod
wife: 10 Blodenwedd
curses bestowed by: 9 Arianhrod

Lloyd
origin: 5 Welsh
form: 8 magician
cast spells upon: 7 Pryderi

Lloyd, Harold
born: 10 Burchard NE
roles: 9 Feet First 10 Safety Last 11 The Freshman 13 The Kid Brother

Llud
also: 4 Ludd, Nudd
origin: 5 Welsh
king of: 7 Britain
rid kingdom of: 6 plague
famous for: 10 generosity

Llyr
origin: 5 Welsh
son: 10 Manawyddan
corresponds to: 3 Ler, Lir

load 3 try, vex 4 care, fill, haul, heap, lade, pack, pile 5 cargo, crush, stack, stuff, worry 6 burden, hamper, hinder, lading, misery, strain, weight 7 afflict, carload, freight, oppress, trouble 8 capacity, contents, encumber, handicap, pressure, shipload, shipment 9 overwhelm, plane load, truckload, wagonload, weigh down 10 affliction, deadweight, depression, misfortune, oppression 11 encumbrance

loads 4 lots, much 5 heaps, piles, scads 6 oodles, plenty 14 more than enough

loaf 4 idle, loll 5 dally 6 be lazy 7 goof off 8 kill time, malinger 9 do nothing, gold brick, laze about, waste time 10 take it easy 12 lounge around

loafer 3 bum 4 shoe 5 idler 6 no-good 7 laggard, shirker, sponger, wastrel 8 deadbeat, loiterer, sluggard 9 goldbrick, lazybones 10 lazy person, malingerer, ne'er-do-well 11 couch potato 12 lounge lizard 15 drugstore cowboy

French: 7 flaneur

loan 4 lend 5 allow 6 credit 7 advance, lending 8 mortgage 9 advancing

loath 4 loth 6 averse 7 against, counter, hostile, opposed 8 inimical 9 reluctant, resisting, unwilling 10 indisposed, set against 11 disinclined

loathe 4 hate 5 abhor, scorn 6 detest, eschew 7 deplore, despise, disdain, dislike 9 abominate 10 blench from, flinch from, recoil from, shrink from 11 keep clear of, shy away from 12 draw back from 14 be unable to bear, find disgusting, view with horror 16 have no stomach for

loathing 4 hate 5 odium 6 hatred 7 disgust, dislike 8 aversion, distaste 9 antipathy, repulsion, revulsion 10 abhorrence, repugnance 11 abomination, detestation

loathsome 4 foul, mean, rank, vile 5 nasty 6 odious 7 hateful 8 abhorrent, invidious, obnoxious, offensive, repugnant, repulsive, revolting, sickening 10 abominable, despicable, detestable, disgusting, nauseating, unbearable 11 distasteful

lobby 5 foyer 8 anteroom, politick 9 vestibule 11 antechamber, pull strings, waiting room 12 entrance hall

local 6 narrow, native, nearby 7 insular, limited 8 citywide, confined, regional 9 adjoining, homegrown, parochial, sectional 10 provincial 11 territorial 12 neighborhood 13 circumscribed

locale 4 area, site, spot, zone 6 region 7 quarter, section, setting 8 locality, location, precinct, province, vicinity 12 neighborhood

locality 4 area, site, spot, zone 5 place 6 locale, region 7 quarter, section 8 district, location, precinct, province, vicinity 9 territory 12 neighborhood

locate 3 fix, put 4 find, live, post, seat, stay 5 dwell, place 6 detect, move to, reside, settle 7 deposit, discern, hit upon, set down, situate, station, uncover, unearth 8 come upon, meet with, pinpoint 9 establish, ferret out, light upon, search out, stumble on, track down 10 settle down 12 put down roots

location 4 site, spot 5 place 6 locale 8 district, position 9 situation 11 whereabouts 12 neighborhood

Lochinvar
character in: 7 Marmion
author: 5 Scott

lock 3 bar, dam, pen 4 bang, bolt, cage, coil, curl, grab, grip, hank, hold, hook, jail, join, link, tuft 5 catch, clamp, clasp, grasp, latch, seize, skein, tress, unite 6 clinch, coop up, fasten, lock up, secure, shut in 7 confine, embrace, entwine, grapple, impound, padlock, ringlet 8 dock gate, imprison 9 canal gate, fastening, floodgate, interlink 10 intertwine, sluice gate 11 incarcerate

lock, cylinder
invented by: 4 Yale

Lockhart, Gene
  daughter: 12 June Lockhart
  granddaughter: 11 Ann Lockhart
  born: 6 Canada, London 7 Ontario
  roles: 12 Madame Bovary 16 Death of a
    Salesman 19 The Inspector General 20
    Abe Lincoln in Illinois
lock horns 4 feud, tiff 5 argue, brawl,
  clash, fight 7 dispute, quarrel, wrangle 8
  squabble 9 altercate
Lockit
  character in: 12 Beggar's Opera
  author: 3 Gay
lockup 3 jug, pen 4 jail, stir 5 clink, pokey
  6 cooler, prison 7 slammer 8 big house,
  hoosegow 11 reformatory 12 penitentiary
lock up 3 pen 4 cage, jail 6 coop up, secure 7 confine, impound 8 imprison, restrain, restrict 11 incarcerate
Lockyer, Joseph Norman
  field: 9 astronomy
  nationality: 7 British
  discovered: 6 helium
loco citato 15 in the place cited
  abbreviation: 6 loc cit
locomotive
  invented by:
  electric: 4 Vail
  experimental: 6 Fenton, Hedley 10
    Stephenson, Trevithick
  first US: 6 Cooper
  practical: 10 Stephenson
Locrian Ajax *see* 4 Ajax
Locrus
  king of: 8 Locrians
locust 7 Robinia
  varieties: 4 moss 5 black, honey, mossy,
    swamp, sweet, water 6 clammy, yellow 7
    African, bristly 8 ship-mast 10 West In-
    dian 13 Allegheny moss, South American
locution 4 term 5 idiom, trope, usage 6
  phrase, saying 7 wording 8 idiolect, phrasing 9 set phrase, utterance, verbalism 10
  expression 11 phraseology, regionalism 12
  turn of phrase 14 figure of speech
lode 3 bed 4 seam 7 deposit
lodge 3 bed, hut 4 camp, file, room, stay 5
  cabin, catch, hotel, house, motel, put up 6
  billet, harbor, resort, submit 7 cottage,
  quarter, shelter, sojourn 8 register
lodging 4 room 8 quarters 13 accommodation
Lofn
  origin: 12 Scandinavian
  goddess of: 18 forbidden marriages
  permission given by: 4 Odin 5 Othin
loft 3 lob 5 attic, pop up 6 belfry, garret 7
  balcony, gallery, hit high, mansard 8 top
  floor 9 attic room, throw high 10 clerestory
loftiness 5 pride 9 arrogance 11 haughtiness 13 imperiousness 16 superciliousness
Lofting, Hugh
  author of: 11 Dr Doolittle
lofty 4 cold, high, tall 5 aloof, grand, great,
  noble, proud 6 lordly, mighty, remote,
  snooty 7 distant, eminent, exalted,
haughty, leading, soaring, stately,
stuck-up, sublime 8 arrogant, elevated, glorious, imposing, insolent, majestic,
puffed-up, scornful, snobbish, superior,
towering 9 conceited, dignified, imperious, important 10 disdainful, hoity-toity,
preeminent 11 high ranking, illustrious, patronizing 12 high-reaching 13 condescending, distinguished, high-and-mighty,
self-important
lofty bearing 7 dignity, majesty 10 augustness 11 stateliness
log 5 block, diary, stump 6 docket, lumber,
  record, timber 7 account, daybook, journal,
  logbook 8 calendar, schedule
loges 5 boxes 7 balcony 9 mezzanine
loggia 5 lanai, porch 6 arcade, piazza 7
  balcony, gallery
Logi
  origin: 12 Scandinavian
  form: 3 man
  personifies: 4 fire
  defeated: 4 Loki
logic 5 sense 6 reason 7 cogency 8 analysis, argument 9 coherence, deduction,
  good sense, induction 10 dialectics
logical 5 clear, sound, valid 6 cogent, likely
  7 germane 8 coherent, rational, relevant,
  sensible 9 deducible, pertinent, plausible
  10 analytical, consistent, most likely, reasonable 11 enlightened, intelligent 13 well-
  organized
logos 4 word 5 ratio 6 saying, speech 7
  thought 9 discourse, reckoning 10 proportion
logy 4 dull 5 inert, tired, weary 6 drowsy,
  groggy, sleepy, torpid 8 comatose, torp-
  less, listless, sluggish 9 enervated, inanimate, lethargic 10 phlegmatic 12 hebetudi-
  nous
Lohengrin
  opera by: 6 Wagner
  character: 4 Elsa 6 Ortrud 9 Gottfried
    (Duke of Brabant) 25 Count Frederick of
    Telramund
Lohengrin
  origin: 8 Germanic
  knight of: 9 Holy Grail
  father: 8 Parsifal, Parzival
loiter 4 idle, laze, loaf, loll, lurk 5 dally,
  skulk, slink, tarry 6 dawdle 10 dillydally,
  hang around 11 hover around 12 shilly-
  shally
Loki
  origin: 12 Scandinavian
  mentioned in: 9 Lokasenna
  god of: 4 fire
  son: 6 Fenrir, Fenris
  daughter: 3 Hel
  fathered: 10 Jormungand 11 Iormun-
    gandr, Jormungandr 14 Midgard Serpent
  mother of his children: 9 Angerboda,
    Angrbodha, Angurboda
  caused death of: 5 Baldr 6 Balder, Bal-
    dur
  form: 5 giant
  extorted treasure from: 7 Andvari

function: 4 evil 6 strife

Lolita
author: 15 Vladimir Nabokov
character: 14 Humbert Humbert
director: 14 Stanley Kubrick
based on novel by: 15 Vladimir Nabokov
cast: 7 Sue Lyon (Lolita) 10 James Mason (Humbert Humbert) 12 Peter Sellers 14 Shelley Winters

loll 3 sag 4 drag, drop, flap, flop, idle, lean, loaf 5 droop, relax, slump 6 dangle, dawdle, lounge, repose, slouch, sprawl 7 goof off, recline 8 flop over, languish

Lollobrigida, Gina
born: 5 Italy 7 Subiaco
roles: 7 Trapeze 14 Anne of Brooklyn, The Wayward Wife 15 Solomon and Sheba 20 Buona Sera Mrs Campbell 27 The World's Most Beautiful Woman

Loman, Willy
character in: 16 Death of a Salesman
author: 6 Miller

Lombard, Carole
real name: 15 Jane Alice Peters
husband: 10 Clark Gable
born: 11 Fort Wayne IN
roles: 12 My Man Godfrey 13 Nothing Sacred, To Be Or Not To Be 16 Twentieth Century

Lome
capital of: 4 Togo

London
airport: 7 Gatwick 8 Heathrow, Stansted
architect: 4 Wren
area: 4 Soho 6 Camden 7 Brixton, Chelsea, Holborn, Pimlico 8 Vauxhall 9 Bayswater, Belgravia, Islington, Southwark 10 Bloomsbury, Kensington, Paddington, Shoreditch 11 Notting Hill, St John's Wood 13 Knightsbridge
capital of: 7 England 12 Great Britain 13 United Kingdom
landmark: 6 Big Ben 8 Hyde Park 9 Whitehall, Wimbledon 11 Regent's Park, Saint James's, Tate Gallery, Tower Bridge 12 Covent Garden, London Bridge 13 British Museum, Tower of London 14 British Library, Speaker's Corner 15 National Gallery, Trafalgar Square 16 Buckingham Palace, Piccadilly Circus, Westminster Abbey 17 Kensington Gardens, Royal Festival Hall, Westminster Palace 18 Houses of Parliament 19 Saint Paul's Cathedral 23 Victoria and Albert Museum
police: 7 bobbies
established by: 13 Sir Robert Peel
prime minister's residence: 16 Ten Downing Street
river: 6 Thames
Roman name: 9 Londinium
subway: 11 Underground

London, Jack
author of: 9 White Fang 10 The Sea Wolf 16 The Call of the Wild

lone 4 only, sole 5 alone 6 single, unique 8 isolated, singular, solitary, unpaired 9 unabetted 10 individual, unattended, unescorted 13 companionless, unaccompanied

loneliness 9 isolation, seclusion 12 lonesomeness, solitariness 14 friendlessness

Loneliness of the Long Distance Runner, The
director: 14 Tony Richardson
cast: 11 Avis Bunnage, Peter Madden 12 Tom Courtenay 15 Michael Redgrave

lonely 6 remote 7 forlorn 8 deserted, desolate, forsaken, hermitic, isolated, lonesome, secluded, solitary, unsocial 9 by oneself, reclusive, withdrawn 10 friendless, unattended 11 uninhabited, unpopulated 12 unfrequented 13 companionless, unaccompanied

Lone Ranger, The
character: 5 Tonto
cast: 8 John Hart 12 Clayton Moore 14 Jay Silverheels
horse: 5 Scout 6 Silver
Lone Ranger used: 13 silver bullets
theme: 19 William Tell Overture

lonesome 5 alone, aloof 6 lonely 7 forlorn, insular 8 desolate, detached, forsaken 9 alienated, withdrawn 10 friendless, unfriended 13 companionless

Lone Star State
nickname of: 5 Texas

long 4 hope, lust, pine, sigh, want, wish 5 covet, crave, yearn 6 aspire, hanker, hunger, thirst 7 lengthy, spun out 8 drawn-out, extended, have a yen, in length, unending 9 elongated, extensive, prolonged 10 be bent on, protracted 11 far-reaching, have a desire 12 from end to end, interminable, outstretched

Long, Crawford Williamson
field: 8 medicine
first used: 5 ether

Longaville
character in: 16 Love's Labour's Lost
author: 11 Shakespeare

Long Day's Journey into Night
author: 12 Eugene O'Neill
director: 11 Sidney Lumet
cast: 13 Dean Stockwell 14 Jason Robards Jr 15 Ralph Richardson 16 Katharine Hepburn

Longest Day, The
director: 10 Ken Annakin 12 Andrew Marton, Bernard Wicki
cast: 9 John Wayne, Mel Ferrer 10 Henry Fonda, Red Buttons, Robert Ryan, Rod Steiger 12 Peter Lawford
setting: 8 Normandy (Allied invasion)

Longevity
goddess of: 11 Anna Perenna

long-faced 4 glum 6 dismal, gloomy 7 doleful, unhappy 8 dejected, mournful 10 lugubrious 14 down in the mouth

Longfellow, Henry Wadsworth
author of: 8 Hyperion, (The Song of) Hiawatha 10 Evangeline 15 Paul Re-

vere's Ride 18 Tales of a Wayside Inn 21 The Wreck of the Hesperus 27 The Courtship of Miles Standish

longing 3 yen 4 wish 6 ardent, pining, thirst 7 craving, wishful 8 desirous, yearning 9 hankering, hungering 10 aspiration 11 languishing

long-lasting 7 chronic, lengthy, tedious 8 enduring, extended 9 prolonged 10 continuing, protracted

long live
    French: 4 vive

long past 3 old 5 olden 6 gone by, of yore 7 ancient, long ago 8 long gone

long-standing 4 long 5 hardy, hoary 6 rooted 7 abiding, ancient, chronic, durable, lasting 8 enduring, habitual, hallowed, unfading 9 confirmed, continual, long-lived, perennial, perpetual, venerable 10 continuous, deep-rooted, deep-seated, inveterate, persistent, persisting 11 long-lasting, time-honored 15 long-established

Longstreet, James
    served in: 8 Civil War
    side: 11 Confederate
    battle: 7 Bull Run 10 Gettysburg 11 Chickamauga 14 Fredericksburg 18 Wilderness Campaign
    after war joined: 10 Republicans
    US minister to: 6 Turkey

Long Voyage Home, The
    director: 8 John Ford
    based on play by: 12 Eugene O'Neill
    cast: 9 Ian Hunter, John Wayne 13 Wilfrid Lawson 14 Thomas Mitchell 15 Barry Fitzgerald

long-wearing 5 tough 6 strong, sturdy 7 durable, lasting 8 enduring 11 substantial

long-winded 5 wordy 6 prolix 7 lengthy, tedious, verbose 8 rambling 9 garrulous 10 digressive, discursive

long-windedness 8 rambling 9 garrulity, prolixity, verbosity, wordiness 14 discursiveness

Lonnrot, Elias
    author of: 8 Kalevala

look 3 air, see 4 cast, face, gape, gaze, mien, ogle, peek, peep, scan, seem, show, view 5 front, glare, guise, sight, stare, study, watch 6 appear, behold, glance, regard, survey 7 bearing, examine, exhibit, glimpse 8 demeanor, manifest, once-over, presence, scrutiny 10 appearance, be directed, cut a figure, expression, scrutinize 11 contemplate, counte nance, observation

look after 4 help 6 assist, defend 7 help out, protect 10 minister to 11 watch out for 17 take under one's wing

look askance at 7 condemn 8 object to 9 frown upon 10 disapprove 14 discountenance 15 take exception to 16 find unacceptable, view with disfavor

look at 3 see 4 view 6 behold, notice, regard 7 examine, inspect, witness 10 scrutinize

Look Back in Anger
    director: 14 Tony Richardson
    based on play by: 11 John Osborne
    cast: 7 Mary Ure 10 Edith Evans 11 Claire Bloom 13 Richard Burton 15 Donald Pleasance

look down on 7 despise, disdain 9 frown upon, patronize 10 condescend 13 put on airs with 14 hold in contempt

looker-on 6 viewer 7 watcher, witness 8 beholder, observer, onlooker 9 bystander, spectator

look for 4 seek 5 await 6 expect, pursue 7 hunt for 9 search for 10 anticipate

look for the woman
    French: 15 cherchez la femme

look forward to 5 await 6 expect 7 long for, wait for 9 pin hope on 10 anticipate 17 count the days until

Look Homeward, Angel
    author: 11 Thomas Wolfe
    character: 7 Ben Gant 9 Eliza Gant 10 Eugene Gant, Laura James, Oliver Gant 15 Margaret Leonard

Looking Backward
    author: 13 Edward Bellamy

look in the eye 4 defy, face 5 brave 8 confront 9 challenge

look into 5 probe 7 examine, explore 10 scrutinize 11 inquire into, investigate

lookout 4 heed 5 guard, scout, vigil 6 patrol, sentry 7 spotter 8 observer, sentinel, watchdog, watchman 9 alertness, attention, awareness, readiness, vigilance 10 precaution 11 guardedness, mindfulness, watchkeeper 12 surveillance, watchfulness

look out 4 mind 6 beware 8 take care, watch out 9 be careful, be on guard 11 take warning 12 be on the alert

look over 4 scan, skim 5 judge 6 assess, peruse, survey 7 dip into 8 appraise, evaluate 13 browse through, glance through

look through 4 scan, skim 6 browse, peruse 7 dip into 8 look over 9 check over 13 glance through

look toward 7 count on 10 anticipate 13 look forward to

look upon 3 see 4 view 6 be hold, gaze at, look at 7 observe, stare at

look upon as 4 deem, hold 5 count, judge, think 6 regard, view as 7 account, believe 8 consider, take to be

look up to 5 honor 6 admire, esteem, revere 7 respect 8 venerate

loom 4 hulk, rise, soar 5 tower 6 appear, ascend, emerge 8 stand out 9 take shape

loom, power
    invented by: 10 Cartwright

loop 3 eye 4 bend, coil, curl, furl, ring, roll, turn 5 braid, curve, noose, plait, twirl, twist, whorl 6 circle, eyelet, spiral 7 opening, ringlet 8 aperture, encircle, loophole 10 wind around 11 convolution, curve around

Loos, Anita
    author of: 22 Gentlemen Prefer Blondes

loose 4 fast, free, lewd, undo, wild 5 freed, let go, slack, untie, vague 6 freely, loosen, unbind, undone, untied, wanton 7 immoral, inexact, loosely, release, set free, slacken, unbound, uncaged, unchain, unleash, unloose, unyoked 8 careless, heedless, liberate, not tight, rakehell, unbridle, unchaste, unfasten, unjoined, untether 9 abandoned, debauched, dissolute, imprecise, liberated, libertine, unbridled, unchained, unleashed, unmanacle, un shackle 10 dissipated, inaccurate, licentious, not binding, profligate, unattached, unexacting, unfastened, unfettered, unhandcuff, untethered 11 not fastened, unconnected 12 unimprisoned 13 unconstrained

loose-fitting 4 limp 5 baggy, loose, slack 6 draped, droopy 7 sagging 9 overlarge, oversized

loosely connected 5 jerky 6 fitful 8 episodic, rambling 9 spasmodic, wandering 10 digressive, discursive, meandering

loosen 3 lax 4 ease, free, undo 5 break, relax, untie 6 limber, unbend, unbind 7 release, relieve, slacken, unchain, unscrew 8 liberate, unbuckle, unfasten, work free 10 emancipate

looseness 8 fastness, lewdness, wildness 9 slackness, vagueness 10 debauchery, immorality, inaccuracy, profligacy, wantonness 11 dissipation, dissolution, imprecision 12 carelessness, heedlessness, inexactitude 14 licentiousness

loot 3 rob 4 haul, raid, sack, swag, take 5 booty, prize, strip 6 boodle, fleece, pilfer, ravage, spoils 7 pillage, plunder, ransack 11 stolen goods

looter 5 thief 6 robber, vandal 7 brigand 8 pillager 9 despoiler, plunderer

lop 3 cut 4 chip, chop, crop, dock, flop, sned, snip, trim 5 droop, prune, sever 6 cut off, deduct, detach, remove, slouch 7 cut back 8 amputate, truncate

Lopez, Nancy
  sport: 4 golf
  husband: 9 Ray Knight
  plays: 8 baseball

lopsided 4 awry 5 askew 6 aslant, tipped, uneven 7 crooked, leaning, listing, slanted, tilting, unequal 8 cockeyed, inclined, slanting 9 irregular 10 asymmetric, off-balance, unbalanced 15 disproportional 16 disproportionate

loquacious 5 gabby, talky, windy, wordy 6 blabby, chatty, prolix 7 prating, verbose, voluble 8 babbling, chattery 9 garrulous, prattling, talkative 10 chattering, long-winded

loquitur 8 he speaks 9 she speaks

lord 4 king 5 chief, crown, ruler 6 leader, master 7 monarch 8 overlord, seignior, superior 9 commander, landowner, sovereign 10 landholder, proprietor
  Japanese: 6 daimyo
  Turkish: 3 beg, bey

Lord
  Latin: 7 Dominus

Lord be with you, the
  Latin: 15 Dominus vobiscum

Lord have mercy
  Greek: 12 Kyrie eleison

Lord Jim
  author: 12 Joseph Conrad
  character: 5 Stein 6 Marlow 9 Dain Waris 14 Gentleman Brown

lordliness 7 disdain 8 contempt 9 arrogance, insolence, loftiness 11 haughtiness 13 imperiousness 16 superciliousness

lordly 4 cold 5 aloof, bossy, grand, lofty, noble, proud, regal 6 august, remote, snooty 7 distant, elegant, eminent, exalted, haughty, stately, stuck-up 8 arrogant, despotic, imposing, majestic, princely, puffed-up, scornful, snobbish 9 conceited, dignified, imperious, sumptuous 10 disdainful, hoity-toity, tyrannical 11 dictatorial, domineering, magisterial, magnificent, patronizing 13 condescending, high-and-mighty, self-important

Lord of the Flies
  author: 14 William Golding

Lord of the Rings, The
  author: 10 J R R Tolkien

Lord Raingo
  author: 13 Arnold Bennett

Lord Weary's Castle
  author: 12 Robert Lowell

lore 7 beliefs, legends 10 traditions

Lorelei
  also: 7 Lurelei
  origin: 8 Germanic
  form: 5 nymph
  dwelling place: 5 cliff, Rhine
  lured: 7 boatmen
  caused shipwrecks by: 7 singing

Loren, Sophia
  real name: 14 Sofia Scicolone
  husband: 10 Carlo Ponti
  born: 4 Rome 5 Italy
  roles: 5 El Cid 8 Two Women (Oscar) 9 Arabesque, Houseboat 13 Man of La Mancha 14 The Black Orchid 18 Desire Under the Elms 20 Marriage Italian Style 21 A Countess from Hong Kong, The Pride and the Passion

Lorentz, Hendrik Anton
  field: 7 physics
  nationality: 5 Dutch
  discovered: 17 special relativity
  named for him: 21 Lorentz transformation 34 Lorentz-Fitzgerald Length Contraction
  awarded: 10 Nobel Prize

Loring, Eugene
  choreographer of: 11 Billy the Kid

Lorna Doone
  author: 11 R D Blackmore
  character: 8 John Ridd 9 Tom Faggus 11 Carver Doone 13 Sir Ensor Doone 14 Jeremy Stickles 15 Reuben Huckaback

Lorre, Peter
  real name: 16 Laszlo Lowenstein
  born: 7 Hungary 9 Rosenberg
  roles: 1 M 7 Mad Love 10 Casablanca,

The Verdict 12 The Big Circus 14 Three
Strangers 16 The Maltese Falcon 18
Crime and Punishment, The Mask of
Dimitrios

Lorry, Jarvis
character in: 16 A Tale of Two Cities
author: 7 Dickens

Los Angeles
airport: 3 LAX 7 Burbank 23 Los Angeles International
area: 6 Watts 6 Bel Air, Downey, Venice
7 Anaheim, Compton, Norwalk 8 Mar
Vista, Pasadena, Torrance, Westwood 9
Brentwood, Hollywood, Inglewood, Long
Beach 10 Culver City 11 Century City,
Garden Grove, Palos Verdes, Santa
Monica 12 Beverly Hills, Marina del Rey
16 Pacific Palisades
San Fernando Valley: 6 Encino 7
Tarzana, Van Nuys, Ventura 10 Northridge 11 Sherman Oaks
baseball team: 7 Dodgers
basketball team: 6 Lakers 8 Clippers
football team: 4 Rams 7 Express, Raiders
hockey team: 5 Kings
landmark: 5 Forum 10 Disneyland 11
Civic Center, Getty Museum, Watts Towers 12 Griffith Park 13 Farmers' Market,
Hollywood Bowl, Hollywood Park, La
Brea Tar Pits, Magic Mountain 15 Knott's
Berry Farm 16 Bonaventure Hotel 17
Norton Simon Museum 22 Grauman's
Chinese Theater 23 Griffith Park Observatory
mountains: 10 San Gabriel 11 Santa
Monica
nickname: 15 City of the Angels
street: 4 Vine 10 Rodeo Drive 12 Olvera
Street 15 Mulholland Drive 16 Van Nuys
Boulevard 17 Wilshire Boulevard 18 Hollywood Boulevard 20 Santa Monica Boulevard
university: 3 USC 4 UCLA 7 Caltech 10
Pepperdine 17 Occidental College 31
California Institute of Technology
lose 4 fail, miss 6 forget, ignore, mislay 7
confuse, forfeit 8 misplace 9 fail to win,
stray from 10 be the loser, fail to heed 11
be thrown off 12 be defeated in, be deprived of, suffer loss of, take a licking
lose control 5 break, crack 7 crack up 9
fall apart 10 go to pieces 15 go off the
deep end
lose faith 6 give up 7 despair 9 lose heart
10 have no hope 18 become disenchanted
lose force 3 die 7 run down 9 lose power
lose heart 6 give up 7 de spair 17 become
discouraged
lose one's cool 12 fly into a rage 13 become enraged, throw a tantrum 14 lose
one's temper 15 fly off the handle
loser 4 flop 7 failure 8 defeated 9 conquered 10 vanquished
lose track of 4 lose 9 let escape 11 lose
sight of

lose vigor 4 flag 5 droop 6 sicken, weaken,
wither 7 decline
Losing Battles
author: 11 Eudora Welty
loss 4 ruin 5 wreck 6 defeat, losing 7 licking, removal, undoing 8 overturn, riddance, wrecking ·9 abolition, mislaying,
privation 10 amount lost, demolition, extinction, forfeiture, misplacing, number lost 11 bereavement, deprivation,
destruction, dissolution, eradication, expenditure, extirpation
loss of life 5 death 8 fatality 9 mortality
lost 5 stray 6 absent, astray, killed, ruined,
wasted 7 lacking, mislaid, missing, misused, strayed, wrecked 8 absorbed,
murdered, perished, vanished, wiped out 9
abolished, destroyed, engrossed, misplaced, off-course 10 demolished, eradicated, extirpated, gone astray, misapplied,
squandered 11 annihilated, misdirected,
obliterated, preoccupied 12 exterminated
Lost Honor of Katharina Blum, The
author: 12 Heinrich Boll
Lost Horizon
author: 11 James Hilton
character: 10 Hugh Conway, Rutherford
12 Henry Barnard, Miss Brinklow 14 Father Perrault 20 Captain Mallison Chang
director: 10 Frank Capra
cast: 5 Margo 8 H B Warner, Sam Jaffe 9
Jane Wyatt 10 John Howard 12 Isabel Jewell, Ronald Colman 14 Thomas
Mitchell 19 Edward Everett Horton
setting: 5 Tibet
Lost Illusions
author: 14 Honore de Balzac
Lost in America
director: 12 Albert Brooks
cast: 12 Albert Brooks, Julie Hagerty
Lost in Space
character: 5 Robot 7 Don West 12
Judy Robinson, Will Robinson 13 Penny Robinson 14 Dr Zachary Smith 15
Maureen Robinson 16 Prof John Robinson
cast: 9 Billy Mumy 11 Guy Williams,
Mark Goddard 12 June Lockhart, Marta
Kristen 14 Jonathan Harris 16 Angela
Cartwright
ship: 9 Jupiter II
Lost in the Funhouse
author: 9 John Barth
Lost in the Stars
author: 15 Maxwell Anderson
lost in thought 7 pensive 8 absorbed 9 engrossed, wrapped up 13 contemplative, in
a brown study, introspective
Lost Lady, A
author: 11 Willa Cather
Lost Ones, The
author: 13 Samuel Beckett
Lost Patrol, The
director: 8 John Ford
cast: 8 Alan Hale 11 Wallace Ford 12
Boris Karloff 14 Victor McLaglen
score: 10 Max Steiner

Lost Weekend, The
   author: **14** Charles Jackson
   director: **11** Billy Wilder
   cast: **9** Jane Wyman, Mary Young **10**
   Frank Falen, Ray Milland **11** Philip Terry
   12 Doris Dowling **13** Howard da Silva
   Oscar for: **5** actor (Milland) **7** picture **8**
   director **10** screenplay
lot 4 fate, lots, many, much, plot **5** field,
patch, quota, share, straw, tract **6** oceans,
oodles, ration **7** counter, measure **8** beaucoup, property **9** allotment, allowance,
great deal
Lot
   grandfather: **5** Terah
   father: **5** Haran
   uncle: **7** Abraham
   son: **5** Ammon
   hometown: **5** Sodom
   rescued by: **6** angels
   fled to: **4** Zoar
lothario 3 rip **4** rake, roue, wolf **5** lover, Romeo, sheik **6** lecher **7** Don Juan, seducer,
swinger **8** Casanova, lover-boy **9** debauchee, debaucher, libertine, womanizer
10 lady-killer, profligate, sensualist **11** philanderer, skirt-chaser
Lothario
   character in: **15** The Fair Penitent
   author: **4** Rowe
Loti, Piere
   author of: **18** An Iceland Fisherman
lotion 4 balm, wash **5** salve **6** liquid **7** unction, unguent **8** cosmetic, liniment, ointment, solution **9** demulcent, emollient,
freshener, skin cream **10** after-shave,
astringent **11** conditioner, embrocation,
moisturizer
Lotis
   form: **5** nymph
   changed into: **4** tree **5** lotus
lotophagi
   means: **11** lotus-eaters
lots 4 much **5** heaps, loads, plots, scads **10**
quantities
lotus 7 Nelumbo **13** Nymphaea lotus
   varieties: **4** blue **5** water, white **6** sacred
   8 American, Egyptian **10** East Indian
lotus-eaters 9 lotophagi
loud 4 gaudy, noisy, showy, vivid **6** bright,
flashy, garish **7** blatant, booming, intense,
splashy **8** colorful, sonorous **9** clamorous, deafening **10** resounding, stentorian, thundering, vociferous **11** ear-
piercing, loudmouthed **12** earsplitting,
ostentatious
loud sound 4 bang, boom, clap, honk,
howl, peal, roar, slam, toot **5** blare, blast,
burst, crash **6** bellow, report, scream,
shriek **7** clatter, thunder **9** explosion **10**
detonation
Lou Grant
   character: **6** Animal **8** Joe Rossi **10** Art
   Donovan **11** Charlie Hume **12** Billie
   Newman **15** Margaret Pynchon
   cast: **10** Jack Bannon, Mason Adams **11**
   Edward Asner, Linda Kelsey **12** Robert

Walden **13** Nancy Marchand **14** Darryl
Anderson
   paper: **17** Los Angeles Tribune
   spinoff of: **18** Mary Tyler Moore Show
Louhi
   origin: **7** Finnish
   form: **9** sorceress
   mistress of: **7** Pohjola
   defeated by: **11** Vainamoinen
   enemy of: **5** Finns
Louis, Joe
   real name: **14** Joe Louis Barrow
   nickname: **11** Brown Bomber
   sport: **6** boxing
   class: **11** heavyweight
Louis, Morris
   born: **11** Baltimore MD
   artwork: **4** Veil **5** Signa **7** Stripes **8** Unfurled **15** Mountains and Sea
Louise
   opera by: **11** Charpentier
   character: **6** Julian
Louisiana
   abbreviation: **2** LA
   nickname: **5** Bayou, Sugar **6** Creole **7**
   Pelican
   capital: **10** Baton Rouge
   largest city: **10** New Orleans
   others: **5** Houma **6** Bunkie, Gretna,
   Kenner, Minden, Monroe, Ruston **7**
   Bastrop **8** Bogalusa **9** Lafayette,
   Opelousas **10** Alexandria, Shreveport **11**
   Lake Charles
   college: **3** LSU **6** Loyola, Tulane **7**
   Dillard, Newcomb **9** Grambling
   explorer: **7** La Salle **9** Iberville **13** Pierre
   Lemoyne
   feature:
     area: **5** bayou **13** French Quarter
     festival: **9** Mardi Gras
     music: **4** jazz
     stadium: **9** Sugar Bowl
     street: **7** Bourbon
   tribe: **4** Adai, Ioni, Rees, Waco **5** Caddo,
   Haini, Washa **6** Eyeish, Pawnee **7**
   Andarko, Arikara, Atakapa **8** Ovachita **9**
   Bayogoula, Nachitoch
   people: **5** Cajun **6** Creole **7** Acadian, pelican **8** Huey Long **14** Lillian Hellman,
   Louis Armstrong
   island: **5** Avery
   lake: **3** lat **4** latt **5** Caddo, Clear, Cross,
   Larto, White **6** Borgne, Saline **8** Dar-
   bonne, Maurepas **9** Bistineau, Calcasieu,
   Catahoula **10** False River **13** Pontchartrain
   land rank: **11** thirty-first
   mountain:
     highest point: **8** Driskill
   physical feature: **15** Head of the Passes
   17 coastal marshlands
     delta: **11** Mississippi
     gulf: **6** Mexico
     salt domes: **11** Five Islands
     river: **3** Red **5** Amite, Bayou, Pearl **6**
   Tensas **8** Ouachita **11** Mississippi
   state admission: **10** eighteenth

state bird: 19 eastern brown pelican
state flower: 8 magnolia
state motto: 5 Union 7 Justice 10 Confidence
state song: 15 Give Me Louisiana 16 You Are My Sunshine
state tree: 11 bald cypress
Louisiana Lightning
   nickname of: 9 Ron Guidry
lounge 4 flop, idle, laze, loaf, loll, rest, sofa 5 couch, dally, divan, lobby, relax, sleep, slump 6 dawdle, daybed, repose, slouch, sprawl 7 recline, slumber 8 kill time, languish 9 davenport, do nothing, lie around, vestibule 10 dillydally, stretch out, take it easy
lourd
   music: 5 heavy
Lourenco Marques
   capital of: 10 Mozambique
louse 3 cad, rat 4 heel 5 churl, knave 6 rascal, rotter, vermin 8 parasite 9 scoundrel
louse up 3 mar 4 goof, muff, ruin 5 botch, spoil 6 bungle, foul up, mess up 7 butcher, do badly, screw up 9 mismanage 11 make a mess of
lousiness 9 nastiness 10 crumminess, horridness, rottenness 11 inferiority, infestation 13 despicability, unsuitability 14 unpleasantness
lousy 3 bad 4 mean 5 awful, nasty 6 crummy, rotten, shabby, unkind 7 hateful, vicious 8 dreadful, inferior, infested, terrible 9 unethical, worthless 10 pediculous, second-rate, unpleasant 12 contemptible
lout 3 ape, oaf 4 boor, clod 5 booby, churl, clown, dummy, dunce, klutz, yokel 6 lummox, rustic 7 bumpkin, dullard
loutish 4 rude 5 crude 6 coarse, gauche, oafish, vulgar 7 boorish, uncouth 9 unrefined 10 unpolished 11 peasantlike
lovable, loveable 4 cute 5 sweet 6 cuddly, lovely, taking 7 darling, winning, winsome 8 adorable, charming, engaging, fetching 9 endearing 10 enchanting 11 captivating
Lovberg, Eilert
   character in: 11 Hedda Gabler
   author: 5 Ibsen
love 3 man 4 beau, bent, dear, girl, mind, turn 5 adore, amity, amour, angel, ardor, enjoy, fancy, flame, honey, lover, savor, taste, woman 6 admire, bask in, choice, esteem, fellow, relish 7 beloved, charity, cherish, concord, darling, dearest, emotion, leaning, passion, rapture, revel in, sweetie 8 affinity, be fond of, devotion, fondness, goodwill, hold dear, loved one, mistress, paramour, penchant, precious, sympathy, treasure, truelove, weakness 9 adoration, affection, boyfriend, delight in, inamorata, rejoice in, sentiment 10 admiration, appreciate, attachment, cordiality, friendship, girlfriend, partiality, proclivity, solicitude, sweetheart, sweetie pie, tenderness 11 amorousness, benevolence, brotherhood, inclination, infatuation

12 be enamored of, congeniality, predilection
   god of: 4 Amor, Eros 5 Cupid 7 Angus Og
   goddess of: 5 Freia, Freya 6 Hathor, Inanna, Ishtar 7 Mylitta 9 Aphrodite
Love, the Magician
   also: 11 El Amor Brujo
   ballet by: 5 Falla
love affair 5 amour 7 liaison, romance 14 affaire de coeur
Love Boat, The
   character: 3 Ace 10 (Cruise Director) Julie McCoy 11 (Dr) Adam Bricker, (Purser Burl) Gopher Smith 14 (Captain) Merrill Stubing 15 (Bartender) Isaac Washington
   cast: 8 Ted Lange 10 Fred Grandy 11 Lauren Tewes 12 Bernie Kopell, Gavin MacLeod
   ship: 15 Pacific Princess
love child 7 bastard 12 natural child 17 illegitimate child
love conquers all
   Latin: 15 omnia vincit amor
loved one 4 love, wife 5 lover 6 fiance, spouse 7 be loved, dearest, fiancee, husband 9 boyfriend 10 girlfriend, sweetheart 12 family member
Love for Three Oranges, The
   opera by: 9 Prokofiev
Love in the Afternoon
   director: 11 Billy Wilder
   cast: 10 Gary Cooper 13 Audrey Hepburn 16 Maurice Chevalier
   setting: 5 Paris
Lovelace, Richard
   author of: 18 To Althea from Prison 23 To Lucasta Going to the Wars
loveliness 6 beauty 9 good looks 11 pulchritude 14 attractiveness
lovely 4 cute, fine, good 5 sweet 6 comely 7 elegant, lovable, winning, winsome 8 adorable, alluring, charming, engaging, fetching, handsome, pleasant, pleasing 9 agreeable, beautiful, endearing, enjoyable, exquisite 10 attractive, delightful, enchanting 11 captivating, fascinating 12 irresistible
Love Machine, The
   author: 16 Jacqueline Susann
Love Me Tonight
   director: 15 Rouben Mamoulian
   cast: 8 Myrna Loy 14 Charlie Ruggles 16 Maurice Chevalier 17 Jeanette MacDonald
   score: 14 Rodgers and Hart
   song: 4 Mimi 5 Lover 14 Isn't It Romantic
love of country
   Latin: 11 amor patriae
Love of One's Neighbor
   author: 14 Leonid Andreyev
lover 3 fan, man, nut 4 beau, buff, dear, girl, love 5 freak, honey, swain, woman, wooer 6 fellow, suitor 7 admirer, beloved, darling, devotee, fanatic, sweetie 8 follower, loved one, lover boy, mistress,

paramour, truelove 9 boyfriend, inamorata
10 aficionado, enthusiast, girlfriend, sweetheart 11 afficionado
French: 6 bon ami 9 bonne amie
Italian: 8 cicisbeo

Lovers and Other Strangers
director: 8 Cy Howard
cast: 8 Gig Young 9 Anne Meara, Bea Arthur 11 Anne Jackson 13 Bonnie Bedelia, Harry Guardino 14 Cloris Leachman, Michael Brandon 17 Richard Castellano

love seat 4 sofa 5 couch 6 settee 13 courting chair

lovesick 7 amorous 8 yearning 10 moonstruck

Love's Labour's Lost
author: 18 William Shakespeare
character: 4 Dull 5 Maria 7 Berowne, Costard, Dumaine 8 Rosaline 9 Ferdinand, Katherine 10 Holofernes, Jaquenetta, Longaville 16 Princess of France 18 Don Adriano de Armado

Love Song of J Alfred Prufrock, The
author: 7 T S Eliot

Love Story
author: 10 Erich Segal

Love-wit
character in: 12 The Alchemist
author: 6 Jonson

loving 4 fond, kind, warm 6 ardent, caring, doting, erotic, tender 7 amatory, amorous, devoted 8 enamored, friendly 10 benevolent, passionate, solicitous 11 sympathetic, warm hearted 12 affectionate

loving word 9 sweet talk 10 endearment 12 sweet nothing

low 4 base, blue, deep, down, evil, glum, mean, soft, vile 5 awful, cruel, dirty, dumpy, faint, gross, lower, lowly, muted, prone, quiet, short, small, squat 6 brutal, coarse, common, cruddy, crummy, feeble, gentle, gloomy, humble, hushed, little, paltry, scurvy, softly, sordid, stubby, stumpy, sunken, vulgar, wicked 7 coastal, concave, corrupt, doleful, heinous, muffled, obscene, quietly, snubbed, squalid, subdued, unhappy 8 cowardly, degraded, dejected, depraved, downcast, inferior, low-lying, low-slung, mediocre, murmured, sawed-off, soothing, terrible, trifling, undersea, unworthy 9 dastardly, depressed, lethargic, nefarious, prostrate, repugnant, repulsive, submarine, submerged, truncated, unethical, whispered 10 abominable, despicable, despondent, dispirited, melancholy, outrageous, scandalous 11 ignominious, scoundrelly, underground, unimportant 12 contemptible, disheartened, dishonorable 14 down in the mouth

lowbred 6 coarse, common, vulgar 7 lowbrow, peasant 10 lower-class, uncultured

low-down 4 base, mean 5 dirty 10 despicable 12 contemptible 13 reprehensible

Lowell, James Russell
author of: 12 The Cathedral 15 The Biglow Papers 16 A Fable for Critics 21 The Vision of Sir Launfal

Lowell, Robert
author of: 8 Day by Day 9 Skunk Hour 10 The Dolphin 11 Life Studies 15 For the Union Dead 16 Lord Weary's Castle

Lowenstein, Laszlo
real name of: 10 Peter Lorre

lower 3 cut, dim 4 damp, drop, duck, mute, pare, sink, sulk 5 frown, glare, pared, prune, scowl 6 deduct, glower, lop off, muffle, reduce, soften, subdue 7 curtail, depress, immerse, let down, put down, reduced, repress, shorten 8 decrease, diminish, grow dark, lessened, make less, pare down, pull down, submerge, take down, tone down 9 curtailed, decreased, make lower, pared down 10 abbreviate, diminished

lower-case letter 9 minuscule 11 small letter

lower-class 4 poor 6 common 7 lowbred, lowbrow, peasant 9 unrefined 10 bluecollar 12 working-class

lower classes 6 proles, rabble 8 canaille, riffraff 9 hoi polloi, peasantry 11 proletariat 13 the common herd, working people 16 the great unwashed

lower depths 4 pits, scum 5 dregs 6 rabble 8 canaille, riffraff 14 scum of the earth

Lower Depths, The
also called: 11 At the Bottom 14 A Night's Lodging
author: 10 Maxim Gorky

lower in rank 4 bust 6 demote 7 degrade

lower in spirits 6 deject, sadden 7 depress 8 dispirit 10 dishearten

low-key 4 soft 5 loose, muted 6 gentle, subtle 7 muffled, relaxed, subdued 8 laidback, softened, soft-sell 9 modulated, toned-down 10 low-pitched, restrained 11 low-pressure, understated, unobtrusive 14 unostentatious

lowliness 8 baseness 9 obscurity 10 humbleness

lowly 3 low 6 humble, modest, simple, softly 7 ignoble, low born, lowbred, obscure 8 baseborn, plebeian 10 unassuming 11 proletarian 13 unpretentious

low-minded 4 lewd, vile 5 crude, gross 6 coarse, smutty, vulgar 7 obscene, uncouth 9 obnoxious, offensive 11 disgraceful 12 contemptible

low point, lowest point 4 base, foot, zero 5 depth, nadir, worst 6 bottom 7 perigee 10 rock bottom

low-priced 5 cheap, token 6 budget, modest 7 bargain, cut-rate, low-cost, nominal, reduced 8 closeout, moderate 9 dirt-cheap 10 discounted, economical, marked-down, reasonable 11 inexpensive 15 bargain-basement

low-ranking 5 minor, petty 11 subordinate, unimportant

low-spirited 3 low, sad 4 blue, down, glum 6 gloomy, morose, woeful 7 doleful, forlorn, unhappy 8 dejected, desolate, downcast 9 depressed, heart sore, sorrowful, woebegone 10 despondent, dispirited, melancholy 11 crestfallen, discouraged, downhearted 12 disconsolate, disheartened 14 down-in-the-mouth

low spirits 4 funk 5 gloom 6 dismay, sorrow 7 despair 8 dejected 9 pessimism 10 depression, desolation, melancholy, moroseness 11 despondency 12 hopelessness 14 discouragement 15 downheartedness

Loxias
 epithet of: 6 Apollo
 means: 9 ambiguous

Loy, Myrna
 real name: 13 Myrna Williams
 co-star: 13 William Powell
 born: 13 Raidersburg MT
 roles: 10 The Thin Man 11 Nora Charles 17 Cheaper by the Dozen 22 The Best Years of Our Lives

loyal 4 firm, true 6 trusty 7 devoted, dutiful, staunch 8 constant, faithful, reliable, resolute, true-blue 9 steadfast 10 dependable, scrupulous, unswerving, unwavering 11 trustworthy 12 tried and true

loyalist 4 tory 12 conservative

Loyalties
 author: 14 John Galsworthy

loyalty 6 fealty 8 devotion, fidelity, firmness 9 adherence, constancy 10 allegiance 11 reliability, staunchness 12 faithfulness 13 dependability, steadfastness 15 trustworthiness

lozenge 4 drop, pill 6 tablet, troche 8 pastille 9 cough drop

Luanda
 capital of: 6 Angola

Lubitsch, Ernst
 director of: 9 Ninotchka 13 Heaven Can Wait, To Be or Not To Be

Lucas, Charlotte
 character in: 17 Pride and Prejudice
 author: 6 Austen

Lucentio
 character in: 19 The Taming of the Shrew
 author: 11 Shakespeare

Lucerne
 German: 6 Luzern
 river: 5 Reuss
 landmark: 9 Hofkirche 11 Am Rhyn House 15 Mariahilf Church

Lucia di Lammermoor
 opera by: 9 Donizetti
 based on novel by: 14 Sir Walter Scott
 called: 20 The Bride of Lammermoor

Luciana
 character in: 17 The Comedy of Errors
 author: 11 Shakespeare

Luciani, Albino 13 Pope John Paul I 20 Pope John Paul the First

lucid 5 clear 6 bright, direct, normal 7 certain, precise, radiant, shining 8 accurate, apposite, dazzling, luminous, lustrous, pellucid, positive, rational, specific 9 brilliant, sparkling 10 articulate, perceptive, responsive, to the point 11 clearheaded, crystalline, illuminated, resplendent, transparent 12 crystal clear, intelligible 13 clear thinking, scintillating, well-organized 14 comprehensible, understandable 15 straightforward

Lucifer
 means: 5 Satan 11 fallen angel, light bearer

Lucina
 origin: 5 Roman
 goddess of: 10 childbirth
 corresponds to: 4 Juno 8 Ilithyia 10 Eileithyia

Lucio
 character in: 17 Measure for Measure
 author: 11 Shakespeare

luck 3 lot 4 fate 5 karma 6 chance, kismet 7 destiny, fortune, success, triumph, victory 8 accident, fortuity, good luck, Lady Luck 11 good fortune, piece of luck 12 happenstance
 god of: 12 Bonus Eventus

lucky 4 good 5 happy 6 in luck, timely 7 blessed, favored 9 favorable, fortunate, opportune, promising 10 auspicious, beneficial, felicitous, of good omen, propitious 12 providential

Lucky Jim
 author: 12 Kingsley Amis

lucky piece 5 charm 6 amulet 8 talisman 10 lucky charm

lucrative 7 gainful 8 fruitful 10 beneficial, high-income, high-paying, profitable 11 moneymaking 12 remunerative

Lucretia
 husband: 26 Lucius Tarquinius Collatinus
 raped by: 16 Sextus Tarquinius
 death by: 7 suicide

Lucretius
 author of: 13 De rerum natura 19 On the nature of things

Lucullan 4 rich 6 lavish 7 gourmet 9 epicurean, luxurious

Lucy Show, The
 also: 9 Here's Lucy
 character: 9 Kim Carter 10 Lucy Carter 11 Craig Carter 12 Harry Conners, Vivian Bagley 13 Mary Jane Lewis, Sherman Bagley 14 Lucy Carmichael 15 Chris Carmichael, Harrison Cheever, Jerry Carmichael, Theodore J Mooney 18 Harrison Otis Carter
 cast: 9 Ralph Hart 10 Candy Moore, Dick Martin, Gale Gordon, Lucie Arnaz, Roy Roberts 11 Desi Arnaz Jr, Lucille Ball, Vivian Vance 12 Jimmy Garrett 13 Mary Jane Croft

Ludd *see* 4 Llud

ludicrous 4 wild 5 comic, crazy, funny 6 absurd, far-out 7 amusing, comical 8 farcical 9 laughable 10 outlandish, ridiculous 11 nonsensical 12 preposterous

Ludlum, Robert
author of: 15 The Matlock Paper 17 The Bourne Identity, The Parsifal Mosaic, The Road to Gandolfo 18 The Osterman Weekend 19 The Gemini Contenders 20 The Rhinemann Exchange 23 The Chancellor Manuscript, The Scarlatti Inheritance

Luftwaffe 9 air weapon 18 German Nazi air force

lug 3 tow, tug 4 bear, drag, draw, haul, pull, tote 5 carry, heave 9 transport

Lug
origin: 5 Irish
habitat: 5 solar

luggage 4 bags, gear 6 trunks 7 baggage, effects, valises 9 suitcases 13 accouterments

Luggnagg
fictional land in: 16 Gulliver's Travels
author: 5 Swift

Lugnasad
origin: 5 Irish
feast date: 11 August first

Lugosi, Bela
real name: 10 Bela Blasko
born: 5 Lugos 7 Hungary
roles: 7 Dracula 21 Murders in the Rue Morgue

lugubrious 4 dour, glum 6 gloomy, morose, rueful, somber, woeful 7 doleful, elegiac 8 dolorous, downcast, funereal, mournful 9 miserable, sorrowful, woebegone 10 depressing, melancholy

Lukas, George
director of: 8 Star Wars 16 American Graffiti

Luke
birthplace: 7 Antioch
companion: 4 Paul
wrote: 6 Gospel

lukewarm 4 cool, mild, warm 5 aloof, tepid 8 detached, uncaring 9 apathetic, temperate 11 halfhearted, indifferent, perfunctory, unconcerned 12 uninterested 13 lackadaisical 14 unenthusiastic 15 body-temperature, room-temperature

lull 3 gap 4 calm, ease, halt, hush 5 break, pause, quell, quiet, still 6 hiatus, lacuna, pacify, recess, soothe, subdue 7 assuage, caesura, compose, mollify, respite 8 breather, calmness 9 interlude 12 brief silence, interruption

Lully, Jean-Baptiste
born: 5 Italy 8 Florence
composer of: 4 Atys, Isis 6 Persee, Psyche, Roland, Thesee 7 Alceste, Phaeton 10 Le Sicilien, Proserpine 11 Bellerophon 13 Acis et Galatee, Amadis de Gaule, L'Amour medecin 14 Acis and Galatea, Armide et Renaud, Le mariage force 16 Cadmus et Hermione 17 Achille et Polyxene, Cadmus and Hermione 19 Achilles and Polyxene 20 Les Amants magnifiques 22 Le Bourgeois Gentilhomme, Monsieur de Pourceaugnac

lulu 3 pip 5 dandy, doozy 8 Jim Dandy 9 allowance, humdinger, wonderful 10 remarkable

lumber 3 log 4 plod, wood 5 barge, clump, stamp 6 boards, planks, trudge, waddle 7 shamble, shuffle 8 flounder 9 fell trees

Lumber State
nickname of: 5 Maine

Lumet, Sidney
director of: 7 Network, Serpico 13 The Pawnbroker 14 Twelve Angry Men 15 Dog Day Afternoon 24 Long Day's Journey Into Night

luminary 3 VIP 5 light, wheel 6 bigwig 7 big shot, notable 8 somebody 9 celebrity, dignitary, personage 10 luminosity 11 illuminator

luminescent 5 aglow 7 glowing 8 gleaming, luminous 9 twinkling 10 flickering, glimmering, glistening, shimmering 11 fluorescent 14 phosphorescent

luminosity 4 glow 5 gleam, sheen, shine 6 luster 8 radiance 10 brightness, brilliance

luminous 6 bright 7 glowing, radiant, shining 8 lustrous 9 brilliant 10 irradiated 11 illuminated, luminescent 15 reflecting light

lump 3 gob, mix 4 bump, cake, clod, fuse, heap, hunk, knob, knot, mass, node, pile, pool 5 amass, batch, blend, bunch, chunk, clump, group, knurl, merge, tumor, unite 6 gather, growth, nodule 7 collect, combine, compile 8 assemble, swelling 9 aggregate 10 protrusion, tumescence 11 excrescence 12 protuberance

lumpish 4 dull, slow 5 bulky, dumpy, heavy, lumpy 6 clumsy 7 awkward 8 clod dish, ungainly, unwieldy 9 corpulent 10 cumbersome, overweight

Lumpkin, Tony
character in: 18 She Stoops to Conquer
author: 9 Goldsmith

lump together 4 fuse, pool 7 combine 10 amalgamate 11 consolidate, incorporate

Luna
personifies: 4 moon

lunacy 5 folly, mania 6 idiocy 7 madness 8 dementia, insanity 9 absurdity, asininity, craziness, silliness, stupidity 10 imbecility, imprudence, insaneness 11 foolishness 13 foolhardiness, senselessness

lunatic 3 mad, nut 4 daft, loco 5 batty, crazy, loony, nutty, potty 6 cuckoo, insane, madman, maniac, screwy 7 bonkers, cracked, touched 8 crackers, demented, demo niac, deranged, maniacal, unhinged 9 psychotic, senseless 10 irrational, psychopath, reasonless, unbalanced 11 crazy person, mentally ill, not all there 12 crackbrained, insane person, psychopathic, round the bend 13 off one's rocker, of unsound mind, out of one's mind

lunch
French: 8 dejeuner

luncheonette 4 cafe 5 diner 7 beanery 8 snack bar 9 hash house, lunchroom 10 coffee shop 11 eating house 12 lunch counter, sandwich shop

lunchroom 4 cafe 5 diner, grill 8 snack bar 9 cafeteria 12 luncheonette

lunge 3 cut, jab 4 dash, dive, pass, rush, stab 5 hit at, lurch, swing, swipe 6 attack, charge, plunge, pounce, thrust 7 set upon 8 fall upon, strike at 9 make a pass

lunkhead 3 ass 4 dope, fool 5 booby, dunce, idiot, moron, ninny 6 dimwit, nitwit 7 fat head, halfwit 8 bonehead, dumb-dumb, imbecile, numskull 9 blockhead, lamebrain, numbskull 10 dunderhead, nincompoop 11 chowderhead

Lunt, Alfred
  wife: 12 Lynn Fontanne
  born: 11 Milwaukee WI
  roles: 12 The Guardsman 13 The Ragged Edge

Lupercalia
  origin: 5 Roman
  event: 8 festival
  honoring: 6 Faunus 8 Lupercus
  to procure: 9 fertility

Lupercus
  origin: 5 Roman
  god of: 9 fertility
  corresponds to: 3 Pan 6 Faunus

Lupino, Ida
  husband: 10 Howard Duff 12 Collier Young, Louis Hayward
  born: 6 London 7 England
  roles: 8 Devotion 10 The Hard Way 12 Junior Bonner, Women's Prison 13 Escape Me Never 15 Strange Intruder 17 On Dangerous Ground 18 The Light That Failed, While the City Sleeps

lurch 4 cant, keel, list, reel, roll, sway, tilt, toss 5 lunge, pitch, slant 6 careen, plunge, swerve, teeter, totter 7 incline, stagger, stumble

lure 4 bait, coax, trap 5 bribe, decoy, snare, tempt 6 allure, cajole, come-on, entice, induce, seduce 7 attract, beguile 8 cajolery, persuade 9 fascinate, tantalize 10 allurement, attraction, enticement, inducement, temptation 11 drawing card 12 blandishment

Lurelei *see* 7 Lorelei

lurid 4 gory, grim 5 eerie, fiery, vivid 6 bloody 7 carmine, flaming, ghastly, glaring, glowing, graphic, scarlet, shining 8 dramatic, rubicund, sanguine, shocking 9 appalling, bright-red 11 sensational 12 melodramatic 13 bloodcurdling

lurk 4 hide 5 prowl, skulk, slink, sneak 9 lie in wait

Lusaka
  capital of: 6 Zambia

luscious 5 tasty 6 savory 7 scented 8 aromatic, fragrant, perfumed 9 delicious, flavorful, succulent, toothsome 10 appetizing, delectable 13 mouth-watering

lush 4 posh, rich 5 dense, fancy, grand 6 ornate 7 elegant, profuse 8 abundant, prolific, splendid 9 elaborate, luxuriant, luxurious, sumptuous 11 flourishing, magnificent

Lusia
  epithet of: 7 Demeter
  means: 6 bather

lust 5 covet, crave 6 be lewd 7 craving, lechery, passion 8 lewdness 9 carnality, hunger for, sexuality 10 satyriasis 14 lasciviousness, libidinousness

lust after 4 want 5 covet, crave 6 desire 11 have a yen for, have an eye on, hunger after, thirst after

luster 4 fame, glow 5 gleam, glory, gloss, honor, merit, sheen, shine 6 dazzle 7 burnish, glimmer, glitter, sparkle 8 prestige, radiance 9 radiation 10 brightness, brilliance, luminosity, notability, refulgence 11 distinction 12 luminousness, resplendence 15 illustriousness

lusterless 3 dim, wan 4 dead, drab, dull, flat 5 faded, matte, muted 7 prosaic 9 colorless, tarnished

Lust for Life
  author: 11 Irving Stone
  director: 16 Vincente Minnelli
  based on story by: 11 Irving Stone
  cast: 11 James Donald, Kirk Douglas (Vincent Van Gogh), Pamela Brown 12 Anthony Quinn (Gaugin)
  Oscar for: 15 supporting actor (Quinn)

lustful 4 lewd 6 carnal 8 prurient 9 lecherous, salacious 10 lascivious, libidinous

lustrous 6 bright, glossy 7 glowing, radiant, shining 8 dazzling, gleaming, luminous, polished 9 burnished, effulgent 10 glistening 11 coruscating, illuminated 12 incandescent

lusty 4 hale 5 husky, sound 6 brawny, hearty, robust, rugged, sturdy, virile 7 healthy 8 vigorous 9 exuberant, strapping 10 full of life 11 uninhibited 12 unrestrained, wholehearted 13 irrepressible

Luther, Martin
  born: 7 Germany 8 Eisleben
  author: 16 Ninety-Five Theses 27 On the Freedom of a Christian Man 46 Address to the Christian Nobility of the German Nation 51 A Prelude Concerning the Babylonian Captivity of the Church
  excommunicated by: 8 Pope Leo X 15 Pope Leo the Tenth
  summoned before: 11 Diet of Worms
  founded: 11 Lutheranism, Reformation 13 Protestantism

lux 5 light

Luxembourg
  other name: 9 Luxemburg 13 Lucilinburhuc
  name means: 10 little fort
  capital/largest city: 10 Luxembourg
  others: 4 Hamm 5 Roodt, Wiltz 6 Mersch, Remich 7 Kopstal, Lintgen, Petange, Redange, Vianden 8 Capellen, Clervaux, Diekirch, Frisange 9 Dudelange

10 Echternach, Ettel bruck, Hesperange, Larochette 11 Differdange, Wormeldange 12 Grevenmacher, Troisvierges, Wasserbillig 14 Esch-sur-Alzette
division: 6 Esleck 7 Bon Pays, Gutland, Oesling
measure: 5 fuder
monetary unit: 5 franc 7 centime
lake: 8 Haut Sure
mountain: 8 Ardennes
highest point: 8 Huldange 9 Burgplatz 11 Wemperhardt
river: 3 Our 4 Sure, Syre 5 Alert, Clerf, Eisch, Mosel, Sauer, Wiltz 6 Chiers 7 Alzette, Moselle 8 Petrusse 11 Ernz Blanche
physical feature:
plateau: 4 Bock 8 Ardennes, Lorraine
valley: 7 Moselle
people: 6 French, German 12 Luxembourger
ruler: 8 Sigefroi, Wencelas 12 Jean l'Aveugle 21 House of Nassau-Weilburg
saint: 10 Willibrord
language: 6 French, German 7 English 13 Letzeburgesch
religion: 13 Roman Catholic
food:
pastry: 20 les pensees brouilees
luxuriant 4 lush, rank 5 dense, fancy, grand 6 florid, ornate 7 elegant, flowery, profuse, teeming 8 abundant, splendid 9 elaborate, exuberant, luxurious, overgrown, sumptuous 10 flamboyant 11 extravagant, flourishing, magnificent
luxuriate 4 bask 6 relish 7 delight 8 wallow in 9 indulge in
luxurious 4 rich 5 grand 6 costly, effete 7 elegant, wealthy 8 decadent, pampered 9 enjoyable, expensive, indulgent, sumptuous 10 gratifying 11 comfortable, pleasurable
luxuriousness 4 ease 6 luxury 7 comfort 8 richness 10 costliness 13 sumptuousness
luxury 5 bliss 6 heaven, riches, wealth 7 delight 8 paradise, pleasure 9 enjoyment 10 high living, indulgence 12 extravagance, nonessential, nonnecessity, satisfaction 13 gratification
LXX *see* 15 Septuagint
Lyaeus
epithet of: 8 Dionysus
means: 8 loosener
Lycaeus
epithet of: 4 Zeus
means: 7 wolfish
Lycaon
king of: 7 Arcadia
father: 8 Pelasgus
son: 8 Maenalus, Tegeates
tested: 4 Zeus
turned into: 4 wolf
Lycidas
author: 10 John Milton
elegy for: 10 Edward King

Lycomedes
king of: 6 Scyrus
daughter: 8 Deidamia
pushed over cliff: 7 Theseus
Lycon
mentioned in: 5 Iliad
vocation: 7 warrior
home: 4 Troy
killed by: 8 Peneleus
Lycophron
origin: 5 Greek
father: 9 Periander
exiled to: 7 Corcyra
killed by: 10 Corcyreans
committed: 6 murder
went to: 4 Troy
killed by: 6 Hector
Lycotherses
king of: 7 Illyria
wife: 5 Agave
killed by: 5 Agave
Lycurgas
king of: 6 Edones, Thrace
son: 5 Dryas
persecuted: 8 Dionysus
killed: 5 Dryas
Lycus
king of: 6 Thebes 7 Cilicia
father: 7 Pandion 9 Chthonius
mother: 5 Pylia
brother: 7 Nycteus
wife: 5 Dirce
niece: 7 Antiope
son: 5 Lycus
succeeded: 8 Sarpedon
killed by: 6 Zethus 7 Amphion 12 Antiope's sons
Lygodesma
epithet of: 7 Artemis
means: 11 willow-bound
lying down 5 in bed, prone 6 supine 7 napping, resting 8 snoozing 9 reclining, recumbent 10 taking a nap 13 taking a snooze
Lyle, Albert Walter
nickname: 6 Sparky
sport: 8 baseball
position: 7 pitcher
team: 12 Boston Red Sox 14 New York Yankees
author of: 11 The Bronx Zoo
Lyly, John
author of: 20 Euphues and His England 22 Euphues the Anatomy of Wit
lynch 4 hang 6 gibbet 8 string up
Lynde, Paul
born: 13 Mount Vernon OH
roles: 12 Bye Bye Birdie 16 Hollywood Squares 17 Beach Blanket Bingo 18 Under the Yum-Yum Tree
Lyngi
origin: 12 Scandinavian
mentioned in: 8 Volsunga
rival of: 7 Sigmund
sought: 7 Hiordis, Hjordis
killed: 7 Sigmund
killed by: 6 Sigurd

lynx 3 cat 6 bobcat 7 wildcat
Lyonnesse
   place in: 16 Arthurian romance
   birthplace of: 8 Tristram
Lyre
   constellation of: 4 Lyra
lyric, lyrical 6 poetic 7 lilting, melodic,
   musical, singing, tuneful 8 songlike 9
   melodious 10 euphonious 11 mellifluent,
   mellifluous 13 sweet-sounding
Lyrical Ballads
   author: 17 William Wordsworth 21 Samuel Taylor Coleridge
lyrics 4 poem 5 words
Lyrus
   father: 8 Anchises
   mother: 9 Aphrodite
Lysander
   character in: 21 A Midsummer Night's
   Dream
   author: 11 Shakespeare
Lysippe
   father: 7 Proetus
   mother: 5 Antia
Lysistrata
   author: 12 Aristophanes
   character: 7 Lampito 8 Cinesias, Cle-
   onice, Myrrhine 10 Magistrate 14 Old
   Men of Athens (Chorus)

M

M
director: 9 Fritz Lang
cast: 10 Peter Lorre 11 Inge Landgut 12 Ellen Widmann 15 Gustav Grundgens
setting: 6 Berlin

Maat
origin: 8 Egyptian
goddess of: 3 law 13 righteousness
symbol: 7 feather

Mabinogian
origin: 5 Welsh
tales of: 7 romance

macabre 4 grim 5 eerie, weird 6 grisly, horrid 7 ghastly, ghostly 8 dreadful, gruesome, horrible, horrific 9 frightful, ghostlike, unearthly 11 frightening

Macao
other name: 5 Ao-men, Macau
territory of: 8 Portugal
monetary unit: 3 avo 6 pataca, pataco
island: 5 Taipa 7 Coloane
highest point: 5 Hag-Sa
river: 5 Pearl 6 Canton
sea: 10 South China
people: 7 Chinese, Macaoan 10 Portuguese
language: 7 Chinese, English 9 Cantonese 10 Portuguese
religion: 6 Taoism 8 Buddhism 13 Roman Catholic
place:
street: 11 Praia Grande
feature:
houseboat: 6 sampan

Macareus
father: 6 Aeolus
mother: 7 Encrete
sister: 6 Canace

MacArthur, Douglas
served in: 3 WWI 4 WWII 9 Korean War, World War I 10 World War II 11 World War One, World War Two
commander of: 15 Rainbow (42nd) Division 19 United Nations forces 24 US Army forces in the Pacific
rank: 15 five-star general 16 army chief of staff
battle: 5 Luzon, Pusan 6 Inchon 9 New Guinea 11 Leyte Island, Philippines 14 Bismark Islands, Solomon Islands 15 Bataan Peninsula 16 Admiralty Islands, Corregidor Island
accepted surrender of: 5 Japan
surrender occurred aboard: 8 Missouri
chairman of: 13 Remington Rand
author of: 13 Reminiscences
smoked: 11 corncob pipe
saying: 12 "I shall return"

Macbeth
author: 18 William Shakespeare
character: 6 Banquo, Duncan (King of Scotland) 7 MacDuff, Malcolm 11 Lady Macbeth 12 Three Witches
director: 13 Roman Polanski
cast: 8 Jon Finch 10 Martin Shaw 13 Nicholas Selby 14 Francesca Annis

Maccabees
title of: 5 Judas
patriarch: 10 Mattathias
means: 8 hammerer

MacDonald, John D
author of: 11 Condominium
character: 11 Travis McGee

MacDonald, Ross
real name: 13 Kenneth Millar
author of: 8 The Chill 10 Black Money 13 The Blue Hammer 14 The Goodbye Look
character: 9 Lew Archer

MacDowell, Edward Alexander
born: 9 New York NY
composer of: 9 Sea Pieces 11 To a Wild Rose 13 Fireside Tales 15 Poems after Heine 16 Hamlet and Ophelia, New England Idylls, Woodland Sketches 17 Idylls after Goethe

MacDuff
character in: 7 Macbeth
author: 11 Shakespeare

mace
origin: 9 Indonesia
from same tree as: 6 nutmeg
tree: 17 Myristica fragrans
use: 4 fish 7 seafood 9 cherry pie, pound cake 16 chicken fricassee

Macedonia
capital/largest city: 6 Skopje
head of state: 9 president
government: 8 republic
monetary unit: 5 denar
river: 6 Struma, Vardar
people: 4 Turk 9 Albanian 10 Macedonian
language: 10 Macedonian
religion: 27 Macedonian Orthodox Christian

macerate 4 fade, mash, pulp, soak 5 souse, steep 6 shrink, soften, squash, wither 7 decline, liquefy, shrivel 8 dissolve, emaciate, fluidize, permeate, saturate 9 liquidize, waste away 10 lose weight

MacGraw, Ali
real name: 12 Alice MacGraw
husband: 8 Bob Evans 12 Steve McQueen
born: 12 Pound Ridge NY

roles: 7 Dynasty 9 Love Story 10 The Getaway 13 The Winds of War 15 Goodbye Columbus

Machaerus
killed: 11 Neoptolemus

Machaon
father: 9 Asclepius
brother: 10 Podalirius
wife: 8 Anticlea
son: 8 Alexanor, Gorgasus 10 Nicomachus
vocation: 9 physician
served in: 9 Trojan War

Macheath, Captain
character in: 12 Beggar's Opera
author: 3 Gay

ma chere 6 my dear

Machiavelli, Niccolo
author of: 9 The Prince 11 The Art of War 16 Discourses on Livy

Machiavellian 6 amoral, crafty 7 cunning, devious 8 scheming 9 deceitful, designing 10 perfidious 11 self-serving, treacherous, underhanded 12 falsehearted, unscrupulous

machination 4 plot, rule, ruse 5 dodge 6 design, device, scheme 8 artifice, intrigue, maneuver 9 stratagem 10 conspiracy 11 contrivance

machine 3 set 4 army, body, camp, club, gang, pool, ring 5 corps, crowd, force, group, setup, trust, union 6 device, system 7 combine, coterie, faction, society 9 apparatus, appliance, machinery, mechanism, structure 11 association 12 organization 13 establishment

machine gun
invented by: 7 Gatling
improved by: 5 Maxim 9 Hotchkiss

machinery 4 gear 5 setup, tools 6 agency, makeup, system, tackle, wheels 9 apparatus, mechanism, resources, structure 12 contrivances, organization

macho 5 he-man, manly 6 strong, virile

Machpelah
location: 6 Hebron
burial place of: 4 Leah 5 Isaac, Jacob, Sarah 7 Abraham, Rebekah

Macilente
character in: 22 Every Man out of His Humour
author: 6 Jonson

MacInnes, Helen
author of: 13 North from Rome 14 Above Suspicion 16 Decision at Delphi 17 The Venetian Affair 21 The Salzburg Connection

macintosh, mackintosh 7 slicker 8 raincoat 10 waterproof

Mack, Connie
real name: 30 Cornelius Alexander McGillicuddy
sport: 8 baseball
position: 7 manager
team: 21 Philadelphia Athletics

MacKellar
character in: 21 The Master of Ballantrae
author: 9 Stevenson

mackerel
young: 5 spike 6 tinker 7 blinker

mackinaw 4 coat 6 jacket 8 overcoat

MacLaine, Shirley
real name: 19 Shirley MacLean Beaty
brother: 12 Warren Beatty
born: 10 Richmond VA
roles: 6 Can Can 10 Being There 11 Irma La Douce 12 Sweet Charity, The Apartment 15 Some Came Running, The Turning Point, Two for the Seesaw 16 The Children's Hour 17 Terms of Endearment (Oscar) 19 The Trouble with Harry 20 The Bliss of Mrs Blossom

MacMurray, Fred
wife: 9 June Haver
born: 10 Kankakee IL
roles: 11 My Three Sons 12 The Apartment 14 Above Suspicion, The Caine Mutiny 15 Double Indemnity 20 The Miracle of the Bells

Macro-Chibchan
language branch: 6 Paezan 8 Chibchan

macrocosm 6 cosmos, nature 7 heavens 8 creation, universe 9 firmament

Macro-Ge
language family: 11 Ge-Pano-Carib
group: 2 Ge 6 Bororo, Caraja

Macro-Panoan
language family: 11 Ge-Pano-Carib
group: 6 Panoan 10 Guaycuruan

mad 4 avid, daft, loco, nuts, wild 5 angry, balmy, crazy, irate, nutty 6 ardent, crazed, cuckoo, fuming, insane, miffed, screwy, ticked 7 cracked, enraged, excited, fanatic, furious, in a huff, lunatic, riled up, teed off, touched 8 crackers, demented, deranged, frenzied, incensed, maniacal, provoked, unhinged, up in arms, worked up, wrathful 9 devoted to, non compos, seeing red, ticked off, wrought up 10 distracted, distraught, infatuated, infuriated, in love with, irrational, unbalanced 11 boiling over, exasperated, impassioned, not all there 12 enthusiastic, round the bend 13 beside oneself, in high dudgeon, not quite right, off one's rocker, out of one's mind

Madagascar
other name: 16 Malagasy Republic
capital/largest city: 10 Tananarive 12 Antananarivo
others: 6 Tulear 7 Majanga, Nossibe, Toliary 8 Manakara, Tamatave 9 Faradofay, Mananjory, Toamasina 10 Antisirabe 11 Antsiranana, Diego-Suarez, Fort Dauphin
measure: 7 gantang
monetary unit: 5 franc 7 centime
island: 6 Barren, Radama 7 Nossi-Be 11 Sainte-Marie 12 Chesterfield
lake: 5 Itasy 7 Alaotra, Kinkony
mountain: 4 Boby 9 Ankaratra 12 High

Plateaus, Tsiafajavona 17 Tsaratanana Massif

highest point: 11 Maromokotro

river: 5 Ikopa, Mania, Sofia 7 Mangoky, Mangoro, Onilahy 8 Ivoloina, Manambao, Mananara 9 Betsiboka, Manambolo 10 Manarandra 11 Tsiribihina

ocean: 6 Indian

physical feature:

bay: 6 Radama 8 Antongil 9 Mahajamba 10 Sahamalaza

cape: 5 Amber 10 Saint-Andre 11 Sainte-Marie 14 Saint-Sebastien

channel: 10 Mozambique

lagoon: 9 pangalane

plateau: 9 Ankaizina

people: 4 Arab, Bara, Hova 5 Malay 6 Merina, Tanala 7 African 8 Betsileo, Mahafaly, Malagasy, Sakalava 9 Antaimoro, Antaisaka, Antandroy, Tsimi-hety 10 Indonesian, Polynesian 13 Betsimisaraka

dynasty: 6 Merina

leader: 9 Ratsiraka, Tsiranana 11 Ranamantsoa

language: 6 French 8 Malagasy, Malgache

religion: 5 Islam 7 animism 10 Protestant 13 Roman Catholic

place:

market: 4 Zoma

royal estate: 4 Rova

feature:

animal: 4 zebu 5 lemur 6 foussa

musical instrument: 11 jego vaotavo

proverb: 8 hainteny

shawl: 5 lamba

food:

vegetable: 7 brettes

madam, madame 3 Mrs 4 dame, lady 6 matron 7 dowager 8 mistress

German: 4 Frau

Spanish: 6 senora

Italian: 5 donna 7 signora

Spanish/Portuguese: 4 dona

Madame Bovary

author: 15 Gustave Flaubert

character: 10 Emma Bovary, Leon Dupuis 13 Charles Bovary 17 Rodolphe Boulanger

Madame Butterfly

also: 15 Madama Butterfly

opera by: 7 Puccini

character: 6 Bonze 6 Suzuki 9 Cho-Cho-San, Cio-Cio-San, Sharpless 14 Prince Yamadori 19 Lieutenant Pinkerton

mad as a hatter 3 mad 4 daft, nuts 5 crazy, nutty 6 insane 7 cracked, touched 8 demented, deranged, unhinged 10 unbalanced 13 off one's rocker, out of one's head 14 off one's trolley 15 mad as a March hare 17 nutty as a fruitcake

mad as a March hare 3 mad 4 daft, nuts 5 crazy, nutty 6 insane 7 cracked, touched 8 demented, deranged, unhinged 10 unbalanced 12 mad as a hatter 13 out of one's

head 14 off one's trolley 17 nutty as a fruit-cake

madcap 4 rash, wild, zany 5 brash, clown, giddy, joker 6 unruly 7 erratic, flighty, foolish 8 reckless 9 hotheaded, impetuous, impulsive, senseless 10 incautious 11 impractical, thoughtless 12 unconsidered 13 inconsiderate, undisciplined

madden 3 vex 4 gall 5 anger, craze, pique, upset 6 enrage, frenzy 7 derange, incense, inflame, outrage, provoke, torment, unhinge 9 aggravate, infuriate, unbalance 10 exasperate

made 5 built 6 formed 7 created 8 composed, produced 9 assembled, developed 10 fabricated 11 constructed 12 manufactured

madeira

type: 4 wine 6 brandy 7 liqueur 8 aperitif

origin: 7 Madeira

Madeira Islands

capital: 7 Funchal

city: 5 Monte

island: 6 Grande 7 Dezerte, Madeira 8 Desertas 9 Selvagens 10 Porto Santo

ocean: 8 Atlantic

owned by: 8 Portugal

stone aqueduct: 7 levadas

wine: 4 Bual 5 Tinta, Tinto 6 Canary, Gomera 7 Malmsey, Marsala, Sercial 8 Verdelho

made-up 5 false 7 assumed, created 8 fanciful, invented 9 fictional, imaginary, pretended, thought-up 10 fictitious 11 make-believe, theoretical 12 hypothetical

Mad Hatter

character in: 28 Alice's Adventures in Wonderland

author: 7 Carroll

madhouse 6 asylum, bedlam, uproar 7 turmoil 8 loony bin, nuthouse

Madison, James

nickname: 23 Father of the Constitution

presidential rank: 6 fourth

party: 20 Democratic-Republican

state represented: 2 VA

defeated: 7 (DeWitt) Clinton 8 (Charles Cotesworth) Pinckney

vice president: 5 (Elbridge) Gerry 7 (George) Clinton

cabinet:

state: 5 (Robert) Smith 6 (James) Monroe

treasury: 6 (Alexander James) Dallas 8 (Abraham Alfonse Albert) Gallatin, (George Washington) Campbell, (William Harris) Crawford

war: 6 (James) Monroe, (William) Eustis 8 (William Harris) Crawford 9 (John) Armstrong

attorney general: 4 (Richard) Rush 6 (Caesar Augustus) Rodney 7 (William) Pinkney

navy: 5 (William) Jones 8 (Paul) Hamilton 13 (Benjamin Williams) Crowninshield

born: 12 Port Conway VA 16 King George County

died/buried: 2 VA 12 Orange County 16 Montpelier estate

education:

tutored at home by: 15 Rev Thomas Martin

school: 15 Donald Robertson

college of: 9 New Jersey (now Princeton University)

religion: 12 Episcopalian

interests: 3 law 11 agriculture 14 natural history

author: 16 Federalist Papers (with Hamilton and Jay) 24 Memorial and Remonstrances 29 Journal of the Federal Convention

political career: 24 US House of Representatives 25 Second Continental Congress

secretary of: 5 state

signed: 12 Constitution

civilian career: 6 farmer 7 planter

military service:

colonel of: 19 Orange County militia

notable events of lifetime/term: 19 War of Eighteen Twelve

battle of: 10 New Orleans

treaty of: 5 Ghent

Washington DC burned by: 7 British

father: 5 James

mother: 7 Eleanor (Rose Conway)

siblings: 5 Sarah 6 Reuben 7 Ambrose, Catlett, Francis, William 9 Elizabeth 11 Nelly Conway 13 Frances Taylor

wife: 5 Dorothea (Payne Todd)

nickname: 6 Dolley

first lady:

saved: 11 state papers 25 George Washington's portrait

madman 3 nut 5 loony 6 maniac 7 lunatic 8 demoniac 9 psychotic 10 psychopath

Mad Max director: 12 George Miller

cast: 9 Mel Gibson

sequel: 14 The Road Warrior 17 Beyond Thunderdome (with Tina Turner)

madness 6 lunacy, oddity 8 delusion, dementia, illusion, insanity 9 craziness 11 derangement

Madonna

nickname: 15 The Material Girl

husband: 8 Sean Penn

recordings: 7 Madonna 8 True Blue 11 Like A Prayer, Like A Virgin

films: 9 Dick Tracy 11 Truth or Dare 12 Who's That Girl 14 Body of Evidence 16 Shanghai Surprise 17 A League of Their Own 23 Desperately Seeking Susan

tour: 6 Girlie 13 Blond Ambition

books: 3 Sex

Madrid

area: 9 Salamanca 19 Ciudad Universitaria

capital of: 5 Spain

landmark: 14 National Palace 18 Biblioteca Nacional

bull ring: 22 Plaza de Toros Monumental

museum: 5 Prado

mountain: 18 Sierra de Guadaramma

river: 10 Manzanares

square: 10 Plaza Mayor 11 Plaza del Sol 13 Plaza de Espana

street: 13 Paseo del Prado

Madwoman of Chaillot

author: 13 Jean Giraudoux

Mael

origin: 5 Irish

father: 5 Ronan

killed by: 5 Ronan

maelstrom 4 eddy 5 shoot, swirl 6 bedlam, rapids, tumult, uproar, vortex 7 riptide, torrent 8 disorder, madhouse, undertow, upheaval 9 confusion, whirlpool 10 white water 11 pandemonium

maenad, menad 5 lenae 7 bacchae, bassara 8 clodones, thyiades 9 bacchante 10 mimallones

companion of: 7 Bacchus 8 Dionysus

Maenalus

father: 6 Lycaon

Maeterlinck, Maurice

author of: 8 The Blind 11 The Blue Bird, The Intruder 19 Pelleas and Melisande

ma foi 6 my word, really 7 my faith

magazine 6 weekly 7 arsenal, journal, monthly 9 quarterly 10 periodical, powder room 13 military depot, munitions room

Magdalene see 4 Mary

magenta 6 maroon 7 carmine, crimson, fuchsia 9 vermilion 12 purplish rose 13 reddish purple

Maggie

character in: 16 Cat on a Hot Tin Roof

author: 8 Williams

Maggie: A Girl of the Streets

author: 12 Stephen Crane

maggot 4 grub, worm 5 larva 8 mealworm

Magi

also called: 7 Wisemen 11 astrologers

followed: 15 Star of Bethlehem

visited: 5 Jesus

gifts: 4 gold 5 myrrh 12 frankincense

singular: 5 magus

magic 4 lure 5 charm, spell 6 hoodoo, voodoo 7 sorcery 8 charisma, jugglery, witchery, wizardry 9 occultism, voodooism 10 allurement, black magic, demonology, divination, hocus-pocus, witchcraft 11 captivation, conjuration, enchantment, fascination, legerdemain, the black art 12 entrancement 13 sleight of hand 16 prestidigitation

god of: 5 Thoth

Magic

nickname of: 13 Earvin Johnson

Magic Flute, The

also: 14 Die Zauberflote

opera: 6 Mozart

character: 6 Pamina, Tamino 8 Papagena, Pageno, Sarastro 10 Monostatos 12 Queen of Night

magician 5 magus 6 shaman, wizard 7 juggler, warlock 8 conjurer, sorcerer 9 alchemist 11 illusionist, medicine man, necromancer, witch doctor 12 escape artist 15 prestidigitator

Magic Mountain, The
  author: 10 Thomas Mann
  character: 6 Naphta 7 Clavdia 11 Hans Castorp, Settembrini 15 Joachim Ziemssen

magisterial 9 imperious 10 autocratic, peremptory 11 dictatorial, domineering, overbearing 13 condescending

Magister Ludi: The Glass Bead Game
  author: 12 Hermann Hesse

magistrate 2 JP 5 judge 7 prefect 17 justice of the peace

magna cum laude 15 with great praise

Magna Graecia 27 ancient Greek colonies in Italy

Magna Mater 3 Ops 4 Rhea 6 Cybele

Magnani, Anna
  nickname: 10 Nannerella
  roles: 8 Open City 13 The Rose Tattoo (Oscar) 15 The Fugitive Kind 21 Secret of Santa Vittoria

magnanimous 7 liberal 8 generous, princely 9 forgiving, unselfish 10 altruistic, beneficent, charitable 12 largehearted 13 philanthropic

magnate 3 VIP 5 giant, mogul, nabob 6 big gun, bigwig, leader, tycoon 7 big shot, notable 8 big wheel, great man 9 celebrity 13 empire builder, industrialist

magnesium
  chemical symbol: 2 Mg

magnetic 8 alluring, charming, inviting 9 of a magnet, seductive 10 attractive, enchanting, entrancing, persuasive 11 captivating, charismatic, fascinating 12 irresistible

magnetism 4 lure 5 charm 6 allure 8 charisma 9 mesmerism, seduction 10 allurement, attraction, enticement 11 captivation, enchantment, fascination

magnification 5 honor 7 worship 9 adoration, blowing up, expansion, inflation, reverence 11 acclamation, enlargement, idolization 12 exaggeration 13 amplification, glorification, overstatement

magnificence 4 pomp 5 glory, state 6 luxury 7 glitter, majesty, royalty 8 grandeur, richness, splendor 10 brilliance 13 sumptuousness

magnificent 4 fine 5 grand, noble 6 august, superb 7 elegant, exalted, stately, sublime 8 glorious, imposing, majestic, splendid 9 brilliant, exquisite, wonderful 10 commanding, impressive 11 resplendent 12 transcendent 13 extraordinary

Magnificent Ambersons, The
  director: 11 Orson Welles
  based on novel by: 15 Booth Tarkington
  cast: 7 Tim Holt 10 Anne Baxter 12 Joseph Cotten 14 Agnes Moorehead 15 Dolores Costello

Magnificent Obsession, The
  author: 13 Lloyd C Douglas

Magnificent Seven, The
  director: 11 John Sturges
  cast: 10 Brad Dexter, Eli Wallach, Yul Brynner 11 James Coburn 12 Robert Vaughn, Steve McQueen 13 Horst Buchholz 14 Charles Bronson
  setting: 6 Mexico
  score: 14 Elmer Bernstein
  remake of: 12 Seven Samurai
  sequel: 16 Return of the Seven 20 Magnificent Seven Ride

magnify 4 laud 5 adore, boost, exalt, extol 6 blow up, double, expand, praise, puff up, revere 7 acclaim, amplify, enlarge, glorify, greaten, inflate, stretch, worship 8 heighten, maximize, overrate 9 embroider, overstate, reverence 10 exaggerate

magniloquence 7 bombast, fustian 8 euphuism, tumidity 9 pomposity, turgidity 10 orotundity 11 fanfaronade, grandiosity 14 grandiloquence 15 pretentiousness

magniloquent 5 tumid, windy, wordy 6 turgid 7 pompous, verbose 8 inflated 9 bombastic 13 grandiloquent

magnitude 4 bulk, fame, mass, size 6 extent, renown, repute, volume 7 bigness, expanse, measure 8 eminence, enormity, hugeness, vastness

magnolia
  varieties: 4 ashe, star 6 saucer 7 Chinese 8 southern, umbrella 11 greatleaved

Magnum, P. I.
  character: 2 TC 4 Rick 7 Higgins 12 Thomas Magnum
  cast: 10 Tom Selleck 12 Roger E Mosley 13 John Hillerman
  setting: 6 Hawaii

Magog
  father: 7 Japheth

Magritte, Rene Francois Ghislain
  born: 7 Belgium 8 Lessines
  artwork: 14 La Belle Captive, The False Mirror, The Key of Dreams 15 Memory of a Voyage 18 L'Empire des Lumieres (The Empire of Light), The Menaced Assassin

Magua
  character in: 20 The Last of the Mohicans
  author: 6 Cooper

Magus see 4 Magi

Magwitch, Abel
  character in: 17 Great Expectations
  author: 7 Dickens

Magyar 9 Hungarian

Mahican see 7 Mohican

Mahler, Gustav
  born: 7 Austria, Bohemia
  composer of: 12 Resurrection (symphony No 2) 15 Das Klagendlied 16 Songs of a Wayfarer 17 Das Lied von der Erde, Kindertotenlieder, The Song of the Earth 19 Des Knaben Wunderhorn 28 Lieder eines fahrenden Gesellen

mahogany 4 tree, wood 5 brown 8 hardwood 9 Swietenia 12 reddish-brown
  varieties: 3 red 5 swamp, white 7 African, big-leaf, Florida, Senegal, Spanish 8 Honduras, mountain 9 Nyasaland, Venezulan 10 West Indian

Mahon, Christopher
character in: 27 The Playboy of the Western World
author: 5 Synge

mahzor, machzor 16 Jewish prayer book

Maia
member of: 8 Pleiades
place in group: 6 eldest
father: 5 Atlas
mother: 7 Pleione
son: 6 Hermes

maid 6 tweeny 7 servant 8 domestic 9 hired girl, housemaid, lady's maid, nursemaid 10 parlor maid 11 maidservant 12 upstairs maid 13 female servant
French: 6 au pair

maiden, maidenly 4 girl, lass, maid, miss 5 chick, first 6 chaste, damsel, lassie, virgin 7 colleen, girlish, ingenue, initial, untried 8 original, virginal, youthful 9 inaugural, soubrette, unmarried 10 demoiselle, initiatory 12 introductory

Maid Marian
beloved of: 9 Robin Hood

maidservant 4 amah, ayah, char, lass, maid 5 bonne 6 au pair, tweeny 7 abigail 8 charlady, domestic 9 hired girl, lady's maid, tirewoman 10 handmaiden, parlormaid

Maidu
language family: 8 Penutian
location: 10 California
noted for: 8 basketry

mail 4 arms, post 5 armor 6 get out 7 airmail, harness, letters, panoply 8 dispatch, packages 9 postcards 10 send by mail, send by post, suit of mail 11 surface mail 12 mail delivery, put in the mail 13 postal service 14 defensive armor, drop in a mailbox 17 post-office service

Mailer, Norman
author of: 15 An American Dream 16 Armies of the Night 18 The Naked and the Dead 19 The Executioner's Song

Maillol, Aristide
born: 6 France 13 Banyuls-sur-mer
artwork: 5 Night, Torso 7 Le Desir (Desire) 11 Ile de France 12 Young Cyclist 14 Action in Chains, The Three Nymphs 16 The Mediterranean (Seated Woman) 17 Monument to Cezanne, Monument to Debussy 18 Venus with a Necklace

maim 3 cut, rip 4 gash, lame, maul, rend, tear 5 slash, wound 6 deface, hobble, injure, mangle, savage 7 cripple, disable 8 lacerate, mutilate 9 disfigure, dismember, hamstring 12 incapacitate

main 4 head 5 chief, prime, vital 6 urgent 7 capital, central, crucial, leading, primary, special, supreme 8 critical, foremost, pressing 9 essential, important, necessary, paramount, principal, requisite 10 particular, preeminent 11 outstanding, predominant 13 consequential, indispensable

Main, Marjorie
real name: 13 Mary Tomlinson
partner: 12 Wallace Beery 13 Percy Kilbride
born: 7 Acton IN
roles: 7 Dead End 8 Ma Kettle

Maine
abbreviation: 2 ME
nickname: 6 Lumber 8 Pine Tree 10 Wonderland
capital: 7 Augusta
largest city: 8 Portland
others: 4 Bath, Saco 5 Hiram, Orono 6 Auburn, Bangor 7 Kittery 8 Boothbay, Lewiston, Ogunquit 9 Bar Harbor, Biddeford, Brunswick, Skowhegan 10 Waterville 11 Millinocket, Presque Isle
college: 5 Bates, Colby 7 Bowdoin
explorer: 6 Cabots 8 Norsemen
feature: 8 lobsters 19 West Quoddy Headlight
beach: 10 Old Orchard
national park: 6 Acadia
waterway: 18 Allagash Wilderness
tribe: 6 Abnaki 7 Wewenoc
people: 10 downeaster 11 Dorothea Dix 19 Edna St Vincent Millay 24 Henry Wadsworth Longfellow
island: 4 Orrs 8 Mt Desert 10 Campobello
lake: 5 Sebec, Wyman 6 Sebago 8 Rangeley, Schoodic 9 Flagstaff, Moosehead 10 Chesuncook
land rank: 11 thirty-ninth
mountain: 5 Kineo, White 7 Bigelow 8 Cadillac
highest point: 8 Katahdin
physical feature:
bay: 5 Casco 9 Penobscot 12 Merrymeeting 13 Passamaquoddy
sand dunes: 13 Desert of Maine
river: 4 Saco 6 St John 7 St Croix 8 Allagash, Kennebec 9 Aroostook, Kennebago, Penobscot 12 Androscoggin
state admission: 11 twenty-third
state bird: 9 chickadee
state fish: 16 land-locked salmon
state flower: 7 thistle 8 pine cone 22 white pine cone and tassel
state motto: 7 I Direct
state song: 16 State of Maine Song
state tree: 16 eastern white pine

mainly 6 mostly 7 chiefly 8 above all 9 in the main, most of all, primarily 10 on the whole 11 principally 13 predominantly 14 for the most part, in great measure 16 first and foremost

main point 3 nut 4 core, crux, gist, meat 5 basis, heart, theme 6 kernel 7 essence 10 brass tacks 11 nitty-gritty 15 sum and substance

mainspring 5 agent, cause 6 motive 9 incentive 10 motivation

mainstay 4 prop 6 anchor, pillar 7 bulwark 8 backbone, buttress 16 pillar of strength

Main Street
  author: 13 Sinclair Lewis
  character: 14 Carol Kennicott 15 Dr Will
    Kennicott
maintain 4 aver, avow, hold, keep 5 claim,
  state, swear 6 affirm, allege, assert, defend, insist, keep up, uphold 7 care for,
  contend, declare, finance, profess, stand
  by, support, sustain 8 conserve, continue,
  preserve 9 keep alive, keep going 10 provide for, take care of
maintenance 4 keep 6 living, repair, upkeep 7 keeping, support 10 livelihood, protection, sustenance 11 safekeeping, subsistence, sustainment 12 conservation,
  preservation, safeguarding
Main-Travelled Road
  author: 13 Hamlin Garland
maison de sante 10 sanitarium 13 house
  of health
maize 4 corn, milo 5 grain 6 cereal, silage,
  yellow 7 zea mays 10 Indian corn
majestic, majestical 5 grand, lofty, noble,
  regal, royal 6 august, famous, superb 7 elegant, eminent, stately, sublime 8 esteemed, glorious, imperial, imposing,
  princely, renowned, splendid 10 impressive 11 illustrious, magnificent 13 distinguished
majesty 4 pomp 5 glory 6 luster 7 dignity 8
  elegance, eminence, grandeur, mobility,
  splendor 9 elevation, loftiness, solemnity,
  sublimity 10 augustness 11 distinction,
  stateliness 12 gloriousness, magnificence
  14 impressiveness
major 4 main 5 chief, prime, vital 6 larger,
  urgent 7 capital, crucial, greater, leading,
  primary, ranking, serious, supreme 8 critical, foremost, pressing 9 essential, important, necessary, paramount, requisite, requisite 10 preeminent 11 outstanding,
  predominant, significant 13 consequential,
  indispensable
Major Barbara
  director: 13 Gabriel Pascal
  based on play by: 17 George Bernard
    Shaw
  cast: 11 Deborah Kerr, Rex Harrison,
    Wendy Hiller 12 Robert Morley, Robert
    Newton 14 Sybil Thorndike
majority 4 bulk, mass 8 best part, legal
  age, maturity 9 adulthood, seniority,
  womanhood 10 lion's share 13 preponderance
major key (in music)
  German: 3 dur
Major prophets see 8 prophets
majuscule 7 capital 11 large letter 13 capital letter 15 upper-case letter
make 3 fix 4 form, kind, mark, meet, pass 5
  beget, brand, build, catch, cause, enact,
  erect, force, frame, impel, press, reach,
  shape, speak, utter 6 attain, compel, create, devise, draw up, effect, foment,
  makeup, oblige, render 7 appoint, compose, deliver, dragoon, fashion, produce,
  require 8 arrive at, assemble, engender 9

cause to be, constrain, construct, establish, fabricate, formation, legislate, pronounce, structure 10 bring about, fashioning 11 composition, manufacture
make a bet 3 bet 4 risk 5 stake, wager 6
  chance, gamble, hazard, plunge 7 venture
make a clean breast of 7 confess, lay
  bare, own up to 8 blurt out 14 come clean
  about
make a dash 3 fly, run 4 flee 6 escape 7
  get away 8 make a run 10 make a break,
  take flight 12 make a getaway
make a deal 5 agree 6 settle 10 compromise 11 come to terms, meet halfway 14
  strike a bargain
make advances 8 approach, come on to,
  sound out 11 proposition 13 make overtures, put the moves on
make a fuss over 6 dote on 7 protest 8
  crow over
make again 4 copy 6 remake, repeat 9 duplicate 11 reconstruct
make a getaway 4 bolt, flee, skip 6 escape
  7 get away, make off, run away 8 make a
  run, slip away 9 break free, cut and run,
  make a dash 10 break loose, fly the coop,
  take flight
make a gift of 4 give 6 donate 7 present 8
  bequeath 10 contribute
make allowance for 6 excuse, pardon 7
  forgive, indulge 8 bear with, pass over
make amends 5 atone 6 make up, square
  7 expiate 9 do penance 10 compensate
make a mess of 3 mar 4 goof, muff, ruin 5
  botch, spoil 6 bungle, foul up, mess up 7
  butcher, do badly, louse up, screw up 9
  mismanage
make a mistake 3 err 4 goof 6 mess up,
  slip up 12 miscalculate
make an effort 3 try 5 essay 6 strive, work
  at 7 attempt 8 endeavor
make appear 5 evoke 6 elicit 7 produce 9
  conjure up 10 bring forth
make a racket 3 cry 4 howl, yell 5 shout 6
  bellow, clamor, holler, scream 7 bluster
  make a din 10 vociferate 12 raise a rumpus
make a stab at 3 try 5 essay, guess 6
  reckon, take on 7 attempt, surmise, venture 8 estimate, give a try 9 undertake 10
  conjecture 11 approximate 12 take a crack
  at, take a fling at
make a stand 9 stand fast 13 refuse to
  yield 17 fight to the last man
make a statement 6 remark 7 clarify, comment, discuss, explain, expound 9 elucidate, talk about
make aware 4 tell 5 edify 6 advise, inform,
  notify, reveal 7 apprise 8 acquaint, disclose 9 divulge to, enlighten, introduce 11
  familiarize 16 bring to (one's) attention
make away with 3 eat 4 kill, take 5 spend,
  steal 6 kidnap, murder 7 abolish, consume, destroy 8 carry off, embezzle, get
  rid of 9 dissipate

make-believe 4 fake, sham 5 false, phony 6 made-up, make-up, unreal 7 assumed, charade, fantasy, feigned, fiction 8 creation, imagined, invented, pretense, spurious 9 fantastic, imaginary, invention, pretended, simulated 10 artificial, fictitious 11 counterfeit, fabrication 13 falsification

make certain of 6 assure, clinch, ensure 8 be sure of 10 make sure of

make damp 5 bedew 6 dampen 7 moisten 8 sprinkle

make dark 5 dim 6 darken 7 blacken, obscure

make different 4 vary 5 alter, amend 6 change, modify, mutate 7 convert, remodel 9 transform, transmute 12 metamorphose

make distinctive 8 set apart 9 single out 11 distinguish 12 characterize 13 differentiate

make easy 4 ease 6 smooth 7 explain, lighten 8 simplify 10 clear a path, facilitate

make eligible 5 allow 6 permit 7 entitle, qualify 9 authorize

make evident 4 show 5 prove 6 reveal 7 exhibit 8 manifest 9 establish, make clear, make plain 11 demonstrate

make fast 3 fix 4 moor 5 affix, tie up 6 attach, fasten, secure 7 connect

make feeble 6 weaken 7 wear out 8 enervate 10 debilitate, devitalize

make furious 5 anger 6 enrage, madden 7 incense, inflame 9 infuriate

make giddy 5 dizzy 12 make unsteady 15 make lightheaded

make good 5 repay 6 arrive, make it 7 fulfill, succeed 11 reach the top 15 make restitution

make happy 5 amuse, cheer 6 please 7 delight, gratify 9 entertain

make haste slowly
  Latin: 12 festina lente

make hostile 5 repel 6 offend 7 provoke 8 alienate 10 antagonize

make ill 5 repel 6 infect, revolt, sicken 7 afflict, disgust, repulse 8 disagree, distress, make sick, nauseate 9 discomfit 14 turn the stomach

make ill at ease 5 upset 6 rattle 7 fluster 8 distress 9 discomfit, embarrass 10 disconcert

make impure 4 foul, soil 5 dirty, spoil, taint 6 befoul, blight, defile, infect, poison 7 corrupt, pollute 10 adulterate 11 contaminate

make inroads 6 invade 7 impinge, intrude 8 encroach, infringe, trespass 9 penetrate

make known 4 tell 6 advise, impart, inform, notify, report, reveal, unveil 7 apprise, divulge, lay bare, publish, uncover 8 disclose 9 broadcast 10 give notice, make public 11 communicate

make less forceful 6 soften, weaken 9 undermine 10 devitalize, emasculate

make light of 8 belittle, minimize, pooh-pooh, sneeze at 9 deprecate, disparage, underrate 10 depreciate, undervalue 13 underestimate

make merry 5 revel 7 carouse, roister 9 celebrate, have a ball 15 paint the town red

make much of 5 honor 6 praise 7 acclaim, applaud, commend, flatter 8 fuss over

make nervous 5 annoy, upset 7 agitate, disturb, perturb, trouble, unnerve 10 disconcert

make off with 5 steal 6 abduct, kidnap, snatch 7 bear off 8 carry off 10 run off with 11 get away with

make one's blood boil 5 anger 6 enrage, madden 7 incense, inflame 9 infuriate

make one's eyes pop 4 stun 5 shock 6 dazzle 7 stagger, startle 8 astonish 9 electrify 11 flabbergast

make out 3 see 4 see 4 espy 6 behold, descry, detect, fill in 7 discern, observe, pick out 8 get along, perceive, write out 12 catch sight of

make plain 7 clarify, clear up, explain, lay open 9 elucidate, explicate, make clear 10 illuminate 11 disentangle, shed light on 12 bring to light

make possible 5 allow 6 enable, permit 7 empower, qualify 10 capacitate

make public 3 air 4 tell, vent 5 print, utter, voice 6 expose, inform, reveal, spread 7 declare, display, divulge, exhibit, express, give out, publish 8 announce, disclose, proclaim, televise 9 broadcast, circulate, publicize

maker, Maker 3 god 4 poet 5 smith 6 author, forger 7 builder, creator, founder 8 declarer, inventor, producer 9 architect, generator 12 originator 12 manufacturer

make ready 5 prime 7 arrange, forearm, prepare

make reparation for 5 atone, repay 6 pay for 10 compensate, recompense, remunerate

make restitution 5 repay 7 pay back 9 reimburse 10 compensate, recompense

make right 3 fix 5 amend, emend 6 remedy, repair 7 correct, improve, rectify

make self-conscious 5 abash 6 rattle 7 chagrin, fluster 9 discomfit, embarrass 10 disconcert

makeshift 6 make-do 7 standby, stopgap 8 slapdash 9 alternate, expedient, temporary, tentative 10 substitute 11 provisional

make sick 6 revolt 7 disgust 8 nauseate

make smaller 6 lessen, reduce, shrink, take in 8 decrease, diminish

make sure 5 cinch 6 assure, clinch, decide, ensure, secure, settle 9 ascertain 11 double-check

make thinner 4 thin 6 dilute 9 water down 10 adulterate

make tracks 2 go 4 scat, shoo 5 be off, leave, scram 6 beat it, cut out, depart, go away 8 withdraw 10 hit the road

make uncomfortable 3 try 7 agitate, perturb 8 disquiet, distress 9 discomfit, embarrass 10 discompose

make uneasy 7 disturb, perturb, trouble, unnerve 8 disquiet, distress 9 discomfit, embarrass 10 discomfort, discompose, disconcert

make uniform 4 even 5 equal 6 smooth 7 balance 8 equalize 10 straighten

makeup 5 frame 9 character, cosmetics, framework, structure 11 composition, personality 12 constitution, organization

make up 4 form 5 cover 6 invent 7 arrange, concoct 8 assemble 9 improvise, reconcile 10 compensate, constitute 11 put together

make up for 5 atone 7 expiate 8 make good 10 make amends 13 compensate for

make up one's mind 6 decide 7 resolve 9 determine

make use of 3 use 5 apply 6 employ, engage, occupy 7 exploit, utilize 8 keep busy, put to use 13 turn to account

make weary 4 do in, poop, tire 7 exhaust, wear out 8 enervate

makeweight 6 weight 7 ballast

make well 4 cure, heal

make wider 5 widen 6 dilate, expand 7 broaden, stretch 9 spread out

make worse 6 worsen 8 heighten, increase 9 aggravate, intensify 10 exacerbate

making excuses 8 alibiing 9 defending 10 justifying 11 apologizing

Making of the President, The (series)
   author: 14 Theodore H White

making the rounds 5 about 6 abroad 11 circulating, going around 13 going the route

Malachi
   means: 11 my messenger
   identified with: 4 Ezra 8 Mordecai, Nehemiah 10 Zerubbabel

maladroit 5 inept 6 clumsy, gauche 7 awkward, unhandy 8 bumbling, bungling, tactless 9 impolitic, unskilled 10 blundering, left-handed, ungraceful

maladroitness 9 gaucherie, inability 10 clumsiness, ineptitude 11 awkwardness, unhandiness 12 incompetence

malady 7 ailment, disease, illness 8 disorder, sickness 9 affection, complaint, infirmity 10 affliction, disability

mala fide 10 in bad faith, not genuine

malaise 4 pang 5 throb 6 twinge 7 anxiety 8 disquiet 9 lassitude 10 uneasiness, discomfort 11 nervousness

Malamud, Bernard
   author of: 8 The Fixer 9 God's Grace 10 The Natural, The Tenants 11 Dubin's Lives 12 The Assistant

Malaprop, Mrs
   character in: 9 The Rivals
   author: 8 Sheridan

Malawi
   other name: 9 Nyasaland
   capital: 8 Lilongwe
   largest city: 8 Blantyre
   others: 4 Bana 5 Dedza, Limbe, Mzuzu, Zomba 6 Kasese, Mzimba, Salima 7 Chipoka, Chiromo, Deep Bay, Karonga, Katumbi 8 Chikwawa, Chilumbe, Kota Kota, Nkata Bay 9 Monkey Bay 10 Port Herald 12 Fort Johnston, Livingstonia
   monetary unit: 6 kwacha 7 tambala
   lake: 5 Nyasa 6 Chilwa, Malawi
   mountain: 11 Livingstone
   highest point: 6 Mlanje 7 Mulanje
   river: 3 Bua 5 Shire 7 Dwangwa 11 South Rukuru
   physical feature:
      highlands: 5 Shire
      plateau: 5 Nyika
      valley: 5 Shire 9 Great Rift
   people: 3 Yao 4 Sena 5 Bantu, Lomwe, Ngoni 6 Cheiva, Maravi, Ngonde, Nyanja 7 Tumbuka
   dynasty: 6 Maravi
   explorer: 16 David Livingstone
   leader: 5 Banda
   language: 3 Yao 4 Cewa 5 Bantu, Ngoni, Tonga 6 Nyanja 7 English, Tumbuka 8 Chichewa 10 Chitumbuka
   religion: 5 Islam 7 animism 10 Protestant 12 Presbyterian 13 Roman Catholic
   feature:
      village: 5 mudzi

Malaysia
   capital/largest city: 11 Kuala Lumpur
   others: 4 Ipoh, Sibu 5 Anson, Davao, Telok 6 Iloilo, Johore, Kupang, Manado, Penang, Pinang 7 Bintulu, Kuantan, Kuching, Melalap 8 Port Weld, Sandakan 10 Georgetown, Kota Baharu 11 Johor Baharu, Port Dickson 12 Kota Kinabulu 14 Port Swettenham
   division: 5 Sabah 6 Malaya 7 Malacca, Sarawak
   head of state:
      supreme head of state: 18 yang dipertuan agong
   measure: 3 pau, tun 4 para, pipe, tael, wang 5 parah 6 chupak, parrah 7 gantang
   monetary unit: 3 sen, tra 4 taro, trah 7 ringgit, tampang
   weight: 4 chee, mace, tael, wang 7 tampang
   island: 6 Banggi, Borneo, Labuan, Penang, Pinang, Tioman 7 Pangkor, Sebatik 8 Langkawi 10 Perhentian 11 Balambangan
   mountain: 4 Bulu, Hose, Iban, Iran, Main, Mulu, Niut, Raja 5 Murjo, Niapa, Ophir 6 Blumut, Kapuas, Leuser, Slamet 7 Binaija, Brassey, Crocker 8 Rindjani 11 Gunong Korbu, Gunong Tahan
   highest point: 8 Kinabalu
   river: 5 Klang, Kutai, Perak 6 Barito, Pahang, Rajang, Rejang 7 Sarawak 12 Kinabatangan
   sea: 4 Sulu 7 Celebes 10 South China
   physical feature:
      bay: 5 Labuk
      cape: 5 Sirik
      highlands: 7 Cameron
      passage: 5 Sibutu
      peninsula: 5 Malay
      point: 13 Tanjong Gelang

strait: 6 Johore 7 Balabac, Malacca
people: 4 Iban 5 Dayak, Malay 6 Indian 7 Chinese, Kadazan 9 Pakistani, Sri Lankan 10 Bangladesh, Indonesian
language: 4 Bugi, Dyak 5 Malay, Tamil 6 Battok, Rejang 7 Chinese, English, Lampong, Niasese 8 Achinese, Javanese, Makassar 14 Bahasa Malaysia
alphabet: 5 tagal
religion: 5 Hindu, Islam 6 Taoism 7 animism 8 Buddhism 12 Christianity, Confucianism
place:
mosque: 8 National
feature:
cap: 7 songkok
cloth: 4 tapa 5 batik
clothing: 4 baju, malo, sari 5 badju, pareu 6 cabaya, kebaya, sam-foo, sarong 9 cheongsam
dance: 4 haka, hula 5 joget
game: 9 sepakraga
hamlet: 7 kampong
parish: 5 mukim
rice paddy: 4 padi
scarf: 9 selendang
self-defense: 5 silat
shadow play: 6 menora
spirit: 5 hantu
food:
drink: 4 kava
fruit: 6 durian 8 rambutan 10 mangosteen
Malcolm
character in: 7 Macbeth
author: 11 Shakespeare
Malcolm X
original name: 13 Malcolm Little
born: 2 NE 5 Omaha
religion: 5 Islam 11 Black Muslim 13 Nation of Islam
assassinated in: 6 Harlem 11 New York City
book about: 26 The Autobiography of Malcolm X
author: 9 Alex Haley
film about: 8 Malcolm X
director: 8 Spike Lee
malcontent 4 glum, sour 5 rebel 6 grouch, grumpy, morose, sullen, uneasy 7 grouchy, growler, repiner, restive 8 dejected, downcast, grumbler, restless 9 insurgent, irritable 10 complainer, despondent 11 faultfinder 12 discontented, dissatisfied, faultfinding, hard to please
mal de mer 11 seasickness
Malden, Karl
real name: 16 Mladen Sekulovich
born: 6 Gary IL
roles: 6 Patton 8 Baby Doll 15 On the Waterfront 21 A Streetcar Named Desire 24 The Streets of San Francisco
Maldives
capital/largest city: 4 Male
government:
legislature: 6 Majlis
monetary unit: 5 laree, rupee

island: 3 Ari, Gan 4 Addu, Male 5 Rasdu 6 Felidu, Hulele, Mulaku 7 Malcolm, Minicoy, Nilandu 8 Maldives, Suvadiva 9 Fadiffolu, Wilingili 10 Haddummati, Kolumadulu 11 Tiladummati 13 Ihavandiffulu, Miladummadulu 16 North Malosmadulu, South Malosmadulu
sea: 6 Indian 7 Arabian 9 Laccadive
physical feature:
channel: 4 Wadu 7 Kardiva 8 Veimandu 10 Equatorial 11 Eight Degree 17 One and a Half Degree
people: 4 Arab 6 Indian 9 Sinhalese 10 Singhalese
ruling family/sultans: 4 Didi
language: 6 Arabic, Divehi
religion: 5 Islam
feature:
coconut fiber: 4 coir
dried coconut: 5 copra
male 3 boy, man, ram 4 bull 5 manly, youth 6 tomcat 7 manlike, rooster 8 stallion 9 billy goat, masculine
Male
capital of: 8 Maldives
male bird 4 cock 5 drake 6 gander 7 rooster
maledict 4 damn 5 curse 8 denounce 9 proscribe 12 anathematize
malediction 5 curse 8 anathema, diatribe 9 damnation, evil spell 10 execration 11 fulmination, imprecation 12 denunciation, proscription
malefactor 5 felon, knave, rogue 6 sinner 7 culprit 8 criminal, evil-doer, offender 9 miscreant, scoundrel, wrongdoer 10 malfeasant
male hairdresser
French: 8 coiffeur
malentendu 7 mistake 16 misunderstanding
male power
god of: 7 Priapus
Malevich, Kasimir Severinovich
born: 4 Kiev 6 Russia
artwork: 11 Black Square 15 The Knife Grinder 18 Eight Red Rectangles 19 Woman with Water Pails 34 Suprematist Composition White on White
malevolence 4 evil, hate 5 spite 6 enmity, grudge, hatred, malice, rancor, spleen 7 despite, ill will 9 hostility, malignity 10 antagonism, malignance, malignancy 12 spitefulness 13 maliciousness
malevolent 5 surly 6 malign, sullen 7 baleful, vicious 8 sinister, spiteful, venomous 9 invidious, malicious, malignant, rancorous, resentful 10 ill-natured, pernicious, revengeful 11 acrimonious, ill-disposed 14 ill-intentioned
malfeasance 5 crime 8 misdeeds 10 misconduct, wrongdoing
malformation 9 deformity 10 aberration, distortion 11 abnormality, monstrosity, peculiarity 12 grotesquerie, irregularity 13 disfigurement

malformed 7 twisted 8 deformed 9 contorted, distorted, grotesque, irregular, misshapen

malfunction 6 glitch, malady 7 problem 9 complaint

malgre lui 16 in spite of himself

Mali

  other name: 11 French Sudan 12 French Soudan 16 Sudanese Republic

  capital/largest city: 6 Bamako

  others: 3 Gao 5 Kayes, Mopti, Segou 6 Djenne 7 Sikasso 8 Taoudeni, Timbuktu 10 Tombouctou

  division: 5 Sahel 7 Azaouad

  monetary unit: 5 franc 7 centime

  lake: 2 Do 4 Debo 5 Garou 7 Korarou 9 Faguibine

  mountain: 4 Mina 6 Iforas 7 Manding

  highest point: 12 Hombori Tondo

  river: 4 Bani 5 Bagoe, Bakoy, Diaka, Niger 6 Bafing, Bakoye, Baoule, Faleme 7 Azaouak, Senegal

  physical feature:

  desert: 6 Sahara 8 Chech Erg 10 Sekkane Erg 13 Haricha Hamada

  plateau: 14 Adrar des Iforas

  valley: 5 Niger 7 Tilemsi

  people: 3 Bwa 4 Fula, Kyan, Moor, Peul 5 Dogon, Dyula, Fulbe, Marka 6 Berber, Dognon, Fulani, Senufo, Tuareg 7 Bambara, Fellata, Malinke, Miniaka, Songhai, Soninke 8 Khasonke, Mandingo, Senoufo

  leader: 4 Umar 5 Keita 6 Traore 9 Mansa Musa

  language: 5 Dogon, Dyula, Feulh, Mande, Marka 6 Berber, French, Fulani 7 Bambara, Malinke, Senoufo, Songhai

  religion: 5 Islam 7 animism

  place:

  ruins: 8 Terhazza

  feature:

  empire: 4 Mali 5 Ghana 7 Bambara, Songhai

malice 4 hate 5 spite, venom 6 enmity, grudge, hatred, rancor 7 ill will 8 acrimony 9 animosity, malignity 10 antagonism, bitterness, evil intent, resentment 11 malevolence 12 spitefulness

malice aforethought

  legal term: 51 planning to commit a crime without just cause or provocation

malicious 7 baleful, harmful, hateful, vicious 8 spiteful 9 invidious, malignant, rancorous, resentful 10 malevolent, revengeful, vindictive 11 acrimonious, ill-disposed

malign 3 bad 4 evil 5 abuse, black 6 defame, revile, vilify 7 baneful, harmful, hateful, noxious, ominous, put down, run down, slander 8 backbite, bad mouth, belittle, derogate, deprecate, disparage, injurious, malicious, malignant 10 malevolent, pernicious, speak ill of 11 deleterious, detrimental, threatening 14 inveigh against

malignancy 5 spite, tumor 6 cancer, malice, rancor 7 ill will, sarcoma 8 acrimony, neoplasm, toxicity 9 carcinoma, hostility, virulence 10 bitterness 11 malevolence, viciousness 12 hard feelings, spitefulness, vengefulness 13 poisonousness

malignant 4 evil 5 fatal, toxic 6 bitter, deadly 7 hateful, hostile, vicious 8 fiendish, spiteful, venomous, virulent 9 invidious, malicious, poisonous, rancorous, resentful 10 diabolical, evil-minded, malevolent, pernicious, revengeful, vindictive 11 acrimonious, ill-disposed

malignant spirit 3 imp 5 demon, devil 7 gremlin

malignity 4 evil 5 spite, venom 6 animus, rancor, spleen 7 ill will 8 acrimony 9 animosity 12 hard feelings, spitefulness, venomousness

malinger 4 loaf 5 dodge, evade, shirk, slack 7 goof off 9 goldbrick

mall 4 yard 5 court, plaza 6 arcade, circus, piazza, square 8 cloister 9 colonnade, esplanade, promenade 10 quadrangle 12 parade ground

Mallarme, Stephane

  author of: 8 Herodias 18 L'Apres Midi d'un faune 19 The Afternoon of a Faun

Malle, Louis

  director of: 10 Pretty Baby 12 Atlantic City 13 Lacombe Lucien 16 Murmur of the Heart

malleable 6 docile, pliant 7 ductile, plastic, pliable 8 flexible, moldable, workable 9 adaptable, compliant, teachable, tractable 10 governable, manageable 12 easily shaped 13 easily wrought 14 impressionable

mallet

  type: 6 rubber, wooden 12 plastic-faced

mallophaga

  class: 8 hexapoda

  phylum: 10 arthropoda

  group: 8 bird lice 10 biting lice

malnutrition 10 emaciation, starvation 16 undernourishment

malodorous 4 rank 5 acrid, fetid, musty 6 putrid, smelly 7 noisome, reeking 8 stinking 12 foul-smelling

Malone, Dorothy

  real name: 20 Dorothy Eloise Maloney

  husband: 15 Jacques Bergerac

  born: 9 Chicago IL

  roles: 11 Peyton Place 14 Too Much Too Soon 16 Written on the Wind

Malory, Sir Thomas

  author of: 14 Le Morte d'Arthur

Malpighi, Marcello

  field: 10 physiology

  nationality: 7 Italian

  founded: 18 microscopic anatomy

malpractice 10 negligence

Malraux, Andre

  author of: 8 Man's Fate 11 Anti-Memoirs, Days of Wrath, The Royal Way 13 The Conquerors 18 The Voices of Silence

Malta
  capital: 8 Valletta
  largest city: 6 Sliema
  others: 5 Marfa, Mdina, Mgarr, Mosta, Nadut, Paola, Rabat 6 Zejtun 7 Senglea, Zeibrun 8 Cospicua, Floriana, Mellieha, Victoria 10 Birkirkara, Birzebbuga, Vittoriosa
  measure: 4 rotl 5 artal, canna, parto, ratel, salma 6 kantar 7 caffiso
  monetary unit: 4 cent 5 grain, grano, pound
  island: 4 Gozo 5 Malta 6 Comino, Filfla 7 Filfola 9 Cominotto 10 Comminotto
  highest point: 12 Dingli Cliffs
  sea: 13 Mediterranean
  physical feature:
  bay: 7 St Paul's 8 Mellieha 10 Marsaxlokk
  channel: 11 North Comino, South Comino
  harbor: 5 Grand 10 Marsamxett
  people: 7 Maltese
  leader: 7 Mintoff 9 Buttigieo 18 Parisot de La Valette
  ruler: 5 Arabs 6 Romans 7 British 8 Napoleon 10 Byzantines 11 Hospitalers, Phoenicians 13 Carthaginians 15 Holy Roman Empire, Knights of St John
  language: 7 English, Italian, Maltese
  religion: 13 Roman Catholic
  feature:
  gondola boat: 7 dghaisa

Maltese Falcon, The
  author: 15 Dashiell Hammett
  director: 10 John Huston
  cast: 9 Mary Astor (Brigid O'Shaughnessy) 10 Peter Lorre (Joel Cairo) 12 Elisha Cook Jr (Wilmer), Gladys George 14 Humphrey Bogart (Sam Spade) 17 Sydney Greenstreet (the Fat Man)
  character: 6 Wilmer 8 Sam Spade 9 Joel Cairo 11 Miles Archer 12 Casper Gutman, Floyd Thursby 18 Brigid O'Shaughnessy
  remade as: 13 Satan Met a Lady

malt liquor 3 ale 4 beer, bock, brew 5 stout 6 porter

maltreat 4 harm, hurt 5 abuse 6 ill-use, injure 8 mistreat

maltreatment 5 abuse 6 ill-use, injury 7 assault, cruelty 10 bodily harm, oppression 11 manhandling, molestation, persecution 12 mistreatment

Malvolio
  character in: 12 Twelfth Night
  author: 11 Shakespeare

Mama
  character: 4 Nels 6 Dagmar, Katrin, TR Ryan 9 Aunt Jenny 10 (Papa) Lars Hansen 11 (Mama) Marta Hansen
  cast: 8 Iris Mann 9 Peggy Wood, Ruth Gates 11 Judson Laire, Robin Morgan 12 Rosemary Rice 13 Dick Van Patten, Kevin Coughlin
  dog: 6 Willie

  based on book: 16 Mama's Bank Account
  setting: 12 San Francisco
  theme: 12 Holverg Suite 13 The Last Spring

Mamers *see* 4 Mars

mamma, mama 2 ma 3 mam, mom, mum 4 wife 5 madre, mammy, mater, mommy, mummy, mumsy, woman 6 mother, parent

mammal
  bat (chiroptera): 4 tomb 5 fruit, naked, smoky 7 mastiff, vampire 9 fisherman, horseshoe, leaf-nosed, sac-winged, slit-faced, thumbless 10 disk-winged, free-tailed, moustached 11 funnel-eared, hollow-faced, mouse-tailed 12 false vampire, sheath-tailed, sucker-footed, yellow-winged 14 vespertilionid 21 New Zealand short-tailed
  carnivore: 3 cat, dog, fox 4 bear, lion, lynx, mink, puma, wolf 5 civet, dingo, fossa, hyena, otter, panda, skunk, tayra, tiger 6 badger, bobcat, coyote, ferret, grison, hyaena, jackal, jaguar, marten, olingo, weasel 7 polecat, raccoon 8 aardwolf, kinkajou, mongoose, suricate 9 wolverine 10 cacomistle, coatimundi
  cetacea: 4 gray 5 pilot, right, whale 6 beluga, killer 7 dolphin, rorqual 8 humpback, narwhale, porpoise 10 sperm whale 11 beaked whale 16 bottle-nosed whale
  edentata: 5 sloth 8 anteater 9 armadillo, tree sloth
  egg-laying: 7 echidna 13 spiny anteater 18 duck-billed platypus
  even-toed ungulate: 2 ox 3 elk, hog, pig 4 deer, goat, oxen 5 bison, camel, llama, moose, okapi, sheep 6 alpaca, cattle, duiker, vicuna 7 buffalo, caribou, gazelle, giraffe, guanaco, muntjak, peccary 8 antelope 9 mouse deer 10 chevrotain 12 hippopotamus
  hyracoidea: 5 hyrax
  insect-eating: 4 mole 5 shrew 6 desman, tenrec 7 gymnure, moon rat 8 hedgehog 9 shrew-mole, solenodon 10 golden mole, otter shrew, water shrew 13 elephant shrew
  lagomorpha: 4 hare, pika 6 rabbit
  marsupials/pouched: 5 koala 6 cuscus, numbat, possum, wombat 7 opossum, wallaby 8 kangaroo 9 bandicoot, phalanger 14 Tasmanian devil
  odd-toed ungulate: 3 ass 5 horse, kiang, tapir, zebra 6 onager, quagga 10 rhinoceros
  pinnipedia: 4 seal 6 walrus 7 sea lion
  primate: 5 lemur, loris, potto 6 avahis, aye-aye, baboon, galago, gibbon, indris, monkey, people 7 gorilla, tamarin, tarsier 8 marmoset, simpoona 9 orangutan, tree shrew 10 chimpanzee
  proboscidea: 8 elephant
  rodent: 4 cavy, vole 5 coypu, gundi, hutia, mouse 6 agouti, beaver, coruro, gerbil, gopher, jerboa, nutria 7 blesmol, cane rat, hamster, lemming, mole-rat, rock rat

8 capybara, chipmunk, dormouse, sewellel, spiny rat, squirrel, tucu-tuco, viscacha 9 chozchori, false paca, pacaranas, porcupine, woodchuck 10 chinchilla, prairie dog, springhare 11 kangaroo rat, pocket mouse, viscacha rat 13 kangaroo mouse 16 Speke's pectinator

sirenia: 6 dugong, sea cow 7 manatee

tubulidentata: 8 aardvark

mammon, Mammon 4 gain, gold 5 money 6 profit, riches, wealth 9 affluence 11 possessions 13 material goods, the god of money

Mammon, Sir Epicure
  character in: 12 The Alchemist
  author: 6 Jonson

mammoth 4 huge 5 great 6 mighty 7 immense, massive 8 colossal, enormous, gigantic, whopping 9 cyclopean, herculean, monstrous, ponderous, very large 10 gargantuan, monumental, prodigious, stupendous, tremendous 11 elephantine, mountainous

Mammy
  character in: 15 Gone With the Wind
  author: 8 Mitchell

Mamoulian, Rouben
  director of: 13 Love Me Tonight, Silk Stockings 14 Queen Christina, The Mark of Zorro

Mamurius
  copied: 6 Ancile

man 3 boy, guy, one 4 chap, gent, hand, male, soul 5 equip, hubby, human, staff 6 anyone, attend, butler, fellow, fit out, helper, outfit, people, person, spouse, waiter, worker 7 footman, husband, laborer, mankind, someone, subject, workman 8 employee, garrison, handyman, henchman, humanity, liegeman, somebody 9 assistant, gentleman, hired hand, humankind 11 Homo sapiens
  Spanish: 6 hombre

Man, first 4 Adam 12 Alalcomeneus
  Nordic: 3 Ask

Man, Woman and Child
  author: 10 Erich Segal

man-about-town 5 blade 7 playboy 8 cavalier, gay blade 12 boulevardier

manacle, manacles 3 ply, run, use 4 cope, fare, head, rule, work 5 bonds, get on, guide, irons, order, pilot, shift, steer, wield 6 chains, direct, fetter, govern, handle, make go 7 command, conduct, control, operate, oversee, shackle, succeed, survive, work out 8 cope with, deal with, dominate, get along, handcuff, maneuver, shackles 9 bracelets, handcuffs, look after, supervise, watch over 10 accomplish, administer, bring about, manipulate, put in irons, take care of 11 be at the helm, hand-fetters, preside over, put in chains, superintend 12 have charge of, hold the reins

manage 4 care, rule 6 bosses, charge, wheels 7 bigwigs, command, conduct, control, dealing, running, tactics 8 big shots, guidance, handling, ordering, plan-

ning, strategy, top brass 9 direction, directors, operation 10 conducting, executives, overseeing, regulation 11 generalship, negotiation, supervision, supervisors, transaction 12 manipulation, organization 14 administration, administrators 15 superintendence

manageable 4 easy 6 docile, pliant, wieldy 8 amenable, flexible 9 compliant, tractable 10 governable, submissive 12 controllable

management 4 boss, head 5 agent, chief 7 foreman, planner 8 overseer 9 budgeteer, majordomo, organizer, tactician 10 impresario, negotiator, supervisor 11 manipulator 13 administrator 14 superintendent

manager 4 boss, head 5 agent, chief 7 foreman, planner 8 overseer 9 budgeteer, majordomo, organizer, tactician 10 impresario, negotiator, supervisor 11 manipulator 13 administrator 14 superintendent

managerial 9 executive 10 management 11 supervisory 14 administrative, organizational

Managua
  capital of: 9 Nicaragua

Manala see 7 Tuonela

Manama
  capital of: 7 Bahrain

manana 6 future 8 tomorrow 11 in the future

Man and Superman
  author: 17 George Bernard Shaw

Manannan
  origin: 5 Irish
  god of: 3 sea
  father: 3 Ler, Lir

Manassa Mauler
  nickname of: 11 Jack Dempsey

Manasseh
  father: 6 Joseph
  mother: 7 Asenath
  great uncle: 4 Esau
  grandfather: 5 Jacob
  descendant of: 9 Manassite

man-at-arms 7 fighter, soldier, warrior 9 combatant 10 cavalryman

Manawyddan
  origin: 5 Welsh
  father: 4 Llyr
  sister: 7 Branwen
  brother: 4 Bran 9 Evnissyen
  wife: 8 Rhiannon
  rescued: 7 Pryderi

Manchester, William
  author of: 11 The Last Lion 14 American Caesar 15 Goodbye Darkness

Manchuria
  also: 7 Manchow
  city: 5 Aigun, Hulan, Kirin, Peian, Penki 6 Anshan, Antung, Dairen, Fu-Shun, Hailar, Harbin, Hokang, Mukden, Penchi, Yenchi 7 Hulutao, Ikuliho, Ssuping, Tantung 8 Chinchao, Paicheng, Shenyang 9 Changchun, Chiamussu, Manchouli, Miuchwang 10 Port Arthur 11 Chichihaerh, Mutanchiang
  peninsula: 8 Liaotung

province: 5 Jehol, Jilin, Kirin 8 Liaoning 12 Heilongjiang, Heilungkiang

river: 4 Amur, Liao, Yalu 5 Argun, Mutan, Nonni, Tumen 6 Ussuri 7 Sungari

tribe: 5 Tungu 6 Manchu, Mongol

Mandalay
  found in: 18 Barrack-Room Ballads
  author: 14 Rudyard Kipling

mandamus
  legal term: 48 writ from a superior court commanding that a thing be done
  literally: 9 we command

Mandan
  language family: 6 Siouan
  location: 11 North Dakota
  ceremony: 5 Okipa

Mandarins, The
  author: 16 Simone de Beauvoir

Mandasuchus
  type: 8 dinosaur
  period: 8 Triassic

mandate 5 edict, order 6 behest, charge, decree 7 bidding, command, dictate 8 approval, sanction 9 authority, direction, directive 10 commission, dependency 11 instruction, requisition 12 protectorate 13 authorization

mandatory 7 binding, exigent, needful 8 required 9 called for, essential, necessary, requisite 10 compulsory, imperative, obligatory, peremptory

Mande
  language family: 16 Niger-Kordofanian
  group: 10 Niger-Congo
  includes: 3 Vai 5 Mende 7 Bambara, Malinke

Mandelbaum Gate, The
  author: 11 Muriel Spark

Manderly
  house in: 7 Rebecca
  author: 9 Du Maurier

mandible 3 jaw 4 beak, bill, jowl 7 maxilla 8 lower jaw
  part: 4 mala 5 angle, molar, ramus 6 corpus

Mandrake the Magician
  creator: 7 Lee Falk 9 Phil Davis
  character: 5 Narda 6 Lothar

Manes
  spirits or souls of: 4 dead

Manet, Edouard
  born: 5 Paris 6 France
  artwork: 7 Olympia 8 The Fifer 9 Emile Zola 10 Argenteuil 12 The Guitarist 19 Le Dejeuner sur l'Herbe (Luncheon on the Grass) 25 The Bar at the Folies-Bergeres 31 Execution of the Emperor Maximilian

Manette, Dr and Lucie
  characters in: 16 A Tale of Two Cities
  author: 7 Dickens

maneuver 4 move, plot, ploy 5 dodge, guide, pilot, steer, trick 6 deploy, device, gambit, scheme, tactic 7 finagle 8 artifice, contrive, intrigue 9 stratagem 10 manipulate 11 contrivance, machination, pull strings

Man for All Seasons, A
  director: 13 Fred Zinnemann
  based on play by: 10 Robert Bolt
  cast: 9 Leo McKern 10 Robert Shaw 11 Orson Welles, Wendy Hiller 12 Paul Scofield (Sir Thomas More), Susannah York 14 Nigel Davenport 15 Vanessa Redgrave
  Oscar for: 5 actor (Scofield) 7 picture 8 director

Manfred
  author: 21 George Gordon Lord Byron

man Friday 4 aide 8 adjutant, employee 9 assistant 10 aide de camp 12 right-hand man

Man from St Petersburg, The
  author: 10 Ken Follett

Man from UNCLE, The
  character: 9 Mr Waverly 12 Napoleon Solo 13 Illya Kuryakin
  cast: 11 Leo G Carroll 12 Robert Vaughn 13 David McCallum
  foe: 6 THRUSH

manful 5 brave 8 resolute 10 courageous

manganese
  chemical symbol: 2 Mn

mangle 3 cut 4 harm, hurt, lame, maim, maul, ruin, tear 5 crush, press, slash 6 damage, impair, injure 7 flatten 8 lacerate, mutilate 9 disfigure

manhandle 4 maul 5 abuse 6 batter 7 rough up 8 maltreat, mistreat 9 pull about, push about 10 knock about, slap around

Manhattan
  director: 10 Woody Allen
  cast: 9 Anne Byrne 10 Woody Allen 11 Diane Keaton, Meryl Streep 13 Michael Murphy 15 Mariel Hemingway

Manhattan Transfer
  author: 13 John Dos Passos

manhood 5 prime 8 legal age, machismo, majority, maleness, maturity, virility 9 adulthood, manliness, mature age 10 manfulness 11 masculinity

mania 4 rage 5 craze 6 frenzy, lunacy, raving 7 craving, madness, passion 8 delirium, delusion, dementia, fixation, hysteria, insanity 9 monomania, obsession 10 aberration, compulsion, enthusiasm, fanaticism 11 fascination, infatuation

maniac 3 ass, nut 4 fool 5 loony 6 cuckoo, madman, nitwit 7 half-wit, lunatic 9 psychotic, screwball, simpleton 10 crackbrain, psychopath

manic 2 up 4 high 7 excited, frantic, hyped up 8 agitated, frenzied, worked up 9 wrought up 10 freaked out, switched on 11 hyperactive

manifest 4 bare, open, show 5 clear, frank, plain 6 candid, evince, expose, patent, reveal, unveil 7 display, divulge, evident, exhibit, express, obvious, uncover, visible 8 apparent, disclose, evidence, indicate, palpable 9 make known 10 noticeable 11 demonstrate, make visible, self-evident, transparent, unconcealed, undisguised

manifestation 4 show 7 display, example, symptom 8 evidence, instance 10 exhibition, expression, indication, revelation 12 illustration, presentation, proclamation, public notice 13 demonstration

manifesto 4 bull 5 edict, ukase 6 notice 9 broadside, statement 10 communique, encyclical 11 declaration 12 announcement, annunciation, notification, proclamation, public notice 13 position paper, pronouncement 14 pronunciamento

manifold 4 many 6 myriad, varied 7 complex, diverse 8 multiple, numerous 9 many-sided, multiform 10 variegated 11 diversified, innumerable 12 multifarious 13 multitudinous

Manila
　capital of: 11 Philippines
　former name: 8 Maynilad
　island: 5 Luzon
　landmark: 9 Rizal Park 16 San Agustin Church
　river: 5 Pasig
　section: 10 Quezon City
　university: 10 Santo Tomas

Man in the Gray Flannel Suit, The
　author: 11 Sloan Wilson

manipulate 3 pat, ply, use 4 feel, work 5 drive, pinch, wield 6 employ, finger, handle, manage, stroke 7 control, deceive, defraud, massage, operate, squeeze

Manitoba
　bay: 6 Hudson
　capital: 8 Winnipeg
　city: 6 Carman, The Pas 7 Brandon, Caribou, Dauphin, Selkirk 8 Flin Flon, Lynn Lake, Wabowden, Winnipeg 9 Churchill, Killarney, Sherridon, Swan River 10 St Boniface 11 Norway House, York Factory 16 Portage La Prairie
　flower: 11 windflower 13 prairie crocus
　Indian tribe: 4 Cree 6 Eskimo, Ojibwa 8 Chippewa 10 Assiniboin
　lake: 4 God's, Swan 5 Cedar, Moose 6 Island 7 Dauphin, Red Deer 8 Manitoba, Reindeer, St Martin, Waterhen, Winnipeg 9 Granville
　mountain: 4 Hart 5 Baldy
　name means: 16 lake of the prairies 18 Great Spirit's strait 19 Great Spirit's narrows
　nickname: 15 Prairie Province 16 Keystone Province
　province of: 6 Canada
　river: 3 Red 4 Seal, Swan 5 Hayes 6 Nelson, Roseau, Souris 7 Pembina 8 Winnipeg 9 Churchill 11 Assiniboine 12 Saskatchewan
　university: 7 Brandon 10 St Boniface

Mankiewicz, Joseph L
　director of: 6 Sleuth 9 Cleopatra 11 All About Eve (Oscar) 12 Guys and Dolls, Julius Caesar 18 The Ghost and Mrs Muir 19 A Letter to Three Wives (Oscar)

mankind 3 man 6 people 7 mortals, persons, society 8 humanity 9 humankind 11 Homo sapiens

manlike 5 macho, manly 6 virile 8 hominoid 9 masculine

manly 4 bold, male 5 brave, hardy, husky, noble 6 brawny, daring, heroic, manful, plucky, robust, strong, sturdy, virile 7 gallant, staunch, valiant 8 athletic, fearless, malelike, muscular, powerful, resolute, stalwart, vigorous 9 masculine, strapping 10 chivalrous, courageous 11 gentlemanly, indomitable, self-reliant 12 stouthearted
　Spanish: 5 macho

man-made 4 mock, sham 6 formed 7 crafted, created 8 produced 9 fashioned, ready-made, simulated, synthetic 10 artificial, fabricated, factitious, originated 11 constructed, handcrafted 12 manufactured

Mann, Delbert
　director of: 5 Marty (Oscar) 14 Separate Tables

Mann, Thomas
　author of: 12 Buddenbrooks 13 Death in Venice, Doctor Faustus 16 The Magic Mountain

manna, Manna 4 boon 5 award 6 reward 7 bonanza 16 divine sustenance

mannequin 4 form 5 dummy, model 6 figure

manner 3 air, way 4 form, kind, make, mode, mold, race, rank, sort, type 5 brand, breed, caste, genre, grade, guise, habit, stamp, style 6 aspect, custom, method, strain 7 bearing, conduct, fashion, species, variety 8 behavior, carriage, category, demeanor, practice, presence 9 character 10 appearance, deportment 14 classification

mannered 6 formal 7 stilted, studied 8 affected 9 contrived, unnatural 10 artificial 11 ceremonious

mannerism 4 airs, pose 5 habit 8 pretense 10 pretension 11 affectation, singularity 12 eccentricity, idiosyncrasy

mannerly 5 civil 6 polite 7 courtly, gallant, genteel, refined 8 well-bred 9 courteous 10 chivalrous 11 gentlemanly, well-behaved

manner of living
　Latin: 12 modus vivendi

manner of looking at the world
　German: 14 Weltanschauung

manner of speaking 7 diction 9 elocution 10 intonation 13 pronunciation

manners 6 polish 7 decorum 8 behavior, breeding, courtesy 9 amenities, deference, etiquette, gallantry, gentility, politesse, priority 10 deportment, politeness, refinement 11 courtliness

Mannix
　character: 9 Joe Mannix, Peggy Fair 10 (Lt) Adam Tobias 13 Lou Wickersham
　cast: 10 Gail Fisher, Robert Reed 11 Mike Connors 16 Joseph Campanella

Mannon family
　members: 4 Ezra, Orin 7 Lavinia 9 Christine
　characters in: 22 Mourning Becomes Electra
　author: 6 O'Neill

Manoah
son: 6 Samson

mano a mano 5 alone 8 conflict 13 confrontation, in a small group
literally: 10 hand to hand

Man of a Thousand Faces
nickname of: 9 Lon Chaney

Man of Nazareth
author: 14 Anthony Burgess

Man of Property, The
author: 14 John Galsworthy

Man of Sorrows see 5 Jesus

Manolin
character in: 18 The Old Man and the Sea
author: 9 Hemingway

Manon Lescaut
author: 11 Abbe Prevost

Manor, The
author: 19 Isaac Bashevis Singer

manor house 6 estate, manoir 7 chateau, mansion 11 stately home

manpower 4 help 5 brawn, labor 9 work force, employees

manque 6 failed, missed 7 lacking 11 fallen short, unfulfilled

Mansart, Francois
architect of: 14 Chateau de Berny 18 Hotel de la Vrilliere 33 Church of Sainte Marie de la Visitation
feature: 11 mansard roof

manservant 5 groom, valet 6 butler 7 footman 8 factotum 9 chauffeur

Man's Fate
author: 12 Andre Malraux

Mansfield, Jayne
real name: 14 Vera Jane Palmer
husband: 7 Mickey Hargitay
born: 10 Bryn Mawr PA
roles: 15 Hell on Frisco Bay 26 Will Success Spoil Rock Hunter

Mansfield, Katherine
author of: 5 Bliss 12 The Dove's Nest 14 The Garden Party

Mansfield Park
author: 10 Jane Austen
character: 5 Yates 8 Mrs Grant 9 Mrs Norris, Rushworth 10 Fanny Price 11 Lady Bertram 12 Mary Crawford 13 Henry Crawford 16 Sir Thomas Bertram
Bertram children: 3 Tom 5 Julia, Maria 6 Edmund

mansion 5 manor, villa 6 castle, estate, palace 7 chateau 10 manor house

manslaughter 6 murder 7 killing 8 homicide

manta 3 ray 4 cape 5 cloak, shawl 9 devilfish

Mantegna, Andrea
born: 5 Italy 14 Isola di Carturo
artwork: 9 Parnassus 16 Camera degli Sposi (Bridal Chamber) 18 The Triumph of Caesar, The Triumph of Virtue 20 Madonna della Vittoria

Man That Corrupted Hadleyburg, The
author: 9 Mark Twain

Mantius
father: 8 Melampus
son: 6 Clitus

mantle 4 cape, film, mask, pall, veil 5 cloak, cloud, cover, scarf, tunic 6 canopy, screen, shroud 7 blanket, curtain, wrapper 8 covering, envelope, mantilla

Mantle, Mickey (Charles)
sport: 8 baseball
position: 8 outfield
team: 14 New York Yankees

manual 6 primer 8 handbook, physical, textbook, workbook 9 guidebook 10 done by hand 12 hand-operated, nonautomatic 15 instruction book

manual skill 8 deftness 9 dexterity, handiness 10 adroitness 12 coordination

manufacture 4 form, make, mold 5 build, frame 6 cook up, create, devise, invent, make up 7 concoct, fashion, produce, think up, trump up 8 assemble 9 construct, fabricate 11 mass-produce, put together

manufacturing 8 devising 9 inventing, producing 10 industrial 11 fabricating, nonagrarian

manumission 7 freeing 10 liberation 11 setting free 12 emancipation

manumit 4 free 7 set free 8 liberate 10 emancipate

manure 4 dung 5 feces 6 ordure 7 compost, excreta 8 dressing 10 fertilizer

manuscript 6 script 10 typescript 14 shooting script 15 written document

Manvah
son: 6 Samson

Man Who Came to Dinner, The
director: 15 William Keighley
based on play by: 8 Moss Hart 14 George S Kaufman
cast: 10 Bette Davis 11 Ann Sheridan, Billie Burke 12 Monty Woolley 13 Richard Travis

Man Who Fell to Earth, The
director: 12 Nicholas Roeg
cast: 7 Rip Torn 9 Buck Henry 10 Candy Clark, David Bowie

Man Who Shot Liberty Valence, The
director: 8 John Ford
cast: 9 John Wayne, Lee Marvin, Vera Miles 12 Edmund O'Brien, James Stewart

Man Who Was Thursday, The
author: 12 G K Chesterton

Man Without a Country, The
author: 17 Edward Everett Hale
character: 11 Philip Nolan

many 4 a lot, lots 5 a heap, heaps, piles 6 divers, dozens, myriad, scores, sundry 7 numbers, several, various 8 numerous 9 countless 10 a profusion, numberless 11 an abundance, innumerable 13 multitudinous

manzanita 14 Arctostaphylos
varieties: 4 dune, Ione, Otay 5 hairy, hoary, Morro, Parry, Pecho 6 island, Sonoma, woolly 7 Mexican, Pajarro, pine-mat 8 big-berry, Del Norte, Eastwood, Mari-

posa, Monterey, shagbark, Stanford 9 Fort Bragg, green-leaf, heart-leaf, little Sur, white-leaf 10 serpentine, silver-leaf 11 brittle-leaf, pink-bracted

map 4 plan, plot 5 chart, graph, ready 6 design, devise, lay out 7 arrange, diagram, prepare, project 8 contrive, organize 9 elevation 10 make a map of, projection 14 representation 18 topographical chart

maple 4 Acer

varieties: 3 red 4 Amur, hard, rock, soft, vine 5 black, chalk, field, hedge, Nikko, river, sugar, swamp, white 6 Balkan, canyon, Norway, Oregon, parlor, sierra, silver, Triden 7 big-leaf, Florida, Persian, scarlet, striped 8 big-tooth, Drummond, full-moon, Hawthorn, Hornbeam, Japanese, mountain, Shantung, Sycamore, Tatarian 9 ash-leaved, eagle-claw, flowering, paperbark, Schwedler, Tartarian 11 Montpellier 12 Pennsylvania 13 Rocky Mountain, Southern sugar 18 Rocky Mountain sugar

map out 3 map 5 chart, draft 6 devise, lay out 7 diagram, outline 8 block out 9 delineate, formulate

Maputo

capital of: 10 Mozambique

mar 4 hurt, maim, mark, nick, ruin, scar 5 botch, spoil, stain, taint 6 blight, damage, deface, defile, impair 7 blemish, destroy, scratch 8 diminish, mutilate 9 disfigure

Marabar Caves

setting in: 15 A Passage to India

author: 7 Forster

Maranatha

means: 9 O Lord come

maraschino

type: 7 liqueur

origin: 5 Italy

flavor: 6 cherry

color: 3 red 5 white

Marathi

language family: 12 Indo-European

branch: 11 Indo-Iranian

group: 5 Indic

spoken in: 5 (northern) India

Marathonian bull see 10 Cretan bull

marauder 6 looter, pirate, ranger 7 corsair, ravager, spoiler 8 pillager 9 buccaneer, despoiler, guerrilla, plunderer, privateer 10 depradator, freebooter

marble 3 jet 4 vein 5 agate 6 basalt, blotch, mottle, streak 7 calcite 8 dolomite 9 limestone 10 serpentine, travertine 12 anthraconite

quarry: 7 Carrara

Marble Faun, The

author: 18 Nathaniel Hawthorne

character: 5 Hilda 6 Kenyon, Miriam 9 Donatello

marbles

type: 3 mib, taw 4 aggy, duck, immy, migg 5 agate, monny, scrap 6 commie, glassy, hoodle, marine 7 cat's eye, rainbow, shooter 9 carnelian 16 peppermint stripe

term: 3 hit 4 shot 6 edgers, ringer 7 bowling, for fair, histing, lagging, lag line, lofting 8 circling, for keeps, hunching 9 pitch line 10 roundsters 11 knuckle down 13 knuckling down

Marc, Franz

born: 6 Munich 7 Germany

artwork: 10 Blue Horses 12 Yellow Horses 13 Fighting Forms

Marceline

character in: 19 The Marriage of Figaro

author: 12 Beaumarchais

march 2 go 4 hike, rise, step, trek, walk 5 tramp 6 file by, growth, parade 7 advance, proceed 8 progress 9 group walk 10 go directly, procession, walk in step 11 advancement, development, progression 12 martial music

March

event: 8 Passover 9 Mardi Gras 11 Ides of March (15) 12 Ash Wednesday 13 vernal equinox (21)

flower: 7 jonquil 8 daffodil

French: 4 Mars

gem: 10 aquamarine, bloodstone

German: 4 Marz

holiday: 6 Easter 12 St Joseph's Day (19) 13 St Patrick's Day (17)

Italian: 5 Marzo

number of days: 9 thirty-one

origin of name: 4 Mars

Roman god of: 3 war

place in year:

Gregorian: 5 third

Roman: 5 first

saying: 20 Beware the Ides of March 40 March comes in like a lion and goes out like a lamb

Spanish: 6 Marcha

Zodiac sign: 5 Aries 6 Pisces

March, Fredric

real name: 29 Ernest Frederick McIntyre Bickel

born: 8 Racine WI

roles: 11 A Star Is Born 12 Anna Karenina, The Buccaneer 13 Les Miserables 14 Anthony Adverse, Inherit the Wind, Mary of Scotland, Seven Days in May 16 Death of a Salesman 17 Alexander the Great, Dr Jekyll and Mr Hyde (Oscar), The Desperate Hours 18 Death Takes a Holiday 19 The Affairs of Cellini 22 The Best Years of Our Lives (Oscar) 23 Barretts of Wimpole Street

Marchen 8 folk tale 9 fairy tale

Marcheshvan 17 eighth Hebrew month

March family

members: 2 Jo 3 Amy, Meg 4 Beth 6 Marmee

characters in: 11 Little Women

author: 6 Alcott

March Hare

character in: 28 Alice's Adventures in Wonderland

author: 7 Carroll

Marchmain family

characters in: 19 Brideshead Revisited

author: 5 Waugh

Marciano, Rocky
   real name: 23 Rocco Francis Marche-
   giano
   nickname: 19 Brockton Blockbuster
   sport: 6 boxing
   class: 11 heavyweight

Marconi, Guglielmo
   nationality: 7 Italian
   nickname: 16 father of wireless
   invented/discovered: 5 radio 12 radio
   signals 16 magnetic detector 30 wireless
   high frequency telegraph
   shared (1919): 20 Nobel Prize for physics

Marcus Welby MD
   character: 11 (Dr) Steven Kiley 13
   Consuelo Lopez
   cast: 11 James Brolin, Robert Young 12
   Elena Verdugo

Mardi (and a Voyage Thither)
   author: 14 Herman Melville
   character: 4 Alma, Jarl, Mohi, Taji 5 Media, Samoa, Yoomy 6 Yillah 7 Annatoo 10
   Babbalanja, Braidbeard 11 Queen Hautia

Mardi Gras 7 holiday 8 carnival, festival,
   jamboree 10 fat Tuesday

Marduk
   also: 8 Merodach 12 Baal Merodach
   origin: 10 Babylonian
   chief of: 4 gods

mare 3 sea 9 brood-mare 11 female horse

mare nostrum 6 our sea
   ancient Roman name for: 13 Mediterranean

mares of Diomedes *see* 8 Diomedes

margin 3 hem, rim 4 edge, side 5 bound,
   skirt, verge 6 border, fringe, leeway 7 confine 8 boundary 9 allowance, extra room,
   safeguard

marginal 9 on the edge 11 in the margin 12
   barely useful

mariage de convenance 21 marriage of
   convenience

Marica
   also: 9 Dea Marica
   origin: 5 Roman
   goddess of: 7 marshes

marigold 7 Tagetes
   varieties: 3 big, bur, fig, pot 4 cape, corn,
   wild 5 Aztec, fetid, field, marsh, water 6
   desert, French, signet 7 African 12
   sweet-scented

marijuana, marihuana 3 boo, kif, pot, tea 4
   hash, hemp, herb, weed 5 bhang, dagga,
   ganja, grass, joint 6 moocah, reefer 7
   hashish 8 cannabis, locoweed, mary jane

Marin, John Cheri (3rd)
   born: 12 Rutherford NJ
   artwork: 8 Sea Piece 12 Maine Islands
   13 Tunk Mountains 16 Beach Flint Island
   19 Movement Fifth Avenue 21 Seaside
   Interpretation 26 Camden Mountain
   across the Bay

marine 3 sea 5 naval 7 aquatic, oceanic, of
   ships, pelagic 8 maritime, nautical, of the

sea, seagoing 9 salt-water, seafaring 10
   oceangoing 13 oceanographic

mariner 3 gob, tar 4 salt 5 pilot 6 sailor, sea
   dog, seaman 7 boatman 8 deck hand,
   helmsman, seafarer 9 navigator, yachtsman 10 bluejacket 12 seafaring man 16
   able-bodied seaman

Marion, Francis
   nickname: 8 Swamp Fox
   served in: 16 Revolutionary War
   type of warfare: 9 guerrilla
   area fought in: 13 South Carolina
   battle: 12 Eutaw Springs

marionette 6 puppet 10 fantoccino

Maris
   companion of: 8 Sarpedon

marital 6 wedded, wifely 7 married, nuptial,
   spousal 8 conjugal 9 connubial, husbandly
   10 of marriage 11 matrimonial

maritime 5 naval 6 marine 7 aquatic,
   coastal, oceanic, of ships 8 nautical, of the
   sea, seagoing 9 seafaring

marjoram
   botanical name: 8 Majorana, O vulgare,
   Origanum 16 M hortensis moench
   origin: 4 Asia 13 Mediterranean
   family: 4 mint
   symbol of: 5 honor 9 happiness
   charm against: 10 witchcraft
   used as: 12 air sweetener
   use: 4 eggs, fish, meat 5 salad 8 stuffing
   9 vegetable

Marjorie Morningstar
   author: 10 Herman Wouk

mark 3 cut, mar, pit 4 dent, goal, harm,
   heed, line, mind, nick, note, pock, rate, scar,
   show, sign, spot 5 badge, brand, grade,
   judge, label, notch, point, proof, score, stain,
   stamp, token, track 6 attend, bruise, deface,
   denote, emblem, evince, injure, intent, rating, regard, reveal, streak, symbol, target,
   typify 7 betoken, blemish, correct, imprint,
   measure, scratch, signify, suggest, symptom, write in, write on 8 bull's-eye, colophon, disclose, evidence, hallmark, indicate,
   manifest, point out, standard, stand for 9 be
   a sign of, criterion, designate, disfigure, objective, symbolize, yardstick 10 impression,
   indication, touchstone 11 distinguish 12
   characterize 13 differentiate

Mark
   also: 8 John Mark
   mother: 4 Mary
   cousin: 8 Barnabas
   wrote: 11 Gospel

Mark (King Mark)
   character in: 16 Arthurian romance

Mark Antony
   also: 14 Marcus Antonius
   character in: 12 Julius Caesar
   author: 11 Shakespeare

mark down 4 note 5 enter, lower 6 record,
   reduce 7 put down 9 write down

marked 5 clear, great, noted, plain 6 dotted, scored, severe, showed, spotty,
   tabbed, tagged, traced 7 branded, labeled,
   pointed, specked, spotted, stained,

tracked 8 destined, speckled, striking, targeted 9 indicated, prominent 10 emphasized, identified, made note of, noticeable, remarkable, singled out 11 conspicuous, distinctive, outstanding 12 considerable 13 distinguished

marker 3 IOU, peg, run, tab 4 chip, flag, sign 5 score 6 etcher, scorer, tablet, ticket 7 counter 8 bookmark, memorial, monument, recorder

market 4 hawk, sell, vend 5 stand 6 bourse, peddle, retail 7 grocery 9 dispose of 10 curb market, meat market 11 butcher shop, grocer's shop, marketplace

marketplace 4 mart 5 agora, arena, plaza 6 bazaar, market, square 8 exchange

Mark of Zorro, The
  director: 15 Rouben Mamoulian
  cast: 11 Tyrone Power 12 Linda Darnell 13 Basil Rathbone 15 Gale Sondergaard
  score: 12 Alfred Newman

mark out 8 describe 9 delineate

marksman 8 dead shot, good shot, sure shot 9 crack shot 12 sharpshooter

marksmanship 3 aim 5 skill 8 accuracy 13 sharpshooting

Marley's Ghost
  character in: 15 A Christmas Carol
  author: 7 Dickens

Marlow
  character in: 7 Lord Jim
  author: 6 Conrad

Marlowe
  character in: 15 Heart of Darkness
  author: 6 Conrad

Marlowe, Christopher
  author of: 8 Edward II 13 Doctor Faustus, The Jew of Malta 14 Hero and Leander 15 Edward the Second 19 Tamburlaine the Great

Marmax
  suitor of: 10 Hippodamia
  murdered by: 8 Oenomaus

Marmee
  character in: 11 Little Women
  author: 6 Alcott

Marmion
  author: 14 Sir Walter Scott
  character: 11 Lord Marmion 13 Ralph de Wilton 14 Clare Fitz-Clare 16 Archibald Douglas 19 Constance de Beverley

Marnie
  director: 15 Alfred Hitchcock
  cast: 10 Diane Baker 11 Sean Connery, Tippi Hedren

maroon 4 plum, wine 6 desert, strand 7 abandon, forsake, magenta 8 cast away, jettison 9 put ashore 10 cast ashore, terra cotta 11 brownish-red, leave behind 15 leave high and dry

Marpessa
  origin: 5 Greek
  father: 6 Euenos
  loved by: 4 Idas 6 Apollo
  chose: 4 Idas

Marple, Miss Jane
  detective created by: 14 Agatha Christie

Marquand, J P
  author of: 13 Wickford Point 18 The Late George Apley
  character: 6 Mr Moto

marquee 4 tent 6 awning, canopy 8 marquise

marred 6 ruined 7 damaged, injured, spoiled 8 impaired 9 blemished, destroyed 10 disfigured

Marrener, Edythe
  real name of: 12 Susan Hayward

marriage 7 wedding, wedlock 8 nuptials 9 matrimony
  god of: 4 Frey 5 Freyr, Hymen 9 Hymenaeus
  goddess of: 3 Fri 5 Frigg, Frija 6 Frigga, Tellus

Marriage a la Mode
  author: 10 John Dryden

marriage broker
  Yiddish: 8 shadchan 9 schatchen

marriage of convenience
  French: 19 mariage de convenance

Marriage of Figaro, The
  also: 15 Le Nozze di Figaro
  opera: 6 Mozart
  character: 7 Susanna 8 Countess 9 Cherubino, Dr Bartolo 10 Marcellina 13 Count Almaviva

Marriage of Figaro, The
  author: 12 Beaumarchais
  character: 6 Figaro 7 Suzanne 8 Cherubin 9 Marceline 10 Dr Bartholo 13 Count Almaviva 16 Countess Almaviva

Marriages Between Zones Three, Four and Five
  author: 12 Doris Lessing

married 3 wed 5 mated 6 joined, united, wedded 7 hitched, marital 8 combined, espoused 9 connubial 11 matrimonial, tied the knot

married woman
  German: 4 frau

marry 3 wed 7 espouse, make one 10 get spliced, tie the knot 13 join in wedlock 14 join in marriage, lead to the altar, take in marriage

Marryat, Frederick
  author of: 11 Peter Simple 16 Mr Midshipman Easy

Mars
  also: 6 Mamers, Mavors
  origin: 5 Roman
  god of: 3 war
  mother: 4 Juno
  wife: 5 Nerio
  epithet: 5 Ultor 8 Gradivus
  corresponds to: 4 Ares

Mars
  position: 6 fourth
  nickname: 9 Red Planet
  satellite: 6 Deimos, Phobos

Marseillaise 20 French national anthem

marsh 3 bog, fen 5 swamp 6 morass, slough 7 bottoms, wetland 8 quagmire 9 everglade, marshland, quicksand

Marsh, Dame Ngaio
   author of: 9 Dead Water 12 Final Curtain 13 Death at the Bar 14 Enter a Murderer 19 Singing in the Shrouds
   character: 10 Troy Alleyn 14 Roderick Alleyn

Marsh, Reginald
   born: 5 Paris 6 France
   artwork: 9 The Bowery 10 Pip and Flip 14 Why Not Use the El? 16 Tattoo and Haircut 17 Twenty-Cent Haircut

marshal 5 align, array, chief, group, order 6 deploy, draw up, gather, leader, line up, muster 7 arrange, collect, manager, sheriff 8 assemble, director, marechal, mobilize, organize 9 fire chief 10 law officer, supervisor 11 police chief 12 chief officer, field marshal 13 generalissimo

Marshall, George C
   served in: 3 WWI 4 WWII 9 Korean War, World War I 10 World War II 11 World War One, World War Two
   rank: 12 chief of staff 16 general of the army
   author of: 12 Marshall Plan
   secretary of: 5 state 7 defense
   winner of: 15 Nobel Peace Prize (1953)

Marshall, Penny
   husband: 9 Rob Reiner
   born: 7 Bronx NY
   roles: 5 Myrna 12 The Odd Couple 14 Laverne DeFazio 17 Laverne and Shirley
   director: 3 Big

marshy 3 wet 4 miry 5 boggy, fenny, muddy 6 swampy 7 paludal, paludic 11 waterlogged

marsupial 5 koala 6 numbat, possum, wombat 7 cuscuse, opossum, wallaby 8 kangaroo 9 bandicoot, phalanger 14 Tasmanian devil

Marsyas
   form: 5 satyr
   played: 5 flute

mart 4 show 6 market 8 exchange 9 trade fair, trade show 10 exposition

Martha
   sister: 4 Mary
   brother: 7 Lazarus
   hometown: 7 Bethany

martial 7 hostile, Spartan, warlike 8 militant, military 9 bellicose, combative, soldierly 10 pugnacious 11 belligerent, contentious

Martian Chronicles, The
   author: 11 Ray Bradbury

Martin, Dean
   real name: 16 Dino Paul Crocetti
   partner: 10 Jerry Lewis
   born: 14 Steubenville OH
   roles: 8 Matt Helm, Rio Bravo, The Caddy 9 The Stooge 10 Living It Up 12 Four for Texas, Sailor Beware 14 Toys in the Attic 15 Some Came Running 16 Artists and Models

Martin, Mary
   son: 11 Larry Hagman
   born: 13 Weatherford TX

   roles: 6 I Do I Do 8 Peter Pan 12 Sound of Music, South Pacific

Martin, Steve
   born: 6 Waco TX
   roles: 7 The Jerk 17 Pennies From Heaven, Saturday Night Live 19 The Man with Two Brains 20 Dead Men Don't Wear Plaid 26 Planes Trains and Automobiles

Martin Chuzzlewit
   author: 14 Charles Dickens
   character: 5 Mercy 7 Charity 8 Tom Pinch 9 Pecksniff, Ruth Pinch, Sarah Gamp 10 Mark Tapley, Mary Graham 15 Jonas Chuzzlewit 17 Anthony Chuzzlewit

martinet 6 despot, tyrant 8 dictator 10 hard master, taskmaster 11 drillmaster, Simon Legree 12 little Caesar 13 authoritarian, drill-sergeant

Marty
   director: 11 Delbert Mann
   cast: 10 Betsy Blair 11 Joe De Santis 14 Ernest Borgnine 15 Esther Minciotti
   Oscar for: 5 actor (Borgnine) 7 picture
   script: 14 Paddy Chayefsky

martyr 5 saint 8 sufferer

martyrdom 5 agony 6 ordeal 7 anguish, torment, torture 9 bitter cup, suffering 10 affliction 11 cup of sorrow 13 crown of thorns

marvel 4 gape 6 be awed, rarity, wonder 7 miracle 8 be amazed 9 spectacle 10 phenomenon

Marvell, Andrew
   author of: 9 The Garden 16 To His Coy Mistress

marvelous, marvellous 4 A-one, fine 5 grand, great, super 6 divine, lovely, superb 7 amazing 8 colossal, fabulous, heavenly, smashing, splendid 9 fantastic, first-rate, wonderful 10 phenomenal, remarkable, stupendous 11 astonishing, magnificent, outstanding, sensational 13 extraordinary

marvelous to relate
   Latin: 13 mirabile dictu

Marwood, Mrs
   character in: 16 The Way of the World
   author: 8 Congreve

Marx, Bernard
   character in: 13 Brave New World
   author: 6 Huxley

Marx, Karl
   author of: 10 Das Kapital 18 Communist Manifesto (with Friedrich Engels)

Marx Brothers 5 Chico (Leonard), Gummo (Milton), Harpo (Adolph, Arthur) Zeppo (Herbert) 7 Groucho (Julius)
   costar: 14 Margaret Dumont
   born: 9 New York NY
   roles: 8 Coconuts, Duck Soup 11 The Big Store 13 Horse Feathers 14 A Day at the Races, Animal Crackers, Monkey Business 16 A Night at the Opera
   Groucho's TV show: 14 You Bet Your Life

Mary 6 Virgin 7 Madonna 8 Holy Mary 9 Magdalene, of Cleopas 10 Virgin Mary 11 Mother of God, Regina Coeli 13 Queen of Heaven 15 Mother of Sorrows 17 Mother of the Church
 mother: 4 Anna, Anne
 husband: 6 Joseph 7 Alpheus, Cleopas
 son: 4 Jude, Mark 5 Jesus, Moses, Simon 12 James the Less
 sister: 6 Martha
 brother: 7 Lazarus 8 Barnabas
 cousin: 9 Elizabeth
 hometown: 8 Nazareth
 visitor: 7 Gabriel
 flower: 4 lily 8 marigold

Mary
 author: 10 Sholem Asch

Maryland
 abbreviation: 2 MD
 nickname: 4 Free 7 Cockade 12 Old Line State
 capital: 9 Annapolis
 largest city: 9 Baltimore
 others: 5 Essex 6 Easton, Laurel, Towson 8 Aberdeen, Bethesda, Pocomoke 9 Frederick, Ocean City, Rockville 10 Cumberland, Hagerstown, Pikesville 11 Catonsville, College Park
 college: 4 Hood 7 Goucher, St John's 10 Washington 11 Towson State 12 Johns Hopkins 21 Annapolis Naval Academy
 feature:
 fort: 7 McHenry
 national battlesite: 8 Antietam
 presidential retreat: 9 Camp David
 race: 9 Preakness 12 Steeplechase
 racetrack: 5 Bowie 6 Butler, Laurel 7 Pimlico
 tribe: 5 Conoy 9 Nanticoke
 people: 6 Wesort 8 Terrapin 9 Spiro Agnew 11 crawthumper 14 Sargent Shriver 15 Francis Scott Key
 explorer: 7 Calvert
 lake: 8 Patapsco 9 Deep Creek, Loch Raven, Pretty Boy 10 Rocky Gorge 11 Triadelphia
 land rank: 11 forty second
 mountain: 4 Dans 8 Piedmont 9 Blue Ridge 11 Appalachian
 highest point: 8 Backbone
 physical feature:
 bay: 10 Chesapeake
 sea: 8 Atlantic
 swamp: 7 Pocoson
 valley: 5 Great 10 Hagerstown
 river: 3 Elk 7 Chester, Potomac 8 Choptank, Patapsco, Patuxent, Pocomoke 11 Susquehanna
 state admission: 7 seventh
 state bird: 15 Baltimore oriole
 state fish: 11 striped bass
 state flower: 14 black-eyed Susan
 state motto: 22 Manly Deeds Womanly Words 43 Thou Hast Crowned Us With the Shield of Thy Good Will
 state song: 18 Maryland My Maryland
 state tree: 8 white oak

Mary Poppins
 director: 15 Robert Stevenson
 based on story by: 9 P L Travers
 cast: 6 Ed Wynn 11 Dick Van Dyke (Bert), Glynis Johns 12 Julie Andrews 14 David Tomlinson 16 Hermione Baddeley
 score: 13 Robert Sherman 14 Richard Sherman
 Oscar for: 4 song 5 score 7 actress (Andrews) 13 visual effects
 song: 14 Chim-chim-cheree

Mary Queen of Scots
 director: 14 Charles Jarrott
 cast: 12 Trevor Howard 13 Glenda Jackson (Elizabeth I), Timothy Dalton 14 Nigel Davenport 15 Patrick McGoohan, Vanessa Redgrave (Mary of Scotland)

Mary Tyler Moore Show, The
 character: 8 Lou Grant 9 Ted Baxter 12 Gordon (Gordy) Howard, Mary Richards, Sue Ann Nivens 13 Bess Lindstrom 14 Marie Slaughter 15 Murray Slaughter 16 Phyllis Lindstrom, Rhoda Morgenstern 23 Georgette Franklin Baxter
 cast: 8 John Amos 9 Ted Knight 10 Betty White 11 Edward Asner 12 Gavin MacLeod, Georgia Engel 13 Joyce Bulifant, Lisa Gerritsen, Valerie Harper 14 Cloris Leachman
 setting: 11 Minneapolis

Mary Worth
 creator: 8 Carey Orr 9 Dale Allen 10 Dale Connor 13 Allen Saunders
 character: 4 Bill, Slim

Masaccio
 real name: 26 Tommaso di Ser Giovanni di Mone
 born: 5 Italy 27 Castel San Giovanni di Valdarno
 artwork: 14 The Holy Trinity 15 The Tribute Money 24 The Expulsion from Paradise

Mascagni, Pietro
 born: 5 Italy 7 Leghorn
 composer of: 4 Iris 6 Nerone 7 Isabeau 10 Le Maschere 11 L'Amico Fritz 14 Il Piccolo Marat 19 Cavalleria Rusticana

masculine 4 bold, male 5 brave, hardy, husky, macho, manly 6 brawny, daring, manful, plucky, robust, strong, sturdy, virile 7 staunch, valiant 8 athletic, fearless, forceful, intrepid, muscular, powerful, resolute, vigorous 9 strapping 10 courageous 11 indomitable, self-reliant 12 stouthearted

Masefield, John
 author of: 7 Cargoes 8 Sea Fever 16 Salt Water Ballads

Maseru
 capital of: 7 Lesotho

mash 4 mush 5 crush, paste, puree, smash 6 squash 8 mishmash 9 pulverize

M*A*S*H
 character: 10 (Capt) BJ Hunnicut, (Lt Col) Henry Blake, (Maj) Frank Burns 12 (Corp) Radar O'Reilly 13 Father (John) Mulcahy, (Capt Benjamin Franklin) Hawkeye Pierce, (Col) Sherman Potter 14

(Corp) Maxwell Klinger 15 (Maj Margaret)
Hot Lips Houlihan 19 (Capt) Trapper
John McIntyre 24 (Maj) Charles Emerson
Winchester

cast: 8 Alan Alda 9 Jamie Farr 11 Harry
Morgan, Loretta Swit, Mike Farrell,
Wayne Rogers 12 Gary Burghoff 13 Larry
Linville 15 McLean Stevenson 16 David
Ogden Stiers 18 William Christopher

war: 6 Korean

MASH stands for: 26 Mobile Army Surgical Hospital

tent: 5 Swamp

theme: 17 Suicide Is Painless

M*A*S*H

director: 12 Robert Altman

cast: 10 Jo Ann Pflug 11 Elliot Gould
(Trapper John McIntyre), Tom Skerritt
(B J Hunnicut) 12 Gary Burghoff (Radar
O'Reilly), Robert Duvall (Frank Burns) 14
Sally Kellerman (Margaret Hot Lips
Houlihan) 16 Donald Sutherland (Hawk-
eye Pierce)

masjid 6 mosque

mask 4 hide, veil 5 blind, cloak, cover 6
domino, screen, shroud 7 conceal,
cover-up, curtain, obscure 8 disguise 9
face guard, false face 10 camouflage,
keep secret

Mask

director: 16 Peter Bogdanovich

cast: 4 Cher 10 Eric Stoltz (Rocky
Dennis), Sam Elliott

masked 9 concealed, covered up, disguised 10 in disguise, masquerade

Masked Ball, A

also: 17 Un Ballo in Maschera

opera by: 5 Verdi

character:

first version: 9 Count Horn 10 King
Gustav 12 Count Ribbing

second version: 3 Sam, Tom 13 Count
Riccardo

masking 6 hiding 7 veiling 8 covering 9
eclipsing, obscuring 10 concealing, covering up

Mason, Bertha

character in: 8 Jane Eyre

author: 6 Bronte

Mason, James

wife: 6 Pamela

born: 7 England 12 Huddersfield

roles: 6 Lolita 7 Lord Jim 9 Bloodline 10
Georgy Girl 13 Heaven Can Wait 14
Humbert Humbert, Murder by Decree,
The Seventh Veil 15 Prisoner of Zenda
16 North by Northwest 17 The Boys from
Brazil

Mason, Marsha

husband: 9 Neil Simon

born: 9 St Louis MO

roles: 10 Chapter Two 11 Blume in Love
14 The Goodbye Girl 15 Max Dugan Returns 17 Cinderella Liberty

Masque of the Red Death, The

author: 13 Edgar Allan Poe

masquerade 4 mask, ruse, veil 5 cloak,
cover, guise, trick 6 masque, pose as,
screen, shroud 7 cover-up, pretext 8 artifice, pretense 9 bal masque 10 camouflage, masked ball, subterfuge 11 impersonate 12 harlequinade

Masquerade Party

host: 9 Bert Parks 10 Bud Collier 11 Peter Donald 12 Eddie Bracken, Robert Q
Lewis 14 Douglas Edwards

mass, Mass 3 jam, lot, mob 4 body, bulk,
cake, clot, heap, host, hunk, knot, lump,
pack, pile 5 amass, batch, block, bunch,
chunk, clump, corps, crowd, crush, group,
horde, press, stack, troop 6 bundle,
gather, matter, throng, weight 7 collect,
pyramid 8 assemble, best part, main body,
majority, material 9 aggregate, Eucharist,
gathering, plurality 10 accumulate, assemblage, assortment, collection, concre-
tion, congregate, cumulation, lion's share
11 aggregation, consolidate, greater part
12 accumulation, congregation 13 Holy
Communion, holy sacrament, preponderance 14 conglomeration

Massachusetts

abbreviation: 2 MA 4 Mass

nickname: 3 Bay 7 Puritan 9 Baked
Bean, Old Colony

capital/largest city: 6 Boston

others: 4 Ayer, Lynn, Otis 5 Athol, Barre,
Lenox, Salem 6 Agawam, Dedham,
Groton, Nahant, Natick, Revere, Saugus,
Woburn 7 Belmont, Beverly, Concord,
Danvers, Everett, Holyoke, Ipswich,
Medford, Peabody, Taunton, Waltham 8
Brockton, Chicopee, Cohasset, Plym-
outh, Scituate, Yarmouth 9 Arlington,
Attleboro, Braintree, Brookline, Cam-
bridge, Lexbridge, Lexington, Worcester
10 Gloucester, New Bedford, Pittsfield 11
Springfield 12 Provincetown, Williams-
town

college: 3 MIT 5 Clark, Curry, Smith,
Tufts 6 Babson 7 Amherst, Harvard,
Simmons, Wheaton 8 Brandeis, Williams
9 Hampshire, Holy Cross, Merrimack,
Radcliffe, Wellesley 11 Springfield 12
Mount Holyoke, Northeastern 13 Boston
College

feature: 10 Walden Pond 12 Plymouth
Rock

national seashore: 7 Cape Cod

village: 13 Old Sturbridge

tribe: 6 Nauset 8 Pocomtuc 10 Wampanoags

people: 8 Pilgrims 9 Amy Lowell, Elias
Howe 10 Cyrus Field, Eli Whitney 11
Clara Barton, John Hancock, Samuel Ad-
ams, Samuel Morse 12 Henry Thoreau,
Robert Lowell, Winslow Homer 13 James
Whistler, Joseph Kennedy, Robert Ken-
nedy 14 Emily Dickinson 15 Henry Cabot
Lodge 16 Benjamin Franklin, Edward
"Ted" Kennedy 17 Ralph Waldo Emerson
18 Bartholomew Gosnold, James Russell
Lowell, Nathanial Hawthorne 19 Oliver

Wendell Holmes, William Cullen Bryant 21 John Greenleaf Whittier

explorer: 8 Norsemen

island: 5 Duke's 9 Nantucket 13 Chappaquidick 15 Martha's Vineyard

lake: 5 Onota 7 Quabbin, Rohunta, Webster 8 Long Pond 11 Watuppa Pond 16 Assawompsett Pond 17 Chaubunagungamaug

land rank: 10 forty-fifth

mountain: 3 Tom 6 Brodie, Potter 7 Alander, Everett, Taconic 10 Berkshires

highest point: 8 Greylock

physical feature:

bay: 8 Buzzard's

cape: 3 Ann, Cod

sea: 8 Atlantic

president: 9 John Adams 14 Calvin Coolidge 15 John Quincy Adams 21 John Fitzgerald Kennedy

river: 6 Nashua 7 Charles, Concord, Quaboag, Taunton 8 Chicopee 9 Deerfield, Merrimack 10 Blackstone, Housatonic 11 Connecticut

state admission: 11 thirty-sixth

state bird: 9 chickadee

state flower: 9 mayflower 15 trailing arbutus

state motto: 37 With the Sword She Seeks Peace Under Liberty 45 By the Sword We Seek Peace But Peace Only Under Liberty

state song: 22 All Hail to Massachusetts

state tree: 11 American elm

massacre 7 butcher, carnage 8 butchery, decimate 9 bloodbath, slaughter 10 mass murder 12 bloodletting

massage 3 rub 4 flex 5 chafe, knead 6 finger, handle, stroke 7 rubbing, rub down, stretch 8 kneading, stroking 10 manipulate 12 manipulation

Massasoit *see* 10 Wampanoags

Massenet, Jules Emile Frederic

born: 6 France 9 St Etienne

composer of: 5 Le Cid, Manon, Thais 7 Werther 9 Herodiade 11 David Rizzio 12 Don Quichotte 13 Le Roi de Lahore 21 Le Jongleur de Notre-Dame

masses 6 plebes, proles, rabble, the mob 7 the many 8 the crowd 9 hoi polloi, plebeians 11 the populace, the riffraff 12 the multitude 13 the common herd 14 the proletariat, the rank and file 15 the common people, the lower classes, the working class 16 the great unwashed

Masset *see* 10 Skidegatta

massive 4 huge, vast 5 ample, bulky, great, heavy, hefty, massy, solid 7 hulking, immense, mammoth, titanic, weighty 8 colossal, enormous, gigantic, imposing, towering, whopping 9 cyclopean, extensive, monstrous, ponderous 10 gargantuan, impressive, monumental, stupendous 11 elephantine, substantial

massiveness 4 bulk, size 6 volume, weight 7 bigness 8 enormity, hugeness, vastness 9 amplitude, bulkiness, greatness, immensity, largeness, magnitude

mast 4 main, nuts, pole, post, spar 5 spirit, staff, stick, stuff 6 acorns, pillar 9 beechnuts, chestnuts

type: 4 fore, main 6 jigger, mizzen

support: 4 bibb

master 3 ace 4 able, A-one, best, boss, curb, deft, head, lord, main, tame, whiz 5 check, chief, crack, grasp, owner, prime, ruler 6 bridle, choice, expert, genius, gifted, govern, leader, manage, subdue, wizard 7 conquer, control, excel at, head man, manager, primary, skilled, skipper, supreme 8 director, dominate, finished, governor, masterly, overcome, overlord, overseer, regulate, suppress, talented, virtuoso 9 authority, conqueror, craftsman, first-rate, paramount, practiced, principal 10 controller, proficient, supervisor 12 get the hang of, ship's captain

Master Builder, The

author: 11 Henrik Ibsen

master craftsman 7 artisan 12 master-worker 13 skilled worker

masterful 4 able, deft 5 bossy 6 expert, superb 7 dynamic, skilled 8 finished, forceful, masterly, resolute, skillful, virtuoso 9 excellent 10 commanding 11 domineering, self-reliant 12 accomplished, strong-willed 13 authoritarian, self-confident

masterfulness 6 genius 10 capability, competence, excellence 11 proficiency

Master Melvin

nickname of: 6 Mel Ott

mastermind 4 plan, sage 6 direct, expert, genius, master, pundit, wizard 7 old hand, planner 8 conceive, director, engineer, organize, virtuoso 9 authority, initiator, organizer 10 specialist 11 moving force

Master of Ballantrae, The

author: 20 Robert Louis Stevenson

character: 4 Chew 5 Teach 9 MacKellar 11 Henry Durrie, James Durrie 12 Alison Graeme, Francis Burke, Secundra Dass

master of the family

Latin: 13 paterfamilias

masterpiece 5 jewel, prize 7 classic, paragon 8 monument, treasure 9 nonpareil 10 brainchild 11 chef d'oeuvre, ne plus ultra, prizewinner

Masterpiece Theater

host: 13 Alistair Cooke

master race

German: 10 Herrenvolk

Masters, Edgar Lee

author of: 19 Spoon River Anthology

Mastersingers of Nuremberg, The

also: 27 Die Meistersinger von Nurnberg

opera by: 9 Wagner

character: 9 Eva Pogner, Hans Sachs 10 Beckmesser 18 Walther von Stolzing

mastery 4 rule, sway 5 grasp 7 ability, command, control 8 deftness, whip hand 9 dominance, supremacy, upper hand 10 adroitness, attainment, domination, leadership 11 achievement, acquirement, proficiency, superiority 14 accomplishment

masticate 4 chew, gnaw 5 chomp, munch 6 nibble

Mastroianni, Marcello
born: 5 Italy 11 Fontana Liri
roles: 13 Eight and a Half 7 La Notte 11 La Dolce Vita, The Stranger, White Nights 19 Divorce Italian Style

mat 3 dim, pad, rug 4 dead, dull, flat 5 doily, muted 6 carpet, matrix, tangle 7 bedding, bolster, coaster, cushion, support 8 entangle 10 lackluster, lusterless
Japanese: 6 tatami

Mata Hari
real name: 21 Gertrud Margarete Zelle
worked as: 3 spy 6 dancer
worked for: 7 Germans
executed by: 6 French

match 3 fit 4 game, join, mate, meet, pair, peer, suit, twin, yoke 5 adapt, agree, equal, event, unite 6 couple, double, oppose 7 be alike, be equal, combine, connect, contend, contest, vie with 8 parallel 9 companion, duplicate, harmonize 10 correspond, equivalent, tournament 11 competition, counterpart

matched 5 equal 8 of a piece 9 identical 11 coordinated

matching 4 twin 5 equal 6 paired 10 equivalent 11 harmonizing 13 corresponding

matchless 4 rare 7 supreme 8 crowning, foremost, peerless, sterling, superior 9 exemplary, first rate, priceless, paramount, unequaled, unmatched, unrivaled 10 invaluable, preeminent, unbeatable, unexcelled 11 inestimable, superlative, unsurpassed 12 incomparable, unparalleled

matchmaker
Yiddish: 8 shadchan 9 schatchen

mate 3 pal 4 chum, twin, wife 5 buddy, crony, hubby, match 6 couple, friend, spouse 7 cohabit, comrade, consort, husband, pair off, partner 8 copulate, coworker, sidekick 9 associate, colleague, companion, duplicate 10 better half, equivalent 11 confederate, counterpart 12 fellow worker, ship's officer

materfamilias 15 mother of a family

material 5 stuff 6 matter 8 elements 9 substance 12 constituents

materialism 5 greed 12 covetousness 15 acquisitiveness

materialistic 6 greedy 8 covetous, grasping 11 acquisitive, unspiritual

materiality 9 existence 11 tangibility

materialization 5 ghost, shade 6 coming, wraith 7 phantom, specter 9 emergence 10 apparition, appearance 13 manifestation

materialize 4 loom, rise, show 5 bob up, issue, pop up 6 appear, crop up, emerge, turn up 9 come forth 10 burst forth 11 come to light, spring forth 12 come into view

materially 7 vitally 8 palpably, tangibly 9 in the main, seriously 10 monetarily 11 corporeally, essentially, financially, in substance 12 considerably, emphatically 13 significantly, substantially 14 for the most part

material possessions 6 assets, estate, wealth 7 fortune 8 property 10 belongings 12 worldly goods

material proof 8 evidence 13 documentation

materials 4 data 5 cloth, facts, notes, tools 6 stocks, stores, timber 7 fabrics, figures 8 concrete, dry goods, supplies, textiles 9 citations, equipment, machinery, yard goods 10 essentials, piece goods, quotations, references 11 impressions 12 observations 15 bricks and mortar

materiel 4 gear 6 stores 8 supplies 9 equipment, materials 10 provisions 16 military supplies

Mater Matuta *see* 6 Matuta

maternal 4 fond 6 doting 8 motherly 9 of a mother, shielding 10 motherlike, protective, sheltering

maternity 5 labor 8 delivery 9 pregnancy 10 childbirth, motherhood 11 parturition 12 accouchement, childbearing

Mater Turrita *see* 6 Cybele

mathematical, mathematic 5 exact, rigid 6 strict 7 precise 8 accurate, rigorous, unerring 10 meticulous, scientific, scrupulous 11 punctilious, well-defined 13 computational

mathematician
American: 5 Aiken 6 Wiener
British: 6 Newton 7 Babbage
French: 6 Fermat 9 D'Alembert, Descartes
German: 5 Frege, Gauss 6 Bessel 7 Hilbert
Greek: 6 Euclid, Thales 11 Anaximander
Norwegian: 4 Abel
Swiss: 5 Euler 9 Bernoulli

Mathewson, Christy
nickname: 5 Matty 6 Big Six
sport: 8 baseball
position: 7 pitcher
team: 13 New York Giants

Matholwych
king of: 7 Ireland
wife: 7 Branwen

matinee 9 early show 16 early performance 20 afternoon performance

Mating Season, The
author: 11 P G Wodehouse

Matisse, Henri Emile Benoit
born: 6 France 16 Chateau Cambresis (Le Cateau)
artwork: 5 Dance, Music 8 The Slave 10 Odalisques 11 Joie de Vivre 12 Harmony in Red, La Serpentine 13 Head with Tiara, The Open Window 15 Bathers by a River, Memory of Oceanie, Woman with the Hat 16 Heads of Jeannette 19 Torso with Arms Raised 20 Goldfish and Sculpture

Matralia
  origin: 5 Roman
  event: 8 festival
matriarch 7 dowager 10 female head,
grande dame 11 female ruler 12 female
leader 13 materfamilias
matriculate 4 join 5 enter 6 enlist, enroll,
sign up 7 check in 8 register
matriculation 9 signing up 10 enrollment
12 registration
matrimonial 6 bridal, wedded, wifely 7
marital, married, nuptial, spousal 8 conjugal, hymeneal 9 affianced, connubial, husbandly 11 epithalamic
matrimony 7 wedlock 8 marriage 11 holy
wedlock
matrix 3 die 4 cast, form, mold 5 frame,
punch, stamp
matron 4 dame 5 madam 7 dowager 8
forelady, mistress, overseer 9 forewoman
10 directress 11 housekeeper 12 married
woman 14 superintendent
Matronalia
  origin: 5 Roman
  event: 8 festival
matter 3 fix 4 gist, snag, text 5 count, drift,
event, sense, stuff, theme, thing, topic 6
affair, crisis, import, moment, object,
scrape, strait, thesis 7 content, dilemma,
episode, essence, purport, signify, subject,
trouble 8 argument, business, elements,
exigency, material, obstacle, quandary 9
adventure, emergency, happening, situation, substance 10 difference, difficulty,
experience, impediment, importance, occurrence, perplexity, proceeding 11 carry
weight, consequence, predicament, transaction 12 circumstance, significance
matter-of-course 5 usual 6 common 7 routine 8 everyday, ordinary, standard 9 customary 11 commonplace, established
matter-of-fact 4 real 5 blunt, frank 6 candid, direct 7 factual, literal, mundane, natural, prosaic 8 ordinary, sensible 9 outspoken, practical, pragmatic, realistic 10
hardheaded, no-nonsense, unaffected,
uninspired, unromantic 11 commonplace,
common-sense, down-to-earth, straight-
out 13 unimaginative, unsentimental 15
straightforward
matter-of-factness 10 detachment 11 impassivity 12 practicality 13 impassiveness
17 unimaginativeness
Matter of Time, A
  author: 12 Jessamyn West
Matthau, Walter
  real name: 13 Walter Matthow 23 Walter
  Matuschanskavasky
  born: 9 New York NY
  roles: 5 Kotch 8 A New Leaf 10 Plaza
  Suite 11 Pete n Tillie 12 Bad News Bears,
  Ensign Pulver, Oscar Madison, The Front
  Page, The Odd Couple 15 California
  Suite, The Sunshine Boys 16 The Fortune Cookie 22 A Guide for the Married
  Man

Matthew 7 apostle
  father: 7 Alpheus
  also called: 4 Levi
  wrote: 6 Gospel
Matthiessen, Peter
  author of: 10 Sand Rivers 14 The Snow
  Leopard
maturation 6 growth 8 fruition, ripening 9
growing up
mature 4 ripe 5 adult, bloom, grown, manly,
of age, ready, ripen 6 flower, grow up, mellow, nubile, virile 7 blossom, develop,
grown-up, matured, womanly 8 finished,
maturate, seasoned 9 come of age, completed, full-blown, full-grown, perfected,
practiced 10 middle-aged 11 become
adult, experienced, full-fledged, in one's
prime 12 marriageable
Mature, Victor
  born: 12 Louisville KY
  roles: 7 The Robe 11 After the Fox, Kiss
  of Death 12 Cry of the City, One Million
  BC 16 Samson and Delilah 19 Androcles
  and the Lion
matured 3 big 4 aged, ripe 5 adult, grown 6
formed 7 ripened 8 flowered, mellowed,
seasoned 9 blossomed, developed, full-
blown, full-grown 11 full-fledged
maturity 7 manhood 8 legal age, majority,
practice, ripeness 9 adulthood, composure, full bloom, readiness, seasoning,
womanhood 10 completion, experience,
full growth, maturation, matureness, perfection 11 culmination, fulfillment 12 age of
consent
Matuschanskavasky, Walter
  real name of: 13 Walter Matthau
Matuta
  origin: 5 Roman
  goddess of: 3 sea 4 dawn 7 harbors 10
  childbirth
  called: 11 Mater Matuta
Maud
  author: 18 Alfred Lord Tennyson
Maude
  character: 5 Carol 7 Phillip 10 Henry Evans 12 Florida Evans, Maude Findlay,
  Mrs Naugatuck 13 Walter Findlay 14 Dr
  Arthur Harmon 20 Vivian Cavender
  Harmon
  cast: 8 Bill Macy, John Amos 10 Conrad
  Bain 11 Esther Rolle 13 Brian Morrison,
  Rue McClanahan 14 Beatrice Arthur,
  Kraig Metzinger 15 Adrienne Barbeau 16
  Hermione Baddeley
  spinoff from: 14 All in the Family
  spinoff: 9 Good Times
maudlin 5 gushy, mushy, teary 6 slushy 7
gushing, mawkish, tearful 8 bathetic 9
emotional 10 lachrymose 11 sentimental
13 overemotional
maudlinism 6 bathos 11 mawkishness 14
sentimentalism, sentimentality
Maugham, W Somerset
  author of: 9 The Circle 10 Our Betters 11
  Cakes and Ale 12 Miss Thompson 13
  The Razor's Edge 14 Of Human Bond-

age 15 The Constant Wife 18 The Moon and Sixpence 21 Lady Frederick Ashenden

maul 4 beat 5 stomp 6 batter, beat up, bruise, mangle, pummel, thrash 7 rough up 9 manhandle 10 knock about

Mauldin, Bill
creator/artist of: 7 Up Front 12 Willie and Joe

maunder 4 loaf 5 drift, run on, stray 6 babble, dawdle, gabble, gibber, ramble, wander 7 blather, meander, prattle, saunter 8 flounder, ramble on, straggle 9 go on and on, hem and haw 10 dillydally

maundering 7 diffuse 8 rambling 9 wandering 10 digressive, disjointed, roundabout 14 drift, run on, stray 6 babble, dawdle, gabble, gibber, ramble, wander 7 blather, meander, prattle, saunter 8 flounder, ramble on, straggle 9 go on and on, hem and haw 10 dillydally

Maupassant, Guy de
author of: 6 Belami 9 Ball of Fat, Mont-Oriol 11 A Woman's Life, The Necklace 12 Ball of Tallow 16 Mademoiselle Fifi

Mauriac, Francois
author of: 8 Genitrix 10 The Egoists 12 Viper's Tangle 15 A Kiss to the Leper, The Desert of Love 20 A Woman of the Pharisees

Mauritania
capital/largest city: 10 Nouakchott
others: 4 Atar 5 Kaedi, Rosso 6 Fderik 7 Akjoujt 10 Nouadhibou
division: 5 Sahel 7 Chemama
monetary unit: 5 khoum 7 ouguiya
highest point: 11 Kediat Idjil
river: 7 Senegal
sea: 8 Atlantic
physical feature:
desert: 6 Sahara
valley: 7 Chemama 12 Senegal River
people: 4 Arab, Fula, Moor 5 Black, Fulbe, Wolof 6 Bafour, Berber, Fulani 7 African, Soninke, Tukulor 8 Sarakole 9 Sarakolle 10 Toucouleur 12 Halphoolaren
leader: 4 Luly 5 Salek 6 Daddah 8 Haidalla
ruler: 6 France 9 Almoravid 14 Kingdom of Ghana
language: 4 Fula 5 Wolof 6 Arabic, French 7 Phoolor, Tukulor 8 Fulfulde, Mandingo 9 Sarakolle, Hassaniya
religion: 5 Islam
place:
mosque: 5 Grand
feature:
beehive hut: 4 ruga
priest-teacher: 8 marabout
waterskin: 6 guerba
food:
dish: 7 meshuri
tea: 5 attay

Mauritius
other name: 11 Ile de France
capital/largest city: 9 Port Louis
others: 6 Reduit 8 Curepipe 9 Mahe-

bourg 13 Quartre Bornes 19 Grande Riviere Sud-Est
head of state: 14 British monarch 15 governor general
monetary unit: 4 cent 5 rupee
island: 3 Est 4 Flat 5 Ambre, Cerf's, Morne, Round 7 Agalega, Serpent 9 Mauritius, Rodrigues, Rodriguez, St Brandon 12 Gunner's Quoin 15 Cargados Carajos
highest point: 27 Piton de la Petite Riviere Noire
sea: 6 Indian
people: 6 Creole, French, Indian 7 African, Chinese 8 European 13 Indo-Mauritian
leader: 8 Jugnauth 9 Ramgoolam
ruler: 5 Dutch 6 French 7 English
language: 4 Urdu 5 Hindi, Tamil 6 Creole, French

mausoleum 10 family tomb 11 stately tomb 18 sepulchral monument

mauve 4 plum, puce 5 lilac 6 violet 8 lavender 11 light purple 12 bluish purple

maverick 5 loner 8 yearling 9 dissenter, dissident, eccentric 11 independent 13 individualist, noncomformist

Maverick
character: 12 Bart Maverick, Bret Maverick 13 Brent Maverick 16 Samantha Crawford 24 Cousin Beauregard Maverick
cast: 9 Jack Kelly 10 Roger Moore 11 James Garner 13 Diane Brewster, Robert Colbert

Mavors see 4 Mars

maw 4 craw, crop, jaws 5 mouth 6 gullet, muzzle, throat

mawkish 5 gushy, mushy, teary 7 maudlin, tearful 9 emotional, nostalgic, schmaltzy 10 lachrymose 11 sentimental 15 oversentimental

mawkishness 4 mush 5 slush 6 bathos 9 mushiness, soppiness 10 maudlinism, slushiness 14 sentimentalism, sentimentality

maxim 3 saw 4 rule 5 adage, axiom, motto 6 old saw, saying, truism 7 proverb 8 aphorism, apothegm 9 platitude

Maximes
author: 23 Francois La Rochefoucauld

Maxims of the Law
author: 12 Francis Bacon

maximum 3 top 4 most 6 utmost 7 highest, largest, maximal, optimum, supreme 8 foremost, greatest 9 paramount 11 unsurpassed

May
characteristic: 7 Maypole 13 queen of the May
flower: 8 hawthorn 15 lily of the valley
French: 3 Mai
gem: 7 emerald
German: 3 Mai
holiday: 6 May Day (1) 10 Mother's Day (2nd Sunday) 11 Memorial Day (last

Monday) **14** Armed Forces Day (3rd Saturday)
Italian: 6 Maggio
number of days: 9 thirty-one
origin of name: 4 Maia
Roman goddess of: **6** spring
place in year:
Gregorian: **5** fifth
Roman: **5** fifth
saying: 27 April showers bring May flowers
Spanish: 4 Mayo
Zodiac sign: 6 Gemini, Taurus

May, Elaine
real name: 12 Elaine Berlin
partner: 11 Mike Nichols
born: 14 Philadelphia PA
roles: 8 A New Leaf **15** California Suite
director of: 16 The Heartbreak Kid
writer/director of: 8 A New Leaf

Maya
city: 4 Coba **5** Tulum, Uxmal **6** Akumal, Cuello, Izamal **8** Calakmul, Palenque **11** Chichen Itza
conqueror: 8 Alvarado
day: 5 uayeb
language family: 5 Mayan **10** Maya-Quiche
location: 5 Tikal **6** Belize, Mexico **7** Chiapas, Mayapan, Tabasco, Yucatan **8** Honduras **9** Guatemala **11** Chichen Itza **14** Central America
month: 5 uinal **6** uinal
noted for: 9 astronomy **12** architecture **19** hieroglyphic writing
rain god: 4 Chac **5** Chaac **7** Chac Mol **8** Chac Mool
ruins: 9 Yaxchilan **20** Temple of Inscriptions
underworld: 7 Xibalba
year: 4 haab

maybe 6 mayhap **7** perhaps **8** feasibly, possibly **9** perchance **10** God willing, imaginably **11** conceivably **12** peradventure

Maybe
author: 14 Lillian Hellman

Mayberry RFD
character: 5 Alice **7** Aunt Bee **8** Sam Jones **9** Mike Jones **10** Goober Pyle **11** Emmett Clark **13** Howard Sprague, Millie Swanson
cast: 8 Ken Berry **10** Jack Dodson **11** Buddy Foster, Paul Hartman **13** Alice Ghostley, Arlene Golonka, Frances Bavier, George Lindsey

mayfly
varieties: 5 small **6** stream **9** burrowing

mayhem 4 maim **6** felony **7** battery, cripple **8** mutilate, violence **9** crippling, dismember **10** mutilation **13** disfigurement

may he rest in peace
Latin: 16 requiescat in pace

may it do good
Latin: 6 prosit

Maylie, Mrs and Rose
characters in: 11 Oliver Twist
author: 7 Dickens

Mayo, Virginia
real name: 13 Virginia Jones
husband: 12 Michael O'Shea
born: 9 St Louis MO
roles: 17 The West Point Story **22** The Best Years of Our Lives **26** The Secret Life of Walter Mitty

Mayor of Casterbridge, The
author: 11 Thomas Hardy
character: 13 Donald Farfrae, Richard Newson **14** Lucetta Le Sueur **15** Michael Henchard **19** Elizabeth Jane Newson, Susan Henchard-Newson

Mays, Willie
nickname: 9 Say Hey Kid
sport: 8 baseball
position: 11 center field
team: 11 New York Mets **13** New York Giants **18** San Francisco Giants

may she live forever
Latin: 12 esto perpetua
motto of: 5 Idaho

may she rest in peace
Latin: 16 requiescat in pace

maze 5 snarl **6** jungle, tangle **7** complex, meander, network **9** labyrinth **11** convolution

mazel tov 8 good luck

Mbabane
capital of: 9 Swaziland

McCambridge, Mercedes
real name: 32 Carlotta Mercedes Agnes McCambridge
born: 8 Joliet IL
roles: 5 Giant **8** Cimarron **11** Touch of Evil **14** All the King's Men **15** A Farewell to Arms **18** Suddenly Last Summer

McCarey, Leo
director of: 8 Duck Soup **10** Going My Way (Oscar) **13** The Awful Truth (Oscar), **15** Ruggles of Red Gap **17** The Bells of St Mary's

McCarthy, Mary
author of: 8 The Group

McCay, Winsor
creator/artist of: 23 Little Nemo in Slumberland

McClellan, George B
nickname: 25 Little Mac the Young Napoleon
served in: 8 Civil War **10** Mexican War
side: 5 Union
commander of: 16 Army of the Potomac
battle: 8 Antietam **18** Peninsular campaign
governor of: 9 New Jersey

McCloud
character: 10 Sam McCloud **13** Chris Coughlin, (Sgt) Joe Broadhurst **14** Peter B Clifford
cast: 8 JD Cannon **11** Terry Carter **12** Dennis Weaver, Diana Muldaur

McClure, Darrell
creator/artist of: 17 Little Annie Rooney

McCrea, Joel
wife: 10 Frances Dee
born: 12 Los Angeles CA
roles: 11 Buffalo Bill 14 Palm Beach
Story 16 Sullivan's Travels, The Great
Man's Lady 17 Reaching for the Sun, The
More the Merrier 20 Foreign Correspondent

McCreary, Fainy (Mac)
character in: 3 USA
author: 9 Dos Passos

McCullers, Carson
author of: 17 The Mortgaged Heart 18
Member of the Wedding 21 The Ballad of
the Sad Cafe 23 Reflections in a Golden
Eye, The Heart Is a Lonely Hunter

McCullough, Colleen
author of: 13 The Thornbirds 19 An Indecent Obsession

McCutcheon, George Barr
author of: 9 Graustark

McEvoy, JP
creator/artist of: 10 Dixie Dugan

McFee, William
author of: 15 Casuals of the Sea

McGillicuddy, Cornelius Alexander
real name of: 10 Connie Mack

McGinley, Phyllis
author of: 12 Three Decades 15 A Pocketful of Wry 24 The Horse Who Lived Upstairs

McHale's Navy
character: 7 Christy 9 Willy Moss 11 Fuji
Kobiaji, Happy Haines 12 Harrison (Tinker) Bell, Lester Gruber 13 Virgil Farrell,
(Ensign) Charles Parker, (Lt Cdr) Quinton
McHale 14 (Lt) Elroy Carpenter 18 (Capt)
Wallace B Binghamton
cast: 8 Joe Flynn 9 Tim Conway 10 Billy
Sands, Gary Vinson, John Wright, Yoshio
Yoda 11 Bob Hastings, Edson Stroll 12
Gavin MacLeod 14 Carl Ballantine, Ernest Borgnine

McKenna, Siobhan
born: 7 Belfast, Ireland
roles: 11 King of Kings 13 Doctor
Zhivago 14 Of Human Bondage 24 Playboy of the Western World

McKim, Charles M
architect of: 27 Lutheran Church of the
Redeemer (Houston)

McKim, Mead, and White
partners: 13 Stanford White 18 Charles
Follen McKim 21 William Rutherford
Mead
architects of: 11 Century Club 14 University Club, Washington Arch 17 Vanderbilt Mansion 18 Columbia University
(NYC) 19 Boston Public Library, Pennsylvania Station (NYC), (first) Madison
Square Garden (NYC) 21 New York Herald Building, Pierpont Morgan Library
(NYC) 31 Madison Square Presbyterian
Church
style: 7 Shingle 18 Italian Renaissance

McKinley, William
nickname: 13 Major McKinley
presidential rank: 11 twenty-fifth
party: 10 Republican
state represented: 2 OH
defeated: 4 (Eugene Victor) Debs 5
(Seth Hockett) Ellis, (William Jennings)
Bryan 6 (John McCauley) Palmer,
(Wharton) Barker 7 (Charles Eugene)
Bentley, (John Granville) Woolley, (Jonah
Fitz Randolph) Leonard 8 (Charles Horatio) Matchett, (Joseph Francis) Malloney,
(Joshua) Levering
vice president: 6 (Garret Augustus) Hobart 9 (Theodore) Roosevelt
cabinet:
state: 3 (John Milton) Hay, (William Rufus) Day 7 (John) Sherman
treasury: 4 (Lyman Judson) Gage
war: 4 (Elihu) Root 5 (Russell Alexander)
Alger
attorney general: 4 (Philander Chase)
Knox 6 (John William) Griggs 7 (Joseph)
McKenna
navy: 4 (John Davis) Long
postmaster general: 4 (James Albert)
Gary 5 (Charles Emory) Smith
interior: 4 (Cornelius Newton) Bliss 9
(Ethan Allen) Hitchcock
agriculture: 6 (James) Wilson
born: 7 Niles OH
died: 9 Buffalo NY
died by: 13 assassination
buried: 8 Canton OH
education:
college: 10 Allegheny
law school: 6 Albany
religion: 9 Methodist
author: 37 The Tariff in the Days of
Henry Clay and Since
political career: 24 US House of Representatives
governor of: 4 Ohio
civilian career: 6 lawyer
military service: 7 captain 8 Civil War 11
brevet major
notable events of lifetime/term:
Act: 13 Dingley Tariff
Peace Conference: 5 Hague
Treaty of: 5 Paris
war with: 5 Spain
father: 7 William
mother: 5 Nancy (Campbell Allison)
siblings: 4 Anna, Mary 5 Abner, Helen,
James 10 Abbie Celia 12 David Allison
14 Sarah Elizabeth
wife: 3 Ida (Saxton)
children: 3 Ida 9 Katherine

McManus, George
creator/artist of: 12 The Newlyweds 16
Bringing Up Father

McMath, Virginia ~~Katherine~~
real name of: 12 Ginger Rogers

McMeekan, Wayne
real name of: 10 David Wayne

McMillan, Edwin Mattison
    field: 7 physics 9 chemistry
    developed: 16 synchrocyclotron
    awarded: 10 Nobel Prize
McMillan and Wife
    character: 7 Mildred 13 Sally McMillan
    14 (Sgt) Charles Enright 15 (Commis-
    sioner) Stewart McMillan
    cast: 10 John Schuck, Rock Hudson 11
    Nancy Walker 15 Susan Saint James
McMurtry, Larry
    author of: 10 Texasville 12 Lonesome
    Dove 14 Horseman Pass By 18 The Last
    Picture Show
McPhee, John
    author of: 16 In Suspect Terrain 20
    Coming into the Country 23 The Curve of
    Binding Energy 26 Encounters with the
    Archdruid
McQueen, Steve
    real name: 21 Terrence Steven Mc-
    Queen
    wife: 10 Ali MacGraw
    born: 8 Slater MO 14 Indianapolis IN
    roles: 7 Bullitt, The Blob 8 Papillon 14
    The Great Escape, The Sand Pebbles 16
    The Cincinnati Kid 17 Thomas Crown Af-
    fair, Wanted Dead or Alive 19 The Mag-
    nificent Seven
McTeague
    author: 11 Frank Norris
mea culpa 7 my fault 14 through my fault
Mead, Margaret
    author of: 14 My Earlier Years 16 Black-
    berry Winter 18 Coming of Age in Samoa
    20 Growing Up in New Guinea 42 Sex
    and Temperament in Three Primitive So-
    cieties
    husband: 14 Gregory Bàteson
Meade, Dr and Mrs
    characters in: 15 Gone With the Wind
    author: 8 Mitchell
Meade, George Gordon
    served in: 8 Civil War 10 Mexican War
    side: 5 Union
    battle: 7 Bull Run 8 Antietam 10 Gettys-
    burg 13 South Mountain 14 Fredericks-
    burg 16 Chancellorsville 18 Peninsular
    campaign
    commander of: 16 Army of the Potomac
meadow 3 lea 4 mead, park 5 field, green 6
    forage 7 herbage, pasture, savanna 9
    grassland, pasturage
meager 4 bare, lean, slim, thin 5 scant,
    short, spare, token 6 little, paltry, scanty,
    scarce, skimpy, slight, sparse 7 scrimpy,
    slender, stinted, wanting 9 deficient 10
    inadequate 12 insufficient 13 insubstantial
meagerness 4 sparsity 9 smallness 10 in-
    adequacy, measliness, scantiness, skimpi-
    ness, sparseness 13 insufficiency 14 insig-
    nificance
Meagles
    character in: 12 Little Dorrit
    author: 7 Dickens

meal 4 bran, chow, diet, eats, fare, food,
    grub, menu 5 feast, flour, grits 6 farina,
    groats, repast, spread 7 banquet, cooking,
    cuisine, oatmeal 8 cornmeal, victuals 10
    bill of fare 11 nourishment, refreshment
mealymouthed 6 unsure 7 devious 8 hesi-
    tant 9 deceptive, insincere
mean 3 low, par, say 4 base, evil, norm,
    plan, poor, rude, rule, vile, want, wish 5
    aim at, cheap, close, cruel, imply, nasty,
    petty, small, tight, venal 6 denote, flimsy,
    greedy, hint at, intend, malign, medium,
    menial, normal, paltry, sleazy, sordid,
    stingy, tell off, trashy, unfair 7 average, bal-
    ance, betoken, dream of, drive at, express,
    hoggish, inhuman, miserly, point to, pro-
    pose, purpose, regular, resolve, selfish,
    signify, squalid, suggest, think of, trivial,
    vicious 8 aspire to, gimcrack, grasping,
    indicate, inferior, inhumane, intimate,
    low-grade, picayune, piddling, pitiless, rub-
    bishy, say truly, shameful, standard, stand
    for, trifling, uncaring, wretched 9 illiberal,
    low-paying, malicious, mercenary, merci-
    less, miserable, niggardly, penurious, sym-
    bolize, unfeeling 10 avaricious, compro-
    mise, despicable, have in mind, have in
    view, jerry-built, low-ranking, malevolent,
    pinchpenny, second-rate, ungenerous, vil-
    lainous 11 closefisted, commonplace,
    disgraceful, happy medium, hardhearted,
    self-seeking, small-minded, tightfisted, un-
    important 12 contemptible, disagreeable,
    dishonorable 13 insignificant, unsympa-
    thetic 15 inconsequential
meander 4 loop, rove, wind 5 snake, stray,
    twist 6 circle, ramble, spiral, wander, zig-
    zag 8 undulate 9 convolute, corkscrew
meandering 7 devious, sinuous, turning,
    winding 8 indirect, rambling, tortuous,
    twisting 9 wandering 10 circuitous, round-
    about, serpentine
meaning 3 aim, end 4 gist, goal, hint, meat,
    pith, plan, view 5 drift, force, point, sense,
    value, worth 6 burden, design, intent, ob-
    ject, scheme, thrust, upshot 7 content, es-
    sence, pointer, purport, purpose 9 inten-
    tion, substance 10 denotation, indication,
    intimation, suggestion 11 implication 12
    significance 15 sum and substance
meaningful 4 deep 5 meaty, pithy 6 useful
    7 pointed, serious 8 eloquent, explicit,
    pregnant 9 designing, important 10 ex-
    pressive, gratifying, portentous, purpose-
    ful, suggestive, worthwhile 11 significant,
    substantial 13 consequential
meaningless 5 trite 6 absurd, paltry, stupid
    7 aimless, fatuous, foolish, idiotic, shallow,
    trivial, useless 8 baffling, piddling, puzzling
    9 enigmatic, facetious, frivolous, illegible,
    senseless, valueless, worthless 10 inco-
    herent, mystifying, perplexing 11 bewilder-
    ing, inscrutable, nonsensical, purposeless,
    unessential, unimportant 12 impenetrable,
    inexplicable, inexpressive, preposterous
    13 insignificant, unsubstantial 14 undeci-
    pherable

Mean Joe

nickname of: 9 Joe Greene

means 3 way 4 jack, mode 5 bread, dough, funds, money 6 avenue, course, income, method, resort, riches, wealth 7 capital, dollars, measure, process, revenue 8 property 9 affluence, long green, resources, substance 11 alternative, wherewithal

mean-spirited 3 low 4 base, poor, vile 5 cheap, nasty, petty, small, snide, sorry, tight, venal 6 abject, measly, paltry, scurvy, shabby, sordid, stingy 7 ignoble, miserly, selfish, vicious 8 tightwad, wretched 9 miserable, penurious 10 ungenerous 12 parsimonious

Mean Streets

director: 14 Martin Scorsese

cast: 11 Amy Robinson, David Proval 12 Harvey Keitel, Robert DeNiro

meantime 7 interim 8 interval 9 meanwhile

meanwhile 8 meantime 12 concurrently, in the interim 13 at the same time 14 simultaneously

measurable 10 assessable, computable, mensurable, reckonable 11 appraisable 12 determinable

measure 3 act, law 4 bill, plan, rule, size, step, time 5 bound, clock, gauge, judge, limit, means, plumb, quota, range, scale, scope, share, sound, value 6 amount, assess, course, degree, design, extent, method, resort, scheme, survey 7 portion, project 8 appraise, evaluate, proposal, quantity 9 allotment, allowance, enactment, procedure, restraint, yardstick 10 limitation, moderation, proceeding, temperance

measure, unit of

of Afghanistan: 3 paw, sir 5 jerib, karoh 6 khurds 7 kharwar

of Algeria: 3 pik 5 rebis, tarri 6 termin

of Argentina: 4 sino 5 legua 6 cuadra, lastre 7 manzana

of Australia: 4 arna, naut, saum

of Austria: 4 fass, fuss, joch, mass, muth, yoke 5 halbe, linie, meile, metze, pfiff, punkt 6 achtel, becher, leipoa, seidel 7 klafter, viertel 8 dreiling 12 futtermassel

of Belgium: 3 vat 4 aune, pied 5 carat 6 perche 8 boisseau

of Bolivia: 6 league 7 celemin

of Borneo: 7 gantang

of Brazil: 2 pe 4 moio, sack, vara 5 braca, legoa, milha, tonel 6 canada, cuarto, quarto, tarefa 7 garrafa 8 alqueire

of Bulgaria: 3 oka, oke 5 krine, lekhe, likhe

of Canada: 3 ton 5 minot, perch, point 6 arpent 7 chainon

of the Canary Islands: 8 fanegada

of Chile: 4 vara 5 legua, linea 6 cuadra 7 fanega

of China: 3 cho, fan, fen, pau, tou, tun, yan, yin 4 chek, chih, fang, kish, papa, quei, shih, teke, tsän, tsun 5 catty, chang, ching, sheng, shing 6 chupak, gungli,

kungho, kungmu, tching 7 kungfen, kungyin 8 kungchih, kungshih 9 kungching

of Colombia: 4 vara 7 azumbre, celemin

of Costa Rica: 4 vara 5 cafiz, cahiz 6 fanega, tercia 7 cajuela, cantaro, manzana 10 caballeria

of Cuba: 4 vara 5 bocoy, cocoy, tarea 6 cordel, fanega 10 caballeria

of Czechoslovakia: 3 lan 4 mira 5 korec, liket, stopa 6 merice, strych

of Denmark: 3 ell, fod, mil, pot 4 alen 5 album, anker, kande, linje, paegl 7 landmil, oltonde, ortonde, skieppe, viertel 8 fjerding 9 ottingkar 10 korntonde

of the Dominican Republic: 3 ona 5 tarea 6 fanega

of Ecuador: 5 libra 6 cuadra, fanega

of Egypt: 3 apt, den, hen, rob 4 arab, dira, draa, khet, nief, ocha, roub, theb, wudu 5 abdat, ardab, cubit, farde, fedan, keleh, kerat, kilah, sahme 6 artaba, aurure, baladi, kantar, keddah, robhah, schene 7 choryos, daribah, malouah, roubouh, toumnah 8 kassabah, kharouba 10 diramimari, diribaladi

of El Salvador: 4 vara 5 cafiz, cahiz 6 fanega 7 batella, botella, cantara, manzana

of England: 3 cut, ell, lea, pin, rod, ton, tun, vat 4 acre, bind, butt, comb, coom, cran, foot, gill, goad, hand, hank, heer, hide, inch, last, line, mile, nail, pace, palm, peck, pint, pipe, pole, pool, rood, rope, sack, seam, span, trug, typp, wist, yard, yoke 5 bodge, chain, cubit, diglt, float, floor, fluid, hutch, jugum, minim, ounce, perch, point, prime, quart, skein, stack, truss 6 barrel, bovate, bushel, cranne, fathom, firkin, gallon, hobbet, hobbit, league, manent, oxgang, pottle, runlet, square, strike, sulung, thread, tierce 7 auchlet, furlong, kenning, quarter, rundlet, seamile, spindle, tertian, virgate 8 carucate, chaldron, hogshead, landyard, puncheon, quadrant, standard

of Estonia: 3 tun 4 elle, liin, sund, toll, toop 5 verst 6 sagene, versta 7 kulimet 8 tonnland

of Ethiopia: 3 tat 4 cubi, kuba 5 derah, messe 6 cabaho, sinjer, sinzer, tanica 7 entelam, farsakh, farsang, ghebeta

of Finland: 5 kannu, verst 6 fathom, kannor 8 ottinger, skalpund, tunnland

of France: 3 pot, sac 4 aune, mine, pied, velt 5 arpen, carat, ligne, minot, pinte, point, pouce, velte 6 arpent, hemine, league, quarte, setier

of Greece: 3 pik 4 bema, piki, pous 5 baril, chous, cubit, diote, doron, maris, pekhe, podos, pygon, xylon 6 acaena, bacile, barile, cotula, dichas, gramme, hemina, koilon, lichas, milion, orgyia, palame, pechys, schene, xestes 7 bacvhel, chenica, choenix, cyathos, diaulos, metreta, stadium, stremma 8 condylos, daktylos, dekapode, dolichos, medimnos, medimnys, metretes, palaiste,

plethron, plethrum, stathmos 9
hemiekton, oxybaphon

of Guatemala: 4 vara 6 cuarta, tercia 7
cajuela, manzana 10 caballeria

of Guinea: 7 jacktan

of Honduras: 4 vara 5 milla 6 mecate 7
cajuela

of Hungary: 3 ako 4 hold, yoke 5 itcze,
marok, metze 7 huvelyk

of Iceland: 3 set 4 alin 5 almud 6
almenn, ferfet, pottur 7 fathmur, fermila,
oltunna

of India: 3 ady, gaz, gez, jow, lan 4 byee,
coss, depa, doph, hath, koss, kunk, raik,
rati, seit, taun, tola 5 bigha, covid, crosa,
danda, depoh, drona, erosa, garce,
hasta, krosa, parah, ratti, salay, yojan 6
adhaka, amunam, covido, cudava,
cumbha, geerah, moolum, mushti,
ouroub, palgat, parran, prasha, ropani,
tipree, unglee, yojana 7 dhanush,
gavyuti, khahoon, niranga, prastha 8
okthabah

of Indonesia: 5 depah, depoh

of Iran: 3 gaz, zar, zer 4 cane 5 gareh,
kafiz, makuk, qasab 6 charac, chebel,
ghalva 7 capicha, chenica, farsakh, mansion, mishara 8 parasang, piamaneh,
stathmos

of Ireland: 4 mile 6 bandle 8 crannock

of Israel: 3 cab, car, hin, kab, kor 4 bath,
ezba, omer, reed 5 cubit, donum, dunam,
ephah, ganeh, homer, kaneh

of Italy: 3 pie 4 orna 5 palma, palmo,
punto, salma, stero 6 barile, miglie,
moggio, rubbio, tomolo 7 braccio, secchio
8 giornata, quadrato

of Japan: 2 go 3 boo, cho, djo, fun, inc,
ken, kin, kon, rin, shi, sho, sun, tan 4 hiro,
isse, kati, koku, niyo, shoo 5 carat, catty,
issho, ittan, momme, picul, shaku 6
kwamme 8 hiyak-kin 9 hiyak-hiro 11
komma-ichida, kujira-shaku

of Java: 3 kan 4 paal, rand 5 palen

of Kenya: 4 wari

of Laos: 3 bak

of Latvia: 3 let 4 stof 5 stoff, verst 6 arshin, kulmet 7 verchoc, verchok 8
krouchka, pourvete 9 deciatine, lofstelle,
pourvette 10 tonnseteel

of Liberia: 4 kuba

of Libya: 3 dra, pik, saa 4 kele 5 bozze,
donum, jabia, teman, uckia 6 barile,
gorrah, misura 7 mattaro, termino 8
kharouba

of Luxembourg: 5 fuder

of Madagascar: 7 gantang

of Malaysia: 3 pau, tun 4 para, pipe, tael,
wang 5 parah 6 chupak, parrah 7
gantang

of Malta: 4 rotl 5 artal, canna, parto, ratel, salma 6 kantar 7 caffiso

of Mexico: 3 bag, pie 4 alma, onza, vara
5 almud, baril, carga, jarra, labor, legua,
libra, linea, marco, sitio 6 adarme, almude, arroba, carega, fanega, ochaua,

terceo 7 pulgada, quintal 9 cuarteron,
cuartillo 10 caballeria

of Morocco: 4 kala, muhd, rotl, saah,
sahh, ueba 5 artal, cadee, gerbe, ratel 6
covado, dirhem, fanega, izenbi, kintar,
tangin, tomini 8 quintral

of Myanmar: 2 ly 3 dha, gon, mau, sao,
tao, tat 4 byee, phan, seit, taun, that 5
shita, thuoc 6 lamany, palgat 7 chaivai 8
okthabah

of the Netherlands: 2 el 3 aam, ahm, ell,
kan, vat 4 duim, mijl, rood, rope 5 anker,
roede, wisse 6 bunder, legger, maatje,
mutsje, streep 7 schepel 8 mimgelen,
steekkan

of Nicaragua: 4 vara 5 cahiz 6 suerte 7
cajuela, manzana 10 cabelleria

of Norway: 3 fot, mal 4 alen 5 kande 6
fathom 7 skieppe 9 korntonde

of Panama: 7 celemin

of Paraguay: 3 pie 4 lino, lira, lire, vara 5
legua 6 cuadra, fanega

of Peru: 4 topo 5 galon 7 celemin 8
fanegada

of the Philippines: 4 loan 5 braza, catty,
cavan, chupa, fardo, ganta, picul, punto 6
apatan, balita, lachsa, quinon 7 quilate 8
chinanta

of Poland: 3 cal 4 mila, pret 5 morga,
sazen, vloka, wloka 6 cwierc, cwierk,
kwarta, lokiec 7 garniec 9 kwarterka

of Portugal: 2 pe 4 bota, moio, vara 5 almud, fanga, geira, linha, milha 6 almude,
covado 7 alquier, ferrado, selamin 8
alqueire

of Puerto Rico: 6 cuerda 10 cabelleria

of Rumania: 7 faltche

of Russia: 3 fut, lof 4 duim, fass, loof,
pood, quar, stof 5 duime, foute, korec,
korek, ligne, osmin, pajak, stoff, stoof, ve-
dro, verst 6 charka, liniya, osmina, paletz,
sagene, stekar, tchast, tsarki, versta,
verste 7 archine, arsheen, botchka,
chkalik, garnetz, verchoc, verchok 8 bou-
tylka, chetvert, krouchka, kroushka 9
chetverik 10 dessiatine 11 polugarnetz

of Scotland: 3 cop 4 boll, cran, fall, mile,
peck, pint, rood, rope, span 5 crane, lippy
6 audlet, davach, firlot, lippie, noggin 7
chalder, choppin 8 mutchkin, stimpart,
stimpert 9 particate, shaftment, shathmont

of Sicily: 5 salma 7 caffiso

of Sierra Leone: 4 load 6 kettle

of Somalia: 3 top 4 caba 5 chela, darat,
tabla 6 cubito 8 parsalah

of South Africa: 4 vara

of Spain: 3 pie 4 codo, dedo, paso, vara
5 braza, cahiz, carga, legua, medio,
palmo, sesma 6 cordel, cuarta, fanega,
racion, yugada 7 azumbre, celemin,
estadel, pulgada 8 fanegada

of Sri Lanka: 4 para, seer 5 parah 6
amunam, parrah

of Sudan: 2 ud

of Suriname: 7 ketting

of Sweden: 3 aln, fot, ref, tum 4 alar,

amar, famn, kapp, last, stop 5 carat, foder, kanna, linje, nymil, spann 6 fathom, jumfru 7 oxhuvud, tunland 8 fjarding, koltunna, tunnland

of Switzerland: 3 imi, pot 4 aune, fuss, muid, pied, zoll 5 lieue, linie, maass, pouce, staab, toise 6 perche, strich 7 klafter, viertel 9 quarteron 10 holzlafter 11 holzklafter

of Syria: 5 makuk 6 garava

of Thailand: 2 wa 3 can, ken, niv, rai, sat, sok, wah 4 cohi, keup, niou, tang 5 kwien, leeng, sesti, vouah 6 kabiet, kanahn 7 chaimeu 8 changawn 9 anukabiet

of Tunisia: 3 saa 4 saah 5 cafiz 6 mettar 8 milerole

of Turkey: 3 dra, oka, pik 4 draa, khat, kile, zira 5 berri, kileh, zirai 6 arshin, chinik, fortin, halebi 7 nocktat

of Uruguay: 4 vara 6 cuadra, suerte

of Venezuela: 5 galon, milla 6 fanega 7 estadel

of Vietnam: 4 gang, phan, thon

of Wales: 5 cover 7 cantred, crannoc, listred

of Yugoslavia: 3 oka, rif 4 akov, ralo 5 donum, khvat, lanaz, plaze, stopa 6 motyka, ralico 9 danoranja

measured 5 equal, exact 6 steady 7 precise, regular, studied, uniform 8 verified 10 calculated, deliberate 11 cold-blooded, intentional, well-planned 12 premeditated 13 predetermined

Measure for Measure

author: 18 William Shakespeare

character: 5 Lucio 6 Angelo, Juliet 7 Claudio, Escalus, Mariana 8 Isabella 9 Vincentio

measureless 7 endless 8 infinite 9 boundless, unlimited 12 immeasurable

measurement 4 area, mass, size 5 depth, width 6 extent, height, length, volume, weight 7 breadth, content, gauging 8 capacity, plumbing, sounding 9 amplitude, appraisal, dimension, magnitude, measuring, reckoning, surveying 10 assessment, estimation, evaluation 11 mensuration

Biblical: 4 omer 5 cubit, ephah 6 shekel

champagne: 6 magnum 8 jeroboam, rehoboam 9 balthazar 10 methuselah, salmanazar 14 Nebuchadnezzar

cloth: 4 bolt

cotton: 4 bale

electricity: 3 ohm 4 volt, watt 5 joule 6 ampere 10 horsepower

energy: 3 BTU 5 joule 7 calorie 11 kilocalorie 18 British thermal unit

firewood: 4 cord

force: 4 dyne 6 newton 7 poundal

gold/jewelry: 5 carat, karat, point

Greek: 4 mina 5 cubit 6 obolos, talent 7 drachma, stadion

gun: 5 gauge 7 caliber

light: 7 candela 11 candlepower

liquor/spirits: 4 pint, pony, shot 5 fifth, quart 6 jigger, magnum

metric system: 5 liter, meter 9 deciliter, decimeter, dekaliter, dekameter, kiloliter, kilometer, nanometer 10 centiliter, centimeter, cubic meter, hectoliter, hectometer, milliliter, millimeter 11 square meter 14 cubic dekameter 15 cubic centimeter, cubic millimeter, square decimeter, square dekameter, square kilometer 16 square centimeter, square hectometer, square millimeter

metric weight: 3 ton 4 gram 5 tonne 7 quintal 8 dekagram, kilogram 9 centigram, hectogram, microgram, milligram

paper: 4 ream 5 quire

pressure: 6 pascal 10 atmosphere

Roman: 2 as 5 cubit, libra 6 pondus 7 stadium

sound: 7 decibel

temperature: 6 degree, Kelvin 7 Celsius 10 Fahrenheit

time: 3 day 4 hour, week, year 5 month, score 6 decade, minute, second 7 century 10 millennium, nanosecond 11 microsecond, millisecond

typography: 2 em, en 4 pica 5 point

unit: 3 cup, rod 4 acre, dram, foot, gill, inch, link, mile, peck, pint, yard 5 chain, minim, ounce, quart 6 barrel, bushel, circle, degree, fathom, gallon 7 furlong, hectare 8 angstrom, hogshead, teaspoon 9 cubic foot, cubic inch, cubic yard, square rod 10 fluid ounce, right angle, square foot, square inch, square mile, square yard, tablespoon 25 international nautical mile

weight: 3 ton 4 dram 5 grain, ounce, pound 7 scruple 8 short ton 9 ounce troy, pound troy 11 pennyweight 13 hundredweight

measure out 6 ration 7 dole out, mete out 9 apportion

meat 3 nut 4 core, fare, food, gist, grub 5 heart, point 6 kernel 7 edibles, essence, nucleus 8 victuals 9 provender, substance 10 provisions, sustenance 11 comestibles, nourishment

Mechaneus

epithet of: 4 Zeus

means: 9 contriver

mechanic 6 joiner 7 artisan 9 automatic, craftsman, machinist 11 uninspired 12 grease monkey

mechanical 4 cold 7 routine 9 automatic, unfeeling 10 impersonal, self-acting, unthinking 11 instinctive, involuntary, machinelike, perfunctory, unconscious 13 machine-driven

mechanism 4 tool 5 motor, works 7 machine, utensil 9 apparatus, appliance, implement, machinery 10 instrument 11 contrivance

Meda

husband: 9 Idomeneus

lover: 6 Leucus

medal 5 award, honor, prize 6 laurel, reward, ribbon, trophy 8 citation 9 medallion 10 decoration

Medawar, Peter Brian
  field: 7 biology
  nationality: 7 British
  discovered: 23 acquired immune tolerance
  awarded: 10 Nobel Prize
meddle 5 mix in 6 butt in, horn in, kibitz 7 intrude, pry into 9 interfere, interlope, intervene 10 tamper with
meddler 3 pry 5 snoop 7 Paul Pry 8 busybody 10 interferer, Nosy Parker
meddlesome 4 nosy 5 pushy 6 prying, snoopy 7 pushing 8 meddling, snooping 9 intrusive, obtrusive, officious 11 impertinent, interfering 12 presumptuous
Medea
  author: 9 Euripides
  character: 5 Creon, Jason 6 Aegeus, Glauce
Medea
  form: 9 sorceress
  father: 6 Aeetes
  mother: 5 Idyia
  aunt: 5 Circe
  brother: 8 Apsyrtus
  sister: 9 Chalciope
  lover: 5 Jason
  son: 6 Medeus, Pheres 8 Mermerus, Tisander 9 Alcimenes, Thessalus
  killed: 7 her sons
  escaped to: 6 Athens
Medeus
  father: 6 Aegeus
  mother: 5 Medea
media 5 press, radio 9 magazines 10 billboards, journalism, newspapers, television 11 journalists
  singular: 6 medium
medial 4 mean 6 median 7 average
median 3 mid, par 4 mean, norm 5 mesne 6 center, medial, medium, middle 7 average, central, halfway 8 middling, midpoint, moderate 12 intermediate
mediate 6 pacify, step in, umpire 7 referee 8 moderate 9 arbitrate, intercede, interpose, intervene, negotiate, reconcile 10 conciliate, propitiate
mediation 6 parley 10 adjustment, compromise, discussion 11 arbitration, give-and-take, negotiation, peacemaking 12 conciliation, intercession, intervention, pacification 14 reconciliation
mediator 6 umpire 7 referee 9 go-between, moderator 10 arbitrator, negotiator, peacemaker, reconciler 12 intermediary
medical 7 healing 8 curative, remedial, salutary, sanative 9 medicinal 10 medicative 11 restorative, therapeutic
medical abbreviation
  a c: 11 before meals
  ad lib: 8 as needed 9 as desired
  agit: 5 shake
  aq: 5 water
  b i d: 9 twice a day
  cap: 4 take 7 capsule
  coch: 8 spoonful
  dil: 6 dilute 8 dissolve
  fldxt: 12 fluid extract
  ft: 4 make
  ft mist: 12 make a mixture
  ft pulv: 11 make a powder
  gr: 5 grain
  gt: 4 drop
  gtt: 5 drops
  h s: 9 at bedtime
  in d: 5 daily
  lot: 6 lotion
  mod praesc: 21 in the manner prescribed
  O: 4 pint
  O D: 8 right eye
  O S: 7 left eye
  O U: 9 in each eye
  ol: 3 oil
  p c: 9 after food 10 after meals
  p o: 7 by mouth
  p r n: 25 as circumstances may require
  pil: 3 pill
  pulv: 6 powder
  q i d: 14 four times daily
  rep: 6 repeat
  s o s: 11 if necessary
  ss: 7 one half
  tab: 6 tablet
  t i d: 15 three times daily
  ut dict: 10 as directed
Medical Center
  character: 9 (Dr) Joe Gannon 11 Nurse Wilcox, (Dr) Paul Lochner 13 Nurse Chambers 14 Nurse Courtland, (Dr) Jeanne Bartlett
  cast: 9 James Daly 11 Chad Everett, Chris Hutson 12 Audrey Totter, Jayne Meadows 14 Corinne Camacho
medical practitioner 6 doctor medico 9 physician
medication 4 balm 5 tonic 6 elixir, remedy 7 nostrum, panacea 8 medicine 10 medicament, palliative 11 restorative
Medici, Giovanni de' 8 Pope Leo X 15 Pope Leo the Tenth
Medici, Giulio 14 Pope Clement VII 21 Pope Clement the Seventh
medicine 4 balm, drug, pill 5 salve, tonic 6 remedy 7 nostrum 10 healing art, medication 11 restorative 12 therapeutics 13 materia medica
  god of: 9 Asclepius 11 Aesculapius
medieval 8 Dark Ages 10 antiquated, Middle Ages 12 old-fashioned 14 pre-Renaissance
mediocre 4 so-so 5 petty 6 common, meager, medium, normal, paltry, slight 7 average 8 inferior, ordinary, passable, trifling 9 tolerable 10 negligible, pedestrian, second-rate 11 commonplace, indifferent, unimportant 12 run-of-the-mill 13 inappreciable, insignificant 14 fair-to-middling, inconsiderable 15 inconsequential, undistinguished
mediocrity 8 poorness 9 pettiness 10 low-quality, meagerness, paltriness, triviality 11 inferiority 12 indifference, ordinariness, un-

importance 14 insignificance 15 commonplaceness

meditate 4 muse, plan 5 aim at, study, think 6 devise, ponder 7 concoct, dream of, propose, reflect 8 cogitate, consider, contrive, mull over, ruminate 9 dwell upon 10 deliberate 11 contemplate

meditation 4 yoga 5 study 6 musing, poring 7 mulling, reverie, thought 8 brooding 9 discourse, pondering 10 cogitation, reflection, rumination 12 deliberation 13 consideration, contemplation

Mediterranean
  called by ancient Romans: 11 mare nostrum
  coast: 7 Riviera
  gulf: 5 Lions, Sidra, Tunis 7 Antalya, Catania, Taranto 8 Hammamet 9 Iskenderon
  island: 4 Elba 5 Capri, Corfu, Crete, Ibiza, Malta 6 Cyprus, Euboea, Lesbos, Rhodes, Sicily 7 Corsica, Majorca, Minorca 8 Balearic, Sardinia
  resort: 4 Nice 5 Capri 6 Cannes 7 Riviera 9 Cote d'Azur 10 Costa Brava
  river into: 2 Po 4 Ebro, Nile 5 Rhone
  sea: 5 Black 6 Aegean, Ionian 8 Adriatric, Ligurian 10 Tyrrhenian
  strait: 8 Bosporus 9 Bosphorus, Gibraltar 11 Dardanelles
  wind: 7 mistral, sirocco

medium 3 way 4 form, mean, mode, tool 5 means, organ 6 agency, avenue, common, milieu, normal 7 average, balance, channel, diviner, psychic, setting, vehicle 8 middling, moderate, ordinary 9 go-between, middle way, mid-course 10 atmosphere, compromise, golden mean, instrument, moderation 11 clairvoyant, environment, happy medium 12 crystal-gazer, intermediary, intermediate, middle ground, spiritualist, surroundings 13 fortuneteller 15 instrumentality

medley 4 hash, mess, olio 6 jumble, mosaic 7 farrago, melange, mixture 8 mishmash, pastiche 9 patchwork, potpourri 10 assortment, hodgepodge, miscellany 11 gallimaufry

Medon
  mentioned in: 5 Iliad 7 Odyssey
  father: 6 Oileus
  mother: 5 Rhene
  position: 6 herald
  friend of: 8 Penelope
  killed by: 6 Aeneas

medulla
  part of: 5 brain
  controls: 6 glands 7 muscles

Medusa
  form: 6 Gorgon
  father: 7 Phorcys
  mother: 4 Ceto
  sisters: 6 Graiae
  loved by: 8 Poseidon
  children: 7 Pegasus 8 Chrysaor
  sight of her caused people to turn to: 5 stone
  killed by: 7 Perseus

meek 4 mild 6 docile, gentle, humble, modest 8 lamblike, retiring, tolerant, yielding 9 compliant, spineless, tractable, weak-kneed 10 spiritless, submissive, unassuming 11 acquiescent, complaisant, deferential, unassertive, unresisting 13 long-suffering, tenderhearted, unpretentious

meekness 7 pliancy, shyness 8 docility, humility 9 passivity 10 diffidence, humbleness 11 bashfulness 13 nonresistance 14 self-effacement

meet 3 apt, fit 4 abut, face, good, heed, obey 5 cross, equal, greet, match, rally, right 6 adjoin, answer, border, follow, gather, muster, proper, seemly 7 abide by, collect, convene, execute, fitting, fulfill, observe, perform, respect, run into, satisfy, welcome 8 assemble, becoming, bump into, confront, converge, decorous, opposite, relevant, suitable 9 agreeable, allowable, befitting, congruous, discharge, encounter, intersect, permitted, pertinent 10 admissable, comply with, congregate, felicitous 11 acknowledge, appropriate, permissible 12 come together

meet eye to eye 4 face 8 confront, face up to 11 meet vis-a-vis

meet halfway 6 settle 9 make a deal 10 compromise 11 come to terms 14 strike a bargain 18 split the difference

meet head on 4 face 5 crash 6 oppose 7 collide, crack up 8 confront, face up to 9 challenge, encounter

meeting 4 date 5 group, tryst 6 caucus 7 council 8 assembly, conclave, congress 9 encounter, gathering 10 conference, convention, engagement, rendezvous 11 assignation, convocation, get-together 12 introduction, presentation 13 confrontation

Meeting at Telgte
  author: 11 Gunter Grass

meeting of the minds 7 concert, concord, harmony 9 agreement 11 concordance 13 understanding

meeting place 5 mecca 10 focal point, rendezvous

Meet Me in St Louis
  director: 16 Vincente Minnelli
  cast: 8 Leon Ames, Tom Drake 9 Mary Astor 11 Judy Garland 12 June Lockhart, Marjorie Main 13 Lucille Bremer 14 Margaret O'Brien
  song: 11 Trolley Song 14 The Boy Next Door 33 Have Yourself a Merry Little Christmas

Meet the Press
  moderator: 9 Ned Brooks 10 Bill Monroe 11 Edwin Newman 14 Lawrence Spivak, Martha Rountree

meet with 4 meet 6 endure 7 undergo 8 come upon 9 encounter 10 come across, experience

Mefitis
  also: 8 Mephitis
  prevented: 5 winds
  kind of winds: 7 harmful

Megaera
  member of: 6 Furies
Megalosaurus
  type: 8 dinosaur
  means: 11 great lizard
  found by: 15 William Buckland
  period: 8 Jurassic
Megamede
  husband: 12 King Thespius
  number of daughters: 5 fifty
Megapenthes
  father: 7 Proetus 8 Menelaus
  mother: 10 Stheneboea
Megara
  father: 5 Creon
  husband: 8 Hercules
  son: 11 Therimachus
Mehuman 6 eunuch
Meilichius
  epithet of: 4 Zeus
  means: 8 gracious
Mein Kampf
  author: 11 Adolf Hitler
  means: 7 my fight 8 my battle
Meitner, Lise
  field: 7 physics
  nationality: 8 Austrian
  contributed to: 21 atomic bomb development
  discovered: 12 protactinium 16 fission of uranium
Melaenis
  epithet of: 9 Aphrodite
  means: 5 black
Melampus
  father: 8 Amythaon
  mother: 7 Idomene
  brother: 4 Bias
  wife: 7 Lysippe
  son: 4 Abas 7 Mantius 10 Antiphates
  vocation: 4 seer 6 healer
melancholia 7 despair 10 depression, desolation, melancholy 11 despondency
melancholy 4 blue, glum 5 blues, dumps, gloom, moody 6 dismal, dreary, gloomy, mopish, morose, somber 7 despair, doleful, forlorn, joyless, unhappy 8 dejected, desolate, doldrums, dolorous, downcast, funereal, mournful 9 cheerless, dejection, depressed, heartsick, moodiness, plaintive 10 calamitous, depressing, depression, despondent, dispirited, gloominess, low spirits 11 despondency, discouraged, downhearted, forlornness, languishing, melancholia, sick at heart, unfortunate 12 disconsolate, heavyhearted 14 down in the dumps, down in the mouth 16 disconsolateness
  French: 6 triste 9 tristesse
melange 3 mix 6 jumble, medley 7 mixture 8 compound, mishmash, pastiche 9 pasticcio, patchwork, potpourri 10 assemblage, assortment, hodgepodge, miscellany 11 gallimaufry
Melanion
  suitor of: 8 Atalanta

Melanippe
  form: 4 foal
  foal born to: 6 Euippe
  transformed into: 4 Arne, girl
  father: 4 Ares
  queen of: 7 Amazons
Melanosaurus
  type: 8 dinosaur
  period: 8 Triassic
Melanthius
  goatherd for: 8 Odysseus
Melantho
  handmaiden for: 8 Penelope
Melas
  father: 7 Phrixus
  mother: 10 Chalciope
  brother: 5 Argus 8 Phrontis 10 Cytissorus
Melbourne
  bay: 7 Hobson's 11 Port Phillip
  landmark: 20 Flemington Racecourse
  river: 5 Yarra 6 Plenty 9 Mary Creek, Patterson 11 Maribyrnong 12 Diamond Creek 13 Kororoit Creek 14 Dandenong Creek, Gardiner's Creek 16 Moonee Ponds Creek
  state: 8 Victoria
  university: 6 Monash 7 La Trobe
Melchizedek
  means: 19 king of righteousness
  hometown: 5 Salem
  contemporary: 7 Abraham
meld 3 mix 4 fuse, join 5 blend, merge, unite 6 jumble, mingle 7 combine 8 coalesce, intermix, scramble 9 commingle 10 amalgamate, intertwine, interweave 11 consolidate, incorporate, intermingle
Meleager
  father: 4 Ares 6 Oeneus
  mother: 7 Althaea
  uncle: 9 Plexippus
  slew: 14 Calydonian boar
  loved: 8 Atalanta
  killed: 15 mother's brothers
  sisters: 11 Meleagrides
Meleagrides
  sisters of: 8 Meleager
  transformed into: 10 guinea hens
  transformed by: 7 Artemis
melee 3 row 4 fray, riot 5 brawl, scrap, set-to 6 fracas, rumpus, tussle 7 scuffle 8 disorder, dogfight 9 commotion, fistfight 10 free-for-all 11 altercation, pandemonium
Melete
  member of: 5 Muses
  personifies: 10 meditation
Melia
  form: 5 nymph
  born from: 5 blood
  blood of: 6 Uranus
Meliad
  form: 5 nymph
  nymph of: 6 flocks 10 fruit trees
Meliae
  nymphs of: 5 Melic
Meliboea
  form: 6 maiden

Melicertes
 father: 7 Athamas
 mother: 3 Ino
 changed into: 8 Palaemon

Melie
 form: 5 nymph
 son: 6 Amycus

Melissa
 sister: 8 Amaethea
 nourished: 4 Zeus

mellifluous 4 soft 5 sweet 6 dulcet, mellow, smooth 7 musical 8 resonant 9 full-toned, melodious 10 euphonious, harmonious, sweet-toned 13 sweet-sounding

Mellors
 character in: 20 Lady Chatterley's Lover
 author: 8 Lawrence

mellow 4 rich, ripe, soft 5 drunk, sweet 6 mature, season, soften 7 matured, relaxed 8 luscious, tolerant 9 delicious 10 full-bodied 11 sympathetic 12 full-flavored 13 compassionate, understanding

mellowness 8 full body, fullness, maturity, richness, ripeness, softness 9 tolerance 10 compassion, smoothness 11 lusciousness, pleasantness

melodic 5 lyric 7 tuneful

melodious 4 rich, soft 5 clear, lyric, sweet 6 dulcet, mellow, smooth 7 melodic, musical, ringing, tuneful 8 resonant 9 full-toned 10 euphonious, sweet-toned 11 mellifluent, mellifluous

melodrama 9 theatrics 12 emotionalism 13 theatricality

melodramatic 5 corny, hammy, hokey, stagy 7 maudlin, mawkish 8 cornball, frenzied 10 flamboyant, histrionic 11 exaggerated, overwrought, sensational, sentimental, spectacular 13 overemotional

melody 3 air 4 aria, song, tune 5 ditty, theme 6 ballad, strain, timbre 7 concord, euphony 10 musicality 11 tunefulness 12 mellifluence 13 melodiousness 14 harmoniousness 15 mellifluousness

melon
 varieties: 4 pear 5 mango, snake, stink 6 casaba, citron, Dudaim, netted, nutmeg, orange, winter 7 Persian, serpent 8 honeydew 10 cantaloupe, preserving, watermelon 11 pomegranate 16 Oriental pickling, Queen Anne's pocket 17 Chinese preserving

Melpomene
 member of: 5 Muses
 personifies: 7 tragedy

melt 4 fade, fuse, pass, thaw 5 blend, merge, shade, touch 6 affect, disarm, dispel, soften, vanish 7 appease, dwindle, liquefy, mollify, scatter 8 dissolve 9 disappear, dissipate, evaporate, waste away 10 arouse pity, conciliate, propitiate

melt away 5 dry up 8 vaporize 9 evaporate

Melus
 father: 7 Cinyras
 mother: 6 Cyprus
 changed into: 9 apple tree

Melville, Herman
 author of: 4 Omoo 5 Mardi, Typee 7 Redburn 8 Moby Dick 9 Billy Budd 12 Benito Cereno 16 The Confidence Man 20 Bartleby the Scrivener

Melville, Julia
 character in: 9 The Rivals
 author: 8 Sheridan

Melvin and Howard
 director: 13 Jonathan Demme
 cast: 9 Paul LeMat 12 Jason Robards 15 Mary Steenburgen
 Oscar for: 6 script 17 supporting actress (Steenburgen)

member 3 arm, leg, toe 4 foot, hand, limb, part, tail, wing 5 bough, digit, organ, piece, shoot 6 branch, finger, pinion 7 element, portion, section, segment 8 fragment 9 appendage, component, extremity 10 ingredient 11 constituent

member
 of the bar: 4 beak 7 counsel 8 advocate, attorney 9 barrister, counselor 10 mouthpiece 12 legal advisor 13 attorney-at-law
 of a crew: 4 hand, mate 6 ensign, ganger, gunner, purser, yeoman 7 bowsman, oarsman, steward, swabbie 8 cabin boy, coxswain, deckhand, helmsman 9 first mate, navigator
 of faculty: 3 don, PhD 4 prof 5 tutor 6 doctor, master 7 teacher 8 lecturer 9 professor 10 instructor
 of family: 3 son 4 aunt 5 niece, uncle 6 cousin, father, mother, nephew, sister 7 brother 8 daughter, grandson 11 grandfather, grandmother 13 granddaughter
 of legislature: 4 whip 6 deputy 7 senator, speaker 8 delegate, lawmaker 10 legislator, politician 11 congressman 12 congresswoman 14 representative
 of religious order: 3 nun 4 dame, monk 5 Clare, friar, priest 6 father, hermit, Jesuit, sister 7 Alexian, ascetic, brother, Cluniac, Templar 8 Capuchin, cenobite, minister, Trappist 9 Carmelite, Dominican 10 Carthusian, Cistercian, Franciscan 11 Augustinian, Benedictine 14 mother superior

Member of the Wedding, The
 author: 15 Carson McCullers
 character: 6 Jarvis 11 Janice Evans 13 Frankie Addams, John Henry West 16 Honey Camden Brown 18 Berenice Sadie Brown

membership 4 club 6 league, roster 7 company, society 9 community, personnel 10 connection, fellowship, fraternity 11 affiliation, association, brotherhood

membrane 3 web 4 film, skin 6 lining, sheath 7 coating 8 envelope, pellicle 9 thin sheet 10 integument

memento 5 favor, relic, token 6 record, trophy 8 keepsake, memorial, reminder, souvenir 11 memorabilia, remembrance 12 remembrancer 13 commemoration

memento mori 23 remember that thou must die 31 object serving as a reminder of death

Memnon
　origin: 8 Oriental 9 Ethiopian
　father: 8 Tithonus
　mother: 3 Eos 4 Dawn
　brother: 8 Emathion
　companions: 10 Memnonides
　fought with: 7 Trojans
　killed by: 8 Achilles

Memnonides see 6 Memnon

memo
　French: 11 aide memoire

memoir 4 life 5 diary 7 journal 9 biography, life story 10 adventures 11 confessions, experiences, reflections 13 autobiography, recollections, reminiscences

Memoirs of a Dutiful Daughter
　author: 16 Simone de Beauvoir

memorabilia 6 papers 7 records 8 archives 9 documents

memorable 6 famous 7 eminent, notable, salient 8 historic, stirring, striking 9 important, momentous, prominent, red-letter 10 celebrated, impressive, noteworthy, remarkable 11 illustrious, outstanding, significant 13 distinguished, extraordinary, unforgettable

memorandum 4 memo, note 5 brief 6 agenda, minute, record 7 jotting 8 reminder 11 brief report, list of items

memorial 6 homage 7 tribute 8 monument 10 monumental 11 testimonial 13 commemorative

memorialization 11 celebration 13 commemoration

memorialize 4 mark 5 honor 9 celebrate 11 commemorate, pay homage to 12 pay tribute to

memory 4 fame, mark, name, note 5 glory, honor, token 6 esteem, recall, regard, renown, repute 7 memento, respect 8 eminence, keepsake, memorial, prestige, reminder, souvenir 10 estimation, reputation 11 distinction, remembering, remembrance, testimonial 12 recollection, remembrancer, reminiscence 13 commemoration

　goddess of: 9 Mnemosyne

Memphis
　football team: 9 Showboats

menace 3 cow 4 risk 5 bully, daunt, peril 6 danger, hazard, threat 7 imperil, pitfall, portend, presage, terrify 8 browbeat, endanger, forebode, jeopardy, threaten 9 terrorize 10 intimidate, jeopardize 11 be a hazard to, imperilment 12 endangerment

menacing 7 hostile 9 dangerous 11 belligerent, threatening, treacherous 12 antagonistic

Menaechmi
　author: 7 Plautus

menage a trois 9 threesome 16 household of three

Menander
　author of: 5 Heros 13 Perikeiromene 14 The Arbitration, The Misanthrope 16 The Rape of the Lock

Men at Arms
　author: 11 Evelyn Waugh

Mencken, H L
　author of: 10 Prejudices 19 The American Language
　editor of: 10 The Mercury 11 The Smart Set

mend 3 fix 4 cure, darn, heal, knit 5 amend, emend, patch 6 better, reform, remedy, repair, revise 7 correct, improve, rectify, restore, retouch, touch up 8 overhaul, renovate 9 meliorate 10 ameliorate 11 recondition

mendacious 5 false, lying 8 spurious 9 deceptive 10 misleading, untruthful

mendacity 5 fraud, lying 6 deceit 7 falsity, perfidy 9 chicanery, deception, duplicity, falsehood, hypocrisy 10 dishonesty 11 insincerity 13 double-dealing, falsification, prevarication 14 untruthfulness 17 misrepresentation

Mendel, Gregor Johann
　field: 6 botany
　nationality: 8 Austrian
　discovered: 14 laws of heredity
　founded: 8 genetics

Mendeleyev (Mendeleev), Dimitri Ivanovich
　field: 9 chemistry
　nationality: 7 Russian
　devised: 11 periodic law 13 periodic table

Mendelssohn, (Jakob Ludwig) Felix
　born: 7 Germany, Hamburg
　composer of: 6 Elijah, St Paul 7 Athalie, Italian (symphony No 4), Lorelei, Ruy Blas 8 Antigone, Scottish (symphony No 3) 11 Reformation (symphony No 5), The Hebrides 12 Hymn of Praise (symphony No 2) 17 Songs without Words 21 A Midsummer Night's Dream

mendicant 6 beggar 10 alms-seeker, panhandler

Mending Wall
　author: 11 Robert Frost

Menelaus
　king of: 6 Sparta
　father: 6 Atreus
　mother: 6 Aerope
　brother: 9 Agamemnon
　wife: 5 Helen
　son: 11 Megapenthes, Nicostratus
　daughter: 8 Hermione

mene mene tekel upharsin 30 numbered numbered weighed divided
　foretells destruction of: 10 Belshazzar
　from Biblical book of: 6 Daniel

Menestheus
　regent of: 6 Athens
　rejected by: 5 Helen
　assisted: 8 Menelaus

Menesthius
father: 9 Areithous
fought with: 6 Greeks
killed by: 5 Paris

menhaden 4 pogy 5 pogie 6 bunker 7 ale-wife, bugfish, eilfish, fatback, herring, old-wife, sardine 8 bonyfish, hardhead, lady-fish 10 mossbunker

menial 3 low 4 mean 5 drone, lowly, slave, toady 6 abject, drudge, flunky, helper, humble, lackey 7 fawning, ignoble, servant, servile, slavish 8 cringing, employee 9 degrading, groveling, sycophant, truckling, underling 10 apprentice, obsequious 11 boot-licking, subordinate, subservient, sycophantic

menial labor 4 toil 5 grind 8 drudgery

Menjou, Adolphe
born: 12 Pittsburgh PA
roles: 9 Golden Boy, Pollyanna 11 A Star Is Born 12 The Front Page 13 A Woman of Paris 15 A Farewell to Arms, State of the Union 16 Little Miss Marker 18 A Bill of Divorcement

meno
music: 4 less

Menodice
form: 5 nymph
son: 5 Hylas

Menoeceus
descendant of: 6 Sparti
father: 5 Creon
son: 5 Creon
daughter: 7 Jocasta
death by: 7 suicide

Menoetes
occupation: 7 cowherd

Menoetius
member of: 6 Titans 9 Argonauts
father: 7 Lapetus
mother: 7 Clymene
brother: 5 Atlas 10 Epimetheus, Prometheus
son: 9 Patroclus

Menominee, Menomini, Menomonie
language family: 9 Algonkian 10 Algonquian
location: 4 Ohio 7 Indiana 8 Illinois, Michigan 9 Wisconsin

menorah 11 candelabrum, candlestick 12 candleholder
number of candles: 5 seven

Menotti, Gian-Carlo
born: 5 Italy 10 Cadigliano
composer of: 9 The Consul, The Medium 12 The Island God, The Telephone 19 Amelia Goes to the Ball 24 Amahl and the Night Visitors

mens sana in corpore sano 22 a sound mind in a sound body

mental 5 crazy, nutty 6 insane, psycho 7 cracked, lunatic, psychic 8 abstract, cerebral, neurotic, rational 9 disturbed, in the mind, of the mind, psychotic 10 disordered, subjective, unbalanced 11 intelligent, mentally ill 12 intellectual, metaphysical 13 psychological

mental application 9 diligence 10 absorption, intentness 11 deep thought, engrossment, fixed regard 13 concentration 14 close attention

mental disorder 5 quirk 6 lunacy, oddity 7 madness 8 delusion, insanity, neurosis 9 craziness, psychosis 10 aberration 11 abnormality, derangement, mental lapse, peculiarity, strangeness 12 eccentricity, idiosyncrasy 13 schizophrenia 15 manic depression

mental hospital 6 asylum 8 madhouse 11 institution

mental institution 6 asylum 8 madhouse 12 insane asylum

mentality 4 mind 6 acumen, brains, wisdom 8 judgment, sagacity 9 intellect 10 gray matter, perception 11 discernment 12 intelligence, perspicacity

mental lapse 5 quirk 6 lunacy, oddity 7 madness 8 rambling, straying 9 wandering 10 aberration 11 derangement, peculiarity 12 eccentricity 13 forgetfulness

mentally incapable
Latin: 15 non compos mentis

mentally sound
Latin: 12 compos mentis

Mentes
origin: 7 Taphian
rank: 7 captain

mention 3 say 4 cite, hint, name, tell 5 imply, state 6 hint at, notice, remark, report, tell of 7 comment, divulge, inkling, narrate, observe, recount, refer to, specify 8 allude to, allusion, disclose, intimate 9 insinuate, make known, reference, statement, touch upon, utterance 10 advisement, indication, suggestion 11 designation, insinuation, observation 12 acquaintance, announcement, notification 13 communication, enlightenment, specification

mentor 4 guru 5 guide, tutor 6 master 7 adviser, monitor, proctor, teacher 9 counselor, preceptor, professor 10 instructor

Mentor
advisor of: 8 Odysseus
educated: 10 Telemachus

Mephibosheth
father: 4 Saul 8 Jonathan
also called: 9 Meribbaal
grandfather: 4 Saul
son: 5 Micha

Mephistopheles
character in: 5 Faust
author of: 6 Goethe

Mephitis see 7 Mefitis

mer 3 sea

Merab
father: 4 Saul
sister: 6 Michal
brother-in-law: 5 David

mercantile 5 trade 8 business 10 commercial 16 buying-and-selling

mercantilism 5 trade 8 business, commerce, exchange 13 commercialism

Mercedes
  character in: 21 The Count of Monte Cristo
  author: 5 Dumas (pere)
mercenary 5 venal 6 for pay, greedy 7 for gain, selfish 8 covetous, grasping, hireling, monetary 10 avaricious 11 acquisitive, paid soldier 12 hired soldier
merchandise 4 sell 5 goods, stock, trade, wares 6 deal in, market 7 effects, staples 8 huckster 9 advertise, publicize, traffic in 10 belongings, buy and sell, distribute 11 commodities 12 stock in trade
merchant 6 broker, dealer, hawker, jobber, monger, trader, vendor 7 peddler 8 chandler, retailer, salesman 9 purchaser, tradesman 10 saleswoman, shopkeeper, wholesaler 11 storekeeper, tradeswoman
Merchant of Venice, The
  author: 18 William Shakespeare
  character: 6 Portia 7 Antonio, Jessica, Lorenzo, Nerissa, Shylock 8 Bassanio, Gratiano
merci 8 thank you
merci beaucoup 16 thank you very much
merciful 4 kind 6 benign, humane, tender 7 clement, feeling, lenient, pitying, sparing 8 gracious 9 forgiving 10 beneficent 11 kindhearted, soft-hearted, sympathetic 13 compassionate, understanding
mercifulness 8 clemency, kindness, leniency, sympathy 9 benignity 10 compassion, humaneness 11 beneficence, forgiveness 13 understanding
merciless 4 fell 5 cruel, harsh 6 fierce, severe 7 callous, inhuman 8 inhumane, pitiless, ruthless 9 ferocious, heartless, unpitying, unsparing 10 relentless, unmerciful 11 cold-blooded, hardhearted, remorseless, unrelenting
Mercouri, Melina
  husband: 11 Jules Dassin
  born: 6 Athens, Greece
  roles: 7 Topkapi 10 Gaily Gaily 13 Never on Sunday 15 Once Is Not Enough
mercurial 6 fickle, lively, mobile 7 erratic, flighty, kinetic, protean 8 electric, spirited, unstable, variable, volatile 9 impetuous, impulsive 10 capricious, changeable, inconstant 11 fluctuating 13 irrepressible, unpredictable
mercury
  chemical symbol: 2 Hg
Mercury
  origin: 5 Roman
  messenger of: 4 gods
  god of: 7 science, thieves 8 commerce 9 eloquence
  corresponds to: 6 Hermes, Ogmios
Mercutio
  character in: 14 Romeo and Juliet
  author: 11 Shakespeare
mercy 4 pity 5 grace 6 lenity 7 charity 8 blessing, clemency, humanity, kindness, lenience, leniency, sympathy 9 good thing, tolerance 10 compassion, humaneness, lucky break 11 benevolence, forbearance, forgiveness, piece of luck 13 commiseration, fellow feeling 15 softheartedness 17 tenderheartedness
  Latin: 12 misericordia
Mercy seat *see* 16 Ark of the Covenant
Merdle
  character in: 12 Little Dorrit
  author: 7 Dickens
mere 4 bald, bare, sole 5 plain, scant, sheer, utter 6 common, paltry 7 mundane 8 nugatory, ordinary, trifling 10 negligible, uneventful 11 commonplace, unmitigated 13 insignificant, unappreciable 14 inconsiderable
mere 6 mother
Meredith, Burgess
  wife: 15 Paulette Goddard
  born: 11 Cleveland OH
  roles: 5 Magic, Rocky 6 Batman (the Penguin) 7 Madame X 8 Foul Play 12 Hurry Sundown, Of Mice and Men 15 Magnificent Doll, Such Good Friends 16 Advise and Consent
Meredith, George
  author of: 9 The Egoist 10 Modern Love 14 Evan Harrington 16 Beauchamp's Career 19 Diana of the Crossways 25 The Ordeal of Richard Feverel
merely 3 but 4 just, only 5 quite 6 barely, in part, purely, simply, solely 7 utterly 8 scarcely, wholly 10 absolutely
meretricious 4 mock, sham 5 bogus, false, phony 6 pseudo, shoddy, tawdry 8 delusive, specious, spurious 9 deceptive 10 fraudulent, misleading 11 counterfeit
merge 4 fuse, join, weld 5 blend, unify, unite 6 link up 7 combine 8 coalesce, converge, intermix 9 associate, become one, integrate, interfuse, interlock 10 amalgamate, synthesize 11 confederate, consolidate 12 band together, interconnect
mergence 3 mix 5 blend 7 merging, mixture 8 mingling 10 concoction 11 combination
Mergenthaler, Ottmar
  nationality: 8 American
  invented: 8 linotype
merger 5 union 7 wedding 8 marriage 9 coalition 12 amalgamation 13 confederation, consolidation
Meribbaal *see* 12 Mephibosheth
meridian 3 tip, top 4 acme, apex, brow, peak 5 crest, crown, point, ridge 6 apogee, climax, summit, vertex, zenith 7 heights 8 pinnacle 11 culmination
Merimee, Prosper
  author of: 6 Carmen 7 Colomba
Meriones
  mentioned in: 5 Iliad
  vocation: 6 archer
  father: 5 Molus
merit 4 earn, rate 5 value, worth 6 credit, desert, invite, prompt, talent, virtue 7 ability, benefit, deserve, quality, stature, warrant 8 efficacy 9 advantage 10 be worthy of, excellence, worthiness 11 distinction 12

be entitled to, have a right to **13** justification

merited 3 due **5** rated **6** earned **8** deserved, rightful

meritorious 4 fine **6** worthy **8** laudable **9** admirable, estimable, excellent, exemplary **10** creditable, noteworthy **11** commendable, exceptional **12** praiseworthy

Mermaid Tycoon
  nickname of: 14 Esther Williams

Merman, Ethel
  real name: 20 Ethel Agnes Zimmermann
  husband: 14 Ernest Borgnine
  born: 9 Astoria NY
  autobiography: 6 Merman
  roles: 11 Call Me Madam **12** Anything Goes, Panama Hattie **15** Annie Get Your Gun **16** Stage Door Canteen **21** Alexander's Ragtime Band

Mermerus
  father: 5 Jason
  mother: 5 Medea

Merodach *see* **6** Marduk

Merope
  member of: 8 Pleiades
  father: 5 Atlas **8** Oenopion
  husband: 7 Polybus **8** Sisyphus **11** Cresphontes, Polyphontes
  son: 7 Aepytus
  raped by: 5 Orion
  raised: 7 Oedipus

merrily 5 gaily **6** gladly **7** briskly, happily, lightly, lustick, quickly **8** blithely, jocundly, jovially, joyfully, joyously **9** festively, gleefully **10** cheerfully, laughingly, mirthfully **11** hilariously, vivaciously **14** lightheartedly

Merrimac *see* **9** Pennacook

merriment 3 fun **4** glee **5** cheer, mirth **6** frolic, gaiety, hoopla, levity **7** good fun, jollity, revelry, whoopee **8** hilarity, laughter **9** amusement, festivity, good humor, jocundity, joviality **10** jocularity, jubilation, liveliness, skylarking **11** celebration, gleefulness, good spirits, merrymaking **12** conviviality, exhilaration, sportiveness **16** lightheartedness

Merriweather, Mrs
  character in: 15 Gone With the Wind
  author: 8 Mitchell

merry 3 gay **5** happy, jolly **6** blithe, cheery, jocund, jovial, joyous, lively **7** festive, gleeful, jocular **8** animated, carefree, cheerful, gladsome, laughing, mirthful, partying, reveling, sportive **9** convivial, fun-loving, sprightly, vivacious **10** froliesome, rollicking, skylarking **12** high-spirited, lighthearted

merrymaking 5 sport **6** frolic, gaiety, hoopla, revels **7** jollity, revelry, whoopee **8** carousal **9** festivity, fun-making, high jinks, merriment, rejoicing, whoop-de-do **10** saturnalia **11** bacchanalia, celebration, festivities **12** conviviality

Merry Wives of Windsor, The •
  author: 18 William Shakespeare
  character: 4 Ford, Page **5** Caius **6** Doctor, Fenton **7** Slender **8** Anne Page **12** Mistress Ford, Mistress Page **15** Mistress Quickly, Sir John Falstaff

mesa 4 hill, peak **5** bench, butte, table **7** plateau, terrace **9** cartouche, tableland

Mescalero
  language family: 6 Apache
  location: 6 Mexico **9** New Mexico
  related to: 5 Lipan **10** Chiricahua

Meserve, Margaret Hamilton
  real name of: 16 Margaret Hamilton

Meservey, Robert Preston
  real name of: 13 Robert Preston

mesh 3 fib, net, web **4** grid, jibe **5** agree, sieve, tally **6** engage, enmesh, grille, plexus, screen **7** connect, engaged, netting, network, webbing, webwork **8** dovetail, interact, lacework, meshwork, openwork **9** grillwork, interlock, intermesh **10** coordinate, correspond, interweave, wickerwork **11** fit together, latticework **12** reticulation

Meshach
  former name: 7 Mishael
  companion: 6 Daniel
  friend: 8 Abednego, Shadrach

Mesmer, Franz (Friedrich) Anton
  nationality: 6 German
  developed: 8 hypnosis

mesmerize 5 charm **7** bewitch **8** enthrall, entrance **9** fascinate, hypnotize, magnetize, spellbind, transport

Mesopotamian mythology
  god of agriculture/earth: 5 Dagan
  corresponds to Phoenician: **5** Dagon

Mesquakie *see* **3** Fox

mess 3 fix **4** hash, stew **5** mix-up, pinch **6** crisis, jumble, litter, muddle, pickle, plight, scrape, strait **7** clutter, dilemma, trouble **8** disarray, disorder, hot water, mess hall, mishmash, quandary **9** cafeteria, confusion, imbroglio, refectory, situation **10** commissary, difficulty, dining hall, dining room, hodgepodge **11** predicament **14** conglomeration

message 4 news, note, word **5** moral, point, theme **6** letter, notice, report **7** meaning, missive, purport, tidings **8** bulletin, dispatch **9** statement **10** communique, memorandum **12** intelligence **13** communication

mess around with 4 test **6** try out **8** fool with, play with **10** tinker with **14** experiment with

Messene
  husband: 8 Polycaon

messenger 5 envoy **6** bearer, runner **7** carrier, courier **8** delegate, emissary **9** deliverer, go-between **11** delivery boy, delivery man **12** intermediary

messenger of gods 4 Iris **6** Hermes **7** Mercury

Messiaen, Olivier Eugene Prosper Charles
  born: 6 France **7** Avignon
  composer of: 11 Exotic Birds, Turangalila **13** Chronochromie **20** Le Nativite du Seigneur **22** Quartet for the End of Time

27 Vingt Regards sur l'Enfant Jesus 33
Et exspecto resurrectionem mortuorum
41 Transfiguration de Notre Seigneur Jesus Christ

Messiah

means: 11 anointed one

see also: 10 Jesus

Messick, Dale

creator/artist of: 19 Brenda Starr Reporter

messiness 5 chaos, mix-up, upset 6 jumble 7 clutter 8 disarray, disorder, scramble, shambles 9 confusion 10 disharmony, sloppiness, untidiness 12 dishevelment 14 disarrangement 15 disorganization

mess up 3 mar 4 goof, muff, ruin 5 botch, spoil 6 bungle, foul up, jumble 7 blunder, butcher, disturb, do badly, louse up, screw up 9 mismanage 10 disarrange 11 disorganize, make a mess of, make an error 12 make a mistake

messy 4 ugly 6 blowsy, frowsy, grubby, sloppy, tricky, untidy 7 awkward, chaotic, jumbled, tangled, unkempt 8 confused, littered 9 cluttered, difficult 10 bedraggled, disheveled, disordered, slatternly, topsy-turvy, unenviable, unpleasant 11 disarranged 12 embarrassing, inextricable 13 uncomfortable

Mesthles

commander of army of: 5 Maeon

mesto

music: 8 mournful

Mestor

father: 7 Perseus

mother: 9 Andromeda

daughter: 9 Hippothoe

Metabus

daughter: 7 Camilla

metal

alloy: 5 brass 6 bronze, nickel, pewter, solder

bar: 3 gad 4 risp 5 ingot

bolt: 5 rivet

box: 8 canister

casting: 3 peg

classification: 5 light, noble 6 alkali, common 7 coinage 8 platinum, precious 9 rare earth 10 low-melting, refractory, transition 11 high-melting 14 semiconductors

clippings: 7 scissel

coarse: 5 matte

corrosion: 4 rust

crude: 3 ore 4 slug

cymbals: 3 tal

deposit: 4 lode, vein

design: 7 chasing

disk or plate: 4 shim 5 medal, paten 6 platen, sequin

eyelet: 7 grommet

filings: 5 lemel

god of: 6 Vulcan 10 Hephaestus

heaviest: 6 osmium

kind: 3 tin 4 gold, iron, lead, zinc 6 barium, cerium, cesium, copper, erbium, nickel, osmium, radium, silver, sodium 7 arsenic, bismuth, calcium, holmium, iridium, lithium, rhodium, silicon, terbium, thulium 8 actinium, aluminum, antimony, europium, lutetium, platinum, rubidium, samarium, selenium, titanium, tungsten 9 beryllium, magnesium, palladium, potassium, ruthenium, strontium 10 molybdenum, phosphorus

layer: 7 plating

leaf: 4 foil

lightest: 7 lithium

liquid: 7 mercury

mass: 3 pid 5 ingot 7 bullion

piece: 4 jack, slug

refuse: 4 slag 5 dross

shaper: 5 swage

suit: 4 mail 5 armor 6 armour

thread: 4 lame, wire

trademark: 5 monel

ware: 4 tole 6 Revere

worker: 5 smith 6 forger, welder 7 armorer, riveter 8 armourer 9 goldsmith, ironsmith 10 blacksmith 11 coppersmith, silversmith 12 metallurgist

Metalious, Grace

author of: 11 Peyton Place

metalworking

god of: 6 Vulcan 10 Hephaestus, Hephaistos

metamorphose 6 change, mutate 7 convert 9 transform 11 transfigure

Metamorphoses

author of: 4 Ovid

metamorphosis 8 mutation 10 alteration, conversion 11 permutation 12 change of form, modification 13 radical change, transmutation 14 transformation 15 series of changes, startling change, transfiguration 18 transmogrification

Metamorphosis, The

author of: 10 Franz Kafka

Metanira

husband: 6 Celeus

son: 4 Abas 9 Demophoon 11 Triptolemus

metaphor 5 image, trope 6 simile 7 analogy 8 metonymy, parallel 11 equivalence 14 figure of speech, representation

metaphysical 5 basic, lofty, vague 6 far-out 7 eternal 8 abstract, abstruse, esoteric, mystical, ultimate 9 essential, high-flown, recondite, universal 10 impalpable, intangible, jesuitical, oversubtle 11 existential, fundamental, ontological, speculative 12 cosmological, intellectual, unanswerable 13 philosophical 15 epistemological

Metaphysics

author of: 9 Aristotle

metaxa

type: 6 brandy 7 liqueur

origin: 6 Greece

mete, mete out 5 allot 6 assign, divide 7 deal out, dole out 8 allocate, disburse, dispense 9 apportion, parcel out 10 administer, distribute, measure out

meteoric 4 fast 5 fiery, rapid, swift 6 speedy, sudden 7 blazing, flaming, instant 8 flashing, unabated 10 inexorable 11 ineluctable, unstoppable

meter
abbreviation: 1 m

Meter
epithet of: 6 Athena
means: 6 mother

method 3 way 4 form, mode, plan, tack 5 means, order, style, usage 6 course, design, manner, scheme, system 7 fashion, formula, process, program, purpose, routine 8 approach, efficacy 9 procedure, technique, viability 13 modus operandi

methodical, methodic 4 neat, tidy 5 exact 7 careful, logical, orderly, precise, regular, uniform 10 analytical, deliberate, meticulous, systematic 12 businesslike 13 well-regulated

methodization 5 order 11 arrangement 12 organization 14 categorization, classification 15 systematization

methodize 5 order 7 arrange 8 classify, organize 11 systematize

Methuselah
father: 5 Enoch
son: 6 Lamech
years lived: 23 nine hundred and sixty-nine
known as: 9 oldest man

meticulous 4 nice 5 exact, fussy 7 finical, finicky, precise 8 exacting, sedulous 10 fastidious, particular, scrupulous 11 painstaking, punctilious 13 conscientious, perfectionist

meticulousness 4 care 5 pains 12 sedulousness, thoroughness 14 fastidiousness, scrupulousness 17 conscientiousness

metier 3 job 4 area, line, work 5 craft, field, forte, trade 7 calling, pursuit 8 activity, business, lifework, province, vocation 9 specialty 10 employment, livelihood, occupation, profession

meting out 8 alloting 9 bestowing, doling out 10 allocating, conferring, consigning, dealing out, dispensing 11 designating 12 apportioning, distributing, measuring out

Metioche
father: 5 Orion
sister: 7 Menippe

Metion
father: 10 Erechtheus
mother: 9 Praxithea
brother: 7 Cecrops

Metis
member of: 6 Titans
father: 7 Oceanus
mother: 6 Tethys
consort of: 4 Zeus
daughter: 6 Athena

Metiscus
charioteer of: 6 Turnus

metrical narrative
French: 5 Roman

Metropolis
director: 9 Fritz Lang
cast: 10 Alfred Abel 12 Brigitte Helm

metropolitan area 4 city 8 core city, downtown, environs 9 inner city, precincts, urban area 10 city limits, metropolis 11 central city 16 business district

mettle 3 vim 4 grit, guts 5 nerve, pluck, spunk, valor, vigor 6 spirit 7 bravery, courage, heroism 8 audacity, backbone, boldness, gameness, temerity 9 derring-do, fortitude, gallantry, manliness 10 enthusiasm, resolution 11 intrepidity 12 fearlessness 13 determination

mettlesome 4 bold, edgy 5 brave, fiery 6 ardent, plucky, spunky 7 gingery, peppery 8 restless, skittish, spirited 9 excitable, impatient 10 courageous, high-strung 12 high-spirited

Mexica see 5 Aztec

Mexico
other name: 8 New Spain
capital/largest city: 10 Mexico City
others: 4 Leon 5 La Paz, Taxco 6 Cancun, Celaya, Merida, Oaxaca, Puebla, Toluca 7 Durango, Guaymas, Tampico, Tijuana, Torreon 8 Acapulco, Culiacan, Ensenada, Irapuato, Mazatlan, Mexicali, Saltillo, Veracruz 9 Chihuahua, Matamoras, Monterrey, Queretaro, Salamanca, Zacatecas 10 Hermosillo 11 Guadalajara, Nuevo Laredo 12 Ciudad Juarez, Villahermosa 13 Coatzacoalcos, Piedras Negras, San Luis Potosi 14 Puerto Vallarta 15 Netzahualcoyotl
ancient city: 4 Tula 7 Texcooo 8 Tlacopan 10 Monte Alban 11 Teotihuacan 12 Tenochtitlan 13 Tula de Allende
division: 6 Colima, Oaxaca, Puebla, Sonora 7 Chiapas, Durango, Hidalgo, Jalisco, Sinaloa, Tabasco, Yucatan 8 Campeche, Coahuila, Tlaxcala, Veracruz 9 Chihuahua, Michoacan, Nuevo Leon, Zacatecas 13 San Luis Potosi 14 Baja California
measure: 3 bag, pie 4 alma, onza, vara 5 almud, baril, carga, jarra, labor, legua, libra, linea, marco, sitio 6 adarme, almude, arroba, carega, fanega, ochaua, terceo 7 pulgada, quintal 9 cuarteron, cuartillo 10 caballeria
monetary unit: 4 onza, peso 5 adobe, claco, tlaco 6 azteca, cuarto, dinero 7 centavo, piaster
weight: 3 bag 4 onza 5 libra, marco 6 arroba, tercio 7 quintal
island: 6 Carmen, Cedros 7 San Jose, Tiburon 8 Cerralvo 10 Tres Marias 13 Espiritu Santo 14 Santa Magdalena, Santa Margarita 15 Angel de la Guarda
lake: 7 Chapala, Texcoco 9 Patzcuaro
mountain: 6 Colima, Tacana, Toluca 9 Paricutin 11 Ixtacihuatl, Sierra Madre 12 Popocatepetl 14 Sierra Zacateca 16 Chiapas Highlands 24 Transverse Volcanic Sierra
highest point: 7 Orizaba 12 Citlaltepetl

river: 4 Mayo 5 Yaqui 6 Balsas, Fuerte, Grande, Panuco 8 Colorado, Grijalva 10 Papaloapan, Usumacinta 13 Bravo del Norte, Coatzacoalcos, Lerma-Santiago
sea: 7 Pacific 8 Atlantic 9 Caribbean
physical feature:
bay: 8 Campeche 9 Olas Atlas
cape: 10 Corrientes
desert: 6 Sonora
gulf: 6 Mexico 8 Campeche 10 California 11 Tehuantepec
isthmus: 11 Tehuantepec
peninsula: 7 Yucatan 14 Baja California
plain: 7 Tabasco
plateau: 7 Mexican
valley: 7 Chiapas
people: 6 Indian 7 Mestizo, Spanish
architect: 7 O'Gorman
artist: 6 Orozco, Rivera, Tamayo 9 Siqueiros
composer: 6 Chavez
emperor: 10 Maximilian
explorer: 6 Cortes, Cortez 7 Cordoba 8 Alvarado, Grijalva
god: 6 Tlaloc 12 Quetzalcoatl 14 Huitzilopochtl
leader: 3 Gil 4 Diaz 5 Lopez, Rubio, Villa 6 Calles, Huerta, Juarez, Madero, Valdes, Zapata 7 Obregon 8 Carranza, Iturbide, Portillo, Santa Ana 9 Diaz Ordaz, Montezuma, Rodriguez 13 Madrid Hurtado 16 Salinas de Gortari
revolutionary/priest: 13 Morelos y Pavon 16 Hidalgo y Costilla
soldier/explorer: 12 conquistador
viceroy: 7 Mendoza
writer: 3 Paz 5 Nervo, Reyes, Yanez 6 Azuela, Guzman, Najera 7 Fuentes
language: 5 Mayan, Otomi 6 Mixtec 7 Mazahua, Mazatec, Nahuatl, Spanish, Totonac, Zapotec 8 Tarascan
religion: 13 Roman Catholic
place:
cathedral: 10 Assumption
center of Mexico City: 6 Zocalo 21 Plaza de la Constitucion
floating gardens: 10 Xochimilco
museum: 28 Shrine of the Virgin of Guadalupe
park: 7 Alameda 11 Chapultepec
ruins: 5 Mitla, Uxmal 8 Palenque 10 Monte Alban 11 Chichen Itza, Teotihuacan 20 Temple of Quetzalcoatl
street: 13 Avenida Juarez 16 Paseo de la Reforma
temple/pyramid: 7 Cholula 8 Castillo
feature:
agreement: 5 NAFTA
Christmas tradition: 6 pinata
coffee plantation: 5 finca
empire: 4 Maya 5 Aztec, Olmec 6 Mixtec, Toltec 7 Zapotec
large estate: 8 hacienda
musician: 8 mariachi
small farm/commune: 6 ejidos
sport: 7 jai alai 12 bullfighting
tree: 9 sapodilla 11 chicozapote

food:
corn cake: 8 tortilla
dish: 4 mole, taco 5 huevo, pollo 6 tamale 7 burrito, chorizo, taquito, tostada 8 empanada 9 enchilada, guacamole, sopadilla 10 chili verde, quesadilla 11 chimichanga 12 chili relleno
drink: 6 pulque 7 tequila
Mexico City
Aztec name: 12 Tenochtitlan
capital of: 6 Mexico
landmark: 13 Mercado Merced 15 Chapultepec Park 19 Basilica of Guadalupe
bull ring: 11 Plaza Mexico
floating gardens: 10 Xochimilco
pyramids: 11 Teotihuacan
square: 6 Zocalo 22 Plaza de las Tres Culturas
street: 16 Paseo de la Reforma
Meyer, David Harold
real name of: 12 David Janssen
Meyerbeer, Giacomo
real name: 17 Jacob Liebmann Beer
born: 6 Berlin 7 Germany
composer of: 7 Dinorah 10 Le Prophete, The African, The Prophet 12 Les Huguenots, The Huguenots, The North Star 14 Robert le Diable, Robert the Devil
Mezentius
king of: 7 Etruria
noted for: 7 cruelty
son: 6 Lausus
killed by: 6 Aeneas
mezza voce
music: 9 half voice 10 half volume
mezzo
music: 4 half
Miami
bay: 8 Biscayne
county: 4 Dade
developer: 7 Flagler
football team: 8 Dolphins
museum: 4 Lowe 12 Villa Viscaya
ocean: 8 Atlantic
people: 5 Cuban 8 Hispanic
section: 7 Hialeah 10 Bal Harbour 11 Coral Gables
stadium: 10 Orange Bowl
tropical garden: 8 Fairchild
university: 5 Barry 8 St Thomas
zoo: 11 Crandon Park
Miami (Twightwee)
language family: 9 Algonkian 10 Algonquian
tribe: 3 Wea 5 Miami 10 Piankashaw
location: 4 Ohio 7 Indiana 8 Illinois, Michigan 9 Wisconsin
leader: 12 Little Turtle
allied with: 6 Peoria
Miami Vice
character: 4 Gina 5 Trudy 8 (Capt) Castillo 13 Riccardo Tubbs, Sonny Crockett
cast: 10 Don Johnson 11 Olivia Brown 15 Saundra Santiago 16 Edward James Olmos 20 Phillip Michael Thomas

Micah Clarke
  author: 19 Sir Arthur Conan Doyle
Micawber, Mr
  character in: 16 David Copperfield
  author: 7 Dickens
Micha
  father: 9 Meribbaal 12 Mephibosheth
  grandfather: 8 Jonathan
  great-grandfather: 4 Saul
Michael
  author: 17 William Wordsworth
Michael
  means: 12 Who is like God
  father: 8 Izrahiah 11 Jehoshaphat
  son: 4 Omri 8 Zabadiah
  also: 9 archangel
Michel
  father: 4 Saul
  husband: 5 David, Palti
  sister: 5 Merab
Michelangelo di Buonarotti (Simoni)
  architect of: 11 Campidoglio (Capitoline Hill) 12 Medici Chapel (Florence) 13 Farnese Palace 21 Palazzo Medici-Riccardi (Florence) 22 Palazzo dei Conservatori (Capitoline Hill) 24 Convent of San Marco Library
  born: 5 Italy 7 Caprese
  patron: 12 Pope Julius II 14 Lorenzo d'Medici 19 Pope Julius the Second 21 Lorenzo the Magnificent
  artwork: 5 David, Moses, Pieta 6 Brutus, Slaves 7 Bacchus 9 The Victor 10 Holy Family 12 Madonna Pitti 15 The Last Judgment 18 Conversion of St Paul 20 Madonna Seated on a Step, Sistine Chapel Ceiling 21 The Flight of the Lapites, The Martyrdom of St Peter
Michelozzo
  architect of: 21 Palazzo Medici-Riccardi (Florence) 24 Convent of San Marco Library
Michelson, Albert A
  field: 7 physics
  established: 12 speed of light 15 velocity of Earth
  awarded: 10 Nobel Prize
Michener, James A
  author of: 5 Space 6 Alaska, Hawaii, Iberia, Legacy, Poland 8 Caravans, Sayonara 9 The Source 10 Centennial, Chesapeake 11 The Covenant, The Drifters 16 The Fires of Spring 18 The Bridges at Toko-ri 22 Tales of the South Pacific
Michigan
  abbreviation: 2 MI 4 Mich
  nickname: 4 Lake 9 Wolverine 10 Automobile 15 Water Wonderland 16 Winter Wonderland
  capital: 7 Lansing
  largest city: 7 Detroit
  others: 4 Caro, Troy 5 Flint, Niles, Wayne 6 Adrien, Alpena, Bad Axe, Monroe, Owosso, Warren, Wassar 7 Bay City, Holland, Jackson, Livonia, Midland, Pontiac, Saginaw, Trenton, Wyoming 8 Ann Arbor, Cadillac, Dearborn, Escan-

aba, Ironwood, Manistee, Muskegon, Petoskey, Royal Oak 9 Cheboygan, Hillsdale, Kalamazoo, Marquette, Port Huron, Roseville, Wyandotte 10 Birmingham, River Rouge 11 Battle Creek, Grand Rapids 12 Benton Harbor, Traverse City 13 Sault Ste Marie, St Clair Shores
  college: 4 Alma, Hope 5 Wayne 6 Adrian, Albion, Calvin, Olivet, Owosso 7 Detroit, Oakland 9 Hillsdale, Kalamazoo, Marygrove
  feature:
  bridge: 8 Mackinac
  canal: 3 Soo 12 Sault St Marie
  festival: 12 Holland Tulip
  national park: 10 Isle Royale
  village: 10 Greenfield
  tribe: 6 Ojibwa, Ottawa 8 Chippewa 10 Potawatomi
  people: 9 Henry Ford, wolverine 11 Bruce Catton, Edgar A Guest, Julie Harris, Ralph Bunche, Ring Lardner 16 Charles Lindburgh
  explorer: 6 Joliet 7 La Salle, Nicolet 9 Marquette 12 Etienne Brule, Sault St Marie
  island: 8 Mackinaw
  lake: 4 Burt, Erie 5 Clear, Huron, Round, Torch 6 Austin, Devils, Moline 7 Bawbees, St Clair 8 Houghton, Michigan, Superior
  land rank: 11 twenty-third
  mountain: 6 Copper 7 Gogebic 9 Menominee, Porcupine
  highest point: 12 Mount Curwood
  physical feature:
  bay: 7 Saginaw, Thunder 8 Keweenaw, Sturgeon
  straits: 8 Mackinac
  president: 10 Gerald Ford
  river: 4 Cass 5 Grand, Huron 6 Raisin 7 Detroit, Saginaw, St Clair, St Mary's 8 Escanaba, Muskegon 9 Menominee
  state admission: 11 twenty-sixth
  state bird: 5 robin
  state fish: 5 trout
  state flower: 12 apple blossom
  state motto: 11 I Will Defend 39 If You Seek a Pleasant Peninsula Look About You
  state song: 18 Michigan My Michigan
  state tree: 16 eastern white pine
Mickey Mouse
  creator: 10 Walt Disney
  character: 5 Morty 6 Ferdie 11 Minnie Mouse
  cow: 10 Clarabelle
Micklewhite, Maurice Joseph
  real name of: 12 Michael Caine
Micmac
  language family: 9 Algonkian 10 Algonquian
  location: 6 Canada 10 Nova Scotia 12 Newfoundland, New Brunswick 14 Gaspe Peninsula 16 Cape Breton Island 18 Prince Edward Island

microbe 4 germ 5 virus 6 gamete, zygote 8 bacillus, parasite 9 bacterium 10 spirochete 13 microorganism, streptococcus 14 staphylococcus

microbiologist
    American: 7 Waksman 9 Baltimore
    Dutch: 11 (van) Leeuwenhoek

Micronesia
    part of: 7 Oceania
    island: 3 Nui 4 Guam, Rota, Truk, Wake 5 Makin, Nauru, Wotho 6 Bikini, Ellice, Majuro, Ponape 7 Gilbert, Mariana 8 Caroline, Kiribati, Marshall

microorganism 3 bug 4 germ 5 virus 7 microbe 8 bacillus, pathogen 9 bacterium

microphobia
    fear of: 12 small objects

microscope
    invented by:
        compound: 7 Janssen
        electronic: 5 Knoll, Ruska
        field ion: 7 Mueller
    single lens model improved by: 11 (van) Leeuwenhoek
    first observed: 8 protozoa 13 red blood cells 19 single-celled animals

microscopic, microscopical 4 tiny 5 teeny 6 atomic, minute 9 invisible 10 diminutive, very little 13 imperceptible, infinitesimal

microscopy
    founder: 11 Robert Hooke 13 Jan Swammerdam 16 Marcello Malpighi 19 Anton van Leeuwenhoek

Midas
    king of: 7 Phrygia
    father: 7 Gordius
    gift: 11 golden touch
    gift from: 7 Silenus
    ears changed to those of: 3 ass
    changed by: 6 Apollo

midday 4 noon 7 noonday 8 meridian, noontide, noontime

middle 3 act, gut, hub, mid 4 core, main 5 belly, heart, midst, waist 6 center, course, medial, median, midway, throes 7 central, halfway, midmost, midriff, nucleus, process, stomach 8 midpoint 9 heartland 10 midsection 12 intermediate

Middle Ages
    French: 8 moyen age

middle-class 4 mass 8 ordinary 9 bourgeois 10 mainstream, middlebrow

middle Europe
    German: 12 Mitteleuropa

middle ground 4 mean 7 balance 8 midpoint 11 equilibrium 12 common ground

Middle Kingdom *see* 5 China

middleman 5 agent 6 broker, dealer, jobber 7 liaison 8 mediator 9 go-between 10 wholesaler 11 distributor, intercessor 12 entrepreneur, intermediary

Middlemarch
    author: 11 George Eliot
    character: 5 Celia 12 Will Ladislaw 13 Rosamond Viney 14 Dorothea Brooke, Edward Casaubon, Tertius Lydgate 15 Sir James Chettam

middlemost 4 mean 5 inner 6 inmost, median 7 central, midmost 8 interior

middle-of-the-road 8 moderate 10 mainstream

middle-of-the-roader 8 moderate 12 mainstreamer

middle way
    Latin: 8 via media

middling 4 fair, so-so 6 medium 7 average, fairish, minimal 8 mediocre, moderate, ordinary, passable 9 tolerable 10 pretty good, second-rate 11 indifferent 12 run-of-the-mill, unremarkable

Midea *see* 9 Licymnius

Midgard
    also: 10 Mithgarthr
    origin: 12 Scandinavian
    means: 10 abode of man
    located between: 8 Niflheim 10 Muspelheim
    connected to Asgard by: 7 bifrost 13 rainbow bridge
    formed from brow of: 4 Ymir

Midgard Serpent *see* 11 Jormungandr

midget 4 doll, runt 5 dwarf, pygmy 6 peewee, puppet, shrimp, squirt 7 manikin 8 half-pint, munchkin, small fry, Tom Thumb 9 pipsqueak 10 fingerling, homunculus 11 hop-o'-my-thumb, lilliputian

Midian
    father: 7 Abraham
    mother: 7 Keturah
    descendant of: 9 Midianite

midlands 8 interior 10 hinterland 13 central region

midmost 5 inner 6 inmost, middle 7 central, pivotal 8 interior 10 middlemost

Midnight Cowboy
    director: 15 John Schlesinger
    cast: 9 Jon Voight 11 John McGiver, Sylvia Miles 13 Brenda Vaccaro, Dustin Hoffman (Ratso Rizzo)
    Oscar for: 7 picture

Midnight Express
    director: 10 Alan Parker
    cast: 8 John Hurt 9 Bo Hopkins, Brad Davis (Billy Hayes) 10 Randy Quaid 12 Irene Miracle
    setting: 13 Turkish prison
    score: 14 Giorgio Moroder
    Oscar for: 5 score 6 script

midori
    type: 7 liqueur
    origin: 5 Japan
    flavor: 5 melon

midpoint 4 core, mean 5 focus 6 center, middle 15 point of no return

midriff 3 gut 4 guts 5 belly, tummy 6 paunch 7 abdomen, stomach 9 diaphragm 10 midsection 11 breadbasket

midst 3 eye, hub 4 core 5 bosom, heart, thick 6 center, depths, middle 7 nucleus 8 interior

Midsummer Night's Dream, A
    author: 18 William Shakespeare
    character: 4 Puck (Robin Goodfellow) 6 Bottom, Helena, Hermia, Oberon 7 The-

seus, Titania 8 Lysander 9 Demetrius, Hippolyta

midterm 4 exam, test 6 review 11 examination

midwife
French: 11 accoucheuse

mien 3 air 4 look 5 guise, style 6 aspect, manner, visage 7 bearing, feature 8 attitude, behavior, carriage, demeanor, presence 9 semblance 10 appearance, deportment, expression 11 countenance

Mies van der Rohe, Ludwig
architect of: 14 German Pavilion (1929 International Exposition, Barcelona), Lake Shore Drive (apartment towers, Chicago), Tugendhat House (Brno Czechoslovakia) 15 National Gallery (West Berlin), Seagram Building (NYC)
style: 13 International
principle: 10 less is more

miff 3 irk, vex 4 rile 5 anger, annoy, chafe, pique 6 nettle, offend, rankle 7 affront, provoke 8 irritate 9 put one off 10 exasperate 11 make one sore 14 rub the wrong way 15 raise one's dander

Mifune, Toshiro
born: 5 China 8 Tsingtao
roles: 6 Midway, Shogun 8 Rashomon 12 Seven Samurai 13 Throne of Blood

Miggs, Miss
character in: 12 Barnaby Rudge
author: 7 Dickens

might 3 may 5 brawn, clout, force, power, vigor 6 energy, muscle 7 potency, prowess 8 strength 9 influence, lustihood, puissance, toughness 10 capability, competence, durability, robustness, sturdiness 11 capableness 12 forcefulness

mighty 4 able, bold, huge, vast, very 5 brave, hardy, husky, lusty, stout, truly 6 brawny, manful, potent, really, robust, strong, sturdy 7 immense, massive, titanic, valiant 8 colossal, enormous, forceful, gigantic, imposing, majestic, powerful, puissant, stalwart, towering, valorous, vigorous 9 monstrous, strapping 10 courageous, gargantuan, invincible, monolithic, monumental, prodigious, stupendous 11 elephantine, exceedingly, indomitable, of great size 12 overpowering, particularly 13 exceptionally 14 Brobdingnagian

Migonitis
epithet of: 9 Aphrodite
means: 6 uniter

migrate 4 move, trek 6 travel 7 journey 8 emigrate, relocate, resettle 9 immigrate

migration 4 trek 6 exodus, flight, moving 7 passage 9 diaspora, movement

mikado 5 ruler 7 emperor, monarch 9 sovereign 15 Japanese emperor

Mikado, The
subtitle: 15 The Town of Titipu
operetta by: 18 Gilbert and Sullivan
character: 4 Ko-Ko 6 Peep-Bo, Yum-Yum 7 Katisha, Pooh-Bah 8 Nanki-Poo, Pish-Tush 9 Pitti-Sing

Mikkelsen, Dahl
also: 3 Mik
creator/artist of: 8 Ferd'nand

mikrophobia
fear of: 5 germs

mikvah 35 public establishment for ritual bathing
used by: 12 Orthodox Jews

mild 4 calm, easy, soft, warm 5 balmy, bland 6 docile, gentle, placid, serene, smooth 7 pacific, summery 8 delicate, moderate, not sharp, pleasant, soothing, tranquil 9 easygoing, emollient, not severe, not strong, temperate 10 forbearing, not extreme, springlike 11 complaisant, uninjurious 12 good-tempered

mildew 4 mold 6 blight, fungus

mildewed 5 fusty, moldy 10 discolored

mildness 8 calmness, delicacy, serenity, softness 9 placidity 10 gentleness, good temper

Mildred Pierce
director: 13 Michael Curtiz
based on novel by: 12 James M Cain
cast: 8 Ann Blyth, Eve Arden 10 Jack Carson 12 Bruce Bennett, Joan Crawford, Zachary Scott
Oscar for: 7 actress (Crawford)

mild-tempered 7 equable, patient 9 easygoing 11 good-natured, unflappable

mile
abbreviation: 2 mi

Miles, Sarah
brother: 11 Christopher
husband: 10 Robert Bolt
born: 7 England 11 Ingatestone
roles: 6 Blow-Up 10 The Servant 11 The Hireling 13 Ryan's Daughter 16 Lady Caroline Lamb

miles gloriosus 15 boastful soldier

Miles Gloriosus
author: 7 Plautus

Milesian
origin: 5 Irish
invaders from: 5 Spain
invaded: 7 Ireland
defeated: 14 Tuatha De Danann
ancestors of: 5 Irish

milestone 7 jubilee 8 milepost, signpost 10 road marker 11 anniversary 12 red-letter day, turning point

Milestone, Lewis
director: 12 Of Mice and Men, The Front Page 13 A Walk in the Sun 17 Mutiny on the Bounty 25 All Quiet on the Western Front (Oscar)

Milestones
author: 13 Arnold Bennett

Miletus
father: 6 Apollo
mother: 4 Aria
son: 6 Caunus
daughter: 6 Byblis

milieu 5 scene 7 culture, element, setting 8 ambience, backdrop 10 background 11 environment, mise-en-scene 12 surroundings

militant 7 defiant, extreme, martial, warlike, warring 8 fighting, military 9 assertive, bellicose, combatant, combative 10 aggressive, pugnacious 11 belligerent, contentious 12 disputatious, paramilitary, warmongering 14 uncompromising

military 4 army 5 armed, crisp 6 strict, troops 7 martial, militia, Spartan, warlike 8 generals, soldiers 9 combative, defensive, regulated, soldierly, warmaking 10 regimented 11 armed forces, belligerent, soldierlike

military force 4 army, navy 6 legion, troops 7 legions, militia 8 military, regiment, soldiers, soldiery 9 battalion 11 fighting men 13 fighting force

military machine 4 army 6 legion, troops 11 armed forces 13 fighting force

military rank abbreviation
   admiral: 3 adm
   brigadier general: 2 bg 7 brig gen
   captain: 3 cpt 4 capt
   chief petty officer: 3 CPO
   colonel: 3 col
   commander: 5 comdr
   corporal: 3 cpl
   ensign: 3 ens
   general: 3 gen
   lieutenant: 2 lt 5 lieut
   lieutenant colonel: 3 ltc 5 lt col
   lieutenant general: 5 lt gen 8 lieut gen
   major: 3 maj
   master sergeant: 4 msgt
   private: 3 pvt
   private first class: 3 pfc
   sergeant: 3 sgt
   sergeant first class: 3 sfc
   sergeant major: 4 smaj 6 sgt maj
   specialist: 4 spec

military storehouse 6 armory 7 arsenal 8 magazine 9 arms depot 13 ordnance depot 14 ammunition dump

military stores 7 arsenal, weapons 8 ordnance 9 munitions 10 ammunition

military unit 4 army, crew, unit 5 corps, force, squad 6 legion, outfit 7 brigade, company 8 regiment, squadron 9 battalion, task force 10 contingent, detachment

milksop 4 baby, wimp 5 mouse, pansy, sissy, softy 6 coward 7 crybaby, nebbish 8 mama's boy, poltroon, weakling 9 fraidycat 10 namby-pamby, pantywaist, scaredycat, weak sister 11 milquetoast, mollycoddle

mill 4 roam, teem 5 crush, grind, shape, swarm, works 6 finish, groove 7 factory, meander 8 converge 9 granulate, pulverize

Mill, John Stuart
   author of: 9 On Liberty 14 Utilitarianism 20 The Subjection of Women 28 Principles of Political Economy

Millais, Sir John Everett
   born: 7 England 12 Southampton
   artwork: 7 Bubbles 9 Blind Girl 12 Autumn Leaves, Chill October 13 My First Sermon 18 Lorenzo and Isabella 25

Christ in the Carpenter's Shop 36 Young Men of Benjamin Seizing Their Brides

Millament, Mrs
   character in: 16 The Way of the World
   author: 8 Congreve

Milland, Ray
   real name: 21 Reginald Truscott-Jones
   born: 5 Neath, Wales
   roles: 9 Beau Geste 11 Blonde Crazy 14 Dial M for Murder, The Lost Weekend (Oscar) 22 Bulldog Drummond Escapes

Millar, Kenneth
   real name of: 13 Ross MacDonald

Millay, Edna St Vincent
   author of: 11 Second April 13 The Harp Weaver 19 Make Bright the Arrows 20 A Few Figs from Thistles

Mille, Agnes de
   choreographer of: 5 Rodeo 15 Fall River Legend

millennium 13 thousand years 9 age of gold 21 one-thousandth anniversary

Miller
   character in: 18 The Canterbury Tales
   author: 7 Chaucer

Miller, Ann
   real name: 17 Lucille Ann Collier
   autobiography: 15 Miller's High Life
   born: 9 Chireno TX
   roles: 9 On the Town, Stage Door 10 Hit the Deck, Kiss Me Kate 11 Sugar Babies 16 The Kissing Bandit

Miller, Arthur
   wife: 13 Marilyn Monroe
   author of: 8 The Price 11 The Crucible 12 After the Fall 16 Death of a Salesman 18 A View from the Bridge

Miller, Henry
   author of: 5 Nexus, Sexus 6 Plexus 14 Tropic of Cancer 17 Tropic of Capricorn 18 The Rosy Crucifixion 21 The Colossus of Maroussi

Milles, Carl
   real name: 23 Wilhelm Carl Emil Anderson
   born: 5 Lagga 6 Sweden
   artwork: 5 Diana, Jonah 6 Europa 12 Man and Nature, Playing Bears 13 Peace Monument 15 Orpheus Fountain 18 Meeting of the Waters, Saltsjobaden Church (bronze doors)

millet 16 Panicum miliaceum
   varieties: 3 hog 5 pearl, Sanwa 6 finger, Indian 7 African, foxtail, Italian 8 barnyard, browntop, Japanese 16 Japanese barnyard

Millet, Jean-Francois
   born: 6 France, Gruchy
   artwork: 5 Sower 7 Angelus 11 The Gleaners, The Winnower 14 Potato Planters, The Man with a Hoe 23 Oedipus Taken from the Tree

Millett, Kate
   author of: 6 Flying 14 Sexual Politics

milligram
   abbreviation: 2 mg

milliliter
 abbreviation: 2 mL
millimeter
 abbreviation: 2 mm
Millionaire, The
 character: 14 Michael Anthony
 cast: 12 Marvin Miller
Mill on the Floss, The
 author: 11 George Eliot
 character: 8 Bob Jakin, Mrs Glegg 9 Lucy Deane, Mrs Pullet 11 Philip Wakem, Tom Tulliver 12 Stephen Guest 14 Maggie Tulliver
Mills, Hayley
 real name: 15 Rose Vivian Mills
 father: 4 John
 sister: 6 Juliet
 husband: 11 Ray Boulting
 born: 6 London 7 England
 roles: 8 Tiger Bay 9 Pollyanna 11 Summer Magic 13 The Parent Trap 14 The Chalk Garden 15 The Moon-Spinners 19 In Search of Castaways 20 The Trouble with Angels
Mills, John
 daughter: 6 Hayley, Juliet
 born: 7 England 10 Felixstowe
 roles: 12 Tunes of Glory 13 Ryan's Daughter 14 The Chalk Garden 17 Great Expectations 19 Swiss Family Robinson
Mills, Robert
 architect of: 10 Post Office (Washington DC) 12 Patent Office (Washington DC) 14 Circular Church (Charleston) 15 Unitarian Church (Philadelphia) 16 Treasury Building (Washington DC) 18 Washington Monument 25 Sansom Street Baptist Church (Philadelphia) 29 Egyptian Revival Monument Church (Richmond VA)
 style: 12 Greek Revival
millstream 3 run 4 race 5 brook, canal, creek, river 6 branch
Milne, A A
 author of: 13 Winnie-the-Pooh 20 The House at Pooh Corner
 character: 3 Roo 4 Pooh 5 Kanga 6 Eeyore, Piglet, Tigger 16 Christopher Robin
Milosz, Czeslaw
 author of: 11 Native Realm, The Usurpers 13 Bells in Winter 14 Seizure of Power, The Captive Mind
milquetoast 4 wimp 7 milksop, nebbish 11 mollycoddle
Milton
 author: 12 William Blake
Milton, George
 character in: 12 Of Mice and Men
 author: 9 Steinbeck
Milton, John
 author of: 7 Lycidas 8 L'Allegro 11 Il Penseroso 12 Areopagitica, Paradise Lost 15 Samson Agonistes 16 Paradise Regained 29 On the Morning of Christ's Nativity

Milton Berle Show, The
 host: 11 Milton Berle
 regulars: 10 Fatso Marco 11 Arnold Stang, Jack Collins, Milton Frome, Ruth Gilbert 12 Irving Benson 13 Bobby Sherwood
 announcer: 8 Sid Stone 11 Jimmy Nelson 13 Jack Lescoulie
 orchestra: 8 Alan Roth, Billy May 11 Victor Young
 theme: 7 Near You
Milton Berle's nickname: 12 Mr Television
 sponsor: 5 Buick 6 Texaco
Milwaukee
 baseball team: 7 Brewers
 basketball team: 5 Bucks
 Indian name: 16 Mahn-a-waukee Seepe
 lake: 8 Michigan
 river: 9 Milwaukee, Menomonee, 12 Kinnickinnic
 university: 9 Marquette
mimic 3 ape 4 aper, copy, echo, mime 6 mirror, parrot 7 copycat, copyist, feigner, imitate, take off 8 imitator, simulate 9 reproduce 10 burlesquer 11 counterfeit, impersonate 13 impressionist
Mimir
 origin: 12 Scandinavian
 god of: 3 sea
 decapitated by: 5 Vanir
 head sent to: 4 Odin 5 Othin
 oracle for: 4 Asar 5 Aesir
mimosa 14 Acacia dealbata 18 Albizia Julibrissin
 varieties: 5 Texas 6 golden 7 prairie 8 Egyptian
mince 4 dice, pose 5 grate, shred 6 refine, soften 7 posture, qualify 8 chop fine, hold back, mitigate, moderate, palliate 9 gloss over, put on airs, whitewash 12 attitudinize 14 affect delicacy, affect primness 15 give oneself airs 16 affect daintiness, soften one's speech 18 cut into small pieces 19 be mealymouthed about 20 cut into tiny particles
mince words 5 dodge, hedge, stall 10 equivocate 11 be ambiguous 13 avoid the issue 17 beat around the bush
mind 4 hate, heed, note, obey, tend, will, wits 5 abhor, bow to, brain, focus, sense, watch 6 brains, choice, detest, eschew, follow, intent, liking, memory, notice, notion, reason, recall, regard, resent, sanity 7 dislike, marbles, observe, opinion, outlook, thought 8 adhere to, attend to, be wary of, judgment, object to, reaction, response, submit to, take care, thinking 9 attention, awareness, be careful, cognition, faculties, intellect, intention, look after, sentiment 10 be cautious, comply with, conception, conclusion, gray matter, impression, perception, propensity, recoil from, reflection, shrink from, take care of 11 acquiesce to, be wary about, inclination, percipience, point of view, rationality, remembrance 12 apprehension, disapprove of, intelligence,

recollection, reminiscence, take charge of, take notice of **13** be conscious of, comprehension, concentration, consciousness, consideration, contemplation, look askance at, preoccupation, ratiocination, retrospection, understanding **14** pay attention to
  German: 5 Geist

mindful 4 wary **5** aware **7** alert to, alive to, careful, heedful **8** cautious, sensible, watchful **9** cognizant, conscious, observant, regardful **10** absorbed in, open-eyed to, thoughtful **11** attentive to, engrossed in, taken up with **12** occupied with **15** preoccupied with

mindfulness 9 alertness, awareness **10** perception **12** acquaintance **13** attentiveness, consciousness, understanding

mindless 6 insane, obtuse, stupid **7** asinine, doltish, idiotic, unaware, witless **8** careless, heedless **9** apathetic, cretinous, imbecilic, oblivious, unattuned, unheeding **10** neglectful, regardless, sophomoric, unthinking **11** inattentive, indifferent, nonsensical, thoughtless, unobservant, unreasoning **12** disregardful, simple-minded **13** inconsiderate, unintelligent **14** indiscriminate

mine 3 pit **4** fund **5** cache, hoard, shaft, stock, store **6** dig for, quarry, supply, tunnel, wealth **7** extract, reserve **8** dig under, excavate, treasure **9** abundance, boobytrap **10** excavation **12** accumulation

Mineo, Sal
  real name: 14 Salvatore Mineo
  born: 7 Bronx NY
  roles: 5 Giant, Tonka **6** Exodus **18** Rebel Without a Cause, Who Killed Teddy Bear?

mineral 3 jet, ore **4** coal, gold, iron, mica, opal, spar, talc **5** beryl, topaz **6** augite, barite, blende, cerine, copper, galena, garnet, iolite, pinite, rutile, sandix, silver, sphene, spinel, sulfur **7** amesite, apatite, azurite, biotite, bornite, calcite, citrine, coesite, crystal, cuprite, cyanite, element, gahnite, helvite, jadeite, kernite, kunzite, niobite, olivine, prasine, zeolite, zircon **8** asbestos, borocite, chlorite, cinnabar, corundum, dolomite, epsomite, fayalite, feldspar, fluorite, graphite, hematite, lazulite, siderite, sodalite, stibnite, triplite, wellsite **9** aragonite, argentite, carnelian, celestite, cerussite, danburite, fosterite, kaolinite, lawsonite, magnetite, malachite, muscovite, petroleum, phenakite, scapolite, tridymite, turquoise, wulfenite **10** calaverite, chalcedony, orthoclase, pyrrhotite, sphalerite, tourmaline, wolfachite **11** alexandrite, chrysoberyl, melanterite **12** brazilianite, chalcopyrite, fincalconite, fluorapatite **13** rhodochrosite

Minerva
  origin: 5 Roman
  goddess of: 3 war **4** arts **6** wisdom **11** handicrafts
  corresponds to: 6 Athena

mingle 3 mix **4** fuse, join **5** blend, merge, unite **6** hobnob **7** combine, consort **8** coalesce, intermix **9** associate, circulate, commingle, interfuse, interlard, socialize **10** amalgamate, fraternize, intertwine, interweave **11** intermingle, intersperse **12** rub shoulders

miniature 3 wee **4** tiny **5** elfin, pygmy **6** bantam, little, petite **9** minuscule **10** diminutive, pocket-size, small-scale **11** lilliputian, microcosmic, microscopic

minim
  abbreviation: 3 min

minimal 5 token **7** minimum, nominal **13** least possible, unappreciable

minimize 5 dwarf **6** reduce, shrink **8** belittle, mitigate **9** underrate **10** depreciate, undervalue

minimum 4 base **5** basic, least **7** modicum **8** smallest

minister 4 abbe, tend **5** padre, rabbi, serve, vicar **6** answer, cleric, father, oblige, parson, pastor, priest **7** care for, cater to **8** attend to, chaplain, pander to, preacher, reverend **9** clergyman, secretary **10** evangelist, revivalist, take care of **11** accommodate **12** ecclesiastic **13** cabinet member

ministerial 6 cleric **8** churchly, clerical, pastoral, priestly **14** ecclesiastical

ministration 3 aid **4** care **6** charge **7** comfort **9** attention **10** protection **11** supervision

Ministry of Fear, The
  author: 12 Graham Greene

Minitari *see* **7** Hidatsa

Minnehaha
  character in: 8 Hiawatha
  author: 10 Longfellow

Minnelli, Liza
  father: 8 Vincente
  mother: 11 Judy Garland
  born: 12 Los Angeles CA
  roles: 6 Arthur **7** Cabaret (Oscar) **14** New York New York **16** The Sterile Cuckoo **17** Flora the Red Menace

Minnelli, Vincente
  director of: 4 Gigi (Oscar) **9** Brigadoon **11** Lust for Life **15** Bells Are Ringing, Meet Me in St Louis **16** Father of the Bride **17** An American in Paris

Minnesota
  abbreviation: 2 MN **4** Minn
  nickname: 6 Gopher **9** North Star **19** Land of Sky-blue Waters **22** Land of Ten Thousand Lakes
  capital: 6 St Paul
  largest city: 11 Minneapolis
  others: 3 Ada, Ely **4** Mora **5** Edina **6** Austin, Duluth, Newulm, Winona **7** Babbitt, Bemidji, Fosston, Hibbing, Mankato, Red Wing, St Cloud **8** Brainerd, Moorhead **9** Albertlea, Blue Earth, Richfield, Rochester, Roseville **10** Minnetonka, Robinsdale **11** Bloomington, St Louis Park **14** Brooklyn Center **18** International Falls
  college: 6 Bethel, St Olaf, Winona **7**

Bemidji, Hamline 8 Adolphus, Augsburg,
Carleton, St Thomas 10 Macalester
feature:
monument: 10 Paul Bunyan
national monument: 9 Pipestone 12
Grand Portage
national park: 9 Voyageurs'
Norse artifact: 19 Kensington Rune
Stone
tribe: 5 Sioux 6 Dakota, Ojibwa, Santee
8 Chippewa 9 Menominee
people: 11 Judy Garland 12 Mayo brothers 13 Harold Stassen, Lauris Norstad,
Sinclair Lewis 16 F Scott Fitzgerald
explorer: 8 Hennepin, Norsemen, Radisson 9 Greysolon 12 Groseilliers 19 Sieur
Duluth or du Lhut
lakes: 4 Red 5 Leech, Rainy 6 Itasca 7
Bemidji 8 Superior 9 Mille Lacs 10
Minnewaska 14 Lake of the Woods,
Winnibigoshish
land rank: 7 twelfth
mountain: 6 Cuyuna, Mesabi 7 Misquah
9 Vermilion
highest point: 5 Eagle
physical feature: 6 Big Bog 14 Northwest Angle
falls: 9 Minnehaha
river: 3 Red 5 Rainy 6 Pigeon 7 St Croix,
St Louis 9 Des Moines, Minnesota 10 St
Lawrence 11 Mississippi
state admission: 12 thirty-second
state bird: 10 common loon
state fish: 7 walleye
state flower: 14 moccasin flower 24 pink
and white lady's slipper
state motto: 17 The Star of the North
state song: 13 Hail Minnesota
state tree: 13 Norway red pine
baseball team: 5 Twins
football team: 7 Vikings
hockey team: 10 North Stars
Minni *see* 7 Armenia
minor 5 child, light, petty, small, youth 6 infant, lesser, paltry, slight 7 trivial 8 nugatory, picayune, piddling, teenager, trifling 9
secondary, youngster 10 adolescent 11
subordinate, unimportant 13 insignificant
14 inconsiderable 15 inconsequential
minority 4 less 5 youth 6 lesser, nonage 7
boyhood, infancy 8 girlhood 9 childhood,
juniority 10 immaturity 11 adolescence
minor-league 4 punk 5 dinky, seedy, tacky
6 cheesy, common, lesser, shabby 8 inferior, small-fry 9 secondary, small-time 10
bush-league, second-rate 13 insignificant
Minos
king of: 5 Crete
father: 4 Zeus
mother: 6 Europa
brother: 8 Sarpedon 12 Rhadamanthys
wife: 8 Pasiphae
daughter: 7 Ariadne, Phaedra
ordered: 9 Labryinth
became: 5 judge
in: 5 Hades

Minotaur
form: 7 monster
combined: 3 man 4 bull
father: 10 Cretan bull
mother: 8 Pasiphae
home: 9 Labyrinth
ate flesh of: 6 humans
killed by: 7 Theseus
minstrel 4 bard, poet 6 dancer, end man,
lyrist, player, singer 8 comedian, songster
9 blackface, poetaster, serenader, versifier
10 troubadour 11 entertainer 12 interlocutor, vaudevillian 15 song-and-dance man
mint
varieties: 3 dog, red 4 wood 5 apple,
field, lemon, stone, water 6 coyote, dotted, orange, Scotch 7 Meehan's 8 bergamot, Corsican, creeping, Japanese,
mountain 9 pineapple
flavor: 7 menthol 9 spearmint 10 peppermint
liqueur: 13 creme de menthe
botanical name: 6 Mentha 8 Labiatae, M
spicata 9 M piperita
origin: 13 Mediterranean
related herb: 7 oregano 8 marjoram,
rosemary
symbol of: 11 hospitality
mythical nymph: 6 Mintha
beloved of: 5 Pluto
Mintha trod underfoot by: 10 Persephone
cure for: 7 hiccups
antidote for: 16 sea serpent stings
use: 4 lamb 5 salad 6 fruits
Minthe
form: 5 nymph
changed into: 9 mint plant
changed by: 10 Persephone
minuscule 3 wee 4 tiny 5 small 6 minute
10 teeny-weeny 11 small letter 13 infinitesimal 15 lower-case letter
minute 3 wee 4 fine, puny, tiny, wink 5
close, exact, flash, jiffy, petty, scant,
shake, teeny, trice 6 breath, little, moment,
petite, second, slight, strict 7 careful, instant, minikin, precise 8 detailed, itemized,
trifling 9 miniature, twinkling 10 a short
time, diminutive, exhaustive, meticulous,
negligible, scrupulous 11 lilliputian, microscopic 12 sixty seconds 13 conscientious,
imperceptible, inappreciable, infinitesimal,
insignificant 14 extremely small, inconsiderable
abbreviation: 3 min
minute portion 3 bit, sip 4 bite 5 crumb,
grain, scrap, shred, speck 6 morsel, sliver
7 swallow 8 fragment, mouthful, particle
minutiae 6 trivia 7 trifles 8 niceties 10 bag-
atelles, pedantries, subtleties 11 odds and
ends, particulars 12 minor details, triviali-
ties 15 particularities
minx 4 jade, slut 5 hussy, huzzy, wench 7
baggage 10 prostitute
Minyades
daughters of: 6 Minyas

Miolnir
hammer of: 4 Thor

mir 5 peace, world 21 Russian village commune

mirabile dictu 12 strange to say 17 marvelous to relate

miracle 4 omen, sign 6 marvel, wonder 7 mystery, portent, prodigy 9 divine act, sensation, spectacle 10 phenomenon 11 masterpiece

Miracle of Morgan's Creek, The
director: 14 Preston Sturges
cast: 9 Diana Lynn 11 Betty Hutton 12 Brian Donlevy, Eddie Bracken 15 William Demarest

Miracle on 34th Street
director: 12 George Seaton
based on story by: 15 Valentine Davies
cast: 9 John Payne 11 Edmund Gwenn (Kris Kringle), Natalie Wood 12 Gene Lockhart, Maureen O'Hara, Thelma Ritter
Oscar for: 12 screenwriter 15 supporting actor (Gwenn)

Miracle Worker, The
director: 10 Arthur Penn
cast: 9 Patty Duke (Helen Keller) 10 Victor Jory 11 Inga Swenson 12 Anne Bancroft (Anne Sullivan)
Oscar for: 7 actress (Bancroft) 17 supporting actress (Duke)

miraculous 6 divine 7 amazing, magical 9 marvelous, visionary, wonderful 10 incredible, mysterious, phenomenal, prodigious, remarkable 11 astonishing, astounding, exceptional, spectacular, supernormal 13 extraordinary, preternatural, wonderworking 14 thaumaturgical

miraculous food 5 manna

Miraculous writing
also: 4 mene 5 perez, tekel 8 upharsin
means: 7 divided, weighed 8 numbered
interpreted by: 6 Daniel

mirage 5 fancy 7 fantasy 8 delusion, illusion, phantasm 9 unreality 12 will-o'-the-wisp 13 hallucinations, misconception 14 castle in the air 15 optical illusion

Miranda
character in: 10 The Tempest
author: 11 Shakespeare

Miranda, Carmen
real name: 26 Maria do Carmo Miranda da Cunha
nickname: 18 Brazilian Bombshell
born: 8 Portugal 16 Marco de Canavezes
roles: 10 Copacabana 14 That Night in Rio 15 Weekend in Havana 16 Down Argentine Way 22 Springtime in the Rockies

mire 3 bog, fen, mud 4 cake, muck, ooze, soil 5 marsh, muddy, slime, slush, smear 6 enmesh, sludge 7 begrime, bog down, ensnare, spatter 8 besmirch, entangle, quagmire

Miriam
father: 5 Amram
mother: 8 Jochebed
brother: 5 Aaron, Moses

Miro, Joan
born: 5 Spain 8 Montroig 9 Barcelona
artwork: 9 Help Spain, The Reaper 13 Dutch Interior 14 Constellations 16 Catalan Landscape 19 Dog Barking at the Moon 20 Still Life with Old Shoe 26 Woman and Bird in the Moonlight

mirror 4 copy, show 5 glass, image, model 7 epitome, example, paragon, reflect 8 exemplar, manifest, paradigm, standard 10 reflection 11 cheval glass 12 looking glass

mirth 4 glee 6 gaiety, levity 7 jollity 8 drollery, hilarity, laughter 9 amusement, festivity, happiness, jocundity, joviality, merriment 10 jocularity 11 good spirits, merrymaking, playfulness 12 cheerfulness

mirthful 3 gay 4 glad 5 happy, jolly, merry 6 blithe, jocose, jovial, joyful, joyous 7 gleeful, jocular, risible

mirthless 3 sad 4 dour, glum 6 gloomy, morose 7 joyless, unhappy 8 dejected 9 cheerless, sorrowful 10 in the dumps, melancholy 14 down in the mouth

miry 3 wet 4 oozy 5 boggy, mucky, muddy, slimy, slushy, soggy 6 claggy, swampy 7 sloughy

misadventure 3 ill 4 slip 6 mishap 7 debacle, failure, reverse, setback 8 bad break, calamity, casualty, disaster 9 adversity, mischance 10 infelicity, misfortune 11 catastrophe, contretemps

misanthrope 5 cynic 7 skeptic 9 pessimist 10 misogynist

Misanthrope, Le
author: 7 Moliere
character: 7 Alceste, Arsinoe, Eliante 8 Celimene, Philinte

misanthropic 4 cold 5 surly 6 morose 7 cynical, distant 10 antisocial, unfriendly, unsociable 11 distrustful 12 discourteous, inhospitable, unneighborly, unpersonable, unresponsive 14 unapproachable 15 unaccommodating

misapplication 5 abuse 6 misuse 11 improper use 13 misemployment

misapply 5 abuse 6 misuse 9 misemploy 13 use improperly

misapprehension 5 mixup 7 mistake 11 misjudgment 13 misconception 14 miscalculation 15 false impression, misconstruction 16 misunderstanding 17 misinterpretation

misappropriate 4 bilk 5 abuse, cheat, mulct, steal 6 misuse 7 defraud, purloin, swindle 8 embezzle, misapply, peculate 9 defalcate, misemploy

misappropriation 6 misuse, taking 11 defalcation 12 embezzlement

misbehave 5 act up 7 disobey, do wrong 10 transgress 15 get into mischief

misbehavior 5 lapse 7 misdeed, offense 8 acting up, trespass 9 impudence 10 bad conduct, bad manners, disrespect, misconduct 11 delinquency, dereliction, impropriety, misdemeanor 12 indiscretion 13 transgression 16 obstreperousness, unmanageableness

misbelief 8 delusion, illusion 13 misconception

miscalculate 3 err 8 misjudge 10 guess wrong 11 misestimate

miscalculation 5 error 10 inaccuracy 13 misestimation

miscarriage 4 slip 5 botch 6 fizzle 7 default, failing, failure, misfire, undoing, washout 8 casualty, collapse

miscarry 4 fail 5 abort, botch 6 fizzle, go awry 9 terminate 12 come to naught

miscellanea 8 analects 9 anthology, gleanings, scrapbook 10 collection, miscellany, selections 11 collectanea

miscellaneous 5 mixed 6 divers, motley, sundry, varied 7 diverse, mingled, various 8 assorted, manifold 9 different 11 diversified 13 heterogeneous

miscellaneous collection
  Latin/pseudo Latin: 14 omnium-gatherum

miscellany 5 blend 6 jumble, medley 7 melange, mixture, variety 8 analects, extracts, mishmash, pastiche 9 anthology, gleanings, potpourri 10 assortment, collection, hodgepodge, salmagundi, selections 11 collectanea, compilation, gallimaufry, miscellanea 14 conglomeration, omnium-gatherum

mischance 6 ill lot, mishap 7 bad luck, ill luck, ill wind 8 accident 9 adversity 10 infelicity, misfortune 12 misadventure

mischief 4 evil 5 wrong 6 injury, malice 7 devilry, knavery, roguery 8 deviltry, foul play, plotting, scheming, villainy 9 depravity, devilment, rascality 10 orneriness, wrongdoing 11 naughtiness, playfulness, roguishness, shenanigans, willfulness 12 prankishness, sportiveness 14 capriciousness

mischief-maker 3 imp 5 demon, devil, scamp 7 gremlin, hellion 9 scoundrel 10 hell-raiser

mischievous 3 sly 5 elfin 6 elfish, impish, malign, vexing, wicked 7 harmful, naughty, noxious, playful, roguish, teasing, vicious, waggish 8 annoying, devilish, prankish, spiteful, sportive 9 injurious, malicious, malignant, uninvited 10 frolicsome, gratuitous, pernicious 11 deleterious, destructive, detrimental, uncalled for 12 exacerbating

misconceive 3 err 4 lose, miss 8 misjudge 12 misinterpret 13 misunderstand

misconception 5 error 8 delusion 11 misjudgment 13 erroneous idea 14 misinformation 15 misapprehension, misconstruction 16 misunderstanding 17 misinterpretation, misrepresentation

misconduct 7 misdeed, misstep 10 misprision, peccadillo, wrongdoing 11 delinquency, dereliction, impropriety, male-

faction, malfeasance, misbehavior, misdemeanor 13 transgression

misconstrue 7 distort, mistake 8 misjudge 9 misreckon, misrender 12 misapprehend, miscalculate, misinterpret, mistranslate 13 misunderstand

miscreant 3 bum 4 heel 5 knave, scamp 6 bad egg, rascal, sinner, wretch 7 villain 8 evildoer, lost soul, scalawag 9 reprobate, scoundrel 10 blackguard, black sheep, malefactor

misdeed 3 sin 4 slip 5 crime, lapse, wrong 6 felony 7 faux pas, offense, outrage 8 atrocity, trespass 9 violation 10 misconduct, peccadillo 11 malfeasance, misbehavior, misdemeanor 12 indiscretion, infringement 13 transgression

misdemeanor 3 sin 5 crime, fault 7 offense, misdeed 8 disorder 10 peccadillo 11 misbehavior 13 transgression

misdoer 5 crook 8 criminal 9 miscreant, wrongdoer 10 delinquent

mise en scene 6 milieu 7 setting 8 ambience 10 atmosphere, background 11 environment 12 stage setting, surroundings

misemployment 6 misuse 14 misapplication

Misenus
  father: 6 Aeolus

miser 5 piker 7 hoarder, niggard, Scrooge, skimper 8 tightwad 9 skinflint 10 cheapskate, pinchpenny 12 pennypincher, stingy person

Miser, The
  also: 6 L'Avare
  author: 7 Moliere
  character: 5 Elise 6 Valere 7 Anselme, Cleante, Mariane 8 Harpagon

miserable 3 sad 4 mean 5 inept, needy, sorry 6 abject, scurvy, shabby, sordid, woeful 7 abysmal, crushed, doleful, forlorn, grieved, hapless, unhappy 8 beggarly, degraded, dejected, desolate, dolorous, feckless, inferior, mournful, pathetic, pitiable, rubbishy, very poor, wretched 9 appalling, atrocious, cheerless, depressed, desperate, heartsick, sorrowful, woebegone 10 chapfallen, deplorable, despicable, despondent, heavy-laden, lamentable, second-rate, unbearable 11 crestfallen, heartbroken, unfortunate 12 contemptible, disconsolate, impoverished 13 brokenhearted 14 down in the mouth

Miserables, Les
  author: 10 Victor Hugo
  character: 6 Javert 7 Cosette, Fantine 10 Thenardier 11 Jean Valjean 15 Father Madeleine, Marius Pontmercy 17 Eponine Thenardier

misericordia 5 mercy 10 compassion

miserliness 6 penury 9 frugality, parsimony 10 stinginess 13 niggardliness, pennypinching 15 tight-fistedness

miserly 4 mean, near 5 cheap, tight 6 frugal, greedy, meager, stingy 7 selfish 8 grasping, grudging, pinching 9 illiberal, niggardly, penurious, scrimping 10 avaricious, ungenerous 11 closefisted, close-handed, tight-fisted 12 parsimonious 13 penny-pinching

misery 3 woe 4 blow 5 agony, curse, grief, trial 6 ordeal, regret, sorrow 7 anguish, bad deal, bad news, chagrin, despair, sadness, torment, trouble 8 bad scene, calamity, disaster, distress, exaction, hardship 9 dejection, heartache, privation, suffering 10 affliction, bitter pill, depression, desolation, melancholy, misfortune 11 catastrophe, despondency, tribulation 12 wretchedness

Misfits, The
   director: 10 John Huston
   based on story by: 12 Arthur Miller
   cast: 10 Clark Gable, Eli Wallach 12 Thelma Ritter 13 Marilyn Monroe 15 Montgomery Clift

misfortune 4 blow, loss 6 misery, mishap 7 bad luck, reverse, setback, tragedy, trouble 8 calamity, casualty, disaster, downfall, hard luck, hardship 9 adversity, hard times, ruination 10 affliction, ill fortune 11 catastrophe, tribulation 12 misadventure

misgiving, misgivings 4 fear 5 alarm, doubt, dread, qualm, worry 7 anxiety, dubiety 8 disquiet, mistrust 9 suspicion 10 foreboding, skepticism 11 dubiousness, uncertainty 12 apprehension, doubtfulness, presentiment, reservations 14 second thoughts

misguided 5 at sea 6 adrift, faulty, misled, unwise 7 in error 8 mistaken 9 erroneous, imprudent, led astray, off course 10 illadvised, indiscreet, misadvised 11 injudicious, misdirected, misinformed

Mishael see 7 Meshach

mishap 4 slip, snag 5 botch 6 fiasco, slipup 7 reverse, setback 8 casualty, disaster 9 mischance 10 difficulty, misfortune 11 miscarriage 12 misadventure

mishmash 3 mix 4 hash, stew 5 salad 6 jumble, medley, muddle 7 melange 8 mixed bag, pastiche, scramble 9 patchwork 10 assemblage, crazy quilt, hodgepodge, miscellany, salmagundi 14 conglomeration, omnium-gatherum

misinform 7 deceive, mislead 8 misguide 9 misdirect 10 lead astray 12 misrepresent

misinterpret 11 misconstrue 12 misapprehend 13 misunderstand

misinterpretation 13 misconception 16 misunderstanding 17 misrepresentation

misjudge 3 err 7 mistake 10 exaggerate, understate 11 misconceive, misconstrue 12 misapprehend, miscalculate, misinterpret, overestimate 13 misunderstand, underestimate

mislay 4 lose, miss 8 displace, misplace

mislead 4 dupe, fool, gull 6 betray, delude, entice, seduce, take in 7 beguile, deceive 8 hoodwink, inveigle, misguide 9 bamboozle, misdirect, misinform, play false, victimize 10 lead astray 11 double-cross, string along

misleading 6 luring 8 deluding 9 deceiving 10 misguiding 11 hoodwinking

mismanage 3 mar 4 flub, muff, ruin 5 botch, spoil 6 bollix, bungle, foul up, mess up 7 louse up, screw up 9 mishandle 11 make a hash of, make a mess of

misnomer 8 misusage, solecism 9 barbarism, misnaming 11 malapropism

misogynic 7 cynical 11 woman-hating 12 misanthropic

misogynist 5 cynic 10 woman-hater 11 misanthrope

misplace 4 lose 5 abuse 6 mislay 11 lose track of

misreckon 8 misjudge 10 guess wrong, miscompute 11 misestimate 12 miscalculate

misrepresent 7 falsify, mislead 8 disguise

misrepresentation 7 mockery 8 altering, travesty, twisting 9 burlesque, doctoring 10 caricature, distortion, falsifying 12 adulteration, exaggeration, misstatement 13 falsification

miss 4 blow, girl, lack, lady, lass, lose, loss, maid, muff, skip, slip, want 5 avert, avoid, error, forgo, let go, woman 6 bypass, damsel, escape, forego, lassie, maiden, miscue, pass by 7 blunder, colleen, default, failure, fly wide, let pass, let slip, long for, mistake, neglect, old maid, overrun, pine for 8 leave out, omission, overlook, pass over, senorita, slip up on, spinster, yearn for 9 disregard, fall short, false step, gloss over, go without, overshoot, oversight, surrender, young lady 10 demoiselle, schoolgirl 12 be absent from 13 feel the loss of, mademoiselle

missal 10 prayer book

missed
   French: 6 manque

misshapen 7 twisted 8 deformed 9 contorted, distorted

missile 4 ball, dart 5 arrow, lance, shaft, shell, spear, stone 6 bullet, rocket 7 harpoon, javelin 10 projectile

missing 4 AWOL, gone, lost 6 absent 7 lacking, left out, not here 8 avoiding, skipping 10 longing for, not present 11 overlooking, yearning for 12 disregarding

Missing
   director: 22 Constantine Costa-Gavras
   cast: 8 John Shea 10 Jack Lemmon 11 Sissy Spacek 13 Melanie Mayron

Missing Persons and Other Essays
   author: 12 Heinrich Boll

mission 3 end, job 4 task 5 quest 6 charge 7 calling, mandate, pursuit 8 legation, ministry 9 objective 10 assignment, commission, delegation, enterprise 11 raison d'etre, undertaking

Mission
   tribe: 7 Chumash, Juaneno, Luiseno 8 Diegueno 9 Costanoan 10 Gabrielino 11 Fernandario
   location: 10 California

Mission: Impossible
  character: 5 Casey, Paris 10 Rollin Hand 11 Dana Lambert, James Phelps 12 Daniel Briggs 13 Barney Collier 14 Cinnamon Carter, Willie Armitage
  cast: 10 Greg Morris, Peter Lupus, Steven Hill 11 Barbara Bain, Peter Graves 12 Leonard Nimoy, Martin Landau 14 Lynda Day George 15 Lesley Ann Warren

Mississippi
  abbreviation: 2 MS 4 Miss
  nickname: 5 Bayou 6 Mudcat 8 Magnolia
  capital/largest city: 7 Jackson
  others: 6 Biloxi, Helena, Laurel, Tupelo, Winona 7 Belzoni, Corinth, Grenada, Natchez 8 Bogalusa, Columbus, Gulfport, Meridian 9 Kosciusko, Vicksburg 10 Clarksdale, Pascagoula 11 Hattiesburg 13 Pass Christian
  college: 4 Rust 6 Alcorn 7 Jackson 8 Belhaven, Millsaps, Tougaloo 11 Mississippi 12 Blue Mountain, William Carey
  feature: 12 Natchez Trace
  national military park: 9 Vicksburg
  national seashore: 11 Gulf Islands
  tribe: 3 Sac 5 Tious 6 Biloxi, Mandan, Tunica 7 Choctaw, Natchez, Tonikan 8 Chicksaw
  people: 11 Eudora Welty 15 William Faulkner 17 Tennessee Williams
  explorer: 6 DeSoto, Joliet 9 Iberville, Marquette
  island: 3 Cat 4 Horn, Ship 9 Petit Bois
  lake: 4 Enid 6 Sardis 7 Barnett, Grenada 8 Pickwick 9 Arkabutla, Okatibbee
  land rank: 12 thirty-second
  highest point: 7 Woodall
  physical feature:
  delta: 10 Yazoo Basin
  hills: 8 Fall Line 9 Tennessee 11 Loess Bluffs
  prairie: 5 Black 7 Jackson
  sound: 11 Mississippi
  river: 4 Leaf 5 Pearl, Yazoo 8 Big Black 9 Tombigbee, Yalobusha 10 Homochitto, Pascagoula 11 Mississippi 12 Tallahatchie
  state admission: 9 twentieth
  state bird: 11 mockingbird
  state flower: 8 magnolia
  state motto: 14 By Valor and Arms
  state song: 13 Go Mississippi
  state tree: 8 magnolia

missive 4 note 6 billet, letter 7 epistle, message 13 communication 14 correspondence

Miss Julie
  author: 16 August Strindberg

Miss Lonelyhearts
  author: 13 Nathanael West

Missouri
  abbreviation: 2 MO
  nickname: 5 Ozark 6 Show-Me 7 Bullion 15 Mother of the West
  capital: 13 Jefferson City
  largest city: 7 St Louis

  others: 5 Eldon, Hayti, Lamar, Macon, Rolla 6 Butler, Joplin, Mexico 7 Bethany, Bolivar, Cameron, Clayton, Lebanon, Moberly, Sedalia 8 Berkeley, Columbia, Hannibal, Kirkwood, Sikeston, St Joseph 10 Bonne Terre, Kansas City 11 Springfield, Warrensburg 12 Independence 13 Cape Girardeau, Webster Groves
  college: 5 Avila, Drury 6 Tarkio 7 Lincoln, St Louis, Webster 8 Stephens 10 Washington 11 Westminster
  feature:
  dam: 5 Osage
  tribe: 3 Fox, Sac 4 Sauk 5 Osage 7 Shawnee 8 Cherokee, Missouri
  people: 7 TS Eliot 9 Mark Twain 10 Jesse James 11 Omar Bradley 12 Helen Traubel, Sara Teasdale 13 John J Pershing, Marianne Moore, Samuel Clemens 15 Reinhold Niebuhr 22 George Washington Carver
  explorer: 6 Joliet 7 La Salle 9 Marquette
  lake: 7 Norfolk 9 Tablerock, Taneycomo 10 Bull Shoals 14 Kaysinger Bluff 15 Lake of the Ozarks
  land rank: 10 nineteenth
  mountain: 6 Ozarks 10 St Francois
  highest point: 8 Taumsauk
  physical feature: 8 Bootheel 9 Big Spring
  plains: 4 Till 5 Osage
  plateau: 5 Ozark
  president: 12 Harry S Truman
  river: 4 Salt 5 Grand, Osage, White 6 Platte 7 Current, Meramec 8 Big Muddy, Chariton, Missouri 9 Des Moines, Gasconade, St Francis 11 Mississippi
  state admission: 12 twenty-fourth
  state bird: 8 bluebird
  state flower: 8 hawthorn
  state motto: 41 The Welfare of the People Shall Be the Supreme Law
  state song: 13 Missouri Waltz
  state tree: 7 dogwood

Miss Peach
  creator: 11 Mell Lazarus
  character: 3 Ira 6 Arthur, Lester, Marcia 8 Francine
  place: 9 Kamp Kelly 11 Kelly School

misspend 5 waste 8 squander 9 dissipate, throw away 11 fritter away

misspent 6 wasted 8 depraved 9 debauched, dissolute, idled away 10 misapplied, profitless, squandered, thrown away

misstate 5 alter 6 bollix, garble 7 confuse, distort, falsify, pervert 8 misquote 9 misreport 12 misrepresent

misstatement 3 fib, lie 4 tale 5 error 7 falsity, untruth 9 falsehood 13 prevarication 17 misrepresentation

misstep 3 sin 4 goof, slip, vice 5 boner, error, fault, gaffe, lapse 6 boo-boo, defect, foul-up 7 blooper, faux pas, offense, screw-up 11 delinquency, dereliction, shortcoming 12 indiscretion 13 transgression

miss the mark 4 fail 9 fall short 11 come up short

miss the point 7 mistake 11 fail to catch, misconceive 12 misapprehend 13 misunderstand

mist 3 fog 4 haze, murk, smog 5 steam, vapor 7 drizzle

mistake 4 slip 5 boner, error, gaffe, mix-up 6 slipup 7 blooper, blunder, confuse, faux pas, misstep 8 confound, misjudge 9 misreckon, oversight 11 misconstrue, misidentify 12 misapprehend, miscalculate, misinterpret 13 misunderstand 14 miscalculation

French: 10 malentendu

mistaken 5 at sea, false, wrong 6 faulty, untrue 7 at fault, in error, unsound 8 deceived 9 erroneous, illogical, incorrect, off course, unfounded 10 fallacious, groundless, inaccurate, ungrounded 11 unjustified

Mister

Yiddish: 3 Reb

Mister Roberts

author of: 12 Thomas Heggen

director: 8 John Ford 11 Mervyn LeRoy

cast: 8 Ward Bond 10 Henry Fonda, Jack Lemmon (Ensign Pulver) 11 Betsy Palmer, James Cagney 13 William Powell

Oscar for: 15 supporting actor (Lemmon)

Mister Saturday Night

nickname of: 13 Jackie Gleason

mistreat 4 harm 5 abuse, bully, hound, wrong 6 harass, ill-use, injure, misuse, molest 7 assault, oppress, outrage, pervert, torment, violate 8 ill-treat, maltreat 9 brutalize, manhandle, mishandle, persecute

mistreatment 5 abuse 6 ill-use, injury 7 assault, cruelty, harming 10 bodily harm, oppression 11 manhandling, molestation, persecution 12 maltreatment

mistress 3 Mrs 4 doxy, lady, Miss 5 lover, Madam 6 matron 8 ladylove, paramour 9 concubine, headwoman, housewife, inamorata, kept woman 10 chatelaine, girlfriend, sweetheart

mistrust 5 doubt, qualm 7 anxiety, dubiety, suspect 8 distrust, question, wariness 9 challenge, chariness, leeriness, misgiving, suspicion 10 disbelieve, skepticism

misty 4 dewy, hazy 5 filmy, foggy, murky 6 cloudy, opaque, steamy 8 nebulous, overcast, vaporous 10 indistinct

misunderstand 7 confuse, misread, mistake 8 misjudge 9 misreckon 11 misconceive, misconstrue 12 misapprehend, miscalculate, misinterpret, miss the point

misunderstanding 4 rift, spat 5 set-to 7 discord, dispute, quarrel, wrangle 8 conflict, squabble 10 difference, dissension, misreading 11 altercation, contretemps, misjudgment 12 disagreement 13 misconception 15 false impression, misapprehension 16 miscomprehension 17 misinterpretation

French: 10 malentendu

misuse 4 harm, hurt 5 abuse, waste, wrong 6 debase, injure 7 corrupt, exploit, outrage, pervert, profane 8 ill-treat, maltreat, misapply, mistreat, wrong use 9 misemploy 10 corruption, perversion, prostitute 11 desecration, profanation, squandering 12 ill treatment, maltreatment, mistreatment, prostitution 13 misemployment 14 misapplication 15 take advantage of

Mitchell, Billy (William Lendrum)

advocate of: 8 air power

court-martialed for: 15 insubordination

served in: 3 WWI

rank: 16 brigadier general

commander of: 15 US army air forces

Mitchell, Margaret

author of: 15 Gone With the Wind

Mitchell, Silas Weir

author of: 9 Hugh Wynne (Free Quaker) 11 Roland Blake

Mitchell, Thomas

born: 11 Elizabeth NJ

roles: 7 Our Town 8 Doc Boone 9 The Outlaw 10 Stagecoach 11 Gerald O'Hara, Lost Horizon 15 Gone With the Wind 19 Only Angels Have Wings

Mitchell, William

real name of: 10 Peter Finch

Mitchum, Robert

born: 12 Bridgeport CT

roles: 6 Midway 10 Winds of War 11 Thunder Road 13 Ryan's Daughter, The Longest Day, The Sundowners 15 The Story of G I Joe 16 Farewell My Lovely 20 Heaven Knows Mr Allison

mite 3 bit, jot 4 atom, iota, whit 5 scrap, speck 6 spider 7 smidgen 8 arachnid, particle

Mitford, Jessica

author of: 21 The American Way of Death 22 Kind and Usual Punishment

Mitford, Nancy

author of: 14 Noblesse Oblige 16 The Pursuit of Love 18 Love in a Cold Climate

Mithgarthr see 7 Midgard

Mithraeum

temple of: 7 Mithras

Mithras

origin: 7 Persian

god of: 5 light, truth

corresponds to: 3 Sol

mitigate 4 ease 5 allay, blunt 6 lessen, reduce, soften, soothe, temper, weaken 7 assuage, lighten, mollify, placate, relieve 8 diminish, moderate, palliate 9 alleviate, extenuate 10 ameliorate

mitigating 6 easing 8 allaying, blunting, reducing 9 assuaging, lessening, relieving, softening, tempering 10 lightening, moderating, palliating, palliative 11 diminishing, extenuating 12 ameliorating

Mitrephorus

epithet of: 8 Dionysus

means: 15 headband-bearing

Mitteleuropa 12 middle Europe

mitzvah, mitsvah 8 good deed 11 commandment

mix 3 add 4 beat, club, fold, fuse, join, stir, whip 5 admix, alloy, blend, merge, put in, unite 6 commix, fusion, hobnob, mingle 7 combine, consort, include, mixture 8 assembly, coalesce, compound, intermix, mingling 9 associate, commingle, interfuse, interlard, introduce, socialize 10 amalgamate, fraternize, intertwine, interweave 11 incorporate, intermingle, intersperse, put together

mixed 4 coed 5 fused 6 hybrid, motley 7 alloyed, blended, inmixed, mingled, mongrel, not pure 8 combined 9 composite, uncertain 10 ambivalent, indecisive, interwoven, variegated 11 adulterated, diversified, half and half, put together 12 conglomerate, inconclusive 13 heterogeneous, male-and-female, miscellaneous

mixed-up 6 addled 7 chaotic, jumbled, muddled, tangled 8 confused, rambling 9 befuddled, illogical, nonplused, perplexed 10 bewildered, disjointed, incoherent, irrational, nonplussed 12 disconnected, disorganized 13 disharmonious, heterogeneous

Mixtec
    tribe: 7 Zapotec

mixture 3 mix 4 hash, stew 5 alloy, blend, union 6 fusion, jumble, medley 7 amalgam, melange 8 compound, mishmash, pastiche 9 admixture, composite, potpourri 10 commixture, hodgepodge, salmagundi 11 association, combination 12 adulteration, amalgamation, intermixture

mixup 4 mess, riot 5 fight, melee 6 fracas, muddle, tangle 7 mistake 8 disorder 9 confusion, imbroglio 11 misjudgment 14 miscalculation 16 miscomprehension, misunderstanding

mix up 5 addle 6 mess up, muddle 7 confuse, nonplus, perplex 8 befuddle, bewilder 10 disarrange

Mneme
    member of: 5 Muses
    personifies: 6 memory

Mnemosyne
    origin: 5 Greek
    member of: 6 Titans
    goddess of: 6 memory
    father: 6 Uranus
    mother: 4 Gaea
    daughters: 5 Muses

Moabite god 7 Chemosh

moan 3 sob 4 keen, wail 5 groan 6 bemoan, bewail, lament, plaint 7 grumble 11 lamentation

moan over 5 mourn 6 bemoan, bewail, lament 7 cry over 8 weep over 10 grieve over

moat 4 foss 5 ditch, fosse, graff 6 gutter, rundel, trench

mob 4 gang, herd 5 crowd, crush, horde, Mafia, swarm 6 masses, rabble, throng 7 flock to 8 assembly, populace, surround 9 gathering, hoi polloi, multitude, plebeians, syndicate 10 converge on 11 proletariat, rank and file 14 organized crime

mobile 6 active, motile 7 kinetic, movable, nomadic 8 portable, rootless 9 footloose, traveling, wandering 10 ambulatory, locomotive

mobilize 6 call up, muster, summon 7 marshal 8 activate, organize 10 call to arms 11 put in motion

mobster 4 hood 6 hitman 7 hoodlum, Mafioso 8 gangster 10 gang member

Moby Dick
    author: 14 Herman Melville
    character: 4 Ahab 5 Stubb 7 Ishmael 8 Fedallah, Queequeg, Starbuck

mock 3 ape 4 copy 5 belie, mimic, scorn, spurn, taunt 6 deride, insult, jeer at, parody, revile, show up 7 imitate, laugh at, let down, profane, scoff at, sneer at 8 ridicule 9 burlesque, frustrate, make fun of, poke fun at 10 caricature, disappoint, make game of 11 make sport of

mockery 4 joke, sham 5 farce, scorn 7 jeering, mimicry, sarcasm 8 derision, raillery, ridicule, scoffing, travesty 9 burlesque, contumely 10 disrespect, ridiculing 13 laughingstock

Mock Turtle
    character in: 28 Alice's Adventures in Wonderland
    author: 7 Carroll

mode 3 cut, fad, way 4 form, rage, rule 5 craze, means, style, taste, trend, vogue 6 course, custom, manner, method, system 7 fashion, process 8 approach, practice 9 condition, procedure, technique 10 appearance

model 4 cast, copy, form, mold, show, type 5 build, dummy, ideal, shape, sport, style 6 design, mirror, mock-up 7 display, example, fashion, outline, paragon, pattern, perfect, replica, subject, variety, version 8 exemplar, paradigm, peerless, standard 9 archetype, criterion, exemplary, facsimile, mannequin, prototype, simulated 10 simulacrum 14 representation, representative

model on 6 base on 7 found on 10 derive from

mode of operating
    Latin: 2 mo 13 modus operandi

moderate 4 calm, cool, curb, fair, hush, mild, tame 5 abate, chair, sober 6 direct, gentle, lessen, manage, medium, modest, soften, subdue, temper 7 average, careful, conduct, control, oversee 8 diminish, measured, mediocre, middling, ordinary, passable, rational, regulate, restrain, tone down 9 judicious, peaceable, temperate, unruffled 10 not violent, reasonable 11 inexpensive, preside over 12 mainstreamer, medium-priced

moderation 7 abating, economy 8 allaying 9 abatement, frugality, lessening, remission, restraint 10 continence, diminution, mitigation, palliation, relaxation, temperance 11 alleviation, forbearance, self-control 12 moderateness 13 temperateness 14 abstemiousness 19 avoidance of extremes

moderator 8 chairman, mediator 10 chairwoman, negotiator

modern 3 new 6 modish, recent 7 current, in vogue 8 up-to-date 10 present-day 11 fashionable, streamlined 12 contemporary 15 contemporaneous 16 twentieth-century

Modern Comedy, A
  author: 14 John Galsworthy

modernistic 6 modern 7 moderne 10 newfangled 12 contemporary

modernity 5 vogue 7 fashion, new look, novelty, the rage 8 last word 14 newfangledness 15 contemporaneity 16 new fashionedness

modernize 4 redo 5 renew 6 do over, revamp, update 7 restore 8 redesign, renovate 9 refurbish 10 regenerate, rejuvenate, streamline 11 recondition 13 bring up to date 16 move with the times

modern times 5 today 8 nowadays 10 the present 13 the here and now

Modern Times
  director: 14 Charles Chaplin
  cast: 12 Henry Bergman 14 Charlie Chaplin, Chester Conklin 15 Paulette Goddard 19 Stanley "Tiny" Sandford

modest 3 coy, shy 4 meek, prim 5 plain, quiet, timid 6 demure, humble, proper, simple 7 bashful, limited, nominal, prudish, unshowy 8 blushing, discreet, moderate, reserved, timorous 9 diffident, shrinking 10 unassuming 11 circumspect, constrained, inexpensive, puritanical, straitlaced, unassertive, unobtrusive 12 medium-priced, not excessive, self-effacing, unpretending 13 unpretentious 14 unostentatious

modesty 7 coyness, prudery, reserve, shyness 8 humility, plainess, timidity 9 propriety, restraint, reticence 10 constraint, demureness, diffidence, humbleness, simplicity 11 bashfulness, naturalness 12 timorousness 14 reasonableness, self-effacement 15 inexpensiveness

modicum 3 bit, dab, jot 4 atom, dash, drop, inch, iota, mite, whit 5 crumb, grain, pinch, scrap, speck, tinge, touch 6 morsel, sliver, snatch, trifle 7 handful, minimum, smidgen 8 fraction, fragment, particle 9 little bit 10 sprinkling 11 small amount 13 small quantity

modification 6 change 8 revision 9 variation 10 adjustment, alteration, conversion, emendation, regulation 14 transformation 15 differentiation

modify 4 redo, vary 5 adapt, alter, limit, lower, remit 6 adjust, change, narrow, reduce, remold, revise, rework, soften, temper 7 control, convert, qualify, remodel, reshape 8 moderate, modulate, restrain, restrict, tone down 9 condition, refashion, transform, transmute 10 reorganize 12 transmogrify

Modigliani, Amedeo
  born: 5 Italy 7 Leghorn, Livorno
  artwork: 10 Seated Nude 13 Reclining Nude, Yellow Sweater 15 Jeanne Hebuterne

modish 2 in 3 now 4 chic 5 natty, nifty, sharp, smart, today 6 dapper, snazzy, spiffy, trendy, with it 7 a la mode, current, faddish, in style, in vogue, stylish, voguish 9 high-style 11 fashionable 13 up-to-the-minute

Modoc
  language family: 12 Shapwailutan
  division: 10 Lutuamnian
  location: 6 Oregon 10 California
  leader: 14 Chief Kintpuash (Captain Jack)
  related to: 7 Klamath

Modred
  character in: 16 Arthurian romance

Mod Squad, The
  character: 9 Linc Hayes, (Capt) Adam Greer 11 Julie Barnes, Pete Cochran
  cast: 11 Michael Cole, Peggy Lipton, Tige Andrews 19 Clarence Williams III

modulate 4 pass 5 lower 6 accord, attune, change, reduce, soften, temper 8 moderate, progress, regulate, tone down, turn down 9 harmonize

modulation 4 tone 5 pitch 6 accent 9 reduction 10 expression, regulation, transition

modus operandi 15 mode of operating
  abbreviation: 2 mo

modus vivendi 14 manner of living

Moerae see 5 Fates

Mogadishu, Mogadiscio
  capital of: 7 Somalia

mogul 3 VIP 4 czar, lord 5 baron, power, wheel 6 bigwig, tycoon 7 big shot, magnate, notable 8 big wheel 9 personage, potentate

Mohammed
  also: 7 Mahomet, Prophet 8 Muhammad
  born: 5 Mecca
  clan: 6 Hashim
  daughter: 6 Fatima
  deity: 5 Allah
  died: 6 Medina
  father: 8 Abdallah, Abdullah
  father-in-law: 7 Abu Bakr, Abubekr
  flight: 4 hadj 6 hegira, hejira
  follower: 6 Moslem, Muslim, Wahbi 10 Mohammedan
  grandfather: 13 Abd al-Muttalib
  horse: 5 Buraq 7 Alborrak
  mother: 5 Amina
  religion: 5 Islam
  shrine: 5 Kaaba
  son: 7 Ibrahim
  adopted: 3 Ali
  successor: 4 imam 5 calif 6 caliph 7 Abu Bakr
  tribe: 7 Koreish, Quraysh
  uncle: 5 Abbas 8 Abu Talib
  wife: 5 Aisha 6 Ayesha, Safiya 7 Khadija 8 Khadidja, Kadijah

Mohammedan 4 Sufi 6 Moslem, Muslim, Shiite 7 Islamic, Moorish, Sunnite 10 Mahometan, Muhammadan, Muhammedan

Mohave, Mojave
language family: 5 Yuman
location: 7 Arizona 10 California

Mohawk (Kaniengehaga)
language family: 9 Iroquoian
location: 6 Canada, Quebec 7 New York 11 Lake Ontario
leader: 8 Hiawatha 11 Joseph Brant
member of: 19 League of the Iroquois

Mohegan, Mohican, Mahican
language family: 9 Algonkian 10 Algonquian
location: 7 New York 9 Wisconsin 11 Connecticut 12 Hudson Valley
leader: 5 Occom, Uncas 12 Chingachgook
allied with: 6 Pequot
with Delaware: 11 Loup Indians, Wolf Indians
subject of novel: 20 The Last of the Mohicans
author: 19 James Fenimore Cooper

Moira
personifies: 4 fate

Moirai *see* 5 Fates

moist 3 wet 4 damp, dank, dewy 5 humid, misty, muggy, rainy 6 clammy, drippy, watery 7 aqueous, drizzly, tearful, wettish, wet-eyed 8 dripping, vaporous 10 lachrymose

moisten 3 dew, wet 4 damp, hose, mist, soak 5 spray, water 6 dampen, douche, splash, sponge 8 humidify, irrigate, saturate, vaporize 10 moisturize

moisture 3 dew, wet 4 damp, mist 5 sweat, vapor 7 drizzle, exudate, wetness 8 dampness, dankness, humidity 9 moistness, mugginess 10 wateriness 11 evaporation 12 perspiration

Mojave *see* 6 Mohave

Moki *see* 4 Hopi

mold 3 cut, die, ilk 4 cast, form, kind, line, make, rust, sort, turn, type 5 brand, frame, knead, model, shape, stamp, train 6 blight, create, figure, fungus, kidney, lichen, matrix, mildew, render, sculpt, shaper 7 contour, convert, develop, fashion, outline, pattern, quality, remodel 9 character, construct, formation, structure, transform

Moldova
other name: 8 Moldavia
capital/largest city: 8 Chisinau, Kishinev
head of state: 9 president
government: 8 republic
monetary unit: 5 ruble
river: 8 Dniester
people: 7 Gagauzi 8 Moldovan 9 Moldavian
language: 8 Romanian 9 Moldavian
religion: 15 Russian Orthodox

moldy 5 fusty, hoary, musty, stale 7 spoiled 8 mildewed

molest 3 irk, vex 4 fret, harm, hurt 5 abuse, annoy, beset, harry, worry 6 attack, bother, harass, hector, injure, pester, plague 7 assault, disturb, torment, trouble 8 maltreat

Moliere (Jean-Baptiste Poquelin)
author of: 6 Scapin 8 Tartuffe, The Miser 10 Amphitryon 13 Le Misanthrope 17 The School for Wives 19 The Imaginary Invalid 20 The School for Husbands 22 Le Bourgeois Gentilhomme

Moll Flanders
author: 11 Daniel Defoe
character: 5 Robin 6 Jemmy E 10 Sea Captain

mollification 8 soothing 9 placation 11 appeasement, assuagement 12 conciliation

mollify 4 calm, curb, dull, ease, lull 5 abate, allay, blunt, check, quell, quiet, still 6 lessen, pacify, reduce, soften, soothe, temper 7 appease, assuage, lighten, placate 8 decrease, mitigate, moderate, palliate, tone down

mollusk 4 clam, slug 5 conch, cowry, murex, snail, squid, whelk 6 chiton, cockle, cowrie, limpet, mussel, oyster, teredo, triton 7 abalone, bivalve, geoduck, octopus, scallop 8 argonaut, nautilus, shipworm 9 shellfish 10 cuttlefish, nudibranch, periwinkle

mollycoddle 3 pet 4 baby, wimp 5 sissy, spoil 6 cosset, coward, pamper 7 cater to, crybaby, indulge, milksop 8 give in to, mama's boy, weakling 9 cream puff 11 milquetoast, overindulge

Molnar, Ferenc
author of: 6 Liliom 7 The Swan 12 The Guardsman

Moloch
3 god 5 diety
also: 6 Molech
worshiped by: 9 Ammonites

Molorchus
form: 7 peasant

Molossus
father: 11 Neoptolemus
mother: 10 Andromache

molt 4 cast, shed, slip 6 change, slough 7 castoff, discard, ecdysis 8 exuviate

molten 6 melted, red-hot 7 fusible, igneous, smelted 8 magmatic 9 liquefied

molto
music: 4 very

Molus
father: 4 Ares
mother: 8 Demonice
son: 8 Meriones

Moly
form: 4 herb
given to: 8 Odysseus
given by: 6 Hermes
to counteract spells of: 5 Circe

Momaday, N Scott
author of: 18 The House Made of Dawn 21 The Way to Rainy Mountain

moment 5 flash, jiffy, trice, value, worth 6 import, minute, second, weight 7 concern, gravity, instant 8 interest, juncture 9 twinkling 10 importance 11 consequence, weightiness 12 significance

momentary 5 brief, hasty, quick, short 6 sudden 7 instant, passing 8 flashing, fleeting, fugitive, imminent 9 ephemeral, immediate, temporary, transient 10 short-lived, transitory 13 instantaneous

momentous 5 grave 7 crucial, fateful, salient, serious, weighty 8 critical, decisive, eventful 9 essential, important, ponderous 11 far-reaching, influential, significant, substantial 12 earthshaking 13 consequential

momentous occurrence 5 event 8 occasion 9 milestone 12 red-letter day, turning point

momentum 2 go 4 dash, push 5 drive, force, speed, vigor 6 energy, moment, thrust 7 headway, impetus, impulse 8 velocity 10 propulsion

Mommsen, Theodor
   author of: 16 The History of Rome

Momus
   also: 5 Momos
   god of: 7 censure 8 ridicule

Monaco
   capital: 11 Monaco-Ville
   largest city: 10 Monte Carlo
   others: 9 Fontville
   division: 9 Fontville 10 Monte Carlo 11 La Condamine, Monaco-Ville
   head of government: 15 minister of state
   head of state: 6 prince
   monetary unit: 5 franc 7 centime
   river: 7 Vesubie
   sea: 13 Mediterranean
   physical feature: 9 Cote d'Azur
   people: 6 French 7 Italian 10 Monegasque
   oceanographer: 15 Jacques Cousteau
   prince: 5 Louis 6 Albert, Honore 7 Antoine, Charles, Rainier 9 Florestan
   princess: 10 Grace Kelly
   ruler: 4 Rome 5 Genoa 6 Greece 8 Grimaldi, Saracens 9 Phoenicia
   language: 6 French 7 English, Italian 10 Monegasque
   religion: 13 Roman Catholic
   place:
   beach: 8 Larvotto
   casino: 10 Monte Carlo
   gardens: 6 Exotic
   museum: 12 Oceanography
   park: 18 Princess Antoinette
   feature:
   auto race: 15 Monaco Grand Prix

Monaco-Ville
   capital of: 6 Monaco

monarch 3 HRH 4 czar, doge, emir, khan, king, rani, shah 5 rajah, ruler, queen 6 kaiser, prince 7 czarina, emperor, empress, majesty, pharaoh 8 kaiserin, princess 9 chieftain, potentate

monarchical 9 czaristic 10 autocratic 11 dictatorial

monastery 5 abbey 6 friary, priory 7 convent, nunnery, retreat 8 cloister

monastic 7 ascetic, monkish, recluse 8 celibate, hermitic, secluded, solitary 9 cloistral, reclusive, unworldly 10 cloistered, hermitlike 11 sequestered 13 contemplative

mon cher 6 my dear

Moncrieff, Algernon (Algy)
   character in: 27 The Importance of Being Earnest
   author: 5 Wilde

Mond, Mustapha
   character in: 13 Brave New World
   author: 6 Huxley

Monday
   French: 5 lundi
   German: 6 montag
   heavenly body: 4 moon
   Italian: 6 lunedi
   means: 12 day of the moon
   Spanish: 5 lunes

Mondrian, Piet
   real name: 23 Pieter Cornelis Mondriaan
   born: 10 Amersfoort 14 The Netherlands
   artwork: 5 Trees 10 The Red Tree 12 Ocean and Pier 17 Evening Landscapes 18 Landscape with a Mill 20 Broadway Boogie-Woogie 29 Composition in Red Yellow and Blue

Monet, Claude Oscar
   born: 5 Paris 6 France
   artwork: 7 Poplars 9 Haystacks, The Thames 11 Water Lilies 14 Rouen Cathedral 16 Women in the Garden 17 Impression Sunrise 18 Mornings on the Seine 21 The Bridge at Argenteuil

Moneta
   epithet of: 4 Juno
   means: 7 advisor

monetary 6 fiscal 9 budgetary, financial, pecuniary, sumptuary

money 4 cash, coin 5 bread, bucks, dough, funds 6 assets, riches, specie, wealth 7 capital, coinage, payment, revenue, scratch 8 currency, hard cash, proceeds 9 affluence, long green 10 collateral, greenbacks 11 wherewithal

money-carrier
   French: 12 porte-monnaie

moneyed, monied 4 rich 5 flush, swell 6 flashy, loaded 7 elegant, opulent, solvent, wealthy 8 affluent 10 prosperous

money-grubbing 5 venal 6 greedy 8 covetous, grasping 9 mercenary 10 avaricious

money lender 6 banker, lender, usurer 7 lombard, shylock 9 loanshark 10 pawnbroker

money saved 7 nest egg, savings 10 investment

money spent 6 outlay 7 payment 8 expenses 11 expenditure

Mongolia
   other name: 13 Outer Mongolia
   capital/largest city: 9 Ulan Bator
   others: 5 Kobdo 6 Darhan 10 Choibalsan, Sukhe Bator, Tsetserlik, Uliassutai
   ancient capital: 9 Karakoram
   government:

legislature: 17 People's Great Hural 18 People's Great Khural

monetary unit: 5 mongo, mungo 6 tugrik 7 tughrik

weight: 3 lan

lake: 3 Uvs 5 Har Us 6 Bor Nor 7 Ghirgis, Ubsa Nor 8 Airik Nor, Durga Nor, Hobsogol, Khara Usu 9 Khubsugul, Khukhu-Nur 10 Khirgis Nor

mountain: 4 Cast, Orog 5 Altai 6 Kentei, Sevrej 7 Ich Ovoo, Khangai, Khentei 8 Tannu-Ola 9 Edrengijn 10 Cagaan Bogd 11 Munky Sardyk 14 Hangayn-Hentiyn, Monch Chajrchan

highest point: 10 Tabun Bogdo

river: 3 Tes 4 Egin, Onon, Tuul, Uldz 5 Kobdo, Tesin 6 Orkhon 7 Kerulen, Selenga, Selenge 8 Dzabkhan, Dzavchan

physical feature:

desert: 4 Gobi 5 Ordos, Shamo

plateau: 8 Mongolia

region: 10 Great Lakes

people: 5 Oirat, Tungu 6 Buryat, Darbet, Khoton, Mongol 7 Kazakhs, Khalkha 8 Tuvinian 9 Dariganga

leader: 8 Jahangir, Jehangir 10 Kublai Khan, Tsendenbal 11 Genghis Khan

ruler: 4 Huns 5 Ching 6 Manchu 7 Kirghiz, Uighurs 8 Hsiung-nu

spiritual/secular ruler: 12 Living Buddha 21 Jebtsun Damba Khutu Khtu

language: 6 Kazakh 16 Khalkha Mongolian

religion: 7 Lamaism 9 Shamanism 15 Tibetan Buddhism

place:

monastery: 6 Gandun

feature:

felt tent: 4 yurt

nomadic herder: 4 arat

food:

fermented mare's milk: 5 airag

Mongolian

language family: 6 Altaic

group: 6 Buryat 7 Khalkha

Mongoose, The

nickname of: 11 Archie Moore

mongrel 3 cur 4 mutt 5 mixed 6 hybrid 7 bastard 8 offshoot 9 anomalous, crossbred 10 crossbreed

moniker 3 tag 4 name 5 label, title 6 eponym, handle 7 epithet, surname 8 cognomen, nickname, taxonomy 9 sobriquet 11 appellation, designation 12 denomination

monitor 2 TV 4 tend 5 guide, teach 6 censor, direct, pickup, police, screen, sensor 7 oversee, proctor, scanner 8 overseer, watchdog 9 supervise 14 disciplinarian

monk 4 abbe 5 abbot, friar 6 hermit 7 brother, holy man, recluse 8 cenobite, monastic 9 anchorite

French: 5 frere

Monk, The

author: 19 Matthew Gregory Lewis

Monkees, The

cast/musician: 9 Davy Jones, Peter Tork 10 David Jones 11 Micky Dolenz, Mike Nesmith

monkey 3 ape, ass, toy 4 butt, dupe, fool, jerk 5 clown, jimmy 6 baboon, fiddle, meddle, simian, tamper, tinker, trifle 7 buffoon, primate 13 laughingstock

group of: 5 troop

god: 7 Hanuman

kind: 3 owl 4 saki, titi 5 aotus, lemur, titis 6 baboon, guenon, howler, langur, rhesus, spider 7 colobus, Goeldi's, guereza, macaque, tamarin, tarsier, uakaris 8 capuchin, mandrill, marmoset, squirrel, talapoin 11 douroucouli

monkey business 6 capers 9 highjinks 11 shenanigans

monkeyshines 6 antics, capers, pranks 7 hijinks 10 buffoonery, tomfoolery 11 foolishness

Monks (Edward Leeford)

character in: 11 Oliver Twist

author: 7 Dickens

monocle 4 quiz 5 glass 7 lorgnon 8 eyeglass

Monoclonius

type: 8 dinosaur 10 ceratopsid

location: 12 North America

characteristic: 6 horned

Monod, Jacques

field: 7 biology

nationality: 6 French

researched: 3 RNA 8 genetics

awarded: 10 Nobel Prize

monograph 8 tractate, treatise 9 discourse 12 disquisition, dissertation

monolith 5 stone 6 column, menhir, pillar, statue 7 obelisk 8 memorial, monument

monologue, monolog 6 screed, sermon, speech 7 address, lecture, oration 9 discourse, soliloquy 11 expatiation 12 disquisition

monopolize 3 own 6 absorb, corner, manage, take up 7 consume, control, preempt 8 arrogate, dominate, regulate, take over 9 cartelize 11 appropriate

monopoly 4 bloc 5 trust 6 cartel, corner 7 combine, control 8 dominion 9 copyright, ownership, syndicate 10 consortium, domination 11 sovereignty 12 jurisdiction 14 proprietorship

monotonous 3 dry 4 dull, flat 5 banal 6 boring, dreary, jejune, stodgy, torpid 7 droning, humdrum, insipid, mundane, prosaic, routine, tedious 8 plodding, singsong, tiresome, toneless, unvaried 9 colorless, soporific, wearisome 10 pedestrian 11 repetitious, somniferous 13 uninteresting

monotony 3 rut 5 ennui 6 tedium 7 boredom, humdrum 8 dullness, flatness, prosaism, sameness 9 iteration 10 dreariness, redundancy, uniformity 11 reiteration, tediousness 13 wearisomeness 14 predictability

Monroe, Earl
 nickname: 12 Earl the Pearl
 sport: 10 basketball
 position: 5 guard
 team: 16 Baltimore Bullets 21 New York
 Knickerbockers
Monroe, James
 presidential rank: 5 fifth
 party: 20 Democratic-Republican
 state represented: 2 VA
 defeated: 4 (Rufus) King 5 (John Quincy)
 Adams
 vice president: 8 (Daniel D) Tompkins
 cabinet:
 state: 5 (John Quincy) Adams
 treasury: 8 (William Harris) Crawford
 war: 7 (John Caldwell) Calhoun
 attorney general: 4 (Richard) Rush,
 (William) Wirt
 navy: 8 (Samuel Lewis) Southard,
 (Smith) Thompson 13 (Benjamin Williams) Crowninshield
 born: 2 VA 18 Westmoreland County
 died: 13 New York City NY
 buried: 10 Richmond VA
 education: 14 William and Mary (did not
 graduate)
 religion: 12 Episcopalian
 author: 67 A View of the Conduct of the
 Executive in the Foreign Affairs of the
 United States
 political career: 8 US Senate
 governor of: 8 Virginia
 minister: 5 Spain 6 France 12 Great Britain
 secretary of: 3 war 5 state
 civilian career: 6 lawyer
 military service: 5 major 7 captain 10
 lieutenant 16 Revolutionary War 17 lieutenant colonel
 wounded in Battle of: 7 Trenton
 notable events of lifetime/term: 5 Panic
 (of 1819) 14 Monroe Doctrine
 Agreement: 9 Rush-Bagot
 Compromise: 8 Missouri
 war: 8 Seminole
 father: 6 Spence
 mother: 9 Elizabeth (Jones)
 siblings: 6 Andrew, Spence 9 Elizabeth
 11 Joseph Jones
 wife: 9 Elizabeth (Kortright)
 nickname: 5 Eliza
 children: 11 Maria Hester 14 Eliza
 Kortright
Monroe, Marilyn
 real name: 23 Norma Jean Mortenson
 Baker
 husband: 11 Joe DiMaggio 12 Arthur
 Miller
 born: 12 Los Angeles CA
 roles: 12 Bus Stop, Niagara 10 The Misfits
 13 Some Like It Hot 16 The Seven-Year
 Itch 22 Gentlemen Prefer Blondes, How
 To Marry a Millionaire 23 The Prince and
 the Showgirl
Monrovia
 capital of: 7 Liberia

monseigneur 6 my lord
monsieur 2 Mr 3 sir 6 mister, my lord
Monsieur Beaucaire
 author: 15 Booth Tarkington
Monsignor Quixote
 author: 12 Graham Greene
monster 4 Fury 5 beast, brute, demon,
 devil, fiend, freak, ghoul, giant, golem,
 harpy, hydra, satyr, titan 6 dragon, gorgon,
 marvel, oddity, savage, threat, wonder,
 wretch, zombie 7 anomaly, caitiff, centaur,
 chimera, deviant, incubus, mammoth, mermaid, vampire, variant, villain 8 bogeyman,
 colossus, gargoyle, succubus, werewolf 9
 barbarian, curiosity, cutthroat, scoundrel
 10 blackguard, phenomenon 11 abnormality, miscreation 12 Frankenstein, lusus na-
 turae
monstrosity 5 freak 7 monster
monstrous 4 bald, evil, huge 5 cruel, giant
 6 grisly, mighty, odious 7 ghastly, harried,
 heinous, hideous, hulking, immense,
 mammoth, obscene, obvious, satanic, titanic, vicious 8 colossal, enormous, fiendish, flagrant, gigantic, gruesome, horrible,
 outright, shocking 9 atrocious, egregious,
 nefarious, revolting 10 diabolical, gargantuan, outrageous, prodigious, scandalous,
 stupendous, tremendous, villainous 14
 Brobdingnagian
monstrousness 8 baseness, enormity,
 evilness, vileness, villainy 9 barbarity, depravity, malignity 10 inhumanity, wickedness 11 heinousness, viciousness 13
 atrociousness, offensiveness 14 outrageousness
Montagnais-Naskapi (Innu)
 language family: 9 Algonkian 10 Algonquian
 tribe: 8 Nascapee 9 Mistassin 10
 Bersiamite, Montagnais 11 Papinachois
 location: 5 Maine 6 Canada, Quebec 17
 Maritime Provinces
 occupation: 7 hunters 10 fur traders
Montague family
 characters in: 14 Romeo and Juliet
 author: 11 Shakespeare
Montaigne, Michel de
 author of: 6 Essais, Essays
Montalban, Ricardo
 born: 6 Mexico 10 Mexico City
 roles: 4 Khan 8 Mr Roarke 9 The Colbys
 13 Fantasy Island 24 Star Trek II The
 Wrath of Khan
Montalvo, Garcia de
 author of: 12 Amadis of Gaul
Montana
 abbreviation: 2 MT 4 Mont
 nickname: 6 Big Sky 7 Bonanza,
 Stubtoe 8 Mountain, Treasure
 capital: 6 Helena
 largest city: 8 Billings
 others: 4 Kipp 5 Butte, Havre, Malta 6
 Hardin 7 Bozeman, Chinook, Choteau,
 Forsyth, Glasgow, Roundup 8 Anaconda,
 Missoula 9 Kalispell 10 Great Falls

college: 7 Carroll 10 Great Falls 13 Rocky Mountain
feature: 17 Continental Divide
cemetery: 6 Custer
national park: 7 Glacier 11 Yellowstone
tribe: 4 Cree, Crow, Hohe 5 Sioux 6 Atsima, Atsina, Salish 7 Arapaho, Bannock, Kutenai, Siksika 8 Cheyenne, Chippewa, Flatfoot, Flathead, Shoshone 9 Blackfeet 11 Assiniboine
people: 8 Myrna Loy 9 Will James 10 Gary Cooper 14 Charles Russell 15 Jeannette Rankin
explorer: 13 Lewis and Clark 16 Pierre Jean de Smet
lake: 5 Tiber 6 Hebgen 8 Flathead, Fort Peck, Medicine 10 Yellowtail 11 Canyon Ferry, Hungry Horse
land rank: 6 fourth
mountain: 4 Ajax 5 Baldy, Cowan, Crazy, Lewis 6 Sphinx, Torrey 7 Bighorn, Big Belt, Hilgard, Purcell, Rockies, Trapper 8 Absaroka, Gallatin, Pentagon, Snowshoe
highest point: 11 Granite Peak
physical feature: 10 Great Falls
river: 3 Sun 4 Milk 5 Clark, Teton 6 Marias, Powder, Tongue, Willow 7 Madison, Shields 8 Columbia, Kootenai, Missouri 9 Blackfoot 10 Bitterroot 11 Musselshell, Yellowstone
state admission: 10 forty-first
state bird: 17 western meadowlark
state fish: 26 black-spotted cutthroat trout
state flower: 10 bitterroot
state motto: 13 Gold and Silver
state song: 7 Montana
state tree: 13 Ponderosa pine
Montana, Bob
creator/artist of: 6 Archie
Montand, Yves
real name: 7 Ivo Livi
wife: 14 Simone Signoret
born: 5 Italy 14 Monsummano Alto
roles: 1 Z 12 Let's Make Love 14 Is Paris Burning?
montani semper liberi 28 mountaineers are always free men
motto of: 12 West Virginia
Montcalm, Louis Joseph
also: 17 Marquis de Montcalm
nationality: 6 French
served in: 18 French and Indian War
battle: 6 Oswego, Quebec (siege) 8 Carillon 11 Ticonderoga 16 Fort William Henry
killed in battle at: 6 Quebec 15 Plains of Abraham
mont-de-piete 10 pawnbroker
literally: 10 bank of pity
Montenegro
name means: 13 black mountain
other name: 4 Zeta 8 Crna Gora
capital: 7 Cetinje 8 Titograd 9 Podgorica
cities: 3 Bar 5 Kotor, Tivat 6 Niksic, Ulcinj 8 Antivari, Dulcigno, Ivangrad, Pljevlja 10 Hercegnovi 11 Sveti Stefan

division:
Roman province: 7 Illyria
governed by: 10 Yugoslavia
monetary unit: 4 para 6 florin 7 perpera
lake: 7 Scutari, Shkoder
mountain: 8 Durmitor 11 Dinaric Alps
river: 3 Lim 4 Piva, Tara, Zeta 6 Moraca 7 Ceotina
sea: 8 Adriatic
physical feature:
gulf: 5 Kotor
people: 4 Serb, Slav 11 Montenegrin
former ruler (Orthodox bishop): 7 vladike 8 vladika
language: 13 Serbo-Croatian
religion: 16 Serbian Orthodoxy
Monteverdi, Claudio
born: 5 Italy 7 Cremona
composer of: 5 Adone, Orfeo 7 Arianna 14 La Favola d'Orfeo 17 The Fable of Orpheus 21 The Coronation of Poppea 22 L'incoronazione di Poppea 24 Il Ritorno d'Ulisse in patria 34 Il Combattimento di Tancredi e Clorinda
Montevideo
capital of: 7 Uruguay
Montgomery, Bernard Law
also: 27 (first) Viscount Montgomery of Alamein
author of: 7 Memoirs 17 A History of Warfare
battle: 9 El Alamein
chief: 19 British general staff
commander of: 17 British Eighth Army 32 British occupation forces in Germany
commando raid: 6 Dieppe
deputy supreme commander: 4 NATO
Eighth Army called: 10 Desert Rats
evacuation of: 7 Dunkirk
fought against: 6 Rommel 11 Africa Corps, Afrika Korps
invasion: 6 Sicily 8 Normandy
member: 12 House of Lords
nationality: 7 British
nickname: 5 Monty
served in: 3 WWI 4 WWII
Montgomery, Robert
real name: 17 Henry Montgomery Jr
daughter: 9 Elizabeth
born: 8 Beacon NY
roles: 11 The Big House 13 Night Must Fall 17 Here Comes Mr Jordan
month
abbreviation: 2 mo
Month in the Country, A
author: 12 Ivan Turgenev
months, Hebrew
first: 4 Ahib, Nisn 6 Ehanim, Tishri
second: 3 Bul, Civ 4 Iyar 7 Heshvan
third: 5 Sivan 6 Kislev
fourth: 5 Tebet 6 Tammuz, Tebeth
fifth: 2 Ab 7 Shelbat
sixth: 4 Adar, Elul 6 Veadar
seventh: 4 Abib 5 Nisan 6 Tishri 7 Ethanim
eighth: 3 Zif 4 Iyar 11 Marchesvan
ninth: 5 Sivan 7 Chislev

tenth: 6 Tebeth, Tammuz
eleventh: 2 Ab 6 Shabat
twelfth: 4 Adar, Elul
Mont-Oriol
  author: 15 Guy de Maupassant
Montreal
  airport: 6 Dorval 8 St Hubert 12 Cartier-ville
  baseball team: 5 Expos
  founder: 11 Maisonneuve
  hill: 10 Mount Royal
  hockey team: 9 Canadiens
  island: 5 Jesus 6 Bizard, Perrot 8 Montreal 9 des Soeurs 14 de Boucherville
  lake: 7 St Louis
  landmark: 12 Place des Arts 13 Molson Stadium 16 Chateau de Ramezay 17 Church of Notre Dame, St Sulpice Seminary 21 Man and His World Exhibit
  original name: 10 Ville-Marie
  province: 6 Quebec
  river: 6 Ottawa 10 St Lawrence 11 des Prairies 14 des Milles Isles
  subway: 5 Metro
  university: 6 McGill
Montresor
  character in: 20 The Cask of Amontillado
  author: 3 Poe
Mont Saint Michel and Chartres
  author: 10 Henry Adams
Monty
  nickname of: 15 Montgomery Clift 17 (General) Bernard Montgomery
monument 4 slab 5 token 6 shrine 7 memento, obelisk, witness 8 cenotaph, memorial, monolith, reminder 9 testament, tombstone 10 gravestone 11 remembrance, testimonial 13 commemoration
monumental 4 huge 5 fatal, heavy 7 awesome, classic, epochal, immense, lasting, massive 8 colossal, decisive, enduring, gigantic, historic, immortal, statuary 9 cyclopean, egregious, memorable 10 horrendous, monolithic, shattering, stupendous 11 inestimable 12 catastrophic 13 unprecedented
mooch 3 beg, bum 5 cadge 6 hustle, sponge 7 solicit 8 freeload
mood 5 blues, dumps, humor 6 spirit, temper 7 feeling 8 doldrums, vexation 9 condition 10 depression, gloominess, melancholy 11 disposition, melancholia, temperament 14 predisposition 16 hypersensitivity
moody 4 mean 5 sulky, surly, testy 6 crabby, dismal, fickle, gloomy, mopish, morbid, morose, sullen 7 erratic, flighty, peevish, unhappy 8 brooding, dejected, notional, variable, volatile 9 impetuous, impulsive, irascible, irritable, mercurial, saturnine, whimsical 10 capricious, changeable, despondent, inconstant, lugubrious, melancholy 11 pessimistic 12 inconsistent 13 temperamental, unpredictable

Mookerjee, Hurree Chunder
  character in: 3 Kim
  author: 7 Kipling
moon 4 gape, lamp, luna, roam 5 dream, month, stare 6 dawdle, wander 8 daydream 9 satellite
  god of: 3 Sin 5 Nanna 6 Meztli
  goddess of: 4 Luna 5 Diana, Holle, Tanit 6 Hecate, Hekate, Phoebe, Selena, Selene, Tanith 7 Artemis, Astarte, Cynthia
  full: 9 plenilune
  new: 5 prime
  waning: 7 waiand
Moon and Sixpence, The
  author: 16 W Somerset Maugham
moonless 4 dark 5 black, murky 7 stygian 9 lightless, unlighted 13 unilluminated
Moonlighting
  character: 11 Maddie Hayes 12 Agnes Dipesto, David Addison
  cast: 11 Bruce Willis 13 Allyce Beasley 14 Cybill Shepherd
  detective agency: 8 Blue Moon
Moon Mullins
  creator: 12 Frank Willard
  character: 4 Kayo 5 Mamie 9 Mushmouth 11 Uncle Willie 15 Lady Plushbottom, Lord Plushbottom 16 Moonshine Mullins
Moon of the Caribbees, The
  author: 12 Eugene O'Neill
moonshine 5 hokum 6 bunkum, humbug 7 bootleg 8 clockade, homebrew, malarky, nonsense 10 balderdash, bathtub gin 11 mountain dew
moonstone
  species: 8 feldspar
  source: 5 Burma, Mogok
Moonstone, The
  author: 13 Wilkie Collins
  character: 7 Dr Candy 12 Lady Verinder, Sergeant Cuff 13 Franklin Blake 14 John Herncastle, Rachel Verinder 15 Rosanna Spearman 16 Godfrey Ablewhite
moor 3 fen 4 dock, down, fell, lash, wold 5 affix, berth, chain, heath, marsh, tie up 6 anchor, attach, fasten, secure, steppe, tether, tundra, upland 7 savanna, tie down 8 make fast 9 wasteland
Moore, Archie
  nickname: 11 The Mongoose
  real name: 18 Archibald Lee Wright
  sport: 6 boxing
  class: 16 light-heavyweight
Moore, Clement C
  author of: 23 A Visit from Saint Nicholas
Moore, Dick
  creator/artist of: 13 Gasoline Alley
Moore, Dudley
  nickname: 12 Cuddly Dudley
  wife: 11 Suzy Kendall, Tuesday Weld
  born: 5 Essex 7 England 8 Dagenham
  roles: 3 Ten 6 Arthur 8 Lovesick, Six Weeks 9 Bedazzled 13 Micki and Maude 16 Arthur on the Rocks 17 Like Father Like Son
  plays: 5 piano

Moore, George
author of: 12 Esther Waters 15 Hail and Farewell

Moore, Henry
born: 7 England 10 Castleford
artwork: 4 Mask 8 Two Forms 9 North Wind 10 Bird Basket 11 Family Group, Head of a Girl 12 Locking Piece 13 Nuclear Energy 15 Reclining Figure 20 Four-Piece Composition

Moore, Marianne
author of: 12 Like a Bulwark, Nevertheless, O To Be a Dragon, Tell Me Tell Me

Moore, Mary Tyler
husband: 11 Grant Tinker
born: 10 Brooklyn NY
roles: 4 Mary 12 Mary Richards 14 Ordinary People 18 The Dick Van Dyke Show 21 The Mary Tyler Moore Show

Moore, Mrs
character in: 15 A Passage to India
author: 7 Forster

Moore, Roger
born: 6 London 7 England
roles: 8 The Saint 12 Simon Templar
as James Bond: 9 Moonraker, Octopussy 13 Live and Let Die 16 The Spy Who Loved Me 22 The Man with the Golden Gun

Moorehead, Agnes
born: 9 Clinton MA
roles: 6 Endora 9 Bewitched 11 Citizen Kane 13 Johnny Belinda 15 Dear Dead Delilah 20 Magnificent Obsession 23 The Magnificent Ambersons

mooring 4 hook, line, rope 5 cable, chain 6 anchor, hawser

moot 4 open 7 eristic 8 arguable, disputed 9 debatable, undecided, unsettled 10 disputable, unresolved 11 conjectural 12 questionable 13 controversial, problematical 14 controvertible

mope 4 fret, pine, pout, sulk 5 brood, worry 6 grieve, grouse, lament, repine 7 grumble 8 languish

Mopsus
occupation: 4 seer
mother: 5 Manto
grandfather: 8 Tiresias
member of: 9 Argonauts
founded: 6 oracle
location: 6 Mallus 7 Cilicia
cofounder: 11 Amphilochus
epithet: 9 Ampycides

moral 3 tag 4 fair, just, pure 5 adage, maxim, motto, noble, right 6 honest, lesson, proper, saying 7 epigram, ethical, message, proverb, saintly 8 aphorism, didactic, personal, virtuous 9 estimable, homiletic, honorable, preaching 10 aboveboard, high-minded, principled 11 meritorious, sermonizing, tendentious 12 conscionable

moral code 6 ethics 9 integrity, standards 10 principles

morale 4 mood 6 spirit, temper 10 confidence, resolution 11 disposition
French: 13 esprit de corps

morality 5 honor 6 ethics, habits, tastes, virtue 7 modesty, probity 8 fairness, goodness 9 integrity, rectitude 10 chasteness 11 uprightness 13 righteousness

moralize 6 preach 7 lecture

moralizing 7 preachy 8 didactic 9 homiletic

morally corrupt 6 effete 8 decadent, depraved 10 degenerate

moral sense 9 integrity 10 conscience

morass 3 bog, fen 4 mire 5 marsh, swamp 6 slough 8 quagmire, wetlands 9 quicksand

morbid 3 sad 4 dour, glum, grim 5 moody 6 gloomy, morose, somber 8 brooding 9 depressed, saturnine 10 despondent, lugubrious 11 melancholic, pessimistic, unwholesome

morbid condition 6 malady 7 ailment, disease, illness 8 sickness 9 infirmity

Morcerf, Comte de (Fernand)
character in: 21 The Count of Monte Cristo
author: 5 Dumas (pere)

mordant 6 biting, bitter 7 acerbic, caustic, cutting, waspish 8 incisive, piercing, scathing, scornful, stinging, venomous, virulent 9 acidulous, malicious, sarcastic, trenchant 11 acrimonious

Mordecai
cousin: 6 Esther
served: 15 Ahasuerus Xerxes
enemy: 5 Haman

more 5 added, extra, other, spare 6 longer 7 further, reserve 10 additional 12 additionally, supplemental 13 supplementary

More, Thomas
author of: 6 Utopia

Moreau, Frederic
character in: 21 A Sentimental Education
author: 8 Flaubert

Moreau, Gustave
born: 5 Paris 6 France
artwork: 7 Orpheus 13 Dance of Salome (Salome Dancing), The Apparition 16 Hesiod and the Muse 18 The Poet and the Siren 19 Oedipus and the Sphinx 27 Diomedes Devoured by His Horses

Morehouse, J Ward
character in: 3 USA
author: 9 Dos Passos

Morel, Paul
character in: 13 Sons and Lovers
author: 8 Lawrence

Moreno, Rita
real name: 20 Rosita Dolores Alverio
born: 7 Humacao 10 Puerto Rico
roles: 13 Pagan Love Song, The Deerslayer, West Side Story 15 Singin' in the Rain

more or less 5 about 6 around 8 somewhat 9 generally, just about 13 approximately

moreover 3 too 4 also 7 besides, further 11 furthermore 12 more than that

mores 4 code **5** ethos, forms, rules **6** usages **7** customs, rituals **9** etiquette, practices, standards **10** traditions **11** conventions, observances, proprieties
more than enough 5 ample **6** excess, plenty **7** copious, profuse **8** plethora **9** abundance, amplitude, bountiful, excessive, profusion **10** oversupply
Morgan, Daniel
   served in: 16 Revolutionary War
   commander of: 8 riflemen **13** sharp-shooters
   battle: 7 Cowpens **8** Saratoga **12** Bemis Heights, Freeman's Farm
   helped suppress: 16 Whiskey Rebellion
Morgan, Thomas Hunt
   founder of: 8 genetics
   awarded: 10 Nobel Prize
Morgan, William De
   author of: 11 Joseph Vance
Morgan family
   characters in: 19 How Green Was My Valley
   members: 4 Beth, Davy, Huur, Ivor, Owen **5** Ianto **6** Gwilym **8** Angharad
   author: 9 Llewellyn
morganite
   color: 4 pink **5** peach
Morgan le Fay
   character in: 16 Arthurian romance
Moriae Encomium (In Praise of Folly)
   author: 7 Erasmus
Moriarty, Professor
   character in: 14 (The Adventures of) Sherlock Holmes
   author: 10 Conan Doyle
moribund 5 dying **6** doomed, waning **10** stagnating
Morier, James
   author of: 18 Hajji Baba of Ispahan
morituri te salutamus 28 we who are about to die salute thee
   said by: 15 Roman gladiators
   said to: 13 Roman emperors
Mork & Mindy
   character: 4 Mork **6** Eugene **10** Cora Hudson **13** Mindy McConnel **17** Frederick McConnel
   cast: 9 Pam Dawber **11** Conrad Janis **13** Elizabeth Kerr, Robin Williams **14** Jeffrey Jacquet
   Mork's planet: 3 Ork
   phrase: 8 nanu nanu
   spinoff from: 9 Happy Days
Morland, Catherine
   character in: 15 Northanger Abbey
   author: 6 Austen
Morley, Robert
   born: 6 Semley **7** England
   roles: 5 Melba **10** Oscar Wilde **11** Beau Brummel, Edward My Son **12** Major Barbara **15** Marie Antoinette, The African Queen **21** The Man Who Came to Dinner
Mormon State
   nickname of: 4 Utah
morning 4 dawn **5** early, sunup **7** sunrise **8** daybreak, daylight, forenoon **9** matutinal

morning-glory 7 Ipomoea **10** Calystegia **11** Convolvulus
   varieties: 3 red **4** wild **5** beach, dwarf **6** Ceylon, common, silver, woolly, yellow **9** Brazilian **16** Imperial Japanese
Morocco
   other name: 7 Barbary **8** Maroquin **9** Al Maghrib **13** Maghrib el Aksa **19** Mauretania Tingitana
   capital: 5 Rabat **6** Rabbat
   largest city: 10 Casablanca
   others: 3 Fes, Fez, Sla **4** Ifni, Safi, Sale, Sali, Taza **5** Ceuta, Oujda, Porte, Saffi **6** Agadir, Meknes, Semara, Tetuan **7** Elarish, Kenitra, Larache, Mazagan, Mililla, Mogador, Tangier, Tetouan **8** Kouribga, Tinerhir **9** Marrakech, Marrakesh **10** Youssoufia **11** Port-Lyautey
   division:
   disputed territory: **13** Western Sahara
   head of state: 4 king
   measure: 4 kala, muhd, rotl, saah, sahh, ueba **5** artal, cadee, gerbe, ratel **6** covado, dirhem, fanega, izenbi, kintar, tangin, tomini **8** quintal
   monetary unit: 4 flue, okia, rial **5** floos, franc, okieh, ounce **6** dirham, miskal **8** mouzouna
   weight: 4 rotl **5** artel, ratel **6** dirhem, kintar **7** quintal
   island: 7 Madeira
   mountain: 3 Rif **4** Bani **5** Abyla, Atlas, Sarro **8** Tidiguin **9** Anti-Atlas, High Atlas, Jebel-Musa **11** Middle Atlas
   highest point: 12 Jebel Toubkal **13** Djebel Toubkal
   river: 3 Dra, Ziz **4** Sous **5** Sebou **6** Gheris **7** Tensift **8** Moulouya **9** Oum er Rbia
   sea: 8 Atlantic **13** Mediterranean
   physical feature:
   cape: **4** Nun, Sim **4** Juby, Noun, Rhir **6** Cantin
   desert: **6** Sahara
   oasis: **8** Tafilelt
   plain: **5** Rharb
   strait: **9** Gibraltar
   valley: **7** Ouergha
   wind: **5** leste **7** charqui
   people: 4 Arab, Moor **6** Berber, French **7** Spanish
   dynasty: **7** Alawite, Almohad **9** Almoravid
   leader: **5** Idris **7** Lyautey **8** Hassan II **9** Abd el-Krim
   philosopher: **8** Averroes
   language: 6 Arabic, Berber, French **7** Spanish
   religion: 5 Islam
   place:
   ruins: **9** Volubilis
   feature:
   clothing: **4** haik **7** jellaba
   hat: **3** fez
   Islamic holy war: **5** jehad, jihad
   shanty town: **10** bidonville
   food:

dish: 8 couscous

moron 3 ass, nut, oaf, sap 4 boob, dolt, dope, fool 5 dummy, dunce, idiot, loony, ninny 6 dimwit, nitwit 7 half-wit, jackass 8 bonehead, dumbbell, dumbhead, imbecile, numskull 9 blockhead, numbskull, simpleton 10 muttonhead, nincompoop

Moroni

capital of: 7 Comoros

Moros

mother: 3 Nyx

personifies: 4 fate

morose 3 low, sad 4 blue, dour, glum, sour 5 cross, moody, sulky, surly, testy 6 cranky, gloomy, grumpy, mopish, solemn, sullen 7 waspish 8 churlish, downcast, mournful 9 depressed, irascible, saturnine 10 despondent, melancholy 11 crestfallen

moroseness 5 gloom 8 glumness 9 pessimism, sulkiness, surliness 10 sullenness

Morpheus

god of: 6 dreams

father: 6 Hypnos

morphology

study of: 9 structure

Morris, Dinah

character in: 8 Adam Bede

author: 5 Eliot

Morris, Willie

author of: 5 Yazoo 10 Good Old Boy 15 North Toward Home

Morris, Wright

author of: 8 Will's Boy 10 Plain's Song 13 Field of Vision, My Uncle Dudley

Morrison, Jeanette Helen

real name of: 10 Janet Leigh

Morrison, Marion Michael

real name of: 9 John Wayne

Morrison, Toni

real name: 19 Chloe Anthony Wofford

author of: 4 Sula, Jazz 7 Beloved, Tar Baby 12 The Bluest Eye 13 Song of Solomon

honor: 10 Nobel Price 13 Pulitzer Prize

Morrow, Vic

born: 7 Bronx NY

roles: 6 Combat 8 Cimarron 14 God's Little Acre 15 The Twilight Zone 18 Portrait of a Mobster 19 The Blackboard Jungle

Morse, Samuel F B

nationality: 8 American

invented: 9 Morse code 17 electric telegraph 24 electromagnetic telegraph

morsel 3 bit, nip, sip 4 bite, drop, iota, whit 5 crumb, grain, piece, scrap, snack, speck, taste, touch, trace 6 dollop, nibble, sliver, tidbit 7 modicum, segment, swallow 8 fraction, fragment, mouthful, particle 9 scintilla

mortal 4 deep, type 5 fatal, grave, human 6 deadly, lethal, living, person, severe 7 earthly, extreme, intense, mundane 8 creature, enormous, fleeting, temporal 9 character, corporeal, ephemeral 10 individual, transitory 12 unimaginable

mortality 7 carnage 8 fatality 9 bloodshed, ephemeral, slaughter 10 transience 11 evanescence 12 impermanence 13 extermination 14 transitoriness

mortar 6 cannon, cement, vessel 7 plaster 8 adhesive

Morte d'Arthur, Le

author: 12 Thomas Malory

Mortgaged Heart, The

author: 15 Carson McCullers

mortification 3 rot 5 decay, shame 7 chagrin, penance 8 ignominy 11 humiliation 12 putrefaction 13 embarrassment

mortified 6 rotted 7 abashed, ashamed, debased 8 dismayed, festered, tortured 9 chagrined, putrefied 11 discomfited, embarrassed

mortify 3 rot 4 deny, fast 5 abash, decay, shame 6 appall, fester 7 chagrin, horrify, putrefy 9 discomfit, embarrass 10 discipline, disconcert

Mosaic law 10 Pentateuch 15 Ten Commandments

Mosan

language family: 14 Algonkian-Mosan

subgroup: 6 Nootka 8 Chemakum, Kwakiutl, Quileute, Salishan, Wakashan 9 Chemakuan

Moscow

airport: 12 Sheremetyevo

canal: 11 Moscow-Volga

capital of: 4 USSR 6 Russia 11 Soviet Union

hills: 5 Lenin

landmark: 7 Kremlin 9 Gorky Park, Red Square 12 Lenin Library 13 Izmailovo Park, Sokolniki Park 14 Bolshoi Theater 16 Moscow Art Theater 21 Luzhniki Sports Complex

museum: 6 Armory 7 Pushkin 10 Historical 16 Tretyakov Gallery 28 Central Museum of the Soviet Army

river: 5 Setun, Volga, Yauza 6 Moscow

Russian: 6 Moskva

Moses father: 5 Amram

mother: 8 Jochebed

sister: 6 Miriam

brother: 5 Aaron

wife: 8 Zipporah

son: 7 Eliezar, Gershom

father-in-law: 6 Jethro

received: 15 Ten Commandments

patriarch of: 10 Israelites

saw: 11 burning bush

successor: 6 Joshua

pertaining to: 6 Mosaic

Moses, Grandma

real name: 17 Anna Mary Robertson, Mary Anne Robertson

born: 11 Greenwich NY

artwork: 23 Out for the Christmas Trees

mosey 4 poke 5 amble 6 stroll 7 saunter, shuffle

Moslem 4 Moor 5 Islam, Sunni 6 Muslim, Shiite 7 Islamic 10 Mohammadan, Muhammadan

mosque 6 temple
   Arabic: 6 masjid, musjid
Mosquito Coast, The
   author: 11 Paul Theroux
Mosquito State
   nickname of: 9 New Jersey
moss
   varieties: 4 ball, club, gold, rose **5** broom, bunch, coral, ditch, fairy, Irish, spike, water **6** Scotch, spring **7** cushion, haircap, peacock, Spanish **8** floating, fountain, Japanese, mat spike **9** dwarf club, flowering **10** little club, pincushion **11** basket spike, meadow spike, shining club **12** treelet spike **13** Douglas's spike
Mossbauer, Rudolph Ludwig
   field: 7 physics
   nationality: 6 German
   discovered: 15 Mossbauer effect **28** recoil-free gamma ray absorption
   awarded: 10 Nobel Prize
Mosses from an Old Manse
   author: 18 Nathaniel Hawthorne
most 4 best, very **6** degree **7** maximum **9** extremely
most distant point 5 limit, reach **8** boundary **9** extremity
Mostel, Zero
   real name: 16 Samuel Joel Mostel
   born: 10 Brooklyn NY
   roles: 8 The Front **10** Rhinoceros **11** The Enforcer **12** The Producers **15** Du Barry Was a Lady **16** Fiddler on the Roof **17** Panic in the Streets
most important 3 key, top **4** head, main **5** chief **7** central, highest, leading **8** cardinal, dominant, foremost, greatest **9** paramount, principal, uppermost **10** preeminent **11** outstanding, predominant
mostly 4 mainly **7** as a rule, chiefly, greatly, largely **8** above all **9** generally, primarily, specially **10** especially **11** principally **12** particularly **13** predominantly
most prominent 7 leading **8** dominant **10** preeminent **11** outstanding
most successful 6 banner, record **7** winning **10** triumphant **11** outstanding
mote 3 dot **4** iota **5** speck **8** particle **9** scintilla
moth
   varieties: 4 hawk, luna, tent **5** ghost, gypsy, plume, royal, swift, yucca **6** hornet, lappet, miller, urania **7** clothes, emperor, flannel, hook tip, leopard, tussock **8** army worm, forester, imperial, polka dot **9** clearwing, clearwing **10** forest tent **11** pseudosphex **12** African peach **13** American tiger, giant Hercules **14** tropical sphinx **15** Chinese silkworm, glover's silkworm **20** striped morning sphinx
moth-eaten 6 holey **6** old-hat **7** worn-out **8** outmoded **10** antiquated, threadbare **11** dilapidated
mother 3 mom, mum **4** bear, mama, mind, mums, rear, tend **5** beget, breed, mater, momma, mommy, mummy, nurse, raise **6** origin, source **7** care for, indulge, nurture,

old lady, produce, protect **8** conceive, stimulus **10** wellspring **11** inspiration
   French: 4 mere
   Spanish: 5 madre
   of wind: 3 Eos
   of stars: 3 Eos
   of gods: 5 Nammu
mother country 8 homeland **10** fatherland, native land, native soil, old country **13** native country
Mother Goose in Prose
   author: 14 Lyman Frank Baum
motherly 4 kind **6** gentle, loving, tender **7** devoted **8** maternal, parental **9** indulgent **10** protective, sheltering
mother of a family
   Latin: 13 materfamilias
Mother of the West
   nickname of: 8 Missouri
mother's helper
   French: 6 au pair
motif 4 form, idea **5** shape, style, theme, topic **6** design, figure, thread **7** pattern, refrain, subject **9** treatment
motion 3 cue, nod **4** flow, flux, move, sign, stir **5** drift **6** action, beckon, signal, stream **7** gesture, kinesis, passage, request **8** mobility, movement, progress **10** indication, suggestion **11** gesticulate, proposition **13** gesticulation **14** recommendation
motionless 4 calm, dead, idle **5** fixed, inert, still **6** at rest, frozen, stable, static **8** immobile, inactive, lifeless, tranquil, unmoving **9** immovable, quiescent **10** stationary, transfixed **11** immobilized **12** unresponsive
motion picture 3 pic **4** cine, film, show **5** flick, movie **6** cinema, talkie **8** flickers **10** photodrama **11** picture show **13** moving picture
motivate 4 goad, move, stir **5** egg on, impel **6** arouse, induce, prompt, stir up, turn on **7** actuate, provoke **8** activate, persuade **9** influence, stimulate
motivation 5 cause **6** reason **7** impetus, impulse **9** causation, impulsion **11** provocation
motive 3 aim, end **4** goal, spur **5** cause **6** design, object, reason **7** grounds, purpose **8** occasion, stimulus, thinking **9** incentive, intention, prompting, rationale **10** enticement, incitement, inducement **11** inspiration, instigation, provocation
motley 4 pied **5** mixed, tabby **6** hybrid, sundry, unlike, varied **7** dappled, piebald, watered **8** assorted, brindled, speckled **9** checkered, composite, different, disparate, divergent, harlequin, patchwork **10** dissimilar, iridescent, polychrome, variegated **11** diversified, incongruous, varicolored **12** multicolored **13** heterogeneous, kaleidoscopic, miscellaneous
motor 3 car **4** auto, ride, tour **5** drive, pilot, wheel **6** engine, turbine **7** machine **8** efferent **10** automobile
motorcar 4 auto, heap **6** jalopy, wheels **7** flivver, machine, vehicle **9** tin lizzie **10** automobile

motor vehicle 3 bus, car, van 4 auto, heap, limo 5 motor, truck, wagon 6 jalopy, pickup, wheels 7 flivver, hardtop, machine, omnibus, town car, vehicle 8 limosine 9 tin lizzie 10 automobile 11 convertible

mottled 4 pied 5 tabby 7 blotchy, flecked, piebald, specked 8 brindled, speckled, stippled 10 iridescent, multicolor, variegated 11 varicolored 12 parti-colored 13 kaleidoscopic, polychromatic

motto 3 saw 4 rule 5 adage, axiom, maxim 6 byword, dictum, saying, slogan, truism 7 epigram, precept, proverb 8 aphorism 9 catchword, principle, watchword

moue 4 pout 7 grimace

Moulin Rouge
director: 10 John Huston
cast: 12 Jose Ferrer (Toulouse-Lautrec) 11 Suzanne Flon, Zsa Zsa Gabor 12 Eric Pohlmann
setting: 5 Paris 10 Montmartre

mound 4 bump, dune, heap, hill, pile, rick 5 knoll, mogul, ridge, stack 7 bulwark, hillock, hummock, rampart 9 earthwork 10 embankment 12 entrenchment

Mound Builders
location: 15 Ohio River Valley 22 Mississippi River Valley
known for: 13 earthen mounds

mount 3 fit, fix, rig, set, wax 4 go up, grow, pony, rise, soar 5 affix, camel, climb, equip, frame, horse, scale, steed, surge, swell 6 ascend, fit out, outfit, set off 7 augment, charger, climb up, get over, get upon, install, set into 8 elephant, increase, multiply, straddle 9 intensify

mountain 3 alp 4 peak 5 bluff, butte, range, ridge 6 height, massif 7 volcano 8 eminence, highland 9 elevation
of Afghanistan: 3 Koh 5 Safeo 6 Chagai, Pamirs 7 Nowshak 8 Koh-i-Baba, Safed Koh, Sulaiman 9 Himalayas, Hindu Kush, Istoro Nal 11 Khwaja Amran, Paropamisus
of Albania: 5 Shala 6 Pindus 8 Koritnjk 10 Mount Korab 12 Albanian Alps
of Algeria: 5 Aissa, Atlas, Aures, Dahra, Tahat 6 Chelia 7 Ahaggar, Kabylia, Mouydir 8 Djurjura 9 Djurdjura, Tell Atlas 12 Saharan Atlas
of Andorra: 6 d'Etats 8 l'Estanyo 8 Pyrenees 10 Cataperdis 11 Como Pedrosa
of Angola: 4 Moco 5 Chela 6 Loviti 8 Humpata Highlands
of Antigua and Barbuda: 9 Boggy Peak
of Argentina: 4 Toro 5 Andes, Chato, Laudo, Potro 6 Conico, Pissis, Rincon 8 Famatina, Murallon, Olivares, Tronador, Zapaleri 9 Aconcagua, Tupungato 10 Cordillera 13 Ojos del Salado 15 Cerro Mercedario, Sierra de Cordoba
of Armenia: 6 Ararat, Taurus 8 Karabekh 7 Aladagh 12 Mount Aragats
of Australia: 3 Ise 4 Blue, Olga, Ossa, Zeil 5 Bruce, Snowy 6 Cradle, Doreen, Garnet, Gawler, Magnet, Morgan 7 Bongong, Gregory 8 Augustus,

Brockman, Cuthbert, Herbert, Jusgrave, Mulligan, Surprise 9 Murchison, Kosciusko, Woodroffe 14 Australian Alps 15 New England Range 18 Great Dividing Range
of Austria: 4 Alps 6 Tirols, Tyrols, Stubai 8 Eisenerz, Rhatikon 9 Dolomites, Kitzbuhel 10 Hohe Tauern 13 Grossglockner 14 Silvretta Group
of Azerbaijan: 8 Caucasus
of Bangladesh: 10 Keokradong 15 Chittagong Hills
of Barbados: 6 Chalky 7 Hillaby
of Belgium: 8 Ardennes 16 Signal de Botrange
of Benin: 7 Atakora
of Bhutan: 5 Black 9 Himalayas 10 Chomo Lhari, Kula Kangri
of Bolivia: 4 Jara 5 Andes, Cusco, Cuzco 6 Sajama, Sorata, Sunsas 7 Illampu 8 Ancohuma, Illimani, Mururata, Sansimon, Santiago, Zapaleri 12 Eastern Range, Western Range 18 Cordillera Oriental 20 Cordillera Occidental
of Borneo: 4 Iran, Raja 5 Saran 6 Kapuas, Muller, Nijaan, Tebang 8 Kinabalu, Kinibalu, Schwaner
of Bosnia-Herzegovina: 11 Dinaric Alps
of Brazil: 3 Mar 5 Geral, Organ, Piaui 6 Acarai, Gurupi, Parima, Urucum 7 Amambai, Carajas, Gradaus, Neblina, Oragaos, Roraima 8 Bandeira, Itatiaia, Roncador, Tombador 9 Pacaraima, Sugar Loaf 10 Tumuc-Humac
of Brunei: 6 Teraja 9 Ulu Tutong 10 Pagon Priok
of Bulgaria: 3 Kom 5 Botev, Pirin, Sapka 6 Balkan, Musala, Sredna 7 Vikhren 8 Musallah 11 Rila-Rhodope
of Burkina Faso: 4 Tema 8 Nakourou 10 Tenakourou, Tenekourou
of Burundi: 8 Nyarwana 9 Nyamisana
of Cambodia: 3 Pan 7 Dangrek, Dong Rek 8 Cardamom, Elephant 10 Phnom Aoral, Phnom Aural
of Cameroon: 5 Mbabo 7 Bambuto, Kapsiki, Mandara 8 Batandji, Cameroon 9 Atlantika
of Canada: 5 Coast, Logan, Royal 6 Robson, Skeena 7 Cariboo, Cascade, Purcell, Rockies, Selkirk, Stelias, St Elias 8 Columbia, Hazelton, Monashee 9 Mackenzie, Notre Dame, Tremblant 10 Laurentian, Richardson, Shickshock 14 Jacques Cartier
of Canary Islands: 5 Teide, Teyde 6 La Cruz 8 El Cumbre, Tenerife
of Cape Verde: 4 Cano, Fogo 10 Pico de Cano
of Central African Republic: 5 Karre, Tinga 6 Mongos 9 Dar Challa 11 Kayagangiri
of Chad: 7 Tibesti, Touside 9 Emi Koussi
of Chile: 4 Maca, Toro 5 Chato, Maipo, Maipu, Paine, Potro, Pular, Torre, Yogan 6 Apiwan, Burney, Conico, Jervis, Poquis, Rincon 7 Chaltel, Copiapo, Fitzroy,

Palpana, Velluda 8 Cochrane, Tronador, Yanteles 9 Tupungato 13 Ojos del Salado
of Colombia: 5 Abibe, Andes, Baudo, Chita, Cocuy, Huila, Pasto 6 Ayapel, Perija, Purace, Tolima, Tunahi 7 Chamusa, del Ruiz 8 Oriengal 10 Santa Marta 14 Cristobal Colon 17 Central Cordillera, Eastern Cordillera, Western Cordillera
of Costa Rica: 4 Poas 5 Barba, Irazu 6 Blanco 7 Central, Gongora 9 Talamanca, Turrialba 10 Guanacaste 14 Chirripo Grande
of Crete: 3 Ida 5 Dikte, Phino 6 Juktas 7 Lasithi, Madaras 8 Leuka Ori, Theodore, Thriphte 9 Psiloriti
of Croatia: 10 Julian Alps 11 Styrian Alps
of Cuba: 6 Copper 7 Cristal, Maestra, Organos 8 Camaguey, Trinidad, Turquino 9 Las Villas 11 Pinar del rio 12 Guaniguanico 14 Sancti-Spiritus
of Czechoslovakia: 3 Ore 5 Grant, Tatra 6 Sumava 7 Gerlach, Sudeten 8 Krkonose 9 High Tatra 10 Carpathian 11 Gerlachovka
of Denmark: 12 Ejer Bavnehoj, Yding Skovhoj 14 Himmelbjaerget
of Djibouti: 5 Gouda 9 Moussa Ali
of Dominican Republic: 4 Tina 5 Gallo, Neiba 6 Duarte 7 Baoruco, Central 8 Bahoruco, Oriental 13 Septentrional
of Ecuador: 5 Andes 6 Condor, Sangay 7 Cayambe 8 Antisana, Cotopaxi 9 Cotacachi, Pichincha 10 Chimborazo
of Egypt: 5 Sinai, Uekia 6 Gharib 8 Katerina 9 Katherina 13 Shayib al-Banat
of El Salvador: 6 Izalco 8 Santa Ana
of England: 5 Black 7 Pennine, Snowdon 8 Cambrian, Cumbrian 11 Scafell Pike
of Equatorial Guinea: 5 Mitra 11 Santa Isabel
of Ethiopia: 4 Amba, Batu, Guge, Guna, Talo 5 Ahmar, Choke 9 Rasdashan, Ras Deshen
of Finland: 6 Haltia 7 Laltiva 10 Saari Selka 11 Haldetsokka
of France: 4 Alps, Jura 5 Blanc, Pelat 6 Vosges 8 Ardennes, Pyrenees 9 Mont Blanc 10 French Alps 11 Pic Montcalm
of Gabon Republic: 5 Mpele 7 Chaillu, Cristal, Mikongo 8 Balaquri, Birougou, Iboundji
of Georgia: 8 Caucasus
of Germany: 3 Ore 4 Harz 8 Feldberg 9 Zugspitze 10 Erzgebirge 11 Black Forest, Fichtelberg 12 Bavarian Alps
of Ghana: 8 Afadjato 12 Akwapim Hills
of Gibraltar: 6 Misery
of Greece: 3 Ida 4 Idhi, Oeta, Oite, Ossa 5 Athos 6 Ithome, Peleon, Pelion, Pindus 7 Grammos, Helicon, Olympus, Rhodope 8 Hymettos, Smolikas, Targetos, Taygetus 9 Parnassus 10 Hagion Oros, Lycabettus, Pentelicus
of Greenland: 5 Forel, Payer 7 Khardyu

8 Peterman 9 Gunnbjorn 15 Petermannsbjerg 16 Gunnbjornsfjaeld
of Guatemala: 4 Agua, Mico 5 Fuego, Madre 6 Pacaya, Tacana 7 Atitlan, Toliman 8 La Candon, Las Minas, Tajumuko 9 Tajamulco 10 Acatenango, Santa Maria 12 Cuchumatanes
of Guinea: 4 Loma 5 Nimba 6 Tamgue 11 Fouta Djalon
of Guyana: 5 Amuku, Ariwa, Kamoa 6 Akarai, Kanuku 7 Caburai 9 Pacaraima
of Haiti: 4 Nord 5 Cahos 6 Macaya, Noires 7 Lahotte, Laselle 8 Troudeau
of Honduras: 4 Pija 6 Agalta 7 Celaque 8 Las Minas 9 Esperanza 25 Central American Cordillera
of Hong Kong: 6 Castle 8 Victoria 9 Tai Mo Shan
of Hungary: 4 Alps, Bukk 5 Kekes, Matra, Tatra, Vetes 6 Bakony, Mecsek 7 Cserhat, Gerecse 8 Borzsony, Zempleni 9 Korishegy 10 Carpathian
of Iceland: 4 Laki 5 Askja, Hekla, Jokul, Katla 7 Surtsey 10 Orafajokul 16 Hvannadalshnukur
of India: 8 Aravalli 9 Broad Peak, Distaghil, Himalayas, Karakoram, Nanda Devi, Rakaposhi 10 Gasherbrum, Masherbrum 11 Nanga Parbat 12 Eastern Ghats, Godwin Austen, Kanchenjunga, Western Ghats
of Iran: 6 Elburz, Zagros 8 Demavend
of Iraq: 6 Qalate, Zagros 7 Halgurd, Qaarade 9 Kurdistan
of Ireland: 5 Galty 6 Croagh, Mourne 7 Errigal, Muckish, Patrick, Wicklow 8 Comeragh 10 Benna Beola, Twelve Bens, Twelve Pins 13 Carrantuohill, Knockmealdown 19 Macgillycuddy's Reeks
of Israel: 4 Nafh, Sagi 5 Harif, Meron, Ramon, Tabor 6 Atzmon, Carmel, Hatira, Meiron
of Italy: 4 Alps, Etna, Rosa, Viso 5 Amaro, Blanc, Corno, Somma 6 Cimone, Ortles 7 Vulcano 8 Vesuvius 9 Apennines, Dolomites, Maritimes, Stromboli 10 Apuane Alps, Carnic Alps, Julian Alps, Otztal Alps 11 Bernina Alps, Gennargentu 12 Gran Paradiso, Ligurian Alps 13 Lepontine Alps 16 Abruzzi Apennines
of Jamaica: 4 Blue 8 Sir Johns
of Japan: 3 Uso, Zao 4 Fuji 5 Asahi, Asama, Hondo, Yesso 6 Asosan, Enasan, Hiuchi, Kiusiu, Yariga 7 Fujisan, Hakusan, Kujusan, Tokachi 8 Fujiyama 9 Japan Alps
of Java: 4 Amat, Gede 5 Lawoe, Murjo, Prahu 6 Raoeng, Semuru, Slamet 7 Semeroe 8 Soembing
of Jordan: 9 Jabal Ramm, Jebel Ramm
of Kenya: 5 Elgon, Kenya, Kulai, Nyira, Nyiru 6 Kinyaa, Matian 7 Logonot 8 Aberdare 9 Kirinyaga
of Korea: 4 Wang 5 Chiri, Halla 6 Kwanmo, Paektu, Sobaek 7 Diamond, Kyebang, Nangnim, Taebaek 8 Chang-

pai, Hamgyong, Myohyang 9 Paektu-san
10 Kumgang-san
of Kyrgyzstan: 8 Tian Shan
of Laos: 3 Bia, Lai, Loi, San 4 Copi, Khat
5 Atwat 6 Khoung, Tiubia 7 Phou Bia 15
Annam Cordillera
of Lebanon: 4 Mzar 5 Aruba 6 Hermon 7
es Sauda, Lebanon, Sannine 8 Kadischa,
Kenisseh 9 Kennisseh 10 al-Mukammal
11 Anti-Lebanon 13 Qurnat al-Sawda
of Lesotho: 6 Maloti, Maluti 7 Central 8
Injasuti, Machache 10 Ben Macdhui 11
Drakensberg, Thaba Putsoa 16 Thabana
Ntlenyana
of Liberia: 3 Uni 4 Bong, Putu 5 Niete,
Nimba 6 Wutivi 9 Bomi Hills
of Libya: 5 Green 9 Bette Peak 13 Jabal
al Akhdar, Tibesti Massif
of Liechtenstein: 4 Alps 8 Naafkopf,
Rhatikon 12 Three Sisters 15 Vorder-
Grauspitz
of Lithuania: 9 Juozapine 15 Samogitian
Hills
of Luxembourg: 8 Ardennes, Huldange
9 Burgplatz 11 Wemperhardt
of Madagascar: 4 Boby 9 Ankaratra 11
Maromokotro 12 High Plateaus, Tsiafaja-
vona 17 Tsaratanana Massif
of Malawi: 6 Mlanje 7 Mulanje 11
Livingstone
of Malaysia: 4 Bulu, Hose, Iban, Iran,
Main, Mulu, Niut, Raja 5 Murjo, Niapa,
Ophir 6 Blumut, Kapuas, Leuser, Slamet
7 Binaija, Brassey, Crocker 8 Kinabalu,
Rindjani 11 Gunong Korbu, Gunong
Tahan
of Mali: 4 Mina 6 Iforas 7 Manding 12
Hombori Tondo
of Mexico: 6 Colima, Tacana, Toluca 7
Orizaba 9 Paricutin 11 Ixtacihuatl, Sierra
Madre 12 Citlaltepetl, Popocatepetl 14 Si-
erra Zacateca 16 Chiapas Highlands 24
Transverse Volcanic Sierra
of Mongolia: 4 Cast, Orog 5 Altai 6
Kentei, Sevrej 7 Ich Ovoo, Khangai,
Khentei 8 Tannu-Ola 9 Edrengijn 10
Cagaan Bogd, Tabun Bogdo 11 Munky
Sardyk 14 Hangayn-Hentiyn, Monch
Chajrchan
of Montenegro: 8 Durmitor 11 Dinaric
Alps
of Morocco: 3 Rif 4 Bani 5 Abyla, Atlas,
Sarro 8 Tidiguin 9 Anti-Atlas, High Atlas,
Jebel-Musa 11 Middle Atlas 12 Jebel
Toubkal 13 Djebel Toubkal
of Mozambique: 5 Binga 7 Lebombo
of Myanmar: 4 Chin, Naga, Pegu, Popa
5 Dawna 6 Arakan, Kachin, Lushai,
Patkai 7 Karenni 8 Nattaung, Peguyoma,
Saramati, Victoria 10 Tenasserim 11
Hkakabo Razi, Manipur Hill 12 Tanen
Taunggi
of Namibia: 9 Brandberg 14 Khomas
Highland, Koakoveld Hills
of Nepal: 6 Cho Oyu, Churia, Makalu 7
Everest, Lhotse I, Manaslu, Siwalik 8
Lhotse II 9 Annapurna, Himalayas 10

Dhaulagiri, Gosainthan, Himalchuli 11
Ganesh Himal 12 Kanchenjunga 14
Mahabharat Lekh
of New Guinea: 4 Snow 6 Orange 7
Bismark, Wilhelm 8 Victoria 9 Carstensz
10 Puncak Jaya 11 Owen Stanley 12 Al-
bert Edward
of New Zealand: 4 Cook, Eden, Flat,
Owen 5 Allen, Chope, Lyall, Mitre,
Ohope, Otari, Young 6 Egmont, Stokes,
Tasman 7 Aorangi, Cameron, Coronet,
Ernslaw, Huiarau, Pihanga, Ruahine,
Ruapehu, Tauhera, Tutamee, Tyndall 8
Aspiring, Richmond, Tauranga 9 Messen-
ger, Murchison, Ngauruhoe, Raukumara,
Tongariro 11 Remarkables 12 Southern
Alps
of Nicaragua: 4 Leon 5 Negro, Viejo 6
Madera, Telica 7 Managua, Mogoton,
Saslaya 9 Momotombo
of Niger: 7 Bagzane, Greboun 9 Air Massif
of Norway: 5 Sogne 6 Kjolen 7 Numedal
8 Blodfjel, Snohetta, Telemark, Ustetind 9
Harteigen, Jotunheim, Langfjell, Ramna-
nosi 10 Dovrefjell, Galdhoepig, Glitretind, Vibmesnosi 11 Myrdalfjell 12
Galdhopiggen 13 Glittertinden 14 Aardangerjokul, Hallingskarvet, Skagastolstind
of Oman: 4 Qara 5 Green, Hafit, Harim,
Nakhl, Tayin 6 al-Sham 8 el-Akhdar 11
Jabal Akhdar 13 Green Mountain
of Pakistan: 3 Pab, Pub 4 Salt 6 Makran
7 Kirthar 8 Himalaya, Safed Koh,
Sulaiman 9 Hindu Kush, Karakoram,
Tirich Mir 11 Makran Coast 12 Godwin
Austin 13 Central Makran 14 Takht-i-
Sulaiman
of Panama: 4 Baru, Maje 5 Chico, Gandi
6 Darien 7 Columan, San Blas, Veragua
8 Chiriqui, Santiago, Tabasara 10 Costa
Rican 14 Serrania de Sapo 15 Aspave
Highlands 17 Cordillera Central
of Peru: 5 Andes 7 El Misti, Huamina 8
Coropuna 9 Huascaran
of Philippines: 3 Apo, Iba 4 Mayo, Taal
5 Albay, Askja, Hibok, Mayon, Pulog 6
Pagsan 7 Banahao, Canlaon
of Poland: 4 Rysy 5 Tatra 6 Beskid 7
Pieniny, Sudeten 9 Beshchady, High
Tatra, Holy Cross 10 Carpathian
of Portugal: 4 Acor, Lapa 5 Gerez,
Marao, Mousa 6 Bornes, Peneda 7
Larouco 8 Caramulo 9 Caldeirao,
Monchique 11 Pico da Serra 14 Serra da
Estrela
of Puerto Rico: 4 Toro 5 Cayey, Punta 6
Yunque 8 Guilarte, Luquilla 10 Torrecilla
17 Cordillera Central
of Romania: 5 Banat, Bihor, Negoi 6
Codrul, Rodnei 7 Apuseni, Balkans,
Caliman, Fagaras 8 Pietrosu 9 Moldavian
10 Carpathian, Moldoveanu 17 Transyl-
vanian Alps
of Russia: 5 Altai, Lenin, Sayan, Urals 6
Anadyr, Elbrus, Koryak, Pamirs, Pobedy

7 Belukha, Crimean, Khibiny, Stanovi, Zhiguli 8 Caucasus, Dzhughur, Stanavoi, Tien Shan 9 Kopet Dagh, Narodnaya, Pamir-Alai, Yablonovy 11 Sikhote-Alin, Verkhoyansk

of Rwanda: 7 Mitumba, Virunga 8 Muhavura 9 Karisimbi

of Samoa: 4 Fito, Vaea 5 Alava 6 Savaii 7 Matafao 8 Silisili 9 Rainmaker

of San Marino: 6 Titano 9 Apennines

of Sardinia: 4 Rasu 5 Ferry, Linas 7 Gallura, Limbara 8 Marghine, Serpeddi, Vittoria 11 Gennargentu

of Saudi Arabia: 5 Razih 6 Tuwayq 10 Jebal Sawda

of Scotland: 5 Attow, Ochil 6 Sidlaw 7 Cheviot 8 Ben Nevis, Grampian 9 Ben Lomond, Highlands, Trossachs

of Senegal: 6 Gounou 12 Fouta Djallon

of Sicily: 4 Erei, Etna, Moro, Sori 5 Aetna, Atlas, Erici, Hybla, Iblei, Ibrei 7 Nebrodi, Vulcano 9 Apennines, Le Madonie, Stromboli 10 Peloritani

of Sierra Leone: 4 Loma 9 Bintimani 10 Tingi Hills

of Sikkim: 7 Dongkya, Donkhya 9 Himalayas, Singalili 10 Darjeeling 12 Kanchenjunga

of Singapore: 6 Mandai 7 Panjang 10 Bukit Timah

of Slovakia: 7 Sudetes 8 Low Tatra 9 High Tatra, Slovak Ore 10 Carpathian, Nizke Tatry 11 Visoke Tatry 15 White Carpathian

of the Solomon Islands: 5 Balbi 11 Popomanasiu

of Somalia: 5 Guban 7 Surud Ad 11 Migiurtinia, Ogo Highland

of South Africa: 3 Aux, Kop 5 Table 7 Kathkin 8 Injasuti 9 Stormberg 10 Devil's Peak, Sneeuwberg 11 Drakensberg 12 Giant's Castle 13 Witwatersrand 14 Mont-aux-Sources 15 Great Escarpment

of Spain: 4 Gata 5 Aneto, Rouch, Teide 6 Cuenca, Estats, Europa, Gredos, Magina, Morena, Nethou, Nevada, Teleno, Toledo 7 Alcaraz, Banuelo, Catalan, Cerredo, Demanda, Iberian, La Sagra, Moncayo, Perdido 8 Almanzor, Asturias, Galician, Maladeta, Monegros, Montseny, Mulhacen, Penalara, Pyrenees 10 Albarracin, Cantabrian, Guadarrama, Torrecilla

of Sri Lanka: 5 Pedro 7 Sri Pada 9 Adams Peak 14 Pidurutalagala

of Sudan: 4 Nuba 6 Red Sea 7 Imatong, Kinyeti 9 Dongotona 10 Jabal Marra, Jebel Marra 18 Ethiopian Highlands

of Surinam: 4 Emma 6 Kayser, Oranje 10 Julianatop, Tumuc-Humac, Wilhelmina 13 Eilert's Il Haan, Van Ach Van Wyck 15 Guiana Highlands

of Swaziland: 7 Emlembe 8 Highveld 11 Drakensberg

of Sweden: 4 Sarv 5 Ammar, Kebne 6 Helags, Kjolen, Ovniks, Sarjek 7 Kjollen 10 Kebnekaise

of Switzerland: 3 Dom 4 Alps, Jura, Rigi, Rosa, Todi 5 Adula, Blanc, Cenis, Eiger, Genis, Karpf, Righi 6 Linard, Pizela, Sentis 7 Bernina, Beverin, Grimsel, Pilatus, Rotondo 8 Balmhorn, Jungfrau 9 Weisshorn 10 Diablerets, Matterhorn, St Gotthard, Wetterhorn 11 Burgenstock 12 Dufourspitze 13 Rheinwaldhorn 14 Finsteraarhorn

of Syria: 6 Carmel, Hermon 7 Alawite, Libanus 10 Nusairiyya 11 Anti-Lebanon

of Taiwan: 5 Tatun 6 Tzukao, Yu Shan 7 Taitung 8 Morrison 10 Sinkao Shan 11 Hsin-Kao Shan 15 Chungyang Shanmo

of Tajikistan: 13 Communism Peak

of Tanzania: 4 Kibo, Mero 8 Usambara 11 Kilimanjaro

of Thailand: 5 Dawna, Khieo 6 Phanom 8 Dang Raek, Inthanon, Kao Prawa, Maelamun 9 Khao Luang 11 Bilauktaung, Doi Inthanon

of Tibet: 5 Kamet, Sajum 6 Kailas, Kunlun 7 Bandala, Everest 9 Himalayas, Karakoram

of Togo: 4 Togo 7 Atakora, Baumann, Koronga

of Tunisia: 5 Atlas 6 Chambi, Mrhila 7 Tebessa 8 High Tell, Zaghouan 12 Northern Tell 18 Dorsale Tunnisienne

of Turkey: 2 Ak 3 Ala 4 Alai, Dagh, Kara 5 Hasan, Hinis, Honaz, Murat, Murit 6 Ala Dag, Ararat, Bingol, Bolgar, Pontic, Suphan, Taurus 7 Aladagh, Erciyas 8 Karacali 10 Kackar Dagi

of Uganda: 4 Oboa 5 Elgon 7 Virunga 9 Mufumbiro, Ruwenzori 10 Margherita 18 Mountains of the Moon

of Ukraine: 7 Crimean 10 Carpathian

of United States: 4 Hood 5 Coast, Green, Kenai, Ozark, Rocky, White 6 Alaska, Brooks, DeLong, Elbert, Helena, Mesabi, Pocono, Shasta 7 Cascade, Chugach, Foraker, Harvard, Kilauea, Massive, Olympic, Olympus, Rainier, St Elias, Whitney 8 Catskill, Davidson, Endicott, Katahdin, Mauna Loa, McKinley, Mitchell, Ouachita, St Helens, Wrangell 9 Allegheny, Blue Ridge, Kuskokwim, North Peak, Pike's Peak 10 Black Hills, Blanca Peak, Grand Teton, Washington, Williamson 11 Appalachian, Santa Monica 12 Sierra Nevada 14 Berkshire Hills

of Uruguay: 6 Animas 10 Grand Hills 14 Cuchilla Grande 15 Mirador Nacional

of Vanuatu: 6 Lopevi 11 Tabwemasana

of Venezuela: 3 Pao 4 Pava, Yair 5 Andes, Duida, Icutu 6 Concha, Cuneva, Merida, Parima, Sierra, Yumari 7 Bolivar, Imutaca, Masaiti, Roraima 8 Gurupira 9 Pacaraima 10 Auyan-Tepui 11 Turimiquire 18 Cordillera del Norte

of Vietnam: 6 Badinh, Badink 7 Nindhoa, Ninhhoa 8 Fansipan, Knontran, Ngoklinh, Ngoklink, Tchepone, Tclepore 18 Annamese Cordillera

of Wales: 6 Berwyn 7 Snowdon 8 Cambrian 9 Prescelly 13 Brecon Beacons

of Western Samoa: 4 Fito, Vaea 13 Mauga Silisili

of Yemen: 6 Shuayb, Thamir 7 Djehaff

of Yugoslavia: 5 Karst 6 Balkan 7 Rhodope, Triglav 8 Crna Gora, Durmitor 9 Sar-Pindus 10 Carnic Alps, Julian Alps, Karawanken 11 Dinaric Alps 13 Slovenian Alps 20 Northern Albanian Alps

of Zaire: 7 Crystal, Mitumba, Virunga 9 Ruwenzori 10 Margherita, Nyaragongo 18 Mountains of the Moon

of Zambia: 8 Muchinga 12 Mafinga Hills

of Zimbabwe: 5 Vumba 6 Manica 7 Inyanga 9 Inyangani 11 Chimanimani, Matopo Hills

Mountain
constellation of: 5 Mensa

mountaineers are always free men
  Latin: 19 montani semper liberi
  motto of: 12 West Virginia

Mountain State
nickname of: 7 Montana 12 West Virginia

Mountbatten, Louis
also: 27 first Earl Mountbatten of Burma
nationality: 7 British
position: 12 first sea lord
supreme allied commander of: 13 Southeast Asia
chief of: 25 British combined operations
viceroy of: 5 India
served in: 3 WWI 4 WWII
directed invasion of: 10 Madagascar
recaptured: 5 Burma

mountebank 5 cheat, fraud, phony, quack 6 con man, humbug 7 hustler, sharper 8 huckster, operator, swindler 9 charlatan, con artist 11 quacksalver

mounted soldier 6 hussar, lancer 7 dragoon 8 cavalier, horseman 10 cavalryman

mourn 3 cry, rue, sob 4 keen, pine, wail, weep 6 bemoan, bewail, grieve, lament, regret, sorrow 7 deplore, despair 8 languish, weep over

mournful 3 sad 5 black, sorry, weepy 6 dismal, rueful, somber, triste, woeful 7 doleful, joyless, unhappy 8 dejected, dirgeful, dolorous, funereal, grevious, saddened 9 depressed, plaintive, sorrowful 10 depressing, dispirited, lamentable, lugubrious, melancholy 11 distressing, melancholic 12 heavy hearted

mourning 3 woe 5 black, crape, dolor, grief, weeds 6 sorrow 7 anguish, despair 8 grieving 9 lamenting, sorrowing 11 bereavement, lamentation

Mourning Becomes Electra
author: 12 Eugene O'Neill
character: 4 Seth 10 Hazel Niles, Peter Niles 16 Captain Adam Brant
Mannon family: 4 Ezra, Orin 7 Lavinia 9 Christine

mourning period
  Hebrew: 6 shibah, shivah

mouser 3 cat 4 puss 5 kitty, pussy 6 feline 8 pussycat

Mousetrap, The
author: 14 Agatha Christie

mousseline 6 muslin

mousy 3 shy 4 drab, dull 5 timid, wimpy 7 bashful, fearful 8 timorous 9 colorless, unnoticed, withdrawn 11 unobtrusive 13 inconspicuous

mouth 3 bay, say 4 bell, jaws, lips 5 inlet, speak, voice 6 outlet, portal 7 declare, estuary, opening 8 aperture, propound 9 pronounce

mouthful 3 dab 4 bite 5 taste 6 morsel, nibble

mouthpiece 4 reed 6 lawyer 7 counsel 8 advocate, attorney 9 counselor

mouth-watering 8 inviting, tempting 9 appealing 10 appetizing 11 tantalizing

movable, moveable 4 free 5 loose 6 mobile, motile, moving 8 portable 10 changeable

movables 4 gear 5 goods 7 baggage, effects, luggage 9 equipment 10 belongings 11 impedimenta, possessions 13 accoutrements, paraphernalia

move 2 go 3 act, ask, get 4 bear, deed, fire, lead, pass, ploy, step, stir, sway, turn, urge 5 begin, budge, carry, cause, drive, impel, plead, rouse, shift, touch 6 action, affect, arouse, attack, convey, excite, exhort, incite, induce, motion, prompt, strike, stroke, switch 7 advance, budging, gesture, go ahead, impress, inspire, measure, operate, proceed, propose, provoke, request, suggest 8 function, interest, locomote, maneuver, motivate, persuade, relocate, start off, stirring, transfer, transmit 9 impassion, influence, recommend, stimulate, transport, transpose 10 transplant 11 opportunity

move downward 3 dip 4 dive, drop, fall, sink 6 plunge, tumble 7 decline, descend, plummet 8 decrease

movement 4 part 5 drive, steps, works 6 action, effort, motion 7 crusade, measure, program, section 8 activity, division, gestures, maneuver, progress, stirring 9 agitation, execution, mechanism, operation 10 locomotion 11 undertaking

move out 5 leave 6 depart, vacate 8 evacuate

move quickly 3 fly, run 4 bolt, dash, race, rush, tear 5 hurry 6 hasten, sprint

move sideways 4 edge 5 sidle 8 sidestep

move slyly 4 edge, lurk 5 sidle, skulk, slink, sneak, steal

move up 5 boost, climb, heave, hoist, raise, scale 6 ascend, uplift 7 advance, elevate, promote, upraise

move upward 4 rise, soar 5 climb, mount 6 ascend 7 take off

movie 4 film, show 5 flick 6 cinema 7 feature, picture, showing 9 screening
  invented by:
    machine: 7 Jenkins
    panoramic: 6 Waller

projector: 6 Edison
talking: 14 Warner Brothers
moving 5 motor 6 mobile, motile 8 exciting, poignant, spurring, stirring, touching 9 affecting, inspiring 10 impressive, locomotive, motivating 11 interacting, stimulating
moving about 5 astir 6. active 7 on the go
Moving Target, A
author: 14 William Golding
Mowgli
character in: 14 The Jungle Books
author: 7 Kipling
moxie 4 grit, guts, sand 5 nerve, pluck, spunk 6 mettle, spirit 7 courage, stamina 8 audacity, backbone 9 hardihood, toughness 10 pluckiness 13 dauntlessness
moyen age 10 Middle Ages
Mozambique
capital/largest city: 6 Maputo 15 Lourenco Marques
others: 4 Tete 5 Beira, Pemba, Zumbo 6 Chemba, Nacala, Pafuri, Sofala 7 Nampula 8 Mutarara 9 Inhambane, Quelimane 11 Porto Amelia
school: 15 Eduardo Mondlane
monetary unit: 6 escudo 7 centavo, metical
island: 6 Inhaca 7 Angoche 8 Bazanuto 9 Benguerua
lake: 5 Nyasa 6 Chuali, Nyassa 8 Nhavarre
mountain: 7 Lebombo
highlands: 6 Namuli 9 Gorongosa
highest point: 5 Binga
river: 4 Buzi, Save 5 Lurio, Msalu 6 Rovuma, Ruvuma 7 Ligonha, Limpopo, Lugenda, Messaio, Zambezi 8 Changane
ocean: 6 Indian
physical feature:
cape: 7 Delgado
channel: 10 Mozambique
people: 3 Yao 5 Bantu, Chopi, Lomue, Lomwe, Macua, Makua, Ngoni, Nguni, Shona 6 Manica, Thouga 7 Maconde, Makonde 10 Portuguese
explorer: 11 Vasco de Gama
leader: 8 Chissano 9 Dos Santos 12 Samora Machel 15 Eduardo Mondlane
language: 3 Yao 5 Makua 6 Nyanji, Thonga 7 Swahili 10 Portuguese
religion: 5 Islam 7 animism 13 Roman Catholic
place:
game reserve: 8 Marromeu 9 Gorongosa, Gorongoza 18 Maputo Elephant Park
reservoir: 11 Cabora Bassa
feature:
bride price: 6 lobolo
Mozart, Wolfgang Amadeus
born: 7 Austria 8 Salzburg
composer of: 4 Linz (symphony No 36) 5 Paris (symphony No 31) 6 Prague (symphony No 38) 7 Don Juan, Haffner (symphony No 35), Jupiter (symphony No 41), Requiem, Turkish (concerto) 8 Idomeneo 9 Credo Mass, Mitridate 10

Lucio Silla 11 Don Giovanni, Hunt Quartet, Il Re Pastore, Sparrow Mass 12 A Musical Joke, Cosi Fan Tutte (So Do They All or Women Are Like That), Haydn Quartet, Spatzenmesse 13 The Magic Flute, Trumpet Sonata, Turkish Sonata 14 Coronation Mass, Stadler Quintet, Die Zauberflote 15 Haffner Serenade, La Finta Semplice, Prussian Quartet 16 Dissonant Quartet, La Clemenza di Tito, Posthorn Serenade, Serenata Notturna 17 A Little Night Music 18 Jeunehomme Concerto, La Finta Giardiniera, The Clemency of Titus 19 Bastien und Bastienne, The Marriage of Figaro 20 Eine Kleine Nachtmusik, The Pretender Gardener 21 Der Schauspieldirektor, Ein Musikalischer Spass 22 The Pretending Simpleton 25 Die Entfuhrung aus dem Serail 27 The Abduction from the Seraglio
Mr, Mister
Russian: 8 gospodin
French: 8 monsieur
Yiddish: 3 Reb
Mr B
character in: 6 Pamela
author: 10 Richardson
Mr Basketball
nickname of: 8 Bob Cousy
Mr Britling Sees It Through
author: 7 H G Wells
Mr Cub
nickname of: 10 Ernie Banks
Mr Deeds Goes to Town
director: 10 Frank Capra
cast: 10 Gary Cooper (Longfellow Deeds), Jean Arthur 14 George Bancroft
Mr Ed
character: 9 Carol Post 10 Kay Addison, Wilbur Post 12 Roger Addison 14 Gordon Kirkwood, Winnie Kirkwood
cast: 8 Leon Ames 9 Alan Young 11 Connie Hines, Edna Skinner 12 Larry Keating 18 Florence MacMichael
Mr Ed was: 12 talking horse
Mr Flood's Party
author: 22 Edwin Arlington Robinson
Mr Midnight
nickname of: 10 Steve Allen
Mr Peepers
character: 9 Mrs Gurney 11 Marge Weskit, Mr Remington 12 Harvey Weskit 14 Nancy Remington 15 Robinson Peepers 20 Superintendent Bascom
cast: 8 Wally Cox 9 Gage Clark 11 Ernest Truex, Marion Lorne, Tony Randall 14 Patricia Benoit 16 Georgiann Johnson
Mr Peepers taught: 7 science
school: 13 Jefferson High
Mr Sammler's Planet
author: 10 Saul Bellow
Mrs Dalloway
author: 13 Virginia Woolf
character: 10 Miss Kilman, Peter Walsh, Sally Seton 15 Richard Dalloway 16 Clarissa Dalloway 17 Elizabeth Dalloway

Mrs Miniver
 director: 12 William Wyler
 cast: 11 Greer Garson 12 Teresa Wright
 13 Dame May Whitty, Walter Pidgeon
 Oscar for: 7 actress (Garson), picture 8
 director 17 supporting actress (Wright)

Mr Smith Goes to Washington
 director: 10 Frank Capra
 cast: 9 Guy Kibbee 10 Jean Arthur 11
 Claude Rains 12 Edward Arnold, James
 Stewart 14 Thomas Mitchell

Mrs Parkington
 author: 14 Louis Bromfield

Mrs Stevens Hears the Mermaids Singing
 author: 9 May Sarton

Mrs Warren's Profession
 author: 17 George Bernard Shaw

Mr Television
 nickname of: 11 Milton Berle

much 3 far 4 a lot, lots 5 about, ample,
 heaps, loads, often 6 almost, indeed,
 nearly, overly, rather, scores 7 copious,
 greatly 8 abundant, good deal, plenty of,
 quantity, somewhat, striking 9 decidedly,
 important, plenteous, plentiful, regularly 10
 frequently, impressive, noteworthy, oftentimes, satisfying, sufficient, worthwhile 11
 appreciable, exceedingly, excessively, sufficiency 12 considerable 13 approximately,
 consequential

Much Ado About Nothing
 author: 18 William Shakespeare
 character: 4 Hero 7 Claudio, Don John,
 Leonato 8 Beatrice, Benedick, Dogberry,
 Don Pedro

much in little
 Latin: 12 multum in parvo

much loved 4 dear 7 beloved, darling,
 dearest 8 precious 9 cherished, treasured

mucilage 3 gum 4 glue 5 paste 6 cement 8
 adhesive

mucilaginous 5 gluey, gummy, gunky 6
 gloppy, sticky 8 adhesive

muck 3 mud 4 dirt, dung, gunk, mire, ooze,
 slop 5 filth, slime 6 sewage, sludge 7 compost, garbage

muck up 4 soil 5 dirty, muddy 7 pollute

mud 4 dirt, muck, soil, wire

Mudcat State
 nickname of: 11 Mississippi

muddied 5 dirty, grimy 6 grubby, soiled 7
 stained 8 begrimed, confused

muddle 3 fog 4 blow, daze, haze, mess,
 muff, ruin 5 botch, chaos, mix up, spoil,
 throw 6 boggle, bungle, fumble, goof up,
 jumble, mess up, pother, rattle 7 blunder,
 clutter, confuse, nonplus, stupefy 8 bewilder, confound, disarray, disorder 13 dis-
 concertion 14 disarrangement

muddlebrained 5 inept 7 witless 8 confused 11 lamebrained

muddled 5 fuzzy 7 bemused 8 confused 10
 bewildered

muddy 4 dull 5 dirty, grimy, vague 6 filthy,
 grubby 7 obscure 8 begrimed, confused

muff 5 botch, spoil 6 bungle 10 hand-
 warmer

muffle 3 gag 4 dull, hush, mask, mute, veil,
 wrap 5 cloak, cover, quell, quiet, still 6
 dampen, deaden, shroud, soften, stifle,
 swathe 7 conceal, enclose, envelop, silence, swaddle

muffled 3 low 4 dull, soft 5 faint, muted 6
 dulled, feeble, hushed, veiled 7 cloaked,
 covered, quelled, quieted, stilled, subdued,
 swathed, wrapped 8 deadened, shrouded,
 silenced, softened, swaddled 9 concealed,
 enveloped, inaudible 10 indistinct, suppressed

mug 3 cup 4 face, puss, toby 5 stein, stoup
 6 beaker, flagon, goblet, kisser, visage 7
 chalice, tankard, toby jug, tumbler 11
 countenance

mugger 8 assailer, attacker 9 assailant, assaulter

mugginess 4 damp 8 dampness, dankness, humidity 9 humidness 10 sultriness
 14 oppressiveness

muggy 5 close, humid 6 clammy, steamy,
 sticky, stuffy, sultry, sweaty 8 steaming, vaporous 10 oppressive, sweltering

Muisca see 6 Chibcha

mulberry 5 Morus
 varieties: 3 red 4 Aino 5 black, paper,
 white 6 French, Indian 7 Russian 8 American, silkworm

Mulciber
 epithet of: 6 Vulcan
 means: 6 melter

mulct 4 bilk 6 extort 7 defraud, swindle

mule 3 ass 5 burro 6 donkey 7 jackass
 group of: 4 span

mulish 5 balky 6 ornery 8 perverse, stubborn 9 fractious, obstinate 10 refractory 11
 intractable 12 recalcitrant

Mulius
 wife: 7 Agamede
 father-in-law: 6 Augeas
 position: 8 spearman
 killed by: 6 Nestor

mull, mull over 5 study, weigh 6 ponder 8
 consider, meditate, pore over, ruminate 10
 deliberate

Muller
 character in: 25 All Quiet on the Western Front
 author: 8 Remarque

Muller, Hermann Joseph
 field: 8 genetics
 researched: 5 X-rays 8 mutation
 awarded: 10 Nobel Prize

Muller, Paul
 field: 9 chemistry
 nationality: 5 Swiss
 established: 16 DDT as insecticide
 awarded: 10 Nobel Prize

Mulligan, Buck
 character in: 7 Ulysses
 author: 5 Joyce

multicolored 10 variegated

multifarious 4 many 5 mixed 6 divers, motley, sundry, varied 7 diverse, protean, several, various 8 manifold, numerous 9 different, multiplex 10 variegated 11 diversified 13 heterogeneous, miscellaneous

multiple 4 many 7 various 8 manifold

multiply 5 add to, beget, breed, raise 6 extend, spread 7 augment, enhance, enlarge, magnify 8 generate, heighten, increase 9 intensify, procreate, propagate, reproduce 11 proliferate

multitude 3 mob 4 army, herd, host, mass, pack, slew 5 array, crowd, crush, drove, flock, flood, horde, troop 6 legion, myriad, scores, throng 7 conflux

multum in parvo 12 much in little 23 a great deal in a small space

mum 4 mute 5 quiet, still, tacit 6 silent 8 taciturn, wordless 9 secretive 12 closemouthed 15 uncommunicative

mumble 5 growl, grunt, mouth 6 murmur, mutter, rumble 7 stammer 9 hem and haw

mumbo jumbo 3 rot 4 blah, bosh, cant, tosh 5 bilge, hokum, hooey, tripe 6 hot air, humbug 7 baloney 8 flummery 9 gibberish, sophistry 10 double talk, hocus pocus 11 doublespeak, jabberwocky, obfuscation 12 fiddle-faddle, gobbledygook, obscurantism

Mummy, The
   director: 10 Karl Freund
   cast: 10 Zita Johann 12 Boris Karloff, David Manners 16 Bramwell Fletcher

munch 4 chew, gnaw 5 champ, chomp, crush, grind 9 masticate

Munch, Edvard
   born: 5 Loten 6 Norway 10 Hedemarken
   artwork: 6 The Cry 7 Puberty, The Kiss 9 The Scream 11 Dance of Life 12 Frieze of Life 21 Death in the Sick Chamber

Munchkins
   characters in: 13 The Wizard of Oz
   author: 4 Baum

mundane 5 petty 7 earthly, humdrum, prosaic, routine, worldly 8 day-to-day, everyday, ordinary 9 practical 10 pedestrian 11 commonplace, down-to-earth, terrestrial

Muni, Paul
   real name: 16 Muni Weisenfreund
   born: 7 Austria, Lemberg (now Lvov USSR)
   roles: 8 Juarez 8 Scarface 10 The Valiant 12 The Good Earth 14 Clarence Darrow, Inherit the Wind 15 The Last Angry Man 18 The Life of Emile Zola 22 The Story of Louis Pasteur (Oscar) 26 I Am a Fugitive from a Chain Gang

municipal 4 city 5 civic 6 public 9 community 14 administrative

municipality 4 city, town 6 parish 7 village 8 township 9 bailiwick

munificence 6 bounty 7 charity 8 largesse 9 patronage 10 generosity, liberality 11 benefaction, beneficence, benevolence 12 philanthropy 13 bounteousness, bountifulness 14 charitableness 15 humanitarianism

munificent 4 free 6 kindly, lavish 7 liberal, profuse 8 generous, princely 9 bounteous, bountiful 10 altruistic, beneficent, benevolent, charitable, freehanded, open-handed 11 extravagant, magnanimous 12 eleemosynary, humanitarian 13 philanthropic

Munin
   origin: 12 Scandinavian
   form: 5 raven
   owned by: 4 Odin 5 Othin
   personifies: 6 memory
   duty: 10 newsbearer
   other raven: 5 Hugin

Munitus
   father: 6 Acamas
   mother: 7 Laodice

Munsters, The
   character: 11 Lily Munster 12 Eddie (Edward Wolfgang) Munster 13 Herman Munster 14 Grandpa Munster, Marilyn Munster
   cast: 7 Al Lewis 9 Pat Priest 10 Fred Gwynne 11 Beverly Owen 12 Butch Patrick 13 Yvonne DeCarlo

Muppet Show, The
   character: 4 Rolf 5 Gonzo 6 Animal, Beaker 7 Scooter 9 Miss Piggy 10 Fozzie Bear 13 Kermit the Frog (Kermie)

Murasaki, Lady
   author of: 14 The Tale of Genji

murder 4 kill, slay 5 abuse, waste 6 mangle, misuse 7 butcher, corrupt, cut down, killing 8 homicide, knock off 9 agonizing, slaughter 10 bastardize, formidable, impossible, oppressive, unbearable 11 assassinate, intolerable 12 manslaughter 13 assassination, very difficult 14 commit homicide, use incorrectly

Murder, She Wrote
   character: 15 Jessica (JB) Fletcher
   cast: 14 Angela Lansbury
   setting: 9 Cabot Cove

murderer 4 Cain 6 killer, slayer 7 butcher 8 assassin, Barabbas, homicide 9 cutthroat

Murder in the Cathedral
   author: 7 T S Eliot

Murder of Roger Ackroyd, The
   author: 14 Agatha Christie

Murder on the Orient Express
   author: 14 Agatha Christie

murderous 4 gory 5 cruel, rough 6 bloody, brutal, deadly, savage, trying 7 killing 9 dangerous, difficult, ferocious 11 devastating 12 bloodthirsty, disagreeable

Murdoch, Iris
   author of: 7 The Bell 11 Under the Net 12 A Severed Head, The Sea the Sea 14 The Black Prince 15 Nuns and Soldiers 17 The Good Apprentice, The Nice and the Good 20 The Philosopher's Pupil 24 The Book and The Brotherhood 30 The Sacred and Profane Love Machine

Murdstone, Mr
   character in: 16 David Copperfield
   author: 7 Dickens

Murillo, Bartolome (Bartolomeo) Esteban
  born: 5 Spain 7 Seville
  artwork: 13 Angels' Kitchen 14 Death of
    St Clare 15 The Two Trinities 17 Vision of
    St Anthony 23 The Immaculate Concep-
    tion 24 Dream of the Roman Patrician
murk 3 fog 4 haze, mist 5 gloom 6 miasma
  8 darkness
murky 3 dim 4 dark, gray, hazy 5 dusky,
  foggy, misty 6 cloudy, dismal, dreary,
  gloomy, somber 7 obscure, sunless 8 lowering, overcast, vaporous 9 cheerless
murmur 3 hum 4 buzz, purl, purr, sigh 5
  drone, sough, swish 6 lament, mumble,
  mutter, rumble, rustle 7 grumble, lapping,
  whimper, whisper 8 low sound, susurrus 9
  complaint, undertone
murophobia
  fear of: 4 mice
Murphy, Eddie
  roles: 3 Raw 13 Trading Places 14 The
    Golden Child 15 Coming to America,
    Forty-Eight Hours 16 Beverly Hills Cop
    17 Saturday Night Live 19 Beverly Hills
    Cop Two
Murray, Bill
  roles: 7 Stripes 9 Meatballs 10 Caddy-
    shack 12 Ghostbusters 13 The Razor's
    Edge 17 Saturday Night Live 27 Not
    Ready for Prime Time Players
Murray, Don
  wife: 9 Hope Lange
  born: 11 Hollywood CA
  roles: 7 Bus Stop 13 A Hatful of Rain 16
    The Bachelor Party, The Hoodlum Priest
Murray, Jeanne
  real name of: 13 Jean Stapleton
Murray, Mina
  character in: 7 Dracula
  author: 6 Stoker
Musaeus
  occupation: 4 poet, seer
Musagetes see 6 Apollo
Muscat, Masqat
  capital of: 4 Oman
muscle 4 grit, thew 5 bicep, brawn, force,
  might, power, sinew, vigor 6 energy, flexor,
  tendon 7 potency, prowess, stamina 8 virility 9 puissance 10 sturdiness 16 muscular
  strength
  kind: 4 limb 5 axial 6 smooth 7 dynamic,
    flexors, special, striped 8 postural, stri-
    ated 9 abductors, extensors, voluntary 11
    involuntary
  fuel: 4 food
  action: 4 pull
  specific: 6 rectus 7 deltoid, oblique 8
    omohyoid 9 abdominal, abdominis, sarto-
    rius 10 pectoralis 11 intercostal, sternohy-
    oid 13 biceps brachii, rectus femoris 14
    vastus medialis 15 brachioradialis, vastus
    lateralis 16 serratus anterior, tensor fas-
    cia lata 17 quadriceps femoris 18 trans-
    verse thoracic 19 sternocleidomastoid 20
    transversus abdominis
  supplementary structure: 6 sheath 10

deep fascia, retinacula 14 synovial bur-
  sae, synovial sheath
muscular 3 fit 5 burly, husky, tough 6
  brawny, sinewy, strong 8 athletic, powerful
  9 strapping
muscular contraction 5 cramp, crick,
  spasm 6 stitch 12 charley horse
musculoskeletal system
  component: 4 bone 6 muscle, tendon 8
    ligament
muse 4 mull 6 ponder, review 7 reflect 8
  cogitate, consider, meditate, ruminate 9
  speculate 10 deliberate 11 contemplate
Musee des Beaux Arts
  author: 7 W H Auden
Muses
  also: 7 the Nine 8 Pierides 10 Castalides
  form: 9 goddesses
  names: 4 Clio 5 Aoede, Erato, Mneme 6
    Melete, Thalia, Urania 7 Euterpe 8 Calli-
    ope 9 Melpomene 10 Polyhymnia 11
    Terpsichore
  father: 4 Zeus
  mother: 9 Mnemosyne
  corresponds to: 7 Camenae
Musgrave, Thea
  born: 8 Scotland 9 Edinburgh
  composer of: 11 The Decision 16 The
    Five Ages of Man 17 Beauty and the
    Beast, The Voice of Ariadne
mush 5 slush 6 drivel 8 porridge 14 sentimentalism, sentimentality
mushiness 5 slush 6 bathos 10 sponginess 11 mawkishness 14 sentimentalism,
  sentimentality
mushroom 4 grow 5 burst, fungi 6 blow up,
  expand, fungus, spread, sprout 7 burgeon,
  explode, shoot up 8 flourish, increase,
  spring up 9 toadstool 11 proliferate
  part: 3 cap 4 veil 5 gills, stalk, tubes,
    volva 6 button, hyphae, spores 7 annu-
    lus, basidia 10 rhizomorph
  non-poisonous: 5 field, honey, morel,
    table 6 oyster 7 inky cap, parasol 8 puff-
    ball, shiitake 9 fairy-ring, morchella,
    shaggy cap, stinkhorn 10 champignon 11
    chanterelle 12 edible bolete, slippery jack
    16 old man of the woods
  poisonous: 7 amanita 8 death cap, sick-
    ener 9 fly agaric 12 jack-o-lantern 13 dev-
    il's boletus 15 destroying angel
  study of: 8 mycology
mushy 4 soft 5 foggy, misty, pappy, pulpy,
  vague 6 cloudy, quaggy, spongy 7 maudlin, mawkish, squashy, squishy 8 effusive,
  romantic, squelchy 10 lovey-dovey 11 sentimental, tear-jerking 12 affectionate
Musial, Stan
  nickname: 10 Stan the Man
  sport: 8 baseball
  team: 16 St Louis Cardinals
music 4 song, tune 5 score 6 melody 7 euphony, harmony 8 lyricism 10 minstrelsy
  11 tunefulness 13 melodiousness
  god of: 5 Brage, Bragi 6 Apollo 7 Phoe-
    bus, Pythius 9 Musagetes

musical 5 lyric, sweet 6 dulcet 7 lilting, lyrical, melodic, tuneful 9 melodious 10 euphonious, harmonious 11 mellifluent

musical instrument 3 lur, sax, saz 4 bass, bell, drum, fife, gong, harp, horn, lute, lyre, oboe, outi, pipe, tuba, viol 5 argul, banjo, bugle, cello, cobza, flute, kazoo, organ, piano, guena, rabob, sansa, shawm, sheng, sitar, viola 6 bagana, chimes, cornet, cymbal, fiddle, guitar, spinet, treble, violin, zither 7 bagpipe, bassoon, cittern, clavier, kithara, marimba, panpipe, pibcorn, piccolo, samisen, strings, tambura, theorbo, timpani, trumpet, ukulele 8 autoharp, bass drum, calliope, clarinet, dulcimer, Jew's harp, mandolin, psaltery, recorder, talharpa, triangle, trombone, virginal 9 accordion, balalaika, castanets, harmonica, harmonium, krummhorn, rommelpot, saxophone, snare drum, xylophone 10 bongo drums, clavichord, concertina, flugelhorn, French horn, kettledrum, sousaphone, tambourine, vibraphone 11 English horn, harpsichord 12 jouhikantele
  classification: 4 horn, reed, wind 5 brass 6 string 8 keyboard, woodwind 10 electronic, percussion

musical terms
  agitated: 7 agitato
  all players/singers together: 5 tutti
  becoming quicker: 11 accelerando
  continue without a break: 5 segue
  disconnected/each note separate: 8 staccato
  end: 4 fine
  expressively: 10 espressivo
  abbreviation: 4 espr
  fast: 6 veloce 7 allegro
  gentle: 5 soave
  gently: 9 doucement
  getting slower: 10 allargando
  getting weaker and slower: 7 calando
  gradually getting louder: 9 crescendo
  abbreviation: 5 cresc
  gradually getting softer: 10 diminuendo 11 decrescendo
  abbreviation: 3 dim 4 decr
  gradually slowing: 11 rallentando
  abbreviation: 4 rall
  half: 5 mezzo
  half voice/half volume: 9 mezza voce
  heavy: 5 lourd
  in an undertone/in a low voice: 9 sotto voce
  leisurely: 6 comodo
  less: 4 meno
  light: 8 leggiero
  little: 4 poco
  lively: 3 vif
  loud: 5 forte
  abbreviation: 1 f
  moderately slow and even: 7 andante
  more: 3 piu
  mournful: 5 mesto
  not too much: 9 non troppo
  plucked instead of bowed: 9 pizzicato
  abbreviation: 4 pizz

  quick/vivacious: 6 vivace
  repeat from beginning: 6 da capo
  abbreviation: 2 D C
  shaking and quavering/rapid alternation of notes: 5 trill
  silent: 4 tace
  singing/songlike/flowing: 9 cantabile
  sliding: 9 glissando
  slow: 5 lento 6 adagio
  slow dignified tempo: 5 largo
  slow down: 5 cedez
  smooth/connected: 6 legato
  soft: 5 piano
  abbreviation: 1 p
  solemn/serious: 5 grave
  sorrowful: 7 dolente
  strict time: 10 tempo gusto
  sudden accent: 9 sforzando
  abbreviation: 2 sf
  sweetly: 5 dolce
  tearful: 9 lacrimoso
  tenderly: 9 affettuoso
  trembling vibrating effect/rapid reiteration of a single pitch: 7 tremolo
  very: 5 molto
  very loud: 10 fortissimo
  abbreviation: 2 ff
  very soft: 10 pianissimo
  abbreviation: 2 pp
  with fire: 8 con fuoco
  with spirit/vigor: 7 con brio
  with style/taste: 8 con gusto
  with the mute: 10 con sordino

musician 4 bard 5 piper 6 artist, player, singer, violer 7 bandman, cellist, drummer, pianist, twanger 8 minstrel, organist, virtuoso 9 performer, trumpeter, violinist 11 saxophonist

Music Man, The
  director: 13 Morton Da Costa
  cast: 12 Buddy Hackett, Shirley Jones (Marian the librarian) 13 Robert Preston (Professor Harold Hill) 15 Hermione Gingold
  setting: 9 River City
  score: 15 Meredith Willson
  song: 15 Till There Was You 19 Seventy-six Trombones

music school 12 conservatory
  French: 13 conservatoire

musing 6 absent, dreamy 7 mulling 8 absorbed 9 pondering 10 meditating, meditative, reflecting, reflective

musjid 6 mosque

Muskogean, Muskhogean
  tribe: 4 Cree 7 Alabama, Alibamu, Choctaw, Natchez 8 Seminole 9 Chickasaw

Muslim *see* 6 Moslem

muslin
  French: 10 mousseline

muss 4 mess 6 foul up, jumble, ruffle, rumple, tangle, tousle 7 crumple, disturb 8 dishevel, disorder 9 bedraggle 10 disarrange

mussed 5 messy 6 frowzy, untidy 7 ruffled, rumpled, tousled, unkempt 8 uncombed 10 disarrayed, disheveled, disordered, disorderly 11 disarranged

Mussorgsky (Moussorgsky), Modest Petrovich
  born: 5 Pskov 6 Russia
  member of: 7 The Five
  composer of: 7 Sunless 10 The Nursery 12 Boris Godunov 13 Khovanshchina 19 Night on Bald Mountain 21 Songs and Dances of Death 22 Pictures at an Exhibition

mustard
  botanical name: 5 B alba 6 B hirta, B nigra 7 B juncea 8 Brassica
  also called: 7 sinapis
  origin: 4 Asia 5 China
  use: 6 hotdog, sauces 7 egg roll 9 hamburger 13 salad dressing

muster 4 call 5 amass, raise, rally 6 gather, line up, summon 7 collect, company, convene, convoke, marshal, meeting, round up, turnout 8 assemble, assembly, mobilize 9 convocate, gathering 10 assemblage, confluence, congregate, inspection 11 aggregation 12 accumulation 13 agglomeration

musty 3 old 4 damp, dank, worn 5 banal, dirty, dusty, moldy, stale, tired, trite 6 frousy, frouzy, frowsy, frowzy, old hat, stuffy 7 worn-out 8 familiar, mildewed 9 hackneyed 10 antiquated, threadbare 11 commonplace

mutable 6 fickle 7 pliable 8 flexible, variable 9 adaptable, alterable, mercurial, versatile 10 adjustable, changeable, inconstant, modifiable, permutable 11 convertible, metamorphic 13 transformable

mutate 4 turn 5 alter 6 change 7 convert 9 transform

mutation 6 change 7 anomaly 9 deviation, variation 10 alteration 12 modification 13 metamorphosis 14 transformation 15 transfiguration 18 transmogrification

mutatis mutandis 30 necessary changes having been made

mute 3 mum 4 dumb 5 quiet, tacit 6 silent 8 aphasiac, nonvocal, reserved, reticent 9 unsounded, unuttered, voiceless 10 speechless 12 inarticulate, noncommittal, unpronounced 13 unarticulated 15 uncommunicative

muted 3 dim, low 4 dull, soft, weak 5 quiet 6 dulled, feeble 7 muffled 8 deadened, softened 10 indistinct, lackluster

mutilate 4 lame, maim 6 cut off, deform, excise, mangle 7 butcher, cripple 8 amputate, lacerate, truncate 9 disfigure, dismember

mutineer 5 rebel 9 dissident, insurgent 10 malcontent 15 insurrectionist

mutinous 6 unruly 10 dissenting, rebellious 13 revolutionary

Mutinus
  origin: 5 Roman 7 Italian
  god of: 9 fertility
  fertility in: 8 marriage
  corresponds to: 7 Priapus

mutiny 4 coup 5 rebel 6 revolt, rise up 8 takeover, upheaval, uprising 9 overthrow, rebellion 10 insurgency 12 insurrection

Mutiny on the Bounty
  author: 15 Charles Nordhoff, James Norman Hall
  character: 6 Tehani 9 Roger Byam 12 William Bligh (Captain Bligh) 13 George Stewart 17 Fletcher Christian
  director: 10 Frank Lloyd
  cast: 10 Clark Gable (Fletcher Christian) 12 Eddie Quillan, Franchot Tone 13 Herbert Mundin 15 Charles Laughton (Captain Bligh)
  Oscar for: 7 picture

mutt 3 cur, dog, pup 5 puppy 7 mongrel

Mutt and Jeff
  creator: 7 Al Smith 9 Bud Fisher
  character: 5 A Mutt 6 Cicero 7 Mrs Mutt

mutter 4 carp 5 gripe, growl, grunt 6 grouch, grouse, kvetch, mumble, murmur, rumble 7 grumble, whisper 8 complain

mutual 5 joint 6 common, shared 7 related 8 communal, returned 10 coincident, reciprocal 11 correlative, interactive

mutual understanding 6 accord 9 agreement

muzzle 3 gag 4 bind, curb 5 check, quiet, still 6 bridle, rein in, stifle 7 harness, silence 8 strangle, suppress, throttle

Myanmar
  former name: 5 Burma
  other name: 16 Land of the Pagodas
  capital: 6 Yangon 7 Rangoon
  ancient capital: 3 Ava 4 Pegu 8 Mandalay
  largest city: 7 Rangoon
  others: 2 Ye 3 Ava 4 Pegu 5 Akyab, Bhamo, Katha, Minbu, Namtu, Papun, Prome, Tavoy 6 Hsenwi, Hsipaw, Lashio, Maymyo, Monywa, Shwebo 7 Bassein, Henzada, Pakokku, Toungoo 8 Moulmein, Myingyan
  measure: 2 ly 3 dha, gon, mau, sao, tao, tat 4 byee, phan, seit, taun, that 5 shita, thuoc 6 lamany, palgat 7 chaivai 8 okthabah
  monetary unit: 3 pya 4 kyat
  weight: 2 ta 3 can, pai, vis 4 binh, kyat, ruay, viss 5 behar, candy, ticul 6 abucco 7 peiktha
  lake: 4 Inle
  mountain: 4 Chin, Naga, Pegu, Popa 5 Davna 6 Arakan, Kachin, Lushai, Patkai 7 Karenni 8 Nattaung, Peguyoma, Saramati, Victoria 10 Tenasserim 11 Manipur Hill 12 Tanen Taunggi
  highest point: 11 Hkakabo Razi
  river: 3 Hka 6 Salwin, Sutang 7 Irawadi, Kaladan, Myitnge, Salween, Schweli, Sittang 8 Chindwin, Indawgyi 9 Irrawaddy
  sea: 7 Andaman

physical feature:
bay: 4 Siam 6 Bengal, Hunter 7 Heanzay 8 Thailand
gulf: 8 Martaban
plateau: 4 Shan
port: 5 Akyab 7 Bassein, Henzada 8 Moulmein
people: 2 Ao, Vu, Wa 3 Kaw, Lai, Lao, Mon, Pyu, Tai, Was 4 Akha, Chin, Juki, Kadu, Laos, Lolo, Miao, Naga, Sema, Shan, Thai, Tsin 5 Karen, Lhota 6 Birman, Burman, Kachin, Peguan, Rengma 7 Akhlame, Burmese, Kakhyen, Palauna, Palaung, Siamese 8 Mon-Khmer 9 Arakanese 12 Tibeto-Berman
language: 3 Lai 4 Chin, Kuki, Pegu, Shan 5 Karen 6 Kachin 7 Burmese, English
religion: 5 Hindu, Islam 8 Buddhism 12 Christianity
place:
mines: 6 Mawchi 7 Bawdwin
pagoda: 9 Shwe Dagon
road: 4 Ledo 5 Burma 9 Stillwell
feature:
ball game: 7 chin-lon
festival: 5 Water 6 Lights 10 Thadin-gyut
silk head band: 10 gaungbaung
skirt: 6 longyi
traveling theatrical group: 4 Pwes

My Antonia
author: 11 Willa Cather
character: 9 Jim Burden 15 Antonia Shimerda

My Darling Clementine
director: 8 John Ford
cast: 7 Tim Holt 8 Ward Bond 10 Henry Fonda (Wyatt Earp) 12 Linda Darnell, Victor Mature (Doc Holliday) 13 Walter Brennan

my dear
French: 7 ma chere, mon cher

My Fair Lady
director: 11 George Cukor
based on play by: 17 George Bernard Shaw (Pygmalion)
cast: 11 Rex Harrison (Professor Henry Higgins) 13 Audrey Hepburn (Eliza Doolittle) 15 Stanley Holloway 16 Wilfrid Hyde-White
score: 14 Lerner and Loewe
Oscar for: 7 picture
song: 14 The Rain in Spain 24 I Could Have Danced All Night

my faith
French: 5 ma foi

my fault
Latin: 8 mea culpa

My Favorite Martian
character: 8 Tim O'Hara 11 Uncle Martin 15 Mrs Lorelei Brown
cast: 9 Bill Bixby 10 Ray Walston 13 Pamela Britton

Mygdon
king of: 8 Bebryces
killed by: 8 Hercules

Myles
king of: 7 Laconia
invented: 9 grain mill

Mylitta *see* 6 Ishtar

My Little Margie
character: 7 Charlie 9 Mrs Odetts 11 Mr Honeywell 13 Freddie Wilson 14 Margie Albright, Vernon Albright 15 Roberta Townsend
cast: 9 Don Hayden, Gale Storm 10 Willie Best 12 Clarence Kolb 13 Hillary Brooke 14 Charles Farrell 15 Gertrude Hoffman

my lord
French: 8 monsieur 11 monseigneur
Italian: 9 monsignor 10 monsignore

My Man Godfrey
director: 13 Gregory La Cava
cast: 10 Alice Brady, Mischa Auer 11 Gail Patrick 13 Carole Lombard, William Powell

Mynes
king of: 9 Lyrnessus
wife: 7 Briseis
killed by: 8 Achilles

myriad 6 untold 7 endless 8 infinite, manifold 9 boundless, countless, limitless, uncounted 11 innumerable, measureless 12 immeasurable, incalculable 13 multitudinous

Myrina
husband: 8 Dardanus

myrmidon 6 cohort 8 follower, henchman

Myrmidons
people of: 6 Aegina 8 Thessaly
created by: 4 Zeus
created from: 4 ants
characteristic: 7 warlike
leader: 6 Peleus 8 Achilles

Myrrha
also: 6 Smyrna
father: 11 King Cinyras
loved: 7 Cinyras
crime: 6 incest
son: 6 Adonis
changed into: 6 myrtle 9 myrrh tree

Myrtilus
charioteer of: 8 Oenomaus

myrtle 6 Myrtus 10 Vinca minor 14 Myrtus communis 18 Cyrilla racemiflora 23 Umbellularia californica
varieties: 3 bog, gum, sea, wax 4 cape, Jew's, sand 5 crape, crepe, downy, dwarf, Greek, honey, scent 6 German, Oregon, Polish, willow 7 box sand, classic, running, Swedish 10 Western tea 11 candleberry, Queen's crape, sandverbena 13 Allegheny sand, bracelet honey, California wax 16 Australian willow

Mysia
epithet of: 7 Demeter

mysophobia
fear of: 4 dirt

Mysteries of Paris, The
author: 9 Eugene Sue

Mysteries of Udolpho, The
author: 15 Mrs Ann Radcliffe

mysterious 4 dark **6** cloudy, covert, hidden, secret **7** cryptic, obscure, strange, unknown **8** baffling, puzzling **9** enigmatic, secretive **10** perplexing, sphinxlike, undercover **11** clandestine, inscrutable **12** impenetrable, inexplicable, supernatural, unfathomable **13** surreptitious **14** undecipherable

Mysterious Stranger, The
  author: **9** Mark Twain

mystery 6 enigma, occult, puzzle, riddle, secret **7** problem, secrecy **9** conundrum, obscurity, symbolism, vagueness **11** ambivalence, elusiveness **12** ineffability, quizzicality **13** ineffableness, mystification

Mystery of Edwin Drood, The see **10** Edwin Drood

mystical, mystic 5 inner **6** hidden, occult **7** cryptic, obscure **8** abstruse, esoteric, ethereal, symbolic **9** enigmatic, secretive **10** cabalistic, symbolical, unknowable **11** inscrutable, nonrational **12** metaphysical, otherworldly **14** transcendental

mystification 9 confusion **10** bafflement, perplexity, puzzlement **12** bewilderment

mystify 4 fool **5** elude **6** baffle, puzzle **7** confuse, deceive, mislead, perplex **8** bewilder, confound **9** bamboozle

myth 3 fib, lie **4** tale, yarn **5** error, fable, story **6** canard, legend **7** fantasy, fiction, hearsay, parable **8** allegory, delusion, illusion, tall tale **9** fairy tale, falsehood **10** shibboleth **13** prevarication

mythical, mythic 6 fabled, unreal **8** illusory **9** imaginary, legendary, pretended **10** conjured-up, fabricated, fantasized, fictitious **13** unsubstantial

mythological, mythologic 6 unreal **8** fabulous, illusory, imagined **9** fantastic, imaginary, legendary, unfactual **10** fictitious

My Three Sons
  character: **11** Chip Douglas, Mike Douglas **12** Steve Douglas **13** Robbie Douglas **18** Katie Miller Douglas, Uncle Charley O'Casey **20** Ernie Thompson Douglas, Michael Francis (Bub) O'Casey
  cast: **8** Don Grady, Tina Cole **12** Tim Considine **13** Fred MacMurray **14** William Frawley **15** Barry Livingston, William Demarest **17** Stanley Livingston
  dog: **5** Tramp

my word
  French: **5** ma foi

N

nab 4 bust, grab, nail, snag 5 catch, pinch, seize, snare 6 arrest, collar, detain, haul in, pick up, pull in, snatch 7 capture 9 apprehend

nabob 4 lord 5 mogul, nawab 6 deputy, tycoon 7 magnate 8 governor 9 plutocrat 10 capitalist 11 billionaire, millionaire

Nabokov, Vladimir
   author of: 3 Ada 6 Lolita 8 Pale Fire

Nabonidus
   son: 10 Belshazzar

Nadab
   father: 5 Aaron 6 Gibeon 7 Shammai 8 Jeroboam
   mother: 8 Elisheba
   brother: 5 Abihu 7 Eleazar, Ithamar

nadir 4 base, zero 5 floor 6 apogee, bottom 7 nothing 8 low point 10 rock bottom 11 lowest point

Nadja
   author: 11 Andre Breton

nag 4 fury, goad, harp 5 annoy, devil, harpy, scold, shrew, vixen 6 badger, bicker, harass, hassle, heckle, hector, nettle, peck at, pester, pick at, pick on, plague, rail at, tartar, virago 7 bedevil, upbraid 8 battle-ax, irritate 9 importune, termagant, Xanthippe

Nahua *see* 5 Aztec

Nahuatl *see* 10 Uto-Aztecan

Naiad
   form: 5 nymph
   location: 5 water

nail 3 fix, pin 4 claw 5 talon 6 fasten, hammer, secure
   part: 3 bed 4 root

Naipaul, V S
   author of: 10 Guerrillas 15 A Bend in the River 17 A House for Mr Biswas 19 The Return of Eva Peron, The Suffrage of Elvira

Nairobi
   capital of: 5 Kenya

naive 4 open 5 green, plain 6 candid, simple, unwary, unwise 7 artless, foolish, natural, unjaded 8 gullible, immature, innocent 9 childlike, credulous, guileless, ingenuous, unspoiled, unworldly 10 unaffected, unassuming 11 susceptible 12 unsuspecting, unsuspicious 15 unsophisticated

naivete, naivete 6 candor 7 modesty 8 openness 9 credulity, frankness, greenness, innocence, sincerity 10 callowness, simplicity 11 artlessness, foolishness, naturalness 12 childishness, inexperience 13 ingenuousness 14 unaffectedness 16 simplemindedness

naked 4 bald, bare, nude, pure 5 bared, frank, plain, sheer 6 patent, simple, unclad 7 blatant, exposed 8 disrobed, laid bare, manifest, palpable, undraped, wide-open 9 in the buff, unclothed, uncovered, undressed 11 perceptible, unapparelled, unqualified, unvarnished 15 in the altogether

Naked and the Dead, The
   author: 12 Norman Mailer

Naked City
   character: 5 Libby 9 (Det) Adam Flint 10 (Det Lt) Dan Muldoon, (Lt) Mike Parker 11 (Det) Jim Halloran, (Ptlm/Sgt) Frank Arcaro 13 Janet Halloran
   cast: 9 Paul Burke 11 Nancy Malone 12 John McIntire 13 Harry Bellaver, Horace McMahon, Suzanne Storrs 15 James Franciscus
   setting: 11 New York City
   theme: 19 Somewhere in the Night

Namath, Joe (Joseph William)
   nickname: 11 Broadway Joe
   sport: 8 football
   position: 11 quarterback
   team: 11 New York Jets

namby-pamby 3 coy 4 dull, prim, weak 5 banal, inane, vapid 6 prissy 7 insipid, mincing, sapless 9 colorless, innocuous, simpering 10 indecisive, wishy-washy 13 characterless

name 3 tag 4 call, term 5 label, title 6 choose, ordain, select 7 appoint, baptize, epithet, specify 8 christen, cognomen, delegate, deputize, nominate, taxonomy 9 authorize, designate, signature, sobriquet 10 commission 11 appellation, designation 12 denomination, nomenclature

nameless 5 minor 7 obscure, unknown, unnamed 8 untitled 9 anonymous, unheard-of, unhonored 12 undesignated

namely
   Latin: 3 viz 9 videlicet

Name of the Game
   character: 8 Andy Hill 9 Joe Sample, Ross Craig 10 Dan Farrell, Jeff Dillon 11 Glenn Howard 12 Peggy Maxwell
   cast: 9 Ben Murphy, Gene Barry 10 Mark Miller 11 Cliff Potter, Robert Stack 13 Tony Franciosa 15 Susan Saint James
   business: 8 magazine 10 publishing

Name of the Rose, The
   author: 10 Umberto Eco

Name That Tune
   host: 9 Red Benson 10 Bill Cullen 12 George de Witt
   orchestra: 11 Harry Salter

Namibia
  other name: 15 South West Africa
  capital/largest city: 8 Windhoek
  others: 6 Tsumeb 8 Luderitz 9 Walvis
    Bay 10 Oranjemund, Swakopmund 12
    Keetmanshoop
  monetary unit: 4 cent, rand
  mountain: 14 Khomas Highland, Koako-
    veld Hills
  highest point: 9 Brandberg
  river: 4 Fish 6 Cunene, Orange 7
    Zambezi 8 Okavango
  sea: 8 Atlantic
  physical feature:
    bay: 6 Walvis
    desert: 5 Namib 8 Kalahari
    region: 12 Caprivi Strip
  people: 4 Nama 5 Bantu 6 Damara, He-
    rero, Ovambo, Tswara 7 Bushman, col-
    ored 8 Okavango 9 Hottentot
  language: 5 Bantu 6 German 7 English,
    Khoisan 9 Afrikaans
  religion: 7 animism 8 Lutheran
  feature:
    homeland: 9 bantustan

Nammu
  origin: 8 Sumerian
  mother of: 4 gods
  personifies: 3 sea

Namtar
  origin: 8 Akkadian, Sumerian
  form: 5 demon
  personifies: 5 death

Nana
  author: 9 Emile Zola

Nana (Nurse)
  character in: 8 Peter Pan
  author: 6 Barrie

Nancy
  character in: 11 Oliver Twist
  author: 7 Dickens

Nancy
  creator: 15 Ernie Bushmiller
  character: 6 Sluggo 10 Aunt Fritzi

Nanna
  origin: 12 Scandinavian
  husband: 5 Baldr 6 Balder, Baldur
  habitat: 4 moon

Nannerella
  nickname of: 11 Anna Magnani

nanometer
  abbreviation: 2 nm

Naoise
  origin: 5 Irish
  wife: 8 Deirdre
  uncle: 9 Conchobar
  killed by: 9 Conchobar
  father: 6 Usnach, Usnech

Naomi
  husband: 9 Elimelech
  daughter-in-law: 4 Ruth
  son: 6 Mahlon 7 Chilion

nap 3 nod 4 doze, rest 6 cat nap, drowse,
  siesta, snooze 7 doze off, drop off, goof
  off, shut-eye, slumber 8 drift off 10 forty
  winks

Napaeae
  form: 6 nymphs
  location: 4 dell

napery 5 doily 6 linens, napkin 10 table-
  cloth

Naphtali
  father: 5 Jacob
  mother: 6 Bilkah
  brother: 3 Dan, Gad 4 Levi 5 Asher,
    Judah 6 Joseph, Reuben, Simeon 7
    Zebulun 8 Benjamin, Issachar
  sister: 5 Dinah
  descendant of: 10 Naphtalite

Napoleon Bonaparte
  also: 9 Napoleon I 18 Emperor of the
    French
  battle: 3 Ulm 5 Eylau 6 Lutzen, Moscow,
    Toulon (siege), Wagram 7 Bautzen, Dres-
    den, Leipzig, Marengo, Mondovi 8
    Borodino, Waterloo 9 Friedland 10
    Austerlitz 13 Aspern-Essling, Jena-
    Auerstadt, Peninsular War 22 War of the
    Fifth Coalition
  born: 7 Corsica
  exile to: 4 Elba 11 Saint Helena
  fought against: 7 Kutuzov 10 von Blu-
    cher, Wellington 14 Barclay de Tolly
  French fleet destroyed at: 9 Trafalgar
    destroyed by: 6 Nelson
  laws: 14 Napoleonic Code
  marshal/general under: 3 Ney 5 Murat 7
    Massena 10 Bernadotte
  position: 7 emperor 11 first consul 13
    consul for life
  tomb: 5 Paris 9 Invalides
  wife: 9 Josephine 20 Marie-Louise of
    Austria

Napoleon of Notting Hill, The
  author: 12 G K Chesterton

Narcaeus
  father: 8 Dionysus
  mother: 7 Physcoa

narcissism 6 egoism, vanity 7 conceit
  8 self-love 11 egocentrism 16 self-
  centeredness

narcissist 6 egoist 7 egotist 11 egocentric
  12 self-absorbed, self-admiring

narcissistic 4 smug, vain 6 vanity 7 conceit, selfish 8 egotistic, puffed-up 9 conceited 10 egocentric, egoistical 11
  egomaniacal, egotistical

narcissus
  varieties: 5 poet's 6 poetaz 7 leedsii,
    trumpet 10 paper-white, polyanthus 16
    primrose peerless

Narcissus
  father: 8 Cephisus
  mother: 8 Leiriope
  loved: 7 himself
  loved by: 4 Echo
  punished by: 9 Aphrodite
  changed into: 6 flower

narcotic 4 drug 6 opiate 8 medicine, sedative 9 soporific 10 medicament, medication, painkiller 12 tranquilizer 14 pharma-
  ceutical

Narragansett
language family: 9 Algonkian 10 Algonquian
location: 11 Connecticut, Rhode Island
related to: 7 Niantic
involved in: 9 Pequot War 14 King Philip's War 15 Great Swamp Fight

narrate 6 detail, recite, relate, render, repeat, retell 7 portray, recount 8 describe, set forth 9 chronicle 10 tell a story 15 give an account of

narration 7 recital, telling 8 relating, speaking 9 voice-over 10 recitation, recounting 11 chronicling, description 12 storytelling

narrative 4 tale 5 story 6 report 7 account, recital 8 dialogue, episodic 9 anecdotal, chronicle, statement 10 historical 12 storytelling

Narrative of Arthur Gordon Pym, The
author: 13 Edgar Allan Poe

narrow 3 set 4 fine, slim 5 close, scant, small, tight 6 biased, scanty 7 bigoted, cramped, pinched, shallow, slender, tapered 8 confined, dogmatic, isolated, squeezed 9 hidebound, illiberal, parochial 10 attenuated, compressed, intolerant, provincial, restricted 11 constricted, incapacious, opinionated, reactionary 12 conservative

narrowing 5 taper 8 tapering 9 squeezing 11 compressing 12 constricting

narrow-minded 5 petty 7 bigoted, prudish 8 one-sided 9 hidebound, parochial, unworldly 10 provincial 11 opinionated, reactionary, straitlaced 12 conservative 15 unsophisticated

narrow-mindedness 4 bias 7 bigotry 9 prejudice 10 unfairness 11 intolerance

narrows 4 neck, pass 5 canal 6 ravine, strait 7 channel, isthmus, passage

Nasca see 5 Nazca

Nascimento, Edson Arantes do
real name of: 4 Pele

Nash, Ogden
author of: 6 Versus 9 Hard Lines 20 The Private Dining Room 21 I'm a Stranger Here Myself

Nashville
director: 12 Robert Altman
cast: 10 Karen Black, Lily Tomlin 11 Henry Gibson 12 Ronee Blakley 13 Barbara Harris, Michael Murphy 14 Keith Carradine 16 Geraldine Chaplin
Oscar for: 4 song
song: 6 I'm Easy

Nassau
capital of: 7 Bahamas

nasty 4 foul, mean, vile 5 awful 6 odious 7 beastly, hateful, vicious 8 horrible 9 repellent, revolting 10 abominable, disgusting, nauseating, unpleasant 11 distasteful 12 disagreeable

Natchez
language family: 10 Muskhogean
tribe: 6 Avoyel, Taensa
location: 11 Mississippi 13 South Carolina

allied with: 7 Choctaw
practiced: 14 head flattening

nates 4 buns, rear, rump, seat 7 rear end 8 buttocks, haunches 9 fundament, posterior 12 hindquarters

Nathan
father: 5 Attai
served: 5 David 7 Solomon

Nathanael see 5 Jesus 8 Apostles 11 Bartholomew

nation 4 host, race 5 realm, state, tribe 6 empire, people 7 country, kingdom 8 republic 9 community 11 sovereignty 12 commonwealth

national park
Alaska: 13 Mount McKinley
Arizona: 11 Grand Canyon 15 Petrified Forest
Arkansas: 10 Hot Springs
California: 7 Redwood, Sequoia 8 Yosemite 11 Kings Canyon 14 Channel Islands, Lassen Volcanic
Canada: 4 Yoho 5 Banff, Fundy 6 Jasper, Kluane 8 Kootenay 9 Auyuittuq 13 Waterton Lakes
Colorado: 5 Estes 9 Mesa Verde 13 Rocky Mountain
Florida: 10 Everglades
Hawaii: 9 Haleakala 15 Hawaii Volcanoes
Kentucky: 11 Mammoth Cave
Maine: 6 Acadia
Michigan: 10 Isle Royale
Minnesota: 9 Voyageurs
Montana: 7 Glacier 11 Yellowstone
New Mexico: 15 Carlsbad Caverns
North Carolina: 19 Great Smoky Mountains (with Tennessee)
North Dakota: 17 Theodore Roosevelt
Oklahoma: 6 Platte
Oregon: 10 Crater Lake
South Dakota: 8 Badlands, Wind Cave
Tennessee: 6 Shiloh 13 Cumberland Gap 19 Great Smoky Mountains (with North Carolina)
Texas: 7 Big Bend 18 Guadalupe Mountains
Utah: 4 Zion 6 Arches 11 Bryce Canyon, Canyonlands, Capital Reef
Virginia: 10 Shenandoah 26 Colonial National Historical
Washington: 7 Olympic 12 Mount Rainier 13 North Cascades
Wyoming: 10 Grand Teton 11 Yellowstone

National Velvet
director: 13 Clarence Brown
cast: 10 Anne Revere 11 Donald Crisp 12 Mickey Rooney 14 Angela Lansbury 15 Elizabeth Taylor
Oscar for: 17 supporting actress (Revere)
sequel: 19 International Velvet

native 4 home 5 basic, local, natal 6 inborn, inbred, innate, savage 7 citizen, endemic, natural 8 domestic, inherent, national, paternal 9 aborigine, elemental, homegrown, ingrained, inherited, intrinsic, primitive 10 congenital, countryman, hereditary, indigenous 11 instinctive 12 countrywoman 13 autochthonous

native country 7 country 8 homeland 10 fatherland 13 mother country

native-grown 5 local 8 domestic 9 homegrown 10 indigenous

native land 8 homeland 10 birthplace, fatherland, native soil 13 mother country, native country

native of Israel
    Hebrew: 5 sabra

native soil 8 homeland 10 fatherland, native land 13 mother country, native country

Native Son
    author: 13 Richard Wright

natty 4 chic, neat, posh, tidy, trim 5 smart 6 dapper, jaunty, snappy, spruce 7 dashing, modish, stylish 11 fashionable

Natty Bumppo
    also: 7 Hawkeye 10 Pathfinder, The Trapper 13 The Deerslayer 15 Leatherstocking 16 Le Longue Carabine
    character in: 23 The Leatherstocking Tales
    friend: 5 Uncas 12 Chingachgook
    author: 6 Cooper

natural 5 plain 6 inborn, native, normal 7 earthly, genuine, regular 8 God-given, inherent 9 essential, intuitive, unstudied 10 unaffected, unmannered 11 instinctive, spontaneous, terrestrial 13 unpretentious 14 characteristic 15 straightforward

Natural, The
    director: 13 Barry Levinson
    based on story by: 14 Bernard Malamud
    cast: 10 Glenn Close 12 Robert Duvall 13 Robert Redford

natural child 7 bastard 9 love child 17 illegitimate child

natural gift 5 flair 6 talent 7 ability, faculty 8 aptitude 9 attribute, endowment

natural habitat 5 range 6 domain, milieu 7 element 9 territory 11 environment

naturalize 5 adapt, adopt 6 adjust 8 accustom 9 acclimate 11 domesticate, familiarize

naturalness 4 ease 9 sincerity 10 simplicity 11 artlessness, genuineness 12 unconstraint 14 unaffectedness

nature 4 bent, kind, mood, sort, type 5 birth, earth, globe, humor, stamp, style, trait 6 cosmos, spirit 7 essence, feature, variety 8 category, creation, instinct, property, universe 9 character 11 disposition, peculiarity 12 constitution 13 particularity 14 characteristic
    goddess of: 6 Cybele 9 Dindymene 10 Berecyntia

Nature
    author: 17 Ralph Waldo Emerson

naught 3 nil 4 zero 5 nihil, zilch 6 cipher 7 nothing, useless 9 worthless

naughty 3 bad 4 blue 5 bawdy, dirty 6 ribald, risque, vulgar 7 wayward, willful 8 devilish, off-color, perverse 9 fractious, obstinate 11 disobedient, misbehaving, mischievous 12 pornographic, recalcitrant, unmanageable 13 disrespectful

Naum
    son: 4 Amos

Nauru
    other name: 14 Pleasant Island
    capital: 13 Yaren District
    cities: 3 Boe, Ewa 4 Aiwo, Ijuw 5 Baiti, Buada, Nibok, Uaboe, Yaren 6 Anabar, Anetan, Meneng 7 Anibare 10 Denigomodu
    monetary unit: 4 cent 6 dollar
    lake: 11 Buada Lagoon
    sea: 7 Pacific
    physical feature:
    bay: 7 Anibare
    lagoon: 5 Buada
    point: 4 Anna 6 Meneng
    people: 7 Chinese 10 Melanesian, Polynesian 11 Micronesian
    explorer: 9 John Fearn
    language: 7 English, Nauruan
    religion: 10 Protestant 13 Roman Catholic
    feature: 9 phosphate

nausea 7 disgust, heaving 8 contempt, loathing, retching, sickness, vomiting 9 repulsion, revulsion 10 queasiness 11 airsickness, biliousness, car sickness, seasickness 12 upset stomach 14 motion sickness, travel sickness

Nausea
    author: 14 Jean-Paul Sartre

nauseate 5 repel, upset 6 offend, revolt, sicken 7 disgust, repulse 8 make sick 15 turn one's stomach

nauseated 3 ill 4 sick 5 upset 6 queasy 8 repelled, revolted 9 disgusted

nauseating 9 offensive, repellent, repulsive, revolting, sickening 10 disgusting

nauseous 4 sick 5 upset 6 queasy 9 abhorrent, nauseated, offensive, repellent, repulsive, revolting, sickening, upsetting 10 disgusting, nauseating 12 unappetizing

Nausicaa
    father: 8 Alcinous
    position: 8 princess
    aided: 8 Odysseus

Nausithous
    father: 8 Poseidon
    mother: 8 Periboea
    occupation: 8 helmsman
    employer: 7 Theseus
    became: 4 king
    realm: 8 Phaeacia

Nautes
    advisor to: 6 Aeneas

nautical 5 naval 6 marine 7 aquatic, boating, oceanic 8 maritime, of the sea, seagoing, yachting

nautical mile
    abbreviation: 3 nmi

Nautilus
   submarine in: 32 Twenty Thousand Leagues Under the Sea
   author: 5 Verne

Navajo, Navaho (Dine)
   language family: 10 Athapascan, Athapaskan
   location: 4 Utah 7 Arizona 9 New Mexico
   noted for: 7 weaving 14 silversmithing
   dwelling: 5 hogan

navigate 3 fly 4 ride, sail, ship 5 cross, steer 6 cruise, voyage 8 maneuver, sail over 11 plot a course 12 chart a course

navigation 7 boating, sailing 8 cruising, piloting, voyaging 9 traveling 10 seamanship
   god of: 5 Niord, Njord

Navigators Islands see 12 Western Samoa

navy 5 fleet 6 armada, convoy 8 flotilla, warships

navy-blue 6 indigo 8 dark blue, deep blue

nay 4 also, deny, vote 5 never 6 denial, refuse 7 against, but also, refusal 8 negative

Nazarene see 5 Jesus

Nazarene, The
   author: 10 Sholem Asch

Nazca, Nasca
   location: 4 Peru 12 South America
   noted for: 8 ceramics, textiles 10 Nazca lines (sketches on plain)

Nazi air force
   German: 9 Luftwaffe

Nazi swastika
   German: 10 Hakenkreuz

N'Djamena
   capital of: 4 Chad

Neaera
   mentioned in: 7 Odyssey
   form: 5 nymph
   father: 6 Pereus
   cousin: 9 King Aleus
   husband: 9 King Aleus
   son: 7 Cepheus
   daughter: 4 Auge 6 Evadne 8 Lampetia

Neal, Patricia
   husband: 9 Roald Dahl
   born: 9 Packard KY
   roles: 3 Hud (Oscar) 15 A Face in the Crowd, The Fountainhead 18 The Subject Was Roses

near 4 nigh 5 about, close 6 all but, almost 7 close by, close to, looming 8 approach, come up to, imminent, next door 9 alongside, close with, impending 10 hereabouts 11 approaching, practically, proximately, threatening 13 approximately

nearby 5 close, handy 6 at hand 7 close by 8 next door 9 adjoining 10 accessible, hereabouts

near death
   Latin: 10 in extremis

near home 5 close 7 close by 10 hereabouts

nearly 4 nigh 5 about 6 all but, almost 7 close to, roughly 11 practically 13 approximately

nearly equal 5 close 7 similar 10 nip-and-tuck 11 approaching

nearly even 5 close 10 head to head, nip-and-tuck 11 neck and neck

nearness 8 intimacy, vicinity 9 adjacency, closeness, handiness, immediacy, proximity 10 contiguity 11 propinquity 12 availability, neighborhood 13 accessibility, approximation

neat 4 tidy 5 clean, great 6 groovy 7 concise, correct, orderly 8 accurate, exciting, original, straight, striking, succinct 9 competent, dexterous, efficient, ingenious, organized, purposive, shipshape 10 controlled, immaculate, methodical, systematic 11 imaginative, intelligent, uncluttered

neatness 5 order 8 tidiness 11 orderliness 12 organization

Nebraska
   abbreviation: 2 NE 4 Nebr
   nickname: 4 Beef 8 Antelope 10 Blackwater, Cornhusker 12 Treeplanter's
   capital: 7 Lincoln
   largest city: 5 Omaha
   others: 5 Cozad 6 Gering 7 Kearney 8 Beatrice, Hastings 9 Broken Bow 11 Grand Island, North Platte, Scottsbluff
   college: 4 Dana 5 Doane 8 Duchesne, Hastings 9 Creighton 15 Midland Lutheran
   feature: 8 Boys' Town
   national monument: 11 Scott's Bluff 15 Agate Fossil Beds
   tribe: 3 Oto 4 Otoe 5 Kiowa, Omaha, Ponca, Sioux 6 Pawnee
   people: 10 Henry Fonda 11 Fred Astaire, Roscoe Pound
   lake: 7 Merritt, Sherman, Swanson 10 McConaughy 13 Lewis and Clark
   land rank: 9 fifteenth
   physical feature: 8 Badlands
   hills: 4 Sand 5 Drift, Loess
   plains: 5 Great
   river: 4 Loup 5 Logan 6 Dismal, Nemaha, Platte 7 Big Blue, Elkhorn 8 Missouri, Niobrara 10 Little Blue, Republican 12 Harlan County
   state admission: 13 thirty-seventh
   state bird: 17 western meadowlark
   state flower: 9 goldenrod
   state motto: 20 Equality Before the Law
   state song: 17 Beautiful Nebraska
   state tree: 3 elm 10 cottonwood

nebris
   skin of: 4 fawn

Nebrophonus see 5 Thoon

Nebuchadnezzar
   father: 12 Nabopolassar
   son: 12 Evilmerodach

nebula 4 Crab, Ring, Veil 5 Great 6 Lagoon 7 Rosette 9 Horsehead

nebulous 3 dim 4 dark, hazy 5 murky, vague 6 cloudy 7 obscure, unclear 8 confused 9 ambiguous, uncertain 10 impalpable, indefinite, indistinct, intangible 13 indeterminate

necessarily 8 perforce 9 naturally 10 inevitably, inexorably 11 accordingly 12 compulsorily 13 automatically, axiomatically, unqualifiedly 16 incontrovertibly

necessary 6 needed, urgent, wanted 7 crucial, desired, exigent, fitting, needful 8 required 9 called for, essential, requisite 10 compulsory, imperative, obligatory 13 indispensable

necessary changes having been made
Latin: 15 mutatis mutandis

necessitate 5 cause, force, impel 6 compel, demand, oblige 7 call for, enforce, require 9 constrain, prescribe

necessitation 5 cause, force 6 demand, duress 8 coercion, pressure 10 compulsion, constraint, obligation 11 enforcement, requirement

necessity, necessities 4 must, need 6 demand, needed 7 urgency 8 exigency, pressure 9 essential, requisite 10 sine qua non 11 requirement 13 indispensable
Latin: 10 sine qua non

neck 3 pet 4 kiss, nape, pass 6 caress, cervix, cuddle, fondle, smooth, strait 7 channel, isthmus, make out 9 narrowing

neckerchief 5 scarf 8 bandanna, kerchief

necklace 3 tie 5 beads, chain, noose 6 choker, collar, locket, pearls, string 7 jewelry, pendant 8 ornament 9 lavaliere

necktie 3 bow 4 band 5 ascot, black, scarf 6 cravat, string 7 Windsor 10 four in hand 11 half Windsor 12 hangman's rope

necromancer 5 hexer, magus, witch 6 wizard 7 charmer, warlock 8 conjurer, exorcist, magician, sorcerer 9 enchanter, occultist, voodooist 10 soothsayer 13 black magician, thaumaturgist

necromancy 5 magic, spell 7 sorcery 8 black art 10 witchcraft 11 enchantment, foretelling

necrophobia
fear of: 5 death 10 dead bodies

necropolis 8 cemetery 9 graveyard 12 burial ground 13 burying ground

Nectar
drink of: 4 gods
gives: 4 life

Neda
form: 5 nymph, river
location: 11 mountaintop

need 4 lack, want, wish 5 crave, exact 6 demand, penury 7 call for, longing, poverty, require, straits 8 distress, exigency, yearn for 9 essential, extremity, indigence, necessity, requisite 10 bankruptcy, insolvency 11 desideratum, destitution, necessitate, requirement 13 impecuniosity, pen+lessness

needed 5 vital 7 crucial 9 essential, necessary, requisite 13 indispensable

needful 7 wishful 8 required 9 essential, necessary, requisite 10 imperative 13 indispensable

needle 3 vex 4 josh, leaf, ride, twit 5 annoy, chaff, harry, taunt, tease 6 badger, harass, hector 7 torment 9 indicator

needle-shaped 5 sharp 6 peaked, spiked 7 pointed 8 piercing 10 bodkin-like

needless 7 useless 9 excessive, pointless, redundant 10 gratuitous, pleonastic, unavailing 11 dispensable, purposeless, superfluous, uncalled-for, unessential, unnecessary 12 overabundant

needlework 6 sewing 7 basting, brocade, darning, tacking, tatting 8 applique, knitting, quilting 9 stitching 10 embroidery 11 cross stitch, needle point

needy 4 poor 5 broke 6 hard-up, in want 8 indigent, strapped 9 destitute, money less, penniless 10 down-and-out 12 impoverished 15 poverty-stricken

ne'er-do-well 3 bum 5 idler, loser 6 loafer, no-good 7 goof-off, sad sack, wastrel 8 layabout 9 do-nothing, no-account 10 black sheep 14 good-for-nothing

nefarious 3 bad, low 4 base, evil, foul, vile 6 odious, wicked 7 beastly, ghastly, heinous, hellish, ungodly, vicious 8 depraved, devilish, infamous, infernal, shameful 9 atrocious, execrable 10 abominable, despicable, detestable, iniquitous, scandalous, villainous 11 disgraceful, opprobrious, unspeakable 12 dishonorable 13 unmentionable

Nefertem
origin: 8 Egyptian
personifies: 5 lotus
true identity: 4 Ptah

negate 4 deny, veto, void 5 quash, quell, rebut 6 defeat, disown, refute, repeal, revoke, squash 7 blot out, destroy, disavow, gainsay, nullify, retract, reverse, squelch, wipe out 8 abrogate, disallow, disclaim, set aside, vanquish 9 overthrow, overwhelm, repudiate 10 contradict, invalidate

negating 7 denying, voiding 8 refuting, revoking 9 reversing 10 cancelling, nullifying 11 disallowing 12 invalidating, setting aside 13 contradicting

negation 6 denial 7 counter 8 reversal 9 rejection 10 abrogation, disclaimer, refutation 11 confutation, repudiation 12 invalidation 13 contradiction, nullification

negative 4 blue, dark 5 bleak 6 at odds, gloomy 7 dubious, opposed 8 contrary, doubtful, downbeat, inimical, opposing, refusing 9 declining, demurring, dissident, jaundiced, objecting, rejecting, reluctant, skeptical, unwilling 10 dissenting, fatalistic 11 disagreeing, pessimistic 12 antagonistic, disapproving 13 uncooperative 14 unenthusiastic

neglect 4 fail, omit 5 let go, shirk 6 forget, ignore, laxity, pass by, pass up, slight 7 abandon, default, laxness, let pass, let ride, let slip 8 be remiss, idleness, let slide, omission, overlook, pass over, shake off 9 disregard, oversight, passivity, slackness 10 inaccuracy, negligence, remissness 11 dereliction, inattention, inexactness 12 carelessness, fecklessness, indifference, slovenliness 13 noncompliance, unful-

fillment 14 nonpreparation 16 under-
achievement

neglected 7 dropped, ignored, omitted,
shirked, unkempt 8 forsaken, untended 9
abandoned, cast aside, forgotten 10 overlooked, uncared for 11 disregarded

neglectful 4 lazy 5 slack 6 remiss, untrue 7
careless, derelict, heedless 9 forgetful,
negligent, oblivious, unheeding, unmindful
10 inconstant, thriftless, unfaithful, unthinking, unwatchful 11 improvident, inattentive,
indifferent, respectless, thoughtless, unobservant 12 devil-may-care, disregardant,
disregardful, happy-go-lucky 15 procrastinating

negligee, neglige 4 robe 6 kimono 7 wrapper 8 bathrobe, peignoir 9 housecoat 12
dressing gown

negligence 6 laxity 7 neglect 11 disregarded 12 carelessness

negligent 3 lax 5 slack 6 remiss, untidy 8
careless, heedless, slovenly 9 forgetful,
unheeding, unmindful 10 neglectful, unthinking, unwatchful 11 inattentive, indifferent, thoughtless, unobservant 13 inconsiderate

negligible 5 minor, petty, small 6 minute,
paltry, slight 7 trivial 8 piddling, trifling 11
unimportant 13 insignificant 15 inconsequential

negotiate 4 cash, make, pass 6 barter,
cash in, convey, dicker, haggle, handle,
manage, redeem, settle 7 arrange, consign, deliver, discuss, get over 8 contract,
cope with, deal with, hand over, make
over, pass over, sign over, transact, transfer, transmit, turn over 10 bargain for 11
come to terms, meet halfway

negotiation 4 deal 6 treaty 8 argument,
haggling 9 dickering 10 bargaining 11 arbitration, arrangement 12 compromising

negotiator 7 arbiter 8 mediator 9 go-
between 10 arbitrator 12 intermediary

Negrette, Lolita Dolores
  real name of: 13 Dólores Del Rio

Nehemiah
  father: 5 Azbuk 14 Hachaliah

neigh 5 hinny 6 nicker, whinny

neighbor 4 abut, meet 5 touch 6 adjoin, be
near, border, friend 7 conjoin 8 borderer,
border on 9 associate 12 acquaintance

neighborhood 4 area, part, side, ward 5
place, range 6 locale, parish, region,
sphere 7 quarter, section 8 confines,
district, environs, precinct, purlieus, vicinity
9 community

neighboring 4 near, next 5 close 6 at hand,
nearby 7 close by 8 abutting, adjacent 9
adjoining, bordering 10 contiguous 11 surrounding 12 circumjacent

neighborly 4 kind 5 civil 6 chummy, kindly,
polite 7 affable, amiable, cordial, helpful 8
amicable, friendly, gracious, obliging 9
courteous 10 hospitable 11 considerate,
warmhearted 12 well-disposed

Neighbors
  author: 12 Thomas Berger

Neith
  origin: 8 Egyptian
  personifies: 10 femininity
  son: 2 Ra
  corresponds to: 6 Athena

Nekhbet
  origin: 8 Egyptian
  form: 7 vulture
  guardian of: 5 Egypt 10 Upper Egypt

Neleus
  king of: 5 Pylos, Pylus
  father: 8 Poseidon
  mother: 4 Tyro
  twin brother: 6 Pelias
  wife: 7 Chloris
  son: 6 Nestor 12 Periclymenus
  daughter: 4 Pero
  refused purification to: 8 Hercules
  killed by: 8 Hercules

Nelides
  epithet of: 6 Nestor

Nelson, Harriet Hilliard
  real name: 14 Peggy Lou Snyder
  husband: 5 Ozzie
  son: 4 Rick 5 David
  born: 11 Des Moines IA
  roles: 30 The Adventures of Ozzie and
    Harriet

Nelson, Horatio
  also: 14 Viscount Nelson
  nationality: 7 British
  battle: 9 Trafalgar 11 Bay of Abukir 15
    Battle of the Nile 16 Cape Saint Vincent
    18 Battle of Copenhagen
  defeated: 5 Danes 6 French 7 Spanish
  flagship: 7 Victory
  killed at: 9 Trafalgar
  lover: 16 Emma Lady Hamilton

Nelson, Ozzie
  real name: 18 Oswald George Nelson
  wife: 15 Harriet Hilliard
  son: 4 Rick 5 David
  born: 12 Jersey City NJ
  roles: 30 The Adventures of Ozzie and
    Harriet

Nemean
  epithet of: 4 Zeus

Nemean lion
  strangled by: 8 Hercules

nemesis 4 ruin 5 match, 6 rival 7 avenger,
justice, revenge, undoing 8 downfall, pun-
isher, Waterloo 9 overthrow, vengeance 10
punishment 11 destruction, retaliation,
retribution 16 instrument of fate

Nemesis *see* 8 Adrastea

nemine contradicente 11 unanimously 18
no one contradicting

nemine dissentiente 11 unanimously 15
no one dissenting

Nemo
  character in: 10 Bleak House
  author: 7 Dickens

Nemo, Captain
  character in: 32 Twenty Thousand
    Leagues Under the Sea
  author: 5 Verne

neologism, neology 7 coinage 9 nonce word

neon
chemical symbol: 2 Ne

neonate 4 baby 6 infant 7 newborn

neophyte 4 tyro 5 pupil 6 novice, rookie 7 convert, entrant, learner, recruit, student, trainee 8 beginner, disciple, newcomer 9 greenhorn, novitiate, proselyte 10 apprentice, tenderfoot 11 probationer

neoplasm 5 tumor 6 cancer, growth 7 sarcoma 9 carcinoma 10 malignancy 14 carcinosarcoma

Nepal
other name: 9 Shangri-La
capital/largest city: 8 Katmandu 9 Kathmandu
others: 5 Patan, Patna 6 Gurkha 7 Birganj 8 Bhadgaon, Lalitpur 9 Bhaktapur 10 Biratnagar
university: 9 Tribhuvan
division: 5 Terai 13 High Himalayas
monetary unit: 4 anna, pice 5 mohar, paisa, rupee
mountain: 6 Cho Oyu, Churia, Lhotse, Makalu 7 Manaslu, Siwalik 9 Annapurna, Himalayas 10 Dhaulagiri, Gosainthan, Himalchuli 11 Ganesh Himal 12 Kanchenjunga 14 Mahabharat hekh
highest point: 9 Mt Everest
river: 4 Kali, Kosi, Mugu, Seti 5 Babai, Bheri, Rapti, Sarda, Tamur 6 Gandak 7 Karnali 8 Narayani
physical feature:
plain: 5 Terai
valley: 5 Nepal 8 Katmandu
people: 3 Rai 4 Aoul 5 Bhote, Limbu, Magar, Murmi, Newar, Tharu 6 Bhutia, Gurkha, Gurung, Nepali, Sherpa, Tamang 7 Kiranti, Tibetan 8 Gorkhali, Nepalese
birthplace of: 6 Buddha 13 Gautama Buddha 17 Siddhartha Gautama
king: 8 Mahendra 9 Tribhuwan 18 Prithwi Narayan Shah 23 Birenda Bir Bikram Shah Dev
ruler: 4 Rana 5 Malla 6 Rajput
language: 6 Nepali, Newari
religion: 8 Buddhism, Hinduism
place:
dam: 6 Gandak
shrine: 9 Swayambhu 10 Gorakhnath
feature:
animal: 3 dzo, yak 7 dzopkyo
arch: 6 Juddha
god/goddess: 5 Indra 6 Kumari
legend: 4 Yeti 17 abominable snowman
soldiers: 6 Gurkha

Nepali
language family: 12 Indo-European
branch: 11 Indo-Iranian
group: 5 Indic
spoken in: 5 Nepal

nepenthe 4 drug 5 drink, opium 6 heroin, opiate 7 hashish 8 narcotic

Nephele
counterfeit of: 4 Hera
formed by: 4 Zeus
husband: 7 Athamas
children: 8 centaurs
son: 7 Phrixus
daughter: 5 Helle

nephrite
variety: 4 jade

ne plus ultra 4 acme 12 highest point

Neptune
origin: 5 Roman
god of: 3 sea
corresponds to: 8 Poseidon

Neptune
position: 6 eighth
satellite: 6 Nereid, Triton
color: 5 green

Nereid
form: 5 nymph
location: 3 sea
father: 6 Nereus

Nereus
god of: 3 sea
father: 6 Pontus
mother: 4 Gaea
father of: 7 Nereids
number of Nereids: 5 fifty
son: 7 Nerites

Nergal
origin: 8 Akkadian
ruler of: 4 dead
consort of: 10 Ereshkigal

Nerissa
character in: 19 The Merchant of Venice
author: 11 Shakespeare

Nerites
father: 6 Nereus
mother: 5 Doris
transformed into: 6 mussel
transformed by: 9 Aphrodite

neritic 7 aquatic, coastal 8 offshore

Nero
name: 18 Nero Claudius Caesar
emperor of: 4 Rome
mother: 9 Agrippina
father: 19 Domitius Ahenobarbus
stepfather: 8 Claudius
tutor: 6 Seneca
son: 11 Britannicus
wife: 7 Octavia 13 Poppaea Sabina

nerve 4 dash, gall, grit, guts, sass 5 brass, cheek, crust, pluck, spunk, valor 6 mettle, spirit 7 bravery, courage 8 backbone, boldness, coolness, gameness, strength, tenacity 9 arrogance, assurance, derring-do, endurance, flippancy, fortitude, gallantry, hardihood, hardiness, impudence, insolence, sauciness 10 assumption, brazenness, confidence, effrontery, steadiness 11 intrepidity, presumption 12 fearlessness, impertinence, resoluteness 13 determination 16 stoutheartedness

nerveless 4 calm, dead, weak 5 brave, frail, inert 6 feeble, flabby 7 flaccid 8 cowardly 9 powerless 10 courageous 12 fainthearted

nervous 4 wild 5 jumpy, shaky, tense 6 touchy, uneasy 7 alarmed, anxious, excited, fearful, fidgety, jittery, peevish, ruffled 8 feverish, neurotic, skittish, startled, timorous, unstrung 9 delirious, disturbed, excitable, impatient, irritable, sensitive, trembling, tremulous, unsettled 10 highstrung, hysterical 12 apprehensive

nervousness 6 tremor 7 anxiety, flutter, shaking, tension 8 hysteria, timidity 9 agitation, quivering, the creeps, the shakes, trembling, twitching 10 the fidgets, touchiness 11 disturbance, fidgetiness, stage fright 12 apprehension, excitability, irascibility, irritability, perturbation, timorousness 16 hypersensitivity

nervous system
   component: 4 ears, eyes 5 brain, taste, touch 7 ganglia 8 nerve end 10 nerve fiber, spinal cord

nervy 4 bold, firm, rude 5 brash, gutty, gutsy, sassy 6 brassy, brazen, cheeky, gritty, plucky, strong 7 assured, nervous 10 courageous, determined 12 stouthearted

Nesbitt, Cathleen
   born: 7 England 8 Cheshire
   roles: 10 My Fair Lady 18 Upstairs Downstairs 23 Three Coins in the Fountain

Nessus
   form: 7 centaur
   shot by: 8 Hercules
   caused death of: 8 Hercules

n'est-ce pas? 10 isn't that so?

nestle 3 lie, pet 4 live, snug, stay 5 clasp, dwell, lodge 6 bundle, caress, coddle, cosset, cuddle, enfold, fondle, huddle, nuzzle, occupy, remain, settle 7 embrace, inhabit, lie snug, snuggle 8 lie close 10 settle down

Nest of Gentlefolk
   author: 23 Ivan Sergeyevich Turgenev

Nest of Simple Folk, A
   author: 12 Sean O'Faolain

Nestor
   origin: 5 Greek
   attributes: 6 oldest, wisest
   father: 6 Neleus
   son: 10 Thasymedes 11 Pisistratus
   epithet: 7 Nelides

net 3 web 4 earn, gain, grab, grid, grip, mesh, snag, take, trap 5 catch, clasp, grate, seize, snare 6 clutch, enmesh, gather, grille, obtain, pick up, screen, snap up, take in 7 acquire, bring in, capture, collect, ensnare, grating, lattice 8 entangle, gather in, gridiron, meshwork 9 apprehend, grillwork, lay hold of, screening 10 accumulate 11 latticework
   constellation of: 9 Reticulum

nether 5 basal, below, lower, under 6 bottom, lowest 8 downward, inferior 9 subjacent 10 bottommost

Netherlands
   other name: 7 Holland 12 Low Countries
   capital/largest city: 9 Amsterdam
   others: 3 Urk 5 Delft, Lisse 6 Almelo, Arnhem, Leiden, Velsen 7 Haarlem, Helmond, Hengelo, Limburg, Tilberg, Tilburg, Utrecht 8 Aalsmeer, Enschede, Ijmuiden, Nijmegen, The Hague 9 Apeldoorn, Dordrecht, Eindhoven, Groningen, Rotterdam 12 Scheveningen
   division: 6 Twente 7 Drenthe, Limburg, Utrecht, Zeeland 9 Friesland, Groningen 10 Gelderland, Overijssel 12 North Brabant, North Holland, South Holland 19 Netherlands Antilles
   government:
      legislature: 4 Raad 11 Eerste Kamer, Tweede Kamer
      head of state: 5 queen
   measure: 2 el 3 aam, ahm, ell, kan, vat 4 duim, mijl, rood, rope 5 anker, roede, wisse 6 bunder, legger, maatje, mutsje, streep 7 schepel 8 mimgelen, steekkan
   monetary unit: 4 doit, oord, raps 5 crown, daler, rider, ryder 6 florin, gulden, stiver, suskin 7 daalder, ducaton, escalan, escalin, guilder, stooter, stuiver 8 albertin, ducatoon 9 dubbeltje 12 rijksdaalder 13 albertustaler
   weight: 3 ons 4 last, pond 5 bahar 6 korrel 7 wichtje
   island: 5 Texel 7 Ameland, Frisian 8 Antilles, Vlieland
   lake: 7 Haarlem 10 Ijsselmeer 11 Grevelingen, Havingvliet
   highest point: 11 Vaalserberg
   river: 3 Eem, Lek 4 Leck, Maas, Waal, Ysel 5 Donge, Hunse, Meuse, Rhine, Schie, Yssel 6 Dintel, Dommel, Ijssel, Kromme 7 Scheldt
   sea: 5 North
   physical feature:
      canal: 6 Oranje 7 Juliana, Merwede 8 Drentsch, North Sea 10 Wilhelmina 11 New Waterway
      former bay: 9 Zuider Zee
      port: 9 Europoort
   people: 5 Dutch 7 Frisian 9 Hollander 10 Surinamese 12 Netherlander 13 South Moluccan
   artist: 4 Eyck, Hals 5 Appel, Bosch 7 Van Gogh, Vermeer 8 Mondrian, Ruisdael 9 Rembrandt
   author: 6 Vondel 7 Erasmus, Grotius, Spinoza 8 Vestdijk 9 Anne Frank
   explorer: 6 Tasman
   king: 7 William
   queen: 7 Beatrix, Juliana 10 Wilhelmina
   ruler: 5 Spain 13 House of Orange 15 Holy Roman Empire
   scientist: 7 Huygens 11 Leeuwenhoek
   language: 5 Dutch 7 English, Frisian
   religion: 13 Dutch Reformed, Protestantism 16 Roman Catholicism
   place:
      airport: 8 Schiphol
      bird sanctuary: 9 Waddenzee
      miniature town: 9 Madurodam
      museum: 9 Frans Hals, Stedelijk 11 Mauritshuis, Rijksmuseum 14 Vincent Van Gogh 19 Boymans-van Beuningen

seat of government: 7 Den Haag 8 The Hague 11 'sGravenhage

tower: 14 Schreierstoren

feature:

  cheese market: 9 kaasmarkt

  earth mounds: 6 terpen

  flower: 5 tulip

  flower parade: 12 Bloemencorso

  pottery: 5 Delft

  reclaimed land: 6 polder

  wooden shoes: 7 klompen

food:

  cheese: 4 Edam 5 Gouda 6´ Leyden 7 cottage

  dish: 10 nasi goreng, rijsttafel

  drink: 3 gin 8 anisette, schnapps

  pea soup: 10 erwtensoep

Netherlands East Indies *see* 9 Indonesia

netherworld 4 hell 5 Hades 10 underworld 14 infernal region

nettle 3 vex 4 bait, gall, miff, rile 5 annoy, beset, chafe, harry, pique, sting 6 bother, harass, ruffle 7 perturb, prickle, provoke 8 irritate 9 displease 10 exasperate

nettle 6 Urtica

  varieties: 4 dead, dumb, hemp, rock 5 false, flame, hedge, horse, Roman 6 spurge 7 painted 8 stinging 9 white dead 11 spotted dead 12 western horse

network 3 web 4 grid, mesh, trap 5 grate, group, snare 6 grille, scheme, system 7 complex, netting, station

Network

  director: 11 Sidney Lumet

  based on story by: 14 Paddy Chayefsky

  cast: 9 Ned Beatty 10 Peter Finch, Wesley Addy 11 Faye Dunaway 12 Robert Duvall 13 William Holden 16 Beatrice Straight

  Oscar for: 5 actor (Finch) 7 actress (Dunaway) 17 supporting actress (Straight)

neuroptera

  class: 8 hexapoda

  phylum: 10 arthropoda

  group: 7 ant lion, fishfly 8 alderfly, lacewing, snakefly

neurotic 4 sick 7 anxious, intense, nervous 8 abnormal, unstable 9 disturbed, obsessive, unhealthy 10 distraught, immoderate 11 overwrought

neuter 5 fixed 6 barren, fallow, gelded, spayed 7 asexual, sexless, sterile 8 impotent 9 infertile

Neutra, Richard J

  architect of: 15 Mathematics Park (Princeton) 16 Lovell Heath House (Los Angeles CA) 17 von Sternberg House (Northridge CA) 22 Orange County Courthouse (Santa Ana CA)

neutral 4 mean 5 aloof 6 medium, middle, normal, remote 7 average 8 pacifist, peaceful, unbiased 9 impartial, in-between, peaceable, withdrawn 10 achromatic, indefinite, of two minds, unaffected, uninvolved 11 half-and-half, indifferent, nonpartisan, unconcerned 12 fence sitting, intermediate, noncombatant 13 disinterested, dispassionate 14 nonbelligerent, noninterfering 16 nonparticipating 18 noninterventionist

neutralize 4 halt, stop 5 annul, block, check 6 cancel, defeat, impede, negate, offset, stymie 7 balance, disable, nullify, prevent 8 overcome, suppress 9 frustrate, overpower 10 counteract 12 counterpoise, incapacitate 14 counterbalance

neutralizer 7 blocker 9 nullifier 12 counteractor, counteragent 15 counterbalancer

Neuvillette, Christian de

  character in: 16 Cyrano de Bergerac

  author: 7 Rostand

Nevada

  abbreviation: 2 NV 3 Nev

  nickname: 6 Silver 9 Sagebrush

  capital: 10 Carson City

  largest city: 8 Las Vegas

  others: 3 Ely, Nye 4 Elko, Reno 6 Fallon, Nellis, Sparks, Storey, Washoe 7 Boulder, Gerlach 9 Hawthorne, Henderson 11 Weed Heights 12 Virginia City

  explorer: 7 Fremont 13 Jedediah Smith

  feature: 12 Comstock Lode

  dam: 5 Davis 6 Hoover

  hot springs: 4 Tule 9 Punch Bowl, Steam Boat

  national monument: 11 Death Valley

  tribe: 5 Modoc, Washo 6 Digger, Mohave, Paiute 7 Klamath 8 Achomawi, Atsugewi, Shoshone

  lake: 4 Mead, Ruby 5 Tahoe, Weber 6 Mohave, Walker 7 Pyramid 8 Lahontan, Rye Patch 9 Wild Horse

  land rank: 7 seventh

  mountain: 4 East, Pine, Ruby 5 White 7 Rockies, Toiyabe, Wasatch 13 Sierra Nevadas

  highest point: 12 Boundary Peak

  physical feature: 7 geysers 10 hot springs

  basin: 5 Great

  cave: 6 Gypsum

  desert: 7 Sonoran

  plateau: 8 Columbia

  river: 5 Reese 6 Carson, Walker 7 Truckee 8 Colorado, Humboldt

  state admission: 11 thirty-sixth

  state bird: 7 sagehen 16 mountain bluebird

  state flower: 9 sagebrush

  state motto: 16 All for Our Country

  state song: 15 Home Means Nevada

  state tree: 9 pinon pine 15 single-leaf pinon

never 4 ne'er 7 not ever 8 at no time, not at all

never-ending 6 steady 7 abiding, eternal, lasting, nonstop 8 constant, enduring, immortal, infinite, repeated, unbroken 9 ceaseless, continual, incessant, perennial, perpetual, recurring, unceasing 10 continuous, persistent, relentless 11 everlasting, unremitting 12 interminable, undiminished 13 uninterrupted

never-failing 4 firm, sure 6 proven, trusty 7 abiding 8 enduring, reliable 9 steadfast 10 dependable 11 trustworthy, undeviating, unfaltering 12 unhesitating, tried-and-true

nevermore 6 no more 10 never again

Never on Sunday
  director: 11 Jules Dassin
  cast: 11 Jules Dassin, Titos Vandis 14 Georges Foundas, Melina Mercouri
  setting: 6 Greece

nevertheless 3 but, yet 6 anyhow, anyway, even so, though 7 however 8 after all, although 10 contrarily, in any event, regardless 12 contrariwise 15 notwithstanding

Neville, Constance
  character in: 18 She Stoops to Conquer
  author: 9 Goldsmith

new 4 late 5 fixed, fresh, green, novel 6 modern, reborn, recent, remote, unused 7 altered, changed, current, just out, rebuilt, resumed, untried 8 original, reopened, repaired, restored, up-to-date 9 recreated, refreshed, remodeled, renovated, uncharted, unessayed, untouched 10 revivified, unexplored, unfamiliar, ungathered, unseasoned, unventured 11 regenerated, uncollected, unexercised 12 unaccustomed 13 reconstructed, reinvigorated

New Atlantis
  author: 12 Francis Bacon

New Brunswick
  abbreviation: 2 NB
  bay: 5 Fundy, Maces 7 Shepody 9 Chignecto, Miramichi 13 Passamaquoddy
  channel: 5 Minas 10 Grand Manan
  city: 7 Moncton 8 Bathurst 9 Riverview 10 Edmundston, Saint John 11 Fredericton
  island: 4 Deer 6 Miscou 7 Machias 10 Campobello, Grand Manan
  known as: 16 Atlantic province, maritime province
  lake: 5 Grand 8 Oromocto 12 Magagudavic 14 Chiputneticook
  people: 5 Irish 6 French 7 Acadian, English 8 American, Scottish 9 Algonkian 10 Anglo Saxon
  religion: 6 Canaan 7 Baptist 8 Anglican 10 Protestant 12 Presbyterian, United Church 13 Roman Catholic
  river: 5 Cains, Green 6 Renous, Salmon 7 Tobique 8 Kedgwick, Nashwak, Oromocto 9 Miramichi, Patapedia, Saint John 10 Nepisiguit, Richibucto, Saint Croix 11 Petitcodiac, Restigouche, Upsalquitch 12 Kennebecasis

New Centurions, The
  author: 14 Joseph Wambaugh

newcomer 4 tyro 5 alien 6 novice 7 entrant 8 intruder, neophyte, outsider, stranger 9 foreigner, immigrant, outlander 10 interloper, trespasser

Newcomes, The
  author: 25 William Makepeace Thackeray

New Deal Agency 3 AAA, CCC, CWA, FCA, FHA, FSA, NRA, NYA, PWA, REA, SEC, SSB, TVA, WPA 4 FCIC, FDIC, FERA, HOLC, NLRD, USHA

New Delhi
  capital of: 5 India
  designed by: 7 Lutyens
  earlier city: 5 Dilli 8 Dhillika, Din Panah, Kilookai 9 Firozabad 11 Tughlukabad 12 Indraprastha 13 Shah Jahanabad
  invader: 5 Timur 6 Abdali 7 British, Rohilas 8 Marathas 9 Nadir Shah
  landmark: 7 Red Fort 9 India Gate, Qutb Minar 10 Iron Pillar, Jama Masjid 12 Humayun's Tomb 14 Connaught Place 15 Rajghat Memorial 17 Rashtrapati Bhavan (Presidential Palace) 23 Jantar Mantar Observatory 30 Gandhi National Museum and Library
  river: 6 Yamuna
  street: 7 Raj Path (Kingsway)
  university: 15 Jawaharlal Nehru

New England
  capital: 6 Boston 7 Augusta, Concord 8 Hartford 10 Montpelier, Providence
  city: 4 Lynn 5 Barre 6 Bangor, Lowell, Nashua 7 Hyannis, Rutland, Warwick 8 Brockton, Cranston, Lawrence, Lewiston, New Haven, Portland, Stamford 9 Cambridge, Fall River, New London, Pawtucket, Waterbury, Worcester 10 Bridgeport, Burlington, Manchester, Pittsfield, Portsmouth, Woonsocket 11 Brattleboro, Springfield
  football team: 8 Patriots
  Indians: 6 Abnaki, Pequot 7 Mahican, Mohegan, Niantic, Nipmuck, Wangunk 8 Algonkin, Iroquois 9 Algonquin, Pennacook 10 Quinnipiac 12 Narraganset
  lake: 6 Sebago, Tiogue 7 Sunapee 9 Champlain, Moosehead 10 Candlewood 11 Pemaduncook 13 Winnipesaukee
  mountain: 5 Green, White 8 Greylock, Katahdin 9 Berkshire, Mansfield 10 Washington 11 Appalachian
  river: 5 Otter 6 Thames 7 Charles 8 Kennebec, Pawtucket, Winooski 9 Merrimack, Missiquoi, Naugatuck, Pawcatuck, Penobscot, Saint John 10 Housatonic, Providence, Quinnipiac 11 Connecticut 12 Androscoggin
  state: 5 Maine 7 Vermont 11 Connecticut, Rhode Island 12 New Hampshire 13 Massachusetts

newfangled 5 novel 6 modern, modish 7 stylish

new-fashioned 6 modern, modish 7 stylish 8 up-to-date

Newfoundland
  abbreviation: 4 Nfld
  capital: 10 Saint Johns
  city: 19 Happy Valley Goose Bay

lake: 7 Jeddore, Melville 8 Meelpaeg 10 Michikamau

mountain: 9 Long Range

river: 5 Eagle 6 Fraser, Gander 8 Exploits, Naskaupi 9 Churchill

section: 8 Labrador

New Granada *see* 8 Colombia

New Guinea

other name: 14 Papua New Guinea

capital/largest city: 11 Port Moresby

others: 3 Lae, Wau 4 Daru 5 Soron, Wewak 6 Aitape, Kikori, Medang, Rabaul 7 Gorolka, Kitbadi

division:

eastern half of island: 9 Indonesia, Irian Jaya

western half of island: 14 Papua New Guinea

government: 22 constitutional monarchy

head of state: 14 British monarch 15 governor-general

monetary unit: 4 kina, toea

island: 3 Aru 4 Aroe, Buka 5 Arroe, Ceram, Japen, Jobie, Manus 6 Cretin, Mussau, Ninigo, Waigeu 7 Sainson, Solomon 8 Bismarck, Kiriwina, Schouten, Woodlark 9 Admiralty, Trobriant 10 Louisiande, New Britain, New Ireland 12 Bougainville 14 D'Entrecasteaux

mountain: 4 Snow 6 Orange 8 Bismarck, Victoria 9 Carstensz 11 Owen Stanley 12 Albert Edward

highest point:

Irian Jaya: 9 Carstensz 10 Puncak Jaya

Papua New Guinea: 7 Wilhelm

river: 3 Fly 4 Hamu, Hany, Ramu 5 Degul, Sepik 6 Kikori, Purari 7 Amberno, Markham

sea: 5 Ceram, Coral, Sepik 6 Indian 7 Arafura, Pacific, Solomon 8 Bismarck

physical feature:

bay: 3 Oro 5 Milne 8 Geelvink

gulf: 4 Huon 5 Papua

strait: 6 Torres, Vitiaz

people: 5 Pygmy 6 Papuan 7 Negrito 10 Melanesian

explorer: 15 Jorge de Menesses

ruler: 7 Germany 9 Australia 12 Great Britain

language: 4 Motu 7 English 16 Melanesian Pidjin

religion: 7 animism 10 Protestant 13 Roman Catholic

feature:

bird: 7 mudlark 9 cassowary

food:

dried coconut meat: 5 copra

New Hampshire

abbreviation: 2 NH

nickname: 7 Granite

capital: 7 Concord

largest city: 10 Manchester

others: 5 Dover, Keene 6 Berlin, Durham, Exeter, Nashua 7 Hanover, Laconia 8 Sandwich 9 Claremont, Rochester 10 Portsmouth 12 Bretton Woods

college: 5 Keene 6 Rivier 9 Dartmouth, St Anselms 10 New England

feature: 14 Great Stone Face

notch: 7 Kinsman, Pinkham 8 Crawford 9 Franconia

tribe: 6 Abnaki 9 Pennacook

people: 11 Robert Frost 12 Daniel French 13 Daniel Webster, Horace Greeley, Mary Baker Eddy

explorer: 9 Champlain 16 Captain John Smith

island: 4 Star 5 White 6 Shoals 7 Lunging

lake: 5 Squam 7 Ossipee, Sunapee, Umbagog 8 Newfound 10 Winnisquam 13 Winnipesaukee

land rank: 11 forty-fourth

mountain: 5 Flume, White 6 Moriah, Paugus 7 Waumbek 8 Chocorua, Sandwich 9 Franconia, Monadnock 11 Profile Peak 12 Presidential

highest point: 10 Washington

physical feature:

bay: 5 Great

president: 14 Franklin Pierce

river: 4 Saco 6 Israel 7 Bellamy 8 Souhegan 9 Merrimack 10 Piscataqua 11 Connecticut, Salmon Falls 12 Androscoggin

state admission: 5 ninth

state bird: 11 purple finch

state flower: 11 purple lilac

state motto: 13 Live Free Or Die

state song: 15 Old New Hampshire 26 New Hampshire My New Hampshire

state tree: 10 paper birch, white birch

Newhart

character: 4 Dick 6 Joanna 7 Michael 9 Stephanie

cast: 9 Mary Frann 10 Bob Newhart, Julia Duffy 12 Peter Scolari

Newhart, Bob

born: 9 Chicago IL

roles: 7 Newhart 10 Cold Turkey 17 The Bob Newhart Show

New Hebrides *see* 7 Vanuatu

New Jersey

abbreviation: 2 NJ

nickname: 6 Garden 8 Mosquito

capital: 7 Trenton

largest city: 6 Newark

others: 4 Lodi 5 Ewing, Ft Lee 6 Camden, Dumont, Haddon, Kearny, Linden, Nutley, Orange, Rahway, Totowa 7 Bayonne, Cape May, Clifton, Hoboken, Hohokus, Keyport, Madison, Matawan, Netcong, Oradell, Paramus, Passaic, Raritan, Teaneck, Tenafly, Wyckoff 8 Carteret, Cranford, Freehold, Garfield, Hillside, Metuchen, Paterson, Secaucus, Watchung 9 Bridgeton, Elizabeth, Englewood, Hawthorne, Irvington, Maplewood, Montclair, Ocean City, Princeton 10 Asbury Park, Belleville, Ft Monmouth, Hackensack, Jersey City, Livingston, Long Branch, Morristown, Perth Amboy

11 Bergenfield **12** Atlantic City, Collingswood, New Brunswick

colleges: 4 Drew **6** Upsala **7** Rutgers **8** Caldwell, Monmouth, St Peter's **9** Princeton, Seton Hall **10** Bloomfield **18** Fairleigh-Dickinson

feature: 9 Boardwalk **16** Delaware Water Gap

tribe: 8 Delaware **11** Lenni-Lanape

people: 9 Aaron Burr **11** Joyce Kilmer, Paul Robeson **12** Stephen Crane, Thomas Edison **13** James Lawrence **19** James Fenimore Cooper

explorer: 6 Hudson **9** Verrazano

lake: 6 Mohawk **9** Greenwood, Hopatcong

land rank: 10 forty-sixth

mountain: 8 Piedmont **10** Kittatinny **13** First Watchung **14** Second Watchung

highest point: **9** High Point

physical feature: 9 Palisades, Sandy Hook

bay: **8** Delaware

cape: **3** May

sea: **8** Atlantic

president: 15 Grover Cleveland

river: 4 Toms **5** Dennis, Haynes, Hudson, Mantua, Ramapo **7** Mullica, Passaic, Raritan **8** Cohansey, Delaware, Tuckahoe **10** Hackensack

state admission: 5 third

state bird: 16 eastern goldfinch

state flower: 6 violet

state motto: 20 Liberty and Prosperity

state tree: 6 red oak

basketball team: 4 Nets

football team: 8 Generals

hockey team: 6 Devils

Newley, Anthony

wife: 11 Joan Collins

born: 6 London **7** England

roles: 11 Oliver Twist **25** Stop the World I Want to Get Off **41** The Roar of the Greasepaint The Smell of the Crowd

newly 4 anew **6** afresh, lately, of late **7** freshly, just now **8** recently

newly rich person

French: **12** nouveau riche

Newlywed Game, The

host: 10 Bob Eubanks

executive producer: 11 Chuck Barris

Newlyweds, The

creator: 13 George McManus

character: 12 Baby Snookums

Newman, Barnett

born: 9 New York NY

artwork: 7 Abraham, The Wild **8** Onement I **18** Stations of the Cross **19** Vir Heroicus Sublimis

Newman, Christopher

character in: 11 The American

author: 5 James

Newman, John Henry (Cardinal)

author of: 18 Apologia pro Vita Sua

Newman, Paul

wife: 14 Joanne Woodward

born: 11 Cleveland OH

roles: 3 Hud **6** Harper, Picnic **8** The Sting **10** The Hustler, The Verdict **12** Cool Hand Luke **15** Absence of Malice, The Color of Money **16** Cat on a Hot Tin Roof, The Left-Handed Gun, The Long Hot Summer, The Silver Chalice **29** Butch Cassidy and the Sundance Kid

New Mexico

abbreviation: 2 NM **4** N Mex

nickname: 8 Sunshine **17** Land of Enchantment

capital: 7 Santa Fe

largest city: 11 Albuquerque

others: 3 Jal **4** Taos **5** Aztec, Belen, Hobbs, Raton **6** Clovis, Deming, Gallup, Grants **7** Artesia, Bananea, Roswell, Socorro, Torreon **8** Carlsbad **9** Las Cruces, Los Alamos **10** Alamogordo **13** Piedras Negras

college: 7 Sante Fe **11** Albuquerque

feature: 11 Four Corners

dam: **5** Butte **8** Elephant

labs: **6** Sandia **17** Los Alamos National

national monument: 10 Aztec Ruins, White Sands **11** Chaco Canyon **17** Gila Cliff Dwelling

national park: 15 Carlsbad Caverns

observatory: **14** Sacramento Peak

tribe: 3 Sia **4** Hano, Piro, Tano, Taos, Tewa, Tiwa, Zuni **5** Acoma, Jemez, Kares, Manso, Pecos, Tiqua, Tonoa **6** Apache, Isleta, Laguna, Navaho, Navajo, Pueblo **7** Anasazi, Picuris **8** Santa Ana **9** Mescalero **12** Santo Domingo

people: 9 Kit Carson, Peter Hurd **11** Bill Mauldin

explorer: 5 Onate **6** de Niza, de Vaca **8** Coronado

lake: 6 El Vado, Navajo, Sumner **7** Conchas **8** McMillan **10** Alamogordo **13** Elephant Butte

land rank: 5 fifth

mountain: 5 Jemez **6** Sandia **7** Manzano, Mimbres, Rockies, Truchas **8** Mogollon **9** Guadalupe, San Andres **10** Nacimiento, Sacramento **11** Mount Taylor **15** Sangre de Christo

highest point: **11** Wheeler Peak

physical feature:

basin: **8** Tularosa

desert: **15** Jornada de Muerto

plains: **5** Great

river: 3 Ute **4** Gila **5** Pecos **7** San Jose, San Juan **8** Canadian **9** Rio Grande

state admission: 12 forty-seventh

state bird: 10 roadrunner

state fish: 14 cutthroat trout

state flower: 5 yucca

state motto: 15 It Grows as It Goes

state song: 14 O Fair New Mexico **16** Asi es Nuevo Mexico

state tree: 5 pinon **8** tarantah **15** velvet ash pinyon

New Orleans

basketball team: Jazz

event: 9 Mardi Gras, Sugar Bowl **25** International Jazz Festival

football team: 6 Saints
landmark: 7 Cabildo 9 Old Square, Superdome 10 Vieux Carre 12 Pirate's Alley 13 French Quarter
noted for: 4 jazz
people: 5 Cajun 6 Creole 7 Acadian
river: 11 Mississippi
street: 5 Royal 7 Bourbon
university: 6 Loyola, Tulane
news 4 dirt, dope, talk, word 5 flash, libel, piece, rumor, story 6 babble, expose, gossip, report 7 account, article, chatter, hearsay, lowdown, mention, message, release, scandal, slander, tidings 8 bulletin, dispatch, exposure 9 statement 10 communique, disclosure, divulgence, revelation 11 information 12 announcement, intelligence
news account 4 item 5 story 6 report 7 release 8 bulletin, dispatch 10 communique
newsmonger 6 gossip 8 busybody, reporter
News of the Day
  also: 12 Neues vom Tage
  opera by: 9 Hindemith
  character: 5 Laura 7 Eduoard
Newsome, Chadwick
  character in: 14 The Ambassadors
  author: 5 James
New Spain *see* 6 Mexico
newspaper 3 rag 5 daily, paper, sheet 6 herald, weekly 7 courant, gazette, journal, tabloid, tribune 10 periodical 11 publication
New Testament
  books of: 4 Acts, John, Jude, Luke, Mark 5 James, Peter, Titus 6 Romans 7 Hebrews, Matthew, Timothy 8 Philemon 9 Ephesians, Galatians 10 Colossians, Revelation 11 Corinthians, Philippians 13 Thessalonians
  books: 12 Humologumena
Newton, Isaac
  field: 11 mathematics
  nationality: 7 British
  discovered laws of: 6 motion 7 gravity 8 calculus
  discovered: 13 color spectrum 15 binomial theorem 16 method of fluxions
  invented: 21 infinitesimal calculus
New York
  abbreviation: 2 NY
  nickname: 6 Empire 9 Excelsior
  capital: 6 Albany
  largest city: 7 New York
  others: 3 Rye 4 Rome, Troy 5 Ilion, Islip, Nyack, Olean, Owego, Utica 6 Attica, Auburn, Cohoes, Elmira, Goshen, Ithaca, Oneida, Oswego, Tappan 7 Ardsley, Babylon, Batavia, Buffalo, Congers, Endwell, Geneseo, Hewlett, Mahopac, Merrick, Messena, Mineola, Montauk, Oneonta, Pennyan, Suffern, Syosset, Wantagh, Yaphank, Yonkers 8 Bethpage, Catskill, Endicott, Herkimer, Kingston, Ossining, Pottsdam, Saratoga, Tuckahoe 9 Rochester, Scarsdale 10 Binghamton, Bronxville, Mamaroneck 11 Cooperstown, New

Rochelle, Schenectady, White Plains 12 Poughkeepsie
  college: 4 Bard, CUNY, Iona, Pace, SUNY 5 Finch, Keuka 6 Hobart, Hunter, Vassar 7 Adelphi, Barnard, Colgate, Cornell, Fordham, St John's 8 Columbia, Skidmore, Syracuse 9 Juilliard, Rochester, West Point 13 Sarah Lawrence 30 Rensselaer Polytechnic Institute
  feature:
  building: 11 Empire State
  hall of fame: 8 baseball
  park: 7 Central
  prison: 6 Attica 8 SingSing
  square: 5 Times 6 Herald
  statue: 7 Liberty
  street/avenue: 4 Park, Wall 5 Fifth 7 Madison 8 Broadway
  tomb: 6 Grant's
  tribe: 4 Erie 6 Cayuga, Mohawk, Oneida, Seneca 7 Mohican, Montauk 8 Iroquois, Onondaga 9 Manhattan, people: 7 John Jay 8 Walloons 9 Jonas Salk 10 Henry James 11 Rockefeller, Walt Whitman 12 Eugene O'Neill 13 DeWitt Clinton, John Burroughs 14 Herman Melville 15 Peter Stuyvesant 16 Eleanor Roosevelt, Washington Irving 17 Fiorello La Guardia
  explorer: 6 Hudson 9 Champlain, Verrazano 16 Dutch West India Co
  island: 4 Fire, Long 5 Ellis 6 Staten 7 Bedloe's, Fisher's, Liberty, Shelter, Welfare 8 Thousand 9 Governors, Manhattan
  lake: 4 Erie 6 Cayuga, Finger, George, Oneida, Otisco, Otsego, Owasco, Placid, Seneca 7 Conesus, Ontario, Saranac, Schroon 8 Saratoga 9 Champlain
  land rank: 9 thirtieth
  mountain: 4 Bear 5 Slide 7 Taconic 9 Catskills 10 Adirondacks
  highest point: 5 Marcy
  physical feature:
  bay: 7 Jamaica, Peconic 8 Moriches
  canal: 4 Erie 7 Gowanus
  falls: 7 Niagara
  valley: 6 Mohawk
  president: 14 Martin Van Buren 14 Teddy Roosevelt 15 Millard Fillmore 17 Theodore Roosevelt 23 Franklin Delano Roosevelt
  river: 4 East 5 Black, Tioga 6 Harlem, Hoosic, Hudson, Mohawk, Oswego 7 Ausable, Genesee, Niagara 10 St Lawrence 11 Susquehanna
  state bird: 8 bluebird
  state fish: 10 brook trout
  state flower: 4 rose
  state motto: 9 Excelsior (Ever upward, Still higher)
  state tree: 10 sugar maple
New York City
  airport: 3 JFK 6 Newark 9 La Guardia 12 John F Kennedy
  area: 4 Soho 6 Harlem 7 Chelsea, Midtown, Tribeca 9 Chinatown, Manhattan 10 Stuyvesant 11 Brownsville, Little Italy 13

Spanish Harlem 16 Greenwich Village 17 Bedford-Stuyvesant

baseball team: 4 Mets 7 Yankees

basketball team: 6 Knicks 14 Knickerbockers

borough: 5 Bronx 6 Queens 8 Brooklyn, Richmond 9 Manhattan

early governor: 10 Stuyvesant

football team: 4 Jets 6 Giants

former name: 12 New Amsterdam

hockey team: 7 Rangers 9 Islanders

island: 4 City, Long 5 Ellis, Ward's 6 Riker's, Staten 7 Liberty 8 Randall's 9 Governor's, Manhattan, Roosevelt

landmark: 5 Macy's 8 Bronx Zoo 11 Battery Park, Central Park, Penn Station, Shea Stadium, Times Square 12 Carnegie Hall 13 Gracie Mansion, Lincoln Center, Port Authority, Trinity Church, United Nations, Yankee Stadium 14 Waldorf-Astoria 15 NY Public Library, NY Stock Exchange, Seagram Building, Statue of Liberty 16 Bellevue Hospital, Chrysler Building, World Trade Center 17 Hayden Planetarium, Rockefeller Center, Woolworth Building 18 Radio City Music Hall 19 Empire State Building, Grand Central Station, Madison Square Garden, St Patrick's Cathedral 22 Metropolitan Opera House 26 Sloan-Kettering Cancer Center 29 Cathedral of Saint John the Divine

mayor: 4 Koch 6 Walker 9 La Guardia

museum: 6 Jewish 7 Whitney 9 Cloisters 10 Guggenheim 12 Cooper-Hewitt, Metropolitan 15 Frick Collection 17 Museum of Modern Art (MoMA) 30 American Museum of Natural History

river: 4 East 6 Harlem, Hudson

street: 6 Bowery 8 Broadway 9 Lexington 10 Park Avenue, Wall Street 11 Central Park, Fifth Avenue, Sutton Place 13 Madison Avenue 17 Forty-Second Street

university: 3 NYU 6 Queens 7 Barnard, Fordham, Yeshiva 8 Brooklyn, Columbia 13 Hunter College 22 Juilliard School of Music 23 City University of New York

New Zealand

other name: 8 Aotearoa 12 Nieuw Zeeland 23 Land of the Long White Cloud

capital: 10 Wellington

largest city: 8 Auckland

others: 5 Leuin, Oreti, Otaki, Taupo 6 Clutha, Foxton, Oamaru, Picton, Timaru 7 Dunedin, Manu Kau, Raetihi, Rotorua 8 Hamilton, Kawakawa, Touranga 9 Lyttelton 10 Queenstown 12 Christchurch, Invercargill, Port Chalmers 13 Port Nicholson 14 Napier-Hastings 15 Palmerston North

school: 5 Otago 6 Massey 7 Waikato 8 Auckland, Victoria 10 Canterbury

division: 11 North Island, South Island

head of state: 14 British monarch 15 governor general

monetary unit: 4 cent 6 dollar

island: 4 Cook, Niue, Otea 5 North, South 6 Bounty, Chatam, Snares 7 Stewart, Tokelau 8 Auckland, Campbell, Kermadec, Puketutu 9 Antipodes 10 Resolution, Three Kings 12 Great Barrier

lake: 3 Ada 4 Gunn, Ohau 5 Hawea, Taupo 6 Pukaki, Pupuke, Te Anau, Tekapo, Wanaka 7 Brunner, Diamond, Kanieri, Okareka, Rotorua 8 Okataina, Paradise, Rotoaira, Wakatipu 9 Manapouri

mountain: 4 Eden, Flat, Owen 5 Allen, Chope, Lyall, Mitre, Ohope, Otari, Young 6 Egmont, Stokes, Tasman 7 Cameron, Coronet, Ernslaw, Huiarau, Pihanga, Ruahine, Ruapehu, Tauhera, Tutamoe, Tyndall 8 Aspiring, Richmond, Tauranga 9 Messenger, Murchison, Ngauruhoe, Raukumara, Tongariro 11 Remarkables 12 Southern Alps

highest point: 4 Cook 7 Aorangi

river: 4 Avon 5 Mokau, Waipa 6 Clutha, Rakaia, Tamaki, Waihou, Wairau, Wairoa 7 Waikato, Waitaki 8 Clarence, Manawatu, Wanganui 10 Rangitikei

sea: 6 Tasman 12 South Pacific

physical feature:

bay: 4 Ohua 5 Evans, Hawke, Lyall 6 Awarua, Cloudy, Golden, Plenty, Tasman 7 Fitzroy, Pegasus, Poverty 8 Halfmoon, Rangaunu

bight: 7 Karamea 10 Canterbury 13 North Taranaki, South Taranaki

cape: 4 East, West 5 North 6 Egmont 8 Farewell, Foulwind, Palliser 9 Southwest

channel: 8 Colville

falls: 10 Sutherland

glacier: 3 Fox 6 Tasman 11 Franz Joseph

gulf: 7 Hauraki

harbor: 7 Kaipara, Manukau 9 Waitemata

peninsula: 5 Mahia, Otago

plains: 10 Canterbury

sound: 8 Doubtful

strait: 4 Cook 7 Foveaux

people: 3 Ati 5 Arawa, Dutch, Maori 7 British, Ringatu 10 Polynesian

author: 5 Frame 9 Mansfield 10 Ngaio Marsh 12 Ashton-Warner

explorer: 4 Cook 6 Tasman

mountain climber: 7 Hillary

language: 5 Maori 7 English

religion: 8 Anglican 9 Methodist 10 Protestant 12 Presbyterian 13 Roman Catholic

place:

national park: 9 Fiordland, Fjordland, Tongariro

feature:

animal: 7 tuatara

bird: 3 kea, tui 4 kiwi, weka 6 takahe 7 apteryx 8 bellbird

tree: 4 rimu, tawa 5 kauri, matai 6 totara

food:

fish: 4 mako

fruit: 4 kiwi 9 tamarillo 17 Chinese gooseberry

next-door 8 adjacent 9 adjoining 10 connecting, contiguous, juxtaposed, side-by-side, 12 conterminous

next to 6 beside 8 abutting, adjacent 9 adjoining, bordering 10 contiguous, juxtaposed 12 conterminous

next world, the 6 Heaven 8 eternity, paradise 12 the hereafter 14 the world to come

Nez Perce (Numipu)
  language family: 10 Shahaptian
  location: 5 Idaho 6 Oregon 10 Washington
  leader: 11 Chief Joseph

Niamey
  capital of: 5 Niger

nib 3 end, tip, top 4 apex, peak 5 point 6 height, tiptop, vertex 7 extreme 8 pinnacle 9 extremity

nibble 3 nip 4 bite, chew, gnaw, peck 5 crumb, munch, speck, taste 6 crunch, morsel, peck, at tidbit 8 fragment, particle

Nibelung, ring of
  origin: 8 Germanic
  mentioned in: 14 Nibelungenlied
  stolen by: 8 Alberich

Nibelungenlied
  origin: 8 Germanic
  form: 4 epic
  date written: 17 thirteenth century
  related to: 8 Volsunga
  author: 7 unknown
  character: 5 Etzel (Attila), Hagen 6 Gernot 7 Gunther 8 Brunhild, Dankwart, Giselher 9 Kriemhild, Siegfried

Nibelungs, Niblungs
  origin: 8 Germanic, Teutonic
  followers of: 9 Siegfried
  race: 6 dwarfs
  possessed: 8 treasure
  captured by: 9 Siegfried
  family of: 7 Gunther

Nicaragua
  capital/largest city: 7 Managua
  others: 4 Leon, Rama 6 Masaya 7 Corinto, Granada 8 Jinotega 9 Matagalpa 10 Bluefields, Chinandega
  division: 13 Mosquito Coast
  measure: 4 vara 5 cahiz 6 suerte 7 cajuela, manzana 10 cabelleria
  monetary unit: 4 peso 7 centavo, cordoba
  weight: 3 bag 4 caha, caja 8 tonelada
  island: 7 Ometepe
  lake: 7 Managua 9 Nicaragua
  mountain: 4 Leon 5 Negro, Viejo 6 Madera, Telica 7 Managua, Saslaya 9 Momotombo
  highest point: 7 Mogoton
  river: 4 Coco, Tuma 5 Wanks 6 Grande, Poteca 7 San Juan 8 Tipitapa 9 Escondido
  sea: 7 Pacific 9 Caribbean
  physical feature:
  gulf: 7 Fonseca
  people: 4 Mico, Mixe, Rama, Smoo, Ulva

5 Cukra, Diria, Lenca, Sambo, Toaca 6 Mangue 7 mestizo, Miskito 8 Mosquito 9 Matagalpa
  author: 5 Dario
  explorer: 6 Davila 7 Cordoba 8 Columbus
  group: 6 Contra 10 Sandinista
  leader: 6 Somoza, Walker, Zelaya 7 Nicardo 8 Chamorro
  language: 7 English, Spanish
  religion: 13 Roman Catholic
  place:
  cathedral: 12 Metropolitan
  feature:
  dance: 5 sones 10 zapateados, zarabandas
  food:
  beans: 8 frijoles
  dish: 10 naca tamale
  drink: 5 tiste 9 pinolillo
  fruit: 6 zapote

nice 4 deft, fine, good, kind 5 dandy, exact, fussy, great, swell 6 divine, genial, lovely, proper, seemly, strict, subtle 7 amiable, amusing, careful, cordial, correct, finicky, genteel, likable, precise, refined, winning 8 accurate, charming, cheerful, delicate, friendly, gracious, jim-dandy, ladylike, pleasant, pleasing, rigorous, skillful, unerring, virtuous, well-bred 9 agreeable, congenial, excellent, fantastic, marvelous, sensitive, wonderful 10 attractive, delightful, enchanting, entrancing, fastidious, methodical, meticulous, scrupulous 11 interesting, painstaking, pleasurable, punctilious, respectable, sympathetic, warmhearted 13 compassionate, understanding, well brought up 17 overconscientious

Nice and the Good, The
  author: 11 Iris Murdoch

nicely 6 neatly 7 exactly, fussily, happily 9 carefully, precisely 10 accurately, critically, pleasantly, unerringly 11 faultlessly, fortunately, opportunely 12 attractively, fastidiously

nicety 4 care, tact 5 flair, grace 6 acumen, polish 7 culture, finesse, insight 8 accuracy, delicacy, elegance, subtlety 9 attention, exactness, precision 10 refinement 11 cultivation, penetration, preciseness, sensitivity 12 per spicacity, subtle detail, taste fulness 13 elaborateness, particularity 14 discrimination, fastidiousness, meticulousness

niche 4 cove, nook, slot 5 berth, trade 6 alcove, cavity, corner, cranny, dugout, hollow, metier, recess 7 calling 8 position, vocation 9 cubby hole 10 depression, pigeon hole 11 proper place 13 hole in the wall

Nicholas Nickleby
  author: 14 Charles Dickens
  character: 5 Smike 11 Arthur Gride, Newman Noggs 12 Kate Nickleby, Madeline Bray 13 Lord Verisopht, Ralph Nickleby 14 Frank Cheeryble 15 Sir Mulberry Hawk, Vincent Crummles, Wackford Squeers 17 Cheeryble Brothers

Nichols, Mike
director of: 7 Catch-22 11 The Graduate
(Oscar) 15 Carnal Knowledge 25 Who's
Afraid of Virginia Woolf?

Nicholson, Ben
born: 6 Denham 7 England
artwork: 9 Fireworks 11 White Relief 12
Tuscan Relief 13 Painted Relief 14 At the
Chat Botte

Nicholson, Jack
born: 9 Neptune NJ
roles: 8 Ironweed 9 Chinatown, Easy
Rider 10 The Shining 12 Prizzi's Honor,
The Passenger 13 The Last Detail 14
Five Easy Pieces 15 Carnal Knowledge
17 Terms of Endearment 20 The Witches
of Eastwick 22 The King of Marvin Gardens 25 One Flew Over the Cuckoo's
Nest (Oscar) 26 The Postman Always
Rings Twice

nicht wahr? 10 isn't that so?

Nicippe
father: 6 Pelops
son: 10 Eurystheus

nick 3 cut, jag, mar 4 chip, dent, gash,
mark, scar 5 cleft, gouge, notch, score,
wound 6 damage, deface, indent, injure,
injury 7 marking, scarify, scoring, scratch 8
incision, lacerate 10 depression 11 indentation

nickel
chemical symbol: 2 Ni

Nickel Mountain
author: 11 John Gardner

nickname 6 handle 7 agnomen, epithet,
moniker, pet name 8 baby name, cognomen 9 pseudonym, sobriquet 10 diminutive 11 appellation, designation

Nicomachean Ethics
author: 9 Aristotle

Nidhogg
origin: 12 Scandinavian
form: 7 serpent
domain: 8 Niflheim
gnaws on lowest root of: 9 Iggdrasil,
Yggdrasil

Nielsen, Carl August
born: 6 Odense 7 Denmark
composer of: 9 Maskarade 12 Saul and
David 16 Inextinguishable (symphony
No 4)

Nietzsche, Friedrich
author of: 14 The Will to Power 17 Beyond Good and Evil, The Birth of Tragedy
20 Thus Spake Zarathustra

Niflheim
origin: 12 Scandinavian
ruler of: 3 Hel
purpose: 10 punish dead
climate: 3 fog 4 cold

nifty 4 chic, fine, neat, posh 5 natty, smart
6 clever, dapper 7 dashing, stylish 8 splendid 10 attractive 11 fashionable

Niger
other name: 6 Joliba, Kworra, Ramtil
capital/largest city: 6 Niamey
others: 5 Goure 6 Agadex, Agadez,
Maradi, Tahoua, Zinder
division:
region: 3 Air 5 Arlit, Sahel
monetary unit: 5 franc 7 centime
lake: 4 Chad
mountain: 7 Bagzane 9 Air Massif
highest point: 7 Greboun
river: 5 Niger 6 Dillia
physical feature:
desert: 6 Sahara
oasis: 6 Kaouar
plateau: 5 Djado 6 Tegama 7 Tchigai 8
Mengueni 11 Adar Doutchi, Djerma
Ganda
people: 4 Daza, Idjo, Idyo, Idzo, Peul,
Teda 5 Hausa, Warri 6 Djerma, Fulani,
Kanuri, Songha, Toubou, Tuareg 13
Djerma-Songhai
conqueror: 13 Usman Dan Fodio
leader: 5 Diori 6 Saibou 7 Ousmane 8
Kountche
language: 5 Hausa, Mande 6 Djerma,
French, Fulani, Tuareg 8 Mandingo, Tamashek
religion: 5 Islam 7 animism 12 Christianity
place:
ruins: 6 Agadez
feature:
cavalry: 5 Dosso
empire: 4 Mali 6 Fulani 7 Songhai 10
Kanem-Borno
tree: 6 acacia, baobab

Nigeria
capital: 5 Abuja
largest city: 5 Lagos
new capital: 5 Abuja
others: 3 Aba, Ado, Ede, Isa, Iwo, Jos,
Oyo 4 Bida, Bidi, Buea, Kano, Offa, Yola
5 Benin, Bonny, Enugu, Warri, Zaria 6
Burutu, Ibadan, Ilesha, Ilorin, Kachia,
Kaduna, Kadune, Kokoto, Mushin, Ta-
koba 7 Calabar, Onitsha, Oshogbo 8
Abeokuta 9 Maiduguri, Ogbomosho 12
Port Harcourt
division: 3 Air, Isa, Oyo 4 Kano, Nupe,
Ondo 5 Asben, Benin, Bornu, Ijebu,
Ogoja, Warri 6 Biafra, Degema, Owerri,
Sokoto 7 Adamawa
monetary unit: 4 kobo 5 naira
lake: 4 Chad
highest point: 7 Dimlang
river: 3 Oli 4 Gana, Yobe 5 Benin,
Benue, Cross, Niger 6 Kaduna, Sokoto 7
Calabar, Gongola 8 Komadugu 9
Sambreiro
sea: 8 Atlantic
physical feature:
bight: 5 Benin, Bonny 6 Biafra
delta: 5 Niger
gulf: 6 Guinea
plains: 5 Bornu 9 Hausaland
plateau: 3 Jos, Udi 6 Bauchi

port: 5 Lagos 7 Calabar 8 Harcourt

people: 3 Abo, Aro, Djo, Ebo, Edo, Ibo, Ijo, Tiv, Vai 4 Beni, Bini, Eboe, Efik, Egba, Ejam, Ekoi, Idyo, Igbo, Ijaw, Nupe 5 Angas, Benin, Gwari, Hausa 6 Chamba, Fulani, Ibibio, Kanuri, Yoruba 11 Hausa-Fulani

author: 6 Achebe

British colonial ruler: 6 Goldie, Lugard

kingdom: 3 Ife, Nok, Oyo 5 Benin 6 Fulani 10 Kanem-Borno

leader: 5 Gowon 6 Balewa, Ojukwu, Schick 7 Awolowo, Azikine, Azikiwe, Shagari 8 Obasanjo 9 Babangida 13 Usman dan Fodio

language: 3 Ibo 4 Efik, Igbo 5 Hausa 6 Yoruba 7 English

religion: 5 Islam 7 animism 12 Christianity

place:

dam: 6 Kainji

mosque/walled city: 4 Kano

feature:

dress: 4 riga 7 agbados

tree: 5 abura, afara 6 obeche 10 terminalia

war: 7 Biafran

niggard 4 mean 5 cheap, miser, tight 6 stingy 7 miserly 8 scrimper 9 skinflint 10 ungenerous 12 parsimonious

niggardliness 6 penury 8 meanness 9 closeness, parsimony 10 stinginess 11 miserliness 13 penny-pinching 15 tightfistedness

niggardly 4 mean, poor 5 cheap, close, sorry, tight 6 flimsy, frugal, meager, measly, paltry, saving, scanty, shabby, stingy, tawdry 7 miserly, scrubby, sparing, thrifty 8 beggarly, grubbing, grudging, stinting, wretched 9 illiberal, mercenary, miserable, penurious 10 hardfisted, second-rate, ungenerous 11 closefisted 12 contemptible, insufficient, parsimonious

Nigger of the Narcissus, The

author: 12 Joseph Conrad

character: 5 Baker 6 Donkin 9 James Wait 12 Old Singleton

niggling 5 fussy, minor, petty, small 7 finicky 8 caviling, nugatory, picayune, piddling, trifling 9 quibbling 10 negligible, nitpicking 12 pettifogging 13 insignificant 15 inconsequential

nigh 4 near 5 close, handy 6 almost, at hand, nearly 7 close by 8 adjacent 9 bordering 11 neighboring, practically

night 4 dark, dusk 7 bedtime, evening, sundown 8 darkness, eventide 9 murkiness, obscurity 13 tenebrousness

goddess of: 3 Nox

nightclub

French: 5 boite 11 boite de nuit

nightfall 4 dark, dusk 6 sunset 7 evening, sundown 8 darkness, eventide 9 gloaming, moonrise, twilight

French: 10 crepuscule

Night Gallery

host: 10 Rod Serling

nightingale

group of: 5 watch

Nightline

host: 9 Ted Koppel

nightly 4 dark 7 evening, obscure 9 nocturnal 11 nocturnally

nightmare 7 incubus 8 bad dream, succubus 13 hallucination

Night of the Iguana, The

director: 10 John Huston

based on play by: 17 Tennessee Williams

cast: 7 Sue Lyon 8 Skip Ward 10 Ava Gardner 11 Deborah Kerr 13 Richard Burton

setting: 6 Mexico

nightshade 16 Solanum dulcamara

varieties: 4 ball 5 black 6 common, deadly, sticky 7 Malabar 8 stinking 9 melon-leaf, poisonous, soda-apple 10 enchanter's

Nights of Cabiria

director: 15 Federico Fellini

cast: 13 Amedeo Nazzari 14 Francois Perier 15 Giulietta Masina

remade as: 12 Sweet Charity

nightstick 3 rod 4 mace, wand 5 baton, staff 6 cudgel 7 scepter 8 bludgeon 9 billy club, truncheon 10 shillelagh

nighttime 4 late 5 night 9 late-night, nighttide, nocturnal

Night to Remember, A

director: 8 Roy Baker

based on story by: 10 Walter Lord

cast: 9 Jill Dixon 11 Kenneth More 13 David McCallum 16 Laurence Naismith

setting: 7 Titanic

nihil 7 nothing

nihilism 5 chaos 6 anomie 7 license 9 amorality, anarchism, emptiness, terrorism 10 alienation, iconoclasm, radicalism, skepticism 11 agnosticism, lawlessness, nothingness 12 nonexistence 16 irresponsibility

nihilist 5 rebel 9 anarchist, terrorist 13 revolutionary

Nihon *see* 5 Japan

Nike

origin: 5 Greek

goddess of: 7 victory

father: 11 Titan Pallas

mother: 4 Styx

brother: 5 Zelos

corresponds to: 6 Athena 8 Victoria

nil 4 none, null, zero 6 cipher, naught 7 nothing, nullity 11 nonexistent

Nile

boat: 5 baris 6 cangia, nuggar, sandal 7 felucca, gaiassa 8 dahabeah

cities: 3 Qus 4 Abri, Argo, Idfu, Isna, Juba, Qina 5 Aswan, Asyut, Cairo, Kokka, Kusti, Luxor, Meroe, Minya, Rejaf, Saite, Tanis, Tanta 6 Atbara, Faiyum 7 Malakel, Mansura, Rosetta 8 Khartoum,

Omdurman, Rusayris 9 Was Madani 10
Alexandria
dam: 6 Sannar 9 Aswan High, White Nile
desert bordering: 6 Libyan, Nubian 7
Arabian
falls: 5 Ripon 8 Kabalega 9 Murchison
feature: 6 Sphinx
pyramid: 4 Giza
temple: 8 Ramses II 9 Abu Simbel 11
Deir el-Bahri, Medinet Habu
flows into: 13 Mediterranean
flows through: 5 Egypt, Kenya, Sudan,
Zaire 6 Rwanda, Uganda 7 Burundi 8
Ethiopia, Tanzania
island: 4 Roda 6 Philae
lake: 4 Tana 5 Kyoga, Tsana 6 Albert,
Edward, Nasser 8 Victoria
other name: 4 Hapi 20 The Father of the
Rivers
people: 3 Jur, Luo, Lwo, Nuo, Suk 4 Bari,
Beja, Golo, Luoh, Madi 5 Nilot 7 Shilluk
plain: 6 Gezira
plant: 4 sudd 5 lotus
starting point: 5 Tsana 8 Victoria
swamp: 4 Sudd
tributary: 4 Arab 5 Rahad, Sobat 6
Atbara, Ghazai, Kagera 7 Rosetta 8 Blue
Nile, Damietta 9 Bahr Jebel, White Nile
Niles, Hazel and Peter
characters in: 22 Mourning Becomes
Electra
author: 6 O'Neill
nil nisi bonum 21 nothing unless it is good
nil sine numine 27 nothing without the divine will
motto of: 8 Colorado
nimble 4 deft, spry 5 agile, fleet, light,
quick, rapid, ready, swift 6 active, expert,
lively, prompt, speedy, supple 8 animated,
skillful, spirited 9 dexterous, mercurial,
sprightly 10 proficient
nimbleness 7 agility 8 alacrity, spryness 9
dexterity, quickness 10 limberness, suppleness
nimble-witted 5 droll, witty 6 clever 11 resourceful
nimbus 4 aura, disk, halo 5 cloud, vapor 7
aureole 8 radiance
Nimitz, Chester
served in: 3 WWI 4 WWII
commander of: 12 Pacific fleet
rank: 12 fleet (five-star) admiral 22 chief
of naval operations
battle: 6 Midway 9 Leyte Gulf 13 Philippine Sea
Nimoy, Leonard
born: 8 Boston MA
roles: 7 Mr Spock 8 Star Trek 17 Mission: Impossible 21 Star Trek: The Voyage Home 22 Star Trek: The Wrath of
Khan 25 Star Trek: The Search for Spock
Nimrod
father: 4 Cush
grandfather: 3 Ham
great grandfather: 4 Noah
founded: 5 Calah, Resen 7 Nineveh 8
Rehoboth

nincompoop 4 boob, dolt, dope, fool, jerk 5
dummy, dunce, idiot, klutz, moron, ninny 6
dimwit, lummox, nitwit 7 half-wit, jackass
8 bonehead, dummkopf, imbecile, lunkhead, numskull 9 blockhead, dumb bunny,
harebrain, numbskull, simpleton 10 dunderhead, dunderpate, muddlehead, noodlehead 11 knucklehead, rattlebrain 12
featherbrain, scatterbrain
Nine, the see 5 Muses
Nineteen Eighty-Four
author: 12 George Orwell
character: 5 Julia 6 O'Brien 11 Char-
rington 12 Winston Smith
1919
author: 13 John Dos Passos
Ninety-Five Theses
author: 12 Martin Luther
Nineveh
founder: 6 Nimrod
Nine worthies
mentioned in: 16 medieval romances
three each of: 4 Jews 6 Pagans 10
Christians
names: 5 David 6 Arthur, Hector, Joshua
11 Charlemagne 12 Julius Caesar 15 Judas Maccabaeus 17 Alexander the Great
18 Godefroy de Bouillon
Ningal
origin: 8 Sumerian
son: 3 Utu
consort of: 5 Nanna
Ninib see 7 Ninurta
Ninlil
origin: 8 Sumerian
goddess of: 3 air
ninny 3 ass, sap 4 fool, simp 5 booby,
dunce, idiot, moron 6 dimwit, nitwit 7 fathead, half-wit 8 bonehead, dumb-dumb,
imbecile, lunkhead, numskull 9 blockhead,
dumb bunny, lamebrain, numbskull 10
dunderhead, nincompoop 11 chowderhead
Ninotchka
director: 13 Ernst Lubitsch
cast: 9 Ina Claire 10 Bela Lugosi, Greta
Garbo 13 Melvyn Douglas
setting: 5 Paris
remade as: 13 Silk Stockings
Ninurta
also: 5 Ninib
origin: 8 Sumerian 10 Babylonian
type of god: 4 hero
personifies: 4 wind 9 south wind
father: 5 Enlil
avenger of: 5 Enlil
Ninus
wife: 9 Semiramis
founder of: 7 Nineveh
Niobe
father: 8 Tantalus
mother: 5 Dione
brother: 6 Pelops
husband: 7 Amphion
children: 9 seven sons 14 seven daughters
children called: 6 Niobid
taunted: 4 Leto

children killed by: 6 Apollo 7 Artemis
changed into: 5 stone
changed by: 4 Zeus
Niord
  also: 5 Njord
  origin: 12 Scandinavian
  god of: 4 wind 10 navigation, prosperity
  king of: 5 Vanir
  son: 4 Frey 5 Freyr
  daughter: 5 Freia, Freya
nip 3 cut, lop 4 bite, clip, crop, dock, grab, grip, ruin, snag, snap, snip 5 blast, check, chill, clamp, clasp, crack, crush, frost, grasp, pinch, quash, seize, sever, shear, snare, tweak 6 benumb, clutch, cut off, freeze, pierce, snatch, sunder, thwart 7 curtail, destroy, shorten, squeeze 8 compress, cut short, demolish 9 frustrate 10 abbreviate
nip-and-tuck 5 close
nip in the bud 7 prevent 8 preclude 9 forestall, frustrate
Nipper, Susan
  character in: 12 Dombey and Son
  author: 7 Dickens
Nippon *see* 5 Japan
nippy 3 raw 5 brisk, chill, crisp, sharp 6 biting, chilly 7 cutting
Nisn 16 first Hebrew month
nit-pick 4 carp, pick 5 cavil 9 criticize
nitrate 4 salt 5 ester 6 sodium 9 potassium 10 fertilizer
nitrogen
  chemical symbol: 1 N
nitty-gritty 4 core, crux, gist, meat, pith 5 heart 7 essence 9 substance
nitwit 3 ass 4 clod, dolt, fool 5 booby, dummy, dunce, idiot, klutz, moron, ninny 7 fathead, pinhead 8 bonehead, dumbdumb, imbecile, lunkhead, meathead, numskull, peabrain 9 birdbrain, blockhead, lamebrain, numbskull 10 dunderhead, nincompoop, noodlehead 11 chowderhead
Niven, David
  real name: 21 James David Graham Niven
  autobiography: 16 The Moon's a Balloon 21 Bring on the Empty Horses
  born: 8 Scotland 10 Kirriemuir
  roles: 11 Phileas Fogg 12 Casino Royale, My Man Godfrey 14 The Pink Panther, Separate Tables (Oscar) 16 Stairway to Heaven, Wuthering Heights 18 The Prisoner of Zenda 26 Around the World in Eighty Days
Nix
  origin: 8 Germanic
  form: 6 spirit
  habitat: 5 water
Nixon, Richard Milhous
  presidential rank: 13 thirty-seventh
  party: 10 Republican
  state represented: 2 NY
  defeated: 7 (George Corley) Wallace 8 (Hubert Horatio) Humphrey
  vice president: 4 (Gerald Rudolph) Ford 5 (Spiro Theodore) Agnew

cabinet:
  state: 6 (William Pierce) Rogers 9 (Henry A) Kissinger
  treasury: 5 (William E) Simon 6 (George P) Shultz 7 (David Matthew) Kennedy 8 (John Bowden) Connally
  defense: 5 (Melvin Robert) Laird 10 (Elliot L) Richardson 11 (James R) Schlesinger
  attorney general: 5 (William B) Saxbe 8 (John Newton) Mitchell 10 (Elliot L) Richardson 11 (Richard G) Kleindienst
  postmaster general: 6 (Winton Malcolm) Blount
  interior: 6 (Rogers Clark Ballard) Morton, (Walter Joseph) Hinkel
  agriculture: 4 (Earl Lauer) Butz 6 (Clifford Morris) Hardin
  commerce: 4 (Frederick B) Dent 5 (Maurice Hubert) Stans
  labor: 6 (George Pratt) Shultz 7 (James Day) Hodgson, (Peter J) Brennan
  HEW: 5 (Robert Hutchinson) Finch 10 (Caspar W) Weinberger, (Elliot Lee) Richardson
  HUD: 4 (James T) Lynn 6 (George Wilcken) Romney
  transportation: 5 (John Anthony) Volpe 8 (Claude S) Brinegar
  born: 2 CA 10 Yorba Linda
  died: 7 New York 11 New York City
education:
  college: 8 Whittier
  law school: 14 Duke University
  religion: 6 Quaker 16 Society of Friends
  interests: 8 football
  vacation spot: 11 Key Biscayne (FL), San Clemente (CA)
  dog: 8 Checkers 11 King Timahoe
  author: 9 Six Crises 10 The Real War 11 Beyond Peace 27 RN: The Memoirs of Richard Nixon
  political career: 8 US Senate 13 Vice President 24 US House of Representatives
  civilian career: 5 lawyer
  military service: 6 US Navy 10 lieutenant, World War II
notable events of lifetime/term:
  Calley court martialed for: 13 Mylai Massacre
  court martial of: 6 Calley
  creation of: 10 Bangladesh
  crisis: 3 oil 6 energy
  embargo on: 3 oil
  first men on: 4 moon
  incident: 11 Wounded Knee
  pardon of Nixon by: 4 Ford
  publication of: 14 Pentagon Papers
  resignation of: 5 Agnew, Nixon
  scandal: 9 Watergate
  student deaths at: 9 Kent State
  treaty: 10 Seabed Arms 32 Nonproliferation of Nuclear Weapons
  trip to: 5 China
  war: 7 Vietnam 10 Middle East 12 East Pakistan

quotes: 31 A respectable Republican cloth coat 35 You won't have Nixon to kick around any more
father: 14 Francis Anthony
mother: 6 Hannah (Milhous)
siblings: 11 Arthur Burdg 12 Harold Samuel 13 Edward Calvert, Francis Donald
wife: 8 (Thelma Catherine) Patricia (Ryan)
nickname: 3 Pat
children: 5 Julie 8 Patricia
Julie married: 15 David Eisenhower
Patricia married: 9 Edward Cox
Patricia's nickname: 6 Tricia
Njord see 5 Niord
no 3 nay, nix, not 4 none, veto
Noah
father: 6 Lamech
grandfather: 10 Methuselah
son: 3 Ham 4 Shem 7 Japheth
grandson: 3 Put 4 Cush 6 Canaan 7 Misraim
great grandson: 6 Nimrod
built: 3 ark
collected: 7 animals
survived: 5 flood
pertaining to: 8 Noachian
Noah's Ark
made of: 10 gopherwood
nob 4 peer, toff 5 swell 9 patrician 10 aristocrat
Nobel, Alfred
nationality: 7 Swedish
invented: 8 dynamite
originated: 10 Nobel Prize
Nobel Prizes
Literature:
1901: 20 Rene F A Sully-Prudhomme
1902: 14 Theodor Mommsen
1903: 20 Bjornstjerne Bjornson
1904: 13 Jose Echegaray 15 Frederic Mistral
1905: 17 Henryk Sienkiewicz
1906: 14 Giosue Carducci
1907: 14 Rudyard Kipling
1908: 13 Rudolf C Eucken
1909: 13 Selma Lagerlof
1910: 12 Paul von Heyse
1911: 18 Maurice Maeterlinck
1912: 16 Gerhart Hauptmann
1913: 21 Sir Rabindranath Tagore
1915: 13 Romain Rolland
1916: 15 Verner von Heidenstam
1917: 11 K A Gjellerup 17 Henrik Pontoppidan
1919: 15 Carl F G Spitteler
1920: 10 Knut Hamsun
1921: 13 Anatole France
1922: 25 Jacinto Benavente y Martinez
1923: 18 William Butler Yeats
1924: 17 Wladyslaw S Reymont
1925: 17 George Bernard Shaw
1926: 13 Grazia Deledda
1927: 12 Henri Bergson
1928: 12 Sigrid Undset
1929: 10 Thomas Mann

1930: 13 Sinclair Lewis
1931: 14 Erik A Karlfeldt
1932: 14 John Galsworthy
1933: 10 Ivan A Bunin
1934: 15 Luigi Pirandello
1936: 12 Eugene O'Neill
1937: 17 Roger Martin du Gard
1938: 10 Pearl S Buck
1939: 15 Frans E Sillanpaa
1944: 15 Johannes V Jensen
1945: 15 Gabriela Mistral
1946: 12 Hermann Hesse
1947: 9 Andre Gide
1948: 7 T S Eliot
1949: 15 William Faulkner
1950: 15 Bertrand Russell (Earl Russell)
1951: 14 Par F Lagerkvist
1952: 15 Francois Mauriac
1953: 21 Sir Winston L S Churchill
1954: 15 Ernest Hemingway
1955: 15 Halldor K Laxness
1956: 16 Juan Ramon Jimenez
1957: 11 Albert Camus
1958: 15 Boris L Pasternak
1959: 18 Salvatore Quasimodo
1960: 14 Saint-John Perse
1961: 9 Ivo Andric
1962: 13 John Steinbeck
1963: 13 George Seferis
1964: 14 Jean Paul Sartre
1965: 17 Mikhail A Sholokhov
1966: 10 Nelly Sachs 17 Samuel Joseph (Shmuel Y) Agnon
1967: 19 Miguel Angel Asturias
1968: 16 Yasunari Kawabata
1969: 13 Samuel Beckett
1970: 22 Aleksandr I Solzhenitsyn
1971: 11 Pablo Neruda
1972: 12 Heinrich Boll
1973: 12 Patrick White
1974: 13 Eyvind Johnson 14 Harry Martinson
1975: 14 Eugenio Montale
1976: 10 Saul Bellow
1977: 17 Vicente Aleixandre
1978: 15 Isaac Bashevis Singer
1979: 14 Odysseus Elytis
1980: 13 Czeslaw Milosz
1981: 12 Elias Canetti
1982: 20 Gabriel Garcia Marquez
1983: 14 William Golding
1984: 15 Jaroslav Seifert
1985: 11 Claude Simon
1986: 11 Wole Soyinka
1987: 13 Joseph Brodsky
1988: 13 Naguib Mahfouz
1989: 10 Camilo Cela
1990: 10 Octavio Paz
1991: 14 Nadine Gordimer
1992: 12 Derek Walcott
1993: 12 Toni Morrison
1994: 11 Kenzaburo Oe
Physiology/Medicine:
1901: 15 Emil A von Behring
1902: 13 Sir Ronald Ross
1903: 12 Niels R Finsen
1904: 11 Ivan P Pavlov

1905: 10 Robert Koch
1906: 12 Camillo Golgi 19 Santiago-Ramon y Cajal
1907: 16 Charles L A Laveran
1908: 11 Paul Ehrlich 15 Elie Metchnikoff
1909: 11 Emil T Kocher
1910: 14 Albrecht Kossel
1911: 16 Allvar Gullstrand
1912: 12 Alexis Carrel
1913: 14 Charles R Richet
1914: 12 Robert Barany
1919: 11 Jules Bordet
1920: 12 Shack A S Krogh
1922: 12 Otto Meyerhof 14 Archibald V Hill
1923: 13 John J R Macleod 20 Sir Frederick G Banting
1924: 15 Willem Einthoven
1926: 15 Johannes Fibiger
1927: 19 Julius Wagner-Jauregg
1928: 16 Charles J H Nicolle
1929: 17 Christiaan Eijkman 20 Sir Frederick G Hopkins
1930: 15 Karl Landsteiner
1931: 12 Otto H Warburg
1932: 12 Edgar D Adrian 21 Sir Charles Sherrington
1933: 13 Thomas H Morgan
1934: 12 George R Minot 14 George H Whipple, William P Murphy
1935: 11 Hans Spemann
1936: 9 Otto Loewi 13 Sir Henry H Dale
1937: 31 Albert Szent-Gyorgyi von Nagyrapolt
1938: 16 Corneille Heymans
1939: 13 Gerhard Domagk
1943: 9 Henrik Dam 12 Edward A Doisy
1944: 14 Herbert S Gasser, Joseph Erlanger
1945: 11 Ernst B Chain 16 Sir Howard W Florey 19 Sir Alexander Fleming
1946: 14 Hermann J Muller
1947: 9 Carl F Cori 10 Gerty T Cori 16 Bernardo A Houssay
1948: 11 Paul H Muller
1949: 11 Walter R Hess 21 Antonio C de A F Egas Moniz
1950: 12 Philip S Hench 14 Edward C Kendall 16 Tadeus Reichstein
1951: 10 Max Theiler
1952: 14 Selman A Waksman
1953: 11 Fritz A Lipmann, Sir Hans A Krebs
1954: 11 John F Enders 13 Thomas H Weller 17 Frederick C Robbins
1955: 14 Axel H T Theorell
1956: 13 Andre Cournand 15 Werner Forssmann 20 Dickenson W Richards Jr
1957: 11 Daniel Bovet
1958: 12 Edward L Tatum 13 George W Beadle 15 Joshua Lederberg
1959: 11 Severo Ochoa 14 Arthur Kornberg
1960: 13 Peter B Medawar 15 Sir Frank M Burnet
1961: 14 Georg von Bekesy

1962: 12 James D Watson 14 Francis H C Crick 16 Maurice H F Wilkins
1963: 16 Alan Lloyd Hodgkin 18 Sir John Carew Eccles 20 Andrew Fielding Huxley
1964: 11 Feodor Lynen 12 Konrad E Bloch
1965: 10 Andre Lwoff 12 Jacques Monod 13 Francois Jacob
1966: 17 Francis Peyton Rous 21 Charles Brenton Huggins
1967: 10 George Wald 12 Ragnar Granit 20 Haldan Keffer Hartline
1968: 13 Robert W Holley 14 H Gobind Khorana 18 Marshall W Nirenberg
1969: 11 Max Delbruck 14 Alfred D Hershey, Salvador E Luria
1970: 11 Ulf von Euler 13 Julius Axelrod 14 Sir Bernard Katz
1971: 14 Earl W Sutherland Jr
1972: 13 Rodney R Porter 14 Gerald M Edelman
1973: 12 Konrad Lorenz 13 Karl von Frisch 17 Nikolaas Tinbergen
1974: 12 Albert Claude 15 Christian de Duve 16 George EmilPalade
1975: 12 Howard M Temin 14 David Baltimore, Renato Dulbecco
1976: 15 Baruch S Blumberg 22 Daniel Carleton Gajdusek
1977: 13 Andrew Schally, Rosalyn S Yalow 14 Roger Guillemin
1978: 11 Werner Arber 13 Daniel Nathans, Hamilton Smith
1979: 13 Allan M Cormack 17 Godfrey Hounsfield
1980: 11 Jean Dausset 12 George D Snell 15 Baruj Benacerraf
1981: 11 David H Hubel 12 Roger W Sperry 14 Torsten N Wiesel
1982: 9 John R Vane 15 Bengt Samuelsson 17 Sune Karl Bergstrom
1983: 17 Barbara McClintock
1984: 11 Niels K Jerne 13 Cesar Milstein 16 Georges J F Koehler
1985: 13 Michael S Brown 16 Joseph L Goldstein
1986: 12 Stanley Cohen 18 Rita Levi-Montalcini
1987: 14 Susumu Tonegawa
1988: 10 James Black 14 Gertrube B Elion 16 George H Hitchings
1989: 12 Harold Varmas 14 J Michael Bishop
1990: 12 Joseph Murray 14 E Donnall Thomas
1991: 10 Edwin Neher 11 Bert Sakmann
1992: 10 Edwin Krebs 12 Edmond Fisher
1993: 12 Phillip Sharp 14 Richard Roberts
1994: 12 Alfred Gilman 13 Martin Rodbell
Chemistry:
1901: 16 Jacobus H van't Hoff
1902: 11 Emil Fischer
1903: 16 Svante A Arrhenius
1904: 16 Sir William Ramsay
1905: 17 J F W Adolf von Baeyer
1906: 12 Henri Moissan

1907: 13 Eduard Buchner
1908: 19 Sir Ernest Rutherford
1909: 14 Wilhelm Ostwald
1910: 11 Otto Wallach
1911: 11 Marie S Curie
1912: 12 Paul Sabatier 14 Victor Grignard
1913: 12 Alfred Werner
1914: 17 Theodore W Richards
1915: 18 Richard Willstatter
1918: 10 Fritz Haber
1920: 13 Walther Nernst
1921: 14 Frederick Soddy
1922: 13 Francis W Aston
1923: 10 Fritz Pregl
1925: 16 Richard Zsigmondy
1926: 15 Theodor Svedberg
1927: 15 Heinrich Wieland
1928: 12 Adolf Windaus
1929: 15 Sir Arthur Harden 19 Hans von Euler-Chelpin
1930: 11 Hans Fischer
1931: 9 Carl Bosch 16 Friedrich Bergius
1932: 14 Irving Langmuir
1934: 11 Harold C Urey
1935: 16 Irene Joliot-Curie 19 Frederic Joliot-Curie
1936: 12 Peter J W Debye
1937: 10 Paul Karrer 17 Sir Walter N Haworth
1938: 11 Richard Kuhn
1939: 14 Adolf Butenandt, Leopold Ruzicka
1943: 14 Georg von Hevesy
1944: 8 Otto Hahn
1945: 16 Artturi I Virtanen
1946: 12 James B Sumner 13 John H Northrop 15 Wendell M Stanley
1947: 17 Sir Robert Robinson
1948: 12 Arne Tiselius
1949: 15 William F Giauque
1950: 9 Kurt Alder, Otto Diels
1951: 13 Glenn T Seaborg 14 Edwin M McMillan
1952: 14 Archer J P Martin, Richard L M Synge
1953: 17 Hermann Staudinger
1954: 13 Linus C Pauling
1955: 17 Vincent du Vigneaud
1956: 15 Nikolai N Semenov 20 Sir Cyril N Hinshelwood
1957: 17 Sir Alexander R Todd (Baron Todd)
1958: 15 Frederick Sanger
1959: 17 Jaroslav Heyrovsky
1960: 13 Willard F Libby
1961: 12 Melvin Calvin
1962: 10 Max F Perutz 12 John C Kendrew
1963: 11 Giulio Natta, Karl Ziegler
1964: 26 Dorothy Mary Crowfoot Hodgkin
1965: 19 Robert Burns Woodward
1966: 15 Robert S Mulliken
1967: 17 Manfred Eigen 15 Sir George Porter 27 Ronald George Wreyford Norrish
1968: 11 Lars Onsager

1969: 9 Odd Hassel 13 Derek H R Barton
1970: 18 Luis Federico Leloir
1971: 15 Gerhard Herzberg
1972: 13 Stanford Moore 18 Christian B Anfinsen, William Howard Stein
1973: 16 Ernst Otto Fischer 17 Geoffrey Wilkinson
1974: 10 Paul J Flory
1975: 14 John W Cornforth, Vladimir Prelog
1976: 16 William N Lipscomb
1977: 13 Ilya Prigogine
1978: 13 Peter Mitchell
1979: 11 Georg Wittig 13 Herbert C Brown
1980: 8 Paul Berg 13 Walter Gilbert 15 Frederick Sanger
1981: 12 Kenichi Fukui 13 Roald Hoffmann
1982: 9 Aaron Klug
1983: 10 Henry Taube
1984: 21 Robert Bruce Merrifield
1985: 11 Jerome Karle 16 Herbert A Hauptman
1986: 8 Yuan T Lee 12 John C Polanyi 16 Dudley Herschbach
1987: 11 Donald J Cram 16 Charles J Pederson
1988: 11 Robert Huber 13 Hartmut Michel 17 Johann Deisenhofer
1989: 10 Thomas Cich 12 Sidney Altman
1990: 10 Elias Corey
1991: 12 Richard Ernst
1992: 13 Rudolph Marcus
1993: 10 Kary Mullis 12 Michael Smith
1994: 10 George Olah
Physics:
1901: 16 Wilhelm K Roentgen
1902: 12 Pieter Zeeman 15 Hendrik A Lorentz
1903: 11 Marie S Curie, Pierre Curie 15 A Henri Becquerel
1904: 11 John W Strutt (Lord Rayleigh)
1905: 13 Philipp Lenard
1906: 16 Sir Joseph Thomson
1907: 16 Albert A Michelson
1908: 15 Gabriel Lippmann
1909: 10 Karl F Braun 16 Guglielmo Marconi
1910: 20 Johannes D van der Waals
1911: 11 Wilhelm Wien
1912: 10 Nils G Dalen
1913: 20 Heike Kamerlingh Onnes
1914: 10 Max von Laue
1915: 16 Sir William H Bragg, Sir William L Bragg
1917: 14 Charles B Barkla
1918: 9 Max Planck
1919: 13 Johannes Stark
1920: 17 Charles E Guillaume
1921: 14 Albert Einstein
1922: 10 Nils H D Bohr
1923: 15 Robert A Millikan
1924: 14 Karl M G Siegbahn
1925: 11 Gustav Hertz, James Franck
1926: 11 Jean B Perrin

1927: 14 Arthur H Compton 15 Charles T R Wilson
1928: 18 Sir Owen W Richardson
1929: 15 Louis V de Broglie
1930: 23 Sir Chandrasekhara V Raman
1932: 16 Werner Heisenberg
1933: 11 Paul A M Dirac 16 Erwin Schrodinger
1935: 16 Sir James Chadwick
1936: 11 Victor F Hess 13 Carl D Anderson
1937: 16 Clinton J Davisson 17 Sir George P Thomson
1938: 11 Enrico Fermi
1939: 15 Ernest O Lawrence
1943: 9 Otto Stern
1944: 11 Isidor I Rabi
1945: 13 Wolfgang Pauli
1946: 14 Percy W Bridgman
1947: 18 Sir Edward V Appleton
1948: 17 Patrick M S Blackett
1949: 12 Hideki Yukawa
1950: 12 Cecil F Powell
1951: 14 Ernest T S Walton 17 Sir John D Cockcroft
1952: 10 Felix Bloch 14 Edward M Purcell
1953: 12 Frits Zernike
1954: 7 Max Born 12 Walther Bothe
1955: 13 Polykarp Kusch, Willis E Lamb Jr
1956: 11 John Bardeen 15 Walter H Brattain 16 William B Shockley
1957: 11 Tsung Dao Lee 12 Chen Ning Yang
1958: 9 Igor Y Tamm 10 Ilya M Frank 15 Pavel A Cherenkov
1959: 11 Emilio Segre 15 Owen Chamberlain
1960: 13 Donald A Glaser
1961: 16 Robert Hofstadter, Rudolf L Mossbauer
1962: 10 Lev D Landau
1963: 11 J Hans Jensen 16 Eugene Paul Wigner 18 Maria Goeppert Mayer
1964: 17 Charles Hard Townes 25 Nikolai Gennadiyevich Basov 30 Aleksandr Mikhailovich Prokhorov
1965: 18 Shinichiro Tomonaga 22 Julian Seymour Schwinger, Richard Phillips Feynman
1966: 13 Alfred Kastler
1967: 17 Hans Albrecht Bethe
1968: 12 Luis W Alvarez
1969: 14 Murray Gell-Mann
1970: 12 Hannes Alfven 15 Louis Eugene Neel
1971: 11 Dennis Gabor
1972: 11 John Bardeen, Leon N Cooper 20 John Robert Schreiffer
1973: 8 Leo Esaki 11 Ivar Giaever 15 Brian D Josephson
1974: 12 Antony Hewish 13 Sir Martin Ryle
1975: 8 Aage Bohr 13 Ben R Mottelson 15 L James Rainwater

1976: 12 Samuel C C Ting 13 Burton Richter
1977: 13 John H Van Vleck, Sir Nevill Mott 15 Philip W Anderson
1978: 12 Arno A Penzias, Peter Kapitza (Pyotr Kapitsa) 13 Robert W Wilson
1979: 10 Abdus Salam 14 Sheldon Glashow, Steven Weinberg
1980: 9 Val L Fitch 12 James W Cronin
1981: 12 Kai M Siegbahn 14 Arthur Schawlow 19 Nicolaas Bloembergen
1982: 14 Kenneth G Wilson
1983: 14 William A Fowler 25 Subrahmanyan Chandrasekhar
1984: 11 Carlo Rubbia 15 Simon van der Meer
1985: 16 Klaus von Klitzing
1986: 10 Ernst Ruska, Gerd Binner 14 Heinrich Rohrer
1987: 12 K Alex Mueller 13 J Georg Bednorz
1988: 13 Leon M Lederman 14 Melvin Schwartz 15 Jack Steinberger
1989: 11 Hans Dehmelt 12 Norman Ramsey, Wolfgang Paul
1990: 12 Henry Kendall 13 Richard Taylor 14 Jerome Friedman
1991: 12 Pierre Gennes
1992: 13 George Charpak
1993: 12 Joseph Taylor, Russell Hulse
1994: 13 Clifford Shull 17 Bertram Brockhouse

Peace:
1901: 13 Frederic Passy 15 Jean Henri Dunant
1902: 12 Elie Ducommun 18 Charles Albert Gobat
1903: 17 Sir William R Cremer
1904: 27 Institute of International Law
1905: 24 Baroness Bertha von Suttner
1906: 17 Theodore Roosevelt
1907: 12 Louis Renault 14 Ernesto T Moneta
1908: 12 Fredrik Bajer 14 Klas P Arnoldson
1909: 16 Auguste Beernaert 35 Paul H Balluat d'Estournelles de Constant
1910: 24 International Peace Bureau
1911: 12 Alfred H Fried 13 Tobias M C Asser
1912: 9 Elihu Root
1913: 15 Henri La Fontaine
1917: 30 International Red Cross Committee
1919: 13 Woodrow Wilson
1920: 13 Leon Bourgeois
1921: 15 Christian L Lange 19 Karl Hjalmar Branting
1922: 14 Fridtjof Nansen
1925: 13 Charles G Dawes 26 Sir Joseph Austen Chamberlain
1926: 14 Aristide Briand 16 Gustav Stresemann
1927: 12 Ludwig Quidde 17 Ferdinand E Buisson
1929: 13 Frank B Kellogg

1930: **15** (Lars Olof Jonathan) Nathan Soderblom
1931: **10** Jane Addams **20** Nicholas Murray Butler
1933: **15** Sir Norman Angell
1934: **15** Arthur Henderson
1935: **16** Carl von Ossietzky
1936: **19** Carlos Saavedra Lamas
1937: **13** E A Robert Cecil (Viscount Cecil)
1938: **36** Nansen International Office for Refugees
1944: **30** International Red Cross Committee
1945: **11** Cordell Hull
1946: **9** John R Mott **11** Emily G Balch
1947: **21** Friends Service Council **31** American Friends Service Committee
1949: **11** John Boyd Orr (Baron Orr)
1950: **12** Ralph J Bunche
1951: **11** Leon Jouhaux
1952: **16** Albert Schweitzer
1953: **15** George C Marshall
1954: **51** Office of the United Nations High Commissioner for Refugees
1957: **14** Lester B Pearson
1958: **28** Rev Dominique Georges Henri Pire
1959: **16** Philip J Noel-Baker
1960: **14** Albert J Luthuli
1961: **13** Dag Hammarskjold
1962: **13** Linus C Pauling
1963: **25** League of Red Cross Societies **30** International Red Cross Committee
1964: **18** Martin Luther King Jr
1965: **26** United Nations Children's Fund (UNICEF)
1968: **10** Rene Cassin
1969: **30** International Labor Organization (ILO)
1970: **14** Norman E Borlaug
1971: **11** Willy Brandt
1973: **8** Le Duc Tho **15** Henry A Kissinger
1974: **10** Eisaku Sato **12** Sean MacBride
1975: **15** Andrei D Sakharov
1976: **13** Betty Williams **15** Mairead Corrigan
1977: **20** Amnesty International
1978: **10** Anwar Sadat **13** Menachem Begin
1979: **12** Mother Teresa
1980: **19** Adolfo Perez Esquivel
1981: **51** Office of the United Nations High Commissioner for Refugees
1982: **10** Alva Myrdal **19** Alfonso Garcia Robles
1983: **10** Lech Walesa
1984: **17** Bishop Desmond Tutu
1985: **51** International Physicians for the Prevention of Nuclear War
1986: **10** Elie Wiesel
1987: **17** Oscar Arias Sanchez
1988: **31** United Nations peacekeeping troops
1989: **9** Dalai Lama
1990: **16** Mikhail Gorbachev

1991: **13** Aung San Suu Kyi
1992: **15** Rigoberta Menchu
1993: **9** F W de Klerk **13** Nelson Mandela
1994: **11** Yasir Arafat, Shimon Peres **12** Yitzhak Rabin
Economics:
1969: **12** Jan Tinbergen, Ragnar Frisch
1970: **14** Paul A Samuelson
1971: **13** Simon S Kuznets
1972: **13** Kenneth J Arrow, Sir John R Hicks
1973: **15** Wassily Leontief
1974: **12** Gunnar Myrdal **18** Friedrich A von Hayek
1975: **17** Tjalling C Koopmans **18** Leonid V Kantorovich
1976: **14** Milton Friedman
1977: **11** Bertil Ohlin, James E Meade
1978: **13** Herbert A Simon
1979: **14** Sir Arthur Lewis **15** Theodore Schultz
1980: **14** Lawrence R Klein
1981: **10** James Tobin
1982: **14** George J Stigler
1983: **12** Gerard Debreu
1984: **15** Sir Richard Stone
1985: **16** Franco Modigliani
1986: **19** James McGill Buchanan
1987: **12** Robert M Solow
1988: **13** Maurice Allais
1989: **14** Trygve Haavelmo
1990: **12** Merton Miller **13** William Sharpe **14** Harry Markowitz
1991: **11** Ronald Coase
1992: **10** Gary Becker
1993: **11** Robert Fogel **12** Douglas North
1994: **8** John Nash **12** John Harsanyi **14** Reinhard Selten

nobility **5** elite, lords **7** dignity, majesty, peerage, primacy, royalty **8** breeding, eminence, grandeur, high rank, prestige, splendor **9** gentility, grandness, greatness, loftiness, sublimity, supremacy **10** blue bloods, mightiness, patricians, patriciate, upper crust **11** aristocracy, distinction, exaltedness, preeminence, stateliness, superiority **12** magnificence

nobility obliges
French: 14 noblesse oblige

noble **3** don **4** high, just, lord, peer **5** famed, grand, great, lofty, moral, regal, royal **6** famous, gentle, honest, knight, lordly, squire, superb, worthy **7** awesome, courtly, eminent, ethical, exalted, grandee, stately, sublime, supreme, upright **8** baronial, cavalier, elevated, glorious, handsome, highborn, imperial, imposing, lordlike, majestic, princely, renowned, selfless, splendid, superior, virtuous **9** chevalier, dignified, estimable, excellent, exemplary, gentleman, honorable, patrician, personage, reputable **10** aristocrat, impressive, preeminent **11** magnanimous, magnificent, meritorious, pureblooded, trustworthy **12** aristocratic, thoroughbred **13** distinguished, incorruptible
French: 6 gentil

Noble House
  author: 12 James Clavell
nobleman 4 lord, peer 7 grandee 9 patrician 10 aristocrat
noblesse oblige 15 nobility obliges
noblewoman 4 dame, lady, rani 5 begum, queen 6 milady 7 czarina, duchess, empress, peeress, sultana 8 baroness, contessa, countess, maharani, princess 11 marchioness

Nobody Knows My Name
  author: 12 James Baldwin
nocturnal 4 dark 5 night 7 nightly, obscure 8 darkling 9 nighttime

Nocturne
  author: 15 Frank Swinnerton
nod 3 bob 4 doze, hail, show, sign 5 agree, greet, lapse, let up 6 assent, beckon, concur, drowse, motion, reveal, salute, signal 7 consent, drop off, fall off, gesture, signify 9 recognize
node 3 bud 4 bump, burl, hump, knob, knot, lump 5 bulge, joint 6 button 8 swelling 10 prominence, tumescence 11 excrescence 12 protuberance

Nodosaurus
  type: 8 dinosaur 10 ornithopod
  location: 12 North America
nodule 3 sac, wen 4 bump, cyst, knob, knot, lump, stud 5 bulge 6 growth 8 swelling 9 outgrowth 10 projection, prominence, protrusion, tumescence 11 excrescence 12 protuberance
noel, Noel 4 yule 5 carol 8 yuletide 9 Christmas 13 Christmastide

Noemon
  mentioned in: 7 Odyssey
  supplied: 4 ship
  supplied ship to: 10 Telemachus
No Exit
  author: 14 Jean-Paul Sartre
noggin 3 cup, mug 4 bean, head, pate 5 gourd 6 noodle
Noggs, Newman
  character in: 16 Nicholas Nickleby
  author: 7 Dickens
Noguchi, Hideyo
  field: 12 bacteriology
  nationality: 8 Japanese
  isolated: 8 syphilis
noise 3 ado, din 4 bang, blab, boom, echo, pass, roar, stir, wail 5 babel, blare, blast, bruit, rumor, sound, voice 6 bedlam, clamor, hubbub, racket, repeat, report, rumble, tumult, uproar 7 barrage, bluster, clatter, thunder 8 brawling, gabbling, rumbling, shouting 9 cacophony, cannonade, circulate, commotion, discharge 10 dissonance, hullabaloo 11 pandemonium 12 caterwauling, vociferation 13 reverberation
noiseless 5 quiet, still, tacit 6 hushed, silent 9 soundless, voiceless
noisemaker 4 bell, horn 5 siren 6 rattle 7 clacker, clapper, snapper, whistle
noisome 4 foul, rank 5 acrid, fetid, toxic 6 putrid, rotten, smelly 7 baneful, harmful, hurtful, noxious, reeking 8 mephitic, stink-

ing 9 injurious, offensive, poisonous, unhealthy 10 malodorous, nauseating, pernicious 11 deleterious, detrimental 12 evil-smelling
noisy 4 loud 5 alive 6 lively, raging, shrill, stormy 7 blaring, blatant, furious, grating, jarring, rackety 8 animated, piercing, strident 9 clamorous, deafening, dissonant, turbulent 10 boisterous, clangorous, discordant, rampageous, resounding, thundering, thunderous, tumultuous, uproarious 11 cacophonous, tempestuous 12 earsplitting

Nolan, George Brendan
  real name of: 11 George Brent
Nolan, Lloyd
  born: 14 San Francisco CA
  roles: 22 Lieutenant Colonel Queeg 26 The Caine Mutiny Court Martial
Nolde, Emil
  real name: 10 Emil Hansen
  born: 5 Nolde 7 Germany
  artwork: 7 Prophet 10 Papua Youth 11 Tropical Sun 12 The Magicians, The Pentecost 13 The Last Supper, Three Russians 14 Doubting Thomas 20 Life of Maria Aegyptica 22 Christ Among the Children, Christ and the Adulteress
nolens volens 10 willy-nilly 19 whether willing or not
noli me tangere 10 touch me not
nolle prosequi 14 do not prosecute 19 be unwilling to pursue
nolo contendere 21 I am unwilling to contend
no longer able to fight
  French: 12 hors de combat
no longer in existence 4 dead, gone, lost 7 defunct, died out, extinct 8 vanished
Nolte, Nick
  born: 7 Omaha NE
  roles: 5 Weeds 7 The Deep 10 Cannery Row 12 I Love Trouble 13 Prince of Tides 14 Rich Man Poor Man 15 Forty-Eight Hours 16 North Dallas Forty
nomad 4 hobo 5 gypsy, mover, rover, stray, tramp 6 roamer 7 migrant, rambler, refugee, runaway, strayer, vagrant 8 bohemian, emigrant, migrator, renegade, traveler, vagabond, wanderer 9 immigrant, itinerant, straggler
nomadic 6 roving 7 migrant, roaming, vagrant 8 drifting, vagabond 9 footloose, itinerant, migratory, strolling, traveling, wandering
nom de guerre 5 alias 7 war name 9 pseudonym 11 assumed name
nom de plume 5 alias 7 pen name 9 false name, pseudonym 11 assumed name, writing name
nomenclature 5 lingo, terms 6 jargon, naming 8 language, taxonomy 10 nomination, vocabulary
nominal 3 low 5 cheap, small 6 puppet 7 minimum, titular 8 baseless, moderate, official, so-called 9 pretended, professed,

purported, suggested **10** groundless, ostensible, reasonable

nominate 3 tag **4** call, name, pick, term **5** elect, label, style **6** choose, invest, select **7** elevate, install, propose, suggest **9** authorize, recommend

nomination 8 election **9** accession, selection **10** suggestion

nominee 7 hopeful **8** aspirant, eligible **9** applicant, candidate **10** competitor, contestant

nonadjustable 5 fixed, rigid **9** immovable **10** inflexible

nonalcoholic 4 soft **15** nonintoxicating

nonattendance 3 cut **7** absence, truancy **11** absenteeism

nonbeliever 5 cynic, pagan **7** atheist, doubter, heathen, infidel, skeptic **8** agnostic, apostate **10** backslider, empiricist, questioner, unbeliever **11** disbeliever, freethinker **14** doubting Thomas

nonbinding 8 optional **9** voluntary **12** unimperative **13** discretionary

nonchalance 9 composure, unconcern **13** offhandedness

   French: **11** insouciance

nonchalant 3 lax **4** cool, idle, lazy **5** blase, slack **6** casual **7** languid, offhand, unmoved **8** careless, heedless, indolent, listless **9** apathetic, collected, easygoing, lethargic, unexcited, unheeding, unmindful, unruffled, unstirred, withdrawn **10** insensible, insouciant, phlegmatic, unaffected

noncombatant 7 neutral **8** civilian

noncommittal 3 mum **4** cool, mute, safe, wary **5** vague **7** careful, evasive, guarded, neutral, politic, prudent **8** cautious, discreet, reserved **9** ambiguous, equivocal, tentative **10** indecisive, indefinite, unspeaking **11** circumspect, temporizing

noncompliance 6 breach **7** failure, neglect **9** disregard **10** resistance **11** dereliction

noncompliant 6 unruly **7** defiant, froward, naughty, wayward **8** contrary, mutinous, perverse, stubborn **9** differing, dissident, fractious, objecting, obstinate, resistant, resistive, undutiful **10** disorderly, dissenting, rebellious, refractory, unorthodox, unyielding

non compos mentis 14 not of sound mind **17** mentally incapable

nonconfirming 7 denying **8** negating, refuting **9** rejecting **10** disavowing **11** disclaiming, repudiating

nonconformist 3 nut **4** beat, card **5** freak, hippy, loner, rebel **6** oddity, weirdo **7** heretic, oddball, radical **8** bohemian, crackpot, deserter, maverick, original, reformer, renegade, vagabond **9** character, dissenter, dissident, eccentric, exception, insurgent, protester, screwball **10** dissenting, iconoclast, rebellious, schismatic **13** individualist, revolutionary

nonconformity 5 quirk **6** oddity **7** anomaly **9** deviation, rebellion **10** aberration, divergence, resistance

noncongenial 6 unlike **8** opposite **9** different, disparate, ill-suited, unrelated **10** dissimilar **11** disagreeing **12** disagreeable, incompatible **13** unsympathetic

nondescript 5 usual, vague **8** ordinary **9** amorphous, colorless **11** stereotyped **12** unimpressive **13** characterless, undistinctive, unexceptional **15** undistinguished

nonentity 4 zero **6** cipher, nobody **7** nothing, no-count, nullity **8** small-fry, unperson **10** mediocrity

nonessential 6 luxury, trivia **7** trivial **9** extrinsic, secondary, trimmings **10** accidental, extraneous, incidental, irrelevant, peripheral, subsidiary

nonexclusive 4 open **6** public, shared **7** divided **12** unrestricted

nonexistence 4 lack, void **7** absence **8** oblivion **11** nothingness

nonexistent 4 gone **5** short **6** absent **7** lacking, missing, wanting **11** unavailable **12** insufficient

nonindulgence 7 refusal **8** eschewal, forgoing **9** avoidance, eschewing **10** abstaining, abstention, refraining **11** forbearance **16** nonparticipation

nonirritating 4 calm **5** bland **6** benign **7** calming **8** soothing, tranquil **9** temperate

non licet 13 it is not lawful **16** it is not permitted

non liquet 12 it is not clear **14** it is not evident

nonmaterialistic 9 spiritual **10** idealistic **12** intellectual

nonmember 5 guest **7** outcast, visitor **8** outsider

nonnatural 7 manmade **9** synthetic **10** artificial, fabricated, factitious **12** manufactured

nonobservance 6 breach **7** failure, neglect **9** disregard **11** dereliction **13** noncompliance

non obstante 15 notwithstanding

no-nonsense 4 grim, hard **5** grave, harsh, rigid, sober, stern **6** ardent, intent, severe, solemn, strict **7** earnest, serious **8** critical, diligent, exacting, resolute **9** committed, dedicated, demanding, hardnosed, practical, pragmatic, unbending, unsparing **10** determined, hardheaded, purposeful, sobersided **12** businesslike

nonpareil 5 elite, ideal, model, super **6** symbol, unique **7** epitome, paragon, pattern, supreme **8** exemplar **9** unequaled, unmatched, unrivaled **10** apotheosis **11** exceptional, unsurpassed **13** extraordinary **14** representative

   French: **11** ne plus ultra **14** creme de la creme

nonparticipation 7 refusal **8** eschewal, forgoing **9** avoidance, eschewing **10** abstaining, abstention, refraining, sitting out **11** forbearance

nonpartisan 4 fair, just **8** unbiased, unswayed **9** equitable, impartial, objective, unbigoted **10** impersonal, uninvolved **12**

freethinking, unaffiliated, unimplicated, un-influenced, unprejudiced 13 disinterested

nonpermissible 9 forbidden 10 disallowed 11 intolerable 12 inadmissible, unacceptable

nonplus 4 balk, faze, foil, halt, stop 5 abash, stump, upset 6 baffle, bother, dismay, muddle, puzzle, stymie 7 astound, confuse, disturb, mystify, perplex 8 astonish, bewilder, confound, deadlock 9 dumbfound, embarrass 10 disconcert 11 flabbergast 14 discountenance

nonplussed, nonplused 5 at sea, fazed 7 at a loss, baffled, floored, mixed-up, muddled, puzzled, stumped 8 confused 9 befuddled, mystified, unsettled 10 bewildered, confounded 12 disconcerted

nonpoisonous 4 safe 8 nontoxic 11 nonvenomous, nonvirulent

non possumus 8 we cannot

nonpresence 3 cut 7 absence, truancy 11 absenteeism

nonprofessional 3 lay 4 laic 7 dabbler
French: 7 amateur 10 dilettante

non prosequitur 15 he does not pursue

non repetatur 11 do not repeat

nonresident 7 tourist, visitor 9 transient 11 out-of-towner

nonresistance 6 assent 7 pliancy 8 docility, giving in, meekness, yielding 9 deference, obedience, passivity 10 compliance, conforming, conformity, pliability, submission 12 acquiescence, complaisance

nonresistant 4 meek 6 docile, pliant 7 passive, pliable 8 deferent, obedient, yielding 9 compliant 10 conforming, submissive 11 acquiescent, complaisant, deferential

nonscholarly 8 untaught 9 unlearned 10 uneducated, unlettered, unpedantic, unschooled

nonsectarian 10 ecumenical 11 interchurch 16 undenominational 17 nondenominational 19 interdenominational

nonsense 3 rot 4 bosh, bunk 5 folly, trash 6 antics, babble, drivel, joking, piffle 7 baloney, blather, bombast, chatter, fooling, garbage, hogwash, inanity, prattle, rubbish, trifles, twaddle 8 claptrap, flummery 9 absurdity, frivolity, gibberish, high jinks, horseplay, moonshine, silliness, stupidity 10 balderdash, flapdoodle, tomfoolery, triviality 11 foolishness, shenanigans 12 childishness, extravagance 13 facetiousness, ludicrousness, senselessness 14 ridiculousness 15 meaninglessness

nonsensical 4 wild 5 crazy, funny, inane, silly 6 absurd, stupid 7 asinine, comical, foolish 8 farcical 9 facetious, laughable, ludicrous 10 irrational, ridiculous

non sequitur 15 it does not follow

nonspecialized 11 generalized

nonspecific 4 hazy 5 vague 7 general, inexact 9 imprecise, uncertain 10 indefinite, undetailed 11 approximate, generalized

nonspiritual 7 earthly, profane, secular, worldly 8 material, temporal 13 materialistic

nonstop 7 endless, express 8 constant, unbroken 9 incessant 10 continuous, unrelieved 11 unremitting 12 interminable

nonstudious 9 unlearned 10 uneducated, unlettered, unpedantic, unschooled

nontaxable 9 sheltered 10 deductible

nontechnical 6 simple 8 academic 13 uncomplicated

nontypical 7 unusual 8 abnormal, uncommon 9 anomalous, irregular 16 unrepresentative

nonuniform 5 mixed 6 unlike 7 altered, changed, erratic, unalike 8 changing, variable 9 deviating, different, irregular, multiform 10 dissimilar 11 fluctuating, nonstandard 12 inconsistent

nonvital 9 accessory, extrinsic 10 disposable, expendable, incidental 11 dispensable, superfluous, unessential, unimportant, unnecessary

nonvocational 8 academic

nonvolitional 6 reflex 8 unwilled 9 automatic 11 instinctive, involuntary, spontaneous 12 uncontrolled

noodle 4 bean, head, pate 5 gourd, pasta 6 noggin 8 practice 9 improvise

nook 3 den 4 cove, lair 5 haven, niche 6 alcove, cavity, corner, cranny, dugout, recess, refuge 7 retreat, shelter 8 hideaway 9 cubbyhole 10 depression 11 hiding place

noon 6 midday, zenith 8 high noon, meridian

no one contradicting
Latin: 19 nemine contradicente

no one dissenting
Latin: 18 nemine dissentiente

noose 3 tie 4 bond, hang, loop 5 catch, hitch, lasso, snare 6 choker, entrap, halter, lariat, tether

Nootka
language family: 8 Wakashan
tribe: 5 Makah 6 Hoiath, Ozette 7 Ahosath, Nitinat 8 Machlath, Otsosath, Tokwaath 9 Ihatisath, Mowachath, Nochalath, Qayokwath, Tsishaath, Yoloilath 10 Hishkwiath, Hochoqtlis, Manohisath, Tlaokwiath 11 Chiqtlisath, Hopachasath, Qiltsamaath
location: 10 Washington 15 Vancouver Island
leader: 8 Maquinna 10 Wikaninish
related to: 5 Makah
noted for: 7 whaling

Nordhoff, Charles
author of: 17 Mutiny on the Bounty (with James Norman Hall)

Nordic Mythology see 21 Scandinavian Mythology

Norge see 6 Norway

norm 3 par 4 rule, type 5 gauge, model 7 average, measure, pattern 8 standard 9 barometer, criterion, yardstick 12 measuring rod

norm, the norm 7 the mean, the rule 9 the median 10 the average 14 the common thing

normal 3 fit, par 4 sane 5 sound, usual 6 steady 7 average, healthy, natural, regular, typical, uniform 8 constant, expected, mediocre, middling, ordinary, rational, reliable, standard 9 incessant, steadfast, unceasing 10 conforming, consistent, continuous, dependable, reasonable, unchanging 11 conformable, right-minded, unremitting 12 conventional 13 uninterrupted 14 representative

Normandy, Normandie
  beach: 4 Gold, Juno, Utah 5 Omaha, Sword
  borders: 7 Picardy 8 Brittany 14 English Channel
  church/shrine: 12 Saint Etienne 15 Mont Saint Michel
  city: 4 Caen 5 Rouen 7 Le Havre 9 Cherbourg
  event: 4 D Day 17 Operation Overlord
  region of: 6 France
  river: 5 Seine

Norma Rae
  director: 10 Martin Ritt
  cast: 9 Pat Hingle 10 Ron Liebman, Sally Field 11 Beau Bridges
  Oscar for: 4 song 7 actress (Field)
  song: 16 It Goes Like It Goes

Norn
  origin: 12 Scandinavian
  form: 6 virgin 7 goddess
  personifies: 4 fate
  original Norn: 5 Urdar
  the three: 3 Urd 5 Skuld 8 Verdandi
  known as: 12 weird sisters

Norris, Frank
  author of: 6 The Pit 8 McTeague 10 The Octopus

Norse Mythology see 21 Scandinavian Mythology

north 5 polar, upper 6 arctic

North America
  nation: 4 Cuba 5 Haiti 6 Belize, Canada, Mexico, Panama 7 Bahamas, Jamaica 8 Barbados, Honduras 9 Costa Rica, Guatemala, Nicaragua 10 El Salvador, Puerto Rico, Saint Lucia 12 Saint Vincent, United States 17 Dominican Republic, Trinidad and Tobago 28 Saint Vincent and the Grenadines
  desert: 7 Sonoran
  island: 4 Long 6 Baffin, Cayman, Kodiak 7 Antigua, Bermuda, Iceland 8 Aleutian, Catalina, Thousand 9 Antilles, Greenland, Nantucket, Vancouver 10 Cape Breton 12 Newfoundland, Prince Edward 14 Queen Charlotte
  ocean/sea/bay: 6 Arctic, Baffin, Bering, Hudson, Mexico 7 Chukchi, Lincoln, Pacific 8 Amundsen, Atlantic, Beaufort, Labrador 9 Caribbean, Greenland 10 California, Chesapeake, St Lawrence
  river: 3 Red 4 Ohio 5 Peace, Snake, Yukon 6 Hudson 8 Arkansas, Colorado, Columbia, Missouri 9 Churchill, Mackenzie, Rio Grande 10 St Lawrence 11 Mississippi 12 Saskatchewan

lake: 4 Erie 5 Huron 7 Ontario 8 Michigan, Superior, Winnipeg 9 Great Bear, Nicaragua 10 Great Lakes, Great Slave
mountain range: 5 Ozark, Rocky 6 Alaska 7 Cascade 9 Blue Ridge 10 Laurentian 11 Appalachian, Sierra Madre 12 Sierra Nevada
highest point: 13 Mount McKinley
lowest point: 11 Death Valley
city: 4 Nome 5 Miami 6 Boston, Dallas, Denver, Havana, Ottawa, Quebec 7 Atlanta, Calgary, Chicago, Detroit, Houston, Memphis, New York, Phoenix, Seattle, Toronto 8 Montreal, Portland, San Diego 9 Anchorage, Milwaukee, Reykjavik, Vancouver 10 Kansas City, Los Angeles, Mexico City, New Orleans, Washington 11 Philadelphia, San Antonio, San Francisco
mineral: 3 oil, tin 4 coal, gold, lead, salt, zinc 6 cobalt, copper, nickel, quartz, silver 7 iron ore, mercury, sulphur, uranium 8 aluminum, antimony, asbestos, chromium, platinum, titanium, tungsten 9 magnesium, manganese, petroleum 10 molybdenum, natural gas

Northanger Abbey
  author: 10 Jane Austen
  character: 9 Mrs Allen 10 John Thorpe 12 James Morland 14 Isabella Thorpe 16 Catherine Morland
  Tilney family: 5 Henry 7 Captain, Eleanor, General

North by Northwest
  director: 15 Alfred Hitchcock
  cast: 9 Cary Grant 10 James Mason 11 Leo G Carroll 12 Martin Landau 13 Eva Marie Saint 17 Jessie Royce Landis
  setting (climax): 13 Mount Rushmore
  score: 15 Bernard Herrmann

North Carolina
  abbreviation: 2 NC 4 N Car
  nickname: 7 Tar Heel 8 Old North 10 Turpentine
  capital: 7 Raleigh
  largest city: 9 Charlotte
  others: 4 Bath 6 Durham, Lenoir, Shelby, Wilson 7 Edenton, Hickory, Kinston, New Bern, Roxboro, Tarboro 8 Gastonia 9 Albemarle, Asheville, Goldsboro, Henderson, Kitty Hawk, Lumberton 10 Chapel Hill, Greensboro, Greenville, Kannapolis, Wilmington 11 Statesville, Thomasville, Williamston 12 Fayetteville, Jacksonville, Winston-Salem
  college: 4 Duke, Elon 7 Catawba 8 Davidson 10 Wake Forest
  feature:
    battle site: 18 Guilford Courthouse
    national park: 19 Great Smoky Mountains (with Tennessee)
    national seashore: 11 Cape Lookout 12 Cape Hatteras
    tribe: 3 Eno 5 Coree 6 Cheraw 7 Buffalo, Moratok, Pamlico 8 Chowanoc, Hatteras 9 Tuscarora
  people: 6 O Henry (William Sidney Por-

ter) 7 tarheel 11 Billy Graham, Thomas Wolfe 13 Dolley (Dolly) Madison, Edward R Murrow 14 Richard Gatling

explorer: 6. de Soto 8 de Ayllon 9 Verrazano

island: 7 Roanoke

lake: 6 Norman, Phelps 7 Fontana 8 Waccamaw 12 Mattamuskeet

land rank: 12 twenty-eighth

mountain: 5 Black, Unaka 6 Harris 9 Blue Ridge 10 Great Smoky 13 Clingman's Dome

highest point: 8 Mitchell

physical feature: 10 Outer Banks 11 French Broad 15 Little Tennessee

cape: 4 Fear 7 Lookout 8 Hatteras

plateau: 8 Piedmont

sea: 8 Atlantic

sound: 4 Core 5 Bogue 7 Croatan, Pamlico

swamp: 6 Dismal

president: 9 James Polk 13 Andrew Johnson

river: 3 Haw, Tar 4 Fear 5 Neuse 6 Chowan, Lumber, Peedee, Yadkin 7 Roanoke, Wateree

state admission: 7 twelfth

state bird: 8 cardinal

state fish: 11 channel bass

state flower: 7 dogwood 9 goldenrod

state motto: 20 To Be Rather Than To Seem

state song: 16 The Old North State

state tree: 4 pine

state dance: 4 shag

North Dakota

abbreviation: 2 ND 4 N Dak

nickname: 5 Sioux 11 Flickertail 16 Land of the Dakotas

capital: 8 Bismarck

largest city: 5 Fargo

others: 5 Minot 6 Bottineau, Jamestown, Williston 10 Grand Forks

college: 4 Mary 9 Jamestown

feature:

dam: 4 Oahe 8 Garrison

garden: 18 International Peace

national park: 17 Theodore Roosevelt

tribe: 5 Sioux 6 Mandan 7 Arikara, Hidatsa 8 Chippewa

people: 12 Eric Sevareid

explorer: 6 Carver 8 Thompson, Varennes 13 Lewis and Clark

lake: 5 Stump 6 Devils 9 Sakakawea

land rank: 11 seventeenth

mountain: 6 Turtle 8 Killdeer 10 Black Butte

highest point: 10 White Butte

physical feature:

basin: 9 Williston

plain: 8 The Slope

valley: 8 Red River

river: 3 Red 4 Park, Rush 5 Cedar, Goose, Heart, James, Knife, Mouse 6 Souris 7 Deslacs, Pembina 8 Missouri, Cheyenne, Wild Rice 9 Otter Tail 10 Cannonball 11 Yellowstone 12 Boise de Sioux

14 Little Missouri 18 Red River of the North

state admission: 8 fortieth 11 thirty-ninth (with South Dakota)

state bird: 17 western meadowlark

state fish: 12 northern pike

state flower: 15 wild prairie rose

state motto: 45 Liberty and Union Now and Forever One and Inseparable

state song: 15 North Dakota Hymn

state tree: 11 American elm

North Dallas Forty

director: 11 Ted Kotcheff

based on story by: 9 Peter Gent

cast: 8 Mac Davis 9 Nick Nolte 11 Dayle Haddon 14 Charles Durning

Northern Crown

constellation of: 14 Corona Borealis

Northern Rhodesia *see* 6 Zambia

North Korea *see* 5 Korea

North Star State

nickname of: 9 Minnesota

North Toward Home

author: 12 Willie Morris

North Vietnam *see* 7 Vietnam

Northwest Passage

director: 9 King Vidor

author: 14 Kenneth Roberts

cast: 10 Ruth Hussey 11 Robert Young 12 Spencer Tracy 13 Walter Brennan

Northwest Territories

abbreviation: 3 NWT

borders: 7 Alberta 8 Manitoba 9 Baffin Bay, Hudson Bay 11 Arctic Ocean, Beaufort Sea, Labrador Sea 12 Saskatchewan 15 British Columbia

city: 6 Inuvik 8 Hay River 9 Fort Smith 11 Yellowknife 12 Frobisher Bay

country: 6 Canada

Inuit land: 7 Nunavut

island: 5 Banks, Devon 6 Baffin 7 Melville 8 Bathurst, Somerset, Victoria 9 Ellesmere 11 King William 13 Prince of Wales, Prince Patrick 14 Queen Elizabeth

mineral: 3 oil 4 gold, lead, zinc 6 silver 8 tungsten 9 petroleum

mountain: 21 Mount Sir James MacBrien

native: 5 Inuit 6 Eskimo

territory: 8 Franklin, Keewatin 9 Mackenzie

North wind

associated with: 6 Boreas

Norton, Thomas

author of: 8 Gorboduc (with Thomas Sackville)

Norway

other name: 5 Norge 20 Land of the Midnight Sun

capital: 4 Oslo 11 Christiania

largest city: 4 Oslo

others: 3 Gol, Nes 4 Bodo, Moss, Odda, Rena, Voss 5 Bjort, Floro, Hamar, Molde, Skien, Skjak, Vadso 6 Bergen, Horton, Larvik, Narvik, Tromso 7 Alesund, Arendal, Drammen, Harstad, Sandnes 8

Aalesund, Kirkenes 9 Stavanger, Trondheim 10 Hammerfest 12 Kristiansand

division: 3 Amt 4 Oslo 5 Fylke, Troms 6 Bergen, Opland, Tromso 7 Finmark, Hedmark, Ostfold 8 Letemark, Nordland, Rogaland, Vestfold 9 Ostlandet

former: 11 Kalmar Union

province called: 6 fylker

government:

legislature: 8 Storting

head of state: 4 king

measure: 3 fot, mal 4 alen 5 kande 6 fathom 7 skieppe 9 korntonde

monetary unit: 3 ore 5 krone

weight: 3 lod 4 mark, pund 10 bismerpund

island: 4 Vega 5 Bomlo, Donna, Froya, Hitra, Hopen, Senja, Smola, Soroy 6 Alsten, Averoy, Bouvet, Hinnoy, Karmoy, Kvaloy, Solund, Vannoy 7 Gurskoy, Lofoten, Mageroy, Seiland 8 Jan Mayen, Svalbard

lake: 4 Alte 5 Ister, Mjosa, Snasa 6 Femund 7 Rostavn, Tunnsjo

mountain: 5 Sogne 6 Kjolen 7 Numedal 8 Blodfjel, Snohetta, Telemark, Ustetind 9 Harteigen, Jotunheim, Langfjell, Ramnanosi 10 Dovrefjell, Galdhoepig, Glitretind, Vibmesnosi 11 Myrdalfjell 14 Aardangerjokul, Hallingskarvet, Skagastolstind

highest point: 12 Galdhopiggen 13 Glittertinden

river: 3 Ena 4 Alta, Klar, Otra, Rana, Tana, Teno 5 Bardu, Begna, Glama, Lagen, Orkla, Otter, Rauma, Reisa 6 Glomma, Lougen, Namsen, Pasvik

sea: 5 North 6 Arctic 7 Barents 8 Atlantic 9 Norwegian, Skagerrak

physical feature:

cape: 4 Naze 7 Nordkyn 8 Nordkapp 9 Lindesnes

fjord: 4 Oslo 5 Sogne

glacier: 12 Jostedalsbre

inlet: 2 ls 3 Kob, Ran 4 Alst, Ands, Bokn, Nord, Ofot, Salt, Sunn, Tyri, Vest 5 fiord, fjord, Folda, Lakse, Sogne 6 Bjorna, Hadsel 7 Hortens 9 Trondheim

plateau: 5 Doure, Dovre, Fjeld 9 Hardanger

people: 4 Lapp 5 Samme 6 Nordic, Viking

artist: 5 Munch

author: 5 Ibsen 6 Hamsun, Undset 7 Holberg 8 Bjornson 9 Wergeland

composer: 5 Grieg 7 Sinding 8 Svendsen

explorer: 4 Eric, Leif, Mohn, Sars 6 Nansen 8 Amundsen

explorer/statesman: 6 Nansen 8 Amundsen 9 Heyerdahl

king: 4 Olaf, Olav 5 Olave, Oscar 6 Haakon, Harold, Magnus, Sverre

Nazi collaborator: 8 Quisling

Norse god/goddess: 3 Sif, Tyr 4 Frey, Idun, Loki, Odin, Thor 5 Bragi, Freya, Ho-

der, Woden 6 Balder, Eostre, Frigga, Hermod

sculptor: 8 Vigeland

language: 4 Lapp 5 Norse 6 Bokmal 7 Nynorsk, Riksmal 8 Landsmal, Samnorsk 9 Landsmaal, Norwegian

religion: 19 Evangelical Lutheran 22 National Church of Norway

place:

castle: 8 Akershus

cathedral: 7 Nidaras

museum: 7 Kon Tiki 10 Viking Ship 15 Polar Expedition

park: 7 Frogner

former colony: 7 Vinland

feature:

dance: 6 gangar 7 halling 8 springar 9 spingleik

literature form: 4 edda, saga

food:

bread: 8 flat brod

cheese: 3 Ost 7 gjetost 9 gammelost, Jarlsberg

drink: 7 aquavit

Norwegian Mythology *see* 21 Scandinavian Mythology

nose

sense of: 5 smell

part: 7 nostril 14 olfactory patch

nosegay 4 posy 7 bouquet 10 tussy-mussy

nosiness 6 prying 9 curiosity 15 inquisitiveness

nostalgia 6 pining, regret 7 remorse 11 languishing, remembrance 12 homesickness 13 regretfulness

Nostradamus

name: 7 Michael 17 Michelde Notredame

occupation: 7 prophet 9 physician 10 astrologer 13 metaphysicist

wrote: 9 Centuries

Nostromo

author: 12 Joseph Conrad

nostrum 4 balm, cure, dose, drug 5 draft 6 elixir, physic, potion, remedy 7 cure-all, formula, panacea 8 medicine 9 treatment 10 medicament 12 prescription

nosy, nosey 6 prying, snoopy 7 all ears, curious 8 snooping 9 intrusive 11 inquisitive, overcurious 13 eavesdropping

nota bene 8 note well 10 take notice

notability 4 fame 6 import, moment, renown 8 eminence 9 celebrity 10 importance, prominence 11 consequence, distinction, preeminence 12 significance

notable 3 VIP 4 name 5 famed, wheel 6 biggie, bigwig, famous, marked 7 eminent, salient 8 luminary, renowned, striking 9 celebrity, dignitary, personage, prominent, reputable 10 celebrated, pronounced, remarkable 11 conspicuous, outstanding, personality 13 distinguished

notably 7 visibly 8 markedly 10 distinctly, strikingly 11 prominently 12 unmistakably 13 conspicuously, outstandingly

not alike 8 distinct 9 different, differing, disparate, divergent 10 dissimilar 11 contrasting

notation 5 entry 10 memorandum

not bright 3 dim 4 dark, dull 5 dense, dusky, murky 6 cloudy, stupid 7 clouded 8 obscured 13 unilluminated

notch 3 cut 4 dent, mark, nick 5 grade, level, score 6 degree 7 scoring, scratch 11 indentation

not disclosed
Italian: 7 in petto

note 4 bill, fame, line, mark 5 bread, draft, enter, green, money, write 6 regard, renown 7 epistle, jot down, lettuce, message, missive, put down, scratch, set down, voucher 8 currency, dispatch, eminence, mark down, perceive 9 bank draft, celebrity, greenback 10 communique, importance, memorandum, prominence, reputation 11 certificate, consequence, distinction

notebook 3 log 5 diary 6 record 7 journal 9 looseleaf
French: 6 cahier

noted 6 famous 7 eminent 8 renowned 9 prominent, reputable 10 celebrated, remarkable 11 illustrious, outstanding 13 distinguished

Notes from the Underground
author: 16 Fyodor Dostoevsky

note well
Latin: 8 nota bene

noteworthy 7 unusual 8 singular 9 important 10 remarkable 11 outstanding, significant, substantial 12 considerable 13 distinguished, exceptionable

not far from 4 near 6 all but, almost, nearly 7 close to 8 not quite 13 approximately

not genuine 4 fake, sham 5 bogus, false, phony 6 ersatz, unreal 7 feigned 8 spurious 9 imitation, insincere, pretended, synthetic 10 artificial, fraudulent 11 counterfeit 12 hypocritical
Latin: 8 mala fide

not germane 9 extrinsic, unrelated 10 extraneous, immaterial, irrelevant 11 incongruous, inconsonant, unconnected 12 incompatible, nonessential 13 inappropriate

not guilty 5 clear 8 innocent 9 blameless 10 inculpable, unblamable

nothing 3 air, nix, zip 4 none, zero 5 stuff, trash, zilch 6 bauble, bubble, cipher, gewgaw, naught, trifle, trivia 7 duck egg, nullity, rubbish, trinket 8 goose egg 9 bagatelle, obscurity 14 insignificance 16 inconsequentials
Latin: 5 nihil

nothing is created from nothing
Latin: 16 ex nihilo nihil fit

nothingness 4 void 5 death 8 oblivion 9 emptiness 10 triviality 12 nonexistence 14 insignificance

Nothing Sacred
director: 14 William Wellman
cast: 13 Carole Lombard, Frederic March 14 Walter Connolly
score: 11 Oscar Levant
remade as: 10 Living It Up
script: 8 Ben Hecht

nothing unless it is good
Latin: 12 nil nisi bonum

nothing without the divine will
Latin: 13 nil sine numine
motto of: 8 Colorado

notice 3 eye, see 4 dope, heed, info, mark 5 goods 6 poster, rating, regard, review, take in 7 leaflet, mention, observe, warning 8 brochure, circular, critique, handbill, pamphlet 9 appraisal, attention, knowledge, statement 10 advisement, cognizance, disclosure 11 declaration, information 12 announcement, intelligence 13 advertisement, communication, specification

noticeable 5 clear, plain 7 evident, obvious 8 definite, distinct, manifest, palpable, striking 10 observable 11 appreciable, conspicuous, perceivable, perceptible 12 unmistakable

notification 4 news, word 6 advice, report 7 message, release 8 bulletin, dispatch 9 statement 10 communique 11 information 12 announcement, intelligence 13 communication

notify 4 tell, warn 6 advise, inform 7 apprise, let know 8 acquaint, send word 9 enlighten

not indigenous 5 alien 6 exotic 7 foreign 8 imported 9 nonnative 10 extraneous 11 naturalized

notion 4 idea, view, whim 5 fancy, humor, quirk 6 belief, vagary, whimsy 7 caprice, conceit, concept, opinion 8 crotchet 9 suspicion 10 conception, intimation 12 eccentricity

not native 5 alien 6 exotic 7 foreign 8 imported 10 extraneous 11 naturalized

not of sound mind
Latin: 15 non compos mentis

not ordinary 4 rare 6 exotic, unique 7 bizarre, foreign, strange, unusual 8 peculiar, singular, uncommon 9 anomalous, different, fantastic 11 distinctive, outstanding 14 unconventional

notoriety 4 blot 5 shame, stain 6 infamy, stigma 7 scandal 8 disgrace, dishonor, ignominy 9 discredit, disrepute 11 degradation

notorious 6 arrant 7 blatant, glaring 8 infamous, renowned 9 egregious 10 celebrated, outrageous 11 outstanding

Notorious
director: 15 Alfred Hitchcock
cast: 9 Cary Grant 11 Claude Rains 12 Louis Calhern 13 Ingrid Bergman

not pertinent 9 unrelated 10 extraneous, immaterial, irrelevant 11 incongruous, unconnected 13 inappropriate

not quite 6 all but, almost, nearly

not required 8 elective, optional 9 voluntary

not too seriously
Latin: 13 cum grano salis

Notus
origin: 5 Greek
personifies: 9 south wind

not wanted
 French: 6 de trop
notwithstanding
 Latin: 11 non obstante
not working 4 dead 8 inactive 10 unemployed 11 inoperative 12 unresponsive
Nouakchott
 capital of: 10 Mauritania
nourish 4 feed 5 nurse 6 suckle 7 nurture, sustain
nourishing 4 rich 6 hearty 7 healthy 9 fostering, nurturing, wholesome 10 nutritious, sustaining 11 maintaining 12 invigorating 13 strengthening
nourishment 4 chow, eats, food, grub, meat 5 bread 6 viands 8 victuals 9 nutriment, nutrition 10 sustenance 11 comestibles
nouveau riche 9 newly rich (person)
Novak, Kim
 real name: 19 Marilyn Pauline Novak
 born: 9 Chicago IL
 roles: 6 Picnic 7 Pal Joey, Vertigo 14 Of Human Bondage 17 Bell Book and Candle 20 The Jeanne Eagels Story 22 The Man with the Golden Arm 31 Amorous Adventures of Moll Flanders
Nova Scotia
 borders: 10 Bay of Fundy 12 New Brunswick 13 Atlantic Ocean 16 Gulf of St Lawrence 20 Northumberland Strait
 city: 5 Truro 6 Sydney 7 Amherst, Halifax 8 Glace Bay, Yarmouth 9 Dartmouth 10 New Glasgow
 country: 6 Canada
 island: 10 Cape Breton
 means: 11 New Scotland
 mineral: 3 oil 4 lead, salt, sand, zinc 6 barite, gravel, gypsum, silver 9 celestite, petroleum 10 natural gas
 mountain: 5 North 8 Cobequid
 part of: 12 Appalachians 17 Maritime Provinces 18 Atlantic Provinces
 river: 4 Avon 5 Clyde 6 LaHave, Medway, Mersey 7 St Mary's 12 Shubenacadie
novel 3 new 6 unique 7 unusual 8 original, singular, uncommon 9 different 10 innovative, unorthodox 14 unconventional
 French: 5 roman
novelty 5 token 6 bauble, change, gewgaw 7 memento, newness, trinket 8 gimcrack, souvenir, surprise 9 bagatelle, variation 10 innovation, knick-knack, uniqueness 11 originality
November
 event: 11 Election Day
 flower: 13 chrysanthemum
 French: 8 Novembre
 gem: 5 topaz
 German: 8 November
 holiday: 11 All Souls' Day (2), Veterans Day (11) 12 All Saints' Day (1), Guy Fawkes Day (5), Thanksgiving (4th Thursday)
 Italian: 8 Novembre
 number of days: 6 thirty

origin of name: 5 novem (Latin meaning nine)
 place in year:
 Gregorian: 8 eleventh
 Roman: 5 ninth
 Spanish: 9 Noviembre
 Zodiac sign: 7 Scorpio 11 Sagittarius
novice 4 tyro 5 pupil 7 amateur, learner, student 8 beginner, disciple, newcomer 9 greenhorn 10 apprentice, tenderfoot
Novum Organum
 author: 12 Francis Bacon
novus ordo seclorum 24 a new order of the ages is born
 author: 6 Vergil, Virgil
 work: 8 Eclogues
 motto of: 11 US Great Seal
Now, Voyager
 director: 12 Irving Rapper
 cast: 10 Bette Davis 11 Claude Rains, Janis Wilson, Paul Henreid 12 Gladys Cooper
 score: 10 Max Steiner
now and then 8 on-and-off, periodic, sometime, sporadic 9 irregular, sometimes, temporary 10 infrequent, occasional 11 irregularly 12 infrequently, occasionally, periodically, sporadically
Now Playing at Canterbury
 author: 14 Vance Bourjaily
Nox
 goddess of: 5 night
noxious 4 foul 6 deadly, lethal, putrid 7 baneful, beastly, harmful, hurtful, noisome 8 damaging, virulent 9 injurious, loathsome, poisonous, revolting 10 abominable, disgusting, pernicious, putrescent 11 deleterious 12 foul-smelling
nth degree 5 limit 6 utmost 7 extreme
nuance 5 shade, touch 6 nicety 7 finesse 8 delicacy, fineness, keenness, subtlety 9 sharpness, variation 10 modulation, refinement 11 discernment
nub 4 core, crux, gist, hump, knob, knot, lump, node 5 bulge, heart 6 kernel 7 essence 8 swelling 10 projection, prominence, tumescence 11 nitty-gritty 12 protuberance
nubbin 3 ear 4 corn, lump, stub 5 bulge, fruit, piece, stump 10 diminutive
Nubbles, Kit
 character in: 19 The Old Curiosity Shop
 author: 7 Dickens
nubbly 5 lumpy, rough 6 coarse, knobby, pebbly
nucleus 3 nub 4 core, pith, seed 5 heart 6 center, kernel
Nudd *see* 4 Llud
nude 3 raw 4 bare 5 bared, naked 6 unclad 7 exposed 8 in the raw, stripped 9 unadorned, unarrayed, unclothed, uncovered, undressed
 French: 9 au naturel
nudge 3 jab, jog, nod 4 bump, jolt, poke, prod, push 5 elbow, press, punch, shove, touch 6 jostle, motion, signal 8 indicate

nugatory 4 idle 5 empty 6 hollow, otiose, paltry 7 trivial, useless 8 piddling, trifling 9 meritless, valueless, worthless 10 profitless 11 ineffectual 12 functionless 15 inconsequential

nugget 4 hunk, lump 5 chunk, piece

nuisance 4 bore, fret, hurt, pain, pest 5 curse, thorn, worry 6 blight, bother, burden, plague 7 scourge, torment, trouble 8 handicap, vexation 9 annoyance, grievance 10 affliction, irritation, misfortune, pestilence 11 aggravation, botheration 13 inconvenience

Nuk
  capital of: 9 Greenland

Nukualofa
  capital of: 5 Tonga

null 2 NG 4 void 6 no good 7 invalid 9 valueless, worthless 10 immaterial 11 inoperative, nonexistent, unimportant 13 insignificant

nullification 6 repeal 7 voiding 8 recision 9 abolition, annulment 10 abrogation, rescinding 11 abolishment 12 cancellation, invalidation

nullify 4 veto, void 5 annul 6 cancel, repeal, revoke 7 abolish, rescind, retract 8 abrogate, make void, override, set aside 10 invalidate

nullity 6 cipher, naught 7 nothing 9 nonentity

Numanus
  brother-in-law: 6 Turnus

numb 4 dead 6 frozen 8 deadened 9 insensate, unfeeling 10 insensible, narcotized 12 anesthetized

number 3 mob, sum, tot 4 army, bevy, book, herd, host, mass, part 5 array, bunch, count, crowd, digit, group, issue, swarm, tally, total 6 amount, cipher, figure, reckon, scores, symbol 7 chapter, company, compute, edition, foliate, integer, numeral, passage, section 8 division, estimate, magazine, numerate, paginate, quantity 9 abundance, aggregate, calculate, character, enumerate, multitude, paragraph, quarterly 10 assemblage, quantities 13 preponderance

numbered numbered weighed divided
  Aramaic: 21 mene mene tekel upharsin
  foretells destruction of: 10 Belshazzar
  Biblical book of: 6 Daniel

numberless 6 myriad 7 copious, umpteen 8 unending, zillions 9 countless, plenteous, unbounded, uncounted 11 illimitable, uncountable 12 immeasurable 13 multitudinous

numbness 8 deadness 11 insentience

numeral 5 digit 6 cipher, figure, letter, number, symbol 7 integer 9 character

numerate 3 add 5 count, tally, total 6 number, reckon 7 compute, tick off 9 calculate

numerophobia
  fear of: 7 numbers

numerous 4 many 6 myriad 7 copious, profuse 8 abundant 9 plentiful 13 multitudinous

Numidia see 7 Algeria

Numipu see 8 Nez Perce

Numitor
  king of: 9 Alba Longa
  father: 5 Proca
  brother: 7 Amulius
  daughter: 10 Rhea Silvia
  grandson: 5 Remus 7 Romulus

numskull, numbskull 3 sap 4 dolt, dope, fool, jerk 5 dummy, dunce, idiot, klutz, ninny 6 dimwit, nitwit 7 dullard, half-wit 8 bonehead, dummkopf, imbecile, lunkhead, silly ass 9 blockhead, simpleton 10 dunderhead, muttonhead, nincompoop, noodlehead 11 chowderhead, knucklehead 12 scatterbrain

Nun see 4 Nunu

nuncio 5 envoy 6 legate 8 diplomat, minister 9 messenger 10 ambassador 11 papallegate 14 representative

nunnery 5 abbey, order 6 priory 7 cenacle, convent 8 cloister 9 hermitage, monastery 10 sisterhood

Nun's Story, The
  director: 12 Fred Zinneman
  based on story by: 12 Kathryn Hulme
  cast: 10 Dean Jagger, Edith Evans, Peter Finch 13 Audrey Hepburn, Peggy Ashcroft 15 Colleen Dewhurst

Nunu
  also: 3 Nun
  origin: 8 Egyptian
  god of: 5 ocean
  personifies: 5 chaos

nuptial 7 marital 8 conjugal, hymeneal 9 connubial 11 matrimonial

nuptials 7 wedding 8 marriage 9 espousals, hymeneals 12 matrimonials

Nurmi, Paavo
  nickname: 13 The Flying Finn
  sport: 5 track
  won: 8 Olympics

nurse 4 feed 5 nanny, treat 6 attend, doctor, foster, harbor, remedy, sister, succor, suckle 7 care for, nourish, nurture, promote 8 attend to, guardian 9 attendant, cultivate, encourage, governess
  Hindi/Indian: 4 ayah

nursery 6 hotbed 9 incubator, preschool 10 greenhouse, schoolroom 12 conservatory, kindergarten

nurture 4 feed, mess, rear, tend 5 breed, raise, teach, train, tutor 6 foster, school 7 bring up, develop, educate, nourish, prepare, sustain, victual 8 instruct, maintain 9 cultivate, provision 10 discipline, strengthen

Nusantara see 9 Indonesia

Nusku
  origin: 8 Sumerian 10 Babylonian
  visier of: 5 Enlil

nut 3 fan, pit 4 buff, seed 5 freak, idiot, loony, stone 6 madman, maniac, zealot 7 devotee, fanatic, lunatic, oddball 8 crackpot 9 eccentric, screwball 10 aficionado, enthusiast, psychopath 11 afficionado

Nut
  origin: 8 Egyptian
  goddess of: 3 sky

nut-brown 5 tawny 6 auburn, brunet 8 brunette, cinnamon

Nutcracker, The
  also: 13 Shchelkunchik
  ballet by: 11 Tchaikovsky
  based on fairy tale by: 11 ETA Hoffmann
  contains: 17 Waltz of the Flowers 24 Dance of the Sugar-Plum Fairy

nutmeg
  botanical name: 17 Myristica fragrans
  from same plant as: 4 mace
  origin: 9 Indonesia
  use: 5 punch 6 eggnog 8 desserts 10 vegetables 11 baked dishes

Nutmeg State
  nickname of: 11 Connecticut

nutriment 4 chow, eats, fare, feed, food, meat, mess 5 board 6 fodder, forage 7 aliment, edibles 8 eatables, victuals 9 foodstuff, groceries, provender 10 provisions, sustenance 11 nourishment, subsistence

nutrition 4 chow, feed, food, grub 6 fodder, forage, silage 7 edibles, rations 8 eatables 9 groceries, pasturage, provender 10 foodstuffs, provisions, sustenance 11 nourishment, subsistence

nutritious 9 wholesome 10 nourishing, sustaining

nuts 3 mad 4 bats, daft 5 balmy, crazy, dotty, loony, potty, wacko, wacky 6 insane 7 bananas, bonkers, cracked, touched 8 demented, deranged, unhinged 10 unbalanced

nutty 3 mad 4 daft 5 balmy, crazy, dippy, dotty, goofy, inane, loony, silly, wacko, wacky 6 cuckoo, insane, screwy, weirdo 7 bonkers, cracked, foolish, lunatic, meshuga, touched 8 bughouse, demented 9 senseless 10 addlepated, squirrelly 11 harebrained 12 crackbrained

nuzzle 3 pat, pet 4 buss, kiss 5 smack 6 caress, coddle, cosset, cuddle, fondle, nestle 7 embrace, snuggle

Nyasaland see 6 Malawi

Nycteus
  father: 9 Chthonios
  brother: 5 Lycus
  daughter: 7 Antiope, Nycteis

Nyctimus
  father: 6 Lycaon

nyctophobia
  fear of: 8 darkness 14 the dark of night

nymph 5 belle, dryad, naiad, sylph 6 beauty 7 charmer

Nymphaea
  epithet of: 9 Aphrodite
  means: 6 bridal

Nyx
  form: 7 goddess
  personifies: 5 night
  originated from: 5 Chaos

children: 3 Ker 4 Eris 5 Fates, Geras, Momus, Moros, Oizys 6 Aether, Hemera, Hypnos, Somnus 7 Nemesis, Oneiroi 8 Thanatos

O

oaf 3 sap 4 boob, boor, clod, dolt, dope, fool, jerk, lout 5 booby, dummy, dunce, idiot, klutz, moron, ninny 6 lummox, nitwit 7 dullard, half-wit 8 bonehead, imbecile, numskull 9 blockhead, ignoramus, numbskull, simpleton 10 dunderhead, nincompoop

oafish 4 rude 5 crude 6 coarse, gauche, vulgar 7 boorish, doltish, loutish, uncouth 9 unrefined 10 unpolished

oak 7 Quercus
  varieties: 3 bur, cow, pin, red, she 4 bear, blue, cork, deer, Holm, jack, live, maul, post, silk 5 black, Emory, holly, scrub, ubame, water, white 6 basket, Belote, canyon, Ceylon, Daimyo, gambel, gander, Havard, Indian, island, Kermes, Konara, laurel, Oregon, poison, possum, Turkey, Turner, valley, willow, yellow 7 Ballota, Bartram, Belloot, Catesby, Durmast, English, Georgia, Italian, Kellogg, leather, Lebanon, overcup, scarlet, shingle, Spanish, tanbark, truffle, western 8 Arkansas, bluejack, chestnut, McDonald, mossy-cup, shinnery, Texas red 9 blackjack, Engelmann, flowering, Jerusalem, Mongolian, pubescent, swamp post 10 Chinquapin, Darlington, ring-cupped, Spanish red, swamp white 11 huckleberry, Japanese red, northern pin, northern red, Shumard's red 12 interior live, laurel-leaved, rock chestnut, southern live, yellow-barked 13 dwarf chestnut, oriental white, swamp chestnut 14 Austrian turkey, California live, yellow chestnut 15 California black, California field, California scrub, California white 16 high-ground willow 17 Japanese evergreen 18 Rocky Mountain scrub

Oak, Gabriel
  character in: 22 Far From the Madding Crowd
  author of: 5 Hardy

Oakie, Jack
  real name: 19 Lewis Delaney Offield
  born: 9 Sedalia (Sadalia) MO
  roles: 16 The Great Dictator 17 Alice in Wonderland

Oakland
  baseball team: 2 A's 9 Athletics
  football team: 8 Invaders

oar 3 row 4 pole 5 blade, rower, scull 6 paddle, propel 9 propeller
  blade: 4 palm, peel
  fulcrum: 5 thole 7 oarlock, rowlock
  part: 4 loom 5 shaft 6 collar

oarsman 5 pilot, rower 6 bowman 7 mariner, sculler 8 helmsman 9 gondolier, propeller

oasis 5 haven 6 asylum, harbor, refuge 7 retreat, sanctum, shelter 9 green spot, sanctuary, water hole 11 fertile area 13 watering place

oast 4 kiln, oven

oat, oats 5 Avena 11 Avena sativa
  varieties: 3 sea 4 wild 6 potato 8 animated 9 Tartarian 11 slender wild

Oates, Joyce Carol
  author of: 4 Them 9 Childwold 10 Bellefleur, Wonderland 11 Unholy Loves, Wheel of Love 15 Son of the Morning 18 A Bloodsmoor Romance 19 Do With Me What You Will

oath 3 vow 5 curse 6 avowal, pledge 8 cuss word, swearing 9 affidavit, blasphemy, expletive, obscenity, profanity 10 adjuration, deposition 11 affirmation, attestation, declaration, imprecation, malediction

oaths
  god of: 6 Horcus, Sancus 10 Dius Fidius, Semo Sancus

oatmeal 6 cereal 7 pottage 8 drammock, porridge

Obadiah 4 Obad 7 prophet 12 minor prophet
  father: 4 Azel 6 Jehiel 8 Izrahiah, Shemaiah
  son: 8 Ishmaiah
  predicted fall of: 4 Edom

Obata, Gyo
  architect of: 20 Dallas–Ft Worth Airport 25 National Air and Space Museum (Smithsonian Institution)

obdurate 5 cruel, harsh 6 mulish 7 adamant, callous, unmoved, willful 8 hardened, pitiless, stubborn, uncaring 9 immovable, merciless, obstinate, pigheaded, unfeeling, unpitying, unsparing, untouched 10 bullheaded, headstrong, inflexible, unmerciful, unyielding 11 cold-blooded, hardhearted, intractable 12 ungovernable, unmanageable 13 unsympathetic 14 uncontrollable 15 uncompassionate

obedience 8 docility, yielding 9 deference, ductility, obeisance 10 accordance, allegiance, compliance, subjection, submission 11 conformance, dutifulness, willingness 12 acquiescence, subservience, tractability 14 conformability, submissiveness

obedient 5 loyal 6 docile 7 devoted, dutiful 8 amenable, faithful, obeisant, yielding 9 compliant, tractable 10 governable, law-abiding, respectful, submissive 11 acquiescent, deferential, subservient

obeisance 3 bow 5 honor 6 curtsy, esteem, fealty, homage, regard 7 loyalty, respect, 8 courtesy, fidelity, humility, kneeling 9 deference, obedience, reverence 10 allegiance, humbleness, subjection, submission, veneration 11 prostration 12 genuflection 13 self-abasement

obelisk 5 pylon, shaft, tower 6 column, dagger, needle, pillar 8 memorial, monolith, monument

Oberon
    character in: 21 A Midsummer Night's Dream
    author: 11 Shakespeare

Oberon
    opera by: 5 Weber
    character: 5 Reiza
    setting: 18 court of Charlemagne 21 court of Haroun al Rashid

Oberon, Merle
    real name: 26 Estelle Merle O'Brien Thompson
    husband: 14 Alexander Korda
    born: 8 Tasmania
    roles: 5 Hotel 7 Desiree 15 A Song to Remember 16 Wuthering Heights 19 The Scarlet Pimpernel 25 The Private Life of Henry VIII 30 The Private Life of Henry the Eighth

obese 3 fat 5 gross, heavy, plump, porky, pudgy, stout, tubby 6 chubby, fleshy, portly, rotund 7 paunchy 9 corpulent 10 overweight, potbellied

obesity 3 fat 7 fatness, liposis 8 adiposis, enormity 9 heaviness, plumpness, stoutness 10 corpulence, overweight

obey 4 heed, mind 5 bow to, serve 6 assent, concur 7 abide by, observe, respect, yield to 8 accede to, submit to 9 acquiesce, conform to, succumb to 10 comply with, toe the line 12 follow orders

obfuscate 4 blur 5 befog 6 garble, mess up, muddle 7 becloud, confuse, distort, fluster, obscure, stupefy 8 confound, scramble 10 complicate

obfuscation 8 flummery 9 confusion 10 doubletalk, mumbo jumbo

obi 4 sash 5 obeah 6 girdle

obiit 6 he died 7 she died

obiter dictum 9 diversion 10 digression, divagation, side remark

object 3 aim, end, use 4 body, butt, dupe, form, gist, goal, pith, prey 5 abhor, basis, cause, knock, point, sense, thing 6 balk at, carp at, design, device, dingus, gadget, intent, loathe, motive, oppose, quarry, reason, target, victim 7 article, cavil at, condemn, dislike, essence, frown on, meaning, mission, protest, purpose, subject 8 be averse, cynosure, denounce 9 abominate, criticize, doohickey, incentive, intention, objective, principle, recipient, substance 10 inducement, phenomenon 11 contrivance, explanation, thingamabob, thingamajig 12 be at odds with, disapprove

of, significance 13 find fault with, take exception 18 remonstrate against

objection 4 beef, kick 5 cavil 7 protest 8 demurral, rebuttal 9 challenge, complaint, criticism, exception 10 dissension, opposition 11 disapproval, reservation 12 disagreement 13 contradiction 14 disapprobation, opposing reason 15 counter argument

objectionable 4 foul, vile 5 nasty 6 odious 8 unseemly 9 abhorrent, loathsome, obnoxious, offensive, revolting 10 abominable, despicable, disgusting, unbearable, unpleasant 11 displeasing, distasteful, intolerable, unendurable 12 disagreeable, unacceptable 13 inappropriate

objective 3 aim, end 4 fair, goal, just, mark, real 6 actual, design, intent, target 7 mission, purpose 8 detached, unbiased, unswayed 9 impartial, intention, uncolored 10 impersonal, open-minded 11 destination 12 uninfluenced, unprejudiced 13 disinterested, dispassionate

objectivity 8 fairness 10 detachment, neutrality 12 impartiality

object to 7 condemn, dislike 9 frown upon 12 disapprove of 14 discountenance 15 take exception to 16 find unacceptable

objet d'art 5 bijou, curio 7 bibelot, trinket 9 art object

oblation 4 gift 8 offering 9 offertory 10 collection

obligated 5 bound 6 forced, liable 7 pledged 8 beholden, indebted 9 committed 11 constrained

obligation 4 bond, care, debt, duty, oath, onus, word 6 charge, pledge 7 compact, promise 8 contract, guaranty, warranty 9 agreement, guarantee, liability 10 a favor owed, commitment, constraint 12 indebtedness 13 answerability, understanding 14 accountability, responsibility

obligatory 7 binding 8 coercive, enforced, required 9 mandatory, necessary, requisite 10 compulsory, imperative, peremptory 11 unavoidable

oblige 3 aid 4 bind, help, make 5 favor, force, impel, serve 6 assist, coerce, compel 7 require, support 8 obligate 9 constrain 11 accommodate, do a favor for, necessitate 13 do a service for, to be duty bound

obliged 5 bound 7 favored, pleased 8 assisted, beholden, indebted, required, thankful 9 compelled 12 accommodated

obliging 4 kind 6 polite 7 amiable, helpful 8 cheerful, friendly, gracious 9 agreeable, courteous 10 solicitous 11 complaisant, considerate, cooperative, good-natured, sympathetic 12 well-disposed 13 accommodating

oblique 3 sly 4 awry 5 askew 6 aslant, covert, hinted, masked, tilted, veiled 7 cloaked, devious, furtive, implied, slanted, sloping 8 allusive, diagonal, inclined, indirect, slanting, sneaking 9 suggested, underhand

obliterate 4 raze **5** erase, level **6** cancel, delete, efface, remove, rub out **7** abolish, blot out, destroy, expunge, wipe out **9** eradicate, write over **10** annihilate, strike over

obliteration 8 deletion **9** abolition, expunging, wiping out **11** blotting out, destruction, eradication **12** annihilation

oblivion 5 limbo **7** the void **9** blankness, disregard, obscurity, unconcern **11** blotting out, nothingness **12** nonexistence **13** forgetfulness, insensibility, obliviousness **14** insignificance **15** unconsciousness

oblivious 8 careless **9** forgetful, unaware of, unmindful **10** heedless of, insensible **11** inattentive, unconcerned, unobservant **12** disregardful, undiscerning **13** unconscious of

Oblonsky, Prince Stepan
   character in: 12 Anna Karenina
   author: 7 Tolstoy

obloquy 5 abuse, odium, shame **6** infamy, rebuke **7** calumny, censure, railing **8** contempt, disfavor, disgrace, ignominy, reviling **9** discredit, invective **10** defamation, opprobrium, scurrility **11** degradation, humiliation, verbal abuse **12** billingsgate, condemnation, denunciation, dressing-down, vilification

obnoxious 4 foul, vile **5** nasty **6** odious **7** hateful **8** unseemly **9** abhorrent, loathsome, offensive, repellent, repugnant, revolting **10** abominable, despicable, detestable, disgusting, nauseating, unbearable, unpleasant **11** displeasing, intolerable, unendurable **12** disagreeable, insufferable **13** inappropriate, objectionable

oboe family
   instruments: 5 shawm **6** curtal, pommer, racket **7** bassoon, bombard, curtall, hautboy **8** crumhorn, schalmey, tenoroon **10** Cor Anglais, oboe d'Amore **11** English horn, heckelphone, sarusophone **12** oboe da caccia, sarrusophone **13** contra bassoon, double bassoon

O'Brian, Hugh
   real name: 11 Hugh J Krampe
   born: 11 Rochester NY
   roles: 9 Wyatt Earp **27** The Life and Legend of Wyatt Earp

O'Brien, Edna
   author of: 5 Night **11** A Pagan Place **13** The Lonely Girl **14** The Country Girl **20** August Is a Wicked Month **24** Girls in Their Married Bliss

O'Brien, Margaret
   real name: 18 Angela Maxine O'Brien
   born: 12 Los Angeles CA
   roles: 8 Jane Eyre **11** Little Women **15** Meet Me in St Louis **24** Our Vines Have Tender Grapes

O'Brien, Pat
   real name: 26 William Joseph Patrick O'Brien
   born: 11 Milwaukee WI
   roles: 12 Hildy Johnson, The Front Page **13** Some Like It Hot, The Last Hurrah **20**

Angels with Dirty Faces **22** Knute Rockne All American
   autobiography: 12 Wind on My Back

obscene 4 blue, foul, lewd **5** dirty **6** filthy, smutty, vulgar **8** indecent, prurient **9** salacious **10** lascivious, lubricious **12** pornographic, scatological **16** morally offensive

obscenity 8 cuss word, lewdness **9** dirtiness, indecency, profanity, prurience, swear word, taboo word, vulgarity **10** filthiness, smuttiness **11** pornography **13** salaciousness **14** four-letter word, lasciviousness

obscuration 7 eclipse, masking, veiling **8** cloaking, clouding, covering **9** darkening, shadowing **10** concealing **11** concealment

obscure 3 dim, fog **4** blur, hide, mask, veil **5** bedim, befog, block, cloak, cloud, cover, dingy, dusky, faint, murky, vague **6** cloudy, darken, hidden, muddle, screen, shadow, shroud, somber, unsung **7** becloud, conceal, confuse, cryptic, curtain, eclipse, shadowy, unclear, unknown, unnoted **8** befuddle, confused, disguise, nameless, puzzling **9** confusing, enigmatic, forgotten, lightless, obfuscate, uncertain, unheard of, unlighted **10** indefinite, indistinct, overshadow, perplexing, unrenowned **11** indefinable, inscrutable, little known, out-of-the-way, unimportant **12** unfathomable **13** inconspicuous, insignificant, unilluminated **15** inconsequential

obscurity 3 fog **4** mist **5** cloud, shade **6** shadow **7** dimness, mystery, opacity, privacy **8** darkness **9** ambiguity, seclusion, vagueness **10** cloudiness

obsequies 5 rites **6** burial **7** funeral **15** memorial service

obsequious 6 menial **7** fawning, servile, slavish **8** cowering, cringing, toadying **9** kowtowing, truckling **11** bootlicking, deferential, subservient, sycophantic **12** ingratiating, mealymouthed **14** apple-polishing

observance 4 rite **6** custom, regard, ritual **7** heeding, keeping, obeying **8** ceremony, practice **9** adherence, attending, attention, following, formality, solemnity **10** ceremonial, compliance **11** celebration, observation **13** commemoration **15** memorialization

observant 5 alert, awake, aware **7** careful, heedful, mindful **8** vigilant, watchful **9** attentive, conscious, regardful, wide-awake **10** perceptive **12** on the lookout

observation 4 heed, idea, view **5** probe **6** eyeing, notice, remark, search, seeing, survey, theory **7** comment, finding, opinion, viewing **8** interest, judgment, scrutiny, spotting, watching **9** assertion, attention, beholding, detection, diagnosis, discovery, glimpsing, observing, statement **10** cognizance, commentary, inspection, reflection **11** description, examination, heedfulness **12** surveillance, watchfulness **13** pronouncement **20** firsthand information

observatory 5 tower 7 lookout 9 satellite 11 planetarium

  name: 4 Hale, Lick 6 Yerkes 7 Palomar, Whipple 8 Kitt Peak, Mt Wilson 11 Las Campanas, Mount Wilson 12 Big Bear Solar 14 Royal Greenwich

observe 3 eye, say, see 4 espy, heed, keep, mark, note, obey, ogle, spot, view 5 honor, opine, state, watch 6 assert, behold, detect, follow, notice, peer at, regard, remark, size up, survey 7 abide by, comment, declare, defer to, execute, fulfill, glimpse, inspect, make out, mention, perform, reflect, respect, stare at 8 adhere to, announce, carry out, discover, perceive, sanctify, theorize 9 celebrate, recognize, solemnize 10 be guided by, comply with, consecrate 11 acknowledge, acquiesce to, commemorate, take stock of 12 catch sight of 14 pay attention to

observer 6 viewer 7 watcher 8 onlooker 9 investigator

obsessed 5 beset 7 haunted 8 hung up on, maniacal 9 dominated, possessed 10 controlled 15 having a fixation

obsession 5 craze, mania, quirk 6 phobia 7 fixation 9 fixed idea, monomania 11 infatuation 13 preoccupation 16 overwhelming fear 18 neurotic conviction

obsolescent 8 dying out 9 declining 11 on the way out 12 disappearing 16 becoming obsolete 17 becoming out-of-date

obsolete 3 out 5 dated, passe 6 bygone 7 antique, archaic, extinct 8 outdated, out of use, outmoded 9 out-of-date 10 antiquated 12 old-fashioned, out of fashion

obstacle 3 bar 4 curb, snag 5 block, catch, check 6 hurdle 7 barrier, problem 8 blockade, stoppage 9 barricade, hindrance, roadblock 10 difficulty, impediment, limitation 11 obstruction, restriction 12 interference 14 stumbling block

obstetrician

  French: 10 accoucheur

obstinacy 4 rigidity 10 mulishness, resistance 11 willfulness 12 stubbornness 13 inflexibility, intransigence, pigheadedness

obstinate 6 dogged, mulish 7 staunch, willful 8 obdurate, resolute, stubborn 9 pigheaded, steadfast, tenacious, unbending 10 headstrong, inflexible, refractory, selfwilled, unyielding 11 intractable 12 recalcitrant, ungovernable, unmanageable 14 controllable 20 unreasonably stubborn

obstreperous 4 loud 5 noisy 6 unruly 8 perverse 9 clamorous, rampaging 10 boisterous, disorderly, refractory, roistering, uproarious, vociferous 11 disobedient 12 uncontrolled, ungovernable, unmanageable, unrestrained 14 uncontrollable

obstruct 3 bar 4 curb, halt, hide, mask, stop 5 block, check, cloak, close, cover, dam up, debar, delay, limit, stall 6 arrest, hinder, hobble, impede, plug up, retard, shroud, stifle, thwart 7 eclipse, inhibit, shut off 8 blockade, choke off, close off, restrict,

suppress, throttle 9 barricade, frustrate 18 bring to a standstill

obstruction 3 bar 4 curb, snag, stop 5 block, check, hitch 6 hurdle 7 barrier 8 blockage, obstacle, stoppage 9 barricade, hindrance 10 bottleneck, impediment 11 encumbrance

obtain 3 get 4 earn, gain, hold, take 5 exist, glean, stand 6 attain, come by, gather, pick up, secure 7 achieve, acquire, prevail, procure, receive 9 get hold of 14 get one's hands on 16 gain possession of

obtainment 11 achievement, acquirement, acquisition, procurement

obtrude 5 eject, expel, force 6 butt in, impose, meddle, thrust 7 presume, project 9 interfere

obtrusive 4 nosy 5 brash 6 prying, snoopy 7 bulging, forward, salient 8 familiar, meddling 9 intruding, intrusive, prominent 10 aggressive, jutting out, meddlesome, projecting, protruding 11 conspicuous, impertinent, interfering, outstanding, protuberant, sticking out, trespassing 12 interrupting, presumptuous

obtuse 4 dull, slow 5 blunt, dense, thick 6 simple, stupid 7 blunted 8 ignorant, not sharp 9 unpointed 10 insensible, not pointed, slow-witted 11 insensitive, unsharpened 12 imperceptive, thickskinned 15 uncomprehending

obtuseness 8 dullness 9 denseness, ignorance, stupidity 13 insensitivity 14 slowwittedness 15 thick-headedness 16 lack of perception, simplemindedness 19 lack of comprehension

obverse 4 face 5 front 10 complement 11 counterpart

  of coin: 4 head

obviate 5 avert, avoid, parry 6 divert, remove 7 fend off, prevent, ward off 8 preclude, stave off 9 forestall, sidetrack, turn aside 10 circumvent, do away with 11 nip in the bud

obvious 5 clear, plain 6 patent 7 evident, glaring, visible 8 apparent, distinct, manifest, palpable, striking, unhidden, unmasked, unveiled 10 undeniable 11 conspicuous, discernible, perceptible, selfevident, unconcealed, undisguised 12 in plain sight, unmistakable 24 plain as the nose on your face

O'Casey, Sean

  author of: 10 Purple Dust 12 The Green Crow 17 Juno and the Paycock 18 The Shadow of a Gunman 20 The Plough and the Stars

occasion 4 base, time 5 basis, cause, event 6 advent, affair, chance, elicit, ground, lead to, motive, prompt, reason 7 episode, grounds, inspire, opening, provoke, venture 8 incident, instance 9 adventure, happening, rationale, situation 10 bring about, experience, motivation, occurrence 11 celebration, explanation, opportunity, provocation 12 circumstance, special event, suitable time 13 justification, opportune time 14 convenient time, important event, particular time

occasional 4 rare 6 fitful, random 8 sporadic, uncommon 9 irregular, recurring, scattered, spasmodic, uncertain 10 incidental, infrequent, now and then, unreliable 12 intermittent

occasionally 6 rarely, seldom 7 at times 8 fitfully 9 sometimes 10 now and then 11 irregularly 12 infrequently, once in a while, periodically, sporadically 14 from time to time, intermittently 15 every now and then, once in a blue moon

occidental 7 Western 8 American, European 9 Hesperian, Westerner

occlude 4 clog, plug 5 block, choke, close 6 shut up, stop up 7 congest, shut off, stopper 8 choke off, obstruct 9 barricade, constrict 11 strangulate

occult 4 dark 5 magic 6 arcane, hidden, mystic, secret, veiled 7 obscure, private 8 esoteric, mystical, shrouded 9 concealed 10 cabalistic, mysterious, unrevealed 11 undisclosed 12 supernatural

occupancy 3 use 6 tenure 7 tenancy 8 lodgment 9 enjoyment, habitancy 10 engagement, habitation, occupation, possession 11 inhabitancy

occupant 5 owner 6 lessee, lodger, native, renter, roomer, tenant 7 dweller, settler 8 colonist, occupier, resident 9 addressee 10 inhabitant 11 householder

occupation 3 job 4 line, work 5 craft, forte, trade 6 career, living, metier, sphere 7 calling, control, pursuit, seizure 8 activity, business, capacity, conquest, lifework, vocation 9 specialty 10 employment, line of work, livelihood, possession, profession, subjection 11 foreign rule, subjugation 14 specialization 15 military control 18 military occupation

occupied 5 in use 6 amused, took up, used up 7 dwelt in, engaged, lived in, overran, overrun, taken up 8 absorbed, tenanted 9 concerned, conquered, inhabited, resided in 12 had control of, held in thrall 13 was situated in 16 took possession of

occupy 3 use 4 be in, be on, busy, fill, hold 5 amuse, sit in 6 absorb, employ, engage, fill up, room in, take up 7 concern, conquer, dwell in, engross, enslave, inhabit, lodge in, overrun, pervade, possess 8 permeate, reside in, saturate 9 entertain, subjugate 10 monopolize 11 have control 12 be situated in, hold in thrall 14 be the tenants of 16 take possession of

occur 3 hit 4 rise 5 arise, ensue 6 appear, befall, crop up, emerge, happen, result, strike, turn up 7 be found, come off, develop 8 spring up 9 come about, eventuate, take place, transpire 10 come to pass 11 materialize 13 cross one's mind, enter one's mind

occurrence 5 event 6 affair 7 episode, venture 8 business, incident, instance, occasion 9 adventure, emergence, happening, situation, unfolding 10 appearance, experience, proceeding 11 development, transaction 12 circumstance 13 manifestation 15 materialization

ocean 3 sea 4 deep, main, pond 5 flood, water 7 big pond, high sea 9 briny deep
   god of: 3 Nun 4 Nanu 7 Neptune, Oceanus 8 Poseidon

Oceania, Oceanica 9 Melanesia, Polynesia 10 Micronesia 11 Australia
   ocean: 12 South Pacific
   island: 4 Cook, Guam, Fiji, Maui, Niue, Wake 5 Aunuu, Bonin, Kauai, Lanai, Tonga 6 Bikini, Futuna, Hawaii, Marcus, Midway, Rurutu, Tahiti, Tubuai, Tuvalu, Wallis 7 Gambier, Gilbert, Iwo Jima, Leeward, Mariana, Molokai, Phoenix, Solomon, Tokelau, Tuamotu, Tutuila, Vanuatu, Volcano 8 Aitu taki, Bismarck, Bora-Bora, Johnston, Kiribati, Marshall, Pitcairn, Windward 9 Australia, Christmas, Marquesas, Trobriand 10 New Zealand 12 New Caledonia, Western Samoa 14 Papua New Guinea 15 French Polynesia

oceanic 6 marine 7 aquatic, pelagic 8 seagoing 9 thalassic

Oceanid
   form: 5 nymph
   location: 3 sea
   father: 7 Oceanus
   mother: 6 Tethys

Oceanus
   member of: 6 Titans
   father: 6 Uranus
   mother: 4 Gaea
   consort of: 6 Tethys
   father of: 8 Oceanids 9 river gods
   son: 7 Proteus
   daughter: 5 Doris, Persa 7 Philyra
   form: 6 stream

ocelot 3 cat 7 wildcat

Ochimus
   king of: 6 Rhodes
   father: 6 Helius
   wife: 9 Hegetoria
   daughter: 7 Cydippe

ochlophobia
   fear of: 6 crowds

Ockelman, Constance Frances Marie
   real name of: 12 Veronica Lake

Ocnus
   origin: 6 Tuscan
   father: 8 river god
   mother: 5 Manto
   founded: 6 Mantua
   personifies: 16 unavailing effort

O'Connor, Carroll
   born: 7 Bronx NY
   roles: 12 Archie Bunker, Archie's Place 14 All in the Family
   restaurant: 12 The Ginger Man

O'Connor, Donald
   born: 9 Chicago IL
   roles: 9 Beau Geste 15 Singin' in the Rain 18 Tom Sawyer Detective 21 Francis the Talking Mule

O'Connor, Flannery
  author of: 9 Wise Blood 15 The Habit of Being 17 Mystery and Manners 20 A Good Man Is Hard to Find, The Violent Bear It Away

Ocrisia
  position: 5 slave
  slave to: 7 Tarquin 8 Tanaquil
  son: 14 Servius Tullius

Octavia
  brother: 8 Augustus
  husband: 4 Nero 10 Mark Antony
  grandson: 8 Caligula

October
  flower: 6 cosmos 9 calendula
  French: 7 Octobre
  gem: 4 opal 10 tourmaline
  German: 7 Oktober
  holiday: 9 Halloween (31), Yom Kippur 11 Columbus Day (12) 12 Rosh Hashanah 16 United Nations Day (24)
  Italian: 7 Ottobre
  number of days: 12 thirty-one
  origin of name: 4 octo (Latin meaning eight)
  place in year:
  Gregorian: 5 tenth
  Roman: 6 eighth
  Spanish: 7 Octubre
  Zodiac sign: 5 Libra 7 Scorpio

October Light
  author: 11 John Gardner

Octopus, The
  author: 11 Frank Norris

odd 4 rare 5 extra, funny, queer, spare, weird 6 casual, far-out, quaint, single, sundry, unique 7 bizarre, curious, not even, strange, surplus, unusual, various 8 freakish, left over, peculiar, periodic, singular, sporadic, uncommon 9 irregular, remaining, spasmodic, unmatched 10 occasional, outlandish 13 miscellaneous 15 being one of a pair 16 out of the ordinary 17 not divisible by two

oddball 3 nut 4 kook 5 freak 6 weirdo 8 crackpot, original 9 character, eccentric, screwball 10 one-of-a-kind

Odd Couple, The
  character: 3 Roy 5 Myrna, Roger, Speed 6 Miriam, Murray, Vinnie 10 Felix Unger 11 Gloria Unger 12 Cecily Pigeon, Oscar Madison 14 Blanche Madison 15 Gwendolyn Pigeon, (Dr) Nancy Cunningham
  cast: 10 Al Molinaro, Archie Hahn 11 Brett Somers, Carol Shelly, Jack Klugman, Larry Gelman, Monica Evans, Tony Randall 12 Garry Walberg, Janice Hansen, Ryan McDonald 13 Elinor Donahue, Joan Hotchkiss, Penny Marshall
  setting: 11 New York City
  Felix's job: 12 photographer
  Oscar's job: 12 sportswriter
  based on play by: 9 Neil Simon

Odd Couple, The
  director: 8 Gene Saks
  based on play by: 9 Neil Simon
  cast: 10 Jack Lemmon (Felix Unger) 11 Herb Edelman, John Fiedler 13 Walter Matthau (Oscar Madison)

oddity 5 freak, sight 6 marvel, rarity, wonder 9 curiosity, queerness 10 phenomenon, uniqueness 11 abnormality, bizarreness, peculiarity, singularity, strangeness, unusualness 12 eccentricity, freakishness 13 individuality, unnaturalness 14 outlandishness
  Latin: 8 rara avis

oddly amusing 5 droll, kooky 9 laughable, whimsical 10 ridiculous

odd person 3 nut 4 kook 5 flake, freak 6 looney, weirdo 7 oddball 8 crackpot 9 character, eccentric, screwball

odds and ends 4 olio 6 scraps 8 remnants 9 leftovers 10 hodgepodge, miscellany 11 this and that 13 bits and pieces 18 miscellaneous items

ode 4 epic, hymn, poem 5 lyric, paean, psalm, verse 6 ballad 8 canticle
  type: 8 Horatian, Pindaric

Ode on a Grecian Urn
  author: 9 John Keats

Ode on Indolence
  author: 9 John Keats

Ode on Melancholy
  author: 9 John Keats

Ode to a Nightingale
  author: 9 John Keats

Ode to Autumn
  author: 9 John Keats

Ode to Duty
  author: 17 William Wordsworth

Ode to Psyche
  author: 9 John Keats

Ode to the West Wind
  author: 18 Percy Bysshe Shelley

Odets, Clifford
  author of: 9 Golden Boy 12 Awake and Sing 14 The Country Girl 15 Waiting for Lefty 17 The Flowering Peach

Odin
  also: 5 Othin
  brother: 2 Ve 4 Vili
  children: 4 Hodr, Thor 5 Baldr 6 Balder, Baldur
  corresponds to: 5 Wotan
  counterpart: 5 Wotan
  court: 8 Valhalla
  father: 3 Bor
  god of: 3 war 6 poetry, wisdom 9 knowledge
  grandson: 7 Volsung
  home: 9 Gladsheim
  horse: 8 Sleipnir
  magic ring: 8 Draupnir
  origin: 12 Scandinavian
  raven: 5 Hugin, Munin
  remaining eye: 3 sun
  ruler of: 5 Aexir
  spear: 7 Gungnir
  throne: 10 Hlidskjalf
  wife: 3 Fri 5 Frigg, Frija 6 Frigga
  wolf: 4 Geri 5 Freki

odious 4 evil, foul, vile **5** hated, nasty **6** rotten **7** hateful, heinous, hideous **8** infamous **9** invidious, loathsome, monstrous, obnoxious, offensive, repugnant, repulsive, revolting, sickening **10** abominable, despicable, detestable, disgusting, nauseating, unbearable **11** intolerable, unendurable **12** contemptible **13** objectionable

odium 5 shame **6** hatred, infamy **7** disgust **8** contempt, disfavor, disgrace, dishonor, ignominy **9** antipathy, discredit, disesteem, disrepute **10** abhorrence, disrespect, opprobrium, repugnance **11** detestation, disapproval **14** disapprobation

odonata
　class: **8** hexapoda
　phylum: **10** arthropoda
　group: **9** damselfly, dragonfly

odor 5 aura **5** aroma, scent, smell, stink **6** flavor, stench **7** bouquet, essence, perfume **9** effluvium, fragrance **10** atmosphere

odoriferous 4 rank **5** acrid, fetid **6** putrid, smelly **7** noisome, odorous, pungent, reeking, scented **8** aromatic, fragrant, perfumed, stinking **10** malodorous

odorous 4 rank **5** acrid, fetid **6** smelly **7** noisome, pungent, reeking, scented **8** aromatic, fragrant, perfumed, stinking

Odysseus
　also: **7** Ulysses
　king of: **6** Ithaca
　father: **7** Laertes
　mother: **8** Anticlea
　hero of: **5** Iliad **7** Odyssey
　wife: **8** Penelope **9** Callidice
　son: **9** Telegonus **10** Polypoetes, Telemachus **11** Polyporthis
　seduced by: **5** Circe
　killed by: **9** Telegonus
　epithet: **10** Laertiades

Odyssey
　author: **5** Homer
　character: **4** Zeus **5** Arete, Circe, Helen **6** Athene, Nestor, Scylla, Sirens **7** Calypso, Cyclops **8** Alcinous, Menelaus, Nausicaa, Odysseus, Penelope, Poseidon, Tiresias **9** Charybdis **10** Telemachus **11** Lotus-eaters

Oedipus
　king of: **6** Thebes
　father: **5** Laius
　mother: **7** Jocasta
　foster father: **7** Polybus
　foster mother: **6** Merope **8** Periboea
　wife: **7** Jocasta
　son: **8** Eteocles **9** Polynices
　daughter: **7** Ismene **8** Antigone
　killed: **5** Laius
　defeated: **6** Sphinx

Oedipus at Colonus
　author: **9** Sophocles
　character: **5** Creon **6** Elders, Ismene **7** Theseus **8** Antigone **9** Polynices

Oedipus Rex (Oedipus Tyrannus)
　author: **9** Sophocles
　character: **5** Creon, Laius **7** Jocasta **8** Tiresias

oeil-de-boeuf 16 small round window
　literally: **8** bull's eye

Oeneus
　king of: **7** Calydon
　wife: **7** Althaea
　son: **8** Meleager

Oenomaus
　king of: **4** Elis, Pisa
　father: **4** Ares
　mother: **7** Sterope
　daughter: **10** Hippodamia
　murdered: **6** Marmax

Oenone
　form: **5** nymph
　father: **6** Cebren
　husband: **5** Paris

Oenopion
　king of: **5** Chios
　father: **8** Dionysus
　mother: **7** Ariadne
　daughter: **6** Merope
　blinded: **5** Orion

Oersted, Hans Christian
　field: **7** physics
　nationality: **6** Danish
　founded: **16** electromagnetism
　isolated: **16** metallic aluminum
　named for him: **11** oersted unit

oeuvre 4 work **5** works **13** artist's output

O'Faolain, Sean
　author of: **15** The Heat of the Sun **17** A Nest of Simple Folk **22** Midsummer Night's Madness

of a piece 5 alike, equal **7** matched, the same **8** all in one **9** analogous, identical **10** equivalent, homogeneous, synonymous **13** evenly matched, one and the same

of bad character 5 shady **8** unsavory **11** of ill repute **12** disreputable, unprincipled

off 2 by **3** bad, far, ill, odd **4** afar, away, down, from, kill, poor, stop **5** amiss, apart, aside, crazy, wrong **6** absent, begone, lessen, remote **7** distant, further, in error, stopped, tainted **8** abnormal, canceled, inferior, mistaken **9** imperfect

offal 4 junk, slag **5** dregs, trash, waste **6** debris, refuse **7** carcass, carrion, garbage, grounds, remains, residue, rubbish **8** leavings

off base 5 amiss, wrong **8** improper, mistaken **10** out of order, unsuitable **13** inappropriate

offbeat 3 odd **7** strange **8** peculiar **9** different, eccentric **14** unconventional

off-center 6 askew **7** strange **9** eccentric **10** imbalanced, nonaligned, unbalanced **12** unreasonable **14** unconventional

off-color 4 blue, lewd, racy, sexy **5** bawdy, dirty, salty, spicy **6** earthy, risque, smutty, wicked **7** naughty, obscene, raunchy **8** improper, indecent, scabrous **9** offensive **10** indelicate, indiscreet, suggestive

off duty 8 inactive 9 at leisure 10 unoccupied 13 on one's own time

Offenbach, Jacques
born: 7 Cologne, Germany
composer of: 13 La Belle Helene 15 Tales of Hoffmann, La Vie Parisienne 22 Orpheus in the Underworld

offend 3 err, sin, vex 4 fret, gall, miff, rile 5 anger, annoy, chafe, lapse, pique, wound 6 insult, madden, nettle, rankle 7 affront, disgust, incense, inflame 8 irritate 9 aggravate, displease, misbehave 10 antagonize, disgruntle, exasperate, transgress 13 fall from grace

offender 5 crook, felon 6 sinner 7 culprit 8 criminal, violator 9 wrong doer 10 malefactor, trespasser

offense 3 sin 4 gibe, harm, slap, slip, snub, twit 5 abuse, crime, lapse, taunt 6 attack, charge, felony, insult 7 affront, assault, misdeed, outrage, umbrage 8 atrocity, enormity, evil deed, rudeness 9 impudence, indignity, insolence, offensive, violation 10 aggression, disrespect, infraction, peccadillo, wickedness 11 delinquency, humiliation, malfeasance, misdemeanor, shortcoming 13 embarrassment, transgression 15 breach of conduct

offensive 4 foul, rank, rude, ugly 5 nasty, onset 6 attack, horrid 7 abusive, assault, hideous, offense, uncivil 8 charging, impudent, insolent, storming 9 abhorrent, assailing, attacking, insulting, loathsome, obnoxious, onslaught, repugnant, repulsive, revolting, sickening, ungallant 10 abominable, aggression, aggressive, assaulting, bombarding, detestable, disgusting, nauseating, unmannerly, unpleasant 11 belligerent, distasteful, intolerable 12 disagreeable, embarrassing, insufferable 13 disrespectful, objectionable

offensiveness 8 rudeness 9 impudence, insolence, nastiness 10 disrespect, horridness, incivility 13 repulsiveness 14 unpleasantness 15 distastefulness

offer 3 bid 5 put up 6 bestow, extend, render, submit, tender 7 advance, hold out, present, proffer, propose, suggest 8 bestow on, offering, overture, proposal, propound, put forth 9 be willing, volunteer 10 invitation, put forward, submission, suggestion 11 make a motion, proposition 12 bring forward 14 put on the market 19 place at one's disposal

offer hospitality 4 host 7 welcome 8 play host to 9 entertain 10 give a party, have guests 13 keep open house

offering 3 bid 4 alms, gift 5 goods, wares 6 course 7 charity, present, tribute 8 anathema, bestowal, donation, oblation 9 sacrifice 11 beneficence 12 contribution
to God: 6 corban 7 deodate
to household deities: 4 bali

offertory 4 gift 8 oblation, offering 10 collection

offhand, offhanded 5 ad-lib, hasty 6 casual, chance, random 7 relaxed 8 careless, cavalier, heedless 9 facetious, haphazard, impromptu, unplanned, unstudied 10 improvised, nonchalant, off-the-cuff, unprepared 11 spontaneous, thoughtless, unconcerned, unrehearsed 12 off-the-record 14 extemporaneous, unpremeditated

office 3 job 4 post, role 8 capacity, function, position 10 commission, occupation 11 appointment

officer 3 cop 4 head 7 manager 8 director, gendarme, governor 9 constable, detective, executive, patrolman, policeman, president, secretary, treasurer 10 bureaucrat 12 commissioner 13 administrator, vice-president

officers 8 managers 10 executives, management 14 administration

Officers and Gentlemen
author: 11 Evelyn Waugh

offices 4 duty, help, task 5 favor, trust 6 charge 7 service 8 function, province 10 assistance

office seeker 7 hopeful, nominee 8 aspirant 9 candidate

office worker 5 clerk, steno 6 typist 9 file clerk, secretary 10 bookkeeper, keypuncher 13 data processor 14 clerical worker

official 5 agent 6 formal, vested 7 manager, officer 8 approved, chairman, director, licensed 9 authentic, certified, dignitary, executive, warranted 10 accredited, authorized, sanctioned, supervisor 11 functionary 13 administrator, authoritative 14 administrative 18 administrative head

official communication 5 edict, order, ukase 6 report 7 release 8 bulletin 10 communique 12 proclamation

officialdom 10 government 11 authorities, bureaucracy 14 administration

official paper 4 writ 5 order 8 document 10 instrument

officiate 3 run 4 head, lead 5 chair, emcee 6 direct, handle, manage 7 oversee, preside 8 moderate, regulate 9 supervise 10 administer 11 superintend 12 be in charge of

officious 6 prying 7 pompous 8 meddling 9 intrusive, kibitzing, obtrusive 10 highhanded, meddlesome 11 domineering, interfering, overbearing, patronizing 13 high and mighty, self-assertive, self-important 16 poking one's nose in

Offield, Lewis Delaney
real name of: 9 Jack Oakie

offset 6 redeem 7 balance, nullify 8 equalize, knock out 9 cancel out, make up for 10 counteract, neutralize 11 countervail 13 compensate for, counterweight 14 counterbalance

offshoot 4 limb 5 scion, shoot 6 branch 7 adjunct 9 aftermath, by-product, outgrowth 10 descendant

offspring 3 fry 4 heir, seed 5 brood, child, issue, scion, spawn, young 6 family, litter 7 progeny 8 children, increase 9 posterity 10 descendant, succession 11 descendants

off the mark 5 amiss 6 afield, astray 9 off target 16 off the right track

off-the-record 5 privy 6 secret 7 private 11 undisclosed 12 confidential 16 not to be disclosed 17 not for publication

off the top of one's head 5 ad-lib 7 offhand 9 extempore, impromptu 10 improvised, unprepared 11 extemporary, unrehearsed 14 extemporaneous, unpremeditated

of good quality 4 good 6 worthy 8 superior 9 excellent 10 creditable

of high rank 5 noble, regal, royal 6 lordly, titled 7 courtly 11 blue-blooded 12 aristocratic

Of Human Bondage
  author: 16 W Somerset Maugham
  director: 12 John Cromwell
  character: 5 Weeks 7 Hayward 11 Louisa Carey, Philip Carey 12 Sally Athelny, William Carey 13 Mildred Rogers, Miss Wilkinson, Thorpe Athelny
  cast: 10 Bette Davis, Frances Dee, Kay Johnson 12 Leslie Howard

of its own kind
  Latin: 10 sui generis

Of Mice and Men
  author: 13 John Steinbeck
  director: 14 Lewis Milestone
  character: 4 Slim 5 Candy 6 Crooks, Curley 11 Lennie Small 12 George Milton
  cast: 10 Betty Field 11 Lon Chaney Jr (Lenny) 15 Burgess Meredith, Charles Bickford
  score: 12 Aaron Copland

of one's own right
  Latin: 8 sui juris

of poor quality 5 junky 6 flimsy, shoddy, sleazy, trashy 8 inferior 11 substandard

of secondary importance 8 nonvital 9 accessory, extrinsic 10 incidental 11 dispensable, unnecessary 12 nonessential

often 3 oft 4 much 7 usually 8 commonly, ofttimes 9 generally, regularly 10 constantly, frequently, habitually, oftentimes, repeatedly 11 continually, customarily, over and over, recurrently 12 periodically, time and again

of the dead say nothing but good
  Latin: 21 de mortuis nil nisi bonum

of the faith
  Latin: 6 de fide

of their own kind
  Latin: 10 sui generis

of the old school 5 passe 8 outdated, outmoded 9 out-of-date 12 conservative, old-fashioned 18 establish-mentarian

Of Time and the River
  author: 11 Thomas Wolfe
  character: 10 Eugene Gant

oft-repeated 5 trite 7 popular 8 constant, familiar, frequent, habitual, well-worn 9 continual, recurring, well-known 10 persistent 11 widely known

of what good
  Latin: 7 cui bono

Ogdoad
  also: 3 Heh
  origin: 8 Egyptian
  number of gods: 5 eight

ogle 3 eye 6 gape at, gawk at, goggle, leer at 7 stare at 8 goggle at 10 give the eye, scrutinize 15 give the once-over, stare at greedily 16 cast sheep's eyes at, gaze at with desire

Ogma
  origin: 5 Irish
  god of: 6 poetry 9 eloquence
  inventor of: 12 Ogham letters

Ogmios
  origin: 6 Gaelic
  god of: 9 eloquence
  corresponds to: 7 Mercury

ogre, ogress 5 brute, demon, fiend, ghoul, harpy 6 despot, tyrant 7 bugbear, monster 8 bogeyman, dictator, martinet 11 slave driver

Ogygia
  island of: 7 Calypso

Ogygus
  king of: 7 Boeotia
  father: 8 Poseidon

O'Hara, John
  author of: 7 Pal Joey 11 A Rage to Live 13 The Instrument 14 From the Terrace, The Hat on the Bed 16 Butterfield Eight 17 Ten North Frederick 19 The Horse Knows the Way 20 Appointment in Samarra

O'Hara, Maureen
  real name: 18 Maureen Fitzsimmons
  nickname: 18 Queen of Technicolor
  born: 7 Ireland 8 Milltown
  roles: 10 Lady Godiva 11 The Quiet Man 13 North to Alaska, The Parent Trap 16 The Foxes of Harrow 19 How Green Was My Valley 20 Hunchback of Notre Dame 27 Miracle on Thirty-fourth Street

O'Hara, Scarlett
  character in: 15 Gone With the Wind
  family: 6 Gerald 7 Carreen, Suellen
  author: 8 Mitchell

O Henry
  real name: 19 William Sidney Porter
  author of: 11 The Last Leaf 16 Cabbages and Kings, The Gift of the Magi 18 The Cop and the Anthem 19 The Ransom of Red Chief

Ohio
  abbreviation: 2 OH
  nickname: 7 Buckeye
  capital: 8 Columbus
  largest city: 9 Cleveland
  others: 3 Ada 4 Kent, Lima 5 Akron, Berea, Cadiz, Niles, Parma, Piqua, Xenia 6 Athens, Canton, Dayton, Elyria, Lorain, Marion, Newark, Tiffin, Toledo, Warren 7

Ashland, Findlay, Fremont, Norwood, Wooster 8 Alliance, Bluffton, Fostoria, Lakewood, Marietta, Sandusky 9 Ashtabula, Kettering, Lancaster, Massillon, Struthers, Vermilion, Willowick 10 Cincinnati, Huntington, Portsmouth, Rocky River, Willoughby, Youngstown, Zanesville 11 Painesville, Springfield 12 Steubenville

college: 4 Kent 5 Akron, Hiram, Miami 6 Dayton, Kenyon, Xavier 7 Antioch, Oberlin, Wooster 8 Defiance, Dennison, Marietta, Ursuline 10 Wittenberg 11 Case Western 12 Bowling Green, Ohio Wesleyan

feature:
hall of fame: 11 Pro Football
race: 12 Soap Box Derby
tribe: 4 Erie 7 Wyandot 13 Mound Builders
people: 7 buckeye, Cy Young 8 Zane Grey 10 Clark Gable, T Hart Crane 11 Annie Oakley, Lillian Gish 12 James Thurber, Lowell Thomas, Norman Thomas 13 Neil Armstrong, Orville Wright, Thomas A Edison 14 Barney Oldfield, Clarence Darrow 15 William T Sherman 16 Sherwood Anderson 18 Norman Vincent Peale
explorer: 7 La Salle
lake: 4 Erie 5 Grand 6 Berlin, Dillon, Hoover, Indian 8 Delaware 13 Mosquito Creek
land rank: 35 thirty-fifth
mountain:
highest point: 12 Campbell Hill
physical feature:
caverns: 4 Ohio, Zane 6 Seneca
spring: 8 Blue Hole
president: 13 Ulysses S Grant 14 James A Garfield, Warren G Harding 15 William McKinley 16 Rutherford B Hayes 17 William Howard Taft 20 William Henry Harrison
river: 5 Grand, Miami 6 Maumee, Scioto, Wabash 7 Hocking 8 Cuyahoga, Sandusky 9 Muskingum, Tennessee 10 Cumberland 11 Monongahela
state admission: 11 seventeenth
state bird: 8 cardinal
state flower: 10 scarlet carnation
state motto: 27 With God All Things Are Possible
state song: 13 Beautiful Ohio
state tree: 7 buckeye

Ohm, Georg Simon
field: 7 physics
nationality: 6 German
discovered: 20 electrical resistance
named for him: 7 ohm unit

oil 4 balm, lard 5 cream, salve 6 anoint, grease, pomade 7 unguent 8 liniment, ointment 9 lubricant, lubricate, melted fat, petroleum 12 melted grease
type: 4 corn, fuel, hair 5 crude, motor, olive, whale 7 cooking, mineral 9 safflower, vegetable

Oilean Ajax *see* 4 Ajax
Oileus
  king of: 6 Locris
  member of: 9 Argonauts
  father: 10 Hodoedocus
  mother: 9 Agrianome
  son: 5 Medon 13 Ajax the Lesser
oily 5 fatty, lardy, slick 6 greasy, smarmy 7 buttery, fawning, servile 8 slippery, slithery, toadying, unctuous 9 groveling, sebaceous 10 lubricous, oleaginous 11 bootlicking, subservient 12 ingratiating
ointment 4 balm 5 salve 6 lotion, pomade 7 pomatum, unguent 8 liniment 9 emollient, spikenard
Oizys
  mother: 3 Nyx
  personifies: 4 pain
Ojibwa, Ojibway *see* 8 Chippawa
OK 4 fine, good 7 approve, endorse 8 all right, approval 9 authorize 11 endorsement 13 authorization
  French: 7 d'accord
O'Keeffe, Georgia
  born: 12 Sun Prairie WI
  artwork: 7 Stables 9 Black Iris 14 Patio with Cloud 15 Lake George Barns 22 Light Coming on the Plains 26 Black Flower and Blue Larkspur
Oklahoma
  abbreviation: 2 OK 4 Okla
  nickname: 6 Boomer, Sooner
  capital/largest city: 12 Oklahoma City
  others: 3 Ada 4 Alva, Enid, Hugo 5 Altus, Miami, Ponca, Tulsa 6 Duncan, El Reno, Guymon, Idabel, Lawton 7 Ardmore, Guthrie, Sapulpa, Shawnee 8 Anadarko, Fort Sill, Muskogee 9 Blackwell, Claremore, McAlester 10 Stillwater 12 Bartlesville
  college: 5 Tulsa 6 Norman 7 Cameron 8 Langston, Phillips 10 Stillwater 11 Oral Roberts 12 Oklahoma City 15 Bethany Nazarene 17 American Christian
  feature:
  hall of fame: 14 American Indian
  national park: 6 Platte
  tribe: 3 Kaw, Oto 4 Iowa, Loup, Otoe, Waco 5 Caddo, Kansa, Osage, Ponca 6 Apache, Ottawa, Pawnee, Quapaw 7 Shawnee, Wichita 8 Arapahoe, Tawakoni
  Five Civilized Tribes: 5 Creek 7 Choctaw 8 Cherokee, Seminole 9 Chickasaw
  people: 4 Okie 6 Sooner 9 Jim Thorpe 10 Will Rogers 12 Mickey Mantle 14 Maria Tallchief
  explorer: 8 Coronado
  lake: 5 Atoka, Grand, Hulah 6 Texoma, Wister 7 Eufaula, Heyburn, Oologah 8 Keystone 9 Pensacola, Tenkiller 10 Fort Gibson 11 Thunderbird 12 Markham Ferry 17 Lake O' The Cherokees
  land rank: 10 eighteenth
  mountain: 6 Ozarks 8 Ouachita
  highest point: 9 Black Mesa
  physical feature: 9 Panhandle
  plains: 5 Great

river: 3 Red 5 Grand 6 Little, Neosho 7 Washita 8 Arkan sas, Canadian, Cimarron 9 Verdigris 15 Muddy Boggy Creek

state admission: 10 forty-sixth

state bird: 23 scissor-tailed flycatcher

state fish: 9 white bass

state flower: 9 mistletoe

state motto: 22 Labor Conquers All Things

state song: 8 Oklahoma

state tree: 6 redbud

Oklahoma!

director: 13 Fred Zinnemann

cast: 10 Rod Steiger 11 Eddie Albert 12 Gordon MacRae, Shirley Jones 13 Gloria Grahame, James Whitmore 18 Charlotte Greenwood

score: 21 Rodgers and Hammerstein

song: 23 People Will Say We're in Love 24 Surrey with the Fringe on Top

Olbers, Heinrich Wilhelm Matthaus

field: 9 astronomy

nationality: 6 German

discovered: 5 Vesta 6 comets, Pellas 9 asteroids

old 3 aged, used 5 hoary, of age 6 beat-up, bygone, of yore 7 ancient, antique, archaic, elderly, outworn, rundown, vintage, wornout 8 battered, decrepit, familiar, grizzled, much-used, obsolete, outdated, timeworn 9 crumbling, hackneyed, out-of-date, venerable, weathered 10 antiquated, broken-down, gray-headed, ramshackle, tumbledown 11 dilapidated, from the past, gray with age, obsolescent, timehonored, traditional 12 deteriorated, oldfashioned, white with age 13 weatherbeaten 14 of long standing 15 long established

Old Aches and Pains

nickname of: 11 Luke Appling

old age 6 dotage 7 ripe age 8 maturity, senility 11 advanced age 15 second childhood

Old and the Young, The

author: 15 Luigi Pirandello

Old Bay State

nickname of: 13 Massachusetts

Old Bulgarian

also: 15 Old Church Slavic

language family: 12 Indo-European

group: 11 Balto-Slavic

status: 7 archaic

used in: 14 Orthodox church

Old Chinook

nickname of: 10 Washington

Old Colony State

nickname of: 13 Massachusetts

Old Curiosity Shop, The

author: 14 Charles Dickens

character: 5 Quilp 9 Fred Trent, Mrs Jarley 10 Kit Nubbles, Sally Brass 11 Grandfather 12 Sampson Brass 13 Dick Swiveller 15 Little Nell Trent 18 The Single Gentleman

Old Dominion

nickname of: 8 Virginia

olden 4 past 6 bygone, former, of yore 7 ancient, long-ago 8 departed

Oldest Man 10 Methuselah

old-fashioned 5 corny, dated, passe 7 antique, archaic 8 obsolete, outdated, outmoded 9 out-of-date 10 antiquated, out of style 11 obsolescent, traditional 12 longstanding, out of fashion 13 unfashionable 14 behind the times

Old-Fashioned Girl, An

author: 15 Louisa May Alcott

Old Franklin State

nickname of: 9 Tennessee

old hand 3 pro 6 expert, master 8 virtuoso 9 authority 12 professional

old hat 5 passe, stale 6 demode 7 archaic, outworn 8 obsolete, outdated, outmoded 9 out-of-date 10 antiquated, superseded 11 obsolescent 12 old-fashioned 13 unfashionable 14 behind the times

old-line 11 established, traditional 12 conservative

Old Line State

nickname of: 8 Maryland

Old Love

author: 19 Isaac Bashevis Singer

Old Maid, The

author: 12 Edith Wharton

Old Man and the Sea, The

author: 15 Ernest Hemingway

character: 7 Manolin 8 Santiago

Old Mortality

author: 14 Sir Walter Scott

character: 5 Edith 11 Henry Morton 12 Basil Olifant, Lord Evandale 19 John Balfour of Burley 21 Lady Margaret Bellenden 27 Colonel Grahame of Claverhouse

Old Mortality

author: 19 Katherine Anne Porter

Old North

nickname of: 13 North Carolina

Old Patagonian Express, The

author: 11 Paul Theroux

old saw 5 adage, maxim 6 cliche, saying, truism 7 bromide, proverb 9 old saying 10 expression 11 old chestnut

oldster 5 elder 6 codger, old man 7 ancient 8 old woman 13 senior citizen

Old Testament

first five books: 10 Pentateuch

first six books: 9 Hexateuch

first seven books: 10 Heptateuch

books of: 3 Job 4 Amos, Ezra, Joel, Ruth 5 Hosea, Jonah, Kings, Micah, Nahum, Songs, Tobit 6 Baruch, Daniel, Esther, Exodus, Haggai, Isaiah, Joshua, Judges, Judith, Psalms, Samuel, Sirach, Wisdom 7 Ezekiel, Genesis, Malachi, Numbers, Obadiah 8 Habakkuk, Jeremiah, Macabees, Nehemiah, Proverbs 9 Leviticus, Zechariah, Zephaniah 10 Chronicles 11 Deuteronomy 12 Ecclesiastes 13 Song of Solomon 14 Ecclesiasticus

Oldtown Folks

author: 19 Harriet Beecher Stowe

Old Wives' Tale, The
  author: 13 Arnold Bennett
old-world 6 formal 7 courtly, gallant, old-line 8 European, orthodox 10 ceremonial, chivalrous, prescribed 11 ceremonious, continental, established, traditional 12 conservative, conventional, old-fashioned
Ole
  character in: 16 Giants of the Earth
  author: 7 Rolvaag
Olen
  occupation: 4 poet
  location: 5 Lycia
Olenska, Ellen
  character in: 17 The Age of Innocence
  author: 7 Wharton
oleoresin 3 gum 5 anime, apiol, elemi 6 balsam 7 solvent 10 turpentine
olio 4 stew 6 jumble, medley 7 melange, mixture 8 mishmash 9 potpourri 10 assortment, collection, hodgepodge, hotchpotch, miscellany
olive 12 Olea europaea
  varieties: 3 tea 4 wild 5 black, false, holly, sweet 6 common, desert, spurge 7 Russian 8 American, fragrant 11 Californian
olive-drab 5 khaki 13 greenish-brown
Oliver
  character in: 11 As You Like It
  author: 11 Shakespeare
Oliver!
  director: 9 Carol Reed
  based on story by: 14 Charles Dickens (Oliver Twist)
  cast: 8 Jack Wild, Ron Moody (Fagin) 10 Mark Lester (Oliver), Oliver Reed 11 Shani Wallis
  Oscar for: 7 picture 8 director
  remake of: 11 Oliver Twist
  song: 16 Consider Yourself, Food Glorious Food 17 As Long As He Needs Me
Oliver Twist
  author: 14 Charles Dickens
  character: 5 Fagin, Monks (Edward Leeford), Nancy 6 Bumble 9 Bill Sikes, Mrs Maylie 10 Mr Brownlow, Rose Maylie
  director: 9 David Lean
  cast: 8 Kay Walsh 12 Alec Guinness (Fagin), Robert Newton 13 Anthony Newley (Artful Dodger) 16 Francis L Sullivan, John Howard Davies
  remade as: 7 Oliver!
Olivia
  character in: 12 Twelfth Night
  author: 11 Shakespeare
Olivier, Sir Laurence
  born: 7 Dorking, England
  wife: 11 Vivien Leigh 13 Joan Plowright
  roles: 6 Becket, Hamlet (Oscar), Henry V, Sleuth 7 Rebecca 11 Marathon Man 16 Wuthering Heights 17 Pride and Prejudice, The Boys from Brazil, The Devil's Disciple 19 Shoes of the Fisherman 23 The Prince and the Showgirl
olivine
  variety: 7 peridot

olla 3 jar, pot 10 earthen pot
Olmsted, Frederick Law
  landscape architect of: 11 Central Park (NYC, with Calvert Vaux) 12 Prospect Park (Brooklyn NY) 13 Fairmount Park (Philadelphia) 14 Biltmore Estate (Asheville NC), Mount Royal Park (Montreal)
Olsen, Merlin (Jay)
  sport: 8 football
  team: 14 Los Angeles Rams
  TV roles: 12 Father Murphy 15 Highway to Heaven 23 Little House on the Prairie
Olsson, Ann-Margret
  real name of: 10 Ann-Margret
O Lucky Man
  director: 15 Lindsay Anderson
  cast: 9 Alan Price 13 Rachel Roberts 15 Malcolm McDowell, Ralph Richardson
  score: 9 Alan Price
Olwen
  origin: 5 Welsh
  form: 8 princess
  father: 16 Yspadaden Penkawr
Olympic Games
  site:
    1896: 6 Athens
    1900: 5 Paris
    1904: 7 St Louis
    1906: 6 Athens
    1908: 6 London
    1912: 9 Stockholm
    1920: 7 Antwerp
    1924: 5 Paris 8 Chamonix
    1928: 8 St Moritz 9 Amsterdam
    1932: 10 Lake Placid, Los Angeles
    1936: 6 Berlin 21 Garmisch-Partenkirchen
    1948: 6 London 8 St Moritz
    1952: 4 Oslo 8 Helsinki
    1956: 9 Melbourne 15 Cortina d'Ampezzo
    1960: 5 Tokyo 15 Squaw Valley
    1968: 8 Grenoble 10 Mexico City
    1972: 6 Munich 7 Sapporo
    1976: 8 Montreal 9 Innsbruck
    1980: 6 Moscow 10 Lake Placid
    1984: 8 Sarajevo 10 Los Angeles
    1988: 6 Seoul 7 Calgary
    1992: 9 Barcelona 11 Albertville
    1994: 11 Lillehammer
    1996: 7 Atlanta
Omaha
  language family: 6 Siouan 7 Dhegiha
  location: 4 Iowa 8 Nebraska, Oklahoma
Oman
  other name: 13 Muscat and Oman
  capital: 6 Masqat, Muscat
  largest city: 5 Matra 6 Matrah
  others: 3 Sur 4 Fida 5 Dubai, Nazwa, Nigwa, Sohar, Wazit 6 Khasab, Marbat, Murbat, Suwaih, Tinouf 7 Khabura, Salalah 8 Ashkhara
  government: 9 Sultanate
  head of state/government: 6 sultan
  monetary unit: 3 gaj, gaz 4 rial 5 baiza, ghazi 7 mahmudi

island: 6 Masera, Masira 7 Masirah 10 Kuria Muria
mountain: 4 Qara 5 Hafit, Harim, Nakhl, Tayin 8 el-Akhdar 11 Jabal Akhdar 13 Green Mountain
highest point: 6 al-Sham
sea: 6 Indian 7 Arabian
physical feature:
cape: 7 Madraka 9 Ras Al Hadd 13 Ras Dharbat 'Ali
gulf: 4 Oman
peninsula: 7 Arabian 8 Musandam
plain: 6 Dhofar 7 Batinah
strait: 6 Hormuz
people: 4 Arab
ruler: 12 Qabus Bin Said 13 Said Bin Taimur
language: 4 Urdu 5 Hindi 6 Arabic 7 Baluchi
religion: 5 Islam
war: 4 Gulf 14 Desert Storm
omega 3 end 4 last 5 final 6 ending 8 terminus
opposite: 5 alpha
omen 4 sign 5 token 6 augury, herald 7 auspice, portent, presage, warning 9 foretaste, harbinger, precursor 10 foreboding, indication
Omet 15 Biblical measure
ominous 7 unlucky 8 menacing, minatory, monitory, sinister 9 dismaying, ill-omened 10 foreboding, ill-starred, portentous
omission 3 gap 4 hole 7 neglect 9 exception, exclusion, oversight 10 leaving out, negligence 11 delinquency, elimination 12 noninclusion 13 neglected item 16 something omitted
omit 3 cut 4 drop, fail, jump, miss, shun, skip 5 avoid, elide 6 bypass, delete, except, forget, ignore, slight 7 excerpt, exclude, let slip, neglect 8 leave out, overlook, pass over, preclude, set aside 11 forget about
omnia vincit amor 15 love conquers all
Omnibus
host: 13 Alistair Cooke
omnipotent 6 mighty 7 supreme 8 almighty, powerful, puissant 11 all-powerful
omniscient 7 all-wise, supreme 8 infinite 9 all-seeing 10 all-knowing, preeminent
omnium gatherum 23 miscellaneous collection
omnivorous 7 hoggish 8 edacious, ravenous 9 crapulous, rapacious, voracious 10 gluttonous, polyphagic, predacious 12 pantophagous
Omoo
author: 14 Herman Melville
character: 10 Captain Bob 15 Doctor Long Ghost
Omphale
queen of: 5 Lydia
father: 8 Iardanus
husband: 5 Tmolus
son: 5 Lamus
served by: 8 Hercules

Omri
father: 6 Becher 7 Michael
son: 4 Ahab
daughter-in-law: 7 Jezebel
on 2 at 4 atop, near, over, upon 5 about, above, ahead, along, anent 7 against, forward, planned 8 abutting, adjacent, attached, intended, touching 9 occurring 10 concerning, juxtaposed
On
father: 6 Peleth
city of: 10 Heliopolis
on-and-off 6 spotty 8 episodic 9 irregular, spasmodic, temporary 10 now-and-then, occasional
On Beginning and Perishing
author: 9 Aristotle
once 7 ages ago, long ago, one time 8 formerly, hitherto, years ago 9 at one time 10 heretofore, previously 11 a single time, for the nonce, in times past, some time ago 12 in the old days, some time back 13 once upon a time, on one occasion
once-in-a-lifetime 6 unique 7 special 8 singular 11 one-time-only
once more 4 anew 5 again 9 once again, over again 11 one more time
on cloud nine 6 elated, joyful, joyous 8 ecstatic, euphoric 9 exuberant, rapturous 15 in seventh heaven
oncoming 5 close 7 looming, nearing 8 imminent 9 advancing, impending, onrushing 11 approaching, bearing down
on course 8 on target 15 on the right track
Ondine
author: 13 Jean Giraudoux
one 2 an 3 you 4 a man, lone, only, sole 5 a body, a soul, whole 6 a thing, entire, single, unique 7 a person, someone 8 complete, singular, solitary, somebody 10 individual, unrepeated
One, Two, Three
director: 11 Billy Wilder
cast: 11 James Cagney 12 Pamela Tiffin 13 Arlene Francis, Horst Buchholz
setting: 10 West Berlin
score: 11 Andre Previn
O'Neal, Ryan
real name: 16 Patrick Ryan O'Neal
born: 12 Los Angeles CA
daughter: 10 Tatum O'Neal
roles: 9 Love Story, Paper Moon 10 What's Up Doc 11 Barry Lyndon, Peyton Place 16 Rodney Harrington
O'Neal, Tatum
born: 12 Los Angeles CA
father: 9 Ryan O'Neal
roles: 9 Paper Moon 12 Bad News Bears 14 Little Darlings 19 International Velvet
husband: 11 John McEnroe
one and the same 5 equal 7 matched 9 identical
one by one 6 singly 10 one at a time, separately, single file 12 individually

One Day at a Time
character: 9 Ann Romano 11 Julie Cooper 13 Barbara Cooper 15 Dwayne Schneider
cast: 14 Bonnie Franklin 15 Pat Harrington Jr 17 Mackenzie Phillips, Valerie Bertinelli

One Day in the Life of Ivan Denisovich
author: 23 Aleksandr Solzhenitsyn Jr

One Fat Englishman
author: 12 Kingsley Amis

One Flew Over the Cuckoo's Nest
director: 11 Milos Forman
based on story by: 8 Ken Kesey
cast: 13 Jack Nicholson 14 Louise Fletcher, Michael Beryman 15 William Redfield
Oscar for: 5 actor (Nicholson) 7 actress (Fletcher), picture 8 director 10 screenplay

One Hour with You
director: 11 George Cukor 13 Ernst Lubitsch
cast: 14 Genevieve Tobin 16 Maurice Chevalier 17 Jeanette MacDonald
remake of: 17 The Marriage Circle
song: 14 What Would You Do

one-hundred percent 5 sheer, total, utter, whole 7 supreme 8 absolute, complete 10 consummate 17 through-and-through

O'Neill, Eugene
author of: 8 The Straw 11 The Hairy Ape 12 Ah Wilderness, Anna Christie 13 Marco Millions 14 Glencairn Cycle 15 The Emperor Jones, The Iceman Cometh 16 Beyond the Horizon, Strange Interlude, The Great God Brown 18 Desire Under the Elms 20 The Moon of the Caribees 22 A Moon for the Misbegotten, All God's Chillun Got Wings, Mourning Becomes Electra 24 Long Day's Journey into Night

Oneiros
also: 6 Oniros
origin: 5 Greek
god of: 6 dreams

oneness 5 union, unity 7 concord, harmony 8 entirety, identity, sameness, totality 9 agreement, aloneness, integrity, wholeness 10 uniformity, uniqueness 11 singularity 12 completeness 13 individuality

one-of-a-kind 4 rare 6 unique 7 strange, unusual 8 original 9 eccentric

onerous 5 heavy 6 taxing 7 arduous, painful, weighty 8 crushing, grievous 9 demanding, wearisome 10 burdensome, exhausting, oppressive 11 distressing 12 hard to endure

one thing in return for another
Latin: 10 quid pro quo

one-time 3 old 4 past 5 early, prior 6 former, recent 7 earlier, quondam 8 previous 9 erstwhile
French: 8 ci-devant

one voice 4 solo 6 unison 7 concert

one who has a fixed income
French: 7 rentier

On First Looking Into Chapman's Homer
author: 9 John Keats

on foot
French: 5 a pied

ongoing 7 endless, lasting 8 enduring, unbroken, unending 10 continuing, proceeding 11 never-ending, unremitting 13 uninterrupted

On Golden Pond
director: 10 Mark Rydell
based on play by: 14 Ernest Thompson
cast: 9 Jane Fonda 10 Doug McKeon, Henry Fonda (Norman Thayer Jr) 16 Katharine Hepburn
setting: 5 Maine
Oscar for: 5 actor (Fonda) 7 actress (Hepburn)

on guard 4 wary 5 alert 7 careful, heedful 8 cautious, vigilant, watchful

on hand 5 handy, on tap 6 at hand 9 available 10 accessible, convenient 14 at one's disposal

on horseback
French: 7 a cheval

onion 6 Allium 10 Allium cepa
varieties: 3 red, sea, top 4 leek, tree, wild 5 green, gypsy, pearl, swamp, Welsh, white 6 German, potato, yellow 7 Bermuda, Danvers, nodding, prairie, shallot, Spanish 8 climbing, Egyptian, false sea, scallion, Valencia 9 Catawissa, ever-ready, flowering, two-bladed 10 multiplier, red-skinned 16 Japanese bunching
origin: 9 Asia Minor
called by Robert Louis Stevenson: 14 rose among roots

Onion Field, The
author: 14 Joseph Wambaugh

Oniros see 7 Oneiros

On Liberty
author: 14 John Stuart Mill

onlooker 5 gazer, ogler 6 viewer 7 watcher, witness 8 beholder, kibitzer, observer 9 bystander, spectator 10 eyewitness, rubberneck

only 4 just, lone, sole 5 alone 6 barely, merely, purely, simply, single, singly, solely, unique 7 at least 8 by itself, singular, solitary 9 by oneself, exclusive, unmatched 10 individual, no more than, nothing but, one and only, unrepeated 11 exclusively 12 individually, unparalleled

on one's uppers 5 broke 9 destitute 10 down and out

On Plants
author: 9 Aristotle

On Revolution
author: 12 Hannah Arendt

onrush 4 flow, flux, gush, tide, wave 5 flood, onset, storm, surge 6 attack, charge, deluge, spring, stream 7 assault, cascade, current, torrent 9 avalanche

onset 4 push, raid 5 birth, sally, start 6 attack, charge, onrush, outset, thrust 7 assault, genesis, infancy, offense 8 founding, invasion, outbreak, storming 9 beginning, inception, incursion, offensive, onslaught

10 incipience, initiation **12** commencement, inauguration

onslaught 4 coup, push, raid **5** blitz, foray, onset, sally **6** attack, charge, putsch, thrust **7** assault, offense **8** invasion **9** incursion, offensive **10** aggression, blitzkrieg

on tap 5 handy **6** at hand, on hand **9** available **10** accessible, convenient

Ontario
  bay: 6 Hudson
  canal: 5 Trent **6** Rideau
  capital: 7 Toronto
  city: 3 Emo **4** Galt **6** London, Ottawa **7** Windsor **8** Hamilton, Kingston **9** Kitchener
  explored by: 5 French **6** British
  industry: 6 mining **11** agriculture **13** manufacturing
  lake: 6 Simcoe
  province of: 6 Canada
  river: 6 Ottawa, Thames **7** Niagara **10** St Lawrence
  settled by: 9 Loyalists
  university: 4 York **5** Brock, Trent **8** McMaster

on the alert 4 wary **7** careful, mindful, on guard **8** cautious, watchful **9** wide awake **12** on the lookout

On the Beach
  author: 10 Nevil Shute
  director: 13 Stanley Kramer
  cast: 10 Ava Gardner **11** Fred Astaire, Gregory Peck **13** Donna Anderson **14** Anthony Perkins

on the contrary
  French: 11 au contraire

on the dot 7 exactly **8** promptly **9** on the nose, precisely **10** punctually

on the face
  Latin: 7 ex facie

on the go 4 busy **6** active, mobile **8** in motion **9** energetic, on the move **13** indefatigable

On the Heavens
  author: 9 Aristotle

On the Morning of Christ's Nativity
  author: 10 John Milton

on the move 5 astir **6** active, mobile **7** on the go **8** in motion

on the nose 5 exact **7** exactly, precise **8** accurate, on target **9** precisely **10** accurately, on the money

on the outer edges
  Latin: 10 in extremis

on the right track 8 on course, on target

On the Soul
  author: 9 Aristotle

On the Town
  director: 9 Gene Kelly **12** Stanley Donen
  cast: 9 Ann Miller, Gene Kelly, Vera-Ellen **12** Betty Garrett, Frank Sinatra
  setting: 11 New York City
  score: 11 Adolph Green, Betty Comden **16** Leonard Bernstein
  song: 14 New York New York

On the Waterfront
  director: 9 Elia Kazan
  cast: 8 Lee J Cobb **10** Karl Malden, Pat Henning, Rod Steiger **12** Lelf Erickson, Marlon Brando **13** Eva Marie Saint
  Oscar for: 5 actor (Brando) **7** picture **8** director **10** screenplay **17** supporting actress (Saint)

on the whole 9 in general **10** by and large **27** considering the circumstances

onto 4 atop, upon **5** aware, privy **6** aboard

onus 4 duty, load **5** cross **6** burden, strain, weight **9** liability **10** obligation **11** encumbrance **13** burden of proof **14** responsibility

onus probandi 13 burden of proof

onward, onwards 5 ahead, along **7** forward, ongoing **9** advancing, frontward **11** moving ahead, progressive
  French: 7 en avant, en route

On Wings of Eagles
  author: 10 Ken Follett

oodles 4 gobs, lots, many **5** heaps, loads, scads **6** plenty

ooze 4 drip, leak, mire, muck, seep, silt **5** bleed, drain, exude, slime, sweat **6** filter, sludge **7** dribble, leakage, seepage, soft mud, trickle **8** alluvium **9** discharge, exudation, percolate, secretion, transpire

oozing 5 leaky, weepy **6** sweaty **7** exuding, seepage, seeping **8** bleeding, sweating

opal
  color: 3 red **5** black, white **6** orange **11** transparent
  source: 6 Mexico **9** Australia **14** Lightning Ridge
  variety: 8 fire opal

opalescent 5 milky **6** pearly **8** irisated, luminous **10** iridescent

opaque 4 dark, dull, hazy **5** muddy, murky **7** clouded, muddied, obscure, unclear **8** abstruse **9** difficult **12** impenetrable, unfathomable **14** nontranslucent, nontransparent, unintelligible **16** incomprehensible

opaqueness 7 opacity **8** dullness **9** denseness, muddiness, murkiness, obscurity **10** cloudiness **11** unclearness **15** impenetrability **17** unintelligibility **19** incomprehensibility

open 4 ajar, fair, just, wide **5** agape, begin, clear, crack, found, frank, plain, unbar **6** candid, create, direct, expand, gaping, honest, launch, unfold, unlock, unseal, unshut **7** artless, exposed, lay open, natural, not shut, sincere, unblock, unclose, yawning **8** commence, extended, outgoing, unbiased, unclosed, unfasten, unfenced, unfolded, unlocked, unsealed **9** available, coverless, establish, expansive, impartial, institute, not closed, objective, originate, receptive, unbigoted, unbounded, uncovered, uncrowded, undertake, welcoming **10** accessible, forthright, impersonal, inaugurate, responsive, unenclosed, unfastened **11** extroverted, uncluttered, uninhabited **12** permit access, unobstructed, unprejudiced **13** disinterested, doing business **15** straightforward

open-air 7 outdoor, outside **10** unconfined
  Italian: 8 al fresco

open and aboveboard 6 candid, honest 7 ethical 10 forthright 12 on the up and up 15 straightforward

Open Boat, The
   author: 12 Stephen Crane

Open City
   director: 17 Roberto Rossellini
   cast: 11 Aldo Fabrizi, Anna Magnani 16 Marcello Pagliero
   setting: 4 Rome

open-eyed 5 alert, awake, aware 7 heedful, mindful 8 vigilant, watchful, wide-eyed 9 attentive, wide-awake

open-handed 6 lavish 7 liberal 8 generous, prodigal 9 bounteous, bountiful 10 altruistic, beneficent, benevolent, ungrudging, unstinting 11 magnanimous

openhandedness 10 generosity, liberality 11 benevolence, generousity, munificence 12 extravagance

openhearted 7 artless, sincere 8 trusting 9 ingenuous

opening 3 gap, job 4 gash, hole, rent, rift, slit, slot, spot, tear, vent 5 break, chink, cleft, crack, place, space, start 6 breach, chance 7 fissure, kickoff, preface, prelude, send-off, vacancy 8 aperture, occasion, overture, position 9 be ginning, first part, launching, situation 10 initiation 11 opportunity, possibility 12 commencement, inauguration, installation, introduction

openly 6 freely 7 frankly 8 directly, honestly, publicly 9 obviously

open-minded 4 fair 7 liberal 8 amenable, flexible, tolerant, unbiased 9 adaptable, impartial, objective, receptive 10 responsive, undogmatic 11 broad-minded 12 unprejudiced 13 disinterested, nonjudgmental

openmouthed 4 agog, awed 5 agape 6 aghast, amazed 8 wide-eyed 9 awestruck, bewitched, marveling, staggered, stupefied, surprised 10 astonished, confounded dumbstruck, enthralled, spellbound 11 dumbfounded 12 wonderstruck 13 flabbergasted, thunderstruck

openness 6 candor 7 honesty 8 daylight 9 frankness, sincerity 11 artlessness 13 guilelessness 14 forthrightness 19 straightforwardness

open sanction 8 free hand, free rein 13 full authority
   French: 12 catre blanche

open the eyes of 8 disabuse 11 set straight

open to choice 8 elective, optional 9 voluntary

openwork 3 net 4 lace 6 eyelet 7 lattice, Madeira, tracery 8 filigree

opera 5 score 7 musical 8 libretto 11 composition
   by Bizet: 6 Carmen
   by Delibes: 5 Lakme
   by Gounod: 5 Faust
   by Leoncavallo: 10 I Pagliacci
   by Mozart: 8 Idomeneo 10 Magic Flute

11 Don Giovanni 12 Cosi fan tutte 16 Marriage of Figaro
   by Offenbach: 15 Tales of Hoffmann
   by Ponchielli: 10 La Gioconda
   by Puccini: 5 Tosca 8 La Boheme 12 Manon Lescaut 15 Madame Butterfly
   by Rossini: 8 Tancredi 11 William Tell 15 The Barber of Seville
   by Smetana: 13 The Bartered Bride
   by Strauss: 6 Salome 7 Elektra 15 Ariadne auf Naxos 16 Der Rosenkavalier
   by Tchaikovsky: 12 Eugene Onegin
   by Verdi: 4 Aida 6 Otello 8 Falstaff 9 Rigoletto 10 La Traviata 11 Il Trovatore
   by Wagner: 8 Parsifal 9 Lohengrin 10 Tannhauser 16 Tristan and Isolde 17 The Flying Dutchman 21 The Ring of the Nibelungs
   comic: 5 buffa 7 comique
   glass: 9 lorgnette
   hat: 5 crush, gibus
   house: 3 Met 6 Sydney 7 La Scala 12 Covent Garden, Metropolitan
   singer: 4 bass, diva 5 buffa, buffo, tenor 7 soprano 10 coloratura, prima donna
   singular: 4 opus
   solo: 4 aria
   text: 8 libretto

operate 2 go 3 run 4 go in, work 6 behave, manage, open up 7 oversee, perform 8 function 11 superintend 14 perform surgery 18 perform an operation

operating 6 active 7 working 8 in motion 9 operative 10 responsive

operation 5 force 6 action, agency, effect 7 conduct, pursuit, running, surgery, working 8 activity, exertion 9 influence, procedure 10 management, overseeing 11 exploratory, performance, supervision 15 instrumentality, superintendence

operative 3 spy 4 dick 5 agent, in use 6 acting, active, shamus, worker 7 in force, working 8 in effect, in motion, workable 9 activated, detective, effective, effectual, operating 10 functional, private eye, responsive 11 efficacious, secret agent

operator 4 doer, user 5 agent, pilot 6 driver, worker 7 manager 9 performer

opere citato 14 in the work cited
   abbreviation: 5 op cit

Ophelia
   character in: 6 Hamlet
   author: 11 Shakespeare

Opheltes
   also: 10 Archemorus

ophidiophobia
   fear of: 6 snakes

Ophion
   form: 7 serpent
   created from: 9 north wind
   created by: 8 Eurynome

Ophir
   father: 6 Joktan
   source of: 4 gold

oplate 4 dope 6 downer 7 anodyne 8 hypnotic, narcotic, nepenthe, sedative 9 analgesic, calmative, soporific, stupefier 10 depressant, painkiller, palliative 12 somnifacient, stupefacient, tranquilizer

opine 3 say 4 deem 5 allow, guess, offer, state, think 6 assume, reckon 7 believe, imagine, presume, suggest, surmise 8 conclude, consider, estimate 9 speculate, volunteer 10 conjecture, have a hunch

opinion 4 idea, view 6 belief, notion, theory 7 surmise 8 estimate, judgment, thinking 9 sentiment, suspicion 10 assessment, assumption, conception, conclusion, conjecture, conviction, estimation, evaluation, impression, persuasion 11 speculation

opinionated 8 dogmatic, obdurate, stubborn 9 obstinate, pigheaded, unbending 10 bullheaded, headstrong, inflexible, unyielding 12 closed-minded 14 uncompromising

O Pioneers!
  author: 11 Willa Cather

Opis
  companion of: 7 Artemis

Opobalsammum 12 Biblical tree

Oppenheimer, Julius Robert
  field: 7 physics
  directed development of: 10 atomic bomb
  location: 9 Los Alamos, New Mexico
  chaired: 3 AEC 22 Atomic Energy Commission

Opper, Frederick
  creator/artist of: 13 Happy Hooligan 17 Alphonse and Gaston, And Her Name Was Maud

opponent 3 foe 5 enemy, rival 8 resister 9 adversary, assailant, contender, disputant 10 antagonist, challenger, competitor, opposition

opportune 3 apt 5 happy, lucky 6 proper, timely 7 fitting 8 suitable 9 expedient, favorable, fortunate, well-timed 10 auspicious, convenient, felicitous, profitable, propitious, seasonable 11 appropriate 12 advantageous

opportunity 4 time, turn 5 means 6 chance, moment 7 opening 8 occasion 9 situation 10 good chance 11 contingency

oppose 4 buck, defy 5 fight 6 battle, combat, resist, thwart 7 contest 8 obstruct 9 withstand 12 be set against, speak against

opposed 3 con 4 anti 6 averse, pitted 7 adverse, against, counter, hostile 8 contrary, disputed, objected, resisted 9 contested, countered 10 confronted, contrasted, reciprocal 12 contradicted

opposer 5 rival 8 opponent 9 adversary 10 antagonist, competitor

opposite 5 other 6 facing 7 adverse, counter, reverse 8 contrary, converse, opposing 9 differing 11 conflicting 12 antagonistic, antithetical 13 contradictory, counteractive

opposite number 5 equal 8 parallel 10 equivalent 11 correlative, counterpart

opposition 3 foe 5 enemy, rival 6 enmity 8 aversion, defiance, opponent 9 adversary, contender, hostility, other side, rejection 10

antagonism, antagonist, competitor, negativism, resistance 11 contrariety, disapproval 12 disagreement

oppress 3 tax, try, vex 4 pain 5 abuse, worry 6 burden, deject, grieve, sadden, sorrow 7 depress, trouble 8 cast down, dispirit, maltreat 9 despotize, persecute, tyrannize, weigh down 10 discourage, dishearten

oppressed 7 crushed 9 exploited 10 tyrannized 11 downtrodden, subservient

oppressive 5 cruel, harsh 6 brutal, severe, trying, vexing 7 onerous, painful, wearing 8 despotic, grievous, pressing 9 worrisome 10 burdensome, depressing, repressive, tyrannical, unbearable 11 distressing, hardhearted, troublesome 12 discouraging 13 uncomfortable

oppressor 6 despot, tyrant 8 autocrat, dictator

opprobrious 4 base 6 wicked 7 abusive, corrupt, damning 8 infamous, reviling, shameful, shocking 9 malicious, maligning, nefarious, vilifying, vitriolic 10 censorious, deplorable, despicable, malevolent, outrageous, scandalous, scurrilous, unbecoming 11 acrimonious, disgraceful, fulminating 12 condemnatory, denunciatory, dishonorable, disreputable, faultfinding 13 hypercritical, objectionable, reprehensible

opprobrium 5 shame 6 infamy 8 disgrace, dishonor 9 disrepute 12 denunciation

Ops
  origin: 5 Roman
  goddess of: 6 plenty
  husband: 6 Saturn
  son: 7 Jupiter
  called: 10 Magna Mater
  corresponds to: 4 Rhea 6 Cybele 9 Dindymene 10 Berecyntia

opt 4 pick, take 5 elect, fix on, go for 6 choose, prefer, select 7 vote for 8 decide on, settle on

opt for 4 pick, take 5 adopt 6 choose, select, take up 7 embrace, espouse, fix upon, pick out 8 decide on, settle on

optimism 10 confidence 11 hopefulness 12 cheerfulness, sanguineness 13 bright outlook, encouragement

optimistic 6 bright 7 hopeful, roseate 8 buoyed up, cheerful, sanguine 9 confident, favorable, heartened, promising 10 auspicious, encouraged, heartening, propitious 11 encouraging, rose-colored 12 enthusiastic

Optimist's Daughter, The
  author: 11 Eudora Welty

optimum 4 acme, A-one, best, peak 5 crest, ideal, prime 6 choice, height, select, zenith 7 capital, perfect, supreme 8 flawless 9 faultless, first-rate 10 perfection, unexcelled 11 superlative 12 quintessence

option 4 will 5 voice 6 choice, liking 8 decision, election, free will, pleasure 9 franchise, privilege, selection 10 discretion, partiality, preference 11 alternative 12 predilection

optional 4 open 8 elective, unforced 9 allowable, open-ended, voluntary 10 volitional 11 not required 12 discretional 13 discretionary, nonobligatory

opulence 6 bounty, plenty, riches, wealth 7 fortune 8 elegance, luxuries, richness 9 abundance, affluence, amplitude, profusion 10 cornucopia, lavishness, plentitude, prosperity 11 copiousness, great wealth 13 sumptuousness

opus 4 work 5 piece 6 effort 7 attempt, product 8 creation 9 handiwork, invention 10 brainchild, production 11 composition

oracle, Oracle 4 sage, seer 5 augur, sibyl 6 wizard 7 adviser, diviner, prophet 9 predictor, Scripture 10 forecaster, soothsayer 11 clairvoyant

oral 5 vocal 6 spoken, verbal, voiced 7 uttered 8 ingested 9 swallowed 10 of the mouth, verbalized 11 articulated, using speech
    Latin: 8 viva voce

orange
    varieties: 4 king, mock, sour, wild 5 blood, hardy, natal, navel, Osage, sweet 6 bitter, common, Panama, Temple 7 Florida, Mexican, Satsuma, Seville, Spanish 8 Bergamot, Mandarin, Otaheite, Valencia 9 Tachibana, vegetable 10 Chinese box, trifoliate 13 African cherry, Mediterranean 15 Jamaica mandarin 17 house-blooming mock
    liqueur: 7 Curacao

orangutan, orang-outang 3 ape 4 mias 5 satyr 6 primate 10 anthropoid
    characteristic: 8 arboreal 11 herbivorous
    native land: 6 Borneo 7 Sumatra
    species: 13 Pongo pygmaeus

ora pro nobis 9 pray for us

orate 6 recite, speak 7 declaim 11 make a speech

oration 4 talk 5 spiel 6 eulogy, sermon, speech 7 address, lecture, recital 9 discourse, monologue, panegyric 10 peroration 11 declamation 12 disquisition, formal speech

orator 6 talker 7 speaker 8 lecturer, preacher 9 declaimer 10 sermonizer 11 rhetorician, speechmaker, spellbinder 12 elocutionist 13 public speaker

oratory 6 speech 7 bombast 8 delivery, rhetoric 9 elocution, eloquence, preaching 11 declamation 12 speechifying, speechmaking 14 grandiloquence

orb 4 ball, moon 5 globe 6 sphere 7 globule 8 spheroid

orbit 3 way 4 path 5 cycle, route, track 6 circle, course 7 channel, circuit, pathway 10 trajectory 13 revolve around 14 circumnavigate

orchards
    god of: 9 Vertumnus

orchestra 3 pit 4 band 6 stalls 7 parquet 8 ensemble, parterre 12 Philharmonic

orchestrate 5 adapt, score 7 arrange, compose

orchestration 5 score 10 adaptation 11 arrangement 12 organization

orchid
    varieties: 3 bat, bee, fen, fly, nun, nut 4 baby, blue, dove, moth, nun's, rein, swan 5 black, chain, cigar, cobra, coral, giant, jewel, pansy, Salep, showy, snowy, spice, tiger, water, widow 6 bamboo, bottle, cradle, dollar, Easter, helmet, mirror, monkey, pigeon, ragged, sawfly, shower, spider, stream, virgin 7 Alaskan, cow-horn, fringed, hooker's, jumping, peacock, rainbow, rosebud, scarlet, soldier 8 beeswarm, Cooktown, cranefly, fried-egg, gold-lace, green-fly, hyacinth, nun's-hood, poor-man's, Savannah, scorpion, white nun, windmill, woodland 9 blunt-leaf, butterfly, chocolate, Christmas, clam-shell, green rein, green swan, white rein 10 buttonhole, five-leaved, golden swan, hay-scented, late spider, leafy white, Sierra rein, slender bog 11 cockle-shell, crested rein, dancing-doll, dancing-lady, early spider, golden chain, green-winged, one-leaf rein, pink slipper, purple-spire, rattlesnake, round-leaved 12 green fringed, pink scorpion, purple-hooded, Southern rein, tall white bog, white fringed 13 crested yellow, golden fringed, green woodland, Northern green, ragged fringed, yellow fringed 14 crested fringed, large butterfly, little club-spur, white butterfly 15 lesser butterfly, lily-of-the-valley 16 downy rattlesnake, Florida butterfly, Northern small bog, purple fringeless, small round-leaved, white-flowered bog 18 large purple fringed, leafy Northern green, small purple fringed, Southern small white 19 lesser purple fringed 20 greater purple fringed

Orcus
    god of: 10 underworld
    punishes: 7 perjury
    corresponds to: 3 Dis 5 Hades, Pluto 8 Dis Pater

ordain 4 name, rule, will 5 elect, enact, frock 6 decree, invest 7 adjudge, appoint, command, dictate 8 delegate, deputize, instruct 9 determine, legislate, prescribe, pronounce 10 commission, consecrate

ordeal 4 care, pain 5 agony, grief, trial, worry 6 burden, misery, sorrow, strain, stress 7 anguish, concern, torment, tragedy, trauma 8 calamity, distress, pressure, vexation 9 heartache, nightmare, suffering 10 affliction, oppression 11 tribulation, unhappiness 12 wretchedness 16 trying experience

Ordeal of Richard Feverel, The
    author: 14 George Meredith

order 3 bid, law 4 body, book, calm, club, fiat, form, kind, rank, rule, sort, type 5 breed, caste, class, grade, group, guild, house, lodge, quiet, ukase 6 adjure, ask for, charge, decree, degree, demand, dictum, direct, engage, enjoin, family, status, stripe, system 7 agree to, bidding, caliber, call for, command, company, control, dictate, harmony, pattern, quality, request, reserve, silence, society, species, station 8 alliance, category, division, grouping, instruct, neatness, position, purchase, sorority, standing, tidiness 9 framework, structure, ultimatum 10 discipline, federation, fraternity, imperative, sisterhood, tabulation 11 arrangement, association, brotherhood, commandment, confederacy, designation, instruction, tranquility 12 codification, organization, peacefulness, tranquillity 13 pronouncement 14 categorization, classification

ordered 4 bade, neat, trim 7 regular, uniform 8 arranged 9 shipshape 10 systematic

orderliness 8 neatness, tidiness 10 discipline 12 organization

orderly 4 neat, tidy 5 civil, quiet 6 proper, spruce 8 peaceful 9 organized, peaceable, shipshape, tractable 10 classified, controlled, methodical, restrained, system atic 11 disciplined, uncluttered, well-behaved

ordinance 3 act, law 4 bull, fiat, rule, writ 5 canon, edict, order 6 decree, dictum, ruling 7 command, mandate, statute 9 enactment 10 regulation 11 commandment

ordinarily 7 as a rule, usually 8 commonly, normally 9 generally, regularly, routinely 10 habitually 11 customarily 12 on the average 14 conventionally

ordinary 4 dull, so-so 5 usual 6 common, normal 7 average, humdrum, routine, trivial, typical 8 everyday, familiar, habitual, mediocre, standard 9 customary 10 pedestrian, uninspired 11 commonplace, indifferent, stereotyped, traditional, unimportant 12 conventional, run-of-the-mill, unimpressive 13 insignificant, unexceptional, unimaginative, uninteresting 15 inconsequential, undistinguished

Ordinary People
director: 13 Robert Redford
author: 11 Judith Guest
cast: 10 Judd Hirsch 13 Timothy Hutton 14 Mary Tyler Moore 16 Donald Sutherland
Oscar for: 7 picture 8 director 12 screenwriter 15 supporting actor (Hutton)

ordinary wine
French: 12 vin ordinaire

ordnance 4 arms 6 cannon 9 armaments, artillery, munitions

ordnance depot 6 armory 7 arsenal 18 military storehouse

ore 3 tin 4 gold, iron, lead, paco, rock, zinc 5 metal 6 bronze, copper, galena, sulfur 7 halvans, mineral 8 aluminum, cinnabar, hematite 9 melachite
byproduct: 6 gangue
deposit: 3 bed 4 lode, mine, vein 7 bonanza
layer: 4 seam 5 stope
trough: 6 strake
worthless: 4 slag 5 dross, matte

Oread
form: 5 nymph
location: 8 mountain
companion of: 7 Artemis

oregano
name means: 16 joy of the mountain
botanical name: 8 O vulgare, Origanum
also: 6 organy, origan 8 marjoram 9 pizza herb 11 Mexican sage, winter sweet
origin: 13 Mediterranean
family: 4 mint
cure for: 11 indigestion 14 loss of appetite
first aid for: 12 spider stings 14 scorpion stings
use: 5 pizza 6 broths 8 stuffing 12 tomato dishes 13 Italian dishes

Oregon
abbreviation: 2 OR 4 Oreg
nickname: 6 Beaver, Sunset 7 Webfoot 13 Sawdust Empire
capital: 5 Salem
largest city: 8 Portland
others: 5 Nyssa 6 Albany, Eugene 7 Ashland, Astoria, Medford 8 Portland, Roseburg 9 Corvallis, Pendleton 10 Grant's Pass, Willamette 12 Klamath Falls
college: 4 Reed 7 Pacific 8 Linfield, Portland 10 Willamette 13 Lewis and Clark
feature:
fort: 5 Boise 6 Casper 7 Kearney, Laramie
national park: 10 Crater Lake
tribe: 4 Coos 5 Alsea, Kusan, Modoc, Wasco, Yanan, Yunca 6 Cayuse, Chetco, Chinoo, Kuitsh, Molala, Siletz, Tenino, Umpqua 7 Bannock, Clatsop, Klamath, Sastean, Shastan, Takelma, Walpapi, Yaquina 8 Clackama, Klikitat, Nez Perce, Sahaptin, Umatilla 9 Kalapuyan, Tillamook 10 Kalapooian, Wallawalla
people: 10 Wayne Morse 12 Linus Pauling 15 Phyllis McGinley
explorer: 13 Lewis and Clark
lake: 5 Abert, Waldo 6 Harney, McNary 7 John Day, Klamath, Malheur
deepest in US: 6 Crater
land rank: 5 tenth
mountain: 6 Mazama, Tacoma, Walker, Wilson 7 Elkhorn, Grizzly, Jackass, Rainier, Tidbits, Wallowa 8 Cascades 9 Blue Coast, Marys Peak 10 Strawberry
highest point: 4 Hood
physical feature:
bay: 4 Coos
caves: 11 Marble Halls
wind: 7 Chinook
river: 5 Rogue, Snake 6 Imnaha, Owyhee, Powder, Umpqua 7 Blitzen, John Day, Klamath, Silvie's 8 Columbia 9 Deschutes 10 Willamette
state admission: 11 thirty-third
state bird: 17 western meadowlark
state fish: 13 Chinook salmon

state flower: 7 mahonia **11** Oregon grape
state motto: 8 The Union
state song: 14 Oregon My Oregon
state tree: 10 Douglas fir
Oregon Trail, The
  author: 14 Francis Parkman
Oresteia
  author: 9 Aeschylus
  trilogy includes: 9 Agamemnon, Eumenides **10** Choephoroe
Orestes
  author: 9 Euripides
  character: 5 Helen **6** Apollo, Furies **7** Electra, Pylades **8** Menelaus
Orestes
  father: 9 Agamemnon
  mother: 12 Clytemnestra
  sister: 7 Electra **9** Iphigenia
  wife: 8 Hermione
  son: 9 Tisamenus
  killed: 9 Aegisthus **12** Clytemnestra
  pursued by: 6 Furies
Orfeo, L'
  also: 17 The Story of Orpheus
  opera by: 10 Monteverdi
Orfeo ed Euridice
  also: 18 Orpheus and Eurydice
  opera by: 5 Gluck
  character: 4 Amor, Zeus **6** Furies
Orff, Carl
  born: 6 Munich **7** Germany
  composer of: 7 Der Mond, The Moon **8** Antigone, Die Kluge **9** Schulwerk **10** Prometheus **13** Carmina Burana, The Clever Girl **14** Catulli Carmina **16** Oedipus der Tyrann, Oedipus the Tyrant
organ 7 agency **7** journal, vehicle **9** harmonium **10** hurdy-gurdy, instrument **11** publication
organic 5 alive, quick **6** living **7** animate, natural, ordered, planned, unified **8** designed, physical **9** patterned **10** anatomical, harmonious, methodical, systematic **12** nonsynthetic **13** physiological **14** constitutional
organism 4 cell **5** plant, whole **6** animal, entity, system **7** complex, network, society **8** creature **9** bacterium **10** federation **11** association, corporation, institution, living thing **13** microorganism
organization 4 club, firm, sect **5** corps, group, order, party, union **6** design, league, making, outfit **7** company, forming, harmony, pattern, society **8** alliance, assembly, business, grouping, ordering **9** arranging, formation **10** federation, fellowship, fraternity **11** arrangement, association, composition, corporation, formulation, structuring **12** constitution, coordination **13** establishment, incorporation
organizational 10 managerial **13** developmental **14** administrative
organize 4 file, form, tidy **5** found, group, index, order, set up **6** codify, create, neaten, tidy up **7** arrange, catalog, develop **8** classify, tabulate **9** establish, formulate,

originate 10 categorize, coordinate **11** make orderly, systematize
organized 4 neat, tidy **7** logical, orderly **8** coherent **10** methodical, systematic
orgiastic 4 wild **6** wanton **7** drunken, riotous **9** abandoned, debauched, Dionysian, dissolute, libertine **10** dissipated, licentious **12** bacchanalian, unrestrained **13** overindulgent, undisciplined
orgy 7 debauch, wassail **8** carousal **9** bacchanal **10** saturnalia **11** bacchanalia
orient, the Orient 3 fix, set **4** Asia, find **6** locate, relate, square **7** situate **8** accustom **9** acclimate, reconcile **10** the Far East **11** Eastern Asia, familiarize
oriental 4 Arab, fine, Thai, Turk **5** Asian **6** bright, Indian, Korean **7** Asiatic, Chinese, Eastern, Iranian, shining **8** Japanese, lustrous, precious, superior **10** Vietnamese
  animal: 4 zebu **5** rasse
  building: 6 pagoda
  dish: 5 pilau, pilaw **6** pilaff
  drum: 6 tomtom
  food fish: 3 tai
  garment: 3 aba **6** sarong
  inn: 4 Khan **5** serai **6** imaret **11** caravansary
  laborer: 6 coolie
  market: 3 suk, sug **4** souk **6** bazaar
  nurse: 4 amah, ayah
  prince: 4 amir, haja
  sail: 6 lateen
  sash: 3 obi
  shrub: 3 tea **5** henna **8** oleander
  wagon: 5 araba
  weight: 2 mo **4** rotl, tael **5** catty, liang **6** cantar
orientation 8 location **9** alignment, direction, situation **10** adjustment **11** acclimation **15** acclimatization, familiarization
orifice 3 gap, pit **4** hole, slit, slot, vent **5** cleft, inlet, mouth **6** cavity, cranny, hollow, lacuna, pocket, socket **7** crevice, fissure, opening, passage **8** alveolus, aperture, entrance
origin 4 base, line, race, rise, root **5** agent, basis, birth, breed, cause, house, stock **6** author, family, father, ground, growth, mother, reason, source, spring, strain **7** creator, descent, genesis, lineage, taproot **8** ancestry, nativity, producer **9** beginning, emergence, evolution, generator, inception, parentage, principle **10** derivation, extraction, foundation **12** commencement, fountainhead
Origin, The
  author: 11 Irving Stone
original 3 new **4** bold **5** basic, basis, first, fresh, novel **6** daring, primal, unique **7** example, initial, pattern, primary, seminal, strange, unusual **8** atypical, creative, earliest, germinal, primeval, singular, uncommon **9** different, essential, first copy, formative, inaugural, ingenious, inventive, prototype **10** aboriginal, newfangled, primordial, underlying, unfamiliar, unorthodox

11 fundamental, imaginative 12 introductory 13 extraordinary 14 unconventional

Original Amateur Hour, The
host: 7 Ted Mack

originality 6 daring 7 newness, novelty 8 boldness 9 freshness, ingenuity 10 cleverness, creativity, uniqueness 11 imagination, singularity, unorthodoxy 13 individuality, inventiveness 17 unconventionality

originally 7 at first, by birth 8 uniquely 9 initially, unusually 10 creatively 11 differently, inventively 13 imaginatively

originate 4 come, flow, rise, stem 5 arise, begin, draft, found, issue, start 6 create, crop up, derive, design, devise, emerge, evolve, father, invent, sprout 7 develop, emanate, proceed 8 commence, conceive, envision, initiate, organize, spring up 9 establish, fabricate, formulate, germinate 10 inaugurate

origination 5 birth 7 genesis 9 inception, invention 10 conception, initiation 11 germination 12 commencement 13 establishment

Origin of Species, The
author: 13 Charles Darwin

Origins of Totalitarianism, The
author: 12 Hannah Arendt

Orion
form: 5 giant
vocation: 6 hunter
pursued: 8 Pleiades
killed by: 7 Artemis
became: 13 constellation

Orithyia
father: 10 Erechtheus
mother: 9 Praxithea
abducted by: 6 Boreas
son: 5 Zetes 6 Calais
daughter: 6 Chione 9 Cleopatra

Oriya
language family: 12 Indo-European
branch: 11 Indo-Iranian
group: 5 Indic
spoken in: 5 (northern) India

Orkney Islands
county seat: 8 Kirkwall
country: 8 Scotland
firth: 8 Pentland
island: 3 Hay 6 Rousay, Sanday 7 Westray 8 Stronsay 14 South Ronaldsay
largest city: 6 Pomona

Orlando
author: 13 Virginia Woolf
character: 5 Sasha 14 Nicholas Greene 28 Archduchess Harriet of Roumania, Marmaduke Bonthrop Shelmerdine

Orlando
character in: 11 As You Like It
author: 11 Shakespeare

Orlando Furloso
author: 7 Ariosto
character: 6 Rogero 7 Rinaldo 8 Agramant, Angelica, Rodomont 9 Bradamant 11 Charlemagne

Orley Farm
author: 15 Anthony Trollope

ormolu 5 alloy, brass, paste 6 bronze 7 gilding 8 ornament
imitation of: 4 gold
used to decorate: 5 clock 9 furniture

ornament 4 deck, gild, trim 5 adorn 6 bedeck, enrich, finery, frills 7 festoon, furbish, garnish 8 beautify, decorate, furbelow, trick out, trimming 9 accessory, adornment, embellish 10 decoration, enrich ment 11 elaboration 13 embellishment 14 beautification

ornamental 4 gilt 5 fancy 6 chichi, rococo 10 decorative
ball: 4 bead 6 pompom
button: 4 stud
grass: 4 neti
loop: 5 picot
metal: 5 niello

ornamentation 7 garnish 8 trimming 9 adornment 10 decoration 13 embellishment

ornate 5 fancy, showy 6 flashy, florid, lavish, rococo 7 adorned, baroque, flowery 9 decorated, elaborate, sumptuous 10 flamboyant 11 embellished, pretentious 12 ostentatious

ornery 4 curt, mean 5 testy 6 crabby, grumpy, shirty 7 grouchy, peevish, waspish 8 snappish 9 dyspeptic, irascible, irritable 10 ill-natured 11 ill-tempered, quarrelsome 12 cantankerous

Orneus
father: 10 Erechtheus
brother: 6 Metion 7 Cecrops
son: 6 Peteos

Ornitholestes
type: 8 dinosaur
period: 8 Jurassic

Ornithomimus
type: 8 dinosaur
period: 10 Cretaceous

ornithophobia
fear of: 5 birds

ornithopod
type of: 8 dinosaur
member: 9 Iguanodon 10 Edmontonia, Nodosaurus 11 Anatosaurus, Polacanthus, Saurolophus, Scolosaurus, Stegosaurus 12 Ankylosaurus, Camptosaurus, Lambeosaurus, Pisanosaurus 13 Acanthopholis, Corythosaurus, Hypsilophodon, Palaeoscincus 14 Thescelosaurus 15 Parasaurolophus, Procheneosaurus 17 Heterodontosaurus

Ornytus see 7 Teuthis

orotund 4 full, rich 5 clear 6 strong 7 pompous, ringing, vibrant 8 resonant, sonorous 9 bombastic 10 resounding, rhetorical, stentorian
Latin: 10 ore rotundo

Orowitz, Eugene Maurice
real name of: 13 Michael Landon

oro y plata 4 gold and silver
motto of: 7 Montana

Orozco, Jose Clemente
born: 6 Mexico 7 Jalisco (Zapotlan) 12 Ciudad Guzman
artwork: 5 Grief 9 Catharsis 11 Omni-

science 12 House of Tears 16 National Allegory, Social Revolution 18 Hidalgo and Castillo

Orphans of the Storm
director: 10 D W Griffith
cast: 11 Dorothy Gish, Lillian Gish 17 Joseph Schildkraut

Orpheus
vocation: 4 poet 8 musician
mother: 8 Calliope
wife: 8 Eurydice
member of: 9 Argonauts
went into: 5 Hades
killed by: 7 Maenads

Orpheus in the Underworld
also: 15 Orphee aux Enfers
operetta by: 9 Offenbach

Orsino
character in: 12 Twelfth Night
author: 11 Shakespeare

ort 3 bit 5 crumb, dregs, scrap 6 morsel, refuse, trifle 7 remnant 8 leavings, leftover

Orthaea
father: 10 Hyacinthus

Orthia
epithet of: 7 Artemis
means: 7 upright

orthodox 5 fixed, pious, usual 6 devout, narrow 7 limited, regular, routine 8 accepted, approved, official, ordinary, standard 9 customary, religious 11 commonplace, conformable, established, traditional 12 conventional 13 authoritative, circumscribed

orthoptera
class: 8 hexapoda
phylum: 10 arthropoda
group: 4 leaf 5 stick 6 locust, mantid 7 cricket 9 cockroach 11 grasshopper

Orwell, George
real name: 15 Eric Arthur Blair
author of: 4 1984 10 Animal Farm 18 Nineteen Eighty-Four 29 Politics and the English Language

oryx 5 beisa 6 pickax 7 gazelle, gemsbok 8 antelope, leucoryx

Osage (Wazhazhe)
language family: 6 Siouan
location: 6 Kansas 8 Arkansas, Missouri, Oklahoma

Oscan
language family: 12 Indo-European
branch: 6 Italic

Oschophoria
origin: 8 Athenian
event: 8 festival
honoring: 7 vintage 8 Dionysus

oscillate 4 vary 5 pulse, swing, waver 6 change, seesaw 7 librate, pulsate, vibrate 8 hesitate 9 alternate, come and go, fluctuate, hem and haw, vacil late 10 ebb and flow, equivocate 12 shilly-shally 16 move back and forth

O'Shaughnessy, Brigid
character in: 16 The Maltese Falcon
author: 7 Hammett

osier 3 rod 4 wand 5 salix, withe 6 willow 7 dogwood, wilgers 9 twigwithy
species: 14 Salix viminalis
use: 6 wicker 8 basketry

Osiris
origin: 8 Egyptian
god of: 4 dead, Nile
judge of: 4 dead
king of: 4 dead
wife: 4 Isis
sister: 4 Isis
son: 5 Horus
brother: 3 Set 4 Seth 5 Horus
killed by: 3 Set 4 Seth

Oskar Matzerath
character in: 7 Tin Drum
author: 5 Grass

Oslo
capital of: 6 Norway
former name: 11 Christiania
landmark: 8 Storting (Parliament) 11 Royal Palace
mountain: 12 Holmenkollen
park: 7 Frogner
peninsula: 8 Akershus
street: 14 Karl Johansgate

Osmond, Gilbert
character in: 18 The Portrait of a Lady
author: 5 James

Ossian
character in: 12 Gaelic poetry

ossify 6 harden 7 stiffen 9 fossilize

ossuary 8 boneyard 10 depository, receptacle

ostensible 6 avowed 7 alleged, assumed, feigned, implied, nominal, outward, seeming, surface, titular, visible 8 apparent, declared, illusory, manifest, specious 10 pretended, professed 10 presumable 11 perceivable

ostentation 4 airs, dash, fuss, pomp, ritz, show 5 glitz, gloss, swank 6 splash 7 display, glitter 8 flourish, pretense 9 pageantry, pomposity, showiness, spectacle
French: 7 etalage

ostentatious 4 loud 5 gaudy, showy 6 flashy, florid, garish 7 pompous 8 affected, immodest, overdone 9 grandiose, obtrusive 10 flamboyant, showing off 11 conspicuous, exaggerated, pretentious 15 flaunting wealth

Osterreich see 7 Austria

ostracize 3 cut 4 oust, shun, snub 5 avoid, expel 6 banish, disown, reject 7 exclude, shutout 9 blackball, blacklist

Ostwald, Wilhelm
field: 9 chemistry
nationality: 6 German
founded: 17 physical chemistry

O'Sullivan, Maureen
born: 5 Boyle 7 Ireland 15 County Roscommon
daughter: 9 Mia Farrow
roles: 4 Jane (Tarzan movies) 16 David Copperfield 17 Pride and Prejudice 19 Hannah and Her Sisters

Otello
also: 7 Othello
opera by: 5 Verdi 7 Rossini
O tempora! O mores! 14 O times! O customs!

Othello
director: 11 Stuart Burge
author: 18 William Shakespeare
character: 4 Iago 6 Cassio, Emilia 9 Desdemona
cast: 11 Frank Finlay, Joyce Redman, Maggie Smith 15 Laurence Olivier

other 4 more 5 added, extra, spare 6 unlike 7 further, reverse 8 contrary, opposite 9 alternate, auxiliary, different, remaining 10 additional, contrasted, dissimilar 11 contrasting 13 contradictory, supplementary 14 differentiated

Other Gods
author: 9 Pearl Buck

Other Side of Midnight, The
author: 13 Sidney Sheldon

other than 3 but 4 save 6 except, saving 7 barring, besides 9 excepting, excluding
otherwise 5 if not 6 or else 9 inversely 10 contrarily 11 differently 12 contrariwise
otherworldly 7 sublime 8 heavenly 9 celestial 14 transcendental

Othin see 4 Odin

Othniel 11 Hebrew judge
father: 5 Kenaz
brother: 5 Caleb
wife: 6 Achsah

O times! O customs!
Latin: 14 O tempora! O mores!

Otionia
father: 10 Erechtheus
sister: 10 Protogonia
death by: 9 sacrifice
for victory of: 9 Athenians
over: 11 Eleusinians

otiose 4 idle, lazy 6 futile 7 laggard, resting, useless, worn-out 8 abortive, impotent, inactive, indolent, listless, slothful, sluggish 9 fruitless, lethargic, powerless, somnolent 10 unavailing 11 incompetent, ineffective, inoperative, unrewarding 12 unproductive

Otomi
tribe: 7 Capotec

O'Toole, Peter
born: 7 Ireland 9 Connemara
roles: 6 Becket 7 Creator, Lord Jim 13 Man of La Mancha 14 Goodbye Mr Chips, My Favorite Year, The Last Emperor 15 The Lion in Winter 16 Lawrence of Arabia, What's New Pussycat 18 How to Steal a Million

O'Trigger, Sir Lucius
character in: 9 The Rivals
author: 8 Sheridan

Ott, Mel
nickname: 9 Boy Wonder 12 Master Melvin
sport: 8 baseball
position: 8 outfield
team: 13 New York Giants

Ottawa
capital of: 6 Canada
early name: 6 Bytown
falls: 6 Rideau 9 Chaudiere
landmark: 18 National Arts Centre 19 Dominion Observatory, Parliament Buildings
river: 6 Ottawa, Rideau 8 Gatineau
university: 8 Carleton

Ottawa
language family: 9 Algonkian 10 Algonquian
location: 4 Ohio 6 Canada, Kansas 7 Ontario 12 Lake Michigan
leader: 7 Pontiac

Otter
origin: 12 Scandinavian
mentioned in: 8 Volsunga
form: 5 otter
father: 8 Hreidmar
killed by: 4 Loki

ottoman, Ottoman 4 seat, Turk 5 couch, divan, stool 7 sultane, Turkish 9 footstool
color: 3 red 9 vermilion
governor: 3 bey, dey 5 pasha
ruler: 5 Osman 8 Suleiman
standard: 4 ale

Otus
form: 5 giant
member of: 7 Aloidae
father: 8 Poseidon
mother: 9 Iphimedia
brother: 9 Ephialtes

Ouagadougou
capital of: 10 Upper Volta 11 Burkina Faso

oui 3 yes

ounce
abbreviation of: 2 oz

ounce troy
abbreviation of: 3 oz t

Our Bill
creator: 14 Harry Haenigsen
character: 6 Walter

Our Crowd
author: 17 Stephen Birmingham

Our Miss Brooks
character: 8 Mrs Davis 12 Connie Brooks, Walter Denton 13 Osgood Conklin, Philip Boynton 14 Harriet Conklin
cast: 8 Eve Arden 10 Dick Crenna, Gale Gordon, Jane Morgan 14 Gloria McMillan, Robert Rockwell
Miss Brooks taught: 7 English
school: 11 Madison High

Our Mutual Friend
author: 14 Charles Dickens
character: 4 Wegg 5 Venus 6 Boffin 11 Bella Wilfer 17 Mortimer Lightwood, Young John Harmon (Handford, Rokesmith)

our sea
Latin: 11 mare nostrum
ancient Roman name for: 13 Mediterranean

Our Town
  author: 14 Thornton Wilder
  character: 12 Simon Stimson
  Gibbs family: 2 Dr 3 Mrs 6 George 7 Rebecca
  Webb family: 2 Mr 3 Mrs 5 Emily, Wally
  director: 7 Sam Wood
  cast: 10 Fay Bainter 11 Martha Scott 13 William Holden

oust 4 fire, sack 5 eject, evict, expel 6 banish, bounce, put out, remove, unseat 7 boot out, cashier, cast out, dismiss, kick out 8 throw out 9 discharge, give the ax 11 give the gate, send packing

ouster 6 firing 7 removal, sacking 8 bouncing, ejection, eviction 9 discharge, dismissal, expelling, expulsion, overthrow 10 banishment, cashiering 11 dislodgment, drumming out, throwing out 13 dispossession

out 2 ex 4 away 5 aloud, eject, forth, not in, passe 6 absent, begone, excuse, public 7 outside 8 exterior, external, revealed 9 in society, in the open, published 10 extinguish

out-and-out 4 pure, sure 5 sheer, total, utter 6 arrant 7 perfect 8 absolute, complete, hardened, outright, positive, thorough 9 confirmed, downright, unlimited 10 inveterate 11 straight out, unequivocal, unmitigated, unqualified 12 unregenerate, unrestricted 13 dyed-in-the-wool, thoroughgoing, unadulterated, unconditional 14 unquestionable

outbrazen 4 dare, defy, face 8 confront 9 challenge, stand up to

outbreak 5 burst 7 display 8 epidemic, eruption, invasion, outburst 9 explosion 10 outpouring 13 demonstration

outbuilding 4 barn, shed 5 privy 6 garage, stable 7 latrine 8 outhouse, woodshed

outburst 5 blast, burst 7 display, thunder 8 eruption, outbreak 9 explosion 10 outpouring 11 fulmination 13 demonstration

outcast 5 exile, rover 6 ousted, outlaw, pariah, roamer 7 refugee, runaway 8 banished, castaway, deportee, derelict, expelled, fugitive, rejected, vagabond 9 discarded 10 expatriate

Outcast of the Islands, The
  author: 12 Joseph Conrad

Outcault, R F
  creator/artist of: 11 Buster Brown 12 The Yellow Kid

outcome 3 end 5 fruit, issue 6 effect, payoff, result, upshot 9 aftermath, outgrowth 11 aftereffect, consequence

outcry 3 cry 4 howl, roar, yell, yelp, yowl 5 noise, shout, whoop 6 bellow, clamor, hubbub, scream, shriek, uproar 7 clangor, protest, screech 9 commotion, complaint, crying out, hue and cry, objection 10 cry of alarm, hullabaloo 12 caterwauling, remonstrance

outdated 5 passe 7 antique 8 outmoded 9 out-of-date 10 antiquated 12 old-fashioned

outdo 3 top 4 beat, best 5 excel, worst 6 better, defeat, exceed, outfox, outwit 7 eclipse, outplay, outrank, surpass 8 outclass, outshine, outstrip, overcome 9 transcend

outdoor festival
  French: 13 fete champetre

outdoor market 5 agora 6 bazaar 10 flea market 11 marketplace

outer 6 distal, remote 7 extreme, farther, outside, outward, without 8 exterior, external, outlying 9 outermost 10 farther out, peripheral

outer edge 3 lip, rim, tip 5 bound 6 margin 8 boundary 9 extremity

Outer Mongolia
  also: 24 Mongolian People's Republic
  border: 5 China 6 Russia 11 Soviet Union
  capital: 4 Urga 5 Kulun 9 Ulan Bator
  currency: 5 mongo 6 tugrik
  desert: 4 Gobi 5 Shamo
  language: 7 Khalka
  mountain range: 5 Altai, Altay 7 Khangai

outermost 5 outer 6 utmost 7 extreme, outside, outward, surface 8 exterior, external 11 farthest out, most distant, superficial

outfit 3 fit, rig 4 gear 5 array, dress, equip, getup, habit, rig up 6 clothe, supply 7 appoint, costume, furnish 8 accouter, ensemble, wardrobe 9 equipment, provision, trappings 13 accoutrements, paraphernalia

outflow 5 issue 7 leakage, seepage 8 drainage 9 discharge

outgo 4 beat, cost, exit, pass 5 excel, issue, outdo 6 efflux, egress, outlay, outlet 7 outflow, surpass 8 outstrip 9 departure 11 expenditure

outgoing 4 warm 6 genial, social 7 amiable, cordial, exiting, leaving 8 friendly, going out, outbound, sociable 9 convivial, departing 10 gregarious 11 extroverted, sympathetic, warmhearted

outgoing person 9 extrovert 17 hail-fellow-well-met

outgrowth 3 end 4 knob, knot, node 5 bulge, fruit, issue, shoot 6 result, sequel, sprout, upshot 7 product 8 offshoot 9 aftermath 10 conclusion, projection 11 aftereffect, consequence, culmination, excrescence, outcropping 12 protuberance

outing 4 hike, ride, spin, tour, trip, walk 5 drive, jaunt, tramp 6 airing, junket, ramble 7 holiday 9 excursion 10 expedition

outlander 5 alien, exile 6 emigre 7 invader, settler 8 intruder, newcomer, stranger, wanderer 9 Auslander, barbarian, foreigner, immigrant 10 tramontane 12 ultramontane

outlandish 3 odd 5 kooky, queer, weird 6 far-out 7 bizarre, curious, strange, unusual 8 freakish, peculiar 9 eccentric, fantastic, grotesque, unheard-of 10 incredible, outrageous, ridiculous 12 preposterous, unbelievable, unimaginable, unparalleled 13 inconceivable 14 unconventional

outlast 6 endure, hold on, keep on, remain, stay on 7 carry on, hold out, outstay, outwear, perdure, persist, prevail, survive 8 continue

outlaw 3 ban, bar 4 deny, stop 5 felon 6 bandit, forbid, pariah 7 exclude, outcast 8 criminal, disallow, fugitive, prohibit, suppress 9 desperado, interdict, miscreant, proscribe 10 highwayman

outlay 3 fee 4 cost 5 outgo, price 6 charge 7 expense, payment 8 spending 11 amount spent, expenditure 12 disbursement

outlet 3 way 4 door, duct, exit, gate, path, vent 5 means 6 avenue, egress, escape, portal 7 channel, conduit, gateway, opening, passage

outline 4 plot 5 brief, trace 6 digest, limits, resume, review 7 contour, diagram, profile, summary, tracing 8 abstract, synopsis 9 blueprint, delineate, lineation, perimeter, periphery, sketch out 10 abridgment, silhouette 11 delineation 12 condensation
   French: 6 apercu

outlook 4 view 5 scene, sight, vista 6 aspect, chance 7 picture, promise 8 attitude, forecast, panorama, prospect 9 spectacle, viewpoint 10 assumption 11 expectation, frame of mind, perspective, point of view, presumption, probability 12 anticipation

outlying 5 outer, rural 6 far-off, remote 7 distant, exurban 8 exterior, suburban 10 peripheral

outmoded 5 corny, dated, passe, tired 6 demode, old hat 7 antique, archaic, vintage 8 obsolete, old-timey, outdated 9 out-of-date 10 antiquated 12 old-fashioned, out-of-fashion 14 behind the times
   French: 6 demode

Out of Africa
   director: 13 Sydney Pollack
   cast: 11 Meryl Streep (Baroness Karen Blixen, Isak Dinesen) 13 Robert Redford (Denys Finch Hatton) 19 Klaus Maria Brandauer (Baron Bror von Blixen)

out of bed 2 up 5 astir 9 up and at 'em 10 on one's feet, up and about 12 rise and shine

out-of-date 5 dated, passe 8 outmoded 10 antiquated 12 old-fashioned
   French: 6 demode

out of doors 3 out 5 forth 6 abroad 7 outside 8 alfresco 12 in the open air

out-of-fashion 5 passe 8 obsolete, outmoded 9 out-of-date 12 old-fashioned
   French: 6 demode

out of hand 4 wild 5 rowdy 6 unruly 10 disorderly 12 obstreperous, out of control, unmanageable, unrestrained 14 uncontrollable

out of keeping 8 atypical, peculiar, unseemly 9 anomalous, irregular 11 incongruous 12 inconsistent 13 inappropriate

out of kilter 4 awry 5 askew 6 uneven 7 crooked, oblique

out of line 6 unruly 9 excessive 10 exorbitant 12 presumptuous, unreasonable

out of many one
   Latin: 13 e pluribus unum
   motto of: 12 United States

out of one's head 3 mad 4 daft, nuts 5 crazy, nutty 6 insane 7 cracked, touched 8 demented, deranged, unhinged 10 unbalanced 12 mad as a hatter, off his rocker 15 mad as a March hare 17 nutty as a fruitcake

out of operation 4 dead, down 8 inactive 10 not working, out of order 11 inoperative

out of order 5 amiss 6 faulty 10 not working 11 inoperative, uncalled-for 13 inappropriate

out of place 3 odd 8 unseemly 10 unsuitable 11 incongruous, inconsonant 13 inappropriate

out of shape 4 bent 5 unfit 6 flabby, warped 7 crooked 8 deformed 9 distorted, untrained

out of sorts 5 cross, huffy, testy 6 crabby, cranky, touchy 7 bearish, grouchy, peevish 8 petulant, snappish 9 crotchety, irritable 10 ill-humored 11 ill-tempered 12 cantankerous 13 short-tempered

out of the books of
   Latin: 8 ex libris

out of the fight
   French: 12 hors de combat

out of the ordinary 4 rare 6 unique 7 notable, unusual 8 singular, uncommon 10 phenomenal, remarkable 11 exceptional 13 extraordinary

Out of the Past
   director: 15 Jacques Tourneur
   based on novel by: 13 Geoffrey Homes (Daniel Mainwaring) (Build My Gallows High)
   cast: 9 Jane Greer 11 Kirk Douglas, Richard Webb 13 Rhonda Fleming, Robert Mitchum

out of touch 7 mixed-up 8 unstable 11 disoriented 12 out of contact 13 incommunicado

out-of-towner 7 tourist, visitor 9 sojourner, transient 11 nonresident

outpace 4 pass 5 outdo 6 exceed, outrun 8 outstrip

outpouring 6 deluge 7 barrage, gushing, outflow 8 effusion

output 4 crop, gain, take 5 yield 6 profit 7 harvest, produce, product, reaping, turnout 8 gleaning, proceeds 9 gathering 10 production 11 achievement 12 productivity 14 accomplishment

outrage 4 evil, gall, rile 5 anger, shock, wrong 6 arouse, enrage, insult, madden, offend, ruffle 7 affront, incense, provoke, steam up 8 atrocity, disquiet, enormity, iniquity 9 barbarity, indignity, infuriate 10 discompose, disrespect, exasperate, gross crime, scandalize 11 desecration, monstrosity, profanation 13 barbarousness, get one's back up, make one see red, slap in the face, transgression 17 make one's blood boil

outraged 3 mad 5 angry, irate, riled 6 fuming, raging 7 enraged, furious 8 incensed, inflamed, offended 9 affronted, indignant 10 displeased, infuriated

outrageous 4 base, foul, rank, rude, vile 5 gross 6 brutal, odious, wicked 7 abusive, extreme, galling, heinous, immense, inhuman 8 enormous, flagrant, inhumane, insolent, scornful, shocking 9 atrocious, barbarous, excessive, insulting, maddening, monstrous, nefarious, offensive, shameless 10 despicable, exorbitant, horrifying, immoderate, iniquitous, scandalous 11 disgraceful, infuriating, unspeakable, unwarranted 12 contemptible, contemptuous, exasperating, preposterous, unreasonable 13 disrespectful, reprehensible 14 unconscionable

outrageousness 8 enormity 9 immensity 10 wickedness 13 atrociousness, monstrousness, offensiveness 16 preposterousness

outre 8 improper

outreach 6 exceed 7 surpass

outright 4 full 5 sheer, total, utter 6 at once, entire, openly 7 utterly, visibly 8 absolute, complete, entirely, patently, promptly, thorough 9 downright, forthwith, instantly, on the spot, out-and-out 10 absolutely, altogether, completely, manifestly, thoroughly, unreserved 11 immediately, unmitigated, unqualified 12 demonstrably, undiminished 13 thoroughgoing, unconditional

outrival 3 dim 5 excel, outdo 6 exceed 7 eclipse, surpass 8 outshine 9 transcend 10 overshadow, tower above

outrush 4 gust 8 overflow

outset 4 dawn 5 birth, start 7 dawning 9 beginning, departure, threshold 12 commencement

outshine 3 dim 5 excel, outdo 6 exceed 7 eclipse, surpass 9 transcend 10 overshadow

outside 4 case, face, skin 5 alien, faint, outer 6 facade, remote, sheath, slight 7 coating, distant, foreign, obscure, outdoor, outward, strange, surface 8 covering, exterior, external, outdoors 9 nonnative, outer side, outermost 10 extraneous, out-of-doors, unfamiliar

outsider 5 alien 7 outcast 8 onlooker, stranger 9 bystander, foreigner, nonmember 14 nonparticipant

outskirts 3 rim 4 edge 6 limits, verges 7 borders, fringes, margins, suburbs 8 environs 9 periphery, precincts 10 perimeters 11 extremities

outspoken 5 blunt, frank 6 candid, direct, honest 7 artless 9 guileless, ingenuous, unsparing 10 forthright, unreserved 11 opinionated, plainspoken 13 undissembling 15 straightforward, undissimulating

outspread 5 broad 6 opened, spread 7 laid out 8 expanded, extended, unfolded, unfurled, unrolled 9 spread out, stretched 12 outstretched

outstanding 3 due 5 famed, great, owing 6 famous, unpaid 7 eminent, notable, payable 8 foremost, renowned, striking 9 best known, exemplary, in arrears, marvelous, memorable, prominent, unsettled 10 celebrated, noteworthy, phenomenal, remarkable 11 exceptional, magnificent, uncollected 13 distinguished, extraordinary, unforgettable

outstrip 4 pass 6 exceed, outrun 7 outpace, surpass 11 leave behind

outward 5 outer 7 evident, outside, surface, visible 8 apparent, exterior, external, manifest 10 observable, ostensible 11 perceivable, perceptible, superficial

outward appearance 4 mien 6 aspect, facade, manner 7 bearing 8 demeanor, exterior

Outward Bound
   author: 10 Sutton Vane

outwardly 7 clearly, visibly 9 evidently, seemingly 10 apparently, manifestly, ostensibly 13 on the face of it 16 to all appearances

outwards 3 out 4 away

outweigh 6 exceed 7 eclipse, surpass 8 override 9 rise above 10 overshadow 11 predominate, prevail over 13 be heavier than, weigh more than

outwit 4 dupe, foil, fool, trap 5 trick 6 baffle, outfox, take in, thwart 7 ensnare 8 outsmart 9 get around 10 circumvent 11 outmaneuver

outworn 5 dated, passe 6 bygone 7 defunct, disused, extinct 8 obsolete, rejected 9 abandoned, discarded, forgotten, out-of-date 10 antiquated, superseded 12 old-fashioned 13 unfashionable

ouzo
   type: 7 liqueur
   origin: 6 Greece
   flavor: 5 anise
   substitute for: 8 absinthe

oval 5 ovate, ovoid 6 curved, ovular 7 obovate, oviform, rounded 9 egg-shaped 10 elliptical 11 ellipsoidal

ovation 6 cheers, homage, hurrah, hurray, huzzah 7 acclaim, fanfare, tribute 8 applause, cheering 9 adulation 11 acclamation

oven 3 umu 4 kiln, oast 5 baker, range, stove 6 hearth 7 broiler, chamber, kitchen, roaster
   clay: 7 tandoor
   fork: 7 fruggan, fruggin
   mop: 6 scovel

over 3 too 4 also, anew, done, else, gone, past 5 above, again, ended, extra, often 6 afresh, bygone, lapsed, no more, to boot 7 at an end, elapsed, expired, settled, surplus 8 finished, in excess, once more, too great 9 completed, concluded, excessive, remaining 10 additional, all through, in addition, passed away, repeatedly, terminated 11 a second time, superfluous

overabundance 4 glut 6 excess 7 surfeit, surplus 8 plethora 9 abundance, profusion 10 oversupply 11 superfluity 14 superabundance 15 supersaturation 21 embarrassment of riches
French: 19 embarras de richesses

over again 4 anew 5 again 7 all over 8 once more 9 once again

overall 5 total 6 entire 7 general 8 complete, long-term, sweeping 9 extensive, long-range, panoramic 10 exhaustive, widespread 12 all-embracing, all-inclusive 13 comprehensive, thoroughgoing

over-and-above 5 added, extra 7 added on, besides 10 additional, in addition 13 supplementary

overawe 6 dazzle 9 overpower, overwhelm 10 intimidate

overbalance 5 upset 6 topple 8 outweigh

overbearing 5 cocky 6 lordly, snooty 7 haughty, high-hat, pompous, stuck-up 8 arrogant, despotic, egoistic 9 conceited, imperious, know-it-all 10 autocratic, disdainful, egoistical, high-handed, tyrannical 11 dictatorial, domineering, egotistical 13 high-and-mighty, self-assertive, self-important

overburden 3 tax 4 load, task, tire 5 whelm 7 exhaust, wear out 8 encumber, overwork, surcharge 9 overwhelm

overcast 4 dark, dull, gray, hazy 5 foggy, misty, murky 6 cloudy, dreary, gloomy, leaden 7 sunless 8 lowering 11 overclouded, threatening

overcharge 3 gyp, pad 4 rook, skin, soak 5 bleed, cheat, gouge, stick, sting, usury 6 extort, fleece 7 exploit 10 exaggerate

overcoat 3 mac 5 parka 6 duster, poncho, raglan, tabard, ulster 7 oilskin, paletot, topcoat 8 burberry, mackinaw 9 greatcoat, inverness, pea jacket 10 mackintosh, trenchcoat 12 chesterfield, Prince Albert

Overcoat, The
author: 12 Nikolai Gogol
character: 9 Petrovich 26 A Certain Important Personage 28 Akakii Akakiievich Bashmachkin

overcome 4 beat, best, lick 5 crush, quell 6 defeat, master, subdue 7 conquer, put down, survive, win over 8 suppress, surmount, vanquish 9 overpower, overthrow, overwhelm, transcend 11 prevail over, triumph over 14 get the better of

overconfident 5 brash 6 cheeky 8 arrogant, cocksure, egoistic, immodest, impudent 9 conceited 10 egoistical 11 egotistical, self-assured 12 presumptuous

overcrowd 3 jam 4 cram, fill, pack 5 stuff 7 congest

overcrowded 6 filled, jammed, packed 7 crammed, stuffed 9 congested, jampacked

overdecorated 5 gaudy, showy 6 flashy, garish 9 unsightly 12 ostentatious

overdelicacy 11 genteelness, prudishness 12 priggishness 14 overrefinement

overdo 4 gild 6 expand 7 amplify, ham it up, magnify, overact 8 overplay 9 embroider, overstate 10 do to excess, exaggerate 11 carry too far, hyperbolize 12 lay it on thick 13 stretch a point

overdue 4 late, slow 5 tardy 7 belated, delayed, past due 8 dilatory 10 behindhand, behind time, unpunctual 11 long delayed

overdue debt 7 arrears 10 balance due 18 balance outstanding

overflow 4 glut 5 flood 6 excess 7 run over, surplus 8 flow over, inundate, plethora, slop over 9 overspill, profusion 10 overspread, oversupply 11 copiousness, superfluity 13 overabundance 14 superabundance

overflowing 4 full 5 flush 7 replete, swamped 8 abundant, flooding 9 abounding, inundated 11 running over

overgarment 4 cape, coat, robe 5 cloak, habit, parka, shawl, smock 6 blazer, blouse, duster, jacket, kimono, mantle, poncho 7 sweater, topcoat, wrapper 8 cardigan, raincoat 9 gaberdine, housecoat

overgrown 4 rank 5 giant 7 blown-up 8 colossal, enlarged, forested, gigantic 9 luxuriant, oversized

overhang 3 jut 4 eave 5 bulge, drape, eaves, jetty 6 beetle, impend, sadden, shelve 7 project, suspend 8 protrude, threaten 9 projection

overhaul 4 beat, pass 5 catch 6 revamp 7 rebuild, remodel, restore, service 8 overtake, renovate 11 catch up with, recondition, reconstruct

overhead 3 nut 4 atop, roof 5 above, aloft, on top, upper 6 upward 7 ceiling, topmost, up above 8 superior 9 overlying, uppermost 11 overhanging

overindulge 4 baby 5 spoil, stuff 6 overdo, pamper, pig out 7 carouse, overeat 9 dissipate 11 mollycoddle

overjoyed 6 elated, joyous 8 ecstatic, euphoric, exultant, jubilant, thrilled 9 delighted, enchanted, exuberant, gratified 10 enraptured, enthralled 11 carried away, tickled pink, transported 12 happy as a lark

overlay 4 coat 5 cover, layer 6 carpet, veneer 7 blanket, coating 8 covering 11 superimpose

overload 3 tax 4 glut 5 flood, whelm 6 deluge, excess 7 burnout, surfeit 8 encumber 9 innundate, surcharge

overlook 4 miss, omit, skip 6 excuse, forget, give on, ignore, pass up, slight, survey, wink at 7 blink at, command, forgive, let ride, neglect 8 leave out, look over, pass over, shrug off 9 disregard, look out on 10 tower above 11 forget about, have a view of, leave undone

overlord 4 czar, tsar 7 emperor, monarch 8 autocrat 12 supreme ruler 13 absolute ruler

overly 3 too 4 very 6 highly, unduly 7 acutely, too much 8 overmuch, severely, to a fault, unfairly 9 extremely, intensely 10 needlessly 11 exceedingly, excessively 12 exorbitantly, immoderately, inordinately, unreasonably 18 disproportionately

overly trusting 5 naive 8 gullible 9 credulous 12 unsuspicious

overmodest 3 coy 4 prim 7 prudish 8 priggish 11 puritanical

overmuch 3 too 6 excess 7 surplus 8 plethora 9 profusion

overpass 4 span 6 bridge 9 crossover

overpower 4 beat, best, move, sway 5 crush, quell, worst 6 defeat, master, subdue 7 conquer 8 overcome, vanquish 9 influence, overwhelm

overpowering 6 mighty, strong 8 crushing 10 astounding 12 overwhelming

overpraise 4 line 7 blarney, fawning 8 flattery 11 fulsomeness

overpriced 6 costly 7 too high 9 expensive 10 exorbitant

overproud 4 vain 8 arrogant, egoistic 9 conceited 10 egoistical 11 egotistical, swell-headed 13 self-important

overrate 9 overprize, overvalue 10 overesteem, overpraise 12 overestimate 13 make too much of

overrefined 7 genteel, prudish 8 priggish 12 overdelicate

override 5 crush, quash 7 reverse 8 set aside 10 commission 11 countermand

overrule 4 veto, vote 5 annul, eject, repel, waive 6 cancel, refuse, reject, revoke 7 dismiss, nullify, outvote 8 disallow, outweigh, override, overturn, preclude, set aside, throw out 9 repudiate 10 invalidate 11 countermand

overrun 4 loot, raid, sack 5 choke 6 deluge, engulf, infest, invade 7 despoil, pillage, plunder, surplus 8 inundate, overgrow, pour in on, rove over 9 overwhelm, surge over, swarm over

overseas, oversea 5 alien 6 abroad, exotic 7 foreign 8 external 11 ultramarine 12 transoceanic 14 in foreign lands

oversee 3 run 4 boss, rule 5 guide, pilot, see to, steer, watch 6 direct, govern, handle, manage 7 carry on, command 8 attend to, overlook, regulate 9 supervise 10 administer 11 keep an eye on, preside over, superintend 12 have charge of

overseeing 7 bossing, guiding, running 8 guidance, handling, managing 9 leadership, management 11 attending to, supervising, supervision 13 administering 14 administrating, administration, superintending 15 superintendence

overseer 4 boss, head 5 chief 7 captain, foreman, manager 8 director, governor 10 supervisor, taskmaster 11 slave driver 13 administrator 14 superintendent

overshadow 3 fog 4 hide, mask, veil 5 cover, dwarf, shade 6 darken, screen, shroud 7 conceal, eclipse, obscure 8 outshine 9 tower over

overshadowing 7 eclipse, masking, shading, veiling 8 cloaking 9 darkening, eclipsing, obscuring 10 concealing, surpassing

11 concealment, obscuration 12 towering over

overshoe 3 gum 4 boot 6 arctic, gaiter, galosh, patten, rubber 7 galoshe

overshoot 4 pass 6 exceed, go over 8 go beyond

oversight 6 laxity, slight 7 blunder, mistake, neglect 8 omission 9 disregard 10 negligence 11 inattention 12 carelessness, heedlessness, inadvertence 13 careless error 14 neglectfulness 15 thoughtlessness

oversized 4 huge, vast 7 immense, mammoth 8 colossal, enormous, gigantic 10 monumental 14 Brobdingnagian

overspending 12 extravagance, throwing away

overspread 3 fog 4 coat, fill, pave 5 bathe, cloud, cover, paint, plate, smear 6 clothe, infest 7 blanket, diffuse, overlay, overrun, pervade, suffuse 8 disperse 9 whitewash

overstate 6 overdo, play up 7 enlarge, inflate, lay it on, magnify, stretch, touch up 8 increase, overdraw, oversell 9 embellish, embroider, enlarge on, overpaint 10 exaggerate, overstress 15 spread it on thick

overstep 6 exceed 7 violate 10 transgress

oversupply 4 glut 6 excess 7 surfeit, surplus, too much 8 plethora 11 undue amount 13 overabundance 14 superabundance

overt 4 open 5 plain 6 public 7 evident, obvious, visible 8 apparent, manifest, palpable, revealed 10 easily seen, noticeable, observable, ostensible 11 perceivable, perceptible, unconcealed, undisguised

overtake 4 go by, pass 5 catch, reach 6 befall, gain on 7 run down 8 approach, overhaul 11 catch up with

overtax 4 tire 5 abuse, hoist 6 burden, exceed, strain, stress 7 exhaust 8 overload, overwork 9 misemploy 10 overburden

over the hill 3 old 4 aged 5 aging 7 elderly 11 past the peak 13 past one's prime

overthrow 4 undo 5 crush 6 defeat, mutiny, topple 7 abolish, undoing 8 downfall, overcome, overturn, toppling 9 abolition, bring down, overpower, rebellion 10 do away with, revolution

overtire 3 fag 4 bush, do in, poop 5 drain 7 exhaust, fatigue, wear out 8 enervate

overtone 3 hue 4 hint 5 drift 8 coloring, innuendo 10 intimation, suggestion 11 connotation, implication, insinuation

overtrustful 8 gullible 9 credulous 12 unsuspecting, unsuspicious 13 unquestioning

overture 3 bid 6 motion, signal, tender 7 advance, gesture, preface, prelude 8 approach, foreword, offering, preamble, prologue, proposal 9 beginning 10 invitation, suggestion 11 opening move, proposition 12 introduction

overturn 4 beat, oust 5 crush, upend, upset 6 defeat, depose, thrash, topple 7 capsize, conquer, turn out 8 overcome, push over, vanquish 9 knock down, knock over, overpower, overthrow, overwhelm **14** turn topsy-turvy, turn upside down

overturning
   French: 14 bouleversement

overweening 5 bossy, cocky, pushy **6** brassy **7** haughty, pompous **8** arrogant, egoistic **9** bigheaded, imperious **10** disdainful, egoistical, high-handed, immoderate **11** domineering, egotistical, overbearing, patronizing **12** presumptuous **13** high-and-mighty, overconfident, self-important

overweight 3 fat **5** dumpy, fatty, gross, hefty, obese, piggy, plump, pudgy, stout, tubby **6** chubby, chunky, fleshy, portly, rotund **7** fattish, well-fed **8** roly-poly **9** corpulent **10** potbellied, well-padded **11** beer-bellied, overstuffed **15** well-upholstered

overwhelm 4 beat, bury **5** crush, quash, quell, swamp **6** defeat, engulf **7** conquer, overrun, stagger **8** bowl over, confound, inundate, overcome, vanquish **9** devastate, overpower, overthrow, subjugate

overwhelming 8 crushing **10** staggering **11** astonishing, devastating **12** overpowering

overwork 3 tax **4** task, tire, toil **5** labor **6** burden, strain **7** exhaust, overtax, wear out **9** misemploy **10** overburden

overwrought 4 wild **5** riled **6** touchy, uneasy **7** excited, nervous, ruffled **8** agitated, frenzied, inflamed, wild-eyed, worked up **9** perturbed, wrought up **10** distracted, highstrung **11** carried away, overexcited

Ovid
   author of: 6 Amores **7** Tristia **8** Heroides **11** Ars Amatoria **12** The Art of Love **13** Metamorphoses

ovule 3 egg, nit **4** germ, ovum **6** embryo **7** seedlet

ovum 3 egg **4** cell, germ, seed **5** spore **6** gamete **8** oosphere

owe 8 be in debt **11** be obligated **12** be beholden to, be indebted to

owed 3 due **5** owing **6** unpaid **9** in arrears **11** outstanding

Owen Marshall, Counselor at Law
   character: 11 Jess Brandon **12** Frieda Krause **15** Melissa Marshall
   cast: 9 Lee Majors **10** Arthur Hill **11** Joan Darling **17** Christine Matchett

owing 3 due **4** owed **6** unpaid **9** in arrears **11** outstanding

own 4 avow, have, hold, keep, tell **5** admit, allow, grant, yield **5** assent, concur, retain **7** concede, possess, private **8** disclose, maintain, personal **9** acquiesce, confess to, consent to, recognize **10** individual, particular **11** acknowledge

owner 6 holder, master **7** partner **8** landlady, landlord, mistress **9** copartner, landowner, possessor **10** landholder, proprietor **11** householder, titleholder **12** proprietress

own up to 5 admit **6** accept **7** confess **8** blurt out **9** recognize **11** acknowledge **14** come clean about

ox 3 oaf **4** bull, clod, musk, urus, zebu **5** aiver, beast, bison, gayal, steer **6** auroch, bantin, bovine **7** banteng, buffalo **10** clodhopper
   Cambodian: 7 Kouprey, Kouproh
   Celebesian: 3 goa, noa **4** anoa
   extinct: 4 urus **7** aurochs
   family: 7 bovidae
   genus: 3 bos
   horned: 4 reem
   hornless: 4 moil
   Indian: 4 gaur
   Paul Bunyan's: 4 Babe
   color: 4 blue
   stall: 4 crib
   team: 4 yoke
   Tibetan: 3 yak
   wild: 3 ure **4** anoa
   young: 4 stot **5** stirk

Ox-Bow Incident, The
   author: 21 Walter Van Tilburg Clark
   character: 5 Canby, Croft **6** Davies, Gerald, Martin, Tetley **9** Gil Carter
   director: 14 William Wellman
   cast: 10 Henry Fonda **11** Dana Andrews **12** Anthony Quinn **13** William Blythe **14** Mary Beth Hughes

oxen
   group of: 4 yoke

oxide 8 compound
   afterburn: 4 calx
   calcium: 4 calx, lime
   cobalt: 6 zaffer, zaffre
   element: 6 oxygen
   iron: 4 rust **8** hematite, limonite **9** colcothar, magnetite
   make by heat: 7 calcine
   sodium: 4 soda
   zinc: 6 cadmia

oxidize 4 burn, char, rust **7** corrode

Oxyderces
   epithet of: 6 Athena
   means: 10 bright-eyed

oxygen
   chemical symbol: 1 O

Oxylus
   origin: 8 Aetolian
   punishment: 5 exile
   chosen leader of: 10 Heraclidae
   led invasion of: 12 Peloponnesus

oyez 4 hear **6** attend
   cry used by: 10 court crier
   preceded: 12 proclamation

Ozark Jubilee
   host: 8 Red Foley **10** Webb Pierce
   theme: 12 Sugarfoot Rag

Ozark State
   nickname of: 8 Missouri

Ozick, Cynthia
   author of: 10 Levitation **17** The Cannibal Galaxy **21** The Messiah of Stockholm

Ozzie and Harriet, The Adventures of
   cast: 11 David Nelson, Ozzie Nelson, Ricky (Eric) Nelson **13** Harriet Nelson

P

pa 3 dad, paw, pop 4 papa 5 daddy 6 father
mate: 2 ma

pace 4 clip, flow, gait, rate, step, walk 5 amble, speed, tread 6 motion, stride, stroll 7 saunter 8 momentum, slow gait, velocity

Pacelli, Eugenio Maria Giuseppe Giovanni 11 Pope Pius XII

pachyderm 5 hippo, rhino 8 elephant, ungulate 10 rhinoceros 12 hippopotamus
characteristic: 4 tusk 5 ivory, trunk 12 thick-skinned
prehistoric: 7 mammoth 8 mastodon

pachydermatous 4 hard 5 horny, tough 7 callous 8 callused, hardened, leathery 12 thick-skinned 13 elephant-hided

pacific 4 calm 5 quiet, still 6 gentle, placid, serene, smooth 7 halcyon, restful 8 dovelike, peaceful, tranquil 9 pacifying, peaceable, reposeful, unruffled 10 harmonious, untroubled 11 inoffensive, undisturbed 12 conciliatory

pacification 8 soothing 11 appeasement, peacemaking 12 conciliation, nonagression 14 reconciliation

pacify 4 calm 5 allay, quiet 6 soothe 7 appease, assuage, compose, mollify, placate 9 reconcile 10 conciliate, propitiate

Pacino, Al
real name: 13 Alberto Pacino
born: 9 New York NY
roles: 7 Serpico 8 Scarface 12 Author Author, The Godfather 15 Dog Day Afternoon, Michael Corleone 16 And Justice for All

pack 3 box, jam, kit, lot, mob, set, tie 4 bevy, bind, cram, fill, heap, herd, load, mass 5 batch, bunch, clump, covey, crowd, drove, flock, group, horde, stuff, swarm, truss 6 bundle, gaggle, gather, packet, parcel, passel, throng 7 cluster, package 8 assemble 9 container, multitude 10 assortment, collection, miscellany 12 accumulation

package 3 box, kit 4 case, pack, wrap 6 bundle, carton, encase, packet, parcel, wrap up 9 container, wrappings

packed 4 full 6 filled, jammed, loaded, massed, rammed, wedged 7 crammed, crowded, crushed, pressed, stuffed 8 overfull, squeezed 10 sandwiched 11 overcrowded

packet 3 bag, box 4 bale, pack, roll 5 pouch, sheaf 6 bundle, parcel, quiver 7 package

pack closely 4 cram, pack 5 press, stuff 7 compact 8 compress

pact 4 bond 6 treaty 7 compact 8 alliance, contract, covenant 9 agreement, concordat 10 convention 11 concordance 13 understanding

pad 3 mat 4 fill 5 stuff 6 blow up, fatten, tablet 7 bolster, cushion, inflate, protect, puff out 8 mattress, notebook 9 upholster 10 cushioning, stretch out

padding 6 filler, lining 7 filling, packing, surfeit, surplus, wadding 8 stuffing, verbiage, wrapping 9 prolixity, verbosity, wordiness 10 redundancy 11 verboseness 12 extravagance 14 superabundance

Paderewski, Ignace (Ignacy Jan)
born: 6 Poland 9 Kurilowka
composer of: 5 Manru 9 Minuet in G

pad out 5 add to 6 expand, extend 7 amplify, augment, enlarge, stretch out 8 elongate, increase, lengthen

padre 6 cleric, father, priest 8 chaplain 9 clergyman

paean 6 anthem, eulogy 7 hosanna 9 laudation, panegyric 10 hallelujah 11 acclamation 12 hymn of praise
form: 4 hymn, song
characteristic: 6 joyful 12 thanksgiving

Paeon
form: 3 god
position: 9 physician
served gods of: 7 Olympia
corresponds to: 6 Apollo

Paeonia
epithet of: 6 Athena
means: 6 healer

Paezan
language family: 13 Macro-Chibchan
group: 4 Paez 5 Choco 6 Warrau 8 Colorado

pagan 7 atheist, heathen, infidel 8 idolator 9 barbarian 10 heathenish, idolatrous, polytheist, unbeliever 11 nonbeliever 12 polytheistic

Paganini, Niccolo
born: 5 Genoa, Italy
played: 6 violin
composer of: 19 The Carnival of Venice

page 3 boy, lad 4 beep, call, girl, leaf 5 folio, groom, sheet, youth 6 knight, number, summon 7 callboy, contact 8 announce 9 attendant, messenger 10 apprentice, manservant
blank: 7 flyleaf
left-hand: 5 verso
right-hand: 5 recto

Page, Geraldine
born: 12 Kirksville MO
husband: 7 Rip Torn
roles: 5 Hondo 9 Interiors 11 Pete-n-Tillie

14 Summer and Smoke **16** A Trip to Bountiful (Oscar), Sweet Bird of Youth

Page and Mistress Page
   characters in: **22** The Merry Wives of Windsor
   author: **11** Shakespeare

pageant 4 pomp, rite, show **6** parade, ritual **7** display **8** ceremony **9** spectacle **10** exhibition, procession **12** extravaganza

pageantry 4 pomp, rite, show **5** drama, flair **6** ritual, splash **7** display, glitter, pageant **8** ceremony, grandeur, splendor **9** showiness, spectacle, theatrics **10** flashiness **11** ostentation **12** extravagance, magnificence

Paget, James
   field: **7** surgery **8** medicine
   nationality: **7** British
   founder of: **9** pathology

Pagliacci, I
   also: **9** The Clowns
   opera by: **11** Leoncavallo
   character: **5** Canio, Nedda, Tonio **6** Silvio

Pagnol, Marcel
   author of: **5** Cesar, Fanny **6** Marius, Topaze

Pago Pago
   capital of: **13** American Samoa

Paige, Leroy
   nickname: **7** Satchel
   sport: **8** baseball
   position: **7** pitcher

pain 3 vex, woe **4** ache, gall, hell, hurt, pang, rile **5** agony, annoy, chafe, grief, pinch, pique, smart, sting, throb, worry **6** aching, grieve, harass, misery, ordeal, sadden, sorrow, stitch, twinge **7** agonize, anguish, disturb, hurting, malaise, sadness, torment, torture, trouble **8** distress, smarting, soreness **9** displease, heartache, suffering **10** affliction, discomfort, exasperate, heartbreak **11** unhappiness **12** wretchedness

Paine, Thomas
   author of: **9** The Crisis **11** Common Sense **14** The Rights of Man

painful 3 sad **4** dire **5** sharp **6** aching, dismal, dreary, trying **7** arduous, hurtful, racking **8** grievous, grueling, pathetic, piercing, smarting, stinging, very sore **9** agonizing, difficult, sorrowful, throbbing, torturous **10** afflictive, disturbing, lamentable, unpleasant **11** disquieting, distasteful, distressful, distressing **12** disagreeable, excruciating

pain in the neck 4 bane **6** bother **7** torment **8** headache, nuisance **9** annoyance **10** affliction

painstaking 5 fussy **7** careful, earnest, finicky, precise **8** diligent, exacting, thorough **9** assiduous, energetic, strenuous **10** meticulous, scrupulous **11** industrious, persevering, punctilious **13** conscientious, thoroughgoing

paint 4 coat, daub, draw, limn, swab, tint **5** adorn, brush, color, cover, horse, rouge, shade, stain **6** depict, enamel, makeup, opaque, sketch **7** pigment, portray, stipple, touch up **8** cosmetic, decorate, describe, variegate **9** delineate, represent

Painted Bird, The
   author: **13** Jerzy Kosinski

painter 6 artist, drawer **8** sketcher **9** old master **10** delineator **11** illustrator, landscapist, miniaturist **13** watercolorist

Painter, Painter's Easel
   constellation of: **6** Pictor

painting 3 art, oil **5** draft, mural, piece **6** canvas, design, tablet **7** cartoon, daubing, drawing, graphic, picture, picture **8** panorama, portrait, seascape **9** depiction, landscape, still life **10** cerography, watercolor **11** perspective **12** illustration
   colloidal: **7** tempera
   method: **9** encaustic
   on plaster: **5** secco **6** fresco
   one-color: **8** monotint **10** monochrome
   opaque: **7** gouache
   religious: **5** Pieta
   style: **5** genre
   tool: **5** brush, easel, knife **6** canvas, roller, sponge **7** palette **8** spraygun

pair 3 duo **4** dyad, mate, span, team, yoke **5** brace, match, unite **6** couple **7** combine, doublet, match up, pair off, twosome

pair off 10 go two by two **11** form couples

Paiute
   language family: **10** Shoshonean
   tribe: **12** Mono-Paviosto, Snake Indians **13** Digger Indians **14** Northern Paiute, Southern Paiute
   location: **4** Utah **5** Idaho **6** Nevada, Oregon **7** Arizona **10** California

Pakistan
   name means: **13** Land of the Holy, Land of the Pure
   capital: **9** Islamabad
   largest city: **7** Karachi
   others: **3** Dir, Sui **4** Mari, Sidi **5** Dacca, Qasim, Ralat **6** Chalna, Khulna, Lahore, Multan, Quetta **7** Larkana, Sialkot **8** Jamalpur, Lyallpur, Peshawar, Sargodha **9** Hyderabad **10** Gujranwala, Rawalpindi
   school: **9** U of Punjab **10** U of Karachi **12** U of Hyderabad **16** Allama Iqbal Open U **22** Pakistan U of Agriculture **39** Pakistan Institute of International Affairs
   division: **3** Dir **4** Sind, Swat **5** Hunza, Kalat **6** Bengal, Kharan, Punjab **7** Chitral **8** Khairpur, Peshawar **10** Bahawalpur, Waziristan **11** Baluchistan
   empire: **5** Gupta, Mogul **6** Kushan, Maurya **7** British, Magadha
   seceded state: **10** Bangladesh
   monetary unit: **4** anna, pice **5** paisa, rupee
   weight: **4** seer, tola **5** maund
   mountain: **3** Pab, Pub **4** Salt **6** Makran **7** Kirthar **8** Himalaya, Safed Koh, Sulaiman **9** Hindu Kush, Karakoram **11** Makran Coast **13** Central Makran **14** Takht-i-Sulaiman
   highest point: **9** Tirich Mir **12** Godwin Austin

river: 3 Nal 4 Bado, Beas, Ravi, Swat, Zhob 5 Dasht, Indus, Kabul 6 Chenab, Ganges, Jamuna, Jhelum, Kundar, Porali, Sutlej 7 Jamunna
sea: 7 Arabian
physical feature:
bay: 8 Soymiani
canal: 4 Nara 5 Rohri
cape: 5 Fasta, Jaddi 6 Jiwani
delta: 6 Ganges 11 Char-Manpura
desert: 4 Sind, Thal, Thar
mountain pass: 5 Bolan 6 Khyber
plateau: 11 Baluchistan
valley: 5 Kohat
people: 5 Sindi, Wazir 6 Afridi, Bengal, Mahsud, Pathan, Sindhi 7 Baluchi, Brahuis, Puktuns, Punjabi, Sherani 8 Khattack, Pushtuns, Shinwari, Yusefazi 11 Mohammedzai
leader: 6 Jinnah 7 Aly Khan 8 Ayub Khan, Zia Ul-Haq 9 Ali Bhutto, Yahya Khan 13 Benazir Bhutto, Mujibur Rahman 15 Mahmud of Ghaznbi
poet: 5 Iqbal, Iqbal
language: 4 Urdu 6 Pushtu, Sindhi 7 Baluchi, Bengali, English, Punjabi
religion: 5 Hindu, Islam 8 Buddhism 12 Christianity
place:
dam: 6 Mangla 7 Tarbela
gardens: 8 Shalamar
mosque: 8 Badshahi
tomb: 15 Emperor Jahangir
feature:
clothing: 5 kurta, pugri, qamis 6 jinnah 7 dupatta, shalwar 8 sherwani 9 churidars
food:
bread: 8 chappati
dish: 5 kebab, pilaf 6 qormas, salans, sautes 10 vermicelli
yogurt: 4 dahi
Pakula, Alan
director of: 19 All the President's Men
pal 4 chum, mate, pard 5 buddy, crony 6 cohort, friend 7 comrade, partner 8 alter ego, intimate, sidekick 9 associate, colleague, companion, confidant 10 accomplice, bosom buddy 13 boon companion
palace 5 villa 6 castle 7 chateau, mansion 8 hacienda
French: 6 palais
Italian: 7 palazzo
Palaeoscincus
type: 8 dinosaur 10 ornithopod
location: 12 North America
period: 10 Cretaceous
palais 6 palace 17 municipal building 18 government building
Palamedes
lieutenant of: 9 Agamemnon
pal around 7 consort, hang out 9 associate, be friends, run around 10 fraternize
palatable 5 tasty 6 savory 8 pleasant 9 agreeable, toothsome 10 appetizing
palatial 6 posh, rich 5 grand, noble, plush, regal, ritzy, showy 6 swanky 7 elegant, opulent, stately 8 imposing, splendid 9 gran-

diose, luxurious, sumptuous 10 monumental 11 magnificent
palaver 3 gab 4 chat, talk 5 prate 6 confer, gossip, parley 7 consult, discuss, prattle 8 chitchat, idle talk 10 chew the fat, chew the rag, conference, discussion
palazzo 6 palace
pale 3 pen, wan 4 fold, post 5 ashen, close, light, pasty, stake, white 6 anemic, blanch, paling, pallid, picket, sallow, whiten 7 closure, confine, deathly, ghastly, upright, whit ish 8 bleached, palisade 9 bloodless, colorless, deathlike, enclosure, ghostlike 10 ash-colored, cadaverous, light-toned
Pale Horse, Pale Rider
author: 19 Katherine Anne Porter
paleness 6 pallor 7 wanness 8 dullness 9 whiteness 13 colorlessness
paleontology
study of: 18 correlation of parts
founder: 13 Georges Cuvier
Palermo
capital of: 6 Sicily
Pales
origin: 5 Roman
protector of: 6 flocks 9 shepherds
festival: 7 Parilia
Palestine see 6 Israel
Palestrina, Giovanni Pierluigi da
born: 5 Italy 10 Palestrina
composer of: 11 Stabat Mater 18 Missa Papae Marcelli
Paley, Grace
author of: 26 The Little Disturbances of Man 30 Enormous Changes at the Last Minute
Palici
origin: 5 Roman
form: 4 gods 5 twins
gods of: 14 sulphur springs
Palilicium see 6 Hyades
paling 4 pale, rail 5 fence, stake 6 picket
Palinurus
steersman of: 6 Aeneas
palisade 5 close, fence 7 bulwark, rampart 8 stockade 9 enclosure
palisades 4 crag 5 ledge 6 bluffs, cliffs 10 escarpment, promontory
pall 4 cloy, haze, sate 5 gloom, weary 6 shadow, sicken 7 dimness, satiate 8 darkness 10 become dull, be tiresome, depression, desolation, melancholy, moroseness, oppression
Palladio, Andrea
real name: 26 Andrea di Pietro della Gondola
architect of: 12 Villa Rotunda (Vicenza Italy) 14 Teatro Olimpico (Vicenza) 19 Church of Il Redentore (Venice) 26 Church of San Giorgio Maggiore (Venice)
style: 9 Palladian
Pallas see 6 Athena
Pallas Athena see 6 Athena
pallet 3 bed, cot 4 bunk, tick 5 berth 8 mattress, platform

palliate 4 calm, curb, ease, hush, lull, tame 5 abate, allay, check, quiet, sooth, still 6 lessen, modify, reduce, soften, subdue, temper 7 assuage, comfort, cushion, lighten, relieve 8 decrease, diminish, minimize, mitigate, moderate 9 alleviate 10 ameliorate

palliative 4 balm 6 solace 7 anodyne, comfort 10 comforting

pallid 3 wan 4 ashy, blah, dull, pale 5 ashen, bland, pasty, vapid, waxen 6 boring, chalky, peaked, sallow 7 ghostly, humdrum, insipid, tedious 8 blanched, lifeless 9 bloodless, colorless 10 monotonous 13 anemic looking, unimaginative, uninteresting

pallor 7 wanness 8 paleness 9 pastiness, whiteness 10 ashen color, pallidness 11 ghostliness 13 bloodlessness, colorlessness

palm
varieties: 3 Fan, Ita, Key, Nut, Oil, Wax 4 Cane, Date, Doom, Doub, Doum, Fern, Hair, Hemp, King, Lady, Nipa, Nypa, Rock, Sago, Step, Tala, Wine 5 Areca, Areng, As sai, Betel, Black, Bread, Broom, Curly, Grass, Honey, Inaga, Ivory, Jelly, Latan, Manac, Nikau, Peach, Queen, Royal, Snake, Spine, Sugar, Syrup, Toddy, Yatay, Zombi 6 Bamboo, Barbel, Barrel, Bottle, Cherry, Cohune, Coyoli, Gebang, Gomuti, Gru-gru, Hesper, Kentia, Licuri, Manila, Mazari, Needle, Nibung, Parlor, Pignut, Raffia, Rattan, Ruffle, Sagisi, Sentry, Silver, Thatch, Thread, Yellow 7 Arikury, Cabbage, Calappa, Coconut, Coquito, Feather, Fiji fan, Funeral, Jaggery, Leopard, Mexican, Moriche, Overtop, Palmyra, Prickly, Spindle, Talipot, Weddell 8 Betel nut, Carnauba, Cucurite, Dwarf fan, Fishtail, Good luck, Ivory-nut, Mangrove, Pandanus, Peaberry, Princess, Roebelin, Umbrella, Wild date, Windmill 9 Alexander, Alexandra, Butterfly, Christmas, Desert fan, Gippsland, Guadalupe, Hurricane, India date, Macarthur, Ouricouri, Panama-hat, Petticoat, Piccabeen, Porcupine, Pygmy date, Silver saw, Solitaire, Spiny-club, Traveler's 10 African oil, Black-fiber, Canary date, Chinese fan, Cuban belly, Cuban royal, Everglades, Franceschi, Saw cabbage, Sealing-wax, Thatch-leaf, Washington 11 American oil, Chilean wine, European fan, Gingerbread, Mexican blue, Morass royal, Senegal date, Slender lady, Woolly butia 12 Caribee royal, Egyptian doum, Florida royal, Miniature fan, Walking-stick 13 Australian fan, Australian ivy, Australian nut, Belmore sentry, Feather-duster, Florida silver, Florida thatch, Forster sentry, Golden feather, Miniature date, San Jose hesper 14 Common princess, East Indian wine, Puerto Rican hat, Tufted fish tail, Yellow princess 15 Burmese fishtail, Chinese fountain, Chinese windmill, Yellow butterfly 16 Hispaniolan royal, Northern bangalow, Puerto Rican royal 17 Australian cabbage, Clustered fishtail, Mexican Washington, Piccabeen bangalow 18 South American royal

Palm Beach Story, The
director: 14 Preston Sturges
cast: 9 Mary Astor 10 Joel McCrea, Rudy Vallee 15 William Demarest 16 Claudette Colbert

Palmer, Arnold
sport: 4 golf
noted for: 10 Arnie's Army

Palmer, Lilli
real name: 17 Lillie Marie (Maria Lilli) Peiser
born: 5 Posen 7 Germany
husband: 11 Rex Harrison 14 Carlos Thompson
roles: 11 Body and Soul
autobiography: 22 Change Lobsters and Dance

Palmer, Vera Jane
real name of: 14 Jayne Mansfield

Palmetto State
nickname of: 13 South Carolina

Palm Sunday
author: 12 Kurt Vonnegut

palmy 4 rosy 5 balmy, sunny 6 golden 7 booming, halcyon 8 blooming, pleasant, thriving 9 agreeable, bounteous, congenial 10 prosperous, successful 11 flourishing, pleasurable

Palmyra
Biblical name: 6 Tadmor

palpable 5 clear, plain 7 evident, obvious, tactile, visible 8 apparent, definite, distinct, feelable, manifest, tangible 9 touchable 10 noticeable 11 discernible, perceivable, perceptible 12 recognizable, unmistakable

palpitate 4 beat 5 pound, shake, throb 6 quaver, quiver, shiver 7 flutter, tremble, vibrate 9 go pit-a-pat

palsied 7 quaking, shaking, spastic 9 trembling

palsy-walsy 5 close, palsy, thick 6 chummy 8 friendly, intimate 10 buddy-buddy 14 thick as thieves

paltriness 10 triviality 12 unimportance 14 insignificance 18 inconsequentiality

paltry 4 poor, puny 5 petty, sorry 6 measly, shabby 7 scrubby, trivial 8 inferior, picayune, piddling, trifling, wretched 11 unimportant 13 insignificant, of little value 14 inconsiderable 15 inconsequential

Pama-Nyungan
language spoken by: 10 aborigines
spoken in: 9 Australia

Pamela
author: 16 Samuel Richardson
character: 3 Mr B 9 Mrs Jervis, Mrs Jewkes 10 Lady Davers 13 Pamela Andrews

pamper 5 humor, spoil 6 coddle, cosset 7 cater to, indulge 8 give in to 11 mollycoddle

pampered 7 coddled, humored 8 indulged 9 catered to, cossetted

pamphlet 5 tract 6 folder 7 booklet, leaflet 8 brochure, bulletin, circular 9 monograph, throwaway

pan 3 boo, map, mug, pot 4 face, hiss 6 kisser 8 ridicule, saucepot 9 criticize

Pan
  also: 7 Sinoeis
  origin: 5 Greek
  form combined: 3 man 4 goat
  god of: 6 flocks 7 forests 8 pastures 9 shepherds
  father: 4 Zeus 6 Hermes
  loved: 4 Echo 5 Pitys 6 Syrinx
  invented: 5 pipes 6 syrinx
  corresponds to: 6 Faunus

panacea 6 elixir 7 cure-all, nostrum 13 universal cure

panache 4 dash, tuft 5 flair, plume, style, verve 11 flamboyance

Panama
  capital/largest city: 10 Panama City
  others: 4 Daid 5 Ancon, Colon 6 Azuero, Balboa, Gamboa 8 Dos Bocas, Penonome, Santiago 9 Cristobal 10 Portobello
  division: 5 Cocle, Colon 6 Darien, Panama 7 Herrera 8 Chiriqui, Veraguas 9 Los Santos 12 Bocas del Toro
  measure: 7 celemin
  monetary unit: 4 cent 6 balboa 10 centesimos
  island: 5 Coiba, Pearl 6 Cebaco, Multas, Taboga 7 San Blas 10 Isla Del Rey 12 Bocas del Toro, Juan Gallegos 13 Barro Colorado
  lake: 5 Gatun
  mountain: 4 Baru, Maje 5 Chico, Gandi 6 Darien 7 Columan, San Blas, Veragua 8 Santiago, Tabasara 13 Costa Rican 14 Serrania de Sapo 15 Aspave Highlands 17 Cordillera Central
  highest point: 8 Chiriqui
  river: 5 Chepo, Sambu, Tuira 6 Bayano, Panugo 7 Chagres
  sea: 7 Pacific 9 Caribbean
  physical feature:
  bay: 5 Limon 6 Panama
  dam: 5 Gatun
  gulf: 6 Darien, Panama, Parita 7 Montijo, San Blas 8 Chiriqui 9 Mosquitos, San Miguel
  isthmus: 6 Darien, Panama 7 San Blas
  lagoon: 8 Chiriqui
  peninsula: 6 Azuero 8 Valjente
  people: 4 Cuna 5 Choco 6 Guaymi 7 mestizo
  canal builder: 7 Lesseps
  explorer: 6 Balboa 8 Bastidas, Columbus
  leader: 4 Royo 5 Arias 7 Noriega 8 Guerrero, Torrijos 9 Espriella 12 Simon Bolivar
  poet: 4 Miro 5 Korsi, Sinan
  language: 7 English, Spanish
  religion: 13 Roman Catholic

place:
  church: 7 San Jose 15 Virgen del Carmen
  plaza: 13 Independencia
  ruins: 9 Old Panama
  feature:
  clothing: 7 montuno, pollera
  dance: 4 caja 7 pujador 9 tamborito
  tree: 4 yaya 5 maria, quira 6 alfaje, cativo
  US operation: 9 Just Cause
  food:
  meat: 6 tazajo
  soup: 8 sancocho

Panama City
  capital of: 6 Panama

pancake 4 blin 5 blini, crepe, kisra, latke, lefse 6 blintz, makeup 7 fritter, hotcake 8 flapjack, slapjack 11 griddlecake 12 silverdollar
  day: 13 Shrove Tuesday

Pancks
  character in: 12 Little Dorrit
  author: 7 Dickens

pancreas
  produces: 7 insulin

Pandareus
  father: 6 Lycaon, Merops
  daughter: 5 Aedon 6 Merope 9 Cleothera
  wounded: 8 Menelaus
  stole: 9 golden dog
  turned to: 5 stone
  killed by: 8 Diomedes

Pandarus
  character in: 18 Troilus and Cressida, Troilus and Criseyde
  author: 7 Chaucer 11 Shakespeare

Pandarus
  son: 7 Alcanor
  companion of: 6 Aeneas

pandemic 4 rife 7 rampant 8 epidemic 10 prevailing, widespread 21 dangerously contagious

pandemonium 3 din 5 chaos 6 bedlam, clamor, hubbub, racket, rumpus, tumult, uproar 7 turmoil 8 disorder 9 commotion 10 hullabaloo 11 disturbance

Pandemos
  epithet of: 9 Aphrodite

pander, panderer 4 mack, pimp 5 cadet 7 hustler 8 procurer 9 maquereau, souteneur 12 flesh-peddler

Pandion the Younger
  king of: 6 Athens
  later reigned in: 6 Megara

Pandora
  form: 10 first woman
  created by: 10 Hephaestus
  presented to: 10 Epimetheus
  daughter: 6 Pyrrha
  given by gods: 3 box
  box contained: 4 hope 5 evils

Pandrosos
  position: 9 priestess
  first priestess of: 6 Athena
  father: 7 Cecrops
  mother: 8 Agraulos

panegyric 6 eulogy, homage, praise **7** tribute **8** citation, encomium, good word **9** extolment, laudation **10** compliment **11** testimonial **12** commendation

panegyrize 4 laud **5** extol **6** praise **8** eulogize

panel 4 jury, pane **5** board, group, piece **6** insert **7** divider **8** bulkhead **9** committee, partition **10** round table **11** compartment, expert group, select group **13** advisory group

pang 4 ache, pain **5** agony, pinch, smart, stick, sting, throb **6** stitch, twinge **7** anguish **8** distress **9** suffering **10** discomfort

Pangloss
   character in: 7 Candide
   author: 8 Voltaire

pang of conscience 5 demur, qualm **6** unease **7** remorse, scruple **9** misgiving **10** uneasiness **11** compunction

panhandle 3 beg, bum **5** cadge, mooch **6** hustle **7** solicit **9** importune

Panhandle State
   nickname of: 12 West Virginia

Panhellenius
   epithet of: 4 Zeus
   means: 14 god of all Greeks

panic 5 alarm, dread, go ape, scare **6** fright, horror, terror **7** anxiety **8** affright, hysteria **9** cold sweat, confusion, fall apart **10** go to pieces **11** nervousness, trepidation **12** apprehension, perturbation **13** consternation

panicky 6 scared **7** alarmed, anxious **9** terrified **10** frightened **13** panic-stricken, scared to death **14** terror-stricken

panic-stricken 6 afraid, scared **7** alarmed, anxious, fearful, panicky **9** terrified **13** scared to death **14** terror-stricken

Panjabi
   language family: 12 Indo-European
   branch: 11 Indo-Iranian
   group: 5 Indic
   spoken in: 5 (northern) India

Pankrits
   language family: 12 Indo-European
   branch: 11 Indo-Iranian
   form of: 5 Indic
   followed use of: 8 Sanskrit

pannier 3 bag **4** hoop **6** basket, dossel, pantry **7** corbeil, drapery **9** framework, overskirt
   literally: 11 breadbasket

Panomphaeus *see* **4** Zeus

Panopeus
   father: 6 Phocus
   mother: 7 Asteria
   twin brother: 6 Crisus

Panoptes
   epithet of: 5 Argus
   means: 7 all eyes

panorama 3 scene, vista **6** survey **7** diorama, picture, scenery, tableau **8** long view, overview, prospect **10** scenic view **11** perspective **12** bird's-eye view

panoramic 3 ide **7** overall **8** bird's-eye, extended, sweeping **9** extensive **10** far-ranging **11** far-reaching **12** all-embracing, all-inclusive **15** all-encompassing

pansy 5 Viola
   varieties: 4 Wild **5** Field **6** Garden, Orchid **8** Japanese **9** Miniature **11** Monkey-faced **12** European wild

pant 4 blow, gasp, huff, puff **6** wheeze

pant after 4 seek **5** covet, crave **6** desire, pursue **7** hope for, long for, lust for, wish for **8** yearn for **9** hanker for, hunger for, lust after **11** thirst after, have a yen for **14** set one's heart on

Pantagruel *see* **22** Gargantua and Pantagruel

panther 3 cat **6** cougar **7** leopard

Panthous
   priest of: 6 Apollo
   counselor of: 5 Priam
   father: 6 Othrys
   son: 9 Euphorbus, Hyperenor, Polydamas

Pantomime Quiz
   host: 10 Mike Stokey **15** Pat Harrington Jr

pantry 5 ambry, store **6** closet, galley, larder **7** butlery, buttery, pannier, spicery **8** cupboard, scullery

pants 5 jeans **6** denims, shorts, slacks **7** drawers, panties **8** breeches, britches, knickers, trousers **9** bluejeans, dungarees **10** underpants **11** undershorts **12** underdrawers

pantywaist 4 wimp **5** sissy, softy **7** crybaby, milksop **8** mama's boy, weakling **10** namby-pamby, sissy-pants, weak sister **11** Milquetoast, mollycoddle **13** sissy-britches

Panurge
   character in: 22 Gargantua and Pantagruel
   author: 8 Rabelais

Panza, Sancho
   character in: 10 Don Quixote
   author: 9 Cervantes

pap 3 rot **4** bosh, junk, mash, mush, pulp, tosh **5** gruel, paste **6** cereal, drivel, Pablum, trivia **7** rubbish, twaddle **8** soft food **10** balderdash, flapdoodle, triviality

papa 2 pa **3** dad, doc, paw, pop **5** daddy, poppy **6** father, priest **9** Hemingway
   mate: 4 mama

Papa Bear
   nickname of: 11 George Halas

Papago
   language family: 5 Piman **10** Uto-Aztecan
   location: 6 Mexico **7** Arizona
   related to: 4 Pima

papal 9 apostolic, of the pope **10** pontifical

Papaleo, Anthony
   real name of: 16 Anthony Franciosa

paper 4 bond, deed, news, opus, pulp, work **5** daily, draft, essay, stock, theme **6** record, report, tissue, weekly **7** article, gazette, journal, monthly, tabloid, writing **8** document, gift wrap **9** cardboard, chroni-

cle, newspaper, newsprint, onionskin 10
instrument, manuscript, paperboard, periodical, stationery, typescript 11 certificate,
com position, publication

Paper Chase, The
   character: 10 James T Hart, Willis Bell
   13 Asheley Brooks 14 Elizabeth Logan,
   Jonathan Brooks 15 Franklin Ford III 19
   Thomas Craig Anderson 29 Professor
   Charles W Kingsfield Jr
   cast: 10 James Keane 11 Robert Ginty
   12 Deka Beaudine, John Houseman 13
   James Stephens, Jonathan Segal 14
   Francine Tacker, Tom Fitzsimmons
   subject: 9 law school
   Kingsfield's specialty: 11 contract law
paper measure 4 ream 5 quire
Paper Moon
   director: 16 Peter Bogdanovich
   cast: 9 Ryan O'Neal 10 Tatum O'Neal 12
   Madeline Kahn (Trixie Delight) 13 John
   Hillerman
   Oscar for: 17 supporting actress
   (O'Neal)
Paphian see 9 Aphrodite
Paphos
   also: 6 Paphus
   father: 9 Pygmalion
   mother: 7 Galatea
Paphus see 6 Paphos
Papua New Guinea
   formerly: 16 British New Guinea
   capital: 11 Port Moresby
   town: 3 Thu, Lae 4 Ioma 6 Kikori,
   Madang
   province of: 9 Indonesia
   province: 9 West Irian
   monetary unit: 4 kina
   island: 6 Misima 10 New Britain
   archipelago: 8 Bismarck
   lake: 6 Murray
   river: 3 Fly 4 Ramu
   sea: 5 Coral 7 Solomon
   strait: 6 Torres
   people: 4 Hula, Kate 5 Kiwai, Kwoma 6
   Banaro 7 Arapesh 10 Melanesian
   language: 7 English
papyrus 4 pith, reed 5 paper, sedge 6
   scroll 7 bulrush 8 document 10 manuscript
   accordion pleated: 6 orihon
   genus: 7 Cyperus
   origin: 5 Egypt 9 Nile delta 10 Nile valley
   use: 3 mat 4 rope, shoe, sail 5 paper
par 5 level, usual 6 normal, parity 7 average, balance, the norm 8 equality, evenness, identity, sameness, standard 9 stability 11 equilibrium, equivalency 12 equal
   footing 13 identicalness
parable 4 myth, tale 5 fable, story 6 homily,
   legend 8 allegory, apologue, folk tale 9 folk
   story 12 morality tale
Paracelsus
   author: 14 Robert Browning
parade 4 line, pomp, show 5 array, march,
   strut, train, vaunt 6 column, defile, flaunt,
   review, string 7 caravan, cortege, display, show off 8 vaunting 9 cavalcade,

flaunting, march past, motorcade, pageantry, put on airs, spectacle 10 exposition, grandstand, procession 11 progression 13 demonstration

paradigm 5 ideal, model 6 matrix, sample 7
   example, paragon, pattern 8 exemplar,
   original, standard 9 archetype, criterion,
   prototype, yardstick
paradise 3 joy 4 Eden 5 bliss 6 heaven,
   utopia 7 delight, ecstasy, nirvana, rapture
   8 pleasure 9 enjoyment, happiness,
   Shangri-la, transport 11 happy valley 12
   Garden of Eden, satisfaction 13 gratification, seventh heaven 15 Land of Cockaigne
Paradise 5 Annwn 6 Annfwn
Paradise
   also: 9 Paradisio
   part three of: 12 Divine Comedy
   author: 14 Dante Alighieri
Paradise Lost
   author: 10 John Milton
   character: 3 Eve, God 4 Adam 5 Satan 6
   Christ 7 Lucifer
Paradise of the Pacific
   nickname of: 6 Hawaii
Paradise Regained
   author: 10 John Milton
paradisiacal 7 elysian, sublime 8 blissful,
   empyreal, empyrean, ethereal, heavenly 9
   celestial, unearthly 12 otherworldly
paradox 5 poser 6 enigma, oddity, puzzle,
   riddle 7 anomaly 11 incongruity 13 inconsistency
paradoxical 9 ambiguous, enigmatic, equivocal 13 contradictory
paragon 4 norm 5 ideal, model 6 symbol 7
   example, pattern 8 exemplar, paradigm,
   standard 9 archetype, criterion, prototype,
   yardstick 10 apotheosis
Paraguay
   capital/largest city: 8 Asuncion
   others: 3 Ita 4 Rica, Yuty 5 Belen,
   Luque, Pilar, Villa 7 Caacupe 8 Trinidad 9
   Paraguari 10 Concepcion, Villarrica 11
   Encarnacion 26 Puerto Presidente
   Stroessner
   division: 6 Guaira, Itapua, Olimpo 7
   Caazapa 8 Boqueron 10 Concepcion
   measure: 3 pie 4 lino, lira, lire, vara 5
   legua 6 cuadra, fanega
   monetary unit: 4 peso 7 guarani, centimo
   weight: 7 quintal
   island:
     floating island: 8 camalote
   lake: 4 Vera, Ypoa 8 Ypacarai
   river: 3 Apa 5 Guazu, Negro, Plata,
   Verde, Ypane 6 Acaray, Parana 7
   Aguaray, Confuso 8 Paraguay 9 Aquida-
   ban, Pilcomayo, Tebicuary, Tibiquare 10
   Monte Lindo 14 Riacho Gonzales 15
   Riacho Mosquitos
   physical feature:
     falls: 6 Guaira
     plains: 5 Chaco
     plateau: 6 Parana

people: 6 Abipon, Moskoi 7 Guarani, mestizo 8 Guayaqui
artist: 7 Bestard
author: 3 Pla 4 Baez 6 Alcala, Bastos, Correa, O'Leary 7 Cervera 8 Casaccia
composer: 8 Asuncion
leader: 5 Lopez 7 Francia 10 Stroessner 16 Antequera y Castro
sculptor: 8 Guggiari
language: 6 German 7 Guarani, Spanish
religion: 9 Mennonite 13 Roman Catholic
place:
church: 10 Villarrica 11 Incarnation
dam: 6 Itaipu
memorial: 16 Pantheon of Heroes
museum: 5 Godoi
palace: 10 Government
feature:
animal: 4 puma 5 tapir 6 iguana, jaguar 7 peccary
bird: 6 toucan
clothing: 5 fajas, typoi 6 poncho 7 rebozos 9 bombachas 10 alpargatas
communes: 11 reducciones
dance: 7 Sante Fe 15 Paraguayan polka
fish: 7 piranha
lace: 7 nanduti
music: 8 quarania
townspeople: 9 comuneros
tree: 5 ceiba 7 lapacho 9 quebracho
food:
bread: 5 chipa, mbeyu
dish: 12 sopa paraguay
tea: 9 yerba mate
vegetable: 8 mandioca
parallel 4 akin, like, same, twin 5 alike, equal, match 6 follow 7 abreast, analogy, be alike, similar 8 analogue, likeness, relation 9 alongside, analogous, corollary, duplicate 10 collateral, comparable, comparison, concurrent, connection, equivalent, similarity 11 coextensive, coincidence, comparative, compare with, correlation, correlative, counterpart, equidistant, resemblance 12 correspond to 13 corresponding 14 correspondence
parallelism 8 affinity, likeness, sameness 9 agreement 10 comparison, similarity, similitude 11 resemblance 14 correspondence
parallelogram 5 rhomb 6 square 7 diamond, rhombus 8 rhomboid 9 rectangle 11 plane figure 13 quadrilateral
paralyze 4 stun 6 benumb, deaden, disarm, freeze, weaken 7 cripple, destroy, disable, petrify, stupefy, wipe out 8 demolish, enfeeble 10 debilitate, immobilize, neutralize 12 incapacitate
Paramaribo
capital of: 8 Suriname
paramount 4 main 5 chief 6 utmost 7 capital, highest, leading, premier, supreme 8 cardinal, dominant, foremost, greatest, peerless, superior 9 essential, principal, unmatched 10 preeminent 11 outstanding, predominant 12 incomparable, preponderant, transcendent

paramour 3 man 4 doxy 5 lover, Romeo 6 gigolo 7 Don Juan 8 Casanova, fancy man, lothario, loverboy, mistress 9 boyfriend, concubine, courtesan, inamorata, inamorato, kept woman 10 girlfriend, lady friend, sugar daddy
paranoid 4 wary 7 deluded 9 paranoiac 11 distrustful 14 oversuspicious
parapet 7 bulwark, rampart 8 abutment, palisade 9 barricade, earthwork 10 battlement, breastwork
paraphernalia 3 rig 4 gear 5 stuff 6 outfit, tackle, things 7 effects, harness, regalia 8 fittings, material, supplies, utensils 9 apparatus, equipment, trappings 10 belongings, implements, properties, provisions 11 accessories, furnishings 13 accoutrements
paraphrase 5 recap 6 rehash, reword 7 restate 8 rephrase 12 recapitulate
Parasaurolophus
type: 8 dinosaur 10 ornithopod
location: 6 Canada
period: 10 Cretaceous
parasite 5 leech 6 beggar, cadger, loafer 7 moocher, shirker, slacker, sponger 8 deadbeat 9 goldbrick, scrounger 10 freeloader 11 bloodsucker
inside host: 12 endoparasite
outside host: 12 ectoparasite
parasol 5 shade 6 shadow 7 roundel 8 sunshade, umbrella
mushroom: 7 lepiota
par avion 5 by air
parboil 4 boil 5 scald 6 blanch 7 precook
Parca
origin: 5 Roman
member of: 6 Parcae
goddess of: 7 destiny 10 childbirth
Parcae see Fates
parcel 3 lot 4 bale, pack, part, plot 5 allot, piece, tract 6 bundle, divide, packet 7 carve up, deal out, dole out, package, portion, section, segment, split up 8 allocate, dispense, disperse, division, fraction, fragment, property 9 allotment, allowance, apportion, partition 10 distribute 11 piece of land
parceling out 9 allotment, doling out, meting out 10 allocation, assignment, dealing out 12 distribution 13 apportionment
parcel out 5 allot 7 dole out, give out, mete out 8 allocate, dispense, divide up 9 apportion 10 distribute, portion out
parch 4 bake, burn, char, sear 5 dry up, singe 6 dry out, scorch, sun-dry, wither 7 blister, shrivel 9 dehydrate, dessicate, evaporate
parched 3 dry 4 arid 6 barren 8 withered 9 shriveled 10 dehydrated, desiccated
parchment 6 scroll, vellum 7 papyrus 8 goatskin 9 sheepskin
pardon 5 grace, mercy 6 excuse, wink at 7 absolve, amnesty, blink at, forbear, forgive, indulge, release, set free 8 overlook, reprieve, shrug off 9 discharge, disregard, exculpate, exonerate, remission, vindicate 10 absolution, indulgence 11 deliverance,

exculpation, forbearance, forgiveness 12
grant amnesty 16 forgive and forget

Pardoner
  character in: 18 The Canterbury Tales
  author: 7 Chaucer

pare 3 cut, lop 4 clip, crop, dock, hull, husk,
peel, skin, trim 5 lower, prune, shave,
shear, shell, shuck, slash, strip 6 lessen,
reduce, shrink 7 curtail, cut back 8 decrease, diminish 11 decorticate

pare down 3 cut 4 trim 5 shave 6 reduce 7
abridge, curtail, cut down, shorten 8 condense, cut short, diminish 10 abbreviate

parent 3 dam 4 sire 5 model 6 father,
mother 7 creator 8 ancestor, begetter, exemplar, original, producer 9 precursor,
prototype 10 antecedent, forerunner, originator, procreator, progenitor 11 predecessor

parentage 5 birth, roots, stock 6 family, origin, strain 7 descent, lineage 8 ancestry,
forbears, heredity, pedigree 9 ancestors,
genealogy 10 background, derivation, extraction, family tree 11 antecedents

Parentalia
  origin: 5 Roman
  event: 8 festival

parenthetical 5 aside 6 braced, casual 8
inserted 9 bracketed 10 extraneous, immaterial, incidental, interposed, irrelevant
11 impertinent, intervening, superfluous

par excellence 8 superior 10 preeminent

parfait d'amour
  type: 7 liqueur
  flavor: 7 violets
  color: 6 purple

Paria
  form: 5 nymph
  loved by: 5 Minos
  children: 7 Chryses 9 Eurymedon,
  Nephalion, Philolaus

pariah 5 exile, rover, stray 6 outlaw, roamer
7 outcast 8 vagabond, wanderer 10 expatriate 11 undesirable, untouchable

paring 4 chip, snip 5 scrap, shred, slice 6
sliver 7 cutting, peeling, shaving 8 fragment

pari passu 6 fairly 7 equably 10 side by
side 13 equal progress 17 without partiality

Paris
  airport: 4 Orly 9 Le Bourget 15 Charles
  de Gaulle
  area: 5 Passy 6 Clichy, Marais, Ternes,
  Wagram 7 Auteuil 8 Chaillot, Gobelins,
  Left Bank, St Honore 9 Les Halles, Right
  Bank, St Germain 10 Montmartre, Rive
  Droite, Rive Gauche, Val de Grace 11 Ile
  de la Cite 12 Hotel de Ville, Latin Quarter,
  Montparnasse
  capital of: 6 France
  city planner: 9 Haussmann
  island: 10 Ile St Louis 11 Ile de la Cite
  landmark: 8 Pantheon 9 Notre Dame 10
  Paris Opera, Sacre Coeur 11 Eiffel Tower,
  La Madeleine, Palais Royal 12 Elysee
  Palace, Hotel de Ville, Place Vendome 13
  Arc de Triomphe, Palais Bourbon 14 Bois

de Boulogne, Place de l'Etoile, Pompidou
  Center, Sainte Chapelle, Tomb of
  Napoleon 15 Bois de Vincennes 16 Lux-
  embourg Palace 17 Hotel des Invalides,
  Place de la Bastille, Place de la
  Concorde 18 Jardin des Tuileries 20
  Place Charles de Gaulle
  nickname: 11 city of light
  river: 5 Seine
  street: 9 Haussmann, Invalides 10 Grand
  Armee 11 Saint Michel 12 Montparnasse,
  Saint Germain 13 Champs Elysees 15
  Charles de Gaulle
  subway: 5 Metro
  university: 8 Sorbonne

Paris
  character in: 14 Romeo and Juliet
  author: 11 Shakespeare

Paris
  position: 6 prince
  father: 5 Priam
  mother: 6 Hecuba
  brother: 6 Hector 9 Polydorus
  sister: 9 Cassandra
  wife: 6 Oenone
  abducted: 5 Helen
  judgment of: 14 apple of discord
  awarded apple to: 9 Aphrodite
  killed by: 11 Philoctetes

parish 4 fold 5 flock, shire 6 canton, county
7 diocese, section 8 brethren, district, precinct, province 9 community, pastorate 10
department 11 archdiocese 12 congregation, neighborhood

parity 7 balance 8 equality, sameness 10
coequality, uniformity 11 equivalence,
equivalency 14 correspondence

park 4 lawn 5 field, green, grove, woods 6
common, meadow, square 7 grounds, reserve 8 parkland, preserve, woodland 9
grassland, sanctuary 10 public park, quadrangle

Parker, Dorothy
  author of: 9 Big Blonde 10 Enough Rope
  13 Death and Taxes 18 After Such
  Pleasures 19 Laments for the Living

Parkman, Francis
  author of: 30 France and England in
  North America

parkway 6 avenue 9 boulevard 12 thoroughfare

parlance 4 talk 5 idiom, lingo 6 speech 16
manner of speaking

Parlement of Fowles, The
  author: 15 Geoffrey Chaucer

parley 4 talk 6 confab, powwow, summit 7
council, meeting, palaver 8 conclave 9 discourse, mediation, peace talk 10 conference, discussion 11 arbitration, negotiation
12 conversation

parliament 4 diet 5 court, house, junta 6
fan-tan, senate, sevens 7 cabinet, council
8 assembly, congress 9 high court 11 legislature 12 three estates
  Communist: 6 Soviet 9 politburo, presid-
  ium

estate: 12 House of Lords **14** House of Commons
Germanic: 9 Bundesrat, Bundestag, Bolksraad **11** Volkshammer
Greek: 5 Boule
Icelandic: 7 Althing
Israeli: 7 Knesset **8** Knesseth
Scandinavian: 7 Lagting, Riksdag **8** Lagthing, Storting **9** Odelsting, Storthing
Spanish: 6 Cortes

parlor 5 salon **6** saloon **8** best room **9** front room **10** living room **11** drawing room, sitting room

Parnopius
epithet of: 6 Apollo
means: 9 locust god

parochial 5 local, petty, small **6** church, little, narrow, parish **7** insular, limited **8** regional **9** hidebound, illiberal, religious, sectional, small-town **10** provincial, restricted **11** countrified **12** narrow-minded

parodos
from Greek drama: 9 choral ode

parody 5 mimic **6** satire **7** lampoon, takeoff **8** satirize, travesty **9** burlesque, take off on **10** caricature

Parolles
character in: 20 All's Well That Ends Well
author: 11 Shakespeare

paroxysm 3 fit **5** spasm, spell **7** seizure **10** convulsion

parrot 3 ape **4** bird, echo, lory **5** macaw, mimer, mimic **6** chorus, monkey **7** copycat, imitate **8** cockatoo, imitator, parakeet **9** reiterate

parry 4 duck, shun **5** avert, avoid, dodge, elude, repel **7** beat off, fend off, repulse, ward off **8** sidestep, stave off **10** circumvent, fight shy of

Parsifal
opera by: 6 Wagner
character: 6 Kundry **8** Amfortas, Klingsor **9** Gurnemanz

Parsifal Mosaic, The
author: 12 Robert Ludlum

parsimonious 5 close, tight **6** frugal, saving, stingy **7** miserly, sparing, thrifty **9** niggardly, penurious **10** economical, ungenerous **11** closefisted, tightfisted **13** money-grubbing, penny-pinching

parsimony 6 thrift **7** economy **8** meanness **10** stinginess **13** niggardliness **15** tightfistedness

parsley 19 Petroselinum crispum
varieties: 5 Horse **7** Chinese, Italian **12** Turnip-rooted
related herb: 4 dill **5** cumin **6** fennel
garland worn by: 8 Hercules
gives speed to: 6 horses
use in: 11 fines herbes **12** bouquet garni

parson 5 clerk, padre **6** cleric, divine, father, pastor, priest, rector **7** dominie **8** minister, preacher, reverend, shepherd, sky pilot **9** clergyman
French: 4 abbe, cure

parsonage 5 glebe, manse **7** deanery, rectory, Vatican **8** vicarage **9** pastorate

part 2 go **3** bit, job **4** care, chip, duty, hunk, item, open, rend, role, slit, task, tear, unit **5** break, chore, crumb, guise, leave, piece, place, scrap, sever, shard, share, sherd, shred, slice, split **6** branch, charge, cleave, depart, detach, detail, divide, go away, member, morsel, region, sector, set out, sliver, sunder **7** concern, cutting, disjoin, element, portion, push off, section, segment, snippet **8** breakoff, business, capacity, disguise, disunite, division, fraction, fragment, function, separate, set forth, start out **9** character, component, disengage, go one's way **10** assignment, break apart, department, disconnect, get up and go, ingredient, mosey along, say good-bye **11** be on one's way, call it quits, constituent, subdivision

partake 5 enjoy, savor, share **6** join in, sample **7** share in **8** engage in **11** participate

part from 5 leave **9** break with **12** separate from

Parthenia
epithet of: 6 Athena
means: 6 virgin

Parthenius *see* **9** Plexippus

Parthenopaeus
father: 10 Hippomenes
mother: 8 Atalanta
member of: 18 Seven against Thebes

Parthenope
form: 5 siren

Parthenos
means: 6 virgin

partial 6 biased, unfair, unjust **7** limited, slanted **8** one-sided, partisan **9** factional **10** fractional, incomplete, interested, prejudiced, subjective, unbalanced, unfinished **11** fragmentary, inequitable, predisposed, uncompleted **12** inconclusive, prepossessed

partiality 4 bent, bias, love, tilt **5** fancy, slant, taste **6** choice, liking **7** leaning **8** affinity, fondness, penchant, tendency, weakness **9** prejudice **10** attraction, favoritism, preference, proclivity, propensity **11** inclination **12** one-sidedness, partisanship, predilection **14** predisposition

partially 6 in part, partly **7** partway **8** somewhat **9** piecemeal **12** fractionally, incompletely

participant 4 ally **5** party **6** cohort, fellow, helper, member, player, sharer, worker **7** partner **8** confrere, partaker **9** accessory, associate, colleague, performer **10** accomplice **11** contributor, shareholder **12** collaborator, participator

participate 5 share **6** join in **7** partake, perform **8** engage in, take part **9** play a part

particle 3 bit, jot **4** atom, iota, mite, snip, whit **5** crumb, grain, scrap, shred, speck, trace **6** morsel, tittle, trifle **7** granule, modicum, smidgen, snippet **9** scintilla

parti-colored 4 pied 5 plaid 6 motley 7 checked, dappled, mottled 8 colorful 9 checkered 10 variegated 11 many-colored 12 multicolored

particular 4 sole 5 exact, fixed, fussy, picky 6 single, strict 7 express, finicky, special 8 concrete, critical, definite, detailed, distinct, especial, exacting, explicit, itemized, personal, separate, specific 9 demanding 10 fastidious, individual, meticulous, scrupulous 11 painstaking, persnickety, punctilious, well-defined 12 hard to please

particularize 6 detail 7 itemize, specify 9 enumerate

particularly 6 mainly 7 notably 8 markedly 9 eminently, expressly, specially, supremely, unusually 10 definitely, distinctly, especially, explicitly, strikingly 11 principally, prominently 13 exceptionally 15 extraordinarily

particulars 5 facts, items 6 events 7 details 9 specifics 13 circumstances

parti pris 15 position decided 20 preconceived attitude

partisan 3 fan 4 ally 6 backer, biased, rooter, zealot 7 booster, devotee, partial, slanted 8 adherent, advocate, champion, follower, one-sided, upholder 9 guerrilla, insurgent, irregular, jayhawker, supporter 10 bushwacker, enthusiast, prejudiced, subjective, unbalanced 11 sympathizer

partition 4 wall 5 allot, fence, panel 6 assign, divide, screen 7 barrier, deal out, divider, mete out, parting, split up 8 allocate, bulkhead, dispense, disperse, dividing, division, separate 9 allotment, apportion, parcel out, separator, severance, splitting, subdivide 10 allocation, assignment, distribute, separation 11 demarcation, segregation 12 distribution, dividing wall 13 apportionment

partly 6 in part 7 part way 8 somewhat 9 not wholly, partially, to a degree 10 relatively 12 fractionally, incompletely 13 after a fashion, comparatively

partly open 4 ajar 5 agape 6 gaping 7 cracked 8 half-open, unclosed 9 squinting 10 half-closed

partner 3 aid, pal 4 ally, chum, mate, wife 5 aider, buddy 6 fellow, friend, helper, sharer, spouse 7 comrade, co-owner, husband 8 confrere, helpmate, partaker, sidekick, teammate 9 accessory, assistant, associate, colleague, companion, co-partner 10 accomplice, better half, joint owner 11 confederate, participant 12 collaborator

Partners, The
  author: 16 Louis Auchincloss

Parton, Dolly
  roles: 10 Nine to Five, Rhinestone 30 The Best Little Whorehouse in Texas

partridge
  group of: 5 covey

Partridge
  character in: 8 Tom Jones
  author: 8 Fielding

Partridge Family, The
  character: 13 Reuben Kinkaid 14 Danny Partridge, Keith Partridge, Tracy Partridge 15 Connie Partridge, Laurie Partridge 20 Christopher Partridge
  cast: 8 Susan Dey 11 David Madden 12 Brian Forster, David Cassidy, Shirley Jones 13 Danny Bonaduce, Suzanne Crough 14 Jeremy Gelbwaks
  song: 14 I Think I Love You

Parts of Animals
  author: 9 Aristotle

parturition 8 birth 8 delivery 10 childbirth 11 giving birth 12 childbearing

party 2 do 4 band, bash, body, crew, fete, gang, team, unit, wing 5 corps, force, group, squad 6 affair, at-home, league, soiree 7 accused, blow out, company, coterie, faction 8 alliance, claimant, conclave, litigant, wingding 9 appellant, coalition, defendant, festivity, gathering, plaintiff, reception 10 contestant, federation, petitioner, respondent 11 celebration, confederacy, get-together, participant, paticipator, perpetrator

party-pooper 4 drag 10 spoilsport, wet blanket

parvenu 4 snob 6 nobody 7 upstart 8 arriviste, mushroom 9 arriviste 12 nouveau riche

Pascal, Blaise
  nationality: 6 French
  invented: 7 syringe 13 adding machine 14 hydraulic press
  author of: 7 Pensees 19 Lettres provinciales 20 Essay pour les coniques

Pascin, Julius
  real name: 6 Pincas
  born: 5 Vidin 8 Bulgaria
  artwork: 6 Femmes 12 Les Deux Amies 17 Ginette et Mireille

Pasiphae
  father: 6 Helios
  mother: 7 Perseis
  husband: 5 Minos
  daughter: 7 Ariadne, Phaedra 9 Acacallis
  became enamored of: 10 Cretan bull
  mother of: 8 Minotaur

Pasithea
  member of: 6 Graces

Pasolini, Pier Paolo
  director of: 13 Arabian Nights

pass 2 go 3 cap, die, end, gap, hit, top, use, way 4 best, busy, fill, flow, give, go by, go on, hand, kick, lane, meet, toss 5 canal, exact, excel, gorge, gulch, leave, outdo, route, spend, throw, trail 6 accept, affirm, avenue, be over, canyon, convey, course, decree, depart, devote, elapse, employ, engage, exceed, expend, expire, finish, go away, go past, occupy, ordain, permit, pickle, plight, ratify, ravine, slip by, strait, take up, vanish 7 achieve, advance, approve, channel, confirm, consume, deliver, die away, eclipse, freebie, glide by, go ahead, let have, narrows, pathway, pre-

sent, proceed, qualify, satisfy, slide by, surpass **8** blow over, dissolve, exigency, fade away, furlough, go beyond, go onward, hand over, juncture, legalize, melt away, outshine, outstrip, passaway, peter out, progress, quandary, sanction, transfer, transmit, turn over **9** authorize, disappear, evaporate, extremity, hand along, legislate, situation, terminate **10** accomplish, difficulty, free ticket, get through, move onward, over shadow, passageway **11** predicament, proposition **12** complication, run its course, solicitation, stand the test **13** authorization **15** amorous overture
　French: 13 laissez passer

passable 4 fair, open, so-so **5** clear **6** not bad **8** adequate, fordable, mediocre, middling **9** allowable, crossable, navigable, tolerable **10** acceptable, admissible, pretty good **11** presentable, respectable, traversable **12** unobstructed

passage 3 way **4** hall, pass, path, road, tour, trek, trip **5** aisle, canal, piece, route, verse **6** access, clause, column, course, junket, tunnel, voyage **7** channel, chapter, hallway, journey, passing, portion, section, transit **8** approach, approval, corridor, movement, sanction, sentence **9** enactment, excursion, paragraph, selection, ship's excursion **10** acceptance, expedition, ordainment **11** affirmation, endorsement, legislation, progression **12** confirmation, legalization, ratification **13** authorization

passage out 4 exit **6** egress, outlet

Passages
　author: 10 Gail Sheehy

Passage to India, A
　author: 9 E M Forster
　character: 6 Dr Aziz **8** Mrs Moore **12** Adela Quested **13** Cecil Fielding, Ronald Heaslop **16** Professor Godbole
　setting: 11 Chandrapore **12** Marabar Caves
　director: 9 David Lean
　cast: 9 Judy Davis **12** Alec Guinness **13** Peggy Ashcroft **15** Victor Bannerjee
　Oscar for: 17 supporting actress (Ashcroft)

passageway 4 exit, hall, lane, path, walk **5** aisle **6** access, arcade, tunnel **7** doorway, gangway, gateway, hallway, passage **8** corridor, entrance, entryway, sidewalk **12** companionway

pass away 3 die **6** depart, expire, pass on, perish **7** decease **8** pass over **13** go to one's glory **14** give up the ghost

pass by 4 go by, pass **5** lapse **6** elapse, roll by, slip by **7** glide by, slide by **8** slip away

passe 4 past **5** faded, hoary, stale **6** demode, lapsed, quaint **7** ancient, antique, archaic, disused, outworn, retired **8** obsolete, outdated, outmoded **9** out-of-date **10** antiquated **11** prehistoric **12** antediluvian, old-fashioned, out of fashion **13** superannuated

passenger 4 fare **5** rider **8** commuter, stowaway, traveler, wayfarer

Passepartout
　character in: 26 Around the World in Eighty Days
　author: 5 Verne

pas seul
　ballet: 9 solo dance
　literally: 8 solo step

passim 12 here and there, repeated item

passing 5 brief, death, dying **6** demise, fickle **7** decease, passage **8** adequate, fleeting **9** enactment, ephemeral, momentary, temporary, transient **10** evanescent, expiration, not failing, short-lived, transitory **11** impermanent, legislating

passing the bounds of propriety
　French: 5 outre

passion 4 fire, idol, love, lust, rage, urge **5** ardor, craze, fancy, flame, gusto, heart, mania **6** desire, fervor, hunger, thirst, warmth **7** beloved, craving, ecstasy, emotion, feeling, rapture **8** loved one **9** carnality, eagerness, inamorata, intensity, obsession, sentiment, transport, vehemence **10** carnal love, enthusiasm **11** amorousness, earnestness, infatuation

passionate 3 hot **4** sexy **5** fiery **6** ardent, carnal, erotic, fervid, fierce, heated, loving, raging **7** amorous, earnest, excited, feeling, fervent, furious, intense, lustful **8** desirous, ecstatic, inflamed, sensuous, vehement **9** emotional, heartfelt, wrought-up **11** tempestuous **12** enthusiastic, intoxicating

passionfruit
　type: 7 liqueur
　origin: 6 Hawaii
　flavor: 5 peach

passionless 4 calm, cold **6** placid, serene **7** passive **8** tranquil **9** apathetic, unfeeling **10** spiritless **11** emotionless, indifferent, unemotional

Passion Play
　author: 13 Jerzy Kosinski

passive 5 inert **6** docile **7** dormant, patient, pliable **8** enduring, inactive, lifeless, listless, resigned, yielding **9** apathetic, compliant, impassive, quiescent, tractable **10** spiritless, submissive **11** acquiescent, unassertive, unresisting **12** nonresistant

passiveness 6 apathy **7** inertia **8** docility **10** quiescence **11** resignation **12** acquiescence, lifelessness **14** submissiveness **16** unresponsiveness

passivity 6 apathy **7** inertia **8** docility, meekness **11** resignation **12** complaisance, lifelessness **13** nonresistance **14** submissiveness

pass muster 2 do **5** serve **6** answer **8** be enough **10** be adequate **12** be sufficient **14** be satisfactory

pass on 3 die **6** depart, expire **7** decease **8** pass away **13** go to one's glory **14** give up the ghost, leave this world **15** breathe one's last

pass over 6 ignore, slight **7** neglect **8** overlook **10** brush aside

pass up 4 miss 6 ignore, refuse

password 3 key 4 word 6 by word, slogan 7 keyword, tessera 9 catchword, watchword 10 open sesame, secret word, shibboleth 11 countersign, passe-parole

Password
host: 11 Allen Ludden

past 2 by 4 gone 5 ended, prior 6 beyond, bygone, former, gone by 7 ancient, earlier, elapsed, expired, history, long ago, through 8 departed, finished, previous 9 antiquity, days of old 10 days gone by, days of yore, historical, olden times, passed away, yesteryear 11 dead and gone, former times, times gone by 12 ancient times

pasta 4 orzo, ziti 6 elbows, shells 7 gnocchi, lasagna, pastina, ravioli, rotelli 8 ditalini, linguini, macaroni, rigatoni, tortelli 9 canelloni, cavatelli, fettucine, manicotti, spaghetti 10 tortellini, vermicelli
ingredient: 3 egg 5 flour

past due 4 late 5 tardy 7 belated, overdue 9 in arrears 10 behindhand

paste 3 gum, hit 4 glue, seal, sock 5 affix, punch, stick 6 attach, cement 7 stickum 8 adhesive, mucilage

pastel 3 dim 4 pale, soft 5 chalk, faded, faint, light, muted 6 crayon 9 washed-out 13 coloring stick 14 coloring pencil

Pasternak, Boris
author of: 9 Dr Zhivago

Pasteur, Louis
field: 9 chemistry
nationality: 6 French
originated: 14 anti-rabies shot, pasteurization
founded: 12 microbiology
disproved: 21 spontaneous generation

pastime 3 fun 4 game, play 5 hobby, sport 9 amusement, avocation, diversion 10 relaxation 11 distraction 13 entertainment 14 divertissement

pastis
type: 7 liqueur
flavor: 8 licorice
substitute for: 8 absinthe

past one's prime 3 old 4 aged 5 aging 7 elderly 9 venerable 11 over the hill 12 in one's dotage

pastor 4 cure, dean 5 padre, vicar 6 cleric, father, parson, priest, rector 8 chaplain, minister, preacher 9 clergyman

pastoral 5 rural 6 rustic 7 bucolic, idyllic 8 arcadian, clerical, priestly 9 episcopal 10 sacerdotal 11 ministerial 14 ecclesiastical

Pastoral Symphony, The
author: 9 Andre Gide

pastorate 6 clergy 8 ministry, the cloth 10 priesthood

pastures
god of: 3 Pan 6 Dumuzi

pasty 3 wan 4 ashy, gray, pale 5 ashen, gluey, gooey, gummy, white 6 anemic, chalky, doughy, pallid, peaked, sallow, sticky 7 deathly, starchy 9 bloodless, color-less, ghostlike, glutinous, like paste 12 mucilaginous

pat 3 apt, dab, hit, pet, rap, tap 4 cake, daub, easy, glib, slap 5 exact, ideal, ready, slick, thump 6 caress, facile, fondle, simple, smooth, stroke, thwack 7 apropos, fitting, perfect, precise, reliant 8 flippant, suitable 9 contrived, pertinent, rehearsed

patch 3 fix, lot 4 area, darn, mend, plot, spot, zone 5 field, sew up, tract 6 garden, repair, stitch 7 expanse, stretch 8 clearing, insignia 9 reinforce 13 reinforcement

patchwork 4 hash, mess 6 jumble, medley, muddle, tangle 7 grab bag, melange, mixture 8 mishmash, mixed bag, pastiche, scramble 9 confusion, potpourri 10 hodgepodge, miscellany, salmagundi 11 gallimaufry 14 conglomeration, omnium-gatherum

pate 3 pie 4 brow, head 5 brain, crown, paste, pastry, patty, skull 6 noddle, noggin, noodle 9 meat paste

patella
bone of: 7 kneecap

patent 4 bald, bold, open, rank 5 clear, gross, overt, plain 6 permit 7 decided, evident, express, glaring, license, obvious 8 apparent, distinct, flagrant, manifest, palpable, registry, striking 9 copyright, downright, prominent 10 pronounced, unreserved 11 conspicuous, copyrighted, indubitable, self-evident, trademarked, transparent, unconcealed, undisguised 12 unmistakable 15 nonprescription

paterfamilias 6 father 17 father of the family, master of the family 20 master of the household

paternal 4 kind 6 tender 8 fatherly, parental, vigilant, watchful 9 concerned, indulgent 10 benevolent, fatherlike, interested, solicitous 11 patriarchal

Pater Patriae 18 father of his country

path 3 way 4 lane, plan, road, walk 5 byway, means, orbit, route, track, trail 6 access, by path, course 7 pathway, process, walkway 8 approach, footpath

pathetic 3 sad 6 moving, rueful, woeful 7 doleful, piteous, pitiful 8 dolorous, grievous, pitiable, poignant, touching, wretched 9 affecting, miserable, plaintive, sorrowful 10 deplorable, lamentable, to be pitied 11 distressing

Pathfinder, The
author: 19 James Fenimore Cooper
character: 9 Arrowhead, Dew-of-June 10 Charles Cap 11 Mabel Dunham, Natty Bumppo 12 Chingachgook 13 Jasper Western 14 Sergeant Dunham 18 Lieutenant Davy Muir

Pathfinders, The
author: 10 Gail Sheehy

pathogen 3 bug 4 germ 5 virus 7 microbe 8 bacillus 9 bacterium 13 microorganism

pathophobia
fear of: 7 disease

pathos 3 woe 5 agony 6 misery 7 anguish, feeling, sadness 8 distress 9 heartache, poignancy, sentiment 10 desolation 12 pitiableness 13 plaintiveness

Paths of Glory
director: 14 Stanley Kubrick
cast: 11 Kirk Douglas, Ralph Meeker 13 Adolphe Menjou

pathway 4 lane, path, road 5 alley, route, track 6 course 7 passage, walkway 8 footpath 10 passageway

patience 5 poise 7 stamina 8 industry, tenacity 9 composure, diligence, fortitude, restraint, tolerance 10 equanimity, resolution, sufferance 11 application, forbearance, longanimity, persistence, self-control 12 perseverance, tirelessness

Patience
author: 9 W S Gilbert

patient 4 case 6 dogged, serene 8 composed, diligent, enduring, resolute, tireless 9 dauntless, tenacious, undaunted 10 determined, forbearing, persistent, sick person, unflagging, unswerving, unwavering 11 industrious, persevering, unfaltering, unperturbed 13 indefatigable, long-suffering, uncomplaining

patio 4 deck 5 lanai, porch 6 piazza 7 terrace, veranda

patois 5 argot, idiom, lingo 6 jargon 7 dialect 10 vernacular

Paton, Alan
author of: 19 Too Late the Phalarope 20 Cry the Beloved Country 24 Ah but Your Land Is Beautiful

pat on the back 6 praise 7 plaudit 10 compliment 12 commendation

patriarch 5 elder, ruler 6 father, leader, old man 8 male head 9 chieftain 13 paterfamilias

patrician 4 lord, peer 5 noble 6 lordly 7 genteel, stately 8 highborn, imposing, noble man, princely, well-bred 9 blueblood, dignified, gentle man 10 aristocrat, upperclass 12 aristocratic, silk-stocking

patrimony 3 lot 5 dower, share 6 devise, estate, legacy 7 portion 8 bestowal, heritage, jointure 9 endowment 10 bequeathal, birthright 11 inheritance 12 hereditament

patriotism
Latin: 11 amor patriae

Patroclus
father: 9 Menoetius
mother: 8 Periapis
friend: 8 Achilles
killed by: 6 Hector

patrol 5 guard, scout, watch 6 ranger, sentry, warden 7 protect 8 sentinel 9 safe guard, walk a beat, watch man, watch over 10 stand watch

patron 5 angel, buyer 6 backer, client, friend, helper 7 habitue, shopper, sponsor, visitor 8 advocate, attender, champion, customer, defender, financer, promoter, upholder 9 protector, spectator, supporter 10 benefactor, encourager, frequenter,

well-wisher 11 sympathizer 12 benefactress 14 philanthropist

patronage 3 aid 4 help 5 favor, plums, trade 6 buying, custom, spoils 7 backing, charity, clients, dealing, support 8 advocacy, auspices, business, commerce 9 clientele, customers, fosterage 10 assistance, friendship, pork barrel, protection, purchasing 11 benefaction, sponsorship 12 philanthropy 13 encouragement

patronize 5 humor 6 shop at 7 buy from 8 deal with, frequent 9 trade with 10 condescend

patsy 4 dupe, pawn, tool 7 cat's-paw, fall guy

patter 3 pad, pat, rap, tap 4 beat, drum 5 pound, thrum 6 tattoo 7 rat-a-tat, spatter, tapping 8 drumming, sprinkle

pattern 4 copy, form, mold, plan 5 draft, guide, ideal, mimic, model, motif, shape 6 design, follow, sample 7 emulate, example, fashion, imitate, paragon 8 exemplar, original, paradigm, parallel, simulate, specimen, standard 9 archetype, criterion, duplicate, prototype 10 apotheosis, stereotype 12 illustration

Patton
director: 17 Franklin Schaffner
cast: 10 Karl Malden (Omar Bradley) 12 George C Scott (George Patton), Stephen Young 13 Michael Strong
Oscar for: 5 actor (Scott), story 7 picture 8 director 10 screenplay (Francis Ford Coppola and Edmund H North)

Patton, George S
nickname: 15 Old Blood and Guts
served in: 3 WWI 4 WWII 11 World War One, World War Two
commander of: 9 Third Army
invasion of: 8 Normandy 11 North Africa
capture of: 6 Sicily
battle: 5 Bulge
wore: 21 ivory-handled revolvers
memoirs: 12 War As I Knew It

Patty Duke Show, The
character: 7 Richard 8 Ross Lane 9 Cathy Lane, Patty Lane 10 Martin Lane 14 Natalie Masters
cast: 9 Jean Byron, Patty Duke 10 Paul O'Keefe 14 Eddie Applegate 16 William Schallert

paucis verbis 10 by few words, in few words 12 with few words

paucity 4 lack 6 dearth 7 fewness, poverty 8 exiguity, poorness, puniness, scarcity, shortage, sparsity, thinness 10 deficiency, meagerness, scantiness, scarceness 13 insufficiency

Paul
former name: 4 Saul
hometown: 6 Tarsus
teacher: 8 Gamaliel
companion: 5 Silas 7 Timothy 8 Barnabas, John Mark 9 Trophimus
cities visited: 4 Rome 5 Derbe, Perga, Troas 6 Lystra, Paphos 7 Antioch, Corinth, Ephesus, Iconium, Miletus, Salamis

8 Caesarea, Damascus, Neapolis, Philippi 9 Macedonia 12 Thessalonica
conversion place: 14 road to Damascus
wrote: 8 epistles

Paul Bunyan
author: 12 James Stevens
character: 9 Shanty Boy 10 Hels Helson 11 King Bourbon 12 Sourdough Sam 13 Babe the Blue Ox 14 Hot Biscuit Slim 16 Johnny Inkslinger

Pauli, Wolfgang
field: 7 physics
researched: 13 quantum theory
established: 14 Pauli principle 18 exclusion principle
awarded: 10 Nobel Prize

Paulina
character in: 14 The Winter's Tale
author: 11 Shakespeare

Pauling, Linus Carl
field: 12 biochemistry
worked on: 8 proteins 18 molecular structure
advocated: 8 Vitamin C
awarded: 10 Nobel Prize
awarded for: 9 peace 9 chemistry

paunch 3 gut, pot 5 belly, tummy 7 abdomen, stomach 8 potbelly 9 bay window, beer belly, spare tire 10 midsection 11 breadbasket, corporation

pauper 6 beggar 7 almsman 8 bankrupt, indigent 9 insolvent, mendicant 10 poor person, starveling 11 charity case 12 down-and-outer

pause 3 gap 4 halt, rest, stop, wait 5 break, cease, delay, let up 6 hiatus 7 interim, time out 8 break off, hesitate, interval 9 cessation, interlude 10 deliberate, suspension 12 intermission, interruption

pave 3 tar 4 face 6 cement 7 asphalt, surface 8 black top 9 resurface 10 macadamize

pavement 4 slab 5 brick 6 cement, hearth, street, tarmac 7 asphalt, cobbles, macadam 8 concrete, driveway, flagging, sidewalk 9 flagstone

pavilion 4 tent, ward, wing 5 arbor, kiosk 6 gazebo 7 pergola 9 bandshell 11 summerhouse

Pavlov, Ivan Petrovich
nationality: 7 Russian
researched: 9 digestion
studied: 20 behavior conditioning 21 Pavlovian conditioning
awarded: 10 Nobel Prize

paw 2 pa 3 dad, pop, toe 4 feel, foot, grab, hand, maul, mitt, papa 5 daddy, flail, touch 6 caress, clutch, father, handle, scrape, strike 7 rough up 8 forefoot 9 mishandle
mate: 3 maw

pawn 4 bond, dupe, hock, tool 5 agent, patsy 6 flunky, lackey, pledge, puppet 7 cat's-paw 8 borrow on, creature, guaranty, henchman, hireling, security 9 assurance, guarantee, underling 10 instrument 12 raise money on 14 give as security

pawnbroker
French: 11 mont-de-piete

Pawnbroker, The
director: 11 Sidney Lumet
cast: 10 Rod Steiger (Sol Nazerman) 11 Brock Peters 12 Jaime Sanchez 19 Geraldine Fitzgerald
setting: 6 Harlem

Pawnee (Chahiksichhiks)
language family: 7 Caddoan
location: 5 Texas 8 Nebraska, Oklahoma 9 New Mexico
related to: 7 Arikara
god: 6 Tirawa

Pawtuxet
location: 13 Massachusetts
leader: 7 Squanto

Pax
origin: 5 Roman
goddess of: 5 peace
corresponds to: 5 Irene

pax vobiscum 14 peace be with you

pay 3 fee 4 foot, give, meet 5 grant, honor, remit, repay, serve, wages, yield 6 ante up, chip in, extend, income, profit, render, return, salary, settle 7 benefit, bring in, cough up, payment, present, proffer, stipend 8 be useful, earnings, paycheck, shell out 9 bear fruit, liquidate, reimburse 10 come across, compensate, make good on, recompense 12 compensation 13 reimbursement

payable 3 due 4 owed 5 owing 6 mature, unpaid 8 to be paid 9 in arrears, spendable 10 demandable, expendable, receivable 11 outstanding

pay attention 4 heed, note 6 attend, notice 7 observe

Payaya
language family: 12 Coahuiltecan
location: 5 Texas

pay back 5 repay 7 counter, get even 9 reimburse, retaliate 10 recompense, remunerate 15 make restitution

pay for 6 redeem 7 expiate 8 atone for 9 answer for, suffer for 10 compensate, recompense, remunerate 13 make amends for 17 make reparation for

pay heed 6 notice 8 consider 11 concentrate 12 pay attention 13 put one's mind to

pay homage 5 defer, honor 7 acclaim 10 pay tribute

paying back 9 repayment 11 getting even 12 making good on 13 reimbursement

paymaster 6 bursar, purser 7 cashier 10 cashkeeper

payment 3 fee, pay 4 debt 6 outlay, paying, salary 7 premium 8 defrayal, spending 9 allowance, discharge 10 recompense, remittance, settlement 11 expenditure, installment, liquidation 12 compensation, contribution, disbursement, remuneration 13 reimbursement

pay no heed to 4 defy 6 ignore, slight 7 disobey, neglect, violate 8 overlook, pass over 9 disregard 10 brush aside, infringe on 14 shut one's eyes to 16 pay no attention to 17 transgress against

payoff 3 end 4 soap 5 bribe, graft 6 climax, crunch, finale, finish, grease, payola, result, upshot, windup 7 outcome 8 clincher 9 hush money 10 bottom line, conclusion, denouement, protection, resolution 11 culmination

pay off 5 bribe 6 buy off, suborn 13 grease the palm

payola 5 bribe, graft 6 grease, payoff

pay out 5 spend 6 expend, lay out 7 fork out 8 allocate, disburse, dispense, shell out 10 distribute

pay suit 3 woo 5 court 8 pay court

Payton, Walter
nickname: 9 Sweetness
sport: 8 football
position: 11 running back
team: 12 Chicago Bears

pay tribute to 4 laud, tout 5 boost, toast 6 praise, salute 7 applaud, commend 8 eulogize 10 compliment 16 sing the praises of

Payuga
tribe: 4 Agaz 6 Magach 7 Cadigue, Payagua, Sarigue, Siacuas, Tacumbu
location: 8 Paraguay 12 South America

pea 3 Pisum 12 Pisum sativum
varieties: 4 Flat, Love, Snow, Wild 5 Beach, Caley, Chick, Congo, Coral, Field, Glory, Green, Heart, Heath, Hoary, No-eye, Rough, Sugar, Sweet 6 Angola, Canada, Desert, Garden, Marble, Pigeon, Rosary, Scurfy, Winged, Winter 7 Catjang, Darling, English, Rabbit's, Seaside 8 Earthnut, Egyptian, Princess, Shamrock 9 Asparagus, Black-eyed, Butterfly, Chaparral, Jerusalem, Partridge, Perennial 10 Australian, Singletary, Wild winter 11 Everlasting, Sturt desert, Two-flowered, Winter sweet 12 Edible-podded 14 Austrian winter 15 Australian flame

peace 4 calm, ease 5 amity, truce 6 accord, repose 7 concord, content, entente, harmony 8 serenity 9 agreement, armistice, composure, placidity 12 pacification, tranquillity 14 reconciliation
god of: 4 Frey 5 Freyr
goddess of: 3 Pax 9 Concordia
Hebrew: 6 shalom
Russian: 3 mir

Peace
author: 12 Aristophanes

peace be with you
Latin: 11 pax vobiscum

peaceful 4 calm 5 quiet, still 6 placid, serene, silent 7 pacific, restful 8 amicable, friendly, tranquil 9 agreeable, peaceable, peacetime 10 harmonious, nonviolent, nonwarring, pacifistic, untroubled 11 undisturbed

peacefulness 4 calm 7 concord, harmony 8 calmness, serenity 9 placidity 11 tranquility

peacemaker 8 diplomat, mediator, placater 9 go-between 10 ambassador, arbitrator, negotiator 11 adjudicator, conciliator, pacificator, peacekeeper, peacemonger 12 intermediary

peacemaking 9 pacifying, placating, placatory 11 reconciling 12 conciliating, conciliatory, pacification

peace offering 6 amends 11 appeasement 12 conciliation

peace of mind 8 security, serenity 11 tranquility 16 freedom from worry

peace to you
Hebrew: 14 shalom aleichem

peach 13 Prunus persica
varieties: 4 Muir, Peak, Sims, Vine, Wild 5 Gaume, Hiley, Pavie 6 Carmen, Crosby, Desert, Foster, J H Hale, Lovell, Orejon, Paloro, Peen-to, Salwey 7 Dixigem, Dixired, Elberta, Persian, Quadong 8 Champion, Crawford, Isabella, Redhaven, Russelet 9 Alexander, Freestone, Halehaven, Rochester, Southland 11 Clingstone, Goldeneast, Heath Cling, Summer Snow 12 Chinese Cling, Iron Mountain, Mountain Rose, Oldmixon Free 13 Golden Jubilee, Old mixon Cling, Phillips Cling 14 Belle of Georgia

peach-like: 7 apricot 9 nectarine

Peach State
nickname of: 7 Georgia

Peachum, Polly
character in: 12 Beggar's Opera
author: 3 Gay

peachy 4 fine, keen 5 dandy, super, swell 9 excellent, marvelous, wonderful

peacock
group of: 6 muster

Peacock
constellation of: 4 Pavo

Peacock, Thomas Love
author of: 12 Headlong Hall 14 Crotchet Castle, Nightmare Abbey

Peacock Spring, The
author: 11 Rumer Godden

peak 3 tip, top 4 acme, apex 5 crest, crown, flood, prime 6 apogee, climax, summit, zenith 8 pinnacle 9 culminate 11 culmination

peaked 3 ill, wan 4 lean, pale, thin, weak 5 ashen, drawn, gaunt, spare, spiked, spiny, white 6 ailing, infirm, pallid, pointy, sallow, sickly, skinny, spiked 7 haggard, pinched, pointed, scrawny, tapered, wizened 9 emaciated, shriveled 11 debilitated

peal 3 din 4 boom, clap, ring, roar, roll, toll 5 blare, blast, clang, crack, crash, knell 6 rumble 7 clangor, resound, ringing 10 resounding 11 reverberate 13 reverberation 14 tintinnabulate 16 tintinnabulation

Peale, Charles Willson
born: 17 Queen Anne County MD
son: 9 Raphaelle, Rembrandt 12 Titian Ramsay
artwork: 26 The Exhumation of the Mastodon
portrait: 8 Franklin 9 Jefferson, John Adams 10 Washington

Peale, Raphaelle
born: 13 Bucks County PA
father: 14 Charles Willson
brother: 9 Rembrandt 12 Titian Ramsay
artwork: 12 After the Bath

Peale, Rembrandt
born: 13 Bucks County PA
father: 14 Charles Willson
brother: 9 Raphaelle 12 Titian Ramsay
artwork: 15 The Court of Death
portrait: 9 Jefferson 10 Washington

peal of bells 7 clangor, ringing 16 tintinnabulation

peanut 3 pod, tot 4 puny, seed 5 petty, small 6 goober, legume, measly, paltry 8 earthpea 9 little one
species: 15 Arachis hypogaea

Peanuts
creator: 13 Charles Schulz
character: 4 Lucy 5 Linus 6 Marcie, Snoopy 9 Schroeder 12 Charlie Brown 15 Peppermint Patty
Halloween figure: 12 Great Pumpkin
Snoopy's plane: 12 Sopwith Camel
Snoopy's foe: 8 Red Baron
saying: 9 Good Grief

pear 5 Pyrus 13 Pyrus communis
varieties: 4 Bosc, Sand 5 Anjou, Asian, Blind, Melon, Smith 6 Balsam, Burrel, Butter, Comice, Common, Garber, Garlic, Orient, Seckel, Warden 7 Chinese, Kieffer, Prickly, Vinegar 8 Bartlett, Japanese, Oriental 9 Alligator, Evergreen, Muscadine 10 Beurre Bosc, Brandywine, Chaumontel 11 Birch-leaved, Bon Chretien, Paper-spined, Winter Nelis 12 Beurre d'Anjou, Easter Beurre, Sacred garlic, Willow-leaved 13 Flemish Beauty, Waite Bergamot 15 Doyenne du Comice 18 Duchesse d'Angouleme

pearl
grows in: 6 oyster
genus: 8 Pinctada
source: 6 Red Sea 9 Caribbean 11 Persian Gulf 12 South Pacific 16 Gulf of California
composed of: 5 nacre 9 aragonite 10 conchiolin 13 mother-of-pearl
quality: 6 luster 11 iridescence
color: 4 blue, rose 5 black, brown, cream, green, white 6 yellow
shape: 5 round 7 baroque
type: 8 cultured, Oriental (saltwater) 9 simulated 10 freshwater

Pearl-Fishers, The
also: 19 Les Pecheurs de Perles
opera by: 5 Bizet
setting: 6 Ceylon

Pearl of the Antilles *see* 4 Cuba

peasant 4 boor, esne, peon, serf 5 churl, knave, yokel 6 farmer, rustic, worker 7 laborer, lowlife, villein 10 countryman, dirt farmer
Arabic: 6 fellah
Indian: 4 ryot 5 kisan 6 raiyat
Irish: 4 kern
Russian: 5 kulak 6 muzhik

Scottish: 6 cotter

peasantlike 5 crude, rough 6 coarse, oafish, rustic, vulgar 7 boorish, loutish, uncouth 9 unrefined 10 unpolished

peccadillo 4 slip 5 lapse 6 boo-boo 7 blunder, faux pas, misdeed, misstep 8 petty sin, trespass 9 false move, wrong step 10 misconduct, wrongdoing 11 misdemeanor 13 transgression

peck 3 pat, rap, tap 4 buss, gobs, lots, mess 5 a slew, batch, bunch, heaps, scads, smack, snack, stack, thump 6 nibble, oodles, pick at, strike, stroke, worlds 8 light jab 9 abundance, light kiss 11 eight quarts
abbreviation of: 2 pk

Peck, Gregory
real name: 17 Eldred Gregory Peck
born: 9 La Jolla CA
roles: 8 Moby Dick 10 On the Beach, Spellbound 11 The Yearling 12 Duel in the Sun, Roman Holiday 15 The Paradine Case 16 Twelve O'Clock High 17 The Boys from Brazil, The Guns of Navarone 18 To Kill a Mockingbird (Oscar) 19 Gentleman's Agreement, The Keys of the Kingdom 21 The Snows of Kilimanjaro 26 The Man in the Gray Flannel Suit
autobiography: 12 An Actor's Life

Peckinpah, Sam
director of: 9 Straw Dogs 12 The Wild Bunch

Pecksniff
character in: 16 Martin Chuzzlewit
author: 7 Dickens

peculiar 3 odd 5 queer, weird 6 far-out, quaint, unique 7 bizarre, curious, erratic, private, special, strange, typical, unusual 8 abnormal, distinct, freakish, personal, singular, specific 9 eccentric, exclusive, whimsical 10 capricious, individual, outlandish, particular 11 distinctive 13 idiosyncratic 14 characteristic, distinguishing, representative, unconventional

peculiarity 4 mark 5 badge, stamp, trait 6 oddity 7 feature, quality 8 odd trait 9 attribute, queerness, weirdness 10 erraticism, uniqueness 11 abnormality, bizarreness, distinction, singularity, strangeness 12 eccentricity, freakishness, idiosyncrasy 13 particularity, unnaturalness 14 characteristic 21 distinguishing quality

pecuniary 6 fiscal 8 economic, monetary 9 budgetary, financial

pedagogic 7 bookish, donnish 8 academic, didactic, pedantic, tutorial 9 scholarly 11 educational 12 professorial 13 instructional

pedagogue, pedagog 5 tutor 7 teacher 8 academic, educator 9 professor 10 instructor, schoolmarm 12 educationist, schoolmaster 13 schoolteacher 14 schoolmistress

pedant 6 purist 8 bookworm 9 dogmatist 13 methodologist

pedantic 5 fussy 7 bookish, finicky, pompous, stilted 8 academic, didactic, dogmatic 10 nitpicking, scholastic 11 doctrinaire, punctilious 13 hairsplitting 14 overparticular

Pedasus
  mentioned in: 5 Iliad
  twin brother: 7 Aesepus
  killed by: 8 Euryalus

peddle 4 hawk, sell, vend 6 retail 7 deal out 8 dispense

Peder Victorious
  character in: 16 Giants of the Earth
  author: 7 Rolvaag

pedestal 4 base, foot 6 bottom, plinth 10 foundation

pedestrian 6 walker 7 mundane, prosaic, tedious, trekker 8 mediocre, ordinary, stroller 9 itinerant 10 ambulatory, for walking, unexciting 11 commonplace, peripatetic, unimportant 12 foot-traveler, run-of-the-mill 13 insignificant, perambulating, perambulatory, unimaginative 15 inconsequential

pedigree 4 line 6 family, strain 7 descent, lineage 8 ancestry 9 bloodline, parentage 10 derivation, extraction, family tree 13 line of descent

peek 3 pry 4 peep, peer 5 watch 6 glance 7 glimpse

peel 4 bark, hull, husk, pare, rind, skin, tear, zest 5 flake, scale, shuck, spade, strip 6 remove 7 undress 11 decorticate

peel off 6 remove 7 veer off 8 strip off

peep 4 peek, peer, skim, word 5 cheep, chirp, tweet 6 emerge, glance, murmur, mutter, squeak 7 chirrup, glimpse, peeping, peer out, twitter, whimper, whisper 9 come forth, quick look

peeper 3 eye 4 frog 6 voyeur 10 peeping Tom

peer 4 gape, gaze, look, lord, peek, peep 5 equal, noble, stare 6 appear, emerge, squint 7 compeer 8 nobleman 9 blue blood, gentleman, patrician 10 aristocrat

peerage 8 nobility 10 blue bloods, patricians 11 aristocracy

Peer Gynt
  author: 11 Henrik Ibsen
  character: 3 Ase 7 Solveig 12 The Great Boyg 16 The Button Moulder

peerless 7 supreme 8 flawless 9 faultless, matchless, unequaled, unmatched, unrivaled 10 consummate, inimitable, preeminent, surpassing, unexcelled 11 superlative, unsurpassed 12 incomparable, transcendent

peeve 3 bug, eat, irk, vex 4 fret, gall, rile 5 annoy, chafe, eat at, frost, gripe 6 gnaw at, nettle 7 dislike, perturb, provoke 8 irritate, vexation 9 aggravate, annoyance, complaint, grievance 10 exasperate, irritation 11 aggravation, provocation 12 exasperation, give one a pain 13 pain in the neck 14 thorn in the side

peevish 4 mean 5 cross, huffy, sulky, surly, testy 6 crabby, cranky, grumpy 7 grouchy, pettish 8 churlish, petulant, snappish 9 fractious, irritable, querulous, splenetic 10 ill-humored, ill-natured 11 bad-tempered, ill-tempered, quarrelsome 12 cantankerous

peewee 4 tiny 5 dwarf, small, teeny 6 little, midget, minute 9 itsy-bitsy, itty-bitty, minuscule 10 diminutive, teeny-weeny 11 Lilliputian

Pee Wee
  nickname of: 11 Harold Reese

peg 3 pin 4 nail 5 cleat, dowel, spike, thole 6 skewer, toggle 8 fastener, tholepin

Pegae
  form: 6 spring
  spring of: 6 Dryope

Pegasus
  form: 5 horse
  characteristic: 6 winged
  mother: 6 Medusa
  ridden by: 11 Bellerophon

Peggotty, Clara
  character in: 16 David Copperfield
  author: 7 Dickens

Pei, I M (leoh Ming)
  architect of: 12 East Building (National Gallery of Art), L'Enfant Plaza (Washington DC) 14 East-West Center (U of Hawaii), Mile High Center (Denver) 15 Place Ville Marie (Montreal) 16 John Hancock Tower (Boston) 18 Everson Museum of Art (Syracuse NY) 22 Kips Bay Plaza Apartments (NYC) 36 National Center for Atmospheric Research (Boulder CO)

peignoir 4 gown 6 kimono 8 negligee 9 nightgown 12 dressing gown

Peiser, Lillie Marie
  real name of: 11 Lilli Palmer

pejorative 7 mocking 8 debasing, negative, scornful 9 degrading, demeaning, slighting 10 belittling, derogatory, detracting, disdainful, ridiculing, unpleasant 11 deprecatory, disparaging, downgrading 12 contemptuous, depreciatory, disapproving 15 uncomplimentary

Peking
  also: 7 Beijing
  means: 15 northern capital
  capital of: 5 China
  landmark: 9 Bell Tower, Drum Tower, Ming Tombs 10 Pei-hai Park 12 Palace Museum 13 Forbidden City 14 Hall of Classics, Temple of Heaven 15 Marco Polo Bridge 17 Temple of Confucius 18 Old Legation Quarter 19 Temple of Agriculture 20 Great Hall of the People, Hall of Supreme Harmony 21 Mausoleum of Mao Tse-tung 22 Palace of Heavenly Purity 26 Monument to the People's Heroes 32 Revolutionary and Historical Museum
  mountain: 7 Taihang
  river: 3 Hai 7 Ch'ao-pai 8 Yungting
  square: 9 T'ien-an Men
  university: 8 Tsinghua

walled city: 5 Inner, Outer, Tatar **7** Chinese

pelagic 6 marine **7** aquatic, oceanic **9** thalassic **11** sea-dwelling

Pelagon
  mentioned in: 5 Iliad
  ally of: 8 Sarpedon

Pelasgus
  also: 9 Corynetes
  son: 6 Lycaon **7** Temenus
  first: 3 man
  founder of: 10 Pelasgians

Pele
  real name: 24 Edson Arantes do Nascimento
  sport: 6 soccer
  team: 13 New York Cosmos
  nationality: 9 Brazilian

Pelegon
  mentioned in: 5 Iliad
  god of: 5 river
  mother: 8 Periboea
  son: 11 Asteropaeus

Peleus
  king of: 6 Phthia **9** Myrmidons
  father: 6 Aeacus
  mother: 6 Endeis
  brother: 7 Telamon
  half-brother: 6 Phocus
  wife: 6 Thetis **8** Antigone
  son: 8 Achilles
  daughter: 8 Polydora

pelf 4 gain **5** booty, lucre, money **6** mammon, riches, spoils

Pelias
  father: 8 Poseidon
  mother: 4 Tyro
  twin brother: 6 Neleus
  wife: 8 Anaxibia
  son: 7 Acastus
  nephew: 5 Jason

Pelican State
  nickname of: 9 Louisiana

Pelides
  descendant of: 6 Peleus

pelisse 4 cape, coat **5** cloak **6** mantle

Pelleas (King Pelleas)
  character in: 16 Arthurian romance
  daughter: 6 Elaine

Pelleas and Melisande
  also: 18 Pelleas et Melisande
  opera by: 7 Debussy
  character: 6 Golaud, Yniold
  author: 18 Maurice Maeterlinck

pellet 3 pea **4** ball, bead, drop, pill **5** pearl, stone **6** marble, pebble, sphere **7** globule

pell-mell 6 rashly **7** hastily **8** slapdash **9** hurriedly, post haste **10** at half cock, carelessly, heedlessly, recklessly **11** hurry-scurry, impetuously, imprudently **12** incautiously **13** helter-skelter, precipitately, thoughtlessly

pellucid 5 clear, lucid **10** articulate **11** crystalline, translucent, transparent **12** intelligible **14** understandable

Pelopia
  father: 8 Thyestes
  raped by: 8 Thyestes
  son: 9 Aegisthus

Pelops
  father: 8 Tantalus
  sister: 5 Niobe
  son: 6 Atreus, Sciron **7** Letreus **8** Pittheus, Thyestes **9** Alcathous **10** Chrysippus
  daughter: 7 Nicippe **8** Lysidice **9** Astydamia
  resurrected by: 6 Hermes

pelt 3 fur, hit, rap **4** belt, coat, hide, skin, sock **5** pound, punch, whack **6** batter, buffet, fleece, pepper, pummel, strike, thrash, thwack **7** clobber

Pemphredo
  member of: 6 Graeae, Graiae

pen 3 sty **4** cage, coop, crib, fold **5** draft, hutch, pound, quill, stall, write **6** corral, pencil, scrawl **7** compose, paddock **8** compound, scribble, stockade **9** ballpoint, enclosure

penal 7 of jails **8** punitive **9** punishing **10** corrective, penalizing **11** castigatory, retributive **12** disciplinary

penalty 4 fine **7** forfeit **8** handicap **9** suffering **10** assessment, forfeiture, infliction, punishment **11** retribution **12** disadvantage

penance 9 atonement, explation, hair shirt, penitence **10** contrition, repentance **12** propitiation **13** mortification

Penates
  protectors of: 4 home
  companions: 5 lares

penchant 4 bent, bias, gift, turn **5** fancy, flair, knack, taste **6** liking, relish **7** leaning **8** affinity, fondness, tendency **9** prejudice, proneness, readiness **10** attraction, partiality, preference, proclivity, propensity **11** disposition, inclination **12** predilection **14** predisposition

pendant 3 fob **6** locket **15** hanging ornament

Pendennis
  author: 25 William Make peace Thackeray
  character: 9 Laura Bell **10** Henry Foker **12** Blanche Amory **13** Emily Costigan **14** Helen Pendennis, Major Pendennis **15** Arthur Pendennis

pendent, pendant 7 hanging, jutting, pensile **8** dangling, swinging **9** extending, pendulous, suspended **10** projecting, protruding **11** overhanging, protuberant

pendente lite 16 during litigation **19** with a lawsuit pending

pending 8 imminent **9** undecided, unsettled **10** in suspense, unfinished, unresolved, up in the air **11** in the offing **12** undetermined

pendulous 7 hanging, pendent, pensile, sagging **8** dangling, drooping, swinging **9** suspended

pendulum
  invented by: 7 Galileo

Penelope
father: 7 Icarius
mother: 8 Periboea
husband: 8 Odysseus 9 Telegonus
son: 6 Ifalus 10 Telemachus 11 Polyporthis
fended off: 7 suitors

penetrate 3 get 4 bore 5 catch, enter, prick 6 decode, fathom, invade, pierce, seep in 7 cut into, discern, pervade, unravel 8 decipher, perceive, permeate, puncture, saturate, traverse 9 figure out, perforate 10 comprehend, cut through, impregnate, infiltrate, see through, understand 11 pass through

penetrating 4 keen 5 acrid, alert, alive, aware, harsh, heady, sharp, smart 6 astute, biting, clever, shrewd, strong 7 caustic, pungent, reeking 8 piercing, redolent, stinging 9 pervading, pervasive, trenchant 10 discerning, perceptive, percipient, permeating, saturating, thoughtful 11 intelligent, sharp-witted 13 perspicacious

penetration 5 foray, grasp 6 access, boring 7 insight, passage 8 infusion, invasion, keenness, piercing 9 intrusion, quickness, sharpness 10 astuteness, cleverness, perception, puncturing, shrewdness 11 discernment, perforation 12 intelligence, perspicacity

Peneus
god of: 5 river
river: 7 Peneus
son: 7 Hypseus
daughter: 6 Daphne

Penguin Island
author: 13 Anatole France

peninsula 4 cape 5 point 8 headland 10 promontory

Peninsular State
nickname of: 7 Florida

penitence 6 regret, sorrow 7 penance, remorse 9 atonement, attrition, expiation 10 contrition, repentance 11 compunction, humiliation

penitent 5 sorry 6 rueful 7 atoning, devotee, pilgrim 8 contrite 9 regretful, repentant 10 remorseful

penitentiary 3 pen 4 jail, stir 5 joint 6 prison 7 slammer 8 big house

Penn, Arthur
director of: 12 Little Big Man 14 Bonnie and Clyde 16 The Miracle Worker

Penn, Sean
wife: 7 Madonna 11 Robin Wright
roles: 7 Bad Boys 15 Shanghai Express 22 The Falcon and the Snowman 24 Fast Times at Ridgemont High

Pennacook (Merrimac)
language family: 9 Algonkian 10 Algonquian
location: 5 Maine 6 Quebec 7 New York, Vermont 10 New England 12 New Hampshire 13 Massachusetts
leader: 11 Wannalancet 12 Passaconaway
related to: 6 Abnaki

pen name
French: 10 nom de plume

pennant 4 flag, jack 6 banner, burgee, colors, ensign, pennon 7 bunting 8 ensignia, standard, streamer 9 banderole, oriflamme

penniless 4 poor 5 broke, needy 6 busted, ruined 8 bankrupt, indigent, strapped, wiped out 9 destitute, flat broke, insolvent, moneyless 10 down-and-out, pauperized 12 impoverished 15 poverty-stricken

pennon 4 flag, jack 6 banner, colors, ensign 7 pennant 8 standard, streamer

Pennsylvania
abbreviation: 2 PA 5 Penna
nickname: 8 Keystone
capital: 10 Harrisburg
largest city: 12 Philadelphia
others: 4 Erie, Etna, Plum, York 5 Avoca, Baden 6 Beaver, Bethel, Butler, Easton, Emmaus, Radnor, Ridley, Sharon 7 Altoona, Baldwin, Bristol, Chester, Ephrata, Hanover, Hershey, Lebanon, Reading 8 Abington, Braddock, Bradford, Bryn Mawr, Carlisle, Clairton, Harrison, Hazelton, Monessen, Scranton, Shamokin 9 Aliquippa, Allentown, Bethlehem, Charleroi, Haverford, Jeannette, Johnstown, Lancaster, Meadville, Mill Creek, Newcastle, Swissvale, Uniontown, Whitehall 10 Carbondale, Gettysburg, McKeesport, Norristown, Pittsburgh 11 Springfield, Wilkes Barre 12 State College, Williamsport
college: 3 PSU 4 Penn, Pitt 5 Gratz, Thiel 6 Drexel, Lehigh, Temple 7 Juniata, LaSalle, Ursinus 8 Alliance, Bryn Mawr, Bucknell, Duquesne, Lycoming 9 Dickinson, Lafayette, Penn State, St Josephs, Villanova 10 Pittsburgh, Swarthmore 12 Carnegie Tech 17 Pennsylvania State
feature:
battle site: 10 Gettysburg
bell: 7 Liberty
hall: 12 Independence
historical site: 11 Valley Forge
tribe: 6 Seneca 7 Shawnee 8 Delaware 11 Lenni-Lanape 13 Susquehannock
people: 5 Amish, Dutch 10 Stan Musial 11 Andrew Wyeth, Ethel Waters, Mary Cassatt, Stuart Davis 12 Andrew Mellon, Anthony Wayne, Margaret Mead, Martha Graham, Samuel Barber, Thomas Eakins 13 Clifford Odets, Gertrude Stein 14 George S Kaufman 15 Maxwell Anderson 19 Stephen Vincent Benet
explorer: 5 Brule 6 Hudson 11 Hendrickson
lake: 4 Erie 7 Harveys 8 Conneaut 10 Pymatuning 13 Wallenpaupack
land rank: 11 thirty-third
mountain: 5 South 6 Pocono 11 Alleghenies
highest point: 5 Davis
physical feature:
peninsula: 11 Presque Isle
valley: 5 Great

president: 13 James Buchanan
river: 4 Ohio 6 Lehigh 7 Clarion, Genesee, Juniata, Licking, Towanda 8 Caldwell, Delaware, Schrader 9 Allegheny 10 Schuylkill 11 Monongahela, Susquehanna
state admission: 6 second
state bird: 12 ruffed grouse
state fish: 10 brook trout
state flower: 14 mountain laurel
state motto: 28 Virtue Liberty and Independence
state tree: 7 hemlock

penny 3 sum 4 cent 5 cheap, pence 6 copper, stiver 7 trivial

penny-pinching 5 close, tight 6 stingy 7 miserly 8 grudging 9 niggardly, penurious 10 ungenerous 11 tight-fisted 12 parsimonious

Penny Serenade
director: 13 George Stevens
cast: 9 Cary Grant 10 Irene Dunne 11 Beulah Bondi 13 Edgar Buchanan

pennyweight
abbreviation of: 3 dwt

Penobscot
language family: 9 Algonkian 10 Algonquian
location: 5 Maine 13 Old Town Island
members of: 17 Abnaki Confederacy

Penrod
author: 15 Booth Tarkington
sequel: 12 Penrod and Sam 13 Penrod Jashber
character: 6 Herman, Verman 9 Sarah Crim 11 Rupe Collins 13 Marjorie Jones 15 Penrod Schofield
dog: 4 Duke

pensee 7 thought 10 reflection

Pensees
author: 12 Blaise Pascal

pension 5 grant 6 income, retire 7 annuity, stipend, subsidy 9 allowance 13 boardinghouse 14 retirement fund

pensive 3 sad 5 grave 6 dreamy, musing, solemn, somber 7 serious, wistful 8 dreaming 10 meditative, melancholy, reflective 11 day dreaming 13 contemplative, introspective 15 sadly thoughtful

Pentateuch 10 Law of Moses 28 first five books of Old Testament
see also: 7 books of 12 Old Testament

Penthesilea
queen of: 7 Amazons
father: 4 Ares
mother: 6 Otrere
sister: 9 Hippolyta
killed by: 8 Achilles

Pentheus
king of: 6 Thebes
father: 6 Echion
mother: 5 Agave
grandfather: 6 Cadmus

pent-up 7 boxed-up, checked, stifled 8 hedged-in, held back, penned-in, penned-up, reined in, stored-up 9

bottled-up, repressed 10 restrained, suppressed

penurious 5 close 6 frugal, stingy 7 miserly, sparing 8 stinting 9 niggardly 12 parsimonious 13 penny-pinching

penury 4 need, want 7 poverty 9 indigence, privation 10 bankruptcy, insolvency 11 destitution 14 impoverishment

Penutian
language branch: 4 Coos 5 Huave, Maidu, Mayan, Miwok 6 Wintun, Yokuts 7 Chinook, Klamath, Takelma, Totonac 8 Sahaptin 9 Mixe-Zoque, Tsimshian
tribe: 5 Maidu 7 Klamath

peon 4 pawn, serf 5 slave 6 drudge, menial, worker 7 footman, laborer, orderly, peasant, servant

peony 7 Paeonia
varieties: 4 Tree 7 Chinese, Tibetan 8 Majorcan 11 Chinese tree 12 Common garden

people 3 kin 5 folks 6 family, humans, the mob 7 kinfolk, mankind, mortals, the herd 8 citizens, humanity, populace, the crowd 9 ancestors, citizenry, commoners, human kind, relatives, the masses, the public, the rabble 10 population 11 Homo sapiens, human beings, individuals, inhabitants, John Q Public, men and women, the millions

People Are Funny
host: 13 Art Linkletter

pep 3 vim, zip 4 dash, life, snap 5 gusto, verve, vigor 6 energy, ginger, spirit 8 vitality, vivacity 9 animation 10 enthusiasm, get-up-and-go, liveliness

Pepe Le Moko
director: 14 Julien Duvivier
cast: 9 Jean Gabin 13 Gabriel Gabrio, Mireille Balin
remade as: 6 Casbah 7 Algiers

peperomia
varieties: 3 Ivy 6 Prayer, Vining 7 Ivyleaf, Leather, Red-edge 8 Coin-leaf, Platinum 9 Flowering 10 Silver-edge, Silverleaf, Watermelon 11 Green-ripple 13 Emerald-ripple, Little fantasy

Pepita
character in: 21 The Bridge of San Luis Rey
author: 6 Wilder

Peppard, George
born: 9 Detroit MI
wife: 15 Elizabeth Ashley
roles: 6 Tobruk 7 Banacek 8 The A-Team 16 The Carpetbaggers 19 Breakfast at Tiffany's

pepper 3 dot 6 shower, strafe 7 bombard 8 sprinkle 9 condiment, vegetable

pepper, peppercorn
botanical name: 5 Piper 7 Pnigrum 8 Capsicum 10 Piperaceae 11 C frutescens
color: 3 red 5 black, green, white
origin: 5 India 6 Brazil, Ceylon 7 Malabar, Sarawak, Sumatra 8 Alleppey, Pandjang, Sri Lanka 11 Tellicherry
varieties: 3 Red 4 Baby, Bell, Bird, Cone,

Long, Wild 5 Betle, Black, Chili, Cubeb,
Green, Japan, Sweet, White 6 Cherry 7
Cayenne, Celebes, Cluster, Tabasco 8
Capsicum 9 Mild water 10 Australian,
Red cluster 12 Mountain long, Tabasco-
sauce
French: 6 poivre
German: 7 pfeffer
Italian: 4 pepe
Latin: 5 piper
Persian: 5 biber 6 pilpil
Spanish: 8 pimienta
Swedish: 6 peppar
Sanskrit: 7 pippali

peppermint 6 Mentha
varieties: 4 Gray 5 Black, River, White 6
Silver, Sydney 9 Blackbutt 10 Robertson's 11 Broad-leaved 15 Mount Wellington 17 Narrow-leaved black 19 Nichol's
willow-leaved

peppermint schnapps
type: 7 liqueur
flavor: 4 mint

peppery 3 hot 5 fiery, sharp, spicy 7 burning, piquant, pungent 14 highly seasoned
peppy 4 spry 5 brisk, perky 6 active,
bouncy, frisky, lively, snappy 7 dynamic 8
animated, spirited, vigorous 9 energetic,
full of pep, sparkling, sprightly, vivacious
12 enthusiastic
pep up 4 fire 6 excite, vivify, wake up 7 animate, enliven, quicken 8 vitalize

Pepys, Samuel
author of: 10 Pepys' Diary

Pepys' Diary
author: 11 Samuel Pepys

Pequot
language family: 9 Algonkian 10 Algonquian
location: 11 Connecticut, Rhode Island
perambulate 4 pace, tour, walk 5 amble,
mosey 6 ramble, stroll 7 meander, saunter
9 promenade
perceivable 7 visible 8 apparent, distinct
10 detectable, noticeable, observable 11
discernible, perceptible 13 ascertainable
perceive 3 get, see 4 feel, hear, know, note
5 grasp, savvy, sense, smell, taste 6 deduce, detect, gather, notice 7 discern,
make out, observe, realize 8 conclude,
discover 9 apprehend, be aware of, recognize 10 comprehend, understand 11 distinguish
perceptible 5 clear, plain 7 evident, notable, obvious, visible 8 apparent, distinct,
manifest, palpable, tangible, unhidden 9
prominent 10 detectable, noticeable, observable 11 conspicuous, discernible, perceivable, unconcealed, well-defined 12
discoverable, unmistakable 13 ascertainable
perception 5 grasp, sense 7 faculty 8 judgment 9 awareness, detection 10 cognizance, conception 11 discernment, recognition 12 apprehension 13 comprehension,
consciousness, understanding 14 discrimination

perceptive 4 keen 5 acute, aware, quick,
sharp 6 astute, shrewd 8 sensible 9 sensitive 10 discerning, insightful, responsive
11 intelligent, penetrating, quick-witted 13
understanding
perch 3 sit 4 land, rest, seat 5 eyrie, light,
roost 6 alight, settle

Perchta
also: 7 Berchta
origin: 8 Germanic
goddess of: 5 death 9 fertility
corresponds to: 5 Holle

Percival, Perceval
character in: 16 Arthurian romance
percolate 4 boil, brew 6 bubble, seethe
percussion instrument 4 gong 5 anvil,
bells, tabor 6 chimes, rattle 7 celesta, cymbals, marimba, taboret, timpani 8 bass
drum, side drum, triangle 9 castanets, dul-
citone, snare drum, tenor drum, typo-
phone, xylophone 10 kettledrum, tambourine 12 Glockenspiel, tubular bells

Percy, Walker
author of: 8 Lancelot 12 The Moviegoer
14 Love in the Ruins 15 The Second
Coming 16 The Last Gentleman

Perdita
character in: 14 The Winter's Tale
author: 11 Shakespeare
perdition 4 Hell, ruin 8 hellfire 9 damnation,
ruination 11 destruction 12 condemnation

Perdix
also: 9 Polycaste
brother: 8 Daedalus
son: 5 Talus
changed into: 9 partridge
pere 6 father, senior

Pere Goriot
author: 14 Honore de Balzac
character: 15 Monsieur Vautrin 17 Eugene de Rastignac, Madame de Beause-
ant 18 Victorine Taillefer 26 Countess
Anastasie de Restaud, Baroness Delphine de Nucingen
peregrination 4 trip 5 jaunt, sally 6 hiking,
junket, roving, travel 7 journey, roaming 8
rambling, trekking 9 excursion, wandering
10 expedition

Peregrine Pickle
author: 14 Tobias Smollett

Pereira, William
architect of: 13 Cape Canaveral 20
Transamerica Building (San Francisco)

Perelman, S J
author of: 10 Eastward Ha 15 One
Touch of Venus (with Ogden Nash and
Kurt Weill) 16 The Road to Miltown 18
Strictly from Hunger 24 Under the
Spreading Atrophy
peremptory 5 final 6 biased, lordly 8 absolute, decisive, dogmatic 9 assertive,
imperious 10 aggressive, high-handed, imperative, obligatory, undeniable 11 dictatorial, domineering, irrevocable, opinionated,
overbearing, unavoidable, unequivocal 12
closed-minded, irreversible 13 authoritative 14 unquestionable 16 incontrovertible

perennial 5 fixed **7** durable, lasting, undying **8** constant, enduring, timeless **9** ceaseless, continual, immutable, incessant, long-lived, permanent, perpetual, unceasing, unfailing **10** changeless, continuous, persistent, unchanging **11** everlasting, long-lasting, unremitting **12** imperishable **14** indestructible

Pereus
　　father: 6 Elatus
　　mother: 7 Laodice

Perez, Manuel Benitez
　　nickname: 10 El Cordobes

perfect 4 pure, true **5** exact, ideal, whole **6** effect, entire, evolve, strict **7** achieve, develop, fulfill, precise, realize, sublime, supreme **8** absolute, accurate, complete, faithful, finished, flawless, peerless, thorough, unbroken, unerring **9** blameless, faultless, matchless, undamaged, unequaled, unrivaled, untainted **10** accomplish, consummate, immaculate, impeccable, scrupulous, unimpaired **11** superlative, unblemished, unmitigated, unqualified

perfection 6 purity **9** achieving, evolution, exactness, precision, sublimity **10** completion, excellence, ideal state **11** development, fulfillment, perfectness, realization, superiority **12** accurateness, consummation, flawlessness **13** faultlessness, impeccability **14** accomplishment

perfectly 5 fully, quite **6** purely, wholly **7** totally, utterly, entirely, superbly **9** downright, supremely **10** absolutely, altogether, completely, flawlessly, impeccably, infinitely, positively, thoroughly **11** faultlessly, wonderfully **12** consummately, preeminently, to perfection, without fault **13** without defect **14** to the nth degree, without blemish

perfidious 5 false, lying **6** shifty, sneaky **7** corrupt **8** cheating, disloyal, two-faced **9** deceitful, dishonest, faithless **10** traitorous, treasonous, unfaithful, untruthful **11** treacherous, treasonable **12** dishonorable, undependable, unscrupulous **13** doubledealing, untrustworthy

perfidy 6 deceit **7** treason **8** bad faith, betrayal **9** falseness, recreancy, treachery, two-timing **10** disloyalty, infidelity **11** double-cross, inconstancy **13** breach of faith, deceitfulness, double-dealing, faithlessness **14** unfaithfulness

perforate 4 bore, gash, hole, slit, stab **5** drill, prick, punch, slash, split, stick **6** pierce **8** puncture **9** lancinate, penetrate

perform 2 do **3** act **4** meet, play **5** enact **6** attain, depict, effect, finish, render, troupe **7** achieve, execute, fulfill, portray, present, pull off, realize **8** carry out, knock off **9** discharge, dispose of, polish off, represent **10** accomplish, bring about, consummate, perpetrate, take part in

performance 4 play, show **5** doing, opera **6** ballet **7** concert, conduct, recital **8** ceremony, dispatch, exercise **9** acquittal, discharge, execution, rendering, spectacle **10** attainment, completion, exhibition, performing, production **11** achievement, fulfillment, realization, transaction **12** consummation, effectuation, perpetration, presentation **13** entertainment **14** accomplishment

perfume 4 odor **5** aroma, scent, smell **7** bouquet, cologne, essence, extract, sweeten **9** aromatize, fragrance

perfumed 7 odorous, scented **8** aromatic, fragrant **11** odoriferous **12** sweet-scented **13** sweet-smelling

perfunctory 3 lax **5** hasty **6** casual **7** cursory, offhand, routine **8** careless, listless, lukewarm **9** apathetic, negligent **10** mechanical, spiritless, unthinking **11** halfhearted, inattentive, indifferent, passionless, superficial, unconcerned **13** disinterested

Pergamus
　　father: 11 Neoptolemus
　　mother: 10 Andromache

pergola 5 arbor, bower **6** ramada **7** balcony, trellis

Per Hanea
　　character in: 16 Giants of the Earth
　　author: 7 Rolvaag

perhaps 5 maybe **6** mayhap **8** peut-etre, possibly **9** perchance **10** God willing, imaginably **11** conceivably **12** peradventure

Perialla
　　form: 9 priestess
　　priestess of: 6 Delphi

Periapis
　　also: 8 Periopis
　　father: 6 Pheres
　　son: 9 Patrocles

Periboea
　　father: 9 Alcathous, Hipponous
　　husband: 6 Oeneus **7** Polybus
　　son: 6 Tydeus **7** Olenias, Pelegon **14** Telamonian Ajax
　　foster son: 7 Oedipus

Perichole, La
　　character in: 21 The Bridge of San Luis Rey
　　author: 6 Wilder

Pericles, Prince of Tyre
　　author: 18 William Shakespeare
　　character: 5 Cleon **6** Marina, Thaisa **7** Dionyza **9** Antiochus **10** Lysimachus

Periclymenus
　　father: 6 Neleus **8** Poseidon
　　grandfather: 8 Poseidon
　　gift: 13 shape-changing
　　killed by: 8 Hercules

periderm 4 bark **8** covering **9** sheathing

peridot
　　species: 7 olivine
　　source: 5 Burma, Mogok **8** Zebirget
　　color: 11 yellow-green

perigee 5 depth, nadir **8** low point

Perikeiromene (The Rape of the Ringlets)
　　author: 8 Menander

peril 4 risk 6 danger, hazard, menace, threat 7 pitfall 8 jeopardy, unsafety 10 insecurity 11 uncertainty 13 cause for alarm, vulnerability

Perilaus
father: 7 Icarius
cousin: 12 Clytemnestra

perilous 5 risky, shaky 6 chancy, unsafe, unsure 7 ominous 8 insecure, slippery, ticklish 9 dangerous, hazardous, uncertain 10 precarious, vulnerable 11 threatening, venturesome

Perimedes
mentioned in: 7 Odyssey
companion of: 8 Odysseus
father: 10 Eurystheus

Perimele
father: 10 Hippodamas
ravished by: 8 Achelous
changed into: 6 island

perimeter 4 edge 6 border, bounds, margin 8 confines 9 periphery 10 borderline 13 circumference

period 3 age, end, eon, era 4 halt, stop, term, time 5 close, epoch, limit 6 finale, finish, season 7 curtain 8 duration, interval 9 cessation, interlude
French: 6 siecle

periodic, periodical 6 cyclic 7 regular, routine 8 frequent, repeated, seasonal 9 recurrent, recurring 12 intermittent

periodical 5 daily, paper 6 annual, review, weekly 7 journal, monthly 8 bulletin, magazine 9 newspaper, quarterly 10 newsletter 11 publication 12 newsmagazine

periodically 5 often 9 regularly, routinely 10 frequently, repeatedly 12 occasionally

Periopis *see* 8 Periapis

peripatetic 6 roving 7 migrant, nomadic, roaming, walking 8 rambling, tramping 9 itinerant, migratory, traveling, wandering 10 ambulating, ambulatory 12 Aristotelian, gallivanting 13 peregrinating

Periphas
mentioned in: 5 Iliad
king of: 6 Attica
father: 6 Epytus
vocation: 6 herald 7 warrior
changed into: 5 eagle
changed by: 4 Zeus

periphery 4 edge 5 bound 6 border 7 fringes 8 boundary 9 outskirts, perimeter 13 circumference

Periphetes
form: 5 giant
father: 7 Copreus
ally of: 7 Trojans
killed by: 7 Theseus

perish 3 die 5 decay 6 expire, vanish 7 crumble 8 pass away 9 disappear 10 come to ruin, wither away 11 be destroyed

perishable 8 fleeting, unstable 9 ephemeral 10 evanescent, short-lived, transitory 12 decomposable

perished 4 dead, died 7 expired 8 lifeless 10 passed away

periwinkle 5 Vinca 12 Catharanthus
varieties: 4 Rose 6 Common, Lesser 7 Greater 10 Madagascar

perjury 13 false swearing 14 lying under oath 20 giving false testimony

Perker
character in: 14 Pickwick Papers
author: 7 Dickens

Perkins, Anthony
born: 9 New York NY
roles: 6 Psycho 11 Norman Bates 14 Catch Twenty-Two 17 Look Homeward Angel 18 Desire Under the Elms, Friendly Persuasion

perk up 4 lift 5 cheer, rally, renew 6 buoy up, lift up, revive 7 animate, enliven, gladden 8 brighten, vitalize 9 stimulate 10 rejuvenate

perky 3 gay 4 pert 5 alert, brisk, happy, saucy, sunny 6 jaunty, lively 7 smiling 8 animated, cheerful, spirited 9 sprightly, vivacious 11 free and easy 12 full of spirit, lighthearted

permanent 3 set 4 perm, wave 6 stable 7 abiding, durable, endless, eternal, lasting, undying 8 constant, enduring, immortal, infinite, unending, unfading 9 deathless, immutable, long-lived, perpetual, unfailing 10 changeless, unyielding 11 everlasting, long-lasting, never-ending, unalterable 12 imperishable

permeate 4 fill 5 imbue 6 infuse 7 pervade 8 saturate 9 penetrate 11 pass through, seep through, soak through

per mensem 12 by the month

permissible 5 legal, licit 6 lawful 7 allowed, granted 8 licensed 9 allowable, permitted, tolerated 10 admissible, authorized, legitimate, sanctioned 12 unprohibited

permission 8 grant, leave 6 assent, permit 7 consent, license 8 approval, sanction 9 agreement, allowance 10 compliance, concession, indulgence 11 approbation, endorsement 12 acquiescence, dispensation 13 authorization

permissive 3 lax 7 lenient 8 allowing, granting, tolerant 9 assenting, easygoing, indulgent 10 consenting, forbearing, permitting 11 acquiescent 13 unprohibitive 14 unproscriptive

permit 2 OK 3 let 5 allow 6 endure, suffer 7 agree to, approve, condone, endorse, let pass, license, warrant 8 bear with, sanction, tolerate 9 authority, authorize, consent to, put up with 11 give leave to 12 give assent to 13 authorization
French: 13 laissez passer

permit to leave 4 free 5 let go 6 excuse 7 dismiss, release, set free 8 liberate 9 allow to go, discharge, send forth

pernicious 5 fatal, toxic 6 deadly, lethal, mortal 7 baneful, harmful, noxious, serious 8 damaging, venomous 9 dangerous, injurious, malignant, poisonous 10 disastrous 11 deleterious, destructive, detrimental

pernod
type: 8 aperitif
flavor: 5 anise
substitute for: 8 absinthe
with gin: 7 Dubarry
with orange juice: 9 Tiger Tail
with rum: 8 Shanghai
with rye: 3 TNT

Pero
father: 6 Neleus
mother: 7 Chloris
husband: 4 Bias

peroration 6 sermon, speech, tirade 7 address, lecture, oration 8 diatribe, harangue, jeremiad 9 discourse, philippic 10 filibuster 11 declamation, exhortation

perpendicular 4 sine 5 erect, plumb, sheer, steep 7 upright 8 vertical 10 right angle

perpetrate 2 do 5 enact 6 commit, pursue 7 execute, inflict, perform, pull off 8 carry out, transact

perpetration 5 doing 9 committal 10 commission, committing, performing 11 carrying out, performance

perpetrator 9 performer 11 participant

perpetual 7 abiding, endless, eternal, lasting 8 constant, enduring, repeated, unending 9 ceaseless, continual, incessant, permanent, sustained, unceasing 10 continuous 11 everlasting, never ending, unremitting 12 interminable 13 inexhaustible, uninterrupted

perpetuate 4 save 7 sustain 8 continue, maintain, make last, preserve 10 eternalize 11 immortalize, memorialize

perpetuity 7 all time, forever 8 eternity, infinity 9 end of time 10 permanence 11 endlessness 12 perpetuation, timelessness 13 perdurability, perennialness

perplex 5 mix up, stump 6 baffle, boggle, muddle, puzzle, rattle 7 confuse, mystify, nonplus 8 befuddle, bewilder, confound 9 dumbfound

perplexed 7 anxious, amazed, baffled, bemused, muddled, puzzled 8 confused, doubtful, involved 9 befuddled, intricate, mystified 10 astonished, bewildered, nonplussed

perplexing 4 hard, mazy 6 thorny 7 complex 10 mysterious
riddle: 9 conundrum

perplexity 9 confusion 10 bafflement, puzzlement 12 bewilderment 13 mystification

perquisite 3 due 4 gift, perk 5 right 6 reward 7 benefit, present 9 advantage, emolument, privilege 10 honorarium, inducement, recompense 13 fringe benefit

Perrine, Valerie
born: 11 Galveston TX
roles: 5 Lenny 8 Superman 18 Slaughterhouse Five

Perry, Matthew Calbraith
served in: 10 Mexican War 19 War of Eighteen Twelve
rank: 9 commodore
helped establish: 7 Liberia
commander of: 17 US African Squadron

gained treaty with: 5 Japan

Perry, Oliver Hazard
nickname: 14 Hero of Lake Erie
served in: 13 Tripolitan War 19 War of Eighteen-Twelve
battle: 8 Lake Erie
commander of ship: 7 Niagara 8 Lawrence
defeated: 7 British
saying: 31 We have met the enemy and they are ours

Perry, William
nickname: 12 Refrigerator
sport: 8 football
team: 12 Chicago Bears

Perry Como Show, The
regulars: 8 Don Adams 9 Jack Duffy, Paul Lynde 10 Pierre Olaf 11 Kaye Ballard 12 Sandy Stewart 14 Fontane Sisters 17 Ray Charles Singers 18 Louis Da Pron Dancers 19 Peter Gennaro Dancers
announcer: 9 Dick Stark, Ed Herlihy 11 Frank Gallop, Martin Block 12 Durward Kirby
orchestra: 13 Mitchell Ayres
theme: 16 Dream Along with Me

Perry Mason
character: 6 Lt Drum 7 Lt Tragg 9 Paul Drake 10 Lt Anderson 11 Della Street 14 Hamilton Burger
cast: 9 Wesley Lau 10 Ray Collins 11 Barbara Hale, Raymond Burr 13 William Hopper, William Talman 15 Richard Anderson

Persa
father: 7 Oceanus
mother: 6 Tethys

persecute 3 vex 4 bait 5 abuse, annoy, bully, harry, hound 6 badger, harass, harrow, hector, plague 7 oppress, torment 8 maltreat 9 tyrannize, victimize

Persephone
also: 4 Cora, Kore 10 Perserpina, Proserpine
queen of: 5 Hades
father: 4 Zeus
mother: 7 Demeter
husband: 5 Hades
abducted by: 5 Pluto
ate seeds of: 11 pomegranate
epithet: 11 Carpophorus
corresponds to: 5 Brimo 6 Libera 8 Despoena

Perseus
father: 4 Zeus
mother: 5 Danae
grandfather: 8 Acrisius
wife: 9 Andromeda
son: 6 Mestor, Perses 7 Alcaeus, Heleius 9 Electryon, Sthenelus
daughter: 10 Gorgophone
saved: 9 Andromeda
killed: 6 Gorgon, Medusa

perseverance 8 tenacity 10 doggedness, resolution 11 persistence 12 resoluteness 13 determination, steadfastness

persevere 6 hang on, keep on 7 persist 8 keep at it, plug away, work hard 9 not give up, stick to it 10 be resolute, be resolved, hammer away 11 be obstinate, be steadfast, hang in there

persevering 6 dogged 8 constant, diligent, resolute, sedulous 9 keeping on, steadfast, tenacious 10 determined, persistent, unflagging 11 hardworking, industrious, unremitting

Pershing, John J
nickname: 9 Black Jack
served in: 3 WWI 11 Philippines, World War One 18 Spanish-American War
commander of: 21 Mexican border campaign
trained: 27 American Expeditionary Forces
battle: 10 Kettle Hill 11 San Juan Hill
fought against: 5 Moros 11 Pancho Villa
rank: 16 brigadier general 18 general of the armies
memoirs: 26 My Experiences in the World War
won: 13 Pulitzer Prize (for history)

Persia see 4 Iran

Persian Gulf War
caused by: 4 Iraq 13 Saddam Hussein 14 Kuwait invasion
took place in: 4 Iraq 6 Kuwait 10 Middle East 11 Saudi Arabia
leaders:
Allies: 11 Colin Powell 15 Khalid bin Sultan 18 H Norman Schwarzkopf
Iraq: 13 Saddam Hussein
operations: 11 Desert Storm 12 Desert Shield
weapons: 4 Scud 5 AWACS 6 Abrams, Apache 7 Bradley, Patriot, Stealth 8 Tomahawk
battle: 6 Khafji 18 mother of all battles

Persian Mythology
god of light/truth: 7 Mithras

Persians, The
author: 9 Aeschylus
character: 6 Atossa, Xerxes 13 Ghost of Darius

persist 4 go on, last, stay 6 endure, hang on, hold on, remain 7 hold out, survive 8 continue, keep at it, not yield 9 not give up, persevere, stand fast, stick to it 10 be resolute 11 be obstinate, be tenacious, hang in there, never say die

persistence 8 tenacity 9 diligence 11 application 12 perseverance 13 determination

persistent 6 dogged 7 abiding, endless, eternal, lasting 8 constant, enduring, obdurate, resolute, stubborn 9 continual, incessant, obstinate, perpetual, steadfast, sustained, tenacious, unceasing, unfailing 10 continuous, determined, persisting, relentless, unshakable, unswerving 11 persevering, unrelenting, unremitting 12 interminable 13 inexhaustible

Perske, Betty Joan
real name of: 12 Lauren Bacall

persnickety 5 fussy 6 choosy 7 finical, finicky 8 picayune 10 fastidious, fuddy-duddy, meticulous, nitpicking, particular, pernickety 11 overprecise, punctilious 13 overdemanding

person 4 body, soul 5 being, human 6 mortal 8 creature 9 earthling 10 human being, individual, living body, living soul

persona 5 being 6 facade 9 character

personable 4 warm 7 affable, amiable, cordial, likable, tactful 8 amicable, charming, friendly, outgoing, pleasant, sociable 9 agreeable 10 attractive, diplomatic 11 complaisant, sympathetic 12 welldisposed, well-mannered

Personae
author: 9 Ezra Pound

personage 3 VIP 5 nabob 6 bigwig 7 big name, big shot, notable 8 big wheel, luminary, somebody 9 celebrity, dignitary 11 heavyweight 12 leading light, public figure 13 high-muck-a-muck

persona grata 16 acceptable person 34 acceptable diplomatic representative

personal 3 own 5 privy 6 bodily, inward, secret 7 private, special 8 intimate, physical 9 corporeal, exclusive 10 individual, particular, subjective 12 confidential

Personal Anthology, A
author: 15 Jorge Luis Borges

personality 5 charm 6 makeup, nature 8 charisma, identity 9 magnetism 10 affability, amiability 11 disposition, temperament 12 friendliness 13 agreeableness, individuality 15 distinctiveness

persona non grata 15 unwelcome person 18 unacceptable person 33 unwelcome diplomatic representative

Personification of
aging: 4 Elli
air: 4 Amen, Amon 5 Ammon 6 Aether
astronomy: 6 Urania
breath: 4 Amen, Amon 5 Ammon
chaos: 4 Nunu
choral song: 11 Terpsichore
comedy: 6 Thalia
confusion: 5 Chaos
conscience: 5 Aidos
courage: 5 Arete 6 Virtus
dance: 8 Polymnia 10 Polyhymnia 11 Terpsichore
death: 4 Mors 6 Namtar 8 Thanatos
desert: 3 Set 4 Seth
desire: 6 Pothos
divine punishment: 3 Ate 7 Nemesis
east wind: 5 Eurus 9 Volturnus
echo: 4 Echo
emulation: 5 Zelos
familial affection: 6 Pietas
fate: 4 Norn 5 Moira, Moras
fear: 6 Deimos
femininity: 5 Neith
fire: 4 Logi
force: 3 Bia
good faith: 5 Fides
grain blight: 7 Robigus
heaven: 6 Uranus

hostile nature: 8 Fomorian
idyllic poetry: 6 Thalia
liberty: 8 Libertas
longing: 6 Pothos
lotus: 8 Nefertem
meditation: 6 Melete
memory: 5 Mneme, Munin
moon: 4 Luna
nature: 7 Eriking
night: 3 Nox
north wind: 6 Boreas
order: 7 Eunomia
pain: 5 Oizys
past: 5 Urd
peace: 5 Irene
prayer: 5 Litae
present: 8 Verdandi
punishment: 5 Poena, Poine
recklessness: 3 Ate
revenge: 5 Poena, Poine
Roman nation: 8 Quirinus
sacred music: 8 Polymnia 10 Polyhymnia
sea: 3 Ler, Lir 5 Nammu 6 Pontus 8 Thalassa
sky: 6 Aether, Hathor
soul: 6 Psyche
southeast wind: 5 Eurus 9 Volturnus
south wind: 5 Notus 7 Ninurta
strength: 6 Cratus
sun: 3 Sol
thought: 5 Hugin
tragedy: 9 Melpomene
truth: 7 Alethia
unavailing effort: 5 Ocnus
wealth: 6 Plutus
west wind: 8 Favonius, Zephyrus
wind: 7 Ninurta
zeal: 5 Zelos

personify 6 embody 7 express 9 exemplify, incarnate, represent, symbolize 11 externalize, incorporate, personalize 12 characterize

personnel 4 crew 5 staff 7 members, workers 8 manpower 9 employees, work force 10 associates

Person to Person
host: 13 Edward R Murrow 18 Charles Collingwood

perspective 4 view 5 scape, scene, vista 7 outlook 8 overview, prospect 9 broad view, viewpoint 12 bird's-eye view

perspicacious 4 keen 5 acute, alert, awake, sharp 6 astute, shrewd 9 clear-eyed, sagacious 10 discerning, perceptive 11 clearheaded, keen-sighted, penetrating, sharp-witted 12 clear-sighted

perspicacity 6 acumen 8 keenness, sagacity 9 acuteness, alertness, sharpness 10 astuteness, perception, shrewdness 11 discernment 14 discrimination

persuadable 7 willing 8 amenable, obliging 9 malleable, tractable 10 open-minded 16 open to suggestion

persuade 3 get 4 coax, lure, move, sway 5 tempt 6 cajole, entice, induce, prompt 7 wheedle, win over 8 convince, inveigle, motivate, talk into 9 influence

Persuasion
author: 10 Jane Austen
character: 7 Mrs Clay 8 Mrs Croft 11 Lady Russell 12 Admiral Croft 25 Captain Frederick Wentworth
Elliot family: 4 Anne 7 William 9 Elizabeth, Sir Walter
Musgrove family: 4 Mary 6 Louisa 7 Charles 9 Henrietta

persuasive 6 cogent 7 coaxing, logical, winning 8 alluring, credible, forceful, inviting 9 effective, plausible, seductive 10 believable, compelling, convincing 11 influential

pert 4 flip, spry 5 alert, brash, brisk, fresh, nervy, perky, quick, saucy 6 brassy, brazen, cheeky, lively, nimble 7 chipper 8 flippant, impolite, impudent, insolent 9 audacious, energetic, insulting, sprightly, wide-awake 11 impertinent, smart-alecky 12 discourteous

pertain 2 be 5 apply, touch 6 befall, belong, relate 7 concern, connect

pertinacious 6 dogged 8 stubborn 9 obstinate, tenacious 10 persistent, unyielding 11 persevering

pertinacity 9 obstinacy 10 mulishness 11 persistence, willfulness 12 contrariness, obdurateness, perverseness, stubbornness 13 determination, inflexibility, intransigence, pigheadedness 14 bullheadedness, intractability

pertinence 9 relevance 11 germaneness 12 appositeness 13 applicability

pertinent 3 apt 4 meet 7 apropos, fitting, germane, related 8 apposite, material, relevant, suitable 9 befitting, concerned, congruent, connected 10 applicable, consistent, to the point
Latin: 5 ad rem

perturb 5 upset, worry 6 bother 7 disturb, fluster, trouble 8 disquiet, distress 10 discompose, disconcert

perturbation 5 alarm, upset, worry 6 dismay 7 anxiety, concern, turmoil 8 distress 9 agitation, commotion 10 excitement 11 disquietude, trepidation 12 apprehension, discomposure 13 consternation

perturbed 5 upset 7 annoyed, worried 8 agitated, troubled 9 disturbed 12 disconcerted

perturbing 6 vexing 7 irksome 8 annoying 9 vexatious 10 bothersome, irritating, unsettling 11 disquieting, distressing, troublesome 13 disconcerting

Peru
capital/largest city: 4 Lima
Inca capital: 5 Cuzco
others: 3 Ica 4 Puno 5 Cuzco, Paita, Pisco, Tacna 6 Callao, Talara 7 Huanuco, Iquitos 8 Arequipa, Castilla, Chiclayo, Chimbote, Mollendo, Pucallpa, Trujillo 9 Cajamarca 10 Yurimaguas

school: 8 Trujillo 8 San Marcos
division: 3 Ica 4 Lima, Puno 5 Cusco,
Cuzco, Junin, Piura, Tacna 6 Ancash,
Loreto, Tumbes
Inca empire: 13 Tahuantinsuyo
measure: 4 topo 5 galon 7 celemin
monetary unit: 3 sol 5 libra 6 dinero,
reseta 7 centavo
weight: 5 libra 7 quintal
island: 6 Chinca 7 Chincha
lake: 8 Titicaca
mountain: 5 Andes 7 El Misti, Huamina
8 Coropuna
highest point: 9 Huascaran
river: 3 Ene, Ica, Ilo 4 Napo, Napu 5
Piura, Rimac 6 Amazon, Oroton, Pampas, Yaguas, Yavari 7 Curaray, Mantaro,
Maranon, Pastaza, Tapiche, Ucayali 8
Apurimac, Huallaga, Urubamba 11 Madre
de Dios, Paucartambo
sea: 7 Pacific
physical feature:
current: 6 el nino
desert: 5 Nazca 7 Atacama, Sechura
drizzling rain: 8 ilovizna
fog: 5 garua
gulf: 9 Guayaquil
plateau: 7 Tablazo
people: 4 Ande, Boro, Cana, Inca, Inka,
Lama, Pano, Peba, Piro, Yutu 5 Campa,
Carib, Chana, Colan, Colla, Jwaro,
Moche, Nasca, Senci, Yagua, Yunca 6
Atalan, Aymara, Canchi, Chanca,
Chanka, Chimer, Cholos, Cocama, Ji-
baro, Kechua, Omagua, Quiche, Quolla,
Setibo, Sipibo 7 Changos, Chincha,
Chuncho, Mestizo, Mochica 8 Amahuaca,
Criollos, Mayoruma, Quechuia 9
Callawaya 10 Tiahuanaca, Tiatinagua 11
Chumpivilca
artist: 4 Lazo 7 Montero, Sabogal,
Szyszlo 8 Codesido
author: 4 Vega 5 Palma, Prada 8
Caviedes 10 Mariategui
explorer: 7 Pizarro
Inca leader: 7 Huascar 9 Atahualpa 10
Manco Capac
leader: 5 Balta, Pardo, Prado, Torre 7
Bolivar 8 Castilla, Fujimori 9 Santa Cruz
13 Belaunde Terry 15 Leguiay y Salcedo,
Morales Bermudez
language: 6 Aymara 7 English, Quechua,
Spanish
religion: 13 Roman Catholic
place:
bullring: 11 Plaza de Acho
center of Lima: 12 Plaza de Armas
church: 10 La Compania
open market/street: 9 Calle Real
ruins: 5 Huaco 8 Chan-Chan 9
Cajamarca 11 Machu- Picchu 22 Fortress
of Sacsayhuaman
feature:
animal: 5 llama 6 alpaca, vicuna 7 guanaco
commune: 6 ayllus
dance: 5 cueca, kaswa 6 cachua

farmers: 10 campesinos
priest: 6 villac
slums: 9 barriadas
tree: 8 cinchona
food:
dish: 3 aji, cuy 7 ceviche 10 anticuchos
drink: 5 pisco 6 chicha 11 aguardiente
Perugino, Pietro
real name: 14 Pietro Vannucci
also called: 10 Il Perugino 14 Pier della
Pieve
born: 5 Italy 15 Citta della Pieve
artwork: 24 The Crucifixion with Saints
26 Delivery of the Keys to St Peter 27
The Giving of the Keys to St Peter 32 Apparition of the Virgin to St Bernard, Christ
Delivering the Keys to St Peter
perusal 5 study 6 review 7 reading 8 scanning, scrutiny 10 inspection, run-through
11 examination, look-through 12 scrutiniz-
ing 13 contemplation
peruse 3 con 4 read, scan 5 study 6
search, survey 7 examine, inspect 10
scrutinize
pervade 4 fill 5 imbue 6 infuse 7 suffuse 8
permeate, saturate 9 penetrate 13 spread
through 17 diffuse throughout
pervasive 4 rife 7 rampant 8 dominant 9
prevalent 10 ubiquitous 11 omnipresent,
predominant
perverse 5 balky 6 dogged, mulish, ornery
7 wayward, willful 8 contrary, obdurate,
stubborn 9 obstinate, pigheaded 10 hardheaded, headstrong, inflexible, rebellious
11 disobedient, intractable, wrongheaded
perversion 9 depravity 10 corruption, degeneracy, immorality 11 dissipation, dissolution
pervert 4 warp 5 abuse 6 debase, misuse 7
contort, corrupt, degrade, deprave, distort,
falsify, subvert 8 misapply 9 desecrate 12
misrepresent
perverted 5 false 6 faulty, untrue, warped 7
corrupt, debased, deviant, twisted, unsound 8 aberrant, abnormal, degraded,
depraved 9 contorted, distorted, erroneous, imperfect, unnatural 10 fallacious, unbalanced 12 misconceived, misconstrued
13 misunderstood
Peschkowsky, Michael Igor
real name of: 11 Mike Nichols
pesky 7 chafing, galling, irksome 8 annoying 9 maddening, obnoxious, offensive,
vexatious 10 bothersome, disturbing, nettlesome 11 aggravating, distasteful, infuriating, pestiferous, troublesome 12 disagreeable, exasperating 13 objectionable
pessimism 5 gloom 7 despair 10 gloominess 12 hopelessness 13 gloomy outlook
14 discouragement 15 downheartedness
pessimist 7 kill-joy 8 sourpuss 9 Cassandra, defeatist, gloomy Gus 10 spoilsport,
wet blanket 11 crepehanger 13 prophet of
doom
pessimistic 5 gloomy 8 hopeless 10 despairing, dispirited 11 discouraged, downhearted

pest 4 bane 5 curse 6 blight, bother 7 scourge 8 nuisance, vexation 9 annoyance 10 irritation 13 pain in the neck

pester 3 irk, nag, vex 4 bait, fret 5 annoy, harry, taunt, worry 6 badger, bother, harass, hector, nettle, plague 7 disturb, provoke, torment, trouble 8 irritate

pesticide 3 DDT 7 biocide 8 fumigant 9 fungicide, germacide, vermicide 11 insecticide
   user: 12 exterminator

pestilence 6 blight, plague 7 disease 8 epidemic
   god of: 4 Irra

pet 3 pat 4 baby, dear 6 caress, choice, fondle, stroke 7 beloved, darling, dearest, favored 8 favorite 9 cherished, preferred 10 sweetheart 14 apple of one's eye

pet activity 5 hobby 7 passion 8 interest 10 enthusiasm, hobbyhorse

Peter 7 apostle
   means: 4 rock
   also called: 5 Simon 6 Cephas
   father: 4 John 5 Jonas
   brother: 6 Andrew
   birthplace: 9 Bethsaida
   hometown: 9 Capernaum
   disciple of: 5 Jesus
   companion: 4 John 5 James
   rebuked: 7 Ananias 8 Sapphira
   secretary: 8 Silvanus
   pertaining to: 7 Petrine

Peter and the Wolf
   composed by: 9 Prokofiev

Peter Grimes
   opera by: 7 Britten
   character: 11 Ellen Orford

Peter Heering, Cherry Heering
   type: 6 brandy 7 liqueur
   origin: 7 Denmark
   flavor: 6 cherry
   color: 3 red

Peter Ibbetson
   author: 15 George Du Maurier

peter out 3 ebb 7 decline, dwindle, fall off, give out 8 diminish

Peter Pan
   author: 11 James Barrie
   character: 9 Nurse Nana 10 Tinker Bell 11 Captain Hook 12 Wendy Darling

Peter Quince at the Clavier
   author: 14 Wallace Stevens

Peters, Jane Alice
   real name of: 13 Carole Lombard

petiole 4 stem 5 spine, stalk, stipe 8 peduncle 9 leafstalk

petite 3 wee 4 tiny 5 small 6 little 9 miniature 10 diminutive

petition 3 ask, beg, sue 4 plea, pray, seek, suit, urge 5 press 6 appeal, invoke, orison, prayer 7 apply to, beseech, entreat 8 appeal to, call upon, entreaty, proposal 9 imploring, plead with, request of 10 invocation, supplicate 11 application, beseechment, requisition 12 solicitation, supplication

petitioner 6 suitor 8 claimant 9 solicitor, suppliant 10 supplicant

pet name 9 nickname 9 sobriquet 10 diminutive, endearment

pet phrase 5 maxim, motto 6 saying, slogan 9 catchword

Petre (Lord)
   character in: 16 The Rape of the Lock
   author: 4 Pope

petrified 4 hard 5 dense, solid, stony 6 frozen 8 hardened, rocklike 9 paralyzed 10 solidified 11 hard as a rock, scared stiff 13 turned to stone

Petrified Forest, The
   director: 10 Archie Mayo
   based on play by: 14 Robert Sherwood
   cast: 9 Dick Foran 10 Bette Davis 12 Leslie Howard 14 Humphrey Bogart (Duke Mantee)
   setting: 7 Arizona

Petronius
   author of: 9 Satyricon

Petruchio
   character in: 19 The Taming of the Shrew
   author: 11 Shakespeare

Petticoat Junction
   character: 10 Floyd Smoot, Sam Drucker 11 Homer Bedloe, Kate Bradley 12 Charlie Pratt, Dr Janet Craig, Steve Elliott, Wendell Gibbs 14 Betty Jo Bradley, Uncle Joe Carson 15 Billie Jo Bradley, Bobbie Jo Bradley
   cast: 9 Frank Cady, Linda Kaye, Mike Minor, Rufe Davis 10 Pat Woodell 11 Charles Lane 12 Bea Benaderet, Byron Foulger, June Lockhart, Lori Saunders 13 Edgar Buchanan, Gunilla Hutton, Jeannine Riley 14 Meredith MacRae, Smiley Burnette
   setting: 11 Hooterville 14 Shady Rest Hotel
   train: 10 Cannonball

petto 5 chest 6 breast

petty 4 mean 5 minor, small 6 flimsy, paltry, shabby, slight 7 ignoble, trivial 8 niggling, picayune, piddling, trifling 10 ungenerous 11 small-minded, unimportant 12 narrow-minded 13 insignificant 14 inconsiderable 15 inconsequential

petulance 9 poutiness, sulkiness 11 fretfulness, peevishness 12 irritability

petulant 4 sour 5 cross, gruff, huffy, sulky, surly, testy 6 grumpy, sullen, tetchy, touchy 7 bearish, crabbed, fretful, grouchy, peevish, pettish, uncivil 8 snappish 9 crotchety, fractious, irascible, irritable 10 ill-natured, out of sorts, ungracious 11 complaining, contentious, ill-tempered, quarrelsome, thin-skinned 12 cantankerous, faultfinding

Petulia
   director: 13 Richard Lester
   cast: 10 Arthur Hill, Pippa Scott 12 George C Scott, Joseph Cotten 13 Julie Christie, Shirley Knight 18 Richard Chamberlain

setting: 12 San Francisco

petunia
varieties: 4 Wild 7 Mexican, Seaside 10 Large white 12 Common garden 14 Violet-flowered

peu a peu 14 little by little

peu de chose 14 trifling matter 17 unimportant matter

pew 4 seat 5 bench 6 settle

Peychaud Bitters
type: 8 aperitif
origin: 10 New Orleans

Peyton Place
author: 14 Grace Metalious
character: 9 Rita Jacks (Harrington) 10 Hannah Cord, Steven Cord 12 Matthew Swain 13 Betty Anderson (Harrington Cord Harrington), Elliott Carson, Julie Anderson 14 Dr Michael Rossi, Dr Robert Morton, George Anderson 16 Allison Mackenzie (Harrington), Leslie Harrington, Norman Harrington, Rodney Harrington 18 Constance Mackenzie (Carson)
cast (television): 8 Ed Nelson 9 Kent Smith, Mia Farrow, Ryan O'Neal 10 Tim O'Connor 11 Kasey Rogers, Paul Langton, Ruth Warrick 12 Henry Beckman, James Douglas 13 Dorothy Malone 14 Barbara Parkins, Patricia Morrow, Warner Anderson 19 Christopher Connelly
director (movie): 10 Mark Robson
cast (movie): 9 Hope Lange 10 Lana Turner, Lloyd Nolan 13 Arthur Kennedy
score: 11 Franz Waxman

Phaeax
father: 8 Poseidon
mother: 7 Corcyra
ancestor of: 10 Phaeacians

Phaedo
author: 5 Plato

Phaedra
father: 5 Minos
mother: 8 Pasiphae
sister: 7 Ariadne
husband: 7 Theseus
son: 6 Acamas 8 Demophon
stepson: 10 Hippolytus
loved: 10 Hippolytus
death by: 7 hanging, suicide

Phaenna
origin: 5 Greek 7 Spartan
member of: 6 Graces

Phaethon
father: 6 Helios
mother: 7 Clymene

phalanx 6 column, parade 9 formation 13 ranks and files

Phallus
image of: 9 male organ
symbol of: 9 fertility
carried in: 6 comedy 9 festivals
associated with: 3 Pan 6 Hermes 7 Demeter 8 Dionysus

phantasm 5 ghost, shade, spook 6 mirage, spirit, vision 7 fantasy, figment, incubus, phantom, specter 8 delusion, illusion, succubus 10 apparition

Phantasus
origin: 5 Greek
god of: 6 dreams

phantom 5 dream, ghost 6 mirage, spirit, vision, wraith 7 chimera, specter 8 illusion, phantasm 10 apparition 13 hallucination

Phantom, The
creator: 7 Lee Falk 8 Ray Moore
nickname: 16 The Ghost Who Walks
mask: 5 black
costume: 6 purple

Phantom of the Opera, The
director:
1925 version: 12 Rupert Julian
1943 version: 11 Arthur Lubin
cast:
1925 version: 9 Lon Chaney 11 Mary Philbin, Norman Kerry
1943 version: 10 Hume Cronyn, Jane Farrar, Nelson Eddy 11 Claude Rains 12 Edgar Barrier 13 Susanna Foster
setting: 10 Paris Opera

Phaon
occupation: 7 boatman
location: 8 Mitylene
given: 9 youth 6 beauty
given by: 9 Aphrodite

pharos 5 light 6 beacon, signal 7 seamark 10 lighthouse, watchtower

phase 4 side, step, view 5 angle, facet, guise, level, slant, stage 6 aspect, degree, period 7 feature 8 attitude, juncture 9 condition, viewpoint 10 appearance 11 development 12 circumstance

pheasant
group of: 4 nest, nide

Phedre, Phaedra
author: 6 Racine
character: 6 Aricia 7 Theseus 10 Hippolytus

Phegeus
king of: 7 Psophis
son: 5 Axion 7 Temenus
daughter: 7 Arsinoe
purified: 8 Alcmaeon
ordered death of: 8 Alcmaeon

Phenix see 7 Phoenix

phenomenal 5 super 6 unique 7 amazing, unusual 8 singular, superior, uncommon 9 fantastic, marvelous, unheard-of 10 incredible, miraculous, prodigious, remarkable, stupendous, surpassing 11 astonishing, exceptional, outstanding, sensational, spectacular 12 overwhelming, unparalleled 13 extraordinary, unprecedented

phenomenon 5 thing 6 marvel, rarity, wonder 7 episode, miracle 8 incident, occasion 9 actuality, curiosity, exception, happening, nonpareil, sensation 10 fact of life, occurrence, proceeding 11 contingency

Phereclus
also: 10 Harmonides
father: 6 Tecton
built: 5 ships

Pheres
  king of: 6 Pherae
  father: 8 Cretheus
  mother: 4 Tyro
  son: 7 Admetus, Idomene
  daughter: 8 Periapis
Pheriphetes
  epithet: 9 Corynetes
phial 4 vial 6 bottle, vessel 9 container
Phidias
  born: 6 Athens, Greece
  artwork: 4 Zeus 6 Amazon 13 Lemnian
  Athene (Athena Lemnia) 15 Apollo
  Parnopios, Athena Parthenos, Athena
  Promachos
Philadelphia
  baseball team: 8 Phillies
  basketball team: 13 Seventy-Sixers
  bay: 8 Delaware
  football team: 5 Stars 6 Eagles
  founded/planned by: 4 Penn
  hockey team: 6 Flyers
  landmark: 6 US Mint 8 City Hall 11 Liberty Bell 12 Christ Church, Congress Hall
  13 Franklin Field, Roosevelt Park 14
  Betsy Ross House, Carpenter's Hall 15
  Gloria Dei Church, Veterans Stadium 16
  Independence Hall
  means: 19 city of brotherly love
  museum: 5 Rodin 15 Fels Planetarium
  16 Barnes Foundation 17 Franklin Institute
  river: 8 Delaware 10 Schuylkill
  university: 4 Penn 6 Drexel, Temple 9
  Jefferson, St Joseph's 22 Curtis Institute
  of Music
Philadelphia Story, The
  director: 11 George Cukor
  based on play by: 11 Philip Barry
  cast: 9 Cary Grant 10 Ruth Hussey 12
  James Stewart 16 Katharine Hepburn
  Oscar for: 5 actor (Stewart)
  remade as: 11 High Society
Philammon
  father: 6 Apollo
  mother: 6 Chione
  half-brother: 9 Autolycus
  son: 8 Thamyris
  vocation: 8 musician
philanderer 3 rip 4 rake, wolf 5 flirt 6
  lecher, tomcat, wanton 7 dallier, Don Juan,
  gallant, swinger, trifler 8 lothario, lover boy,
  rakehell 9 adulterer, libertine, womanizer
  10 lady-killer 11 woman-chaser
philanthropic, philanthropical 7 liberal 8
  generous 9 bounteous 10 almsgiving, beneficent, benevolent, charitable, munificent
  11 magnanimous 12 eleemosynary, humanitarian
philanthropist 5 donor, giver 8 do-gooder
  9 almsgiver 11 contributor 12 humanitarian
  13 Good Samaritan
philanthropy 6 bounty 7 charity 8 goodness 10 almsgiving, generosity, liberality
  11 beneficence, benevolence, munificence
  13 unselfishness 14 charitableness, open-

handedness 15 humanitarianism 16 large-
heartedness 18 public-spiritedness
Philaster
  author: 30 Francis Beaumont and John
  Fletcher
Philemon
  friend: 4 Paul
  slave: 8 Onesimus
  wife: 6 Baucis
  entertained: 4 Hera, Zeus
  became: 12 temple priest
Philip
  hometown: 9 Bethsaida
  disciple of: 5 Jesus
Philippines
  named for: 15 Philip II of Spain
  capital/largest city: 6 Manila
  others: 3 Iba 4 Agoa, Bogo, Cebu, Debu,
  Naga, Palo 5 Albay, Davao, Gapan, Iriga,
  Lanao, Laoag, Pasay, Vigan 6 Aparri, Ba-
  guio, Cavite, Ilagan, Iloilo, Tarlac 7 Baco-
  lod, Basilan, Calapan, Dagupan, Legaspi
  8 Batangas, Caloocan, Cotabato, Tac-
  loban 9 Zamboanga 10 Cabanutuan,
  Dumaguette, Quezon City
  school: 10 Santo Tomas 14 Ateneo de
  Manila
  division: 4 Abra, Cebu 5 Aklan, Albay,
  Bohol, Capiz, Davao, Lanao, Leyte, Rizal, Samar 6 Agusan, Bataan, Cavite, Iloilo, Laguna, Quezon, Tarlac 7 Isabela,
  Lepanto, Surigao
  measure: 4 loan 5 braza, catty, cavan,
  chupa, fardo, ganta, picul, punto 6
  apatan, balita, lachsa, quinon 7 quilate 8
  chinanta
  monetary unit: 4 peso 6 conant, peseta
  7 centavo
  weight: 5 catty, picul 6 lachsa 7 quilate 8
  chinanta
  island: 4 Cebu, Cuyo, Jolo, Poro, Sulu 5
  Batan, Bohol, Leyte, Luzon, Panay, Samar, Ticao 6 Culion, Lubang, Negros 7
  Babuyan, Batanes, Bisayan, Masbate,
  Mindoro, Palawan, Paragua, Polillo,
  Visoyan 8 Mindanao 10 Corregidor,
  Marinduque
  lake: 4 Taal 5 Lanao
  mountain: 3 Iba 4 Mayo, Taal 5 Albay,
  Askja, Hibok, Mayon, Pulog 6 Pagsan 7
  Banahao, Canlaon
  highest point: 3 Apo
  river: 4 Abra, Agno 5 Magat, Pasig 6
  Agusan, Laoang 7 Cagayan 8 Mindanao,
  Pampanga
  sea: 4 Sulu 5 Samar 7 Celebes, Pacific,
  Visayan 10 Philippine, South China
  physical feature:
  bay: 6 Manila
  falls: 9 Pagsanjan 14 Maria Christina
  gulf: 4 Moro 5 Albay, Davao, Leyte,
  Ragay 8 Lingayen
  hot springs: 8 Los Banos
  national park: 12 Mayon Volcano
  ocean trench: 8 Mindanao
  peninsula: 6 Bataan
  storm: 6 bagyos 7 monsoon, typhoon

volcano: 8 Pinatubo
people: 3 Ati, Eta, Ita, Tao 4 Aeta, Ifil, Moro, Sulu, Tino 5 Abaca, Aripa, Batak, Batan, Bicol, Bikol, Busao, Lutao, Mundo, Sinay, Tagal, Vicol, Yakan 6 Apayao, Baluga, Bilaan, Biscol, Bontoc, Bontok, Busaos, Ibanag, Ibilao, Ifugao, Igalot, Igorot, Illano, Isinai, Lutayo, Manabo, Manobo, Montes, Sambal, Tagala, Timaua, Timawa, Zambal 7 Bagoboo, Bisayan, Cagayan, Ilocano, Itanega, Malanoa, Mangyan, Naboloi, Negrito, Tagalog, Tirurai, Visayan 8 Arupaata, Babaylan, Bukidono, Filipino, Igorotte, Manguian, Pampanga 9 Arupaatta, Dulangane, Macajambo, Pampangao, Tinguiane 10 Magindanao, Pangasinan 11 Calalangane
author: 5 Rizal
explorer: 7 Legazpe 8 Magellan 10 Villalobos
leader: 5 Ramos 6 Aquino, Marcos, Osmena, Quezon 9 Aguinaldo, Bonifacio, Macapagal, Magsaysay 11 Roxas y Acuna
language: 4 Moro 5 Bicol, Bikol 6 Ibanag 7 Cebuano, English, Ilocano, Spanish, Tagalog, Visayan 8 Filipino, Pilipino 9 Pampangan 10 Samar-Leyte 13 Bamboo-English
religion: 7 animism 9 Aglipayan 10 Protestant 13 Roman Catholic 15 Iglesia ni Kristo
place:
church: 14 Saint Augustine
esplanade: 6 Luneta
fort: 4 Cota, Gota, Kota 5 Lotta 10 Corregidor
president's palace: 10 Malacanang
street: 7 Escolta
US bases: 5 Clark 8 Subic Bay
walled city: 10 Intramuros
feature:
animal: 7 carabao, tamarau, tarsier 9 mouse deer
bird: 7 creeper
clothing: 4 saya 6 camisa 10 balintawak 12 mestiza terno 13 barong tagalog
dance: 9 tinikling
drama: 8 moro-moro
guerrilla fighter: 3 huk
musicians: 12 musikongbuho
naval base: 6 Cavite
song: 8 kundiman
village: 8 barangay
food:
dish: 3 poi 4 baha, sabu, taro 5 balut
drink: 4 beno, vino 5 bubud 6 tampoy 7 pangasi
philistine 5 yahoo 6 savage 7 Babbitt, lowbrow, prosaic 8 ignorant 9 barbarian, bourgeois, unrefined, untutored 10 conformist, uncultured, uneducated, uninformed, unlettered 11 commonplace 12 conventional, uncultivated 13 unenlightened 15 conventionalist 16 anti-intellectual

Philistine city 4 Gath
Philius
   epithet of: 4 Zeus
   means: 8 friendly
Phillotson, Richard
   character in: 14 Jude the Obscure
   author: 5 Hardy
Philoctetes
   author: 9 Sophocles
   character: 8 Heracles, Odysseus 11 Neoptolemus
   inherits arms of: 8 Hercules
   father: 5 Poeas, Poias
   killed: 5 Paris
philodendron
   varieties: 5 Dubia, giant 6 common 7 cut-leaf, red-leaf 8 blushing 9 black-gold, heart-leaf, horsehead, spade-leaf, split-leaf 10 fiddle-leaf, variegated, velvet-leaf 11 leather-leaf
Philoetius
   cowherd of: 8 Odysseus
Philomela
   position: 8 princess
   realm: 6 Athens
   father: 7 Pandion
   sister: 6 Procne
   brother-in-law: 6 Tereus
   raped by: 6 Tereus
   transformed into: 7 swallow 11 nightingale
Philomelides
   king of: 6 Lesbos
   defeated by: 8 Odysseus
Philonome *see* 9 Phylonome
philosopher/theologian 4 sage 6 savant 7 thinker, wise man 8 logician, reasoner 9 theorizer 11 rationalist, truth seeker 12 dialectician 13 metaphysician
   Alsatian: 10 Schweitzer
   American: 4 Eddy 5 Dewey, James, Royce, Smith, Young 6 Mather, Peirce 7 Edwards, Niebuhr, Russell, Tillich 8 Williams 9 McPherson 14 Elijah Muhammad
   Austrian: 12 Wittgenstein
   British: 3 Fox 4 Hume, Inge, Knox, More, Owen 5 Bacon, Burke, Locke, Moore 6 Biddle, Cotton, Hobbes, Huxley, Newman, Wesley 7 Bentham, Bradley, Carlyle, Cranmer, Russell, Spencer 8 Berkeley, Wycliffe 9 Whitehead 13 Thomas a Becket 14 William of Occam
   Chinese: 6 Lao-tzu 9 Confucius
   Christian: 6 Calvin, Luther, Origen, St Paul 7 Abelard 8 St Anselm 9 St Patrick 10 Duns Scotus, St Benedict 11 St Augustine 14 William of Occam 15 St Thomas Aquinas 16 St Albertus Magnus
   Czech: 3 Hus
   Danish: 11 Kierkegaard
   Dutch: 7 Erasmus, Spinoza
   El Salvadorian: 9 Masferrer
   French: 5 Comte 6 Calvin, Pascal, Sartre 7 Abelard, Bergson, Diderot 8 Maritain, Rousseau, Voltaire 9 Descartes, Levy-Bruhl, Montaigne 11 Montesquieu
   German: 4 Kant, Marx 5 Buber, Hegel 6

Boehme, Fichte, Herder, Luther **7**
Husserl, Jaspers, Leibniz **9** Heidegger,
Nietzsche, Schelling **10** Muhlenberg **11**
Melanchthon **12** Schopenhauer **13**
Thomas a Kempis **14** Schleiermacher
Greek: 5 Plato **6** St Paul, Thales **8**
Socrates **9** Aristotle **10** Anaxagoras,
Anaximenes, Heraclitus, Parmenides, Pythagoras **11** Anaximander
Indian: 6 Buddha **16** Siddharta Gautama
Islamic: 7 al Kindi **8** al-Farabi, Averroes,
Avicenna **9** al Ghazali **10** Ibn Khaldun
Italian: 5 Bruno **7** Aquinas, Mazzini **10** St
Benedict, Zeno of Elea **17** St Francis of
Assisi
Japanese: 6 Suzuki
Jewish: 7 Spinoza **10** Maimonides
Latin: 8 Plotinus **11** St Augustine
Spanish: 8 Averroes **10** Maimonides **13**
Ortega y Gasset **16** Ignatius of Loyola
Swedish: 10 Swedenborg
Swiss: 7 Zwingli

Philosopher's Pupil, The
   author: 11 Iris Murdoch

philosophic, philosophical 4 calm **5** quiet,
stoic **6** serene **7** erudite, learned, logical,
patient, stoical **8** abstract, composed, rational, resigned, tranquil **9** impassive, judicious, sagacious, unexcited, unruffled **10**
complacent, fatalistic, reasonable, theorizing, thoughtful **11** imperturbed, theoretical,
unemotional **14** self-restrained

philosophy 4 calm, view **5** ideas, logic **6**
reason **7** beliefs, opinion, thought **8** doctrine, fatalism, patience, serenity, stoicism,
thinking **9** basic idea, composure, esthetics, principle, reasoning, restraint,
viewpoint **10** conception, theorizing **11**
complacency, convictions, forbearance,
impassivity, metaphysics, rationalism, resignation
   means: 12 love of wisdom
   branch: 6 ethics **8** ontology **10** aesthetics
   11 metaphysics **12** epistemology
   term: 8 noumenon **9** causality, dialectic,
   solipsism
   school of: 7 Sophism **8** idealism, Milesian, Stoicism **9** Epicurean, pantheism,
   Platonism **10** empiricism, pragmatism,
   Skepticism **11** rationalism **12** Aristotelian,
   neoplatonism **13** Phenomenology, scholasticism **14** existentialism **17** logical positivism

Phil Silvers Show, The
   character: 6 Fender **7** Col Hall, Henshaw
   8 Doberman **9** Sgt Ritzik **12** Sgt Joan Hogan **13** Rocco Barbella, Sgt Ernie Bilko
   cast: 8 Joe E Ross, Paul Ford **10** Alan
   Melvin, Herbie Faye **13** Harvey Lembeck
   15 Elisabeth Fraser, Maurice Gosfield
   setting: 6 Kansas **10** Fort Baxter

Philyra
   father: 7 Oceanus
   mother: 6 Tethys
   mother of: 6 Chiron
   changed into: 10 linden tree

Phlegethon
   also: 14 Pyriphlegethon
   form: 5 river
   location: 10 underworld

phlegmatic 4 calm, cool, dull **6** serene **7**
languid, passive, stoical **8** listless, sluggish, tranquil **9** apathetic, impassive, lethargic, unfeeling **10** nonchalant, spiritless
11 indifferent, insensitive, unconcerned,
unemotional, unexcitable **12** unresponsive
13 imperturbable, unimpassioned **15** undemonstrative

Phlegyas
   king of: 8 Lapithae
   condemned: 6 Apollo

Phlias
   father: 8 Dionysus
   member of: 9 Argonauts

phlox
   varieties: 4 blue, fall, moss, sand, star **6**
   annual, smooth **7** prickly **8** creeping,
   drummond, mountain, trailing **9** perennial,
   sword-leaf, thick-leaf **15** summer perennial

Phnom-Penh
   airport: 10 Pochentong
   also: 8 Pnom Penh
   capital of: 8 Cambodia **9** Kampuchea
   pagoda: 12 Preah Morokot
   river: 6 Mekong **8** Tonle Sap

Phobetor
   epithet of: 6 Icelus
   means: 9 terrifier

phobia 5 dread **6** horror, terror **7** bugaboo,
bugbear **8** aversion, loathing **12** apprehension **16** unreasonable fear **19** overwhelming anxiety
   fear of animals: 9 zoophobia
   fear of birds: 13 ornithophobia
   fear of blushing: 13 erythrophobia
   fear of bridges: 13 gephyrophobia
   fear of cats: 10 gatophobia **12** aelurophobia, ailurophobia
   fear of closed/confined spaces: 14
   claustrophobia
   fear of crowds: 11 ochlophobia
   fear of darkness/the dark of night: 11
   nyctophobia
   fear of death: 13 thanatophobia
   fear of death/dead bodies: 11 necrophobia
   fear of dirt: 10 mysophobia
   fear of disease: 11 pathophobia
   fear of fire: 10 pyrophobia
   fear of flowers: 11 anthophobia
   fear of flying: 10 aerophobia
   fear of germs: 11 mikrophobia
   fear of hair: 12 trichophobia
   fear of heights: 10 acrophobia
   fear of insanity: 13 dementophobia
   fear of lightning: 11 astraphobia
   fear of men: 11 androphobia
   fear of mice: 10 murophobia
   fear of numbers: 12 numerophobia
   fear of open spaces: 11 agoraphobia
   fear of pain: 10 algophobia
   fear of people: 12 anthrophobia

fear of reptiles: 13 herpetophobia
fear of snakes: 13 ophidiophobia
fear of speaking aloud: 11 phonophobia
fear of spiders: 13 arachnophobia
fear of strangers: 10 xenophobia
fear of thunder: 12 brontophobia
fear of the number thirteen: 17 triskaidekaphobia
fear of vehicles/driving: 11 amaxophobia
fear of water: 10 aquaphobia 11 hydrophobia
fear of women: 10 gynophobia

Phobos
also: 6 Phobus
father: 4 Ares

Phocus
father: 6 Aeacus 8 Ornytion
mother: 8 Psamathe
half-brother: 6 Peleus 7 Telamon
wife: 7 Antiope
killed by: 7 Telamon
burial place: 8 Tithorea

Phoebe
member of: 6 Titans
father: 6 Uranus
mother: 4 Gaea
sister: 6 Themis
daughter: 4 Leto 7 Asteria
identified with: 4 moon
corresponds to: 5 Diana 7 Artemis

Phoebus see 6 Apollo

Phoenicia see 7 Lebanon

Phoenician Mythology
god of agriculture/earth: 5 Dagon
corresponds to Mesopotamian: 5 Dagan
bird: 6 Phenix 7 Phoenix 8 Phoeenix
goddess of fertility/reproduction: 7 Astarte

Phoenissae (The Phoenician Maidens)
author: 9 Euripides
character: 7 Creon 7 Jocasta, Oedipus 8
Adrastus, Antigone, Eteocles, Tiresias 9
Polynices 10 Menoikieus

Phoenix
basketball team: 4 Suns
capital of: 7 Arizona
event: 5 rodeo
feature: 10 Papago Park 22 Desert Botanical Gardens
football team: 9 Wranglers, Cardinals
river: 4 Salt

Phoenix, Phoeenix
also: 6 Phenix
origin: 10 Phoenician
form: 4 bird
gift: 11 immortality
king of: 9 Dolopians
father: 7 Amyntor
mother: 8 Cleobule
brother: 6 Cadmus
sister: 4 Europa
foster son: 8 Achilles
ancestor of: 11 Phoenicians

Pholus
form: 7 centaur
guarded: 4 wine
wine a gift from: 8 Dionysus
phonograph 4 hi-fi 5 phono 6 stereo 8 Vic-
trola 9 turntable 10 gramophone 12 record
player

phonophobia
fear of: 13 speaking aloud

phony, phoney 4 fake, hoax, mock, sham
5 bogus, false, fraud, trick 6 forged,
pseudo, unreal, untrue 7 forgery 8 specious, spurious 9 deceptive, imitation, pretended, synthetic 10 artificial, fraudulent,
not genuine 11 counterfeit, make-believe,
unauthentic

Phorbas
son of: 8 Lapithes
dispelled: 6 plague
plague of: 8 serpents
leader of: 4 Troy
allies of: 9 Phygians
killed by: 4 Ajax
form: 5 boxer
killed: 8 pilgrims
killed by: 6 Apollo

Phorcids
father: 7 Phorcys
mother: 4 Ceto

Phorcys
god of: 3 sea
sister: 4 Ceto
children: 5 Ladon 6 Graiae 7 Echidna,
Gorgons 8 Phorcids
harbor in: 6 Ithaca

Phormio
author: 7 Terence

phosphorus
chemical symbol: 1 P
photograph 3 pic 4 film, snap 5 image,
print, shoot, still 6 candid, glossy 7 mug-
shot, picture, tintype 8 likeness, portrait,
snapshot 12 daguerrotype
bath: 5 fixer, toner 7 reducer 9 developer
book: 5 album

photographer
American: 4 Haas, Hine, Penn, Riis,
Rose, Tice 5 (Ansel) Adams, Annan, Ar-
bus, Brady, Evans, Hawes, Lange, Lynes,
Smith, White 6 Avedon, Coburn, Eakins,
Man Ray, Strand, Turner, Weston 7 Bur-
rows, Eastman, Gardner, Jackson, Wat-
kins 8 Bogardus, Davidson, Steichen 9
Muybridge, O'Sullivan, Rothstein, Stieg-
litz 10 Cunningham, Southworth 11
Bourke-White, Eisenstaedt, Turberville 13
Watson-Schutze
British: 5 Evans, Frith 6 Bailey, Beaton,
Fenton, Mayall, Talbot 7 Cameron 8
Brewster, Robinson 9 Rejlander 10
MacPherson
French: 5 Marey, Nadar 6 Baldus,
DuCamp, Le Secq, Newton, Niepce 7 Lu-
miere 8 Daguerre 12 Sabatier-Blot 14
Cartier-Bresson
German: 4 Hoch 5 Ernst 7 Hausman 8
Stelzner 13 Renger-Patzsch

Hungarian: 7 Kertesz 10 Moholy-Nagy
Japanese: 4 Ikko
Scottish: 4 Hill 7 Adamson
Spanish: 7 Picabia

photostat 4 copy 7 replica 9 duplicate, facsimile 12 reproduction

phrase 3 put, say 4 word 5 couch, idiom,
maxim, state, utter, voice, words 6 cliche,
dictum, impart, remark, saying, truism 7
declare, express, proverb 8 aphorism, banality, locution 9 enunciate, find words,
platitude, utterance, verbalize, word group
10 articulate, expression 11 communicate

phraseology 5 style 7 diction, wording 13
choice of words 18 manner of expression

Phrixus
  father: 7 Athamas
  mother: 7 Nephele
  stepmother: 3 Ino
  sister: 5 Helle
  wife: 9 Chalciope
  son: 5 Argus, Melas 8 Phrontis 10 Cytissorus

Phrontis
  father: 7 Phrixus
  mother: 9 Chalciope
  brother: 5 Argus, Melus 10 Cytissorus
  husband: 8 Panthous

Phthia
  mentioned in: 5 Iliad
  concubine of: 7 Amyntor
  seduced by: 7 Phoenix
  son: 5 Dorus 8 Laodocus 10 Polypoetes

Phyleus
  king of: 6 Ephyra
  father: 6 Auglas
  wife: 8 Timandra
  children: 5 Meges 10 Astyocheia

Phyllis
  father: 8 Phylleus
  husband: 8 Demophon
  loved: 6 Acamas

Phylomache
  son: 7 Acastus
  daughter: 8 Alcestis

Phylonome
  also: 9 Philonome
  husband: 6 Cycnus
  stepson: 6 Tenes

physical 4 real 5 human, solid 6 actual, animal, bodily, carnal, living 7 fleshly, natural,
sensual 8 apparent, concrete, corporal,
existent, existing, external, material, palpable, tangible 9 corporeal, essential, of the
body 11 substantive

physical checkup 4 exam 8 physical 11
examination 19 physical examination

physical condition 5 shape 7 fitness,
stamina 12 constitution

physical disorder 6 malady 7 ailment, disease, illness 8 sickness 9 ill health, infirmity

physical training 3 gym 6 sports 8 exercise 9 athletics, shaping up 10 gymnastics,
working out 12 conditioning

physician 2 GP, MD 3 doc 5 medic 6 doc-
tor, medico 7 surgeon 8 sawbones 10 spe-
cialist 11 medicine man, pill peddler 13
medical doctor
  Alsatian: 10 Schweitzer
  American: 4 Long, Rush, Salk 5 Sabin 6
  Dooley, Gorgas 7 Huggins, Whipple 8
  Williams 9 Blackwell 11 Landsteiner
  British: 5 Paget 6 Adrian, Harvey, Jen-
  ner, Lister
  Canadian: 4 Best 7 Banting
  Dutch: 7 Eijkman
  French: 7 Charcot
  German: 6 Mesmer 7 Fechner, Virchow
  10 Blumenbach
  Greek: 10 Herophilus 11 Hippocrates 12
  Erasistratus
  Italian: 8 Malpighi
  Russian: 6 Pavlov
  Scottish: 4 Lind
  South African: 7 Barnard

Physician to Olympian gods 5 Paeon 6
Apollo

physicist
  American: 4 Hess, Rabi 5 Bethe, Ga-
  mow, Pauli, Yalow 6 Bekesy, Teller,
  Townes, Watson 7 Richter, Seaborg 8
  Einstein, Lawrence, Van Allen 9 Michel-
  son 11 Chamberlain, Oppenheimer
  Austrian: 7 Doppler, Meitner
  British: 4 Born 5 Bragg, Hooke, Joule 6
  Kelvin 7 Gilbert, Thomson 8 Chadwick,
  Rayleigh 9 Cockcroft 10 Rutherford
  Danish: 4 Bohr 7 Oersted
  Dutch: 6 Zeeman 7 Lorentz
  French: 6 Ampere 7 Broglie, Coulomb,
  Fresnel 8 Foucault 9 Becquerel 11 Joliot-
  Curie
  German: 3 Ohm 5 Hertz, Stark 6 Planck
  7 Rontgen, Wegener 8 Humboldt, Roent-
  gen 9 Kirchhoff, Mossbauer 10 Fahren-
  heit, Fraunhofer
  Indian: 5 Raman
  Irish: 7 Tyndall 10 Fitzgerald
  Italian: 5 Fermi
  Russian: 6 Landau 8 Cerenkov, Sak-
  harov
  Scottish: 7 Rankine

Physics
  author: 9 Aristotle

physiognomy 4 face 5 shape 6 facade,
visage 7 contour, outline, profile 8 features
10 silhouette 11 countenance

physiology
  founder: 13 William Harvey
  study of: 8 function
  study of nervous sytem: 15 neurophysi-
  ology

Phytalus
  hospitable to: 7 Demeter
  given: 7 fig tree

Phyteus
  epithet of: 6 Apollo

pianissimo
  music: 8 very soft
  abbreviation: 2 pp

pianist 4 Hess 5 Liszt, Watts 6 Busoni, Chopin, Gilels, Serkin 7 Cliburn, Hofmann, Richter 8 Backhaus, Horowitz, Schnabel, Schumann, Thalberg, von Bulow 9 Barenboim, Casadesus, Gieseking 10 Gottschalk, Rubinstein 12 Rachmaninoff

piano
  invented by: 10 Cristofori
  player piano: 9 Fourneaux

piano
  music: 4 soft
  abbreviation: 1 p

piazza 5 patio, porch 6 square 7 gallery, portico, veranda

Piazzi, Giuseppe
  field: 9 astronomy
  nationality: 7 Italian
  discovered: 5 Ceres
  catalogued: 5 stars

picaresque 6 daring 7 raffish, roguish, waggish 8 devilish, prankish, rascally, scampish 9 foolhardy 10 roistering 13 adventuresome 14 mischief-loving

Picasso, Pablo
  born: 5 Spain 6 Malaga
  artwork: 4 Dove 6 Guitar, Jester 7 Ma Jolie, Rooster, She-Goat 8 Guernica 9 Bull's Head, Notre Dame 11 Seated Woman, Woman Diving 12 Head of a Woman 13 Seated Bathers 14 Minotauromachy, Mother and Child, Women of Algiers 15 Ambroise Vollard, Man Holding a Lamb, The Charnel-House, The Large Profile, The Three Dancers 16 Nude in an Armchair 17 Girl Before a Mirror, The Glass of Absinth, The Three Musicians 20 Still Life with a Candle 22 Les Demoiselles d'Avignon 23 Portrait of Gertrude Stein

picayune, picayunish 5 dinky, petty, small 6 flimsy, little, measly, paltry, slight 7 trivial 8 niggling, nugatory, piddling, trifling 11 unimportant 13 insignificant 14 inconsiderable 15 inconsequential

Piccini, Nicola (Piccinni, Niccola)
  born: 4 Bari 5 Italy
  composer of: 5 Didon 6 Roland 11 The Good Girl 15 La buona figliola 18 Iphigenie en Tauride

pick 3 cut 4 crop 5 cream, elect, elite, pluck, prize 6 choice, choose, detach, flower, gather, opt for, select 7 collect, fix upon, harvest, pull off, pull out, the best 9 single out 10 decide upon, favored one, preference, settle upon

picket 4 pale, post 5 fence, go out, guard, hem in, pen in, stake, watch 6 corral, paling, patrol, sentry, shut in, strike, tether, wall in 7 boycott, enclose, hedge in, lookout, striker, upright, walk out 8 blockade, palisade, restrain, restrict, sentinel 9 blockader, boycotter, protester, restraint, stanchion

picketing 5 march 7 protest 8 marching, on strike, striking 10 protesting 12 protest march 13 demonstrating, demonstration

Pickett, George E
  served in: 8 Civil War 10 Mexican War
  side: 11 Confederate
  battle: 10 Gettysburg
  famous for: 6 charge

Pickford, Mary
  real name: 15 Gladys Mary Smith
  nickname: 18 America's Sweetheart
  born: 6 Canada 7 Toronto
  husband: 16 Douglas Fairbanks 18 Charles Buddy Rogers
  roles: 4 Rags 8 Coquette (Oscar) 9 Pollyanna 19 The Taming of the Shrew 21 The Poor Little Rich Girl 23 Rebecca of Sunnybrook Farm
  home: 8 Pickfair
  memoirs: 17 Sunshine and Shadow
  formed: 13 United Artists
  partners: 10 D W Griffith 14 Charlie Chaplin 16 Douglas Fairbanks

pickings 4 loot 5 booty 6 scraps, spoils 7 plunder, takings 9 leftovers

pickle 3 fix, jam 4 corn, dill, mess, sour 6 crisis, plight, scrape 7 dilemma, gherkin, mustard 8 cucumber, hot water, quandary 9 emergency, extremity, tight spot 10 difficulty, kosher dill, pretty pass 11 predicament 14 bread-and-butter

pickled 5 drunk 6 soused 8 powdered

pick on 5 annoy, bully 6 harass, jibe at 7 torment 8 browbeat

pick out 3 see 4 espy 6 choose, descry, detect, notice, select 7 discern, make out 8 perceive 12 catch sight of

pickup 4 rise 5 boost, truck 7 advance 9 impromptu 11 improvement 12 acceleration

pick up 3 buy, get 6 gather, lift up, look up, obtain, secure 7 acquire, develop, improve, procure 8 contract, retrieve 9 cultivate, get better

Pickwick Papers
  author: 14 Charles Dickens
  character: 6 Perker, Tupman, Wardle, Winkle 9 Sam Weller, Snodgrass 10 Mrs Bardell 11 Emily Wardle 12 Alfred Jingle, Rachel Wardle 13 Arabella Allen

picky 5 fussy 6 choosy 7 finicky 10 fastidious, particular 11 persnickety 14 discriminating

Picrochole
  character in: 22 Gargantua and Pantagruel
  author: 8 Rabelais

picture 3 see 4 copy, draw, film 5 fancy, flick, image, model, movie, paint, photo, study 6 cinema, depict, double, mirror, sketch 7 believe, drawing, essence, etching, feature, imagine, paragon, portray, tintype 8 envision, likeness, painting, snapshot 9 delineate, duplicate, facsimile, portrayal, represent 10 call to mind, carbon copy, conceive of, dead ringer, embodiment, illustrate, photograph 11 delineation 12 illustration, see in the mind 13 daguerreotype, motion picture, moving picture, spitting image 14 representation 15 exemplification, personification

Picture of Dorian Gray, The
    author: 10 Oscar Wilde
    character: 9 James Vane, Sibyl Vane 13 Basil Hallward 15 Lord Henry Wotton

picturesque 6 exotic, quaint 7 unusual 8 artistic, charming, colorful, striking 9 beautiful, pictorial 10 attractive 11 distinctive, imaginative, interesting

Picumnus
    also: 8 Pilumnus
    origin: 5 Roman
    god of: 9 fertility 11 agriculture

Picus
    origin: 5 Roman 7 Italian
    god of: 11 agriculture
    father: 6 Saturn
    associated with: 10 woodpecker
    loved by: 5 Circe
    changed into: 10 woodpecker
    son: 6 Faunus

piddling 4 puny 5 petty, small 6 flimsy, little, measly, modest, paltry, skimpy, slight 7 trivial 8 picayune, trifling 9 niggardly 11 unimportant 13 insignificant 15 inconsequential

pie 4 tart 6 pastry, quiche 7 cobbler, dessert 8 turnover
    liner: 5 crust, shell
    top: 7 lattice 8 meringue

piebald 6 motley 7 dappled, flecked, mottled, spotted 8 many-hued, speckled 10 variegated 11 many-colored, varicolored 12 multicolored, parti-colored

piece 4 bit, cut, fix, pat 4 blob, case, hunk, item, lump, mend, part, play, unit, work 5 chunk, drama, essay, patch, scrap, shard, share, shred, slice, story, study, thing 6 amount, entity, length, member, paring, repair, review, sample, sketch, sliver, swatch 7 article, cutting, example, patch up, portion, restore, section, segment 8 creation, division, fraction, fragment, instance, quantity, specimen 9 component, selection 11 composition

piece de resistance 13 principal dish 14 principal event

piece goods 5 cloth, goods 6 fabric 8 dry goods, material 9 yard goods

piecemeal 9 gradually 10 fragmented, one at a time 14 little by little

piece of the action 3 cut, fee 5 piece 7 portion, rake-off 10 commission, percentage

pied 6 motley 7 checked, dappled, mottled, piebald 8 colorful 9 checkered 10 variegated 11 many-colored 12 parti-colored

pied-a-terre 17 temporary dwelling
    literally: 12 foot on ground

Pied Piper of Hamlin, The
    author: 14 Robert Browning

Pielus
    father: 11 Neoptolemus
    mother: 10 Andromache

pier 4 anta, dock, mole, quay, slip 5 jetty, levee, wharf 6 pillar 7 landing, support 10 breakwater

pierce 3 cut 4 hurt, pain, stab 5 drill, lance, prick, spear, spike, stick, sting, wound 6 grieve, impale 7 affront 8 distress, puncture 9 penetrate, perforate 10 cut through, run through

Pierce, Franklin
    nickname: 29 Young Hickory of the Granite Hills
    presidential rank: 10 fourteenth
    party: 8 Democrat
    state represented: 2 NH
    defeated: 4 (John Parker) Hale 5 (Winfield) Scott
    vice president: 4 (William Rufus Devane) King (died in office)
    cabinet:
        state: 5 (William Learned) Marcy
        treasury: 7 (James) Guthrie
        war: 5 (Jefferson) Davis
        attorney general: 7 (Caleb) Cushing
        navy: 6 (James Cochran) Dobbin
        postmaster general: 8 (James) Campbell
        interior: 10 (Robert) McClelland
    born: 14 Hillsborough (Hillsboro) NH
    died/buried: 9 Concord NH
    education:
        academy: 7 Hancock 11 Francestown
        college: 7 Bowdoin
        studied: 3 law
    religion: 12 Episcopalian
    political career: 8 US Senate 16 state legislature 24 US House of Representatives
    civilian career: 6 lawyer
    military service: 6 US Army 10 Mexican War 16 brigadier general
    notable events of lifetime/term:
        Act: 6 Tariff (of 1857)
        bill: 14 Kansas-Nebraska
        civil war in: 6 Kansas
        first US: 10 World's Fair
        Manifesto: 6 Ostend
        Purchase: 7 Gadsden
        treaty of: 8 Kanagawa
    father: 8 Benjamin
    mother: 4 Anna (Kendrick)
    siblings: 5 Henry, Nancy 7 Charles, Harriet 9 Charlotte 12 John Sullivan 16 Benjamin Kendrick
    half sister: 9 Elizabeth
    wife: 4 Jane (Means Appleton)
    children: 8 Benjamin, Franklin 11 Frank Robert

piercing 3 raw 4 keen, loud 5 angry, cruel, sharp 6 biting, bitter, fierce, shrill 7 caustic, cutting, furious, grating, hurtful, intense, painful, probing 8 strident 9 agonizing, deafening, searching, shrieking, torturous 10 screeching 11 penetrating 12 earsplitting, excruciating 13 ear-shattering

Pierian
    pertains to: 5 Muses

Pierian Spring
　form: 8 fountain
Pierides see 5 Muses
**Piero della Francesca (Piero dei Fran-
ceschi)**
　born: 5 Italy 16 Borgo San Sepolcro
　artwork: 12 Duke of Urbino 15 The Resurrection 18 Federigo and His Wife 19 St
John the Evangelist 20 Flagellation of
Christ 23 The Compassionate Madonna,
The Legend of the True Cross, The Old
Age and Death of Adam 24 The History
of the True Cross 45 The Madonna and
Saints with Frederigo da Montefeltro
Pierre
　author: 14 Herman Melville
Piers Plowman
　author: 15 William Langland
Pietas
　personifies: 17 familial affection
piety 7 loyalty, respect 8 devotion, humility
9 godliness, piousness, reverence 10 devoutness 11 dutifulness, religiosity 13 reli-
giousness
pig 3 hog 5 piggy, porky, swine 6 porker 7
glutton, guzzler 8 gourmand 9 chowhound
11 gormandizer
　male: 4 boar
　female: 3 sow
　young: 5 shoat 6 piglet 11 suckling pig
pigeon
　young: 5 squab 8 squeaker
pigeonhole 4 rank, rate, type 5 brand,
cubby, group, label, niche 6 category, classify 9 cubbyhole 10 categorize 11 compartment
pigheaded 6 dogged, mulish 7 willful 8
contrary, obdurate, perverse, stubborn 9
insistent, obstinate, unbending 10 bullheaded, inflexible, refractory, unyielding 11
opinionated, wrongheaded
Piglet
　character in: 13 Winnie-the-Pooh
　author: 5 Milne
pigment 3 dye 4 tint 5 color 8 coloring, dyestuff 14 coloring matter
pigmentation 5 color 9 skin color 10 coloration
pigtail 5 braid, plait, queue 8 ponytail
pike 4 bill 5 lance, spear, spike 6 poleax 7
assegai, freeway, halberd, harpoon, highway, javelin, parkway, thruway 8 autobahn,
hard road, speedway, toll road, turnpike 10
expressway, interstate, throughway 12 superhighway
　British: 12 King's Highway 13 Queen's
highway
　German: 8 autobahn
piker 5 miser 7 niggard, trifler 8 tightwad 9
skinflint 10 cheapskate, pinchpenny 12
penny pincher
Pilar
　character in: 19 For Whom the Bell Tolls
　author: 8 Hemingway
pilaster 4 pier 6 column, pillar 7 support,
upright 8 baluster

pile 3 nap 4 heap, mass, pier, post, shag,
warp 5 amass, batch, fluff, grain, hoard,
mound, plush, stack, store 6 fleece,
gather, piling, pillar 7 collect, pyramid, support, surface, upright 8 assemble, quantity
9 abundance, amassment, profusion, stanchion 10 accumulate, assortment, collection, foundation 11 agglomerate, aggregation, fibrousness 12 accumulation
pile up 4 bank, heap 5 amass, hoard,
mound, stack 7 collect 10 accumulate
pile-up 3 jam, mob 4 mass 5 snarl 8 crowding, gridlock 10 bottleneck, congestion 11
obstruction 12 overcrowding
pilfer 3 cop, rob 4 hook, lift 5 boost, filch,
heist, pinch, steal, swipe 6 finger, pirate,
snitch, thieve 7 purloin 8 shoplift 10 plagiarize
pilferer 5 thief 6 robber 7 burglar 10 shoplifter, sneak thief
pilgrim, Pilgrim 4 haji 5 exile, hadji 6
palmer 7 pioneer, Puritan, settler 8 newcomer, traveler, wanderer, wayfarer 9 foreigner
　father: 5 Alden
　founder: 10 Separatist
　interpreter: 7 Squanto
　leader: 8 Standish
　protector: 7 Templar
　ship: 9 Mayflower, Speedwell
Pilgrim, Billy
　character in: 18 Slaughterhouse Five
　author: 8 Vonnegut
pilgrimage 4 hadj, trek 6 ramble, roving,
voyage 7 journey, roaming, sojourn 8 long
trip 9 excursion, wandering 13 peregrination
Pilgrim's Progress, The
　author: 10 John Bunyan
　character: 7 Despair, Hopeful 8 Apollyon, Faithful 9 Christian, Ignorance 10
Evangelist 14 Worldly Wiseman
pill 3 rob 4 ball, pell 5 bolus 6 bullet, pellet,
tablet, pilule 7 capsule 8 medicine 9 cigarette
pillage 3 rob 4 loot, raid, sack 5 booty, rifle,
strip 6 fleece, maraud, piracy, ravage,
spoils 7 despoil, looting, plunder, robbery 9
filchings 10 plundering
pillager 6 looter, vandal 7 brigand 9 despoiler, plunderer
pillar 3 VIP 4 pile, post, rock 5 shaft, wheel
6 column, piling 7 obelisk, support, upright
8 champion, mainstay, pilaster, somebody
9 colonnade, stanchion
Pillars of Society, The
　author: 11 Henrik Ibsen
pillow 3 pad 7 bolster, cushion 8 headrest
pilot 4 lead 5 flyer, guide, steer 6 airman,
direct, escort, fly-boy, handle, leader, manage 7 aviator, birdman, conduct, control 8
aeronaut, coxswain, helmsman, navigate,
wheelman 9 accompany, sky jockey,
steersman
Pilot, The
　author: 19 James Fenimore Cooper

Pima (Aatam, Pima Alto)
  language family: 10 Uto-Aztekan
  location: 7 Arizona
  related to: 6 Papago
  descendants of: 7 Hohokam
Pima Alto *see* 4 Pima
Piman
  tribe: 6 Papago
pin 4 bind, clip, tine 5 affix, badge, clasp,
  dowel, medal, prong 6 brooch, fasten, pinion, secure, skewer 8 hold down, hold fast,
  restrain 10 decoration
  type: 3 hat 4 push 5 stick, thole 6 breast,
  common, diaper, safety 8 straight
pincer 4 claw 5 chela
pinch 3 bit, cop, jam, jot, nab, nip 4 bust,
  crib, grab, iota, lift, mite, pain, snip, spot 5
  catch, cramp, crimp, crush, filch, run in,
  speck, steal, swipe, trace, trial, tweak 6 arrest, clutch, collar, crisis, misery, ordeal,
  pickle, plight, snatch, snitch, strait, tittle 7
  capture, purloin, squeeze, tighten 8 compress, exigency, hardship 9 apprehend,
  emergency 10 affliction, difficulty, discomfort 11 predicament
Pinch, Tom
  character in. 6 Martin Chuzzlewit
  author: 7 Dickens
pinch hitter 5 proxy 7 stand-in 9 alternate
  10 substitute
pinchpenny 5 miser 6 frugal, stingy 7 niggard, prudent, thrifty
  Dickensian: 7 Scrooge
Pindar
  author of: 4 Odes 8 Epinicea
pine 3 die, ebb 4 flag, long, sigh, wilt 5
  covet, crave, droop, yearn 6 desire, expire,
  hanker, weaken, wither 7 decline, dwindle,
  pant for 8 languish 9 hunger for, waste
  away 11 have a yen for, thirst after 12 fail
  in health
pine 5 Pinus
  varieties: 3 air, nut, red 4 blue, chir, gray,
  hoop, Huon, Imou, Jack 5 beach, cedar,
  Cuban, Emodi, giant, house, Kauri, pitch,
  Scots, screw, scrub, shore, slash, stone,
  sugar, white 6 Aleppo, Apache, Bhutan,
  Bishop, celery, Dammar, digger, ground,
  Jersey, Korean, limber, Mallee, Norway,
  Parana, Pinyon, Scotch, spruce, Torrey,
  Totara, yellow 7 Amboina, Benguet, big-
  cone, Chilean, Chinese, cluster, Cypress,
  Formosa, Georgia, Gerard's, hickory,
  jointed, long-tag, poverty, prickly, prince's,
  running, Soledad 8 Austrian, Buddhist,
  cow's-tail, knob-cone, lace-bark, Loblolly,
  longleaf, mahogany, Monterey, mountain,
  Nepal nut, old-field, princess, umbrella 9
  Brazilian, Calabrian, Chilghoza, Jerusalem, lodgepole, Oyster Bay, shortleaf,
  white-bark 10 Australian, Bunya-bunya,
  dwarf stone, Macedonian, Moreton Bay,
  red cypress, Swiss stone, Tenasserim 11
  African fern, bristlecone, common screw,
  Japanese red, Parry pinyon, Port Jackson, thatch screw, twisted-leaf, Veitch
  screw 12 black cypress, Canary Island,

Chinese water, eastern white, frankincense, Italian stone, Mexican stone, Mexican white, two-leaved nut, western white
  13 dwarf Siberian, Japanese black, Japanese white, Mexican yellow, New Caledonian, Norfolk Island, Swiss mountain, table mountain 14 Himalayan white,
  Rottnest Island, southern yellow 15
  Mueller's cypress 16 Japanese umbrella,
  single-leaf pinyon 19 Rough-barked Mexican 19 Rocky Mountain yellow
Pine Tree State
  nickname of: 5 Maine
pin hope on 6 bank on 7 count on, long for,
  wish for 8 aspire to, yearn for 10 anticipate
pink 8 Dianthus
  varieties: 3 Sea 4 fire, moss, pine, rose,
  wild 5 cameo, clove, dairy, grass, marsh,
  swamp 6 button, ground, indian, Kirtle,
  maiden 7 cheddar, cottage, cushion, Mul-
  lein, rainbow 8 Childing, Deptford, election 11 cluster-head 13 fringed indian,
  spottle kirtle 16 California indian
pinnacle 3 cap, top 4 acme, apex, peak 5
  crest, crown, spire, tower 6 belfry, height,
  summit, tiptop, vertex, zenith 7 steeple 9
  bell tower, campanile
pinochle
  also known as: 7 binocle, pinocle 8 pe-
  nuchle
  derived from: 7 bezique
  points/game: 11 one thousand
pinpoint 3 dot, jot 4 iota, spot 5 speck 6
  detail 8 home in on, localize, zero in on 12
  characterize
pint
  abbreviation of: 2 pt
pinxit 11 he painted it 12 she painted it
pioneer 5 found, start 6 create, father, herald, invent, leader 7 develop, founder 8
  colonist, discover, explorer 9 be a leader,
  developer, establish, harbinger, innovator,
  precursor 10 antecedent, forerunner, lead
  the way, pathfinder, show the way 11 establisher, predecessor, trailblazer 12 first
  settler, frontiersman 13 blaze the trail 14
  early immigrant, founding father
  Hebrew: 6 halutz 7 chalutz
Pioneers, The
  author: 19 James Fenimore Cooper
  character: 10 Indian John 11 Judge
  Temple, Natty Bumppo 13 Oliver
  Edwards 14 Hiram Doolittle 15 Elizabeth
  Temple
pious 4 holy 5 godly 6 devout, divine 7
  sainted, saintly 8 faithful, reverent, unctuous 9 dedicated, insincere, pietistic, religious, spiritual 10 worshipful 11 reverential
  12 hypocritical 13 rationalizing, sanctimonious, self-righteous 14 holier-than-thou
Pip
  character in: 17 Great Expectations
  author: 7 Dickens
pipe 4 duct, main, peep, sing, tube 5
  cheep, chirp, trill, tweet 6 warble 7 conduit,
  twitter, whistle 8 conveyor 9 conductor 10
  play a flute 12 play a bagpipe

Pippa Passes
author: 14 Robert Browning

piquant 3 hot 4 acid, racy 5 peppy, salty, sharp, spicy, tangy, zesty 6 biting, bitter, bright, clever, lively, savory 7 mordant, peppery, pungent, rousing 8 animated, incisive, piercing, spirited, stinging, vigorous 9 sparkling, trenchant 11 interesting, provacative, stimulating 13 scintillating 14 highly seasoned, strong-flavored

pique 3 ire, irk, vex 4 gall, goad, miff, snit, spur, stir 5 annoy, peeve, rouse, spite 6 arouse, excite, grudge, kindle, malice, nettle, offend 7 affront, incense, perturb, provoke, quicken, umbrage 8 disquiet, irritate, vexation 9 annoyance, displease, stimulate 10 discomfort, exasperate, irritation, resentment 11 displeasure, humiliation, ill feelings, indignation 12 exasperation, hurt feelings 13 embarrassment, mortification, put one's back up 14 vindictiveness

piqued 5 angry, riled, vexed 6 galled, miffed, peeved 7 annoyed, aroused, excited, kindled, nettled, stirred 9 affronted, irritated 10 displeased, stimulated

Pirandello, Luigi
author of: 17 The Old and the Young 18 Tonight We Improvise 19 The Late Mattia Pascal 31 Six Characters in Search of an Author

pirate 3 rob 5 steal 6 raider, robber, sea dog 7 brigand, corsair, plunder 8 marauder 9 buccaneer, privateer 10 freebooter
flag: 9 blackjack 10 Jolly Roger
name: 4 Kidd 6 Morgan 7 Lafitte 10 Blackbeard

Pirate Coast *see* 18 United Arab Emirates

Pirates of Penzance, The
author: 9 W S Gilbert
comic opera by: 18 Gilbert and Sullivan
character: 4 Kate, Ruth 5 Edith, Mabel 6 Isabel 8 Frederic, Sergeant 10 Pirate King 14 General Stanley

Pirithous
prince of: 8 Lapithae
father: 4 Zeus
mother: 3 Dia
son: 10 Polypoetes
friend of: 7 Theseus

Pirous
led allies of: 6 Thrace

pis aller 10 last resort 12 last resource

Pisan Cantos
author: 9 Ezra Pound

Pisander
rank: 7 captain
member of: 9 Myrmidons

Pisanio
character in: 9 Cymbeline
author: 11 Shakespeare

Pisanosaurus
type: 8 dinosaur 10 ornithopod
location: 12 South America
period: 8 Triassic

Pisces
symbol: 4 fish
planet: 7 Jupiter, Neptune
rules: 7 secrets
born: 13 February-March

Pisistratidae
sons of: 11 Pisistratus
names: 7 Hippias 10 Hipparchus

Pisistratus
tyrant of: 6 Athens
father: 11 Hippocrates
son: 7 Hippias 10 Hipparchus

Pissarro, Camille
born: 8 St Thomas 16 Danish West Indies
artwork: 8 Red Roofs 15 Morning Sunlight 21 Lower Norwood Snow Scene 28 Peasant Woman with a Wheelbarrow

pistol (revolver)
invented by: 4 Colt

pit 3 dip, nut 4 dent, hole, nick, pock, scar, seed 5 gouge, gully, match, notch, stone 6 cavity, crater, dimple, furrow, hollow, indent, kernel, oppose, trough 7 scratch 8 contrast, pockmark 9 concavity, juxtapose 10 depression, set against 11 indentation

Pit, The
author: 11 Frank Norris

Pitana
form: 5 nymph
daughter: 6 Evadne

Pit and the Pendulum, The
author: 13 Edgar Allan Poe

pitch 3 bob, dip, fix, lob, set, shy, top 4 apex, cant, cast, fall, fire, hurl, jerk, jolt, peak, rock, tone, toss 5 angle, chuck, crown, erect, fling, grade, heave, level, lurch, place, plant, point, raise, set up, shake, slant, sling, slope, sound, throw 6 degree, height, let fly, locate, plunge, propel, settle, summit, topple, tumble, zenith 7 bobbing, incline, rocking, station 8 delivery, harmonic, lurching, pinnacle, undulate 9 declivity, establish, oscillate 10 undulation 11 oscillation 12 fall headlong
speed of: 9 vibration

pitcher 3 jar, jug 4 ewer 6 carafe 8 decanter 9 container 10 spitballer
and catcher: 7 battery
award: 7 Cy Young
brother duo: 4 Dean 5 Perry 6 Niekro
Hall of Famer: 4 Ford, Wynn 6 Koufax 8 Drysdale
left-hander: 8 southpaw
relief staff: 7 bullpen
reliever: 7 fireman

pitch in 5 begin 7 share in 8 take part 9 co-operate, get to work, join hands 10 act jointly, contribute, get started 11 collaborate, participate 12 make an effort, pull together, work together

pitch into 5 fly at 6 assail, have at 7 assault, set upon

piteous 3 sad 6 moving, woeful 7 pitiful 8 pathetic, pitiable, poignant, touching 9 affecting 10 deplorable 11 distressing 12 heart-rending 13 heartbreaking

pitfall 4 risk, trap **5** peril, snare **6** ambush, danger, hazard **7** springe **8** quagmire **9** booby trap, quicksand **14** stumbling block

pith 4 core, gist, meat **5** heart, point **7** essence, meaning **12** significance

pithy 5 terse **6** cogent **7** concise **8** forceful, succinct **9** effective, trenchant **10** expressive, meaningful, to the point **12** concentrated

pitiful 3 sad **4** poor **5** sorry **6** abject, measly, moving, paltry, shabby **7** doleful, forlorn, piteous **8** dreadful, god-awful, mournful, pathetic, pitiable, poignant, touching, wretched **9** miserable, plaintive, worthless **10** abominable, despicable, lamentable **11** distressing **12** arousing pity, contemptible, heartrending

pitiless 5 cruel **6** brutal **7** inhuman, unmoved **8** ruthless, uncaring **9** heartless, merciless, unpitying, unsparing, untouched **10** implacable, relentless, unmerciful **11** cold-blooded, hardhearted, indifferent, insensitive, unrelenting

pittance 4 mite **5** crumb **6** little, trifle **7** minimum, modicum, smidgen

Pittheus
 father: 6 Pelops
 mother: 10 Hippodamia
 brother: 7 Troezen
 daughter: 6 Aethra

Pittsburgh
 baseball team: 7 Pirates
 feature: 14 Fort Pitt Museum **15** Buhl Planetarium
 football team: 8 Steelers
 formerly: 8 Fort Pitt **12** Fort Duquesne
 hockey team: 8 Penguins
 noted for: 5 steel
 river: 4 Ohio **9** Allegheny **11** Monongahela
 university: 8 Duquesne **14** Carnegie-Mellon

Pittypat, Aunt
 character in: 15 Gone With the Wind
 author: 8 Mitchell

pituitary
 located in: 5 brain
 known as: 11 master gland

pity 5 mercy, shame **6** lament, lenity, regret **7** charity, feel for, weep for **8** bleed for, clemency, humanity, leniency, sad thing, sympathy **10** compassion, condolence, indulgence, kindliness, tenderness **11** crying shame, forbearance, magnanimity **12** feel sorry for **13** commiseration

Pityocamptes
 epithet of: 5 Sinis
 means: 10 pine-bender

Pitys
 form: 5 nymph
 loved by: 3 Pan
 changed into: 8 pine tree

piu
 music: 4 more

pivot 4 axis, axle, hang, rely, spin, turn **5** focus, hinge, twirl, wheel, whirl **6** center, circle, depend, rotate, swivel **7** fulcrum, hinge on, revolve **9** pirouette

pivotal 5 vital **7** crucial **8** critical, decisive **9** climactic **11** determining

pivotal point 4 axis **12** turning point **13** crucial moment

pixy 3 elf **5** fairy **6** sprite **10** leprechaun

pizzicato
 music: 21 plucked instead of bowed
 abbreviation: **4** pizz

placable 7 lenient **8** flexible, tolerant, yielding **9** indulgent, relenting **10** appeasable, forbearing **12** reconcilable

placard 4 bill, sign **6** notice, poster **8** bulletin **13** advertisement

placate 4 calm, lull **5** quiet **6** pacify, soothe **7** appease, assuage, mollify, win over **9** alleviate **10** conciliate, propitiate

placatory 9 appeasing, pacifying **10** mollifying **12** conciliatory **13** accommodative

place 3 fix, job, put, set **4** area, city, digs, duty, farm, firm, home, land, plot, post, rank, rest, shop, site, spot, town, zone **5** abode, affix, array, berth, house, lodge, niche, plant, point, ranch, space, stand, state, store, venue **6** assign, attach, county, harbor, invest, locale, locate, office, region, settle **7** appoint, borough, company, concern, country, deposit, install, quarter, shelter, situate, station, village **8** building, business, classify, district, domicile, dwelling, ensconce, find hire, function, identify, locality, location, lodgings, position, premises, property, province, quarters, remember, standing, township, vicinity **9** recognize, residence, situation, territory **10** commission, get a job for, habitation **11** appointment, find work for, whereabouts **12** neighborhood **13** establishment
 Latin: 4 situ

Place in the Sun, A
 director: 13 George Stevens
 based on novel by: 15 Theodore Dreiser (An American Tragedy)
 cast: 14 Keefe Brasselle, Shelley Winters **15** Elizabeth Taylor, Montgomery Clift
 Oscar for: 5 score **9** direction **10** screenplay

placement 8 grouping, location **10** assignment, employment **11** arrangement, disposition, positioning

place of residence 4 home **5** abode, house **7** address, lodging **8** domicile, dwelling **9** residence **10** habitation **14** living quarters

place to stand on
 Greek: 6 pou sto

place upright 5 erect, raise **7** stand up

placid 4 calm, mild **5** quiet **6** gentle, poised, serene, smooth **7** pacific, restful **8** composed, peaceful, tranquil **9** collected, unexcited, unruffled **10** untroubled **11** undisturbed, unexcitable **13** imperturbable, self-possessed **15** undemonstrative

plague 3 irk, vex, woe 4 bane, evil, fret, gall, pain, pest 5 agony, chafe, curse, harry, haunt, peeve, worry 6 badger, blight, bother, burden, cancer, harass, misery, nettle 7 afflict, disturb, perturb, scourge, torment, trouble 8 aggrieve, calamity, disquiet, distress, hardship, pandemic 9 embarrass, persecute, suffering 10 affliction, Black Death, pestilence, visitation
French: 5 peste

Plague, The
  author: 11 Albert Camus
  character: 7 Rambert 10 Jean Tarrou 11 Joseph Grand 14 Father Paneloux, Raymond Cottard 15 Dr Bernard R Rieux

Plague Dogs, The
  author: 12 Richard Adams

plain 4 bald, bare, open 5 blunt, clear, frank, naked, vivid 6 candid, common, direct, homely, honest, modest, simple 7 average, glaring, legible, obscure, obvious, plateau, prairie, sincere, visible 8 apparent, clear-cut, distinct, everyday, explicit, manifest, ordinary, palpable, specific, straight, striking, uncomely, unlovely 9 grassland, outspoken, prominent, tableland, unadorned, undiluted 10 forthright, pronounced, unaffected, unassuming, unhandsome, unreserved, well-marked 11 commonplace, conspicuous, discernible, not striking, open country, outstanding, plain-spoken, unambiguous, undecorated, undisguised, unequivocal, ungarnished, unvarnished, well-defined 12 matter-of-fact, not beautiful, unattractive, unmistakable, unornamented 13 unembellished, unpretentious, without frills 14 comprehensible, understandable 15 straightforward, undistinguished

Plain Dealer, The
  author: 16 William Wycherley

plainly 6 baldly, openly, simply 7 bluntly, clearly, frankly, visibly, vividly 8 candidly, directly, honestly, markedly, modestly 9 doubtless, obviously 10 apparently, definitely, distinctly, explicitly, manifestly, ordinarily, positively, strikingly, undeniably 11 beyond doubt, discernibly, prominently, undoubtedly 12 unaffectedly, unassumingly, unmistakably, without doubt 13 conspicuously, unambiguously, unequivocally 14 comprehensibly, unquestionably

plainness 10 homeliness, simplicity 12 ordinariness

plainspoken 4 open 5 bluff, blunt, frank, plain 6 candid, direct, honest 7 genuine, sincere 8 explicit, straight 9 open-faced, outspoken, unsparing 10 above board, forthright, point-blank 11 straight-out 15 straightforward

plaint 3 cry, sob 4 beef, moan, wail 5 gripe 6 charge, grouse, grudge, lament, regret, squawk 7 grumble, reproof 8 reproach 9 complaint, grievance, objection 10 accusation, resentment 12 remonstrance

plaintive 3 sad 6 rueful 7 doleful, moaning, piteous, pitiful, tearful 8 dolorous, grievous, mournful, pathetic, wretched 9 lamenting, sorrowful, woebegone 10 lugubrious, melancholy 12 heartrending

plait 5 braid, queue, twine, twist, weave 7 pigtail 10 intertwine

plan 3 aim, map, way 4 form, idea, plot 5 frame, shape 6 design, devise, intend, lay out, map out, method, scheme, sketch 7 diagram, outline, prepare, program, project, propose, purpose 8 block out, conceive, contrive, organize, proposal, strategy, think out 9 blueprint, fabricate, procedure, stratagem 10 conception, suggestion 11 proposition
French: 8 demarche

Planchet
  character in: 18 The Three Musketeers
  author: 5 Dumas (pere)

Planck, Max
  field: 7 physics
  nationality: 6 German
  developed: 13 quantum theory 15 Planck's constant
  awarded: 10 Nobel Prize

Planctae
  form: 5 rocks
  characteristic: 8 shifting

plane 3 jet 4 bird, flat 5 level, plumb 6 degree, status 7 regular, station 8 aircraft, airplane, position, standing 9 condition, elevation
  type: 4 jack 5 block

planet, planets 13 celestial body
  first: 7 Mercury
  second: 5 Venus
  third: 5 Earth
    satellite: 4 Moon
  fourth: 5 Mars
    satellite: 6 Deimos, Phobos
    nickname: 9 Red Planet
  fifth: 7 Jupiter
    satellite: 2 Io 6 Europa 8 Amalthea, Callisto, Ganymede
    characteristic: 7 red spot
  sixth: 6 Saturn
    satellite: 4 Rhea 5 Dione, Janus, Mimas, Titan 6 Phoebe, Tethys 7 Iapetus 8 Hyperion 9 Enceladus
    characteristic: 5 rings
  seventh: 6 Uranus
    satellite: 5 Ariel 6 Oberon 7 Miranda, Titania, Umbriel
    color: 9 blue-green
    characteristic: 5 rings
  eighth: 7 Neptune
    satellite: 6 Nereid, Triton
    color: 5 green
  ninth: 5 Pluto
    satellite: 6 Charon
  asteroid/minor planet/planetoid: 4 Eros, Juno 5 Ceres, Vesta 6 Chiron, Hermes, Icarus, Pallas 7 Astraea, Hidalgo

planetary 6 astral 7 earthly 9 celestial 11 terrestrial 12 astronomical

Planet of the Apes
 director: 18 Franklin J Schaffner
 based on novel by: 12 Pierre Boulle
 cast: 9 Kim Hunter 12 Maurice Evans 13 Roddy McDowall 14 Charlton Heston
 script: 10 Rod Serling
plank 4 deal, deck, slab 5 board, shole, stone 8 platform
planned 7 devised, schemed 8 designed, expected, foreseen, intended, prepared 9 mapped out, organized, projected, rehearsed 10 calculated, purposeful, thought out 11 intentional, prearranged, prepared for 12 premeditated
planner 6 author, framer 7 creator, deviser 8 arranger, designer 9 architect, organizer
plant 4 bush, herb, mill, moss, shop, slip, tree, vine, weed, wort, yard 5 algae, flora, fungi, grass, set in, shrub, works 6 flower, foster, infuse, set out 7 factory, foundry, herbage, implant, inspire, instill, scatter, sow seed 8 business, engender, seedling 9 broadcast, cultivate, establish, inculcate, propagate, vegetable 10 transplant, vegetation 13 establishment, sow the seeds of 14 put in the ground
plaster 4 coat, daub, sand 5 grout, smear 6 bedaub, gypsum, lather, stucco 7 overlay, spackle
 mixture of: 4 lime 5 water 6 gypsum
plastered 5 drunk 6 coated, daubed, soused 7 covered, crocked, smeared, swacked 8 mortared, polluted, stuccoed 10 inebriated 11 intoxicated
plastic 4 soft 6 pliant, supple 7 ductile, elastic, pliable 8 flexible, formable, moldable, shapable, yielding 9 malleable, tractable
Platanistius
 epithet of: 6 Apollo
 means: 22 god of the plane-tree grove
plate 4 dish 6 saucer 7 helping, platter, portion, serving 10 platterful 11 serving dish
plateau 4 mesa 5 table 6 upland 8 highland 9 tableland
Plateosaurus
 type: 8 dinosaur, sauropod
 location: 6 Europe 7 Germany
 period: 8 Triassic
platform 4 dais, goal, plan 5 creed, plank, stage, stand 6 podium, policy, pulpit, tenets 7 program, rostrum
Plath, Sylvia
 author of: 5 Ariel 10 The Bell Jar
platinum
 chemical symbol: 2 Pt
platitude 3 saw 6 cliche, old saw, truism 7 bromide 8 banality, chestnut 11 commonplace
platitudinous 5 banal, corny, stale, tired, trite, vapid 6 jejune 8 bromidic, ordinary 9 hackneyed 10 pedestrian, unexciting, unoriginal 12 cliche-ridden, conventional 13 unimaginative
Plato
 author of: 4 Laws 5 Crito 6 Phaedo 7 Apology, Gorgias, Sophist, Timaeus 8

Philebus, Republic 9 Symposium 10 Parmenides
platoon 4 band, body, crew, team, unit 5 corps, force, group 10 detachment
platter 4 dish, disk, lanx 6 salver 7 record 8 trencher 9 recording
plaudit, plaudits 4 rave 5 cheer, kudos 6 hurrah, huzzah, praise 7 acclaim, bouquet, ovation 8 applause, approval, cheering 10 compliment, hallelujah 11 approbation 12 commendation
plauditory 8 admiring, praising 9 extolling, laudatory, praiseful 12 commendatory 13 complimentary
plausible 5 sound, valid 6 likely 7 logical, tenable 8 credible, feasible, possible, probable, rational, sensible 10 acceptable, believable, convincing, persuasive, reasonable 11 conceivable, justifiable
Plautus
 author of: 7 Stichus 8 Mercator 9 Amphitruo, Menaechmi, Pseudolus 10 Amphitryon 14 Miles Gloriosus
play 3 act, fun, toy 4 jest, lark, romp, room, show 5 antic, caper, drama, enact, farce, frisk, revel, space, sport, sweep, swing 6 act out, cavort, comedy, frolic, gambol, leeway, trifle 7 disport, have fun, pageant, perform, skylark, tragedy, vie with 8 pleasure, take part 9 amusement, diversion, elbowroom, enjoyment, make merry, melodrama, perform on, personify, represent, spectacle 10 recreation 11 impersonate, merrymaking
playboy 4 rake, wolf 5 Romeo, sheik 6 lecher 7 Don Juan, swinger 8 Casanova, hedonist, Lothario, party boy 9 jet-setter, ladies' man, partygoer, womanizer 10 lady-killer, profligate 14 pleasure seeker 15 good-time Charlie
Playboy of the Western World, The
 author: 19 John Millington Synge
 character: 8 Old Mahon 9 Widow Quin 10 Shawn Keogh 16 Christopher Mahon, Margaret Flaherty (Pegeen)
play down 9 underplay 11 de-emphasize
played out 4 beat 5 all in, spent, weary 6 bushed, done in, pooped 7 drained, wearied, worn out 8 depleted, dog tired, fatigued, tired out, unreeled 9 dead tired, exhausted
player 4 jock, mime 5 actor 6 mummer 7 actress, athlete, trouper 8 gamester, opponent, thespian 9 adversary, contender, performer 10 antagonist, competitor, contestant, team member 11 entertainer, participant
play false 4 dupe 5 trick 6 betray 7 deceive, two-time 10 be disloyal 12 be unfaithful 13 be treacherous
playfellow 3 pal 4 chum 5 buddy 6 friend 8 playmate
playful 6 frisky, impish, lively 7 amusing, coltish, jesting, waggish 8 humorous, mirthful, prankish, sportive 9 fun-loving, sprightly 10 capricious, frolicsome, rollicking 12 lighthearted

French: 8 espiegle

playful trick
French: 11 espieglerie

play host 4 host 9 entertain 10 give a party, have guests 13 keep open house

playing field 4 bowl 5 arena 7 diamond, stadium 8 gridiron 10 playground 12 amphitheater

playing piece 3 man 4 disk 5 piece 7 counter

play in water 3 dip 4 swim 6 dabble, paddle, splash

play Judas 6 betray 7 sell out, two-time 9 play false 11 double-cross

playmate 3 pal 4 chum 5 buddy 6 friend 10 playfellow

play of spirit
French: 10 jeu d'esprit

play on words
French: 9 jeu de mots

plaything 3 toy 4 dupe 5 patsy, sport 6 bauble, trifle 9 diversion

play truant 3 cut 4 skip 8 be absent 9 play hooky

play with 5 bandy 7 torment, toy with 11 have fun with

playwright 6 author, writer 9 dramatist, scenarist 10 dramatizer, dramaturge, librettist, play doctor 12 dramatic poet, dramaturgist, scriptwriter 13 melodramatist

plea 4 suit 5 alibi 6 appeal, excuse, prayer 7 apology, begging, defense, pretext, request 8 argument, entreaty, petition 10 adjuration, beseeching 11 explanation, extenuation, vindication 12 solicitation, supplication 13 justification

plead 3 ask, beg 6 adjure, enjoin 7 beseech, entreat, implore, request, solicit 8 appeal to, petition 9 importune 10 supplicate

pleader 6 beggar 8 advocate, defender, implorer 9 apologist, beseecher 10 importuner, supplicant

plead with 3 beg 4 pray 6 adjure 7 beseech, implore 10 supplicate

Pleasance, Donald
born: 7 England, Worksop
roles: 12 The Caretaker 14 The Great Escape 16 You Only Live Twice 17 The Eagle Has Landed 24 The Greatest Story Ever Told

pleasant 4 fine, good, mild, nice, soft, warm 6 genial, gentle, lovely, polite 7 affable, amiable, cordial, likable, tactful 8 amicable, charming, cheerful, friendly, inviting, pleasing, sociable 9 agreeable, congenial, enjoyable 10 attractive, felicitous, gratifying, gregarious, satisfying 11 good-humored, good-natured, pleasurable 13 companionable

Pleasant Island see 5 Nauru

pleasantry 4 jape, jest, joke, quip 5 sally 6 bon mot 8 greeting 9 wisecrack, witticism 10 salutation

pleasant-tasting 4 mild 5 sweet, tasty 6 savory 8 luscious 9 delicious, palatable, succulent 10 appetizing, delectable 11 scrumptious 13 mouth-watering

please 3 opt 4 like, suit, want, will, wish 5 amuse, charm, elate, elect 6 choose, desire, divert, prefer, thrill, tickle 7 content, delight, gladden, gratify, satisfy 8 enthrall, entrance 9 enrapture, entertain, fascinate, make happy 10 be inclined 14 give pleasure to
French: 12 s'il vous plait
German: 5 bitte
Spanish: 8 por favor

pleased 4 glad 5 happy, proud 6 elated 8 thrilled 9 delighted, gratified

please reply
French: 4 rsvp 20 repondez s'il vous plait

pleasing 6 genial, polite 7 affable, amiable, amusing, likable, winning 8 charming, cheerful, friendly, inviting, mannerly 9 agreeable, congenial, diverting, enjoyable 10 attractive, delightful, gladdening, gratifying, satisfying 11 captivating, fascinating, good-humored, good-natured, pleasurable 12 entertaining, well-mannered

pleasing inactivity
Italian: 14 dolce far niente

pleasurable 8 pleasing 9 agreeable, enjoyable 10 delightful

pleasure 3 fun, joy 4 like, will, wish 5 bliss, cheer, mirth 6 choice, desire, gaiety, option 7 delight, elation, rapture 9 amusement, diversion, enjoyment, festivity, happiness, merriment, selection 10 exultation, jubilation, preference, recreation 11 high spirits, inclination 13 entertainment, gratification 15 beer and skittles 16 lightheartedness
goddess of: 8 Voluptas

pleasure-giving 7 amusing 8 pleasing 9 agreeable, enjoyable 10 delightful 11 pleasurable 12 entertaining

Pleasure of His Company, The
author: 19 Cornelia Otis Skinner

pleasure trip 4 tour 5 jaunt 6 outing 8 vacation 9 excursion

pleat 4 fold 5 crimp, frill 6 crease

pleated 6 fluted, folded 7 creased, crimped 10 corrugated

plebeian 3 low 4 base, mean 5 banal 6 coarse, common, vulgar 7 lowborn, lowbrow, popular 8 commoner, everyman, low-class, ordinary 9 bourgeois, common man, unrefined 10 average man, uncultured 11 bourgeoisie, commonplace, proletarian 12 uncultivated

plebs 5 demos 6 masses 7 commons 8 populace 9 commoners, hoi polloi, plebeians 11 bourgeoisie 12 common people

plecoptera
class: 8 hexapoda
phylum: 10 arthropoda
group: 8 stone fly

pledge 3 vow 4 bail, bond, oath, pact, pawn, word 5 swear, troth 6 assert, avowal, surety 7 compact, promise, warrant 8 contract, covenant, guaranty, security, warranty **9** agreement, assurance, guarantee **10** adjuration, collateral

Pleiades
  father: 5 Atlas
  mother: 7 Pleione
  half-sisters: 6 Hyades
  names: 4 Maia 6 Merope 7 Alcyone, Celaeno, Electra, Sterope, Taygete
  number of daughters: 5 seven

plenary 4 full 6 entire 7 perfect 8 absolute, complete

plenitude 4 glut, heap, mass 5 flood 6 bounty, plenty, wealth 7 quality, surfeit, surplus 8 fullness, plethora, totality 9 abundance, amplitude, profusion, repletion, wholeness 10 cornucopia, entireness, quantities 11 ample supply, copiousness, full measure, sufficiency 12 completeness 14 more than enough

plenteous 6 lavish 7 copious, profuse 8 abundant 9 bountiful, plentiful

plentiful 4 lush 5 ample, large 6 lavish 7 copious, liberal, profuse 8 abundant, generous, infinite, prolific 9 abounding, bounteous, bountiful, plenteous, unsparing, unstinted 11 overflowing 13 inexhaustible

plenty 4 gobs, lots, slew 5 scads 6 luxury, oceans, oodles, riches, wealth, worlds 8 opulence 9 abundance, affluence, good times, great deal, plenitude, profusion, well-being 10 prosperity 11 ample amount, good fortune, sufficiency 12 a full measure
  goddess of: 3 Ops

plethora 4 glut 5 flood 6 excess, wealth 7 overage, surfeit, surplus 8 fullness 9 abundance, amplitude, plenitude, profusion 10 oversupply, redundancy, surplusage 11 superfluity 13 overabundance 14 more than enough, superabundance

Plexippus
  also: 10 Parthenius
  father: 7 Phineus 8 Thestius
  brother: 7 Pandion
  sister: 8 Althaea
  nephew: 8 Meleager
  killed by: 8 Meleager

pliable 5 lithe 6 limber, pliant, supple 7 elastic, plastic, springy, willing 8 flexible, yielding 9 adaptable, compliant, receptive, resilient, tractable 10 manageable, responsive, submissive 11 acquiescent 13 accommodating 14 easily bendable, impressionable

pliancy 8 docility, meekness, yielding 9 passivity 10 compliance, pliability, submission, suppleness 11 flexibility 12 complaisance

pliant 4 meek 6 supple 7 pliable 8 flexible, yielding 9 compliant 10 submissive 11 deferential

pliers
  type: 10 fixed-joint 11 combination, needle-nosed, side-cutting 17 offset combination

plight 3 fix, jam 5 pinch, state, trial 6 crisis, muddle, pickle, scrape 7 dilemma, impasse, straits, trouble 8 distress, exigency

9 condition, emergency, extremity, situation 10 difficulty 11 predicament, tribulation, vicissitude 12 circumstance

Plisthenes
  brother/half-brother: 8 Menelaus 9 Agamemnon
  father: 6 Atreus
  mother: 6 Cleola
  sister/half-sister: 8 Anaxibia
  sister-in-law: 12 Clytemnestra
  uncle: 8 Thyestes

plod 4 drag, grub, moil, plug, slog, toil 5 grind, sweat, tramp 6 drudge, lumber, trudge, waddle 7 peg away, shuffle 8 struggle 9 persevere

plodding 4 dull 6 clumsy 8 trudging 9 laborious 10 pedestrian

plot 3 lot, map 4 area, draw, mark, plan, tale, yarn 5 chart, draft, field, patch, space, story, tract 6 action, design, scheme, sketch 7 collude, compute, diagram, outline, section 8 clearing, conspire, contrive, evil plan, intrigue, maneuver 9 blueprint, calculate, determine, incidents, narrative, story line, stratagem 10 conspiracy, secret plan 11 machination

plotting 4 wily 6 artful, crafty 7 cunning 8 scheming 9 conniving, designing 10 intriguing

Plough and the Stars, The
  author: 10 Sean O'Casey

plover
  group of: 4 wing 12 congregation

plow, plough 3 cut, dig 4 push, till, work 5 break, dig up, drive, forge, press, shove, spade 6 furrow, harrow, loosen, plunge, turn up 7 break up 8 bulldoze 9 cultivate
  invented by:
    cast iron: 7 Ransome
    disc: 5 Hardy

plowable 6 arable 7 friable 8 farmable, tillable 10 cultivable

Plowright, Joan
  born: 5 Brigg 7 England
  husband: 15 Laurence Olivier
  roles: 13 A Taste of Honey 15 The Entertainers

ploy 4 game, ruse, wile 5 trick 6 design, gambit, scheme, tactic 7 gimmick 8 artifice, maneuver, strategy 9 stratagem 10 subterfuge

pluck 4 draw, grab, grit, guts, jerk, pick, sand, yank 5 spunk, valor 6 daring, mettle, pull at, snatch, spirit, uproot 7 bravery, courage, pull off, pull out, resolve 8 boldness, temerity, tenacity 9 extirpate, fortitude 10 doggedness, resolution 11 persistence 12 perseverance 13 determination

pluck out 7 extract, pick out, pull out

plucky 4 bold, game 5 brave, gutsy 6 daring, spunky 7 doughty, valiant 8 fearless, intrepid, spirited, unafraid, valorous 9 audacious, dauntless, undaunted 10 courageous, mettlesome 11 lionhearted, unflinching 12 stouthearted

plug 4 bung, cork 5 close, stuff 6 fill up, stanch, stop up 7 shut off, stopper, stopple

plug up 3 dam **4** clog, plug **5** block, choke, dam up, stuff **6** stop up **7** congest **8** obstruct

plum

varieties: 3 hog **4** Coco, date, Duhr, gage, Java, sand, sloe, wild **5** beach, black, goose, Islay, Jaman, Lansa, Moxie, nanny, Natal, shore, Simon **6** August, Batoko, Canada, Cheney, cherry, common, Damson, ground, Indian, Jambul, Kaffir, Kelsey, Lomboy, Pigeon, Sapote, Sierra, Sisson **7** apricot, Burbank, Cheston, Jambosa, Malabar, Orleans, Pacific, Spanish, Wickson **8** American, Assyrian, Burdekin, European, Hortulan, Jambolan, Japanese, Oklahoma, Prunello, Victoria **9** Allegheny, Chickasaw, Governor's, greengage, marmalade, Myrobalan, wild-goose **10** Madagascar **13** Queensland hog

plumb 4 lead, test, true **5** gauge, level, probe, sheer, sound **6** fathom **7** examine, measure, plummet **8** plumb bob, straight, vertical **9** penetrate

plume 3 pen **4** down **5** egret, pique, preen, pride, prize, quill **7** feather

military: 7 panache

Plumed Serpent, The

author: 10 D H Lawrence

Plummer, Christopher

real name: 28 Arthur Christopher Orme Plummer

born: 6 Canada **7** Toronto

wife: 11 Tammy Grimes **12** Elaine Taylor

roles: 14 Murder by Decree **15** The Sound of Music **18** Baron Georg von Trapp **20** The Man Who Would Be King **25** The Return of the Pink Panther

plummet 4 dive, fall **6** plunge, tumble **8** nosedive **12** fall headlong

plump 4 drop, firm, flop, plop, sink **5** blunt, buxom, obese, plunk, pudgy, solid, spill, stout **6** abrupt, chubby, direct, fleshy, portly, rotund, sprawl, stocky, tumble **7** rounded **8** collapse, outright **9** corpulent

plumpness

French: 10 embonpoint

plunder 3 rob **4** haul, loot, raid, sack, swag, take **5** booty, rifle, prize, strip **6** fleece, maraud, pilfer, ravage, spoils **7** despoil, pillage, ransack, takings **9** filchings **10** pilferings

plunderer 6 looter, vandal **7** brigand **8** pillager **9** despoiler

plunge 3 dip, fly, run **4** bolt, cast, dart, dash, dive, drop, duck, fall, jerk, roll, jump, leap, push, reel, rock, rush, sink, sway, tear, toss **5** douse, drive, heave, lunge, lurch, pitch, press, shoot, speed, surge, swarm, whisk **6** charge, hasten, hurtle, hustle, scurry, sprint, streak, thrust, tumble **7** descend, immerse, scuttle **8** scramble, submerge, submerse **12** fall headlong

plunk 4 pick, thud **5** pluck, plumb, strum, twang **6** dollar **7** exactly **8** squarely **9** precisely

plurality 4 bulk, most **8** majority **13** preponderance

plus 5 added, extra, other, spare **6** useful **7** helpful **9** auxiliary, desirable **10** additional, beneficial **12** advantageous, supplemental **13** supplementary

plush 4 lush, posh, rich **5** fancy, grand, ritzy, swank, thick **6** classy, deluxe, lavish, snazzy, swanky **7** elegant, opulent **8** palatial **9** luxurious, sumptuous **11** extravagant

plushy 4 soft **5** cushy, swank **7** opulent, velvety **9** luxurious, sumptuous

Plutarch

author of: 13 Parallel Lives

Plutarch's Lives

author: 8 Plutarch

Pluto

also: 5 Hades

god of: 10 underworld

corresponds to: 3 Dis **5** Orcus **8** Dis Pater

Pluto

position: 5 ninth

satellite: 6 Charon

plutocrat 5 mogul **6** fat cat, tycoon **9** financier **10** capitalist

plutonic 7 abyssal, igneous **9** cimmerian, intrusive, vulcanian

plutonium

chemical symbol: 2 Pu

Plutus

author: 12 Aristophanes

character: 5 Cario **9** Chremylus **11** Blepsidemus

god of: 6 wealth

Plutus

personifies: 6 wealth

father: 6 Iasion

mother: 7 Demeter

Pluvius

epithet of: 7 Jupiter

ply 3 fly, run **4** leaf, sail, work **5** layer, offer, plait, plate, press, sheet, slice, twist, wield **6** employ, follow, handle, lamina, pursue, sheath, strand, supply **7** besiege, carry on, labor at, operate, stratum, utilize **8** exercise, navigate, practice, put to use, urge upon **9** thickness **10** manipulate

poach 3 rob **4** cook **5** shirr, steal **6** plunge, simmer **7** trample **8** encroach, trespass

pocket 3 bag, get, pit **4** gain, lode, sack, vein **5** pouch, purse, pygmy, small, steal, strip, usurp **6** attain, bantam, cavity, come by, hollow, little, obtain, pilfer, strain, streak **7** chamber, compact, handbag, placket, receive **8** arrogate, envelope, portable **9** miniature **10** diminutive, receptacle **11** appropriate, compartment

Pocket, Herbert

character in: 17 Great Expectations

author: 7 Dickens

pocketbook 3 bag **5** pouch, purse **6** clutch, wallet **7** handbag, satchel **8** moneybag, notecase **9** coin purse **10** money purse **11** shoulder bag

French: 12 porte-monnaie

pocket flask 5 flask 6 bottle 7 canteen

pocket-sized 3 wee 4 tiny 5 dwarf, pygmy, small 6 bantam, little, midget, minute, petite 7 compact 9 miniature 10 diminutive, vest-pocket

poco
    music: 6 little

Pocock, Mamie
    character in: 14 The Ambassadors
    author: 5 James

pod 4 case, hull, husk 5 shell 6 jacket, sheath 8 pericarp, seed case 10 seed vessel

Podarces
    mentioned in: 5 Iliad
    father: 8 Iphiclus
    brother: 11 Protesilaus
    commanded: 8 Pythians

Podes
    home: 4 Troy
    occupation: 7 warrior
    killed by: 8 Menelaus

Podgorica
    capital of: 10 Montenegro

podium 4 dais, foot, wall 5 stipe 7 lectern 8 pedestal, platform 9 footstalk

Poe, Edgar Allan
    author of: 6 Ligeia 7 Israfel, To Helen 8 The Bells, The Raven 11 Annabel Lee, The Gold Bug 18 The Purloined Letter 20 The Cask of Amontillado, The Pit and the Pendulum 22 The Masque of the Red Death 24 The Fall of the House of Usher, The Murders in the Rue Morgue 29 The Narrative of Arthur Gordon Pym

Poeas
    also: 5 Poias
    lit: 11 funeral pyre
    pyre of: 8 Hercules
    son: 11 Philoctetes

poem 3 lay, ode 4 epic, song 5 elegy, idyll, lyric, rhyme, verse 6 ballad, jingle, sonnet 8 doggerel, limerick, madrigal

Poema del Cid see 6 The Cid

Poems Chiefly in the Scottish Dialect
    author: 11 Robert Burns

Poena
    also: 5 Poine
    personifies: 7 revenge 10 punishment

poet 4 bard 5 maker 6 lyrist, rhymer, singer 7 reciter 8 lyricist, minstrel, verseman 9 balladeer, balladist, poetaster, rhymester, sonneteer, versifier 10 improviser, librettist, songwriter

poetaster 4 bard, poet 6 rhymer, writer 8 poetizer, rimester 9 rhymester, versifier

poetic, poetical 5 lyric 7 lilting, lyrical, melodic, musical 8 metrical, rhythmic, songlike 9 melodious 11 imaginative

Poetics
    author: 9 Aristotle

poetizer 4 bard, poet 6 rhymer, writer 8 rhymster 9 poetaster, versifier

poetry 5 poesy, rhyme, verse 13 versification
    god of: 4 Odin, Ogma 5 Brage, Bragi,

Othin 6 Apollo 7 Phoebus, Pythius 9 Musagetes

Pogo
    creator: 9 Walt Kelly
    character: 9 Porkypine, Wiley Catt 10 Boll Weevil 12 PT Bridgeport 13 Deacon Mushrat, Mole MacCarony
    alligator: 6 Albert
    fox: 11 Seminole Sam
    frog: 15 Moonshine Sonata
    hound: 18 Beauregard Bugleboy
    possum: 4 Pogo
    skunk: 16 Ma'm'selle Hepzibah
    snake: 7 Snavely
    sorcerer: 10 Howland Owl
    turtle/pirate captain: 14 Churchy La Femme
    place: 15 Okefenokee Swamp

Pohjola
    origin: 7 Finnish
    identified with: 7 Lapland
    location: 12 North Finland

poignant 3 sad 5 sharp 6 biting, moving, rueful, woeful 7 cutting, doleful, piquant, piteous, pitiful, pungent, tearful 8 grievous, pathetic, piercing, pitiable, touching 9 affecting, sorrowful, trenchant 10 lamentable 11 distressing, penetrating 12 heartrending

Poine see 5 Poena

point 3 aim, end, hit, nib, run, tip, use 4 apex, bend, bode, core, game, gist, goal, item, mark, meat, pike, pith, spur, time, turn, unit 5 argue, cause, guide, heart, imply, level, limit, place, prong, prove, score, sense, slant, spike, stage, steer, tally, train, value 6 aspect, basket, degree, detail, direct, hint at, kernel, marrow, moment, number, object, reason 7 essence, feature, instant, portend, presage, purpose, quality, signify, suggest, testify 8 indicate, intimate, juncture, main idea, manifest, offshoot, position, sharp end 9 condition, extension, intention, objective, outgrowth 10 foreshadow, particular, projection, prominence, promontory 11 demonstrate 12 protuberance

point-blank 5 blunt 6 direct 10 forthright 11 plainspoken

Point Counter Point
    author: 12 Aldous Huxley

point d'appui 4 prop, stay 24 point of battle line support

pointed 5 acute, blunt, sharp 6 biting, direct, peaked, pointy 7 cutting, fitting, hinting, telling 8 accurate, incisive, piercing 9 aciculate, acuminate, cuspidate, pertinent, trenchant 10 emphasized, forthright 11 appropriate, conspicuous, insinuating, penetrating

pointer 3 arm, tip 4 hand, hint 5 arrow, guide, stick 6 needle 7 caution, warning 9 indicator 10 admonition, advisement, suggestion 13 piece of advice 14 recommendation
    dog breed: 16 German wirehaired 17 German shorthaired 25 wirehaired pointing griffon

pointless 4 dull 5 blunt 6 absurd, futile, obtuse, stupid 7 aimless, invalid, rounded, unedged, useless 8 bootless, worn down 9 fruitless, illogical, senseless, unpointed, worthless 10 irrational, irrelevant, ridiculous, unavailing 11 ineffectual, meaningless, purposeless, unsharpened 12 inapplicable, preposterous, unproductive, unprofitable, unreasonable

point of view 4 side 5 angle, slant 6 aspect 7 outlook 8 attitude 9 viewpoint 10 standpoint 11 frame of mind, perspective

point the way 4 guide, pilot, usher 6 direct 8 indicate, navigate 14 give directions

point to 5 argue, imply 6 denote 7 express 8 indicate

point up 6 stress 9 emphasize, underline 10 accentuate, underscore

Poirot, Hercule
   detective created by: 14 Agatha Christie
   nationality: 7 Belgian
   famed for: 10 moustaches
   phrase: 15 little grey cells
   played by: 12 Peter Sellers

poise 4 calm 5 raise 6 aplomb 7 balance, elevate 8 presence 9 assurance, composure, hold aloft, sangfroid 10 equanimity 11 savoir faire, self-command, self-control 13 self-assurance 14 presence of mind, self-confidence 15 be in equilibrium

poised 7 assured 8 composed 9 confident 10 controlled 11 self-assured 13 self-possessed

poison 4 bane, evil, harm 5 curse, taint, toxin, venom 6 cancer, canker, debase, defile, impair, infect, plague, weaken 7 corrode, corrupt, degrade, disease, outrage, pollute 8 enormity, make sick 9 malignity 10 adulterate, corruption, debilitate, malignancy, pestilence 11 abomination, contaminate

poisonous 5 fatal, toxic 6 deadly, lethal, mortal 7 baneful, noxious 8 venomous, virulent 10 pernicious 11 deleterious 12 pestilential

Poitier, Sidney
   born: 7 Miami FL
   wife: 13 Joanna Shimkus
   roles: 11 Virgil Tibbs 12 A Patch of Blue, For Love of Ivy, Porgy and Bess 13 To Sir with Love 14 The Defiant Ones 15 A Raisin in the Sun 16 Lilies of the Field (Oscar) 17 They Call Me Mr Tibbs 19 In the Heat of the Night, The Blackboard Jungle, Uptown Saturday Night 23 Guess Who's Coming to Dinner?

Pokanoket *see* 10 Wampanoags

poke 3 dig, hit, jab 4 butt, drag, gore, idle, jolt, prod, push, stab 5 crawl, dally, delay, mosey, nudge, punch, stick, thump 6 dawdle, fiddle, potter, thrust 7 meander, saunter, shamble, shuffle 8 hang back 10 dilly-dally 12 shilly-shally

poker
   derived from: 5 as nas, gilet 6 brelan 7 primero 11 brouillotte
   cards/hand: 4 five 5 seven
   bets: 4 ante 5 chips
   hand: 4 pair 5 flush 8 straight, two pairs 9 full house 10 royal flush 11 four of a kind 12 three of a kind 13 straight flush
   term: 4 call, fold 5 check, raise 6 ante up 7 reraise
   variation: 4 draw, stud 5 jacks 8 jackpots 12 five-card draw 13 seven-card stud

poky, pokey 4 dull, jail, slow 5 dowdy, small 6 dreary, shabby, stodgy, stuffy 7 cramped 8 confined, dawdling, dilatory, frumpish 9 puttering 10 monotonous
   creature: 5 sloth, snail 6 turtle 8 slow-poke, tortoise

Polacanthus
   type: 8 dinosaur 10 ornithopod

Poland
   other name: 6 Polska 17 the land of the plain
   capital/largest city: 6 Warsaw
   medieval capital: 6 Cracow, Krakow
   others: 3 Lwo 4 Kodz, Kolo, Lida, Lodz, Lvov, Lyck, Nysa, Oels, Pila 5 Brest, Bytom, Chelm, Dukla, Narev, Opole, Posen, Radom, Sroda, Torun, Vilna 6 Danzig, Elblag, Gdansk, Gdynia, Gnesen, Grodno, Kalisz, Kielce, Kracow, Lublin, Poznan, Tarnow, Zabrze 7 Beuthen, Breslau, Chorzow, Garocin, Gliwice, Litousk, Litovsk, Lyublin, Oleztyn, Stettin, Wroclaw 8 Frombork, Gleiwitz, Katowice, Lidzbark, Liegnitz, Oswiecim, Przemysl, Szczecin, Tarnopol 9 Auschwitz, Bialogard, Bialystok, Bydgoszcz, Sosnowiec, Szczecin, Walbrzych 11 Czestochowa
   school: 6 Warsaw 12 Jagiellonian
   division: 7 Galicia, Silesia 8 Podlesia, Volhynia 9 Lithuania, Pomerania
   measure: 3 cal 4 mila, pret 5 morga, sazen, vloka, wloka 6 cwierc, cwierk, kwarta, lokiec 7 garniec 9 kwarterka
   monetary unit: 4 abia 5 dalar, ducat, grosz, marka, zloty 6 fennig, groszy, gulden, halerz, ko rona 8 groschen
   weight: 3 lut 4 funt 6 kamian 7 skrupul
   island: 5 Wolin
   lake: 5 Goplo, Mamry 8 Niegocin, Sniardwy 13 Stettin Lagoon
   mountain: 5 Tatra 6 Beskid 7 Pieniny, Sudeten 9 Beshchady, High Tatra, Holy Cross 10 Carpathian
   highest point: 4 Rysy
   river: 3 Bug, San 4 Alle, Brda, Gwda, Lyna, Nysa, Oder, Styr 5 Biala, Drana, Dwina, Narev, Narew, Notec, Podra, Seret, Warta, Wista 6 Neisse, Niemen, Nyeman, Pilica, Pripet, Prosna, Styrpa, Wieprz 7 Nemunas, Vistula, Wistoka 8 Dniester
   sea: 6 Baltic
   physical feature:
   forest: 10 Bialowieza
   gulf: 6 Danzig, Gdansk
   lagoon: 7 Stettin 12 Frischeshaff
   plain: 7 Silesia
   plateau: 6 Lublin

people: 4 Pole, Slav 5 Mazur 8 Silesian
astronomer: 10 Copernicus
author: 7 Reymont 8 Zeromski 10 Mickiewicz, Wyspianski 11 Sienkiewicz
composer: 6 Chopin 10 Paderewski
dynasty: 5 Piast 7 Jagello
king: 7 Casimir 8 Augustus
leader: 5 Kania 6 Gierek 7 Gomulka, Mieszko 8 Boleslaw 9 Pilsudski, Stanislaw 10 Jaruzel ski, Kosciuszko, Lech Walesa
pope: 10 John Paul II 20 Cardinal Carol Wojtyla
queen: 7 Jadwiga
language: 6 Kaszub, Polish 10 Pomeranian
religion: 13 Roman Catholic
place:
 castle: 5 Wawel
 church: 6 St John 10 Panna Maria
 monastery: 9 Jasna Gora
 monument: 17 Heroes of the Ghetto
 national park: 5 Ojcow 10 Bialowieza
 palace: 7 Casimir
feature:
 folk dance: 5 polka 7 mazurka 9 krakowiak, polonaise
 union: 10 Solidarity
food:
 dish: 5 bigos 7 kolduny
 drink: 5 vodka 7 Krupnik
 sausage: 8 kielbasa
 soup: 7 barszca
Polanski, Roman
 director of: 4 Tess 7 Macbeth 9 Chinatown 13 Rosemary's Baby
polar 3 icy 6 arctic, frigid, wintry 7 glacial, ice-cold 8 freezing 9 antarctic 11 nothernmost 12 southernmost
pole 3 rod 4 mast, spar 5 shaft, staff, stick 6 tongue 9 pikestaff
 flax holder: 7 distaff
 pertaining to: 5 nodal
 sacred: 7 Asherah
 Scottish: 5 caber
 tribal: 5 totem
 vehicular: 4 neap
Polias, Poliatas
 epithet of: 6 Athena
police, police officer 4 cops, dick, fuzz, tidy 5 clean, guard 6 neaten, patrol, tidy up 7 clean up, control, marshal, officer, protect, sheriff 8 blue coat, flatfoot, gendarme, regulate, spruce up, troopers 9 gendarmes, men in blue, patrolmen 10 traffic cop 11 arm of the law, keep in order 12 constabulary, cop on the beat
 French: 8 gendarme
 Italian: 11 carabiniere
Police Woman
 character: 9 (Det) Joe Styles, (Lt) Paul Marsh 11 (Det) Pete Royster, (Lt) Bill Crowley 12 (Sgt Suzanne) Pepper Martin
 cast: 9 Ed Bernard 11 Val Bisoglio 12 Earl Holliman 14 Angie Dickinson, Charles Dierkop

policy 3 way 4 plan, rule 5 habit, style 6 custom, design, method, scheme, system 7 program, routine, tactics 8 behavior, platform, practice, strategy 9 principle, procedure
Polieus
 epithet of: 4 Zeus
 means: 5 urban
polish 3 oil, wax 4 buff, sand 5 class, emend, glaze, gloss, grace, rouge, rub up, shine 6 pumice, refine, smooth 7 burnish, correct, culture, enhance, finesse, improve, perfect, sauvity, touch up, varnish 8 abrasive, courtesy, elegance, round out, urbanity 9 gentility, politesse, sandpaper 10 politeness, refinement 11 cultivation, good manners
polished 4 able, deft, fine, oily 5 oiled, suave, waxed 6 buffed, expert, glassy, glazed, glossy, polite, rubbed, sanded, shined, urbane 7 capable, elegant, genteel, refined, skilled 8 cultured, finished, mannerly, masterly, skillful, smoothed 9 brilliant, burnished, courteous, masterful, practiced, varnished 10 cultivated, proficient 11 experienced 12 accomplished
polish off 6 finish 8 complete, get rid of 9 dispose of
polite 4 high 5 civil, elite 6 proper 7 courtly, elegant, gallant, genteel, refined 8 cultured, mannerly, polished, well-bred 9 civilized, courteous, diffident, patrician 10 cultivated, respectful 11 ceremonious, fashionable, gentlemanly, well-behaved 12 well-mannered
politeness 7 decorum 8 courtesy 9 gentility, propriety 10 refinement 11 good manners
Polites
 character in: 7 Odyssey
 brother: 5 Paris 6 Hector
 companion: 8 Odysseus
 father: 5 Priam
 mother: 6 Hecuba
 sister: 9 Cassandra
 transformed by: 5 Aeaea, Circe
 transformed into: 3 hog, pig 5 swine
politic 4 wily, wise 5 chary, suave 6 artful, astute, shrewd, subtle 7 mindful, prudent, tactful 8 cautious, discreet, scheming 9 designing, expedient, judicious, opportune 10 contriving, diplomatic 11 calculating, circumspect, machinating 13 Machiavellian
political party 3 GOP 4 Tory, Whig 5 Labor 7 faction 9 Communist, Greenback, Socialist 10 Democratic, Republican 11 Know-Nothing
political refugee 2 DP 5 exile 6 emigre 10 expatriate 15 displaced person
politician 8 politico 9 incumbent, statesman 10 campaigner, legislator 12 officeholder, office seeker 13 public servant
politics 10 government, statecraft 11 party policy 13 statesmanship 14 affairs of state
Politics
 author: 9 Aristotle

Politic Would-Be, Lord and Lady
 characters in: 7 Volpone
 author: 6 Jonson
Poliuchus
 epithet of: 6 Athena
 means: 14 city-protecting
Polixenes
 character in: 14 The Winter's Tale
 author: 11 Shakespeare
Polk, James Knox
 presidential rank: 8 eleventh
 party: 8 Democrat
 state represented: 2 TN
 defeated: 4 (Henry) Clay 6 (James Gillespie) Birney
 vice president: 6 (George Mifflin) Dallas
 cabinet:
 state: 8 (James) Buchanan
 treasury: 6 (Robert John) Walker
 war: 5 (William Learned) Marcy
 attorney general: 5 (John Young) Mason 6 (Isaac) Toucey 8 (Nathan) Clifford
 navy: 5 (John Young) Mason 8 (George) Bancroft
 postmaster general: 7 (Cave) Johnson
 born: 2 NC 17 Mecklenburg County
 died/buried: 2 TN 9 Nashville
 education: 11 prep schools 16 tutored privately
 University: 13 North Carolina
 religion: 9 Methodist
 political career: 16 state legislature 17 Speaker of the House 24 US House of Representatives
 governor of: 9 Tennessee
 civilian career: 6 lawyer
 notable events of lifetime/term:
 boundary dispute: 9 Northwest
 discovery in California of: 4 gold
 Proviso: 6 Wilmot
 treaty of: 16 Guadalupe Hidalgo
 war: 7 Mexican
 father: 6 Samuel
 mother: 4 Jane
 siblings: 7 John Lee 9 Jane Maria, Naomi Tate 10 Lydia Eliza 12 Marshall Tate, Samuel Wilson 14 William Hawkins 15 Franklin Ezekiel, Ophelia Clarissa
 wife: 5 Sarah (Childress)
 children: 4 none
polka 5 dance 10 round dance 13 Bohemian dance
poll 4 head, vote 5 count, tally 6 census, survey, voting 7 canvass, figures, returns 8 register, sampling 9 interview, nose count 10 count noses, voting list 11 voting place
Pollack, Sydney
 director: of: 11 Out of Africa (Oscar) 12 The Way We Were 15 Absence of Malice 23 They Shoot Horses Don't They?
Pollock, Jackson
 born: 6 Cody WY
 artwork: 5 Scent 9 Blue Poles 10 The She-Wolf 11 Convergence 12 Autumn Rhythm 13 Eyes in the Heat 17 Easter and the Totem 20 Guardians of the Secret

pollutant 5 fumes, smoke, waste 7 exhaust 8 emission, impurity
pollute 4 foul, soil 5 dirty, sully 6 befoul, debase, defile 7 deprave, profane 9 desecrate 10 adulterate, make filthy 11 contaminate
polluted 4 foul 5 dirty, drunk 6 impure, soiled 7 corrupt, profane, smashed, unclean 9 poisonous 12 contaminated
pollution 7 fouling, soiling 8 defiling, dirtying, foulness, impurity 9 befouling, pollutant 11 uncleanness 12 adulteration 13 contaminating, contamination
Pollux see 15 Castor and Pollux
Pollyanna
 director: 10 David Swift
 based on story by: 13 Eleanor Porter
 cast: 9 Jane Wyman 10 Karl Malden 11 Hayley Mills, Richard Egan
polo
 equipment: 6 mallet
 period of play: 7 chukker
 championship: 10 Camacho Cup 13 Coronation Cup 16 Cup of the Americas
Polonius
 character in: 6 Hamlet
 author: 11 Shakespeare
Polska see 6 Poland
poltergeist 5 ghost 6 spirit
 literally: 10 noise-ghost
 manifestation: 5 knock, noise, prank
Poltergeist
 director: 10 Tobe Hooper
 cast: 12 Craig T Nelson 14 Jobeth Williams 16 Beatrice Straight
 co-writer/producer: 15 Steven Spielberg
poltroon 6 coward, craven 7 caitiff, chicken, dastard 11 yellow-belly
Polybates
 member of: 8 Gigantes
Polycaste see 6 Perdix
Polydora
 father: 6 Peleus
 mother: 8 Antigone
 husband: 5 Borus
 son: 10 Menestheus
Polydorus
 mentioned in: 5 Iliad
 father: 5 Priam 10 Hippomedon
 mother: 6 Hecuba
 killed by: 10 Polymestor 11 Polymnestor
 avenged by: 6 Hecuba
 member of: 7 Epigoni
 descendant of: 18 Seven against Thebes
polygon 10 multiangle 11 plane figure
 eight-sided: 7 octagon
 equal angled: 6 isogon
 five-sided: 8 pentagon
 four-sided: 6 square 7 rhombus 8 tetragon 9 rectangle, trapezoid
 nine-sided: 7 nonagon
 seven-sided: 8 heptagon
 six-sided: 7 hexagon
 ten-sided: 7 decagon
 three-sided: 8 triangle
 twelve-sided: 9 dodecagon

Polyhymnia
  also: 8 Polymnia
  member of: 5 Muses
  personifies: 5 dance 11 sacred music
  mother: 9 Mnemosyne
Polyidus
  revived: 7 Glaucus
Polymastus
  epithet of: 7 Artemis
  means: 12 many-breasted
polymer 5 dimer, nylon 6 hydrol 7 hexamer
  8 oligomer
Polymnestor
  king of: 6 Thrace
  killed: 9 Polydorus
Polymnia see 10 Polyhymnia
Polyneices see 9 Polynices
Polynesia
  name means: 11 many islands
  cities: 4 Apia 7 Papeete 8 Auckland,
    Pago Pago 9 Nukualofa
  island: 4 Cook, Line 5 Samoa, Tonga 6
    Easter, Ellice, Hawaii, Midway, Tahiti,
    Tubuai, Tuvalu 7 Austral, Maupiti,
    Phoenix, Society, Tokelau, Tuamotu 8
    Pitcairn 9 Marquesas 10 New Zealand 15
    French Polynesia
  sea: 7 Pacific
  people: 3 Ati 5 Maori 6 Kanaka, Nivean,
    Samoan, Tongan 9 Nesogaean 10 Poly-
    nesian
  explorer: 4 Cook 6 Tasman, Wallis 8 Ma-
    gellan 9 Roggeveen 12 Bougainville
  language: 4 Niue, Uvea 5 Maori 6 Sa-
    moan, Tongan 7 Austral, Tagalog,
    Tokelau 8 Hawaiian, Tahitian 9 Marque-
    san, Tuamatuan 10 Mangarevan
  religion: 12 Christianity
  place:
  legendary origin: 8 Hawaiiki
  feature:
  chief: 5 matai
  clothing: 5 pareu 6 sarong 8 lavalava
  dance: 4 hula, siva
  dwelling: 4 fale
  family social unit: 4 aiga
  priest: 7 kahunas
  supernatural power: 4 mana
  food:
    dish: 3 kai, poi 4 taro 8 palusami
    drink: 3 ava 4 kava, kawa
Polynices
  also: 10 Polyneices
  father: 7 Oedipus
  mother: 7 Jocasta
  uncle: 5 Creon
  brother: 7 Oedipus 8 Eteocles
  sister: 6 Ismene 8 Antigone
  killed by: 8 Eteocles
polyp 5 coral, hydra, tumor 6 growth, isopod 7 octopod 10 sea anemone
Polypemon see 10 Procrustes
Polyphemus
  form: 7 Cyclops 12 one-eyed giant
  father: 6 Elatus 8 Poseidon
  mother: 6 Thoosa
  joined: 9 Argonauts

  killed: 4 Acis
  blinded by: 8 Odysseus
  loved: 7 Galatea
Polyphides
  king of: 6 Sicyon
  vocation: 4 seer
  protected: 8 Menelaus 9 Agamemnon
Polyphontes
  brother: 11 Cresphontes
  killed: 11 Cresphontes
polyphony 7 organum 8 faburden 11 faux-
  bourdon 12 counterpoint
Polypoetes
  king of: 10 Thesprotia
  father: 6 Apollo 8 Odysseus 9 Pirithous
  mother: 6 Phthia 9 Callidice 10 Hippo-
    damia
  leader of: 6 Greeks
Polyporthis
  father: 8 Odysseus
  mother: 8 Penelope
polysaccharide 6 insulin, starch 7 dextrin 8
  galactin, lichenin 9 cellulose 12 carbohydrate
Polytechnus
  wife: 5 Aedon
Polyxena
  father: 5 Priam
  mother: 6 Hecuba
  loved by: 8 Achilles
Polyxenus
  grandfather: 6 Augeas
Polyxo
  advisor to: 9 Hypsipyle
Pomaria see 7 Algeria
Pomerania
  capital: 7 Stettin
  city: 5 Thorn, Torun 6 Anklam
  country: 6 Poland 7 Germany
  island: 5 Rugen 6 Usedom
  province: 7 Pomorze
pommel, pummel 4 beat, hilt, horn, knob,
  pake 6 finial, strike 9 saddlebow
Pomona
  origin: 5 Roman
  goddess of: 10 fruit trees
pomp 4 show 5 front, glory, style 7 display
  8 ceremony, flourish, grandeur, splendor 9
  pageantry, showiness, solemnity, spectacle 10 brilliance 11 affectation, grandiosity,
  ostentation, pompousness 12 magnificence 14 stately display 15 pretentiousness
pompous 4 vain 5 proud 6 lordly, uppish 7
  haughty 8 affected, arrogant, mannered,
  overdone, puffed-up, snobbish 9 conceited, egotistic, grandiose, imperious 10
  blustering, swaggering 11 overbearing, patronizing, pretentious 12 ostentatious, presumptuous, supercilious, vainglorious 13
  condescending, high and mighty, self-
  important
Ponchielli, Amilcare
  born: 5 Italy 7 Cremona
  composer of: 10 La Gioconda 15 Dance
    of the Hours

poncho 4 cape 5 cloak, shawl 6 mantle, serape

pond 4 pool, tarn 5 basin 6 lagoon 9 small lake, water hole

ponder 4 muse 5 study 6 wonder 7 examine, reflect 8 cogitate, consider, mull over, ruminate 9 brood over, cerebrate, reflect on, speculate, think over 10 deliberate, meditate on, puzzle over 11 contemplate

ponderous 3 big 4 dull 5 bulky, heavy, hefty, large, wordy 6 boring, bovine, dreary 7 awkward, droning, hulking, labored, lumpish, massive, tedious, weighty 8 cumbrous, enormous, sluggish, unlively, unwieldy 9 corpulent, graceless, lumbering, wearisome 10 burdensome, cumbersome, long-winded, lusterless, monotonous, unexciting, ungraceful 11 heavy-handed

pontiff 4 pope 6 bishop, priest 8 pontifex

pontifical 7 pompous 8 churchly, clerical, dogmatic, priestly 9 apostolic, episcopal, imperious 11 opinionated, overbearing, patronizing, pretentious 13 authoritarian, condescending 14 ecclesiastical

Pontus
 personifies: 3 sea
 father: 2 Ge
 son: 6 Nereus 7 Phorcys

pony 3 nag 4 trot 5 glass, horse, pinto 7 mustang 9 racehorse
 breed: 6 Exmoor 8 Shetland

pooh-pooh 5 knock 7 disdain, put down, run down, sneer at 8 belittle 9 disparage

Pooka see 4 Puca

pool 3 pot 4 ally, bank, lake, mere, pond, tarn 5 group, kitty, merge, share, union, unite 6 puddle, splash, stakes 7 combine 8 alliance, fishpond, millpool 9 coalition 10 amalgamate, collective 11 association, consolidate, cooperative 13 confederation

Poole, Grace
 character in: 8 Jane Eyre
 author: 6 Bronte

poop 3 fag 4 bush, deck, do in, tire 7 exhaust, fatigue, wear out 8 enervate

pooped 4 beat 5 all in, spent, tired, weary 6 bushed, done in 7 drained, wearied, worn out 8 fatigued, tired out 9 dead tired, exhausted, played out

poor 3 sad 4 bare, dead, vain, worn 5 broke, empty, needy, sorry 6 barren, fallow, faulty, futile, hard up, in need, in want, meager, paltry, wasted 7 forlorn, sterile, unhappy, unlucky, wanting 8 badly off, bankrupt, beggarly, depleted, desolate, devoid of, grieving, indigent, inferior, pathetic, pitiable, strapped, unworthy, wretched 9 defective, deficient, destitute, exhausted, fruitless, imperfect, infertile, insolvent, in straits, miserable, moneyless, penniless, unfertile, worthless 10 distressed, inadequate, pauperized 11 impecunious, unfortunate 12 impoverished, uncultivable, unproductive, unprofitable 15 poverty-stricken

Poor People
 author: 16 Fyodor Dostoevsky

Poor Richard's Almanac
 author: 16 Benjamin Franklin

Poor White
 author: 16 Sherwood Anderson

pop 4 bang, boom, come, shot, snap, soda 5 arise, blast, burst, crack 6 appear, report 7 explode 8 detonate 9 discharge, explosion, soft drink 10 detonation

pope 3 Leo 4 John, Paul, Pius 5 Peter, Urban 6 Adrian, Eugene, Julius, Martin, Sixtus 7 Clement, Gregory 8 Benedict, Innocent, John Paul, Nicholas 9 Alexander, Callistus
 also: 12 Bishop of Rome 13 Vicar of Christ 14 Primate of Italy, Supreme Pontiff 16 Archbishop of Rome 18 Metropolitan of Rome, Patriarch of the West 25 Servant of the Servants of God
 office: 6 Papacy 7 Holy See 11 Seat of Peter
 elected by: 18 College of Cardinals
 elected in: 8 conclave
 signal that election is concluded: 10 white smoke
 resides: 3 Rome 10 the Vatican 11 Vatican City
 former residence: 13 Lateran Palace
 summer residence: 14 Castel Gondolfo
 papal land holding: 9 patrimony 21 patrimony of Saint Peter
 first pope: 10 Saint Peter
 pope who crowned Charlemagne: 6 Leo III
 pope who excommunicated Luther: 4 Leo X
 pope who authorized Michelangelo to paint Sistine Chapel: 8 Julius II
 "September Pope": 9 John Paul I
 real name of pope:
 Alexander VI: 15 Rodrigo de Borgia
 Callistus III: 15 Alfonso de Borgia
 Clement VII: 14 Giulio de' Medici
 John XXIII: 22 Angelo Giuseppe Roncalli
 John Paul I: 13 Albino Luciani
 John Paul II: 12 Karol Wojtyla 18 Archbishop of Krakow
 Leo X: 16 Giovanni de' Medici
 Pius XI: 12 Achille Ratti
 Pius XII: 35 Eugenio Maria Giuseppe Giovanni Pacelli
 popes of Avignon papacy: 6 Urban V 8 Clement V, John XXII 9 Clement VI, Gregory XI, Nicholas V 10 Innocent VI 11 Benedict XII
 popes during Great Western Schism:
 Avignon: 10 Clement VII 12 Benedict XIII
 Pisa: 9 John XXIII 10 Alexander V
 Rome: 7 Urban VI 10 Boniface IX, Gregory XII 11 Innocent VII
 papal bull/encyclical: 11 Unam sanctam 12 Humanae vitae, Rerum novarum, Vox in excelso 13 Pacem in terris 15 Mater et magistra 19 Populorum progressio 22 Sacerdotalis caelibatus

Pope, Alexander
  author of: 10 The Dunciad 12 An Essay on Man 15 Eloisa to Abelard 16 The Rape of the Lock 18 An Essay on Criticism 20 Epistle to Dr Arbuthnot
Pope, John Russell
  architect of: 17 Jefferson Memorial 20 National Gallery of Art 23 Temple of the Scottish Rite 24 National Archives Building
Popeye
  character in: 9 Sanctuary
  author: 8 Faulkner
popinjay 3 fop 4 beau 5 dandy 7 coxcomb
poplar 7 Populus 22 Liriodendron tulipifera
  varieties: 4 gray 5 black, downy, tulip, white 6 balsam, Eugene, yellow 8 Carolina, Lombardy, necklace 10 Queensland 12 Chinese white, silver-leaved 13 Western balsam
poppy 7 Papaver
  varieties: 3 sea 4 blue, bush, corn, snow, tree, wind, wood 5 field, opium, plume, satin, tulip, water, Welsh 6 arctic, desert, horned 7 Asiatic, flaming, Iceland, Mexican, prickly, Shirley, Western 8 Flanders, harebell, Matilija, oriental 9 Celandine 10 California, island tree 12 Mexican tulip 13 yellow Chinese 14 California tree
  drug: 5 opium 6 heroin 8 morphine
poppycock 3 rot 4 bosh, bunk, jive, tosh 5 froth, fudge, hooey, stuff, trash 6 drivel, humbug 7 baloney, blabber, blather, eyewash, fustian, garbage, hogwash, inanity, prattle, rubbish, twaddle 8 falderal, flummery, nonsense, tommyrot, wish-wash 9 absurdity, gibberish, moonshine, rigmarole 10 applesauce, balderdash, flapdoodle, hocus-pocus, mumbo-jumbo, rigamarole 11 abracadabra, jabberwocky 12 fiddlefaddle, gobbledygook
poppy seed
  botanical name: 7 Papaver 11 P somniferum (sleep-bearing poppy)
  color: 4 blue 5 white
  origin: 4 Asia 6 Europe
  guards against: 9 creditors
  use: 5 bread, cakes, rolls 6 sweets 10 vegetables 11 butter sauce
populace 4 folk 6 people, public 7 society 9 citizenry, community 10 population
popular 5 cheap, civic, civil, stock 6 famous, public, social 7 admired, current, general, in favor 8 accepted, approved, communal, familiar, favorite, in demand, national, orthodox 9 community, preferred, prevalent, well-known, well-liked 10 affordable, celebrated, democratic 11 established, fashionable, inexpensive, of the people, sought-after
popularity 4 fame, note 5 favor, glory, kudos, vogue 6 esteem, regard, renown, repute 7 acclaim, fashion 8 approval 9 celebrity, notoriety 10 acceptance, admiration, notability, reputation 11 acclamation

popular opinion
  Latin: 9 vox populi
popular whim 3 fad 4 rage 5 craze, mania 7 passion 11 infatuation
populate 6 occupy, people, settle 7 inhabit
populated 5 urban 7 peopled, settled 8 citified, occupied 9 inhabited
population 4 folk 6 people, public 8 citizens, populace 9 citizenry, habitancy, residents 11 body politic, commonality, inhabitants
populous 5 dense 6 jammed 7 crowded, peopled, teeming 8 swarming, thronged
porcelain 5 china 11 ceramic ware
porch 4 stoa 5 lanai, plaza, stoop 7 balcony, narthex, portico, veranda 8 solarium, verandah 9 colonnade, vestibule
pore 4 hole, read, scan 5 probe, study 6 outlet, peruse, ponder, review, search, survey 7 dig into, examine, explore, inspect, orifice 8 aperture, consider 9 delve into
Porfiry
  character in: 18 Crime and Punishment
  author: 10 Dostoevsky
Porgy
  author: 13 DuBose Heyward
Porgy and Bess
  opera by: 14 George Gershwin
  character: 4 Bess 5 Porgy 11 Sportin' Life
pornographic 4 blue, lewd 5 bawdy, dirty, gross 6 coarse, filthy, smutty, vulgar 7 obscene 8 indecent, off-color, prurient 9 salacious 10 lascivious, licentious
porous 4 lacy 6 spongy 7 riddled 8 cellular, pervious 9 absorbent, permeable, sievelike 10 penetrable 11 honeycombed
Porphyrion
  member of: 8 Gigantes
porpoise 4 leap 5 whale 6 palach, puffer, seahog 7 cowfish, dolphin, surface 8 cetacean
  genus: 8 Phocaena 9 Delphinus
porridge 4 pobs, samp 5 atole, brose, brout, gruel 6 cereal 7 crowdie, oatmeal, polenta 8 flummery
Porrima see 9 Antevorta
porringer 4 bowl, dish 6 vessel 9 container 10 receptacle
port 4 dock, pier, quay 5 haven, wharf 6 harbor, refuge 7 dry dock, landing, mooring, seaport, shelter 9 anchorage, harborage 11 destination
port
  type: 4 wine 6 brandy
  origin: 8 Portugal
  variety: 4 ruby 5 tawny 7 vintage
  with brandy: 9 Betsy Ross
  with vermouth: 10 Broken Spur
portable 5 handy, light, small 6 bantam, pocket 7 compact, folding, movable 8 cartable, haulable, liftable 9 ready-to-go 10 convenient, conveyable, manageable, vest-pocket 11 pocket-sized

portal, portals 4 adit, arch, door, gate 5 entry 6 wicket 7 doorway, gateway, portico 8 approach, entrance 9 threshold, vestibule 10 portcullis 11 entranceway

Port-au-Prince
  capital of: 5 Haiti

porte-monnaie 5 purse 10 pocketbook 12 money-carrier

portend 4 bode 5 augur 6 denote, herald, warn of 7 bespeak, betoken, point to, predict, presage, signify, suggest 8 forebode, forecast, foretell, forewarn, prophesy 9 foretoken, prefigure 10 foreshadow

portent 4 omen, sign 5 token 6 augury, boding, threat 7 presage, warning 9 harbinger 10 foreboding 11 forewarning

portentous 6 superb 7 amazing, fateful, ominous, pompous 8 alarming, menacing 9 bombastic, grandiose, prophetic 10 foreboding, incredible, prodigious, remarkable, stupendous, surprising 11 astonishing, exceptional, frightening, pretentious, significant, superlative, threatening 12 inauspicious, intimidating, unpropitious

porter 4 brew 5 stout 6 bearer, coolie, redcap, skycap 7 carrier 8 conveyer 9 conductor

Porter, Katherine Anne
  author of: 11 Ship of Fools 12 Old Mortality 14 Flowering Judas 15 The Leaning Tower 18 Pale Horse Pale Rider

Porter, William Sidney
  real name of: 6 O Henry

portfolio 4 case, file 5 album 6 binder, folder 7 dossier 8 envelope 9 scrapbook 10 securities

Porthos
  character in: 18 The Three Musketeers
  author: 5 Dumas (pere)

Portia
  character in: 12 Julius Caesar 19 The Merchant of Venice
  author: 11 Shakespeare

portico 4 stoa 5 lanai 6 piazza 7 balcony, veranda, walkway

portion 3 cut, lot, sum 4 dole, doom, fate, luck, part 5 carve, cut up, moira, piece, sever, share, slice, split 6 amount, divide, kismet, parcel, ration, sector 7 break up, deal out, destiny, fortune, helping, measure, section, segment, serving 8 allocate, disperse, division, fraction, fragment, quantity, separate 9 allotment, allowance, demarcate, partition 10 allocation, distribute, percentage

portion out 5 allot 6 ration 7 dole out, mete out, prorate 8 allocate, dispense, divide up 9 apportion, parcel out 10 distribute, measure out

Portland
  basketball team: 12 Trail Blazers
  football team: 8 Breakers
  river: 8 Columbia 10 Willamette
  university: 4 Reed

Port Louis
  capital of: 9 Mauritius

portly 3 big, fat 4 full 5 beefy, burly, heavy, large, obese, plump, pudgy, round, stout, tubby 6 brawny, chubby, fleshy, rotund, stocky 9 corpulent

Portman, John
  architect of: 15 Peachtree Center (Atlanta)

portmanteau 3 bag 4 grip 5 cloak 6 mantle, valise 8 suitcase 9 gladstone

Port Moresby
  capital of: 9 New Guinea

Portnoy's Complaint
  author: 10 Philip Roth

Port of Spain
  capital of: 17 Trinidad and Tobago

Porto-Novo
  capital of: 5 Benin

portrait 5 cameo 6 sketch 7 drawing, picture 8 likeness, painting, vignette 9 depiction 10 impression, photograph 11 description

Portrait of a Lady, The
  author: 10 Henry James
  character: 11 Madame Merle, Pansy Osmond 12 Isabel Archer 13 Gilbert Osmond, Lord Warburton, Ralph Touchett 14 Caspar Goodwood 18 Henrietta Stackpole

Portrait of the Artist as a Young Man
  author: 10 James Joyce
  character: 4 Emma 12 Simon Dedalus 14 Stephen Dedalus

portray 3 ape 4 draw, play 5 carve, enact, mimic, model, paint 6 depict, detail, figure, pose as, sketch 7 imitate, narrate, picture 8 describe, set forth, simulate 9 delineate, represent, sculpture 10 illustrate, photograph 11 impersonate 12 characterize

portrayal 7 picture 8 portrait 9 picturing 11 delineation, description 14 representation 16 characterization

ports
  god of: 8 Portunus

Portugal
  capital/largest city: 6 Lisbon
  others: 4 Beja, Faro, Ovar 5 Braga, Evora, Olhao, Porto, Viseu 6 Aveiro, Guarda, Leiria, Oporto, Sintra 7 Algarve, Amadora, Bragama, Cascoes, Coimbra, Covilha, Estoril, Funchal, Granada, Setubal 8 Barreiro, Portimao 9 Lusitania 10 Portalegre 14 Vila Nova de Gaia
  Roman city: 10 Portus Cale
  school: 5 Minho 6 Aveiro, Lisbon, Oporto 7 Coimbra
  division: 3 Goa 4 Tejo, Tete 5 Beira, Evora, Macao, Minho, Timor 6 Azores, Loanda 7 Algarve, Madeira 8 Alemtejo, Rebatejo 9 Cape Verde 10 Mozambique 11 Estremadura
  Roman district: 9 Lusitania
  measure: 2 pe 4 bota, moio, vara 5 almud, fanga, geira, linha, milha 6 almude, covado 7 alquier, ferrado, selamin 8 alqueire

monetary unit: 3 avo, rei 4 peca, real 5 conto, crown, dobra, indio, justo, rupia 6 escudo, macuta, octave, pataca, testad, tostao, vintem 7 angalar, centavo, crusado, miereis, testone 8 equipaga, johannes

weight: 4 onca, once 5 libra, marco 6 arroba 7 arratel 9 excropulo

island: 6 Azores 7 Madeira 8 Terceira

mountain: 4 Acor, Lapa 5 Gerez, Marao, Mousa 6 Bornes, Peneda 7 Larouco 8 Caramulo 9 Caldeirao, Monchique 14 Serra da Estrela

highest point: 11 Pico da Serra

river: 3 Sor, Tua 4 Lima, Mino, Mira, Sado, Seda, Tago, Tajo, Tejo, Vara 5 Douro, Duero, Le goa, Micha, Minho, Sabar, Tagus, Vouga, Zatas 6 Cavado, Chanca, Quarto, Tamega, Zezere 7 Mondego, Selamin, Sorraia 8 Quadiana, Tonelada

ocean: 8 Atlantic

physical feature:

bay: 7 Setubal

cape: 4 Roca 7 Mondego 8 Espichel 9 St Vincent

peninsula: 7 Iberian

port: 4 Faro 6 Aveiro, Lisbon, Oporto 7 Leixoes

people: 4 Celt, Moor 7 Iberian 10 Portuguese

artist: 7 Pereira 9 Goncalves 13 Soares dos Reis

author: 5 Dinis 6 Camoes, Vieiva 7 Garrett, Vicente 8 Deus-Ramos

explorer: 3 Cam, Cao 4 Dias, Diaz 6 Cabral, Da Gama 7 Almeida 8 Magellan 11 Albuquerque 23 Prince Henry the Navigator

king: 6 Manuel, Philip, Sancho 7 Alfonso 9 Ferdinand, Sebastian

leader: 5 Eanes 6 Dombal, Soares 7 Caetano, Carmona, Salazar, Spinola

queen: 5 Maria 9 Elizabeth

language: 10 Portuguese

religion: 13 Roman Catholic

place:

church: 5 Jesus 6 Christ 11 Os Jeronimos, Sao Lourenco 12 Old Cathedral 13 Santa Engracia 16 Sao Vicente de Fora

city square: 15 Praca do Comercio

dam: 6 Belver, Idanha 13 Castelo do Bode

fortress-church: 12 Leco do Bailio

monastery: 8 Alcóbaca 12 Hieronymites 20 Santa Maria da Victoira

monument: 11 Discoveries

museum: 13 Soares dos Reis

palace: 6 Cintra

shrine: 6 Fatima

colony: 5 Macad, Macao

former colony: 3 Goa 5 Timor 6 Angola 7 Sao Tome 8 Principe, St Thomas 9 Cape Verde 10 Mozambique 12 Guinea Bissau

feature:

song: 4 fado

food:

dish: 8 bacalhau, bucellas 10 calcavella 11 carcavellos

sausage: 8 linguica

wine: 4 port 7 madeira

Portuguese Guinea *see* 12 Guinea-Bissau

Portuguese West Africa *see* 6 Angola

Portunus

origin: 5 Roman

god of: 5 ports 7 harbors

posada 3 inn 12 halting place

pose 3 air, set 4 cast, mien 5 group, order, state, style 6 line up, stance, submit 7 advance, arrange, bearing, bring up, posture, present, propose, show off, suggest 8 attitude, carriage, position, propound, set forth, throw out 9 mannerism, postulate 10 put forward

Poseidon

also: 9 Asphalius

origin: 5 Greek

god of: 3 sea

caused: 11 earthquakes

father: 6 Cronos

mother: 4 Rhea

brother: 4 Zeus

wife: 10 Amphitrite

lover: 2 Ge 6 Aethra, Medusa, Thoosa 7 Demeter

child: 5 Arion 6 Triton 7 Antaeus, Pegasus, Theseus 8 Chrysaor 10 Polyphemus

symbol: 5 horse 7 trident

epithet: 11 Ennosigaeus, Hippocurius 12 Prosclystius

corresponds to: 7 Neptune

poser 5 facer 6 puzzle 7 problem 8 examiner, stickler

posh 4 chic 5 fancy, ritzy, smart, swell 6 chi-chi, classy, deluxe, lavish, swanky 7 elegant, opulent, refined, stylish 9 high-class, luxurious 11 extravagant

position 3 fix, job, put, set 4 duty, pose, post, role, site 5 array, caste, class, locus, lodge, order, place, stand, state 6 career, charge, ground, locate, office, plight, stance, status 7 arrange, deposit, opinion, outlook, posture, situate, station, vantage 8 attitude, capacity, eminence, function, locality, location, prestige, standing 9 condition, elevation, establish, placement, situation, viewpoint 10 assignment, commission, importance, notability, prominence 11 appointment, consequence, disposition, distinction, frame of mind, point of view

position decided upon

French: 9 parti pris

positive 4 firm, good, real, sure 5 total 6 narrow, useful 7 assured, certain, gainful, helpful 8 absolute, cocksure, complete, decisive, definite, dogmatic, explicit, obdurate, salutary 9 assertive, confident, convinced, effective, immovable, practical, satisfied, veritable 10 applicable, autocratic, beneficial, conclusive, definitive, optimistic, undisputed, undoubting 11 affirmative, cooperative, dead certain, dictatorial, irrefutable, opinionated, overbearing, practicable, progressive, self-assured, serviceable, unequivocal, unqualified 12 confirmatory, constructive, contributory, unchangeable 13 corroborative, thoroughgoing 16 incontrovertible

positively 9 assuredly, certainly, decidedly, literally 10 absolutely, definitely 11 confidently, indubitably 12 emphatically, indisputably, unmistakably, without doubt 13 affirmatively, categorically, unqualifiedly 14 beyond question, unhesitatingly, unquestionably

possess 3 own 4 grab, have, hold 5 boast, enjoy 6 absorb, fixate, obsess, occupy 7 acquire, bedevil, bewitch, command, conquer, consume, control, enchant, overrun 8 dominate, maintain, take over, vanquish 9 fascinate, hypnotize, influence, mesmerize

Possessed, The
author: 16 Fyodor Dostoevsky
character: 5 Marya, Pyotr 6 Shatov 7 Nikolay 16 Varvara Stavrogin 17 Stepan Verhovensky

possession 4 hold 5 asset, poise, title 6 effect, owning 7 command, control, control, custody, tenancy 8 calmness, coolness, dominion, province, resource 9 belonging, composure, occupancy, ownership, placidity, sangfroid, territory 10 equanimity, even temper, occupation, possessing 11 equilibrium, self-control 12 accoutrement, protectorate

possibility 4 hope, odds, risk 6 chance, gamble, hazard 7 promise 8 prospect 9 prospects 10 likelihood 11 contingency, eventuality, feasibility, probability, workability 12 potentiality 14 practicability

possible 8 credible, feasible, workable 9 potential, thinkable 10 achievable, admissible, attainable, cognizable, compatible, contingent, imaginable, manageable, obtainable, reasonable 11 conceivable, performable, practicable 12 hypothetical

possibly 5 at all, maybe 6 mayhap 7 could be, perhaps 8 in any way, normally 9 at the most, perchance 10 by any means, God willing 11 conceivably

post 2 PX 3 fix, job, put, set 4 base, beat, camp, pale, part, pile, pole, role, seat, send, spot, work 5 brace, house, lodge, place, put up, round, shaft, stake 6 advise, column, inform, locate, notify, office, picket, report, settle, splint, tack up 7 apprise, declare, install, mission, publish, quarter, routine, situate, station, support, upright 8 acquaint, announce, capacity, disclose, exchange, fasten up, function, instruct, mainstay, position, proclaim 9 advertise, broadcast, circulate, enlighten, establish, make known, situation 10 assignment, settlement

postdate 6 follow 7 succeed 9 come after
poster 4 bill, sign 6 notice 7 placard 8 bulletin 13 advertisement
posterior 3 bum, can 4 back, butt, prat, rear, rump, seat, tail, tush 5 fanny, stern, tushy 6 behind, bottom, caudal, dorsal, hinder 7 keister 8 backside, buttocks, derriere, hindmost, rearward 9 aftermost

Posterior Analytics
author: 9 Aristotle

posterity 5 heirs, issue, young 6 family 7 descent, history, lineage, progeny 8 children 9 offspring 10 succession, successors 11 descendants

post hoc, ergo propter hoc 29 after this therefore be cause of it
describes: 14 logical fallacy

Posthumus, Leonatus
character in: 9 Cymbeline
author: 11 Shakespeare

Postman Always Rings Twice, The
director: 10 Tay Garnett
based on story by: 10 James M Cain
cast: 10 Hume Cronyn, Lana Turner 12 John Garfield 13 Cecil Kellaway

postpone 4 stay 5 defer, delay, table, waive 6 put off, remand, shelve 7 adjourn, lay over, reserve, suspend

postponement 4 stay 5 delay 6 recess 7 tabling 8 abeyance, deferral 9 deferment, extension 10 suspension

postscript 2 ps 5 rider 7 codicil 8 addendum 10 attachment

postulate 5 axiom, guess 6 assume, hazard, submit, theory 7 premise, presume, propose, surmise, theorem 8 put forth, theorize 9 speculate 10 assumption, conjecture, hypothesis, presuppose 11 hypothesize, presumption

posture 3 air, set 4 case, mien, mood, pose, post, tone 5 phase, place, shape, state, tenor 6 aspect, stance, status 7 bearing, contour, station 8 attitude, carriage, position, standing 9 condition, situation 11 predicament 12 circumstance

Postvorta
form: 5 nymph
member of: 7 Camenae
knowledge of: 4 past

posy 5 bloom, motto 6 flower, phrase 7 blossom, bouquet, corsage, garland, nosegay

pot 3 pan 4 ruin 5 crock, kitty 6 vessel 9 container, marijuana 11 rack and ruin
Spanish: 4 olla

potable 3 ale 5 clean, drink, water 6 liquor 8 beverage, quencher 9 drinkable

potage 4 soup 9 thick soup

potassium
chemical symbol: 1 K

potato 16 Solanum tuberosum
varieties: 3 air, yam 4 duck, swan, wild, Zulu 5 Idaho, Irish, Maine, rural, swamp, sweet, white 6 Russet 7 Burbank, epicure, prairie, Telinga
dish: 4 chip 5 baked, salad 6 mashed 8

au gratin 9 lyonnaise, scalloped 11 french fries 12 baked stuffed

Potawatomi
language family: 9 Algonkian 10 Algonquian
location: 4 Ohio 6 Kansas 7 Indiana 8 Illinois, Michigan, Oklahoma 9 Wisconsin
leader: 7 Pontiac
united with: 6 Ojibwa, Ottawa 7 Ojibway

Potemkin
director: 17 Sergei Eisenstein
cast: 14 Vladimir Barsky 16 Alexander Antonov 17 Grigori Alexandrov
famous segment: 11 Odessa Steps

potency 3 vis 5 force, power 6 energy 8 efficacy, strength, virility, vitality

potent 5 solid, tough 6 mighty, strong 7 dynamic 8 forceful, forcible, powerful, vigorous 9 effective, operative 10 compelling, convincing, formidable, impressive, persuasive 11 efficacious, influential 12 overpowering

potentate 4 lord 5 chief, mogul, ruler 6 prince, satrap, sultan 7 emperor, monarch 8 overlord, suzerain 9 chieftain, sovereign

potential 6 covert, hidden, latent 7 dormant, lurking, passive 8 implicit, possible 9 concealed, quiescent, unexerted 10 unapparent, unrealized 11 conceivable, undisclosed, unexpressed

potentiality 7 ability 10 capability 13 possibilities

potentially
Latin: 7 in posse

pother 3 ado 4 fuss, stir, to-do 6 bustle, flurry, hustle, tumult 8 activity 9 agitation, commotion

Pothos
companion of: 9 Aphrodite
personifies: 6 desire 7 longing

potion 4 brew, dram 5 draft, tonic 6 elixir 7 mixture, philter 8 libation, potation 10 concoction

Pot of Gold, The
author: 7 Plautus

Potok, Chaim
author of: 9 The Chosen 10 Wanderings 15 The Book of Lights

potpourri 4 hash, mess, olio, stew 6 jumble, medley, mosaic, motley 7 farrago, goulash, melange, mixture 8 mishmash, pastiche 9 patchwork 10 hodgepodge, miscellany, salmagundi 11 gallimaufry, olla podrida

pottage 4 soup, stew 6 brewis 8 porridge

Potter, Beatrix
author of: 11 (The Tale of) Peter Rabbit 21 The Tailor of Gloucester

Potter, Muff
character in: 9 Tom Sawyer
author: 5 Twain

potter's field 8 boneyard, cemetery 9 graveyard 12 burial ground 13 burying ground

pottery 5 china 8 clayware, crockery 11 ceramic ware, earthenware

pouch 3 bag, kit, sac 4 sack 5 purse 6 pocket, wallet 7 handbag, satchel 8 carryall, ditty bag, reticule, rucksack 9 container 10 pocketbook, receptacle

Poulenc, Francis
born: 5 Paris 6 France
member of: 6 Les Six, The Six
composer of: 9 Les Biches 13 The Carmelites 22 Dialogues des Carmelites

poultice 7 plaster 8 dressing 10 medicament

poultry 3 hen 4 cock, duck, fowl, swan 5 capon, geese, goose, quail 6 grouse, layers, pigeon, turkey 7 chicken, peacock, rooster 8 pheasant 9 partridge 10 guinea fowl
breed: 6 Ancona, Bantam 7 Cornish, Dorking, Leghorn 9 Wyandotte 12 Plymouth Rock 14 Rhode Island Red
disease: 3 pip 4 roup, tick
farm: 7 hennery
house: 4 coop

pounce 4 jump, leap 5 fly at, swoop 6 ambush, dash at, jump at, plunge, snatch, spring 8 downrush, fall upon, surprise

Pounce, Peter
character in: 13 Joseph Andrews
author: 8 Fielding

pound 4 bang, beat, drub, drum, maul 5 clomp, clout, crush, grind, march, paste, smack, stomp, throb, thump, tramp 6 batter, bruise, cudgel, hammer, pummel, strike, thrash, thwack, wallop 7 clobber, crumble, pulsate, thunder, trounce 8 lambaste 9 fustigate, palpitate, pulverize 13 sixteen ounces
abbreviation: 2 lb

Pound, Ezra
author of: 6 Cantos 8 Personae 11 Exultations, Pisan Cantos

pound troy
abbreviation: 3 lb t

pour 3 tap 4 drip, drop, flow, gush, ooze, rain, seep, slop 5 drain, flood, issue, spill, spout 6 decant, deluge, drench, effuse, squirt, stream 7 cascade, draw off, dribble, lade out 15 rain cats and dogs 16 come down in sheets 17 come down in buckets

pourboire 3 tip 8 gratuity
literally: 11 for drinking

pourparler 29 informal preliminary conference
literally: 10 for talking

Poussin, Nicholas
born: 6 France 10 Les Andelys
artwork: 10 The Seasons 14 Birth of Bacchus, St John on Patmos 17 Bacchanalian Revel 18 The Burial of Phocion 19 The Poet's Inspiration 20 The Arcadian Shepherds 23 Landscape with Polyphemus, The Holy Family on the Steps 27 The Adoration of the Golden Calf

pou sto 14 place to stand on, where I may stand 16 base of operations

pout 4 crab, fret, fume, mope, sulk 5 brood, frown, lower, scowl 6 glower
French: 4 moue

poverty 4 lack, need, want 6 dearth, penury 7 beggary, deficit, paucity 8 scarcity, shortage 9 indigence, neediness, pauperism, privation 10 bankruptcy, deficiency, insolvency, meagerness, mendicancy 11 destitution 13 insufficiency, pennilessness 14 impoverishment

poverty-stricken 4 poor 5 broke, needy 8 indigent 9 destitute, penniless 10 down and out

powder 4 dust, talc 5 emery 6 pollen, talcum 7 crumble 9 pulverize
  antiseptic: 6 formin 7 aristol
  applier: 4 puff
  cookery: 4 soda
  cosmetic: 5 blush, rouge 7 compact
  poisonous: 5 robin

powder-blue 5 azure 6 pastel 7 sky-blue 8 pale-blue 9 light-blue, robin's egg

powdery 5 dusty, mealy 6 chalky, floury, grated, ground, milled 7 crushed, pestled 8 shredded 10 comminuted, pulverized, triturated

Powell, Dick
  real name: 14 Richard E Powell
  born: 14 Mountain View AR
  wife: 11 June Allyson 12 Joan Blondell
  costar: 9 Ruby Keeler
  roles: 7 Mrs Mike 8 Cornered 12 Johnny O'Clock 13 Murder My Sweet 15 Footlight Parade 17 Forty-second Street 32 Gold Diggers of Nineteen Thirty-three

Powell, Jane
  real name: 12 Suzanne Burce
  born: 10 Portland OR
  roles: 5 Irene 12 Royal Wedding 13 A Date with Judy 27 Seven Brides for Seven Brothers

Powell, John
  nickname: 4 Boog
  sport: 8 baseball
  team: 16 Baltimore Orioles

Powell, Michael
  codirector: 17 Emeric Pressburger
  director of: 11 The Red Shoes 14 Black Narcissus 16 Stairway to Heaven

Powell, SR
  creator/artist of: 22 Sheena Queen of the Jungle

Powell, William
  born: 12 Pittsburgh PA
  wife: 13 Carole Lombard
  costar: 8 Myrna Loy
  roles: 10 Philo Vance, The Thin Man 11 Nick Charles 12 My Man Godfrey 13 Mister Roberts 14 Life with Father 16 The Great Ziegfeld 22 How to Marry a Millionaire

power 4 gift, sway 5 brawn, force, might, right, ruler, skill, vigor 6 energy, genius, muscle, status, talent 7 faculty, license, operate, potency, quality 8 activate, aptitude, capacity, energize, iron grip, pressure, prestige, property, strength, vitality 9 attribute, authority, endowment, influence, puissance 10 capability, competence
  Latin: 3 vis

Power, Tyrone
  born: 12 Cincinnati OH
  wife: 9 Annabella 14 Linda Christian
  roles: 10 Jesse James 12 Blood and Sand 13 The Razor's Edge 14 Nightmare Alley, The Mark of Zorro 15 The Sun Also Rises 18 Captain from Castile

Power and the Glory, The
  author: 12 Graham Greene

powerful 5 hardy, husky, stout 6 brawny, cogent, mighty, moving, potent, robust, sturdy 7 intense, rousing 8 athletic, emphatic, exciting, forceful, incisive, muscular, stalwart, vigorous 9 effective, energetic, herculean, strapping 10 able-bodied, commanding, invincible

powerhouse 9 strongman 10 power plant 15 generating plant

powerless 4 weak 6 feeble, infirm 7 unarmed 8 crippled, disabled, feckless, helpless, impotent 9 incapable, pregnable, prostrate 10 impuissant, vulnerable, weaponless 11 debilitated, defenseless, immobilized 13 incapacitated

powerlessness 8 debility, weakness 9 impotence, inability, infirmity 10 enervation, feebleness, inadequacy, incapacity 12 helplessness, incapability, inefficiency 13 vulnerability

Power Politics
  author: 14 Margaret Atwood

powers that be 9 higher-ups 10 government 11 authorities 13 establishment 14 administration

Powhatan
  language family: 9 Algonkian 10 Algonquian
  tribe: 11 Confederacy
  location: 8 Atlantic, Maryland, Virginia
  leader: 8 Powhatan 11 Opechancano 13 Wahunsonacock
  member: 10 Pocahontas

powwow 4 meet, talk 5 forum 6 caucus, confer, huddle, parley 7 consult, convene, council, discuss, meeting, palaver 8 assembly, colloquy, conclave, congress 9 discourse, interview 10 colloquium, conference, convention, discussion, round table 12 consultation

Poyser, Martin
  character in: 8 Adam Bede
  author: 5 Eliot

practicable 6 doable, viable 8 feasible, possible, workable 9 practical 10 achievable, attainable, functional

practical 4 able 5 solid, sound 6 expert, useful, versed 7 skilled, trained, veteran, working 8 seasoned, sensible, skillful 9 efficient, judicious, practiced, pragmatic, qualified, realistic 10 functional, hardheaded, instructed, proficient, systematic, unromantic 11 down-to-earth, experienced, pragmatical, serviceable, utilitarian 12 accomplished, businesslike, matter-of-fact 13 unsentimental

practical joke 4 jape 5 caper, prank, stunt, trick

practically 6 all but, almost, nearly **8** actually, in effect **9** basically, in the main, just about, virtually **11** essentially **13** fundamentally, substantially

practice 2 do **3** use, way **4** deed, mode, play, rule, ruse, ways, wont **5** apply, dodge, drill, habit, train, trick, usage **6** action, custom, device, effect, follow, manner, method, pursue, ritual, work at **7** conduct, fashion, perform, process, qualify, routine, utilize **8** carry out, engage in, exercise, live up to, maneuver, rehearse, tendency, training **9** execution, operation, perform in, procedure, rehearsal, seasoning, set to work, turn to use **10** discipline, observance, prepare for, repetition **11** application, be engaged in, performance, preparation

practiced 4 able, fine **5** adept **6** adroit, expert **7** capable, drilled, pursued, skilled, trained **8** masterly, polished, seasoned, skillful, worked at **9** competent, engaged in, masterful, qualified, rehearsed **10** cultivated, proficient **11** experienced, prepared for **12** accomplished

practice sorcery 5 charm **7** bewitch, conjure, enchant **9** work magic **10** cast a spell

Practicing History
  author: **15** Barbara W Tuchman

practitioner 6 doctor **7** dentist **9** performer **12** professional

pragmatic 5 sober **8** sensible **9** hard-nosed, practical, realistic **10** hardheaded, hard-boiled **11** down-to-earth, utilitarian **12** businesslike, matter-of-fact, unidealistic **13** materialistic, unsentimental

Praia
  capital of: **9** Cape Verde

prairie 3 bay **5** llano, pampa, plain **6** camass, meadow, steppe **7** quamash **9** grassland
  apple: **9** breadroot
  berry: **9** trampillo
  chicken: **6** grouse
  dog: **6** gopher, marmot
  schooner: **12** covered wagon
  state: **8** Illinois
  wolf: **6** coyote

Prairie, The
  author: **19** James Fenimore Cooper
  character: **4** Inez **9** Dr Battius, Ellen Wade, Hard-Heart, Paul Hover **10** Esther Bush **11** Abiram White, Ishmael Bush, Natty Bumppo **16** Captain Middleton

Prairie State
  nickname of: **8** Illinois

praise 4 laud, tout **5** cheer, exalt, extol, honor **6** esteem, eulogy, hurrah, regard, revere **7** acclaim, applaud, approve, build up, commend, glorify, plaudit, respect, root for, tribute, worship **8** accolade, applause, approval, encomium, eulogize, venerate **9** adoration, celebrate, good words, laudation, panegyric **10** admiration, compliment, panegyrize **11** approbation, compliments, testimonial **12** appreciation, commendation, congratulate **14** congratulation

Hebrew: 6 hallel
praise be to God
  Latin: **7** laus Deo

praiseful 8 praising **9** extolling, laudatory **10** plauditory **12** commendatory **13** complimentary

praiseworthiness 5 merit **10** excellence **12** admirability, desirability **14** commendability

praiseworthy 4 fine **6** worthy **8** laudable **9** admirable, estimable, excellent, exemplary **11** commendable, meritorious

pram, praam, prahm 4 boat **5** buggy **6** vessel **7** rowboat **8** carriage, stroller **12** perambulator

prance 4 jump, leap, romp, skip **5** bound, caper, dance, frisk, strut, vault **6** bounce, cavort, frolic, gambol, spring **7** swagger

prank 4 joke, lark **5** antic, caper, spoof, stunt, trick **6** gambol **8** escapade, mischief **9** horseplay **10** shenanigan, tomfoolery

prate 3 gab, yak **4** blab, brag, chat, crow, talk **5** boast **6** babble, gabble, jabber **7** blabber, chatter, prattle, twaddle, twattle

Prathet Thai *see* **8** Thailand

Pratt, William Henry
  real name of: **12** Boris Karloff

prattle 3 gab, yak **4** blab **5** prate **6** babble, gabble, hot air, jabber **7** blather, chatter, twaddle **8** cackling, chitchat, gabbling **9** gibbering, jabbering

Pravda 16 Russian newspaper
  literally: **5** truth

Praxithea
  husband: **10** Erechtheus
  daughters: **8** Orithyia **10** Protogonia

pray 3 beg, bid, sue **4** urge **5** cry to, plead **7** beseech, entreat, implore, request, solicit **8** call upon, invocate, petition **9** importune **10** supplicate

prayer 6 litany, orison, praise **7** worship **9** adoration **12** thanksgiving **13** glorification

prayerful 4 holy **5** godly, pious **9** devout, solemn **8** reverent **9** pietistic, religious, spiritual **10** worshipful **11** reverential

prayers 4 hope, plea, suit **5** dream **6** appeal **7** request **8** entreaty, petition **10** aspiration, invocation **11** beseechment **12** solicitation, supplication

prayer service 9 devotions **13** prayer meeting **14** worship service

pray for us
  Latin: **11** ora pro nobis

pray to 3 beg **5** plead **7** address, entreat, worship **8** call upon, petition, venerate **10** supplicate

preach 4 urge **6** advise, exhort **7** counsel, declare, expound, profess **8** admonish, advocate, homilize, proclaim, stand for **9** discourse, hold forth, preachify, prescribe, pronounce, propagate, sermonize **10** evangelize, promulgate

preacher 5 vicar **6** curate, parson, pastor **8** chaplain, homilist, minister, reverend, sky pilot **9** churchman, clergyman **10** evangelist, prebendary, sermonizer **12** ecclesiastic **13** man of the cloth

preachy 8 didactic, pedantic 10 moralistic, moralizing

prearranged 7 planned 10 calculated, deliberate, purposeful 11 intentional 12 premeditated

pre-Cambrian 5 Azoic 6 Eozoic 7 primary 10 Archeozoic 11 Proterozoic

precarious 5 risky, shaky 6 chancy, unsafe 7 dubious 8 alarming, critical, doubtful, insecure, perilous, sinister, ticklish, unstable, unsteady 9 hazardous, uncertain 10 touch-and-go, unreliable, vulnerable 12 questionable, uncontrolled, undependable 13 problematical

precaution 4 care 7 caution, defense 8 prudence, security, wariness 9 foresight, provision, safeguard 10 protection 11 carefulness, forethought, heedfulness 12 anticipation 14 circumspection

precede 8 antecede, antedate, go before 9 go ahead of 10 come before

precedence, precedency 8 priority 10 importance, preference, prevalence 11 antecedence, preeminence 12 predominance, preexistence

precedent 5 model 7 example, pattern 8 standard 9 criterion, guideline

preceding 5 prior 6 former 7 earlier 8 anterior, previous 9 aforesaid, foregoing 10 antecedent, first-named, precursory 11 preexistent, preliminary 14 abovementioned, aforementioned, first-mentioned

precept 3 law 4 bull, code, rule 5 axiom, canon, edict, maxim, motto, tenet, truth, ukase 6 byword, decree, dictum 7 dictate, mandate, statute 8 standard, teaching 9 ordinance, principle, yard stick 10 regulation 11 commandment, declaration

preceptor 5 coach, tutor 6 mentor 7 advisor, teacher 8 director 9 admonitor, counselor, principal 10 headmaster 12 headmistress

precincts 7 suburbs 8 environs 9 districts, outskirts 10 boundaries 12 subdivisions 15 surrounding area

precious 4 dear, rare 5 fussy, sweet 6 adored, choice, costly, dainty, prissy, prized, valued 7 beloved, darling, finical, finicky, lovable 8 adorable, affected, uncommon, valuable 9 cherished, expensive, exquisite, priceless, treasured 10 fastidious, high-priced, invaluable, meticulous, particular 11 beyond price, inestimable, overrefined, pretentious

Precious Bane
   author: 8 Mary Webb

precipice 4 crag 5 bluff, cliff, ledge 8 headland, palisade 9 cliff edge, declivity 10 escarpment

precipitate 4 cast, hurl, rash, spur 5 drive, fling, hasty, throw 6 abrupt, hasten, launch, let fly, propel, rushed, speedy, thrust 7 advance, bring on, hurried, quicken, speed up 8 catapult, expedite, headlong, reckless 9 discharge, foolhardy, impetuous, imprudent, impulsive 10 accelerate, incautious 11 thoughtless

precipitation 4 hail, rain, rush, snow 5 haste, sleet 8 rainfall, rashness 9 hastiness 11 impetuously

precipitous 5 hasty, sharp, sheer, steep 6 abrupt 9 impetuous

precis 5 brief 6 apercu, digest, resume, sketch 7 epitome, outline, rundown, summary 8 abstract, synopsis 10 abridgment, compendium 12 condensation 14 recapitulation

precise 4 true 5 exact, fussy, rigid 6 strict 7 careful, express, finicky, literal 8 accurate, clear-cut, definite, distinct, explicit, incisive, specific 9 unbending 10 fastidious, inflexible, meticulous, particular, to the point 11 painstaking, unequivocal

precision 5 rigor 8 accuracy, fidelity 9 attention, exactness 11 factualness, preciseness 12 authenticity, truthfulness 14 meticulousness

preclude 3 bar, dam 4 balk, curb, foil, stop 5 avert, avoid, block, check, debar, deter 6 arrest, hamper, hinder, thwart 7 head off, inhibit, prevent 8 stave off 9 forestall, frustrate 11 nip in the bud

preclusion 9 exclusion, restraint 10 prevention

precocious 3 apt 5 quick, smart 6 bright, clever, gifted, mature 8 advanced 9 brilliant

preconception 4 bias 6 notion 9 fixed idea, prejudice 11 prejudgment, presumption 14 predisposition

precursor 4 mark, omen, sign 5 token, usher 6 herald 7 portent, symptom, warning 8 vanguard 9 harbinger, messenger 10 antecedent, forerunner 11 predecessor

precursory 5 prior 8 anterior, previous 9 precedent 10 antecedent 11 preexistent

predaceous, predacious 9 predatory, rapacious 10 meat-eating 11 carnivorous, flesh-eating

predate 7 precede 8 antecede, antedate, go before

predatory 8 thievish 9 larcenous, marauding, pillaging, piratical, rapacious, raptorial, vulturine 10 plunderous, predacious

predecessor 7 forbear 8 ancestor, forebear, foregoer 10 antecedent, forefather, forerunner

predestination 4 fate 6 kismet 7 destiny, fortune 8 God's will 10 providence 13 inevitability, preordination 16 predetermination

predetermined 5 fated 7 decided, planned 8 destined 10 calculated, deliberate, preplanned 11 intentional, prearranged, predestined 12 foreordained, premeditated

predicament 3 fix, jam 4 bind, mess 5 pinch 6 corner, crisis, pickle, plight, scrape, strait 7 dilemma, trouble 8 hot water, quandary 9 imbroglio, sad plight 10 difficulty, perplexity

predicate 4 base, real, rest, true 5 found, imply 6 affirm, assert 7 commend, connote, declare 8 proclaim

predict 4 omen 5 augur 6 divine 7 betoken, foresee, presage 8 envision, forecast, foretell, prophesy 10 anticipate 13 prognosticate

prediction 6 augury 7 portent 8 forecast, prophecy 10 divination 11 declaration, foretelling, soothsaying 12 announcement, anticipation, proclamation 13 crystal gazing 15 prognostication

predilection 4 bent, bias, love 5 fancy, favor, taste 6 desire, hunger, liking, relish 7 leaning 8 appetite, fondness, penchant, tendency 9 prejudice, proneness 10 attraction, partiality, preference, proclivity, propensity 11 inclination 13 prepossession 14 predisposition

predispose 4 bias, lure, sway, urge 5 tempt 6 entice, induce, prompt, seduce 7 dispose, incline, win over 8 persuade 9 encourage, influence, prejudice

predisposed 3 apt 5 given, prone 8 inclined

predisposition 7 leaning 8 tendency 11 inclination

predominance 7 command, control 8 currency 9 dominance, supremacy 10 ascendancy, importance, prevalence 11 preeminence, superiority 12 universality

predominant 4 main 5 chief, major 6 potent, ruling, strong 7 leading, supreme 8 dominant, forceful, powerful, reigning, vigorous 9 ascendant, important, paramount, sovereign 11 controlling, influential 13 authoritative

predominate 4 lead 7 prevail 8 dominate

predominating 5 chief 6 ruling 8 dominant, superior 9 principal 10 commanding, prevailing 11 controlling, predominant 13 authoritative

preeminence 9 greatness, supremacy 10 ascendancy, importance, leadership, notability, prominence 11 distinction, superiority 12 predominance

preeminent 4 best 5 famed 6 famous 7 eminent, honored, supreme 8 dominant, foremost, greatest, peerless, renowned, superior 9 matchless, paramount, unequaled, unrivaled 10 celebrated, consummate 11 illustrious, predominant, unsurpassed 12 incomparable, second to none, unparalleled 13 distinguished

    French: 13 par excellence

preempt 4 take 5 seize, usurp 8 arrogate, take over 10 commandeer, confiscate 11 appropriate, expropriate

preen 3 pin 4 perk, trim 5 adorn, dress, groom, plume, pride, primp, prink 6 brooch, smooth

    wings: 4 whet

preexistent 5 prior 8 anterior, previous 9 precedent 10 antecedent, precursory

preface 4 open 5 begin, proem, start 6 launch 7 prelude 8 commence, foreword, initiate, lead into, overture, preamble, prologue 9 introduce 12 introduction

prefer 3 opt 4 file 5 adopt, elect, exalt, fancy, favor, lodge, offer 6 select, take to, tender 7 dignify, elevate, ennoble, fix upon, pick out, present, proffer, promote 8 graduate, set forth 9 single out

preference 4 bent, bias, pick 5 fancy 6 liking, option 7 leaning 8 favoring, priority 9 advantage, prejudice, proneness, selection, supremacy 10 ascendancy, partiality, precedence, proclivity, propensity 11 first choice, inclination 12 predilection 13 predomination 14 predisposition

    French: 4 gout

prefigure 4 hint, type 6 shadow, typify 7 foresee, imagine, presage, suggest 9 adumbrate 10 foreshadow

pregnant 4 full, rich 6 fecund, filled, gravid 7 copious, fertile, fraught, replete, seminal, teeming, weighty 8 forceful, fruitful, prolific 9 abounding, expecting, gestating, important, luxuriant, momentous, plenteous, potential, with child, with young 10 impressive, life-giving, meaningful, parturient, productive, suggestive 11 having a baby, proliferous, provocative, significant 12 fructiferous, in a family way

    French: 8 enceinte

prehistoric 3 old 7 ancient 10 immemorial

    continent: 8 Atlantis

    epoch: 6 Eocene 7 Miocene 8 Pliocene 9 Oligocene, Paleocene 11 Pleistocene

    era: 8 Cenozoic, Mesozoic 9 Paleozoic 10 Archeozoic 11 Proterozoic

    implement: 4 celt 6 eolith

    period: 7 Neogene, Permian 8 Cambrian, Devonian, Jurassic, Silurian, Triassic 9 Paleogene 10 Cretaceous, Ordovician, Quaternary

    reptile: 8 dinosaur

prehistoric era 6 Ice Age 8 Cenozoic, Jurassic, Mesozoic, Triassic 9 Paleozoic 10 Cenomanian, Cretaceous 11 Precambrian 15 Upper Cretaceous 16 Pleistocene Epoch

prehistoric man *see* 8 early man

prejudice 3 ill, mar 4 bias, harm, hurt, loss, sway 5 slant, spoil, taint 6 damage, impair, infect, injure, injury, poison 7 bigotry 8 jaundice 9 detriment 10 favoritism, impairment, partiality, predispose, unfairness 11 contaminate, intolerance, prejudgment 12 disadvantage, one-sidedness, predilection 13 preconception 14 discrimination, predisposition

prejudiced 6 biased, unfair, unjust 7 bigoted, slanted 9 arbitrary 10 intolerant 11 close-minded, opinionated 12 narrow-minded

prejudicial 3 bad 6 biased 7 harmful, hurtful 8 damaging, inimical, sinister 9 injurious 11 deleterious, detrimental

prelate 5 abbot 6 bishop, cleric 9 churchman, clergy man 12 ecclesiastic

preliminary 9 prelusive, prelusory 10 initiatory, precursory, prefactory 11 preparative, preparatory 12 introductory

prelude 7 opening, preface 8 overture, preamble, prologue 9 beginning 11 preliminary, preparation 12 introduction

Prelude, The
  author: 17 William Wordsworth

premature 3 raw 5 green, hasty 6 callow, unripe 7 too soon, unready 8 abortive, ill-timed, immature, previous, too early, untimely 9 embryonic, overhasty, unfledged, unhatched, vestigial 10 incomplete, unprepared 11 inopportune, precipitate, rudimentary, undeveloped 12 unseasonable

premeditated 7 planned, plotted, studied, willful 8 intended 9 conscious, contrived, voluntary 10 calculated, considered, deliberate, predevised, purposeful 11 in cold blood, intentional, prearranged, predesigned 13 predetermined 22 with malice aforethought

premeditation 4 plan 6 design 7 purpose 11 calculation, forethought, preplanning 12 deliberation

premier 3 bet 4 head 5 chief, first 6 oldest 7 leading, supreme 8 earliest, foremost 9 principal 13 prime minister

Preminger, Otto
  director of: 5 Laura 11 Carmen Jones 16 Anatomy of a Murder

premise 6 theory 8 argument 9 postulate, principle 10 assumption, hypothesis 11 presumption, proposition, supposition 14 presupposition

premises 4 site 8 environs, property, vicinity 9 precincts

premium 4 gain, gift 5 award, bonus, prize 6 bounty, return, reward 7 benefit, payment 8 priority 9 high value, incentive 10 great stock, recompense, reparation 11 overpayment 12 appreciation, compensation, inflated rate, remuneration 13 consideration, encouragement

premonition 4 omen, sign 5 hunch, token 6 augury 7 auspice, feeling, inkling, portent, presage 9 foretoken 10 foreboding, indication, prediction 11 forewarning 12 presentiment

Prendergast, Maurice Brazil
  born: 6 Canada 7 St John's 12 Newfoundland
  artwork: 6 Dieppe 8 Seashore 11 Picnic Grove 12 The Promenade 16 Ponte della Paglia 17 Along the Boulevard, Four Girls in Meadow 24 Umbrellas in the Rain Venice

Prentice, John
  creator/artist of: 8 Rip Kirby

preoccupation 9 immersion, obsession 10 absorption, detachment, dreaminess, employment 11 abstraction, involvement 16 absent-mindedness

preoccupied 6 absent, dreamy 8 absorbed, immersed, involved, obsessed 9 engrossed, wrapped up 10 abstracted, distracted 12 absent-minded

preoccupy 6 absorb, arrest, obsess, take up, wrap up 7 engross, immerse 9 fascinate

preparation 8 prudence, readying 9 foresight, preparing, provision, safeguard 10 precaution 11 expectation, forethought 12 anticipation

preparations 5 plans 7 elixirs 8 guidance, measures, mixtures, training, tutelage 9 dressings, education, seasoning, tinctures 11 concoctions, confections 12 arrangements 13 preliminaries, prepared foods, prescriptions 14 qualifications

prepare 3 fix 5 adapt, prime, ready 7 arrange, be ready, provide 8 get ready 9 make ready, rearrange, take steps

prepared 4 done 5 fixed, ready 6 cooked, primed 7 planned 8 arranged, finished 9 made ready, rehearsed 11 provided for

prepayment 6 credit 7 advance 9 allowance 11 downpayment

preponderance, preponderancy 4 bulk, glut, mass 6 excess 7 surfeit, surplus 8 majority, plethora 9 dominance, plurality, profusion 10 domination, lion's share, oversupply, prevalence, redundance 12 predominance 14 superabundance

preponderant 3 key 4 main 5 chief, first, major, prime 7 highest, leading, primary, supreme 8 dominant, foremost, greatest 9 paramount, principal, uppermost 10 prevailing 11 outstanding, predominant

prepossessing 4 nice 7 winsome 8 alluring, charming, engaging, inviting, pleasant, striking 9 beguiling 10 attractive, bewitching, enchanting, entrancing, personable 11 captivating, fascinating, tantalizing

preposterous 5 inane, outre, silly 6 absurd, stupid 7 asinine, bizarre, fatuous, foolish, idiotic 9 imbecilic, laughable, ludicrous 10 irrational, outrageous, ridiculous 11 nonsensical, unthinkable 12 unreasonable

prerequisite 4 need 6 demand 8 demanded, exigency, required 9 called for, condition, de rigueur, essential, mandatory, necessary, necessity, postulate, requisite 10 imperative, sine qua non 11 requirement, stipulation 13 indispensable, qualification

prerogative 3 due 5 claim, grant, right 6 choice, option 7 freedom, liberty, license, warrant 9 advantage, exemption, franchise, privilege 10 birthright

presage 4 bode, omen, osse, sign 5 augur, token 6 augury, herald 7 betoken, portend, portent, predict 8 forecast, foreshow, foretell, indicate 9 foresight 10 foreboding, foreshadow, indication, prediction, prescience, prognostic 11 premonition 12 presentiment

presbyter 5 elder 13 church officer

prescience 7 presage 9 foresight, prevision 13 foreknowledge

prescribe 3 fix, set 4 rule, urge 5 enact, order 6 assign, decree, demand, direct, enjoin, impose, ordain, settle 7 appoint, command, dictate, require, specify 8 advocate, proclaim 9 authorize, establish, institute, legislate, recommend, stipulate

prescribed 3 set 5 fixed 6 thetic 9 formulary

prescript 3 law 4 rule 5 order 7 precept, statute 10 regulation

prescriptive 7 binding 8 demanded, dictated, didactic, required 9 customary, mandatory, requisite 10 compulsory, imperative, obligatory

presence 3 air 4 life, look, mien 5 being, curse, favor, ghost, group, midst 6 aspect, entity, figure, manner, shadow, spirit, vision, wraith 7 bearing, company, eidolon, phantom, specter 8 carriage, charisma, demeanor, features, phantasm, revenant, vitality 9 character, existence 10 apparition, attendance, deportment, expression, lineaments 11 reification, subsistence 12 neighborhood 13 manifestation

presence of mind 6 aplomb 8 calmness, coolness 9 composure, sangfroid 10 equanimity, steadiness 14 self-possession 16 imperturbability

present 2 in 3 fee, now, tip 4 alms, aver, boon, cite, gift, give, here, near, nigh, read, show, tell 5 about, award, frame, grant, offer, state, today 6 accord, allege, assert, at hand, bestow, bounty, call up, chip in, coeval, confer, donate, hand in, impart, legacy, nearby, on hand, recite, relate, render, rooted, submit, summon, supply, tender, turn in 7 advance, bequest, bring on, current, declare, deliver, display, dole out, exhibit, expound, give out, instant, largess, mete out, not away, produce, profess, proffer, propose, provide, recount, vicinal 8 donation, embedded, existent, existing, give away, give over, gratuity, hand over, nowadays, oblation, offering, propound, put forth 9 apprise of, attending, draw forth, endowment, ensconced, hold forth, immediate, implanted, in the room, introduce, make known, not absent, on-the-spot, prevalent, pronounce, surrender, the moment, unremoved 10 asseverate, come up with, contribute, here and now, liberality, perquisite, put forward 11 benefaction, communicate 12 accounted for, bring forward, contemporary, in attendance

presentable 4 chic, so-so 6 decent, modish, not bad, proper 7 stylish 8 becoming, passable, suitable 9 tolerable 10 acceptable, good enough 11 appropriate, fashionable, fit to be seen, respectable

presentation 3 fee, tip 4 boon, gift, show 5 favor, grant, offer 6 bounty 7 advance, display, exhibit, largess, present, proffer 8 bestowal, exposure, gratuity, oblation, offering, overture, proposal 9 unfolding 10 appearance, compliment, disclosure, exhibition, exposition, liberality, production, proffering, submission, unfoldment 11 benefaction, performance, proposition 13 demonstration

Present at the Creation
  author: 11 Dean Acheson

presentiment 7 feeling 10 foreboding 11 forewarning, premonition 12 apprehension

presently 3 now 4 anon, soon 7 shortly 8 directly, in a while, this week, this year 9 at present, currently, forth with 10 any time now, before long, pretty soon 11 after a while, at the moment 12 in a short time
  French: 11 tout a l'heure

preservation 6 saving 7 defense 9 salvation 10 protection 11 maintenance, safekeeping 12 conservation, safeguarding

preservative 4 salt 5 brine, spice 8 marinade 12 formaldehyde

preserve, preserves 3 can, dry, jam 4 corn, cure, park, salt, save, seal 5 guard, haven, jelly, nurse, put up, smoke, sweet 6 comfit, defend, embalm, foster, freeze, pickle, refuge, season, secure, shield 7 care for, compote, mummify, protect, reserve, shelter 8 conserve, insulate, keep safe, maintain, marinate 9 dehydrate, keep sound, marmalade, safeguard, sanctuary, sweetmeat, watch over 10 confection, keep intact, perpetuate 11 refrigerate, reservation

preside 4 boss, host, rule 5 chair, watch 7 direct, govern, manage 7 command, conduct, control, hostess, oversee 8 chairman, overlook, regulate 9 keep order, supervise 10 administer 11 superintend 12 administrate, take the chair

president, President 4 head 5 ruler 8 chairman 12 chief officer, chief of state, first citizen 14 chief executive 16 commander in chief, executive officer, head of government

president of US
  first: 16 George Washington
  second: 9 John Adams
  third: 15 Thomas Jefferson
  fourth: 12 James Madison
  fifth: 11 James Monroe
  sixth: 15 John Quincy Adams
  seventh: 13 Andrew Jackson
  eighth: 14 Martin Van Buren
  ninth: 20 William Henry Harrison
  tenth: 9 John Tyler
  eleventh: 10 James K Polk
  twelfth: 13 Zachary Taylor
  thirteenth: 15 Millard Fillmore
  fourteenth: 13 Franklin Pierce
  fifteenth: 13 James Buchanan
  sixteenth: 14 Abraham Lincoln
  seventeenth: 13 Andrew Johnson
  eighteenth: 13 Ulysses S Grant
  nineteenth: 16 Rutherford B Hayes
  twentieth: 14 James A Garfield
  twenty-first: 17 Chester Alan Arthur
  twenty-second: 15 Grover Cleveland
  twenty-third: 16 Benjamin Harrison
  twenty-fourth: 15 Grover Cleveland
  twenty-fifth: 15 William McKinley
  twenty-sixth: 17 Theodore Roosevelt
  twenty-seventh: 17 William Howard Taft
  twenty-eighth: 13 Woodrow Wilson
  twenty-ninth: 14 Warren G Harding
  thirtieth: 14 Calvin Coolidge
  thirty-first: 13 Herbert Hoover
  thirty-second: 18 Franklin D Roosevelt

thirty-third: 12 Harry S Truman
thirty-fourth: 17 Dwight D Eisenhower
thirty-fifth: 12 John F Kennedy
thirty-sixth: 14 Lyndon B Johnson
thirty-seventh: 13 Richard M Nixon
thirty-eighth: 11 Gerald R Ford
thirty-ninth: 11 (James E) Jimmy Carter (Jr)
fortieth: 12 Ronald Reagan
forty-first: 10 George Bush
forty-second: 11 (William Jefferson) Bill Clinton

President's Analyst, The
director: 16 Theodore J Flicker
cast: 8 Will Geer 11 James Coburn 12 Severn Darden 16 Godfrey Cambridge
preside over 5 chair, guide 6 direct, govern, manage 7 conduct 8 dominate 9 supervise 10 administer 11 superintend
presentiment 11 forewarning, premonition
Presley, Elvis Aron
nickname: 14 Elvis the Pelvis 15 King of Rock n Roll
born: 6 Tupelo 11 Mississippi
wife: 9 Priscilla
daughter: 9 Lisa Marie
father: 6 Vernon
mother: 6 Gladys
twin brother: 11 Jessie Garon
manager: 16 Colonel Tom Parker
home: 9 Graceland
location: 7 Memphis 9 Tennessee
song: 8 Hound Dog 10 All Shook Up 11 Don't Be Cruel 12 Love Me Tender 13 Jailhouse Rock 14 Blue Suede Shoes 15 Heartbreak Hotel 17 That's All Right Mama
film: 7 G I Blues 9 Loving You 10 Blue Hawaii, King Creole 12 Love Me Tender, Viva Las Vegas 13 Jailhouse Rock
press 2 TV 3 beg, bug, dun, hit, hug, jam, mob, pet, tap, tax 4 army, body, cram, duty, heap, herd, host, iron, mash, mill, pack, prod, push, rush 5 beset, bunch, clasp, crowd, crush, drove, exact, flick, force, horde, hound, hurry, media, plead, radio, set on, steam, stuff, surge, swarm 6 appeal, bother, burden, caress, compel, duress, enjoin, exhort, extort, fondle, gather, huddle, legion, mangle, push in, reduce, smooth, strain, stress, throng 7 cluster, collect, depress, embrace, entreat, flatten, implore, newsmen, oppress, snuggle, squeeze, trouble 8 assemble, bear down, bear upon, calender, compress, condense, hot-press, insist on, pressure, printing, push down 9 annoyance, be hard put, constrain, constrict, final form, force down, force from, importune, multitude, reporters 10 compulsion, congregate, newspapers, obligation, supplicate, television, thrust down 11 journalists, periodicals, publication 12 bear down upon, broadcasting, come together, news services, newspapermen 14 Fourth Estate
Pressburger, Emeric see 13 Michael Powell

press down 7 compact, depress 8 push down
press forward 5 drive 6 push on 7 advance 10 forge ahead
press home 5 stress 9 emphasize, underline 10 accentuate, underscore
pressing 5 vital 6 crying, needed, urgent 7 crucial, exigent, needful 8 critical 9 clamoring, demanding, essential, important, insistent, necessary 10 imperative 11 importunate 13 indispensable
pressing necessity 6 crisis 7 urgency 8 exigency 9 emergency
press on 9 move ahead, persevere 10 accelerate, forge ahead 11 move forward
pressure 4 bias, care, load, need, pull, sway, want 5 force, hurry, pinch, power, press, trial 6 burden, demand, strain, stress, weight 7 anxiety, density, gravity, potency, squeeze, straits, tension, trouble, urgency 8 coercion, distress, exigency, interest 9 adversity, grievance, heaviness, influence, necessity 10 affliction, compaction, compulsion, difficulty, oppression
pressure measurement 6 pascal 10 atmosphere
prestige 4 fame, mark, note 5 glory, honor 6 esteem, import, regard, renown, report, repute 7 account, respect 8 eminence 9 authority, celebrity 10 importance, notability, prominence, reputation 11 consequence, distinction, preeminence 12 significance
prestigious 5 famed 6 famous 7 eminent, honored, notable 8 esteemed, renowned 9 acclaimed, important, prominent, reputable, respected, well-known 10 celebrated 11 illustrious, outstanding 13 distinguished
Preston, Robert
real name: 21 Robert Preston Meservey
born: 17 Newton Highlands MA
roles: 4 Mame 9 Semi-Tough 11 The Music Man 12 Junior Bonner 14 Victor Victoria 16 How the West Was Won
presumable 6 likely 8 apparent, probable 10 ostensible
presumably 6 likely 8 probably 9 assumably, doubtless 10 apparently, ostensibly 13 presumptively 14 unquestionably 15 in all likelihood 16 in all probability
presume 4 dare 5 fancy, guess, posit 6 assume, deduce, gather, have it, impose, take it 7 believe, imagine, suppose, surmise, suspect, venture 8 be so bold, conceive, make bold, make free 9 postulate, take leave 11 hypothesize, rely too much, think likely 12 take a liberty
presumed 7 assumed, deduced, posited 8 believed, imagined, supposed, surmised 9 suspected 10 postulated 13 took advantage 15 taken for granted
presumption 3 lip 4 gall 5 brass, cheek, guess, nerve, pride 6 belief, daring 7 egotism, premise, surmise 8 audacity, boldness, chutzpah, rudeness 9 arrogance, flippancy, impudence, insolence, postulate 10 assumption, conjecture, effrontery 11

forwardness, haughtiness, prejudgment, speculation, supposition 12 impertinence 13 preconception 14 presupposition

presumptuous 4 bold 5 brash, cocky, fresh, lofty, nervy, proud 6 brassy, brazen, daring, lordly 7 forward, haughty, pompous 8 arrogant, assuming, snobbish 9 audacious, imperious, shameless 10 disdainful 11 dictatorial, domineering, overbearing, patronizing 12 contemptuous, overfamiliar 13 overconfident

presuppose 6 assume 7 presume, suppose 9 speculate 10 conjecture 11 hypothesize

presupposed 7 assumed 8 presumed, supposed 10 speculated 11 conjectured

presupposition 7 premise 10 assumption 11 postulation, presumption

pretend 4 fake, sham 5 claim, fancy, feign, mimic, put on 6 affect, assume 7 imagine, imitate, playact, purport, suppose 8 simulate 9 dissemble 10 masquerade 11 counterfeit, dissimulate, impersonate, make believe

pretended
  French: 9 soi-disant

pretender 5 faker, fraud, phony 8 claimant, imposter

pretense 4 airs, fake, hoax, mask, sham, show 5 cloak, cover, feint, guile, trick, vaunt 6 deceit 7 bluster, bombast, display, pretext 8 boasting, bragging, disguise, trickery 9 deception, false show, imposture, invention, pomposity 10 camouflage, pretension, showing off, subterfuge 11 affectation, counterfeit, fabrication, fanfaronade, make-believe, ostentation 12 affectedness

pretension 4 airs, pomp, show 5 claim, right, title 7 bombast, display 8 ambition, pretense, snobbery 9 hypocrisy, pomposity, showiness 10 aspiration, showing off 11 affectation, ostentation 13 grandioseness 14 self-importance 16 ostentatiousness

pretentious 4 airy, smug 5 gaudy, lofty, showy, stagy 6 flashy, florid, garish, ornate, tawdry 7 blown-up, fatuous, pompous, stuck-up 8 affected, assuming, boastful, inflated, overdone, pedantic, puffed-up, snobbish 9 bombastic, flaunting, insincere, presuming, unnatural 10 hoity-toity, theatrical 11 exaggerated, extravagant, overbearing 12 ostentatious, self-praising 13 high-and-mighty, self-important

pretentiousness 4 cant 6 humbug 9 hypocrisy 11 insincerity 17 sanctimoniousness

preternatural 5 eerie, weird 6 arcane, occult 7 bizarre, strange, uncanny 8 esoteric, mystical 9 unearthly, unworldly 10 miraculous, mysterious, superhuman 11 hypernormal, preterhuman, supernormal 12 extramundane, metaphysical, supernatural, supranatural 14 transcendental

pretext 5 basis, bluff, feint 6 excuse, ground 8 pretense 9 semblance 10 pretension, subterfuge 11 vindication

pretty 4 fair 5 bonny 6 comely, dainty, fairly, goodly, lovely, rather 7 shapely, sightly, well-set 8 alluring, charming, delicate, engaging, fetching, graceful, handsome, somewhat, well-made 9 beauteous, beautiful 10 adequately, attractive, moderately, reasonably 11 captivating, good-looking, symmetrical, well-favored

pretty child 4 doll 5 cutie 10 living doll

prevail 3 win 4 rule 5 exist, reign 6 abound, obtain, win out 7 conquer, succeed, triumph 8 have sway, hold sway, overcome 9 be a winner, be current 11 be prevalent, be the victor, carry the day, gain the palm, predominate 12 be victorious, be widespread, preponderate

prevailing 3 set 4 main 5 fixed, usual 6 normal 7 current, general, in style, popular 8 definite, dominant 9 customary, prevalent, principal 10 accustomed, widespread 11 established, predominant 12 conventional, preponderant

prevail over 4 beat 5 outdo 6 defeat 7 eclipse, surpass 8 overcome

prevail upon 4 sway 8 convince, persuade 9 influence

prevalent 4 rife 5 usual 6 common, normal 7 general, popular, rampant 8 abundant, everyday, familiar, frequent, habitual, numerous 9 customary, extensive, pervasive, universal 10 prevailing, ubiquitous, widespread 11 commonplace 12 conventional

prevaricate 3 fib, lie 4 fake 6 palter 7 deceive, distort, falsify, mislead, perjure 8 hoodwink, misstate 9 be evasive, dissemble 10 equivocate, tell a story 11 counterfeit 12 be untruthful, misrepresent

prevarication 3 fib, lie 5 fable 7 fiction, untruth, whopper 9 fairy tale, falsehood, fish story, invention 11 fabrication 12 equivocation 16 cock-and-bull story 17 misrepresentation

prevent 3 bar, dam 4 balk, foil, halt, stop, veto 5 avert, avoid, block, deter 6 arrest, forbid, thwart 7 deflect, draw off, fend off, obviate, rule out, ward off 8 hold back, preclude, prohibit, stave off, turn away 9 forestall, frustrate, intercept, sidetrack, turn aside 10 anticipate, counteract 11 nip in the bud

prevention 6 defeat 8 stoppage 9 avoidance, hindrance, obviation, restraint, thwarting 10 deterrence, inhibition, preclusion 11 elimination, frustration 12 interception 13 forestallment

preview 5 sneak 6 sample, survey 8 futurama 9 foretaste 10 inspection

previous 5 early, prior 6 before, former 7 earlier 8 foregone 9 aforesaid, erstwhile, foregoing, preceding 10 antecedent 14 aforementioned

previously 4 once 6 before 7 earlier, long ago 8 back when, formerly 9 at one time, a while ago, earlier on 10 a while back, heretofore 11 in times past 12 sometime back

Prevost, Abbe
  author of: 12 Manon Lescaut

prey 3 eat 4 dupe, food, game, gull, kill 5 patsy, prize, quest 6 devour, infest, pigeon, quarry, sucker, target, victim 7 cat's-paw, consume, fall guy, live off 8 feed upon 9 feast upon 10 fasten upon, fatten upon, parasitize

Priam
  king of: 4 Troy
  father: 8 Laomedon
  brother: 8 Tithonus
  wife: 6 Hecuba
  son: 5 Paris 6 Hector 9 Polydorus
  daughter: 8 Polyxena 9 Cassandra
  number of sons: 5 fifty
  number of daughters: 5 fifty
  killed by: 11 Neoptolemus

Priamid
  father: 5 Priam

Priapus
  god of: 5 herds 7 gardens 9 fertility, male power 11 procreation
  father: 8 Dionysus
  mother: 9 Aphrodite
  corresponds to: 7 Mutinus

price 3 fee 4 cost, fine, rate 5 value, worth 6 amount, assess, charge, outlay 7 expense, penalty 8 appraise, evaluate, par value 9 face value, list price 10 forfeiture, punishment

Price, Fanny
  character in: 13 Mansfield Park
  author: 6 Austen

Price, Vincent
  born: 9 St Louis MO
  wife: 11 Coral Browne 12 Edith Barrett
  roles: 6 The Fly 8 The Raven 10 House of Wax 13 Tower of London 15 The House of Usher 20 The Pit and the Pendulum 22 The Masque of the Red Death
  expert in: 3 art

Price Is Right, The
  host: 9 Bob Barker 10 Bill Cullen

priceless 4 dear, rare 6 costly, prized, valued 8 peerless, precious, valuable 9 cherished, expensive, treasured 10 high-priced, invaluable 11 beyond price 12 incomparable, without price 13 irreplaceable 17 worth a king's ransom

prick 5 stick 6 pierce 8 puncture

prickle 4 barb, itch 5 point, quill, smart, sting, thorn 6 tingle 7 barbule, bristle, spicule

prickly 5 itchy 6 coarse, thorny 8 scratchy, stinging 9 vexatious

pride 3 joy 4 airs, pomp, show 5 honor 6 egoism, parade, vanity 7 comfort, conceit, delight, dignity, display, egotism, swagger 8 pleasure, self-love, smugness 9 arrogance, be proud of, enjoyment, happiness, immodesty, pomposity, vainglory 10 pretension, self-esteem 11 haughtiness, ostentation, self-respect 14 self-importance

Pride and Prejudice
  author: 10 Jane Austen
  character: 7 Mr Darcy 9 Mr Bingley, Mr Collins, Mr Wickham 14 Charlotte Lucas 15 Caroline Bingley 21 Lady Catherine de Bourgh
  Bennet daughters: 4 Jane, Mary 5 Kitty, Lydia 9 Elizabeth
  director: 14 Robert Z Leonard
  cast: 10 Mary Boland 11 Edmund Gwenn, Greer Garson, Karen Morley 13 Ann Rutherford, Edna May Oliver 15 Laurence Olivier 16 Maureen O'Sullivan

Pride of the Yankees, The
  director: 7 Sam Wood
  cast: 8 Babe Ruth 9 Dan Duryea 10 Gary Cooper (Lou Gehrig) 12 Teresa Wright 13 Walter Brennan

priest 5 padre 6 cleric 8 minister, preacher 9 churchman 10 man of the cloth

priesthood 5 cloth 6 clergy 8 ministry, the cloth 9 pastorage

Priestley, J B
  author of: 9 Bright Day 11 Lost Empires 13 Angel Pavement 17 The Good Companions

Priestley, Joseph
  field: 9 chemistry
  nationality: 7 British
  discovered: 6 oxygen 7 ammonia 13 nitrogen oxide
  invented: 11 carbonation

priestly 8 churchly, clerical 10 sacerdotal 14 ecclesiastical

prig 5 bigot, prude 6 pedant 7 puritan 8 bluenose 9 formalist, hypocrite, nitpicker, pretender 10 fuddy-duddy 11 faultfinder 12 bluestocking, precisionist, stuffed shirt 14 attitudinarian

priggish 4 prim, smug 6 stuffy 7 prudish 9 blue-nosed 10 tight-laced 11 puritanical, straitlaced 13 self-righteous, self-satisfied

prim 4 smug, tidy 5 fussy 6 prissy, proper, strict, stuffy 7 haughty, prudish 8 priggish, starched 9 squeamish, unbending 10 fastidious, fuddy-duddy, inflexible, nononsense, particular 11 overprecise, puritanical, stiff-necked, straitlaced

prima donna 4 diva, lead, star 6 singer 9 principal
  literally: 9 first lady

primarily 6 mainly, mostly 7 chiefly, largely 9 basically, generally, in the main 11 essentially, principally 13 fundamentally, predominantly 14 for the most part 16 first and foremost

primary 3 key 4 main, star 5 basal, basic, chief, first, prime, vital 6 innate, native, oldest, primal, ruling, utmost 7 highest, initial, leading, nascent, natural 8 cardinal, dominant, earliest, greatest, inherent, original, primeval 9 beginning, elemental, essential, important, necessary, primitive, principal, prominent 10 aboriginal, elementary, indigenous, primordial, rudimental 11 fundamental, predominant, preparatory, rudimentary 12 introductory

primary constituent 5 basic 9 basic need, essential, necessity, requisite 10 sine qua non

primate 3 ape, man 5 avahi, indri, lemur, loris, potto 6 aye-aye, baboon, bishop, galago, gibbon, mammal, monkey 7 gorilla, tamarin, tarsier 8 marmoset, simpoona 9 orangutan, tree shrew 10 archbishop, chimpanzee

prime 2 A1 3 ace, fit 4 best, main, peak, pink 5 adapt, basal, basic, bloom, breed, brief, chief, coach, early, first, groom, guide, lucky, raise, ready, train, tutor, vital 6 adjust, choice, fill in, flower, Grade A, height, heyday, inform, innate, native, oldest, primal, prompt, ruling, school, seemly, select, timely, utmost, zenith 7 educate, fitting, highest, leading, maximal, natural, prepare, primary, quality, supreme, tophole 8 best days, cardinal, crowning, earliest, get ready, greatest, inherent, instruct, maturity, original, peerless, suitable, superior 9 befitting, elemental, essential, expedient, important, intrinsic, make ready, matchless, necessary, opportune, paramount, preferred, principal, provident, topdrawer, top-flight, unmatched, well-timed 11 superlative, unsurpassed, without peer 12 unparalleled

prime example 5 model 7 classic 8 exemplar 9 archetype

prime mover 6 author 9 initiator, organizer 10 originator
Latin: 12 primum mobile

Prime of Miss Jean Brodie, The
author: 11 Muriel Spark

primer 3 cap 4 book 5 paint 6 manual, reader 8 hornbook, textbook 9 undercoat

primeval 5 early 6 oldest, primal 7 ancient, archaic 8 earliest, original 9 ancestral, legendary, primitive 10 aboriginal, indigenous, primordial 11 fundamental, prehistoric 12 antediluvian, mythological

primitive 4 bare 5 crude, early, first 6 native, simple 7 antique, archaic, artless, ascetic, austere, primary, Spartan 8 backward, earliest, original 9 beginning, unlearned, unrefined, unskilled 10 aboriginal, elementary 11 rudimentary, uncivilized, undeveloped

primordial 5 first 6 primal 7 initial 8 original, primeval 9 beginning, primitive 10 elementary 11 fundamental, prehistoric

primp 5 groom, plume, preen 6 doll up, make up 7 gussy up 8 prettify, spruce up

primrose 7 Primula 15 Primula vulgaris
varieties: 4 baby, cape, star 5 fairy 6 German, poison 7 Chinese, English, evening 8 bird's-eye 9 buttercup 12 beach evening, white evening 13 desert evening 14 Mexican evening

primum mobile 10 prime mover 16 first moving thing

primus inter pares 16 first among equals

prince
Italian: 8 principe
Turkish: 3 beg, bey

Prince
original name: 18 Prince Rogers Nelson
nickname: 12 Royal Badness
born: 2 MN 11 Minneapolis
recording: 6 For You, Parade, Prince 9 Dirty Mind 10 Purple Rain 11 Controversy 20 Around the World in a Day
film: 10 Purple Rain 13 Sign o' the Times 14 Graffiti Bridge 18 Under the Cherry Moon

Prince, The
author: 18 Niccolo Machiavelli

Prince and the Pauper, The
author: 9 Mark Twain
character: 4 Hugo 8 Tom Canty 9 John Canty 10 Hugh Hendon 11 Miles Hendon 19 Edward Prince of Wales

Prince Edward Island
abbreviation: 3 PEI
bay: 5 Rollo 6 Egmont 7 Bedeque 8 Cardigan, Malpeque 9 Cascumpec 12 Hillsborough
capital: 13 Charlottetown
gulf: 10 St Lawrence
people: 4 Scot 5 Irish, Scots 6 French 7 English
discoverer: 7 Cartier
province of: 6 Canada
river: 4 Dunk 5 Eliot, Yorke 12 Hillsborough
strait: 14 Northumberland

Prince Igor
also: 9 Kniaz Igor
opera by: 7 Borodin
character: 11 Khan Konchak
contains: 17 Polovetsian dances

princely 3 big 5 noble, royal 8 generous 11 magnificent

prince of darkness 5 Satan 7 Lucifer 8 the Devil 9 Beelzebub

Prince of Peace 5 Jesus 6 Christ

Princess and the Pea, The
author: 21 Hans Christian Andersen

Princess Casamassima
author: 10 Henry James

Princess Daisy
author: 12 Judith Krantz

Princesse de Cleves, La
author: 14 Mme de LaFayette

Princess Flavia
character in: 15 Prisoner of Zenda
author: 4 Hope

Prince Valiant
creator: 12 Harold Foster
character: 5 Ilene 9 Prince Arn 10 King Arthur
wife: 5 Aleta
nickname: 3 Val

principal 4 dean, fund, main, star 5 basic, chief, first, money, prime 6 master 7 capital, leading, primary, supreme 8 cardinal, dominant, foremost, greatest, superior, ultimate 9 essential, paramount, preceptor, prominent 10 capital sum, headmaster, leading man, preeminent 11 fundamental, predominant, protagonist 13 most important

principal constituent 4 base 12 chief feature 14 main ingredient

principal dish of a meal
French: 17 piece de resistance

principal event
French: 17 piece de resistance

principality 5 angel 9 princedom 14 celestial being, heavenly spirit

principally 6 mainly, mostly 7 chiefly, largely 8 above all 9 basically, primarily 10 especially 12 particularly 13 fundamentally, predominantly 14 for the most part 16 first and foremost

principe 6 prince

principle 3 law 4 code, fact, rule, view 5 axiom, basis, canon, credo, creed, dogma, honor, maxim, tenet, truth 6 belief, dictum, ethics, morals, theory, virtue 7 element, formula, honesty, precept, probity, scruple, theorem 8 attitude, doctrine, goodness, morality, position, rudiment, scruples, teaching 9 direction, integrity, rectitude, standards 10 assumption, regulation 11 fundamental, proposition, uprightness

principled 6 honest 7 upright 9 honorable 10 aboveboard, forthright

Pringle, John
real name of: 11 John Gilbert

prink 4 deck, fuss 5 adorn, preen, primp 6 spruce

print 3 die 4 copy, text, type 5 issue, plate, press, stamp, write 7 compose, edition, engrave, etching, gravure, impress, picture, publish, woodcut 10 lithograph, silkscreen 11 letterpress

printing press
invented by:
rotary: 3 Hoe
web: 7 Bullock

prior 6 former 7 earlier 8 anterior, previous 9 aforesaid, erstwhile, foregoing, prefatory 10 antecedent, precursory 11 going before, preexistent, preexisting, preparatory 14 aforementioned

Prior Analytics
author: 9 Aristotle

Prioress
character in: 18 The Canterbury Tales
author: 7 Chaucer

priority 7 urgency 9 immediacy, seniority 10 ascendancy, precedence, precedency, preference 11 antecedence, preeminence, superiority

priory 5 abbey 6 friary 7 convent, nunnery 8 cloister 9 hermitage, monastery

Prism, Letitia
character in: 27 The Importance of Being Earnest
author: 5 Wilde

prison 3 can, jug, pen 4 brig, gaol, jail, stir, tank 5 clink, joint, pokey, tower 6 cooler 7 dungeon, slammer 8 bastille, big house 9 calaboose, jailhouse

Prisoner of Zenda
author: 11 Anthony Hope
character: 14 Princess Flavia 17 Lady Rose Burlesdon, Rudolph Rassendyll 18 Antoinette de Mauban, Fritz von Tarlenheim 21 Michael Duke of Strelsau 22 Rudolph King of Ruritania
director: 12 John Cromwell
cast: 9 Mary Astor 10 David Niven 12 C Aubrey Smith, Ronald Colman (Rudolf Rassendyll) 16 Madeleine Carroll 18 Douglas Fairbanks Jr (Rupert of Hentzau)
setting: 9 Ruritania

prissy 4 prim 5 fussy 6 proper, stuffy 7 finicky, prudish 8 overnice 9 sissified 10 effeminate 11 strait-laced

Prissy
character in: 15 Gone With the Wind
author: 8 Mitchell

pristine 4 pure 8 unmarred, virginal 9 undefiled, unspoiled, unsullied, untouched 10 unpolluted 11 untarnished 14 uncontaminated

Pritchett, V S
author of: 11 Midnight Oil 16 Collected Stories, The Spanish Temper 19 On the Edge of the Cliff

privacy 6 secret 7 privity, retreat, secrecy 8 security, solitude 9 integrity, isolation, seclusion 10 retirement, withdrawal 11 privateness 12 dissociation, solitariness 13 sequestration

private 4 dark 5 fixed, privy 6 buried, closed, covert, hidden, lonely, remote, secret 7 cryptic, express, limited, obscure, special 8 confined, desolate, esoteric, hush-hush, isolated, lonesome, personal, secluded, solitary 9 concealed, exclusive, inviolate, invisible, nonpublic, not public, reclusive 10 classified, indistinct, mysterious, restricted, undercover, under wraps, unofficial, unrevealed 11 clandestine, nonofficial, sequestered, underground, undisclosed 12 confidential, off-the-record, unfrequented

privateer 6 pirate 7 brigand, corsair 9 buccaneer

private eye 4 dick 6 shamus 7 gumshoe 9 detective 12 investigator

Private Life of Henry VIII, The
director: 14 Alexander Korda
cast: 11 Merle Oberon, Robert Donat 12 Binnie Barnes 14 Elsa Lanchester (Anne of Cleves) 15 Charles Laughton (Henry VIII)

Private Life of the Master Race, The
author: 13 Bertold Brecht

Private Lives
author: 10 Noel Coward
character: 10 Elyot Chase, Sibyl Chase 12 Amanda Prynne, Victor Prynne

Private Lives of Elizabeth and Essex, The
director: 13 Michael Curtiz
cast: 10 Bette Davis (Elizabeth I), Errol Flynn (Essex) 11 Donald Crisp 12 Vincent Price 13 Nanette Fabray 17 Olivia de Havilland
also known as: 17 Elizabeth the Queen

privately 7 sub rosa 8 in secret, secretly 9 between us, entre nous, in private 12 in confidence 14 confidentially 15 between you and me 16 between ourselves 17 behind closed doors

privation 4 lack, need, want 5 pinch 6 misery, penury 7 beggary, poverty, straits 8 distress, exigency, hardship 9 indigence, neediness, pauperism 10 bankruptcy, mendicancy 11 destitution 14 impoverishment 15 impecuniousness

privilege 3 due 4 boon 5 allow, favor, grant, honor, power, right, title 6 patent, permit 7 benefit, charter, empower, entitle, freedom, liberty, license 8 pleasure 9 advantage, authority, franchise 10 birthright 11 entitlement, prerogative 12 prerequisite

privileged 4 free 6 exempt, immune 7 allowed, excused, granted, limited, special 8 entitled, licensed 9 empowered, not liable, permitted, warranted 10 authorized, sanctioned 13 unaccountable

prize 3 cup, gem, pip 4 like, lulu 5 award, catch, crown, dandy, honey, honor, jewel, medal, peach, pearl, value 6 admire, esteem, honors, regard, reward, ribbon, trophy 7 cherish, diamond, guerdon, honored, laurels, premium, respect, winning 8 accolade, champion, citation, hold dear, look up to, pure gold, treasure 9 humdinger, medallion 10 appreciate, blue ribbon, decoration, set store by 11 crackerjack, masterpiece

prized 4 dear 8 esteemed, precious 9 cherished, treasured

prizefight 2 go 4 bout 5 match 6 boxing 7 contest 15 fisticuffs

prizefighter 3 pug 5 boxer 7 slugger 8 pugilist 9 flyweight 11 heavyweight, lightweight 12 bantamweight, middleweight, welterweight 13 featherweight 16 light heavyweight

pro 3 for 5 forth 6 before, expert, master 8 favoring 9 authority 11 affirmative

opposite: 3 con 7 amateur

probability 4 odds 6 chance 10 likelihood

probable 6 likely 7 logical, seeming, tenable 8 apparent, assuring, credible, expected, possible, presumed, supposed 9 plausible, promising, thinkable 10 believable, in the cards, ostensible, presumable, reasonable 11 conceivable, encouraging, presumptive

probably 6 likely 10 most likely, presumably, supposedly 11 as like as not 15 in all likelihood

probe 4 hunt, quiz, seek, test 5 query, study, trial 6 pursue, review, search, survey 7 examine, fish for, inquest, inquire, inquiry, inspect, pry into, rummage 8 analysis, look into, question, research 9 penetrate 10 inspection, scrutinize 11 examination, exploration, interrogate, investigate 13 investigation

probity 5 honor 6 virtue 7 decency, honesty 8 goodness, morality 9 character, integrity, principle 11 uprightness 12 straightness 13

righteousness 14 high-mindedness 15 trustworthiness 16 incorruptibility

problem 5 poser, query 6 puzzle, riddle, unruly 8 question, stubborn 9 conundrum, difficult 10 difficulty 11 intractable 12 disagreement, hard to manage, incorrigible, unmanageable

problematic 7 dubious, unknown 8 doubtful, puzzling 9 difficult, enigmatic, uncertain, unsettled, worrisome 10 perplexing 11 paradoxical, troublesome 12 questionable, undetermined

pro bono publico 16 for the public good

proboscis 4 beak, nose 5 snoot, snout, trunk 6 siphon, sucker, syphon 7 rostrum

monkey: 4 kaha 5 kahua

procedure 2 MO 3 way 4 mode 6 course, manner, method 7 process, routine 8 approach, strategy 9 technique 11 methodology 13 modus operandi

proceed 2 go 3 act 4 come, flow, go on, grow, move, stem, work 5 arise, begin, ensue, issue, start 6 derive, follow, move on, push on, result, set out, spring 7 advance, carry on, emanate, go ahead, operate, press on, succeed 8 be caused, commence, continue, function, progress, take rise 9 be derived, go forward, move ahead, originate, undertake

proceedings 4 case, suit 5 cause, trial 6 doings, events, report 7 account, actions, affairs, lawsuit, matters, minutes, records, returns 8 activity, archives, goings on 9 incidents, memoranda 10 happenings, litigation, operations 11 occurrences 12 transactions

proceeds 4 net 4 gain, gate, pelf, take 5 gross, lucre, money, yield 6 assets, income, profit, reward 7 returns, revenue 8 earnings, pickings, receipts, winnings 9 box office

process 3 can, dry 4 fill, flow, flux, mode, plan, ship, step, writ 5 alter, candy, smoke, treat, usage 6 change, course, freeze, handle, manner, method, motion, policy, scheme, system 7 convert, measure, passage, prepare, project, summons 8 deal with, function, movement, practice, preserve, progress, subpoena 9 dehydrate, dispose of, freeze-dry, procedure, transform, unfolding 10 court order, proceeding

procession 4 file, line, rank 5 array, march, train 6 column, course, parade 7 caravan, cortege, pageant, passage 8 progress, sequence 9 cavalcade, motorcade 10 succession 11 progression

Procheneosaurus

type: 8 dinosaur 10 ornithopod

location: 6 Canada

period: 10 Cretaceous

proclaim 3 cry 4 tell 5 blare, state, voice 6 affirm, assert, blazon, herald, report, reveal 7 call out, declare, divulge, give out, profess, publish, release, sing out, trumpet 8 announce, disclose, set forth 9 advertise, broadcast, circulate, enunciate, hawk about, make known, publicize 10 make public, promulgate

proclamation 5 edict, ukase 6 decree 12 announcement 13 pronouncement

Proclea
 husband: 6 Cycnus
 son: 5 Tenes

Procles
 twin of: 11 Eurysthenes

proclivity 3 yen 4 bent, bias 5 taste 6 desire, liking 7 impulse, leaning 8 affinity, appetite, penchant, soft spot, tendency 9 affection, prejudice, proneness 10 partiality, propensity 11 disposition, inclination 12 predilection 14 predisposition

Procne
 sister: 9 Philomela
 husband: 6 Tereus
 changed into: 7 swallow

procrastinate 3 lag 5 dally, defer, delay, stall, tarry 6 dawdle, linger, loiter 7 adjourn 8 hang back, hesitate, hold back, kill time, postpone, put on ice 9 temporize, waste time 10 be dilatory, dillydally 11 play for time 12 drag one's feet

procrastinating 4 slow 5 tardy 6 remiss 8 dilatory 9 reluctant 12 foot-dragging 13 dillydallying

procreate 3 get 4 bear, sire 5 beget, breed, spawn 6 create, father, mother 7 produce 8 conceive, engender, generate, multiply 9 propagate, reproduce 10 bring forth 11 give birth to, proliferate

procreation
 god of: 7 Priapus

procreator 4 sire 6 father 8 begetter

Procris
 father: 8 Thespius 10 Erechtheus
 husband: 8 Cephalus

Procrustes
 also: 8 Damastes 9 Polypemon
 robber who: 6 maimed
 killed by: 7 Theseus

procure 3 buy, get, win 4 earn, gain, take 5 evoke, seize 6 attain, come by, effect, elicit, gather, incite, induce, obtain, pick up, secure 7 achieve, acquire, receive 8 contrive, purchase 10 accumulate, bring about, commandeer, lay hands on 11 appropriate

procurement 4 gain 7 seizure 8 purchase 10 attainment, purchasing 11 achievement, acquirement, acquisition 12 accumulation 13 appropriation

prod 3 jab, nag 4 flog, goad, lash, move, poke, push, spur, stir, urge, whip 5 egg on, impel, prick, rouse, shove, speed 6 excite, exhort, incite, needle, prompt, propel, stir up 7 actuate, animate, provoke, quicken 8 motivate, pressure 9 encourage, instigate, stimulate

prodigal 4 lush 5 ample 6 lavish, myriad, wanton 7 copious, profuse, replete, spender, teeming, wastrel 8 abundant, generous, numerous, reckless, swarming, wasteful 9 abounding, bounteous, bountiful, countless, excessive, exuberant, im-petuous, luxuriant, plentiful, unthrifty 10 exorbitant, gluttonous, immoderate, inordinate, numberless, profligate, squanderer, thriftless 11 dissipating, extravagant, improvident, innumerable, intemperate, overliberal, precipitate, spendthrift 13 multitudinous

prodigality 10 imprudence, lavishness 12 extravagance, improvidence, overspending, wastefulness

prodigious 3 big 4 huge, rare, vast 5 grand, great, large 6 mighty, unique 7 amazing, immense 8 colossal, enormous, gigantic, renowned, singular, striking, terrific, uncommon, unwonted, wondrous 9 marvelous, monstrous, startling, wonderful 10 astounding, impressive, miraculous, monumental, noteworthy, remarkable, stupendous, surprising, tremendous 11 astonishing, exceptional, far-reaching, uncustomary, unthinkable 12 dumbfounding, overwhelming, unimaginable 13 extraordinary, inconceivable, unprecedented

prodigiously 10 enormously, incredibly, remarkably 12 inordinately, tremendously 13 astonishingly, exceptionally, extravagantly, outstandingly, spectacularly 14 overwhelmingly

prodigiousness 6 rarity 8 enormity, hugeness, vastness 10 uniqueness 11 singularity 12 extravagance

prodigy 4 whiz 6 expert, genius, marvel, master, rarity, wizard, wonder 7 stunner, whiz kid 8 rara avis 9 sensation 10 mastermind, phenomenon, wunderkind 11 wonder child

Prodromia
 epithet of: 4 Hera
 means: 7 pioneer

produce 4 bear, form, give, make, show 5 beget, bloom, cause, found, frame, hatch, set up, shape, yield 6 adduce, afford, create, devise, effect, evince, evolve, flower, fruits, greens, invent, reveal, sprout, supply, unmask, unveil 7 achieve, advance, bring in, compose, concoct, develop, display, divulge, exhibit, fashion, furnish, present, provide, staples, turn out, uncover 8 bring off, bring out, conceive, disclose, discover, generate, manifest, set forth 9 bear fruit, construct, fabricate, institute, make plain, originate, procreate, put on view, show forth 10 accomplish, bring about, come up with, effectuate, foodstuffs, give life to, give rise to, put in force, vegetables 11 bring to pass, give birth to, manufacture, materialize 14 bring into being

Producers, The
 director: 9 Mel Brooks
 cast: 9 Dick Shawn 10 Gene Wilder, Zero Mostel 11 Kenneth Mars

production 4 film, play, show 5 drama, movie 6 cinema, circus, making 7 display, exhibit, musical, showing 8 building, carnival, creation 9 execution, formation, producing, stage show 10 appearance, disclosure, revelation 11 fabrication, fulfillment, manufacture, origination, performance 12 construction, effectuation, introduction, presentation 13 demonstration, entertainment, manifestation, manufacturing, motion picture 15 materialization

productive 4 busy, rich 6 active, fecund, paying, useful 7 causing, copious, dynamic, fertile, gainful, teeming 8 creating, creative, fruitful, prolific, valuable, vigorous, yielding 9 effectual, luxuriant, plenteous, plentiful, producing 10 invaluable, profitable, worthwhile 11 efficacious, moneymaking, proliferous 12 contributing, fructiferous, remunerative

Proetus
  father: 4 Abas
  mother: 6 Aglaia
  twin brother: 8 Acrisius
  wife: 5 Antia 10 Stheneboea
  son: 11 Megapenthes
  daughter: 7 Iphinoe, Lysippe 10 Iphianassa
  invented: 6 shield
  enemy: 8 Acrisius

profanation 9 sacrilege 10 defilement 11 desecration

profane 3 lay 4 evil, foul, lewd, mock, vile 5 abuse, bawdy, crude, nasty, scorn, waste 6 coarse, debase, filthy, ill-use, impure, misuse, offend, revile, ribald, sinful, unholy, vulgar, wicked 7 abusive, earthly, godless, impious, obscene, outrage, pervert, pollute, satanic, secular, ungodly, violate, worldly 8 agnostic, diabolic, off-color, temporal, unchaste, undevout, unseemly 9 atheistic, blaspheme, desecrate, hellbound, heretical, misemploy, shameless, unsaintly 10 irreverent, prostitute 11 blasphemous, contaminate, irreligious, terrestrial, unbelieving 12 nonreligious, sacrilegious

profanity 5 filth, oaths 7 cursing, cussing, impiety 8 swearing 9 blasphemy, obscenity, scatology 10 dirty words, execration, expletives, scurrility, swearwords 11 irreverence, obscenities, ungodliness 12 billingsgate 15 four-letter words

profess 3 act, own, say 4 aver, avow, fake, sham, tell 5 admit, claim, feign, offer, put on, state, vouch 6 affirm, allege, assert, assume, depose 7 advance, certify, confess, confirm, contend, declare, embrace, pretend, purport 8 announce, lay claim, maintain, practice, proclaim, propound, simulate 9 believe in, dissemble, enunciate, hold forth 10 asseverate, put forward 11 acknowledge, counterfeit, dissimulate

professed 6 avowed 7 alleged 8 admitted 9 confessed, purported 12 acknowledged, self-declared 14 self-proclaimed

profession 3 job, law, vow 4 line, post, word, work 5 claim, craft, field, trade, troth 6 avowal, career, metier, office, pledge, plight, sphere 7 calling, promise, pursuit, service 8 averment, business, endeavor, industry, medicine, position, practice,

teaching, vocation 9 assertion, assurance, guarantee, situation, specialty, statement, testimony 10 allegation, confession, deposition, employment, line of work, occupation, walk of life 11 affirmation, attestation, declaration, undertaking, word of honor 12 announcement, confirmation 13 pronouncement 15 acknowledgement

professional 4 paid 5 adept 6 expert 9 authority, competent, practiced 10 specialist 11 experienced

professionalism 5 savvy, skill 7 know-how 9 expertise 10 expertness

professor 3 don 6 regent 7 adjoint, teacher 8 lecturer 10 instructor
  retired: 8 emeritus

Professor, The
  author: 15 Charlotte Bronte

professorial 6 teachy 7 bookish, donnish, preachy 8 academic, didactic, pedantic, teachery 11 pedagoguish 13 schoolmarmish 15 schoolmasterish 16 schoolteacherish

Professor's House, The
  author: 11 Willa Cather

proffer 5 offer 6 extend, tender 7 advance, hold out, present

proficiency 5 knack, skill 6 acumen 7 ability, know-how 8 aptitude, capacity, deftness, facility 9 adeptness, dexterity, expertise, handiness 10 adroitness, capability, competence 13 qualification 14 accomplishment

proficient 3 apt 4 able, deft, good 5 adept, handy, quick, ready, sharp 6 adroit, clever, expert, gifted 7 capable, skilled, trained 8 masterly, polished, skillful, talented 9 competent, dexterous, effective, efficient, masterful, practiced, qualified, versatile 11 experienced 12 accomplished, professional

profile 4 form, side, tale 5 shape 6 figure, sketch 7 contour, drawing, outline, picture, skyline 8 half face, portrait, side view, vignette 9 biography 10 lineaments, silhouette 11 delineation 13 configuration

Profiles in Courage
  author: 12 John F Kennedy

profit 3 pay, use 4 boon, earn, gain, good, help 5 avail, favor, money, serve, value 6 income, return 7 account, benefit, revenue, service, utility, utilize 8 earnings, interest, proceeds, receipts 9 advantage, make money 11 advancement

profitable 6 paying, useful 7 gainful 8 fruitful, salutary, valuable 9 favorable, lucrative, rewarding 10 beneficial, invaluable, productive, well-paying, worthwhile 11 moneymaking, serviceable 12 advantageous, remunerative

profitmaking 8 business 11 moneymaking 13 noncharitable

profits 4 gate, take 5 gains, yield 6 assets, income 7 returns, revenue 8 earnings, receipts

profligacy 10 lavishness 11 dissipation, dissolution, prodigality, unrestraint 12 extravagance, immoderation, improvidence, recklessness, wastefulness 13 excessiveness

profligate 4 evil, fast, rake, roue, wild 5 loose, satyr 6 erotic, lavish, sinful, sinner, wanton, wicked 7 corrupt, immoral, pervert, satyric, wastrel 8 degraded, depraved, prodigal, reckless, wasteful 9 abandoned, debauched, debauchee, dissolute, libertine, reprobate, sybaritic, unbridled, unthrifty, wrongdoer 10 degenerate, dissipated, dissipater, iniquitous, lascivious, licentious 11 extravagant, improvident, promiscuous, spendthrift 12 unprincipled, unrestrained

pro forma 15 according to form, as a matter of form

profound 4 deep, keen, sage, wise 5 acute, sober, utter 6 abject, hearty, moving, severe 7 decided, erudite, extreme, intense, knowing, learned, radical, serious, sincere 8 complete, educated, informed, piercing, positive, thorough 9 heartfelt, out-and-out, recondite, sagacious, scholarly 10 all-knowing, consummate, deep-seated, omniscient, pronounced, reflective, thoughtful 11 enlightened, far-reaching, penetrating 12 intellectual, soul-stirring 13 comprehensive, knowledgeable, philosophical, thoroughgoing

profundity 5 abyss, depth 6 wisdom 8 deepness, sagacity, sapience 9 erudition 11 learnedness, penetration 12 abstractness, abstruseness, profoundness 13 reconditeness, sagaciousness 16 impenetrableness

profuse 4 rich 5 ample, wordy 6 lavish, prolix 7 copious, diffuse, verbose 8 abundant, generous, prodigal, rambling, wasteful 9 bounteous, bountiful, excessive, garrulous, unthrifty 10 digressive, discursive, immoderate, inordinate, long-winded, loquacious, munificent 11 extravagant, improvident, intemperate, spendthrift

profuseness 9 abundance, diffusion, profusion, prolixity, verbosity, wordiness 10 lavishness 11 copiousness, diffuseness

profusion 4 glut 5 waste 6 excess 7 surfeit, surplus 8 plethora 9 abundance, multitude 10 oversupply 11 superfluity 12 extravagance, multiplicity

progenitor 8 ancestor, forebear 10 forefather

progeny 3 kin, son 4 clan, heir, line, race, seed 5 blood, breed, child, heirs, issue, scion, stock, young 6 family 7 kindred, lineage 8 children, offshoot 9 offspring, posterity 10 descendant

prognosticate 7 predict, presage 8 forecast, foretell, prophesy 9 foretoken

prognostication 6 augury 8 forecast, prophecy 9 divination, prediction

prognosticator 4 seer 5 augur 7 prophet 9 predictor 10 forecaster

program 4 bill, book, card, list, plan, show 5 slate 6 agenda, design, docket, expect, intend, line up, notice, series, sketch 7 arrange, outline 8 bulletin, calendar, playbill, register, schedule, syllabus 9 timetable 10 curriculum, production, prospectus 12 presentation

progress 4 gain, grow, rise 5 climb, get on, mount, ripen 6 action, course, grow up, growth, mature, stride 7 advance, develop, headway, improve, proceed, process, success 8 get ahead, increase, movement 9 get better, go forward, move ahead, promotion, unfolding 10 betterment, enrichment, gain ground 11 achievement, advancement, development, enhancement, furtherance, improvement, make headway, make strides

progression 3 run 5 chain, climb, order 6 ascent, course, series, strain, string 7 advance 8 progress, sequence 10 succession 11 advancement, continuance, furtherance 12 continuation 14 continuousness 15 consecutiveness

progressive 7 dynamic, gradual, liberal, ongoing 8 activist, advanced, populist, up-to-date 9 advancing, enlarging, reformist, spreading, traveling 10 ameliorist 11 incremental 12 enterprising

prohibit 3 ban, bar 4 curb, deny, stay, stop, veto 5 block, check, delay, limit 6 enjoin, forbid, hamper, hinder, impede, negate 7 inhibit, obviate, prevent, repress 8 disallow, obstruct, preclude, restrain, restrict, suppress, withhold 9 proscribe

prohibited
  German: 8 verboten

prohibition 3 ban 4 veto 5 edict 7 embargo, sanction 10 temperance 11 forbiddance 12 interdiction

prohibitive, prohibitory 9 enjoining, hindering 10 forbidding, inhibitive, injunction, preventative, repressive 11 disallowing, obstructive, restraining, restrictive, suppressive 12 inadmissible, unacceptable 13 disqualifying 15 circumscriptive

project 3 aim, job 4 cast, emit, fire, goal, plan, send, task, work 5 draft, eject, expel, fling, frame, shoot, throw 6 beetle, design, devise, extend, hurtle, invent, jut out, launch, map out, propel, scheme 7 concoct, outline, propose 8 activity, ambition, bend over, contrive, forecast, overhang, protrude, stand out, stick out, throw out, transmit 9 calculate, discharge, ejaculate, intention, objective, plan ahead 10 assignment 11 extrapolate, undertaking 12 predetermine

projected 6 hurled 7 hurtled, planned 8 extended, forecast, launched, overhung, proposed, stood out, stuck out 9 mapped out, propelled, protruded 10 catapulted 11 conjectural

projectile 4 dart 5 arrow, spear 6 rocket 7 javelin, missile

projecting part 3 arm, ell, leg 4 eave, limb, tail 6 branch, feeler, member 7 antenna 8 tentacle 9 appendage

projection 4 brow, bump, eave 5 bulge, guess, jetty, jutty, ledge, ridge, shelf 8 estimate, forecast, overhang 9 extension, extrusion 10 estimation, prediction, prospectus, protrusion 11 guesstimate 12 protuberance 13 approximation, extrapolation

Prokofiev, Serge
   born: 6 Russia 9 Sontsovka
   composer of: 6 Lt Kije 10 Cinderella, The Gambler 11 War and Peace 13 Scythian Suite, The Fiery Angel 14 Lieutenant Kije, Romeo and Juliet, The Prodigal Son 15 Alexander Nevsky, Peter and the Wolf 17 Classical Symphony 22 The Love for Three Oranges 57 Cantata for the Twentieth Anniversary of the October Revolution

proletarian 6 worker 7 laborer 10 working man

proletariat 5 plebs 6 rabble, the mob 7 populus 8 canaille, laborers, populace 9 commonage, commoners, hoi polloi, the masses 10 commonalty 11 lower orders, rank and file, wage earners 12 lower classes, vulgus mobile, working class 15 the common people 16 the great unwashed

proliferate 4 teem 5 breed, hatch, spawn, swarm 8 increase, multiply 9 procreate, propagate, pullulate 10 regenerate 11 overproduce

prolific 4 lush 6 fecund 7 copious, fertile, profuse 8 abundant, breeding, creative, fruitful, yielding 9 luxuriant 11 germinative, multiplying, procreative, progenitive, proliferous, propagating 12 reproductive

prolix 5 wordy 7 verbose 10 long-winded

prolixity 9 verbosity, wordiness 11 profuseness 14 long-windedness

prologue 7 opening, preface, prelude 8 foreword, overture, preamble 9 beginning 12 introduction

prolong 5 delay 6 extend, retard 7 drag out, draw out, spin out, stretch, sustain 8 continue, elongate, lengthen, maintain, protract 9 attenuate 10 perpetuate

prolongation 5 delay 9 extending, extension 10 drawing out 11 attenuation, dragging out, lengthening, protraction, retardation 12 perpetuation 13 streching out

prolonged 7 lengthy 8 drawn-out, extended 9 continued, long-lived 10 continuing, lengthened, persistent, protracted 11 long-lasting

prom 3 hop 4 ball 5 dance 9 cotillion, promenade

Promachorma
   epithet of: 6 Athena
   means: 25 protectress of the anchorage

Promachus
   member of: 7 Epigoni
   leader of: 9 Boeotians
   epithet of: 6 Athena

   means: 8 defender 9 protector

promenade 3 hop 4 ball, prom, walk 5 dance 6 soiree, stroll 9 cotillion

Prometheus
   member of: 6 Titans
   father: 7 Iapetus
   mother: 6 Themis 7 Clymene
   brother: 5 Atlas 10 Epimetheus
   son: 9 Deucalion
   created mankind from: 4 clay
   stole: 4 fire
   punished by: 4 Zeus
   chained to: 4 rock
   released by: 8 Hercules

Prometheus Bound
   author: 9 Aeschylus
   character: 2 Io 3 Bia 6 Hermes, Kratos 7 Oceanus 10 Hephaestus

Prometheus Unbound
   author: 18 Percy Bysshe Shelley
   character: 4 Asia, Ione 5 Earth 7 Jupiter, Mercury, Panthea 8 Hercules 9 Demogoron

prominence 3 tor 4 bump, dune, fame, hill, hump, knob, lump, mark, mesa, name, node, peak, rise, spur 5 bluff, bulge, cliff, crest, honor, jetty, jutty, knoll, knurl, might, mound 6 credit, height, renown, rising, summit, weight 7 dignity, hillock, majesty, process 8 eminence, grandeur, mountain, nobility, outshoot, overhang, pinnacle, prestige, salience, splendor, swelling 9 celebrity, convexity, elevation, extension, extrusion, greatness, influence, notoriety, precipice 10 brilliance, importance, notability, popularity, projection, promontory, protrusion, reputation, tumescence 11 distinction, excrescence, excurvature, preeminence, superiority 12 protuberance, significance

prominent 6 convex, famous 7 bulging, eminent, evident, glaring, honored, jutting, leading, notable, obvious, salient, staring, swollen 8 apparent, definite, excurved, extended, renowned, striking, swelling 9 arresting, important, respected, well-known 10 celebrated, easily seen, jutting out, noticeable, preeminent, projecting, pronounced, protruding, protrusive, remarkable 11 conspicuous, discernible, illustrious, outstanding, prestigious, protuberant 12 recognizable 13 distinguished

promiscuous 3 lax 4 fast, lewd, wild 5 loose, mixed 6 casual, impure, medley, motley, rakish, wanton 7 aimless, chaotic, diverse, immoral, jumbled, mingled, mixed-up, satyric 8 careless, confused, immodest, sweeping, unchaste 9 composite, desultory, dissolute, haphazard, perplexed, scrambled, wholesale 10 commingled, disordered, disorderly, dissipated, intermixed, lascivious, licentious, uncritical, undirected, unvirtuous, variegated 11 disarranged, incontinent, indifferent, intemperate, unselective 12 disorganized, of easy virtue, undiscerning 13 helter-skelter, heterogeneous, miscellaneous 14 indiscriminate

promise 3 vow 4 aver, avow, oath, word 5 agree, augur, imply, swear, troth, vouch 6 assure, avowal, hint of, parole, pledge, plight 7 be bound, betoken, suggest, warrant 8 covenant, indicate, warranty 9 agreement, assurance, guarantee, potential, undertake 11 declaration, stipulation, swear an oath, word of honor

Promised Land 6 Canaan
  nickname of: 10 California 6 Israel

Promises
  author: 16 Robert Penn Warren

promising 4 rosy 5 happy, lucky 6 bright, rising 7 hopeful 8 assuring, cheerful, cheering 9 advancing, favorable, fortunate, looking up 10 auspicious, of good omen, optimistic, propitious, reassuring 11 encouraging, inspiriting, up-and-coming

promissory note 3 IOU 4 bond, chit 6 pledge 7 promise 9 agreement 10 obligation 11 certificate

promontory 4 cape, hill, ness, spur 5 bluff, cliff, jetty, jutty, point 6 height 8 headland, overhang 9 peninsula, precipice 10 embankment, projection

promote 3 aid 4 abet, ease, help, plug, push 5 raise 6 assist, foster, prefer, refine 7 advance, develop, elevate, enhance, forward, further, upgrade, work for 8 advocate, expedite, graduate 9 advertise, cultivate, encourage, publicize

promoter 6 backer 8 advocate, champion 9 proponent, supporter

promotion 4 hype 5 raise 7 advance, fanfare, puffery 8 ballyhoo, boosting, progress 9 elevation, publicity, upgrading 10 preferment 11 advancement, advertising, furtherance 12 promulgation 13 advertisement, encouragement

promotive 7 helpful 9 conducive 10 beneficial 12 contributive, contributory, instrumental

prompt 3 cue 4 goad, keen, move, prod, push, spur, stir 5 alert, alive, cause, drive, eager, force, impel, press, quick, ready, sharp 6 active, assist, bright, excite, incite, induce, intent, lively, on time, propel, remind, thrust, timely 7 actuate, animate, dispose, help out, incline, inspire, instant, on guard, provoke, zealous 8 activate, inspirit, motivate, occasion, open-eyed, persuade, punctual, vigilant, watchful 9 attentive, determine, efficient, immediate, influence, instigate, observant, open-eared, stimulate, wide-awake 10 on one's toes 12 jog the memory, unhesitating 13 instantaneous

prompting 6 cueing, urging 7 goading 8 egging on 10 motivation 11 exhortation

promptly 3 pat 4 anon, soon, tite 6 pronto 7 quickly, swiftly 10 punctually 11 immediately

promptness 5 haste 8 alacrity, celerity, dispatch 9 quickness, readiness, swiftness 11 punctuality 15 expeditiousness

promulgate 6 foster 7 explain, expound, present, promote, sponsor 8 instruct, set forth 9 elucidate, enunciate, interpret 11 communicate

promulgation 9 fostering, promotion 11 circulation, instruction, sponsorship 12 distribution, presentation, transmission 13 communication 14 interpretation

Pronaus
  epithet of: 6 Athena
  means: 12 of the pronaos
  pronaos: 15 before the temple

prone 3 apt 4 flat 5 level 6 liable, likely 7 subject, tending 8 disposed, face-down, inclined 9 prostrate, reclining, recumbent 10 accustomed, habituated, horizontal 11 predisposed, susceptible

proneness 4 bent, bias, turn 7 leaning 8 penchant, tendency 9 prejudice 10 proclivity, propensity 11 inclination 12 predilection 14 predisposition

prong 4 barb, hook, horn, spur, tine 5 point, spike, tooth 6 branch 10 projection

Pronoea
  epithet of: 6 Athena
  means: 11 forethought

pronoun 2 he, it, me, my, us, we, ye 3 all, any, few, her, his, one, she, thy, who, you 4 hers, mine, ours, some, thee, them, they, that, this, thou, what, whom 5 no one, their, these, thine, those, which, whose, yours 6 anyone, itself, myself, nobody 7 anybody, herself, himself, nothing, someone, whoever 8 somebody, whomever 9 everybody, something, whosoever 10 everything, themselves
  French: 2 il, je, tu 3 lui, mes, moi 4 elle, vous
  German: 2 er, es, du 3 ich, mir, sie 4 mein, mich
  Italian: 2 io, me, mi, ti, tu, vi 3 cio, lei, lui, mio, tei, voi 4 egli, ella, essa, esse, essi, loro
  Spanish: 2 el, la, lo, me, mi, tu, yo 4 ella, ello, suyo, tuyo 5 usted

pronounce 3 say 4 emit, form, rule 5 frame, judge, orate, sound, speak, state, utter, voice 6 decree 7 declare, enounce 8 announce, proclaim, vocalize 9 enunciate 10 articulate

pronounced 4 bold 5 broad, clear, plain, vivid 6 patent 7 decided, evident, obvious, visible 8 apparent, clear-cut, definite, distinct, manifest, positive, unhidden 9 arresting 10 noticeable 11 conspicuous, outstanding, undisguised, well-defined 12 recognizable, unmistakable 14 unquestionable

pronouncement 6 decree 11 declaration 12 announcement, proclamation

pronto 3 now 4 asap, fast, stat 5 quick 7 quickly 8 promptly 11 immediately

Pronuba
  epithet of: 4 Juno

pronunciamento 5 edict 12 proclamation 13 pronouncement

pronunciation 6 accent 10 inflection 11 enunciation 12 articulation 16 manner of speaking

proof 4 test 5 essay, proof, sheet, trial 6 galley, ordeal 8 scrutiny, weighing 9 probation 10 assessment 11 attestation, examination 12 confirmation, ratification, verification 13 certification, corroboration, documentation 14 substantiation

proofreader's mark 3 cap, rom 4 dele, ital, stet 5 caret, space

prop 3 set 4 lean, rest, stay 5 brace, stand 6 hold up, pillar 7 bolster, shore up, support 8 buttress, mainstay, shoulder, underpin 9 stanchion, supporter, sustainer 13 reinforcement

  French: 11 point d'appui

propaganda 6 hoopla 8 ballyhoo 9 party line, promotion, publicity 10 persuasion 11 advertising

propagandist 6 zealot 8 activist, exponent 9 apologist, proponent, publicist 12 spokesperson

propagate 3 air, sow 4 bear, tell 5 beget, breed, hatch, issue, rumor, spawn, spray 6 blazon, herald, impart, notify, preach, purvey, repeat, report, spread 7 bestrew, give out, implant, instill, publish, scatter, trumpet 8 disperse, engender, generate, increase, multiply, proclaim, put forth 9 broadcast, circulate, enunciate, give birth, inculcate, make known, procreate, publicize, reproduce

propagation 6 laying, siring 7 bearing 8 breeding, hatching, issuance, spawning, yielding 9 begetting, diffusion, gestation, pregnancy, spreading 10 dispersion, generation 11 circulation, engendering, giving birth, procreation, publication 12 distribution, reproduction, transmission 13 dissemination

pro patria 14 for one's country

propel 4 cast, goad, hurl, poke, prod, push, send, toss 5 drive, eject, force, heave, impel, pitch, shoot, shove, sling, start 6 launch, thrust 7 project 8 catapult 9 discharge 11 precipitate, set in motion

propeller, screw
  invented by: 7 Stevens 8 Ericsson

propensity 4 bent, bias, turn 5 fancy, favor, taste 6 liking 7 leaning 8 affinity, penchant, pleasure, sympathy, tendency, weakness 9 prejudice 10 attraction, partiality, preference, proclivity 11 disposition, inclination 12 predilection 14 predisposition

proper 3 apt, fit, own 4 meet, nice, true 5 per se, right 6 decent, marked, modest, polite, seemly 7 apropos, correct, express, fitting, germane, precise, typical 8 assigned, becoming, decorous, orthodox, peculiar, relevant, specific, suitable 9 befitting, courteous, pertinent 10 acceptable, applicable, individual, particular, respective 11 appropriate, conformable, distinctive 12 conventional 14 characteristic, distinguishing, representative

  French: 11 comme il faut

properly 5 aptly, right 7 exactly 8 decently, politely, suitably 9 correctly, perfectly, precisely 10 acceptably, accurately, decorously, tastefully 12 without error 13 appropriately 14 conventionally

property 4 hold, land, mark 5 acres, badge, funds, goods, means, point, stock, title, trait 6 aspect, assets, estate, moneys, realty, wealth 7 acreage, capital, earmark, effects, estates, feature, grounds, quality 8 chattels, holdings, treasure 9 attribute, ownership, resources, territory 10 belongings, real estate 11 investments, peculiarity, possessions, singularity 12 appointments, idiosyncrasy 13 individuality, particularity 14 characteristic, proprietorship

prophecy 6 augury 7 portent 8 forecast 10 divination, prediction, revelation 15 prognostication
  god of: 6 Apollo 7 Phoebus, Pythius 9 Musagetes

prophesy 4 warn 5 augur 6 divine 7 forbode, foresee, portend, predict, presage 8 forecast, foretell, forewarn, soothsay 9 apprehend, premonish 13 prognosticate

prophet 4 seer 5 augur, guide, sibyl 6 oracle 7 diviner, palmist, seeress 8 preacher, sorcerer 9 Cassandra, divinator, geomancer, predictor, sorceress 10 evangelist, forecaster, foreteller, prophesier, prophetess, soothsayer 11 clairvoyant, intercessor, interpreter 12 crystal gazer 13 fortuneteller 14 prognosticator

Prophet, major 6 Baruch, Daniel, Elijah, Isaiah 7 Ezekiel 8 Jeremiah

Prophet, minor 3 Gad 4 Amos, Joel 5 Hosea, Jonah, Micah, Nahum 6 Haggai, Nathan 7 Malachi, Obadiah 8 Habakkuk 9 Zechariah, Zephaniah

Prophetess 4 Anna 6 Miriam 7 Deborah

prophetic, prophetical 5 vatic 6 mantic 7 fateful, ominous 8 oracular 10 portentous, predictive, presageful

Prophetic Books
  author: 12 William Blake

Prophet of famine 11 Agabus

prophylactic 8 hygienic 10 preventive 13 contraceptive

propinquity 7 kinship 8 affinity, nearness, vicinity 9 closeness, proximity 10 similarity

propitiate 4 calm 5 allay 6 pacify, soothe 7 appease, assuage, mollify, placate 10 conciliate 11 accommodate

propitiation 8 soothing 11 appeasement 12 conciliation, pacification

propitious 3 fit 5 bonny, happy, lucky 6 benign, golden 8 suitable 9 agreeable, favorable, fortunate, opportune, promising, welltimed 10 auspicious, beneficial, felicitous 12 advantageous, providential

Propoetides
  form: 7 maidens
  home: 6 Cypria
  changed into: 5 stone
  angered: 9 Aphrodite
  denied her: 8 divinity

proponent 6 backer, friend, patron, votary 7 booster 8 advocate, champion, defender, endorser, espouser, exponent, partisan, upholder 9 apologist, spokesman, supporter 10 enthusiast, vindicator 14 representative

proportion 5 ratio 7 balance, harmony 8 evenness, symmetry 9 agreement 11 consistency, correlation, perspective 12 distribution, relationship 14 commensuration, correspondence

proportionate 5 equal 8 balanced 10 comparable, equivalent 12 commensurate 13 commensurable, corresponding

proportions 3 fit, lot 4 area, bulk, form, gear, mass, part, size, span 5 adapt, gauge, grade, match, order, poise, quota, range, ratio, scope, shape, share, width 6 amount, degree, equate, extent, spread, volume 7 balance, breadth, conform, correct, expanse, measure, portion, rectify, segment 8 capacity, division, equalize, fraction, graduate, modulate, regulate 9 amplitude, apportion, greatness, harmonize, magnitude 10 dimensions 12 measurements

proposal 3 bid 4 idea, plan, plot, suit 5 draft, offer 6 appeal, course, design, motion, scheme, sketch, theory 7 outline, proffer, program, project 8 overture, prospect 9 stratagem 10 conception, invitation, nomination, prospectus, resolution, suggestion 11 proposition 12 presentation 14 recommendation

propose 3 aim, woo 4 hope, mean, plan, plot 6 aspire, design, expect, intend, scheme, submit, tender 7 advance, present, proffer, purpose, suggest, venture 8 affiance, propound, put forth, set about, set forth 9 determine, have a mind, introduce, recommend, undertake 10 come up with, have in mind, have in view, put forward 11 contemplate 14 pop the question 21 offer for consideration

proposition 4 deal, pass, plan 5 issue, offer, point, topic 6 matter, scheme 7 advance, bargain, solicit, subject 8 contract, proposal, question 9 agreement, assurance, guarantee 10 resolution, suggestion 11 make a pass at, negotiation, stipulation, undertaking 14 recommendation

propound 4 pose 5 boost 6 assert 7 advance, profess, propose 8 put forth, set forth

proprieties 7 decorum, manners 8 protocol 9 amenities, etiquette 10 civilities 11 conventions

proprietor 5 owner 6 holder, master 7 manager 8 landlord 9 landowner, possessor 10 landholder 11 titleholder 12 proprietress

propriety 7 aptness, decorum, dignity, fitness 8 courtesy 9 etiquette, formality, rightness 10 seemliness 11 correctness, good manners, savoir faire 12 becomingness, decorousness, good behavior, suitableness 13 applicability 14 respectability 15 appropriateness

propulsion 6 launch, thrust 9 launching 10 propelling

prop up 5 brace 7 bolster, support 8 buttress

prorate 6 divide 9 apportion 10 distribute

Prorsa see 9 Antevorta

prosaic 3 dry 4 blah, dull, flat 5 prosy, stale, trite, vapid, wordy 6 common, jejune 7 humdrum, tedious 8 ordinary, plebeian, tiresome 9 hackneyed 10 monotonous, pedestrian, spiritless, unpoetical 12 matter-of-fact 13 platitudinous, unimaginative, uninteresting

Prosclystius
epithet of: 8 Poseidon
means: 7 flooder

proscribe 3 ban 4 damn 5 curse, exile 6 banish, forbid, outlaw 7 boycott, censure, condemn 8 denounce, prohibit 9 interdict, repudiate 10 disapprove 12 anathematize 13 excommunicate

proscription 3 ban 7 barring, censure 8 anathema 9 interdict 11 forbiddance, prohibition 12 condemnation, denunciation, interdiction 15 excommunication

prose 3 dry 4 dull 5 novel 7 fiction, quality, tedious, writing 8 sequence 9 discourse 10 expression 11 commonplace 13 unimaginative

prosecute 3 sue, try 4 wage 6 direct, go with, handle, indict, manage, pursue 7 arraign, carry on, conduct, execute, go to law, perform, prolong, stick to, sustain 8 continue, deal with, follow up, maintain 9 discharge, persist in 10 administer, put on trial, see through 11 take to court 12 bring to trial 14 bring to justice

prosecution 4 suit 6 action 7 conduct, pursuit 11 performance 14 administration

Proserpina see 10 Persephone

prosit 11 may it do good
used as: 5 toast

prospect, prospects 4 hope, plan, seek, view 5 scene, vista 6 aspect, design, search, vision 7 chances, explore, go after, look for, outlook, picture, promise, scenery 8 ambition, panorama, proposal 9 candidate, foretaste, intention, landscape, work a mine 10 expectancy, likelihood 11 expectation, possibility, probability 12 anticipation 13 contemplation

prospective 4 to be 6 coming, future, in view, likely, to come 7 looming 8 destined, eventual, expected, foreseen, hoped-for, intended, possible 9 about to be, impending, in the wind, looked-for, potential, promising 10 in prospect 11 approaching, forthcoming, threatening

prosper 4 gain 5 get on 6 flower, thrive 7 advance, succeed 8 fare well, flourish, fructify, get ahead, grow rich, increase, make good, progress 9 bear fruit 15 make one's fortune

prosperity 4 ease, gain 6 luxury, plenty, profit, wealth 7 advance, success, welfare 8 good luck, progress 9 abundance, advantage, affluence, blessings, golden age,

good times, palmy days, run of luck, well-being 11 advancement, good fortune
god of: 4 Frey 5 Freyr, Niord, Njord 12 Bonus Eventus
goddess of: 5 Salus

Prospero
character in: 10 The Tempest
author: 11 Shakespeare

prosperous 4 fair, good, rich, rosy 5 happy, lucky, sunny 6 bright, golden, timely 7 hopeful, moneyed, opulent, smiling, wealthy, well-off 8 affluent, cheering, pleasing, thriving, well-to-do 9 favorable, fortunate, opportune, promising 10 auspicious, heartening, of good omen, propitious, reassuring, successful 11 comfortable, encouraging, flourishing 12 on easy street

Pross, Miss
character in: 16 A Tale of Two Cities
author: 7 Dickens

prostitute 4 bawd, jade, slut, tart 5 abuse, hussy, lower, spoil, whore 6 chippy, debase, defile, demean, floozy, harlot, hooker, misuse 7 cheapen, corrupt, debauch, degrade, hustler, pervert, profane, sell out, trollop 8 call girl, misapply, strumpet 9 courtesan, desecrate, misdirect, misemploy 12 streetwalker 14 lady of the night

prostrate 4 deck, flat 5 abase, floor, prone, spent 6 fagged, kowtow 7 bow down, flatten, laid out, worn out 8 bowed low, overcome 9 bone weary, crouching, dead tired, exhausted, kneel down, lying flat, overthrow, recumbent 10 beseeching, horizontal 11 on one's knees 12 on bended knee, stretched out, supplicating 13 lying face down 15 fall to one's knees

prostration 3 bow, woe 5 grief 6 misery, sorrow 7 anguish, despair 8 distress, kneeling, weakness 9 abasement, dejection, heartache, impotence, lowliness, paralysis, weariness 10 depression, desolation, enervation, exhaustion, subjection, submission 11 desperation, despondency 12 genuflection, helplessness, wretchedness 13 depth of misery

prosy 4 dull, flat 5 banal, inane 6 stupid 7 humdrum, prosaic, tedious 9 wearisome 11 commonplace 13 uninteresting

protagonist 4 diva, hero, lead, star 7 heroine 9 headliner, principal, superstar, title role 10 leading man, prima donna 11 leading lady 12 danseur noble, jeune premier 13 jeune premiere, main character 14 prima ballerina 16 central character

protect 4 hide, keep, save, tend, veil 5 cover, guard 6 defend, harbor, screen, secure, shield 7 care for, shelter, sustain 8 conserve, maintain, preserve 9 look after, safeguard, watch over 10 take care of

protected 4 safe 5 saved 6 immune, secure 7 guarded, secured 8 anchored, defended, shielded 9 sheltered 10 inviolable 12 invulnerable

protection 3 aid 4 care, keep, wall 5 cover, fence, guard, haven, shade 6 asylum, buffer, charge, harbor, refuge, safety, saving, screen, shield 7 barrier, custody, defense, shelter, support 8 guarding, immunity, preserve, security 9 preserver, safeguard, sanctuary 10 assistance 11 safekeeping 12 championship, conservation, guardianship, preservation

protective 7 careful, heedful 8 fatherly, guarding, maternal, motherly, paternal, sisterly, vigilant, watchful 9 avuncular, brotherly, defensive, shielding 10 preventive, sheltering, solicitous 11 safekeeping 12 big-brotherly, safeguarding

protective covering 4 coat, husk, mail 5 armor, shell 6 shield 7 coating, plating 8 carapace 10 coat of mail 11 suit of armor 12 armor plating

protectorate 6 colony 7 mandate 8 province, dominion 9 satellite, territory 10 dependency, possession, settlement

protege 4 ward 5 pupil 6 charge 7 student, trainee 9 dependent

pro tempore 9 temporary 11 temporarily 15 for the time being

Protesilaus
father: 8 Iphiclus
brother: 8 Podarces
wife: 8 Laodamia

protest 3 vow 4 aver, avow, beef, deny, kick 5 gripe, march, offer, sit-in, speak, state 6 affirm, allege, assert, assure, attest, avouch, cry out, insist, object, oppose, strike 7 boycott, contend, declare, dispute, dissent, hold out, profess, testify 8 announce, complain, demurral, disagree, maintain, propound, put forth, set forth 9 enunciate, objection, picketing, pronounce 10 asseverate, contradict, controvert, disapprove, disclaimer, dissidence, opposition, put forward, resistance 11 beg to differ, deprecation 12 disaffection, disagreement, remonstrance, renunciation 13 contradiction, demonstration, remonstration, take exception 14 discountenance

Protestant 5 Amish 6 Mormon, Quaker, Shaker 7 Baptist, Puritan 8 Anglican, Huguenot, Lutheran 9 Adventist, Calvinist, Methodist, Unitarian 12 Episcopalian, Presbyterian 17 Congregationalist 18 Christian Scientist

protest meeting 5 rally 13 demonstration

Proteus
character in: 20 Two Gentlemen of Verona
author: 11 Shakespeare

Proteus
god of: 3 sea
king of: 5 Egypt
father: 7 Oceanus
mother: 6 Tethys
wife: 8 Psamathe
son: 12 Theoclymenus
daughter: 7 Theonoe
gift: 8 prophesy 12 form-changing 13 shape-changing

Prothoenor
leader of: 9 Boeotians

Protoceratops
type: 8 dinosaur 10 ceratopsid
period: 10 Cretaceous
location: 8 Mongolia 10 Gobi Desert
characteristic: 6 horned 7 armored

protocol 5 usage 7 customs, decorum, manners 8 good form 9 amenities, etiquette, formality, standards 11 conventions, proprieties 14 code of behavior, court etiquette, diplomatic code 17 dictates of society

Protogonia
father: 10 Erechtheus
mother: 9 Praxithea
sister: 7 Otionia

prototypal 5 model 7 classic 9 exemplary 10 archetypal, definitive 12 prototypical

prototype 5 model 7 example 8 original 9 archetype

protozoan 4 cell 5 ameba, cilia 6 amoeba 7 euglena 8 flagella, protista 9 eukaryote, pseudopod 10 paramecium, plasmodium 11 microscopic, unicellular 17 nonphotosynthetic

protract 6 extend, keep up 7 drag out, draw out, prolong, spin out 8 lengthen 9 keep going 10 stretch out

protracted 4 long 7 lengthy 8 drawn-out, extended 9 continued, long-lived, prolonged 10 lengthened, persistent 11 long-lasting

protraction 4 stay 7 lasting 9 extension 10 continuing, drawing out 11 continuance, dragging out, persistence 12 perseverance, prolongation

protrude 5 belly, bulge, swell 6 jut out 7 project 8 stand out, stick out 11 push forward

protrusion 4 bump, hump 6 hernia 8 swelling 9 extension 10 projection 12 prolongation, protuberance

protuberance 3 bow 4 bump, hump, knob, knot, lump, node, weal, welt 5 bulge, gnarl, ridge 6 rising 8 swelling 9 convexity, elevation, roundness 10 projection, prominence 11 excrescence, excurvature

protura
class: 8 hexapoda
phylum: 10 arthropoda
characteristic: 5 small 6 minute 7 eyeless 8 wingless

proud 4 fine, smug, vain 5 aloof, cocky, grand, great, happy, lofty, noble 6 august, lordly, snooty, snotty, strict, uppish, uppity 7 bloated, exalted, haughty, high-hat, pleased, pompous, revered, stately, storied, stuck-up, swollen 8 affected, arrogant, assuming, boastful, braggart, bragging, elevated, euphoric, glorious, inflated, insolent, majestic, prideful, puffed up, reserved, snobbish 9 admirable, cherished, conceited, contented, delighted, dignified, flaunting, gratified, honorable, imperious, know-it-all, satisfied, venerable 10 complacent, disdainful, high-minded, intolerant,

principled, scrupulous 11 egotistical, independent, magnificent, overbearing, patronizing, punctilious 12 contemptuous, self-praising, supercilious, vainglorious 13 condescending, distinguished, high-and-mighty, self-important, self-satisfied 14 self-respecting, self-sufficient

Proudie, Dr
character in: 16 Barchester Towers
author: 8 Trollope

Proust, Marcel
author of: 23 Remembrance of Things Past 24 A la Recherche du Temps Perdu

prove 3 try 4 test 5 check, end up, probe 6 affirm, attest, result, try out, uphold, verify, wind up 7 analyze, bear out, certify, confirm, examine, justify, support, sustain, warrant, witness 8 document, evidence, look into, make good, manifest, result in, validate 9 ascertain, establish, eventuate, testify to 11 corroborate, demonstrate 12 authenticate, substantiate

proved 5 known 6 proven, upheld 8 affirmed, attested, borne out, verified 9 certified, confirmed, supported, sustained, warranted; witnessed 10 documented 11 established 12 corroborated, demonstrable 13 authenticated, substantiated

prove false 5 belie 6 refute, reject 7 explode 8 disprove 9 discredit 10 invalidate

proven 5 known 6 proved, upheld 8 accepted, affirmed, attested, borne out, verified 9 certified, confirmed, supported, sustained, warranted, witnessed 10 documented, verifiable 11 established 12 corroborated, demonstrable 13 authenticated, substantiated

provender 3 hay 4 chow, corn, eats, feed, food, grub, oats 5 grain 6 fodder, forage, ration, viands 7 nurture 10 provisions 11 subsistence

proverb 3 mot, saw 5 adage, axiom, maxim, moral, motto 6 byword, cliche, dictum, saying, truism 7 bromide, epigram, precept 8 aphorism, apothegm 9 platitude 11 commonplace 13 accepted truth, popular saying

prove wrong 5 belie 6 expose, refute 7 explode 8 disprove 9 discredit

provide 3 arm, fit, pay 4 give, plan 5 allow, award, cater, equip, grant, offer, state, yield 6 accord, afford, bestow, confer, donate, impart, outfit, render, save up, submit, supply, tender 7 arrange, deliver, furnish, prepare, present, produce, require, specify 8 dispense, get ready 9 make plans, postulate, stipulate 10 accumulate, contribute

provide for 7 care for 8 attend to, wait upon 9 look after 10 minister to, take care of

providence 8 prudence 9 foresight, husbandry, provision 11 forethought 14 circumspection, farsightedness, forehandedness

provident 4 wary 5 chary, ready 6 frugal, saving 7 careful, prudent, thrifty 8 cautious, discreet, equipped, vigilant 9 farseeing, judicious 10 discerning, economical, farsighted, forehanded, foreseeing, thoughtful 11 circumspect, foresighted, precautious 12 parsimonious, well-prepared

province 3 job 4 area, duty, part, role, zone 5 field, place, state 6 canton, charge, county, domain, office, region, sphere 7 section, station 8 business, capacity, function 9 authority, bailiwick, territory 10 assignment, department 11 subdivision 12 jurisdiction 13 scope of duties 14 arrondissement, responsibility

provincial 4 rude 5 crude, gawky, local, rough, rural 6 clumsy, gauche, homely, narrow, oafish, rustic 7 awkward, boorish, bucolic, country, hayseed, insular, loutish 8 cloddish, clownish, down-home, homespun, regional, yokelish 9 backwoods, parochial, small-town, unrefined 10 unpolished 11 clodhopping, countrified, territorial 15 unsophisticated

provision 6 giving 8 donation 9 endowment, providing, supplying 10 furnishing

provisional 6 acting, pro tem 7 interim 9 surrogate, temporary, tentative 10 substitute 11 conditional 12 probationary 15 for the time being

provisions 4 feed, food, term 6 clause, fodder, forage, stores, string, viands 7 article, commons, edibles, proviso 8 eatables, supplies, victuals 9 condition, groceries, provender, readiness, requisite 10 limitation, obligation, precaution, sustenance 11 arrangement, comestibles, forethought, preparation, requirement, reservation, restriction, stipulation, wherewithal 12 anticipation, modification 13 qualification 14 forehandedness, prearrangement

proviso 5 rider 6 clause, string 8 addition 9 amendment, condition 10 limitation 11 requirement, restriction, stipulation 12 modification 13 qualification

provocation 4 goad, spur 5 cause, pique 6 insult, slight 7 affront, offense 8 prodding, stimulus, vexation 9 actuation, annoyance 10 excitation, incitement, irritation, motivation 11 aggravation, fomentation, instigation, stimulation 12 perturbation

provocative 4 sexy 6 vexing 7 irksome 8 alluring, annoying, arousing, exciting, inviting, tempting 9 beguiling, provoking, ravishing, seductive, thrilling, vexatious 10 attractive, bewitching, enchanting, entrancing, intriguing, irritating 11 aggravating, captivating, fascinating, stimulating, tantalizing 12 intoxicating, irresistible

provoke 3 irk, vex 4 fire, gall, move, rile, stir 5 anger, annoy, cause, chafe, evoke, grate, impel, pique, rouse 6 arouse, awaken, compel, create, effect, elicit, enrage, excite, foment, incite, induce, kindle, madden, prompt, put out, stir up 7 actuate, agitate, animate, bring on, incense, in-flame, inspire, outrage, produce, quicken 8 generate, get to one, irritate, motivate 9 aggravate, call forth, establish, galvanize, infuriate, instigate, stimulate 10 bring about, exasperate, give rise to 11 get one's goat, put in motion 15 try one's patience 16 get under one's skin

prow 3 bow 4 stem 5 front 10 forward end

prowess 4 grit, guts 5 knack, might, nerve, power, skill, spunk, valor, vigor 6 daring, genius, mettle, spirit, talent 7 ability, bravery, courage, faculty, heroism, know-how, stamina 8 aptitude, boldness, strength 9 adeptness, derring-do, endurance, fortitude, gallantry, hardihood 10 competence, expertness 11 intrepidity, proficiency 12 fearlessness, skillfulness 13 dauntlessness 14 accomplishment

prowl 4 hunt, lurk, roam 5 creep, range, skulk, slink, snack, stalk, steal 6 ramble 8 scavenge

prowler 7 burglar 10 peeping Tom 16 suspicious person

proximate 4 near 5 close 6 beside, nearby, next to 8 adjacent, imminent, next-door 11 forthcoming

proximity 7 presence 8 locality, nearness, vicinity 9 closeness 10 contiguity 11 propinquity 12 togetherness

proxy 3 sub 4 vote 5 agent 6 ballot, deputy 7 stand-in 9 alternate 10 substitute

prude 4 prig 6 prissy 7 puritan 8 hypocrite 10 goody-goody 13 prim and proper

prudence 4 care, tact 5 thrift, wisdom 7 caution, economy 9 austerity, foresight, frugality, parsimony 10 discretion, precaution 11 calculation, thriftiness 14 thoughtfulness

prudent 4 sage, sane, wary, wise 5 chary 6 frugal, saving, shrewd 7 careful, guarded, heedful, politic, sapient, sparing, thrifty 8 cautious, discreet, prepared, rational, sensible, vigilant 9 expedient, judicious, provident, sagacious, wideawake 10 discerning, economical, farsighted, prudential, reflecting, thoughtful 11 circumspect, considerate, foresighted, levelheaded, precautious, well-advised 13 self-possessed

Prud'hon, Pierre-Paul
    born: 5 Cluny 9 France
    artwork: 14 Venus and Adonis 15 The Rape of Psyche 16 Empress Josephine 33 Crime Pursued by Vengeance and Justice 38 Justice and Divine Vengeance Pursuing Crime

prudish 3 shy 4 prim, smug 5 timid 6 demure, modest, prissy, queasy, stuffy 7 finical, mincing, precise, stilted 8 pedantic, priggish, skittish, starched 9 squeamish, Victorian 10 fastidious, old-maidish, overmodest, particular 11 punctilious, puritanical, straitlaced 13 sanctimonious, self-righteous

prudishness 8 primness 10 prissiness, puritanism 11 overmodesty 12 overdelicacy, priggishness 14 overrefinement

prudish phrase 9 euphemism 10 bowdlerism

prune 3 cut, lop 4 clip, crop, pull, snip, thin, trim 5 shear 6 reduce 7 abridge, clarify, curtail, shorten, thin out 8 condense, simplify 10 abbreviate

prunelle
  type: 7 liqueur
  origin: 6 France
  flavor: 4 plum

pruning 6 digest 8 clipping, snipping, synopsis, trimming 10 shortening 11 abridgement, cutting back, cut-down form 12 abbreviation, condensation

prurient 4 lewd, sexy 6 carnal 7 fleshy, goatish, immoral, lustful, obscene, priapic, satyric 9 lecherous, salacious 10 hot-blooded, lascivious, libidinous, licentious, lubricious, passionate 12 concupiscent

pry 4 butt, nose, peek, peer, poke, tear, work, worm 5 break, crack, delve, force, jimmy, lever, mix in, prize, probe, smoke, sniff, snoop, wrest, wring 6 butt in, ferret, horn in, meddle, search, winkle, wrench 7 explore, extract, inquire, intrude, squeeze 9 interfere, intervene 15 stick one's nose in

Pryderi
  origin: 5 Welsh
  father: 5 Pwyll
  mother: 8 Rhiannon
  stolen by: 5 Gwawl
  wife: 5 Kicva

prying 4 busy, nosy 7 peering, raising, seeking 8 levering, snooping 9 searching 10 intrusive, meddling 11 inquisitive

Prylis
  father: 6 Hermes

Prynne, Hester
  character in: 16 The Scarlet Letter
  author: 9 Hawthorne

Pryor, Richard
  born: 8 Peoria IL
  roles: 6 The Wiz 9 Stir Crazy 12 Silver Streak 17 Lady Sings the Blues 19 Uptown Saturday Night

Prytanis
  ally of: 8 Sarpedon
  killed by: 8 Odysseus

psalm 3 ode 4 hymn, poem, song 5 canon, chant, verse 6 praise 7 cantata, glorify, introit 8 canticle

Psalter 12 Book of Psalms

Psamathe
  member of: 6 Nereid
  form: 8 princess
  husband: 7 Proteus
  son: 5 Linus 6 Phocus 12 Theoclymenus
  daughter: 7 Theonoe

pseudo 4 fake, mock, sham 5 bogus, false, phony 6 forged 7 feigned 8 spurious 9 pretended, simulated, soi-disant 10 fictitious, fraudulent, self-styled 11 counterfeit, make-believe 13 self-described

pseudonym 5 alias 6 anonym 7 pen name 8 cognomen, nickname 9 false name, sobriquet, stage name 11 assumed name 16 professional name
  French: 10 nom de plume 11 nom de guerre 12 nom de theatre

pseudonymic 7 assumed 10 fictitious 12 pseudonymous

pseudonymous 7 assumed 10 fictitious 11 pseudonymic

Psittacosaurus
  type: 8 dinosaur 10 ceratopsid
  period: 10 Cretaceous

psocoptera
  class: 8 hexapoda
  phylum: 10 arthropoda
  group: 8 booklice

psyche 2 id 3 ego 4 mind, self, soul 5 anima 6 bowels, make up, spirit 8 superego 10 penetralia 11 personality, unconscious 12 subconscious

Psyche
  personifies: 4 soul
  loved by: 4 Eros 5 Cupid
  daughter: 8 Voluptas

psychic 5 augur 6 medium, mental, mystic, occult, voyant 7 diviner, prophet, voyante 8 cerebral 9 paragnost, sensitive, spiritual 10 soothsayer, telepathic 11 clairvoyant, telekinetic, telepathist 12 extrasensory, intellectual, spiritualist, supernatural, supersensory 13 preternatural

Psycho
  director: 15 Alfred Hitchcock
  cast: 9 John Gavin, Vera Miles 10 Janet Leigh 12 Martin Balsam 14 Anthony Perkins
  score: 15 Bernard Herrmann

psychoanalysis 7 therapy 8 analysis 14 physchotherapy

psychoanalyst 6 shrink 7 analyst 12 headshrinker

psychologist/psychiatrist
  American: 4 Hall, Hull 5 Dewey, James, Lewin 6 Harlow, Horney, Miller, Rogers, Terman, Tolman, Watson, Witmer 7 Cattell, Chomsky, Erikson, Goddard, Guthrie, Johnson, Masters, Skinner 8 Brothers, Wechsler 9 Thorndike 10 Westheimer
  Austrian: 5 Adler, Freud, Reich
  British: 5 Ellis 7 Eysenck 9 Titchener
  French: 5 Binet
  German: 5 Wundt 6 Koffka, Kohler 7 Fechner 9 Helmholtz, Kraepelin 10 Ebbinghaus, Wertheimer 11 Krafft-Ebing
  Russian: 6 Pavlov
  Swiss: 4 Jung 6 Piaget

psychology 4 head, mind 6 makeup 7 feeling 8 attitude 15 mental processes
  problem/illness: 6 phobia 7 obesity, smoking 8 hysteria, neuroses, paranoia, schizoid 9 drug abuse, obsession, psychoses 10 alcoholism, compulsion, depression 11 sociopathic 13 schizophrenia 14 sexual deviance 15 anxiety reaction 17 passive-aggressive
  term: 2 id 3 ego 6 libido 7 empathy 8

neuroses, superego 9 catatonic, cognition, psychoses 10 inhibition, repression 11 behaviorism, unconscious 12 conditioning, transference 13 actualization, Rorschach test 14 identification, Oedipus complex 19 operant conditioning 20 behavior modification

type: 4 social 7 Gestalt 8 abnormal, clinical 9 cognitive 10 industrial 11 educational 12 experimental 13 developmental, physiological, psychometrics, psychophysics

psychopomp
  conductor of spirits to: 5 Hades 10 otherworld
  epithet: 12 psychopompus
  epithet of: 6 Charon, Hermes

psychosis 8 dementia, insanity, neurosis, paranoia 9 paranomia, unreality 10 pathomania 12 hallucinosis 13 schizophrenia 14 mental disorder

psychotherapy 7 therapy 8 analysis 14 psychoanalysis

psychotic 3 mad, nut 4 kook, loon 5 crazy, kooky, loony, nutty 6 insane, madman, maniac 7 lunatic 8 demented, deranged 9 disturbed 10 psychopath 12 insane person, psychopathic 15 non compos mentis

Ptah
  origin: 8 Egyptian
  diety of: 17 universal creation
  worshiped at: 7 Memphis

Pterelaus
  descendant of: 8 Poseidon
  mother: 9 Hippothoe
  daughter: 8 Comaetho

Ptolemy
  author of: 8 Almagest 9 Geography

Ptous
  father: 7 Athamas
  mother: 8 Themisto

pub 3 bar, inn 5 local 6 bistro, saloon, lounge, tavern 7 bar room, ginmill, rummery, rum shop, taproom 8 alehouse, grogshop, pothouse 9 road house, speakeasy 10 beer parlor 11 public house

pubescent 7 teenage 8 immature, juvenile 10 adolescent

public 3 mob 4 folk, open 5 civic, civil, frank, overt, plain, state, trade 6 buyers, common, in view, masses, nation, patent, people, shared, social 7 evident, exposed, general, in sight, obvious, outward, patrons, popular, society, visible 8 apparent, audience, communal, divulged, everyone, manifest, national, passable, populace, revealed, societal, unbarred, unfenced 9 available, citizenry, clientele, community, disclosed, followers, following, free to all, hoi polloi, multitude, notorious, political, statewide, unabashed, unashamed, unbounded, used by all 10 accessible, attendance, nationwide, not private, observable, population, purchasers, recognized, supporters, unenclosed 11 body politic, bourgeoisie, commonality, conspicuous, countrywide, discernible, perceivable, pro-

letariat, rank and file, unconcealed, undisguised 12 acknowledged, constituency, unobstructed, unrestricted 14 community-owned

publication 4 book, news 5 issue, paper 6 digest, report 7 edition, gazette, journal, tabloid 8 bulletin, magazine, pamphlet 9 broadcast, newspaper 10 periodical 11 circulation, information 12 announcement, notification

public disturbance 4 riot 6 fracas, ruckus, uproar 7 turmoil 9 commotion

public house 3 bar, pub 5 local 6 saloon, tavern 7 gin mill, taproom 8 alehouse 9 roadhouse

publicity 4 hype, plug, puff 5 blurb, flack 7 build-up, puffery, write-up 8 ballyhoo, currency 9 attention, notoriety, promotion 10 propaganda, publicness 11 advertising, circulation, information 12 promulgation, public notice, salesmanship

publicize 4 hype, plug, puff, push, sell 6 herald 7 acclaim, promote 8 announce, ballyhoo, emblazon, proclaim 9 advertise, broadcast, make known, propagate 10 make public, promulgate 11 circularize 12 propagandize

publicly
  Latin: 11 coram populo

public matter
  Latin: 10 res publica

public notice 5 edict, ukase 6 decree 8 bulletin 9 manifesto 12 proclamation 13 pronouncement 14 pronunciamento
  French: 7 affiche

public speaking 7 oratory 9 lecturing 12 speechmaking

public-spirited 8 generous 10 altruistic, benevolent 12 humanitarian

publish 3 air 4 tell, vent 5 issue, print, utter 6 herald, impart, put out, spread 7 declare, diffuse, divulge, give out, placard, promote, release, trumpet 8 announce, bring out, disclose, proclaim 9 advertise, broadcast, circulate, make known, propagate, publicize 10 make public, promulgate, put to press 11 communicate, disseminate

Puca
  also: 5 Pooka
  origin: 5 Irish
  form: 6 spirit
  corresponds to: 4 Puck

Puccini, Giacomo
  born: 5 Italy, Lucca
  composer of: 5 Tosca 8 La Boheme, Turandot 12 Manon Lescaut 14 Madam Butterfly 15 Madama Butterfly 18 La Fanciulla del West 22 The Girl of the Golden West

puce 3 red 7 dark red 13 purplish-brown

Puck
  also: 15 Robin Goodfellow
  character in: 21 A Midsummer Night's Dream
  author: 11 Shakespeare
  form: 6 spirit
  characteristic: 11 mischievous

corresponds to: 4 Puca 5 Pooka

pucker 4 fold, tuck 5 pinch, pleat, prune 6 crease, gather, ruffle, rumple, shrink 7 crinkle, crumble, squeeze, wrinkle 8 compress, contract 12 draw together

puckered 6 pursed, rucked, tucked 7 creased, crinkly, pinched, pleated 8 crinkled, gathered, wrinkled 10 compressed, corrugated

puckish 5 elfin 6 impish 7 playful 8 annoying 9 whimsical 11 mischievous

pudding 5 jello 6 junket 7 custard, dessert, tapioca 8 pandowdy 9 charlotte, yorkshire 14 floating island

pudgy, podgy 3 fat 5 buxom, dumpy, obese, plump, squat, stout, tubby 6 chubby, chunky, fleshy, rotund, stocky, stubby 7 paunchy 8 roly-poly, thickset

Pueblo (Cliff Dwellers)
language family: 4 Tewa, Zuni 6 Queres, Tanoan 10 Shoshonean
tribe: 4 Hopi, Tiwa, Towa, Tuei 5 Acoma, Kiowa 6 Isleta
location: 4 Utah 7 Arizona 8 Colorado 9 New Mexico
noted for: 5 adobe 12 architecture
spirit: 7 Kachina 8 Katchina

puerile 3 raw 5 green, inane, petty, silly, vapid 6 callow, simple 7 babyish, foolish, trivial 8 childish, immature, juvenile, piddling 9 childlike, frivolous, infantile, senseless, worthless 10 irrational, ridiculous, sophomoric 11 harebrained, nonsensical

Puerto Rico
name means: 8 rich port
other name: 9 Borinquen 15 San Juan Bautista
capital/largest city: 7 San Juan
others: 5 Cayey, Coamo, Lares, Ponce 6 Caguas, Dorado, Manati, Utuado 7 Arecibo, Bayamon, Fajardo, Guanica, Guayama, Humacao 8 Adjuntas, Cabo Rojo, Mayaguez 9 Aquadilla 11 Santa Isabel
government: 32 self-governing commonwealth of the U S
measure: 6 cuerda 10 caballeria
island: 4 Mona 7 Culebra, Vieques 13 Caja de Muertos 15 Greater Antilles
lake: 5 Loiza 6 Carite 8 Dos Bocas 9 Caonillas, Guatajaca
mountain: 4 Toro 5 Cayey 6 Yunque 8 Guilarte, Luquilla 10 Torrecilla 17 Cordilera Central
highest point: 5 Punta
river: 5 Camuy, Canas, Loiza, Yauco 6 Anasco, Manati, Tanama 7 Arecibo, Fajardo, La Plata 9 Caonillas
sea: 8 Atlantic 9 Caribbean
physical feature:
bay: 5 Sucia 6 Rincon 8 Boqueron 9 Aquadilla 14 Phosphorescent
sound: 7 Vieques
people: 6 gibaro 10 borinqueno
explorer: 8 Columbus 11 Ponce de Leon
leader: 10 Munoz Marin
language: 7 English, Spanish

religion: 10 Protestant 13 Roman Catholic

place:
area of San Juan: 7 Hato Rey 10 Rio Piedras
beach: 7 Condado
cathedral: 15 San Juan Bautista
fortress: 7 El Morro 11 San Jeronimo 12 San Cristobal
governor's residence: 11 La Fortaleza
museum: 14 El Museo de Porice
reservoir: 5 Loiza
tomb: 11 Ponce de Leon
feature:
bird: 4 rola 7 yeguita
festival: 6 Casals
housing development: 14 urbanizaciones
song: 9 aguinaldo
strolling musicians: 9 parrandas
tree: 4 mora 5 yafua, yaray 8 emajagua, guayrote 10 guaranguao
food:
dish: 4 sama, sisi 9 moreillas 11 lechon asado
drink: 3 rum 10 anis-golila

puff 3 bow 4 blow, draw, emit, gasp, hump, node, pant, plug, suck, wisp 5 bloat, blurb, bulge, heave, smoke, swell, whiff 6 blow up, breath, dilate, exhale, expand, extend, flurry, inhale, rising, wheeze 7 bluster, bombast, distend, inflate, puffery, stretch 8 ballyhoo, be winded, dilation, encomium, flattery, flummery, swelling 9 convexity, discharge, elevation, euphemism, extension, inflation, panegyric, publicity, sales talk 10 be inflated, distention, exhalation, overpraise, protrusion, tuberosity 11 be distended, breathe hard, excrescence, excurvature 12 exaggeration, inflammation, protuberance, protuberancy 13 overlaudation 16 overcommendation 17 misrepresentation

puffed 5 baggy 7 bulbous, swollen 9 ballooned

puffed up 4 vain 5 proud, puffy 7 swollen 8 inflated 9 conceited 11 swell-headed 12 vainglorious 13 self-important

puffery 4 hype 7 big talk, bluster, bombast 9 hyperbole 11 braggadocio

puff out 5 bloat, bulge, swell 6 billow, expand 7 balloon, distend, enlarge, inflate

puffy 3 fat 5 round 6 fleshy 7 bloated, bulging, swollen 8 enlarged, expanded, inflamed; inflated, puffed up 9 corpulent, distended

pugilist 3 pug 5 boxer 7 battler, bruiser, fighter 12 prizefighter

pugnacious 7 defiant, hostile, warlike 8 menacing, militant 9 bellicose, combative, fractious 10 aggressive, unfriendly 11 belligerent, contentious, quarrelsome, threatening 12 antagonistic, disputatious 13 argumentative

pugnacity 9 hostility 10 antagonism 12 belligerence 13 combativeness 14 aggressiveness, fighting spirit 15 contentiousness

puissance 5 force, might, power 6 energy 7 potency, prowess 8 strength

pulchritude 6 beauty 8 fairness 9 bonniness, good looks 10 comeliness, loveliness, prettiness 12 gorgeousness, handsomeness 13 beauteousness, exquisiteness 14 attractiveness, personableness

pulchritudinous 4 fair, fine 5 bonny 6 comely, lovely, pretty 8 gorgeous, handsome 9 beauteous, beautiful, ravishing 10 attractive 11 good-looking

Pulitzer
  author: 10 W A Swanberg

Pulitzer Prize
  originator: 14 Joseph Pulitzer
  administered by: 18 Columbia University
  awarded for: 4 play 5 drama, music, novel 6 poetry 7 cartoon, feature, fiction, letters 9 biography, criticism, editorial, reporting 10 commentary, journalism, literature, nonfiction 11 photography 13 autobiography

pull 2 go 3 lug, rip, tow, tug 4 drag, draw, grab, haul, jerk, lure, move, rend, rive, tear, yank 5 drive, sever, shake, split, trawl, troll, twist, wrest, wring 6 allure, appeal, detach, dig out, entice, remove, sprain, strain, uproot, wrench 7 attract, draw out, extract, gravity, stretch, weed out 8 withdraw 9 extirpate, influence, magnetism, take in tow 10 allurement, attraction, enticement 11 fascination 14 attractiveness

pull apart 3 rip, tug 4 drag, rend, tear 6 detach, wrench 7 extract 8 separate 9 criticize, disengage 10 disconnect

pull away 5 wrest 7 remove 8 drawback, withdraw

pull back 7 back off, retreat 8 fall back, withdraw

Pullman, George Mortimer
  nationality: 8 American
  developed: 9 (railroad) dining car 11 (railroad) sleeping car

pull off 4 pull 6 commit, effect 7 execute, perform 8 carry out 10 perpetuate 13 participate in

pull on 3 don 5 put on 7 get into

pull one's leg 3 kid 4 fool, hoax 5 tease, trick 7 deceive 9 make fun of

pull out 5 leave 7 draw out, extract 8 withdraw

pull over, pullover 4 cite, stop 5 shirt 6 arrest, jersey, slip on, ticket, t-shirt 7 maillot, sweater 8 slip over

pull together 4 join 5 unite 7 pitch in, share in 8 take part 9 cooperate, join hands 10 act jointly, join forces 11 collaborate, participate

pull to pieces 5 shred 6 tear up 7 destroy 9 tear apart

pull up 4 halt, rein, stop, weed 5 check, hoist 6 arrest, uplift, uproot 7 extract, reprove

pulp 4 curd, mash, mush, pith 5 crush, flesh, paste, puree, slush, smash 6 squash, tissue 7 journal 8 magazine 9 masticate

pulsate 4 beat, tick, wave 5 pound, pulse, shake, throb, thump, waver 6 quaver, quiver, shiver 7 flutter, shudder, tremble, vibrate 8 undulate 9 alternate, come and go, oscillate, palpitate 10 ebb and flow 11 reverberate

pulse 4 beat 5 throb, thump 6 quiver, rhythm, stroke 7 cadence, pulsate, shudder, tremble, vibrate 9 oscillate, palpitate, pulsation, vibration 10 recurrence, undulation 11 oscillation, palpitation

pulverize 4 mash, mill 5 crumb, crush, grind, mince, pound 6 powder 7 atomize, crumble 9 comminate, granulate, triturate 12 reduce to dust

pulverized 6 ground, milled 7 crumbed, crushed, pounded 8 atomized, crumbled, crunched, powdered 10 granulated 12 ground to dust

pummel 4 beat, maul 5 pound 6 batter, thrash 7 trounce

pump 4 quiz, shoe, well 5 grill 7 inflate, slipper 8 question 9 draw water

Pump
  constellation of: 6 Antlia

Pump House Gang, The
  author: 8 Tom Wolfe

pumpkin 5 fruit, gourd, melon 6 squash 9 vegetable 12 jack o'lantern

pun
  French: 9 jeu de mots

punch 3 box, hit, jab 4 beat, blow, chop, clip, conk, cuff, pelt, plug, poke, slam, sock, swat 5 baste, clout, knock, paste, pound, smite, thump, whack 6 pummel, strike, stroke, thrust, thwack, wallop 7 clobber 8 haymaker 10 roundhouse

punchy 3 fat 5 dazed 6 stubby 8 confused, forceful 9 befuddled

punctilious 5 exact, fussy, picky, rigid 6 proper, strict 7 correct, finicky, precise 8 exacting, rigorous 9 demanding 10 meticulous, particular, scrupulous 11 painstaking

punctual 5 early, quick, ready 6 on time, prompt, steady, timely 7 instant, not late, regular 8 constant, on the dot 9 immediate, well-timed 10 in good time, seasonable 11 expeditious 13 instantaneous

punctuate 4 lace 5 break 6 pepper 7 scatter 8 separate, sprinkle 9 interrupt 11 intersperse

punctuation mark 4 dash 5 colon, comma, pause, point, slash 6 accent, ending, hyphen, parens, period, quotes 7 bracket 8 ellipsis 9 semicolon 10 apostrophe 11 parenthesis 12 question mark 13 quotation mark 16 exclamation point

puncture 3 cut 4 bite, hole, nick, pink 5 break, prick, stick, sting, wound 6 pierce 7 deflate, let down, opening, rupture 9 knock down, shoot down 10 depreciate 11 perforation

pundit 4 guru, sage 5 guide 6 critic, expert, master, mentor, savant, wizard 7 thinker 9 authority 13 learned person

pungent 3 hot 4 acid, keen, racy, sour, tart 5 acrid, acute, nippy, salty, sharp, smart, spicy, tangy, tasty, witty 6 biting, bitter, clever, savory, snappy, strong 7 acetous, caustic, cutting, mordent, peppery, piquant, pointed 8 incisive, piercing, poignant, smarting, stinging, stirring, vinegary, wounding 9 brilliant, flavorful, invidious, palatable, sarcastic, sparkling, trenchant 10 astringent, flavorsome, keenwitted 11 acrimonious, penetrating, provocative, stimulating, tantalizing 12 sharptasting 13 scintillating, sharp-smelling 14 highly flavored, highly seasoned

punish 4 beat, fine, flog, whip 6 avenge, rebuke 7 chasten, correct, reprove 8 admonish, chastise, imprison, penalize, sentence 9 castigate, dress down, retaliate 10 discipline, take to task 11 get even with, take revenge 14 bring to account 15 take vengeance on

punishing 5 harsh, penal 6 brutal, severe 7 abusive 8 scolding 9 torturing 10 chastizing, tormenting 11 castigating

punishment 4 fine 5 price 7 damages, deserts, flaying, forfeit, hanging, payment, penalty, penance, redress 8 flogging, punition, spanking, whipping 10 chastening, correction, crucifying, discipline, reparation 11 castigation, retribution 12 chastisement, penalization

punk 4 hood, lout, poor 5 bully, lousy, rowdy, tough 6 crummy, rotten 7 hoodlum, ruffian 8 hooligan 9 barbarian, roughneck 10 delinquent

Punt *see* 7 Somalia

Puntarvolo
  character in: 22 Every Man Out of His Humour
  author: 6 Jonson

punt e mes
  type: 8 aperitif
  origin: 5 Italy
  flavor: 6 orange
  color: 12 reddish-brown

puny 4 poor, thin, tiny, weak 5 frail, light, petty, runty, small 6 bantam, feeble, flimsy, infirm, little, meager, measly, paltry, sickly, slight, weakly 7 fragile, shallow, tenuous, trivial 8 delicate, impotent, picayune, piddling, runtlike, sawed-off, trifling 9 emaciated, miniature, mite-sized, pint-sized, worthless 10 diminutive, inadequate, picayunish, under sized 11 unimportant 12 insufficient 13 insignificant 14 inconsiderable, underdeveloped

pupa 3 egg 5 larva, nymph 6 cocoon 7 wiggler 9 chrysalis 14 transformation

pupil 4 coed, tyro 6 novice 7 learner, scholar, student, trainee 8 beginner, disciple, initiate 9 schoolboy 10 apprentice, schoolgirl 11 probationer 13 undergraduate

puppet 3 toy 4 doll, dupe, pawn, tool 6 flunky, lackey 7 cat's-paw, manikin, servant 8 creature, henchman, hireling 9 jackstraw, lay figure, underling 10 figurehead, instrument, man of straw, marionette 11 subordinate

puppy 3 dog, pet, pup 6 canine

Purcell, Henry
  born: 6 London 7 England
  composer of: 9 Fantasias 10 Bell Anthem, Dioclesian, King Arthur (The British Worthy), The Tempest 12 Golden Sonata 13 Dido and Aeneas 14 The Indian Queen

purchase 3 buy 4 edge, hold 6 buying, pay for, pick up 7 footing, support, toehold 8 foothold, leverage 9 advantage, influence 11 acquirement, acquisition

pure 4 full, mere, neat, true 5 basic, clean, fresh, moral, sheer, stark, utter, whole 6 chaste, decent, entire, higher, virgin 7 angelic, ethical, perfect, sincere, sinless, sterile, unmixed, upright 8 absolute, abstract, complete, flawless, germfree, innocent, positive, purebred, sanitary, spotless, straight, thorough, unmarred, virginal, virtuous 9 blameless, downright, faultless, guileless, guiltless, healthful, inviolate, out-and-out, pedigreed, righteous, unalloyed, undefiled, unmingled, unspoiled, unsullied, untainted, wholesome 10 antiseptic, immaculate, inviolable, sterilized, uninfected, unmodified, unpolluted 11 conjectural, disinfected, fundamental, pure-blooded, speculative, theoretical, unblemished, uncorrupted, unqualified, untarnished 12 full-strength, hypothetical, thoroughbred 13 unadulterated, unimpeachable 14 above suspicion, uncontaminated

puree 4 bisk, pulp, soup 5 paste 6 bisque

purely 4 only 5 fully 6 merely, simply, solely, wholly 7 cleanly, morally, piously, totally 8 chastely, devoutly, entirely, worthily 9 admirably 10 absolutely, completely, flawlessly, in all honor, innocently, virginally, virtuously 11 essentially, faultlessly 13 incorruptibly

Purgatory, Purgatorio
  part II of: 12 Divine Comedy
  author: 14 Dante Alighieri

purge 4 kill, oust 5 crush, expel 6 banish, emetic, pardon, physic, purify, remove, uproot 7 clean up, cleanse, cleanup, clyster, dismiss, expiate, purging, rout out, shake up 8 aperient, atone for, clean out, get rid of, laxative, sweep out, wash away 9 cathartic, discharge, eliminate, eradicate, liquidate, purgation, purgative 10 do away with 11 exterminate 12 obtain pardon (from), purification 15 obtain remission (from) 16 obtain absolution (from) 17 obtain forgiveness

purification 7 baptism 9 cleansing 13 sterilization

purify 4 boil 5 clear 6 filter 7 clarify, distill 8 make pure, sanitize 9 disinfect, sterilize 10 chlorinate, pasteurize 13 decontaminate

Puritani, I
also: 11 The Puritans
opera by: 7 Bellini
character: 14 Oliver Cromwell, Queen Henrietta 16 Lord Arthur Talbot

puritanical 4 prim 5 rigid, stiff 6 narrow, prissy, severe, strict, stuffy 7 ascetic, austere, bigoted, prudish, puritan, stilted 8 dogmatic, priggish 9 bluenosed, fanatical 11 stiff-necked, straitlaced 13 sanctimonious

Puritan State
nickname of: 13 Massachusetts

purity 5 honor, piety 6 virtue 7 clarity, decency, honesty, modesty 8 chastity, fineness, holiness, lucidity, morality, pureness, sanctity 9 cleanness, clearness, innocence, integrity, limpidity, plainness, rectitude, virginity 10 brilliance, chasteness, directness, excellence, immaculacy, simplicity, temperance, uniformity 11 cleanliness, homogeneity, saintliness, uprightness 12 virtuousness 13 guilelessness, guiltlessness 14 immaculateness 15 clear conscience 16 incorruptibility

purlieu 4 area 5 haunt, limit 6 border, locale, region, resort 7 district, environ 8 outskirt 11 surrounding 12 neighborhood

purloin 3 rob 5 steal 6 pilfer 11 appropriate, make off with

Purloined Letter, The
author: 13 Edgar Allan Poe

purloiner 5 thief 6 robber 7 burglar 8 pilferer

purple 4 plum, puce, racy 5 color, grape, lilac, lurid, mauve, royal 6 florid, orchid, turgid, violet 7 crimson, flowery, furious, fuchsia, magenta 8 amethyst, burgundy, imperial, lavender 9 gastropod

Purple Land see 7 Uruguay

Purple Rose of Cairo, The
director: 10 Woody Allen
cast: 9 Mia Farrow 11 Danny Aiello, Jeff Daniels

purport 3 aim, end 4 gist 5 claim, drift, point, sense, tenor, trend 6 allege, burden, design, import, intent, object, reason 7 bearing, meaning, profess, purpose 9 intention, objective, rationale, substance 11 implication 12 significance 13 signification

purpose 3 aim 4 goal, hope, mean, plan, will, wish 5 elect, point, sense 6 aspire, choose, decide, design, desire, intend, intent, motive, object, reason, scheme, target 7 drive at, meaning, mission, persist, project, propose, resolve, think to 8 ambition, conclude, endeavor, function, proposal, set about 9 determine, intention, objective, persevere, rationale, undertake 10 aspiration, motivation, resolution 11 contemplate, disposition, expectation, fixed intent, have a mind to, raison d'etre 13 commit one self, determination

purposeful 7 decided, studied 8 resolute, resolved 9 committed, conscious 10 calculated, considered, deliberate, determined 11 intentional 12 premeditated, strong-willed

purposefulness 7 purpose, resolve 10 resolution 11 decidedness 12 decisiveness, resoluteness 13 determination

purposeless 6 random 7 aimless, useless 8 needless, plotless 9 desultory, driftless, haphazard, irregular, senseless, unplanned 11 meaningless 12 functionless, undetermined, unprofitable

purposely 8 by design 9 advisedly, expressly, knowingly, on purpose, willfully, wittingly 10 designedly, with intent 11 consciously, voluntarily 12 calculatedly, deliberately 13 intentionally

purse 3 bag 4 fold, fund, knit 5 award, bunch, pinch, pleat, pouch, prize, stake 6 clutch, coffer, gather, pucker, wallet 7 handbag, sporran, wrinkle 8 contract, moneybag, proceeds, treasury, winnings 10 pocketbook 11 shoulder bag
French: 12 porte-monnaie

purser 6 bursar 7 cashier 9 paymaster 10 cashkeeper

pursue 4 seek 5 aim at, chase, track, trail 6 aim for, follow, try for 7 be after, carry on, go after, perform 8 aspire to, engage in, labor for, run after 9 race after, strive for 10 chase after, push toward

pursuer 5 pupil 6 seeker 7 devotee, student 8 disciple, follower, searcher 10 aficionado

pursuit 4 hunt 5 chase 6 search 7 pastime 8 activity 9 following 10 occupation

purvey 3 get 4 give, hand 5 cater, equip, yield 6 obtain, outfit, supply 7 deliver, furnish, procure, provide

purveyor 4 pimp 6 seller 8 procurer, provider, supplier

purview 3 ken 4 area 5 field, range, reach, realm, savvy, scope, sweep 6 domain, extent 7 compass, horizon, outlook 8 dominion, overview 9 territory, viewpoint 10 commission, experience 11 mental grasp 13 comprehension, understanding 14 responsibility

push 2 go 3 dun, ram 4 butt, goad, jolt, move, plug, prod, spur, sway, urge, work, worm 5 boost, drive, egg on, elbow, fight, foray, force, forge, harry, hound, impel, nudge, press, rouse, shove, stick, stuff, vigor, wedge 6 arouse, badger, coerce, compel, energy, exhort, harass, heckle, hustle, incite, induce, inroad, jostle, plunge, prompt, propel, thrust, wiggle 7 advance, animate, buffalo, inspire, promote, provoke, squeeze 8 ambition, browbeat, motivate, persuade, shoulder, struggle, vitality 9 advertise, constrain, encourage, importune, incursion, instigate, make known, publicize, stimulate, strongarm 10 get-up-and-go 11 make one's way, prevail upon, vim and vigor 12 force one's way, propagandize 13 determination

pushcart 5 wagon 6 barrow 8 handcart 10 handbarrow 11 wheelbarrow

push forward 4 goad, prod, spur 5 drive, impel, press 9 urge along

Pushkin, Alexander (Aleksandr)
author of: 12 Boris Godunov, Eugene Onegin 16 The Queen of Spades 17 The Bronze Horseman 19 The Captain's Daughter

push through 6 hasten 7 advance, forward 8 dispatch, expedite 10 accelerate, facilitate

pushy 8 forceful 9 assertive, insistent 10 aggressive 11 domineering 12 strong-willed 13 self-assertive

pusillanimous 7 fearful 8 cowardly, timorous 10 spiritless 11 lily-livered 12 apprehensive, fainthearted, mean-spirited

pusillanimousness 8 timidity 9 cowardice 12 yellow streak 13 yellow feather 16 faint heartedness 18 chickenheartedness

puss 3 cat, mug, pan 4 face 5 kitty 6 feline, kisser, kitten

pussyfoot 5 dodge, evade, hedge, sneak 6 tiptoe, weasel 8 sidestep 13 evade the issue 14 beg the question 15 walk on eggshells 16 straddle the fence

put 3 fix, lay, set 4 cast, pose, rest, word 5 bring, drive, force, heave, offer, pitch, place, state, throw 6 assign, employ, impute, phrase, submit 7 ascribe, deposit, express, present, propose 8 position 9 attribute, enunciate 10 articulate

put a damper on 4 cool, dull 7 depress, squelch 10 discourage, dishearten

put an edge on 4 hone, whet 6 excite 7 sharpen 9 stimulate

put an end to 4 halt, stop 5 annul, quash 6 cancel, finish, repeal, revoke 7 abolish, blot out, rescind, squelch, wipe out 8 abrogate, demolish, dispatch, stamp out 9 eliminate, eradicate, finish off 10 discourage, do away with, put a stop to 12 write finis to

put aside 5 table 6 forget 7 discard, lay away 10 relinquish

put away 3 eat 4 down, stow 5 stash 6 commit 7 confine, consume 9 drink down

put back 4 rout 5 delay 6 defeat, demote, impair, reject, return 7 replace, restore 9 reinstate

put down 4 note, post 5 crush, enter, knock, quash, quell 6 dispel, enlist, record, subdue 7 deposit, disdain, sneer at, squelch 8 belittle, derogate, laugh off, pooh-pooh, suppress 9 denigrate, disparage, humiliate, write down 10 depreciate

put forth 5 offer 6 extend, put out 7 proffer, send out

put forward 4 pose 6 assert 7 advance, profess, propose 8 propound

put in irons 5 chain 6 fetter 7 manacle, shackle 8 handcuff

put in motion 4 move 5 begin, start 6 arouse, launch 8 activate, carry out, commence, initiate 9 instigate, undertake

put in order 5 array 6 neaten, tidy up 7 arrange 8 organize 10 straighten

put in plain sight 4 show 6 set out 7 display, exhibit

put in shackles 6 fetter, hobble 7 enchain, enslave, manacle 8 handcuff, imprison

put into circulation 4 move 5 issue, print 7 publish 10 pass around

put into effect 6 effect 7 achieve, enforce, execute, fulfill, realize 8 carry out, complete 10 accomplish, administer, consummate, effectuate, perpetrate 12 carry through

put into words 5 voice 7 express 8 describe 9 verbalize 10 articulate 11 communicate

Putnam, Abbie
character in: 18 Desire Under the Elms
author: 6 O'Neill

put off 5 delay, repel, stall 6 offend, rebuff, recess 7 adjourn, repulse, set sail, suspend 8 hold back, launched, offended, postpone, rebuffed, repelled, repulsed 9 interrupt 11 discontinue 13 procrastinate

put off guard 4 lull 6 disarm 10 make unwary

put on 3 don 5 affix 6 attach 7 dress in, get into, stick on 8 fasten to

put-on 8 pretense 11 affectation

put on guard 4 warn 5 alert 6 advise, tip off 7 caution 8 forewarn 9 make ready 10 precaution

put out 3 irk 5 annoy, issue 6 quench, retire 7 produce, publish 8 irritate 9 strike out 10 extinguish 11 manufacture 13 leave the shore

put out of order 5 mix up, upset 6 jumble, mess up, muddle 7 confuse, scatter 8 disarray, disorder, displace, put askew, scramble 10 disarrange 11 disorganize

putrefaction 3 rot 5 decay 7 rotting 8 spoilage, spoiling 10 rottenness 12 decomposition

putrefy 3 rot 4 turn 5 decay, spoil, taint 6 molder 8 putresce, stagnate 9 decompose 10 biodegrade 11 deteriorate 12 disintegrate

putrescent 4 foul, rank 5 fetid 6 smelly 7 rotting 8 decaying, spoiling, stinking 9 offensive 10 malodorous, putrefying 11 decomposing

putrid 3 bad 4 foul, rank 5 fetid 6 rancid, rotten, spoiled 7 tainted 8 decaying, polluted, purulent, stinking 9 putrefied 10 putrescent 11 decomposing 12 contaminated, putrefactive

putridity 5 decay, filth, taint 8 foulness, impurity 9 dirtiness, pollution, purulence, rancidity 10 rottenness 11 putrescence, uncleanness 13 contamination, decomposition

putsch 6 revolt 8 uprising

putter 4 fool, idle, laze, loaf, loll 5 dally, drift 6 dawdle, diddle, fiddle, loiter, lounge, piddle, potter, tinker 9 golf club, lallygag 10 dillydally

put to death 4 do in, hang, kill, slay 5 slain 6 done in, hanged, killed, murder, poison, rub out 7 bump off, butcher, execute 8 dispatch, executed, massacre, murdered, poisoned, strangle 9 bumped off, butchered, finish off, massacred, strangled, suffocate 11 assassinate, electrocute, exterminate 12 assassinated, electrocuted, exterminated

put to flight 4 rout, shoo 5 chase 6 dispel 7 cast out, scatter 8 drive off, send away 11 send packing

put together 4 join 5 unite 7 combine 8 assemble

put to shame 6 ashame 7 chagrin, mortify 9 discomfit, embarrass, humiliate

put to sleep 4 lull 5 quiet 6 sedate 8 knock out 9 narcotize 11 anesthetize

put to use 3 use 5 apply 6 employ, engage, occupy 7 exploit, utilize 9 make use of

put under a spell 5 charm 7 bewitch, enchant 8 entrance 9 fascinate, mesmerize, spellbind

put up 3 can 4 hang 5 erect, house, lodge, raise, store 6 billet 7 shelter 8 preserve 11 accommodate 14 furnish room for

put up with 4 bear, take 5 abide, brave, brook, stand 6 endure, suffer 7 stomach, sustain, undergo 8 stand for, submit to, tolerate 9 withstand 11 countenance

Puvis de Chavannes, Pierre Cecile
   born: 5 Lyons 6 France
   artwork: 6 Summer 13 Shepherd's Song 14 Ludus pro patria 16 The Poor Fisherman 17 Life of St Genevieve, The Inspiring Muses 21 Science Arts and Letters

Puyallop
   language family: 8 Salishan, Wakashan 9 Algonkian 10 Algonquian
   location: 10 Washington

Puzo, Mario
   author of: 12 The Godfather

puzzle 4 foil, mull 5 brood, stump 6 baffle, enigma, outwit, ponder, riddle, wonder 7 confuse, dilemma, mystery, mystify, nonplus, perplex, problem 8 bewilder, confound, hoodwink 9 conundrum 10 bafflement, difficulty, perplexity 12 bewilderment, complication 13 mystification

puzzled 6 amazed 7 baffled 8 befogged, confused, troubled 9 astounded, befuddled, mystified, perplexed 10 bewildered, confounded, nonplussed

puzzling 7 elusive 8 baffling 9 confusing, enigmatic 10 mysterious, mystifying, perplexing 11 bewildering, confounding, enigmatical 12 unfathomable 16 hard to understand, incomprehensible

Pwyll
   origin: 5 Welsh
   form: 6 prince
   steals: 8 Rhiannon
   wife: 8 Rhiannon
   son: 7 Pryderi

Pyanepsia
   origin: 5 Greek 8 Athenian
   event: 8 festival
   honoring: 6 Apollo 7 harvest

Pygmalion
   author: 17 George Bernard Shaw
   character: 12 Henry Higgins 14 Eliza Doolittle
   basis for: 10 My Fair Lady
   director: 14 Anthony Asquith
   cast: 11 Wendy Hiller (Eliza Doolittle) 12 Leslie Howard (Professor Henry Higgins) 13 Wilfrid Lawson

Pygmalion
   king of: 6 Cyprus
   avocation: 8 sculptor
   statue named: 7 Galatea
   loved: 7 Galatea
   statue changed to: 5 woman
   wife: 7 Galatea
   daughter: 6 Paphos 8 Metharme

pygmy 3 elf, toy, wee 4 mite, runt, tiny 5 dwarf, elfin, short, small 6 bantam, midget, peewee, shrimp 7 manikin 8 dwarfish, halfpint, Tom Thumb 9 miniature, pipsqueak 10 diminutive, homun culus, undersized 11 Lilliputian

Pylades
   father: 9 Strophius
   mother: 8 Anaxibia
   cousin: 7 Orestes
   wife: 7 Electra
   son: 5 Medon 9 Strophius
   friend: 7 Orestes

Pylaemenes
   king of: 13 Paphlagonians
   killed by: 8 Menelaus

Pylaeus
   mentioned in: 5 Iliad
   rank: 7 captain

Pylas
   king of: 6 Megara
   uncle: 4 Bias
   gave throne to: 17 Pandion the Younger

Pyncheon family
   character in: 24 The House of the Seven Gables
   members: 6 Phoebe 8 Clifford, Hepzibah 12 Judge Jaffrey
   author: 9 Hawthorne

Pynchon, Thomas
   author of: 1 V 15 Gravity's Rainbow 23 The Crying of Lot Forty-Nine

Pyongyang
   capital of: 10 North Korea

Pyramus
   form: 5 youth
   location: 7 Babylon
   loved: 6 Thisbe
   died at tomb of: 5 Ninus

Pyrigenes
   epithet of: 8 Dionysus
   means: 10 born of fire

Pyriphlegethon *see* 10 Phlegethon

pyromaniac 7 firebug 8 arsonist 10 incendiary 11 firestarter

Pyronia
  epithet of: 7 Artemis
  means: 11 fire goddess
pyrope
  species: 6 garnet
  color: 3 red
pyrophobia
  fear of: 4 fire
pyrotechnics 9 fireworks 16 brilliant display 19 dazzling performance
Pyrrha
  father: 10 Epimetheus
  mother: 7 Pandora
  husband: 9 Deucalion
Pythia
  priestess of: 6 Apollo
  location: 6 Delphi
  delivered: 7 oracles
Pythias
  friend: 5 Damon
Pythius see 6 Apollo
Python see 8 Delphyne

Q

Qatar
capital/largest city: 4 Doha 7 al-Dawha
others: 3 Juh 5 Wagra 6 Dukhan, Umm-
Bab 7 al-Khawr, Musayid, Umm Said
government: 7 emirate
head of state/government: 4 emir
monetary unit: 5 riyal 6 dirham
highest point: 13 Aba al-Bawl Hill
physical feature:
bay: 5 Salwa
cape: 5 Rakan 6 Laffan 8 Ushayriq 9 al-
Matbakh
gulf: 7 Bahrain, Persian
people: 4 Arab 6 Pushtu, Yemeni 7 Baluchi, Iranian 9 Pakistani
rulers: 12 Great Britain, Ottoman Turks
sheik/sheikh: 18 Ahmad bin Ali al-Thani
22 Khalifa bin Hamad al-Thani
language: 6 Arabic
religion: 5 Islam
sect: 7 Wahhabi
war: 4 Gulf 11 Desert Storm

quack 4 fake, sham 5 phony 6 pseudo 9
charlatan, pretender 10 fake doctor, fraudulent 11 counterfeit, quacksalver 15 medical impostor

quackery 5 bluff, guile 6 deceit 7 cunning 9
deception, duplicity 12 charlatanism

quaff 4 down, gulp, swig 5 drink, lap up,
swill 6 guzzle, imbibe, tipple 7 swallow,
toss off 8 belt down, chug-a-lug 9 knock
back 11 drink deeply

quagmire 3 bog, fen, fix, jam 4 mess, mire,
ooze, quag, sump 5 marsh, pinch, swamp
6 crisis, morass, muddle, pickle, plight,
scrape, slough, sludge, strait 7 dilemma 8
hot water, quandary 9 imbroglio, intricacy,
quicksand 10 difficulty, perplexity 11 Gor-
dian knot, involvement, predicament 12
entanglement

quail 3 shy 5 cower, quake, shake 6
blanch, flinch, recoil, shrink 7 run away,
shudder, tremble 8 fight shy, turn tail 9
lose heart 10 be cowardly, lose spirit, take
fright 11 lose courage 12 have cold feet 16
shake in one's boots 17 shiver in one's
shoes, show a yellow streak

quail
group of: 4 bevy 5 covey

quaint 3 odd 4 rare 5 droll, queer 6 unique
7 antique, bizarre, curious, strange, unusual 8 charming, fanciful, old-timey, original, peculiar, singular, uncommon 9 eccentric, whimsical 10 antiquated, outlandish
11 out-of-the-way, picturesque 12 old-
fashioned 13 extraordinary 14 unconventional

quake 4 wave 5 quail, shake, spasm, throb
6 blanch, quaver, quiver, ripple, shiver,
thrill, tremor 7 shudder, tremble 9 trembling 10 earthquake 18 seismic disturbance

qualification 4 gift 5 forte, skill 6 talent 7
ability, faculty, fitness, proviso 8 aptitude,
bona fide, capacity, property, standard 9
attribute, condition, endowment, exception, exemption, objection, postulate, provision, requisite 10 capability, competency,
credential, limitation 11 achievement, arrangement, eligibility, requirement, reservation, restriction, stipulation 12 escape
clause, modification, prerequisite, suitableness 13 certification 14 accomplishment

qualified 3 fit 4 able, meet 5 adept, equal 6
expert, fitted, suited, versed 7 capable,
guarded, hedging, knowing, limited,
skilled, trained 8 eligible, equipped, licensed, reserved, skillful, talented 9 ambiguous, certified, competent, efficient,
equivocal, practiced 10 authorized, indefinite, proficient, restricted 11 conditional,
efficacious, experienced, provisional 12
accomplished

qualify 3 fit 4 ease 5 abate, adapt, alter,
endow, equip, limit, ready, train 6 adjust,
enable, ground, modify, narrow, permit, reduce, soften, temper 7 assuage, certify,
empower, entitle, license, make fit, prepare 8 describe, diminish, mitigate, moderate, restrain, restrict, sanction 9 authorize,
condition, give power, measure up 10 be
accepted, be eligible, commission, legitimate 11 accommodate 12 characterize,
circumscribe, make eligible

qualifying 9 tempering 10 mitigating 11 eligibility, extenuating, preparatory

quality 4 mark, rank 5 blood, class, grade,
merit, trait, value, worth 6 aspect, family,
nature 7 caliber, dignity, faculty, feature 8
capacity, eminence, position, property,
standing 9 attribute, character 11 disposition, distinction, high station, temperament
12 constitution, social status 13 qualification 14 characteristic

Quality Street
author: 12 James M Barrie

qualm 4 turn 6 nausea 7 scruple; vertigo 9
faintness, giddiness, misgiving 10 dizzy
spell, hesitation, queasiness, reluctance,
uneasiness 11 compunction, reservation,
sick feeling 13 indisposition, unwillingness
14 disinclination 18 twinge of conscience

quandary 3 fix, jam 4 mire 5 pinch 6 crisis, morass, pickle, plight, scrape, strait 7 dilemma, impasse 8 hot water, quagmire 9 imbroglio 10 difficulty 11 involvement, predicament 12 entanglement, kettle of fish

quantities 4 lots, much 5 heaps, loads 7 amounts

quantity 3 sum 4 area, bulk, dose, mass, size 5 quota, share 6 amount, dosage, extent, length, number, volume 7 expanse, measure, portion 8 vastness 9 abundance, aggregate, allotment, amplitude, extension, greatness, magnitude, multitude 10 proportion 11 measurement 13 apportionment

quarantine 7 confine, isolate 9 isolation, segregate, sequester 13 sequestration 15 cordon sanitaire 18 medical segregation

Quare Fellow, The
  author: 12 Brendan Behan

quarrel 3 jar, nag, row 4 carp, feud, fuss, spat, tiff 5 argue, brawl, cavil, clash, fight, scrap 6 bicker, differ, strife 7 contend, discord, dispute, dissent, fall out, wrangle 8 argument, be at odds, conflict, squabble 9 altercate, bickering, complaint, find fault, have words, objection 10 contention, difference, dissension, dissidence, falling out 11 controversy 12 disagreement 13 breach of peace, contradiction, misunderstand 14 apple of discord 15 be at logger heads 16 bone of contention, misunderstanding

quarreling 6 strife 7 discord 8 clashing, conflict, disunity, friction 9 bickering, disputing, scrapping, wrangling 10 contention, dissension, dissidence, squabbling 11 discordance 12 disagreement

quarrelsome 7 peevish 8 captious, churlish, contrary, militant, petulant 9 bellicose, combative, fractious, irascible, querulous, truculent 10 pugnacious 11 belligerent, contentious 12 antagonistic, cantankerous, disagreeable, disputatious 13 argumentative

quarry 3 bed, dig, pit 4 game, lode, mine, prey 5 catch, stone 6 source, victim 8 excavate

quart
  abbreviation: 2 qt

quarter, quarters 4 area, part, pity, post, side, spot, zone 5 board, house, lodge, mercy, place, put up, realm, rooms 6 billet, domain, fourth, locale, region, sphere 7 housing, install, lodging, shelter, station, terrain 8 clemency, district, humanity, leniency, locality, location, lodgings, position, precinct, province, sympathy 9 percent, direction, one-fourth, situation, territory 10 compassion, fourth part, indulgence, quadrisect 11 place to live, place to stay, three months 13 quarter dollar, specific place 14 accommodations 15 twenty-five cents

quarterstaff 4 pole 5 staff 6 cudgel

quartz
  varieties: 4 sard 5 agate, topaz 8 amethyst 9 carnelian, tiger's-eye 11 rock crystal

quash 4 ruin, stop, undo, void 5 annul, crush, erase, quell, smash, wreck 6 cancel, delete, dispel, efface, quench, recall, revoke, squash, subdue, vacate 7 blot out, destroy, expunge, nullify, put down, repress, rescind, retract, reverse, squelch 8 abrogate, dissolve, override, overrule, overturn, set aside, suppress 9 devastate, eradicate, extirpate, overthrow, overwhelm, repudiate, strike out 10 annihilate, extinguish, invalidate, obliterate, put an end to 11 countermand, exterminate

quasi 4 near, part, semi 6 almost, ersatz 7 halfway, seeming, virtual 8 apparent, somewhat, so-called 9 imitation, synthetic 10 resembling

Quasimodo
  character in: 23 The Hunchback of Notre Dame
  author: 4 Hugo

Quatermain, Allan
  character in: 17 King Solomon's Mines
  author: 7 Haggard

quaver 4 beat, sway, wave 5 quake, shake, throb, trill, waver 6 falter, quiver, shiver, teeter, totter, tremor, wobble, writhe 7 pulsate, shudder, tremble, tremolo, vibrate, vibrato, wriggle 9 oscillate, trembling, vibration 14 tremulous shake

quay 4 dock, mole, pier 5 basin, jetty, levee, wharf 6 marina 7 landing 10 waterfront

queasy 5 giddy, upset 6 uneasy 7 bilious, sickish 8 nauseous, qualmish, troubled 9 nauseated, sickening, uncertain 10 nauseating 13 uncomfortable 16 sick to the stomach

Quebec
  borders: 7 Ontario 8 Labrador 9 Hudson Bay 12 Newfoundland, United States 13 Atlantic Ocean 16 Gulf of St Lawrence
  cape: 5 Gaspe
  city: 6 Quebec 8 Montreal 10 Chicoutimi, Sherbrooke 13 Trois Rivieres
  highest point: 18 Mont Jacques Cartier
  hockey team: 9 Canadiens, Nordiques
  island: 9 Anticosti
  lake: 5 Gouin 9 Bienville, Eau Claire, Saint Jean 10 Mistassini 11 Manicouagan
  mineral: 4 gold, zinc 6 copper 7 iron ore 8 asbestos 9 limestone
  mountain: 5 Otish 10 Laurentian, Shickshock 11 Appalachian 12 Monteregians
  province of: 6 Canada

Quechua
  tribe: 4 Inca

Quedens, Eunice
  real name of: 8 Eve Arden

queen 5 ranee 7 czarina, empress 8 princess 13 female monarch
  French: 5 reine
  German: 7 Konigin

Latin: 6 regina
Spanish: 5 reina
queen/empress/princess
  of Egypt: 9 Cleopatra, Nefertari, Nefertiti
  10 Hatshepsut, Hetepheres
  of England: 3 Mab 4 Anne, Bess, Jane,
  Mary 7 Eleanor 8 Boadicea, Victoria 9
  Catherine, Charlotte, Elizabeth,
  Guinevere 10 Bloody Mary, Elizabeth I 11
  Elizabeth II, Jane Seymour
  of France: 7 Eugenie 9 Josephine 11
  Marie Louise 14 Marie de Medicis 15 Marie Antoinette
  of Italy/Rome: 7 Poppaea 9 Agrippina,
  Messalina 13 Livia Drusilla
  of Monaco: 8 Caroline 9 Stephanie 10
  Grace Kelly
  of the Netherlands: 7 Beatrix, Juliana 10
  Wilhelmina
  of Poland: 7 Jadwiga
  of Portugal: 5 Maria 9 Elizabeth
  of Russia: 9 Alexandra, Catherine 17
  Catherine the Great
  of Scotland: 4 Mary 13 Saint Margaret
  16 Mary Queen of Scots
  of Spain: 8 Isabella 16 Elizabeth
  Farnese
  of Sweden: 9 Christina
  of Syria: 7 Zenobia
Queen Christina
  director: 15 Rouben Mamoulian
  cast: 8 Ian Keith 10 Greta Garbo, Lewis
  Stone 11 John Gilbert 12 C Aubrey Smith
Queen Mab
  author: 18 Percy Bysshe Shelley
Queen of Amazons 9 Hippolyta, Hippolyte
Queen of Hearts
  character in: 28 Alice's Adventures in
  Wonderland
  author: 7 Carroll
Queen of Heaven 4 Hera, Mary 6 Ishtar 7
  Mylitta
Queen of Spades, The
  also: 12 Pikovaya Dama
  opera by: 11 Tchaikovsky
  character: 4 Lisa 6 Herman 8 Countess
Queen of Spades, The
  author: 16 Alexander Pushkin
Queen of Technicolor
  nickname of: 12 Maureen O'Hara
Queen of the Surf
  nickname of: 14 Esther Williams
Queen's Necklace, The
  author: 14 Alexandre Dumas (pere)
  character: 5 Oliva 13 Count de Charny
  15 Cardinal de Rohan, Count Cagliostro,
  Marie Antoinette 16 Andree de Taverney
  18 Philippe de Taverney 21 Jeanne de la
  Motte Valois
Queequeg
  character in: 8 Moby Dick
  author: 8 Melville
queer 3 odd 4 daft, harm, hurt, rare, ruin 5
  crazy, dizzy, droll, faint, fishy, funny, giddy,
  shady, spoil, weird, woozy, wreck 6 absurd, damage, exotic, impair, injure,
  quaint, qualmy, queasy, thwart, unique 7

bizarre, comical, curious, disrupt, erratic,
reeling, strange, touched, unusual 8 abnormal, bohemian, doubtful, fanciful, freakish, original, peculiar, uncommon, unhinged 9 eccentric, fantastic, grotesque,
irregular, laughable, ludicrous, unnatural
10 capricious, compromise, farfetched,
irrational, outlandish, remarkable, ridiculous, suspicious, unbalanced, unexampled, unorthodox 11 astonishing,
exceptional, light-headed, out of the way,
slightly ill, vertiginous 12 preposterous,
questionable, unparalleled 13 extraordinary, nonconforming, unprecedented 14
unconventional
  French: 5 outre
quell 4 calm, dull, ease, hush, lull, rout,
  ruin, stay, stem 5 abate, allay, blunt, crush,
  quash, quiet, still, worst, wreck 6 becalm,
  deaden, defeat, pacify, quench, reduce,
  soften, soothe, subdue 7 appease, assuage, compose, conquer, destroy, mollify,
  put down, scatter, silence, squelch 8 beat
  down, disperse, mitigate, overcome, palliate, stamp out, suppress, vanquish 9 alleviate, overpower, overthrow, overwhelm,
  subjugate 10 extinguish 11 tranquilize
quench 4 cool, sate 5 allay, crush, douse,
  quell, slake 6 dampen, put out, stifle 7 appease, blow out, put down, satiate, satisfy,
  smother 8 stamp out, suppress 10 annihilate, extinguish
Quentin Durward
  author: 14 Sir Walter Scott
  character: 8 Isabelle 9 Le Balafre 10
  Jacqueline 11 King Louis XI 12 Lady
  Hameline 13 Ludovic Lesley 15 Countess
  of Croye 16 William de la Marck 18
  Hayraddin Maugrabin 20 King Louis the
  Eleventh 21 Charles Duke of Burgundy
  23 Count Philip de Crevecoeur
querulous 4 sour 5 cross, fussy, testy,
  whiny 6 cranky, touchy 7 crabbed, finical,
  finicky, fretful, grouchy, peevish, pettish,
  waspish, whining 8 captious, exacting, petulant, shrewish 9 difficult, grumbling,
  irascible, irritable, long-faced, obstinate,
  resentful, splenetic 10 nettlesome 11 complaining, quarrelsome 12 disagreeable,
  discontented, disputatious, dissatisfied,
  faultfinding
query 3 ask 4 quiz 5 doubt, issue, quest 6
  demand, impugn, search 7 dispute, examine, impeach, inquest, inquiry, inspect,
  problem, request, suspect 8 distrust, look
  into, mistrust, question, sound out 9 catechize, challenge, inquire of 10 controvert
  11 examination, inquisition, interrogate,
  investigate, make inquiry 13 interrogation,
  investigation
quest 4 hunt, seek 6 pursue, search, voyage 7 crusade, journey, mission, pursuit,
  seeking 9 adventure 10 enterprise, pilgrimage 11 exploration
Quested, Adela
  character in: 15 A Passage to India
  author: 7 Forster

Quest for Fire
 director: 17 Jean-Jacques Annaud
 cast: 10 Ron Perlman 12 Rae Dawn
 Chong 13 Everett McGill
question 3 ask, rub 4 pump, quiz, test 5
 doubt, drill, grill, issue, query 6 impugn,
 matter, motion, oppose 7 dispute, dubiety,
 examine, problem, subject, suspect 8 distrust, look into, mistrust, proposal, sound
 out 9 catechize, challenge, inquire of, misgiving, moot point, objection 10 difficulty,
 disbelieve 11 controversy, interrogate, investigate, proposition, uncertainty 12
 cross-examine 13 consideration
questionable 4 moot 5 fishy, shady 6 unsure 7 dubious, in doubt, suspect 8 arguable, doubtful, puzzling, unproven 9 ambiguous, confusing, debatable, enigmatic,
 equivocal, in dispute, uncertain, undecided
 10 apocryphal, disputable, indefinite, mysterious, mystifying, perplexing, suspicious
 12 hypothetical 13 controversial, problematical
queue 3 row 4 file, line, rank 5 chain, train
 6 column, string
quibble 3 nag 4 carp, spar 5 argue, cavil,
 dodge, fence, fudge, shift 6 bicker, haggle,
 hassle, nicety, niggle, waffle 7 evasion,
 nitpick, shuffle 8 artifice, pretense, squabble, subtlety, white lie 9 be evasive, duplicity 10 equivocate, pick a fight, subterfuge
 11 distraction 12 equivocation 13 dodge
 the issue, prevarication
Quiche
 language family: 5 Mayan
 location: 9 Guatemala 12 South America
 14 Central America
quick 3 apt 4 able, deft, fast, keen, spry 5
 acute, adept, agile, alert, brief, brisk,
 eager, fiery, fleet, hasty, rapid, sharp,
 smart, swift, testy 6 abrupt, active, adroit,
 astute, brainy, bright, clever, expert, facile,
 flying, frisky, lively, nimble, prompt,
 shrewd, speedy, sudden, touchy, winged 7
 hurried, peppery, waspish 8 animated,
 choleric, headlong, petulant, skillful, snappish, spirited, vigilant, vigorous 9 dexterous, energetic, excitable, impatient,
 impetuous, impulsive, irascible, irritable,
 sagacious, splenetic, sprightly, vivacious,
 whirlwind, wide-awake 10 discerning, high-
 strung, hot-blooded 11 accelerated, expeditious, hot-tempered, intelligent, light-
 footed, penetrating, precipitate 12
 nimble-footed 13 perspicacious, temperamental
quicken 4 fire, goad, move, rush, spur, stir,
 urge 5 drive, egg on, hurry, impel, pique,
 press, rouse, speed 6 affect, arouse, excite, hasten, hustle, incite, kindle, propel,
 revive, vivify 7 actuate, advance, animate,
 enliven, further, hurry on, inspire, provoke,
 refresh, sharpen 8 activate, dispatch,
 energize, enkindle, expedite, inspirit, vitalize 9 galvanize, instigate, stimulate 10 accelerate, invigorate 11 precipitate

quick glance
 French: 9 coup d'oeil
quickly 4 anon, fast, soon 6 keenly, presto,
 pronto 7 briefly, hastily, rapidly, swiftly 8
 promptly, speedily 9 instantly 11 immediately 12 lickety-split
Quickly, Mistress
 character in: 22 The Merry Wives of
 Windsor
 author: 11 Shakespeare
quickness 5 haste, speed 6 acuity 8 alacrity, celerity, keenness, rapidity 9 acuteness, alertness, dexterity, sharpness 10
 cleverness, nimbleness, promptness 15
 expeditiousness
quick-tempered 5 cross, testy 6 cranky,
 shirty, touchy 7 grouchy, peevish, waspish
 8 choleric, churlish, shrewish, snappish 9
 emotional, excitable, irascible, irritable 10
 ill-humored 11 bad-tempered, hot-
 tempered, quarrelsome 12 cantankerous
 13 temperamental
quick-witted 4 keen 5 acute, alert, aware,
 quick, ready, sharp, smart, witty 6 astute,
 bright, clever, shrewd 8 incisive 9 brilliant,
 wide-awake 10 discerning, perceptive 11
 clear-headed, intelligent, penetrating 13
 perspicacious
quid pro quo 4 swap 5 trade 8 exchange 9
 tit for tat 21 something for something
quien sabe 8 who knows?
quiescence 7 latency 8 dormancy, inaction
 10 inactivity
quiescent 6 latent 7 dormant 8 inactive 10
 in abeyance
quiet 3 low, mum 4 calm, curb, dull, ease,
 hush, lull, meek, mild, mute, rest, soft,
 stay, stop 5 abate, allay, blunt, check,
 fixed, inert, peace, plain, quell, still 6 arrest, at rest, deaden, docile, dozing, gentle, humble, hushed, lessen, mellow, modest, muffle, pacify, placid, repose, sedate,
 serene, settle, silent, simple, soften,
 soothe, stable, steady, stifle, subdue,
 weaken 7 assuage, clement, comfort,
 compose, dormant, halcyon, mollify, not
 busy, pacific, passive, patient, relieve,
 restful, silence, smother, subdued, suspend, unmoved 8 becalmed, calmness,
 comatose, composed, decrease, immobile, inactive, mitigate, moderate, muteness, not rough, not showy, palliate,
 peaceful, quietude, reserved, reticent, retiring, serenity, sleeping, stagnant, taciturn,
 tranquil 9 alleviate, collected, contented,
 easygoing, immovable, lethargic, make-
 quiet, noiseless, not bright, peaceable,
 placidity, quietness, set at ease, soundless, stillness, temperate, terminate, unruffled, voiceless 10 coolheaded, gentleness, motionless, phlegmatic, put a stop
 to, relaxation, slumbering, speechless,
 stationary, stock-still, unassuming, untroubled 11 discontinue, tranquility, tranquilize, undisturbed, unexcitable, unobtrusive,
 unperturbed 12 bring to an end, even-
 tempered, inarticulate, peacefulness, tran-

quillity 13 at a standstill, dispassionate, imperturbable, noiselessness, soundlessness, unimpassioned, unpretentious 14 unostentatious, unpresumptuous 15 uncommunicative, undemonstrative

quietly 5 coyly 6 calmly, humbly, meekly, mildly, mutely, softly, tamely 8 demurely, modestly, placidly, serenely, silently 9 bashfully, inaudibly, patiently 10 composedly, moderately, peacefully, tranquilly 11 collectedly, contentedly, diffidently, noiselessly, pacifically, soundlessly, temperately, unexcitedly 12 speechlessly, unassumingly, unboastfully 13 unobtrusively, unperturbedly 15 dispassionately, unpretentiously, without ceremony 16 unostentatiously 17 undemonstratively

Quiet Man, The
director: 8 John Ford
author: 13 Liam O'Flaherty
cast: 9 John Wayne 12 Maureen O'Hara 14 Mildred Natwick, Victor McLaglen 15 Barry Fitzgerald
setting: 7 Ireland
score: 11 Victor Young
Oscar for: 8 director

quietness 5 peace, quiet 7 silence 8 softness 9 stillness 12 peacefulness

quietude 4 calm, rest 6 repose 8 easiness 9 composure

Quigley, Jane
real name of: 13 Jane Alexander

quill 3 pen 4 fold, hair, pick, seta, stem, tube 5 pluck, plume, spike, spine, spool 6 bobbin, needle 7 bristle, feather, spindle 9 toothpick

Quilp
character in: 19 The Old Curiosity Shop
author: 7 Dickens

quilt 5 cover 6 spread 7 blanket 8 coverlet 9 bedspread, comforter

Quin, Widow
character in: 24 Playboy of the Western World
author: 5 Synge

Quincy, M. E.
character: 3 Lee 5 Danny, (Sgt) Brill 11 Sam Fujiyama, (Dr) Robert Astin 12 (Lt) Frank Monahan
cast: 9 Robert Ito 10 John S Ragin 11 Jack Klugman, Joseph Roman, Val Bisoglio 12 Garry Walberg 13 Lynette Mettey
setting: 10 Los Angeles 11 Danny's Place

Quinn, Anthony
born: 6 Mexico 9 Chihuahua
wife: 16 Katherine DeMille
roles: 8 La Strada 10 Viva Zapata 11 Lust for Life 13 Zorba the Greek 17 The Guns of Navarone 22 Requiem for a Heavyweight, The Shoes of the Fisherman
autobiography: 14 The Original Sin

Quintana and Friends
author: 16 John Gregory Dunne

quintessence 4 core, gist, pith, soul 5 heart 6 elixir, marrow, nature 7 essence 8 exemplar, quiddity, sum total 9 substance 10 embodiment 12 distillation 15 personification, sum and substance

quip 3 gag, pun 4 barb, gibe, jape, jeer, jest, joke 5 crack, sally, spoof, taunt 6 banter, retort 7 epigram, putdown, riposte, sarcasm 8 badinage, raillery, repartee, wordplay 9 wisecrack, witticism
French: 6 bon mot 14 double entendre

Quirinus
origin: 5 Roman
god of: 3 war
personifies: 11 Roman nation
identified with: 7 Romulus

quirk 4 kink, turn, whim 6 fetish, foible, oddity, vagary, whimsy 7 caprice 8 crotchet, odd fancy 9 mannerism 10 aberration 11 abnormality, affectation, peculiarity, sudden twist 12 eccentricity, idiosyncrasy

quisling 6 puppet 7 traitor 12 collaborator 16 collaborationist

quit 3 end, rid 4 free, stop 5 cease, clear, forgo, leave, let go, waive, yield 6 depart, desist, disown, exempt, forego, give up, reject, resign, retire 7 abandon, disavow, drop out, forsake, take off 8 abdicate, absolved, forswear, renounce, withdraw 9 acquitted, foreswear, leave a job, surrender, terminate 10 discharged, exculpated, exonerated, relinquish 11 discontinue

quite 4 very 5 fully, truly 6 highly, hugely, indeed, in fact, in toto, really, surely, vastly, verily, wholly 7 exactly, in truth, totally, utterly 8 actually, entirely, outright 9 assuredly, certainly, extremely, in reality, out-and-out, perfectly, precisely, unusually, veritably 10 absolutely, altogether, completely, enormously, positively, remarkably, throughout 11 exceedingly, excessively 12 considerably 13 exceptionally

Quito
capital of: 7 Ecuador

quiver 3 tic 4 jerk, jolt, jump, pant 5 quake, shake, spasm, throb 6 quaver, shiver, totter, tremor, twitch, wobble 7 flicker, flutter, pulsate, seizure, shudder, tremble, vibrate, wriggle 8 convulse 9 fluctuate, oscillate, palpitate, pulsation, quivering, twitching, vibration 10 convulsion 11 palpitation

Quiverful, Mr
character in: 16 Barchester Towers
author: 8 Trollope

quivering 7 shaking 9 agitating, quavering, shimmying, shivering, trembling, vibrating 10 flittering, fluttering, shuddering, twittering 11 palpitating

qui vive? 12 who goes there?

quixotic 4 wild 6 absurd, dreamy, madcap, poetic 7 utopian 8 fanciful, romantic 9 fantastic, impulsive, visionary, whimsical 10 chimerical, idealistic, ridiculous, starryeyed 11 impractical, ineffective, sentimental, unrealistic 12 preposterous 13 inefficacious

quiz 3 ask, rib **4** exam, joke, mock, pump, test **5** prank, query, taunt, tease **6** banter **7** examine, inquest, inquiry **8** question, ridicule, sound out **9** catechism, eccentric, inquire of **11** examination, inquisition, interrogate, investigate, questioning **12** cross-examine **13** interrogation, investigation **16** cross-examination

Quiz Kids
   host: 8 Joe Kelly **14** Clifton Fadiman

quizzical 3 coy **4** arch **6** joking **7** baffled, curious, mocking, puzzled, teasing **8** derisive, impudent, insolent **9** bantering, inquiring, perplexed, searching **11** inquisitive, questioning

quoad hoc 12 as much as this, to this extent

quod erat demonstrandum 17 which was to be shown **24** which was to be demonstrated
   abbreviation: 3 QED

quod erat faciendum 16 which was to be done

quod vide 8 which see
   abbreviation: 2 qv

quo jure? 11 by what right?

quo modo 3 how **9** in what way **19** in the same manner that

quondam 4 erst, late, once, past **6** bygone, former **8** formerly, sometime **9** erstwhile

quota 4 part **5** share **6** ration **7** measure, minimum, portion **8** quantity **9** allotment **10** allocation, assignment, percentage, proportion **12** distribution **13** apportionment

quotation 5 quote **7** cutting, excerpt, extract, passage **8** citation, clipping **9** reference, selection **12** illustration

quote 4 cite, name **6** adduce, recall, repeat, retell **7** excerpt, extract, refer to **8** instance **9** exemplify, recollect, reproduce **10** paraphrase

quoted passage 7 excerpt, extract **9** quotation

quotidian 5 daily **6** common **8** everyday, ordinary **11** commonplace

Quo Vadis?
   author: 17 Henryk Sienkiewicz
   character: 4 Nero **5** Chilo, Lygia, Peter **8** Vinitius **9** Petronius, Tigellius
   director: 11 Mervyn LeRoy
   cast: 7 Leo Genn **11** Deborah Kerr **12** Peter Ustinov, Robert Taylor
   setting: 11 ancient Rome

R

Ra
also: 2 Re
origin: 5 Greek 10 Heliopolis
god of: 3 sun
also worshipped by: 9 Egyptians

Rabat, Rabbat
capital of: 7 Morocco

rabbi 6 master, rabbin 7 scholar, teacher 9 clergyman 15 spiritual leader

rabbinical, rabbinic 8 clerical

rabbit 4 cony, hare, jack, lure 5 bunny, coney, lapin 6 novice, rodent 8 beginner 10 cottontail, pacesetter

Rabbit Is Rich
author of: 10 John Updike

Rabbit Redux
author of: 10 John Updike

rabble 3 mob 5 swarm 7 the herd 8 populace, riffraff 9 commoners, hoi polloi, the masses 11 proletariat, rank and file 12 lower classes 15 disorderly crowd 16 the great unwashed
French: 8 canaille
German: 17 Lumpenproletariat

Rabelais, Francois
author of: 22 Gargantua and Pantagruel

rabid 4 wild 6 ardent, crazed, raging 7 berserk, fervent, frantic, violent, zealous 8 deranged, frenzied, maniacal, wild-eyed 9 fanatical 11 hydrophobic 17 foaming at the mouth

race 3 fly, run 4 dart, dash, heat, rush 5 hurry 6 hasten, hustle 7 contest, operate 8 campaign 11 competition

racecourse 4 turf 5 track 6 course 9 racetrack

Rachel
father: 5 Laban
husband: 5 Jacob
sister: 4 Leah
son: 6 Joseph 8 Benjamin
slave: 6 Bilhah

Rachmaninov (Rachmaninoff, Rakhmaninov), Sergei
born: 6 Russia 8 Novgorod
composer of: 15 Symphonic Dances 16 The Isle of the Dead 19 Second Piano Concerto 26 Rhapsody on a Theme by (of) Paganini

Racine, Jean Baptiste
author of: 6 Phedre 7 Athalie 8 Berenice 10 Andromache 11 Britannicus

racism 7 bigotry 8 color bar 9 color line 10 race hatred, racial bias 11 segregation 15 racial prejudice 20 racial discrimination

rack 4 buck, gait, hurt, neck, pace, pain, path 5 agony, cloud, exert, frame, raise, track, trail, worry, wreck, wring 6 can-ter, holder, strain 7 afflict, agonize, draw off, oppress, stretch, torment, torture 8 distress 9 suffering 10 destruction, excruciate, iron maiden

racked 4 torn 5 paced 6 framed, pained, traced, walked 7 annoyed, tracked, trotted, wronged, worried 8 cantered, suffered, tortured 9 afflicted, anguished, destroyed, oppressed, tormented 10 persecuted

racket 3 din 4 game, line, roar, stir 5 babel 6 clamor, hubbub, rumpus, tumult, uproar 7 clangor, clatter, turmoil 8 business, shouting 9 commotion, loud noise 10 hullabaloo, hurly-burly, occupation, turbulence 11 disturbance, pandemonium 12 caterwauling, vociferation

racketeer 4 hood 5 crook 6 bagman, bandit, extort 7 hoodlum, mafioso, mobster 8 criminal, gangster 12 extortionist

racking 7 painful 9 agonizing, torturous 10 tormenting, unbearable 11 intolerable, unendurable 12 excruciating, insufferable

raconteur 8 fabulist, narrator, romancer 10 anecdotist 11 storyteller 13 teller of tales 14 spinner of yarns

racy 4 keen 5 bawdy, crude, heady, lurid, zesty 6 erotic, lively, ribald, risque, smutty, vulgar 7 buoyant, glowing, obscene, zestful 8 animated, exciting, immodest, indecent, off-color, prurient, spirited, vigorous 9 energetic, fast-paced, salacious, sparkling 10 suggestive 11 stimulating 12 exhilarating, pornographic

radar
invented by: 4 Watt 6 Watson

Radcliffe, Mrs Ann
author of: 10 The Italian 21 The Mysteries of Udolpho

raddle 3 rod 4 reed, scar, twig 5 fence, hedge, rouge, stick, weave 6 branch, ruddle 8 hematite, red ocher, red ochre 10 interweave

radiance, radiancy 3 joy 5 gleam, gleem, sheen 6 dazzle, luster 7 glitter, rapture, sparkle 8 lambency, splendor 9 animation, happiness 10 brightness, brilliance, brilliancy, effulgence, luminosity, refulgence 11 coruscation, iridescence 12 luminousness, resplendence 13 incandescence
god of: 5 Baldr 6 Balder, Baldur

radiant 5 aglow, happy, sunny 6 bright, elated, joyous 7 beaming, glowing, pleased, shining 8 blissful, dazzling, ecstatic, flashing, gladsome, gleaming, luminous, lustrous 9 brilliant, delighted, effulgent, overjoyed, rapturous, refulgent, sparkling 10 glittering 12 incandescent 13 scintillating

radiate 4 beam, pour, shed 5 carry 6 spread 7 diffuse, diverge, give off, give out, scatter 8 disperse, emit heat, transmit 9 branch out, circulate, emit light, spread out 11 disseminate

radical 4 rash 5 basic, rebel 6 severe 7 drastic, extreme 8 left-wing, militant 9 extremist, firebrand 10 immoderate, inordinate 11 freethinker, fundamental, precipitate 13 revolutionary 22 antiestablishmentarian

radio
   invented by: 7 Donovan, Fleming, Marconi 8 De Forest, Nicolson 9 Armstrong, Fessenden 12 Alexanderson

radium
   chemical symbol: 2 Ra

radon
   chemical symbol: 2 Rn

raffish 3 low 4 fast, wild 5 cheap, rowdy, showy 6 common, flashy, rakish, tawdry, vulgar 7 boorish 8 rakehell 9 worthless 10 dissipated 12 devil-may-care, disreputable

raft 3 lot 4 mass 5 barge, float 6 plenty 7 carrier, pontoon 8 flatboat, platform, quantity 9 abundance, multitude

Raft, George
   real name: 11 George Ranft
   born: 9 New York NY
   roles: 8 Scarface 11 Johnny Angel 12 Guido Rinaldo 13 Some Like It Hot

rag 3 kid, rib 4 scap, song, tune, twit 5 cloth, taunt, taunt, tease 6 harass 7 torment 8 magazine 9 newspaper 11 ragtime tune 14 worn-out garment

ragamuffin 3 bum 4 hobo, waif 5 gamin, tramp 6 beggar, gamine, hoyden, sloven, urchin, wretch 7 vagrant 8 derelict, vagabond 9 itinerant, ragpicker 10 panhandler, street arab 11 guttersnipe 14 tatterdemalion

rage 3 fad, ire 4 boil, fume, fury, mode, rant, rave, roar 5 craze, furor, mania, pique, storm, vogue, wrath 6 blow up, choler, frenzy, seethe, spleen, temper 7 explode, fashion, ferment, flare up, madness, passion, rampage, umbrage 8 paroxysm, the thing 9 animosity, fulminate, raise cain, throw a fit, vehemence 10 bitterness, excitement, irritation, resentment, the "in" thing 11 displeasure, high dudgeon, indignation, the last word 12 current style, le dernier cri, perturbation, violent anger 13 temper tantrum 14 the latest thing 15 fly off the handle, froth at the mouth

Rage of Angels
   author: 13 Sidney Sheldon

ragged 4 rent, torn, worn 5 seedy, tacky 6 beat up, frayed, shabby, shaggy, shoddy 7 patched, run down, worn-out 8 battered, shredded, strained, tattered 9 overtaxed 10 aggravated, threadbare, worn to rags 11 exacerbated

ragging 5 chaff 6 banter 7 kidding, ribbing, teasing 8 chaffing, needling, raillery, taunting, twitting

raging 3 mad 4 wild 5 angry, livid, rabid, rough 6 fierce, raving, stormy 7 fervent, frantic, furious, rampant, violent 8 frenzied, incensed, storming 9 turbulent 10 blustering, ferocious, infuriated 11 tempestuous

Raging Bull
   director: 14 Martin Scorsese
   cast: 8 Joe Pesci 12 Frank Vincent, Robert De Niro (Jake La Motta) 13 Cathy Moriarty
   Oscar for: 5 actor (De Niro)

Ragnarok
   also: 15 Gotterdammerung 17 Twilight of the Gods
   origin: 12 Scandinavian
   event: 11 final battle
   battlefield: 6 Vigrid

ragout 4 hash, stew 7 borscht, goulash 9 fricassee

Ragtime
   author: 10 E L Doctorow

Rahab
   hometown: 7 Jericho
   husband: 6 Solmon
   hid: 12 Joshua's spies

raid 4 bust 5 foray, onset, sally, storm 6 attack, inroad, invade, razzia, sortie 7 assault, round-up 8 invasion 10 pounce upon 14 surprise attack

Raiders of the Lost Ark
   director: 15 Steven Spielberg
   cast: 10 Karen Allen, Wolf Kahler 11 Paul Freeman 12 Harrison Ford
   sequel: 30 Indiana Jones and the Temple of Doom

rail 3 bar 4 rage, rant 5 scold, fence, train 6 blow up, scream, take on 7 barrier, carry on, declaim, inveigh, railing, railway, the cars 8 banister, railroad 9 fulminate 10 vituperate, vociferate 11 rant and rave 14 foam at the mouth

rail at 5 scold 6 berate 7 chew out 9 castigate 14 inveigh against

railing 3 bar 5 fence, grate, rails 6 fender 7 barrier, parapet, support 8 banister 9 enclosing 10 balustrade

raillery 5 chaff, sport 6 banter, japing, joking, satire 7 fooling, jesting, joshing, kidding, ragging, razzing, ribbing, teasing 8 badinage, chaffing, roasting, twitting 10 lampoonery, persiflage, pleasantry

railroad sleeping car
   French: 8 wagon-lit

railroad station 5 depot 8 terminal, terminus

railway 4 tube 5 track, train 6 cogway, subway 7 cograod, trolley 8 elevated, monorail, railroad 9 streetcar

raiment 4 duds, togs 5 dress 6 attire 7 apparel, clothes, costume, threads 8 clothing, garments 11 habiliments

rain, rains 4 down, drop, mist, pour 5 spate 6 deluge, lavish, shower, squall 7 drizzle, monsoon, torrent 8 downpour, drencher,

plethora, rainfall, send down, sprinkle 9 hurricane, rainstorm 10 cloudburst 13 precipitation, thundershower 15 rain cats and dogs 16 come down in sheets 17 come down in buckets
   god of: 4 Thor

Rainbow
   goddess of: 4 Iris

Rainbow, The
   author: 10 D H Lawrence
   character: 10 Anna Lensky 11 Lydia Lensky, Tom Brangwen 12 Will Brangwen 14 Ursula Brangwen 15 Anton Skrebensky

Rainbow Bridge see 7 bifrost

raincoat 3 mac 4 mack 6 poncho, ulster 7 oilskin, slicker 8 burberry 9 tarpaulin 10 mackintosh, trenchcoat, waterproof

rainless 3 dry 4 arid, sere 10 desertlike

Rains, Claude
   born: 6 London 7 England
   wife: 11 Isabel Jeans
   roles: 9 Notorious 10 Casablanca, Now Voyager 13 Mr Skeffington 14 Anthony Adverse 15 The Invisible Man 16 Lawrence of Arabia 17 Here Comes Mr Jordan 20 The Phantom of the Opera 23 Mr Smith Goes to Washington 24 The Adventures of Robin Hood

rain shower 6 shower 7 drizzle 8 sprinkle 12 thundershower

rainstorm 6 deluge, shower 8 downfall, downpour 10 cloudburst 12 thunderstorm

rainy 3 wet 4 damp 7 drizzly, showery 11 pouring rain 18 raining cats and dogs

raise 3 end 4 grow, hike, lift, rear, spur, urge 5 amass, boost, breed, build, erect, nurse, pique, put up, rouse, set up, spark 6 arouse, awaken, excite, foster, hike up, jack up, kindle, obtain, stir up 7 advance, bring in, bring up, canvass, collect, develop, elevate, inflame, inflate, inspire, nurture, procure, produce, sharpen, solicit 8 increase, summon up 9 construct, cultivate, elevation, promotion, stimulate, terminate 10 make higher, put forward 11 advancement

raise aloft 5 boost, hoist 6 lift up, uplift 7 elevate, upraise

raised 4 bred, grew 5 anted, built, grown 6 anteed, convex, jacked, lifted, reared, roused 7 aroused, erected, exalted, hoisted, honored, incited 8 elevated, embossed, leavened, mustered 9 brought up, collected 10 cultivated 11 resurrected

Raisin in the Sun, A
   director: 12 Daniel Petrie
   based on play by: 17 Lorraine Hansberry
   cast: 7 Ruby Dee 9 Ivan Dixon 10 Diana Sands 13 Claudia McNeil, Sidney Poitier
   setting: 7 Chicago

rake 4 comb, goat, roue 5 rogue, satyr, scour, sport 6 lecher, pepper, rascal 7 Don Juan, playboy, ransack, seducer, swinger 8 Casanova, Lothario, enfilade, prodigal, rakehell 9 debauchee, libertine, womanizer 10 immoralist, profligate, sensualist, voluptuary

rake-off 3 cut, fee 5 piece 10 percentage 16 piece of the action

Rake's Progress, The
   opera by: 10 Stravinsky
   character: 10 Ann Trulove, Nick Shadow 11 Baba the Turk, Mother Goose, Tom Rakewell

rakish 4 airy 6 breezy, dapper, jaunty, sporty 7 dashing, gallant, immoral, lustful 8 cavalier, debonair, depraved, sporting 9 bumptious, debauched, dissolute, lecherous, libertine 10 dissipated, lascivious, profligate, sauntering, swaggering

rally 4 meet, rush 5 score, unite 6 caucus, gather, muster, pick up, powwow, revive 7 catch up, collect, get well, improve, recruit, reunite, revival 8 assemble, assembly, recovery 9 come round, gathering, get better, reconvene 10 assemblage, convalesce, convention, reassemble, recuperate 11 convocation, improvement, mass meeting, pull through, restoration 12 call together, congregation, recuperation 13 convalescence

ram 3 hit, jam 4 beat, bump, butt, dash, goat, slam 5 crash, drive, force, smash 6 batter, hammer, hurtle, strike, thrust 7 run into

Ram
   constellation of: 5 Aries

ramble 3 gad 4 hike, roam, rove, wind 5 amble, drift, range, snake, twist 6 stroll, wander, zigzag 7 meander, saunter, traipse 8 gad about, idle walk 9 gallivant 11 perambulate, peregrinate

rambling 6 prolix, uneven 7 diffuse 10 circuitous, digres sive, discursive, disjointed

rambunctious 4 wild 5 noisy, rowdy 6 active, unruly 7 raucous, untamed, violent 9 irascible 10 boisterous, pugnacious 11 quarrelsome 14 uncontrollable

Rameau, Jean-Philippe
   born: 5 Dijon 6 France
   composer of: 6 Platee 8 Dardanus 13 Les Fetes d'Hebe 14 Castor et Pollux 15 Castor and Pollux 16 Les Indes Galantes, The Indigo Suitors 17 Hippolyte et Aricie 20 La Princesse de Navarre

ramification 3 arm 4 part, spur 5 prong 6 branch 8 division, offshoot 9 branching, outgrowth 10 divergence, separation 11 consequence, subdivision

rampage 4 rage 5 storm 7 run amok, run riot

rampant 4 rife 5 erect 6 raging 8 epidemic, pandemic 9 prevalent, unchecked, universal 10 on hind legs, standing up, widespread 12 ungovernable, unrestrained 14 uncontrollable

rampart 7 barrier, bastion, bulwark, parapet 9 barricade, earthwork 10 breastwork 13 defensive wall, fortification 14 protective wall

Ramsay, William
  field: 9 chemistry
  nationality: 7 British
  discovered: 4 neon 5 argon (in air) 6 helium 7 krypton
  awarded: 10 Nobel Prize
ramshackle 5 shaky 6 flimsy, shabby 7 rickety, run-down 8 decrepit, unstable, unsteady 9 crumbling, tottering 10 tumbledown 11 dilapidated 13 deteriorating
Ramtil *see* 5 Niger
Ran
  origin: 12 Scandinavian
  goddess of: 3 sea
  husband: 5 Aegir
ranch 4 farm 5 range 6 grange, spread 7 acreage, station 8 hacienda 10 plantation
rancher 6 cowboy, farmer, gaucho 7 cowhand, cowpoke 8 herdsman, sheepman, stockman 9 cattleman 10 cowpuncher
rancid 3 old 4 foul, gamy, high, rank 6 putrid, strong 8 mephitic, stinking 10 malodorous
rancor 4 hate 5 spite 6 animus, enmity, hatred, malice, spleen 7 ill will 8 acrimony 9 animosity, antipathy, hostility 10 antagonism, bitterness, ill feeling, resentment 11 malevolence 12 spitefulness
rancorous 5 nasty 6 bitter 7 hostile 8 churlish, spiteful, vengeful, venomous 9 splenetic 10 ill-natured 11 acrimonious 12 antagonistic
Rand, Ayn
  author of: 13 Atlas Shrugged 15 The Fountainhead 17 Romantic Manifesto
Randall, Tony
  real name: 16 Leonard Rosenberg
  born: 7 Tulsa OK
  roles: 9 Mr Peepers 10 Felix Unger, Pillow Talk 12 Harvey Weskit, The Odd Couple 13 The Mating Game 20 The Seven Faces of Dr Lao
random 5 stray 6 casual, chance 7 aimless, offhand 9 haphazard, hit-or-miss, unplanned 10 accidental, fortuitous, occasional, undesigned, unexpected, unintended 12 adventitious 13 unintentional 14 unpremeditated
Ranft, George
  real name of: 10 George Raft
range 3 run 4 roam, rove 5 field, gamut, limit, orbit, reach, ridge, scope 6 bounds, domain, extend, massif, plains, radius, sierra, sphere, wander 7 explore, pasture, purview, stretch, variety 8 province 9 selection 11 grazing land 16 chain of mountains
Rangoon
  capital of: 5 Burma
  former name: 5 Dagon 6 Yangon
  founder: 10 Alaungpaya
  landmark: 10 Sule Pagoda 15 Shwe Dagon Pagoda
  name means: 11 end of strife
  river: 7 Rangoon
  square: 12 Independence

rangy 4 tall 5 broad, lanky 9 expansive, extensive
rank 3 row 4 bald, file, foul, line, lush, rate, sort, tall, type, wild 5 class, crass, dense, grade, gross, level, nasty, order, sheer, stale, stand, total, utter 6 arrant, coarse, column, estate, filthy, jungly, lavish, rancid, status 7 come out, echelon, glaring, profuse, quality, rampart 8 absolute, complete, flagrant, position, standing, tropical 9 atrocious, be classed, come first, downright, have place, luxuriant, monstrous, overgrown 10 outrageous, scurrilous 11 highgrowing, ill smelling, unmitigated 12 over abundant 14 classification, social standing, strong smelling
rank and file 6 troops 17 enlisted personnel, general membership
Rankine, William John Macquorn
  field: 7 physics
  nationality: 8 Scottish
  devised: 12 Rankine Cycle, Rankine Scale 26 Fahrenheit temperature scale
  author of: 22 Manual of the Steam Engine
rankle 4 gall, rile 5 chafe, gripe, pique 6 fester 8 irritate 10 not sit well
ransack 3 gut 4 comb, loot, raid, rake, sack 5 rifle, scour, strip 6 ravage, search 7 despoil, pillage, plunder 8 lay waste 9 devastate, vandalize 14 rummage through, turn upside down
ransom 3 buy 4 free, save 5 atone, price 6 redeem, rescue 7 deliver, expiate, reclaim, recover, release 8 liberate, retrieve 10 liberation, redemption
Ransom, John Crowe
  member of: 12 the Fugitives
  author of: 14 I'll Take My Stand 16 Captain Carpenter 30 Bells for John Whiteside's Daughter
rant 4 fume, rage, rave, yell 5 orate, scold, spout, storm 6 bellow 7 bluster, bombast, bravado, explode 8 harangue 11 declamation 12 exaggeration
rap 3 jaw, pan, tap 4 bang, chat, drum, talk 5 blame, knock, roast, speak, thump 6 dump on 7 clobber 8 converse 9 criticize 10 come down on 11 communicate 14 responsibility, shoot the breeze
rapacious 6 greedy 7 looting, wolfish 8 covetous, grasping, ravenous, thievish 9 marauding, mercenary, pillaging, predatory, voracious 10 avaricious, insatiable, plundering, ransacking
rapacity 5 greed 7 avarice 10 greediness 12 covetousness, graspingness 13 mercenariness
Rape of Lucrece
  author of: 18 William Shakespeare
  character: 7 Tarquin 9 Collatine
Rape of the Lock, The
  author: 13 Alexander Pope
  character: 5 Ariel 7 Belinda, Umbriel 9 Lord Petre 10 Thalestris

Raphael 9 archangel

Raphael
   real name: 14 Raffaello Santi 15 Raffaello Sanzio
   born: 5 Italy 6 Urbino
   artwork: 7 Disputa 8 Julius II 10 Entombment 14 Sistine Madonna 17 The School of Athens, The Virgin and Child 18 Madonna di Casa Tempi, The Transfiguration 19 The Triumph of Galatea 21 Baldassare Castiglione 22 The Marriage of the Virgin 24 The Expulsion of Heliodorus 28 The Madonna and Child with St John (La Belle Jardiniere)
   architect of: 11 Villa Madama (Rome) 16 Pandolfini Palace (Florence) 22 Vidoni-Caffarelli Palace (Rome)

rapid 4 fast 5 brisk, fleet, hasty, quick, swift 6 active, flying, prompt, speedy 7 express, hurried, instant, rushing 8 agitated, feverish 9 galloping, unchecked 11 accelerated, expeditious, precipitate

rapidity 5 haste, speed 8 celerity, velocity 9 fleetness, quickness, swiftness 10 promptness

rapidly 4 fast 5 apace 7 briskly, hastily, quickly, swiftly 8 pell-mell, speedily 9 hurriedly, like a shot, overnight 10 in high gear 11 at full speed 13 expeditiously, helter-skelter

rapids 5 chute 7 current 10 white water

rapport 3 tie 4 link 10 connection, fellowship 11 affiliation, camaraderie 12 relationship 13 understanding 17 interrelationship

rapprochement 6 accord 7 detente, entente 9 agreement 10 adjustment, compromise, settlement 11 appeasement, arrangement 12 conciliation, pacification 13 accommodation, harmonization, reconcilement, understanding 14 reconciliation 16 mutual concession

rapscallion 5 knave, rogue, scamp 6 rascal 7 low-life, villain 8 scalawag 9 scoundrel 10 blackguard, ne'er-do-well, rascallion 14 good-for-nothing

rapt 6 dreamy, enrapt, intent 7 bemused, charmed 8 absorbed, ecstatic 9 attentive, bewitched, delighted, enchanted, engrossed, entranced, rapturous 10 captivated, enraptured, enthralled, fascinated, interested, moonstruck, spellbound 11 transported

rapture 3 joy 5 bliss 6 thrill 7 delight, ecstasy, elation 8 euphoria, felicity 9 beatitude

rapturous 4 rapt 8 beatific, blissful, ecstatic 10 enraptured, enthralled

rare 3 few 6 scarce, unique 7 unusual 8 uncommon 10 hard to find, infrequent 11 exceptional, seldom found 16 few and far between

rarefied 4 thin 6 dilute, purify, rarify, reduce, refine, subtle 7 inflate 8 diminish 9 attenuate, extenuate

rarely 6 hardly, seldom 8 not often 10 hardly ever, uncommonly 12 infrequently, scarcely ever 15 once in a blue moon, on rare occasions 17 once in a great while

raring 4 agog, avid, keen 5 eager 8 desirous 9 impatient 12 enthusiastic

rarity 6 oddity 7 anomaly 8 scarcity 11 unusualness 12 uncommonness 14 remarkableness

rascal 3 cad, imp 4 rake 5 devil, knave, rogue, scamp 7 villain 8 rakehell, scalawag 9 prankster, reprobate, scoundrel, trickster 10 blackguard, delinquent 11 rapscallion

rash 5 brash, hasty 6 abrupt 7 foolish 8 careless, headlong, heedless, reckless 9 foolhardy, impetuous, imprudent, impulsive, premature, unadvised, unchecked 10 incautious, indiscreet, ungoverned, unthinking 11 adventurous, harebrained, injudicious, precipitate, thoughtless 12 devil-may-care, uncontrolled 13 irresponsible

rashness 8 audacity, boldness 9 riskiness 12 heedlessness, indiscretion, recklessness 13 foolhardiness, impulsiveness 15 precipitousness, thoughtlessness

Rashomon
   author: 18 Ryunosuke Akutagawa
   director: 13 Akira Kurosawa

Raskolnikov
   character in: 18 Crime and Punishment
   author: 10 Dostoevsky

rasp 3 irk, nag, rub, vex 4 file 5 chafe, grate, worry 6 abrade, scrape, wheeze 7 grating, scraper, scratch 8 abrasive, irritate 9 huskiness 10 hoarseness

raspberry 11 Rubus idaeus
   varieties: 3 red 4 hill 5 black, dwarf 6 Mysore, purple 8 European 9 flowering, Mauritius 11 American red 13 Rocky Mountain 15 Purple-flowering 22 Rocky Mountain flowering
   brandy: 9 Framboise

rasping 5 harsh, raspy, rough 6 hoarse 7 chafing, grating, nagging 8 abrading, scraping, worrying 9 offensive 10 irritating

Rasselas
   author: 13 Samuel Johnson
   character: 5 Imlac 6 Pekuah 7 Nekayah
   Rasselas's title: 17 Prince of Abyssinia

Rassendyll, Rudolph
   character in: 15 Prisoner of Zenda
   author: 4 Hope

rat 3 cad, cur 4 fink, heel 5 churl, knave, louse 6 betray, rascal, rotter, squeal, vermin 7 bounder, villain 8 informer, inform on 9 scoundrel 10 blackguard 11 stool pigeon

rate 3 fee 4 cost, deem, dues, levy, pace, rank, toll 5 class, count, price, speed, tempo 6 charge, figure, look on, regard, tariff 7 expense, measure 8 classify 10 assessment

rate highly 5 prize, value 6 admire, esteem 7 cherish, respect 8 treasure

Rathbone, Basil

real name: 25 Philip St John Basil Rathbone

born: 11 South Africa 12 Johannesburg

roles: 6 Tybalt 7 Karenin 10 Dawn Patrol 11 Mr Murdstone 12 Anna Karenina 14 Romeo and Juliet, Sherlock Holmes, The Mark of Zorro 16 A Tale of Two Cities, David Copperfield 20 The Last Days of Pompeii 24 The Adventures of Robin Hood 25 The Hound of the Baskervilles

rather 4 a bit, very 5 quite 6 fairly, kind of, pretty, sort of 8 slightly, somewhat 10 moderately, more or less, relatively 13 comparatively

ratification 2 OK 4 okay 7 consent 8 approval, sanction 10 validation 11 affirmation, endorsement 12 confirmation 13 authorization, corroboration 14 seal of approval

ratify 2 OK 4 okay 6 affirm, uphold 7 agree to, approve, certify, confirm, endorse, support 8 accede to, make good, sanction, validate 9 authorize, consent to, make valid 11 acknowledge 12 authenticate

rating 4 mark, rank 5 class, grade, ratio, value 6 degree, rebuke, sailor, seaman 7 ranking 8 standing 9 appraisal 10 assessment, evaluation, percentage 14 classification

ratio 5 equation 10 proportion 11 arrangement 12 distribution 13 apportionment, fixed relation 15 proportionality 17 interrelationship 20 proportional relation

ration, rations 3 due 4 dole, food 5 allot 6 stores 7 measure, mete out 8 allocate 9 allotment, apportion, food share, provender, provision 10 provisions 13 apportionment

rational 4 sage, sane, wise 5 lucid, solid, sound 6 normal 7 logical 8 all there, balanced, credible, feasible 9 advisable, judicious, plausible, sagacious 10 reasonable 11 clearheaded, responsible 12 composmentis 13 perspicacious 15 in one's right mind

rationale 5 basis, logic 6 excuse, reason 7 grounds 9 reasoning 10 key concept, philosophy 11 explanation, foundations 16 underlying reason

rationalize 6 excuse 7 explain, justify 8 palliate 9 whitewash 10 account for 11 explain away 13 put a gloss upon 14 make excuses for 16 make allowance for

rattan, ratan 4 cane, lash, palm, whip 5 thong 6 switch, wicker

Ratti, Achille 10 Pope Pius XI

rattle 3 gab, jar 4 faze 5 clang, clank, clink, prate, shake, throw, upset 6 bounce, flurry, jangle 7 agitate, blather, chatter, clatter, confuse, disturb, fluster, maunder, nonplus, perturb 8 bewilder, clacking, distract 9 discomfit 10 discompose, disconcert 11 roll loosely

rattlebrained 4 dumb 5 silly 6 stupid 7 asinine, doltish, foolish, idiotic, moronic, witless 9 brainless, imbecilic 10 fool-headed, half-witted 11 harebrained, lamebrained

rattled 5 fazed, upset 7 annoyed 9 disturbed, flustered, perturbed, thrown off 10 distracted 11 discomposed 12 disconcerted

rattle on 3 gab 4 blab 5 prate, run on 6 babble, gabble 7 blabber, chatter, prattle 16 run off at the mouth

ratty 4 poor, worn 5 angry, cross, nasty, testy 6 cranky, shabby, touchy 7 tangled, unkempt 8 wretched 9 irascible, motheaten 11 dilapidated

raucous 4 loud 5 harsh, raspy, rough 6 hoarse, shrill 7 blaring, grating, jarring 8 grinding, jangling, piercing, strident 9 dissonant 10 discordant, stertorous 11 cacophonous 12 earsplitting, inharmonious

raunchy 4 lewd 5 dirty, gross 6 coarse, smutty, vulgar 8 off-color

Rauschenberg, Robert

born: 12 Port Arthur TX

artwork: 3 Bed 5 Barge 7 Jammers 8 Monogram 11 Retroactive

ravage 3 gut 4 loot, raid, rape, raze, ruin, sack 5 strip, waste, wreck 6 maraud 7 despoil, destroy, overrun, pillage, plunder, ransack, shatter 8 demolish, desolate, lay waste, spoliate 9 devastate 10 lay in ruins

rave 3 wax 4 fume, go on, gush, rage, rant 5 be mad, kudos, storm 6 babble, bubble, ramble 7 be angry, bluster, carry on, explode, flare up, run amok, sputter, thunder 8 flattery 9 be furious, expatiate, go on and on, good press, laudatory 10 effervesce, high praise, rhapsodize 11 blow one's top, compliments

ravel 4 undo 6 unknit 7 unravel, untwine, untwist

Ravel, Maurice

born: 6 France 7 Ciboure

composer of: 6 Bolero 7 La Valse, Mirrors 8 Jeux d'eau 9 Fountains 11 Mother Goose, Sheherazade 14 Daphnis et Chloe 15 Gaspard de la Nuit, L'Heure Espagnole 17 Rapsodie Espagnole, The Tomb of Couperin 20 Pavane for a Dead Infant 21 Don Quichotte a Dulcinee 22 L'Enfant et les Sortileges, Pavane for a Dead Princess 27 Pavane pour une infante de funte, Valses nobles et sentimentales

raven 3 jet 4 crow, dark, inky, rook 5 black, ebony, sable 6 devour 9 coal-black

Raven, The

author: 13 Edgar Allan Poe

ravenous 6 greedy, hungry 7 piggish, starved 8 covetous, famished, grasping, ravening, starving 9 insatiate, predatory, rapacious, voracious 10 avaricious, gluttonous, insatiable

Ravenshoe

author: 13 Henry Kingsley

ravine 3 gap 4 pass, rift, wadi 5 abyss, break, chasm, cleft, crack, gorge, gulch, gully, split 6 arroyo, breach, canyon, clough, divide, valley 7 fissure 8 crevasse

raving 3 mad 4 wild 6 insane 7 ranting 8 frenzied 9 delirious

ravish 4 rape 5 abuse, charm, cheer 6 defile, snatch, tickle 7 delight, enchant, gladden, outrage, overjoy, violate 8 deflower, enthrall, entrance, knock out 9 captivate, enrapture, fascinate, transport

ravishing 8 alluring, charming, gorgeous, smashing, splendid, striking 9 beautiful 10 bewitching, delightful, enchanting, entrancing 11 captivating, fascinating, sensational

raw 4 bare, cold, damp, rare 5 basic, bleak, crude, frank, fresh, green, harsh, plain, rough, young 6 biting, bitter, brutal, callow, chilly, rookie, unripe 7 cutting, natural, nipping, numbing, unbaked, untried 8 blustery, freezing, ignorant, immature, inexpert, piercing, pinching, uncooked, untaught, untested 9 inclement, underdone, undrilled, unfledged, unrefined, unskilled, untrained, windswept 10 amateurish, unprepared, unseasoned 11 not finished, undercooked, undeveloped, unexercised, uninitiated, unpracticed, unprocessed, unvarnished 13 inexperienced, undisciplined, unembellished 15 not manufactured

rawboned 4 lean 6 gaunt, lanky, spare 7 angular

Rawdon, Captain
　character in: 10 Bleak House
　author: 7 Dickens

Rawhide
　character: 5 Mushy 8 Gil Favor, Ian Cabot, Wishbone 9 Jim Quince, Pete Nolan 10 Rowdy Yates 11 Joe Scarlett, Solomon King 13 Clay Forrester 14 Hey Soos Patines
　cast: 10 Sheb Wooley 11 Charles Gray, David Watson, Eric Fleming, Robert Cabal, Rocky Shahan, Steve Raines 12 James Murdock, Paul Brinegar 13 Clint Eastwood 16 Raymond St Jacques

Rawlings, Marjorie Kinnan
　author of: 11 The Yearling

rawness 3 nip 4 bite 5 chill 8 rudeness 9 crudeness, greenness, roughness, sharpness, vulgarity 10 chilliness 12 inexperience

ray 3 arm 4 beam, fish, line 5 gleam, light, shaft, shine, skate, trace 6 branch, streak, stream, stripe 7 radiate 8 particle, plowfish, radiance 9 emanation, radiation

Ray, Man
　born: 14 Philadelphia PA
　artwork: 4 Gift (Le Cadeau) 7 Manikin 9 The Lovers 13 Observing Time 45 The Rope Dancer Accompanies Herself with Her Shadows

Rayleigh, John William Strutt
　field: 7 physics
　nationality: 7 British
　discovered: 5 argon
　awarded: 10 Nobel Prize

rayon
　invented by: 4 Swan

raze 4 fell, ruin 5 level, smash, wreck 6 reduce, remove, topple 7 destroy, flatten, wipe out 8 demolish, pull down, tear down 9 break down, dismantle, knock down 10 obliterate

razor
　invented by: 6 Schick 8 Gillette

Razorback State
　nickname of: 8 Arkansas

Re see 2 Ra

reach 3 get, hit 4 find, go to, grab, make, move 5 climb, enter, get to, grasp, seize, touch 6 attain, clutch, come to, extend, grab at, land at, secure, spread 7 contact, stretch 8 amount to, approach, arrive at 9 get hold of, set foot in 10 get as far as, outstretch, stretch out

reachable 6 at hand 8 possible 10 accessible, achievable, attainable, obtainable, procurable

reach the top 6 arrive 7 prosper, succeed 8 make good 13 hit the big time

react 4 work 6 answer, behave, resist, return 7 respond 11 reverberate

reaction 5 reply 6 answer, reflex 8 backlash, response 11 restoration 13 counteraction 14 chemical change 17 counterrevolution, right-wing comeback

reactionary 7 diehard 8 mossback, rightist 9 right-wing 10 regressive 11 right-winger 12 reversionary 17 ultraconservative 20 counterrevolutionary

react to 5 reply 6 answer 7 respond 11 acknowledge

read 2 go 3 say 4 note, scan, show 5 study, utter 6 adduce, peruse, recite 7 analyze, deliver, discern, explain, present 8 construe, decipher, indicate, perceive, pore over 9 apprehend, interpret, translate 10 comprehend, glance over, understand 11 extrapolate

Read, Piers Paul
　author of: 5 Alive 9 Polonaise 10 Monk Dawson, The Junkers, The Upstart 18 Professor's Daughter

Reade, Charles
　author of: 13 Peg Woffington 23 The Cloister and the Hearth

readily 6 at once, easily, freely, pronto 7 quickly 8 in no time, promptly, smoothly, speedily 9 expressly, hands down, instantly, willingly 10 graciously 11 immediately, straightway 12 effortlessly, ungrudgingly

readiness 8 alacrity, dispatch 9 alertness 10 promptness 12 preparedness

Reading on the Statute of Uses
　author: 12 Francis Bacon

read the riot act 5 chide, scold 6 berate, rebuke 7 censure, chasten, correct, lecture, reprove 8 admonish 9 dress down, reprimand 10 take to task

ready 3 apt, fit, set 4 deft, keen, ripe, up to 5 acute, alert, eager, equip, handy, on tap, prone, sharp 6 adroit, all set, artful, astute, at hand, bright, clever, expert, facile, fit out, liable, mature, on hand, primed, prompt, shrewd, speedy 7 cunning, equal to, prepare, present, tending, willing 8 disposed, inclined, masterly, punctual, skillful

9 attentive, dexterous, fitted out, furnished, ingenious, in harness, versatile, wide-awake **10** accessible, discerning, perceptive, put in order **11** acquisitive, expeditious, predisposed, quick-witted, resourceful, serviceable

ready for use 5 handy, on tap **6** at hand, on hand **9** available **10** accessible, convenient **11** at one's elbow **14** at one's disposal

ready-made 10 off-the-rack **11** ready-to-wear, store-bought **17** store manufactured

ready money 4 cash **8** currency **10** cash on hand

ready to go 5 peppy **9** full of pep **10** raring to go **17** full of vim and vigor **24** bright-eyed and bushy-tailed

Reagan, Ronald Wilson
　nickname: **5** Dutch **6** Ronnie
　presidential rank: **8** fortieth
　party:
　　current: **10** Republican
　　former: **10** Democratic
　state represented: **2** CA
　defeated: **6** (James Earl) Carter (Jr) **7** (Walter Frederick "Fritz") Mondale **8** (John Bayard) Anderson
　vice president: **4** (George Herbert Walker) Bush
　cabinet:
　　state: **4** (Alexander M) Haig (Jr) **6** (George P) Shultz
　　treasury: **5** (Donald T) Regan
　　defense: **10** (Caspar W) Weinberger
　　attorney general: **5** (William French) Smith
　　interior: **4** (James) Watt **5** (William P) Clark
　　agriculture: **5** (John R) Block
　　commerce: **8** (Malcolm) Baldrige
　　labor: **7** (Raymond J) Donovan
　　health and human services: **7** (Margaret M) Heckler **9** (Richard S) Schweiker
　　education: **4** (Terrel H) Bell
　　HUD: **6** (Samuel R) Pierce (Jr)
　　transportation: **4** (Elizabeth H) Dole **5** (Andrew L) Lewis (Jr)
　　energy: **5** (Donald P) Hodel **7** (James B) Edwards
　born: **9** Tampico IL
　education:
　　college: **6** Eureka
　religion: **17** Disciples of Christ
　interests: **2** TV **5** track **6** movies **8** football **9** chops wood **10** basketball, jelly beans **13** weightlifting **15** horseback riding
　vacation spot: **14** Rancho del Cielo (Santa Barbara CA)
　dog: **5** Lucky
　author: **18** Where Is the Rest of Me?
　political career:
　　governor of: **10** California
　civilian career: **5** actor **17** radio sportscaster
　　host: **15** Death Valley Days **22** General Electric Theater

　president of: **17** Screen Actors Guild
　roles: **8** King's Row **10** Brother Rat **13** John Loves Mary, The Hasty Heart **15** Bedtime for Bonzo **19** The Voice of the Turtle **20** Cattle Queen of Montana **21** The Girl from Jones Beach **22** Knute Rockne All American
　military service: **6** US Army **7** captain **10** World War II
　notable events of lifetime/term:
　　approval of: **10** MX missiles
　　assassination attempt on: **6** Reagan **14** Pope John Paul II
　　attempted assassination on Reagan by: **15** John W Hinckley Jr
　　bombing of: **5** Libya
　　hostages freed in: **4** Iran
　　invasion of: **7** Grenada
　　marines sent to: **7** Lebanon
　　nuclear disaster at: **9** Chernobyl
　　Russians shot down: **14** Korean airliner
　　scandal: **8** Irangate
　father: **10** John Edward
　nickname: **4** Jack
　mother: **5** Nelle (Wilson)
　siblings: **4** (John) Neil
　wife: **4** Jane (Wyman) **5** Nancy (Davis)
　Nancy Davis born: **18** Anne Frances Robbins
　children: **6** Ronald **7** Maureen, Michael (adopted) **8** Patricia
　Patricia also actress known as: **10** Patti Davis
　first lady:
　　program: **9** Drug abuse, Just Say No **12** Alcohol abuse **18** Foster Grandparents

real 4 pure, true **5** solid, valid **6** actual, honest **7** certain, factual, genuine, sincere **8** absolute, bona fide, positive, rightful, tangible, truthful **9** authentic, unalloyed, unfeigned, veracious, veritable **10** legitimate, unaffected **11** not affected, substantial, substantive, unvarnished **12** well-grounded **13** unadulterated **14** unquestionable

realistic 4 real **7** genuine, graphic, natural, precise **8** faithful, lifelike, truthful **9** authentic, depictive, objective, pragmatic **10** true-to-life **11** descriptive, down-to-earth **12** naturalistic **16** representational

reality 4 fact **5** truth **6** verity **9** actuality **11** materiality, tangibility **12** corporeality **14** substantiality **17** physical existence

realization 7 success **8** grasping **10** attainment, perception **11** achievement, culmination, fulfillment **12** appreciation, consummation **13** comprehension, understanding **14** accomplishment

realize 2 do **3** get, net **4** gain **5** clear, grasp **6** absorb, attain, fathom, gather, profit **7** achieve, acquire, cognize, discern, execute, fulfill, imagine, make out, perform, produce **8** carry out, complete, conceive, make good, perceive **9** actualize, apprehend, discharge, make money, penetrate, recognize **10** accomplish, appreciate, bring about, comprehend, consummate, effectuate, understand 11 bring to pass 12 carry through

realized 3 got 6 gained, netted, proved, proven 7 cleared, grasped, made out, saw into 8 absorbed, accepted, effected, executed, existing, fathomed, gathered, imagined, made good, profited 9 completed, conceived, discerned, fulfilled, perceived, performed 10 actualized, penetrated, recognized, understood 11 appreciated, apprehended, consummated, established 12 accomplished, comprehended

really 5 truly 6 indeed, in fact, surely, verily 8 actually 9 certainly, genuinely, literally, veritably 10 absolutely, positively, truthfully 13 categorically 14 unquestionably

realm 4 land 5 field, orbit, state 6 domain, empire, nation, region, sphere 7 country, demesne, kingdom 8 dominion, monarchy, province 11 royal domain

real McCoy, the 4 real 7 genuine 9 authentic 12 the real thing

reap 3 get, win 4 earn, gain 5 glean, score 6 derive, gather, obtain, profit, secure, take in 7 acquire, bring in, harvest, procure, realize

rear 3 aft, end 4 back, heel 5 after, nurse, raise, stern, train 6 dorsal, foster 7 bring up, care for, cherish, develop, educate, nurture, postern, tail end 8 back part, hind part, hindmost 9 aftermost, after part, at the back, cultivate, in the back, posterior

Rear Window
   director: 15 Alfred Hitchcock
   based on story by: 15 Cornell Woolrich
   cast: 10 Grace Kelly 11 Raymond Burr 12 James Stewart, Thelma Ritter, Wendell Corey

Rea Silvia
   also: 4 Ilia 10 Rhea Silvia
   form: 12 vestal virgin
   lover: 4 Mars
   son: 5 Remus 7 Romulus

reason 3 wit 4 head 5 cause, logic, sense, solve 6 acumen, brains, figure, motive, sanity 7 grounds, insight 8 lucidity, occasion 9 awareness, faculties, intellect, normality, rationale, reasoning 10 perception 11 common sense, discernment, exhortation, explanation, penetration, rationality 12 apprehension, intelligence, perspicacity, think through 13 argumentation, comprehension, justification, mental balance, understanding 15 clearheadedness

reasonable 4 fair, just, sage, sane, wise 5 sound 6 likely, proper 7 fitting, knowing, lenient, logical, natural, patient, prudent 8 credible, moderate, possible, probable, rational, sensible, suitable, thinking 9 equitable, impartial, judicious, objective, plausible, temperate, tolerable 10 admissible, coolheaded, legitimate, not extreme, reflective, thoughtful 11 circumspect, intelligent, justifiable, levelheaded, not unlikely, of good sense, predictable, well-founded 12 not excessive, well-grounded 13 understanding 14 understandable 15 of sound judgment

reasonableness 5 logic 6 sanity, wisdom 8 fairness, prudence 9 good sense 10 moderation 11 credibility, objectivity, rationality 12 good judgment, impartiality, intelligence 13 judiciousness 14 circumspection, thoughtfulness 15 clearheadedness

reasonably 6 almost, fairly 8 passably, somewhat 10 moderately, more or less 13 approximately

reasoning 5 basis, logic 6 ground 7 thought 8 analysis, argument, thinking 9 deduction, inference, rationale 10 cogitation, reflection 11 penetration 13 ratiocination 14 interpretation

reason out 8 mull over 10 deliberate 12 think through

reassure 7 cheer 6 buoy up, uplift 7 bolster, comfort 8 inspirit 9 encourage 13 inspire hope in

reassured 6 buoyed 9 bolstered, comforted, heartened 10 emboldened, encouraged, inspirited

reassuring 7 hopeful 10 auspicious, comforting, heartening 11 encouraging

Reb 2 Mr 5 Rabbi 6 Mister

rebate 6 refund 8 discount 9 abatement

Rebecca
   author: 15 Daphne du Maurier
   character: 10 Jack Favell, Mrs Danvers (Danny) 12 Frank Crawley 13 Colonel Julyan, Maxim de Winter
   house: 9 Manderley
   director: 15 Alfred Hitchcock
   cast: 10 Nigel Bruce 12 Joan Fontaine 13 George Sanders 14 Judith Anderson (Mrs Danvers) 15 Laurence Olivier (Maxim de Winter)
   Oscar for: 7 picture

Rebecca
   character in: 7 Ivanhoe
   author: 5 Scott

Rebecca see 7 Rebekah

Rebecca of Sunnybrook Farm
   author: 17 Kate Douglas Wiggin
   character: 4 Cobb 8 Adam Ladd 11 Aunt Miranda 14 Rebecca Randall 15 Emma Jane Perkins

Rebekah
   also: 7 Rebecca
   father: 7 Bethuel
   husband: 5 Isaac
   brother: 5 Laban
   son: 4 Esau 5 Isaac, Jacob

rebel 3 shy 4 riot 5 avoid, quail, react, wince 6 flinch, mutiny, recoil, revolt, rise up, shrink 7 seceder, traitor, upstart 8 deserter, maverick, resister, turncoat 9 anarchist, dissenter, insurgent 10 iconoclast, malcontent, separatist 12 secessionist 13 nonconformist, revolutionary, revolutionist 15 insurrectionist

rebellion 6 mutiny, putsch, revolt 8 defiance, sedition, upheaval, uprising 9 coup d'etat 10 insurgency, revolution 12 insurrection

rebellious 6 unruly 7 defiant 8 contrary, mutinous, up in arms 9 alienated, fractious, insurgent, seditious, truculent, turbulent 10 disorderly, pugnacious, refractory 11 disobedient, intractable, quarrelsome 12 contumacious, recalcitrant, ungovernable, unmanageable 13 insubordinate, revolutionary 14 uncontrollable 15 insurrectionary

rebelliousness 8 defiance 9 rebellion 12 disobedience

Rebel Without a Cause
director: 11 Nicholas Ray
cast: 8 Sal Mineo 9 James Dean, Jim Backus 11 Natalie Wood

Rebirth
god of: 4 Gwyn

rebound 3 bob 6 bounce, recoil, re-echo 7 flounce 8 recovery, ricochet 10 spring back

rebounding 7 rubbery, springy 9 resilient 11 ricocheting 12 bouncing back

rebuff 4 deny, snub 5 check, repel, spurn 6 ignore, put off, refuse, reject, slight 7 decline, put-down, refusal, repulse 8 turn down 9 disregard, rejection 10 putting off 12 cold shoulder 13 slap in the face 15 keep at a distance

rebuke 3 blame, chide, scold, score 6 berate 7 censure, chew out, chiding, lecture, reproof, reprove, upbraid 8 admonish, berating, call down, reproach, reproval, scolding 9 dress down, reprimand 10 admonition, chewing out, take to task, upbraiding 11 castigation, disapproval 12 admonishment, dressing down, remonstrance, reprehension, take down a peg 13 find fault with, tongue-lashing 15 remonstrate with

rebuttal 5 reply 6 answer, denial, retort 7 defense, riposte 8 disproof, negation, response 9 disproval, rejoinder 10 refutation 11 confutation 12 counterreply, disagreement, surrejoinder 13 contradiction 15 counterargument

recalcitrant 5 balky 6 mulish, unruly 7 willful 8 contrary, stubborn 9 obstinate, pigheaded, unwilling 10 bullheaded, headstrong, refractory 11 disobedient, intractable 12 unsubmissive

recall 5 place 6 memory, revive 8 call back, remember 9 reanimate, recognize, recollect 10 reactivate, remobilize 11 reinstitute, remembrance 12 recollection 17 ability to remember

recant 4 deny 5 unsay 6 abjure, disown, recall, renege, repeal, revoke 7 disavow, rescind, retract 8 disclaim, forswear, renounce, take back, withdraw 9 foreswear, repudiate 10 apostatize 12 eat one's words 14 change one's mind

recantation 6 denial 9 disavowal 10 refutation, retraction, revocation 11 repudiation 12 renunciation

recapitulate 5 recap, sum up 6 relate, repeat, reword 7 recount, restate 8 rephrase 9 epitomize, reiterate, summarize 15 repeat in essence

recapture 6 retake 7 reprise 15 experience again

recede 3 ebb 5 abate 6 back up, go back, retire 7 regress, retreat, subside 10 retrogress

receipt 7 arrival, release, voucher 9 admission, discharge, receiving, reception 10 acceptance, admittance, possession, recipience 11 acquisition, transferral

receipts 3 pay 4 gain, gate, take 5 share, split, wages 6 income, recipe, return 7 formula, payment, profits, returns, revenue 8 earnings, proceeds 9 emolument 10 net profits 12 remuneration 13 reimbursement

receive 3 get 4 meet 5 admit, greet, put up 6 accept, come by, obtain, regard, secure, suffer, take in 7 acquire, adjudge, approve, be given, react to, sustain, undergo, welcome 8 meet with, submit to 9 encounter, entertain 10 experience 11 accommodate

receive willingly 6 accept 10 take gladly 16 accept with thanks 18 accept with open arms

receive with favor 6 praise 7 approve 10 appreciate

receive with open arms 6 invite 7 embrace, welcome 13 accept eagerly 19 roll out the red carpet

recent 3 new 4 late 5 fresh, novel 6 modern 8 up-to-date 9 latter-day 12 contemporary 13 up-to-the-minute

receptacle 3 bag, bin, box, can, jar 4 file, tray 6 basket, bottle, hamper, holder, hopper, vessel 7 carrier 8 receiver 9 container 10 depository, repository 11 compartment

reception 2 do 4 fete 5 party 6 affair, soiree 7 welcome 8 greeting 11 recognition 15 social gathering

receptive 8 amenable, friendly 10 accessible, hospitable, interested, open-minded, responsive 11 susceptible 12 approachable 17 favorably disposed

recess 3 bay, gap 4 bend, cell, cove, fold, gulf, lull, nook, pass, rest, slot 5 break, cleft, gorge, inlet, letup, niche, pause 6 alcove, corner, harbor, hiatus, hollow 7 holiday, interim, respite, time out 8 interval, vacation 9 interlude 10 pigeonhole 11 coffee break, indentation 12 intermission 14 breathing spell

recessed 4 sunk 6 paused, sunken 7 delayed 8 deferred, extended, indented 9 adjourned, dissolved, postponed, prolonged, withdrawn 10 terminated
church wall: 5 ambry
wall: 6 alcove

recesses 6 depths 10 inmost part, penetralia

recession 10 depression 11 recessional 16 economic downturn

recherche 4 rare 5 prize 6 choice, exotic, scarce, select, unique 7 special, unusual 8 original, superior, uncommon, valuable 9 different, priceless 10 one of a kind 11 exceptional

recipe 2 Rx 4 cure, rule 5 axiom 6 elixir, remedy 7 formula, receipt 12 instructions, prescription

recipient 4 heir 5 donee, taker 6 getter 7 legatee 8 accepter, acquirer, obtainer, receiver 9 presentee 11 beneficiary

reciprocal 6 common, linked, mutual, shared 8 returned 9 bilateral, exchanged, one for one 10 equivalent 11 give-and-take 12 interchanged, interrelated 13 complementary, corresponding, given in return 14 interdependent 15 interchangeable

reciprocate 4 feel 6 return 7 requite, respond 9 retaliate 10 make return 11 act likewise, give and take, interchange 12 give in return 19 return the compliment

reciprocity 8 exchange 11 give and take, interchange

recital 4 talk 6 report 7 concert, telling 8 delivery, reciting 9 discourse, narration, narrative, rendition 10 recitation 11 description, particulars, performance 12 dissertation, oral exercise 13 public reading 14 graphic account, recapitulation

recite 4 tell 5 quote, speak 6 relate, repeat 7 declaim, deliver, narrate, perform, recount 10 say by heart 11 communicate

reckless 4 rash, wild 5 giddy, hasty 6 daring, fickle, madcap, unwary 7 flighty, foolish, unaware 8 careless, cavalier, heedless, mindless, unsteady, volatile 9 daredevil, desperate, foolhardy, imprudent, impulsive, negligent, oblivious, unheeding, unmindful 10 incautious, indiscreet, insensible, neglectful, regardless, unthinking, unwatchful 11 harebrained, inattentive, precipitate, thoughtless, unconcerned 12 devil-may-care, unsolicitous 13 inconsiderate, irresponsible, uncircumspect 14 scatterbrained

recklessly 4 fast 5 blind 6 rashly, wildly 7 hastily 8 headlong 9 headfirst 10 carelessly, heedlessly 11 audaciously, desperately, impetuously, impulsively 12 unmindfully 13 irresponsibly, unconcernedly

recklessness 7 abandon 8 rashness 9 disregard, unconcern 10 imprudence, profligacy 11 impetuosity 12 heedlessness, immoderation 13 foolhardiness 15 thoughtlessness 16 irresponsibility

reckon 3 add 4 bank, cope, deal, deem, plan, rank, rate 5 add up, class, count, fancy, guess, judge, tally, think, total, value 6 assess, decide, esteem, expect, figure, handle, regard 7 account, adjudge, balance, bargain, compute, imagine, presume, suppose, surmise 8 appraise, consider, estimate 9 calculate, determine, speculate

reckoning 3 tab 4 bill, doom 5 count, tally, total 6 adding, charge 7 account 8 estimate, judgment 9 appraisal, summation 10 estimation, evaluation 11 calculation, computation 13 final judgment 19 settling of an account

reclaim 6 reform, rescue 7 correct, recover, rectify, restore

recline 4 lean, loll, rest 6 lounge, repose, sprawl 7 lie back, lie down 12 take one's ease

reclining 7 lolling, resting 8 lounging, reposing 9 lying down, recumbent

recluse 3 nun 4 monk 5 crank, loner 6 hermit, hidden, secret 7 ascetic, eremite, erratic, oddball 8 cenobite, crackpot 9 eccentric 10 cloistered 11 sequestered 13 nonconformist

recognition 6 notice 9 discovery 10 acceptance, validation 13 comprehension, understanding 14 acknowledgment, identification 19 diplomatic relations

recognizable 5 clear, plain 8 distinct 10 detectable 11 discernable, perceivable, perceptible 12 identifiable, intelligible 13 ascertainable 14 comprehensible, understandable 15 distinguishable

recognizance 4 bond 6 pledge 10 obligation 11 recognition 15 acknowledgement

recognize 3 see 4 know, spot 5 admit, place, sight 7 discern, make out, pick out, realize, respect, yield to 8 identify, submit to 9 be aware of, concede to 10 appreciate, comprehend, understand 11 acknowledge 14 give the floor to

recognized 5 known 8 accepted, admitted, approved, familiar, realized 9 customary 10 accredited 11 traditional 12 acknowledged, conventional

recoil 4 fail, kick 5 blink, cower, demur, quail, shirk, start, wince 6 blench, cringe, falter, flinch, revolt 7 fly back, rebound, retreat 8 draw back, hang back, jump back 9 bound back 10 shrink back, spring back

recoil at 4 hate 5 abhor 6 detest, eschew, loathe 7 despise 9 abominate, shudder at 10 shrink from 12 be revolted by 14 view with horror 18 feel aversion toward

recoiling 7 wincing 9 flinching 10 rebounding 11 drawing back 13 shrinking back, springing back

recollect 5 place 6 recall 8 remember 10 call to mind

recollection 4 mind 6 memoir, memory, recall, record 11 remembrance 12 reminiscence 13 retrospection
  French: 8 souvenir

recommend 4 urge 5 favor, order 6 advise 7 counsel, endorse, propose, suggest 8 advocate, vouch for 9 encourage, prescribe 10 put forward 11 speak well of

recommendable 9 advisable, favorable 10 worthwhile

recommendation 4 plug 6 behest, praise 8 approval, good word 9 reference 11 endorsement 12 commendation

recompense 3 pay 5 repay 6 return, reward 7 payment 9 reimburse, repayment 10 compensate, remunerate, reparation 12 compensation, remuneration 15 indemnification

reconcile 5 fix up 6 adjust, make up, resign, settle, square 7 correct, patch up, rectify, reunite, win over 8 persuade 9 harmonize 10 conciliate, propitiate 11 set straight

reconcile oneself 6 submit 9 acquiesce 13 resign oneself

reconciliation 8 fixing up, making up, settling, squaring 10 adjustment, correction, patching up, rectifying 11 resignation, winning over 12 conciliation 13 justification, rectification 15 setting straight

recondite 4 deep 6 arcane, hidden 7 obscure 8 abstruse, esoteric 9 concealed 10 mysterious 16 incomprehensible

reconnaissance 6 survey 7 viewing 8 scouting, scrutiny 10 inspection 11 exploration, observation 12 surveillance 13 investigation 14 reconnoitering

reconnoiter 4 look 5 probe, scout 6 patrol, picket, survey 7 examine 8 remember, traverse

reconsider 5 amend 6 modify, ponder, review, revise 7 correct, rethink, sleep on 8 mull over, reassess 9 reexamine, think over 10 reevaluate 13 think better of 15 think twice about

reconstitute 7 restore 9 recompose 10 add water to 11 reconstruct

reconstruct 7 rebuild 8 make over, recreate 10 reassemble 11 reestablish 12 reconstitute

record 3 log 4 copy, file, list, memo, note, post, show, tape 5 admit, enter 6 annals, career, docket, enroll, report 7 account, archive, catalog, conduct, history, jot down, jotting, journal 8 document, indicate, register, take down 9 chronicle, introduce, write down 10 adventures, background, memorandum, transcribe 11 experiences, make an entry, performance, proceedings 12 unbeaten mark 14 top performance

French: 11 compte rendu

record
  invented by: 4 Bell 6 Edison 7 Tainter 8 Berliner 10 Goldenmark

recount 4 tell 6 detail, recite, relate 7 explain, narrate 8 describe 9 count over

recoup 5 atone 6 redeem, regain 7 recover, replace 8 make good, retrieve 9 make up for, reacquire 13 make amends for

recourse 6 choice, option, resort 11 alternative, other choice

recover 4 heal, mend 5 rally 6 offset, pick up, recoup, redeem, regain, retake, revive 7 balance, get back, get well, improve, reclaim, restore, win back 8 make good, retrieve, revivify 9 make up for, reacquire, recapture, reconquer, repossess 10 come around, compensate, convalesce, recuperate, rejuvenate 11 pull through, resuscitate

recovery 4 cure 5 rally 6 recoup, rescue, upturn 7 revival, salvage 8 comeback 9 retrieval 10 betterment, regainment 11 improvement, reclamation, reformation, res-

toration 12 recuperation 13 business cycle, convalescence

recreancy 8 apostasy 9 cowardice, desertion 10 cravenness, disloyalty, infidelity 13 faithlessness, pusillanimity 14 unfaithfulness

recreant 6 coward, craven, yellow 8 apostate, cowardly, deserter, disloyal, renegade 9 undutiful 10 unfaithful 11 lily-livered 12 dishonorable 13 pusillanimous, yellow-bellied

recreation 4 play 5 hobby, sport 7 pastime 9 amusement, avocation, diversion 10 relaxation 13 entertainment 15 leisure activity

recrimination 5 blame 6 charge 10 accusation 13 countercharge

recruit 4 hire 5 raise, renew 6 employ, enlist, enroll, muster, novice, recoup, revive, rookie 7 draftee, provide, recover, restore 8 beginner, newcomer 9 conscript 10 recuperate

rectangle 3 box 6 oblong, square 7 polygon 10 quadrangle 13 parallelogram, quadrilateral

rectangular 4 long 6 square 7 boxlike 11 right-angled 12 quadrangular 13 quadrilateral

rectification 6 fixing, reform 7 redress 8 righting, squaring 9 remedying, repairing 10 adjustment, correction, regulation 13 setting right 15 putting straight, putting to rights 16 straightening out

rectify 3 fix 4 cure, mend 5 amend, emend, focus, right 6 adjust, attune, reform, remedy, repair, revise, square 7 correct, redress 8 put right, regulate, set right 9 make right 10 straighten

rectitude 5 honor 7 decency, probity 8 morality 9 integrity, principle 11 uprightness 12 virtuousness 13 righteousness 14 high-mindedness 15 trustworthiness 16 incorruptibility 17 irreproachability

rector 6 cleric, parson, pastor, priest 8 minister, preacher 9 churchman, clergyman 12 ecclesiastic

recumbent 4 flat 5 prone 6 supine 7 leaning 8 couchant 9 lying down, prostrate, reclining 10 horizontal 12 stretched out

recuperate 4 heal, mend 7 get well, improve, recover 8 come back 9 get better 10 come around, convalesce 11 be on the mend, pull through 14 return to health 16 regain one's health

recuperation 8 recovery 11 restoration 13 convalescence

recuperative 11 restorative 15 health-restoring

recur 6 repeat, resume, return 7 persist 8 come back, continue, reappear 9 come again 10 occur again

recurrence 5 cycle, round 6 repeat, return 7 relapse, renewal, reprise, routine 8 iterance, rotation 10 continuity, repetition 11 periodicity 12 reappearance

recurrent 7 regular 8 frequent, periodic 9 recurring, repeating 10 repetitive 11 reappearing 12 intermittent 14 appearing again

red 4 pink, rose, rosy, ruby, wine 5 aglow, coral, flame, ruddy 6 auburn, cherry, florid, maroon 7 burning, crimson, flaming, flushed, glowing, scarlet 8 blooming, blushing, cardinal, inflamed, reddened, rubicund 9 rubescent, vermilion 12 blood-colored

Red and the Black, The (Le Rouge et le Noir)
   author: 8 Stendhal
   character: 6 Fouque 8 M de Renal 11 Julien Sorel 16 Mathilde de la Mole

Red Badge of Courage, The
   author: 12 Stephen Crane
   character: 6 Wilson 10 Jim Conklin 12 Henry Fleming

red-blooded 5 lusty, peppy, vital 6 ardent, robust, strong, sturdy 7 dynamic, intense 8 forceful, powerful, spirited, vigorous 9 energetic 10 hot-blooded, passionate

Red Branch
   origin: 5 Irish
   warriors of: 9 Conchobar

Redburn
   author: 14 Herman Melville

red-cheeked 4 rosy 5 ruddy 6 robust 8 blushing 12 apple-cheeked

Red Cross Knight
   character in: 15 The Faerie Queene
   author: 7 Spenser

redden 4 burn, glow 5 blush, color, flame, flush 9 go crimson 12 become florid

reddish 4 rosy, ruby 5 ruddy, rufus 6 flushy, rufous 7 roseate 8 rubicund

reddish-brown 4 rust 5 henna 6 auburn, copper, russet, sienna 8 chestnut, cinnamon

Red Earth People *see* 3 Fox

redeem 4 keep, save 5 cover 6 defray, ransom, recoup, reform, regain, rescue, settle 7 buy back, convert, fulfill, reclaim, recover, satisfy 8 atone for, make good, retrieve 9 discharge, make up for, repossess 10 evangelize, repurchase

redeemed 5 saved 7 claimed, rescued 8 made good, ransomed, reformed 9 atoned for, delivered, fulfilled, recovered 10 carried out, regenerate 11 repossessed

redemption 6 excuse, pardon, ransom, reform, rescue 7 salvage 8 recovery 9 amendment, atonement, exemption, expiation, salvation 10 conversion 11 deliverance, reformation

Redford, Robert
   real name: 20 Charles Robert Redford
   born: 13 Santa Monica CA
   roles: 8 The Sting 10 The Natural 11 Legal Eagles 12 The Candidate, The Way We Were 13 Downhill Racer 14 The Great Gatsby 15 Jeremiah Johnson 17 Barefoot in the Park 19 All the President's Men 20 Three Days of the Condor 29 Butch Cassidy and the Sundance Kid

director: 14 Ordinary People (Oscar)

Redgrave, Lynn
   born: 6 London 7 England
   father: 18 Sir Michael Redgrave
   sister: 15 Vanessa Redgrave
   roles: 10 Georgy Girl 14 The Happy Hooker

Redgrave, Sir Michael
   born: 7 Bristol, England
   daughter: 4 Lynn 7 Vanessa
   roles: 11 Dan Peggotty 15 The Lady Vanishes 16 David Copperfield 22 Mourning Becomes Electra 27 The Importance of Being Earnest

Redgrave, Vanessa
   born: 6 London 7 England
   father: 18 Sir Michael Redgrave
   sister: 12 Lynn Redgrave
   husband: 14 Tony Richardson
   roles: 5 Julia, Yanks 6 Agatha, Blow-Up, Morgan 7 Camelot, Isadora 9 Guinevere 16 Mary Queen of Scots 17 The Lady from the Sea

red-hot 5 aglow, fiery 6 heated, raging 7 blazing, burning, glowing, intense 12 all-consuming

red-letter 5 happy, lucky 6 banner 10 auspicious, felicitous

redness 4 glow 5 blush, flush 8 rosiness 9 ruddiness 10 floridness

redolence 5 aroma, savor 7 bouquet 9 fragrance, good smell 12 pleasant odor

redolent 5 balmy, spicy 6 savory, smelly 7 mindful, odorous, reeking, scented 8 aromatic, fragrant, perfumed, stinking 9 evocative, odiferous 10 expressive, indicative, suggestive 11 odoriferous, reminiscent 13 sweet-smelling

Redon, Odilon
   born: 6 France 8 Bordeaux
   artwork: 10 In the Dream, The Cyclops 11 Le Vieil Ange 13 Flowers of Evil 15 Violette Heymann

redouble 7 augment, magnify 8 heighten, multiply 9 intensify

redoubtable 7 awesome 8 alarming, imposing 10 formidable 11 illustrious 12 awe-inspiring

redound 4 lead, tend 5 cause, surge 6 abound 7 conduce, incline 8 overflow 10 contribute 11 reverberate

redress 4 ease 5 amend, right 6 amends, reform, relief, remedy 7 correct, payment, rectify, relieve 8 easement, set right 9 make up for 10 recompense, reparation 11 restitution 12 compensation, satisfaction 13 compensate for, rectification 15 indemnification 18 make retribution for

Red River
   director: 11 Howard Hawks
   cast: 9 Joanne Dru, John Wayne 11 John Ireland 13 Walter Brennan 15 Montgomery Clift

Red Rover, The
   author: 19 James Fenimore Cooper

Reds
director: 12 Warren Beatty
cast: 11 Diane Keaton (Louise Bryant),
Paul Sorvino 12 Warren Beatty (John
Reed) 13 Jack Nicholson, Jerzy Kosinski
14 Edward Herrmann 16 Maureen
Stapleton
Oscar for: 8 director 17 supporting actress (Stapleton)

Red Shoes, The
author: 21 Hans Christian Andersen
director: 13 Michael Powell 17 Emeric
Pressburger
cast: 12 Marius Goring, Moira Shearer
13 Anton Walbrook 14 Robert Helpmann

Red Skelton Show, The
character: 8 Gertrude 10 Heathcliff 13
Mean Widdle Kid 14 San Fernando Red,
Sheriff Deadeye, Willie Lump-Lump 16
Bolivar Shagnasty 17 Cauliflower
McPugg 18 Clem Kadiddlehopper 20
Freddie the Freeloader
saying: 7 I dood it
closing line: 8 God bless

Red Sky at Morning
author: 15 Richard Bradford

reduce 3 cut 4 bust, curb, diet, dull, ease,
thin 5 abate, blunt, break, check, force,
lower, slash, water 6 damage, demote, dilute, lessen, retard, soften, temper,
weaken 7 assuage, atrophy, cripple, cut
down, leave in 8 diminish, discount, enfeeble, mark down, minimize, mitigate, moderate, modulate, slim down, slow down,
tone down, trim down 9 bring down,
checkmate, undermine 10 debilitate, devitalize, slenderize 11 lower in rank 12 incapacitate

reduced form 6 digest 7 summary 9 short
form 11 abridgement, contraction 12 abbreviation, condensation

reduce speed 4 slow 5 brake 6 rein in 8
slow down 10 decelerate

reduce to nothing 5 erase 7 abolish, destroy, wipe out 8 lay waste 9 eradicate,
liquidate 10 annihilate 11 exterminate

reductio ad absurdum 22 reduction to an
absurdity

reduction 3 cut 5 break 8 decrease, discount 9 abatement, lessening 10 concession 11 abridgement, subtraction

reduction to an absurdity
Latin: 18 reductio ad absurdum

redundancy 6 excess 7 surplus 8 verbiage
9 tautology 10 repetition 11 diffuseness,
superfluity 13 overabundance 14 circumlocution, repetitiveness

redundant 5 extra 6 excess 7 surplus 10
pleonastic 11 dispensable, inessential,
overflowing, repetitious, superfluous, unnecessary 12 tautological 13 superabundant

redwood 19 Adenanthera pavonina, Sequoia sempervirens
varieties: 4 dawn 5 coast, giant 7 Madeira

reed
varieties: 3 bur 4 vine 5 Burma, giant 6
common 14 Mauritania vine

reed 9 six cubits

Reed, Sir Carol
director of: 6 Oliver (Oscar) 11 The
Third Man

Reed, Walter S
field: 12 bacteriology
discovered cause of: 11 yellow fever

reef 3 bar 4 bank, flat, spit 5 shelf, shoal 7
sandbar, shallow

reek 4 fume 5 smell, smoke, steam, stink 6
stench 7 give off 9 effluvium, emanation

reel 4 rock, roll, spin, sway 5 lurch, pitch,
swirl, waver, whirl 6 rotate, teeter, totter,
wobble 7 revolve, stagger, stumble

reeling 5 dizzy, giddy, shaky 6 whirly 8
spinning, unsteady 10 staggering 11 vertiginous

Reese, Harold
nickname: 6 Pee Wee
sport: 8 baseball
position: 9 shortstop
team: 15 Brooklyn Dodgers

Reeve
character in: 18 The Canterbury Tales
author: 7 Chaucer

Reeve, Christopher
born: 9 New York NY
roles: 8 Superman 9 Deathtrap 13 The
Bostonians 19 Somewhere in Time

refer 2 go 4 cite, send, turn 6 advert, allude, direct, submit 7 consult, deliver, mention 8 hand over, transfer, transmit 9 pass
along

referee 5 judge 6 decree, settle, umpire 7
arbiter, mediate 8 judgment, mediator,
moderate 9 arbitrate, determine, intercede,
intervene, moderator, pronounce 10 adjudicate, arbitrator 11 adjudicator, intercessor 12 intermediary

reference 4 hint 7 inkling, mention 8 allusion, good word, innuendo 10 deposition,
intimation, suggestion 11 affirmation, credentials, endorsement, implication, testimonial 13 certification 14 recommendation

reference book 5 atlas, bible 6 manual 9
guidebook 10 dictionary 12 encyclopedia

refine 6 filter, purify, strain 7 cleanse, develop, improve, perfect, process 9 cultivate

refined 5 clean, suave 6 gentle, polite, urbane 7 courtly, elegant, genteel 8
cleansed, cultured, delicate, finished,
graceful, ladylike, mannerly, polished, purified, well-bred 9 civilized, clarified, courteous 10 cultivated, fastidious 11 gentlemanly 14 discriminating

refinement 5 grace 6 finish, nicety, polish,
step up 7 advance, culture, dignity, finesse, suavity 8 breeding, civility, cleaning, courtesy, delicacy, elegance, fineness,
revision, urbanity 9 amendment, cleansing, gentility, propriety 10 betterment, filtra-
tion, gentleness, politeness 11 advancement, cultivation, development, discernment, enhancement, good manners,

improvement, progression, savoir faire, step forward **12** amelioration, distillation, graciousness, purification, tastefulness **13** courteousness, rectification **14** discrimination, fastidiousness

refitting 8 adapting **10** adaptation, remodeling **11** reequipping, resupplying

reflect 4 cast, copy, muse, show, undo **5** image, study, think, throw **6** betray, evince, expose, mirror, ponder, reason, return, reveal **7** condemn, display, exhibit, express, imitate, present, rebound, uncover **8** cogitate, consider, disclose, give back, indicate, manifest, meditate, mull over, register, ruminate, send back, set forth **9** bring upon, cerebrate, dwell upon, represent, reproduce, speculate, throw back, undermine **10** deliberate **11** concentrate, contemplate, demonstrate

reflection 4 blot, idea, slur, view **5** image, study **6** insult, musing, notion **7** opinion, reproof, thought **8** reproach, thinking **9** attention, pondering, sentiment **10** cogitation, conviction, derogation, impression, imputation, meditation, rumination **11** cerebration, insinuation, mirror image, pensiveness **12** deliberation **13** concentration, consideration, disparagement

French: **6** pensee

reflective 7 pensive **8** thinking **9** judicious, pondering **10** meditative, ruminative, thoughtful **11** speculative **13** contemplative

Reflex
   author: **11** Dick Francis

reform 4 mend **5** amend, atone, emend **6** better, remedy, repair, repent, revise **7** convert, correct, improve, rebuild, rectify, remodel, restore **8** progress **9** amendment **10** correction **12** mend one's ways, rehabilitate **13** rectification **16** set straight again, turn over a new leaf

reformation 6 change, reform **9** amendment, reforming **10** alteration, conversion **11** improvement **12** modification **14** reorganization

refractory 5 balky **6** mulish, unruly **7** restive, wayward, willful **8** contrary, stubborn **9** fractious, obstinate, pigheaded **10** rebellious **11** disobedient, intractable **12** unmanageable

refrain 5 avoid, forgo **6** desist, eschew, forego, refuse, resist **7** abstain, forbear, hold off **8** leave off, renounce **11** curb oneself, keep oneself **12** stay one's hand **15** restrain oneself

refrain from 5 avoid, forgo **6** desist, eschew, forego **7** abstain, forbear **8** leave off, renounce

refresh 3 jog **4** prod **5** brace, renew, rouse **6** arouse, awaken, prompt, revive, stir up, vivify **7** cool off, freshen, quicken, recruit, restore **8** activate, energize, recreate **9** reanimate, stimulate **10** invigorate, rejuvenate, strengthen

refreshed 7 revived **8** animated, restored, vivified **9** enlivened, freshened **11** invigorated

refreshing 7 bracing **11** revivifying **12** invigorating **13** strengthening **15** thirst-quenching

refreshment 4 bite, eats **5** drink, snack **6** bracer **7** potable **8** beverage, cocktail, pick-me-up, potation **9** appetizer, drinkable, refresher **10** recreation, relaxation **11** hors d'oeuvre, nourishment, restoration, restorative **12** food and drink, invigoration, rejuvenation **14** reinvigoration, thirst quencher

refrigerate 4 cool **5** chill **6** freeze **7** congeal **8** keep cold, keep cool, put on ice **9** keep on ice

Refrigerator, The
   nickname of: **12** William Perry

refuge 2 home **5** haven **6** asylum, harbor, resort **7** hideout, retreat, shelter **8** safehold **9** anchorage, harborage, sanctuary **10** protection **12** port in a storm **14** help in distress, place of shelter

refugee 2 DP **5** exile **6** bolter, eloper, emigre **7** escapee, evacuee, runaway **8** emigrant, fugitive **9** absconder **10** expatriate **15** displaced person

refulgent 6 bright, lucent **7** glowing, lambent, radiant, shining **8** luminous, relucent **9** brilliant

refund 5 remit, repay **6** rebate, return **7** pay back **9** reimburse, repayment **10** recompense, remittance, remunerate **12** amount repaid **13** give back money, reimbursement **18** make restitution for **19** make compensation for

refurbish 4 mend, redo **5** clean, fix up, renew **6** repair, tidy up **7** freshen, improve, remodel, restore **8** overhaul, renovate, spruce up **11** recondition

refusal 2 no **3** nay **4** veto **6** denial **7** regrets **8** turndown **9** declining, rejection **10** nonconsent **11** declination, disapproval **13** nonacceptance, noncompliance, unwillingness

refuse 2 no **4** deny, junk, veto **5** spurn, trash, waste **6** forbid, litter, reject **7** decline, garbage, rubbish, say no to **8** disallow, prohibit, turn down, withhold

refuse pile 4 dump **6** midden **11** rubbish heap

refuse to submit 4 defy **5** rebel **6** resist **7** disobey, hold out, violate **10** transgress **12** fail to comply

refutation 4 veto **6** denial **7** counter **8** negation, rebuttal **9** disavowal **11** confutation, repudiation **12** invalidation **13** contradiction

refutatory 8 contrary, opposing **10** discrepant **11** conflicting, disagreeing **12** antithetical, inconsistent **13** contradictory **14** countervailing, irreconcilable

refute 4 deny **5** rebut **6** answer **7** confute, counter **8** disprove **9** challenge **10** contradict, invalidate **12** give the lie to

regain 6 recoup, redeem, retake **7** get back, reclaim, recover, win back **8** gain anew, get again, retrieve **9** recapture, repossess

regal 5 grand, noble, proud, royal **6** august, kingly, lordly **7** queenly, stately **8** imposing, kinglike, majestic, princely, splendid **9** queenlike **10** princelike **11** magnificent **13** splendiferous

regale 3 ply **4** fete **5** amuse, feast **6** divert, please **7** banquet, delight, lionize **8** enthrall **9** entertain **10** serve nobly **11** wine and dine **15** feed sumptuously

Regan
  character in: 8 King Lear
  author: 11 Shakespeare

regard 3 eye, see **4** care, heed, hold, mind, note, rate, scan, view **5** judge, point, think, value, watch **6** accept, admire, aspect, behold, detail, esteem, follow, gaze at, look at, matter, notice, reckon, survey, take in **7** account, believe, concern, put down, respect, set down, subject, thought **8** consider, estimate, listen to, look upon, look up to, note well, relation **9** attention, hearken to, reference **10** admiration, connection, estimation, meditation, reflection, scrutinize **11** contemplate, observation, think well of **12** appreciation **13** cast the eyes on, consideration, think highly of **14** pay attention to

regardful 5 civil **6** polite **7** mindful **8** reverent **9** courteous, observant **10** respectful **11** deferential, reverential

regard highly 6 admire, esteem **7** respect **10** appreciate

regarding 4 in re **5** about, anent **7** apropos **10** concerning, respecting

regardless 6 anyhow, anyway **10** for all that **11** nonetheless **12** nevertheless **15** notwithstanding **19** in spite of everything

regard with repugnance 4 hate **5** abhor **6** detest, loathe **7** despise **8** execrate **9** abominate, can't stand, shudder at **10** recoil from, shrink from **11** can't stomach **12** be revolted by **13** be nauseated by, find repulsive **18** feel aversion toward

regard with suspicion 5 doubt **7** suspect **8** distrust, mistrust, question

regenerate 5 renew **6** redeem, reform, revive, uplift **7** restore **8** inspirit, reawaken, retrieve, revivify **9** enlighten, resurrect **10** rejuvenate **11** resuscitate **12** generate anew **13** give new life to, make a new man of

regent 4 king **5** queen, ruler **8** governor **9** protecter, protector

regime 4 rule **5** power, reign **7** command, control, dynasty **8** dominion **9** direction **10** government, leadership, management **12** jurisdiction **14** administration

regimen 4 diet, rule **6** system **10** government

regimentation 5 order, rigor **6** method, system **7** control, regimen **9** orthodoxy **10** discipline, regulation, uniformity **12** rigorousness **13** methodization **19** doctrinaire approach

Regiment of Women
  author: 12 Thomas Berger

Regin
  origin: 12 Scandinavian
  mentioned in: 8 Volsunga
  brother: 6 Fafnir
  raised: 6 Sigurd

region 4 area, land, zone **5** field, range, realm, space, tract **6** domain, sphere **7** country, expanse **8** district, locality, province, vicinity **9** territory **12** neighborhood

regional 5 areal, local, zonal **7** dialect **10** locational, provincial **11** territorial **12** geographical

register 3 log **4** dial, mark, roll, show **5** diary, gauge, meter, range, scale **6** betray, enlist, enroll, master, ledger, record, sign up **7** betoken, check in, compass, counter, daybook, exhibit, express, logbook, point to, portray, set down **8** disclose, heat duct, heat vent, indicate, manifest, note down, radiator, recorder, registry, take down **9** indicator, write down **10** calculator, heat outlet, hot-air vent, record book **12** put in writing

Regius 16 Greek unical codex

regnat populus 16 let the people rule
  motto of: 8 Arkansas

regress 3 ebb **4** back, exit, fall **6** go back, recede, return, revert **7** relapse, retreat, reverse **8** fall back, pass back, withdraw **9** backslide **10** lose ground, retrogress **11** deteriorate **12** move backward

regressive 8 backward **9** declining, worsening **10** retrograde **13** retrogressive

regret 3 rue, woe **4** moan **5** grief, mourn, qualm **6** bemoan, bewail, lament, repent, sorrow, twinge **7** anguish, apology, deplore, eat crow, remorse, scruple **8** be rueful, grieve at, weep over **9** apologies, grievance, heartache, rue the day **10** be sorry for, contrition, repentance, ruefulness **11** be ashamed of, compunction, lamentation, reservation **12** be remorseful, eat humble pie, eat one's words, self-reproach **13** feel sorry for, regretfulness, second thought **14** disappointment, feel remorse for, remorsefulness **15** dissatisfaction **16** feel distress over, pang of conscience, self-condemnation

regretful 6 rueful **8** contrite **9** sorrowful **10** apologetic, remorseful **15** self-reproachful

regrettable 6 woeful **7** unhappy **8** grievous, pitiable **10** calamitous, deplorable, lamentable **11** unfortunate

regular 3 set **4** even, fine, real **5** daily, fixed, plain, usual **6** common, normal, proper, smooth, steady, trusty **7** classic, correct, genuine, habitue, natural, typical, uniform **8** absolute, accepted, complete, constant, everyday, faithful, familiar, frequent, habitual, loyalist, ordinary, orthodox, periodic, stalwart, standard, thorough, true blue **9** customary, recurrent, recurring, unvarying **10** consistent, dependable, invariable, periodical, unchanging **11** commonplace, down-to-earth, established, old reliable, symmetrical, undeviating **12** well-balanced **16** well-proportioned

regulate 3 fix 5 guide 6 adjust, direct, govern, handle, manage 7 balance, control, monitor, oversee, rectify 8 moderate, modulate, organize 9 supervise 10 regularize 11 superintend

regulation 4 rule 5 edict, order 6 decree 7 command, control, dictate, statute 8 handling 9 adjusting, direction, ordinance 10 adjustment 11 commandment 13 standing order

regulator 5 guide 7 manager 8 director, governor, overseer 9 moderator, modulator 10 adjustment, supervisor 14 superintendent 15 adjusting device

regurgitate 4 barf 5 vomit 7 throw up 8 disgorge

rehabilitate 3 fix 4 save 6 redeem, remake 7 restore, salvage 8 make over, readjust, renovate 9 reeducate, refurbish, reinstate 11 recondition, reconstruct, resocialize, set straight 13 straighten out 16 restore to society

rehash 6 repeat, retell, reword 7 restate 8 rephrase 9 iteration, rechauffe

rehearsal 5 drill, recap 6 tryout 7 hearing, reading, test run 8 audition, exercise, practice, trial run 9 polishing 10 perfecting, repetition, run-through 11 preparation, reiteration, walk-through 14 recapitulation

rehearse 5 drill, ready, train 6 go over, polish, recite, relate, repeat, retell 7 narrate, prepare, recount 8 practice 9 reiterate 10 run through 13 read one's lines 14 give a recital of, study one's lines

Rehoboam
   father: 7 Solomon
   mother: 6 Naamah
   son: 6 Abijah

Rehoboth
   founder: 6 Nimrod

Reich, Charles
   author: 20 The Greening of America

Reichsfuhrer 11 Reich leader
   chief: 8 SS troops

reign 4 rule 6 govern, regime, regnum, tenure 7 command 8 dominion, hold sway, regnancy, tutelage 9 dominance, influence 10 government, incumbency 11 sovereignty, supervision 12 wear the crown 13 hold authority 14 have royal power, sit on the throne 15 occupy the throne 17 exercise authority 19 exercise sovereignty
   Hindu: 3 raj

reign over 4 rule 6 govern 7 command, control 8 dominate

reimburse 5 pay up, remit, repay 6 rebate, refund 7 pay back 8 square up 9 indemnify 10 compensate, recompense, remunerate 15 make restitution

reimbursement 6 refund 9 indemnity, repayment 12 compensation, remuneration

rein, reins 4 curb, hold 5 check, limit, watch 6 bridle 7 control, harness 8 hold back, restrict, suppress 9 restraint 11 keep an eye on

Reiner, Carl
   born: 7 Bronx NY
   son: 9 Rob Reiner
   roles: 15 Your Show of Shows 21 It's a Mad Mad Mad Mad World
   created: 15 Dick Van Dyke Show
   director: 5 Oh God 7 The Jerk 8 The Comic 11 Where's Poppa?
   novel: 13 Enter Laughing

Reiner, Rob
   father: 10 Carl Reiner
   roles: 8 Meathead 10 Mike Stivik 14 All in the Family

reinforce 4 prop 5 steel 7 bolster, brace up, fortify, support 8 buttress 10 strengthen 12 make stronger

reinforcement 4 stay 5 brace, strut 7 bracing, support 10 assistance 11 buttressing 13 strengthening

reinstate 5 renew 6 revive 7 readmit, restore 11 reestablish, reinstitute, reintroduce

reinstatement 7 renewal, revival 11 restoration 13 reinstitution 14 reintroduction 15 reestablishment

reintroduce 6 revive 9 recreate 9 reinstate 11 reestablish, reinstitute

reintroduction 7 revival 10 recreation 11 restoration 13 reinstatement 15 reestablishment

reiterate 5 resay 6 hammer, rehash, repeat, retell, reword, stress 7 iterate, reprise, restate 8 rephrase 11 pound away at 12 recapitulate 13 go over and over

reject 4 deny 5 repel, spurn 6 rebuff, refuse 7 castoff, decline, discard, disdain, dismiss, flotsam, repulse, say no to 8 castaway, disallow, shrug off, turn down, turn from 9 repudiate

rejected 6 denied, dumped, jilted 7 cast off, outcast, refused, spurned, unloved 8 disowned, forsaken, lovelorn 9 abandoned, discarded, disproved 10 unaccepted, repudiated 11 invalidated

rejection 6 rebuff 7 disdain, refusal 8 scorning, spurning 9 declining, dismissal, rebuffing, rejecting, ruling out

rejoice 5 exult, glory, revel 6 be glad 7 be happy, delight 8 be elated, jubilate 9 be pleased, celebrate, make merry 10 exhilarate, sing for joy 11 be delighted, be overjoyed 13 be transported

rejoice in 5 eat up, enjoy, savor 6 relish 7 revel in 9 delight in 13 be pleased with, get a kick out of 14 take pleasure in

rejoicing 5 mirth 6 gaiety 7 delight, ecstasy, elation, jollity, jubilee, revelry, triumph 8 cheering, gladness, pleasure, reveling 9 festivity, good cheer, happiness, jubilance, merriment 10 exultation, joyfulness, jubilation, liveliness 11 celebration, merrymaking

rejoin 6 answer, retort 7 respond

rejoinder 5 reply 6 answer, retort, return 7 riposte 8 backtalk, comeback, retaliate, repartee, response 10 refutation 11 surrebuttal 12 counterblast, remonstrance, sur-

rejoinder 13 countercharge 16 counterstatement

rejuvenate 6 revive 7 restore 8 revivify 9
reanimate 10 revitalize 12 reinvigorate 14
put new life into 17 make youthful again

relapse 4 fall 5 lapse 6 revert, worsen 7 decline, regress, reverse 8 fall back, sink
back, slip back, turn back 9 backslide, reversion, worsening 10 degenerate, recurrence, regression, retrogress 11 backsliding, falling back 13 deterioration,
retrogression 15 return to illness, turn for
the worse

relate 3 say 4 link, tell 5 apply, refer, speak,
state, utter 6 attach, belong, convey, detail, impart, recite, report, reveal 7 concern,
connect, divulge, narrate, pertain, recount
8 describe, disclose 9 appertain, associate, feel close, make known 10 be relevant
11 communicate, have rapport 12 be responsive, interact well, recapitulate 13 be
sympathetic, have reference, particularize
15 feel empathy with, give an account of

related 3 kin 4 akin, said, told 7 kindred, recited 8 narrated, reported 9 recounted 15
of the same family

related by blood 3 kin 4 akin 7 kindred 14
consanguineous, of the same stock 21
having a common ancestor

relation 3 kin, tie 4 bond, link 5 tie-in 6 regard, report 7 account, bearing, concern,
kinsman, recital, telling, version 8 relative
9 narrating, narration, narrative, reference,
relevance, retelling 10 connection, pertinence, recitation 11 affiliation, application,
association, correlation, description 13 applicability, communication 17 interrelationship

relationship 3 kin 5 blood, union 6 affair 7
kindred, kinship, liaison, sibship, society 8
affinity, alliance 10 connection 11 affiliation, association, correlation 13 consanguinity

relative 3 kin 4 clan, kith 5 blood, folks,
tribe 6 allied, cousin, family, people 7 cognate, germane, kinfolk, kinsman, related 8
relation, relevant 9 connected, dependent,
kinswoman, pertinent, referable 10 affiliated, applicable, associated, comparable,
connection, connective, correlated, kith
and kin, pertaining, relational, respective
11 appropriate, comparative, correlative,
not absolute 12 interrelated 13 flesh and
blood 14 interconnected

relax 4 bend, calm, ease, idle, laze, loaf,
rest 5 let up, slack 6 be idle, be lazy, ease
up, loosen, soften, soothe, unbend, unwind 7 cool off, holiday, make lax, slacken
8 decrease, loosen up, vacation 9 lie
around 10 take it easy 13 enjoy oneself 13
make less tense 14 make less severe,
make less strict

relaxation 3 fun 5 games, hobby, sport 6
repose 7 bending, leisure, pastime 8 pleasure 9 abatement, amusement, avocation,
diversion, enjoyment, loosening, remission

10 recreation, slackening 11 refreshment
12 rest from work 13 entertainment

relaxed 3 lax 4 calm, cool, easy, slow, soft
5 loose, slack 6 at ease, casual, gentle, remiss 7 flaccid, lenient 8 informal, laid back,
unstrict 9 easygoing, leisurely, negligent,
nerveless, unnervous 10 unstrained 11
free and easy, thoughtless

    French: 6 degage

relaxed manner 4 ease 5 poise 6 aplomb 9
composure 10 confidence 11 naturalness
12 unconstraint 14 unaffectedness

relay 3 leg 4 race, tour 5 shift 6 length 8
transfer, transmit 9 conductor, regulator,
satellite 10 retransmit

    cylinder: 5 baton

    part: 8 armature, receiver 11 transmitter
    13 electromagnet

    race: 6 medley 10 track event

release 4 free 5 let go, loose, untie 6 detach, let out, unbind 7 freeing, present, relieve, set free, unloose 8 liberate, set
loose, unfasten 9 circulate, discharge,
disengage, dismissal, extricate, letting go,
releasing 10 distribute, liberating, liberation 11 circulation, communicate, extrication, publication, setting free 12 distribution, emancipation, set at liberty, setting
loose

relegate 3 bar 5 eject, expel 6 assign, banish, charge, commit, demote, reject 7 cast
out, consign, discard, dismiss, exclude,
keep out, shut out 8 delegate 9 ostracize

relent 4 bend, melt 5 let up, relax, yield 6
give in, soften, unbend, weaken 7 give
way 8 have pity 10 be merciful, capitulate,
come around 11 give quarter, grow lenient
12 become milder 14 grow less severe

relentless 4 hard 5 harsh, rigid, stern, stiff
6 severe 7 adamant 8 pitiless, rigorous,
ruthless 9 merciless 10 implacable, inexorable, inflexible, unyielding 11 remorseless, undeviating, unrelenting 14 uncompromising

relevance 7 aptness, fitness, meaning 9
propriety 10 pertinence 11 materiality,
relatedness, suitability 12 significance 13
applicability 15 appropriateness

relevant 3 apt, fit 6 allied, suited, tied in 7
apropos, bearing, cognate, fitting, germane, related 8 apposite, material, suitable 9 connected, intrinsic, pertinent, refer-
ring 10 applicable, associated, concerning,
to the point 11 appropriate, significant 12
on the subject, to the purpose

reliable 4 true 5 solid, sound 6 trusty 8
faithful 9 unfailing 10 dependable 11 responsible, trustworthy 12 tried and true 13
conscientious

reliance 5 faith, trust 6 belief, credit 8 credence 9 assurance 10 confidence, dependence

relic 5 scrap, token, trace 7 antique, memento, records, remnant, vestige 8 artifact, fragment, heirloom, keepsake, reminder, souvenir 11 remembrance

relief 4 balm, cure, dole, rest 5 break, cheer 6 remedy 7 anodyne, elation, panacea, respite, welfare 8 antidote, easement, lenitive 9 abatement, reduction 10 mitigation, palliation, palliative 11 alleviation, assuagement, peace of mind 12 amelioration 13 encouragement 16 public assistance 17 welfare assistance
    Italian: 7 rilievo

relieve 3 aid 4 calm, ease, free, help, mark 5 abate, allay, cheer, spell 6 assist, let out, pacify, remove, set off, solace, soothe, subdue, succor, temper 7 appease, assuage, break up, comfort, console, lighten, mollify, release, replace, support, take out 8 contrast, mitigate, palliate, reassure 9 alleviate, encourage, interrupt, punctuate 12 free from fear

relieved 5 freed 6 calmed, exempt 7 cheered, excused, solaced 8 consoled 9 comforted, reassured 10 encouraged

Religio Medici
    author: 15 Sir Thomas Browne

religion 4 cult, sect 5 canon, creed, dogma, faith, piety 6 belief, church, homage 7 worship 8 devotion, theology 9 adoration, godliness, reverence 10 devoutness, persuasion, veneration 11 affiliation, belief in God 12 belief in gods, denomination, spirituality 13 system of faith 15 system of worship

religionist 8 believer 16 God-fearing person

religiosity 5 piety 8 devotion 10 fanaticism 15 religious fervor

religious 3 nun 4 holy, monk 5 exact, friar, godly, rigid 6 ardent, devout, divine, priest, sacred 7 devoted, staunch 8 constant, faithful, unerring 9 spiritual, steadfast 10 devotional, fastidious, God-fearing, meticulous, scrupulous, unswerving 11 punctilious, theological, undeviating 12 wholehearted 13 conscientious 14 denominational 15 spiritual-minded

religious belief 5 canon, credo, creed, dogma, tenet 8 doctrine

religious fervor 5 piety 7 ecstasy 8 holiness 9 godliness 10 devoutness 12 religiousity, spirituality

religious group 4 sect 12 denomination

religious orders
    Christian: 6 Jesuit 7 Cluniac, Templar 8 Capuchin, Theatine, Trappist, Ursuline 9 Carmelite, Dominican 10 Carthusian, Cistercian, Franciscan 11 Augustinian, Benedictine, Camaldolite 16 Sisters of Charity 20 Order of the Visitation
    non-Christian: 4 Sufi 7 Jainism 8 Dasanami

relinquish 4 cede, deny, drop, quit, shed 5 forgo, leave, let go, waive, yield 6 forego, give up, resign, vacate 7 abandon, cast off, discard, dismiss, forbear, forsake, release 8 abdicate, break off, disclaim, hand over, lay aside, put aside, renounce, sign away 9 deliver up, repudiate, surrender

relinquishable 9 forgoable 10 expendable, foregoable 11 dispensable 12 renounceable

relinquished 5 ceded, let go 6 gave up 7 forgone, given up, yielded 8 cast away, foregone, forsaken 9 abandoned, given away, renounced 10 left behind

relinquishment 7 cession 8 giving up, yielding 9 letting go, rejection, surrender 10 abnegation 11 repudiation 12 renunciation

relish 3 dig 4 like, love, tang, want, wish, zest 5 enjoy, fancy, gusto, savor, spice, taste 6 accent, desire, dote on, flavor, liking, palate 7 delight, longing, stomach 8 appetite, fondness, groove on, penchant, piquancy, pleasure 9 condiment, delight in, enjoyment, hankering, rejoice in 10 appreciate, ebullience, enthusiasm, exuberance, partiality, propensity 11 luxuriate in 12 appreciation, be crazy about, predilection, satisfaction 13 gratification
    type: 4 beef, corn 5 sweet 7 chutney 6 pickle, tomato 10 chili sauce, piccalilli 11 horseradish

reluctance 10 hesitation 13 unwillingness 14 disinclination

reluctant 3 shy 4 slow 5 loath 6 averse 7 laggard 8 hesitant 9 diffident, unwilling 10 indisposed 11 disinclined

rely 3 bet 4 bank, lean, rest 5 count, swear, trust 6 credit, depend, reckon 7 believe 10 feel sure of 11 be dependent 12 give credence

remain 4 go on, last, stay, wait 5 abide, stand 6 be left, endure, hang on, hold up, linger 7 not move, not stir, persist, prevail, stay put, subsist, survive 8 continue, stand pat 10 be left over, stay behind

remainder 4 rest 5 waste 6 excess, refuse 7 balance, overage, remains, remnant, residue, surplus, wastage 8 leavings, residual, residuum 9 leftovers, scourings 10 surplusage 11 superfluity

remains 4 body 5 stiff 6 corpse, scraps 7 cadaver 8 dead body 9 leftovers

remark 3 say, see 4 espy, mark, mind, note, view, word 6 behold, look at, notice, regard, survey 7 comment, mention, observe, pay heed 8 perceive 9 attention 10 commentary, give heed to, make note of, reflection, take note of 11 contemplate, observation 12 fix the mind on, say in passing, take notice of 13 consideration 14 pay attention to

remarkable 6 signal 7 notable, unusual 8 singular, striking 9 memorable 10 impressive, noteworthy, phenomenal 11 conspicuous, exceptional, outstanding 13 distinguished, extraordinary, unforgettable

Remarque, Erich Maria
    author of: 25 All Quiet on the Western Front

Rembrandt (Harmensz) van Rijn
    born: 6 Leiden, Leyden 14 The Netherlands
    artwork: 6 Balaam 9 Bathsheba 13 The

Night Watch (The Sortie of the Company of Captain Banning Cocq) 14 The Jewish Bride 15 Old Woman Reading, The Bridal Couple 19 The Blinding of Samson 20 Christ Healing the Sick 21 The Stoning of St Stephen 22 Man with the Golden Helmet, Self-Portrait with Saskia, The Descent from the Cross 24 The Anatomy Lesson of Dr Tulp, The Syndics of the Cloth Hall 36 Aristotle Contemplating the Bust of Homer

remedial 7 healing, helpful, mending 8 curative, salutary, sanative 10 beneficial, corrective 11 meliorative, reformative, restorative, therapeutic 12 advantageous, correctional, prophylactic

remedy 3 aid, fix 4 calm, cure, ease, heal, help, mend 5 amend, emend, right 6 relief, repair, soothe 7 assuage, correct, cure-all, improve, mollify, nostrum, panacea, rectify, redress, relieve, restore 8 make easy, medicine, mitigate, palliate, regulate, set right 9 alleviate, make sound, treatment 10 ameliorate, assistance, corrective, make better, medicament, medication, preventive 13 rectification 15 restore to health

remember 3 tip 6 recall, reward 9 not forget, recognize, recollect 10 appreciate, bear in mind, call to mind, have in mind, keep in mind, take care of, take note of 11 bring to mind 12 bear in memory

remember that thou must die
  Latin: 11 memento mori

remembrance 5 favor, relic, token 6 memory, recall 7 memento 8 keepsake, memorial, reminder, souvenir 9 nostalgia 11 recognition, remembering 12 recognizance, recollection, reminiscence 13 commemoration

Remembrance of Things Past
  author: 12 Marcel Proust

Remembrance Rock
  author: 12 Carl Sandburg

Remick, Lee
  born: 8 Quincy MA
  roles: 16 Anatomy of a Murder, The Long Hot Summer 18 Days of Wine and Roses

remind 9 put in mind, suggest to 11 bring back to, bring to mind, put in memory 16 awaken memories of

reminder of death
  Latin: 11 memento mori

Remington, Frederic Sackrider
  born: 8 Canton NY
  artwork: 12 Bronco Buster 23 Roping Horses in the Corral 32 Cavalry Charge on the Southern Plains

reminisce 4 mull, muse 6 ponder 7 reflect 8 hark back, look back, remember 9 recollect, think back 12 tell old tales 16 exchange memories, swap remembrances

reminiscent 9 nostalgic, remindful, similar to 11 analogous to, remembering 12 recollecting 13 retrospective

remiss 3 lax 4 idle, lazy, slow 5 loose, slack 6 sloppy 7 laggard, loafing 8 careless, derelict, dilatory, inactive, indolent, slipshod, slothful, uncaring 9 do-nothing, forgetful, negligent, oblivious, shiftless, undutiful, unmindful 10 delinquent, neglectful, unthinking, unwatchful 11 inattentive, indifferent, thoughtless

remission 4 cure 5 lapse, pause 6 hiatus, pardon 7 respite, retreat 8 decrease 9 abatement, acquittal, cessation, reduction, shrinkage 10 absolution, diminution, hesitation, moderation, modulation, subsidence 11 exoneration, forgiveness, vindication

remit 3 pay 4 free, send, ship 5 clear, let go, relax, slack 6 excuse, let out, pardon, reduce 7 absolve, forgive, forward, release, set free, slacken 8 decrease, diminish, dispatch, liberate, make good, moderate, overlook, pass over, transmit 9 discharge, reimburse 10 compensate 11 put to rights 13 send in payment

remnant 3 bit 5 piece, relic, scrap, shred, token, trace 7 discard, remains, residue, vestige 8 fragment, leavings, leftover, monument, residuum, survival 9 remainder 11 odds and ends

remodel 4 redo 5 adapt, alter, fix up 6 change, modify 7 convert, reshape 8 overhaul, renovate 9 refashion, transform 11 recondition

remodeling 6 change 10 alteration, conversion 12 modification 13 transmutation 14 transformation

remonstrance 6 rebuke 7 censure 8 reproach, scolding 9 criticism, reprimand 10 admonition

remonstrate 5 argue, chide, demur, scold 6 differ, object, rebuke 7 censure, chasten, contend, dispute, dissent, protest, reprove, upbraid 8 admonish, complain, reproach 9 criticize 10 take to task 11 expostulate 13 call to account

remorse 3 rue 4 pang 5 grief, guilt, qualm 6 regret, sorrow 7 anguish 9 penitence 10 contrition, repentance, ruefulness 11 compunction, lamentation, self-reproof 12 self-reproach 13 regretfulness 14 second thoughts

remorseful 8 contrite, penitent 9 chastened, regretful, repentant, sorrowful 10 apologetic 13 grief-stricken 18 conscience-stricken

remote 3 far 4 slim 5 alien, alone, aloof, faint, quiet 6 exotic, far-off, lonely, meager, slight 7 distant, dubious, faraway, foreign, removed, strange 8 detached, doubtful, isolated, secluded, separate, set apart, solitary, unlikely 9 withdrawn 10 far-removed, segregated 11 God-forsaken, implausible, out of the way, sequestered, standoffish

removal 6 moving, ouster 7 doffing 8 deletion, ejection 9 discharge, dismissal, expulsion, taking off, taking out 10 amputation, carting off, cutting away, dislodging, evacuation, lopping off 11 carrying off, chopping off, elimination, transferral 12 cancellation, displacement 14 transportation 15 transplantation

remove 4 doff, drop, fire, move, oust, quit 5 eject, erase, expel, leave, shift 6 cancel, change, cut off, delete, depart, go away, lop off, retire, unseat, vacate 7 blot out, boot out, cart off, chop off, cut away, dismiss, extract, kick out, retreat, take off, take out, wipe out 8 amputate, carry off, dislodge, displace, evacuate, get rid of, sweep out, take away, transfer, withdraw 9 discharge, eliminate, take leave, transport 10 make an exit, transplant

removed 3 off 4 away, took 5 alone, aloof, apart 6 remote 7 distant, faraway 8 abstract, detached, isolated, reticent, secluded 9 alienated, separate, unrelated, withdrawn 10 segregated, unsociable 11 interspaced, standoffish

remove from office 4 oust 6 depose, unseat 9 discharge

remunerate 3 pay 5 award, grant, repay 6 reward 7 requite, satisfy 9 indemnify, reimburse, vouchsafe 10 compensate, recompense 15 make restitution

remuneration 7 payment 9 repayment 10 recompense, reparation 12 compensation 13 reimbursement 15 indemnification

Remus
   father: 4 Mars
   mother: 4 Ilia 9 Rea Silvia 10 Rhea Silvia
   twin brother: 7 Romulus
   raised by: 7 she-wolf

renaissance 7 rebirth, renewal, revival 9 rekindling, renascence, resurgence 11 reawakening, reemergence, restoration 12 regeneration, rejuvenation, resurrection, risorgimento 14 revitalization, revivification 15 reestablishment

rend 3 cut, rip 4 hurt, pain, rive, sear, tear 5 break, crack, sever, split, wound 6 cleave, divide, pierce, sunder 7 afflict, rupture, shatter 8 dissever, fracture, lacerate, polarize, splinter 12 disintegrate, fall to pieces 15 break into pieces

render 2 do 4 cede, give, make, play 5 allot, grant, remit, yield 6 accord, donate, give up, supply, tender 7 deal out, dole out, execute, hand out, pay back, perform, present, requite 8 construe, dispense, fork over, hand over, pay as due, shell out, turn over 9 cause to be, interpret, surrender, translate 10 relinquish 12 give in return, make requital 13 cause to become, make available, make payment of

render impotent 6 defuse, weaken 7 disable, unnerve 8 paralyze 9 undermine 10 devitalize, emasculate

render inoperable 6 damage, impair 7 cripple, disable 12 incapacitate

render null and void 4 void 5 annul 6 cancel, repeal, revoke 7 abolish, nullify, rescind, retract, reverse 8 abrogate, dissolve 10 invalidate

rendezvous 4 date 5 focus, haunt, mecca, tryst 6 gather, muster 7 retreat 8 assemble 9 encounter, tete-a-tete 10 engagement, focal point 11 appointment, assignation, get together 12 meeting place, watering hole 14 gathering place, stamping ground 15 agreement to meet 17 meet by appointment 18 prearranged meeting

rendition 7 edition, reading, version 9 depiction, portrayal, rendering 11 arrangement, performance, translation 14 interpretation

rend the air 3 cry 4 bawl, howl, wail 6 clamor, scream, shriek, squeal 7 screech 9 caterwaul

Renee Mauperin
   author: 24 Edmond and Jules de Goncourt

renegade 5 rebel 6 outlaw 7 heretic, runaway, slacker, traitor 8 apostate, betrayer, defector, deserter, forsaker, fugitive, mutineer, mutinous, quisling, recreant, turncoat 9 dissenter, insurgent 10 backslider, traitorous, treasonist, unfaithful

renege 7 back out, fink out, pull out 8 back down, fall back, withdraw 9 repudiate, weasel out 11 get cold feet 12 turn one's back 13 break a promise, break one's word 16 go back on one's word

renew 4 save 6 extend, pick up, redeem, resume, retain, revive 7 prolong, refresh, restore, salvage 8 continue, maintain 9 make sound, reinstate, sign again 10 begin again, offer again, regenerate, rejuvenate, revitalize 11 reestablish, take up again 12 reinvigorate 16 put back into shape

renewal 7 revival 9 extension 10 redemption 11 restoration 12 regeneration 13 reinstatement 14 revitalization

Renoir, Pierre-Auguste
   born: 6 France 7 Limoges
   artwork: 4 Lise 6 La Loge 10 The Bathers 12 Margot Berard, The Umbrellas 14 La Grenouillere 19 Le Moulin de la Galette 28 Mme Charpentier and Her Children, The Luncheon of the Boating Party

renounce 4 cede, deny, quit 5 forgo, waive 6 abjure, disown, eschew, forego, give up, recant, reject, resign 7 abandon, cast off, disavow, discard, dismiss 8 abdicate, abnegate, abrogate, disclaim, forswear, lay aside, part with, put aside, turn from, write off 9 cast aside, foreswear, repudiate 10 relinquish 13 give up claim to 15 wash one's hands of

renovate 3 fix 4 mend 6 remake, repair, revamp 7 improve, remodel, restore 8 make over 9 modernize, refurbish 10 redecorate

renown 4 fame, mark, note 6 repute, status 7 acclaim 8 eminence 9 celebrity, notoriety 10 popularity, prominence, reputation 11 distinction

renowned 5 famed, noted 6 famous 7 eminent, notable, popular 9 acclaimed, prominent, well-known 10 celebrated, noteworthy 11 outstanding 13 distinguished

rent 3 fee, gap, let, rip 4 dues, gash, hire, hole, rift, slit, tear 5 break, chasm, chink, cleft, crack, lease, split 6 breach, hiatus, rental, schism, tatter, wrench 7 charter, fissure, opening, payment, rent out, rupture 8 cleavage, crevasse, division, fracture 11 buy the use of 12 sell the use of

rente 6 income 7 revenue 12 annual income

rentier 21 one who has a fixed income

renunciation 6 denial 7 refusal 8 forgoing, spurning 9 disavowal, eschewing, foregoing, rejection, repulsion 10 abjuration, renouncing 11 abandonment, disclaiming, forswearing, repudiation 12 foreswearing 14 relinquishment

Renwick, James, Jr
　architect of: 8 Main Hall (Vassar College) 11 Grace Church (NYC) 15 Corcoran Gallery (now Renwick Gallery, Washington, DC) 19 St Patrick's Cathedral (NYC) 22 Smithsonian Institution (Washington DC)
　style: 13 Gothic Revival

reopen 7 restart 9 begin anew, reconvene, start anew 10 recommence, reinitiate 11 reestablish, reinstitute 12 reinaugurate

repair 2 go 3 fix 4 mend, move 5 amend, emend, patch, renew, shape, state 6 fixing, remedy, remove, retire 7 correct, mending, patch up, rebuild, rectify, redress, restore 8 make good, overhaul, patching, set right, withdraw 9 condition, make up for, refurbish, repairing 10 rebuilding 11 recondition 12 refurbishing 14 reconditioning

reparation 6 amends, return 7 damages, redress 8 requital 9 quittance 10 recompense 11 restitution 12 compensation, satisfaction 13 peace offering

repartee 6 banter, bon mot 7 riposte 8 badinage, chit chat, word play 10 persiflage, witty reply 11 witty retort 12 pleasantries 14 snappy comeback

repast 4 food, meal 5 board, feast, snack, table 6 spread 7 banquet 8 victuals 9 provision 11 nourishment, refreshment

repay 5 match 6 refund, return, reward 7 pay back, requite 9 get back at, indemnify, pay in kind, reimburse 10 recompense, remunerate 11 get even with, reciprocate 12 make requital 14 give in exchange, make a return for 15 make restitution, make retribution 19 return the compliment

repayment 10 paying back, recompense 12 compensation 13 reimbursement 17 making restitution

repeal 4 void 5 annul 6 cancel, revoke 7 abolish, nullify, rescind, voiding 8 abrogate, set aside 9 abolition, annulment 10 abrogation, invalidate, revocation 11 termination 12 cancellation, invalidation 13 nullification 18 declare null and void

repeat 4 echo, redo, tell 5 mimic, quote, rerun 6 pass on, recite, relate, retell 7 imitate, recount, restate, retread, say over 8 say again 9 duplicate, reiterate, reproduce

10 repetition 11 duplication, reiteration 12 perform again

repeated exercises 4 rote 5 drill 8 practice, training

repel 4 foil, rout 5 check 6 dispel, offend, oppose, put off, rebuff, resist, revolt, sicken 7 deflect, disgust, fend off, forfend, hold off, keep off, keep out, repulse, scatter, turn off, ward off 8 alienate, beat back, disperse, nauseate, push back, stave off, throw off 9 chase away, drive away, drive back, force back, frustrate, keep at bay, withstand

repellent 5 proof 9 abhorrent, loathsome, offensive, repelling, repugnant, repulsive, resisting, revolting, sickening 10 disgusting, nauseating 11 distasteful, impermeable

repent 3 rue 6 bemoan, bewail, lament, regret, repine 7 deplore 8 mea culpa, weep over 9 be ashamed 10 be contrite, be penitent 11 be regretful, feel remorse

repentance 5 grief, guilt 6 regret, sorrow 7 remorse 9 penitence 10 contrition 11 compunction 12 self-reproach 16 self-condemnation 17 pangs of conscience

repercussion 4 echo 6 effect, result 8 backlash, reaction 10 concussion, side effect 11 aftereffect, consequence 13 reverberation 15 boomerang effect

repetition 6 repeat 9 iteration, retelling 11 reiteration, restatement 14 recapitulation

repetitious 5 wordy 6 prolix 8 repeated 9 redundant 10 repetitive

Repin, Ilya Efimovich
　born: 6 Russia 8 Chugeyev
　artwork: 15 The Volga Boatmen 18 Zaporozhye Cossacks 19 They Did Not Expect Him 26 Ivan the Terrible Kills His Son

replace 5 spell 6 return 7 put back, restore, succeed 8 supplant 9 supersede

replaceable 10 disposable, expendable 11 dispensable

replenish 5 renew 6 refill, reload 7 refresh, reorder, replace, restock, restore

replenished 7 renewed 8 refilled, replaced, restored 9 restocked

replenishment 7 renewal 9 refilling 10 restocking 11 replacement, restoration

replete 4 full 5 sated 6 gorged, loaded 7 crammed, fraught, stuffed, teeming 8 brimming, satiated 9 abounding, jam-packed, surfeited 11 well-stocked

repletion 4 glut 6 excess 7 surfeit, surplus 9 abundance, plenitude, profusion, satiation 11 sufficiency

replica 4 copy 5 model 6 double 8 likeness 9 duplicate, facsimile, imitation 12 reproduction

reply 5 react 6 answer, rejoin, retort 7 counter, respond 8 reaction, response 9 rejoinder 14 acknowledgment

reply if you please
　French: 4 rsvp 20 repondez s'il vous plait

reply to 6 answer 7 counter, react to 8 retort to 9 respond to 11 acknowledge

repondez s'il vous plait 11 please reply 16 reply if you please
   abbreviation: 4 rsvp

report 4 bang, boom, note, talk, tell, word 5 crack, noise, rumor, sound, state, story 6 appear, detail, expose, gossip, recite, record, relate, reveal, show up, tell on 7 account, article, check in, divulge, hearsay, message, missive, recount, summary, version, write-up 8 announce, denounce, describe, disclose, dispatch, relation 9 discharge, narration 10 communique, detonation, memorandum 11 communicate, description, information
   French: 11 compte rendu

reporter 7 newshen, newsman 8 newshawk 9 anchorman, announcer, columnist, newshound, newswoman 10 journalist, newscaster 11 commentator 12 newspaperman 13 correspondent 14 newspaperwoman

repose 3 lie 4 calm, ease, rest 5 quiet, relax 6 be calm, settle 7 leisure, recline, respite 8 quietude 10 inactivity, quiescence, relaxation 11 tranquility 12 peacefulness, tranquillity

repository 5 depot 8 magazine 9 warehouse 10 storehouse

reprehend 5 decry 7 censure, condemn, reprove 8 denounce, reproach 9 criticize 10 disapprove

reprehensible 3 bad 4 base, evil, foul, vile 6 guilty, wicked 7 heinous, ignoble 8 blamable, culpable, infamous, shameful, unworthy 9 nefarious 10 censurable, despicable, villainous 11 blameworthy, condemnable, disgraceful, inexcusable, opprobrious 12 unpardonable 13 objectionable, unjustifiable

reprehension 6 rebuke 7 censure, reproof 8 reproach 9 criticism 11 disapproval 12 condemnation, denunciation 14 disapprobation

represent 2 be 4 mean, show 5 enact, equal, state 6 denote, depict, pose as, sketch, typify 7 betoken, express, outline, picture, portray, present, serve as 8 appear as, describe, indicate, stand for 9 delineate, designate, symbolize 10 illustrate 11 emblematize, impersonate 12 characterize

representation 5 image 6 effigy, emblem, symbol 7 epitome, essence, picture 8 likeness 9 depiction, portrayal 10 embodiment 12 illustration 15 exemplification 16 characterization

representative 2 MP 3 rep 5 agent, envoy, proxy 6 deputy, varied 7 deputed, elected, proctor, typical 8 balanced, delegate, elective, emissary, symbolic 9 delegated, exemplary, spokesman, surrogate, typifying 10 delegatory, democratic, denotative, emblematic, legislator, mouthpiece, republican, substitute, symbolical 11 assemblyman, congressman, delineative, descriptive 12 exemplifying, illustrative 13 assemblywoman, congresswoman 14 characteristic, cross-sectional

repress 4 curb, hide, mask, veil 5 box up, check, cloak, cover, crush, pen up, quash, quell 6 hold in, muffle, shut up, squash, stifle, subdue 7 conceal, control, inhibit, put down, silence, smother, squelch 8 bottle up, hold back, keep down, restrain, strangle, suppress

repression 8 muffling 9 holding in, restraint, retention 10 inhibition, throttling 11 concealment, holding back, suppression

reprieve 4 lull, stay 5 delay, pause 6 pardon, parole 7 amnesty, respite 8 breather 9 remission 10 moratorium, suspension 11 adjournment 12 postponement 14 breathing spell

reprimand 4 trim 5 chide, scold 6 berate, rail at, rebuff, rebuke, revile 7 censure, chew out, chiding, lecture, obloquy, tell off, upbraid 8 admonish, berating, chastise, denounce, reproach, reproval, scolding, take down, trimming 9 castigate, criticism, criticize, disparage, dispraise, dress down, reprehend, reprobate 10 admonition, chewing out, opprobrium, take to task, upbraiding 11 castigation 12 admonishment, denunciation, dressing down, remonstrance 13 disparagement 16 rap on the knuckles

reprisal 7 redress, revenge 8 requital 9 tit for tat, vengeance 11 counterblow, retaliation, retribution 13 counterattack 16 counteroffensive
   Latin: 10 quid pro quo

reproach 4 blot, slur, spot 5 blame, chide, scold, shame, stain, taint 6 charge, insult, malign, rail at, rebuke, revile, stigma, tirade, vilify 7 asperse, blemish, censure, condemn, offense, reproof, reprove, scandal, tarnish, upbraid 8 admonish, denounce, diatribe, disgrace, dishonor, scolding 9 castigate, criticism, criticize, discredit, disparage, indignity, reprimand 10 stigmatize, take to task, tongue-lash, upbraiding 11 degradation, humiliation 12 remonstrance 13 call to account, embarrassment

reprobate 3 bad, low 4 base, evil, rake, roue, vile 5 scamp 6 pariah, rascal, rotter, sinner, wanton, wicked 7 corrupt, outcast 8 castaway, depraved, derelict, evildoer, prodigal, rakehell 9 abandoned, dissolute, miscreant, shameless, wrongdoer 10 black sheep, degenerate, immoralist, profligate, voluptuary 11 rapscallion, untouchable 12 incorrigible, transgressor, wicked person

reproduce 4 copy, redo, sire 5 beget, breed, match, spawn 6 mirror, repeat, reecho 7 imitate, reflect 8 generate, multiply 9 duplicate, procreate, propagate, replicate, represent 11 counterfeit, proliferate

reproduction 4 copy 7 replica 8 breeding, likeness 9 duplicate, facsimile, imitation 10 carbon copy, generation, simulation 11 procreation, propagation 13 progeneration, proliferation 14 multiplication, representation

goddess of: 7 Astarte

reproductive system
component: 5 penis 6 testes, uterus, vagina 7 ovaries

reproof 5 blame 6 rebuke 7 censure, chiding 8 reproach, scolding 9 criticism, reprimand 10 admonition 12 condemnation, dressing-down, remonstrance

reprovable 7 at fault 8 blamable, culpable 10 censurable 11 blameworthy 12 reproachable

reprove 5 chide, scold 6 rebuke 7 censure, chasten 8 admonish, reproach 9 castigate, reprimand

reptile 3 asp, eft 4 newt, teju 5 agama, anole, gecko, skink, snake, viper 6 dragon, iguana, lizard, mugger, turtle 7 crawler, creeper, serpent, tuatara 8 basilisk, dinosaur, groveler, terrapin, tortoise 9 alligator, chameleon, crocodile, pterosaur 10 salamander, vertebrate 11 Gila monster, pterodactyl

republic 9 democracy
Latin: 10 res publica

Republic
author: 5 Plato

Republican Party
also called: 3 GOP 13 Grand Old Party
president belonging to: 4 Bush, Ford, Taft 5 Grant, Hayes, Nixon 6 Arthur, Hoover, Reagan 7 Harding, Lincoln, (Andrew) Johnson 8 Coolidge, Garfield, Harrison, McKinley 9 (Theodore) Roosevelt 10 Eisenhower
symbol: 8 elephant

Republic of China see 6 Taiwan

repudiate 4 deny, void 5 annul 6 cancel, desert, disown, reject, repeal, revoke 7 abandon, abolish, cast off, disavow, discard, forsake, nullify, protest, rescind, retract, reverse 8 abrogate, disclaim, dissolve, renounce

repudiation 6 denial 9 disavowal, rejection 10 abrogation, disclaimer, retraction

repugnance 4 hate 5 odium 6 hatred 7 disgust 8 aversion, loathing 9 antipathy, revulsion 10 abhorrence 11 abomination, detestation

repugnant 4 foul, vile 5 nasty 6 odious 7 adverse, counter, hateful, opposed 8 contrary, unsavory 9 abhorrent, loathsome, obnoxious, offensive, repellent, repulsive, revolting, sickening 10 abominable, detestable, disgusting, nauseating, unpleasant 11 distasteful, uncongenial, undesirable, unpalatable 12 antipathetic, disagreeable, insufferable, unacceptable, unappetizing 13 objectionable

repulse 4 shun 5 avoid, repel, spurn 6 ignore, rebuff, refuse, reject 7 refusal 8 shunning, spurning 9 rejection

repulsion 6 hatred 7 disgust, dislike 8 aversion, distaste, loathing 9 antipathy 10 abhorrence, repugnance 11 abomination, detestation 13 indisposition 14 disinclination

repulsive 4 vile 5 nasty 6 odious 7 hateful 9 abhorrent, loathsome, obnoxious, offensive, repellent, repugnant, revolting 10 abominable, detestable, disgusting, nauseating 11 distasteful 13 disagreeable 13 objectionable

repulsiveness 8 ugliness 13 loathsomeness, offensiveness 14 disgustingness, unpleasantness 16 disagreeableness

reputable 7 honored 8 esteemed, reliable 9 respected 10 creditable 11 respectable, trustworthy

reputation 4 name 7 stature 8 standing

repute 3 say 4 deem, fame, hold, view 5 judge, think 6 esteem, reckon, regard, renown 7 account, believe, suppose 8 consider, estimate, standing 9 celebrity, notoriety 10 prominence 14 respectability

request 3 ask 4 seek 6 ask for, bid for, desire, sue for 7 call for, entreat, solicit 8 petition 9 importune 11 application 12 solicitation

requiem 5 dirge 6 lament 8 threnody
requiescat in pace 11 rest in peace 16 may he rest in peace 17 may she rest in peace

require 3 bid 4 lack, miss, need, want 5 crave, imply, order 6 charge, compel, desire, direct, enjoin, entail, oblige 7 command, dictate 9 constrain 11 necessitate

required 6 forced, needed 7 obliged 9 compelled, essential, necessary 10 compulsory, imperative, obligatory

requirement 4 must 8 standard 9 criterion, essential, guideline, requisite 12 prerequisite 13 specification
Latin: 10 sine qua non 11 desideratum

requisite 4 must, need 6 needed 8 required 9 essential, mandatory, necessary, necessity 10 compulsory, imperative, obligatory 11 requirement 12 prerequisite 13 indispensable
Latin: 10 sine qua non 11 desideratum

requisition 4 form 7 request 11 application

requital 7 redress 9 repayment 11 retaliation 12 compensation 15 indemnification

rescind 4 void 5 annul, quash 6 cancel, recall, repeal, revoke 7 abolish, discard, nullify, retract, reverse 8 abrogate, dissolve, override, overrule 10 invalidate 11 countermand 12 counterorder

rescinding 6 recall 7 voiding 8 recision 9 abolition 10 abrogation, retraction, revocation 11 abolishment, dissolution 12 cancellation, invalidation 13 nullification

rescue 4 save 6 ransom, saving 7 deliver, freeing, recover, release, salvage 8 liberate, recovery 9 extricate 10 liberation 11 deliverance, extrication

research 5 probe, study 7 delving, inquiry 8 analysis, scrutiny 10 inspection 11 examination, exploration, factfinding, investigate, scholarship 13 investigation

resemblance 7 analogy 8 affinity, likeness, parallel 10 congruence, similarity, similitude 14 correspondence

resemble 5 favor 6 be like 8 be akin to, look like, parallel 9 take after

Resen
  founder: 6 Nimrod

resent 7 dislike

resentful 5 angry 6 bitter 7 annoyed 8 grudging, offended, provoked 10 displeased 12 dissatisfied

resentfulness 5 anger, spite 10 bitterness 15 dissatisfaction

resentment 3 ire 4 huff 5 anger, pique, spite 6 animus, malice, rancor 7 dudgeon, ill will, offense, umbrage 8 acerbity, acrimony, asperity, jealousy, soreness, sourness 9 animosity, crossness 10 bitterness, irritation 11 displeasure, indignation 12 irritability, vengefulness 14 vindictiveness

reservation 4 date 5 doubt 7 booking, proviso, scruple, strings 8 preserve 9 condition, hesitancy, provision 10 encampment, reluctance, settlement 11 appointment, compunction, stipulation, uncertainty 12 installation 13 accommodation, establishment, qualification 14 prearrangement

reserve 4 book, hold, keep, save 5 amass, delay, extra, hoard, lay up, spare, stock, table 6 backup, engage, retain, shelve, unused 7 husband, nest egg, savings 8 conserve, keep back, postpone, preserve, salt away, schedule, withhold 9 aloofness, reticence, stockpile 10 additional, prearrange

reserved 5 aloof, taken 6 booked, formal 7 distant, engaged 8 bespoken, retained, reticent, strained, unsocial 9 inhibited, spoken for 10 restrained, unsociable 11 ceremonious, constrained, standoffish 12 unresponsive 15 uncommunicative, undemonstrative

reservoir 4 fund, pool, tank, well 5 basin, fount, hoard, stock, store 6 supply 7 backlog, cistern 8 millpond 9 container, stockpile 10 depository, receptacle, repository 12 accumulation

res gestae 5 deeds 10 things done 15 accomplishments

reshape 4 redo 5 adapt, alter, block 6 change, modify, reform, remold, rework 7 convert, reframe, remodel 9 refashion, transform

reside 3 lie 4 live, rest, room 5 dwell, exist, lodge 6 belong, occupy 7 inhabit, sojourn 8 domicile

residence 3 pad 4 digs, flat, home, room, stay 5 abode, house, place 7 address, lodging, sojourn 8 domicile, dwelling, quarters 9 apartment, homestead, household 10 habitation
  French: 10 pied a terre

resident 5 local 6 lodger, tenant 7 citizen, denizen, dweller 8 occupant, townsman 9 sojourner 10 inhabitant 11 housekeeper

residual 5 extra 7 abiding, lasting, surplus 8 enduring, leftover 9 lingering, remaining 10 continuing 13 supplementary

residue 4 rest 5 dregs 6 scraps 7 balance, remains, remnant 8 leavings 9 remainder
  Latin: 8 residuum

resign 4 quit 5 leave 6 give up, submit 8 abdicate, disclaim, renounce 9 reconcile 10 relinquish

resignation 8 fatalism, patience, quitting, stoicism 9 departure 10 equanimity, retirement, submission, withdrawal 11 passiveness 12 acquiescence 13 nonresistance 14 submissiveness

resign oneself 5 yield 6 submit 9 acquiesce

resilience 6 recoil 7 rebound 8 buoyancy 10 elasticity 11 flexibility 12 adaptability 13 changeability, nonuniformity 16 lightheartedness

resilient 5 hardy 6 supple 7 buoyant, elastic, rubbery, springy 8 flexible 9 adaptable, expansive, resistant, tenacious 10 rebounding, responsive 13 irrepressible

resist 5 balk, foil, stem, stop 5 fight, repel 6 baffle, combat, oppose, refuse, reject, thwart 7 contest, counter, weather 8 beat back, turn down 9 frustrate, withstand 10 counteract

resistance 6 mutiny, rebuff 7 refusal 8 defiance, struggle 9 obstinacy, rebellion, rejection 10 contention, insurgency, opposition 11 obstruction 12 insurrection 13 intransigence, noncompliance, recalcitrance

resolute 5 stern 6 dogged, steady 7 earnest, staunch, zealous 8 decisive, diligent, intrepid, stubborn, untiring, vigorous 9 assiduous, obstinate, purposive, steadfast, tenacious, unbending 10 deliberate, determined, inflexible, persistent, relentless, unflagging, unswerving, unwavering, unyielding 11 industrious, persevering, undeviating, unfaltering, unflinching 12 pertinacious, strong-minded, strong-willed 13 indefatigable 14 uncompromising

resoluteness 7 purpose, resolve 8 decision, tenacity 11 decidedness, persistence 12 decisiveness, perseverance 13 determination, steadfastness 14 purposefulness

resolution 3 aim 4 goal, plan, zeal 6 design, energy, intent, mettle, motion, object, spirit 7 promise, purpose, resolve 8 ambition, proposal, solution, tenacity 9 constancy, intention, objective, resolving, stability 10 resilience, steadiness 11 earnestness, persistence 12 perseverance, resoluteness 13 determination, steadfastness 14 aggressiveness 16 indefatigability

resolve 4 plan 6 answer, decide, design, intend, set out, settle, vote on 7 adjudge, clear up, explain, purpose 8 decision 9 determine, elucidate 10 commitment, resolution 12 resoluteness 13 determination 14 make up one's mind

resonant 4 full, rich 7 booming, orotund, ringing, vibrant 8 sonorous 9 bellowing 10 resounding, stentorian, thunderous 11 reverberant

resort 3 use 4 hope 5 apply, avail 6 chance, employ, take up 7 utilize 8 exercise, recourse 9 expedient

resound 4 echo, peal, ring 5 clang 6 re-echo 7 vibrate 11 reverberate 14 tintinnabulate

resounding 7 echoing, ringing 9 re-echoing 10 thundering, thunderous 13 reverberating

resource 8 recourse 9 expedient 11 wherewithal

resourceful 4 able 5 ready, sharp, smart 6 adroit, artful, bright, shrewd 7 capable, cunning 8 creative, original, skillful, talented 9 competent, effectual, ingenious, inventive 10 innovative, proficient 11 imaginative 12 enterprising

resourcefulness 9 ingenuity 10 creativity, enterprise 13 inventiveness

resources 5 funds, means, money 6 assets, income 7 capital, effects, revenue 10 belongings, collateral 11 possessions, wherewithal

respect 5 honor, point, sense 6 detail, esteem, matter, notice, praise, regard 7 bearing, feature, viewing 8 approval, courtesy, relation 9 affection, attention, deference, laudation, reference, relevance, reverence 10 admiration, connection, particular, veneration 11 point of view, recognition 12 appreciation, circumstance 13 consideration

respectability 7 decency, decorum 9 gentility, propriety 11 correctness, genteelness

respectable 4 fair 5 ample, civil, noble 6 decent, honest, polite, proper, worthy 7 correct, courtly, passing, refined, upright 8 becoming, decorous, estimable, honorable, reputable 10 aboveboard, admissible, sufficient 11 presentable 12 considerable, praiseworthy, satisfactory

respected 4 valued, worthy 7 admired, honored, revered 8 esteemed 9 admirable, venerated

respectful 5 civil 6 formal, genial, polite 7 amiable, winning 8 admiring, decorous, gracious, mannerly, obliging, reverent 9 attentive, courteous, regardful 10 personable, solicitous 11 ceremonious, deferential, reverential 13 accommodating

respects 4 heed, obey 5 honor, prize, value 6 admire, esteem, fealty, follow, regard, revere 7 abide by, cherish, defer to, observe, regards, tribute 8 adhere to, consider, venerate 9 greetings 10 appreciate, understand 11 acknowledge, compliments 12 remembrances 13 consideration

Respighi, Ottorino
   born: 5 Italy 7 Bologna
   composer of: 8 La Fiamma, The Birds 14 The Pines of Rome 18 The Fountains of Rome 19 La Boutique Fantasque, The Fantastic Toyshop 27 Ancient Airs and Dances for Lute

respiration 9 breathing

respiratory system
   component: 4 lung, nose 6 larynx 7 pharynx, trachea 8 voice box, windpipe 9 bronchius, diaphragm
   action: 9 breathing

respire 7 breathe

respite 4 lull 5 break, delay, letup, pause 6 recess 8 reprieve 9 extension 12 intermission

resplendence 6 dazzle, luster 7 glitter 8 lambency, radiance 10 brilliance, luminosity, refulgence 12 circumstance, magnificence

resplendent 6 bright 7 beaming, blazing, glowing, lambent, radiant 8 dazzling, gleaming, luminous, lustrous, splendid 9 brilliant, refulgent, sparkling 10 glittering 11 coruscating

respond 5 react, reply 6 answer, rejoin 7 speak up 9 recognize 11 acknowledge

respond to 6 answer 7 act upon, react to, reply to 8 thank for 11 acknowledge

response 5 reply 6 answer, retort, return 7 riposte 8 comeback, feedback, reaction, rebuttal 9 rejoinder 10 impression 13 countercharge 14 acknowledgment 16 counterstatement

responsibility 4 duty, task 5 blame, order, trust 6 burden, charge 8 function 9 liability 10 obligation 11 culpability, reliability 13 answerability, dependability 14 accountability 15 trustworthiness

responsible 5 adult, of age 6 guilty, liable, mature 7 at fault, capable 8 culpable, reliable 9 demanding, executive, important 10 answerable, creditable, dependable 11 accountable, challenging, trustworthy 13 conscientious 14 administrative

responsive 5 alive, awake, sharp 8 reactive 9 receptive, sensitive 11 retaliative, retaliatory, susceptible, sympathetic 13 compassionate, understanding 14 impressionable

responsiveness 6 action 7 concern 8 interest 9 attention, awareness 11 sensitivity 13 understanding

res publica 8 republic, the state 12 commonwealth, public matter

rest 2 be 3 end, lay, lie, nap, set 4 base, ease, halt, hang, keep, laze, lean, loaf, loll, lull, prop, rely, stay, stop 5 break, death, exist, hinge, let up, pause, peace, place, quiet, relax, sleep, stand 6 demise, depend, holder, lounge, others, recess, remain, repose, reside, scraps, snooze, trivet 7 balance, be based, be found, be quiet, decease, deposit, holiday, leisure, lie down, recline, remains, remnant, residue, respite, set down, slumber, support 8 breather, platform, vacation 9 cessation, departure, leftovers, remainder, stillness 10 complement, quiet spell, relaxation, standstill, suspension 11 hibernation, take time out 12 intermission, interruption 13 take a breather
   Spanish: 6 siesta

Latin: 8 residuum

restaurant 5 diner 6 eatery 7 beanery, tearoom 9 cafeteria, chophouse, grillroom, hashhouse, luncheonette

French: 4 cafe 6 bistro 9 brasserie
German: 11 rathskeller

restful 4 calm 5 quiet 6 placid, serene 7 pacific, relaxed 8 peaceful, soothing, tranquil 10 unagitated 11 comfortable, undisturbed

restfulness 4 ease 5 quiet 6 repose 8 serenity, softness 10 relaxation 11 tranquility 12 tranquillity

rest in peace
Latin: 16 requiescat in pace

restitution 6 amends 7 redress, replevy 8 replevin, requital, restoral 9 atonement, indemnity, repayment 10 recompense, reparation 11 restoration 12 compensation, remuneration, satisfaction 13 reimbursement, reinstatement 15 indemnification

restive 5 balky 6 mulish, ornery, unruly 7 fidgety, wayward, willful 8 contrary, stubborn 9 fractious, pigheaded 10 rebellious, refractory 11 disobedient, intractable 12 recalcitrant, unmanageable

restless 5 awake, jumpy 6 fitful, uneasy 7 anxious, fidgety, fretful, jittery, nervous, on the go, unquiet, wakeful, worried 8 agitated 9 excitable, impatient, incessant, insomniac, on the move, sleepless, transient, unsettled 10 disquieted, highstrung 11 hyperactive 13 uncomfortable

restoration 7 revival 8 recovery 12 recuperation 13 convalescence, reinstatement 14 rehabilitation, reintroduction, reinvigoration 15 reestablishment

restorative 5 tonic 6 elixir 7 bracing, healing 8 curative 10 beneficial, energizing, fortifying 11 revivifying 12 invigorating, revitalizing 13 strengthening

restore 3 fix 4 cure, dose, heal, mend 5 rally, renew, treat 6 do over, recoup, remedy, repair, rescue, return, revive 7 convert, get back, patch up, put back, rebuild, reclaim, recover, refresh, remodel, retouch, touch up 8 energize, give back, make over, make well, medicate, renovate, retrieve, revivify, recreate 9 reanimate, refurbish, reinstall, reinstate, stimulate 10 exhilarate, revitalize, strengthen 11 recondition, reconstruct, reestablish, reinstitute, resuscitate 12 rehabilitate, reinvigorate

restored 4 kept 5 saved 7 revived 8 replaced 9 conserved, pressured 11 replenished 13 rehabilitated

restrain 3 gag 4 bind, curb, hold, stop 5 check, leash, limit 6 arrest, bridle, fetter, muzzle, pinion, temper, tether 7 chasten, contain, curtail, harness, inhibit, prevent, shackle, trammel 8 handicap, hold back, restrict, suppress, withhold

restrained 4 cool 5 aloof 6 curbed 7 checked, distant 8 held back, reined in, reserved 10 controlled, unfriendly

restraint 4 curb 5 check 7 control 10 limitation

restrict 4 curb, hold 5 check, cramp, crimp, hem in, limit 6 hamper, impede, narrow, thwart 7 confine, inhibit, prevent, squelch 8 hold back, obstruct, straiten, suppress 9 constrain, frustrate 12 circumscribe

restricted 7 cramped, limited 8 confined, hampered, held back 9 exclusive 10 suppressed 13 circumscribed

restriction 4 rule 7 control, curbing, proviso 9 condition, provision 10 limitation, regulation 11 requirement, reservation, stipulation 13 consideration, qualification

restrictive 8 limiting 9 confining, exclusive 12 constraining

result 4 stem 5 arise, end up, ensue, fruit, issue, owe to 6 derive, effect, happen, pan out, report, sequel, spring, upshot, wind up 7 finding, opinion, outcome, product, turn out, verdict 8 decision, judgment, reaction, solution 9 aftermath, culminate, eventuate, originate, outgrowth 10 resolution 11 aftereffect, consequence, development, eventuality 13 determination

resume 2 CV 3 bio 4 go on 5 brief 6 digest 7 epitome, proceed, summary 8 abstract, continue, reembark, synopsis 9 biography, summation 10 abridgment, recommence 11 reestablish 12 condensation

Latin: 15 curriculum vitae
French: 6 precis

resumption 11 recommenced, restoration 12 continuation

resurgam 15 I shall rise again

resurgence 6 return 7 rebirth, renewal, revival 10 renascence 11 reemergence, renaissance 12 rejuvenation 13 recrudescence

retailer 5 store 6 dealer, seller, trader 8 merchant, provider, supplier 9 tradesman 10 wholesaler 11 distributor, storekeeper, tradeswoman 12 merchandiser

French: 9 vivandier 10 vivandiere

retain 4 hold, keep 5 grasp 6 absorb, recall 7 possess 8 hang on to, hold on to, maintain, memorize, remember 9 recollect

retainer 7 servant 8 employee 9 attendant

retainership 4 hire 6 employ 7 service 10 employment

retaliate 5 repay 6 avenge, pay off, return 7 counter, pay back, requite, revenge 11 reciprocate

retaliation 6 talion 7 deserts, revenge 8 reprisal, requital 9 vengeance 10 recompense 11 comeuppance, eye for an eye, interchange, just deserts, lex talionis, retribution 12 compensation 13 reciprocation 14 tooth for a tooth

retard 4 clog, drag 5 block, brake, check, delay 6 arrest, baffle, detain, fetter, hamper, hinder, hold up, impede, slow up 7 draw out, inhibit, prevent, prolong, slacken 8 hold back, obstruct, slow down 10 decelerate

retarded 4 dull, slow 6 simple 7 idiotic, moronic, unsound 8 backward, disabled 9 imbecilic, mongoloid, subnormal 10 slow-witted 11 handicapped 12 simpleminded

reticent 3 shy 5 quiet 6 closed, silent 7 subdued 8 reserved, retiring, taciturn 9 diffident, withdrawn 10 restrained 11 tight-lipped 12 close-mouthed 15 uncommunicative

retinue 5 court, staff, suite, train 6 convoy 9 courtiers, employees, entourage, followers, following, personnel, retainers 10 associates, attendance, attendants

retire 6 depart, go away, remove, resign, resort, secede, turn in 7 drop out, retreat 8 abdicate, flake out, withdraw

retired
French: 8 ci-devant

retiring 3 shy 4 meek 5 quiet, timid 6 demure, humble, modest 7 bashful 8 reserved, reticent, sheepish, timorous, unsocial 9 diffident, shrinking, withdrawn 10 unassuming 11 unassertive 12 self-effacing 13 inconspicuous, unpretentious 15 uncommunicative

retort 3 say 4 quip 5 rebut, reply 6 answer, rejoin, return 7 counter, respond, riposte 8 fire back, rebuttal 9 rejoinder

retract 4 deny 6 abjure, disown, draw in, recall, recant, recede, recoil, reel in, repeal, revoke 7 disavow, rescind, retreat, reverse 8 abnegate, abrogate, disclaim, draw back, forswear, peel back, pull back, renounce, take back, withdraw 9 foreswear, repudiate

retraction 6 recall 8 recision 9 disavowal 10 disclaimer, refutation, withdrawal

retreat 2 go 3 den 4 bolt, flee, port 5 haunt, haven, leave 6 asylum, depart, escape, flight, harbor, recoil, refuge, resort, retire, shrink 7 abscond, getaway, privacy, sanctum, shelter, shy away 8 back away, draw back, fall back, hideaway, move back, solitude, turn tail, withdraw 9 departure, isolation, reclusion, sanctuary, seclusion 10 evacuation, immurement, retirement, withdrawal 11 hibernation, rustication

retrench 5 slash 6 reduce, scrape, scrimp 7 curtail, cut back, cut down 8 conserve, cut costs 9 economize 15 tighten one's belt

retribution 6 amends, return, reward 7 justice, penalty, redress, revenge 8 reprisal, requital 9 vengeance 10 punishment, recompense, reparation 11 just deserts, restitution, retaliation, vindication 12 satisfaction 13 reciprocation, recrimination

retrieve 4 snag 5 fetch 6 ransom, recoup, redeem, regain, rescue 7 get back, reclaim, recover, salvage 9 recapture, repossess

retriever
dog breed: 5 Irish 6 golden, Gordon 7 English 8 Labrador 10 flat-coated 11 curly-coated 13 Chesapeake Bay

retrograde 5 worse 6 worsen 7 inverse, retreat, reverse 8 backward 10 regressive 13 retrogressive

retrogress 6 worsen 9 backslide

retrogression 7 decline, setback 9 worsening 11 backsliding

retrogressive 8 backward 9 declining, worsening 11 backsliding

retrospect 6 review 9 flashback, hindsight 11 remembrance 12 afterthought, reminiscence 15 reconsideration

return 3 net 4 earn, gain 5 gross, recur, repay, yield 6 advent, come to, go back, income, profit, render, reseat, reward 7 arrival, benefit, produce, provide, put back, requite, restore, revenue 8 announce, come back, earnings, proceeds, reappear, recovery, restoral, send back 9 advantage, reinstall, reinstate, retrieval, reversion 10 homecoming, recurrence 11 reciprocate, reestablish, restoration 12 compensation, reappearance 13 reinstatement 15 reestablishment

Return, The
author: 14 Walter de la Mare

Return of the Native
author: 11 Thomas Hardy
character: 11 Diggory Venn, Eustacia Vye 12 Damon Wildeve 13 Clym Yeobright 17 Thomasin Yeobright

Return to Thebes
author: 10 Allan Drury

Reuben
father: 5 Jacob
mother: 4 Leah
brother: 3 Dan, Gad 4 Levi 5 Asher, Judah 6 Joseph, Simeon 7 Zebulun 8 Benjamin, Issachar, Naphtali
sister: 5 Dinah
descendant of: 9 Reubenite

reunite 5 rewed 7 remarry 9 reconcile

reveal 4 bare, show 6 betray, expose, impart, let out, unfold, unmask, unveil 7 display, divulge, exhibit, give out, lay bare, publish, uncover, unearth 8 disclose, evidence, manifest, point out

revealed 4 open 5 clear, known 7 evident, obvious 8 manifest

revel 4 romp 5 caper, enjoy 6 bask in, frolic, gambol, relish 7 carouse, delight, indulge, rejoice, roister, skylark 8 wallow in 9 celebrate

revelation 6 expose, vision 7 shocker 8 exposure, prophecy 9 admission, bombshell, discovery, eyeopener, unveiling 10 apocalypse, confession, disclosure, divulgence 11 divulgation, divulgement

revelatory 10 expressive 11 informative 13 communicative

reveler 6 barfly, ranter, player 7 drinker 8 bacchant, carouser, drunkard 9 roisterer, rollicker, skylarker 10 merrymaker

revelry 5 spree 6 carnival, carousal, festival, jamboree 9 high jinks, merriment, rejoicing 10 exultation, roistering 11 cele-

brating, celebration, merrymaking 12 conviviality 13 jollification 14 boisterousness
   god of: 5 Comus
revenge 5 repay 7 pay back, requite 8 reprisal, requital 9 repayment, retaliate, vengeance, vindicate 10 recompense 11 eye for an eye, reciprocate, retaliation, retribution 12 satisfaction
revenue 3 pay 4 take 5 gains, wages, yield 6 income, profit, return, salary 7 annuity, pension, subsidy 8 earnings, interest, pickings, proceeds, receipts 9 allowance, emolument 12 compensation, remuneration
revenue, annual
   French: 5 rente
reverberate 4 boom, echo, ring 5 carry 6 rumble 7 resound, thunder, vibrate
reverberation 4 boom, echo 6 rumble 7 ringing, thunder 8 rumbling 9 vibration 10 resounding, thundering
revere 5 honor 6 esteem 7 defer to, respect 8 venerate
revered 6 adored 7 admired, honored 9 estimable, respected, venerated, worshiped 10 worshipped
reverence 3 awe 4 fear 5 honor, piety 6 esteem, homage, regard 7 respect, worship 8 devotion 9 adoration, deference 10 admiration, devoutness, observance, veneration 11 prostration, religiosity 12 genuflection
reverent 4 pure 5 pious 6 devout, humble, solemn 7 adoring, awesome, devoted 8 faithful 9 religious, spiritual 10 respectful, worshipful
reverential 4 awed 10 respectful, worshipful 11 deferential
reverie 5 dream, fancy 6 musing 7 fantasy 8 daydream 9 dreamland, quixotism 10 brown study, meditation 12 extravagance 13 woolgathering 14 fantasticality
reverse 4 back, rear, tail, undo, void 5 annul, upend, upset 6 cancel, change, defeat, invert, mishap, negate, recall, recant, repeal, revoke, unmake, upturn 7 counter, failure, nullify, rescind, retract, setback, trouble 8 abrogate, backward, contrary, converse, hardship, inverted, opposite, override, overrule, set aside, turn over, withdraw 9 adversity, mischance, posterior, transpose 10 antithesis, invalidate, misfortune 11 countermand, counterpart, frustration 14 disappointment
revert 5 lapse 6 go back, repeat, return 7 regress, relapse 9 backslide 10 recidivate, retrogress
review 4 show 5 study, sum up 6 notice, parade, rehash, survey 7 analyze, journal, retrace, run over 8 critique, evaluate, hash over, magazine, reassess, report on, scrutiny 9 criticism, criticize, reexamine, reiterate, summarize 10 commentary, evaluation, exhibition, exposition, procession, reconsider, reevaluate, reflection, scrutinize 11 examination 12 presentation, reassessment, recapitulate, reevaluation 13

demonstration, retrospection 14 recapitulation 15 reconsideration
   French: 11 compte rendu
revile 4 slur 5 abuse, curse, scold, scorn 6 berate, defame, deride, malign, rebuke, vilify 7 bawl out, chew out, slander, upbraid 8 belittle, denounce, execrate, reproach, sail into 9 blaspheme, castigate, denigrate, disparage 10 vituperate
reviler 6 critic, curser 8 vilifier 9 backbiter, slanderer 10 blasphemer
revise 4 edit, redo 5 alter, amend, emend, fix up 6 change, doctor, modify, recast, redact, revamp, review, update 7 correct, rectify, rewrite 8 emendate, overhaul
revision 6 change 7 edition 9 amendment, recension 10 alteration, correction, emendation 11 improvement 12 modification
revival 7 renewal 11 restoration 13 reinstatement, reinstitution, resuscitation
revive 5 dig up, renew 6 drag up, repeat 7 freshen, refresh, restage 8 reawaken 9 reanimate, reproduce, resurrect 11 resuscitate
revived 7 renewed 8 animated, repeated, restaged 9 enlivened, freshened, refreshed 10 reanimated, reawakened, reproduced 11 invigorated, resurrected 12 resuscitated
revocation 6 repeal 8 recision 9 abolition, annulment 10 abrogation, retraction 11 abolishment, elimination, repudiation 12 cancellation 13 nullification
revoke 4 void 5 annul, erase, quash 6 abjure, cancel, negate, recall, repeal, vacate 7 abolish, dismiss, expunge, nullify, rescind, retract, reverse 8 abrogate, call back, disallow, disclaim, override, overrule, renounce, set aside, take back, withdraw 9 repudiate 10 invalidate 11 countermand
revolt 4 coup, rise 5 rebel, repel, shock 6 appall, mutiny, offend, rise up, sicken 7 disgust, dissent, horrify, repulse 8 disorder, distress, nauseate, sedition, uprising 9 rebellion 10 insurgency, opposition, 12 factiousness, insurrection
   German: 6 Putsch
revolting 4 foul, grim, vile 5 nasty 6 horrid, odious 7 hateful, noisome, noxious 8 dreadful, horrible, horrific, shocking, stinking 9 abhorrent, appalling, frightful, invidious, loathsome, obnoxious, offensive, repellent, repugnant, repulsive, sickening 10 abominable, disgusting, malodorous, nauseating 11 distasteful 12 disagreeable 13 objectionable
Revolt of the Angels, The
   author: 13 Anatole·France
revolution 6 mutiny, revolt, rising 8 circling, gyration, rotation, uprising 9 rebellion 12 insurrection 14 circumrotation, circumvolution
   French: 4 coup 9 coup d'etat
   German: 6 Putsch

revolutionary 7 radical 8 mutinous 9 extremist, insurgent, seditious 10 dissenting, rebellious, subversive 13 superadvanced, unprecedented 15 insurrectionary

revolve 4 spin, turn 5 twist, wheel 6 circle, gyrate, rotate 12 circumrotate

revolver 3 gat, gun, rod 4 colt 6 pistol, weapon 7 firearm, handgun, rotator, sidearm 10 six-shooter 20 Saturday night special

revulsion 8 aversion, distaste, loathing 10 abhorrence, repugnance 11 detestation

reward 3 due 5 bonus, prize, repay, wages 6 bounty 7 deserts, guerdon, payment, premium, requite 9 reckoning 10 compensate, recompense, remunerate 12 compensation, remuneration 13 consideration
Latin: 10 quid pro quo

rewarding 8 pleasant, valuable 9 enjoyable 10 delightful, gratifying, satisfying 11 pleasurable

rework 4 redo 5 adapt, alter 6 modify 7 remodel, reshape 9 refashion, transform

rex 4 king

Reykjavik
  capital of: 7 Iceland

Reynolds, Burt
  born: 10 Waycross GA
  wife: 9 Judy Carne 12 Loni Anderson
  roles: 6 Shamus 9 Dan August, Semi-Tough 11 Deliverance 14 The Longest Yard 18 Smokey and the Bandit

Reynolds, Debbie
  real name: 19 Mary Frances Reynolds
  born: 8 El Paso TX
  husband: 11 Eddie Fisher
  roles: 13 The Singing Nun, The Tender Trap 15 Singin' in the Rain 19 Tammy and the Bachelor 23 The Unsinkable Molly Brown

Reynolds, Sir Joshua
  born: 7 England 8 Plympton
  artwork: 14 Lord Heathfield, Miss Jane Bowles 15 Commodore Keppel 18 Mrs Francis Beckford 21 Mrs Abington as Miss Prue 25 Mrs Siddons as the Tragic Muse 38 Lady Sarah Bunbury Sacrificing to the Graces

Rhadamanthus, Rhadamanthys
  father: 4 Zeus
  mother: 6 Europa
  brother: 5 Minos 6 Aeacus 8 Sarpedon
  became a judge in: 5 Hades

rhapsodic 6 elated 7 beaming, excited 8 blissful, ecstatic, thrilled 9 delirious, overjoyed, rapturous 11 exhilarated, transported

Rhea
  member of: 6 Titans
  father: 6 Uranus
  mother: 4 Gaea
  brother: 6 Cronos, Cronus, Kronos
  husband: 6 Cronos, Cronus, Kronos
  son: 4 Zeus 5 Hades 8 Poseidon
  daughter: 4 Hera 6 Hestia 7 Demeter
  called: 10 Magna Mater

  corresponds to: 3 Ops 6 Cybele 9 Dindymene 10 Berecyntia
  epithet: 6 Antaea

Rhea Silvia *see* 9 Rea Silvia

Rhene
  mistress of: 6 Oileus
  son: 5 Medon

Rhesus
  owned: 6 horses
  horses captured by: 8 Diomedes, Odysseus

rhetoric 4 bunk, wind 5 hokum, hooey 6 bunkum, hot air 7 fustian, oratory 8 euphuism 9 discourse, elocution, eloquence, hyperbole 10 hocus-pocus 11 flamboyance 13 magniloquence 14 grandiloquence

Rhetoric
  author: 9 Aristotle

rhetorical 5 showy, windy 6 florid, ornate, purple, verbal 7 aureate, flowery 8 eloquent, inflated 9 bombastic, grandiose, highflown, stylistic 10 decorative, discursive, euphuistic, expressive, flamboyant, linguistic, oratorical, ornamental 11 disputative, embellished, extravagant 12 disputatious, elocutionary, magniloquent 13 argumentative, grandiloquent

Rhiannon
  origin: 5 Welsh
  husband: 5 Pwyll 10 Manawyddan
  son: 7 Pryderi
  accused of devouring: 7 Pryderi

Rhigmus
  origin: 8 Thracian
  ally of: 7 Trojans
  killed by: 8 Achilles

rhinoceros
  group of: 5 crash

Rhoda
  character: 8 Gary Levy 9 Joe Gerard 12 Benny Goodwin 14 Ida Morgenstern, Sally Gallagher 17 Brenda Morgenstern, Martin Morgenstern 22 Rhoda Morgenstern Gerard
  cast: 9 Anne Meara, David Groh, Ron Silver 11 Julie Kavner, Nancy Walker 12 Harold J Gould, Ray Buktenica 13 Valerie Harper

Rhode Island
  abbreviation: 2 RI
  nickname: 11 Little Rhody
  capital/largest city: 10 Providence
  others: 7 Bristol, Newport 8 Cranston, Kingston, Westerly 9 Pawtucket, Wakefield 10 Woonsocket
  college: 5 Brown 6 Bryant 8 Pembroke 10 Barrington, Providence 11 Salve Regina 13 Mount St Joseph, Roger Williams 15 Johnson and Wales, Naval War College
  feature: 7 Newport
  tribe: 7 Niantic 9 Wampanoag 12 Narragansett
  people: 8 Puritans 12 George M Cohan 13 Gilbert Stuart, Matthew C Perry, Roger Williams 15 Ambrose Burnside,

Nathanael Greene 17 Oliver Hazard
Perry
island: 5 Block, Rhode 8 Prudence 9
Aquidneck, Conanicut
lake: 8 Scituate
pond: 7 Wordens 8 Stafford, Watchaug
land rank: 8 fiftieth
mountain: 10 Durfee Hill
highest point: 12 Jerimoth Hill
physical feature:
bay: 12 Narragansett
sea: 8 Atlantic
sound: 11 Block Island
river: 7 Seekonk 8 Pawtuxet 9 Pawcatuck, Pawtucket, Potowomut 10 Blackstone, Providence
state admission: 10 thirteenth
state bird: 14 Rhode Island Red
state flower: 6 violet
state motto: 4 Hope
state song: 11 Rhode Island
state tree: 8 red maple
Rhodesia *see* 8 Zimbabwe
rhodium
chemical symbol: 2 Rh
rhododendron
varieties: 4 tree 5 Bluet 6 Indian, Yunnan
7 catawba, fringed, Lapland, silvery,
Smirnow 8 Carolina, Chapman's, Fortune's, Fujiyama, piedmont 9 Caucasian,
honey-bell, West Coast 11 leather-leaf 12
willow-leaved
rhodolite
species: 6 garnet
Rhodope
companion of: 7 Artemis
skill: 7 hunting
Rhodopis
also: 7 Rhodope
form: 9 courtesan
origin: 5 Greek 8 Thracian
slave in: 5 Egypt
lost: 7 slipper
slipper found by: 12 Psammetichus
husband: 12 Psammetichus
Rhodus
father: 8 Poseidon
mother: 9 Aphrodite
Rhoeo
father: 9 Staphylus
mother: 12 Chrysothemis
seduced by: 6 Apollo
Rhoetus
member of: 8 Gigantes
rhubarb 5 Rheum 16 Rheum rhabarbarum
varieties: 4 wild 5 monk's 6 garden, Sikkim 7 spinach 8 mountain
rhyme 3 pun 4 poem, rune, song 5 chime,
clink, meter, poesy, verse 6 jingle, poetry,
rhythm 7 measure, poetize, versify 8 asso-
nate, doggerel 10 consonance 12 allitera-
tion
game: 6 crambo
rhymer, rhymester 4 bard, poet 6 writer 8
minstrel, poetizer 9 poetaster, versifier 10
troubadour

Rhys, Jean
author of: 7 Quartet 15 Voyage in the
Dark, Wide Sargasso Sea
rhythm 4 beat, lilt, time 5 meter, pulse,
swing, throb 6 accent, number, stress 7
cadence, measure 8 emphasis, movement
9 pulsation 10 recurrence 11 fluctuation,
syncopation 12 accentuation
riant 3 gay 4 airy 5 jolly, merry 6 blithe,
bright, jocund, jovial 7 smiling 8 cheerful, laughing, mirthful
ribald 4 lewd, racy, rude 5 bawdy, crude,
gross 6 coarse, earthy, rakish, risque, vulgar, wanton 7 raffish, uncouth 8 improper,
indecent, off-color, prurient, shocking 9 salacious, unrefined 10 lascivious, libidinous,
licentious, suggestive
ribbon 3 bow, ray 4 band, sash 5 award,
braid, prize, reins, strip 6 cordon, riband 7
binding, rosette 8 memorial, streamer 10
decoration
rice 5 Oryza 11 Oryza sativa
varieties: 4 wild 6 Indian, pampas 8
mountain 9 Tennessee 10 annual wild
dish: 5 grits, pilaf 7 pudding, risotto 8
porridge 9 jambalaya
liquor: 4 sake
Rice, Elmer
author of: 11 Street Scene 16 The Adding Machine
Riceyman Steps
author: 13 Arnold Bennett
rich 4 dark, deep, fine, lush 5 flush, heavy,
loamy, sweet, vivid 6 bright, costly, fecund,
lavish, mellow 7 fertile, filling, intense,
moneyed, opulent, wealthy, well-off 8
abundant, affluent, fruitful, in clover, precious, prodigal, resonant, sonorous, splendid, valuable, well-to-do 9 abounding, estimable, expensive, luxuriant, luxurious,
priceless, sumptuous 10 euphonious, productive, propertied, prosperous 11 mellifluous 12 on easy street
Rich, Adrienne
author of: 18 Diving into the Wreck
Richard, Maurice
nickname: 6 Rocket
sport: 6 hockey
position: 7 forward
team: 17 Montreal Canadiens
Richard Cory
author: 22 Edwin Arlington Robinson
Richard Diamond, Private Detective
character: 3 Sam 6 Lt Kile 9 Lt McGough
10 Karen Wells
cast: 10 Russ Conway 11 Barbara Bain,
Regis Toomey 12 David Janssen 13
Roxanne Brooks 14 Mary Tyler Moore
viewers saw only Sam's: 4 legs
Richard II
author: 18 William Shakespeare
character: 11 John of Gaunt 13 Edmund
Langley, Thomas Mowbray 16 Henry
Bolingbroke 20 Earl of Northumberland
Duke of: 4 York 7 Aumerle, Norfolk 8
Hereford 9 Lancaster

Richard III
author: 18 William Shakespeare
character: 6 George 7 Richard 8 Edward IV, Lady Anne 10 Henry Tudor (Earl of Richmond) 11 Lord Stanley 12 Lord Hastings 13 Queen Margaret 14 Queen Elizabeth 15 Edward the Fourth 17 Sir William Catesby 19 Edward Prince of Wales
Duke of: 4 York 8 Clarence 10 Buckingham, Gloucester

Richardson, Henry Hobson
architect of: 9 Sever Hall (Harvard) 11 Grace Church (West Medford MA) 13 Trinity Church (Boston) 23 State Asylum for the Insane (Buffalo NY) 27 Marshall Field Wholesale Store (Chicago)

Richardson, Samuel
author of: 6 Pamela (or Virtue Rewarded) 8 Clarissa (Harlowe) 19 Sir Charles Grandison

Richardson, Sir Ralph
born: 7 England 10 Cheltenham
roles: 6 Exodus 10 Oscar Wilde, Richard III, The Heiress 11 A Doll's House 12 Anna Karenina 13 Doctor Zhivago 15 Richard the Third 20 Little Lord Fauntleroy 24 Long Day's Journey into Night 26 Greystoke The Legend of Tarzan

Richardson, Tony
director of: 8 Tom Jones (Oscar) 15 Look Back in Anger 36 The Loneliness of the Long Distance Runner

riches 4 pelf 5 lucre, means 6 assets, mammon, wealth 7 fortune 8 opulence, treasure 9 resources 10 prosperity 11 possessions

richness 6 wealth 8 fullness, lushness, opulence 9 amplitude, intensity 10 lavishness, mellowness 12 completeness 13 luxuriousness

Richter, Charles Francis
field: 10 geophysics, seismology
developed: 12 Richter scale 24 measurement of earthquakes

rickety 4 weak 5 frail, shaky 6 feeble, flimsy, infirm, wasted, weakly, wobbly 7 fragile 8 decrepit, unsteady, withered 9 tottering 10 brokendown, tumbledown 11 debilitated, dilapidated, weakjointed 12 deteriorated

rid 4 free 5 clear, purge 6 remove 8 disabuse, liberate, unburden 9 disburden, eliminate 11 disencumber

Ridd, John
character in: 10 Lorna Doone
author: 9 Blackmore

riddance 6 ouster, relief 7 freeing, removal 8 ejection 9 clearance, expulsion 11 deliverance, dislodgment

riddle 5 poser, rebus 6 enigma, puzzle, secret 7 mystery, problem, puzzler, stumper 9 conundrum

ride 4 move 5 annoy, carry, drive, harry, hound 6 badger, handle, harass, hector, manage, needle, travel 7 control, journey, support 8 progress 9 transport

rider 5 affix 6 suffix 7 adjunct, codicil 8 addendum, addition, appendix 9 amendment, appendage 10 attachment, supplement

Riders to the Sea
author: 19 John Millington Synge

ridge 3 bar, rib, rim 4 bank, fret, hill, hump, rise, wale, weal, welt 5 bluff, crest, crimp, knoll, mound, spine 6 ripple 7 crinkle, hillock, wrinkle 10 promontory 11 corrugation

ridicule 3 guy, rib 4 gibe, jeer, josh, mock, razz, ride, twit 5 mimic, scorn, taunt, tease 6 deride, gibe at, parody 7 lampoon, laugh at, mockery, ribbing, sarcasm, scoff at, sneer at, snicker, teasing 8 belittle, derision, sneering, travesty 9 aspersion, burlesque, disparage, humiliate, make fun of, poke fun at 10 caricature, derogation, lampoonery 13 disparagement
god of: 5 Momos, Momus

ridiculous 3 odd 5 crazy, droll, funny, inane, nutty, queer, silly 6 absurd, screwy 7 amusing, asinine, bizarre, comical, fatuous, foolish, idiotic 8 farcical 9 fantastic, frivolous, grotesque, laughable, ludicrous, screwball, senseless 10 hysterical, incredible, irrational, outlandish 11 astonishing, nonsensical 12 preposterous, unreasonable

Rienzi
author: 18 Edward Bulwer-Lytton

Riesling, Paul
character in: 7 Babbitt
author: 5 Lewis

rife 5 close, dense, solid, thick 6 common, packed 7 crowded, general, studded, teeming 8 epidemic, pandemic, populous, swarming 9 chock-full, extensive, plumbfull, prevalent, universal 10 prevailing, widespread 11 predominant

riffraff 3 mob 4 herd, scum 5 crowd, dregs, trash 6 masses, proles, rabble, vermin 9 peasantry 10 commonalty 11 proletariat
French: 8 canaille

rifle 3 rob 4 loot, sack 6 ravage 7 despoil, pillage, plunder, ransack 8 spoliate 10 burglarize

rifle, repeating
invented by: 7 Spencer

Rifleman, The
character: 10 Lou Mallory, Mark McCain 11 Lucas McCain 14 Miss Milly Scott 20 Marshal Micah Torrance
cast: 7 Paul Fix 10 Joan Taylor 12 Chuck Connors 13 Patricia Blair 14 Johnny Crawford
setting: 9 New Mexico, North Fork

rift 3 cut, gap 4 gash, gulf, rent, slit 5 abyss, break, chasm, chink, cleft, crack, fault, gorge, gulch, gully, split 6 breach, cranny, ravine 7 breakup, crevice, fissure, quarrel, rupture 8 aperture, crevasse, division, fracture 12 disagreement 16 misunderstanding

rig 4 gear 5 equip 6 fit out, outfit 8 carriage 9 apparatus, equipment, machinery

Rigaud
   character in: 12 Little Dorrit
   author: 7 Dickens

Rigg, Diana
   born: 7 England 9 Doncaster
   roles: 6 Helena 8 Emma Peel 10 Bleak
   House 11 Lady Dedlock, The Avengers
   12 Julius Caesar 21 A Midsummer
   Night's Dream 26 On Her Majesty's
   Secret Service

right 2 OK 3 due 4 deed, fair, good, just,
   meet, nice, real, sane, true, well 5 amend,
   emend, exact, grant, honor, ideal, legal,
   licit, moral, power, solve, sound, valid 6
   actual, at once, decent, honest, lawful,
   morals, normal, proper, remedy, seemly,
   square, virtue 7 certain, correct, ethical,
   exactly, factual, fitting, freedom, genuine,
   liberty, license, perfect, precise, probity, redress, regular, standup, warrant 8 accurate, becoming, clear-cut, definite, directly,
   goodness, morality, promptly, properly, rational, sanction, straight, suitable, suitably,
   truthful, virtuous 9 allowable, authentic,
   authority, correctly, desirable, equitable,
   exemplary, favorable, favorably, honorable, integrity, nobleness, opportune, ownership, perfectly, precisely, presently, privilege, propriety, rectitude, veracious,
   veridical, vindicate 10 aboveboard, accurately, admissible, completely, convenient,
   infallible, legitimate, permission, preferable, reasonable, recompense, scrupulous,
   undisputed, unmistaken 11 inheritance,
   immediately, irrefutable, prerogative, punctilious 12 advantageous, jurisdiction, satisfactory 13 appropriately, authorization, incontestable, justification, unimpeachable
   14 proprietorship, satisfactorily, unquestionable
   Latin: 3 jus

right beside 6 next to 8 abutting, adjacent,
   touching

righteous 4 fair, good, holy, just 5 godly,
   moral, pious 6 chaste, devout, honest 7
   ethical 8 elevated, innocent, reverent, virtuous 9 blameless, equitable, honorable,
   incorrupt, religious, spiritual, unsullied

righteousness
   goddess of: 4 Maat

righteous person
   Hebrew: 6 zaddik

rightful 3 due 4 just, true 5 legal, valid 6
   lawful, proper 7 allowed, condign, correct,
   fitting, merited 8 deserved 9 deserving, equitable 10 authorized, designated, legitimate, prescribed, sanctioned 11 appropriate, inalienable 14 constitutional

right hand 4 aide, ally 6 helper 7 partner 8
   adjutant 9 assistant
   French: 10 aide-de-camp

right of blood
   Latin: 12 jus sanguinis

right of soil/land
   Latin: 7 jus soli

Right People, The
   author: 17 Stephen Birmingham

right side up 7 upright 10 on one's feet

Right Stuff, The
   director: 13 Philip Kaufman
   author: 8 Tom Wolfe
   cast: 8 Ed Harris 10 Sam Shepard
   Oscar for: 5 score

right-wing 7 old-line 10 nonliberal 11 reactionary 12 conservative 14 nonprogressive

right-winger 8 rightist 11 reactionary 12
   conservative

rigid 3 set 4 firm, hard, taut 5 fixed, harsh,
   sharp, stern, stiff, tense 6 formal, severe,
   strict, strong, wooden 7 austere 8 exacting, obdurate, rigorous, stubborn, unpliant
   9 inelastic, stringent, unbending 10 inflexible, unyielding 11 puritanical, unrelenting
   14 uncompromising

Rigoletto
   opera by: 5 Verdi
   character: 5 Gilda 9 Maddalena 11 Spa-
   rafucile 12 Duke of Mantua 15 Countess
   Ceprano 16 Count of Monterone

rigorous 5 exact, harsh, stern, tough 6 severe, strict, trying 7 austere, correct, precise 8 accurate, exacting 9 demanding,
   stringent 10 meticulous, scrupulous 11
   challenging, punctilious

rig out 4 garb 5 array, dress 6 attire, clothe

rile 3 irk, vex 4 gall, mlff, roil 5 anger, annoy, chafe, gripe, peeve, pique 6 bother,
   enrage, nettle, offend, plague 7 incense,
   inflame, provoke 8 irritate 9 aggravate, infuriate

Riley, James Whitcomb
   author of: 18 Little Orphant Annie 25
   When the Frost Is on the Punkin

rilievo 6 relief

Rilke, Rainer Maria
   author of: 11 Book of Hours 12 Duino Elegies, Life and Songs 13 Divine Elegies
   16 Sonnets to Orpheus 19 Letters to a
   Young Poet

rill 5 brook, cleft, creek 6 furrow, groove,
   runnel, stream 7 channel, rivulet 9 streamlet

rim 3 lip 4 edge, side 5 brink, ledge, verge
   6 border, margin 9 outer edge

Rima
   character in: 13 Green Mansions
   author: 6 Hudson

Rimbaud, Arthur
   author of: 12 Le Bateau Ivre 13 A Season in Hell 14 The Drunken Boat 16 Les
   Illuminations 17 Sonnet of the Vowels

rime 3 ice 4 hoar 5 chink, cleft, crack, crust,
   frost 7 crevice, fissure 9 hoarfrost

Rime of the Ancient Mariner, The
   author: 21 Samuel Taylor Coleridge
   character: 6 Hermit 9 Albatross 12 Wedding Guest 14 Ancient Mariner

Rimsky-Korsakov, Nikolai (Nicholas)
   born: 6 Russia 8 Novgorod
   member of: 7 The Five
   composer of: 5 Mlada, Sadko 6 Kitezh
   10 Night in May, Snow Maiden, Tzar
   Saltan 11 Sheherazade 12 Christmas
   Eve, Scheherazade 16 Spanish Capriccio

17 Capriccio Espagnol, The Golden Cockerel **21** Russian Easter Overture **29** Russian Easter Festival Overture

rind 4 bark, hull, husk, peel, skin **5** crust, shell **6** cortex, fringe **7** epicarp, surface **8** exterior
  pork: 9 crackling

ring 4 aura, band, bloc, buzz, call, echo, gang, hoop, loop, peal, toll, tone **5** cabal, chime, clang, knell, party, sound **6** cartel, circle, cordon, herald, jangle, jingle, league, signal, strike, summon, tinkle **7** besiege; circuit, combine, enclose, quality, resound, seal off, vibrate **8** announce, blockade, encircle, proclaim, striking, surround **9** broadcast, encompass, perimeter, resonance, syndicate, ting-a-ling, vibration **10** federation **11** reverberate **12** circumscribe **13** circumference, reverberation **14** tintinnabulate **16** tintinnabulation

Ring and the Book, The
  author: 14 Robert Browning

Ring des Nibelungen, Der
  also: 12 The Ring Cycle **20** The Ring of the Nibelung(s)
  opera by: 6 Wagner
  part one: 12 Das Rheingold, The Rhine Gold
  part two: 10 Die Walkure **11** The Valkyrie
  part three: 9 Siegfried
  part four: 15 Gotterdammerung **17** Twilight of the Gods
  character: 4 Erda, Mime **5** Freia, Hagen, Wotan **6** Fafner, Fasolt **7** Gunther, Gutrune, Hunding **8** Alberich, Siegmund **9** Siegfried, Sieglinde, Valkyries **10** Brunnhilde

ring down the curtain 3 end **4** halt **6** finish **8** conclude **9** terminate

ringleader 6 chief **6** master **10** mastermind

ringlet 4 curl **6** circle

ring-shaped 5 round **8** circular

Rin Tin Tin, The Adventures of
  character: 4 Rusty, (Cpl) Boone **9** (Sgt) Biff O'Hara **10** (Lt) Rip Masters
  cast: 8 Lee Aaker **9** Joe Sawyer **10** James Brown, Rand Brooks

Rio Bravo
  director: 11 Howard Hawks
  cast: 8 Ward Bond **9** John Wayne **10** Dean Martin **11** Ricky Nelson **13** Walter Brennan **14** Angie Dickinson

Rio de Janeiro
  airport: 6 Galeao
  architect: 5 Costa, Reidy **8** Niemeyer
  area: 4 Caju, Lapa **6** Catete, Gamboa, Gloria, Grajau, Tijuca **7** Catumbi, Ipanema **8** Botafogo **10** Copacabana, Vila Isabel **12** Sao Cristovao
  bay: 8 Botafogo, Jurujuba **9** Guanabara
  bridge: 11 Costa e Silva
  celebration: 8 Carnival **9** Mardi Gras
  discovered by: 6 Coelho
  former capital of: 6 Brazil
  island: 6 Governador
  lake: 16 Rodrigo de Freitas
  landmark: 10 Candelaria **14** Mount

Corcovado **15** Maracana Stadium **17** Sugarloaf Mountain
  statue of: 17 Christ the Redeemer
  means: 14 river of January
  ocean: 8 Atlantic
  people: 8 Cariocas
  replaced as capital by: 8 Brasilia
  slums: 7 favelas
  suburb: 7 Niteroi

riot 4 rage **5** act up, arise, melee, rebel **6** fracas, mutiny, resist, revolt, rumpus, strife, tumult, uproar **7** rampage, run amok, trouble, turmoil **8** disorder, outburst, uprising, violence **9** commotion, confusion, rebellion **10** Donnybrook, turbulence **11** lawlessness, pandemonium **12** insurrection

rioting 6 tumult, uproar **7** turmoil **8** disorder, outbreak, violence **9** commotion **11** disturbance

riotous 4 loud, wild **5** arroar, noisy, randy **6** stormy, unruly, wanton **7** bacchic, rampant, violent **8** bacchian **9** debauched, dissolute, insurgent, plentiful, tumultuous, turbulent **10** boisterous, dissipated, licentious, rebellious **11** intemperate, overcopious **12** unrestrained **13** superabundant **15** insurrectionary
  party: 4 orgy

rip 3 cut, gap **4** rend, rent, rift, rive, slit, tear **5** burst, sever, shred, slash, split **6** cleave **7** fissure, rupture **8** cleavage, cut apart, fracture, incision, tear open **10** laceration

ripe 3 due, fit **4** come **5** ideal, ready **6** mature, mellow, primed, timely **7** perfect **8** complete, finished, seasoned **9** maturated **10** consummate **12** accomplished

ripen 3 age **4** grow **5** bloom, fruit **6** flower, mature, mellow **7** develop

Rip Kirby
  creator: 11 Alex Raymond **12** John Prentice

Ripley, Robert L
  author of: 14 Believe It or Not

Rip Van Winkle
  author: 16 Washington Irving

rise 4 bank, defy, dune, face, gain, go up, grow, hill, lift, meet, soar **5** climb, get up, knoll, march, mount, rebel, ridge, spire, stand, surge, swell, tower **6** ascend, growth, mutiny, resist, revolt, rocket, strike, thrive **7** advance, balloon, burgeon, disobey, elevate, headway, improve, prosper, stand up, succeed, upswing **8** addition, flourish, increase, progress **9** expansion, extension **10** embankment **11** advancement, enlargement

Rise and Fall of the Third Reich, The
  author: 14 William L Shirer

Rise of Silas Lapham, The
  author: 18 William Dean Howells
  character: 5 Irene **8** Mr Rogers, Penelope, Tom Corey **9** Mrs Lapham

risible 4 rich **5** comic, droll, funny, merry, silly, witty **6** absurd, jocose, jovial **7** amusing, comical, jocular **8** farcical, humorous, mirthful **9** facetious, laughable, ludicrous, whimsical **10** ridiculous **11** nonsensical

rising sun
  god of: 5 Janus

risk 4 dare **5** peril **6** chance, danger, gamble, hazard **7** imperil, venture **8** endanger, jeopardy **9** speculate **10** jeopardize **11** imperilment, speculation, uncertainty **12** endangerment

risky 6 chancy, daring, unsafe **8** insecure, perilous, ticklish **9** dangerous, daredevil, haphazard, hazardous, hit or miss, uncertain **10** precarious **11** adventurous, unprotected, venturesome

risque 4 blue, lewd, racy **5** bawdy, dirty, gross, spicy **6** coarse, daring, ribald, smutty, vulgar **7** immoral, obscene **8** immodest, improper, indecent, off-color **9** offensive, salacious **10** indecorous, indelicate, lascivious, licentious, suggestive **12** pornographic

rite 6 ritual **7** liturgy, service **8** ceremony **9** formality, solemnity **10** ceremonial, observance

rite of passage 6 ritual **7** baptism **8** ceremony, marriage **10** bar mitzvah, bat mitzvah, initiation **11** christening **12** confirmation

Rites of Passage
  author: 14 William Golding

Ritt, Martin
  director of: 3 Hud **7** Sounder **8** Norma Rae, The Front **26** The Spy Who Came in From the Cold

Ritter, John
  born: 9 Burbank CA
  father: 9 Tex Ritter
  roles: 9 Hooperman **11** Americathon, Jack Tripper **13** Three's Company **14** Captain Avenger

Ritter, Thelma
  born: 10 Brooklyn NY
  roles: 10 Pillow Talk, Rear Window, The Misfits **11** All About Eve **15** The Mating Season **17** Birdman of Alcatraz **18** With a Song In My Heart **19** A Letter to Three Wives, Pickup on South Street **21** The Proud and the Profane **27** Miracle on Thirty-Fourth Street

ritual 4 rite **7** service **8** ceremony **10** observance

ritual bathing place
  Jewish Orthodox: 6 mikvah

ritualistic 6 formal, solemn **10** ceremonial **11** ceremonious

ritualize 7 observe **9** celebrate, solemnize **13** ceremonialize

ritzy 4 chic, posh, tony **5** sharp, swank **6** classy, snazzy, spiffy **7** elegant, stylish **9** high-class, high-toned, luxurious, sumptuous

rival 4 foe **5** enemy, equal, excel, fight, match, outdo, touch **6** strive **7** eclipse, surpass **8** approach, opponent, opposing, outshine **9** adversary, competing, contender, disputant **10** antagonist, competitor, contending, contestant

Rivals, The
  author: 23 Richard Brinsley Sheridan
  character: 8 Bob Acres **9** Faulkland **11** Mrs Malaprop **13** Julia Melville, Lydia Languish **17** Sir Lucius O'Trigger **18** Sir Anthony Absolute **19** Captain Jack Absolute (Ensign Beverley)

rive 4 rend **5** crack, split **6** cleave, detach, divide, sunder **7** shatter **8** fracture

riven 4 rent, torn **5** split **7** cleaved, cracked **8** sundered **9** fractured, shattered

River, The
  director: 10 Jean Renoir
  based on novel by: 11 Rumer Godden
  cast: 5 Radha **13** Adrienne Corri, Arthur Shields, Nora Swinburne **15** Patricia Walters
  setting: 5 India **6** Bengal

Rivera, Diego
  born: 6 Mexico **10** Guanajuato
  artwork: 5 Sleep **13** Creation **11** Mother Earth **14** The Fecund Earth **15** Detroit Industry **18** Man at the Crossroads **21** Carnival of Mexican Life **23** Life in Pre-Hispanic Mexico

river mouth 5 delta, firth **7** estuary

rivers
  god of: 6 Peneus, Simois **7** Inachus

Rivers, Reba
  character in: 9 Sanctuary
  author: 8 Faulkner

rivet 3 fix, pin **6** absorb, clinch, engage, fasten, occupy **7** engross **8** fastener **9** fascinate

Rivieres du Sud *see* **6** Guinea

rivulet 3 run **4** rill **5** brook, creek **6** stream **9** streamlet

Riyadh
  capital of: 11 Saudi Arabia

Rizzuto, Phil
  nickname: 7 Scooter
  position: 9 shortstop
  sport: 8 baseball
  team: 14 New York Yankees

road 3 way **4** lane, path **5** byway, route, trail **6** avenue, street **7** freeway, highway, parkway **8** turnpike **9** boulevard **10** expressway, throughway **12** thoroughfare

Road Not Taken, The
  author: 11 Robert Frost

roads
  god of: 6 Hermes

road safety
  god of: 6 Sancus **10** Semo Sancus

Road to Gandolfo, The
  author: 12 Robert Ludlum

roam 3 gad **4** rove **5** drift, jaunt, prowl, range, stray, tramp **6** ramble, stroll, travel, wander **7** meander, traipse **8** divagate **9** gallivant **11** peregrinate

roan 5 horse **7** grayish, reddish, tannish **8** blackish, brownish

Roan Stallion
  author: 15 Robinson Jeffers

roar 3 bay, cry, din **4** bawl, boom, howl, roll, yell **5** blare, growl, grunt, noise, shout, snort **6** bellow, clamor, guffaw, outcry, racket, rumble, scream, shriek **7** bluster, resound, thunder **8** outburst **10** vociferate

roast 3 pan **4** bake **6** berate **7** scourge **8** barbecue **9** criticize

rob 4 bilk, lift, loot, raid, sack, skin **5** cheat, filch, heist, rifle, seize, steal **6** burgle, fleece, forage, hold up, pilfer, thieve **7** despoil, pillage, plunder, purloin, ransack, stick up, swindle **8** carry off, embezzle **9** bamboozle **10** burglarize **11** appropriate

Robards, Jason
  born: 9 Chicago IL
  wife: 12 Lauren Bacall
  roles: 5 Julia **7** Isadora **9** Dick Diver **10** Ben Bradlee **11** Jamie Tyrone **12** Hour of the Gun **15** A Thousand Clowns, Dashiell Hammett, Melvin and Howard, The Disenchanted **16** Tender Is the Night **19** All the President's Men **24** Long Day's Journey into Night

Robbe-Grillet, Alain
  author of: 8 Jealousy **9** The Voyeur **10** The Erasers **14** In the Labyrinth **19** Last Year at Marienbad

robber, Robber 4 yegg **5** crook, thief **6** bandit, con man, outlaw, pirate, raider **7** brigand, burglar, forager, rustler, sharper **8** Barabbas, marauder, swindler **9** buccaneer, despoiler, embezzler, larcenist, plunderer **10** highwayman, pickpocket

Robbins, Harold
  author of: 8 The Betsy **13** The Inheritors **14** Dreams Die First, The Adventurers **16** The Carpetbaggers **17** The Dream Merchants **18** Never Love a Stranger **20** A Stone for Danny Fisher **21** Seventy-Nine Park Avenue

Robbins, Jerome
  choreographer of: 8 Les Noces **9** Fancy Free, Interplay
  director of: 13 West Side Story (with Robert Wise, Oscar)

robe 4 gown **5** dress, habit, smock **6** duster **7** costume, garment **8** bathrobe, vestment **9** housecoat
  French: 8 negligee
  Japanese: 6 kimono

Robe, The
  author: 13 Lloyd C Douglas

robe-de-chambre 12 dressing-gown

Robert Kennedy and His Times
  author: 20 Arthur M Schlesinger Jr

Roberts, Kenneth
  author of: 16 Northwest Passage

Roberts, Rachel
  born: 5 Wales **8** Llanelly
  husband: 11 Rex Harrison
  roles: 8 Foul Play **10** Oh Lucky Man **16** This Sporting Life **24** Murder on the Orient Express **29** Saturday Night and Sunday Morning

Robertson, Cliff
  real name: 23 Clifford Parker Robertson
  born: 9 La Jolla CA
  wife: 11 Dina Merrill
  roles: 5 PT-109 **6** Charly (Oscar) **9** Obsession **11** Falcon Crest

Robertson, Oscar
  nickname: 7 The Big O
  sport: 10 basketball
  position: 5 guard
  team: 14 Milwaukee Bucks **16** Cincinnati Royals

Robeson, Paul
  born: 11 Princeton NJ
  roles: 7 Othello **8** Show Boat **11** Brutus Jones **15** The Emperor Jones **17** King Solomon's Mines **22** All God's Chillun Got Wings

Robigo
  goddess of: 5 grain

Robigus
  spirit of: 9 red mildew **11** grain blight

Robin, Christopher
  character in: 13 Winnie-the-Pooh
  author: 5 Milne

Robin Hood's Adventures
  author: 7 unknown
  character: 9 Friar Tuck **10** Little John **11** Will Scarlet **14** Band of Merry Men **18** Sir Richard of the Lea **19** Sheriff of Nottingham

robin's-egg-blue 4 aqua **5** azure **7** sky-blue **8** cerulean **9** light blue **10** aquamarine, powder-blue

Robinson, Edward G
  real name: 18 Emmanuel Goldenberg
  born: 7 Romania **9** Bucharest
  roles: 8 Key Largo **12** Little Caesar, Rico Bandello **13** Scarlet Street **15** Double Indemnity, Flesh and Fantasy **16** House of Strangers **19** The Woman in the Window **20** A Dispatch from Reuters **21** Dr Ehrlich's Magic Bullet

Robinson, Edwin Arlington
  author of: 6 Merlin **8** Amaranth, Tristram **10** King Jasper **11** Richard Cory **12** Captain Craig **13** Miniver Cheevy, Mr Flood's Party

Robinson, Jackie
  sport: 8 baseball
  team: 15 Brooklyn Dodgers
  first black in: 12 major leagues

Robinson, Sugar Ray
  real name: 19 Walker Smith Robinson
  sport: 6 boxing
  class: 12 middleweight, welterweight

Robinson Crusoe
  author: 11 Daniel Defoe
  character: 6 Friday

Rob Roy
  author: 14 Sir Walter Scott
  character: 11 Diana Vernon **18** Sir Frederick Vernon **21** Rob Roy MacGregor Campbell
  Osbaldistone family: **5** Frank **7** William **9** Rashleigh **13** Sir Hildebrand

robust 3 fit **4** firm, hale, well, wiry **5** hardy, husky, lusty, sound, stout, tough **6** active, brawny, hearty, mighty, potent, rugged, sinewy, strong, sturdy, virile **7** healthy, staunch **8** athletic, forceful, muscular, powerful, stalwart, vigorous **9** energetic,

healthful, strapping, wholesome 10 able-bodied 12 in fine fettle
French: 8 puissant

robustness 5 vigor 8 strength 10 good health, ruggedness, sturdiness 11 healthiness

Roche, Kevin
architect of: 13 Oakland Museum (CA) 14 Fine Arts Center (U of MA), Ford Foundation (NYC) 17 Knights of Columbus (New Haven CT) 21 One United Nations Plaza (NYC) 24 Union Carbide Headquarters (Danbury CT) 31 Power Center for the Performing Arts (U of Michigan)

Rochester
football team: 8 Panthers

Rochester, Edward
character in: 8 Jane Eyre
author: 6 Bronte

rock 3 bob, jar 4 crag, reef, roll, stun, sway, toss 5 cliff, flint, pitch, quake, shake, stone, swing, upset 6 gravel, marble, pebble, totter, wobble 7 agitate, bobbing, boulder, disturb, shaking 8 convulse, flounder, undulate, wobbling 9 limestone, oscillate, tottering 10 convulsion, undulation

Rock & Rye
type: 7 liqueur
flavor: 6 citrus
ingredient: 3 rye 9 rock candy

rock crystal
species: 6 quartz
color: 9 colorless

Rocket
nickname of: 14 Maurice Richard

rocket engine
invented by: 7 Goddard

Rockford Files, The
character: 10 John Cooper 11 Angel Martin, Jim Rockford 12 (Det) Dennis Becker 13 Beth Davenport, (Joseph) Rocky Rockford
cast: 9 Bo Hopkins, Joe Santos, Noah Beery 11 James Garner 14 Stuart Margolin 15 Gretchen Corbett

rock of Tarik see 9 Gibraltar

Rockwell, Norman
born: 9 New York NY
artwork:
covers: 19 Saturday Evening Post
mural: 15 Freedom of Speech

Rocky
director: 13 John G Avildsen
cast: 9 Burt Young 10 Talia Shire 11 Thayer David 12 Carl Weathers 15 Burgess Meredith 17 Sylvester Stallone (Rocky Balboa, the Italian Stallion)
setting: 12 Philadelphia
Oscar for: 7 editing, picture 8 director
sequel: 7 Rocky II, Rocky IV 8 Rocky III, Rocky Two 9 Rocky Four 10 Rocky Three

rod 4 cane, lash, mace, pale, pole, wand, whip 5 baton, birch, crook, staff, stake, stick 6 cudgel, rattan, switch 7 penalty, scepter, scourge 8 caduceus 9 stanchion

10 alpenstock, punishment 11 retribution 12 swagger stick
abbreviation: 2 rd

rod, Aaron's see 9 Aaron's rod

rodent 4 cavy, vole 5 coypu, gundi, hutia, mouse 6 agouti, beaver, cururo, gerbil, gopher, jerboa, nutria 7 blesmol, cane rat, hamster, lemming, mole-rat, rock rat 8 capybara, chipmunk, dormouse, pacarana, sewellel, spiny rat, squirrel, tucu-tuco, viscacha 9 chozchori, false paca, porcupine, woodchuck 10 chinchilla, prairie dog, springhare 11 kangaroo rat, pocket mouse, viscacha rat 13 kangaroo mouse 16 Speke's pectinator

Roderick Hudson
author: 10 Henry James

Roderick Random
author: 14 Tobias Smollett
character: 5 Strap 8 Narcissa 10 Tom Bowling 12 Miss Williams

Rodin, (Francois) Auguste Rene
born: 5 Paris 6 France
artwork: 7 The Kiss 10 Head of Iris, The Thinker, Victor Hugo, Walking Man 14 John the Baptist, The Age of Bronze, The Gates of Hell 16 Monument to Balzac 19 The Burghers of Calais 23 The Man with the Broken Nose

rodomontade 4 rant 5 boast 6 hot air 7 blather, bluster, bombast, fustian 8 bragging, folderol, nonsense, rhetoric 10 balderdash, doubletalk 11 braggadocio 12 boastfulness

roe 3 doe, elk, hen 4 buck, deer, eggs, fawn, fish, hart, hind, milt 5 spawn, sperm 6 caviar 8 fish eggs
of lobster: 5 coral

Roentgen, Rontgen, Wilhelm Konrad
field: 7 physics
nationality: 6 German
discovered: 5 X-rays
awarded: 10 Nobel Prize

Roethke, Theodore
author of: 9 Open House, The Waking 11 The Far Field 15 Straw for the Fire, Words for the Wind

Rogers, Ginger
real name: 23 Virginia Katherine McMath
born: 14 Independence MO
husband: 8 Lew Ayres 15 Jacques Bergerac, William Marshall
partner: 11 Fred Astaire
roles: 6 Top Hat 9 Stage Door 10 Hello Dolly, Kitty Foyle (Oscar) 12 Shall We Dance? 14 The Gay Divorcee 15 Flying Down to Rio, Tom Dick and Harry 17 Forty-Second Street 19 The Major and the Minor 21 The Barkleys of Broadway 30 The Story of Vernon and Irene Castle

Rogers, James Gamble
architect of: 22 Northwestern University (Chicago) 33 Columbia-Presbyterian Medical Center (NYC)

Rogers, Roy
 real name: 11 Leonard Slye
 born: 12 Cincinnati OH
 wife: 9 Dale Evans
 sidekick: 10 Gabby Hayes
 singing group: 17 Sons of the Pioneers
 horse: 7 Trigger
 roles: 10 Apache Rose 11 Song of Texas
 12 My Pal Trigger 13 Song of Arizona,
 Son of Paleface 17 Heart of the Rockies,
 Under Western Stars 18 Billy the Kid Returns 19 Tumbling Tumbleweeds 20 The
 Yellow Rose of Texas 22 Springtime in
 the Sierras
rogue 3 cur 5 devil, fraud, knave, scamp 6
 bad man, rascal, rotter, varlet, wretch 7
 bounder, hellion, villain 8 deceiver, evildoer, scalawag 9 miscreant, reprobate,
 scoundrel 10 blackguard, malefactor,
 mountebank, scapegrace 11 rapscallion
 13 mischief-maker 14 good-for-nothing 15
 snake in the grass
Rogue Herries
 author: 11 Hugh Walpole
roguish 3 sly 4 arch 5 saucy 8 devilish,
 rascally 11 mischievous
Rohe, Vera-Ellen
 real name of: 9 Vera-Ellen
roil 3 irk, vex 4 mill, rile, stir 5 annoy,
 muddy 6 ruffle, seethe 7 agitate, disturb,
 perturb, provoke, turmoil 8 irritate 9 aggravate 10 exasperate
role 3 job 4 duty, part, pose, post, task,
 work 5 chore, guise 7 posture, service 8
 capacity, function 9 character, portrayal 10
 assignment 13 impersonation 14
 representation 15 personification 16 characterization
 Latin: 7 persona
roll 4 boom, coil, curl, echo, flip, flow, furl,
 knot, list, loop, reel, roar, rock, spin, sway,
 toss, tube, turn, wind 5 coast, crack, lurch,
 pitch, sound, spool, surge, swell, swing,
 swirl, throw, twirl, twist, wheel, whirl 6 billow, gyrate, muster, roster, rotate, rumble,
 scroll, tumble 7 booming, catalog, entwine,
 resound, revolve, rocking, thunder, toss-
 ing, turning 8 cylinder, drumbeat, drumming, rumbling, schedule, tumbling, undulate 9 inventory 10 undulation 11
 reverberate 13 reverberation 15 turn over
 and over
Rolland, Romain
 author of: 14 Jean-Christophe 16 The
 Soul Enchanted
rollicking 3 gay 5 happy, jolly, merry, sunny
 6 bright, hearty, jocund, jovial, joyous,
 lively 7 gleeful, jocular, playful, romping 8
 cheerful, mirthful, spirited 9 exuberant,
 gamboling, sparkling, sprightly 10 frolicking, frolicsome, hysterical, rip-roaring 12
 lighthearted
Rolvaag, Ole Edvart
 author of: 15 Peder Victorious, Their Father's God 16 Giants in the Earth
roly-poly 3 fat 5 obese, plump, pudgy,
 round 6 chubby, rotund 9 corpulent

Roma
 father: 7 Evander
roman 5 novel 17 metrical narrative
Roman Catholic church
 council/synod: 4 Pisa 5 Basel, Trent 6
 Nicaea, Vienne, Whitby 7 Ephesus,
 Pistoia, Sardica 9 Chalcedon, Constance
 12 First Vatican 13 Fourth Lateran, Second Vatican 14 Constantinople 15
 Ferrara-Florence
 official Vatican yearbook: 18 Annuario
 Pontificio
 first Christian emperor: 11 Constantine
 **gifts of territory/sovereignty to pa-
 pacy:** 15 Donation of Pepin 21 Donation
 of Constantine
romance 4 bosh, call, pull 5 amour, idyll,
 novel 6 affair, allure 7 fantasy, fiction 8 illusion 9 courtship, exoticism, fairy tale, fish
 story, invention, love story, melodrama,
 moonshine, tall story 10 attachment, concoction, flirtation, love affair 11 fabrication,
 fascination, imagination 12 exaggeration,
 relationship, self-delusion 13 flight of
 fancy, tender passion 16 affair of the heart
Romance language see 5 Latin
Romance of the Forest
 author: 12 Ann Radcliffe
Romances sans paroles
 author: 12 Paul Verlaine
Romancing the Stone
 director: 7 Robert Zemeckis
 cast: 11 Danny De Vito 14 Kathleen
 Turner, Michael Douglas
 sequel: 17 The Jewel of the Nile
Roman Holiday
 director: 12 William Wyler
 cast: 11 Eddie Albert, Gregory Peck 13
 Audrey Hepburn
 Oscar for: 7 actress (Hepburn)
Romania see 7 Rumania
Roman measure 2 as 5 cubit, libra 6
 pondus 7 stadium
Roman Mythology
 collective name for gods: 6 Superi
 goddess of anguish: 8 Angerona
 goddess of agriculture: 5 Ceres 6 Dea
 Dia, Vacuna 13 Acca Laurentia
 Ceres corresponds to Greek: 7 Demeter
 goddess of the arts: 7 Minerva
 corresponds to Greek: 6 Athena
 goddess of baking: 6 Fornax
 goddess of chastity: 5 Fauna 7 Bona
 Dea
 goddess of childbirth: 5 Parca 6 Lucina, Matuta, Parcae 11 Mater Matuta
 goddess of the dawn: 6 Aurora, Matuta
 11 Mater Matuta
 Aurora corresponds to Greek: 3 Eos
 goddess of destiny: 5 Parca 6 Parcae
 goddess of discord: 9 Discordia
 goddess of door hinges: 6 Cardea
 goddess of the earth: 5 Tellus
 corresponds to Greek: 4 Gaea
 goddess of the family: 6 Cardea

goddess of fertility: 5 Fauna 6 Libera, Tellus 7 Bona Dea

Libera corresponds to Greek: 10 Persephone

Tellus corresponds to Greek: 4 Gaea

goddess of flowers: 5 Flora

goddess of fortune: 7 Fortuna

corresponds to Greek: 5 Tyche

goddess of fruit trees: 6 Pomona

goddess of gardens: 5 Venus

corresponds to Greek: 9 Aphrodite

goddess of grain/protectress against grain blight: 5 Robigo

goddess of harbors: 6 Matuta 11 Mater Matuta

goddess of harmony: 9 Concordia

goddess of the hearth: 4 Caca 5 Salus, Vesta

Salus corresponds to Greek: 6 Hygiea

goddess of heaven: 4 Juno

corresponds to Greek: 4 Hera

goddess of hunting: 5 Diana

corresponds to Greek: 6 Phoebe 7 Artemis

goddess of longevity: 11 Anna Perenna

goddess of love: 5 Venus

corresponds to Greek: 9 Aphrodite

goddess of marriage: 4 Juno 6 Tellus

corresponds to Greek: 4 Gaea, Hera

goddess of marshes: 6 Marica 9 Dea Marica

goddess of the moon: 5 Diana

corresponds to Greek: 6 Phoebe 7 Artemis

goddess of peace: 3 Pax 9 Concordia

Pax corresponds to Greek: 5 Irene

goddess of pleasure: 8 Voluptas

goddess of plenty: 3 Ops 10 Magna Mater

goddess of prosperity: 5 Salus

corresponds to Greek: 6 Hygeia

goddess of the sea: 6 Matuta 11 Mater Matuta

goddess of sleeping infants: 6 Cunina

goddess of the spring: 5 Venus

corresponds to Greek: 9 Aphrodite

goddess of storms: 11 Tempestates

goddess of victory: 8 Victoria

corresponds to Greek: 4 Nike

goddess of vineyards: 6 Libera

corresponds to Greek: 10 Persephone

goddess of war: 7 Bellona

corresponds to Greek: 5 Enyon

goddess of wine: 6 Libera

corresponds to Greek: 10 Persephone

goddess of wisdom: 7 Minerva

corresponds to Greek: 6 Athena

god of agriculture: 5 Picus 6 Saturn 7 Eventus 12 Bonus Eventus

corresponds to Greek: 6 Cronos, Cronus, Kronos

god of beginnings: 5 Janus

god of boundaries: 8 Terminus

god of commerce: 7 Mercury

corresponds to Greek: 6 Hermes

god of the dead: 7 Veiovis

god of doorways: 5 Janus

god of drinking/revelry: 5 Comus

god of eloquence: 7 Mercury

corresponds to Greek: 6 Hermes

god of farm boundaries: 8 Silvanus, Sylvanus

god of fertility: 7 Mutinus, Priapus 8 Lupercus, Picumnus

god of fire/metalworking: 6 Vulcan

corresponds to Greek: 10 Hephaestus, Hephaistos

god of forest: 7 Virbius

god of gardens: 9 Vertumnus

god of good counsel: 3 Ops 6 Consus

god of grain/protector against grain blight: 7 Robigus

god of healing: 11 Aesculapius

corresponds to Greek: 9 Asclepius

god of heavens: 4 Jove 7 Jupiter

corresponds to Greek: 4 Zeus

god of herds: 8 Silvanus, Sylvanus

god of horse racing: 3 Ops 6 Consus

god of hospitality: 6 Sancus 10 Dius Fidius, Semo Sancus

god of the house: 8 Silvanus, Sylvanus

god of hunting: 7 Virbius

god of international affairs: 6 Sancus 10 Dius Fidius, Semo Sancus

god of landmarks: 8 Terminus

god of light: 6 Apollo

god of love: 4 Amor 5 Cupid

corresponds to Greek: 4 Eros

god of luck: 7 Eventus 12 Bonus Eventus

god of medicine: 11 Aesculapius

corresponds to Greek: 9 Asclepius

god of music: 6 Apollo

god of oaths: 6 Sancus 10 Dius Fidius, Semo Sancus

god of orchards: 9 Vertumnus

god of ports/harbors: 8 Portunus

god of prosperity: 7 Eventus 12 Bonus Eventus

god of the rising sun: 5 Janus

god of science: 7 Mercury

corresponds to Greek: 6 Hermes

god of sea: 7 Neptune

corresponds to Greek: 8 Poseidon

god of seasons: 9 Vertumnus

god of the setting sun: 5 Janus

god of sleep: 6 Somnus

corresponds to Greek: 6 Hypnos, Hypnus

god of springs: 4 Fons

gods of sulphur springs (twins): 6 Palici

god of the sun: 3 Sol

corresponds to Greek: 6 Helios 8 Hyperion

god of thievery: 7 Mercury

corresponds to Greek: 6 Hermes

god of thunder: 7 Taranis

god of thunderstorms: 8 Summanus

god of the Tiber: 9 Tiberinus

god of uncultivated land: 8 Silvanus, Sylvanus

god of underworld: 3 Dis 5 Orcus 8 Dis Pater

corresponds to Greek: 5 Pluto

god of war: 4 Mars 6 Mamers, Mavors 8 Quirinus

corresponds to Greek: 4 Ares

god of weather: 4 Jove 7 Jupiter

god of weddings: 8 Talassio

corresponds to Greek: 5 Hymen 9 Hymenaeus

god of the woods: 6 Faunus 8 Silvanus, Sylvanus

house spirits: 5 lares 7 penates

nymphs/deities with gift of prophecy: 7 Camenae

names: 6 Egeria 8 Carmenta 9 Antevorta, Postvorta

corresponds to Greek: 5 Muses

protectress of childbirth: 8 Carmenta

protectress of cows/oxen: 6 Bubona

protector of flocks/shepherds: 5 Pales

protectress of military age men: 8 Juventas

corresponds to Greek: 4 Hebe

protectress of women: 5 Diana

corresponds to Greek: 6 Phoebe 7 Artemis

protectress of women/marriage: 4 Juno

queen of heaven: 4 Juno

corresponds to Greek: 4 Hera, Here

staff of Mercury: 8 Caduceus

troublesome ghosts: 7 lemures

romantic 4 fond 5 mushy, soppy 6 ardent, dreamy, loving, tender, unreal 7 amorous, devoted, fervent, flighty, idyllic, utopian 8 enamored, fanciful, quixotic 9 fantastic, idealized, imaginary, sensitive, visionary, whimsical 10 idealistic, improbable, passionate 11 extravagant, impassioned, impractical, rhapsodical, sentimental, unrealistic, warmhearted 12 melodramatic, preposterous

Romantic Comedians, The

  author: 12 Ellen Glasgow

romanticize 8 idealize 9 embroider

Romantic Manifesto

  author: 7 Ayn Rand

Romany Rye, The

  author: 17 George Henry Borrow

Rome, ancient

  emperor: 4 Nero, Otho 5 Galba, Nerva, Titus 6 Trajan 7 Hadrian 8 Augustus, Caligula, Claudius, Commodus, Domitian, Tiberius 9 Caracalla, Vespasian, Vitellius 10 Diocletian 11 Constantine, Lucius Verus 13 Antoninus Pius 14 Marcus Aurelius

  emperor's bodyguard: 15 Praetorian Guard

  first citizen title: 8 princeps

  first triumvirate: 6 Caesar, Pompey 7 Crassus

  foe: 4 Gaul 5 Spain 6 Cimbri 7 Perseus, Philip V, Pyrrhus, Teutons 8 Carthage, Hannibal, Iberians, Jugurtha, Samnites, Tarentum, Umbrians 9 Etruscans, Macedonia, Seleucids 11 Latin League

12 Antiochus III 13 Achaean League, Hamilcar Barca

  general: 5 Sulla 6 Brutus, Marius, Pompey 7 Crassus 8 Octavian 10 Flamininus, Mark Antony 12 Julius Caesar 14 Caesar Augustus 20 Quintus Fabius Maximus, Scipio Africanus Major, Scipio Africanus Minor

  king: 12 Ancus Marcius 13 Numa Pompilius 16 Sextus Tarquinius 17 Tarquinius Priscus (Tarquin the Elder) 18 Tarquinius Superbus (Tarquin the Proud)

  reformer: 8 Gracchus

  republican ruler: 6 consul 7 senator, tribune 8 plebeian 9 optimates, patrician, populares 10 magistrate

  Roman peace: 9 Pax Romana

  second triumvirate: 6 Antony 7 Lepidus 8 Octavian (Caesar Augustus)

Rome, Roma

  airport: 8 Ciampino 15 Leonardo da Vinci

  area: 9 Cinecitta (Cinema City) 10 Trastevere 11 Vatican City

  capital of: 5 Italy 6 Latium 11 Papal States, Roman Empire

  church: 8 St Peter's 11 San Giovanni 18 Santa Maria Maggiore 19 San Paolo Fuori le Mura

  Italian: 4 Roma

  landmark: 5 Forum 7 Capitol 8 Pantheon 9 catacombs, Colosseum 12 Palazzo Doria 13 Circus Maximus, Lateran Palace, Sistine Chapel, Vatican Palace, Villa Borghese 14 Palazzo Corsini, Villa Farnesina 16 Baths of Caracalla, Castel Sant'Angelo, Palazzo Barberini 17 Arch of Constantine 19 Saint Peter's Basilica

  legendary founders: 5 Remus 6 Aeneas 7 Romulus

  nickname: 11 Eternal City

  mountain: 8 Apennine

  museum: 5 Doria 7 Colonna, Corsini, Vatican 8 Borghese, National 10 Capitoline

  river: 5 Tiber

  school: 33 Conservatorio di Musica Santa Cecilia

  sea: 10 Tyrrhenian

  seven hills: 7 Caelian, Viminal 8 Aventine, Palatine, Quirinal 9 Esquiline 10 Capitoline

  square/piazza: 6 Popolo, Spagna 7 Colonna, Venezia 9 Quirinale 11 Campidoglio

  state within: 11 Vatican City

  street: 9 Appian Way, Emmanuele 11 Via del Corso 13 Corso Vittorio

  subway: 13 Metropolitana

Rome Haul

  author: 14 Walter D Edmonds

Romeo 4 beau 5 lover, sheik, swain, wooer 7 Don Juan, gallant 8 Casanova, cavalier, Lothario 9 boyfriend, Lochinvar

  French: 8 paramour

  Latin: 9 inamorato

Romeo and Juliet
  author: 18 William Shakespeare
  character: 5 Nurse, Paris 6 Tybalt 8 Benvolio, Mercutio 13 Friar Laurence
  family: 7 Capulet 8 Montague
  setting: 6 Verona

Romeo and Juliet
  director:
  1936 version: 11 George Cukor
  1968 version: 16 Franco Zeffirelli
  based on play by: 18 William Shakespeare
  cast:
  1936 version: 12 Leslie Howard, Norma Shearer 13 Basil Rathbone, Edna May Oliver, John Barrymore
  1968 version: 9 Milo O'Shea 11 John McEnery, Michael York 12 Olivia Hussey 14 Leonard Whiting
  score: 8 Nino Rota

Romeo and Juliet
  symphony by: 7 Berlioz
  opera by: 6 Gounod
  orchestral piece by: 11 Tchaikovsky
  ballet by: 9 Prokofiev

Romney, George
  born: 7 England 15 Dalton-in-Furness
  artwork: 5 Circe 9 Joan of Arc 11 Mrs Robinson, Sensibility 12 Mrs Davenport, Saint Cecilia 19 Mrs Carwardine and Son 22 The Death of General Wolfe 24 The Levenson-Gower Children 26 Sir Christopher and Lady Sykes

Romola
  author: 11 George Eliot
  character: 5 Bardo, Tessa 10 Tito Melema 15 Baldasarre Calvo

romp 3 hop 4 skip 5 caper, cut up, frisk, sport 6 frolic, gambol 7 disport, rollick

Romulus
  father: 4 Mars
  mother: 4 Ilia 9 Rea Silvia 10 Rhea Silvia
  twin brother: 5 Remus
  raised by: 7 she-wolf 9 Faustulus 12 Acca Larentia
  first king of: 4 Rome
  founder of: 4 Rome

Romus
  father: 6 Aeneas 8 Ascanius
  possible founder of: 4 Rome

Ronan
  origin: 5 Irish
  form: 4 king
  son: 4 Mael
  killed: 4 Mael
  killed by: 13 grandchildren

Roncalli, Angelo Giuseppe 13 Pope John XXIII 22 Pope John the Twenty-Third

Ronsard, Pierre de
  author of: 17 Sonnets pour Helene
  member of: 7 Pleiade

roofing 4 tile, turf 5 slate, terne 6 thatch 7 asphalt, ceiling, pantile, shingle 8 housetop

Roof of the World see 5 Tibet

rook 3 gyp 4 bilk, crow, dupe, gull 5 cheat, cozen, raven, trick 6 castle, fleece 7 deceive, defraud, swindle 8 chessman 9 bamboozle, victimize

rookie 4 tyro 6 novice 8 beginner 9 fledgling, greenhorn 10 apprentice, tenderfoot

Rookies, The
  character: 9 Jill Danko, (Officer) Mike Danko 10 (Lt) Eddie Ryker, (Officer) Chris Owens 12 (Officer) Terry Webster, (Officer) Willie Gillis
  cast: 11 Kate Jackson, Sam Melville 14 Bruce Fairbairn, Michael Ontkean 16 Gerald S O'Loughlin 18 Georg Stanford Brown

room 4 area 5 range, scope, space 6 chance, extent, leeway, margin, volume 7 chamber, cubicle, expanse, lodging 9 allowance, provision, territory 11 compartment
  French: 5 salle
  Spanish: 4 sala

Room at the Top
  director: 11 Jack Clayton
  based on novel by: 10 John Braine
  cast: 12 Heather Sears 14 Laurence Harvey, Simone Signoret 16 Hermione Baddeley
  Oscar for: 7 actress (Signoret)
  sequel: 11 Man at the Top 12 Life at the Top

Room 222
  character: 6 Bernie 9 Pete Dixon 11 Liz McIntyre 12 Alice Johnson 14 Seymour Kaufman
  cast: 11 Lloyd Haynes 13 David Jolliffe 14 Denise Nicholas, Karen Valentine 18 Michael Constantine
  school: 15 Walt Whitman High

roomy 3 big 4 huge, long, vast, wide 5 ample, broad, large 7 immense, lengthy, sizable 8 generous, spacious 9 boundless, capacious, expansive, extensive, unlimited 10 commodious

Rooney, Mickey
  real name: 9 Joe Yule Jr
  born: 10 Brooklyn NY
  wife: 10 Ava Gardner 13 Martha Vickers
  co-star: 11 Judy Garland
  roles: 4 Puck 8 Boys' Town 9 Andy Hardy 11 Sugar Babies 13 Mickey McGuire 14 Baby Face Nelson, National Velvet, The Human Comedy 21 A Midsummer Night's Dream 30 The Adventures of Huckleberry Finn

Roosevelt, Franklin Delano
  presidential rank: 12 thirty-second
  party: 10 Democratic
  state represented: 2 NY
  defeated: 5 (Jacob Sechler) Coxey, (John W) Aiken, (Thomas Edmund) Dewey, (William) Lemke 6 (Alfred Mossman) Landon, (Claude A) Watson, (David Leigh) Colvin, (Herbert Clark) Hoover, (Norman) Thomas, (Roger Ward) Babson, (William David) Upshaw, (Wil-

liam Hope) Harvey, (William Zebulon) Foster 7 (Earl Russell) Browder, (Wendell Lewis) Willkie 8 (Edward A) Teichert, (Verne L) Reynolds

vice president: 6 (Harry S) Truman, (John Nance) Garner 7 (Henry Agard) Wallace

cabinet:

state: 4 (Cordell) Hull 10 (Edward Reilly) Stettinius (Jr)

treasury: 6 (William Hartman) Woodin 10 (Henry) Morgenthau (Jr)

war: 4 (George Henry) Dern 7 (Henry Lewis) Stimson 8 (Harry Hines) Woodring

attorney general: 6 (Francis) Biddle, (Frank) Murphy 7 (Robert Houghwout) Jackson 8 (Homer Stille) Cummings

navy: 4 (Frank) Knox 6 (Charles) Edison 7 (Claude Augustus) Swanson 9 (James Vincent) Forrestal

postmaster general: 6 (Frank Comerford) Walker, (James Aloysius) Farley

interior: 5 (Harold LeClaire) Ickes

agriculture: 7 (Claude Raymond) Wickard, (Henry Agard) Wallace

commerce: 5 (Daniel Calhoun) Roper, (Jesse Holman) Jones 7 (Henry Agard) Wallace, (Henry Lloyd) Hopkins

labor: 7 (Frances) Perkins (Wilson)

born: 10 Hyde Park NY

died: 13 Warm Springs GA 16 Little White House

buried: 10 Hyde Park NY

education:

prep school: 6 Groton

university: 7 Harvard

law school: 8 Columbia

religion: 12 Episcopalian

interests: 3 art 4 polo 6 tennis, travel 7 fishing, hunting 8 shooting

vacation spot: 13 Warm Springs GA 16 Campobello Island (Canada)

dog: 4 Fala

author: 27 The Happy Warrior: Alfred E Smith

political career: 12 state senator

assistant secretary of: 4 Navy

governor of: 7 New York

civilian career: 6 lawyer 11 bank officer

notable events of lifetime/term: 4 D-Day, WWII 7 New Deal 10 atomic bomb, Depression, World War II 11 World War Two 13 United Nations 15 Atlantic Charter

act: 9 Lend-Lease

attack on: 10 Pearl Harbor

conference: 5 Cairo, Yalta 7 Arcadia, Crimean, Teheran

scandal: 11 Tammany Hall

quote: 24 A day that will live in infamy 31 Meet every day's troubles as they come 36 The only thing we have to fear is fear itself 50 This generation of Americans has a rendezvous with destiny 53 I pledge you I pledge myself to a new deal for the American people

father: 5 James

mother: 4 Sara (Delano)

siblings:

half-brother: 5 James

wife: 7 (Anna) Eleanor (Roosevelt)

children: 5 James 7 Elliott 11 Anna Eleanor 13 John Aspinwell 14 Franklin Delano

first lady:

author: 7 On My Own 13 This I Remember, This Is My Story 34 The Autobiography of Eleanor Roosevelt

chairwoman: 25 UN Commission on Human Rights

codirector: 23 Office of Civilian Defense

member: 35 Democratic National Campaign Committee

newspaper column: 5 My Day

US delegate to: 2 UN

Roosevelt, Theodore

nickname: 5 Teddy

presidential rank: 11 twenty-sixth

party: 10 Republican

state represented: 2 NY

succeeded: 8 McKinley

defeated (second term): 4 (Eugene Victor) Debs 6 (Alton Brooks) Parker, (Thomas Edward) Watson 7 (Austin) Holcomb, (Silas Comfort) Swallow 8 (Charles Hunter) Corregan

vice president: 4 none (1st term) 9 (Charles Warren) Fairbanks

cabinet:

state: 3 (John Milton) Hay 4 (Elihu) Root 5 (Robert) Bacon

treasury: 4 (Leslie Mortier) Shaw, (Lyman Judson) Gage 9 (George Bruce) Cortelyou

war: 4 (Elihu) Root, (William Howard) Taft 6 (Luke Edward) Wright

attorney general: 4 (Philander Chase) Knox 5 (William Henry) Moody 9 (Charles Joseph) Bonaparte

navy: 4 (John Davis) Long 5 (William Henry) Moody 6 (Paul) Morton 7 (Victor Howard) Metcalf 8 (Truman Handy) Newberry 9 (Charles Joseph) Bonaparte

postmaster general: 5 (Charles Emory) Smith, (George von Lengerke) Meyer, (Henry Clay) Payne, (Robert John) Wynne 9 (George Bruce) Cortelyou

interior: 8 (James Rudolph) Garfield 9 (Ethan Allen) Hitchcock

agriculture: 6 (James) Wilson

commerce and labor: 6 (Oscar Solomon) Straus 7 (Victor Howard) Metcalf 9 (George Bruce) Cortelyou

born: 13 New York City NY

died/buried: 2 NY 9 Oyster Bay 10 Long Island

education:

university: 7 Harvard

law school: 8 Columbia (did not graduate)

religion: 13 Dutch Reformed

interests: 7 hunting (African game), writing **9** exploring (South America) **14** natural history

author: **11** Rough Riders **14** Oliver Cromwell **16** Gouverneur Morris, Thomas Hart Benton **17** African Game Trails, The New Nationalism **19** The Winning of the West **20** Letters to His Children **21** America and the World War **24** The Foes of Our Own Household **25** Fear God and Take Your Own Part **27** A Booklover's Holiday in the Open, Ranch Life and the Hunting Trail, The Naval War of Eighteen-Twelve **28** Hero Tales from American History **29** Through the Brazilian Wilderness **33** Life Histories of African Game Animals

political career: **13** Vice President **15** NY State Assembly **24** US Civil Service Commission

assistant secretary: **4** Navy

governor of: **7** New York

organized party: **9** Bull Moose **11** Progressive

civilian career: **6** author **7** rancher **14** public lecturer

military service: **15** NY National Guard **18** Spanish-American War

organized cavalry regiment: **11** Rough Riders

led charge up: **11** San Juan Hill

notable events of lifetime/term: **5** Panic (of 1907) **10** Square Deal **15** Nobel Peace Prize **22** San Francisco earthquake

Act: **11** Reclamation **14** Meat Inspection **15** Hepburn Railroad, Pure Food and Drug

bureau of: **12** Corporations **28** Immigration and Naturalization

first flight by: **14** Wright Brothers

revolution: **6** Panama

treaty: **13** Hay-Pauncefote **15** Hay-Bunau-Varilla

quotes: **25** Hasten forward quickly there **28** Speak softly and carry a big stick

father: **8** Theodore

mother: **6** Martha (Bulloch)

siblings: **4** Anna **7** Corinne, Elliott

wife: **4** Alice (Hathaway Lee), Edith (Kermit Carow)

children: **6** Kermit **7** Quentin **8** Alice Lee, Theodore **10** Ethel Carow **16** Archibald Bulloch

rooster

young: **8** cockerel

root 3 fix, set **4** back, base, bind, bulb, clap, hail, nail, rise, stem **5** basis, boost, cheer, fount, radix, start, stick, tubes **6** bottom, fasten, ground, motive, origin, reason, second, source, spring **7** acclaim, applaud, bolster, cheer on, pull for, radicle, support **8** fountain, occasion, shout for **9** beginning, encourage, establish, inception, rationale **10** derivation, foundation, mainspring **11** fundamental **12** commencement, fountainhead

Root, John Wellborn

partner: **14** Daniel H Burnham

architect of: **10** The Rookery **12** Hotel Statler (Washington DC), Montauk Block **13** Hotel Tamanaco (Caracas) **17** Monadnock Building, Palmolive Building (Chicago) **19** Rand-McNally Building

root for 5 boost **6** urge on **7** cheer on, pull for

root out 5 dig up **6** remove **7** extract, pull out, uncover, unearth **8** discover **9** extirpate, ferret out **12** bring to light

Roots

author: **9** Alex Haley

character: **3** Tom **4** Ames, Bell, Noah **5** Binta, Fanta, Grill, Irene, Kizzy, Lewis, Mingo, Omoro **6** Justin, Martha, Ordell **7** Fiddler, Gardner, Nyo Boto **8** Kintango, Mathilda, Mrs Moore, Tom Moore **9** Evan Brent, Missy Anne **10** Brima Cesay, Capt Davies, Carrington, Jemmy Brent, Kadi Touray, Kunta Kinte, Sam Bennett, Sister Sara **11** Mrs Reynolds, Squire James **12** John Reynolds **13** Chicken George **14** Sir Eric Russell, Stephen Bennett **15** Ol' George Johnson, Third Mate Slater **17** Dr William Reynolds

cast: **8** Burl Ives, John Amos, Ren Woods **9** Ben Vereen, Brad Davis, Moses Gunn, O J Simpson, Vic Morrow **10** Billy Hicks, Ian McShane, John Schuck, Lynne Moody, Olivia Cole, Paul Shenar, Ralph Waite, Robert Reed **11** Beverly Todd, Cicely Tyson, Doug McClure, Edward Asner, Gary Collins, Harry Rhodes, Lane Binkley, LeVar Burton, Lorne Greene, Maya Angelou, Sandy Duncan **12** Carolyn Jones, Chuck Connors, Leslie Uggams, Lloyd Bridges **13** Louis Gosset Jr, Madge Sinclair, William Watson **14** George Hamilton, Lynda Day George, Macdonald Carey **15** Lillian Randolph, Scatman Crothers, Thalmus Rasulala **16** Raymond St Jacques, Richard Roundtree **18** Georg Stanford Brown **20** Lawrence Hilton-Jacobs

rope 3 gad, guy, tie, tow **4** bind, cord, fast, guss, hemp, line, lure, snag, trap, wire, yarn **5** cable, catch, chord, lasso, noose, riata, shank, strap, twine **6** corral, entice, hawser, lariat, seduce, string, tether **7** bobstay, cordage, halyard, lanyard, lashing, painter **8** dragline, restrain

fiber: **5** sisal

Rosaline

character in: **16** Love's Labour's Lost

author: **11** Shakespeare

rose 4 Rosa

varieties: **3** bog, dog, sun, tea, wax **4** baby, gold, moss, musk, rock, rush, sand, wood **5** briar, brier, China, fairy, field, malva, Ophir, pygmy, swamp **6** Alpine, Burnet, copper, cotton, damask, desert, French, ground, Karroo, Lenten, mallow, Nootka, Scotch, velvet **7** baby sun, Banksia, Bourbon, cabbage, cluster, Guelder, Manetti, pasture, prairie, rambler 8 Burgundy, Champney, Cherokee, chestnut, cinnamon, climbing, Japanese, Memorial, mountain, Noisette 9 Christmas, evergreen, hybrid tea, McCartney, Polyantha, Remontant, Turkestan 10 California, Chinquapin, shaggy-rock, underwater 11 confederate, giant velvet, hairy alpine 12 green Mexican, Hawaiian wood, Seven-sisters, white Mexican 13 Himalayan musk, Hybrid Bourbon, Persian yellow, Stuart's desert 15 hybrid perpetual 16 York-and-Lancaster

Rose, Pete (Peter Edward)
　nickname: 13 Charlie Hustle
　sport: 8 baseball
　position: 7 baseman 8 outfield
　team: 14 Cincinnati Reds 20 Philadelphia Phillies

Rosedale, Mr
　character in: 15 The House of Mirth
　author: 7 Wharton

Rosemary's Baby
　director: 13 Roman Polanski
　based on novel by: 8 Ira Levin
　cast: 9 Mia Farrow 10 Ruth Gordon 14 John Cassavetes, Sidney Blackmer
　Oscar for: 17 supporting actress (Gordon)

Rosenberg, Stuart
　director of: 12 Cool Hand Luke

Rosenbloom, Maxie
　nickname: 12 Slapsie Maxie
　sport: 6 boxing
　class: 16 light heavyweight

Rosencrantz
　character in: 6 Hamlet
　author: 11 Shakespeare

Rosenkavalier, Der
　also: 18 The Knight of the Rose
　opera by: 7 (Richard) Strauss
　character: 6 Sophie 8 Octavian 9 Baron Ochs 11 Marschallin (Princess von Werderberg)

Rose of Sharon
　character in: 16 The Grapes of Wrath
　author: 9 Steinbeck

Rose Tattoo, The
　director: 10 Daniel Mann
　based on play by: 17 Tennessee Williams
　cast: 11 Anna Magnani 13 Burt Lancaster
　Oscar for: 7 actress (Magnani)

Roseanne
　former name: 4 Barr 6 Arnold
　husband: 3 Tom 6 Thomas
　television:
　show: 8 Roseanne
　family:
　husband: 3 Dan
　children: 2 DJ 5 Becky 7 Darlene
　sister: Jackie
　town: Lanford

rosiness 5 bloom, blush, flush 7 redness 8 pinkness

Rosmersholm
　author: 11 Henrik Ibsen

Rosofsky, Barnet
　real name of: 10 Barney Ross

Ross, Barney
　real name: 14 Barnet Rosofsky
　sport: 6 boxing
　class: 12 welterweight

Ross, Herbert
　director of: 14 The Goodbye Girl 15 The Turning Point

Ross, Katharine
　born: 12 Los Angeles CA
　aunt: 16 Katharine Hepburn
　roles: 9 The Colbys 11 The Graduate 13 Stepford Wives 29 Butch Cassidy and the Sundance Kid

Rossellini, Roberto
　director of: 6 Paisan 8 Open City 9 Stromboli 10 The Miracle 15 Germany Year Zero
　wife: 13 Ingrid Bergman

Rossen, Robert
　director of: 11 Body and Soul 14 All the King's Men

Rossetti, Dante Gabriel
　author of: 17 The Blessed Damozel
　born: 6 London 7 England
　group: 14 Pre-Raphaelites
　artwork: 12 Beata Beatrix 15 The Annunciation 17 Ecce Ancilla Domini

Rossini, Gioacchino Antonio
　born: 5 Italy 6 Pesaro
　composer of: 5 Moise 6 Otello 8 Tancredi 10 Le Comte Ory, Semiramide 11 William Tell 12 Mose in Egitto 13 Guillaume Tell, La Cenerentola 15 Barber of Seville 20 Il Barbiere di Siviglia 22 La Cambiale di Matrimonio

Rossner, Judith
　author of: 11 Attachments 14 Ordinary People 19 Looking for Mr Goodbar

Rostand, Edmond
　author of: 7 L'Aiglon 10 Chantecler 12 The Romancers 16 Cyrano de Bergerac

roster 4 list, roll 5 cadre, panel, slate 6 agenda, docket, muster, record 7 catalog, listing, posting 8 register, schedule 9 catalogue, directory

rostrum 4 dais 5 stage, stand, stump 6 podium, pulpit 7 lectern, soapbox 8 platform

rosy 4 pink 5 ruddy 6 bright, florid 7 flushed, glowing, hopeful, reddish 8 blooming, blushing, cheerful, cheering, flushing, inflamed, rubicund 9 confident, favorable, promising, reddening, rubescent 10 auspicious, felicitous, optimistic, propitious, reassuring 11 encouraging, high-colored, inspiriting 13 full of promise

Roszak, Theodore
　born: 6 Poland, Poznan
　artwork: 5 Raven, Surge 7 Anguish 9 Chrysalis, Scavenger, Sea Quarry 11 Sea Sentinel 12 Amorphic Form, Thorn Blossom 18 Specter of Kitty Hawk 20 The Whaler of Nantucket 27 Recollections of the Southwest

rot 3 mar **4** bosh, bull, bunk, harm, hurt, warp **5** decay, go bad, spoil, stain, taint, trash **6** damage, debase, defile, drivel, impair, infect, injure, jabber, molder, poison **7** blather, corrupt, crumble, deprave, inanity, pervert, pollute, putrefy, rubbish, twaddle **8** flummery, folderol, nonsense, putresce **9** absurdity, decompose, gibberish, moonshine, poppycock, purulence, putridity **10** balderdash, corruption, degenerate, flapdoodle **11** contaminate, deteriorate, putrescence **12** disintegrate, fiddle-faddle, gobbledygook, putrefaction **13** contamination, decomposition, deterioration **14** disintegration **16** stuff and nonsense

rotate 4 eddy, reel, roll, spin, turn **5** pivot, swirl, twirl, twist, wheel, whirl **6** change, circle, gyrate, swivel **7** revolve **9** alternate, circulate, pirouette **11** interchange

Roth, Philip
   author of: 8 The Facts **15** Goodbye Columbus **16** The Anatomy Lesson, Zuckerman Unbound **17** Portnoy's Complaint

Rothko, Mark
   born: 6 Dvinsk, Latvia, Russia **16** Daugavpils Latvia
   artwork: 5 Light **12** Central Green, Earth and Blue **14** Four Darks in Red

rotten 3 bad **4** base, foul, rank **5** dirty, fetid, nasty, reeky, venal **6** filthy, putrid, rancid, scurvy **7** corrupt, crooked, decayed, devious, immoral, tainted, very bad, vicious **8** criminal, decaying, indecent, purulent, two-faced **9** deceitful, dishonest, dissolute, faithless, insincere, mercenary, moldering, putrefied, worm-eaten **10** decomposed, iniquitous, putrescent, scurrilous, unpleasant, villainous **11** decomposing, disgraceful, treacherous **12** contemptible, dishonorable, unforgivable, unscrupulous **13** double-dealing, untrustworthy

rotter 3 cad, cur, rat **4** heel **5** knave, louse, rogue **6** no-good, rascal **7** bounder, caitiff, villain **9** scoundrel

rotund 3 fat **5** obese, ovate, ovoid, plump, pudgy, round, stout, tubby **6** chubby, curved, fleshy, portly **7** bulbous, lumpish, rounded **8** circular, globular **9** corpulent, egg-shaped, spherical **10** potbellied **11** full-fleshed

Rouault, Georges
   born: 5 Paris **6** France
   artwork: 3 Mr X **5** Clown **8** Le Chahut, Miserere, Twilight **9** The Mirror **10** The Old King **11** Fleurs du mal, The Holy Face **12** Head of a Clown **13** Little Olympia **14** The Three Judges **19** Small Family of Clowns **22** Christ Mocked by Soldiers **26** Les Reincarnations du Pere Ubu **28** The Child Jesus among the Doctors

roue 3 cad, rip **4** rake, wolf **6** lecher, wanton **7** bounder, dallier, Don Juan, playboy, seducer, trifler **8** Casanova, debauche, Lothario, rakehell **9** libertine, womanizer **10** profligate **11** philanderer, skirt-chaser

rough 3 raw **4** beat, hard, rude, wild **5** bluff, blunt, bumpy, crude, cruel, draft, green, gruff, harsh, hasty, husky, quick, raspy, rocky, scaly, sharp, surly, tough, vague **6** abrupt, beat on, broken, brutal, callow, choppy, clumsy, coarse, craggy, crusty, gauche, hoarse, jagged, knotty, ragged, raging, roiled, rugged, savage, severe, stormy, thrash, turbid, uneven, vulgar **7** austere, awkward, bearish, boorish, brusque, chapped, coarsen, drastic, extreme, general, gnarled, grating, ill-bred, inexact, jarring, loutish, outline, rasping, raucous, scraggy, sketchy, stubbly, uncouth, unlevel, untamed, violent **8** agitated, churlish, rigorous, scabrous, scratchy, strident, ungentle, unsmooth **9** brutalize, difficult, ferocious, imperfect, imprecise, inelegant, irregular, manhandle, sketch out, stringent, turbulent, uncourtly, unfeeling, ungenteel, unmusical, unrefined **10** discordant, incomplete, indelicate, push around, tumultuous, unfinished, ungracious, unmannerly, unpleasant, unpolished **11** approximate, cacophonous, ill-mannered, preliminary, rudimentary, tempestuous, unluxurious **12** inharmonious **13** inconsiderate, uncomfortable, ungentlemanly

rough going 8 struggle **10** difficulty **11** arduousness **13** laboriousness

Roughing It
   author: 9 Mark Twain
   character: 12 Brigham Young, Hank Erickson **16** Slade the Terrible

rough it 4 camp **7** camp out

roughneck 4 hood, lout, punk **5** bully, rowdy, tough **6** vandal **7** hoodlum, ruffian **8** hooligan **9** barbarian **10** delinquent

roughness 7 crudity **8** acrimony, aviation, pungency, violence **9** gruffness, harshness, vulgarity **10** coarseness, inelegance, unevenness, unkindness **11** raucousness **12** irregularity, unsmoothness, unrefinement **13** undevelopment

rough sketch 5 draft **7** cartoon, outline

rough-textured 5 harsh **6** coarse, nubbly, shaggy, tweedy **7** bristly, prickly **8** scratchy **9** bristling **10** sandpapery

round 3 fat **4** full, oval **5** cycle, obese, orbed, ovate, ovoid, plump, pudgy, stout, total, tubby, whole **6** chubby, circle, curved, entire, fluent, intact, portly, rotund, series, smooth **7** flowing, globoid, perfect, rounded **8** circular, complete, globular, resonant, sonorous, spheroid, thorough, unbroken **9** corpulent, egg-shaped, spherical, undivided **10** ball-shaped, elliptical, harmonious, pear-shaped, procession, succession **11** cylindrical, full-fleshed, mellifluent, progression

roundabout 5 wordy **6** random, zigzag **7** devious, erratic, oblique, sinuous, winding **8** indirect, rambling, tortuous, twisting **9** desultory **10** circuitous, discursive, meandering, serpentine **12** labyrinthine **14** circumlocutory

roundaboutness 9 wandering 10 digression, meandering 11 indirection 14 circuitousness, circumlocution

rounded 6 convex 7 curving 11 protuberant

rounding out 10 developing 12 augmentation 13 amplification

rounding-out 10 complement, completion, perfecting 12 consummation

rounds 4 beat 5 route, skirt, watch 7 circuit

roundup 6 muster, resume 7 meeting, summary 8 assembly 9 gathering 11 convocation

round up 6 gather, muster, summon 7 collect, convene, convoke, marshal 8 assemble 10 accumulate 12 call together

rouse 4 call, goad, move, prod, spur, stir, wake 5 arise, awake, get up, pique, rally, waken 6 awaken, excite, foment, kindle, incite, stir up, summon, turn on, wake up 7 animate, inflame, inspire, provoke, shake up 8 activate 9 galvanize, instigate, stimulate

roused 2 up 5 astir, awake 7 excited, incited, kindled, rallied, shook up 8 awakened, inflamed, inspired, out of bed, shaken up 9 stirred up 10 up and about

rousing 5 brisk, peppy 6 active, lively 8 animated, exciting, stirring, vigorous 9 awakening, inspiring 10 energizing, refreshing, remarkable 11 provocative, stimulating 12 exhilarating, intoxicating 13 extraordinary

Rousseau, Henri Julien Felix
 nickname: 10 Le Douanier
 born: 5 Laval 6 France
 artwork: 3 War 8 The Dream 12 Child on Rocks, The Waterfall 13 The Hungry Lion 15 Carnival Evening, The Snake Charmer 16 Bouquet of Flowers, The Sleeping Gypsy 17 The Poet and his Muse

Rousseau, Jean Jacques
 author of: 5 Emile 11 Confessions 17 La Nouvelle Heloise, The Social Contract

Rousseau, (Pierre Etienne) Theodore
 born: 5 Paris 6 France
 artwork: 7 Evening 12 After the Rain 15 Edge of the Forest, Under the Birches 18 Descent of the Cattle, Oak Trees at Apremont 19 The Marsh in the Landes 20 The Valley of Tiffauges 21 Meadow Bordered by Trees

roust 4 bust 5 rouse 6 arrest, hassle 7 capture, seizure 12 apprehension

rout 4 beat, drub, lick, ruin, trim 5 chaos, cream, crush, panic, quell, repel, worst 6 defeat, subdue, thrash 7 beating, clobber, conquer, licking, repulse, scatter 8 drive off, drubbing, lambaste, overcome, vanquish 9 chase away, drive away, overpower, overthrow 11 put to flight 15 disorganization 18 throw into confusion

route 3 run 4 beat, pass, path, road, ship, tack 5 remit, round, track 6 artery, course, detour, direct 7 circuit, highway, parkway, passage, roadway 8 dispatch, transmit, turnpike 9 boulevard, itinerary 10 throughway 12 thoroughfare

Route 66
 character: 8 Linc Case 9 Tod Stiles 10 Buz Murdock
 cast: 12 Glenn Corbett, Martin Milner 13 George Maharis
 car: 8 Corvette

routine 4 dull 5 order, usual 6 boring, custom, method, normal, system 7 formula, regular, tedious, typical 8 habitual, ordinary, periodic, practice 9 customary, operation, technique 11 arrangement, predictable 12 conventional, run-of-the-mill 13 unexceptional

rove 4 roam 5 drift, prowl, range 6 ramble, stroll, travel, wander 7 meander, traipse 9 gallivant

roving 6 errant 7 aimless, gadding, migrant, nomadic, roaming, vagrant 8 errantry, rambling, restless 9 desultory, itinerant, traveling, uncertain, wandering 10 changeable, discursive, meandering, inconstant 11 peripatetic 14 discursiveness

row 4 file, line, rank, spat, tier, tiff 5 brawl, chain, melee, queue, range, scrap, set-to, train, words 6 column, fracas, scrape, series, string 7 echelon, quarrel, wrangle 8 argument, disorder, sequence, squabble 9 imbroglio, wrangling 10 difference, succession 11 altercation, contretemps

rowboat 3 gig 4 bark, dory 5 barge, canoe, dingy, scull, skiff 6 barque, caique, dinghy, wherry
 seat: 4 taft

rowdy 6 unruly 7 lawless, raffish 9 roughneck 10 boisterous, disorderly 11 mischievous 12 obstreperous

Rowena, Lady
 character in: 7 Ivanhoe
 author: 5 Scott

rowing
 athlete: 10 James Dietz 14 Anthony Johnson

Rowlands, Gena
 real name: 23 Virginia Cathryn Rowlands
 born: 9 Cambria WI
 husband: 14 John Cassavetes
 roles: 5 Faces 12 Opening Night 23 A Woman Under the Influence

Roxana
 subtitle: 20 The Fortunate Mistress
 author: 11 Daniel Defoe

royal 5 grand, regal 6 august, lavish, superb 7 stately 8 imposing, majestic, splendid 9 monarchal, sovereign 10 munificent 11 fit for a king, magnificent, resplendent

royalty 4 sway 7 command, majesty 8 dominion, hegemony, kingship, regality 9 queenship, supremacy 11 divine right, sovereignty

Royaume de Belgique see 7 Belgium

Roy Rogers
 ingredient: 9 ginger ale, grenadine
 also called: 13 Shirley Temple

Roy Rogers Show, The
   regular: 8 Pat Brady 9 Dale Evans
   theme: 16 Happy Trails to You
   horse: 7 Trigger
   dog: 6 Bullet
   jeep: 10 Nellybelle
   ranch: 10 Double R Bar
Ruanda *see* 6 Rwanda
rub 4 buff, swab, wipe 5 annoy, braze, catch, chafe, clean, hitch, knead, pinch, scour, scrub, smear, thing, touch, trick 6 abrade, finger, handle, polish, secret, smooth, spread, strait, stroke 7 burnish, dilemma, massage, problem, rubdown, setback, slather, trouble 8 handling, hardship, kneading, obstacle, stroking 10 difficulty, impediment, manipulate 12 manipulation
Rubaiyat of Omar Khayyam, The
   author: 11 Omar Khayyam
   translator: 16 Edward FitzGerald
rubber, vulcanized
   invented by: 8 Goodyear
rubber plant 13 Ficus elastica
   varieties: 4 baby 5 dwarf 7 Chinese 8 American, creeping, Japanese 9 mistletoe 11 small-leaved 16 broad-leaved India
rubberstamp 6 affirm 7 approve, endorse
rubber tree 10 Schefflera
   varieties: 4 Para 5 India 8 Castilla 11 West African
rubbery 5 tough 6 supple 7 elastic 8 flexible 9 resilient 11 stretchable
rubbing 7 chafing 8 abrading, scraping 12 manipulation
rubbish 3 rot 4 bosh, junk 5 dross, offal, trash, waste 6 babble, debris, drivel, idiocy, jetsam, litter, refuse, rubble 7 blather, garbage, inanity, twaddle 8 folderol, nonsense 9 gibberish, rigmarole, silliness 10 balderdash, flapdoodle, rigamarole
rubbish heap 4 dump 6 midden 10 refuse pile
rubble 4 junk, rock 5 brash, chalk, stent, stone, talus, trash 6 debris, refuse 7 rubbish 8 nonsense 9 fragments 11 foolishness
rube 3 oaf 4 boor, clod, hick 5 yokel 6 rustic 7 bumpkin, hayseed, peasant 10 clodhopper
rub elbows 3 mix 4 club 6 hobnob, mingle 7 consort, hang out 9 associate 10 fraternize
Rubens, Peter Paul
   born: 6 Siegen 10 Westphalia
   artwork: 8 Lion Hunt 10 The Rainbow 15 The Garden of Love 17 Laocoon and his Sons 18 Battle of the Amazons 20 The Raising of the Cross 21 Landscape with Het Steen 22 The Descent from the Cross 23 Altarpiece of St Aldefonso 26 The Adoration of the Shepherds 27 Marchesa Brigida Spinola-Doria, Mystic Marriage of St Catherine 29 Rape of the Daughters of Leucippus 34 Helene Fourment with Two of her Children

rubicund 3 red 4 rosy 5 ruddy 6 florid 7 flushed, reddish
rubidium
   chemical symbol: 2 Rb
rub out 4 do in, kill, slay 5 erase 6 efface, murder 7 bump off, destroy, execute, expunge 8 massacre 10 obliterate, put to death 11 assassinate, exterminate
ruby
   species: 8 corundum
   source: 5 Burma, India, Mogok 7 Bangkok, Kashmir 8 Sri Lanka, Thailand
   kind: 4 star
   color: 3 red
ruckus 3 row 4 fray, to-do 5 brawl, broil, clash, fight, melee 6 battle, fracas, rumpus, uproar 7 scuffle 9 imbroglio 10 donnybrook, free-for-all 11 embroilment
ruddy 3 red 4 rosy 6 florid 7 flushed, reddish, roseate, scarlet 8 blushing, rubicund, sanguine 11 rosy-cheeked
rude 3 raw 4 wild 5 blunt, crude, fresh, green, gross, gruff, rough, saucy, sulky, surly 6 abrupt, callow, clumsy, coarse, crusty, gauche, homely, rugged, rustic, sullen, uneven, vulgar 7 abusive, artless, awkward, boorish, brusque, brutish, illbred, loutish, profane, scraggy, uncivil, uncouth 8 churlish, homebred, ignorant, impolite, impudent, indecent, insolent, slapdash, untaught 9 inelegant, insulting, makeshift, primitive, roughhewn, uncourtly, ungallant, unlearned, unrefined, untrained, untutored 10 illiterate, indecorous, indelicate, peremptory, provincial, uncultured, uneducated, ungraceful, ungracious, unladylike, unmannerly, unpolished 11 badmannered, countrified, impertinent, uncivilized, uncourteous, undignified 12 discourteous, roughly built 13 disrespectful, inconsiderate, ungentlemanly
rudeness 9 bluntness, impudence, insolence, sauciness 10 bad manners, coarseness, disrespect, incivility 11 boorishness, discourtesy 12 impertinence, impoliteness 14 ungraciousness 17 inconsiderateness
rudimentary 5 basic 6 simple 7 initial, primary 8 immature 9 elemental, formative, imperfect, premature, primitive, vestigial 10 elementary, incomplete, prototypal 11 undeveloped
rudiments 6 basics 7 essence 8 elements 9 beginning 10 principles 12 fundamentals
Rudkus, Jurgis and Antanas
   characters in: 9 The Jungle
   author: 8 Sinclair
Rudolph, Paul
   architect of: 16 Jewett Arts Center (Wellesley College) 24 Government Services Center (Boston) 28 School of Architecture Building (Yale)
rue 4 Ruta
   varieties: 4 bush, lady, wall 5 goat's 6 common, meadow 10 tall meadow 11 early meadow 12 Alpine meadow
rue 5 mourn 6 bemoan, lament, regret, repent, repine 7 deplore

rueful 3 sad 5 sorry 6 woeful 7 doleful 8 contrite, mournful, dolorous, penitent, repining 9 depressed, plaintive, regretful, sorrowful, sorrowing 10 deplorable, lamentable, melancholy, remorseful, unpleasant

ruffian 4 hood, thug 5 brute, bully, crook, knave, rogue, rough, rowdy, tough 6 mugger 7 hoodlum, villain 8 gangster, hooligan 9 cutthroat, roisterer, roughneck, scoundrel 10 blackguard

ruffle 4 fold, muss, wave 5 frill, plait, pleat, ruche, upset 6 edging, excite, muss up, pucker, rimple, ripple, rumple 7 agitate, confuse, crinkle, disturb, flounce, perturb, roughen, trouble, wrinkle 8 dishevel, disorder, disquiet, furbelow, unsettle 9 aggravate, agitation, commotion, corrugate 10 disarrange, discompose, disconcert 11 disturbance

ruffled 5 upset, vexed 7 annoyed, frilled, nettled, pleated 8 agitated, flounced, troubled 9 nonplused, unsettled 10 nonplussed

ruffle one's feathers 3 vex 5 anger, annoy, pique 6 enrage, madden, nettle 7 incense, outrage, provoke 9 displease, infuriate

Rugg
    character in: 12 Little Dorrit
    author: 7 Dickens

rugged 4 hale, hard, rude, wiry, worn 5 bumpy, hardy, harsh, husky, lined, rocky, rough, stern, tough 6 brawny, coarse, craggy, jagged, ridged, robust, severe, sinewy, sturdy, taxing, trying, uneven, virile 7 arduous, cragged, onerous, scraggy, uncouth 8 athletic, furrowed, muscular, stalwart, vigorous, wrinkled 9 difficult, graceless, irregular, laborious, masculine, roughhewn, strenuous, unrefined, weathered 12 uncultivated 13 weather-beaten

Ruggles of Red Gap
    director: 10 Leo McCarey
    cast: 9 ZaSu Pitts 10 Mary Boland 14 Charlie Ruggles 15 Charles Laughton
    remade as: 10 Fancy Pants

ruin, ruins 3 gut, pot 4 doom, fall, fell, harm, raze, seed 5 break, crush, decay, level, quash, quell, shell, spoil, upset, wreck 6 beggar, defeat, ravage, squash 7 destroy, failure, remains, shatter, undoing 8 bankrupt, demolish, downfall, lay waste, make poor, overturn, remnants, wreckage 9 breakdown, devastate, disrepair, overthrow, pauperize 10 impoverish 11 destruction, devastation, dissolution 14 disintegration

ruination 4 ruin 5 wreck 6 fiasco 7 trouble 8 disaster 9 adversity, cataclysm 11 destruction, devastation 12 misadventure

ruinous 4 dire 5 fatal 6 deadly 7 adverse, baneful 8 damaging, ravaging 10 calamitous, disastrous, pernicious 11 cataclysmic, deleterious, destructive, devastating 12 catastrophic

Ruisdael, Jacob (Jakob) van
    born: 7 Haarlem 14 The Netherlands
    uncle: 18 Salomon van Ruysdael

    artwork: 5 Dunes 12 The Waterfall 13 View of Haarlem 14 Bentheim Castle 15 Winter Landscape 17 The Jewish Cemetery 28 View on the Amstel near Amsterdam

rule 3 law, run 4 find, form, head, lead, sway 5 adage, axiom, canon, guide, judge, maxim, model, order, reign 6 custom, decide, decree, direct, empire, govern, manage, method, policy, regime, settle, system 7 adjudge, command, control, declare, formula, precept, prevail, resolve, routine 8 conclude, doctrine, dominate, domineer, dominion, pass upon, practice, regnancy, regulate, standard 9 authority, criterion, determine, direction, establish, guideline, influence, ordinance, precedent, principle, pronounce, supremacy 10 adjudicate, administer, convention, domination, government, leadership, regulation, suzerainty 11 predominate, preside over, sovereignty 12 jurisdiction, prescription 14 administration
    type: 5 bench 7 folding 9 steel tape
    constellation of: 5 Norma

rule out 4 omit 6 delete, except 7 exclude 9 eliminate

ruler 4 boss, czar, emir, head, khan, king, lord, shah, tsar, tzar 5 chief, judge, queen, rajah, sheik 6 dynast, leader, prince, satrap, shogun, sultan 7 arbiter, emperor, manager, measure, monarch, pharaoh, referee, viceroy 8 chairman, director, governor, suzerain 9 chieftain, commander, potentate, president, sovereign, yardstick 10 controller, supervisor 11 coordinator, crowned head, head of state, tape measure 12 straightedge 13 administrator

rules of conduct 6 ethics 9 moral code 10 principles 12 code of ethics

Rules of the Game
    director: 10 Jean Renoir
    cast: 10 Jean Renoir, Mila Parely, Nora Gregor 11 Marcel Dalio

ruling 6 decree 7 regnant 8 decision, dominant, reigning 9 enactment, governing, prescript 10 commanding, widespread 11 controlling, predominant 13 authoritative, predominating

ruling class 11 aristocracy 13 Establishment

Ruling Class, The
    director: 10 Peter Medak
    cast: 10 Arthur Lowe 11 Alastair Sim, Peter O'Toole 12 Harry Andrews

rum
    drink: 4 Bolo, Grog 6 Mojito 7 Gauguin 8 Daiquiri, Navy Grog, Pina Fria 9 Borinquen, Hurricane 10 Pina Colada 12 Boston Cooler 13 Planter's Punch 14 Fish House Punch 15 Bacardi Cocktail 18 Barbados Rum Swizzle
    ingredient: 8 molasses 9 sugar cane
    origin: 10 West Indies
    type: 4 dark 5 light
    with apple brandy: 6 Bolero 8 Apple Pie
    with apricot brandy: 11 Apricot Lady
    with black coffee: 9 Black Rose

with bouillon: 6 Creole
with bourbon: 14 Artillery Punch
with brandy: 15 Quaker's Cocktail
with Cointreau: 8 Acapulco 10 Casa Blanca 11 Beachcomber 12 Blue Hawaiian
with cola: 9 Cuba Libre
with creme de cacao: 6 Panama
with curacao: 6 Mai-Tai 8 Blue Lady 12 Blue Hawaiian
with Dubonnet: 3 BVD 10 Bushranger
with Galliano: 9 Bossa Nova
with gin: 3 BVD
with guava: 8 Ocho Rios
with kahlua: 10 Black Maria
with milk: 6 Rum Cow 11 Tom-and-Jerry
with Pernod: 8 Shanghai
with sloe gin: 11 Shark's Tooth
with Tia Maria: 10 Black Maria
with vermouth: 6 Bolero 8 Apple Pie 10 Black Devil 11 Shark's Tooth
Rumania
 other name: 7 Romania
 capital/largest city: 9 Bucharest
 others: 4 Aiud, Arad, Cluj, Deva, Iasi 5 Bacau, Balta, Cerna, Jassy, Neamt, Sibiu, Turnu, Yassy 6 Braila, Brasov, Brasso, Eforie, Galatz, Galeti, Lupeni, Mamaia, Oradea, Sighet 7 Bendery, Craiova, Focsani, Giurgiu, Ploesti, Severin 8 Bloiesti, Cernavti, Chisinau, Irongate, Kishenef, Satu-Mare, Temesvar 9 Constanta, Kolozsvar, Timisoara 10 Czernowitz 11 Klausenburg
 school: 4 Cuza
 division: 4 Alba, Iasi 5 Banat, Bihor, Jassy 6 Ardeal 7 Dobruja 8 Bucovina, Bukovina, Dobrogea, Moldavia, Walachia 9 Maramures 10 Bessarabia 12 Transylvania
 Roman province: 5 Dacia
 measure: 7 faltche
 monetary unit: 3 ban, lei, leu, lev, ley 4 bani 5 uncia 6 triens
 lake: 5 Sinoe 6 Snagov
 mountain: 5 Banat, Bihor 6 Codrul, Rodnei 7 Apuseni, Balkans, Caliman, Fagaras 8 Pietrosu 9 Moldavian 10 Carpathian, Moldoveanu 17 Transylvanian Alps
 highest point: 11 Moldoveanul
 river: 3 Alt, Jui, Olt 4 Prut 5 Aluta, Arges, Buzdu, Moros, Mures, Oltul, Schyl, Siret, Somes, Timis, Vedea 6 Crasna, Danube 7 Argesul 8 Bistrita, Ialomita, Iniester 9 Dimbovita, Jiul Mures
 sea: 5 Black
 physical feature:
  canal: 4 Bega
  forest: 6 Snagov 7 Baneasa
  gorge: 8 Iron Gate
  peninsula: 6 Balkan
  plain: 5 Banat 9 Moldavian, Walachian 13 Prahova Valley
  plateau: 7 Dobruja
  wind: 6 crivat
 people: 6 Dacian 8 Romanian, Rumanian

 artist: 8 Brancusi
 author: 7 Ionesco
 composer: 6 Enesco
 leader: 6 Carol I 7 Michael, Iliescu 8 Ioan Cuza 9 Ceausescu 12 Gheorghiu-Dej, Ion Antonescu
 language: 6 French, Magyar 7 Russian 8 Romanian, Rumanian 9 Hungarian
 religion: 7 Judaism 8 Lutheran 9 Calvinism, Unitarian 10 Protestant 13 Roman Catholic 16 Rumanian Orthodox
 place:
  castle: 4 Bran 7 Huniady
  church: 5 Golia 9 Mihaivoda 10 Cretulescu, Patriarchy 11 Curtea Veche, Stavropdeos, Trei Ierarhi
  monastery: 5 Humor 6 Arbore 7 Voronet 8 Sucerita 9 Moldovita
  museum: 11 Peles Castle
  palace: 9 mogosoaia
  park: 7 Baneasa
  resort: 5 Venus 6 Eforie, Mamaia, Neptun 7 Jupiter 10 Costinesti
 feature:
  community gathering: 9 sezatoare
  game: 4 oina
  food:
   dish: 6 ciorba 7 mititei, sarmala 8 mamaliga 11 imam bayildi
   plum brandy: 5 tuica
rumble 4 bang, boom, clap, roar, roll 7 booming, resound, thunder 8 drumming 9 resonance 11 reverberate 13 reverberation
Rumford, Benjamin Thomson
 invented: 10 photometer 11 calorimeter
Rumina
 protectress of: 14 nursing mothers
ruminant 3 cow, elk, yak 4 deer, oxen 5 bison, camel, llama, moose, sheep 6 alpaca, cattle, vicuna 7 buffalo, giraffe, pensive 8 antelope 10 chevrotain, meditative, thoughtful 13 contemplative
ruminate 4 mull, muse 5 brood, study, think, weigh 6 ponder 7 reflect 8 cogitate, consider, meditate, mull over 9 speculate, think over 10 deliberate, think about 11 contemplate
ruminating 6 musing 7 pensive 8 thinking 10 meditating, meditative, reflecting, reflective, thoughtful 11 chewing over, mulling over, speculative 13 contemplating, contemplative, introspective
rumination 5 study 6 musing 7 mulling, reverie, thought 8 brooding, thinking 9 pondering 10 cogitation, meditation, reflection 11 speculation 12 deliberation 13 consideration, contemplation 15 reconsideration
rummage 4 root 5 probe 7 examine, explore, ransack 10 disarrange, poke around 11 look through
rummy 3 sot 4 lush, soak 5 drunk, souse, toper 6 barfly, boozer 7 tippler 8 card game, drunkard 9 alcoholic 11 dipsomaniac
 also known as: 3 gin, rum 4 rhum 5 romme 8 gin rummy

derived from: 8 conquien

rumor 4 talk 5 story 6 babble, gossip, report 7 hearsay, whisper 8 innuendo, intimate 9 circulate, insinuate 11 insinuation, scuttlebutt, supposition

rump 4 rear, seat 5 croup, stern 6 behind, bottom, pother, breech, dorsum 7 rear end 8 backside, buttocks, derriere, haunches 9 posterior 12 hindquarters

Rumpelstiltskin
origin: 8 Germanic
form: 5 dwarf
spun: 4 flax
made: 4 gold

rumple 4 fold, muss 5 crimp, crush 6 crease, pucker, rimple, ruffle, tousle 7 crinkle, crumple, wrinkle 8 dishevel, disorder 9 corrugate 10 disarrange

rumpus 3 ado, row 4 fray, fuss, stir, to-do 5 brawl, melee, noise 6 affray, fracas, hubbub, pother, racket, ruckus, tumult, uproar 7 rhubarb, scuffle, tempest 8 brouhaha, upheaval 9 agitation, commotion, confusion, imbroglio 10 hullabaloo 11 disturbance, embroilment

run 2 be, go 3 fly, get, hie, jog, pen, ply 4 bolt, boss, cost, dart, dash, defy, flee, flow, go by, head, kind, last, meet, melt, pass, pour, push, race, roll, rush, sort, tear, tour, trip, trot, type, vary 5 bleed, bound, class, court, drift, drive, genre, glide, hurry, impel, incur, issue, leave, pilot, print, speed, spell, split, stand, surge, total, while 6 become, canter, course, decamp, direct, elapse, endure, escape, extend, gallop, hasten, hustle, invite, ladder, manage, motion, move on, outing, period, pierce, propel, scurry, series, sprint, streak, stream, thrust, vanish, voyage, wander 7 abscond, add up to, advance, bring on, compete, current, display, freedom, get past, journey, liquefy, meander, operate, oversee, passage, proceed, publish, running, scamper, stretch, take off, vamoose 8 amount to, campaign, continue, dissolve, duration, evanesce, maneuver, meet with, navigate, progress, scramble, separate, tendency 9 direction, disappear, enclosure, encounter, excursion, go quickly, lose color, penetrate, skedaddle, supervise 10 coordinate, pilgrimage 11 continuance 12 beat a retreat, continuation, perpetuation
baseball: 5 point, score, tally 17 circuit of the bases

run aground 7 founder 8 collapse

runaround 4 slip 5 dodge 6 bypass 7 evasion 8 shunning, sidestep 9 avoidance 11 elusiveness, evasiveness 12 equivocation

run around 7 consort, hang out 9 associate, pal around 10 fraternize

runaway 4 pure 6 bolter 7 escapee, perfect, refugee 8 absolute, complete, deserter, fugitive 9 out-and-out, unalloyed 10 skedaddler 11 unmitigated, unqualified

run away 3 fly 4 flee 5 elope 6 decamp, escape, run off 7 abscond, make off 8 sneak off 10 fly the coop, make a break, take flight 12 make a getaway

rundown 5 brief 6 digest, precis, resume, review, sketch 7 outline, summary 8 abstract, synopsis 12 capitulation, condensation

run-down 5 frail, seedy, tacky, tired, weary 6 ailing, beat-up, feeble, shabby, sickly 7 rickety, worn out 8 fatigued, tattered 9 crumbling, exhausted 10 broken-down, tumbledown 11 dilapidated 12 deteriorated

run down 4 scan 5 knock 6 slight 7 detract, put down, run over 8 belittle, derogate, ridicule 9 denigrate, deprecate, discredit, disparage, downgrade, enumerate, underrate 10 depreciate, undervalue

run-in 5 brush, set-to 6 battle, fracas 7 scuffle 8 skirmish 9 encounter 10 engagement

run into 4 meet 8 flow into 9 encounter 10 chance upon, meet up with 11 collide with

run off 3 fly 4 flee 5 elope 6 escape 7 abscond, make off, runaway 9 steal away 10 take flight 15 head for the hills

run off at the mouth 3 gab 5 prate 6 babble, gabble 8 rattle on 11 talk too much

run off with 5 seize 6 abduct, kidnap 7 bear off 8 carry off 9 elope with 11 abscond with, make off with

run-of-the-mill 4 dull, so-so 5 banal, stock, usual 6 common, modest 7 average, humdrum, mundane, routine, typical 8 everyday, mediocre, middling, ordinary, passable, standard 10 second-rate 11 commonplace, indifferent, nondescript 12 unimpressive 13 unimaginative 15 undistinguished

runt 3 elf 4 chit 5 dwarf, pygmy 6 midget, peewee, shrimp 8 half-pint, Tom Thumb 11 Lilliputian
Latin: 10 homunculus

run through 5 spend, waste 6 expend, pierce 7 deplete, exhaust 8 rehearse, squander

runty 5 short 6 bantam 7 dwarfed, squatty, stunted 9 pint-sized

Runyon, Damon
author of: 12 Guys and Dolls 16 Blue Plate Special

rupture 3 pop 4 part, rent, rift, snap 5 break, burst, clash, cleft, crack, split 6 breach, divide, schism, sunder 7 discord, disrupt, fissure 8 breaking, bursting, cleavage, dissever, disunion, disunite, fracture, friction, puncture 9 severance 10 dissension, falling out, separation 12 disagreement

R U R
author: 10 Karel Capek

rural 4 hick 5 rustic 7 bucolic, country 8 pastoral 10 provincial 11 countrified

rural area 6 sticks 7 boonies, country 8 farmland 9 backwater, backwoods, boondocks 10 hinterland 11 countryside

Rural Dionysia *see* 14 Lesser Dionysia

ruse 4 hoax 5 blind, dodge, feint, shift, trick 6 deceit, device, scheme 8 artifice, maneuver 9 deception, stratagem 10 subterfuge 11 contrivance, machination

rush 3 hie, run 4 dart, dash, goad, leap, push, race, spur, tear, urge, whip 5 drive, haste, hurry, press, speed, storm 6 charge, hasten, hustle, plunge, scurry, sprint, urgent 7 scamper, urgency 8 dispatch, expedite, pressure, scramble 9 emergency 10 accelerate 11 top priority

rush 6 Juncus
> **varieties:** 3 bog 4 salt, soft, wood 5 spike 6 grassy 8 scouring 9 field wood, flowering 10 common wood, least spike 11 chair-maker's, greater wood, Japanesemat 12 slender spike 13 dwarf scouring 14 common scouring 18 variegated scouring

Rush, Benjamin
> **field:** 8 medicine
> **established first:** 21 free medical dispensary
> **signer of:** 25 Declaration of Independence

rush light 3 dip 5 torch 6 candle, tallow

Rushworth
> **character in:** 13 Mansfield Park
> **author:** 6 Austen

Ruskin, John
> **author of:** 13 Fors Clavigera 14 Modern Painters 17 The Stones of Venice 27 The Seven Lamps of Architecture

Russell, Bertrand
> **author of:** 19 Why I Am Not a Christian 20 Principia Mathematica (with Alfred North)

Russell, Jane
> **real name:** 29 Ernestine Jane Geraldine Russell
> **born:** 9 Bemidji MN
> **discovered by:** 12 Howard Hughes
> **roles:** 4 Waco 9 The Outlaw 13 The French Line 22 Gentlemen Prefer Blondes, The Revolt of Mamie Stover

Russell, Rosalind
> **born:** 11 Waterbury CT
> **roles:** 5 Gypsy 6 Picnic 8 The Women 9 Hired Wife 10 Auntie Mame 11 Sister Kenny 13 His Girl Friday 14 My Sister Eileen 22 Mourning Becomes Electra

russet 5 apple, umber 6 auburn, copper 10 terra-cotta 11 rust-colored 12 reddish-brown

Russia (includes constituent republics of the former USSR)
> **other name:** 17 Russian Federation
> **former name:** 4 USSR 11 Soviet Union 31 Union of Soviet Socialist Republics
> **member of:** 3 CIS 31 Commonwealth of Independent States
> **capital/largest city:** 6 Moscow
> **others:** 4 Baku, Eisk, Kiev, Okha, Omsk, Poti, Riga 5 Anapa, Batum, Gorki, Gorky, Memel, Minsk, Sochi, Vilna, Yeisk 6 Batumi, Erevan, Frunze, Odessa, Rostov, Samara, Tiflis 7 Alma-Ata, Derbent, Donetsk, Kharkov, Liepaja, Petsamo, Pivonia, Saratov, Tallinn, Tbilisi, Yerevan 8 Dushanbe, Kishinev, Murmansk, Pechenga, Taganrog, Tashkent 9 Ashkhabad, Astrakhan, Balaklava, Kronstadt, Kuibyshev, Leningrad, Nikolayev, Petrograd, Ulyanovsk, Volgograd, Yaroslavl 10 Kronshtadt, Sevastopol, Stalingrad, Sverdlovsk 11 Chelyabinsk, Kaliningrad, Makhachkala, Novorossisk, Novosibirsk, Vladivostok 12 St Petersburg, Vladisvostok 14 Dnepropetrovsk
> **division/country:** 6 Latvia 7 Armenia, Belarus, Estonia, Georgia, Moldova, Siberia, Ukraine 8 Moldavia 9 Kirghizia, Lithuania, Turkmenia 10 Azerbaijan, Belorussia, Kazakhstan, Kyrgyzstan, Tajikistan, Uzbekistan 12 Tadzhikistan, Turkmenistan
> **former:** 4 Kiev 8 Novgorod
> **government:**
> > **legislature:** 4 Duma, Rada 7 Zemstvo 8 Congress
> **measure:** 3 fut, lof 4 duim, fass, loof, pood, quar, stof 5 duime, foute, korec, korek, ligne, osmin, pajak, stoff, stoof, vedro, verst 6 charka, lineya, osmina, paletz, sagene, stekar, tchast, tsarki, versta, verste 7 archine, arsheen, botchka, chkalik, garnetz, verchoc, verchok 8 boutylka, chetvert, krouchka, kroushka 9 chetverik 10 dessiatine 11 polugarnetz
> **monetary unit:** 5 altin, bisti, copec, denga, grosh, kopek, ruble, shaur 6 abassi, copeck, grivna, kopeck, piatak, rouble 7 poltina, valiuta 8 auksinas, deneshka, imperial, polushka 9 poltinnik 10 altininink, chervonets
> **weight:** 3 lof, lot 4 dola, funt, lana, last, loof, loth, once, pood, poud 5 dolia
> **island:** 5 Kuril 7 Hiiumaa, Karagin, Shantar, Vaygach, Wrangel 8 Kolguyev, Saaremaa, Sakhalin 9 Andreanof 12 Novaya Zemlya 13 Komandorskiye 14 Franz Josef Land, Novosibirskiye 15 Severnaya Zemlya
> **lake:** 3 Seg 4 Aral, Azov, Kola, Sego, Topo, Vigo 5 Chany, Elton, Erara, Ilmen, Lacha, Onega, Pskov, Vozhe 6 Baikal, Byeloe, Ladoga, Peipus, Selety, Taymyr, Tengiz, Zaysan 8 Balkhash 10 Caspian Sea
> **mountain:** 5 Altai, Lenin, Sayan, Urals 6 Anadyr, Elbrus, Koryak, Pamirs, Pobedy 7 Belukha, Crimean, Khibiny, Stanovi, Zhiguli 8 Caucasus, Dzhughur, Stanavoi, Tien Shan 9 Kopet Dagh, Narodnaya, Pamir-Alai, Yablonovy 10 Carpathian 11 Sikhote-Alin, Verkhoyansk
> **highest point:** 9 Communism
> **river:** 3 Don, Ili 4 Amur, Lena, Neva, Ural 5 Dvina, Kuban, Neman, Volga 6 Kolyma, Moskva 7 Dnieper, Pechora, Yenisei 8 Amu Darya, Dniester, Ob-Irtysh, Syr Darya 9 Indigirka

sea: 4 Aral, Azov, Kara 5 Black, Japan, White 6 Arctic, Baltic, Bering, Laptev 7 Barents, Caspian, Chukchi, Okhotsk, Pacific

physical feature:

gulf: 4 Azov 5 Mezen 9 Kara-Bogaz, Shelikhov

peninsula: 4 Kola 5 Yamal 6 Crimea, Taymyr 7 Chukchi, Karelia 9 Kamchatka 10 Mangyshlak

strait: 5 Tatar 6 Bering 8 Bosporus 11 Dardanelles

people: 3 Jew 4 Slav 5 Ersar, Kulak, Tatar, Uzbec 6 Kazakh, Soviet, Velika 7 Chukchi, Cossack, Kirghiz, Latvian, Russian, Tadzhik, Turkmen 8 Armenian, Estonian, Georgian, Siberian 9 Moldavian, Ukrainian 10 Lithuanian 11 Azerbaijani, Belorussian

actor: 12 Stanislavsky

author: 5 Gogol 7 Nabokov, Pushkin, Tolstoy 8 Turgenev 9 Ehrenburg, Pasternak, Sholokhov 10 Dostoevsky 12 Solzhenitsyn

composer: 6 Glinka 7 Borodin 9 Prokofiev 10 Mussorgsky, Stravinsky 11 Tchaikovsky 12 Rachmaninoff, Shostakovich 14 Rimsky-Korsakov

cosmonaut: 11 Yuri Gagarin

czar/tsar/tzar: 4 Ivan, Paul 5 Peter 6 Alexis 7 Michael 8 Nicholas 9 Alexander 12 Boris Godunov

dancer: 7 Nureyev, Pavlova 8 Danilova, Nijinsky 11 Baryshnikov

dynasty: 7 Romanov

early people: 3 Hun 4 Goth 5 Tatar 6 Khazar, Mongol, Tartar 8 Norsemen, Scythian 9 Cimmerian, Sarmatian, Varangian

empress: 9 Alexandra, Catherine

hereditary noble: 5 boyar

leader: 5 Beria, Lenin 6 Stalin, Suslov 7 Gromyko, Kosygin, Molotov, Trotsky, Yeltsin 8 Andropov, Brezhnev, Bukharin, Bulganin, Kerensky, Malenkov, Podgorny 9 Chernenko, Gorbachev 10 Khrushchev

monk: 8 Rasputin

prince: 4 Oleg 5 Rurik 8 Vladimir

revolutionary: 9 bolshevik 10 Decembrist

ruler: 5 Tatar 6 Mongol 8 Batu Khan

scientist: 6 Pavlov 9 Mendeleev 11 Tsiolkovsky

language: 5 Evenk, Tatar, Uzbek 6 Buriat, Kalmyk, Kazakh 7 Finnish, Kirghiz, Latvian, Russian, Tadzhik, Turkmen 8 Armenian, Estonian, Georgian, Ossetian 9 Moldavian, Ukrainian 10 Lithuanian 11 Belorussian

alphabet: 8 cyrillic

religion: 5 Islam 7 Judaism 8 Buddhism, Lutheran 10 Protestant 13 Roman Catholic 15 Russian Orthodox 16 Armenian Orthodox, Georgian Orthodox

place: 7 Kremlin 11 Red Square

art gallery: 9 Tretyakov

castle: 8 Starosty

cathedral: 5 Sobor 7 Zagorsk 8 St Basils

cemetery: 11 Piskarevsky

museum: 9 Hermitage 12 Petrodvorets 18 Cathedral of St Isaac

palace: 6 Winter

park: 5 Gorky

ruins: 7 Bukhara 10 Echmiadzin 15 Gediminas Castle

prison: 8 Lubyanka

street: 11 Kreshchatik 14 Nevski Prospekt

theater: 7 Bolshoi

feature:

collective farm: 7 kolkhoz

country house: 5 dacha

dance: 4 kolo 5 gopac, hopak, saber 6 cossac, trepak 7 cosaque, ziganka 8 kozachok 9 tzazatski

dance company: 5 Kirov 7 Bolshoi

labor camp: 5 gulag

musical instrument: 9 balalaika

secret police: 3 KGB, MGB 4 NKVD, OGPU 5 Cheka

state farm: 7 sovkhoz

food:

caviar: 13 ikra zernistia

cereal: 5 kasha

sour cream: 7 smetana

dessert: 8 vareniki

dish: 4 plov 5 pirau 6 pelemo 8 osetrina, shashlyk 16 kotleta po kievski

drink: 4 kvas 5 kvass, vodka 6 chacha, kumiss

filled pastries: 8 piroshki, pirozhki

soup: 5 shchi 6 borshch 7 borscht, borsch

Russian Hide-and-Seek

author: 12 Kingsley Amis

Russian village commune 3 mir

rust 3 rot 5 decay, stain 6 auburn, blight, russet 7 corrode, crumble, decline, oxidize 9 corrosion, oxidation 11 deteriorate 12 reddish-brown 13 reddish-yellow

rust-colored 5 henna 6 auburn, russet 8 cinnamon 12 reddish-brown

rustic 4 rube, rude 5 crude, plain, rough, rural, yokel 6 coarse, gauche, simple 7 awkward, boorish, bucolic, bumpkin, country, hayseed, loutish, peasant, uncouth 8 agrarian, churlish, cloddish, pastoral 9 inelegant, unrefined 10 clodhopper, countryman, provincial, uncultured, unpolished 11 countrified 13 country person 15 unsophisticated

rustle 3 rub 4 hiss, stir 5 swish, whish 6 riffle

rustler 5 thief 6 bandit, outlaw 7 brigand 9 desperado

rusty 5 moldy, stiff 6 rotten, rusted 7 reddish, tainted 8 corroded, sluggish 11 rust-colored 13 out of practice

rut 3 cut 4 mark 5 ditch, habit, score, tread 6 furrow, groove, gutter, hollow, trench, trough 7 channel, depress, dig into, pattern 8 monotony 9 deep track 10 depression 11 dull routine

Ruth
  husband: 4 Boaz 6 Mahlon
  son: 4 Obed
  father-in-law: 9 Elimelech
  mother-in-law: 7 Naomi
  brother-in-law: 7 Chilion

Ruth, George Herman
  nickname: 4 Babe 12 Sultan of Swat
  sport: 8 baseball
  position: 8 outfield
  team: 14 New York Yankees

Rutherford, Dame Margaret
  born: 6 London 7 England
  roles: 7 The VIPs 10 Jane Marple 12
  Blithe Spirit 27 The Importance of Being
  Earnest

Rutherford, Ernest
  field: 7 physics
  nationality: 7 British
  discovered: 6 proton 13 atomic nucleus,
  beta radiation 14 alpha radiation, gamma
  radiation
  awarded: 10 Nobel Prize

ruthless 5 cruel, harsh 6 brutal, deadly,
  savage 7 bestial, brutish, callous, inhuman, vicious 8 pitiless 9 barbarous, ferocious, heartless, merciless, murderous,
  unfeeling, unpitying, unsparing 10 relentless, sanguinary, unmerciful 11 cold-
  blooded, hardhearted, remorseless, unforgiving, unrelenting 12 bloodthirsty

ruthlessness 7 cruelty 9 barbarity, brutality,
  harshness 10 inhumanity, savageness 11
  viciousness

Ruysdael, Salomon van
  born: 7 Naarden 14 The Netherlands
  nephew: 16 Jacob van Ruisdael
  artwork: 9 River Bank 10 River Scene 14
  River Landscape 18 River with Ferry
  Boat

Rwanda
  other name: 6 Ruanda
  capital/largest city: 6 Kigali
  others: 6 Biumba, Butare, Kibuye,
  Nyanza 7 Astrida, Gisenyi, Kibungu 8
  Cyangugu 9 Ruhengeri
  division:
  ·colonial: 12 Ruanda-Urundi
  monetary unit: 5 franc 7 centime
  lake: 4 Kivu 5 Ihema 6 Bufera, Bulera,
  Mohasi 7 Rugwero, Ruhnodo 8
  Mugesera, Tshohoha
  mountain: 7 Mitumba, Virunga 8
  Muhavura
  highest point: 9 Karisimbi
  river: 6 Kagera, Ruzizi 7 Akagera 8
  Akanyaru 9 Luvironza 10 Nyawarongo
  physical feature:
  forest: 7 Nyungwe
  valley: 11 Western Rift
  people: 3 Twa 4 Hutu 5 Batwa, Pygmy,
  Tutsi 6 Bahutu, Watusi 7 Batutsi
  explorer: 5 Speke 6 Gotzen
  leader: 9 Kayibanda 11 Habyarimana
  language: 6 French 7 Swahili 11
  Kinyarwanda
  religion: 7 animism 13 Roman Catholic

  place:
  game reserve: 6 Gabiro
  park: 6 Albert, Kagera 16 Virunga Volcanoes
  feature:
  clothing: 5 pagne
  king: 5 mwami

Ryan, Cornelius
  author of: 13 A Bridge Too Far, The Last
  Battle, The Longest Day

Ryan, Robert
  born: 9 Chicago IL
  roles: 6 Caught 8 The Set-Up 9 Billy
  Budd, Crossfire 12 Clash by Night, The
  Wild Bunch 13 Act of Violence, The
  Longest Day 14 About Mrs Leslie, God's
  Little Acre 17 Bad Day at Black Rock 18
  The Woman on the Beach

Ryder, Albert Pinkham
  born: 12 New Bedford MA
  artwork: 12 The Race Track (Death on a
  Pale Horse) 15 Toilers of the Sea 27
  Siegfried and the Rhine Maidens

rye 6 Secale
  varieties: 4 wild 5 giant 6 common 8 Aral
  wild, blue wild 9 Altai wild, giant wild,
  Volga wild 10 Canada wild 11 Chinese
  wild, Russian wild 12 Siberian wild, Virginia wild
  type: 6 liquor 7 whiskey
  origin: 7 Ireland 8 Scotland
  ingredient: 10 mash grains
  drink: 9 Cablegram 11 John Collins,
  Whiskey Sour
  with Cointreau: 10 Temptation
  with Pernod: 3 TNT
  with vermouth: 8 Brooklyn 9 Algonquin

S

Saarinen, Eero
  father: 5 Eliel
  architect of: 11 St Louis Arch 20 Gateway to the West Arch (St Louis) 26 Trans World Airlines Terminal (NYC) 28 General Motors Technical Center (Warren MI) 39 Columbia Broadcasting Company Headquarters (NYC)
  style: 13 International

Saarinen, Eliel
  son: 4 Eero
  architect of: 16 Cranbrook Academy (Bloomfield Hills MI) 18 Kleinhaus Music Hall (Buffalo) 19 Tanglewood Music Shed (MA) 20 Christ Lutheran Church (Minneapolis MN), First Christian Church (Columbus IN)

Saba *see* 5 Sheba

Sabaoth 6 armies

Sabbath 8 Lord's Day 9 day of rest

Sabbatical: A Romance
  author: 9 John Barth

saber, sabre 3 cut 4 kill, stab 5 blade, sword, wound 6 cutlas, rapier, strike 7 cutlass, soldier 8 scimitar 10 broadsword

Sabin, Albert Bruce
  field: 8 medicine
  developed: 16 oral polio vaccine

sable 3 fur, jet 4 dark, inky 5 black, ebony, raven

sabotage 3 sap 6 retard 7 cripple, destroy, disable, disrupt, subvert 8 paralyze 9 undermine, vandalize 10 subversion 12 incapacitate

sabra 11 Israeli-born 14 native of Israel

Sabra
  type: 7 liqueur
  origin: 6 Israel
  flavor: 6 orange 9 chocolate

Sac *see* 4 Sauk

saccharine 5 gooey, mushy, soppy, sweet 6 sugary, syrupy 7 candied, cloying, honeyed, maudlin, mawkish, sugared 9 offensive, oversweet, revolting, sickening 10 disgusting, nauseating 11 sentimental

sacerdotal 5 papal 8 clerical, pastoral, priestly 9 apostolic, canonical, episcopal 10 pontifical 11 ministerial 12 hierarchical 14 ecclesiastical

sack 3 bag, rob 4 loot, pack, raid 5 pouch, spoil, store, waste 6 duffel, maraud, rapine, ravage, tear up 7 despoil, pillage, plunder, ransack 8 spoliate 9 depredate, duffel bag, gunnysack, haversack, marauding 10 plundering, ravishment 11 depredation, devastation 12 despoliation

sackbut 18 Biblical instrument

Sackville, Thomas
  author of: 8 Gorboduc (with Thomas Norton)

sacrament 3 vow 4 rite 5 troth 6 pledge, plight, ritual 7 liturgy, promise, service 8 ceremony, contract, covenant 9 solemnity 10 ceremonial, obligation, observance 11 affirmation 12 ministration

sacramental 4 holy 6 ritual 7 blessed 10 ceremonial, liturgical

Sacraments, Seven 7 Baptism, Penance 9 Eucharist, Last Rites, Matrimony 10 Holy Orders 12 Confirmation 13 Holy Communion 14 Extreme Unction, Reconciliation 18 Anointing of the Sick

sacred 4 holy 6 church 7 blessed, revered 8 Biblical, hallowed; hieratic 9 religious, venerable 10 sanctified, scriptural 11 consecrated 14 ecclesiastical

Sacred and Profane Love Machine, The
  author: 11 Iris Murdoch

Sacred writings 5 Bible 11 Bibliotheca

sacrifice 4 cede, loss 5 forgo, waive 6 forego, give up, homage 7 cession, forfeit, offer up 8 immolate, oblation, offering, renounce 9 surrender 10 concession, immolation, lustration, relinquish 12 renunciation 14 relinquishment

sacrilege 3 sin 7 impiety, mockery, outrage 8 iniquity 9 blasphemy, profanity, violation 10 irreligion, sinfulness, wickedness 11 desecration, impiousness, irreverence, profanation, profaneness

sacrilegious 7 impious, profane 10 irreverent 11 blasphemous, irreligious

sacrosanct 4 holy 5 godly 6 divine, solemn 8 hallowed, heavenly 9 celestial, inviolate, religious, spiritual 10 inviolable, unexamined 11 consecrated 12 unquestioned

sacrum
  bone of: 11 base of spine

sad 3 low 4 blue, grim, hard, hurt 5 grave 6 dismal, solemn, taxing, tragic, trying, woeful 7 adverse, crushed, doleful, forlorn, grieved, joyless, maudlin, pitiful, serious, unhappy 8 dejected, desolate, downcast, grievous, mournful, pathetic, touching, troubled, wretched 9 cheerless, depressed, difficult, miserable, sorrowful 10 calamitous, chapfallen, despairing, despondent, dispirited, distressed, lachrymose, lamentable, melancholy 11 crestfallen, distressing, pessimistic, troublesome, unfortunate 12 disconsolate, heartrending, heavyhearted, inconsolable 13 brokenhearted, griefstricken, heartbreaking 14 down in the dumps, down in the mouth

French: 6 triste
Sadat, Anwar el-
  president of: 5 Egypt
  awarded: 15 Nobel Peace Prize
  author of: 18 In Search of Identity
sadden 4 damp, dash 5 crush 6 burden,
  deject, grieve, sorrow, subdue 7 depress 8
  aggrieve, dispirit 10 discourage, dishearten
saddle with 9 stick with 10 burden with 12
  encumber with 18 make responsible for
Sade, Marquis de
  author of: 7 Justine 8 Juliette
sadistic 6 brutal 7 vicious 8 fiendish, perverse 9 perverted 12 bloodthirsty
Sadness
  author: 15 Donald Barthelme
sadness
  French: 9 tristesse
sad poem 5 elegy 6 lament
Sad Sack
  creator: 11 George Baker
Saehrimnir
  origin: 12 Scandinavian
  form: 4 boar
  served in: 8 Valhalla
  feat: 12 regeneration
safe 4 firm, sure, wary 5 sound, vault,
  whole 6 intact, modest, secure, stable,
  steady, unhurt 7 certain, guarded, prudent
  8 cautious, defended, discreet, harmless,
  reliable, unbroken, unharmed 9 innocuous,
  protected, undamaged, unexposed, unscathed 10 dependable, protecting 11 circumspect, impregnable, out of danger,
  trustworthy, unscratched 12 conservative,
  invulnerable, noncommittal
safeguard 4 ward 5 armor, charm 6 amulet,
  buffer, defend, harbor, screen, secure,
  shield 7 bulwark, defense, fortify, protect,
  shelter 8 conserve, garrison, preserve, security, talisman 12 precaution, protection
safekeeping 4 care 6 charge 7 custody 8
  security 9 husbandry 10 protection 12 conservation, guardianship, preserving
Safety Net, The
  author: 12 Heinrich Boll
saffron
  botanical name: 13 Crocus sativus
  also called: 6 Krokus
  Moorish: 6 Zafran
  of all spices most: 6 costly
  color: 6 orange, yellow 12 yellow-orange
  used as: 8 coloring, cosmetic, medicine
  9 fabric dye
  origin: 5 Egypt, Syria 8 Holy Land 9 Palestine
  use: 4 rice 5 bread, rolls
sag 3 bow, dip 4 drop, fail, flag, flap, flop,
  keel, lean, list, sink, sway, tilt, tire 5 droop,
  pitch, slump, weary 6 billow, plunge, settle,
  weaken 7 decline, descend, give way 8 diminish
saga 4 epic, myth, tale, yarn 6 legend 7 history, romance 9 adventure, chronicle, narrative
  French: 11 roman-fleuve

sagacious 4 foxy, wise 5 acute, canny,
  sharp, smart, sound 6 astute, brainy,
  clever, shrewd 7 cunning, knowing, prudent, sapient, tactful 8 discreet, rational,
  sensible 9 judicious, practical 10 diplomatic, discerning, perceptive 11 calculating, intelligent 13 perspicacious 14
  discriminating
sagacity 6 acumen, brains, smarts, wisdom
  8 sapience 9 canniness, smartness 10
  astuteness, braininess, cleverness,
  shrewdness 11 discernment 12 intelligence, perspicacity 13 judiciousness 14
  discrimination
Sagan, Carl
  author of: 6 Cosmos 7 Contact 16 The
  Dragons of Eden
Sagan, Francoise
  real name: 16 Francoise Quoirez
  author of: 13 A Certain Smile 15 Aimez-
  vous Brahms 16 Bonjour Tristesse
sage 4 guru, wise 5 sound 6 astute, pundit,
  savant, shrewd 7 egghead, knowing, prudent, sapient, scholar, wise man 8 mandarin, sensible 11 intelligent, philosopher
  French: 6 savant
  Latin: 5 magus, solon
sage 6 Salvia 12 S officinalis
  varieties: 3 bog 4 baby, blue, gray, rose,
  sand, wood 5 black, lilac, Texas, white 6
  autumn, common, desert, garden, purple,
  silver, yellow 7 bladder, gentian, scarlet,
  Spanish, thistle, Vervain 8 creeping,
  gray ball, mealy-cup, rose-leaf 9 Bethlehem, Jerusalem 11 Mexican bush 16
  pineapple-scented
  means: 6 to heal, to save
  strengthens: 6 memory, wisdom 8 prudence
  makes men: 8 immortal
  origin: 7 Albania 10 Yugoslavia 13 Mediterranean
  use: 4 pork 6 breads, cheese 7 chicken,
  poultry, seafood 8 stuffing
Sage of Concord
  nickname: 17 Ralph Waldo Emerson
Sagittarius
  symbol: 6 archer 7 centaur
  planet: 7 Jupiter
  rules: 10 philosophy 15 higher education
  born: 8 November, December
Sagittary
  form: 7 centaur
  carried: 3 bow
said 5 above, quoth 6 quoted, spoken,
  stated 7 related, uttered 8 repeated
Saigon
  capital of: 7 Vietnam
sail 3 fly 4 boat, scud, skim, soar 5 drift,
  float, glide, steam 6 course, cruise, voyage
  8 navigate 9 excursion
sailboat 4 saic, yawl 5 craft, ketch, sloop,
  yacht 6 vessel 7 sunfish 8 schooner 9 cat-
  amaran
  part: 4 boom, mast 6 canvas 7 rigging 9
  mainsheet

sailcloth 4 duck 6 canvas
Sailing to Byzantium
   author: 7 W B Yeats
sailor 3 gob, tar 4 salt 6 sea dog, seaman
7 mariner, voyager 8 deckhand, seafarer 9
navigator, yachtsman
sailors
   goddess of: 5 Brizo 11 Britomartis
Sails (of Argo)
   constellation of: 4 Vela
saint 6 martyr
   Buddhist: 5 arhat 11 bodhisattva
   Chinese: 8 immortal
   Islamic: 3 pir
   lives of the saints: 8 menology 9 hagiol-
   ogy 11 hagiography 13 acta sanctorum
   process of becoming: 12 canonization
   relic box: 6 chasse
   remains: 5 relic
   symbol: 4 halo
Saint, Eva Marie
   born: 8 Newark NJ
   roles: 6 Exodus 15 On the Waterfront 16
   North by Northwest
saint, patron
   acolytes: 13 John Berchmans
   actors: 8 Genesius
   artists: 4 Luke
   astronomers: 7 Dominic
   athletes: 9 Sebastian
   authors: 14 Francis de Sales
   aviators: 15 Our Lady of Loreto 16
   Therese of Lisieux 17 Joseph of
   Cupertino
   bakers: 8 Nicholas 18 Elizabeth of Hungary
   bankers: 7 Matthew
   barbers: 5 Louis 6 Cosmas, Damian
   barren women: 9 Felicitas 14 Anthony of
   Padua
   beggars/cripples: 5 Giles
   blind: 6 Odilia 7 Raphael
   bodily ills: 16 Our Lady of Lourdes
   boy scouts: 6 George
   brides: 14 Nicholas of Myra
   builders: 13 Vincent Ferrer
   butchers: 4 Luke 7 Hadrian 14 Anthony
   of Egypt
   carpenters: 6 Joseph
   cancer patients: 9 Peregrine
   children: 10 Santa Claus 14 Nicholas of
   Myra
   comedians: 5 Vitus
   cooks: 6 Martha 8 Lawrence
   deaf: 14 Francis de Sales
   dying: 6 Joseph 7 Barbara
   emigrants: 14 Frances Cabrini
   England: 6 George
   eye sufferers: 4 Lucy
   falsely accused: 15 Raymond Nonnatus
   farmers: 6 George 7 Isidore
   fishermen: 5 Peter 6 Andrew
   foreign missions: 13 Francis Xavier 16
   Therese of Lisieux
   foundlings: 13 Holy Innocents
   France: 5 Denis

   gardeners: 6 Fiacre, Phocas 7 Adelard,
   Dorothy, Tryphon
   heart patients: 9 John of God
   hospitals: 9 John of God 12 Jude
   Thaddeus 16 Camillus de Lellis
   housewives: 4 Anne
   hunters: 6 Hubert 10 Eustachius
   invalids: 4 Roch
   Ireland: 7 Patrick
   Italy: 7 Anthony
   laborers: 5 James 7 Isidore 9 John
   Bosco
   lawyers: 3 Ivo 4 Ives 8 Genesius 10
   Thomas More
   librarians: 6 Jerome
   lovers: 9 Valentine
   mariners: 7 Michael 19 Nicholas of
   Tolentino
   mentally ill: 6 Dympna
   merchants: 14 Nicholas of Myra 15
   Francis of Assisi
   metalworkers: 7 Eligius
   miners: 7 Barbara
   mothers: 6 Monica
   musicians: 7 Cecilia, Dunstan 15
   Gregory the Great
   Norway: 4 Olaf
   nurses: 6 Agatha 7 Alexius, Raphael 9
   John of God 16 Camillus de Lellis
   painters: 4 Luke
   philosophers: 6 Justin 21 Catherine of
   Alexandria
   physicians: 4 Luke 6 Cosmas, Damian 7
   Raphael 9 Pantaleon
   pilgrims: 5 James 7 Alexius
   poets: 5 David 7 Cecilia
   policemen: 7 Michael
   poor souls: 19 Nicholas of Tolentino
   postal workers: 7 Gabriel
   priests: 19 Jean-Baptiste Vianney
   printers: 8 Genesius 9 John of God 16
   Augustine of Hippo
   prisoners: 6 Dismas 7 Barbara 13 Joseph Cafasso
   rheumatism: 15 James the Greater
   sailors: 4 Elmo 7 Brendan, Erasmus, Eu-
   lalia 8 Cuthbert, Nicholas 11 Christopher
   13 Peter Gonzales
   scholars: 6 Brigid
   scientists: 6 Albert
   Scotland: 6 Andrew
   sculptors: 6 Claude
   seamen: 14 Francis of Paolo
   sick: 7 Michael 9 John of God 16
   Camillus de Lellis
   singers: 7 Cecilia, Gregory
   skiers: 7 Bernard
   shoemakers: 7 Crispin
   soldiers: 6 George 7 Hadrian 8 Ignatius
   9 Joan of Arc, Sebastian 13 Martin of
   Tours
   Spain: 5 James 8 Santiago
   students: 13 Thomas Aquinas 21 Catherine of Alexandria
   surgeons: 6 Cosmas, Damian
   tailors: 9 Homobonus
   tax collectors: 7 Matthew

teachers: 15 Gregory the Great 21 Catherine of Alexandria, Jean Baptiste de la Salle

theologians: 9 Augustine 16 Alphonsus Liguori

throat sufferers: 6 Blaise

travelers: 7 Raphael 11 Christopher 14 Anthony of Padua, Nicholas of Myra

Wales: 5 David

winegrowers: 7 Vincent

workingmen: 6 Joseph

writers: 14 Francis de Sales

youth: 13 John Berchmans 15 Aloysius Gonzaga, Gabriel Possenti

Saint, The
author: 16 Antonio Fogazzaro

Saint, The
author: 15 Leslie Charteris
character: 12 Simon Templar 26 Inspector Claude Eustace Teal
cast: 10 Roger Moore

Saint Anthony's fire 6 herpes 8 ergotism, shingles 10 erysipelas

Sainte-Beuve, Charles Augustin
author of: 19 Monday Conversations

Saint Elmo's fire 5 flame, hermo 6 castor, corona, furole, helena 9 corposant 12 luminescence

Saint Esprit 9 Holy Ghost 10 Holy Spirit

Saint-Exupery, Antoine de
author of: 11 Night Flight 12 Southern Mail 15 The Little Prince 16 Wind Sand and Stars

Saint Francis
born: 6 Assisi
called: 9 Poverello

Saint-Gaudens, Augustus
born: 6 Dublin 7 Ireland
artwork: 7 Puritan 13 Mrs Henry Adams (Grief) 14 General Sherman 15 Admiral Farragut 16 President Lincoln

Saint Jack
author: 11 Paul Theroux

Saint Joan
author: 17 George Bernard Shaw

Saint John's bread 5 carob

Saint John's wort 5 amber 6 tutsan 7 ascyrum, cammock 9 androseme, hypericum, rosin-rose 10 broombrush 11 Aaron's-beard

saintliness 6 purity 8 goodness, holiness 9 beatitude, godliness 11 blessedness 12 spirituality

Saint Lucia, St Lucia
capital: 8 Castries
highest point: 5 Gimie
island group: 8 Windward 14 Lesser Antilles
language: 6 patois
location: 9 Caribbean

saintly 4 good, holy 5 godly, moral, pious 6 devout 7 angelic, blessed, exalted, sinless, upright 8 beatific, faithful, reverent, virtuous 9 believing, religious, righteous, spiritual 10 benevolent

Saint Paul
born: 6 Tarsus
companion: 4 Luke
epistle: 5 Titus 6 Romans 7 Hebrews, Timothy 8 Philemon 9 Ephesians, Galatians 10 Colossians 11 Corinthians, Philippians 13 Thessalonians

Saint Paul's Cathedral (London)
architect: 4 Wren

Saint Peter
called: 4 Rock 5 Simon 6 Cephas
brother: 6 Andrew

Saint-Saens, (Charles) Camille
born: 5 Paris 6 France
composer of: 12 Danse Macabre 14 Samson et Dalila 16 Samson and Delilah 18 La Jeunesse d'Hercule 20 Carnival of the Animals

Saints' lives
writer of: 12 hagiographer

Saint Vincent, St Vincent
capital: 9 Kingstown
highest point: 9 Soufriere
Indian: 5 Carib 6 Arawak
island group: 8 Windward 14 Lesser Antilles
islands: 10 Grenadines
language: 6 patois
location: 9 Caribbean
volcano: 9 Soufriere

Saint Vitus' dance 6 chorea

Saitis *see* 6 Athena

sake 3 end 4 care, gain, good 5 cause 6 behalf, object, profit, regard 7 account, benefit, concern, purpose, respect, welfare 8 interest 9 advantage 11 enhancement 13 consideration

sake
type: 4 wine 6 spirit
origin: 5 Japan
ingredient: 4 rice

Sakharov, Andrei Dimitrievich
field: 7 physics
nationality: 7 Russian
researched: 14 nuclear fission
defended: 12 civil liberty
exiled to: 5 Gorky
awarded: 10 Nobel Prize

Saki
real name: 7 H H Munro
author of: 8 Reginald 20 Beasts and Super-Beasts 21 The Chronicles of Clovis 23 The Unbearable Bassington

salaam 3 bow 6 homage 9 obeisance

Salacia
partner of: 7 Neptune

salacious 4 lewd, sexy 7 lustful, obscene 8 indecent 9 lecherous 10 lascivious, libidinous 12 pornographic

salad days 5 prime, youth 6 heyday 9 flowering

salamander 3 eft 4 newt 5 giant, siren, tiger 6 lizard, red eft 7 axolotl, urodela 8 congo eel, mudpuppy 9 amphibian, fireeater, proteidae 10 hellbender, necturidae 14 red-spotted newt

Salamis
  father: 6 Asopus
  mother: 6 Metope
  son: 8 Cychreus

Salammbo
  author: 15 Gustave Flaubert
  character: 5 Matho 8 Hamilcar, Spendius
    9 Narr Havas
  setting: 8 Carthage

salary 3 pay 5 wages 6 income 7 stipend 8
  earnings 9 allowance, emolument 10 recompense 12 remuneration

sale 3 cut 7 bargain, selling, special 8 discount, exchange, markdown, transfer 9 reduction

Salem
  home of: 11 Melchizedek

salesperson 5 agent, clerk 6 vendor 8
  huckster

salient 6 arrant, marked 7 glaring, notable,
  obvious 8 flagrant, manifest, palpable,
  striking 9 egregious, important, prominent
  10 noteworthy, noticeable, pronounced,
  protruding, remarkable 11 conspicuous,
  outstanding, substantial 12 considerable

Salil
  also: 6 Salian
  form: 7 priests
  priests of: 4 Mars
  guarded: 7 ancilia 13 sacred shields

saline 4 salt 5 briny, salty 8 brackish

Salinger, J D
  author of: 14 Franny and Zooey 18 The
    Catcher in the Rye

Salisbury
  capital of: 8 Zimbabwe

Salisbury, Harrison E
  author of: 16 American in Russia 19 A
    Journey for Our Times, Black Night White
    Snow

Salish (Flatheads)
  language family: 8 Salishan
  location: 5 Idaho 6 Oregon 7 Montana
    10 Washington 15 British Columbia

Salishan
  tribe: 6 Salish 8 Puyallop 9 Flatheads

Salk, Jonas Edward
  field: 8 medicine
  developed: 12 (inactivated) polio vaccine

salle a manger 10 dining room
  literally: 13 hall for eating

sallow 3 wan 4 gray, pale 5 ashen, livid 6
  anemic, pallid, sickly, yellow 7 bilious 9
  jaundiced, washed-out, yellowish

sallowness 6 pallor 7 wanness 8 paleness
  10 sickliness 11 biliousness 13 colorlessness, yellowishness

Sallust
  author of: 9 Histories 13 War of Jugurtha
    20 Conspiracy of Catiline

sally 3 mot 4 flow, pour, quip, raid, trip 5
  erupt, foray, surge 6 attack, banter,
  charge, outing, retort, sortie, spring, thrust
  7 debouch, journey 8 badinage, repartee 9
  excursion, wisecrack, witticism 10 expedition 13 counterattack

Salmacis
  form: 5 nymph
  loved: 14 Hermaphroditus
  joined with: 14 Hermaphroditus
  became: 13 hermaphrodite 14 bisexual
    person

Salmagundi
  author: 16 Washington Irving

salmon 4 fish, king 5 cohoe 6 silver 7 chinook, Pacific, quinnat, sockeye, spawner 8
  Atlantic, humpback
  enclosure: 4 yair
  female: 4 raun 6 baggit
  genus: 12 Oncorhynchus
  hatchling: 4 pink 6 alevin
  male: 3 gib 4 buck, cock
  post-spawning: 4 kelt 7 shedder
  pre-spawning: 7 gilling, girling
  young: 4 parr 7 essling

Salmoneus
  father: 6 Aeolus
  mother: 7 Enarete
  brother: 8 Sisyphus
  wife: 6 Sidero 8 Alcidice
  daughter: 4 Tyro
  struck by: 9 lightning

Salome
  father: 11 Herod Philip
  mother: 8 Herodias
  husband: 7 Zebedee
  opera by: 7 (Richard) Strauss
  character: 5 Herod (the Tetrarch) 8
    Herodias, Jokanaan (John the Baptist) 9
    Narraboth

salon 4 hall 7 gallery 11 drawing room 13
  establishment

saloon 3 bar, inn, pub 6 bistro, tavern 7
  barroom, ginmill, taproom 8 alehouse 9
  roadhouse, speakeasy

salt 3 wit 4 best, corn, cure, pick, save 5
  brine, briny, cream, elect, humor, savor,
  smack, souse, spice 6 choice, flavor,
  pickle, saline, season, select 8 brackish,
  marinate, piquancy, pungency 9 seasoning
  12 quintessence

Salten, Felix
  author of: 5 Bambi

saltwater 3 sea 5 brine, ocean

salty 4 racy 5 briny, funny, spicy, terse,
  witty 6 corned, ribald, risque, saline 7 pungent, zestful 8 brackish, improper

salubrious 7 bracing, healthy 9 healthful,
  wholesome 10 beneficial, lifegiving 11
  therapeutic 12 invigorating

salubriousness 11 healthiness 13 healthfulness, wholesomeness

Salus
  origin: 5 Roman
  goddess of: 6 health 10 prosperity
  corresponds to: 6 Hygeia

salutary 4 good 5 tonic 6 useful 7 healing,
  healthy 8 curative, sanitary 9 healthful,
  wholesome 10 beneficial, profitable 12 advantageous

salutation 3 bow 5 hello, howdy, toast 6 curtsy 7 address, welcome 8 greeting 9 reception
  Hawalian: 5 aloha
  Italian: 4 ciao
  Latin: 3 ave
salute 3 ave 4 hail, kiss 5 bow to, cheer, greet, honor, nod to, salvo 6 accost, homage, praise, wave to 7 address, applaud, respect, welcome 8 accolade, applause, greeting 9 laudation, reverence 11 acclamation, recognition 12 congratulate
Salvador
  author: 10 Joan Didion
salvage 4 junk, save 5 scrap 6 debris, rescue 7 recover, remains, restore 8 recovery, retrieve 9 retrieval 11 reclamation 12 rehabilitate
salvation 4 rock 5 grace 6 rescue, saving 8 election, lifeline, mainstay, recovery, survival 9 retrieval 10 protection, redemption 11 deliverance, reclamation 12 preservation
salve 4 balm, calm, ease, hail 5 hello 6 lessen, lotion, pacify, reduce, soothe, temper 7 anodyne, assuage, mollify, relieve, unguent 8 dressing, liniment, mitigate, moderate, ointment 9 alleviate, emollient, greetings 11 alleviative
salver 4 bowl, dish, tray 6 waiter 7 coaster
salvia 4 herb, mint, sage 5 shrub 8 mejorana 9 artemisia
salvo 5 burst 6 volley 7 barrage, battery 8 shelling 9 cannonade, fusillade 11 bombardment
sambuca
  type: 7 liqueur
  origin: 5 Italy
  flavor: 5 anise 10 elderberry
same 4 like, twin, very 5 alike, equal 6 on a par 7 similar, uniform 8 parallel 9 identical, unchanged 10 consistent, equivalent, invariable 13 corresponding
same as previously given
  Latin: 4 idem
sameness 6 parity 8 equality, evenness, likeness, monotony 10 similarity, uniformity 11 homogeneity 14 homogenousness
Samoa
  capital:
    American Samoa: 8 Pago Pago
    Western Samoa: 4 Apia
  cities: 6 Utulei 7 Palauli 8 Fagatogo
  division: 12 Western Samoa 13 American Samoa
  monetary unit: 4 tala
  island: 3 Ofu, Tau 4 Rose 5 Aunuu, Manua, Namua, Upolu 6 Manono, Nuulua, Savaii, Swains 7 Apolima, Nuutele, Olosega, Tutuila 8 Nuusafee
  mountain: 4 Vaea 5 Alava 6 Savaii 7 Matafao 9 Rainmaker
  highest point: 4 Fito 8 Silisili
  sea: 12 South Pacific
  physical feature:
    bay: 5 Afono, Leone 6 Fagasa, Falefa,

Safata 7 Lafanga, Masefau, Matautu 8 Massacre, Salealua 9 Saluofata
  people: 6 Samoan 10 Polynesian
  explorer: 9 Roggeveen 12 Bougainville
  language: 6 Samoan 7 English
  religion: 6 Mormon 9 Methodist 13 Roman Catholic 15 Latter Day Saints 19 Seventh-Day Adventist 26 Congregational Christianity
  feature:
    bird: 3 iao 4 lulu, lupe 6 manuao, manuma, maomao 7 manuali 8 manusina, manutagi
    chief: 5 matai
    chief's daughter: 5 taupo
    cloth: 4 para, tapa
    clothing: 5 pareu 8 lavalava, puletasi
    dance: 4 siva
    dwelling: 4 fale
    food:
    drink: 3 ava
Samoyed
  language family: 6 Uralic
  spoken in: 7 Siberia
sample 3 try 4 test 5 model, taste 7 dip into, examine, example, pattern, portion, segment 8 instance, paradigm, specimen 10 experience 12 cross section, illustration 14 representative 15 exemplification
Sampo
  origin: 7 Finnish
  stolen by: 9 Ilmarinen 11 Vainamoinen 12 Lemminkainen
  stolen from: 5 Louhi
Samson 11 Hebrew judge
  father: 6 Manoah
  mistress/betrayer: 7 Delilah
  hometown: 5 Zorah
Samson Agonistes
  author: 10 John Milton
Samuel 11 Hebrew judge
  father: 7 Elkanah
  mother: 6 Hannah
  hometown: 5 Ramah
  anointed: 4 Saul 5 David
Sana, Sanaa
  capital of: 10 North Yemen
San Antonio
  basketball team: 5 Spurs
  football team: 11 Gunslingers
  landmark: 8 The Alamo 9 River Walk
sanctification 8 blessing 9 hallowing 12 consecration
  Hebrew: 7 Kiddush
sanctified 4 holy 6 sacred 7 blessed 8 hallowed 11 consecrated
sanctify 5 bless, exalt 6 anoint, hallow, purify, uphold 7 absolve, beatify, cleanse 8 dedicate, enshrine, make holy 10 consecrate, legitimate, legitimize 12 legitimatize
sanctimonious 6 solemn 7 canting, pompous, preachy 8 unctuous 9 overblown, pietistic 11 pharisaical, pretentious 14 holier-than-thou
sanctimoniousness 4 cant, sham 6 humbug 9 hypocrisy 11 insincerity 15 pretentiousness

sanction 5 allow, favor, leave 6 accept, assent, permit, ratify 7 agree to, approve, consent, endorse, liberty, license, penalty, support 8 approval, coercion, pressure 9 authority, authorize 10 legitimate, permission 11 countenance, endorsement 12 commendation, confirmation, ratification 13 authorization

sanctuary 4 park 5 cover, haven 6 asylum, chapel, church, refuge, safety, shrine, temple 7 reserve, retreat, shelter 8 preserve 10 protection

Sanctuary
  author: 15 William Faulkner
  character: 5 Tommy 6 Popeye 9 Ruby Lamar 10 Lee Goodwin, Reba Rivers 11 Temple Drake 12 Gowan Stevens, Horace Benbow

sanctum sanctorum 12 holy of holies

sanctus 4 holy

Sancus
  also: 10 Semo Sancus
  origin: 5 Roman
  god of: 5 oaths 10 road safety 11 hospitality 20 international affairs
  corresponds to: 8 Hercules 10 Dius Fidius

sand 4 grit, guts 5 pluck, spunk 6 mettle 7 bravery, courage, resolve 8 backbone 9 fortitude 10 resolution 12 resoluteness

Sand, George
  real name: 14 Aurore Dudevant
  author of: 5 Lelia 7 Indiana 8 Consuelo 9 Valentine 13 Story of My Life 14 The Country Waif, The Haunted Pool 17 Fanchon the Cricket 18 Les Maitres Sonneurs 23 The Countess of Rudolstadt

sandal 4 clog, flat, shoe, zori 5 scuff, thong 6 loafer 7 slipper 8 flipflop, huarache, moccasin, overshoe 10 espadrille

sandalwood 5 Algum, Almug

sandbank 4 dune, reef 5 shelf, shoal 7 shallow

sandbar 4 bank, flat, reef, spit 5 shelf, shoal 7 shallow

Sandbox, The
  author: 11 Edward Albee

Sandburg, Carl
  author of: 3 Fog 7 Chicago 12 Harvest Poems 15 Smoke and Steel 14 Abraham Lincoln, The Cornhuskers 15 Remembrance Rock

Sanders, George
  born: 9 Russia 12 St Petersburg
  wife: 10 Benita Hume, Magda Gabor 11 Zsa Zsa Gabor
  roles: 6 The Fan 7 Ivanhoe, Rebecca 8 The Saint 9 The Falcon 11 All About Eve 12 Forever Amber, The Gay Falcon 18 The Moon and Sixpence 20 Foreign Correspondent 22 The Picture of Dorian Gray 24 The House of the Seven Gables
  autobiography: 25 Memoirs of a Professional Cad

San Diego
  airport: 14 Lindbergh Field
  area: 7 La Jolla, Old Town 8 Coronado 9

Point Loma 10 Balboa Park, Mission Bay 13 Mission Valley 14 Gaslamp Quarter
  baseball team: 6 Padres
  football team: 8 Chargers
  founder: 13 Junipero Serra
  landmark: 11 San Diego Zoo 14 Wild Animal Park 30 Scripps Institute of Oceanography

sandpiper 3 ree 4 bird, ruff 5 reeve, stint, wader 6 common, oxbird, plover 7 fiddler, haybird, spotted, tipbird 8 graybird, sandpeep, shadbird 10 beachrobin

Sands of Iwo Jima
  director: 9 Allan Dwan
  cast: 8 John Agar 9 Adele Mara, John Wayne 13 Forrest Tucker

sandwich 3 sub 4 club, deli, hero 5 hogie 6 burger, hoagie, insert 7 grinder, western 8 laminate 9 interpose, submarine 10 lamination 11 combination

sane 5 lucid, sober 7 logical 8 all there, balanced, credible, rational, sensible 9 judicious, plausible, sagacious 10 farsighted, reasonable 11 clearheaded, responsible
  Latin: 12 compos mentis

Sanford and Son
  character: 5 Bubba 6 Melvin 10 Aunt Esther 11 Donna Harris, Fred Sanford, Grady Wilson, Rollo Larson 12 Julio Fuentes, Officer Smith (Smitty) 13 Lamont Sanford
  cast: 8 Redd Foxx 9 Don Bexley 11 Hal Williams, LaWanda Page, Slappy White, Whitman Mayo 12 Demond Wilson, Lynn Hamilton 13 Gregory Sierra 15 Nathaniel Taylor

San Francisco
  baseball team: 6 Giants
  bay: 12 San Francisco
  county: 5 Marin 8 San Mateo 12 San Francisco
  football team: 11 Forty-Niners
  known as: 12 City by the Bay 19 City by the Golden Gate
  landmark: 8 Alcatraz 16 Golden Gate Bridge
  noted for: 8 cable car 9 earthquake (1906) 26 crookedest street in the world
  street/section: 6 Market 7 Lombard, Nob Hill 8 Presidio 9 Chinatown 10 Montgomery 11 Embarcadero, Russian Hill

Sangallensis 16 Greek uncial codex

sangaree, sangria
  flavor: 5 fruit, spice

sangfroid 5 poise 6 aplomb 7 balance 8 coolness 9 composure 10 confidence, equanimity 11 tranquility 12 tranquillity 16 imperturbability

sanguine 3 red 4 rosy 5 happy, ruddy, sunny 6 bright, elated, florid 7 buoyant, crimson, flushed, glowing, hopeful, reddish, scarlet 8 blooming, cheerful, inflamed, rubicund 9 confident 10 optimistic 12 lighthearted

Sanhedrin 7 council

sanitarium, sanitorium 8 hospital 11 institution
  French: 13 maison de sante

sanitary 5 clean 7 aseptic, healthy, sterile 8 germ-free, hygienic 9 healthful, wholesome 10 salubrious, sterilized, uninfected, unpolluted 11 disinfected 12 prophylactic

sanitorium *see* 10 sanitarium

sanity 5 sense 6 reason 8 lucidity, saneness 9 coherence, normality 11 rationality 12 sensibleness 14 reasonableness 15 clearheadedness

San Jose
  capital of: 9 Costa Rica

San Juan
  capital of: 10 Puerto Rico

San Juan Bautista *see* 10 Puerto Rico

San Marino
  capital/largest city: 9 San Marino
  others: 10 Serravalle 13 Borgo Maggiore
  division: 8 Castelli
  government:
    legislature: 22 Great and General Council
  monetary unit: 4 lira, lire 9 centesimi
  mountain: 9 Apennines
  highest point: 6 Titano
  people: 7 Italian 11 San Marinese
  founder: 7 Marinus
  language: 7 Italian
  religion: 13 Roman Catholic
  place: 13 Valloni Palace 17 Palazzo del Governo 19 Basilica of San Marino
  church: 5 Pieve 11 St Francis

San Salvador
  capital of: 10 El Salvador

sans doute 12 without doubt

Sansovino, Andrea
  real name: 14 Andrea Contucci
  born: 5 Italy 14 Monte San Savino
  artwork: 15 Baptism of Christ 20 Virgin Child and St Anne

Sansovino, Il
  real name: 11 Jacopo Tatti
  born: 5 Italy 7 Caprese
  artwork: 4 Mars 7 Bacchus, Logetta, Neptune 10 Old Library 15 Madonna del Parto 16 St John the Baptist

sans pareil 12 without equal

sans peur et sans reproche 29 without fear and without reproach

sans souci 8 carefree 11 without care

Santa Cruz de Tenerife
  capital of: 13 Canary Islands

Santayana, George
  author of: 14 The Last Puritan 16 The Realms of Being, The Sense of Beauty 24 Skepticism and Animal Faith

Santiago
  capital of: 5 Chile

Santiago
  character in: 18 The Old Man and the Sea
  author: 9 Hemingway

Santo Domingo
  capital of: 17 Dominican Republic

Santo Domingo *see* 5 Haiti

Sao Tome
  capital of: 18 Sao Tome and Principe

Sao Tome and Principe
  capital/largest city: 7 Sao Tome
  others: 8 Trindade 11 Porto Alegre 12 Santo Antonio
  monetary unit: 5 dobra 6 escudo 7 centavo
  highest point: 7 Sao Tome
  sea: 8 Atlantic
  physical feature:
    bay: 11 Ana de Chaves
    gulf: 6 Guinea
  people: 7 African 10 Portuguese 11 Cape Verdean
  explorer: 7 Escobar 8 Santarem
  language: 10 Portuguese
  religion: 7 animism 13 Roman Catholic 19 Seventh Day Adventist 21 Evangelical Protestant

sap 3 rob, tax 4 ruin, wear 5 bleed, drain 6 impair, reduce, weaken 7 afflict, cripple, deplete, destroy, disable, exhaust, subvert 8 enervate, enfeeble 9 devastate, undermine 10 debilitate, devitalize

sapient 4 wise 7 knowing 8 profound 9 sagacious 10 discerning, perceptive 11 intelligent 13 knowledgeable

sap one's energy 3 fag 4 bush, poop, tire 5 drain, weary 6 tucker, weaken 7 deplete, exhaust, fatigue, wash out 8 enervate, enfeeble 10 debilitate, devitalize

Sapphira
  husband: 7 Ananias
  lied to: 5 Peter

sapphire 3 gem 4 blue 5 azure, jewel 6 indigo
  species: 8 corundum
  source: 5 Burma, Mogok 6 Ceylon 7 Kashmir 8 Sri Lanka, Thailand 9 Australia
  kind: 4 star

Sappho
  author: 14 Alphonse Daudet

Sarah, Sarai
  father: 5 Asher
  former name: 5 Sarai
  husband: 7 Abraham
  son: 5 Isaac
  slave: 5 Hagar
  burial place: 9 Machpelah

sarcasm 3 rub 4 gibe, jeer, jest 5 irony, scorn, sneer, taunt 7 mockery 8 contempt, derision, ridicule, scoffing 13 disparagement

sarcastic 5 acerb 6 biting, bitter, ironic 7 caustic, cutting, mocking, mordant 8 derisive, piercing, sardonic, scornful, sneering, stinging, taunting 11 disparaging 12 contemptuous

sarcoma 5 tumor 6 cancer, growth 8 neoplasm 10 malignancy

sarcophagus 4 pall 6 coffin

sard
  species: 6 quartz

sardine 4 bang, cram, fish, lile, lour, pack 5 crowd 7 alewife, anchovy, herring 8 pilchard

Sardinia
  other name: 8 Sardegna
  capital: 8 Cagliari
  cities: 4 Bono, Bosa 5 Nuoro, Olbia 7 Alghero, Bonorva, Sassari, Thatari 8 Iglesias, Oristano 11 Porto Torres
  division: 5 Nuoro 7 Arborea, Gallura, Sassari 8 Cagliari, Logudoro
  government: 13 region of Italy
  monetary unit: 7 carline
  island: 7 Caprera 8 Tavolara 9 Maddalena
  lake: 6 Omodeo
  mountain: 4 Rasu 5 Ferry, Linas 7 Gallura, Limbara 8 Marghine, Serpeddi, Vittoria 11 Gennargentu
  river: 5 Mannu, Tirso 6 Lascia 7 Coghinas 10 Flumendosa
  sea: 13 Mediterranean
  physical feature:
    gulf: 6 Orosei, Palmas 7 Asinara 8 Cagliari, Oristano
    plain: 7 Sassari 9 Campidano
    strait: 9 Bonifacio
  people:
    king: 12 Charles Felix 13 Charles Albert 14 Victor Emmanuel
    leader: 6 Cavour
    ruler: 4 Pisa 5 Genoa, Spain 7 Austria, Vandals 9 Byzantium, Phoenicia 12 House of Savoy
  language: 7 Italian
  religion: 13 Roman Catholic
  feature:
    towers: 7 nuraghi
  food:
    cheese: 6 romano 8 pecorino

Sardius 8 gemstone
sardonic 6 biting 7 caustic, cynical, jeering, mocking, mordant, satiric 8 derisive, scornful, sneering, taunting 9 sarcastic 11 disparaging 12 contemptuous
Sardonyx 8 gemstone
Sargent, John Singer
  born: 5 Italy 8 Florence
  artwork: 6 Madam X (Madame Gautreau) 7 El Jaleo 17 The Wyndham Sisters 20 Robert Louis Stevenson 21 Carnation Lily Lily Rose 22 Daughters of Edward D Boit 24 Oyster Gatherers of Cancale
Sargom
  captured: 5 Accad
  successor: 11 Sennacherib
Saron
  king of: 7 Troezen
Saroyan, William
  author of: 12 My Name Is Aram 14 The Human Comedy 17 The Time of Your Life 22 My Heart's in the Highlands
Sarpedon
  prince of: 5 Lycia
  father: 4 Zeus
  mother: 6 Europa 8 Laodamia
  uncle: 5 Cilix
  brother: 5 Minos 12 Rhadamanthys
  ally of: 4 Troy
  friend: 7 Glaucus
  killed by: 9 Patroclus
Sarton, May
  author of: 5 Anger 11 Kinds of Love 17 Plant Dreaming Deep 20 Faithful Are the Wounds 33 Mrs Stevens Hears the Mermaids Singing
Sartor Resartus
  author: 13 Thomas Carlyle
Sartre, Jean-Paul
  author of: 6 Nausea, No Exit 8 The Words 17 The Roads to Freedom 19 Being and Nothingness
  philosophy: 14 Existentialism
  quote: 17 Hell is other people
sash 3 tie 4 band, belt 5 frame, scarf, strip 6 casing, corset, girdle, ribbon, window 7 baldric 8 casement 9 doorframe, waistband 10 cummerbund 11 windowframe
  Japanese: 3 obi
  pulley weight: 5 mouse
  window: 5 chess
sashay 4 move, skip 5 glide, mince 6 chasse, travel
Saskatchewan 5 river 8 province
  boundary: 7 Alberta, Montana 8 Manitoba 11 North Dakota 12 Old Northwest 20 Northwest Territories
  capital: 6 Regina
  city: 8 Moose Jaw 9 Saskatoon 12 Prince Albert, Swift Current
  country: 6 Canada
  Indian: 4 Cree 9 Chipewyan 10 Assiniboin
  lake: 8 Reindeer 9 Athabasca, Wollaston
  mountain: 7 Cypress, Pasquia 9 Porcupine 14 Missouri Coteau
  river: 9 Churchill, Frenchman
  river mouth: 12 Lake Winnipeg
Sassoon, Siegfried
  author of: 26 The Memoirs of a Fox-Hunting Man 26 The Memoirs of George Sherston 29 The Memoirs of an Infantry Officer
sassy 4 bark, bold, flip, rude, tree 5 brash, fresh, saucy 6 mouthy, snippy 7 forward 8 impolite, impudent, insolent 12 discourteous 13 disrespectful
Satan 6 Belial, Moloch 7 Lucifer, Old Nick 8 Apollyon, the Devil 9 Beelzebub 10 Old Scratch, the Evil One, the Tempter 11 fallen angel 12 the Foul Fiend 13 the Old Serpent 14 Mephistopheles 19 the Prince of Darkness
satanic 3 bad 4 evil, vile 5 cruel 6 wicked 7 demonic, heinous, hellish, inhuman, vicious 8 devilish, fiendish, infamous, infernal, sadistic 9 malicious, malignant 10 demoniacal, diabolical, malevolent
satchel, Satchel 3 bag 4 case, grip, sack 5 purse 6 valise 7 handbag 8 reticule, suitcase 9 carpetbag, Gladstone, schoolbag
  pitcher, Hall of Famer: 5 Paige

sate 4 cloy, fill, glut 5 gorge, stuff 7 surfeit

satellite 4 moon 5 crony, toady 6 menial, puppet, vassal 7 servant 8 disciple, follower, hanger-on, parasite, retainer 9 assistant, attendant, companion, sycophant, tributary, underling

satellite state 6 colony 8 dominion 10 possession 12 protectorate

satiate 4 bore, cloy, fill, glut, jade 5 slake, stuff, weary 6 overdo, quench, sicken 7 content, disgust, gratify, suffice, surfeit 8 nauseate, overfill, saturate

Satie, Erik
  born: 6 France 8 Honfleur
  composer of: 6 Parade 13 Pieces froides 16 The Three Gymnasts 19 Limp Preludes for a Dog 20 Pieces en forme de poire 23 Pieces in the Shape of a Pear

satiny 4 fine 5 shiny, silky 6 smooth

satire 5 irony 6 banter, parody, send up 7 lampoon, mockery, sarcasm, takeoff 8 acrimony, derision, raillery, ridicule, travesty 9 burlesque 10 caricature, persiflage

satirical 5 comic 6 biting, bitter 7 caustic, mocking, mordant 8 derisive, humorous, ironical, sardonic, scornful, sneering 9 malicious, sarcastic

satirize 4 mock 6 parody 7 lampoon 9 burlesque 10 caricature

satisfaction 5 pride 6 amends 7 comfort, content, damages, deserts, justice, payment, redress 8 pleasure, requital 9 answering, atonement, happiness, quittance, reckoning, repayment 10 correction, recompense, remittance, settlement 11 contentment, fulfillment, restitution 12 compensation, remuneration 13 gratification, rectification, reimbursement

satisfactory 2 OK 4 okay 8 adequate, all right, passable, suitable 9 competent 10 acceptable, sufficient

satisfied 5 happy 7 content, pleased 9 gratified 10 complacent 11 comfortable

satisfy 3 pay 4 fill, meet 5 annul, clear, remit, repay, serve, slake 6 answer, assure, pacify, pay off, please, quench, remove, settle 7 appease, content, delight, fulfill, gratify, mollify, requite, suffice 8 convince, persuade, reassure 9 discharge, reimburse 10 compensate, recompense

satisfying 8 pleasant, pleasing 9 agreeable, enjoyable, rewarding 10 delightful, fulfilling, gratifying 11 pleasurable

saturate 4 fill 5 cover, douse, imbue, souse 6 drench, infuse 7 immerse, pervade, suffuse 8 permeate, submerge 10 impregnate, infiltrate

saturated 3 wet 4 full 5 drunk, soggy, soppy 6 soaked, sodden 8 bursting

Saturday
  day of: 15 Biblical Sabbath
  French: 6 samedi
  from: 8 Saturnus
  German: 7 samstag
  heavenly body: 6 Saturn
  Italian: 6 sabato

  observance: 13 Jewish Sabbath 20 Seventh Day Adventists
  Spanish: 6 sabado

Saturday Night Fever
  director: 10 John Badham
  cast: 11 Barry Miller 12 John Travolta 15 Karen Lynn Gorney
  setting: 8 Brooklyn
  score: 7 Bee Gees
  sequel: 12 Staying Alive

Saturday Night Live, NBC's
  regular: 10 Bill Murray, Chevy Chase, Dan Aykroyd, Jane Curtin 11 Eddie Murphy, Gilda Radner, John Belushi 13 Garrett Morris, Laraine Newman
  group: 27 Not Ready For Prime Time Players
  bits: 4 Bees 7 Samurai 9 Coneheads 10 Church Lady 13 Blues Brothers, Weekend Update 16 Pathological Liar 18 Rosanne Rosanna-Dana

Saturn
  origin: 5 Roman
  god of: 11 agriculture
  consort of: 3 Ops
  son: 5 Picus
  corresponds to: 6 Cronos, Cronus, Kronos

Saturn
  position: 5 sixth
  satellite: 4 Rhea 5 Dione, Janus, Mimas, Titan 6 Phoebe, Tethys 7 Iapetus 8 Hyperion 9 Enceladus
  characteristic: 5 rings

saturnalia, Saturnalia 4 orgy 5 revel, spree 7 carouse, debauch, revelry 8 carousal 9 bacchanal 10 debauchery
  origin: 5 Roman
  event: 8 festival
  honoring: 6 Saturn 13 sowing of crops

saturnine 4 dour, glum, grim 5 grave, staid, stern, sulky 6 gloomy, moping, morose, solemn, somber, sullen 7 austere, serious 8 dejected, downcast, reserved, sardonic, taciturn 9 apathetic, cheerless, withdrawn 11 downhearted 15 uncommunicative

satyr
  form: 5 deity
  location: 8 woodland

Satyricon
  author: 9 Petronius
  character: 4 Gito 8 Ascyltus, Eumolpus 9 Encolpius 10 Trimalchio

sauce 3 dip 4 sass 5 booze, gravy 6 fillip, flavor 7 alcohol 8 dressing, pertness 9 condiment, flippancy 12 impertinence
  basil: 5 pesto
  fish: 4 alec
  hot: 7 Tabasco
  Indian: 5 curry
  salty: 3 soy

saucy 4 bold, pert, rude, trim 5 brash, cocky, fresh, natty, smart 6 brazen, cheeky, jaunty, lively, spruce 7 forward 8 flippant, impolite, impudent, insolent 9 audacious, barefaced, unabashed 11 impertinent, smart-alecky 12 discourteous 13 disrespectful

Saudi Arabia
capital/largest city: 6 Riyadh
others: 4 Abha, Hail, Taif 5 Hofuf, Hufuf, Jedda, Jidda, Yanbu, Yenbo 6 Anaiza, Dammam, Jiddah, Jubail 7 Alhofuf, Buraido, Dhahran 9 Ras Tanura
holy city: 5 Mecca 6 Medina
school: 5 Islam 13 King Abd al-Aziz 19 Imam Muhammad bin Saud 20 Petroleum and Minerals
division: 4 Asir, Nejd 5 Hejaz 6 El Hasa
government: 8 monarchy
head of state/government: 4 king
monetary unit: 5 girsh, gursh, pound, riyal
weight: 3 oke
mountain: 6 Tuwayq
highlands: 4 Asir 5 Hejaz
highest point: 5 Razih 10 Jebal Sawda
sea: 3 Red
physical feature:
desert: 3 Red 5 Dahna, Nafud, Nefud, Nufud 6 al-Dahy, Dahana 10 Rub al Khali
gulf: 5 Aqaba 7 Persian
peninsula: 7 Arabian
plain: 6 Tihama
plateau: 4 Nejd
people: 4 Arab 7 Bedouin
king: 4 Fahd, Saud 6 Faisal, Khalid 7 Ibn Saud 9 Abdul Aziz
religious leader: 8 Mohammed, Muhammad
language: 6 Arabic
religion: 5 Islam
sect: 5 Sunni 6 Shiite 7 Wahhabi
place:
shrine: 5 Kaaba 10 Black Stone
feature:
annual pilgrimage: 4 hadj, hajj
clothing: 3 aba 4 agal 5 thobe 6 ghutra
kingdom: 5 Hejaz 7 Minaean, Ottoman, Sabaean 9 Himyarite
laws of Islam: 6 sharia
village school: 6 kuttab
war: 4 Gulf 11 Desert Storm 12 Desert Shield

Sauguet, Henri
born: 6 France 8 Bordeaux
composer of: 6 La Nuit 10 Les Forains, Les Mirages

Sauk, Sac
family: 9 Algonkian 10 Algonquian
tribe: 3 Fox, Sac 8 Kickapoo
location: 4 Iowa, Ohio 6 Kansas 7 Indiana 8 Illinois, Michigan, Oklahoma 9 Wisconsin
leader: 9 Blackhawk
related to: 8 Kickapoo 9 Mesquakie 11 Potawatomie
involved in: 12 Black Hawk War

Saul
king of: 4 Edom 6 Israel
father: 4 Kish
daughter: 5 Merab 6 Michal

son: 7 Abinoam 8 Jonathan 10 Ishbosheth
succeeded: 6 Samlah
anointed by: 6 Samuel
hometown: 6 Gibeah 8 Rehoboth
successor: 5 David
former name: 4 Paul

Saunders, Allen
creator/artist of: 9 Mary Worth

saunter 4 roam 5 amble, mosey, stray 6 loiter, ramble, stroll, wander 7 meander, traipse 8 straggle 9 promenade

Saurolophus
type: 8 dinosaur 10 ornithopod
location: 6 Canada 7 Alberta

sauropod
type of: 8 dinosaur
member: 9 Euhelopus 10 Diplodocus 11 Apatosaurus 12 Brontosaurus, Camarasaurus, Plateosaurus 13 Brachiosaurus, Hypselosaurus

sausage 5 frank, gigot, wurst 6 hot-dog, salami, weenie, wiener 7 baloney, bologna 8 kielbasa 9 bratwurst, pepperoni 10 liverwurst 11 frankfurter
British: 6 banger

sauve qui peut 4 rout 8 stampede 18 every man for himself 23 let him save himself who can

savage 4 boor, wild 5 brute, cruel, feral, fiend, harsh, rough, yahoo 6 animal, bloody, brutal, fierce, maniac, native, rugged, unkind 7 brutish, hoodlum, ruffian, untamed, violent 8 barbaric, hooligan, pitiless, ruthless, sadistic 9 aborigine, barbarian, barbarous, ferocious, merciless, murderous, primitive 10 aboriginal, heathenish, relentless, uncultured, unmerciful 11 uncivilized 12 uncultivated 14 undomesticated

savagery 7 cruelty 8 ferocity 9 barbarism, barbarity, brutality 10 fierceness, inhumanity 12 pitilessness, ruthlessness

savanna, savannah 5 campo, plain 9 grassland

savant 6 genius 7 scholar 13 learned person

save 3 but 4 bank, free, help, hold, keep 5 amass, guard, hoard, lay by, lay up, put by, spare, stock, store 6 defend, except, garner, heap up, redeem, rescue, shield 7 deliver, deposit, husband, protect, put away, recover, reserve, salvage 8 conserve, preserve, retrench, withhold 9 economize, safeguard 10 accumulate

save up 5 amass, hoard 7 collect, put away 8 salt away, sock away 10 accumulate 12 squirrel away

saving 5 close, tight 6 frugal, stingy 7 careful, miserly, prudent, sparing, thrifty 8 markdown, stinting 9 illiberal, niggardly, provident, redeeming, restoring 10 economical, reclaiming, redemptory, reparative 12 compensating, conservative

savings 5 hoard 7 nest egg, reserve

savior 5 freer 7 rescuer 8 champion, defender, guardian, redeemer 9 deliverer, liberator, preserver, protecter, protector, salvation 11 emancipator

Savior 5 Jesus 6 Christ 8 Redeemer 10 the Messiah 11 Jesus Christ, the Son of God 13 Prince of Peace

Savior anointed 5 Jesus

savoir-faire 4 tact 5 poise 6 aplomb, polish 7 finesse, know-how, suavity 8 presence, urbanity 9 assurance, composure 10 adroitness, discretion, smoothness 11 worldliness 12 complaisance, graciousness 14 self-possession

savoir-vivre 16 knowing how to live 19 knowledge of the world

savor 3 try 4 aura, gist, like, odor, soul, tang, zest 5 aroma, enjoy, scent, smack, smell, spice, taste, trait 6 flavor, nature, relish, sample, season, spirit 7 essence, quality 8 piquancy, property, pungency 9 character, fragrance, substance 10 appreciate, experience 11 peculiarity 13 particularity 14 characteristic

savory 5 tangy, tasty, yummy 6 honest 7 odorous, piquant, pungent 8 alluring, aromatic, charming, edifying, fragrant, luscious, tasteful 9 delicious, flavorous, palatable, reputable, toothsome 10 appetizing, attractive, delectable 11 inoffensive, respectable, scrumptious 13 mouthwatering

savory
  botanical name: 8 Satureia, S montana 10 S hortensis
  origin: 13 Mediterranean
  varieties: 6 summer, winter
  use: 4 eggs, meat 5 beans, salad 6 sauces 8 dressing 11 chicken soup

savvy 5 catch, get it 7 know-how 10 comprehend, understand 13 understanding

saw 3 cut 4 tool 5 adage, maxim, slash 6 saying 7 proverb 8 aphorism
  type: 3 jig, rip 4 back, band, hack 5 miter 6 coping 7 keyhole 8 circular, crosscut

sawfly
  varieties: 4 stem, wood 5 cedar 6 pergid 7 conifer 8 horntail 11 web spinning

say 2 do 4 hint, hold, read, tell, vote, word 5 bruit, claim, guess, imply, judge, mouth, rumor, speak, state, utter, voice 6 allege, assert, assume, chance, convey, phrase, reason, recite, remark, render, repeat, report, reveal, spread 7 comment, contend, declare, deliver, divulge, express, imagine, mention, perform, suggest, suppose, surmise 8 announce, disclose, intimate, maintain, rehearse, vocalize 9 circulate, franchise, insinuate, pronounce, verbalize 10 articulate, conjecture 11 communicate

Sayers, Dorothy L
  author of: 9 Whose Body 12 Strong Poison 14 Have His Carcase, The Nine Tailors, Unnatural Death 15 Clouds of Witness, Five Red Herrings 16 Busman's Honeymoon 19 Murder Must Advertise 30 Unpleasantness at the Bellona Club
  character: 6 Bunter 11 Harriet Vane 15 Lord Peter Wimsey

Say Hey Kid
  nickname of: 10 Willie Mays

saying 3 saw 5 adage, maxim, moral, motto 6 byword, dictum, truism 7 epigram, precept, proverb 8 aphorism, apothegm 10 expression

Sayonara
  director: 11 Joshua Logan
  author: 13 James Michener
  cast: 9 Miiko Taka 10 Red Buttons 11 James Garner, Martha Scott 12 Marlon Brando, Miyoshi Umeki 16 Ricardo Montalban
  score: 12 Irving Berlin
  Oscar for: 15 supporting actor (Buttons) 17 supporting actress (Umeki)

scabrous 5 dirty, rough, scaly 7 immoral, leprous 8 indecent, off-color 9 salacious 10 suggestive 12 pornographic

scalding 3 hot 5 harsh 7 boiling, caustic 8 seething, steaming 9 sarcastic

scale, scales 3 key, set 4 chip, film, husk, peel, rise, rule, skin 5 crust, flake, layer, mount, order, plate, range, ratio, scour, shave, shell, weigh 6 adjust, ascend, goupen, ladder, lamina, octave, rub off, scrape, series, spread 7 balance, chip off, clamber, climb up, coating, lamella, measure 8 escalade, membrane, register, regulate, spectrum, surmount 9 continuum, gradation 10 delaminate, graduation, proportion 11 calibration, progression 14 classification

scale down 4 trim 6 reduce 7 abridge, curtail, shorten 8 compress, condense, decrease, diminish, downsize, moderate 10 abbreviate

scale insects
  varieties: 3 lac, pit, wax 5 giant 6 ensign 7 armored 8 mealybug, tortoise 12 ground pearls

Scamandrius *see* 8 Astyanax

scamp 3 imp, rip 5 cut-up, knave, rogue, tease 6 rascal, rotter 7 bounder, villain 8 blighter, scalawag 9 miscreant, prankster, scoundrel 10 scapegrace 11 rapscallion 13 mischief-maker

scamper 3 fly, run, zip 4 dart, dash, flit, race, romp, rush, scud 5 frisk, hurry, scoot 6 frolic, gambol, hasten, scurry, sprint 7 scuttle 9 skedaddle 21 running about playfully

scan 4 skim 5 check, probe, scour, study, sweep 6 peruse, search, size up, survey 7 analyze, examine, explore, inspect 10 scrutinize

scandal 4 blot 5 abuse, libel, odium, shame, stain 6 expose, smirch, stigma 7 calumny, obloquy, outrage, slander 8 disgrace, dishonor, ignominy 9 aspersion, discredit, disesteem, sensation 10 debasement, detraction, opprobrium, revilement

12 vituperation **13** disparagement, embarrassment

scandalize 5 shock **6** appall, defame, insult, offend **7** horrify, outrage **10** calumniate

scandalmonger 6 gossip **8** busybody **10** talebearer, tattletale

scandalous 8 libelous, shameful, shocking **9** gossiping, offensive **10** defamatory, outrageous, scurrilous, slanderous **11** disgraceful **12** disreputable **13** reprehensible

Scandinavian
  language family: **12** Indo-European
  branch: **8** Germanic
  group: **15** Western Germanic
  language: **6** Danish **7** Swedish **9** Icelandic, Norwegian

Scandinavian Mythology
  abode of man: **7** Midgard **10** Mithgarthr
  afterworld: **6** Manala **7** Tuonela
  began race of giants: **4** Ymir
  blacksmith/hero: **9** Ilmarinen
  boar: **10** Saehrimnir
  bridge of gods: **7** Bifrost
  dragon: **6** Fafnir
  dwarf: **5** Skuld **7** Andvari
  earth is made from: **4** Ymir
  elf: **4** Norn **8** Verdandi
  epic: **8** Kaleva
  final battle: **15** Gotterdammerung **17** Twilight of the Gods
  first god: **4** Buri **7** Forsete, Forseti
  first man: **3** Ask
  first woman: **5** Embla
  folk hero: **8** Kalevala
  giant: **4** Loki **5** Jotun, Thrym **6** Thiazi, Thjazi **7** Skrymir
  giantess: **3** Urd **5** Thokk **9** Angerboda, Angrbodha, Angurboda
  giant's realm: **9** Jotunheim
  goat: **7** Heidrun
  goddesses: **7** Asynjur
  goddess of death: **3** Hel
  goddess of forbidden marriages: **4** Lofn
  goddess of marriage: **4** Frey **5** Freyr
  goddess of peace: **4** Frey **5** Freyr
  goddess of prosperity: **4** Frey **5** Freyr
  goddess of spring: **4** Idun **5** Iduna, Ithun **6** Ithunn
  goddess of the sea: **3** Ran
  god of beauty/radiance: **5** Baldr **6** Balder, Baldur
  god of dawn: **8** Heimdall
  god of farming: **4** Thor
  god of fire: **4** Loki
  god of knowledge: **4** Odin **5** Othin
  corresponds to Germanic: **5** Wotan
  god of justice: **7** Forseti
  god of light: **8** Heimdall
  god of music: **5** Bragi
  god of navigation: **5** Niord, Njord
  god of poetry: **4** Odin **5** Bragi, Othin
  corresponds to Germanic: **5** Wotan
  god of prosperity: **5** Niord, Njord
  god of rain: **4** Thor
  god of sea: **5** Aegir, Mimir

  god of thunder: **4** Thor
  god of underworld: **8** Niflheim
  god of victory: **3** Tyr
  god of war: **4** Odin **5** Othin
  corresponds to Germanic: **5** Wotan
  god of wind: **5** Niord, Njord
  god of wisdom: **4** Odin **5** Othin
  corresponds to Germanic: **5** Wotan
  hero: **11** Vainamoinen **12** Lemminkainen
  home of dead: **3** Hel
  king: **5** Gjuki
  magician: **11** Joukahainen
  magic necklace: **11** Brisingamen
  misty void: **11** Ginnungagap
  mountain: **11** Hindarfjall
  nature spirit: **7** Eriking
  oak tree: **9** Barnstock, Branstock
  Odin's court/hall: **8** Valhalla
  Odin's father: **3** Bor
  Odin's horse: **8** Sleipnir
  Odin's magic ring: **8** Draupnir
  Odin's palace: **9** Gladsheim
  Odin's raven: **5** Hugin, Munin
  Odin's spear: **6** Gungni
  Odin's throne: **10** Hlidskjalf
  Odin's wolf: **4** Geri **5** Freki
  race of gods: **5** Vanir
  saga: **8** Vulsunga
  sea monster: **6** Kraken
  serpent: **7** Nidhogg **11** Jormungandr
  Sigmund's sword: **4** Gram
  slave: **8** Kullervo
  sorceress: **5** Louhi **8** Grimhild
  Thor's hammer: **7** Miolnir
  Thor's servant: **9** Thialfi
  tree with three roots: **9** Iggdrasil, Yggdrasil
  Valkyrie: **8** Brynhild **9** Brunhilde, Sigrdrifa **11** Brunnehilde
  virgin goddess: **3** Urd **4** Norn **5** Skuld, Urdar **8** Verdandi
  warrior: **8** Baresark **9** Berserker
  watchdog: **4** Garm
  wolf monster: **6** Fenrir, Fenris

scant 3 cut **4** bare **5** limit, short, small, stint **6** in need, meager, paltry, reduce, sparse **7** limited **8** exiguous, hold back **9** deficient **10** inadequate, incomplete **12** insufficient

scantiness 10 deficiency, inadequacy, meagerness, skimpiness **13** insufficiency

scanty 4 thin **5** short, small **6** meager, modest, paltry, skimpy, sparse **7** slender, stunted **9** deficient **10** inadequate, undersized **12** insufficient

scapegoat, Scapegoat 4 butt, dupe, gull **5** patsy **6** Azazel, victim **7** fall guy **11** whipping boy **13** laughingstock

scapolite
  source: **5** Burma, Mogok

scapula
  bone of: **13** shoulder blade

scar 3 cut, pit **4** dent, flaw, gash, hurt, mark, pock, seam **5** brand, wound **6** affect, bruise, damage, deface, defect, impair, mangle **7** blemish, scratch **8** cicatrix, lacerate, mutilate **9** disfigure, influence

scarce 4 rare 6 scanty, sparse 7 unusual, wanting 8 uncommon 9 deficient

scarcely 4 just 6 at most, barely, hardly 7 but just, faintly 8 slightly

scarcity 4 lack, want 5 stint 6 dearth, rarity 7 fewness, paucity 8 rareness, shortage, sparsity, thinness 10 deficiency, scantiness, sparseness 12 uncommonness 13 insufficiency

scare 4 turn 5 alarm, daunt, panic, shake, shock, start 6 harrow, shiver 7 horrify, jitters, startle, terrify 8 disquiet, frighten 9 terrorize 10 disconcert, dishearten, intimidate 11 nervousness, palpitation 13 consternation

scarecrow 6 effigy 8 straw man

Scarecrow
character in: 13 The Wizard of Oz
author: 4 Baum

scared 5 shaky, timid, upset 6 afraid 7 alarmed, fearful, nervous, spooked 8 startled, timorous 9 diffident, terrified, tremulous 10 frightened 12 apprehensive, fainthearted 13 panic-stricken

scarf 3 boa 4 sash, veil, wrap 5 ascot, shawl, stole 6 choker, cravat, tippet 7 foulard, muffler, overlay 8 babushka, bandanna, mantilla 11 neckerchief

Scarface
director: 11 Howard Hawks
cast: 8 Paul Muni 9 Ann Dvorak 10 George Raft 12 Boris Karloff

scarify 3 cut 6 incise, loosen 7 break up, scratch 8 lacerate 9 cultivate

Scarlatti, Alessandro
born: 6 Sicily 7 Palermo
composer of: 11 Stabat Mater 17 Mitridate Eupatore, The Triumph of Honor 18 Il Trionfo dell Onore 23 Gli equivoci nel sembiante

Scarlatti, Domenico
born: 5 Italy 6 Naples
composer of: 7 Sonatas 9 Cat's Fugue, Essercizi 18 Le Donne di Buon Umore 20 The Good-Humored Ladies 23 Ottavia risituita al trono

scarlet 3 red 6 cherry, claret 7 carmine 8 cardinal

Scarlet Letter, The
author: 18 Nathaniel Hawthorne
character: 5 Pearl 12 Hester Prynne 16 Arthur Dimmesdale 18 Roger Chillingworth

scary 3 bad 5 awful, hairy 6 creepy 7 fearful 8 alarming, menacing, shocking 9 difficult 10 disturbing, terrifying 11 frightening, goosepimply, hair-raising, threatening 12 discomfiting

scat 3 off, out 4 away, shoo 5 be off, leave, scram 6 beat it, be gone, depart, get out, go away 7 get lost, vamoose

scathing 4 keen, tart 5 sharp 6 biting, brutal, savage 7 caustic, cutting, hostile, mordant, pointed, searing 8 incisive, stinging, virulent 9 ferocious, rancorous, scorching, trenchant, vitriolic, withering 10 lacerating 11 acrimonious, excoriating

scatter 3 sow 4 cast, flee, rout 5 strew, throw 6 dispel 8 disperse, sprinkle 9 broadcast, circulate, dissipate 10 distribute 11 disseminate

scatterbrained 4 rash, wild, zany 5 crazy, dizzy, giddy, nutty, silly 6 madcap, stupid 7 flighty, foolish 8 careless, heedless, reckless, unstable, unsteady 9 foolhardy, forgetful, frivolous, imprudent 11 birdbrained, empty-headed, harebrained 12 absentminded, muddleheaded 13 irresponsible

scattered 6 random, spotty 7 diffuse 9 irregular 10 infrequent, occasional

scattering 6 sowing 7 casting 8 strewing 9 dispersal 10 dispersing, sprinkling 12 broadcasting, distribution 13 dissemination

scavenger 6 magpie 8 salvager 9 collector

scenario 4 book, idea, plan 6 scheme 7 concept, outline, summary 8 abstract, game plan, synopsis, teleplay 10 conception, manuscript, screenplay
French: 6 precis

scene 3 act 4 fuss, part, show, site, spot, to-do, view 5 place, sight, vista 6 locale, region, survey, vision 7 display, episode, picture, scenery, setting 8 backdrop, division, locality, location, panorama, position, prospect, sequence 9 commotion, spectacle 10 background 11 whereabouts

scenery 4 sets, view 5 vista 7 terrain 9 backdrops, landscape, spectacle 11 backgrounds

Scenes from a Marriage
director: 13 Ingmar Bergman
cast: 10 Liv Ullmann 13 Bibi Andersson 15 Erland Josephson

scent 4 odor, path, wake, wind 5 aroma, smell, sniff, spoor, trace, track, trail 6 course, detect, inhale 7 bouquet, breathe, discern, essence, perfume, pursuit, suspect 9 aromatize, fragrance, get wind of, recognize 11 distinguish

scented 5 spicy 7 odorous, piquant, pungent 8 aromatic, fragrant, perfumed 9 odiferous 13 sweet-smelling

Scephrus
father: 8 Tegeates
brother: 5 Limon
killed by: 5 Limon

Schaffner, Franklin
director of: 6 Patton (Oscar) 15 Planet of the Apes

Schedius
father: 7 Iphitus
mother: 9 Hippolyte
suitor of: 5 Helen

schedule 3 fix 4 book, list, plan, roll 5 fit in, slate, table 6 agenda 7 appoint, program, put down, set down 8 calendar 9 inventory, timetable

Scheele, Karl Wilhelm
field: 9 chemistry
nationality: 7 Swedish
discovered: 6 oxygen 8 chlorine 9 glycerine

Scheider, Roy
 born: 8 Orange NJ
 roles: 4 Jaws 11 All That Jazz, Blue
 Thunder, The Seven-Ups 14 Fifty-two
 Pickup 19 The French Connection
Schell, Maria
 real name: 15 Margarete Schell
 born: 6 Vienna 7 Austria
 brother: 16 Maximilian Schell
 roles: 8 Cimarron, Gervaise 11 End of
 Desire, White Nights 13 The Last Bridge
 20 The Brothers Karamazov
Schell, Maximilian
 born: 6 Vienna 7 Austria
 sister: 11 Maria Schell
 roles: 5 Julia 13 The Young Lions 19
 Judgment at Nuremberg (Oscar) 21 The
 Man in the Glass Booth
scheme 3 map, way 4 plan, plot, ruse 5 cabal, chart, frame, means, shift, study 6
 course, design, device, devise, layout,
 method, policy, sketch, system 7 complot,
 concoct, connive, drawing, network, outline, program, project, tactics 8 conspire,
 contrive, grouping, intrigue, maneuver, organize, strategy 9 machinate, procedure,
 stratagem 10 connivance, conspiracy 11
 arrangement, contrivance, delineation, disposition, machination 12 organization
scheming 3 sly 4 arch, wily 6 artful, crafty,
 shrewd, tricky 7 cunning 8 slippery 9 conniving, designing, insidious 10 contriving,
 intriguing 11 calculating 13 Machiavellian
Schiller, (Johann) Friedrich von
 author of: 8 Ode to Joy 9 Don Carlos 11
 Maria Stuart, William Tell 17 The Bride of
 Messina 18 The Maiden of Orleans
schism 5 break, split 8 division 10 separation 14 disassociation
Schlegel family
 characters in: 10 Howard's End
 members: 5 Helen 8 Margaret, Theobald
 author: 7 Forster
schlepp 3 lug 4 cart, haul, tote 5 carry 6
 convey 9 transport
Schlesinger, Arthur M, Jr
 author of: 13 A Thousand Days 15 The
 Age of Jackson 21 The Imperial Presidency 24 Robert Kennedy and His Times
Schlesinger, John
 director of: 7 Darling 14 Midnight Cowboy (Oscar) 22 The Falcon and the
 Snowman
Schlesinger, Leon
 creator/artist of: 9 Bugs Bunny
schmaltz 4 corn 14 sentimentalism, sentimentality
**Schmeling, Max (Maxmillian Adolph Otto
 Siegfried)**
 nickname: 10 Black Uhlan
 sport: 6 boxing
 class: 11 heavyweight
Schneider, Romy
 real name: 20 Rosemarie Albach-Retty
 born: 6 Vienna 7 Austria
 roles: 8 The Trial 11 The Cardinal 16
 Boccaccio Seventy

Schoenberg, Arnold
 born: 6 Vienna 7 Austria
 composer of: 9 Erwartung 11 De Profundis, Expectation, Gurrelieder 12 The
 Lucky Hand 13 Moses and Aaron, Ode to
 Napoleon 14 Verklarte Nacht 16 Die
 Glucklich Hand, Resplendent Night 17
 Transfigured Night 19 A Survivor from
 Warsaw, Pelleas and Melisande 26 The
 Book of the Hanging Gardens
Schoenius
 father: 7 Athamas
 mother: 8 Themisto
 wife: 7 Clymene
 daughter: 8 Atalanta
scholar 4 coed, sage 5 brain, grind, pupil 6
 pundit, savant 7 egghead, learner, student,
 studier, wise man 8 bookworm, humanist,
 mandarin 9 collegian, schoolboy 10
 schoolgirl 11 matriculant 12 intellectual 13
 undergraduate
Scholar Gypsy, The
 author: 13 Matthew Arnold
scholarly 6 humane 7 erudite, learned, liberal 8 academic, educated, informed, lettered, literate, well-read 12 intellectual
scholarship 5 grant 7 stipend 8 learning 9
 education, endowment, erudition 12 intelligence, thoroughness 13 enlightenment
scholastic 8 academic, pedantic 9 pedagogic 11 educational 12 professorial 13 instructional
school 3 ism 4 view 5 bunch, crowd, faith,
 order, style, teach, train 6 belief, lyceum,
 method, system, theory 7 academy, college, educate, faction, thought 8 doctrine,
 instruct, seminary 9 institute 10 persuasion, university 12 denomination, kindergarten
schoolbook 3 abc 4 text 5 atlas 6 manual,
 primer, reader 7 grammar, lessons, speller
School for Scandal, The
 author: 23 Richard Brinsley Sheridan
 character: 5 Maria 6 Rowley 10 Lady
 Teazle 13 Joseph Surface, Lady
 Sneerwell 14 Charles Surface, Sir Peter
 Teazle 16 Sir Oliver Surface
School for Wives, The
 author: 7 Moliere
 character: 5 Agnes 6 Horace, Oronte 7
 Enrique 8 Arnolphe 9 Chrysalde
schooling 5 drill 8 drilling, training 9 education 11 instruction, preparation 14 indoctrination
schoolmaster 4 head 5 tutor 7 dominie,
 pedagog, scholar, teacher 9 pedagogue,
 principal, professor 10 headmaster, instructor 12 disciplinarian
 fish: 7 snapper
 genus: 8 Lutianus
 species: 6 apodus
Schubert, Franz Peter
 born: 6 Vienna 7 Austria
 composer of: 6 Little (symphony), Tragic
 (symphony No 4) 8 Sad Waltz 9
 Rosamunde 11 Winterreise 12 Trout
 Quintet 13 Mourning Waltz 17 Die

Schone Mullerin 18 Unfinished Symphony (No 8) 24 Death and the Maiden Quartet, Symphony of Heavenly Length

Schulz, Charles
creator/artist of: 7 Peanuts

Schuman, William
born: 9 New York NY
composer of: 8 Undertow 9 Credendum 14 The Mighty Casey 16 American Festival 18 New England Triptych

Schumann, Robert Alexander
born: 7 Germany, Zwickau
composer of: 6 Myrten, Spring (symphony No 1) 7 Rhenish (symphony No 3) 8 Arabeske, Carnival 9 Papillons 10 Novelettes 11 Blumenstuck, Butterflies, Nachtstucke, Nightpieces, Novelletten 12 Bunte Blatter, Dichterliebe, Flower Pieces, Kinderscenen, Kreisleriana, Motley Leaves 14 Fantasiestucke 16 David's Band Dances, Symphonic Studies 18 Davidsbundlertanze 19 Frauenliebe und Leben

Schwann, Theodor
field: 7 biology
nationality: 6 German
established: 10 cell theory

Schwarzenegger, Arnold
roles: 5 Twins 7 Red Heat 8 Commando, Predator, Red Sonja 11 Total Recall 13 The Terminator 15 Kindergarten Cop 17 Conan the Barbarian, Conan the Destroyer
wife: 12 Maria Shriver

Schweitzer, Albert
field: 8 medicine
worked in: 5 Gabon 6 Africa
founded: 17 Lambarene Hospital
awarded: 15 Nobel Peace Prize

Schwitters, Kurt
born: 7 Germany 8 Hannover
artwork: 7 Merzbau
collages called: 10 Merzbilden

science 3 art 5 skill 6 method 7 finesse 8 aptitude, facility 9 technique 10 discipline 11 acquirement
god of: 7 Mercury

scintilla 3 dot 4 atom, iota 5 shred, spark, speck, trace 7 glimmer 10 smithereen

scintillate 4 joke, snap 5 amuse, charm, flash, gleam, glint, shine, spark 7 glimmer, glisten, glitter, shimmer, sparkle, twinkle 9 coruscate 10 effervesce

scintillating 5 witty 6 bright, lively 8 animated, charming, dazzling 9 brilliant, ebullient, exuberant, sparkling 10 glittering 11 stimulating 12 effervescent

scion 3 son 4 heir, seed 5 child, issue 7 heiress, progeny 8 daughter, offshoot 9 offspring, posterity, successor 10 descendant 11 progeniture

Sciron
vocation: 6 robber
killed by: 7 Theseus

Scirophoria
also: 11 Skirophoria
origin: 5 Greek
event: 8 festival
honoring: 6 Athena

scissors 5 snips 6 blades, cutter, shears 7 clipper, snipper, trimmer
French: 8 secateur

scoff 4 jeer, mock, razz 5 flout, knock, taunt 6 deride, rail at, revile 7 condemn, laugh at, put down, run down 8 belittle, ridicule

Scofield, Paul
real name: 13 David Scofield
born: 7 England 14 Hurstpierpoint
roles: 8 King Lear 13 Sir Thomas More 17 A Man for All Seasons (Oscar)

scold 3 nag 5 chide, shrew 6 berate, carp at, nagger, rail at, rebuke, virago 7 censure, reprove, upbraid 9 castigate, criticize, dress down, reprehend, reprimand, termagant 10 complainer
Yiddish: 6 kvetch

scolding 7 chiding, reproof 8 berating, rebuking 9 reprimand, talking-to 10 admonition, upbraiding 11 castigation 12 admonishment 13 tongue-lashing

Scolosaurus
type: 8 dinosaur 10 ornithopod
location: 12 North America

sconce 11 candlestick 12 candleholder

scoop 4 bail, beat 5 clean, clear, gouge, ladle, spoon 6 burrow, dig out, dipper, hollow, shovel, trowel 7 dish out, lade out, lift out 8 excavate

scoop out 3 dig 5 gouge 8 excavate

scoot 3 run 4 dash, rush 6 scurry, sprint

Scooter
nickname of: 11 Phil Rizzuto

scope 3 aim 4 area, goal, rein, room, span, vent 5 field, force, grasp, range, reach 6 bounds, effect, margin, motive, spread, vision 7 bearing, compass, freedom, liberty, purpose, stretch 8 ambition, confines, latitude 9 extension, influence, intention 10 competence 11 application, destination 13 determination

scorch 3 dry 4 char, sear 5 parch, singe 6 dry out, scathe, wither 7 blacken 8 discolor 9 dehydrate

score, scores 3 cut, mar, run, tab, win 4 bill, debt, gain, gash, goal, lots, make, mark, nick, slit 5 amass, count, facts, grade, hosts, judge, notch, point, slash, tally, truth 6 basket, charge, damage, deface, droves, groove, grudge, masses, pile up, strike, swarms, twenty 7 account, achieve, arrange, legions, reality, scratch, throngs 8 evaluate, incision, register 9 grievance 10 amount owed, difference, multitudes, obligation 11 orchestrate

scoria 4 slag 5 dross 6 cinder, refuse

scorn 5 spurn 6 ignore, rebuff, refuse, reject, slight 7 condemn, despise, disdain, mockery, repulse, sarcasm 8 contempt, derision, ridicule, scoffing, spit upon 9 arrogance, contumely, disregard, ostracize

10 look down on, opprobrium 11 haughtiness

scorned 7 derided, refused 8 despised, rebuffed, rejected, repulsed 9 disdained 10 deprecated, disparaged

scornful 6 lordly 7 cynical 8 arrogant, derisive, insolent, sardonic, scoffing, sneering 9 sarcastic 10 disdainful, ridiculing 11 disparaging 12 contemptuous, supercilious

Scorpio
  symbol: 8 scorpion
  planet: 4 Mars 5 Pluto
  rules: 5 death 7 passion
  born: 7 October 8 November

Scorpion 4 whip 7 scourge
  constellation of: 8 Scorpius

Scorsese, Martin
  director of: 10 After Hours, Raging Bull, Taxi Driver 11 Mean Streets 12 The Last Waltz

scotch 4 foil, kill, stop 5 crush, quash 6 thwart 7 destroy 8 confound, obstruct, sabotage, suppress 9 undermine 11 nip in the bud

scotch
  type: 6 whisky 7 whiskey
  origin: 8 Scotland
  ingredient: 12 cereal grains
  drink: 10 Scotch Mist 14 Highland Cooler
  with amaretto: 9 Godfather
  with cherry brandy: 12 Blood and Sand
  with Drambuie: 9 Rusty Nail
  with gin: 12 Barbary Coast
  with vermouth: 6 Rob Roy 8 Affinity 10 Bobby Burns

Scotia
  epithet of: 9 Aphrodite
  means: 7 dark one

Scotland
  Roman name: 9 Caledonia
  capital: 9 Edinburgh
  largest city: 7 Glasgow
  others: 3 Ayr 4 Duns, Oban 5 Alloa, Banff, Brora, Burgh, Cupar, Ellon, Leith, Perth, Salen, Troon 6 Dundee, Girvan, Hawick 7 Airdrie, Alloway, Dunkeld, Falkirk, Frunock, Mallaig, Paisley, Renfrew 8 Aberdeen, Dumfries, Greenock, Hamilton, Kirkwall, Rothesay, Stirling 9 Clydebank, Dumbarton, Greenlock, Inverness, Kirkcaldy, Peter head, St Andrews 10 Coatbridge, Kilmarnock, Motherwell 11 Dunfermline, Grangemouth
  school: 7 Glasgow 8 Aberdeen 9 Edinburgh 12 Saint Andrew's
  division: 3 Ayr 4 Bute, Fife, Ross 5 Angus, Banff, Moray, Nairn, Perth 6 Argyll, Lanark, Orkney 7 Berwick, Kinross, Lothian, Peebles, Renfrew, Selkirk, Wigtown 8 Aberdeen, Ayrshire, Cromarty, Dumfries, Roxburgh, Shetland, Stirling 9 Buteshire, Caithness, Dumbarton 10 Kincardine, Midlothian, Sutherland 11 Clackmannan, Kincudbight 12 Renfrewshire 13 Stirlingshire

kingdom: 8 Dalriada 11 Northumbria, Strathclyde
government: 13 United Kingdom
measure: 3 cop 4 boll, cran, fall, mile, peck, pint, rood, rope, span 5 crane, lippy 6 audlet, davach, firlot, lippie, noggin 7 chalder, choppin 8 mutchkin, stimpart, stimpert 9 particate, shaftment, shathmont
monetary unit: 3 ecu 4 demy, doit, lion, mark, rial, ryal 5 bodle, broad, groat, plack, rider, turne 6 bawbee, folles 7 unicorn 8 atchison, hardhead 9 halfpenny 11 bonnetpiece
weight: 4 boll, drop 5 trone 6 bushel
island: 3 Rum 4 Aran, Bute, Eigg, Fair, Inch, Iona, Jura, Lona, Muck, Mull, Rhum, Skye 5 Arran, Barra, Islay, Lewis 6 Harris, Orkney, Staffa 7 St Kilda 8 Berneray, Cumbraes, Hebrides, Shetland 9 North Uist, South Uist
lake/loch: 3 Awe, Dee, Lin, Tay 4 Earn, Fyne, Gair, Gare, Linn, Ness, Oich, Ryan, Sloy 5 Duich, Leven, Lochy, Lough, Morar, Maree, Nevis 6 Laggan, Linnhe, Lomond 7 Katrine, Rannoch, St Mary's
mountain: 4 Hope 5 Attow, Dearg, Nevis, Tinto, Wyvis 7 Cheviot, Macdhui, Merrick 8 Grampian 9 Ben Lomond, Cairngorm, Highlands, Trossachs
hills: 5 Ochil 6 Calton, Sidlaw 7 Cheviot
highest point: 8 Ben Nevis
river: 3 Ayr, Dee, Don, Esk, Tay 4 Doon, Glen, Nith, Norn, Spey 5 Afton, Annan, Clyde, Forth, Garry, North, Tweed, Ythan 6 Affric, Teviot, Tummel 7 Deveron 8 Findhorn
sea: 5 Irish, North 8 Atlantic, Hebrides
physical feature:
bay: 5 Scapa
canal: 10 Caledonian
channel: 5 Minch, North
firth: 3 Tay 4 Kyle, Lorn 5 Clyde, Forth, Lorne, Moray 6 Linnhe, Solway 7 Comarty, Dornoch 8 Pentland
glen: 8 Glen More 9 Great Glen
moor: 7 Rannoch
valley: 8 Trossach
people: 4 Gael, Pict, Scot 5 Norse
artist: 7 Raeburn
author: 5 Burns, Scott 6 Dunbar 7 Barbour, Douglas 8 Henryson 9 Stevenson 10 Conan-Doyle, MacDiarmid, Macpherson
economist: 5 Smith
historian: 7 Carlyle
inventor: 4 Bell
king: 5 David, James 6 Duncan 7 Kenneth, Macbeth, Malcolm, Stuarts, William 9 Alexander 14 Robert the Bruce
philosopher: 4 Hume
prime minister: 9 Macdonald, MacMillan 11 Douglas-Home
prince: 19 Bonnie Prince Charlie
queen: 4 Mary 13 Saint Margaret
religious leader: 8 John Knox
scientist: 7 Fleming

language: 4 Erse 6 Celtic, Gaelic, Keltic, Lallan 7 English, Lalland

religion: 12 Episcopalian, Presbyterian 13 Roman Catholic

place:

abbey: 5 Kelso 7 Melrose 8 Dryburgh, Jedburgh

castle: 8 Stirling 9 Edinburgh 11 Eilean Donan

church/kirk: 7 St Giles 11 St Cuthbert's

royal residence: 8 Balmoral

Scott's home: 10 Abbotsford

street: 7 Prince's 9 Royal Mile 11 Sauchiehall

feature:

bird: 3 bae, cae 4 hern, muir, smeu 6 grouse, smeuth, snabby 7 jackdaw 8 throstle 9 swinepipe

clothing: 4 kilt 6 tartan 12 Harris tweeds 13 Shetland knits 15 Fair Isle sweater

dance: 3 bob 4 reel 7 walloch 9 ecossaise 10 petronella 11 strathsprey 12 gilliecallum 13 Highland fling

game: 4 golf

monster: 6 Nessie 8 Loch Ness

musical instrument: 7 bagpipe

symbol: 7 thistle

food:

bread: 5 scone

cheese: 7 crowdie

dish: 6 haggis 12 finnan haddie 15 kippered herring

drink: 12 Scotch whisky

soup: 11 cock-a-leekie

Scott, George C

born: 6 Wise VA

wife: 14 Trish Van Devere 15 Colleen Dewhurst

roles: 4 Rage 6 Patton (Oscar, refused) 8 Jane Eyre 16 The New Centurions 18 The Day of the Dolphin

Scott, Sir Walter

author of: 6 Rob Roy 7 Ivanhoe, Marmion 8 The Abbot, Waverley 10 Kenilworth 11 The Talisman 12 Guy Mannering, Old Mortality, The Antiquary 14 Quentin Durward 16 The Lady of the Lake 20 The Bride of Lammermoor, The Heart of Midlothian 23 The Lay of the Last Minstrel

Scottish Mythology

spirit/horse: 6 kelpie

scoundrel 3 cad, cur 5 crook, knave, rogue, scamp, thief 6 rascal, rotter, varlet, weasel 7 bounder, ruffian, sharper, varmint, villain 8 scalawag, swindler, turncoat 9 miscreant, trickster 10 blackguard, copperhead, mountebank, ne'er-do-well 11 fourflusher, rapscallion 12 carpetbagger

scoundrelly 3 low 4 mean 7 debased 8 rascally 10 degenerate, despicable, villainous 12 contemptible, disreputable 13 reprehensible

Scoundrel Time

author: 14 Lillian Hellman

scour 4 buff, comb, rake, scan 5 scrub, shine 6 abrade, polish, scrape 7 burnish, cleanse, ransack, rummage 8 brighten, traverse

scourge, Scourge 3 rod 4 bane, beat, cane, flog, lash, whip 5 birch, blast, curse, flail, strap 6 punish, switch, terror, thrash 7 censure, chasten 8 chastise, scorpion, vexation 9 castigate, excoriate 10 affliction, discipline, flagellate 11 troublement 13 cat-o'-nine-tails

scout 3 spy 4 case 5 guide, pilot 6 escort, spy out, survey 7 lookout, observe 8 outrider, point man, vanguard 9 recruiter 11 reconnoiter 13 reconnoiterer

scowl 4 pout 5 frown, glare, lower 6 glower 7 grimace

scrabble 3 paw 4 claw, rake 5 climb 6 drudge, jostle, scrape, scrawl 7 clamber, grapple, scratch 8 struggle

scram 3 out 4 scat, shoo 5 be off, leave 6 beat it, begone, depart, get out, go away 7 get lost, vamoose 10 make tracks

scramble 3 run, vie 4 race, rush 5 clash, fight, mix up, scrap, upset 6 battle, combat, engage, garble, jostle, jumble, mess up, scurry, strive, tussle 7 collide, confuse, disturb, scatter, scuffle, shuffle 8 disorder, struggle, unsettle 9 scrimmage 10 disarrange, free-for-all 11 competition, disorganize

scramble up 5 climb, mount, scale 7 clamber

scrap 3 bit, dab, jot, row 4 atom, drop, iota, junk, spat 5 brawl, crumb, fight, grain, melee, speck, trace, trash 6 fracas, morsel, refuse, ruckus, sliver 7 abandon, glimmer, minimum, modicum, quarrel, snippet 8 brouhaha, fraction, fragment, jettison, molecule, particle, squabble 10 free-for-all, smattering, sprinkling

scrapbook 5 album 9 portfolio 11 memorabilia, miscellanea

scrape 3 dig 4 buff, gash, mark, rasp, save, skin 5 amass, clean, fight, glean, gouge, grate, graze, grind, plane, run-in, score, scour, scuff, stint 6 abrade, bruise, forage, gather, groove, obtain, pick up, plight, scrimp, secure, smooth, tussle 7 acquire, burnish, dilemma, procure, rub hard, scratch, scuffle, straits 8 abrasion 9 economize, tight spot 10 difficulty 11 predicament 13 confrontation

scratch 3 cut, mar, rub 4 claw, etch, gash, nick, omit, rasp 5 dig at, erase, grate, graze, grind, score 6 cancel, delete, incise, remove, rub out, scrape, scrawl, streak, strike 7 blemish, blot out, exclude, expunge, rule out 8 abrasion, cross out, lacerate, scribble, withdraw 9 eliminate 10 laceration

scratchy 5 rough 6 coarse 7 bristly, prickly 9 irritated 10 irritating

scrawl 4 draw 5 write 6 doodle 7 scratch, writing 8 scrabble, scribble, squiggle 10 penmanship 11 handwriting

scrawniness 8 lankness, leanness, slimness, thinness 10 skinniness, slightness 11 slenderness

scrawny 4 bony, lank, lean, puny 5 drawn, gaunt, lanky, runty, spare 6 sinewy, skinny, wasted 7 angular, scraggy, spindly, stunted 8 rawboned, skeletal 9 emaciated, fleshless 10 attenuated, undersized 11 underweight

screak 4 rasp 5 grate, grind 6 shriek, squeak 7 screech

scream 4 howl, loud, roar, wail, yell, yelp, yowl 5 shout, whine 6 bellow, cry out, holler, outcry, shriek, squawk, squeal 7 screech 11 lamentation

screech 3 cry 4 howl, rasp 6 screak, scream, shriek 9 caterwaul

screen 3 see, web 4 cull, mask, mesh, rate, show, sift, sort, veil, view 5 class, cloak, cover, eject, films, grade, grate, group, guard, order, shade, sieve 6 buffer, cinema, defend, filter, mantle, movies, secure, shield, shroud, sifter, size up, strain, winnow 7 arrange, conceal, curtain, defense, discard, lattice, present, preview, project, protect, secrete, shelter, shutter, weed out 8 colander, coverage, evaluate, jalousie, separate, strainer, withhold 9 eliminate, partition, safeguard 10 protection 11 concealment

screw 4 bolt, join, knot, turn, warp 5 clamp, exact, force, gnarl, rivet, twist, wrest, wring 6 adjust, attach, deform, driver, extort, fasten, garble, wrench 7 contort, distort, pervert, squeeze, tighten 8 fastener, misshape 9 propeller

screwball 3 nut 4 kook 5 flake, freak 6 looney 7 lunatic 8 crackpot 9 character, eccentric

screwdriver
type: 6 rachet 11 spiral-drive 12 Phillips-head

screwy 3 odd 4 daft 5 batty, dotty, flaky, funny, kinky, kooky, nutty, queer, wacky, weird 6 weirdo 7 oddball 8 peculiar 9 eccentric 10 unbalanced

Scriabin, Aleksandr (Scriabine, Skryabin)
born: 6 Moscow, Russia
composer of: 7 Mystery 10 Prometheus 12 Vers la flamme 13 Poem of Ecstasy, The Divine Poem, The Poem of Fire

scribble 4 tear 5 squib 6 doodle, scrawl 7 scratch 8 squiggle 9 pull apart
fiber: 4 wool
procedure: 7 carding

scribe, Scribe 3 cut 4 mark, tool 5 clerk, score 6 author, copier, penman, writer 7 copyist, teacher 8 recorder 9 archivist, scrivener, secretary 10 amanuensis, translator 12 newspaperman, stenographer 13 calligraphist
Biblical: 4 Ezra 6 Esdras
French dramatist: 8 Augustin
Palestinian: 5 sofer 6 sopher

scribe of gods 5 Thoth

scrimp 4 save 5 hoard, pinch, skimp, stint 8 begrudge 9 besparing 12 pinch pennies

scrimping 6 frugal 7 sparing 10 economical 11 economizing 12 cheeseparing 15 pinching pennies

scrip 5 paper 8 document 11 certificate

scripsit 7 he wrote 8 she wrote

script 4 book, hand 5 lines, score 6 dialog 7 cursive 8 dialogue, libretto, longhand, scenario 10 manuscript, penmanship 11 calligraphy, chirography, handwriting

Scriptures, the 5 Bible 6 the Law, oracle 8 holy writ, the Bible, the Torah 10 the Gospels 11 The Good Book 12 New Testament, Old Testament, the Word of God 13 the Pentateuch, the Septuagint 14 sacred writings

scroll of the Torah
Hebrew: 11 Sepher Torah

Scrooge, Ebenezer
character in: 15 A Christmas Carol
author: 7 Dickens

scrub 4 swab 5 brush, scour 8 scouring 9 brushwood, scrubbing

scrubby 4 base 6 brushy 7 stunted 8 inferior 10 undersized

scrumptious 5 juicy, tasty 6 savory, tender 8 luscious, pleasant, pleasing 9 agreeable, delicious, enjoyable, flavorful, succulent, toothsome 10 appetizing, delectable, delightful, flavorsome 13 mouth-watering

scruple 3 shy 4 balk, care, halt 5 demur, pause, qualm, waver 6 blench, ethics, falter 7 anxiety, concern, refrain 8 hesitate 9 fluctuate, misgiving, principle 10 conscience, hesitation 11 compunction, fearfulness, uncertainty 12 apprehension, doubtfulness, protestation 13 squeamishness 17 conscientiousness

Scruples
author: 12 Judith Krantz

scrupulous 5 exact 6 honest 7 careful, dutiful, precise, upright 8 cautious, exacting, sedulous 9 honorable 10 deliberate, fastidious, meticulous, principled 11 painstaking, punctilious 13 conscientious

scrupulousness 4 care 5 pains 9 exactness 14 meticulousness 17 conscientiousness

scrutinize 4 scan 5 probe, study 6 peruse, search, survey 7 explore, inspect, observe 11 investigate

scrutiny 5 study, watch 7 inquiry, perusal 9 attention 10 inspection 11 examination 12 surveillance 13 investigation

scuffle 3 row 4 spar 5 brawl, clash, fight, melee, scrap 6 fracas, jostle, rumpus, tussle 8 squabble, struggle 9 commotion, imbroglio 10 donnybrook, free-for-all

sculpsit 10 he carved it 11 she carved it 12 he engraved it 13 she engraved it 14 he sculptured it 15 she sculptured it

sculptor 6 artist, carver, caster, imager, molder 7 marbler, modeler 8 chiseler, engraver
constellation: 19 Apparatus Sculptoris

French: 5 Rodin
Greek: 7 Phidias 10 Praxiteles
Irish-American: 12 Saint-Gaudens
Italian: 7 Cellini 12 Michelangelo
tool: 6 chisel, graver 7 spatula 9 ebau-
choir
sculpture 3 cut 4 bust, cast, head, work 5
cameo, carve, erode, model, mould 6
chisel, relief, statue 7 carving, erosion, fai-
ence 8 intaglio, statuary 9 cloissone, medallion, statuette
   medium: 4 clay 5 china, stone 6 bronze,
enamel, marble 7 ceramic 9 porcelain 10
terra cotta 11 earthenware
scum 4 film, slag 5 crust, dregs, dross,
trash 6 rabble, refuse 7 deposit, rubbish,
surface 8 riffraff
scurrility 5 abuse 8 rudeness 9 indecency,
obscenity, profanity 13 offensiveness,
salaciousness
scurrilous 3 low 5 gross 6 coarse, vulgar 7
obscene 8 churlish, derisive, indecent,
reviling 9 insulting, offensive, shameless
10 derogatory, detracting, indelicate, slanderous 11 disparaging, foulmouthed 12
contemptuous
scurry 3 hie 4 race, rush, skim 5 haste,
hurry, scoot, speed 6 bustle, hasten, hustle, spring 7 rushing, scamper, scuttle 8
hurrying, scooting, scramble 9 confusion,
dispersal 10 scattering
scurvy 3 low 4 base, mean, vile 6 shabby
7 ignoble 9 worthless 10 despicable 12
contemptible, dishonorable
scuttle 4 sink 5 abort, hurry, scrap, speed,
wreck 6 hasten, scurry 7 destroy, discard,
scamper 8 dispatch, scramble
scuttlebutt 4 talk 5 rumor 6 gossip 7 hearsay, prattle, scandal 8 chitchat
Scylaceus
   origin: 6 Lycian
   ally of: 7 Trojans
   death by: 7 stoning
Scylla
   form: 5 nymph 7 monster
   location: 3 sea 16 Straits of Messina 20
Whirlpool of Charybdis
   father: 7 Phorcys
   mother: 6 Hecate
   loved by: 8 Poseidon
   rival: 10 Amphitrite
Scyphius
   first: 5 horse
   created by: 8 Poseidon
sea 3 bay, ton 4 deep, gulf, host, lake, leap,
lots, main, mass, slew, wave 5 bight, flock,
flood, ocean, scads, spate, surge, swarm,
swell, waves 6 legion, roller, scores,
waters 7 breaker 9 abundance, multitude,
profusion
   French: 3 mer
   god of: 5 Aegir, Memir 6 Nereus, Triton 7
Glaucus, Neptune, Phorcys, Proteus 8
Poseidon 9 Asphalius
   goddess of: 3 Ino, Ran 6 Graeae,
Graiae, Matuta 8 Dictynna, Menannan 9
Leucothea 10 Amphitrite

Sea, the Sea, The
   author: 11 Iris Murdoch
Sea Around Us, The
   author: 13 Rachel L Carson
seaboard 5 coast 9 shoreline
Seaborg, Glen Theodore
   field: 7 physics
   worked with: 14 actinide series 19 trans-
uranic elements
   headed: 3 AEC 22 Atomic Energy Commission
   awarded: 10 Nobel Prize
seacoast 5 beach, coast, shore 7 seaside
8 littoral 9 coastland, coastline, shoreline,
waterside
   French: 4 cote
   Italian: 4 lido 7 riviera
seafarers 5 salts 7 sailors, seadogs 8 mariners
Seagull, The
   author: 12 Anton Chekhov
   character: 5 Masha 6 Polina 10 Pyotr
Sorin 11 Yevgeny Dom 12 Ilya Shamraev,
Irina Arkadin 13 Boris Trigorin, Nina
Zaretchyn 16 Semyon Medvedenko 17
Konstantin Treplev
Seah 15 Biblical measure
Sea Hawk, The
   director: 13 Michael Curtiz
   cast: 10 Errol Flynn 11 Claude Rains,
Donald Crisp 14 Brenda Marshall
   score: 21 Erich Wolfgang Korngold
seal 2 OK 3 dam, fix 4 cork, lock, mark,
plug, shut, stop 5 brand, close, stamp 6
accept, affirm, emblem, fasten, figure,
ratify, secure, settle, shut up, signet, stop
up, symbol, verify 7 approve, certify, confirm, endorse, imprint 8 colophon,
conclude, fastener, hallmark, insignia,
sanction, validate 9 determine, establish,
trademark 10 impression 12 authenticate
   Latin: 10 imprimatur
seal
   young: 3 pup
   group of: 3 pod
sea lion
   young: 3 pup
seam 3 gap 4 line, lode, mark, scar, vein 5
break, chink, cleft, crack, joint, layer, notch
6 breach, furrow, incise, suture 7 crevice,
fissure, joining, opening, rupture, stratum,
wrinkle 8 junction, juncture 9 interface
seaman 3 gob, tar 4 hand, mate, salt 5 bo-
sun, middy 6 lubber, merman, sailor, sea
dog 7 mariner 9 boatswain 10 bluejacket,
midshipman
seamark 5 light 6 beacon, pharos, signal
10 lighthouse, watchtower
sea monster 6 dragon 9 Leviathan
seamstress 10 dressmaker
   French: 9 midinette 10 couturiere
seamy 3 raw 4 dark 5 dirty, nasty, rough 6
coarse, sordid 7 squalid, unclean 10 unpleasant 11 unwholesome 12 disagreeable
Sea of Grass, The
   author: 13 Conrad Richter

sear 4 burn, char, scar 5 blast, singe, steel 6 harden, scorch 7 blister 9 cauterize 10 caseharden

search 4 comb, drag, fish, hunt, look, seek, sift 5 check, frisk, probe, quest, rifle, scour, snoop, study 6 survey, tracer 7 dragnet, examine, explore, inquiry, inspect, pry into, pursuit, ransack, rummage 8 overhaul, scrutiny 10 inspection, scrutinize 11 examination, exploration 13 investigation

Search, The
  director: 13 Fred Zinnemann
  cast: 9 Ivan Jandl 13 Aline MacMahon 14 Jarmila Novotna 15 Montgomery Clift
  setting: 6 Berlin

Searchers, The
  director: 8 John Ford
  cast: 8 Ward Bond 9 John Wayne, Vera Miles 11 Natalie Wood 13 Jeffrey Hunter

searching 4 dour, keen, nosy 5 sharp 6 prying, shrewd, snoopy 7 curious, groping 8 exacting, piercing, rigorous, thorough 9 observant, quizzical, unsparing 11 inquisitive, penetrating 13 investigative

Seascape
  author: 11 Edward Albee

seashore 5 beach, coast

seasick 3 ill 5 barfy, dizzy, faint, giddy, woozy 6 queasy 8 qualmish, vomitous 9 nauseated, squeamish 11 vertiginous

seasickness
  French: 8 mal de mer

seaside 5 beach, coast, shore 9 shoreline

season 3 age, dry 4 fall, lace, tame, term 5 adapt, color, drill, inure, prime, ripen, shape, spell, spice, stage, train 6 accent, autumn, finish, flavor, inform, leaven, mature, mellow, period, refine, soften, spring, summer, temper, winter 7 enhance, enliven, prepare, quarter, stretch 8 accustom, duration, heighten, interval, ornament, practice 9 condition, cultivate, embellish 10 discipline

seasoned 6 herbed, inured, salted, spiced 7 veteran 8 flavored, hardened, peppered 9 competent, qualified 10 acclimated, accustomed, habituated 11 experienced 12 familiarized

seasoning 4 dill, herb, mace, sage, salt, zest 5 aging, basil, clove, gusto, onion, spice, thyme 6 drying, garlic, ginger, nutmeg, pepper, relish 7 oregano, paprika, parsley 8 allspice, cinnamon, marjoram, practice, ripening, rosemary, training 9 condiment, flavoring 10 maturation 11 orientation, preparation 15 familiarization

Season in Hell, A
  author: 13 Arthur Rimbaud

seasons
  god of: 9 Vertumnus
  goddess of: 4 Hour 5 Horae

seat 3 box, hub 4 axis, core, home, rump, site, sofa 5 abode, bench, chair, couch, croup, divan, fanny, heart, house, locus, place 6 behind, bottom, center, locale, settle 7 address, capital, cushion, habitat, housing, nucleus, rear end, situate 8 backside, buttocks, derriere, domicile, dwelling, haunches, location, quarters 9 posterior, residence 10 incumbency, membership 12 hindquarters

seat of justice 5 bench, court 8 tribunal 9 judiciary 10 courthouse

Seattle
  baseball team: 8 Mariners
  basketball team: 11 Supersonics
  bay: 7 Elliott
  football team: 8 Seahawks
  lake: 10 Washington
  landmark: 11 Space Needle
  site of: 10 World's Fair
  sound: 5 Puget

Sea Wolf, The
  author: 10 Jack London

Sebastian
  character in: 12 Twelfth Night
  author: 11 Shakespeare

Seberg, Jean
  born: 14 Marshalltown IA
  husband: 10 Romain Gary
  roles: 6 Lilith 7 Airport 9 Saint Joan 10 Breathless 16 Bonjour Tristesse

Secchi, Angelo
  field: 9 astronomy
  nationality: 7 Italian
  classified: 5 stars

secede 4 quit 5 leave 6 resign, retire 7 forsake 8 withdraw 12 disaffiliate

secession 10 separation, withdrawal 14 disaffiliation

seclude 4 hide 6 retire 7 isolate 8 separate 9 sequester 10 dissociate

secluded 6 covert, cut off, lonely, remote, shut in 7 private 8 closeted, confined, isolated, shut away, solitary 9 reclusive, sheltered, unvisited, withdrawn 10 cloistered 11 out-of-the-way, sequestered 12 unfrequented

seclusion 5 exile 6 asylum, hiding 7 retreat 8 cloister, hideaway, solitude 9 hermitage, isolation, reclusion, sanctuary 10 quarantine, retirement, withdrawal 11 concealment 13 sequestration

second 3 aid 4 abet, back, help, wink 5 agent, favor, flash, jiffy, other, proxy, trice 6 assist, back up, deputy, fill-in, helper, minute, moment, uphold 7 advance, another, endorse, further, instant, one more, outdone, promote, stand by, stand-in, support 8 advocate, delegate, exceeded, inferior 9 alternate, assistant, attendant, encourage, surpassed, twinkling 10 additional, lieutenant, substitute, understudy 11 alternating, subordinate 14 representative
  abbreviation: 1 s 3 sec

secondary 5 lower, minor, other 6 backup, lesser 7 smaller 8 inferior, mediocre, middling 9 alternate, ancillary, auxiliary, following, resultant 10 consequent, subsequent, subsidiary 11 subordinate

second childhood 6 dotage 8 senility

secondhand 4 used 8 indirect 10 derivative

second-in-command 6 deputy 8 adjutant 9 assistant 10 lieutenant 13 vice president

second-rate 3 bad 4 poor, so-so 5 cheap, tacky 6 shabby 7 average 8 everyday, inferior, mediocre, middling 9 imperfect 10 inadequate, outclassed, pedestrian 11 commonplace, substandard 15 undistinguished

Second Sex, The
  author: 16 Simone de Beauvoir
second-story man 5 thief 6 robber 7 burglar 9 cracksman 10 cat burglar
second string 4 subs 5 bench 11 substitutes
second team 5 bench 11 substitutes
secrecy 6 hiding 7 mystery, privacy, private, silence, stealth 8 muteness, solitude 9 closeness, seclusion 10 covertness 11 concealment, furtiveness 13 sequestration 15 clandestineness, confidentiality, underhandedness 17 surreptitiousness 19 uncommunicativeness
secret 3 key, mum 4 dark 6 arcane, covert, enigma, hidden, mystic, occult, puzzle, recipe, unseen 7 formula, furtive, mystery, private, unknown 8 discreet, esoteric, hush-hush, secluded, stealthy 9 concealed, disguised, invisible, secretive 10 confidence, mysterious, undercover, unrevealed 11 camouflaged, clandestine, undisclosed, unpublished 12 confidential, unrevealable 13 surreptitious

Secret Agent
  character: 9 John Drake
  cast: 15 Patrick McGoohan
  theme: 14 Secret Agent Man
secretary 4 aide, desk 5 clerk 6 scribe 7 officer 8 recorder 10 amanuensis 12 stenographer
  French: 10 escritoire
secret council 8 conclave
secrete 4 hide, veil 5 cache, cloak, cover, stash 6 screen, shroud 7 conceal, curtain 8 disguise
secretive 3 mum, sly 4 mute 6 covert, silent 7 cryptic, evasive, furtive, laconic, private 8 discreet, reserved, reticent, stealthy, taciturn 9 enigmatic, withdrawn 10 mysterious 11 tight-lipped, underhanded, unrevealing 13 surreptitious 15 uncommunicative
secretiveness 7 mystery, stealth 9 reticence 11 furtiveness 14 inscrutability, mysteriousness 19 uncommunicativeness

Secret Life of Walter Mitty, The
  author: 12 James Thurber
sect 4 camp, cult 7 faction 8 division 10 persuasion 11 affiliation 12 denomination
sectarian 6 narrow 7 limited 8 clannish 9 exclusive, parochial 10 provincial, restricted
section 4 area, part, side, unit, ward, zone 5 piece, range, share, slice 6 region, sample, sphere 7 chapter, cutting, measure, passage, portion, segment, terrain 8 district, division, province, specimen, vicinity 9 allotment, increment, territory 10 department, proportion 11 installment 12 neighborhood

sector 4 area, zone 7 theater 8 district
secular 3 lay 4 laic 6 carnal 7 earthly, fleshly, mundane, profane, sensual, worldly 8 material, temporal 9 nonsacred 11 nonclerical 12 nonreligious, nonspiritual 17 nonecclesiastical
secundum 11 according to
secure 3 get, set 4 bind, easy, safe, sure 5 fixed, tight 6 at ease, defend, ensure, fasten, immune, insure, obtain 7 acquire, assured, certain, protect, shelter, tie down 8 absolute, carefree, composed, defended, definite, in the bag, positive, surefire 9 confident, guarantee, protected, reassured, safeguard, sheltered 10 guaranteed 11 impregnable 12 invulnerable, unassailable, unattackable, unthreatened
securities 5 bonds, title 6 stocks 12 certificates
security 4 bond, care, hope, keep 5 faith, trust 6 guards, pledge, police, safety, surety, troops 7 defense, deposit, promise, support 8 reliance, sureness, warranty 9 assurance, certainty, guarantee 10 collateral, confidence, conviction, protection, safeguards 11 maintenance, safekeeping 12 absoluteness, decisiveness, definiteness, positiveness, preservation
sedate 4 calm, cool 5 grave, quiet, sober, staid, still 6 poised, serene, solemn, steady 7 serious, subdued 8 composed, decorous, reserved 9 collected, dignified, impassive, unexcited, unruffled 10 coolheaded 11 levelheaded 13 imperturbable 15 undemonstrative
sedateness 7 decorum, dignity, gravity, reserve 8 calmness 9 composure, soberness, solemnity 11 impassivity, seriousness
sedative 6 easing, opiate 7 anodyne, calming 8 allaying, lenitive, narcotic, relaxing, soothing 9 analgesic, assuasive, calmative, composing, mitigator, soporific 10 comforting, palliative 11 alleviative 12 tranquilizer 13 tranquilizing
sedentary 5 fixed, inert, still 6 seated 7 resting, sitting 8 inactive, unmoving 9 quiescent 10 stationary, unstirring
sedge 4 reed 5 grass 10 marsh grass
sediment 4 lees, scum, slag 5 dregs, dross, waste 6 debris, sludge 7 grounds, remains, residue 8 leavings 9 settlings
sedition 6 mutiny, revolt 7 treason 8 defiance, uprising 9 rebellion 10 disloyalty, insurgency, subversion, unruliness 11 lawlessness 12 disobedience, insurrection 14 rebelliousness, subversiveness

Sedley, Amelia and Joseph
  characters in: 10 Vanity Fair
  author: 9 Thackeray
seduce 4 lure, ruin 5 abuse, charm, tempt 6 allure, defile, entice, ravish 7 attract, conquer, corrupt, debauch, deprave, pervert, violate, win over 8 deflower, disgrace, dishonor, persuade 9 captivate

seducer 3 cad 4 wolf 5 letch, Romeo 7 defiler, Don Juan, playboy 8 Casanova, Lothario, lover-boy, ravisher, violater 9 corrupter, debaucher, ravisher, violater 9 corrupter, debaucher, womanizer 10 deflowerer 11 philanderer 12 heartbreaker

French: 4 roue

seductive 4 sexy 8 alluring, charming, enticing, tempting 9 beguiling, disarming 10 attractive, bewitching, come-hither, enchanting, voluptuous 11 captivating, provocative

seductress 4 vamp 5 siren 7 charmer, Jezebel, Lorelei, mantrap 9 temptress 11 adventuress, enchantress

French: 7 cocotte 11 femme fatale

sedulous 6 dogged 8 diligent, thorough 9 assiduous, steadfast 10 determined, persistent 11 industrious, painstaking, persevering 13 conscientious, indefatigable

sedulousness 4 zeal 8 industry, tenacity 9 assiduity, diligence 11 persistence 12 perseverance

see 3 dig, eye, spy, woo 4 date, espy, know, meet, mind, spot, view 5 court, grasp, sight, visit, watch 6 attend, behold, descry, escort, fathom, notice, regard, survey 7 consult, discern, glimpse, observe, picture, realize, receive, undergo, witness 8 conceive, consider, discover, envision, meditate, perceive, register, ruminate 9 accompany, apprehend, ascertain, determine, encounter, entertain, interview, recognize, visualize 10 appreciate, comprehend, experience, understand 11 contemplate, distinguish

Latin: 4 vide

see above

Latin: 9 vide supra

see after

Latin: 8 vide post

see as above, see as stated above

Latin: 11 vide ut supra

see before

Latin: 8 vide ante

see below

Latin: 9 vide infra

seed 3 pit, sow 4 germ 5 basis, grain, heirs, issue, ovule, plant, stone 6 embryo, origin, source 7 progeny 8 children 9 beginning, offspring, posterity 11 descendants

seedy 4 worn 5 dingy, faded, lousy, mangy, ratty, spent, tacky 6 scuffy, shabby 7 haggard, sickish, squalid 8 slovenly 10 threadbare 11 debilitated

see eye to eye 5 agree 6 concur 11 be of one mind

see fit 5 deign 6 choose, please

see further

Latin: 8 vide post

seek 3 try 4 hunt 5 court, essay, trace 6 demand, invite, pursue 7 attempt, examine, explore, inspect, request, solicit, venture 8 endeavor 9 undertake 11 scrutinize 11 investigate

seek out 4 find 6 pursue 7 embrace, look for, solicit

seek proof 4 test 6 try out 7 analyze, examine 8 research 10 experiment 11 investigate

seem 4 look 6 appear

seeming 7 evident, obvious, surface 8 apparent, presumed, putative, supposed 10 ostensible 11 superficial

seemly 3 due 5 right 6 decent, polite, proper 7 correct, fitting, prudent, refined 8 becoming, decorous, suitable, tasteful, well-bred 9 befitting, courteous 10 acceptable, felicitous 11 appropriate 12 conventional

French: 11 comme il faut

seep 4 drip, leak, ooze, soak 7 diffuse, dribble, suffuse, trickle 8 permeate 9 penetrate

seepage 4 ooze 5 flour, issue 7 leakage, outflow 9 discharge, dribbling, secretion, trickling

seer 4 sage 5 augur 6 medium, oracle 7 diviner, prophet, psychic 8 conjurer, sorcerer 9 sorceress, stargazer 10 astrologer, soothsayer 11 clairvoyant, necromancer 13 fortuneteller 14 prognosticator

seesaw 5 waver 6 teeter 9 alternate, fluctuate, up-and-down, vacillate 12 teeter-totter

seethe 4 boil, brew, cook, fume, rage, rant, rave, roil, stew 5 churn, storm 6 blow up, bubble, simmer 7 bluster, smolder

seething 3 mad 7 boiling 8 agitated, bubbling, frenzied 10 distraught

see through 3 get 6 detect, effect, finish 7 achieve, execute, perform 8 carry out, complete, conclude 9 catch onto, figure out, penetrate 10 comprehend, understand

Segal, Erich

author of: 9 Love Story 12 Oliver's Story 16 Man Woman and Child

Segal, George

born: 9 New York NY

roles: 11 Blume in Love, Where's Poppa? 13 A Touch of Class 18 Fun with Dick and Jane 25 Who's Afraid of Virginia Woolf?

segment 3 leg 4 part 5 cut up, piece, stage 6 cleave 7 disjoin, portion, section, split up 8 disunite, division, separate 9 increment 11 installment

segmented 5 cut up 7 split up 9 sectioned, separated

segregate 6 cut off, detach, divide 7 divorce, isolate, seclude, sort out 8 disunite, insulate, separate 9 sequester 10 disconnect, quarantine

segue

music: 21 continue without a break

seine 3 net 4 drag, fish 5 trawl 7 dragnet

seism 5 quake, shock 6 tremor 8 temblor, upheaval 10 earthquake

seize 3 bag, nab 4 grab, read 5 catch, glean, grasp, pinch, pluck, usurp 6 arrest, clutch, collar, gather, snatch 7 capture, embrace, impound, possess, utilize 8 arrogate 9 apprehend, overpower, overwhelm 10 commandeer, comprehend, confiscate, understand 11 appropriate

seize the day
   Latin: 9 carpe diem
seizure 3 fit 5 onset, spell, throe 6 access, arrest, attack, crisis, stroke, taking 7 capture, episode 8 grasping, paroxysm 9 abduction, snatching 10 convulsion, kidnapping, possession, usurpation, visitation 11 impressment 12 apprehension, confiscation 13 appropriation, commandeering
Sejanus
   author: 9 Ben Jonson
Sekhmet
   origin: 8 Egyptian
   goddess of: 4 evil
Selden, Mr
   character in: 15 The House of Mirth
   author: 7 Wharton
seldom 6 rarely 8 scarcely 10 uncommonly 12 infrequently, occasionally, sporadically
select 3 tap 4 A-one, pick, posh 5 elect, elite, fancy 6 choice, choose, opt for, picked, prefer 8 four-star, superior, topnotch 9 exclusive, first-rate, preferred 10 first-class, privileged
selection 4 pick 5 range 6 choice, medley, option 7 program, variety 8 choosing, decision 9 potpourri 10 collection, miscellany, preference
selective 5 fussy, picky 6 choosy 7 careful, finicky 8 cautious 10 discerning, fastidious, meticulous, particular 14 discriminating
Selemnus
   vocation: 8 shepherd
   loved: 6 Argyra
   changed into: 5 river
   changed by: 9 Aphrodite
Selene
   goddess of: 4 moon
   father: 8 Hyperion
   mother: 5 Theia
   brother: 6 Helios
   sister: 3 Eos
   loved: 8 Endymion
   daughter: 5 Herse 6 Pandia
   corresponds to: 5 Diana 7 Artemis
self 3 ego 6 person, psyche 8 identity 10 individual 11 homogeneity, personality
   inner: 5 anima 6 animus
   Universal: 5 Atman
self-abnegation 7 modesty 8 humility 10 diffidence 11 bashfulness
self-absorbed 4 vain 8 egoistic 9 egotistic 10 egocentric 11 egotistical 12 narcissistic
self-absorption 6 egoism, vanity 7 conceit 11 egocentrism, selfishness 16 self-centeredness
self-admiration 6 vanity 7 conceit, egotism 8 smugness 9 immodesty, vainglory
self-assertive 4 bold 7 dynamic 8 forceful 9 ambitious, confident 10 aggressive
self-assuming 4 vain 8 arrogant, egoistic 9 conceited 10 egoistical 11 egotistical
self-assurance 6 aplomb 9 brashness 12 cocksureness
   French: 9 sangfroid
self-assured 5 brash, cocky 8 cocksure 9 confident

self-centered 4 vain 8 egoistic, immodest 9 conceited, egotistic 10 egocentric 11 egotistical, swellheaded 12 narcissistic
self-centeredness 6 egoism, vanity 7 conceit 10 narcissism 11 egocentrism
self-composure 6 poise 8 aplomb 8 calmness 10 equanimity
self-confidence 5 nerve, pluck 6 mettle, spirit 8 boldness, gameness 9 cockiness 10 resolution 12 cocksureness
self-conscious 7 awkward 8 affected 9 chagrined, ill at ease, unnatural 11 discomposed, embarrassed 12 disconcerted
self-consciousness 7 modesty, reserve, shyness 8 timidity 9 abashment, hesitancy, reticence 10 constraint, demureness, diffidence 11 bashfulness, fearfulness 12 apprehension, sheepishness
self-control 5 poise 6 aplomb 8 firmness, patience, sobriety 9 composure, soberness, soundness, stability, willpower 10 temperance 11 forbearance 14 coolheadedness, unexcitability 15 levelheadedness 16 imperturbability
   French: 9 sangfroid 11 savoir faire
self-critical 6 humble, modest 9 diffident 13 perfectionist
self-criticism 7 modesty 8 humility 10 diffidence 13 perfectionism
self-deception 7 fantasy 8 delusion, illusion 13 hallucination
self-declared 5 sworn 6 avowed 8 admitted 9 confessed, professed 12 acknowledged
self-denial 8 eschewal 10 abnegation, abstention, abstinence, continence 11 forbearance 12 renunciation 14 abstemiousness
self-deprecation
   also: 16 self-depreciation 7 modesty 8 humility, meekness 10 humbleness
self-doubt 11 uncertainty
self-effacement 7 modesty, shyness 8 humility, meekness 10 diffidence 11 bashfulness
self-esteem 5 pride 10 confidence
self-evident 5 plain 6 patent 7 glaring, obvious 8 apparent, distinct, explicit, manifest, palpable 10 unarguable, undeniable 11 unambiguous, unequivocal 12 unmistakable 16 incontrovertible
self-explanatory 5 clear, lucid, plain 7 obvious 8 manifest 12 intelligible 15 straightforward
self-governing 4 free 9 sovereign 10 autonomous 11 independent
self-government 8 autonomy, home rule 11 sovereignty 12 independence
self-gratifying 11 intemperate
self-importance 6 egoism, vanity 8 smugness 9 arrogance, immodesty, pomposity, vainglory 11 egocentrism
self-important 4 smug, vain 7 pompous 8 egoistic, immodest 10 egocentric 11 egotistical 12 vainglorious
self-indulgence 12 extravagance, incontinence, intemperance

self-indulgent 9 libertine,
sybaritic 10 hedonistic, voluptuous 11 extravagant, incontinent, intemperate

selfish 4 mean 5 tight, venal 6 greedy, stingy 7 miserly 8 covetous, egoistic, grasping, grudging 9 egotistic, illiberal, mercenary, rapacious 10 avaricious, egocentric, ungenerous 11 egotistical 12 parsimonious, uncharitable

self-love 6 egoism, vanity 7 conceit, egotism 9 vainglory 10 narcissism 11 complacency, egocentrism, haughtiness 13 conceitedness 15 swellheadedness
French: 11 amour propre

self-possessed 4 calm, cool 6 poised 7 assured, courtly, refined 8 balanced, composed, polished, resolute 9 collected, confident 12 aristocratic 13 distinguished

self-possession 5 poise 6 aplomb 7 dignity 8 calmness, coolness 9 composure 10 confidence, equanimity, steadiness 16 imperturbability
French: 9 sangfroid

self-praise 6 vanity 7 conceit, egotism 8 bragging, smugness 9 arrogance, immodesty, vainglory 12 boastfulness
Italian: 11 braggadocio

self-propelling 9 automatic

self-questioning 10 uneasiness 13 soul-searching

self-reliance 8 sureness 9 assurance 12 independence

Self-Reliance
author: 17 Ralph Waldo Emerson

self-reliant 5 hardy 6 plucky 7 assured 8 resolute, spirited 10 mettlesome 11 independent 12 enterprising

self-reproachful 8 contrite 9 regretful 10 apologetic, remorseful

self-respecting 5 proud 7 upright 8 decorous 9 dignified, honorable 10 upstanding 11 circumspect 13 distinguished

self-restraint 9 willpower 10 continence 11 forbearance

self-righteous 4 smug 5 pious 7 pompous 9 insincere, pietistic 10 complacent, moralizing 11 pharisaical, pretentious 12 hypocritical, mealymouthed 13 sanctimonious 14 holier-than-thou

self-sacrificing 6 heroic 7 gallant 9 unselfish 10 altruistic, martyrlike

self-satisfaction 5 pride 6 vanity 8 smugness 11 complacency

self-satisfied 4 smug, vain 8 cocksure, priggish 9 overproud 10 complacent 11 egotistical 12 narcissistic, vainglorious 13 overconfident

self-secure 4 smug 7 content 9 contented 10 complacent

self-seeking 6 greedy 8 covetous

self-styled
French: 9 soi-disant

self-willed 8 obdurate, stubborn 9 obstinate, pigheaded 10 headstrong, refractory 11 intractable 12 ungovernable, unmanageable

sell 4 dump, hawk, vend 6 barter, betray, deal in, enlist, handle, market, peddle, unload 7 deceive, trade in, win over 8 convince, dispense

Selleck, Tom
roles: 8 Lassiter, Magnum PI 12 Thomas Magnum 15 High Road to China 16 Three Men and A Baby

seller 6 dealer, jobber, monger, trader, vendor 7 peddler 8 merchant, retailer, salesman 9 middleman, salesgirl, saleslady, tradesman 10 saleswoman, shopkeeper, wholesaler 11 salesperson, storekeeper

Sellers, Peter
real name: 19 Richard Henry Sellers
born: 7 England 8 Southsea
wife: 11 Britt Ekland
roles: 10 Being There 12 Casino Royale 13 Dr Strangelove, Murder by Death 14 A Shot in the Dark, The Pink Panther 16 What's New Pussycat? 17 Inspector Clouseau 18 The Mouse that Roared 21 The World of Henry Orient

Selli
priests of: 4 Zeus

sell out 6 betray 11 double-cross

semblance 3 air 4 cast, copy, look, show 5 image 6 aspect 7 bearing, replica 8 likeness, pretense 9 duplicate, facsimile 10 simulacrum 11 counterpart 12 reproduction 14 representation
French: 4 mien

Semele
also: 6 Thyone
father: 6 Cadmus
mother: 8 Harmonia
loved by: 4 Zeus
son: 8 Dionysus
sister: 3 Ino 5 Agave 7 Autonoe

seminal 7 primary 8 creative, fruitful, germinal, original 9 formative 10 generative, productive 11 germinative, originating

Seminole
language family: 9 Muskogean
tribe: 8 Cow Creek, Mikasaki
location: 6 Mexico 7 Florida, Georgia 10 Everglades
leader: 7 Osceola, Wild Cat 10 Coacoochie

Semiramis
queen of: 7 Assyria
husband: 5 Ninus
founder of: 7 Babylon

Semitic
language family: 11 Afro-Asiatic 13 Hamito-Semitic
eastern branch: 8 Akkadian, Assyrian 10 Babylonian
western branch: 4 Geez 5 Tigre 6 Arabic, Gurage, Harari, Hebrew, Minean, Sabean, Syriac 7 Amharic, Aramaic, Argobba, Moabite 8 Ethiopic, Tigrinya, Ugaritic 9 Canaanite 10 Himyaritic, Phoenician, Qatabanian
southwest branch: 6 Minean, Sabean 7 Amharic 10 Himyaritic, Qatabanian 11 North Arabic 19 South Arabic-Ethiopic

Semo Sancus *see* 6 Sancus

senatus consultum 17 Roman senate decree

send 4 cast, emit, head, hurl, lead, show, toss 5 drive, fling, guide, refer, relay, shoot, throw 6 convey, direct, launch, propel 7 conduct, deliver, forward, give off, project 8 dispatch, transmit 9 broadcast, cause to go, discharge 11 disseminate

send away 4 oust, rout, shoo 5 chase, evict

send forth 4 emit, gush 5 erupt, expel, issue, let go 7 dismiss, release 8 disgorge, dispatch 9 discharge

send off 4 post 7 forward 8 dispatch, disperse, transmit

send out 4 beam, emit 8 dispatch, transmit 9 discharge

send packing 3 axe, can 4 fire, oust, rout, sack, shoo 5 evict 6 bounce 7 cast out, dismiss

send to Coventry 3 cut 5 eject, expel 6 banish, ignore 7 cast out, exclude 9 ostracize

Seneca
    language family: 9 Iroquoian
    location: 7 New York 15 Canandaigua Lake
    leader: 9 John Abeel, John O'Bail 11 Cornplanter
    member: 19 League of the Iroquois

Senegal
    capital/largest city: 5 Dakar
    others: 5 Bakel, Matam, Thies 7 Bignona, Kaolack, Kaollak 8 Diourbel, Kedougou, Linguere, Rufisque 10 Saint-Louis, Ziguinchor 11 Richard-Toll, Tambacounda
    division: 7 Sudanic 8 Sahelian 9 Casamance
    empire: 4 Mali 5 Jolof 6 Tekrur
    monetary unit: 5 franc 7 centime
    island: 5 Goree
    lake: 6 Guiers
    mountain: 6 Gounou
    highest point: 12 Fouta Djallon
    river: 4 Sine 6 Faleme, Gambia, Saloum 7 Senegal 9 Casamance
    sea: 8 Atlantic
    physical feature:
    desert: 5 Ferlo
    peninsula: 9 Cape Verde
    people: 4 Lebu, Peul, Soce 5 Diola, Dyola, Foula, Laobe, Peulh, Serer, Wolof 6 Fulani, Serere 7 Bambara, Malinke, Tukuler, Tukulor 8 Mandingo
    leader: 7 Senghor
    language: 5 Wolof 6 French
    religion: 5 Islam 7 animism 13 Roman Catholic
    feature:
    musical instrument: 4 kora
    tree: 6 acacia, baobab 7 juniper, oil palm 10 raffia palm

senile 6 doting, infirm 7 foolish 8 decrepit 9 doddering, senescent 13 superannuated

senior, Senior 4 head, over 5 above, chief, doyen, elder, older 6 better 7 veteran 8 superior

seniority 6 tenure 9 longevity 10 precedence
    French: 4 pere

senor 2 Mr 3 don 5 title 6 mister 8 Spaniard

senora 3 Mrs 4 lady, wife 5 madam, woman 8 mistress

senorita 4 lass, miss
    abbreviation: 4 srta

senorita 6 wrasse
    genus: 8 Oxyjulis
    species: 11 californica

sensation 3 hit 4 stir, to-do 6 thrill, uproar 7 feeling, scandal 9 agitation, awareness, commotion, detection 10 impression, perception

sensational 5 cheap, lurid 6 superb 8 dramatic, exciting, galvanic, shocking, striking 9 emotional, excellent, thrilling 10 electrical, scandalous 11 exaggerated, exceptional, extravagant, outstanding, spectacular 12 meretricious 13 extraordinary 14 heartthrobbing

sensationalism 7 scandal 9 luridness, melodrama 13 grandstanding 15 blood and thunder 16 yellow journalism

sense 3 see, use 4 aura, espy, feel, good, mind, note 5 grasp, guess, point, sight, smell, taste, touch, value, worth 6 descry, detect, divine, reason, regard, take in, wisdom 7 benefit, discern, faculty, feeling, hearing, meaning, purpose, realize, suspect 8 efficacy, function, judgment, perceive, sagacity 9 apprehend, awareness, intuition, recognize 10 atmosphere, comprehend, definition, denotation, impression, understand 11 connotation, premonition, realization, recognition 12 appreciation, intelligence, perspicacity, practicality, presentiment 13 consciousness, signification, understanding 14 reasonableness

Sense and Sensibility
    author: 10 Jane Austen
    character: 10 Lucy Steele 13 Edward Ferrars, Robert Ferrars 14 Colonel Brandon, John Willoughby 16 Sir John Middleton
    Dashwood family: 4 John 5 Fanny 6 Elinor 8 Marianne

senseless 4 dumb, idle, numb 5 crazy, inane, nutty, silly 6 stupid, unwise 7 aimless, foolish, stunned, useless, witless 8 comatose, deadened 9 brainless, foolhardy, illogical, insensate, pointless 10 groundless, ill-advised, insensible, irrational, ridiculous 11 harebrained, meaningless, purposeless, unconscious 12 unreasonable 13 irresponsible

sense of duty 15 moral obligation 21 sense of responsibility

sensibilities 8 feelings, sore spot, thin skin 12 Achilles' heel 14 susceptibility

sensibility 7 feeling 10 perception 11 temperament 14 responsiveness

sensible 4 just, sage, sane, wise 5 aware, plain, sound 7 evident, knowing, logical, obvious, prudent, visible 8 apparent, apprised, credible, discreet, informed, palpable, possible, rational, tangible 9 cognitive, cognizant, conscious, judicious, plausible, sagacious 10 detectable, discerning, farsighted, noticeable, perceiving, perceptive, reasonable, responsive, thoughtful 11 discernible, enlightened, intelligent, perceptible, susceptible 13 perspicacious 14 discriminating

sensitive 4 fine, keen, sore 5 acute, exact 6 tender, touchy 7 painful, precise 8 accurate, delicate, faithful, sentient 10 perceptive, responsive 11 susceptible, thin-skinned 14 impressionable

sensitiveness 8 delicacy 10 touchiness

sensual 4 lewd, sexy 6 carnal, earthy, erotic 7 fleshly, lustful 9 lecherous 10 hedonistic, licentious, voluptuous

sensualist 8 hedonist, sybarite 9 libertine 10 voluptuary

sensuous 9 delicious, exquisite 10 delightful

sententious 7 orotund, pompous, preachy, stilted 8 didactic, pedantic 9 grandiose, high-flown, pietistic 10 judgmental, moralistic 13 sanctimonious

sentient 5 aware 7 alert to, alive to, awake to, mindful 8 sensible 9 conscious

sentiment, sentiments 4 idea 5 heart 6 notion 7 emotion, feeling, opinion, romance, thought 8 attitude 9 nostalgia, viewpoint 10 tenderness 11 romanticism 12 emotionalism 15 softheartedness

sentimental 5 mushy, weepy 7 maudlin, mawkish, tearful 8 pathetic, romantic 9 emotional, nostalgic 10 lachrymose 12 melodramatic, romanticized

Sentimental Education, A
  author: 15 Gustave Flaubert
  character: 6 Arnoux 9 Dambreuse, Rosanette 11 Des Lauriers, Louise Roque 14 Frederic Moreau

sentimentalism 4 corn, mush 5 slush 6 bathos, pathos 8 schmaltz 9 mushiness, soppiness 10 maudlinism, slushiness 11 mawkishness

sentimentality 4 mush 5 heart 6 bathos, pathos 10 sloppiness 11 mawkishness, temperament 12 emotionalism
  Yiddish: 6 kitsch

Sentimental Journey, A
  author: 14 Laurence Sterne
  character: 5 Maria 6 Yorick 7 La Fleur

sentinel 4 ward 5 guard, scout, watch 6 patrol, picket, ranger 7 lookout 8 guardian, watchman 9 guardsman

sentry 5 guard, watch 7 lookout, vedette, vidette 8 sentinel, watchman
  greeting: 4 halt

Seoul
  capital of: 10 South Korea

separate 3 cut 4 cull, fork, part, sift 5 break, crack, sever, split 6 bisect, detach, divide, ramify, remove, single, spread, sunder 7 crumble, disjoin, diverge, diverse, divorce, isolate, radiate 8 detached, discrete, distinct, disunite 9 bifurcate, break away, come apart, different, disunited, partition, segregate, subdivide 10 autonomous, disconnect, dissimilar, divaricate, individual 11 distinguish, independent

separated 6 cut off 7 severed 8 detached 10 disengaged 12 disconnected, disentangled

separate from 5 apart, leave

separately 5 apart 6 singly 7 asunder 9 severally 12 individually

Separate Tables
  director: 11 Delbert Mann
  based on play by: 15 Terence Rattigan
  cast: 10 David Niven 11 Deborah Kerr, Wendy Hiller 12 Rita Hayworth 13 Burt Lancaster
  Oscar for: 5 actor (Niven) 17 supporting actress (Hiller)

separation 3 gap 4 fork 5 break, space, split 6 breach, divide, schism 7 divider, divorce, good-bye, opening, parting, removal, sorting 8 boundary, distance, disunion, division, farewell, interval 9 branching, isolation, partition, severance 10 detachment, divergence 11 bifurcation, disjunction, segregation 12 estrangement 13 disconnection, disengagement 14 disassociation

Sepharvite god 10 Anammelech 11 Adrammelech

Sepharvites
  residents of: 6 Sippar

Sepher Torah 16 scroll of the Torah
  literally: 9 book of law

September
  characteristic: 11 harvest moon
  event: 14 aurora borealis, Northern lights 15 autumnal equinox
  flower: 5 aster 12 morning glory
  French: 9 Septembre
  gem: 8 sapphire 12 star sapphire
  German: 9 September
  holiday: 8 Labor Day (1st Monday) 9 Yom Kippur 10 Michaelmas (29) 12 Rosh Hashanah 15 Grandparents' Day
  Italian: 9 Settembre
  number of days: 6 thirty
  origin of name: 6 septum (Latin meaning seven)
  place in year:
    Gregorian: 5 ninth
    Roman: 7 seventh
  Spanish: 10 Septiembre
  Zodiac sign: 5 Libra, Virgo

septentrional 6 arctic 8 northern 11 hyperborean

Septuagint
  abbreviation: 3 LXX
  author: 10 the Seventy

sepulcher 4 tomb 5 crypt, grave, vault 7 ossuary 8 cenotaph 9 mausoleum, reliquary 10 necropolis

sepulchral 6 hollow 7 charnel 8 funereal, mournful, tomblike 10 lugubrious

sequel 3 end 6 finish, result, upshot 7 outcome, product 8 addendum, epilogue, follow-up, offshoot 9 aftermath, corollary, outgrowth 10 conclusion, postscript 11 consequence, culmination 12 continuation
French: 10 denouement

sequence 3 run 4 flow 5 chain, cycle, order, round, train 6 course, parade, series, string 7 routine 8 schedule 9 cavalcade 10 procession, succession 11 arrangement, progression 14 successiveness 15 consecutiveness

sequester 6 banish, lock up, retire 7 confine, isolate, seclude 8 separate, withdraw 9 segregate 10 quarantine

sequestered 8 closeted, confined, isolated, secluded 9 insulated, sheltered, withdrawn 10 cloistered 11 dissociated

sequin 4 coin, disk 5 ducat 7 spangle 8 ornament
French: 9 paillette

seraglio 3 oda 5 harem, serai 6 zenana 9 gynaeceum

Seraiah
son: 4 Ezra

serape 4 cape 5 shawl 6 mantle, poncho

seraph 5 angel

seraphic 7 angelic 8 beatific, ethereal, heavenly 9 celestial

Seraphim 6 angels

Serapis
origin: 5 Greek 8 Egyptian
form: 5 deity
combination of: 4 Apis, Hapi 6 Osiris

Serbia see 10 Yugoslavia

sere 3 dry 4 arid 6 barren 7 parched, wizened 8 droughty, scorched, withered 9 shriveled, unwatered, waterless 10 dehydrated, desiccated 12 dehumidified, moistureless

serene 3 calm, cool, fair 5 clear, quiet, still 6 bright, limpid, placid, poised, sedate, smooth 7 halcyon 8 composed, peaceful, pellucid, tranquil 9 dignified, unruffled 10 nonchalant, unobscured, untroubled 11 undisturbed, unexcitable, unperturbed 13 unimpassioned

serenity 7 dignity 8 calmness, coolness, quietude 9 composure, placidity 10 equanimity, quiescence 11 complacence, nonchalance, tranquility 12 peacefulness, tranquillity 13 collectedness
French: 9 sangfroid

serf 6 cotter, thrall, vassal 7 bondman, peasant, villein

serfdom 4 yoke 6 thrall 7 bondage, slavery 9 servitude, thralldom, vassalage 11 enslavement, subjugation

Sergeant York
director: 11 Howard Hawks
cast: 10 Gary Cooper, Joan Leslie 12 George Tobias 13 Walter Brennan
Oscar for: 5 actor (Cooper)

Sergestus
origin: 6 Trojan
companion to: 6 Aeneas

serial 7 regular 9 continued, piecemeal, recurring 10 continuous, sequential, successive 11 consecutive, incremental

series 3 set 5 chain, cycle, group, order 6 course, number, parade, string 8 sequence 10 procession, succession 11 progression

serious 3 bad, sad 4 grim 5 grave, heavy, sober, staid 6 rueful, sedate, severe, solemn, somber 7 crucial, decided, earnest, fateful, harmful, pensive, sincere, weighty 8 alarming, critical, dejected, downcast, frowning, perilous, resolute, resolved 9 crippling, dangerous, important, momentous, saturnine 10 determined, portentous, purposeful, thoughtful 13 consequential 14 incapacitating

seriousness 7 gravity 8 severity 9 sincerity, soberness, solemnity 10 importance 11 earnestness

sermon 6 homily, rebuke, tirade 7 lecture, reproof 8 diatribe, harangue 9 preaching 10 admonition, preachment 11 exhortation

serpent, Serpent 3 asp 5 cheat, devil, rogue, Satan, snake, viper 7 reptile, traitor 8 deceiver 9 trickster
constellation of: 7 Serpens

Serpent Holder
constellation of: 9 Ophiuchus

serpentine 4 mazy 6 spiral, zigzag 7 coiling, crooked, devious, sinuous, snaking, winding 8 flexuous, tortuous, twisting 10 circuitous, convoluted, meandering, round about, undulating 12 labyrinthine

Serpico
director: 11 Sidney Lumet
based on story by: 9 Peter Maas
cast: 8 Al Pacino 9 Jack Kehoe 12 John Randolph
setting: 11 New York City

serrate 5 notch 6 jagged, pinked, ridged 7 dentate, grooved, notched, toothed 10 sawtoothed

serration 5 notch, ridge, teeth, tooth 8 notching, sawtooth

servant 3 man 4 cook, girl, help, maid 5 valet 6 butler, flunky, helper, lackey, menial, minion, slavey 7 footman 8 domestic, employee, factotum, henchman, hired man, retainer, scullion 9 attendant, chauffeur, hired girl, hired help, man Friday, underling 10 girl Friday 11 housekeeper

serve 2 do 3 act, aid 4 help, pass, suit, tend, work 5 avail, spend, treat 6 assist, attend, be used, do duty, oblige, supply, wait on 7 content, deliver, further, perform, present, promote, satisfy, suffice, work for 8 carry out, complete, function, hand over, minister 9 officiate 11 fill the bill

service, services 3 aid, use 4 help, mend, rite 5 avail, labor 6 adjust, agency, bureau, effort, employ, profit, repair, ritual, system 7 benefit, support, utility, waiting 8 ceremony, facility, maintain, military 9 advantage, provision, treatment 10 assistance, attendance, ceremonial, department, employment, observance, usefulness 11 cele-

bration, convenience, maintenance 12
ministration 13 accommodation

serviceable 5 tough 6 rugged, strong,
sturdy, usable, useful 7 durable, lasting 8
workable 9 effective, operative, practical
10 functional 11 utilitarian

serviceman 6 marine, sailor 7 soldier 9 re-
pairman

servile 4 oily 6 abject, humble, menial 7
fawning, in bonds, slavish 8 cringing,
scraping, toadying, unctuous 9 groveling,
truckling 10 obsequious, submissive 11
bootlicking, subservient, sycophantic

serving 6 acting 7 dishful, helping, portion,
waiting 8 plateful 9 assisting, attending,
sufficing 11 ministering

serving counter 3 bar 6 buffet 9 sideboard

servitude 5 bonds 6 chains 7 bondage, fetters, serfdom, slavery 8 shackles 9 thralldom, vassalage 10 oppression 11 enslavement, subjugation 12 enthrallment,
imprisonment

Servius Tullius
  also: 7 Tullius
  king of: 4 Rome
  daughter: 6 Tullia
  son-in-law: 7 Tarquin
  killed by: 6 Tullia 7 Tarquin

sesame
  also called: 10 benne seeds
  botanical name: 14 Sesamum indicum
  fairy tale: 10 "open sesame" 25 Ali Baba
    and the Forty Thieves
  high in: 7 protein
  former/mythical use: 3 oil 8 medicine 10
    opens locks 11 lighting oil 16 discovers
    secrets 21 discovers secret places
  use: 5 bread 6 salads 10 casseroles
  use like: 8 nutmeats 11 chopped nuts

Sesame Street
  character: 4 Bert, Elmo 5 Ernie, Herry,
    Oscar 6 Snuffy 7 Barkley, Big Bird,
    Muppets 8 the Count 12 Telly Monster 13
    Cookie Monster 15 Mr Snuffleupagus

Sesostris
  king of: 5 Egypt

session 4 bout, term 5 round, synod 6
course, period 7 meeting, quarter, sitting 8
assembly, conclave, semester 10 conference, convention

set 3 cut, fit, fix, gel, kit, lay, put, sic 4 club,
drop, firm, line, make, plop, post, rate,
sink, stud, suit 5 adapt, align, array, banal,
bunch, crowd, embed, fixed, group, imbed,
order, place, plunk, ready, rigid, scene,
stale, stiff, stock, style, trite, usual 6 adjust,
assess, assign, attach, common, confer,
create, decree, frozen, harden, line up, locale, locate, ordain, outfit, studio 7 arrange, bearing, complex, congeal, decided, faction, install, jellify, machine,
prepare, profile, regular, release, routine,
scenery, service, setting, situate, station,
thicken, unleash 8 arranged, assembly,
backdrop, carriage, definite, estimate, everyday, familiar, firmness, habitual, hardened, location, ornament, position, pre-

pared, regulate, rigidity, solidify, stubborn 9
apparatus, calibrate, customary, determine, establish, hackneyed, immovable,
obstinate, prescribe, represent, steadfast
10 accustomed, assortment, collection, inflexible 11 anticipated, commonplace, consolidate, established, prearranged 12 conventional
  French: 6 clique 7 coterie

Set
  also: 4 Seth
  origin: 8 Egyptian
  form: 6 animal
  personifies: 6 desert
  brother: 6 Osiris
  killed: 6 Osiris

set about 5 begin 6 assume 9 undertake
10 surrounded

set against 8 alienate, estrange

set apart 6 allot 6 detach, divide 7 earmark,
isolate 8 allocate, separate 9 apportion,
segregate 11 appropriate

set aside 4 kill 5 allot, annul 6 abjure, cancel, repeal, revoke 7 abandon, abolish, call
off, destroy, discard, earmark, nullify, put
away, rescind, retract, reverse 8 abrogate,
allocate, override, overturn 9 designate,
repudiate 10 invalidate 11 discontinue

set at ease 5 cheer 6 please 7 appease,
comfort, content, gratify

set at liberty 4 free 5 let go 6 parole 7
manumit, release, unchain 8 liberate, unfetter 9 unshackle 10 emancipate

setback 4 flop, loss, snag 5 hitch, slump 6
defeat, mishap, rebuff 7 failure, relapse,
reverse, undoing 8 reversal 9 adversity,
mischance, worsening 10 misfortune, regression 13 retrogression 14 disappointment

set down 6 record 7 deposit

set forth 2 go 5 be off, leave 6 assert,
avouch, depart 7 advance 8 advocate,
propound 10 sally forth

set free 5 let go, loose, untie 6 acquit,
loosen, pardon, parole, unbind, uncage,
unlock 7 deliver, release 8 liberate,
unfetter 9 discharge, disengage, extricate
10 emancipate

Seth see 3 Set

Seth
  means: 12 compensation
  father: 4 Adam
  mother: 3 Eve
  son: 4 Enos

set in 5 arise, ensue, occur 6 arrive

set in motion 5 begin, start 6 launch 8 initiate 9 instigate, originate 10 inaugurate

set in order 4 rank, sort 5 align 6 line up 7
arrange, marshal 8 classify, organize 9
methodize 11 systematize

set of beliefs 5 credo, creed, dogma, ethos
6 ethnic, tenets 8 doctrine 10 philosophy,
principles 11 convictions

set off 6 depart 7 explode, go forth 8 detonate, start out 10 sally forth

set on fire 4 burn 5 light 6 ignite, kindle
set out 4 pose 5 array, begin, be off, place, range 6 deploy, embark, intend 7 arrange, display 9 undertake
set right 7 correct 8 disabuse
set store by 5 prize, value 6 esteem 7 respect 8 treasure
set straight 5 edify 6 advise, inform 7 educate 8 disabuse 9 enlighten
settee 4 seat, sofa 5 bench
setting 5 scene 6 fixing, locale 7 jelling 8 aligning, ambiance, locating, location, mounting 9 adjusting, arranging, decreeing, hardening, ordaining 10 congealing, regulating, thickening 11 arrangement, determining, environment, prescribing, solidifying 12 establishing, surroundings
    French: 6 milieu 11 mise-en-scene
setting sun
    god of: 5 Janus
settle 3 fix, pay, sag 4 calm, drop, land, sink 5 agree, allay, clear, droop, light, lodge, perch, quiet 6 alight, choose, decide, locate, move to, pacify, people, soothe 7 arrange, clarify, clear up, compose, inhabit, rectify, resolve, satisfy, sit down, situate 8 colonize, make good, populate, take root 9 determine, discharge, establish, reconcile 11 precipitate
settled 4 sure 7 certain, decided
settlement 3 sum 4 camp, post 6 amount, colony, hamlet 7 bequest, outpost, payment, village 8 clearing, peopling 9 clearance, discharge 10 adjustment, colonizing, encampment, resolution 11 acquittance, arrangement, liquidation 12 amortization, colonization, compensation, satisfaction 14 reconciliation
settler 7 pioneer 8 colonist, squatter 9 colonizer, immigrant 11 homesteader 12 frontiersman
settle upon 6 bestow 7 consign 8 bequeath
settlings 4 lees 5 dregs 7 deposit, grounds, remains, residue 9 leavings
set-to 4 spat 5 brush, clash, run-in 6 battle, fracas 7 dispute, quarrel, scuffle 8 argument, skirmish, squabble 10 engagement, falling out 12 disagreement 13 confrontation
    French: 11 contretemps
setup 4 plan 6 scheme, system 8 practice 9 apparatus 11 arrangement 12 organization
set up 3 rig 5 erect, found 7 arrange, install 9 construct, establish, institute 10 inaugurate, prearrange
set upon 3 mug 5 beset, fly at 6 assail, attack 7 besiege, lunge at 9 pitch into
Seurat, Georges Pierre
    born: 5 Paris 6 France
    artwork: 9 The Chahut, The Circus, The Models, The Parade, The Uproar 10 The Bathers 12 Le Grand Jatte, The Yoked Cart 19 Une Baignade Asnieres 23 A Bathing Scene at Asnieres, The Bec du Hoc at Grand champ 40 Sunday Afternoon on the Island of La Grand Jatte

Seuss, Dr
    real name: 19 Theodore Seuss Geisel
    author of: 12 If I Ran the Zoo 14 The Cat in the Hat 15 Green Eggs and Ham, Horton Hears a Who, If I Ran the Circus 19 Horton Hatches the Egg 23 Mister Brown Can Moo Can You? 26 Thidwick The Big-Hearted Moose, How the Grinch Stole Christmas
Seve
    nickname of: 20 Severiano Ballesteros
Seven Against Thebes
    author: 9 Aeschylus
    character: 6 Ismene 8 Antigone, Eteocles 9 Polynices 11 Theban Women
    seven heroes: 6 Tydeus 8 Adrastus, Capaneus 9 Polynices 10 Amphiaraus, Hippomedon 13 Parthenopaeus
Seven Beauties
    director: 14 Lina Wertmuller
    cast: 11 Fernando Rey 13 Shirley Stoler 17 Giancarlo Giannini
Seven Brides for Seven Brothers
    director: 12 Stanley Donen
    cast: 9 Tammy Rall 10 Howard Keel, Jane Powell 11 Julie Newmar (Newmeyer), Russ Tamblyn 12 Jeff Richards 14 Virginia Gibson
    score: 11 Saul Chaplin 12 Johnny Mercer
    choreography: 11 Michael Kidd
Seven Pillars of Wisdom
    author: 10 T E Lawrence
Seven Samurai
    director: 13 Akira Kurosawa
    cast: 11 Yoshio Inaba 13 Toshiro Mifune 14 Takashi Shimura
    remade as: 19 The Magnificent Seven
seven seas 6 Arctic, Indian 9 Antarctic 12 North Pacific, South Pacific 13 North Atlantic, South Atlantic
Seven Sisters colleges 5 Smith 6 Vassar 7 Barnard 8 Bryn Mawr 9 Radcliffe, Wellesley 12 Mount Holyoke
Seventeen
    author: 15 Booth Tarkington
    character: 7 Genesis 9 Miss Pratt, Mrs Baxter 10 Jane Baxter, May Parcher 21 William Sylvanus Baxter
Seventh Seal, The
    director: 13 Ingmar Bergman
    cast: 9 Nils Poppe 11 Max von Sydow 13 Bibi Andersson 17 Gunnar Bjornstrand
77 Sunset Strip
    character: 6 J R Hale, Kookie (Gerald Lloyd Kook son III), Roscoe 7 Suzanne 11 Jeff Spencer, Rex Randolph 12 Stuart Bailey
    cast: 9 Edd Byrnes 10 Louis Quinn, Roger Smith 11 Richard Long, Robert Logan 14 Jacqueline Beer 16 Efrem Zimbalist Jr
    Kookie's sayings: 10 a dark seven 12 the ginchiest 13 piling up the Z's 14 lend me your comb 15 play like a pigeon 17 headache grapplers 22 keep the eyeballs rolling

seven wonders of the world 8 pyramids (Egypt) 12 Olympian Zeus (sculpted by Phidias) 15 Temple of Artemis (at Ephesus) 16 Colossus of Rhodes 22 Lighthouse at Alexandria 23 hanging gardens of Babylon (of Semiramis) 24 Mausoleum at Halicarnassus

Seven Year Itch, The
 director: 11 Billy Wilder
 cast: 8 Tom Ewell 10 Sonny Tufts 11 Evelyn Keyes, Victor Moore 13 Marilyn Monroe
 setting: 11 New York City

sever 3 saw 4 part, rend, rive, tear 5 slice, split 6 bisect, cleave, cut off, lop off 7 disjoin, rupture, split up 8 amputate, break off, cut in two, dissolve, disunite, separate, truncate 9 dismember, terminate 10 disconnect 11 discontinue

several 3 own 4 a few, some 6 divers, single, sundry 7 certain, diverse, express, private, special 8 assorted, distinct, peculiar, personal, separate, specific 9 different, exclusive 10 individual, particular, respective 11 distinctive, independent

severe 5 cold, dour, grim, wild 5 cruel, grave, harsh, plain, rough, sober, stern, stiff 6 biting, bitter, brutal, chaste, fierce, fuming, raging, savage, sedate, simple, somber, strict, taxing 7 austere, cutting, drastic, extreme, furious, intense, painful, serious, uniform, violent 8 piercing, rigorous, ruthless, stinging, vigorous 9 dangerous, demanding, difficult, draconian, merciless, saturnine, turbulent, unadorned, unsparing 10 forbidding, restrained, tumultuous 11 distressing, undecorated, unrelenting 12 conservative

severed 6 cut off 8 detached 9 uncoupled, unhitched 10 unfastened 11 unconnected 12 disconnected

Severini, Gino
 born: 5 Italy 7 Cortona
 artwork: 9 Harlequin 15 The Armored Train 25 Dancer Sea and Vase of Flowers 32 Dynamic Hieroglyph of the Bal Tabarin

severity 5 rigor 7 cruelty 8 acrimony, violence 9 austerity, gruffness, harshness, sternness 10 asceticism, difficulty, strictness, stringency 11 seriousness 12 grievousness

Seville
 former name: 8 Hispalis
 landmark: 7 Alcazar, Giralda
 plain: 9 Andalusia
 river: 12 Guadalquivir
 ruler: 5 Moors 6 Romans 7 Vandals 8 Abbasids, Almohads, Iberians 9 Visigoths 10 Almoravids
 Spanish: 7 Sevilla

sew 3 hem 4 mend, seam, tack 5 unite 6 fasten, ground, stitch, suture 10 run aground
 loosely: 5 baste

sewage 5 waste 6 efflux, refuse 8 effluent 9 effluence

Seward, Dr
 character in: 7 Dracula
 author: 6 Stoker

sewing machine
 invented by: 4 Howe

sex 4 Eros, love 6 coitus, gender, libido 7 coition 8 maleness 10 copulation, femaleness, femininity, generation, lovemaking 11 masculinity, procreation 12 reproduction

Sexton, Anne
 author of: 15 All My Pretty Ones 22 To Bedlam and Part Way Back 23 The Awful Rowing Toward God

sexual 6 coital, erotic 7 amatory, genital, marital, sensual 8 conjugal, intimate, venereal 10 copulatory, generative, libidinous 11 procreative 12 reproductive

sexually stimulating 4 sexy 6 erotic, risque 9 salacious 10 suggestive 12 pornographic

sexy 4 lewd 5 bawdy 6 erotic 8 prurient 9 seductive 10 come-hither, coquettish, suggestive, voluptuous 11 flirtatious, provocative

Seychelles
 capital/largest city: 8 Victoria
 monetary unit: 4 cent 5 rupee
 island: 4 Mahe 7 Aldabra, La Digue, Praslin 8 Farquhar 9 Desroches 10 Silhouette
 highest point: 16 Morne Seychellois
 sea: 6 Indian
 people: 5 Asian 6 Creole, French, Indian 7 African, Chinese
 leader: 4 Rene 7 Mancham
 language: 6 Creole, French 7 English
 religion: 8 Anglican 13 Roman Catholic

sforzando
 music: 12 sudden accent

Shabbas 7 Sabbath

shabby 3 low 4 mean, poor, torn, worn 5 cheap, dirty, mangy, raggy, ratty, seedy, sorry, tatty, tight 6 frayed, meager, ragged, sordid, unfair 7 ignoble, rundown, scruffy 8 beggarly, decaying, inferior, slovenly, unworthy, wretched 9 illiberal, miserable, neglected 10 ramshackle, threadbare, tumbledown, ungenerous 11 dilapidated 12 contemptible, deteriorated, dishonorable, impoverished

shabby bar 4 dive 5 joint 7 gin mill 9 honky-tonk

shack 3 hut 5 cabin 6 lean-to, shanty

shackle 3 bar, tie 4 balk, bind, cuff, curb, foil, rein 5 block, bonds, chain, check, cramp, cuffs, deter, irons, limit, stall 6 chains, fetter, hamper, hinder, hobble, hogtie, impede, pinion, retard, secure, tether, thwart 7 inhibit, manacle, prevent 8 encumber, handcuff, restrict 9 forestall, frustrate, hamstring, handcuffs 12 circumscribe

shackled 7 chained, in irons 8 in chains, manacled 10 handcuffed

shadchan, schatchen 10 matchmaker 14 marriage broker

Shaddai 3 God
shade 3 bit, dim, hue, jot 4 atom, cast, hint,
hood, iota, tint, tone, veil, whit 5 blind,
color, drape, tinge, touch, trace 6 awning,
canopy, darken, screen, shadow, shield 7
curtain, modicum, shadows, shutter 8
darkness, particle, semidark 9 scintilla 10
suggestion
  French: 7 soupcon
  form: 6 spirit
  location: 5 Hades
shadow, shadows 3 bit, dog 4 blot, hint,
tail 5 cloud, ghost, hound, shade, smear,
stain, stalk, taint, tinge, touch, trace, track,
trail 6 blight, follow, pursue, smirch,
smudge, threat 7 blemish, specter,
whisper 8 penumbra 10 reflection, silhouette, suggestion
Shadow of a Doubt
  director: 15 Alfred Hitchcock
  cast: 10 Hume Cronyn 12 Joseph
  Cotten, Teresa Wright 14 Macdonald
  Carey 16 Patricia Collinge
  remade as: 16 Step Down to Terror
Shadow of the Moon
  author: 6 M M Kaye
Shadows on the Rock
  author: 11 Willa Cather
shadowy 3 dim 5 shady 6 gloomy, unreal 7
obscure 8 illusory 9 tenebrous 10 indistinct
13 insubstantial
Shadrach
  former name: 8 Hananiah
  friend: 6 Daniel
  companion: 7 Meshach 8 Abednego
shady 5 fishy 7 crooked, devious, dubious,
shadowy 9 dishonest, unethical 10 suspicious 11 underhanded 12 disreputable,
questionable 13 untrustworthy
shady dealings 5 fraud, graft 7 bribery 10
corruption, dishonesty
shaft 3 cut, pit, ray 4 barb, beam, dart,
duct, flue, gibe, hilt, stem, vent, well 5
abyss, arrow, chasm, gleam, lance, patch,
pylon, quill, shank, spear, spire, stalk,
tower, trunk 6 cavity, column, funnel, handle, insult, pillar, streak, stream 7 affront,
chimney, conduit, minaret, obelisk,
spindle, steeple 8 brickbat, monolith, pilaster 9 aspersion 10 excavation
shaggy 5 bushy, downy, fuzzy, hairy,
nappy, piled, wooly 6 tufted, woolly 7
bearded, hirsute, shagged, unshorn 9
whiskered 11 bewhiskered
shah 4 king 5 ruler 7 emperor, monarch 8
autocrat 9 sovereign
Shahaptian
  tribe: 6 Numipu 8 Nez Perce
Shahn, Ben
  born: 6 Kaunas 9 Lithuania
  artwork: 5 Epoch 8 Handball 12 Seurat's
  Lunch, The Physicist 16 Pacific Land
  scape 18 Willis Avenue Bridge 28 The
  Passion of Sacco and Vanzetti
shake 3 jar, jog, mix 4 jerk, jolt, move, stir,
stun, sway, wave 5 elude, quake, swing,
touch 6 affect, bounce, jiggle, joggle, jostle, jounce, quaver, quiver, rattle, ruffle,
shimmy, shiver, slough, totter, twitch,
wobble 7 agitate, disturb, flicker, flutter,
perturb, quaking, shudder, stagger, startle,
tremble, unnerve, vibrate 8 brandish, disquiet, distress, flourish, frighten, throw off,
unsettle, unstring 9 quivering, shivering,
trembling 10 discompose, flickering, fluttering
shakedown 6 extort, payoff, search, tryout
7 testing 8 thorough 9 blackmail, extortion,
hush money
Shakespeare, William
  also: 10 bard of Avon 12 immortal bard
  author of: 6 Hamlet, Henry V 7 Henry IV,
  Henry VI, Macbeth, Othello 8 King John,
  King Lear, Pericles (Prince of Tyre) 9
  Cymbeline, Henry VIII, Richard II 10
  Coriolanus, Richard III, The Tempest 11
  As You Like It 12 Julius Caesar, Twelfth
  Night 13 Rape of Lucrece, Timon of Athens 14 Romeo and Juliet, The Winter's
  Tale, Venus and Adonis 15 Titus
  Andronicus 16 Love's Labour's Lost 17
  Measure for Measure, The Comedy of
  Errors 18 Antony and Cleopatra, Troilus
  and Cressida 19 Much Ado About Nothing, The Merchant of Venice, The Taming
  of the Shrew 20 All's Well That Ends Well
  21 A Midsummer Night's Dream 22 The
  Merry Wives of Windsor 23 The Two
  Gentlemen of Verona
  birthplace: 15 Stratford-on-Avon
  theater: 4 Swan 5 Globe
  wife: 12 Anne Hathaway
shakeup 5 purge 7 cleanup 8 turnover 10
clean sweep 11 realignment 13 rearrange-
ment, redisposition, restructuring 14 redis-
tribution, reorganization
shake up 3 mix 4 stir 5 churn 7 agitate, disturb
shakiness 6 tremor 10 insecurity 11 instability, uncertainty 12 unsteadiness
shaky 4 weak 5 frail, jumpy 6 flimsy, unsafe, unsure, wobbly 7 dubious, fidgety,
fragile, halting, jittery, nervous, teetery 8
hesitant, insecure, unstable, unsteady, wavering 9 faltering, hazardous, quivering,
teetering, tottering, trembling, tremulous,
uncertain, undecided 10 inconstant, irresolute, precarious, unreliable, unresolved 11
vacillating 12 undependable
shallow 5 shoal 6 frothy, slight 7 surface,
trivial 8 knee-deep, skin-deep, trifling 9
frivolous 11 meaningless, superficial, unimportant 13 insubstantial 15 inconsequential
shalom 5 peace
shalom aleichem 10 peace to you
sham 3 act 4 copy, fake 5 bogus, false,
feign, fraud, phony, put on, trick 6 affect,
assume, forged 7 feigned, forgery, imitate,
pretend 8 pretense, simulate, spurious 9
imitation, pretended, simulated, synthetic
10 artificial, fraudulent 11 counterfeit,
make-believe

Shamash
   origin: 8 Akkadian
   god of: 3 sun
shamble, shambles 4 limp 5 hitch, lurch, stall 6 hobble 7 shuffle 8 butchery 14 slaughterhouse
shame 5 guilt, odium 6 humble, stigma 7 chagrin, mortify, remorse, scandal 8 contempt, disgrace, dishonor, ignominy 9 disrepute, embarrass, humiliate 10 debasement, disrespect 11 degradation, humiliation, self-disgust 12 unworthiness 13 embarrassment, mortification 14 disappointment
shamed be the one who thinks evil of it
   Latin: 20 honi soit qui mal y pense
shamefaced 5 sorry 7 abashed, crushed, humbled, put-down 8 blushing, sheepish 9 chagrined, disgraced, mortified 10 humiliated, remorseful 11 embarrassed
shameful 3 low 4 base, mean, vile 6 odious 7 heinous, ignoble 8 shocking, unworthy 9 dastardly, degrading 10 deplorable, despicable, inglorious, iniquitous, outrageous, villainous 11 disgraceful, ignominious, opprobrious 12 contemptible, dishonorable 13 reprehensible
shameless 4 pert 5 brash, saucy 6 brazen, wanton 7 forward, immoral 8 degraded, flagrant, immodest, impudent, indecent 9 abandoned, audacious, barefaced, boldfaced, dissolute, unabashed 10 indecorous, unblushing, unreserved 11 disgraceful 12 dishonorable
shamelessness 4 gall 5 brass, cheek 8 audacity 10 brazenness, effrontery 11 forwardness, presumption
Shamgar 11 Hebrew judge
shamus 7 gumshoe 9 detective 10 private eye 12 investigator
Shane
   director: 13 George Stevens
   cast: 8 Alan Ladd 9 Van Heflin 10 Jean Arthur 11 Jack Palance 12 Elisha Cook Jr 13 Edgar Buchanan 14 Brandon de Wilde
Shanghai
   area: 23 International Settlement
   landmark: 13 Long Hua Temple 17 People's Opera House 28 Shanghai Industrial Exhibition
   river: 6 Wusung 7 Huang-P'u, Yangtze
Shangri-La see 5 Nepal
shanty 3 hut 5 cabin, hovel, shack 6 lean-to
shape 4 form, make, mold, trim 5 array, build, frame, guide, model, order 6 create, fettle, figure, health 7 contour, develop, fashion, outline, profile 8 physique 9 condition, construct, determine 10 silhouette 12 conformation 13 configuration
shapeless 5 baggy 8 formless 9 amorphous, irregular
shapely 3 fit 4 neat, trim 6 comely, gainly 11 symmetrical
shaper 9 architect, innovator 10 instigator, prime mover

Shapley, Howard
   field: 9 astronomy
   studied: 6 galaxy
Shapwailutan
   tribe: 5 Modoc 11 Kiowa Apache
Shardik
   author: 12 Richard Adams
share 3 cut 4 dole, part 5 allot, cut up, quota, split 6 ration 7 deal out, divvy up, mete out, percent, portion 8 allocate 9 allotment, allowance, apportion 10 percentage 13 apportionment
shared 5 joint 6 common, public 7 general 8 communal 10 collective
share one's sorrow 7 condole 10 sympathize 11 commiserate
Sharif, Omar
   real name: 15 Michael Shalhoub
   born: 5 Egypt 10 Alexandria
   roles: 3 Che 9 Dr Zhivago, Funny Girl, Funny Lady 11 Genghis Khan 12 Nick Arnstein 16 Lawrence of Arabia
   expert on: 6 bridge
shark 3 ace 4 fish 5 cheat 6 expert, usurer, wizard 8 predator 9 trickster 12 extortionist
sharp 3 sly 4 acid, curt, fine, foxy, high, keen, sour, tart, wily 5 acrid, acute, alert, angry, awake, blunt, clear, cruel, edged, gruff, harsh, nippy, piked, quick, rapid, salty, sheer, spiny, steep 6 abrupt, artful, astute, barbed, biting, bitter, clever, crafty, crusty, fierce, keenly, marked, pointy, severe, shrewd, shrill, strong, sudden, thorny, tricky, unkind 7 acutely, alertly, angular, bearish, bristly, brusque, caustic, closely, crabbed, cunning, cutting, drastic, exactly, extreme, galling, intense, nipping, piquant, pointed, prickly, quickly, raucous, toothed, violent 8 abruptly, distinct, on the dot, piercing, promptly, scathing, serrated, spiteful, stinging, strident, suddenly, venomous, vertical, vigilant, vinegary 9 conniving, deceptive, excessive, on the nose, precisely, rancorous, unethical, vitriolic 10 contriving, discerning, immoderate, inordinate, perceptive, punctually 11 attentively, calculating, on the button, penetrating, precipitous 12 unprincipled, unscrupulous 13 precipitously
   French: 5 juste
   Spanish: 7 en punto
Sharp, Becky
   character in: 10 Vanity Fair
   author: 9 Thackeray
sharp-cornered 6 jagged 7 angular
sharp dresser 3 fop 4 dude 5 dandy 12 Beau Brummell, clotheshorse, fashion plate
sharpen 4 edge, hone, whet 5 grind, strop
sharply pointed 4 keen 5 acute 6 spiked 7 tapered 8 piercing 10 rapierlike 11 needle-nosed
sharpness 3 nip, wit 4 edge, tang 6 acuity, acumen 7 acidity, insight 8 acerbity, acridity, acrimony, keenness, pungency, saliency, tartness 9 acuteness, alertness,

quickness 10 causticity, craftiness 12 perspicacity

sharp pain 4 pang, stab 5 cramp 6 twinge

sharpshooter
French: 10 tirailleur

sharp-sighted 5 acute 6 shrewd 8 piercing 9 far-seeing 10 discerning, perceptive 11 penetrating 13 perspicacious

sharp-witted 4 keen 5 acute, alert, canny, quick, smart 6 astute, brainy, clever

Shatner, William
born: 6 Canada 8 Montreal
roles: 8 Star Trek, T J Hooker 17 Captain James T Kirk

shatter 4 rive, ruin 5 break, burst, crack, crash, crush, quash, smash, split, spoil, upset, wreck 6 squash, sunder, topple 7 crumble, destroy, explode, scuttle 8 demolish, fracture, overturn, splinter 9 devastate, pulverize

shattered 6 broken, dashed 7 crushed, smashed 8 crumbled, decrepit 9 flustered 10 demolished, fragmented, splintered, tumbledown 11 crestfallen, demoralized 13 disillusioned, disintegrated

shave 3 cut, lop, mow 4 clip, crop, dock, pare, skin, snip, trim 5 brush, graze, prune, shear 6 barber, cut off, fleece, glance, scrape 7 scissor

Shaw, George Bernard
author of: 7 Candida 9 Pygmalion, Saint Joan 12 Major Barbara 13 Arms and the Man 14 Man and Superman 15 Heartbreak House 16 Back to Methuselah 17 The Devil's Disciple, The Doctor's Dilemma 18 Caesar and Cleopatra 19 Androcles and the Lion 20 Mrs Warren's Profession
member of: 13 Fabian Society

Shaw, Irwin
author of: 12 Top of the Hill 13 The Young Lions 14 Beggarman Thief, Rich Man Poor Man

Shaw, Robert
born: 7 England 12 Westhoughton
wife: 7 Mary Ure
roles: 4 Jaws 7 The Deep 8 The Sting 12 Swashbuckler 13 The Caretakers 17 A Man for All Seasons 20 Force Ten from Navarone 28 The Taking of Pelham One-Two-Three
author of: 14 The Hiding Place 21 The Man in the Glass Booth

Shawabti
origin: 8 Egyptian
form: 8 figurine
where used: 6 burial

shawl 4 wrap 5 scarf 6 mantle 7 paisley 10 fascinator
Mexican: 6 serape
Spanish: 8 mantilla

Shawnee
language family: 9 Algonkian 10 Algonquian
location: 4 Ohio 6 Kansas 8 Missouri, Oklahoma 9 Tennessee 12 Pennsylvania 13 South Carolina

leader: 8 Tecumseh 11 Tenskwatawa
related to: 8 Delaware

She
author: 13 H Rider Haggard

shear 3 cut, lop 4 clip, crop, snip, trim 5 prune, shave 6 fleece, remove 7 deprive, relieve, scissor

Shearer, Norma
real name: 17 Edith Norma Shearer
born: 6 Canada 8 Montreal
husband: 14 Irving Thalberg
roles: 8 The Women 9 A Free Soul 11 The Divorcee (Oscar) 14 Romeo and Juliet, Their Own Desire 15 Marie Antoinette 26 The Barretts of Wimpole Street

shears 5 clips, trims 6 prunes 7 pruners 8 clippers, scissors, trimmers

sheath 3 pod 4 case, coat, skin 6 casing, jacket 7 capsule, coating, wrapper 8 covering, envelope, membrane, scabbard, slipcase, wrapping 9 container 10 receptacle

sheathing 6 casing, siding 8 covering

Sheba
father: 6 Bichri, Joktan, Raamah 7 Jokshan
grandfather: 4 Cush 7 Keturah
people of: 7 Sabeans

Shebat 19 eleventh Hebrew month

she carved it
Latin: 8 sculpsit

shed 3 hut 4 cast, doff, drop, emit, molt 5 exude, hovel, shack, spill, strew, throw 6 lean-to, shanty, shower, slough, spread 7 cast off, discard, let fall, let flow, radiate, scatter 8 disperse, lose hair, toolshed 9 broadcast, discharge, tool house 10 distribute 11 disseminate, outbuilding

she died
Latin: 5 obiit

shed light on 7 clarify, explain 9 elucidate, explicate, make clear, make plain 10 illuminate

She Done Him Wrong
director: 13 Lowell Sherman
cast: 7 Mae West (Diamond Lil) 9 Cary Grant, Noah Beery 13 Gilbert Roland

shed tears 3 cry, sob 4 bawl, weep 6 boohoo 7 blubber

Sheehy, Gail
author of: 8 Passages 14 The Pathfinders

Sheeler, Charles
born: 14 Philadelphia PA
artwork: 9 Landscape, Upper Deck 11 Incantation 12 City Interior, Rolling Power 15 Bucks County Barn, River Rouge Plant 31 American Landscape Nineteen Thirty

sheen 4 glow 5 glaze, gleam, glint, gloss, shine 6 luster, patina, polish 7 burnish, glister, glitter, shimmer 8 radiance 9 shininess 10 brightness, brilliance, effulgence, glossiness, luminosity, refulgence 12 luminousness, resplendence

Sheen, Martin
   real name: 12 Ramon Estevez
   born: 8 Dayton OH
   son: 12 Charlie Sheen 13 Emilio Estevez
   roles: 8 Badlands 12 The Believers 13
   Apocalypse Now 14 Catch Twenty-two 18
   The Subject Was Roses 27 The Execution of Private Slovik
Sheena, Queen of the Jungle
   creator: 8 SR Powell 13 W Morgan
   Thomas
   character: 3 Bob 4 Chim
she engraved it
   Latin: 8 sculpsit
sheep
   breed: 5 Iraqi 6 Hirrik, Merino, Panama,
   Romney, Somali 7 Cheviot, Karakul,
   Lincoln, Suffolk, Targhee 8 Columbia,
   Cotswold, Tatarian 9 Montadale, Romel-
   dale, Southdown 10 Corriedale, Dorset
   Down, Dorset Horn, Shropshire, Sikkim
   Bera 11 Rambouillet 13 Hampshire Down
   15 Border Leicester
   female: 3 ewe
   family: 7 Bovidae
   genus: 4 Ovis
   group of: 5 drove, flock 6 cosset
   meat: 4 lamb 6 mutton
   oil from: 7 lanolin
   wild: 5 urial 6 argali 7 bighorn, mouflon
   young: 4 lamb 7 lambkin 8 yearling
sheepish 3 shy 4 meek 5 timid 6 docile,
   guilty, humble 7 abashed, ashamed, bashful, fearful, hangdog, passive, servile 8
   blushing, obedient, obeisant, timorous,
   yielding 9 chagrined, chastened, diffident,
   mortified, shrinking, tractable 10 shamefaced, submissive 11 embarrassed, subservient, unassertive, unresisting
sheepishness 7 chagrin 8 docility, meekness 10 diffidence 11 bashfulness 12 tractability 13 embarrassment 14 submissiveness 15 unassertiveness
Sheep Well, The
   also: 13 Fuente Ovejuna
   author: 10 Lope de Vega
sheer 4 fine, pure, thin 5 bluff, filmy, gauzy,
   plumb, sharp, steep, total, utter 6 abrupt 7
   perfect, unmixed 8 absolute, complete,
   gossamer, vertical 9 out and out, unalloyed, unbounded, unlimited 10 consummate, diaphanous 11 precipitous, transparent, unmitigated, unqualified 12 unrestrained 13 perpendicular, unadulterated,
   unconditional
sheet 3 top 4 coat, film, leaf, pane, slab 5
   layer, panel, piece, plate 6 sheath, square
   7 blanket, coating, overlay 8 bed sheet,
   covering, membrane 9 rectangle
shegetz 12 non-Jewish boy, non-Jewish
   man
Sheldon, Sidney
   author of: 9 Bloodline 12 Rage of Angels, The Naked Face 15 If Tomorrow
   Comes 20 A Stranger in the Mirror 22
   The Other Side of Midnight

shelf 4 bank, prop, reef, slab 5 ledge, shoal
   6 mantel, mantle 7 bedrock, bracket, stratum 9 supporter 11 mantelpiece, mantle-
   piece
shell 3 pod 4 bomb, case, hulk, hull, husk,
   shot 5 pound, round, shuck 6 bullet, fire
   on, pepper, rocket 7 barrage, bombard,
   grenade, missile 8 carapace, skeleton 9
   cartridge, framework 10 projectile
shellac 4 beat, drub, lick, whip 7 clobber,
   lacquer, trounce, varnish
Shelley, Mary Wollstonecraft
   father: 13 William Godwin
   husband: 18 Percy Bysshe Shelley
   author of: 12 Frankenstein
Shelley, Percy Bysshe
   author of: 7 Adonais, Alastor 8 Queen
   Mab, The Cenci 10 To a Skylark 16 A
   Defence of Poetry, Ode to the West Wind
   17 Prometheus Unbound
shellfish 4 clam, crab 5 prawn 6 cockle,
   mussel, oyster, shrimp 7 abalone, lobster,
   mollusk, scallop 8 barnacle, crawfish,
   crayfish 9 trunkfish 10 crustacean 13
   softshell crab
   spawn: 4 spat
shell out 3 pay 6 expend 8 allocate, disburse, dispense 10 contribute
shelter 5 cover, guard, haven, house, lodge
   6 asylum, defend, harbor, refuge, safety,
   shield, take in 7 care for, housing, lodging,
   protect 8 quarters, security 9 safeguard,
   sanctuary 10 protection
Sheltered Life
   author: 12 Ellen Glasgow
shelve 5 defer, table 6 put off 7 suspend 8
   lay aside, postpone, put aside, put on ice,
   set aside 10 pigeonhole
Shem
   father: 4 Noah
   brother: 3 Ham 7 Japheth
   son: 8 Arphazed
   descendant of: 6 Semite
shenanigans 5 sport 6 antics, capers,
   hijinx, pranks, stunts, tricks 8 deviltry, mischief, nonsense 9 highjinks, horseplay, silliness 10 buffoonery, tomfoolery 11 roguishness 12 monkeyshines, sportiveness
   14 monkey business 15 mischievousness
she painted it
   Latin: 6 pinxit
shepherd 4 herd, lead, show, tend 5 guard,
   guide, pilot 6 direct, escort, herder, keeper,
   patron, shield 7 protect, shelter 8 champion, defender, guardian, herdsman, provider 9 custodian, protector, safeguard 10
   benefactor
Shepherdess and the Sweep, The
   author: 21 Hans Christian Andersen
shepherds
   god of: 3 Pan 6 Tammuz
sherbet 3 ade, ice 5 sorbet 7 dessert
Shere Khan
   character in: 14 The Jungle Books
   author: 7 Kipling

Sheridan, Ann
  real name: 16 Clara Lou Sheridan
  nickname: 9 Oomph Girl
  born: 8 Denton TX
  husband: 10 Scott McKay 11 George
    Brent 12 Edward Norris
  roles: 8 King's Row 11 Silver River 12
    Nora Prentiss 16 Wings for the Eagle 20
    Angels with Dirty Faces

Sheridan, Philip H
  served in: 8 Civil War 10 Indian Wars
  side: 5 Union
  commander of: 19 Army of the Shenan-
    doah
  rank: 22 general in chief of US army
  battle: 9 Five Forks 10 Cedar Creek,
    Winchester 11 Chattanooga, Chicka-
    mauga, Fisher's Hill 12 Sayler's Creek 18
    Wilderness Campaign

Sheridan, Richard Brinsley
  author of: 9 The Critic, The Duenna, The
    Rivals 18 A Trip to Scarborough 19 The
    School for Scandal

sheriff 7 officer 9 constable

Sheriff of Nottingham
  character in: 9 Robin Hood

Sherman, William Tecumseh
  nickname: 4 Cump
  served in: 8 Civil War 10 Mexican War
  side: 5 Union
  battle: 6 Shiloh 7 Atlanta, Bull Run 8 Sa-
    vannah 9 Vicksburg 11 Chattanooga 15
    Kenesaw Mountain
  fought against: 8 Johnston
  rank: 20 general in chief of army
  famous for: 13 march to the sea (Geor-
    gia)
  established: 29 Command and General
    Staff College
  saying: 9 War is hell

sherry
  type: 4 wine 6 brandy
  origin: 5 Spain
  varieties: 4 fino (dry) 7 amoroso (sweet),
    oloroso (medium dry)
  drink: 6 Adonis, Bamboo 9 Andalusia
  with gin: 11 Renaissance
  with vermouth: 6 Brazil

Sherwood, Robert E
  author of: 13 Idiot's Delight 15 Reunion
    in Vienna 18 The Petrified Forest 19 Roo-
    sevelt and Hopkins, There Shall Be No
    Night 20 Abe Lincoln in Illinois
  screenplay: 22 The Best Years of Our
    Lives

she sculptured it
  Latin: 8 sculpsit

she speaks
  Latin: 8 loquitur

She Stoops to Conquer
  author: 15 Oliver Goldsmith
  character: 6 Marlow 8 Hastings 10 Sir
    Charles 11 Tony Lumpkin 12 Mr
    Hardcastle 13 Mrs Hardcastle 14 Kate
    Hardcastle 16 Constance Neville

she wrote (it)
  Latin: 8 scripsit

shibah, shivah 14 mourning period
  literally: 9 seven days

shibboleth 6 byword, saying, slogan 8 apothegm 9 catchword

Shibboleth 17 Gileadite password

shield 4 keep, star 5 aegis, badge, cover,
  guard, house, shade 6 buffer, button, emblem, ensign, fender, harbor, screen, secure 7 buckler, defense, protect, shelter 8
  insignia, keep safe, preserve 9 medallion,
  protecter, protector, safeguard 10 escutcheon, protection

Shield (of Sobieski)
  constellation of: 6 Scutum

shielded 6 hidden 7 guarded 9 concealed,
  protected, sheltered

Shields, Brooke
  real name: 20 Christa Brooke Shields
  born: 9 New York NY
  roles: 10 Pretty Baby 11 Endless Love
    13 The Blue Lagoon

shift 2 go 4 move, slip, vary, veer 5 hitch,
  stint 6 change, swerve, switch 7 chemise,
  turning, veering 8 exchange, straight,
  transfer 9 deviation, transpose, variation
  10 alteration, assignment, reposition 11 alternating, fluctuation, interchange 12 modification
  French: 8 camisole

shiftless 3 lax 4 idle, lazy 8 careless, inactive, indolent, slothful 10 ne'er-do-well 13
  lackadaisical 14 good-for-nothing 15 unconscientious

shifty 4 foxy, wily 6 crafty, sneaky, tricky 7
  cunning, evasive 8 scheming, slippery 9
  conniving, deceitful, dishonest 10 contriving, unreliable 11 maneuvering, treacherous 13 untrustworthy

Shikasta
  author: 12 Doris Lessing

shiksa 13 non-Jewish girl 14 non-Jewish
  woman

shillelagh 4 club 5 stick 6 cudgel 9 truncheon

shilly-shally 5 stall, waver 6 dawdle, dither,
  falter, seesaw 8 hesitate 9 fluctuate, hem
  and haw, oscillate, vacillate

shilly-shallying 8 dawdling, wavering 9 uncertain, undecided 10 indecision, indecisive, irresolute 11 vacillation

Shimazaki Toson
  author of: 5 Hakai 20 The Broken Com-
    mandment

shimmer 4 beam, glow 5 blink, dance,
  flash, gleam, quake, shine, waver 6 quiver,
  shiver 7 flicker, flutter, glisten, sparkle,
  tremble, twinkle, vibrate 8 blinking 9 coruscate 11 scintillate 12 phosphoresce

shindig 3 hop 4 ball, bash, prom 5 dance,
  party 6 affair, shindy 7 blowout, revelry 9
  barn dance, festivity, record hop 10
  masked ball, the dansant
  French: 4 fete, gala 6 soiree 9 bal
    masque 10 bal costume

shine 3 wax 4 beam, buff, glow 5 blink,
  flash, glare, gleam, glint, gloss, light, rub
  up, sheen 6 dazzle, luster, polish, waxing

7 buffing, burnish, flicker, glimmer, glisten, glister, glitter, radiate, shimmer, sparkle, twinkle **8** brighten, radiance **9** coruscate, irradiate, polishing **10** brightness, brilliance, burnishing, luminosity **11** scintillate **12** illumination, luminousness **13** incandescence

shininess 5 gleam, glint, gloss, sheen **6** luster, polish **7** shimmer

shining 5 aglow **6** glossy **7** glowing, radiant **8** gleaming, luminous, lustrous **9** brilliant, effulgent **11** illustrious **12** incandescent

Shining, The
   author: **11** Stephen King

shiny 6 bright, glossy **7** glaring, glowing, radiant **8** gleaming, luminous, lustrous, polished **9** brilliant, burnished, effulgent, sparkling **10** glistening, glittering, shimmering **12** incandescent **13** scintillating

ship 4 crew, send **5** craft, liner, route, tramp, yacht **6** packet, tanker, vessel **7** carrier, cruiser, forward, steamer **8** dispatch **9** destroyer, freighter, steamship, transport **10** ocean liner

Ship of Fools
   author: **9** Katherine Anne Porter
   director: **13** Stanley Kramer
   cast: **9** Jose Greco, Lee Marvin **10** Jose Ferrer **11** George Segal, Oscar Werner, Vivien Leigh **14** Simone Signoret **15** Elizabeth Ashley

shipshape 4 neat, snug, taut, tidy, trip, trim **5** tight **6** spruce **7** orderly

Shirer, William L
   author of: **28** The Collapse of the Third Republic **29** The Rise and Fall of the Third Reich

shirk 4 duck, shun **5** avoid, dodge, elude, evade **6** escape, eschew, ignore **7** goof off, neglect **8** malinger, sidestep **9** goldbrick

shirker 5 piker **6** dodger, evader, loafer, rotter, truant **7** deserter, quitter, slacker **9** goldbrick **10** backslider, malingerer

Shirley Temple
   ingredient: **9** ginger ale, grenadine
   also called: **9** Roy Rogers

shirr 5 crimp, smock **6** gather, pucker **8** bake eggs

shirt 3 top **4** sark **5** frock, waist **6** blouse, bodice **10** underwaist

shirty 5 angry, irked, testy, vexed **7** annoyed **9** irritated **11** disgruntled

Shittimwood 12 Biblical tree

shiver 5 quake, shake **6** quaver, shimmy **7** shudder, tremble

shivers 3 bit **5** piece, shard **6** sliver **8** fragment

shivery 3 icy, raw **4** cold, cool **5** brisk, chill, crisp, nippy **6** arctic, biting, bitter, chilly, frigid, frosty, wintry **7** quaking, trembly **8** chilling **9** quivering **11** penetrating

shoal 3 bar **4** bank, flat **5** crowd, shelf **6** school **7** sand bar, shallow **8** sand bank

shock 3 jar, mat, mop **4** blow, bush, cock, crop, daze, jolt, mane, mass, pile, rick, rock, stun, turn **5** scare, shake, sheaf,

stack, start, upset **6** appall, bundle, dismay, impact, offend, revolt, thatch, trauma **7** astound, disgust, disturb, horrify, outrage, perturb, stagger, startle, stupefy **8** astonish, bowl over, disquiet, distress, paralyze, surprise, unsettle **9** collision, overwhelm **10** concussion, discompose, disconcert **11** disturbance **13** consternation

shocking 4 foul **5** awful **6** grisly, horrid, odious **7** ghastly, hideous, jarring, jolting **8** gruesome, horrible, indecent, terrible, wretched **9** abhorrent, appalling, frightful, monstrous, offensive, repellent, repugnant, revolting, startling, upsetting **10** abominable, astounding, detestable, disgusting, disturbing, horrifying, outrageous, perturbing, scandalous, staggering, stupefying, surprising, unsettling **11** astonishing, disgraceful, disquieting **12** insufferable, overwhelming **13** disconcerting, reprehensible

shoddy 3 low **4** base, mean, poor **5** dirty, nasty, tacky **6** shabby, sloppy, stingy **7** lowdown, miserly **8** careless, inferior, slipshod **9** haphazard, negligent, niggardly **10** second-rate, ungenerous **11** inefficient **12** contemptible **13** inconsiderate, reprehensible

shoe
   French: **9** chaussure

shoemaker 7 cobbler **8** bootmaker

Shoemaker's Holiday, The
   author: **12** Thomas Dekker

Shoes of the Fisherman, The
   author: **11** Morris L West

Shogun
   author: **12** James Clavell

Sholokhov, Mikhail
   author of: **19** And Quiet Flows the Don **21** The Virgin Soul Upturned

shoo 3 out **4** away, oust, rout, scat **5** be off, chase, leave, scram **6** beat it, be gone, depart, get out, go away **7** cast out, get lost, vamoose

shoot 3 bud, fly, hit **4** bolt, cast, dart, dash, drop, fell, fire, hurl, jump, kill, leap, nick, pelt, plug, race, rain, rush, stem, tear, toss, twig, wing **5** eject, fling, go off, hurry, shell, sling, speed, spray, sprig, spurt, sweep, throw, waste **6** charge, launch, let fly, pepper, propel, riddle, shower, spring, sprout **7** bombard, explode, pick off, tendril **8** catapult, detonate, open fire **9** discharge

Shootist, The
   director: **9** Don Siegal
   cast: **9** John Wayne, Ron Howard **10** Hugh O'Brien **11** Harry Morgan, Sheree North **12** James Stewart, Lauren Bacall, Richard Boone **13** John Carradine **15** Scatman Crothers

Shoot the Piano Player
   director: **16** Francois Truffaut
   cast: **11** Marie Dubois **12** Nicole Berger **14** Michele Mercier **15** Charles Aznavour
   setting: **5** Paris

shoot up 4 rise, soar 6 rocket

shop 3 buy 4 hunt, look, mart, mill 5 plant, store, works 6 browse, market, studio 7 factory 8 emporium, purchase, workshop 9 patronize 10 windowshop 13 establishment

French: 7 atelier 8 boutique

shopkeeper 6 dealer, monger, trader, vendor 8 merchant, purveyor, retailer 9 tradesman

shopworn 5 banal, corny, faded, stale, tired, trite, vapid 6 jejune 10 threadbare

shore 4 bank, hold, land, prop 5 beach, brace, brink, coast 6 hold up, margin, strand 7 bolster, bulwark, seaside, support, sustain 8 buttress, mainstay, seaboard, seacoast, underpin 9 reinforce, riverbank, waterside 10 strengthen

Latin: 10 terra firma

shorebird 3 auk 4 rail, sora 5 snipe, stilt, wader 6 avocet, curlew, plover, puffin 7 lapwing 8 woodcock 9 guillemot, sandpiper 13 oyster catcher

shore up 4 prop 5 brace 6 prop up 7 bolster, support 8 buttress 9 reinforce

short 3 low 4 curt, lean, slim, thin 5 brief, cross, elfin, fleet, gruff, hasty, pygmy, quick, runty, scant, sharp, small, squat, terse, testy, tight 6 abrupt, bantam, little, meager, scanty, scarce, skimpy, slight, sparse, stubby 7 brusque, compact, concise, cursory, lacking, limited, not long, not tall, slender, stunted, summary, wanting 8 abridged, abruptly, dwarfish, fleeting, impolite, snappish, succinct, suddenly, unawares 9 condensed, curtailed, deficient, impatient, momentary, niggardly, pintsized, truncated 10 by surprise, diminutive, short-lived 11 abbreviated, ill-tempered, Lilliputian, pocket-sized 12 insufficient 13 precipitously 14 without warning

shortage 4 lack, want 6 dearth 7 deficit 8 leanness, scarcity, sparsity 9 shortfall 10 deficiency, inadequacy, scantiness, sparseness 13 insufficiency

shortcoming 4 flaw 5 fault 6 defect, foible 7 blemish, failing, failure, frailty 8 drawback, handicap, weakness 10 deficiency, inadequacy 12 imperfection

shorten 3 cut 4 clip, pare, trim 5 prune, shave, shear 6 lessen, reduce 7 abridge, curtail, cut down 8 condense, contract, cut short, decrease, diminish 10 abbreviate

shortening 3 fat, oil 4 lard, oleo 6 butter, digest 7 cutting, summary 8 abstract, synopsis, trimming 9 hemming up, margarine, reduction 11 abridgement, compression, contraction, curtailment 12 abbreviation, condensation

short form 6 digest, precis 7 summary 8 abstract, synopsis 11 abridgement, contraction 12 abbreviation, condensation

Short Happy Life of Francis Macomber, The

author: 15 Ernest Hemingway

short journey 5 jaunt 6 outing 7 day trip 9 excursion

short-lived 5 brief 7 passing 8 fleeting 9 ephemeral, momentary, temporary, transient 10 evanescent, transitory, unenduring 11 impermanent 24 here today and gone tomorrow

shortly 4 anon, soon 7 by and by 8 directly, in a trice, promptly 9 forthwith, presently 10 before long 11 immediately

short narrative 5 essay, story 6 sketch 8 anecdote 10 short story

shortsighted 4 rash 6 myopic 7 foolish 8 careless, heedless, purblind, reckless, weak-eyed 9 amblyopic, imprudent 10 ill-advised, incautious, unthinking 11 improvident, injudicious, nearsighted, thoughtless 12 undiscerning 13 uncircumspect

short-tempered 4 curt 5 cross, huffy, sharp, testy 6 abrupt, cranky, crusty, grumpy, shirty, touchy 7 bearish, grouchy, peevish, waspish 8 choleric, snappish 9 irascible, irritable, splenetic 10 ill-humored, out of sorts, short-fused 11 hot-tempered, ill-tempered 12 cantankerous

Shosha

author: 19 Isaac Bashevis Singer

Shoshone (Snake)

language family: 10 Shoshonean

location: 4 Utah 5 Idaho 6 Nevada 7 Wyoming

translator: 9 Sacagawea

Shoshonean

tribe: 4 Hopi, Moki 5 Snake 6 Hopitu, Paiute 7 Bannock 8 Comanche, Shoshoni

Shostakovich, Dmitri (Dimitri)

born: 6 Russia 12 St Petersburg

composer of: 7 The Nose 9 Leningrad (symphony No 7) 11 May the First 12 The Golden Age 17 Katerina Ismailova 19 Lady Macbeth of Mzensk

shot 2 go 3 hit, try 4 dose, move, play, toss 5 balls, blast, crack, drive, essay, guess, salvo, slugs, throw 6 beat-up, archer, bowman, chance, report, ruined, shabby, stroke, volley 7 attempt, bullets, gunfire, shooter, surmise, worn-out 8 decrepit, marksman, rifleman 9 discharge, explosion, fusillade, injection 10 ammunition, conjecture, detonation 11 dilapidated, projectiles 12 falling apart, sharpshooter

shot in the arm 4 lift 5 boost 6 uplift 8 stimulus 13 encouragement

shot in the dark 5 guess 6 notion, theory 9 guesswork, suspicion 10 assumption, conjecture, hypothesis

shoulder 3 rim 4 bank, bear, brow, bump, edge, push, side, take 5 brink, carry, crest, elbow, lunge, shove, skirt, verge 6 assume, border, jostle, margin, take on, thrust, uphold 7 scapula, support, sustain 8 clavicle 9 undertake

shoulder blade 7 scapula 8 omoplate 9 bladebone

shout 3 cry 4 bawl, call, hoot, howl, roar, yell, yelp 5 burst, cheer, hollo, whoop 6 bellow, chorus, clamor, cry out, holler, hurrah, huzzah, outcry, scream, shriek 7 call out, exclaim, screech, thunder 8 outburst 9 hue and cry 10 hullabaloo

shout down 3 boo 4 hiss 6 hoot at, revile 7 catcall, condemn 8 denounce, drown out

shove 4 bump, butt, jolt, prod, push 5 boost, crowd, drive, elbow, force, impel, nudge 6 joggle, jostle, propel, thrust 8 shoulder

show 4 bare, bill, fair, give, lead, mark, play, pomp, pose, sham, sign 5 argue, coach, drama, endow, favor, front, grant, guide, movie, opera, prove, teach, token, tutor, usher 6 appear, attest, ballet, bestow, comedy, direct, effect, evince, expose, hint at, impart, inform, lavish, reveal, school, tender, unveil 7 bear out, bespeak, certify, conduct, confirm, display, exhibit, explain, lay bare, musical, picture, pretext, proffer, program, suggest, uncover 8 ceremony, delusion, disclose, dispense, evidence, illusion, indicate, instruct, intimate, manifest, operetta, point out, pretense, vaunting 9 establish, make clear, make known, represent, spectacle 10 appearance, disclosure, distribute, exhibition, exposition, expression, impression, indication, pretension, production, revelation 11 affectation, attestation, corroborate, counterfeit, demonstrate, performance, testimonial 12 bring to light, substantiate 13 demonstration, entertainment, manifestation, motion picture

Showboat
author: 10 Edna Ferber

showcase 7 cabinet, counter, display, exhibit, vitrine

showdown 3 war 6 battle, climax, combat, crisis 7 face-off 8 clashing, conflict 9 collision, encounter 13 confrontation

shower 3 wet 4 fall, pour, rain, rush 5 flood, salvo, spray, surge 6 deluge, lavish, splash, stream, volley, wealth 7 barrage, bombard, drizzle, torrent 8 downpour, plethora, sprinkle 9 profusion 10 cloudburst, inundation 11 bombardment

showiness 7 glitter 8 splendor 9 jazziness 10 flashiness 11 ostentation 14 grandiloquence

Show-me State
nickname of: 8 Missouri

show-off 6 egoist 7 boaster, egotist, windbag 8 braggart, fanfaron, flaunter, strutter 9 extrovert, swaggerer 11 braggadocio 13 cock of the walk, exhibitionist 14 life of the party

showpiece 3 gem 5 jewel, pearl, pride, prize 6 rarity, wonder 7 classic, paragon 8 treasure 10 masterwork 11 chef d'oeuvre, masterpiece, prizewinner 17 piece de resistance

show up 4 come 5 outdo 6 appear, arrive, attend, crop up, expose, loom up, reveal, turn up 9 be present 11 come to light, make a fool of 12 come into view 13 become visible

showy 4 loud 5 gaudy, vivid 6 flashy, florid, garish, ornate 7 pompous 8 colorful, gorgeous, imposing, splendid, striking 9 brilliant 11 magnificent, pretentious 12 ostentatious

Shqyptare, Shqiprija, Shqlperi see 7 Albania

shred 3 bit, ion, jot, rag 4 atom, band, hair, iota, spot, whit 5 grain, piece, scrap, speck, strip, trace 6 morsel, ribbon, sliver, tatter 7 snippet 8 fragment, molecule, particle 9 scintilla

shrew 3 hag, nag 5 harpy, scold, vixen, yenta 6 kvetch, virago 7 she-wolf 8 battle-ax, fishwife, harridan, spitfire 9 termagant, Xanthippe

shrewd 3 sly 4 foxy, keen, wily, wise 5 acute, cagey, canny, quick, sharp, slick, smart 6 artful, astute, clever, crafty, shifty, smooth, tricky 7 careful, cunning, knowing, probing, prudent 8 cautious, piercing, scheming, sensible, slippery 9 designing, farseeing, sagacious 10 contriving, discerning, farsighted, perceptive 11 calculating, circumspect, intelligent, penetrating, quick-witted, self-serving, sharp-witted 12 disingenuous 13 Machiavellian, perspicacious

shrewdness 6 acumen 7 cunning, slyness 8 foxiness, keenness, wiliness 9 acuteness, cageyness, sharpness, slickness, smartness 10 artfulness, astuteness, cleverness, craftiness, smoothness, trickiness 11 carefulness, discernment 12 slipperiness 16 disingenuousness

shriek 3 cry 4 call, hoot, howl, peal, yell, yelp 5 shout, whoop 6 cry out, holler, outcry, scream, squawk, squeak, squeal 7 screech

shrift 7 penance 9 atonement, expiation 10 confession

shrill 4 high, loud 6 piping 7 blaring, raucous 8 piercing, strident 9 clamorous 10 screeching 11 high-pitched, penetrating

shrine 6 altar 8 chapel, church, temple 7 sanctum 8 monument 9 sanctuary

shrink 3 ebb, shy 4 balk, duck, wane 5 cower, demur, dry up, quail, stick, wince 6 blench, bridle, cringe, flinch, lessen, pucker, recoil, reduce, refuse, retire 7 curtail, decline, deflate, dwindle, retreat, shorten, shrivel, shudder 8 compress, condense, contract, decrease, diminish, draw back, hang back, make less, withdraw 9 constrict 11 make smaller 12 draw together 13 become smaller

shrink from 4 hate, shun 5 abhor, evade 6 balk at, detest, eschew, loathe, resist 7 despise 8 recoil at 9 abominate, shudder at 12 be revolted by 13 find repulsive

shrinking 3 shy 5 timid 6 ebbing, waning 7 bashful 8 reticent, retiring, timorous 9 declining, dwindling 10 decreasing, shriveling 11 contraction, diminishing

shrive 6 pardon 7 absolve, forgive

shrivel 5 dry up, parch, wizen 6 pucker, scorch, shrink, wither 7 wrinkle

Shropshire Lad, A
  author: 9 A E Housman
shroud 4 hide, pall, veil, wrap 5 cloak, cloud, cover, sheet 6 clothe, mantle, screen, swathe 7 blanket, conceal, envelop 8 covering 9 cerecloth, cerements 11 burial cloth 12 graveclothes, winding sheet
shrub 4 bush 5 brush 8 beverage 10 fruit drink
shrubbery 4 bush 5 brush 6 bushes, shrubs 9 brushwood 10 underbrush 11 undergrowth
Shuara see 6 Jivaro
shuck 4 husk, peel, shed 5 chaff, shell, strip
shudder 4 jerk, pang 5 quake, shake, spasm, throb 6 quaver, quiver, shimmy, shiver, tremor, twitch 7 flutter, tremble 8 paroxysm 9 pulsation, trembling 10 convulsion
shudder at 4 hate 5 abhor 6 detest, loathe 8 recoil at 9 abominate, can't stand 10 recoil from, shrink from
shuffle 3 mix 4 drag, gimp, limp, step 5 scuff, slide 6 clumsy, jumble, scrape 7 shamble 8 scramble 9 rearrange 10 disarrange 11 interchange
shul, schul 9 synagogue
shun 5 avoid, dodge, elude, evade, forgo 6 eschew, forego, ignore, refuse, reject 7 boycott, disdain 10 circumvent, fight shy of, shrink from 11 keep clear of, shy away from 12 have no part of, keep away from, steer clear of, turn away from
shut 3 box 4 cage, coop, draw, fold, lock, snap 5 clasp, close, drawn, latch 6 closed, closet, corral, draw to, fasten, intern, locked, lock in, secure 7 confine, drawn to, enclose, fence in, impound, latched, secured 8 cloister, closed up, fastened, imprison 9 barricade, constrain 11 incarcerate
shut down 4 halt, stop 5 cease 7 suspend 9 close down, interrupt 11 discontinue
Shute, Nevil
  author of: 10 On the Beach
shut in 4 cage 5 caged, pen in 6 coop up, encage, lock up 7 confine, encaged, enclose 8 cornfined, cooped up, enclosed, locked up, restrain, restrict 10 restrained, restricted
shut one's eyes to 5 allow 6 ignore, wink at 8 overlook 9 connive in, disregard 11 pay no heed to 14 turn one's back on
shut out 3 bar 5 debar 6 defeat 7 exclude 8 obstruct, prohibit
shutter 5 blind, close, shade 6 screen 7 curtain
shut the door on 3 ban, bar 6 forbid, refuse, reject 7 exclude, keep out, shut out 8 prohibit
shut up 4 cage, coop, hush, lock, pent 5 close, pen in 6 immure 7 be quiet, confine, silence 8 imprison 11 incarcerate

shy 4 balk, meek, wary 5 chary, cower, dodge, leery, minus, scant, short, timid, under, wince 6 blench, demure, flinch, in need, modest, shrink, swerve 7 anxious, bashful, careful, fearful, lacking, needing, nervous, wanting 8 cautious, draw back, jump back, reserved, reticent, skittish, timorous 9 deficient, diffident, shrinking, tremulous 10 suspicious 11 distrustful 12 apprehensive 13 self-conscious
shy away from 4 duck, shun 5 avoid, dodge, spurn 6 balk at, refuse, reject 10 shrink from 12 steer clear of
Shylock
  character in: 19 The Merchant of Venice
  author: 11 Shakespeare
shyness 8 meekness, timidity 9 reticence 10 diffidence, insecurity 11 bashfulness 12 sheepishness, timorousness 14 self-effacement 15 unassertiveness
shyster 5 rogue 6 lawyer 8 attorney 10 mouthpiece 11 pettifogger 15 ambulance chaser
si 3 yes
Siam see 8 Thailand
Sibelius, Jean
  born: 7 Finland 10 Tavastehus
  composer of: 6 En Saga 7 Karelia, Legends, Tapiola, The Band 8 Kalevala 9 Finlandia 10 The Tempest 12 The Oceanides, Voces Intimae 14 Ride and Sunrise
Siberia, Siber 8 disfavor 10 punishment 14 undesirability
  city: 4 Omsk 5 Chita, Tomsk 6 Kurgan 7 Irkutsk, Yakutsk
  conqueror: 9 Timafeyev 11 Genghis Khan
  continent: 4 Asia
  gulf: 2 Ob
  inhabitant: 4 Yaku 5 Sagai, Tatar 6 Tartar 7 Yukagir 8 prisoner 17 political prisoner
  mountain range: 4 Ural 5 Altai, Altay
  river: 2 Ob 3 Ket, Ili, Taz 4 Amga, Amur, Lena, Onon 5 Ishim, Tobol 6 Olekma
  sea: 4 Kara 6 Laptev 7 Okhotsk
sibyl 4 seer 5 augur 6 oracle 7 diviner 9 predictor, sorceress 10 forecaster, prophetess, soothsayer 13 fortune teller 14 prognosticator
Sibyls
  form: 10 prophetess
  inspired by: 5 deity 6 Apollo
  names: 6 Libyan 7 Cumaean 10 Erythraean
  prophecies: 14 Sibylline Books
sic 2 so 4 thus
Sicilian Vespers, The
  also: 20 Les Vepres Siciliennes
  opera by: 5 Verdi
  character: 5 Elena 6 Arrigo 7 Procida 8 Monforte
Sicily
  other name: 7 Sicilia 9 Trinacria, Triquetra
  capital/largest city: 7 Palermo
  others: 3 Aci 4 Enna, Noto 6 Ragusa 7

Augusta, Catania, Marsala, Messina, Trapani 8 Syracuse 10 Montelepre
division: 4 Enna 6 Ragusa 7 Catania, Messina, Palermo, Trapani 8 Siracusa, Syracuse 9 Agrigento 13 Caltanissetta
government: 13 region of Italy
measure: 5 salma 7 caffiso
monetary unit: 5 litra, oncia, uncia 6 carlin 7 carline, oncetta
island: 5 Egadi 6 Lipari, Ustica 7 Pelagie 11 Pantelleria
lake: 7 Pergusa 8 Camarina
mountain: 4 Erei, Moro, Sori 5 Atlas, Erici, Hybla, Iblei, Ibrei 7 Nebrodi, Vulcano 9 Apennines, Le Madonie, Stromboli 10 Peloritani
highest point: 4 Etna 5 Aetna
river: 4 Acis 5 Salso, Torto 6 Belice, Simeto 7 Mazzaro, Platani
sea: 6 Ionian 10 Tyrrhenian 13 Mediterranean
physical feature:
cape: 4 Boeo, Faro 7 Lilibeo, Passaro, Passero, Pelorus
gulf: 4 Noto 7 Catania
strait: 7 Messina
wind: 7 sirocco
people: 5 Elymi, Sican, Sicel 6 Sicani, Siculi
author: 9 Lampedusa 10 Pirandello
composer: 7 Bellini
king: 4 Eryx 5 Bomba, Henry, Peter, Roger 7 Charles, Cocalus, Leontes 9 Ferdinand, Frederick
ruler: 4 Rome 5 Arabs, Goths, Spain 6 Greeks 7 Germans, Normans, Vandals, Vikings 8 Carthage, Saracens 9 Aragonese, Byzantium, Egyptians, Phoenicia 15 Holy Roman Empire
language: 7 Italian
religion: 13 Roman Catholic
place:
cathedral: 8 Monreale
resort: 4 Enna 8 Taormina
ruins: 14 Villa Imperiale 15 Temple of Concord 18 Valley of the Temples
feature:
brigands: 5 Mafia
evening stroll: 11 passeggiata

sick 3 ill 4 weak 5 frail, tired, weary 6 ailing, infirm, laid up, poorly, queasy, sickly, uneasy, unwell 7 crushed, grieved, invalid, unsound 8 delicate, stricken, troubled, wretched 9 afflicted, bored with, disturbed, miserable, nauseated, perturbed, suffering, unhealthy 10 disquieted, distressed, indisposed 11 discomposed, heartbroken 15 under the weather
sicken 5 repel, shock, upset 6 offend, revolt 7 disgust, horrify, make ill, repulse 9 nauseate 14 turn the stomach
sickening 4 foul, vile 5 nasty 7 noisome 8 horrible, unsavory 9 abhorrent, loathsome, offensive, repellent, repugnant, repulsive, revolting 10 disgusting, nauseating 11 distasteful

sickly 3 ill, wan 4 drab, flat, lame, pale, sick, weak 5 ashen, faint, frail, silly 6 ailing, feeble, flimsy, guilty, infirm, leaden, peaked, poorly, sneaky, torpid, unwell 7 insipid, invalid, unsound 8 delicate, smirking 9 afflicted, apathetic, bloodless, simpering, unhealthy 10 cadaverous, lackluster, namby-pamby, snickering, spiritless, uninspired, wishy-washy 11 ineffective 12 unconvincing 13 self-conscious
sickness 6 malady, nausea 7 ailment, disease, illness 8 debility, disorder, vomiting 9 complaint, frailness, ill health, infirmity 10 affliction, disability, invalidism, poor health, queasiness 11 unsoundness 12 qualmishness 13 indisposition
sic passim 12 so throughout
sic semper tyrannis 19 thus always to tyrants
motto of: 8 Virginia
sic transit gloria mundi 33 thus passes away the glory of this world
Siddhartha
author: 12 Hermann Hesse
story of: 6 Buddha
siddur 16 Jewish prayer book
literally: 5 order
side 3 hem, rim 4 area, body, brim, edge, half, hand, part, sect, team, view 5 angle, bound, cause, facet, flank, group, house, light, limit, minor, party, phase, skirt, slant, stand, stock 6 allied, aspect, behalf, belief, border, circle, clique, fringe, lesser, margin, region, sector, strain 7 askance, coterie, faction, lateral, lineage, oblique, opinion, postern, quarter, related, section, segment, surface 8 alliance, attitude, boundary, division, indirect, marginal, position, skirting 9 accessory, bloodline, coalition, on one side, perimeter, periphery, secondary, territory, viewpoint 10 collateral, contingent, federation, incidental, standpoint, subsidiary 11 affiliation, association, unimportant 13 insignificant
Side
origin: 5 Irish
form: 7 fairies
owner: 14 Tuatha De Danann
sideboard 6 buffet 8 credenza
side by side 7 abreast 8 abutting, together 9 adjoining 11 cheek by jowl, in proximity
Latin: 9 pari passu
Side Effects
author: 10 Woody Allen
sidekick 3 pal 4 aide 5 buddy 6 deputy, friend 9 assistant 10 lieutenant
sideline 5 bench, hobby 8 boundary 9 avocation 14 put out of action
sidestep 4 duck 5 avert, avoid, dodge, elude, evade, skirt 6 bypass, escape 10 circumvent, fight shy of 12 steer clear of
sidestepping 7 dodging, ducking, eluding, evasion 8 skirting 9 avoidance 13 circumvention
sidewalk 4 curb 8 footpath, pavement 9 promenade

sideways, sideway 6 aslant 7 askance, lateral, oblique 8 orabwise, edgeways, edgewise, sidelong, sideward, sidewise 9 crosswise, laterally, obliquely, to the side 11 from one side

side with 5 agree 7 stand by, stick by, support 8 champion 12 take one's part

sidle 4 cant, edge, skew, veer 10 lateralize

Sidney, Sir Philip
   author of: 7 Arcadia 15 Defence of Poesie, Defence of Poetry 18 Apologie for Poetrie, Astrophel and Stella

Sidney, Sylvia
   real name: 11 Sophia Kosow
   born: 7 Bronx NY
   husband: 11 Luther Adler 12 Bennett A Cerf
   roles: 4 Fury 7 Dead End 11 Street Scene 13 Les Miserables 15 Madame Butterfly 17 An American Tragedy 24 Summer Wishes Winter Dreams

Sidrophel
   character in: 8 Hudibras
   author: 6 Butler

siecle 3 age 6 period 7 century

Siegel, Jerry
   creator/artist of: 8 Superman

Siegfried
   origin: 8 Germanic
   mentioned in: 14 Nibelungenlied
   father: 7 Sigmund
   mother: 9 Sieglinde
   wife: 9 Kriemhild
   killed by: 5 Hagen
   same as: 6 Sigurd
   killed: 6 Fafnir
   won for Gunther: 10 Brunnhilde
   stole: 9 Tarnkappe

Sieg Heil 13 hail to victory
   salute used by: 5 Nazis

Sieglinde
   origin: 8 Germanic
   mentioned in: 14 Nibelungenlied
   husband: 7 Sigmund
   son: 9 Siegfried

Sienkiewicz, Henryk
   author of: 8 Quo Vadis?

Sierra Leone
   name means: 12 lion mountain
   other name: 9 Gold Coast 10 Grain Coast, Ivory Coast
   capital/largest city: 8 Freetown
   others: 2 Bo 5 Hepel, Kissi, Lungi, Pepel 6 Bonthe, Kenema, Makeni, Shenge, Sulima
   school: 6 Njaia U 9 Fourah Bay
   measure: 4 load 6 kettle
   monetary unit: 4 cent 5 leone
   island: 4 York 6 Banana, Turtle 7 Sherbro
   mountain: 4 Loma 10 Tingi Hills
   highest point: 9 Bintimani
   river: 3 Moa 4 Jong, Mano, Meli, Ribi, Sewa, Taia 5 Bagbe, Mongo, Morro, Rokel 6 Mabole, Rokkel, Scarcy, Waanje 13 Great Scarcies 14 Little Scarcies
   sea: 8 Atlantic
   physical feature:
     bay: 5 Yawri 7 Sherbro
     cape: 8 Shilling 11 Sierra Leone
     peninsula: 7 Turners 11 Sierra Leone
     wind: 9 harmattan
   people: 3 Vai 4 Kono, Loko, Susu 5 Bulom, Kissi, Limba, Mende, Mendi, Temne 6 Creole, Fulani, Syrian 7 Gallina, Koranko, Kuranko, Sherbro, Yalunka 8 Lebanese, Mandingo
   explorer: 6 Cintra
   leader: 6 Margai 7 Stevens
   language: 4 Krio 5 Limba, Mende, Mendi, Temne 6 Creole 7 English
   religion: 5 Islam 7 animism 12 Christianity
   place:
     wharf: 10 King Jimmys
   feature:
     cloth: 5 garra
     clothing: 5 lappa 6 caftan
     secret society: 4 poro
   food:
     dish: 4 fufu 7 cassava
     sauce: 7 palaver

siesta 3 nap 4 rest 5 break, sleep 6 cat nap, snooze 10 forty winks

sieve 4 sift 6 filter, riddle, screen, sorter, strain 7 tattler 8 colander, strainer 9 separator 12 blabbermouth

sift 4 sort 5 drift, probe, study 6 filter, review, screen, search, winnow 7 analyze, inspect, scatter, sort out 8 separate 10 scrutinize 11 distinguish, investigate 12 discriminate

Siggeir
   origin: 12 Scandinavian
   king of: 5 Goths
   wife: 5 Signy
   causes death of: 7 Volsung

sigh 3 sob 4 hiss, long, moan, pine, weep 5 brood, groan, mourn, whine, yearn 6 grieve, lament, sorrow

sight 3 ken, see, spy 4 bead, espy, gaze, spot, view 5 image, scene, vista 6 behold, seeing, survey, vision 7 display, exhibit, eyeshot, glimpse, observe, pageant, scenery, viewing 8 eyesight, perceive, prospect, scrutiny 9 peepsight, sighthole, spectacle 10 appearance, visibility

sighted 3 saw 4 seen 6 seeing 8 not blind, observed

sightless 5 blind 8 unseeing 9 unsighted

sightly 4 fair 6 lovely, pretty 8 handsome, pleasing 9 appealing, beautiful 10 attractive

Sigmund
   origin: 8 Germanic 12 Scandinavian
   mentioned in: 8 Volsunga 14 Nibelungenlied
   king of: 11 Netherlands
   father: 7 Volsung
   mother: 4 Liod, Ljod 5 Hliod
   wife: 7 Hiordis, Hjordis 8 Borghild 9 Sieglinde
   sister: 5 Signy
   lover: 5 Signy

son: 6 Sigurd 9 Siegfried, Sinfiotli

sign 3 nod 4 clue, hint, mark, note, omen, wave 5 badge, brand, index, stamp, token, trait 6 emblem, ensign, figure, herald, motion, signal, symbol 7 earmark, endorse, feature, gesture, go-ahead, placard, portent, presage, symptom, warning 8 evidence, forecast, inscribe, neon sign, road sign, signpost 9 autograph, billboard, guidepost, harbinger, indicator, nameplate, trademark 10 indication, intimation, prognostic, suggestion, underwrite 11 forewarning 12 manifestation 14 characteristic

signal 3 cue, nod 4 sign 6 beckon, famous, motion, unique 7 command, eminent, gesture, guiding, honored, notable, warning 8 high sign, password, pointing, renowned, singular, striking 9 arresting, directing, direction, important, indicator, memorable, momentous, prominent, watchword 10 commanding, impressive, indicating, indication, noteworthy, one-of-a-kind, remarkable 11 conspicuous, distinctive, exceptional, illustrious, outstanding, significant 12 considerable 13 consequential, distinguished, extraordinary, unforgettable

significance 3 aim 4 note 5 drift, force, merit, sense, value, worth 6 import, intent, moment, object, virtue, weight 7 concern, gravity, meaning, portent, purpose 8 eminence, interest, priority 9 authority, direction, influence, intention, relevance 10 excellence, importance, notability, prominence 11 consequence, distinction, implication

significant 4 main 5 chief, grave, great, major, prime, vital 6 cogent, signal 7 eminent, knowing, notable, serious, telling, weighty 8 critical, distinct, eloquent, eventful, material, pregnant, symbolic 9 important, momentous, paramount, principal, prominent 10 emblematic, expressive, indicative, meaningful, noteworthy, portentous, remarkable, suggestive 11 exceptional, influential, outstanding, substantial, symptomatic 12 considerable 13 consequential, demonstrative 14 representative

signify 4 mean, omen, show, tell 5 argue, augur, imply 6 convey, denote, evince, herald, hint at, import, reveal, typify 7 bespeak, betoken, connote, declare, exhibit, express, portend, predict, presage, promise, suggest 8 announce, disclose, evidence, forebode, foretell, indicate, intimate, manifest, proclaim, set forth, stand for 9 be a sign of, designate, represent, symbolize 10 foreshadow 11 communicate, demonstrate

signing up 7 joining 9 enlisting, enrolling 10 enlistment, enrollment 11 registering 12 registration 13 matriculating, matriculation

Sign of Four, The
author: 19 Sir Arthur Conan Doyle
character: 11 Mary Morstan 12 Dr John Watson 13 Jonathan Small 14 Sherlock Holmes, Thaddeus Sholto

Signoret, Simone
real name: 32 Simone-Henriette-Charlotte Kaminker
born: 7 Germany 9 Wiesbaden
husband: 11 Yves Montand 12 Yves Allegret
roles: 10 Madame Rosa 11 Ship of Fools 12 Room at the Top (Oscar) 14 Is Paris Burning?
autobiography: 27 Nostalgia Isn't What It Used to Be

sign up 4 join 6 enlist, enroll, join up 8 register 9 volunteer 11 matriculate

Signy
origin: 12 Scandinavian
mentioned in: 8 Volsunga
father: 7 Volsung
brother: 7 Sigmund
son: 9 Sinfiotli
husband: 7 Siggeir

Sigrdrifa
also: 18 Brynhildr Sigrdrifa
origin: 9 Icelandic
mentioned in: 9 Elder Edda
member of: 9 Valkyries
disobeyed: 4 Odin 5 Othin
sleeps in circle of: 4 fire
awakened by: 6 Sigurd

Sigurd
origin: 12 Scandinavian
mentioned in: 8 Volsunga
father: 7 Sigmund
mother: 7 Hiordis, Hjordis
wife: 6 Gudrun, Kudrun 7 Guthrun
killed: 6 Fafnir
acquired treasure of: 8 Andavari
won for Gunnar: 8 Brynhild

Sigyn
origin: 12 Scandinavian
husband: 4 Loki

Sikes, Bill
character in: 11 Oliver Twist
author: 7 Dickens

Sikkim
capital/largest city: 7 Gangtok
others: 6 Dikchu, Lachen, Namchi, Rangpo, Rumtek 9 Lachung 9 Chungtang
government: 12 state of India
mountain: 7 Dongkya, Donkhya 9 Himalayas, Singalili 10 Darjeeling 12 Kanchenjunga
river: 5 Tista 6 Ranjit 9 Lachen Chu 10 Lachung Chu
physical feature:
mountain pass: 6 Natu La 7 Jelep La
storm: 7 monsoon
people: 4 Rong 5 Bhote 6 Bhotia, Bhutia, Indian, Lepcha 7 Tibetan 8 Nepalese 9 Mongoloid
king: 7 chogyal
religion: 5 Hindu 7 Lamaism 15 Tibetan Buddhism

Sikorsky, Igor
nationality: 7 Russian 8 American
invented: 10 helicopter

Silas Marner
    author: 11 George Eliot
    character: 5 Eppie 11 Dunstan Cass,
    Godfrey Cass 13 Aaron Winthrop, Nancy
    Lammeter

silence 3 gag 4 calm, curb, halt, hush, kill,
    rout, stop 5 allay, check, crush, peace,
    quash, quell, quiet, still 6 banish, deaden,
    defeat, muffle, muzzle, repose, squash,
    stifle, subdue 7 conquer, nullify, put down,
    quieten, repress, reserve, squelch 8 choke
    off, dumbness, muteness, overcome, se-
    renity, suppress, vanquish 9 lay to rest,
    placidity, quietness, reticence, stillness,
    tongue-tie 10 extinguish, placidness, put
    an end to, strike dumb 11 taciturnity, tran-
    quility 12 tranquillity 13 noiselessness,
    secretiveness, soundlessness 14 speech-
    lessness 16 closemouthedness 19 uncom-
    municativeness

silent 3 mum 4 calm, dumb, idle, mute 5 in-
    ert, muted, quiet, still, tacit 6 covert, hid-
    den, hushed, placid, serene, unsaid 7 dor-
    mant, implied, muffled 8 discreet, implicit,
    inactive, inferred, lifeless, peaceful, re-
    served, reticent, taciturn, tranquil, un-
    spoken, wordless 9 concealed, intimated,
    noiseless, quiescent, secretive, soundless,
    suggested, unsounded, unwritten 10 insin-
    uated, mysterious, speechless, tongue-
    tied, undeclared, understood, unrevealed,
    unstirring, untalked-of 11 close-lipped,
    tight-lipped, unexpressed, unmentioned,
    unpublished, untalkative, unvocalized 12
    closemouthed, unpronounced 15 uncom-
    municative

Silent Spring
    author: 13 Rachel L Carson

Silenus
    god of: 6 forest
    oldest: 5 satyr
    father: 3 Pan 6 Hermes
    foster father of: 8 Dionysus
    teacher of: 8 Dionysus
    companion of: 8 Dionysus
    sons: 6 Sileni

silicon
    chemical symbol: 2 Si

silk
    fabric: 4 crin 5 crepe, ninon, satin, surah,
    tulle 6 faille, pongee, sendal, tussah 7
    chiffon, foulard, organza, raw silk, taffeta
    8 organzie, paduasoy 10 peau de soie 12
    crepe de chine
    lining: 7 sarsnet 8 sarcenet
    measure: 6 denier
    raw silk: 5 grege 6 greige 8 marabout
    source: 6 cocoon 9 silkworms
    waste: 4 noil 5 floss
    watered: 5 moire
    yarn/thread: 4 tram 5 floss

silk-stocking 6 uptown 8 highborn, high-
    bred, wellborn 9 patrician 10 upper-class
    11 blue-blooded 12 aristocratic

Silk Stockings
    director: 15 Rouben Mamoulian
    cast: 10 Janis Paige, Peter Lorre 11 Cyd
    Charisse, Fred Astaire
    setting: 5 Paris
    score: 10 Cole Porter
    remake of: 9 Ninotchka

silky 4 fine, soft 6 satiny, smooth 11 fine-
    grained

silliness 5 folly 6 drivel, idiocy 7 inanity 9
    absurdity, asininity, frivolity 10 buffoonery,
    tomfoolery 11 foolishness 13 pointless-
    ness 14 playing the fool, ridiculousness

Sillitoe, Alan
    author of: 10 Her Victory 29 Saturday
    Night and Sunday Morning 36 The Lone-
    liness of the Long-Distance Runner

silly 3 mad 4 dumb 5 crazy, giddy, inane 6
    absurd, frothy, insane, stupid, unwary, un-
    wise 7 aimless, asinine, fatuous, foolish,
    idiotic, shallow, witless 8 childish, farcical 9
    brainless, foolhardy, frivolous, laughable,
    ludicrous, pointless, senseless 10 ill-
    advised, irrational, ridiculous 11 empty-
    headed, harebrained, meaningless, non-
    sensical, purposeless 12 muddleheaded,
    preposterous, simpleminded, unreason-
    able 13 inappropriate, irresponsible, mud-
    dlebrained, rattlebrained 14 featherbrained
    15 inconsequential

Silmarillion, The
    author: 10 J R R Tolkien

Silone, Ignazio
    real name: 17 Secondo Tranquilli
    author of: 9 Fontamara 12 Bread and
    Wine 26 The Story of a Humble Christian

Silvanus
    also: 8 Sylvanus
    god of: 5 herds, house, woods 12 farm
    boundary 16 uncultivated land

silver 5 coins, plate 6 argent, change 7
    jewelry 8 argentum, platinum 9 argentine
    10 silverware
    chemical symbol: 2 Ag

Silver, Long John
    character in: 14 Treasure Island
    author: 9 Stevenson

Silver, Mattie
    character in: 10 Ethan Frome
    author: 7 Wharton

Silvers, Phil
    real name: 17 Philip Silversmith
    born: 10 Brooklyn NY
    roles: 9 Top Banana 13 Sergeant Bilko
    15 High Button Shoes 22 A Guide for the
    Married Man 37 A Funny Thing Hap-
    pened on the Way to the Forum
    autobiography: 14 The Laugh Is on Me

Silvius
    father: 6 Aeneas
    s'il vous plaît 6 please 11 if you please

Simenon, Georges
    author of: 8 The Train 12 Act of Passion
    14 The Little Saint 15 Maigret's Memoirs
    28 The Strange Case of Peter the Lett
    character: 21 Inspector Jules Maigret

Simeon
 father: 5 Jacob
 mother: 4 Leah
 brother: 3 Dan, Gad **4** Levi **5** Asher, Judah **6** Joseph, Reuben **7** Zebulun **8** Benjamin, Issachar, Naphtali
 sister: 5 Dinah
 canticle: 12 nunc dimittis
 descendant of: 9 Simeonite
similar 4 akin, like, twin **5** close **6** allied **7** cognate, kindred **8** agreeing, matching, parallel **9** analogous, duplicate **10** comparable, equivalent, resembling **11** approximate, correlative, much the same, nearly alike **13** correspondent, corresponding
similarity 7 harmony, kinship, oneness **8** affinity, likeness, nearness, sameness **9** agreement, closeness, congruity, semblance **10** congruence, similitude **11** concordance, conformance, equivalence, parallelism, reciprocity, resemblance **13** comparability **14** conformability, correspondence
similarly 4 thus **5** alike **7** equally **8** likewise **11** furthermore, identically **15** correspondingly
similitude 7 analogy **8** likeness, sameness **10** similarity **11** parallelism, resemblance
simmer 3 boil, burn, foam, fume, stew **5** chafe, smart **6** bubble, burble, gurgle, seethe, sizzle
simmer down 7 cool off **8** calm down **14** collect oneself, compose oneself
Simmons, Jean
 born: 6 London **7** England
 husband: 13 Richard Brooks **14** Stewart Granger
 roles: 4 Trio **6** Hamlet **7** Desiree, Ophelia, The Robe **9** Spartacus, Young Bess **11** Elmer Gantry **12** Guys and Dolls **14** The Happy Ending **17** Great Expectations **19** Androcles and the Lion
Simois
 god of: 5 river
Simoisius
 killed by: 14 Telamonian Ajax
Simon
 also known as: 5 Peter
 son: 13 Judas Iscariot
 disciple of: 5 Jesus
Simon, Neil
 author of: 10 Chapter Two, Plaza Suite **11** Biloxi Blues **12** The Odd Couple **15** The Sunshine Boys **16** Come Blow Your Horn **17** Barefoot in the Park **21** Last of the Red Hot Lovers **25** The Prisoner of Second Avenue
Simon & Simon
 character: 7 AJ Simon **9** Rick Simon **12** Cecilia Simon **13** Downtown Brown
 cast: 7 Tim Reid **10** Mary Carver **13** Gerald McRaney, Jameson Parker
 setting: 8 San Diego
Simon Boccanegra
 opera by: 5 Verdi
 setting: 5 Genoa
 character: 5 Maria, Paolo **6** Andrea,

Fiesco, Pietro **14** Amelia Grimaldi, Gabriele Adorno
Simonov, Konstantin
 author of: 13 Days and Nights
simpatico 7 likable **9** agreeable, congenial, gemutlich
simper 5 smirk **6** giggle, tee-hee, titter **7** snicker, snigger
simple 4 bare, dull, dumb, easy, open, slow, soft, true **5** basic, blunt, dense, frank, green, homey, naive, naked, plain, quiet, sheer, stark, thick **6** callow, candid, common, direct, honest, modest, obtuse, rustic, stupid **7** artless, foolish, natural, sincere **8** absolute, innocent, not fancy, ordinary, peaceful, straight, workaday **9** downright, elemental, guileless, ingenuous, out-and-out, unadorned, unfeigned, untrimmed, unworldly **10** elementary, manageable, not complex, unaffected, uninvolved **11** commonplace, fundamental, plain-spoken, rudimentary, thick-witted, undecorated, unvarnished **12** not difficult, not elaborate, uncompounded **13** inexperienced, uncomplicated, unembellished, unpretentious **15** straightforward, unsophisticated
simple house 3 cot, hut **5** shack **6** chalet **7** cottage **8** bungalow
simpleminded 4 dull, dumb, slow **5** dense, silly, thick **6** stupid **7** asinine, fatuous, foolish, idiotic, moronic, witless **9** retarded **9** brainless, dim-witted, imbecilic **10** dull-witted, half-witted **11** empty-headed, harebrained, lamebrained **12** feeble-minded
simpleton 3 ass, oaf **4** dolt, dope, fool, hick, jerk, rube **5** booby, dummy, dunce, goose, idiot, ninny, stupe **6** donkey, rustic **7** dullard, jackass **8** dumbbell, imbecile, numskull **9** blockhead, greenhorn, ignoramus, numbskull **10** nincompoop
simplicity 6 candor, purity **7** clarity, honesty, naivete **8** easiness, openness, serenity **9** austerity, clearness, innocence, plainness, restraint, sincerity **10** directness **11** artlessness, cleanliness, naturalness, obviousness **12** truthfulness **13** guilelessness, unworldliness **19** straightforwardness
simply 7 clearly, lucidly, plainly, starkly **8** directly, modestly **9** naturally **10** explicitly **11** ingenuously **12** intelligibly, unaffectedly **15** uncomplicatedly, unpretentiously **17** straightforwardly
Simpson, O J (Orenthal James)
 nickname: 5 Juice
 sport: 8 football
 position: 11 running back
 team: 10 USC Trojans **12** Buffalo Bills **23** San Francisco Forty-Niners
simulate 3 act, ape **4** copy, fake, play, pose, sham **5** feign, mimic, put on **6** affect, assume, invent **7** imitate, playact, pretend **9** dissemble, fabricate **11** counterfeit, make believe

simulated 4 fake, sham 5 phony 6 forged 7 manmade, pretend 9 imitation, synthetic 10 artificial, fabricated 11 counterfeit, make-believe

simultaneous 6 coeval 10 coexistent, coexisting, coincident, concurrent, synchronal, synchronic 11 concomitant, synchronous 12 accompanying, contemporary 15 contemporaneous

sin 3 err 4 evil, fall, slip, vice 5 crime, error, lapse, shame, stray, wrong 6 breach, do evil, offend 7 do wrong, misdeed, offense, scandal 8 disgrace, evil deed, iniquity, trespass, villainy 9 violation 10 infraction, transgress, wrongdoing 13 transgression

Sin
  origin: 8 Akkadian
  god of: 4 moon

Sinaiticus 16 Greek uncial codex

Sinatra, Frank
  real name: 20 Francis Albert Sinatra
  nickname: 8 The Voice 11 Old Blue Eyes
  born: 9 Hoboken NJ
  wife: 9 Mia Farrow 10 Ava Gardner
  daughter: 12 Nancy Sinatra
  son: 14 Frank Sinatra Jr
  leader of: 7 Rat Pack
  roles: 8 Tony Rome 12 Angelo Maggio, Guys and Dolls, The Detective 14 The Joker Is Wild 17 The First Deadly Sin 18 From Here to Eternity 22 The Man with the Golden Arm

Sinbad the Sailor
  character in: 27 Arabian Nights' Entertainments

since 2 as 3 ago, for, yet 4 ergo, from 5 after, hence, later 6 thence, whence 7 because, whereas 8 in as much 9 therefore 10 afterwards 11 accordingly, considering 12 subsequently
  archaic: 4 sith
  prefix: 3 cis
  Scottish: 4 syne

sincere 4 real 5 frank 6 candid, honest 7 artless, earnest, genuine, natural, serious 8 truthful 9 authentic, guileless, heartfelt, ingenuous, unfeigned 10 forthright, unaffected 11 in good faith, undeceitful 12 wholehearted 15 straightforward

sincerely 5 truly 6 really 8 honestly 9 earnestly, genuinely, seriously 10 truthfully 14 wholeheartedly

sincerity 6 candor 7 honesty, probity 8 openness 9 frankness, good faith 11 artlessness, earnestness, genuineness, seriousness 12 truthfulness 13 guilelessness, ingenuousness 14 forthrightness, unaffectedness 16 wholeheartedness 19 straightforwardness

Sinclair, Upton
  author of: 9 The Jungle, World's End 12 Dragon's Teeth
  character: 9 Lanny Budd

Sindhi
  language family: 12 Indo-European
  branch: 11 Indo-Iranian
  group: 5 Indic

  spoken in: 13 Northern India

sine die 17 without fixing a day (for future action or a future meeting)
  literally: 13 without the day

sine prole 14 without progeny 16 without offspring

sine qua non 15 without which not 18 something essential 22 indispensable condition

sinew, sinews 4 grit, thew 5 fiber, nerve, power, vigor 6 muscle, tendon 7 stamina 8 ligament, strength, virility, vitality 10 resilience, strengthen

sinewy 4 wiry 5 beefy, nervy, thewy, tough 6 brawny, robust, strong 7 fibrose, stringy 8 muscular, powerful, vigorous

Sinfiotli
  origin: 12 Scandinavian
  mentioned in: 8 Volsunga
  mother: 5 Signy
  father: 7 Sigmund

sinful 3 bad 4 evil, vile 5 wrong 6 errant, unholy, wicked 7 corrupt, heinous, immoral, impious, ungodly, wayward 8 criminal, depraved, shameful 9 miscreant 10 degenerate, despicable, iniquitous, profligate, villainous 11 disgraceful, irreligious, unrighteous

sing 3 hum 4 lilt, pipe 5 carol, chant, chirp, croon, trill, tweet 6 intone, warble 7 chirrup, whistle 8 melodize

Sing Along with Mitch
  regulars: 10 Diana Trask 11 Mitch Miller 12 Leslie Uggams, Louise O'Brien, Sandy Stewart 13 Gloria Lambert, Sing Along Gang, Sing Along Kids

Singapore
  other name: 8 Singa Pur
  name means: 13 city of the lion
  capital/largest city: 9 Singapore
  others: 4 Tuas 6 Changi, Jurong 7 Nee Soon 9 Paya Lebar, Woodlands 10 Bukit Timah, Queenstown 12 Bukit Panjang 15 Toa Payoh New Town
  medieval town: 7 Temasek
  school: 7 Nanyang 8 National 9 Singapore
  monetary unit: 4 cent 6 dollar
  island: 4 Ubin 5 Brani, Bukum, Pesek 7 Semakau 8 Merlimau, Southern 10 Ayer Chawan, Ayer Merbau 11 Blakang Mati, Tekong Besar 12 Tekong Kechil
  mountain: 6 Mandai 7 Panjang
  highest point: 10 Bukit Timah
  river: 6 Jurong, Sungei 7 Kallang, Seletar 9 Singapore
  sea: 6 Indian 10 South China
  physical feature:
  harbor: 6 Keppel 9 Serangoon
  strait: 6 Johore, Pandan 8 Sembilan 9 Singapore
  people: 5 Malay 6 Indian 7 Chinese 9 Malaysian, Pakistani, Sri Lankan
  founder: 7 Raffles
  leader: 10 Lee Kwan Yew
  language: 5 Malay, Tamil 7 Chinese, English 8 Mandarin

religion: 4 Sikh 5 Hindu, Islam 6 Taoism 8 Buddhism 12 Christianity, Confucianism

place:

amusement park: 8 New World 10 Great World, Happy World

aquarium: 8 Van Kleef

cathedral: 9 St Andrews

gardens: 7 Botanic

hall: 16 Victoria Memorial

industrial park: 6 Jurong

mosque: 8 Sultan

park: 6 Farber 7 Merlion 12 Raffles Place

street: 16 Raffles Boulevard

temple: 17 One Thousand Lights

feature:

boat: 4 junk 6 sampan

clothing: 4 sari

singe 4 burn, char, sear 5 brand 6 scorch

singer 4 alto, bard, bass, diva, lark 5 tenor 7 crooner, soprano 8 baritone, minstrel, songbird, songster, vocalist 9 chanteuse, chantress, contralto 10 songstress, troubadour 11 nightingale 12 countertenor, mezzo-soprano

singer, female

French: 9 chanteuse

Singer, Isaac Bashevis

author of: 6 Shosha 7 Old Love 8 The Manor 9 The Estate 13 Gimpel the Fool 15 The Family Moskat 16 In My Father's Court 24 The Spinoza of Market Street

singer, professional

French, Italian: 10 cantatrice

singing group 4 trio 5 choir 6 chorus 7 quartet 8 glee club 13 choral society 17 barbershop quartet

Singin' in the Rain

director: 9 Gene Kelly 12 Stanley Donen

cast: 9 Gene Kelly, Jean Hagen 11 Cyd Charisse 13 Donald O'Connor 14 Debbie Reynolds

song: 11 Make 'em Laugh

single 3 one 4 lone, sole 5 unwed 6 maiden 7 only one 8 bachelor, singular, solitary, spinster, wifeless 10 unmarried 11 individual, spouseless 11 husbandless

single file 8 one by one 10 Indian file, one at a time 13 in a single line 16 one behind another

single-handedly 5 alone 7 unaided 9 by oneself, on one's own 10 unassisted 11 without help

single-minded 4 firm 6 dogged 7 devoted, intense, staunch, zealous 8 resolved, tireless, untiring 9 dedicated, steadfast, tenacious 10 determined, inflexible, persistent, relentless, unswerving, unwavering 11 persevering, unflinching

singleness 12 bachelorhood, spinsterhood 14 unmarried state 17 single blessedness

single out 4 pick, take 6 choose, opt for, select 7 call out, extract, fix upon, pick out 8 decide on, set apart, settle on 11 distinguish

sing the praises of 4 hail, laud, tout 5 boost, cheer, exalt, extol, honor 6 praise 7 acclaim, applaud, approve, commend 8 eulogize 9 celebrate 10 compliment

singular 3 odd 4 rare 5 queer 6 choice, quaint, select, unique 7 bizarre, curious, strange, unusual 8 aberrant, abnormal, atypical, freakish, peculiar, peerless, superior, uncommon, unwonted 9 anomalous, different, eccentric, fantastic, marvelous, matchless, unequaled, unnatural, wonderful 10 noteworthy, outlandish, prodigious, remarkable, surpassing, unfamiliar 11 exceptional, uncustomary 12 unparalleled 13 extraordinary, unaccountable, unprecedented 14 unconventional 16 out-of-the-ordinary

Sinhalese

language family: 12 Indo-European

branch: 11 Indo-Iranian

group: 5 Indic

spoken in: 6 Ceylon 8 Sri Lanka

sinister 4 dark, dire, evil, foul, rank, vile 5 black 6 cursed, malign, wicked 7 adverse, fearful, hellish, ominous, unlucky 8 accursed, alarming, damnable, devilish, infernal, menacing, rascally 9 dismaying, insidious, malignant 10 despicable, detestable, diabolical, disturbing, malevolent, perfidious, villainous 11 disquieting, frightening, threatening, treacherous, unfavorable, unpromising 12 blackhearted, inauspicious, unpropitious 13 Machiavellian, reprehensible

sink 3 dig, dip, ebb, lay, sag, set 4 bore, bowl, bury, drop, fall, seep, slip, soak, tilt, wane 5 basin, drill, drive, droop, drown, gouge, lower, slant, slope, slump, stoop, yield 6 engulf, go down, lessen, plunge, reduce, shrink, worsen 7 decline, descend, give way, go to pot, go under, put down, regress, subside, succumb 8 diminish, excavate, languish, lavatory, scoop out, submerge, submerse, washbowl 9 hollow out, wash basin 10 degenerate, depreciate, go downhill, retrogress 11 deteriorate, go to the dogs

sinless 4 good, holy, pure 6 chaste 7 upright 8 innocent, spotless, virtuous 9 reputable, righteous

sinner 8 apostate, evildoer, offender 9 miscreant, misfeasor, reprobate, wrongdoer 10 backslider, malefactor, malfeasant, recidivist, trespasser 12 transgressor

Sinnis see 5 Sinis

Sinoeis see 3 Pan

Sinon

pretended to be: 13 Greek deserter

told Trojans of: 11 Trojan Horse

Sino-Tibetan

language branch: 7 Sinitic 12 Tibeto-Burman

includes: 4 Naga 5 Karen 7 Burmese, Chinese 8 Kuki-Chin, Mandarin

Sins, Seven 4 envy, lust 5 anger, pride, sloth 8 gluttony 12 covetousness

sinuosity 10 slinkiness 11 convolution, sinuousness 12 tortuousness

sinuous 6 curved, folded, volute, zigzag 7 bending, coiling, curving, twisted, winding 8 indirect, mazelike, rambling, tortuous, twisting 9 wandering 10 circuitous, convoluted, meandering, roundabout, serpentine, undulating 12 labyrinthine

sinuousness 9 sinuosity 10 slinkiness 11 convolution 12 tortuousness

Sinus
  also: 6 Sinnis
  vocation: 6 robber
  daughter: 8 Perigune
  killed by: 7 Theseus
  epithet: 12 Pityocamptes

Siouan
  tribe: 4 Crow, Iowa 5 Ioway, Omaha, Osage, Sioux 6 Dakota, Mandan 7 Hidatsa 8 Minitari, Wazhazhe 10 Assiniboin, Gros Ventre 11 Assiniboine

Sioux see 6 Dakota

Sioux State
  nickname of: 11 North Dakota

sip 3 lap, nip, sup 4 dram, drop 5 drink, savor, taste 6 sample 7 soupcon, swallow 10 thimbleful

siphon 4 tube 5 drain 7 draw off

siphonaptera
  class: 8 hexapoda
  phylum: 10 arthropoda
  group: 4 flea

Sippar residents 11 Sepharvites

Siqueiros, David Alfaro
  born: 6 Mexico 9 Chihuahua
  artwork: 12 New Democracy 13 Echo of a Scream 14 Trial of Fascism 15 Ascent of Culture, Burial of a Worker 16 Towards the Cosmos 17 Death to the Invader 18 Polyforum Siqueiros 22 March of Humanity on Earth 24 Cuauhtemoc Against the Myth

sir
  French: 8 monsieur

sire 4 king, lord 5 beget, breed 6 create, father 7 creator 9 originate 10 originator, progenitor

siren, Siren 4 horn, vamp 5 alarm, nymph, witch 6 sexpot 7 charmer, whistle 8 deceiver, sea nymph 9 temptress 10 seductress 11 enchantress 13 warning signal 15 bewitching woman
  French: 11 femme fatale
  form: 5 nymph
  location: 3 sea
  lured sailors by: 7 singing

Sir Gawain and the Green Knight
  author: 7 unknown
  character: 10 King Arthur 22 Sir Bernlak de Hautdesert
  horse: 9 Gringalet

Sirian Experiments, The
  author: 12 Doris Lessing

Sisera
  commander for: 5 Jabin
  defeated by: 5 Barak

sissified 6 prissy 7 unmanly 8 womanish 10 effeminate

sissy 6 coward 8 weakling 9 fraidy-cat 10 scaredy-cat

sister 3 nun, kin, sib 5 nurse 6 female 7 sibling 8 feminist, relation, relative
  nautically: 6 secure 10 strengthen
  society: 8 sorority

Sister Carrie
  author: 15 Theodore Dreiser
  character: 11 G W Hurstwood 12 Carrie Meeber 13 Charles Drouet

Sister Woman
  character in: 16 Cat on a Hot Tin Roof
  author: 8 Williams

Sisyphean 4 hard 5 tough 6 uphill 7 arduous, onerous 8 toilsome 9 demanding, difficult, strenuous, wearisome 10 exhausting

Sisyphus
  king of: 7 Corinth
  father: 6 Aeolus
  mother: 7 Enarete
  brother: 9 Salmoneus
  wife: 6 Merope
  son: 5 Almus 7 Glaucus 8 Ornytion 10 Thersander
  founded: 6 Ephyra 7 Corinth
  rolled: 5 stone

sit 3 lie 4 loll, meet, mind, rest, rule, stay 5 abide, chair, nurse, perch, reign, roost, squat, stand, teach, watch 6 attend, endure, gather, govern, linger, remain, reside, settle, sprawl 7 baby-sit, care for, convene, preside 8 assemble, be placed, be seated, chaperon 9 have a seat, officiate 10 deliberate 11 be in session

site 4 area, post, spot, zone 5 field, locus, place, point, scene 6 ground, locale, region, sector 7 section, setting, station 8 district, locality, location, position, province 9 territory 11 whereabouts

sit in judgment 5 judge 6 decide, settle 7 adjudge, mediate 9 arbitrate, reconcile 10 adjudicate 12 bring to terms

situ 5 place

situate 3 put, set 4 post 5 build, house, lodge, place, plant, stand 6 billet, locate, settle 7 install, station 8 ensconce, position 9 construct, establish

situation 3 fix, job 4 case, duty, post, role, seat, site, work 5 berth, place, state 6 locale, office, plight, status 7 dilemma, posture, station 8 capacity, function, locality, location, position, quandary 9 condition 10 assignment, livelihood 11 predicament 13 circumstances 14 state of affairs

sit upon 5 brood, cover, hatch 8 incubate

Sivan 16 third Hebrew month

Six Characters in Search of an Author
  author: 15 Luigi Pirandello

six cubits 4 reed

Six Million Dollar Man
  character: 11 Dr Rudy Wells, (Col) Steve Austin 12 Oscar Goldman
  cast: 9 Lee Majors 13 Martin E Brooks 15 Alan Oppenheimer, Richard Anderson
  spinoff: 11 Bionic Woman

Sixty Minutes

correspondent: 9 Dan Rather 10 Andy Rooney 11 Diane Sawyer, Mike Wallace, Morley Safer 13 Harry Reasoner

sizable 5 ample, broad, large, roomy 7 immense 8 spacious 9 capacious, good-sized

size 3 sum 4 area, bulk, mass, sort 5 array, grade, group, scope, total 6 amount, extent, spread, volume 7 arrange, bigness, content, expanse, stretch 8 capacity, classify, quantity, totality 9 aggregate, amplitude, greatness, largeness, magnitude 10 dimensions 11 measurement, proportions

sizzle 3 fry 4 hiss, spit 7 crackle, frizzle, hissing, sputter 8 splutter 10 sputtering

skate 3 nag, ray 4 skid, skim, slip 5 blade, coast, glide, horse, slide 6 rotter
female: 4 maid
genus: 4 Raja
mark: 4 cusp

skein 4 coil, hank, reel, yarn 5 twist 6 tangle, thread 9 filaments, twistings
members: 4 fowl 5 ducks, flock, geese 6 flyers

skeletal 4 bony, thin 5 gaunt 6 wasted 9 emaciated 10 cadaverous

skeleton 4 hulk 5 bones, frame, shell 9 framework
purpose: 7 support 8 protects 9 framework

Skelton, Red

real name: 21 Richard Bernard Skelton
born: 11 Vincennes IN
roles: 7 I Dood It 8 Ship Ahoy 12 Panama Hattie 16 Neptune's Daughter 17 The Fuller Brush Man 18 Clem Kadiddlehopper, Whistling in the Dark 20 Freddie the Freeloader

skeptic, sceptic 7 atheist, doubter, scoffer 8 agnostic 10 questioner, unbeliever 14 doubting Thomas

skeptical, sceptical 6 unsure 7 cynical, dubious 8 doubtful, doubting, scoffing 9 uncertain 11 incredulous, questioning, unbelieving, unconvinced 12 disbelieving 13 hypercritical

skepticism 5 doubt 7 dubiety 8 distrust, mistrust, unbelief 9 disbelief, suspicion 11 agnosticism, incredulity 12 doubtfulness 13 faithlessness

sketch 3 map 4 draw, plot, skit 5 chart, draft, graph, scene 6 depict, digest, precis, satire 7 drawing, lampoon, mark out, outline, picture, portray, summary, takeoff 8 abstract, rough out, synopsis, vignette 9 blueprint, burlesque, delineate, short play, summarize 11 preliminary 16 characterization

Sketch Book, The

author: 16 Washington Irving

sketchy 4 bare, hazy 5 brief, crude, light, rough, short, vague 6 meager, skimpy, slight 7 cursory, outline, shallow, slender 9 essential, rough-hewn, unrefined 10 incomplete, undetailed, unfinished, unpo-

lished 11 preliminary, preparatory, provisional, superficial

skewed 5 slued 6 veered, warped 7 oblique, sheered, slanted, swerved, twisted 9 distorted

skewer 3 pin, rod 4 spit, stab 5 truss 6 pierce, skiver 7 impale 9 brochette 10 run through

skid 3 ski 4 drag, dray, skim, skip, sled, slip 5 coast, glide, skate, slide 6 runner, sledge 7 skitter 8 glissade, platform, sideslip

Skidbladnir

origin: 12 Scandinavian
ship of: 4 Frey 5 Freyr
feature: 11 collapsible

Skidegatta

tribe: 5 Haida

Skidmore, Owings, and Merrill

partners: 13 John Merrill Sr, Louis Skidmore 15 Nathaniel Owings
architects of: 10 Lever House (NYC) 11 AEC town site (Oak Ridge TN) 13 Banque Lambert (Brussels) 16 John Hancock Tower (Chicago) 17 Terrace Plaza Hotel (Cincinnati), US Air Force Academy (CO) 18 Mauna Kea Beach Hotel (Kamuela HI) 19 Istanbul Hilton Hotel (Turkey) 23 Beinecke Rare Book Library (Yale) 26 Chase Manhattan Bank Building (NYC) 33 American Republic Insurance Building (Des Moines IA)
world's tallest building: 10 Sears Tower (Chicago)

skiff 4 boat 6 dinghy 7 rowboat

skiing

athlete: 9 Phil Mahre 11 Bill Johnson, Cindy Nelson 13 Gustavo Thoeni, Robert Cochran 14 Marilyn Cochran, Martha Rockwell 15 Debbie Armstrong, Ingemar Stenmark, Jean Claude Killy 16 Michael Gallagher 17 Barbara Ann Cochran 20 Annemarie Proell Moser

Skikne, Larushka Misch

real name of: 14 Laurence Harvey

skill 4 gift 5 craft, knack 6 acumen, talent 7 ability, cunning, faculty, knowhow, mastery, prowess 8 artistry, capacity, deftness, facility 9 adeptness, dexterity, expertise, handiness, ingenuity 10 adroitness, cleverness, competence, experience, expertness 11 proficiency 12 skillfulness 13 inventiveness

skilled 6 adroit, expert 7 trained 8 skillful 9 competent, masterful, practiced 10 proficient 12 accomplished

skilled worker 7 artisan 9 craftsman 10 technician 15 master craftsman

skillful 3 apt 4 able, deft, keen 5 adept, handy, sharp, slick 6 adroit, clever, expert, facile, gifted 7 capable, cunning, skilled, trained, veteran 8 masterly, talented 9 competent, dexterous, ingenious, masterful, practiced, qualified 10 proficient, well-versed 11 experienced 12 accomplished, professional

skim 3 fly 4 flip, ream, sail, scan, scud, skid, skip 5 coast, float, glide, skate, sweep 6 bounce, scrape 7 dip into 8 glissade 10 glance over 11 leaf through, move lightly 12 thumb through

skimp 5 pinch, stint 6 scrimp, slight 8 be frugal, be stingy, hold back, withhold 9 economize 11 cut expenses, scrape along

Skimpole, Harold
  character in: 10 Bleak House
  author: 7 Dickens

skimpy 5 close, scant, small, spare, tight 6 frugal, meager, modest, scanty, slight, sparse, stingy 7 miserly, scrimpy, sparing, wanting 8 exiguous, grudging, smallish, stinting 9 illiberal, niggardly, penurious, scrimping 10 inadequate, incomplete, too thrifty 11 close fisted, tightfisted 12 insufficient, parsimonious 13 pennypinching 14 inconsiderable

skin 3 fur, pod 4 bark, case, coat, flay, hide, hull, husk, peel, pelt, rind, shell, abrade, casing, fleece, jacket, scrape, sheath, lay bare, epidermis, complexion, integument, body covering, outer coating
  outer layer: 9 epidermis
  contains: 3 fat 4 hair, pore, root 5 nerve 6 vessel 8 oil gland 10 sweat gland
  body's largest: 5 organ
  sense of: 4 cold, heat, pain 5 touch 8 pressure, tickling

skinflint 5 miser 7 hoarder, niggard, scrooge 8 tightwad 10 pinchpenny 12 penny pincher

Skinner, Cornelia Otis
  author of: 23 The Pleasure of His Company (with Samuel Taylor) 24 Our Hearts Were Young and Gay (with Emily Kimbrough)

skinny 4 lank, lean, thin, wiry 5 gaunt, gawky, lanky, spare 6 slight 7 angular, scraggy, scrawny, slender, spindly 8 gangling, rawboned, shrunken, skeletal 9 emaciated

Skin of Our Teeth, The
  author: 14 Thornton Wilder

skip 3 bob, cut, hop 4 flee, flit, jump, leap, miss, omit, romp, shun, trip 5 bound, caper, dodge, elude, evade 6 bounce, escape, eschew, gambol, ignore, prance, spring 7 abscond, make off, neglect 8 leap over, leave out, overlook, pass over 9 disappear, disregard, do without, play hooky, skedaddle 10 fly the coop 12 be absent from

skirmish 4 fray, tilt 5 brush, clash, joust, run-in, scrap, set-to 6 action, affray, battle, fracas, tussle 7 scuffle 8 struggle 9 encounter, firefight, scrimmage 10 engagement

skirmisher
  French: 10 tirailleur

Skirnir
  origin: 12 Scandinavian
  servant of: 4 Frey 5 Freyr

Skirophoria see 11 Scirophoria

skirt 3 hem, rim 4 edge, gird, kilt, maxi, mini, ring, shun 5 avoid, evade, flank, hem in, verge 6 border, bounds, circle, dirndl, fringe, girdle, margin 7 enclose, envelop 8 boundary, encircle, go around, lie along 9 crinoline, outer area, perimeter, periphery 10 circumvent, fight shy of 12 circumscribe, detour around

skittish 3 shy 4 wary 5 chary, jumpy, leery, shaky, timid 6 fitful, unsure 7 bashful, fearful, fidgety, flighty, guarded, jittery, nervous, restive 8 cautious, restless, unstable, unsteady, volatile 9 demurring, excitable, impulsive, mercurial, reluctant 10 suspicious 11 distrustful

skittles
  equipment: 4 pins 6 cheese
  also called: 5 closh 6 cloddy 8 roly-poly 10 Dutch bowls
  tabletop version: 15 Enfield skittles

Skrymir
  also: 10 Utgardloki
  origin: 12 Scandinavian
  form: 5 giant
  took to Jotunheim: 4 Loki, Thor 7 Thialfi

Skuld 4 Norn
  origin: 12 Scandinavian
  form: 5 dwarf
  personifies: 6 future
  developed from: 5 Urdar
  companions: 3 Urd 8 Verdandi

skulduggery, skullduggery 7 knavery 8 trickery 9 chicanery, deception 10 dirty trick 12 pettifoggery

skulk 4 hide, lurk 5 cower, creep, prowl, slink, sneak 9 pussyfoot

skull
  contains: 5 brain
Skull place 7 Calvary 8 Golgotha

sky 5 space 9 firmament 10 atmosphere, outer space, the heavens 12 arch of heaven
  goddess of: 3 Fri, Nut 5 Frigg, Frija 6 Frigga

sky blue 5 azure 8 cerulean, pale blue 9 clear blue, light blue

Sky King
  character: 5 Penny 7 Clipper
  cast: 10 Kirby Grant 11 Ron Haggerty 13 Gloria Winters
  ranch: 11 Flying Crown
  plane: 8 Songbird

skylarking 5 sport 6 antics 7 hijinks, romping 10 frolicking

skypilot 5 padre, rabbi 6 cleric, parson, priest 8 chaplain, minister 9 clergyman

skyward 2 up 6 upward 8 to the sky 10 heavenward 12 to the heavens

slab 3 wad 4 hunk, slat 5 block, board, chunk, plank, slice, wedge 10 thick slice

slack 3 lax 4 dull, easy, free, lazy, limp, slow, soft 5 baggy, loose, quiet, relax 6 easily, flabby, freely, limply, loosen, pliant, remiss, slowly, untied 7 flaccid, let up on, loosely, not busy, not firm, not taut, offhand, relaxed, slacken 8 careless, dilatory, flexible, heedless, inactive, indolent, listless, not tight, slapdash, slipshod, slothful, sluggish 9 leisurely, lethargic, negligent, slow-paced, unmindful, untighten 10 neglectful, nonchalant, permissive, slow-moving, sluggishly, unexacting, unfastened, unthinking 11 inattentive, indifferent, thoughtless, unconcerned, undemanding

slacken 4 curb, ease, flag, free, slow 5 abate, check, let go, let up, limit, loose, relax, slack 6 arrest, go limp, lessen, loosen, reduce, retard, soften, temper, weaken 7 dwindle, inhibit, release 8 decrease, diminish, keep back, mitigate, moderate, restrain, slow down, taper off 9 untighten

slacker 5 idler 6 dodger, loafer, truant 7 dallier, dawdler, goof-off, laggard, quitter, shirker 9 do-nothing, goldbrick 10 malingerer 14 good-for-nothing, procrastinator

slag 5 dross 6 cinder, scoria 8 clinkers

slake 4 calm, cool, curb, ease, hush, sate 5 allay, quell, quiet, still 6 modify, quench, soothe, subdue, temper 7 appease, assuage, compose, gratify, mollify, relieve, satiate, satisfy 8 decrease, mitigate, moderate 9 alleviate 11 tranquilize 14 take the edge off

slake off 4 wane 5 abate 6 lessen, reduce, weaken 7 decline, subside 8 diminish, fade away, slack off

slam 3 hit 4 bang, bump, slap 5 crash, smack, smash, throw

slammer 3 jug, pen 4 jail, stir 5 clink 6 cooler, lockup, prison 8 big house, hoosegow 9 calaboose, jailhouse 12 penitentiary

Slammin' Sammy
  nickname of: 8 Sam Snead

slander 4 soil 5 libel, smear, sully 6 defame, malign, revile, vilify 7 calumny 8 besmirch 9 falsehood 10 defamation, distortion 12 vilification 14 false statement 17 misrepresentation

Slaney, Mary see 10 Mary Decker

slang 4 cant, jive 5 argot, idiom, lingo 6 jargon 7 dialect

slant 4 bias, lean, list, rake, tilt, view 5 angle, color, pitch, slope 7 distort, incline, leaning 8 attitude 9 prejudice, viewpoint

slanted 4 awry 6 biased, tilted 7 colored, crooked, leaning, pitched, sloping 8 inclined 9 on an angle, on the bias 10 prejudiced

slanting 4 bias 5 alean, atilt 7 oblique, sloping 8 diagonal, glancing, inclined 10 distorting

slap 3 cut, hit 4 blow, clap, cuff, snub, swat 5 smack, whack 6 insult, rebuff, strike, wallop 9 rejection

slapdash 6 casual, sloppy 8 careless, slipshod, slovenly 9 haphazard

Slapsie Maxie
  nickname of: 15 Maxie Rosenbloom

slash 3 cut, rip 4 drop, gash, mark, pare, rend, rent, slit, tear 5 lower, slice 6 reduce, stroke 8 decrease, lacerate, lowering 9 reduction 10 laceration

slate 4 list 6 ballot, tablet, ticket 10 blackboard, chalkboard

slattern 4 drab, slob, slut 5 bitch, frump 6 harlot, sloven 7 trollop

slatternly 6 frowsy, frumpy, sloppy, untidy 7 unkempt 8 slipshod, slovenly

slaughter 4 kill, slay 6 pogrom 7 butcher, destroy, killing, wipe out 8 decimate, massacre 9 bloodbath 10 annihilate, butchering, mass murder 11 exterminate

Slaughterhouse Five
  author: 12 Kurt Vonnegut
  character: 12 Billy Pilgrim
  setting: 7 Dresden

Slav 4 Pole, Serb, Sorb, Wend 5 Croat, Czech 6 Bulgar, Slovak 7 Russian, Serbian, Slovene, Sorbian 8 Bohemian, Croatian, Moravian 9 Bulgarian, Ruthenian, Slavonian, Slovadian, Ukrainian

slave 4 prey, serf, toil 6 addict, drudge, menial, thrall, toiler, vassal, victim 7 chattel, plodder 8 bondsman 9 workhorse 11 bond servant

slaver 5 drool 6 drivel 7 slobber

slavery 4 toil 5 grind, labor, sweat 6 strain 7 bondage, serfdom, travail 8 drudgery, struggle 9 captivity, treadmill, vassalage 11 enslavement, impressment, subjugation 12 enthrallment

Slavic
  language family: 12 Indo-European
  group: 11 Balto-Slavic
  subgroup: 12 Old Bulgarian 13 Eastern Slavic, Western Slavic 14 Southern Slavic 15 Old Church Slavic

slavish 5 exact 6 strict 7 literal, servile 9 imitative, slavelike 10 derivative, obsequious, submissive, unoriginal 11 subservient 13 unimaginative

slay 4 do in, kill 6 murder 7 destroy, execute 8 massacre 9 slaughter 10 annihilate

slayer 6 hit man, killer 7 butcher 8 assassin, murderer 11 executioner 12 exterminator

slaying 6 murder 7 killing 8 homicide 9 execution

sleazy 5 cheap, tacky 6 flimsy, shabby, shoddy, trashy, vulgar 7 schlock 13 insubstantial

sleek 4 oily 5 shiny, silky, slick, suave 6 glossy, satiny, smooth 7 fawning, velvety 8 lustrous, unctuous 12 ingratiating

sleep 3 nap 4 doze, rest 5 death, peace 6 repose, snooze 7 slumber
  god of: 6 Hypnos, Hypnus, Somnus

sleeping 6 asleep, dozing 7 dormant, napping, resting 8 snoozing 9 quiescent, somnolent 11 hibernating 19 in the arms of Morpheus

Sleeping Beauty, The
  composer: 11 Tchaikovsky

sleeping car (railroad)
  invented by: 7 Pullman

sleeping infants
  goddess of: 6 Cunina

sleeping place 3 bed, cot **4** bunk **5** berth **6** pallet **7** bedroom **9** dormitory **10** bedchamber

sleepless 5 alert **7** wakeful **8** restless, watchful **9** insomniac, wide awake **11** industrious

sleeplessness 8 insomnia **9** alertness, attention **11** wakefulness **12** restlessness

sleep lightly 3 nap, nod **4** doze **6** catnap, snooze **15** catch forty winks

sleepy 4 dull **5** quiet, tired, weary **6** drowsy **8** fatigued, inactive **9** exhausted

sleigh 4 dray, sled **6** cutter, sledge, troika **8** transport

Sleipnir
origin: **12** Scandinavian
horse of: **4** Odin **5** Othin
legs: **5** eight

slender 4 lean, poor, slim, thin, weak **5** faint, scant, small, spare **6** feeble, little, meager, narrow, remote, skinny, slight **7** willowy **8** delicate

Slender
character in: **22** The Merry Wives of Windsor
author: **11** Shakespeare

Sleuth
director: **17** Joseph L Mankiewicz
based on play by: **14** Anthony Shaffer
cast: **12** Michael Caine **15** Laurence Olivier

slew 3 lot, ton **4** gang, heap, load, lots, peck, pile, raft **5** batch, did in **6** killed **8** murdered **12** assassinated

Slezak, Walter
born: **6** Vienna **7** Austria
father: **9** Leo Slezak
roles: **5** Fanny **8** Lifeboat **11** Dr Coppelius

slice 3 cut **4** pare **5** carve, piece, sever, shave **6** cut off, divide **7** portion, section, segment, whittle **8** separate **9** dismember

slick 3 sly **4** coat, film, foxy, oily, scum, waxy, wily **5** sharp, shiny, sleek **6** clever, glassy, glossy, greasy, satiny, smooth, tricky **7** coating, cunning **8** slippery **10** make glossy **11** fast-talking **13** smooth-talking

slicker 8 raincoat **9** sou'wester **10** mackintosh, waterproof

slide 4 fall, pass, ramp, skid, slip, veer **5** chute, coast, glide, lapse, slope **7** slither **8** sideslip **11** diapositive **12** transparency

slide by 4 go by **5** lapse **6** elapse, roll by, slip by **7** glide by **8** slip away

slight 3 cut **4** lean, slap, slim, snub, thin, tiny **5** frail, small, spare **6** insult, little, modest, rebuff **7** fragile, limited, slender **8** moderate **10** incivility, negligible, restricted **11** unimportant **13** imperceptible, inappreciable, infinitesimal

slight amount 3 bit **4** dash, drop **5** pinch, touch, trace **6** little **7** smidgen, smidgin, soupcon **8** smidgeon **9** little bit **10** smattering

slightly 6 feebly, rarely **8** meagerly, scantily, scarcely, somewhat **10** negligibly **13** superficially **15** insignificantly

slim 4 lean, thin **5** faint, small **6** meager, remote, skinny, slight, svelte **7** distant, slender, thready, willowy **10** negligible

slime 3 mud **4** mire, muck, ooze **6** sludge

slimy 4 foul, vile **5** gummy, mucky, nasty **6** creepy, putrid, sticky **7** viscous **9** glutinous, loathsome, obnoxious, offensive, repulsive

sling 3 net **4** cast **5** fling, throw **9** slingshot **10** arm support

Slingin' Sammy
nickname of: **10** Sammy Baugh

slingshot 5 sling **8** catapult

slink 4 slip **5** creep, prowl, skulk, sneak, steal **6** tiptoe

slip 3 put **4** dock, drop, fail, fall, leak, pass, sink, skid **5** berth, error, glide, lapse, scrap, shoot, shred, slide, sneak, sprig, steal, strip **6** escape, sprout, ticket, worsen **7** blunder, chemise, cutting, decline, faux pas, receipt, sapling, voucher **9** petticoat, stripling, youngling, youngster **10** be revealed, get clear of, imprudence, underdress **12** indiscretion

slip away 4 go by **5** lapse **6** elapse, escape **7** run away, slide by **8** creep off **9** tiptoe off

slip by 4 go by, pass **5** lapse **6** elapse, pass by, roll by **7** glide by, slide by

slip of the tongue, a
Latin: **13** lapsus linguae

slipper 4 mule, shoe **5** scuff **6** sandal

slippery 4 foxy, oily, waxy, wily **5** slick, soapy **6** crafty, glassy, greasy, shifty, smooth, sneaky, tricky **7** devious **9** deceitful **10** contriving, unreliable **11** treacherous **13** untrustworthy

slipshod 3 lax **5** loose, messy **6** casual, sloppy, untidy **7** offhand **8** careless, slovenly **11** thoughtless

slip-up 4 flub, goof **5** botch, error, gaffe, lapse **6** boo-boo, bungle, foul-up, mess-up, miscue **7** blooper, blunder, clinker, faux pas, mistake, screw-up **9** oversight

slit 3 cut **4** gash **5** crack, slash **7** crevice, fissure **8** incision

slither 5 glide, slide **25** move with a side-to-side motion

sliver 5 crumb, shred, slice, snick **6** morsel **8** splinter

slivovitz
type: **6** brandy **7** liqueur
origin: **10** Yugoslavia
flavor: **4** plum

Sloan, John F
born: **11** Lock Haven PA
artwork: **12** McSorley's Bar **14** Wake of the Ferry **18** Hairdresser's Window **25** Backyards Greenwich Village

slob 6 sloven **8** slattern

slobber 4 slop **5** drool **6** drivel, slaver **7** dribble, sputter **8** salivate, splutter

sloe gin
- **type:** 7 liqueur
- **flavor:** 9 sloe berry 15 blackthorn berry
- **drink:** 11 Sloe Gin Fizz
- **with bourbon:** 9 Black Hawk
- **with rum:** 11 Shark's Tooth
- **with vermouth:** 10 Blackthom

slogan 5 motto 6 byword 9 battle cry, catchword, watchword

sloop 4 boat, brig, ship 5 smack 8 sailboat, schooner

slop 3 mud 4 mire, muck, ooze 5 filth, slosh, slush, spill, swash, swill, waste 6 refuse, sludge, splash 7 garbage, spatter 8 splatter

Slop, Dr
- **character in:** 14 Tristram Shandy
- **author:** 6 Sterne

slope 3 tip 4 bank, bend, lean, tilt 5 angle, pitch, slant 7 descent, incline 9 downgrade 11 inclination

sloping 5 alean, steep 6 aslant 7 leaning, oblique, tilting 8 diagonal, inclined, on a slant, slanting 9 slantways 11 declivitous

sloppiness 5 chaos, mix-up, upset 6 jumble 7 clutter 8 disarray, disorder, shambles 9 messiness 10 disharmony, untidiness 12 dishevelment 14 disarrangement 15 disorganization

sloppy 3 wet 5 dirty, messy, muddy 6 marshy, sloshy, slushy, sodden, soiled, swampy, untidy, watery 7 unclean 10 disorderly

sloppy person 4 slob 6 sloven

slosh 3 lap 4 drop, mire, stir 5 slush, spill, swash 6 splash 8 flounder

slot 3 gap 4 slit 5 crack, niche, notch
- **machine:** 14 one-armed bandit

sloth 6 phlegm, torpor 7 languor 8 idleness, laziness, lethargy 9 indolence, lassitude, torpidity 12 listlessness, sluggishness 13 do-nothingness, shiftlessness

slothful 3 lax 4 idle, lazy 5 inert 6 drowsy, otiose, supine, torpid 8 indolent, listless, sluggish 9 do-nothing, lethargic, negligent, shiftless 10 sluggardly 11 unambitious

slouch 4 bend 5 droop, hunch, idler, slump, stoop 6 loafer 7 laggard, shirker, slacker 8 sluggard 9 goldbrick, lazybones

Slovakia
- **formerly part of:** 14 Czechoslovakia
- **capital/largest city:** 10 Bratislava
- **others:** 6 Kosice
- **head of state:** 9 president
- **government:** 8 republic
- **monetary unit:** 5 crown 6 koruna
- **mountain:** 7 Sudetes 8 Low Tatra 9 High Tatra, Slovak Ore 10 Carpathian, Nizke Tatry 11 Visoke Tatry 15 White Carpathian
- **river:** 2 Uh 3 Vah 4 Hron 5 Nitra, Slana 6 Danube, Hornad, Ondava, Poprad 7 Laborec 8 Latorica
- **people:** 5 Czech 6 Slavik, Slovak 9 Hungarian
- **language:** 6 Slavik, Slovak
- **religion:** 9 Christian 13 Roman Catholic

Slovenia
- **capital/largest city:** 9 Ljubljana
- **others:** 5 Celje, Koper, Kranj 7 Maribor
- **head of state:** 9 president
- **government:** 8 republic
- **monetary unit:** 5 tolar
- **river:** 4 Sava 5 Drava
- **sea:** 8 Adriatic
- **people:** 8 Slovenes
- **language:** 7 Slovene
- **religion:** 13 Roman Catholic

slovenly 5 dirty, dowdy, messy 6 frowzy, sloppy, untidy 7 unclean, unkempt 8 careless, slapdash, slipshod 10 disorderly, slatternly 11 indifferent, unconcerned

slow 3 dim, off 4 curb, dull, dumb, flag, late, long 5 brake, check, dense, heavy, loath, quiet 6 averse, boring, falter, hinder, hold up, impede, obtuse, retard, stupid, torpid 7 belated, delayed, laggard, lumpish, not busy, overdue, tedious, unhasty 8 backward, cautious, dawdling, dilatory, dragging, drawn out, extended, hesitant, inactive, obstruct, sluggish, tarrying 9 dimwitted, leisurely, lingering, ponderous, prolonged, reluctant, snail-like, unhurried 10 behind time, decelerate, deliberate, dullwitted, indisposed, protracted, unexciting, unpunctual

slowdown 4 curb, flag 5 brake, delay, letup, slump 6 ease-up, falter, hinder, impede, lessen, retard, slow-up 7 decline, fall off, letdown, setback, slowing, subside 8 diminish, downturn, flagging 9 grind down 10 decelerate, slackening, stagnation 11 reduce speed, retardation 12 deceleration

slow-moving 4 poky 5 pokey 6 idling 8 crawling, creeping, dawdling, sluggish 9 leisurely, snaillike 10 turtlelike 12 tortoiselike
- **creature:** 4 slug 5 loris, sloth, snail 6 turtle 8 tortoise

slowness 6 tedium 8 dullness 9 torpidity 10 snail's pace 12 backwardness, sluggishness

slow-paced 4 easy 7 gradual, laggard 8 sluggish 9 leisurely, lethargic, unhurried 10 deliberate

slowpoke 4 slug 5 idler, snail 7 dallier, dawdler, laggard, lie-abed, plodder 8 lingerer, slugabed, tortoise 9 saunterer, straggler 11 foot-dragger

slow to learn 4 dull 5 dense, inapt 6 stupid 8 retarded 10 slow-witted

slow up 4 stem 5 delay 6 detain, hinder, impede, retard 8 slow down

slow-witted 4 dull 5 dense 7 doltish, idiotic, moronic 8 backward, retarded 9 imbecilic

sludge 3 mud 4 mire, muck, ooze, slop 5 dregs, slime, slush 8 sediment

slug 3 bat, hit 4 bash, belt, sock 5 baste, clout, pound, punch, smite, thump, whack, whale 6 batter, strike, wallop 7 clobber 8 lambaste

sluggard 4 lazy 5 drone, idler, sloth, snail 6 loafer, truant, turtle 7 dawdler, laggard 8 loiterer, slothful, slowpoke, tortoise 9 do-nothing, lazybones 11 couch potato 12 lounge lizard 13 stick-in-the-mud

sluggish 4 lazy, slow 5 inert 6 torpid 7 languid 8 inactive, indolent, lifeless, listless, slothful 9 leisurely, lethargic, soporific, unhurried 10 phlegmatic, protracted, spiritless

sluggishness 6 torpor 7 inertia 8 lethargy, slowness 9 lassitude 10 inactivity 12 listlessness

slum
   Portuguese: 6 favela

slumber 3 nap 4 doze 5 sleep 6 snooze 8 vegetate 9 hibernate 10 be inactive, lie dormant

slump 3 dip, sag 4 drop, fall, slip 5 droop, lapse 6 plunge, slouch, tumble 7 decline, give way, reverse, setback 8 collapse

slur 3 cut, dig 4 mark, skip, spot 5 smear, stain, sully, taint 6 defame, ignore, insult, malign, mumble, mutter, slight 7 affront, blacken, blemish, let pass 8 mumbling, overlook, pass over 9 disregard, gloss over, muttering 11 run together

slush 4 slop 6 bathos 9 soppiness 11 mawkishness, melting snow 14 sentimentalism, sentimentality

slushiness 5 slush 10 sponginess 11 mawkishness 14 sentimentalism, sentimentality

slut 4 doxy, jade 5 bimbo, frump, hussy, tramp, wench, whore 6 floozy, harlot, sloven, wanton 7 jezebel, trollop 8 slattern, strumpet 10 prostitute

sly 4 foxy, wily 6 artful, covert, crafty, secret, shrewd, sneaky, tricky 7 cunning, furtive, playful, private 8 stealthy 9 conniving 11 dissembling, mischievous 12 confidential

Slye, Leonard
   real name of: 9 Roy Rogers

slyness 5 craft 7 cunning, stealth 8 archness, foxiness, subtlety, wiliness 10 artfulness, craftiness, shrewdness, trickiness 11 furtiveness 15 underhandedness

smack 3 bit, hit, rap 4 blow, buss, clap, cuff, dash, hint, kiss, slap 5 savor, smell, smite, spank, taste, tinge, touch, trace, whack 6 buffet, flavor 7 suggest

small 4 mean, tiny, weak 5 faint, minor, petty, scant 6 feeble, lesser, little, meager, modest, narrow, petite, slight 7 bigoted, fragile, ignoble, trivial 8 not great, trifling 10 diminutive, provincial, undersized 11 of no account, opinionated, superficial, unimportant 13 insignificant 15 inconsequential

Small, Lennie
   character in: 12 Of Mice and Men
   author: 9 Steinbeck

small details
   Latin: 8 minutiae

smaller 4 less 5 lower 6 lesser, tinier 7 dinkier, littler, pettier, reduced, shorter 8 inferior

smallest 5 least 6 lowest 7 tiniest 8 dinkiest, pettiest, shortest 9 slightest

Small House at Allington, The
   author: 15 Anthony Trollope

small intestine
   part of: 15 digestive system
   lined with: 5 villi

small-minded 4 mean 5 petty 6 narrow 7 bigoted 9 parochial 10 prejudiced 12 mean-spirited

smallness 8 meanness, tininess 9 pettiness 10 meagerness, triviality 12 dwarfishness 14 insignificance 18 inconsequentiality

small piece 3 bit, dab 4 chip, drop, snip 5 crumb, grain, piece, pinch, scrap, shred, speck 6 dollop, morsel 7 granule, smidgen, smidgin 8 fragment, particle, smidgeon

small quantity 3 bit, dab, few 5 touch 7 smidgen, smidgin, soupcon 8 smidgeon 9 little bit

small round window
   French: 11 oeil-de-boeuf

small spot 3 dab, dot 5 fleck, speck

small talk 6 banter, gossip 7 chatter, prattle 8 chitchat, idle talk, repartee 9 bavardage, prattling 12 tittle-tattle

smart 4 ache, burn, chic, hurt, keen, neat, trim 5 brash, brisk, quick, sassy, sharp, sting, wince, witty 6 astute, blench, brainy, bright, clever, flinch, modish, shrewd, suffer 7 elegant, stylish 8 feel pain, vigorous 9 be painful, energetic 10 smart-aleck 11 fashionable, intelligent

smart aleck 6 smarty 7 show-off, windbag, wiseass, wise guy 8 blowhard, braggart, saucebox, wiseacre 9 know-it-all 11 smarty-pants 12 grand stander 13 exhibitionist

smarten up 7 dress up, improve 8 beautify, spruce up

smartness 6 acumen, wisdom 8 keenness, sagacity 9 acuteness 10 astuteness, cleverness, perception, shrewdness 12 intelligence, perspicacity

smash 3 hit 4 bang, bash, beat, blow 5 break, clout, crack, crash, crush 6 batter, strike, winner 7 clobber, crack-up, destroy, shatter, success, triumph 8 accident, demolish, splinter 9 collision, sensation 12 disintegrate

smash against 4 beat, lash 5 crash, pound, smite 6 batter, buffet 7 break on

smashed 5 drunk 6 soused, wasted, zapped, zonked 7 crashed, crushed 8 squashed 9 plastered, shattered 10 inebriated 11 intoxicated 17 under the influence 20 three sheets to the wind

smashing 5 great, super 6 superb 8 fabulous, terrific 9 fantastic, marvelous, wonderful 10 stupendous 11 magnificent, sensational 13 extraordinary

smashup 5 crash, wreck 7 crackup 8 accident 9 collision 12 fender bender

smattering 3 bit, dab 4 dash, drop 5 scrap 7 smidgen, smidgin, snippet 8 smidgeon 10 sprinkling

smear 3 mar, rub 4 blur, coat, daub, soil 5 cover, lay on, libel, stain 6 blotch, injure, malign, smirch, smudge, spread, streak 7 blacken, blemish, degrade, slander, splotch, tarnish 8 besmirch, besmudge 9 denigrate 10 accusation, obliterate

smell 4 feel, nose, odor, reek 5 aroma, fetor, scent, sense, sniff, stink 6 detect, stench 7 bouquet, perfume, suspect 8 perceive 9 emanation, fragrance, get wind of

smelly 4 rank 5 fetid 6 putrid 7 noisome, odorous, reeking 8 stinking 10 malodorous

Smerdyakov
　character in: 20 The Brothers Karamazov
　author: 10 Dostoevsky

Smetana, Bedrich
　born: 7 Bohemia 8 Litomysl 11 Leitomischl 14 Czechoslovakia
　composer of: 7 Ma Vlast 9 My Country 10 From My Life 11 Czech Dances 12 The Two Widows 16 The Bartered Bride

smidgen, smidgin, smidgeon 3 bit, dab 4 mite, snip 5 crumb, pinch, scrap, shred, speck, trace 6 dollop, morsel

Smike
　character in: 16 Nicholas Nickleby
　author: 7 Dickens

smile 4 beam, grin 5 favor, shine, smirk 6 simper

Smiles of a Summer Night
　director: 13 Ingmar Bergman
　cast: 11 Eva Dahlbeck 13 Ulla Jacobsson 15 Margit Carlquist 16 Harriet Andersson
　remade as: 17 A Little Night Music

Smiley's People
　author: 11 John Le Carre

Smintheus
　epithet of: 6 Apollo

smirch 4 blot, mark, soil, spot 5 dirty, smear, stain, sully, taint 6 blotch, damage, smudge, stigma 7 begrime, blacken, blemish, slander, tarnish 8 besmirch, besmudge, dishonor 9 discredit

smirk 4 grin, leer 5 sneer 6 simper 7 grimace

Smirke, Sir Robert
　architect of: 12 King's College (U of London) 13 British Museum (London) 19 Covent Garden Theater (London)
　style: 12 Greek Revival

smite 3 hit 4 swat 5 knock, smack, whack 6 enamor, strike, wallop 7 clobber

Smith, Adam
　author of: 18 The Wealth of Nations

Smith, Al
　creator/artist of: 11 Mutt and Jeff

Smith, Betty
　author of: 20 A Tree Grows in Brooklyn

Smith, Charles Aaron
　nickname: 5 Bubba
　sport: 8 football
　team: 14 Baltimore Colts

Smith, David
　born: 8 Decatur IN
　artwork: 3 Zig 4 Cubi 6 Oculus 8

Agricola, Main View, Sentinel, Star Cage 9 Australia, Royal Bird, Tank Totem 10 The Banquet 12 Detroit Queen 15 Lectern Sentinel 17 Medals for Dishonor 20 Hudson River Landscape 23 Song of an Irish Blacksmith

Smith, Gladys Mary
　real name of: 12 Mary Pickford

Smith, Harriet
　character in: 4 Emma
　author: 6 Austen

Smith, Lillian
　author: 12 Strange Fruit

Smith, Maggie
　born: 6 Ilford 7 England
　husband: 14 Robert Stephens
　roles: 7 Othello 15 California Suite, The Pumpkin Eater 17 Travels with My Aunt 24 The Prime of Miss Jean Brodie (Oscar)

Smith, Winston
　character in: 18 Nineteen Eighty-Four
　author: 6 Orwell

smithereen 3 bit 4 atom 5 crumb, shard 8 fragment, particle 9 scintilla

Smithson, James
　field: 9 chemistry
　nationality: 7 British
　discovered: 11 smithsonite 13 zinc carbonite
　funded: 22 Smithsonian Institution

smitten 8 enamored 9 bewitched 10 enraptured, infatuated

smoke 4 draw, fume, pipe, puff, reek, suck 5 cigar, fumes 6 billow, smoke 7 light up, smolder 9 cigarette, have a drag

Smoke
　author: 12 Ivan Turgenev
　character: 5 Irina 7 Potugin 13 Tanya Shestoff 16 General Ratmiroff, Grigory Litvinoff 18 Kapitolina Shestoff

smoke screen 4 ruse 5 cover, dodge, front 6 screen 9 deception 10 camouflage, subterfuge

smoky 5 dingy, grimy, sooty 6 fuming, smudgy 7 reeking 10 smoldering

smolder 4 burn, fume, rage 5 smoke 6 seethe

Smollett, Tobias George
　author of: 14 (The Expedition of) Humphry Clinker, Roderick Random 15 Peregrine Pickle

smooch 3 pet 4 buss, kiss, neck 5 smack, spoon 7 make out

smooth 4 calm, ease, easy, even, flat, glib, help, mild, open, pave 5 allay, level, silky, sleek, suave 6 facile, mellow, placid, polish, refine, serene, soften, soothe, steady 7 appease, assuage, flatten, mollify, orderly, perfect, prepare, velvety 8 civilize, composed, make even, mitigate, peaceful, pleasant 9 collected, cultivate, easygoing, make level 10 facilitate, flattering, harmonious, methodical, uneventful 11 well-ordered 12 ingratiating 13 self-possessed, well-regulated

smoothness 8 evenness, fineness, flatness 9 silkiness, sleekness

smooth the feathers 4 calm 6 pacify, soothe 7 appease, assuage, mollify, placate 10 conciliate

smooth-tongued 4 glib 5 suave 6 fluent 8 unctuous 10 flattering 11 fast-talking 12 hypocritical, ingratiating

smother 4 hide, mask, wrap 5 choke, quash, snuff 6 deaden, quench, shower 7 conceal 8 keep down, strangle, suppress, surround 9 choke back, envelop in, suffocate 10 asphyxiate, extinguish

Smothers Brothers Comedy Hour, The
  regulars: 10 Don Novello, Pat Paulsen 11 Bob Einstein, Leigh French, Steve Martin, Tom Smothers 12 Betty Aberlin, Dick Smothers, John Hartford, Nino Senporty, Spencer Quinn 13 Mason Williams 14 Jennifer Warren, Sally Struthers 16 Anita Kerr Singers 17 Jimmy Joyce Singers 18 Louis DaPron Dancers 19 Marty Paich Orchestra 20 Denny Vaughn Orchestra, Ron Poindexter Dancers 21 Nelson Riddle Orchestra

smudge 4 blot, mark, soil, spot 5 dirty, smear, stain 6 smutch

smudgy 5 dirty, messy 6 filthy, grubby, smeary 7 sullied 8 befouled, unwashed 9 besmeared

smug 8 superior, virtuous 10 complacent 13 self-righteous, self-satisfied

smuggle 5 sneak 15 export illegally, import illegally

smuggled goods 10 contraband 14 illegal exports, illegal imports 18 prohibited articles

smuggler 6 runner 9 gunrunner, rumrunner 10 bootlegger 13 contrabandist

smugness 7 egotism 9 immodesty 11 superiority 12 virtuousness 16 selfsatisfaction 17 self-righteousness

smut 4 dirt, porn, soot 5 filth, grime 6 smudge 9 obscenity, scatology 11 pornography

smutty 4 lewd 5 dirty, grimy, sooty 6 filthy, soiled, vulgar 7 obscene 8 indecent 12 pornographic

Smyrna see 6 Myrrha

Smythe, Reginald
  creator/artist of: 8 Andy Capp

sneck 3 eat, tea 4 bite, nosh 5 munch 6 nibble, tidbit 7 take tea 8 lap lunch, munchies, nibblies, pick-me-up, snackies 9 collation, crunchies, elevenses 10 finger food, light lunch 11 casse-croute, coffee break, light repast, refreshment

snag 3 bar, rip 4 grab, stub, tear 5 block, catch, hitch, stump 7 barrier 8 obstacle 9 hindrance 10 difficulty, impediment, projection, protrusion 11 encumbrance, obstruction 14 stumbling block

Snagsby
  character in: 10 Bleak House
  author: 7 Dickens

snail
  French: 8 escargot

snake 5 sneak, viper 7 reptile, serpent, traitor 8 ophidian 9 reptilian
  combining form: 4 ophi 5 ophio, ophis 6 herpes 7 herpeto
  expert: 13 herpetologist
  fear of: 13 herpetophobia
  genus: 7 Ophidia
  kind: 3 asp, boa, sea 4 file, habu, wart, whip 5 aboma, adder, cobra, coral, krait, mamba, tiger, viper 6 bongar, elapid, garter, gopher, python, taipan 7 rattler, sunbeam 8 anaconda, cerastes, moccasin, pit viper, ringhals 9 boomslang, colubrina, mole viper, puff adder 10 black mamba, bushmaster, copperhead, fer-de-lance, sidewinder 11 cottonmouth, diamondback, Gaboon viper, rattlesnake 12 slender blind 13 elephant-trunk, water moccasin 14 boa constrictor
  shedding: 7 ecdysis 8 moulting
  skin: 6 exuvia
  snake killer: 8 mongoose

Snake see 8 Shoshoni

snake, poisonous 9 Coactrice

Snake, the
  nickname of: 10 Ken Stabler

Snake Pit, The
  author: 12 Sigrid Undset

snap 3 nip, pop 4 bark, bite, grab, lock, yelp 5 break, catch, cinch, clasp, click, close, crack, growl, hasty, latch, quick, snarl, spell 6 breeze, period, secure, snatch, sudden 8 careless, fastener, fracture 9 impulsive 11 thoughtless

snapdragon 11 Antirrhinum
  varieties: 4 wild 5 dwarf 6 common, garden, lesser 7 spurred 8 withered

snappish 4 edgy 5 cross, huffy, surly, testy 6 crabby, cranky, shirty, touchy 7 grouchy, huffish, peevish, waspish 8 captious, petulant 9 irascible, irritable, querulous 10 illhumored, ill-natured, out of sorts 11 hottempered 12 cantankerous 13 quicktempered, short-tempered

snappy 4 fast, tony 5 hasty, quick, rapid, ritzy, sharp, smart, swank, swift, swish 6 classy, dapper, jaunty, speedy, spiffy 7 stylish 12 lickety-split

snare 3 net 4 bait, hook, lure, ruse, trap 5 catch, decoy, noose, seize, trick 6 entrap 7 capture, ensnare, pitfall 9 deception 12 entanglement

snarl 3 mat 4 bark, clog, kink, knot, mess, snap 5 chaos, growl, ravel, twist 6 hinder, impede, jumble, muddle, tangle 7 confuse, lash out 8 disorder, entangle 9 confusion

snatch 3 bit, nab 4 grab, part, pull, take 5 catch, grasp, piece, pluck, seize, wrest 7 snippet 8 fragment

Snead, Sam
  nickname: 12 Slammin' Sammy
  sport: 4 golf
  won: 7 Masters

sneak 3 sly 4 slip 5 creep, knave, rogue, scamp, steal 6 lurker, rascal, secret, spirit 7 bounder, furtive, skulker, slinker, smuggle 8 scalawag, surprise 9 miscreant,

scoundrel, secretive, underhand 11 rapscallion 13 surreptitious

sneak attack 4 raid 6 ambush 7 assault 9 ambuscade, incursion

sneak off 5 elope 6 decamp 7 abscond 9 steal away

sneaky 3 sly 4 mean 7 devious, furtive, vicious 9 malicious, secretive, underhand 10 traitorous 11 treacherous

sneer 4 jeer, leer, mock 5 scoff, scorn, smirk 6 deride, rebuff 7 disdain 8 belittle, ridicule

sneer at 5 knock, scorn 6 deride, malign 7 disdain, put down, run down 8 pooh-pooh 16 cast aspersions on

Sneerwell, Lady
  character in: 19 The School for Scandal
  author: 8 Sheridan

snicker 5 snort 6 cackle, giggle, simper, titter 7 snigger

snide 5 nasty 7 mocking 8 scoffing 9 malicious, sarcastic 11 insinuating 12 contemptuous

Snider, Edwin
  nickname: 4 Duke
  sport: 8 baseball
  position: 7 fielder
  team: 15 Brooklyn Dodgers

sniff 4 jeer, mock, odor 5 aroma, scoff, smell, snort, snuff, whiff 6 snivel 7 disdain, sniffle, snuffle 9 disparage

snip 3 bit, bob, cut, lop 4 brat, clip, crop, punk, snap, trim 5 clack, click, piece, prune, scrap, shear, twerp 6 sample, shrimp, swatch 7 cutting 8 fragment

snippy 4 curt, rude 5 sassy, saucy, short 6 cheeky, snotty 7 brusque 8 flippant, impudent, insolent, snippety 11 ill-mannered, impertinent, smart-alecky

snivel 3 cry 5 sniff, whine 6 boohoo 7 sniffle 8 complain

sniveler 6 coward, whiner 7 crybaby 10 complainer

snob 7 elitist 13 social climber

snobbish 4 vain 6 snooty, snotty 7 haughty, high-hat, stuck-up 8 arrogant, superior 10 disdainful 11 overbearing, patronizing, pretentious 13 condescending

Snodgrass
  character in: 14 Pickwick Papers
  author: 7 Dickens

snoop 3 pry 7 meddler, Paul Pry 8 busybody 10 Nosy Parker 12 eavesdropper

snoopy, Snoopy 4 nosy 6 beagle, prying 7 curious 8 meddling 10 meddlesome 11 inquisitive
  brother: 5 Spike
  creator: 6 Schulz
  friend: 9 Woodstock
  master: 12 Charlie Brown

snooze 3 nap 4 doze 5 sleep 6 catnap, drowse, siesta 7 slumber 10 forty winks

Snopes family
  characters in: 9 The Hamlet
  members: 2 Ab 4 Flem, Mink 5 Isaac
  author: 8 Faulkner

snort 4 blow, gasp, huff, jeer, pant, puff, rage 5 blast, grunt, scoff, sneer, storm

snout 3 neb 4 beak, bill, nose 5 snoot, spout 6 muzzle, nozzle 9 proboscis

Snow, C P (Charles Percy Snow, Lord Snow)
  author of: 9 The New Men 10 Last Things, The Masters 14 A Coat of Varnish 16 Corridors of Power 20 Strangers and Brothers

Snow-Bound
  author: 21 John Greenleaf Whittier

snowfall 4 firn, neve 6 flurry 8 blizzard
  Scottish: 6 onding

Snow Leopard, The
  author: 16 Peter Matthiessen

Snow Queen, The
  author: 21 Hans Christian Andersen

Snows of Kilimanjaro, The
  author: 15 Ernest Hemingway

snow-white 4 pure 5 snowy 9 lily-white, pure white 11 white as snow

Snow White
  author: 15 Donald Barthelme

snowy 4 pure 5 white 7 nievous 8 pristine, spotless 9 blizzardy

snub 3 cut 5 blunt, check, scorn, short 6 ignore, rebuff, slight, stubby 7 disdain 9 retrousse 11 repudiation 12 cold shoulder 16 turn up one's nose at 19 give the cold shoulder

snuff 5 scent, smell, sniff, whiff 7 sniffle, snuffle

snuff out 5 crush 8 suppress 10 extinguish, put an end to

snug 4 cozy, neat, safe 5 close, tight 6 secure 7 compact 8 tranquil 9 sheltered, skin-tight 11 comfortable 12 close-fitting, tight-fitting 13 well-organized

snuggle 3 hug 4 nest 6 cuddle, curl up, enfold, nestle, nuzzle

Snyder, Peggy Lou
  real name of: 21 Harriet Hilliard Nelson

so
  Latin: 3 sic

soak 3 wet 4 seep 5 bathe, enter, steep 6 absorb, drench, sink in, take in, take up 7 immerse, pervade 8 permeate, saturate 9 penetrate

soaked 5 soggy 6 sodden, soused 7 sopping 8 drenched 9 saturated 11 waterlogged, wringing wet

soak up 4 blot 6 absorb, take up 8 sponge up

soak up warmth 4 bask 11 warm oneself 12 toast oneself

Soames Forsyte
  character in: 14 The Forsyte Saga
  author: 10 Galsworthy

Soap
  character: 5 Major 6 Benson 9 Billy Tate 10 Eunice Tate 11 Chester Tate, Corrine Tate, Danny Dallas, Jessica Tate, Jodie Dallas 12 Burt Campbell 18 Mary Dallas Campbell
  cast: 7 Ted Wass 9 Jimmy Baio 11 Diana Canova 12 Billy Crystal, Cathryn Damon,

Jennifer Salt, Robert Mandan **14** Arthur Peterson **15** Richard Mulligan, Robert Guillaume **16** Katherine Helmond

soar 3 fly **4** rise, wing **5** climb, float, glide, mount, tower **8** take wing

soave
    music: 6 gentle

sob 3 cry **4** howl, wail, weep **6** lament, plaint, snivel **7** blubber, whimper

so be it 4 amen **7** let it be **9** let it be so

sober 3 dry, sad **4** cool, drab, dull, grim, sane **5** grave, sound, staid **6** dreary, sedate, solemn, somber, steady **7** joyless, prudent, serious, subdued **8** moderate, not drunk, rational **9** judicious, realistic, sorrowful, temperate **10** abstemious **11** level-headed **13** dispassionate

So Big
    author: 10 Edna Ferber

sobriety 10 abstention, abstinence, continence, temperance **13** nonindulgence **14** abstemiousness

sobriquet 7 epithet, pet name **8** nickname **11** appellation

so-called
    French: 9 soi-disant

soccer
    athlete: 4 Pele **11** Johan Cruyff
    players/team: 6 eleven
    position: 6 goalie **7** forward **8** fullback, halfback **10** goalkeeper
    championship: 8 World Cup **11** European Cup, National Cup **13** Cup Winner's Cup
    violation: 5 hands **7** hacking, offside **11** obstructing
    gaining control of ball: 4 trap

sociable 6 social **7** affable, cordial **8** friendly, gracious, outgoing **9** agreeable, congenial, convivial **10** gregarious, neighborly **11** extroverted **13** companionable

social 2 in **5** smart **7** stylish **8** friendly, pleasant, sociable **9** agreeable **10** gregarious, neighborly **11** cooperative, fashionable **14** interdependent

Social Contract, The
    author: 19 Jean-Jacques Rousseau

social order
    goddess of: 4 Hour **5** Horae

society 4 body, club **5** elite, group **6** circle, gentry, league **7** mankind **8** alliance, humanity, nobility **9** community, humankind **10** blue bloods **11** aristocracy, association, high society, social order **12** organization **14** the four hundred **16** the general public

sociologist
    American: 4 Mead, Park, Ward **5** Coser, Gerth, Mills, Small, Wirth **6** Bendix, Cooley, Merton, Speier, Sumner, Thomas **7** Parsons, Sorokin **8** Eberhard **10** Lazarsfeld
    British: 4 Webb **8** Hobhouse, Mannheim **12** Carr-Saunders
    Danish: 6 Geiger
    French: 4 Aron **5** Comte **8** Durkheim, Gurvitch **9** Friedmann
    German: 5 Konig, Weber, Wiese **6**

Simmel **8** Habermas, Luckmann **10** Dahrendorf, Horkheimer
    Hungarian: 6 Lukacs **8** Mannheim
    Israeli: 5 Buber **10** Eisenstadt
    Norwegian: 6 Aubert **7** Galtung
    Swedish: 8 Carlsson

sociopathic 9 alienated **10** antisocial, rebellious

sock 3 box, hit, sox **4** belt, blow, slap **5** punch, smack, smash **6** strike, wallop **7** clobber **8** knee sock **9** ankle sock **13** short stocking

sod 4 soil, turf **5** divot, earth, grass, sward **10** greensward

soda 3 pop **4** base, cola **5** tonic **6** bicarb, sodium **7** barilla, seltzer **8** beverage, root beer **9** ginger ale, soft drink **11** bicarbonate **12** sarsaparilla
    ash: 6 alkali
    in faro: 9 first card
    maker: 4 jerk

sodden 4 dull **5** heavy, lumpy, mushy, pasty, soggy, soppy **6** doughy, soaked **7** sopping **8** besotted, drenched, dripping, listless **9** saturated **10** wet through **14** expressionless

Soddy, Frederick
    field: 9 chemistry
    nationality: 7 British
    discovered: 8 isotopes
    worked with: 13 William Ramsay **16** Ernest Rutherford
    awarded: 10 Nobel Prize

sodium
    chemical symbol: 2 Na

Sodom
    destroyed with: 5 Admah **6** Zeboim **8** Gomorrah

sofa 5 couch, divan **6** canape, lounge, settee **8** love seat **9** davenport **12** chesterfield

Sofia
    Roman name: 12 Ulpia Serdica
    Byzantine name: 9 Triaditsa
    capital of: 8 Bulgaria
    landmark: 13 Buyuk Dzhamiya **16** Saint Sofia Church **17** Saint George Church **24** Alexander Nevsky Cathedral **32** Cyril and Methodius National Library

soft 4 easy, kind, mild, pale, weak **5** downy, faint, furry, muted, quiet, silky, sleek **6** feeble, gentle, hushed, pliant, satiny, shaded, silken, smooth, supple, tender **7** lenient, not hard, pitying, pliable, restful, subdued, velvety **8** delicate, not sharp, shadowed, tolerant, tranquil, twilight **9** malleable, not strong **10** harmonious **11** sentimental, sympathetic **12** easily molded, low intensity **13** compassionate, pleasantly low **16** easily penetrated **19** having a breathy sound **21** requiring little effort **25** incapable of great endurance

soften 5 lower **6** lessen, subdue, temper **7** cushion, mollify **8** make soft, mitigate, moderate, palliate, tone down, turn down **10** ameliorate, make softer

softhearted 4 kind, soft, warm 6 benign, gentle, humane, kindly, tender 8 generous 9 forgiving, indulgent 10 benevolent 11 considerate, kindhearted, sympathetic, warmhearted 13 compassionate, tenderhearted

softly 6 easily, gently, mildly, weakly 7 quietly

softness 8 mildness 9 downiness, silkiness 10 fluffiness, gentleness, smoothness, tenderness 11 tranquility 12 tranquillity

soft soap 7 blarney 8 cajolery, flattery 10 persuasion

sogginess 7 wetness 8 dampness 9 mushiness 10 soddenness

soggy 5 heavy, mushy, pasty, soppy 6 doughy, soaked, sodden 7 sopping 8 drenched, dripping 9 saturated

Sogliardo
character in: 22 Every Man out of His Humour
author: 6 Jonson

Soglow, Otto
creator/artist of: 13 The Little King

Sohrab and Rustum
author: 13 Matthew Arnold

soi-disant 8 so-called 9 pretended 10 self-styled 18 calling oneself thus

soigne, soignee 4 chic, neat, tidy 5 sleek, smart 6 classy, modish 7 elegant 11 well-groomed

soil 4 dirt, foul, land, loam, ruin, soot, spot 5 dirty, earth, grime, humus, muddy, smear, stain, sully 6 debase, defile, ground, region, smudge 7 blacken, country, tarnish 8 disgrace

soiled 5 dirty, grimy, messy 6 filthy, grubby, smudgy 7 muddied, sullied, unclean 8 begrimed, unwashed 9 besmeared

soiree 4 ball, prom 5 dance, party 9 cotillion, promenade

sojourn 4 stay 5 abide, pause, visit 6 stay at 7 holiday, layover 8 stay over, stopover, vacation

sojourner 6 lodger, tenant 7 pilgrim, tourist, visitor 8 traveler 9 transient, weekender 10 daytripper, vacationer

Sol
origin: 5 Roman
form: 3 god
personifies: 3 sun
corresponds to: 6 Helios 7 Mithras 8 Hyperion

sola, solus 5 alone 9 by oneself

solace 4 calm 5 cheer 6 soothe 7 assuage, comfort, console 8 reassure 10 help in need 11 consolation, reassurance 18 relief in affliction

solder 4 fuse, join, weld 5 braze, stick

soldier 3 GI 3 PFC 5 major 6 worker, zealot 7 colonel, general, private, servant, trooper, veteran, warrior 8 follower, partisan, sergeant 10 lieutenant, serviceman 11 enlisted man, military man 14 militant leader 16 brigadier general

Soldier of Orange
director: 13 Paul Verhoeven
based on novel by: 13 Erik Hazelhoff
cast: 10 Peter Faber 11 Derek De Lint, Eddy Habbema, Rutger Hauer 12 Jeroen Krabbe 15 Susan Penhaligon
setting: 14 The Netherlands

Soldier's Embrace, A
author: 14 Nadine Gordimer

soldiery 4 army 6 legion, troops 7 legions, militia 8 military, soldiers 11 fighting men

sole 4 lone, only 6 single 8 solitary 9 exclusive

solely 5 alone 6 merely, purely, singly 8 uniquely 11 exclusively 14 single-handedly

solemn 4 dark, drab, grim, holy 5 grave, sober, staid 6 formal, gloomy, sacred, sedate, somber 7 earnest, serious, sincere 8 absolute 9 dignified, religious, spiritual, steadfast 10 ceremonial, depressing, determined 11 ceremonious 12 awe-inspiring

solemnity 3 awe 7 dignity 8 ceremony 9 formality, reverence 11 seriousness 12 circumstance

solemnize 4 mark 5 honor 6 hallow 7 observe 9 celebrate 10 consecrate 11 commemorate

solicit 3 ask 4 seek 5 plead 7 entreat, request 9 appeal for, importune

solicitation 6 appeal 7 request 8 entreaty 11 importuning

solicitor 6 beggar, lawyer 7 counsel 8 salesman 10 supplicant

solicitous 4 avid, keen 5 eager 6 ardent, intent 7 anxious, intense, longing, mindful, zealous 8 desirous 9 attentive, concerned, regardful 10 thoughtful 12 enthusiastic

solicitude 4 care, zeal 5 worry 7 anxiety, avidity, concern 9 attention 10 enthusiasm, inquietude, uneasiness 11 disquietude, fearfulness, overconcern 12 apprehension

solid 4 firm, hard, pure, real 5 dense, massy, sober, sound, tough 6 rugged, stable, steady, strong, sturdy 7 durable, genuine, lasting, unmixed 8 complete, concrete, constant, rational, reliable, sensible, tangible, thorough, unbroken 9 not hollow, unalloyed, unanimous, undivided, well-built 10 continuous, dependable, solidified 11 impermeable, levelheaded, substantial, trustworthy 12 impenetrable 13 uninterrupted 15 well-constructed

solidarity 5 union, unity 7 harmony 9 closeness 11 cooperation, unification

solidify 3 fix, gel, set 4 cake, jell 6 cement, harden 7 congeal, stiffen, thicken 9 coagulate 11 crystallize 12 agglomerate

soliloquy 9 monologue 10 solo speech

Sollnus
character in: 17 The Comedy of Errors
author: 11 Shakespeare

solitariness 8 solitude 9 aloneness, seclusion 13 reclusiveness

solitary 4 lone 6 hidden, lonely, remote, single 8 desolate, isolated, lonesome, secluded 9 concealed 10 cloistered 11 out-of-the-way, uninhabited 13 companionless

solitude 9 aloneness, isolation, seclusion, wasteland 10 desolation, loneliness, remoteness, wilderness

solo 5 alone 8 solitary 9 by oneself 10 unattended 12 singlehanded 13 unaccompanied

   operatic: 4 aria

solo dance

   ballet: 7 pas seul

Solomon

   father: 5 David

   mother: 9 Bathsheba

   wife: 6 Naamah

   son: 8 Rehoboam

   brother: 5 Amnon 7 Absalom, Chileab 8 Adonijah

   sister: 5 Tamar

   visitor: 5 Sheba

   wrote: 8 Proverbs 12 Ecclesiastes 13 Song of Solomon

   built: 6 temple

Solomon Islands

   capital/largest city: 7 Honiara

   others: 4 Auki, Bina, Gizo, Luti 5 Kieta, Munda 6 Tulagi 7 Yandina 8 Kira Kira 9 Tangarare 10 Sasamungga

   head of state: 14 British monarch 15 governor-general

   member of: 14 Spearhead Group

   monetary unit: 4 cent 6 dollar

   island: 4 Buka, Gizo, Savo 5 Ndeni, Ulawa 6 Tulagi 7 Malaita, Rennell, Solomon, Vangunu 8 Choiseul, Sikaiana, Vanikoro 9 Santa Cruz 10 New Georgia, Ontong Java 11 Guadalcanal, Santa Isabel 12 Bougainville, San Cristobal

   mountain: 5 Balbi

   highest point: 11 Popomanasiu

   ocean: 7 Pacific

   physical feature:

     gulf: 4 Huon, Kula

     sound: 10 New Georgia

     strait: 13 Indispensable

   people: 7 Chinese 8 European 10 Melanesian, Polynesian

   explorer: 14 Mendana de Neyra

   leader: 8 Mamaloni 9 Kenilorea

   language: 7 English 13 Pidgin English 16 Melanesian pidgin

   religion: 8 Anglican 13 Roman Catholic

so long

   Spanish: 12 hasta la vista

solution 3 key 5 blend 6 answer, cipher 7 mixture, solving 8 emulsion 9 resolving 10 resolution, suspension, unraveling 11 explanation

solve 7 resolve, unravel, work out 8 decipher, unriddle, untangle 9 figure out 10 find the key 13 find the answer

solvent 7 diluent, soluble 9 dilutable 10 dissoluble, dissolvent 11 dissolvable 16 financially sound

Solymi

   origin: 9 Asia Minor

   occupation: 8 warriors

Solzhenitsyn, Aleksandr

   author of: 13 The Cancer Ward 14 The First Circle 19 The Gulag Archipelago 22 August Nineteen-Fourteen 31 One Day in the Life of Ivan Denisovich

Somalia

   other name: 4 Punt 10 Somaliland 12 Horn of Africa

   capital/largest city: 9 Mogadishu 10 Mogadiscio

   others: 5 Burao, Merca 6 Mereka 7 Berbera, Galkayu, Kismayu 8 Belet Uen, Hargeisa 9 Chisimaio

   division: 6 Hawiya 9 Mijirtein 10 Midjertein

   colonial: 17 British Somaliland, Italian Somaliland

   measure: 3 top 4 caba 5 chela, darat, tabla 6 cubito 8 parsalah

   monetary unit: 4 besa 6 somalo 8 shilling 9 centesimi

   weight: 8 parsalah

   mountain: 5 Guban 11 Migiurtinia, Ogo Highland

   highest point: 7 Surud Ad

   river: 4 Juba 5 Daror, Nogal 9 Nugaaleed 11 Webi Shebeli 13 Webi Shabeelle

   sea: 6 Indian

   physical feature:

     bay: 5 Negro

     cape: 9 Guardafui

     desert: 4 Aror

     gulf: 4 Aden

     plateau: 3 Ogo 4 Haud

   people: 3 Sab 4 Asha 5 Galla 6 Hawiya, Isbaak, Somali 7 Danakil, Hamitic, Marehan, Samaale, Shuhali 8 Rahanwin

   leader: 9 Siad Barre 12 Ali Shermarke

   language: 6 Arabic, Somali 7 English, Italian

   religion: 5 Islam

   feature:

     boat: 4 dhow

     cloth: 7 banadir

     clothing: 4 futa, toga 6 sarong

     tree: 6 acacia, baobab 7 incense

Somaliland *see* 7 Somalia

somber 4 dark, drab, gray, grim 5 grave, sober 6 dreary, gloomy, solemn 7 serious 8 funereal, mournful, toneless 9 cheerless 10 depressing, melancholy

Sombrero Fallout

   author: 16 Richard Brautigan

Some Like It Hot

   director: 11 Billy Wilder

   cast: 9 Joe E Brown, Pat O'Brien 10 George Raft, Jack Lemmon, Tony Curtis 13 Marilyn Monroe

Somers Islands *see* 7 Bermuda

something essential

   Latin: 10 sine qua non

something for something

   Latin: 10 quid pro quo

Something Happened

   author: 12 Joseph Heller

sometime 4 late, once 5 later 6 former 7 quondam 8 formerly, previous 9 erstwhile 10 occasional

sometimes 7 at times 10 now and then, on occasion 12 occasionally, once in a while

somewhat 6 fairly, kind of, partly, sort of 8 passably 9 tolerably 10 moderately, more or less, reasonably 13 approximately

somnolent 4 dozy, dull 5 dopey 6 drowsy, groggy, sleepy, torpid 7 languid, nodding, out of it, yawning 8 hypnotic, sluggish 9 half-awake, lethargic, sopoforic 10 half-asleep, slumberous 11 heavy-lidded 13 semiconscious

Somnus
  origin: 5 Roman
  god of: 5 sleep
  mother: 3 Nyx
  brother: 4 Mors
  corresponds to: 6 Hypnos, Hypnus

son
  French: 4 fils

song 4 call, poem, tune 5 ditty, lyric, verse 6 ballad, melody, number, piping
  French: 7 chanson

songbird 4 chat, lark, wren 5 robin, veery, vireo 6 canary, singer, thrush 7 warbler 11 nightingale

Song of Bernadette, The
  author: 11 Franz Werfel
  character: 13 Dean Peyramale 18 Sister Marie Therese 19 Bernadette Soubirous
  director: 9 Henry King
  cast: 8 Lee J Cobb 12 Vincent Price, William Eythe 13 Jennifer Jones 15 Charles Bickford
  Oscar for: 7 actress (Jones)

Song of Hiawatha see 8 Hiawatha

Song of Roland, The see 15 Chanson de Roland

Song of Solomon
  author: 12 Toni Morrison

Song of Solomon
  bride: 9 Shulamite

Song of Songs, The
  author: 16 Hermann Sudermann

Song of the Lark, The
  author: 11 Willa Cather

Songs of Experience
  author: 12 William Blake

Songs of Innocence
  author: 12 William Blake

Sonnets from the Portuguese
  author: 24 Elizabeth Barrett Browning

Sonnets to Orpheus
  author: 16 Rainer Maria Rilke

Sonny
  nickname of: 13 Charles Liston

Son of the Morning
  author: 15 Joyce Carol Oates

sonorous 4 deep, rich 6 florid 7 ringing, vibrant 8 eloquent, resonant 9 full-toned, grandiose 10 flamboyant, impressive, resounding 13 reverberating

Sons and Lovers
  author: 10 D H Lawrence
  character: 10 Clara Dawes 11 Baxter Dawes 13 Miriam Leivers
  Morel family: 4 Paul 5 Annie 6 Arthur, Walter 7 William 8 Gertrude

Sons of thunder 4 John 5 James
  also: 9 Boanerges

soon 4 anon 6 pronto 7 betimes, by and by, early on, ere long, quickly, shortly 8 directly 9 any minute, forthwith, instantly, presently, right away 10 before long 12 without delay 14 in a little while

sooner 6 before, in time 7 earlier 9 before now, in advance 10 beforehand 11 ahead of time

sooner or later 6 one day 7 finally, someday 8 in the end, sometime 10 eventually, ultimately 17 in the course of time, sometime or another

Sooner State
  nickname of: 8 Oklahoma

soot 4 dirt, smut 5 crock, grime 6 carbon, smudge, smutch 7 residue 9 lampblack

soothe 4 calm, ease 6 lessen, pacify 7 appease, comfort, console, mollify, placate, relieve 8 mitigate, moderate 9 alleviate 11 tranquilize

soothing 4 mild 7 calming, healing, salving 9 appeasing, consoling, emollient, pacifying, placating 10 comforting, mitigating 13 tranquilizing

soothsayer 4 seer 5 sibyl 7 diviner, prophet 10 forecaster 13 fortune-teller

soothsaying 6 augury 8 divining, prophecy 10 divination, predicting, prediction 11 foretelling, prophesying

sooty 4 inky 5 black, dingy, dirty, grimy 6 smudgy, smutty 9 coal-black

sop 3 dip, tip, wet 4 dunk, soak 5 bribe 6 absorb, drench, payoff, payola, take up 8 gratuity, saturate 9 baksheesh, become wet, hush money

Sophie's Choice
  author: 13 William Styron

Sophisms
  author: 9 Aristotle

sophisticate 8 civilize 11 cosmopolite, disillusion, make worldly 12 cosmopolitan

sophisticated 6 subtle 7 complex, studied, worldly 8 advanced, cultured, highbrow, mannered, precious, seasoned 9 difficult 10 artificial, cultivated 11 complicated, experienced, worldly-wise 12 cosmopolitan, intellectual

sophistry 6 deceit 7 fallacy 8 subtlety 9 casuistry, chicanery, deception 10 distortion 12 speciousness

Sophocles
  author of: 4 Ajax 7 Electra, Oedipus 8 Antigone 10 Oedipus Rex, Trachiniae 11 Philoctetes 16 Oedipus at Colonus 18 The Trachinian Women

sophomoric 6 callow 7 foolish, puerile 8 childish, immature, juvenile 9 infantile 10 adolescent 12 schoolboyish

soporific 4 lazy 5 balmy, heavy 6 drowsy, sleepy 8 hypnotic, sedative, sluggish 9 lethargic, somnolent 10 slumberous 11 somniferous 12 sleep-inducer 13 sleep-inducing

soppiness 4 corn, mush 5 slush 6 bathos 7 wetness 9 mushiness 10 slushiness 11 mawkishness 14 sentimentalism, sentimentality

sopping 3 wet 5 soggy, soppy 6 soaked, sodden 8 drenched, dripping 9 saturated 10 bedraggled, soaking wet

sorcerer 5 witch 6 shaman, wizard 7 warlock 8 magician 11 medicine man

sorceress 5 siren, witch 11 enchantress

sorcery 8 witchery, wizardry 9 shamanism 10 black magic, necromancy, witchcraft 11 enchantment

Sordello
    author: 14 Robert Browning

sordid 3 low 4 base, rank, vile 5 dirty, gross 6 filthy, putrid, rotten, vulgar, wicked 7 corrupt, ignoble, squalid, unclean 8 degraded, depraved 9 debauched 12 disreputable

Sordido
    character in: 22 Every Man out of His Humour
    author: 6 Jonson

sordino, con
    music: 11 with the mute

sore 4 hurt 5 acute, angry, great, harsh, irked, sharp, upset, wound 6 aching, pained, severe, tender 7 bruised, extreme, grieved, hurting, painful 8 agonized, critical, grievous, smarting, sorespot, wounding 9 agonizing, desperate, indignant, irritated, sensitive 10 distressed, unbearable 11 distressing 12 inflammation

So Red the Rose
    author: 10 Stark Young

Sorel, Julien
    character in: 17 The Red and the Black
    author: 8 Stendhal

sorely 5 badly 7 greatly 8 severely 9 extremely 10 critically 11 desperately

soreness 4 ache, pain 10 discomfort, irritation, tenderness

sorrel 3 bay 4 herb, roan, weed 5 brown, plant, Rumex 8 chestnut 12 reddish-brown
    varieties: 3 red 4 dock, tree, wood 5 lady's, sheep 6 common, French, garden, In dian 7 redwood 8 Jamaican, mountain 10 violet wood 12 European wood

Sorrel, Hetty
    character in: 8 Adam Bede
    author: 5 Eliot

sorrow 3 woe 4 loss, weep 5 be sad, mourn, trial 6 grieve, lament 7 despair, sadness, travail, trouble 8 disaster, hardship 10 affliction, bad fortune, misfortune 11 catastrophe, unhappiness
    French: 9 tristesse

sorrowful 3 sad 6 woeful 7 unhappy 8 affected, grieving, mournful 9 lamenting

Sorrows of Young Werther, The
    author: 6 Goethe
    character: 6 Albert 9 Charlotte (Lotte)

sorry 3 sad 6 woeful 7 grieved, pitiful, unhappy 8 contrite, pathetic, pitiable, wretched 9 miserable, regretful, repentant, sorrowful 10 deplorable, melancholy, remorseful, ridiculous 11 crestfallen 13 brokenhearted

sort 4 kind, list, make, sift, type 5 brand, class, grade, group, index, order 6 divide, person 7 arrange, catalog, species, variety 8 classify, organize, separate take from 9 segregate 10 categorize, individual 11 systematize 14 classification

sortie 4 rush 5 onset 6 attack, charge 7 assault 8 storming 9 onslaught

sortilege 6 augury 7 auspice, sorcery 10 divination, witchcraft

sorting 8 dividing, grouping 9 arranging 10 organizing 11 classifying 12 categorizing

so-so 4 blah, fair 5 ho-hum 6 casual, modest 7 average, humdrum 8 adequate, bearable, mediocre, middling, ordinary, passable 9 tolerable 10 second-rate 11 commonplace, indifferent 12 run-of-the-mill 13 unexceptional 15 undistinguished

Sospita
    epithet of: 4 Juno

sot 4 lush, soak 5 drunk, rummy, souse, toper 8 drunkard, rumhound 9 alcoholic, inebriate 11 dipsomaniac

Soter
    epithet of: 4 Zeus
    means: 6 savior

Sothern, Ann
    real name: 13 Harriette Lake
    born: 12 Valley City ND
    husband: 10 Roger Pryor 14 Robert Sterling
    roles: 6 Maisie 8 Cry Havoc 10 Lady Be Good 16 Private Secretary 19 A Letter to Three Wives

so throughout
    Latin: 9 sic passim

sotto voce
    music: 11 in a low voice 13 in an undertone, under the voice

sought 6 hunted 7 pursued, quested 9 attempted, looked for 11 endeavored

soul 5 being, force 6 person, spirit 7 essence 8 creature, vitality 9 inner core 10 embodiment, individual, vital force 11 inspiration 12 quintessence

soul-searching 10 discontent, insecurity, uneasiness 15 dissatisfaction, self-questioning

soul-stirring 7 rousing 8 electric, exciting, stirring 9 inspiring, thrilling 11 galvanizing

sound 3 fit 4 deep, firm, good, seem, tone, wise 5 drift, hardy, noise, range, sober, solid, tenor, utter, voice 6 intact, robust, severe, signal, stable, strong, sturdy 7 durable, earshot, healthy, lasting, perfect, solvent 8 announce, rational, reliable, sensible, thorough, unmarred 9 come off as, competent, enunciate, pronounce, undamaged, well-built 10 articulate, dependable, make a noise, reasonable, suggestion, untroubled 11 implication, penetrating, responsible, substantial 13 thoroughgoing 15 hearing distance, well-constructed

Sound and the Fury, The
author: 15 William Faulkner
character: 6 Dilsey 17 Sydney Herbert Head
Compson family: 5 Jason 7 Candace (Caddy), Quentin 8 Benjamin (Benjy)

Sounder
director: 10 Martin Ritt
cast: 8 Taj Mahal 10 Kevin Hooks 11 Cicely Tyson 12 Paul Winfield 13 Carmen Mathews
sequel: 13 Sounder Part II

sound measure 7 decibel

sound mind in a sound body
Latin: 21 mens sana in cor pore sano

soundness of mind 6 reason, sanity 9 normality 12 mental health

Sound of Music, The
director: 10 Robert Wise
cast: 9 Peggy Wood 12 Julie Andrews (Maria Von Trapp) 13 Eleanor Parker 18 Christopher Plummer
setting: 7 Austria
score: 21 Rodgers and Hammerstein
Oscar for: 7 picture 8 director
song: 5 Maria 6 Do-Re-Mi 9 Edelweiss 16 My Favorite Things

sound out 3 ask 8 approach 15 make a proposal to, make overtures to, put out feelers to

soup
French: 6 potage

soupcon 3 bit, dab, jot, tad 4 clue, dash, drop, hint 5 pinch, shade, taint, taste, tinge, touch, trace, whiff 6 little, trifle 7 smidgen, smidgin, vestige 8 smidgeon 9 little bit, suspicion 10 smattering, sprinkling, suggestion 12 slight amount

Soupy Sales
character: 9 White Fang 10 Black Tooth 13 Herman the Flea, Hippy the Hippo, Pookie the Lion, Willie the Worm 14 Marilyn Monwolf

sour 3 bad 4 acid, dour, keen, tart, turn 5 nasty, sharp, spoil, surly, tangy, testy 6 crabby, cranky, curdle, rancid, sullen, turned 7 acerbic, bilious, crabbed, curdled, ferment, grouchy, peevish, spoiled, turn off, uncivil, waspish 8 alienate, choleric, embitter, jaundice, petulant, unsavory, vinegary 9 acidulous, clabbered, fermented, irritable, jaundiced, offensive, prejudice, repugnant 10 astringent, ill-dispose, ill-humored, unpleasant 11 bad-tempered, distasteful, ill-tempered 12 disagreeable

sourball 4 crab 5 crank, grump 6 grouch 9 hard candy 10 curmudgeon

source 4 font, head, root 5 basis, cause, fount 6 author, father, origin, rising, spring 8 begetter, fountain 9 authority, beginning, headwater 10 antecedent, derivation, foundation, prime mover, wellspring

source and origin
Latin: 11 fons et origo

Sourdough State
nickname of: 6 Alaska

sourness 7 acidity, vinegar 8 acerbity, acrimony, ill humor, pungency, tartness 9 acridness, greenness 10 bitterness

sourpuss 4 bear, crab 5 crank, grump 6 griper, grouch 7 grouser, killjoy 8 grumbler, sorehead 10 bellyacher, complainer, crosspatch, curmudgeon, spoilsport

Sousa, John Philip
born: 12 Washington DC
composer of: 9 El Capitan 14 Washington Post 25 The Stars and Stripes Forever

souse 3 dip, sot 4 duck, dunk, lush, soak 5 douse, drunk, rummy, steep, toper 6 barfly, boozer, drench, pickle 7 immerse, tippler 8 drunkard, inundate, marinate, saturate, submerge 9 alcoholic, inebriate 11 dipsomaniac

soused 5 drunk 6 dunked, potted, zapped, zonked 7 pickled, sloshed, smashed 8 immersed 9 plastered 10 inebriated 11 intoxicated 17 under the influence 20 three sheets to the wind

South Africa
capital: 8 Cape Town, Pretoria 12 Bloemfontein
largest city: 12 Johannesburg
others: 3 Aus 4 Mara, Stad 6 Benoni, Bononi, Braker, Durban, Garies, Severn, Soweto, Umtata, Untata 7 Brakpan, Kokstad 8 Kaapstad, Mafeking, Modjadji 9 Germiston, Kimberley 10 East London, Oudtshoorn 11 Krugersdorp, Vereeniging 13 Port Elizabeth 16 Pietermaritzburg
school: 5 Natal 8 Capetown 13 Witwatersrand 15 Orange Free State
division: 5 Natal 8 Backveld 9 Transvaal 10 Basutoland 12 Cape Province 14 Cape of Good Hope 15 Orange Free State
independent homelands: 5 Venda 6 Ciskei 8 Transkei 10 bantustans 14 Bophuthatswana
goverment:
legislature: 4 Raad
measure: 4 vara
monetary unit: 4 cent, pond, rand 5 pound 6 florin 7 daalder 9 krugerand
mountain: 3 Aux, Kop 5 Table 7 Kathkin 9 Stormberg 10 Devil's Peak, Sneeuwberg 11 Drakensberg 12 Giant's Castle 13 Witwatersrand 14 Mont-aux-Sources 15 Great Escarpment
highest point: 8 Injasuti
river: 3 Hex 4 Vaal 5 Nosob 6 Modder, Molopo, Orange, Tugela 7 Caledon, Kurumam, Limpopo 8 Olifants 9 Crocodile, Great Fish
ocean: 6 Indian 8 Atlantic
physical feature:
bay: 5 Algoa, False, Table 6 Mossel, Walvis 7 Walfish 8 Richard's, Saldanha 11 Saint Helena
cape: 7 Agulhas 8 Good Hope
current: 8 Benguela

desert: 5 Namib 8 Kalahari
plateau: 6 Karroo
region: 8 Highveld, Zululand 9 Kaffraria
11 Great Karroo 12 Little Karroo
people: 3 San 4 Boer, Yosa, Zulu 5
Asian, Bantu, Namas, Nguni, Pondo, Sotho, Swazi, Tembu, Venda, Xhosa 6 Damara, Kaffir 7 African, British, Bushmen,
English, Swahili 8 Bechuana, Coloured,
Khoikhoi 9 Afrikaner, Hottentot
author: 5 Paton 7 Luthuli 8 Gordimer
civil rights advocate: 6 Gandhi
explorer: 8 Riebeeck
leader: 4 Biko, Tutu 5 Botha, Malan,
Smuts, Tomba 6 Kruger, Rhodes 7 de
Klerk, Hertzog, Mandela, Vorster 8
Verwoerd 9 Buthelezi, Pretorius
language: 4 Taal, Zulu 5 Bantu, Hindi,
Nguni, Sotho, Swazi, Tamil, Venda,
Xhosa 6 Telegu, Thonga 7 English,
Khoisan, Ndebele, Sesotho 8 Bujarati,
Fanakalo 9 Afrikaans
religion: 5 Hindu, Islam 7 animism, Judaism 8 Anglican 9 Methodist 12 Episcopalian, Presbyterian 13 Dutch Reformed,
Roman Catholic
place:
Cecil Rhodes' estate: 11 Groote Shuur
game reserve: 5 Mkuze 6 Kruger 8
Hluhluwe
monument: 11 Voortrekker
feature:
bird: 4 taha
bride price: 6 lobolo
flower: 5 coral 6 clivia, protea 7 cowslip,
fuchsia 9 phygelius 10 lachenalia
organization: 3 ANC 7 Inkatha 23 African
National Congress
segregation: 9 apartheid
tree: 7 assagai 9 jacaranda
food:
corn: 6 mealie
drink: 9 sundowner
meat: 7 biltong 8 sosaties 9 boerewors

South America

bird: 5 macaw 7 seriema, tinamou 8 caracara
cape: 4 Horn
country: 4 Peru 5 Chile 6 Brazil, Guyana
7 Bolivia, Ecuador, Surinam, Uruguay 8
Colombia, Paraguay 9 Argentina, Venezuela 12 French Guiana
desert: 7 Atacama
explorer: 16 Francisco Pizarro 18 Pedro
Alvares Cabral
hero: 12 Simon Bolivar 15 Jose de San
Martin 16 Bernardo O'Higgins 18 Antonio
Jose de Sucre
highest mountain: 9 Aconcagua
islands: 8 Falkland 9 Galapagos
lake: 8 Titicaca 9 Maracaibo
mountain range: 5 Andes
native: 2 Ge 3 Ona 4 Inca 5 Carib, Mayan 7 Quechua 10 Araucanian
plain: 5 llano, pampa
region: 9 Patagonia
river: 3 Apa 5 Plata 6 Amazon 7 Orinoco

South Carolina

abbreviation: 2 SC
nickname: 7 Calinky 8 Palmetto
capital/largest city: 8 Columbia
others: 5 Aiken, Greer, Union 6 Belton,
Camden, Cheraw, Conway, Dillon, Seneca, Sumter 7 Bamberg, Laurens,
Manning 8 Beaufort, Florence, Newberry,
Rock Hill, Walhalla 9 Greenwood 10
Charleston, Greenville, Orangeburg 11
Spartanburg
college: 5 Allen, Coker 6 Furman, Lander 7 Claffin, Clemson, Erskine, Wofford
8 Benedict, Bob Jones, Columbia,
Winthrop 13 Francis Marion 15 Citadel
Military
explorer: 6 Ayllon, Ribaut
feature:
beach: 6 Myrtle
dam: 6 Saluda
fort: 6 Sumter
gardens: 7 Cypress
tribe: 5 Pedee, Sewee 6 Cusabo, Santee, Waxhaw, Yamasi 7 Catawba, Shawnee, Sugeree, Wateree 8 Congaree
people: 11 James Byrnes 12 Althea Gibson, John C Cal houn 13 Bernard Baruch, Francis Marion 14 Dizzy Gillespie
island: 3 Sea 6 Parris 10 Hilton Head
lake: 6 Marion, Murray 7 Catawba,
Wateree 8 Hartwell, Moultrie 9 Clark Hill
land rank: 8 fortieth
mountain: 5 Kings 6 Little 9 Blue Ridge,
Sassafras
physical feature:
bay: 8 Carolina
plateau: 8 Piedmont
president: 13 Andrew Jackson
river: 5 Broad 6 Edisto, Pee Dee,
Saluda, Santee 7 Ashepoo 8 Savannah
state admission: 6 eighth
state bird: 12 Carolina wren
state flower: 13 yellow jasmine 17 Carolina jessamine
state motto: 18 While I Breathe I Hope
26 Prepared in Mind and Resources
state song: 8 Carolina
state tree: 8 palmetto

South Dakota

abbreviation: 2 SD 4 S Dak
nickname: 6 Coyote 8 Blizzard, Sunshine
capital: 6 Pierre
largest city: 10 Sioux Falls
others: 4 Lead, Leap 5 Huron 6 Custer,
Eureka, Lemmon, Miller, Winner 7
Sturgis, Webster, Yankton 8 Aberdeen,
Deadwood, Sisseton 9 Brookings, Rapid
City 10 Vermillion
college: 5 Huron 7 Yankton 9 Augustana
10 Mount Marty, Sioux Falls 14 Dakota
Wesleyan
explorer: 8 Varennes 13 Lewis and Clark
feature: 8 Deadwood
battlefield: 11 Wounded Knee
dam: 4 Oahe
mine: 9 Homestake

monument: 13 Mount Rushmore
national park: 8 Badlands, Wind Cave
tribe: 5 Brule, Sioux 6 Dakota, Sutaio 8 Cheyenne
people: 10 Crazy Horse 11 Sitting Bull 14 George McGovern, Hubert Humphrey
lake: 4 Oahe 5 Sharp 8 Big Stone, Traverse 11 Francis Case 13 Lewis and Clark
land rank: 9 sixteenth
mountain: 4 Bear 5 Sheep, Table 6 Crook's, Moreau
highest point: 6 Harney
hills: 5 Black 7 Prairie
physical feature:
butte: 7 Thunder 9 Deer's Ears 10 Castle Rock
cave: 5 Jewel
river: 3 Bad 5 Grand, James, White 6 Moreau 8 Big Sioux, Cheyenne, Missouri 10 Vermillion
state admission: 8 fortieth 11 thirty-ninth (with North Dakota)
state bird: 18 ring-necked pheasant
state flower: 12 pasqueflower
state animal: 6 coyote
state motto: 21 Under God the People Rule
state song: 15 Hail South Dakota
state tree: 11 white spruce 16 Black Hills spruce
southeast wind
associated with: 5 Eurus 9 Volturnus
Southern Comfort
type: 7 liqueur
origin: 10 New Orleans
flavor: 5 peach
base: 7 bourbon
drink: 13 Scarlett O'Hara 15 Plantation Punch
with bourbon: 14 Blended Comfort
Southern Cross
constellation of: 4 Crux
Southern Crown
constellation of: 15 Corona Australis
Southerner, The
director: 10 Jean Renoir
cast: 10 Betty Field 11 Beulah Bondi 12 Zachary Scott 13 Bunny Sunshine
Southern Fish
constellation of: 15 Piscis Austrinus
Southern Fly
constellation of: 5 Musca
Southern Rhodesia see 8 Zimbabwe
Southern Slavic
language family: 12 Indo-European
group: 11 Balto-Slavic
branch: 6 Slavic
language: 8 Slovene 9 Bulgarian 10 Macedonian 13 Serbo-Croatian
Southern Triangle
constellation of: 18 Triangulum Australe
South Korea see 5 Korea
South Vietnam see 7 Vietnam
South West Africa see 7 Namibia
south wind
associated with: 5 Notus

South Wind
author: 13 Norman Douglas
South Yemen see 5 Yemen
souvenir 4 scar 5 relic, token 6 emblem, memory, trophy 7 memento 8 keepsake, reminder 11 remembrance
sovereign 4 czar, free, king, lord, main, tsar 5 chief, major, prime, queen, regal, royal 6 kingly, potent, prince, ruling, utmost 7 emperor, highest, leading, monarch, queenly, supreme 8 absolute, autocrat, dominant, foremost, imperial, overlord, powerful, princely, reigning 9 chieftain, governing, paramount, potentate, prepotent, principal, uppermost 10 autonomous, self-ruling 11 all-powerful, crowned head, independent, monarchical 12 supreme ruler 13 self-directing, self-governing
sovereignty 4 sway 5 crown, power 6 throne 7 command, control, freedom, primacy, scepter 8 autonomy, dominion, home rule, kingship, lordship, self-rule 9 authority, supremacy 10 ascendancy 11 paramountcy 12 independence, jurisdiction, predominance 14 self-government 17 self-determination
Soviet Union see 6 Russia
sow 4 cast, seed 5 lodge, plant, set in, strew 6 inject, spread 7 implant, instill, scatter 8 disperse, sprinkle 9 broadcast, establish, introduce 11 disseminate
space 3 gap, sky 4 area, part, rank, room, seat, span, spot, term, time 5 berth, blank, break, chasm, ether, field, order, place, range, reach, scope, sweep, swing, width 6 hiatus, lacuna, line up, margin, period, set out, spread 7 arrange, breadth, compass, expanse, mark out, the void 8 distance, duration, infinity, interval, latitude, omission, organize, schedule, separate 9 amplitude, emptiness, keep apart, territory 10 distribute, interspace, interstice, outer space, separation, the heavens 11 nothingness, reservation, the universe 12 interruption, the firmament 13 accommodation
Space
author: 13 James Michener
spacecraft 4 ship 6 rocket 7 orbiter, shuttle 9 satellite 10 rocketship
space flight
US mission: 6 Apollo, Gemini, Skylab 7 Mercury
US rocket: 5 Atlas, Titan 6 Saturn 8 Redstone
US space shuttle: 8 Columbia 9 Discovery 10 Challenger
Soviet mission: 5 Soyuz 6 Salyut, Vostok 7 Voskhod
Soviet astronaut:
first man in space: 11 Yuri Gagarin
first woman in space: 19 Valentina Tereshkova
first space walk by: 13 Aleksei Leonov
American astronaut: 9 John Glenn, John Young 11 Alan Shepard, Edward White, Edwin Aldrin, Frank Borman, James Lovell 12 Roger Chaffee, Wally

(Walter) Schirra 13 Charles Conrad, L
Gordon Cooper, Virgil Grissom 14 Scott
Carpenter, Thomas Stafford

first man on moon: 13 Neil Armstrong

Challenger seven: 12 Michael Smith,
Ronald McNair 13 Francis Scobee,
Gregory Jarvis, Judith Resnick 14 Ellison
Onizuka 16 Christa McAuliffe

Spacek, Sissy

real name: 19 Mary Elizabeth Spacek

born: 9 Quitman TX

roles: 6 Carrie 7 Missing 8 Badlands,
The River 10 Raggedy Man 16 Crimes of
the Heart 18 Coal Miner's Daughter (Oscar)

spacious 4 vast, wide 5 ample, broad,
large, roomy 7 immense, sizable 8 enormous 9 capacious, expansive, extensive,
uncrowded 10 commodious

spaciousness 9 amplitude, largeness,
roominess 13 capaciousness 14 commodiousness

Spade, Sam

character in: 16 The Maltese Falcon

author: 7 Hammett

Spain

other name: 6 Iberia 8 Hispania

capital/largest city: 6 Madrid

others: 4 Adra, Aspe, Baza, Elda, Horo,
Irun, Jaen, Leon, Noya, Olot, Reus, Rota,
Sama, Vigo 5 Baena, Bejar, Cadiz, Cieza,
Cueta, Ecija, Eibar, Elche, Gades, Gadir,
Gijon, Ibiza, Jerez, Jodar, Liego, Lorca,
Oliva, Palma, Palos, Ronda, Siero,
Ubeda, Xeres, Yecla, Zafra 6 Abdera,
Aviles, Azuaga, Bilbao, Burgos, Coruna,
Duenca, Gandia, Gerona, Getafe, Gua-
dix, Hellin, Huelva, Huesca, Jativa,
Lerida, Lucena, Malaga, Mataro, Merida,
Murcia, Orense, Oviedo, Termel, Toledo,
Utrera, Zamora 7 Almeria, Badajos, Cor-
doba, Daimiel, Granada, Jumilla, Linares,
Logrono, Manresa, Segovia, Sevilla, Se-
ville, Tarrasa, Vitoria 8 Alicante, Bada-
lona, Figueras, Pamplona, Sabadell,
Santiago, Torrente, Valencia, Zaragoza 9
Barcelona, Las Palmas, Saragossa

school: 6 Ciudad, Madrid

division: 4 Jaen, Leon, Lugo 5 Alava,
Avila, Cadiz, Soria 6 Basque, Burgos,
Coruna, Cuenca, Gerona, Huelva,
Huesca, Lerida, Madrid, Malaga, Murcia,
Orense, Oviedo, Teruel, Toledo, Zamora
7 Almeria, Caceres, Cordoba, Granada,
Logrono, Navarra, Segovia, Sevilla,
Vizcaya, Zadajoz 8 Albacete, Alicante,
Baleares, Palencia, Valencia, Zaragoza 9
Catalonia

kingdom: 4 Leon 6 Aragon 7 Castile,
Galicia, Granada, Navarre 8 Asturias 9
al-Andalus, Catalonia 12 Spanish March

government: 8 monarchy

legislature: 6 Cortes

head of state: 4 king

measure: 3 pie 4 codo, dedo, paso, vara
5 braza, cahiz, carga, legua, medio,
palmo, sesma 6 cordel, cuarta, fanega,

racion, yugada 7 azumbre, celemin,
estadel, pulgada 8 fanegada

monetary unit: 3 cob 4 duro, peso 5 dobla 6 cuarto, dinero, escudo 7 alfonso,
centimo, pistole 8 doubloon

weight: 4 onza 5 frail, libra, marco, tomin
6 arroba, dinero, dracma 7 arienzo,
quilate, quintal 8 tonelada

island: 5 Ceuta, Ibiza, Iviza, Palma 6 Ca-
nary, Gomera, Hierro 7 Alboran, Majorca,
Melilla, Minorca 8 Balearic, Mallorca,
Tagomago, Tenerife 9 Lanzarote 13
Fuerteventura

lake: 4 lago 8 Albufera

mountain: 4 Gata 5 Aneto, Rouch 6
Cuenca, Estats, Europa, Gredos, Magina,
Morena, Nethou, Nevada, Teleno, Toledo
7 Alcaraz, Banuelo, Catalan, Cerredo,
Demanda, Iberian, La Sagra, Moncayo,
Perdido 8 Almanzor, Asturias, Galician,
Maladeta, Monegros, Montseny,
Penalara, Pyrenees 10 Albarracin, Can-
tabrian, Guadarrama, Torrecilla

highest point: 5 Teide 8 Mulhacen

river: 3 Sil, Ter 4 Cega, Ebro, Esla, Lima,
Mino, Muga, Tajo, Ulla 5 Adaja, Cinca,
Douro, Duero, Genil, Jalon, Jucar, Navia,
Odiel, Riaza, Segie, Tagus, Tinto, Turia
6 Alagon, Aragon, Eresma, Huerva,
Jarama, Orbigo, Segura, Torote 7 Al-
meria, Almonte, Arlanza, Barbate,
Cabriel, Gallego, Henares, Mijares,
Perales 8 Duration, Guadiana 12
Guadalquivir

sea: 8 Atlantic, Balearic 13 Mediterranean

physical feature:

bay: 5 Bahia 6 Biscay

cape: 9 Trafalgar

gulf: 5 Cadiz 8 San Jorge, Valencia

peninsula: 7 Iberian

plateau: 6 meseta

strait: 9 Gibraltar

people: 5 Diego, Gente, Latin 6 Basque,
Espana 7 Catalan, Espanol, Iberian 8 Galician, Gallegos, Maragato

architect: 5 Gaudi

artist: 4 Dali, Goya, Gris, Miro 6 Ribera 7
El Greco, Murillo, Picasso 8 Zurbaran 9
Velazquez

author: 4 Cela, Vega 5 Barea, Cueva,
Rojas 6 Aleman, Alonso, Azorin, Baroja,
Castro, Encina, Felipe, Ibanez, Miguel 7
Alarcon, Becquer, Cernuda, Ercilla,
Gongora, Guillen, Jimenez, Machado,
Unamuno 8 Montalvo, Zorrilla 9
Benavente, Cervantes, Goytisola 10
Aleixandre, Espronceda, Lope de Vega,
Pardo Bazan 11 Garcia Lorca 12 Lopez
de Ayala 13 Tirso de Molina 17 Calderon
de la Barca

composer: 7 Albeniz 8 Granados, Victoria 13 Manuel de Falla

converted Moslem: 7 morisco

dynasty: 7 Almohad, Umayyad 9 Almoravid

explorer: 6 Balboa, Cortes 7 Pizarro 8 Columbus

Jesuit founder: 14 Ignatius Loyola

king: 6 Pelayo, Philip, Ramiro, Sancho, Witiza 7 Alfonso, Charles 8 al-Mansur, Reccared, Roderick 9 Ferdinand, Leovigild 10 Juan Carlos 11 Abd al-Rahman, Reccosvinth

leader: 4 Prim 5 Godoy 6 Franco 7 Canovas 11 Calvo Sotelo 13 Primo de Rivera 14 Suarez-Gonzalez

queen: 8 Isabella 16 Elizabeth Farnese

ruler: 4 Rome 5 Celts, Moors 6 Greece 7 Almeria, Vandals 8 Carthage 9 Phoenicia, Visigoths

scholar: 8 Averroes

warrior: 14 El Cid Campeador

language: 6 Basque 7 Catalan, Spanish 8 Balearic, Galician 9 Castilian, Valencian

religion: 7 Judaism 10 Protestant 13 Roman Catholic

place:

aqueduct: 7 Segovia

bridge: 7 Cordoba

castle: 7 Alcazar 12 Santa Barbara

cathedral bell tower: 7 Giralda

center of Madrid: 12 Puerto del Sol

church/cathedral: 4 Leon 6 Burgos, Gerona, Toledo 7 Seville 9 Barcelona, San Isidro 10 Santa Maria 14 Sagrada Familia

fountain: 6 Cibele

library: 8 Columbus

minaret: 7 Seville

mosque: 11 Great Mosque 19 Santo Cristo de la Cruz

museum: 5 Prado 15 Museo de Pinturas

palace: 7 Granada, Naranco 8 Alhambra, Escorial 12 Real Mayor

park: 6 Retiro

resort: 8 Marbella 10 Costa Brava 12 Torremolinos

shrine: 32 Saint James at Santiago de Compostela

street: 7 Ramblas 13 Paseo del Prado 16 Plaza de la Cibeles 19 Paseo de la Castellana

synagogue: 10 El Transito

theater: 6 Merida

wall paintings/caves: 8 Altamira

possession: 5 Ceuta 6 Melill

feature:

bar: 6 tascas

dance: 5 tango 8 fandango, flamenco

estate: 10 latifundia

matador's suit: 12 traje de luces

political party: 7 Falange

food:

dish: 6 cocido, paella 8 zarzuela

soup: 8 gazpacho

span 4 arch, area, last, term, wing 5 cover, cross, range, reach, scope, spell, sweep, vault 6 bridge, endure, extent, length, period 7 archway, breadth, measure, stretch, survive, trestle 8 distance, duration, interval 9 extension, reach over, territory 10 bridge over, dimensions 11 proportions,

reach across, stretch over 12 extend across

spangle 4 star 5 bedew 6 sequin 7 glisten, glitter, shimmer, twinkle 9 bugle bead, coruscate, paillette

spaniel

dog breed: 5 field 6 cocker, Sussex 7 clumber, Tibetan 10 Irish water 13 American water, English cocker, Welsh springer 15 English springer

Spanish (language, person) 7 espanol

Spanish Guinea *see* 16 Equatorial Guinea

Spanish Sahara *see* 13 Western Sahara

Spanish Tragedy, The

   author: 9 Thomas Kyd

   character: 7 Horatio, Lorenzo, Villupo 9 Alexandro, Balthazar, Hieronimo 10 Bel-Imperia 16 Ghost of Don Andrea

spank 3 hit, tan 4 beat, belt, blow, cane, flog, hide, lick, slap, whip, whop 5 birch, strap, whale 6 paddle, strike, switch, thrash, wallop 8 paddling 10 flagellate

spanking 4 very 5 brisk, fresh 7 beating 8 paddling, whipping 9 extremely, thrashing 10 punishment 12 chastisement

spanking new 5 fresh 6 unused 8 brand new 9 untouched

spar 4 boom, mast, pole 5 argue, fight, sprit 6 bicker 7 dispute, quarrel, wrangle 8 crossbar 10 crosspiece

spare 3 odd 4 bony, cede, free, give, keep, lank, lean, save, thin 5 amass, extra, forgo, gaunt, grant, guard, hoard, lanky, lay up, limit, pinch, rangy, scant, stint, weedy 6 acquit, afford, defend, donate, excess, exempt, forego, let off, meager, not use, pardon, scanty, shield, skimpy, skinny, slight, unused 7 forgive, haggard, husband, let go of, protect, release, relieve, reserve, scraggy, scrawny, shelter, skimp on, slender, surplus 8 conserve, hold back, leftover, liberate, part with, reprieve, set aside, skeletal, withhold 9 auxiliary, emaciated, exonerate, fleshless, safeguard, show mercy 10 additional, extraneous, relinquish, substitute, unconsumed 11 economize on, have mercy on, superfluous, unnecessary, use frugally 12 be merciful to, dispense with, supplemental 13 supernumerary, supplementary

spared 5 freed 6 exempt, immune 7 excused 8 absolved, excepted, relieved

sparing 4 near 5 close, scant 6 frugal, meager, saving, scanty, stingy 7 careful, miserly, thrifty 8 grudging, stinting 9 niggardly, penurious 10 economical, ungenerous 11 closefisted, tightfisted 12 parsimonious

spark 3 bit, jot 4 atom, beam, fire, iota, life 5 brand, ember, flash, gleam, pique, trace 6 arouse, excite, incite, spirit 7 flicker, glimmer, glitter, inspire, provoke, sparkle 8 vitality 9 animation, instigate, stimulate 10 get-up-and-go

Spark, Muriel

   author of: 11 Memento Mori 14 The Driver's Seat, The Only Problem 17 The

Mandelbaum Gate, Territorial Rights 19 Loitering with Intent 21 A Far Cry from Kensington 24 The Prime of Miss Jean Brodie

sparkle 3 pep, pop, vim 4 dash, elan, fizz, foam, glow, life 5 be gay, brand, cheer, ember, flash, froth, gleam, glint, light, shine, verve 6 bubble, dazzle, fizzle, gaiety, spirit 7 be witty, flicker, glimmer, glisten, glitter, jollity, rejoice, shimmer, twinkle 8 radiance, vitality, vivacity 9 alertness, animation, briskness, coruscate, quickness 10 be cheerful, brilliance, ebullience, effervesce, effulgence, exuberance, liveliness, luminosity 11 be vivacious, scintillate 12 cheerfulness, exhilaration, luminousness 13 effervescence, scintillation

sparkling 5 fizzy 6 bubbly 7 fizzing, twinkly 8 bubbling, dazzling, glittery 9 twinkling 10 glistening, glittering 11 coruscating 12 effervescent 13 scintillating

Sparky Lyle
nickname of: 16 Albert Walter Lyle

sparse 3 few 4 thin 5 scant, spare 6 meager, scanty, scarce, skimpy, spotty, strewn 7 diffuse 8 exiguous, sporadic 9 dispersed, scattered, spaced-out, uncrowded 10 infrequent 16 few and far between

sparseness 7 paucity 8 sparsity, thinness 10 meagerness, scantiness

Sparsit, Mrs
character in: 9 Hard Times
author: 7 Dickens

Spartacus
director: 14 Stanley Kubrick
cast: 8 Nina Foch 9 John Gavin 10 Tony Curtis 11 Jean Simmons, Kirk Douglas 12 Peter Ustinov 15 Charles Laughton, Laurence Olivier
setting: 4 Rome
score: 9 Alex North

spartan 4 hard 5 plain, stark, stern, stiff 6 frugal, severe, simple, strict 7 ascetic, austere 8 exacting, rigorous 9 stringent 10 abstemious, inexorable, inflexible, restrained, restricted 11 disciplined, self-denying 15 self-disciplined

Sparti
occupation: 8 warriors

spasm 3 fit, tic 4 grip, jerk, pang 5 burst, cramp, crick, flash, onset, spell, spurt, start, storm, throe 6 access, attack, frenzy, twitch 7 seizure, shudder, tempest 8 eruption, paroxysm 9 explosion 10 convulsion

spasmodic 6 fitful 7 erratic, flighty 8 fleeting, periodic, sporadic 9 desultory, irregular, mercurial, transient 10 capricious, inconstant, occasional 12 intermittent 13 discontinuous

spat 4 tiff 5 argue, fight, scrap, set-to 6 bicker, differ 7 contend, dispute, dissent, quarrel, wrangle 8 disagree, squabble 10 difference 11 altercation 12 disagreement 16 misunderstanding

spatter 4 slop, soil, spot 5 fleck, plash, spray, spurt, stain, swash 6 mottle, shower, splash 7 speckle, stipple 8 splatter, sprinkle

spawn 4 eggs, seed, teem 5 beget, breed, brood, fruit, yield 7 lay eggs, produce, product 8 engender, generate, multiply 9 offspring, propagate, reproduce 10 bring forth, give rise to 11 deposit eggs, give birth to, proliferate

speak 3 air, say 4 call, chat, deal, talk, tell 5 imply, orate, refer, shout, sound, state, treat, voice 6 advise, confer, convey, cry out, dilate, impart, mumble, murmur, mutter, preach, recite, relate, remark, report, reveal 7 bespeak, comment, consult, declaim, declare, discuss, divulge, expound, express, lecture, mention, suggest, whisper 8 announce, converse, disclose, harangue, indicate, proclaim, vocalize 9 discourse, enunciate, expatiate, hold forth, make known, pronounce, sermonize 10 articulate 11 communicate, give a speech

speakeasy 3 bar 6 saloon, tavern 7 gin mill 14 cocktail lounge

speaker 5 voice 6 orator, reader, talker 7 reciter 8 advocate, lecturer, preacher 9 declaimer, spokesman 10 discourser, monologist, mouthpiece, sermonizer 11 rhetorician, speechmaker, spokeswoman 13 valedictorian

speak highly of 4 laud 5 exalt, extol 6 praise 7 commend 8 eulogize 10 compliment 16 sing the praises of

speak ill of 4 slur 5 curse, knock, libel 6 defame, insult, malign, vilify 7 slander 8 bad-mouth 9 criticize, denigrate, discredit, disparage 13 find fault with 14 inveigh against

speak loudly 3 cry 4 bawl, call, hail, roar, yell 5 shout 6 bellow, clamor, cry out, halloo, holler 7 call out, speak up

speak of 7 mention, refer to 8 allude to 9 talk about, touch upon

speak to 6 talk to 7 address, lecture

speak together 3 gab, jaw, rap 4 chat, chin, talk 6 confer 7 chatter, palaver 8 chitchat, converse 10 chew the fat, chew the rag 11 communicate, confabulate

speak well of 4 laud 5 boost, extol 6 praise 7 acclaim, approve, commend, flatter, root for 8 eulogize 9 sweet talk 10 compliment, stick up for 13 speak highly of 16 sing the praises of 17 put in a good word for

spear 4 bolt, dart, gaff, gore, pike, spit, stab 5 lance, prick, shaft, spike, stick 6 impale, pierce 7 harpoon, javelin 8 puncture, transfix 9 penetrate 10 run through

spearhead 4 iron, lead 5 begin, found, start 6 launch, leader 7 creator, develop, founder, pioneer 8 begetter, conceive, initiate 9 establish, initiator, institute, originate, spokesman 10 inaugurate, instituter, prime mover 11 establisher, inaugurator, spokeswoman 12 avant-gardist

special 4 fast, good, rare 5 close, great, novel 6 ardent, proper, select, signal, unique 7 bargain, certain, devoted, endemic, feature, staunch, typical, unusual 8 distinct, especial, intimate, peculiar, personal, sale item, singular, specific, uncommon 9 headliner, high point, highlight, important, momentous, specialty, steadfast 10 attraction, individual, noteworthy, particular, remarkable 11 distinctive, exceptional, outstanding, specialized 12 extravaganza distinguished, extraordinary 14 representative, unconventional 16 out of the ordinary 17 piece de resistance

specialist 4 buff 5 adept, maven 6 expert, master 9 authority 10 past master 11 connoisseur

specialization 5 focus, forte, major 6 metier 8 province 10 speciality 13 concentration

specialize 5 adapt, focus, major 6 pursue 10 narrow down 11 concentrate

specialty 4 bent, mark, turn 5 badge, focus, forte, hobby, major, stamp 6 genius, talent 7 earmark, faculty, feature, pursuit, special 8 aptitude 9 endowment, trademark 10 competence, profession 11 claim to fame, distinction

species 4 form, kind, make, sort, type 5 breed, class, genre, group, order 6 kidney, nature, stripe 7 variety 8 category, division 11 designation, subdivision 14 classification

specific 5 exact, fixed 6 minute, stated, unique 7 bounded, certain, endemic, limited, pointed, precise, special, typical 8 clear-cut, concrete, confined, definite, detailed, especial, peculiar, personal, relevant, singular, tied-down 9 intrinsic, pertinent, specified 10 individual, particular, pinned-down, restricted 11 categorical, determinate, distinctive, unequivocal 13 circumscribed 14 characteristic

specification 6 detail 7 clarity 9 condition, precision, substance 11 enumeration, itemization, requirement, stipulation 12 concreteness 13 particularity, qualification 17 particularization

specifics 4 cure, fact, item 5 datum 6 detail, physic 10 medication, particular 12 circumstance

specify 4 cite, name 5 order 6 adduce, define, denote, detail 7 call for, focus on, itemize 8 describe, indicate, set forth 9 designate, enumerate, stipulate 13 particularize

specimen 4 case, type 5 model 6 sample 7 example, exemplar, instance 9 prototype 14 representative 15 exemplification

specious 5 false 6 faulty, tricky, untrue 7 dubious, in valid, unsound 8 slippery, spurious 9 casuistic, deceptive, illogical, incorrect, unfounded 10 fallacious, inaccurate, misleading 11 sophistical 12 questionable 15 unsubstantiated

speck 3 bit, dot, jot, pin 4 drop, hair, iota, mark, mite, mote, spot, whit 5 fleck, grain, pinch, trace 6 shadow, trifle 7 glimmer, modicum, speckle 8 farthing, flyspeck, particle 9 scintilla

speckled 4 pied 6 dotted 7 flecked, spotted, studded 8 freckled, peppered 9 sprinkled

spectacle 5 scene, sight 6 marvel, parade, rarity, wonder 7 display, exhibit, pageant 9 curiosity, rare sight 10 exhibition, exposition, phenomenon, production 12 extravaganza, presentation 13 demonstration

spectacles 6 lenses, shades 7 glasses 8 bifocals, pince-nez 10 eyeglasses

spectacular 4 gala, rich 5 grand, showy 6 daring 7 jeweled, opulent, stately 8 dramatic, fabulous, glorious, gorgeous, splendid, striking 9 daredevil, elaborate, marvelous, spectacle, sumptuous, thrilling 10 astounding, bespangled, eye-filling, impressive, theatrical 11 ceremonious, hair-raising, magnificent, sensational 12 extravaganza, overwhelming 16 ostentatious show 19 elaborate production

spectator 3 fan 5 house 6 viewer 7 gallery, witness 8 audience, beholder, kibitzer, observer, onlooker 9 bystander, sightseer 10 aficionado, eyewitness 11 afficionado, theatergoer 12 rubbernecker

Spectator, The
author: 13 Joseph Addison, Richard Steele

specter 5 demon, ghost, ghoul, shade, spook 6 spirit, sprite, vision, wraith 7 banshee, fantasy, phantom 8 phantasm, presence, revenant 9 hobgoblin 10 apparition

spectral 4 airy 5 eerie, weird 6 creepy, spooky, unreal 7 ghastly, ghostly, phantom, shadowy, uncanny 8 ethereal, gossamer, vaporous 9 unearthly 10 chimerical, phantasmal, wraithlike 11 incorporeal 12 otherworldly, supernatural 13 insubstantial

speculate 4 muse 5 brood, dream, fancy, guess, study, think, wager 6 chance, gamble, hazard, ponder, reason, wonder 7 imagine, reflect, suppose, surmise, venture 8 cogitate, consider, meditate, ruminate, theorize 10 conjecture, deliberate, excogitate, play a hunch 11 contemplate, hypothesize, take a chance 13 play the market

speculation 4 risk 7 venture 8 gambling 9 guesswork 10 conjecture, estimation 11 supposition

speculative 4 iffy 5 dicey, risky 6 chancy 8 academic 11 conjectural, theoretical 12 experimental, hypothetical 13 suppositional

speculator 7 gambler, plunger 8 investor, operator, theorist 10 adventurer, arbitrager 11 arbitrageur

speech 4 talk 5 idiom, lingo, slang, voice 6 appeal, gossip, homily, jargon, sermon, tirade, tongue 7 address, chatter, comment, dialect, diction, lecture, oration, palaver, prattle, remarks, talking 8 chitchat, colloquy, converse, dialogue, diatribe, harangue, language, parlance, rhetoric, speaking 9 discourse, elocution, monologue, soliloquy, statement, utterance 10 discussion, expression, recitation, salutation 11 declamation, declaration, enunciation, exhortation, observation, valedictory 12 articulation, conversation, dissertation, vocalization 13 colloquialism, confabulation, pronouncement, pronunciation, verbalization

speechless 3 mum 4 dumb, mute 6 silent 7 aphonic 8 wordless 9 stupefied 10 tongue-tied

speed 3 aid, hie, run, zip 4 dart, dash, help, race, rate, rush, tear, zoom 5 boost, favor, gun it, haste, hurry, impel, speed, tempo 6 assist, barrel, gallop, hasten, hurtle, hustle, pick up, plunge, propel, scurry, step up 7 advance, further, hurry up, promote, quicken, tear off 8 alacrity, celerity, dispatch, expedite, high tail, make time, momentum, rapidity, step on it, velocity 9 bowl along, briskness, fleetness, give a lift, hastiness, make haste, move along, quickness, rapidness, swiftness 10 accelerate, expedition, get a move on, go hellbent, lose no time, promptness, spurt ahead 11 push forward 12 acceleration 13 burn up the road

speedily 4 fast 5 apace, quick 6 pronto 7 hastily, rapidly, swiftly 8 in no time, promptly 9 post haste, right away, summarily 11 on the double 12 lickety-split

speed up 4 rush 5 hurry 6 hasten, step up 7 hop to it, quicken 8 expedite, multiply, step on it 9 encourage, intensify 10 accelerate, facilitate, get a move on 12 step on the gas

speedy 4 fast 5 brisk, early, fleet, hasty, quick, rapid, ready, swift 6 abrupt, lively, sudden 7 express, hurried, running, summary 8 headlong 9 quick-fire, rapid-fire 10 not delayed 11 precipitate

Spelaites
  epithet of: 6 Hermes
  means: 9 of the cave

spell 2 go 3 bit, hex 4 bout, free, lull, mean, omen, snap, term, time, tour, turn, wave 5 augur, break, charm, hitch, imply, magic, pause, round, stint, trick, while 6 allure, course, denote, herald, hoodoo, make up, period, recess, tenure, typify, voodoo 7 bespeak, betoken, connote, glamour, portend, presage, promise, purport, rapture, release, relieve, respite, signify, sorcery, stretch, suggest 8 amount to, cover for, duration, forebode, forecast, foretell, indicate, interval, stand for, witchery 9 form a word, influence, interlude, represent, symbolize 10 assignment, invocation, mumbo jumbo, open-sesame 11 abracadabra, bewitchment, enchantment, fascination, incantation, pinch-hit for, take over for 12 magic formula

spellbind 5 charm 7 bewitch, enchant 8 enthrall, entrance, intrigue, transfix 9 enrapture, fascinate, hypnotize, mesmerize, transport

spellbound 4 rapt 5 agape 7 charmed 8 wordless 9 awestruck, bewitched, enchanted, entranced, possessed 10 breathless, dumbstruck, enraptured, enthralled, fascinated, hypnotized, mesmerized, speechless, tongue-tied, transfixed 11 openmouthed, transported

Spellbound
  director: 15 Alfred Hitchcock
  cast: 9 John Emery 11 Gregory Peck, Leo G Carroll 13 Ingrid Bergman 14 Michael Chekhov
  score: 11 Miklos Rosza
  Oscar for: 5 score
  dream sequences by: 12 Salvador Dali

spell out 6 define, detail 7 clarify, clear up, explain, expound, specify 8 describe 9 delineate, designate, elucidate, explicate, interpret, make plain 10 illustrate

Spemann, Hans
  field: 7 zoology
  nationality: 6 German
  worked in: 20 embryonic development
  awarded: 10 Nobel Prize

Spencer, Sir Stanley
  born: 7 Cookham, England 9 Berkshire
  artwork: 22 Resurrection of Soldiers, The Resurrection Cookham 31 Christ Preaching at Cookham Regatta 43 Double Nude Portrait—the Artist and his Second Wife

spend 3 pay, use 4 dole, fill, give, pass 5 drain, empty, use up, waste 6 devote, employ, expend, invest, occupy, outlay, pay out, take up 7 burn out, consume, deplete, destroy, exhaust, fork out, scatter, wear out 8 allocate, disburse, dispense, shell out, squander 9 dissipate, while away 10 impoverish

spendable 9 available 10 expendable 13 discretionary

spend foolishly 5 waste 8 misspend, squander 9 dissipate, throw away 11 fritter away

spendthrift 6 lavish, waster 7 wastrel 8 prodigal, spend-all, wasteful 10 big spender, profligate, squanderer 11 extravagant, improvident 12 overgenerous

Spengler, Oswald
  author of: 19 The Decline of the West

Spenlow, Dora
  character in: 16 David Copperfield
  author: 7 Dickens

Spenser, Edmund
  author of: 8 Amoretti 12 Epithalamion 15 The Faerie Queene 22 The Shephearde's Calendar

spent 4 beat, done, weak 5 faint, weary 6 bushed, done in, used up 7 laid low, wearied, worn out 8 drooping, fatigued, tired out 9 enfeebled, exhausted, fagged out, played out, powerless, prostrate 11 debilitated, ready to drop **12** strengthless **14** on one's last legs

Sperry, Elmer Ambrose
  invented: 11 gyrocompass **22** airplane automatic pilot

spew 5 eject, expel, heave, vomit **6** cast up **7** spit out **8** disgorge, throw out **11** regurgitate

spew up 4 spew **5** eject, expel, spout, vomit **6** cast up **7** cough up, throw up **8** disgorge **11** regurgitate

sphere 3 orb **4** area, ball, beat, pale **5** globe, orbit, range, realm, scope **6** domain **7** compass, globule **8** province, spheroid **9** bailiwick, round body, territory **10** experience

spherical 5 orbic, round **6** global, rotund **7** globate, globose, orbical **8** globular **9** orbicular **11** globe-shaped
  nearly: 8 obrotund

spheroid 3 orb **4** ball **5** globe **6** sphere **7** globule

spherule 4 ball, bead, drop **6** pellet **7** droplet, globule

Sphinx
  form: 7 monster
  bust of: 5 woman
  body of: 4 lion
  father: 6 Typhon **7** Orthrus
  mother: 7 Echidna **8** Chimaera
  proposed: 7 riddles
  location: 6 Thebes
  answered by: 7 Oedipus

spice 3 zip **4** herb, kick, snap, tang, zest **5** savor **6** accent, flavor, relish, stacte **7** pizzazz **8** piquancy, pungency **9** condiment, flavoring, seasoning **10** excitement

spicule 4 barb **5** point, spine **7** prickle

spicy 3 hot **4** keen, racy **5** acute, bawdy, fiery, nippy, pithy, salty, sharp, tangy, witty, zippy **6** clever, ribald, risque, snappy, strong **7** gingery, peppery, piquant, pungent **8** aromatic, improper, incisive, indecent, off-color, piercing, redolent, spirited **9** sparkling, trenchant **10** indelicate, scandalous, suggestive **11** provocative **12** questionable **13** scintillating

spider
  black widow marking: 9 hourglass
  class: 9 Arachnida
  combining form: 6 arachn **7** arachno
  family: 7 Attidae **9** Drassidae **10** Citigradae, Pisauridae
  famous: 9 Charlotte
  fear of: 13 arachnophobia
  kind: 4 crab, wolf **5** taint **7** jumping **8** trap-door **9** orb weaver, solpugida, tarantula **10** black widow **13** daddy longlegs
  mythology: 7 Arachne
  nest: 5 nidus
  order: 7 Araneae
  part: 4 claw, coxa **5** femur, tibia **6** tarsus **7** abdomen, mammula, patella, pedicel, scopula **9** chelicera, protarsis, spinneret **10** pedipalpus, trochanter **11** calamistrum **13** cephalothorax
  study of: 10 araneology **11** arachnology

  young: 11 spiderlings

Spielberg, Steven
  director of: 4 Jaws **14** The Color Purple **19** Raiders of the Lost Ark **21** ET The Extra Terrestrial (in his adventures on earth) **29** Close Encounters of the Third Kind

spike.**3** peg, pin **4** barb, nail, spur, tine **5** briar, point, prong, rivet, spine, stake, thorn **6** needle, skewer **7** bramble, bristle, hobnail **8** spikelet

spill 3 run **4** blab, drip, drop, dump, fall, flow, shed, slop, tell, toss **5** slosh, throw, waste **6** reveal, splash **7** let flow, pour out **8** disclose, overflow, overturn

Spillane, Mickey
  real name: 13 Frank Morrison
  author of: 8 I the Jury **12** Kiss Me Deadly **14** The Girl Hunters **15** The Death Dealers
  character: 10 Mike Hammer

spin 4 roll, tell, turn **5** swirl, twirl, whirl, wheel, whirl **6** gyrate, invent, relate, render, rotate, unfold **7** concoct, narrate, recount, revolve **8** rotation, spinning **9** fabricate, pirouette

spinach 3 rot **4** bull, bunk **5** hokum, hooey, stuff **6** bunkum, hot air, humbug **7** baloney, blather, hogwash, potherb **8** claptrap, nonsense, tommyrot **9** poppycock, vegetable **10** applesauce **11** foolishness **16** stuff and nonsense

spinach 16 Spinacia oleracea
  varieties: 4 wild **5** Cuban **6** Indian **7** Malabar **8** mountain **10** New Zealand **11** round-seeded **13** prickly-seeded

spinal column 4 back **5** spine **8** backbone

spindly 4 puny **5** frail, leggy **6** skinny **7** scraggy **8** skeletal

spine 4 barb, horn, spur **5** briar, point, prong, quill, spike, thorn **6** needle **7** bramble, bristle, prickle **8** backbone **9** vertebrae **12** spinal column

spinel
  source: 5 Burma, Mogok
  color: 3 red **5** mauve

spineless 4 weak **5** timid **7** fearful **8** cowardly, cowering, cringing, timorous, wavering **10** indecisive, irresolute, spiritless, weak-willed **11** lily-livered, vacillating **12** fainthearted **13** pusillanimous **14** chickenhearted

spinelessness 8 timidity, weakness **9** cowardice **10** indecision **11** fearfulness **12** cowardliness, irresolution **13** pusillanimity

spine-tingling 7 rousing **8** exciting **9** thrilling **11** hair-raising, sensational **12** breathtaking, electrifying

spinning jenny
  invented by: 10 Hargreaves

spinoff 5 issue **6** result **7** ad junct, outcome **8** offshoot **9** byproduct, outgrowth **10** descendant, side effect, supplement **11** aftereffect, consequence

spin out 4 skid **7** draw out **8** lengthen **9** attenuate

spinster 6 virgin **7** old maid **14** unmarried woman

spinsterhood 8 celibacy 9 virginity 11 old maidhood

spiral 4 coil, curl, gyre 5 helix, screw, whirl, whorl 6 coiled, curled 7 helical, ringlet, spiroid, whorled, winding 8 curlicue, twisting 9 corkscrew 11 screw-shaped

Spiral Staircase, The
  director: 13 Robert Siodmak
  based on story by: 14 Ethel Lina White (Some Must Watch)
  cast: 9 Kent Smith 11 George Brent 13 Rhonda Fleming 14 Dorothy McGuire, Ethel Barrymore

spire 3 cap, tip 4 apex, cone, peak 5 crest, point, shaft, tower 6 belfry, summit, turret, vertex 7 minaret, obelisk, steeple 8 pinnacle 9 bell tower, campanile

spirit 3 elf 4 mind, soul, urge, will 5 fairy, ghost, ghoul, heart, shade, spook 6 animus, dybbuk, goblin, psyche, sprite, wraith 7 banshee, bugaboo, bugbear, impulse, phantom, resolve, specter 8 phantasm, presence 9 hobgoblin, intellect 10 apparition, motivation, resolution
  German: 9 Geist

spirited 4 bold 5 fiery, nervy 6 frisky, lively, plucky 8 fearless, intrepid 10 courageous, mettlesome

spiritless 4 dull, limp, tame 6 abject 8 cowardly, lifeless, listless 9 apathetic, spineless 10 unanimated, world-weary 11 passionless

spirit of the time
  German: 9 Zeitgeist

spirits 3 aim, vim 4 bond, elan, fire, gist, glow, grit, guts, mood, sand, tone, vein, zeal, zest 5 ardor, drive, humor, pluck, sense, spunk, tenor, valor, verve, vigor 6 daring, effect, elixir, energy, fervor, intent, liquor, mettle, morale, stripe, temper, warmth 7 alcohol, avidity, bravery, courage, essence, extract, feeling, loyalty, meaning, purport, purpose, sparkle 8 attitude, audacity, backbone, boldness, devotion, emotions, feelings, tincture, vitality, vivacity 9 animation, eagerness, fortitude, intention, sentiment, stoutness, substance 10 allegiance, attachment, enterprise, enthusiasm, liveliness 11 disposition, doughtiness, staunchness 12 fearlessness, significance 13 dauntlessness, sprightliness 16 stoutheartedness 17 alcoholic solution

spiritual 4 holy 5 godly, inner, moral, pious 6 divine, mental 7 blessed, churchy, ghostly, phantom, psychic 8 cerebral, hallowed, heavenly, platonic, priestly, spectral, supernal 9 celestial, Christian, innermost, of the soul, religious, unearthly, unfleshly, unworldly 10 devotional, immaterial, intangible, sacrosanct, sanctified 11 consecrated, incorporeal 12 metaphysical, otherworldly, supernatural 13 insubstantial, psychological 14 ecclesiastical

spirituality 5 piety 8 devotion, holiness 9 godliness, reverence 10 devoutness

spirituous 4 hard 6 strong 9 alcoholic, distilled 12 intoxicating

spit 3 bar, pop, rod 4 foam, hiss, reef, spew 5 atoll, drool, eject, fling, froth, shoal, throw 6 saliva, shower, shriek, skewer, slaver, sputum 7 dribble, scatter, slobber, spatter, spittle, sputter 8 headland, sandbank, turnspit 9 brochette, peninsula 10 promontory 11 expectorate

spite 3 irk, vex 4 gall, hate, hurt, pain 5 annoy, odium, sting, venom, wound 6 animus, enmity, grudge, harass, hatred, injure, malice, misuse, nettle, put out, rancor 7 ill will, mortify, provoke 8 bad blood, illtreat, irritate, loathing, meanness 9 animosity, antipathy, hostility, humiliate, malignity, nastiness, vengeance 10 bitterness, resentment 11 detestation, malevolence 12 vengefulness 13 maliciousness, slap in the face 14 revengefulness, vindictiveness

spiteful 4 evil 5 nasty 6 bitter, malign, wicked 7 caustic, envious, hateful, hostile, vicious 8 grudging, vengeful, venomous 9 malicious, merciless, rancorous, resentful, sarcastic, splenetic 10 ill-natured, malevolent, vindictive 11 acrimonious, unforgiving 12 antagonistic

spitting image (the) 4 copy, mate, twin 6 double 9 duplicate 15 perfect likeness

splash 3 ado, hit 4 cast, dash, daub, soil, stir, toss, wash 5 bathe, break, fling, plash, slosh, smack, smear, stain, strew, surge, swash 6 batter, blazon, buffet, effect, impact, paddle, plunge, shower, spread, streak, strike, uproar, wallow, welter 7 bestrew, scatter, spatter, splotch 8 besmirch, discolor, disperse, splatter, sprinkle 9 bespatter, broadcast, commotion, sensation 10 spattering 11 splattering

splashy 5 jazzy, showy 6 flashy 10 glittering 11 spectacular 12 ostentatious

splatter 4 dash 6 splash 7 spatter

splay 4 awry 5 askew, broad 6 aslant, clumsy, extend, tilted, warped 7 awkward, crooked, fanlike, slanted, sloping, turn out 8 inclined, slanting 9 distorted, fanshaped, irregular, outspread, spread out 10 stretch out

spleen 4 bile, gall 5 anger, spite, venom 6 animus, enmity, hatred, malice, rancor 7 ill will 8 acrimony, ill humor, vexation 9 animosity, bad temper, hostility 10 bitterness, resentment 11 malevolence, peevishness 12 irritability, spitefulness

splendid 4 fine, high, rare, rich 5 grand, lofty, noble, regal, royal 6 august, costly, ornate, superb 7 elegant, eminent, exalted, stately 8 dazzling, elevated, flashing, gleaming, glorious, gorgeous, imposing, majestic, palatial, peerless, terrific 9 admirable, beautiful, brilliant, effulgent, estimable, excellent, marvelous, sumptuous, wonderful 10 glittering, preeminent, remarkable, surpassing 11 exceptional, illustrious, magnificent, outstanding, resplendent, splendorous **12** transcendent **13** distinguished, splendiferous

Splendid Splinter
nickname of: 11 Ted Williams

splendor 4 fire, pomp **5** gleam, glory, light, sheen, shine **6** beauty, dazzle, luster, renown **7** burnish, glitter **8** grandeur, nobility, opulence, radiance **9** intensity, sublimity **10** augustness, brilliance, effulgence, irradiance, luminosity **11** preeminence, stateliness **12** gorgeousness, luminousness, magnificence, resplendence **13** incandescence

Splendor in the Grass
director: 9 Elia Kazan
based on story by: 11 William Inge
cast: 9 Pat Hingle **11** Natalie Wood **12** Sean Garrison, Warren Beatty **14** Audrey Christie

splenetic 5 cross, nasty, surly, testy **6** cranky, malign **7** bilious, hostile, peevish **8** choleric, spiteful, venomous **9** irascible, rancorous **11** acrimonious, ill-tempered **12** cantankerous, disagreeable

splice 3 wed **4** join, knit **5** graft, merge, plait, unite **7** connect **8** dovetail **9** interlace **10** intertwine, interweave **12** interconnect

splinter 4 chip **5** smash, split **6** needle, shiver, sliver **7** break up, crumble, explode, shatter **8** fly apart, fracture, fragment **9** pulverize **12** disintegrate

split 3 hew **4** deal, dole, dual, mete, part, rent, rift, rive, snap, tear, torn **5** allot, break, burst, cleft, crack, halve, mixed, riven, sever, share **6** bisect, breach, broken, cleave, differ, divide, ripped, schism, shiver, sunder, varied **7** be riven, cracked, diverge, divided, divorce, divvy up, fissure, give way, opening, portion, quarrel, rupture, severed, twofold **8** alienate, allocate, cleavage, disagree, dispense, disperse, dissever, disunion, disunite, division, fracture, ruptured, splinter **9** apportion, fractured, parcel out, partition, segmented, segregate, separated, set at odds, subdivide, undecided **10** alienation, ambivalent, break apart, difference, dissension, dissevered, distribute, divergence, falling out, separation, splintered **11** come between, part company, tear asunder **12** disagreement, estrangement

split off 7 deviate, diverge **8** separate **9** draw apart

split the difference 5 agree **6** settle **9** make a deal **10** compromise **11** come to terms, meet halfway **14** strike a bargain

splitting off 9 diverging **10** separating **12** drawing apart

splitting up 8 dividing **9** divorcing **10** breaking up, separating **11** subdividing **12** partitioning

splotch 4 blot, daub, mark, spot **5** smear, stain **6** blotch, smudge **13** discoloration

splurge 4 binge, spree **6** bender **8** live it up **10** indulgence, showing off **12** showy display **13** be extravagant, shoot the works

14 indulge oneself, self-indulgence **22** throw caution to the winds

splutter 4 hiss, spew, spit **5** burst, spray **6** gibber, jabber, mumble, seethe **7** bluster, slobber, spatter, sputter, stammer, stumble, stutter **9** hem and haw **11** expectorate

Spodius
epithet of: 6 Apollo
means: 10 god of ashes

spodumene
variety: 7 kunzite

spoil 3 mar, rot **4** baby, flaw, harm, mold, ruin, sour, turn **5** addle, botch, decay, go bad, humor, taint **6** blight, bungle, coddle, damage, deface, foul up, impair, injure, mess up, mildew, muddle, pamper **7** blemish, destroy, disrupt, putrefy **8** mutilate **9** decompose, disfigure **11** deteriorate, mollycoddle, overgratify, overindulge

spoiled 3 bad, off **6** putrid, rotten, ruined **7** coddled, corrupt, decayed, gone bad, went bad **8** indulged, overripe, pampered **9** putrefied **10** decomposed, frustrated **12** deteriorated **15** rotten to the core

spoiler 6 vandal **8** underdog **9** deflector

Spoilers, The
author: 8 Rex Beach

spoils 4 haul, loot, swag, take **5** booty **6** bounty, prizes, quarry **7** plunder, profits **8** benefits, comforts, pickings **9** amenities, patronage **11** perquisites **12** acquisitions

spoilsport 4 drag **10** wet blanket **11** party-pooper

spoken 4 oral, said **5** parol **6** verbal, voiced **7** uttered **9** expressed **10** pronounced **11** articulated

spokesman 5 agent, PR man, proxy **6** backer, deputy **7** speaker **8** delegate, promoter **9** middleman, proponent, supporter, surrogate **10** mouthpiece, negotiator, press agent **11** protagonist

sponge 3 bum, dry, mop, rub **4** blot, swab, wash **5** cadge, clean, leech, mooch, towel **6** borrow, live on **7** cleanse, moisten **8** freeload, impose on, scrounge **9** panhandle

sponger 5 leech **6** cadger, sponge **7** moocher **8** barnacle, borrower, deadbeat **9** scrounger **10** freeloader **11** bloodsucker

sponsor 4 back **5** angel, set up **6** backer, patron, uphold **7** finance, promote, support **8** advocate, champion, defender, financer, guardian, partisan, promoter, start out, upholder, vouch for, warranty **9** guarantee, financier, guarantor, proponent, protecter, protector, supporter **10** advertiser, stand up for, underwrite

sponsorship 5 aegis **7** support **8** advocacy, auspices **9** patronage **12** championship

spontaneity 7 freedom **11** impetuosity, naturalness **12** unconstraint **13** impulsiveness, offhandedness **18** extemporaneousness

spontaneous 4 free **5** ad lib **7** natural, offhand, willing **8** unbidden **9** automatic, extempore, impetuous, impromptu, impulsive, ingenuous, unplanned, unstudied,

voluntary 10 gratuitous, improvised, off the cuff, unprompted 11 independent, instinctive, uncontrived 12 unhesitating 13 unconstrained 14 extemporaneous, unpremeditated

spoof 3 kid 4 joke, josh, twit 6 parody, satire, sendup 7 joshing, kidding, lampoon, mockery, ribbing, takeoff 8 satirize, travesty 9 burlesque, take off on 10 caricature

spook 5 alarm, bogey, ghost, haunt, scare, shade 6 goblin, shadow, spirit 7 disturb, phantom, specter, startle, terrify, unnerve 8 disquiet, frighten, unsettle 9 hobgoblin, terrorize 10 apparition, intimidate

spooky 5 eerie, jumpy, scary, weird 6 creepy 7 ghostly, nervous 8 skittish 10 mysterious

sporadic 3 few 4 rare, thin 6 fitful, meager, random, scarce, sparse, spotty 8 isolated, periodic, uncommon 9 haphazard, irregular, scattered, spasmodic 10 infrequent, now and then, occasional 11 fragmentary 12 intermittent, widely spaced 13 discontinuous 16 few and far between

sport 3 fun, toy 4 bear, butt, game, goat, jest, joke, lark, play, romp, trip 5 abuse, caper, carry, chaff, dally, frisk, hobby, mirth, revel 6 antics, cavort, frolic, gaiety, gambol, misuse, monkey, take in, trifle 7 buffoon, contest, display, disport, exhibit, gambler, jesting, jollity, kidding, mockery, rollick, show off, skylark 8 badinage, derision, fair game, flourish, hilarity, ill-treat, raillery, ridicule, scoffing, trifling 9 amusement, athletics, daredevil, diversion, festivity, joviality, make merry, play games, scapegoat 10 persiflage, pleasantry, recreation, relaxation, skylarking 11 competition, distraction, merrymaking 12 depreciation 13 entertainment, laughingstock 14 divertissement

sporting house 4 stew 5 house 6 bagnio, bordel 7 brothel 8 bordello, cathouse 10 bawdy house, fancy house, whorehouse 14 house of ill fame 16 house of ill repute 19 house of prostitution

sportive 6 blithe, frisky 7 playful 8 animated 10 frolicsome

sportsman 6 hunter 9 fisherman

Sportsman's Notebook, A
author: 12 Ivan Turgenev

sporty 6 casual, flashy, jaunty 8 informal

spot 3 dot, fix, see, spy 4 area, bind, blot, daub, espy, flaw, mark, part, seat, site, slur, soil 5 brand, fleck, grime, locus, patch, place, point, smear, space, speck, stain, sully, taint, tract 6 blotch, defect, detect, locale, locate, plight, region, sector, smirch, smudge, splash, stigma 7 blemish, dilemma, discern, light on, pick out, quarter, section, spatter, speckle, splotch, station 8 discolor, discover, disgrace, district, flyspeck, locality, location, position, premises, reproach, sprinkle 9 aspersion, discredit, recognize, situation, territory 10 difficulty, imputation 11 predicament 12 bad situation, neighborhood 13 discoloration

spotless 4 pure 5 clean, snowy 7 perfect, shining 8 flawless, gleaming, pristine, unflawed, unmarred, unsoiled 9 faultless, stainless, unspotted, unstained, unsullied, untainted 10 immaculate, impeccable 11 unblemished, untarnished 14 irreproachable 15 unexceptionable

spotted 3 saw 6 dotted, espied, soiled 7 dappled, located, mottled, stained 8 detected, speckled 9 blemished, discerned, spattered 10 discovered 13 caught sight of

spotty 6 fitful, pimply, random, uneven 7 blotchy, dappled, erratic, flecked, mottled, spotted 8 episodic, freckled, splotchy, sporadic, unsteady, variable, wavering 9 broken out, desultory, irregular, spasmodic, uncertain 10 capricious, inconstant, unreliable, variegated 11 full of spots 12 disorganized, intermittent, undependable, unmethodical, unsystematic

spouse 4 mate, wife 7 consort, husband, partner 8 helpmate 10 better half

spout 3 jet, lip 4 beak, flow, go on, gush, nose, pipe, rant, spew, tube, vent, well 5 eject, erupt, expel, exude, issue, mouth, shoot, snout, spray, spurt, surge, vomit 6 nozzle, outlet, sluice, squirt, stream, trough 7 bluster, carry on, channel, conduit, pour out 8 disgorge, fountain, harangue 9 discharge, hold forth 10 waterspout 11 pontificate 12 emit forcibly 14 speak pompously

sprawl 4 flop, lean, loll, wind 5 slump 6 branch, extend, lounge, slouch 7 gush out, meander, recline 8 languish, reach out, straggle 9 spread out 10 stretch out 11 spread-eagle

spray 4 coat, mist, posy, twig 5 bough, burst, shoot, sprig, treat, vapor 6 dampen, nozzle, shower, splash, switch, volley 7 atomize, barrage, blossom, bouquet, drizzle, moisten, nosegay, scatter, spatter, sprayer, syringe 8 atomizer, disperse, droplets, moisture, sprinkle 9 discharge, fusillade, sprinkler, vaporizer

spread 3 air, lay 4 area, cast, coat, open, pave, shed, span, vent 5 apply, bruit, cloak, cover, feast, field, issue, range, reach, scope, smear, spray, story, strew, sweep, table, tract, width 6 bedaub, beshed, blazon, extend, extent, herald, length, notice, repeat, report, unfold, unfurl, unroll 7 account, advance, article, banquet, besmear, bestrew, breadth, circuit, compass, declare, diffuse, divulge, expanse, overlay, overrun, pervade, plaster, publish, radiate, scatter, spatter, stretch, suffuse, trumpet, untwine, write-up 8 announce, coverage, disperse, distance, increase, permeate, proclaim, sprinkle 9 broadcast, circulate, diffusion, expansion, extension, make known, penetrate, pervasion, propagate, publicize, radiation, spreading, suffusion, ventilate 10 dispersion, distribute, make public, permeation, promulgate, stretch out 11 communicate, disseminate, noise abroad, proliferate 13 amplification, dissemination, proliferation

spread out 5 broad, widen **6** expand, extend **7** broaden, diffuse, enlarge, radiate, stretch **8** expanded, extended, open wide **9** dispersed, outspread, scattered **10** distribute, unhampered **11** unconfirmed **12** unrestricted **14** unconcentrated

spree 4 bout, orgy, toot **5** binge, drunk, fling, revel **6** bender **7** carouse, debauch, revelry, splurge, wassail **8** carousal **9** bacchanal **10** saturnalia

sprightliness 8 buoyancy, spryness, vivacity **9** animation, briskness **10** breeziness, liveliness **16** lightheartedness

sprightly 3 gay **4** keen, spry **5** agile, alive, brisk, jolly, merry **6** active, blithe, breezy, cheery, jaunty, jovial, lively, nimble **7** buoyant, chipper, dashing, dynamic, playful **8** animated, cheerful, spirited, sportive **9** energetic, vivacious **10** blithesome, frolicsome **12** lighthearted

spring 3 hop, jet, pop, spa **4** come, dart, flow, gush, jump, kick, leap, loom, pool, pour, rise, rush, stem, well **5** arise, baths, begin, bound, caper, ensue, fount, issue, lunge, shoot, spout, spurt, start, surge, vault **6** appear, bounce, derive, gambol, recoil, reflex, result, sprout, stream **7** burgeon, crop out, descend, emanate, proceed, release, shoot up, start up, stretch, trigger **8** buoyancy, commence, fountain, mushroom **9** come forth, entrechat, germinate, originate, saltation, waterhole **10** break forth, burst forth, elasticity, resiliency **11** flexibility

    goddess of: 4 Hebe **5** Venus

spring back 6 bounce, recoil **7** rebound **8** ricochet

spring flowers

    goddess of: 6 Thallo

Springhaven

    author: 11 R D Blackmore

springlike 4 mild, soft, warm **5** balmy

springs

    god of: 4 Fons **6** Palici

    goddess of: 4 Idun **5** Idura, Ithun **6** Ithunn

spring up 4 grow, rise **5** arise, occur, pop up **6** crop up, emerge, happen, sprout **9** originate **10** burst forth

springy 6 bouncy, spongy, supple **7** elastic **9** resilient **16** rebounding

sprinkle 4 dash, dust, rain **5** spray, strew, water **6** powder, shower, splash, spread, squirt **7** bestrew, diffuse, drizzle, moisten, scatter, spatter **8** splatter

sprinkling 4 dash, drop, hint **5** pinch, touch **7** droplet, minimum, modicum, soupcon **8** sprinkle **10** smattering

sprint 3 run **4** dart, dash, kick, race, rush, tear, whiz **5** burst, shoot, spurt, whisk **7** scamper

sprit 3 bar **4** spar **8** crossbar **10** crosspiece

sprite 3 elf **5** fairy, pixie **10** leprechaun

sprout 3 bud, wax **4** grow **5** bloom, shoot, sprig **6** come up, flower, spread, thrive **7** blossom, burgeon **8** multiply, offshoot, put forth, spring up **9** germinate, outgrowth

spruce 4 chic, neat, tidy, trim **5** kempt, natty, sharp, smart **6** dapper **7** conifer, elegant **9** evergreen, shipshape **11** well-groomed **12** spick-and-span

    French: 6 soigne

spruce 5 Picea

    varieties: 3 bog, cat, red **4** blue **5** black, Hondo, Sitka, snake, white, Yeddo **6** double, Norway **7** Alberta, big-cone, Finnish, hemlock **8** Colorado, Sakhalin, Siberian **9** Himalayan, tiger-tail **10** Black Hills **12** Colorado blue, Japanese bush

spry 4 deft, hale **5** agile, brisk, quick **6** active, frisky, hearty, jaunty, lively, nimble, supple **7** buoyant, chipper, playful **8** animated, spirited, sportive, vigorous **9** energetic, sprightly, vivacious **11** lightfooted

spunk 4 fire, grit, guts, salt, sand **5** heart, nerve, pluck **6** daring, ginger, mettle, pepper, spirit **7** bravery, courage **8** backbone, boldness, gumption **9** feistiness

spur 3 arm, leg **4** fork, goad, prod, whet, whip, wing **5** prick **6** branch, feeder, fillip, hasten, motive, siding **7** impetus, impulse **8** excitant, stimulus **9** boot spike, encourage, incentive, stimulant, stimulate, tributary **10** incitement, inducement **11** instigation, provocation, stimulation **13** encouragement

spurge 9 Euphorbia **11** Pachysandra

    varieties: 5 caper, leafy, melon **6** ipecac, myrtle, tramp's **7** cypress, mottled, seaside, slipper **8** fiddler's, Japanese **9** Allegheny, flowering **10** Indian tree

spurious 4 fake, mock, sham **5** bogus, false, phony **6** faulty, forged, hollow **7** feigned, unsound **8** specious **9** imitation, simulated **10** fallacious, fraudulent, not genuine **11** counterfeit, make-believe, unauthentic **12** illegitimate

spurn 4 mock, snub **5** flout, repel, scorn **6** rebuff, refuse, reject, slight **7** condemn, decline, disdain, dismiss, repulse, scoff at, sneer at **8** turn down **9** cast aside, disparage, repudiate **12** coldshoulder, look down upon **16** turn up one's nose at

spur-of-the-moment 5 ad-lib **7** offhand **9** extempore, impromptu **10** improvised, unprepared **11** extemporary, spontaneous, unrehearsed **14** extemporaneous, unpremeditated

spurt 3 jet **4** dart, dash, emit, flow, gush, gust, rush, tear, whiz **5** burst, flash, issue, lunge, scoot, shoot, speed, spout, spray, surge **6** access, spring, sprint, squirt, stream **7** pour out **8** disgorge, ejection, eruption, fountain, outbreak, outburst **9** discharge, explosion, spring out **10** outpouring

spy 3 pry, see 4 find, peep, spot, view 5 scout, sight, snoop 6 behold, descry, detect, notice, shadow 7 discern, glimpse, make out, observe 8 discover, informer, Mata Hari, perceive, saboteur 9 keep watch, operative, recognize 11 reconnoiter, secret agent 12 catch sight of 13 undercover man, watch secretly 14 espionage agent, fifth columnist 16 agent provocateur 17 intelligence agent

Spy 5 Caleb

Spy, The
   author: 19 James Fenimore Cooper

Spy Who Came In from the Cold, The
   director: 10 Martin Ritt
   based on novel by: 11 John LeCarre
   cast: 11 Claire Bloom, Oskar Werner 12 Peter Van Eyck 13 Richard Burton

Spy Who Loved Me, The
   author: 10 Ian Fleming
   director: 12 Lewis Gilbert
   cast: 10 Bernard Lee (M), Roger Moore (James Bond) 11 Barbara Bach, Curt Jurgens (Stromberg), Richard Kiel (Jaws)

squabble 3 row, war 4 spat, tiff 5 argue, brawl, clash, fight, run-in, scrap, set-to, words 6 battle, bicker, differ 7 contend, contest, dispute, quarrel, wrangle 8 argument 9 have words, lock horns 10 bandy words, contention, difference, dissension 11 altercation, controversy 12 disagreement

squadron 5 fleet 6 armada 8 flotilla 9 naval unit 10 escadrille 11 cavalry unit 12 military unit

squalid 4 foul, mean 5 dirty, nasty 6 abject, filthy, horrid, rotten, shabby, sloppy, sordid 7 decayed, reeking, run-down, unclean 8 battered, degraded, slovenly, wretched 9 miserable 10 broken-down, disheveled, ramshackle, slatternly, tumbledown 11 dilapidated 12 deteriorated

squalidness 4 dirt 5 filth 7 squalor 8 foulness, meanness, vileness 9 dirtiness 10 sordidness 11 degradation, uncleanness

squalor 4 dirt 5 filth 6 misery 7 neglect, poverty 8 foulness, meanness, ugliness 9 dinginess, dirtiness, nastiness, seediness 10 abjectness, grubbiness, sordidness 11 squalidness, uncleanness 12 wretchedness 13 uncleanliness

squander 4 blow 5 spend, waste 6 lavish, misuse 7 consume, deplete, exhaust 8 misspend 9 dissipate, throw away 10 run through 11 fritter away 14 spend like water

squanderer 6 waster 7 wastrel 8 prodigal 10 dissipater, profligate 11 spendthrift

squandering 7 wasting 8 prodigal, wasteful 9 imprudent 10 profligate 11 dissipating, extravagant, improvident, spendthrift 12 overspending, throwing away 14 frittering away 17 spending like water

square 3 box, fit 4 even, fogy, heal, hick, jerk, jibe, just, mend, park, prig 5 agree, align, blend, block, close, equal, green, match, place, plane, plaza, prude, tally 6 accord, adjust, candid, circus, cohere, common, concur, even up, fall in, honest, pay off, settle, smooth 7 arrange, balance, clear up, compose, conform, even out, flatten, mediate, patch up, rectify, resolve 8 block out, cornball, make even, quadrate, set right, settle up, truthful 9 arbitrate, discharge, equitable, harmonize, liquidate, make level, reconcile 10 clodhopper, correspond, quadrangle, straighten 11 marketplace 12 apple knocker, conservative 13 quadrilateral, stick-in-the-mud 15 straightforward
   type: 1 T 3 try 11 combination

Square
   character in: 8 Tom Jones
   author: 8 Fielding

Square
   constellation of: 5 Norma

square centimeter
   abbreviation: 4 sq cm

square decimeter
   abbreviation: 4 sq dm

square dekameter
   abbreviation: 5 sq dam

square foot
   abbreviation: 4 sq ft

square hectometer
   abbreviation: 4 sq hm

square inch
   abbreviation: 4 sq in

square kilometer
   abbreviation: 4 sq km

square meter
   abbreviation: 3 sq m

square mile
   abbreviation: 4 sq mi

square millimeter
   abbreviation: 4 sq mm

square rod
   abbreviation: 4 sq rd

square yard
   abbreviation: 4 sq yd

squash 3 jam 4 cram, mash, pulp 5 crowd, crush, level, quash, quell, smash, upset 6 dispel, squish 7 compact, destroy, flatten, put down, ram down, repress, squeeze, squelch, trample 8 compress, suppress 9 dissipate, overthrow, prostrate, undermine 10 annihilate, obliterate 11 concentrate

squash 9 Cucurbita
   varieties: 4 bush 5 acorn 6 autumn, banana, summer, turban, winter 7 Hubbard, scallop 8 pattypan, zucchini 9 cocozelle, crookneck 12 Boston marrow 13 sweet dumpling 15 Canada crookneck, summer crookneck, winter crookneck

squat 5 cower, dumpy, dwell, kneel, pudgy 6 chunky, cringe, crouch, encamp, hunker, lie low, locate, move in, shrink, square, stocky, stubby, stumpy 8 thickset

squawk 5 blare, croak, gripe 6 scream, squall 7 grumble, protest, screech 8 complain

squeak 3 cry 4 peep, yelp 5 cheep, chirp, creak, grate 6 shriek, shrill, squeal 7 screech

squeal 3 cry 4 bawl, blab, fink, peep, sing, wail, yell, yelp 5 cheep, whine 6 inform, scream, shriek, shrill, squeak 7 screech

squealer 3 pig, rat 4 fink 6 canary, piglet, snitch 7 stoolie, tattler, traitor 8 informer 10 tattletale 11 stool pigeon 12 blabbermouth

squeamish 3 coy 4 prim, sick 5 fussy 6 demure, modest, proper, queasy 7 finical, finicky, mincing, prudish, sickish 8 delicate, nauseous, priggish, qualmish 9 finicking 10 fastidious 11 puritanical, straitlaced 13 sanctimonious

Squeers, Wackford
    character in: 16 Nicholas Nickleby
    author: 7 Dickens

squeeze 3 hug, jam, pry, ram 4 butt, cram, edge, grip, hold, pack, push 5 clasp, cramp, crowd, drive, elbow, grasp, press, shove, stuff, wedge, wrest, wring 6 clutch, coerce, compel, defile, elicit, extort, jostle, thrust, wrench 7 compact, draw out, embrace, extract, passage, pull out, tear out 8 compress, crowding, crushing, force out, pinching, press out, pressure, shoulder, withdraw 9 extricate, narrowing, stricture 10 bottleneck 11 compression, concentrate, consolidate 12 constriction

squelch 4 hush 5 abort, crush, quash, quell, quiet, smash 6 retort, squash 7 put down, riposte, silence 8 silencer, suppress

squire 4 date, take 5 court 6 attend, escort 7 consort, gallant, planter 8 cavalier, chaperon 9 accompany, attendant, boyfriend, chauffeur, companion, landowner 14 lord of the manor 16 country gentleman

Squire
    character in: 18 The Canterbury Tales
    author: 7 Chaucer

squirm 4 bend, jerk, toss, turn 5 pitch, shift, smart, sweat, twist, wince 6 blench, fidget, flinch, shrink, twitch, wiggle, writhe 7 agonize, contort, wriggle 8 flounder

squirt 3 jet 4 dash, gush, punk, runt 5 piker, shoot, spout, spray, spurt 6 shower, splash, stream 7 spatter 8 sprinkle 9 discharge, pipsqueak 10 besprinkle

Sri Lanka
    other name: 6 Ceylon 8 Serendib 9 Taprobane
    capital/largest city: 7 Colombo
    ancient capital: 11 Polonnaruwa 12 Anuradhapura
    others: 3 Uva 5 Galle, Kandy 6 Jaffna, Mannar, Matale, Matara 7 Badulla, Kegalle, Negombo 8 Kalutara, Mankulem, Moratuwa, Puttalam 9 Ratnapura 10 Batticaloa, Mullaitivu 11 Ambalangoda, Trincomalee
    division: 8 Dambulla, Sri Lanka 9 Taprobane
    measure: 4 para, seer 5 parah 6 amunam, parrah
    monetary unit: 4 cent 5 rupee
    island: 5 Delft 6 Mannar 8 Sri Lanka
    mountain: 5 Pedro 7 Sri Pada 9 Adam's Peak
    highest point: 14 Pidurutalagala

    river: 4 Kala 6 Deduru, Gal Ova 8 Aruvi Aru 9 Deburu Ova 11 Kelani Ganga 13 Mahaweli Ganga
    sea: 6 Indian
    physical feature:
    bay: 6 Bengal 8 Koddiyar
    falls: 8 Lazapana
    gulf: 6 Mannar
    peninsula: 6 Jaffna
    plateau: 6 Hatton
    strait: 4 Palk
    people: 5 Malay, Tamil, Vedda 6 Veddah, Weddah 7 Burgher, Mahinda, Malabar 8 Eurasian 9 Cingalese, Dravidian, Sinhalese 10 Singhalese
    leader: 11 Jayawardene 12 Bandaranaike
    ruler: 5 Dutch 7 British, Chinese 10 Portuguese
    language: 4 Pali 5 Tamil 7 English 9 Sinhalese
    religion: 5 Hindu, Islam 8 Buddhism
    place:
    fortress: 8 Sigiriya
    gardens: 8 Hakgalle 10 Peradiniya
    national park: 6 Ruhuna 8 Wilpattu
    temple: 5 Tooth 6 Gal Oya 7 Kelanya 8 Runaweli 9 Ruanvelli 10 Dankahlaka 12 Asokharamaya
    feature:
    animal: 5 loris 12 wild elephant
    clothing: 4 sari 5 camba 6 sarong 7 cambaya 8 sherwani
    dancer: 7 Kandyan
    drama: 5 kolam 7 nadagam
    festival: 8 Perahera
    shrine: 6 dagoba
    tree: 4 doon, hora, palu, tala 5 domba, ebony 7 talipot 8 halmilla, ironwood 9 satinwood 11 allaeanthus 12 shimohabodhi

SS-GB
    author: 11 Len Deighton

SS troops, chief of 12 Reichsfuhrer

stab 2 go 3 cut, jab, try 4 ache, bite, gash, gore, hurt, pain, pang, pass, shot, spit 5 essay, gouge, knife, lance, lunge, prick, qualm, slash, spear, spike, stick, sting, trial, wound 6 cleave, dagger, effort, impale, pierce, shiver, stroke, thrill, thrust, twinge 7 attempt, bayonet 8 endeavor, lacerate, transfix 10 laceration, run through

stability 5 poise 6 aplomb, fixity 7 balance 8 evenness, firmness, security, solidity 9 constancy, fixedness, solidness, soundness 10 continuity, durability, permanence, stableness, steadiness, sturdiness 11 abidingness, equilibrium, reliability 13 steadfastness 14 changelessness 16 unchangeableness

stabilize 7 balance 8 hold firm, make firm 10 hold steady, make steady

stabilizer 7 balance, ballast 8 additive 9 equipoise, gyroscope 10 ballasting 12 airplane part 14 counterbalance

stable 4 barn, byre, even, firm, mews, safe, true **5** fixed, loyal, solid, sound **6** moored, secure, steady, sturdy **7** abiding, durable, staunch, uniform **8** anchored, constant, cowhouse, cowshed, enduring, faithful, reliable, resolute, stalwart **9** immovable, steadfast **10** dependable, persisting, stationary, unchanging, unwavering **11** established, unfaltering **12** indissoluble, unchangeable

Stabler, Ken
  nickname: 8 the Snake
  sport: 8 football
  position: 11 quarterback
  team: 13 Houston Oilers **14** Oakland Raiders

staccato
  music: 12 disconnected **16** each note separate

stack 4 bank, flue, heap, load, lump, mass, pile, rick **5** amass, batch, bunch, clump, hoard, mound, sheaf **6** bundle, funnel, gather **7** chimney **8** assemble, mountain **9** amassment **10** accumulate **11** aggregation **12** accumulation

Stack, Robert
  born: 12 Los Angeles CA
  roles: 9 Eliot Ness **13** Name of the Game **15** The Untouchables **16** Written on the Wind **19** The High and the Mighty **24** The Bullfighter and the Lady

Stackpole, Henrietta
  character in: 18 The Portrait of a Lady
  author: 5 James

Stacte 5 spice

stadium 4 bowl, park **5** arena, field, stade **6** circus **8** ballpark, coliseum **9** palaestra **10** hippodrome **12** amphitheater

Stael, Madame de
  author of: 7 Corinne **8** Delphine **9** On Germany **35** The Influence of Literature upon Society

staff 3 bat, man, rod **4** cane, crew, help, pole, team, tend, wand, work **5** cadre, force, group, stave, stick **6** crutch, cudgel, manage **7** retinue, scepter, service, support **8** advisors, bludgeon, flagpole **9** billy club, employees, flagstaff, personnel **10** alpenstock, assistants, shillelagh **12** walking stick

staff member 4 aide **6** worker **8** employee

stage 3 act **4** dais, play, spot, step **5** arena, drama, grade, level, phase, put on, sight, stump **6** acting, locale, period, podium, pulpit **7** perform, present, produce, rostrum, setting, show biz, soapbox, theater **8** bearings, locality, location, position, scaffold **9** dramatize, the boards

Stagecoach
  director: 8 John Ford
  cast: 9 John Wayne **10** Andy Devine **11** Louise Platt **12** Claire Trevor **13** John Carradine **14** George Bancroft, Thomas Mitchell
  Oscar for: 15 supporting actor (Mitchell)

stagecraft 5 drama **7** theater **9** theatrics **10** dramaturgy **11** thespianism **12** dramatic arts

Stage Door
  author: 10 Edna Ferber **14** George S Kaufman
  director: 13 Gregory La Cava
  cast: 11 Andrea Leeds, Gail Patrick **12** Ginger Rogers **13** Adolphe Menjou **16** Katharine Hepburn

stage setting
  French: 11 mise en scene

stagger 3 jar **4** jolt, reel, stun, sway **5** amaze, lurch, shake, shock, waver **6** hobble, totter, wobble **7** astound, blunder, nonplus, overlap, shamble, startle, stumble, stupefy **8** astonish, bewilder, bowl over, confound, flounder, unsettle **9** alternate, dumbfound, give a turn, overwhelm, spread out **10** disconcert, knock silly, strike dumb **11** cause to reel, cause to sway, consternate, flabbergast, take in turns **12** make unsteady **15** throw off balance

staggering 7 amazing **8** shocking, stunning **9** startling **10** astounding **11** astonishing **12** breathtaking

stagnant 4 dead, dull, foul, lazy, slow **5** close, inert, quiet, slimy, stale, still **6** filthy, leaden, putrid, static, supine, torpid **7** dormant, dronish, languid, tainted **8** inactive, lifeless, listless, polluted, sluggish, standing **9** lethargic, ponderous, putrefied, quiescent **10** monotonous, motionless, not flowing, not running, stationary, unstirring, vegetative **13** uncirculating

stagnate 7 go to pot, lie idle, putrefy **8** go to seed, lie still, vegetate **10** stand still **11** cease to flow, deteriorate, stop growing **14** become inactive, become polluted, become sluggish

stagy 5 phony **8** affected, mannered **9** unnatural **10** artificial, factitious, theatrical

staid 5 grave, quiet, sober, stiff **6** decent, demure, proper, sedate, seemly, solemn, somber **7** earnest, prudish, serious, settled, subdued **8** decorous, priggish, reserved **9** dignified **10** complacent **15** undemonstrative

stain 3 dye, mar **4** blot, daub, flaw, foul, mark, ruin, slur, soil, spot, tint **5** brand, color, dirty, grime, libel, patch, shame, smear, speck, spoil, sully, taint **6** befoul, blotch, debase, defile, impair, malign, smirch, smudge, stigma, vilify **7** blacken, blemish, pigment, slander, splotch, subvert, tarnish **8** besmirch, coloring, discolor, disgrace, dishonor, dyestuff, tincture **9** denigrate, discredit, disparage, undermine **10** imputation, stigmatize **13** discoloration

stainless 5 clean, moral **6** chaste, decent **8** spotless, unsoiled **9** exemplary, unspotted, unsullied, untainted **11** unblemished

Stairway to Heaven
  director: 13 Michael Powell **17** Emeric Pressburger
  cast: 9 Kim Hunter **10** David Niven **12** Roger Livesey **13** Raymond Massey

original title: 21 A Matter of Life and Death

stake 3 bar, bet, peg, pot, rod 4 ante, back, grab, haul, lash, loot, moor, pale, pawn, pile, play, pole, post, prop, risk, stay, take 5 booty, brace, hitch, kitty, prize, purse, share, spike, stand, stick, treat, wager 6 chance, column, define, fasten, fetter, hazard, hold up, marker, picket, pillar, reward, secure, spoils, tether 7 delimit, finance, jackpot, mark off, mark out, outline, peg down, returns, sponsor, support, trammel, venture 8 interest, make fast, pickings, standard, winnings 9 delineate, demarcate, speculate, subsidize 10 investment, jeopardize, underwrite 11 involvement, speculation

Stalag 17
  director: 11 Billy Wilder
  cast: 9 Don Taylor 11 Peter Graves 12 Neville Brand 13 Harvey Lembeck, Otto Preminger, Richard Erdman, Robert Strauss, William Holden
  Oscar for: 5 actor (Holden)

stale 4 dull, flat 5 banal, close, fusty, musty, trite, vapid 6 common 7 humdrum, insipid, prosaic, tedious, worn-out 8 mediocre, not fresh, ordinary, stagnant, unvaried 9 hackneyed, savorless, tasteless 10 monotonous, pedestrian, threadbare 11 commonplace 13 unimaginative, uninteresting

stalemate 3 tie 4 draw, halt 7 dead end, impasse 8 blockage, cul-de-sac, dead heat, deadlock, standoff 10 standstill

stalk 4 hunt, lurk, stem 5 haunt, march, prowl, shaft, spire, stamp, steal, stomp, strut, track, tramp, trunk 6 column, menace, stride 7 pedicel, pervade, swagger 8 hang over, threaten 9 creep up on, go through, sneak up on

stall 3 box, pen 4 cell, coop, halt, shed, shop, stop 5 block, booth, check, delay, kiosk, stand 6 arcade, arrest, hobble, impede, pull up, put off 7 bed down, confine, cubicle, disable, trammel 8 obstruct, paralyze, postpone 9 be evasive, interrupt, stop short, temporize 10 equivocate 11 compartment, play for time, stop running 12 incapacitate 13 orchestra seat

Stallone, Sylvester
  born: 9 New York NY
  nickname: 3 Sly
  roles: 4 FIST 5 Rambo, Rocky 9 John Rambo 10 First Blood, Rhinestone 11 Rocky Balboa 18 The Lords of Flatbush

stalwart 4 bold, firm, hale 5 beefy, brave, hardy, hefty, husky, manly, sound 6 brawny, gritty, heroic, mighty, plucky, robust, rugged, spunky, stable, strong, sturdy 7 gallant, staunch, valiant 8 constant, intrepid, muscular, powerful, resolute, valorous, vigorous 9 steadfast, strapping, unbending, undaunted 10 ablebodied, courageous, persistent, unflagging, unshakable, unswerving, unwavering, unyielding 11 indomitable, lionhearted, undeviating, unfaltering, unflinching, un-

shrinking 12 intransigent, stouthearted, strong-willed 14 uncompromising

stamina 4 pith 5 vigor 6 energy 8 vitality 9 endurance, hardiness, stoutness 10 ruggedness, sturdiness 12 perseverance, staying power

stammer 6 falter, fumble, mumble 7 sputter, stumble, stutter 8 splutter 9 hem and haw

stamp
  collecting: 9 philately
  first: 10 Penny Black
  issued by: 12 Great Britain
  inscribed with: 8 One Penny
  picture of: 13 Queen Victoria
  first-day hand stamper: 6 cachet
  hole measurer: 16 perforation gauge
  mounting paper: 5 hinge
  not perforated: 11 imperforate
  paper design: 9 watermark
  rolls: 4 coil
  tear holes: 12 perforations
  tear slit: 8 roulette
  unseparated group: 5 block
  used mark: 8 postmark 12 cancellation
  value suspended: 11 demonetized

stamp, stamp out 2 OK 3 die, tag 4 cast, kind, make, mark, mint, mold, seal, sort, type 5 brand, breed, clump, crush, erase, genre, label, march, order, print, pound, punch, quash, smash, stalk, stomp, strut, thump, tramp 6 banish, betray, emblem, expose, matrix, nature, put out, reveal, rub out, signet, step on, strain, stride, trudge 7 abolish, blot out, display, engrave, exhibit, impress, imprint, put down, squelch, trample, variety, voucher 8 get rid of, hallmark, identify, inscribe, intaglio, manifest, suppress, typecast 9 character, eliminate, engraving, eradicate, personify, signature, trademark 10 annihilate, do away with, extinguish, imprimatur, stigmatize, validation 11 attestation, certificate, demonstrate, distinguish, endorsement, exterminate, 12 characterize, official mark, ratification 13 certification 14 authentication, characteristic, identification

stampede 4 bolt, dash, flee, race, rout, rush 5 chaos, flood, panic 6 engulf 7 overrun, retreat, scatter 8 inundate 10 take flight 11 crowd around, pandemonium 12 beat a retreat
  French: 12 sauve qui peut

stanchion 4 post, prop, stay 5 brace, strut 7 support, upright

stand 2 be 3 put, set 4 draw, face, hold, last, move, rank, rear, rest, rise, stay, step, take, tent 5 abide, argue, booth, brook, erect, exist, get up, hoist, honor, kiosk, mount, place, put up, raise, shift, stall, treat 6 bear up, effort, endure, obtain, pay for, policy, remain, remove, stance, suffer, uphold 7 carry on, commend, counter, defense, endorse, finance, hold out, opinion, persist, posture, prevail, provide, stick up, stomach, support, survive, sustain, undergo, weather 8 advocate, be placed, champion, continue, pavilion, position, sanction, submit to, tolerate 9 be located, be present, be upright, persevere, put up with, sentiment, undertake, viewpoint 10 resistance, set upright 11 be permanent, countenance, disposition, point of view 13 remain in force, take a position

Stand, The
  author: 11 Stephen King

standard 3 leg 4 base, flag, foot, jack, post 5 basic, canon, guide, ideal, stock, usual 6 banner, column, common, ensign, normal, pillar 7 measure, pennant, regular, support, typical, upright 8 accepted, ordinary, streamer 9 criterion, customary, guideline, principle, prototype, stanchion, universal, yardstick 10 foundation, touchstone 11 requirement 13 specification

stand behind 4 back 7 endorse, support 8 champion, vouch for 9 recommend

standby 6 backup 9 alternate, available 10 substitute, understudy 11 old reliable 12 tried-and-true

stand by 4 keep 5 cling 6 adhere, be true, defend, hold to, keep to 7 be loyal, stick by 8 cleave to, maintain 10 be constant, be faithful, stick up for

stand fast 4 hold 6 resist 8 stand pat

stand for 4 bear 5 abide, favor, stand 6 embody 7 signify 8 advocate, submit to, tolerate 9 personify, put up with, represent, symbolize

stand-in 3 sub 5 agent, proxy 6 backup, deputy, double, fill-in, second 9 alternate, assistant, surrogate 10 substitute, understudy 11 pinch hitter, replacement

standing 3 age 4 life, rank, term, time 5 erect, fixed, grade, inert, order, place, still 6 at rest, static, status, tenure 7 dormant, footing, lasting, station, upended, upright 8 duration, inactive, position, stagnant, vertical 9 immovable, permanent, perpetual, quiescent, renewable 10 continuing, importance, motionless, reputation, stationary, unstirring 11 continuance 13 perpendicular

standoff 7 impasse 8 deadlock

standoffish 4 cool 5 aloof 6 formal, remote 7 distant, haughty 8 detached, reserved, solitary, taciturn 9 reclusive, withdrawn 10 antisocial, restrained, unfriendly, unsociable 12 inaccessible, misanthropic, unresponsive 14 unapproachable 15 uncommunicative, uncompanionable

standpoint 4 side 5 angle, slant 6 aspect 9 viewpoint 11 point of view

standstill 3 end 4 halt, stop 5 pause 6 hiatus 7 dead end, impasse 8 abeyance, deadlock, dead stop, full stop 9 breakdown, cessation, stalemate 10 suspension 11 termination 14 discontinuance

stand up for 4 back 5 boost 6 defend 7 further, promote, support 8 advocate, champion

stand up to 4 defy, face 5 brave 6 resist 8 confront 9 challenge

Stant, Charlotte
  character in: 13 The Golden Bowl
  author: 5 James

Stan the Man
  nickname of: 10 Stan Musial

Stanton, Adam
  character in: 14 All the King's Men
  author: 6 Warren

Stanwyck, Barbara
  real name: 11 Ruby Stevens
  born: 10 Brooklyn NY
  husband: 8 Frank Fay 12 Robert Taylor
  roles: 9 Big Valley, The Colbys 10 Ball of Fire, The Lady Eve 11 Meet John Doe 12 Stella Dallas 15 Double Indemnity 16 Sorry Wrong Number 20 Cattle Queen of Montana 22 Christmas in Connecticut

staple 3 key 4 main 5 basic, chief, major, prime, vital 6 leader 7 feature, primary, product 8 resource, vendible 9 commodity, essential, necessary 11 fundamental, raw material 13 indispensable

Stapleton, Jean
  real name: 12 Jeanne Murray
  born: 9 New York NY
  roles: 7 Dingbat 11 Edith Bunker 14 All in the Family

Stapleton, Maureen
  born: 6 Troy NY
  roles: 7 Airport 9 Interiors 12 Lonelyhearts 13 The Rose Tattoo 18 A View from the Bridge

star, stars 3 god, sun, VIP 4 diva, fate, hero, idol, lead, lion, name 5 comet, excel, giant, great, omens, shine 6 big wig, do well, galaxy, meteor, nebula, planet 7 destiny, feature, fortune, goddess, heroine, notable, soloist, starlet, succeed, top draw 8 asteroid, cynosure, eminence, immortal, luminary, mainstay, Milky Way, portents, showcase, stand out, virtuoso 9 celebrity, headliner, meteoroid, principal, satellite, top banana 10 prima donna 11 All-American, drawing card, play the lead, protagonist 12 famous person, gain approval, heavenly body 13 celestial body, constellation 14 main attraction, predestination, prima ballerina
  brightest: 6 Sirius
  brightness measure: 9 magnitude 10 luminosity
  color: 3 red 4 blue 5 black, white 6 orange, yellow
  distance measure: 6 parsec 9 light year
  double star: 6 binary
  exploding star: 4 nova 9 supernova
  French: 6 etoile
  name: 4 Mira, Ross, Vega, Wolf 5 Cygni, Deneb, Rigel, Spica 6 Altair, Luyten, Pollux 7 Antares, Canopus, Capella, Lalande, Polaris, Procyon, Regulus, Tau Ceti 8 Achernar, Arcturus, Barnard's, Lacaille, Pleiades 9 Aldebaran, Fomalhaut 10 Beta Crucis, Betelgeuse 11 Delta Cephei, Epsilon Indi, Groombridge 12 Beta Centauri 14 Epsilon Eridani
  nearest: 13 Alpha Centauri

position/motion: 7 azimuth 8 parallax 11 declination

type: 5 dwarf, giant 6 pulsar 7 cluster, neutron 8 variable 9 black hole, collapsed

Starbuck

character in: 8 Moby Dick

author: 8 Melville

starch 5 vigor 6 sizing 8 backbone, gumption 10 stiffening

starched 5 crisp, sized, stiff 7 starchy 9 stiffened

starchy 5 rigid, stiff 6 formal, proper 7 correct 10 meticulous

stare 3 eye 4 gape, gawk, gaze, ogle, peep, peer 5 glare, lower, watch 6 gaping, glower, goggle, ogling, regard 7 staring 8 once-over, scrutiny 9 fixed look 10 inspection, rubberneck

stare at 3 eye 4 ogle 5 watch 6 behold, gaze at, look at, regard 7 inspect, observe 10 scrutinize 11 contemplate

Star Is Born, A

director:

1937 version: 14 William Wellman

1954 version: 11 George Cukor

1976 version: 12 Frank Pierson

cast:

1937 version: 11 Janet Gaynor 13 Adolphe Menjou, Frederic March

1954 version: 10 Jack Carson, James Mason 11 Judy Garland 15 Charles Bickford

1976 version: 9 Gary Busey 11 Oliver Clark 15 Barbra Streisand 17 Kris Kristofferson

Oscar for:

1937 version: 5 story

song:

1954 version: 17 The Man That Got Away

stark 4 bare, bold, cold, grim, pure 5 bleak, blunt, clean, empty, fully, gross, harsh, naked, plain, plumb, quite, sheer, total, utter 6 arrant, barren, chaste, patent, severe, simple, vacant, wholly 7 austere, evident, forlorn, glaring, obvious, staring, utterly 8 absolute, complete, deserted, desolate, entirely, flagrant, forsaken, outright, palpable 9 abandoned, downright, out-and-out, unadorned, unalloyed, veritable 10 absolutely, altogether, completely, consummate 11 conspicuous, unmitigated 12 unmistakable

Stark, Johannes

field: 7 physics

nationality: 6 German

described: 11 Stark Effect 14 dispersed light

awarded: 10 Nobel Prize

Stark, Willie

character in: 14 All the King's Men

author: 6 Warren

starlet 7 actress, ingenue 9 bit player, pinup girl

Starsky and Hutch

character: 5 Hutch (Ken Hutchinson) 7 (Dave) Starsky 9 Huggy Bear 11 (Capt) Harold Dobey

cast: 9 David Soul 13 Antonio Fargas 14 Bernie Hamilton 17 Paul Michael Glaser

car: 10 Ford Torino

start 3 aid, shy 4 dawn, drop, edge, form, gush, jerk, jolt, jump, lead, leap, odds, rush, turn 5 beget, begin, birth, blink, bound, eject, erupt, evict, flush, forge, found, issue, leave, leg up, onset, rouse, set up, shoot, spasm, spurt, wince 6 blench, broach, chance, create, depart, embark, emerge, fall to, father, flinch, ignite, kindle, launch, origin, outset, pop out, propel, recoil, set off, set out, spring, take up, twitch 7 advance, backing, disturb, genesis, make off, opening, push off, scatter, set sail, support, take off, turn out, usher in 8 advocacy, commence, creation, dis place, embark on, engender, generate, get going, initiate, organize, priority, set about, set going, touch off 9 advantage, beginning, establish, fabricate, first step, inception, institute, introduce, originate, propagate, undertake, venture on 10 assistance, break forth, bring about, buckle down, burst forth, give rise to, inaugurate, initiation, plunge into, sally forth, venture out 11 break ground, put in motion, set in action 12 commencement, inauguration, introduction 14 set in operation

starting point 5 onset, start 8 zero hour 9 beginning

Latin: 12 terminus a quo

startle 3 jar 4 faze 5 alarm, scare, shake, shock, upset 7 perturb, unnerve 8 disquiet, frighten, surprise, unsettle 9 give a turn 10 discompose, disconcert, intimidate

Star Trek

character: 4 Sulu 5 Uhura 6 Scotty (Engineer Montgomery Scott), (Ensign) Chekov 7 Mr Spock 10 (Captain) James T Kirk, (Yeoman) Janice Rand 12 (Dr) Leonard McCoy 15 (Nurse) Christine Chapel

cast: 11 George Takei, James Doohan 12 Leonard Nimoy, Majel Barrett, Walter Koenig 13 DeForest Kelly 14 William Shatner 15 Grace Lee Whitney, Nichelle Nichols

ship: 10 (USS) Enterprise

aliens: 8 Klingons, Romulans

Spock's planet: 6 Vulcan

pet: 7 tribble

starve 3 yen 4 burn, deny, fast, gasp, long, lust, pine 5 crave, raven, yearn 6 aspire, cut off, famish, hunger, refuse, thirst 7 deprive 8 be hungry, go hungry, languish

Star Wars

director: 11 George Lucas

cast: 10 Kenny Baker, Mark Hamill (Luke Skywalker) 12 Alec Guinness, Carrie Fisher (Princess Leia), Harrison Ford (Han Solo), Peter Cushing 14 Anthony Daniels

voice of Darth Vader: 14 James Earl
Jones
score: 12 John Williams
Oscar for: 5 score
sequel: 15 Return of the Jedi **20** The
Empire Strikes Back
stasimon 9 choral ode
literally: 8 standing
state 3 put **4** form, land, mind, mode,
mood, pass, pomp **5** guise, offer, phase,
realm, shape, stage **6** aspect, luxury,
morale, nation, people, plight, recite, relate, report, ritual, status **7** comfort, country, declare, explain, expound, express,
kingdom, narrate, posture, present, recount, spirits **8** attitude, ceremony, describe, dominion, monarchy, official, position, propound, republic, set forth **9**
condition, elucidate, formality, full dress,
high style, situation, structure **10** ceremonial, government **11** body politic, frame of
mind, predicament, state of mind **12** com-
monwealth, constitution, governmental,
principality **13** circumstances
state abbreviations
Alabama: **2** AL **3** Ala
Alaska: **2** AK **3** Alas
Arizona: **2** AZ **4** Ariz
Arkansas: **2** AR **3** Ark
California: **2** CA **3** Cal **5** Calif
Colorado: **2** CO **4** Colo
Connecticut: **2** CT **4** Conn
Delaware: **2** DE **3** Del
Florida: **2** FL **3** Fla
Georgia: **2** GA
Hawaii: **2** HI
Idaho: **2** ID **3** Ida
Illinois: **2** IL **3** Ill
Indiana: **2** IN **3** Ind
Iowa: **2** IA
Kansas: **2** KS **4** Kans
Kentucky: **2** KY
Louisiana: **2** LA
Maine: **2** ME
Maryland: **2** MD
Massachusetts: **2** MA **4** Mass
Michigan: **2** MI **4** Mich
Minnesota: **2** MN **4** Minn
Mississippi: **2** MS **4** Miss
Missouri: **2** MO
Montana: **2** MT
Nebraska: **2** NE **4** Nebr
Nevada: **2** NV **3** Nev
New Hampshire: **2** NH
New Jersey: **2** NJ
New Mexico: **2** NM **4** N Mex
New York: **2** NY
North Carolina: **2** NC **4** N Car
North Dakota: **2** ND **4** N Dak
Ohio: **2** OH
Oklahoma: **2** OK **4** Okla
Oregon: **2** OR **4** Oreg
Pennsylvania: **2** PA **4** Penn **5** Penna
Rhode Island: **2** RI
South Carolina: **2** SC
South Dakota: **2** SD **4** S Dak
Tennessee: **2** TN **4** Tenn

Texas: **2** TX **3** Tex
Utah: **2** UT
Vermont: **2** VT
Virginia: **2** VA
Washington: **2** WA **4** Wash
West Virginia: **2** WV **3** W Va
Wisconsin: **2** WI **3** Wis
Wyoming: **2** WY **3** Wyo
state admittance
first: **8** Delaware
second: **12** Pennsylvania
third: **9** New Jersey
fourth: **7** Georgia
fifth: **11** Connecticut
sixth: **13** Massachusetts
seventh: **8** Maryland
eighth: **13** South Carolina
ninth: **12** New Hampshire
tenth: **8** Virginia
eleventh: **7** New York
twelfth: **13** North Carolina
thirteenth: **11** Rhode Island
fourteenth: **7** Vermont
fifteenth: **8** Kentucky
sixteenth: **9** Tennessee
seventeenth: **4** Ohio
eighteenth: **9** Louisiana
nineteenth: **7** Indiana
twentieth: **11** Mississippi
twenty-first: **8** Illinois
twenty-second: **7** Alabama
twenty-third: **5** Maine
twenty-fourth: **8** Missouri
twenty-fifth: **8** Arkansas
twenty-sixth: **8** Michigan
twenty-seventh: **7** Florida
twenty-eighth: **5** Texas
twenty-ninth: **4** Iowa
thirtieth: **9** Wisconsin
thirty-first: **10** California
thirty-second: **9** Minnesota
thirty-third: **6** Oregon
thirty-fourth: **6** Kansas
thirty-fifth: **12** West Virginia
thirty-sixth: **6** Nevada
thirty-seventh: **8** Nebraska
thirty-eighth: **8** Colorado
thirty-ninth/fortieth: **11** North Dakota,
South Dakota
forty-first: **7** Montana
forty-second: **10** Washington
forty-third: **5** Idaho
forty-fourth: **7** Wyoming
forty-fifth: **4** Utah
forty-sixth: **8** Oklahoma
forty-seventh: **9** New Mexico
forty-eighth: **7** Arizona
forty-ninth: **6** Alaska
fiftieth: **6** Hawaii
state capitals
Alabama: **10** Montgomery
Alaska: **6** Juneau
Arizona: **7** Phoenix
Arkansas: **10** Little Rock
California: **10** Sacramento
Colorado: **6** Denver
Connecticut: **8** Hartford

Delaware: 5 Dover
Florida: 11 Tallahassee
Georgia: 7 Atlanta
Hawaii: 8 Honolulu
Idaho: 5 Boise
Illinois: 11 Springfield
Indiana: 12 Indianapolis
Iowa: 9 Des Moines
Kansas: 6 Topeka
Kentucky: 9 Frankfort
Louisiana: 10 Baton Rouge
Maine: 7 Augusta
Maryland: 9 Annapolis
Massachusetts: 6 Boston
Michigan: 7 Lansing
Minnesota: 8 St Paul
Mississippi: 7 Jackson
Missouri: 13 Jefferson City
Montana: 6 Helena
Nebraska: 7 Lincoln
Nevada: 10 Carson City
New Hampshire: 7 Concord
New Jersey: 7 Trenton
New Mexico: 7 Santa Fe
New York: 6 Albany
North Carolina: 7 Raleigh
North Dakota: 8 Bismarck
Ohio: 8 Columbus
Oklahoma: 12 Oklahoma City
Oregon: 5 Salem
Pennsylvania: 10 Harrisburg
Rhode Island: 10 Providence
South Carolina: 8 Columbia
South Dakota: 6 Pierre
Tennessee: 9 Nashville
Texas: 6 Austin
Utah: 12 Salt Lake City
Vermont: 10 Montpelier
Virginia: 8 Richmond
Washington: 7 Olympia
West Virginia: 10 Charleston
Wisconsin: 7 Madison
Wyoming: 8 Cheyenne
State Fair
author: 9 Phil Stong
state in detail 7 explain, expound **8** describe, spell out **9** explicate **16** give a full account
stateliness 7 dignity, majesty **10** augustness
stately 5 grand, lofty, noble, proud, regal, royal **6** august, formal, lordly **7** awesome, elegant, eminent **8** glorious, imperial, imposing, majestic **9** dignified, grandiose **10** ceremonial, impressive **11** magnificent
statement 3 tab **4** bill **5** check, claim, count, tally **6** avowal, charge, record, remark, report, speech **7** account, comment, invoice, mention, recital **8** relation, sentence **9** assertion, manifesto, reckoning, testimony, utterance, valuation **10** accounting, allegation, communique, exposition, profession, recitation **11** declaration, delineation, explanation, observation **12** pronouncement, balance sheet **13** pronouncement, specification

state of affairs 5 state **6** status **9** condition, situation **13** circumstances
State of the Union
director: 10 Frank Capra
cast: 10 Van Johnson **12** Spencer Tracy **13** Adolphe Menjou **14** Angela Lansbury **16** Katharine Hepburn
stateroom 5 cabin **8** quarters **11** compartment
statesman 3 diplomat **15** political leader
statesmanship 9 diplomacy **19** political leadership
static 5 fixed, inert, still **8** immobile, inactive, stagnant, unmoving **9** crackling, suspended **10** changeless, motionless, stationary, unchanging **12** interference
station 4 post, rank, site, spot, stop **5** caste, class, depot, grade, level, place **6** assign, degree, locate, sphere, status **7** footing, install **8** ensconce, facility, location, position, prestige, terminal, terminus **9** condition, firehouse, place ment **10** dispensary, guardhouse, importance **11** emplacement, whistle-stop **12** headquarters
stationary 4 even, firm **5** fixed, inert **6** intact, moored, stable, steady **7** riveted, uniform **8** constant, immobile, standing **9** dead-still, immovable, immutable, unchanged, unvarying **10** motionless, stockstill, transfixed **11** not changing, undeviating **12** unchangeable **13** standing still
Statius
author of: 6 Silvae **10** The Thebaid **12** The Achilleid
statue 8 monument **9** sculpture **14** representation
statuesque 5 regal **7** stately **8** majestic **9** dignified
stature 4 rank, size **5** place **6** height, regard **8** eminence, position, prestige, standing, tallness **9** elevation **10** importance, prominence, reputation **11** distinction
status 4 rank **5** caste, class, grade, place, state **6** degree **7** caliber, footing, station **8** eminence, position, prestige, standing **9** condition, situation **10** estimation **11** distinction
statute 3 law **7** precept **9** prescript
statute law
Latin: 10 lex scripta
staunch, stanch 3 dam **4** firm, stem, true **5** check, loyal, solid, sound, stout **6** impede, rugged, steady, strong, sturdy **7** contain, zealous **8** constant, faithful, hold back, obstruct, resolute, stalwart **9** steadfast, wellbuilt **10** watertight **11** substantial
stave off 7 beat off, fend off, keep off, ward off **9** keep at bay
stay 3 aim, guy, rib, rod **4** bunk, curb, foil, halt, live, pole, prop, rest, room, stem, stop **5** abide, block, brace, check, delay, dwell, lodge, quell, shore, stick, tarry, visit **6** endure, keep in, linger, rein in, remain, reside, splint, stifle, thwart **7** carry on, hold out, holiday, last out, persist, sojourn, support, ward off **8** abeyance, buttress, con-

tinue, hold back, mainstay, postpone, reprieve, restrain, standard, stopover, suppress, vacation, withhold 9 deferment, frustrate, persevere, staunchion 10 hang around, see through, suspension 12 postponement, reinforcement

stay put 4 stay 6 remain 8 stand pat

St Clare, Eva
  character in: 14 Uncle Tom's Cabin
  author: 5 Stowe

steadfast 4 keen, rapt 5 fixed 6 direct, intent, steady 8 resolute 9 attentive, obstinate, tenacious, undaunted 10 deep-rooted, deep-seated, inflexible, unchanging, unflagging, unwavering, unyielding 11 indomitable, persevering, unalterable, undeviating, unfaltering, unflinching 12 intransigent, single-minded, unchangeable, undistracted 14 uncompromising

steadfastness 8 tenacity 10 resolution 11 persistence 12 perseverance, resoluteness 13 determination

Steadfast Tin Soldier, The
  author: 21 Hans Christian Andersen

steadiness 4 care 5 poise 6 aplomb 8 calmness, coolness, evenness, firmness 9 composure, sangfroid, stability 10 equanimity, resolution 11 carefulness, persistence, self-control, tranquility 12 resoluteness, tranquillity 13 dependability, steadfastness 14 presence of mind, self-possession 16 imperturbability

steady 4 even, firm, sure 5 sober 6 secure, stable 7 balance, careful, devoted, regular, serious, staunch 8 constant, faithful, frequent, habitual, hold fast, reliable, resolute, unending, untiring 9 ceaseless, confirmed, dedicated, immovable, incessant, stabilize, steadfast, tenacious, unceasing 10 continuing, continuous, coolheaded, deliberate, dependable, methodical, persistent, unflagging, unwavering 11 levelheaded, persevering, substantial, undeviating, unfaltering, unremitting 12 single-minded 13 conscientious

steal 3 buy, cop 4 copy, crib, filit, flow, lift, slip, take 5 creep, drift, filch, glide, pinch, skulk, slide, slink, sneak, swipe, usurp 6 borrow, elapse, escape, extort, filter, pilfer, pocket, rip off, snatch, snitch, thieve 7 bargain, defraud, diffuse, good buy, imitate, purloin, swindle 8 abstract, embezzle, good deal, liberate 10 burglarize, plagiarize 11 abscond with, appropriate, make off with 14 misappropriate

steal away 3 fly 4 bolt, flee, skip 5 elope 6 escape 7 get away, make off, slip out 8 creep off, slip away, sneak off 9 break free, tiptoe out 10 break loose, fly the coop 12 make a getaway

stealth 7 secrecy, slyness 10 covertness, sneakiness, subterfuge 11 furtiveness 12 stealthiness 13 secretiveness 15 unobtrusiveness 17 surreptitiousness

stealthy 3 sly 5 shady 6 covert, shifty, sneaky 7 devious, furtive 8 slippery, sneaking 9 secretive, underhand 11 clandestine, underhanded 12 hugger-mugger 13 surreptitious

steamboat
  invented by: 6 Fulton 9 Symington

steamed up 5 angry, het up, irate 6 raging 7 enraged, furious, riled up 8 heated up, inflamed 10 infuriated 12 mad as a wet hen 14 hot and bothered 17 hot under the collar

steamer 4 boat, clam, ship 5 liner, trunk 10 paddleboat 11 side-wheeler 12 sternwheeler 13 paddle-wheeler

steel 4 dirk, foil, gird 5 blade, brace, knife, nerve, saber, sword 6 dagger, rapier 7 bayonet, cutlass, fortify, machete 8 falchion, scimitar 10 broadsword
  process invented by: 8 Bessemer

Steele, Sir Richard
  pseudonym: 16 Isaac Bickerstaff
  author of: 9 The Tatler (with Joseph Addison) 10 The Funeral 12 The Spectator (with Joseph Addison) 13 The Lying Lover 16 The Tender Husband 18 The Conscious Lovers

steely 4 hard 5 stony 6 flinty 9 heartless, unfeeling 10 forbidding 11 cold-hearted

Steen, Jan
  born: 6 Leiden, Leyden 14 The Netherlands
  artwork: 7 Cabaret 11 The Egg Dance 12 Merry Company 14 Garden of the Inn 15 The Doctor's Visit, The Rhetoricians 16 The Morning Toilet 17 The Skittle Players 18 The World Topsy-Turvy, Young Woman Dressing

Steenburgen, Mary
  roles: 10 Cross Creek 13 Time After Time

steep 4 brew, bury, fill, soak 5 imbue, sharp, sheer, souse 6 abrupt, drench, engulf, infuse, plunge 7 immerse, pervade, suffuse 8 marinate, saturate, submerge 10 impregnate 11 precipitous

steeple 5 spire, tower 6 belfry 9 campanile

steer 3 aim, lay, run 4 bear, head, lead, make, sail 5 coach, guide, pilot 6 direct, govern, manage 7 conduct, proceed 8 navigate 9 supervise

steer clear of 4 shun 5 avert, avoid, dodge, evade, forgo, skirt 6 escape, eschew, forego 8 sidestep 9 keep shy of 11 abstain from, refrain from 16 give a wide berth to

Steerforth
  character in: 16 David Copperfield
  author: 7 Dickens

Steffens, Lincoln
  author of: 19 The Shame of the Cities

Stegosaurus
  type: 8 dinosaur 10 ornithopod
  location: 12 North America
  period: 8 Jurassic
  characteristic: 6 plated

Steiger, Rod
   real name: 20 Rodney Stephen Steiger
   born: 13 Westhampton NY
   wife: 11 Claire Bloom
   roles: 8 Waterloo 13 The Longest Day,
   The Pawnbroker, W C Fields and Me 15
   On the Waterfront 19 In the Heat of the
   Night (Oscar)

Stein, Clarence S
   architect of: 13 Temple Emanu-El (NYC)

Stein, Gertrude
   author of: 10 Three Lives 13 Tender Buttons 20 The Making of Americans 27 Autobiography of Alice B Toklas
   coined phrase: 14 lost generation

Steinbeck, John
   author of: 8 The Pearl 10 Cannery Row,
   East of Eden, The Red Pony 12 Of Mice
   and Men, Tortilla Flat 15 In Dubious Battle 16 The Grapes of Wrath 18 Travels
   with Charley 24 The Winter of Our
   Discontent

Steinmetz, Charles P
   field: 11 engineering
   developed: 2 AC 18 alternating current

Stella, Frank
   born: 8 Malden MA
   artwork: 4 Jill 5 Itata 14 Jasper's Dilemma 15 Guadalupe Island

Stella, Joseph
   born: 5 Italy 6 Naples
   artwork: 8 Full Moon (Barbados) 9 Sunflower, The Bridge 14 Brooklyn Bridge 16
   Pittsburgh Winter 18 New York Interpreted 28 Battle of the Lights Coney Island

Stella Dallas
   director: 9 King Vidor
   cast: 9 John Boles 11 Anne Shirley 12
   Barbara O'Neil 15 Barbara Stanwyck

stellar 6 astral, starry 7 leading 8 starring 9
   brilliant, celestial, principal 11 outstanding

stem 3 dam 4 buck, cane, come, curb,
   grow, halt, rise, stay, stop 5 arise, block,
   check, deter, ensue, issue, quell, shank,
   shoot, speak, spire, stalk, stall, stock,
   trunk 6 arrest, derive, hinder, impede, oppose, resist, result, retard, spring, stanch,
   thwart 7 counter, pedicel, petiole, prevent,
   proceed, tendril 8 hold back, obstruct, peduncle, restrain, surmount 9 leafstalk,
   originate, withstand

stem from 5 arise, begin, start 6 derive 9
   originate

stench 4 odor, reek 5 fetor, stink 8 bad
   smell 9 fetidness

Stendhal (Henri Marie Beyle)
   author of: 17 The Red and the Black 18
   Memoirs of an Egotist 22 The Charterhouse of Parma

Stengel, Charles Dillon
   nickname: 5 Casey
   sport: 8 baseball
   position: 7 manager
   team: 11 New York Mets 14 New York
   Yankees 15 Brooklyn Dodgers

Stentor
   vocation: 6 herald
   characteristic: 10 loud-voiced
   voice as loud as: 8 fifty men

step 3 act 4 clip, gait, move, pace, rank,
   rung, span, walk 5 notch, phase, point,
   riser, stage, stair, strut, track, tramp, tread
   6 action, degree, hobble, period, remove,
   stride 7 footing, measure, process, shamble, shuffle, swagger, trample 8 footfall,
   foothold, maneuver, purchase 9 footprint,
   gradation, procedure 10 proceeding

step down 4 quit 5 leave 6 resign, retire

Stephens, James
   author of: 7 Deirdre 14 The Crock of
   Gold 21 The Charwoman's Daughter

Stephenson, George and Robert
   nationality: 7 English
   developed: 15 steam locomotive

Steppenwolf
   author: 12 Hermann Hesse
   character: 5 Maria, Pablo 7 Hermine 11
   Harry Haller

Steps
   author: 13 Jerzy Kosinski

step up 4 spur 6 come up 7 quicken, speed
   up 8 ap proach, escalate, expedite, increase 9 intensify 10 accelerate

stereotype 4 type 6 cliche 7 formula 8 typecast 10 categorize, pigeonhole 13 preconception

stereotyped 5 stale, trite 9 hackneyed 11
   commonplace 13 unimaginative

sterile 4 bare, pure, vain 5 empty 6 barren,
   fallow, futile 7 aseptic, useless 8 abortive,
   bootless, impotent, infecund, sanitary 9
   childless, fruitless, infertile, worthless 10
   antiseptic, profitless, sterilized, unavailing,
   unfruitful, uninfected 11 disinfected, ineffective, ineffectual, unrewarding 12 unproductive, unprofitable 13 free from germs
   14 uncontaminated

sterilize 6 purify 9 autoclave, disinfect 13
   decontaminate

sterling 4 pure, true 5 noble 6 silver, superb, worthy 7 genuine, perfect 8 flawless,
   superior 9 admirable, estimable, first-rate,
   honorable 10 invaluable 11 meritorious,
   superlative

stern 4 cold, grim, hard 5 cruel, grave,
   harsh, rigid, sharp, stiff 6 brutal, gloomy,
   severe, somber, strict, unkind 7 austere,
   serious 8 coercive, despotic, frowning, pitiless, rigorous, ruthless, ungentle 9 reprov-
   ing, stringent, unfeeling 10 forbidding, implacable, ironfisted, ironhanded,
   tyrannical, unmerciful 11 admonishing,
   cold-blooded, reproachful 12 unreasonable 13 unsympathetic 14 unapproachable

Stern (of Argo)
   constellation of: 6 Puppis

Sterne, Laurence
   author of: 14 Tristram Shandy 19 A Sentimental Journey
   character: 9 Uncle Toby 12 Parson
   Yorick, Walter Shandy

sternum
  bone of: 6 breast

Sterope
  also: 8 Asterope
  member of: 8 Pleiades
  son: 8 Oenomaus

Steve Canyon
  creator: 12 Milton Caniff
  character: 7 Cheetah 9 Madam Lynx 10 Doe Redwood, Miss Mizzou 11 Savannah Gay 13 Copper Calhoun 14 Herself Muldoon 17 Princess Sun Flower
  wife: 6 Summer
  ward/cousin: 12 Poteet Canyon
  Summer's son: 13 Leigh ton Olson

Stevens, George
  director of: 5 Giant (Oscar), Shane 8 Gunga Din 9 Swing Time 13 I Remember Mama, Penny Serenade 14 A Place in the Sun (Oscar), Woman of the Year 16 The Talk of the Town 19 The Diary of Anne Frank

Stevens, Gowan
  character in: 9 Sanctuary
  author: 8 Faulkner

Stevens, James
  author of: 10 Paul Bunyan

Stevens, Ruby
  real name of: 15 Barbara Stanwyck

Stevens, Wallace
  author of: 7 The Rock 9 Harmonium 13 Sunday Morning 17 Transport to Summer 23 Peter Quince at the Clavier, The Idea of Order at Key West, The Man with the Blue Guitar

Stevenson, Robert
  director of: 8 Jane Eyre 10 Back Street 11 Mary Poppins

Stevenson, Robert Louis
  author of: 9 Kidnapped 13 The Black Arrow 14 Treasure Island 18 Travels with a Donkey 21 A Child's Garden of Verses, Doctor Jekyll and Mr Hyde, The Master of Ballantrae

St Evremond, Marquis
  character in: 16 A Tale of Two Cities
  author: 7 Dickens

stew 4 fret, fume, fuss 5 chafe, gripe, steep, tizzy, worry 6 grouse, ragout, seethe, simmer 7 agonize, fluster, flutter, grumble, mixture 10 miscellany

steward 5 agent, proxy 6 deputy, factor, waiter 7 bailiff, manager, trustee 8 executor, overseer 10 controller, supervisor 11 comptroller 13 administrator 14 representative, ship's attendant 15 flight attendant

Stewart, James
  born: 9 Indiana PA
  roles: 4 Rope 6 Harvey 7 Vertigo 10 Rear Window, Shenandoah 11 Elwood P Dowd 14 Cheyenne Autumn 16 Anatomy of a Murder, Destry Rides Again, The Stratton Story 17 Bell Book and Candle, It's a Wonderful Life 18 It's a Wonderful World, The Spirit of St Louis 19 The Glenn Miller Story 20 The Philadelphia Story (Oscar), You Can't Take It with You 22 The Greatest Show on Earth 23 Mr Smith Goes to Washington

Stewart, Mary
  real name: 22 Florence Rainbow Stewart
  author of: 11 Crystal Cave 14 The Hollow Hills 15 The Moon-Spinners 16 My Brother Michael, The Gabriel Hounds 18 Airs Above the Ground, The Last Enchantment

St George's
  capital of: 7 Grenada

Sthenelaus
  vocation: 7 warrior
  killed by: 9 Patroclus

Sthenele
  father: 7 Acastus
  son: 9 Patroclus

Sthenelus
  king of: 7 Mycenae
  father: 5 Actor 7 Perseus
  mother: 9 Andromeda
  brother: 6 Mestor 9 Electryon
  son: 10 Eurystheus
  daughter: 6 Medusa 7 Alcyone
  member of: 7 Epigoni
  companion of: 8 Hercules

Sthenius
  epithet of: 4 Zeus
  means: 6 strong

Stheno
  member of: 7 Gorgons

Stichius
  origin: 8 Athenian
  rank: 7 captain
  killed by: 6 Hector

stick 3 bar, bat, cue, dig, fix, jab, pin, put, rod, set 4 balk, bind, cane, club, curb, fuse, glue, hold, join, last, mire, nail, pink, poke, pole, seal, snag, stab, stop, tack, twig, wand, weld 5 abide, affix, baton, billy, block, catch, check, fagot, leave, lodge, paste, place, plant, prick, punch, shift, snarl, spear, spike, staff, stall, stake, stand, stave, stump 6 adhere, attach, boggle, branch, burden, cement, cudgel, detain, endure, fasten, hamper, hinder, hogtie, impede, insert, pierce, puzzle, scotch, skewer, stymie, switch, thrust, thwart 7 confuse, crosier, inhibit, perplex, shackle, trammel 8 bewilder, bludgeon, caduceus, continue, obstruct, puncture 9 checkmate, constrain, perforate, truncheon, victimize 10 immobilize, shillelagh

stick fast 4 hold 5 cling, stick 6 adhere, cleave

stickler 3 bug, nut 5 crank, poser 6 enigma, purist, puzzle, riddle, zealot 7 devotee, dilemma, fanatic, mystery, stumper 8 martinet 10 enthusiast, monomaniac

sticks 4 skis 5 bonds, glues, twigs 6 pastes, Podunk 7 adheres, boonies, catches, cements, country 8 kindling 9 backwoods, boondocks, golf clubs, provinces 10 hicksville, hinterland 11 countryside, hinterlands

stick together 4 bind, fuse, glue, hold, join 5 cling, stick, unite 6 cement, cohere

stick-to-itiveness 8 tenacity 9 endurance 10 resolution 11 persistence 12 perseverance, resoluteness 13 determination, tenaciousness

stickum 3 gum 4 glue 5 paste 6 cement 8 adhesive, mucilage 12 rubber cement

stick up for 5 boost 6 defend 7 root for 11 speak well of 17 put in a good word for

stick with 4 stay 5 abide 6 keep at 7 stand by 9 accompany, persevere

sticky 3 wet 4 damp, dank 5 gluey, gooey, gummy, humid, moist, muggy, pasty, tacky 6 clammy, clingy, steamy, sultry, viscid 7 viscous 8 adherent, adhesive, clinging, cohesive, sticking 9 glutinous, tenacious 10 gelatinous 12 mucilaginous

stiff 4 body, cold, cool, firm, grim, hard, high, iron, keen, prim, sore, taut 5 aloof, awful, brave, brisk, crisp, cruel, dense, fixed, gusty, harsh, heavy, rigid, sharp, smart, solid, steep, stern, tense, thick, tight, tough, undue 6 bitter, brutal, chilly, clumsy, corpse, dogged, forced, formal, raging, severe, steady, steely, strong, uneasy, viscid, wooden 7 austere, awkward, cadaver, clotted, decided, distant, drastic, extreme, fearful, intense, jellied, labored, precise, remains, settled, starchy, stately, staunch, steeled, stilted, uptight, valiant, violent, viscous 8 affected, constant, dead body, exacting, forceful, grievous, mannered, pitiless, pounding, powerful, resolute, resolved, rigorous, ruthless, spanking, stubborn, ungainly, unlimber, unshaken, vigorous 9 difficult, draconian, excessive, graceless, inelastic, inelegant, laborious, merciless, obstinate, resistant, steadfast, stringent, tenacious, unnatural 10 artificial, courageous, determined, exorbitant, formidable, gelatinous, immoderate, inflexible, inordinate, persistent, solidified, unswerving, unyielding 11 ceremonious, constrained, extravagant, indomitable, straitlaced, unfaltering, unflinching, unwarranted 12 strong-willed, unreasonable 14 uncompromising

stiff-necked 6 mulish 7 will ful 8 contrary, obdurate, stubborn 9 obstinate, pigheaded, unbending 10 bullheaded, refractory, self-willed, unshakable, unyielding 11 intractable 12 intransigent, pertinacious

stiffness 7 tension 8 firmness, rigidity 9 aloofness, formality, tenseness, tightness 10 constraint 11 starchiness

stifle 3 gag 4 curb 5 check, choke 6 muffle, subdue 7 garrote, inhibit, repress, smother, squelch, swelter 8 keep back, restrain, strangle, suppress, throttle 9 suffocate 10 asphyxiate

stifling 3 hot 6 stuffy 7 airless 10 overheated

stigma 4 blot, flaw, mark, scar 5 brand, odium, shame, stain, taint 6 smirch, smudge 7 blemish, tarnish 8 disgrace, dishonor 11 mark of shame 12 besmirchment

stigmatize 5 brand, smear 6 debase, defame, smirch 7 villify 9 discredit, disparage

still 4 calm, hush 5 inert, quiet 6 at rest, hushed, pacify, settle, silent 7 appease, assuage, gratify, put down, repress, silence, turn off 8 immobile, overcome, restrain, suppress, unmoving 9 noiseless, soundless 10 motionless, put an end to, stationary, unstirring

stillness 4 calm, hush 5 quiet 6 repose 7 silence 8 calmness, inaction, quietude 9 composure 10 immobility, inactivity, quiescence 11 tranquility 12 tranquillity

Stillness at Appomattox, A
author: 11 Bruce Catton

stilted 4 cold, prim 5 rigid, stiff 6 forced, formal, stuffy, wooden 7 awkward, labored, pompous, starchy, studied, uptight 8 mannered, priggish, starched 9 graceless, unnatural 10 artificial 11 ceremonious, constrained

Stilwell, Joseph W
nickname: 10 Vinegar Joe
served in: 3 WWI 4 WWII
chief of staff for: 13 Chiang Kai-shek
driven out of: 5 Burma

stimulant 5 tonic, upper 6 bracer 8 excitant 9 energizer

stimulate 3 fan 4 spur, stir, wake 5 alert, rouse 6 arouse, awaken, excite, incite, prompt, vivify 7 actuate, animate, inflame, inspire, quicken, sharpen 8 activate, enkindle, initiate, inspirit

stimulating 5 tonic 7 piquing 8 arousing, exciting, spurring, stirring, whetting 9 animating, provoking 10 energizing, refreshing 11 interesting, provocative

stimulus 4 goad, spur, whet 5 tonic 6 bracer, fillip, motive 7 impetus 8 excitant 9 activator, energizer, incentive, quickener, stimulant 10 incitement, inducement 11 provocation 13 encouragement

sting 3 cut, nip, rub, vex 4 ache, barb, bite, blow, burn, fire, gall, gnaw, goad, grip, hurt, itch, lash, move, pain, prod, rack, rasp, rile, sore, spur, stab, whip 5 anger, chafe, cross, egg on, grate, impel, pinch, pique, prick, shake, shock, smart, venom, wince, wound 6 arouse, awaken, excite, harrow, incite, insult, kindle, madden, nettle, offend, pierce, prompt, propel, stir up, tingle, twinge 7 actuate, agonize, disturb, incense, inflame, prickle, provoke, quicken, scourge, stinger, torment, torture 8 irritate, motivate, vexation 9 infuriate, instigate, penetrate 10 affliction, irritation

Sting, The
director: 13 George Roy Hill
cast: 10 Paul Newman, Ray Walston, Robert Shaw 13 Eileen Brennan, Robert Redford 14 Charles Durning
score: 11 Scott Joplin
Oscar for: 7 picture 8 director

stinginess 6 penury 9 parsimony 11 miserliness 13 niggardliness, penny-pinching 15 tight-fistedness

stinging 4 acid 5 harsh, sharp 6 biting, bitter 7 burning, caustic, cutting, pungent 8 piercing 9 sarcastic, satirical 10 astringent

stingy 4 lean, mean, thin 5 close, scant, small, tight 6 frugal, meager, modest, paltry, scanty, skimpy, sparse 7 miserly, scrimpy, slender, sparing 8 piddling, stinting 9 illiberal, niggardly, penurious 10 inadequate, ungenerous 11 closefisted, tightfisted 12 cheeseparing, insufficient, parsimonious 13 penny-pinching

stink 4 odor, reek 5 fetor 6 stench 8 bad smell 17 smell to high heaven

stint 3 job 4 curb, duty, part, save, task, term, turn 5 check, chore, limit, quota, shift 6 reduce, scrimp 8 hold back, restrain, restrict, withhold 9 constrain, cut down on, economize 10 assignment, engagement 12 circumscribe, pinch pennies

stipend 5 grant, wages 6 income, salary 7 pension 8 fixed pay 9 allowance, emolument 10 honorarium, recompense 11 scholarship 12 compensation, remuneration

stipulate 4 cite, name 5 agree, allow, grant, state 6 assure, insure, pledge 7 promise, provide, specify, warrant 8 indicate, set forth 9 designate, guarantee

stipulation 4 term 7 proviso 9 condition 10 limitation 11 requirement, restriction

stipulative 7 limited 9 qualified, tentative 10 contingent, restricted 11 conditional, provisional 16 with reservations

stir 3 act, mix 4 beat, fire, goad, jolt, move, prod, rush, spur, to-do, whip 5 blend, rouse, shake, sough, start 6 arouse, awaken, bustle, commix, excite, flurry, hasten, hustle, kindle, mingle, mixing, moving, pother, quiver, rustle, shiver, tumult, twitch, uproar, vivify, work up 7 agitate, animate, enflame, flutter, inspire, provoke, quicken, scamper 8 energize, inspirit, intermix, mingling, movement, prodding, rustling, scramble, stirring 9 agitation, commingle, commotion, electrify, stimulate 10 get a move on, step lively 11 set in motion 12 exert oneself, make an effort

Stirla
also: 8 Stiritis
epithet of: 7 Demeter

Stiritis see 6 Stiria

stirred up 5 riled, upset 7 aroused, excited, kindled, ruffled 8 agitated, inflamed 9 disturbed 10 stimulated

stirring 5 astir, awake 6 moving 7 rousing 8 electric, exalting, exciting, in motion, spirited 9 inspiring, thrilling 10 up and about 11 galvanizing, stimulating 12 electrifying

stir up 5 upset 6 arouse, awaken, excite, kindle, ruffle 7 agitate, disturb 9 call forth, stimulate 10 antagonize

stir vigorously 3 mix 4 beat, whip 7 agitate

stitch 3 bit, jot, sew 4 ache, iota, kink, mend, pain, pang, seam, tack 5 baste, cramp, crick, piece, scrap, shoot, shred 6 suture, tingle, twinge, twitch 7 article, garment 8 particle 9 embroider 12 charley horse

St John's
capital of: 17 Antigua and Barbuda

St Louis
baseball team: 9 Cardinals
football team: 9 Cardinals
founded by: 13 Pierre Laclede
hockey team: 5 Blues
landmark: 11 Gateway Arch
newspaper: 12 Post-Dispatch
river: 11 Mississippi
site of: 10 Exposition (1904)
university: 10 Washington

stock 4 butt, clan, form, fund, haft, herd, hold, kind, line, pull, race, root, type 5 array, basic, birth, blood, breed, broth, cache, caste, equip, goods, grasp, hoard, house, offer, shaft, store, tribe, wares 6 cattle, family, fit out, formal, handle, origin, people, shares, source, staple, strain, supply 7 appoint, capital, descent, dynasty, furnish, lineage, provide, regular, reserve, routine 8 accoutre, ancestry, bouillon, heredity, pedigree, pro forma, quantity, standard 9 forebears, genealogy, inventory, livestock, ownership, parentage, provision, reservoir, selection 10 assortment, background, extraction, family tree, investment 11 merchandise, nationality, progeniture 12 accumulation 13 capital shares

Stockhausen, Karlheinz
born: 7 Germany, Modrath
composer of: 5 Cycle, Tempi 6 Groups, Hymnen, Mantra, Zyklus 7 Anthems, Gruppen, Momente 8 Attuning, Gold Dust, Kontakte, Stimmung 9 Goldstaub, Zeitmasze 10 Procession, Prozession 12 Kontrapunkte 13 Klavierstücke 16 From the Seven Days 17 Aus den Sieben Tagen

Stockholm
nickname: 16 Venice of the North
capital of: 6 Sweden
sea: 6 Baltic
lake: 7 Malaren
section: 8 Norrmalm 9 Sodermalm 11 Gamla Staden
landmark: 7 Skansen 8 City Hall 11 Great Church
site of: 10 Nobel Prize

stockpile 5 cache, hoard, stock, store 10 accumulate

stocky 5 dumpy, husky, pudgy, solid, squat, stout 6 blocky, chunky, stubby, stumpy, sturdy 8 thickset

stodgy 4 dull, flat 5 dated, heavy, lumpy, passe, staid, thick 6 boring, clumsy, dreary, narrow, prolix, stuffy 7 humdrum, pompous, prosaic, serious, starchy, tedious 8 lifeless, pedantic, tiresome 9 laborious, lumbering, wearisome 10 antiquated, inflexible, monotonous 12 indigestible, old-fashioned 13 uninteresting

stoic 4 calm 8 detached, fatalist, quietist, tranquil 9 impassive, unruffled 11 philosophic 13 dispassionate, imperturbable, unimpassioned

stoicism 8 fatalism 9 fortitude 11 impassivity, tranquility 12 tranquillity 16 imperturbability

stole 3 fur 4 cape, robe, took, wrap 5 crept, orary, scarf 6 swiped 7 filched, pinched, sneaked, tiptoed 8 mantilla, pilfered, snatched, vestment 9 embezzled, purloined

stolen 3 hot 5 taken 6 swiped 7 filched, pinched 8 pilfered, snatched 9 embezzled, ill-gotten, purloined

stolid 4 dull 5 dense 6 bovine, obtuse 7 lumpish 8 sluggish 9 apathetic, impassive, lethargic 10 phlegmatic 11 insensitive, unemotional

stolidity 6 apathy 8 lethargy 9 inertness 11 impassivity 12 sluggishness

stomach 3 maw, pot 4 bear, bent, bias, craw, crop, guts, mind, take 5 abide, belly, brook, fancy, humor, stand, taste, tummy 6 desire, endure, hunger, liking, middle, paunch, relish, retain, suffer, temper, thirst 7 abdomen, gizzard, leaning, midriff, swallow 8 affinity, appetite, bear with, keenness, overlook, pass over, pleasure, potbelly, sympathy, tolerate 9 put up with 10 attraction, midsection, partiality, proclivity, propensity 11 breadbasket, countenance, disposition, inclination 12 predilection

stone 3 gem, nut, pip, pit 4 rock, seed 5 bijou, jewel 6 kernel, pebble 9 brilliant 10 throw rocks

Stone, Edward Durell
architect of: 9 US Embassy 17 Museum of Modern Art 33 Kennedy Center for the Performing Arts

Stone, Irving
author of: 9 The Origin 11 Lust for Life 12 Those Who Love 17 Sailor on Horseback, The President's Lady 19 Adversary in the House 21 The Agony and the Ecstasy

Stone, Oliver
born: 9 New York NY
profession: 6 writer 8 director
films: 3 JFK 7 Platoon 10 Wall Street 13 Heaven and Earth 15 Midnight Express 21 Born on the Fourth of July

stoned to death 5 Achan

stonefly
varieties: 5 giant, green 6 spring, winter 8 perlodid 9 roachlike 11 green-winged 12 rolled-winged

stoneware 5 china 7 ceramic, pottery 8 crockery

stony 3 icy 4 cold 5 blank, bumpy, chill, rocky, rough, stern 6 coarse, craggy, flinty, frigid, jagged, marble, pebbly, rugged, severe, steely, stolid, uneven 7 austere, callous, granite, lithoid, stoical 8 concrete, deadened, gravelly, hardened, indurate, obdurate, ossified, pitiless, rocklike, soulless, uncaring 9 bloodless, heartless, merciless, petrified, unfeeling, untouched 10 ada mantine, forbidding, fossilized, hardboiled, inexorable, insensible, unaffected, unyielding

stool 5 bench 7 cricket, has sock, ottoman

stool pigeon 3 rat, spy 4 fink 5 decoy, patsy 6 snitch 7 peacher, stoolie, tattler 8 informer, squealer 10 tale-bearer, tattletale

stoop 3 bow, sag 4 bend, fall, sink 5 deign, droop, porch, slump, steps, yield 6 resort, slouch, submit 7 concede, descend, succumb 8 doorstep 9 acquiesce 10 condescend 11 entranceway 19 round-shoulderedness

stooped 4 bent 5 bowed 7 deigned, hunched 9 contorted 12 condescended

stop 3 ban, bar, end 4 curb, fill, halt, hold, idle, plug, quit, rest, seal, stay, stem, wait 5 abide, block, brake, break, caulk, cease, check, close, depot, deter, dwell, lapse, lodge, pause, put up, spell, stall, stand, tarry, visit 6 alight, arrest, cut off, desist, draw up, expire, falter, finish, hamper, hiatus, hinder, pull up, recess, rein in, repose, run out, stanch, stop up, thwart 7 close up, halting, layover, occlude, prevent, respite, sojourn, sta ion, suspend 8 abeyance, break off, conclude, cut short, hold back, intermit, interval, leave off, obstruct, pass away, peter out, postpone, preclude, restrain, suppress, surcease, terminal, terminus, wind down 9 cessation, frustrate, interlude, stand fast, terminate 10 desistance, drop anchor, put an end to, standstill, suspension 11 come to a halt, come to an end, destination, discontinue, prohibition, termination 12 intermission, interruption 17 come to a standstill 18 bring to a standstill

stopgap 7 stand-by 9 contrived, emergency, expedient, impromptu, makeshift, temporary, tentative 10 improvised, substitute 11 provisional
Latin: 5 ad hoc 6 pro tem

stop in 4 call 5 visit 6 drop in, look in

stop off 4 call 5 visit 6 drop in, look in, stop by

stoppage 4 halt 5 check, tieup 6 arrest 7 barrier, embargo, staying 8 blockage, checking, clogging, gridlock, obstacle 9 checkmate, hindrance, restraint, stricture 10 disruption, impediment 11 curtailment, obstruction 12 interruption

Stoppard, Tom
author of: 10 Travesties 33 Rosencrantz and Guildenstern Are Dead

stopper 3 lid 4 bung, cock, cork, plug 5 spile

Stopping by Woods on a Snowy Evening
author: 11 Robert Frost

Stop the Music
host: 9 Bert Parks
orchestra: 11 Harry Salter
vocalist: 9 June Valli 11 Jaye P Morgan, Jimmy Blaine 12 Marion Morgan 13 Betty Ann Grove, Estelle Loring

stop up 3 jam 4 clog 5 block, choke 8 obstruct

Storax 12 Biblical tree

store 3 lot **4** fund, hold, host, keep, mart, pack, pile, save, shop **5** amass, array, cache, faith, hoard, lay by, lay in, lay up, stash, stock, trust, value, wares **6** credit, esteem, gather, heap up, legion, market, plenty, regard, riches, scores, supply, volume, wealth **7** deposit, effects, husband, put away, reserve, satiety **8** emporium, lay aside, overflow, plethora, quantity, reliance, richness, salt away, sock away, stow away **9** abundance, inventory, multitude, profusion, provision, reservoir, stockpile **10** accumulate, confidence, cornucopia, dependence, estimation, exuberance, luxuriance **11** copiousness, full measure, prodigality, supermarket **12** accumulation **13** establishment

storehouse 4 bank, silo **5** depot, vault **7** arsenal, granary **8** elevator, magazine, treasury **9** stockroom, warehouse **10** depository, repository

storied 4 epic **6** fabled **8** fabulous **9** legendary

Stories and Texts for Nothing
　　author: **13** Samuel Beckett

storm 3 ado, row **4** blow, fume, fuss, gale, rage, rant, rave, roar, rush, stir, tear, to-do **5** burst, furor, snarl, stalk, stamp, stomp, tramp **6** assail, attack, charge, clamor, deluge, flurry, hubbub, pother, ruckus, squall, strike, tumult, uproar **7** assault, besiege, bluster, carry on, cyclone, rampage, tempest, tornado, torrent, turmoil, twister, typhoon **8** blizzard, brouhaha, downpour, eruption, fall upon, outbreak, outburst, upheaval **9** agitation, commotion, explosion, fulminate, hurricane, raise hell **10** cloudburst, hullabaloo **11** blow one's top, disturbance **12** blow one's cool, vent one's rage

storm and stress
　　German: **13** Sturm und Drang
　　name of 18th century: **16** literary movement

storms
　　goddess of: **11** Tempestates

storm troopers
　　German: **14** Sturmabteilung

stormy 4 foul, wild **5** rainy, rough, snowy, windy **6** raging, rugged **7** howling, roaring, squally, violent **8** blustery **9** inclement, turbulent **10** blustering **11** tempestuous

story 3 fib, lie **4** news, plot, tale, word, yarn **5** alibi, fable, piece **6** excuse, legend, report, sketch **7** account, article, parable, romance, tidings, version **8** allegory, anecdote, argument, dispatch, news item, white lie **9** falsehood, narrative, statement, testimony **10** allegation **11** fabrication, information **13** prevarication

Story of a Bad Boy, The
　　author: **19** Thomas Bailey Aldrich

Story of G I Joe, The
　　director: **14** William Wellman
　　cast: **13** Freddie Steele, Robert Mitchum **15** Burgess Meredith (Ernie Pyle)

Story of Louis Pasteur, The
　　director: **15** William Dieterle
　　cast: **8** Paul Muni (Pasteur) **11** Anita Louise **19** Josephine Hutchinson
　　Oscar for: **5** actor (Muni)

stout 3 big, fat, fit **4** able, bold, firm, true **5** brave, bulky, burly, hardy, heavy, hefty, husky, large, obese, plump, pudgy, round, solid, tough, tubby **6** brawny, chubby, daring, fleshy, heroic, mighty, plucky, portly, robust, rotund, rugged, spunky, steady, stocky, strong, sturdy **7** doughty, gallant, staunch, valiant **8** athletic, constant, enduring, faithful, fearless, intrepid, leathery, muscular, resolute, resolved, stalwart, thickset, untiring, valorous, vigorous **9** confident, corpulent, dauntless, steadfast, strapping **10** able-bodied, courageous, determined, inflexible, unshakable, unswerving, unwavering **11** indomitable, lionhearted, unfaltering, unflinching, unshrinking

Stout, Rex
　　author of: **10** Fer-de-Lance **12** Too Many Cooks **16** If Death Ever Slept
　　character: **5** Fritz **9** Nero Wolfe **13** Archie Goodwin

stouthearted 4 bold **5** brave, gutsy, hardy **6** heroic, plucky, spunky **7** valiant **8** fearless, intrepid, resolute, spirited, stalwart, unafraid, valorous **9** dauntless, undaunted **10** courageous **11** indomitable, lionhearted, unblenching

stouteartedness 4 grit, guts, sand **5** nerve, pluck, spunk, valor **6** daring, mettle **7** bravery, courage **8** boldness **12** fearlessness **13** dauntlessness

stoutness
　　French: **10** embonpoint

stow 3 jam, put, set **4** cram, load, pack, tuck **5** cache, crowd, place, stash, store, stuff, wedge **7** deposit, squeeze **8** ensconce, salt away

Stowe, Harriet Beecher
　　author of: **12** Oldtown Folks **14** Uncle Tom's Cabin

Strachey, Lytton
　　author of: **13** Queen Victoria **17** Elizabeth and Essex, Eminent Victorians
　　member of: **15** Bloomsbury Group

strafe 7 bombard **8** fire upon **10** machine-gun

straggle 4 rove **5** drift, stray **6** sprawl, wander **7** deviate, meander **8** divagate

straight 4 even, neat, tidy, true **5** clear, frank, right, solid, sound **6** candid, direct, evenly, honest, square, unbent **7** aligned, erectly, in order, orderly, upright **8** accurate, adjusted, arranged, directly, on a level, reliable, squarely, truthful, unbroken **9** ceaseless, forthwith, incessant, instantly, not curved, shipshape, sorted out, sustained, veracious **10** aboveboard, continuous, forthright, four-square, methodical, persistent, straightly, successive, unrelieved, unswerving, unwavering **11** consecutive, coordinated, immediately, trustworthy, undeviating 13 uninterrupted

straighten 4 tidy 5 align 6 adjust, neaten, unbend 7 even out 8 level out, square up 9 put in line 10 put in order, stand erect

straightening 7 tidying 9 adjusting, alignment, evening up, unbending 10 evening out 11 leveling out 13 putting in line 14 putting in order

straighten out 6 unbend 7 realign 8 redirect 10 discipline

straighten up 4 tidy 5 align, clean, order 6 neaten, tidy up 7 arrange, stand up 8 organize

straightforward 4 open 5 blunt, frank 6 candid, direct, honest, square 7 ethical, upright 8 straight 9 guileless, honorable 10 aboveboard, creditable, forthright, scrupulous 11 plainspoken, trustworthy

straightforwardness 6 candor 7 honesty 12 truthfulness 14 forthrightness

straight from the shoulder 4 open 5 frank 6 candid, direct, openly 7 bluntly, frankly, sincere 8 candidly, directly 9 downright

straightness 7 honesty 8 evenness 10 directness 11 uprightness

strain 3 air, tax, tug 4 kind, line, pull, sift, song, sort, toil, tune, type, vein 5 blood, breed, drain, force, grain, grind, group, heave, labor, people, press, sieve, streak, stock, trait, twist 6 burden, drudge, effort, extend, family, filter, genius, injure, injury, melody, overdo, purify, refine, screen, sprain, stress, weaken, winnow, wrench 7 descent, distend, exhaust, fatigue, lineage, overtax, species, stretch, tension, tighten, try hard, variety, wear out 8 ancestry, bear down, elongate, exertion, hardship, heredity, make taut, overwork, pressure, protract, struggle, tendency 9 draw tight, make tense, overexert, parentage 10 buckle down, derivation, extraction, overburden 11 disposition, huff and puff, inclination 12 do double duty, drive oneself, exert oneself 14 predisposition, work like a horse, work like a slave

strained 5 tense 6 touchy 8 volatile 9 explosive 10 precarious

strait 7 channel, narrows, passage

straitened 5 broke, needy 6 hard-up 7 pinched 8 bank rupt, indigent, strapped, wiped-out 9 destitute, penniless, penurious 10 distressed, pauperized, restricted 11 embarrassed 12 impoverished 15 poverty-stricken

Strait Is the Gate
author: 9 Andre Gide

straitlaced 4 prim 5 rigid, stiff 6 formal, narrow, proper, severe, strict 7 austere, prudish, uptight 8 reserved 9 inhibited 11 puritanical 14 overscrupulous 15 undemonstrative

straits 3 fix 4 hole 6 pickle, plight 8 distress 9 extremity 10 difficulty 11 predicament 13 embarrassment

strand 4 bank, cord, lock, rope 5 beach, braid, coast, fiber, leave, shore, tress, twist 6 desert, ground, maroon, string, thread 8 filament, necklace, seacoast, seashore 9 component, go aground, riverside, shipwreck 10 ingredient, run aground 15 leave high and dry, leave in the lurch

stranded 5 stuck 6 ashore 7 aground, beached 8 grounded 9 foundered 11 shipwrecked 14 left high and dry, left in the lurch

strange 3 new, odd 4 lost 5 alien, queer 6 uneasy, unused 7 awkward, bizarre, curious, erratic, foreign, unknown, unusual 8 aberrant, abnormal, freakish, peculiar, singular, uncommon 9 alienated, anomalous, eccentric, estranged, fantastic, ill at ease, irregular, unnatural 10 bewildered, far-fetched, out of place, outlandish, unexplored, unfamiliar 11 discomposed, disoriented, out-of-the-way 12 unaccustomed, undiscovered, unhabituated 13 extraordinary, unaccountable, uncomfortable 14 unconventional

Strange Fruit
author: 12 Lillian Smith

Strange Interlude
author: 12 Eugene O'Neill

strangeness 7 anomaly, oddness 9 queerness 10 aberration 11 abnormality, peculiarity 12 eccentricity, idiosyncrasy, irregularity, unconformity 13 nonconformity

stranger 5 alien 8 newcomer, outsider 9 auslander, foreigner, immigrant, outlander

Stranger, The
author: 11 Albert Camus

Strangers on a Train
director: 15 Alfred Hitchcock
cast: 9 Ruth Roman 11 Leo G Carroll, Marion Lorne 12 Robert Walker 13 Farley Granger 17 Patricia Hitchcock
remade as: 20 Once You Kiss a Stranger

strange to say
Latin: 13 mirabile dictu

strangle 3 gag 4 stop 5 burke, check, choke, crush, quell 6 muzzle, stifle 7 garrote, put down, repress, smother, squelch 8 choke off, snuff out, suppress, throttle 9 suffocate 10 asphyxiate, extinguish

strangulate 8 choke off, compress, strangle 9 constrict

strap 3 tie 4 band, beat, belt, bind, cord, flog, lash, whip 5 flail, leash, thong, truss 6 tether, thrash 7 scourge

strapped 8 bankrupt, wiped out 9 insolvent, penniless 12 impoverished, without funds

strapping 5 burly, hardy, husky, stout 6 brawny, robust, strong, sturdy 8 muscular, powerful, stalwart

stratagem 4 game, plan, plot, ploy, ruse, wile 5 blind, dodge, feint, trick 6 deceit, device, scheme, tactic 8 artifice, intrigue, maneuver, trickery 9 deception 10 subterfuge 11 contrivance, machination

strategic 3 key 4 wary 5 vital 6 clever 7 careful, crucial, cunning, guarded, planned, politic, prudent, turning 8 cautious, critical, decisive, military, tactical, vigilant **9** important, momentous, principal **10** calculated, deliberate, diplomatic **11** significant **13** consequential, precautionary

strategy 4 game **5** craft, wiles **6** policy, scheme **7** cunning, devices, tactics **8** artifice, art of war, game plan, plotting **9** war policy **10** artfulness, craftiness **11** grand design, machination, maneuvering **12** military plan **15** military science

stratosphere 3 sky **5** ozone **7** heavens **8** upper air **12** high altitude **14** wild blue yonder

stratum 4 band, belt, seam, zone **5** layer

Strauss, Johann (the Elder)
    composer of: 13 Radetzky March

Strauss, Johann (the Younger)
    composer of: 6 The Bat **13** Die Fledermaus, The Gipsy Baron **16** Der Zigeunerbaron
    waltz: **12** Emperor Waltz **13** The Blue Danube **23** Tales from the Vienna Woods

Strauss, Joseph
    composer of: 17 Music of the Spheres **27** The Village Swallows in Austria

Strauss, Richard
    born: 6 Munich **7** Germany
    composer of: 6 Salome **7** Don Juan, Elektra **8** Arabella **9** Capriccio **10** Don Quixote **14** Ein Heldenleben **15** Ariadne auf Naxos **16** Der Rosenkavalier, Domestic Symphony, Till Eulenspiegel **19** Die Frau ohne Schatten **20** Die Aegyptische Helena, Thus Spake Zarathustra **21** Also Sprach Zarathustra **23** Death and Transfiguration

Stravinsky, Igor Feodorovich
    born: 6 Russia **10** Oranienbaum
    composer of: 4 Agon **6** Threni **7** Orpheus **8** The Flood **9** Card Party, Fireworks **10** Oedipus Rex, Petrouchka, Petruschka, Pulcinella **11** Jeu de Cartes, The Firebird **13** Dumbarton Oaks, Psalm Symphony **14** The Nightingale **15** Abraham and Isaac, The Rite of Spring **16** Requiem Canticles, The Rake's Progress **18** Le Sacre du Printemps

straw 3 hay **4** tube **5** chaff **7** pipette

strawberry 8 Fragaria
    varieties: 4 mock **5** beach **6** barren, Dunlap, garden, Indian **7** sow-teat **8** Klondike, Rosacean, Virginia, woodland
    liqueur: 13 creme de fraise

Straw Dogs
    director: 12 Sam Peckinpah
    cast: 9 T P McKenna **11** Susan George **12** Peter Vaughan **13** Dustin Hoffman

straw man 6 effigy **9** scapegoat, scarecrow

stray 4 lost, roam, rove, waif **5** drift **6** random, wander **7** digress, drifter **8** go astray, sepa rate, set apart, straggle, straying, vagabond, wanderer **9** itinerant, misplaced, scat tered, straggler **10** lost animal, lost person **11** lose one's way

straying 5 lapse **8** drifting, rambling **9** departure, deviation, wandering **10** aberration, digression, divergence

streak 3 bar, bed, fly **4** band, blot, blur, cast, dart, dash, daub, line, lode, race, rush, seam, tear, vein, whiz, zoom **5** layer, level, plane, smear, speed, strip, touch **6** blotch, hurtle, smirch, smudge, strain, stripe **7** portion, splotch, stratum

stream 3 jet, run **4** blow, file, flow, flux, gush, pour, race, rill, rush, teem, tide, waft, wave **5** brook, burst, creek, float, flood, issue, river, shoot, spate, spill, spout, spurt, surge **6** abound, branch, course, deluge, extend, feeder, onrush, sluice **7** current, flutter, freshet, rivulet, torrent **8** effusion, fountain, overflow **9** profusion, tributary **11** watercourse

streamer 4 flag **6** banner, burgee **7** pennant

streamlet 3 run **4** rill **5** brook, creek **7** rivulet

streamlined 4 racy **5** clean, sleek **7** compact **8** up-to-date **9** organized **10** futuristic, modernized, simplified **11** aerodynamic

stream of abuse 6 tirade **8** diatribe, harangue **9** contumely, invective **12** vituperation

streams
    goddess of: 7 Juturna

Streep, Meryl
    real name: 16 Mary Louise Streep
    born: 14 Basking Ridge NJ
    roles: 8 Ironweed, Silkwood **11** Out of Africa **13** Falling in Love, Sophie's Choice (Oscar), The Deer Hunter **14** Kramer vs Kramer **25** The French Lieutenant's Woman

street 3 way **4** lane, mews, road **5** alley, block, route **6** avenue **7** highway, roadway, terrace, thruway **8** turnpike **9** boulevard **10** expressway **12** thoroughfare

Streetcar Named Desire, A
    author: 17 Tennessee Williams
    director: 9 Elia Kazan
    cast: 9 Kim Hunter (Stella Dubois Kowalski) **10** Karl Malden **11** Vivien Leigh (Blanche Dubois) **12** Marlon Brando (Stanley Kowalski)
    setting: 10 New Orleans
    score: 9 Alex North
    Oscar for: 7 actress (Leigh) **15** supporting actor (Malden) **17** supporting actress (Hunter)

Streets of San Francisco, The
    character: 9 (Det Lt) Mike Stone **10** (Inspector) Dan Robbins **11** (Inspector) Steve Keller
    cast: 10 Karl Malden **12** Richard Hatch **14** Michael Douglas

strega
    type: 7 liqueur
    origin: 5 Italy
    flavor: 6 spices **10** orange peel
    with brandy: 10 Strega Flip

Streisand, Barbra
    real name: 20 Barbara Joan Streisand
    born: 10 Brooklyn NY
    husband: 11 Elliot Gould
    roles: 5 Yentl **9** Funny Girl (Oscar),

Funny Lady 10 Fanny Brice, Hello Dolly, What's Up Doc? 11 A Star Is Born 12 The Main Event, The Way We Were

strength 4 beef, grit, kick, pith, sand, size 5 brawn, force, forte, might, pluck, power, sinew, spice, vigor 6 anchor, mettle, number, purity, spirit, succor, virtue 7 bravery, muscles, potency, stamina, support 8 backbone, buttress, efficacy, firmness, mainstay, security, solidity, tenacity, vitality 9 endurance, fortitude, hardiness, intensity, lustiness, puissance, stoutness, toughness, viability 10 robustness, sturdiness, sustenance 13 concentration, effectiveness 16 stoutheartedness

Latin: 3 vis

strengthen 4 prop 5 brace, renew, steel 6 harden 7 build up, enhance, fortify, improve, restore, shore up, support, sustain 8 buttress 9 reinforce

strength of character 4 grit, guts 5 pluck, spunk 6 mettle 7 resolve 8 backbone 9 fortitude 10 resolution 12 resoluteness 13 steadfastness

Strength of Fields

author: 11 James Dickey

strenuous 4 hard 5 eager 6 active, ardent, dogged, taxing, uphill 7 arduous, dynamic, earnest, intense, zealous 8 animated, diligent, sedulous, spirited, untiring, vigorous 9 assiduous, difficult, energetic, laborious, punishing 10 exhausting, on one's toes 11 hardworking, industrious, painstaking 12 enterprising 13 indefatigable

stress 4 beat, mark 5 force, value, worth 6 accent, affirm, assert, burden, moment, repeat, strain, weight 7 anxiety, concern, feature, gravity, meaning, sawdust, tension, urgency 8 emphasis, pressure 9 emphasize, necessity, underline 10 accentuate, importance, insist upon, oppression, prominence, underscore 11 consequence, seriousness 12 accentuation, significance 13 consideration

stretch 4 span, term, tire 5 cover, reach, spell, stint, tract, while, widen 6 burden, deepen, expand, extend, period, sprawl, spread, spring, strain 7 distend, draw out, ex panse, fatigue, lie over, over tax, pull out 8 distance, draw taut, duration, elongate, interval, lengthen, overtask, over work, protract, put forth, reach out, tautness, traverse 9 be elastic, draw tight, make tense, make tight, overexert 10 elasticity, exaggerate, overburden, overcharge, overstrain, push too far, resiliency 11 carry too far 12 be expandable, be extendable 14 push to the limit

stretchable 7 elastic, rubbery 8 flexible 9 resilient

stretching 9 extending, extension 10 drawing out, elongation 11 attenuation, enlargement, lengthening, protraction 12 prolongation 13 amplification

stretching out 8 outreach 9 expansion, extending, extension 10 elongation 11 attenuation, lengthening 12 prolongation

stretch out 6 expand, extend 7 amplify, augment, draw out 8 elongate, lengthen, protract

Strether

character in: 14 The Ambassadors

author: 5 James

strew 3 sow 6 litter 7 scatter 8 disperse 9 broadcast 11 disseminate

stricken 3 ill 4 hurt, sick 7 injured, smitten, wounded 8 blighted, diseased 9 afflicted, taken sick 13 incapacitated

strict 4 nice 5 exact, rigid, stern 6 severe 7 austere, perfect 8 absolute, complete, exacting, rigorous, unerring 9 stringent 10 fastidious, inflexible, meticulous, scrupulous, unyielding 13 authoritarian, conscientious 14 uncompromising

strictly required

French: 9 de rigueur

stride 4 gait, lope, pace, step 5 march, stalk 7 advance, headway 8 long step, progress 11 advancement, improvement 13 take long steps

strident 5 harsh 6 shrill 7 grating, jarring, rasping, raucous 8 clashing, grinding, jangling, piercing, twanging 9 dissonant 10 discordant, screeching 11 cacophonous, high-pitched

Striebel, John H

creator/artist of: 10 Dixie Dugan

strife 6 unrest 7 discord, trouble, turmoil, warfare 8 conflict, disquiet, fighting, struggle, upheaval, violence 10 contention, convulsion, disharmony, dissension 11 altercation, disturbance

Strife

author: 14 John Galsworthy

strike 3 bat, box, hit, run, tap 4 bang, beat, belt, bump, clap, clip, club, come, cuff, drub, find, flog, lash, make, meet, pelt, ring, slam, slap, slug, sock, toll, whip, wipe 5 chime, clout, erase, flail, knell, knock, light, pound, punch, reach, smash, smite, sound, thump, whack, whale 6 affect, arrive, assail, attack, batter, buffet, cancel, chance, charge, cudgel, delete, effect, fold up, hammer, pommel, remove, seem to, thrash, wallop 7 achieve, arrange, assault, boycott, impress, occur to, protest, put away, ram into, run into, scourge, scratch, stumble, unearth, walk out 8 appear to, bump into, come upon, cross out, dawn upon, discover, fall upon, lambaste, pull down, take down 9 burst upon, devastate, eliminate, encounter, eradicate, knock into, take apart 10 come across, flagellate, meet head-on 11 beat against, collide with, dash against 12 labor dispute, work stoppage

strike a bargain 5 agree 6 settle 9 make a deal 10 compromise 11 come to terms, meet halfway 18 split the difference 20 reach an understanding

strike back 7 counter, get even, hit back, pay back, riposte 9 fight back, retaliate 13 counterattack

strike dumb 4 daze, stun 5 amaze, shock 7 astound, stagger, stupefy 8 astonish, dumfound 9 dumbfound, electrify 11 flabbergast

strike noisily 4 bang, beat, clap, slam 5 thump

strike out 6 delete, fan out, set off, set out 7 take out 10 sally forth

strike sharply 3 rap 4 slap 5 crack

striking 6 marked 7 notable 9 prominent 10 astounding, impressive, noteworthy, noticeable, remarkable, surprising 11 conspicuous, outstanding 13 extraordinary

Strindberg, August
    author of: 9 Miss Julie, The Father 10 A Dream Play 12 The Creditors 14 The Ghost Sonata 15 The Dance of Death

string 3 row 4 cord, file, line, rope 5 chain, queue, train, twine 6 column, extend, parade, series, spread, strand, thread 7 binding, stretch 8 necklace, sequence 10 procession, succession

stringent 5 close, harsh, spare, stern, stiff, tight 6 cogent, frugal, severe, strict 7 sparing 8 exacting, forceful, rigorous 9 demanding, effectual, unbending 10 inflexible, unyielding 14 uncompromising

strip 3 rob 4 band, flay, loot, peel, raid, sack, skin, slip, tear 5 field, flake, rifle, shave 6 denude, divest, length, ravage, remove, ribbon, stripe, unwrap 7 deprive, despoil, disrobe, draw off, lay bare, measure, plunder, pull off, ransack, uncover, undrape, undress 8 airstrip, desolate, lay waste, spoliate, unclothe 9 steal from 11 disencumber

stripe 3 bar 4 band, line, tape 5 braid, strip, swath 6 ribbon, streak 7 chevron 8 insignia 9 striation

stripling 3 boy, lad 5 minor, youth 8 teenager, young man 9 schoolboy, youngster 10 adolescent

stripped 4 bare, nude 5 naked 6 peeled, unclad 7 denuded, exposed, unrobed 8 disrobed, divested 9 unclothed, uncovered, undressed

strive 3 vie 4 push 5 essay, fight, labor 6 battle, strain 7 contend, try hard 8 endeavor, struggle 9 take pains, undertake 10 do one's best 12 apply oneself, do one's utmost, exert oneself, spare no pains 15 work like a Trojan 18 move heaven and earth 20 leave no stone unturned

striving 4 toil 5 exert, labor 6 effort, strain 7 toiling, travail 8 exertion, struggle 9 straining 10 struggling

stroke 3 bat, hit, pat, pet, tap 4 blow, chop, coup, deed, feat, poke, slap, sock, swat 5 brush, chime, fluke, punch, whack 6 caress, chance, wallop 7 massage, ringing, seizure, tolling 8 accident, apoplexy, flourish, movement, sounding, striking 11 achievement, coincidence, piece of luck, transaction 15 brain hemorrhage

stroll 4 tour, turn, walk 5 amble, mosey 6 ramble, wander 7 meander, saunter 9 poke along, promenade 14 constitutional

stroller 4 pram 5 buggy 6 ambler, walker 7 rambler 8 carriage 9 itinerant, pushchair, saunterer 10 promenader 12 perambulator

strong 3 hot 4 able, bold, deep, keen, tart 5 burly, clear, close, fiery, hardy, nippy, sharp, solid, sound, stout, tangy, tough, vivid 6 ardent, biting, brawny, bright, cogent, fervid, fierce, gritty, hearty, mighty, moving, plucky, potent, robust, savory, severe, sinewy, sturdy 7 buoyant, capable, devoted, earnest, fervent, healthy, intense, piquant, pungent, skilled, violent, zealous 8 animated, athletic, definite, diligent, distinct, emphatic, faithful, forceful, muscular, powerful, puissant, sedulous, spirited, stalwart, tireless, vehement, vigorous 9 assiduous, competent, confirmed, effective, energetic, herculean, resilient, tenacious, undiluted 10 compelling, convincing, courageous, deep-seated, persistent, proficient 11 impassioned, persevering, resourceful 12 advantageous, concentrated, highly spiced, high-spirited, unmistakable 13 indefatigable, well-qualified 14 highly flavored, highly seasoned
    Spanish: 5 macho

Strong
    character in: 7 Erewhon
    author: 6 Butler

strong-arm 3 cow 5 bully, force 6 coerce, compel 8 browbeat, threaten 10 intimidate

strong feeling 4 fear, hate, heat, love, zeal 5 anger, ardor 6 fervor, sorrow, warmth 7 despair, emotion, passion, sadness 8 jealousy 9 happiness, vehemence 12 satisfaction

stronghold 4 fort, hold, home, keep 6 bunker, center, locale, refuge 7 bastion, bulwark, citadel, rampart, redoubt 8 fastness, fortress, safehold, stockade 10 battlement, blockhouse 13 fortification

strongly committed 4 true 5 loyal 6 ardent 7 devoted, staunch, zealous 8 adhering, faithful 9 dedicated, steadfast 10 passionate, unwavering

strong point 5 forte 6 anchor 8 mainstay, strength

strong-willed 5 pushy 8 forceful, positive 9 assertive 10 aggressive 11 domineering, self-assured 13 self-assertive

Strophius
    king of: 6 Phocis
    reared by: 7 Orestes

structural support 3 bar 4 beam, prop, stud 5 brace, joist 6 girder, rafter, timber 7 trestle 12 underpinning

structure 4 form, plan 6 design, makeup 7 arrange, edifice, pattern 8 assemble, building, conceive, organize 9 construct, formation 11 arrangement, composition, put together 12 conformation, construction, organization 13 configuration

struggle 3 vie, war 4 duel, feud, pull, push, spar, tilt 5 argue, brawl, brush, clash, fight, grind, joust, labor, match, scrap, trial 6 action, battle, combat, differ, effort, engage, jostle, oppose, resist, strain, stress, strife, strive, tussle 7 compete, contend, contest, grapple, quarrel, scuffle 8 conflict, endeavor, exertion, long haul, skirmish, work hard 9 encounter, lock horns, take pains 10 engagement 11 altercation, cross swords 15 work like a Trojan 18 move heaven and earth 20 leave no stone unturned

strut 4 sail 6 parade, sashay 7 peacock, swagger 9 promenade

Struthiomimus
　type: 8 dinosaur, theropod
　known as: 15 ostrich dinosaur
　period: 10 Cretaceous
　characteristic: 9 toothless

Stryver
　character in: 16 A Tale of Two Cities
　author: 7 Dickens

Stuart, Gilbert
　born: 15 North Kingston RI
　artwork: 16 George Washington

Stuart, J E B
　served in: 8 Civil War
　side: 11 Confederate
　commander of: 7 cavalry
　battle: 7 Bull Run 8 Antietam 10 Gettysburg 14 Fredericksburg 16 Chancellorsville 18 Peninsular campaign

Stuart Little
　author: 7 E B White

stub 3 end 4 bump, butt, dock, tail 5 crush, knock, snuff, stump 6 fag end, scrape 7 receipt, remains, tamp out, voucher 10 extinguish, torn ticket 11 counterfoil

stubble 5 beard 6 stumps 8 bristles, whiskers 9 cut stalks 16 five-o'clock shadow

stubborn 6 dogged, mulish, strong, sturdy 7 willful 8 forceful, obdurate, perverse, resolute 9 concerted, immovable, obstinate, pigheaded, resistant, tenacious, unbending, unmovable 10 bullheaded, headstrong, inflexible, persistent, purposeful, refractory, self-willed, unshakable, unyielding 11 indomitable, intractable, opinionated, uncompliant 12 hard to handle, recalcitrant, ungovernable, wholehearted

stubbornness 10 mulishness, obstinacy, resistance 11 willfulness 13 intransigence, pigheadedness

stubby 5 dumpy, pudgy, squab, squat, tubby 6 chubby, chunky, stocky, stodgy, stumpy 7 squatty 8 thickset

Stubtoe State
　nickname of: 7 Montana

stuck 3 dug, put 4 held 5 bound, fixed, fused, glued, mired, poked 6 balked, curbed, jabbed, joined, nailed, pasted, pinned, placed, sealed, spiked, tacked, thrust, welded 7 adhered, affixed, boggled, impeded, planted, pricked, punched, saddled, snarled, speared, stabbed, stalled, stumped, stymied 8 attached, burdened,

cemented, fastened, inserted 9 punctured 10 obstructed, perforated 11 immobilized

stuck-up 4 vain 5 cocky 6 snooty, uppish, uppity 7 haughty, high-hat 8 arrogant, snobbish 9 bigheaded, conceited 10 disdainful, egocentric, hoity-toity 11 overbearing, swellheaded 13 self-important, self-satisfied

stud 3 dot 4 beam, buck, dude, sire 5 board, rivet 6 button 7 upright 8 fastener, macho man, nailhead

student 4 coed 5 pupil 6 reader 7 analyst, learner, scholar, watcher 8 disciple, examiner, follower, observer, reviewer 9 collegian, schoolboy, spectator 10 schoolgirl 11 commentator, interpreter, matriculant 13 undergraduate

studied 8 measured 10 calculated, deliberate, purposeful 11 intentional 12 premeditated

studious 6 brainy, intent 7 bookish, earnest, erudite 8 academic, cerebral, diligent, literate, well-read 9 laborious, scholarly 10 determined, purposeful, scholastic 11 painstaking 12 intellectual

Studs Lonigan
　series includes: 11 Judgment Day 12 Young Lonigan 29 The Young Manhood of Studs Lonigan
　author: 13 James T Farrell

study 3 den 4 cram, read 5 grind, probe 6 office, peruse, review, search, studio, survey 7 examine, explore, inquiry, library, observe, reading 8 analysis, consider, learning, pore over, read up on, research, scrutiny 9 delve into, education 10 glance over, inspection, scrutinize 11 examination, exploration, hit the books, inquire into, instruction, investigate, read closely, reading room, scholar ship 13 consideration, investigation, school oneself, search through

Study in Scarlet, A
　author: 19 Sir Arthur Conan Doyle
　character: 12 Dr John Watson 13 Jefferson Hope, Tobias Gregson 14 Sherlock Holmes 17 Inspector Lestrade

Study of History, A
　author: 14 Arnold J Toynbee

stuff 3 act, bit, jam, pad, wad 4 best, bosh, bunk, cram, fill, gear, heap, load, pack, pile, sate, stow 5 cache, crowd, gorge, hokum, hooey, stash, store, thing, trash, wedge 6 burden, fill up, humbug, matter, staple, tackle, things, thrust, tricks, utmost 7 effects, essence, hogwash, overeat, rubbish, satiate, spinach, twaddle 8 darndest, falderal, material, nonsense 9 component, empty talk, substance 10 balderdash, belongings, gluttonize, ingredient, make a pig of 11 constituent, foolishness, overindulge, performance, possessions, raw material 12 quintessence 13 paraphernalia

stuff-and-nonsense 3 rot 4 bosh, bull, bunk 5 hokum, hooey, trash 6 bunkum, drivel, humbug 7 baloney, hogwash, spinach, twaddle 8 buncombe, claptrap, non-

sense, tommyrot 9 poppycock 10 applesauce, balderdash, tomfoolery 11 foolishness 12 fiddlesticks 13 horsefeathers

stuffed 4 full 6 filled, jammed, loaded,
packed, rammed, wadded 7 crammed,
crushed, replete 8 overfull, satiated,
squeezed 10 sandwiched

stuff in 4 cram, pack 6 devour 8 bolt down,
compress, gobble up, wolf down

stuffing 5 farce 7 filling, pack ing, padding,
wadding 8 dressing 9 forcemeat

stuffy 4 cold, smug 5 close, fusty, heavy,
muggy, musty, staid 6 stodgy, sultry 7 airless, pompous 8 reserved, stagnant, stifling 9 clogged-up, congested, high-flown,
stopped-up, stuffed-up 10 old-fogyish, oppressive, sweltering 11 pretentious, straitlaced, suffocating 12 supercilious, unventilated 13 ill-ventilated, self-satisfied, stale-
smelling

stultify 4 balk 6 hinder, impair, impede,
thwart 7 cripple, inhibit, nullify, vitiate 8
suppress 9 frustrate, hamstring 11 make
useless

stumble 3 hit 4 fall, reel, roll, sway, trip 5
botch, lurch, pitch, spill 6 bungle, falter,
happen, hash up, hobble, mess up, slip
up, sprawl, topple, totter 7 blunder, misstep, shamble, stagger 8 flounder 10 take
a spill 12 come by chance, make mis-
takes, pitch forward

stumble upon 4 find 7 learn of 8 come
upon, discover 10 chance upon, happen
upon 14 find by accident

stumbling block 3 bar, rub 4 snag 5 block,
catch, hitch 6 hamper, hurdle 7 barrier,
problem 8 drawback, obstacle 9 detriment,
hindrance 10 difficulty, impediment 11 obstruction 12 complication, interference

stump 3 end 4 butt, foil, stub, thud 5 befog,
clomp, clonk, clump, clunk, stamp, stomp,
tramp 6 baffle, nubbin, stymie 7 confuse, mystify, nonplus, perplex 8 bewilder,
confound, dumfound, footfall, stomping,
tramping 9 bamboozle, dumbfound

stun 4 daze, numb 5 amaze, shock 7 astound, stagger, startle, stupefy 8 astonish,
dumfound 9 dumbfound 11 flabbergast

stunner 4 doll 5 beaut, Venus 6 beauty,
eyeful 8 knockout 9 dreamboat 10 good-
looker

stunning 6 dazing, lovely 7 amazing,
numbing 8 shocking, striking 9 beautiful,
exquisite, startling 10 astounding, staggering, stupefying 11 astonishing, dum-
founding 12 dumbfounding, electrifying 14
flabbergasting

stunt 3 act 4 curb, feat 5 abort, check,
cramp, dwarf, limit, stint, trick 6 impede,
number, stifle 7 curtail, delimit 8 restrain,
restrict, suppress

stunted 5 dumpy, runty 6 bantam 7
dwarfed, squatty, wizened 9 pint-sized 13
foreshortened

Stunt Man, The
  director: 11 Richard Rush
  cast: 9 Alex Rocco 11 Peter O'Toole (Eli

Cross) 13 Allen Goorwitz, Sharon Farrell
14 Barbara Hershey, Steve Railsback

stupefaction 5 shock 8 numbness, surprise 9 amazement 12 astonishment

stupefied 5 dazed 6 amazed 7 shocked,
stunned 8 benumbed 10 dumbstruck,
dumfounded 11 dumbfounded 13 flabbergasted, thunderstruck

stupefy 4 daze, stun 5 amaze, shock 7 astound, nonplus, stagger 8 astonish, confound, dumfound, surprise 9 dumbfound,
overwhelm 11 flabbergast

stupefying 8 shocking, stunning 11 dum-
founding 12 dumbfounding, electrifying,
overwhelming 14 flabbergasting

stupendous 3 big 4 huge, vast 5 giant,
great, jumbo 6 mighty 7 amazing, immense, mammoth, massive, titanic, unusual 8 colossal, enormous, fabulous, gigantic, imposing, stunning, terrific 9
cyclopean, herculean, marvelous, monstrous, very great, very large, wonderful 10
astounding, gargantuan, incredible, monumental, phenomenal, prodigious, remarkable, surprising, tremendous, unexpected
11 astonishing, elephantine 13 extraordinary

stupid 4 dull, dumb 5 dense, inane, inept,
silly 6 absurd, oafish, obtuse, simple, unwise 7 aimless, asinine, boorish, doltish,
fatuous, foolish, idiotic, moronic, witless 8
backward, childish, heedless, mistaken,
reckless, tactless 9 brainless, cretinous,
dimwitted, duncelike, foolhardy, ill-judged,
imbecilic, imprudent, pointless, senseless
10 half-witted, ill-advised, indiscreet, irrelevant, weak-minded 11 empty-headed,
meaningless, nonsensical, purposeless,
thoughtless 12 absentminded, muddleheaded, preposterous, simpleminded,
slow-learning, unreasonable 13 ill-
considered, inappropriate, irresponsible,
rattlebrained, unintelligent

stupor 4 daze 5 faint 6 apathy, torpor 7 inertia 8 blackout, lethargy, numbness 9
inertness 10 somnolence 12 stupefaction
13 insensibility

sturdy 4 able, firm 5 brave, burly, gutsy,
hardy, heavy, solid, sound, stout, tough 6
daring, dogged, gritty, heroic, mighty,
plucky, robust, rugged, secure, sinewy,
spunky, strong 7 defiant, doughty, durable,
gallant, lasting, valiant 8 enduring, fearless, forceful, intrepid, muscular, powerful,
resolute, spirited, stalwart, stubborn, vigorous, well-made 9 dauntless, strapping,
unabashed, undaunted, well-built 10 courageous, determined, invincible 11 indomitable, substantial, unshrinking 12 high-
spirited, stouthearted 15 well-constructed

Sturges, John
  director of: 14 The Great Escape 19 The
  Magnificent Seven

Sturges, Preston
  director of: 10 The Lady Eve 16 Sullivan's Travels 17 The Palm Beach Story,

Unfaithfully Yours 21 Hail the Conquering Hero 24 The Miracle of Morgan's Creek

Sturmabteilung 13 storm troopers

Sturm und Drang 22 German literary movement (18th century)
literally: 14 storm and stress

stygian 3 dim 4 dark 5 black, murky 6 dreary, gloomy, somber 7 hellish 8 funereal, infernal, starless 9 tenebrous, unlighted

style 3 fad 4 call, elan, kind, mode, name, pomp, rage, sort, type 5 charm, class, craze, favor, flair, grace, model, taste, trend, vogue 6 design, luxury, manner, polish 7 arrange, comfort, fashion, pattern 8 currency, elegance 9 affluence, designate 10 smoothness 11 savoir faire
French: 4 gout

stylish 3 hip, new 4 chic 5 natty, smart, swank 6 dapper, latest, modern, modish, with-it 7 a la mode, elegant, in vogue, voguish 8 up-to-date 9 in fashion 11 fashionable 13 sophisticated, up-to-the-minute

stymie 4 balk 5 block, check, stump 6 baffle, hinder, puzzle, thwart 7 confuse, mystify 8 confound, obstruct 9 frustrate

Stymphalides
origin: 8 Arcadian
form: 5 birds
attribute: 9 dangerous

Stymphalus
king of: 7 Arcadia
killed by: 6 Pelops
form: 4 lake
home of: 12 Stymphalides

Styracosaurus
type: 8 dinosaur 10 ceratopsid
location: 12 North America
period: 10 Cretaceous
characteristic: 6 horned

Styron, William
author of: 12 The Long March 13 Sophie's Choice 17 Lie Down in Darkness 18 Set This House on Fire 25 The Confessions of Nat Turner

Styx
form: 5 river
location: 5 Hades 10 underworld
father: 7 Oceanus
ferryman: 6 Charon

suave 5 silken, smooth, urbane 7 affable, elegant, politic 8 charming, gracious, mannerly, polished, unctuous 9 civilized 10 diplomatic, flattering 12 ingratiating 13 smooth-tongued

sub 5 below, proxy, under 6 backup, deputy, second 7 beneath, standby, stand-in 9 alternate, submarine, surrogate 10 substitute, understudy 11 pinch-hitter

subaltern 4 aide 6 helper 9 assistant 10 lieutenant 11 subordinate

subconscious 3 dim 7 dawning 9 intuitive 10 subliminal 11 instinctive

subdivide 4 divide 7 split up 8 separate 9 partition

subdivision 3 arm 4 wing 6 branch 7 chapter, section 8 offshoot 11 development 12 neighborhood

subdue 3 bow 4 calm, curb, down, drub, ease, foil, mute, rout, trim, whip 5 allay, break, check, crush, floor, quell, salve, smash, still 6 deaden, defeat, master, mellow, muffle, reduce, soften, soothe, temper, thrash 7 appease, assuage, conquer, mollify, oppress, overrun, put down, relieve, slacken, subject, trample 8 mitigate, moderate, overcome, palliate, surmount, tone down, vanquish 9 meliorate, overpower, overwhelm, quiet down, soft-pedal, subjugate 10 ameliorate 11 triumph over 12 tranquillize

subdued 4 dull 5 cowed, muted, quiet 7 abashed, crushed, humbled, muffled, quelled 8 deadened, overcame 10 humiliated, indistinct, lackluster 11 intimidated, overpowered

subduer 6 victor, winner 9 conqueror, overcomer 10 subjugator, vanquisher 11 intimidator

subject 4 bare, case, gist, open, pith, text 5 field, issue, liege, motif, prone, study, theme, topic 6 affair, expose, liable, matter, submit, thesis, vassal 7 bound by, citizen, concern, exposed, lay open 8 business, disposed, follower, obedient, question 9 dependent, subjected, substance 10 answerable, discipline, in danger of, make liable, put through, vulnerable 11 stipulatory, subordinate, subservient, susceptible

subjection 11 subjugation 12 subservience 13 regimentation, subordination

subjective 5 inner 6 biased 7 partial 8 partisan, personal 9 emotional 10 individual, prejudiced 12 nonobjective

subjoin 5 add on, affix, annex 6 append, attach, tack on

subjugate 4 tame 5 crush, quell 6 subdue 7 conquer, put down 8 dominate, suppress, vanquish 10 overmaster

subjugation 6 chains, thrall 7 bondage, slavery 9 dominance, mastering, servitude, thralldom 10 conquering, domination 11 enslavement, vanquishing

subjugator 6 master, victor 7 subduer 9 conqueror, dominator 10 vanquisher 11 slavemaster

sublimate 4 turn 5 exalt, shift 6 divert, purify 7 channel, convert, elevate, ennoble 8 redirect, transfer 9 transform, transmute 12 spiritualize

sublime 4 high 5 grand, great, lofty, noble 6 superb 7 exalted, stately 8 elevated, imposing, majestic, splendid, terrific, very good 9 estimable, excellent, marvelous, wonderful 12 awe-inspiring, praiseworthy

submarine
invented by: 7 Holland
even keel: 4 Lake
torpedo: 8 Bushnell

submerge 4 dive, sink 5 douse, drown, flood, souse 6 deluge, engulf, go down, plunge 7 go under, immerse 8 inundate, pour over, submerse

submerse 5 drown 6 engulf 7 immerse 8 inundate, submerge

submersion 7 sinking 8 drowning 9 immersion 10 inundation 11 submergence

submission 8 giving in, meekness, tameness, yielding 9 handing in, obedience, passivity, surrender, tendering 10 compliance, remittance, submitting 11 passiveness 12 acquiescence, capitulation, presentation, subservience, tractability 13 nonresistance 14 submissiveness

submissive 4 meek, mild 6 docile, humble, pliant 7 dutiful, fawning, passive, servile, slavish 8 crawling, obedient, toadying, yielding 9 compliant, malleable, tractable, truckling 10 obsequious 11 acquiescent, bootlicking, complaisant, deferential, subservient, unassertive 12 capitulating, ingratiating, nonresisting 13 accommodating

submissiveness 8 docility, meekness 9 passivity 10 compliance 11 resignation 12 complaisance, tractability

submit 3 bow 4 bend, cede 5 agree, argue, claim, defer, kneel, offer, stoop, yield 6 accede, assert, commit, comply, give in, give up, resort, tender 7 contend, hold out, present, proffer, propose, succumb, suggest 8 back down, put forth 9 acquiesce, surrender, volunteer 10 capitulate, put forward 12 knuckle under

submit an offer 3 bid 6 tender 7 proffer, propose

submit to 4 bear, take 5 abide, brave, brook, stand 6 endure, suffer 7 stomach, undergo 8 stand for, tolerate 9 put up with

subnormal 3 bad, low 5 seedy, sorry 6 crummy, dismal, shabby, sleazy, subpar 7 abysmal 8 below par, inferior, mediocre, wretched 9 defective, deficient 10 inadequate, second-rate 11 below normal, substandard 12 insufficient

subordinate 4 help 5 lower 6 junior, lackey, lesser, menial, worker 7 servant, subject 8 hireling, inferior 9 ancillary, assistant, attendant, auxiliary, dependent, of low rank, outranked, secondary, subaltern, underling 10 subsidiary 11 subservient

subordination 10 subjection 11 inferiority, subjugation 12 subservience 13 regimentation

suborn 5 bribe 6 buy off, pay off

sub rosa 8 covertly, in secret, on the sly, secretly 9 in private, privately 12 off-the-record 14 confidentially 15 behind-the-scenes 17 behind closed doors

subscribe 4 help, sign 6 assent, chip in, donate 7 consent, endorse, support 8 hold with 9 undersign 10 contribute

subsequent 4 next 7 ensuing 9 following, proximate 10 consequent, succeeding, successive

subsequently 2 so 5 after, later, since 9 afterward, following 10 succeeding 12 consequently

subservient 6 docile, menial 7 fawning, servile, slavish, subject 8 cringing, toadying 9 accessory, ancillary, auxiliary, prostrate, truckling 10 obsequious, subsidiary 11 bootlicking, subordinate, sycophantic 12 contributory, ingratiating

subside 3 ebb, sag 4 calm, drop, ease, sink, wane 5 abate, let up 6 cave in, lessen, recede, settle, shrink 7 descend, dwindle 8 decrease, diminish, level off, melt away, moderate

subsidence 5 letup 6 easing, ebbing, waning 7 calming 9 abatement, dwindling, lessening, recession, shrinking 10 decreasing, inactivity, moderation 12 diminishment

subsidiary 5 extra, lower, minor 6 branch, junior, lesser 7 adjunct 8 addition, division, inferior 9 accessory, affiliate, auxiliary, secondary 10 additional, supplement 11 subordinate 12 supplemental 13 supplementary

subsidy 3 aid 4 gift 5 award, grant 7 backing, support 9 allotment, provision 10 fellowship, grant-in-aid, honorarium, subvention 11 scholarship, sponsorship 13 appropriation, assistantship

subsist 4 live 5 exist 7 survive 9 stay alive 11 feed oneself, support life 12 make ends meet 23 keep body and soul together

subsistence 6 living, upkeep 7 support 8 survival 10 livelihood, sustenance 11 maintenance, nourishment

substance 4 body, core, germ, gist, pith, soul 5 force, heart, means, money, sense, stuff 6 burden, import, intent, marrow, matter, riches, thrust, wealth 7 element, essence, keynote, purport, reality 8 backbone, material, property, solidity 9 actuality, affluence, basic idea, main point 10 ingredient 11 connotation, constituent, corporality 12 corporeality, quintessence 13 corporealness

substandard 3 bad 4 poor 5 awful, lousy 6 crummy, shoddy 8 below par, inferior, terrible 9 imperfect 10 second-rate 11 second-class 12 below average

substantial 3 big 4 firm, full 5 ample, bulky, large, massy, solid, sound 7 massive, sizable 8 abundant 9 plenteous, plentiful 10 monumental 12 considerable

substantiate 5 prove 6 verify 7 confirm, support, sustain 11 corroborate, demonstrate 12 authenticate

substantiated 6 proved, proven 7 factual 8 verified 9 supported 11 well-founded 12 corroborated, demonstrated, well-grounded 13 authenticated

substantiation 5 proof 8 evidence 11 affirmation 12 verification 13 corroboration, demonstration, documentation 14 authentication

substitute 3 act 6 backup, change, ersatz, fill in, switch 7 standby, stand in, stopgap 8 deputize, exchange, pinch-hit, take over 9 alternate, makeshift, surrogate, temporary 10 understudy 11 alternative, pinch hitter, replacement

substitution 5 shift 6 change, switch 8 exchange, swapping 9 variation 10 alteration 11 replacement

substructure 4 base 6 ground 10 foundation, groundwork 12 underpinning

subsume 5 cover 6 assume, deduce 7 explain, include, involve 8 consider 13 subcategorize

subterfuge 4 ruse, sham, wile 5 blind, dodge, guile, shift, trick 6 scheme 7 evasion 8 artifice, intrigue, pretense, scheming 9 casuistry, chicanery, deception, duplicity, imposture, sophistry, stratagem 10 camouflage, sneakiness 11 deviousness, evasiveness, game-playing, machination, make-believe, smoke screen

subtle, subtile 3 sly 4 cagy, deft, fine, foxy, keen, wily 5 light, quick, sharp, slick 6 artful, astute, clever, crafty, expert, shifty, shrewd, tricky 7 cunning, devious, elusive, refined 8 delicate, indirect, masterly, skillful 9 deceptive, designing, ingenious, underhand 10 discerning 11 understated 13 perspicacious, sophisticated 14 discriminating

Subtle
   character in: 12 The Alchemist
   author: 6 Jonson

subtleties 7 nuances 10 fine points 11 refinements 12 distinctions

subtract 6 deduct, detach, lessen, reduce, remove 8 decrease, diminish, take away, withdraw

subtraction 7 removal 8 decrease 9 deduction, lessening, reduction 10 diminution, taking away, withdrawal 11 diminishing

suburbs 8 environs, vicinity 9 outskirts, periphery, precincts

sub verbo 12 under the word 15 under the heading

subversion 4 fall, ruin 6 defeat, mutiny 8 disorder, sabotage 9 overthrow, rebellion 10 corruption, disruption 11 destruction

subversive 7 traitor 8 quisling 9 insurgent, seditious 10 incendiary, traitorous, treasonous 11 seditionary 12 collaborator 13 revolutionary 14 fifth columnist 15 insurrectionary 16 collaborationist

subvert 3 mar 4 ruin, undo 5 smash, spoil, upset, wreck 6 baffle, poison, ravage 7 despoil, destroy, disrupt, shatter 8 demolish, overturn 9 devastate, overthrow, undermine 11 contaminate

sub voce 21 under the specified word
   literally: 15 under the voice

succeed 3 hit, win 5 avail, catch, click 6 accede, do well, follow, move up 7 inherit, prevail, prosper, replace, triumph 8 make a hit, make good, supplant, take over 9 bear fruit, strike oil

succeed at 2 do 6 attain 7 execute, fulfill, perform, realize 8 carry out 9 make a go of 10 accomplish

succeeding 5 later 6 coming, future 7 ensuing 8 oncoming 9 following, impending, posterior 10 consequent, subsequent, successive

succeed to 6 follow 7 inherit 15 ascend the throne

succes d'estime 15 critical success

success 3 hit 4 fame 5 smash 7 triumph, victory 8 conquest 9 affluence 10 ascendancy, attainment, prosperity 11 achievement, advancement, fulfillment, good fortune

successful 4 rich 6 proven 7 perfect, wealthy, well-off 8 achieved, affluent, complete, fruitful, thriving 9 effective 10 prosperous, triumphant 11 efficacious, flourishing 12 accomplished, acknowledged

successful completion 7 success, victory, winning 9 execution 10 making good 11 achievement, culmination, fulfillment, realization 12 consummation 14 accomplishment

succession 3 run 5 chain, cycle, round, train 6 course, series 8 sequence 9 accession 10 assumption, procession, stepping-up, taking over 11 inheritance, progression

successive 7 ensuing 10 continuous, succeeding 11 consecutive

successor 4 heir 5 donee 7 devisee, heiress, heritor, legatee 8 follower, parcener 9 heritress, joint heir 10 coparcener, substitute 11 beneficiary, replacement, reversioner 12 heir apparent

succinct 4 neat 5 brief, crisp, pithy, short, terse, tight 6 direct, gnomic 7 clipped, compact, concise, summary 9 condensed 10 aphoristic, to the point 12 epigrammatic

succinctness 7 brevity 9 crispness, terseness 11 compactness, conciseness 12 condensation

succor 3 aid 4 help 5 nurse 6 assist, back up, relief, shield, wait on 7 comfort, nurture, protect, relieve, support, sustain 8 befriend 10 assistance, minister to, sustenance, take care of 11 give a lift to, helping hand, lend a hand to, maintenance 13 accommodation

succulent 5 juicy 6 fleshy 9 toothsome 10 appetizing

succumb 3 die 5 yield 6 accede, expire, give in, submit 7 defer to, give way, go under 8 pass away 9 surrender 10 capitulate, comply with 12 fall victim to

such as
   Latin: 2 eg 13 exempli gratia

such is life
   French: 9 c'est la vie

sucker 3 sap 4 boob, butt, dupe, fool, goat, gull, jerk, mark 5 chump, patsy 6 pigeon, victim 7 cat's-paw, fall guy 8 easy mark, fair game, pushover 9 schlemiel, soft touch 11 sitting duck

Sucker State
   nickname of: 8 Illinois

suck up 6 absorb, soak up 7 drink in 8 sponge up 9 swallow up

Sucre
   legal capital of: 7 Bolivia

Sudan
   capital/largest city: 8 Khartoum
   others: 3 Waw, Yei 4 Juba 5 Kosti, Meroe, Nyala, Obeid, Opari, Segon 6 Atbara, Suakin 7 Aluboyd, Elobeid, Geneina, Kassala, Malakal 8 Elfasher, Omdurman 9 al-Ubayyid, Elgeneina, Port Sudan, Wad Medani
   division: 7 Jonglei 9 Upper Nile 12 Bahr el Ghazal 16 Eastern Equatoria, Western Equatoria
   ancient kingdom: 4 Alwa, Funj, Kush 7 Maqurra
   measure: 2 ud
   monetary unit: 5 pound 8 piastres
   weight: 5 habba
   lake: 2 No 4 Chad, Toad 6 Nasser
   mountain: 4 Nuba 7 Imatong 9 Dongotona 10 Jabal Marra, Jebel Marra 18 Ethiopian Highlands
   highest point: 7 Kinyeti
   river: 4 Nile 5 Sobat 6 Atbara 8 Blue Nile 9 White Nile 10 Bahr el-Arab 11 Bahr el-Jebel 12 Bahr el-Ghazal
   sea: 3 Red
   physical feature:
   desert: 6 Libyan, Nubian
   gum forest: 8 Kordofan
   plain: 6 Gezira
   sandstorm: 6 haboob
   plateau: 8 Kordufan
   swamp: 4 Sudd
   people: 3 Bor, Dor, Fur 4 Arab, Bari, Beri, Bobo, Daza, Egba, Fula, Golo, Nuba, Nuer, Poul, Sere 5 Anuak, Bongo, Dinka, Fulah, Hausa, Joluo, Junje, Mosgu, Mossi, Negro, Tibbu, Volta 6 Acholi, Azande, Gurusi, Hamite, Lotuho, Makari, Nilote, Nubian, Senufo, Surhai, Tuareg 7 Balante, Baqqara, Gubayna, Jaaliin, Nilotes, Shilluk, Songhai, Songhay, Songhoi, Sourhai 8 Kababish, Mandingo, Menkiera 9 Sarakille 10 Gurmantshi, Shaiquiyya
   leader: 5 Mahdi 9 al-Nimeiry 10 Mehemet Ali 22 Jaafar Mohammed al-Nemery
   language: 2 Ga 3 Efe, Ewe, Ibo, Kru, Vak, Vei 4 Efik, Mole, Tshi 6 Arabic, Nubian, Yoruba 7 English 8 Mandango, Mandingo 9 Ta Bedawie
   religion: 5 Islam 7 animism 12 Christianity
   place:
   canal: 7 Jonglei
   dam: 6 Sennar 8 Roseires 10 Jebel Aulia
   temple: 4 Lion
   tomb: 5 Mahdi
   feature:
   boat: 6 murkab
   food: 4 dura 5 dukhn, kisra

Sudanese Republic see 4 Mali

sudden 4 rash 5 hasty, quick, rapid 6 abrupt, speedy 7 instant 9 immediate, impetuous 10 surprising, unexpected, unforeseen 11 precipitate, unlooked-for 13 instantaneous, unanticipated, unforeseeable

sudden development
   French: 10 coup de main

suddenly 7 quickly 8 abruptly, in no time 9 all at once, instantly, on the spot 11 in an instant 12 all of a sudden, unexpectedly 13 at short notice 14 without warning 20 on the spur-of-the-moment 21 in the twinkling of an eye

sudden movement 4 dart, jolt 5 flash, spurt

sudden noise 3 pop 4 bang, clap, slam 5 burst, crash 6 report 9 explosion

Sudermann, Hermann
   author of: 5 Honor 8 Dame Care 14 The Song of Songs

suds 3 ale 4 beer, brew, foam 5 draft, froth, lager 10 malt liquor

sue 3 beg 4 pray 5 plead 6 appeal 7 beseech, entreat, implore 8 petition 9 importune 10 supplicate

Sue, Eugene (Marie-Joseph)
   author of: 15 The Wandering Jew 19 The Mysteries of Paris

suffer 4 ache, bear, hurt, pine 5 stand 6 endure, grieve, lament 7 agonize, despair, drop off, fall off, stomach, sustain, undergo 8 bear with, feel pain, tolerate 9 go through, put up with, withstand 10 be impaired 11 deteriorate

suffer for 6 pay for 8 atone for 9 answer for

suffering 3 woe 4 ache, care, hurt, pain, pang 5 agony, dolor, grief, throe, trial 6 misery, sorrow, twinge 7 anguish, anxiety, torment, torture, travail 8 distress, soreness 9 heartache 10 affliction, discomfort, heavy heart, irritation 11 tribulation

suffice 2 do 4 last, meet, pass 5 avail, get by, serve 6 answer, make do 7 fulfill, qualify, satisfy

sufficiency 6 enough, plenty 7 surfeit 8 adequacy 9 abundance, ampleness, profusion

sufficient 5 ample 6 enough, plenty 7 copious, minimal 8 abundant, adequate 9 plenteous, plentiful 11 up to the mark 12 satisfactory

suffocate 3 gag 5 choke 6 quench, stifle 7 garrote, smother 8 snuff out, strangle, throttle 10 asphyxiate, extinguish

suffuse 4 fill, soak 5 cover, steep 6 infuse 7 diffuse, overrun, pervade 8 overflow, permeate, saturate 9 transfuse 10 impregnate, infiltrate, overspread

Sugar State
   nickname of: 9 Louisiana

sugary 5 mushy, sweet 6 syrupy 7 cloying, fulsome, gushing, honeyed, mawkish 8 cajoling, unctuous 10 flattering, saccharine

suggest 3 bid 4 move, urge 5 imply, posit 6 advise, hint at, submit 7 advance, counsel, propose 8 advocate, indicate, intimate, propound 9 give a clue, recommend 16 lead one to believe

suggested 6 hinted 7 implied, oblique 8 implicit, indirect, possible, proposed

suggestion 3 dab, tip 4 dash, hint, tint 5 grain, shade, taste, tinge, touch, trace 6 advice, urging 7 counsel, feeling, pointer, soupcon 9 prompting, suspicion 10 intimation, sprinkling 11 exhortation 14 recommendation

suggestive 4 lewd, racy 5 bawdy, loose 6 risque, sexual, wanton 8 allusive, improper, indecent, off-color, prurient, unseemly 9 evocative, remindful, seductive, shameless 10 expressive, indelicate, licentious 11 provocative, reminiscent, stimulating

sui generis 6 unique 12 of her own kind, of his own kind, of its own kind 14 of their own kind

sui juris 14 of one's own right 31 capable of managing one's own affairs 36 capable of assuming legal responsibility

suit 3 fit 4 duds, garb, plea, togs 5 befit, court, getup, habit, match 6 appeal, attire, become, beseem, follow, livery, oblige, outfit, please, prayer, wooing 7 apparel, begging, clothes, content, costume, delight, gladden, gratify, raiment, satisfy, uniform 8 clothing, entreaty, jell with, make glad, petition 9 addresses, agree with, conform to, courtship, do one good, overtures, tally with, trappings 10 accord with, attentions, comply with, fall in with, habiliment, lovemaking, square with 11 accommodate, go along with 12 be becoming to, blandishment, correspond to, dovetail with, solicitation, supplication 13 accoutrements, be agreeable to, harmonize with 14 be acceptable to, be convenient to 15 be appropriate to 16 be appropriate for

suitable 3 apt, fit 4 meet 5 right 6 proper, seemly, worthy 7 apropos, fitting, germane 8 adequate, becoming, relevant 9 befitting, congruous, cut out for, pertinent, qualified 10 applicable, seasonable 11 appropriate 12 commensurate

suitcase 3 bag 4 grip 6 valise 7 satchel 8 knapsack, rucksack 9 duffel bag, gladstone, two-suiter 11 portmanteau 12 overnight bag, traveling bag

suite 3 set 4 flat 5 chain, court, group, rooms, round 6 convoy, series 7 company, cortege, retinue 8 servants 9 apartment, followers, following 10 attendants 11 progression

suited 3 fit 7 adapted, attired, clothed, dressed, good for, matched 8 adjusted, agreeing, becoming 9 agreeable 11 appropriate, harmonizing

suit of armor 4 mail 5 armor 9 chain mail 10 coat of mail

suitor 4 beau, love 5 flame, lover, swain, wooer 6 fellow 7 admirer, gallant 8 young man 9 boyfriend 10 sweetheart

sulfur
  chemical symbol: 1 S

sulk 4 crab, fret, fume, mope, pout 5 brood, chafe, frown, grump, scowl 6 glower, grouch 7 grumble 8 be in a pet, be miffed, be put out, be sullen, look glum 9 be in a huff 11 be resentful 12 be out of humor

sulky 6 morose, sullen 7 pouting 8 petulant

sullen 4 blue, dark, glum, grim, sore, sour 5 cross, heavy, moody, sulky, surly 6 crabby, dismal, dreary, gloomy, grumpy, morose, somber, touchy 7 crabbed, doleful, forlorn, grouchy, peevish 8 brooding, desolate, dolorous, funereal, mournful, petulant, scowling 9 cheerless, glowering, resentful, saturnine, splenetic, unamiable 10 depressing, foreboding, ill-humored, ill-natured, melancholy, out of humor, out of sorts, unsociable 11 ill-tempered 13 temperamental
  French: 8 farouche

sullied 5 dirty 6 impure, soiled 7 defiled, stained, unclean 9 tarnished

Sullivan, Elizabeth
  real name of: 14 Elsa Lanchester

Sullivan, John Florence
  real name of: 9 Fred Allen

Sullivan, John L (Lawrence)
  nickname: 15 Boston Strong Boy
  sport: 6 boxing
  class: 11 heavyweight
  fought: 12 bareknuckled

Sullivan, Louis H
  architect of: 16 Guaranty (now Prudential) Building (Buffalo NY) 18 Auditorium Building (Chicago), Wainwright Building (St Louis MO) 21 Carson Pirie Scott Store (Chicago), Stock Exchange Building (Chicago), Merchants' National Bank (Grinnell, IA), National Farmers' Bank (Owatonna, MN)
  principle: 21 "form follows function"
  student: 16 Frank Lloyd Wright

Sullivan, Pat
  creator/artist of: 11 Felix the Cat

Sullivan's Travels
  director: 14 Preston Sturges
  cast: 10 Joel McCrea 12 Veronica Lake 13 Robert Warwick 15 William Demarest

sully 4 ruin, soil, spot 5 dirty, spoil, stain 6 befoul, defame, defile, smudge 7 begrime, besmear, blemish, corrupt, pollute, tarnish 8 disgrace, dishonor 10 adulterate 11 contaminate

Sully, Thomas
  born: 7 England 10 Horncastle
  artwork: 13 Queen Victoria 23 The Passage of the Delaware 28 Colonel Thomas Handasyd Perkins 29 Washington Crossing the Delaware

sultan 4 king 5 ruler 7 emperor, monarch 9 sovereign

sultana 5 grape 6 raisin 7 empress 11 sultan's wife

sultry 3 hot **4** sexy **5** close, humid, muggy **6** erotic, stuffy, sweaty **7** sensual **8** stifling **10** oppressive, sweltering, voluptuous **11** provocative, suffocating

sum 4 cash, coin, jack **5** bread, bucks, dough, funds, score, tally, whole **6** amount, moolah **7** lettuce, measure **8** currency, entirety, quantity, sum total, totality **9** aggregate, summation **12** entire amount **13** amount of money

sumac 4 Rhus
  varieties: 5 dwarf, lemon, scrub, sugar, swamp **6** desert, laurel, poison, smooth, velvet **7** scarlet, shining, tanner's, tobacco, wing-rib **8** fragrant, lemonade, Sicilian, staghorn, Venetian **9** elm-leaved, evergreen, Virginian **11** small-leaved **12** sweet-scented

sum and substance 4 core, crux, gist, guts, meat **5** heart **7** essence **10** brass tacks **11** nitty-gritty

Sumatra
  chevrotain: 4 napu
  city: 5 Medan **6** Padang **9** Palembang
  country: 9 Indonesia
  crop: 3 tea **6** coffee, rubber
  currency: 6 rupiah
  empire: 9 Srivijaya
  highest point: 10 Mt Kerintji
  inhabitant: 5 Batak, Malay **11** Minangkabau
  mountain range: 7 Barisan
  river: 4 Musi, Siak **6** Asahan
  squirrel shrew: 4 tana
  strait: 5 Sunda **7** Malacca

Sumerian Mythology *see* **19** Babylonian Mythology

Summa Catholicae Fidei Contra Gentiles
  author: 13 Thomas Aquinas

summa cum laude 17 with highest praise

Summanus
  origin: 5 Roman
  god of: 13 thunderstorms

summarily 6 at once **7** quickly **8** directly, promptly, speedily **9** forthwith, on the spot **11** arbitrarily, immediately, straightway **12** straightaway, with dispatch, without delay **13** at short notice, precipitately **14** unhesitatingly **20** on the spur of the moment

summarize 5 sum up **6** digest **7** abridge, outline **8** abstract, compress, condense **9** capsulize, epitomize, synopsize **10** abbreviate **11** concentrate **12** recapitulate

summary 4 curt **5** brief, hasty, rapid, short, terse, token **6** apercu, digest, precis, resume, sketch, sudden, survey **7** concise, cursory, epitome, hurried, rundown **8** abridged, abstract, analysis, succinct, syllabus, synopsis **9** breakdown, condensed **10** abridgment, peremptory **11** perfunctory **12** abbreviation, condensation, short version **13** instantaneous

Summa Theologiae
  author: 13 Thomas Aquinas

summation 5 total **6** review **7** summary **8** addition **9** reckoning **19** concluding statement

Summer and Smoke
  author: 17 Tennessee Williams
  director: 14 Peter Glenville
  cast: 9 Una Merkel **10** Rita Moreno **12** Earl Holliman **13** Geraldine Page **14** Laurence Harvey

summer fruit
  goddess of: 5 Carpo

summerhouse 5 arbor, cabin, kiosk **6** cabana, gazebo, pagoda **7** cottage

Summerson, Esther
  character in: 10 Bleak House
  author: 7 Dickens

Summertime
  director: 9 David Lean
  based on story by: 14 Arthur Laurents (The Time of the Cuckoo)
  cast: 10 Isa Miranda **13** Darren McGavin, Rossano Brazzi **16** Katharine Hepburn
  setting: 6 Venice

summery 3 hot **4** warm **5** balmy, close, humid, muggy, sunny **6** stuffy, sultry, torrid, vernal **8** aestival, roasting, stifling, sunshiny **9** scorching, temperate **10** oppressive, summerlike

summit 3 tip, top **4** acme, apex, peak **5** crest, crown **6** apogee, climax, height, vertex, zenith **8** pinnacle **11** culmination **12** highest point **13** crowning point

summon 4 call **5** rouse **6** beckon, call on, draw on, gather, invoke, muster, strain **7** call for, call out, command, send for **8** activate, subpoena **9** call forth **12** call together **14** call into action, serve with a writ

summons 4 call **8** citation, subpoena **12** notification

summon up 4 stir **5** evoke **6** arouse, excite **7** collect, marshal, provoke **8** assemble **9** call forth, stimulate

summum bonum 9 chief good **11** highest good

sumptuous 4 dear, posh, rich **5** grand, plush, regal **6** costly, deluxe, lavish, superb **7** elegant **8** splendid **9** elaborate, expensive, luxurious **10** exorbitant, munificent **11** extravagant, magnificent, spectacular

sumptuousness 4 luxe **6** luxury **8** elegance, grandeur, richness, splendor **12** magnificence **13** expensiveness, luxuriousness

sum total 6 amount **8** totality **9** aggregate **11** final result

sum up 3 add **5** tally, total, tot up **6** reckon **7** compute, count up **9** calculate, enumerate, summarize

sun
  god of: 2 Ra, Re **3** Sol, Utu **5** Horus **6** Apollo, Helios **7** Shamesh **8** Hyperion

Sun Also Rises, The
  author: 15 Ernest Hemingway
  character: 10 Bill Gorton, Jake Barnes, Robert Cohn **11** Pedro Romero **15** Lady Brett Ashley, Michael (Mike) Campbell

sunbathe 3 tan **4** bask **12** soak up the sun **13** catch some rays

Sunday
 means: 11 day of the sun
 heavenly body: 3 sun
 day of: 4 rest 7 worship 8 blue laws
 observance: 16 Christian Sabbath
 French: 8 dimanche
 Italian: 8 domenica
 Spanish: 7 domingo
 German: 7 sonntag

Sunday best 6 finery 8 glad rags 11 fine clothes 16 best bib and tucker

Sunday Morning
 author: 14 Wallace Stevens

sunder 4 rend, rive 5 crack, sever 6 cleave, divide 7 separate 9 tear apart 10 break in two 11 break in half

sundown 4 dusk 6 sunset 7 evening 8 eventide, twilight 9 nightfall

Sundowners, The
 director: 13 Fred Zinnemann
 cast: 11 Deborah Kerr, Dina Merrill, Glynis Johns 12 Peter Ustinov 13 Robert Mitchum
 setting: 9 Australia

sundry 4 many 5 mixed 6 divers, motley, myriad, varied 7 diverse, several, various 8 assorted, manifold, numerous 9 different 10 dissimilar 12 multifarious 13 heterogeneous, miscellaneous

sun-filled 4 fair 5 clear, sunny 6 bright, cheery 8 cheerful 9 cloudless

sunfish 5 dwarf, perch, pigmy, sunny 6 redear 7 lepomis, longear, teleost 8 bluegill, sailboat 9 blackband 10 Sacramento 11 bluespotted, centrarchid, pumpkinseed, yellowbelly

sunflower 10 Helianthus 12 Balsamorhiza
 varieties: 4 ashy 5 giant, showy, stiff, swamp 6 common, desert, Oregon 7 dark-eye, Mexican 8 thin-leaf 10 Maximilian 12 cucumber-leaf

Sunflower State
 nickname of: 6 Kansas

sunless 4 dark, dull, gray, hazy 5 bleak, foggy, misty, murky, rainy 6 cloudy, dismal, dreary, gloomy, leaden, somber 8 overcast 9 cheerless 10 depressing

sunny 4 fair, fine 5 clear, happy, jolly, merry 6 blithe, breezy, bright, cheery, genial, jovial, joyful, joyous, sunlit 7 affable, amiable, buoyant, shining, smiling 8 cheerful, sunshiny 9 brilliant, cloudless, sparkling, unclouded 10 optimistic 12 lighthearted

sunrise 4 dawn 5 sunup 6 aurora 7 dawning 8 cockcrow, daybreak, daylight 10 break of day, crepuscule, newborn day 15 dawn's early light 16 rosy-fingered dawn

sunset 4 dusk 7 sundown 8 blue hour, eventide, gloaming, twilight 9 nightfall 10 close of day, crepuscule

Sunset Boulevard
 director: 11 Billy Wilder
 cast: 8 Jack Webb 9 Fred Clark 11 Hedda Hopper 12 Buster Keaton 13 Cecil B DeMille, Gloria Swanson (Norma Desmond), William Holden 16 Erich von Stroheim

Sunset State
 nickname of: 6 Oregon

sunshade 3 hat 5 visor 6 awning 7 parasol, roundel 8 sombrero, umbrella 9 sunscreen

Sunshine State
 nickname of: 7 Florida 9 New Mexico

sunstone
 species: 8 feldspar

suntan 3 tan 5 brown 6 bronze 7 sunburn

suo jure 14 in one's own right

suo loco 14 in one's own place 19 in one's rightful place

Suomen Tasavalta see 7 Finland

Suomi see 7 Finland

sup 3 eat, sip 4 dine, feed 5 drink, feast, supra 6 absorb, supper, supply 7 consume 8 superior 10 supplement 11 superlative 13 supplementary

Supai see 9 Havasupai

super 4 A-one, fine 5 grand, great, prime, prize, swell 6 grade-A, superb, tip-top 7 capital 8 peerless, superior, terrific, top-notch 9 excellent, fantastic, first-rate, marvelous, matchless, non pareil, superfine, wonderful 10 first-class, tremendous, unexcelled, world-class 11 outstanding, superlative 12 incomparable 13 extraordinary

superabound 4 teem 5 swarm 6 thrive 7 burgeon 8 be rich in, flourish, overflow

superabundance 4 glut, riot 5 flood, spate 6 deluge, excess, plenty 7 surfeit, surplus 8 overdose, overflow, pleonasm, plethora 9 avalanche 10 inundation, oversupply, redundance 11 superfluity 12 extravagance 13 overabundance 14 more than enough
 French: 19 embarras de richesses

superabundant 4 lush 6 lavish 7 copious, profuse, teeming 8 swarming, thriving 9 exuberant, luxuriant 10 burgeoning 11 flourishing, overflowing

superb 4 A-one, rare, rich 5 elect, grand, regal 6 choice, costly, deluxe, golden, lordly, select, tip-top 7 elegant, stately 8 gorgeous, imposing, laudable, majestic, peerless, precious, princely, splendid, topnotch, very fine 9 admirable, excellent, expensive, exquisite, first-rate, luxurious, marvelous, matchless, priceless, sumptuous, top-drawer 10 first-class 11 crackerjack, magnificent 12 breathtaking, praiseworthy 15 of the first water

Super Bowl
 1967:
 winner: 15 Green Bay Packers
 loser: 16 Kansas City Chiefs
 site: 8 Coliseum 10 Los Angeles
 1968:
 winner: 15 Green Bay Packers
 loser: 14 Oakland Raiders
 site: 5 Miami 10 Orange Bowl
 1969:
 winner: 11 New York Jets
 loser: 14 Baltimore Colts
 site: 5 Miami 10 Orange Bowl
 1970:
 winner: 16 Kansas City Chiefs
 loser: 16 Minnesota Vikings

site: 10 New Orleans 13 Tulane Stadium
1971:
winner: 14 Baltimore Colts
loser: 13 Dallas Cowboys
site: 5 Miami 10 Orange Bowl
1972:
winner: 13 Dallas Cowboys
loser: 13 Miami Dolphins
site: 10 New Orleans 13 Tulane Stadium
1973:
winner: 13 Miami Dolphins
loser: 18 Washington Redskins
site: 8 Coliseum 10 Los Angeles
1974:
winner: 13 Miami Dolphins
loser: 16 Minnesota Vikings
site: 7 Houston 11 Rice Stadium
1975:
winner: 18 Pittsburgh Steelers
loser: 16 Minnesota Vikings
site: 10 New Orleans 13 Tulane Stadium
1976:
winner: 18 Pittsburgh Steelers
loser: 13 Dallas Cowboys
site: 5 Miami 10 Orange Bowl
1977:
winner: 14 Oakland Raiders
loser: 16 Minnesota Vikings
site: 8 Pasadena, Rose Bowl
1978:
winner: 13 Dallas Cowboys
loser: 13 Denver Broncos
site: 9 Superdome 10 New Orleans
1979:
winner: 18 Pittsburgh Steelers
loser: 13 Dallas Cowboys
site: 5 Miami 10 Orange Bowl
1980:
winner: 18 Pittsburgh Steelers
loser: 14 Los Angeles Rams
site: 8 Pasadena, Rose Bowl
1981:
winner: 14 Oakland Raiders
loser: 18 Philadelphia Eagles
site: 9 Superdome 10 New Orleans
1982:
winner: 23 San Francisco Forty-Niners
loser: 17 Cincinnati Bengals
site: 7 Pontiac 10 Silverdome
1983:
winner: 18 Washington Redskins
loser: 13 Miami Dolphins
site: 8 Pasadena, Rose Bowl
1984:
winner: 17 Los Angeles Raiders
loser: 18 Washington Redskins
site: 12 Tampa Stadium
1985:
winner: 23 San Francisco Forty-Niners
loser: 13 Miami Dolphins
site: 8 Palo Alto 15 Stanford Stadium
1986:
winner: 12 Chicago Bears
loser: 18 New England Patriots
site: 9 Superdome 10 New Orleans
1987:
winner: 13 New York Giants

loser: 13 Denver Broncos
site: 8 Pasadena, Rose Bowl
1988:
winner: 18 Washington Redskins
loser: 13 Denver Broncos
site: 8 San Diego 17 Jack Murphy Stadium
1989:
winner: 23 San Francisco Forty-Niners
loser: 17 Cincinnati Bengals
site: 5 Miami 16 Joe Robbie Stadium
1990:
winner: 23 San Francisco Forty-Niners
loser: 13 Denver Broncos
site: 9 Superdome 10 New Orleans
1991:
winner: 13 New York Giants
loser: 12 Buffalo Bills
site: 5 Tampa 12 Tampa Stadium
1992:
winner: 18 Washington Redskins
loser: 12 Buffalo Bills
site: 9 Metrodome 11 Minneapolis
1993:
winner: 13 Dallas Cowboys
loser: 12 Buffalo Bills
site: 8 Pasadena, Rose Bowl
1994:
winner: 13 Dallas Cowboys
loser: 12 Buffalo Bills
site: 7 Atlanta 11 Georgia Dome

supercilious 5 proud 6 lordly, snooty, uppity 7 haughty, pompous, stuck-up 8 arrogant, prideful, snobbish 10 disdainful 11 egotistical, magisterial, overbearing, patronizing 12 vainglorious 13 condescending, high-and-mighty, self-important

superciliousness 4 airs 7 hauteur 8 snobbery 9 arrogance, pomposity 10 lordliness, snootiness 11 haughtiness 12 snobbishness 14 disdainfulness

superficial 4 slim 5 faint, outer, silly, trite 6 flimsy, hollow, myopic, slight 7 cursory, minimal, nodding, partial, passing, shallow, summary, surface 8 exterior, mindless, skin-deep 9 desultory, frivolous 10 incomplete 11 empty-headed, perfunctory 12 lacking depth, narrow-minded, on the surface, shortsighted

superficiality 6 myopia 9 frivolity 11 cursoriness, shallowness 13 desultoriness 16 narrow-mindedness, shortsightedness

superfine 4 A-one 6 choice, grade-A, superb, tip-top 8 superior, top-notch 9 excellent, extra fine, first-rate 10 first-class 11 outstanding, overrefined, superlative 13 extraordinary

superfluity 3 fat 5 extra, frill 6 excess, luxury 7 greater, surfeit, surplus 8 overflow, overmuch, plethora 11 gingerbread 12 extravagance 13 embellishment 14 superabundance

superfluous 5 extra, spare 6 excess 7 surplus 8 needless 9 excessive, redundant 10 extraneous, gratuitous, pleonastic 11 inessential, unnecessary 12 nonessential, overgenerous 13 superabundant, supernumerary 14 supererogatory

superhuman 4 epic 5 great 6 divine, heroic 7 godlike, supreme 8 superior 9 herculean, unearthly 10 miraculous, omnipotent 12 otherworldly, supermundane, supernatural, supranatural, transcendent 13 preternatural

Superi
  origin: 5 Roman
  collective name for: 4 gods

superintend 3 run 4 boss 6 direct, govern, manage 7 oversee 9 supervise, watch over 10 administer 12 administrate, have charge of

superintendence 6 charge 7 bossing, running 9 direction, governing 10 leadership, management, overseeing 12 jurisdiction 14 administration

superintendent 4 boss, head 5 chief 6 warden 7 foreman, headman, manager, proctor, steward 8 director, guardian, overseer 9 custodian 10 supervisor

superior 4 boss, fine 5 chief 6 better, choice, deluxe, leader, lordly, senior 7 greater, haughty, notable 8 arrogant, foremost, higher-up, peerless, snobbish 9 commander, excellent, first-rate, imperious, matchless, nonpareil, unrivaled 10 inimitable, noteworthy, preeminent, supervisor 11 exceptional, illustrious, patronizing 12 incomparable, more advanced, vainglorious 13 condescending, distinguished, high-and-mighty
  French: 13 par excellence

superlative 4 best 5 crack, prime 6 expert 7 supreme 8 foremost, greatest, peerless, superior 9 exquisite, first-rate, matchless, nonpareil, paramount, unequaled, unmatched, unrivaled 10 consummate, preeminent, surpassing 11 magnificent, unsurpassed 12 incomparable, transcendent, unparalleled 15 of the first water 17 of the highest order

superman
  German: 10 Ubermensch

Superman
  creator: 11 Jerry Siegel
  character: 4 Lara 5 Jor-el, Kal-el 8 Eben Kent, Lois Lane, Sy Horton 9 Clark Kent 10 Jimmy Olsen, Martha Kent, Perry White 22 Inspector Bill Henderson 23 Professor JJ Pepperwinkle
  place: 7 Krypton 10 Metropolis, Smallville 14 telephone booth
  nickname: 10 Man of Steel
  director: 13 Richard Donner
  cast: 9 Glenn Ford, Ned Beatty 11 Gene Hackman 12 Jackie Cooper, Margot Kidder (Lois Lane), Marlon Brando 14 Valérie Perrine 16 Christopher Reeve

supernatural 6 mystic, occult 7 psychic 9 spiritual, unearthly 10 miraculous, paranormal 12 otherworldly, supranatural 13 preternatural, superphysical 14 transcendental

superpatriotism 8 jingoism 10 chauvinism 11 nationalism

supersede 7 discard, replace, succeed 8 displace, set aside, supplant

supervise 4 boss, head 5 guide 6 direct, govern, handle, manage, survey 7 conduct, control, oversee 8 regulate 9 look after, watch over 10 administer 11 preside over, superintend 12 have charge of

supervision 6 orders 7 control 8 guidance 9 direction 10 governance, government, management, regulation 12 surveillance 15 superintendence

supervisor 4 boss, head 5 chief 7 foreman, manager, steward 8 director, overseer 9 commander 13 administrator 14 superintendent

supper club 4 cafe 6 bistro 7 cabaret 9 nightclub, night spot

supplant 6 depose 7 replace 8 displace 9 supersede 14 take the place of

supple 5 lithe 6 limber, pliant 7 elastic, lissome, plastic, pliable 8 amenable, bendable, flexible, graceful, yielding 9 adaptable, compliant, malleable, tractable 10 submissive 11 acquiescent, complaisant, coordinated

supplement 5 add to, annex, extra, rider 6 extend, insert 7 adjunct, augment, codicil, section 8 addendum, addition, appendix, increase 9 added part, corollary, extension 10 attachment, complement, postscript 12 augmentation

supplementary 5 added, extra 6 backup 7 added on, reserve 8 appended, attached, expanded, extended 9 ancillary, auxiliary, enlarging, secondary 10 additional, amplifying, augmenting 11 subordinate 13 complementary

suppliant 5 asker 6 beggar, cadger, seeker, suitor 7 almsman 8 claimant 9 almswoman, appellant, beseecher, entreater, mendicant 10 petitioner, supplicant 11 supplicator

Suppliants, The
  author: 9 Aeschylus
  character: 6 Danaus 8 Pelasgus 19 Fifty Sons of Aegyptus 20 Fifty Maiden Daughters

Suppliants, The
  author: 9 Euripides
  character: 6 Aethra, Evadne 7 Theseus 8 Adrastus

supplicate 3 ask, beg 4 pray 5 plead 6 ask for 7 entreat 8 appeal to, call upon, petition

supplication 3 cry 4 plea, suit 6 appeal, orison, prayer 7 bumming, cadging, request 8 entreaty, mooching, petition 10 invocation 11 application, beseechment, imploration, imprecation, panhandling 12 solicitation

supplies 4 gear 5 goods, items 8 material 9 equipment, foodstuff, trappings 10 provisions 13 accoutrements

supply 4 fund, give 5 cache, equip, grant, quota, stock, store, yield 6 bestow, outfit, render 7 deal out, deliver, furnish, present,

provide, reserve 9 providing, provision, reservoir **10** allocation, come up with, contribute, furnishing **12** provisioning

support 3 aid **4** base, bear, help, hold, keep, lift, pile, post, prop, stay **5** abide, boost, brace, brook, carry, favor, means, shore, stand **6** assist, back up, bear up, clinch, column, defend, endure, foster, hold up, pay for, pillar, ratify, second, succor, suffer, uphold, upkeep, verify **7** backing, bear out, bolster, comfort, confirm, defense, endorse, espouse, finance, further, keeping, nurture, shore up, sustain, warrant **8** abutment, accredit, advocacy, advocate, buttress, champion, espousal, maintain, pedestal, pilaster, sanction, strength, tolerate, vouch for **9** establish, guarantee, patronage, patronize, promotion, put up with, reinforce, stanchion, subsidize **10** assistance, livelihood, provide for, stand up for, stick up for, strengthen, sustenance, underwrite **11** buttressing, consolation, corroborate, countenance, furtherance, go along with, involvement, maintenance, subsistence **12** substantiate, underpinning **13** encouragement

supportable 9 endurable **10** defensible, verifiable **11** sustainable **12** demonstrable, maintainable

supporter 4 ally **6** backer, helper, patron **8** adherent, advocate, champion, defender, disciple, follower, partisan, upholder **10** benefactor, well-wisher **11** sympathizer

supposable 8 credible **9** thinkable **10** believable, imaginable **11** conceivable, perceivable

suppose 5 fancy, guess, judge, posit **6** assume, divine, gather, reckon **7** believe, imagine, presume, surmise, suspect **8** conceive, consider **9** predicate **11** hypothesize **14** take for granted

supposed 5 given **7** alleged, assumed **8** probable, putative **9** imaginary **11** conjectural, speculative, theoretical **12** hypothetical

supposition 4 idea, view **5** given, guess **6** belief, notion, theory, thesis **7** opinion, surmise **9** guesswork, postulate, suspicion **10** assumption, conjecture, hypothesis **11** predication, presumption, proposition, speculation

suppress 4 bury, curb, hide **5** check, crush, quash, quell, still **6** keep in, muffle, quench, squash, stifle, subdue **7** conceal, control, cover up, inhibit, put down, repress, silence, smother, squelch **8** hold back, keep back, overcome, restrain, restrict, snuff out, withhold **9** overpower **10** extinguish, keep secret, put an end to **11** hold in leash, keep private **12** put a damper on **13** put under wraps

suppressant 4 curb **5** brake **7** control **9** restraint

suppressed feelings 7 reserve **9** restraint **10** constraint, diffidence

supremacy 5 power **7** mastery, primacy **10** ascendancy, domination, precedence **11** omnipotence, paramountcy, preeminence, sovereignty, superiority **13** transcendency

supreme 4 tops **5** chief, first, prime **6** ruling **7** extreme, highest, leading, perfect, topmost **8** absolute, dominant, foremost, peerless **9** matchless, nonpareil, paramount, principal, sovereign, unequaled, unlimited, unmatched, unrivaled, uppermost **10** commanding, consummate, unexcelled **11** all-powerful, superlative, unqualified, unsurpassed **12** front-ranking, immeasurable, incomparable, second to none, unparalleled **13** unconditional

Supreme Court

Chief Justices: 3 Jay (John) **4** Taft (William Howard) **5** Chase (Salmon), Stone (Harlan Fiske), Taney (Roger Brooke), Waite (Morrison), White (Edward) **6** Burger (Warren), Fuller (Melville), Hughes (Charles Evans), Vinson (Frederick), Warren (Earl) **8** Marshall (John), Rutledge (John) **9** Ellsworth (Oliver), Rehnquist (William)

Associate Justices: 5 Black (Hugo), Story (Joseph), White (Byron) **6** Breyer (Stephen), Fortas (Abe), Holmes (Oliver Wendell), Powell (Lewis), Scalia (Antonin), Souter (David), Thomas (Clarence) **7** Brennan (William), Cardozo (Benjamin), Douglas (William O), Kennedy (Anthony), O'Connor (Sandra Day), Stevens (John), Stewart (Potter) **8** Blackmun (Harry), Brandeis (Louis), Ginsburg (Ruth Bader), Goldberg (Arthur), Marshall (Thurgood) **11** Frankfurter (Felix)

Cases: 15 Marbury v Madison **17** Gideon v Wainwright **18** McCulloch v Maryland **20** Griswold v Connecticut

 abortion: **8** Roe v Wade

 antitrust: **8** E C Knight **11** Standard Oil **15** Swift and Company **22** American Tobacco Company

 civil rights: **9** Bakke Case **15** Plessy v Ferguson **30** Brown v Board of Education of Topeka

 Japanese internment: **22** Korematsu v United States **24** Hirabayashi v United States

 rights of accused: **15** Miranda v Arizona **17** Escobedo v Illinois

 slavery: **13** Dred Scott Case **14** Scott v Sandford

surcease 4 quit, rest, stop **5** abate, cease, pause **7** die away, respite **8** conclude, leave off **11** come to an end, discontinue **17** come to a standstill

surcharge 3 tax **4** levy **6** excise, impost

surcingle 4 band, belt **5** girth **6** girdle **8** cincture

sure 4 fast, firm, true **5** solid, sound **6** stable, steady **7** assured, certain **8** accurate, fail-safe, faithful, flawless, positive, reliable, surefire, unerring **9** confident, con-

vinced, unfailing **10** dependable, infallible, undoubting **11** trustworthy **12** never-failing
sure bet **4** fact **5** cinch **7** reality **9** actuality, certainty, sure thing **13** inevitability **14** inescapability
surely **7** no doubt **8** of course, to be sure **9** assuredly, certainly, doubtless **10** by all means, definitely, for certain, infallibly, positively **11** come what may, indubitably, undoubtedly, without fail **12** emphatically, without doubt **14** unquestionably
sureness **6** surety **9** assurance, certainty, certitude **10** confidence **11** assuredness **12** positiveness **13** self-assurance **14** conclusiveness, self-confidence, self-possession
sure thing **4** fact **5** cinch **7** reality, sure bet **9** actuality, certainty **13** inevitability **14** inescapability
surety **4** bail, bond **8** sureness **9** certainty, certitude, guarantee **10** confidence **12** positiveness
surface **3** top **4** coat, face, skin **5** crust, shell **6** facade, finish, veneer **7** coating, outside **8** covering, exterior **11** superficies
Surface family

>   **characters in:** **19** The School for Scandal
>   **member:** **6** Joseph **7** Charles **9** Sir Oliver
>   **author:** **8** Sheridan

surfeit **4** cloy, glut, sate **5** gorge, stuff **6** excess **7** satiate, satisfy, surplus **8** overmuch, plethora **9** plenitude, profusion, repletion, satiation **10** oversupply, surplusage **11** exorbitance, overindulge, prodigality, superfluity **12** extravagance **13** overabundance **14** more than enough, superabundance **15** supersaturation
surfeited **4** full **5** sated **6** gorged **7** glutted, replete, stuffed **8** overfull, satiated **9** satisfied
surge **4** rush, wave **5** flood, swell **7** torrent
Suriname

>   **other name:** **7** Surinam **11** Dutch Guiana
>   **capital/largest city:** **10** Paramaribo
>   **others:** **6** Albina **7** Totness **9** Groningen **10** Brokopondo, Onverwacht **13** Nieuw Nickerie **14** Nieuw Amsterdam
>   **measure:** **7** ketting
>   **monetary unit:** **4** cent **5** guilder
>   **lake:** **14** Van Blommestein
>   **mountain:** **4** Emma **6** Kayser, Oranje **10** Tumuc-Humac, Wilhelmina **13** Eilerts Il Haan, Van Ach Van Wyck **15** Guiana Highlands
>   **highest point:** **10** Julianatop
>   **river:** **6** Maroni **7** Surinam **8** Nickerie, Suriname **9** Coppename **10** Courantijn, Courantyne, Tapanahoni
>   **ocean:** **8** Atlantic
>   **physical feature:**
>   *falls:* **7** Kaiteur
>   **people:** **4** Boni, Bush, Trio **5** Djuka, Dutch **6** Creole, Wayana **7** African, Chinese **10** Amerindian, Boschneger, West Indian **11** Asian Indian
>   *settler:* **22** Lord Willoughby of Parham

>   **language:** **5** Carib, Dutch, Hindi **6** Arawak **7** English **8** Javanese, Taki-Taki **10** Hindustani **11** Sranan Tongo **12** Sranang Tongo
>   **religion:** **5** Hindu, Islam **10** Protestant **13** Roman Catholic
>   **feature:**
>   *canoe:* **6** corial
>   *clothing:* **4** sari **5** dhoti **6** kamisa, sarong **10** koto-missie
>   *hat:* **3** fez
>   *hut:* **5** benab
>   *scarf:* **9** selendong
>   *tree:* **4** dali, lana, mora **5** dalli, genip, icica **7** acuyari, quassia **9** bethabara
>   **food:**
>   *drink:* **7** paiwari

surliness **8** ill humor, rudeness **9** bad temper **11** discourtesy, grouchiness **12** irascibility
surly **4** rude, sour **5** cross, gruff, harsh, testy **6** abrupt, crusty, grumpy, sullen, touchy **7** bearish, crabbed, grouchy, hostile, peevish, uncivil, waspish **8** choleric, churlish, insolent, petulant, snappish, snarling **9** irascible, splenetic, unamiable **10** ill-humored, ill-natured, unfriendly **11** bad-tempered **12** discourteous
surmise **4** deem, idea **5** guess, infer, judge, opine, posit, think **6** belief, notion **7** believe, imagine, opinion, presume, suppose, suspect, thought **8** conclude, consider, theorize **9** suspicion **10** assumption, conjecture, hypothesis, presuppose **11** hypothesize, presumption, speculation, supposition **13** shot in the dark
surmount **3** top **4** best **5** clear, climb, scale, worst **6** defeat, master **7** conquer, get over **8** overcome, vanquish **11** prevail over, triumph over **14** get the better of
surpass **3** top **4** beat, best **5** excel, outdo **6** exceed, outrun **7** eclipse **8** go beyond, outclass, outshine, outstrip, override **9** rise above, transcend **10** overshadow **11** go one better, leave behind, outdistance, triumph over **12** be better than, be superior to **13** have it all over
surplus **4** glut **5** extra **6** excess **7** overage, surfeit **8** leftover, overflow, plethora, residual **10** oversupply, surplusage **11** superfluity, superfluous **14** overproduction
surprise **4** stun **5** amaze, shock **6** ambush, wonder **7** astound, nonplus, set upon, stagger, startle, stupefy **8** astonish, confound, discover, dumfound, fall upon **9** amazement, bombshell, burst in on, dumbfound, take aback **10** defy belief, pounce upon, revelation, wonderment **11** flabbergast, incredulity **12** astonishment, take unawares **13** boggle the mind **16** bolt out of the blue
surprise attack

>   **French:** **10** coup de main

surrender **4** cede **5** forgo, let go, waive, yield **6** accede, forego, give up, render, submit, vacate **7** abandon, concede, forsake **8** delivery, forgoing, give over, giving up, hand over, part with, renounce, turn over, yielding 9 deliver up, foregoing 10 capitulate, relinquish, submission 11 lay down arms 12 capitulation, renunciation 14 relinquishment 15 throw in the towel 16 show the white flag

surreptitious 6 covert, hidden, secret, veiled 7 furtive 8 hush-hush, stealthy 9 concealed, secretive 10 undercover 11 clandestine

surrogate 6 acting, deputy 7 interim, stand-in 9 temporary 10 substitute 11 provisional

surround 4 belt, ring 5 hedge, hem in 6 circle, enfold, engird, girdle, shut in 7 close in, compass, enclose, envelop, fence in, hedge in 8 encircle 9 encompass 12 circumscribe

surrounding area 7 suburbs 8 environs, vicinity 9 outskirts, precincts

surroundings 5 scene 6 milieu 7 habitat, setting 8 ambience, environs 10 atmosphere, conditions 11 environment 13 circumstances

French: 11 mise en scene

Surt
origin: 12 Scandinavian
ruler of: 10 Muspelheim

surveillance 5 vigil, watch 8 scrutiny, trailing 11 observation 13 eavesdropping

survey 4 plot, poll, scan 5 gauge, graph, plumb, probe, scout, study 6 fathom, review 7 canvass, delimit, examine, inspect, measure, observe 8 analysis, block out, consider, look over, overview 10 scrutinize 11 contemplate, reconnoiter 12 pass in review 13 investigation

survival 5 relic 6 living 7 atavism, vestige 8 hangover 9 carry-over, throwback 11 subsistence 12 continuation, keeping alive

survive 4 last 5 abide, exist 6 endure, hang on, live on 7 hold out, outlast, outlive, persist, prevail, subsist 8 be extant, continue 9 keep alive 11 live through

surviving 6 extant 7 abiding, lasting 8 enduring, existent, existing, living on 9 hanging on, outliving, to be found 10 continuing, holding out, outlasting, persistent, persisting, subsisting 11 in existence 13 living through

Susann, Jacqueline
author of: 14 The Love Machine 15 Once Is Not Enough 16 Valley of the Dolls

Susanna
husband: 6 Joakim
accused of: 8 adultery
saved by: 6 Daniel

susceptible 4 open 5 prone 7 alive to, subject 8 liable to, sensible 9 sensitive 10 disposed to, responsive, vulnerable 11 conducive to, receptive to, sensitive to, sympathetic

suspect 5 doubt, fancy, guess, judge, opine, posit, think 7 believe, imagine, presume, suppose, surmise 8 distrust, misdoubt, mistrust, question, theorize 9 speculate 10 conjecture 11 hypothesize, wonder about 14 alleged culprit, be suspicious of 19 have one's doubts about

suspend 4 halt, hang, quit, stay, stop 5 cease, check, defer, delay, sling, swing, table 6 append, arrest, dangle, put off, shelve 7 reserve 8 break off, cut short, leave off, postpone, withhold 9 interrupt, stop short 10 put an end to 11 discontinue 12 bring to a stop 18 bring to a standstill

suspenders 6 braces, straps 7 gallows, garters, hangers 8 elastics, galluses 10 supporters

suspense 7 anxiety, tension 8 edginess 9 curiosity 10 indecision 11 expectation, incertitude, uncertainty 12 anticipation 15 indetermination

suspenseful 7 anxious 8 dramatic, exciting 9 climactic, uncertain

suspension 4 stay 5 pause 6 hiatus, recess 7 tabling 8 abeyance, deferral 12 postponement 14 discontinuance

suspicion 4 idea 5 guess, hunch 6 notion 7 feeling, surmise 8 distrust, mistrust 10 conjecture, hypothesis 11 supposition

Suspicion
director: 15 Alfred Hitchcock
cast: 9 Cary Grant 10 Nigel Bruce 12 Joan Fontaine 13 Dame May Whitty 15 Cedric Hardwicke
Oscar for: 7 actress (Fontaine)

suspicious 4 wary 5 shady 7 dubious, suspect 8 doubtful, doubting, slippery 9 ambiguous 10 untrusting 11 distrustful, incredulous, mistrustful, open to doubt 12 disbelieving, questionable 13 untrustworthy

sustain 4 bear, feed, prop 5 abide, brave, brook, stand 6 bear up, endure, hold up, keep up, suffer, uphold 7 nourish, nurture, prolong, support, undergo 8 maintain, protract, tolerate, underpin 9 keep alive, withstand 10 experience 12 carry on under 14 hold out against

sustenance 4 food, gear 5 bread, means 6 living 7 aliment, support 9 provender 10 provisions 11 maintenance, nourishment, subsistence
heaven-sent: 5 manna

sustineo alas 16 I sustain the wings
motto of: 10 US Air Force

Sutherland, Donald
born: 6 Canada, St John 12 New Brunswick
roles: 4 MASH 5 Klute 13 Hawkeye Pierce 14 Eye of the Needle, Ordinary People 16 Fellini's Casanova 17 The Eagle Has Landed 26 Invasion of the Body Snatchers

Sutpen, Colonel Thomas
character in: 14 Absalom Absalom
author: 8 Faulkner

Suva
capital of: 4 Fiji

Suzanne
character in: 19 The Marriage of Figaro
author: 12 Beaumarchais

svelte 4 fine, lean, neat, slim, thin, trim 5 lithe, spare 7 elegant, lissome, shapely, slender, willowy 8 graceful 9 sylphlike

Svengali
  character in: 6 Trilby
  author: 9 Du Maurier

Sverige see 6 Sweden

swab 3 dab, mop 4 daub, lout, wipe 5 clean, cloth, patch, scrub 6 cotton, sponge 7 cleanse 8 specimen
  brand name: 4 Q-tip

swagger 5 strut, sweep 6 parade, sashay, stride 7 saunter 11 swashbuckle

swaggerer 6 gascon 7 boaster, bragger 8 blowhard, braggart, strutter 11 braggadocio

swain 4 beau 6 fellow, suitor 7 admirer, gallant 8 cavalier, young man 9 boyfriend 10 sweetheart

swallow 3 bit, nip, sip 4 down, gulp, swig 5 drink, quaff, swill, taste 6 credit, devour, gobble, guzzle, hold in, imbibe, ingest, tipple 7 believe, fall for, repress 8 gulp down, hold back, keep back, mouthful, suppress, withhold

swallow up 5 drown, eat up, swamp 6 absorb, engulf 7 consume, envelop 8 inundate 9 overwhelm 10 assimilate

swallow words 6 mumble, mutter

swamp 3 bog, fen 4 fill, mire, moor, ooze, quag, sink, slew, slue 5 bayou, beset, flood, marsh, swale 6 deluge, engulf, morass, slough 7 besiege, bottoms, envelop 8 inundate, quagmire, submerge, wash over 9 everglade, marshland, overwhelm, snow under, swallow up

swamped 7 deluged, flooded, glutted, overrun 9 inundated 11 overwhelmed

Swan
  constellation of: 6 Cygnus

swan
  young: 6 cygnet
  group of: 4 bevy

swank 4 airs 5 ritzy 6 la-di-da, snooty, swanky 9 high-class, top-drawer 11 pretensions, pretentious 12 affectations, ostentatious 15 pretentiousness 16 superciliousness

swanky 4 chic, posh, rich 5 fancy, grand, jazzy, plush, ritzy, sharp, showy, smart, swank 6 flashy, snazzy, spiffy, sporty 7 dashing, elegant, splashy, stylish 9 sumptuous 11 fashionable

Swan Lake
  composer: 11 Tchaikovsky

Swanson, Gloria
  real name: 25 Gloria Josephine Mae Swenson
  born: 9 Chicago IL
  husband: 12 Wallace Beery
  roles: 13 Sadie Thompson, The Trespasser 16 Sunset Boulevard

swap 5 trade 6 barter, dicker, switch 7 bargain 8 exchange 11 give and take

sward 3 sod 4 lawn, rind, skin, turf 5 grass

swarm 4 herd, host, mass, rush, teem 5 cloud, crowd, drove, flock, horde, press, surge 6 abound, legion, myriad, stream, throng 7 cluster, overrun 8 stampede 9 multitude

swarthy 4 dark 5 dusky, swart, tawny 6 brunet 8 brunette 11 dark-skinned 12 brown-colored, brown-skinned, olive-skinned 14 dark-complected 16 dark-complexioned

swashbuckler 9 buccaneer, daredevil 10 adventurer

swashbuckling 4 bold 7 dashing 8 boasting 9 audacious, daredevil

swat 3 hit, tap 4 bash, belt, slam, slap, slug, sock 5 clout, knock, smack, smite, whack 6 buffet, strike, thwack, wallop 7 clobber

swathe 4 bind, wrap 5 cloak, cover 6 encase, enfold, enwrap 7 envelop, sheathe, swaddle

sway 4 bend, grip, hold, lead, list, move, reel, rock, roll, rule, spur, vary, wave 5 alter, clout, impel, power, reign, rouse, shift, swing, waver 6 change, domain, incite, induce, prompt, swerve, totter, waving, wobble 7 command, control, dispose, mastery, stagger, swaying 8 hesitate, iron hand, motivate, persuade, swinging, to-and-fro, undulate 9 authority, direction, encourage, fluctuate, influence, oscillate, pendulate, pulsation, stimulate, vacillate 10 domination, government, predispose, suzerainty, undulation 11 fluctuation, oscillation 12 back and forth, dictatorship, jurisdiction, manipulation

Swaziland
  capital/largest city: 7 Mbabane
  others: 5 Bunya, Hluti, Mpaka, Nsoko, Stegi 6 Gollel, Mhlume 7 Big Bend, Lobamba, Manzini 8 Havelock, Malkerns 9 Geodgegun, Hlatikulu, Mankaiana, Mankayana, Nhlangano, Pigg's Peak, Rocklands
  government: 22 constitutional monarchy
  head of state: 4 king
  monetary unit: 4 rand 9 lilangeni
  mountain: 8 Highveld 11 Drakensberg
  highest point: 7 Emlembe
  river: 5 Usutu 6 Komati, Lomati 8 Mhlatuze, Ngwavuma, Umbeluzi, Umbuluzi
  physical feature:
    forest: 5 Usutu
    plateau: 7 Lebombo, Lubombo
  people: 5 Asian, Bantu, Swazi 11 Eurafricans
  king: 3 Kbe 5 Nyama 6 Mswati 7 Sobhuza
  prince: 6 Sozisa
  language: 5 Ngumi 7 English, Siswati 9 Afrikaans 10 Portuguese
  religion: 7 animism 10 Protestant 13 Roman Catholic
  feature:
    bride payment: 6 lobolo

god: 14 Mkhulumngcandi
ritual dance: 7 Incwala

swear 3 vow 4 aver, avow, cuss 5 curse, vouch 6 adjure, assert, attest, pledge 7 certify, promise, warrant 9 blaspheme 10 take an oath, utter oaths 11 bear witness

swear by 7 believe, count on 9 believe in 10 put faith in

sweat 4 ooze, toil 5 exude, worry 6 effort 7 agonize 8 drudgery, hard work, perspire 9 exudation 12 perspiration

sweaty 3 wet 6 clammy, sticky 10 perspiring

Sweden
  other name: 7 Sverige
  capital/largest city: 9 Stockholm
  others: 4 Lund, Umea 5 Boden, Boras, Edane, Falun, Gavle, Lulea, Malmo, Pitea, Visby 6 Arvika, Kiruna, Orebro 7 Uppsala 8 Goteborg, Jokkmokk, Vasteras 9 Jonkoping, Linkoping, Sundsvall 10 Eskilstuna, Gottenburg, Norrkoping, Skelleftea 11 Halsingborg
  school: 4 Lund 7 Uppsala 8 Goteborg 9 Stockholm
  division: 3 Lan 4 Laen 5 Skane 6 Kalmar, Orebro 7 Dalarna, Gotland, Lapland 8 Alvsborg, Blekinge, Elfsborg, Gotaland, Jamtland, Malmohus, Norrland, Svealand
  government: 22 constitutional monarchy
  legislature: 7 Riksdag
  head of state: 4 king
  measure: 3 aln, fot, ref 4 alar, amar, famn, kapp, last, stop 5 carat, foder, kanna, linje, nymil, spann 6 fathom, jumfru 7 oxhuvud, tunland 8 fjarding, koltunna, tunnland
  monetary unit: 3 ore 5 krona, krone 7 carolin 8 skilling 9 rigsdaler
  weight: 3 ass, lod 4 last, mark, sten 5 carat 6 nylast 7 centner, lispund 8 skalpund, skeppund 9 shippound
  island: 5 Oland 7 Gotland
  lake: 4 Ster 5 Asnen, Malar, Silja, Vaner 6 Vanern, Vetter, Wenner 7 Hielmar, Malaren, Vattern 8 Dalalven 9 Hjalmaren
  mountain: 4 Sarv 5 Ammar 6 Helags, Kjolen, Ovniks, Sarjek 7 Kjollen
  highest point: 5 Kebne 10 Kebnekaise
  river: 3 Dal 4 Gota, Klar, Lule, Pite, Umea 5 Indal, Kalix, Lulea, Pitea, Ranea, Torne 6 Lainio, Muonio 7 Ljusnan 8 Angerman
  sea: 6 Baltic 8 Atlantic
  physical feature:
    canal: 4 Gota
    gulf: 7 Bothnia
    sound: 6 Kalmar
    strait: 7 Oresund 8 Kattegat 9 Skagerrak
  people: 4 Lapp 5 Norse, Swede 6 Viking
  actress: 5 Liv Ullman 10 Greta Garbo 13 Ingrid Bergman
  astronomer: 7 Celsius 8 Angstrom
  author: 8 Lagerlof 10 Lagerkvist, Strindberg
  diplomat: 12 Hammarskjold

director: 13 Ingmar Bergman 14 Arne Sucksdorff
inventor: 5 Nobel
king: 4 Vosa, Wasa 5 Oscar 6 Gustav 8 Gustavus 10 Carl Gustav 12 Gustav Adolph 13 Charles Gustav 22 Jean Baptiste Bernadotte
philosopher/scientist: 10 Swedenborg
queen: 9 Christina
scientist: 8 Linnaeus
language: 4 Lapp 7 Swedish
religion: 19 Evangelical Lutheran
place:
  castle: 9 Gripsholm
  center of Stockholm: 11 Gamla Staden
  park: 7 Skansen 12 Millesgarden
  theater: 18 Drottningholm Court
  walled city: 5 Visby
  food: 11 smorgasbord
  cheese: 7 fontina 8 jarlberg 9 jarlsberg
  dish: 10 kottbullar
  drink: 5 glogg 7 aquavit

Swedish Punch
  type: 7 liqueur
  origin: 6 Sweden
  base: 3 rum
  with gin: 5 Biffy
  with vermouth: 9 Grand Slam

Sweeney Among the Nightingales
  author: 7 T S Eliot

sweep 3 arc, fly 4 dart, dash, race, rush, scud, tear, zoom 5 hurry, spell, swing, swish, swoop, whisk 6 charge, gather, scurry, stroke 7 stretch 8 distance

sweeping 5 broad 7 blanket, radical 9 extensive, out-and-out, wholesale 10 exhaustive, large-scale, widespread 11 far-reaching, wide-ranging 12 all-inclusive 13 comprehensive, thoroughgoing

sweepings 4 dirt, dust 6 refuse

sweep off one's feet 7 enchant 8 bedazzle 9 captivate, overpower, overwhelm

sweet 4 dear, kind, nice 5 candy, fresh 6 dulcet, mellow, smooth, sugary 7 amiable, cloying, darling, dessert, lovable, nonsalt, not salt, tuneful 8 fragrant, pleasant, pleasing 9 agreeable, melodious, sweetmeat, wholesome 10 attractive, confection, euphonious, saccharine 11 good-natured, mellifluous, silver-toned, sympathetic 12 nonfermented

Sweet Bird of Youth
  director: 13 Richard Brooks
  based on play by: 17 Tennessee Williams
  cast: 8 Ed Begley 10 Paul Newman 13 Geraldine Page, Shirley Knight 17 Madeleine Sherwood
  Oscar for: 15 supporting actor (Begley)

sweetheart 4 beau, dear, love 5 flame, honey, lover, swain 6 fiance, old man, steady, suitor 7 beloved, darling, fiancee, old lady 8 ladylove, mistress, true love 9 boyfriend, inamorata, valentine 10 girlfriend, lady friend 15 gentleman friend
  French: 6 cherie

sweet life
   Italian: 9 dolce vita
Sweet Mama Stringbean
   nickname of: 11 Ethel Waters
sweetmeats 5 candy 6 sweets 7 bonbons 10 sugar candy 11 confections 13 confectionery
sweet-natured 5 sweet 6 benign, gentle, kindly 7 likable, lovable 8 pleasant 13 compassionate
sweetness
   French: 7 douceur
sweet roll 3 bun 6 Danish 7 cruller 8 doughnut 10 coffee cake 11 cinnamon bun
sweets 5 candy 7 goodies 8 desserts 10 sugar candy, sweetmeats 11 confections 13 confectionery
sweet-scented 8 aromatic, fragrant, perfumed, redolent
sweet-smelling 5 spicy 7 scented 8 aromatic, fragrant, perfumed, redolent 9 odiferous
sweet talk 6 cajole, praise 7 blarney, flatter 8 cajolery, flattery, soft soap 10 compliment 11 endearments, loving words 13 blandishments 14 fond utterances
Sweetwater
   nickname of: 16 Nathaniel Clifton
sweet words 7 blarney 8 flattery, soft soap 9 sweet talk 12 honeyed words
swell 3 fop, wax 4 A-one, fine, good, grow, okay, puff, rise, wave 5 bloat, bulge, dandy, great, heave, mount, super, surge, throb, widen 6 billow, blow up, comber, expand, extend, fatten, puff up 7 amplify, breaker, burgeon, distend, inflate, stretch, thicken 8 fabulous, heighten, increase, lengthen, splendid, terrific 9 excellent, firstrate, intensify, marvelous, spread out 10 delightful, first-class, tremendous, undulation 11 pleasurable 12 clotheshorse, fashion plate, smart dresser
swell-headed 8 egoistic, puffed up 9 conceited 10 egoistical 11 egotistical 12 vainglorious 13 self-important
swelling 4 bump, lump 5 bulge, swell 8 dilation 9 puffiness 10 distension 11 enlargement 12 protuberance
swell out 5 bloat, bulge 6 billow, expand 7 distend, inflate, puff out
swelter 3 fry 4 boil, cook 5 be hot, broil, sweat 8 languish, perspire
sweltering 3 hot 5 humid, muggy 6 sultry, torrid 7 burning 8 sweating 10 oppressive, perspiring
sweltry 3 hot 4 dank 5 humid, muggy 6 baking, clammy, steamy, sticky, sultry, torrid 7 boiling 8 broiling, roasting, sizzling, stifling 9 scorching 10 blistering 11 suffocating
Swenson, Gloria Josephine Mae
   real name of: 13 Gloria Swanson
Swept Away
   subtitle: 38 by an unusual destiny in the blue sea of August
   director: 14 Lina Wertmuller

   cast: 16 Mariangela Melato 17 Giancarlo Giannini
swerve 3 shy, yaw 4 tack, turn, veer 5 avert, dodge, sheer, shift, stray 6 careen, change 7 deviate, digress, diverge 9 turn aside
swift 4 fast 5 brisk, fleet, hasty, quick, rapid 6 abrupt, flying, prompt, speedy 8 headlong 9 immediate 11 expeditious, precipitate
Swift, Jonathan
   author of: 11 A Tale of a Tub 15 A Modest Proposal 16 Battle of the Books, Gulliver's Travels
   fictional places: 6 Laputa 8 Lilliput 11 Brobdingnag
   character: 6 Yahoos 10 Houyhnhnms 14 Lemuel Gulliver
swiftness 5 haste, speed 8 alacrity, celerity, dispatch, rapidity 9 quickness
swill 4 mash, slop, swig 5 quaff, waste 6 guzzle, refuse, scraps, soak up, tipple 7 garbage 8 chugalug, gulp down, leavings
swimming
   athlete: 9 Diana Nyad, John Naber, Mark Spitz 10 Dawn Fraser, Kim Linehan, Linda Jezek 11 Claudia Kolb, Debbie Meyer, John Hencken 12 Brian Goodell, Bruce Furniss, Greg Louganis, John Kinsella 13 Jim Montgomery, Kornelia Ender, Michael Burton, Tracy Caulkens 14 Charles Hickcox, Duke Kahanamoku, Esther Williams, Gertrude Ederle 15 Cynthia Woodhead 16 Shirley Babashoff 17 Johnny Weissmuller
Swinburne, Algernon Charles
   author of: 16 Hymn to Perserpine 17 Atalanta in Calydon 18 Songs Before Sunrise
swindle 2 do 3 con, gyp 4 bilk, dupe, gull, hoax, rook 5 cheat, cozen, fraud, mulct, steal, trick 6 delude, fleece, racket, rip-off 7 con game, deceive, defraud 8 embezzle, hoodwink 9 bamboozle, defalcate 12 embezzlement 13 confidence game
swindler 3 gyp 5 cheat, crook, faker, fraud 6 con man 7 sharper 8 chiseler, deceiver 9 charlatan, embezzler 10 mountebank 12 rip-off artist
swine 3 cad, cur, rat 4 pigs 5 beast, brute 6 animal
   group of: 5 drift 7 sounder
Swineherd, The
   author: 21 Hans Christian Andersen
swing 4 drop, hang, loop, move, rein, rock, sway, turn 5 pivot, rally, scope, sweep, whirl 6 dangle, decide, handle, manage, rotate, seesaw, stroke, wangle 7 compass, extract, freedom, inveigh, liberty, license, listing, pull off, rocking, rolling, suspend, swaying 8 maneuver, pitching, undulate 9 determine, influence, oscillate 10 accomplish, manipulate 11 be suspended, oscillation
Swing Time
   director: 13 George Stevens
   cast: 9 Eric Blore 11 Fred Astaire, Victor

Moore 12 Betty Furness, Ginger Rogers 14 Helen Broderick
score: 10 Jerome Kern 13 Dorothy Fields
Oscar for: 4 song
song: 12 A Fine Romance 14 Pick Yourself Up 20 The Way You Look Tonight

swirl 4 bowl, eddy, reel, roll, spin, swim, turn 5 churn, twirl, twist, wheel, whirl 6 gyrate, rotate 7 revolve

Swiss Family Robinson
  director: 10 Ken Annakin
  cast: 9 John Mills 14 Janet Munro 14 Dorothy McGuire, James MacArthur, Sessue Hayakawa
  author: 16 Johann Rudolf Wyss
  character: 13 Emily Montrose
  Robinson family: 4 Jack 5 Fritz 6 Ernest 7 Francis

switch 3 box, rod, tan 4 cane, jerk, lash, move, whip 5 birch, lever, shift, shunt, stick, swing, trade, whisk 6 button, change, handle 8 exchange 9 sidetrack 11 alternation

Switzerland
  capital: 4 Bern
  largest city: 6 Zurich
  others: 3 Zug 4 Bale, Bern, Biel, Brig, Chur, Nyon, Sion, Thun 5 Basel, Basle, Berne, Coire, Surat, Vevey 6 Geneva, Geneve, Glarus, Lugano, Sarnen, Schwyz 7 Altdorf, Fyzabad, Herisau, Locarno, Lucerne, Luzerne, Zermatt 8 Lausanne, Montreux, St Moritz 9 Neuchatel, Solothurn 10 Bellinzona, Interlaken, Winterthur 12 Schaffhausen
  school: 4 Bern 5 Basel 8 Catholic, Lausanne 28 Federal Institute of Technology
  division: 3 Uri, Zug 4 Bern, Chur, Nyon, Vaud 5 Aarau, Basel, Basle, Berne, Sankt, Waadt 6 Aargau, canton, Gallen, Geneva, Geneve, Glaris, Glarus, Luzern, Obwald, Schwyz, St Gall, Tessin, Ticino, Valais, Wallis, Zurich 7 Atldorf, Grisons, Lucerne, Nidwald, Thurgau 8 Fribourg, Obwalden, St Gallen 9 Appenzell, Neuchatel, Neuenberg, Solothurn 10 Graubunden 11 Unterwalden 12 Schaffhausen
  measure: 3 imi, pot 4 aune, fuss, muid, pied, zoll 5 lieue, linie, maass, pouce, staab, toise 6 perche, strich 7 klafter, viertel 8 quarteron 10 holzlafter 11 holzklafter
  monetary unit: 5 franc, rappe 6 hallar, rappen 7 centime, duplone 8 baetzner
  weight: 4 fund 5 pfund 7 centner, quintal 12 zugthierlast
  lake: 3 Uri, Zug 4 Biel, Thon, Thun 5 Ageri, Leman, Morat 6 Bienne, Brienz, Geneva, Lugano, Sarnen, Wallen, Zurich 7 Hallwil, Lucerne, Lungern 8 Maggiore, Viervald 9 Bielersee, Constance, Neuchatel, Sarnersee, Thunersee
  mountain: 3 Dom 4 Alps, Jura, Rigi, Rosa, Todi 5 Adula, Blanc, Cenis, Eiger, Genis, Karpf, Righi 6 Linard, Pizela, Sentis 7 Bernina, Beverin, Grimsel, Pilatus, Rotondo 8 Balmhorn, Jungfrau 9 Weisshorn 10 Diablerets, Matterhorn, St Gotthard, Wetterhorn 11 Burgenstock 12 Dufourspitze 13 Rheinwaldhorn 14 Finsteraarhorn
  mountain pass: 5 Cenis, Furka, Gemmi 6 Albula, Kinzig, Maloja, Usteri 7 Bernina, Brenner, Grimsel, Simplon, Splugen 8 Lotschen 10 St Gotthard
  highest point: 12 Dufourspitze
  river: 2 Po 3 Aar, Inn 4 Aare, Arve, Thur, Toss 5 Broye, Doubs, Linth, Reuss, Rhine, Rhone, Saane 6 Limmat, Maggia, Safane, Sarine, Ticino 8 Engadine, Pratigau
  physical feature:
  glacier: 5 Rhone
  plateau: 5 Swiss
  people: 5 Swiss
  artist: 4 Klee
  author: 5 Hesse, Spyri 6 Keller 8 Gotthelf, Rousseau 10 Durrenmatt
  educational reformer: 10 Pestalozzi
  hero: 4 Tell
  psychologist: 4 Jung 6 Piaget
  religious leader: 6 Calvin 7 Zwingli
  scientist: 9 Bernoulli
  language: 5 Ladin 6 French, German 7 Italian 8 Romansch 14 Switzerdeutsch
  religion: 9 Calvinism 10 Protestant 13 Roman Catholic
  place:
  castle: 7 Chillon
  fountain: 7 Jet d'Eau
  playhouse: 6 Zurich
  resort: 5 Arosa, Davos 6 Gstaad 7 Zermatt 8 St Moritz 9 Schwagalp 10 Interlaken
  street: 14 Bahnhofstrasse
  tower: 5 Clock
  feature:
  animal: 4 ibex 7 chamois
  flower: 9 edelweiss
  pageant: 9 Alpenfest
  food:
  cheese: 6 bagnes, sbrinz 7 Gruyere 10 Emmentaler 11 Appenzeller
  dish: 5 rosti 6 fondue 8 raclette 11 grisons beef 14 bundnerfleisch
  drink: 11 cheri-suisse 14 marmotchocolat

Swiveller, Dick
  character in: 19 The Old Curiosity Shop
  author: 7 Dickens

swollen 5 puffy 7 bloated, bulging, swelled 8 inflated, puffed-up 9 distended

swoon 5 faint 8 collapse, keel over 13 fall prostrate 17 become unconscious

swoop 4 dive, drop, rush 5 pitch, sweep 6 plunge, pounce, spring 7 descend, plummet 8 nose-dive, swooping 9 sweep down 12 rush headlong

sword 4 epee, foil 5 blade, saber, steel 6 rapier 7 cutlass 8 scimitar 10 broadsword

sybarite 8 hedonist 10 sensualist, voluptuary

sybaritic 4 rich 6 lavish 7 sensual 9 dissolute, epicurean, luxurious 10 dissipated, hedonistic, voluptuous 12 luxury-loving, pleasure-bent 13 self-indulgent 14 pleasure-loving 15 pleasure-seeking

Sycamire 12 Biblical tree

sycamore 8 Platanus 18 Acer pseudoplatanus
   varieties: 7 eastern 8 Egyptian

Sychaeus
   also: 7 Acerbas
   priest of: 8 Hercules
   wife: 4 Dido
   brother-in-law: 9 Pygmalion
   murdered by: 9 Pygmalion

sycophant 4 tool 5 slave, toady 6 fawner, flunky, jackal, lackey, puppet, stooge, yes-man 7 cat's-paw 8 hanger-on, parasite, truckler 9 flatterer 10 bootlicker 11 lickspittle, rubber stamp 13 apple-polisher

Sydney
   bay: 5 Walsh 11 Rushcutter's 13 Woolloomooloo
   capital of: 13 New South Wales
   cove: 4 Farm
   founder: 7 Phillip
   harbor: 7 Darling 11 Port Jackson
   island: 4 Goat 6 Garden
   landmark: 10 Opera House 11 Wynyard Park 13 Harbour Bridge 14 Fitzroy Gardens 15 Mitchell Library 16 Australian Museum, Hyde Park Barracks, Saint James Church 18 Rushcutter's Bay Park 21 Royal Botanical Gardens
   river: 10 Parramatta
   university: 9 Macquarie 13 New South Wales

Syleus
   position: 4 king
   killed by: 8 Hercules

sylvan 5 bushy, leafy, woody 6 wooded, woodsy 8 arcadian, forested, timbered, woodland 9 luxuriant, overgrown 10 forestlike

Sylvanus *see* 8 Silvanus

Sylvia
   character in: 20 Two Gentlemen of Verona
   author: 11 Shakespeare

Symaethis
   form: 5 nymph
   location: 3 sea
   mother of: 4 Aeis

symbol 4 mark, sign 5 badge, token 6 emblem, figure, signal 10 indication 14 representation 15 exemplification

symbolize 4 mean 5 imply 6 denote, embody, symbol 7 betoken, connote, express, signify 8 stand for 9 emblemize, exemplify, personify, represent, signalize 10 allegorize 11 emblematize

symmetrical 7 orderly, regular 8 balanced 9 congruent 12 well-balanced 16 well-proportioned

symmetry 4 form 5 order 7 balance, harmony 9 congruity 10 conformity, regularity 11 equilibrium, orderliness, parallelism, shapeliness 15 proportionality

sympathetic 6 benign, humane, kindly 7 feeling, pitying 8 friendly, merciful 9 agreeable, approving, benignant, sensitive 10 benevolent, comforting 11 softhearted, warmhearted 12 sympathizing, well-disposed 13 commiserative, compassionate, tenderhearted, understanding

sympathize 4 back, pity, side 5 agree, favor 7 approve, feel for, go along, support 8 sanction 9 empathize 10 appreciate, be in accord, be sorry for 11 condole with, have pity for, stand behind

sympathy 4 pity 5 amity, favor, grief 6 accord, regard, sorrow 7 concern, concert, concord, empathy, feeling, harmony, rapport, support 8 advocacy, affinity, approval, sanction 9 agreement, communion, patronage, unanimity 10 compassion, consonance, fellowship, friendship, tenderness 11 well-wishing 12 congeniality, partisanship 13 commiseration, consanguinity, fellow feeling, understanding

Symplegades
   form: 5 rocks
   location: 8 Bosporus 9 Euxine Sea
   characteristic: 8 clashing, dark-blue

symposium 5 forum, synod 6 debate, parley, powwow 7 meeting 8 colloquy, congress 10 conference, discussion, round table 12 deliberation 15 panel discussion

Symposium
   author: 5 Plato
   character: 7 Agathon 8 Phaedrus, Socrates 9 Pausanias 10 Alcibiades 11 Aristodemus 12 Aristophanes

symptom 4 mark, sign 5 token 6 signal 7 earmark, warning 8 evidence, giveaway 10 indication 15 prognostication

synagogue
   Yiddish: 4 shul 5 schul

synchronal 11 concomitant, synchronous 12 contemporary, simultaneous

synchronous 10 synchronal 11 concomitant 12 contemporary, simultaneous

syndicalist 5 rebel 9 anarchist, insurgent 13 revolutionary

syndicate 5 group, trust, union 6 cartel, league, merger 7 combine 8 alliance 9 coalition 10 consortium, federation 11 association

Synge, John Millington
   author of: 14 Riders to the Sea 19 Deirdre of the Sorrows 20 In the Shadow of the Glen 27 The Playboy of the Western World

synod 4 diet 13 governing body 15 advisory council 21 ecclesiastical council

synonym 8 analogue 10 equivalent 11 another name

synonymous 4 like, same 5 alike, equal 7 coequal 10 equivalent

synopsis 5 brief 6 apercu, digest, precis, resume 7 epitome, outline, rundown, summary 8 abstract, argument 11 abridgement

synopsize 6 digest 7 abridge, outline 8 abstract, condense 9 summarize

Synoptist 12 Gospel writer

synthesize 3 mix 4 fuse 5 blend 7 combine 8 compound 10 amalgamate

synthetic 4 fake, sham 5 phony 6 ersatz 7 man-made 9 unnatural 10 artificial 11 counterfeit 12 manufactured

Syri 16 Greek uncial codex

Syria
other name: 4 Aram
capital/largest city: 8 Damascus
others: 5 Hama, Homs, Nawa 5 Busra, Calno, Derra, Emesa, Halab, Hamah, Idlib, Jerud, Raqqa 6 Aleppo, Calneh, Dumeir, Fajami, Tadmor, Ugarit 7 Antioch, Latakia, Palmyra 8 Seleucia 9 Ghabaghib
school: 6 Aleppo, Syrian 11 Arab Academy
measure: 5 makuk 6 garava
monetary unit: 4 lira 5 pound 6 talent 7 piaster
weight: 4 cola 5 artal, ratel 6 talent
lake: 5 Merom 7 Djeboid 8 Tiberias
mountain: 6 Carmel 7 Alawite, Libanus 10 Nusairiyya 11 Anti-Lebanon
highest point: 6 Hermon
river: 3 Asi 6 Balikh, Barada, Jordan, Khabur, Yarmuk 7 Orontes 9 Asi Knabur, Euphrates
sea: 13 Mediterranean
physical feature:
desert: 5 Hamad 6 Hauran, Syrian
heights: 5 Golan
people: 4 Arab, Kurd, Turk 5 Alawi, Aptal, Druse, Druze 6 Afshar, Aissor, Aushar, Avshar, Awshar 7 Amorite, Ansarie, Bedouin, Nosaris, Saracen, Shemite 8 Ansarieh, Armenian 9 Ansariyah 10 Circassian 12 Khachaturian
king: 5 Rezin 6 Faisal, Hazael 8 Benhadad 9 Antiochus
leader: 10 T E Lawrence 12 Hafiz al-Assad 16 Lawrence of Arabia
queen: 7 Zenobia
ruler: 4 Rome 5 Arabs 6 France, Greeks, Persia 7 Mongols 8 Abbasids 9 Mamelukes, Phoenicia, Seleucids 11 Seljuk Turks 12 Ottoman Turks
language: 6 Arabic, French, Syriac 7 Aramaic, English, Kurdish, Turkish 8 Armenian
religion: 5 Druze, Islam 7 Alawite 12 Christianity 13 Greek Orthodox 23 Eastern Rite Christianity
place:
dam: 5 Tabqa 9 Euphrates
ruins: 7 Palmyra
square: 7 Martyrs'
feature:
animal: 9 dromedary
clothing: 3 aba 4 abah 7 abayyah 8 kafiyyah

marketplace: 4 souk
tent: 8 bayt shar
village common: 6 maidan

Syrinx
form: 5 nymph
location: 8 mountain
transformed into: 4 reed
transformed by: 3 Pan
made into: 7 panpipe
pipes called: 6 syrinx

system 4 body, unit 5 setup 6 method, scheme, theory 7 program, regimen, routine 8 organism 9 procedure, structure 10 hypothesis 11 arrangement 12 constitution, organization 13 modus operandi 15 mode of operation

systematic 4 neat, tidy 7 ordered, orderly, planned, precise, regular 8 constant 9 organized 10 methodical 12 businesslike, systematized 13 well-organized, well-regulated

systematization 5 order 8 ordering 9 gradation 10 organizing 11 arrangement 12 categorizing, codification, organization 13 methodization 14 categorization, classification

systematize 5 order 7 arrange 8 classify, organize 9 methodize

systematized 7 ordered 8 arranged, codified 9 organized 10 classified, methodized, systematic

T

tab 3 lip 4 bill, cost, flap, loop 5 check, price, strip, tally 6 tongue 7 eyehole 10 projection

tabard 4 cape, coat 5 cloak, tunic

Tabard Inn
  starting point in: 18 The Canterbury Tales

tabernacle 6 church, temple 14 house of worship

Tabeth 16 tenth Hebrew month

Tabitha
  also called: 6 Dorcas
  revived by: 5 Peter
  hometown: 5 Joppa

table 4 fare, list, roll 5 board, chart, index 6 record, roster, shelve, spread 7 catalog 8 lay aside, postpone, put aside, register, schedule, syllabus, synopsis 9 inventory 10 tabulation

Table
  constellation of: 5 Mensa

tableau 4 view 5 scene 7 pageant, picture, setting 8 grouping 9 depiction, spectacle, still life 11 arrangement, delineation 12 illustration 13 picturization

tableau vivant 13 living picture

tablespoon
  abbreviation: 4 tbsp

tablet 3 pad 4 leaf 5 bolus, panel, sheet, wafer 6 pellet, plaque, troche 7 lozenge, memo pad, surface 8 flat cake, thin slab 9 tablature 10 pad of paper, writing pad

tableware 5 china 6 dishes, plates 7 cutlery 8 crockery, utensils 9 chinaware, glassware 10 dinnerware, silverware 14 cups and saucers

taboo, tabu 3 ban 4 no-no 6 banned 8 anathema, outlawed, verboten 9 forbidden, social ban 10 in bad taste, prohibited, proscribed 11 disapproved, prohibition, unthinkable 12 interdiction, proscription, religious ban, unacceptable 13 unmentionable

tabulate 4 file, list, rank, rate, sort 5 chart, grade, group, index, order, range 6 codify 7 arrange, catalog, compute, diagram, sort out 8 classify, organize 9 methodize 10 categorize, make a table 11 systematize

tace
  music: 6 silent

tacit 7 assumed, implied 8 implicit, inferred, unspoken, unstated, wordless 10 undeclared, understood 11 unexpressed 15 taken for granted

taciturn 5 aloof, quiet 6 silent 7 laconic 8 reserved, reticent 9 secretive 11 tight-lipped 12 close-mouthed 15 uncommunicative

tack 3 add, peg, pin, way 4 clap, nail, slap, veer 5 affix, sheer, shift, spike, thole 6 append, attach, change, fasten, method, swerve, switch, zigzag 7 go about 8 approach, tholepin 9 short nail 12 change course 14 course of action

tackle 3 try 4 gear, lift 5 assay, begin, crane, hoist, jenny, throw, tools, winch 6 accept, assume, attack, take on, take up 7 attempt, capstan, derrick, embrace, go about, halyard, rigging 8 endeavor, engage in, material, set about, windlass 9 apparatus, enter upon, equipment, trappings, undertake 10 appliances, embark upon, implements 11 instruments 12 appointments 13 accoutrements, paraphernalia

tack on 3 add 5 annex 6 adjoin, append, attach 7 stick on, subjoin 8 fasten to

tacky 5 dowdy, gluey, gooey, gucky, gummy, messy, ratty, seedy, tatty 6 grubby, shabby, shoddy, sloppy, sticky, untidy, viscid 7 stringy, unkempt, viscous 8 adhesive, frazzled, slipshod, slovenly 10 disordered

tact 7 finesse, suavity 8 delicacy 9 diplomacy, suaveness 10 discretion 11 savoir faire, sensibility 13 consideration 14 circumspection
  French: 11 savoir-faire

tactful 5 suave 6 polite, smooth, subtle 7 politic 8 decorous, delicate, discreet, mannerly 9 sensitive 10 diplomatic, thoughtful 11 considerate

tactic 3 way 4 line, plan, tack 6 method, policy, scheme 8 approach 9 stratagem 14 course of action

tactics 9 maneuvers 18 battle arrangements, military operations

tactless 4 curt, rude 5 blunt, brash, rough 6 abrupt, clumsy, gauche, stupid 7 boorish 8 impolite 9 ham-handed, impolitic, imprudent, untactful 10 blundering, indelicate, indiscreet 11 insensitive, thoughtless 12 undiplomatic 13 ill-considered, inconsiderate
  French: 6 gauche

tactlessness 8 curtness 9 bluntness, gaucherie 10 abruptness, clumsiness, indelicacy 13 insensitivity, tastelessness

taedium vitae 5 ennui 12 tedium of life 22 feeling life is wearisome

Taft, William Howard
  presidential rank: 13 twenty-seventh
  party: 10 Republican
  state represented: 2 OH
  defeated: 4 (Eugene Victor) Debs 5 (William Jennings) Bryan 6 (Daniel Braxton) Turney, (Eugene Wilder) Chafin, (Thomas

Edward) Watson, (Thomas Louis) Hisgen
8 (August) Gillhaus
vice president: 7 (James Schoolcraft)
Sherman
cabinet:
state: 4 (Philander Chase) Knox
treasury: 8 (Franklin) MacVeagh
war: 7 (Henry Lewis) Stimson 9 (Jacob
McGavock) Dickinson
attorney general: 10 (George Woodward) Wickersham
navy: 5 (George von Lengerke) Meyer
postmaster general: 9 (Frank Harris)
Hitchcock
interior: 6 (Walter Lowrie) Fisher 9 (Richard Achilles) Ballinger
agriculture: 6 (James) Wilson
commerce and labor: 5 (Charles) Nagel
born: 12 Cincinnati OH
died: 12 Washington DC
buried: 25 Arlington National Cemetery
education:
university: 4 Yale
law school: 10 Cincinnati
religion: 9 Unitarian
interests: 4 golf
author: 22 Four Aspects of Civic Duty 23
The United States and Peace 30 Our
Chief Magistrate and His Powers 33 The
Anti-Trust Act and the Supreme Court 65
The Presidency: Its Duties Its Powers Its
Opportunities and Its Limitation
political career: 18 US Solicitor General
judge: 19 Federal Circuit Court
president of: 21 Philippines Commission
civil governor of: 11 Philippines
secretary of: 3 War
US Supreme Court: 12 Chief Justice
civilian career:
law professor: 4 Yale
president: 22 American Bar Association
notable events of lifetime/term: 19
Postal Savings System
Act: 10 Webb-Kenyon 11 Mann-Elkinst
12 Payne-Aldrich
sinking of: 7 Titanic
father: 8 Alphonso
mother: 6 Louisa (Maria Torrey)
siblings: 5 Fanny 11 Henry Waters 12
Horace Dutton 15 Samuel Davenport
half-brothers: 11 Peter Rawson 13
Charles Phelps
wife: 5 Helen (Herron)
nickname: 6 Nellie
children: 11 Helen Herron 13 Charles
Phelps 14 Robert Alphonso
first lady:
author: 24 Recollections of Full Years
tag 3 add, dog, tab 4 card, heel, mark,
name, slip, stub, tail, term 5 add on, affix,
annex, hound, label, title, trail 6 append,
attach, attend, fasten, follow, handle, join
to, marker, shadow, tack on, ticket 7 earmark, moniker, pendant 8 cognomen,
identify, nickname 9 accompany, appendage, sobriquet

Tahiti
artist: 7 Gauguin
author: 9 Stevenson
capital: 7 Papeete
formerly: 8 Otaheite
island group: 7 Society
isthmus: 7 Taravao
ocean: 7 Pacific
volcano: 5 Roniu 7 Orohena

tail 3 dog 4 butt, seat 5 fanny, stalk, track,
trail 6 follow, shadow 7 back end, rear end
8 buttocks
tail end, tail-end 4 back, butt, rear, rump,
tail 6 caudal 7 hind end, rear end 8 backside, buttocks, last part 9 posterior
tailor 3 fit, sew 4 make, redo 5 adapt, alter,
build, shape 6 change, create, design, devise, modify 7 convert, fashion, produce 8
clothier, costumer 9 construct, couturier,
fabricate, transform 10 dressmaker, seamstress
taint 3 mar, rot 4 blot, flaw, ruin, soil, spot,
turn 5 dirty, fault, go bad, smear, spoil,
stain, sully 6 damage, debase, defect, defile, smudge, stigma 7 blemish, putrefy,
tarnish 8 besmirch 12 imperfection
tainted 5 dirty 6 impure, rotten 7 spoiled,
stained, unclean 9 blemished, tarnished
10 besmirched
Taipei
capital of: 6 Taiwan
Taiwan
name means: 11 terraced bay
other name: 7 Formosa 11 Ilha Formosa
15 Republic of China
capital/largest city: 6 Taipei
others: 4 Suao 5 Shoka, Takao 6 Tainan
7 Chilung, Hualien, Keelong, Keelung,
Taoyuan 8 Fengshan, Kaohiung, Tai-
chung 9 Kaohsiung
school: 7 Soochow, Tunghai 14 National
Taiwan
monetary unit: 4 yuan 6 dollar
island: 5 Matsu 6 Lan Hsu, Penghu,
Quemoy, Taiwan 7 Hungtou, Huoshao 10
Pescadores
mountain: 5 Tatun 6 Tzukao 7 Taitung
15 Chungyang Shanmo
highest point: 6 Yu Shan 8 Morrison 10
Sinkao Shan 11 Hsin-Kao Shan
river: 5 Wuchi 6 Tachia 7 Choshui,
Hualien, Tanshui
sea: 7 Pacific 9 East China 10 Philippine,
South China
physical feature:
cape: 7 Olwanpi
channel: 5 Bashi
gorge: 6 Taroko
storm: 7 monsoon, typhoon
strait: 6 Taiwan 7 Formosa
people: 4 Yami 5 Hakka, Hoklo 7 Chinese, Malayan 9 Fukienese, Taiwanese
10 Indonesian, Polynesian 12 Kwangtungese
goddess: 5 Matsu
leader: 7 Koxinga 9 Sun Yat-sen 10 Yen

Chia-Kan 13 Chiang Kai-shek 14 Cheng Cheng-Kung, Chlang Ching-kuo
language: 4 Amon, Amoy 5 Hakka, Kuo Yu 6 Minnan 9 Taiwanese 15 Mandarin Chinese
religion: 6 Taoism 7 animism 8 Buddhism 12 Christianity, Confucianism
place:
   museum: 14 National Palace
   square: 12 Presidential
feature:
   festival: 5 Ghost
   political party: 10 Kuomintang
food:
   feast: 6 pal-pai

Tajikistan
   other name: 12 Tadzhikistan
   capital/largest city: 8 Dushanbe
   head of state: 9 president
   government: 8 republic
   monetary unit: 5 ruble
   mountain: 13 Communism Peak
   people: 5 Tajik, Uzbek 7 Tadzhik
   language: 7 Tadzhik
   religion: 11 Sunni Muslim

take 3 buy, get, lug, nab, net, see, use 4 bear, bilk, deem, draw, feel, gain, grab, grip, haul, have, heed, hire, hold, know, lead, look, mark, mind, move, need, obey, read, rent, sack, tote, work 5 bring, brook, carry, catch, cheat, claim, clasp, filch, grasp, gross, guide, infer, lease, seize, stand, steal, use up, usher, usurp 6 accept, assume, attain, clutch, convey, deduce, deduct, demand, derive, divest, employ, endure, escort, fleece, follow, look on, obtain, pilfer, pocket, profit, regard, remove, secure, snatch, suffer 7 acquire, agree to, believe, call for, capture, conduct, consume, deliver, make out, observe, pillage, plunder, purloin, receive, require, respect, stomach, succeed, suppose, undergo 8 accede to, assent to, conceive, conclude, consider, listen to, perceive, proceeds, purchase, submit to, subtract, take away, tolerate, transfer 9 ascertain, be ruled by, consent to, deprive of, eliminate, get hold of, interpret, lay hold of, put up with, respond to, transport, undertake 10 commandeer, comply with, comprehend, confiscate, experience, lay hands on, take effect, understand 11 appropriate, begin to work, go along with, necessitate 13 help oneself to 14 avail oneself of, misappropriate

take aback 5 amaze 7 astound 8 astonish, surprise 9 overwhelm

take a crack at 3 try 5 essay 6 hazard, tackle, take on 7 at- tempt, venture 9 have a go at, undertake 11 make a stab at

take advantage of 3 use 5 avail 7 exploit, utilize 10 profit from

take after 4 copy, echo 6 follow, repeat 7 imitate 8 resemble, simulate 9 duplicate, reproduce

take apart 7 destroy 8 demolish 9 dismantle, knock down 11 disassemble

take a powder 4 blow, exit 5 go out, leave, scram, split 6 cut out, depart, escape 8 withdraw

take away 5 seize 6 lessen, reduce 7 abridge, bear off, curtail, detract 8 carry off, decrease, subtract 9 deprive of 11 make off with

take a whack at 3 try 5 essay 6 hazard, tackle 7 attempt, venture 8 give a try 9 have a go at 10 give a whirl 12 take a crack at

take back 6 abjure, recall, recant, renege 7 disavow, retract, reverse 8 forswear, withdraw

take captive 3 bag 4 snag, take, trap 5 catch, seize, snare 7 capture, ensnare 9 apprehend, lay hold of 12 take prisoner

take care 6 beware, be wary 9 be careful 10 be cautious 17 look before you leap

take care of 4 tend 6 assume 7 nurture 8 attend to, shoulder 10 minister to

take exception 5 demur 6 object, resent 11 look askance

take flight 3 fly 4 flee 6 escape, run off 7 abscond, fly away, run away, run free, take off 9 make a dash 10 fly the coop 12 make a getaway

take for granted 6 assume 10 undervalue

take heed 4 mind 6 beware 7 look out 8 take care, watch out 11 take warning

take hold 4 bite, grab, grip 5 grasp 6 clutch 7 catch on

take in stride 12 not skip a beat 13 be unperturbed

take into custody 3 bag, nab 4 book, bust, hold 5 catch, pinch, seize 6 arrest, collar, detain, secure 7 capture 9 apprehend 12 take prisoner

take into service 4 hire 6 employ, engage, retain, secure, take on

take issue 5 demur 6 differ 8 disagree 12 be at variance, stand opposed

take no notice of 6 ignore 9 disregard 11 pay no heed to 15 fail to recognize 16 pay no attention to 17 fail to acknowledge

take notice
   Latin: 8 nota bene

take notice of 3 see 4 heed, mark, note 6 call on, regard 7 observe 8 call upon 9 recognize 10 get a load of 11 acknowledge 14 pay attention to

take nourishment 3 eat 4 feed 10 break bread 14 take sustenance

takeoff 5 spoof 6 parody, satire 7 lampoon 9 burlesque 10 caricature

take off 4 doff, lift 5 leave 6 decamp, depart, detach, remove 7 lift off, peel off, run away 8 strip off 14 leave the ground

take off guard 5 catch 8 surprise 14 take by surprise

take on 4 bear, hire 6 accept, assume, engage 8 shoulder 9 undertake

take one's breath away 4 daze, stun 5 shock 7 stupefy 8 astonish, dumfound 9 dumbfound, electrify 11 flabbergast 15 make one's eyes pop

take out 4 date 5 court 6 delete, escort, remove 7 extract, isolate 8 abstract, separate, take home, withdraw 9 strike out

take over 4 take 5 assume, take on, take up 8 shoulder 10 commandeer, confiscate 11 appropriate, expropriate, gain control

take pains 6 strive 7 attempt, try hard 8 endeavor, go all out 10 do one's best 11 give one's all 12 make an effort 15 knock oneself out 16 give one's best shot

take pleasure in 4 like, love 5 adore, eat up, enjoy, fancy, savor 6 dote on, relish, relish 7 revel in 9 rejoice in 10 appreciate 13 be pleased with, get a kick out of

take possession of 5 claim 10 confiscate 11 appropriate, expropriate

take prisoner 3 bag, nab 4 book, bust 5 catch, pinch, seize 6 arrest, collar 7 capture 9 apprehend 11 take captive 15 take into custody

take sick 3 ail 6 sicken 8 collapse 9 become ill 10 be stricken

take stock of 5 audit, check 6 assess, review, survey 7 examine, inspect 8 look over 9 inventory

take sustenance 3 eat 4 feed 10 break bread 15 take nourishment

take the cake 5 excel 7 beat all, surpass 12 beat the devil, win hands down

take the edge off 6 lessen, pacify, soothe, temper 7 appease, assuage, lighten, mollify 8 tone down

take the first step 5 begin, start 6 launch, set out 8 commence, embark on, initiate 9 undertake 10 inaugurate

take the place of 7 replace 8 displace, supplant 9 supersede

take to 4 deem, hold 5 count, judge, think 6 assume, regard, view as 7 account, believe 8 consider 10 look upon as

take to heart 4 heed, mind 6 attend 8 consider 9 hearken to 13 give thought to 14 pay attention to

take to one's heels 3 fly 4 flee 6 escape 7 get away, run away 10 fly the coop, make a break, take flight 12 make a getaway 15 head for the hills

take to task 5 chide, scold 6 accuse, berate, charge, rail at, rebuke 7 bawl out, censure, chasten, chew out, reprove, upbraid 8 admonish, chastise, reproach 9 castigate, criticize, dress down, reprimand 10 tongue-lash 11 remonstrate 13 call to account

take turns 5 share 6 rotate 9 alternate

take under one's wing 6 assist, defend 7 protect 8 befriend 9 look after

take unfair advantage of 5 abuse 6 misuse 7 exploit

take up 4 lift 6 absorb, accept, assume, occupy, pick up, resume, soak up, suck up 7 discuss, drink in 8 consider, continue, sponge up, talk over 9 cultivate, swallow up

taking a siesta 6 dozing 7 napping 8 snoozing 10 taking a nap 18 catching forty winks

takings 4 loot 5 booty 6 spoils 7 plunder 8 pickings

Talamancan
  tribe: 7 Cabecar

Talaria
  form: 7 sandals
  owner: 6 Hermes 7 Mercury
  characteristic: 6 winged

Talassio
  origin: 5 Roman
  form: 3 god
  invoked at: 8 weddings
  corresponds to: 5 Hymen 9 Hymenaeus

tale 3 fib, lie 4 epic, myth, saga, yarn 5 fable, novel, rumor, story 6 legend, report 7 account, fiction, hearsay, recital, romance, scandal, untruth 8 anecdote 9 falsehood, fish story, narration, narrative, tall story 10 short story 11 fabrication, scuttlebutt 12 tittle-tattle 13 falsification, piece of gossip 16 cock-and-bull story

talebearer 6 gossip 7 blabber, reciter, tattler 8 busybody, informer, reporter, telltale 10 newsmonger, tattletale 11 storyteller 12 blabbermouth 13 scandalmonger

talent 4 bent, gift, turn 5 flair, forte, knack, skill 6 genius 7 faculty 8 aptitude, capacity, facility, strength 9 endowment 10 capability 11 proficiency

Talent 14 Biblical weight

talented 4 able 5 adept 6 expert, gifted 7 born for, capable, endowed, skilled 8 artistic, polished 9 brilliant, competent 10 proficient 11 well-endowed 12 accomplished

Tale of a Tub, A
  author: 9 Ben Jonson 13 Jonathan Swift

Tale of Genji
  author: 19 Lady Murasaki Shikibu

Tale of Two Cities, A
  author: 14 Charles Dickens
  character: 7 Gaspard, Stryver 9 Dr Manette, Miss Pross 11 Jarvis Lorry, John Barstad 12 Lucie Manette, Sydney Carton 13 Charles Darnay, Jerry Cruncher, Madame Defarge 18 Marquis St Evremonde
  director: 10 Jack Conway
  cast: 12 Blanche Yurka, Isabel Jewell, Reginald Owen, Ronald Colman (Sydney Carton) 13 Basil Rathbone, Edna May Oliver 14 Elizabeth Allan
  setting: 16 French Revolution

Tales Before Midnight
  author: 19 Stephen Vincent Benet

Talese, Gay
  author of: 14 Honor Thy Father 16 Thy Neighbor's Wife

Tales of a Fourth Grade Nothing
  author: 9 Judy Blume

Tales of a Wayside Inn
  author: 24 Henry Wadsworth Longfellow

Tales of Hoffmann, The
  also: 18 Les Contes d'Hoffmann
  opera by: 9 Offenbach

character: 6 Stella 7 Antonia, Olympia 9 Dr Miracle, Giulietta 11 E T A Hoffmann

Tales of Manhattan

author: 16 Louis Auchincloss

talisman 5 charm 6 amulet, fetish 10 lucky piece

Talisman, The

author: 14 Sir Walter Scott

character: 7 Conrade, El Hakim 10 Sir Kenneth 15 Queen Berengaria 19 Theodorick of Engaddi 20 Lady Edith Plantagenet 21 Richard the Lion-Hearted 31 Grand Master of the Knights Templars

talk 3 gab, jaw, rap, say 4 cant, chat, word 5 argot, idiom, lingo, noise, prate, rumor, slang, speak, state, utter 6 babble, bunkum, confab, confer, gossip, hot air, intone, jargon, parley, patois, powwow, preach, report, sermon, speech, tirade 7 address, blarney, blather, chatter, consult, declare, deliver, dialect, discuss, express, hearsay, lecture, oration, palaver, prattle, twaddle 8 chitchat, colloquy, converse, dialogue, harangue, language, proclaim, rattle on, verbiage 9 discourse, enunciate, negotiate, pronounce, tete-a-tete, utterance 10 bandy words, conference, discussion, rap session, recitation, speak about 11 declamation, exhortation, pontificate, scuttlebutt 12 blatherskite, consultation, conversation, tittle-tattle 13 confabulation

talkative 5 gabby, talky, windy, wordy 6 babbly, chatty, prolix 7 gossipy, verbose, voluble 8 effusive 9 garrulous 10 longwinded, loquacious

talk big 4 brag, crow 5 boast, vaunt 13 puff oneself up 15 blow one's own horn 19 pat oneself on the back

talk down to 9 patronize 10 condescend

talker 6 gabber, gossip, magpie, orator 7 babbler, speaker, windbag 8 lecturer, prattler 9 chatterer, converser 10 chatterbox, mouthpiece 11 rumormonger, speechifier, speechmaker 12 blatherskite, spokesperson 13 scandalmonger 17 conversationalist

talk nonsense 6 babble, drivel, ramble

Talk of the Town, The

director: 13 George Stevens

cast: 9 Cary Grant 10 Jean Arthur 12 Ronald Colman 13 Edgar Buchanan, Glenda Farrell

talk out of 4 balk 6 thwart 8 dissuade 10 discourage

talk over 6 confer, review 7 consult, discuss, hash out

talk to 7 address, lecture, speak to 12 converse with

talk together 4 talk 6 confer 7 discuss 8 converse 9 discourse

tall 3 big 4 high 5 lanky, lofty, rangy 6 absurd 7 soaring, stringy 8 elevated, gangling, towering 10 incredible, long-limbed 11 embellished, exaggerated, implausible 12 preposterous, unbelievable 13 hard to believe, hard to swallow

tallow 3 fat, tip 5 taper 6 bougie, candle, cierge 9 rushlight

Tall State

nickname of: 8 Illinois

tall story 3 fib, lie 4 yarn 5 fable 7 fiction, untruth, whopper 9 fairy tale, falsehood, fish story, invention 11 fabrication 16 cock-and-bull story

tally 3 add, sum 4 jibe, list, mark, poll, post 5 agree, count, match, score, sum up, total 6 accord, census, concur, muster, reckon, record, square 7 catalog, compute, conform 8 coincide, mark down, register, scorepad, tabulate 9 calculate, harmonize, reckoning, scorecard 10 correspond 11 enumeration

talon 4 claw, nail, spur

Talos

form: 5 youth 7 monster

made of: 5 brass 6 bronze

made by: 10 Hephaestus

guarded: 5 Crete

destroyed by: 5 Medea

uncle: 8 Daedalus

killed by: 8 Daedalus

Talthybius

occupation: 6 herald

employer: 9 Agamemnon

Tamar

author: 15 Robinson Jeffers

Tamar

father: 5 David 7 Absalom

mother: 6 Maacah

husband: 2 Er 4 Onan 5 Judah, Uriah

brother: 5 Amnon 7 Absalom, Chileab, Solomon 8 Adonijah

son: 5 Zarah 6 Pharez

daughter: 8 Maachiah

father-in-law: 5 Judah

Tamburlaine the Great

author: 18 Christopher Marlowe

character: 6 Cosroe 7 Mycetes, Orcanes 8 Bajazeth 9 Callepine, Techelles, Zenocrate 10 Theridamas, Usumcasane

tame 4 curb, damp, dull, flat, meek, mild, rein 5 break, check, quiet, timid, train 6 boring, bridle, broken, docile, gentle, govern, manage, master, placid, pliant, serene, subdue 7 conquer, control, pliable, prosaic, repress, subdued, tedious 8 amenable, domestic, dominate, lifeless, overcome, regulate, restrain, suppress, timorous, tranquil 9 tractable 10 made docile, submissive, unexciting 11 complaisant, domesticate, unresisting 12 domesticated 13 uninteresting

tameness 8 docility 9 placidity 10 gentleness, insipidity 12 complaisance, tractability 13 domestication 14 submissiveness

Taming of the Shrew, The

author: 18 William Shakespeare

character: 6 Bianca, Gremio, Tranio 8 Baptista, Lucentio 9 Hortensio, Katharina, Petruchio, Vincentio

director: 16 Franco Zeffirelli

cast: 11 Michael York, Natasha Pyne 13 Richard Burton (Petruchio) 14 Michael

Hordern 15 Elizabeth Taylor (Katharina), Vernon Dobtcheff
  score: 8 Nino Rota

Tammuz
  origin: 8 Sumerian
  god of: 9 shepherds
  Hebrew month: 6 fourth

Tam O'Shanter
  author: 11 Robert Burns

Tampa Bay
  football team: 7 Bandits 10 Buccaneers

tamper 3 mix 4 muck 6 butt in, fiddle, horn in, meddle, tinker 7 intrude, obtrude 9 interfere, intervene 10 fool around, mess around 12 monkey around

tamper with 5 alter 6 change, doctor 7 falsify

tan 4 roan 5 beige, brown, khaki, sandy, tawny 6 bronze, sorrel, suntan 7 bronzed 8 brownish, cinnamon, sunburnt 9 sunburned, suntanned 10 light brown 11 yellow-brown

Tanah Airkita see 9 Indonesia

Tananarive, Antananarivo
  capital of: 10 Madagascar

Tanaquil
  origin: 5 Roman
  form: 5 queen
  husband: 7 Tarquin 17 Tarquinius Priscus

Tandy, Jessica
  born: 6 London 7 England
  husband: 10 Hume Cronyn 11 Jack Hawkins
  roles: 8 The Birds 10 The Gin Game 12 Forever Amber 21 A Streetcar Named Desire

tang 3 bit 4 bite, hint, odor, reek 5 aroma, punch, savor, scent, smack, smell, sting, tinge, touch, trace 6 flavor 8 acridity, piquancy, pungency, tartness 9 acridness, sharpness, spiciness 10 suggestion

Tange, Kenzo
  architect of: 11 Press Center (Kofu) 16 Shizuoka Building (Tokyo) 19 Olympic Sports Stadia (Tokyo) 24 Kagawa Prefectural Offices (Takamatsu) 30 Imabara Municipal Office Building

tangibility 11 materiality, palpability 12 touchability

tangible 4 real 5 solid 6 actual 7 obvious 8 clear-cut, concrete, manifest, material, palpable, physical, positive 9 corporeal, touchable 10 verifiable 11 indubitable, substantial

tangle 3 fix, net, web 4 knot, maze, mesh, muss 5 ravel, skein, snarl, twist 6 jumble, jungle, ruffle, rumple, tousle 7 impasse, network 8 disheval, disorder 9 labyrinth 10 disarrange

tangled 6 knotty 7 chaotic, complex, jumbled, mixed-up, snarled 11 complicated, intertwined

Tanguy, Yves
  born: 5 Paris 6 France
  artwork: 4 Fear 17 Mama Papa is Wounded, Untitled Landscape 18 Rose of the Four Winds 20 Slowly Toward the North 22 Four O'Clock in Summer Hope, Indefinite Divisibility 23 Multiplication of the Arcs 25 Extinction of Useless Lights

tank 3 vat 6 boiler 7 cistern 8 aquarium, fish tank 9 container, reservoir 10 armored car, receptacle 11 storage tank

Tannhauser and the Tournament of Song at Wartburg
  opera by: 6 Wagner
  also: 41 Tannhauser und der Sangerkrieg auf dem Wartburg
  character: 5 Venus 7 Wolfram 9 Elizabeth

Tanoan
  tribe: 4 Tuei 5 Kiowa 6 Isleta

tantalize 4 bait 5 charm, taunt, tease, tempt 6 entice, lead on 7 bewitch, provoke, torment 8 intrigue 9 captivate, fascinate, titillate 15 whet the appetite 18 make one's mouth water

tantalizing 7 teasing 8 inviting, tempting 9 appealing, leading on 10 intriguing 11 fascinating

Tantalus
  king of: 4 Pisa 7 Phrygia
  father: 8 Thyestes
  wife: 12 Clytemnestra
  son: 6 Pelops
  daughter: 5 Niobe
  punishment in Hades: 6 hunger, thirst

tantamount 4 like 5 equal 9 analogous 10 comparable, equivalent, on a par with 12 commensurate 13 commensurable

tantrum 3 fit 5 storm 7 flare-up, rampage 8 outburst, paroxysm 9 explosion 12 fit of passion 13 burst of temper, conniption fit

Tanystropheous
  type: 8 dinosaur
  period: 8 Triassic

Tanzania
  other name: 12 isle of cloves
  capital/largest city: 11 Dar es Salaam
  new capital: 6 Dodoma
  others: 4 Wete, 5 Kilwa, Lindi, Moshi, Tanga, Ujiji 6 Arusha, Kigoma, Mwadui, Mwanza, Tabora 7 Korogwe, Mtawara 8 Morogoro, Zanzibar 12 Kwasemangube, Zanzibar Town
  division: 8 Zanzibar 17 union of Tanganyika
  monetary unit: 4 cent 8 shilling
  weight: 8 farsalah
  island: 5 Mafia, Pemba 6 Latham 8 Zanzibar
  lake: 5 Eyasi, Nyasa, Rukwa 6 Malawi, Natron, Nyassa 7 Manyara 8 Victoria 10 Tanganyika
  mountain: 4 Kibo, Mero 8 Usambara
  highest point: 11 Kilimanjaro
  river: 4 Lupa, Ruvu, Wami 5 Ruaha 6 Kagera, Luwegu, Mbaesa, Rufiji, Rungwa, Ruvuma 7 Nkululu, Pangani 8 Mbenkuru 11 Mbarangandu
  sea: 6 Indian
  physical feature:
  crater: 10 Ngorongoro

gorge: 7 Olduvai
national park: 9 Serengeti
plains: 9 Serengeti
steppe: 5 Masai 8 Iwembere
valley: 9 Great Rift
people: 2 Ha 4 Arab, Gogo, Goma, Haya, Hehe 5 Asian, Bantu, Masai 6 Arusha, Chagga, Sukuma, Wagogo, Wagoma 7 African, Makonde, Sambara, Sandawe, Shirazi, Swahili, Wabunga, Zongora 8 Nyakyusa, Nyamwezi
early man: 13 zinjanthropus
explorer: 6 Da Gama 7 Rebmann 11 Livingstone
leader: 5 Sayid 6 Karume 7 Nyerere 16 Sultan of Zanzibar
language: 5 Bantu 6 Arabic 7 English, Khoisan, Nilotic, Swahili 8 Cushitic, Gujarati
religion: 5 Islam 7 animism 12 Christianity
feature:
animal: 6 dik-dik
cattle barn: 4 byre
clothing: 4 sari 6 bui bui
fly: 6 tsetse
holiday: 8 Saba Saba
homestead: 8 manyatta
food:
dish: 5 ugali

Tao Te Ching
author: 6 Lao-tzu

Taotieh
origin: 7 Chinese
form: 6 animal

tap 3 pat, rap, use 4 cock, drum, peck, thud 5 spout, touch, valve 6 broach, employ, faucet, hammer, spigot, stroke, uncork, unplug 7 draw off, exploit, utilize 8 draw upon, stopcock 9 put to work, unstopper

taper 3 dip, wax 4 wick 5 light 6 candle, cierge, narrow 8 decrease 9 narrowing 10 diminution 12 come to a point

taper off 4 wane 5 abate 6 weaken 7 slacken, subside 8 decrease, diminish, fade away, slack off

tapestry 3 rug 5 arras, tapis 6 Bruges, fabric, mosaic 7 Gobelin, hanging, montage, weaving 8 Aubusson 12 wallcovering

Tapley, Mark
character in: 16 Martin Chuzzlewit
author: 7 Dickens

Tappertit, Simon
character in: 12 Barnaby Rudge
author: 7 Dickens

Taprobane *see* 8 Sri Lanka

taproom 3 bar, pub 6 lounge, saloon, tavern 8 alehouse 11 bar and grill, public house 14 cocktail lounge

Taranis
god of: 7 thunder

Taras Bulba
author: 12 Nikolai Gogol
character: 5 Ostap 6 Andrii, Yankel 26 Daughter of the Polish Waiwode

Tarascans, Tarascos
location: 6 Mexico 9 Michoacan 14 Central America
leader: 8 Zincicha 9 Tangaxoan, Tariacuri

Tarawa
capital of: 8 Kiribati

Tar Baby
author: 12 Toni Morrison

Tarchetius
king of: 9 Alba Longa

tardy 4 late, slow 5 slack 6 remiss 7 belated, languid, overdue 8 crawling, creeping, dilatory, slowpoke, sluggish 9 leisurely, not on time, reluctant, slow-paced, snail-like 10 behindhand, behind time, unpunctual 14 slow as molasses 15 procrastinating

tare 12 Biblical weed

target 3 aim, end 4 butt, dupe, goal, goat, gull, mark, plan, prey 5 patsy 6 design, intent, object, pigeon, victim 7 purpose 8 ambition 9 intention, objective 13 laughingstock

Targitaus
father: 4 Zeus
first inhabitant of: 7 Scythia

Tar Heel State
nickname of: 13 North Carolina

tariff 3 fee 4 cost, duty, fare, levy, rate, rent 5 price 6 charge, excise, impost 7 expense 8 input tax 9 excise tax, export tax 10 assessment, commission, freightage

Tarkington, Booth
author of: 6 Penrod 9 Seventeen 10 Alice Adams 13 Kate Fennigate 14 The Man from Home 17 Monsieur Beaucaire 19 The World Does Not Move 23 The Magnificent Ambersons

Tarleton, Stuart and Brent
characters in: 15 Gone With the Wind
author: 8 Mitchell

tarnish 3 dim 4 blot, dull, foul, soil, spot 5 dirty, erode, stain, sully, taint 6 befoul, darken, defame, defile, smirch, vilify 7 blacken, blemish, corrode, degrade, oxidize 8 besmirch, discolor, disgrace, dishonor 9 denigrate, discredit 10 lose luster, stigmatize 17 drag through the mud

tarnished 5 dirty 6 soiled 7 stained, sullied 8 oxidized 10 discolored

Tarnkappe
origin: 8 Germanic
mentioned in: 14 Nibelungenlied
form: 5 cloak
gives wearer: 8 strength 12 invisibility
stolen by: 9 Siegfried
stolen from: 8 Niblungs 9 Nibelungs

tarot
Italian: 6 naibes 7 attutti 8 tarocchi
German: 5 tarok
French: 5 tarau, tarot
cards/deck: 12 seventy-eight
division: 11 major arcana, minor arcana 12 lesser arcana 13 greater arcana
suit: 3 cup 4 coin, wand 5 baton, money, sword 6 cudgel 8 pentacle

face card: 4 king, page 5 knave, queen, valet 6 knight

major arcana: 4 Fool, Moon 5 Death 7 Justice 8 Judgment 9 Hanged Man 14 Wheel of Fortune

tarpaulin 4 tarp 6 canvas 9 dropcloth 15 waterproof cover

Tarpeia

form: 12 vestal virgin

father: 15 Spurius Tarpeius

betrayed: 4 Rome

betrayed to: 7 Sabines

killed by: 7 Sabines

Tarquin

king of: 4 Rome

origin: 8 Etruscan

also called: 17 Tarquinius Priscus 18 Tarquinius Superbus

wife: 8 Tanaquil

tarragon

botanical name: 20 Artemisia dracunculus

means: 6 dragon 12 little dragon

Arab: 7 tarkhum

French: 8 estragon

origin: 7 Siberia

used as: 8 purifier

flavor: 8 licorice

use: 4 fish 5 salad, sauce 10 mayonnaise 14 Bearnaise sauce

tarry 3 lag 4 bide, rest, stay, wait 5 abide, dally, delay, pause, stall 6 dawdle, linger, put off, remain 7 be tardy 8 hang back, postpone, stave off, take time 9 temporize 10 hang around 13 cool one's heels, procrastinate

tarsal

bone of: 5 ankle

Tarshish

father: 5 Javan 6 Bilhan

tart 3 pie 4 acid, sour 5 acerb, acrid, sharp, spicy, tangy 6 acetic, barbed, biting, bitter, crusty 7 caustic, cutting, piquant, pungent, sourish 8 vinegary 10 astringent 11 pastry shell

Tartarean see 8 infernal

Tartarin of Tarascon

author: 14 Alphonse Daudet

Tartarus

form: 5 abyss

below: 5 Hades

imprisoned: 6 Titans

tartness 7 acidity, sarcasm 8 acerbity 9 sharpness 11 astringency

Tartuffe

author: 7 Moliere

character: 5 Damis, Orgon 6 Dorine, Elmire, Valere 7 Cleante, Mariane 14 Madame Pernelle

Tarzan

author: 18 Edgar Rice Burroughs

character: 3 Boy 4 Jane 7 Cheetah

Tarzan also called: 15 Lord of Greystoke, Lord of the Jungle

comic strip creator: 9 Hal Foster 12 Burme Hogarth

task 3 job 4 duty, work 5 chore, labor, stint 6 charge, errand 7 mission 8 business 10 assignment 11 undertaking 14 responsibility

Task, The

author: 13 William Cowper

taskmaster 4 boss 6 despot, master, tyrant 7 foreman, headman, manager 8 director, martinet, overseer, stickler 10 supervisor 11 Simon Legree, slave driver 14 disciplinarian, superintendent

Tasmania

bay: 5 Storm 6 Oyster

capital: 6 Hobart

city: 10 Launceston

country: 9 Australia

formerly: 14 Van Diemen's Land

island: 4 Echo 6 Sorell

mountain: 4 Ossa 6 Cradle

river: 3 Esk

strait: 4 Bass

Tasso, Torquato

author of: 6 Aminta 7 Rinaldo 18 Jerusalem Delivered

taste 3 bit, nip, sip, try, yen 4 bent, bite, feel, meet, tang, test, whim 5 crumb, enjoy, fancy, savor, smack 6 desire, flavor, hunger, liking, morsel, relish, sample, thirst 7 craving, decorum, discern, forkful, insight, leaning, longing, savor of, smack of, swallow, undergo 8 appetite, delicacy, fondness, judgment, mouthful, penchant, piquancy, spoonful, yearning 9 encounter, hankering, partake of, propriety 10 experience, partiality, propensity, take a sip of 11 correctness, discernment, disposition, inclination, take a bite of 12 eat a little of, predilection 14 discrimination, drink a little of

French: 4 gout

tasteful 7 elegant, refined 8 artistic, becoming, cultured, esthetic, handsome, suitable 9 beautiful, exquisite 10 attractive, wellchosen

tasteless 3 low 4 flat, mild, rude, weak 5 bland, cheap, crass, crude, gaudy, gross, tacky 6 coarse, common, flashy, garish, ribald, watery 7 insipid, uncouth 8 improper, indecent, unseemly 9 inelegant, offensive, unrefined 10 disgusting, flavorless, indecorous, indelicate, uncultured, unesthetic, unflavored, unsuitable 11 distasteful, insensitive

tastemakers 7 leaders 10 avant-garde, innovators 12 stylesetters, trendsetters

tasty 3 hot 5 spicy, tangy, yummy 6 savory 7 piquant, zestful 8 luscious 9 delicious, flavorful, palatable, toothsome 10 appetizing, delectable, flavorsome 11 goodtasting, scrumptious 12 full-flavored, wellseasoned

Tatar, Mr

character in: 22 The Mystery of Edwin Drood

author: 7 Dickens

Tatius
also: 5 Titus
co-ruler with: 7 Romulus

Tatler, The
author: 13 Joseph Addison, Richard Steele

tattered 4 torn 6 broken, ragged, ripped, shabby, shaggy 10 disheveled 11 dilapidated

tatters 4 rags 6 shreds 7 patches

tattle 3 rat 4 blab 5 prate 6 gabble, gossip, snitch, squeal, tell on 7 blather, chatter, hearsay, prattle, twaddle 8 inform on 9 loose talk 11 mudslinging 12 tittle-tattle 13 tongue-wagging

tattletale 3 rat 4 fink 5 sneak 6 gossip, snitch 7 ratfink, stoolie, tattler 8 betrayer, busybody, informer, squealer, telltale 8 informer 10 newsmonger, talebearer 11 rumormonger, stool pigeon 12 blabbermouth, troublemaker 13 scandalmonger

Tatum, Edward Lawrie
field: 8 genetics 12 biochemistry
discovered: 19 gene characteristics
awarded: 10 Nobel Prize

taunt 3 guy, rag 4 gibe, jeer, jive, mock, slur, twit 5 scoff, sneer, tease 6 deride, harass, insult, jeer at 7 provoke, ragging, sneer at, snigger, torment 8 chaffing, derision, ridicule 9 make fun of, poke fun at, snigger at 10 harassment, make game of, tormenting 11 provocation

Taura
form: 3 cow
attribute: 6 sacred

taurobolium
rite of: 7 baptism

Taurog, Norman
director of: 6 Skippy (Oscar) 8 Boys' Town

Taurus
symbol: 4 bull
planet: 5 Venus
rules: 5 money 9 resources
born: 3 May 5 April

taut 4 neat, snug, tidy, trig, trim 5 rigid, smart, tense, tight 6 spruce 7 orderly 8 not loose, not slack 9 shipshape, unbending, unrelaxed 10 drawn tight, inflexible, nonsense 11 under strain 12 businesslike 13 well-regulated 15 well-disciplined

tavern 3 bar, pub 4 dive 6 bistro, saloon 7 barroom, gin mill, taproom 8 alehouse, drinkery, grogshop 9 beer joint, brasserie, honky-tonk, roadhouse 10 restaurant 11 public house 12 watering hole 14 cocktail lounge
French: 7 auberge
German: 8 Brauhaus

tawdry 4 loud 5 cheap, crass, gaudy, showy, tacky 6 flashy, garish, tinsel, vulgar 7 raffish 8 gimcrack 9 inelegant, obtrusive, tasteless 10 flamboyant 11 conspicuous, pretentious 12 meretricious, ostentatious

tawny 3 tan 4 fawn 5 beige, dusky, olive, sandy 6 bronze 7 swarthy 8 brownish 10 light brown 14 yellowish-brown

tax 3 sap, try 4 duty, lade, levy, load, tire, toll 5 drain, weigh 6 assess, burden, charge, custom, excise, impost, saddle, strain, tariff, weight 7 deplete, exhaust, stretch, wear out 8 exertion, overwork 10 assessment, obligation, overburden
kind: 4 city 5 sales, state 6 county, excise, income, luxury 8 property 11 inheritance 12 excess profit

Taxi
character: 9 John Burns, Tony Banta 10 Alex Rieger 11 Elaine Nardo, Latka Gravas 12 Bobby Wheeler, Louie De Palma
cast: 9 Tony Danza 10 Judd Hirsch 11 Andy Kaufman, Danny DeVito, Jeff Conaway 12 Marilu Henner 13 Randall Carver
company: 11 Sunshine Cab

taxicab 4 hack 6 jitney 7 droshky, hackney 8 hired car, rickshaw 10 automobile 11 jinrickshaw

Taxi Driver
director: 14 Martin Scorsese
cast: 10 Peter Boyle 11 Jodie Foster 12 Albert Brooks, Harvey Keitel, Robert De Niro 13 Leonard Harris 14 Cybill Shepherd
setting: 11 New York City
score: 15 Bernard Herrmann
script: 12 Paul Schrader

taxonomy
study of: 17 structure contrast 19 structure comparison

Taygete
member of: 8 Pleiades
father: 5 Atlas
son: 10 Lacedaemon

Taylor, Elizabeth
born: 6 London 7 England
husband: 8 Mike Todd 10 John Warner 11 Eddie Fisher, Nicky Hilton 13 Richard Burton 14 Michael Wilding
roles: 5 Giant 7 Ivanhoe 9 Cleopatra 11 Little Women 12 The Sandpiper 14 A Place in the Sun, National Velvet, Raintree County 16 Butterfield Eight (Oscar), Cat on a Hot Tin Roof, Father of the Bride 18 Suddenly Last Summer 19 The Taming of the Shrew 25 Who's Afraid of Virginia Woolf (Oscar)

Taylor, Robert
real name: 22 Spangler Arlington Brugh
wife: 12 Ursula Thiess 15 Barbara Stanwyck
roles: 7 Camille, Ivanhoe 8 Quo Vadis 11 Billy the Kid 14 Waterloo Bridge 20 Magnificent Obsession

Taylor, Zachary
nickname: 16 Old Rough and Ready
presidential rank: 7 twelfth
party: 4 Whig
state represented: 2 LA
defeated: 4 (Lewis) Cass 8 (Martin) Van Buren
vice president: 8 (Millard) Fillmore
cabinet:
state: 7 (John Middleton) Clayton
treasury: 8 (William Morris) Meredith

war: 8 (George Walker) Crawford
attorney general: 7 (Reverdy) Johnson
navy: 7 (William Ballard) Preston
postmaster general: 8 (Jacob) Collamer
interior: 5 (Thomas) Ewing
born: 12 Montebello VA 12 Orange County
died: 12 Washington DC
buried: 12 Louisville KY
education: 9 no college 16 privately tutored
religion: 12 Episcopalian
political career: 21 none prior to presidency
civilian career: 7 planter, soldier
military service: 6 US Army 12 major general
War: 7 Mexican 9 Black Hawk 19 War of Eighteen-Twelve 14 Second Seminole
notable events of lifetime/presidency:
treaty: 13 Clayton-Bulwer
father: 7 Richard
mother: 5 Sarah (Dabney Strother)
siblings: 6 George 7 Hancock 11 Sarah Bailey 12 Elizabeth Lee, Emily Richard 13 Joseph Pannill 21 William Dabney Strother
wife: 8 Margaret (Mackall Smith)
children: 7 Richard 9 Sarah Knox 10 Ann Mackall 13 Margaret Smith, Mary Elizabeth, Octavia Panill

Tchad *see* 4 Chad

Tchaikovsky, Peter (Piotr Ilyich Chaikovsky)
born: 6 Russia 8 Votkinsk
composer of: 7 Manfred, Mazeppa 8 Iolanthe, Pathetic (symphony No 6), Swan Lake 9 Joan of Arc 10 Nutcracker 12 Eugene Onegin, Winter Dreams 14 Italian Caprice, Romeo and Juliet, The Enchantress 16 The Queen of Spades 17 Francesca da Rimini, The Sleeping Beauty 22 Eighteen-Twelve Overture

Tchile *see* 5 Chile

tea 16 Camellia sinensis
varieties: 5 Assam, Bohea, China, green, pekoe, Yerba 6 Ceylon, Oolong, Oswego, Tisane 7 African, Arabian, cambric, crystal, Lapsang, Mexican, redroot, Spanish 8 bergamot, camomile, Earl Grey, Labrador, mountain, Paraguay, Siberian, Souchong, Woodruff 9 gunpowder, lemon balm, New Jersey, sassafras 10 Darjeeling, Philippine 11 Appalachian, Orange Pekoe 14 Irish breakfast 16 English breakfast

teach 5 coach, drill, edify, prime, tutor 6 inform, school 7 educate, implant, prepare 8 exercise, instruct 9 enlighten, inculcate 10 discipline 12 indoctrinate

Teach
character in: 21 The Master of Ballantrae
author: 9 Stevenson

teacher 3 don 5 coach, tutor 6 master, mentor 7 maestro, trainer 8 educator 9 preceptor, professor 10 instructor, school-

marm 12 schoolmaster 13 schoolteacher 14 schoolmistress

teaching 5 dogma, tenet 6 belief 7 nurture, precept 8 doctrine, pedagogy, training, tutelage, tutoring 9 education, principle, schooling 10 conviction, philosophy 11 inculcation, instructing, instruction, preparation 14 indoctrination

tea dance
French: 10 the dansant

teal
group of: 5 ducks
color: 4 blue 5 green

team 3 rig, set 4 ally, band, crew, five, gang, join, nine, pair, side, unit, yoke 5 force, group, merge, party, squad, staff, unify, unite 6 circle, clique, couple, eleven, league, tandem 7 combine, company, coterie, faction 8 alliance, federate 9 coalition, cooperate 10 amalgamate, federation, sports team, yoked group 11 association, consolidate, get together, incorporate 12 band together, join together 13 confederation

teammate 4 ally 7 partner 8 co-player, coworker 9 associate, colleague, co-partner 11 confederate 12 collaborator

team spirit 10 group pride, solidarity 13 esprit de corps

team up 4 ally 5 unite 9 cooperate 10 join forces 11 collaborate

tear 3 fly, gap, hie, rip, run 4 bolt, dart, dash, grab, hole, mist, pull, race, rend, rent, rift, rive, rush, scud, slit, snag, swim, whiz, yank 5 abuse, break, crack, fault, pluck, scoot, seize, sever, shoot, shred, speed, split, spurt, sweep, whisk 6 breach, cleave, damage, divide, gallop, hasten, hustle, injury, plunge, ravage, scurry, snatch, sprint, sunder, wrench 7 disrupt, fissure, hard use, opening, rupture, scamper, scuttle 8 disunite, teardrop, scramble, splinter 9 come apart, hotfoot it, pull apart, skedaddle 10 impairment, make tracks 11 destruction 12 pull to pieces

tear down 4 raze 5 level, smash, wreck 7 destroy, flatten 8 demolish 9 dismantle, take apart

tearful 5 teary, weepy 6 crying 7 bawling, crushed, sobbing, wailing, weeping 8 mournful 9 lamenting, sniveling 10 blubbering, lachrymose, whimpering 11 heartbroken 12 inconsolable 13 brokenhearted

tear off 5 sever 6 detach, rip off 7 pull off 8 break off, separate 10 wrench away

Teasdale, Sara
author of: 8 Love Song 11 Helen of Troy 13 Dark of the Moon 14 Flame and Shadow, Rivers to the Sea, Strange Victory

tease 3 guy, irk, nag, rag, vex 4 bait, gall, gibe, goad, haze, jeer, josh, mock, pest, rile, twit 5 annoy, chafe, harry, mimic, pique, scoff, sneer, taunt, worry 6 badger, bother, harass, hazing, heckle, hector, mocker, needle, pester, plague, teaser 7 bedevil, chafing, laugh at, needler, provoke, razzing, snigger, taunter, torment, worrier 8 derision, heckling, irritate, needling, ridicule 9 aggravate, make fun of, mimicking, persecute, tantalize, tormentor 10 harassment, tantalizer 11 persecution

teaspoon
abbreviation: 3 tsp

Teazle, Sir Peter and Lady
characters in: 19 The School for Scandal
author: 8 Sheridan

technical 5 trade 10 mechanical, vocational 11 complicated, nonacademic 13 technological

technique 3 art, way 4 form 5 craft, knack, style 6 manner, method, system 7 formula, know-how 8 approach, facility 9 procedure 10 adroitness, expertness, technology 11 proficiency 12 skillfulness

Tecmessa
father: 8 Teuthras
son: 9 Eurysaces
carried off by: 14 Telamonian Ajax

tedious 3 dry 4 drab, dull, long, slow 5 vapid 6 boring, dismal, dreary, jejune, tiring 7 humdrum, insipid, irksome, onerous, prosaic 8 drawn-out, lifeless, tiresome, wearying 9 fatiguing, laborious, wearisome 10 burdensome, exhausting, monotonous, oppressive, unexciting 13 time-consuming, unimaginative, uninteresting

tediousness 5 ennui 7 boredom 8 dullness, monotony

tedium 3 rut 5 ennui 7 boredom 8 drabness, dullness, monotony, sameness 10 dreariness 11 routineness 12 tiresomeness

tedium of life
Latin: 12 taedium vitae

teem 4 brim, gush 5 swarm 6 abound 8 be full of, overflow 9 be overrun 15 burst at the seams

teeming 4 full 7 crowded 8 swarming 9 abounding, bounteous 11 overflowing

teeny-weeny 3 wee 4 tiny 5 dwarf 6 little, minute, petite 9 miniature, minuscule 10 diminutive, pocket-size 11 lilliputian, microscopic, pocket-sized

teeter 4 reel, sway 5 lurch, waver 6 seesaw, totter, wobble 7 stagger 8 hesitate 9 vacillate

teetotaler 3 dry 9 abstainer 10 nondrinker 14 prohibitionist

Tegeates
father: 6 Lycaon

Tegucigalpa
capital of: 8 Honduras

Tegyrius
king of: 6 Thrace

Tehani
character in: 17 Mutiny on the Bounty
authors: 4 Hall 8 Nordhoff

Tehran, Teheran
capital of: 4 Iran
landmark: 10 Melaat Park 12 Marble Palace, Marmar Palace 14 Azadai Monument, Gulestan Palace, Saadabad Pal-

ace 15 Freedom Monument, Hosseineh Mosque, Shahyad Monument 23 Center for Islamic Studies
means: 9 warm place
mountain: 6 Elburz 8 Demavend
ruler: 8 Khomeini 23 Muhammad Reza Shah Pahlavi

te igitur 13 thee therefore

Teiresias see 8 Tiresias

Telamon
king of: 7 Salamis
member of: 9 Argonauts
father: 6 Aeacus
mother: 6 Endeis
brother: 6 Peleus
half-brother: 6 Phocus
wife: 6 Glauce 7 Eriboea
son: 4 Ajax 6 Teucer
friend: 8 Hercules

Telchines
form: 6 beings
characteristic: 9 malicious

Telegonus
father: 7 Proteus 8 Odysseus
mother: 5 Circe
wife: 2 Io 8 Penelope
killed: 8 Odysseus
killed by: 8 Hercules

telegraph
invented by: 5 Morse, Woods 6 Edison 7 Marconi

Telemachus
father: 8 Odysseus
mother: 8 Penelope
son: 7 Latinus

Telemann, Georg Philipp
born: 7 Germany 9 Magdeburg
composer of: 9 Fantasias 10 Times of Day 12 Don Quichotte 14 Die Tageszeiten, Musique de Table

Telemus
vocation: 4 seer
father: 7 Eurymus
warned: 10 Polyphemus

telepathy 3 ESP 10 sixth sense 11 second sight 12 clairvoyance 19 spirit communication, thought transference 22 extrasensory perception

Telephassa
husband: 6 Agenor

telephone
invented by: 4 Bell

Telephus
king of: 5 Mysia
father: 8 Hercules
mother: 4 Auge

telescope
invented by: 7 Galileo 10 Lippershey
astronomical: 6 Kepler

Telesphorus
god of: 15 illness recovery

telesterion
form: 8 building
purpose: 8 religion 11 celebration

television
invented by: 5 Baird 8 Zworykin 10 Farnsworth

tell 3 ask, bid, own, say, see **4** blab **5** bruit, count, order, speak, spout, state, utter, weigh, write **6** advise, babble, betray, blazon, depict, detail, direct, figure, impart, inform, number, recite, reckon, relate, report, reveal, sketch, unfold **7** apprise, command, compute, confess, declare, discern, divulge, express, find out, mention, narrate, portray, predict, publish, recount, request **8** acquaint, count off, describe, disclose, estimate, forecast, foretell, identify, instruct, perceive, register, set forth **9** apprehend, ascertain, broadcast, calculate, chronicle, enumerate, enunciate, influence, make known, pronounce, recognize **10** take effect **11** communicate, distinguish **12** discriminate **17** breathe a word about

Teller, Edward
    field: **7** physics
    developed: **8** atom bomb **12** hydrogen bomb

telling 5 solid, valid **6** cogent, potent **7** decided, weighty **8** decisive, definite, forceful, material, positive, powerful, striking **9** effective, effectual, important, momentous, trenchant **10** conclusive, definitive, impressive **11** efficacious, influential, significant **13** consequential

telltale 6 gossip **7** tattler **8** busybody, giveaway, informer, squealer **9** affirming, betraying, divulging, revealing, verifying **10** confirming, disclosing, newsbearer, talebearer, tattletale **11** informative **12** blabbermouth, enlightening **13** scandalmonger

Tellus
    called: **10** Terra Mater
    origin: **5** Roman
    goddess of: **5** earth **8** marriage **9** fertility **11** agriculture
    corresponds to: **4** Gaea

Telphusa
    form: **5** nymph
    location: **6** spring
    characteristic: **7** cunning

Temenus
    father: **8** Pelasgus **12** Aristomachus
    brother: **11** Aristodemus, Cresphontes
    reared by: **4** Hera

temerity 4 gall **5** brass, cheek, nerve **8** audacity, boldness, chutzpah, rashness **9** brashness, freshness, impudence, insolence, pushiness, sauciness **10** brazenness, effrontery **11** forwardness **12** impertinence, indiscretion **13** foolhardiness, intrusiveness

Temin, Howard Martin
    field: **8** genetics, oncology
    discovered: **20** reverse transcriptase
    awarded: **10** Nobel Prize

temper 3 ire **4** bile, calm, fury, gall, mood, rage **5** allay, anger, humor, pique, quiet, still, wrath **6** animus, anneal, choler, dander, harden, pacify, soften, soothe, spleen **7** appease, balance, compose, dudgeon, emotion, ferment, passion, toughen, umbrage **8** acrimony, bad humor, calmness, mitigate, moderate, palliate, vexation **9**

annoyance, composure, huffiness **10** irritation, strengthen **11** displeasure, disposition, equilibrium, frame of mind, indignation, peevishness, tranquilize **12** churlishness, irascibility, irritability

temperament 4 bent, cast, mood, soul, tone **5** humor, tenor **6** makeup, nature, spirit, temper **7** leaning, quality **8** tendency **9** character **10** complexion **11** disposition, frame of mind, personality

temperamental 5 fiery, moody **6** fickle **7** erratic, peppery, willful **8** unstable, volatile **9** emotional, excitable, explosive, hotheaded, mercurial, sensitive, turbulent **10** capricious, headstrong, high-strung, hysterical, mettlesome, passionate, unreliable **11** tempestuous, thin-skinned **12** undependable **13** unpredictable

temperance 8 prudence, sobriety **9** restraint **10** abstention, abstinence, discretion, moderation, self-denial **11** forbearance, prohibition, self-control, teetotalism **14** abstemiousness, self-discipline

temperate 4 calm, cool, even, mild, sane, soft, warm **5** balmy, sober, sunny **6** gentle, mellow, sedate, steady **7** clement, patient, sparing **8** composed, moderate, pleasant, rational, tranquil **9** collected, easygoing, unruffled **10** coolheaded, reasonable **11** levelheaded **13** dispassionate, self-possessed, unextravagant, unimpassioned **14** self-controlled, self-restrained

temperature measurement 6 degree, Kelvin **7** Celsius **10** Fahrenheit

tempest 5 chaos, furor, storm **6** hubbub, tumult, uproar **8** brouhaha, outbreak, upheaval **9** agitation, cataclysm, commotion **10** hurly-burly, turbulence **11** disturbance

Tempest, The
    author: **18** William Shakespeare
    character: **5** Ariel **6** Alonso **7** Antonio, Caliban, Gonzalo, Miranda **8** Prospero **9** Ferdinand, Sebastian

Tempestates
    origin: **5** Roman
    goddesses of: **6** storms

tempestuous 3 hot **5** fiery **6** raging, stormy **7** excited, frantic, furious, violent **8** agitated, feverish, frenzied **9** emotional, explosive, turbulent, wrought-up **10** hysterical, passionate, tumultuous **11** impassioned, overwrought

Templar, Simon
    character in: **8** The Saint
    author: **9** Charteris

temple 4 fane, kirk **6** chapel, church, mosque, pagoda, priory, shrine **7** convent **8** basilica, pantheon **9** cathedral, joss house, monastery, sanctuary, synagogue **10** house of God, tabernacle **12** meetinghouse

Temple, Shirley
    married name: **18** Shirley Temple Black
    born: **13** Santa Monica CA
    roles: **5** Heidi **10** Bright Eyes **15** Wee Willie Winkie **16** Little Miss Marker, The Little Colonel, The Littlest Rebel **18** Poor

Little Rich Girl 21 Susannah of the Mounties 23 Rebecca of Sunnybrook Farm

Temple, The
author: 13 George Herbert

Temple Beau, The
author: 13 Henry Fielding

tempo 4 clip, gait, pace, rate, time 5 meter, speed 6 pacing, stride, timing 8 momentum, velocity

tempo giusto
music: 10 strict time

temporal 3 lay 5 civil 6 mortal 7 mundane, passing, profane, secular, worldly 8 day-to-day, fleeting, fugitive 9 ephemeral, temporary, transient 10 evanescent, noneternal 11 impermanent, nonclerical 12 nonspiritual 17 nonecclesiastical

temporary, temporarily 5 brief, fleet 7 interim, passing, stopgap 8 fleeting, fugitive 9 ephemeral, momentary, provisory, transient 10 evanescent, short-lived, transitory 11 impermanent, provisional 13 flash-in-the-pan
Latin: 10 pro tempore

temporary dwelling
French: 10 pied-a-terre

temporize 5 delay, hedge, stall, tarry, waver 8 hang back, maneuver 9 hem and haw, vacillate 10 equivocate 11 play for time 12 drag one's feet, tergiversate 13 procrastinate

tempt 3 try, woo 4 bait, draw, goad, lure, pull, risk 5 charm, decoy, prick, rouse 6 allure, arouse, entice, incite, invite, seduce 7 attract, bewitch, provoke 8 appeal to, intrigue, inveigle 9 captivate, tantalize 12 put to the test 13 take one's fancy 14 fly in the face of 15 whet the appetite

temptation 4 bait, draw, lure, pull, urge 5 charm, snare, spell 8 stimulus, tempting 9 incentive, seduction 10 allurement, attraction, enticement, incitement, inducement 11 captivation, fascination, provocation

tempter 5 Satan 7 enticer, seducer 8 the Devil

temptress 4 vamp 5 Circe, flirt, siren 7 charmer, Delilah, Jezebel, Lorelei, vampire 8 coquette 9 odalisque, sorceress 10 seductress 11 enchantress, femme fatale

tempus fugit 9 time flies

Ten (10)
director: 12 Blake Edwards
cast: 7 Bo Derek 11 Dudley Moore 12 Julie Andrews

tenable 6 viable 8 arguable, rational, sensible, workable 9 excusable 10 condonable, defendable, defensible, vindicable 11 justifiable, warrantable 12 maintainable

tenacious 3 set 4 fast, firm, hard, iron 6 dogged, mulish 7 adamant, staunch 8 clinging, constant, obdurate, resolute, stalwart, stubborn 9 immovable, obstinate, pigheaded, steadfast, unbending 10 determined, inexorable, inflexible, persistent, relentless, unswerving, unwavering, unyielding 11 persevering, undeviating, unfal-

tering, unremitting 12 intransigent, unchangeable 14 uncompromising

tenaciousness 8 tenacity 9 endurance 10 resolution 11 persistence 12 perseverance, resoluteness 13 determination 16 stick-to-itiveness

tenacity 8 strength 9 toughness 10 resolution 11 persistence 12 cohesiveness, perseverance, resoluteness 13 determination, tenaciousness 16 stick-to-itiveness

tenant 6 lessee, lodger, renter, roomer 7 boarder, denizen, dweller 8 occupant, resident 10 inhabitant 11 householder, leaseholder, paying guest

Tenant of Wildfell Hall, The
author: 10 Anne Bronte

Tenants, The
author: 14 Bernard Malamud

Ten Commandments
also: 9 Decalogue
given to: 5 Moses
where given: 10 Mount Sinai
inscribed on: 12 stone tablets
first: 32 Thou shalt have no other Gods before me
second: 37 Thou shalt not bow down before graven images
third: 44 Thou shalt not take the name of the Lord thy God in vain
fourth: 34 Remember the Sabbath Day and keep it holy
fifth: 26 Honor thy father and thy mother
sixth: 16 Thou shalt not kill
seventh: 26 Thou shalt not commit adultery
eighth: 17 Thou shalt not steal
ninth: 46 Thou shalt not bear false witness against thy neighbor
tenth: 17 Thou shalt not covet

Ten Commandments, The
director: 13 Cecil B DeMille
cast: 8 Nina Foch 9 John Derek 10 Anne Baxter, Debra Paget, Yul Brynner 11 Martha Scott 12 Vincent Price 13 John Carradine, Yvonne De Carlo 14 Charlton Heston (Moses), Judith Anderson 15 Cedric Hardwicke, Edward G Robinson

tend 3 aim 4 bear, head, lead, lean, mind, move 5 be apt, guide, nurse, point, watch 6 extend, foster, manage, wait on 7 care for, nurture 8 attend to, be liable, be likely 9 bid fair to, gravitate, look after, supervise, watch over 10 minister to, predispose, take care of 11 keep an eye on

tendency 3 aim, set 4 bent 5 drift, drive, habit, trend 6 course 7 heading, impulse, leaning, turning 8 penchant 9 direction, proneness, readiness 10 proclivity, propensity 11 disposition, gravitation, inclination 14 predisposition

tender 3 raw 4 fond, give, good, kind, soft, sore, weak 5 frail, green, place, young 6 aching, benign, callow, caring, dainty, extend, feeble, gentle, hand in, loving, prefer, submit, weakly 7 advance, fragile, hold out, painful, present, proffer, propose, suggest, swollen 8 delicate, generous, immature, inflamed, juvenile, merciful, propound, underage, youthful **9** lay before, sensitive, volunteer **10** benevolent, put forward, thoughtful, vulnerable **11** considerate, sentimental, softhearted, sympathetic, warmhearted **12** affectionate **13** compassionate, inexperienced, understanding **14** impressionable **15** unsophisticated

tenderfoot 4 tyro **6** novice, rookie **8** beginner, neophyte **9** fledgling, greenhorn **10** apprentice

tenderhearted 4 mild **6** benign, gentle, humane **8** generous, merciful **10** altruistic, benevolent, responsive, thoughtful **11** considerate, kindhearted, softhearted, sympathetic, warmhearted **13** compassionate, understanding

tenderheartedness 4 pity **5** heart **7** empathy **8** sympathy **10** compassion

tendering 6 giving **8** offering **9** advancing, extending, proposing **10** holding out, preferring, proffering, submitting, suggesting **11** propounding **12** volunteering

Tender Is the Night
   author: 16 F Scott Fitzgerald
   character: 8 Abe North **9** Dick Diver **11** Nicole Diver, Tommy Barban **12** Rosemary Hoyt

tenderness 4 love **6** aching, warmth **7** rawness **8** delicacy, fondness, goodness, humanity, kindness, mildness, smarting, softness, soreness, sympathy **9** affection **10** compassion, gentleness, humaneness, kindliness, lovingness **11** beneficence, benevolence, painfulness, sensitivity **12** mercifulness **14** loving kindness

tendon
   part of: 21 musculoskeletal system

tendril 4 coil, curl **5** crook, shoot, sprig, twist **6** winder **7** climber, ringlet

tenebrous 3 dim **4** dark **5** murky **6** gloomy **7** obscure, shadowy **8** darkened, obscured **13** unilluminated

Tenes
   father: 6 Cycnus
   mother: 7 Proclea
   stepmother: 9 Phylonome
   sister: 8 Hemithea

tenet 4 rule, view **5** canon, credo, creed, dogma, maxim **6** belief, thesis **7** opinion **8** doctrine, ideology, position, teaching **9** principle **10** conviction, persuasion

Tennessee
   abbreviation: 2 TN **4** Tenn
   nickname: 7 Big Bend **9** Volunteer **11** Old Franklin
   capital: 9 Nashville
   largest city: 7 Memphis
   others: 5 Alcoa, Paris **6** Camden, Sparta **7** Bristol, Dickson, Pulaski **8** Franklin, Gallatin, Oak Ridge **9** Cedar Hill, Cleveland, Inglewood, Kingsport, Knoxville, Lexington **10** Greenbrier, Morristown, Old Hickory **11** Chattanooga, Clarksville, Springfield **12** Fayetteville, Murfreesboro **14** Hendersonville
   college: 4 Fisk, Lane **5** Bryan, Siena **6** Bethel **7** Belmont, Lambuth, Lemoyne **8** Milligan, Tusculum **10** Vanderbilt **12** Southwestern **13** David Lipscomb **14** Meharry Medical **17** Tennessee Wesleyan
   feature: 12 The Hermitage
   dam: 6 Norris, Wilson **7** Douglas
   fort: 5 Henry **8** Donalson, Nashboro
   national park: 6 Shiloh **13** Cumberland Gap **19** Great Smoky Mountains (with North Carolina)
   national parkway: 12 Natchez Trace
   tribe: 7 Shawnee **8** Cherokee **9** Chickasaw
   people: 7 Sequoya **8** John Bell **9** James Agee **10** Grace Moore **11** Bessie Smith, Cordell Hull **12** Davy Crockett **18** Carey Estes Kefauver **23** Alvin Cullum "Sergeant" York **32** Ernest Jennings "Tennessee Ernie" Ford
   explorer: 6 Arthur, De Soto **7** Jolliet, La Salle, Needham **9** Marquette
   lake: 7 Douglas **8** Barkeley, Cherokee, Reelfoot, Watts Bar **10** Center Hill **11** Chickamauga
   land rank: 12 thirty-fourth
   mountain: 5 Guyot **7** Lookout, Smokies **9** Blue Ridge **10** Cumberland, Great Smoky
   highest point: 13 Clingman's Dome
   physical feature:
      basin: 9 Nashville
      highlands: 11 Appalachian
      plain: 7 Coastal
      plateau: 10 Cumberland
   president: 10 James K Polk **13** Andrew Jackson, Andrew Johnson
   river: 3 Elk **4** Duck **5** Caney, Obion, Stone **6** Clinch **7** Hatchie, Holston **8** Hiwassee **9** Tennessee **10** Cumberland **11** French Broad, Mississippi **15** Little Tennessee
   state admission: 9 sixteenth
   state bird: 11 mockingbird
   state flower: 4 flag, iris **6** maypop **13** passion flower
   state motto: 16 America at Its Best **22** Agriculture and Commerce
   state song: 11 My Tennessee **17** The Tennessee Waltz **19** My Homeland Tennessee **26** When It's Iris Time in Tennessee
   state tree: 11 tulip poplar **12** yellow poplar

tennis
   athlete: 8 Don Budge, Jan Kodes, Rod Laver, Tom Okker **9** Bjorn Borg, Ivan Lendl, Stan Smith **10** Arthur Ashe, Bill Tilden, Jack Kramer, Maria Bueno, Pam Shriver, Roy Emerson, Steffi Graf **11** Alice Marble, Andre Agassi, Edward Dibbs, Ilie Nastase, John McEnroe, Ken Rosewall, Tracy Austin **12** Althea Gibson, Darren Cahill, Francois Durr, Jimmy Connors, John Newcombe, Mats Wilander, Roscoe Tanner, Virginia Wade **13** Dennis Ralston, Harold Solomon, Manuel

Orantes, Manuel Santana, Martin Riessen, Wendy Turnbull **14** Brian Gottfried, Guillermo Vilas, Hana Mandlikova, Pancho Gonzalez, Rosemary Casals **15** Charles Pasarell, Chris Evert Lloyd, Maureen Connolly, Richard Stockton, Vitas Gerulaitis **17** Donald Schollander, Nancy Richey Gunter **18** Margaret Smith Court, Martina Navratilova **20** Helen Wills Moody Roark **21** Billie Jean Moffitt King, Evonne Goolagong Cawley

Tennyson, Alfred, Lord
   author of: 4 Maud **7** Mariana, Ulysses **10** Enoch Arden, In Memoriam (A A H) **12** Locksley Hall, Morte d'Arthur **16** The Lady of Shalott **18** The Idylls of the King **26** The Charge of the Light Brigade

tenor 4 gist **5** drift, sense, trend **6** course, import, intent, nature, object **7** content, essence, meaning, purport, purpose **8** argument, tendency **9** direction, intention, substance **11** connotation, implication **12** significance

tense 4 taut **5** brace, drawn, rigid, shaky, stiff, tight **6** braced, draw up, on edge, uneasy **7** anxious, excited, fearful, fidgety, jittery, nervous, restive, stiffen, uptight **8** agitated, make taut, restless, strained, timorous **9** tighten up, tremulous, wrought-up **10** high-strung, inflexible, unyielding **12** apprehensive

tension 5 dread **6** spring, strain, stress **7** anxiety, pulling, tugging **8** bad vibes, exertion, pressure, rigidity, tautness, traction **9** hostility, misgiving, stiffness, straining, tightness **10** stretching **11** fearfulness, nervousness, restiveness, trepidation **12** apprehension, elastic force, perturbation **13** bad vibrations, combativeness

tent 3 pup **4** care, hard **5** gauze, probe, tepee **6** bigtop, canvas, search, teepee, wigwam **7** shelter **8** pavilion **10** tabernacle

tentacle 3 arm **6** feeler **9** appendage

tentative 4 iffy **5** trial **6** acting **8** not final, proposed **9** ad interim, temporary, undecided, unsettled **10** contingent, indefinite, not settled **11** conditional, probational, provisional, speculative, unconfirmed **12** experimental, probationary **15** subject to change **18** under consideration

tentative procedure 4 test **5** flier, trail **6** feeler, tryout **7** venture **10** experiment **12** trial balloon

tenuous 4 slim, thin, weak **5** frail, shaky **6** flimsy, paltry, slight **7** fragile, shallow, slender **8** delicate, gossamer **9** uncertain **10** indefinite **11** halfhearted, unsupported **12** unconvincing **13** unsubstantial

tenure 4 rule, term, time **5** reign **7** tenancy **9** occupancy, retention **10** incumbency, occupation, permanency, possession **11** entitlement, job security **14** administration

tepee, teepee 4 chum, tent **5** lodge **6** wigwam **7** wickiup

tepid 4 cool, mild **7** languid, warmish **8** lukewarm, moderate **9** apathetic, impassive, temperate **10** nonchalant, phlegmatic

11 halfhearted, indifferent, unemotional **13** lackadaisical **14** unenthusiastic

tequila
   type: 6 spirit
   origin: 6 Mexico
   made from: 5 agave **6** maguey
   used with: 4 lime, salt **5** lemon
   drink: 7 Chapala **8** El Diablo
   with creme de cacao: 8 Toreador
   with kahlua: 9 Brave Bull
   with orange juice: 7 Sunrise
   with Tia Maria: 9 Brave Bull
   with triple sec: 9 Margarita

Terah
   son: 5 Abram, Haran, Nahor

Teraphim
   origin: 6 Hebrew
   form: 4 idol

Ter Borch, Gerard (Terburg)
   born: 6 Zwolle **14** The Netherlands
   artwork: 8 Flea Hunt **10** The Concert **14** Peace of Munster **21** The Parental Admonition

Terbrugghen, Hendrick
   born: 8 Deventer **14** The Netherlands
   artwork: 14 The Flute Player **19** Liberation of St Peter **21** The Calling of St Matthew

terefah, trefah 9 not kosher

Tereus
   prince of: 6 Thrace
   father: 4 Ares
   wife: 6 Procne
   sister-in-law: 9 Philomela
   raped: 9 Philomela
   son: 4 Itys

tergal 4 back **6** dorsal

Terkel, Studs
   author of: 7 Working **9** Hard Times **14** American Dreams

term, terms 3 age, dub, era, tag **4** call, cite, item, name, span, time, word **5** catch, cycle, epoch, idiom, reign, spell, stage, state, style, while **6** clause, course, detail, period, phrase, status, string **7** dynasty, footing, proviso **8** duration, interval, position, standing **9** condition, designate, provision, relations, requisite **10** expression, span of time **11** appellation, designation, requirement, stipulation **12** characterize, circumstance, prerequisite **14** administration

termagant 3 nag **4** fury **5** scold, shrew, vixen **6** ogress, virago **7** hellcat, hellion, she-wolf, tigress **8** battle-ax, fishwife, harridan, spitfire **9** Xanthippe

Termagant
   character in: 21 medieval morality plays

terminal 4 end **4** last **5** depot, fatal, final, stand **6** deadly, lethal, mortal **7** station **8** terminus **10** concluding

terminate 3 end **4** stop **5** cease, close, lapse **6** expire, finish, run out, wind up **8** complete, conclude **11** come to an end, discontinue **12** bring to an end

termination 3 end **4** halt **5** close, finis, lapse **6** ending, finale, finish, windup **7** closing **8** stoppage **9** cessation **10** completion, concluding, conclusion, expiration **15** discontinuation

terminus 3 end **4** stop **5** depot, limit **6** ending **7** extreme, station **8** boundary, last stop, terminal **9** extremity **10** conclusion

Terminus
origin: 5 Roman
god of: 9 landmarks **10** boundaries

terminus ad quem 10 end to which, final limit **11** ending point

terminus a quo 9 beginning **12** end from which **13** starting point

termite
variety: 6 desert **7** dry wood **8** damp wood **10** powderpost, rotten wood **11** soldierless **12** subterranean

Terms of Endearment
director: 12 James L Brooks
based on novel by: 13 Larry McMurtry
cast: 11 Debra Winger **13** Jack Nicholson **15** Shirley MacLaine
Oscar for: 7 actress (MacLaine), picture **8** director **15** supporting actor (Nicholson)

Terpsichore
member of: 5 Muses
personifies: 7 dancing **10** choral song

Terra
goddess of: 5 Earth
Greek: 4 Gaea
mother: 5 Chaos
offspring: 6 Pontus, Titans, Uranus **7** Erinyes, Oceanus **8** Cyclopes **9** mountains **13** Hecatonchires

terrace 4 roof **5** level, patio, plane, porch **6** street **7** balcony, plateau **9** esplanade, promenade **10** embankment

Terraced Bay *see* **6** Taiwan

terra-cotta 4 clay **6** russet **8** brownish **12** reddish-brown **14** brownish-orange

terrain 4 area, zone **5** tract **6** ground, milieu, region **7** setting **8** district **9** territory **10** topography **11** countryside, environment **12** surroundings

terra incognita 11 unknown land **14** unexplored land, unknown subject **16** unknown territory

Terra Mater *see* **6** Tellus

terrapin 3 box **4** emyd, emys **6** slider, turpin, turtle **8** tortoise **11** diamond back
family: 8 Emydidae
female: 6 heifer
male: 4 bull

terrestrial 4 land **6** earth's, global, ground **7** earthly, mundane, worldly **8** riparian **10** earthbound

terrible 3 bad **4** dire, huge **5** awful, great, harsh, rough, scary **6** brutal, fierce, horrid, odious, severe, strong **7** beastly, extreme, fearful, ghastly, hateful, heinous, hideous, intense **8** alarming, dreadful, enormous, fearsome, horrible, shocking, terrific **9** appalling, excessive, harrowing, monstrous, obnoxious, offensive, repulsive, revolting, upsetting **10** disturbing, formidable, horrifying, immoderate, inordinate, terrifying, tremendous, unpleasant **11** distasteful,

distressing, frightening, intolerable **12** insufferable **13** objectionable

terrier
dog breed: 3 fox **4** bull, Skye **5** Cairn, Irish, Welsh **6** border, Boston **7** Norfolk, Tibetan, wire fox **8** Airedale, Lakeland, Scottish, Sealyham **9** Kerry Blue **10** Australian, Bedlington, Manchester **13** Dandie Dinmont **17** soft-coated wheaten, Staffordshire bull, West Highland white **18** miniature schnauzer **21** American Staffordshire

terrific 3 fab **4** fine, good, huge **5** awful, great, harsh, marvy, scary, super **6** bang-up, fierce, severe, superb **7** extreme, fearful, intense, sensash **8** alarming, dreadful, enormous, fabulous, fearsome, smashing, splendid, terrible **9** excellent, excessive, fantastic, harrowing, marvelous, monstrous, upsetting, wonderful **10** disturbing, horrifying, immoderate, inordinate, remarkable, stupendous, superduper, terrifying, tremendous **11** distressing, exceptional, frightening, sensational **13** extraordinary **14** out of this world

terrified 6 afraid, scared **7** alarmed, panicky **9** petrified **10** frightened **11** scared stiff **13** panic-stricken **14** terror-stricken **17** frightened to death

terrify 3 cow **5** abash, alarm, daunt, panic, scare, unman, upset **6** appall, dismay **7** agitate, disturb, horrify, overawe, petrify **8** disquiet, frighten **10** intimidate **17** make one's skin crawl **20** make one's blood run cold **22** make one's hair stand on end

terrifying 5 awful, dread **7** fearful **8** alarming, dreadful **9** frightful **11** frightening, hair-raising

territory 4 area, land, pale, zone **5** clime, realm, state, tract **6** bounds, colony, domain, empire, limits, locale, nation, region, sector **7** acreage, kingdom, mandate, terrain **8** confines, district, dominion, province **9** bailiwick **10** dependency **11** countryside **12** commonwealth, principality, protectorate

terror 3 awe **4** fear **5** alarm, dread, panic **6** dismay, fright, horror **7** anxiety **8** affright, disquiet **9** agitation **11** disquietude, trepidation **12** apprehension, perturbation **13** consternation **16** fear and trembling

terrorize 3 cow **5** abash, force **6** menace **7** terrify **8** browbeat, bulldoze, threaten **10** intimidate

terror-stricken 6 afraid, scared **7** alarmed, panicky **9** horrified, petrified, terrified **11** scared green, scared stiff **13** panic-stricken, scared to death

Terry and the Pirates
creator: 12 Milton Caniff
character: 7 Pat Ryan **8** Terry Lee **10** Dragon Lady

terse 4 curt, neat **5** brief, clear, crisp, pithy, short **6** abrupt **7** clipped, compact, concise, laconic, pointed, summary **8** clearcut, incisive, succinct **9** axiomatic, condensed,

trenchant 10 compressed 11 unambiguous
12 epigrammatic 18 brief and to the point
terseness 7 brevity 8 curtness 9 crispness
10 abruptness 11 compactness, conciseness 12 succinctness
Tesman family
 characters in: 11 Hedda Gabler
 members: 5 Hedda 6 George 7 Juliana
 author: 5 Ibsen
Tess (of the D'Urbervilles)
 author: 11 Thomas Hardy
 director: 13 Roman Polanski
 cast: 8 John Bett 10 Peter Firth, Tom
 Chadbon 14 Rosemary Martin 15 Nastas-
 sia Kinski (Tess)
test 4 exam, quiz 5 check, final, flyer,
probe, proof, prove, trial 6 dry run, feeler,
try out, verify 7 analyze, confirm, examine,
midterm 8 analysis, validate 9 catechism
11 corroborate, examination, investigate,
questioning 12 confirmation, substantiate,
verification 13 comprehensive, corroboration, investigation, questionnaire
Testament 5 Bible 7 the Book 10 Scriptures 12 New Testament, Old Testament
testament 6 legacy 7 bequest 10 settlement
tester 6 canopy 8 examiner 10 questioner
testify 4 show 5 prove, swear 6 affirm, attest, evince 7 declare, signify 8 evidence,
indicate, manifest 11 bear witness, demonstrate 12 give evidence
testimonial 5 medal 6 ribbon, trophy 7 tribute 8 citation, memorial, monument 9
affidavit, reference 10 deposition 11 certificate, endorsement 12 commendation 14
recommendation
testimony 5 proof 6 avowal 7 witness 8
averment, evidence 9 affidavit, statement
10 deposition, indication, profession 11 affirmation, attestation, endorsement 12
confirmation, verification 13 certification,
corroboration, demonstration, documentation, manifestation 14 acknowledgment
testy 5 cross, moody 6 crabby, cranky,
crusty, filthy, grumpy, snappy, sullen,
touchy 7 fretful, peevish, waspish 8 captious, caviling, choleric, churlish, perverse,
petulant, snappish, snarling 9 fractious,
impatient, irascible, irritable, splenetic 10
ill-humored 11 acrimonious, contentious
12 cantankerous, faultfinding, sharp-
tongued 13 quick-tempered, temperamental
tete-a-tete 4 chat, talk 6 parley 9 interview
12 conversation 13 confabulation
tether 3 tie 4 cord, rein, rope 5 chain, leash
6 fasten, halter, hobble, secure
Tethys
 member of: 6 Titans
 father: 7 Uranus
 mother: 4 Gaea
 husband: 7 Oceanus
 mother of: 8 Oceanids 9 river gods
 daughters: 13 three thousand
 foster child: 4 Hera

Teucer
 king of: 4 Troy
 father: 7 Telamon 9 Scamander
 mother: 5 Idaea 7 Hesione
 half-brother: 9 Great Ajax 14 Tele-
 monian Ajax
 daughter: 5 Batia
 skilled in: 7 archery
 founded: 7 Salamis
Teuthis
 also: 7 Ornytus
 rank: 7 general
 wounded: 6 Athena
Teuthras
 mentioned in: 5 Iliad
 king of: 5 Mysia 7 Phrygia
 mother: 8 Leucippe
 daughter: 8 Tecmessa
 killed: 4 boar
 boar sacred to: 7 Artemis
 killed by: 6 Hector
Teutonic 5 Dutch 6 German, Gothic, Nordic
7 British, English 8 Germanic 12 Scandinavian
 alphabet character: 4 rune
 demon: 3 alp
 goddess of death: 3 Hel, Ran
 goddess of peace: 7 Nerthus
 god of peace: 6 Balder
 god of thunder: 4 Thor
 god of war: 3 Tiu, Tyr
 god of wisdom: 4 Odin
Teutonic Mythology *see* 17 Germanic Mythology
Texas
 abbreviation: 2 TX 3 Tex
 nickname: 8 Lone Star
 capital: 6 Austin
 largest city: 7 Houston
 others: 4 Gail, Rice, Vega, Waco 5
 Bryan, Marfa, Ozona, Pampa, Tyler,
 Wiley 6 Baylor, Borger, Dallas, Denton, El
 Paso, Kileen, Laredo, Odessa, Quanah,
 Sonora 7 Abilene, Denison, Lubbock 8
 Amarillo, Beaumont, Floydada 9 Fort
 Worth, Galveston 10 San Antonio 13 Corpus Christi
 college: 3 SMU, TCU 4 Rice 5 Lamar,
 Wiley 6 Austin, Baylor 7 St Mary's, Trinity
 10 Texas A and M 12 Southwestern 14
 Texas Christian 16 Abilene Christian 17
 Southern Methodist
 feature:
 fort: 5 Alamo
 national park: 7 Big Bend 18 Guadalupe
 Mountains
 national seashore: 11 Padre Island
 state park: 10 San Jacinto
 tribe: 4 Adar, Waco 5 Caddo, Lipan 6
 Apache, Biloxi, Jumano, Kichai, Shuman,
 Tejano 7 Alabama, Hasinai, Tonkawa 8
 Comanche, Querecho 9 Coushatta, Ka-
 rankawa
 people: 10 James S Hogg 12 Edward M
 House, Thomas C Clark 13 John B
 Connally, Samuel Houston 14 Chester W
 Nimitz, Mirabeau B Lamar, Samuel T

Rayburn, Stephen F Austin, William B Travis **15** John Nance Garner, Thomas T Connally **19** Katherine Anne Porter
explorer: **4** Vaca **7** La Salle
island: **5** Padre
lake: **6** Falcon, Sabine, Texoma **7** Amistad
river: **3** Red **5** Pecos **6** Brazos, Neches, Nueces, Sabine **7** Trinity **8** Colorado **9** Rio Grande **10** San Jacinto
land rank: **12** second
physical feature:
bay: **13** Corpus Christi
port: **7** Houston **9** Galveston **13** Corpus Christi
president: **14** Lyndon B Johnson **17** Dwight D Eisenhower
Republic of Texas: **10** Sam Houston
state admission: **12** twenty-eighth
state bird: **11** mockingbird
state flower: **10** bluebonnet, yellow rose
state motto: **10** Friendship
state song: **13** Texas Our Texas
state tree: **5** pecan
baseball team: **7** Rangers

text 5 motif, theme, topic, verse, words **6** manual, primer, sermon, thesis **7** content, passage, subject, wording **8** argument, sentence, textbook, workbook **9** paragraph, quotation **10** schoolbook **13** subject matter

textile 4 yarn **5** cloth, fiber **6** fabric **8** filament, material **9** yard goods **10** piece goods

texture 3 nap **4** feel, look **5** grain, touch, weave **6** makeup **7** quality, surface **8** fineness **9** character, structure **10** coarseness **11** composition

Tey, Josephine
  real name: **19** Elizabeth MacKintosh
  author of: **10** Brat Farrar **15** Miss Pym Disposes, The Singing Sands **17** The Daughter of Time **19** A Shilling for Candles
  character: **9** Alan Grant

Thackeray, William Makepeace
  author of: **9** Pendennis **10** Vanity Fair **11** Barry Lyndon, Henry Esmond, The Newcomes **13** The Virginians

Thaddeus of Arimathea *see* **5** Judas

Thaddeus of Warsaw
  author: **10** Jane Porter

Thai-Austronesian
  language branch: **9** Thai-Kadai **12** Austronesian
  includes: **5** Batak, Malay **6** Fijian, Samoan **7** Tagalog **8** Hawaiian, Javanese **15** Bahasa Indonesia
  spoken in: **4** Fiji, Java **5** China, Samoa **6** Hawaii, Taiwan **7** Sumatra **9** Indonesia, Polynesia **10** Madagascar **11** Philippines **12** Easter Island

Thailand
  name means: **13** land of the free
  other name: **4** Siam **11** Prathet Thai
  capital/largest city: **6** Bankok **7** Bangkok

old capital: **8** Thonburi **9** Ayutthaya
others: **4** Ubon **5** Puket **6** Nakhon, Ranong **7** Ayudhya, Ayuthea, Lampang, Lamphur, Lopburi, Rahaeng, Singora, Songkla **8** Khonkaen, Kiangmai, Songkhla, Sukhotai, Thonburi **9** Ayutthaya, Chiangmai, Chiengmai **10** Ratchasima **11** Phitsanulok **14** Ubonratchthani
kingdom: **5** Funan **6** Khymer **8** Thonburi **9** Ayutthaya, Chiang Mai, Dvaravati, Sukhothai **12** Subarnabhumi
school: **9** Thammasat **13** Chulalongkorn
head of state: **4** king
measure: **2** wa **3** can, ken, niv, rai, sat, sok, wah **4** cohi, keup, niou, tang **5** kwien, leeng, sesti, vouah **6** kabiet, kanahn **7** chaimeu **8** changawn **9** anukablet
monetary unit: **2** at **3** att **4** baht **5** cutty, fuang **6** pynung, salung **11** bullet money
weight: **3** bat, hap, pay, sen, sok **4** baht, haph, kati, klam **5** catty, chang, fuang, picul, pilul, tical **6** fluang, graini, salung, **7** tamlung
island: **2** Ko **3** Kut, Tao **4** Chan, Rawi **5** Chang, Lanta, Samui, Thalu **6** Libong, Phuket **7** Phangan, Terutao
lake: **9** Nong Lahan
mountain: **5** Dawna, Khieo **6** Phanom **8** Dang Raek, Kao Prawa, Maelamun **9** Khao Luang **11** Bilauktaung
highest point: **8** Inthanon **11** Doi Inthanon
river: **3** Chi, Mun, Nan, Yom **4** Ping **5** Menam **6** Mekong, Meping **7** Salween **10** Chaophraya
sea: **7** Andaman
physical feature:
gulf: **4** Siam **8** Thailand
isthmus: **3** Kra
pass: **12** Three Pagodas
peninsula: **5** Malay
plateau: **5** Korat **6** Khorat
people: **3** Lao, Mon **4** Lawa, Shan, Thai **5** Malay **6** Indian, Khymer **7** Chinese, Siamese **9** Cambodian **10** Vietnamese
king: **4** Rama **7** Chakkri, Mongkut **10** Chao Phraya **12** Prahjadhipok **13** Chulalongkorn **17** Bhumibol Adulyadej
leader: **9** Phraruang **12** Kukrit-Pramoj
language: **3** Lao, Tai **4** Ahom, Shan, Thai **5** Kadai, Malay **7** Bangkok, Chinese, English **9** Krung Thep
religion: **5** Islam **8** Buddhism **12** Christianity, Confucianism **17** Theravada Buddhism
place:
dam: **8** Bhumibol
palace: **5** Grand
ruins: **7** Ayuthia **9** Ayutthaya
street: **7** Yawarai
temple: **4** Dawn **7** Trimitr **10** Wat Phra Keo **11** Royal Chapel **13** Emerald Buddha
feature:
canal: **5** klong

clothing: 6 panung, sarong 12 saffron robes
festival: 12 Surin Round Up
houseboat: 6 sampan
temple: 3 wat
tree: 4 teak
food:
fruit: 5 camut 6 durian, litchi, pomelo 8 rambutan 10 mangosteen

Thais
author: 13 Anatole France
character: 8 Athanael
composer: 8 Massenet

Thalassa
personifies: 3 sea

thalassic 6 marine 7 aquatic, deep-sea, neritic, oceanic, pelagic

Thales
field: 11 mathematics
nationality: 5 Greek
discovered: 18 geometry principles
predicted: 11 sun's eclipse

Thalestris
character in: 16 The Rape of the Lock
author: 4 Pope

Thalia
member of: 5 Muses 6 Graces
personifies: 6 comedy 13 idyllic poetry
lover: 4 Zeus
killed by: 5 Erato

Thallo
member of: 5 Horae
goddess of: 13 spring flowers

Thamyris
vocation: 4 poet 8 musician
father: 9 Philammon
mother: 7 Argiope
punished for: 9 arrogance
punished by: 5 Muses
punishment: 7 maiming 8 blinding

thanatophobia
fear of: 5 death

Thanatos
personifies: 5 death

thank 5 bless 12 be grateful to 13 be much obliged 18 express gratitude to

thankful 7 obliged 8 beholden, grateful 10 indebted to 12 appreciative, full of thanks 16 feeling gratitude 22 expressing appreciation

thankfulness 6 thanks 9 gratitude 12 appreciation, gratefulness

thankless 4 vain 7 ingrate, useless 8 bootless, caviling, critical, heedless 9 fruitless, unmindful, unwelcome 10 profitless, ungracious, ungrateful, uninviting, unpleasant, unrewarded, unthankful 11 distasteful, thoughtless, undesirable, unrewarding 12 disagreeable, faultfinding 13 inconsiderate, unappreciated 14 unacknowledged, unappreciative

thanks 5 grace 8 blessing 9 gratitude 11 benediction 12 appreciation, gratefulness

thanks be to God
Latin: 10 Deo gratias

thanksgiving 6 thanks 8 blessing

Thanksgiving
started by: 8 Bradford, Pilgrims
traditional food: 4 corn, yams 6 turkey 10 pumpkin pie 13 sweet potatoes 14 cranberry sauce
symbol: 9 ear of corn 12 horn of plenty

thank you
French: 5 merci
German: 5 danke
Spanish: 7 gracias
Italian: 6 grazie
Japanese: 4 domo

Thank You, Fog
author: 7 W H Auden

Thank You, Jeeves
author: 11 P G Wodehouse

thank you very much
French: 9 merci bien 13 merci beaucoup
German: 10 danke schon
Japanese: 11 domo arigato
Spanish: 13 muchas gracias

That Certain Feeling
author: 12 Kingsley Amis

Thatcher, Becky
character in: 9 Tom Sawyer
author: 5 Twain

Thatcher, Judge
character in: 15 (The Adventures of) Huckleberry Finn
author: 5 Twain

That Girl
character: 8 Ann Marie, Lou Marie 10 Helen Marie, Ruth Bauman 11 Jerry Bauman 12 Don Hollinger, Judy Bessemer 14 Dr Leon Bessemer
cast: 9 Lew Parker 10 Ted Bessell 11 Alice Borden, Bonnie Scott, Marlo Thomas 12 Bernie Kopell 13 Dabney Coleman 14 Carolyn Daniels, Rosemary DeCamp

that is
Latin: 2 ie 5 id est

that is to say
Latin: 3 viz 9 videlicet

that's life
French: 9 c'est la vie

thaw 4 melt, warm 5 relax 6 soften, unbend, warm up 7 liquefy, melting, thawing 8 dissolve 11 break the ice

Thea
companion of: 7 Artemis
ravished by: 6 Aeolus
changed into: 4 mare
mare named: 6 Euippe

Theale, Milly
character in: 17 The Wings of the Dove
author: 5 James

theater 4 site 5 arena, drama, house, movie, odeum, place, scene, stage 6 cinema, lyceum 7 gallery, setting 8 assembly, audience, coliseum 9 colosseum, music hall, playhouse 10 assemblage, auditorium, movie house, spectators 11 histrionics, lecture hall, theatricals 12 amphitheater, show business

theatrical 4 film 5 hammy, movie, showy, stage, stagy 6 flashy 7 fustian, show-biz, stilted 8 affected, dramatic, mannered, thespian 9 grandiose, unnatural 10 artificial, histrionic 11 exaggerated, extravagant, pretentious, spectacular 12 magniloquent, ostentatious, show-business 13 entertainment, grandiloquent 14 larger-than-life

theatrical trick
    French: 13 coup de theatre

Thebaid
    author: 7 Statius
    character: 4 Atys 5 Creon 6 Ismene, Tydeus 7 Jocasta, Theseus 8 Antigone, Capaneus, Eteocles, Opheltes, Tiresias 9 Menoeceus, Polynices 10 Amphiaraus, Hippomedon, Melanippus

the bottle 5 booze, drink, sauce 6 liquor 7 alcohol 8 demon rum

the dansant 8 tea dance

thee therefore
    Latin: 8 te igitur

theft 5 fraud 7 larceny, looting, robbery 8 burglary, filching, rustling, stealing, thievery 9 hijacking, pilfering, swindling 10 purloining 11 shoplifting 12 embezzlement
    god of: 6 Hermes 7 Mercury

Theia
    also: 4 Thia
    member of: 6 Titans
    father: 6 Uranus
    mother: 4 Gaea
    brother: 8 Hyperion
    mother of: 8 Cercopes
    son: 6 Helios
    daughter: 3 Eos 6 Selene

the life of the land is maintained by righteousness
    Hawaiian: 52 ua mau ke ea o ka aina i ka pono
    motto of: 6 Hawaii

Them
    author: 15 Joyce Carol Oates

theme 3 air 4 song, text, tune 5 essay, focus, motif, point, topic, tract 6 melody, report, review, strain, thesis 7 keynote, premise, subject 8 argument, critique, question, treatise 9 discourse, leitmotif, monograph 10 commentary 11 composition, proposition 12 dissertation

Themis
    member of: 6 Titans
    father: 6 Uranus
    mother: 4 Gaea
    sister: 6 Phoebe
    consort of: 5 Zeus
    husband: 7 Iapetus
    mother of: 5 Fates, Horae 6 Moerae 7 Seasons
    son: 10 Prometheus
    personifies: 7 justice

Themiste
    father: 8 Laomedon
    mother: 8 Eurydice
    son: 8 Anchises

Then Again, Maybe I Won't
    author: 9 Judy Blume

thence 6 whence 9 from there, therefore 11 accordingly, in due course 13 from that place

the next world 6 Heaven 8 eternity, paradise 12 the hereafter 14 the world to come

the norm 7 the mean, the rule 9 the median 10 the average 14 the common thing

the Occident 7 the West 20 the western hemisphere

Theoclymenus
    king of: 5 Egypt
    father: 7 Proteus
    mother: 8 Psamathe
    vocation: 4 seer

theologian see 22 philosopher/ theologian

theological 4 holy 6 sacred 8 Biblical, dogmatic 9 apostolic, canonical, doctrinal, religious, spiritual 10 scriptural 14 ecclesiastical

theology 5 dogma 8 divinity, doctrine, religion

Theonoe
    father: 7 Proteus, Thestor

Theophane
    bore: 3 ram
    fleece of ram: 6 golden

theoretical 8 abstract, academic, putative 11 conjectural, postulatory, speculative 12 hypothetical, nonpractical 13 suppositional

theorize 5 infer, posit, think 6 assume 7 imagine, presume, propose, suppose, surmise 8 propound 9 formulate, postulate, predicate, speculate 10 conjecture 11 hypothecate, hypothesize

theory 3 law 4 idea, view 5 guess 6 belief, notion, thesis 7 concept, opinion, science, surmise, thought 8 doctrine, ideology, judgment 9 deduction, postulate, principle 10 conclusion, conjecture, hypothesis, persuasion, philosophy 11 presumption, speculation, supposition

therapeutic, therapeutical 7 healing 8 curative, remedial, salutary, sanative 11 restorative 12 ameliorative

Therapne
    means: 12 burial ground

therapy 7 healing 9 treatment 14 rehabilitation

thereafter 5 later 9 after that, afterward 10 afterwards, from then on 11 thenceforth 12 subsequently 14 from that time on

therefore 2 so 4 ergo, thus 5 hence 11 accordingly 12 consequently, on that ground 13 for that reason, in consequence, on that account 14 for which reason

there is no disputing about tastes
    Latin: 27 de gustibus non est disputandum

there it is
    French: 5 voila

Therese Raquin
    author: 9 Emile Zola
    character: 7 Camille, Laurent

There Shall Be No Night
    author: 15 Robert E Sherwood

thereupon 4 then 6 at once 7 thereon 8 directly, suddenly, upon that 9 forthwith, in a moment, upon which 11 immediately 12 straightaway, without delay

Therimachus
father: 8 Hercules
mother: 6 Megary
killed by: 8 Hercules

Theritas see 4 Ares

Thermasia
epithet of: 7 Demeter
means: 6 warmth

thermometer
invented by: 7 Galileo, Reaumur
mercury: 10 Fahrenheit

Thero
nurse of: 4 Ares

theropod
type of: 8 dinosaur
member: 10 Allosaurus, Antrodemus 11 Coelophysis, Gorgosaurus 13 Albertosaurus, Compsognathus, Struthiomimus, Tyrannosaurus

Theroux, Paul
author of: 9 Saint Jack 16 The Mosquito Coast 20 Riding the Iron Rooster 21 The Great Railway Bazaar 23 The Old Patagonian Express

Thersander
member of: 7 Epigoni

Thersilochus
mentioned in: 5 Iliad
killed by: 8 Achilles

Thersites
mentioned in: 5 Iliad
origin: 5 Greek
characteristics: 4 ugly 8 deformed 11 quarrelsome
accused Agamemnon of: 5 greed
accused Achilles of: 9 cowardice
fought in: 9 Trojan War
killed by: 8 Achilles

the same as 4 like 7 equal to 9 a match for 12 comparable to, equivalent to, tantamount to 16 commensurate with

thesaurus 8 synonymy 10 word finder 11 synonymicon 12 word treasury 13 synonym finder 17 synonym dictionary 18 semantic dictionary

Thescelosaurus
type: 8 dinosaur 10 ornithopod
location: 6 Canada 12 United States
period: 10 Cretaceous

These Three
director: 12 William Wyler
based on play by: 14 Lillian Hellman (The Children's Hour)
cast: 10 Alma Kruger, Joel McCrea 11 Merle Oberon 13 Miriam Hopkins 15 Bonita Granville, Catherine Doucet

These Twain
author: 13 Arnold Bennett

Theseus
king of: 6 Athens
father: 6 Aegeus 8 Poseidon
mother: 6 Aethra
wife: 7 Phaedra

consort: 9 Hippolyta
lover: 7 Ariadne
son: 6 Acamas 8 Demophon 10 Hippolytus, Melanippus
helmsman: 10 Nausithous
killed: 5 Sinis 6 Sciron 8 Minotaur 10 Cretan bull, Procrustes

thesis 5 essay, paper, tract 6 notion, theory 7 article, concept, surmise 8 argument, critique, proposal, treatise 9 discourse, monograph, postulate, term paper 10 commentary, conjecture, hypothesis 11 composition, proposition, speculation, supposition 12 disquisition, dissertation

Thesmia
epithet of: 7 Demeter
means: 12 goddess of law

Thesmophorus
epithet of: 7 Demeter
means: 8 lawgiver

Thesophoria
origin: 5 Greek
event: 8 festival

thespian 3 ham 4 star 5 actor, extra 6 costar, player, walk-on 7 actress, ingenue, trouper 8 juvenile 9 bit-player, guest star, performer, tragedian 10 leading man 11 leading lady, stage player

Thespian Lion
attacked: 6 flocks
flock owner: 10 Amphitryon
killed by: 8 Hercules

Thespius
founded city of: 8 Thespiae
wife: 8 Megamede
daughters: 5 fifty

Thessalus
king of: 8 Thessaly
father: 5 Jason 8 Hercules
mother: 5 Medea 9 Chalciope

the state
Latin: 10 res publica

Thestius
king of: 7 Aetolia
father: 4 Ares
mother: 8 Demonice

Thestor
son: 7 Calchas
daughter: 7 Theonoe 8 Leucippe

Thetis
member of: 7 Nereids
husband: 6 Peleus
sister: 8 Eurynome
son: 8 Achilles

the very words
Latin: 14 ipsissima verba

the world over 10 every place, everywhere, far and wide, near and far 11 in all places

They Shoot Horses, Don't They?
director: 13 Sydney Pollack
cast: 8 Gig Young 9 Bruce Dern, Jane Fonda 10 Red Buttons 12 Susannah York 13 Bonnie Bedelia 15 Michael Sarrazin
Oscar for: 15 supporting actor (Young)

They Won't Forget
  director: 11 Mervyn LeRoy
  cast: 10 Lana Turner, Otto Kruger 11 Allyn Joslyn, Claude Rains 12 Elisha Cook Jr 13 Gloria Dickson

Thia *see* 5 Theia

Thialfi
  origin: 12 Scandinavian
  servant of: 4 Thor
  talent: 8 fastness

Thiasos *see* 7 Thiasus

thiasus
  also: 7 thiasos
  group worshipping: 11 patron deity
  followers of: 8 Dionysus
  followers called: 6 satyrs 7 maenads

Thiazi
  also: 6 Thjazi
  origin: 12 Scandinavian
  form: 5 giant
  carried away: 4 Iden 6 apples

thick 3 big, fat 4 deep, dull, dumb, slow, wide 5 broad, bulky, close, dense, fuzzy, great, heavy, husky, piled, solid 6 chummy, heaped, hoarse, lavish, obtuse, packed, strong, stupid, viscid, wooden 7 blurred, clotted, compact, copious, crowded, decided, devoted, doltish, extreme, intense, liberal, muffled, profuse, teeming, throaty, viscous 8 abundant, familiar, friendly, generous, guttural, intimate, profound, sisterly, swarming 9 brotherly, condensed, fatheaded, glutinous, plenteous, unstinted 10 coagulated, dull-witted, gelatinous, indistinct, munificent, pronounced, slow-witted 11 inseparable, overflowing 12 concentrated, impenetrable, inarticulate

thicken 3 set 4 cake, clot, jell 5 muddy 6 darken, deepen, muddle 7 compact, congeal, jellify 8 condense 9 coagulate, intensify 10 gelatinize

thicket 4 bush, wood 5 brake, brush, copse, grove, scrub 6 bushes, covert, forest, shrubs 7 bracken 9 shrubbery 10 underbrush 11 undergrowth

thickheaded 4 dull, dumb, slow 5 blank, dense, dopey, thick 6 obtuse, stupid 8 ignorant 9 dim-witted, fatheaded 10 boneheaded, dull-witted, half-witted, slow-witted 11 blockheaded, thick-witted 12 dunderheaded, thick-skulled 13 chuckleheaded, knuckleheaded

thickset 5 bulky, close, dense, dumpy, husky, solid, squat, stout, tubby 6 chunky, packed, stocky, stubby, sturdy 8 close-set, heavyset, roly-poly

thickskinned 4 hard 5 horny, tough 6 inured 7 callous 8 callused, hardened 9 unfeeling, unmovable 10 impervious, insensible 11 insensitive, unconcerned 13 imperturbable, unsusceptible 14 pachydermatous

thick-skulled 4 dull 5 dense 6 stupid 11 thickheaded 12 dunderheaded

thick-witted 4 dull, slow 5 dense 6 stupid 7 idiotic, moronic 9 dim-witted, imbecilic 11 thickheaded 12 dunderheaded, simpleminded

thief 5 crook 6 bandit, mugger, robber 7 burglar, filcher, rustler 8 hijacker, pilferer, swindler 9 defrauder, embezzler, holdup man, larcenist, purloiner, racketeer 10 highwayman, pickpocket, shoplifter 12 housebreaker, kleptomaniac 13 confidence man, purse-snatcher 14 second-story man

Thief of Bagdad, The
  director: 9 Tim Whelan 12 Ludwig Berger 13 Michael Powell
  cast: 4 Sabu 9 Rex Ingram 10 John Justin, June Duprez 11 Conrad Veidt

Thieves' Carnival
  also: 15 Le Bal des Voleurs
  author: 11 Jean Anouilh

thievish 3 sly 6 sneaky 7 furtive 8 stealthy, thieving 9 dishonest, larcenous, secretive, thieflike 13 light-fingered, surreptitious 14 sticky-fingered

thigh 3 ham, leg 4 hock 5 femur, flank, ilium 6 gammon
  pain: 8 meralgia

Thimbu, Thimphu
  capital of: 6 Bhutan

thin 4 fine, lank, lean, slim, weak 5 faint, gaunt, lanky, prune, runny, scant, sheer, spare, water 6 dilute, feeble, narrow, not fat, reduce, skinny, slight, sparse, watery 7 curtail, diluted, fragile, scrawny, slender, spindly 8 delicate, diminish, finespun 9 emaciated, water down 10 inadequate, threadlike 11 transparent 12 insufficient 13 unsubstantial

thin-blooded 3 wan 4 pale, weak 6 anemic, sickly

thing, things 3 act 4 deed, feat, gear, item 5 event, gizmo, goods, point 6 action, affair, aspect, detail, dingus, entity, gadget, matter, object, person 7 article, clothes, concern, effects, feature, thought 8 business, clothing, creature, movables 9 doohickey, equipment, happening, statement 10 belongings, human being, occurrence, particular, proceeding 11 eventuality, living being, possessions, thingamabob, thingamajig, transaction 12 circumstance 13 paraphernalia

thing already done
  French: 12 fait accompli

thingamajig 5 gizmo 6 doodad, gadget 11 contraption, contrivance, thingamabob 15 whatchamacallit

thing of no value
  Latin: 5 nihil

things done
  Latin: 9 res gestae

think 4 deem, mean, plan 5 brood, fancy, guess, judge 6 design, expect, intend, ponder, reason, recall, reckon 7 believe, dwell on, imagine, presume, propose, purpose, reflect, suppose, surmise 8 cogitate, conceive, conclude, contrive, meditate, mull over, remember, ruminate 9 recollect, speculate 10 anticipate, deliberate, have in mind, keep in mind 11 contemplate, use one's mind, use one's wits 13 rack one's brain

thinkable 8 knowable 10 imaginable 11 conceivable, perceivable

think about 4 mull 6 debate, ponder 7 reflect 8 consider, mull over 10 deliberate

think alike 5 agree 11 be of one mind, see eye to eye

thinker 4 sage 6 savant, wizard 7 egghead, scholar 9 intellect 10 mastermind 11 mental giant, philosopher 13 metaphysician

think fit 4 deem 5 deign, stoop 7 consent 10 condescend

think highly of 5 favor, honor, value 6 admire, esteem, revere 7 approve, respect 8 look up to, venerate 10 set store by

think ill of 4 hate 5 decry 6 detest 7 condemn, deplore, despise, dislike 8 object to 9 abominate, disparage, frown upon 10 disapprove 13 look askance at 14 discountenance 15 take exception to 16 find unacceptable, view with disfavor

thinking 4 view 5 smart, stand, study 6 belief, bright 7 concept, surmise, thought 8 cultured, educated, judgment, position, rational, studious 9 brainwork, deduction, inference, reasoning 10 conclusion, cultivated, impression, meditation, meditative, reflection, reflective, rumination, thoughtful 11 intelligent, speculation 12 deliberation 13 consideration, contemplation, contemplative, philosophical, sophisticated, using one's head 15 paying attention

Thinking Reed, The
author: 15 Dame Rebecca West

think over 5 study, weigh 8 cogitate, consider, mull over 11 reflect upon 12 deliberate on

think through 5 weigh 6 ponder 7 analyze 8 appraise, consider, evaluate

think up 5 frame, hatch 6 create, invent 7 concoct, dream up 8 conceive, contrive

think well of 4 like 6 admire 8 look up to 10 appreciate

Thin Man, The
author: 15 Dashiell Hammett
character: 7 Morelli 11 Nick Charles, Nora Charles 13 Arthur Nunheim, Mimi Jorgensen 15 Herbert Macaulay 18 Christian Jorgensen
Wynant family: 5 Clyde 7 Dorothy, Gilbert
director: 11 W S Van Dyke II
cast: 4 Asta 8 Myrna Loy (Nora Charles) 13 William Powell (Nick Charles)
sequel (film): 14 Another Thin Man 15 After the Thin Man 16 Song of the Thin Man 18 The Thin Man Goes Home

Thin Mountain Air, The
author: 10 Paul Horgan

thin out 5 prune 6 dilute, reduce, weaken 7 weed out 9 water down 10 adulterate

thinskinned 5 cross, huffy, sulky, testy 6 grumpy, sullen, touchy 7 crabbed, peevish 8 petulant, snappish 9 irascible, irritable, sensitive, squeamish 11 ill-tempered, quarrelsome, susceptible 12 cantankerous 13 oversensitive 14 hypersensitive

third estate
French: 9 tiers etat

Third Man, The
director: 9 Carol Reed
based on story by: 12 Graham Greene
cast: 10 Alida Valli 11 Orson Welles (Harry Lime) 12 Joseph Cotten, Trevor Howard 16 Wilfrid Hyde-White
setting: 6 Vienna

Third Wave, The
author: 12 Alvin Toffler

thirst 3 yen 4 itch, lust, pant 5 ardor, covet, crave, yearn 6 desire, fervor, hunger, relish 7 craving, passion, stomach 8 appetite, keenness, voracity, yearning 9 hanker for, hankering 11 thirstiness

thirsty 3 dry 4 avid 5 eager 7 parched 9 thirsting

Thirteen O'Clock
author: 19 Stephen Vincent Benet

Thirty-Nine Steps, The (The 39 Steps)
author: 10 John Buchan
director: 15 Alfred Hitchcock
cast: 11 Robert Donat 13 Godfrey Tearle, Lucie Mannheim, Peggy Ashcroft 16 Madeleine Carroll

This Above All
author: 10 Eric Knight

Thisbe
loved: 7 Pyramus
location: 7 Babylon
death by: 7 suicide
death at tomb of: 5 Ninus

this is
Latin: 6 hoc est

This Is Your Life
host: 12 Ralph Edwards
announcer: 9 Bob Warren

Thisoa
form: 5 nymph
tended: 4 Zeus

thistle 7 Cirsium
varieties: 3 Oat 4 Bull, Holy, Milk, Star 5 Glove, Plume, White 6 Canada, Cotton, Golden, Scotch, Silver 7 Blessed, St Mary's 8 Fishbone, Mountain, Plumless 9 Argentine, Thornless 10 Great globe, Small globe 11 Mountain sow 14 Acanthus-leaved

Thjazi *see* 6 Thiazi

Thoas *see* 5 Thoon

Thokk
origin: 12 Scandinavian
form: 8 giantess
refused to weep for: 5 Baldr 6 Balder, Baldur
possible disguise of: 4 Loki

Thomas 7 apostle
means: 4 twin
also called: 7 Didymus, Doubter 8 Doubting

Thomas, Ambroise
born: 4 Metz 6 France
composer of: 6 Mignon

Thomas, Danny
real name: 16 Amos Muzyad Jacobs
born: 11 Deerfield MI
daughter: 11 Marlo Thomas
roles: 13 The Jazz Singer 16 Make Room for Daddy 19 I'll See You in My Dreams

Thomas, Dylan
author of: 8 Fern Hill 13 Under Milk Wood 23 A Child's Christmas in Wales

Thomas, George H
nickname: 20 The Rock of Chickamauga
served in: 8 Civil War 10 Mexican War
side: 5 Union
commander of: 19 Army of the Cumberland
battle: 9 Nashville 11 Chattanooga, Chickamauga

Thomas, Marlo
real name: 14 Margaret Thomas
born: 9 Detroit MI
father: 11 Danny Thomas
husband: 11 Phil Donahue
roles: 8 That Girl

Thomas, W Morgan
creator/artist of: 22 Sheena Queen of the Jungle

Thomas a Kempis
author of: 20 The Imitation of Christ

Thompson, Estelle Merle O'Brien
real name of: 11 Merle Oberon

Thomson, Joseph John
field: 7 physics
nationality: 7 British
discovered: 8 electron
awarded: 10 Nobel Prize

Thomson, Thomas John
born: 6 Canada 9 Claremont
artwork: 9 Spring Ice 11 The Jack Pine 12 Northern Lake 13 Northern River

Thomson, Virgil
born: 12 Kansas City MO
composer of: 9 Portraits 16 The Mother of Us All 21 Four Saints in Three Acts

thong 4 band 5 strap, strip 6 sandal 7 binding

Thoon
also: 5 Thoas 11 Nebrophonus
member of: 8 Gigantes
attacked wall of: 6 Greeks
killed by: 8 Hercules 10 Antilochus

Thor
origin: 12 Scandinavian
god of: 4 rain 7 farming, thunder
rode: 7 chariot
chariot pulled by: 5 goats
wielded: 6 hammer 7 Miolnir
father: 4 Odin 5 Othin

thorax 5 chest, trunk 6 breast, cavity 8 forebody

Thoreau, Henry David
author of: 6 Walden (Life in the Woods) 17 Civil Disobedience

thorium
chemical symbol: 2 Th

thorn 3 woe 4 bane, barb, care, gall, spur 5 cross, curse, spike, spine, sting 6 plague 7 prickle, scourge, torment, trouble 8 nuisance, vexation 9 annoyance, sore point 10 affliction, bitter pill, infliction, irritation

thorn 9 Crataegus
varieties: 3 Box 4 Lily, Pear 5 Camel, Hedge, White 6 Christ, Karroo, Mysore, Sallow, Sickle, Winter 7 Thirsty 8 Cockspur, Egyptian, Kangaroo, Quick-set 9 Jerusalem, Paper-bark 10 Washington 11 Crucifixion 13 Yellow-fruited

Thornbirds, The
author: 17 Colleen McCullough

Thornburg, Betty June
real name of: 11 Betty Hutton

Thornfield
house in: 8 Jane Eyre
author: 6 Bronte

Thornhill, Squire
character in: 19 The Vicar of Wakefield
author: 9 Goldsmith

thorn in the side 4 bane 7 torment 9 annoyance 10 irritation

thorny 4 dire, hard 5 spiny, tough 6 barbed, spiked, sticky, trying 7 arduous, brambly, complex, crucial, irksome, prickly 8 annoying, critical, involved, ticklish 9 bristling, dangerous, difficult, vexatious 10 formidable, nettlesome, perplexing 11 complicated, troublesome

thorough 4 full, pure 5 sheer, total, utter 6 entire 7 careful, perfect, uniform 8 absolute, complete, of a piece 9 downright, out-and-out 10 consistent, definitive, exhaustive, meticulous 11 painstaking, unmitigated, unqualified 12 all-embracing, all-inclusive

thoroughbred, Thorough bred 7 unmixed 8 purebred 9 blueblood, pedigreed, racehorse 10 aristocrat 11 full-blooded, pureblooded 12 silkstocking

thoroughfare 4 road 6 avenue, street 7 freeway, highway, parkway, roadway, thruway 8 main road, turnpike 9 boulevard, concourse 10 expressway, interstate 12 superhighway 13 through street

thoroughgoing 5 utter 6 arrant 7 extreme 8 outright 9 confirmed, notorious, out-and-out 11 undisguised, unmitigated

thoroughly 5 fully 7 totally, utterly 8 entirely 9 carefully, downright, out-and-out, perfectly, uniformly 10 absolutely, completely, throughout 11 inclusively 12 consistently, exhaustively, meticulously 13 in all respects 15 from top to bottom 17 through and through 18 from beginning to end

Thorpe, Isabella
character in: 15 Northanger Abbey
author: 6 Austen

Thorpe, Jim (James Francis)
sport: 8 football 13 track and field
won: 8 Olympics
named: 11 All-American

Thorvaldsen, Albert Bertel
born: 7 Denmark 10 Copenhagen
artwork: 4 Hope 9 Lord Byron 14 Cupid
and Psyche 16 The Lion of Lucerne 22
Cupid and the Three Graces 24 Jason
with the Golden Fleece

Thoth
origin: 8 Egyptian
god of: 5 magic 6 wisdom 8 learning
scribe of: 4 gods
inventor of: 6 letter 7 numbers
corresponds to: 6 Hermes
head of: 4 ibis 6 baboon

though 3 tho, yet 4 even, that 5 still 6 al-
beit, even if 7 granted 8 although, granting
9 admitting 12 nevertheless 15 notwithstanding

thought 3 aim, end 4 goal, idea, plan, view
5 credo, dogma, fancy, tenet 6 belief, caring, design, intent, musing, notion, object,
regard, scheme 7 concept, concern, opinion, purpose, reverie, surmise 8 doctrine,
judgment, kindness, thinking 9 attention,
intention, objective, sentiment 10 brown
study, cogitation, conception, conclusion,
meditation, reflection, rumination 11 expectation, imagination, speculation, supposition 12 anticipation, deliberation 13 consideration, contemplation, introspection
French: 6 pensee

thoughtful 4 kind 6 caring, loving, musing
7 pensive, probing, serious, wistful 8 thinking 9 attentive 10 meditative, neighborly,
reflective, solicitous 11 considerate, kindhearted 13 contemplative, introspective

thoughtfulness 7 probing, thought 8 kindness, thinking 10 meditation, reflection 11
questioning 13 attentiveness, consideration, contemplation 14 solicitousness 15
kindheartedness

thoughtless 4 dumb, rash, rude 5 silly 6
stupid, unkind 7 foolish 8 careless, heedless, impolite, reckless 9 imprudent 10 ill-
advised, indiscreet, neglectful, unthinking
11 harebrained, improvident, inadvertent,
inattentive, insensitive 12 absent-minded,
unreflecting 13 ill-considered, inconsiderate, rattlebrained 14 scatterbrained

thoughtlessness 7 neglect 8 rashness,
rudeness 9 oversight, unconcern 10 imprudence, negligence, unkindness 11 inattention 12 carelessness, heedlessness,
impoliteness, recklessness 13 insensitivity
15 inattentiveness 16 absentmindedness

Thousand Clowns, A
director: 7 Fred Coe
based on play by: 11 Herb Gardner
cast: 11 Barry Gordon 12 Jason Robards, Martin Balsam 13 Barbara Harris
setting: 11 New York City
Oscar for: 15 supporting actor (Balsam)

Thousand Days, A
author: 20 Arthur M Schlesinger Jr

thou too
Latin: 8 tu quoque

thrall 4 serf 5 slave 6 chains 7 bondage,
serfdom, servant, slavery 9 servitude 11
enslavement, subjugation

thralldom 6 chains 7 bondage, serfdom,
slavery 9 servitude 11 enslavement, subjugation

thrash 4 beat, cane, drub, flog, jerk, lash,
maul, toss, whip 5 birch, flail, heave, solve,
spank, strap 6 jiggle, joggle, plunge, pommel, squirm, switch, thresh, tumble, wiggle, writhe 7 flounce, resolve, scourge,
trounce 8 argue out, lambaste 9 thresh out
10 flagellate

Thrasydemus
also: 11 Thrasymelus
squire of: 8 Sarpedon
killed by: 9 Patroclus

Thrasymedes
father: 6 Nestor
brother: 10 Antilochus

Thrasymelus see 11 Thrasydemus

threadbare 4 dull, worn 5 banal, stale,
stock, tacky, trite 6 boring, frayed, jejune,
ragged, shabby 7 cliched, humdrum, harmless, prosaic, raveled, routine, worn-out 8
bromidic, everyday, pileworn 9 hackneyed,
well-known 11 commonplace, stereotyped
12 conventional, overfamiliar 15 the worse
for wear

threads 4 duds, togs 6 attire 7 apparel,
clothes, strands, strings 8 clothing, garments 9 filaments

threat 4 omen, risk 5 peril 6 danger, hazard, menace 7 ill omen, portent, warning 8
jeopardy 10 foreboding 11 commination,
premonition 12 intimidation

threaten 3 cow 4 warn 6 impend, menace 7
imperil 8 endanger, forewarn, hang over 9
terrorize 10 be imminent, intimidate, jeopardize

threatening 4 grim 7 baleful, ominous,
warning 8 alarming, imminent, menacing,
sinister 9 ill-omened, impending 10 forbidding, foreboding 11 approaching, forewarning, terrorizing 12 inauspicious, intimidating, unpropitious

three
French: 5 trois

Three-Cornered Hat, The
author: 21 Pedro Antonio de Alarcon

Three Faces of Eve, The
director: 15 Nunnally Johnson
cast: 8 Lee J Cobb 9 Nancy Kulp 10 David Wayne 12 Vince Edwards 14 Joanne
Woodward
narration by: 13 Alistair Cooke
Oscar for: 7 actress (Woodward)

Three Lives
includes: 9 Melanctha 11 The Good
Anna 13 The Gentle Lena
author: 13 Gertrude Stein

Three Men in a Boat
author: 13 Jerome K Jerome

Three Musketeers, The
author: 14 Alexandre Dumas (pere)
director: 13 Richard Lester
character: 5 Athos 6 Aramis 7 Porthos 8

Planchet 9 D'Artagnan 12 Lady de Winter 17 Cardinal Richelieu 18 Constance Bonacieux

cast: 10 Oliver Reed 11 Faye Dunaway (Milady), Michael York (D'Artagnan), Raquel Welch 12 Frank Findlay 14 Charlton Heston, Christopher Lee 16 Geraldine Chaplin 18 Richard Chamberlain

sequel: 17 The Four Musketeers

Three's Company
character: 5 Larry 9 Janet Wood 10 Helen Roper 11 Chrissy Snow, Jack Tripper 12 Stanley Roper

cast: 10 John Ritter, Norman Fell 11 Joyce DeWitt 12 Audra Lindley, Richard Kline 13 Suzanne Somers

Three Sisters
director: 10 John Sichel 15 Laurence Olivier

author: 12 Anton Chekhov

character: 13 Fyodor Kuligin 14 Baron Tusenbach, Vassily Solyony 17 Alexandr Vershinin

Prozorov family: 4 Olga 5 Irina, Masha 6 Andrey 7 Natasha

cast: 9 Alan Bates 11 Derek Jacobi, Jeanne Watts 13 Joan Plowright, Louise Purnell 15 Laurence Olivier

Three Soldiers
author: 13 John Dos Passos

threnody 5 dirge, elegy 6 lament 7 requiem

threshold 4 dawn, door, edge, sill 5 brink, limen, onset, start, verge 6 portal 7 doorway, gateway, opening, prelude 8 doorsill, entrance 9 beginning, groundsel, inception 10 groundsill 11 entranceway 12 commencement 13 starting point

Thriae
form: 6 nymphs
nursed: 6 Apollo
taught: 6 Hermes

Thriambus
epithet of: 8 Dionysus

thrift 7 economy 8 prudence 9 frugality, husbandry, parsimony 10 moderation 11 sparingness, thriftiness 14 reasonableness 15 closefistedness 16 parsimoniousness

thriftiness 5 tight 6 thrift 7 economy 8 prudence 9 frugality, parsimony 13 penny-pinching 15 closefistedness, tightfistedness 16 parsimoniousness

thriftless 6 lavish 8 feckless, prodigal, wasteful 11 extravagant, improvident

thrifty 6 frugal, saving, stingy 7 sparing 9 niggardly, penny-wise 10 economical 11 closefisted, economizing, tightfisted 12 parsimonious 13 penny-pinching

thrill 4 fire, glow, kick, stir 5 flush, rouse, throb 6 arouse, excite, quiver, tickle, tingle, tremor 7 delight, impress, inspire, tremble 9 adventure, electrify, enrapture, galvanize, stimulate, transport 12 satisfaction

thrilled 4 agog 7 excited 9 delighted, overjoyed 11 transported

thrilling 7 awesome 8 engaging, exciting, riveting, stirring 9 absorbing, exquisite 10 delightful 11 fascinating, pleasurable, provocative, sensational, tantalizing, titillating 12 electrifying

thrip
variety: 6 banded 10 tube tailed 11 heterothrip, merothripid

thrive 3 wax 4 boom 5 bloom, get on 6 fatten 7 burgeon, prosper, succeed 8 flourish, get ahead, grow rich

thriving 4 busy, lush, rank, rich 7 wealthy, well-off 8 blooming, in clover, vigorous, well-to-do 9 flowering, luxuriant 10 blossoming, prospering, prosperous, succeeding, successful 11 flourishing

throat 3 maw 4 craw, gula, neck 5 gorge 6 gullet 7 chamber, jugulum, passage, pharynx
lozenge: 6 pastil
nautical: 3 jaw 4 jaws, nock
part: 6 fauces, larynx, tonsil 7 glottis, trachea
pertaining to: 5 gular
seizing: 4 knot 5 hitch 12 cuckold's knot
swelling: 6 goiter

throaty 3 dry, low 4 base, deep 5 gruff, husky, thick 6 hoarse 7 cracked, grating, rasping 8 croaking, guttural, resonant, sonorous 9 full-toned

throb 4 beat, jerk, pant 5 heave, pulse, shake 6 quiver, tremor, twitch 7 beating, flutter, pulsate, shaking, tremble, vibrate 9 palpitate, pulsation, quivering, throbbing, trembling, vibration 10 fluttering 11 oscillation, palpitation 13 reverberation

throes 5 agony, chaos, pangs 6 ordeal, spasms, tumult 7 anguish, turmoil 8 disorder, paroxysm, upheaval 9 confusion, paroxysms 10 convulsion, disruption

thrombus 4 clot 9 blood clot 11 coagulation

throng 3 jam 4 army, cram, herd, host, mass, mill, pack, rush 5 bunch, crowd, crush, flock, flood, horde, press, surge, swarm 6 deluge, gather, huddle, stream 7 cluster, collect 8 assemble, converge 9 multitude 10 assemblage, congregate

thronged 4 full 6 jammed, mobbed, packed 7 crammed, crowded, flocked, swarmed, teeming 8 swarming 9 congested, jampacked 11 overflowing

throttle 3 gag, gas 4 stop 5 block, burke, check, choke 6 stifle 7 garrote, seal off, shut off, silence, smother 8 choke off, gas pedal, strangle 9 fuel lever, fuel valve 11 strangulate

through, thru 4 done, past 5 ended 6 direct 7 express 8 finished, from A to Z, to the end 9 all the way, completed, concluded 10 terminated 12 long-distance 15 from first to last 18 from beginning to end 20 from one end to the other

through and through 5 total 6 wholly 7 totally, utterly 8 complete 10 completely, thoroughly 15 from top to bottom 18 from beginning to end 20 from one end to the other

through my fault
Latin: 8 mea culpa

throughout 7 all over 10 all the time, everywhere 11 in every part 16 all the way through 18 from beginning to end

Through the Looking Glass
sequel to: 17 Alice in Wonderland
author: 12 Lewis Carroll
character: 4 Gnat, Lion 5 Alice, Dinah 7 Red King, Unicorn 8 Red Queen 9 Red Knight, White King 10 Tweedledee, Tweedledum, White Queen 11 Black Kitten, White Kitten, White Knight 12 Humpty Dumpty

throw 3 lob, pit, put, shy 4 cast, hurl, shot, toss 5 chuck, fling, floor, heave, impel, pitch, place, put in, put on, sling 6 hurtle, launch, let fly, propel, unseat 7 project 8 delivery 9 knock down, put around

throw away 7 cast off, discard 8 get rid of
throw down 5 let go 8 drop hard, hurl down, toss down 9 fling down
throw into disorder 5 upset 7 agitate, disrupt 10 disarrange
throw off 4 emit, gush 5 exude 7 abandon, cast off, mislead 8 get rid of, shake off, shrug off 9 cast aside, discharge, give forth, pour forth
throw off the scent 7 confuse, mislead 8 confound 19 throw out a red herring
throw out 4 beam, emit, oust 5 eject, evict, expel, exude 6 banish, bounce, remove 7 discard, dismiss, toss out 8 get rid of, jettison 9 cast aside, throw away
throw overboard 4 dump 7 cast off, discard 8 jettison, toss over
throw suspicion upon 11 cast doubt on 17 bring into question
throw up 4 barf, spew 5 eject, expel, spout, vomit 6 cast up, spew up 7 cough up 8 disgorge 9 discharge 11 regurgitate
thrust 3 jab, jam, ram 4 butt, pass, poke, prod, push, raid, stab 5 boost, drive, foray, force, impel, lunge, press, sally, shove, swipe 6 attack, charge, pierce, plunge, propel, sortie, strike, stroke 7 assault, impetus, impulse, riposte 8 momentum 9 incursion 10 aggression
thrust aside 4 dump 6 shelve 7 discard 8 get rid of, throw off, throw out 9 cast aside, dispose of, throw away
thrust at 6 assail, attack 7 lunge at 8 strike at
thrust out 4 spew, spit 5 eject, expel, vomit 6 extend, propel 7 protrude

Thrym
origin: 12 Scandinavian
form: 5 giant
killed by: 4 Thor
demanded return of: 5 Freia, Freya

Thucydides
author of: 28 History of the Peloponnesian War

thud 4 bang 5 clunk, knock, smack, thump
thug 4 hood 6 bandit, gunman, hit man, killer, mugger, robber 7 hoodlum, mobster, ruffian 8 assassin, gangster, murderer 9 cutthroat

thumb 5 hitch 6 finger, handle 9 hitchhike 10 catch a ride, hitch a ride 11 flip through, leaf through

Thumbelina
author: 21 Hans Christian Andersen

thumbnail 5 brief, short 7 compact, concise
thump 3 hit, jab, rap 4 bang, beat, clip, cuff, poke, slam, slap, swat, thud 5 clout, clunk, knock, pound, punch, smack, whack 6 batter, bounce, buffet, pommel, strike, thwack 8 collapse, lambaste

thunder 4 boom, clap, echo, peal, roar, roll 5 crack, crash 6 rumble 7 explode, resound 8 rumbling 9 discharge, explosion 11 reverberate, thunderbolt, thunderclap
god of: 4 Thor 5 Donar 7 Taranis

thunderbolt 4 dart 5 flash, shaft 8 stroke

Thunderstorms, god of 8 Summanus

thunderstruck 4 agog, awed 5 agape 6 aghast, amazed 8 confused, overcome 9 astounded, awestruck, perplexed, surprised 10 astonished, bewildered 11 dumbfounded 13 flabbergasted

Thunder-ten-Tronckh
character in: 7 Candide
author: 8 Voltaire

Thurber, James
author of: 12 The New Yorker 14 Is Sex Necessary (with E B White), The Catbird Seat 16 The Owl in the Attic 18 My Life and Hard Times, The Thurber Carnival 26 The Secret Life of Walter Mitty

Thurber Carnival, The
author: 12 James Thurber

Thurio
character in: 20 Two Gentlemen of Verona
author: 11 Shakespeare

Thursday
French: 5 jeudi
from: 4 Thor
German: 10 donnerstag
heavenly body: 4 Jove 7 Jupiter
Italian: 7 giovedi
Latin: 9 Dies Jovis
observance: 12 Holy Thursday, Thanksgiving 13 Corpus Christi 14 Maundy Thursday 17 Ascension Thursday
Scandinavian: 7 torsdag
Spanish: 6 jueves

Thurso's Landing
author: 15 Robinson Jeffers

thus 2 so 4 ergo 5 hence 6 like so 8 like this 9 as follows, in this way, therefore, wherefore 11 accordingly 12 consequently, in this manner 13 for this reason
Latin: 3 sic

thus always to tyrants
Latin: 17 sic semper tyrannis
motto of: 8 Virginia

thus passes away the glory of this world
Latin: 21 sic transit gloria mundi

Thus Spake Zarathustra
also: 21 Also Sprach Zarathustra
author: 18 Friedrich Nietzsche

thwack 3 box, hit, rap 4 bang, blow, slam, slap 5 baste, clout, knock, smack, thump, whack 6 buffet, paddle, strike, wallop

Thwackum
character in: 8 Tom Jones
author: 8 Fielding

thwart 3 bar 4 balk, foil, stop 5 check, cross 6 baffle, hinder, oppose 7 inhibit, prevent, ward off 8 obstruct, stave off 9 frustrate 10 contravene

Thyestean banquet
meal of: 10 human flesh

Thyestes
author: 6 Seneca

Thyestes
father: 6 Pelops
mother: 10 Hippodamia
brother: 6 Atreus
half-brother: 10 Chrysippus
sister-in-law: 6 Aerope
son: 9 Aegisthus
daughter: 7 Pelopia

Thyiad see 9 bacchante

Thymbraeus
father: 7 Laocoon

thyme
botanical name: 6 Thymus 9 T vulgaris
varieties: 4 Wild 5 Basil, Lemon, Water 6 Common, Garden, Golden 7 Caraway, Spanish
symbol of: 8 activity
attracts: 4 bees
conjures: 9 fairy folk
use: 4 fish 7 poultry 8 stuffing 10 Creole food 21 New England clam chowder

Thymoetes
king of: 6 Athens
elder of: 7 Trojans

Thyone see 6 Semele

Thyoneus
epithet of: 8 Dionysus
means: 11 son of Thyone

Thyrsis
author: 13 Matthew Arnold

Thyrus
staff of: 8 Dionysus
tipped with: 8 pine cone
twined with: 3 ivy 5 vines

thysanoptera
class: 8 hexapoda
phylum: 10 arthropoda
group: 5 thrip

thysanura
class: 8 hexapoda
phylum: 10 arthropoda
group: 8 firebrat 10 silverfish 11 bristle-tail

Tia Maria
type: 6 brandy 7 liqueur
origin: 7 Jamaica
flavor: 6 coffee
with rum: 10 Black Maria
with tequila: 9 Brave Bull
with vodka: 12 Black Russian

Tiamat
origin: 8 Akkadian
consort of: 4 Apsu
children: 4 gods

tiara 4 band 5 crown, miter 6 diadem 7 coronet 8 frontlet, ornament 9 headdress

Tiaxcaltec
language family: 5 Nahua
location: 6 Mexico 14 Central America

Tiber
god of: 9 Tiberinus

Tiberinus
origin: 5 Roman
god of: 5 Tiber

Tibet
other name: 3 Bod 4 Bhot 5 Tobet 8 Hsitsang 10 Land of Snow 14 Roof of the World
capital: 5 Lassa, Lhasa
city: 3 Noh 5 Karak 6 Chamdo, Gartok 7 Changtu, Totling 8 Gyangtse, Jihkatse, Shigatse 9 Chiangtzu
government: 23 autonomous region of China
monetary unit: 5 tanga
lake: 3 Aru, Bam, Bun, Nam 4 Mema, Tosu 5 Jagok, Tabia 6 Dagtse, Garhur, Kashun, Nam Iso, Seling, Tangra, Yamdok 7 Kyaring, Teriman, Tsaring, Zilling 8 Jiggitai 9 Tengrinor 11 Manasarowar
mountain: 5 Kamet, Sajum 6 Kailas, Kunlun 7 Bandala 8 Himalaya 9 Karakoram
highest point: 7 Everest
river: 3 Nak, Nau, Sak 4 Song 5 Hwang, Indus 6 Mekong, Sutlej, Yellow 7 Hwang Ho, Matsang, Melsang, Salween, Tsangpo, Yangtze 11 Brahmaputra
physical feature:
    plain: 4 Kham 9 Chang Tang
    valley: 7 Tsangpo
people: 5 Asian, Balti, Bodpa, Drupa 6 Bhotia, Champa, Drokpa, Khamba, Khambu, Panaka, Sherpa, Tangut 7 Bhotiya, Bhutani, Gyarung, Taghlik, Tibetan 9 Mongoloid
patron god: 14 Avalokitesvara
ruler: 4 Yuan 6 Mongol 9 dalai lama 13 Songtsan Gampo
language: 5 Balti 6 Ladkhi 7 Bhutani, Bodskad 8 Sanskrit 9 Bhutanese
religion: 5 Bonko 7 Lamaism
place:
    Indian border: 11 McMahon Line
    palace: 7 Potalaf
    temple: 7 Jokhang 10 Tashi Lumpo 11 Tashi Lhunpo
feature:
    animal: 3 dzo, yak 5 kiang 7 mastiff 8 musk deer 10 giant panda
    clothing: 5 chuba
    dance: 4 cham 9 achelhamo
    dog: 9 lhasa apso
    leader: 9 dalai lama
    legend: 4 yeti 17 abominable snowman
    monastery: 8 lamasery
    monk: 4 lama

food:
dish: 6 tsamba, tsampa
drink: 5 chang

tibia
bone of: 4 shin

tic 6 twitch 12 facial twitch 13 tic douloureux 19 trigemi nal neuralgia

tick 3 dot, tap 4 beat, line, list, mark, nick, note 5 blaze, check, clack, click, enter, notch, swing, throb 6 record, slight, stroke 7 scratch, vibrate 8 mark down, register, ticktock 9 checkmark, chronicle, oscillate, pulsation, vibration

ticket 3 tag 4 card, mark, pass, slip, stub 5 label, slate 6 ballot, coupon, marker, roster 7 sticker, voucher 14 list of nominees, traffic summons
type: 4 trip 7 parking, traffic 9 admission

tickle 4 itch 5 amuse, cheer, prick, sting, throb 6 divert, please, regale, stroke, thrill, tingle, twitch 7 delight, enchant, enliven, gladden, gratify, prickle, rejoice 8 enthrall, entrance 9 captivate, fascinate, titillate 12 scratchiness 15 do one's heart good

ticklish 4 hard 5 itchy, tough 6 knotty, thorny, tickly, touchy, tricky 7 awkward, prickly 8 critical, delicate, scratchy, tingling 9 difficult, intricate, sensitive, uncertain 11 complicated

tidal basin 3 bay 5 inlet, sound 6 lagoon 7 estuary 11 arm of the sea

tidbit 3 bit 4 item 5 treat 6 morsel 8 delicacy, mouthful 9 choice bit

tide 4 flow, neap, wave 5 drift, state 7 current 8 movement, tendency, undertow 9 direction 10 ebb and flow, wax and wane 11 rise and fall

tidings 4 news, word 6 advice, notice, report 8 good word 11 declaration, information 12 announcement, intelligence, notification

tidy 4 neat, trig, trim 5 ample, array, clean 6 goodly, neaten, tidy up 7 arrange, careful, clean up, orderly, precise, regular, sizable 8 neaten up, spotless, spruce up 9 organized, regulated, shipshape 10 immaculate, methodical, meticulous, put in order, straighten, systematic 11 substantial 12 businesslike, considerable, straighten up 15 in apple-pie order

tidy up 5 clean 6 neaten 9 freshen up 10 put in order, straighten

tie 3 rod 4 ally, band, beam, belt, bind, bond, cord, draw, duty, join, knot, lash, line, link, rope, sash, yoke 5 brace, cable, cinch, limit, marry, match, truss, unite 6 attach, bow tie, clinch, couple, cravat, engage, fasten, girdle, hamper, hinder, ribbon, secure, string, tether 7 confine, connect, kinship, necktie, support 8 affinity, cincture, dead heat, make a bow, make fast, relation, restrain, restrict, tied vote 9 constrain, crossbeam, fastening 10 allegiance, connection, cummerbund, obligation 11 affiliation, come out even 12 relationship 13 connecting rod 15 divide the honors

Tiepolo, Giovanni Battista (Giambattista)
born: 5 Italy 6 Venice
artwork: 10 Kaisersaal (salon) 11 Treppenhaus (staircase) 14 The Crucifixion 16 Ronaldo and Armida 20 Madonna of Mount Carmel 21 The Communion of St Lucia, The Triumph of Aphrodite 24 St Thekla and the Pestilence 28 Apotheosis of Francesco Barbaro 28 The Worship of the Bronze Serpent

tier 3 row 4 bank, file, line, rank, step 5 layer, level, range, story 7 stratum 14 stratification

Tierney, Gene
born: 10 Brooklyn NY
husband: 11 Oleg Cassini
roles: 5 Laura 10 Belle Starr 11 Tobacco Road 13 A Bell for Adano 16 Leave Her to Heaven 18 The Ghost and Mrs Muir

tiers etat 11 third estate
in French politics: 7 commons

tie-up 3 jam 4 snag 5 block, hitch, snarl 6 slow-up 7 failure 8 blockage, gridlock, stop page 9 breakdown 10 bottleneck, disruption 11 malfunction 13 embouteillage

tie up 3 tie 4 bind, gird, lash, rope 5 hitch, snarl, strap, truss 6 engage, fasten, hinder, impede, occupy, secure, tangle 8 entangle

tiff 4 huff, miff, rage, snit, spat 5 clash, run-in, scrap, tizzy, words 6 hassle 7 dispute, quarrel, rhubarb, wrangle 8 argument, ill humor, squabble 10 difference 11 altercation 12 disagreement 16 misunderstanding

tiger 3 cat 6 cougar, jaguar 7 fighter, wildcat
young: 5 whelp

Tiger Joy
author: 19 Stephen Vincent Benet

tiger's-eye
species: 6 quartz

Tigger
character in: 13 Winnie-the-Pooh
author: 5 Milne

tight 4 busy, firm, full, hard, high, snug, taut 5 blind, close, dense, drunk, exact, happy, harsh, lit up, rigid, scant, solid, stern, stiff, tense, tipsy, tough 6 firmly, frugal, gorged, hard-up, jammed, juiced, loaded, scarce, secure, severe, skimpy, sloppy, soused, stewed, stingy, stoned, strict, trying, zonked 7 austere, closely, compact, crammed, crowded, drunken, miserly, onerous, pickled, pie-eyed, smashed, solidly, sparing, stuffed 8 grudging, rigorous, securely, too small 9 deficient, difficult, illiberal, jam-packed, niggardly, penurious, plastered, skintight, stringent, worrisome 10 burdensome, compressed, glassy-eyed, impassable, inadequate, inebriated, inflexible, in one's cups, nip-and-tuck, nose-to-nose, tyrannical, ungenerous, unyielding 11 closefisted, constricted, dictatorial, impermeable, intoxicated, troublesome, well-matched 12 close-fitting, impenetrable, insufficient, parsimonious 13 closely fitted, feeling no pain

14 fitting closely, uncompromising **20** three sheets to the wind

tighten 5 pinch **6** anchor, fasten, narrow, secure **7** squeeze **8** contract, make fast, make taut **9** constrict **14** take up the slack

tighten one's belt 4 save **5** skimp, stint **6** scrimp **8** conserve, cut costs **9** economize **11** cut expenses **12** pinch pennies

tightfisted 5 cheap, mingy, tight **6** greedy, stingy **7** miserly **9** illiberal, niggardly, penurious **10** avaricious **11** closefisted **12** cheeseparing, parsimonious **13** penny-pinching

tightfistedness 6 penury **9** parsimony **10** stinginess **11** miserliness **13** niggardliness, penny-pinching

tight-fitting 4 snug **5** tight **8** too small **9** skintight **11** constricted **12** constricting **15** like a second skin

tight-laced 4 prim **6** prissy, stuffy **7** prudish **8** priggish **9** inhibited, repressed, Victorian **11** puritanical, standoffish, straitlaced **13** self-righteous

tight-lipped 3 mum **4** curt **5** brief, quiet, short, terse **8** discreet, reserved, reticent, taciturn **10** unsociable **11** untalkative **12** close-mouthed **15** uncommunicative

tightly packed 5 dense **6** jammed **7** compact, crammed, stuffed **10** compressed **12** concentrated

tightwad 5 miser, piker **7** niggard, Scrooge **9** lickpenny, skinflint **10** cheapskate, pinch-penny **12** moneygrubber

till 3 sow **4** even, farm, plow, seed, tray, unto up to **6** before, coffer, drawer, harrow, plough **7** as far as, develop, prepare **8** moneybox, treasury **9** cultivate **12** cash register
    geological: 5 drift

tillable 6 arable **8** farmable, plowable **10** cultivable

tillage 7 farming, plowing **11** agriculture, cultivation

Till Eulenspiegel
    also: 16 Tyll Eulenspiegel
    origin: 8 Germanic
    means: 14 practical joker

Tillie the Toiler
    creator: 12 Russ Westover
    character: 3 Mac **7** Mr Chase

Tilney, Henry
    character in: 15 Northanger Abbey
    author: 6 Austen

tilt 3 row, tip **4** cant, lean, list, rake, spar, tiff **5** brawl, fence, fight, grade, joust, pitch, slant, slope **6** affray, battle, combat, oppose **7** contest, dispute, incline, quarrel **8** argument, skirmish, squabble **9** encounter **10** tournament **11** altercation

Timaeus
    author: 5 Plato

Timandra
    father: 9 Tyndareus
    mother: 4 Leda
    brother: 6 Castor, Pollux
    sister: 5 Helen **12** Clytemnestra
    husband: 7 Echemus, Phyleus

    son: 5 Meges
    cursed by: 9 Aphrodite

timber 4 bush, logs, wood **5** copse, trees, woods **6** boards, forest, lumber **7** thicket

timberland 5 woods **6** forest, sticks **8** woodland

timbre 4 tone **5** pitch **9** resonance

time, times 3 age, day, eon, era **4** beat, days, hour, term, week, year **5** clock, cycle, epoch, event, match, month, phase, spell, stage, tempo, while, years **6** adjust, chance, decade, moment, period, rhythm, season **7** century, episode, freedom, instant, liberty, measure, stretch **8** duration, incident, interval, occasion **10** experience, generation **11** opportunity, synchronize

time flies
    Latin: 11 tempus fugit

time-honored 6 common, normal **7** regular, revered **8** accepted, standard **9** customary, respected, universal

timeless 7 abiding, durable, endless, eternal, lasting, undying **8** enduring, immortal, infinite, unending **9** boundless, ceaseless, deathless, immutable, incessant, permanent, perpetual **10** continuous, persistent **11** everlasting, never-ending **12** interminable, unchangeable **13** never-stopping **14** indestructible

timely 6 prompt **8** punctual **9** opportune, well-timed **10** convenient, felicitous, seasonable **12** providential

Time Machine, The
    author: 7 H G Wells
    character: 4 Eloi **5** Weena **8** Morlocks **12** Time Traveler

Time of Your Life, The
    author: 14 William Saroyan
    director: 8 H C Potter
    cast: 8 Ward Bond **11** James Cagney, Wayne Morris **12** Jeanne Cagney **13** William Bendix **17** Broderick Crawford

timepiece 5 clock, watch **8** horologe **11** chronometer

Time Remembered
    author: 11 Jean Anouilh

Timerman, Jacobo
    author of: 38 Prisoner Without a Name Cell Without a Number

timesaving 5 quick **6** speedy **9** efficient **11** expeditious

time without end 7 forever **8** eternity, infinity

timeworn 3 old **4** aged, worn **5** dated, hoary, passe, stale, trite **6** age-old, beat-up, old-hat, shabby **7** ancient, antique **8** battered, dog-eared, obsolete, overused **9** hackneyed, out of date, venerable, weathered **10** antiquated **12** antediluvian

timid 3 coy, shy **6** afraid, humble, modest, scared **7** bashful, fearful **8** cowardly, retiring, sheepish, timorous **9** diffident, shrinking, spineless, weak-kneed **10** unassuming **12** apprehensive, fainthearted **13** pusillanimous

timidity 7 modesty, shyness 8 cold feet, humility 9 cowardice, timidness 10 diffidence 11 bashfulness, fearfulness, trepidation 12 sheepishness, timorousness 13 spinelessness 16 faint-heartedness

timidness 7 shyness 8 meekness, timidity 10 diffidence, insecurity 11 bashfulness 12 timorousness 14 submissiveness 15 unassertiveness 16 faintheartedness

Timon of Athens
author: 18 William Shakespeare
character: 6 Lucius 7 Flavius 8 Lucullus 9 Apemantus, Ventidius 10 Alcibiades, Sempronius

Timor
capital: 4 Dili
country: 8 Portugal 9 Indonesia
islands: 5 Sunda 11 Lesser Sunda
strait: 5 Ombai

timorous 3 shy 4 meek 5 timid 6 afraid 7 anxious, bashful, fearful 8 retiring 9 shrinking 10 submissive 12 fainthearted

timorousness 7 shyness 8 cold feet, meekness, timidity 9 cowardice 11 fearfulness, trepidation 16 faintheartedness

Timothy
mother: 6 Eunice
grandmother: 4 Lois
companion: 4 Paul 8 Silvanus

tin
chemical symbol: 2 Sn

tincture 6 elixir 7 essence, extract, spirits 8 solution 11 concentrate

Tinder Box, The
author: 21 Hans Christian Andersen

Tin Drum, The
author: 11 Gunter Grass
director: 17 Volker Schlondorff
character: 14 Oskar Matzerath
cast: 10 Mario Adorf 12 David Bennett (Oskar) 13 Angela Winkler 16 Daniel Olbrychski 17 Katharina Tahlbach
Oscar for: 11 foreign film

tine 3 die, tip 4 barb, lose, tyne 5 point, prong, spike 6 bodkin, branch, perish, skewer 7 destroy, forfeit

tinge 3 dye 4 cast, dash, hint, lace, tint, tone, vein 5 color, imbue, shade, smack, stain, taste, touch, trace 6 flavor, infuse, nuance, season 7 instill, soupcon 9 suspicion

tingle 5 sting, throb 6 thrill, tickle, tremor 7 flutter, prickle 9 prickling, pulsation 11 palpitation

Tinia
origin: 8 Etruscan
chief: 3 god

Tinker, Tailor, Soldier, Spy
author: 11 John Le Carre

Tinker Bell
character in: 8 Peter Pan
author: 6 Barrie

tinkle 4 ding, peal, ping, ring 5 chime, chink, clank, clink, plink 6 jingle 9 ting-a-ling

tin lizzie 3 car 4 auto, heap 5 motor 6 jalopy, wheels 7 flivver, machine, motocar, vehicle 10 automobile 12 motor vehicle

Tin Man, Tin Woodsman
character in: 13 The Wizard of Oz
author: 4 Baum

tinsel 4 sham, show 5 gloss 6 sequin 7 glitter, spangle 8 pretense 9 gaudiness 10 camouflage, decoration, masquerade 11 affectation, false colors, make-believe, ostentation

tint 3 dye, hue 4 hint, tone, wash 5 color, frost, shade, stain, tinge, touch, trace 6 nuance 7 pigment 8 coloring, tincture 10 suggestion

Tintern Abbey
author: 17 William Wordsworth

tintinnabulate 4 peal, ring, toll 5 chime, clang, knell, sound 6 jingle, tinkle

tintinnabulation 4 gong, peal, ring, toll 5 chime, knell 6 jingle 7 clangor, pealing, ringing 8 clanging, ding-dong, jingling, tinkling 11 peal of bells

Tintoretto, Jacopo
real name: 13 Jacopo Robusti
born: 5 Italy 6 Venice
artwork: 8 Paradise 13 The Last Supper 14 The Crucifixion 16 The Road to Calvary 17 Bacchus and Ariadne 18 Apotheosis of St Roch, The Flight into Egypt 20 Susannah and the Elders 21 The Temptation of Christ 26 St Mark Frees a Christian Slave 27 The Finding of the Body of St Mark 32 The Miracle of St Mark Rescuing a Slave

tiny 3 wee 5 pygmy, runty, small, teeny 6 bantam, little, midget, minute, petite 8 dwarfish 9 itsy-bitsy, miniature, minuscule, pint-sized 10 diminutive, teeny-weeny, undersized 11 Lilliputian, microscopic, pocket-sized 12 teensy-weensy

Tiny Alice
author: 11 Edward Albee

Tiny Tim
character in: 15 A Christmas Carol
author: 7 Dickens

tip 3 cap, pat, tap, top 4 acme, apex, barb, brow, cant, clue, head, hint, hook, lean, list, peak, rake, tilt 5 crest, crown, pitch, point, prong, slant, slope, spike, upend, upset 6 advice, reward, stroke, summit, tip-off, topple, upturn, vertex, zenith 7 capsize, incline, leaning, lowdown, pointer, sharpen, tilting, tipping, warning 8 gratuity, over turn, pinnacle, slanting 9 baksheesh, lagniappe 10 admonition, inside dope, perquisite, suggestion, turn turtle 11 forewarning 13 word to the wise
French: 7 douceur

tipcart 4 cart 8 dumpcart, pushcart

Tiphys
member of: 9 Argonauts
occupation: 9 steersman

tip off 3 tip 4 warn 5 alert 6 caveat 7 caution, warning 8 forewarn 11 forewarning

tip over 5 upend, upset **7** capsize **8** flip over, keel over, overturn, turn over **10** turn turtle

Tippett, Michael Kemp
  born: 6 London **7** England
  composer of: 9 King Priam **13** The Knot Garden **15** A Child of Our Time **20** The Midsummer Marriage **22** The Vision of St Augustine **32** Concerto for Double String Orchestra

tipple 5 drink, quaff **6** guzzle, imbibe, liquor **8** beverage

tippler 3 sot **4** lush, soak, wino **5** drunk, rummy, souse, toper **6** bibber, boozer, sponge **7** guzzler, imbiber, swiller, tosspot **8** drunkard **9** alcoholic, inebriate **10** booze hound **11** dipsomaniac

tipsy 4 high **5** awash, blind, drunk, happy, lit-up, stiff, tight **6** juiced, loaded, sloppy, sodden, soused, stewed, stoned **7** drunken, pickled, pie-eyed, smashed **9** inebriate, plastered **10** glassy-eyed, inebriated, in one's cups **11** intoxicated **12** half seas over **13** feeling no pain **20** three sheets to the wind

tip-top 4 A-one **5** elite, super **7** supreme **8** very fine **10** consummate **11** exceptional, superlative **13** extraordinary

tirade 5 curse **6** screed **7** lecture **8** diatribe, harangue, jeremiad, scolding **9** invective, reprimand **11** castigation, fulmination **12** condemnation, denunciation, dressing-down, vilification, vituperation

tirailleur 10 skirmisher **12** sharpshooter

Tirane, Tirana
  capital of: 7 Albania

tire 3 fag, irk **4** bore **5** annoy, weary **6** bother, tucker **7** disgust, exhaust, fatigue, wear out **8** be sick of **10** make sleepy **11** be fed up with **12** lose interest, lose patience

tire
  invented by: 6 Dunlop **7** Thomson

tired 4 beat **5** all in, weary **6** bushed, drowsy, fagged, pooped, sleepy **7** wearied, worn out **8** dog-tired, fatigued, tuckered **9** enervated, exhausted, played out

tireless 6 steady **7** devoted, staunch **8** constant, faithful, resolute, untiring **9** steadfast, unceasing, unwearied **10** determined, unflagging, unswerving **11** hard-working, industrious, never-tiring, persevering, unfaltering, unremitting **13** indefatigable

Tiresias
  also: 9 Teiresias
  vocation: 7 prophet
  father: 6 Everes
  mother: 8 Chariclo
  grandfather: 6 Udaeus
  home: 6 Thebes
  struck: 5 blind
  character in: 7 Odyssey **10** Oedipus Rex
  characteristic: 9 blind seer

tiresome 4 drab, dull, hard **6** boring, deadly, dismal, tiring, trying, vexing **7** arduous, fagging, humdrum, irksome, tedious, wearing **8** annoying, wearying **9** difficult,

fatiguing, laborious, wearisome **10** bothersome, exhausting, monotonous **13** uninteresting

Tisamenus
  leader of: 9 Boeotians
  father: 7 Orestes
  mother: 8 Hermione
  vocation: 4 seer
  killed by: 10 Heraclidae

Tishri 18 seventh Hebrew month

Tisiphone
  member of: 6 Furies

'Tis Pity She's a Whore
  author: 8 John Ford
  character: 6 Donado, Florio, Putana **7** Soranzo, Vasques **8** Bergetto, Giovanni, Grimaldi **9** Annabella, Hippolita **11** Richardetto **16** Friar Bonaventura

tissue
  kind: 4 bone, skin **5** nerve **6** muscle

titan 5 giant, great, mogul **7** magnate

Titan
  race of: 4 gods
  father: 6 Uranus
  mother: 2 Ge **4** Gaea
  names: 5 Coeus, Crius **6** Cronus **7** Iapetus, Oceanus **8** Hyperion
  sisters: 8 Titaness
  names of sisters: **4** Rhea **5** Theia **6** Phoebe, Tethys, Themis **9** Mnemosyne

Titan, The
  sequel to: 12 The Financier
  author: 15 Theodore Dreiser
  character: 13 Peter Laughlin **15** Berenice Fleming, Stephanie Platow **16** Aileen Cowperwood **23** Frank Algernon Cowperwood

Titan, the *see* **6** Helios

Titaness *see* **5** Titan

Titania
  character in: 21 A Midsummer Night's Dream
  author: 11 Shakespeare

titanic 4 huge, vast **5** giant, great, stout **6** mighty, strong **7** immense, mammoth **8** colossal, enormous, gigantic, whopping **9** herculean, humongous, monstrous **10** gargantuan, monumental, prodigious, stupendous

titanium
  chemical symbol: 2 Ti

Titanomachy
  revolt of: 7 Iapetus

tit for tat 8 exchange **10** quid pro quo **13** an eye for an eye

Tithonus
  father: 8 Laomedon
  brother: 5 Priam
  loved by: 3 Eos
  son: 6 Memnon **8** Emathion

Titian
  real name: 15 Tiziano Vecellio
  born: 5 Italy **13** Pieve di Cadore
  artwork: 5 Pieta **12** The Bacchanal, Tribute Money **13** Noli Me Tangere **15** Diana and Actaeon, The Rape of Europa **16** The Pesaro Madonna, The Venus of

Urbino 17 Bacchus and Ariadne, The
Death of Actaeon, The Girl in a Fur Wrap,
The Three Ages of Man 18 Charles V at
Muhlberg, The Adrian Bacchanal, The
Young Englishman 19 Francis I Roi de
France 20 Sacred and Profane Love 21
Venus and the Lute Player 23 The Ma-
donna of the Cherries 24 Pope Paul III
and his Nephews, The Assumption of the
Virgin

titillate 5 charm, rouse, tease, tempt 6 allure, arouse, excite, seduce, tickle, turn on
7 attract, provoke 8 entrance 9 captivate,
fascinate, stimulate 15 whet the appetite

titillating 8 alluring, exciting, tempting 9 seductive 10 suggestive 11 provocative

title 3 dub 4 deed, name, rank, term 5
claim, crown, grade, label, place, right 6
status, tenure 7 entitle, epithet, station 8
christen, nobility, position 9 condition, designate, ownership 10 legal right, lordly
rank, noble birth, possession 11 appellation, designation 12 championship

titled 5 named, noble, regal, royal 6 called,
lordly 7 courtly 8 entitled 10 designated 11
blue-blooded 12 aristocratic

Titograd
  capital of: 10 Montenegro

titter 5 chirp, smirk 6 cackle, giggle, simper,
teehee 7 chuckle, snicker, snigger

tittle 3 bit, dot, jot 4 atom, iota, mite 5
speck 8 particle

Tittle, Y A (Yelberton Abraham)
  sport: 8 football
  position: 11 quarterback
  team: 13 New York Giants 14 Baltimore
  Colts 23 San Francisco Forty-Niners

titular 7 known as, nominal 8 so-called 10
in name only, ostensible 11 in title only

Titus
  surname: 6 Justus
  hometown: 7 Corinth
  companion: 4 Paul

Titus see 6 Tatius

Titus Andronicus
  author: 18 William Shakespeare
  character: 5 Aaron 6 Chiron, Marcus,
  Tamora 7 Alarbus, Lavinia 9 Bassianus,
  Demetrius 10 Saturninus

Tityus
  form: 5 giant
  father: 4 Zeus
  mother: 2 Ge 5 Elara
  home: 6 Euboea
  threatened: 4 Leto
  killed by: 6 Apollo 7 Artemis

tizzy 4 snit 6 dither, swivet 7 dudgeon 8 tail-
spin
  British: 8 sixpence

Tjaden
  character in: 25 All Quiet on the Western Front
  author: 8 Remarque

Tlepolemus
  father: 8 Hercules
  mother: 10 Astyocheia
  wife: 6 Polyxo

  son: 8 Deiphylus
  killed by: 8 Sarpedon

Tmolus
  king of: 5 Lydia

to 2 ad, on 3 for 4 into, near, unto, upon,
with 5 about, until 6 at hand, closed, toward 7 against, forward 8 together 10 concerning, included in 11 contained in
  prefix: 2 ac, ad
  Scottish: 3 tae

toad
  group of: 4 knot

toady 4 fawn 6 fawner, flunky, stooge, yes-
man 8 hanger-on, kowtow to, parasite,
truckler 9 flatterer, sycophant 10 bootlicker, curry favor 11 apple-polish, lickspittle 13 apple-polisher, backscratcher

To Althea, From Prison
  author: 15 Richard Lovelace

to a man 3 all 8 every one 9 one and all 10
completely 12 to the last man

To a Skylark
  author: 18 Percy Bysshe Shelley

toast 3 dry 4 heat, warm 5 brown, grill,
honor 6 salute, warm up 9 celebrate 10
compliment 11 commemorate 12 browned
bread, clink glasses 15 drink one's health

tobacco
  varieties: 4 tree, wild 6 Indian 7 jasmine,
  Turkish 9 broadleaf, flowering, Nicotiana
  12 long-flowered 16 Nicotiana rustica,
  Nicotiana tabacum

Tobacco Road
  author: 15 Erskine Caldwell
  character: 3 Ada 4 Dude 5 Pearl 6
  Bessie 8 Ellie May 9 Lov Bensey 12
  Jeeter Lester

To Be or Not To Be
  director: 13 Ernst Lubitsch
  cast: 9 Jack Benny 11 Robert Stack 12
  Lionel Atwill 13 Carole Lombard, Felix
  Bressart
  setting: 6 Poland

Tobias
  father: 5 Tobit
  grandfather: 6 Tobiel
  son: 8 Hycranus

Tobit
  father: 6 Tobiel
  son: 6 Tobias

To Catch a Thief
  director: 13 Alfred Hitchcock
  cast: 9 Cary Grant 10 Grace Kelly 12
  John Williams 17 Jessie Royce Landis
  setting: 13 French Riviera

Tocharian
  language family: 12 Indo-European
  spoken in: 11 Central Asia

Tocqueville, Alexis de
  author: 18 Democracy in America

tocsin 4 bell 5 alarm 7 warning

today 3 now 7 this day, this era 8 nowadays, this time 9 in this era, on this day,
this epoch 10 the present 11 in this epoch,
modern times 13 in modern times, the
present age, the present day 15 in this day
and age

Todd, Richard
  real name: 27 Richard Andrew Pale-
  thorpe-Todd
  born: 6 Dublin 7 Ireland
  roles: 13 The Hasty Heart, The Longest
  Day 14 The Virgin Queen 15 A Man
  Called Peter

toddle 6 waddle, wobble 14 take short
steps, walk unsteadily

toddler 3 tot 4 babe, baby, tyke 5 child 6 infant 9 little one

to-do 3 ado 4 fuss, stir 5 furor, noise 6 bustle, flurry, hubbub, hustle, pother, racket,
ruckus, rumpus, tumult, uproar 7 turmoil 8
activity 9 agitation, commotion 10 excitement, hullabaloo, hurly-burly 11 disturbance

Toe, The
  nickname of: 8 Lou Groza

to err is human
  Latin: 16 errare humanum est

toff 3 nob 4 beau 5 dandy, swell 10 young
blood

Toffler, Alvin
  author of: 11 Future Shock 12 The Third
  Wave

toga 3 aba 4 garb, gown, robe 6 trabea 7
garment 12 outergarment
  virilis: 9 white robe 11 manhood robe

Togo
  other name: 14 French Togoland
  capital/largest city: 4 Lome
  others: 5 Badon, Kpeme 6 Anecho,
  Ansoho, Blitta, Klonto, Nuatja, Palime,
  Sokode 7 Bassari, Dopango, Pagonda 8
  Atakpame, Tabligbo 10 Niamtougou
  school: 5 Benin 6 Mawuli
  monetary unit: 5 franc 7 centime
  mountain: 4 Togo 7 Atakora, Koronga
  highest point: 7 Baumann
  river: 3 Oti 4 Anie, Haho, Mono, Ogou
  sea: 8 Atlantic
  physical feature:
    bight: 5 Benin
    gulf: 6 Guinea
    plain: 4 Mono
  people: 3 Ana, Ewe, Twi 4 Mina 5 Hausa
  6 Akposa, Kabrai 7 Bassari, Cabrais,
  Kabrais, Ouatchi 8 Konkomba, Kotokoli,
  Lotokoli
  leader: 7 Eyadema 15 Sylvanus Olympio
  16 Nicolas Grunitzky
  language: 3 Ana, Ewe, Twi 4 Mina 5
  Hausa 6 French, Kabrai, Kabrie 7
  Bassari, Dagomba, Ouatchi 8 Kotokoli,
  Lotocoli
  religion: 5 Islam 7 animism 12 Christianity

togs 4 duds 6 attire, outfit 7 apparel,
clothes, threads 8 clothing, garments

To Have and Have Not
  director: 11 Howard Hawks
  based on novel by: 15 Ernest Hemingway
  cast: 12 Dolores Moran, Lauren Bacall
  13 Walter Brennan 14 Humphrey Bogart
  15 Hoagy Carmichael

remade as: 13 The Gunrunners 16 The
Breaking Point

To His Coy Mistress
  author: 13 Andrew Marvell

toil 4 grub, moil, work 5 grind, labor, pains,
slave, sweat 6 drudge, effort 7 travail 8
drudgery, exertion, hardship, hard work,
industry, struggle, work hard 11 application, elbow grease 12 apply oneself, exert
oneself 14 work like a horse

toiler 4 peon, serf, swot 5 navvy, prole,
slave 6 drudge, flunky, menial, slavey,
worker 7 grubber, laborer, servant, slogger
9 workhorse 10 wage earner 11 galley
slave

toilet 2 WC 3 can, loo 4 john 5 privy 7 commode, latrine 8 facility, lavatory, men's
room, outhouse, rest room, washroom 10
ladies' room 11 convenience, water closet

toilet water 5 scent 7 cologne, essence,
perfume 9 fragrance

toilsome 4 hard 5 tough 6 tiring, uphill 7 arduous, onerous, tedious 8 wearying 9 difficult, effortful, fatiguing, herculean, laborious, strenuous, wearisome 10
burdensome, exhausting 12 backbreaking

To Jerusalem and Back
  author: 10 Saul Bellow

token 4 mark, sign 5 index, proof 6 jetton,
symbol 7 for show, memento, minimal,
nodding, nominal, passing 8 evidence,
keepsake, reminder, souvenir, symbolic 9
vestigial 10 expression, indication 11 perfunctory, remembrance, superficial, testimonial 13 manifestation

To Kill a Mockingbird
  director: 14 Robert Mulligan
  based on novel by: 9 Harper Lee
  cast: 9 John Megna 10 Mary Badham 11
  Gregory Peck 12 Philip Alford
  Oscar for: 5 actor (Peck)

Tokyo
  airport: 6 Haneda
  capital of: 5 Japan
  district: 5 Ginza 6 Keihin 7 Chiyoda 8
  Yokohama 10 Marunouchi 18 Tama New
  Town Project
  former name: 3 Edo
  island: 6 Honshu
  landmark: 8 Ueno Park 11 Meiji Shrine
  12 National Diet 14 Imperial Palace,
  Kitanomaru Park 19 Komazawa Olympic
  Park
  means: 14 Eastern capital

Tola 11 Hebrew judge

Told in the Dog Watches
  author: 12 Frank T Bullen

tolerable 4 fair, so-so 7 allowed, average 8
abidable, accepted, adequate, bearable,
mediocre, middling, ordinary, passable 9
allowable, endurable, innocuous, permitted 10 acceptable, admissible, fairly good,
sufferable 11 commonplace, indifferent,
permissible 12 run-of-the-mill 14 fair-to-
middling

tolerance 7 charity 8 fairness, goodwill, patience, sympathy 9 endurance 10 compassion, sufferance 11 forbearance 13 brotherly love, fair treatment, fellow feeling, power to endure 15 lack of prejudice

tolerant 4 easy, fair, soft 7 lenient, liberal, patient, sparing 8 moderate 9 easygoing, forgiving, indulgent, unbigoted 10 charitable, forbearing, permissive 11 broadminded, kindhearted, softhearted, sympathetic 12 unprejudiced 13 compassionate, uncomplaining, understanding

tolerate 3 let 4 bear, take 5 abide, admit, allow, brook, stand 6 endure, permit, suffer, wink at 7 indulge, stomach, undergo 8 be easy on, be soft on, sanction, submit to 9 consent to, put up with, recognize, vouchsafe

To Let
  author: 14 John Galsworthy

to life
  Hebrew: 7 lehayim 8 lechayim

Tolkien, J R R
  author of: 9 The Hobbit 12 Silmarillion 17 The Lord of the Rings
  fictional setting: 11 Middle Earth

Tolstoy, Leo
  author of: 11 War and Peace 12 Anna Karenina, Resurrection 17 The Kreutzer Sonata 18 Death of Ivan Ilyitch

Toltec
  tribe: 4 Itza

To Lucasta, Going to the Wars
  author: 15 Richard Lovelace

Tolumnius
  vocation: 5 augur

tom 3 cat 6 tomcat 10 male turkey

tomato 12 Lycopersicon 24 Lycopersicon lycopersicum
  varieties: 4 Husk, Pear, Tree 6 Cherry 7 Currant 10 Gooseberry, Strawberry 11 Mexican husk
  soup: 8 gazpacho
  sauce: 6 catsup 7 ketchup

tomb 5 crypt, grave, vault 8 monument 9 mausoleum, sepulcher 11 burial place 12 resting place 13 burial chamber

tomboy 3 meg 4 girl, romp 5 rowdy 6 female, gamine, hoiden, hoyden, tomrig 8 strumpet

Tom Brown's School Days
  author: 12 Thomas Hughes

tombs
  god of: 6 Anubis

tomcat 3 cat, tom 9 womanizer

To-meri *see* 5 Egypt

tomfoolery 4 play 6 antics 8 drollery, nonsense 9 high jinks, horseplay, silliness 10 goofing off, skylarking 11 foolishness 12 lollygagging, monkeyshines, prankishness

13 fooling around, messing around, playing around

Tom Jones
  also: 29 The History of Tom Jones Foundling
  author: 13 Henry Fielding
  character: 6 Square 7 Bridget, Western 8 Mrs Honor, Thwackum 9 Mrs Miller, Partridge 11 Black George, Nightingale 12 Master Blifil 13 Lady Bellaston, Sophia Western 15 Squire Allworthy
  director: 14 Tony Richardson
  cast: 11 Joyce Redman 12 Albert Finney, Diane Cilento, Hugh Griffith, Susannah York 14 Dame Edith Evans
  score: 11 John Addison
  Oscar for: 5 score 7 picture 9 direction 10 screenplay

Tomlin, Lily
  real name: 14 Mary Jean Tomlin
  born: 9 Detroit MI
  roles: 7 Laugh-In 8 Edith Ann 9 Ernestine, Nashville 10 The Late Show 14 Moment By Moment 27 The Incredible Shrinking Woman

Tomlinson, Mary
  real name of: 12 Marjorie Main

tommyrot 3 rot 4 bosh, bull, bunk, crap, tosh 5 bilge, hokum, hooey, trash 6 bunkum, drivel, humbug 7 baloney, hogwash, spinach, rubbish, twaddle 8 buncombe, claptrap, folderol, malarkey, nonsense 9 poppycock 10 applesauce, balderdash, tomfoolery 11 foolishness 12 bullfeathers, fiddle-faddle 13 horsefeathers 16 stuff-and-nonsense

tomorrow 9 the future, the morrow 11 in the future 12 in days to come 16 the day after today 17 the next generation
  Spanish: 6 manana

Tompkins, Yewell
  real name of: 8 Tom Ewell

Tom Sawyer
  author: 9 Mark Twain
  character: 8 Huck (Huckleberry) Finn, Injun Joe 9 Aunt Polly, Joe Harper 10 Muff Potter 13 Becky Thatcher

Tom Thumb the Great
  author: 13 Henry Fielding

ton
  abbreviation: 1 t

tone 3 hue 4 cast, lilt, mood, note, tint 5 color, pitch, shade, sound, style, tenor, tinge 6 accent, chroma, firm up, manner, soften, spirit, stress, subdue, temper 7 cadence, quality 8 attitude, harmonic, make firm, moderate, modulate, overtone, tonality 10 inflection, intonation, make supple, modulation

Tone, Franchot
  real name: 27 Stanislas Pascal Franchot Tone
  born: 14 Niagara Falls NY
  wife: 11 Jean Wallace 12 Joan Crawford 13 Barbara Payton 15 Dolores Dorn-Heft
  roles: 10 Uncle Vanya 11 Phantom Lady 13 Three Comrades 16 Advise and

Consent 17 Five Graves to Cairo, Mutiny on the Bounty 23 The Lives of a Bengal Lancer

tone up 7 make fit, shape up 9 condition 10 put in shape

Tonga
other name: 15 Friendly Islands
capital/largest city: 9 Nukualofa
others: 3 Mua, Pea 6 Neiafu 7 Haakame, Kolonga, Kolovai 8 Fuaamotu
division: 5 Vavau 6 Haapai 9 Tongatapu
government: 8 monarchy
head of state: 4 king
monetary unit: 6 paanga, seniti
island: 3 Eua, Kao, Ono 4 Kotu 5 Tofua, Vavau 6 Haapai, Lifuka, Nomuka 7 Otu Tolu 9 Tongatapu
highest point: 3 Kao
sea: 7 Pacific
people: 10 Polynesian
explorer: 4 Cook 5 Bligh 6 Tasman
king: 11 George Tupou 14 Taufaahau Tupou
missionary: 12 Shirley Baker
queen: 6 Salote
language: 6 Tongan 7 English
religion: 9 Methodist 12 Christianity 25 Wesleyan Free Church of Tonga
feature:
fabric: 4 tapa
spiritual king: 8 tui tonga

tongue 3 lap 4 flap, lick, spit 5 point, shaft 6 lingua, patois, speech 7 dialect, lingula 8 language 10 promontory, vernacular, vocabulary 13 organ of speech, power of speech, style of speech
tastes: 4 salt, sour 5 sweet 6 bitter

tongue-lash 5 scold 6 berate, rail at, rebuke 7 bawl out, chew out, reprove, upbraid 8 reproach 9 castigate, reprimand 10 take to task

tongue-lashing 6 rebuke 7 censure, chiding, reproof 8 reproach, scolding 9 reprimand 10 bawling-out, chewing-out, upbraiding 11 castigation, reprobation 12 dressing-down, remonstrance

tonic 6 bracer, pickup 7 keynote 8 pick-me-up 9 analeptic, refresher, stimulant 10 invigorant 11 restorative

tonne
abbreviation: 1 t

Tono-Bungay
author: 7 H G Wells

tonsure 3 cut 4 trim 8 bald spot 11 shaven patch

too
French: 4 trop

tool 4 dupe, pawn 5 agent, means 6 device, medium, puppet, stooge 7 cat's-paw, machine, utensil, vehicle 8 hireling 9 apparatus, appliance, implement, mechanism 10 instrument 11 contrivance, wherewithal 12 intermediary 15 instrumentality
carpenter's: 3 adz, awl, bit, peg, saw 4 adze, nail, rasp, vise 5 auger, brace, edger, gouge, knife, lathe, plane, ruler, screw 6 bodkin, chisel, gimlet, hammer, pliers, router, sander 7 bradawl, scraper 9 hand drill, try square 11 screwdriver
cutting/shaping: 2 ax 3 adz, axe, saw 4 adze, burr, file, froe, frow, rasp 5 burin, croze, gouge, knife, plane, razor, shave, wedge 6 chisel, sander, shears, trepan 7 hatchet, scraper 8 scissors
drilling/boring: 3 awl, bit, zax 4 pick 5 chuck, drill 6 gimlet, wimble 7 bradawl 11 countersink
farmer's: 2 ax 3 axe, hoe 4 plow, rake 5 spade 6 cradle, harrow, pickax, plough, scythe, seeder, shovel, sickle, tiller, trowel 7 hayfork 9 plowshare 10 cultivator
gripping/turning: 6 pliers, wrench 11 screwdriver
holding: 4 vise 5 clamp
measuring: 4 rule 5 gauge, level 6 square 7 caliper 8 dividers 10 micrometer
mechanic's: 3 awl, zax 4 burr, file, vise 5 bevel, lathe 6 bodkin, pliers 7 bradawl, crowbar 8 calipers 9 jackscrew 11 screwdriver 12 monkey wrench
pounding/striking: 4 maul 5 punch, wedge 6 hammer, mallet

too little 4 lack 6 dearth, scanty, scarce 7 paucity 8 scarcity, shortage 9 deficient, not enough, scantness 10 deficiency, inadequacy, inadequate 12 insufficient 13 insufficiency

too many
French: 6 de trop

too much 4 glut 5 flood 6 excess 7 profuse, surfeit, surplus 8 fullness, overflow, plethora 9 avalanche, excessive, profusion, repletion 10 inundation, oversupply 12 overabundant 13 overabundance 14 superabundance
French: 4 trop

Toonerville Folks
creator: 11 Fontaine Fox
character: 7 skipper 13 Aunt Eppie Hogg 15 Little Scorpions, Powerful Katrina, Suitcase Simpson 20 Mickey Himself McGuire 22 Terrible Tempered Mr Bang
rode on: 7 trolley

to one side 4 over 5 aloof, apart, aside 6 aslant 14 on the sidelines

to one's liking 7 fitting 8 pleasant, pleasing, suitable 9 agreeable 10 acceptable, gratifying 11 appropriate, to one's taste 12 satisfactory

toot 4 blow, honk 5 binge, blare, blast, spree 6 bender 7 trumpet 8 wingding

tooth 3 cog, nib 4 barb, cusp, fang, spur, tang, tine, tusk 5 molar, point, spike, thorn 6 canine, cuspid 7 grinder, incisor 8 bicuspid, sprocket 9 serration

toothed 6 fanged, tusked 7 dentate, notched, serrate, virgate

toothsome 6 savory 8 luscious 9 delicious, palatable 10 appetizing

Toots
character in: 12 Dombey and Son
author: 7 Dickens

top 3 cap, lid, van 4 acme, apex, best, brow, cork, fore, head, lead, peak 5 chief, cover, crest, crown, excel, front, noted, outdo, upper 6 better, exceed, famous, summit, tiptop, vertex, zenith 7 eclipse, eminent, highest, notable, put over, stopper, surpass, topmost 8 complete, foremost, greatest, outshine, outstrip, pinnacle, renowned 9 paramount, principal, put a top on, transcend, uppermost, upper part 10 celebrated, first place, overshadow, preeminent

topaz
   color: 4 blue 5 brown 6 yellow
   source: 5 Japan 6 Brazil, Mexico, Saxony 13 Ural Mountains 18 Cairngorm Mountains
   month: 8 November

Topaze
   author: 12 Marcel Pagnol

topaz quartz
   species: 6 quartz
   color: 4 blue, pink 5 brown, green 6 sherry

toper 3 sot 4 lush, soak 5 drunk 6 boozer 7 tippler 8 drunkard 9 alcoholic 11 dispomaniac

Top Hat
   director: 12 Mark Sandrich
   cast: 9 Eric Blore 11 Fred Astaire 12 Ginger Rogers 14 Helen Broderick 19 Edward Everett Horton
   score: 12 Irving Berlin
   song: 12 Cheek to Cheek 22 Top Hat White Tie and Tails

topic 4 text 5 theme 6 thesis 7 keynote, subject

topical 5 local 6 timely 7 current, limited 9 localized, parochial 10 particular, restricted 12 contemporary

Topkapi
   director: 11 Jules Dassin
   cast: 12 Peter Ustinov, Robert Morley 14 Melina Mercouri 16 Maximilian Schell
   setting: 8 Istanbul
   Oscar for: 15 supporting actor (Ustinov)

topknot 4 comb, tuft 5 crest 9 cockscomb, headdress, headpiece

topmost 3 top 4 head 5 chief 7 highest, leading, supreme 8 foremost 9 paramount, principal, uppermost 10 preeminent

topnotch 3 ace 4 best 5 prime 6 choice, finest, tip-top 7 supreme 8 superior, very fine 9 excellent, first-rate, nonpareil, unequaled, unrivaled 10 preeminent 11 outstanding, unsurpassed 12 incomparable, unparalleled

top of the head 4 dome, pate 5 crown 6 noggin, noodle

Topper
   director: 13 Norman Z McLeod
   based on novel by: 11 Thorne Smith
   cast: 9 Cary Grant 11 Alan Mowbray, Billie Burke, Hedda Hopper, Roland Young 16 Constance Bennett
   sequel: 13 Topper Returns 16 Topper Takes a Trip

topple 4 fall 5 crush, quash, quell, smash, upset 6 defeat, sprawl, tumble 7 abolish, shatter, tip over 8 fall over, over come, overturn, turn over, vanquish 9 bring down, overpower, overthrow 12 pitch forward

tops 4 aces, A-one, fine 5 great, prime, super, swell 6 choice, grade-A, superb, tiptop 7 capital 8 peerless, sterling, superior, terrific, top-notch 9 excellent, first-rate, marvelous, matchless, superfine, wonderful 10 first-class, inimitable, out-of-sight, tremendous 11 outstanding, superlative 12 incomparable 13 extraordinary

top-secret 5 privy 7 private 8 eyes-only, hush-hush 12 confidential

topsoil 4 dirt, loam 5 earth

Topsy
   character in: 14 Uncle Tom's Cabin
   author: 5 Stowe

topsy-turvy 5 messy 6 untidy 7 chaotic 8 confused, inverted, reversed 9 confusing, inside out 10 disorderly, upside down 11 disarranged, wrong side up 12 disorganized

Torah 10 law of Moses

torch 5 brand 7 cresset 8 arsonist, flambeau 9 firebrand 9 set fire to 10 flashlight

torment 3 nag, vex 4 bane, pain, rack 5 agony, annoy, curse, worry 6 harass, harrow, misery, pester, plague 7 afflict, agonize, anguish, despair, scourge, torture, trouble 8 distress, irritate 9 annoyance, persecute, suffering 11 irritation

tormenter 5 bully, tease 6 despot, tyrant 7 coercer 9 oppressor 10 browbeater 11 intimidator

tormenting 7 painful, racking 9 agonizing, torturous 10 unbearable 11 unendurable 12 excruciating, insufferable

torn 4 rent, slit 5 split 6 ragged, ripped 8 ruptured, shredded 9 unraveled

tornado 4 wind 5 storm 6 funnel, squall, vortex 7 cyclone, twister, typhoon 8 outburst 9 hurricane, whirlwind, windstorm 10 waterspout 12 thunderstorm
   belt: 7 Midwest
   cloud: 4 tuba

torn apart 4 rent 6 ripped 7 asunder 8 in pieces, in shreds, shredded

toro 4 bull

Toronto
   baseball team: 8 Blue Jays
   bay: 6 Humber
   football team: 9 Argonauts
   former name: 4 York
   harbor: 5 Inner
   hockey team: 10 Maple Leafs
   lake: 7 Ontario
   landmark: 7 CN Tower 12 Ontario Place, O'Keefe Centre 13 Dufferin Grove 14 Dominion Centre 15 Roy Thompson Hall 16 Maple Leaf Stadium, St Lawrence Centre 17 Commerce Court West 18 Royal Ontario Museum 20 Nathan Phillips Square
   park: 7 Chorley, Stanley, Trinity 8 Winthrow 9 Cedarvale 12 Center Island 16 Winston Churchill

street: 5 Yonge
university: 4 York
Torosaurus
  type: 8 dinosaur 10 ceratopsid
torpedo 4 sink 5 wreck 7 destroy, missile, scuttle 9 explosive 10 projectile
torpedo (marine)
  invented by: 6 Fulton
torpid 4 dull, lazy 5 inert 6 drowsy, sleepy 7 dormant, languid, passive 8 inactive, indolent, listless, sluggish 9 apathetic, lethargic, somnolent 10 half asleep, languorous, slow-moving, spiritless 12 slow-thinking 13 lackadaisical
torpor, torpidity 6 apathy 7 inertia, languor 8 dullness, laziness, lethargy 9 indolence, lassitude 10 drowsiness, inactivity, sleepiness, somnolence 11 languidness, passiveness 12 listlessness, sluggishness
torrent 4 gush, rain, rush 5 burst, flood, salvo 6 deluge, rapids, stream, volley 7 barrage, cascade, Niagara 8 cataract, downpour, effusion, eruption, outburst 9 discharge, heavy rain, rapid flow, waterfall 10 cloudburst, outpouring, white water
Torrey, John
  field: 6 botany
  developed: 16 botanical library
Torricelli, Evangelista
  nationality: 7 Italian
  discovered concept leading to development of: 9 barometer
torrid 3 hot 4 sexy 5 fiery 6 ardent, erotic, fervid, heated, sexual, sultry 7 amorous, boiling, burning, excited, fervent, intense, lustful 8 broiling, desirous, parching, sizzling, spirited, tropical, vehement 9 hot and dry, scorching 10 passionate, sweltering 11 hot and heavy, impassioned
torte 4 cake 7 dessert 9 layer cake
tortilla 7 tostada 8 corncake 11 Mexican cake
  griddle: 5 comal
Tortilla Flat
  author: 13 John Steinbeck
tortuous 4 bent 5 snaky 6 spiral, zigzag 7 crooked, devious, sinuous, turning, winding, wriggly 8 indirect, involved, twisting, wrongful 9 ambiguous 10 circuitous, convoluted, meandering, roundabout, serpentine 11 complicated 12 full of curves, hard to follow, labyrinthine
tortuousness 9 sinuosity 11 indirection, sinuousness 12 convolutions 14 circuitousness
torture 4 pain, rack 5 abuse, agony, prick, smite, trial, wring 6 harrow, ordeal 7 anguish, cruelty, torment 8 distress, maltreat, mistreat 9 brutality, suffering 10 infliction, punishment 11 tribulation 12 put to the rack
torturous 5 cruel 7 galling, irksome, painful, racking 8 annoying 9 agonizing, anguished, harrowing, miserable, tormented, torturing 10 anguishing, distressed, tormenting, unpleasant 11 distressful, distressing 12 disagreeable, excruciating

tory 8 loyalist, royalist 12 conservative
Tosca
  opera by: 7 Puccini
  character: 7 Scarpia 9 Angelotti 16 Mario Cavaradossi
To Sir With Love
  director: 12 James Clavell
  cast: 4 Lulu 10 Judy Geeson 11 Suzy Kendall 13 Sidney Poitier 16 Christian Roberts
  setting: 6 London
toss 3 lob 4 cast, flip, hurl, jerk, rock, roll, sway 5 churn, fling, heave, pitch, shake, sling, throw 6 joggle, let fly, propel, tumble, wiggle, writhe 7 agitate, flounce, wriggle 8 flourish, undulate 9 oscillate
toss about 4 roil 5 bandy 6 jostle, jounce
toss back and forth 5 bandy 8 exchange
total 3 add, sum 4 full 5 add up, gross, sheer, solid, sum up, utter, whole 6 entire, figure, reckon, tote up 7 add up to, compute, perfect, total up 8 absolute, combined, complete, entirety, figure up, integral, outright, sum total, sweeping, thorough, totality 9 aggregate, calculate, down right, out-and-out, unlimited, wholesale 10 full amount, undisputed, unmodified 11 unqualified, whole amount 13 comprehensive, unconditional
totaling 8 addition, coming to 9 reckoning 10 adding up to
totalitarian 7 fascist 8 despotic 9 fascistic, tyrannous 10 autocratic, tyrannical 11 dictatorial 12 undemocratic 16 unrepresentative
totally 7 solidly, utterly 8 entirely 9 downright, out-and-out, perfectly 10 absolutely, completely, thoroughly, throughout 15 unconditionally 18 from beginning to end 20 without qualification
tote 3 lug 4 bear, cart, drag, haul, move, pack, pull 5 carry, fetch 6 convey 7 schlepp 9 transport
to the city and the world
  Latin: 10 urbi et orbi
  form of address used on: 10 papal bulls
to the four winds 7 all over 10 everywhere, far and wide 26 to the four corners of the world
to the letter 5 exact, right 7 correct, precise 8 accurate, explicit, specific 9 on the nose
To the Lighthouse
  author: 13 Virginia Woolf
  character: 4 Prue 5 James 7 Camilla 8 Mr Ramsey 9 Mr Tansley, Mrs Ramsey 11 Lily Briscoe 12 Mr Carmichael
To the North
  author: 14 Elizabeth Bowen
to the point 6 direct 7 apropos, germane 8 explicit, relevant 9 pertinent 12 to the purpose
to the rear 3 aft 4 back 5 abaft 6 astern, behind 8 backward, rearward 9 backwards, sternward 10 to the stern 14 toward the stern
to the stern 6 astern, behind 8 rearward 9 sternward 10 to the stern

to the word
   Latin: 8 ad verbum
to this extent
   Latin: 8 quoad hoc
Toto
   dog in: 13 The Wizard of Oz
   author: 4 Baum
totter 4 reel, rock, sway 5 lurch, shake, waver 6 falter, teeter, waddle, wobble 7 shuffle, stagger, stumble 9 oscillate, vacillate
tottering 5 shaky 6 wobbly 7 rickety, shaking 8 insecure, topheavy, unstable, unsteady, wobbling 9 doddering, quivering, trembling 10 ramshackle, staggering
Toucan
   constellation of: 6 Tucana
touch 3 art, bit, paw, pet, rub, use 4 abut, cite, dash, feel, fire, form, gift, hand, hint, join, meet, melt, move, note, stir, sway, tint, work 5 equal, flair, match, pinch, rival, rouse, skill, smack, speck, style, taste, thumb, tinge, trace, unite 6 adjoin, affect, arouse, border, broach, caress, excite, finger, finish, fondle, handle, hint at, manner, method, pawing, polish, sadden, soften, strike, stroke, thrill 7 concern, consume, contact, feeling, finesse, impress, inflame, inspire, mastery, mention, quality, refer to, soupcon, surface, texture, utilize 8 allude to, artistry, bear upon, come near, come up to, converge, deal with, deftness, fineness, fondling, handling, inspirit, resort to, thumbing 9 awareness, direction, electrify, fingering, influence, palpation, pertain to, suspicion, technique 10 adroitness, intimation, manipulate, perception, sprinkling, suggestion, virtuosity 11 be in contact, compare with, familiarity, guiding hand, realization 12 acquaintance, manipulation 13 communication, comprehension, understanding
touched 3 mad 4 daft, felt, nuts 5 crazy, moved, nutty 6 insane, joined 7 abutted, cracked, handled 8 demented, deranged, unhinged 10 unbalanced 12 mad as a hatter 13 off one's rocker, out of one's head 14 off one's trolley 15 mad as a March hare
Touchett, Ralph
   character in: 18 The Portrait of a Lady
   author: 5 James
touching 3 sad 6 moving, tender 7 pitiful 8 dramatic, pathetic, poignant, stirring 9 affecting, emotional, heartfelt, saddening, sorrowful 11 distressing, sentimental 12 heartrending 13 heartbreaking
touch me not
   Latin: 13 noli me tangere
Touch of Evil
   director: 11 Orson Welles
   cast: 10 Janet Leigh, Ray Collins 11 Joanna Moore, Orson Welles, Zsa Zsa Gabor 12 Akim Tamiroff, Dennis Weaver 13 Joseph Calleia 14 Charlton Heston
   cameo: 15 Marlene Dietrich 19 Mercedes McCambridge

touch off 5 shoot 6 set off 7 explode, fire off, trigger 8 activate, detonate 9 discharge
touch on 4 pose 6 broach, submit 7 advance, bring up, mention, propose, suggest 9 introduce
touchstone 4 norm, rule 5 basis, gauge, guide, model, proof 7 example, measure, pattern 8 standard 9 benchmark, criterion, guideline, precedent, principle, yardstick
Touchstone
   character in; 11 As You Like It
   author: 11 Shakespeare
touch upon 7 apply to, concern, mention, refer to 8 allude to, bear upon, relate to 9 appertain
touchy 5 cross, huffy, surly, testy 6 bitter, crabby, grumpy 7 awkward, fragile, grouchy, peevish, waspish 8 captious, critical, delicate, petulant, snappish, ticklish 9 concerned, difficult, irascible, irritable, querulous, resentful, sensitive 10 precarious 11 thinskinned 12 cantankerous 13 quick-tempered
tough 4 cold, firm, hard, hood, lout, mean, punk, wily 5 bully, cagey, canny, cruel, hardy, rigid, rough, rowdy, solid, stern 6 brutal, crafty, dogged, knotty, mulish, rugged, savage, strict, strong, sturdy, thorny, trying 7 adamant, arduous, callous, complex, durable, hoodlum, inhuman, irksome, lasting, onerous, ruffian, vicious 8 baffling, barbaric, enduring, exacting, grievous, hooligan, involved, leathery, obdurate, perverse, pitiless, puzzling, ruthless, stubborn, ticklish, toilsome 9 barbarian, confusing, difficult, enigmatic, heartless, heavy-duty, intricate, laborious, obstinate, pigheaded, resistant, roughneck, strenuous, unbending, unfeeling 10 bullheaded, delinquent, exhausting, formidable, hardheaded, inflexible, perplexing, unyielding 11 bewildering, calculating, cold-blooded, complicated, hardhearted, hard-to-solve, infrangible, insensitive, troublesome 12 bloodthirsty, impenetrable 13 unsympathetic 14 uncompromising
toughen 4 firm 5 inure, steel 6 firm up, harden, season, temper 7 fortify, stiffen 8 accustom 9 acclimate, habituate 10 discipline, strengthen 11 acclimatize
Toulouse-Lautrec, Henri Marie Raymond de
   born: 4 Albi 6 France 8 Albigois
   artwork: 7 Friends 13 The Inspection 16 At the Moulin Rouge 24 Au Salon de la Rue des Moulins 27 Jane Avril at the Jardin de Paris 29 Cirque Fernando The Equestrienne 29 In the Parlor at the Rue des Moulins 29 The English Girl at Le Star Le Havre 30 La Goulue Entering the Moulin Rouge
toupee 3 rug, wig 6 carpet, peruke 7 periwig 9 hairpiece
tour 4 trek, trip 5 jaunt, visit 6 junket, safari, travel, voyage 7 inspect, journey 8 sightsee 9 excursion, itinerary

tourist 7 pilgrim, tripper, voyager 8 traveler, vagabond, wanderer, wayfarer 9 journeyer, sightseer 10 rubberneck 12 excursionist, globetrotter

tourmaline
    color: 3 red 4 blue, pink 5 green

tournament 4 game 5 event, match 7 contest, rivalry, tourney 11 competition

Tourneur, Cyril
    author of: 19 The Revenger's Tragedy

tourney 4 game 5 event, match 7 contest, rivalry 10 tournament 11 competition

tousled 5 messy 6 mussed, untidy 7 rumpled, tangled, unkempt 8 mussed-up, uncombed 10 disheveled, disordered

tout 4 plug, push 5 boost, exalt, extol, vaunt 6 praise, talk up 7 acclaim, commend, glorify, promote, tipster 8 ballyhoo, eulogize, give a tip 9 advertise, brag about, celebrate, publicize, recommend 10 aggrandize, noise about

tout a fait 8 entirely
    literally: 12 wholly to fact

tout a l'heure 7 just now 8 very soon 9 presently 14 just a moment ago
    literally: 15 wholly to the hour

tout de suite 6 at once 11 immediately
    literally: 19 wholly consecutively

tout ensemble 11 all together

tout le monde 8 everyone 9 everybody 13 the whole world

tovarich 7 comrade

tow 3 lug 4 drag, draw, haul, lift, pull 5 hoist, trail

toward the end
    Latin: 5 ad fin

toward the front 5 ahead 6 before 7 forward 9 to the fore 13 in the vanguard 14 in the forefront

toward the rear 4 back 6 astern 8 backward, rearward 9 sternward

toward the stern 6 astern 8 rearward 9 sternward 10 to the stern

tower 4 keep, loom, rock, soar 5 mount, outdo, spire, surge 6 ascend, belfry, castle, column, exceed, pillar, refuge, turret 7 bulwark, eclipse, minaret, obelisk, overtop, shoot up, steeple, surpass 8 mainstay, outclass, outshine, overhang, rise high 9 bell tower, rise above, transcend 10 foundation, overshadow, skyscraper, stronghold, wellspring 12 fountainhead

towering 4 high, tall 5 lofty 6 alpine 7 soaring, sublime, supreme 8 dominant, foremost, mounting, peerless, snowclad, superior 9 ascending, matchless, paramount, principal, unequaled, unmatched, unrivaled 10 cloud-swept, preeminent, surpassing, unexcelled 11 cloud-capped, overhanging 12 incomparable, second to none, transcendent, unparalleled 13 extraordinary

Tower of London, The
    author: 24 William Harrison Ainsworth

tower over 5 dwarf 7 surpass 8 dominate 9 rise above

town 4 burg, city 6 hamlet, parish 7 borough, village 9 citizenry, residents 10 settlement 11 inhabitants, townspeople 12 municipality

Town, The
    author: 13 Conrad Richter

Townes, Charles Hard
    field: 7 physics
    invented: 5 maser
    awarded: 10 Nobel Prize

town hall
    German: 7 Rathaus

town house 8 row house 10 pied-a-terre 13 city residence

township 4 town 7 village 11 subdivision 12 municipality

Toxeus
    father: 6 Oeneus
    mother: 7 Althaea
    killed by: 6 Oeneus

toxic 5 fatal 6 deadly, lethal, mortal 7 noxious 8 poisoned, venomous 9 poisonous, unhealthy 10 pernicious

toxin 4 bane 5 venom 6 poison 8 pathogen

toy 4 play, tiny 5 dally, pygmy, sport 6 bantam, bauble, fiddle, gadget, gewgaw, little, midget, trifle 7 dwarfed, for play, stunted, trinket 8 gimcrack 9 miniature, plaything, small-size 10 diminutive, small-scale 11 Lilliputian

Toy Bulldog
    nickname of: 12 Mickey Walker

Toynbee, Arnold
    author of: 15 A Study of History

to your health
    French: 11 a votre sante

toy with 8 play with 9 flirt with 10 trifle with 16 amuse oneself with

trace 3 bit, jot, map 4 draw, drop, find, hint, hunt, iota, mark, seek, sign 5 dig up, relic, shade, tinge, token, touch, track, trail 6 depict, flavor, trifle 7 diagram, hunt for, look for, mark out, nose out, outline, remains, uncover, unearth, vestige 8 describe, discover, draw over, evidence 9 delineate, ferret out, footprint, light upon, little bit, search for, suspicion, track down 10 come across, indication, suggestion 11 small amount

trace to 6 credit 7 ascribe 8 charge to 9 attribute

Trachiniae
    author: 9 Sophocles
    characters: 4 Iole 6 Hyllus, Nessus 8 Deianira, Heracles

track 3 way 4 mark, path, rail, sign, tack 5 dirty, route, scent, spoor, trace, trail 6 course, follow 9 footprint, guide rail

track and field
    athlete: 7 Jim Ryun, Ray Ewry 8 Al Oerter, Lee Evans, Zola Budd 9 Bob Beamon, Carl Lewis, Henry Rono, Jim Thorpe 10 Ben Johnson, Bob Mathias, Bob Seagren, Edwin Moses, Grete Waitz, James Hines, Jesse Owens, John Carlos, Lasse Viren, Mac Wilkins, Paavo Nurmi, Peter Snell, Steve Ovett, Wyomia

Tyus 11 Bill Rodgers, Bruce Jenner, Marty Liouri, David Wottle, Dick Fosbury, Doug Padilla, Emil Zatopek, Joni Huntley, Ralph Boston, Randy Matson, Tommie Smith 12 Dwight Stones, Frank Shorter, Harvey Glance, Jay Silvester, Kathy Hammond, Maren Seidler, Rafer Johnson, Sebastian Coe, Willie B White, Wilma Rudolph 13 Allan Feurbach, Arnie Robinson, Janice Merrill, Kathy McMillan, Kipchoge Keino, Rodney Milburn, Ronny Ray Smith, Rosalyn Bryant, William Toomey 14 Alberto Salazar, Francie Larrieu, Roger Bannister 15 Martha Rae Watson, Renaldo Nehemiah, Willie Davenport 16 Madeleine Manning, Mary Decker Slaney, Harold Wohlhuter, Steve Prefontaine 17 Alberto Juantoreno 18 Jackie Joyner-Kersee, Stephanie Hightower 21 Babe Didrikson Zaharias 22 Florence Griffith-Joyner

tract 3 lot 4 area, plot, zone 5 essay 6 parcel, region 7 booklet, expanse, leaflet, quarter, stretch 8 brochure, district, pamphlet, treatise 9 monograph, territory 12 disquisition

tractable 4 tame 6 docile 8 amenable, obedient, yielding 9 compliant, teachable, trainable 10 governable, manageable, submissive 12 controllable, easy to manage 13 easy to control

tractate 8 treatise 9 discourse, monograph 12 disquisition, dissertation

Tracy, Spencer
    born: 11 Milwaukee WI
    costar: 16 Katharine Hepburn
    roles: 7 Desk Set 8 Adam's Rib, Boys' Town (Oscar) 10 Pat and Mike 12 San Francisco, Tortilla Flat 13 The Last Hurrah 14 Cass Timberlane, Inherit the Wind, Woman of the Year 15 State of the Union 16 Father of the Bride, Keeper of the Flame 17 Bad Day at Black Rock 18 Captains Courageous (Oscar), The Old Man and the Sea 19 Judgment at Nuremberg 23 Guess Who's Coming to Dinner

Traddles
    character in: 16 David Copperfield
    author: 7 Dickens

trade 3 buy 4 deal, line, shop, swap 5 craft 6 barter, buyers 7 calling, patrons, pursuit 8 business, commerce, exchange, shoppers, vocation 9 clientele, customers, patronize 10 buy and sell, do business, employment, handicraft, line of work, occupation, profession 12 transactions 13 merchandising 16 business dealings, buying and selling

trade commodity 5 goods, wares

trademark 6 emblem 7 feature 8 property 9 specialty 11 peculiarity 14 characteristic

trade off 4 swap 5 trade 6 barter 8 exchange

trader 6 dealer, monger, seller 7 drummer 8 merchant, retailer 10 shopkeeper, trafficker, wholesaler 11 salesperson, storekeeper 12 merchandiser, tradesperson 14 businessperson

tradesman 6 dealer, seller 8 merchant, retailer 9 craftsman 10 shopkeeper 11 storekeeper

Trade Wind
    author: 6 M M Kaye

tradition 4 lore, myth, saga, tale 5 habit, usage 6 custom, legend 8 folklore, practice 10 convention 12 superstition

traditional 3 old 5 fixed, usual 7 typical 8 habitual, historic 9 ancestral, customary 10 accustomed, inveterate 11 established 12 acknowledged, conventional

traduce 5 abuse, libel, smear, sully 6 defame, malign, vilify 7 run down, slander 8 backbite, bad-mouth, besmirch 9 deprecate, disparage 10 calumniate

traffic 4 cars, deal 5 buses, ships, trade 6 barter, doings, planes, riders, trains, trucks 7 bootleg, contact, freight, smuggle 8 business, commerce, dealings, exchange, tourists, voyagers 9 commuters, relations, smuggling, travelers 10 buy and sell, enterprise, passengers 11 bootlegging, intercourse, pedestrians, proceedings 12 transactions, vacationists 13 excursionists

tragedy 3 woe 4 blow 5 grief 6 misery, sorrow 7 anguish, setback 8 accident, calamity, disaster, reversal, sad thing 9 heartache 10 affliction, heartbreak 11 catastrophe

tragic 3 sad 4 dire 5 awful, fatal 6 deadly, dreary, woeful 7 piteous, pitiful, ruinous, serious, unhappy 8 dramatic, dreadful, grievous, horrible, mournful, pathetic, pitiable, shocking, terrible 9 appalling, frightful 10 calamitous, deplorable, disastrous, lamentable 11 destructive, devastating, unfortunate 12 catastrophic 13 heartbreaking

trail 3 dog, tow, way 4 drag, draw, fall, flow, hunt, mark, path, poke, sign, tail 5 float, hound, scent, spoor, trace, track 6 down, course, dangle, dawdle, follow, lessen, shrink, stream 7 dwindle, pathway, subside 8 decrease, diminish, footpath, grow weak, hand down, peter out, taper off 9 drag along, grow faint, grow small, lag behind 10 bridle path, drag behind, footprints, move slowly 11 beaten track 14 bring up the rear

trailblazers 7 leaders 8 pioneers 10 avantgarde, innovators 11 forerunners, originators, tastemakers 12 trendsetters

train 2 el 3 aim, set 4 line 5 break, chain, drill, focus, level, point, queue, sight, teach, trail, tutor 6 column, direct, escort, school, series, subway 7 caravan, cortege, educate, prepare, retinue 8 elevated, exercise, instruct, practice, rehearse, sequence 9 afterpart, appendage, entourage, followers 10 attendants, discipline, get in shape, procession, succession 11 bring to bear, domesticate, progression 12 continuation

Train, The
    director: 17 John Frankenheimer
    cast: 10 Albert Remy 11 Michel Simon
    12 Jeanne Moreau, Paul Scofield 13 Burt
    Lancaster

trained 4 able 6 expert, master 7 capable, skilled 8 schooled, seasoned 9 competent, qualified 11 experienced 12 accomplished

trainee 4 boot 5 cadet 6 rookie 7 private, rookie, student 9 greenhorn 10 apprentice

trainer 5 coach, tutor 7 teacher 16 athletic director

training 5 drill 8 coaching, drilling, practice, teaching 9 education, schooling 10 discipline 11 preparation 14 apprenticeship, indoctrination

traipse 3 gad 4 roam, walk 5 range, tramp, tread 6 stroll, trapes, wander 7 meander, saunter 8 gadabout 9 gallivant

trait 4 mark 5 quirk 6 earmark, feature, quality 8 hallmark 9 attribute, mannerism 11 peculiarity 12 idiosyncrasy 14 characteristic

traitor 3 rat 5 Judas, rebel 6 ratter 7 ratfink, serpent 8 apostate, betrayer, deceiver, deserter, mutineer, quisling, renegade, turncoat 9 hypocrite 11 false friend 12 doubledealer 13 double-crosser, revolutionary 14 fifth columnist 15 snake in the grass 20 wolf in sheep's clothing

traitorous 5 false 7 corrupt 8 disloyal, renegade 9 betraying, faithless 10 perfidious, treasonous, unfaithful 11 treacherous

tramp 3 bum 4 hike, hobo, roam, rove, slog, trek, walk 5 march, prowl, stamp, stomp 6 ramble, trudge, wander 7 floater, meander, traipse, trample, vagrant 8 derelict 9 gallivant, itinerant 10 panhandler 11 perambulate, peregrinate 15 knight-of-the-road

trample 5 crush, stamp, stomp 6 squash 7 flatten, run over 14 grind under foot 15 step heavily upon

trance 4 coma, daze 5 dream, spell 6 stupor, vision 7 reverie 8 daydream, hypnosis 9 pipe dream 10 absorption, brown study 11 abstraction 12 sleepwalking 13 concentration, preoccupation, woolgathering

tranquil 4 calm, cool, mild 5 quiet, still 6 gentle, placid, serene 7 halcyon, restful 8 composed, peaceful 9 unexcited, unruffled 11 undisturbed, unperturbed 13 self-possessed

tranquility 4 calm, hush 5 peace, quiet 6 repose 7 concord, harmony 8 quietude, serenity 9 composure, placidity, stillness 11 restfulness 12 peacefulness

tranquilize 4 calm, drug, lull 5 allay, quiet, relax, still 6 becalm, pacify, sedate, settle, soothe 7 appease, assuage 9 alleviate

transact 2 do 5 exact 6 handle, manage, settle 7 achieve, carry on, conduct, execute, perform 8 carry out, exercise 9 discharge 10 accomplish, take care of 12 carry through

transaction 4 deal 6 affair 7 bargain, dealing, venture 8 exchange 9 operation 10 enterprise, settlement 11 negotiation 15 business dealing, piece of business

transcend 5 excel, outdo 6 exceed 7 eclipse, outrank, surpass 8 go beyond, outrival, outshine, outstrip, overleap, overstep, surmount 9 rise above 10 overshadow 11 outdistance

transcendence 5 merit 8 eminence 9 exceeding, greatness 10 exaltation, excellence, surpassing 11 distinction, preeminence, superiority

transcendental 5 great 6 mental 7 supreme, unusual 8 elevated, peerless, superior, uncommon 9 exceeding, intuitive, matchless, spiritual, unequaled, unrivaled 10 surpassing 11 unsurpassed 12 incomparable, metaphysical 13 extraordinary

transfer 4 cede, deed, move, send 5 bring, carry, shift 6 change, convey, moving, remove 7 consign, deeding, removal, sending 8 bringing, carrying, hand over, make over, relegate, relocate, shifting, shipment, transmit, turn over 9 conveying, transport 10 delivering, relegation, relocating, relocation 11 consignment, transmittal 12 transporting 14 transportation

transferable 8 catching 10 contagious, infectious 12 communicable 13 transmissible, transmittable

transferal 8 delivery, transfer 10 giving over 11 handing over, transmittal 12 transmission

transference 5 shift 6 change 7 passage, removal 9 transport 11 transmittal 12 dislodgement, displacement, transmission 13 transmittance

transfiguration 10 conversion 13 metamorphosis, transmutation 14 transformation

transfigure 6 change . transform 12 metamorphose

transfix 3 pin 4 hold, stab, stun 5 rivet, spear, spike, stick 6 absorb, impale, pierce, skewer 7 astound, bewitch, enchant, engross, fix fast, terrify 8 astonish, hold rapt, intrigue 9 captivate, fascinate, hypnotize, mesmerize, penetrate, spellbind 10 run through

transform 4 turn 5 alter 6 change, recast, remold 7 convert, remodel 8 make over 9 refurbish, transmute 11 reconstruct, transfigure 12 metamorphose, transmogrify

transformation 6 change 9 restyling 10 alteration, conversion, remodeling 13 metamorphosis, transmutation 15 transfiguration

transgress 3 err, sin 4 slip 5 break, cross, fault, lapse, wrong 6 exceed, impose, offend 7 digress, infract, violate 8 infringe, trespass

transgression 3 sin 5 crime, error, lapse, wrong 6 breach 7 misdeed, offense 8 evil deed, iniquity, trespass 9 violation 10 immorality, infraction, wrongdoing 11 lawbreaking 12 encroachment, infringement, overstepping 13 contravention

transgressor 5 felon 6 sinner 7 culprit 8 criminal, evildoer, offender, violator 9 miscreant, wrongdoer 10 lawbreaker, malefactor, trespasser

transience 7 brevity 11 evanescence 12 ephemerality, impermanence

transient 5 brief 7 passing 8 fleeting, soon past, temporal 9 ephemeral, momentary, short-term, temporary 10 evanescent, perishable, short-lived, transitory, unenduring 11 impermanent 14 passing through 24 here today and gone tomorrow

transistor invented by: 7 Bardeen 8 Brattain, Shockley

transition 4 jump, leap 6 change 7 passage, passing 8 shifting 9 gradation, variation 10 alteration, changeover, conversion, graduation 11 progression 13 transmutation 14 transformation

transitory 5 brief 7 passing 8 fleeting, fugitive 9 ephemeral, temporary, transient 10 evanescent, not lasting, short-lived, unenduring 11 impermanent 24 here today and gone tomorrow

translate 4 turn 5 alter, apply 6 change, decode, explain 6 decipher, rephrase, simplify, recast, render, reword 7 clarify, convert, explain 8 decipher, rephrase, simplify, spell out 9 elucidate, interpret, make clear, transform, transmute 10 paraphrase

translucence 7 clarity 8 lucidity 10 luminosity 12 transparency 16 semitransparency

translucent 8 pellucid 10 semiopaque, translucid 15 semitransparent

transmissible 8 catching 10 contagious, infectious 12 communicable, transferable 13 transmittable

transmission 4 note 7 message, passage, passing, sending 8 delivery, dispatch, transfer 9 broadcast 10 conveyance, forwarding, remittance 11 handing over, transmittal 12 transference, transferring 13 communication 14 transportation

transmit 4 send, ship 5 carry, issue, relay, remit 6 convey, pass on, spread 7 deliver, forward 8 dispatch, televise, transfer 9 broadcast 11 communicate, disseminate

transmittable 8 catching 10 contagious, infectious 12 communicable, transferable

transmittal 7 sending 8 delivery, transfer 10 giving over, transferal 11 handing over 12 transmission

transmutation 6 change 10 conversion 13 metamorphosis 14 transformation 15 transfiguration

transmute 5 alter 6 change 7 convert 9 transform 12 metamorphose

transparency 6 purity 7 clarity 8 lucidity 9 clearness, sheerness 11 obviousness 14 diaphanousness

transparent 4 thin 5 clear, gauzy, lucid, plain, sheer 6 glassy, limpid, patent 7 evident, obvious, visible 8 apparent, clearcut, distinct, explicit, manifest, palpable, peekaboo, pellucid 10 diaphanous, see-

through 11 perceptible, self-evident, translucent, unambiguous, unequivocal 12 crystal-clear, unmistakable

transpire 5 arise, occur 6 appear, befall, chance, crop up, evolve, happen, turn up 7 come out, leak out 9 be met with, eventuate, take place 10 be revealed, come to pass, make public 11 become known, be disclosed, come to light, show its face

transplant 5 graft, repot, shift 7 replant 8 displace, relocate, resettle, transfer 9 transport, transpose

transport 3 bus, lug 4 bear, cart, lift, move, send, ship, take, tote 5 bring, carry, charm, fetch, train, truck 6 convey, moving, remove, thrill 7 bearing, bewitch, carting, delight, deliver, enchant, freight, removal, sending, vehicle 8 airplane, carrying, delivery, dispatch, enthrall, entrance, shipment, shipping, transfer, transmit, trucking 9 captivate, cargo ship, carry away, conveying, electrify, enrapture, freighter, overpower 10 cargo plane, conveyance 12 freight train

transportation 7 cartage, haulage, portage, removal, transit 8 delivery, dispatch, movement, shipment 9 transport 10 conveyance, transferal 12 transference, transmission 13 transmittance

transported 5 moved 6 lifted 7 charmed 8 ecstatic, thrilled, uplifted 9 bewitched, entranced 10 captivated, enthralled 11 carried away, electrified 13 beside oneself

transverse 5 cross 6 across 7 athwart, oblique, transom 8 crossbar, crossing, diagonal, traverse 9 crosswise 10 crosspiece, horizontal

transversely 9 crossways, crosswise, laterally

trap 3 net, pit 4 lure, ploy, ruse, seal, stop, wile 5 catch, feint, snare, trick 6 ambush, device, enmesh, entrap, lock in 7 ensnare, pitfall, springe 8 artifice, entangle, hold back, hunt down, maneuver 9 booby trap, stratagem 11 machination 16 compartmentalize

trappings 4 garb, gear 5 array, dress 6 attire, outfit, things 7 apparel, clothes, costume, effects, raiment, vesture 8 adjuncts, clothing, fittings 9 ornaments, trimmings 10 adornments, habiliment, investment 11 decorations 13 accoutrements, paraphernalia 14 embellishments

trash 3 rot 4 bums, crap, junk, scum 5 dregs, dross, tripe, waste 6 debris, drivel, idlers, litter, refuse, rubble, tramps 7 garbage, hogwash, loafers, residue, rubbish, twaddle 8 castoffs, leavings, nonsense, riffraff 9 poppycock, sweepings 10 balderdash 11 foolishness, ne'er-do-wells, odds and ends 15 good-for-nothings, unsavory element

trashy 4 vile 5 cheap, inane, junky, tacky 6 flashy, flimsy 7 rubbish, trivial, useless 8 riff-raff, trumpery 9 wasteful 10 worthless 13 insignificant

trauma 4 hurt **5** shock, wound **6** injury, stress

travail 4 pain, toil **5** labor, worry **6** strain, stress **7** anguish **8** delivery, distress, drudgery, exertion, hard work, hardship **9** suffering **10** birth pains, childbirth, labor pains **11** parturition **12** accouchement

travel 2 go **4** be on, move, roam, rove, sail, tour, trek, wend **5** cross, drive, range, visit **6** cruise, junket, voyage, wander **7** journey, proceed **8** pass over, progress, sightsee, traverse **9** globetrot, hitchhike, take a trip **11** pass through, press onward

traveler 5 gypsy, nomad, rover **7** drummer, migrant, pilgrim, tourist, trekker, tripper, voyager **8** vagabond, wanderer, wayfarer **9** itinerant, journeyer, sightseer **10** vacationer **12** excursionist, globetrotter

Traveller Without Luggage
   author: 11 Jean Anouilh

Travels with a Donkey
   author: 20 Robert Louis Stevenson
   donkey: 9 Modestine

Travels with My Aunt
   author: 12 Graham Greene

travel through 2 do **5** cover, cross, visit **8** traverse **9** negotiate **11** pass through

traverse 4 span **5** cross **6** bridge, travel **8** go across, move over, overpass **9** cross over, cut across, intersect, move along, negotiate, reach over **10** extend over, run through, travel over **11** move through, pass through, reach across

travesty 4 sham **5** farce, spoof **6** parody, satire **7** lampoon, mockery, takeoff **8** disgrace **9** burlesque **10** caricature, distortion, perversion **17** misrepresentation

Traviata, La
   also: 9 The Misled **23** The Woman Who Was Led Astray
   opera by: 5 Verdi
   based on a story by: 14 Alexandre Dumas (fils)
   called: **7** Camille **17** La Dame aux Camelias
   character: 8 Violetta **14** Alfredo Germont

Travolta, John
   born: 11 Englewood NJ
   roles: 6 Carrie, Grease **10** Tony Manero **11** Urban Cowboy **12** Staying Alive **14** Moment By Moment **15** Vinnie Barbarino **17** Welcome Back Kotter **18** Saturday Night Fever

trawl 3 net **4** drag, fish, haul, line **5** seine, troll **6** dredge **7** dragnet

Treacher, Arthur
   real name: 11 Arthur Veary
   born: 7 England **8** Brighton
   roles: 11 Mary Poppins **14** National Velvet, Thank You Jeeves **16** David Copperfield **20** Magnificent Obsession

treacherous 5 false, risky **6** tricky, unsafe, untrue **7** devious **8** disloyal, perilous, two-faced **9** dangerous, deceitful, deceptive, faithless, hazardous **10** misleading, perfidious, precarious, traitorous, treasonous, unfaithful **12** falsehearted **13** untrustworthy

treachery 5 guile **6** deceit **7** perfidy, treason **8** apostasy, betrayal, trickery **9** deception, duplicity, falseness **10** disloyalty, infidelity **11** double cross **13** breach of faith, deceitfulness, double-dealing, faithlessness **15** underhandedness **17** untrustworthiness

tread 4 gait, hike, pace, roam, rove, step, walk **5** prowl, range, stamp, stomp, tramp **6** step on, stride, stroll, trudge, walk on **7** trample **8** footfall, footstep

treason 6 mutiny, revolt **7** perfidy **8** apostasy, betrayal, sedition **9** duplicity, rebellion, treachery **10** conspiracy, disloyalty, insurgence, revolution, subversion **12** insurrection

treasonable 9 faithless, seditious **10** perfidious, subversive, traitorous **11** treacherous

treasure 3 gem **4** gold **5** hoard, jewel, prize, store, value **6** esteem, jewels, regard, revere, riches, silver **7** cherish, deposit, paragon **8** bank upon, dote upon, gold mine, hold dear **11** pride and joy **14** apple of one's eye **17** pearl of great price

treasure chest 3 box **4** case **5** chest, trunk **6** coffer

treasured 4 dear **5** loved **6** adored, valued **7** beloved **8** precious **9** cherished

Treasure Island
   author: 20 Robert Louis Stevenson
   character: 7 Ben Gunn **8** Smollett **9** Dr Livesey **10** Jim Hawkins **14** Long John Silver **15** Squire Trelawney
   director:
   1934 version: **13** Victor Fleming
   1950 version: **11** Byron Haskin
   based on novel by: 20 Robert Louis Stevenson
   cast:
   1934 version: **10** Lewis Stone **12** Jackie Cooper (Jim Hawkins), Wallace Beery (Long John Silver) **15** Lionel Barrymore
   1950 version: **11** Basil Sydney **12** Robert Newton (Long John Silver) **13** Bobby Driscoll (Jim Hawkins) **16** Walter Fitzgerald

Treasure of the Sierra Madre, The
   director: 10 John Huston
   cast: 7 Tim Holt **12** Bruce Bennett, Walter Huston **13** Alfonso Bedoya, Barton MacLane **14** Humphrey Bogart
   Oscar for: 8 director **10** screenplay **15** supporting actor (Huston)

treasurer 6 banker, bursar, purser, teller **7** auditor, cashier **9** financier **10** accountant, bookkeeper, cash-keeper, controller **16** financial officer **17** minister of finance **22** secretary of the treasury **24** Chancellor of the Exchequer

Treasure State
   nickname of: 7 Montana

treasury 4 bank, safe, till **5** funds, purse, vault **6** coffer **8** money box **9** anthology, exchequer, strongbox, thesaurus **10** collection, compendium, depository, repository, storehouse **11** bank account, compilation

treasury note 4 bill 8 bank note 9 greenback 12 currency note 17 silver certificate

treat 3 joy 4 blow, coat, give 5 apply, cover, favor, grant, imbue, stand 6 attend, divert, doctor, handle, manage, remedy, spring, thrill 7 comfort, delight, discuss, patch up, take out 8 consider, deal with, look upon, medicate, pleasure, relate to 9 act toward, small gift, try to cure, try to heal 10 impregnate, minister to, speak about, write about 12 prescribe for, satisfaction 13 gratification

treat as inferior 7 disdain 9 patronize 12 condescend to 18 look down one's nose at 19 discriminate against

treatise 4 text 5 essay, study, tract 6 manual, memoir, report, thesis 8 textbook, tractate 9 discourse, monograph 12 dissertation

treatment 3 way 4 cure 6 course, remedy 7 conduct, process, regimen, therapy 8 antidote, approach, handling, treating 9 doctoring, operation, procedure 10 management, medication 11 application, medical care 12 manipulation

treaty 4 deal, pact 6 accord 7 bargain, compact, entente 8 covenant 9 concordat 13 understanding 15 formal agreement 22 international agreement

tree 3 ash, elm, fir, oak 4 bush, palm, pine, wood 5 beech, birch, chase, maple, plane, plant, scrub, staff, stake, stick 6 corner, cudgel, redbud, spruce, timber, willow 7 gallows, lineage, live oak, sapling 8 ancestry, chestnut, hardwood, mahogany, pedigree, seedling 9 ailanthus, evergreen 10 cottonwood, eucalyptus

Tree Grows in Brooklyn, A
  author: 10 Betty Smith
  character:
    Nolan family: 5 Katie 6 Neeley 7 Francie, Johnnie
    director: 9 Elia Kazan
    cast: 9 James Dunn 10 Lloyd Nolan 12 Joan Blondell 14 Dorothy McGuire, Peggy Ann Garner
    Oscar for: 7 special (Garner) 15 supporting actor (Dunn)

treeless 4 bald, bare 6 barren 7 denuded 8 unwooded 10 unforested

Treeplanters State
  nickname of: 8 Nebraska

trek 4 hike, plod, roam, rove, sail, slog, trip 5 jaunt, march, range, tramp 6 junket, outing, travel, trudge, voyage, wander 7 journey, odyssey, passage 8 traverse 9 excursion, migration 10 expedition, pilgrimage 11 peregrinate 13 peregrination

trellis 5 arbor, bower, cross, frame, grill, trail 6 gazebo, screen 7 lattice, network, pergola 8 espalier 10 interweave 11 summerhouse

tremble 5 quail, quake, shake, waver 6 quaver, quiver, shiver 7 flutter, pulsate, shudder 9 palpitate

trembling 5 shaky 7 quaking, shaking 8 unsteady 9 doddering, quavering, quivering, shivering 10 shuddering 11 palpitating

tremblor 5 quake, seism, shock 6 tremor 8 upheaval 10 earthquake

tremendous 4 fine, huge, vast 5 giant, great, major 7 amazing, awesome, immense, mammoth, sizable, titanic, unusual 8 colossal, enormous, fabulous, gigantic, terrific, towering, uncommon 9 excellent, fantastic, first-rate, humongous, important, marvelous, monstrous, wonderful 10 formidable, gargantuan, incredible, noteworthy, stupendous 11 elephantine, exceptional 12 considerable 13 consequential, extraordinary

tremolo
  music: 9 trembling, vibrating 30 rapid reiteration of a single pitch

tremor 3 jar 4 jolt 5 quake, shake, shock, spasm, throb, waver 6 quiver, shiver 7 flutter, shaking, shudder, tremble 8 paroxysm 9 pulsation, quavering, quivering, shivering, trembling, vibration 10 convulsion 11 palpitation

tremulous 5 jumpy, shaky, timid 6 wobbly 7 aquiver, excited, fearful, jittery, keyed-up, nervous, panicky, quaking 8 aflutter, agitated, atremble, hesitant, restless, wavering, worked-up 9 faltering, impatient, quivering, trembling, uncertain 10 irresolute, stimulated 13 on tenterhooks, panic-stricken

trench 3 cut, rut 4 scar 5 canal, ditch, drain, fosse, slash, slice 6 dugout, furrow, gutter, trough 7 channel, wrinkle 8 aqueduct 9 earthwork 10 depression

trenchant 4 acid, keen, tart 5 crisp 6 bitter 7 acerbic, caustic, concise, mordant, probing 8 clear-cut, distinct, incisive, scathing 9 sarcastic, scorching 10 razor-sharp 11 acrimonious, penetrating, well-defined

trend 4 bent, flow, mode 5 drift, style 7 fashion, impulse, leaning 8 movement, tendency 9 direction 10 proclivity, propensity 11 inclination

trendsetters 7 leaders 8 trendies, vanguard 10 avant-garde, innovators 11 pacesetters, tastemakers 12 advance guard, stylesetters, trailblazers

trendy 2 in 4 chic, tony 5 swank 6 modern, modish, with-it 7 current, faddish, popular, stylish, voguish 8 up-to-date 10 all the rage 11 fashionable 13 up-to-the-minute

Trenor, Gus and Judy
  characters in: 15 The House of Mirth
  author: 7 Wharton

Trent, Little Nell
  character in: 19 The Old Curiosity Shop
  author: 7 Dickens

trepidation 4 fear 5 alarm, dread, panic, worry 7 anxiety, jitters 8 cold feet, disquiet 10 uneasiness 11 butterflies, disquietude, jitteriness, nervousness 12 apprehension 13 consternation

trespass 3 sin 5 error, wrong 6 invade 7 impinge, intrude, misdeed, offense 8 encroach, infringe, iniquity, invasion 9 evildoing, intrusion, violation 10 immorality, infraction, misconduct, wrongdoing 11 delinquency, misbehavior 12 encroachment, infringement, overstepping 13 transgression, unlawful entry, wrongful entry

tress 4 curl, hair, lock, mane 5 braid, plait 6 strand 7 ringlet, wimpler 8 spitcurl

trestle 4 beam 5 board, brace, frame, table 6 timber 9 framework

trial 2 go 3 try, woe 4 care, pain, shot, test 5 agony, essay, flyer, whirl, worry 6 burden, effort, misery, ordeal, trying, tryout 7 anguish, attempt, bad luck, hearing, testing, test run, torment, trouble, venture 8 accident, distress, endeavor, hardship, vexation 9 adversity, court case, heartache, suffering 10 affliction, litigation, misfortune 11 cross to bear 12 misadventure, wretchedness

Trial, The
    author: 10 Franz Kafka
    character: 4 Leni 7 Joseph K 9 Titorelli 11 The Advocate

trial and error 10 experiment 13 investigation 15 experimentation 20 process of elimination

Triassic period
    dinosaur from: 11 Coelophysis, Mandasuchus 12 Melanosaurus, Pisanosaurus, Plateosaurus 13 Tanystropheus 17 Heterodontosaurus

tribe *see* 11 ethnic group

Tribes of Israel *see* 6 Israel

tribulation 3 woe 4 care, pain 5 agony, grief, trial, worry 6 misery, ordeal, sorrow 7 anguish, bad luck, torment, trouble 8 distress, hardship, vexation 9 adversity, heartache, suffering 10 affliction, ill fortune, misfortune 11 unhappiness 12 wretchedness

Tribulation Wholesome
    character in: 12 The Alchemist
    author: 6 Jonson

tribunal 3 bar 5 bench, court, forum 6 judges 9 authority, judiciary 10 ruling body 11 judge's bench, judge's chair 14 seat of judgment

tributary 6 branch, feeder, source, stream 7 helping, subject 8 affluent 9 ancillary, auxiliary, confluent, secondary 10 subjugated, subsidiary 11 subordinate 12 contributing, contributory

tribute 3 tax 4 duty, levy, toll 5 bribe, honor, kudos 6 esteem, eulogy, excise, impost, payoff, praise, ransom 7 payment, respect 8 accolade, encomium, memorial 9 extolling, gratitude, laudation, panegyric 10 assessment, blood money, compliment, settlement 11 recognition, testimonial 12 commendation, pound of flesh 13 consideration, peace offering 14 acknowledgment

trice 3 sec 4 jiff, wink 5 blink, flash, jiffy, shake 6 minute, moment, second 7 instant 9 coup d'oeil, twinkling 11 split second

trichophobia
    fear of: 4 hair

trichoptera
    class: 8 hexapoda
    phylum: 10 arthropoda
    group: 3 fly 6 caddis

trick 3 art, gag 4 bait, dupe, feat, gift, gull, have, hoax, joke, ploy, ruse, trap, wile 5 antic, blind, bluff, caper, cheat, dodge, feint, fraud, knack, prank, put-on, skill, stunt 6 deceit, device, number, outfox, outwit, resort, secret, take in 7 deceive, gimmick, know-how, mislead, swindle 8 artifice, deftness, flimflam, hoodwink, maneuver 9 bamboozle, chicanery, deception, dexterity, imposture, sophistry, stratagem, technique 10 adroitness, hocus-pocus, manipulate, subterfuge 11 contrivance, machination, outmaneuver 13 practical joke, sleight of hand 16 prestidigitation

trickery 5 guile 6 bunkum, deceit 8 artifice, flimflam, pretense, quackery, wiliness 9 chicanery, deception, duplicity, imposture, rascality, stratagem 10 artfulness, craftiness, hocus-pocus, shiftiness 11 crookedness, deviousness 12 charlatanism, skullduggery, slipperiness 13 deceitfulness

trickiness 6 deceit 7 cunning, slyness 8 trickery 9 duplicity 10 craftiness 15 underhandedness

trickle 4 drip, leak, ooze, seep 5 exude 7 dribble, seepage 9 percolate

trickster 5 cheat, joker 6 dodger, rascal 8 deceiver, impostor, sleeveen 9 prankster

tricky 3 sly 4 foxy, wily 5 risky 6 artful, crafty, shifty, unsafe 7 cunning, devious 8 rascally, slippery, unstable 9 dangerous, deceptive, difficult, hazardous 10 touch-and-go, unreliable 11 complicated, underhanded 12 hard to handle, undependable 13 temperamental, unpredictable

trident
    form: 5 spear
    number of prongs: 5 three

trifle 3 bit, dab, jot, nip, toy 4 dash, drop, idle, iota, mite, play 5 crumb, dally, pinch, scrap, speck, tinge, touch, trace 6 bauble, dawdle, gewgaw, linger, little, morsel, sliver 7 modicum, nothing, trinket 8 fragment, gimcrack, kill time 9 bagatelle, plaything, waste time 10 dillydally, knickknack, sprinkling, triviality 11 deal lightly, small matter 12 amuse oneself, treat lightly 13 small quantity

trifler 5 flirt, idler 6 coquet 7 dabbler, dallier 8 coquette 10 dilettante

trifling 4 puny 5 petty, small, sorry, token 6 paltry, slight 7 nominal, trivial 8 beggarly, niggling, nugatory, picayune, piddling 9 worthless 10 negligible 11 unimportant 13 beneath notice, inappreciable, insignificant 14 inconsiderable 15 inconsequential

trifling circumstances
    Latin: 8 minutiae

trifling matter
French: 10 peu de chose

trigger 5 shoot 6 set off 7 fire off 8 activate, detonate, touch off 9 discharge

trikerion 11 candelabrum, candlestick 12 candleholder

Trilby
author: 15 George du Maurier
character: 5 Gecko, Sandy, Taffy 8 Svengali 12 Little Billee 14 Trilby O'Ferrall

trill
music: 7 shaking, tremolo 9 quavering

trim 3 cut, fit, lop 4 clip, crop, deck, form, lean, pare, slim, thin 5 adorn, array, lithe, prune, shape, shave, shear, shift, sleek, state 6 adjust, bedeck, border, change, fettle, kilter, limber, paring, piping, supple, svelte 7 arrange, balance, bedizen, compact, cutting, fitness, furbish, garnish, lissome, pruning, shapely, slender, willowy 8 athletic, beautify, clipping, cropping, decorate, equalize, ornament, shearing, trick out, trimming 9 adornment, condition, embellish, embroider, shipshape 10 decoration, distribute 11 streamlined 13 embellishment, ornamentation

Trim, Corporal
character in: 14 Tristram Shandy
author: 6 Sterne

trimming 4 trim 5 frill 7 cutting, pruning, slicing 8 clipping 9 adornment 10 decoration, shortening, truncation 11 abridgement, contraction, curtailment 12 abbreviation 13 embellishment

Trinacria see 6 Sicily

Trinidad and Tobago
capital/largest city: 11 Port of Spain
others: 4 Debe, Toco 5 Arima 6 Canaan, Coryal, Labrea 7 San Juan, Siparia 8 Rio Claro, Tunapuna 10 Roxborough 11 San Fernando, Scarborough 12 Princess Town, Sangre Grande 14 Charletteville
school: 6 Fatima 7 St Mary's 11 Queen's Royal
head of state: 14 British monarch 15 governor general
monetary unit: 4 cent 6 dollar
island: 12 Chacachacare, Little Tobago 14 Bird of Paradise
lake: 5 Pitch
mountain:
hills: 7 Trinity 10 Montserrat 12 Three Sisters
highest point: 5 Aripo
river: 6 Caroni 7 Ortoire 8 Oropuche, Trinidad
sea: 8 Atlantic 9 Caribbean
physical feature:
bay: 5 Cocos, Guapo 6 Matura, Mayaro
channel: 12 Dragon's Mouth 13 Serpent's Mouth
gulf: 5 Paria
point: 5 Radix 6 Arenal, Galera 7 Chupara, Galeota 8 Columbus
people: 5 Irish 6 French, Syrian 7 African, Chinese, English, Spanish 8 European, Lebanese 10 East Indian, Portuguese, Venezuelan 11 Asian Indian 13 Latin American
explorer: 8 Columbus
leader: 8 Williams
language: 6 French 7 Chinese, English, Spanish 10 Portuguese 12 French Patois
religion: 5 Hindu, Islam 8 Anglican 10 Protestant 12 Christianity 13 Roman Catholic
place:
asphalt lake: 9 Pitch Lake
mansions: 16 Magnificent Seven
park: 18 Queen's Park Savannah
feature:
bird: 7 oilbird 8 cocorico
clothing: 4 sari 5 dhoti
dance: 6 Dragon, Shango
festival: 6 Hosein, Lights
fish: 5 guppy
music: 7 calypso, goombay
tree: 4 mora
food:
drink: 16 Angostura Bitters

Trinity
author: 8 Leon Uris

trinket 3 toy 5 bijou, charm, jewel 6 bauble, gewgaw, notion, trifle 8 gimcrack, ornament 9 bagatelle, plaything 10 knickknack

trip 3 bob, err 4 flip, flub, fool, muff, pull, skip, slip, tour, trek, undo 5 caper, catch, dance, fluff, foray, jaunt, outdo, throw, upset 6 bungle, cruise, frolic, gambol, junket, outfox, outing, prance, safari, set off, slip up, voyage 7 blunder, commute, confuse, flounce, journey, misstep, release, scamper, stumble 8 activate, fall over, flounder, hoodwink, throw off 9 excursion 10 disconcert, expedition, pilgrimage 11 step lightly

Triple Crown 7 Belmont 9 Preakness 13 Kentucky Derby
winner: 5 Omaha 7 Assault 8 Affirmed, Citation 9 Sir Barton, Whirlaway 10 Count Fleet, Gallant Fox, War Admiral 11 Seattle Slew, Secretariat

Triple Sec see 9 Cointreau

Tripoli
capital of: 5 Libya

Triptolemus, Triptolemus
favorite of: 7 Demeter
inventor of: 4 plow 5 wheel
patron of: 11 agriculture

Triquetra see 6 Sicily

triskaidekaphobia
fear of: 14 number thirteen

Trismegistus see 5 Thoth

Tristan and Isolde
also: 16 Tristan und Isolde
opera by: 6 Wagner
character: 5 Melot 8 Brangane, Kurwenal 18 King Mark of Cornwall

triste 3 sad 10 melancholy

tristesse 6 sorrow 7 sadness 10 melancholy

Tristram
author: 22 Edwin Arlington Robinson
character in: 16 Arthurian romance

Tristram Shandy
 author: 14 Laurence Sterne
 character: 6 Dr Slop 8 Mr Yorick 10 Toby
 Shandy 11 Widow Wadman 12 Corporal
 Trim, Walter Shandy

trite 5 banal, silly, stale 6 common 7 cliched, humdrum, routine, shallow, worn-out
 8 bromidic, everyday, ordinary, overdone,
 shopworn 9 frivolous, hackneyed 10 pedestrian, threadbare 11 commonplace, oft-
 repeated, stereotyped, unimportant 12
 run-of-the-mill 13 platitudinous

Tritogeneia see 6 Athena

Triton
 god of: 3 sea
 father: 8 Poseidon
 mother: 10 Amphitrite
 shape: 6 merman
 trumpet: 10 conch-shell

triumph 3 hit, win 4 best, coup 5 smash 6
 subdue 7 conquer, mastery, prevail, succeed, success, surpass, victory 8 conquest, overcome, smash hit, vanquish 9
 overwhelm 10 ascendancy, attainment,
 gain the day 11 achievement, superiority
 12 come out on top, take the prize 14
 accomplishment, get the better of

triumphal 5 proud 6 joyous 8 exultant 9 ascendant, rewarding 10 fulfilling, gratifying,
 successful, triumphant, victorious 11 spectacular

triumphant 6 elated, joyful 7 winning 8 exultant, jubilant 9 rejoicing 10 conquering,
 first-place, successful, victorious 11 celebrating 12 prizewinning

Triumph of Death, The
 author: 17 Gabriele D'Annunzio

trivia
 Latin: 8 minutiae

trivial 4 idle, puny, slim 5 banal, petty,
 small, trite 6 common, flimsy, little, meager, paltry, slight, two-bit 7 foolish 8
 beggarly, everyday, niggling, nugatory, ordinary, picayune, piddling, trifling 9 rinky-
 dink, worthless 10 incidental, pedestrian
 11 commonplace, meaningless, unessential, unimportant 13 inappreciable, insignificant, of little value 14 inconsiderable 15
 inconsequential

triviality 5 frill 6 trifle 9 frivolity 10 paltriness
 12 nonessential, unimportance 14 insignificance 18 inconsequentiality

troglodyte 5 brute 6 hermit 9 barbarian 11
 cave dweller

Troilus
 father: 5 Priam
 mother: 6 Hecuba

Troilus and Cressida
 author: 18 William Shakespeare
 character: 4 Ajax 5 Priam 6 Hector 7
 Ulysses 8 Achilles, Diomedes, Pandarus
 9 Agamemnon

Troilus and Criseyde
 author: 15 Geoffrey Chaucer
 character: 8 Diomedes, Pandarus

trois 5 three

Trojan Horse
 made of: 4 wood
 made by: 7 Epeiosk
 contained: 8 Odysseus, warriors

Trojans, The
 also: 10 Les Troyens
 opera by: 7 Berlioz
 part one: 14 La Prise de Troie 16 The
 Capture of Troy
 part two: 19 Les Troyens a Carthage 20
 The Trojans in Carthage
 character: 4 Dido 6 Aeneas, Hector

Trojan War
 length: 8 ten years
 combatants: 6 Greeks 7 Trojans
 cause: 5 Helen, Paris 14 Apple of Discord

Trojan Women, The
 author: 9 Euripides
 character: 5 Helen 6 Hecuba 8 Astyanax, Menelaus, Odysseus, Polyxena 9
 Agamemnon, Cassandra 10 Andromache, Talthybius 11 Neoptolemus

troll 3 imp 4 ogre 5 dwarf, gnome 6 goblin
 origin: 12 Scandinavian
 form: 12 supernatural
 inhabits: 10 subterrain

trollop 4 doxy, slut 5 bitch, doxie, frump,
 hussy, trull, whore 6 floozy, harlot, wanton
 7 baggage 8 slattern, strumpet 10 prostitute

Trollope, Anthony
 author of: 9 Orley Farm, The Warden 15
 The Way We Live Now 16 Barchester
 Towers, Framley Parsonage
 character: 11 Phineas Finn

troop, troops 4 army, band, file, gang,
 herd, step, unit 5 bunch, crowd, crush,
 drove, flock, horde, march, press, swarm,
 tramp 6 parade, stride, throng, trudge 7
 cavalry, company, militia 8 infantry, soldiers, soldiery, troopers 9 aggregate, gathering 10 armed force, assemblage 11 cavalry unit, fighting men, police force 12
 congregation 13 military force

trop 3 too 7 too many, too much

Tropaean
 epithet of: 4 Zeus
 means: 14 giver of victory

Trophonius
 vocation: 7 builder
 father: 7 Erginus
 brother: 8 Agamedes
 god of: 5 earth
 killed: 8 Agamedes
 became: 6 oracle
 oracle called: 14 Zeus Trophonius

trophy 4 palm 5 award, booty, honor, kudos, medal, prize, relic, spoil 6 wreath 7
 laurels, memento 8 citation, souvenir 9
 loving cup 10 blue ribbon 11 testimonial

tropical 5 muggy 6 sultry, torrid 8 stifling 10
 sweltering 11 hot and humid

troppo, non
 music: 10 not too much

Tros
 king of: 4 Troy
 father: 12 Erichthonius
 mother: 8 Astyoche
 wife: 10 Callirrhoe
 son: 4 Ilus 8 Ganymede 9 Assaracus

trot 3 jog 9 go briskly 11 step quickly, walk smartly

troth 8 fidelity 9 betrothal 10 affiancing, engagement 12 faithfulness

Trotwood, Betsey
 character in: 16 David Copperfield
 author: 7 Dickens

trouble 3 fix, row, vex, woe 4 blow, care, fuss, heed, mess, pain, pass, snag, work 5 agony, annoy, grief, harry, labor, pains, pinch, think, trial, upset, worry 6 affect, attend, badger, bother, burden, crisis, defect, dismay, effort, grieve, harass, misery, ordeal, pester, pickle, plague, pother, put out, scrape, sorrow, strain, strait, stress, strife, unrest 7 afflict, agitate, ailment, attempt, concern, depress, dilemma, discord, disturb, ferment, ill wind, oppress, perturb, reverse, setback, torment 8 disaster, disorder, disquiet, distress, disunity, exertion, hardship, hot water, quandary, rainy day, struggle, take time, unsettle, vexation 9 adversity, agitation, annoyance, attention, breakdown, challenge, commotion, deep water, hard times, suffering 10 affliction, convulsion, difficulty, disability, discommode, discompose, disconcert, discontent, dissension, irritation, make uneasy, misfortune, opposition 11 competition, disturbance, embroilment, instability, malfunction, predicament, tribulation 12 entanglement, exert oneself 13 inconvenience, make the effort 14 discontentment 15 dissatisfaction

troubled 5 upset 7 worried 8 bothered, careworn 9 disturbed, perturbed 10 distressed 12 heavyhearted

troublemaker 6 gossip 7 inciter 8 agitator, fomenter, provoker 9 miscreant 10 incendiary, instigator 11 rumormonger, scaremonger 12 rabble-rouser 13 mischief-maker, scandalmonger 16 agent provocateur

troublesome 4 hard 5 heavy, pesky, tough 6 cursed, knotty, taxing, thorny, tiring, trying, vexing 7 arduous, irksome, onerous, tedious 8 annoying, tiresome, unwieldy 9 demanding, difficult, fatiguing, harassing, herculean, laborious, wearisome, worrisome 10 bothersome, burdensome, cumbersome, disturbing, irritating, oppressive, tormenting, unpleasant 11 disobedient, distressing 12 disagreeable, exasperating, inconvenient, uncontrolled 13 undisciplined

troublesomeness 5 trial 10 difficulty 11 arduousness 13 inconvenience, laboriousness, vexatiousness, worrisomeness 14 bothersomeness

Trouble with Harry, The
 director: 15 Alfred Hitchcock
 cast: 11 Edmund Gwenn 12 John For-

sythe 14 Mildred Dunnock, Mildred Natwick 15 Shirley MacLaine

troubling 6 vexing 8 worrying 9 worrisome 10 bothersome, disturbing, unsettling

trough 4 duct, moat, race, tray 5 canal, ditch, flume, gorge, gully 6 furrow, hollow, ravine, trench 7 channel 8 aqueduct 10 depression

trounce 4 beat, drub, lick, trim, whip 5 cream, skunk 6 humble 7 clobber 8 vanquish 9 overpower, overwhelm 10 take care of 11 carry the day 14 get the better of

troupe 4 band, cast 5 group, troop 6 actors 7 company, players 10 performers 11 road company

trouper 5 actor 7 actress 8 thespian 9 performer 13 touring player 15 repertory player

trousers 5 jeans, pants 6 chinos, slacks 7 drawers 8 breeches, britches, jodhpurs, knickers, overalls 9 dungarees 10 pantaloons 11 bellbottoms 12 pedal pushers 14 knickerbockers

Trovatore, Il
 also: 13 The Troubadour
 opera by: 5 Verdi
 character: 7 Azucena, Leonora, Manrico 11 Count di Luna

Troy
 abducted queen: 5 Helen
 archaeologist: 6 Blegen 8 Dorpfeld 10 Schliemann
 defender: 5 Eneas 6 Aeneas
 Greek name: 5 Ilion
 hero: 6 Hector
 king: 5 Priam
 Latin name: 5 Ilium
 modern name: 9 Hissarlik
 mountain: 3 Ida
 neighboring city: 6 Albany 10 Watervliet
 river: 6 Hudson
 state: 7 Alabama, New York 8 Michigan
 story: 5 Iliad 7 Odyssey
 surrounding region: 5 Troad, Troas

Troy, Sergeant
 character in: 22 Far From the Madding Crowd
 author: 5 Hardy

truancy 3 cut 7 absence 11 absenteeism, nonpresence 12 playing hooky 13 nonappearance, nonattendance 14 cutting classes, skipping school

truant 4 gone 5 idler 6 absent, dodger, evader, loafer, no show 7 drifter, goof-off, missing, not here, shirker, slacker, vagrant 8 absentee, deserter, layabout 9 goldbrick 10 delinquent, malingerer, nonpresent, not present 11 boondoggler, hooky-player 12 nonattendant, playing hooky

truce 4 halt, lull, rest, stay, stop 5 break, pause 7 respite 9 armistice, cease-fire 12 interruption 14 breathing spell, discontinuance 23 suspension of hostilities

Trucial Oman, Trucial States *see* 18 United Arab Emirates

truck 3 rig, van 5 lorry 15 eighteen-wheeler
  type: 5 panel 6 pickup 7 trailer 8 delivery
truckle 3 bow 4 fawn 5 court, defer, yield 6
grovel, pander, submit 7 flatter 8 bootlick,
butter up, suck up to 9 shine up to 10 curry
favor, take orders 11 apple-polish, fall all
over 12 knuckle under 17 ingratiate oneself
truculence 8 defiance, ill humor 9 hostility,
ill temper, pugnacity, surliness 10 fierceness 11 bellicosity 12 belligerence, churlishness 14 aggressiveness
truculent 4 rude, sour 5 cross, nasty, sulky,
surly 6 fierce, touchy 7 defiant, hostile,
peevish 8 churlish, insolent, petulant,
snappish, snarling 9 bellicose 10 aggressive, ill-humored, ill-natured, pugnacious,
ungracious 11 bad-tempered, belligerent,
ill-tempered
Trudeau, Garry
  creator/artist of: 10 Doonesbury
trudge 4 drag, limp, plod 5 clump, march,
tramp 6 hobble, lumber 7 shamble
true 4 even, firm, full, just, pure, real 5 exact, legal, loyal, right, usual, valid 6 actual,
lawful, normal, proper, steady, strict, trusty
7 correct, devoted, factual, genuine, literal,
precise, regular, staunch, typical 8 absolute, accurate, bona fide, constant, faithful,
official, positive, reliable, rightful, true-blue,
truthful 9 authentic, simon-pure, steadfast
10 dependable, legitimate, unswerving,
unwavering 11 trustworthy 14 unquestionable
true being 4 core, soul 6 nature, psyche,
spirit 7 essence
True Grit
  director: 13 Henry Hathaway
  based on novel by: 13 Charles Portis
  cast: 8 Kim Darby 9 John Wayne 11
  Jeremy Slate 12 Glen Campbell, Robert
  Duvall 14 Strother Martin
  Oscar for: 5 actor (Wayne)
Truffaut, Francois
  director of: 11 Day for Night, Jules and
  Jim 19 Shoot the Piano Player, The Four
  Hundred Blows
truism 3 saw 5 adage, axiom 6 cliche, dictum, saying 9 platitude
truly 6 indeed, in fact, really, surely, verily 7
exactly, in truth, no doubt 8 actually, honestly, to be sure 9 assuredly, certainly, correctly, factually, genuinely, literally, precisely, sincerely 10 absolutely, accurately,
definitely, faithfully, positively, truthfully,
upon my word 11 beyond doubt, in actuality, indubitably, so help me God 12 indisputably 13 incontestably, unequivocally 14
beyond question, unquestionably 15 all
kidding aside, without question
Truman, Harry S
  nickname: 15 Give Em Hell Harry
  presidential rank: 11 thirty-third
  party: 10 Democratic
  state represented: 8 Missouri
  succeeded upon death of: 9 Roosevelt
  defeated: 5 (Farrell) Dobbs, (Thomas

Edmund) Dewey 6 (Claude A) Watson,
(Norman) Thomas 7 (Henry Agard) Wallace 8 (Edward A) Teichert, (James
Strom) Thurmond
  vice president: 7 (Alben William)
Barkley
  cabinet:
    state: 6 (James Francis) Byrnes 7 (Dean
    Gooderham) Acheson 8 (George Catlett)
    Marshall 10 (Edward Reilly) Stettinius (Jr)
    treasury: 6 (Frederick Moore) Vinson,
    (John Wesley) Snyder 10 (Henry)
    Morgenthau (Jr)
    war: 6 (Kenneth Claiborne) Royall 7
    (Henry Lewis) Stimson 9 (Robert Porter)
    Patterson
    defense: 6 (Robert Abercrombie) Lovett
    7 (Louis Arthur) Johnson 8 (George
    Catlett) Marshall 9 (James Vincent) For-
    restal
    attorney general: 5 (Thomas Campbell)
    Clark 6 (Francis) Biddle 7 (James How-
    ard) McGrath 9 (James Patrick)
    McGranery
    navy: 9 (James Vincent) Forrestal
    postmaster general: 6 (Frank
    Comerford) Walker 8 (Robert Emmet)
    Hannegan 9 (Jesse Monroe) Donaldson
    interior: 4 (Julius Albert) Krug 5 (Harold
    LeClaire) Ickes 7 (Oscar Littleton) Chap-
    man
    agriculture: 7 (Charles Franklin) Bran-
    nan, (Claude Raymond) Wickard 8 (Clin-
    ton Presba) Anderson
    commerce: 6 (Charles) Sawyer 7 (Henry
    Agard) Wallace 8 (William Averell)
    Harriman
    labor: 5 (Maurice Joseph) Tobin 7
    (Frances), Perkins (Wilson) 13 (Lewis
    Baxter) Schwellenbach
  born: 2 MO 5 Lamar 8 Missouri
  died: 2 MO 8 Missouri 10 Kansas City
  buried: 2 MO 8 Missouri 12 Independence
  education:
    law school: 21 Kansas City School of
    Law (did not graduate)
  religion: 7 Baptist
  interests: 5 piano 7 history
  vacation spot: 2 FL 7 Florida, Key West
  author: 14 Year of Decision 19 Years of
  Trial and Hope
  political career: 8 US Senate 13 Vice
  President
  presiding judge of: 13 Jackson County
  civilian career: 6 farmer
  owned: 9 men's store 12 haberdashery
  military service: 5 major 9 World War I
  15 MO National Guard 18 Army Reserve
  colonel
  notable events of lifetime/term: 4
  NATO 5 V-E Day 8 Fair Deal 9 Korean
  War 17 iron-curtain speech 20 assassination attempt 31 North Atlantic
  Treaty Organization
  act: 11 Taft-Hartley 12 Bretton-Woods
  airlift to: 6 Berlin

conference: 7 Potsdam

dropping of first: 5 A-bomb 8 atom bomb

plan: 8 Marshall 9 Point Four

signing of: 9 UN charter

Treaty of: 12 Rio de Janeiro

trial of: 9 Alger Hiss

father: 12 John Anderson

mother: 6 Martha (Ellen Young)

siblings: 8 Mary Jane 10 John Vivian

wife: 9 Elizabeth (Virginia Wallace)

nickname: 4 Bess

children: 12 Mary Margaret

Trumbull, John

born: 9 Lebanon CT

artwork: 21 The Battle of Bunker Hill 26 The Resignation of Washington 28 The Declaration of Independence 29 The Surrender of General Burgoyne 32 The Capture of the Hessians at Trenton 38 The Surrender of Lord Cornwallis at Yorktown 46 The Death of General Montgomery in the Attack of Quebec, The Death of General Warren at the Battle of Bunker Hill

trumpery 5 showy, trash 6 deceit, trashy, trivia 7 rubbish, twaddle, useless 8 frippery, nonsense, trifling 9 deception, worthless 11 nonsensical

trumpet 4 honk, horn 5 blare, bugle 6 cornet 7 clarion 8 proclaim 10 hearing aid

Trumpet of the Swan, The

author: 7 E B White

trump up 4 fake 6 invent, make up 7 concoct, falsify 9 fabricate

truncate 3 bob, lop, nip 4 clip, crop, dock, snub, trim 5 prune 7 abridge, curtail, shorten 8 amputate, condense, cut short 10 abbreviate

truncheon 3 bat 4 club 5 baton, billy, stick 6 cudgel 8 bludgeon 9 billyclub

trunker 3 box, die 4 body, bole, dado, line, main 5 chief, pants, shaft, snout, stock, torso 6 coffer, engine, locker, shut up, thorax 7 baggage, close in

Truscott-Jones, Reginald

real name of: 10 Ray Milland

truss 3 tie 4 beam, bind, prop, stay 5 brace, hitch, shore, strap, tie up 6 bind up, fasten, girder, pinion, secure 7 confine, support 8 make fast 9 constrict, framework, stanchion 12 underpinning

trust 4 care, duty, hope 5 faith, hands 6 accept, assume, belief, charge, credit, expect, look to, rely on 7 believe, count on, custody, keeping, presume, swear by 8 credence, feel sure, reliance, sureness 9 certainty, certitude, count upon 10 anticipate, confidence, conviction, depend upon, obligation, protection 11 assuredness, contemplate, have faith in, safekeeping, subscribe to, take on faith, take stock in 12 guardianship 14 give credence to, responsibility, take for granted

trusted 6 trusty 8 reliable 9 unfailing 10 dependable 11 trustworthy

trustee 8 guardian 9 caretaker, custodian, protector

trusteeship 4 care 6 charge 7 custody 10 protection 11 safekeeping 12 guardianship

trusting 8 gullible, trustful 9 believing, credulous 12 unsuspicious

trustworthy 4 true 5 loyal 6 honest 7 ethical, trusted, upright 8 faithful, reliable, true-blue 9 honorable, steadfast 10 aboveboard, dependable, scrupulous 11 responsible 12 tried and true 13 incorruptible, unimpeachable 14 high-principled

trusty 7 trusted 8 reliable 9 unfailing 10 dependable 11 trustworthy

trusty companion 3 pal 5 buddy, crony 6 friend 8 intimate, sidekick 9 confidant 10 bosom buddy, confidante

truth 3 law 4 fact 5 facts 6 verity 7 reality 8 accuracy, fidelity, trueness, veracity 9 actuality, exactness, integrity 11 reliability 12 authenticity, faithfulness, truthfulness 15 proven principle, trustworthiness

Russian: 6 Pravda

also name of: 9 newspaper

god of: 7 Mithras

truth conquers all things

Latin: 18 vincit omnia veritas

truthful 4 open, true 5 exact, frank 6 candid, honest 7 artless, correct, factual, precise, sincere 8 accurate, faithful, reliable 9 authentic, guileless, veracious 10 aboveboard, meticulous, scrupulous 11 trustworthy, undeceitful, unvarnished 13 unadulterated 15 straightforward

truthfulness 6 candor 7 honesty 8 veracity

Truth or Consequences

host: 10 Jack Bailey, Steve Dunne 12 Ralph Edwards

try 2 go 3 aim, use 4 risk, seek, shot, test, turn 5 crack, essay, fling, prove, trial, whack 6 effort, sample, strain, strive, tackle 7 adjudge, attempt, venture 8 endeavor 9 have a go at, partake of, undertake 10 adjudicate, deliberate, put to a test 11 opportunity 12 have a fling at, make an effort, take a crack at

Trygon

nurse of: 9 Asclepius

trying 4 hard 5 pesky, tough 6 taxing, vexing 7 arduous, irksome, onerous, tedious 8 tiresome 9 difficult, fatiguing, harrowing, wearisome 10 bothersome, burdensome, exhausting, irritating 11 aggravating, distressing, troublesome 12 exasperating

tryout 4 test 5 trial 7 hearing 8 audition 10 experiment

try out 3 fry 6 render 7 compete 8 audition 9 give a test 11 performance

tryst 4 date 7 meeting, vis-a-vis 9 tete-a-tete 10 engagement, rendezvous 11 appointment, assignation

try the patience of 5 annoy 7 provoke 8 irritate 10 exasperate

try to equal 5 rival 7 compete, emulate

Tuatha De Danann 4 gods

origin: 5 Irish

mother: 4 Danu

tub 3 keg, kit, pot, tun, vat 4 bath, boat, butt, cask, ship, tank, tram, wash 5 barge, bathe, fatso, fatty, keeve, tramp 6 barrel, bucket, firkin, ore car, vessel 7 cistern, tankard 8 cauldron, slow boat 9 container, freighter

Tubalcain
  father: 6 Lamech
  mother: 6 Zillah
  half-brother: 5 Jabal, Jubal
  progenitor of: 12 metalworkers

tube 4 duct, hose, pipe 7 conduit 8 cylinder

tuber 3 anu, yam 4 beet, bulb, corm, eddo, root, taro 5 jalop, shoot 6 potato, turnip 8 rutabaga, swelling 11 enlargement

Tuchman, Barbara W
  author of: 14 A Distant Mirror, The First Salute 15 The Guns of August, The March of Folly 17 Practicing History

tuck 3 put 4 cram 5 pleat, shove, stick, stuff 6 enwrap, gather, insert, pucker, roll up, ruffle, shroud, swathe, thrust 7 crinkle, swaddle

tucker 3 fag 4 bush, poop, tire 5 weary 7 exhaust, fatigue

tuckered out 5 all in, tired, weary 6 bushed, done in, pooped 8 fatigued 9 exhausted, fagged out

Tudor, Antony
  choreographer of: 11 Lilac Garden 12 Pillar of Fire

tuebor 11 I will defend

Tuei see 6 Isleta

Tuesday
  from: 3 Tiw
  heavenly body: 4 Mars
  French: 5 mardi
  Italian: 7 martedi
  Spanish: 6 martes
  German: 8 dienstag

tuft 4 wisp 5 batch, brush, bunch, clump, crest, plume, sheaf 6 bundle, tassel 7 cluster, topknot

tug 3 lug, tow 4 drag, draw, haul, jerk, pull, yank 6 wrench 7 wrestle

tulip 6 Tulipa
  varieties: 4 lady, star 5 globe 7 Turkish 9 butterfly, guinea-hen, waterlily 10 Sierra star 11 golden globe, purple globe 16 common late garden 17 common early garden

Tulkinghorn
  character in: 10 Bleak House
  author: 7 Dickens

Tullia
  father: 14 Servius Tullius
  husband: 7 Tarquin

Tullius see 14 Servius Tullius

Tulsa
  football team: 7 Outlaws

tumble 3 mix 4 dive, drop, fall, flip, roll, toss 5 whirl 6 bounce, jumble, plunge, stir up, topple 7 descend, shuffle, stumble 9 cartwheel 10 somersault

tumbledown 5 shaky 7 rickety, run-down 8 decaying, decrepit, unstable 9 crumbling, tottering 10 broken-down, jerry-built, ram-

shackle 11 dilapidated, falling-down 14 disintegrating

tumbler 3 cog, dog 5 drier, glass, lever 6 goblet, vessel 7 acrobat, athlete, gymnast, juggler 12 somersaulter

tumbrel 4 cart 5 wagon 7 tipcart 8 dumpcart

tumbril
  French: 7 fourgon

tumid 5 puffy 6 turgid 7 bloated, bulging, dilated, pompous, swollen 8 enlarged, expanded, inflated 9 bombastic, distended, edematous, tumescent 11 protuberant 12 magniloquent 13 grandiloquent

tummy 3 gut 5 belly 6 paunch, tum-tum 7 abdomen, midriff, stomach 9 bay window 11 breadbasket

tumor 3 wen 4 cyst, lump, wart 5 pride 6 cancer, growth 7 bombast, sarcoma 8 hematoma, neoplasm, swelling, tubercle 9 carcinoma, papilloma, pomposity 11 tumefaction

tumult 3 ado, din 6 bedlam, bustle, clamor, hubbub, racket, uproar 7 turmoil 8 disorder, upheaval 9 agitation, commotion, confusion 10 excitement, hullabaloo 11 disturbance, pandemonium

tumultuous 4 loud 5 noisy, rough, rowdy 6 stormy, unruly 7 chaotic, furious, lawless, raucous, riotous, violent 8 agitated, confused 9 clamorous, disturbed, turbulent 10 boisterous, disorderly, uproarious 11 tempestuous

tun 3 keg, tub, vat 4 butt, cast, drum 6 barrel 8 hogshead

tune 3 air 4 aria, line, song, step 5 adjust, ditty, motif, pitch, theme 6 accord, adjust, melody, number, strain, unison 7 concert, concord, harmony 9 agreement 10 conformity

tuneful 6 catchy, dulcet 7 lyrical, musical 9 melodious

tungsten
  chemical symbol: 1 W

Tungusic
  language family: 6 Altaic
  includes: 6 Manchu

tunic 4 robe 5 cloak 6 jacket, mantle, poncho, tabard 7 garment, surcoat

Tunica
  tribe: 10 Chitimacha

Tunis
  capital of: 7 Tunisia

Tunisia
  other name: 8 Carthage 9 Ifriqiyah
  capital/largest city: 5 Tunis
  others: 4 Beja, Sfax, Susa 5 Gabes, Gofsa 6 Djerba, Mateur, Nabeul, Remada, Sousse, Tozeur 7 Bizerte, Kairwan 8 Carthage, Jendouba, Kairouan, Monastir, Tebourba, Zaghouan 9 Grombalia 10 Ferryville
  empire: 8 Carthage 13 Barbary States
  school: 5 Tunis 16 Pasteur Institute
  measure: 3 saa 4 saah 5 cafiz 6 mettar 8 milerole
  monetary unit: 5 dinar 6 dollar 7 millime

weight: 3 saa 4 rotl 5 artal, ratel, uckia

island: 6 Djerba, Galite

lake: 6 Achkel, Djerid 7 Bizerte

mountain: 5 Atlas 6 Mrhila 7 Tebessa 8 High Tell, Zaghouan 12 Northern Tell 17 Dorsale Tunisienne

highest point: 6 Chambi

river: 8 Medjerda, Mellegue

sea: 13 Mediterranean

physical feature:

cape: 3 Bon 5 Blanc 8 Rasaddar

desert: 6 Sahara

gulf: 5 Gabes, Tunis 8 Hammamet

oasis: 5 Gabes, Gafsa, Nefta 6 Djerba, Tozeur 9 El Oudiane 13 El Hamma Djerid

plains: 5 Sahel

salt lake: 11 Chott Djerid, Shatt Djerid

valley: 8 Medjerda

wind: 5 chile 6 chilli 7 sirocco

people: 3 Jew 4 Arab 6 Berber

artist: 5 Gorgi, Turki

dynasty: 6 Hafsid 7 Fatimid 8 Aghlabid, Almohade 10 Husseinite

leader: 6 Ben Ali 9 Bourguiba

language: 6 Arabic, Berber, French

religion: 5 Islam 7 Judaism 12 Christianity

place:

center of Tunis: 13 Place d'Afrique

mosque: 5 Great 7 Zitouna

museum: 5 Bardo, Kouba 6 Sousse

palace: 14 Dar Ben Abdallah

ruins: 8 Carthage

street: 14 Habib Bourguiba

feature:

cap: 7 chechia

clothing: 5 jebba 7 safasri 9 babbouche

market: 4 souk

food:

dish: 7 mesfouf 8 couscous

drink: 4 iban 5 legmi

fruit: 12 deglet en nour

Tunney, Gene

real name: 17 James Joseph Tunney

nickname: 14 Fighting Marine

sport: 6 boxing

class: 11 heavyweight

Tuonela

also: 6 Manala

origin: 7 Finnish

name of: 10 afterworld

form: 6 island

lacked: 3 sun 4 moon

Tupman

character in: 14 Pickwick Papers

author: 7 Dickens

tu quoque 7 thou too

Turandot

opera by: 7 Puccini

character: 3 Liu 4 Pang, Ping, Pong 5 Calaf, Timur 8 Turandot (Princess of China)

turbid 5 muddy, murky 6 cloudy, opaque, roiled 7 clouded, unclear 8 agitated 9 disturbed, stirred up, unsettled

turbulence 4 fury 6 frenzy, hubbub, tumult, unrest, uproar 7 ferment, rioting, torrent, turmoil 8 disorder, violence 9 agitation, commotion 10 excitement, unruliness 11 disturbance

turbulent 5 rowdy 6 fierce, raging, stormy, unruly 7 chaotic, furious, riotous, violent 8 agitated, restless 9 clamorous, disturbed 10 blustering, boisterous, disorderly, tumultuous, uproarious 11 tempestuous

tureen 4 bowl, dish 9 casserole, container 10 receptacle

turf 3 sod 4 area, peat, plot, soil 5 divot, grass, haunt, sward, track 7 verdure 9 racetrack, territory 10 greensward

Turgenev, Ivan

author of: 5 Smoke 9 First Love 10 Virgin Soil 14 Fathers and Sons 18 A Month in the Country 19 A Sportsman's Notebook, A Sportsman's Sketches, The Torrents of Spring

turgid 5 puffy, showy 6 florid, ornate 7 flowery, pompous, swollen 8 inflated, puffed up 9 bombastic, grandiose, overblown 10 hyperbolic

Turkey

capital: 6 Angora, Ankara

largest city: 8 Istanbul

others: 4 Enos, Troy, Urfa 5 Adana, Bursa, Izmir, Konya, Maras, Siirt, Sivas 6 Aintab, Edessa, Edirne, Elaziz, Marash, Samsun, Smyrna 7 Antakya, Antioch, Erzurum, Kayseri, MMersin, Scutari, Trabzon, Uskudar 8 Stamboul 9 Byzantium, Eskisehir, Gaziantep 10 Adrianople 14 Constantinople

school: 6 Aegean, Ankara 8 Istanbul

division: 4 Pera, Sert 5 Siirt, Troad 6 Angora, Eyalet, Thrace 7 Anadolu, Beyoglu, Cilicia 8 Anatolia 9 Asia Minor, Kurdistan

measure: 3 dra, oka, pik 4 draa, khat, kile, zira 5 berri, kileh, zirai 6 arshin, chinik, fortin, halebi 7 nocktat

monetary unit: 4 lira, para 5 akcha, asper, kurus, pound, rebia 6 akcheh, zequin 7 aetilik, beshlik, piaster 8 medjidie

weight: 3 oka, oke 4 aqui, dram, rotl 5 artal, cheke, kerat, obolu, ratel 6 batman, dirhem, kantar, maunch, miskal 7 drachma, quintal, yusdrum

island: 6 Cyprus, Kibris

lake: 3 Tuz, Van 7 Egridir 8 Beysehir

mountain: 2 Ak 3 Ala 4 Alai, Dagh, Kara 5 Hasan, Hinis, Honaz, Murat, Murit 6 Ala Dag, Bingol, Bolgar, Pontic, Suphan, Taurus 7 Aladagh, Erciyas 8 Karacali 10 Kackar Dagi

highest point: 6 Ararat

river: 4 Aras, Kura 5 Araks, Dicle, Firat, Gediz, Goksu, Halys, Irmak, Kizil, Mesta, Murat, Sarus 6 Araxes, Ceyhan, Seihan, Seyhan, Seylan, Tigris 7 Kurucay, Muradsu, Orontes, Sakarya 8 Granicus, Macestus, Maeander, Menderes 9 Euphrates 13 Buyukmenderes

sea: 4 Aral 5 Black 6 Aegean 7 Marmara 13 Mediterranean

physical feature:
cape: 4 Baba, Ince 5 Bafra 6 Anamur, Helles, Hinzir 7 Karatas, Kerempe
gulf: 3 Cos 5 Izmir 7 Antalya
inlet: 10 Golden Horn
peninsula: 9 Anatolian, Gallipoli
plateau: 9 Anatolian
strait: 8 Bosporus 9 Bosphorus 11 Dardanelles
people: 4 Arab, Kurd, Turk 6 Seljuk
king: 8 Mausolus
leader: 5 Inonu, Osman 6 Ecevit 7 Demirel 8 Menderes, Suleiman 12 Kemal Ataturk
poet: 5 Homer
language: 6 Arabic 7 Kurdish, Turkish
religion: 5 Islam 7 Judaism 12 Christianity 13 Greek Orthodox, Roman Catholic
place:
bridge: 6 Galata
dam: 9 Gokcekaya
mosque: 4 Blue, Yeni 8 Selimiye 11 Hagia Sophia, Sultan Ahmed
ruins: 4 Troy 7 Ephesus 8 Pergamum
tomb: 12 Kemal Ataturk
feature:
cap: 3 fez 6 calpac 7 calpack
clothing: 6 caftan, dolman, jelick 7 yashrak 8 charshaf, maharmah, shakseer
goat hair: 6 mohair
grill: 6 mangal
harem: 5 serai 8 seraglio
musical instrument: 5 canum, kanum 6 canoon, johnie, kussir, zither 8 crescent, jingling
pipe: 10 meerschaum
food:
dish: 5 halva, pilaw 10 doner kebab, shish kebab
drink: 4 boza, raki 5 airan, pasha, rakee 6 mastic
pastry: 7 baklava
turkey: 4 hind
Turkic
language family: 6 Altaic
group: 5 Kazak, Nogai, Uigur, Uzbek, Yakut 7 Chuvash, Kirghiz 8 Turkoman 10 Karakaipak 11 Azerbaijani 14 Osmanli Turkish
Turkmenistan
capital/largest city: 9 Ashkhabad
head of state: 9 president
government: 8 republic
monetary unit: 5 ruble
river: 8 Amu Darya
sea: 7 Caspian
physical feature: 13 Kara Kum Desert
people: 7 Turkmen 10 Turkmenian
language: 6 Turkic 10 West Turkic
religion: 11 Sunni Muslim
feature: 9 Altyn Depe
turmeric
botanical name: 12 Curcuma longa
also called: 7 tumeric 13 Crocus indicus, Indian saffron
family: 6 ginger
color: 6 yellow

used as: 3 dye 6 amulet 8 cosmetic, medicine
origin: 4 Asia 9 Caribbean, East India
charm against: 5 ghost 10 tree spirit
turmoil 4 mess 5 chaos 6 tumult, uproar 7 ferment 8 disorder 9 agitation, commotion, confusion 10 convulsion 11 disturbance, pandemonium
French: 14 bouleversement
turn 2 do, go 3 act, arc, lie, put 4 bend, coil, come, deed, flex, hang, look, loop, make, rest, ride, roll, send, shot, sour, spin, time, veer, walk, wing 5 alter, apply, crack, curve, drive, eject, fling, hinge, pivot, round, scare, shift, shock, spell, spoil, start, stint, swing, throw, twist, whack, wheel, whirl 6 action, become, chance, change, curdle, depend, direct, effort, fright, gyrate, invert, period, reside, rotate, sprain, stroll, swerve, swivel, wrench, zig-zag 7 acidify, attempt, convert, deliver, execute, ferment, perform, reverse, revolve, service, winding 8 gyration, overturn, roll over, rotation, surprise 9 cause to go, deviation, discharge, transform 10 accomplish, alteration, revolution
turn a deaf ear to 6 ignore, slight 9 disregard
turn aside 5 avert 6 divert 7 deflect, deviate 8 turn away
turn away 5 avert 6 give up 8 alienate, estrange, send away 9 turn aside 12 turn one's back
turnback 4 fold, quit, tack 5 repel 6 defect, desert, return, revert 7 forsake, regress, relapse, repulse, retrace, retreat, reverse 9 backslide
turncoat 5 Judas 6 bolter 7 traitor 8 apostate, betrayer, defector, deserter, quisling, renegade 12 double-dealer
turn down 5 spurn 6 refuse, reject 14 lower the volume, refuse to accept
Turner, Joseph Mallord William
born: 6 London 7 England
artwork: 12 The Shipwreck, The Slave Ship, Tintern Abbey 17 Dawn After the Wreck 20 Dido Building Carthage 22 Venice S Giorgio Maggiore 24 The Sun of Venice Going to Sea 25 The Thames near Walton Bridge, Ulysses Deriding Polyphemus 30 Burning of the Houses of Parliament 32 Snowstorm Hannibal Crossing the Alps 32 The Falls of the Rhine at Schaffhausen 34 The Bay of Baiae with Apollo and the Sibyl 37 Fighting Temeraire Tugged to her Last Berth 47 The Parting of Hero and Leander from the Greek of Musaeus 50 The Shipwreck Fishing Boats Endeavoring to Rescue the Crew
Turner, Kathleen
roles: 8 Body Heat 12 Prizzi's Honor 17 Romancing the Stone, The Jewel of the Nile 18 Peggy Sue Got Married

Turner, Lana
  real name: 29 Julia Jean Mildred Frances Turner
  nickname: 11 Sweater Girl
  born: 9 Wallace ID
  discovered at: 16 Schwab's Drugstore
  husband: 9 Artie Shaw, Lex Barker 10 Bob Topping 12 Stephen Crane
  roles: 7 Madame X 11 Peyton Place 15 By Love Possessed, Imitation of Life 26 The Postman Always Rings Twice
turning 4 bend 5 curve 7 bending, curving, winding 8 pivoting, rotating, spinning, twisting, whirling 9 revolving, swiveling
turnip 12 Brassica rapa
  group: 8 Rapifera
  varieties: 6 Indian 7 Italian, Swedish 8 seven-top
turn off 4 bore, exit 5 douse, leave, repel 6 revolt, sicken 7 disgust, repulse 8 alienate, turn away 9 switch off 10 deactivate
turn of phrase 5 idiom 8 locution, phrasing 10 expression 11 phraseology
Turn of the Screw, The
  author: 10 Henry James
  character: 5 Flora, Miles 7 Mr Quint 8 Mrs Grose 10 Miss Jessel 12 The Governess
turn on 5 start, tempt 6 allure, attack, entice, excite 7 actuate, attract 8 activate, energize, interest, switch on
turn one's stomach 6 revolt, sicken 7 disgust 8 nauseate
turnout 5 crowd 6 output, throng 8 assembly, audience 9 gathering 10 assemblage, production
turn out 4 garb, oust 5 array, dress, eject, end up, evict, exile, expel 6 appear, attend, attire, banish, clothe, evolve, fit out, invest, rig out, show up, unfold 7 cast out, come out, costume, develop, kick out 8 drive out, send away 9 switch off 11 come to light
turn over 4 flip 5 upset 6 bestow, rotate 7 deliver 8 flipflop, give over, hand over, overturn 9 surrender 10 relinquish, somersault
turn pale 4 fade 6 blanch, whiten 7 lighten
turn tail 4 flee 7 retreat, run away 8 back away 12 beat a retreat
turn to account 7 exploit, utilize 8 profit by, put to use 9 make use of 12 capitalize on
turn topsy turvy 5 upset 7 capsize, confuse, tip over 8 flip-flop, overturn, put askew 10 disarrange, turn turtle 11 disorganize
turn turtle 5 upset 7 capsize, tip over 8 flip over, keel over, overturn, turn over 14 turn upside down
turn up 4 come 6 appear, arrive, crop up, drop in, emerge, loom up, show up 7 develop, surface 11 come to light
Turnus
  father: 6 Daunus
  mother: 7 Venilia
  sister: 7 Juturna
  sought to win: 7 Lavinia

  killed by: 6 Aeneas
Turpentine State
  nickname of: 13 North Carolina
turpitude 4 evil, vice 8 baseness, lewdness, vileness 9 depravity 10 corruption, debauchery, defilement, degeneracy, immorality, perversion, sinfulness, wickedness, wrongdoing 13 dissoluteness 14 licentiousness
turquoise 4 aqua 5 stone 7 mineral, skyblue 10 aquamarine 12 greenish-blue, Prussian-blue
  source: 12 United States
turret 5 tower 6 belfry, cupola, garret, gazebo, louver, terret 7 minaret, rotator, steeple 8 gunhouse, gunmount 9 belvedere, pepperbox 10 watchtower
  tool: 5 lathe
turtle 3 box 4 musk, wood 6 slider 7 painted, reptile, snapper, spotted 8 slowpoke, terrapin, tortoise 10 turtledove 11 leatherback
  dorsal shell: 8 carapace
  nautical: 5 upset 6 pocket 7 capsize 8 overturn
  order: 8 Chelonia
  ventral shell: 8 plastron
  young: 7 turtlet
Turveydrop
  character in: 10 Bleak House
  author: 7 Dickens
tussle 4 fray 5 brawl, fight, melee, scrap, set-to 6 battle, fracas 7 grapple, scuffle, wrestle 8 conflict, struggle 10 donnybrook, free-for-all 11 altercation
tussock 4 hair, tuft 5 brush, bunch, clump, grass, sedge 7 bulrush, cluster, thicket 8 feathers
tutelage 8 coaching, guidance, teaching, training, tutoring 9 direction, education, schooling 10 discipline 11 inculcation, instruction, supervision, trusteeship 12 guardianship 14 indoctrination
tutor 4 guru 5 coach, drill, teach 6 master, mentor, school 7 prepare, teacher 8 instruct 10 instructor 11 give lessons
tutorial 5 class 8 didactic, edifying 11 educational, instructive 12 prescriptive
tutti
  music: 3 all 18 all players together, all singers together
Tuvalu
  other name: 13 Ellice Islands, Lagoon Islands
  capital: 8 Funafuti
  head of state: 14 British monarch 15 governor general
  monetary unit: 4 cent 6 dollar
  island: 3 Nui 6 Niutao 7 Nanumea, Vaitupu 8 Funafuti 9 Nanumanga, Niulakita, Nukufetau 10 Nukulaelae
  highest point: 5 Nuwak
  sea: 7 Pacific
  people: 6 Samoan 10 Polynesian
  leader: 5 Lauti
  language: 6 Samoan 7 English 8 Tuvaluan 10 Polynesian

religion: 10 Protestant 12 Tuvalu Church

Tuvim, Judith
   real name of: 12 Judy Holliday

twaddle 3 rot 4 bosh, bunk 5 trash, tripe 6 babble, drivel, gabble, jabber, piffle 7 chatter, prattle, rubbish 8 claptrap, idle talk, nonsense, tommyrot 9 jabbering, silly talk 10 balderdash 16 stuff-and-nonsense

Twain, Mark
   real name: 13 Samuel Clemens
   author of: 9 Tom Sawyer 10 Roughing It 12 A Tramp Abroad, The Gilded Age 15 (Adventures of) Huckleberry Finn 18 The Innocents Abroad 20 Life on the Mississippi 21 The Mysterious Stranger, The Prince and the Pauper 29 The Man That Corrupted Hadleyburg 36 A Connecticut Yankee in King Arthur's Court 41 The Celebrated Jumping Frog of Calaveras County

twang 9 resonance, vibration 10 nasal sound 13 reverberation

Tweedledee
   character in: 22 Through the Looking Glass
   author: 7 Carroll

Tweedledum
   character in: 22 Through the Looking Glass
   author: 7 Carroll

tweet 4 peep 5 cheep, chirp 7 chirrup, chitter, twitter

Twelfth-Night
   author: 18 William Shakespeare
   character: 5 Feste, Maria, Viola (Cesario) 6 Olivia, Orsino 7 Antonio 8 Malvolio 9 Sebastian 12 Sir Toby Belch 18 Sir Andrew Aguecheek

Twelve Angry Men
   director: 11 Sidney Lumet
   cast: 8 Ed Begley, Lee J Cobb 10 E G Marshall, Henry Fonda, Jack Warden 11 Jack Klugman, John Fiedler 12 Martin Balsam

Twelve O'Clock High
   director: 9 Henry King
   cast: 10 Dean Jagger 11 Gary Merrill, Gregory Peck, Hugh Marlowe 15 Millard Mitchell
   Oscar for: 15 supporting actor (Jagger)

Twentieth Century
   director: 11 Howard Hawks
   based on play by: 8 Ben Hecht 16 Charles MacArthur
   cast: 11 Roscoe Karns 13 Carole Lombard, John Barrymore 14 Walter Connolly

Twentieth Century, The
   narrator: 14 Walter Cronkite

twenty-one see 9 blackjack

Twenty Questions
   host: 10 Bill Slater, Jay Jackson
   panelist: 11 Herb Polesie 12 Bobby McGuire 13 Johnnie McPhee 14 Dickie Harrison, Florence Rinard 15 Fred Van De Venter

Twenty Thousand Leagues Under the Sea
   author: 10 Jules Verne
   character: 7 Conseil, Ned Land 11 Captain Nemo 22 Professor Pierre Aronnax
   submarine: 8 Nautilus

Twenty Years After
   author: 14 Alexandre Dumas (pere)

Twice-Told Tales
   author: 18 Nathaniel Hawthorne

Twightwee see 5 Miami

twilight 3 ebb, eve 4 dusk 6 sunset 7 decline, evening, sundown 8 eventide, gloaming, moonrise 9 half-light, last phase, nightfall 14 edge of darkness

Twilight of the Gods 8 Ragnarok
   German: 15 Gotterdammerung

Twilight Zone, The
   host: 10 Rod Serling

twin 4 dual, like 5 alike 6 double, paired 7 matched, twofold 9 duplicate, identical

Twin 6 Thomas

twine 4 coil, cord, rope, wind 5 braid, cable, plait, twist, weave 6 string, thread 7 binding, entwine 9 interlace 10 intertwine

twinge 4 pain, pang, stab 5 cramp, spasm, throb 6 stitch, tingle, twitch

twinkle 4 glow 5 blaze, flare, flash, gleam, shine 7 flicker, glimmer, glisten, shimmer, sparkle 11 scintillate

Twinkleton, Miss
   character in: 22 The Mystery of Edwin Drood
   author: 7 Dickens

Twins
   constellation of: 6 Gemini

twirl 4 spin 5 pivot, twine, wheel, whirl 6 gyrate, rotate 7 revolve 9 pirouette

twist 3 arc, way 4 bend, coil, curl, idea, kink, knot, pull, roll, spin, turn, veer, wind, wrap, yank 5 curve, pivot, ravel, slant, snake, swing, twine, whirl, wrest 6 change, method, notion, rotate, spiral, sprain, swerve, swivel, system, tangle, wrench, zigzag 7 contort, distort, entwine, meander 8 approach, rotation, surprise 9 corkscrew, interlace, treatment 10 intertwine, involution 11 convolution, development

twisted 4 bent 6 warped 7 crooked, gnarled 8 deformed 9 contorted, distorted, misshapen

twisting 7 crooked, curving, turning 9 contorted, revolving, spiraling, swiveling

twist out of shape 4 warp 6 deform 7 contort, distort

twitch 3 tic 4 jerk 5 shake, spasm, throb 6 quaver, quiver, squirm, tremor, wiggle, writhe 7 tremble 8 paroxysm 10 convulsion

twitter 4 fuss, peep, stew 5 cheep, chirp, tizzy, tweet, whirl 6 bustle, flurry, pother, uproar, warble 7 chatter, chirrup, ferment, fluster, flutter 8 chirping 10 turbulence 11 chirrupping

two-faced 5 false 7 devious 8 slippery 9 deceitful, deceptive, dishonest, insincere 10 perfidious 11 dissembling, double-faced, duplicitous, fork-tongued, treacherous, underhanded 12 dishonorable, disingenuous, falsehearted, hypocritical 13 double-dealing, untrustworthy

twofold 4 dual 6 double 7 two-part

Two Gentlemen of Verona, The
author: 18 William Shakespeare
character: 5 Julia 6 Silvia, Thurio 7 Proteus 9 Valentine 11 Duke of Milan

Two Lands, The see 5 Egypt

two of a kind 4 pair 5 twins 6 couple 7 doublet

two-part 4 dual, twin 6 double, paired 9 bipartite

twosome 3 duo 4 pair 5 brace 6 couple

2001: A Space Odyssey
author: 13 Arthur C Clarke
director: 14 Stanley Kubrick
character: 5 Dave 5 Steve
computer: 3 HAL
cast: 3 HAL 10 Keir Dullea 12 Gary Lockwood 16 William Sylvester
song: 20 Thus Spake Zarathustra (Richard Strauss)
sequel: 24 Two Thousand Ten: Odyssey Two

two-time 6 betray 10 be disloyal 11 doublecross 12 be unfaithful 13 be treacherous, play false with 14 break faith with

two-timing 5 false 6 tricky 7 perfidy 8 bad faith, betrayal, disloyal, trickery 9 deceiving, deception, duplicity, falseness, treachery 10 disloyalty, perfidious 11 doublecross, duplicitous, treacherous 13 breach of faith, double-dealing, faithlessness 14 double-crossing

two-wheeler 4 bike 5 cycle 7 bicycle

Two Years Before the Mast
author: 18 Richard Henry Dana Jr

Tybalt
character in: 14 Romeo and Juliet
author: 11 Shakespeare

Tyche
origin: 5 Greek
goddess of: 7 fortune
corresponds to: 7 Fortuna

tycoon 4 boss 5 mogul, nabob 6 big gun, bigwig 7 big shot, magnate 8 big wheel 9 potentate 12 entrepreneur 13 industrialist 17 captain of industry

Tydeus
father: 6 Oeneus
mother: 8 Periboea
uncle: 5 Melas 6 Agrius 9 Alcathous
son: 8 Diomedes

tyke 3 kid, tad, tot 5 child 6 shaver, squirt, wee one 9 little one

Tyler, John
presidential rank: 5 tenth
party: 4 Whig 20 Democratic-Republican
state represented: 2 VA 8 Virginia
defeated: 5 no-one
succeeded upon death of: 8 Harrison
vice president: 4 none
cabinet:
state: 6 (Abel Parker) Upshur 7 (Daniel) Webster, (John C) Calhoun
treasury: 4 (George Mortimer) Bibb 5

(Thomas) Ewing 7 (John Canfield) Spencer, (Walter) Forward
war: 4 (John) Bell 7 (John Canfield) Spencer, (William) Wilkins
attorney general: 6 (Hugh Swinton) Legare, (John) Nelson 10 (John Jordan) Crittenden
navy: 5 (John Young) Mason 6 (Abel Parker) Upshur, (George Edmund) Badger, (Thomas Walker) Gilmer
postmaster general: 7 (Francis) Granger 9 (Charles Anderson) Wickliffe
born: 2 VA 8 Greenway, Virginia 17 Charles City County
died/buried: 2 VA 8 Richmond, Virginia
education: 14 William and Mary
religion: 6 Episcopalian
vacation spot: 2 VA 7 Hampton 8 Virginia
political career: 8 US Senate 12 State Council 13 vice president 24 US House of Representatives
delegate to: 13 State Assembly
governor of: 8 Virginia
civilian career: 6 farmer, lawyer
military service: 19 War of Eighteen Twelve
notable events of lifetime/term:
act: 6 Tariff (of 1842)
annexation of: 5 Texas
treaty: 16 Webster-Ashburton
father: 4 John
mother: 4 Mary (Marott Armistead)
siblings: 7 William 8 Wat Henry 10 Maria Henry 12 Anne Contesse 14 Christina Booth 15 Martha Jefferson 18 Elizabeth Armistead
wife: 5 Julia (Gardiner) 7 Letitia (Christian)
children: 4 John, Mary 5 Alice, Julia, Pearl 6 Robert 7 Lachlan, Letitia 8 Tazewell 9 Elizabeth 12 Anne Contesse, Lyon Gardiner 13 David Gardiner, John Alexander 16 Robert FitzWalter

Tyll Eulenspiegel see 16 Till Eulenspiegel

Tyndall, John
field: 7 physics
nationality: 5 Irish
studied diffusion of: 5 light

Tyndareus
wife: 4 Leda
daughter: 6 Phoebe 8 Philonoe, Timandra 12 Clytemnestra

Tyndaridae see 15 Castor and Pollux

type 4 font, kind, race, sort 5 brand, class, genus, group, model, order, print 6 design, family, phylum, sample 7 pattern, species, variety 8 category, division, specimen, typeface 9 archetype, prototype 10 typography

type, movable
invented by: 9 Gutenberg

Typee
author: 14 Herman Melville
character: 3 Tom (Melville) 4 Toby 6 Marnoo, Mehevi 7 Fayaway 8 Kory-Kory

typewriter
    invented by: 5 Soule 6 Sholes 7 Glidden

Typhoeus
    form: 7 monster
    father: 8 Tartarus
    mother: 2 Ge
    number of heads: 10 one hundred

Typhon
    form: 7 monster
    father: 8 Typhoeus
    son: 5 Ladon

typhoon 4 gale, gust, wind 5 storm 7 cyclone, tempest, tornado, twister 9 hurricane, whirlwind

Typhoon
    author: 12 Joseph Conrad

typical 5 model, stock, usual 6 normal 7 average, regular 8 ordinary, orthodox, standard 9 exemplary, in keeping 10 individual, prototypal, true to type 11 distinctive, in character 12 conventional, to be expected 14 characteristic, representative

typify 5 sum up 6 embody 7 betoken, connote, pass for 8 instance, stand for 9 epitomize, exemplify, incarnate, personify, represent 10 illustrate 12 characterize

typography measure 2 em, en 4 pica 5 point

Tyr
    origin: 12 Scandinavian
    god of: 7 victory
    father: 4 Odin 5 Othin
    mother: 3 Fri 5 Frigg, Frija 6 Frigga
    killed by: 4 Garm

tyrannical 7 fascist 8 despotic 9 imperious 10 oppressive 11 dictatorial, domineering 13 authoritarian

tyrannize 7 oppress 8 domineer, overlord 10 slave drive

tyrannized 9 exploited, oppressed 11 downtrodden, subservient 12 harshly ruled

Tyrannosaurus
    type: 8 dinosaur, theropod
    location: 7 Montana 12 North America
    period: 10 Cretaceous

tyrannous 8 despotic 9 imperious 10 ironhanded, oppressive, repressive, tyrannical

tyranny 7 cruelty, fascism 8 coercion, iron fist, iron hand, iron rule, severity 9 despotism, harshness 10 domination, oppression, repression 11 persecution 12 dictatorship 13 reign of terror 15 totalitarianism

tyrant 5 bully 6 despot 8 dictator, martinet 10 persecutor, taskmaster 11 cruel master, slave driver

Tyre
    king of: 5 Hiram

tyro 6 intern, novice, rookie 7 learner, recruit, trainee 8 beginner, initiate, neophyte, newcomer 9 greenhorn 10 apprentice, tenderfoot

Tyro
    father: 9 Salmoneus
    loved by: 8 Cretheus, Poseidon
    son: 5 Aeson 6 Neleus, Pelias
    grandson: 5 Jason 6 Nestor

Tyrrheus
    occupation: 8 shepherd

Tyson, Cicely
    born: 9 New York NY
    roles: 5 Roots 7 Sounder 33 The Autobiography of Miss Jane Pittman

Tyson, Mike
    original name: 7 Michael
    nickname: 8 Iron Mike
    born: 2 NY 8 Brooklyn 17 Bedford-Stuyvesant
    wife: 11 Robin Givens
    manager: 9 Cus D'Amato 10 Bill Cayton 11 Jimmy Jacobs
    trainer: 12 Angelo Dundee
    promoter: 7 Don King
    boxing title: 3 IBF, WBA, WBC 11 heavyweight
    defeated: 6 Holmes, Spinks, Thomas, Tillis, Tucker 7 Berbick
    defeated by: 7 Douglas (Buster)
    convicted of: 4 rape

tzimmes 4 fuss 6 uproar 10 hullabaloo
    literally: 4 stew 9 mixed dish

U

Ubangi-Shari *see* 22 Central African Republic
Ubermensch 8 superman
ubiquitous 7 allover 9 pervading, pervasive, prevalent, universal, worldwide 10 everywhere, widespread 11 everpresent, omnipresent 12 all-pervading
ubiquitously 10 everywhere 11 extensively
ubi supra 19 where mentioned above
Ucalegon
  counselor to: 5 Priam
Uccello, Paolo
  real name: 11 Paolo di Dono
  born: 5 Italy 8 Florence
  artwork: 8 The Flood 12 The Night Hunt 15 Sir John Hawkwood 18 The Rout (Battle) of San Romano 20 St George and the Dragon
Udaeus
  member of: 6 Sparti
  grandson: 8 Tiresias
Udall, Nicholas
  author of: 19 Ralph Roister Doister
Uganda
  capital/largest city: 7 Kampala
  others: 4 Arua, Gulu, Lira 5 Atiak, Jinja, Mbale, Mengo 6 Kasese, Kiboga, Kitgum, Masaka, Moroto, Pajule, Soroti, Tororo 7 Entebbe, Kachung, Kilembe, Mbarara, Mombasa 8 Kyenjojo 11 Port Masindi
  school: 8 Makerere
  division: 4 Toro 6 Ankole, Busoga 7 Buganda, Bunyoro
  monetary unit: 4 cent 8 shilling
  island: 4 Sese
  lake: 5 Kioga, Kyoga 6 Albert, Edward, George 8 Victoria
  mountain: 4 Oboa 5 Elgon 7 Virunga 9 Mufumbiro, Ruwenzori 18 Mountains of the Moon
  highest point: 10 Margherita
  river: 4 Aswa, Kafu 5 Pager 7 Katonga 9 White Nile 10 Albert Nile 12 Victoria Nile
  physical feature:
  falls: 5 Owens 6 Kabalega 9 Murchison
  plateau: 6 Ankole 11 East African
  valley: 9 Great Rift
  people: 4 Alur, Gisu, Soga, Teso 5 Ateso, Bantu, Chiga, Ganda, Langi, Lango, Nkole, Pygmy 6 Acholi, Ankole, Bagisu, Bakega, Basiga, Batoro 7 Baganda, Banyoro, Bunyoro, Hamitic, Lugbara, Nilotic, Sudanic 9 Nyoro-Toro 10 Banyankole, Karamojong
  explorer: 5 Baker, Speke 7 Stanley
  king: 6 Mutesa, Mwanga 8 Kabarega
  leader: 5 Obote 6 Mutesa 7 Omukama 11 Idi Amin Dada
  language: 5 Ateso, Ganda 7 English, Luganda, Swahili
  religion: 5 Islam 7 animism 8 Anglican 10 Protestant 13 Roman Catholic
  place:
  airport: 7 Entebbe
  dam: 10 Owens Falls
  national park: 6 Kidepo 14 Murchison Falls, Queen Elizabeth
  feature:
  clothing: 7 busuuti
  council of chiefs: 6 lukiko
  dance group: 17 Heart Beat of Africa
  king: 6 kabaka
  food:
  drink: 6 waragi
ugliness 8 ill-favor 9 grossness 10 homeliness 11 hideousness, monstrosity 12 unseemliness 13 frightfulness, grotesqueness, monstrousness, repulsiveness, unsightliness 14 unpleasantness 16 unattractiveness
ugly 4 foul, mean, vile 5 nasty 6 homely, horrid, odious 7 hideous, hostile, ominous 8 dreadful, horrible, menacing, unseemly 9 abhorrent, dangerous, difficult, frightful, grotesque, monstrous, obnoxious, offensive, repellent, repugnant, repulsive, sickening, unsightly 10 abominable, disgusting
ugly as sin 7 hideous 9 frightful, grotesque, monstrous, repulsive
Ugly Duckling, The
  author: 21 Hans Christian Andersen
ukase 4 fiat 5 edict, order 6 decree, dictum, ruling 7 command, mandate, statute 9 directive, manifesto, ordinance 10 injunction 12 proclamation 13 pronouncement
Ukraine
  capital/largest city: 4 Kiev
  others: 4 Lviv (Lvov), 6 Odessa 7 Donetsk, Kharkov, Lugansk (Voroshilovgrad) 8 Mariupol (Zhdanov) 9 Krivoi Rog, Zaporozhe 14 Dnepropetrovsk
  head of state: 9 president
  government: 8 republic
  monetary unit: 6 grivna 10 karbovanet
  mountain: 7 Crimean 10 Carpathian
  river: 3 Bug 5 Donets 7 Dnieper
  sea: 5 Black
  people: 7 Russian 9 Ukrainian
  language: 9 Ukrainian
  religion: 17 Ukrainian Catholic, Ukrainian Orthodox
  feature: 25 Askaniya Nova Nature Reserve
Ulan Bator
  capital of: 8 Mongolia

ulcer 4 sore 6 canker
Uller
  also: 4 Ullr
  origin: 8 Teutonic
  god of: 12 winter sports
  stepfather: 4 Thor
Ullmann, Liv
  born: 5 Japan, Tokyo
  nationality: 9 Norwegian
  roles: 7 Persona 10 Face to Face 11
    Forty Carats, Lost Horizon 12 The Emi-
    grants 16 Cries and Whispers 19 Scenes
    from a Marriage
Ullr see 5 Uller
Ulman, Douglas Elton
  real name of: 16 Douglas Fairbanks
ulna
  bone of: 8 lower arm
ulterior 6 covert, hidden, secret 7 selfish 9
  concealed 10 undivided, unrevealed 11
  self-serving, undisclosed, unexpressed 13
  opportunistic
ultimate 3 end 4 acme, apex, last, peak 5
  final 6 height, utmost 7 extreme, maximum, supreme 8 crowning, eventual,
  greatest, terminal 9 at the peak, high point,
  last straw, long-range, resulting 10 conclusive, definitive
  French: 7 dernier
Ultor
  epithet of: 7 Jupiter
  means: 7 avenger
ultramodern 8 advanced, brand-new 10
  avant-garde, newfangled 13 in the vanguard, up-to-the-minute
Ulysses
  author: 10 James Joyce
  character: 10 Molly Bloom 12 Blazes
    Boylan, Buck Mulligan, Leopold Bloom 14
    Stephen Dedalus
Ulysses see 8 Odysseus
umber 7 brown 7 pigment 9 dark-brown 14
  yellowish-brown
umbrage 5 pique, shade 6 leaves, shadow
  7 foliage, offense, outrage 10 resentment
Umbrellas of Cherbourg, The
  director: 11 Jacques Demy
  cast: 10 Anne Vernon 15 Nino
    Castelnuovo 16 Catharine Deneuve
  score: 13 Michel Legrand
Umbrian
  language family: 12 Indo-European
  branch: 6 Italic
umpire 5 judge 7 arbiter, mediate, referee 8
  mediator, moderate 9 arbitrate, go-
  between, moderator 10 adjudicate, arbitrator, negotiator 11 adjudicator, intercessor
Una
  character in: 15 The Faerie Queene
  author: 7 Spenser
unabbreviated 5 uncut 8 complete, un-
  docked, unpruned 9 uncropped, unre-
  duced, unsnipped, untrimmed 10 unabridged 11 uncondensed, uncurtailed,
  unshortened 12 uncompressed, unexpur-
  gated

unable 5 unfit 6 cannot 8 helpless, impotent 9 incapable 10 inadequate, unequipped 11 incompetent, unqualified
  to tell pitch: 8 tone deaf
unabridged 5 uncut 6 entire, intact 8 complete 10 full-length 11 uncondensed
unacceptable 8 below par, improper, unseemly, unworthy 9 deficient, out of line,
  unwelcome 10 disallowed, inadequate, unsuitable 11 displeasing, intolerable 12 inadmissible, not allowable, not up to snuff
  13 insupportable 14 unsatisfactory 15 not
  up to standard
unacceptableness 8 disfavor, disgrace, ignominy 18 unsatisfactoriness
unaccommodating 4 rude 8 churlish 9 difficult, unhelpful 10 inflexible, intolerant, unyielding 11 disobliging 13 inconsiderate
unaccompanied 4 lone, solo 5 alone, apart
  6 single, singly 8 isolated, lonesome, separate, solitary 9 a cappella, by oneself 10
  unattended, unescorted 12 all by oneself
  13 companionless
unaccountable 3 odd 4 free 5 clear, queer,
  weird 6 exempt, immune 7 bizarre, curious, excused, strange, unusual 8 baffling,
  innocent, peculiar 9 blameless, not liable,
  unheard-of 10 inculpable, intriguing, mysterious, surprising 11 astonishing, unex-
  plained 12 inexplicable, unfathomable 13
  extraordinary, not answerable 14 not responsible 16 incomprehensible
unaccustomed 3 new, odd 4 rare, wild 5
  green, new to, novel, queer 6 quaint,
  unique, unused 7 amazing, bizarre, curious, foreign, not used, strange, ungiven,
  untried, unusual 8 original, peculiar, singular, uncommon 9 fantastic, startling,
  unheard-of 10 remarkable, surprising,
  unfamiliar, unversed in 11 astonishing, out-
  of-the-way, unpracticed 12 unacquainted,
  unhabituated, unimaginable 13 extraordinary, inexperienced 14 unfamiliar with 16
  out of the ordinary
unacknowledged 9 anonymous 10 unanswered 11 disregarded 12 unidentified, unrecognized
unadorned 4 bald, bare 5 naked, plain,
  stark 6 simple 7 austere 11 undecorated
  12 unornamented 13 unembellished 15
  straightforward
unadulterated 4 pure, true 5 clear, uncut 7
  genuine 9 unalloyed, untainted 14
  untampered-with
unadventurous 5 chary, timid 7 careful 8
  cautious, hesitant 11 circumspect
unadvisable 5 silly 6 stupid, unwise 8 unseemly 9 imprudent 11 inadvisable,
  inexpedient, injudicious, undesirable 15
  disadvantageous
unaesthetic 9 tasteless 10 inartistic 11 insensitive 16 undiscriminating
unaffected 4 open 5 frank, naive, plain 6
  candid, direct, honest, simple 7 genuine,
  natural, sincere, unmoved 8 innocent 9
  childlike, guileless, ingenuous, unfeeling,
  unstirred, untouched, unworldly, whole-

some 10 impervious, unbothered, unreserved 11 indifferent, insensitive, openhearted, plain-spoken, unconcerned, undesigning, undisturbed 12 unresponsive 13 unsympathetic 15 straightforward, unsophisticated

unaffectedness 4 ease 11 naturalness 12 unconstraint

unafraid 4 bold 5 brave 6 daring, heroic, plucky 7 valiant 8 fearless, intrepid, stalwart, valorous 9 audacious, daredevil, dauntless 10 courageous 11 indomitable, lionhearted, venturesome 12 stouthearted 13 adventuresome

unaggressive 3 shy 4 meek 5 timid 7 passive 8 peaceful, timorous 9 peaceable, shrinking 11 unambitious 14 unenterprising

unagitated 4 calm 6 gentle, placid, serene 8 composed, tranquil 9 collected, unexcited, unruffled 10 untroubled 11 undisturbed, unperturbed 13 self-possessed

unalloyed 4 pure 7 unmixed 11 unqualified 13 unadulterated

unalterable 5 fixed, rigid 6 stable 8 constant 9 immutable, indelible, obstinate, permanent, perennial 10 inflexible, persistent 11 irrevocable 12 indissoluble, unchangeable 13 irretrievable

unambitious 4 easy, lazy 6 humble, modest, simple 8 slothful 10 unaspiring 12 unaggressive 14 unenterprising

unamiable 4 sour 5 cross, surly, testy 6 sullen 7 grouchy, hostile, peevish 8 churlish 9 irascible 10 ill-humored, unfriendly, unpleasant, unsociable 11 bad-tempered, uncongenial 12 disagreeable

unamorous 4 cold, cool 6 frigid 8 unloving 11 passionless

unanimated 4 dull, flat, limp 5 inert, vapid 7 insipid 8 lifeless 10 insentient 11 unconscious

unanimity 6 accord 7 concord, harmony 9 agreement, consensus 11 concordance, concurrence 17 meeting of the minds

unanimous 6 allied, united 9 accordant, consonant, of one mind 10 harmonious, like-minded

unannounced 6 secret, sudden 8 surprise, withheld 10 suppressed, unheralded 11 undisclosed, unlooked for, unpublished 12 unadvertised 13 unanticipated

unanticipated 6 sudden 8 surprise 10 unexpected, unforeseen, unheralded 11 unannounced, unlooked-for, unpredicted

unappealing 10 disgusting, uninviting, unpleasant 11 displeasing 12 disagreeable, unappetizing, unattractive

unappetizing 6 horrid 7 insipid 10 bad-tasting, disgusting, uninviting 11 unpalatable 12 disagreeable

unapproachable 4 cold, cool 5 aloof 6 remote, unique 7 austere, awesome, distant, supreme 8 foremost, peerless, superior 9 matchless, nonpareil, unequaled, unrivaled 10 forbidding, inimitable, preeminent 11 beyond reach, stand-offish, unreach-able 12 inaccessible, incomparable, intimidating, second to none, unattainable, unparalleled 13 beyond compare

unasked 6 wanton 8 unbidden, unsought, unwanted 9 uninvited, unwelcome 10 gratuitous 11 uncalled-for, undesirable, unrequested, unsolicited

unassertive 3 shy 5 timid 6 humble, modest 7 bashful 8 sheepish 9 diffident, shrinking

unassertiveness 7 modesty, shyness 8 docility, timidity 9 timidness 10 diffidence, humbleness 11 bashfulness 12 sheepishness

unassuming 5 muted, plain 6 homely, modest, simple 7 natural 9 easygoing 11 unassertive, unobtrusive 13 unpretentious 14 unostentatious

unattached 5 apart, split 6 single 8 detached, separate 9 separated 11 unconnected 12 disconnected

unattractive 3 dull, ugly 5 plain 6 homely 8 frumpish 11 unappealing, undesirable 12 unappetizing

unauthentic 4 fake, mock, sham 5 bogus, false, phony 6 untrue 7 dubious 8 doubtful 9 imitation, synthetic 10 fraudulent 11 counterfeit 12 questionable

unauthenticated 8 disputed 10 apocryphal, unverified 15 unsubstantiated

unauthorized 6 banned, covert 7 furtive 8 outlawed, unlawful 9 concealed, unallowed, underhand 10 prohibited, unapproved, unofficial 11 clandestine, uncertified, unpermitted, unwarranted 12 unaccredited, unsanctioned 13 under-the-table

unavailable 5 taken 6 scarce 7 lacking, married 9 not at hand 10 nonpresent 11 nonexistent

unavailing 4 idle, vain, weak 5 empty, inept 6 futile, no good 7 invalid, useless 8 bootless, impotent 9 fruitless, worthless 11 ineffective, ineffectual 12 unproductive, unsuccessful

unavoidable 4 sure 5 fated, fixed 7 certain 9 necessary, requisite 10 compulsory, imperative, inevitable, obligatory 11 inescapable 13 unpreventable 14 uncontrollable

unaware 4 heedless, ignorant, unwarned 9 in the dark, unalerted, unknowing, unmindful 10 unapprised 11 incognizant, unconscious 12 off one's guard, unacquainted, unsuspecting 13 unenlightened

unawares 8 abruptly, by chance, suddenly 9 by mistake 10 by accident, by surprise, mistakenly 11 unknowingly, unwittingly 12 accidentally, out of nowhere, unexpectedly, unthinkingly 13 inadvertently, involuntarily, unconsciously 14 without warning 15 unintentionally 16 like a thunderbolt 20 like a bolt from the blue, like a thief in the night

unbalanced 3 mad 4 daft, loco 5 batty, nutty, wacky 6 crazed, uneven, warped 7 bonkers, cracked, leaning, unequal, unglued, unsound 8 demented, deranged, lopsided, unhinged, unpoised, unstable,

unsteady 9 disturbed, illogical, psychotic, unsettled 10 irrational, unadjusted 11 not all there 12 psychopathic

unbearable 11 intolerable, unendurable, unthinkable 12 inadmissible, insufferable, unacceptable 13 insupportable

unbecoming 4 ugly 6 homely, vulgar 8 improper, unfitted, unseemly, unsuited 9 offensive, tasteless, unsightly 10 indecorous, unsuitable 11 unappealing, unbefitting 12 unattractive 13 inappropriate

unbelief 5 doubt 7 dubiety 9 disbelief 10 skepticism 11 incredulity 12 doubtfulness

unbelievable 5 false 6 absurd, insane 7 amazing, asinine, idiotic 10 astounding, farfetched, incredible, irrational, remarkable, ridiculous 11 astonishing 12 preposterous, unimaginable, unreasonable 13 hard to swallow

unbeliever 7 atheist, heathen infidel, skeptic 8 apostate 10 godless one 11 disbeliever, nonbeliever

unbelieving 7 dubious 8 doubting 9 quizzical, skeptical 10 suspicious 11 distrustful, incredulous, questioning, unconvinced 12 disbelieving, nonbelieving

unbend 5 relax 6 relent, unflex 10 straighten 12 straighten up 13 straighten out

unbending 4 firm 5 rigid, stiff, tough 6 severe, strict 8 stubborn 9 obstinate 10 inflexible, stone-faced, unyielding 11 hard as nails 14 uncompromising

unbent 5 erect 7 relaxed, unbowed, upright, yielded 8 relented, straight, uncurved, unflexed 9 unstooped 12 straightened

unbiased 4 fair, just 7 liberal, neutral 8 detached, tolerant 9 impartial, unbigoted 10 fair-minded, open-minded, undogmatic 11 broad-minded 12 uninfluenced, unprejudiced 13 disinterested, dispassionate

unbigoted 8 tolerant, unbiased 10 open-minded 11 broad-minded 12 unprejudiced

unbind 4 free, undo 5 loose, untie 6 detach, loosen, ungird 7 deliver, release, undress 9 let loose, unfasten

unblamable 5 clear 8 innocent 9 blameless, guiltless, not guilty 10 inculpable, not at fault 14 not responsible

unblemished 4 pure 7 perfect 8 flawless, spotless, unmarred, unsoiled 9 unsullied 10 immaculate, unvitiated 11 white as snow 13 unadulterated 14 uncontaminated 15 clean as a whistle

unblock 4 free, open 5 unbar, unjam 6 unclog, unstop

unborn 5 fetal, later 6 coming, future, to come 7 in utero 9 embryonic 10 subsequent, succeeding 11 prospective

unbosom oneself 7 confess, confide, lay bare 15 unburden oneself

unbound 4 free 5 freed, loose 6 loosed, untied 8 detached, let loose, loosened, released 10 unconfined, unfastened 12 unrestrained

unbounded 8 absolute 9 boundless, unbridled, unlimited 12 uncontrolled, unrestrained, unrestricted 13 unconditional, unconstrained

unbreakable 5 tough 6 strong

unbroken 5 whole 6 entire, intact 7 endless 8 complete 9 ceaseless, continual, incessant, uncracked, undivided, unsmashed 10 continuous, sequential, successive, unruptured 11 consecutive, progressive, unremitting, unshattered 12 undiminished 13 uninterrupted

unbuckle 4 undo 6 loosen 7 release, unhitch, unstrap 8 uncouple, unfasten

unburden 4 free 6 reveal 7 confess, confide, relieve, unbosom 8 disclose 9 disburden 10 unencumber 11 disencumber 15 get off one's chest 18 get out of one's system

uncalculated 9 unplanned 10 accidental, unintended 11 inadvertent 14 unpremeditated

uncalled-for 6 wanton 7 unasked 8 needless, unneeded, unsought, unwanted 9 redundant, uninvited 10 gratuitous, unprompted 11 unjustified, unnecessary, unsolicited 12 nonessential 14 supererogatory

uncanny 5 eerie, weird 6 spooky 7 curious, strange 8 inspired 9 fantastic, intuitive, marvelous, unearthly, unheard-of, unnatural 10 incredible, mysterious, prodigious, remarkable, unexampled 11 astonishing, exceptional 12 unbelievable, unimaginable 13 extraordinary, uncomfortable

uncanonical 12 unauthorized, unscriptural

Uncas
    character in: 20 The Last of the Mohicans
    author: 6 Cooper

unceasing 7 endless, eternal 8 constant 9 continual, incessant, perpetual, sustained 10 continuous, persistent, without end

uncelebrated 6 unsung 7 obscure, unknown 9 anonymous 14 uncommemorated

unceremonious 4 curt, rude 5 hasty, rough 6 abrupt 7 brusque 8 informal 11 precipitate

uncertain 4 hazy 6 fitful, unsure 7 dubious, erratic, not sure, obscure, unclear 8 doubtful, hesitant, nebulous, not fixed, variable, wavering 9 debatable, undecided, unsettled 10 disputable, indefinite, indistinct, in question, irresolute, unresolved, up in the air 11 conjectural, fluctuating, not definite, speculative, unconfirmed, vacillating 12 not confident, questionable, undetermined 13 indeterminate, unpredictable

uncertainty 4 odds, risk 5 doubt 6 chance, gamble 8 quandary 9 ambiguity, confusion, hesitancy, vagueness 10 hesitation, indecision, perplexity, unsureness 11 ambivalence, vacillation 12 equivocation, irresolution, shilly-shally 14 indefiniteness

unchain 4 free 7 release, set free 8 liberate, unfetter 9 unshackle

unchangeable 5 rigid 6 stable 7 uniform 8 stubborn 9 immutable, obstinate, permanent 10 inflexible, invariable 11 unalterable 12 intransigent

unchanging 4 fast, firm 5 fixed 6 stable, static 7 abiding, durable, lasting 8 constant 9 immutable, permanent, steadfast 10 monotonous 11 everlasting 12 indissoluble

unchaperoned 10 unattended, unescorted 12 unsupervised 13 unaccompanied

uncharacteristic 8 atypical 12 out of keeping 16 unrepresentative

uncharitable 5 tight 6 stingy, unkind 7 miserly 9 illiberal, niggardly, unfeeling 10 unfriendly, ungenerous, ungracious 11 closefisted, insensitive, tightfisted 12 parsimonious 13 unsympathetic 15 uncompassionate

unchaste 4 lewd 5 loose 6 erotic, impure 7 corrupt, immoral 8 immodest 9 abandoned, debauched 10 dishonored

unchecked 4 free 5 loose 6 unruly 7 liberal, rampant 8 reinless, unreined 9 out of hand, unbridled, unmuzzled 10 unhindered 12 out of control, unrestrained, unsuppressed

uncivil 4 curt, rude 5 blunt, surly 6 abrupt, gauche 7 boorish, brusque 8 impolite 10 ungracious 11 ill-mannered 12 disagreeable, discourteous

uncivilized 4 rude 6 savage, vulgar 7 boorish, brutish, ill-bred, uncouth, untamed 8 barbaric, churlish 9 barbarous, obnoxious, ungenteel 10 uncultured, unpolished 12 uncultivated

unclad 4 bare, nude 5 naked 7 exposed, unrobed 8 disrobed, in the raw, starkers, stripped 9 in the nude, unclothed, uncovered, undressed 10 stark-naked 15 in the altogether

unclean 4 evil, foul, tref, vile 5 dirty, dusty, grimy, messy, muddy, sooty 6 filthy, impure, soiled 7 defiled, immoral, obscene, smutted, stained 8 polluted, unchaste 9 blemished 10 besmirched

unclear 3 dim 4 hazy 5 blear, faint, foggy, fuzzy, misty, vague 6 bleary, cloudy, vapory 7 clouded, obscure, shadowy 8 shrouded, vaporous 9 ambiguous, uncertain 10 indefinite, indistinct

Uncle Remus
   author: 18 Joel Chandler Harris

Uncle Tom's Cabin
   author: 19 Harriet Beecher Stowe
   character: 5 Eliza, Topsy 10 Eva St Clare 11 Simon Legree

Uncle Vanya
   author: 12 Anton Chekhov
   character: 6 Marina 12 Mihail Astrov 13 Ivan Voynitsky (Uncle Vanya) 14 Marya Voynitsky 15 Sonya Andreyevna 16 Yelena Andreyevna 19 Alexandr Serebryakov

unclose 4 open 6 reveal, unclog, unfold, unshut, unstop, unwrap 7 unblock
   poetic: 3 ope

unclothed 4 bare, nude 5 naked 6 unclad 7 exposed, unrobed 8 stripped 9 in the nude, uncovered, undressed

unclouded 5 clear, light, sunny 6 bright, serene 10 unobscured

uncollected 4 owed 5 owing, upset 6 shaken 8 agitated, troubled 9 disturbed, perturbed 11 discomposed, outstanding

uncolored 4 bald, bare, true 5 plain, stark 6 simple 9 unadorned 11 unvarnished 12 unelaborated 13 unembellished 15 straightforward

uncombed 5 messy 6 blowsy, frowzy, matted, mussed, untidy 7 ruffled, rumpled, snarled, tangled, tousled, unkempt 11 disarranged

uncomfortable 4 edgy 5 tense, upset 6 on edge, uneasy 7 awkward, keyed up, nervous, painful 8 confused, strained, troubled 9 ill at ease 10 bothersome, disquieted, irritating, out of place 11 discomfited, discomposed, distressful 13 on tenterhooks

uncommitted 9 unpledged 11 undedicated

uncommon 4 rare 5 novel 6 scarce, unique 7 bizarre, curious, notable, supreme, unusual 8 peculiar, peerless, superior 9 matchless, unmatched 10 infrequent, remarkable, unexcelled, unfamiliar 11 exceptional, outstanding, superlative 12 incomparable, unparalleled 13 extraordinary 14 unconventional 15 once in a lifetime 16 few and far between

uncommunicative 3 mum, shy 4 dumb, mute 5 quiet 6 silent 8 reserved, reticent, retiring, taciturn 9 secretive, withdrawn 10 speechless, tongue-tied, unsociable 11 untalkative 12 close-mouthed, inexpressive

uncomplicated 4 easy 5 clear, plain 6 simple 10 uninvolved

uncomplimentary 8 critical, derisive, negative 9 insulting 10 unadmiring 11 disparaging 12 disapproving, unflattering

uncompromising 4 firm 5 rigid, stiff 6 strict 8 exacting, hardline, obdurate 9 immovable, unbending, unvarying 10 inexorable, inflexible, scrupulous, unyielding 11 unrelenting

unconcealed 4 bald, bare, open 5 overt 6 in view 7 exposed, in sight, obvious, visible 8 apparent, manifest, revealed 9 uncovered 11 discernible, perceivable, perceptible 12 in plain sight, out in the open

unconcentrated 4 weak 7 diffuse, diluted, thinned 9 dispersed, scattered, spread out 11 watered down

unconcern 10 dispassion 11 insouciance, nonchalance 12 indifference

unconcerned 4 cold 5 aloof 6 serene 7 distant, unaware, unmoved 8 composed, uncaring 9 apathetic, oblivious, unfeeling, unmindful 10 impervious, nonchalant, uninvolved, untroubled 11 indifferent, insensitive, passionless, unperturbed 12 unresponsive 13 unsympathetic

unconditional 5 utter 6 entire 8 absolute, complete, outright 9 downright, unlimited 10 conclusive 11 categorical, unqualified 12 unrestricted 13 thoroughgoing

Unconditional Surrender
author: 11 Evelyn Waugh

unconfident 3 shy 5 timid 7 bashful 8 reticent, retiring, timorous 9 diffident, shrinking, uncertain

unconfirmed 7 dubious 8 unproved 10 unapproved, unverified 11 unvalidated 12 questionable 14 uncorroborated 15 unsubstantiated

unconformity 7 anomaly 9 deviation 10 aberration, divergence 11 abnormality, peculiarity 12 eccentricity, idiosyncrasy, irregularity 13 nonconformity

uncongenial 9 ill-suited, unamiable 10 dissimilar, unfriendly, unpleasant 12 disagreeable, incompatible 13 unsympathetic

unconnected 7 severed 8 detached, discrete, separate 9 uncoupled, unhitched, unrelated 12 disconnected

unconquerable 6 innate 8 ingrained 10 inveterate, invincible, unbeatable 12 impenetrable, invulnerable, undefeatable 14 insurmountable, unvanquishable

unconscionable 7 extreme 9 excessive 10 immoderate, inordinate, outrageous 11 inexcusable, unjustified, unwarranted 12 indefensible, preposterous, unforgivable, unpardonable, unreasonable 13 unjustifiable

unconscious 3 out 6 latent 7 in a coma, out cold 8 comatose, in a faint 9 insensate, senseless, unknowing, unmindful 10 suppressed, unrealized 11 incognizant 12 unsuspecting 14 dead to the world

unconstitutional 7 illegal 8 unlawful 12 unauthorized

unconstrained 4 bold, easy 7 natural, relaxed 8 unforced 9 abandoned 10 unaffected 11 spontaneous, uninhibited
French: 6 degage

unconstraint 4 ease 7 abandon 8 boldness, free will, openness 9 frankness 11 naturalness, spontaneity

uncontrollable 6 unruly 7 wayward 12 ungovernable, unmanageable

uncontrolled 4 free, wild 8 absolute 9 abandoned, unlimited 10 ungoverned 12 unrestrained

unconventional 3 odd 4 rare 5 crazy, kinky, nutty, queer, wacky, weird 6 far-out, quaint, unique 7 bizarre, curious, offbeat, strange, unusual 8 aberrant, atypical, bohemian, freakish, original, peculiar, singular, uncommon 9 different, eccentric, fantastic, irregular 10 newfangled, outlandish, unorthodox 11 exceptional 12 unaccustomed 13 extraordinary, idiosyncratic, nonconforming, nonconformist 15 individualistic

unconvinced 7 dubious 8 doubtful 9 skeptical, uncertain, unsettled

unconvincing 5 false, fishy 7 dubious, suspect 10 suspicious 11 implausible 12 questionable, unbelievable

uncooked
French: 9 au naturel

uncooperative 6 ornery 7 selfish 8 perverse, stubborn 9 difficult, unhelpful, unwilling 11 intractable 12 intransigent

uncoordinated 6 clumsy 7 awkward 8 ungainly 9 graceless

uncouple 4 undo 6 detach, loosen, unhook 7 release, unhitch 8 unbuckle

uncoupled 8 detached, loosened 9 separated, unhitched 10 disengaged 11 unconnected 12 disconnected

uncourageous 6 timid 8 cowardly, timorous 9 dastardly, shrinking 13 pusillanimous

uncourtly 7 ill-bred, uncivil, uncouth 9 ungallant 10 ill-behaved, ungracious, unmannerly 11 uncourteous 12 discourteous 13 ungentlemanly

uncouth 4 rude 5 crass, crude, gross, rough 6 callow, coarse 7 boorish, brutish, ill-bred, loutish, uncivil 8 barbaric, churlish, impolite 9 unrefined 10 indelicate, uncultured, unmannerly 11 ill-mannered, uncivilized 12 uncultivated

uncover 4 bare, undo 5 dig up, strip 6 denude, dig out, expose, reveal, unmask, unveil, unwrap 7 disrobe, lay bare, uncloak, undrape, undress, unearth 8 disclose, unclothe 9 make known, unsheathe 11 make visible 12 bring to light

uncovered 4 bare 5 bared, dug up, naked 7 exposed, noticed 8 detected, revealed 9 disclosed, made known 10 discovered 13 brought to view 14 brought to light

uncovering 8 exposure 9 divulging, unmasking 10 disclosure, divulgence, laying open, revelation 15 bringing to light 20 bringing out in the open

uncritical 4 dull, dumb 6 casual, obtuse, stupid 7 inexact, offhand, shallow 8 careless, ignorant, slipshod 9 imprecise, untutored 10 inaccurate, uneducated, unschooled, unthinking 11 perfunctory, superficial 12 unreflecting 16 undiscriminating

unctuous 4 oily, smug 6 smarmy 7 fawning, honeyed, servile 8 slippery, too suave 9 pietistic, too smooth 10 flattering, obsequious 11 sycophantic 12 honey-tongued, ingratiating 13 sanctimonious, self-righteous

uncultivated 3 raw 4 wild 7 uncouth 8 unfarmed, unplowed, untilled 9 unrefined 10 unimproved 11 undeveloped

uncultivated land
god of: 8 Silvanus, Sylvanus

uncultured 5 crass 6 coarse, common, vulgar 7 low-bred 9 inelegant, unrefined 10 unpolished 12 uncultivated

uncustomary 4 rare 6 unique 7 amazing, unusual 8 singular, uncommon, unwonted 9 unheard-of 10 incredible, unexpected 11 astonishing, exceptional 12 unaccustomed, unbelievable 13 extraordinary, unanticipated

undaunted 5 brave 6 gritty, heroic, plucky 7 unfazed, valiant 8 fearless, intrepid, resolute, stalwart, valorous 9 not put off 10 courageous, undismayed 11 indomitable, unflinching, unperturbed, unshrinking 12 stouthearted 13 undiscouraged

undeceive 8 disabuse 10 disenchant 11 disenthrall, disillusion 12 open one's eyes 13 break the spell 15 burst one's bubble 19 bring one down to earth 20 shatter one's illusions

undecided 4 open 5 vague 6 unsure 7 dubious, pending 8 not final, wavering 9 tentative, uncertain, unsettled 10 indecisive, indefinite, in abeyance, in a dilemma, irresolute, of two minds, open-minded, unresolved, up in the air 11 fluctuating, vacillating 12 undetermined, unformulated 16 hemming and hawing 17 blowing hot and cold 20 going around in circles

undecorated 4 bare 5 blank, plain, stark 6 simple 7 austere 9 unadorned 13 unembellished

undedicated 11 indifferent, uncommitted

undefiled 4 pure 5 clean 6 chaste, intact, virgin 7 natural 8 innocent, spotless 9 stainless, unsullied 10 unpolluted

undemanding 4 easy 6 low-key, simple 7 patient, relaxed 9 easygoing 10 submissive 12 easy to please, laissez-faire 14 live-and-let-live

undemonstrative 3 shy 4 cold 5 aloof 7 distant, stoical 8 reserved 9 impassive 11 unemotional 12 inexpressive, unresponsive 14 self-controlled

undeniable 4 sure 6 patent, proven 7 certain, obvious 8 decisive, manifest 10 conclusive 11 established, indubitable, irrefutable 12 beyond a doubt, demonstrable, indisputable 13 incontestable 14 unquestionable 16 incontrovertible

undeniably 6 surely 9 certainly 10 decisively, definitely 11 irrefutably 12 conclusively, demonstrably, indisputably 13 incontestably 14 beyond question, unquestionably 16 incontrovertibly

undependable 6 fickle 7 erratic, flighty 8 unstable, variable, wavering 10 capricious, changeable, inconstant, unreliable 13 irresponsible, unpredictable, untrustworthy

under 3 sub 5 below, lower, neath, short 7 beneath 8 inferior, less than 9 because of 11 subordinate

undercover 3 sly 6 covert, hidden, secret 7 furtive, sub rosa 8 hush-hush, stealthy 9 concealed, disguised, incognito 10 unrevealed 11 clandestine, undisclosed 12 confidential 13 surreptitious
French: 8 a couvert

undercurrent 4 aura, hint, mood 5 sense, tinge, vibes 7 quality, riptide 8 undertow 9 undertone 10 atmosphere, intimation, suggestion, vibrations 12 crosscurrent

undercut 9 discredit, undermine, undersell 10 compromise

underestimate 7 dismiss, put down 8 belittle, minimize, misjudge 9 deprecate, discredit, disparage, disregard, sell short, underrate, undersell 10 depreciate, undervalue 11 detract from 12 miscalculate

undergarment 3 bra 4 BVDs, slip 5 pants, shift, teddy 6 corset, girdle, shorts 7 chemise, panties 8 bloomers, camisole, knickers, lingerie, skivvies 9 brassiere, petticoat, union suit 12 jockey shorts

undergo 5 brave, stand 6 endure, suffer 7 sustain, weather 8 submit to 9 encounter, go through, withstand 10 experience

undergraduate 4 coed, soph 5 frosh, plebe 6 junior, senior 7 scholar, student 8 freshman 9 sophomore, undegreed 10 degreeless, nondegreed 13 underclassman, upperclassman

underground 6 buried, covert, secret 7 sub-rosa 10 undercover 11 belowground, clandestine 12 subterranean 13 surreptitious 15 below the surface

underground chamber 4 tomb 5 crypt, vault 6 cellar 8 catacomb 9 sepulcher

underhand, underhanded 6 covert, crafty, sneaky, tricky 7 corrupt, crooked, cunning, devious, evasive, furtive, illegal 8 sneaking, stealthy 9 conniving, dishonest, unethical 10 fraudulent 12 unprincipled, unscrupulous 13 surreptitious

underhandedness 4 guile 6 deceit 7 slyness 8 trickery 9 chicanery, deception, duplicity 10 sneakiness, trickiness 13 secretiveness

underline 6 accent, stress 7 dwell on, point up 9 emphasize, press home 10 accentuate, underscore 15 bring into relief

underling 4 serf 6 flunky, lackey, menial, minion, thrall, vassal 7 servant, subject 8 employee, hireling, inferior 9 attendant, hired hand 11 subordinate

underlying 5 basic 6 covert 7 beneath, radical 8 implicit 9 elemental, essential 10 subtending 11 fundamental

undermine 4 foil, ruin 5 erode 6 injure, riddle, scotch, thwart, weaken 7 cripple, destroy, subvert, torpedo 8 sabotage 9 eat away at, frustrate, hamstring 10 neutralize 11 burrow under, tunnel under

underneath 5 below, lower 6 bottom, hidden 9 disguised, subject to 14 misrepresented

undernourished 8 starving, underfed 12 malnourished

under obligation 5 bound 6 liable 7 obliged 8 beholden, indebted 9 obligated 10 answerable, in one's debt 11 accountable, responsible

underpart 4 sole 5 belly, tails 6 bottom 9 lower side, underside

underpin 4 bear 7 bolster, support 10 strengthen 12 substantiate

underpinning 4 base 5 basic 6 ground 7 support 9 essential 10 foundation, groundwork 11 fundamental 12 substructure

underplay 8 play down 11 deemphasize

underprivileged 4 poor 5 needy 6 in need 7 hapless, unlucky 8 badly-off, deprived, ill-fated, indigent 9 destitute, penniless, penurious 10 ill-starred, pauperized 11 handicapped, unfortunate 12 impoverished 13 disadvantaged 22 in adverse circumstances

underrate 6 slight 8 belittle, derogate, minimize 9 denigrate, deprecate, disparage 10 depreciate, undervalue 13 underestimate

underscore 4 mark 6 accent, deepen, play up, stress 7 feature, point up 8 heighten 9 emphasize, intensify, press home, underline 10 accentuate 15 draw attention to

underscoring 6 stress 8 emphasis 11 underlining

underside 4 back, sole 5 belly, tails 6 bottom 7 reverse 9 lower side, underpart

undersized 4 tiny 5 elfin, short, small 6 little, petite, slight 7 stunted 8 dwarfish 10 diminutive 11 lilliputian

underskirt 4 slip 7 pannier 9 crinoline, hoopskirt, petticoat

understand 3 dig, get, see 4 hear, know, read, take 5 grasp, learn 6 absorb, accept, assume, can see, fathom, gather, take it 7 be aware, discern, make out, presume, realize 8 conclude, perceive 9 apprehend, interpret, recognize 10 appreciate, comprehend, take to mean 14 sympathize with, take for granted

understandable 8 apparent 12 recognizable, unmistakable 14 comprehensible

understanding 4 pact 5 grasp 7 empathy, insight, knowing 8 sympathy, tolerant 9 agreement, awareness, intuition, knowledge, sensitive 10 cognizance, compassion, compromise, discerning, perception, perceptive, responsive 11 concordance, sensitivity, sympathetic 12 appreciation, appreciative, apprehension 13 compassionate, comprehension 17 meeting of the minds

understate 8 minimize 11 deemphasize

understated 9 minimized 10 restrained 12 conservative, deemphasized

understatement 7 litotes 10 minimizing 20 conservative estimate

understudy 3 sub 6 backup, double, fill-in, relief 7 stand-by, stand-in 9 alternate, surrogate 10 substitute 11 pinch hitter; replacement

undertake 3 try 5 begin, essay, start 6 assume, strive, tackle, take on 7 attempt 8 commence, embark on, endeavor, set about, shoulder 9 agree to do, enter upon 11 promise to do 13 get involved in

undertaking 3 job 4 task 6 effort 7 concern, project, pursuit, venture 8 endeavor 10 commitment, enterprise

Under the Greenwood Tree
   author: 11 Thomas Hardy

under the influence 5 drunk 6 sodden, soused, wasted, zapped, zonked 7 smashed 8 besotted 9 plastered 10 inebriated 11 intoxicated 20 three sheets to the wind

under the weather 3 bad, ill 4 sick 6 ailing, sickly, unwell 9 unhealthy 10 indisposed

undertone 4 aura, hint, mood 5 scent, sense, tinge, trace 6 flavor, mumble, murmur, nuance 7 feeling, inkling, low tone, quality, whisper 8 coloring 10 atmosphere, intimation, suggestion 11 connotation, implication 12 subdued voice, undercurrent

undervalue 6 slight 8 belittle, derogate 9 discredit, disparage, underrate 10 depreciate 13 underestimate

underwear 3 bra 4 BVDs, slip 5 pants, teddy 6 briefs, corset, girdle, shorts 7 chemise, panties 8 bloomers, camisole, knickers, lingerie, skivvies 9 brassiere, petticoat, union suit 12 jockey shorts, smallclothes 14 unmentionables

underweight 4 bony, lank 5 gaunt, lanky 6 skinny 7 scrawny, spindly 8 skeletal, underfed 9 emaciated 12 skin-and-bones 13 hollow-cheeked 14 spindle-shanked, undernourished

underworld 4 Hell 5 Hades, limbo 6 the mob 8 mobsters, the Mafia 9 criminals, gangsters, purgatory 10 Cosa Nostra 11 shades below 12 the syndicate 13 bottomless pit, nether regions 14 organized crime 15 criminal element, infernal regions 16 abode of the damned
   god of: 3 Dis 5 Hades, Orcus, Pluto 8 Dis Pater

under wraps 6 hidden, secret 9 concealed 10 suppressed, under cover

underwrite 3 aid 4 back 7 approve, endorse, finance, sponsor, support, warrant 8 invest in, sanction, validate 9 guarantee, subsidize 11 countersign

underwriter 5 angel 6 backer, patron 7 sponsor 8 investor 9 financier, guarantor

undeserving 3 bad 8 inferior, unworthy

undesirable 5 unfit 8 disliked, improper, unbidden, unsavory, unseemly, unwanted, unworthy 9 offensive, unpopular 10 unbecoming, uninviting, unsuitable, unwelcomed 11 distasteful, unbefitting, unwished-for 12 disagreeable, inadmissible, unacceptable, unattractive 13 inappropriate, objectionable 14 unsatisfactory

undetectable 12 unnoticeable, unobservable 13 imperceptible, unsubstantial

undetermined 6 chance 7 unfixed, unknown 8 unproved, unproven 9 uncertain, undecided 10 indefinite, irresolute 13 indeterminate, unascertained

undeveloped 3 raw 5 crude, green 6 callow, unripe 8 immature, inchoate, unformed 9 embryonic, half-baked 10 unfinished 11 rudimentary, unexploited 12 uncultivated

undignified 3 low 7 boorish 8 improper, shameful, unseemly, unworthy 9 degrading, inelegant, tasteless, unrefined 10 beneath one, indecorous, indelicate, in bad taste, unbecoming, unladylike, unsuitable 11 unbefitting 13 discreditable, inappropri-

ate, ungentlemanly 18 beneath one's dignity
Latin: 8 infra dig 15 infra dignitatem
undiluted 4 neat, pure 5 sheer 7 unmixed 8 straight 11 unfortified 12 full-strength 13 unadulterated
Undine
form: 6 spirit
location: 5 water
sex: 6 female
undiscerning 11 insensitive 12 unperceptive 14 indiscriminate
undisciplined 4 wild 6 fickle, fitful 7 erratic, wayward, willful 8 unsteady, untaught 9 mercurial, untrained, untutored 10 capricious, changeable, inconstant, uneducated, unfinished, unreliable, unschooled 11 unpracticed 12 obstreperous, uncontrolled, undependable, unrestrained 13 unpredictable
undisclosed 6 hidden, secret 7 private 9 concealed 10 unrevealed 12 confidential
undisguised 4 open 5 clear, utter 7 evident, obvious 8 complete, distinct, manifest, unhidden 9 out-and-out 10 plain as day, pronounced, unreserved 11 unconcealed 12 unmistakable, wholehearted 13 thoroughgoing 24 plain as the nose on one's face
undismayed 7 uncowed 8 unafraid, unscared 9 confident, unabashed, unalarmed, undaunted 12 unfrightened 13 undiscouraged, unintimidated
undisputed 4 sure 7 certain, granted 8 accepted 9 undoubted 10 conclusive, undeniable 11 beyond doubt, indubitable, irrefutable, past dispute, uncontested 12 acknowledged, indisputable, unchallenged, unquestioned 13 a matter of fact, incontestable 14 beyond question, freely admitted, unquestionable 15 without question 16 incontrovertible
undistinguished 5 plain, usual 6 common 7 prosaic 8 everyday, mediocre, ordinary 10 pedestrian, unexciting 11 commonplace 12 run-of-the-mill, unremarkable 13 unexceptional 18 nothing to rave about
undistracted 4 calm 6 serene, stolid 7 unfazed 9 impassive, unruffled 10 untroubled 11 undisturbed
undisturbed 4 calm, cool 5 quiet 6 placid, serene, steady 7 equable, unmoved 8 composed, peaceful, tranquil 9 collected, inviolate, unexcited, unruffled, untouched 10 of solitude, unagitated, unbothered, untroubled 11 left in order, unperturbed 13 imperturbable, self-possessed, uninterrupted
undivided 5 solid, whole 6 entire, united 7 unified, unsplit 8 complete 9 of one mind, unanimous 10 not divided, unstinting 12 wholehearted
undo 3 end 4 free, open, ruin, void 5 annul, erase, loose, quash, untie 6 cancel, defeat, loosen, offset, repair, unbind, unfold, unhook, unknot, unlace, unlock, unwrap 7 destroy, nullify, rectify, reverse, subvert,

unchain, unravel, wipe out 8 demolish, overturn, unbutton, unfasten 9 disengage, eliminate, make up for, undermine 10 counteract, invalidate, neutralize 11 disentangle 13 compensate for 14 counterbalance
undogmatic 7 liberal 8 flexible, tolerant 10 open-minded 11 broad-minded
undoing 4 doom, jinx, ruin 5 upset 6 defeat 7 erasure, nemesis 8 collapse, downfall, negation, reversal, weakness 9 annulment, breakdown, overthrow, ruination, thwarting, wiping out 11 cause of ruin, destruction 12 Achilles' heel, cancellation, invalidation 13 counteraction, nullification 14 neutralization
undomesticated 4 wild 5 feral 6 ferine, savage 7 untamed 8 barbaric 9 barbarous 11 uncivilized
undone 6 ruined 9 come apart, destroyed 10 incomplete, unfastened 12 not completed
undoubted 4 sure 5 utter 7 certain 8 absolute, complete, definite, positive 11 indubitable, unequivocal 12 indisputable 13 unimpeachable 14 unquestionable
undoubtedly 6 surely 7 no doubt 9 assuredly, certainly, decidedly, doubtless 10 absolutely, definitely, positively, undeniably 11 indubitably 12 beyond a doubt, unmistakably, without doubt 13 unequivocally 14 beyond question, unquestionably 15 without question
undress 5 strip 6 nudity 7 disrobe, uncover, undrape 8 disarray, unclothe 9 nakedness 10 dishabille 18 take off one's clothes
undressed 4 bare, nude 5 naked 6 unclad 7 denuded, exposed, unrobed 8 disrobed, stripped, undraped 9 unclothed, uncovered
Undset, Sigrid
author of: 6 The Axe 20 Kristin Lavransdatter, The Master of Hestviken
undue 6 unmeet 8 impolite, improper, needless, overmuch, too great, unseemly, unworthy 9 excessive, tasteless 10 illadvised, indiscreet, in bad taste, inordinate, not fitting, unbecoming, unsuitable 11 superfluous, uncalled-for, unjustified, unnecessary, unwarranted 13 inappropriate, objectionable
undulate 4 coil 5 slink, weave 9 fluctuate 11 rise and fall
undulating 4 wavy 5 bumpy 6 uneven
undulation 7 coiling 8 slinking, twisting 10 contortion 11 convolution 16 rising and falling
undutiful 6 remiss 8 disloyal 11 disobedient
undying 6 steady 7 abiding, endless, eternal, lasting 8 constant, enduring, immortal, unending, unfading, untiring 9 continual, deathless, incessant, perennial, permanent, perpetual, unceasing 10 continuing 11 everlasting, never-ending, unfaltering, unrelenting, unremitting 12 imperishable,

never-failing, undiminished 13 uninterrupted 14 indestructible

unearth 4 find, show 5 dig up 6 dig out, exhume, expose, reveal 7 display, divulge, exhibit, root out, uncover 8 disclose, discover, disinter, dredge up, excavate 9 disentomb, ferret out 10 come across, come up with 12 bring to light

unearthly 5 awful, eerie, weird 6 absurd 7 extreme, ghostly, phantom, strange, uncanny, ungodly, unusual 8 abnormal, ethereal, spectral, terrible 10 horrendous, unpleasant 11 disembodied, incorporeal, unspeakable 12 disagreeable, extramundane, supernatural 13 extraordinary, preternatural

unease 5 worry 7 tension 8 disquiet 9 misgiving 10 discomfort, uneasiness 11 disquietude 12 apprehension

uneasiness 5 dread 6 dismay 7 anxiety 9 agitation, misgiving 10 discomfort, foreboding 11 disquietude, distraction, nervousness 12 apprehension, discomfiture, discomposure, perturbation 16 apprehensiveness

uneasy 4 edgy 5 nervy, tense, upset 6 on edge, queasy, unsure 7 awkward, irksome, nervous, uptight, worried 8 strained, troubled, worrying 9 disturbed, ill at ease, perturbed, upsetting 10 bothersome, disquieted, disturbing, unpleasant 11 constrained, disquieting 12 apprehensive 13 uncomfortable

uneatable 8 inedible 11 not fit to eat

uneconomical 4 dear 6 costly 8 wasteful 9 expensive 10 exorbitant, high-priced, immoderate, overpriced 11 extravagant 12 unreasonable

uneducated 8 ignorant, untaught 9 unlearned, untrained, untutored 10 illiterate, uncultured, unlettered, unschooled 12 uncultivated, uninstructed 13 unenlightened

unelaborated 4 bald, bare 5 plain, stark 6 simple 9 essential, unadorned, uncolored 11 fundamental, unvarnished 13 unembellished 15 straightforward

unembellished 4 bald, bare 5 naked, plain, stark 7 austere 9 unadorned 11 undecorated 12 unornamented

unemotional 4 cold, cool 6 formal, remote 7 distant 8 lukewarm, reserved 9 apathetic, impassive, unfeeling 11 indifferent, passionless, unconcerned 12 unresponsive 15 undemonstrative

unemployed 4 axed, idle 5 fired 6 canned, sacked, unused 7 bounced, jobless, laid-off 8 workless 9 at leisure, at liberty, booted-out, dismissed, on the dole, on welfare, out of a job, out of work 10 discharged, unoccupied 11 pink-slipped

unencumbered 4 free 6 vacant 7 unladen 8 expedite 10 unburdened, unhindered 13 unhandicapped

unending 6 steady 7 endless, eternal, lasting 8 constant, enduring 9 continual, incessant, perennial, permanent, perpetual, unceasing 10 continuous, unwavering 11

everlasting, never-ending, unremitting 12 undiminished 13 uninterrupted

unendurable 7 racking 9 agonizing, torturous 10 tormenting, unbearable 11 intolerable 12 excruciating, insufferable

unenlightened 8 ignorant 9 in the dark, unlearned 10 uneducated, uninformed 11 uninitiated 12 unabstructed

unenterprising 4 lazy 11 unambitious 12 unaggressive

unenthusiastic 8 lukewarm 10 unspirited 11 halfhearted, indifferent 13 unimpassioned

unequal 6 biased, uneven, unfair, unjust, unlike 7 bigoted, partial 9 different, disparate, unmatched 10 dissimilar, not uniform, prejudiced 11 inequitable

unequaled 7 supreme 8 peerless 9 matchless, paramount, unmatched, unrivaled 10 consummate, unexcelled 11 ne plus ultra, unsurpassed 12 incomparable, second to none, unapproached, unparalleled 13 beyond compare 16 beyond comparison

unequivocable 4 bald 5 utter 8 outright 9 out-and-out 11 categorical, unqualified

unequivocal 5 clear, final 7 certain 8 absolute, clear-cut, decisive, definite, emphatic 11 unambiguous 12 indisputable 13 incontestable 16 incontrovertible

unequivocally 7 clearly 9 certainly, downright 10 completely, decisively, definitely, thoroughly 12 emphatically, indisputably, unmistakably 13 incontestably 14 unquestionably, wholeheartedly 16 incontrovertibly

unerring 4 sure 7 certain, precise 8 constant, faithful, reliable 9 faultless, unfailing 10 infallible, unchanging

unessential 8 nonvital 9 accessory, extrinsic 10 disposable, expendable 11 dispensable, superfluous, unimportant, unnecessary 12 nonessential

unethical 5 dirty, shady, wrong 6 shoddy, unfair 7 devious 8 unworthy 9 dishonest, underhand 10 unladylike 12 dishonorable, disreputable, questionable, unprincipled 13 ungentlemanly 14 unconscionable

uneven 4 awry, bent 5 bumpy, lumpy, rough 6 angled, coarse, craggy, curved, jagged, tilted, unfair, unjust, unlike 7 crooked, not flat, slanted, sloping, unequal 8 lopsided, not level, not plumb, one-sided, unsmooth 9 different, disparate 10 dissimilar, ill-matched, unbalanced

unevenness 7 oddness 9 bumpiness, lumpiness, roughness 10 jaggedness, ruggedness 11 crookedness 12 irregularity 14 changeableness

uneventful 4 dull 5 quiet, usual 6 boring 7 average, humdrum, prosaic, routine, tedious 8 ordinary, standard, tiresome 10 monotonous 11 commonplace 12 conventional 13 insignificant, unexceptional, uninteresting

unexcelled 7 supreme 8 flawless, peerless, superior, unbeaten 9 faultless, matchless, unequaled, unmatched, unrivaled 10 consummate 11 unsurpassed 12 incomparable, second to none, transcendent, unapproached, unparalleled 13 beyond compare

unexceptional 5 usual 6 normal 7 mundane, typical 8 ordinary, standard 9 customary 12 conventional, run of the mill

unexcited 4 calm, cool 6 placid, serene 7 unmoved 8 composed, detached 9 collected, unruffled 11 undisturbed, unemotional 13 dispassionate, unimpassioned

unexciting 4 dull, flat 5 vapid 6 boring 7 insipid 10 lackluster

unexpected 6 sudden 9 startling, unplanned 10 accidental, surprising, undesigned, unforeseen, unintended 11 astonishing, unlooked-for, unpredicted 12 out of the blue 13 unanticipated, unintentional

unextinguished 5 alive 10 unquenched 12 still burning

unfaded 5 fresh 6 bright 8 undimmed 10 unwithered

unfailing 4 true 5 loyal 6 steady 7 endless 8 constant, enduring, faithful, reliable 9 continual 10 continuous, dependable, infallible, unchanging, unwavering 12 never-failing 13 inexhaustible

unfair 4 foul 5 dirty 6 biased, unjust 7 corrupt, crooked, partial, unequal 8 not right, onesided, partisan 9 dishonest, underhand, unethical 10 not cricket, prejudiced 11 inequitable 12 dishonorable, unprincipled, unreasonable, unscrupulous 14 unconscionable

unfaithful 5 false 6 faulty, untrue 7 inexact 8 disloyal, unchaste 9 deceitful, distorted, erroneous, faithless, imperfect 10 adulterous, inaccurate, inconstant, perfidious 11 not accurate, treacherous 12 falsehearted 13 untrustworthy

Unfaithfully Yours
director: 14 Preston Sturges
cast: 10 Rudy Vallee 11 Rex Harrison 12 Edgar Kennedy, Linda Darnell 15 Barbara Lawrence

unfaithfulness 7 falsity, perfidy 9 falseness, treachery 10 disloyalty, fickleness, infidelity 11 inconstancy 13 faithlessness 14 perfidiousness

unfaltering 4 firm, sure 6 steady 8 enduring, resolute 9 obstinate, steadfast, unfailing 10 dependable, persistent, undeviating, unswerving, unwavering 11 persevering 12 never-failing, wholehearted

unfamiliar 3 new 5 novel 6 exotic, unique 7 curious, foreign, strange, unknown, unusual 9 different 10 ignorant of, unversed in 11 a stranger to, little known, out-of-the-way, unexposed to, uninitiated, unskilled in 12 not well-known, unacquainted, unconversant 13 not acquainted, unpracticed in 14 unaccustomed to 15 inexperienced in, uninformed about 18 unenlightened about

unfamiliarity 9 ignorance 11 strangeness 12 inexperience 15 lack of knowledge

unfashionable 5 dated, dowdy, passe 6 frumpy, old-hat 8 outmoded 9 out-of-date, unstylish 12 old-fashioned

unfasten 4 undo 5 unpin, untie 6 detach, unbind, unbolt, unhook, unlace, unlash, unlink, unlock 7 unclose, unhitch, unlatch, unstick 8 unbutton, uncouple

unfastened 5 apart, undid 6 undone, untied 7 severed, unlaced, unstuck 8 detached, unhooked 9 unbuckled, uncoupled, unhitched 11 unconnected 12 disconnected

unfathomable 4 deep, vast 6 arcane, remote, subtle 7 complex, extreme, obscure 8 abstract, abstruse, esoteric, profound, puzzling 9 enigmatic 10 bottomless, perplexing 16 hard to understand, incomprehensible

unfavorable 3 bad 4 poor 7 adverse, unhappy 8 unsuited, untimely 9 ill-suited 10 ill-favored, regretable 11 inopportune, regrettable, unfortunate, unpromising 12 inauspicious, inconvenient, infelicitous, unpropitious, unseasonable 15 disadvantageous

unfeasible 10 impossible, infeasible, unsuitable, unworkable 11 impractical 12 unachievable 13 impracticable

unfeeling 4 cold 5 cruel 9 heartless 11 hardhearted, insensitive 13 unsympathetic

unfeigned 4 real, true 7 genuine, sincere 10 unaffected

unfetter 4 free 7 release, set free, unchain 8 liberate 9 unshackle

unfilled 4 open 5 blank, empty 6 hollow, vacant 7 drained 9 available 10 unoccupied

unfinished 5 crude, rough 6 undone 7 lacking, sketchy, wanting 8 immature 9 deficient, imperfect, unnatural, unpainted, unrefined, unstained 10 incomplete, unexecuted, unpolished 11 uncompleted, unfulfilled, unlacquered, unvarnished

unfit 4 sick, weak 5 frail 6 infirm, not fit, sickly 7 not up to, unequal, unready, unsound, useless 8 delicate, disabled, unsuited 9 incapable, not suited, unhealthy, unskilled, untrained 10 inadequate, ineligible, not equal to, unequipped, unprepared, unsuitable 11 debilitated, ill-equipped, incompetent, ineffective, inefficient, not designed, unqualified 12 ill-contrived, not cut out for 13 inappropriate, incapacitated

unflagging 4 firm 5 fixed 6 steady 7 staunch 8 constant, enduring, resolute, tireless, unshaken, untiring 9 steadfast, tenacious, undaunted 10 determined, persistent, relentless, undrooping, unswerving, unwavering, unyielding 11 indomitable, persevering, undeviating, unfaltering, unremitting 13 indefatigable 14 uncompromising

unflappable 4 calm, cool 6 placid, serene 8 composed 9 collected 10 cool-headed 11 unexcitable 13 imperturbable, self-possessed

unflinching 4 firm, game 6 gritty, plucky, steady, strong 7 staunch 8 fearless, resolute, stalwart, unshaken 9 steadfast, tenacious, unabashed, undaunted **10** persistent, unswerving, unwavering, unyielding **11** indomitable, unfaltering, unshrinking **12** unhesitating

unfold 4 bare, show, tell **6** open up, reveal, unfurl, unroll, unveil, unwrap **7** divulge, explain, expound, lay open, open out, present, recount, uncover **8** describe, disclose, set forth **9** elucidate, explicate, make known, spread out **10** stretch out

unfolding 4 rise **5** birth, start **9** beginning, evolution, inception, unfurling **10** revelation **11** development

unforced 4 easy **5** frank **6** candid, casual **7** natural, relaxed **8** informal **9** easygoing **10** unaffected **13** unconstrained

unforeseen 6 abrupt, sudden **8** surprise **9** unplanned **10** accidental, surprising, unexpected, unintended **11** unlooked-for, unpredicted **12** out of the blue **13** unanticipated

unforeseen danger 7 pitfall **8** exigency **9** emergency **11** contingency

unforgettable 7 notable **8** eventful, exciting **9** important, memorable, thrilling **10** noteworthy **11** significant

unfortunate 5 sorry **6** cursed, jinxed, woeful **7** hapless, unblest, unhappy, unlucky **8** ill-fated, ill-timed, luckless, untimely, wretched **10** disastrous, ill-advised, ill-starred **11** inopportune, regrettable, unfavorable **12** inauspicious, infelicitous, unpropitious, unprosperous, unsuccessful

unfounded 4 idle **5** false **6** untrue **8** baseless, spurious **9** erroneous **10** fabricated, groundless

unfrequented 5 empty **6** lonely **7** remote, uncouth **8** isolated, solitary **9** unvisited **11** out-of-the-way **16** off the beaten path

unfriendly 4 cold **5** aloof **6** at odds, chilly **7** distant, haughty, hostile, warlike **8** inimical, snobbish **9** on the outs, reclusive, withdrawn **10** ungracious, unsociable **11** belligerent, contentious, quarrelsome, uncongenial **12** antagonistic, disagreeable, disputatious, inhospitable **13** at loggerheads, at sword's point, unsympathetic

unfruitful 4 vain **6** barren, fallow, futile **7** useless, worn-out **8** infecund **9** fruitless **10** unavailing **11** purposeless, unrewarding **12** impoverished, unproductive, unprofitable **14** unremunerative

unfulfilled 8 thwarted **10** frustrated, unrealized **11** unsatisfied
  French: 6 manque

unfurl 4 open **6** expand, spread, unfold, unroll **7** develop, roll out **8** shake out **9** spread out

ungainly 5 stiff **6** clumsy, klutzy **7** awkward **9** lumbering, maladroit **10** ungraceful **13** uncoordinated

ungallant 4 rude **7** boorish, uncivil, uncouth **8** impolite **9** uncourtly **10** ill-behaved, ungracious, unmannerly **11** ill-mannered, uncourteous **12** discourteous **13** ungentlemanly

ungenerous 4 mean, near **5** close, cruel, petty, small, venal **6** greedy, shabby, sordid, stingy **7** miserly, selfish, sparing **8** churlish, covetous, cowardly, grudging **9** illiberal, mercenary, niggardly, penurious, rapacious **10** avaricious **11** small-minded **12** narrow-minded, parsimonious, uncharitable

ungifted 8 mediocre **9** unskilled **10** amateurish, unskillful, untalented **14** unaccomplished

unglue 6 unseal **7** peel off, unstick **9** pull apart

ungodly 4 base, vile **5** awful **6** rotten, sinful, wicked **7** corrupt, ghastly, godless, heinous, immoral, impious **8** depraved, dreadful, terrible **9** dissolute **10** degenerate, horrendous, iniquitous, outrageous, villainous **11** blasphemous **12** dishonorable, unreasonable

ungovernable 6 unruly **7** defiant, froward, naughty, wayward **8** contrary, mutinous, perverse, stubborn **9** fractious, obstinate **10** disorderly, rebellious, refractory **11** disobedient, intractable **12** noncompliant, recalcitrant, unmanageable, unsubmissive

ungraceful 5 inept **6** clumsy **7** awkward **9** inelegant

ungracious 4 rude **5** bluff, blunt, gruff, harsh, short **6** abrupt, coarse, crusty, vulgar **7** boorish, brusque, loutish, uncivil, uncouth **8** churlish, grudging, impolite **9** uncourtly, ungallant **10** ill-behaved, unladylike, unmannerly **11** bad-mannered, ill-mannered, impertinent, uncourteous **12** disagreeable, discourteous, inhospitable **13** disrespectful, ungentlemanly

unguarded 6 unwary **8** careless, tactless, too frank **9** imprudent, unmindful, unwatched **10** incautious, indiscreet, undefended **11** defenseless, unpatrolled, unprotected **12** undiplomatic, unrestrained **13** ill-considered, uncircumspect

unguent 4 balm **5** cream, salve **6** lotion **8** ointment **9** emollient

ungulate 2 ox **3** cow, gnu, hog, pig, yak **4** boar, calf, deer, goat, ibex **5** camel, daman, horse, llama, tapir **6** hoofed, vicuna **7** buffalo, caribou, giraffe, peccary **8** antelope, elephant, hooflike, ruminant **9** dromedary **10** hartebeest, rhinoceros, wildebeest **12** hippopotamus

unhampered 4 free **8** expedite **9** unimpeded **10** unconfined **12** unencumbered, unrestrained, unrestricted

unhandy 5 inept **6** clumsy, gauche, klutzy **7** awkward **8** bumbling, fumbling, inexpert, unwieldy **9** all thumbs, ham-handed, maladroit, unskilled **10** cumbersome, unskillful **11** inefficient **12** inconvenient, unmanageable **14** butterfingered

unhappiness 3 woe **5** grief **6** misery, sorrow **7** anguish, sadness **8** distress **9** heartache

unhappy 3 bad, sad **4** blue, poor **5** inapt, sorry **6** gloomy, somber, unwise **7** adverse, awkward, doleful, foolish, forlorn, hapless, joyless, unlucky 8 dejected, downcast, luckless, unseemly 9 depressed, imprudent, long-faced, sorrowful, woebegone 10 despondent, dispirited, ill-advised, melancholy, unbecoming, unsuitable 11 crestfallen, injudicious, regrettable, unbefitting, unfortunate 12 heavyhearted, infelicitous, unsuccessful 13 inappropriate 14 down in the mouth

unharmed 5 whole 6 unhurt 9 uninjured, unscathed, untouched 10 in one piece, unaffected 14 with a whole skin

unhealthy 3 bad 4 sick, weak 6 ailing, feeble, infirm, morbid, poorly, sickly, unwell 7 harmful, hurtful, invalid, not well, noxious, unsound 8 depraved, diseased, negative, perilous 9 dangerous, degrading, hazardous 10 corrupting, indisposed, morally bad 11 destructive, detrimental, undesirable, unhealthful, unwholesome 12 demoralizing, in poor health, insalubrious 13 contaminating

unheard-of 3 odd 4 rare 6 unique 7 amazing, curious, unknown, unusual 8 freakish, original, singular, uncommon 9 irregular, matchless 10 incredible, outlandish, outrageous, phenomenal, unexpected 11 exceptional 12 incomparable, preposterous, unbelievable, unparalleled, unreasonable 13 extraordinary, inconceivable, unprecedented

unheated 3 icy 4 cold 6 chilly, drafty, frosty 7 ice-cold 8 unwarmed

unheeding 7 ignored 8 mindless 12 disregarding

unhelpful 7 of no use, useless 8 in the way 9 hindering 11 disobliging 13 inconsiderate, uncooperative

unheralded 6 unsung 10 unexpected, unforeseen 11 unacclaimed, unannounced, unlooked-for 12 unproclaimed, unpublicized, unrecognized 13 unanticipated

unhesitating 5 eager, quick, ready 6 direct, prompt 9 immediate 10 unreserved 11 unflinching 12 wholehearted, without delay 13 instantaneous 18 without reservation

unhinge 6 detach 7 disrupt 8 separate, unsettle 9 disengage, dislocate, disorient, unbalance 10 disconnect 13 disarticulate

unhitch 6 detach 8 separate, uncouple, unfasten 9 disengage 10 disconnect

unhitched 8 detached 9 uncoupled 10 unfastened 12 disconnected

unholy 4 base, evil, vile 5 awful 6 rotten, sinful, wicked 7 corrupt, heinous, immoral, ungodly 8 depraved, dreadful, shocking 9 dishonest 10 horrendous, iniquitous, outrageous, villainous 12 dishonorable, unreasonable

Unholy Loves
  author: 15 Joyce Carol Oates

unhurried 4 easy, slow 7 gradual 9 leisurely 10 deliberate, slow-moving

unicorn
  form: 5 horse
  feature: 4 horn
  symbolizes: 6 purity 8 chastity

  constellation of: 9 Monoceros

unidentified 5 vague 7 unknown, unnamed 8 nameless 9 anonymous, unlabeled 11 unspecified 12 undesignated, unrecognized

unification 5 union, unity 6 fusion, merger 7 uniting 8 alliance, junction 9 coalition, combining 11 coalescence, combination, confederacy 12 amalgamation 13 confederation, consolidating, consolidation, incorporation

uniform 4 even, garb 5 alike, array, at one, dress, equal, habit 6 attire, in line, in step, livery 7 apparel, costume, regalia, regular, similar, the same 8 agreeing, constant, in accord, of a piece, unvaried, vestment 9 consonant, identical, of one mind, unaltered, unvarying 10 conforming, consistent, harmonious, unchanging 11 regimentals, undeviating

uniformity 8 equality, monotony, sameness 10 consonance 11 consistency, equivalency, homogeneity 15 standardization

unify 3 wed 4 ally, fuse, join 5 blend, merge, unite 6 couple, link up 7 combine 8 coalesce, federate 10 amalgamate 11 confederate, consolidate, form into one, incorporate 12 lump together 13 bring together

unilluminated 3 dim 4 dark 5 murky, unlit 6 gloomy 7 obscure 8 darkened 9 lightless, unlighted

unimaginable 10 incredible 12 unbelievable 13 inconceivable 16 incomprehensible

unimaginative 4 dull 5 stale, stock, trite, usual, vapid 6 dreary 7 cliched, humdrum, prosaic, routine, tedious 8 everyday, mediocre, ordinary 9 hackneyed 10 pedestrian, uncreative, unexciting, uninspired, unoriginal, unromantic 11 commonplace, predictable 12 run-of-the-mill, unremarkable 13 uninteresting

unimpaired 4 good 5 clear, sound 6 intact, unhurt 8 unbroken, unharmed 9 uninjured, unscathed, unspoiled 10 undeformed

unimpassioned 4 calm, cool 6 placid, serene, stolid 7 unmoved 8 detached, unloving 9 apathetic, impassive, objective, unexcited 11 indifferent, unemotional 13 dispassionate

unimpeachable 4 pure 5 clean, solid 7 perfect 8 reliable, spotless, unmarred 9 blameless, faultless, inviolate, stainless, undefiled, untainted 10 immaculate, impeccable, inculpable, infallible 11 trustworthy, unblemished 12 unassailable 13 above reproach, totally honest 14 beyond question, irreproachable, unquestionable 15 beyond criticism, unchallengeable

unimportant 5 minor 6 lesser, meager, paltry, slight 7 trivial 8 inferior, mediocre, not vital, nugatory, piddling, trifling 10 immaterial, irrelevant, low-ranking, negligible, of no moment, second-rate 11 subordinate 12 nonessential, not important 13 insignificant 14 inconsiderable 15 inconsequential, of no consequence

uninformed 6 unread 7 unaware 8 ignorant 9 in the dark, not with it, unadvised, unknowing, unlearned 10 uneducated, unschooled 12 unconversant, uninstructed 13 unenlightened

uninhabited 5 empty 6 vacant 8 deserted, forsaken 9 abandoned, unlived in, unpeopled, unsettled 10 unoccupied, untenanted 11 unpopulated

uninhibited 4 fast, free, open, rash 5 frank 6 candid, daring, madcap, not shy, unwary 8 careless, heedless, immodest, reckless, uncurbed, unreined 9 abandoned, impetuous, impulsive, outspoken, unbridled, unchecked, unguarded, unimpeded, unstopped 10 capricious, flamboyant, forthright, headstrong, incautious, indiscreet, unhampered, unhindered, unreserved 11 instinctive, plainspoken, spontaneous 12 free-spirited, uncontrolled, unobstructed, unrestrained, unrestricted 13 unconstrained 15 straightforward, unself-conscious

uninjured 5 whole 6 intact, unhurt 8 unharmed 9 unscathed, untouched 10 in one piece 14 with a whole skin

uninspired 4 dull 5 stale, stock, trite, vapid 7 cliched, humdrum, prosaic, unmoved 8 ordinary 9 hackneyed, unexcited, unstirred, untouched 10 pedestrian, unaffected, unexciting, unoriginal 11 commonplace, indifferent, predictable, unemotional, unimpressed 12 run-of-the-mill, uninfluenced, unstimulated 13 unimaginative, uninteresting

uninspiring 4 dull 5 bland, stale 6 boring 7 insipid, prosaic 10 lackluster 13 uninteresting

uninstructive 6 barren 9 unhelpful 10 unedifying 12 unproductive 13 uninformative

unintelligent 4 dull, dumb, slow 5 blank, dense, dopey, thick 6 obtuse, stupid 7 asinine, doltish, idiotic, moronic 8 retarded 9 cretinous, dim-witted, imbecilic 10 dullwitted, half-witted, slow-witted 11 blockheaded, thickheaded 12 simpleminded

unintelligible 8 baffling, puzzling 9 confusing, illegible, insoluble 10 incoherent, perplexing 11 meaningless 12 impenetrable, inarticulate, unfathomable 14 undecipherable 16 incomprehensible

unintentional 9 unplanned, unwitting 10 accidental, fortuitous, undesigned, unintended, unthinking 11 inadvertent, involuntary, unconscious 14 unpremeditated

uninterested 5 aloof, blase 6 remote 8 heedless, listless, uncaring 9 apathetic, incurious, unmindful 10 above it all, uninvolved 11 indifferent, unconcerned 13 unimpressible

uninteresting 3 dry 4 drab, dull 5 trite, vapid 6 boring, dreary, jejune 7 humdrum, insipid, prosaic, tedious 8 lifeless, ordinary, tiresome, unmoving 9 colorless, wearisome 10 monotonous, pedestrian, uneventful 11 uninspiring 12 unsatisfying 13 insignificant

uninterrupted 8 unbroken 9 ceaseless, continual, incessant 10 continuous 11 unremitting

uninviting 8 annoying 9 offensive 10 unalluring, unpleasant, untempting 11 displeasing, distasteful, unappealing, undesirable, unwelcoming 12 disagreeable, unappetizing, unattractive

uninvolved 4 easy 5 clear 6 simple 7 neutral, obvious, outside 8 detached 9 impartial 10 unaffected 13 disinterested, dispassionate, uncomplicated

union 5 blend, guild, unity 6 fusion, league, merger 7 amalgam, joining, mixture, oneness, uniting, wedding 8 alliance, marriage, unifying 9 synthesis 10 federation, fraternity 11 affiliation, association, combination, corporation, partnership, unification 12 amalgamation 13 confederation, consolidation

type: 5 craft, labor, trade

unique 8 by itself, peerless, singular 9 matchless, nonpareil, unequaled, unmatched, unrivaled 10 inimitable, one of a kind, surpassing, unexampled, unexcelled 11 distinctive, unsurpassed 12 incomparable, unapproached, unparalleled

unit 4 part 5 group, whole 6 entity, member 7 element, measure, package, section, segment 8 category, division, quantity 9 component 10 detachment 11 constituent, measurement 12 denomination

Unitas, Johnny
  nickname: 7 Johnny U
  sport: 8 football
  position: 11 quarterback
  team: 14 Baltimore Colts

unite 4 ally, fuse, join, pool 5 blend, merge, unify 6 couple 7 combine 8 coalesce, federate, lock arms, organize 10 amalgamate, homogenize, join forces 11 confederate, consolidate, incorporate 12 join together, lump together 13 stand together

united 3 one 5 fused 6 allied, joined, merged, pooled 7 blended, coupled, leagued, unified 8 combined 9 federated, of one mind, unanimous 10 collective 11 amalgamated, in agreement 12 consolidated, incorporated 14 joined together, lumped together

United Arab Emirates
  other name: 11 Pirate Coast, Trucial Oman 13 Trucial States
  capital/largest city: 8 Abu Dhabi
  others: 5 Ajman, Dubai, Kalba, Tarif 6 Sharja 7 Fujaira 11 Ras al Khaima 12 Umm al Qaiwain
  division: 5 Ajman, Dibai, Dubai 6 Sharja 7 Fujaira, Sharjah 8 Abu Dhabi, Fujairah 11 Ras al Khaima, Umm al Qaiwan 12 Ral al Khaimah, Umm al-Qaiwain
  monetary unit: 3 fil 6 dirham
  highest point: 5 Hafit
  physical feature:
  desert: 10 Rub al Khali
  gulf: 4 Oman 7 Persian
  oasis: 7 Buraimi 9 Al Buraymi

peninsula: 7 Arabian
people: 4 Arab 6 Indian 7 African, Iranian 9 Pakistani 10 South Asian
leader: 22 Zaid Bin Sultan al-Nahayan
language: 5 Farsi 6 Arabic 7 English, Persian
religion: 5 Islam
war: 4 Gulf 11 Desert Storm
United Kingdom *see* 7 England
United States
capital: 12 Washington DC
largest city: 11 New York City
others: 4 Nome 5 Miami 6 Boston, Dallas, El Paso 7 Chicago, Detroit, Houston, Memphis, Phoenix, San Jose, Seattle 8 Columbus, Honolulu, San Diego 9 Anchorage, Baltimore, Cleveland, Milwaukee 10 Los Angeles, New Orleans, San Antonio 12 Indianapolis, Jacksonville, Philadelphia, Salt Lake City, San Francisco
school: 3 MIT 4 Penn, Yale 5 Brown 6 Baylor, Drexel, Vassar 7 Amherst, Colgate, Cornell, Fordham, Harvard, Oberlin 8 Bryn Mawr, Columbia, Stanford, Wesleyan 9 Dartmouth, Princeton, Radcliffe 10 Bennington 12 Johns Hopkins, Mount Holyoke
division: 4 Iowa, Ohio, Utah 5 Idaho, Maine, Texas 6 Alaska, Hawaii, Kansas, Nevada, Oregon 7 Alabama, Arizona, Florida, Georgia, Indiana, Montana, New York, Vermont, Wyoming 8 Arkansas, Colorado, Delaware, Illinois, Kentucky, Maryland, Michigan, Missouri, Nebraska, Oklahoma, Virginia 9 Louisiana, Minnesota, New Jersey, New Mexico, Tennessee, Wisconsin 10 California, Puerto Rico, Washington 11 Connecticut, Mississippi, North Dakota, Rhode Island, South Dakota 12 New Hampshire, Pennsylvania, West Virginia 13 Massachusetts, North Carolina, South Carolina 18 District of Columbia
island: 4 Guam, Long, Maui, Oahu 5 Block, Ellis, Kauai, Lanai, Umnak 6 Hawaii, Kodiak, Niihau, Unimak, Virgin 7 Baranof, Key West, Long Key, Molokai, Nunivak, Sanibel 8 Aleutian, Hawaiian, Key Largo, Shumagin, Unalaska 9 Atka Amlia, Canal Zone, Chichagof, Kahoolawe, Nantucket, Snipe Keys 10 Islamorada, Oyster Keys, Puerto Rico, St Lawrence 11 Longboat Key 12 Santa Barbara 13 American Samoa, Marquesas Keys, Prince of Wales, Santa Catalina, Summerland Key 15 Martha's Vineyard 16 Cantout Enderbury 26 Trust Territory of the Pacific
lake: 4 Erie, Mead 5 Huron, Tahoe 6 Cayuga, Finger, George, Itasca, Oneida, Seneca 7 Iliamma, Ontario 8 Michigan, Superior 9 Champlain, Great Salt, Salton Sea, Teshekpuk, Winnebago 10 Okeechobee 11 Yellowstone 13 Pontchartrain, Wallenpaupack, Winnipesaukee 14 Lake of the Woods

mountain: 4 Hood 5 Coast, Green, Kenai, Ozark, Rocky, White 6 Alaska, Brooks, DeLong, Elbert, Helena, Mesabi, Pocono, Shasta 7 Cascade, Chugach, Foraker, Harvard, Kilauea, Massive, Olympic, Olympus, Rainier, St Elias, Whitney 8 Catskill, Davidson, Endicott, Katahdin, Mauna Loa, Mitchell, Ouachita, St Helens, Wrangell 9 Allegheny, Blue Ridge, Kuskokwim, North Peak, Pikes Peak 10 Black Hills, Blanca Peak, Grand Teton, Washington, Williamson 11 Appalachian, Santa Monica 12 Sierra Nevada 14 Berkshire Hills
highest point: 6 Denali 8 McKinley
river: 3 New, Red 4 Gila, Iowa, Milk, Ohio, Rock 5 Black, Cedar, Coosa, Flint, Grand, Green, James, Neuse, Osage, Pearl, Pecos, Snake, White, Yukon 6 Brazos, Hudson, Neches, Neosho, Nueces, Owybee, Pee Dee, Platte, Powder, Sabine, Salmon, Wabash 7 Alabama, Big Horn, John Day, Klamath, Potomac, Roanoke, San Juan, St Johns, Trinity 8 Arkansas, Big Black, Canadian, Cheyenne, Cimarron, Colorado, Columbia, Delaware, Humboldt, Illinois, Kentucky, Kootenay, Missouri, Niabrana, Ouachita, Savannah 9 Allegheny, Deschutes, Des Moines, Minnesota, Rio Grande, Smoky Hill, St Francis, Tennessee, Tombigbee, Wisconsin 10 Cumberland, Republican, Sacramento, San Joaquin, St Lawrence, Tallapoosa 11 Connecticut, Mississippi, North Platte, South Platte, Susquehanna, Yellowstone 12 Tallahatchie 14 Little Colorado, Little Missouri
sea: 6 Arctic, Bering 7 Pacific 8 Atlantic, Beaufort
physical feature:
bay: 5 Tampa 7 Bristol, Prudhoe 8 Biscayne, Monterey 9 Apalachee 10 Chesapeake 12 San Francisco
desert: 4 Gila 6 Mojave 7 Painted 8 Colorado, Vizcaino 9 Black Rock 11 Death Valley
falls: 7 Niagara
gulf: 6 Alaska, Mexico 10 California
plain: 5 Great
plateau: 8 Colorado, Piedmont 10 Cumberland 11 Appalachian
strait: 6 Bering 7 Florida
people:
architect: 4 Root 5 Davis 6 Upjohn, Wright 7 Burnham, Downing, Furness, Gilbert, Gropius, Latrobe 8 Bogardus, Holabird, Sullivan 9 Bullfinch, Jefferson 10 Richardson 14 Mies van der Rohe
artist: 5 Henri, Homer, Leutz, Moses, Peale, Wyeth 6 Copley, Durand, Millet, Rothko, Stuart 7 Audubon, Cassatt, O'Keeffe, Pollock, Sargent 8 Whistler
author: 3 Poe 4 Grey, Inge, Loos, Luce, West, Wouk 5 Aiken, Albee, Beach, Benet, Crane, Eliot, Frost, Guest, Harte, Hecht, James, Lewis, Oates, Odets,

O'Hara, Paine, Pound, Stowe, Twain, Vidal, Welty, Wolfe, Wylie **6** Bellow, Bierce, Bryant, Cabell, Capote, Cather, Cooper, Cullen, Ferber, Holmes, Hughes, Irving, Kilmer, Lanier, London, Lowell, Mather, Millay, Miller, Norris, O'Neill, Porter, Styron, Updike, Wilder **7** Angelou, Baldwin, Clemens, Costain, Dreiser, Emerson, Gallico, Hammett, Hellman, Howells, Jeffers, Kerouac, Lardner, Malamud, Nabokov, Roethke, Stevens, Thoreau, Webster, Wharton, Whitman **8** Anderson, Bradbury, Caldwell, Cummings, Faulkner, Macleish, McCarthy, Melville, Michener, Mitchell, Morrison, Rawlings, Robinson, Sandburg, Schwartz, Sherwood, Sinclair, Teasdale, Whittier, Williams **9** Burroughs, Dickinson, Dos Passos, Hawthorne, Hemingway, McCullers, Steinbeck **10** Fitzgerald, Longfellow, Tarkington

composer: **4** Ives, Kern **5** Cohan, Loewe, Sousa **6** Berlin, Foster, Joplin, Lerner, Porter **7** Copland, Gilbert, Rodgers **8** Gershwin, Sullivan **9** Bernstein **11** Hammerstein

explorer: **4** Byrd, Pike **5** Boone, Cabot, Clark, Lewis, Perry **6** Hudson, Joliet **7** Jolliet **8** Columbus **9** Marquette **10** Eric the Red

leader: **3** Jay **4** Clay, King, Penn **5** Bryan, Davis, Henry, Paine **6** Revere, Sumner **7** Stevens, Webster **8** Franklin, Humphrey **9** Goldwater

military leader: **3** Lee **4** Pike **5** Clark, Gates, Grant, Meade, Tyler **6** Austin, Custer, Marion, Patton **7** Bradley, Houston, Jackson, Sherman **8** Marshall, Pershing **9** MacArthur, Roosevelt, Stillwell **10** Eisenhower, Vandenburg, Washington **11** Schwarzkopf

president: **4** Bush, Ford, Polk, Taft **5** Adams, Grant, Hayes, Nixon, Tyler **6** Arthur, Carter, Hoover, Monroe, Pierce, Reagan, Taylor, Truman, Wilson **7** Clinton, Harding, Jackson, Johnson, Kennedy, Lincoln, Madison **8** Buchanan, Coolidge, Fillmore, Garfield, Hamilton, Harrison, McKinley, Van Buren **9** Cleveland, Jefferson, Roosevelt **10** Eisenhower, Washington

sculptor: **4** Rush **6** Calder, French, Rogers **7** Borglum **9** Greenough, Remington **12** Saint-Gaudens

language: **7** English, Spanish

religion: **5** Amish **6** Mormon **7** Baptist, Judaism, Shakers **8** Lutheran **9** Methodist **10** Protestant **11** Pentacostal **12** Episcopalian, Presbyterian **13** Roman Catholic **14** Church of Christ, Congregational **15** Eastern Orthodox, Latter Day Saints **19** Seventh Day Adventist

place:

national park: **4** Zion **5** Platt **6** Acadia **7** Big Bend, Glacier, Olympic, Redwood, Sequoia **8** Wind Cave, Yosemite **9** Haleakala, Mesa Verde, Multnomah **10** Crater Lake, Everglades, Grand Teton, Hot Springs, Isle Royale, Shenandoah **11** Bryce Canyon, Canyonlands, Grand Canyon, Kings Canyon, Mammoth Cave, Yellowstone **12** Mount Rainier **13** Mount McKinley, Virgin Islands **14** Lassen Volcanic, Rocky Mountains **15** Carlsbad Caverns, Petrified Forest **19** Great Smoky Mountains

possession: **4** Guam **10** Puerto Rico **13** American Samoa, Virgin Islands **14** Mariana Islands **15** Caroline Islands, Marshall Islands

feature:

colony: **7** Roanoke **8** Plymouth **9** Jamestown **11** Rhode Island **12** New Amsterdam, New Hampshire **14** New Netherlands **16** Massachusetts Bay

festival: **9** Mardi Gras

national symbol: **9** bald eagle

tree: **7** redwood, sequoia

unity 5 peace, union **6** accord, entity, fusion, league, merger **7** concord, harmony, joining, oneness, rapport **8** alliance, goodwill **9** synthesis, unanimity, wholeness **10** federation, fellowship, friendship **11** affiliation, association, cooperation, partnership, unification **12** amalgamation, amicableness **13** compatibility, confederation, consolidation, understanding **14** like-mindedness

universal 7 general **9** worldwide **10** ubiquitous, widespread **11** omnipresent **12** affecting all, all-embracing, all-inclusive **13** international

Universal creator

Egyptian: **4** Ptah

universality 8 currency **10** prevalence **12** predominance **17** comprehensiveness

universe

god of: **6** Amen Ra, Amon Ra

university 6 campus, school **7** academy, college **11** institution

British: **6** Oxford **9** Cambridge

Cambridge: **7** Harvard

former: **9** alma mater

French: **8** Sorbonne

Hanover: **9** Dartmouth

lecturer: **9** prelector

New Haven: **4** Yale

New Jersey: **9** Princeton

New York: **8** Columbia

Providence: **5** Brown

session: **4** term **7** seminar **8** semester

Wit: **4** Lyly, Nash **5** Peele **6** Greene

unjust 6 biased, unfair, warped **7** partial **8** one-sided, partisan, wrongful **9** unmerited **10** prejudiced, unbalanced, undeserved **11** inequitable, unjustified, unwarranted

unjustifiable 11 inexcusable **12** indefensible

unjustly 7 falsely, wrongly **8** unfairly **10** wrongfully **11** dishonestly, faithlessly, inequitably **12** undeservedly

unkempt 5 messy 6 sloppy, untidy 7 rumpled, tousled 8 mussed-up, slovenly, uncombed 9 ungroomed 10 disheveled, disordered 11 disarranged

unkind 4 mean 5 nasty 7 abusive 8 uncaring 9 malicious, unfeeling 10 unfriendly, ungenerous, ungracious 11 insensitive, thoughtless 12 inhospitable, uncharitable 13 inconsiderate, unsympathetic

unknot 5 untie 7 unsnarl 8 untangle 11 disentangle

unknowable 12 inaccessible 13 inconceivable

unknown 7 obscure, unnamed 8 nameless 9 anonymous, unheard-of 10 unrenowned 12 uncelebrated, undesignated, undetermined, undiscovered, unidentified

Unknown authors
author of: 4 Edda (elder) 7 Beowulf 8 Everyman, King Horn, Stasimon 10 Cinderella 11 Poema del Cid 12 Panchatantra, Vercelli Book, Volsunga Saga 14 Gesta Romanorum, Sibylline Books 15 Chanson de Roland, The Forty Thieves, The Song of Roland 16 Grettir the Strong 17 The Nibelungenlied 20 Aucassin and Nicolette, Robin Hood's Adventures 23 The Dream of the Red Chamber, The Thousand and One Nights 26 Sir Gawain and the Green Knight 29 Collection of Ten Thousand Leaves 29 The Arabian Nights' Entertainment

unladylike 4 rude 6 coarse, common, vulgar 7 ill-bred, uncouth 8 impolite 10 unmannerly 12 discourteous

unlawful 7 illegal, illegit, illicit, lawless 8 criminal 9 forbidden 10 prohibited, unlicensed, unofficial 12 unauthorized 13 against the law 16 unconstitutional

unlawful act 5 crime 6 felony 10 wrongdoing 11 lawbreaking, malfeasance, misdemeanor

unleash 4 free 5 let go 7 release, set free 8 let loose, liberate 12 give free rein

unlettered 8 ignorant, untaught 9 unlearned, untutored 10 illiterate, uneducated, unschooled 11 unscholarly

unlighted 3 dim 4 dark 5 murky, unlit 6 gloomy 7 stygian, sunless 8 moonless 9 lightless 13 unilluminated

unlikable, unlikeable 7 hateful 9 offensive, unlovable 10 hard to like, unloveable, unpleasant 11 displeasing, unappealing 12 disagreeable

unlike 7 diverse, unalike, unequal 9 different, disparate 10 dissimilar

unlikelihood 12 doubtfulness, unlikeliness 13 improbability

unlikely 8 hopeless 10 improbable 11 unpromising 12 questionable, unbelievable, unpropitious 19 scarcely conceivable

unlikeness 8 contrast, variance 9 disparity, variation 10 difference, divergence 13 dissimilarity, dissimilitude

unlimited 4 huge, vast 5 total 7 endless, immense 8 absolute, complete, infinite 9 boundless, limitless, unbounded, unchecked 11 unqualified 12 immeasurable, totalitarian, uncontrolled, unrestrained, unrestricted 13 comprehensive, inexhaustible, unconstrained 15 all-encompassing

unload 4 dump 7 off-load 8 get rid of, unburden 9 dispose of 10 unencumber

unlooked for 6 sudden 7 unasked 8 surprise 10 unexpected, unforeseen, unheralded 11 unannounced, uncalled for, unpredicted, unsolicited 13 serendipitous, unanticipated

unlovable, unloveable 7 hateful 9 unlikable 10 hard to like, unlikeable, unpleasant 11 displeasing, unappealing 12 disagreeable

unloving 4 cold, cool 6 frigid 11 indifferent, passionless 13 unimpassioned

unlucky 6 cursed, jinxed 7 hapless, unhappy 8 ill-fated, luckless, untoward 9 ill-omened 10 ill-starred 11 star-crossed, unfortunate 12 inauspicious, misfortunate

unman 7 unnerve 8 castrate 10 discourage, emasculate

unmanageable 5 balky, bulky 6 mulish, unruly 7 awkward, unhandy, wayward, willful 8 ungainly, unwieldy 9 fractious, pigheaded 10 cumbersome, rebellious, refractory 11 disobedient, intractable, troublesome 12 incorrigible 14 uncontrollable

unmanly 5 timid 6 yellow 8 cowardly, sissyish, womanish 9 sissified, weak-kneed 10 effeminate 11 lily-livered, unmasculine, weakhearted 12 fainthearted 13 pusillanimous 14 chickenhearted

unmannerly 5 crude, gross, surly 6 coarse 7 boorish, ill-bred, loutish, uncivil, uncouth 8 impolite 10 ungracious, unladylike 11 ill-mannered 12 badly behaved, discourteous 13 ungentlemanly

unmarked 5 clean, clear 9 undamaged, undefaced, unnoticed 10 unobserved 11 unblemished 15 undistinguished

unmarried 4 free 5 unwed 6 maiden, single 7 old maid, widowed 8 bachelor, divorced, spinster, unwedded, virginal, wifeless 9 available, fancy free 10 spouseless, unattached 11 husbandless 21 footloose and fancy-free

unmarried girl
French: 10 jeune fille
German: 8 fraulein
Spanish: 8 senorita

Unmarried Woman, An
director: 12 Paul Mazursky
cast: 9 Alan Bates 11 Cliff Gorman 13 Jill Clayburgh, Michael Murphy

unmask 4 bare, show 6 betray, expose, reveal, unveil 7 lay open, uncover 8 disclose, discover 12 bring to light

unmasking 6 baring 8 betrayal, exposure 9 discovery, unveiling 10 disclosure, laying open, revelation, uncovering 15 bringing to light

unmatched 6 unlike 7 diverse, supreme, unequal 8 peerless, variable 9 differing, disparate, matchless, unequaled 10 dissimilar 12 second to none, unparalleled 13 beyond compare

unmerciful 4 cold, evil 5 cruel, harsh 6 brutal, severe, unkind 7 brutish, extreme, inhuman 8 inhumane, pitiless, ruthless 9 excessive, heartless, inclement, merciless, unfeeling, unpitying, unsparing 10 malevolent, relentless 11 hardhearted 14 unconscionable

unmindful 3 lax 6 remiss 7 unaware 8 careless, derelict, heedless 9 forgetful, negligent, oblivious, unheeding 11 thoughtless, unconscious

unmistakable 5 clear, plain 6 patent 7 evident, glaring, obvious 8 apparent, distinct, manifest, palpable 9 prominent 10 pronounced, undeniable 11 conspicuous, unequivocal 12 indisputable 14 unquestionable

unmistakably 7 clearly, plainly 8 palpably, patently 9 certainly, decidedly, downright, evidently, glaringly, obviously 10 definitely, distinctly, manifestly, positively, thoroughly, undeniably 11 prominently 12 indisputably 13 conspicuously, unequivocally 14 unquestionably 17 beyond all question

unmitigated 6 arrant 8 absolute, unabated, unbroken 9 downright, out-and-out 10 persistent, unrelieved 11 unqualified 12 unalleviated 13 uninterrupted

unmixed 4 neat, pure 5 sheer 6 simple 8 straight 9 unalloyed, unblended, undiluted, unmingled 13 unadulterated

unmoved 4 calm, cold, firm 5 aloof 6 dogged 7 devoted, staunch 8 resolute, resolved, uncaring, unshaken 9 dedicated, obstinate, steadfast, unfeeling, unpitying, unstirred, untouched 10 determined, inflexible, not shifted, persistent, relentless, unaffected, unswerving, unwavering 11 indifferent, unconcerned, undeviating, undisturbed, unfaltering 12 stonyhearted, uninterested, unresponsive 14 uncompromising

unmoving 4 dead, dull 5 fixed, inert, still 6 boring, serene 8 immobile 9 powerless 10 motionless, stationary 11 emotionless 13 at a standstill

unnamed 8 nameless, unsigned 9 anonymous, incognito 10 innominate, uncredited, unreported, unrevealed 11 undisclosed, unspecified 12 pseudonymous, undesignated, undiscovered, unidentified 14 unacknowledged

unnatural 4 fake 5 phony, put-on 6 forced 7 assumed, stilted, studied, unusual 8 aberrant, abnormal, affected, freakish, mannered, peculiar 9 anomalous, contrived 10 artificial, theatrical 13 self-conscious

unnecessary 5 extra 6 excess 7 surplus 8 needless, overmuch 9 auxiliary, excessive 10 expendable, gratuitous, unrequired 11 dispensable, superfluous, uncalled-for, unessential 13 supplementary

unnerve 5 daunt, scare, upset 7 agitate, unhinge 8 frighten, unsettle 10 intimidate

unnerving 5 scary 8 daunting 9 upsetting 10 enervating, unsettling 11 frightening

unnoticeable 3 dim 5 faint 6 hidden 7 obscure 9 concealed 10 indistinct, unassuming, unemphatic, unobserved 11 unobtrusive 12 undetectable 13 imperceptible, inconspicuous, insignificant, undiscernible 14 unostentatious

unnoticed 6 unfelt, unseen 7 unheard, unnoted 8 unheeded, untasted 10 not smelled, overlooked, unobserved 11 disregarded, unperceived 12 undiscovered

unobservant 4 dull 5 blind 8 unseeing 9 unmindful 11 incognizant

unobstructed 4 fair, free, open 5 clear 8 apparent 9 unimpeded 10 unhampered, unhindered 11 unprevented

unobtainable 9 hard to get 10 impossible, out of reach, out of touch 11 unavailable, unreachable 12 improcurable, inaccessible

unobtrusive 3 shy 6 humble, modest 7 bashful 8 reserved, reticent, retiring 9 diffident 10 unassuming 11 unassertive 13 inconspicuous, unpretentious 14 unostentatious

unoccupied 4 idle 5 empty 6 vacant 8 unfilled 9 abandoned, unengaged 10 untenanted 11 uninhabited

unofficial 8 informal 12 unauthorized

unorganized 5 loose 6 casual, random 7 aimless, chaotic 8 confused 9 haphazard, orderless, unordered 10 disjointed, unarranged, undirected 11 harum-scarum 12 unclassified, unsystematic 13 helter-skelter 14 unsystematized

unornamented 4 bald, bare 5 blank, naked, plain, stark 6 simple 7 austere 9 unadorned 11 undecorated 13 unembellished

unorthodox 7 erratic 9 eccentric, irregular 14 unconventional

unostentatious 3 shy 5 plain, quiet 6 humble, modest, simple 9 unadorned, unaffected 10 unassuming 11 constrained 13 inconspicuous, unpretentious 14 unpresumptuous

unpaid 3 due 4 owed 5 owing 9 in arrears 11 outstanding

unpaid debt 5 debit 7 arrears 9 liability 10 balance due, obligation 12 indebtedness

unpalatable 5 nasty 8 inedible, unsavory 9 repellent, repulsive 10 bad-tasting, unpleasant 11 displeasing, distasteful 12 disagreeable, unappetizing 13 hard to swallow

unparalleled 4 best, rare 5 alone, crack, elect 6 unique 8 gilt-edge, peerless, singular 9 matchless, superfine, unequaled, unmatched, unrivaled 10 crackajack, inimitable, unimitated 11 unsurpassed 12 unapproached 13 unprecedented 15 of the first water

unperceptive 5 blind 9 unfeeling 11 insensitive, unobservant 12 imperceptive, impercipient 13 unsympathetic

unperturbed 4 calm, cool 6 poised 8 composed, tranquil 9 collected, unexcited, unruffled 10 coolheaded, nonchalant, unagitated, undismayed, untroubled 11 level-headed, undisturbed 13 unimpassioned

unplanned 9 impromptu 10 accidental, fortuitous, improvised, unexpected, unforeseen 11 spontaneous 12 uncalculated 13 unintentional 14 extemporaneous, unpremeditated 15 spur-of-the-moment

unpleasant 5 nasty, pesky 7 irksome, noisome 8 annoying, churlish 9 obnoxious, offensive, repugnant, repulsive, unlikable, vexatious 10 ill-humored, ill-natured 11 displeasing, distasteful 12 disagreeable, unattractive 13 objectionable

unpleasantness 8 ugliness 9 ill nature, nastiness 12 churlishness 13 obnoxiousness, offensiveness, repulsiveness 15 distastefulness 16 disagreeableness, unattractiveness

unpointed 4 dull 5 blunt 6 dulled 11 unsharpened

unpolished 3 raw 5 gawky, inept, rough 6 cloudy, clumsy 7 amateur, awkward, unwaxed 8 inexpert, unbuffed, unglazed, unshined 9 inelegant, unrefined, unskilled 10 uncultured, unfinished, unskillful 11 unburnished, unpracticed 12 uncultivated 13 inexperienced 15 unaccomplished 15 unsophisticated

unpopular 7 snubbed 8 disliked, rebuffed, rejected, slighted, unwanted 9 disdained, neglected, unwelcome 10 unaccepted 11 disapproved, undesirable 12 looked down on, unacceptable

unpopulated 5 rural 9 backwoods, unpeopled, unsettled

unprecedented 5 novel 6 unique 9 unheard-of 10 unexampled 11 exceptional 12 unparalleled 13 extraordinary 15 hitherto unknown

unpredictable 6 fitful 7 erratic 8 fanciful, unstable, variable 9 arbitrary, eccentric, impulsive, mercurial, uncertain, whimsical 10 capricious, changeable, inconstant

unprejudiced 4 fair, just 8 unbiased, unswayed 9 impartial, objective, unbigoted 10 even-handed, fair-minded, open-minded, undogmatic 11 broad-minded 12 uninfluenced 13 disinterested

unpremeditated 5 ad-lib 9 impetuous, impromptu, impulsive, unplanned 10 accidental, improvised, unintended 11 involuntary, spontaneous 12 uncalculated, unthought-out 13 unintentional 14 extemporaneous 15 spur-of-the-moment

unprepared 5 ad-lib 7 offhand, unready 8 off guard 9 extempore, impromptu 10 flatfooted, improvised 11 spontaneous, unrehearsed 14 extemporaneous 15 spur-of-the-moment

unprepossessing 4 grim 5 seedy 10 ill-favored, ill-looking 12 unattractive

unpressed 5 baggy 6 mussed, sloppy 7 creased, rumpled 8 unironed, wrinkled 9 shapeless, uncreased

unpretentious 5 plain 6 homely, humble, modest, simple 10 unassuming, unimposing 11 unelaborate, unobtrusive 14 unostentatious

unprincipled 6 amoral 12 unscrupulous 14 conscienceless, unconscionable

unproductive 4 poor 6 barren 7 sterile, useless 8 bootless 9 infertile 10 unfruitful, unyielding 11 ineffective, ineffectual, inefficient 12 unprofitable

unprofessional 6 shoddy, sloppy 7 amateur 8 bungling, careless 9 negligent, unethical 10 amateurish 11 incompetent, inefficient, unpracticed 12 unprincipled 13 inexperienced, undisciplined, unworkmanlike 14 unbusinesslike

unprofitable 4 vain 7 useless 8 bootless 11 ineffective, ineffectual

unprogressive 7 diehard 8 backward, standpat, stubborn 9 benighted, right-wing 11 reactionary, reactionist 12 conservative 17 ultraconservative

unprolific 6 barren 7 sterile 9 infertile, unfertile 10 nonbearing 12 unproductive

unpromising 5 bleak 9 ill-omened 10 forbidding 11 unfavorable 12 inauspicious, unpropitious

unpropitious 7 adverse 8 contrary 9 unfitting 10 unsuitable 11 unfavorable 12 antagonistic, inauspicious, infelicitous

unprotected 4 open 5 naked 6 unsafe 7 exposed, unarmed 8 helpless, insecure, perilous 9 dangerous, hazardous, unguarded 10 undefended, vulnerable 11 defenseless

unproven 7 in doubt 8 arguable, doubtful 10 indefinite, in question, up in the air 11 open to doubt, unconfirmed 12 experimental, inconclusive, questionable 13 unestablished 14 open to question

unpunctual 4 late 5 tardy 7 belated 10 behindhand, behindtime

unqualified 5 total, unfit, utter 8 absolute, complete, inexpert, positive, thorough, unsuited 9 downright, out-and-out, unskilled, untrained 10 consummate, undisputed, uneducated, unprepared, unschooled 11 ill-equipped, incompetent 13 inexperienced, unconditional

unquenched 8 unslaked 11 unsatisfied 14 unextinguished

unquestionable 4 sure 5 clear, plain 6 proven 7 certain, evident, obvious, perfect 8 definite, flawless 9 blameless, errorless, faultless 10 impeccable, undeniable 11 beyond doubt, irrefutable, self-evident, unequivocal 12 indisputable, uncensurable 13 uncontestable, unimpeachable 14 irreproachable

unquestionably 6 surely 7 totally 9 certainly, doubtless 10 absolutely, completely, definitely, positively, unarguably 12 conclusively, indisputably, without doubt 13 unequivocally

unravel 4 undo 5 feaze, solve 6 unfold, unfurl, unknit 7 clear up, resolve 8 decipher, separate, untangle 9 pull apart 10 disinvolve 11 disentangle

unreachable 10 impossible, out of touch 11 out of the way, unavailable, unrealistic 12 inaccessible, unobtainable 14 unapproachable

unreal 4 airy 5 dream 6 dreamy 7 ghostly, not real, phantom, shadowy 8 ethereal, illusive, illusory, imagined, spectral 9 dreamlike, fantastic, imaginary, legendary 10 chimerical, fictitious, idealistic, intangible 11 nonexistent 13 insubstantial 16 phantasmagorical

unrealistic 4 wild 5 crazy, silly 6 absurd 7 asinine, foolish 8 crackpot, delusory, fanciful 9 illogical 10 idealistic, improbable, infeasible, starry-eyed 11 impractical 12 unreasonable

unrealized 8 thwarted 10 frustrated, incomplete 11 nonexistent, unfulfilled, unsatisfied 14 unaccomplished

unreasonable 5 undue 6 absurd, biased, mulish, unfair 7 bigoted 8 obdurate, stubborn, too great 9 excessive, fanatical, illogical, obstinate, pigheaded, senseless, unbending 10 bullheaded, exorbitant, far-fetched, headstrong, immoderate, inflexible, inordinate, irrational, prejudiced, unyielding 11 extravagant, intractable, nonsensical, opinionated, uncalled-for, unwarranted 12 closed-minded, preposterous, ungovernable, unmanageable 13 unjustifiable

unreasoning 8 careless, heedless 9 impulsive 10 irrational, unthinking 11 thoughtless 13 unintelligent

unrecognizable 9 disguised, incognito 10 in disguise 11 camouflaged 14 unidentifiable

unrecognized 6 unsung 7 cryptic, unknown 9 incognito, unnoticed

unrefined 3 raw 5 crude, rough 6 coarse, vulgar 7 boorish, low-bred 9 inelegant

unrehearsed 7 offhand 8 informal 9 extempore, impromptu, impulsive, unplanned, unstudied 10 improvised, off-the-cuff, unprepared 11 extempory, spontaneous 14 extemporaneous, unpremeditated 15 improvisational, spur-of-the-moment 19 off the top of one's head

unrelated 6 not kin, unlike 7 foreign 8 unallied 10 dissimilar, extraneous, irrelevant, non-germane 11 unconnected 12 inapplicable, incompatible, unassociated 13 inappropriate

unrelenting 5 rigid 6 steady 7 adamant, endless 8 constant, unabated, unbroken 9 ceaseless, incessant, tenacious, unbending 10 implacable, inexorable, inflexible, relentless, unrelieved, unswerving, unwavering, unyielding 11 undeviating, unremitting 14 uncompromising

unreliable 4 fake 5 false, phony 6 fickle 8 fallible, mistaken, unstable 9 deceitful, erroneous, uncertain 10 capricious, change-able, inaccurate, inconstant 12 questionable, undependable 13 irresponsible, untrustworthy

unremarkable 5 usual 6 common 7 average 8 everyday, mediocre, ordinary 11 commonplace 12 unimpressive, unsurprising 13 insignificant, unexceptional 15 undistinguished

unremitting 6 dogged 8 constant, tireless, untiring 9 ceaseless, continual, incessant, unceasing 10 continuous, persistent 11 persevering

unrepentant 7 callous 8 hardened, obdurate, unatoned 9 unashamed 10 uncontrite, unexpiated 11 remorseless 12 incorrigible, unregenerate

unrepressed 4 free, open 7 liberal 8 effusive, outgoing 9 expansive, exuberant 11 extroverted, uninhibited 12 unrestrained

unreserved 4 full, open 5 frank 6 entire 11 unqualified 12 wholehearted

unresolved 4 moot 5 vague 7 pending 8 doubtful, unsolved 9 tentative, uncertain, undecided, unsettled 10 disputable, unanswered 11 contestable, speculative 12 questionable, undetermined 13 problematical, unascertained

unresponsive 4 cold, cool, dull, limp 5 inert 6 frigid 7 passive 8 lifeless 9 apathetic, unfeeling 11 cold-blooded, inattentive, indifferent, unemotional 13 dispassionate, unsympathetic

unresponsiveness 6 apathy 7 inertia 9 lassitude, passivity 11 inattention, passiveness 12 indifference

unrest 5 chaos 6 tumult 7 anarchy, discord, ferment, protest, turmoil 8 disorder, disquiet, upheaval 9 agitation, rebellion 10 discontent, turbulence 12 restlessness 15 dissatisfaction

unrestrained 8 uncurbed 9 abandoned, boundless, excessive, unbridled, unchecked, unlimited 10 immoderate, inordinate, unfettered, ungoverned, unhampered, unhindered, unreserved 11 extravagant, intemperate, uninhibited, unrepressed 12 uncontrolled, unrestricted, unsuppressed 13 irrepressible

unrestraint 6 excess 7 abandon 9 uncontrol 10 unruliness 12 extravagance, immoderation, recklessness 13 excessiveness, impulsiveness

unrestricted 8 absolute, complete 9 out-and-out, unbounded, unlimited 11 unqualified 12 unrestrained 13 unconditional

unrigid 3 lax 4 easy, limp, soft 5 loose 6 giving, limber, mobile, pliant, supple 7 elastic, lenient, plastic, pliable 8 flexible, informal, merciful, tolerant, yielding 9 indulgent, malleable 11 conformable

unrigorous 4 easy 5 loose, slack 6 casual, sloppy 7 inexact 8 careless, slapdash 9 imprecise

unripe 5 green 8 immature 10 unseasoned 11 undeveloped 14 underdeveloped

unrivaled 8 superior, topnotch 9 unequaled 10 undisputed 11 unsurpassed

unroll 6 reveal, uncoil, unfold, unfurl, unwind 7 display, lay open, play out 9 spread out

unruffled 4 calm, cool, even, mild 5 quiet, still 6 placid, serene, smooth 8 composed, tranquil 9 collected 10 coolheaded, nonchalant, unagitated, untroubled 11 undisturbed, unperturbed 13 self-possessed

unruly 4 wild 5 rowdy 7 restive, wayward, willful 8 contrary, perverse 9 fractious, unbridled 10 boisterous, disorderly, headstrong, refractory 11 disobedient, intractable 12 obstreperous, ungovernable, unmanageable 13 undisciplined 14 uncontrollable

unsafe 5 risky 7 exposed 8 insecure, perilous 9 dangerous, hazardous, unguarded 10 undefended, unreliable, vulnerable 11 defenseless, treacherous, unprotected 13 untrustworthy

unsatisfactory 4 poor 5 inept, unfit 8 below par, inferior, unworthy 9 deficient 10 inadequate, ineligible, unsuitable 12 inadmissible, unacceptable 13 inappropriate

unsavory 3 bad 4 flat, foul 5 nasty 7 insipid, tainted 9 tasteless 10 bad-tasting, nauseating, unpleasant 11 distasteful, unpalatable 12 disagreeable, unappetizing

unscathed 5 sound, whole 6 entire, intact, unhurt 7 perfect 8 unharmed 9 uninjured, untouched 10 unimpaired 11 unscratched 13 all in one piece

unscholarly 8 ignorant 9 unlearned 10 illiterate, uneducated, uninformed 11 ill-informed 13 unintelligent

unschooled 3 raw 5 green 6 callow 8 ignorant, untaught 9 unlearned 10 illiterate, uneducated, uninformed, unlettered, unseasoned 11 uninitiated 13 inexperienced

unscrupulous 5 sharp 6 amoral 7 crooked, devious, immoral 9 unethical 12 dishonorable, unprincipled

unseasonable 6 too hot 7 too cold, too warm 8 abnormal, untimely

unseasoned 3 raw 5 bland, green, plain 6 callow 7 untried 8 immature 13 inexperienced

unseeing 5 blind 7 unaware 9 oblivious, sightless 11 unobservant

unseemly 4 rude 5 crude, gross 6 coarse, vulgar 7 boorish, loutish 8 churlish, improper, indecent, unworthy 9 incorrect, offensive, tasteless 10 indecorous, indelicate, out of place, unbecoming, unladylike, unsuitable 11 distasteful, ill-mannered, unbefitting, undignified 12 discourteous, disreputable 13 discreditable, inappropriate, reprehensible, ungentlemanly

unselfconscious 7 artless 10 unaffected 13 unpretentious

unselfish 7 liberal 8 generous, handsome, princely, selfless 10 altruistic, benevolent, big-hearted, charitable, open-handed 11 considerate, magnanimous, magnificent 12 humanitarian 13 philanthropic 15 self-sacrificing

unserviceable 7 useless 8 unusable

unsettle 5 upset 6 bother, rattle, ruffle 7 agitate, confuse, disturb, fluster, perturb, trouble, unhinge 8 bewilder, confound, disorder 9 unbalance 10 disconcert 13 throw off guard

unsettled 5 fazed 7 anxious, nervous, ruffled 8 agitated, confused, doubtful 9 disturbed, nonplused, perturbed, undecided 10 disquieted, distracted, nonplussed, up in the air 11 discomfited 12 disconcerted 16 at sixes and sevens

unshackle 4 free 7 release, set free, unchain 8 liberate, unfetter

unshakable 4 fast 6 stable 7 abiding, staunch 8 constant, enduring 9 dauntless, permanent, steadfast, unruffled 10 changeless, inflexible, unsinkable, unwavering 11 levelheaded, unflappable 13 imperturbable

unshaken 4 calm, cool 6 poised, serene, stable 7 staunch, unmoved 8 composed, constant, resolved 9 steadfast, tenacious, undaunted, unexcited, unruffled 10 controlled, determined, inflexible, relentless, unaffected, unswerving, untroubled, unwavering 11 levelheaded, undeviating, undisturbed, unemotional, unfaltering, unflinching, unperturbed 13 self-possessed 14 uncompromising

unshapely 5 baggy 9 amorphous, shapeless

unshaven 5 hairy 7 bearded, bristly, hirsute, stubbly, unkempt 9 whiskered 11 bewhiskered

unsheathe 4 bare 6 expose 7 pull out 8 withdraw

unsightly 4 ugly 6 horrid, odious 7 hideous u9 obnoxious, offensive, repellent, repulsive, revolting, sickening 11 distasteful 12 unattractive

unsigned 9 anonymous 13 bearing no name

unskilled 5 green, inept 7 untried 9 untrained 10 amateurish, apprentice 11 incompetent, unqualified 13 inexperienced

unskillful 5 inept 6 clumsy, unable 7 awkward 8 inexpert 9 incapable, maladroit, untrained 10 amateurish 11 incompetent, ineffective, unpracticed 13 inexperienced

unsmiling 3 sad 4 glum, grim 5 grave 6 dismal 7 austere, joyless, serious 9 cheerless, grim-faced

unsociable 7 haughty 9 withdrawn 10 antisocial, unfriendly, ungracious 11 introverted 14 unapproachable

unsoiled 4 pure 5 clean, fresh, white 6 chaste 8 innocent, pristine, spotless 9 unstained, unsullied 10 immaculate 11 unblemished, untarnished

unsolicited 8 unforced, unsought, unwanted 9 undesired, uninvited, unwelcome, voluntary 10 gratuitous, unasked for 11 spontaneous, unnecessary, unrequested, unwished for, volunteered

unsophisticated 4 open 5 green, naive 6 candid 7 artless, natural 8 homespun, innocent, trusting 9 ingenuous, unstudied, unworldly 10 unaffected, unassuming 11 uncontrived 13 undissembling, unpretentious 15 straightforward

unsound 3 mad, off 4 weak 5 risky, shaky, unfit, wrong 6 absurd, ailing, faulty, feeble, flawed, infirm, insane, marred, sickly, unsafe 7 foolish, invalid, rickety, tottery 8 confused, crippled, decrepit, deranged, diseased, drooping, impaired, insecure, not solid, not valid, perilous, specious, spurious, unhinged, unstable, unsteady 9 blemished, dangerous, defective, erroneous, hazardous, illogical, imperfect, incorrect, senseless, uncertain, unfounded, unhealthy, unsettled, untenable 10 disordered, fallacious, groundless, irrational, precarious, unbalanced, unreliable 11 languishing, mentally ill 12 in poor health 13 off one's rocker, unsubstantial

unsoundness 7 frailty 8 delicacy, weakness 9 fragility, frailness, shakiness 11 decrepitude, derangement, instability 12 unsteadiness

unsparing 4 full 6 giving, lavish 7 copious, liberal, profuse 8 abundant, generous 9 bountiful, plenteous, plentiful, unlimited 10 big-hearted, munificent, ungrudging, unstinting 11 extravagant, magnanimous, unqualified 13 unconditional

unspeakable 4 huge, vast 5 awful, great 6 odious 7 fearful, immense 8 enormous, shocking 9 abhorrent, frightful, loathsome, monstrous, repellent, repulsive, revolting, sickening, unheard-of 10 abominable, disgusting, incredible, nauseating, prodigious 11 astonishing, unutterable 12 overwhelming, unimaginable 13 extraordinary, inconceivable, inexpressible, indescribable

unspecified 5 vague 7 general, unnamed 9 undefined, unsettled 10 indefinite 11 unannounced, unindicated, unmentioned 12 undesignated, undetermined, unpublicized, unstipulated

unspoiled 4 open 7 artless, natural, perfect 8 pristine, spotless, trusting, unharmed, unmarred 9 preserved, undamaged, unscarred, unspotted, unstudied, unworldly 10 unaffected, unassuming, unimpaired, unpampered 11 unblemished, uncorrupted 13 unpretentious 15 unself-conscious, unsophisticated

unspoken 5 tacit 6 silent 7 implied 8 implicit 9 ineffable, not voiced, unuttered 10 understood 11 unexpressed

unspotted 5 clean 6 spotless, unsoiled 9 undefiled, unstained, unsullied 11 unblemished

unstable 4 weak 5 frail, shaky, tippy 6 fickle, fitful, flimsy, wobbly 7 erratic, fragile, rickety 8 changing, insecure, shifting, unsteady, volatile 9 emotional, mercurial, tottering 10 capricious, changeable, fly-by-night, irrational 11 fluctuating, vacillating 12 inconsistent 13 irresponsible, unpredictable, unsubstantial

unstained 5 clean 8 spotless 9 unspotted, unsullied, untainted 11 unblemished, uncorrupted

unsteady 6 fickle, wobbly 7 rickety 8 doubtful, unstable 10 unreliable 12 questionable, undependable 13 untrustworthy

unstinting 11 unqualified 12 enthusiastic, unrestrained, wholehearted

unstooped 5 erect 6 unbent 7 upright 8 straight, vertical

unstudied 4 glib 6 casual 7 artless, natural 8 informal, unforced, unversed 9 guileless, unuttered 10 unaffected 11 spontaneous 12 uncalculated

unsubmissive 6 unruly 7 defiant, froward, naughty, wayward 8 contrary, mutinous, perverse, stubborn 9 fractious, insurgent, obstinate, seditious, undutiful 10 disorderly, rebellious, refractory, unyielding 11 disobedient, intractable 12 noncompliant, recalcitrant, ungovernable, unmanageable 13 insubordinate

unsubstantial 4 airy, weak 5 filmy 6 feeble, flimsy 7 unsound 8 ethereal, fanciful, illusory 9 idealized, imaginary 10 jerrybuilt 11 lightweight 12 undetectable 13 imperceptible 17 indistinguishable

unsubstantiated 8 disputed 10 unverified 15 unauthenticated

unsuccessful 4 poor, vain 6 foiled, futile, hard up 7 baffled, hapless, unlucky, useless 8 abortive, badly off, luckless, strapped, thwarted 9 fruitless, moneyless, penniless 10 ill-starred, profitless, unavailing, unfruitful 11 ineffectual, unfortunate 12 unproductive, unprofitable, unprosperous 14 unremunerative

unsuitability 9 unfitness, wrongness 11 impropriety, uselessness 12 unseemliness 13 inconsistency 14 incompatibility, unacceptability 17 inappropriateness

unsuitable 5 inapt, unfit 7 unhappy, useless 8 improper, unseemly 9 unfitting, worthless 10 inadequate, indecorous, out of place, unbecoming, unsuitable 11 incongruous, unbefitting 12 inadmissible, incompatible, inconsistent, infelicitous, out of keeping, unacceptable 13 inappropriate

unsuited 5 inapt, wrong 9 unfitting 10 out of place 13 inappropriate

unsullied 5 clean 8 spotless, unsoiled 9 undefiled, uninjured, untainted 10 unpolluted 11 unblackened, unblemished, uncorrupted, untarnished 14 uncontaminated

unsupportable 6 faulty 9 unfounded, untenable 12 indefensible

unsure 3 shy 5 timid 7 bashful 8 hesitant, insecure, reserved 9 unassured, uncertain, undecided 11 in a quandary, unconfident, unconvinced 12 self-doubting 15 self-distrustful

unsurpassed 4 best 7 highest, supreme 8 greatest, peerless, superior 9 matchless, nonpareil, paramount, unequaled, unmatched, unrivaled 10 consummate, unexcelled 11 exceptional 12 incomparable, transcendent, unparalleled

unsuspecting 5 naive 6 unwary 7 unaware 8 gullible, off guard, trusting 9 believing, credulous 12 overtrustful, unsuspicious 13 overcredulous

unsuspicious 5 naive 8 gullible, trustful, trusting 9 credulous 12 unsuspecting 13 unquestioning

unswerving 4 firm 6 steady, strong 7 devoted, staunch 8 faithful, resolute, resolved, unshaken, untiring 9 dedicated, steadfast, undaunted 10 determined, inflexible, unflagging, unwavering, unyielding 11 undeviating, unfaltering, unflinching, unremitting 12 single-minded 14 uncompromising

unsympathetic 7 callous 8 pitiless, uncaring 9 heartless, repellent, repugnant, unfeeling, unlikable 10 hard-boiled, unlikeable, unmerciful, unpleasant 11 coldhearted, displeasing, hardhearted, indifferent, uncongenial 12 antipathetic, unattractive 15 uncompassionate

unsystematic 6 sloppy 7 chaotic, jumbled, muddled 8 confused 9 haphazard, unplanned 10 disordered, disorderly 12 disorganized, unmethodical

untainted 4 pure 5 clear 9 unsullied 11 uncorrupted 13 unadulterated

untalented 5 inept 8 mediocre, ungifted 9 unskilled 10 amateurish, unskillful 14 unaccomplished

untamed 4 wild 5 feral 6 savage 9 unsubdued 11 uncivilized 12 uncultivated

untangle 5 solve 7 clear up, unravel, unsnarl, untwist 9 extricate 11 disentangle 13 straighten out

untarnished 6 bright 7 perfect, shining 8 flawless, polished, spotless, unsoiled 9 faultless, undefiled, unstained, unsullied, untainted 10 immaculate, impeccable, undisputed, unoxidized 11 unblackened, unblemished 12 unbesmirched 13 unimpeachable

untaught 6 unread 7 natural 8 ignorant 9 untutored 10 illiterate, uneducated, unlettered, unschooled 11 spontaneous 12 uninstructed

untenable 4 weak 6 faulty, flawed 7 invalid, unsound 8 baseless, specious, spurious 9 debatable, erroneous, illogical 10 fallacious, groundless, unreliable 11 contestable 12 indefensible, questionable 13 insupportable, unjustifiable, unsustainable 14 unmaintainable

unthinkable 11 unwarranted 12 unimaginable 13 inconceivable, insupportable, unjustifiable 16 incomprehensible, out of the question

unthinking 7 witless 8 careless, heedless, mindless, tactless 9 imprudent, negligent, senseless 11 inadvertent, insensitive, thoughtless 12 undiplomatic 13 inconsiderate, uncircumspect

untidiness 5 chaos, mix-up, upset 6 jumble 7 clutter 8 disarray, disorder, scramble, shambles 9 confusion, messiness 10 sloppiness 12 dishevelment 14 disarrangement 15 disorganization

untidy 5 dowdy, messy 6 frowsy, mussed, sloppy 7 chaotic, rumpled, tousled, unkempt 8 careless, confused, littered, mussed up, slipshod, slovenly 9 cluttered 10 bedraggled, disarrayed, disheveled, disorderly, slatternly, topsy-turvy 12 unmethodical 14 helter-skelter

untie 4 free, undo 5 loose 6 loosen, unbind, unlace 7 unchain, unstrap 8 make free, unfasten 11 disentangle

untilled 6 fallow 8 unplowed 12 uncultivated

until we meet again
  French: 5 adieu 8 au revoir
  German: 14 auf Wiedersehen
  Hawaiian: 5 aloha
  Italian: 4 ciao 5 addio 11 arrivederci
  Japanese: 8 sayonara
  Spanish: 5 adios

untimely 5 inapt 7 unhappy 8 ill-timed, mistimed, unseemly 9 imprudent, premature, unfitting 10 ill-advised, malapropos, out of place, unbecoming, unexpected, unsuitable 11 inopportune, unbefitting, unfortunate 12 inconvenient, infelicitous 13 inappropriate

untiring 5 fresh 6 steady 7 devoted, earnest, patient, staunch, zealous 8 constant, diligent, resolute, sedulous, tireless 9 assiduous, dedicated, steadfast, tenacious, unceasing, unwearied 10 determined, persistent, relentless, unflagging 11 never tiring, persevering, unfaltering, unremitting 12 wholehearted 13 indefatigable

untold 6 myriad, secret, unsaid 7 endless, private, unknown 8 hushed up, infinite, numerous, unspoken, withheld 9 concealed, countless, limitless, unbounded, uncounted, unrelated 10 numberless, suppressed, unnumbered, unreported, unrevealed 11 innumerable, undisclosed, unexpressed, unpublished 12 immeasurable, incalculable, undetermined

Untouchables, The
  character: 7 Rossman 9 Eliot Ness, Lee Hobson 10 Cam Allison, Frank Nitti 11 Enrico Rossi 14 Martin Flaherty 18 William Youngfellow
  cast: 10 Jerry Paris 11 Bruce Gordon, Paul Picerni, Robert Stack, Steve London 13 Abel Fernandez, Anthony George, Nick Georgiade
  narrator: 14 Walter Winchell

untouched 3 new 4 pure 5 alone 6 intact, virgin 8 pristine, unharmed 9 uninjured 10 unaffected, unmolested

untoward 5 amiss 6 unruly 7 adverse 8 contrary 9 difficult 11 unfavorable 12 inauspicious, unpropitious

untrainable 6 unruly 11 intractable, unteachable 12 ungovernable

untrained 3 raw 5 green 7 untried 9 unskilled 11 unqualified 13 inexperienced

untried 3 raw 5 green 6 callow 8 immature, untested 10 unseasoned 13 inexperienced

untroubled 4 calm 6 placid, serene 7 halcyon, relaxed 8 carefree, careless, peaceful, tranquil 9 easygoing, unworried 10 unbothered 11 free-and-easy, undisturbed, unperturbed 12 happy-go-lucky, lighthearted

untrue 4 fake, sham 5 false 6 made up 7 not true 8 disloyal, spurious, unchaste 9 dishonest, erroneous, faithless, falsified, incorrect, unfounded 10 adulterous, fallacious, fictitious, fraudulent, groundless, inaccurate, inconstant, perfidious, unfaithful, untruthful 11 promiscuous, treacherous 12 meretricious 13 double-dealing

untrustworthy 5 false 6 fickle, shifty, untrue 7 corrupt, crooked, devious 8 disloyal, fallible, slippery, two-faced 9 corrupted, deceitful, dishonest, faithless, insincere, uncertain, unethical 10 capricious, inconstant, perfidious, unfaithful, unreliable, untruthful 11 treacherous 12 dishonorable, disreputable, questionable, undependable, unprincipled, unscrupulous 13 irresponsible 15 unauthenticated

untruth 3 fib, lie 4 hoax, tale, yarn 5 fable, story 6 canard, humbug 8 flimflam 9 deception, falsehood, fish story, invention 11 fabrication 12 equivocation 13 falsification, prevarication 16 cock-and-bull story 17 misrepresentation

untruthful 5 false, lying 8 specious, spurious 9 deceptive, dishonest 10 fraudulent, mendacious

untutored 5 naive 6 native, unread 8 ignorant, untaught 10 illiterate, uneducated, unlettered, unschooled 12 uninstructed 15 unsophisticated

untypical 3 odd 4 rare 5 alien 7 bizarre, deviant, strange, unusual 8 aberrant, abnormal, atypical, uncommon 9 anomalous, irregular, unnatural 10 unfamiliar 16 unrepresentative

unused 3 new 7 strange, untried 8 left over, not given, pristine, unopened 9 remaining, untouched 10 unemployed 12 unaccustomed, unacquainted, unhabituated

unusual 4 rare 5 novel 6 unique 7 curious, offbeat, strange 8 atypical, peculiar, singular, uncommon 9 unequaled, unheard-of, unmatched, untypical 10 noteworthy, one of a kind, phenomenal, remarkable, surprising, unfamiliar 11 exceptional 12 incomparable, unparalleled 13 extraordinary, unprecedented 16 out of the ordinary

unvaried 4 even 5 fixed 6 steady 7 regular, uniform 8 all alike, constant 9 identical, unchanged 10 all the same, invariable, monotonous, unchanging 11 homogeneous, unalterable, undeviating

unvarnished 3 raw 4 bald, bare 5 blunt, crude, frank, naked, plain, stark 6 candid, direct, honest, simple 7 sincere 8 straight 9 unadorned, uncolored 10 unfinished 11

fundamental, undisguised 13 unembellished 15 straightforward 23 straight-from-the-shoulder

unvarying 4 even 6 steady 7 regular, uniform 8 constant 10 unwavering

unveil 4 bare 6 reveal 7 divulge, publish, uncloak, uncover 8 announce, disclose 9 broadcast, make known, unsheathe 12 bring to light

unveiled 5 bared 8 divulged, laid bare, revealed 9 announced, broadcast, disclosed, made known, published, uncovered 14 brought to light

unveiling 4 show 5 array 7 display, exhibit, showing 10 exhibition, exposition 13 demonstration

unverified 7 alleged, rumored 8 disputed 15 unauthenticated, unsubstantiated

unwarranted 7 illegal 8 culpable, unlawful 9 arbitrary, unfounded 10 censurable, groundless, unapproved 11 inexcusable, uncalled-for, unjustified 12 indefensible, unauthorized, unreasonable, unsanctioned

unwary 4 rash 5 hasty 7 unalert 8 careless, headlong, heedless, reckless 9 imprudent, unguarded 10 incautious, indiscreet, unwatchful 11 precipitate 12 disregardful 13 uncircumspect

unwashed 4 foul 5 dirty, grimy, muddy 6 filthy, grubby, smudgy, soiled 7 unclean 8 begrimed

unwasteful 6 frugal 7 thrifty 9 effective, effectual, efficient 10 productive

unwavering 4 firm 6 steady, strong 7 staunch 8 faithful, resolute, unshaken, untiring 9 dedicated, steadfast, tenacious 10 determined, persistent, unflagging, unswerving 11 persevering, undeviating, unfaltering, unflinching, unremitting 12 single-minded 14 uncompromising

unwelcome 7 outcast 8 excluded, rejected, unwanted 9 thankless, uninvited, unpopular 10 uncared for, unpleasant, unrequired 11 displeasing, distasteful, undesirable, unessential, unnecessary, unwished for 12 disagreeable, unacceptable

unwell 3 ill, low 4 sick 5 frail 6 ailing, infirm, laid up, poorly, queasy, sickly 7 run-down 8 delicate, qualmish 10 indisposed 11 off one's feed 15 under the weather

unwholesome 3 bad 4 evil, foul 5 toxic 6 deadly, filthy, sinful, wicked 7 baneful, harmful, hurtful, immoral, noxious, ruinous 8 depraved, venomous 9 corrupted, dangerous, degrading, poisonous, polluting, unhealthy 10 corrupting, pernicious 11 deleterious, detrimental, undesirable, unhealthful 12 demoralizing, dishonorable, insalubrious, unnourishing 13 contaminating

unwieldy 5 bulky, heavy 6 clumsy 7 awkward, weighty 8 not handy 10 burdensome, cumbersome 12 hard to handle, incommodious, inconvenient 13 uncomfortable

unwilled 6 reflex 9 automatic 11 involuntary, unconscious 12 uncontrolled 13 nonvolitional

unwilling 5 loath 6 averse 7 against, opposed 9 demurring, reluctant, resistant 10 dissenting, indisposed, undesirous 11 disinclined 12 not in the mood, recalcitrant 14 unenthusiastic

unwillingness 8 aversion 10 opposition, reluctance, resistance 13 indisposition 14 disinclination

unwise 4 dumb 5 crazy, silly 6 stupid 7 foolish, unsound 8 reckless 9 foolhardy, imprudent, senseless 10 ill-advised 11 improvident, inadvisable, injudicious 12 shortsighted, unreasonable 13 irresponsible, unintelligent

unwitting 7 unaware, unmeant 9 unknowing, unplanned 10 accidental, undesigned, unexpected, unthinking 11 inadvertent, involuntary 12 unconsenting 13 unintentional 14 unpremeditated

unwonted 4 rare 7 unusual 8 atypical, uncommon 10 infrequent, remarkable, unexpected, unfamiliar 11 exceptional 12 unaccustomed 13 extraordinary

unworkmanlike 6 clumsy, sloppy 11 inefficient

unworldly 4 holy, pure 5 godly, green, moral, naive, pious 6 callow, devout, divine, sacred, solemn 7 ethical 8 ethereal, heavenly, innocent, trusting 9 aesthetic, celestial, religious, spiritual, unearthly 10 idealistic, immaterial, provincial 12 intellectual, metaphysical, overtrusting 13 inexperienced, philosophical 14 transcendental 15 unsophisticated

unworried 4 calm 6 serene 7 relaxed 8 carefree, composed, peaceful, tranquil 9 easygoing, unruffled 10 untroubled

unworthy 5 unfit 7 ignoble 8 improper, shameful, unseemly 9 degrading, unethical 10 unbecoming, unsuitable 11 unbefitting 12 dishonorable, disreputable, unacceptable 13 discreditable, inappropriate, objectionable

unwrap 4 open 6 loosen, unbind 7 uncover

unwrinkled 4 even, flat 6 ironed, smooth 7 unlined 8 smoothed 9 uncreased, unrumpled

unwritten 4 oral 5 tacit, vocal 7 assumed, implied 8 implicit, inferred, unstated 9 customary 10 spoken only, understood, unrecorded 11 traditional, unexpressed 12 unformulated, unregistered 13 by word of mouth

unwritten law
Latin: 13 lex non scripta

unyielding 4 firm, hard 5 rigid, stiff, stony, tough 6 wooden 8 resolute, rocklike, stubborn 9 obstinate, steadfast, unbending, unpliable 10 determined, inexorable, inflexible, persistent, unswerving, unwavering 11 undeviating 14 uncompromising

up 4 atop, lift, over, rear 5 about, above, aloft, along, aside, astir, at bat, built, close, equal, erect, raise 6 apiece, ascend,

higher, lifted 7 abreast, batting, forward, promote, skyward, through 8 advanced, cheerful, increase, out of bed, overhead, standing, together, windward 9 northward 10 optimistic 11 constructed

up and about 5 afoot, astir 6 active, mobile, roused 7 walking 8 out of bed 10 ambulatory, on one's feet

up-and-down 6 fitful, seesaw, uneven 7 bobbing 8 jouncing, wavering 11 alternating, fluctuating, vacillating

upbraid 5 scold 6 berate, rebuke, revile 7 bawl out, censure, chew out, reprove 8 admonish, chastise, denounce, reproach 9 castigate, dress down, reprimand 10 tongue-lash

upbringing 7 rearing 8 breeding, training 10 background

upcoming 6 coming, nearby 7 looming, nearing, pending 8 imminent 9 impending, momentary 11 approaching, drawing nigh, forthcoming, in the offing, prospective

update 5 amend, emend, renew 6 recast, revamp, revise, rework 7 restore, touch up, upgrade 8 overhaul, renovate 9 refurbish 10 rejuvenate, reorganize, streamline

up for grabs 4 open 9 available

upgrade 5 raise, slope 6 ascent, better 7 advance, dignify, elevate, incline, inflate, promote 8 gradient

upheaval 5 flood, quake 6 blowup, tumult 7 turmoil 8 disorder, upthrust 9 cataclysm, explosion, tidal wave 10 disruption, earthquake, revolution 11 catastrophe, disturbance

uphill 4 hard 5 tough 6 rising, taxing, tiring, upward 7 arduous, onerous 8 toilsome, wearying 9 ascending, difficult, fatiguing, strenuous, wearisome 10 burdensome, enervating, exhausting 12 backbreaking

uphill work 8 struggle, tough job 10 difficulty, rough going 11 arduousness 12 hard sledding 13 laboriousness

uphold 4 bear, prop 5 brace, carry, raise, shore 6 defend, hold up, prop up 7 approve, bolster, confirm, elevate, endorse, protect, shore up, support, sustain 8 advocate, buttress, champion, maintain, preserve, underpin 9 encourage 10 stand up for, underbrace 11 acknowledge, corroborate

upholder 7 devotee 8 adherent, advocate, defender, partisan 9 supporter

up in the clouds 6 elated, joyful, joyous 8 ecstatic, euphoric 9 exuberant, rapturous 11 on cloud nine 15 in seventh heaven

Upis
goddess of: 10 childbirth

Upjohn, Richard
architect of: 13 Trinity Church (NYC)
style: 13 Gothic Revival

upkeep 4 keep 6 living 7 support 8 expenses, overhead 10 management, sustenance 11 maintenance, subsistence 12 conservation, preservation

upland 4 high, rise **5** ridge **6** height **7** plateau **8** eminence, highland **9** elevation, high place, high point **10** prominence

uplift 5 edify, raise **6** better, refine **7** advance, bracing, elevate, improve, inspire, lifting, shoring, support, upgrade **8** civilize, propping **9** cultivate, elevation **10** betterment, bolstering, enrichment, refinement **11** advancement, buttressing, cultivation, edification, enhancement, improvement **12** underpinning

uplifting 9 elevating, elevation, improving, inspiring **11** improvement **12** enlightening **13** enlightenment, inspirational

upon 2 at, on **4** atop **5** about **6** toward **7** against, thereon **9** by means of, thereupon **10** after which, thereafter

upper 3 top **4** high **5** major **6** higher, inland **7** eminent, greater, topmost **8** elevated, northern, superior **9** important

upper-case letter 7 capital **9** majuscule **13** capital letter

upper class 5 elite **6** gentry, uptown **7** (high) society **8** highborn, highbred, wellborn **9** beau monde, haut monde, highclass, patrician, top drawer **10** upper crust **11** aristocracy, blue-blooded **12** aristocratic, silk-stocking **14** creme de la creme, to the manor born **15** to the manner born

upper crust 5 elite **6** gentry **7** (high) society **9** beau monde, haut monde, top drawer **10** upper class **11** aristocracy **14** creme de la creme

upper hand 4 edge, sway **5** power **7** command, control, mastery **8** whip hand **9** advantage, authority, supremacy **10** domination **12** predominance

upper house 6 Senate **12** House of Lords

uppermost, upmost 3 top **4** main **5** chief, first, major, prime **7** highest, leading, primary, supreme, topmost **8** crowning, dominant, foremost, greatest, loftiest **9** essential, paramount, principal **10** preeminent **11** predominant **12** transcendent **13** most important

Upper Volta
other name 11 Burkina Faso (Fasso)
capital/largest city: 11 Ouagadougou
others: 4 Kaya **7** Banfora **9** Koudougou **10** Ouahigouya
division: 7 Yatenga **9** Tenkodogo **11** Fada Ngourma
monetary unit: 5 franc **7** centime
mountain: 4 Tema
highest point: 8 Nakourou **10** Tenakourou, Tenekourou
river: 5 Komoe **6** Mekrou, Sourou **8** Pendjari, Red Volta **10** Black Volta, White Volta
physical feature:
plateau: **5** Sahel **7** Sikasso, Voltaic
wind: **9** harmattan
people: 4 Bobo, Lobi, Samo **5** Bella, Bissa, Dyula, Fulbe, Hausa, Mande, Marka, Mossi, Puehl **6** Fulani, Senufo, Tuareg **7** Grunshi, Voltaic, Yatenga **8**
Mandingo **9** Gourounsi **15** Bunsansi Gambaga
French governor: 7 Hesling
god: 4 Wuro **5** Tenga
king: 4 Naba **5** Mogho
leader: 5 Oubri, Zerbo **7** Yameogo **8** Lamizana **9** Mogho Naba
language: 4 Bobo, Lobi, More, Samo **5** Dyula, Mande, Mossi **6** French
religion: 5 Islam **7** animism **12** Christianity
place:
game reserve: **11** Arlyand Pama
feature:
animal: **5** hyena **6** duiker, jackal **7** gazelle, warthog **10** hartebeest
tree: **4** shea **6** acacia, baobab, karite, locust

upright 3 rib **4** fair, good, just, pale, pier, pile, pole, post, prop **5** erect, moral, shaft, stake, strut **6** column, honest, picket, pillar **7** ethical, support, upended **8** reliable, standard, vertical **9** honorable, righteous, stanchion **10** aboveboard, high-minded, principled, standing-up, upstanding **11** trustworthy **12** on the up-and-up **13** perpendicular

uprightness 5 honor **7** dignity, honesty **8** morality **9** integrity **13** righteousness **15** trustworthiness

uprising 4 riot **6** mutiny, revolt **8** outbreak **9** rebellion **10** insurgence, revolution **12** insurrection

uproar 3 ado **4** stir, to-do **5** furor **6** clamor, tumult **7** turmoil **9** agitation, commotion **11** disturbance, pandemonium **16** state of confusion

uproarious 4 loud, wild **5** noisy **6** raging, stormy **7** furious, intense, riotous **9** clamorous, hilarious, turbulent, very funny **10** boisterous, disorderly, hysterical, tumultuous **11** tempestuous **13** sidesplitting

uproot 6 banish **7** abolish, cast out, destroy, root out, wipe out **8** dislodge, displace, force out **9** eliminate, extirpate **10** annihilate, do away with **11** exterminate

upset 3 ire, irk, mad, vex **4** beat **5** anger, annoy, crush, irked, messy, mix up, pique, quash, smash, upend, vexed, worry **6** bother, cancel, change, defeat, enrage, grieve, invert, jumble, muddle, mussed, rattle, thrash, untidy **7** agitate, angered, annoyed, capsize, chaotic, confuse, conquer, disturb, enraged, fluster, furious, grieved, incense, jumbled, mixed-up, perturb, reverse, tip over, trouble, trounce, unnerve, upended, worried **8** agitated, bothered, capsized, confused, demolish, disorder, distress, incensed, inverted, overcome, overturn, slovenly, troubled, turn over, unnerved, upturned, vanquish **9** discomfit, disturbed, infuriate, overpower, overthrow, overwhelm, perturbed **10** discompose, disconcert, disheveled, disordered, disorderly, disquieted, distressed, hysterical, overturned, tipped over, topple over, topsy-turvy, turned over, upside-

down 11 disarranged, disorganize, overwrought, wrong side up 12 disorganized
13 make miserable 14 turn topsy-turvy

upsetting
French: 14 bouleversement

upshot 3 end 6 effect, payoff, result, sequel
7 outcome 8 offshoot 9 aftermath, outgrowth 10 conclusion 11 aftereffect, consequence, culmination, eventuality 16 final
development

upside down 7 chaotic 8 reversed 10 disorderly 11 topsy turvey 12 bottomside up
16 at sixes and sevens

upstairs 2 up 11 above stairs, second floor

upstanding 4 good, tall, true 5 erect,
moral, on end 6 honest 7 ethical, upright 8
straight, truthful, vertical, virtuous 9 honorable, righteous 11 trustworthy 13 incorruptible, perpendicular

upstart 4 snip, snob, snub 6 nobody 7
bounder, parvenu 8 mushroom 9 conceited, newly-rich 10 adventurer 12 nouveau riche 13 self-assertive

upsurge 4 gain, push, rise 5 spurt 6 pickup,
thrust, upturn 7 advance, upswing 8 increase 11 improvement

upswing 4 rise 6 pickup 7 upsurge 11 improvement, upward trend

uptight 5 tense 7 anxious, fearful, nervous,
worried, wound up 8 insecure, neurotic,
troubled 9 unbending 10 unyielding 12 apprehensive

up-to-date 2 in 3 new 5 today 6 modern,
modish, timely, trendy, with-it 7 current,
stylish 9 in fashion 12 contemporary 13
up-to-the-minute
French: 9 au courant

upturn 4 gain, push 6 thrust 7 advance, upsurge 8 increase 9 expansion 11 improvement

upward 4 high, more 5 above, aloft 7 skyward 9 ascending, uppermost

upward movement 4 rise 5 climb 6 ascent,
rising, upturn 7 scaling, takeoff 8 climbing,
mounting 9 ascension

upward trend 4 rise 5 boost 6 pickup 7 advance, upsurge, upswing 8 increase 11 improvement

Uralic
language branch: 7 Samoyed 10 Finno-
Ugric

Urania
also: 9 Aphrodite
member of: 5 Muses
personifies: 9 astronomy

uranium
chemical symbol: 1 U

Uranus
mother: 4 Gaea
wife: 4 Gaea
father of: 6 Giants, Titans 8 Cyclopes 10
Titanesses 13 Hecatonchires
castrated by: 6 Cronos, Cronus Kronos

Uranus
position: 7 seventh
satellite: 5 Ariel 6 Oberon 7 Miranda, Titania, Umbriel

color: 9 blue-green
characteristic: 5 rings

Urartu see 7 Armenia

urban 4 city, town 5 civic 8 citified 9 municipal 11 worldly-wise 12 cosmopolitan, metropolitan 13 sophisticated

urban area 4 city 9 inner city 10 metropolis
11 megalopolis 16 metropolitan area

urbane 5 civil, suave 6 polite, smooth 7
courtly, elegant, gallant, genteel, politic, refined, tactful 8 debonair, gracious, mannerly, polished, well-bred 9 civilized, courteous 10 chivalrous, cultivated, diplomatic
11 gentlemanly 12 cosmopolitan, well-
mannered 13 sophisticated

urchin 3 boy, imp, lad 4 brat, waif 5 gamin,
stray, whelp, youth 6 gamine, laddie 8
young pup 9 stripling, young punk, youngster 10 young rogue, young tough 11 guttersnipe

Urd 4 Norn
origin: 12 Scandinavian
form: 8 giantess
personifies: 4 past
developed from: 5 Urdar
companion: 5 Skuld 8 Verdandi

Urdar 12 original Norn
origin: 12 Scandinavian
form: 8 giantess
children: 3 Urd 5 Skuld 8 Verdandi

Urey, Harold Clayton
field: 9 chemistry
isolated: 9 deuterium
awarded: 10 Nobel prize

urge 3 yen 4 back, coax, goad, itch, poke,
prod, push, spur, sway, wish 5 drive, egg
on, fancy, force, press, prick, speed 6 advise, desire, exhort, hasten, hunger, motive, reason, thirst 7 beseech, counsel,
craving, dictate, entreat, implore, impulse,
longing, passion, push for, quicken, request, solicit, suggest 8 advocate, appeal
to, argue for, champion, convince, persuade, petition, pressure, stimulus, yearning 9 hankering, importune, incentive,
plead with, prescribe, prompting, recommend 10 accelerate, inducement, motivation, supplicate 11 prevail upon, provocation

urgency 4 need, urge, want 5 press 6
stress 8 exigency, pressure 9 necessity 10
importance, insistence 11 persistence 14
imperativeness 15 importunateness

urgent 5 grave 6 ardent 7 crucial, earnest,
fervent, intense, serious, weighty, zealous
8 critical, pleading, pressing, required,
spirited 9 demanding, essential, heartfelt,
important, insistent, momentous, necessary 10 beseeching, compelling, compulsory, imperative, obligatory, passionate 12
wholehearted 13 indispensable

urge on 4 push 5 boost 7 cheer on, pull for,
root for

urging 7 bidding, counsel, goading 8
egging on 9 prompting 11 exhortation

Uriah
    father: 7 Shemiah
    wife: 9 Bathsheba
    served: 5 David
urinary system
    component: 6 kidney, ureter 7 bladder, urethra
    rids body of: 5 salts, waste, water 8 minerals
Uris, Leon
    author of: 5 Topaz 6 Exodus 7 Trinity 9 Battle Cry 10 Armageddon
urn 3 jar, pig 4 ewer, kist, tomb, vase 5 grave, steen 6 teapot 7 samovar 9 coffeepot
    botanical: 7 capsule 11 spore-bearer
    in keno: 5 goose
Urn Burial
    author: 15 Sir Thomas Browne
Uruguay
    other name: 10 Purple Land
    capital/largest city: 10 Montevideo
    others: 4 Fray, Melo 5 Minas, Rocha, Salto 6 Bentos, Rivera 7 Artigas, Colonia, Dolores, Durazno, Florida, San Jose 8 Mercedes, Paysandu, Trinidad 9 Maldonado 10 Las Piedras, Santa Lucia, Tacuarembo 12 Treinta y Tres 13 San Jose de Mayo
    measure: 4 vara 6 cuadra, suerte
    monetary unit: 4 peso 9 centesimo, centisimo
    weight: 7 quintal
    island: 5 Lobos
    lake: 5 Merin, Mirim 18 Embalse del Rio Negro
    mountain: 6 Animas 10 Grand Hills 14 Cuchilla Grande
    highest point: 15 Mirador Nacional
    river: 4 Malo 5 Mirim, Negro, Plata 6 Parana, Ulimar 7 Cuareim, Queguay, Uruguay 8 Yaguaron 9 Cebollati 10 Tacauerembo
    sea: 8 Atlantic
    physical feature:
    estuary: 5 Plata
    people: 4 Yaro 5 Swiss 6 Indian 7 Italian, mestizo, Russian, Spanish 8 Charruas
    artist: 6 Figari
    author: 4 Rodo 5 Reyes 6 Onetti 7 Sanchez 9 San Martin 10 Ibarbourou
    leader: 5 Oribe 6 Rivera 7 Artigas 9 Lavelleja 10 Bordaberry 14 Batlle y Ordonez
    language: 7 Italian, Spanish
    religion: 13 Roman Catholic
    place:
    resort: 12 Punta del Este
    square: 13 Independencia
    feature:
    animal: 4 puma 6 jaguar 8 capybara 9 armadillo
    bird: 4 rhea 5 nandu 7 hornero, ostrich
    cattle ranch: 8 estancia
    cowboy: 6 gaucho
    dance: 5 tango 7 milonga
    festival: 8 Carnival 13 Semana Criolla

    lasso: 10 boleadoras
    metal straw: 8 bombilla
    music: 9 candomble
    musical drama: 7 tablado
    ruling class: 10 Patriciado
    food:
    barbecue: 5 asado
    dish: 7 puchero 9 churrasco 13 asado con cuero
    drink: 4 mate
U S A
    author: 13 John Dos Passos
    character: 10 Ben Compton, Mary French 11 Joe Williams 12 Margo Dowling 13 Fainy McCreary (Mac), Janey Williams 14 J Ward Morehouse 15 Charley Anderson, Eleanor Stoddard, Eveline Hutchins 18 Anne Elizabeth Trent 22 Richard Ellsworth Savage
usable 5 handy 6 useful 9 adaptable 10 functional 11 serviceable
usage 3 use 4 care, mode 5 habit 6 custom, manner, method, system 7 control 8 good form, habitude, handling, practice 9 etiquette, operation, tradition, treatment 10 convention, employment, management 12 manipulation
use 3 aid, ply, sap 4 good, help, work 5 apply, avail, drain, exert, spend, treat, usage, value, waste, wield, worth 6 devour, employ, expend, handle, profit 7 benefit, consume, deplete, exhaust, exploit, operate, service, utilize 8 deal with, exercise, function, handling, profit by, put to use, resort to, squander 9 act toward, advantage, dissipate, enjoyment, make use of, operation, swallow up, throw away 10 employment, manipulate, run through, usefulness 11 application, convenience, fritter away, utilization 12 behave toward, capitalize on 13 make the most of 14 serviceability
used 3 old 5 eaten, spent 7 applied, treated 8 actuated, consumed, depleted, employed, occupied, operated, utilized 9 customary, exercised, exhausted, exploited, practiced 10 accustomed, habituated, secondhand 11 implemented, manipulated
used up 4 beat, shot 5 all in, spent 6 wasted 7 worn out 8 depleted, tired out 9 exhausted
useful 5 handy 7 helpful 8 valuable 9 effective, practical, rewarding 10 beneficial, convenient, functional, profitable, timesaving, worthwhile 11 serviceable, utilitarian 12 advantageous
usefulness 5 avail, value, worth 6 profit 7 benefit, purpose, utility 9 advantage 11 convenience, helpfulness, suitability 12 adaptability, practicality 13 effectiveness 14 serviceability
useless 4 vain 6 futile 7 of no use 8 bootless, unusable 9 fruitless, unhelpful, worthless 10 inadequate, profitless, unavailing 11 incompetent, ineffectual, inefficient 12 unproductive 13 impracticable, inefficacious, nonfunctional, unserviceable

uselessness 6 vanity 8 futility, idleness 9 inutility 10 inefficacy 13 fruitlessness, worthlessness

Uses of Enchantment, The
author: 15 Bruno Bettelheim

use sparingly 4 save 5 hoard, stint 6 scrimp 7 cut back, dole out 8 conserve, not waste, preserve

use to advantage 7 exploit 8 profit by 12 capitalize on 13 turn to account

use up 5 drain, spend 6 expend, finish 7 consume, deplete, exhaust 9 dissipate 10 run through

Ushant
author: 11 Conrad Aiken

usher 4 lead, show 5 guide, steer 6 attend, convoy, direct, escort, herald, launch, leader, porter, ring in, squire 7 conduct, precede, preface 8 announce, director, proclaim 9 conductor, introduce 10 doorkeeper, gatekeeper, inaugurate

Usnach
also: 6 Usnech
origin: 5 Irish
daughter: 6 Naoise

Usnech see 6 Usnach

USSR see 6 Russia

Ustinov, Peter
born: 6 London 7 England
roles: 7 Topkapi 8 Quo Vadis? 9 Billy Budd, Spartacus 12 We're No Angels

usual 5 stock, trite 6 common, normal, wonted 7 popular, regular, routine, typical 8 expected, familiar, habitual, ordinary, orthodox, standard 9 customary, hackneyed 10 accustomed, prescribed, threadbare 11 commonplace, established, oft-repeated, traditional 12 conventional, run-of-the-mill 15 well-established

usurp 4 grab 5 steal 7 preempt 8 arrogate 10 commandeer 11 appropriate 12 encroach upon, infringe upon

usurpation 6 taking 7 seizure 8 grabbing, stealing 9 arrogation, preemption 13 appropriation

Utah
abbreviation: 2 UT
nickname: 6 Mormon 7 Beehive
capital/largest city: 12 Salt Lake City
others: 3 Roy 4 Moab, Orem 5 Delta, Heber, Kanab, Logan, Magna, Manti, Nepli, Ogden, Price, Provo 6 Beaver, Eureka, Kearns, Layton, Murray, Tooele, Vernal 7 Bingham 8 American 9 Bountiful 11 Brigham City
college: 5 Weber 11 Westminster 12 Brigham Young
feature:
bridge: 7 Rainbow
dam: 6 Hoover 10 Glen Canyon
gorge: 7 Flaming
national historic site: 11 Golden Spike
national monument: 8 Dinosaur 14 Natural Bridges
national park: 4 Zion 6 Arches 11 Bryce Canyon, Canyonlands, Capital Reef
reef: 7 Capital
tribe: 3 Ute 5 Piute, Uinta(h), Yampa 6 Navajo, Paiute 7 Gosiute 8 Paviotso, Shoshoni
people: 7 Mormons 10 Maude Adams 11 Karl G Maeser 12 Brigham Young 13 John M Browning 15 Latter-Day Saints 16 George Sutherland 19 Daniel Cowan Jackling
explorer: 9 Dominguez, Escalante
lake: 4 Mead, Swan, Utah 6 Powell, Sevier 9 Great Salt
land rank: 8 eleventh
mountain: 4 Lena, Lion, Waas 5 Cedar, Henry, Hogup, Peale, Rocky, Trail, Uinta 6 Frisco, Navajo, Swasey, Wahwah 7 Granite, Griffin, Hawkins, Pennell, Terrace, Wasatch 8 Linnaeus 9 Confusion
highest point: 9 Kings Peak
physical feature:
basin: 5 Great
canyon: 4 Echo
desert: 6 Sevier
plateau: 7 Wasatch 8 Colorado, Tavaputs
river: 4 Bear 5 Grand, Green, Weber 6 Jordan, Sevier, Virgin 7 San Juan 8 Colorado
state admission: 10 forty-fifth
state bird: 7 seagull
state flower: 8 sego lily
state motto: 8 Industry
state song: 14 Utah We Love Thee
state tree: 10 blue spruce

utensils 4 gear 5 tools 6 outfit, silver, tackle 8 flatware 9 apparatus 10 implements, silverware 11 instruments 13 paraphernalia

Utgard
origin: 12 Scandinavian
realm of: 7 Skrymir 10 Utgardloki
location: 9 Gatunheim

Utgardloki see 7 Skrymir

utilitarian 5 handy 6 usable, useful 8 sensible, valuable, workable 9 effective, efficient, practical, pragmatic 10 beneficial, convenient, functional, profitable 11 serviceable 12 advantageous

utility 3 aid, gas, use 4 help 5 avail, extra 6 backup 7 benefit, reserve, service 8 function 9 accessory, advantage, alternate, auxiliary, secondary, surrogate, telephone 10 additional, substitute, usefulness 11 convenience, electricity 12 availability, supplemental 13 public service 14 serviceability

utilization 3 use 10 employment 11 application 12 exploitation

utilize 3 use 6 employ 7 exploit 8 profit by, put to use, resort to 9 make use of 12 capitalize on 13 bring into play, make the most of, turn to account 14 avail oneself of, have recourse to, put into service 15 take advantage of

utmost, uttermost 4 acme, best, main, peak, tops 5 chief, first, major, prime 6 tiptop, zenith 7 capital, highest, leading, maximum, primary, supreme, the most 8 cardinal, foremost, greatest, last word, ultimate 9 paramount, principal, sovereign 10 preeminent 11 predominant

Uto-Aztecan (Nahuatl)
　tribe: 4 Pima 5 Aatam, Aztec, Nahua 6 Mexica, Papago 8 Pima Alto

utopia 4 Eden 6 heaven 7 Erewhon 8 paradise 9 ideal life, Shangri-la 12 perfect bliss, perfect place 13 seventh heaven

utopian 9 visionary 10 idealistic, unfeasible, unworkable 11 unrealistic 12 otherworldly, unattainable, unrealizable 13 impracticable, insubstantial, unfulfillable

Utrillo, Maurice
　born: 5 Paris 6 France
　mother: 14 Suzanne Valadon
　artwork: 16 The Church at Deuil, The Church of Blevy 17 Church at St Hilaire 19 La Petite Communiante 22 Sacre Coeur de Montmartre

ut supra 7 as above

utter 3 say 4 emit, pure, talk, tell, yell 5 sheer, shout, speak, state, total, voice 6 entire, mutter, reveal 7 declare, deliver, divulge, exclaim, express, perfect, whisper 8 absolute, complete, disclose, outright, proclaim, thorough, vocalize 9 downright, enunciate, out-and-out, pronounce, unchecked 10 articulate, unmodified, unrelieved 11 categorical, unequivocal, unmitigated, unqualified

utterance 4 talk, word 6 answer, remark, speech 7 opinion 9 discourse, statement 10 expression 11 declaration, exclamation 12 articulation, proclamation, vocalization 13 pronouncement, verbalization

utterly 4 just 5 fully 6 wholly 7 totally 8 entirely, outright 9 downright, extremely, perfectly 10 absolutely, completely, thoroughly 14 to the nth degree

uttermost 6 utmost 7 extreme, maximum, supreme 9 outermost, sovereign 12 extreme limit

Utu
　origin: 8 Sumerian
　god of: 3 sun

Uzbekistan
　capital/largest city: 8 Tashkent
　others: 9 Samarkand
　head of state: 9 president
　government: 8 republic
　monetary unit: 5 ruble
　river: 8 Amu Darya, Syr Darya
　sea: 4 Aral
　people: 5 Uzbek
　language: 5 Uzbek
　religion: 5 Islam 11 Sunni Muslim

Uzziah
　also: 7 Azariah
　king of: 5 Judah
　father: 7 Amaziah
　son: 6 Jotham 7 Jehoram 8 Jonathan

V

vacancy 3 gap 4 hole, void 5 abode, place 6 breach, cavity, hollow 7 crevice, fissure, housing, lodging, opening 9 emptiness, situation 10 empty space, vacantness 11 room for rent 12 house for rent

vacant 4 dull, free, idle, open 5 aloof, blank, blase, clear, empty, vapid 6 unused, wooden 7 deadpan, for rent, leisure, vacuous 8 deserted, detached, for lease, forsaken, not in use, unfilled 9 abandoned, apathetic, incurious, oblivious, poker-face, unengaged 10 tenantless, unemployed, unoccupied, untenanted 11 indifferent, unconcerned, unfurnished, uninhabited 12 unencumbered 14 expressionless 15 uncomprehending

vacate 4 quit 5 empty, leave 6 give up, resign 8 abdicate, evacuate, hand over 9 surrender 10 depart from, relinquish

vacate the throne 4 cede, flee, quit 5 yield 6 give up, resign, retire 7 abandon 8 abdicate 10 relinquish

vacation 4 rest 5 leave, R and R 6 recess 7 holiday 8 furlough, holidays 10 sabbatical 12 intermission 13 take a vacation 14 leave of absence 17 rest-and-recreation
  French: 8 vacances

vacillate 4 reel, rock, roll, sway, toss 5 pitch, shift, waver 6 falter, teeter, totter, wobble 7 flutter, vibrate 8 hesitate 9 fluctuate, hem and haw, oscillate 12 shilly-shally 14 blow hot and cold

vacillating 7 swaying 8 wavering 9 diffident, uncertain, vibrating 10 hesitating, irresolute, on the fence 11 fluctuating, uncertainty 12 irresolution 15 shilly-shallying

vacillation 7 swaying 8 wavering 9 faltering, vibration 10 indecision 11 fluctuation, uncertainty 12 irresolution 15 shilly-shallying

Vacuna
  origin: 6 Sabine
  goddess of: 11 agriculture

vacuous 4 dull, idle, void 5 blank, empty, inane, silly 6 stupid, vacant 7 fatuous, foolish 8 indolent, unfilled 9 senseless 11 empty-headed, purposeless

Vaduz
  capital of: 13 Liechtenstein

vae victis 18 woe to the vanquished

vagabond 4 hobo 5 gypsy, nomad, rover, tramp 6 roamer, roving 7 drifter, floater, migrant, nomadic, rambler, roaming, vagrant 8 bohemian, carefree, homeless, rambling, wanderer, wayfarer 9 footloose, itinerant, transient, traveling, wandering, wayfaring 10 journeying 11 beachcomber

Vagabond Lover
  nickname of: 10 Rudy Vallee

vagary 4 kink, whim 5 fancy, humor, quirk 6 notion, oddity, whimsy 7 caprice, fantasy, impulse 8 crotchet, daydream 10 brainstorm, erraticism 11 peculiarity 12 eccentricity, idiosyncrasy, passing fancy

vagrant 3 bum 4 hobo 5 nomad, rover, tramp 6 beggar, loafer, roamer, roving 7 floater, migrant, nomadic, roaming 8 homeless, rambling, vagabond, wanderer 9 itinerant, transient, wandering 10 panhandler 11 peripatetic 15 knight-of-the-road

vague 4 hazy 5 fuzzy, loose 6 casual, random, unsure 7 general, unclear 8 confused, nebulous 9 imprecise, uncertain, unsettled 10 ill-defined, indefinite, inexplicit, undetailed, unspecific 11 not definite, unspecified 12 undetermined

vaguely 5 dimly 6 hazily 7 loosely 8 dreamily, slightly, vacantly 9 obscurely, sketchily 10 nebulously 11 ambiguously 12 indistinctly

vagueness 8 haziness 9 ambiguity, confusion, fuzziness 11 uncertainty 13 lack of clarity 14 indefiniteness

vain 4 idle 5 cocky, proud, silly 6 futile 7 foolish, pompous, stuck-up, useless 8 arrogant, boastful, bootless, dandyish, egoistic, nugatory, puffed-up, trifling 9 conceited, egotistic, fruitless, pointless, worthless 10 disdainful, profitless, swaggering, unavailing 11 egotistical, ineffective, ineffectual, superficial, time-wasting 12 self-admiring, supercilious, unprofitable, unsuccessful, vainglorious 13 self-important, self-satisfied

Vainamoinen
  origin: 7 Finnish
  hero of: 8 Kalevala
  form: 8 magician
  opposes: 5 Louhi 11 Joukahainen

vainglorious 5 cocky 7 haughty, pompous, stuck-up 8 affected, arrogant, boastful, bragging, insolent 9 conceited 10 egoistical, pretentious, swaggering 11 egotistical, swell-headed 12 narcissistic, supercilious 13 full of oneself, self-important

vainglory 6 vanity 7 conceit, swagger 9 cockiness 10 pretension 11 braggadocio 14 self-importance 16 overbearing pride

vale 6 good-by 8 farewell

valedictory 4 last 5 final 7 parting 8 farewell, terminal, ultimate 9 departing 10 conclusive 11 leavetaking 14 farewell speech 19 commencement address

Valentine
   character in: 20 Two Gentlemen of Verona
   author: 11 Shakespeare

Valentino, Rudolph
   real name: 16 Rodolfo (Alfonzo Raffaele Pierre Philibert) Guglielmi
   born: 5 Italy 12 Castellaneta
   wife: 9 Jean Acker 14 Natasha Rambova
   roles: 8 The Sheik 12 Blood and Sand 16 The Son of the Sheik 17 Monsieur Beaucaire 30 The Four Horsemen of the Apocalypse

valerian 9 Valeriana
   varieties: 3 red 5 Greek 6 common 7 African 8 American 11 long-spurred

Valery, Paul
   author of: 7 Cahiers, Charmes 12 The Young Fate 13 Le Jeune Parque 16 Sketch of a Serpent 20 The Graveyard by the Sea

Valhalla
   origin: 8 Teutonic
   hall of: 4 Odin 5 Othin

valiant 4 bold 5 brave, noble 6 daring, heroic 7 gallant 8 fearless, intrepid, knightly, resolute, stalwart, unafraid, valorous 9 audacious, dauntless, undaunted 10 chivalrous, courageous 11 lionhearted, unflinching 12 bold-spirited, great-hearted, stouthearted

valid 4 good 5 legal, licit, sound 6 lawful, proper, strong 7 fitting, genuine, logical, weighty 8 accurate, decisive, forceful, official, powerful, suitable, truthful 9 authentic, effective, legalized, realistic 10 acceptable, applicable, compelling, convincing, legitimate 11 substantial, well-founded 12 well-grounded 13 authoritative, being in effect 14 constitutional, legally binding

validate 4 enact, prove, stamp 5 ratify, verify 7 certify, confirm, sustain, warrant, witness 8 legalize, sanction 9 authorize, make legal, make valid 10 make lawful 11 corroborate, countersign 12 authenticate, make official, substantiate

validation 8 sanction 12 confirmation, legalization, ratification 13 authorization, certification

validity 5 force, logic, power, right 6 weight 7 grounds, potency 8 accuracy, legality, strength 9 authority, soundness, substance 10 legal force, legitimacy, properness 11 suitability 12 authenticity, truthfulness 13 acceptability, applicability, effectiveness 14 conclusiveness, convincingness

valise 3 bag 4 grip 7 handbag, luggage, satchel 8 suitcase 9 briefcase, Gladstone 11 portmanteau

Valjean, Jean
   character in: 13 Les Miserables
   author: 4 Hugo

Valkyrie
   origin: 8 Teutonic
   home: 8 Valhalla
   attendant of: 4 Odin 5 Othin

   queen: 8 Brunhild, Brynhild 10 Brunnhilde

Vallee, Rudy
   real name: 17 Hubert Prior Vallee
   nickname: 16 The Vagabond Lover
   born: 13 Island Point VT
   played: 9 saxophone
   wife: 9 Jane Greer
   roles: 16 The Vagabond Lover 17 The Palm Beach Story, Unfaithfully Yours 41 How to Succeed in Business Without Really Trying

Valletta
   capital of: 5 Malta

valley 3 cut, dip, gap 4 dale, dell, glen, vale 5 basin, chasm, glade, gorge, gulch, gully 6 bottom, canyon, divide, hollow, ravine 8 water gap

Valley Forge
   author: 15 Maxwell Anderson

Valley of Horses, The
   author: 9 Jean M Auel

Valley of the Dolls
   author: 16 Jacqueline Susann

valor 4 grit, guts 5 nerve, pluck, spunk 6 daring, mettle 7 bravery, courage, heroism 8 boldness, chivalry 9 fortitude, gallantry 11 intrepidity 12 fearlessness 13 dauntlessness

valorous 4 bold 5 brave, gutsy 6 heroic, plucky 7 valiant 8 fearless, intrepid, stalwart, unafraid 9 dauntless 10 courageous 11 indomitable, lionhearted 12 stouthearted

valse 5 waltz

valuable 4 dear, good 6 costly, prized, useful, valued 7 admired, helpful 8 esteemed, fruitful, precious 9 expensive, important, priceless, respected, treasured 10 beneficial, high-priced, invaluable, profitable, worthwhile 11 serviceable, significant, utilitarian 12 advantageous

valuation 9 appraisal 10 assessment, evaluation 14 estimated value

value, values 3 use 4 cost, help, rate 5 assay, count, judge, merit, price, prize, rules, weigh, worth 6 admire, amount, assess, charge, esteem, ideals, profit, reckon, revere, size up 7 beliefs, benefit, cherish, compute, customs, respect, service, utility 8 appraise, evaluate, prestige, treasure 9 advantage, appraisal, greatness, moral code, practices, standards 10 admiration, appreciate, assessment, estimation, excellence, importance, set store by, usefulness 11 conventions, market price, superiority 12 code of ethics, institutions, significance

valued 6 prized 7 revered 8 esteemed 9 cherished, respected, treasured 11 appreciated 14 highly regarded

valueless 7 trivial, useless 9 worthless 11 of no account, unimportant 13 insignificant 14 good for nothing 15 inconsequential

vamoose 3 out 4 away, scat, shoo 5 be off, leave, scram 6 beat it, begone, depart, get out, go away 7 get lost

vamp 5 siren 9 temptress 10 seductress 11 enchantress, femme fatale 12 introduction

Vamp
nickname of: 9 Theda Bara

vampire 3 bat 7 Dracula 11 bloodsucker

van 4 cart, dray, head 5 lorry, scout, truck, wagon 6 camper, picket 7 trailer 8 sentinel, vanguard 9 first line, forefront, front rank 10 avant-garde, large truck 12 advance guard, covered truck 13 front of an army 16 foremost division
french: 7 fourgon

Van, Bobby
real name: 10 Robert King
born: 9 New York NY
roles: 10 Kiss Me Kate, On Your Toes 11 No No Nanette 12 It's Only Money, The Ladies' Man 13 Small Town Girl 23 The Affairs of Dobie Gillis

van Alen, William
architect of: 16 Chrysler Building (NYC)

Van Allen, James Alfred
field: 7 physics
invented: 18 radio proximity fuse
discovered: 22 Van Allen radiation belts

Van Buren, Martin
nicknames: 9 The Red Fox 17 The Little Magician 18 The Careful Dutchman
presidential rank: 6 eighth
party: 8 Democrat
state represented: 7 New York
defeated: 5 (Hugh Lawson) White 6 (William Person) Mangum 7 (Daniel) Webster 8 (William Henry) Harrison
vice president: 7 (Richard Mentor) Johnson
cabinet:
state: 7 (John) Forsyth
treasury: 8 (Levi) Woodbury
war: 8 (Joel Roberts) Poinsett
attorney general: 6 (Benjamin Franklin) Butler, (Felix) Grundy, (Henry Dilworth) Gilpin
navy: 8 (James Kirke) Paulding 9 (Mahlon) Dickerson
postmaster general: 5 (John Milton) Niles 7 (Amos) Kendall
born/died/buried: 12 Kinderhook NY
education:
Academy: 10 Kinderhook
college: 4 none
studied: 3 law
religion: 13 Dutch Reformed
vacation:
toured: 6 Europe (1853-1855)
author: 64 Inquiry into the Origin and Course of Political Parties in the United States
political career: 8 US Senate 11 state Senate 13 vice presi dent 20 state Attorney General
governor of: 7 New York
secretary of: 5 State
minister: 12 Great Britain
civilian career: lawyer
notable events of lifetime/term: 5 Panic (of 1837)

treaty: 16 Webster-Ashburton
war: 9 Aroostook
father: 7 Abraham
mother: 5 Maria (Hoes Van Alen)
siblings: 6 Derike, Hannah 7 Abraham 8 Lawrence
wife: 6 Hannah (Hoes)
children: 4 John 6 Martin 7 Abraham 13 Smith Thompson

Vance, Vivian
real name: 11 Vivian Jones
born: 12 Cherryvale KS
roles: 9 I Love Lucy 10 Ethel Mertz

Vancouver
hockey team: 7 Canucks

vandal 6 looter, raider 7 ravager, wrecker 8 marauder, pillager, saboteur 9 barbarian, despoiler, destroyer, plunderer 10 demolisher

vandalism 6 damage 10 de facement 11 destruction 17 malicious mischief

vandalize 3 mar 5 trash, wreck 6 damage, deface 7 despoil, destroy

Vanderlyn, John
born: 10 Kingston NY
artwork: 14 Ariadne on Naxos 20 The Death of Jane McCrea 28 Marius Amid the Ruins of Carthage 31 Ariadne Asleep on the Island of Naxos

Van Dyck, Sir Anthony
born: 7 Antwerp 8 Flanders
artwork: 8 Charles I (in Hunting Dress) 11 Iconography 18 Madonna of the Rosary 19 Blessed Herman Joseph, Cardinal Bentiroglio 20 Ecstasy of St Augustine 21 Marchesa Elena Grimaldi

Van Dyke, Dick
born: 12 West Plains MO
roles: 11 Mary Poppins 12 Bye Bye Birdie 15 Dick Van Dyke Show

Vane, Sutton
author of: 12 Outward Bound

Vanessa
author: 11 Hugh Walpole

Van Gogh, Vincent
born: 12 GrootZundert 14 The Netherlands
artwork: 10 Pere Tanguy 11 Cafe at Night, L'Arle sienne 13 The Olive Grove 14 The Starry Night 15 The Potato Eaters 16 The Bridge at Arles 18 Portrait of Dr Gachet, The Chair and the Pipe 22 Cornfield with Cypresses

vanguard 3 van 7 leaders 8 forerank 9 first line, forefront, front line, front rank, spearhead 10 avant-garde, in novators, leadership, modernists 11 pacesetters, tastemakers 12 advance guard, trailblazers, trendsetters

Van Helsing, Dr
character in: 7 Dracula
author: 6 Stoker

Vanir
origin: 12 Scandinavian
race: 4 gods
conflicting with: 4 Asar 5 Aesir

vanish 3 die, end 5 cease 6 die out, expire, perish 7 die away 8 dissolve, fade away, melt away, pass away 9 disappear, evaporate, terminate 13 dematerialize 15 become invisible

vanished 4 dead, gone, lost 7 defunct, died out, extinct 11 disappeared

vanishing 8 dying out 10 ex tinction, fading away 11 passing away 12 disappearing 13 disappearance 15 dematerialization

vanitas vanitatum 16 vanity of vanities

vanity 4 sham 5 folly, pride 6 mirage 7 compact, conceit, egotism, falsity, inanity 8 de lusion, futility, idleness, self-love 9 emptiness, powder box, vainglory, vanity bag 10 hollowness, narcissism, self-praise, vanity case 11 makeup table, mirror table, self-conceit, uselessness 13 dressing table, fruitlessness, worthlessness 14 self-admiration, superficiality

Vanity Fair
   author: 25 William Make peace Thackeray
   character: 10 Becky Sharp 11 Miss Crawley 12 Amelia Sedley, Joseph (Jos) Sedley 13 George Osborne, Rawdon Crawley 14 Sir Pitt Crawley 20 Captain William Dobbin

vanity of vanities
   Latin: 16 vanitas vanitatum

vanquish 4 beat, best, drub, lick, rout 5 crush 6 defeat, master, subdue, thrash 7 conquer 8 overcome 9 overpower, overthrow, overwhelm, subjugate 11 triumph over

vanquisher 6 master, victor, winner 7 subduer 8 champion 9 conqueror 10 subjugator

vanquishment 6 defeat 7 mastery, triumph, victory, winning 8 conquest 10 conquering, overcoming

Van Slyke, Helen
   author of: 10 No Love Lost 15 A Necessary Woman, The Heart Listens 18 Always Is Not Forever

Van Tassel, Katrina
   character in: 23 The Legend of Sleepy Hollow
   author: 6 Irving

Vanuatu
   other name: 11 New Hebrides
   capital/largest city: 4 Vila
   others: 5 Santo 6 Forari 10 Luganville
   school: 7 Malapoa
   monetary unit: 5 franc 7 centime
   island: 3 Api, Epi 4 Aoba, Gaua, Malo, Tana, Vate 5 Banks, Efate, Maewo, Santo, Tanna 6 Ambrym, Mabrim, Torres 8 Anei tyum, Malekula 9 Erromanga, Pentecost, Vanua Lava 13 Espiritu Santo
   mountain: 6 Lopevi
   highest point: 11 Tabwemasana
   sea: 7 Pacific
   people: 8 European 10 Melanesian, Polynesian 11 Micronesian
   explorer: 4 Cook 7 Queiros
   leader: 4 Lini

   language: 6 French 7 Bislama, English 16 Melanesian Pidgin
   religion: 7 animism 8 Anglican, John Frum 10 Protestant 12 Presbyterian 13 Roman Catholic
   feature:
   cult: 5 cargo

vapid 4 dull, flat, lame, tame 5 bland, empty, stale 7 insipid 8 lifeless 9 colorless, pointless 10 flavorless, wishy-washy 11 meaningless, uninspiring 12 unsatisfying 13 characterless

vapor 3 dew, fog 4 haze, mist, smog 5 fumes, smoke, steam 6 miasma 8 moisture

vaporize 5 dry up 7 distill 8 condense, melt away 9 dissipate, evaporate

Varden, Gabriel/Dolly
   character in: 12 Barnaby Rudge
   author: 7 Dickens

Vargas Llosa, Mario
   author of: 13 The Green House 16 The Time of the Hero 26 Conversation in the Cathedral 27 Aunt Julia and the Scriptwriter 34 Captain Pantoja and the Special Service

variable 6 fickle, fitful, uneven, unlike 7 diverse, mutable 8 changing, shifting, unstable, wavering 9 alterable, different, spasmodic, unsettled 10 capricious, changeable, inconstant, indefinite 11 fluctuating

variance 4 odds 6 change 7 dispute, quarrel 9 deviation, disparity 10 contention, difference, dissension, divergence, unlikeness 11 discrepancy, incongruity 12 disagreement, modification 13 dissimilarity, inconsistency

variant 7 altered, derived, take off 8 modified 9 departure, different, divergent, variation 10 alteration 11 transformed 12 modification 14 transformation

variation 6 change 7 variant, variety 8 mutation, variance 9 departure, deviation, diversity 10 aberration, alteration, difference, divergency, innovation 11 discrepancy 12 disagreement, modification 13 metamorphosis 14 transformation

varicolored 6 calico, motley, tartan 7 dappled, flecked, marbled, mottled, piebald 9 multi hued 10 iridescent, opalescent, variegated 11 rainbowlike, technicolor 12 multicolored, parti-colored 13 polychromatic

varied 5 mixed 6 motley, sundry 7 diverse, various 8 assorted 9 different 10 variegated 11 diversified 13 heterogeneous, miscellaneous

variegated 4 pied 6 motley 7 checked, dappled, mottled, piebald 9 checkered 12 parti-colored

variety 4 hash, kind, race, sort, type 5 brand, breed, class, genre, genus, group, stock, tribe 6 change, family, jumble, medley, motley, strain 7 melange, mixture, species 8 category, division, pastiche 9 diversity, patchwork, variation 10 assortment, collection, difference, hodgepodge, innovation, miscellany, subspecies 11 subdivision 12 denomination, multiplicity, unconformity 13 dissimilarity, heterogeneity, nonuniformity 14 classification, omniumgatherum 15 diversification

various 3 few 4 many, some 5 other 6 divers, myriad, sundry, varied 7 diverse, several 8 assorted, manifold, numerous 9 countless, different 10 dissimilar 11 innumerable 12 multifarious 13 miscellaneous, multitudinous

varlet 3 cur 6 rascal, wretch 7 villain 9 scoundrel 10 blackguard

Varner, Will
  character in: 9 The Hamlet
  author: 8 Faulkner

varnish 4 gilt 5 adorn, cover, gloss, stain 6 excuse, soften 7 conceal, lacquer 8 disguise, mitigate 9 embellish, gloss over 10 smooth over

vary 4 veer 5 alter, shift 6 change, depart, differ, modify 7 deviate, dissent, diverge 8 be unlike, contrast, disagree 9 alternate, disaccord, diversify, fluctuate

vase 3 jar, jug, pot, urn 5 crock, diota 8 canister 9 container 10 jardiniere

Vashti
  husband: 9 Ahasuerus
  replaced by: 6 Esther

vassal 4 serf 5 helot, liege, slave 6 tenant, thrall 7 bondman, servant, subject, villein 8 retainer 9 bondslave, bondwoman, dependent 11 subordinate

vassalage 4 yoke 7 bondage, serfdom, slavery 9 servitude 11 enslavement

vast 4 huge, wide 5 great, jumbo 7 endless, immense, titanic, very big 8 colossal, enormous, far-flung, gigantic, infinite, spacious 9 boundless, capacious, extensive, limitless, monstrous, unbounded, unlimited, very large 10 monumental, prodigious, stupendous, tremendous, voluminous, widespread 11 far-reaching, measureless, significant, substantial 12 immeasurable, interminable

vastness 7 bigness 8 enormity, hugeness 9 immensity, largeness 12 enormousness

Vathek
  author: 15 William Beckford

Vaticanus 16 Greek uncial codex

Vaughan Williams, Ralph
  born: 7 Britain 10 Down Ampney
  composer of: 3 Job 8 The Wasps 9 Flos Campi 10 Antarctica (symphony No 7), 11 Old King Cole 12 A Sea Symphony 13 Hugh the Drover, On Wenlock Edge, Sir John in Love, Songs of Travel 14 Riders to the Sea, The House of Life, The Sons of Light 15 A London Symphony, The Poisoned Kiss 16 The Lark Ascending 17 A Pastoral Symphony 18 Five Tudor Portraits, Sinfonia Antarctica 19 The Pilgrim's Progress 22 Toward the Unknown Region

Vaughn, Robert
  born: 9 New York NY
  roles: 7 Bullitt 12 Napoleon Solo 15 The Man from UNCLE 19 The Magnificent Seven 22 The Young Philadelphians

vault 4 arch, dome, jump, leap, safe, tomb 5 bound, clear, crypt 6 arcade, cupola, hurdle, spring 7 ossuary 8 catacomb, jump over, leapfrog, leap over, wall safe 9 mausoleum, pole-vault, sepulcher, strongbox 10 arched roof, spring over, strongroom 13 arched ceiling, burial chamber

vaunt 5 strut 6 brag of, flaunt 7 exult in, show off, swagger 9 crow about, gasconade, gloat over 10 boast about

vaunted 7 exalted, praised 11 gloated over, overpraised 12 boasted about

Veary, Arthur
  real name of: 14 Arthur Treacher

veer 3 yaw 4 jibe, tack, turn 5 curve, dodge, drift, shift, wheel 6 swerve, zigzag 7 go about 9 come round, turn aside 15 change direction

Vegas
  character: 5 Angie 6 Binzer 8 Beatrice, Dan Tanna 10 Bernie Roth 11 (Sgt) Bella Archer
  cast: 10 Tony Curtis 11 Judy Landers, Robert Urich 14 Naomi Stevens, Phyllis Davis 13 Bart Braverman

vegetable 3 pea 4 bean, beet, corn 6 carrot, greens, legume, squash, turnip 7 cabbage, lettuce, parsnip, produce, spinach 8 broccoli, eggplant, lima bean, rutabaga, zucchini 10 string bean 11 cauliflower

vegetarian 5 vegan 8 meatless 9 herbivore 11 herbivorous

vegetation 5 flora, grass, sloth, weeds 6 leaves, plants, torpor 7 foliage, herbage, languor, loafing, verdure 8 dormancy, idleness, lethargy 9 flowerage, indolence, plant life, shrubbery 10 inactivity 11 hibernation, languidness, rustication 12 sluggishness
  god of: 6 Dumuzi

vehemence 4 heat, zeal 5 ardor 6 fervor, warmth 7 passion 9 intensity

vehement 3 hot 4 wild 5 eager, fiery, rabid 6 ardent, fervid, fierce, heated, stormy 7 earnest, excited, fanatic, fervent, furious, intense, violent, zealous 8 agitated, forceful, frenzied, vigorous 9 emotional, fanatical, hotheaded 10 passionate 11 impassioned, tempestuous 12 enthusiastic

vehemently 5 hotly 6 wildly 7 eagerly 8 ardently, fiercely, strongly 9 earnestly, excitedly, fervently, furiously, intensely, violently, zealously 10 vigorously 11 emotionally, fanatically 12 passionately 13 tempestuously 16 enthusiastically

vehicle 3 bus, car 4 tool 5 agent, means, organ, plane, train, truck 6 agency, device, medium 7 bicycle 9 mechanism 10 automobile, conveyance, instrument, motorcycle, rocket ship 12 intermediary 14 transportation

veil 3 dim 4 hide, mask 5 cloak, cloud, cover 6 enwrap, mantle, screen, shroud 7 blanket, conceal, curtain, envelop, obscure 8 covering 10 camouflage

veiled 4 dim 5 murky 6 draped, hidden 7 muffled 8 obscured, shrouded 9 concealed, covered up, disguised, enveloped, enwrapped 11 camouflaged

veiling 3 net 4 mesh 8 cloaking, covering 9 obscurity 10 concealing

vein 3 rib, web 4 bent, hint, line, lode, mark, mood, seam, tone 5 fleck, layer, stria, style, touch 6 furrow, manner, marble, nature, strain, streak, stripe, temper, thread 7 stra tum 8 tendency 9 capillary, character 10 complexion, propensity 11 blood vessel, disposition, inclination, temperament 12 predilection 14 predisposition

Veiovis
   god of: 4 dead

Velazquez (Velasquez), Diego Rodriguez de Silvay
   born: 5 Spain 7 Seville
   artwork: 8 Philip IV 10 Las Meninas 13 Luis de Gongora, Pope Innocent X, Venus and Cupid 14 Cardinal Borgia 17 Don Gaspar de Guzman, Isabella of Bourbon 18 Adoration of the Magi, The Tapestry Weavers 19 The Infanta Margarita, The Surrender of Breda 20 Infanta Maria Theresia 21 An Old Woman Cooking Eggs 22 Portrait of a Court Jester, Portrait of Juan de Pareja 23 The Immaculate Conception 30 Prince Balthasar Carlos at the Hunt

veloce
   music: 4 fast

velocity 4 pace 5 haste, speed 8 alacrity, celerity, rapidity 9 fleetness, quickness, swiftness 10 expedition, speediness

venal 5 shady 6 greedy 7 corrupt, crooked, selfish 8 bribable, covetous, grasping 9 dishonest, mercenary, rapacious 10 avaricious 11 corruptible 12 unprincipled, unscrupulous 13 money-grubbing

venality 7 avarice 10 corruption 11 bribe-taking 13 mercenariness, money-grubbing

vend 4 hawk, sell 5 trade 6 barter, deal in, market, peddle, retail 7 auction, trade in 8 huckster 11 merchandise

Vendetta, La
   author: 14 Honore de Balzac

vendor, vender 6 dealer, hawker, monger, seller, trader 7 peddler 8 huckster, merchant, purveyor, retailer, salesman, supplier 9 tradesman 10 wholesaler 12 merchandiser 13 street peddler

veneer 4 coat, mask, show 5 front, layer 6 casing, facade, facing, jacket, sheath 7 coating, overlay, wrapper 8 covering, envelope, pretense 10 outer layer

venerable 3 old 4 aged 5 hoary 6 august 7 admired, ancient, elderly, honored, revered 8 esteemed 9 respected, venerated 11 patriarchal, white-haired

venerate 5 adore, extol, honor 6 admire, esteem, hallow, revere 7 cherish, glorify, idolize, respect, worship 8 look up to 9 reverence 11 pay homage to

venerated 4 holy 5 loved 6 adored, sacred 7 honored, revered 8 hallowed 9 respected 10 reverenced, worshipped 12 paid homage to

veneration 3 awe 5 honor 6 esteem, homage, wonder 7 respect, worship 8 devotion 9 adoration, adulation, reverence 10 admiration, exaltation 11 idolization 13 glorification

venereal 6 carnal, sexual 7 genital

Venezuela
   name means: 12 little Venice
   capital/largest city: 7 Caracas
   others: 4 Aroa, Coro 6 Atures, Cumana, Merida 7 Barinas, Barines, Cabello, Guaware, Maracay, Maturin 8 Asuncion, Carupano, La Guaira, La Gyayra, Tacupita, Valencia 9 Barcelona, Maracaibo, Tacarigua 12 Barquisimeto, Puerto La Cruz, San Cristobal 13 Ciudad Bolivar, Puerto Cabello 18 Santo Tome de Guayana
   division: 4 Lara 5 Apure, Sucre, Zulia 6 Aragua, Falcon, Merida 7 Barinas, Bolivar, Cojedes, Guarico, Monagas, Tachira, Yaracuy 8 Carabobo, Trujillo
   measure: 5 galon 6 fanega 7 estadel
   monetary unit: 4 peso 5 medio 6 fuerte 7 bolivar, centimo 8 morocota 10 venezolano
   weight: 3 bag 5 libra
   island: 4 Aves 7 Cubagua, Tortuga 9 La Orchila, Los Roques, Margarita 11 Los Hermanos 12 La Blanquilla
   lake: 9 Maracaibo, Tacarigua
   mountain: 3 Pao 4 Pava, Yair 5 Andes, Duida, Icutu 6 Concha, Cuneva, Merida, Parima, Sierra, Yumari 7 Imutaca, Masaiti, Roraima 8 Gurupira 9 Pacaraima 10 Auyan-Tepui 11 Turimiquire 18 Cordillera del Norte
   highest point: 7 Bolivar
   river: 3 Oro, Pao 4 Meta 5 Apure, Caura, Negro, Suata, Tigre, Unare, Zulia 6 Amazon, Arauca, Caroni, Cuyuni 7 Guanare, Guanipa, Guarico, Orinoco, Oritueo, Paragua, Suapure, Vichada, Yuruari 8 Guaviare, Manapire, Ventuari 9 Cuchivero 10 Casiquiare, Portuguesa
   sea: 8 Atlantic 9 Caribbean
   physical feature:
   falls: 5 Angel
   gulf: 5 Paria 6 Triste 9 Venezuela
   highlands: 6 Guiana 7 Guayana, Segovia
   plains: 6 Llanos
   people: 4 Bare, Pume 5 Bello, Carib, pardo, zambo 6 Arawak, Creole, Timote 7 Charoya, Guahibo, Kaliana, mestizo, mulatto, Otomaca, Timotex 8 Caquetio, Guarauno, Matilone 11 Maquiritare
   artist: 7 Marisol

author: 5 Bello 8 Gallegos 13 Diaz-Rodriguez

explorer: 8 Columbus

god: 5 Tsuma

leader: 4 Paez 5 Gomez, Leoni 6 Castro 7 Bolivar, Miranda 10 Betancourt 12 Guzman Blanco 14 Herrera Campins

language: 4 Pume 7 Spanish

religion: 5 Islam 7 Judaism 10 Protestant 13 Roman Catholic

feature:

animal: 4 puma 5 sloth 6 jaguar, ocelot 7 manatee, peccary 8 anteater, capybara 9 armadillo

cowboy: 7 llanero

dance: 6 joropo 16 diablos danzantes

folk entertainment: 10 burriquita

musical instrument: 6 cuatro 7 maracas

street performance: 8 parranda

food:

black beans: 8 caraotas

bread: 5 arepa

dish: 7 hallaca 8 cachapos, pabellon

soup/stew: 8 sancocho

vengeance 7 revenge 8 avenging, reprisal, requital 11 malevolence, retaliation, retribution 12 ruthlessness 13 an eye for an eye, implacability 14 revengefulness, vindictiveness 15 a tooth for a tooth

veni, vidi, vici 19 I came I saw I conquered

author: 12 Julius Caesar

venial 5 minor 6 slight 7 trivial 9 allowable, excusable 10 defensible, forgivable, not serious, pardonable 11 justifiable, unimportant, warrantable

Venice

art exhibition: 8 Biennale

artist: 7 Bellini, Codussi 8 Fabriano, Longhena, Mantegna, Palladio, Scamozzi, Veronese 9 Canaletto, Carpaccio, Giorgione, Sansovino 10 Tintoretto

capital of: 6 Veneto 15 Venezia province

church: 18 San Giorgio Maggiore, Santa Maria dei Frari 19 Santi Giovanni e Paolo

Italian: 7 Venezia

landmark: 6 Ca' d'Oro 9 Campanile 10 Grand Canal 11 Doge's Palace 13 Bridge of Sighs 15 Libreria Vecchia 16 Palazzo Rezzonico, Saint Mark's Church 20 Accademia di Belle Arti 21 Palazzo dei Procuratori 22 Scuola Grande di San Rocco 23 Palazzo Vendramin-Calergi

port: 8 Marghera

resort: 9 Lido Beach

sea: 8 Adriatic

small canal: 3 rii

tomb: 5 Titan

traveler: 9 Marco Polo

Venn, Diggory

character in: 17 Return of the Native

author: 5 Hardy

venom 3 ire 4 gall, hate 5 anger, spite, toxin, virus 6 choler, enmity, grudge, hatred, malice, poison, rancor, spleen 7 ill will 8 acrimony, savagery 9 animosity, barbarity, brutality, hostility 10 bitterness, resentment 11 malevolence 12 spitefulness 13 maliciousness, rancorousness

venomous 5 cruel, fatal, toxic 6 bitter, brutal, deadly, lethal, malign, savage 7 abusive, caustic, hostile, noxious, vicious 8 spiteful, virulent 9 malicious, malignant, poisonous, rancorous, resentful 10 malevolent 11 ill-disposed 12 bloodthirsty

vent 3 air, tap 4 bare, drip, emit, flue, gush, hole, ooze, pipe 5 exude, spout, utter, voice 6 effuse, escape, faucet, let out, outlet, reveal, spigot 7 air hole, chimney, debouch, declare, divulge, express, opening, orifice, release 8 aperture, disclose, exposure, venthole 9 discharge, let escape, pour forth, utterance 10 disclosure, expression, revelation, smoke stack, ventilator 11 communicate, declaration

ventilate 3 air, sow 5 voice 6 aerate, air out, report, review, spread 7 analyze, declare, discuss, dissent, divulge, examine, express 9 broadcast, circulate, comment on, criticize, oxygenate, publicize, talk about 10 bandy about 11 disseminate, noise abroad

ventilator 3 fan 4 flue 7 aerator 10 exhaust fan, smoke stack 14 air conditioner

venture 2 go 3 bet, try 4 dare, risk 5 flyer, offer, wager 6 chance, gamble, hazard, plunge, submit, tender, travel 7 advance, attempt, hold out, presume, proffer, project 8 endeavor, make bold 9 adventure, risk going, strive for, undertake, volunteer 10 enterprise, put forward, take a flyer 11 speculation, uncertainty, undertaking

venturesome, adventuresome 4 bold, rash 5 risky 6 daring, tricky, unsafe, unsure 7 dubious 8 doubtful, insecure, perilous, reckless, ticklish 9 ambitious, audacious, dangerous, daredevil, energetic, foolhardy, hazardous, impetuous, impulsive, uncertain 10 aggressive, precarious 11 adventurous, speculative 12 enterprising, questionable

venturesomeness 6 daring 8 audacity, boldness 9 derring-do 11 impetuosity 12 recklessness

Venus

origin: 5 Roman 7 Italian

goddess of: 6 spring 7 gardens

son: 6 Aeneas

grandson: 5 Iulus

epithet: 7 Erycina 8 Gene trix 10 Erticordia

corresponds to: 9 Aphrodite

Venus and Adonis

author: 18 William Shakespeare

veracious 4 true 6 honest 7 sincere 8 accurate, faithful, truthful 10 scrupulous 11 punctilious

veracity 5 truth 6 candor, verity 7 honesty, probity 8 accu racy, openness 9 exactness, frankness, integrity, sincerity 10 exactitude 11 correctness 12 truthfulness 13 guileless ness, ingenuousness 14 verisimilitude

Vera-Ellen
  real name: 13 Vera-Ellen Rohe
  born: 12 Cincinnati OH
  roles: 9 On the Town 14 White Christmas

veranda
  Hawaiian: 5 lanai

verbal 4 oral, said 5 vocal 6 spoken, voiced 7 in words, of verbs, of words, uttered 9 expressed, unwritten

verbal exchange 6 dialog 8 dialogue 10 discussion 12 conversation

verbalize 5 speak, utter, voice 7 express 10 articulate 12 put into words

verbal thrust 3 dig 4 gibe, jeer 5 taunt 13 cutting remark

verbatim 5 exact 7 exactly, literal, precise 8 accurate, faith ful 9 literally, literatim, precisely 10 accurately, faithfully 11 to the letter, word for word 15 chapter and verse, letter for letter
  Latin: 14 ipsissima verba

verbatim et literatim 21 in exactly the same words 29 word for word and letter for letter

verbena
  varieties: 4 moss, rose, sand 5 clump, lemon, shrub 7 red sand 8 pink sand 9 beach sand 10 desert sand, Mojave sand, yellow sand 12 common garden

verbiage 9 logorrhea, loquacity, prolixity, verbosity, wordiness 10 volubility 11 verboseness 12 effusiveness 14 circumlocution, grandiloquence, long-windedness

verbose 5 gabby, wordy 6 prolix 7 voluble 8 effusive 9 garrulous, talkative 10 long-winded, loquacious 13 grandiloquent 14 circumlocutory

verbosity 9 diffusion, prolixity, talkiness, wordiness 11 diffuseness 13 talkativeness 14 long-windedness

verboten 9 forbidden 10 prohibited

Verdandi 4 Norn
  origin: 12 Scandinavian
  form: 3 elf
  personifies: 7 present
  developed from: 5 Urdar
  companions: 3 Urd 5 Skuld

verdant 4 lush 5 green, leafy, shady, turfy 6 grassy 7 meadowy 8 blooming, thriving 9 luxuriant 10 burgeoning, springlike 11 flourishing

Verdi, Giuseppe
  born: 5 Italy 7 Busseto
  composer of: 4 Aida 6 Otello 7 Macbeth, Nabucco, Othello 8 Falstaff 9 Don Carlos, Il Corsaro, Rigoletto, The Misled 10 La Traviata 11 Il Trovatore 13 The Troubadour 14 Manzoni Requiem 15 Simon Boccanegra

verdict 6 answer, decree, ruling 7 finding, opinion 8 decision, judgment, sentence 9 valuation 10 assessment, estimation 11 arbitrament, arbitration 12 adjudication 13 determination

Vere, Captain
  character in: 9 Billy Budd
  author: 8 Melville

Vereen, Ben
  born: 7 Miami FL
  roles: 5 Roots 6 Pippin 13 Chicken George 20 Jesus Christ Superstar

verge 3 end, hem, lip, rim 4 brim, edge 5 bound, brink, ledge, limit, skirt 6 be near, border, flange, fringe, margin 7 confine, extreme 8 approach, boundary, frontier, terminus 9 threshold 11 approximate 12 be on the brink

verge upon 4 abut 5 flank 6 adjoin, border 8 be next to 10 neighbor on

Vergil, Virgil
  author of: 6 Aeneid 8 Bucolics, Eclogues, Georgics

verification 5 proof 7 support 9 guarantee 10 validation 12 confirmation 13 accreditation, certification, corroboration, documentation 14 authentication, substantiation

verify 5 prove 7 certify, confirm, support, sustain, witness 8 accredit, attest to, document, validate, vouch for 9 establish, guarantee, testify to 11 corroborate 12 authenticate, substantiate

verily 4 amen 5 truly 6 really 9 certainly, yes indeed 10 positively

veritable 4 real, true 5 utter, valid 6 actual 7 genuine, literal 8 absolute, bona fide, complete, positive, true-blue 9 authentic 13 incontestable, unimpeachable 14 unquestionable 17 through-and-through

Verlaine, Paul
  author of: 6 Wisdom 7 Sagesse 8 Langueur 17 Songs Without Words 19 Romances sans Paroles

Vermeer, Jan
  born: 5 Delft 7 Holland
  artwork: 11 View of Delft 12 The Lace Maker, The Procuress 13 Drinking Scene 14 A Street in Delft, The Head of a Girl 15 Alle gory of Faith, Girl with a Red Hat 16 The Artist's Studio 18 Girl Reading a Letter, Girl with a Wine-glass 19 A Girl Asleep at a Table, A Painter in his Studio 20 A Woman Weighing Pearls 22 Maidservant Pouring Milk 23 Young Woman with a Water Jug 24 A Soldier and a Laughing Girl 31 Christ in the House of Mary and Martha

vermilion 3 red 7 scarlet 8 cinnabar 9 bright red 15 mercuric sulfide

vermin 4 ants, lice, mice, owls, rats 5 crows, fleas, foxes, pests 6 snakes, wolves 7 bed bugs, coyotes, roaches, spiders, weasels 8 termites, varmints 9 water bugs 10 centipedes, silverfish 11 birds of prey 18 pestiferous insects

Vermont
  abbreviation: 2 VT
  nickname: 13 Green Mountain 20 Four-Season Recreation
  capital: 10 Montpelier
  largest city: 10 Burlington
  others: 5 Barre, Stowe 7 Grafton, Newfane, Newport, Rutland 8 St Albans, Winooski 9 Bountiful, Vergennes 10 Bennington 11 Brattleboro

college: 7 Goddard, Norwich, Trinity, Windham 8 Marlboro 10 Bennington, Middlebury, St Michaels
feature:
covered bridge: 5 Scott
house: 15 Old Constitution
monument: 6 Battle
people: 9 John Deere, John Dewey 10 Ethan Allen 12 Brigham Young 13 Warren R Austin 15 Stephen A Douglas
lake: 7 Caspian, Dunmore, Seymour 8 Bomoseen 9 Champlain 10 Willoughby 12 Memphremagog
land rank: 10 forty-third
mountain: 5 Green, White 7 Bromley, Hogback, Taconic 8 Prospect, Stratton
highest point: 9 Mansfield
physical feature:
uplands: 10 New England
valley: 9 Champlain
president: 14 Calvin Coolidge, Chester A Arthur
river: 4 West 5 Otter, White 7 Saxtons 8 Lamoille, Nulhegan, Winooski 10 Missisquoi 11 Connecticut
state admission: 10 fourteenth
state bird: 12 hermit thrush
state animal: 11 Morgan horse
state flower: 9 red clover
state motto: 15 Freedom and Unity
state song: 11 Hail Vermont
state tree: 10 sugar maple
vermouth
type: 4 wine 6 brandy 8 aperitif
origin: 5 Italy 6 France
varieties: 3 dry 5 sweet
drink: 9 Boomerang 11 Bittersweet
with bourbon: 9 Allegheny
with brandy: 3 BVD
with Dubonnet: 3 BVD
gin: 5 Bijou, Bronx, Tango 6 Caruso 7 Bermuda, Caberet, Martini 10 Bloodhound
with rum: 6 Bolero 8 Apple Pie 10 Black Devil 11 Shark's Tooth
with rye: 8 Brooklyn 9 Algonquin
with scotch: 8 Affinity 10 Bobby Burns
with sherry: 6 Bamboo, Brazil
with sloe gin: 10 Blackthorn
with vodka: 8 Kangaroo 9 Corkscrew
with whiskey: 9 Manhattan
vernacular 4 cant 5 idiom, lingo, slang 6 jargon, patois 7 dialect 8 parlance, shoptalk 9 the vulgar 12 common speech, native tongue 13 natural speech 14 informal speech, native language
vernal 3 new 5 fresh, green 6 spring 8 youthful 10 springlike
Verne, Jules
author of: 19 Five Weeks in a Balloon 21 From the Earth to the Moon 26 Around the World in Eighty Days 32 Twenty Thousand Leagues Under the Sea
character: 11 Captain Nemo, Phineas Fogg 12 Passepartout

Veronese, Paolo (Cagliari)
born: 5 Italy 6 Verona
artwork: 12 Book of Esther 13 The Last Supper 14 Supper at Emmaus 15 The Rape of Europa, Triumph of Venice 17 Mary with the Saints, The Finding of Moses, The Marriage at Cana, Wisdom and Strength 19 Martyrdom of St George, The Choice of Hercules 21 Esther before Ahasuerus 22 Feast at the House of Simon 24 Mars and Venus United in Love, The Feast in the House of Levi, The Temptation of St Anthony 31 Jesus and the Centurion of Capernaum 32 The Family of Darius before Alexander
Verrocchio, Andrea del
real name: 31 Andrea di Michele di Francesco Cione
born: 5 Italy 8 Florence
artwork: 5 David 15 Boy with a Dolphin 17 Christ and St Thomas 18 The Baptism of Christ 19 Bartolommeo Colleoni 23 Christ and Doubting Thomas 25 Beheading of John the Baptist
versatile 3 apt 4 able 5 handy 6 adroit, clever, expert, gifted 7 protean 8 talented 9 adapta ble, all-around, ingenious, many-sided 10 proficient 11 many-skilled, resourceful 12 accomplished, multifaceted
verse 4 poem 5 meter, rhyme, stave 6 jingle, poetry, stanza 7 measure, strophe
versed 4 able 5 adept 6 expert, taught 7 erudite, learned, skilled, tutored 8 lettered, schooled, skillful, well-read 9 competent, practiced, scholarly 10 at home with, instructed, proficient 11 enlightened, experienced 12 accomplished, familiar with, well-informed 14 acquainted with, conversant with
versifier 4 bard 6 rhymer, writer 8 minstrel, poetizer, poetling, rhymster 9 poetaster, rhymester 10 rhymesmith, troubadour, versemaker, versesmith 11 versemonger 12 balladmonger
version 4 side 5 story 6 report 7 account 9 depiction, rendering 10 adaptation, paraphrase, re-creation 11 description, re statement, translation 14 interpretation
vers libre 9 free verse
vertebral column
bone of: 5 spine 8 backbone
vertex 3 cap, tip 4 apex, peak 5 crown 6 summit, zenith 8 pinnacle 12 highest point 13 crowning point
vertical 5 plumb, sheer 7 up right 12 ninety-degree 13 perpendicular
vertiginous 5 dizzy, giddy, shaky 6 whirly 7 reeling 11 lightheaded
vertigo 7 reeling 8 fainting 9 dizziness, giddiness 12 unsteadiness 15 lightheadedness
Vertigo
director: 15 Alfred Hitchcock
cast: 8 Kim Novak 12 James Stewart 16 Barbara Bel Geddes
setting: 12 San Francisco
score: 15 Bernard Herrmann

Vertumnus
  also: 9 Vortumnus
  origin: 5 Roman
  god of: 5 fruit 7 gardens, sea sons 8 orchards
  wife: 6 Pomona

verve 3 vim, zip 4 dash, elan, fire, zeal 5 ardor, drive, force, gusto, punch, vigor 6 energy, fervor, relish, spirit, warmth 7 abandon, feeling, passion, rapture, sparkle 8 vitality, vivacity 9 animation, eagerness, vehemence 10 enthusiasm, liveliness

Verver, Maggie
  character in: 13 The Golden Bowl
  author: 5 James

very 4 bare, mere, most, much, pure 5 exact, extra, plain, quite, sheer, truly 6 deeply, highly, hugely, mighty, really, simple, vastly 7 awfully, exactly, fitting, greatly, notably, perfect, precise, totally 8 actually, entirely, markedly, specific, suitable, terribly 9 assuredly, certainly, decidedly, eminently, essential, extremely, immensely, intensely, necessary, obviously, perfectly, precisely, unusually, veritably 10 abnormally, absolutely, abundantly, completely, defi nitely, especially, particular, profoundly, remarkably, strikingly, thoroughly, uncommonly, undeniably 11 appropriate, exceedingly, excessively 12 emphatically, surpassingly, tremendously 13 exceptionally, significantly 14 unquestionably

very best
  French: 14 creme de la creme

Very Easy Death, A
  author: 16 Simone de Beauvoir

very great 4 huge 6 severe 7 extreme, intense, mammoth, titanic 8 colossal, enormous, gigantic 9 excessive, monstrous 10 gargantuan, immoderate, inordinate, prodigious 11 magnificent, spectacular 14 Brobdingnagian

very nearly 6 almost 7 close to 9 just about 10 more or less, not far from 13 approximately

very old 4 aged 6 primal 7 ancient, antique, archaic 8 primeval 10 antiquated, primordial 11 prehistoric 12 antediluvian

very soon
  French: 11 tout a l'heure

vessel 3 cup, jar, jug, keg, mug, pot, tub, vat 4 boat, bowl, butt, cask, dish, duct, scow, ship, tube, vase, vein 5 barge, craft, crock, flask, glass, liner, plate, yacht 6 artery, barrel, beaker, carafe, flagon, goblet, packet, tanker, whaler 7 caldron, collier, cruiser, platter, tankard, trawler, tugboat, tumbler, utensil 8 decanter, paquebot, sailboat 9 capillary, container, ferry boat, freighter, houseboat, steamboat, steamship 10 ocean liner, receptacle

vest 3 rig 4 garb, robe 5 array, drape, dress 6 attire, clothe, enwrap, fit out, jacket, jerkin 7 apparel, deck out, doublet, envelop 8 accouter 9 waistcoat

Vesta
  origin: 5 Roman
  goddess of: 6 hearth
  festival: 8 Vestalia
  corresponds to: 4 Caca 6 Hestia

vestal 4 pure 6 chaste, maiden, simple, virgin 8 maidenly, virginal, virtuous 9 pure woman, undefiled, unmarried, unworldly 10 immaculate 15 unsophisticated

vested 5 fixed 7 settled 8 absolute, complete 9 permanent 10 guaranteed 11 established, inalienable 12 indisputable 14 unquestionable

vestibule 4 hall 5 entry, foyer, lobby 6 lounge 7 hallway, passage 8 anteroom, corridor 10 passageway 11 antecham ber, entrance way, waiting room 12 entrance hall

vestige 4 sign 5 relic, token, trace 6 record 7 memento, remnant 8 evidence, souvenir

vestments 4 garb, gear 5 dress 6 livery, outfit 7 apparel, clothes, costume, rai ment, regalia, uniform 8 clothing 9 trappings 13 accoutrements

vesture 4 robe 5 robes 7 apparel, clothes, garment, raiment 8 clothing, garments 9 vestments

vetch 5 Vicia
  varieties: 3 cow 4 bard, bird, milk 5 crown, hairy, Sitka 6 bitter, common, kidney, purple, smooth, spring, tufted, winter 8 Narbonne 9 horseshoe, Hungarian, woolly-pod 12 large Russian

veteran 3 vet 6 expert, master 7 old hand 8 old-timer, seasoned 9 ex-soldier 10 campaigner, old soldier, war veteran 11 experienced 12 ex-serviceman 13 long-practiced

veto 4 deny, void 6 denial, enjoin, forbid, negate, reject 7 nullify, prevent, refusal 8 disallow, prohibit, turn down 9 rejection 10 prevention 11 disallowing, prohibition 12 disallowance 16 turn thumbs down on

vex 3 bug, irk 4 fret, gall, miff, pain, rile 5 anger, annoy, chafe, harry, pique, upset, worry 6 badger, bother, grieve, harass, hassle, nettle, pester, plague, ruffle 7 chagrin, disturb, provoke, torment, trouble 8 distress, irritate 9 displease 10 exasperate 18 ruffle one's feathers

vexation 5 pique, trial 6 hassle 7 torment 8 headache, nuisance 9 annoyance 10 affliction, harassment, irritation 11 aggravation 13 pain in the neck

vexatious 5 pesky 6 thorny, vexing 8 annoying, nettling 9 badgering, harassing, hectoring, provoking, troubling, worrisome 10 bothersome, irritating 11 disquieting, pestiferous, troublesome

vexed 3 irked, riled, testy 6 galled, miffed, piqued 7 annoyed, nettled, peevish 8 provoked 9 irritated 11 disgruntled, exasperated

viable 6 usable 8 feasible, workable 9 adaptable, practical 10 applicable 11 practicable

viaduct 4 ramp, span 8 overpass

vial 5 ampul, flask, phial 7 ampoule

via media 10 a middle way

viands 4 cate, diet, eats, fare, food 7 cuisine, edibles, vittles 8 victuals 9 provender 10 foodstuffs, provisions

vibrancy 4 fire 5 ardor 7 ela tion 8 vitality, vivacity 9 animation 10 enthusiasm 11 high spirits

vibrant 4 deep, loud 5 alive, eager, vital, vivid 6 ardent, bright, florid, lively 7 fervent, glowing, intense, orotund, pealing, pulsing, radiant, ringing 8 animated, bell-like, colorful, forceful, luminous, lustrous, resonant, sonorous, spirited, vehement 9 brilliant, deep-toned, energetic, quivering, thrilling, throbbing, vibrating, vivacious 10 fluttering, glittering, resounding, shimmering 11 full of vigor, resplendent, reverber ant 12 electrifying, enthusiastic

vibrate 4 beat, sway 5 quake, swing, throb, waver 6 quaver, quiver, ripple, wobble 7 flut ter, pulsate, tremble 8 undulate 9 oscillate, palpitate, pendulate 11 reverberate

vibration 5 quake 6 quiver, tremor 7 quaking 9 quivering, throbbing, trembling

vicar 4 cleric, parson, pastor 8 preacher 9 churchman, clergyman 12 ecclesiastic

vicarious 6 mental 7 by proxy 8 imagined, indirect 9 imaginary, surrogate 10 empathetic, fantasized, secondhand 11 at one remove, sympathetic

Vicar of Wakefield, The
　　author: 15 Oliver Goldsmith
　　character: 6 George, Olivia, Sophia 7 Deborah 10 Dr Primrose, Mr Burchill 14 Arabella Wilmot 15 Squire Thornhill 19 Sir William Thornhill

vice 4 flaw 5 fault 6 defect 7 blemish, failing, frailty 8 iniquity, weakness 9 depravity, weak point 10 corruption, debauchery, degeneracy, profligacy, wantonness, wickedness 11 shortcoming 12 imperfection 14 licentiousness

vice president
　　resigned: 10 Spiro Agnew 12 John C Calhoun
　　accused of treason: 9 Aaron Burr 17 John C Breckinridge
　　youngest elected: 17 John C Breckinridge
　　elected by Senate: 14 Richard Johnson
　　elected but did not serve: 11 William King
　　rejected nomination: 11 Frank Lowden, Silas Wright
　　lived longest: 15 John Nance Garner
　　succeeded to presidency: 9 John Tyler 10 Gerald Ford 12 Harry S Truman 13 Andrew Johnson 14 Calvin Coolidge, Chester A Arthur, Lyndon B Johnson 15 Millard Fillmore 17 Theodore Roosevelt

vice versa 9 in reverse 10 conversely 12 contrariwise 16 the other way round 18 in the opposite order

vicinity 4 area 6 region 8 environs, locality, vicinage 9 adjoining, precincts, proximity 11 environment, propinquity 12 neighborhood, surroundings

vicious 3 bad 4 base, evil, foul, mean, vile, wild 5 awful, cruel, gross, nasty, surly 6 brutal, fierce, horrid, savage, sullen, wicked 7 hateful, heinous, hellish, immoral, inhuman, untamed, violent 8 churlish, depraved, fiendish, libelous, shocking, spiteful, terrible, venomous 9 abhorrent, atrocious, barbarous, dangerous, ferocious, invidious, malicious, monstrous, nefarious, offensive, predatory, rancorous 10 abominable, defamatory, diabolical, ill-humored, ill-natured, malevolent, pernicious, slanderous, villainous, vindictive 11 acrimonious, ill-tempered, treacherous 12 bloodthirsty

viciousness 4 evil 6 malice 7 cruelty 8 ferocity, savagery, villainy, violence 9 barbarity, brutality, ill nature 10 fierceness, wickedness 11 heinousness

vicissitude 6 change 8 mutation 9 variation 10 difficulty, mutability, succession 11 fluctuation

Vicomte of Bragelonne, The
　　author: 14 Alexandre Dumas (pere)

victim 4 butt, dead, dupe, gull, mark, pawn, prey, tool 5 patsy 6 pigeon, quarry, sucker, target 7 injured, wounded 8 casualty, fatality, innocent 9 scapegoat

victimize 3 con 4 dupe, gull, hoax 5 bully, cheat, cozen 6 betray, delude 7 deceive, defraud 8 hoodwink 9 bamboozle

victor 6 winner 8 champion, medalist 9 conqueror 10 vanquisher 11 prizewinner

Victoria
　　capital of: 8 Hong Kong 10 Seychelles

Victoria
　　origin: 5 Roman
　　goddess of: 7 victory
　　corresponds to: 4 Nike

Victorian 4 prim, smug 6 narrow, proper, stuffy 7 insular, prudish 8 priggish 9 pietistic 10 tight-laced 11 puritanical, straitlaced 12 conventional, hypocritical 13 sanctimonious

victorious 7 winning 8 champion 10 conquering, successful, triumphant 11 vanquishing 12 championship, prizewinning

Victor Victoria
　　director: 12 Blake Edwards
　　cast: 10 Alex Karras 11 James Garner 12 Julie Andrews 13 Robert Preston 14 John Rhys-Davies 15 Lesley Ann Warren
　　setting: 5 Paris

victory 7 laurels, success, the palm, triumph 8 conquest, the prize 9 supremacy 10 ascendancy 11 superiority
　　god of: 3 Tyr
　　goddess of: 4 Nike 8 Victoria

Victory
　　author: 12 Joseph Conrad
　　character: 4 Lena, Wang 5 Jonas, Pedro 8 Davidson 9 Axel Heyst, Schomberg 13 Martin Ricardo

victuals 4 chow, diet, eats, fare, feed, food, grub, meat **5** meals **6** fodder, forage, repast, stores, viands **7** cooking, cuisine, edibles, rations, vittles **8** supplies **9** groceries, provender **10** foodstuffs, provisions **11** comestibles, nourishment, refreshment

Vidal, Gore
  author of: 4 Burr **5** Kalki **6** Julian **8** Creation **16** Myra Breckinridge **18** Eighteen Seventy-Six, The Judgment of Paris **19** Visit to a Small Planet

Vidar
  origin: 12 Scandinavian
  father: 4 Odin **5** Othin
  killed: 6 Fenrir, Fenris

vide 3 see
vide ante 9 see before
vide infra 9 see below
videlicet 6 namely **11** that is to say
  abbreviation: 3 viz
vide post 8 see after **10** see further
vide supra 8 see above
vide ut supra 10 see as above **16** see as stated above

Vidor, King
  director of: 8 The Crowd **12** Stella Dallas, The Big Parade **16** Northwest Passage

vie 4 life **5** fight **6** strive **7** compete, contend, contest **8** be a rival, struggle, tilt with **9** challenge

Vienna
  airport: 9 Schwechat
  area: 11 Innere Stadt
  capital of: 7 Austria
  early name: 4 Wena **9** Vindobono
  German: 4 Wein
  landmark: 7 Hofburg **10** Stadtsoper **13** Saint Ste phen's **15** Albertina Museum, Belvedere Palace **16** Historical Museum, Schonbrunn Palace
  river: 6 Danube
  ruler: 8 Hapsburg
  street: 11 Ringstrasse

Vientiane, Viengchan
  capital of: 4 Laos

vi et armis 20 with force and with arms
Vietnam
  other name: 5 Annam **15** French Indochina
  capital: 5 Hanoi **6** Saigon
  largest city: 6 Saigon **13** Ho Chi Minh City
  others: 3 Hue, Ron **4** Ngai, Vinh **5** Dalat, Hoa Da, Hoian **6** Annhon, Cholon, Danang, Hongay **7** Bacninh, Cam Ranh, Caobang, Donghoi, Hoabinh, Namdinh, Quinhon, Songoan, Tayninh, Viettri, Vinhloi **8** Binhdinh, Haiphong, Nhatrang, Panthiet, Phan Rang, Quangtri, Quangyen, Thanhhoa, Vinhlong **9** Haiphoang, Longxuyen **11** Dienbienphu
  school: 3 Hue **5** Hanoi **9** Ho Chi Minh
  division: 5 Annam, North, South **6** Tonkin **11** Cochin China
  measure: 4 gang, phan, thon
  monetary unit: 2 xu **4** dong **7** piaster
  weight: 3 can, yet **4** uyen
  mountain: 6 Badinh, Badink **7** Nindhoa, Ninhhoa **8** Fansipan, Knontran, Ngoklinh, Ngoolink, Tchepone, Tclepore **18** Annamese Cordillera
  highest point: 8 Fan Si Pan
  river: 2 Bo, Ca, Da, Lo, Ma **3** Chu, Gam, Koi, Red **4** Chay **5** Nhiha **6** Mekong **7** Dongnai
  sea: 10 South China
  physical feature:
  delta: **6** Mekong **8** Red River
  gulf: **4** Siam **6** Tonkin **7** Tonking **8** Thailand
  peninsula: **11** Indochinese
  people: 3 Hoa, Man, Meo, Tai, Tay **4** Cham, Kinh, Nung, Thai **5** Khmer, Malay, Muong **7** Chinese **8** Annamese, Annamite **9** Cambodian **10** montagnard, Vietnamese
  leader: **5** Le Loi **8** Le Duc Tho **9** Ho Chi Minh **11** Ngo Dinh Diem, Pham Van Doug **14** Nguyen Van Thieu
  language: 3 Yue **4** Cham **5** Khmer, Rhade **6** French **7** Chinese, English **9** Cantonese **10** Vietnamese
  religion: 6 Cao Dai, Hoa Hao, Taoism **7** animism **8** Buddhism **12** Christianity, Confucianism **13** Roman Catholic
  place:
  ruins: **10** Nguyen tomb
  feature:
  army: **4** ARVN **5** COSVN **8** Communsi, Viet Cong, Viet Minh
  clothing: **5** ao dai
  new year: **3** Tet
view 3 eye, ken, see **4** gaze, look, note, peek, peep, scan **5** judge, scene, sight, study, vista, watch **6** behold, belief, gaze at, glance, look at, notion, regard, survey, take in, theory, vision **7** diorama, examine, explore, feeling, glimpse, inspect, observe, opinion, outlook, picture, scenery, thought, witness **8** attitude, consider, glance at, judgment, panorama, perceive, pore over, prospect **9** landscape, sentiment, spectacle **10** conception, conviction, scrutinize, think about **11** contemplate, perspective
view as 4 deem, hold **5** count, judge, think **6** regard **7** account, believe **8** consider, take to be **10** look upon as
viewpoint 4 bias, side **5** angle, slant **6** aspect, belief **7** feeling, opinion **8** attitude, position **9** sentiment **10** conviction, standpoint **11** orientation, perspective **12** vantage point **16** frame of reference
view with disfavor 7 condemn, dislike **8** object to **9** frown upon **10** disapprove, think ill of **13** look askance at, regard as wrong **14** discountenance **15** take exception to
view with horror 5 abhor **6** eschew **8** sicken at **9** abominate, shudder at **10** recoil from, shrink from
vif
  music: 6 lively

vigilance 4 care, heed 7 caution, concern 8 prudence 9 alertness, attention 10 precaution 11 carefulness, forethought, guardedness, heedfulness 12 cautiousness, watchfulness 14 circumspection

vigilant 4 wary 5 alert, chary 7 careful, guarded, heedful, on guard, prudent 8 cautious, watchful 9 attentive, observant, wide-awake 10 on one's toes, on the alert 11 circumspect, on one's guard 12 on the lookout, on the qui vive

vigor 3 pep, vim, zip 4 dash, elan, fire, zeal 5 ardor, drive, force, might, power, verve 6 energy, fervor, spirit 7 passion, stamina 8 haleness, strength, vitality, vivacity 9 animation, hardiness, intensity, vehemence 10 enthusiasm, liveliness, robustness 11 earnestness 12 forcefulness

vigorous 4 bold, hale 5 hardy, lusty, vital 6 active, ardent, brawny, lively, mighty, robust, strong, sturdy, virile 7 dynamic, intense, vibrant 8 forceful, muscular, powerful, spirited 9 assertive, energetic 10 aggressive

vigorously 4 hard 7 briskly, lustily 8 actively, cogently, forcibly, robustly, strongly, sturdily 9 with force 10 forcefully, powerfully 11 strenuously 13 energetically

Vigrid
origin: 12 Scandinavian
final battlefield of: 4 gods

Viking, viking 4 Dane 6 pirate 7 mariner 8 Norseman, Northman, searover 9 plunderer 12 Scandinavian
boat: 8 long ship
burial: 9 ship grave
chieftain: 4 jarl
exploration: 5 Italy, Spain 6 France, Russia 7 England, Germany, Iceland, Ireland, Vinland 9 Greenland
famous: 4 Eric 8 Eirikson, Ericsson 10 Eric the Red 11 Leif Ericson
governing council: 4 Ting 5 Thing 8 Folkmoot
legend: 4 Edda, saga
origin: 6 Norway, Sweden 7 Denmark, Finland
warrior: 7 beserk 9 berserker
writing: 4 rune

Vila
capital of: 7 Vanuatu

vile 3 bad, low 4 base, evil, foul, lewd, mean, ugly 5 awful, gross, nasty 6 coarse, filthy, odious, sinful, smutty, sordid, vulgar, wicked 7 beastly, hateful, heinous, ignoble, immoral, obscene, vicious 8 depraved, shameful, shocking, wretched 9 abhorrent, degrading, execrable, invidious, loathsome, nefarious, obnoxious, offensive, perverted, repellent, repugnant, repulsive, revolting, salacious 10 abominable, degenerate, despicable, detestable, disgusting, iniquitous, unpleasant, villainous 11 disgraceful, foul mouthed, humiliating 12 contemptible 13 objectionable

Vile Bodies
author: 11 Evelyn Waugh

vileness 4 evil 8 foulness, iniquity, villainy 9 depravity, nastiness 10 immorality, odiousness 11 degradation, heinousness, viciousness 12 wretchedness 13 offensiveness

Vili
origin: 12 Scandinavian
brother: 4 Odin 5 Othin

vilification 5 libel 7 calumny, slander 10 defamation 13 disparagement

vilifier 5 scold 6 carper, critic 7 reviler 9 backbiter

vilify 5 abuse 6 defame, revile 7 slander 8 bad-mouth, dis honor 9 criticize, disparage 14 inveigh against

vilifying 7 abusive 8 libelous 9 malignant 10 calumnious, defamatory, slanderous

villa, Villa 5 aldea, dacha 6 castle, Pancho 7 chateau, mansion 9 residence 13 country estate

village 4 burg 6 hamlet, suburb 8 hick town 9 smalltown 11 whistlestop 12 municipality

Village, A
author: 10 Sholem Asch

villain 3 cad, cur, rat 5 knave, louse, rogue 6 rascal, rotter, varlet 7 caitiff, stinker 8 evil doer, scalawag 9 miscreant, scoundrel 10 blackguard, malefactor 11 rapscallion 12 transgressor, wicked person 15 snake in the grass

villainous 4 base, evil, foul, vile 6 wicked 7 caddish, heinous 8 horrible, infamous 9 monstrous, nefarious 10 abominable, despicable, detestable, maleficent 12 blackguardly 13 reprehensible

villainy 4 evil 8 vileness 9 depravity, rascality 10 wickedness 11 viciousness, maleficence

Villa-Lobos, Heitor
born: 6 Brazil 12 Rio de Janeiro
composer of: 6 Choros 20 Bachianas Brasileiras

Villefort
character in: 21 The Count of Monte Cristo
author: 5 Dumas (pere)

villein 4 carl, esne, serf 5 ceorl, churl, slave 6 drudge 7 bondman, peasant 9 bondwoman

Villette
author: 15 Charlotte Bronte

Villon, Francois
author of: 9 The Legacy 16 Le grand testament, Le petit testament
quote: 25 Mais ou sont les neiges d'antan 31 But where are the snows of yesteryear

Villuppo
character in: 17 The Spanish Tragedy
author: 3 Kyd

vim 2 go 3 pep, zip 4 dash, fire, snap, zeal 5 ardor, drive, force, might, power, punch, verve, vigor 6 energy, fervor, spirit 7 passion, potency 8 strength, vitality, vivacity 9 animation, intensity, vehemence 10 enthusiasm, liveliness

vin 4 wine

Vincentio
   character in: 17 Measure for Measure
   author: 11 Shakespeare

vincit omnia veritas 16 truth conquers all 22 truth conquers all things

vindicate 4 free 5 clear 6 acquit, assert, defend, excuse, uphold 7 absolve, bear out, bolster, justify, support 8 advocate, champion, maintain 9 discharge, exculpate, exonerate 11 corroborate 12 substantiate

vindication 6 excuse 7 apology, defense 11 explanation 13 justification

vindictive 6 bitter, malign 8 avenging, punitive, spiteful, vengeful 9 malicious 10 malevolent, revengeful 11 retaliative, retaliatory, unforgiving

vinegarish 4 acid, sour, tart 5 harsh 6 acidic, biting 7 acerbic, pungent 9 acidulous 10 astringent

vin ordinaire 12 ordinary wine 20 inexpensive table wine

vintage 3 era, old 4 aged, date, fine, rare 5 epoch, great, prime, prize 6 choice, period 7 ancient, antique 8 sterling, superior 9 excellent, out-of-date, wonderful 11 outstanding 12 old-fashioned

Viola (Cesario)
   character in: 12 Twelfth Night
   author: 11 Shakespeare

violate 4 rape 5 abuse, break 6 defile, invade, ravish 7 disobey, outrage, profane 8 dishonor, infringe, trespass 9 blaspheme, desecrate, disregard, trample on 10 contravene, transgress 12 encroach upon

violation 5 abuse 6 breach 8 trespass 9 sacrilege 10 defilement, infraction 11 desecration, dishonoring 12 encroachment, infringement 13 contravention, nonobservance, transgression

violence 4 fury, rage 5 force, might, power 6 impact 7 out rage 8 ferocity, savagery, severity 9 brutality, intensity, onslaught 10 bestiality, fierceness 11 desecration, profanation 13 ferociousness, physical force 16 bloodthirstiness

violent 3 hot 4 wild 5 cruel, fiery 6 brutal, fierce, insane, raging, savage, severe, strong, unruly 7 berserk, furious, intense, rampant 8 maniacal, vehement 9 explosive, ferocious, hotheaded, murderous, unbridled 10 passionate 11 full of force, intractable, tempestuous 12 ungovernable 14 uncontrollable

Violent Bear It Away, The
   author: 15 Flannery O'Connor

Violent Land, The
   author: 10 Jorge Amado

violet 5 Viola
   varieties: 3 dog, red 4 bush, pale, pine, rock, tree, wood 5 coast, cream, dame's, false, flame, green, marsh, pansy, sweet, water 6 Alaska, alpine, Canada, garden, German, horned, plains, stream 7 African, English, Mexican, Olympic, Persian, redwood, scarlet, striped, two-eyed 8

bird-foot, crowfoot, dog-tooth, florist's, hook-spur, Labrador, larkspur, Missouri, trailing 9 early blue, evergreen, ivy-leaved, marsh blue, sage brush, tall white 10 Australian, great basin, Philippine, sweet white, western dog, woolly blue, yellow wood 11 Alpine marsh, American dog, arrow-leaved, Confederate, downy yellow, early yellow, lance-leaved, long-spurred, northern bog, strap-leaved 12 eastern water, great-spurred, kidney-leaved, northern blue, smooth yellow 13 common African, Halberd-leaved, northern downy, northern white, purple prairie, southern coast, white dog-tooth, yellow prairie 14 primrose-leaved, triangle-leaved 16 California golden, large-leaved white 17 round-leaved yellow, western sweet white 18 western round-leaved

violin family
   instruments: 3 kit 5 cello, rebec, viola 7 baryton 8 bass viol, lyra viol, violetta 10 hurdy-gurdy 11 viola d'a more, violoncello 12 tromba marina, viola pomposa 13 lira da braccio 14 violino piccolo 15 hardanger fiddle

viper
   group of: 4 nest

Viper's Tangle, The
   author: 15 Francois Mauriac

virago 3 nag 4 fury 5 harpy, scold, shrew, vixen 6 dragon, gorgon 7 she-wolf 8 battle-ax, fishwife, harridan 9 termagant, Xanthippe

Virbius
   origin: 5 Roman
   god of: 6 forest 7 hunting

Virchow, Rudolf
   field: 8 medicine 9 pathology
   nationality: 6 German
   completed formulation of: 10 cell theory

Virgil see 8 Vergil

virgin 4 girl, lass, maid, pure 6 chaste, damsel, maiden, unused 7 unmixed 8 pristine 9 unalloyed, undefiled, unsullied, untouched 10 unpolluted 13 unadulterated 14 uncontaminated
   constellation of: 5 Virgo

Virgin see 4 Mary

Virginia
   abbreviation: 2 VA
   nickname: 11 Old Dominion
   capital: 8 Richmond
   largest city: 7 Norfolk
   others: 5 Galax, Luray, Salem 6 Marion 7 Bedford, Bristol, Emporia, Fairfax, Pulaski, Roanoke 8 Danville, Hopewell, Manassas, Staunton, St Albans, Tazewell, Yorktown 9 Arlington, Lexington, Lynchburg 10 Alexandria, Appomattox, Petersburg, Portsmouth, Waynesboro, Winchester 11 Newport News 12 Hampton Roads, Martinsville, Williamsburg 13 Virginia Beach 14 Fredericksburg 15 Charlottesville
   college: 3 Lee 7 Hampton, Madison,

Radford 8 Longwood, Richmond 10
Washington 11 Mary Baldwin, Old Dominion 13 Randolph Macon 14 Averett Hol-
lins, Mary Washington, William and Mary
feature:
battle site: 7 Bull Run 8 Fair Oaks,
Manassas, Richmond, Yorktown 10
Petersburg, Seven Pines, Wilderness 12
Spotsylvania 14 Fredericksburg 16
Chancellorsville
dam: 4 Kerr
historical site: 10 Monticello 11 Mount
Vernon 12 Williamsburg 13 Stratford Hall
national monument: 26 George Washington Birthplace
national park: 10 Shenandoah 26 Colonial National Historical
tribe: 6 Saponi, Tutelo 7 Monacan 8
Manahoac, Meherrin, Nottaway, Pamun-
key, Powhatan 9 Matchotic 10 Ap-
pomuttoc
people: 9 Henry Clay, John Rolfe, John
Smith 10 Robert E Lee, Walter Reed 11
George Mason 12 John Marshall, Patrick
Henry 13 Samuel Houston 14 Cyrus
McCormick 15 Meriwether Lewis 17
Booker T Washington, Richard Evelyn
Bird 18 Light-Horse Harry (Henry) Lee
lake: 4 Kerr 5 Smith
land rank: 11 thirty-sixth
mountain: 5 Cedar 6 Clinch, Elliot 8
Baldknob 9 Alleghany, Blueridge
highest point: 6 Rogers
physical feature:
bay: 10 Chesapeake
bridge: 7 Natural
caverns: 5 Luray
port: 7 Norfolk 8 Richmond 10 Portsmouth 11 Newport News
tunnel: 7 Natural
valley: 10 Shenandoah
president: 9 John Tyler 11 James Monroe 12 James Madison 13 Woodrow Wilson, Zachary Taylor 15 Thomas Jefferson
16 George Washington 20 William Henry
Harrison
river: 3 Dan 4 York 5 James 7 Potomac,
Rapidan, Roanoke 10 Appomattox,
Shenandoah 12 Rappahannock
state admission: 5 tenth
state bird: 8 cardinal
state flower: 16 flowering dogwood
state motto: 17 Thus Ever To Tyrants
state song: 24 Carry Me Back to Old Virginia
state tree: 7 dogwood
Virginian, The
author: 10 Owen Wister
character: 8 Betsy, Randy, Steve 6
Shorty 7 Trampas 9 Molly Wood 10
Judge (Henry) Garth
cast: 8 Lee J Cobb 10 Gary Clarke,
James Drury, Pippa Scott, Randy Boone
11 Doug McClure 12 Roberta Shore
setting: 11 Shiloh Ranch 16 Wyoming
Territory

Virginians, The
author: 25 William Makepeace Thackeray
Virgin Mary
ingredient: 11 tomato juice
Virgin Soil
author: 12 Ivan Turgenev
Virgo
symbol: 6 virgin
planet: 7 Mercury
rules: 7 service
born: 6 August 9 September
virile 4 bold 5 brave, hardy, husky, lusty,
manly 6 brawny, heroic, manful, mighty,
potent, robust, strong 7 valiant 8 fearless,
forceful, muscular, powerful, resolute, stalwart, vigorous 9 audacious, masculine,
masterful, strapping, undaunted 10 courageous 12 stouthearted
virtual 5 tacit 7 implied 8 implicit, indirect 9
essential, practical 11 substantial
virtually 8 in effect 9 in essence 11 essentially, in substance, practically 13 substantially 14 for the most part 23 for all practical purposes, to all intents and purposes
virtue 5 honor, value 6 purity, reward 7 benefit, decency, honesty, modesty, probity 8
chastity, goodness, morality, strength 9 advantage, good point, innocence, integrity,
principle, rectitude, virginity 11 strong
point, uprightness
virtuosity 7 mastery 8 artistry, wizardry 14
accomplishment
virtuoso 4 whiz 6 expert, genius, master,
wizard 7 artiste, prodigy 10 master hand
virtuous 4 good, just, pure 5 moral 6
chaste, decent, modest 7 ethical, upright 8
innocent, laudable, virginal 9 continent, exemplary, honorable, righteous, unsullied
11 commendable, meritorious 12 praiseworthy 14 high-principled
virtuous person
Hebrew: 6 zaddik
Virtus
personifies: 7 courage
virtute et armis 15 by virtue and arms
motto of: 11 Mississippi
virulent 5 toxic 6 bitter, deadly, lethal, malign 7 harmful, hostile, hurtful, noxious,
vicious 8 spiteful, venomous 9 injurious,
malicious, poisonous, rancorous, resentful,
unhealthy 10 malevolent, pernicious 11 acrimonious, deleterious
virus 3 bug 4 germ 7 microbe 13 microorganism
vis 5 force, power 8 strength
visage 3 air 4 face, look, mien 5 image 6
aspect 7 profile 8 demeanor, features 9
semblance 10 appearance 11 countenance, physiognomy
vis-a-vis 8 eye to eye, together 9 in company, privately, tete-a-tete 10 face-to-face,
side by side 11 as opposed to 12 in contrast to 14 as compared with, confidentially
19 as distinguished from
viscera 4 guts 6 bowels 7 innards, insides
8 entrails 10 intestines

visceral 3 gut 5 crude 6 earthy 11 instinctive

viscous 5 gluey, gooey, gummy, slimy, tacky, thick 6 sticky, syrupy, viscid 9 glutinous

visibility 7 ceiling, clarity, horizon 10 definition, prominence 11 range of view 12 distinctness 14 perceptibility 15 conspicuousness, discernibleness

visible 4 open 5 clear, plain 6 in view, marked, patent 7 blatant, evident, glaring, in focus, in sight, obvious, pointed, salient, seeable 8 ap parent, distinct, manifest, palpable, revealed 9 prominent 10 noticeable, observable, pronounced 11 conspicuous, discernible, inescapable, perceivable, perceptible, well-defined 12 unmistakable

vision 4 idea 5 dream, fancy, ghost, sight 6 notion 7 concept, fantasy, phantom, specter 8 daydream, eyesight, illusion 9 foresight 10 apparition, conception, perception, revelation 11 discernment, imagination 15 materialization

visionary 4 seer 6 dreamy, unreal, zealot 7 dreamer, fanatic, fancied, utopian 8 delusive, fanciful, idealist, illusory, romantic, theorist 9 imaginary, unfounded 10 chimerical, daydreamer, idealistic, starry-eyed 11 imaginative, impractical 13 insubstantial

Vision of Judgement, The
    author: 9 Lord Byron

visit 4 call, stay 5 haunt, smite 6 affect, assail, attack, befall, call on, punish 7 afflict, assault, go to see, sojourn 8 drop in on, frequent, happen to, look in on, stay with 9 sojourn at 10 be a guest of

Visit, The
    author: 19 Friedrich Durrenmatt

visitant 5 alien 7 arrival, visitor

visitor 5 guest 6 caller 7 company, tourist, tripper, voyager 8 traveler 9 journeyer, sightseer, sojourner, transient 10 houseguest, vacationer

vista 4 view 5 scene 6 vision 7 outlook, picture, scenery 8 panorama, prospect 9 landscape 11 perspective

visual 5 optic 6 ocular 7 optical, seeable, visible 9 for the eye 10 noticeable, observable, ophthalmic 11 perceptible

visualize 5 fancy, image 7 dream of, foresee, imagine, picture 8 envision 10 conceive of, daydream of 16 see in the mind's eye

vital 4 life, live 5 alive, basic, chief, quick 6 lively, living, urgent, viable 7 animate, crucial, dynamic, primary, serious, vibrant 8 animated, cardinal, critical, existing, forceful, foremost, material, pressing, spirited, vigorous 9 breathing, energetic, essential, important, necessary, paramount, requisite, vivifying 11 fundamental, significant 13 indispensable

vitality 3 pep, vim, zip 4 zeal, zest 5 verve, vigor 6 energy 8 dynamism, strength, vivacity 9 animation, life force 10 ebullience,

enthusiasm, exuberance, liveliness 13 animal spirits

vitalize 6 excite, vivify 7 animate, quicken 8 activate, energize 9 stimulate 10 invigorate, strengthen 11 bring to life

vital part 9 essential, necessity, requisite 10 key element, sine qua non 11 requirement

Vital Parts
    author: 12 Thomas Berger

vital principle 5 blood 6 source 9 lifeblood 10 sine qua non

vitals 5 belly 6 bowels 10 in testines 11 vital organs 14 liver and lights

Vita Nuova
    author: 14 Dante Alighieri

vitiate 3 mar 4 thin, undo, void 5 spoil, taint 6 blight, cancel, debase, defile, dilute, impair, infect, injure, poison, weaken 7 abolish, corrupt, pervert, pollute 8 sabotage 9 discredit, undermine 10 adulterate, depreciate, invalidate, make faulty, obliterate 11 contaminate

vitriolic 4 acid 5 acerb, nasty, sharp 6 biting 7 abusive, acerbic, caustic, cutting 8 sardonic, scathing 9 sarcastic, satirical, withering 11 acrimonious 13 hypercritical

vituperate 5 abuse 6 carp at, defame, malign, rail at, rebuke, revile, vilify 7 censure 9 castigate 10 speak ill of 14 inveigh against

vituperation 5 abuse, blame, scorn 6 insult, rebuke, tirade 7 censure, obloquy, slander 8 acrimony, scolding 9 invective 10 defamation, revilement, scurrility 11 castigation, deprecation 12 calumniation, denunciation, faultfinding, vilification 13 tongue-lashing

vituperative 5 harsh 7 abusive 8 scornful 9 insulting, maligning, vilifying 10 censorious, defamatory, scurrilous, slanderous 11 acrimonious, deprecatory

vivace
    music: 5 quick 9 vivacious

vivacious 3 gay 5 jolly, merry, sunny, vital 6 active, bright, bubbly, cheery, genial, lively 7 buoyant 8 animated, bubbling, cheerful, spirited 9 convivial, ebullient, sparkling, sprightly 10 frolicsome, full of life 12 effervescent, lighthearted

vivacity 3 zip 4 dash, elan 5 gaity, verve, vigor 6 energy, spirit 8 buoyancy, vitality 9 animation 10 ebullience, liveliness 13 effervescence

Vivaldi, Antonio
    born: 5 Italy 6 Venice
    composer of: 10 Gloria Mass 14 L'Estro Armonico, The Four Seasons 16 Judith Triumphant 17 Juditha Triumphans, Le Quattro Stagioni 19 Harmonic Inspiration

Viva Zapata!
    director: 9 Elia Kazan
    cast: 10 Jean Peters 12 Anthony Quinn, Marlon Brando
    Oscar for: 15 supporting actor (Quinn)
    script: 13 John Steinbeck

vive 8 long live (whomever)

vive valeque 15 live and keep well

Vivian
- also: 16 The Lady of the Lake
- character in: 16 Arthurian romance
- lover: 6 Merlin

Vivian Grey
- author: 16 Benjamin Disraeli

vivid 3 gay 4 deep, loud, rich 5 clear, shiny, showy 6 bright, florid, garish, lively, moving, strong 7 glowing, graphic, in tense, radiant, shining 8 colorful, definite, distinct, dramatic, emphatic, forceful, lifelike, luminous, lustrous, powerful, stirring, striking, true-life, vigorous 9 brilliant, effulgent, energetic, marvelous, memorable, pictorial, realistic 10 astounding, expressive, impressive, remarkable 11 astonishing, conspicuous, descriptive, inescapable, luminescent, picturesque, resplendent 12 unmistakable 13 extraordinary

vividness 9 intensity 10 brightness, brilliance

vivified 7 revived 8 animated, awakened 9 enlivened, quickened, vitalized 11 invigorated

vivify 6 revive, wake up 7 animate, enliven, quicken 8 vitalize 10 invigorate

vixen 4 fury 5 scold, shrew, witch 6 virago 8 fishwife, harridan, spitfire 9 female fox, termagant

Vladimir
- character in: 15 Waiting for Godot
- author: 7 Beckett

Vlaminck, Maurice de
- born: 5 Paris 6 France
- artwork: 8 Red Trees, The Storm 15 Hamlet in the Snow, Winter Landscape 17 The Bridge at Chatou 18 Picnic in the Country, Street at Marly-le-Roi 21 Landscape with Red Trees

vocabulary 4 cant 5 argot, idiom, lingo, slang, style 6 jargon, patois, speech, tongue 7 dialect, lexicon 8 language, phrasing 9 word stock 10 vernacular 11 phraseology, terminology

vocal 4 open, oral, sung 5 blunt, frank, lyric 6 candid, choral, direct, spoken, voiced 7 uttered, voluble 8 operatic 9 outspoken, vocalized 10 forthright, of the voice 11 articulated, plainspoken

vocalize 3 air, say 4 vent 5 speak, utter 7 express 9 ventilate 10 articulate 12 put into words

vocation 3 job 4 line, post, role, task 5 berth, field, stint, trade 6 career, estate, metier 7 calling, pursuit, station 8 business, lifework 9 situation 10 assignment, employment, line of work, occupation, profession

vocational 3 job 5 trade 6 career 9 technical 11 specialized 12 occupational

vociferate 4 howl, yell, yelp 5 shout, shout 6 bellow, clamor, cry out, holler, shriek, squeal 7 bluster, call out, exclaim, screech 9 ejaculate 11 make a racket 12 raise a rumpus

vociferation 3 cry 4 howl, yell, yelp 5 noise, shout 6 bellow, clamor, outcry, shriek, squeal, uproar 7 screech 11 ejaculation, exclamation

vociferous 4 loud 5 noisy, vocal 6 shrill 7 blatant 8 piercing, shouting, strident, vehement 9 clamorous, outspoken 10 boisterous, loud-voiced, uproarious 11 importunate

vodka
- origin: 6 Poland, Russia
- drink: 10 Moscow Mule
- with amaretto: 9 Godmother
- with bouillon: 8 Bullshot
- with cider: 15 Brewster Special
- with Cognac: 7 Cossack
- with cranberry juice: 10 Cape Codder
- with creme de cacao: 7 Barbara 9 Ninotchka 11 Russian Bear 12 Velvet Hammer, White Russian
- with curacao: 8 Aqueduct
- with Galliano: 16 Harvey Wallbanger
- with gin: 15 Russian Cocktail
- with kahlua or Tia Maria: 12 Black Russian
- with kirsch: 12 Volga Boatman
- with orange juice: 11 screwdriver
- with tomato juice: 10 Bloody Mary
- with vermouth: 8 Kangaroo 9 Corkscrew

Vogt, Carl Henry
- real name of: 12 Louis Calhern

vogue 3 fad 4 mode, rage 5 craze, style, trend 6 custom 7 fashion 8 currency, practice, the thing 10 acceptance, popularity 11 the last word 12 popular favor 14 the latest thing 15 prevailing taste

voguish 4 chic 5 smart 6 modish 7 faddish, stylish 11 fashionable

voice 3 air, say 4 alto, bass, part, role, tone, vent, vote, will, wish 5 speak, state, tenor, utter 6 choice, desire, option, reveal, singer, speech 7 declare, divulge, express, opinion, singers, soprano 8 announce, baritone, delivery, disclose, proclaim, vocalize 9 contralto, enunciate, pronounce, ventilate 10 articulate, intonation, modulation, prefer, serve, vocal sound 11 communicate 12 articulation, mezzo-soprano 13 participation, power of speech

voiceless 3 mum 4 deaf, mute, surd 6 silent 7 anaudia, aphonic, spirate

voice of the people
- Latin: 9 vox populi

void 4 bare, emit, free, null, pass 5 annul, blank, clear, drain, eject, empty, purge 6 barren, cancel, devoid, recant, repeal, revoke, vacant, vacuum 7 abolish, drained, emptied, exhaust, invalid, lacking, nullify, pour out, rescind, reverse, vacuity, wanting 8 depleted, evacuate, nugatory, renounce, throw out 9 destitute, discharge, emptiness, exhausted, repudiate 10 empty space, invalidate, not in force 11 countermand, inoperative

voidance 7 voiding 8 ejection, emission 9 discharge, expulsion

Voight, Jon
born: 9 Yonkers NY
roles: 7 Joe Buck 8 The Champ 10 Coming Home (Oscar) 11 Deliverance 13 The Odessa File 14 Catch Twenty-Two, Midnight Cowboy

voila 3 see 4 look 9 there it is

volatile 4 rash, wild 5 brash, giddy, moody 6 fickle, fitful 7 erratic, flighty, gaseous 8 eruptive, reckless, unstable, unsteady, vaporous, variable 9 explosive, frivolous, mercurial, spasmodic, unsettled 10 capricious, changeable, evaporable, inconstant, irresolute, vaporizing 12 undependable 13 temperamental, unpredictable

volition 4 will 6 choice, option 8 choosing, decision, free will 10 discretion, resolution 13 determination

volley 5 burst, salvo 6 shower 7 barrage 8 outbreak, outburst 9 broadside, discharge, fusillade 10 outpouring

Volpone (The Fox)
author: 9 Ben Jonson
character: 5 Celia, Mosca 7 Bonario, Corvino, Voltore 9 Corbaccio, Peregrine 18 Lady Politic Would-Be, Lord Politic Would-Be

Volsung
origin: 12 Scandinavian
mentioned in: 8 Volsunga
grandfather: 4 Odin 5 Othin
son: 7 Sigmund
daughter: 5 Signy

Volsunga
origin: 9 Icelandic 12 Scandinavian
form: 4 saga
time: 17 thirteenth century
subject: 8 Volsungs

Volta, Alessandro, Count
nationality: 7 Italian
invented: 15 electric battery
discovered: 10 methane gas

Voltaic
also: 3 Gur
language family: 16 Niger-Kordofanian
group: 10 Niger-Congo
includes: 5 Mossi

Voltaire, Francois
real name: 19 Francois Marie Arouet
author of: 5 Zadig, Zaire 6 Alzire, Merope 7 Candide, L'Ingenu, Mahomet 11 The Henriade 16 The Maid of Orleans 23 Philosophical Dictionary
member of: 11 Philosophes

Volturnus
origin: 5 Roman
personifies: 4 wind 8 east wind 13 southeast wind

voluble 4 glib 5 wordy 6 chatty, fluent 7 twining 8 effusive, flippant, rotating, twisting 9 garrulous, talkative 10 loquacious

volume 4 book, bulk, heap, mass, size, tome 5 folio, sound, tract 6 amount, extent, quarto 7 measure 8 capacity, loudness, quantity, treatise, vastness 9 abundance, aggregate, magnitude, monograph 10 dimensions

voluminous 5 ample, large 7 copious, massive, sizable 8 abundant 9 extensive

Volund see 7 Wayland

voluntary 6 willed 8 free-will, intended, optional, unforced 10 deliberate 11 intentional, volunteered 13 discretionary, noncompulsory

volunteer 5 offer 6 extend, tender, unpaid 7 advance, present, proffer, recruit 8 enlistee 9 voluntary 10 put forward 11 step forward 12 unpaid worker 13 charityworker

Voluptas
origin: 5 Roman
goddess of: 8 pleasure

voluptuary 4 rake, roue 7 epicure, gourmet, seducer 8 gourmand, hedonist, sybarite 9 bon vivant, debauchee, high liver, libertine, womanizer 10 gastronome, sensualist 14 pleasure seeker

voluptuous 4 soft 6 carnal, erotic, sexual, smooth, wanton 7 fleshly, lustful, sensual 8 sensuous 9 debauched, dissolute, luxurious, sybaritic 10 dissipated, hedonistic, lascivious, licentious, profligate 11 self-indulgent 14 pleasure-loving 15 pleasure-seeking

vomit 4 barf, emit, puke 5 eject, expel, heave, retch 7 bring up, throw up, upchuck 8 disgorge 9 spew forth 10 belch forth 11 regurgitate 15 toss one's cookies

Vonnegut, Kurt, Jr
author of: 8 Jailbird 9 Slap stick 10 Cat's Cradle, Palm Sunday 11 Player Piano 18 Slaughterhouse Five 20 Breakfast of Champions 22 Happy Birthday Wanda June

Von Sternberg, Josef
director of: 12 The Blue Angel

Von Sydow, Max
real name: 18 Carl Adolph von Sydow
born: 4 Lund 6 Sweden
roles: 12 The Emigrants 14 The Seventh Seal 15 The Virgin Spring 16 Wild Strawberries 24 The Greatest Story Ever Told

voracious 6 greedy 7 hoggish 8 edacious, ravenous 10 gluttonous, insatiable, omnivorous

Voragine, Jacobus de
author of: 12 Legenda Aurea (Golden Legend)

vortex 4 eddy 7 cyclone, twister 9 maelstrom, whirlpool, whirlwind

votary 3 fan 4 buff 6 zealot 7 admirer, devotee, fanatic, habitue 8 adherent, champion, disciple, follower, partisan 10 aficionado, enthusiast 11 afficionado

vote 3 say 4 poll 5 voice 6 ballot, choice, option, ticket 8 approval, decision, election, judgment, suffrage 9 franchise, selection 10 plebiscite, preference, referendum 11 cast a ballot 13 determination

vouch 4 back 6 affirm, attest, back up, uphold, verify 7 certify, confirm, endorse, support, sustain, swear to, warrant, witness 8 attest to, maintain 9 guarantee 11 corroborate 12 authenticate

voucher 4 chip, chit 5 check, proof 6 surety, ticket 7 receipt, warrant 8 warranty 9 affidavit, debenture 10 credential 11 certificate 12 verification 14 authentication

vouchsafe 4 give 5 allow, deign, favor, grant 6 bestow, convey, tender 7 concede 10 condescend

vow 4 oath, word 5 swear, troth, vouch 6 affirm, assert, assure, parole, pledge, plight, stress 7 declare, promise, resolve 8 contract 9 emphasize 11 word of honor 13 solemn promise

vox populi 14 popular opinion 16 voice of the people

voyage 4 sail 6 cruise 7 passage 8 crossing, navigate 9 ocean trip 10 sea journey

Voyage of the Beagle, The
   author: 13 Charles Darwin

voyager 5 rover 7 cruiser, pilgrim, rambler, tourist 8 traveler, wayfarer 9 jet-setter, journeyer, sightseer 10 adventurer 12 excursionist, globe-trotter, peregrinator 13 world traveler

Voyage to the Bottom of the Sea
   character: 6 Doctor 8 Kowalsky, Stu Riley, (Cdr/Capt) Lee Crane 9 Patterson 10 (Lt Cdr) Chip Morton 11 (Chief Petty Officer) Curley Jones 12 Chief Sharkey 14 (Adm) Harriman Nelson
   cast: 9 Allan Hunt, Del Monroe 10 Henry Kulky, Paul Trinka 11 Richard Bull, Terry Becker 12 David Hedison 13 Robert Dowdell 15 Richard Basehart
   submarine: 7 Seaview
   explorer: 7 Sea Crab
   mini-sub: 10 Flying Fish

Vronsky, Count Alexei
   character in: 12 Anna Karenina
   author: 7 Tolstoy

Vulcan
   origin: 5 Roman
   god of: 4 fire 12 metalworking
   epithet: 8 Mulciber
   corresponds to: 10 Hephaestus, Hephaistos

vulgar 3 low 4 base, rude 5 crude, dirty, gross, rough 6 coarse, common, filthy, ribald, risque, smutty 7 boorish, ill-bred, lowbrow, obscene, uncouth 8 impolite, indecent, off-color, ordinary, plebeian 9 offensive, tasteless, unrefined 10 suggestive 11 ill-mannered, proletarian 12 pornographic, uncultivated

vulgarian 3 oaf 4 boor, lout 5 brute, yahoo 7 Babbitt 9 ignoramus 10 philistine 16 anti-intellectual

vulgarity 8 bad taste, rudeness 9 crudeness, grossness, indecency, indecorum, obscenity 10 coarseness, ill manners, indelicacy, smuttiness 11 boorishness, pornography 12 impoliteness 13 tastelessness

vulnerable 4 weak 7 exposed 8 helpless, insecure 9 sensitive, unguarded 10 easily hurt, undefended 11 defenseless, susceptible, thin-skinned, unprotected

Vye, Eustacia
   character in: 17 Return of the Native
   author: 5 Hardy

W

wacky, whacky 3 odd 4 nuts 5 crazy, kooky 6 cuckoo, insane, kookie 7 cracked, foolish, touched 9 eccentric, senseless 10 irrational 12 crackbrained

wad 3 bat, pad 4 cram, head, heap, lump, mass, tuft 5 money, stuff 6 bundle, riches, stop up 7 fortune 8 bankroll, plumbago

waddle 3 wag 4 sway 6 hobble, toddle, totter, wobble

wade 4 ford, plod, plow, toil, trek 5 labor 6 drudge, trudge 9 walk in mud 11 walk in water

wafer 4 chip 5 candy, flake 6 cookie 7 cracker 15 unleavened bread

waft 4 blow, puff 5 drift, float

wag 3 bob, wit 4 card, move, stir, wave 5 clown, droll, flick, joker, shake 6 jester, jiggle, switch, twitch, waggle, wiggle, wigwag 7 buffoon, farceur, flicker, flutter 8 comedian, humorist, jokester 9 oscillate 11 wisecracker 14 life of the party

wage 3 fee, pay 6 income, salary 7 carry on, conduct, payment, revenue, stipend 8 earnings, engage in, maintain, practice 9 emolument, undertake 10 recompense 12 compensation, remuneration

wage earner 6 worker 8 employee 9 job holder 12 hourly worker

wager 3 bet, pot 4 ante, pool, risk 5 fancy, guess, stake 6 assume, gamble, hazard 7 imagine, jackpot, presume, suppose, surmise, venture 8 make a bet, theorize 9 speculate 10 conjecture, take a flyer 11 speculation, try one's luck 12 tempt fortune 15 hazard an opinion

wages 3 bet, fee, pay 4 gage, hire 6 fights, reward, return, salary 7 engages, payment, stipend 8 conducts, earnings 9 emolument 10 prosecutes, recompense 12 remuneration

wage war 5 fight 6 combat 7 contend, make war 8 do battle 12 march against

waggery 5 chaff 6 banter, riding 7 joshing, kidding, ragging, ribbing 8 chaffing, drollery, raillery, twitting
   French: 8 badinage

waggish 5 droll, funny 7 comical, puckish 8 humorous

waggle 4 wave 5 wield 8 brandish

Wagner, Honus
   real name: 15 John Peter Wagner
   nickname: 14 Flying Dutchman
   sport: 8 baseball
   position: 9 shortstop
   team: 17 Pittsburgh Pirates

Wagner, Richard
   born: 7 Germany, Leipzig
   composer of: 5 Faust 6 Rienzi 7 Die

Feen 8 Parsifal 9 Lohengrin 10 Tannhauser, The Fairies 14 Siegfried Idyll 16 The Mastersingers, Tristan and Isolde, Wesendonck Lieder 17 The Flying Dutchman 20 Der Ring des Nibelungen, The Ring of the Nibelungs 27 Die Meistersinger von Nurnberg
   the Ring Cycle Part 1: 12 Das Rheingold, The Rhine Gold
   the Ring Cycle Part 2: 10 Die Walkure 11 The Valkyrie
   the Ring Cycle Part 3: 9 Siegfried
   the Ring Cycle Part 4: 15 Gotterdammerung 17 Twilight of the Gods

Wagner, Robert
   born: 9 Detroit MI
   wife: 11 Natalie Wood
   roles: 6 Switch 10 Hart to Hart 13 It Takes a Thief, Prince Valiant, The Longest Day 24 All the Fine Young Cannibals

wagon 3 car, van 4 cart, dray, tram, wain 5 coach, lorry, tonga, truck 7 caisson 10 automobile, battleship
   covered: 15 prairie schooner
   maker: 10 wainwright
   police: 10 Black Maria
   Russian: 6 telega
   sideless: 6 rolley
   track: 3 rut

Wagon Train
   character: 9 Bill Hawks 11 Barnaby West, Cooper Smith, Duke Shannon 14 Charlie Wooster, Major Seth Adams 15 Christopher Hale, Flint McCullough
   cast: 8 Ward Bond 11 Scott Miller, Terry Wilson 12 Frank McGrath, John McIntire, Michael Burns, Robert Fuller, Robert Horton

waif 5 gamin, stray 6 gamine, urchin 7 mudlark 9 foundling 10 ragamuffin, street arab 11 guttersnipe 13 homeless child 14 tatterdemalion

wail 3 cry 4 bawl, howl, keen, moan, roar, weep, yell 5 groan, shout, whine 6 bellow, bemoan, bewail, cry out, lament, outcry, plaint 7 keening, moaning, wailing 9 caterwaul 10 rend the air 11 lamentation

waist 3 top 5 blouse, bodice, middle 7 midriff 9 mid-region, waistband, waistline 10 middle part, midsection, shirtwaist

waistband 4 belt, sash 5 cinch 6 girdle

waistcoat 4 vest 5 benjy 6 jacket, jerkin, veskit, vestee, weskit 7 singlet
   French: gilet

wait 4 halt, stay, stop 5 dally, delay, pause, tarry 6 linger, put off 7 suspend 8 postpone, stopover 9 deferment 10 suspension 11 continuance 12 postponement

wait for 6 expect 10 anticipate
Waiting for Godot
  author: 13 Samuel Beckett
  character: 8 Estragon, Vladimir
wait on 5 serve 6 assist, attend
waive 4 stay 5 defer, forgo, let go, table, yield 6 give up, not use, put off, shelve 7 forbear, lay over 8 disclaim, forswear, postpone, renounce 9 surrender
waiver 9 dismissal 10 abdication, disclaimer 11 abandonment 12 renunciation 14 relinquishment
Wakashan
  tribe: 6 Nootka 8 Kwakiutl, Puyallup
wake 4 fire, path, stir, wash 5 rally, rouse, trail, train, vigil 6 arouse, course, excite, kindle, revive 7 enliven, provoke, quicken 8 backwash 9 galvanize, stimulate 11 resuscitate
wakeful 4 wary 5 alert, astir 7 careful, heedful 8 cautious, restless, vigilant, watchful 9 insomniac, observant, sleepless 10 unsleeping 11 circumspect
wake up 4 rise 5 arise 6 vivify 7 animate, enliven 8 vitalize 9 stimulate
Walcott, Joe
  real name: 18 Arnold Raymond Cream
  nickname: 9 Jersey Joe
  sport: 6 boxing
  class: 11 heavyweight
Walden, or Life in the Woods
  author: 17 Henry David Thoreau
Wales
  other name: 5 Cymru 7 Cambria
  capital: 7 Cardiff
  cities: 4 Rhyl, Ross 5 Flint, Towyn 6 Amlwch, Bangor, Brecon, Sidney 7 Cwmbran, Herford, Newport, Rhondda, Swansea 8 Aberdare, Caerleon, Holyhead, Pembroke 9 Fishguard, Glamorgan 10 Caernarvon, Caerphilly, Carmarthen 11 Aberystwyth 12 Milford Haven 13 Kidderminster, Merthyr-Tydfil
  division: 5 Clwyd, Dyfed, Flint, Gwent, Powys 6 Radnor 7 Denbigh, Gwynedd 8 Anglesey, Cardigan, Monmouth, Pembroke 9 Brecknoch, Glamorgan, Merioneth 10 Caernarvon, Carmarthen, Montgomery
  government: 29 constituent part of Great Britain
  measure: 5 cover 7 cantred, crannoc, listred
  island: 4 Mona 5 Caldy 8 Anglesey, Holyhead
  lake: 4 Bala 6 Vyrnwy
  mountain: 6 Berwyn 8 Cambrian 9 Prescelly 13 Brecon Beacons
  highest point: 7 Snowdon
  river: 3 Dee, Usk, Wye 4 Alun, Taff, Tawe, Teme, Towy 5 Clwyd, Conwy, Dovey, Neath, Teifi 6 Conway, Severn, Vyrnwy
  sea: 5 Irish 8 Atlantic
  physical feature:
  bay: 7 Swansea 8 Cardigan, Tremadoc, Tremadog

  channel: 7 Bristol 9 St George's
  hills: 7 Malvern
  peninsula: 5 Lleyn
  strait: 5 Menai
  valley: 7 Rhondda
  people: 4 Celt, Kelt 5 Cymry, Kymry, Welsh 7 Brython, Silures, Taffies 8 Awabokal, Cambrian 9 Siluridan
  actor: 6 Burton 8 Williams
  artist: 4 John
  author: 3 Map 5 Jones, Lewis, Mapes, Parry 6 Machan, Thrale 9 Llewellyn 11 Dylan Thomas 14 Dafydd ap Gwilym
  god: 3 Deu, Dew 4 Bran, Gwyn 5 Dylan 7 Gwydion
  leader: 5 Bevan 6 Rhodri 8 Hywel Dwa 11 Cadwallader 12 Bishop Morgan 13 Owen Glendower 16 David Lloyd George 18 Llewelyn ap Gruffydd
  language: 5 Welsh 6 Celtic, Cymric, Keltic, Kymric 7 Cymraeg, English
  religion: 8 Anglican 9 Methodist 10 Protestant 12 Presbyterian
  place:
  bridge: 6 Severn
  castle: 6 Conway 7 Harlech 9 Beaumaris 10 Caernarvon, Caerphilly 11 Aberystwyth
  feature:
  festival: 10 Eisteddfod
  stories: 10 Mabinogion
  food:
  dish: 8 flummery
wander aimlessly 5 amble, stray 6 ramble, stroll 7 meander, saunter
Wanderer, The
  author: 13 Alain Fournier
wandering 5 lapse 8 rambling, straying 9 deviation 10 aberration, digressive, discursive, maundering, meandering, roundabout 11 abnormality 12 idiosyncrasy 13 nonconformity 14 circumlocutory
Wandering Jew, The
  author: 9 Eugene Sue
Wanderings
  author: 10 Chaim Potok
wane 3 ebb 4 fade, sink 5 abate, droop, waste 6 ebbing, fading, lessen, weaken, wither 7 abating, decline, dwindle, subside 8 decrease, diminish, fade away 9 dwindling, lessening, recession, subsiding, weakening, withering
wangle 4 worm 5 trick 6 jockey, scheme 7 finagle, wheedle 8 engineer, intrigue, maneuver 9 machinate 10 manipulate
wanness 6 pallor 8 grayness, paleness 9 ashenness 10 sallowness, sickliness 13 colorlessness
want 4 hunt, lack, need, seek, wish 5 covet, crave, fancy 6 dearth, demand, desire, hunger, penury 7 be needy, craving, hope for, long for, paucity, pine for, poverty, require, wish for 8 scarcity, shortage, yearn for, yearning 9 indigence, necessity, pauperism, privation, requisite 10 deficiency, insolvency 11 destitution, require-

ment 13 impecuniosity, insufficiency, penilessness 14 impoverishment

Wanted: Dead or Alive
  character: 11 Josh Randall
  cast: 12 Steve McQueen
  job: 12 bounty hunter
  gun: 8 Mare's Leg

wanting 5 short 6 absent 7 lacking, missing 9 defective, deficient, imperfect 10 inadequate 11 substandard 12 insufficient

wanton 4 bawd, fast, jade, lewd, rake, roue, slut, tart 5 gross, hussy, loose, satyr, whore 6 chippy, harlot, lecher 7 bestial, immoral, lustful, obscene, seducer, trollop, willful 8 careless, heedless, mindless, needless, strumpet, sybarite, unchaste 9 abandoned, adulterer, concubine, debauched, debauchee, dissolute, lecherous, libertine, malicious, senseless, womanizer 10 deliberate, fornicator, groundless, licentious, malevolent, profligate, prostitute, sensualist, unprovoked, voluptuary 11 fornicatrix, promiscuous, unjustified, whoremaster 13 inconsiderate, irresponsible

wapiti 3 elk 4 deer 11 American elk
  female: 3 cow
  literally: 9 white rump
  male: 4 bull
  species: 16 Cervus canadensis

Wapshot Chronicle
  author: 11 John Cheever

war 5 clash, fight 6 attack, battle, combat, invade 7 contend 8 conflict, fighting, struggle 10 opposition 11 hostilities
  god of: 4 Ares, Odin 5 Othin 8 Quirinus
  goddess of: 4 Enyo 5 Athena, Athene, Inanna, Ishtar, Pallas, Saitis 7 Bellona, Mylitta 11 Tritogeneia 12 Pallas Athena 18 Alalcomenean Athena

War and Peace
  author: 10 Leo Tolstoy
  character: 7 Kutuzov 8 Napoleon 13 Natasha Rostov, Nikolay Rostov, Pierre Bezuhov 14 Anatole Kuragin 15 Andrey Bolkonsky 19 Ellen Kuragin Bezuhov 22 Princess Marya Bolkonsky

War and Remembrance
  author: 10 Herman Wouk

warble 4 lump, purl, sing 5 carol, larva, trill, tumor, yodel 6 growth, quaver, ripple 7 twitter, vibrate, whistle

war cry 6 slogan 8 Geronimo

ward 4 zone 5 avert, block, repel 6 charge, thwart 7 beat off, fend off, prevent, quarter 8 pavilion, precinct, stave off, turn away 9 dependent, forestall
  French: 7 protege

warden 5 guard 6 keeper, ranger, sentry 7 curator, manager 8 guardian, watchman 9 protector 14 superintendent

Warden, The
  author: 15 Anthony Trollope

ward off 5 avert 7 prevent

wardrobe 4 togs 5 chest 6 attire, closet, outfit 7 apparel, clothes 8 clothing, garments 10 cedar chest 12 clothespress

French: 6 bureau 7 armoire, commode 10 chiffonier 11 habillement

wares 4 line 5 stock 7 staples 8 supplies 9 inventory 11 commodities, merchandise

warfare 5 fight 6 battle, combat 8 conflict, fighting 11 hostilities

Warhol, Andy
  born: 14 Philadelphia PA
  artwork: 9 Brillo Box, Liz Taylor 13 Marilyn Monroe 16 Campbell's Soup Can 20 Green Coca-Cola Bottles

wariness 7 caution 9 alertness, suspicion, vigilance 11 carefulness, guardedness, heedfulness 12 watchfulness 14 circumspection

warlike 7 hostile, martial, valiant 8 inimical, militant, military 9 bellicose, combative 10 unfriendly 11 belligerent, contentious, threatening
  Indian: 8 Arapahoe

warlike attitude 9 hostility, pugnacity 11 bellicosity 12 belligerence, belligerency 13 combativeness 14 aggressiveness

warm 3 hot 4 cook, heat, kind, melt, thaw 5 cheer, happy, sunny, tepid, vivid 6 bright, heated, heat up, joyful, joyous, kindly, lively, loving, simmer, tender 7 affable, cordial, earnest, fervent, glowing, intense 8 animated, cheerful, friendly, gracious, outgoing, pleasant, spirited, vehement, vigorous 9 brilliant 10 passionate 11 kindhearted, sympathetic 12 affectionate, enthusiastic 13 compassionate, tenderhearted

warmhearted 4 kind 6 genial, kindly, loving 7 cordial 10 solicitous 11 sympathetic 12 affectionate 13 compassionate

warm-hued 3 red 4 rosy 5 ruddy, vivid 6 golden, orange, yellow 7 crimson, roseate, scarlet 8 blushing

warmish 5 tepid 7 cooling

warm oneself 4 bask 12 soak up warmth, toast oneself

warmth 3 joy 4 fire, heat, zeal 5 ardor, cheer, verve, vigor 6 fervor, spirit 7 hotness, passion 8 kindness, sympathy 9 animation, happiness, intensity, vehemence 10 affability, compassion, cordiality, enthusiasm, excitement, joyfulness, kindliness, liveliness, lovingness, tenderness 11 earnestness 12 cheerfulness, friendliness, graciousness 15 kindheartedness 17 tenderheartedness

warn 5 alert 6 advise, inform, notify, signal 7 apprise, caution, counsel 8 admonish

warning 4 hint, omen, sign 5 alarm, token 6 advice, notice, signal 7 portent, presage 8 apprisal 9 foretoken 10 intimation 12 notification

War of the Worlds, The
  author: 7 H G Wells
  invasion by: 8 Martians

war of words 7 dispute, quarrel 8 argument 11 altercation, controversy 12 disagreement

warp 4 bend, bent, bias 5 quirk, twist 6 debase, deform, infect 7 contort, corrupt, distort, leaning, mislead, pervert 8 misguide, misshape, tendency 9 prejudice, proneness 10 contortion, distortion, partiality, proclivity, propensity 11 deformation, disposition, inclination 14 predisposition

warrant 3 vow 4 aver, avow 5 swear 6 affirm, assert, assure, attest, permit, pledge 7 certify, declare, justify, license, promise 9 authorize, guarantee 10 asseverate, permission 13 authorization

warranty 6 pledge 9 agreement 11 certificate

Warren, Robert Penn
  author of: 5 Flood 7 Audubon 8 Promises 10 Now and Then 12 Incarnations 14 All the King's Men 18 World Enough and Time
  member of: 12 the Fugitives

warring 7 hostile 8 battling, clashing, fighting, opposing 9 combatant 10 contending 11 belligerent, conflicting, contentious

warrior 7 fighter, soldier, veteran 9 combatant, man-at-arms 10 campaigner 11 legionnaire

Warsaw
  area: 11 Stare Miasto
  capital of: 6 Poland
  landmark: 14 Kazimierzowski 25 Palace of Culture and Science
  Polish: 8 Warszawa
  river: 7 Vistula
  square: 5 Rynek

warship 5 Maine, U-boat 6 corvet 7 Alabama, cruiser, frigate, gunboat, Monitor 8 Bismarck, corvette, Graf Spee, ironclad, man-of-war 9 destroyer, ironsides, Merrimack, submarine 11 dreadnought, torpedo boat 12 Constitution, Old Ironsides 13 Constellation 15 aircraft carrier 16 superdreadnought
  fleet: 6 armada
  part: 6 turret
  plating: 5 armor

wary 5 alert 7 careful, guarded, heedful, mindful, prudent, wakeful 8 cautious, discreet, vigilant, watchful 10 suspicious 11 circumspect

War Within and Without
  author: 19 Anne Morrow Lindbergh

wash 3 mop, rub, wet 4 bath, lave, soak, swab, wipe 5 bathe, clean, float, flood, rinse, scour, scrub 6 drench, shower, sponge 7 cleanse, immerse, launder, laundry, moisten, mopping, shampoo 8 ablution, cleaning, inundate, irrigate, lavation, scouring 9 cleansing 10 laundering

washbasin 3 tub 4 bowl 5 laver 6 lavabo 8 lavatory

washed out 4 drab, dull, pale 5 dingy, faded, white 6 dreary, grayed 8 bleached 9 colorless

washed up, washed-up 4 lost, shot 6 bathed, broken, ruined, undone 7 done for, preened, through 8 bankrupt, done with,

fatigued, finished, scrubbed 9 played out, showered

washing 6 laving 7 bathing, laundry, purging, rinsing, soaking 8 cleaning, scouring 9 ablutions, drenching, scrubbing, showering 10 laundering, shampooing

Washington
  abbreviation: 2 WA 4 Wash
  nickname: 7 Chinook 9 Evergreen
  capital: 7 Olympia
  largest city: 7 Seattle
  others: 4 Omak 5 Pasco 6 Renton, Tacoma, Yakima 7 Ephrata, Everett, Hoquiam, Othello, Pullman, Spokane 8 Aberdeen, Bellevue, Longview, Puyallup, Richland 9 Anacortes, Bremerton, Kennewick, Vancouver, Wenatchee 10 Bellingham, Burlington, Walla Walla 11 Port Angeles
  college: 7 Gonzaga, Seattle, Whitman 9 Evergreen, Whitworth 10 Puget Sound 14 Seattle Pacific 15 Pacific Lutheran
  feature:
  dam: 10 Bonneville, 11 Grand Coulee
  fort: 5 Lewis
  national park: 7 Olympic 12 Mount Rainier 13 North Cascades
  tribe: 3 Hoh 5 Lummi, Makah, Twana 6 Cayuse, Samish, Skagit, Suwax 7 Chinook, Clallam, Clatsop, Cowlitz, Dwamish, Nooksak, Palouse, Quaitso, Sanpoil, Spokane, Squaxon, Tulalip 8 Chehalis, Chimakum, Colville, Nespelim, Nez Perce, Okanagon, Pishquow, Puyallup, Quileute, Quinault, Sahaptin, Salishan, Sinkiuse 9 Nisqually, Quinaielt, Semiahmoo, Skokomish, Swinomish 10 Senijextee, Shoalwater 11 Shahaptaine
  people: 7 Seattle 10 Bing Crosby 11 Hank Ketcham 12 Elisha P Ferry 13 Marcus Whitman 15 William O Douglas 19 Isaac Ingalls Stevens
  explorer: 4 Cook, Gray 6 Heceta 9 Vancouver 13 Lewis and Clark
  lake: 4 Soap 5 Moses, Union 6 Chelan, Ozette 7 Cle Elum, Cushman, Kachess 8 Crescent, Quinault 9 Keechelus, Wenatchee 10 Washington
  land rank: twentieth
  mountain: 4 Blue, Jack, Tunk 5 Adams, Baker, Lemei, Logan, Moses, Sloan 6 Kettle, Quartz, Simcoe, Stuart 7 Shuksan 8 Cascades, Olympics, St Helens 11 Kettle River
  highest point: 7 Rainier
  physical feature:
  falls: 10 Snoqualmie
  port: 6 Tacoma 7 Everett, Seattle 10 Bellingham
  sound: 5 Puget 7 Rosario
  river: 5 Snake, White 6 Yakima 7 Spokane 8 Columbia, Quinault 9 Snohomish 10 Snoqualmie 11 Pend Oreille
  state admission: 11 forty-second
  state bird: 15 willow goldfinch
  state fish: 14 steelhead trout

state flower: 17 coast rhododendron 19 western rhododendron
state motto: 7 By and By (Alki)
state song: 16 Washington My Home
state tree: 14 western hemlock

Washington, George
nickname: 18 Father of His Country
presidential rank: 5 first
party: 10 Federalist
state represented: 2 VA
elected: 11 unanimously
vice president: 5 (John) Adams
cabinet:
state: 9 (Thomas) Jefferson
treasury: 8 (Alexander) Hamilton
war: 4 (Henry) Knox 7 (James) McHenry 9 (Timothy) Pickering
attorney general: 3 (Charles) Lee 8 (Edmund Jennings) Randolph, (William) Bradford
born: 2 VA 9 Wakefield 18 Westmoreland County
died/buried: 11 Mount Vernon
religion: 12 Episcopalian
interests: 7 fishing, hunting, theater 17 scientific farming
vacation: 11 Mount Vernon
author: 33 The Journal of Major George Washington
political career: 9 president 16 House of Burgesses 24 First Continental Congress 25 Second Continental Congress
signed: 12 Constitution
civilian career: 6 farmer 8 surveyor
military service:
war: 13 Revolutionary 15 French and Indian
notable events of lifetime/term: 18 American Revolution
crossed: 13 Delaware River
rebellion: 7 Whiskey
winter at: 11 Valley Forge
father: 9 Augustine
mother: 4 Mary (Ball)
siblings: 5 Betty 6 Samuel 7 Charles, Mildred 13 John Augustine
half-brother: 6 Butler 8 Lawrence 9 Augustine
half-sister: 4 Jane
wife: 6 Martha (Dandridge Custis)
children:
stepchildren: 15 John Parke Custis 17 Martha Parke Custis

Washington DC
airport: 6 Dulles 8 National
basketball team: 7 Bullets
capital of: 12 United States
designed by: 7 L'Enfant
football team: 8 Redskins
landmark: 4 Mall 7 Capitol, Ellipse 8 Pentagon 10 White House 11 National Zoo 12 Ford's Theatre, Franklin Park, Supreme Court 13 Lafayette Park, Rock Creek Park 14 Farragut Square, Reflecting Pool, Watergate Hotel 15 Lincoln Memorial, McPherson Square 16 National Archives 17 Jefferson Memorial, Library

of Congress, National Arboretum 18 Washington Monument 21 Frederick Douglass Home, Robert F Kennedy Stadium 22 Smithsonian Institution 23 National Sculpture Garden 25 Arlington National Cemetery 33 Kennedy Center for the Performing Arts
museum: 5 Freer 7 Renwick 8 Corcoran 9 Hirshhorn 10 African Art 11 Smithsonian 13 Dumbarton Oaks 15 National Gallery 17 Folger Shakespeare 18 Phillips Collection 23 National Portrait Gallery
river: 7 Potomac 9 Rock Creek
street/avenue: 4 Ohio 7 New York, Potomac 12 Constitution, Independence, Pennsylvania 13 Massachusetts
university: 6 Howard 8 American, Catholic 10 Georgetown 11 George Mason 16 George Washington

Washington Square
author: 10 Henry James

wash one's hands of 4 deny, quit 6 give up 7 abandon, decline, disavow, forsake 8 abnegate, cast away, disclaim, forswear, renounce 9 repudiate 10 relinquish

washout 6 fiasco, fizzle 7 failure, letdown 8 disaster 14 disappointment

wash out 4 fade, fail 6 bleach 7 deplete, fatigue 8 enervate, enfeeble 10 debilitate, devitalize

wasp
variety: 5 paper 6 cuckoo, ensign, hornet, potter, spider 12 yellow jacket

waspish 5 huffy, testy 6 crabby, cranky, ornery, shirty 7 bearish, fretful, peevish, pettish 8 petulant, snappish 9 crotchety, fractious, irascible, irritable, querulous 12 cantankerous

Wasps, The
author: 12 Aristophanes
character: 10 Bdelycleon, Philocleon
dog: 5 Labes

wassail 5 drink, punch, revel, toast 6 liquor, tipple 7 carouse, revelry 8 beverage, carousal

waste 3 die, ebb, rob 4 fade, loot, melt, rape, raze, ruin, sack, sink, void, wane 5 abate, crush, decay, drain, dregs, droop, empty, offal, smash, spoil, strip, trash, wreck 6 barren, burn up, debris, devour, litter, misuse, ravage, razing, refuse, scraps, steppe, tundra, weaken, wither 7 crumble, decline, deplete, despoil, destroy, dwindle, exhaust, garbage, looting, pillage, plunder, rubbish, shatter, subside 8 badlands, decrease, demolish, diminish, leavings, misapply, misspend, needless, prey upon, remnants, squander, wrecking 9 devastate, disappear, dissipate, emptiness, evaporate, excrement, leftovers, misemploy, ruination, sweepings 10 demolition, plundering, remainders, wilderness 11 destruction, devastation, dissipation, expenditure, fritter away, prodigality, squandering 12 despoliation, extravagance 14 misapplication

waste away 4 fail, rust 7 corrode, decline, eat into

wasted 5 spent 6 used-up 7 ravaged 8 emaciated, exhausted 12 unproductive

wasteful 8 prodigal 9 unthrifty 10 thriftless 11 extravagant, improvident, spendthrift, squandering 12 uneconomical

wastefulness 10 imprudence, lavishness 11 prodigality, squandering 12 extravagance, improvidence

wasteland 6 desert

Waste Land, The
author: 7 T S Eliot

waste time 5 dally 6 dawdle, loiter 10 dilly-dally

watch 3 eye, see 4 heed, look, mark, mind, note, ogle, save, tend 5 alert, guard, scout, stare 6 attend, be wary, gaze at, guards, look at, look on, notice, patrol, peep at, peer at, picket, regard, sentry, survey, tend to 7 be chary, care for, examine, lookout, observe, oversee, protect, stare at 8 pore over, preserve, sentinel, sentries, take heed 9 attention, patrolman, vigilance 10 observance, scrutinize 11 contemplate, observation, superintend, supervision 15 superintendence

watch fire 6 beacon
kinds: 4 bale 6 signal

watchful 4 wary 5 alert, aware, canny, chary 6 shrewd 7 careful, guarded, heedful, mindful, prudent 8 cautious, openeyed, vigilant 9 attentive, observant 11 circumspect

watchfulness 4 care, heed 9 attention, diligence, vigilance 13 attentiveness

watchman 5 guard, scout 6 patrol, picket, sentry 7 lookout 8 sentinel 9 patrolman

Watch on the Rhine
director: 13 Herman Shumlin
based on play by: 14 Lillian Hellman
cast: 9 Paul Lukas 10 Bette Davis 19 Geraldine Fitzgerald
Oscar for: 5 actor (Lukas)

watch over 5 guard 6 attend 7 oversee, protect 11 superintend

watchtower 6 beacon, pharos, signal 7 seamark 8 landmark 10 lighthouse

watchword 5 motto 6 byword, slogan

water 3 cut, dip, sea, wet 4 damp, lake, pond, pool, soak, tear, thin 5 douse, flood, H two O, ocean, river, souse 6 dampen, deluge, dilute, drench, lagoon, splash, stream 7 immerse, moisten 8 inundate, irrigate, sprinkle, submerge 10 adulterate
goddess of: 4 Enki

Water Carrier (Water Bearer)
constellation of: 8 Aquarius

watercolor
French: 9 aquarelle

watercourse 5 canal, river 6 strait 7 channel, conduit, narrows, passage 8 aqueduct

water down 3 cut 6 censor, dilute, weaken 7 thin out 9 expurgate 10 adulterate

watered down 4 weak 6 dilute 7 diluted 8 weakened 11 adulterated

waterfall 7 cascade, Niagara 8 cataract

waterfront 4 dock, mole, pier, quay 5 basin, jetty, levee, wharf 6 marina 7 landing

waterless 3 dry 4 arid, sere 6 barren 7 parched, thirsty 10 desertlike

Waterloo Bridge
director: 11 Mervyn LeRoy
cast: 11 Vivien Leigh 12 Lucile Watson, Robert Taylor 13 Virginia Field
remade as: 4 Gaby

Water Monster (Sea Serpent)
constellation of: 5 Hydra

water of life
Latin: 9 aqua vitae

Waters, Ethel
nickname: 19 Sweet Mama Stringbean
born: 9 Chester PA
roles: 5 Pinky 6 Beulah 21 The Member of the Wedding

Watership Down
author: 12 Richard Adams

Water Snake
constellation of: 6 Hydrus

watertight 9 nonporous 10 impervious 11 impermeable

waterway 5 canal, inlet, river, route 6 gutter, strait, strake, stream 7 channel

Water Wonderland
nickname of: 8 Michigan

watery 3 wet 4 damp, thin, weak 5 fluid, moist, teary 6 liquid, rheumy 7 aqueous, diluted, tearful, tearing 11 adulterated

Watling, Belle
character in: 15 Gone With the Wind
author: 8 Mitchell

Watt, James
nationality: 8 Scottish
developed: 11 steam engine 12 piston engine

Watteau, Jean Antoine
born: 6 France 12 Valenciennes
artwork: 6 Gilles 8 Mezzetin 9 La Finette 10 La Toilette 12 Joys of Living, L'indifferent 13 La Gamme d'Amour 16 Company in the Park, La Lecon de Musique 18 Enseigne de Gersaint, Gersaint's Signboard, La Comedie Francaise, La Concert de Famille 20 Le Dejeuner en plein air, L'assemblee dans un parc 21 Harlequin and Columbine 23 Embarquement pour Cythere, Italian and French Theater, Jupiter Surprises Antiope, Les Amusements Champetres 24 Conversation in the Open Air, The Embarkation for Cythera

wattle 6 Acacia
varieties: 5 black, broom, cedar, glory, green, hairy, oven's, Sally, swamp 6 frosty, golden, mudgee, orange, silver, sticky 7 bramble, buffalo, coastal, prickly, weeping, Wyalong 8 blue-leaf, cinnamon, graceful, screw-pod, sunshine 9 red-leaved 10 golden-rain, needle-bush 11 Cootamundra, Mount Morgan, Wallangarra 12 Sydney golden 14 Peppermint-tree 16 Queensland silver

Watts, Sir George Frederic
 born: 6 London 7 England
 artwork: 4 Hope 14 Physical Energy 17
 Paolo and Francesca 19 Anastasio
 degl'Onesti 45 Caractacus Led in Triumph Through the Streets of Rome 54
 Alfred Inciting his Subjects to Prevent the
 Landing of the Danes

Waugh, Evelyn
 author of: 9 Men at Arms 10 Vile Bodies
 11 The Loved One 13 Black Mischief, Edmund Campion 14 A Handful of Dust, Decline and Fall 15 A Little Learning 19
 Brideshead Revisited 20 Officers and
 Gentlemen 22 Unconditional Surrender

wave 4 coil, curl, file, flap, line, rank, rise,
 roll, rush, sway, tier 5 curve, flood, pulse,
 shake, surge, swell, swing, train, twirl,
 wield 6 billow, column, comber, deluge,
 motion, quiver, ripple, roller, signal, spiral,
 string 7 breaker, flutter, gesture, pulsate, tremble, vibrate, winding 8 brandish,
 flourish, increase, undulate, whitecap 9
 advancing, oscillate, pulsation, vibration
 10 salutation, undulation 11 gesticulate,
 heightening 13 gesticulation

wave at 4 hail 6 signal 7 gesture

wave on 6 beckon, signal 7 gesture 11 gesticulate

waver 4 flap, reel, sway, vary 5 pause,
 shake, swing, weave 6 careen, change,
 falter, quiver, totter, wobble 7 flutter, stagger, tremble 8 hesitate, undulate 9 fluctuate, vacillate 10 dillydally 12 shilly-shally

wavering 8 hesitant, waffling 9 undecided
 10 hesitating, indecisive, irresolute 11 vacillating

Waverley
 author: 14 Sir Walter Scott
 character: 12 Flora Maclvor 14 Donald
 Bean Lean, Edward Waverley 15 Rose
 Bradwardine 16 Baron Bradwardine 17
 Evan Dhu MacCombich 24 Fergus
 Maclvor Vich Ian Vohr 25 Prince Charles
 Edward Stuart

wavy 5 curly 6 coiled, curved 7 rolling, sinuous, winding 8 mazelike, rippling, tortuous 10 meandering, serpentine, undulating
 11 curvilinear 12 labyrinthine

wax 4 grow 5 swell, widen 6 become, blow
 up, dilate, expand, extend, thrive 7 balloon, develop, enlarge, fill out, inflate, puff
 out 8 increase

way 3 far, off 4 area, form, lane, pass, path,
 road, room, wont 5 habit, means, route,
 space, trail, usage 6 course, custom, far
 off, manner, method, nature, region, system 7 conduct, passage, pathway, process
 8 behavior, distance, practice, remotely, vicinity 9 direction, procedure, technique 12
 neighborhood

wayfarer 9 traveler, wanderer 9 sojourner

Wayfaring Stranger
 nickname of: 8 Burl Ives

way in 4 door, gate 5 entry 6 access, portal
 7 doorway, gateway, ingress 8 approach,
 entrance

Wayland
 also: 6 Volund 7 Wieland
 origin: 8 European
 king of: 5 elves

waylay 4 lure 5 decoy 6 ambush, assail, attack, entrap 7 assault, ensnare, set upon 8
 inveigle

Wayne, Anthony
 nickname: 10 Mad Anthony
 served in: 10 Indian Wars 16 Revolutionary War
 captured: 10 Stony Point
 battle: 10 Brandywine, Germantown 13
 Fallen Timbers

Wayne, David
 real name: 13 Wayne McMeekan
 born: 14 Traverse City MI
 roles: 6 Sakini 8 Adam's Rib 12 The
 Front Page 13 Mister Roberts, Tonight
 We Sing 15 Huckleberry Finn 16 Portrait
 of Jennie 26 The Teahouse of the August
 Moon

Wayne, John
 real name: 21 Marion Michael Morrison
 nickname: 4 Duke
 born: 11 Winterset IA
 roles: 5 Hondo 6 Chisum 8 Ringo Kid,
 Rio Bravo, The Alamo, True Grit (Oscar)
 9 McLintock, Rio Grande 10 Stagecoach
 11 The Quiet Man, The Shootist 12 The
 Searchers 14 Rooster Cogburn, The
 Green Berets 16 How the West Was Won
 17 The Sands of Iwo Jima 27 The Man
 Who Shot Liberty Valance

Way of All Flesh, The
 author: 12 Samuel Butler
 character: 9 Mr Overton
 Pontifex family: 5 Ellen 6 Althea, Ernest,
 George 8 Theobald 9 Christina

Way of the World, The
 author: 15 William Congreve
 character: 6 Foible 7 Fainall, Witwoud 8
 Mirabell, Waitwell 10 Mrs Fainall, Mrs
 Marwood 12 Lady Wishfort, Mrs Milla-
 mant 17 Sir Wilfull Witwoud

way of thinking 7 beliefs 9 principle 10
 conviction 11 persuasions

way out 4 exit 6 egress, escape, outlet

Ways of Escape
 author: 12 Graham Greene

wayward 5 balky 6 fickle, fitful, mulish, unruly 7 erratic, restive, willful 8 contrary,
 perverse, stubborn, variable 9 mercurial, obstinate, whimsical 10 capricious,
 changeable, headstrong, inconstant, rebellious, refractory, self-willed 11 disobedient,
 fluctuating, intractable, troublesome 12 inconsistent, incorrigible, recalcitrant, undependable, ungovernable, unmanageable
 13 insubordinate

Wazhazhe *see* 5 Osage

weak 4 lame, poor, puny, soft, thin 5 faint,
 frail, shaky, spent 6 feeble, flimsy, unsafe,
 wasted, watery 7 brittle, diluted, exposed,
 fragile, insipid, lacking, unmanly 8 cowardly, delicate, helpless, timorous, unsteady, wide open 9 breakable, enervated,

exhausted, frangible, powerless, spineless, tasteless, unguarded, untenable 10 assailable, effeminate, irresolute, namby-pamby, vulnerable, wishy-washy 11 adulterated, debilitated, defenseless, ineffective, ineffectual, inefficient, unprotected, unsupported 12 unconvincing 13 inefficacious, unsubstantial, untrustworthy 14 unsatisfactory

weaken 3 sap 4 fade, fail, flag, thin, wane 5 abate, droop, lower, unman, waste 6 dilute, expose, impair, lessen, soften 7 cripple, dwindle, exhaust, thin out 8 diminish, enervate, mitigate, moderate 9 undermine 10 devitalize, emasculate

weakened 5 frail 6 dilute, faulty, flawed, watery 7 diluted 8 delicate, disabled 9 enfeebled 10 undermined 11 adulterated, debilitated, watered down

weakling 4 twit, wimp 5 mouse, sissy 6 coward 7 chicken, milksop 9 cream puff, jellyfish 10 namby-pamby, pantywaist 11 milquetoast, mollycoddle

weak-minded 4 daft, dull 7 foolish 8 backward, mindless 10 irresolute 11 addleheaded, vacillating 12 feeble-minded, muddleheaded, thick-skulled

weakness 4 bent, bias 5 fault 6 defect, hunger, thirst 7 failing, frailty, leaning, passion 8 appetite, debility, fondness, lameness, penchant, tendency 9 prejudice, proneness, shakiness 10 deficiency, feebleness, flimsiness, proclivity, propensity 11 inclination 12 debilitation, imperfection, unsteadiness 13 vulnerability 14 susceptibility 15 ineffectiveness 16 unconvincingness, unsubstantiality 17 untrustworthiness

weak point 4 flaw 5 break, crack, fault 6 defect 10 deficiency 11 shortcoming

weak position 8 handicap 12 disadvantage

weak-willed 8 hesitant, wavering 10 hesitating, indecisive, irresolute

wealth 4 fund, mine 5 goods, means, money, store 6 assets, bounty, estate, luxury, mammon, riches 7 capital, fortune 8 chattels, fullness, opulence, property, richness 9 abundance, affluence, amplitude, plenitude, profusion, resources 10 easy street, prosperity 11 copiousness 12 independence 13 luxuriousness

wealthy 4 rich 5 flush 6 loaded 7 moneyed, well-off 8 affluent, well-to-do 9 well-fixed 10 prosperous, well-heeled

weapon 3 arm 5 guard, means 6 attack, resort 7 bulwark, defense, measure, offense 8 armament, resource, security 9 offensive, safeguard 10 protection 14 countermeasure

weaponry 4 arms, guns 8 armament, materiel, ordnance

wear 3 don, tax, use 4 duds, fray, last, tire, togs, wrap 5 drain, erode, put on, shred, weary 6 abrade, attire, damage, endure, injury, shroud, slip on, swathe 7 apparel, clothes, corrode, dress in, eat away, exhaust, fatigue, frazzle, rub away, service, swaddle, utility 8 clothing, costumes, garments, overwork, wash away 9 disrepair 10 employment, overburden 11 application, consumption, utilization 12 dilapidation 13 deterioration 14 disintegration

wear away 4 rust 5 erase, erode 7 corrode, eat into

weariness
French: 5 ennui

wearing apparel 4 duds, garb, rags, togs, wear 5 dress 6 attire, finery 7 clothes, costume, raiment, regalia, threads 8 clothing, ensemble, garments, wardrobe
French: 11 habillement

wearing away 7 erosion 8 abrasion, friction, grinding, scraping 9 corrosion

wearing down 6 tiring 7 eroding, erosion 8 abrasion, friction, grinding, scraping 10 overcoming

wearisome 4 dull 6 boring, dreary, tiring, trying 7 arduous, irksome, tedious 8 annoying, tiresome, toilsome 9 fatiguing, laborious, vexatious 10 bothersome, burdensome, exhausting, irritating, monotonous, oppressive

wear out 4 tire 7 exhaust, fatigue 8 enervate, enfeeble 10 debilitate

weary 3 fag 4 beat, dull, tire 5 all in, blase, bored, fed up, jaded, spent, tired 6 boring, bushed, done in, drowsy, pooped, sleepy, tiring, tucker 7 annoyed, drained, exhaust, fatigue, humdrum, overtax, play out, routine, tedious, tire out, worn-out 8 dog tired, fatigued, overwork, tiresome 9 disgusted, exhausted, fatiguing, impatient, soporific, wearisome 10 dispirited, exhausting, monotonous, overburden 11 somniferous 12 discontented, dissatisfied

weather 3 dry, tan 4 face, rust 5 brave, clime, stand 6 bleach, season 7 climate, oxidize, toughen 8 confront, windward 9 withstand 11 temperature

god of: 4 Jove 7 Jupiter

weave 4 fuse, join, knit, lace, link, loom, meld, wind 5 blend, braid, curve, plait, snake, twist, unify, unite 6 mingle, writhe, zigzag 7 combine, entwine, meander, texture 9 interlace 10 crisscross, intertwine 11 incorporate

Weaver, Earl
nickname: 15 Earl of Baltimore
sport: 8 baseball
position: 7 manager
team: 16 Baltimore Orioles

Weaver, Dennis
born: 8 Joplin MO
roles: 7 Chester, McCloud 8 Gunsmoke 9 Gentle Ben 13 Kentucky Jones

Weaver, Sigourney
born: 12 Los Angeles CA
roles: 5 Alien 6 Aliens 10 Eyewitness 12 Ghostbusters 17 Gorillas in the Mist 26 The Year of Living Dangerously

Weavers, The
author: 16 Gerhart Hauptmann

web 3 net 4 maze, mesh, trap 5 snare 6 screen, tangle, tissue 7 complex, netting, network 8 gossamer 9 labyrinth, screening

Web and the Rock, The
  author: 11 Thomas Wolfe
  character: 10 Esther Jack 12 George Webber

Webb, Jack
  born: 13 Santa Monica CA
  wife: 11 Julie London
  roles: 6 The Men 7 Dragnet 9 Joe Friday 15 Sunset Boulevard

Webber, George
  character in: 16 The Web and the Rock 18 You Can't Go Home Again
  author: 5 Wolfe

Webb family
  characters in: 7 Our Town
  member: 5 Emily, Wally
  author: 6 Wilder

Weber, Karl Maria Friedrich Ernst von
  born: 6 Lubeck 7 Germany
  composer of: 6 Oberon 9 Euryanthe 13 Der Freischutz 20 Invitation to the Dance

Weber, Max
  born: 6 Russia 9 Bialystok
  artwork: 11 The Geranium 17 Chinese Restaurant 18 Adoration of the Moon

Webfoot State
  nickname of: 6 Oregon

Webster
  character: 6 George 7 Webster 9 Katherine
  cast: 10 Alex Karras, Susan Clark 13 Emmanuel Lewis

Webster, John
  author of: 13 The White Devil 17 The Duchess of Malfi

we cannot
  Latin: 11 non possumus

we command
  Latin: 8 mandamus

wed 3 tie 4 bind, fuse, link, mate, meld 5 blend, hitch, marry, merge, unify, unite, weave 6 attach, commit, couple, devote, pledge, splice 7 combine, espouse, make one, win over 8 dedicate 11 incorporate

wedded 4 tied 5 bound, fused 6 joined, linked, melded, merged, united 7 blended, devoted, marital, married, pledged, unified 9 committed, connected 12 incorporated

wedding 8 marriage, nuptials

wedding anniversaries
  first: 5 clock, paper
  second: 5 china 6 cotton
  third: 5 glass 7 crystal, leather
  fourth: 4 silk 5 linen 20 electrical appliances
  fifth: 4 wood 10 silverware
  sixth: 4 iron, wood
  seventh: 4 wool 6 copper 8 desk sets 16 pen and pencil sets
  eighth: 4 lace 6 bronze, linens
  ninth: 5 china 7 leather, pottery
  tenth: 3 tin 8 aluminum 14 diamond jewelry
  eleventh: 5 steel 11 accessories 14 fashion jewelry
  twelfth: 4 silk 6 pearls 11 colored gems
  thirteenth: 4 furs, lace 8 textiles
  fourteenth: 5 ivory 11 gold jewelry
  fifteenth: 7 crystal, watches
  twentieth: 5 china 8 platinum
  twenty-fifth: 6 silver 21 sterling silver jubilee
  thirtieth: 5 pearl 7 diamond
  thirty-fifth: 4 jade 5 coral
  fortieth: 4 ruby
  forty-fifth: 8 sapphire
  fiftieth: 4 gold 13 golden jubilee
  fifty-fifth: 7 emerald
  sixtieth: 7 diamond

weddings
  god of: 8 Talassio

wedge 3 jam, ram 4 cram, pack, rend, rive 5 chock, chunk, crowd, force, press, split, stuff 6 cleave 7 squeeze

wedlock 8 marriage 9 matrimony

Wednesday
  Dutch: 8 woensdag
  French: 8 mercredi
  German: 8 mittwoch
  heavenly body: 7 Mercury
  Italian: 9 mercoledi
  name comes from: 4 Odin 5 Woden
  observance: 12 Ash Wednesday
  Spanish: 9 miercoles
  Swedish: 6 onsdag

wee 4 tiny 5 dwarf, scant, teeny 6 little, minute, petite, scanty 9 itty-bitty, miniature, minuscule 10 diminutive, teeny-weeny, undersized 11 Lilliputian, microscopic

weed 3 bur, hoe, nag, pot 4 burr, butt, cull, dock, hemp, rake 5 cigar, joint, vetch 6 darnel, harrow, pull up, root up, uproot 7 tobacco 8 nuisance, plantain, purslane, toadflax 9 cigarette, crabgrass, cultivate, dandelion, eliminate, extirpate, marijuana 12 mourning band

weed out 6 banish 7 abolish, discard 8 get rid of, throw out 9 eliminate

Weena
  character in: 14 The Time Machine
  author: 5 Wells

weeny 3 wee 4 tiny 5 frank, small, teeny 6 hotdog, little, teensy, wiener 11 frankfurter

weep 3 cry, orp, sob 4 bawl, bend, drip, leak, lerm, ooze, shed, tear, wail 5 exude, mourn 6 bewail, boohoo, lament, shower 7 blubber, lapwing, whimper 8 sweating 9 exudation
  genus: 8 Vanellus

weep over 5 mourn 6 bemoan, bewail, lament

weevil
  variety: 4 boll, rice

Wegener, Alfred L
  field: 10 geophysics 11 meteorology
  nationality: 6 German
  theory of: 16 continental drift

Wegg
  character in: 15 Our Mutual Friend
  author: 7 Dickens

weigh 4 lift 5 count, hoist, raise, scale 6 burden, charge, ponder, regard 7 balance, compare, measure 8 consider, encumber, evaluate, ruminate 11 contemplate 12 counterbalance

weigh anchor 4 sail 7 cast off, set sail, ship out

weigh down 4 load 6 anchor, burden 7 oppress 8 encumber, obligate, overload

weight 3 tax 4 heft, load, mass 5 value 6 burden, import, saddle, strain, stress 7 ballast, concern, oppress, tonnage, urgency 8 emphasis, encumber, poundage, pressure 9 heaviness, influence, magnitude 10 importance 11 consequence 12 significance 13 consideration, ponderousness

weight, unit of
of Afghanistan: 3 pau, paw, ser, sir
of Algeria: 4 rotl
of Argentina: 4 last 5 grano, libra 7 quintal 8 tonelada
of Austria: 4 marc, saum, unze 5 denat, karch, pfund, stein 7 centner, pfennig 8 vierling 9 quantchen
of Belgium: 4 last 5 carat, livre, pound 6 charge 7 chariot 9 esterling
of Bolivia: 5 libra, marco
of Borneo: 4 para 6 chapah
of Brazil: 3 bag 4 onca, onza 5 libra 6 arroba, oitava 7 arratel, quilate, quintal 8 tonelada
of Bulgaria: 3 oka, oke 5 tovar
of Cambodia: 4 mace, tael
of Chile: 5 grano, libra 7 quintal
of China: 3 fan, fen, hao, kin, ssu, tan, yin 4 chee, chin, dong, shih, tael, tsin 5 catty, chien, picul, tchin, tsien 6 kungli 7 haikwan, kungfen, kungssu, kungtun 8 kungchin 9 candareen 10 kupingtael
of Colombia: 3 bag 4 saco 5 carga, libra 7 quilate, quintal
of Costa Rica: 3 bag 4 caja 5 libra
of Cuba: 5 libra 6 tercio
of Ecuador: 5 libra
of Egypt: 3 kat, ket, oka, oke 4 dera, heml, khar, okia, rotl 5 artal, artel, deben, kerat, minae, minas, okieh, pound, ratel, uckia 6 hamlah, kantar 7 drachma, quintal
of El Salvador: 3 bag 4 caja 5 libra
of England: 3 bag, kip, tod, ton 4 keel, last, mast, maun 5 barge, fagot, grain, maund, pound, score, stand, stone, truss 6 bushel, cental, fangot, firkin, fother, fotmal, pocket 7 quarter, quintal, sarpler
of Estonia: 4 lood, nael, puud
of Ethiopia: 3 pek 4 kasm, natr, oket, rotl 5 alada, artal, mocha, neter, ratel, wakea 6 wogiet 8 farasula 9 mutagalla
of France: 3 sol 4 gros, kilo, marc, once 5 carat, livre, pound, tonne, uckia 6 gramme, passir 7 tonneau 8 esterlin 9 esterling
of Greece: 3 mna, oka, oke 4 mina, obol 5 litra, livre, maneh, pound 6 diobol, dramme, obolos, obolus, stater,

talent 7 chalcon, chalque, drachma 8 diobolon, talanton
of Guatemala: 4 caja 5 libra
of Guinea: 4 akey, piso, uzan 5 benda, seron 6 quinto 8 aguirage
of Hungary: 7 vamfont 8 vammazsa
of Iceland: 4 pund 5 pound, tunna 6 smjors
of India: 3 mod, pai, ser, vis 4 dhan, drum, hoen, kona, myat, pala, pank, pice, raik, ruay, tael, tali, tank, tola, wang, yava 5 adpad, bahar, hubba, masha, maund, tical 6 abucco, karsha 8 mangelin
of Indonesia: 5 catty, ounce, thail 6 soekoe
of Iran: 3 ser 4 dram, dung, rotl, sang, seer 5 abbas, artel, maund, pinar, ratel 6 dirhem, gandum, karwar, miscal, nakhod, nimman 7 abbassi 8 tcheirek
of Italy: 5 carat, libra, oncia, pound 6 carato, denaro, libbra, ottava
of Japan: 2 mo 3 fun, kin, kon, rin, shi 4 kati, kwan, niyo 5 carat, catty, momme, picul 6 kwamme 8 hiyakkin
of Java: 4 amat, pond, tali 5 pound 6 soekel
of Korea: 3 won
of Latvia: 9 liespfund
of Libya: 3 pik, saa 4 kele 5 teman, uckia 6 gorraf, misura 7 mattaro, termino 8 kharouba
of Malaysia: 4 chee, mace, tael, wang 7 tampang
of Mexico: 3 bag 4 onza 5 carga, libra, marco 6 adarme, arroba, ochava, tercio 7 quintal
of Mongolia: 3 lan
of Morocco: 4 rotl 5 artal, artel, gerbe, ratel 6 dirhem, kintar 7 quintal
of Myanmar: 2 ta 3 can, mat, moo, pai, vis 4 binh, dong, kyat, ruay, viss 5 bahar, behar, candy, tical, ticul 6 abucco 7 peiktha
of the Netherlands: 3 ons 4 last, lood, pond 5 bahar, grein 6 korrel 7 wichtje 8 esterlin
of Nicaragua: 3 bag 4 caha, caja 8 tonelada
of Norway: 3 lod 4 mark, pund 9 skaalpund 10 bismerpund
of Pakistan: 4 seer, tola 5 maund
of Paraguay: 7 quintal
of Peru: 5 libra 7 quintal
of the Philippines: 5 catty, fardo, picul, punto 6 lachsa 7 quilate 8 chinanta
of Poland: 3 lut 4 funt 5 uncya 6 kamian 7 centner, skrupul
of Portugal: 4 grao, onca, once 5 libra, marco 6 arroba, oitava 7 arratel, quintal 9 excropulo
of Russia: 3 lof, lot 4 dola, funt, lana, last, loof, loth, once, pood, poud 5 dolia
of Saudi Arabia: 3 oke
of Scotland: 4 boll, drop 5 trone 6 bushel
of Somalia: 8 parsalah
of Spain: 4 onza 5 frail, grano, libra, marco, tomin 6 adarme, arroba, dinero,

dracma, ochava 7 arienzo, quilate, quintal 8 caracter, tonelada
of Sudan: 5 habba
of Sweden: 3 ass, lod, ort 4 last, mark, sten 5 carat 6 nylast 7 centner, lispund 8 skalpund, skeppund 9 shippound
of Switzerland: 4 fund 5 pfund 7 centner, quintal 12 zugthierlast
of Syria: 4 cola, rotl 5 artal, artel, ratel 6 talent
of Tanzania: 8 farsalah
of Thailand: 3 bat, hap, pai, pay, sen, sok 4 baht, haph, kati, klam, klom 5 catty, chang, coyan, fuang, picul, pilul, tical 6 fluang, graini, salung, sompay 7 tamlung
of Tunisia: 3 saa 4 rotl 5 artal, artel, ratel, uckia 6 kantar
of Turkey: 3 oka, oke 4 aqui, dram, kile, rotl 5 artal, artel, cheke, kerat, obolu, ratel 6 batman, dirhem, kantar, maunch, miskal 7 drachma, quintal, yusdrum
of Uruguay: 7 quintal
of Venezuela: 3 bag 5 libra
of Vietnam: 3 can, yet 4 uyen
of Yugoslavia: 3 oka 5 dramm, tovar, wagon 7 satlijk
weightlessness 8 buoyancy 9 lightness 11 zero gravity
weighty 5 grave, heavy, hefty, vital 6 solemn, taxing, trying, urgent 7 arduous, crucial, earnest, massive, onerous, serious 8 critical, crushing, cumbrous, pressing 9 difficult, essential, important, ponderous 10 burdensome, cumbersome, oppressive 11 significant, substantial, troublesome 12 considerable 13 consequential
Weill, Kurt
  born: 6 Dessau 7 Germany
  composer of: 8 Happy End 13 Lady in the Dark 15 Down in the Valley 18 The Lindbergh Flight, The Threepenny Opera 19 Die Dreigroschenoper 31 Rise and Fall of the City of Mahagonny 32 Aufstieg und Fall der Stadt Mahagonny
Weir, Peter
  director of: 7 Witness 9 Gallipoli 11 The Last Wave 26 The Year of Living Dangerously
weird 3 odd 4 wild 5 crazy, eerie, kooky, nutty, queer 6 far-out, mystic, spooky 7 bizarre, curious, ghostly, magical, strange, unusual 8 abnormal, freakish, peculiar 9 eccentric, grotesque, irregular, unearthly, unnatural 10 mysterious, outlandish, phantasmal, unorthodox 12 supernatural 14 unconventional
weirdo 3 nut 4 kook 5 flake, freak 6 looney 7 lunatic, oddball 8 crackpot, original 9 character, eccentric, screwball 10 one-of-a-kind
Weird sisters 5 Fates, Norns
Weisenfreund, Muni
  real name of: 8 Paul Muni
Weismuller, Johnny
  real name: 20 Peter John Weissmuller
  born: 9 Windbar PA
  Olympic sport: 8 swimming

  Olympic gold medals: 4 five
  wife: 9 Lupe Velez
  roles: 6 Tarzan 9 Jungle Jim
Weiss, Peter
  author of: 10 Marat/Sade 14 Vanishing Point
welcome 4 meet 5 admit, greet 6 at home, salute, wanted 7 embrace, receive, usher in, winning 8 accepted, admitted, charming, engaging, enticing, greeting, inviting, pleasant, pleasing 9 agreeable, entertain, reception 10 delightful, gratifying, salutation 11 comfortable
Weld, Tuesday
  real name: 12 Susan Ker Weld
  born: 9 New York NY
  husband: 11 Dudley Moore
  roles: 12 I Walk the Line 14 Play It as It Lays 16 The Cincinnati Kid, Wild in the Country 19 Looking for Mr Goodbar
welfare 4 good 6 health, profit, relief 7 benefit, success, the dole 9 advantage, happiness
well 3 jet, run 4 flow, fund, good, gush, hale, mine, ooze, pool, pour, rise 5 amply, fount, fully, issue, lucky, right, shaft, sound, spout, spurt, store, surge 6 easily, fairly, hearty, justly, kindly, nicely, proper, robust, source, spring, stream, strong, warmly 7 chipper, fitting, healthy, readily, rightly 8 famously, fountain, laudably, properly, suitably, very much, vigorous 9 agreeably, capitally, carefully, correctly, favorable, favorably, fortunate, promising, quite well 10 abundantly, acceptably, adequately, auspicious, completely, familiarly, felicitous, intimately, personally, prosperous, splendidly, successful, thoroughly 11 approvingly, commendably 12 advantageous, auspiciously, considerably, propitiously, satisfactory, successfully, sufficiently 13 substantially 14 advantageously, satisfactorily 15 sympathetically 16 enthusiastically
  hole drilled in ground for: 3 gas, oil 5 water
well-adjusted 6 normal, secure 8 sensible
Welland, May
  character in: 17 The Age of Innocence
  author: 7 Wharton
well-behaved 6 polite, sedate 8 decorous
well-being 4 ease, good, luck, weal 6 health, profit 7 benefit, comfort, fortune, success, welfare 8 felicity, good luck 9 advantage, affluence, happiness 10 prosperity
wellborn 8 highbred 9 patrician 10 upper-class 12 aristocratic, silk-stocking
Wellbred
  character in: 19 Every Man in His Humour
  author: 6 Jonson
well-bred 5 civil, suave 6 polite, urbane 7 elegant, gallant, genteel, refined 8 cultured, ladylike, mannerly, polished 9 civilized, courteous 10 cultivated 11 gentlemanly 13 sophisticated

well-chosen 3 apt 4 fine 5 prize 6 choice, seemly, select 7 apropos, correct, fitting, special 8 superior 9 excellent 11 appropriate

well-considered 7 careful, prudent 8 cautious 10 thoughtful 11 circumspect

well-coordinated 6 smooth 8 graceful 9 dexterous 10 effortless

well-defined 5 clear, plain 8 clear-cut, definite, distinct, palpable 10 pronounced

well-dressed 4 chic 5 natty, smart 6 dapper 11 fashionable

well-educated 7 erudite, learned 8 cultured, literate 9 scholarly 10 cultivated 13 knowledgeable

Weller, Sam
  character in: 14 Pickwick Papers
  author: 7 Dickens

Welles, Orson
  real name: 17 George Orson Welles
  born: 9 Kenosha WI
  wife: 9 Paola Mori 12 Rita Hayworth
  formed: 14 Mercury Theatre
  radio show: 14 War of the Worlds
  roles: 8 Jane Eyre 11 Citizen Kane, The Third Man, Touch of Evil
  director of: 7 Macbeth, Othello 8 Falstaff 11 Citizen Kane, The Stranger, Touch of Evil 23 The Magnificent Ambersons

well-favored 4 fair 5 bonny 6 comely, pretty 7 sightly, winsome 8 fetching, handsome 9 beautiful 10 attractive 11 good looking

well-fed 5 hefty, plump, stout 6 portly, rotund 9 corpulent

well-fixed 4 rich 7 moneyed, wealthy 8 affluent 10 prosperous

well-founded 7 factual 9 supported 12 corroborated 13 substantiated

well-groomed 4 neat, tidy 5 natty 6 spruce 10 impeccable

well-grounded 5 valid 7 factual 8 reliable 9 supported 10 undeniable, undisputed, unshakable 11 irrefutable 12 corroborated, indisputable 13 incontestable, substantiated 16 incontrovertible

well-heeled 4 rich 7 moneyed, wealthy 8 affluent 10 in the chips, in the money, prosperous

Wellington
  capital of: 10 New Zealand

Wellington, Duke of
  also: 15 Arthur Wellesley
  nickname: 6 Hookey 12 The Great Duke
  nationality: 7 British
  served in: 5 India 14 Napoleonic Wars
  battle: 6 Assaye 7 Vitoria 8 Talavera, Waterloo 9 Salamanca
  served as: 13 prime minister
  memoirs: 20 Wellington Dispatches

well-kept 4 heat, neat, tidy 7 orderly 9 organized 10 systematic 11 disciplined, uncluttered

well-known 4 open 5 famed, noted 6 common, famous 7 big-time, eminent, evident, leading, obvious, popular 8 familiar, infamous, renowned 9 important, notorious, prominent 10 celebrated, scandalous, understood 11 established, illustrious, outstanding

well-lighted 5 lit up 6 ablaze, bright 11 illuminated

well-made 4 fine 7 perfect 8 executed, flawless 9 faultless 11 beautifully

Wellman, William
  director of: 5 Wings 9 Beau Geste 11 A Star Is Born 13 Nothing Sacred 15 The Story of GI Joe 16 The Ox-Bow Incident

well-mannered 6 polite 7 genteel, refined 8 cultured, decorous, ladylike, polished 9 courteous, dignified 10 cultivated 11 gentlemanly

well-matched 5 close 10 nip-and-tuck

well-off 4 rich 5 flush 6 loaded 7 moneyed, ·wealthy 8 affluent 10 prosperous 11 comfortable

well-padded 5 plump, stout 6 chubby, fleshy, portly, rotund 9 corpulent

well-proportioned 7 classic, elegant, shapely 8 graceful 11 symmetrical

well-read 7 erudite, learned 8 cultured, literate 9 scholarly 10 cultivated

well-reasoned 4 wise 10 perceptive, thoughtful 11 intelligent

well-rehearsed 6 smooth 7 planned 8 prepared 9 practiced

Wells, H G (Herbert George)
  author of: 5 Kipps 10 Tono-Bungay 11 Ann Veronica 14 The Time Machine 15 The Invisible Man 16 Outline of History 17 Love and Mr Lewisham, The War of the Worlds 19 The History of Mr Polly 22 The Shape of Things to Come 23 Mr Britling Sees It Through

Wells, Julia Elizabeth
  real name of: 12 Julie Andrews

wellspring 4 font 6 origin, source 9 beginning 10 birthplace 12 fountainhead

well-stocked 4 full 11 overflowing

well-suited 6 proper 7 correct, fitting 8 suitable 9 congenial, congruous 10 compatible, harmonious 11 appropriate

well-to-do 4 rich 7 moneyed, wealthy 8 affluent 10 in the chips, in the money, prosperous

well up 4 boil, rise 6 bubble 7 surface

well-ventilated 4 airy 5 windy 6 breezy, drafty

well-versed 7 knowing 9 qualified 10 conversant 11 experienced 13 knowledgeable
  French: 9 au courant

well-wisher 6 friend 8 advocate, champion 9 supported

Welsh Mythology
  goddess: 3 Don
  goddess of fire/fertility/agriculture/household/wisdom: 6 Brigit
  king: 4 Bran, Llud, Ludd, Nudd
  magician: 5 Lloyd
  paradise: 5 Annwn 6 Annfwn
  prince: 5 Pwyll 7 Kilwich
  princess: 5 Olwen
  romantic tales: 10 Mabinogian

welt 4 bump, lump, mark, wale, weal 6 bruise, streak, stripe 8 swelling 9 contusion

Weltanschauung 25 manner of looking at the world

Weltansicht 9 world view

welter 4 heap, mass, mess, pile, roll, toss 5 heave, storm 6 bustle, grovel, hubbub, jumble, racket, tumult, wallow, writhe 7 tempest, turmoil 9 commotion, confusion 10 hodgepodge, turbulence

Welter, Blanca Rosa
   real name of: 14 Linda Christian

Weltschmerz 6 sorrow 9 world pain 20 sentimental pessimism

Welty, Eudora
   author of: 12 Delta Wedding, Golden Apples 13 Losing Battles 14 The Ponder Heart 15 A Sweet Devouring 19 The Robber Bridegroom 20 The Optimist's Daughter

wench 4 doxy, girl, lass, maid, slut 5 whore 6 damsel, lassie, maiden 8 strumpet 10 prostitute

wend 4 make 5 hie to

went 3 ran 4 flew, left 5 faded, got on 6 flew by, lapsed, passed 7 elapsed, sallied 8 departed, filed off, passed by, took wing, vanished 9 proceeded, took leave 10 shuffled on, took flight 11 disappeared, forged ahead 12 sallied forth 13 pressed onward

Wentworth, Captain Frederick
   character in: 10 Persuasion
   author: 6 Austen

Werfel, Franz
   author of: 9 Mirror Man 19 Forty Days of Musa Dagh, The Song of Bernadette

Werle, Gregers
   character in: 11 The Wild Duck
   author: 5 Ibsen

Werner, Oskar
   real name: 24 Oskar Josef Bschliessmayer
   born: 6 Vienna 7 Austria
   roles: 11 Jules and Jim, Ship of Fools 17 Voyage of the Damned 22 Fahrenheit Four Fifty One, The Shoes of the Fisherman 26 The Spy Who Came in from the Cold

Wertmuller, Lina
   director of: 9 Swept Away (by an unusual destiny in the blue sea of August) 13 Seven Beauties

Wescott, Glenway
   author of: 14 The Grandmother, The Pilgrim Hawk 16 The Apple of the Eye 17 Apartment in Athens

Wessex
   fictional place created by: 5 Hardy

West, Benjamin
   born: 13 Springfield PA
   artwork: 17 Death on a Pale Horse 19 Death of General Wolfe 22 Saul and the Witch of Endor

West, Dame Rebecca
   real name: 28 Cicily Isabel Fairfield Andrews
   author of: 8 The Judge 11 Harriet Hume 13 Birds Fall Down 15 The Thinking Reed 19 The Strange Necessity 20 The Fountain Overflows 21 The Return of the Soldier 22 Black Lamb and Grey Falcon

West, Jessamyn
   author of: 11 Leafy Rivers 13 A Matter of Time 18 Except for Me and Thee 21 The Friendly Persuasion 22 The Massacre at Fall Creek

West, Mae
   born: 10 Brooklyn NY
   roles: 3 Sex 8 Sextette 9 I'm No Angel 10 Diamond Lil 13 Klondike Annie 14 Go West Young Man 15 Night After Night, She Done Him Wrong 16 Myra Breckinridge 17 My Little Chickadee
   autobiography: 28 Goodness Had Nothing To Do With It
   quote: 18 Beulah peel me a grape 22 Come up and see me sometime

West, Morris L
   author of: 7 Proteus 9 Harlequin 13 The Salamander 14 The Clowns of God 15 The Tower of Babel 17 The Devil's Advocate 22 The Shoes of the Fisherman

West, Nathanael
   author of: 12 A Cool Million 16 Miss Lonelyhearts 17 The Day of the Locust

Westcott, Edward Noyes
   author of: 10 David Harum

Westenra, Lucy
   character in: 7 Dracula
   author: 6 Stoker

Western, Sophia
   character in: 8 Tom Jones
   author: 8 Fielding

Western Sahara
   other name: 13 Spanish Sahara
   capital: 6 Al Aiun 7 El Aaiun
   city: 3 Zug 5 Daora, Smara 6 Aargub, Dakhla, Tichla 9 Asqueimat, Bir Gandus 10 Bir Enzaran 12 Guelta Zemmur
   government: 33 disputed territory claimed by Morocco
   river: 7 Uad Atui 8 Uad Assag 13 Saguia el Hamra
   sea: 8 Atlantic
   physical feature:
   cape: 6 Barbas 7 Bojador
   desert: 6 Sahara
   wind: 5 Ieste 6 gibleh
   people: 4 Arab 6 Berber
   language: 16 Hassaniyya Arabic
   religion: 5 Islam
   feature:
   political group: 14 Polisario Front

Western Samoa
   other name: 17 Navigator's Islands
   capital/largest city: 4 Apia
   others: 6 Safotu, Sataua 7 Faleolo, Palauli, Poutasi, Tuasivi 8 Fagamalo, Falelima, Lufilufi 9 Falealupo, Mulifanua 10 Samalaeulu, Satupaitea
   monetary unit: 4 sene, tala
   island: 5 Upolu 6 Manono, Savaii 7 Apolima

mountain: 4 Fito, Vaea
highest point: 13 Mauga Silisili
sea: 7 Pacific
physical feature:
bay: 4 Asau, Salu 6 Safata 7 Lafanga, Matautu 8 Fangaloa, Salealua 9 Saluofata
strait: 7 Apolima
people: 6 Samoan 10 Melanesian, Polynesian
author: 20 Robert Louis Stevenson (Tusitala, Teller of Tales)
explorer: 6 Wilkes 9 Roggeveen 12 Bougainville
language: 6 Samoan 7 English
religion: 9 Methodist 10 Protestant 13 Roman Catholic 14 Congregational
place:
observatory: 4 Apia
tomb: 9 Stevenson
feature:
chief: 5 matai
clothing: 5 pareu 8 lavalava, puletasi
dance: 4 siva
daughter of chief: 5 taupo
house: 4 fale
food:
dish: 8 palusami
drink: 3 ava

Western Star
author: 19 Stephen Vincent Benet

Westhus, Hale
character in: 25 All Quiet on the Western Front
author: 8 Remarque

West Indies 11 archipelago
Associated States: 7 Antigua, Grenada, St Lucia 8 Anguilla, Dominica 12 St Kitts-Nevis
bird: 4 tody 6 mucaro
channel: 7 Jamaica 9 Old Bahama
component: 4 Cuba 5 Haiti 6 Tobago 7 Bahamas, Jamaica 8 Barbados, Trinidad 10 Hispaniola, Puerto Rico 13 Virgin Islands 14 Leeward Islands, Lesser Antilles 15 Greater Antilles, Windward Islands 17 Dominican Republic
crop: 6 coffee 9 sugarcane
fish: 4 pega 5 pelon
formerly: 10 federation
fruit: 5 papaw 6 pawpaw 7 genipap
islands: 5 Turks 6 Caicos, Cayman, Virgin 7 Bahamas, Leeward 8 Windward
kale: 7 malanga
lizard: 6 arbalo
music: 7 calypso
passage: 4 Mona 8 Windward
rodent: 5 hutia
sea: 9 Caribbean
shark: 4 gata
sorcery: 3 obi 5 obeah
tree: 5 genip 6 aralie
tribesman: 5 Carib 6 Arawak 7 Ciboney
vessel: 6 droger, drogher
volcano: 5 Pelee

Westinghouse, George
nationality: 8 American
invented: 8 air brake 12 railroad frog 20 railroad signal system

Westlake, Donald E
author of: 8 Bank Shot 10 The Hot Rock 13 Dancing Aztecs 15 Brothers Keepers
as Richard Stark: 9 The Hunter 10 The Seventh
as Tucker Coe: 19 Murder Among Children

Westover, Russ
creator/artist of: 15 Tillie the Toiler

West Side Story
director: 10 Robert Wise 13 Jerome Robbins
cast: 10 Rita Moreno 11 Natalie Wood, Russ Tamblyn 13 Richard Beymer 14 George Chakiris
score: 15 Stephen Sondheim 16 Leonard Bernstein
Oscar for: 7 picture 8 director 15 supporting actor (Chakiris) 17 supporting actress (Moreno)

West Virginia
abbreviation: 2 WV 3 W Va
nickname: 8 Mountain 9 Panhandle
capital: 10 Charleston
largest city: 10 Huntington
others: 5 Logan 6 Elkins, Keyser, Ripley, Vienna, Weston 7 Beckley, Grafton, Spencer, Weirton 8 Fairmont, Wheeling 10 Clarksburg 11 Moundsville, Parkersburg
college: 5 Salem 7 Bethany, Concord 8 Marshall, Wheeling 9 Bluefield 10 Charleston 14 Davis and Elkins 16 Alderson Broaddus 20 West Virginia Wesleyan
feature:
historical site: 12 Harper's Ferry
national road: 10 Cumberland
tribe: 7 Moneton
people: 9 Pearl Buck 14 Arthur I Boreman 19 Walter Philip Reuther 24 Thomas "Stonewall" Jackson
explorer: 12 Morgan Morgan
island: 14 Blennerhassett
lake: 4 Lynn
land rank: 10 forty-first
mountain:
highest point: 10 Spruce Knob
physical feature:
cavern: 6 Seneca
plateau: 9 Allegheny
rock: 6 Seneca
spring: 8 Berkeley 12 White Sulphur
river: 3 Elk 4 Ohio 6 Gauley 7 Kanawha, Potomac, Tug Fork 8 Big Sandy, Guyandot 11 Monongahela
state admission: 11 Thirty-fifth
state bird: 8 cardinal
state fish: 10 brook trout
state flower: 11 great laurel 15 big rhododendron 17 great rhododendron
state motto: 25 Mountaineers Are Always Free
state song: 17 West Virginia Hills 20

This Is My West Virginia **27** West Virginia My Home Sweet Home
  state tree: 10 sugar maple
Westward Ho!
  author: 15 Charles Kingsley
west wind
  associated with: 8 Favonius, Zephyrus
wet 3 dip **4** damp, dank, rain, soak **5** humid, moist, rainy, soggy, steep, storm, water **6** clammy, dampen, drench, liquid, shower, soaked, sodden, splash, stormy, watery **7** immerse, moisten, showery, soaking, sopping, squishy, wetness **8** dampened, dampness, dankness, drenched, dripping, inundate, irrigate, moisture, sprinkle, submerge **9** exudation, liquified, moistness, rainstorm **10** clamminess **11** waterlogged **12** condensation **13** precipitation
wet blanket 4 drag **6** damper **10** spoilsport **11** party-pooper
wet down 5 spray **6** dampen **7** moisten **8** sprinkle
wettish 4 damp **5** moist **6** clammy
we who are about to die salute thee
  Latin: 19 morituri te salutamus
  said by: 15 Roman gladiators
  said to: 13 Roman emperors
whack 2 go **3** box, hit, rap, try **4** bang, belt, blow, cuff, slam, slap, slug, sock, stab, turn **5** baste, clout, crack, knock, pound, punch, smack, smite, thump, trial **6** strike, wallop **7** attempt, venture **8** endeavor
whale 4 beat, cane, drub, flog, orca, whip **6** baleen, thrash **9** bastinado
  constellation of: 5 Cetus
  group of: 3 gam, pod
whammy 3 hex **4** jinx **5** curse **7** evil eye **9** evil spell
wharf 3 key **4** dock, pier, quai, quay, slip **5** jetty **6** marina **7** landing **10** breakwater
Wharton, Edith
  author of: 10 Ethan Frome, The Old Maid **15** The House of Mirth **17** The Age of Innocence **21** The Custom of the Country
Whatever Happened to Baby Jane?
  director: 13 Robert Aldrich
  cast: 10 Bette Davis **11** Victor Buono **12** Joan Crawford **15** Marjorie Bennett
What Every Woman Knows
  author: 12 James M Barrie
  character: 9 John Shand **15** Charles Venables **18** Comtesse de la Briere, Lady Sybil Tenterden
  Wylie family: 5 Alick, David, James **6** Maggie
what it takes 5 skill **7** ability, mastery **9** expertise **10** capability, competence, expertness **11** proficiency **13** the right stuff
What Mrs McGillicuddy Saw!
  author: 14 Agatha Christie
What Price Glory?
  author: 15 Maxwell Anderson
What's Happening!!
  character: 5 Rerun **6** Dwayne **7** Shirley **9** Dee Thomas, (Mama) Mrs Thomas **11** Roger (Raj) Thomas

cast: 9 Fred Berry, Mabel King **12** Ernest Thomas **13** Haywood Nelson **15** Danielle Spencer, Shirley Hemphill
What's My Line?
  host: 8 John Daly
  panelist: 8 Hal Block **9** Fred Allen **10** Steve Allen **11** Bennett Cerf **13** Arlene Francis **15** Louis Untermeyer **16** Dorothy Kilgallen
wheat 8 Triticum
  varieties: 4 club, rice **5** durum, dwarf, India, river **6** Alaska, common, German, Polish, starch **7** English, poulard **8** hedgehog **10** one-grained, two-grained **13** Mediterranean
  product: 4 bran **5** bread, flour, pasta **6** cereal **8** macaroni **9** spaghetti
Wheat State
  nickname of: 6 Kansas
wheedle 4 coax, lure **5** charm **6** cajole, entice, induce **7** beguile, flatter **8** butter up, inveigle, persuade, soft soap
wheel 4 disk, drum, hoop, ring, roll, spin **5** pivot, round, swirl, twirl, whirl **6** caster, circle, gilgal, gyrate, roller, rotate, swivel **7** revolve **9** pirouette
Wheel of Fortune
  host: 8 Pat Sajak
  assistant: 10 Vanna White
wheels 3 car **4** auto, heap **5** motor **6** jalopy **7** flivver, vehicle **8** motorcar **9** tin lizzie **10** automobile
wheeze 4 gasp, hiss, pant, puff **7** panting, whistle
whelp 3 boy, cub, kid, lad, pup **4** brat **5** child, puppy, youth **6** urchin **9** stripling, youngster **14** whippersnapper
whence 9 from where **10** antecedent **14** from what source
Where Eagles Dare
  director: 12 Brian G Hutton
  based on novel by: 15 Alistair MacLean
  cast: 7 Mary Ure **12** Robert Beatty **13** Clint Eastwood, Patrick Wymark, Richard Burton **14** Michael Hordern
wherefore 2 so **3** why **7** because **13** for what reason
where I may stand
  Greek: 6 pou sto
where mentioned above
  Latin: 8 ubi supra
whereupon 8 upon what **10** after which **14** upon which point
wherewithal 4 cash **5** funds, means **6** assets **7** capital **9** financing, resources
whet 4 edge, hone, stir **5** grind, pique, strop, tempt **6** allure, arouse, awaken, entice, excite, induce, kindle **7** animate, provoke, quicken, sharpen **9** stimulate **11** put an edge on
whether willing or not
  Latin: 12 nolens volens
which see
  Latin: 2 qv **8** quod vide
which was to be demonstrated
  Latin: 3 QED **21** quod erat demonstrandum

which was to be done
Latin: 17 quod erat faciendum

which was to be shown
Latin: 3 QED 21 quod erat demonstrandum

whiff 4 hint, odor, puff 5 aroma, draft, scent, smell, sniff, trace 6 breath, breeze, zephyr 7 **French:** 7 soupcon

Whig Party
president belonging to: 5 Tyler 6 Taylor 8 Fillmore, Harrison

while 2 as 3 yet 4 idle, till, time, when 5 until 6 during, effort, whilst 7 filling, interim, trouble, whereas 8 although, occasion

whim 4 urge 5 fancy, quirk 6 notion, vagary 7 caprice, conceit, impulse 8 crotchet 11 inspiration 12 eccentricity

whimper 3 sob 4 pule 5 whine 6 snivel 7 blubber, sniffle, sobbing 9 cry softly, sniveling 11 sob brokenly 14 whine plaintively

whimsical 5 droll 6 fickle, fitful, quaint 7 amusing, erratic, waggish 8 fanciful, notional, quixotic 9 eccentric 10 capricious, changeable, chimerical 12 inconsistent

whimsy, whimsey 4 bent, wish 5 fancy, humor, prank, quirk 6 notion, vagary 7 caprice, fantasy 8 escapade, drollery 11 make-believe

whine 3 cry, sob 4 fret, mewl, moan, wail 6 grouse, murmur, mutter, snivel 7 grumble, whimper 8 complain 9 complaint 11 gripe meekly 12 plaintive cry 14 cry plaintively

whip 3 rod 4 beat, cane, drub, flap, flog, jerk, jolt, lash, lick, maul, rout 5 birch, flick, spank, strap, thong, whisk 6 rattan, snatch, switch 7 cowhide, rawhide, scourge, trounce birch rod, vanquish 9 horsewhip, toss about 10 blacksnake, flagellate 13 cat-o'-nine-tails, defeat soundly, move violently 14 beat decisively, beat into a froth

Whip 8 scorpion

whip hand 4 sway 5 power 7 control, mastery 9 advantage, authority, dominance, supremacy, upper hand 10 ascendancy, domination

whipped 5 caned, waled 6 beaten, darted, flayed, frothy, lashed, roused 7 flogged, frothed, incited, revived, spanked, subdued, swished, whisked 8 defeated, overlaid, punished, scourged, switched 9 chastised 10 vanquished

whir 3 hum 4 buzz, purr 5 drone 7 whisper

whirl 2 go 3 try 4 reel, spin, stab, turn 5 crack, fling, pivot, swirl, trial, twirl, whack, wheel 6 circle, dither, flurry, gyrate, rotate 7 attempt, revolve, turning 8 circling, gyration, pivoting, rotation, spinning, swirling, twirling, wheeling 9 feel dizzy, feel giddy, pirouette, revolving, turn round 10 dizzy round, rapid round, revolution 12 merry-go-round 17 state of excitement 18 dizzying succession

whirlpool 4 eddy 5 swirl, whirl 6 vortex 9 maelstrom 15 whirling current

whirlwind 4 rash 5 hasty, quick, rapid, short, swift 7 cyclone, tornado, twister 8 headlong 9 breakneck, impetuous, impulsive 10 waterspout

whirly 5 dizzy, giddy, shaky 7 reeling 8 spinning 11 vertiginous

whisk 3 fly, zip 4 beat, bolt, dart, dash, race, rush, tear, whip, whiz 5 bound, brush, flick, hurry, scoot, shoot, speed, spurt, sweep 6 hasten, scurry, spring, sprint
type: 4 wire 6 French 8 omelette

whiskbroom 5 brush

whiskered 5 bushy, hairy 6 shaggy 7 bearded, bristly, hirsute 8 unshaven 11 bewhiskered, mustachioed

whiskers 5 beard 7 stubble 8 bristles

whiskey, whisky 3 gin, rum, rye 4 corn, shot 5 booze, hooch, Irish, juice, vodka 6 liquor, red eye, rotgut, Scotch 7 alcohol, aquavit, blended, bourbon, spirits 8 eau-de-vie 9 aquavitae, firewater, moonshine, unblended 10 sneaky pete, usquebaugh 11 mountain dew 14 John Barleycorn, white lightning
type: 3 rye 6 Scotch 7 bourbon
drink: 8 hot toddy 14 Klondike Cooler
with beer: 11 Boilermaker
with Benedictine: 10 Frisco Sour
with Cointreau: 16 Canadian Cocktail
with vermouth: 9 Manhattan

whisper 3 hum 4 blab, buzz, hint, purr, sigh, tell 5 blurt, bruit, drone, rumor 6 gossip, murmur, mutter, reveal, rustle 7 breathe, confide, divulge, inkling 8 disclose, innuendo, intimate 9 undertone 10 suggestion 11 insinuation

whist
derived from: 8 triomphe
descendant: 6 bridge
number of players: 4 four
six tricks: 4 book

Whistle
author: 10 James Jones

Whistler, James Abbott McNeill
born: 8 Lowell MA
artwork: 6 Etudes 9 Harmonies, Nocturnes 10 Rosa Corder 12 Arrangements, The White Girl 13 Thomas Carlyle 15 Cicely Alexander, Wapping-on-Thames 24 Venetian Palaces Nocturnes 28 Arrangement in Grey and Black No 1 (The Artist's Mother) 29 Chelsea Nocturne in Blue and Green 31 Princess of the Land of the Porcelain 35 Falling Rocket Nocturne in Black and Gold 37 Cremorne Lights Nocturne in Blue and Silver

whistle-stop 5 stump 8 campaign 11 electioneer

whit 3 dab, dot, jot 4 chip, dash, drop, iota, mite, snip 5 crumb, grain, pinch, speck 6 morsel, tittle, trifle 7 modicum, smidgen 8 fragment, particle, splinter 9 scintilla

white 3 wan 4 ashy, fair, gray, pale, pure 5 ashen, blond, clean, filmy, hoary, ivory, milky, pasty, pearl, smoky, snowy 6 benign, chalky, chaste, cloudy, frosty, leaden, pallid, pearly, sallow, silver 7 ghostly, silvery 8 blanched, bleached, grizzled, harmless, innocent, spotless, virtuous 9 alabaster, bloodless, Caucasian, colorless, stainless, undefiled, unspotted, unstained, unsullied 10 cadaverous, immaculate 11 translucent, unblemished, unmalicious

White, E B (Elwyn Brooks)
  author of: 11 One Man's Meat 12 Stuart Little 13 Charlotte's Web 14 Is Sex Necessary? (with James Thurber) 19 The Trumpet of the Swan
  column: 13 Talk of the Town

White, Stanford see 17 Mead McKim and White

White, T H (Terence Hanbury)
  author of: 15 The Book of Merlyn 16 The Ill-Made Knight 17 The Witch in the Wood 18 The Candle in the Wind, The Sword in the Stone 20 The Once and Future King

White Album
  author: 10 Joan Didion

White Company, The
  author: 19 Sir Arthur Conan Doyle

White Heat
  director: 10 Raoul Walsh
  cast: 11 James Cagney 12 Edmond O'Brien, Virginia Mayo 16 Margaret Wycherly

White-Jacket
  author: 14 Herman Melville

whiten 4 pale 5 clean, frost 6 blanch, bleach, silver 7 lighten

whiteness 6 pallor 7 wanness 8 paleness 9 snowiness 10 sallowness 13 colorlessness

White Nights
  director: 14 Taylor Hackford
  cast: 12 Gregory Hines 18 Mikhail Baryshnikov
  choreographer: 10 Twyla Tharp

White Rabbit
  character in: 28 Alice's Adventures in Wonderland
  author: 7 Carroll

whitewash 6 excuse 7 absolve, cover up, justify 8 downplay, minimize, play down 9 calcimine, exonerate, vindicate
  paint made by mixing: 12 lime and water

Whitewater
  author: 10 Paul Horgan

whitish 4 buff, pale 6 chalky, creamy 7 grayish

Whitman, Bert
  creator/artist of: 14 The Green Hornet

Whitman, Walt
  author of: 12 Song of Myself 13 Leaves of Grass 18 Oh Captain My Captain 33 When Lilacs Last in the Dooryard Bloom'd

Whitmore, James
  born: 13 White Plains NY
  roles: 4 Them 5 Bully 8 Oklahoma 9 Battlecry 10 Will Rogers 11 Black Like Me 12 Battleground, Harry S Truman, Tora Tora Tora 15 Command Decision,

Give 'em Hell Harry 19 The Next Voice You Hear

Whitney, Eli
  nationality: 8 American
  invented: 9 cotton gin
  pioneered use of: 14 mass production

Whittier, John Greenleaf
  author of: 9 Snow-Bound 10 Maud Muller 14 The Barefoot Boy 16 Barbara Frietchie

whittle 3 cut 4 clip, pare 5 carve, shave, slash 7 curtail, shorten 8 decrease

whiz 3 fly, hum, zip 4 bolt, buzz, dart, dash, hiss, race, rush, scud, tear, whir, zoom 5 adept, drone, scoot, shark, shoot, speed, spurt, sweep, swish, whine, whisk 6 expert, genius, hasten, master, scurry, sizzle, sprint, wizard 7 prodigy, scuttle, whistle 11 crackerjack

who goes there?
  French: 7 qui vive

who knows?
  Spanish: 9 quien sabe

whole 4 body, bulk, full, hale, unit, well 5 sound, total, uncut 6 entire, intact, robust, system 7 essence, healthy, perfect 8 complete, ensemble, entirety, totality, unbroken, unharmed, vigorous 9 aggregate, undivided, uninjured 10 assemblage, unabridged 12 completeness, quintessence, undiminished

wholehearted 4 true 7 earnest, serious, sincere, zealous 8 complete, emphatic 9 unfeigned 10 unreserved, unstinting 12 enthusiastic

wholesome 4 hale, nice, pure, well 5 clean, fresh, hardy, moral, sound 6 decent, honest, worthy 7 chipper, dutiful, ethical, healthy, upright 8 blooming, hygienic, innocent, sanitary, vigorous, virtuous 9 exemplary, healthful, honorable, uplifting 10 nourishing, nutritious, principled 11 meritorious, responsible 12 invigorating 13 strengthening

whole world, the
  French: 11 tout le monde

wholly 5 fully, quite 7 totally, utterly 8 as a whole, entirely 9 perfectly 10 altogether, completely, thoroughly
  Latin: 6 in toto

whoop 3 cry 4 hoot, howl, roar, yell 5 cheer, hollo, shout 6 bellow, cry out, holler, hurrah, outcry, scream, shriek 7 screech 9 hue and cry

whopper 3 fib, lie 6 big one 7 fiction 9 falsehood, fish story, tall story 16 cock-and-bull story

whopping 4 huge 5 giant, large 8 thumping, whacking, whapping 10 incredible 13 extraordinary

whore 3 pro 4 bawd, doxy, jade, slut, tart 5 hussy, tramp 6 chippy, harlot, hooker, prosty, wanton 7 demirep, hustler, trollop 8 call girl, mistress, strumpet 9 concubine 10 prostitute 12 streetwalker
  French: 9 courtesan 12 demimondaine

whorl 4 coil, curl, roll 5 helix 6 circle, spiral 9 corkscrew 11 convolution

Who's Afraid of Virginia Woolf?
author: 11 Edward Albee
director: 11 Mike Nichols
cast: 11 George Segal, Sandy Dennis 13 Richard Burton 15 Elizabeth Taylor
Oscar for: 7 actress (Taylor) 17 supporting actress (Dennis)

Who Said That?
host: 8 John Daly 11 Robert Trout 13 Walter Kiernan
panelist: 9 Bill Henry 12 Bob Considine, H V Kaltenborn, June Lockhart 14 John Mason Brown, Morey Amsterdam 17 John Cameron Swayze

Who's on First?
author: 17 William F Buckley Jr

wicked 3 bad, low 4 base, evil, foul, vile 5 acute, awful, gross, rowdy 6 cursed, fierce, impish, raging, severe, sinful 7 corrupt, extreme, fearful, galling, heinous, hellish, immoral, intense, knavish, naughty, painful, rampant, Satanic, serious, vicious 8 depraved, devilish, dreadful, fiendish, infamous, rascally, shameful 9 atrocious, malicious, monstrous, nefarious 10 abominable, bothersome, degenerate, iniquitous, malevolent, scandalous, villainous 11 disgraceful, mischievous, troublesome 12 blackhearted, dishonorable, incorrigible 13 reprehensible

wickedness 4 evil 6 infamy 8 baseness, foulness, iniquity, vileness 9 depravity, malignity 10 immorality, sinfulness 11 malevolence 13 maliciousness, nefariousness

Wicked Witch of the West
character in: 13 The Wizard of Oz
author: 4 Baum

Wickfield, Agnes
character in: 16 David Copperfield
author: 7 Dickens

Wickford Point
author: 13 John P Marquand

Wickham, Mr
character in: 17 Pride and Prejudice
author: 6 Austen

wide 4 vast 5 ample, broad, fully, great, large, roomy 7 dilated, immense 8 expanded, extended, spacious 9 boundless, capacious, distended, extensive, outspread 10 commodious, completely

wide-awake 2 up 5 alert, aware, quick 8 vigilant, watchful 9 attentive, insomniac, observant, sleepless

widely 3 far 5 broad 6 abroad 7 broadly, greatly, largely 10 by and large, far and near 11 extensively

widely known 6 common 7 popular 8 familiar 9 universal, worldwide

widen 6 expand, extend, spread 7 broaden, enlarge, stretch

widened 7 swelled, swollen 8 enlarged, expanded, extended 9 broadened, distended, stretched

wide open 4 ajar, vast 5 agape 6 gaping 7 exposed, yawning 8 extended, unfenced 9 cavernous, expansive, outspread, unbounded 12 outstretched, unobstructed

wide open spaces 7 boonies, country 9 boondocks 11 countryside, hinterlands

wide-ranging 5 broad 7 immense 8 sweeping 9 extensive, universal, unlimited 10 exhaustive 11 diversified, far-reaching 12 encyclopedic 13 comprehensive

Wide Sargasso Sea
author: 8 Jean Rhys

widespread 5 broad 9 extensive, outspread, pervasive, worldwide 10 nationwide 11 far-reaching

Widmark, Richard
born: 9 Sunrise MN
roles: 4 Coma 7 Madigan 8 The Alamo 11 Kiss of Death 12 The Long Ships 16 Halls of Montezuma, How the West Was Won 19 Judgment at Nuremberg

Widow Douglas
character in: 15 (The Adventures of) Huckleberry Finn
author: 5 Twain

wie geht's 9 how are you?

Wieland
author: 20 Charles Brockden Brown

wield 3 ply, use 4 wave 5 apply, exert, swing 6 employ, handle, manage 7 display, utilize 8 brandish, exercise, flourish 10 manipulate

wife 3 rib 4 mate 5 bride, squaw, woman 6 missus, spouse 7 consort, old lady 8 helpmate, helpmeet 9 companion
French: 5 femme
German: 4 frau

Wife of Bath
character in: 18 The Canterbury Tales
author: 7 Chaucer

Wifey
author: 9 Judy Blume

wig 3 rug 4 fall 6 carpet, peruke, switch, topper, toupee, wiglet 9 hairpiece

Wiggin, Kate Douglas
author of: 23 Rebecca of Sunnybrook Farm

wiggle 3 wag 4 jerk 5 shake, twist 6 quiver, squirm, twitch, writhe 7 flutter 8 writhing 9 squirming

wigwam, Wigwam 3 hut 4 tent, tipi 5 hogan, lodge, tepee 6 teepee 7 weekwam, wickiup 11 Tammany Hall

Wilcox family
characters in: 10 Howard's End
members: 4 Paul, Ruth 5 Henry 7 Charles
author: 7 Forster

wild, wilds, the wild 3 mad 4 bush, rash 5 bleak, feral, giddy, madly, nutty, rabid, rough, waste 6 choppy, crazed, fierce, insane, madcap, raging, raving, rugged, savage, unruly, wooded 7 berserk, bizarre, flighty, frantic, furious, howling, lawless, natural, untamed, violent 8 barbaric, blustery, demented, desolate, fanciful, forested, frenzied, insanely, maniacal, reckless, unbroken, unhinged 9 abandoned, fanatical, fantastic, ferocious, furiously, illogical, lawlessly, naturally, overgrown, primitive, rampantly, screwball, turbulent, violently, wasteland 10 disorderly, manically, uninformed 11 harebrained, impractical, tempestuous, uncivilized, uninhabited 12 uncultivated, ungovernable, unrestrained 13 rattlebrained, undisciplined 14 undomesticated

wild animal 9 beast, brute

Wild Ass's Skin
author: 14 Honore de Balzac

Wild Bunch, The
director: 12 Sam Peckinpah
cast: 10 Ben Johnson, Robert Ryan 11 Warren Oates 12 Edmond O'Brien 13 William Holden 14 Ernest Borgnine

wildcat 3 cat 4 lynx 6 ocelot

Wild Duck, The
author: 11 Henrik Ibsen
character: 5 Werle 8 Old Ekdal 9 Gina Ekdal 12 Gregers Werle, Hjalmar Ekdal 13 Hedvig Relling

Wilde, Cornel
real name: 19 Cornelius Louis Wilde
born: 9 New York NY
wife: 11 Jean Wallace
roles: 9 Maracaibo 11 Omar Khayyam 12 Forever Amber, The Naked Prey 15 A Song to Remember 21 A Thousand and One Nights 22 The Greatest Show on Earth

Wilde, Oscar
author of: 6 Salome 17 The Critic as Artist 18 Lady Windermere's Fan 22 The Ballad of Reading Gaol, The Picture of Dorian Gray 27 The Importance of Being Earnest

Wilder, Billy
director of: 11 One Two Three 12 The Apartment (Oscar) 13 Some Like It Hot 14 The Lost Weekend (Oscar) 15 Double Indemnity, Stalag Seventeen, Sunset Boulevard 16 The Seven Year Itch 18 Love in the Afternoon 24 Witness for the Prosecution

Wilder, Gene
real name: 14 Jerry Silberman
born: 11 Milwaukee WI
roles: 12 Silver Streak, The Producers 14 Blazing Saddles, Bonnie and Clyde 17 Young Frankenstein 22 The World's Greatest Lover 27 Start the Revolution Without Me 43 The Adventures of Sherlock Holmes' Smarter Brother

Wilder, Laura Ingalls
author of: 26 The Little House on the Prairie

Wilder, Thornton
author of: 7 Our Town 9 The Cabala 13 The Matchmaker 14 The Ides of March 16 The Woman of Andros 17 The Skin of Our Teeth 20 Heaven's My Destination 21 The Bridge of San Luis Rey

wilderness 4 bush 5 waste 6 barren, desert, forest, plains, tundra 7 barrens 8 badlands, wasteland 9 mountains

Wildeve, Damon
character in: 17 Return of the Native
author: 5 Hardy

Wild Is the River
author: 14 Louis Bromfield

Wild Kingdom
host/narrator: 9 Jim Fowler, Stan Brock 13 Marlin Perkins

Wild One, The
director: 12 Laslo Benedek
cast: 9 Lee Marvin 10 Mary Murphy 12 Marlon Brando

Wild Strawberries
director: 13 Ingmar Bergman
cast: 12 Ingrid Thulin 13 Bibi Andersson 14 Victor Sjostrom 17 Gunnar Bjornstrand

Wild Wild West
character: 10 James T West 13 Artemus Gordon
cast: 10 Ross Martin 12 Robert Conrad
traveled by: 5 train

wile, wiles 4 coax, lure, ploy, ruse, trap 5 charm, guile 6 cajole, entice, gambit, seduce 7 cunning 8 artifice, maneuver, persuade, subtlety, trickery 9 chicanery, expedient, stratagem 10 artfulness, craftiness, subterfuge 11 contrivance, machination

Wilfer, Bella
character in: 15 Our Mutual Friend
author: 7 Dickens

Wilhelm, Kate
author of: 10 City of Cain, Fault Lines 11 The Planners 14 The Infinity Box 16 The Clewiston Test 19 More Bitter than Death 26 Where Late the Sweet Birds Sang

Wilhelm Meister
author: 6 Goethe

Wilhelm Tell
also: 11 William Tell
author: 17 Johann von Schiller

wiliness 5 guile 7 cunning, slyness 8 artifice, foxiness, scheming, trickery 10 artfulness, craftiness 11 machination

Wilkes family
characters in: 15 Gone With the Wind
members: 4 John 5 Honey, India 6 Ashley 15 Melanie Hamilton
author: 8 Mitchell

will 4 want, wish 5 endow 6 bestow, confer, desire 7 craving, feeling, longing, resolve, wish for 8 attitude, bequeath, pleasure, yearning 9 hankering, testament 10 conviction, preference, resolution 11 disposition, inclination 12 resoluteness 13 determination

Willard, Frank
creator/artist of: 11 Moon Mullins

Willet, John
character in: 12 Barnaby Rudge
author: 7 Dickens

willful 6 mulish, unruly 7 planned, studied 8 designed, intended, obdurate, perverse, stubborn 9 obstinate, pigheaded 10 bullheaded, deliberate, determined, headstrong, inflexible, persistent, purposeful, unyielding 11 intentional, intractable 12 contemplated, premeditated, ungovernable 13 undisciplined 14 uncompromising

Williams, Esther
nickname: 13 Mermaid Tycoon 14 Queen of the Surf 17 Hollywood's Mermaid
born: 12 Los Angeles CA
husband: 13 Fernando Lamas
roles: 13 Bathing Beauty 15 Jupiter's Darling, Ziegfeld Follies 16 Dangerous When Wet, Neptune's Daughter 20 Million Dollar Mermaid

Williams, Janey
character in: 3 USA
author: 9 Dos Passos

Williams, Myrna
real name of: 8 Myrna Loy

Williams, Robin
born: 9 Chicago IL
roles: 6 Popeye 12 Mork and Mindy 18 Good Morning Vietnam 23 The World According to Garp

Williams, Ted
nickname: 6 the Kid 16 Splendid Splinter
sport: 8 baseball
position: 8 outfield
team: 12 Boston Red Sox

Williams, Tennessee
author of: 10 Camino Real 13 The Rose Tattoo 14 Summer and Smoke 16 Cat on a Hot Tin Roof, Night of the Iguana, Sweet Bird of Youth 17 Orpheus Descending, The Glass Menagerie 18 Small Craft Warnings, Suddenly Last Summer 21 A Streetcar Named Desire 24 The Roman Spring of Mrs Stone

Williams, William Carlos
author of: 7 Tempers 8 Paterson 9 White Mule 11 Al Que Quiere 20 Pictures from Brueghel

William Tell
also: 13 Guillaume Tell
opera by: 7 Rossini
character: 6 Arnold 7 Gessler

William the Conqueror
also: 17 William of Normandy 21 William I King of England
fought against: 8 Harold II
battle: 8 Hastings
succeeded by: 6 Henry I 9 William II

Willie and Joe
creator: 11 Bill Mauldin

willing 4 game 5 ready 7 content 8 amenable 9 agreeable, compliant, not averse 10 responsive

willingly 4 gain, lief, soon 6 freely, gladly, liefly 7 eagerly, happily, readily 8 by choice 10 cheerfully, graciously 11 voluntarily 12 with pleasure

willingness 4 zeal 8 alacrity 9 eagerness, readiness 10 enthusiasm 11 inclination

Willoughby, John
character in: 19 Sense and Sensibility
author: 6 Austen

willow 5 Salix
varieties: 3 bay, red 4 bush, goat, gray, seep 5 black, crack, false, Niobe, Pekin, pussy, silky, water, white 6 Arctic, arroyo, basket, desert, golden, laurel, puzzle, woolly, yellow 7 brittle, prairie, sandbar, scouler, shining, weeping 8 creeping, florist's, polished, Virginia 9 bay-leaved, bearberry, flowering, sprouting 10 cricket-bat, dragon-claw, large pussy, small pussy 11 green-scaled, heart-leaved, peach-leaved, Port Jackson 13 halberd-leaved 16 Wisconsin weeping

willowy 5 lithe 6 limber, pliant, supple, svelte 7 lissome 8 flexible 9 sylphlike

Wills, Chill
born: 12 Seagoville TX
group: 26 Chill Wills and the Avalon Boys
voice of: 21 Francis the Talking Mule
roles: 5 Giant 8 The Alamo 10 Way Out West 11 The Yearling 15 Meet Me in St Louis

Wills, Garry
author of: 14 Nixon Agonistes, Reagan's America 16 Inventing America

Will Scarlet
character in: 9 Robin Hood

willy-nilly 8 perforce 10 helplessly, inevitably 11 inescapably, unavoidably 12 compulsively, irresistibly 14 uncontrollably
Latin: 12 nolens volens

Wilmer
character in: 16 The Maltese Falcon
author: 7 Hammett

Wilson, Edmund
author of: 11 Axel's Castle 19 To the Finland Station

Wilson, Myrtle
character in: 14 The Great Gatsby
author: 10 Fitzgerald

Wilson, Sloan
author of: 26 The Man in the Gray Flannel Suit

Wilson, Woodrow
name at birth: 19 Thomas Woodrow Wilson
nickname: 5 Tommy
presidential rank: 12 twenty-eighth
party: 10 Democratic
state represented: 2 NJ
defeated: 4 (Eugene Victor) Debs, (William Howard) Taft 5 (James Franklin) Hanly 6 (Allen Louis) Benson, (Arthur Edward) Reimer, (Charles Evans) Hughes, (Eugene Wilder) Chafin 9 (Theodore) Roosevelt
vice president: 8 (Thomas Riley) Marshall
cabinet:
state: 5 (Bainbridge) Colby, (William Jennings) Bryan 7 (Robert) Lansing
treasury: 5 (Carter) Glass 6 (William Gibbs) McAdoo 7 (David Franklin) Houston
war: 5 (Newton Diehl) Baker 8 (Lindley Miller) Garrison

attorney general: 6 (Alexander Mitchell) Palmer 7 (Thomas Watt) Gregory 10 (James Clark) McReynolds
navy: 7 (Josephus) Daniels
postmaster general: 8 (Albert Sidney) Burleson
interior: 4 (Franklin Knight) Lane 5 (John Barton) Payne
agriculture: 7 (David Franklin) Houston 8 (Edwin Thomas) Meredith
commerce: 8 (William Cox) Redfield 9 (Joshua Willis) Alexander
labor: 6 (William Bauchop) Wilson
born: 2 VA 8 Staunton
died/buried: 2 DC 10 Washington
education:
college: 8 Davidson 18 College of New Jersey (later known as Princeton U)
law School: 20 University of Virginia
university: 12 Johns Hopkins
religion: 12 Presbyterian
author: 8 The State 16 George Washington 18 Division and Reunion 27 A History of the American People 28 More Literature and Other Essays 34 An Old Master and Other Political Essays 41 President Wilson's Case for the League of Nations 47 Congressional Government: A Study in American Politics
political career:
governor of: 9 New Jersey
civilian career: 6 lawyer
professor of history: 15 Bryn Mawr College 18 Wesleyan University
professor of jurisprudence: 9 Princeton
president of: 9 Princeton
notable events of lifetime/term: 14 Fourteen Points 15 League of Nations
Act: 7 Adamson 8 Sedition 9 Espionage 10 Child Labor 11 Liberty Loan, Panama Canal 14 Federal Reserve 15 Federal Farm Loan 16 Clayton Antitrust, Selective Service 22 Federal Trade Commission
conference: 3 ABC 10 Paris Peace
18th Amendment: 11 Prohibition
program: 10 New Freedom
sinking of: 9 Lusitania
Treaty: 10 Versailles
won: 15 Nobel Peace Prize
quote: 34 The world must be made safe for democracy
father: 13 Joseph Ruggles
mother: 5 Janet (Woodrow)
siblings: 13 Joseph Ruggles 14 Annie Josephson 16 Marion Williamson
wife: 5 Edith (Bolling Galt), Ellen (Louise Axson)
children: 13 Jessie Woodrow 15 Eleanor Randolph, Margaret Woodrow

wilt 3 die, ebb, sag 4 fade, flag, sink, wane 5 droop 6 recede, weaken, wither 7 decline, dwindle, shrivel, subside 8 decrease, diminish, languish 10 degenerate 11 deteriorate

Wilt the Stilt
nickname of: 15 Wilt Chamberlain

wily 3 sly 4 foxy 5 alert, sharp 6 artful, crafty, shifty, shrewd, tricky 7 crooked, cunning, devious 8 guileful, scheming 9 deceitful, deceptive, designing, underhand 10 intriguing 11 calculating, treacherous

win 3 bag, get, net 4 earn, gain, sway 6 attain, induce, master, obtain, pick up, secure 7 achieve, acquire, collect, conquer, convert, prevail, procure, realize, receive, success, triumph, victory 8 conquest, convince, overcome, persuade, vanquish 9 influence 10 accomplish

win acceptance 9 establish 10 ingratiate

wince 5 cower, quail 6 cringe, flinch, recoil, shrink 7 grimace, shudder 8 cowering, cringing, draw back, quailing 9 shrinking

wind 3 air, lap 4 bend, blow, clue, coil, curl, fold, gale, gust, hint, loop, news, puff, roll 5 blast, bluff, curve, draft, scent, smell, snake, twine, twirl, twist, whiff 6 breath, breeze, hot air, ramble, report, wander, zephyr, zigzag 7 bluster, bombast, cyclone, entwine, inkling, meander, sinuate, tempest, tidings, tornado, twaddle, twister, typhoon, whisper 8 boasting, idle talk 9 aerophone, hurricane, knowledge, whirlwind 10 intimation, suggestion 11 braggadocio, fanfaronade, information 12 intelligence
god of: 5 Eurus, Niord, Njord, Notus 6 Aquilo, Auster, Boreas 8 Favonius, Zephyrus
father: 8 Astraeus
mother: 3 Eos

windfall 7 bonanza

Windhoek
capital of: 7 Namibia

Wind in the Willows, The
author: 14 Kenneth Grahame
character: 4 Mole, Toad 6 Badger 8 Water Rat

windless 4 calm 5 still 8 stifling

window 3 bay 5 oriel 6 dormer 7 opening, orifice, transom 8 aperture, casement, porthole, skylight

Winds of War, The
author: 10 Herman Wouk

windstorm 4 gale 6 squall 7 cyclone, tempest, tornado, twister, typhoon 9 hurricane, whirlwind

windswept 4 bare 5 bleak 6 barren 8 desolate 13 weatherbeaten

windup 3 end 5 close 6 ending, finish 10 completion, conclusion, expiration 11 termination

wind up 3 end 4 halt, stop 5 cease, close 6 finish, settle 8 complete, conclude 9 terminate

windy 5 blowy, empty, gabby, gusty, wordy 6 breezy 7 verbose 8 blustery, rambling 9 bombastic, garrulous, talkative 10 loquacious, meandering, rhetorical 13 grandiloquent

wine
French: 3 vin
Italian: 4 vino
god of: 7 Bacchus

goddess of: 6 Libera
wine-colored 6 claret 8 burgundy, cardinal
winemaking
god of: 9 Aristaeus
Winesburg, Ohio
author: 16 Sherwood Anderson
wing 3 ala, fly, set 4 band, clip, flap, knot, nick, soar, zoom 5 annex, graze, group 6 circle, clique, pennon, pinion 7 adjunct, aileron, coterie, faction, section, segment 8 addition, coulisse 9 appendage, extension 10 fraternity
Winged Horse
constellation of: 7 Pegasus
Winger, Debra
husband: 13 Timothy Hutton
roles: 10 Black Widow, Cannery Row 11 Urban Cowboy 17 Terms of Endearment 22 An Officer and a Gentleman
Wingert, Dick
creator/artist of: 6 Hubert
Wingfield family
characters in: 17 The Glass Menagerie
member: 3 Tom 5 Laura 6 Amanda
author: 8 Williams
Wings
director: 15 William A Wellman
cast: 8 Clara Bow 10 Gary Cooper 12 Richard Arlen 18 Charles Buddy Rogers
Oscar for: 7 picture
Wings of the Dove, The
author: 10 Henry James
character: 8 Kate Croy, Lord Mark 9 Mrs Lowder 11 Milly Theale 12 Mrs Stringham 13 Merton Densher, Sir Luke Strett
wink at 6 ignore 7 condone, let pass 8 overlook 9 disregard
Winkle
character in: 14 Pickwick Papers
author: 7 Dickens
winner 5 champ 6 master, victor 8 champion 9 conqueror 10 vanquisher
Winnie-the-Pooh
author: 7 A A Milne
character: 3 Owl 5 Kanga 6 Eeyore, Piglet, Rabbit, Tigger 7 Baby Roo 16 Christopher Robin
winning 7 amiable 8 charming, engaging, pleasing 9 appealing, beguiling, disarming 10 attractive, bewitching, entrancing 11 captivating 12 ingratiating, irresistible
Winnipeg
hockey team: 3 Jets
win over 4 beat, best 5 charm 6 defeat, seduce 7 convert 8 overcome, vanquish 9 captivate, overpower
winsome 5 sweet 6 comely 7 amiable, likable, lovable 8 charming, cheerful, engaging, pleasing 9 agreeable, appealing, endearing 10 attractive, bewitching, delightful
Winter, Lady de
character in: 18 The Three Musketeers
author: 5 Dumas (pere)
Winter, Maxim de
character in: 7 Rebecca
author: 9 Du Maurier

Winterbourne
character in: 11 Daisy Miller
author: 5 James
Winter of Our Discontent, The
author: 13 John Steinbeck
Winters, Shelley
real name: 14 Shirley Schrift
born: 9 St Louis IL
husband: 13 Tony Franciosa 15 Vittorio Gassman
roles: 11 A Double Life 12 A Patch of Blue 14 A Place in the Sun 16 A House Is Not a Home 19 The Diary of Anne Frank 20 The Poseidon Adventure
Winterset
author: 15 Maxwell Anderson
winter sports
god of: 4 Ullr 5 Uller
Winter's Tale, The
author: 18 William Shakespeare
character: 7 Camillo, Leontes, Paulina, Perdita 8 Florizel, Hermione 9 Autolycus, Polixenes
Winter Wonderland
nickname of: 8 Michigan
wintry 3 icy, raw 4 cold 5 bleak, chilly, harsh, polar, snowy, stark 6 arctic, chilly, dreary, frigid, frosty, frozen, gloomy, stormy 7 glacial 8 Siberian 9 cheerless
wipe 3 dry, mop, rub 4 swab 5 apply, brush, clean, erase, rub on, scour, scrub, swipe, towel 6 banish, remove, rub off, sponge, stroke
wiped out 5 broke 6 failed, ruined 8 bankrupt, indigent, strapped 9 destitute, insolvent, penniless 12 impoverished
wipe out 4 ruin 5 erase 7 abolish, destroy, eclipse 8 bankrupt 9 devastate, eliminate, eradicate, extirpate, liquidate 10 annihilate, obliterate 11 exterminate
wiping out 7 erasing 9 eclipsing, expunging 10 abolishing, destroying 11 eliminating, eradicating 12 annihilating, obliterating
wire 5 cable 8 filament, telegram 9 cablegram, telegraph
wiry 4 lean 5 agile, kinky, lanky, spare, stiff 6 limber, pliant, sinewy 7 brittle
Wisconsin
abbreviation: 2 WI 3 Wis
nickname: 6 Badger
capital: 7 Madison
largest city: 9 Milwaukee
others: 5 Ripon 6 Antigo, Beloit, Cudahy, Neenag, Racine, Wausau 7 Ashland, Baraboo, Bloomer, Kenosha, Menasha, Oshkosh, Portage, Shawano 8 Appleton, Boscobel, Green Bay, Lacrosse, Superior, Waukesha 9 Eau Claire, Fond du Lac, Sheboygan, Shorewood, Wauwatosa, West Allis 10 Brookfield, Janesville 12 Steven's Point
college: 5 Ripon 6 Beloit 7 Alverno, Carroll, Viterbo 8 Carthage, Lawrence 9 Marquette, Northland
feature:
fort: 6 Howard 8 Crawford 9 Winnebago

national lakeshore: 14 Apostle Islands
tribe: 3 Fox, Sac 4 Sauk 5 Huron 6 Oneida, Ottawa 8 Chippewa, Kickapoo 9 Winnebago 10 Potawatomi
people: 11 Orson Welles 12 Fredric March, Harry Houdini, Spencer Tracy 13 Hamlin Garland 14 Joseph McCarthy, Georgia O'Keeffe, Thornton Wilder 16 Frank Lloyd Wright 17 Robert M LaFollette
explorer: 6 Joliet 7 Allouez, Nicolet 8 Radisson 9 Marquette 12 Groseilliers
island: 8 Madeline
lake: 6 Geneva, Poygan 7 Kenosha, Mendota, Wissota 8 Michigan, Superior 9 Winnebago
land rank: 11 twenty-sixth
mountain: 7 Baraboo 9 Sugarbush 10 Blue Mounds
highest point: 9 Timm's Hill
physical feature:
glacial hills: 13 Kettle Moraine
rock formations: 8 The Dells
river: 3 Fox 4 Wolf 7 St Croix 8 Chippewa 9 Black Rock, Wisconsin 11 Mississippi
state admission: 9 thirtieth
state bird: 5 robin
state fish: 11 muskellunge
state flower: 5 pansy 6 violet 10 wood violet
state motto: 7 Forward
state song: 11 On Wisconsin
state tree: 10 sugar maple

wisdom 6 brains 8 sagacity 9 teachings 10 philosophy, principles, profundity 11 discernment, penetration 12 apperception, intelligence 13 comprehension, judiciousness, understanding
    god of: 2 Ea 4 Enki, Odin 5 Othin, Thoth
    goddess of: 6 Athena, Athene, Brigit, Pallas, Saitis 7 Minerva 11 Tritogeneia 12 Pallas Athena 18 Alalcomenean Athena
wise 3 way 4 sage 6 manner 7 knowing, respect, sapient 8 profound 9 judicious, sagacious 10 discerning, perceptive 11 intelligent 13 knowledgeable, perspicacious, understanding
Wise, Robert
    director of: 11 I Want to Live 13 West Side Story (with Jerome Robbins, Oscar) 15 The Sound of Music (Oscar)
wiseacre 4 fool, sage 5 idiot 7 tomfool 9 know-it-all, simpleton 10 smart aleck
Wise Blood
    author: 15 Flannery O'Connor
wisecrack 4 jest, joke, quip 5 flash, sally 8 cut jokes 9 witticism 11 smart saying
Wise men *see* 4 Magi
wise up 5 edify 6 advise, in form 7 apprise 9 enlighten, make aware
wish 3 yen 4 hope, long, love, pine, want, whim, will 5 crave, yearn 6 aspire, desire, hunger, thirst 7 command, craving, leaning, longing, request 8 ambition, appetite, fondness, penchant, yearning 10 aspiration, partiality 11 inclination 12 predilection

wishes 11 compliments 13 felicitations 15 congratulations
wish for 4 want 5 covet, crave 6 desire
Wishfort, Lady
    character in: 16 The Way of the World
    author: 8 Congreve
wishful 4 avid 5 eager 6 keen on, pining 7 anxious, craving, hopeful, longing, wanting, wistful 8 aspiring, bent upon, desirous, fanciful, yearning 9 ambitious, expectant
wish well 10 felicitate 12 congratulate
wishy-washy 4 dull, weak 5 inane, vapid, wimpy 6 jejune 7 insipid 8 wavering 10 indecisive, irresolute 11 ineffective, ineffectual, vacillating 12 equivocating, noncommittal 14 tergiversating 15 shilly-shallying
wisp 4 lock, tuft 5 bunch, shred, torch, twist 6 bundle, rumple 8 fragment 10 whisk broom 11 ignis fatuus 13 friar's lantern
wispy 4 thin 5 frail 6 slight 8 fleeting, nebulous
wistaria, wisteria
    varieties: 4 pink, wild 5 silky, water 7 Chinese 8 Japanese 9 Rhodesian
Wister, Owen
    author of: 12 The Virginian
wistful 3 sad 6 musing, pining 7 craving, doleful, forlorn, longing, pensive 8 desirous, mournful, yearning 9 hankering, sorrowful, woebegone 10 meditative, melancholy, reflective 12 disconsolate 13 contemplative, introspective
wit 3 wag 4 gags 5 comic, humor, joker, jokes, quips, sense 6 acumen, banter, brains, jester, joking, levity, wisdom 7 cunning, funster, gagster, insight, punster, sparkle, waggery 8 comedian, drollery, humorist, jokester, judgment, raillery, sagacity, satirist, vivacity 9 funniness, intellect 10 astuteness, brightness, cleverness, jocularity, perception, shrewdness, witticisms 11 discernment, penetration, wisecracker 12 intelligence, perspicacity 13 comprehension, epigrammatist, sagaciousness, understanding
    French: 8 badinage 9 bel-esprit 10 persiflage
witch 3 hag 4 fury 5 crone, scold, shrew, vixen 6 ogress, virago 7 seeress 8 battle-ax, harridan 9 sorceress, temptress, termagant 10 prophetess 11 enchantress
    French: 6 beldam
witchcraft 6 hoodoo, voodoo 7 sorcery 8 black art, witchery, wizardry 9 diabolism, fetishism, voodooism 10 black magic, divination, necromancy 11 conjuration, enchantment
with
    French: 4 avec, chez
with a grain of salt
    Latin: 13 cum grano salis
with a lawsuit pending
    Latin: 12 pendente lite
with authority
    Latin: 10 ex cathedra

withdraw 2 go 5 leave, split 6 depart, go away, recall, recant, remove, retire 7 extract, rescind, retract, retreat, take off, vamoose 9 disappear, unsheathe

withdrawal 4 exit 6 egress 7 leaving, retreat 9 departure 10 retirement, retraction 14 discontinuance

withdrawn 3 shy 5 quiet 8 reserved, retiring, unsocial 9 reclusive 10 unfriendly 11 introverted 15 uncommunicative

wither 4 fade, wilt 5 abash, blast, droop, dry up, shame 7 cut down, mortify, shrivel 9 dehydrate, desiccate, humiliate

withered 3 dry 4 arid, sere 5 dried, faded 6 shrunk, wilted 7 decayed, dried up, drooped, stunned, wizened 9 petrified, shriveled 10 languished

withering 6 biting 7 caustic 8 scathing 9 shrinkage, shrinking, wrinkling 10 shriveling 11 contracting, contraction, devastating

with few words
   Latin: 12 paucis verbis

with force and with arms
   Latin: 9 vi et armis

with great praise
   Latin: 13 magna cum laude

withheld 4 kept 7 checked, forbore, refused, starved 8 kept back 9 boycotted, refrained

with highest praise
   Latin: 13 summa cum laude

withhold 4 hide, keep 6 hush up, retain 7 conceal, cover up 8 suppress

withhold from 4 deny 6 refuse

within 2 on 4 into 5 inner 6 during, inside 7 indoors 8 inwardly
   combining form: 3 eso 4 endo
   prefix: 5 intra

within an inch of 4 near 6 all but, almost, nearly

with-it 7 current 8 up-to-date
   French: 9 au courant

with one's own two hands 7 oneself, unaided 10 unassisted

without 4 save 5 minus 6 beyond, except, unless 7 lacking, nowhere, outside, wanting 8 exterior, external, free from, outdoors 9 excepting 10 externally
   appointment: 7 sine die
   care: 8 sine cure
   charge: 4 free 6 gratis 8 sine cure
   combining form: 4 ecto
   doubt: 9 sine dubio
   feet: 4 apod 6 apodal
   French: 4 sans
   horns: 7 acerous
   Latin: 4 sine
   law: 8 anarchic
   light: 7 aphotic
   life: 5 amort 9 inanimate
   luster: 3 mat 5 matte
   offspring: 9 sine prole
   prefix: 2 in
   roads: 7 invious
   saddles: 8 asellate, bareback
   subcalyx leaves: 9 bractless
   teeth: 5 morne 8 edentate
   this: 7 sine hoc
   tongue, teeth, or claws: 5 morne
   which not: 10 sine qua non
   wings: 7 apteral 8 apterous

without a doubt 6 surely 8 of course 9 certainly 10 absolutely, positively 11 indubitably 12 indisputably 14 unquestionably

without basis 7 unsound 9 unfounded 10 groundless, ungrounded 11 unjustified, unsupported 15 unsubstantiated

without care
   French: 9 sans souci

without charge 4 free 10 gratuitous, on the house 13 complimentary
   Latin: 6 gratis

without doubt
   French: 9 sans doute

without end 7 endless, eternal, forever 8 immortal, infinite, timeless, unending 9 ceaseless, continual, endlessly, eternally, perpetual 10 immortally, infinitely, timelessly, unendingly 11 ceaselessly, continually, everlasting, never-ending 13 everlastingly 14 lasting forever

without equal
   French: 10 sans pareil

without error 4 true 5 exact, right 7 correct, perfect, precise, sinless 8 accurate, truthful, unerring 9 faultless 10 infallible

without exception 5 never 6 always, wholly 8 entirely 10 absolutely, completely, invariably, positively

without fear and without reproach
   French: 22 sans peur et sans reproche

Without Feathers
   author: 10 Woody Allen

without funds 5 broke 6 ruined 8 bankrupt, indigent, strapped, wiped out 9 destitute, flat broke, insolvent, penniless 10 stone broke 12 impoverished

without light 3 dim 4 dark 5 black, dusky, murky, shady 6 opaque 7 obscure, shadowy, stygian, sunless

without limit
   Latin: 11 ad infinitum

without limitation 6 wholly 7 totally, utterly 8 entirely 9 endlessly 10 absolutely, completely, definitely, positively, thoroughly 11 boundlessly 13 unequivocally 15 unconditionally
   French: 12 carte blanche

without notice 5 ad-lib 9 impromptu 10 improvised 11 extemporary 14 extemporaneous
   Latin: 9 extempore

without offspring, without progeny
   Latin: 9 sine prole

without the day
   Latin: 7 sine die

without which not
   Latin: 10 sine qua non

with praise
   Latin: 8 cum laude

withstand 4 bear, defy 5 brave 6 endure, resist, suffer 7 weather 8 confront, cope with, tolerate

witless 3 mad 5 crazy 6 insane, stupid 7 fatuous, foolish, unaware 9 slaphappy

witness 3 see 4 mark, note, sign, view 5 proof 6 attend, behold, look on, notice, verify 7 bear out, certify, confirm, endorse, initial, observe 8 attester, attest to, beholder, deponent, document, evidence, looker-on, observer, onlooker, perceive, validate, vouch for 9 establish, spectator, testifier, testimony 10 validation 11 corroborate, countersign 12 authenticate, confirmation, substantiate, verification 13 corroboration, documentation 14 authentication, substantiation

Witness for the Prosecution
   director: 11 Billy Wilder
   based on play by: 14 Agatha Christie
   cast: 11 Tyrone Power 14 Elsa Lanchester 15 Charles Laughton, Marlene Dietrich

wits 4 mind 6 sanity 9 composure 14 coolheadedness

witticism 4 jest, joke, quip 5 sally 7 epigram
   French: 6 bon mot 10 jeu d'esprit

witty 5 comic, droll, funny 6 bright, clever, jocose 7 amusing, jocular, waggish 8 humorous, mirthful 9 brilliant, sparkling, whimsical 11 quick-witted 13 scintillating

witty saying 4 jest, quip 6 bon mot 7 epigram 9 witticism 13 clever comment

Witwoud, Sir Wilfull
   character in: 16 The Way of the World
   author: 8 Congreve

wizard 4 sage, seer, whiz 5 adept, shark 6 expert, genius, oracle 7 diviner, prodigy, wise man 8 conjurer, magician, sorcerer, virtuoso 9 enchanter 10 soothsayer 11 clairvoyant, necromancer

Wizard of Id, The
   creator: 10 Johnny Hart 11 Brant Parker
   character: 4 King 5 Spook 6 jester, Rodney, Tyrant

Wizard of Oz, The
   director: 13 Victor Fleming
   author: 10 L Frank Baum
   cast: 4 Toto 8 Bert Lahr (Cowardly Lion) 9 Jack Haley (Tin Woodsman), Ray Bolger (Scarecrow) 11 Billie Burke (Good Witch of the North), Frank Morgan (wizard), Judy Garland (Dorothy) 13 Clara Blandick 15 Charley Grapewin 16 Margaret Hamilton (Wicked Witch of the West), The Singer Midgets (Munchkins)
   score: 9 E Y Harburg 11 Harold Arlen
   remade as: 6 The Wiz
   place: 6 Kansas 8 Land of Oz 11 Emerald City
   Dorothy wore: 8 red shoes

wizened 3 dry 5 dried 7 dried up 8 shrunken, withered, wrinkled 9 shriveled

WKRP in Cincinnati
   character: 10 Andy Travis, Herb Tarlek, Les Nessman 12 Venus Flytrap 13 Arthur Carlson, Dr Johnny Fever 14 Bailey Quarters 15 Jennifer Marlowe
   cast: 7 Tim Reid 9 Gary Sandy 10 Gor-

don Jump 11 Frank Bonner, Jan Smithers 12 Loni Anderson 14 Howard Hesseman, Richard Sanders

wobble 4 reel, sway 5 quake, shake, waver 6 shimmy, teeter, totter 7 quaking, shaking, stagger, swaying 8 wavering 9 shimmying, teetering, tottering 12 unsteadiness

wobbly, Wobbly 5 loose, shaky 7 doubtful 8 hesitant, insecure, unstable, unsteady, wavering 9 quavering, trembling 11 vacillating
   union: 17 Industrial Workers

Wodehouse, P G (Pelham Grenville)
   author of: 8 Full Moon 14 Thank You Jeeves 15 The Mating Season
   character: 6 Jeeves 13 Bertie Wooster

Woden
   origin: 10 Anglo-Saxon
   chief of: 4 gods

woe 5 agony, gloom, grief, trial, worry 6 misery, sorrow 7 anguish, anxiety, despair, torment, torture, trouble 8 calamity, distress 9 adversity, dejection, heartache, suffering 10 affliction, depression, melancholy, misfortune 11 tribulation 12 wretchedness

woebegone 3 sad 4 glum 6 gloomy 7 doleful, forlorn 8 dejected, funereal, mournful, tortured, troubled, wretched 9 agonizing, anguished, miserable, sorrowful, suffering 10 distressed

woeful 3 bad, sad 5 awful, cruel 6 tragic 7 doleful, painful, unhappy 8 crushing, dreadful, grievous, hopeless, horrible, terrible, unlikely, wretched 9 agonizing, appalling, miserable, sorrowful 10 calamitous, deplorable, depressing, disastrous, lamentable 11 distressing, unpromising 12 catastrophic, heartrending 13 disheartening, heartbreaking

woe to the vanquished
   Latin: 9 vae victis

Wofford, Chloe Anthony
   real name of: 12 Toni Morrison

Wojtyla, Karol
   real name of: 14 Pope John Paul II 18 Archbishop of Krakow

wolf 4 bolt, gulp 5 scarf 6 devour, gobble 7 consume
   constellation of: 5 Lupus
   group of: 4 pack

Wolf, The
   author: 11 Frank Norris

Wolfe, Thomas
   author of: 14 The Hills Beyond 16 The Web and the Rock 17 Look Homeward Angel, Of Time and the River 18 You Can't Go Home Again
   character: 10 Eugene Gant 12 George Webber

Wolfe, Tom
   author of: 11 Radical Chic 13 The Right Stuff 14 The Painted Word 16 The Pump House Gang 21 From Bauhaus to Our House 23 The Bonfire of the Vanities 24 Mau-mauing the Flak Catchers 26 The Electric Kool-Aid Acid Test 43 The Kandy Kolored Tangerine Flake Streamline Baby

Wollstonecraft, Mary
  husband: 13 William Godwin
  daughter: 25 Mary Wollstonecraft Shelley
  author of: 30 A Vindication of the Rights of Women

Wolverine State
  nickname of: 8 Michigan

woman 4 girl, lady, maid, wife 5 flame, lover 6 damsel, maiden, matron 7 beloved, darling, dowager, females, fiancee, sweetie 8 ladylove, mistress 9 charwoman, concubine 10 girlfriend, hand maiden, sweetheart, sweetie pie 11 chambermaid, housekeeper, maidservant
  French: 5 femme 8 paramour
  Latin: 9 inamorata

Woman, first
  Scandinavian: 5 Embla

Woman in White, A
  author: 13 Wilkie Collins

womanish 7 unmanly 8 feminine, ladylike 9 sissified 10 effeminate

womanlike 8 feminine 10 effeminate

womanly 8 feminine, matronly

Woman of Substance, A
  author: 21 Barbara Taylor Bradford

Woman of the Year
  director: 13 George Stevens
  cast: 10 Fay Bainter 12 Reginald Owen, Spencer Tracy 16 Katharine Hepburn

Woman's Life, A
  author: 15 Guy de Maupassant

Women, The
  director: 11 George Cukor
  based on play by: 15 Clare Boothe Luce
  cast: 11 Hedda Hopper 12 Joan Crawford, Joan Fontaine, Marjorie Main, Norma Shearer 15 Paulette Goddard, Rosalind Russell
  remade as: 14 The Opposite Sex

Women at Point Sur, The
  author: 15 Robinson Jeffers

Women in Love
  director: 10 Ken Russell
  based on novel by: 10 DH Lawrence
  character: 11 Gerald Crich 12 Rupert Birkin 14 Gudrun Brangwen, Ursula Brangwen
  cast: 9 Alan Bates 10 Oliver Reed 11 Eleanor Bron 12 Jennie Linden 13 Glenda Jackson
  Oscar for: 7 actress (Jackson)

wonder 3 awe 4 gape 5 sight, stare 6 marvel, ponder, rarity 7 miracle 8 cogitate, meditate, question 9 amazement, spectacle, speculate 10 conjecture, phenomenon 11 fascination 12 astonishment, stupefaction

wonder child
  German: 10 wunderkind

wonderful 4 fine, good 5 great, super 6 divine, superb, tiptop, unique 7 amazing, capital 8 fabulous, singular, smashing, striking, terrific 9 admirable, excellent, fantastic, marvelous 10 astounding, incredible, miraculous, phenomenal, staggering,

surprising 11 astonishing, crackerjack, fascinating, magnificent, sensational, spectacular 13 extraordinary

Wonderland State
  nickname of: 5 Maine

wonderstruck 4agog 6 amazed 8 thrilled 9 astounded, stupefied 10 astonished, enthralled, spellbound 11 dumbfounded 13 flabbergasted

Wonder Woman
  character: 9 (Corp) Etta Candy 11 Diana Prince, Joe Atkinson, (Maj) Steve Trevor 13 Gen Blankenship
  cast: 11 Lynda Carter 12 Lyle Waggoner 13 Beatrice Colen, Normann Burton 14 Richard Eastham

wont 3 apt, use 4 used, vain 5 habit, haunt, usage 6 custom, desire 8 accustom, inclined, practice 10 accustomed

wonted 3 apt 5 prone 6 likely 7 given to 10 accustomed, habituated

woo 3 sue 5 chase, court 6 cajole, pursue 7 address, entreat, solicit 8 petition 9 importune

wood 3 log 4 bush 5 brake, brush, copse, grove 6 boards, forest, lumber, planks, siding, timber 7 thicket 8 firewood, kindling 9 clapboard, wallboard 10 timberland

Wood, Grant
  born: 9 Anamosa IA
  artwork: 12 Spring in Town 13 Stone City Iowa 14 American Gothic 15 Woman with Plants 16 Parson Weems' Fable 18 Dinner for Threshers, John B Turner Pioneer 21 Daughters of Revolution

Wood, John, Sr
  architect of: 6 Circus (Bath)

Wood, Natalie
  real name: 13 Natasha Gurdin
  born: 14 San Francisco CA
  husband: 12 Robert Wagner
  roles: 5 Gypsy 10 Brainstorm 12 The Great Race, The Searchers 13 West Side Story 17 Inside Daisy Clover 18 Rebel Without a Cause, Splendor in the Grass 19 Sex and the Single Girl 23 This Property Is Condemned 25 Love with the Proper Stranger 27 Miracle on Thirty-fourth Street

wooded 5 treed 8 forested

wooden 4 dull 5 frame, rigid, stiff 6 clumsy, vacant 7 awkward, deadpan 8 lifeless, ungainly 9 impassive, unbending 10 inflexible, ungraceful 11 unemotional 14 expressionless

Woodhouse, Emma
  character in: 4 Emma
  author: 6 Austen

woodland 5 copse, grove, treed 6 forest 7 coppice, thicket 8 forested

wood of life
  Latin: 11 lignum vitae

woods
  god of: 8 Silvanus, Sylvanus

Woods, Sara
  real name: 13 Sara Bowen-Judd
  author of: 11 Done to Death 12 My Life

Is Done 13 Yet She Must Die 15 A Show of Violence, Knives Have Edges 16 And Shame the Devil 17 The Third Encounter, Trusted Like the Fox 18 Bloody Instructions

character: 15 Anthony Maitland

Woodstock

also called: 11 The Cavalier

author: 14 Sir Walter Scott

Woodstock

director: 15 Michael Wadleigh

cast: 6 The Who 7 Santana 8 Joan Baez 9 Joe Cocker 12 Richie Havens 13 John Sebastian, Ten Years After 17 Jefferson Airplane 19 Crosby Stills and Nash 20 Country Joe and the Fish, Sly and the Family Stone

Oscar for: 11 documentary

Woodward, Bob

author of: 4 Veil 19 All the President's Men (with Carl Bernstein)

Woodward, Joanne

born: 13 Thomasville GA

husband: 10 Paul Newman

roles: 12 A Fine Madness, Rachel Rachel 15 Three Faces of Eve (Oscar) 16 The Long Hot Summer 43 The Effect of Gamma Rays on Man-in-the-Moon Marigolds

woodwind instrument 4 oboe **5** flute **7** bassoon, piccolo **8** clarinet **9** bass flute **10** cor anglais **12** bass clarinet **13** double bassoon

wooer 4 beau, love **5** flame, lover, swain **6** adorer, suitor **7** admirer, courter **8** paramour **10** sweetheart

wool

fabric: 4 felt **5** crepe, llama, serge, tweed, twill **6** alpaca, angora, boucle, covert, faille, melton, vicuna, woolen **7** challis, doeskin, Donegal, worsted **8** cashmere, homespun, shetland **9** Astrakhan, camelhair, gabardine, sharkskin **10** hopsacking **11** Harris tweed, herringbone

Woolf, Virginia

author of: 7 Orlando **8** The Waves, The Years **10** Jacob's Room **11** Mrs Dalloway **14** A Room of One's Own **15** To the Lighthouse

member of: 15 Bloomsbury Group

wool-gather 8 daydream, muse idly

woolly, wooly 5 downy, furry, fuzzy, hairy, sheep, vague **6** fleecy, lanate, lanose **7** blurred, muddled, unclear **8** confused, floccose, peronate **10** flocculent, indistinct **12** disorganized

woozy 4 hazy **5** dizzy, faint, foggy, fuzzy, giddy, shaky **6** punchy **7** muddled **9** befuddled **11** light-headed

word, words 3 vow **4** chat, dirt, news, poop, term **5** edict, order, rumor, set-to, voice **6** advice, avowal, decree, gossip, letter, notice, phrase, pledge, remark, report, ruling, signal **7** command, comment, dictate, dispute, explain, express, hearsay, lowdown, mandate, message, promise, quarrel, summons, tidings **8** argument, audience, bulletin, chitchat, colloquy, decision, describe, dialogue, dispatch, locution, telegram **9** assertion, assurance, bickering, direction, discourse, interview, sobriquet, ultimatum, utterance, wrangling **10** articulate, communique, conference, contention, discussion, expression **11** altercation, appellation, declaration, designation, information, scuttlebutt **12** consultation, intelligence, tittle-tattle **13** communication, pronouncement

French: 9 tete-a-tete

word for word and letter for letter

Latin: 19 verbatim et literatim

wordiness 9 diffusion, prolixity, verbosity **11** diffuseness, profuseness

wording 8 language, phrasing **11** phraseology

wordless 4 dumb, mute **5** tacit **6** silent **8** implicit, taciturn **10** speechless **11** unexpressed

word of honor 3 vow **4** oath **6** pledge **9** assurance

word play 6 banter **7** jesting, kidding

French: 8 badinage, repartee

Words, The

author: 14 Jean-Paul Sartre

Wordsworth, William

author of: 7 Michael **9** Ode to Duty **11** The Prelude **12** Tintern Abbey **14** Lyrical Ballads (with Coleridge) **16** The Ruined Cottage **24** Intimations of Immortality **25** Resolution and Independence

home: 11 Dove Cottage

wordy 5 windy **6** prolix, turgid **7** fustian, gushing, verbose **8** effusive, mumbling **9** bombastic, garrulous, redundant, talkative **10** discursive, loquacious, rhetorical, roundabout **12** tautological **13** grandiloquent

work, works 2 do, go **3** act, job, run, win **4** book, deed, duty, feat, form, gain, line, make, mill, mold, move, shop, song, task, toil, yard **5** beget, cause, chore, craft, enact, labor, opera, piece, plant, shape, slave, solve, sweat, trade **6** drudge, effect, effort, office, output **7** achieve, calling, drawing, execute, exploit, factory, fashion, foundry, innards, insides, operate, perform, produce, product, pursuit, succeed, trouble **8** building, business, concerto, contents, creation, drudgery, endeavor, engender, exertion, function, industry, maneuver, painting, progress, symphony, transmit, vocation **9** originate, sculpture, structure **10** assignment, employment, enterprise, manipulate, occupation, production, profession **11** achievement, composition, performance, transaction

Latin: 4 opus

French: 6 metier

work, artistic or literary

French: 6 oeuvre

workaday 5 plain **6** common **7** humdrum, prosaic, routine **8** ordinary **10** unexciting **11** commonplace

work at 3 try 5 essay 6 tackle 7 attempt 8 endeavor

workbench 5 board, table 7 counter

work conquers all
  Latin: 16 labor omnia vincit
  motto of: 8 Oklahoma

worker 4 doer, hand 5 grind 6 drudge, toiler 7 artisan, hustler, laborer, plodder 8 achiever, employee, producer 9 craftsman, performer 11 breadwinner, eager beaver, proletarian

work for 6 assist 7 support 8 champion

working 3 job 4 duty, toil 5 labor, tasks 6 action, chores, fluent, usable, useful 8 business, drudgery, employed, exertion, industry, laboring 9 effective, operation, operative, practical 10 employment, occupation, profession 11 assignments, functioning, performance

Working
  author: 11 Studs Terkel

working-class 5 labor 8 plebian 10 blue-collar 11 proletarian

working class 9 commoners, common man 11 blue collars, proletariat
  Greek: 9 hoi polloi

workmanlike 5 adept 8 skillful 9 efficient 10 productive

workmanship 5 skill 9 handcraft, handiwork, technique 10 handicraft 11 manufacture 12 construction

work out 5 solve, train 6 figure, reckon 7 compute, resolve 8 exercise, practice 9 ascertain, calculate, determine

Works and Days
  author: 6 Hesiod

work saver 9 appliance 11 convenience

work-saving 4 easy 6 simple 9 efficient

worktable 4 desk 5 bench, board, table 7 counter

work together 5 unite 7 pitch in, share in 8 take part 9 cooperate 11 collaborate, participate

work toward 3 try 4 seek 6 aim for 7 attempt 8 aspire to, endeavor, reach for

work up 4 goad, urge 5 upset 6 excite 7 agitate, ferment, provoke

work with 5 coach, drill, teach, train 6 assist 8 exercise, instruct 11 collaborate

world 3 age, era, orb 4 gobs, lots, span 5 class, Earth, epoch, globe, group, heaps, realm, times 6 domain, nature, oodles, people, period, planet, sphere, system 7 mankind, society 8 creation, division, duration, everyone, humanity, industry, universe 9 everybody, humankind, macrocosm 10 profession
  Latin: 6 cosmos
  Russian: 3 mir

World According to Garp, The
  author: 10 John Irving
  director: 13 George Roy Hill
  cast: 10 Glenn Close, Hume Cronyn 11 John Lithgow 12 Jessica Tandy, Mary Beth Hurt 13 Robin Williams

World Enough and Time
  author: 16 Robert Penn Warren

worldly 5 blase 6 astute, shrewd, urbane 7 callous, earthly, fleshly, knowing, mundane, profane, secular 8 material, physical, temporal 9 corporeal, mercenary 11 experienced, terrestrial 12 cosmopolitan 13 sophisticated

world pain
  German: 11 Weltschmerz

world view
  German: 11 Weltansicht

world-weary 5 blase, bored, jaded 9 unexcited

worldwide 4 rife 6 global 8 catholic, ecumenic, globular, planetal, sweeping 9 universal

worm 4 edge, inch 5 crawl, creep, steal 6 writhe 7 wriggle 9 penetrate 10 infiltrate
  kinds: 4 inch, tape 5 angle, earth

worn 4 weak 5 dingy, drawn, faded, seedy, spent, tired, weary 6 frayed, shabby, wasted 7 abraded, haggard, pinched, rickety, wearied 8 battered, decrepit, dog-tired, drooping, fatigued 9 enfeebled, exhausted 10 threadbare, tumbledown 11 debilitated, dilapidated

worn-out 4 dead, shot 5 spent, tired 6 beat-up, effete, shabby, used-up 7 rundown 9 exhausted 10 threadbare 11 dilapidated 12 deteriorated

worn thin 9 motheaten 10 threadbare 11 dilapidated

worried 6 afraid, scared 7 anxious, fearful 9 concerned 10 distressed 12 apprehensive

worrisome 5 fussy, pesty 6 trying, uneasy, vexing 7 anxious, fretful, irksome 8 annoying 10 bothersome, despairing, disturbing, irritating, tormenting 11 aggravating, troublesome 12 apprehensive

worry 3 vex, woe 4 care, fret, stew 5 agony, beset, dread, grief, harry, upset 6 badger, bother, dismay, harass, hector, misery, pester, plague 7 agitate, agonize, anguish, anxiety, bugaboo, concern, despair, disturb, perturb, problem, torment, trouble 8 distress, vexation 9 misgiving, persecute 10 difficulty, uneasiness 12 apprehension 13 consternation

worsen 4 fail, slip 5 erode, lapse, slide 7 decline 10 degenerate, retrogress 11 deteriorate 12 disintegrate

worsening 7 setback 9 inflaming 10 increasing, regressing, regression 11 aggravating, heightening 12 exacerbating, intensifying 13 retrogressing, retrogression

worship 5 adore, exalt, extol 6 admire, esteem, praise, pray to, revere 7 adulate, glorify, idolize, lionize 8 dote upon, venerate 9 adoration, reverence 10 exaltation, veneration 11 devotionals

worshipful 5 pious 6 devout 8 reverent

worshiping 7 adoring 8 exalting 9 adoration, adulation, adulating, idolizing, reverence 10 exaltation, glorifying, magnifying, venerating, veneration 11 idolization 13 glorification, magnification

worst 3 bad 4 beat, best, rout 5 floor, outdo 6 defeat, lowest, outwit 7 conquer, poorest, triumph 8 inferior, overcome, vanquish 9 discomfit 10 overmaster, unpleasant

worth 3 use 4 cost, good 5 merit, price, value 6 assets, estate, wealth 7 benefit, effects, utility 8 holdings 9 appraisal, resources, valuation 10 importance, usefulness 11 consequence, possessions

worth having 4 good 9 desirable

Worthing, Jack
    character in: 27 The Importance of Being Earnest
    author: 5 Wilde

worthless 6 futile, paltry 7 trivial, useless 8 bootless, piddling, unusable 9 fruitless, meritless, pointless 10 unavailing 11 ineffectual, undeserving, unimportant 12 meretricious, unproductive 13 insignificant 14 good-for-nothing

worthless objects 4 junk 5 trash 7 garbage, rubbish 8 discards 11 odds and ends

worthwhile 4 good 6 usable, useful 8 valuable 9 rewarding 10 beneficial, profitable

worthy 3 fit, VIP 4 good, name 5 moral, noble 6 bigwig, decent, honest, leader, proper 7 big shot, ethical, fitting, notable, upright 8 big wheel, great man, immortal, laudable, luminary, official, reliable, suitable, virtuous 9 admirable, befitting, deserving, dignitary, estimable, excellent, honorable, personage, reputable 10 creditable 11 appropriate, commendable, meritorious, respectable

worthy of imitation 5 model 9 emulative, exemplary

Wotan
    origin: 8 Germanic
    chief of: 4 gods
    corresponds to: 4 Odin 5 Othin

Wouk, Herman
    author of: 13 The Winds of War 14 The Caine Mutiny 17 War and Remembrance 19 Marjorie Morningstar
    character: 12 Captain Queeg

wound 3 cut 4 gash, harm, hurt, pain, slit, tear 5 slash, sting 6 bruise, damage, grieve, injure, injury, lesion, offend, pierce, trauma 7 anguish, mortify, torment 8 distress, lacerate, vexation 9 contusion 10 affliction, irritation, laceration 11 provocation

wounded 3 cut 4 hurt 6 mauled 7 damaged, injured, pierced, stabbed 8 impaired, ruptured, stricken 11 traumatized

wrack 4 kelp, ruin 5 ruins, trash 6 clouds, refuse 7 de stroy, seaweed, torment 8 downfall, eelgrass, wreckage 9 cloud rack 11 destruction, storm clouds

wraith 5 ghost, shade, spook 6 spirit 7 phantom, specter 8 phantasm 10 apparition 15 materialization
    Irish: 7 banshee
    German: 12 doppelganger
    French: 8 revenant

wrangle 4 tiff 5 argue, brawl 6 bicker 7 dispute, quarrel 8 squabble

wrangling 6 strife 7 arguing, discord 8 clashing, friction 9 bickering 10 contention 11 quarrelling

wrap 4 bind, cape, coat, fold, gird, hide, mask, veil, wind 5 cloak, cover, scarf, shawl, stole 6 bundle, clothe, encase, enfold, girdle, jacket, mantle, shroud, swathe 7 conceal, en close, envelop, sweater 8 surround

wrapper, wrapping paper 4 case 6 casing, jacket, sheath 8 covering, envelope, slipcase 9 container

wrapping 6 caping, hiding 7 veiling 8 cerement, bundling, swathing 9 embracing, packaging, shrouding 10 engrossing, enswathing, enveloping 11 enshrouding, surrounding

wrap up 3 end 4 pack 6 finish, wind up 7 engross, envelop, involve, package 8 bundle up, complete, conclude 9 polish off 11 dress warmly

wrath 3 ire 4 bile, fury, gall, rage 5 anger 6 animus, choler, rancor, spleen 8 vexation 9 animosity, hostility 10 irritation, resentment 11 displeasure, indignation 13 irritableness

wrathful 3 mad 5 angry, irate 6 bitter, raging 7 furious 8 incensed, virulent

wreak 4 vent, work 5 visit 7 execute, indulge, inflict, unleash

wreak vengeance 6 avenge 7 get even, revenge 9 retaliate

wreath 5 crown 6 diadem, laurel 7 chaplet, coronet, festoon, garland
    Hawaiian: 3 lei

wreathe 4 bend, coil, wind 5 curve, twist 7 entwine, envelop 8 encircle 10 intertwine, interweave

wreck 3 end 4 mess, raze, ruin 5 break, crash, death, level, ruins, smash, total, up set 6 finish, ravage, wretch 7 breakup, crack-up, destroy, shatter, undoing 8 demolish, derelict 9 devastate, over throw 10 disruption 11 destruction, devastation, dissolution 12 annihilation

wreckage 4 ruin 5 ruins 6 jet sam 7 flotsam, remains 8 shambles 11 destruction

Wren, P C
    author of: 9 Beau Geste

wrench 3 rip 4 jerk, pull, tear, warp 5 force, twist, wrest, wring 6 sprain, strain 7 distort, pervert 12 misrepresent
    type: 6 monkey, socket 7 spanner

wrest 3 get, rip 4 earn, gain, grab, jerk, make, pull, take, tear 5 force, glean, twist, wring 6 attain, obtain, secure, wrench 7 achieve, extract, squeeze

wrestle 4 toil 5 labor 6 battle, strive, tussle 7 contend, grapple, scuffle 8 struggle 10 struggling

wrestling
    athlete: 8 Dan Gable

wretch 3 cur, pig, rat 4 hobo, waif, worm 5 knave, louse, rogue, swine, tramp 6 misfit, rascal, rotter, varlet 7 castoff, outcast, stinker, villain 8 derelict, scalawag, sufferer, vagabond 9 scoundrel 10 blackguard 11 unfortunate

wretched 3 low 4 base, mean, vile 5 awful, lousy, sorry 6 abject, gloomy, rotten, shabby, sleazy 7 crushed, doleful, forlorn, hapless, pitiful, scruffy, unhappy, worried 8 dejected, downcast, dreadful, hopeless, inferior, pathetic, pitiable, terrible 9 cheerless, depressed, miserable, nig gardly, sorrowful, woebegone, worthless 10 abominable, despairing, despicable, despondent, melancholy 11 crestfallen, unfortunate 12 contemptible, disconsolate, disheartened, inconsolable 13 brokenhearted

wretchedness 4 pain 6 misery, sorrow 7 despair, torment, trouble 8 distress, hardship 9 adversity 10 affliction, melancholy, misfortune 11 un happiness 12 hopelessness

wriggle 5 twist 6 squirm, wangle, writhe 7 meander

Wright, Archibald Lee
   real name of: 11 Archie Moore

Wright, Frank Lloyd
   architect of: 8 Taliesin (Spring Green WI) 10 Robie House (Chicago) 11 Martin House (Buffalo NY), Unity Church (Oak Park IL) 12 Fallingwater (Kaufmann House Bear Run PA), Taliesin West (near Phoenix AZ) 13 Imperial Hotel (To kyo) 16 Guggenheim Museum (NYC) 22 Marin County Civic Center (CA) 35 Larkin Company Administration Building (Buffalo NY) 45 S C Johnson and Son Wax Company Administration Center (Racine WI)
   style: 6 Modern 7 Organic, Prairie

Wright, Orville and Wilbur
   invented: 8 airplane
   first plane: 6 Flyer I 9 Kitty Hawk

Wright, Richard
   author of: 8 Black Boy 9 Native Son 17 Uncle Tom's Children

wring 4 hurt, pain, rend, stab 5 choke, force, press, twist, wrest 6 coerce, grieve, pierce, sadden, wrench 7 agonize, extract, squeeze, torture 8 compress, distress

wrinkle 4 fold, idea 5 crimp, fancy, pleat, slant, trick 6 crease, device, furrow, gather, notion, pucker, rimple, rumple 7 crumple, gimmick 9 crow's-feet, viewpoint 11 corrugation

wrinkled 3 old 4 aged 5 lined 6 folded, ridged, rucked, rugate, rugose, rugous, seamed 7 creased, crimped, rimpled, rippled, ruckled, rumpled 8 crimpled, furrowed, puckered 9 shriveled

writ 10 court order 11 sealed order 14 mandatory order

write 3 pen 4 copy, show 5 draft 6 author, draw up, record, scrawl 7 compose, dash off, jot down, make out, produce, set down, turn out 8 inscribe, scribble 10 transcribe

write down 3 jot 4 note, post 5 enter 6 record

write in full 5 add to 6 expand, extend, pad out 7 amplify, augment, stretch 9 expatiate

write out 6 expand, extend 7 amplify, enlarge, stretch 8 lengthen

writer 4 hack, poet 6 author, critic, penman, scribe 7 copy ist 8 essayist, novelist, reporter, reviewer, scrawler 9 columnist, dramatist, scribbler 10 journalist, librettist, playwright, songwriter 11 penny-a-liner 12 calligrapher, newspaperman 13 correspondent 14 newspaperwoman
   French: 11 litterateur

write to 7 address 8 send word 9 drop a line, send a card, send a note 10 correspond 11 send a letter

write-up 4 item 5 piece, story 7 article

write up 5 cover 6 report

writhe 4 jerk 5 flail 6 squirm, thrash, thresh, wiggle 7 contort, wriggle

writing 4 book, play, poem, tome, work 5 diary, essay, novel, print, story 6 column, letter, report, script, volume 7 article, copying, journal, penning 8 critique, document, drafting, libretto, longhand 9 authoring, composing, editorial, recording 10 inscribing, manuscript, penmanship 11 calligraphy, composition, publication 12 transcribing
   Latin: 4 opus

writings
   Hebrew: 7 Ketubim

written agreement 6 treaty 7 compact 8 contract

written law
   Latin: 10 lex scripta

written-out form 9 extension 12 augmentation 13 amplification

wrong 3 bad, sin 4 awry, bilk, evil, harm, hurt, ruin, vice 5 abuse, amiss, cheat, crime, false, inapt, kaput, unfit 6 faulty, fleece, injure, injury, ruined, sinful, unfair, unjust, untrue, wicked 7 crooked, defraud, illegal, illicit, immoral, inexact, inverse, misdeed, offense, reverse, swindle, unhappy, unsound 8 criminal, dishonor, evil deed, ill-treat, immodest, improper, iniquity, maltreat, mistaken, mistreat, opposite, trespass, unlawful, unseemly, villain 9 dishonest, erroneous, felonious, illogical, incorrect, injustice, unethical, unfitting 10 dishonesty, fallacious, illegality, immorality, inaccurate, indecorous, indelicate, iniquitous, malapropos, mistakenly, sinfulness, unbecoming, unfairness, unsuitable, wickedness, wrongdoing 11 blameworthy, erroneously, incongruous, incorrectly, inexcusable, unbefitting, undesirable, unwarranted 12 dishonorable, inaccurately, infelicitous, unlawfulness 13 inappropriate, reprehensible, transgression, unjustifiable 15 unrighteousness

wrongdoer 5 crook, felon, knave, rogue 6 rascal, sinner 7 culprit, misdoer, villain 8 evildoer, offender 9 miscreant, scoundrel 10 blackguard, delinquent, lawbreaker, malefactor, trespasser 11 perpetrator 12 transgressor

wrongdoing 3 sin 4 evil, vice 5 crime 8 misdeeds 10 misconduct 11 delinquency, malfeasance, misbehavior

wrongful 3 bad 6 unfair, unjust 7 illegal 8 criminal, unlawful 10 iniquitous, inequitable 12 illegitimate
act: 4 tort
dispossession: 6 ouster

wrongheaded 3 wry 8 perverse, stubborn 9 misguided

wrong side out 9 backwards 10 topsy-turvy

wrought 4 made 6 beaten, formed, worked 7 crafted 8 hammered 9 fashioned 11 constructed, handcrafted

wrought-up 7 excited 8 agitated 9 emotional 10 hysterical

wry 3 dry 5 askew, droll 6 bitter, ironic, warped 7 amusing, caustic, crooked, cynical, satiric, twisted 8 perverse, sardonic 9 contorted, distorted, sarcastic

Wunderkind 11 wonder child 12 child prodigy

Wurster, William
architect of: 13 Cowell College (UC Berkeley) 17 Ghirardelli Square (San Francisco CA)

Wuthering Heights
character: 9 Ellen Dean 10 Heathcliff, Mr Lockwood 11 Edgar Linton 14 Isabella Linton 15 Catherine Linton, Frances Earnshaw, Hareton Earnshaw, Hindley Earnshaw 16 Linton Heathcliff 17 Catherine Earnshaw
director: 12 William Wyler
author: 11 Emily Bronte
cast: 10 David Niven 11 Donald Crisp, Flora Robson, Leo G Carroll, Merle Oberon (Cathy) 15 Laurence Olivier (Heathcliff) 19 Geraldine Fitzgerald

Wyatt, James
architect of: 8 Pantheon (London) 9 Lee Priory (Kent) 10 Stoke Poges (Buckinghamshire) 13 Fonthill Abbey (Wiltshire) 14 Dodington House Gloucestershire) 15 Heveningham Hall (Suffolk) 16 Sandleford Priory (Berkshire)
style: 13 Gothic Revival

Wyatt, Jane
born: 9 Campgaw NJ
roles: 9 Boomerang 11 Lost Horizon 15 Father Knows Best 17 Great Expectations 19 Gentleman's Agreement 21 None But the Lonely Heart

Wyatt Earp, The Life and Legend of
character: 10 Morgan Earp, Virgil Earp 11 Ben Thompson, Doc Holliday 12 Bat Masterson, Bill Thompson 13 Old Man Clanton
cast: 9 Hal Baylor 10 Denver Pyle, Dirk London, Hugh O'Brien 12 John Anderson 13 Douglas Fowley 14 Trevor Bardette 20 Mason Alan Dinehart III
setting: 8 OK Corral 9 Dodge City, Ellsworth, Tombstone
Wyatt's pistols: 15 Buntline Special

Wyeth, Andrew Newell
born: 2 PA 10 Chadds Ford
father: 7 N C Wyeth
artwork: 9 Grape Wine, River Cove 12 Nick and Jamie 14 Christina Olson, Distant Thunder 15 Christina's World 22 Winter Nineteen Forty-six

Wyler, William
director of: 6 Ben Hur (Oscar) 7 Jezebel 9 Dodsworth, Funny Girl, The Letter 10 Mrs Miniver (Oscar), The Heiress, These Three 12 Roman Holiday 14 The Little Foxes 15 Counsellor-at-Law 15 Wuthering Heights 18 Friendly Persuasion 22 The Best Years of Our Lives (Oscar)

Wylie, Philip
author of: 13 Opus Twenty-one 19 A Generation of Vipers

Wyman, Jane
real name: 14 Sarah Jane Fulks
born: 10 St Joseph MO
husband: 12 Ronald Reagan
daughter: 13 Maureen Reagan
son: 13 Michael Reagan
roles: 5 So Big 9 Pollyanna 11 Falcon Crest, The Blue Veil, The Yearling 13 Johnny Belinda (Oscar) 14 Angela Channing, The Lost Weekend 17 The Glass Menagerie 20 Magnificent Obsession

Wyndham, John
real name: 16 John Beynon Harris
author of: 14 The Kraken Wakes 15 Consider Her Ways 17 The Midwich Cuckoos, Trouble with Lichen 19 The Day of the Triffids

Wyoming
abbreviation: 2 WY 3 Wyo
nickname: 8 Equality
capital: 8 Cheyenne
largest city: 6 Casper
others: 4 Cody, Lusk 7 Bighorn, Buffalo, Laramie, Rawlins, Worland 8 Gillette, Greybull, Kemmerer, Riverton, Sheridan, Sundance 11 Rock Springs
feature:
center: 11 Buffalo Bill
dam: 8 Shoshone
fort: 7 Laramie
historical preserve: 11 Fort Bridger
national grassland: 11 Tunder Basin
national monument: 11 Devil's Tower, Fossil Butte
national park: 10 Grand Teton 11 Yellowstone
reservoir: 12 Flaming Gorge
tribe: 4 Crow 5 Kiowa, Sioux 7 Arapaho, Bannock 8 Cheyenne
people: 11 Buffalo Bill 14 Jackson Pollock 16 Nellie Tayloe Ross 18 Francis Emroy Warren
explorer: 6 Colter, Stuart 7 Bridger 10 Bonneville
lake: 7 Jackson 11 Yellowstone
land rank: 5 ninth
mountain: 3 Elk 5 Cloud, Moran 6 Absaro, Hoback, Tetons 7 Bighorn, Fre-

mont, Laramie, Rockies 8 Atlantic,
Sheridan 9 Wind River 10 Black Hills 11
Rattlesnake
highest point: 11 Gannett Peak
physical feature: 11 Jackson Hole
basin: 7 Wyoming
cave: 8 Shoshone
hot springs: 11 Thermopolis
plains: 5 Great
river: 4 Bear, Wind 5 Green, Snake 6
Platte, Powder, Tongue 7 Bighorn 8
Cheyenne, Shoshone 10 Sweetwater 11
Yellowstone 12 Belle Fourche
state admission: 11 forty-fourth
state bird: 17 western meadowlark
state flower: 10 painted cup 16 Indian
paintbrush
state motto: 11 Equal Rights
state song: 7 Wyoming
state tree: 10 cottonwood

Wyss, Johann Rudolf
    author of: 22 The Swiss Family Robin-
    son
    adaptation of: 14 Robinson Crusoe

X

Xanthippe, Xantippe 3 hag 4 fury 5 scold,
shrew, vixen 6 dragon, virago 7 scolder 8
spitfire 9 termagant
   husband: 8 Socrates
Xanthus and Balius
   horses of: 8 Achilles
   trait: 8 immortal
Xenia
   epithet of: 6 Athena
   means: 10 hospitable
Xenoclea
   form: 9 priestess
xenon
   chemical symbol: 2 Xe
xenophobia
   fear of: 9 strangers
Xerxes *see* 9 Ahasuerus
x-ray 9 radiogram 10 radiograph 13 roent-
genogram 14 roentgenograph
X-ray tube
   invented by: 8 Coolidge
Xuthus
   father: 6 Hellen
   mother: 6 Orscis
   wife: 6 Creusa
   son: 3 Ion 7 Achaeus

Y

yacht 4 boat, race, sail, ship, yawl 5 ketch, sloop 6 cruise, cutter 7 catboat 8 schooner
  race: 11 America's Cup
yachting
  athlete: 9 Ted Turner 11 Lowell North
yahoo 4 lout 5 brute, yokel 7 lowbrow 9 barbarian, ignoramus, vulgarian
Yahoos
  fictional people in: 16 Gulliver's Travels
  author: 5 Swift
Yahweh 3 God 4 Lord 5 Jahve, Jahwe, Yahve 6 Author, I am I am, Jahveh 7 Creator, Eternal, Jehovah 8 Absolute, Almighty, Infinite
  component: 2 he 3 yod, vav
  pronunciation: 6 Adonai, Elohim 9 forbidden
  transliteration: 4 YHVH
Yale, Linus, Jr
  invented: 12 cylinder lock 27 dial-operated combination lock
yam 9 Dioscorea 14 Ipomoea batatas
  varieties: 4 wild 5 Negro, water, white 6 Attoto, potato, yellow 7 Chinese 11 sweet potato
Yamasaki, Minoru
  architect of: 14 St Louis Airport (MO) 16 World Trade Center (NYC) 21 Woodrow Wilson Building (Princeton NJ)
yammer 3 cry 4 carp, harp, howl, wail, yell 5 whine 7 grumble, whimper 8 complain
yank 3 tug 4 jerk, pull 5 pluck, wrest 6 snatch, wrench 7 draw out, extract, pull out
Yankee, Yank 2 GI 5 teddy 6 gringo 8 American, doughboy 10 Northerner
  Spanish: 6 yanqui
Yankee Doodle Dandy
  director: 13 Michael Curtiz
  cast: 10 Joan Leslie 11 James Cagney (George M Cohan) 12 Irene Manning, Walter Huston
  Oscar for: 5 actor (Cagney)
yanqui 6 Yankee 9 US citizen
Yaounde
  capital of: 8 Cameroon
yap 3 yip 4 blab, gush, rave, talk, yawp, yelp 5 scold 6 babble, gabble, gossip, jabber, rave on, tattle 7 blather, chatter, lecture, palaver, prattle 8 complain, converse
Yaqui
  language family: 6 Cahita
  location: 6 Mexico, Sonora 7 Arizona
yard 4 lawn 5 close, court 6 garden 7 confine, grounds, pasture 8 compound 9 enclosure, three feet
  abbreviation: 2 yd

yardbird 3 con 5 felon 7 convict 8 prisoner
yard goods 5 cloth 6 fabric 8 material, textiles
Yard of Sun
  author: 14 Christopher Fry
yardstick 4 rule 7 measure 8 standard 9 criterion
Yaren District
  capital of: 5 Nauru
yarn 4 tale 5 story 7 account 8 anecdote 9 adventure, narrative 10 experience
Yastrzemski, Carl
  nickname: 3 Yaz
  sport: 8 baseball
  team: 12 Boston Red Sox
Yates, Peter
  director of: 7 Bullitt 12 Breaking Away
yawn 3 gap 4 bore, gape 5 chasm 8 open wide, oscitate
yawp 4 roar, yelp 5 noise 6 clamor, squawk, yammer
Yaz
  nickname of: 15 Carl Yastrzemski
Yazoo
  author: 12 Willie Morris
year, years 3 age, era 4 time 5 cycle, epoch 6 period
  abbreviation: 2 yr
Yearling, The
  director: 13 Clarence Brown
  author: 22 Marjorie Kinnan Rawlings
  cast: 9 Jane Wyman 10 Chill Wills 11 Gregory Peck 14 Claude Jarman Jr
  character: 9 Ora Baxter 10 Jody Baxter 11 Oliver Hutto, Penny Baxter 12 Grandma Hutto 14 Twink Weatherby 19 Fodder-Wing Forrester
Year of Living Dangerously, The
  director: 9 Peter Weir
  cast: 9 Linda Hunt (Billy Kwan), Mel Gibson 15 Sigourney Weaver
  setting: 7 Jakarta
  Oscar for: 17 supporting actress (Hunt)
year of wonders
  Latin: 14 annus mirabilis
yearn 4 ache, long, pine, sigh, want, wish 5 crave 6 hanker, hunger, thirst 8 languish
yearning 3 yen 4 ache, want, wish 5 fancy 6 desire, hunger, thirst 7 craving, longing, passion 9 hankering 10 aspiration 11 inclination
Yeats, William Butler
  author of: 7 A Vision 8 The Tower 9 Last Poems 14 Leda and the Swan 15 The Winding Stair 18 Sailing to Byzantium 19 Among School Children, The Wild Swans at Coole 21 Easter Nineteen Sixteen 22

The Lake Isle of Innisfree **29** An Irish Airman Foresees His Death

yegg 6 bomber **9** cracksman **11** safecracker

yell 3 boo, cry **4** bawl, hoot, howl, roar, yowl **5** cheer, hollo, shout, whoop **6** bellow, clamor, cry out, holler, hurrah, huzzah, outcry, scream, shriek, squall, squeal **7** screech

yellow 4 gold **5** blond, lemon, ocher **6** afraid, canary, craven, flaxen **7** chicken, fearful, saffron **8** cowardly, timorous **10** frightened **12** apprehensive, fainthearted **13** pusillanimous **14** chickenhearted

yellow-belly 6 coward **7** caitiff, chicken, dastard **8** poltroon

Yellowhammer State
nickname of: **7** Alabama

yellowish 4 buff **5** blond, cream **6** blonde, creamy, flaxen

Yellow Kid, The
creator: **10** R F Outcault
trademark: **10** nightshirt
place: **5** slums **11** Hogan's Alley
coined term: **16** yellow journalism
first: **10** comic strip

yelp 3 yap, yip **4** bark, howl **5** shout **6** clamor, holler, scream, shriek, squeal **7** screech

Yemen, North
other name: **4** Sana
capital/largest city: **4** Sana **5** Sanaa
others: **4** Moka, Taiz **5** Dahhi, Damar, Jibla, Mocha, Mukha, Taizz, Umram **7** Hodeida, Hudayda
monetary unit: **4** fils, rial **5** riyal
island: **5** Zugar **6** Hanish
highest point: **6** Shuayb
river: **5** Abrad, Zabid **6** al-Jawf, Surdud
sea: **3** Red
physical feature:
desert: **10** Rub al Khali
gulf: **4** Aden
lowlands: **6** Tihama
peninsula: **7** Arabian
strait: **11** Bab el Mandeb
people: **4** Arab **5** Zaidi **6** Shafai, Yemeni **8** Yemenite
leader: **16** Ali Abdallah Saleh **19** Abd al-Aziz Abd al-Ghani
language: **6** Arabic
religion: **5** Islam
place:
ruins: **5** Marib
feature:
dagger: **7** jambiya
king: **4** imam
kingdom: **4** Saba **5** Sheba **11** Arabia Felix
tree: **3** fig **5** carob, mango, myrrh
food:
coffee: **5** mocha

Yemen, South
capital: **4** Aden **14** Madinat al-Shaab
largest city: **4** Aden
others: **5** Ahwar, Shihr, Tarim **6** Balhaf, Damqut, Seiyun, Shabwa, Shibam, Zamakh **7** Mukalla
monetary unit: **4** fils **5** dinar
island: **5** Perim **7** Kamaran, Socotra
mountain: **7** Djehaff
highest point: **6** Thamir
river: **4** Bana **6** Tibban **7** Masilah **9** Hadramaut
sea: **6** Indian **7** Arabian
physical feature:
desert: **10** Rub al Khali **12** Empty Quarter
gulf: **4** Aden
peninsula: **7** Arabian
valley: **9** Hadramawt
people: **4** Arab
language: **6** Arabic
religion: **5** Islam
feature:
animal: **4** ibex, oryx
clothing: **4** futa

yen 4 ache, long, pine, sigh, want, wish **5** crave, fancy, yearn **6** aching, desire, hanker, hunger, relish, thirst **7** craving, longing, passion **8** appetite, languish, yearning **9** hankering **10** aspiration **11** inclination

yenta 3 hen **6** gossip **8** busybody **12** blabbermouth

Yentl
director: **15** Barbra Streisand
based on story by: **19** Isaac Bashevis Singer
cast: **13** Mandy Patinkin **15** Barbra Streisand

Yeobright, Thomasin and Clym
characters in: **17** Return of the Native
author: **5** Hardy

yeoman 4 chap, exon **5** churl, clerk, swain **6** farmer, fellow **7** granger, plowman, servant **8** graycoat, retainer **9** beefeater **10** freeholder **12** petty officer

Yerby, Frank
author of: **8** Fair Oaks **10** Health Card **11** Griffin's Way **12** Pride's Castle **16** The Foxes of Harrow **21** Hail the Conquering Hero

yes 3 aye, yea **4** amen, okay, true **5** truly **6** assent, indeed, it is so, just so, really, so be it, surely, verily **7** consent, exactly, granted, no doubt **8** ap proval, of course, to be sure **9** agreement, assuredly, certainly, doubtless, precisely **10** acceptance, positively **11** affirmation, undoubtedly **12** acquiescence, emphatically **13** affirmatively, authorization
French: **3** oui
German: **2** ja
Spanish: **2** si

yesterday 7 the past **10** bygone days, days of yore, olden times, time gone by **11** former times **13** the recent past **14** the good old days **17** the day before today **22** on the day preceding today

yet 3 but **4** also, even, then, up to **5** again, still, while, until **6** no less, though **7** besides, earlier, even now, further, however, thus far **8** although, hitherto, moreover **9**

presently 10 eventually, ultimately 12 nevertheless 15 notwithstanding

yew 5 Taxus
varieties: 4 plum 5 Irish 6 golden 7 Chinese, California, Florida, Western 8 American, Japanese, Southern 11 Chinese plum, Plum-fruited 12 Japanese plum, Prince Albert 14 Harrington plum

Yggdrasil
also: 9 Iggdrasil
origin: 12 Scandinavian
kind of tree: 12 evergreen ash
roots: 5 three
binds: 6 Asgard 7 Midgard 8 Niflheim 10 Mithgarthr

yield 3 pay, sag 4 bear, crop, earn, gain, give 5 beget, break, burst, defer, droop, forgo, grant, spawn, split, waive 6 accede, cave in, give in, give up, kotow, render, return, submit, supply 7 bow down, concede, forbear, furnish, give way, harvest, pay ment, premium, produce, product, provide, revenue, succumb, truckle 8 collapse, cry uncle, earnings, generate, interest, proceeds, renounce 9 acquiesce, gleanings, procreate, surrender 10 capitulate, relinquish

yielding 3 lax 4 soft 6 ceding, spongy 7 sagging 8 flexible, obedient 9 compliant 11 complaisant 13 accommodating

Yigdal 22 Jewish liturgical prayer
literally: 12 becomes great

Yizkor 33 Jewish service to commemorate the dead
literally: 9 be mindful

Ymir
origin: 12 Scandinavian
progenitor of: 6 giants
earth made from: 5 flesh
water made from: 5 blood
heavens made from: 5 skull

yogi 5 Hindu 6 mystic 7 ascetic

Yogi Bear
creator: 12 Hanna-Barbera
character: 6 BooBoo
setting: 14 Jellystone Park

yoke 3 tax 4 bond, join, link, load, pair, span, team 5 brace, clasp, hitch, trial, unite 6 at tach, burden, collar, couple, fasten, strain, weight 7 bondage, coupler, harness, serfdom, slavery 8 distress, pressure, troubles 9 servitude, thralldom, vassalage 10 oppression 11 enslavement, tribulation

yokel 4 clod, hick, rube 7 bumpkin, hayseed, peasant, plowboy 10 clodhopper, provincial

yolk 6 yellow

yonder 3 yon 5 there 6 far-off 7 faraway, farther, thither

Yorick
skull in: 6 Hamlet
author: 11 Shakespeare

Yorick, Mr
character in: 14 Tristram Shandy
author: 6 Sterne

York, Michael
born: 6 Fulmer 7 England
roles: 6 Tybalt 7 Cabaret 11 Lost Horizon 14 Four Musketeers, Romeo and Juliet, The Forsyte Saga 15 Three Musketeers 19 The Island of Dr Moreau 24 The Last Remake of Beau Geste

York, Susannah
real name: 23 Susannah Yolande Fletcher
born: 6 London 7 England
roles: 5 Freud 6 Images 8 Jane Eyre, Tom Jones 12 The Awakening
author of: 18 In Search of Unicorns

Yossarian
character in: 14 Catch-Twenty-two
author: 6 Heller

You Asked for It
host: 8 Art Baker 9 Jack Smith

You Bet Your Life
host: 11 Groucho Marx
announcer: 14 George Fenneman

You Can't Go Home Again
author: 11 Thomas Wolfe
character: 10 Esther Jack 11 Lloyd McHarg 12 George Webber 13 Else von Kohler 14 Foxhall Edwards

You Can't Take It With You
author: 8 Moss Hart 14 George S Kaufman
director: 10 Frank Capra
cast: 10 Jean Arthur, Mischa Auer 12 Edward Arnold, James Stewart 15 Lionel Barrymore
Oscar for: 7 picture 8 director

young 3 cub, pup 4 baby, kids 5 child, issue, minor, whelp 6 boyish, callow, junior, kitten, youths 7 budding, girlish, growing, progeny, puerile, teenage 8 childish, children, immature, juvenile, underage, youthful 9 beardless, infantile, juveniles, offspring, teenagers 10 adolescent, descendant, sophomoric, youngsters 11 adolescents, undeveloped 13 inexperienced
god of: 7 Angus Og
goddess of: 4 Hebe

Young, Chic
creator/artist of: 7 Blondie

Young, Denton True
nickname: 2 Cy 7 Cyclone
sport: 8 baseball
position: 7 pitcher
team: 12 Boston Braves, Boston Red Sox 16 Cleveland Indians, St Louis Cardinals

Young, Loretta
real name: 13 Gretchen Young
husband: 12 Grant Withers
roles: 13 Cause for Alarm 14 The Bishop's Wife 15 Come to the Stable 18 The Farmer's Daughter (Oscar) 20 Rachel and the Stranger

Young, Robert
born: 9 Chicago IL
roles: 10 Relentless 11 H M Pulham Esq

13 Marcus Welby M D **15** Father Knows Best **16** Strange Interlude

Young Adventure
  author: **19** Stephen Vincent Benet
Young Frankenstein
  director: **9** Mel Brooks
  cast: **8** Teri Garr **10** Gene Wilder, Peter Boyle **11** Gene Hackman **12** Madeline Kahn, Marty Feldman **14** Cloris Leachman
  score: **10** John Morris
young girl
  French: **10** jeune fille
young lady
  German: **8** fraulein
Young Lonigan
  author: **13** James T Farrell
Young Manhood of Studs Lonigan
  author: **13** James T Farrell
youngster 3 boy, kid, tot **4** baby, girl **5** child, minor, youth **7** progeny **8** juvenile, teenager **9** fledgling, offspring **10** adolescent
young Turks 6 rebels **8** radicals, upstarts **9** activists **10** insurgents **15** revolutionaries
young woman
  French: **10** demoiselle
you're welcome
  German: **5** bitte
Your Show of Shows
  regular: **9** Bill Hayes, Jerry Ross, Sid Caesar **10** Carl Reiner **11** Imogene Coca **12** Howard Morris, Nellie Fisher **13** James Starbuck, Robert Merrill **16** Marguerite Piazza
youth 3 boy, kid, lad **4** kids **5** bloom, child, minor, prime, teens **6** heyday **7** boyhood **8** children, girlhood, juvenile, minority, teenager **9** childhood, fledgling, juveniles, schoolboy, stripling, teenagers, youngster **10** adolescent, pubescence, youngsters **11** adolescence, adolescents
youthful 5 fresh, young **6** boyish, callow **7** girlish, puerile, teenage **8** childish, immature, juvenile **10** adolescent, sophomoric **12** enthusiastic, light hearted **13** inexperienced
yowl 3 bay, cry **4** bawl, roar, wail, yelp **5** shout, whine **6** bellow, holler, scream, shriek, squeal **7** screech **9** caterwaul
yucca
  varieties: **4** blue **6** banana **9** San Angelo, spineless **11** twisted-leaf
Yugoslavia
  other name: **8** Dalmatia **34** Kingdom of the Serbs Croats and Slovenes
  capital/largest city: **7** Beograd **8** Belgrade
  others: **3** Nis **4** Pola, Pula, Savo, Zara **5** Agram, Bosna, Budva, Fiume, Kotor, Pirot, Rieka, Rtanj, Senta, Split, Tuzla, Uskub, Zadar **6** Bitola, Bitolj, Ca Haro, Maglaj, Morava, Mostar, Osijek, Prilep, Ragusa, Rijeka, Skopje, Trogir, Visoko, Zagreb **7** Cetinje, Laibach, Maribor, Novisad, Skoplje, Spalato **8** Monastir, Pristina, Sarajevo, Subotica, Titograd **9**

Banja Luka, Dubrovnik, Ljubljana, Podgorica, Smederevo
  divisioin/former division: **6** Bosnia, Serbia **7** Croatia **8** Crna Gora, Slovenia **9** Macedonia, Vojvodina, Voyvodina **10** Montenegro **11** Hercegovina, Herzegovina **14** Kosovo-Metohija
  measure: **3** oka, rif **4** akov, ralo **5** donum, khvat, lanaz, plaze, stopa **6** motyka, ralico **9** danoranja
  monetary unit: **4** para **5** dinar
  weight: **3** oka **5** dramm, tovar, wagon **7** satlijk
  island: **3** Rab **4** Arbe, Brac, Cres, Hvar, Pago **5** Mljet, Solta, Susac, Susak **7** Korcula
  lake: **4** Bled **5** Ohrid **6** Prespa **7** Ochrida, Scutari
  mountain: **5** Karst **6** Balkan **7** Rhodope **8** Crna Gora, Durmitor **9** Sar-Pindus **10** Karawanken
  Alps: **6** Carnic, Julian **7** Dinaric **9** Slovenian **16** Northern Albanian
  highest point: **7** Triglav
  river: **3** Una **4** Drim, Drin, Ibar, Krka, Kupa, Sava, Tisa **5** Anube, Bosna, Cazma, Drava, Drina, Raska, Tamis, Timok, Tisza, Vrbas **6** Danube, Morava, Vardar, Velika **7** Neretva **9** Vojvodina
  sea: **8** Adriatic
  physical feature:
  bay: **5** Kotor
  cave: **8** Postojna
  channel: **7** Narento
  gulf: **5** Kotor **7** Kvarner, Trieste
  hot springs: **16** Krapinske Toplice
  peninsula: **6** Balkan **7** Istrian
  people: **4** Serb, Slav **5** Croat **7** Slovene **8** Albanian **10** Macedonian **11** Montenegrin
  author: **6** Andric, Djilas, Krleza **7** Dedijer
  leader: **4** Tito **5** Dusan, Pasic **6** Djilas **7** Nemanja **9** Milosevic, Obrenovic **13** Mikhailovitch
  ruler: **5** Peter **9** Hapsburgs **12** Ottoman Turks
  sculptor: **9** Mestrovic
  language: **7** Bosnian, Slovene **8** Albanian, Croatian **9** Hungarian, Slovenian **10** Macedonian **11** Montenegrin **13** Herzegovinian, Serbo-Croatian
  alphabet: **5** Latin **8** Cyrillic
  religion: **5** Islam **13** Roman Catholic **15** Eastern Orthodox, Serbian Orthodox
  place:
  amphitheater: **4** Pula
  bridge: **9** Stari Most
  fortress: **10** Kalemedgan
  monastery: **8** Sopocani
  mosque: **6** Begova **15** Bajrakli Dzamija
  ruins: **14** Hadrian's Palace
  square: **8** Republic
  feature:
  coffee house: **7** kafanas
  fields: **5** polje
  military governor: **7** vojvodi
  musical instrument: **5** gusla
  poems: **5** pesme

slippers: 6 opanki
food:
dessert: 4 pita
drink: 5 rakia 6 rakija 7 maraska 9 slivovitz 10 sljivovice 13 Turkish coffee
meat: 7 shaslik 9 cevapcici 10 culbastija
soup: 6 corbas
Yult *see* 6 Eskimo
Yukon Territory
  border: 6 Alaska 15 British Columbia,
  Selwyn Mountains 18 Mackenzie Mountains
  capital: 10 Whitehorse
  country: 6 Canada
  event: 8 gold rush (1897)
  Indian: 4 Dene 6 Eskimo 7 Kutchin 8
  Loucheux 9 Athabasca
  lake: 6 Kluane 9 Great Bear
  mineral: 4 gold 6 silver
  mountain: 3 Joy 5 Logan 6 Harper 7
  Kennedy 8 Campbell
  region: 8 Klondike
  river: 5 Pelly 9 Porcupine
  sea: 8 Beaufort
  town: 4 Elsa, Faro, Mayo, Snag 5 Rocky
  6 Dawson 8 Franklin, Wernecke 9
  Mackenzie
yule 4 Noel 9 Christmas
Yule, Joe, Jr
  real name of: 12 Mickey Rooney
Yuman
  tribe: 6 Mohave, Mojave 8 Hualapai

Z

Zachariah
   father: 4 Babi, Elam 9 Barachias
   wife: 9 Elizabeth
   son: 3 Abi 14 John the Baptist
   succeeded: 8 Jeroboam
   visitor: 7 Gabriel
zaddik 14 virtuous person 15 righteous person

Zadkine, Ossip
   born: 6 Russia 8 Smolensk
   artwork: 4 Stag 6 Christ 7 Orpheus 9 Musicians 10 The Prophet 13 Woman with a Fan 14 Mother and Child 16 The Destroyed City

Zadok
   father: 5 Baana, Immer 6 Ahitub
   son: 7 Shallum
   daughter: 7 Jerusha
   served: 5 David
zaftig 5 buxom, plump 6 bosomy

Zagreus
   form: 5 child, deity
   father: 4 Zeus
   mother: 6 Semele 10 Persephone

Zaire
   other name: 5 Congo 12 Belgian Congo 13 Congo-Kinshasa 17 Congo-Leopoldville
   capital/largest city: 8 Kinshasa
   others: 4 Baya, Boma, Lebo 5 Aketi, Ilebo 6 Banana, Kamina, Kasaji, Kikwit, Matadi, Sandoa 7 Butembo, Kananga, Kolwezi 8 Bakwanga, Yangambi 9 Kisangani 10 Lubumbashi, Luluabourg, Mutshatsha 12 Port-Franc qui, Stanleyville 14 Elisabethville
   school: 5 Zaire 8 Lovanium
   division: 4 Kivu 5 Kasai, Shaba 7 Equator, Katanga 8 Oriental
   monetary unit: 5 zaire 6 makuta
   lake: 4 Kivu 5 Mweru, Tumba 6 Albert, Edward, Upemba 9 Mai-Ndombe 10 Tanganyika
   mountain: 7 Crystal, Mitumba, Virunga 9 Ruwenzori 10 Nyaragongo 18 Mountains of the Moon
   highest point: 10 Margherita
   river: 4 Ruki, Uele 5 Congo, Dengu, Ibina, Kasai, Lindi, Zaire 6 Likati, Lomami, Lukuga, Ubangi 7 Aruwimi, Lualaba, Lulonga
   sea: 8 Atlantic
   physical feature:
   falls: 4 Kivu 6 Tshopo 7 Stanley
   forest: 5 Ituri
   valley: 9 Great Rift
   people: 4 Kuba, Luba, Yaka 5 Bantu, Bashi, Bemba, Kongo, Lulue, Lunda,

Mongo, Pygmy 6 Azande, Baluba, Watusi 7 Bakongo, Nilotes, Tshokwe 8 European, Mangbetu, Sudanese
   explorer: 3 Cao 7 Stanley
   leader: 6 Mobutu (Sese Seko) 7 Lumumba, Tshombe 8 Kasavubu
   ruler: 7 Belgium, Leopold
   language: 5 Bantu 6 French 7 Chiluba, Kikongo, Lingala, Swahili 8 Sudanese, Tshiluba
   religion: 5 Islam 7 animism, Kimbang 10 Protestant 13 Roman Catholic
   place:
   dam: 4 Inga 9 Le Marinee 10 Del Commune
   national park: 6 Albert, Upemba 7 Garamba
   feature:
   animal: 5 hyena, okapi 7 giraffe, gorilla 10 rhinoceros
   fish: 11 electric eel

Zambia
   other name: 16 Northern Rhodesia
   capital/largest city: 6 Lusaka
   others: 4 Kafu 5 Choma, Isoka, Kabwe, Kitwe, Mansa, Mbala, Mongu, Mpika, Mumba, Ndola 6 Mwenda 7 Chipata, Luapula, Mankoya 8 Balovale, Chingola, Luanshya, Mazabuka, Mufulira, Mulobezi 11 Livingstone
   division: 7 Puapula 10 Copperbelt 11 Barotseland
   monetary unit: 5 ngwee 6 kwacha
   lake: 5 Mweru 6 Kariba 9 Bangweulu 10 Tanganyika
   mountain: 8 Muchinga
   highest point: 12 Mafinga Hills
   river: 5 Congo, Kafue 7 Luangwa, Luapula, Zambezi 8 Chambezi 9 Chambeshi
   physical feature:
   cave: 5 Nsalu 14 Chifabwa Stream
   falls: 7 Kalambo 8 Victoria
   gorge: 6 Kariba
   plateau: 7 Zambian
   swamp: 7 Lukanga 9 Bangweulu 12 Mweru Wantipa
   valley: 8 Chambezi 9 Great Rift
   people: 4 Lozi 5 Bantu, Bemba, Ngoni, Tonga
   developer: 6 Rhodes
   explorer: 11 Livingstone
   hero: 11 Chitimukulu
   leader: 6 Kaunda
   language: 4 Lozi 5 Bemba, Lunda, Tonga 6 Luvale, Nyanja 7 English 9 Afrikaans

religion: 5 Hindu, Islam 7 animism 10 Protestant 13 Roman Catholic

place:

botanical garden: 10 Munda Wanga

dam: 5 Kafue 6 Kariba

game reserve: 6 Valley

library: 20 Hammerskjold Memorial

museum: 11 Livingstone

national park: 5 Kafue, Sumbu 12 South Luangwa

feature:

canoe: 10 nalikwanda

king: 7 litunga

king's aide: 5 sungu, twite 8 inabanza

taxi: 6 zamcab

zany 3 nut 4 wild 5 balmy, batty, booby, buffo, clown, comic, crazy, cutup, daffy, dizzy, goofy, inane, nutty, silly, wacky 6 jester, nitwit, screwy, weirdo 7 buffoon, half-wit, lunatic 8 bonehead, clownish, imbecile, lunkhead, numskull 9 blockhead, eccentric, harlequin, ludicrous, pantaloon, simpleton, slapstick 10 nincompoop, noodlehead, outlandish 11 nonsensical person

French: 7 farceur

Zapotec

language family: 5 Otomi 6 mixtec

location: 6 Mexico, Oaxaca

zapped 5 drunk 6 killed, soused, wasted, zonked 7 smashed 8 plas tered 10 inebriated 11 annihi lated,intoxicated

zeal 4 fire, zest 5 ardor, gusto, verve, vigor 6 fervor, relish 7 passion 8 devotion, industry 9 animation, eagerness, intensity, vehemence 10 enthusiasm, fanaticism, fierceness, intentness 11 earnestness

zealot 3 fan, nut 4 buff 5 bigot, crank 6 pusher 7 devotee, fanatic, hustler 8 believer, champion, crackpot, go-getter, livewire, partisan 9 extremist 10 enthusiast

zealous 5 eager, rabid 6 ardent, fervid, fierce, gung ho, raging, raving 7 devoted, earnest, fanatic, fervent, intense 8 animated, vehement, vigorous 10 passionate 11 impassioned, industrious 12 enthusiastic

Zebedee

wife: 6 Salome

son: 4 John 5 James

Zeboim

destroyed with: 5 Admah, Sodom 8 Gomorrah

Zebulun

father: 5 Jacob

mother: 4 Leah

brother: 3 Dan, Gad 4 Levi 5 Asher, Judah 6 Joseph, Reuben, Simeon 8 Benjamin, Issachar, Naphtali

sister: 5 Dinah

descendant of: 10 Zebulunite

Zechariah

father: 5 Bebai, Hosah 6 Jehiel, Pashur 7 Isshiah 8 Jehoiada, Jonathan 9 Berechiah 11 Jeberechiah, Meshelemiah

grandfather: 4 Iddo

mother: 6 Merari

son: 8 Jahaziel

daughter: 6 Abijah

Zeffirelli, Franco

director of: 14 Romeo and Juliet 19 The Taming of the Shrew 20 Brother Sun Sister Moon

Zeitgeist 18 the spirit of the time

Zelos

origin: 5 Greek

personifies: 4 zeal 9 emulation

father: 11 Titan Palles

mother: 4 Styx

brother: 3 Bia 6 Cratus

sister: 4 Nike

Zemeckis, Robert

director of: 15 Back to the Future 17 Romancing the Stone

zenith 4 acme, apex, best, peak 6 apogee, climax, summit, vertex 7 maximum 8 pinnacle 11 culmination

Zenobia (Zeena)

character in: 10 Ethan Frome

author: 7 Wharton

Zephaniah

father: 8 Masseiah

son: 3 Hen 6 Josiah

succeeded: 8 Jehoiada

deathplace: 6 Riblah

zephyr 8 west wind 9 puff of air 10 gentle wind 11 breath of air, light breeze

Zephyrus

personifies: 8 west wind

father: 8 Astraeus

mother: 3 Eos

loved: 10 Hyacinthus

son: 6 Balius 7 Xanthus

Zeppelin, Ferdinand Graf von

nationality: 6 German

invented: 9 dirigible 21 rigid dirigible airship

famous ship: 10 Hindenberg

Zernbbabel

father: 7 Pedaiah 9 Shealtiel

zero 2 no 3 nil, zip 5 aught, nadir, zilch 6 cipher, naught 7 nothing 8 goose egg 11 nonexistent, nothingness

zero hour 5 onset, start 7 liftoff 9 beginning 12 commencement

zest 3 joy, zip 4 salt, tang, zeal, zing 5 gusto, savor, spice, taste, verve 6 flavor, relish, thrill 7 delight, passion 8 appetite, piquancy, pleasure 9 eagerness, flavoring, seasoning 10 enthusiasm, excitement 12 exhilaration, satisfaction

zestful 6 active, lively 7 dynamic, vibrant 8 animated, spirited, vigorous 9 vivacious 12 invigorating

zesty 5 spicy, tangy 7 piquant 9 flavorful

Zetes

origin: 5 Greek

member of: 9 Argonauts

father: 6 Boreas

mother: 8 Orithyia

twin brother: 6 Calais

Zethus
  father: 4 Zeus
  mother: 7 Antiope
  wife: 5 Thebe
  twin brother: 7 Amphion
Zeus
  also: 7 Cenaean 9 Atabyriam, Ithomatas
    10 Anchesmius 11 Panomphaeus 12
    Cithaeronian
  birthplace: 5 Crete
  brother: 5 Hades 8 Poseidon
  corresponds to: 4 Amen, Amon, Jove 5
    Ammon 6 Amen Ra, Amon Ra 7 Jupiter
  daughter: 4 Hebe 6 Athene 10 Eileithyia,
    Persephone
  epithet: 5 Areus, Arius, Sotor 6 Aqueus,
    Nemean, Philus 7 Alastor, Apemius,
    Ctesius, Lycaeus, Polieus, Stenius 8
    Agoraeus, Aphesius, Apomyius, Cathar-
    ius, Chthonius, Coccygius, Hecaleius,
    Lecheates, Mechaneus 10 Cataebates,
    Coryphaeus, Homagyrius, Laphystius,
    Meilichius 11 Eleutherius 12 Panhellenius
  father: 6 Cronus
  form: 5 deity
  god of: 7 heavens
  lover: 4 Leto 7 Demeter
  mother: 4 Rhea
  position: 7 supreme
  sister: 4 Hera 6 Hestia 7 Demeter
  son: 4 Ares 6 Apollo, Hermes
  wife: 4 Hera 5 Metis
zigzag 4 awry, tack 6 angles, forked, jagged 7 chevron, crankle, crooked, notched,
  sinuous, stagger 8 crotched, serrated,
  sideling, traverse 9 bifurcate 10 circuitous,
  deflection
Zillah
  husband: 6 Lamech
  son: 9 Jubal-cain, Tubul-cain
Zilpah
  slave of: 4 Leah
  concubine of: 5 Jacob
  son: 3 Gad 5 Asher
Zimbabwe
  other name: 8 Rhodesia 16 Southern
    Rhodesia
  capital/largest city: 6 Harare 9 Salisbury
  others: 5 Gwelo, Gweru 6 Kariba,
    KweKwe, Mutare, QueQue, Umtali 7
    Gatooma, Rusambo, Selukwe, Shabani 8
    Bulawayo, Zimbabwe 10 Beitbridge
  monetary unit: 4 cent 6 dollar
  lake: 4 Kyle 6 Kariba
  mountain: 5 Vumba 6 Manica 7 Inyanga
    11 Chimanimani, Matopo Hills
  highest point: 9 Inyangani
  river: 4 Sabi, Save 5 Lundi 6 Shashi 7
    Limpopo, Umniati, Zambezi
  physical feature:
  falls: 8 Victoria
  grassland: 4 veld
  plateau: 8 Highveld 11 Mashonaland
  people: 3 Ila 4 Sena 5 Asian, Bantu,
    Bemba, Sotho, Tongo, White 6 Indian 7
    Barotse, Chinese, English, Mashoma,
    Mashona, Ndebele 8 Coloured, Japa-

nese, Matabele 9 Afrikaner 10 Balokwa-
  kwa
  developer: 6 Rhodes
  explorer: 11 Livingstone
  king: 9 Lobengula, Mzilikaze
  leader: 5 Nkomo 6 Mugabe 7 Sithole 8
    Muzorewa 9 Ian D Smith
  language: 3 Ila 5 Bantu, Shona 7 En-
    glish, Ndebele
  religion: 7 animism 8 Anglican 12 Chris-
    tianity, Presbyterian 13 Dutch Reformed,
    Roman Catholic
  place:
  dam: 6 Kariba
  national park: 6 Hwange, Wankie 7
    Matopos 9 Inyan gani 13 Victoria Falls
  ruins: 5 Khami 6 Temple 8 Zimbabwe 9
    Acropolis 13 Valley of Ruins
  feature:
  cattle pen: 5 kraal
  game: 5 tsoro 7 mandani
  hut: 4 kala
  kingdom: 5 Rozwi 10 Monomotapa
  tree: 4 teak 6 baobab, mopani
Zimbalist, Efrem, Jr
  born: 9 New York NY
  father: 14 Efrem Zimbalist
  mother: 9 Alma Gluck
  daughter: 18 Stephanie Zimbalist
  roles: 3 FBI 13 Wait Until Dark 15 By
    Love Possessed 16 The Chapman Re-
    port 62 Seventy-seven Sunset Strip
Zimmerman, Ethel Agnes
  real name of: 11 Ethel Merman
zinc
  chemical symbol: 2 Zn
zing 3 pep, vim, zap, zip 4 dash, snap,
  tang, whiz, zest 5 gusto, speed, vigor,
  whine 6 energy, spirit 7 liven up 8 satirize,
  vitality 9 animation, criticize 10 enthusiasm, liveliness
zingara, zingaro 5 gypsy
Zinnemann, Fred
  director of: 5 Julia 8 High Noon, Okla-
    homa 9 The Search 12 The Nun's Story
    13 The Sundowners 17 A Man for All
    Seasons (Oscar) 18 From Here to Eterni-
    ty (Oscar)
Zion 6 utopia 9 city of God 11 City of David
    13 ancient Israel
  hill in: 9 Jerusalem
  built on the hill: 6 Temple
zip 3 fly, nil, pep, run, vim 4 buzz, dart,
  dash, hiss, life, nada, rush, zero, zest 5
  aught, close, drive, force, gusto, hurry,
  power, punch, speed, verve, vigor, whine,
  zilch 6 cipher, energy, impact, naught,
  spirit, streak 7 nothing, whistle 8 goose
  egg, strength, vitality, vivacity 9 animation,
  intensity 10 enthusiasm, exuberance, liveliness 13 effervescence
zipper
  invented by: 6 Judson
Zipporah
  father: 5 Reuel 6 Jethro
  husband: 5 Moses
  son: 7 Eliezer, Gershom

zircon
  source: 5 Burma 6 Ceylon 8 Cambodia, Sri Lanka 9 Kampuchea
zirconium
  chemical symbol: 2 Zr
zodiac 4 belt, zone 5 stars 7 circuit
  fire sign: 3 Leo 5 Aries 11 Sagittarius
  earth sign: 5 Virgo 6 Taurus 9 Capricorn
  air sign: 5 Libra 6 Gemini 8 Aquarius
  water: 6 Cancer, Pisces 7 Scorpio
  division: 4 sign 5 decan 6 trigon
  number of houses: 6 twelve
  falling between two signs: 4 cusp
Zoimo, Vincent Edward
  real name of: 12 Vince Edwards
Zola, Emile
  author of: 4 Nana 7 The Soil 8 Germinal 10 L'Assommoir 11 The Downfall, The Dram Shop 13 Therese Raquin 14 The Human Animal 20 The Experimental Novel
zone 4 area, belt, ward 5 tract 6 region, sector 7 quarter, section, terrain 8 district, locality, location, precinct 9 territory
zonked 5 drunk 6 soused, wasted, zapped 7 smashed 9 plastered 10 inebriated 11 intoxicated
zoo 8 vivarium 9 menagerie
zoom 3 fly, zip 4 buzz, race, rise, soar 5 climb, flash, shoot, speed 6 ascend, rocket, streak 7 advance, take off 9 sky-rocket
zoophobia
  fear of: 7 animals
Zophar
  friend: 3 Job 5 Elihu 6 Bildad 7 Eliphaz
Zorba the Greek
  director: 17 Michael Cacoyannis
  based on the story by: 11 Kazantzakis
  cast: 9 Alan Bates 11 Irene Pappas, Lila Kedrova 12 Anthony Quinn
  score: 16 Mikis Theodorakis
  Oscar for: 17 supporting actress (Kedrova)
Zosteria
  epithet of: 6 Athena
  means: 20 one who girds with armor
zucchini 5 gourd 6 squash 12 summer squash
Zuck, Alexandra
  real name of: 9 Sandra Dee
Zuckerman Unbound
  author: 10 Philip Roth
Zurich
  festival: 12 Sechselanten
  landmark: 8 Rietberg 9 Kunsthaus 15 CG Jung Institute 17 Centre Le Corbusier, Fraumunster Kirche 21 Grossmunster Cathedral
  religious figure: 7 Zwingli 9 Bullinger
  river: 6 Limmat
  Roman name: 7 Turicum
Zweig, Arnold
  author of: 7 Claudia 24 The Case of Sergeant Grischa